The ...
Br...
Guid...

Edited by Alisdair Aird

Deputy Editor: Fiona Stapley

Associate Editors: Karen Fick, Robert Unsworth

Research Officer: Tom Smith

Walks Consultant: Tim Locke

Additional Research: Fiona Wright, Elinor Breman

EBURY PRESS
LONDON

Please send reports to:

The Good Britain Guide
FREEPOST TN1569
WADHURST
E Sussex
TN5 7BR

This edition published in 1999 by
Ebury Press
Random House, 20 Vauxhall Bridge Road
London SW1V 2SA

1 3 5 7 9 10 8 6 4 2

Copyright © 1999 by Alisdair Aird
Maps copyright © 1999 Perrott CartoGraphics
Cover design by Button

ISBN 0 09 187095 X

Typeset from author's disks by Textype Typesetters, Cambridge
Printed and bound in Great Britain by Cox & Wyman Ltd, Reading, Berkshire

Contents

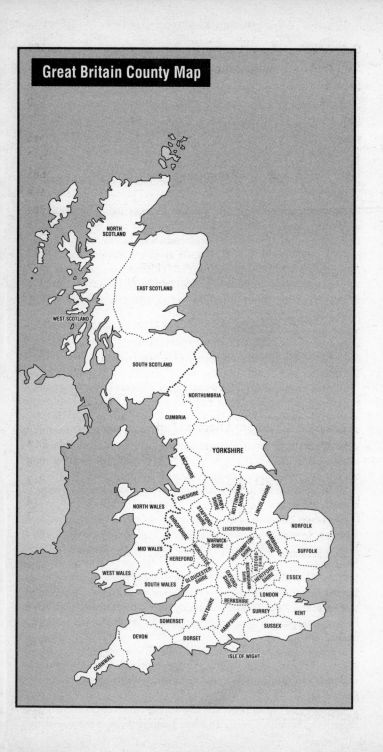

Great Britain County Map

INTRODUCTION

This year we have taken a close look at how those places that charge admission are limbering up for the millennium. How do prices compare in different parts of the country? And, with almost zero inflation now, are they holding their prices steady to match? In all, we compared prices in 2,073 *Guide* entries which charged an admission fee both this year and last (this obviously excludes places which have just opened). This very large number helps to even out regional variations in the style of tourist attractions.

There are indeed huge differences in average admission price, from county to county, around the £3.50 average ticket price for all attractions. For a cheap day out, head for Herefordshire or Northumbria. Rounding prices to the nearest 5p, the cheapest areas are Herefordshire (£2.65), Northumbria (£2.70), Hertfordshire (£2.85), Lincolnshire, Nottinghamshire, Worcestershire and Yorkshire (£3.05), Suffolk (£3.15), Essex and the Isle of Wight (£3.20), Scotland (£3.25) and Cumbria, Gloucestershire and Shropshire (£3.30).

London – hardly a surprise – tops the price chart, with an average admission price of £5.15. Also very expensive are Surrey (£4.80), Bedfordshire (£4.50), Berkshire (£4.45), Lancashire (£4.15), Northamptonshire (£4.10) and Derbyshire (£4).

What is a surprise is that so many places are increasing their prices. In the country as a whole, tourist attractions are bumping up their prices by an average of 5.8% this year – nearly three times the background inflation rate. Places in Somerset, Cumbria, Hampshire and London are averaging an 8% increase. By contrast, most places in Suffolk, Norfolk, Wales and Herefordshire are holding their prices steady, with Lincolnshire, West and South Yorkshire, Lancashire and Dorset nearly as good.

So this year we are looking particularly at the value aspect, in selecting our annual award winners.

Heritage Building of the Year 2000 is Colchester Castle in Essex. Spanning two millennia (the massive Norman fortress is built over a Roman temple's vaults – which you can still see), this is now a splendidly lively museum.

Garden of the Year 2000 is Groombridge Place in Kent: not cheap, but this spectacular garden gives a really good day out for all the family.

Zoo of the Year 2000 is Bristol Zoo: very enjoyable, with a fascinating new seal and penguin area, lots of activities for children – and good-value pricing.

National Museum of the Year 2000 is the staggering Museum of Science and Industry in Manchester, covering its vast field with real verve, and the very latest interactive display technology: great fun, quite fascinating.

Living Museum of the Year 2000 is the North of England Open-air Museum in Beamish, County Durham, perhaps Britain's most rewarding paid attraction, its hundreds of acres devoted to an intricately detailed re-creation of northern working life a century ago, full of interest and action.

Local Museum of the Year 2000 is the Rhondda Heritage Park in Porth, South Wales, vividly showing work and life in a valley's coal-mining community.

Attraction Shop of the Year 2000 is the shop attached to Buckfast Abbey at Buckfastleigh in Devon, worth a special journey for the monks' honey, and for the produce of other Benedictine monasteries throughout Europe.

Tour of the Year 2000 – well, of the year 1750 or thereabouts – is the extraordinary experience Dennis Severs takes you through in his 18th-century house at 18 Folgate Street, London E1, totally immersing you in the feel and atmosphere of the period.

Children's Outing of the Year 2000 is the Cotswold Farm Park at Kineton in Gloucestershire, with all sorts of animals and activities spread over 1,000 acres, at a very attractive price.

New Family Attraction of the Year 2000 is Our Dynamic Earth in Edinburgh, Scotland: a vividly exciting involvement with this living world, from jungles and glaciers to volcanoes and earthquakes.

Gallery of the Year 2000 is the Tate Modern, opening on Bankside in South London in May 2000: great works shown to perfection in a stunning conversion of a redundant power station, linked to St Paul's by a graceful new footbridge across the River Thames.

Family Attraction of the Year 2000 has to be the Millennium Dome in London. At £20 a ticket, you ask? Ah, but the point is that those ticket prices have been so heavily subsidised, mainly by lottery grants, that for each visitor the Dome has actually cost closer to £65. Someone taking four children along on a family ticket is in effect getting an experience that has cost £315 to produce for them, for 'only' £57.

CELEBRATING TWENTY CENTURIES

As this year does end the second millennium, we list here our personal selection of places in Great Britain which give a whirlwind tour of the first two millennia – one for each century.

The 1st century AD has a marvellous monument: **Hadrian's Wall**, still striding massively and evocatively across Northumbria.

For the 2nd century, we choose **Lullingstone Roman Villa** in Kent: started in the 1st century, in its prime then, and unique for its Christian chapel.

The 3rd century has **Chedworth Roman Villa** tucked into the woods of Gloucestershire, near Yanworth: the best surviving of its day, flourishing for some 200 years around then.

In the 4th century, the **Roman Baths** in Bath, Somerset, founded over a century earlier, were at their peak; restored, they give a remarkable impression of life here then.

For the 5th century, the Anglo-Saxon Village in **West Stow Country Park** in Suffolk re-creates the life of the local inhabitants then.

The 6th century is St Columba's, bringing Christianity to Scotland and the North of England from Ireland; his base on **Iona** off Mull in West Scotland has no buildings of his time (except for a kiln, they were all wooden and superseded by later stone ones), but it still has a powerful sense of spirituality that seems to descend from that era.

For the dark days of the 7th century, we choose the little **Escomb Church** in County Durham, built then from stones ransacked from the nearby Binchester Fort after the Romans had abandoned it to a rising tide of barbarism.

A fine memorial to the 8th century is **Bede's World** at Jarrow in Northumbria, on the site of the monastery where he painstakingly recorded the area's recent history; besides actual material of that time, this has some interesting re-creations.

In the 9th century the Vikings were starting to make their mark on much of Britain. The **Jorvik Viking Centre** in York brings their days there in this and the following century to life – sounds and even smells, as well as sights to experience.

As a memento of the 10th century, the final century of the first Christian millennium, the finely carved **Celtic cross** at Kilmartin church in West Scotland could not be bettered.

The 11th century sees a bold start to that new millennium, with the **Tower of London**; its many later additions give a sense of continuity that matches London's own continuing development and change since then, without actually losing its underlying identity.

The 12th century has **Skipton Castle** in North Yorkshire, one of the best-preserved medieval castles in Europe.

Salisbury Cathedral in Wiltshire soars over the 13th century – and over the nearby meadows, much as it has done ever since.

Bodiam Castle in Sussex, a proper story-book castle complete with moat, is a classic 14th-century fortress; a real war machine.

In the 15th century **York Minster**, started over 200 years earlier, was completed.

Ripley Castle, also in North Yorkshire, is a picturesque yet entirely accurate evocation of the 16th century (and the same family still live there, as they had for centuries before).

The 17th century saw the founding of our first public library: **Chetham's Library** in Manchester, in an older building, but still using its 17th-century reading tables.

The swaggering 18th century is epitomised by sumptuous **Blenheim Palace** at Woodstock in Oxfordshire, a reward for the Duke of Marlborough victoriously battling his way across Europe (and later to be the birthplace of Churchill).

A fitting memorial to the 19th century is the **Ironbridge Gorge Museum** in Shropshire: an interlocked series of museums bringing to life the days in which this was the iron heart of new British industry.

For our own past century, we considered the Heritage Motor Centre at Gaydon in Warwickshire and Duxford Airfield in Cambridgeshire, unrivalled collections of the cars and aircraft which have made this century their own, and the new Big Idea inventions museum at Stevenston in South Scotland. However, perhaps the most poignantly accurate memorial to this closing century of the second millennium is Stanley Spencer's moving masterpiece, the **Sandham Memorial Chapel** at Burghclere in Hampshire.

Alisdair Aird

USING THE GUIDE

THE COUNTIES

England has been split alphabetically into county chapters. Scotland and Wales have each been covered in single chapters, and London appears immediately before them at the end of England.

WHERE TO STAY

In each section, hotels, inns and other places to stay such as farmhouses are listed alphabetically.

The price we show is the total for two people sharing a double or twin-bedded room with its own bathroom, for one night in high season. It includes full English breakfast (unless only continental is available, in which case we say so), VAT and any automatic service charge that we know about. So the price is the total price for a room for two people. We say if dinner is included in this total price. It is included in some of the more remote places, especially in Scotland and Wales, and may also be in some other places where the quality of the food is a main attraction; in these cases, the establishment concerned does not normally offer B & B on its own. In some of the places we list, some or occasionally even all the bedrooms share bathrooms; we say if this is the case.

An asterisk beside the price means that the establishment concerned assured us that that price would hold until the end of summer 2000. Many establishments were unable to give us this assurance; this last year, bedroom prices outside London have been holding very steady, but to be on the safe side it would be prudent to allow for an increase of around 5% by then. In London, allow 10%.

A few hotels will do a bargain break price at weekends even if you're staying for just one night. If so, that's the price we give, and we show this with a **w** beside the price. Many more hotels have very good-value short break prices, especially out of season, if you stay a minimum of at least two nights; if you plan to stay in one area rather than tour around, it's well worth asking if there's a special price for short breaks when you book. Many hotels also offer short-notice bargains which don't appear on their tariffs if they are underbooked on a particular night, so as to fill their rooms even at a discount. So, especially if you are not booking in advance, ask what price they can quote you for that particular night.

If there's a choice of rooms at different prices, we always give the cheapest, and if we know that maybe the back rooms are the quietest or the front ones have the best views or the ones in the new extension are more spacious then we say so. If you want a room with a sea view or whatever, you should always ask specifically for this, and check whether it costs extra.

If the hotel closes for any day or part of the year, we say so. But especially in outlying areas hotels have been known to close at other times if their business is very slack. And this last year or two we've found some go out of business altogether. So don't head off into an area where there are no nearby alternatives without checking by telephone first.

We always mention a restaurant if we know the inn or hotel has one. Note that we always commend food if we have information supporting a positive recommendation. So a bare mention that food is served shouldn't be taken to imply a recommendation of the food.

WHERE TO EAT

The price in **bold type** is for one person having a typical three-course restaurant meal with half a bottle of wine, including any automatic service charge. So double it to get a meal for two. The second price, in normal type after the |, is for a more informal single-dish meal, if that's available.

We list any scheduled closing dates. We have found quite a few instances of unscheduled closures in the last year or two, and recommend booking if your plans would be thrown into turmoil by finding a place unexpectedly closed. Moreover, many of the restaurants we list are very popular, and without a booking you may find there's no room for you.

If you want a good meal out in any area, look at the places to stay as well as the restaurants, especially in country areas. When we praise a hotel or inn for its food, that means it's well worth consideration as a place for a good meal out. In some parts of the country, it's in these hotel restaurants that you'll find the best food.

Our brief mentions of places to eat in the text of the **To see and do** sections are based on our own inspections or firm recommendations from readers.

CHILDREN

We asked all hotels, restaurants and other places to stay in and eat at which have full entries in the *Guide* whether they allow children. If the entry doesn't mention children, that means the establishment has told us that it welcomes them, with no restrictions. If there are restrictions (either an age limit, or segregated early evening meals for them), we spell these out. We have found that very occasionally establishments turn out in practice to be more restrictive about children than they claim. And, of course, managements change, and so do their policies. If you are travelling with children, to avoid misunderstandings it's always worth checking ahead that there will be no problem. Please let us know if you find any difference from what we say. Obviously, too, you should bear in mind the character of the hotel or restaurant, as described, and in relation to your own children. While some children might fit perfectly into the atmosphere of a dignified and old-fashioned country house, others might be fractiously ill at ease there – no fun for you, or for the other guests.

LOCATIONS

Generally, we list places to see (and hotels and restaurants) under the name of the nearest village or town. We use **BOLD CAPITALS** to name the locality, and **bold type** like this to name the establishment. If the village is so small that you probably wouldn't find it on a road map, we've listed it under the name of the nearest sizeable village or town instead.

Places well known in their own right – famous castles, great houses, for example – are sometimes shown in **BOLD CAPITALS** instead of the locality name. The maps use the same locality name as the text.

We include places in their true geographical locations – so if a village is actually in Buckinghamshire that's where we list it, even if its postal address is via some town in Oxfordshire.

DAYS OUT

In each chapter except London, we have suggested several full days out, based around places or walks that we recommend in the main text, and which are close enough together to fit well into a day.

Most of the itineraries we have suggested make very full days indeed. While a determined and energetic sightseer might well pack everything into one long day, we expect most people would prefer to treat each day out as a sort of mini-menu, picking the things they'd enjoy most and skipping over the rest.

CALENDAR

Each chapter ends with a list of events we have been able to pin down dates for in 2000; even so, some of these dates are provisional, so best to phone the numbers shown for confirmation if your holiday depends on it.

On Heritage Open Days, not included in the Calendars, many notable buildings will be open to the public which are normally closed. The main date for England and Wales is National Heritage Weekend, 16–17 September, when some 2,000 properties will be open. As we go to press individual details are undecided, but if 1999 was anything to go by they will range from intriguing follies through all sorts of official and office buildings to even the Chancellor of the Exchequer's office. For regional directories write to Civic Trust, 17 Carlton House Terrace, London, SW1Y 5AW with six 2nd-class stamps; for Wales, ring (01222) 484606.

On London Open House Weekend, 23–24 September, there will be free admission to around 100 buildings; in 1999 these included The Ark at Hammersmith, the College of Arms, Lancaster House and the former County Hall. For more details write to London Open House, PO Box 6984, London, N6 6PY.

The Scottish equivalent will be Doors Open Days – again during September, but precise dates were undecided as we went to press; ring (0141) 221 1466.

PRICES AND OTHER FACTUAL DETAILS

Information about opening times and so forth is for 2000. In some cases establishments were uncertain about these when the *Guide* went to press during the autumn of 1999; if so, we say in the text. (And of course there's always the risk of changed plans and unexpected closures.) When we say 'cl Nov–Mar' we mean closed from the beginning of November to the end of March, inclusive; however when we say 'cl Nov–Easter' we mean that the establishment re-opens for Easter.

Where establishments were able to guarantee a price for 2000, we have marked this with an asterisk. In many cases establishments could not rule out an unscheduled price increase, and in these cases – i.e. no asterisk against the price – it's probably prudent to allow for a 5% increase in around April 2000. If you find a significantly different price from that shown, *please let us know*.

⊞ OUR DISCOUNT VOUCHER

Places to visit which have a ⊞ symbol immediately after their name have said they will honour our discount voucher until the end of 2000 (or of course the end of their season, if they close earlier). To get the discount, you must hand one of the vouchers in at the admissions kiosk; there are six vouchers on the tear-out card in the centre of the book. Usually, the discount is that one child will be admitted free for two adults paying the full price. Please check the text for that entry carefully. If there are any variations from the usual, or any special conditions, we spell them out within brackets immediately after the ⊞ symbol. Please also note the general conditions on the voucher itself.

NATIONAL TRUST

NT after price details means that the property is owned by the National Trust, and that for members of the Trust admission is free. There is a similar arrangement for properties owned by the National Trust for Scotland (NTS); the two Trusts have a reciprocal arrangement, so that members of one may visit the properties of the other free. Membership is therefore well worth while if you are likely to visit more than a very few properties in the year – quite apart from its benefit to the Trusts' valuable work. NT membership is £28 a year (£48 for joint membership); details from National Trust, PO Box 39, Bromley, Kent BR1 1NH; (0181) 315 1111. NTS membership is £26 (£42 for a family); details from National Trust for Scotland, 5 Charlotte Sq, Edinburgh EH2 4DU; (0131) 226 5922.

FRIENDS OF HISTORIC HOUSES

The Friends of Historic Houses Association has NT-style membership offering free entry to 283 historic houses and gardens in private ownership throughout Britain – including a high proportion of those we recommend which aren't NT, English Heritage or any other national equivalent. Membership is £28 a year (£40 for joint membership), so you only have to go to four or five houses and you've got your money back. Details from Historic Houses Association, Heritage House, PO Box 21, Baldock, Herts SG7 5SH; (01462) 896688.

ENGLISH HERITAGE

A similar membership scheme now gives free access to those EH properties (about half) which charge admission. It costs £26 (£42 for two adults, £45.50 for a family). Details from English Heritage Membership Dept, PO Box 1BB, London W1A 1BB; (020) 7973 3000. CADW (for Wales) (01222) 500200 and Historic Scotland (0131) 668 8600 have similar schemes.

OTHER MONEY SAVERS

In the relevant sections we mention any notable travel bargains and other sightseeing bargains we know of, such as the *London for Less* guide. You can save the cost of it almost straightaway, and it covers some of the main attractions rather than just peripheral ones. It's also worth knowing about the Slow Travel Networks, especially if you're young and on a budget. Very popular with backpackers from overseas, these are coach runs linking all the main tourist cities around the country – a £129 ticket gets you the whole circuit, though you can get on or off at any stage for as long as you like – there's no time limit, and the drivers are very flexible; (020) 7373 7737.

MAP REFERENCES

Most place names are given four-figure map references, looking like this: NT4892. The NT means it's in the square labelled NT on the map for that area. The *first* figure, 4, tells you to look along the grid at the top and bottom of the NT square for the figure 4. The *third* figure, 9, tells you to look down the grid at the side of the square to find the figure 9. Imaginary lines drawn down and across the square from these figures should intersect near the locality itself.

The second and fourth figures, the 8 and the 2, are for more precise pinpointing, and are really for use with larger-scale maps such as road atlases or the Ordnance Survey 1:50,000 maps, which use exactly the same map reference system. On the relevant Ordnance Survey map, instead of finding the 4 marker on the top grid you'd find the 48 one; instead of the 9 on the side grid you'd look for the 92 marker. This makes it very easy to locate even the smallest village.

DISABLED ACCESS

We always ask establishments if they can deal well with disabled people. We mention disabled access if a cautious view of their answers suggests that this is reasonable, though to be on the safe side anyone with a serious mobility problem would be well advised to ask ahead (many establishments made clear that this helped them to make any special arrangements needed). There may well be at least some access even when we or the establishment concerned have not felt it safe to make a blanket recommendation – again, well worth checking ahead. There are, of course, many places where we can't easily make this sort of assessment – particularly the less formal 'attractions' such as churches, bird reserves, waterside walks and viewpoints. In such cases (which should be obvious from the context) the absence of any statement about disabled access doesn't mean that a visit is out of the question, it simply means we have no information about that aspect. We're always grateful to hear of readers' own experiences. An important incidental point: many places told us that they would give free admission to a wheelchair user and companion.

OUR WEB SITE – NEW

We are working on a new Internet web site which we hope will be open at least in its first version by the time this book is published. It will use and we hope combine material from *The Good Britain Guide* and its sister publication *The Good Pub Guide* in a way that gives people who do not yet know the books at least a taste of them. We also hope that we can use it to give readers of the books extra information (and allow them to report quickly to us), and hope to expand and improve the site significantly (for instance with pictures of places to visit or stay in) over the next year or two. You can try the site yourself at www.goodguides.com.

CHANGES DURING THE YEAR – PLEASE TELL US

Changes are inevitable during the course of the year. Managements change, and so do their policies. We very much hope that you will find everything just as we say. But if you find anything different, please let us know, using the report card in the middle of the book, the forms at the end of the book, or just a letter. For letters posted in Britain you don't need a stamp: the address is *The Good Britain Guide*, FREEPOST TN1569, WADHURST, E. Sussex TN5 7BR.

REPORTS

This *Guide* depends very heavily indeed on readers reporting back to it. In that sense it's very much a collaborative venture: and the more people that send us reports, the better the book will be. So please do help us by telling us about places you think should be added to the book, or removed from it, or even just confirming that places still deserve their entry. We try to answer all letters (though there may be a delay – and between the end of May and October we put all letters aside until after the end of the hectic editorial rush). People who help us do get a special offer discount price on the next edition. There's a note on the sort of information we need at the back of the book, with report forms; and a tear-out report card in the middle of the book.

SYMBOLS

We have used the same symbols in the text and on the maps to pick out all the main types of places to visit. Though you don't need to pay any attention to the symbols, you can if you like use them to scan the text or a map quickly, to see what castles, say, or gardens a particular area has. These are what we have used the symbols to denote :

★ Attractive village or town

🏛 Interesting house – anything from an intimate cottage to the stateliest of stately homes

🏰 Castle, ruined abbey or other romantic ruin

🏚 More or less archaeological site such as Roman remains, Neolithic stone circles, early medieval maze, Iron Age hill fort

✝ Church, cathedral, minster, inhabited abbey

✗ Watermill, windmill or other type of mill

Ⅴ Nature conservation, including wildlife reserves

🐦 Bird reserve, bird centre (including falconry)

🐘 Zoo, safari park, anywhere keeping exotic animals

🐖 Farm animals, farm park, country centre, farm museum

🐟 Anything to do with fish, including both fishing and aquariums

🦋 Butterfly park

❀ Garden, plant centre, arboretum, landscaped park

🗼 Lighthouse

⌂ Walk

🌳 Wood, forest

❋ Viewpoint

🍎 Orchard, fruit farm, pick-your-own; also a vineyard

⍟ Cave, cavern

🏛 Museum

🖼 Art gallery, sculpture park, notable painting collections

⚓ Boat museum

✈ Air museum

🚗 Motor museum

⚙ Open-air museum (including industrial museums)

♄ Heritage centre such as Jorvik Centre in York

🚂 Steam locomotives, railway

⛵ Boat trip

☺ Amusement park, theme park, leisure park, permanent funfair

✂ Craft centre or craft workshop: potters, glass-blowers, weavers, etc

🏭 Factory visit (including power station visits and breweries)

! Anything odd, unusual or decidedly different

⊖ London Underground

⇌ Surface rail – former British Rail

🎫 Our special offer discount (see details above and on the tear-out card in the middle of the book)

Some places embrace all sorts of different attractions in just the one locality. With these, instead of cluttering the maps with lots of different symbols, we show a ✪ on the map.

On the maps, a bed symbol indicates recommended places to stay; a knife-and-fork symbol indicates recommended places to eat.

BEDFORDSHIRE

A good mix of things to do – some outstanding days out.

Several places here have a real variety of appeal. Woburn Abbey stands out, with plenty to keep all sorts of people interested, and more than enough for a day visit – from the exciting safari park to the quieter glories of the abbey and its collections. On a much smaller scale, the Stockwood Craft Museum and Gardens have surprisingly wide appeal, and the charming village of Old Warden glories in both the Shuttleworth Collection of vintage aeroplanes, and the unusual Swiss Garden. The animals in their fine setting at Whipsnade are, of course, a perennial family favourite.

The museum at Leighton Buzzard is one of the better heritage museums (and includes fun train rides). The Cecil Higgins art gallery in Bedford is impressive. Wrest Park has beautiful gardens. After its opening in the spring of 1999, readers quickly tipped us off to the merits of the Bedford Butterfly Park at Wilden – a good mix of pleasure with education, if that's not too harsh a word for such an enjoyable outing. Woodside Farm at Slip End and (another newcomer to the *Guide*) Mead Open Farm at Billington have great family appeal. There are some charming villages to stroll through.

Dunstable Downs have decent walking and remarkable views, though otherwise the county's scenery is generally not memorable. The relative flatness is a boon to cyclists; a tourist board leaflet details good circular cycle routes. You can get this from local tourist information centres, which stand out in this county for their wide range of helpful information. Other good leaflets cover year-round weekend activities and guided walks through some of the prettier villages and countryside; and the Ivel Valley Countryside Project's Kingfisher Way circular walks and Skylark Ride horse trek.

Where to stay

FLITWICK TL0335 **Flitwick Manor** *Church Rd, Flitwick, Bedford MK45 1AE* (01525) 712242 **£160,** plus special breaks; 17 thoughtfully decorated rms. 17th-c country house surrounded by interesting gardens; with log fire in entrance hall, comfortable lounge and library, and smart restaurant with fine French wines and imaginative food using home-grown and local produce; tennis, putting, croquet; children over 12 in evening restaurant; limited disabled access.

LEIGHTON BUZZARD SP9225 **Swan** *High St, Leighton Buzzard LU7 7EA* (01525) 372148 ***£102;** 38 rms. Handsome Georgian coaching inn with pleasant lounge, relaxed bars, and attractive conservatory restaurant with English cooking.

SANDY TL1749 **Highfield Farm** *Great North Rd, Sandy SG19 2AQ* (01767) 682332 ***£50;** 6 rms (2 in former stables), 4 with own bthrm. Neatly kept whitewashed house set well away from A1 and surrounded by attractive arable farmland; friendly helpful owner, open fire in the comfortable sitting room, and communal breakfasts in the pleasant dining room.

WOBURN SP9433 **Bell** *Woburn, Milton Keynes, Bucks MK17 9QD (01525) 290280*
£70, plus wknd breaks; 24 attractively decorated rms, some with antiques. Lovely,
friendly old inn, carefully restored, with beamed evening restaurant, long narrow
bar/dining area, good changing food, and well kept ales; also, residents' own lounge
and bar.

To see and do

BEDFORDSHIRE Family Attraction of the Year

🦋 **WILDEN** TL0954 **Bedford Butterfly Park** 🖼 (off B660 just N of
town) We had our first glowing report on this well organised place just two
weeks after it first opened in spring 1999. They've put a fair bit of thought into
ensuring children enjoy their visit – there's a very good adventure playground,
with climbing frames, log walks and an aerial runway, a separate play area for
younger children, with sandpit, swings and so on, and even colouring books in
the restaurant. The butterfly house is the centre of attention, full of exotic
plants and flowers, as well as the colourful butterflies and caterpillars; above
ponds with carp and waterlilies is a cascading waterfall. The temperature in
here is kept at a snug 28 degrees, so although the whole site is best on a dry day,
it's still useful when cool or wet. Children enjoy the bugs room, with its
tarantulas, cockroaches, scorpions and other creepy-crawlies, all kept safely
behind glass, and various other displays gently put across the centre's
conservation message. An outdoor nature trail goes through a hay meadow
that's a mass of purple flowers in July, and full of meadow brown butterflies on
calm sunny days; it's livened up for children by quiz sheets from the gift shop.
Wear wellies in wet weather, as it can get muddy. There may be a few pygmy
goats outside as well. Staff are helpful and knowledgeable. Older children won't
find it too exciting, but for families with younger children this is a very pleasant,
undemanding detour. Good-value meals and snacks, shop, disabled access;
open daily late Mar–Nov (last admission is at 4pm, 3pm in Nov); (01234)
772770; £4 (£2.50 children over 3). There may be discounts if you come by
bike.

AMPTHILL PARK TL0239
🌾 ⌂ Former hunting grounds of Henry
VIII, surprisingly heathy but landscaped
by Capability Brown, with lovely trees
and a waterlily lake.
BEDFORD TL0549
Really a straightforward modern town
despite its long history, but there are
decent riverside gardens and a few nice
buildings. The Corn Exchange (St Paul's
Sq) has a bronze bust of Glenn Miller,
who made many of his morale-boosting
broadcasts from here. Lincolns
(Goldington Green) is an interesting old
place for lunch.
👶 **Bedford Museum** (Castle Close)
Traditional museum next to the Cecil
Higgins; cl am Sun, all Mon, and 25 Dec;
(01234) 354954; free.
📷👶 **Cecil Higgins Art Gallery &
Museum** (Castle Close) Bedford's
outstanding attraction, very rewarding,

boasting the kind of paintings most
other museums can only dream about,
inc great works by Turner, Constable,
Rembrandt, Matisse, Picasso, and Dali.
The Victorian mansion's beautifully
furnished rooms make it look as if the
family that lived here have just popped
out – it's clear lots of thought has gone
into the displays, and nothing seems
unnatural or out of place. An award-
winning extension has collections of
local lace, glass and ceramics. Snacks,
shop, disabled access; cl am Sun, all day
Mon (exc pm bank hols), 25–26 Dec,
1 Jan, Good Fri; (01234) 211222; free.
👶✝ **John Bunyan Museum** (Bunyan
Meeting Free Church, Mill St) Housed in
a building in the grounds of the church
where John Bunyan was minister,
visitors can walk through a series of
tableaux of his life (there's also a trail
around Bunyan-related sites in the

town). Snacks, shop, disabled access; cl Sun, Mon, Good Fri, Dec–Mar; (01234) 213722; free.

BILLINGTON SP9422
🐄 ⭐ **Mead Open Farm** 🖼
(Stanbridge Road) Plenty of fun for children here including trailer rides, indoor and outdoor play areas and a variety of hands-on activities; falconry displays twice a month exc Jan. Meals, snacks, shop, disabled access; cl Weds–Fri, Nov–Mar, 24–27 Dec, 1 Jan; (01525) 852954; £3.50.

BROMHAM TL0050
✂ 🖋 **Bromham Mill** (Bridge End) Picturesque working 17th-c watermill on River Ouse, with Sunday milling demonstrations (summer, weather permitting), and a gallery with local art and crafts. Lots of events throughout the year, esp in school hols – phone for more information. Snacks, shop, disabled access to ground floor only; open Sun, pm Weds–Sat, and bank hols, Mar–Oct; (01234) 824330; £1.50. The Swan is a popular food pub.

COLMWORTH TL1160
🏰 **Bushmead Priory** Ruins of late 12th-c Augustinian priory, well preserved, with medieval wall paintings and timber-framed roof. Open wknds and bank hols, July and Aug; (01234) 376614; £1.75; EH.

DUNSTABLE TL0019
✝ **Priory Church of St Peter** (Church St) This remarkable priory church incorporates part of a 12th-c abbey (where Henry VIII's first marriage was dissolved); shop, disabled access; cl bank hols; free. The Old Sugarloaf (High St) is useful for lunch.

DUNSTABLE DOWNS TL0019
🐑 ❀ ✂ ⌂ 🎠 Very popular with kite-fliers and gliders at weekends or in summer; there's a countryside centre (cl Mon and winter wkdys), two car

parks, and lots of space to run around. The downs give great views from a spectacular escarpment path, amid ancient grasslands. The downs can be linked to a circuit incorporating Whipsnade village and the nearby Tree Cathedral – the best walk in Beds. **Five Knolls** is an important Bronze Age burial mound, excavated by Agatha Christie's husband Sir Mortimer Wheeler and Gerald Dunning. The Horse & Jockey (A5183) is a decent family food pub.

ELSTOW TL0546
★ ✝ The county's finest village, with a very attractive core of fine old timbered houses by the green. Bunyan was baptised in the attractive church, which has an unusual detached tower and a 'Pilgrims Progress' window. The Three Tuns at Biddenham is the closest good place for lunch.

🏛 ☕ **Moot Hall** (Elstow) Outstanding brick-and-timber medieval market house with a collection of John Bunyan's works (he was born nearby), and a reconstruction of his writing room. Shop; cl am, all day Mon (exc bank hols) and Fri, and Oct–Apr; £1.

FELMERSHAM SP9957
✝ ★ A lovely church by a medieval tithe barn, a fine old thatched pub and some other attractive old houses, with the River Ouse below. Nearby Pavenham is also pretty, with a stroll down to the river.

HARROLD SP9456
★ ✝ Pretty riverside village with 13th-c church and pack-bridge, and an early 19th-c lock-up on the village green. The Magpie is useful for lunch, and in Odell the Bell is good.

⭐ ⌂ **Harrold and Odell Country Park** (Carlton Rd) Highly recommended for birdwatching; with a lake and nature reserve, it's especially

---

Days Out

Fresh air and animals: Walk on Dunstable Downs; Tree Cathedral, Whipsnade; lunch at the Bell, Studham (or picnic at Whipsnade); Whipsnade Wild Animal Park or Woodside Farm, Slip End.

Bedfordshire's quieter side: Elstow; Bromham Mill; lunch at the Bell, Odell, or at the Swan, Bromham; stroll in Harrold and Odell Country Park.

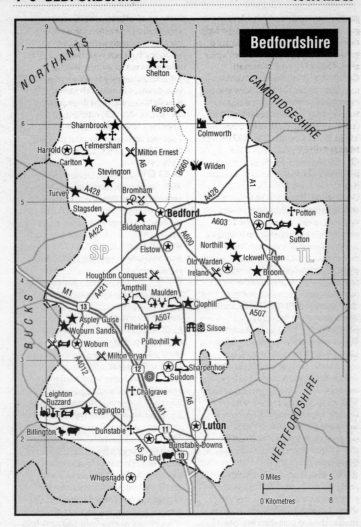

Bedfordshire

NORTHANTS

CAMBRIDGESHIRE

Shelton

Keysoe

Sharnbrook
Colmworth

Felmersham

Harrold Milton Ernest

Carlton Wilden

Stevington

Turvey Bromham

Stagsden Bedford Sandy Potton

Biddenham Sutton

SP Northill

Elstow Ickwell Green

Old Warden Broom

Houghton Conquest Ireland

TL

Ampthill

Maulden Clophill

Aspley Guise

Woburn Sands Flitwick Silsoe

Woburn Pulloxhill

Milton Bryan

Sharpenhoe

Sundon

Chalgrave

Leighton
Buzzard Eggington

Billington Dunstable Luton

Dunstable Downs

Slip End

Whipsnade

BUCKS

HERTFORDSHIRE

0 Miles   5

0 Kilometres   8

good for waterfowl, particularly in winter. Bedfordshire County Council publish a circular route with 3 waymarked walks up to 13 miles long. Snacks, disabled access; visitor centre; cl Christmas wk; (01234) 720016; free.

LEIGHTON BUZZARD SP9225

Leighton Buzzard Railway (Pages Park Station, Billington Rd) Good collection of over 50 locomotives from around the world, with a fleet of 11 steamtrains to trundle you through gently varied countryside. The Stonehenge Works terminus has industrial heritage displays. Snacks, shop, disabled access; open Sun and bank hols Easter–Sept, plus Weds Jun–Aug, Tues, Thurs and Sat in Aug, and wknds in Dec; (01525) 373888 for timetable; £4.50. The Globe in Linslade is a nicely set canalside food pub, with pleasant nearby walks.

LUTON TL0921

Stockwood Craft Museum & Gardens (Stockwood Country Park, Farley Hill) Ideal for a restrained and uncomplicated day out. Besides a museum and several lovely period garden settings (inc a 17th-c knot garden and a Victorian cottage garden), there's a refreshingly witty sculpture garden, and an adjacent children's play area. Also here, the **Mossman Collection** of restored old vehicles has plenty of vintage cars. Pony and cart rides through the park at weekends. Snacks, shop, disabled access; cl Mon (exc bank hols), wkdys Nov–Mar, 25–26 Dec, 1 Jan; (01582) 738714; free.

MAULDEN WOOD TL0358

⚘ ⌂ ❦ Ancient woodland with a picnic site, marked walks and muntjac deer.

OLD WARDEN TL1343

★ ✝ An attractive village in its own right, built deliberately quaintly in the 19th century, and especially worth visiting for the Shuttleworth Collection. The village church has a number of European wood carvings, inc some from the private chapel of Henry VIII's wife, Anne of Cleves. The Hare & Hounds is a useful food pub.

✝ **Shuttleworth Collection** Nearly 40 working historic aeroplanes covering the early history of aviation, from a 1909 Blériot to a 1942 Spitfire in purpose-built hangars on a classic grass aerodrome. Several exhibits are the only surviving examples of their type, and it's worth trying to go on one of the days when some of them are flown (usually the first Sun of the month and Sat evenings, May–Oct). Meals, snacks, shop, disabled access; cl Christmas wk; (01767) 627288; £6, higher charges on flying days.

❁ ⌂ **Swiss Garden** Early 19th-c romantic wilderness garden, with pretty vistas and colourful trees and shrubs – a nice place for a stroll. Meals, snacks, shop, disabled access; open Sun and bank hols Jan–Oct, plus pm daily Mar–Sept; (01234) 228671; £3. Now approached from Old Warden Park via Shuttleworth Mansion; open some Sun pms May–Oct; (01767) 626203; £2.

SANDY TL1749

❁ ❦ ⚘ ⌂ **The Lodge (RSPB Nature Reserve)** The elegant 19th-c Tudor-style house is the headquarters of the RSPB, and isn't open to the public, but is surrounded by formal gardens, a newly developed wildlife garden, and a nature reserve covering 106 acres of heath, lake and woodland, with plenty of birds, animals and trails spread all over. Perfect for watching rare species undisturbed, but even if bird spotting's not your thing, this is a relaxing place to wander through, especially charming in spring when the woods are carpeted with bluebells. Snacks, shop, some disabled access; cl 25–26 Dec; (01767) 680551; £2.50 (free for RSPB members). The Locomotive nearby is useful for lunch.

SHARPENHOE CLAPPERS TL0629

🦋 ⚘ �📷 ❈ ⌂ Steep-sided downland with chalkland flora and butterflies, crowned with a fine beechwood and Iron Age hill fort; the area is owned by the National Trust and is laced with paths.

SHELTON TL0368

★ ✝ Pretty little cottages, hall and rectory grouped around the quite delightful church, with 13th-c work inside, wall paintings, and a 14th-c font on seven legs.

SILSOE TL0835

📷 ❈ **Wrest Park House and Gardens** (off A6) Inspired by French châteaux, the 19th-c house has several ornately plastered rooms open to visitors, but it's the enormous formal gardens that are the main attraction. They go on for over 90 acres and give a good example of the changes in gardening styles between 1700 and 1850. Perhaps best of all is the Great Garden, designed by the Duke of Kent between 1706 and 1740 and later modified by Capability Brown, with lovely views down the water to the baroque pavilion. Snacks, shop, the grassed gardens may be a struggle for wheelchairs; open wknds and bank hols Apr–Oct; (01525) 860152; £3.20; EH. The George Hotel is a friendly place for family lunches.

SLIP END TL0818

🐾 **Woodside Farm & Wildlife Park** 📷 (Mancroft Rd) A good-value day out, it's particularly nice for children, with plenty of friendly and feedable farmyard animals, a playground and tractor rides; you can handle rabbits and collect eggs straight from the hen house. Also rare breeds, poultry and wildfowl, a new lemur house, and a farm shop. They sell pets and poultry, along with all the accessories you'll need to look after them. Meals, snacks, shop, disabled access; cl Sun, 25–26 Dec, 1 Jan; (01582) 841044; £2.50. The Farmer's Boy at Kensworth is an appealing family-minded pub, not far.

SUNDON HILLS COUNTRY PARK TL0528

❋ ⌂ Sheep-cropped downland with good views and marked walks (some quite steep).

SUTTON TL2247

★ Notable for its picturesque, steeply humped packhorse bridge, looking more like a part of Devon or Derbys; ironically, cars have to use a more ancient crossing, the shallow ford beside it. A decent pub nearby is named after John o' Gaunt, the village's former owner.

WHIPSNADE TL0117

! ✿ **Tree Cathedral** Tucked just off the village road is this most unusual war memorial, trees planted in the plan of a cathedral in the 1930s.

🐘 🦛 🐃 **Whipsnade Wild Animal Park** Plenty of space for the animals at this splendid 600-acre zoo; the elephant paddock is reckoned to be Europe's biggest. Altogether 2,500 creatures roam the beautiful downs-edge parkland, from tigers, lions, giraffes and rhinos to monkeys, wallabies, peafowl and Chinese water deer. You'll need a full day to see everything, and it's too big to get round completely on foot – you can drive round the perimeter road and walk from various stopping-points, or there's an open-topped tour bus, but the best way of getting around is on their railway, which takes you past herds of Asian animals. Younger visitors enjoy the elephant walk, penguin feed and sealion demonstrations, and there's a hands-on children's farm, as well as indoor discovery centre with dwarf crocodiles, snakes and spiders. Play areas include a bear-themed maze. Meals, snacks, shop, disabled access; cl 25 Dec; 0990 200123; £9.50. The Bell at Studham is the best nearby place for lunch; the Old Hunters Lodge is very handy.

WILDEN TL0954

🦋 **Bedford Butterfly Park** See separate family panel on p.2.

WOBURN SP9433

★ Some lovely 18th-c houses and good antique shops.

🏛 🖼 🎭 ⚘ 🦌 🐾 **Woburn Abbey & Deer Park** One of England's grandest stately homes – everything from the lovely English and French 18th-c furniture to the splendid range of silver seems to have the edge over most assemblages elsewhere, and the art collection, taking in sumptuous paintings by Rembrandt, Van Dyck and Gainsborough, is outstanding (where else can you see 21 Canalettos in just one room?). The 3,000 acres of surrounding parkland were landscaped by Humphrey Repton, and today are home to several varieties of deer. Swans, ducks and other waterfowl on the lake and aviary with free flying budgies; pottery and huge antique centre. Meals, snacks, shop, disabled access by arrangement; cl Nov–Dec and wkdys Oct and Jan–Mar; (01525) 290666; £7.50.

🐘 ⛵ **Woburn Safari Park** Always exciting, the highlight here is still the drive-through safari – you can almost imagine you are driving through African plains, with lions and tigers (if you're lucky) just on the other side of the windscreen – pick your day carefully however: readers who've visited on bank hols have found themselves in traffic jams so slow-moving it's ruined their enjoyment, so probably best to avoid coming then if you can. The 300 acres of abbey parkland also feature giraffes, rhinos, bears and monkeys, sealion, penguin and elephant shows, a pet's corner, fairground attractions and a boating lake. Birds swoop down and feed from your hand in a walk-through aviary, and there's a new woodland walk among fallow and sika deer. Meals, snacks, shop, disabled access; cl wkdys Nov–Feb; (01525) 290407; £11.50 (£8 children, free for under-3s).

★ **Other attractive villages** include Aspley Guise SP9335, spacious Biddenham TL0249 (nice 12th-c church), Broom TL1743, Clophill TL0837, Eggington SP9525, Northill TL1546, Sharnbrook SP9959 (interesting specialist shops), Pulloxhill TL0634, Turvey SP9452 (the interesting church has Saxon origins) and Woburn Sands (good wooded walks nearby) SP9235; all have pubs we can recommend for lunch. Carlton SP9555

is also pleasant. Ickwell Green TL1545 nr Northill is well worth a look, too, with its colourful thatched houses around a broad green; Stagsden SP9849 is attractive, with a good few thatched houses, and strolls in the woods nearby. Stevington SP9853 has a handsomely restored windmill, and a holy well opposite the church.
✝ **Other churches** worth investigating include Chalgrave TL0027 and Potton TL2449 (it's the gravestones that are worth the visit).

Where to eat

HOUGHTON CONQUEST TL0441 **Knife & Cleaver** *(01234) 740387* Civilised 17th-c dining pub with a welcoming and comfortable bar, blazing winter fire, attentive, friendly service, and smartly stylish bar food (lovely fresh fish and shellfish); 23 good wines by the glass, well kept real ales, good choice of whiskies, no smoking conservatory restaurant, and neat garden; bdrms; cl pm Sun, 27–30 Dec; disabled access. **£20.95 lunch, £27 dinner**|£6.25.

IRELAND TL1341 **Black Horse** *(01462) 811398* Busy and attractive beamed pub in lovely setting, with a good choice of plentiful piping hot food in sizeable lounge or family dining area; helpful, friendly staff, and lots of tables in lovely front garden with play area; disabled access. **£21**|£6.

KEYSOE TL0762 *Chequers (01234) 708678* Friendly and unpretentious village local with two comfortably modernised beamed bars; consistently good food, well kept beer, and terrace and garden with children's play equipment; cl Tues; disabled access. **£16.50**|£6.

MILTON BRYAN SP9730 **Red Lion** *(01525) 210044* Relaxed, comfortable pub with spotless beamed bar area, fresh flowers, good popular food inc quite a few fresh fish dishes and very good-value OAP weekday lunches; no smoking dining areas, real ales, and pretty hanging baskets and plenty of seats on terrace and lawn. **£20**|£7.50.

MILTON ERNEST TL0156 **Strawberry Tree** *Radwell Rd (01234) 823633* 18th-c thatched cottage with low beams and open fires; very good interesting lunchtime and evening food using the best ingredients from a sensibly short menu in the no smoking dining room, and very popular afternoon teas, too; cl Mon, Tues, all Jan; disabled access. **£23 lunch, £35 dinner**.

WOBURN SP9433 **Paris House** *(01525) 290692* Lovely black and white timbered house in Woburn's deer park with a neat garden for pre-meal drinks, and serving enjoyable modern French food with exotic touches and a mainly French wine list; cl pm Sun, Mon, all Feb; disabled access. **£26 lunch, £58 dinner**.

Special thanks to Mrs Y Campion.

Bedfordshire Calendar

Some of these dates were provisional as we went to press. Please check information with the telephone numbers provided.

FEBRUARY

26 Bedford Festival of Music, Speech and Drama – *till 4 March* (01234) 720481

APRIL

2 Old Warden Air Show at the Shuttleworth Collection (01767) 627288

16 Woburn Abbey Open Gardens (01525) 290666

21 Leighton Buzzard Easter Steam Weekend at Leighton Buzzard Railway – *till 24 April* (01525) 373888

22 Silsoe St George's Day Festival at Wrest Park – *till 23 April* (01767) 682728; **Whipsnade** Easter Weekend at the Wild Animal Park – *till 24 April* (01582) 872171

29 Leighton Buzzard Teddy Bears' Outing at Leighton Buzzard Railway – *till 1 May* (01525) 373888; **Whipsnade** Steam Event at the Wild Animal Park – *till 1 May* (01582) 872171

MAY

1 Dunstable Carnival (01582) 607895; **Ickwell Green** May Festival (01767) 640588

2 Luton Open Garden at Seal Point, Wendover Way (01512) 611567

7 Old Warden Air Show at the Shuttleworth Collection (01767) 627288

27 Bedford River Festival – *till 28 May* (01234) 227392

28 Luton International Carnival – *till 29 May* (01582) 546091

JUNE

4 Old Warden Air Show at the Shuttleworth Collection (01767) 627288; **Woburn Abbey** Stationary Engine Cub Rally (01525) 290666

6 Luton Open Garden at Seal Point, Wendover Way (01512) 611567

9 Ampthill 13th Ampthill Music Festival – *till 25 June* (01525) 714049

10 Woburn Abbey Garden Show – *till 11 June* (01525) 290666

11 Luton Festival of Transport at Stockwood Park (01582) 873460

17 Flitwick Carnival (020) 7492 2535

24 Ampthill Festival Gala Day (01582) 402304

25 Woburn Abbey Stud Day (01525) 290666

26 Luton Festival at Lewsey Park (01582) 402034

JULY

1 Silsoe Jazz Festival (01525) 860491

2 Bedford 'Lazy Sunday': free festival with live bands, children's entertainments, street theatre and circus (01234) 360601; **Old Warden** Air Show at the Shuttleworth Collection (01767) 627288; **Woburn Abbey** Open Garden (01525) 290666

4 Luton Open Garden at Seal Point, Wendover Way (01512) 611567

Bedfordshire Calendar (cont.)

7 Cranfield Air Rally and Exhibition at Cranfield Airfield – *till 8 July* (01273) 461616

8 Bedford Bunyan 17th-c Fair (01234) 227392

9 Bromham Show (01234) 825684

22 Luton Festival at Lewsey Park (01582) 696355

30 Leighton Buzzard Model Event at Leighton Buzzard Railway (01525) 373888

AUGUST

1 Luton Open Garden at Seal Point, Wendover Way (01512) 611567

5 Bedford Proms in the Park (01234) 269099

6 Old Warden Air Show at the Shuttleworth Collection (01767) 627288

12 Luton Country Fair at Stockwood Park – *till 13 August* (01582) 876005

13 Leighton Buzzard Family Fun Day at Leighton Buzzard Railway (01525) 373888; **Woburn Abbey** Merlin Classic Car Run (01525) 290666

26 Kempston Fun Day (01234) 356846

30 Biddenham Show at St James School Field (01234) 350644

SEPTEMBER

1 Leighton Buzzard Autumn Steam-up at Leighton Buzzard Railway – *till 3 September* (01525) 373888

3 Old Warden Air Show at the Shuttleworth Collection (01767) 627288

5 Luton Open Garden at Seal Point, Wendover Way (01512) 611567

17 Leighton Buzzard Mad Hatter's Tea Party at Leighton Buzzard Railway (01525) 373888

OCTOBER

1 Old Warden Air Show at the Shuttleworth Collection (01767) 627288

29 Leighton Buzzard Halloween at Leighton Buzzard Railway (01525) 373888

NOVEMBER

4 Podington Fireworks and Drag Racing at Santa Pod Raceway – *till 5 November* (01234) 782828

5 Bedford Fireworks at Bedford Rugby Ground (01234) 347980
Luton Fireworks at Popes Meadow (01582) 876083

DECEMBER

7 Bedford Victorian Christmas Fair – *till 9 December* (01234) 227392

BERKSHIRE

Windsor and its surroundings are the county's biggest draw, but some lesser known places have great charm too – and the west of the county has possibilities for quiet breaks.

Some newcomers to the *Guide* here this year are Period Plants (a nursery with a new–old twist) at Hamstead Marshall, a prettily set new farm park at Bucklebury, and the Household Cavalry Museum in Windsor. The county's greatest draw is Windsor Castle, and the town has plenty to fill a day or more's busy sightseeing. For a complete change of pace nearby, Dorney Court is a fine ancient building with the deep charm of a proper family home. Windsor Great Park, the Savill Garden and the Valley Gardens have memorable vistas, and can be returned to again and again without exhausting their possibilities.

Legoland is a favourite day out for children – outstanding when it first opened, it's improved significantly each year since. Children also really enjoy the Look Out discovery park in Bracknell, a good combination of hands-on science with nature and outdoor adventure.

The innovative Wyld Court Rainforest at Hampstead Norreys is quite an eye-opener, and Beale Park at Lower Basildon is also most rewarding for anyone with an interest in wildlife. Both these are towards the west of the county. This part has quite a good range of walking possibilities, from gentle strolls to long hikes – with some comfortable and attractive places to stay in, and plenty of decent food, it makes for a relaxing short break. Its rolling downland and civilised small villages linked by pleasant minor roads make for attractive drives – the Lambourn Valley and Lambourn Downs, the B4009 and B4494, and the back road from Pangbourne to Aldworth are among the best.

Besides the county's great racecourses, horse-lovers can choose between opposite ends of the speed scale, at Lambourn and at Littlewick Green. The rural life museum on the edge of Reading is one of the best in Britain.

The finest stretch of the Thames is between Marlow and Henley, with easy towpath sauntering and plenty of boating activity. In holiday time the river does get very busy, but is idyllic on a fine early summer or autumn afternoon. Away from the Thames, there are also boat trips in Hungerford, Newbury and Kintbury.

Where to stay

BRAY SU9079 **Monkey Island** *Bray, Maidenhead SL6 2EE (01628) 623400* **£159**, plus wknd breaks; 26 comfortable rms. Set on an island in the River Thames and reached only by footbridge or boat, this peaceful 18th-c former fishing lodge built by the 3rd Duke of Marlborough is made up of two smart white buildings surrounded by beautifully kept gardens with peacocks, ducks and geese; some fine original features inc an original painted ceiling in the lounge showing monkeys in

18th-c sporting gear, helpful friendly staff, and enjoyable food in restaurant overlooking the water; cl 26 Dec–15 Jan.

EAST ILSLEY SU4981 **Crown & Horns** *East Ilsley, Newbury RG16 0LH (01635) 281205* **£58;** 8 rms, some in converted stable block. Bustling and friendly old pub in horse-training country; interesting beamed rooms, well liked bar food, 160 whiskies from all over the world, and a pretty paved stable yard.

HAMSTEAD MARSHALL SU4165 **White Hart** *Hamstead Marshall, Newbury RG20 0HW (01488) 658201* **£80;** 6 beamed, comfortable rms in converted barn. Civilised country inn in quiet village; with a log fire open on both sides of the L-shaped bar, a partly no smoking restaurant, good Italian food (the daily specials are the thing to go for), decent Italian wines, friendly service, and a very pleasant walled garden; cl 25–26 Dec, 1 Jan.

HUNGERFORD SU3368 **Bear** *Charnham St, Hungerford RG17 0EL (01488) 682512* **£93w,** plus special breaks; 41 comfortable, attractive rms with antiques and beams in older ones. Civilised hotel with fresh flowers, open fires, a fantastic huge clock, plentiful bar food, well kept real ales, and a relaxing restaurant; disabled access.

HUNGERFORD SU3368 **Marshgate Cottage** *Marsh Lane, Hungerford RG17 0QX (01488) 682307* ***£49.50;** 10 individually decorated rms. Newly refurbished, family-run little hotel backing on to the Kennet & Avon Canal; with residents' lounge and bar, super breakfasts, a friendly atmosphere, and seats overlooking water and marsh and in the sheltered courtyard; plenty to see nearby; disabled access.

LAMBOURN SU3278 **Lodge Down** *Lambourn, Newbury RG17 7BJ (01672) 540304* **£45;** 3 rms. Country house in lovely grounds with views over the gallops of Lambourn Downs; open fire in the spacious elegant sitting room, friendly owners, and good breakfasts around communal table; visits to stables on request; tennis court and swimming pool.

MAIDENHEAD SU8783 **Fredricks Hotel & Restaurant** *Shoppenhangers Rd, Maidenhead SL6 2PZ (01628) 581000* **£210,** plus wknd breaks; 37 luxurious rms, many with garden views. Smart red brick hotel next to the greens of Maidenhead Golf Club; champagne on arrival in reception with its stylishly modern chandeliers and marble waterfall, plush cocktail bar, fine professional cooking in the luxurious restaurant, and good formal service from long-standing staff; lush wintergarden overlooking gardens; cl Christmas/New Year; disabled access.

STREATLEY SU5980 **Swan Diplomat** *High St, Streatley, Reading RG8 9HR (01491) 878800* **£105w,** plus special breaks; 46 attractive rms, many overlooking the water. Well run, friendly riverside hotel with comfortable, relaxed lounges, consistently good food in the attractive restaurant, popular leisure club, restored Magdalen College barge, and a flower-filled garden; disabled access.

WINDSOR SU9676 **Oakley Court** *Windsor Rd, Water Oakley, Windsor SL4 5UR (01753) 609988* **£156,** plus special breaks; 115 spacious, individually furnished rms. Splendid Victorian country-house hotel in 35 acres of grounds by the Thames, with 9-hole golf course, croquet lawn, tennis, fishing, boating, and health club; log fires in the elegant lounges, a panelled library, and very good cooking in the relaxed bistro and more formal restaurant; used in 200 films, notably the St Trinians series and Hammer House Dracula films; disabled access.

YATTENDON SU5574 **Royal Oak** *The Square, Yattendon, Newbury RG16 0UF (01635) 201325* **£134,** plus special breaks; 5 pretty rms. Elegant and comfortable old inn in peaceful village; fresh flowers and log fire in the prettily decorated panelled bar, a relaxed atmosphere, interesting modern food, real ales, a good wine list, and a pleasant walled garden.

Please let us know what you think of places in the *Guide*. Use the report forms at the back of the book or simply write us a letter.

To see and do

BERKSHIRE Family Attraction of the Year

☺ **WINDSOR** SU9676 **Legoland** (B3022, 2m SW of the town centre; shuttle-bus from the station at Windsor and Eton Riverside, which connects with London Waterloo) Try as we might, we haven't found anywhere in the county that children under 12 enjoy visiting quite as much as this truly imaginative place. It's been our favourite family destination in Berkshire for four years now, and one of the things that really stands out about it is the way that each season they add new features and attractions, so there's always something different to see. Additions last year included an exciting new water ride, miniature rollercoaster for younger visitors, and a Balloon School, where you can control the height of your flight above the park by a pulley system. Don't be put off by the price: comparatively speaking it's not bad value, as you'll need a full day to stand even a chance of seeing everything (it stays open later in the summer holidays). If you'd prefer not to rush, a two-day ticket is £5 extra. As at any theme park you can expect a fair amount of standing in line, though you can avoid this as much as possible by booking in advance – you'll miss the long wait at the entrance, and be able to plan beforehand which bits you most want to see (essential for getting the best out of the place). It also removes the risk of not seeing anything at all – they close the doors when they feel there are enough visitors. The park is divided into several differently themed areas (all built with those amazingly versatile coloured building bricks), with the driving school at Lego Traffic one of the most popular; children who best negotiate the simulated roads and traffic systems earn their own driving licence. The Wild Woods is ideal for lively boys: its Rat Trap is a first-class labyrinth of wooden walkways, climbing nets and slides, and the Pirate Falls is an excellent steep water chute. Children over nine can create robotic models in the more sophisticated Mindstorms Centre; this area can get busy (particularly mid-afternoon), so entrance is by timed ticket – try and sort out your slot as soon as you arrive. Younger children enjoy the colourful Duplo Gardens, while My Town has some jolly fairground rides, a circus, and some splendidly put-together scenes and tableaux in the Explorer's Institute. Best of all though is Miniland, where 20 million Lego bricks charmingly re-create Amsterdam, Brussels, London and Paris in miniature, with moving people, vehicles and animals, and wonderful attention to detail (even down to the 'Mind the Gap' on the London Underground). Several snack bars and restaurants (and very good picnic area), decent shops, good disabled access; open daily from mid-Mar–end of Oct, (01753) 626111; £17 (£14 children).

ARBORFIELD SU7567

❀ **Henry Street Garden Centre** (Arborfield) Specialist rose and bedding plant grower, with a well stocked garden centre. From Jun–Sept you can wander through the fragrant rose fields. Meals, snacks, shop, disabled access; (01189) 761223; free. The George & Dragon over at Swallowfield is good for lunch.

ASCOT SU9268

! **Royal Ascot** Probably the most famous racecourse in the world, though most visitors spend as much time watching the people as the horses. The four-day Royal Meeting in mid-Jun is still one of the highlights of the English season; to try for admission to the Royal Enclosure, British citizens should apply to Ascot Races (Royal Enclosure and Members' Stand), St James's Palace, London SW1, foreign citizens to their embassy. For the other stands contact the racecourse; tickets must be booked in advance and are available from 1 Jan. Plenty of other top-class races throughout the year, when ticket prices range from £5 to £44 depending on the enclosure (the Silver Ring is the cheapest). Meals, snacks, shop, disabled access; (01344) 622211 for dates. The Thatched Tavern at Cheapside is the best nearby place for lunch.

BISHAM SU8485
✝ **Bisham church** Well worth a look; sitting on a seat in the churchyard by the Thames on a fine evening is rather special.

BOULTER'S LOCK SU9082
⌒ An excellent starting-point for leisurely strolls by the River Thames (head upstream).

BRACKNELL SU8769
☺ **Coral Reef** Across the road from the Look Out centre, this is an unusually wacky swimming pool complex, and great for younger members of the family; the Wild Water Rapids are the best bit. Meals, snacks, shop, disabled access; wkdys outside school holidays slides only operate from 3.30pm; cl 2 wks prior to Boxing Day; (01344) 862484; £5.30.

! ⚘ 🏛 ❋ **Look Out** (off B3430, southern edge of Bracknell) A lively centre that's the starting-point for 2,600 acres of woodland. Families love the hands-on science centre, now very much the main feature of the place, and a very full timetable of events includes some particularly well organised children's activities. Mainly conifer plantations, the forest is full of nature trails and wildlife (as well as an Iron Age hill fort); as the name suggests, there's an elevated platform with good views of the surrounding area. You can hire mountain bikes and the many tracks, some based on Roman roads, allow long though not particularly varied walks and rides. Snacks, shop, disabled access; cl Christmas wk; (01344) 354400; *£3.75. The Old Manor (Grenville Pl, High St) has decent food all day, and there's a dry-ski centre with toboggan run at the Leisuresport Complex at Amen Corner.

BUCKLEBURY SU5570
🐑 ⚘ ⌒ ✿ **Bucklebury Farm Park** Perhaps the best time to visit this friendly place, attractively set in the Pang Valley, is in Jun when the red deer calves are born. A free tractor-drawn trailer takes you right up to the herd (some are tame enough to feed), which now numbers around 100 animals. Children can bottle-feed lambs and

calves in the spring, handle rabbits and guinea pigs in the pets corner or watch a sow suckle her litter; also chickens, geese, goats and donkeys. They own five acres of woodland and a two-mile way-marked walk crosses an ancient common; two adventure playgrounds. You can pick your own strawberries between mid-Jun and mid-July. Snacks, shop, disabled access; cl mid-Sept–mid-Mar; (01189) 714002; £3 (£2 children).

BURGHFIELD SU6668
❀ **Old Rectory** Plantsman's garden inc oriental rarities and cottage-garden plants. Plant centre selling plants from other gardens in the area. Snacks, disabled access to most of garden; open last Weds of month Feb–Oct; (01189) 833200; *£2. The Hatch Gate here is a friendly pub for lunch.

COOKHAM SU8985
★ ⌒ ❋ ✿ The village, leading down to the Thames, is attractive, and has several decent pubs of which the very smart if expensive Bel & the Dragon, and Uncle Tom's Cabin at Cookham Dean, are the current pick. There are plenty of opportunities in this area for **walks** combining the Thames with its hinterland, inc great views from the chalk escarpment of Winter Hill. Cock Marsh (NT), by the Thames, is a fine lowland marsh, with breeding wading birds and wetland flora. Paths in this area are very well kept, and it is hard to lose the way seriously, although woodland walking sometimes means you have to keep your eyes skinned for arrow markers painted on trees.

🖼 **Stanley Spencer Gallery** (King's Hall) Cookham really made its mark on Spencer and his art: it was his birthplace and he spent most of his working life here. This rewarding little gallery has a good range of his unique work, with highlights including *The Last Supper* and the curious *Christ Preaching at Cookham Regatta*. Shop, disabled access; cl wkdys Nov–Easter; (01628) 520890; *50p.

DORNEY SU9278
🏛 ❀ ✿ **Dorney Court** Engaging partly 15th-c timber-framed manor house with pleasant gardens and some very fine furniture, as well as the Elizabethan Palmer Needlework tapestry. The same family have lived

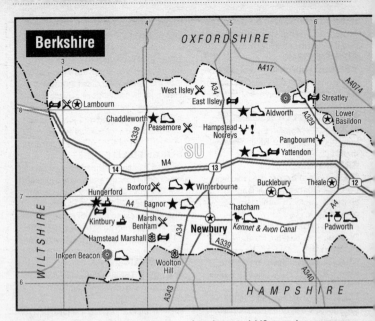

here for over 450 years. In the 16th c they grew the first pineapple raised in England, and still have pick-your-own fruit and vegetables every day in season (usually daily Jun–Sept – discounts on Mon, Tues or Weds). There's also a plant centre, with plants from Blooms of Bressingham, and teas with their own honey. Meals, snacks, shop; open pm Mon–Thurs Jun–Aug, pm bank hols and preceding Sundays in May; (01628) 604638; £5. The Pickwick at Eton Wick is handy for lunch.

EASTHAMPSTEAD SU8666
† Easthampstead church The church here is particularly notable for the fine Pre-Raphaelite stained glass by William Morris, Edward Burne-Jones and others.

ETON SU9677
🏛†🖰🔳 So close to Windsor it's pretty much part of it, this has a restrained and decorous High St with a mix of interesting old shops and houses. Its glory is **Eton College**, the famous public school, whose stately Tudor and later buildings in graceful precincts are marvellously calm during the school's holidays. The chapel is an outstanding late Gothic building in the Perpendicular style, and a museum tells the story of the school from its

foundation in 1440 up to the present, with fascinating videos on life for pupils here today (inc Prince William). Bizarre information is turned up by the various historical documents – in the 17th c, for example, smoking was compulsory for all scholars as a protection against bubonic plague. The Brewhouse Gallery has some good watercolour drawings and changing exhibitions, and next door there's an exhaustive collection of Egyptian antiquities. Shop, some disabled access; cl am in term-time, and all Oct–Mar; (01753) 671177; from £2.60 (guided tours from £3.80). The college runs residential courses in summer on topics as diverse as rowing and choral singing. The Pickwick at Eton Wick has good-value food.

FINCHAMPSTEAD RIDGES
SU7863
🔔🌼🗁 A steepish chunk of heather and pinewood, not big but with a good natural character, fine views and sheltered picnic spots; the avenue of Wellingtonias just above it is well worth seeing too. To the N, Simons Wood NT woodland, with a walk to Heath Pool and Devil's Highway Roman Road, now a track.
HAMPSTEAD NORREYS SU5376
🏠! **Wyld Court Rainforest** (B4009

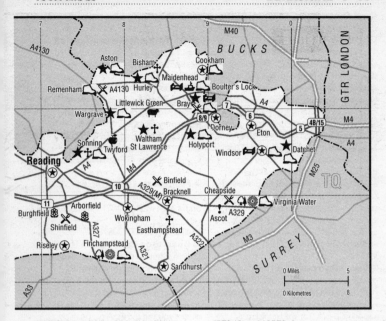

slightly out of village) Very highly praised by readers – an unusual and quite fascinating tropical rainforest reconstructed under glass, with thousands of weird-looking plants currently in danger of extinction. They're spread over three different areas, Lowland Tropical, Amazonica and Cloudforest, each with its own climate and atmosphere. Particularly strange are the giant 8-ft lily pads (best from Jun–Oct), which start life the size of a pea, and the orchid collection is exceptional. Quite a few of these plants can't be seen anywhere else in Europe. Also squirrel monkeys, varied fish, and terrapins. As it's so warm, this is particularly handy on a cold day. Snacks, good shop (with plants for sale), mostly disabled access (though hard work in gravel car park); cl 25–26 Dec; (01635) 200221; £3.50. The White Hart has good-value food.

HAMSTEAD MARSHALL SU4667

🏵 **Period Plants** Small nursery laid out in the style of a 16th-c garden producing plants grown in British gardens until 1700. Dated beds show garden-sized samples of each plant (all for sale); rough farmland may prove difficult for wheelchairs; to check opening times phone either (01488)

657248 or 668572; free.

HUNGERFORD SU3368

★ ⚓ Attractive small town with some interesting antique shops (there's a large arcade on the High St (tel: 01488 683701), some of them general, others specialising in items as diverse as fireplaces, kitchen furnishings and billiard tables; antique fairs in the town hall. The Kennet & Avon Canal Trust run **canal trips** from the Wharf at 2.30pm wknds Easter–Oct (also Weds Jun–Sept, from £3; maybe also 4.30pm trips July and Aug). The Tally Ho towards the motorway is a friendly place for lunch.

INKPEN BEACON SU3562

🌼 ⛰ The high escarpment between here and Walbury Hill gives some dramatic ridgeway walking; best reached from the minor road S of Inkpen (where the Swan is handy for lunch). The gibbet on top of the hill is a macabre relic from highwayman days. Immediately south lie some lovely rolling downlands laced with gentle and mostly well marked tracks, field paths and woodland paths overlapping into Hants and Wilts.

KINTBURY SU3866

⚓ **Horse-drawn barge trips** 1½ hr trips along the restored Kennet & Avon

Canal, Easter–Sept; (01635) 44154;
£4.50.

LAMBOURN SU3278

✝ Quiet streamside racehorse-training
village below the downs. The parish
**Church of St Michael and All
Angels** is worth a look (originally
Norman, with Perpendicular additions),
and the Hare & Hounds (on the B4000
S), with strong racing connections, is
good for lunch.

❗ **Lambourn Trainers Association**
(Windsor House) Guided tours around
this successful racehorse training
centre; you meet individual horses and
see them put through their paces. Wear
suitable shoes, and you must make an
appointment. Snacks, shop, disabled
access; open 10–12 noon, daily exc Sun
and bank hols; (01488) 71347; £5 plus
VAT.

🏛 **Seven Barrows** Up on the downs
off the Lambourn–Kingston Lisle rd
(OS Sheet 174 SU329827) this Bronze
Age cemetery has at least 32 barrows –
a spectacle even for the uninitiated.

LITTLEWICK GREEN SU8580

🐎 **Courage Shire Horse Centre**
♿ (A4, 2m W of Maidenhead) You can
go right up to the horses at this friendly
place, and watch them being groomed
and plaited up; there are also small
animals and birds, working forge on
some days, children's playground, daily
dray rides at 12 noon and 3pm. Meals,
snacks, shop, disabled access; cl
Nov–Feb; (01628) 824848; £3.

LOWER BASILDON SU6078

🏠 ✿ **Basildon Park** (off A329)
Elegant Bath-stone Palladian mansion
with delicate plasterwork on the
ceilings and walls, unusual Octagon
Room, and intriguing collection of rare
sea shells in the Shell Room. Outside
are old-fashioned roses, a pretty
terrace, and pleasant grounds beyond.
The classical frontage is particularly
impressive. Summer teas, light lunches
wknds and bank hols, shop, disabled
access to garden and grounds only;
open pm Weds–Sun and bank hols,
Apr–Oct; (01189) 843040; £4.10, £1.80
grounds only; NT.

✤ ✦ 🐾 ❋ ⚓ **Beale Park** (Church
Farm) Good, reliable and informative
wildlife gardens, with a varied range of
birds and mammals – many rare. Just

about all their animals were born here
in conditions as near as possible to the
wild. The surroundings well deserve
their listing as an Area of Outstanding
Beauty, and there's a lot going on –
attractions include a narrow-gauge
railway, a model boat collection with
exhibits displayed both in and out of the
water, paddling pools and a children's
playground. Readers get a great deal of
pleasure from coming here. Meals,
snacks, shop, disabled access; cl
Christmas–Feb; (01189) 845172; £4. In
summer there are short river cruises
and you can get a boat to here from
Caversham Bridge in Reading (two
hours each way, (01189) 481008, £7
return).

MAIDENHEAD SU8783

⚓ **Boating on the Thames** Though
busy in summer, this is a lovely stretch
of the river, flowing through lively
towns and villages, past grand houses in
imposing grounds to idyllic reaches by
steep quiet woodland – with islets
where you can picnic. A particularly
pretty trip is from Wargrave to Henley
to Medmenham Abbey to Hambleden,
Hurley and Marlow Reach. A good
shorter stretch is Cliveden Reach (the
two miles between Cookham and
Boulter's Lock). As well as motor
launches, you can hire very attractive
(not to mention silent and quite
environmentally friendly) electric
launches, though for the purists – and
the energetic – only a rowing boat will
do. Bray Boats in Maidenhead, (01628)
637880, have small boats/motor
launches ranging from £20 an hour to
around £130 a day; they also run half-
hour or two-hour trips as far as
Cookham. Kris Cruisers in Datchet
have rowing boats from £7 an hour and
electric launches from around £15 –
they do good discounts during the
week; (01753) 543930. A recorded
information service (updated weekly)
has details of events and estimated
conditions on the river; (01189)
535520.

NEWBURY SU4667

✝ ⚓ ❗ 🏛 Busy shopping town famed for
its notorious bypass, which generally
seems to have reduced congestion in
the centre. Some nice old parts, with
interesting older buildings among the

high-street shops. **St Nicolas** is a fine early 16th-c Perpendicular church with a magnificent pulpit. West Mills is the best evocation of the town's 18th-c prosperity, and leads to the attractively rejuvenated canal. **Boat trips** occasionally run from the old wharf, beyond the market square on the other side of the High St; (01635) 44154. The town has an excellent **racecourse**, with mid-week and weekend races all year; (01635) 40015 for dates; prices from £4–£18. **Donnington Castle** (just N off B4494) is actually the tall, ruined medieval gatehouse of a much larger fortress destroyed in the Civil War. The Old Waggon & Horses (Market Pl) has a friendly family dining area above the river, and the Lock Stock & Barrel (also waterside) an afternoon coffee shop as well as bar meals.

☐ **West Berkshire Museum** (The Wharf) Handsome museum, good on the Civil War battles fought here, and on the development of ballooning. Shop, disabled access to ground floor only; open Mon–Sat, exc Weds in term-time, plus pm Sun and bank hols April–Sept; free.

PADWORTH SU6166

☐ † ⌂ **Kennet & Avon Canal Visitor Centre** (Aldermaston Wharf) Set in a nice little house beside the canal, exhibitions on the history and usage of the waterway, and useful information on things to do along its various stretches (of which some would say the Berkshire bits are the prettiest). Good trails and walks. Snacks (in picnic garden), shop, limited disabled access; cl Nov–Mar; (01189) 712868; free. Nearby quietly placed **Padworth church** feels very ancient and peaceful, and the Round Oak has decent food. See also Hungerford, Kintbury and Newbury entries for boat trips. And besides other places we mention, there's good access from Aldermaston Wharf SU6067, Marsh Benham SU4267, Thatcham SU5167 and Woolhampton SU5767, all of which have decent pubs. The railway makes a useful method of return, especially after an energetic walk along the canal from Hungerford to Kintbury, for example.

PANGBOURNE SU6376

⋎ **Pangbourne Meadow** Traditional meadow by the Thames, scythed after flowering and seeding to preserve its wide range of wild flowers. The riverside Swan has food all day, and the village has some decent shops; it was the home of Kenneth Grahame, who perhaps found inspiration here for *The Wind in the Willows*.

READING SU7173

🏛 ! Berkshire's county town, largely 19th-c red brick, and not really a tourist town, but with museums worth visiting. The abbey ruins in Forbury Gardens are worth a look if passing. In West St, Vicars & Sons is an old-fashioned game butchers' established in the 19th century, an interesting shop with good food. For the extravagant, a **balloon trip** gives a very different view of Berkshire; lift off from town-centre parks daily (weather permitting) in summer, dawn and dusk; (020) 8840 0108; £130. Sweeney & Todd in Castle St has excellent-value home-made pies, and the canalside Fisherman's Cottage (Kennet Side – walk through from Orts Rd off Kings Rd) is also very popular for lunch.

↓T **Blake's Lock Museum** (Gasworks Rd) Very well organised, concentrating on Reading's waterways, trade and industries, with reconstructed bakery (the town was well known for biscuit-making), barber's shop and printer's workshop, and a Victorian turbine house. Shop, snacks, disabled access; open pm wknds and bank hols, plus all day Tues–Fri in school hols; (01189) 390918; free.

☐ **Museum of English Rural Life** (University of Reading, Whiteknights Park; 2m SE on A327, so you don't have to go into the busy centre) You won't find a better exploration of life in the English countryside over the last couple of centuries than this, taking in farm tools, rural crafts, and domestic room settings. Shop, disabled access; cl 1–2pm, all day Sun and Mon, and 25 Dec–1 Jan; (01189) 318663; £1.

☐ **Museum of Reading** (Blagrave St) Housed in a showy neo-Gothic building, with hands-on displays and good reconstructions, and a unique Victorian copy of the Bayeux Tapestry. Meals,

snacks, shop, disabled access; cl Mon,
Tues and am Sun; (01189) 399800; free.

REMENHAM SU7684

⌒ A good start for gentle strolls along
the Thames towpath, showing to full
effect the river's nostalgic qualities of
boating and Edwardian England. There
are spectacular period riverside
mansions towards Maidenhead. This
reach is the course of the Henley
regatta; you can instead start from
Henley itself (coming back over the
bridge).

RISELEY SU7263

❀ ✿ ✿ ✿ 𝄞 ⌒ **Wellington
Country Park** (off B3349
Reading–Basingstoke rd) Plenty for
families in this big country park; the 350
acres of meadows, woodland and lakes
include marked nature trails, a
miniature railway, deer park, collection
of small domestic animals, and an
adventure playground. You can fish and
hire rowing and pedal boats on the lake.
Meals, snacks, shop, some disabled
access, cl Nov–Feb; (01189) 326444;
£3.90. The George & Dragon at
Swallowfield does good lunches.

SANDHURST SU8361

❀ ✿ ✿ 𝄞 **Trilakes Country
Park and Fishery** (Yateley Rd) Not
just for fishermen, these attractive lakes
and surrounding park and woodland
have lots of animals and birds, some of
which you can feed. Shetland pony rides
for children on summer Suns, and in
spring you can bottle-feed the lambs.
Also a model railway. Meals, snacks,
shop, limited disabled access; cl wkdys
Nov–Mar; (01252) 873191; £2.25,
£7.50 fishing. The Bird in Hand at Little
Sandhurst is useful for lunch.

SONNING SU8377

★ † ⌒ A charming village, with a
pleasant walk through the churchyard
and past the lovely **church** to the River
Thames, and to Sonning Lock.

STREATLEY HILL SU5580

❀ ⌒ The NT car park below here
gives access to NT downland for fine
views over the Thames valley. The long-
distance downs-top Ridgeway Path, one
of the oldest tracks in England, follows
surfaced farm roads in places
hereabouts, but also takes in some
quiet stretches of countryside –
pleasant scenery for a gentle stroll.

THATCHAM MOOR SU5066

🦆 ⌒ Surprisingly, the largest area of
inland freshwater reed beds in England;
lots of birds (some rare), moths, and
marshland and aquatic plants. Car park
S of A4. The **Nature Discovery
Centre** explains more about the
environment and has a good
programme of special events. Snacks,
shop, disabled access; cl Mon; free.

THEALE SU6371

🏛 ✿ ✿ **Englefield House** (A340)
The striking house itself is open only to
groups, but the surrounding woodland
is attractive, with interesting trees,
water and formal gardens, and deer
park. Some disabled access; open Mon
all year, plus Tues–Thurs Apr–July;
(01189) 302221; £2. The Old Boot over
at Stanford Dingley has very good food.

TWYFORD SU7876

🍷 **Thames Valley Vineyard**
(Stanlake Park, B3018) English wines
made by a pioneering blend of tradition
and technology. Snacks, shop; cl Sun
am, 25 Dec–2 Jan; (01189) 340176; free.
The Bull nr the Thames at Sonning is
pleasant for lunch.

VIRGINIA WATER SU9768

✿ ❀ ⌒ Very beautiful, particularly in
autumn; the Long Walk gives glorious
perspectives of Windsor Castle. Best
access via Valley Gardens or Savill
Garden car parks.

WALTHAM ST LAWRENCE
SU8377

† ★ **Shottesbrooke church** A
magnificent 14th-c building, unusually
set in a park just east of Waltham St
Lawrence – itself an attractive quiet
village with an ancient centre.

WINDSOR SU9676

★ ⚓ ! Well worth an expedition
(though a tremendous magnet for
visitors), the town is dominated by its
famous castle, the largest inhabited one
in the world. The little streets to the
south have many pretty timber-framed
or Georgian-fronted houses and shops.
The High St, by contrast, is wide and
busy. You can walk by the Thames (for
example, from Home Park, beyond the
station); or across to Eton. The good
evening racecourse is best approached
by boat – shuttle services run from
Barry Avenue Promenade; (01753)
865234 for race dates. The Trooper in

St Leonards Rd and Two Brewers in Park St (handy for Royal Mews) are useful for a bite to eat, but for a better meal we'd recommend going out to the Thatched Tavern in Cheapside – handy for the various Windsor Park attractions. The Union and Oxford Blue are good pubs in the quieter nearby Thames-side village of Old Windsor.

🏛 **Frogmore House** (Home Park) This lesser known former Royal residence is definitely worth catching on one of its few open days – usually spring and summer bank hols; (01753) 868286 ext 2347 for dates, (children under 8 not admitted); £4.90. It was a favourite with Queen Victoria, who is buried in a mausoleum in the grounds (open annually on Weds nearest to the 24 May), alongside her beloved Albert.

♿ **Household Cavalry Museum** (St Leonards Road) Only small, but interesting to the military minded: full of memorabilia such as uniforms, medals, weapons; outside is a small armoured vehicle display. Shop, disabled access; open Mon-Fri (exc bank hols); free.

☺ **Legoland** See separate family panel on p.12.

🌸 **Savill Garden** (Wick Lane, Englefield Green – where the Sun is a good lunch break) On the eastern edge of Windsor Great Park, 35 peaceful acres taking in woodland, formal rose garden, rock plants, herbaceous borders and so forth, and punctuated with a number of rare trees, shrubs and perrenials. The range of colours can be quite dazzling. Perhaps best in spring but quite stunning at any time of year. Meals, snacks, good shop with plant sales, disabled access; cl 25–26 Dec; (01753) 860222; *£5 Apr–May, *£4 Jun–Oct, *£3 Nov–Mar.

◠ 🌸 🍃 **Valley Gardens** Lovely for a relaxing stroll, with over 400 acres of woodland – 50 of which are devoted to rhododendrons, making this the largest planting of the species in the world. Also an outstanding collection of trees and shrubs, a heather garden, waterfowl lakes, and attractive landscaping. It's free for pedestrians (the mile-long walk from Savill Garden is pleasant), though cars can enter by a gate on Wick Rd, Englefield Green, for a fee of £4, £3 outside summer – change needed for the automatic barrier).

🏰 ❀ ✝ ♿ 🖼 ! **Windsor Castle** A mass of towers, ramparts and pinnacles, this splendid palace is the official residence of the monarch, though it's changed considerably since William the Conqueror built his original wooden fort here. Henry II constructed the first stone buildings, inc the familiar Round Tower, from the top of which, on a good day, you can see 12 counties. For many the highlight is the magnificent **St George's Chapel**, (where the Earl and Countess of Wessex were married last June), a splendid example of Perpendicular architecture, with intricate carvings on the choir stalls, fine ironwork, an amazing fan-vaulted ceiling, and the arms and pennants of every knight entered into the Order of the Knights of the Garter. This is closed Sun and occasional other dates, often at short notice – best to check on the number below. The **State Apartments**, used for ceremonial and official occasions, are decorated with carvings by Grinling Gibbons and ceilings by Verrio, and full of superb paintings from the Royal Collection (inc notable Rembrandts and Van Dycks), porcelain, armour, and exceptionally fine furniture. This area (which may be closed when the Queen is in residence)

Days Out

Regal splendour: Windsor Castle (get there early to avoid the crowds); stroll into Windsor Great Park; lunch at Oakley Court, Windsor – or drive to the Fish in Bray (Old Mill Lane) or Thatched Tavern, Cheapside; Eton College.

Orchids and exotica: Walk by Thames at Streatley; Wyld Court Rainforest, Hampstead Norreys; lunch at the White Hart there, or at the unspoilt Bell, Aldworth; Beale Park, Lower Basildon.

was badly damaged by the disastrous fire in 1992, but you'd hardly know it now, with St George's Hall restored beyond its former glory. Entrance to **Queen Mary's Dolls House**, an exquisite creation by Edwin Lutyens, built for Queen Mary in the 1920s, with perfectly scaled furniture and decoration, is now also included in the general admission price. Shop, disabled access (exc Dolls House); (01753) 831118 or (01753) 868286 ext 2235 for full details of opening times; £10 (£8.50 when St George's Chapel is closed). The guards generally change daily Mon–Sat (alternate days only in winter), at 11 o'clock – again, phone for exact dates.

🕮 ◔ **Windsor Great Park** Miles of well kept parkland, so sensitively landscaped that it takes the occasional surprising find (statues, even a totem pole) to remind you that it's not natural. It's the only real prospect in this eastern part of the county for walks that'll make you feel genuinely exercised.

WOKINGHAM SU8068

🐟 **California Country Park** (B3016 S of Wokingham, turning right at Wick Hill opposite B3430) These woods and open spaces are very useful for young children to let off steam in.

🌳 ◔ **Holme Grange Craft Village** (Heathlands Rd) Expanding craft centre with paintings, sculpture, rugs, and even a circus shop; Widget the pot bellied pig is a favourite with children. Snacks, disabled access; cl 25 Dec–1 Jan; (0118) 977 6753; free. Heathlands Rd has a couple of farm shops and pick-your-own plots; the Crooked Billet on Gardeners Green, Honey Hill, just SE of Wokingham, is a friendly place for lunch.

WOOLTON HILL SU4261

🕮 **Hollington Herb Garden** Tranquil and relaxed walled gardens. Snacks, shop; open Mar–Sept, Weds–Sat, pm Sun and bank hols; £1.

★ **Other attractive villages**, all with decent pubs and pleasant local walks, include Aldworth SU5579, Aston SU7884, Bagnor SU4569 (with a well regarded theatre in a lovely old watermill), Bray SU9079, Chaddleworth SU4177, Datchet SU9876, Holyport SU8977, Hurley SU8283, Wargrave SU7878, Winterbourne SU4572 and Yattendon SU5574.

Where to eat

BINFIELD SU8571 **Stag & Hounds** (01344) 483553 Little low-beamed rooms with log fires, interesting furnishings and pictures, some fine sporting prints, and a good bustling atmosphere; real ales, decent wines, daily papers, and lots of good modern daily specials – plenty of fish and vegetarian dishes, too. **£21|£8.**

BOXFORD SU4271 **Bell** (01488) 608721 Civilised and neatly kept mock Tudor village inn with long snug bar, a nice mix of racing pictures, smaller old advertisements, and interesting bric-à-brac; a rather smart restaurant, thoughtful modern cooking, well kept real ales, and decent wines; bdrms; cl 26 Dec. **£25|£5.50.**

BRAY SU9079 **Fat Duck** 1 The High St (01628) 580333 Really innovative food cooked with immense care and based on traditional French cooking (some perfectly cooked more straightforward dishes as well) in this black and white former pub; a relaxed if slightly sophisticated feel, knowledgeable helpful staff, and a well chosen wine list; cl Mon, 2 wks Christmas; disabled access. **£55|3-course lunch £23.**

BRAY SU9079 **Fish** Old Mill Lane (01628) 781111 Relaxed dining pub with two stylish rooms and a no smoking conservatory, candles and fresh flowers; good, friendly service, particularly fine fish dishes, lovely puddings, real ales, and a good wine list; cl pm Sun, Mon, Christmas; children over 12 in evening; disabled access. **£33|2-course lunch £12.**

BRAY SU9079 **Waterside** Ferry Rd (01628) 620691 Famous restaurant-with-rooms on a quiet stretch of the Thames with big windows overlooking the water; exquisitely presented, superb classical French cooking using the best luxury ingredients, lovely puddings, fine French cheeses, an outstanding (if pricey) wine list, and impeccable service; pretty bdrms; cl pm Sun (in winter), Mon, am Tues, 26 Dec–27 Jan; children over 12; disabled access (restaurant only). **£40**.

CHEAPSIDE SU9469 **Thatched Tavern** *Cheapside Rd (01344) 20874* Smartly civilised dining pub (not actually thatched!) with low old beams, polished flagstones, and a big inglenook; pretty gingham cloths on the tables in the long dining room, a large choice of good food inc local game and fresh fish, well kept real ales, and polite, friendly service. **£29|£10.50**.

LAMBOURN SU3278 **Hare & Hounds** *(01488) 71386* Stylish dining pub in the heart of horse country; with colourful and idiosyncratically decorated rooms leading off the narrow bar, imaginative food, well kept real ales, good wines, and friendly service. **£23|£10**.

MARSH BENHAM SU4267 **Water Rat** *(01635) 582017* Attractively set, old thatched pub with cheerful 'Wind in the Willows' mural in the comfortable bar, no smoking dining room and a new front orangery restaurant; especially good, carefully cooked food, well kept ales, decent wines, lots of malt whiskies, and quite a few brandies and ports; seats on the terrace and long lawns that slope down to water meadows and River Kennet. **£20.50|£7.50**.

PEASEMORE SU4577 **Fox & Hounds** *(01635) 248252* Tucked-away downland pub with hunting prints and fox masks in the two bars; a relaxed atmosphere, enjoyable bar food, real ales, and seats outside with far-reaching views; cl Mon. **£20|£5.50**.

REMENHAM SU7683 **Little Angel** *(01491) 574165* Cosy little restaurant with good seafood, splendid range of wines by glass, and helpful service; also bar food and well kept real ales in the old low-beamed and panelled bar; floodlit terrace; cl pm winter Sun; children must be well behaved. **£25|£7.95**.

SHINFIELD SU7368 **L'Ortolan** *Church Lane (01189) 883783* Smartly refurbished Victorian rectory with two plant-filled conservatories; exceptional innovative French cooking inc delicious puddings and a fine cheeseboard, an excellent wine list, and courteous service; cl pm Sun, Mon; disabled access. **£30 lunch, £55 dinner**.

WEST ILSLEY SU4782 **Harrow** *(01635) 281260* Popular white-tiled village inn overlooking duck pond and green; with very good home-made bar food (super vegetables), no smoking dining area, real ales, a relaxed and welcoming atmosphere, and a big garden; no food winter pm Sun; disabled access. **£25|£9.50**.

Special thanks to MDN, Mrs C Dewell, Mr Ian Smith.

Berkshire Calendar

Some of these dates were provisional as we went to press. Please check information with the telephone numbers provided.

JANUARY

8 **Savernake Forest** Icicle Hot-air Balloon Meet – *till 9 January* (01672) 562277

MARCH

25 **Burchetts Green** Lambing Weekend at Berkshire College of Agriculture – *till 26 March* (01628) 824444
26 **Riseley** Husky Day at Wellington Country Park (01189) 326444

Berkshire Calendar (cont.)

APRIL

21 Lambourn Open Day at Lambourn Racing Stables (01235) 751693
23 Riseley Easter Fun Days at Wellington Country Park – *till 24 April* (01189) 326444
28 Reading Real Ale Festival at Kings Meadow – *till 1 May* (01189) 390375
29 Newbury Steam Funtasia at the Showground – *till 1 May* (01663) 732750; **Wokingham** Fun Day (01189) 783185

MAY

1 Hungerford Raft Race from Hungerford to Newbury (01635) 44688; **Riseley** Pet Day at Wellington Country Park (01189) 326444; **Wokingham** May Fair in the town centre with Green Man, Sun God, and maypole dancing (01344) 423147
2 Hungerford Hocktide (01488) 682317
6 Newbury Spring Festival, also in surrounding villages – *till 20 May* (01635) 32421; **Pangbourne** Beale Park Model Boat Show – *till 7 May* (01189) 845172; **Windsor** Savill Garden Plant Fair (01753) 847518
7 Burchetts Green Berkshire College of Agriculture Country Fair and Open Day (01628) 824444
9 Windsor Frogmore Gardens and Mausoleum Open Day – *till 11 May* (01483) 211535
11 Windsor Royal Horse Show at Windsor Home Park – *till 14 May* (020) 7370 8206
19 Pangbourne Beale Park 'Boats 2000': International Boat Show – *till 21 May* (01189) 845172
20 Reading Children's Festival: free events – *till 18 June* (01189) 390900
21 Riseley Dragon Boat Racing at Wellington Country Park (01189) 326444
25 Windsor International Three-day Event at Windsor Great Park – *till 28 May* (01753) 860222
29 Sandhurst Donkey Derby at Memorial Hall (01252) 879060

JUNE

3 Burchetts Green Garden Open Day at Berkshire College of Agriculture (01628) 824444
4 Newbury Summer Fair at Watermill Theatre (01635) 46044
10 Woodley Carnival (01189) 690581
11 Riseley Teddy Bears' Picnic at Wellington Country Park (01189) 326444
19 Windsor Garter Ceremony at St George's Chapel after procession from Windsor Castle (apply for limited tickets between 1 Jan and 28 Feb to the Superintendent, Windsor Castle, SL4 1NJ)
20 Ascot Royal Ascot at the Racecourse – *till 23 June* (01344) 622211
24 Chieveley Garden and Leisure Show at Newbury Showground – *till 25 June* (01635) 247111; **Hurst** Country Fair and Horse Show – *till 25 June* (01189) 345253; **Newbury** Garden and Leisure Show – *till 25 June* (01635) 247111; **Reading** Waterfest – *till 25 June* (01189) 390375
30 Bracknell Festival at the Wilde Theatre – *till 2 July* (01344) 427272

JULY

2 Newbury Carnival (01635) 40748

Berkshire Calendar (cont.)

9 **Riseley** Heavy Horse Show at Wellington Country Park (01189) 326444; **Winnesh** Millenium Party: family fun day (01189) 794482

15 **Thatcham** Kite Festival – *till 16 July* (01635) 528400

17 **River Thames** Swan Upping from Sunbury to Abingdon: colourful 13th-c ceremony of swan-marking by Swan Masters and their assistants – *till 21 July* (01628) 528034

20 **Reading** Real Ale and Jazz Festival – *till 22 July* (01189) 390375

21 **Reading** WOMAD at Rivermead – *till 23 July* (01189) 390375

29 **Ascot** Diamond Day at the Racecourse (01344) 22211

AUGUST

6 **Riseley** Heckfield Horticultural Show at Wellington Country Park (01189) 326444

12 **Knowl Hill** Steam Fair – *till 13 August* (01628) 823393; **Pangbourne** Beale Park Medieval Craft Fair – *till 13 August* (01189) 845172

13 **Riseley** Animal Day at Wellington Country Park (01189) 326444

25 **Reading** Music Festival – *till 27 August* (01189) 390373

26 **Newbury** Orchid Fair at Jarvis Elcot Country Hotel – *till 27 August* (01488) 658100

27 **Spencers Wood** Swallowfield Horticultural Show – *till 28 August* (01189) 988 2736

SEPTEMBER

2 **Riseley** Shetland Pony Show at Wellington Country Park (01189) 326444

4 **Spencers Wood** Wokingham and Reading Agricultural Show (01189) 833395

9 **Wokingham** Heritage Day – *till 10 September* (020) 7930 0914

16 **Chieveley** Newbury and Royal County Show at Newbury Showground – *till 17 September* (01635) 247111; **Reading** Heritage Open Weekend – *till 17 September* (01189) 390900

23 **Ascot** Festival at the Racecource – *till 24 September* (01344) 22211

24 **Burchetts Green** Shrub Sunday at Berkshire College of Agriculture (01628) 824444

OCTOBER

1 **Wokingham** Victorian Day: arts, crafts and entertainments at the Holme Grange Craft Village (01189) 776753

14 **Pangbourne** Beale Park Model Boat Trade Show – *till 15 October* (01189) 845172

NOVEMBER

4 Beale Park Fun and Fireworks Party (01189) 845172; **Reading** Firework Fiesta at King's Meadow (01734) 390358

25 **Pangbourne** Beale Park Christmas Craft Fair – *till 26 November* (01189) 845172

DECEMBER

3 **Wokingham** Winter Carnival and Victorian Street Fair (01189) 746467

10 **Woodley** Winter Extravaganza (01189) 690356

BUCKINGHAMSHIRE

Some entertaining family outings, as well as the county's lovely Chilterns scenery and great houses and gardens.

Gulliver's Land in Milton Keynes is a good new outing for young children, and the Roald Dahl Gallery in Aylesbury is outstanding. Odds Farm Park at Wooburn Common, St Tiggiwinkles Wildlife Centre in Haddenham, the Bucks Goat Centre at Stoke Mandeville and the unusual zoo at Weston Underwood are all really good animal attractions. Many older children join adults in enjoying the Chiltern Open-air Museum in Chalfont St Giles, the railway centre at Quainton and the extraordinary Hell Fire Caves at West Wycombe. Conversely, people who take children to see the Bekonscot Model Village in Beaconsfield tend to end up fascinated themselves.

Claydon House at Middle Claydon is basking in the attention brought by its role in the recent BBC TV adaptation of *Vanity Fair*. Waddesdon Manor and Ascott at Wing are both rich testaments to the Rothschild alliance of wealth with taste; Chenies Manor has a quieter charm. The landscape gardens of Stowe and Cliveden are memorable fine-weather outings. Bletchley Park has intriguing memories of World War II secrets, presented at the moment in a friendly and untouristy way; it is now building an up-to-the-minute new museum devoted to its key role in code-cracking. A smaller place, the Old Gaol Museum in Buckingham, is also benefiting from some careful upgrading.

The Chiltern Hills give the south of the county a special charm: quiet valleys, lovely tucked-away villages with pretty brick and flint houses, endless walking possibilities. This scenery is at its best in spring and autumn through to November, when the beechwoods are at their most beautiful. Some of the best stretches of the Thames are in this area – the finest reaches of all are best seen from a boat.

Where to stay

ASTON CLINTON SP8712 **Bell** *London Rd, Aston Clinton, Aylesbury HP22 5HP* (01296) 630252 **£84,** plus special breaks; 20 comfortable rms, some in main building with antiques, some (more modern but spacious) in converted stables around a flower-filled courtyard. Early 17th-c coaching inn with an elegant panelled drawing room, flagstoned smoking room, restaurant with pretty murals and excellent modern French cooking, and formal but kind service; pretty, mature gardens; disabled access.

AYLESBURY SP8213 **Hartwell House** *Oxford Rd HP17 8NL* (01296) 747444 ***£236.80,** plus special breaks; 47 rms, some huge and well equipped, others with four-posters and fine panelling, and 10 secluded suites in separate building with private garden and statues. Elegant Grade I listed building with Jacobean and Georgian façades, wonderful decorative plasterwork and panelling, fine paintings and antiques, marvellous Gothic central staircase, a splendid morning room and library; exceptional service, and excellent food; 80 acres of parkland with a ruined church, lake and statues, and spa with indoor swimming pool, saunas, gym and so forth, as well as an informal restaurant; croquet, fishing; cl 3–6 Jan; children over 8; dogs accepted; good disabled access.

FAWLEY SU7586 **Walnut Tree** *Fawley, Henley-on-Thames, Oxon RG9 6JE (01491) 638360* **£50;** 2 rms with showers. Popular dining pub in lovely spot with Chilterns all around; attractively furnished bars, imaginative food and decent wines in the separate restaurant and no smoking conservatory.

HAMBLEDEN SU7886 **Stag & Huntsman** *Hambleden, Henley-on-Thames, Oxon RG9 6RP (01491) 571227* **£68;** 3 newly refurbished. Peaceful brick and flint pub opposite the church in a very pretty village surrounded by Chilterns beechwoods; with compact half-panelled lounge, a large fireplace, attractively simple public bar and cosy snug, good food, well kept real ales, and a spacious pretty garden (summer barbecues); cl pm bank hols; no children.

MARLOW SU8586 **Compleat Angler** *Marlow Bridge, Marlow SL7 1RG (01628) 484444* **£100w,** plus special breaks; 65 pretty, individually furnished rms overlooking garden or river. Famous Thames-side hotel with a comfortable panelled lounge, balconied bar, and spacious beamed restaurant with marvellous view; imaginative food, and friendly, prompt service; tennis, croquet, coarse fishing and boating; disabled access.

MURSLEY SP8128 **Richmond** *Lodge Mursley, Milton Keynes MK17 0LE (01296) 720275* **£50;** 3 attractive rms, some with own bthrm. Carefully run Edwardian house in big neat garden with tennis and croquet; open fire in sitting room, lovely breakfasts (super dinner if ordered in advance), and friendly owners; no smoking; cl Christmas; children over 6.

TAPLOW SU9185 **Cliveden** *Taplow, Maidenhead SL6 0JF (01628) 668561* **£324** (plus £5.50 per person paid to the National Trust), plus special breaks; 39 luxurious, individual rms with maid unpacking service and a butler's tray. Superb Grade I listed stately home with gracious, comfortable public rooms, fine paintings, tapestries and armour, and a surprisingly unstuffy atmosphere; lovely views over the magnificent NT Thames-side parkland and formal gardens (open to the public); daily-changing imaginative food in the two no smoking restaurants, with lighter meals in the conservatory, friendly breakfasts around a huge table, and impeccable bright staff; pavilion with swimming pool, gym and so forth, tennis, squash, croquet, riding, coarse fishing, and boats for river trips; good disabled access.

WINSLOW SP7627 **Bell** *Market Sq, Winslow, Buckingham MK18 3AB (01296) 714091* **£52;** 43 rms. Elegant black and white timbered inn with beams and open fires; plush hotel bar, all-day coffee lounge, decent bar food, good lunchtime carvery in the restaurant; also, a pleasant inner courtyard; cl 31 Dec; disabled access.

WOOBURN COMMON SU9187 **Chequers** *Kiln Lane, Wooburn Common HP10 0JQ (01628) 529575* **£97.50,** plus special breaks; 17 stripped pine rms in mock Tudor wing. Popular inn with a cheerful traditional atmosphere in the cosy, low-beamed bar, standing timbers and alcoves, log fires and comfortable sofas, well kept real ales; good tasty food in the busy dining room, nice breakfasts, and a spacious garden.

To see and do

BUCKINGHAMSHIRE Family Attraction of the Year

⌚† CHALFONT ST GILES TQ0193 **Chiltern Open-air Museum**
(Newland Park, Gorelands Lane) A good few traditional Chilterns buildings that would otherwise have been demolished have found their way here in the last 20 years, painstakingly dismantled and rebuilt again piece by piece. That may not sound too exciting for children, but in fact they work hard at bringing the buildings and their heritage to life. Every weekend they have different activities themed around a different house or period of history, so, depending on when you visit you might come across historic cooking on an open hearth, or be able to join in brick- or candle-making (ring in advance for what's on when). During school holidays they have a whole range of special hands-on activities and demonstrations designed with children in mind; it's especially lively in the summer holidays, when they have around 50 extra things to do. The buildings are fascinating; dotted about the 45 acres are structures as diverse as an Iron Age house, a Victorian farmyard, an Edwardian public convenience and a 1940s prefab, with useful displays on their original use. You can explore the site in a couple of hours, but even when there's nothing special going on it's easy to spend a bit longer – there's a pretty woodland walk, nature and sculpture trails, some shire horses and farm animals, and a children's playground. One barn is a centre of the Hawk and Owl Trust, and though they don't keep any captive birds you may be lucky enough to see some of the wild birds of prey that live in the grounds. It's not really a place to come in wet weather. The special event days around Christmas and Halloween are fun – though you'll need to book for the latter. Snacks, shop, some disabled access; open Feb half-term and then Apr–Nov, Tues–Sun (daily in Aug) and bank hols; (01494) 872163; £4.50 (£2.50 children 5–16). A family ticket is £13. Some special events may have extra charges. Nearby, the smart Ivy House (London Rd) has good food.

AYLESBURY SP8113
♨! **Buckinghamshire County Museum & Roald Dahl Children's Gallery** (St Mary's Sq, Church St) Roald Dahl lived in Buckinghamshire for most of his life and this museum celebrates the connection with a gallery of hands-on displays that use Dahl's novels and characters to teach children about insects, light and any number of other topics; visitors can crawl through the tunnel of Fantastic Mr Fox, discover Willy Wonka's inventions, and even go inside the Giant Peach to find out what things look like under the microscope. Also a good collection of regional art and a walled garden. Snacks, shop, good disabled access; cl am Sun and 25–26 Dec (Dahl gallery cl until 3pm wkdys in term-time); (01296) 331441; £3.50 (£1 without Dahl gallery). The Bottle & Glass out on the A418 at Gibraltar is the closest good dining pub.

BEACONSFIELD SU9391
! **Bekonscot Model Village** (Warwick Rd) Popular with readers, this miniature portrayal of rural Britain in the 1930s includes scaled-down churches, castles, zoo and even a racecourse, as well as a gauge-1 model railway. Snacks, shop, disabled access; cl Nov–mid-Feb; (01494) 672919; *£4. The Greyhound is handy for lunch.

BLETCHLEY SP8633
♨ 🎖 **Bletchley Park** (turn off B4034 at Eight Bells pub, then turn right into Wilton Ave) Good news for fans of this World War II code-breaking centre, featured in the Robert Harris novel *Enigma*: a recent heritage deal means that a high-tech museum should open in the D-block hut (where intelligence was gathered before D-day) within the next five years. During the war 12,000 men and women worked in and around the Victorian mansion, cracking German

codes. It now has a series of genuine, untouristy wartime exhibitions and displays, warmly praised by contributors. Some of the code-breaking bits are a little technical, but there's plenty more to see, inc a toy collection, landscaped grounds, wartime fire engines and a tank. Snacks, shop, disabled access; open alternate wknds; (01908) 640404; *£3.50. The Crooked Billet (Westbrook End, Newton Longville) has decent food.

BOARSTALL SP6214

! ⌲ ◠ **Boarstall Duck Decoy** Displays and working demonstrations of one of only three remaining 17th-c working duck decoys. Also woodland walks and nature trail. Open wknds and bank hols plus 4–7pm Weds, Apr–Aug; (01844) 237488; £2.10; NT. Brill is the nearest useful place for lunch.

BOOKER SU8390

♙ ✝ **Blue Max Collection** (Wycombe Air Park) The 15 or so aircraft here, include a 1917 Sopwith Camel and 1940 Battle of Britain Spitfire, are all veterans of films or TV, from *Indiana Jones* to *Poirot*. There are some displays of film props and memorabilia. Snacks, shop, disabled access; open Mon–Fri and Sun, April–Nov; (01494) 529432; £2.75. The Chequers at nearby Wheeler End seems a very appropriately chatty sort of place for lunch.

BRADENHAM SU8297

★ ⌲ ◠ This pretty village is surrounded by ancient woodland, with pleasant strolling possibilities.

BRILL SP6514

✗ ❄ ★ ◠ The **windmill** (open pm summer Suns) is in a magnificent position right on the edge of the Chilterns, with distant views across Oxford; there's been a mill on this site for over 700 years. In the distinctive and quietly attractive village the Pheasant (with a view of the windmill) is good for lunch. There's a decent walk up nearby Muswell Hill, or along the ridge and down to Boarstall.

BUCKINGHAM SP6934

Quite a lot of attractive early 18th-c brick buildings, and much of the nostalgic charm of a once important town that has been eclipsed by rivals (in this case Aylesbury and Milton Keynes).

The thatched Wheatsheaf out at Maids Moreton does good steaks.

♙ **Old Gaol Museum** (Market Hill) Lottery-funded improvements such as the glazing over of the exercise courtyard and a lift for disabled people should be completed by the time this small local history museum opens in Apr. Housed in an extraordinary early Gothic-Revival gaol, the museum has a good audio-visual show in an intact original cell. Shop, disabled access; open Mon–Sat April–Dec, plus pm Sun April–Sept; (01280) 823020; *£1.50.

BURNHAM BEECHES SU9485

⌲ ◠ A supreme example of a Chilterns beechwood, splendid in spring and autumn colours, and with maybe a glimpse of deer; maps are posted throughout the forest, but it is quite easy to lose one's bearings. The main starting-point is at East Burnham Common car park, opposite the west end of Beeches Rd at Farnham Common. There are several decent pubs dotted around the forest.

CHALFONT ST GILES TQ0193

↓✝ **Chiltern Open Air Museum** *See separate family panel on p.26.*

🏠♙✿ **Milton's Cottage** (Deanway) The writer brought his family to this timber-framed 16th-c cottage to escape the Plague in 1665, and while here completed *Paradise Lost* and began *Paradise Regained*. Displays of first editions, other rare books and memorabilia, and a charming cottage garden full of plants and flowers mentioned by Milton in his poetry. Shop, disabled access to ground floor; cl 1–2pm, all day Mon (exc bank hols), and Nov–Feb; (01494) 872313; *£2. The nearby White Hart (Three Households) has decent food.

CHENIES TQ0198

🏠✿ ✝ **Chenies Manor House** Rewarding 15th-c house with Tudor rooms, doll collection, tapestries, priest's hole, and 13th-c crypt; the gardens include a physic garden, herbs and a maze. Home-made teas, shop (good for dried flowers and herbs); open pm Weds, Thurs and bank hols Apr–Oct; (01494) 762888; £4.50 house and garden, £2.20 garden only. The neighbouring **church** has the rich family monuments of the Bedfords (viewed through a glass panel), 15th-c brasses, and a Norman font. The Red Lion is good for lunch.

CHESS VALLEY TQ0298

⌂ Shared between Bucks and Herts, this is miniature and unspoilt, and handily reached from Chalfont & Latimer station on the Metropolitan Underground line; Chenies and Latimer in Bucks, and Sarratt just over the Herts border, are the villages to head for.

CHETWODE SP6429

✝ **Chetwode church** A handsome church, notable for its fine Early English windows.

THE CHILTERNS SU7295

⌂ ⌘ ❋ The well wooded Chiltern Hills offer plenty of easy-going walks, with a good scattering of rural pubs and pretty villages, though sometimes you have to choose your path carefully to avoid the numerous suburban developments. Even so, it's easy to escape into idyllic landscapes which some rate above all others for weekend walks. The escarpment where the hills drop sharply down to the plain gives some very distant views, for instance from above Bledlow (good pub). The signposted Ridgeway takes in the most dramatic features.

CHURCH WOOD SU9786

⌘ ❧ On the edge of the immaculate village of Hedgerley, this is a **nature reserve** managed by the RSPB, with over 80 species of birds in 34 acres.

COOMBE HILL SP8506

❋ ⌘ ⌂ The highest point in the Chilterns, with its Boer War Memorial (an excellent place for views – and for kiteflying). Wendover Woods with some well marked nature trails are adjacent. The town of Wendover (the Red Lion Hotel here is walker-friendly) gives nearby access, or you can follow paths from Ellesborough and sneak views of Chequers, the Prime Minister's country retreat (emphatically private); an alternative path in is from Dunsmore.

FAWLEY SU7684

🏠 ✵ ⏀ **Fawley Court** Not the typical English stately home it appears to be; though it does boast some fine Wyatt interiors and an elaborate ceiling by Grinling Gibbons, it's owned by a Polish religious group, and has a unique museum dedicated to their homeland, particularly strong on Polish military history. The grounds (landscaped by Capability Brown) run down to the river, and you can stay here, B & B or half and full board. Shop, limited disabled access; open pm Weds, Thurs and Sun Mar–Oct (exc weeks of Easter and Whitsun); (01491) 574917; *£4. The Walnut Tree has very good food.

FINGEST SU7791

✝ ✗ **Fingest church** This brick and flint church is famous for its huge Norman tower with a twin saddleback roof. The Chequers opposite is nice for lunch, and, below the landmark windmill to the north, this is a particularly delectable valley – try the road round through Turville.

FORTY GREEN SU9291

🏠 **Royal Standard of England** The pub stands out as a quite remarkable old building, full of interesting furniture – crowded at weekends, it's well worth a quiet prowl during the week.

Days Out

Nature managed, manicured – and liberated: Odds Farm Park; Cliveden; picnic at Burnham Beeches; Church Wood nature reserve; (lunch options: Cliveden for the grand, Blackwood Arms, Littleworth Common, for the merry).

A stroll into hellfire: Chilterns woodland walk from Bradenham to West Wycombe, lunch at the George & Dragon there; West Wycombe Park, Hell Fire Caves.

Some Chilterns history: Chiltern Open-air Museum and Milton's Cottage, Chalfont St Giles; lunch at the Ivy House there; walk in Chess Valley.

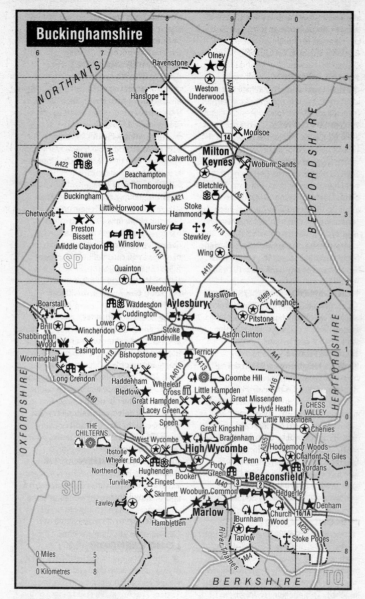

Buckinghamshire

NORTHANTS

Ravenstone
Olney
Weston Underwood
Hanslope
Moulsoe
Stowe
Calverton
Milton Keynes
Woburn Sands
Beachampton
Thornborough
Bletchley
Buckingham
Stoke Hammond
Chetwode
Little Horwood
Preston Bissett
Mursley
Stewkley
Middle Claydon
Winslow
Wing
Quainton
Weedon
Marsworth
Boarstall
Waddesdon
Aylesbury
Ivinghoe
Cuddington
Pitstone
Brill
Lower Winchendon
Stoke Mandeville
Shabbington Wood
Aston Clinton
Easington
Dinton
Terrick
Worminghall
Bishopstone
Long Crendon
Haddenham
Whiteleaf Cross
Coombe Hill
Bledlow
Little Hampden
Great Hampden
Great Missenden
Lacey Green
Hyde Heath
Little Missenden
Speen
Chenies
Great Kingshill
THE CHILTERNS
Bradenham
West Wycombe
Hodgemoor Woods
Ibstone
High Wycombe
Chalfont St Giles
Wheeler End
Penn
Jordans
Northend
Hughenden
Beaconsfield
Turville
Booker
Forty Green
Fingest
Hedgerley
Skirmett
Wooburn Common
Denham
Fawley
Marlow
Church Wood
Hambleden
Burnham
Taplow
Stoke Poges
River Thames
BERKSHIRE

BEDFORDSHIRE

HERTFORDSHIRE

OXFORDSHIRE

SP

SU

CHESS VALLEY

0 Miles 5
0 Kilometres 8

TQ

HADDENHAM SP7408
♈ St Tiggywinkles Wildlife Hospital Visitor Centre (Aston Road) A video system in the new visitor centre at this wildlife hospital allows you to watch the animals being treated without disturbing them. Outdoors there are gardens with enclosures for the animals that they can't release back into the wild, inc hedgehogs, ducks, badgers and foxes. Snacks, shop, disabled access; cl wknds Christmas–Easter; (01844) 292292; £1.50.

HAMBLEDEN SU7886
⌂ Thames Walk The footbridge over

the weir below the charming Chilterns village of Hambleden is attractive, and is the best starting-point on the Buckinghamshire bank for riverside walks.

HANSLOPE SP8046
† Hanslope church Attractive in its own right, but the most striking feature is its unusually tall spire.

HIGH WYCOMBE SU8593
Chair Museum (Castle Hill House) 18th-c house telling the history of the town's furniture industry which started with chair-making, using beechwood from the Chilterns. There's an unusual collection of various styles of chair produced nearby, as well as pretty landscaped gardens; new local history displays (inc hands-on exhibits) complete the museum's refurbishment. Shop; disabled access to ground floor; cl am Sun and all day bank hols; (01494) 421895; free.

HODGEMOOR WOODS SU9693
(W of Chalfont St Giles) This ancient woodland has three colour-coded nature trails, giving enjoyable walks of varying lengths.

HUGHENDEN SU8695
Hughenden Manor The home of Benjamin Disraeli until his death in 1881, this imposing old house still has many of the ex-Prime Minister's books and other possessions, as well as related memorabilia, portraits of friends, and formal gardens; he's buried in the grounds. Snacks, shop, some disabled access; open pm Weds–Sun and bank hol Mons, Apr–Oct, wknds only in Mar; (01494) 755565; £4.10, garden only £1.50, NT. The Red Lion at Great Kingshill does good fish lunches.

IVINGHOE TQ0120
★ Attractive old village giving its name to the 760-ft-high beacon hill above, with splendid views (especially to the north) and an Iron Age earthwork on top. The Rose & Crown does fresh bar lunches. This enclave is a fragment of Buckinghamshire almost encircled by Hertfordshire.
Ford End Watermill (Station Rd) 18th-c, the only remaining working watermill in the county. An unusual feature is the sheep wash, a special pool into which sheep were dropped and cleaned to make shearing easier. Shop;

mill only open this year on Sun 14 May, and at other times by appointment – phone (01582) 600391 to arrange; £1.

IVINGHOE BEACON SP9616
This is a protruding finger of the Chilterns, and the finish of the long-distance Ridgeway Path which begins in Wiltshire. The slopes, too steep for ploughing, comprise woodland, scrub and unspoilt downland; from the beacon itself you look down over eight counties. The Old Swan at Cheddington is the nearest good pub.

JORDANS SU9791
★ Interesting as a quiet tree-filled village built mainly this century in honour of the first 17th-c Quaker meeting-place here – a simple, evocative building. The nearby Mayflower Barn is built with timbers from the famous ship.

LACEY GREEN SP8100
Lacey Green Windmill (off A4010) The oldest surviving smock mill in the country, and indeed the third oldest windmill of any type, built in 1650 at Chesham and moved here in 1821. It's been well restored. Open pm Sun and bank hols May–Sept; (01844) 343560; 70p. The Pink & Lily does good food – and has kept its little tap room much as Rupert Brooke enjoyed it. Other well restored windmills can be seen at nearby Pitstone and Loosley Row. The mill at Ibstone is unusual for having 12 sides.

LITTLE MISSENDEN SU9298
† ★ The **church** of this pretty village has some wall paintings from the 12th c and some pre-Norman traces, and the village itself has charming old timbered and tiled houses. The attractive old Crown does good sandwiches.

LONG CRENDON SP6909
★ The cottages in the High St are very pretty, some little changed since the village was a rich wool centre in the 15th c. The Angel is a good dining pub.
Courthouse A particularly lovely timber-framed building, early 15th-c; probably built as a wool store. Open wknds, bank hols and pm Weds, Apr–Sept; £1; NT. There are snacks in the nearby church house.

LOWER WINCHENDON SP7312
★ † ✿ This secluded old place has

carefully restored houses and a charming, simple church – the walk over the hill to Upper Winchendon gives interesting views.

MARLOW SU8586

⚓ **Thames Boating** Marlow Reach is lively and attractive, and a good centre for trips in either direction. Salters (01865) 243421 operate 40-minute cruises May–Sept, £3.75. The Compleat Angler right on the river is a fine place for lunch; on a humbler plane, the Two Brewers back over the bridge and the Hare & Hounds out towards Henley are good bets.

MARSWORTH SP9114

◌ **Canalside walk** Marsworth gives good towpath access to an imposing flight of locks; there's a useful family pub at Startops End.

MIDDLE CLAYDON SP7125

🏛 **Claydon House** The wonderfully over-the-top rococo décor is the prime attraction of this mainly 18th-c house (featured in BBC's *Vanity Fair*) – quite a surprise given the classical simplicity of the exterior. Highlights are the carvings by Luke Lightfoot and the fantastic walls, ceilings and overmantels, though there are also portraits by Lely and Van Dyck, and mementos of Florence Nightingale, a frequent guest. The original owner's tastes were considerably richer than his pockets; but though his ambitious plans for the house eventually bankrupted him, his family still live here. Snacks, disabled access to ground floor; open pm Sat-Weds Apr–Oct; (01296) 730349; £4.10; NT. The Seven Stars between Twyford and Calvert is a pleasant place for lunch.

MILTON KEYNES SP8239

Britain's largest New Town is perhaps also the most successful example of the idea, with roads well laid out to keep traffic moving easily and well away from pedestrians, and a lot of greenery. Locals are proud of the remarkable number of public sculptures dotted around, from the endearing Wounded Elephant, to the famous concrete cows in a field on the N side of the H3 road (Monks Way, or A422) nr the A5 junction. There's a very swish shopping centre at Midsummer Boulevard, named for its alignment with the summer solstice. Tucked around the city are various villagey corners, and the Swan (Broughton Rd in the Old Village) and canalside Black Horse at Great Linford are both pleasant retreats for lunch.

🏛👶♿🍴 **City Discovery Centre** (Bradwell Abbey) Tells you all you could need to know about the New Town development (lots of slides, maps and old photographs), in a 16th-c farmhouse in the 17-acre grounds of a former abbey. Also, a 14th-c barn and chapel, medieval fishponds, herb gardens and nature trail. Meals, snacks, shop, disabled access; open wknds Apr–Sept, and all year Mon-Fri, but advisable to phone in advance to avoid large school groups; (01908) 227229; free.

☺ **Gulliver's Land** (Newlands, junction14 of M1) Like its sister ventures in Matlock Bath and Warrington (see *Derbyshire and Lancashire chapters*), this new theme park, designed around Swift's classic story, is aimed at under-13s. As well as fairground-style entertainment, rides include a log flume, pirate ship and magic carpet ride. Meals, snacks, shop, disabled access; open wknds Easter–Jun, daily Jun–mid-Sept; (01908) 609001; £8.

🚂 **Milton Keynes Museum** (McConnell Drive, H2 Millers Way, Wolverton) Includes Victorian and Edwardian room settings, a school-room, a steamtram, print shop and a transport hall. A Victorian Christmas week (pm) starts on the first Sat in Dec. Snacks, shop, disabled access; open pm Weds–Sun, Easter–Oct; £3.

♿🕊 **Willen Lakeside Park** (Brickhill St, SP8241) Has two lakes – one with water sports, hotel and restaurant, and the other for birdwatching; also a Japanese peace pagoda built by Buddhist monks, turf maze, and a nature trail.

OLNEY SP8851

★ Pleasant stone-built extended village with a Thursday market and a nice riverside stroll to the Robin Hood at Clifton Reynes; the Bull, HQ for the town's famous Shrove Tuesday pancake race, is an alternative for lunch, as are the Swan and Two Brewers.

♨ **Cowper and Newton Museum** (Market Pl) Enthusiastically run, in the former home of hymn-writer William Cowper. Several of his personal possessions, manuscripts and poems are on display, along with some belonging to his friend John Newton, curate of Olney and composer of *Amazing Grace*. There's a notable lace-making exhibition, and a restored period summerhouse in the little garden. Shop, limited disabled access to garden; cl 1–2 pm all Sun and Mon, and Christmas–Feb; (01234) 711516; £2.

PITSTONE SP9416

♨ † ✕ ⚱ As well as a decent little **agricultural museum** (open some summer Suns and bank hols, (01296) 662151) and an interesting old **church**, this small village has the oldest **windmill** in the country, built in 1627. Open pm Sun and bank hols Jun–Aug; £1, NT. You can hire canal boats for a day from the Wharf (over the B489), and there are pleasant canal walks from there to the Red Lion or White Lion at Marsworth.

QUAINTON SP7419

🚂 **Bucks Railway Centre** (Quainton Rd Station) One of the largest collections of engines and rolling stock we know of, with examples from all over the world attractively displayed in a restored country station; also vintage steamtrain rides, workshops, miniature railway, and small museum. Regular half-day steam driving courses (not cheap at £155, but people come away converted for life). Snacks, picnic area, shop; open Sun and bank hols Easter–Oct, plus Weds July–Aug and some wknds in Dec; (01296) 655720; £3.50 (£4.50 bank hols). The Five Arrows at Waddesdon is the closest good place for lunch.

❋ ⌂ **Quainton Hill** This prominent viewpoint is one of the main features on the 30-mile North Bucks Way, a long distance footpath from Chequers Knap above Great Kimble to Wolverton in Milton Keynes; the Way also runs past Waddesdon.

✕ **Quainton Tower Mill** Particularly tall 19th-c mill on the edge of the village green; you can watch the continuing restoration work. Open am Sun and bank hols; (01296) 655348; £1.50.

SHABBINGTON WOOD SP6210

🦋 (nr Oakley) This has been designated a Site of Special Scientific Interest because of its rich butterfly habitats; a special butterfly trail has been created to help you spot some of the 40-odd species here.

† ❗ **STEWKLEY** SP8426

The **church** in this unusually long village has good examples of late Norman work; the village also has two decent pubs, and hour-long **balloon trips** over the whole county; (01525) 240451; £130 per person.

STOKE MANDEVILLE SP8309

🐐 **Bucks Goat Centre** (Layby Farm, just off A4010) Goats galore as well as a pig, poultry, sheep, donkeys and pets; you can feed the animals (they sell bags of cut up vegetables in the shop.) Many animals are under cover, so good for a rainy day. Donkey rides most weekends. Also plant nursery, farm shop (with cheese and fudge made from goats' milk), pet shop and a specialist motor bike shop. Meals, snacks, shop, disabled access; cl Mon (exc bank hols); (01296) 612983; £2.50. The Chequers over at Weston Turville does good lunches.

🐐 **Oak Farm Rare Breeds Park** (off A41, eastern edge of Aylesbury) Friendly little working farm, with animals to feed, walks and nature trails. Snacks, shop, disabled access; open Weds–Sun (plus bank hol Mons) mid-Feb–Oct; (01296) 415709; £2.50. The Chequers in Weston Turville has enjoyable food.

STOKE POGES SU9782

† **Stoke Poges church** The grave-yard inspired Thomas Gray's elegy (he's buried here); the church has 17th-c stained heraldic glass in the 16th-c chapel.

STOWE SP6737

❀ 🏛 **Stowe Landscape Gardens** Stunning gardens stretching over a staggering 580 acres, first laid out between 1713 and 1725. Capability Brown was head gardener for 10 years, and the monuments and temples that adorn the grounds are by the likes of James Gibb, Sir John Vanbrugh and William Kent. Several suitably grand events throughout the year, but at any time this is a spectacular place to visit, the scale of its artistry quite staggering.

Meals, snacks, shop, disabled access (inc electric-powered cars at no extra charge). Open daily during school hols (inc over Christmas), plus Mon, Weds, Fri and Sun mid-Apr–Oct; (01280) 822850; £4.50; NT. The house itself (a public school since 1923) is open pm daily (exc some wknds) during the Easter and summer hols (phone to check extra opening times this year). You may feel it's outclassed by its surroundings, though it is very elegant from the outside; *£2. The Bull & Butcher at Akeley has a good-value buffet lunch (not Sun, when the Wheatsheaf at Maids Moreton would be a good substitute).

TAPLOW SU9185

❀ ⌁ ⌂ ★ **Cliveden** Nearly 400 acres of lovely formal gardens, woodland and parkland overlooking the Thames. The magnificent house used to belong to the Astors and is now a luxury hotel (and extremely enjoyable as such), although non-resident visitors can see three of the rooms with their family portraits and elegant furnishings and décor. Meals and snacks (not Mon or Tues), shop, very good disabled access; gardens open daily mid-Mar–Dec, house open only Thurs and Sun Apr–Oct from 3–6pm; (01628) 605069; £5, house £1 extra; NT. The village too is attractive.

TERRICK SP8308

⌂ **Chiltern Brewery** Small traditional brewery with guided tours at noon every Sat. Shop, disabled access; cl Sun, 25–26 Dec, 1 Jan; tour *£3.50.

THORNBOROUGH BRIDGE SP7433

⌂ (A421) A 4½-mile walk starting and ending here, and well described in a leaflet from Bucks County Council, takes in a mill, the site of a medieval village, and the Buckingham Arm Canal. Leaflets (25p) from information centres, or from the County Hall; (01280) 823020.

WADDESDON SP7316

⌂ ❀ **Waddesdon Manor** The most spectacular of the mansions built for Baron Ferdinand de Rothschild. Plenty of rooms to see, each as lavish as the last, and filled with a dazzling array of furnishings, porcelain, portraits, and other objects; there's an unrivalled display of Sèvres china. Parts of the Bachelors' Wing are now fully restored and other improvement work continues. Quite splendid late Victorian formal gardens surround the house, and there's a cast-iron rococo aviary (still in use). The fabled wine cellars have huge vintage bottles, and a collection of labels designed or painted by some of the century's greatest artists. A very satisfying place to visit, but it does get busy; they operate a timed ticket system for the house (can be bought in advance, but £2.50 booking charge), so if you arrive too late it's possible you won't get in at all. Good meals and snacks, shop, disabled access; house open Thurs–Sun, Apr–Oct, plus Weds and bank hols in July and Aug, grounds open Weds–Sun Mar–20 Dec; (01296) 651282; £7, Bachelors' Wing £1, £3 grounds only; NT. No under-5s in house. The Five Arrows does very good lunches (and has some fine Rothschild wines in all price ranges).

WEEDON SP8118

★ This is a lovely little village, well worth walking around for the variety of its 17th- and 18th-c houses.

WEST WYCOMBE SU8294

★ ⌂ The whole village was bought by the NT in 1929 when it was threatened with road-widening. It's still beleaguered by traffic, and you risk getting run over as you step back to admire the architecture along the village street – all the sites we mention are just off-street. The busy George & Dragon is useful for lunch. A visit to the caves and village here can be easily combined with a walk into the beechwoods just N; the pretty village of Bradenham makes a good objective for longer circular walks.

❦ ! **Hell Fire Caves** Great fun, these spooky old caves were extended in the 1750s by Sir Francis Dashwood to provide work for the unemployed. Legend has it that the Hell Fire Club he founded met in the tunnels for their drinking, whoring and sorcery. Once through the atmospheric Gothic entrance the tunnels extend for about a third of a mile underground, and are filled with colourful models and tableaux. Underground café, shop; cl wkdys Nov–Feb; *£4.

† ❀ **St Lawrence Church** On the site of an Iron Age fort, adapted by Dashwood, and crowned with a golden ball so big (it can seat six people) that it too served as a meeting-place for the Hell Fire Club. The view from the top of the tower is impressive, and the church's interior has a number of unusual features.

🏛 ❀ **West Wycombe Park** 300 acres of beautifully laid out parkland surround this splendid 18th-c Palladian house, currently closed for refurbishment. The magnificent rooms have a good collection of tapestries, furniture and paintings, and the Italianate painted ceilings are particularly notable. Tel for opening times and prices (01628) 488675; NT.

WESTON UNDERWOOD SP8650

🌱 🐘 ❀ **Flamingo Gardens and Zoological Park** Not just flamingos, but a notable collection of rare and endangered birds from all over the world, inc unusual pink-backed pelicans, vultures, cockatoos and toucans. Also mammals such as bison, llamas and a unique herd of white wallabies. William Cowper wrote many of his poems in the area now patrolled by peacocks and cranes, and extracts appear on several of the statues and urns. Popular with readers, the staff are particularly helpful. Shop; disabled access, open pm Weds–Sun and bank hols May–Jun and Sept, pm daily July and Aug; (01234) 711451; *£4.50. The village is attractive, with Cowpers Oak good value for lunch.

WHITELEAF CROSS SP8203

🏛 A large ancient hill cross dug out of the chalk on the Chilterns escarpment, above which is a Neolithic barrow. The Red Lion below is nice for lunch, and the houses of the surrounding hamlet are quite pretty.

WING SP8922

🏛 🖼 ❀ † **Ascott** Another Rothschild mansion, its black and white timbers and jutting gables quite a contrast to the luxuriant opulence of nearby Waddesdon. Once again it's crammed full of treasures, but it feels more like a home and less like a museum; indeed it's still lived in. Ming and K'ang Hsi porcelain, paintings by Hogarth, Rubens and Gainsborough, Dutch art by Hobbema, Cuyp and others, and French and Chippendale furniture. The 260-acre grounds have extensive gardens with rare trees and shrubs, and some intriguing astrological topiary. Open Apr and Sept, pm Tues–Sun, plus garden only May–Aug, Weds and last Sun in month; (01296) 688242; £5.60 (£4 garden only), NT. **All Saints Church** has a fine monument to Sir Robert Dormer (died 1552), a 10th-c apse, crypt and nave, and a 12th-c font. The Queen's Head has good-value home cooking.

WINSLOW SP7627

† **Keach's Meeting House** Fine example of a 17th-c dissenters' chapel, nr the market square; you'll need to get the key from Wilkinson's the estate agent on Market Sq, or from Mrs Williams; (01296) 715746. The Bell is useful for lunch.

🏛 **Winslow Hall** Striking house almost certainly designed by Wren, and unusually surviving without any major structural changes. A modest but friendly place, with a collection of Chinese art. Open pm bank hol wknds, Easter–Aug, plus pm Weds and Thurs, July and Aug, or by appointment; (01296) 712323; £5.

WOOBURN COMMON SU9387

🐖 **Odds Farm Park** Cheery rare breeds centre developed with children in mind. They can go right up to the rare breeds, and join in bottle-feeding the lambs, hand-milking the goats, or collecting the chickens' eggs. Younger children can pet rabbits and guinea-pigs in the pets corner, while older ones can learn a lot about farm life – displays are instructive as well as fun; also quite a bit of thought has gone into the indoor and outdoor play areas. Special events range from sheepdog demonstrations to parachuting teddy bears! Snacks, shop, disabled access; cl 25–26 Dec, and Mon–Weds mid-Nov–Feb; (01628) 520188; £3.75 (£2.75 children over 2).

★ **Other attractive villages**, all with decent pubs, include Beachampton SP7737 (stream along main street), Bishopstone SP8010 (pleasant country walks), Bledlow SP7702 (great views; Norman church with early wall paintings), Calverton SP7939, Cuddington SP7311, Denham TQ0386,

Dinton SP7611, Great Missenden SP8901, Hedgerley SU9686, Hyde Heath SU9399, Ibstone SU7593, Little Hampden SP8503, Little Horwood SP7930, Marlow SU8586, Northend SU7392, Penn SU9193 (interesting church), Preston Bissett SP6529, Ravenstone SP8450, Speen SU8399, Stoke Hammond SP8829, Turville SU7690 (perhaps the most lovely valley of all here) and Worminghall SP6308.

Where to eat

EASINGTON SP6810 **Mole & Chicken** *(01844) 208387* Bustling country dining pub with a very attractively furnished, beamed bar, winter log fires, candles on tables and a relaxed atmosphere; particularly good food served by neatly dressed young staff, and a fine range of drinks; cl 25 Dec; disabled access. **£24|£7**.

GREAT HAMPDEN SP8401 **Hampden Arms** *(01494) 488255* Comfortable two-room country pub by the cricket green; with civilised atmosphere, interesting, reasonably priced food, real ales, quietly obliging service, and a tree-sheltered garden; good for nearby walks; partial disabled access. **£20|£4.95**.

GREAT KINGSHILL SU8798 **Red Lion** *(01494) 711262* Little brick and flint cottage with simple furnishings, very fresh fish from Billingsgate served by the friendly Spanish landlord and his staff, and good house wines; cl Mon. **£20|£8**.

GREAT MISSENDEN SP8900 **George** *(01494) 862084* Attractive 15th-c inn originally built as a hospice for the nearby abbey; with beams, alcoves, and a big log fire in the cosy two-roomed bar, interesting daily specials, huge Sun roast, no smoking restaurant, and prompt, cheerful service; pretty bdrms; cl pm Sun, pm 25–26 Dec. **£16.50|£6**.

HADDENHAM SP7408 **Green Dragon** *(01844) 291403* Civilised dining pub with particularly imaginative food in its two attractively decorated, high-ceilinged rooms; a French brasserie-type atmosphere, well chosen wines, real ales, a winter log fire, and seats outside on the big sheltered terrace; cl pm Sun children over 6; disabled access. **£29.50|£8.75**.

LITTLE HAMPDEN SP8503 **Rising Sun** *(01494) 488393* Secluded upmarket dining pub surrounded by fine walks; with consistently excellent and interesting food, a short but decent wine list, real ales, and an attractive terrace; bdrms; cl pm Sun, Mon (open am bank hols); disabled access. **£23|£4.95**.

LONG CRENDON SP6908 **Angel** *Bicester Rd (01844) 208268* Carefully restored and civilised partly 17th-c dining pub with big sofas in the comfortable lounge, very good interesting food in both the bar and no smoking conservatory dining room, real ales, and friendly staff; cl pm Sun. **£28.50|£6.95**.

LONG CRENDON SP6908 **Churchill Arms** *(01844) 208344* Cheery village pub with over 50 kinds of sausages – all properly made with no artificial ingredients, and notes on the menu to say which sausage is best accompanied by beer or wine, and a good range of drinks too, inc well kept ales; the nicest part for eating is in a neat room to the left of the entrance with a big fireplace – to the right is a comfortable drinking area with newspapers and fresh flowers. **£5.95**.

MOULSOE SP9041 **Carrington Arms** *(01908) 218050* Well refurbished old brick house with comfortable traditional furnishings, delicious meat and fish displayed in a refrigerated glass case, with friendly staff who guide you through what is on offer (it is then sold in pounds and ounces and cooked on a sophisticated indoor barbecue); separate bar menu as well, an oyster bar, well kept real ales, a decent range of wines inc champagne by the glass, and good coffee; bdrms; disabled access. **£25|£6**.

PRESTON BISSETT SP6529 **White Hart** *(01280) 847969* Friendly 18th-c thatched and timbered house with three cosy little rooms, traditional atmosphere and furnishings, tasty often interesting bar food inc lunchtime snacks, real ales and a dozen malt whiskies; helpful staff. **£21.35|£6.95**.

SKIRMETT SU7790 **Frog** *(01491) 638996* Brightly modernised country inn with the atmosphere of a smart rural local, a mix of comfortable furnishings and an open fire in the neat beamed bar area; good, popular and interesting food, efficient service, no smoking restaurant, real ales, a fair range of wines, and lovely garden; bdrms. **£21.45|£8.95**.

WEST WYCOMBE SU8394 **George & Dragon** High St *(01494) 464414* Striking, partly Tudor inn with a cheerful bustling atmosphere in the rambling main bar, big log fire, popular food inc very good home-made pies, and a big peaceful garden; bdrms (not Christmas, New Year or Easter). **£20|£7.25**.

WHEELER END SU8093 **Chequers** *(01494) 883070* Pleasant old pub with welcoming licensees, a good inglenook, simple furnishings, and small hunting prints in the little bar; good-value homely bar food, and well kept real ales; cl pm Sun, Mon; disabled access. **£16.50|£5**.

WOBURN SANDS SP9235 **Spooners** *61 High St (01908) 584385* Smart, pretty restaurant with good-value French and English cooking, and a welcoming atmosphere; worthwhile snacks downstairs; cl Sun, Mon, Christmas; disabled access. **£15 lunch, £30 dinner|£8**.

Special thanks to Mrs C Dewell.

Buckinghamshire Calendar

Some of these dates were provisional as we went to press. Please check information with the telephone numbers provided.

FEBRUARY

13 **Milton Keynes** Brass Band Festival at Stantonbury Leisure Centre (01908) 510809

MARCH

7 **Olney** Pancake Race: since 1455 (01234) 712176

APRIL

23 **Quainton** Circus Weekend at Bucks Railway Centre – *till 24 April* (01296) 655720
29 **Chalfont St Giles** Live Craft Show at Chiltern Open-air Museum – *till 1 May* (01494) 871117
30 **High Wycombe** Carnival (01494) 522808; **Quainton** Miniature Railway Gala at Bucks Railway Centre – *till 1 May* (01296) 655720

MAY

1 **Bradwell** May Day at Bradwell Windmill: Fête with maypole dancing, Morris Men, bands and stalls (01908) 651263; **Marlow** Millennium Spring Regatta (01628) 477787; **Pitstone** Pitstone Green Farm Museum Open Day (01296) 661997; **Quainton** May Day Fair (01296) 655348; **Wendover** Whitchurch Morris Men at Coombe Hill at 6.30am (01865) 766191
7 **High Wycombe** Carnival (01494) 422104
18 **High Wycombe** Mayor-making and Weighing at the Guildhall (01494) 421134
28 **Quainton** Veterans' Cycle Rally at Bucks Railway Centre (01296) 655720
29 **Quainton** Bus Rally at Bucks Railway Centre (01296) 655720

Buckinghamshire Calendar (cont.)

JUNE

4 Milton Keynes National Bagpipe Annual Festival – *till 6 June* (01327) 705265

9 Quainton Thomas the Tank Engine and Friends at Bucks Railway Centre – *till 11 June* (01296) 655720

11 Pitstone Pitstone Green Farm Museum Open Day (01296) 661997; **Stony Stratford**: Music Festival – *till 17 June* (01908) 566407; also, Folk on the Green (01908) 565653

16 Great Linford Waterside Festival: free theatre, music events and park entertainments – *till 18 June* (01908) 608108

17 Marlow Millennium Regatta in Higginson Park (01628) 477787

18 Marlow Millennium Musical (01628) 483597

23 Stokenchurch Festival 2000 with celebrity show, carnival, procession and static displays – *till 26 June* (01628) 477787

24 Milton Keynes City Spectacular and Carnival at Campbell Park – *till 25 June* (01908) 651259

30 Milton Keynes International Festival – *till 2 July* (01908) 610564 and City Spectacular in Campbell Park – *till 2 July* (01908) 870284; **Newport Pagnell** Festive Fortnight – *till 16 July* (01908) 610526

JULY

1 Aylesbury Massed Morris Men in Market Sq, *10am* (01865) 766191; **Milton Keynes** Floral Fiesta Week (01234) 241076; **Stowe** North Buckinghamshire Show at Stowe Park (01280) 821191

9 Flackwell Heath Millennium Event (01628) 523599; **Pitstone** Pitstone Green Farm Museum Open Day (01296) 661997

14 West Wycombe Millennium Festival – *till 16 July* (01494) 461000

15 Burnham Carnival at Burnham Park (01628) 605772; **Newport Pagnell** Carnival – *till 16 July* (01908) 617903; **Stony Stratford** Blues and Jazz Festival (01908) 563307

16 Silverstone British Grand Prix at Silverstone Circuit (01327) 857177

25 Marlow Children's Giant Party (01628) 484024

AUGUST

12 Milton Keynes Festival of Flight at Campbell Park (01908) 397190

13 Pitstone Pitstone Green Farm Museum Open Day (01296) 661997

14 Rye Asian Mela festival: Asian cultural event accessible to every member of the community; music, theatre, sport, food and exhibitions – *till 15 August* (01628) 477787

27 Quainton Veteran Car Event at Bucks Railway Centre – *till 28 August* (01296) 655720

28 Pitstone Pitstone Green Farm Museum Open Day (01296) 661997; **Stony Stratford** Town Fair: stalls, Morris dancers, children's events (01908) 563143; **Winslow** Show: parade, horses and horticultural show (01280) 823020

31 Weedon Buckinghamshire County Show at Weedon Park (0860) 394495

Buckinghamshire Calendar (cont.)

SEPTEMBER

 2 **High Wycombe** Millennium Show (01494) 532229
 9 **Quainton** Thomas the Tank Engine and Friends at Bucks Railway Centre
   – *till 10 September* (01296) 655720
10 **Marlow** Millennium 'Best of British' Grand Prix Raft Race in Higginson
   Park (01628) 477787; **Pitstone** Pitstone Green Farm Museum Open Day
   (01296) 661997
11 **Thame** Agricultural Show – *till 14 September* (01844) 212737
16 **Marlow** Millennium Carnival (01628) 477787
17 **Quainton** Fire Engine Rally at Bucks Railway Centre (01296) 655720;
   Wolverton Fête (01908) 563143

NOVEMBER

 4 **Milton Keynes** Fireworks in Campbell Park (01908) 870284
 5 **Downley** Torchlight Procession and Bonfire (01494) 421892
11 **Fenny Stratford** Firing the Poppers: since 1730 in celebration of St
   Martin, patron saint of Fenny Stratford church. Poppers are quart-size
   metal vessels filled with gunpowder and fired with a hot rod (01908)
   372825

DECEMBER

 9 **Quainton** Santa Steaming – *till 10 December*; also *16–17 December*,
   23–24 December (01296) 655720

We welcome reports from readers

This *Guide* depends on readers' reports. Do help us if you can – in return, we offer a discount on the next edition to people who've helped us with reports for it. Tell us what you think about places already in it, and anything extra you think we should say about them. And send us your ideas for inclusion in the next edition: places to visit, eat at or stay in, attractive drives or walks, maybe even unusual interesting shops you know of. Use the card in the middle, the report forms at the end, or just write – no stamp needed: *The Good Britain Guide*, FREEPOST TN1569, Wadhurst, E Sussex TN5 7BR.

CAMBRIDGESHIRE

A lot to see and do, for all ages and most tastes; Cambridge city is great for a short visit, with plenty of interest as well as its world-class museums.

The city of Cambridge is arguably Britain's most attractive ancient university city, graceful and charming, with plenty of interest to fill a short stay – and it's an easy day out from London. Its museums are not only outstanding but also mainly free. We have added several new places to visit here this year. The city is at its best during the university terms, when the college students put life and context into the medieval lanes, buildings and gardens. In summer, when it is host instead to foreign language students, its popularity with coach tours means that particular places can suddenly overflow with visitors, so perhaps the best time of all is spring or autumn. Spring is a particular delight in the University Botanic Garden. In winter, like the rest of the county, it can be very chill.

Elsewhere, newcomers to this edition of the *Guide* are the Raptor Foundation at Woodhurst (hundreds of birds of prey), the haunting American War Cemetery at Coton, Elgoods Brewery in the attractive old town of Wisbech, and medieval Denny Abbey at Chittering, with its associated village reconstructions.

Stately Wimpole Hall and its friendly farm wrap together plenty of variety for a good day out. The Duxford Air Museum goes from strength to strength; flying history on a massive scale, right up to the present. Linton Zoo is another first-class family attraction, and the Nene Valley Railway is also an enjoyable family outing. Flag Fen just east of Peterborough is intriguing for anyone interested in the Iron Age and Stone Age. Some great wildlife reserves include Wicken Fen and parts of Grafham Water, and the waterfowl at Peakirk have some enthusiastic admirers. Older people like quiet Ely with its graceful cathedral and most unusual stained-glass museum, Anglesey Abbey at Lode, and Elton Hall. There are some lovely villages to stroll through, often with fine churches.

The countryside is a touch monotonous – especially the north's flat silt fens and vast level fields. But there are those who love the misty bleakness in autumn, say, and this area has a lot to offer birdwatchers. To the west, the land's drier and more rolling, with stonebuilt villages more reminiscent of Leicestershire.

Cambridgeshire's tourist information centres are among the best – very helpful with information, maps and trails.

Where to stay

CAMBRIDGE TL4658 **Arundel House** *53 Chesterton Rd CB4 3AN (01223) 367701* **£87.90;** 105 comfortable rms, 3 without bthrm, some overlooking the river. Carefully preserved terrace of fine early Victorian houses overlooking the River Cam and parkland; comfortable, attractive bar with two fires, elegant restaurant, large and airy plant-filled conservatory, good imaginative food, and seats in the pleasant garden.

CAMBRIDGE TL4658 **Cambridge Lodge** *Huntingdon Rd, Cambridge CB3 0DQ* *(01223) 352833* ***£80;** 14 rms, 10 with own bthrm. Mock Tudor house on the outskirts; with an open fire in the relaxed and comfortable lounge, friendly service, and good freshly prepared food in the popular restaurant; cl 26–30 Dec.

DUXFORD TL4745 **Duxford Lodge** *Ickleton Rd, Duxford, Cambridge CB2 4RU* *(01223) 836444* **£85w;** 15 good-sized rms. Carefully run Victorian hotel in an acre of neatly kept gardens; with a restful little lounge, spacious bar, relaxed atmosphere, and enjoyable modern cooking in the airy, no smoking restaurant; cl 25 Dec–3 Jan.

ELY TL5380 **Lamb** *2 Lynn Rd, Ely CB7 4EJ (01353) 663574* ***£88;** 32 comfortable rms. Pleasant, neatly kept old coaching inn nr the cathedral; two smart bars, enjoyable food in an attractive restaurant, very friendly staff, and good car parking.

HUNTINGDON TL2371 **Old Bridge** *1 High St, Huntingdon PE18 6TQ (01480) 452681* **£89.50,** plus wknd breaks; 25 excellent rms. Creeper-covered Georgian hotel with pretty lounge, log fire in panelled bar, imaginative British cooking and extensive wine list in the partly no smoking restaurant and more informal lunchtime room (nice murals), and quick courteous service; riverside gardens; cl pm 25 Dec.

LITTLE GRANSDEN TL2754 **Gransden Lodge** *Farm Little Gransden, Sandy, Beds SG19 3EB (01767) 677365* **£40;** 4 rms. Set on a working farm of 860 acres with pedigree Gelbwieh cattle, this friendly house has a big lounge, dining room, and gardens with fish ponds; no evening meals (plenty of pubs and restaurants locally).

NEEDINGWORTH TL3472 **Pike & Eel** *Needingworth, St Ives, Huntingdon PE17 3TW (01480) 463336* **£70;** 9 rms. Very peaceful riverside spot with spacious lawns and marina; roomy plush bar, big open fire and easy chairs in smaller room, glass-walled restaurant, carvery, real ale, good breakfasts, and friendly staff.

SIX MILE BOTTOM TL5757 **Swynford Paddocks** *Six Mile Bottom, Newmarket, Suffolk CB8 0UE (01638) 570234* **£127,** plus wknd breaks; 15 individually furnished rms with good bthrms. Gabled mansion in neat grounds; carefully furnished, panelled rooms, fresh flowers and log fires, a relaxed atmosphere, good food, and friendly service; tennis, putting, croquet, and giant chess.

STILTON TL1689 **Bell** *High St, Stilton, Peterborough PE7 3RA (01733) 241066* ***£66.50;** 19 rms. Elegant, carefully restored coaching inn with attractive rambling bars, big log fire, generous helpings of good food using the famous cheese (which was first sold from here), and seats in the sheltered cobbled and flagstoned courtyard; cl 25 Dec; disabled access.

WANSFORD TL0799 **Haycock** *Wansford, Peterborough PE8 6JA (01780) 782223* **£120w,** plus special breaks; 50 attractively decorated rms. Old-fashioned golden stone inn with relaxed, comfortable, carefully furnished lounges and pubby bar; pretty lunchtime café, smart restaurant with good food, excellent wines and efficient, friendly service; garden with boules, fishing and cricket; disabled access. The little village it dominates is attractive, with a fine bridge over the Nene, and a good antique shop.

To see and do

CAMBRIDGESHIRE Family Attraction of the Year

🐾 🏠 ⚘ ⌂ WIMPOLE TL3350 **Wimpole Hall & Home Farm** (off A603) The varied attractions at this huge estate can easily fill most of a day. It's the farm that children like best, its thatched and timbered buildings designed by Sir John Soane when it was at the forefront of agricultural innovation; it remains a working stock farm today. A restored barn shows off machinery and tools from those days, and there are plenty of farm animals, including various rare breeds. Children can usually handle some of the animals, and you can buy feed from the ticket office. They have separate play areas for older and younger children – smaller visitors can get quite attached to the mini pedal tractors. As ever on a farm, be prepared for mud if it's been raining. The heavy-horse wagon rides are popular, running the short distance to the mainly 18th-c house, one of the most striking mansions in the whole of East Anglia. Behind its imposing and harmonious Georgian façade is a lovely trompe l'oeil chapel ceiling, and rooms by James Gibbs and Sir John Soane. Perfect for a relaxing stroll, the gardens are good for spring daffodils and summer roses; a walled garden is currently being restored, and they hold the National Walnut Collection. Best of all perhaps are the 360 acres of parkland, designed by several different notable landscapers including Capability Brown and Repton; the remains of a medieval village are under the pasture. There's a good programme of concerts and events throughout the year, ranging from lambing weekends and children's fun days to evening jazz with fireworks. Dogs are welcome in the park, but not on the farm. Meals and snacks (and picnic area), shops, some disabled access (not to house). The hall is open only Mar–Oct, pm wknds and Tues–Thurs, plus bank hols and pm Fri in Aug. The farm is open the same times, plus mornings, wknds in winter, and Fris in July; (01223) 207257; £8 hall, farm and garden (£4 children); NT. You can buy tickets for just the hall (£5.70 adults, £2.50 children) or to the farm (£4.50, £2.50 children). The surrounding park is open all year, with walkers welcomed free of charge to the extensive paths and tracks through its farmland and woodland, past a folly and up to a surprisingly elevated ridge path.

BARNACK TF0704

★ ✂ † Barnack has interesting dotted-about clusters of stone-built houses, a **windmill**, a part-Saxon **church**, and a fine pub (the Millstone).

BARRINGTON TL3949

★ Superb village green surrounded by pretty timbered houses, an interesting church and a good pub; the nearby village of Foxton is especially interesting if you know the book *The Common Stream* by Rowland Parker (an intricate account of the village through the ages).

BOURN TL3158

✂ The working **windmill** here is thought to be the oldest trestle post mill in the country. Usually open pm last Sun of month, Mar–Oct; (01223) 243830; £1. The Duke of Wellington has good food.

BURWELL TL5866

† ✂ **Burwell church & windmill** This handsome and airy building has a fine oak roof. The village also has a restored windmill.

CAMBRIDGE TL4458

Quieter and prettier than Oxford (which the colleges here were founded to escape), the centre is dominated by ancient and graceful university buildings: you get a real sense of centuries of study. It still has the character of a small, old-fashioned market town, almost untouched by the modern world; Cambridge's hi-tech light industry is kept firmly on the outskirts. Between the colleges and university buildings are numerous less imposing but attractive old buildings, often grouped together quite picturesquely. The architecture has a striking diversity (continuous development of the colleges means that most have much-loved or maligned modern blocks), though isn't always shown off at its best, thanks to layers of muck and grime that rather spoil some of the libraries and faculty buildings. Happily, one of the most delightful parts of town, **The Backs**, where the river snakes through the colleges, never looks less than charming, with its delightful lawns, trees, college gardens, punts gliding past the weeping willows and sometimes even grazing cattle opposite King's. Don't try to drive around town; there really is no parking, and apart from the pedestrianised centre there's a frustrating tangle of congested one-way streets. Head for one of the big NCPs. If you don't plan to take a car at all, it's worth noting that the railway station is far from central, although there is a frequent bus service into the historic centre. Chauffeured trishaws can offer a pleasant alternative way to get around. For a first-time visit, the Tour Bus (about an hour) is a good introduction. Walking tours set off from the Tourist Information Centre (Wheeler St) five times a day in summer. Cyclists will enjoy the towpaths here; nettle-free, and safe if you have children with you. Quite a few shops are that bit different and worth popping into. In term-time, there are countless events; any college notice-board will show what's on. West Road concert hall has outstanding acoustics, while a concert in one of the smaller college chapels can be a charmingly intimate experience.

⚲ **Cambridge & County Folk Museum** (2–3 Castle St) Useful exploration of local life in a handsome 16th-c former inn nr the river – a touch-screen database, inc contemporary residents' diaries and 'virtual' city tours, will be installed in summer. Shop; cl winter Mon; (01223) 355159; £2.

✝ ❀ **Cambridge churches** Of the many churches here, it's worth noting **St Bene'ts**, one of the city's oldest, the popular **Holy Sepulchre** or Round Church (which has brass-rubbing), and **Great St Mary's** with its fine roof and good city views from the tower.

🏛 ❀ **Cambridge colleges** The colleges look private, but you can usually wander into the courtyards (not at exam time, and expect to be charged by many during the summer). Be warned though, college porters will get terribly agitated if you even look at the grass let alone accidently step on it. Several of the dining halls and chapels are worth seeking out. The largest, finest and richest college is Trinity, where the imposing Great Court is usually open to the public and the Wren Library (open wkdys 12–2pm in Nevilles Court is definately worth a visit. King's is probably the best known, with its magnificent chapel, and is pleasant to walk through. Gonville & Caius (pronounced 'keys') is small and slightly snooty, but very pretty. Queen's has a half-timbered courtyard and an eye-catchingly gaudy painted hall, as well as the famous Mathematical Bridge (reputedly built without any bolts or fastenings, until curiosity got the better of some engineers who dismantled it and found they couldn't put it back together in the same way). Peterhouse is the oldest, founded in 1284; the buildings carry their years very gracefully, although these days its deer park is devoid of deer. Opposite, Pembroke's chapel is one of Wren's first buildings. St John's has the very photographed Bridge of Sighs. Jesus, a bit off the main beat, is huge and grandly impressive, and Emmanuel has notable gardens. Clare and Trinity Hall are smaller yet charming colleges, next to each other by The Backs.

⚲ 🖼 **Fitzwilliam Museum** (Trumpington St) This is a wonderful place, a grand and impressive building, crammed with more dazzling treasures than you could hope to examine in one visit. Downstairs are Greek, Egyptian, and Roman antiquities, European ceramics, English glass, carvings, and armour, while upstairs paintings include works by Titian, Canaletto and French Impressionists; if you've not been for a couple of years you'll be pleased to hear both galleries are now open all day. Decent café, shop, disabled access; cl Mon (exc bank hols), 24 Dec–1 Jan, Good Fri; (01223) 332900; free.

🏛 🖼 **Kettle's Yard** (Castle St) Lively arts centre with temporary exhibitions in the gallery and permanent displays in the avant-garde yet surprisingly welcoming house, taking in 20th-c paintings and sculptures (interesting St Ives connections), lovely 18th-c furniture and oriental carpets, and collections of shells and stones. Lots of activities and workshops, several designed especially for the blind or hard of hearing. Devotees say the sunlight on winter afternoons illuminates the exhibits to extraordinary effect. Shop, some disabled access; cl am, all Mon (exc bank hols); (01233) 352124; free.

✝ **King's College Chapel** The annual Festival of Nine Lessons and Carols has made the interior and something of the atmosphere familiar to most visitors, but you're still not fully prepared for the grandeur and scale of the fan-vaulted ceiling, or the miraculously preserved 16th-c stained glass. The overall effect is marred slightly by the unique dark oak screen added by Henry VIII, but the chapel's other famous feature – Rubens's *Adoration of the Magi* – is quite breathtaking. Try and attend choral evensong at 5.30pm Tues–Sat in term-time, or one of the Sun services (10.30am and 3.30pm). Shop, disabled access; cl most of Sun during term-time, and 24 Dec–3 Jan; (01223) 331155; *£3.50.

🖪🏛 **Other Cambridge museums** Most of the town's other museums have a rather academic bent, but are no less rewarding for that: the **Sedgwick Museum** (Downing St) is the university geology museum, with an outstanding collection of fossils, and rocks from Darwin's journey in HMS *Beagle*. The curator not so long ago proved that iguanadons were put together differently from how scientists had previously thought; the bones of his museum's 20-ft specimen have not been rearranged for historical reasons although theoretically, he claims, it is currently in agony. Shop, limited disabled access; cl 1–2pm, pm Sat, all Sun, Christmas–New Year, Easter; (01223) 333456; free. Down the same street is the **Museum of Archaeology & Anthropology**, home to a 50-ft totem pole (open pm Tues–Sat, cl Christmas, Easter) and a **Museum of Zoology**, where a 70-ft whale skeleton hangs above the entrance inside (cl wknds and 1–2pm

outside term-time; free). The **Museum of Classical Archaeology** on Sidgwick Ave has one of the few surviving collections of casts of Greek and Roman sculpture (cl wknds; free), while the various scientific instruments and apparatus at the **Whipple Museum of Science** (Free School Lane) quickly make you thankful we need no longer rely on sundials and abacuses (open pm wkdys; free). The newly re-opened **Scott Polar Research Institute** (Lensfield Rd) houses fascinating exhibits from the fateful polar expedition inc diaries, letters, clothing and an Eskimo carving. Shop, disabled access; open pm Mon–Sat (exc bank hols); (01223) 336540; free. The new exhibition centre at the towering and austere **University Library** (West Rd) has occasional displays of rare and ancient manuscripts. Forthcoming exhibitions will be looking at modern Germany and time; tel (01223) 333122 for details.

⛵ **Punting** The only way to travel, though if your skills in this department were picked up in Oxford you'll find they do things a little back to front here. You can punt right along The Backs, and even down to Grantchester, a pleasant little village still much as described in Rupert Brooke's poem of the same name, with the civilised Orchard Tea Gardens (lovely in summer – and does other drinks too, inc champagne) and three pubs. Hire punts from Scudamores on Mill Lane (01223) 359750 or other stations along the water; prices are generally around £10 an hour (£25 if you require a chauffeur). Bumps races (several rowing eights start off in a line and have to catch up with the one in front) take place on the river in Feb, Jun and July.

🛍 **Shopping** There are lots of **secondhand bookshops** worth a look. Heffers children's bookshop is particularly good, and the general bookshops are as fine as you'd expect in this university town. On the first Sat of the month there's a **craft fair** on St John's Green and **Primavera Contemporary Craftwork** (10 King's Parade) has changing exhibitions of contemporary British painting and craftwork. The **Cambridge**

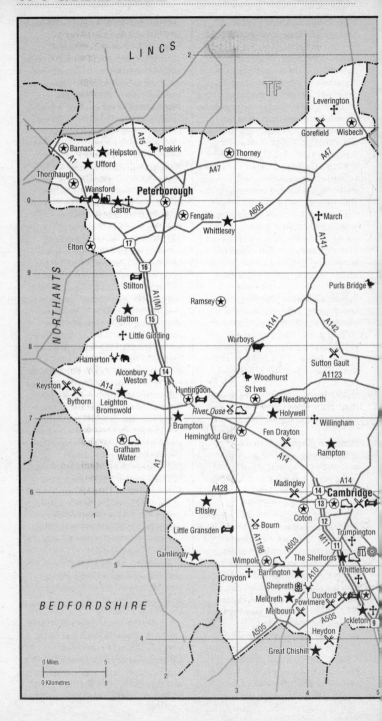

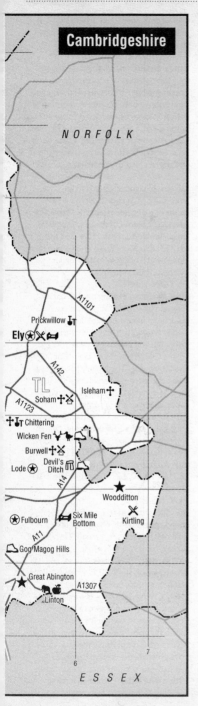

Darkroom (Gwydir St, off Mill Rd) is worth the trek if you're keen on photography; gallery, workshops, darkroom facilities; open Weds–Sun; (01223) 566725.

Snacks in Cambridge Many attractive snack places include Clowns (King St, off Sidney St), Roof Garden (top floor of Arts Theatre – side entrance in St Edward's Passage opposite King's), Boards (down a floor), the tiny Little Tea Room (All Saints Green), Copper Kettle (King's Parade), King's Pantry (King's Parade), Hobbs Pavilion (fantastic pancakes, Parker's Piece) and Browns (Trumpington St). Decent **riverside pubs** include the Anchor (Silver St Bridge), Boathouse (Chesterton Rd), Fort St George (Midsummer Common) and the Mill (Mill Lane). The best pubs away from the river are the smoke-free Free Press (Prospect Row) and atmospheric Eagle (Bene't St).

☁ **Towpath walks** From Magdalene Bridge right in Cambridge itself there's a pleasant walk by the towpath out into the meadows – tranquil, with only punts as far as the lock. Beyond that, you could walk as far as Ely, with oarsmen setting an altogether more vigorous tone – though the Ancient Shepherds or the Plough at Fen Ditton might be a gentler target. Another pleasant stroll out – in the opposite direction – from Cambridge is the walk along the Cam to Grantchester.

❀ **University Botanic Garden** (Cory Lodge, Bateman St) Founded in 1762 and moved to its present site in 1831, now covering 40 acres, with some marvellous mature trees, a geographic rock garden, scented garden, water and winter gardens, and many rare plants inc several National Collections. Rarely crowded, and very pleasant to stroll through. Snacks, shop, disabled access; cl 25–26 Dec, (01223) 336265; *£2.

CASTOR TL1298
★ ✝ Ancient village with a pleasantly relaxed mood. It has a fine **church**, several handsome, thatched stone-built houses, and two pleasant pubs – both thatched too.

CHITTERING TL4970
✝ ⬩ᴛ **Denny Abbey & Farmland**

Museum (off A10) 12th-c Benedictine abbey with some impressive Norman remains and a 14th-c nuns' refectory. The museum focuses on farming and the county's rural history, with reconstructions of a village shop, pub, kitchen and dairy. Workshops and events from Easter–Sept; wknd snacks, shop, disabled access; open pm Apr–Oct; (01223) 860489; £3.40. The Travellers Rest has decent food.

COTON TL4054

† ! **Cambridge American War Cemetery** Built in 1944 on land donated by Cambridge University, this beautiful haunting tribute to the American servicemen and women who lost their lives in both World Wars, covers 30 acres and is framed by woodlands to the W and S. The Portland stone memorial chapel has some intriguing features inc a map of air assaults over the Atlantic and stained-glass windows depicting the seals of the States arranged from left to right in the order that they entered the Union. Disabled access; (01954) 210350; free. The John Barleycorn in the village is a useful lunch stop.

🍴 🚶 **Coton Orchard** (Madingley Rd) Busy 60-acre site with garden centre, pick-your-own soft and top fruits, orchard, and small vineyard. Snacks, farm and gift shop, some disabled access; (01954) 210234; free.

CROYDON TL3149

† **Croydon church** Quietly charming, a proper country church with a timeless feel. The Queen Adelaide is a popular dining pub.

DEVIL'S DITCH TL5765

🏛 🌿 This miles-long ancient embankment lets you fuel a walk with thoughts of whether it was built to fight off the Romans, or some centuries later to protect the riches of East Anglia from Midlands warlords. A good start or finish might be the King's pub in Reach, at its N end: expert German cooking. It's not much of a topographical feature, and is crossed by one or two very busy roads.

DUXFORD TL4546

† ! 🛩 **Duxford Airfield** Very handy from Cambridge, this branch of the Imperial War Museum is home to Europe's best collection of military and civil aircraft, with over 140 flying machines from flimsy-looking biplanes to state-of-the-art Gulf War jets. Children particularly enjoy the fun hands-on section, where they can go into the cockpits of some exhibits, and preserved hangers, control towers and operations rooms create something of the atmosphere Duxford must have had when it was a working World War II air base. A realistic hi-tech flight simulator re-creates a Battle of Britain dogfight, and there's also the prototype Concorde, a summer narrow-gauge railway, pleasure flights, and an adventure playground; airshows in summer – phone for details. Meals and snacks (or plenty of space for picnics), shop, disabled access; cl 24–26 Dec; (01223) 835000; £7.20. The Green Man close by at Thriplow makes for an interesting pub lunch.

ELTON TL0892

🏰 🖼 🌼 **Elton Hall** From the back a splendid 'gothick' fantasy, this is a fascinating lived-in house dating back to Tudor times, with lovely furnishings, porcelain and paintings, inc works by 15th-c Old Masters and Gainsborough and Constable. The library has a Prayer Book that belonged to Henry VIII (his writing is inside), and the gardens are especially pleasant in summer when the roses are in bloom. They may open a shop this year, adjacent garden centre and tearoom; open pm 28–29 May, pm Weds Jun–Aug, plus pm Thurs and Sun July–Aug, and pm 28 Aug; (01832) 280468; £4.50, £2.50 garden. The Black Horse is very handy for lunch.

ELY TL5480

Busy little market town with good shops and some lovely old buildings; it well repays a leisurely stroll. The Prince Albert, handy for the cathedral, has a nice garden. The Cutter, out at Annesdale off the A10, is an attractively placed riverside family pub.

† **Ely Cathedral** One of England's most striking, its distinctive towers dominating the skyline for miles; especially good views coming in on the Soham rd. Complete by the late 12th c, it was restored in a surprisingly sympathetic manner mainly in the mid-19th c. The façade, covered in blind arcading, is fantastic, but most

remarkable perhaps is the Octagonal Tower, over 400 tons suspended in space without any visible means of support; it looks especially impressive from inside. The Lady Chapel has the widest medieval vault in the country and the walls are carved with hundreds of tiny statues which were all somewhat brutally beheaded in the Reformation. The splendid Norman nave seems even longer than it really is because it's so narrow. Also not to be missed are a couple of elaborately sculpted medieval doors – and see if you can spot the railwayman's epitaph, with its unique imagery. Evensong every day except Weds, at 5.30pm. Meals, snacks, shop, disabled access; (01353) 667735; £3.50.

🏺 **Ely Museum** (Old Gaol, Market St) Displays on Hereward the Wake, who led the Anglo-Saxon resistance to the Norman Conquest from here. Shop; disabled access; (01353) 666655; £2.

🏛 **Oliver Cromwell's House** 🖼 (St Mary's St) Next to the unexpectedly grand church of St Mary's, this fine old house was the home of Oliver Cromwell and his family from 1636 until shortly before he became Lord Protector. Period furnished rooms, useful videos (one on the draining of the Fens), and information centre in the downstairs front room. Shop; cl 25–26 Dec, 1 Jan; (01353) 662062; £2.70.

🏺 **Stained Glass Museum** Housed in the cathedral's south triforium, this preserves fine medieval and more modern stained glass rescued from redundant buildings and churches. Good displays on how the windows are made, and a bonus is the unusual view down over the church. Shop; cl am Sun, 25 Dec and Good Fri; (01353) 667735; £2.50.

FENGATE TL2098
🏛🏺🐄 **Flag Fen Bronze Age Excavation** (Fengate, 2m E of Peterborough) Fascinating and well organised prehistoric site, with an excellent Bronze Age museum displaying finds from the ongoing excavations. In summer you should be able to watch archaeologists painstakingly uncovering more secrets, and a reconstructed Bronze Age farm (inc primitive breeds of sheep and pigs) puts the discoveries in context. Snacks, shop, disabled access; cl 25 Dec–2 Jan;

(01733) 313414; *£3.50, EH.
FULBOURN TL5155
★ ✗ 🍺 ✝ 🏛 This is an attractive largely thatched village, with a windmill on the Cambridge rd, a farm shop with pick-your-own fruit, and a pretty church; a path eastwards takes you to the wooded line of the Fleam Dyke, a miles-long Dark Ages defence earthwork.

GOG MAGOG HILLS TL4953
⌂ 🏛 ✾ Not exactly a towering range, these are worth a passing visit; among tall trees you can trace the main rampart and ditch of **Wandlebury Iron Age fort**, and there are good views of the city's distant towers and spires.

GRAFHAM WATER TL1667
🚣 ⚓ 🐦 ⌂ Well liked by readers this offers fishing and sailing, cycle hire, nature reserve with birdwatching hides and trails (you'll see a lot more birds in winter); exhibition centre. There's an attractive waterside path along the northern shore. Snacks, good disabled access; £2 car parking charge, (01480) 812154; free. The Wheatsheaf at West Perry is a popular refreshment stop, and if you're travelling on the B661 from here to Staunton, look out for the roadside stall at the Dillington crossroads – excellent pickled onions and the like, reasonably priced.

HAMERTON TL1481
✌ 🐾 **Hamerton Wildlife Centre** Some of our correspondents seem to make monthly visits to this expanding centre, as there is always something new to see. Providing sanctuary for over 120 different kinds of animal, some extinct in the wild, enclosures include meerkats, wallabies, wolves, gibbons, cheetahs and many more, inc the only breeding group of two-toed sloths in the country. There are frequent exchanges with other zoos, so the inmates change quite often. Regular visitors recommend bringing wellies in winter, though there are concrete paths. Not much under cover but if it rains they will give you free tickets to come back another day. Sensibly priced tearoom (cl winter), shop, disabled access (when dry); cl 25 Dec; (01832) 293362; £4.50. The Green Man pub over at Leighton Bromswold is a useful food stop.

HEMINGFORD GREY TL2970

★ ✝ 🏠 Charming village with a peaceful view of the church over the willow-bordered river (the odd church tower is the result of its spire being lopped off by an 18th-c storm); one stone house among the thatched brick ones is Norman and said to be England's oldest. Nearby Hemingford Abbots is also pretty, and the Axe & Compass here is useful for lunch.

HUNTINGDON TL2371

After considerable recent growth the old centre now feels a bit sidetracked, but has one or two fine buildings such as the George, a particularly handsome Georgian coaching inn. The Old Bridge is a good, civilised place for lunch.

👜 **Cromwell Museum** (Grammar School Walk) Two of Huntingdon's MPs can claim to have run the country for a while, and this commemorates the first. The restored Norman building is where the future Lord Protector went to school (as did Pepys), and many of his possessions are on display. Shop; cl 1–2pm, all Mon, am winter Sun and wkdys, 24–26 Dec; (01480) 425830; free.

🎇 **Hinchingbrooke Country Park** (a couple of miles W) Good for a walk, a run-about or picnic. Guided walks or events most wknds, and there are water sports on the lake. Snacks, disabled access; (01480) 451568; free.

🏠 **Hinchingbrooke House** Now a school, this is where some reckon Cromwell and Charles I met as children. Snacks, disabled access; open pm summer Suns from first May bank hol–Aug bank hol; (01480) 451121; £2. The Olde Mill opposite is a delightfully set family dining pub.

ICKLETON TL4944

★ ✝ This attractive village has a fine church, with Roman columns as bases for its arches, and interestingly carved pews. The churchyard is lovely, and around the church and small green are several beautiful old houses – often a good deal older than their Georgian refacing suggests.

ISLEHAM TL6474

✝ **Isleham church** Attractive from the outside, but its best feature is its wonderful roof.

LEVERINGTON TF4411

✝ **Leverington church** The tower and its spire are noteworthy, as is the very unusual two-storey 14th-c porch.

LINTON TL5646

👜 **Chilford Hall Vineyard** (towards Balsham) A friendly 18-acre winery with interesting old buildings and tours on the hour. Snacks, shop, disabled access; cl Nov–Easter; (01223) 892641; £4.50 (inc tastings and a little souvenir glass). The Pear Tree in Hildersham does decent family food.

🦜 **Linton Zoological Gardens** (B1052, just off A604) Well liked by readers, this friendly family-run zoo has a firm emphasis on conservation and breeding. Current residents include giant tortoises, snow leopards, a couple of Grevy's zebras, Sumatran tigers, and Marabou storks, all housed in enclosures as close to their natural habitats as possible. Family quiz trails in school holidays, play area for smaller

---

Days Out

Cambridge: Climb Great St Mary's Tower for the view; King's College Chapel and colleges; lunch in the Eagle, Bene't St; on a sunny day punt (or walk) along Cam to the tearoom at Granchester – otherwise University Botanic Garden, and Fitzwilliam Museum.

A busy family day: Duxford Airfield/American Air Museum; lunch at the Green Man, Thriplow; Linton Zoo.

Country life: Willers Mill Wildlife Park and Docwra Manor gardens, Shepreth; stroll through Foxton and Barrington – lunch at the Royal Oak there; Wimpole Hall, Home Farm and/or stroll in the estate; if it's the last Sun of the month you may have time to fit in Bourn windmill.

children, picnic areas around the prettily landscaped grounds (some under cover), and children's pony rides on summer wknds. Snacks, shop, disabled access; cl 25 Dec; (01223) 891308; £4.50.

LITTLE GIDDING TL1281

✝ **Little Gidding church** Archetypal small-village country church, well worth a look inside; if it's closed, ask at the farmhouse.

LODE TL5362

🏠 📷 🦋 ✕ **Anglesey Abbey** All that remains of the original priory is a medieval undercroft, but the handsome 17th-c house has an engaging collection of clocks and eclectic range of furniture and paintings; it's definitely worth pausing at Constable's view of the Thames and the landscapes by Claude. The bookshelves in the library are made from Rennie's Waterloo Bridge. The lovely gardens were laid out in Georgian style from 1926 by the first Lord Fairhaven, and a restored **watermill** in the grounds still produces flour. Varied events and activities, inc highly regarded open-air theatre and opera. Meals, snacks, shop, some disabled access; house open pm Weds–Sun and bank hols late Mar–mid-Oct, grounds open from 11am (and are also open Mon and Tues most of July–mid-Sept). Shop, restaurant and plant centre; (01223) 811200; £6 (£7 Sun and bank hols), £3.50 grounds only; NT. The Red Lion at attractive Swaffham Prior does decent fresh food.

MARCH TL4195

✝ Pleasant country town, market day Weds; a good base for exploring the Fens. **St Wendreda's Church** with its wonderful angel roof was described by Betjeman as being 'worth cycling 40 miles in a headwind to see'. The Acre (Acre Rd) has good home cooking.

PEAKIRK TF1606

🦢 **Waterfowl World** Over 150 different species of waterfowl inc rare and unusual breeds, all in a lovely setting. Most were reared in captivity and can be fed by hand – always fun; they sell corn in the gatehouse but the birds seem to prefer bread, so take some along. A good outing even if you're not exactly a twitcher, fascinating if you are. Snacks, shop, disabled access; cl 24–25 Dec,

(01733) 252271; £3.50. The Ruddy Duck is popular for lunch.

PETERBOROUGH TL1998

Has preserved much of its long history and fine old buildings, though it expanded hugely in the mid-1970s and is now a thriving industrial town (with a good pedestrianised shopping centre). A network of cycleways, footpaths and bridleways linking tourist attractions and nature reserves with residential areas is due to be completed by Sept. Charters (by Town Bridge) is an enjoyable floating pub/restaurant in a converted barge. The best place for lunch is some miles outside the town – the Haycock, along the A47 at Wansford.

👶 🖼 **City Museum & Art Gallery** (Priestgate) Among other interesting exhibits are some unusual models made from fishbones by Napoleonic prisoners of war. Shop, disabled access; open Tues–Sat; (01733) 343329; free.

🏠 **Longthorpe Tower** (Thorpe Rd, W of centre) 13th/14th-c fortified house with rare wall paintings (open wknds and bank hols Apr–Oct; £1.40), EH.

✝ **Peterborough Cathedral** One of the most dramatic in the country, its extraordinary west front a medieval masterpiece, with a trio of huge arches. Despite the damage inflicted by Cromwell (he is said to have looked on approvingly as prayer books were torn up and the organ smashed), the richly Romanesque interior has preserved its original fabric to a remarkable degree; especially worth a look are the elaborately vaulted retro-choir and the fine early 13th-c painted wooden nave ceiling – though you'll probably need good light and glasses to see this at its best. Snacks, shop, some disabled access; cl 26 Dec; *£3 guided tour.

🚂 **Railworld** 🔖 (Oundle Rd) Friendly railway museum; cl wknds Nov–Feb; (01733) 344240; £2.50.

✝ **St Margaret's Church** (Fletton) On the southern edge of Peterborough, this has some exceptionally fine little Anglo-Saxon sculptures.

👶 🚂 🦢 **Ferry Meadows Country Park** (Wandsworth TL1329; off A605 W of Peterborough) Useful for children to let off steam; 500 acres with children's play areas, two big lakes with water sports and boat trips, bird reserves, pony and trap rides, miniature railway, two golf courses and pitch and putt.

PRICKWILLOW TL5982

↓T **Drainage Engine Museum** 🖼
The story of water, pumping and fen drainage in the area since the last Ice Age, especially interesting when the engines are running, phone for dates. Snacks, shop, disabled access; open daily Apr–Oct, and wknds Nov and Mar; (01353) 688360; £2 (£3 when engines running).

PURLS BRIDGE TL4787

🐦 Highly recommended for diehard birdwatchers; there's an **RSPB reserve** off the B1093 with several hides (one with disabled access) and big mugs of coffee.

RAMSEY TL2984

🏛 ✝ ♿ ✗ **Abbey Gatehouse** The ruins of an ornate Gothic gatehouse with buttresses and friezes, along with the 13th-c Lady Chapel (all that's left of the abbey itself). Cl Nov–Mar; free. Some of the stone from the abbey is thought to have made up the nearby local history **museum** (open pm Thurs and Sun Apr–Sept; (01487) 815715; £1). The Cross Keys at Upwood (where there's a windmill) has good-value food.

RIVER OUSE TL2772

⌂ ✗ The stretch between St Ives and Hemingford Grey is a popular weekend stamping-ground, with **Houghton Mill** as a charming set piece – a lovely building in pretty setting; the Three Horseshoes nearby has decent food.

ST IVES TL3171

★ ✝ ♿ Pleasant little town, with a graceful church, small local museum, and walks by the curving river. There's an unusual tiny chapel on the old bridge, rising straight out of the water; key from museum. In the town, the Royal Oak does generous food, and the riverside Pike & Eel out at Needingworth is attractively placed for lunch.

THE SHELFORDS TL4552

★ ⌂ The interlinked villages of Great and Little Shelford will reward a slow stroll for those with an eye for architectural detail, and even a quick drive through will show up several delightful timbered houses.

SHEPRETH TL3947

🌺 **Docwra Manor Gardens**
Tranquil gardens, at their best Apr–Jun, but always with a variety of unusual plants grown and for sale. The highlight is perhaps the lovely intimate walled garden. Disabled access (although gravel paths may be hard work); open Weds and Fri, plus, Apr–Oct pm first Sun of month; (01763) 261557; *£2. The Plough is popular for lunch.

✌ **Willers Mill Wildlife Park**
Genuine little wildlife rescue centre with all sorts of unwanted or injured animals and birds. There's a monkey house, and fish farm where the koi will feed from your hand; pony rides summer weekends. The entrance isn't that well signed, so keep an eye out. Snacks (in elevated tree-top café), shop, disabled access (exc café); cl 25 Dec; (01763) 262226; £4.50.

SOHAM TL5872

✝ ✗ As well as a rather grand **church**, this has two surviving mills – you can buy flour ground here.

THORNEY TF2804

★ ✝ ♪ Rises from the flatlands like an island – which it was, when this was all half-submerged marsh. Much older than most villages in the area, it has a Norman-modified Saxon **church** on its green, and some interesting yellow-brick workers' houses put up by the Duke of Bedford. The friendly **Heritage Museum** has good displays, and organises tours of the village and abbey. Shop, limited disabled access; open pm wknds Easter–Oct, or by appointment; (01733) 270908; museum free, tours £1.50. The Rose & Crown does freshly made food.

THORNHAUGH TF0700

🚗 ✗ ✿ 🌺 🌾 **Sacrewell Farm & Country Centre** (off A47) Based around an old working watermill, demonstrations and displays of rural crafts, tools and machinery, as well as gardens, maze and nature trails, lots of animals, and pick-your-own fruit in season. Pleasantly simple and undeveloped, this is a friendly place, well liked by visitors, and very organised for children. Snacks, shop, disabled access; cl 25–26 Dec; (01780) 782254; £3. Wansford is very handy for lunch.

TRUMPINGTON TL4454
✝ **Trumpington church** Attractive in its own right, but perhaps most famous for having the second oldest memorial brass in England.

WANSFORD TL0997
🚂👿 **Nene Valley Railway** 15-mile round trip on steam trains through delightful countryside to Peterborough. Also a fine collection of steam locomotives and rolling stock, and a small museum. The railway is a favourite with film-makers. Meals, snacks, shop, disabled access; cl Mon exc bank hols, best to phone for train times, (01780) 784444; £2 site admission (refundable against train fare), £7.50 for the train. It's easy to extend this into an all-day trip by breaking your journey at one of the country parks alongside stations en route, or by taking a stroll around Peterborough. At the Wansford end (pretty village), the Haycock is particularly good for lunch.

WARBOYS TL3583
🐝🐾 **Grays Honey Farm** (Cross Drove, 5m NE of Warboys, off A141) Buzzing little place with bees at work in an observation hive, an ingenious model railway, aviary, and guinea-pig sty. Tearoom (speciality honey ice-cream), shop (lots of honey-based products), disabled access; cl Sun and Mon (exc bank hols) and Nov–Mar (though shop usually open then); (01354) 693798; free.

WHITTLESFORD TL4748
✝ **Whittlesford church** The interior is a rich testament to the former agricultural wealth of this area. The Tickell Arms, a little way off, is a most unusual pub.

WICKEN TL5670
✤🐾◿ **Wicken Fen** (Lode Lane) After an absence of 60 years, otters have been spotted again at this, the last of the undrained fens. Surrounded in plastic to prevent it from drying out, it is an outstanding area for birdwatching (there are hides). The marshy and open fen landscape is one of the oldest nature reserves in the country, originally safeguarded in 1899 as an example of what the fens were like before they were turned over to intensive agriculture. Beautiful at all times of year,

it's home to a remarkable range of plants, insects, birds and other wildlife; some good trails (one for wheelchairs), along with the last fenland windpump (moved here from elsewhere), and tiny fen cottage. Snacks, shop, disabled access; cl 25 Dec; (01353) 720274; £3.50; NT. The Maid's Head overlooking the village green is a handy dining pub.

WILLINGHAM TL4070
✝ **Willingham church** Lots to notice here: outside are the fine tower and spire, and inside it has many early wall paintings, and some fine early screens.

WIMPOLE TL3350
🐷🏚🕸◿ **Wimpole Hall & Home Farm** *See separate family panel on p.41.*

WISBECH TF4609
The North Brink along the River Nene has handsome Georgian houses (among them the Red Lion has decent food, and serves beer from the nearby brewery – see below – in fine condition).

🍺🕸 **Elgoods Brewery Museum & Gardens** (North Brink) Watch traditional brewing methods in practice at this 200-year-old Georgian brewery on the banks of the River Nene. Behind, four acres of gardens include a hot house, lake and lawns leading to a maze. Snacks, shop, disabled access to gardens only; open pm Weds–Sun May–Oct, brewery tours pm Weds–Fri Jun–Sept; (01945) 583160; £5 inc tasting (£2 gardens only).

🏚📷🕸 **Peckover House** (North Brink) Lovely early 18th-c house with rococo decoration, art exhibitions, and a two-acre Victorian garden with a pond, ornamental ironwork arches, rose gardens, kitchen garden and greenhouses – where orange trees are still fruiting after 250 years. Afternoon teas when house open, shop; open Apr–Oct, pm Weds, wknds and bank hols, plus garden only pm Mon, Tues and Thurs; (01945) 583463; £3.50 (£2 on garden only days), NT.

👿 **Wisbech & Fenland Museum** (Museum Sq) Honest and thorough local history museum, with several early manuscripts, and an exhibition on the slave trade. Shop; cl Sun, Mon; (01945) 583817; free.

WOODHURST TL3176
🐾 **Raptor Foundation** 🔲 Sanctuary

and breeding centre for over 300 birds of prey inc owls, buzzards and falcons; flying displays three times a day. Snacks, shop, disabled access; cl 25 Dec, 1 Jan; (01487) 741140; donations encouraged.

★ **Other attractive villages** include Alconbury Weston TL1776, Brampton TL2170, Eltisley TL2659, Helpston TF1205 (John Clare's village), Elton TL0893, Glatton TL1585, Leighton Bromswold TL1175, Gamlingay TL2452, Great Abington TL5348, Great Chishill TL4239 (well restored windmill), Holywell TL3370, Meldreth TL3746, Rampton TL4268, Ufford TF0904 (the surrounding area can be lovely at bluebell time), Whittlesey TL2797 and Woodditton TL6659.

Where to eat

BYTHORN TL0575 **White Hart** (01832) 710226 Civilised dining pub with a friendly welcome, several linked smallish rooms, magazines and cookery books to read, open fire, imaginative food, real ales, and a sensible wine list; cl pm Sun, Mon, New Year. **£28.40|£7.50.**

CAMBRIDGE TL4658 **Twenty Two** Chesterton Rd (01223) 351880 Simple and pretty candlelit evening restaurant with good modern cooking from a set menu, a fine wine list, and friendly service; cl Sun, Mon, 1 wk Christmas; children over 10. **£28.30.**

DUXFORD TL4745 **John Barleycorn** (01223) 832699 Pretty, early 17th-c thatched country pub, attractively furnished, with a quietly chatty bar, good food and courteous service; fine hanging baskets and a flower-filled back garden; no children. **£25|£8.**

ELY TL5380 **Old Fire Engine House** 25 St Mary's St (01353) 662582 Former fire engine station next to the cathedral; with good hearty English cooking inc nice puddings, an interesting wine list, simple furnishings and a relaxed atmosphere; large walled garden; also, an art gallery; cl pm Sun, 14 days from 24 Dec. **£26|£10.**

FEN DRAYTON TL3368 **Three Tuns** (01954) 230242 Pretty thatched inn with two ingelnook fireplaces and heavy Tudor beams and timbers in its unpretentious and cosy bar; well kept real ales, generous helpings of good, reasonably priced bar food, and a neat back garden with children's play equipment; children until 8pm. **£12|£5.**

FOWLMERE TL4245 **Chequers** (01763) 208369 Civilised old coaching inn with smartly dressed waiters, ambitious food in galleried restaurant, good puddings, and excellent wines; two comfortably furnished rooms with open log fire, some interesting photographs of local World War I and II airfields, and a no smoking conservatory overlooking the garden; cl 25 Dec; disabled access. **£22|£8.80.**

GOREFIELD TF4111 **Woodmans Cottage** (01945) 870669 Very cheerfully run busy village pub specialising in puddings (up to 50 at weekends) as well as a wide choice of other good food in the spacious modernised bar; a comfortable eating area, and separate restaurant; cl 25 Dec; well behaved children only; disabled access. **£23|£7.**

HEYDON TL4340 **King William IV** (01763) 838773 Bustling village pub with nooks and crannies in the rambling rooms, neatly kept agricultural implements on standing props, wall timbers and dark oak beams, and a log fire; notably interesting vegetarian dishes (plus some meaty dishes, too), well kept real ales, and friendly efficient staff. **£24|£7.95.**

KEYSTON TL0475 **Pheasant** (01832) 710241 Pretty thatched former smithy, full of character, with a nice civilised atmosphere; a relaxed bar with informal service, a slightly more formal no smoking room with linen napkins, delicious imaginative food, a particularly good wine list, and real ales; cl pm 25 Dec; partial disabled access. **£25|£5.95.**

KIRTLING TL6857 **Queens Head** (01638) 731737 Peacefully set and charming 16th-c pub discreetly refurbished in period style with delicious, imaginative food from a splendid blackboard, decent wine list and real ales; cl pm Sun. **£20|£6.50.**

MADINGLEY TL3960 **Three Horseshoes** (01954) 210221 Smart, thatched, well run dining pub with a relaxed and civilised atmosphere, open fire in the charming bar, and an attractive conservatory; very good imaginative food, well kept real ales, decent wine list (many by the glass inc champagne), and efficient, attentive service; pretty summer garden; restaurant cl pm Sun (bar open); cl pms 25 and 26 Dec; disabled access. **£29**|£7.95.

MELBOURN TL3844 **Pink Geranium** *Station Rd (01763) 260215* Very pretty 15th-c thatched cottage, pink inside and out, with consistently good, sophisticated cooking; a cosy and relaxed atmosphere, a carefully chosen wine list with helpful notes, cottagey garden, and chauffeur service; good-value set lunches, and cookery courses, too; cl Sun and Mon; disabled access. **£19 lunch, £45 dinner**|£5.

MELBOURN TL3844 **Sheene Mill** *(01763) 261393* Lovely late 17th-c watermill on the River Mel and just 200 yards from its sister restaurant, the Pink Geranium; relaxed and informal bar and conservatory, airy restaurant decorated in yellow and terracotta, with pretty blue dining chairs around yellow-clothed tables, and lovely gardens with seats on the terrace; delicious modern cooking inc vegetarian and fish dishes, and light lunches or snacks; bdrms; cl 26 Dec; disabled access. **£26**|£10 for 2 courses.

SUTTON GAULT TL4279 **Anchor** *(01353) 778537* Popular dining pub with gas lamps and candles in four heavily beamed rooms (two are no smoking), log fires and stripped pine furniture; delicious home-made food, real ales, very good wine list (10 by the glass), and riverbank tables; bdrms; cl 25–26 Dec; no children under 7 after 8pm; disabled access. **£26**|£6.50.

Special thanks to Michael and Jenny Back.

Cambridgeshire Calendar

Some of these dates were provisional as we went to press. Please check information with the telephone numbers provided.

JANUARY

7 **Whittlesey** Straw Bear Festival: folk song, music and dance, with street procession and evening barn dance *on 8 January* and straw bear burning on 9 January (01733) 208245

15 **Alwalton** East of England Agricultural Society: Sheepdog Nursery Trials (01733) 234451

FEBRUARY

5 **Lode** Snowdrops at Anglesey Abbey – *till 6 February; also 12–13 February and 19–20 February* (01223) 811200

MARCH

2 **Ely** Millennium Pageant at Ely Cathedral – *till 4 March* (01353) 667735

18 **Alwalton** National Shire Horse Show at the East of England Showground – *till 19 March* (01733) 452353; **Cambridge** National Science Week: events and displays throughout the town – *till 25 March* (01954) 210636; **Ely** Britten Sinfonia and Ely Cathedral Choir at Ely Cathedral (01353) 667735

25 **Arrington** Lambing Weekend at Wimpole Hall and Home Farm – *till 26 March* (01223) 207257

Cambridgeshire Calendar (cont.)

APRIL

1 Arrington Lambing Weekend at Wimpole Hall and Home Farm – *till 2 April; also 8-9 April* (01223) 207257

8 Elton Craft Fair at Elton Hall – *till 9 April* (01832) 280468; **Thriplow** Daffodil Weekend: gardens open, crafts, rural pursuits – *till 9 April* (01763) 208132

14 Alwalton National Motorhome Show at the East of England Showground – *till 16 April* (01733) 452353

22 Peterborough St George's Day Celebrations inc town criers' contest, Pearly kings and queens, maypole and Morris dancing (01733) 700035

23 Elton Garden Show at Elton Hall – *till 24 April* (01832) 280468

24 Arrington Children's Fun Day at Home Farm, Wimpole Hall (01223) 208987

30 Alwalton Truckfest at the East of England Showground – *till 1 May* (01733) 452353

MAY

1 Stilton Cheese-rolling Contest: wooden replicas are rolled down the High Street; stalls and May Day celebrations (01733) 241206

5 Elton Home Design and Interiors Exhibition at Elton Hall – *till 7 May* (01832) 280468

21 Alwalton British Motorcyclists Federation Rally: largest outdoor motorcycle festival in Europe at East of England Showground (0116) 254 8818

29 Arrington Children's Fun Day at Home Farm, Wimpole Hall (01223) 208987

JUNE

4 Cambridge Trinity College Choir sing from the college towers *from noon*, and from lamplit punts on the river *from 8.45pm* (01223) 338400

8 Cambridge Strawberry Fair on Midsummer Common (01223) 560160

11 Peterborough Kite Festival at Ferry Meadows Country Park (01733) 700718

16 Alwalton East of England Show at the East of England Showground – *till 18 June* (01733) 452353

21 Cambridge Midsummer Fair on Midsummer Common; funfair – *till 26 June* (01223) 463363

22 Cambridge Millennium Flower Festival at Wesley Church, Christ's Piece (01223) 425948

24 Peterborough Festival – *till 9 July* (01733) 452353

28 Wisbech Rose Fair: flower festival, jazz, musical entertainments, stalls and cream teas – *till 1 July* (01945) 583263

JULY

1 Cambridge Open Studios: around 200 exhibiting members at various venues – look out for the yellow flags – *till 2 July* (01223) 249394

2 Ely Aquafest: Riverside Gala and Raft Race at Willow Walk (01638) 780491; **Peterborough** Fête at Thorpe Hall (01733) 330060

Cambridgeshire Calendar (cont.)

7 Ely Folk Festival: family dance and music event – *till 9 July* (01353) 740999

8 Arrington Open-air Concert with fireworks at Wimpole Hall and Home Farm – *till 9 July* (01223) 207257; **Cambridge** Open Studios: around 200 exhibiting members at various venues – look out for the yellow flags – *till 9 July* (01223) 249394; **Witcham** World Pea-shooting Championships: stalls and games (01353) 778363

14 Cambridge Pop in the Park (free) at Parker's Piece (01223) 457521

15 Cambridge Big Day Out: free family day with bands, performers, displays, fireworks at Parker's Piece (01223) 457521; also, Open Studios: around 200 exhibiting members at various venues – look out for the yellow flags – *till 16 July* (01223) 249394

16 Brinkley Millennium Fête at Brinkley Hall (01223) 290951

18 Alwalton East of England Championship Dog Show at the East of England Showground – *till 20 July* (01733) 452353

22 Cambridge Open Studios: around 200 exhibiting members at various venues – look out for the yellow flags – *till 23 July* (01223) 249394

28 Cherry Hinton Folk Festival: one of Europe's top acoustic festivals – *till 30 July* (01223) 457521

AUGUST

12 Peterborough Summer Regatta – *till 13 August* (01733) 563966

19 Arrington Open-air Concerts with fireworks at Wimpole Hall and Home Farm – *till 20 August* (01223) 207257

22 Peterborough Beer Festival on the river embankment: over 200 real ales – *till 27 August* (01733) 574331

30 Alwalton British Show Ponies at the East of England Showground – *till 2 September* (01733) 452353

SEPTEMBER

9 Haddenham Steam Rally inc heavy horse show – *till 10 September* (01487) 841893; **Wisbech** Open Weekend: private historical buildings open to the public – *till 10 September* (01945) 583263; and Folk Festival – *till 10 September* (01945) 583263

23 Soham Pumpkin Fair: pumpkins, sunflowers and large vegetables (01223) 236236

OCTOBER

8 Alwalton Autumn Exhibition at the East of England Showground (01733) 452353

NOVEMBER

4 Cambridge Fireworks at Midsummer Common, first rocket *at 7.30pm* (01223) 463363

11 Cambridge 2000 Music Festival – *till 29 November* (01223) 350544

19 Ely County Brass Band Championships (01353) 662062

30 Peterborough Christmas Street Festival (01733) 452280

CHESHIRE

**Great variety, both in its landscapes and in interesting places to visit –
one of Britain's relatively undiscovered corners.**

With many charming thatched and timbered villages, Cheshire's countryside varies from the picturesque castle-topped wooded hills of the west, through the lush parkland, leafy lanes and meres (shallow lakes) of the central plain to the rugged eastern Peak District – small steep stone-walled pastures, shaggy sheep, deep twisty valleys, austere moorland. An intricate network of canals takes in some of the most interesting countryside, with well kept towpaths.

Two outstanding wildlife features are Chester Zoo (an interesting, threatened islands' project hot on the heels of its fascinating new bat cave, and lovely gardens around the animals), and Blue Planet in Ellesmere Port, Europe's largest aquarium (new shark feature, more space for the popular frogs, lots of unusual conservation projects).

Good heritage centres here include the Salt Museum in Nantwich, the lively Paradise Mill and Silk Museum in Macclesfield, and the thriving Quarry Bank industrial heritage site at Styal.

Tatton Park in Knutsford, with its lovely grounds and working historic farm, has lowered its all-in-one ticket price dramatically this year – very good value now. Lyme Park near Disley is another good day out, and other rewarding places include Tabley House (not to mention the remarkable nearby clock and fairground organ collection), Arley Hall near Northwich, Little Moreton Hall near Congleton, Gawsworth Hall, Norton Priory in Runcorn, the Ness botanic gardens, and the spectacular garden centre at Bridgemere. Jodrell Bank, and Catalyst in Widnes, both have plenty to intrigue an inquiring mind.

Chester itself is a must. Very pedestrian-friendly, it has beautifully restored and preserved medieval buildings, lots of interest, and a lively feel. The city's tourist information department couldn't be more helpful.

Industry is largely confined to the Mersey, with chemical works at Northwich and engineering around Crewe.

Where to stay

BEESTON SJ5459 **Wild Boar** *Whitchurch Rd, Beeston, Tarporley CW6 9NW* (01829) 260309 **£90,** plus special breaks; 37 rms with complimentary extras such as fresh fruit and sherry. Attractive, half-timbered, 17th-c former hunting lodge, carefully extended over the years, beneath the 12th-c castle; with relaxed and comfortable bars and lounges, enjoyable food in the beamed restaurant, and good helpful service; disabled access.

BICKLEY MOSS SJ5549 **Cholmondeley Arms** *Bickley Moss, Malpas SY14 8BT* (01829) 720300 ***£65,** plus special breaks; 2 rms with bath, 4 with showers. Airy, converted Victorian schoolhouse close to castle and gardens; lots of atmosphere, very friendly staff, interesting furnishings, open fire, excellent imaginative bar food, and a very good choice of wines; disabled access.

CHESTER SJ4166 **Castle House** *23 Castle St, Chester CH1 2DS (01244) 350354* ***£46;*** 5 comfortable rms, 3 with own bthrm. Small, carefully preserved 16th-c guesthouse in the middle of the city; with helpful friendly owners, and fine breakfasts.

COTEBROOK SJ5765 **Alvanley Arms** *Cotebrook, Tarporley CW6 9DS (01829) 760200* ***£50;*** 7 rms. Handsome, creeper-covered Georgian inn with pleasant beamed bars (one area is no smoking), big open fire, a chintzy little hall, generous helpings of good food, and a garden with pond and geese.

FULLERS MOOR SJ4954 **Frogg Manor** *Nantwich Rd, Fullers Moor, Broxton, Tattenhall, Chester CH3 9JH (01829) 782629* **£105,** plus special breaks; 6 lavishly decorated rms. Enjoyable Georgian manor house full of ornamental frogs and antique furniture, open fires, a restful upstairs sitting room, little bar, old-time music, and good English cooking in the elegant dining room which leads to a conservatory overlooking the gardens; dogs by arrangement.

HIGHER BURWARDSLEY SJ5256 **Pheasant** *Higher Burwardsley, Chester CH3 9PF (01829) 770434* ***£70,*** plus special breaks; 10 rms in comfortably converted sandstone-built barn. Pretty, half-timbered 17th-c inn on top of Peckforton Hills with marvellous views; interesting decorations, a huge fireplace, and a parrot called Sailor in the attractive old-fashioned bar, no smoking conservatory, good food, and friendly staff; lots of walks nearby; disabled access.

HIGHER WYCH SJ4943 **Mill House** *Higher Wych, Malpas SY14 7JR (01948) 780362* ***£40;*** 2 rms, 1 with own bthrm. Very welcoming and friendly B & B in a former farmhouse on the Welsh/English border; good breakfasts – evening meals by arrangement; self-catering cottage; cl Christmas–New Year.

HOOLE SJ4368 **Hoole Hall** *Warrington Rd, Hoole, Chester CH2 3PD (01244) 350011* ***£90,*** plus special breaks; 97 well equipped rms, some no smoking. Extended and attractively refurbished 18th-c hall with 5 acres of gardens; good food in two restaurants, and friendly service; good disabled access.

KNUTSFORD SJ7578 **Longview** *51–55 Manchester Rd, Knutsford WA16 0LX (01565) 632119* ***£70;*** 23 rms. Warm, friendly Victorian hotel with attractive period and reproduction furnishings, open fires in original fireplaces, pleasant cellar bar, ornate restaurant, and good, well presented food; cl 24 Dec–8 Jan.

MACCLESFIELD SJ9271 **Sutton Hall** *Bullocks Lane, Sutton, Macclesfield SK11 0HE (01260) 253211* **£90;** 9 marvellous rms. Welcoming and secluded historic baronial hall, full of character; stylish rooms with tall black beams, stone fireplaces, suits of armour and so forth, friendly service, and good food; can arrange clayshooting, golf and fishing.

MACCLESFIELD FOREST SJ9471 **Hardingland Farm** *Macclesfield Forest, Macclesfield SK11 0ND (01625) 425759* ***£46;*** 3 rms. Neatly kept Georgian stone farmhouse set in the Peak National Park with wonderful views; an elegantly furnished lounge and Regency-style dining room, helpful owners, and delicious food using their own lamb and beef; cl Nov–Jan; no children.

MOBBERLEY SJ7879 **Laburnum Cottage** *Knutsford Rd, Mobberley, Knutsford WA16 7PU (01565) 872464* **£50;** 5 pretty rms, 3 with own bthrm. Neatly kept and friendly no smoking house set in a flower-filled, landscaped garden with croquet; a relaxed atmosphere in the comfortable lounge with log fire and books, generous breakfasts with home-made jams, and good, freshly cooked food; disabled access.

MOLLINGTON SJ3870 **Crabwall Manor** *Parkgate Rd, Mollington, Chester CH1 6NE (01244) 851666* **£120w;** 48 very comfortable, individually decorated rms. Partly castellated, historic hotel in landscaped grounds; with restful, attractive day rooms, open fires, very good modern British cooking in the elegant restaurant, and friendly, professional service; disabled access.

POTT SHRIGLEY SJ9479 **Shrigley Hall** *Shrigley Park, Pott Shrigley, Macclesfield SK10 5SB (01625) 575757* **£140,** plus special breaks; 150 smart, well equipped rms, some with country views. Set in over 260 acres of parkland, this impressive country house has a splendid entrance hall with several elegant rooms leading off, enjoyable food in the orangery and restaurant, and good service from friendly staff; championship golf course, fishing, tennis, and leisure centre in a former church building; plenty to do nearby; disabled access.

PRESTBURY SJ9077 **White House** *The Village, Prestbury, Macclesfield SK10 4HP (01625) 829376* **£110,** plus wknd breaks; 11 individual, stylish and well equipped rms with antiques, in a separate brick manor. Exceptionally friendly and pretty restaurant-with-rooms, lots of plants, silk and lace, and very good modern British cooking in the restaurant (a short walk into the village centre); breakfast in small conservatory lounge or in room; cl 24–26 Dec; children over 10.

ROWTON SJ4564 **Rowton Hall** *Whitchurch Rd, Rowton, Chester CH3 6AD (01244) 335262* **£150,** plus wknd breaks; 38 attractive rms; 18th-c country house in 8 acres of award-winning gardens; with conservatory lounge, comfortable bar, log fires, a relaxed atmosphere, and smart restaurant; leisure club with swimming pool, gym, sauna and solarium; may be closed over Christmas; disabled access.

SANDBACH SJ7661 **Old Hall** *Newcastle Rd, Sandbach CW11 0AL (01270) 761221* **£75;** 14 comfortable rms. Fine Jacobean timbered hotel with lots of original panelling and fireplaces; relaxing lounge, pianist, friendly welcome, and a popular restaurant; disabled access.

SANDIWAY SJ6071 **Nunsmere Hall** *Tarporley Rd, Sandiway, Northwich CW8 2ES (01606) 889100* **£140w;** 37 individually decorated rms. Luxurious lakeside hotel on wooded peninsula; with an elegantly furnished lounge and library, oak-panelled cocktail bar, very good modern cooking, and a warm welcome from courteous staff; children over 12 in evening restaurant; disabled access.

TARPORLEY SJ5563 **Swan** *50 High St, Tarporley CW6 0AG (01829) 733838* **£72.50;** 20 rms. Well managed Georgian inn with a pleasant mix of individual tables and chairs in the attractive bar, well kept real ales, decent wines, and quite a few malt whiskies; good food from a brasserie menu with lighter lunchtime choices, nice breakfasts, and friendly staff; disabled access.

TILSTON SJ4651 **Tilston Lodge** *Tilston, Malpas SY14 7DR (01829) 250223* ***£64;** 3 thoughtfully equipped rms. Warm, friendly and beautifully restored Victorian house in 16 acres, a collection of rare breed farm animals; comfortable and attractive public rooms, open fire in the dining room, and good breakfasts; evening meal by arrangement.

WESTON SJ7352 **White Lion** *Main Rd, Weston, Crewe CW2 5NA (01270) 500303* **£65;** 16 comfortable rms. Pretty 17th-c timbered inn with low beams (several no smoking areas), a friendly relaxed atmosphere, well kept real ales, and popular food; own bowling green; no accommodation 25 Dec; disabled access.

WETTENHALL SJ6261 **Boot & Slipper** *Wettenhall, Winsford CW7 4DN (01270) 528238* **£48;** 4 attractive rms with showers. Cosily refurbished 16th-c coaching inn on a small country lane; with low beams and open fire in the quiet bars, a relaxed friendly atmosphere, and good breakfasts.

WHEELOCK SJ7559 **Grove House** *Mill Lane, Wheelock, Sandbach CW11 0RD (01270) 762582* **£60w;** 8 rms. Family-run, Georgian restaurant-with-rooms, with a relaxed homely atmosphere, quietly furnished lounge and restaurant, personal, friendly service, and very good modern cooking in the popular restaurant; plenty to do nearby; cl Christmas–New Year; partial disabled access.

WORLESTON SJ6556 **Rookery Hall** *Worleston, Nantwich CW5 6DQ (01270) 610016* **£130w,** plus special breaks; 45 individually decorated rms. Fine, early 19th-c hotel in 200 acres of lovely parkland; with elegant lounges, log fires, an intimate panelled restaurant with enjoyable food, and friendly service; disabled access.

Please let us know what you think of places in the *Guide*. Use the report forms at the back of the book or simply write us a letter.

To see and do

CHESHIRE Family Attraction of the Year

🐾 **CHESTER** SJ4166 **Chester Zoo** 🖼 (A41, 2m N of Chester) Very well liked by readers, this is the biggest zoo in Britain, and undoubtedly one of the best, constantly developing and improving. Its several thousand animals are housed in spacious, near natural enclosures spread over 80 acres of glorious gardens, with 11 miles of pathways. Over 200 of the species here are classed as rare or endangered, and they put a great deal of effort into breeding, so there's usually quite a range of baby animals. Highlights include the splendidly laid out Chimpanzee Island (feeding time 2.15pm), the penguin pool with underwater viewing panels, and the remarkable bat cave – no crime-fighting gadgets, but the biggest free-flying bat enclosure in the world, with around 200 inhabitants. About to open as we went to press was the new Islands in Danger area, a tropical habitat with threatened creatures like komodo dragons and Amazon parrots. There's a full programme of feeding sessions throughout the day: the lions eat at noon (not Fri), the sealions at 10.30am, 2.15pm and 3.30pm, and the elephants between 2.30pm and 4pm. Times can change, so best to check the day's events on the main information boards when you arrive; these also detail the zoo's latest arrivals. A sensibly organised children's farm offers more close-up animal encounters. An overhead train zips around the grounds, or in summer a waterbus can ferry you between the attractions, (both £1 extra). The guide book is exemplary, combining useful information and maps with itineraries to suit variously lengthed visits. Everywhere is suitable for wheelchairs, and they have tactile maps and Braille guides. It's just as well they're so organised – on the busiest of summer days there can be 25,000 people here, but it's big enough to absorb the crowds. It's one of those places where keeping note of where you left the car can reap dividends. You can easily spend the whole day here without feeling drained at the end (anything less than half a day won't do the place justice), and there are lots of summer activities for children. In winter some features may be closed, and some animals (just like people) might be reluctant to venture outside. Meals and snacks (readers prefer the various indoor and outdoor picnic areas), shops, good disabled access; cl 25 Dec, 1 Jan; (01244) 380280; £9 (£6.50 children 3–15). The family ticket, covering 2 adults and up to 3 children, is good value at £30.

ARLEY SJ6781

🏠 🦌 ⚘ ✝ 🐄 🌿 **Arley Hall & Gardens and Stockley Farm** The dramatic-looking house is Victorian Jacobean, but the same family have lived on the estate for over 500 years, so there are older furnishings and mementos. Outside, the award-winning grounds include walled, scented, and herb gardens, shrub rose collection, a more informal woodland area, and craft workshops; also an interesting private chapel. Meals, snacks, shop and nursery, disabled access; open Easter to Sept, Tues–Sun, house open pm Tues and Sun only; (01565) 777353; £4 grounds and gardens, hall £2.50 extra. From the car park, tractor and trailer rides take you to nearby **Stockley Farm**, a friendly working dairy farm that's ideal for children; falconry displays at wknds in school hols. Open pm Weds, Sat, Sun and bank hols Easter–Sept, plus daily exc Mon in Aug; (01565) 777323; £4.

ASTBURY SJ8461

★ ✝ This is a delightful village, and its **church** is well worth a look if you're in the area. It has a graceful detached spire, spectacular roofing and carving.

AUDLEM WHARF SJ6543

⛵ For walkers, a good access point for the **Shropshire Union Canal** which threads through this area giving interesting stretches for strolls; just outside the village is an impressive flight of over a dozen locks.

BARTHOMLEY SJ7752

★ † This charming village has lots of thatch, black and white timbering, quiet up-and-down lanes, and a fine church.

BEESTON SJ5459

🏰 ❋ **Beeston Castle** Well worth the steep climb, there are wonderful views from this ruined 13th-c fortress, perched atop dramatically rising crags, and said to be where Richard III left buried treasure. Good exhibition covers 4,000-year history of site. Snacks, shop; cl 24–26 Dec, 1 Jan; (01829) 260464; £2.80, EH. The pub of the same name, handy for the canal, does good-value generous food.

BOLLINGTON SJ9377

★ ⌂ ❋ Bollington is well worth a stroll: handsome stone milltown buildings, unchanged 19th-c shops and houses, and overhead a great stone aquaduct and its later rival the railway viaduct. Useful pubs include the Church House and Vale. In summer you can hire bikes along a traffic-free 10-mile stretch of the Middlewood Way bordering the Peak District (£5 for three hours – £9 full day), (01625) 572681. Just outside, the Cheshire Hunt in Spurley Lane at Pott Shrigley is a good place for lunch, and near it you can pick up the long-distance Gritstone Trail for walks among high stone-walled pastures (the Cheshire Hunt pub in Spurley Lane has good food). The Poachers (Ingersley Rd) or Redway (Kerridge) are good start points for the viewpoint Kerridge Hill (crowned by a curious folly known as White Nancy) just E of the town.

BRIDGEMERE SJ6352

❋ **Bridgemere Garden World** (A51) A garden-lover's paradise – 25 acres of gardens (inc the WI cottage garden), plants, glasshouses, and garden furniture, with more plants in more varieties than anywhere else in Britain (indoor and outdoor), and professional help on hand for any sort of query. Best to visit in the morning before the coach parties arrive. Good meals and snacks, excellent shop, disabled access; cl 25–26 Dec; (01270) 520381; free (exc Garden Kingdom, *£1.50).

BUNBURY SJ5758

★ † ✗ Bunbury has pretty cottages around its 14th-c church, and a well

restored 19th-c watermill.

BURWARDSLEY SJ5156

✿ 🏠 **Cheshire Candle Workshops** Popular demonstrations of candle-making and other crafts, and a big craft shop. Meals, snacks, disabled access; cl 25 Dec; (01829) 770401; free. The Pheasant is good for lunch, with great views.

CAPESTHORNE SJ8472

🏛 🖼 † ❀ **Capesthorne Hall** 18th-c family home of the Bromley-Davenports, who have lived on the site since Domesday; fine paintings include Lowry's unusual interpretation of the house's striking exterior, and there's a good collection of Roman and Greek busts and vases. Also a lovely Georgian chapel and 60 acres of gardens and woodland. Snacks, disabled access; open pm Weds, Sun and bank hols Apr–Oct; (01625) 861221; £6, £3.50 garden and chapel only. The Blacksmiths Arms at Henbury (A537 towards Macclesfield) is a decent family dining pub, if you don't want the longer trip to the Dog over at Peover Heath.

CHESTER SJ4166

One of Britain's most rewarding cities, Chester was the site of an important fort in Roman times, and later plentiful river traffic kept it rich. The old centre is ringed by a medieval town wall that's more complete than any other in Britain. You can walk the whole way round, enjoying marvellous views; there are summer exhibitions in some of the towers along the way. Partly because of the limit set by the wall, the centre of town is easy to get around on foot, not too big, and with the main streets pretty much free of cars (there may be a few buses), although in summer the sheer number of tourists and shoppers can still make them appear congested. Guided walks leave the tourist information centre on Town Hall Sq at 10.45am each day. If you're driving in, you'll be shunted round to one of the big car parks, and you may have to queue a while to get a space. Chester's racecourse, the Roodee, is the oldest in the world; it still has fashionable races in May and a summer Sun meet that's become a lively event for families. The quaint Albion (Park St) has good food, and Watergates (Watergate St), in a fine medieval crypt, is useful for lunch. The ancient Blue Bell (Northgate St) has been licensed to sell alcohol since 1494.

♨ ♿ Chester Castle Though now largely moated by car parks and occupied by civil servants, this has some impressive buildings, both medieval and grand-manner, late 18th c. There are plans to develop the small military museum here.

† Chester Cathedral Not unlike an ordinary church at first glance, this is far more impressive inside, with some marvellous medieval carving in and above the choir stalls, and some fine vaulting. Many of the former abbey buildings survived the Reformation, so the precincts still include peaceful arcaded flagstoned cloisters, a medieval chapter house, and older Norman parts include a refectory – brought back into use as an excellent café (which even has a resident pianist Tues, Fri and Sat lunchtimes). All the carved bosses have been gilded since last year, and a new model of the cathedral has a Braille text. Shop, disabled access; (01244) 324756; free. There are quiet cobbled Georgian lanes around Abbey Sq, behind the cathedral a little way down Northgate.

❀ ♣ Chester viewpoints The tree-shaded Groves look out to the medieval bridge over the River Dee – very photogenic and a pleasant place for a stroll or picnic. Several companies offer **boat trips** on the river from here (01244 400327). The bridge at the N end of Northgate gives a close view of the so-called Bridge of Sighs over the canal far below.

🐾 Chester Zoo See separate family panel on p.59.

♪ Dewa Roman Experience (Pierpoint Lane, off Bridge St) Re-creation of Chester's Roman heyday, with the sights, sounds and smells of streets, fortresses, and even bath-houses. It starts off as though you're on board a Roman galley, and at the end is an exhibition of Roman, Saxon and medieval relics found on the site. Shop, disabled access; cl 25–26 Dec; (01244) 343407; £3.95.

♿ 🏛 🖼 Grosvenor Museum (Grosvenor St) There will be more interactive displays here when it re-opens after refurbishment for disabled access, sometime in the summer. Its surprising highlight is a gallery of huge Roman tombstones. A passage from here leads to a Georgian house with restored Georgian and Victorian rooms, an art gallery, and displays of locally made silver and furniture. Shop; tel for opening times; (01244) 402008; free.

♿ ! On the Air (Bridge St Row) Evocative exhibition of radio equipment and broadcasts from the 20s through to the 90s, with a reconstructed 1920s living room, 1930s shop, and wartime air-raid shelter brought to life with period recordings. Displays of television and other broadcast equipment too – you can play on the cameras. Shop (sells vintage radios), good disabled access; cl Sun and Mon Christmas–Easter; (01244) 348468; £1.95.

♨ 🏛 Roman Chester Recent research has led to speculation that Emperor Hadrian ordered Chester to be built as a 'beautiful new city' – a reflection of Rome's glory. This certainly helps to explain the city's grandiose walls, constructed with unusually large sandstone blocks in a manner designed to impress, with imposing, ornamental gateways. Other remains include some broken Roman columns in a neat and peaceful garden running along the town wall by the gate at the bottom of Pepper St. Nearby is the excavated part of a very large Roman amphitheatre – probably big enough to seat nearly 10,000 people. Other relics can pop up in unexpected places: Spud-U-Like and Miss Selfridge show off well preserved sections of hypocaust.

🏛 The Rows Giving Chester's heart a magnificently Tudor look, these are sets of timbered two-storey shops – with open upper arcaded galleries – radiating from the central Cross. Parts are thought to be at least 700 years old. Besides being attractive to look at and charming to walk through, they form the heart of the city's shopping centre (and include a useful pub, the Boot, on Eastgate Row north). Watergate is one of the finest stretches, with some of

Chester's most glorious timber-framed buildings, though more fine buildings jetty out over the pavement in Lower Bridge St (for instance, the late 17th-c Falcon, once a house used by the Duke of Westminster's ancestors but now a good pub), and in St Werbergh St off Eastgate (built in the 1890s, despite their Elizabethan look).

🛢 **Toy & Doll Museum** (Lower Bridge St Row, Chester) One of the best such collections we've come across, not least because of the hard-to-beat assemblage of Matchbox cars and toys (the company's HQ are here). Lots of Dinky toys and Hornby trains, as well as dolls, teddies, and some vintage amusement machines. Shop (good for dolls house furniture); cl 25–26 Dec, 1 Jan; (01244) 346297; *£2.

CHOLMONDELEY SJ5351

✱ 🐄 † **Cholmondeley Castle Gardens** Very pretty to stroll through, with acres of colourful ornamental gardens around elegant castle buildings (not open). Famously, it's pronounced Chumley. There are also fine woodland and lakeside walks, llamas and entertaining pygmy goats among the rare breeds, and an ancient private chapel. Snacks, shop and plant centre, limited disabled access; open pm Sun, Weds, Thurs and bank hols Apr–Sept; (01829) 720383; £3. The Cholmondeley Arms is an excellent place for lunch.

CHRISTLETON SJ4465

★ Though now almost part of Chester, this is still very much a distinct village, with a classic green, pond, almshouses, and medieval packhorse bridges.

CONGLETON SJ8358

🏠 ⚓ **Little Moreton Hall** (Scholar Green; A34 S) One of Britain's best-preserved half-timbered buildings, its splendid black and white exterior pretty much unchanged since it was built in 1580, and covered with such a profusion of lines the effect is almost dizzying. The inside, though largely unfurnished, has some interesting features too, especially the wainscoted Long Gallery, Great Hall and chapel. There's a re-creation of a typical 17th-c knot garden – and make sure you don't miss the built-in dog kennel. Regular open-air theatre and concerts. Meals, snacks, shop, disabled access to ground floor only; open pm Weds–Sun mid-Mar–Oct, then pms up to Christmas; (01260) 272018; £4.20; NT. The Brownlow Arms nearby or Rising Sun in Scholar Green itself are popular for lunch. **Heritage Narrow Boats** at Kent Green have electric narrow boats to hire by the day; maybe cl Nov–Easter; (01782) 785700; £60–£80 wkdys for up to 12 people (£75–£95 wknds) – very satisfying, gliding along in silence.

CREWE SJ7055

A 19th-c railway town, smartened up a lot in the last decade or two, with bargains especially china in the market, a pedestrianised centre, colourful Queen's Park and useful foyer restaurant in the Victorian theatre. The Crewe Arms is good value for a comfortable lunch.

🚂 **Railway Age** (Vernon Way) Rapidly developing exhibition with one of the widest ranges of preserved electric and diesel locomotives in the country, along with models, miniature and standard gauge railways and other displays. Shop (not always open), some disabled access; cl Nov–mid-Feb; (01270) 212130; £2.50 wkdys, £3.50 wknds (when there's more going on).

DARESBURY SJ5882

† ⌂ **Daresbury church** The 'Alice in

Days Out

Gems of the South Wirral: Ellesmere Port aquarium and/or boat museum; lunch at the Wheatsheaf, Raby; Ness Gardens; Parkgate, Little Neston and Burton villages, with a walk along the Dee estuary.

Romance of the Peckforton Hills: Beeston Castle; lunch at Cholmondeley Arms, Cholmondeley or at the Pheasant, Higher Burwardsley; Cholmondeley Castle gardens (Sun, Weds or Thurs) or walk in the Peckforton Hills.

Wonderland' stained-glass window commemorates Lewis Carroll, who was born here. There are pleasant canalside strolls, and the Ring o' Bells is useful for lunch.

DELAMERE FOREST SJ5571

⚑ ◲ Several square miles of mainly coniferous plantation, with some older oak and other woodland, inc plenty of open stretches and picnic places, and some small stretches of reedy water. A section of the 30-mile **Sandstone Trail** long-distance path takes in much of the best bits, with good access from several places inc Delamere and Hatchmere, with decent, prettily placed pubs in both villages.

DISLEY SJ9784

🏠 ✿ ◲ **Lyme Park** Wonderful country estate outside the pleasant hillside village of Disley. The Hall at its centre is a magnificent blend of Elizabethan, Georgian and Regency architecture and styles. Tours are unguided, so you can take your time looking at the intricate carvings, and lovely tapestries, paintings and furniture. There's a particularly grand staircase, and a fine collection of English clocks. Around the house (its exterior used as Pemberley in the BBC's *Pride and Prejudice*) are 17 acres of Victorian gardens with orangery, sunken Dutch garden and wilderness garden, and an ancient park with herds of red deer and nature trails. Pleasant walk down to the canal. Snacks, shop, disabled access (with notice); house and gardens open Apr–Oct, garden cl am Weds and Thurs, house cl every am and all Weds and Thurs, gardens also open some winter wknds – ring for dates; the park is open all year; (01663) 762023; £3.50 per car to go in the park, then £4.50 house and garden, £2 garden only; NT. The White Horse is a useful food stop (with OAP lunch days). The long-distance **Gritstone Trail** starts from the park and runs along the western flanks of the Peak District. It's well marked and offers a few days' walking of the highest quality.

EATON SJ5763

★ Eaton is a classic Cheshire village, with unassuming but charming picture-postcard combinations of thatch, stone and timbering.

ECCLESTON SJ4162

★† This romantically eclectic estate village was built in the last century for the Duke of Westminster, with a richly expansive sandstone church that's a culmination of Victorian ecclesiastical architecture.

ELLESMERE PORT SJ4077

✺ ⚒ ⚓ 🏛 **Boat Museum** (Dockyard Rd) Nicely set in a historic dock complex, a huge floating collection of canal boats, as well as steam engines, a blacksmith's forge, workers' cottages, stables, big indoor exhibitions, and boat trips. Snacks, shop, disabled access; cl winter Thurs and Fri, Christmas and New Year; (0151) 355 5017; £5.50. Parts of the surrounding docks have been redeveloped with craft workshops and the like. The Woodland (Chester Rd) is a useful pub/restaurant (with its own bowling green). On the southern edge of town (nr M56 junction 10) **Cheshire Oaks** claims to be Europe's biggest factory outlet shopping village, with familiar brands and good bargains.

♪ ! **Blue Planet Aquarium** (SJ4174; off A5117, near junction 10 of M53) The most obviously dramatic feature at this splendid aquarium is the 71-metre (233-ft) walk-through tunnel, surrounded by sharks, stingray, and 3½ million gallons of water; a moving walkway lets you trundle along gawping without having to look where you're going. Knowledgeable staff (inc marine biologists) are on hand at each exhibit to answer questions and give talks at various times of the day. A big draw is the Aquatheatre, rather like a cinema with the screen replaced by a window into one of their biggest tanks; divers regularly go down to feed the creatures, and have microphones to chat with the audience as they do it. The main sections represent water environments and their occupants from trout streams to mangroves, with touchpools in some areas, where children can handle starfish and the like. As well as fish they have reptiles and insects – who would have thought touching hissing cockroaches would prove so popular? Most displays are at a height younger children can appreciate, and there's free face-painting. Meals,

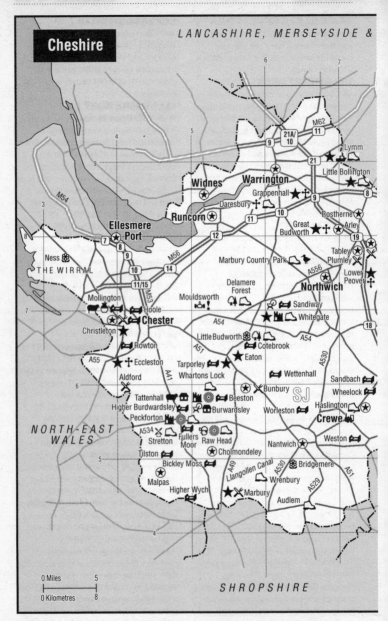

snacks, shop, good disabled access; cl 25 Dec; (0151) 357 8800; £7.50 (£5 children over 3). Various good-value family tickets.

GAWSWORTH SJ8969

🏚 🕸 ★ **Gawsworth Hall**
Exceptionally pretty timbered manor house dating back to Norman times, the former home of Mary Fitton, possibly the Dark Lady of Shakespeare's sonnets; plenty of fine furniture, stained glass, pictures and sculptures. In summer the open-air theatre has a well chosen range of concerts and plays;

Hotel over at Sutton Lane Ends is quite handy for lunch.

GRAPPENHALL SJ6386

★✝ This attractive village is worth a visit for the ancient grinning cat on its church tower; there are peaceful canalside strolls here.

GREAT BUDWORTH SJ6677

★ ✝ Set in attractive rich countryside, this is a quaint, purpose-built estate village; the church is imposing (as is the pub), and there are many pretty cottages.

HASLINGTON SJ7456

🦗🐄🐾🏠 **Lakemore Country Park** (Lane End Farm) Readers enjoy this country park with rare breeds inc miniature donkeys and endangered birds of prey. Nature trails link five man-made lakes; pets corner, outdoor and indoor playgrounds – extra charge for children's rides. Open Weds–Sun plus bank hols Apr–Oct; (01270) 253556; £2.50. The friendly Fox nearby has decent food.

JODRELL BANK SJ7970

⬆✝! 🦗 **Jodrell Bank Centre & Arboretum** Plenty to do at this lively place: the centrepiece is still the huge radio telescope, the second largest in the world and as big as the dome of St Paul's, but they also have a fun Science Centre, with hands-on displays and exhibitions examining subjects as diverse as plants, prisms and planets. Outside is an arboretum with 2,500 types of tree, as well as nature trails, picnic spots, and an Environmental Discovery Centre. Regular shows in the Planetarium. Meals, snacks, shop, disabled access; cl Mon Nov–mid-Mar, 20–26 and 31 Dec, 1 Jan; (01477) 571339; £4.30. The Dog at Peover Heath is quite handy for lunch.

KERRIDGE HILL SJ9477

※ 🏠 Above Bollington, and with fine views, this is topped by the curious folly known as White Nancy. Good walks here, and to the E – where the quaint Highwayman pub (B5470 N of Rainow) also has nice views, and is handy for the long-distance Gritstone Trail path.

KETTLESHULME SJ9879

🦗 🏠 **Dunge Valley Gardens** (off B5470) Prices have actually come down at these colourful gardens in Peak District countryside, especially good

good gardens and park too. Snacks, shop; cl am, and all Oct–Mar; (01260) 223456; £4.20. The village has fine houses in parkland, ponds, an interesting church, and an unusual unspoilt farm pub, while the Sutton Hall for rhododendrons (May, Jun), roses and unusual perennials. Teas, plant sales; cl Sept–Mar and Mon exc bank hols; (01663) 733787; £2.50 wknds and bank hols, £2 wkdys. The Crag at nearby Wildboarclough does decent food, and fits in well with a walk to the Three Shires Head and the summit of Shutlingsoe.

KNUTSFORD SJ7578

Despite obvious present-day prosperity and some rather heavy traffic, this has a pleasantly old-world feel, with lots of striking Georgian and other period buildings. It quickly conjures up schoolday memories of reading Mrs Gaskell's *Cranford*, its alias. 🏠🖼️🏵️🎣🛶🚂 **Tatton Park** On Knutsford's northern edge, a busy estate with a handsome neo-classical Georgian mansion at its centre. Magnificent collection of furnishings, porcelain and paintings (inc two Canalettos) in the opulent state rooms, and restored kitchens and servants' quarters; the medieval old hall hints at the long history of the estate. The lovely grounds boast an Edwardian rose garden, Italian and Japanese gardens, orangery and fern house, leading to a big country park with mature trees, lakes, signposted walks and deer and waterfowl; you can fish, hire bikes, or take a carriage ride. There's also a Home Farm that works as it did 60 years ago, with vintage machinery and rare breeds of animals; children's playground. You could easily spend most of an undemanding day here (good family activities in summer school hols), or take a carload for a picnic in the park. Meals, snacks, shop, some disabled access; park and gardens open all year (except winter Mons), rest cl Mon (exc bank hols), all Nov–Mar (exc farm open Sun), mansion and old hall also cl am, (mansion open some wknds Dec with seasonal decorations); (01625) 534435; entry to park £3 per car (free for cyclists and pedestrians), then £3 for the mansion or gardens, and £2.50 for the farm or old hall. An all-in ticket is £4.50; NT (though as the site is managed by the county council members still have to pay for all exc the mansion and garden).

LITTLE BOLLINGTON SJ7286

★⌂ This peaceful hamlet gives strolls by the Bridgewater Canal and in Dunham Massey deer park.

LITTLE BUDWORTH SJ5867

🏵️ **Cheshire Herbs** Award-winning specialist herb nursery growing and selling over 200 different varieties from agrimony to yellow melilot. Shop, disabled access; cl 24 Dec–2 Jan; (01829) 760578; free. The Shrewsbury Arms has good-value food. 🐾⌂ **Little Budworth Common** This country park is a strong (and oddly refreshing) contrast to most of this area's richly manicured countryside: poor wild heath with young bogs and scrawny birchwoods.

LOWER PEOVER SJ7474

★✝ Many people's favourite Cheshire village: cobbled lanes, glorious 14th-c black and white timbered **church**, quiet watermeadows and a fine pub.

LOWER WITHINGTON SJ8663

🛶✝♘ **Welltrough Dried Flowers** (signed off A34) Well praised by readers, a helpful and friendly dried flowers specialist based on a working dairy farm, with waterfowl and calves for children. Snacks, shop, disabled access; cl 25–27 Dec, 1–3 Jan; (01477) 571616; free. Further along the A34 at Marton is a simple 14th-c shingle-roofed black and white timbered **church** in unpromising surroundings; readers recommend the adjacent **craft centre**, where a farm shop sells home-made ice-cream.

LYMM SJ6887

★⚓⌂ There are pretty cottages in **The Dingle**, and you can take **boat trips** on the Bridgewater Canal, for example from the new Admiral Benbow pub at Agden Wharf. The walk up to the lake at Lymm Dam is a pleasant stroll.

MACCLESFIELD SJ9173

🏠✳️ Away from the modern shopping streets are plenty of fine old buildings associated with the early Industrial Revolution and the silk industry, the weavers' cottages, on Paradise St, with their wide garret windows are of especial note. Behind St Michael's Church is a more ancient core with quaint little cobbled alleys, the famous 108 steps, and fine views across the town to the Pennines. The teashop at Arighi Bianci is highly recommended.

The Sutton Hall Hotel just S is best for lunch, and the moorland pubs are in fairly easy reach.

❀ ⌂ **Hare Hill** (off B5087 NW of Macclesfield) Acres of lovely parkland with walled garden, pergola, fine spring flowers and rhododendrons and azaleas in May. Some disabled access; cl Nov–mid-May, plus Mon (exc bank hols), Tues and Fri Jun–Oct; £2.50; NT. A footpath leads to Alderley Edge.

⚙ ♔ **Paradise Mill** (Park Lane) Good fun; enthusiastic guides (many of whom are former silk workers) demonstrate the silk production process on the mill's restored handlooms, and room settings give a good idea of 1930s working conditions. Shop, good disabled access; cl am, all Mon (exc bank hols), 24–26 Dec, 1 Jan, Good Fri; (01625) 618228; £2.70. A joint ticket with the Silk Museum is £4.75.

⚙ ♔ **Silk Museum** (Roe St) The best place to learn about the industry, and has some fine examples of the end product. Snacks, shop, some disabled access; cl am Sun, Good Fri, 24–26 Dec, 1 Jan; (01625) 613210, £2.70.

⚙ **West Park Museum** (Prestbury Rd) Small refurbished museum with a decent range of decorative arts and a collection of interesting Egyptian antiquities. Adjacent West Park is pleasant and has one of the largest bowling greens in the country. Shop; cl am, all Mon (exc bank hols), 24–26 Dec, 1 Jan, Good Fri; free.

MACCLESFIELD CANAL SJ8965
⌂ With good more or less level towpath walks, this tracks through fine high countryside from the Cheshire county boundary nr Disley to pass Bollington, Macclesfield and Congleton, with plenty of access points. One of the most interesting places is S of the A54 just W of its junction with the A523, where a staggering flight of 10 locks leads down to a sturdily elegant iron aqueduct.

MALPAS SJ4847
★ ✝ ⛪ The most striking thing in this attractive place is the extraordinarily uplifting ceiling in its 14th-c hilltop **church**. There's also a fragmentary castle ruin nearby, as well as pretty cottages and almshouses, and some grander buildings.

MARBURY SJ5645
★ ✝ Some delightful landscapes open up in this village, with its attractive **church**, lake, wood and canal surroundings.

MARBURY COUNTRY PARK SJ6576
⌂ ✎ With some quiet short walks, this gives on to the extensive **Budworth Mere**, with sailing, and herons, ducks, grebes and coots pottering around the rushes; good pubs nearby at Comberbach (pronounced Comberbatch) and Great Budworth.

MIDDLEWOOD WAY SJ9482
⌂ A sort of linear country park near Macclesfield, this runs along a former railway; attractively bordered with wild flowers and trees, with tracks too for cyclists (bicycle hire at Lyme Park or Bollington) and horse rides (can also be hired by the hour, about £10); several decent pubs in Bollington, one at Whiteley Green. The pleasant stretches around the Poynton inclines are underrated, and the Boar's Head here is a good-value refreshment.

MOBBERLEY SJ7879
✎ ✝ **Hillside Ornamental Fowl** (Damson Lane) Excellent private collection of wildfowl with rare species such as magpie geese, white-headed stifftail and the Abyssinian black duck, as well as aviaries of softbills, flamingos and other exotic birds. Children should enjoy the penguin pool, and they have a pair of white wallabies. Undercover picnic area, snacks, shop; open Apr–Oct exc Thurs; (01565) 873282; £4.50. The **church** has a magnificently carved Tudor rood screen. The Bird in Hand and Church Inn are useful for lunch.

MOLLINGTON SJ3870
🐄 ⚙ **Cheshire Cheese Experience** (The Grange) This Cheshire cheese-making centre has relocated to Mollington, where you should be able to watch demonstrations from around the start of Dec; which stages of the process you see depends on the time of day you visit, but a museum will fill you in on the rest. Shop, disabled access; (01244) 851226; free, tours inc samples £1.

MOULDSWORTH SJ5171
🚗 ! **Mouldsworth Motor Museum** (Smithy Lane) Splendid changing

collection of cars, everything from vintage Bentleys to gleaming Ferraris: they hope to have 1920s land speed record-setter Babs (buried for over 40 years beneath Pendine sands after it overturned, tragically killing its driver) this summer. It's a notably friendly place, and you really don't have to be a car fiend to enjoy it – the 1930s Art Deco building and its grounds are very attractive in themselves, and there's plenty to amuse children, with quizzes, play areas and space to run around. There's also a collection of unusual teapots, many from the 1920s and 30s. Shop; disabled access; open pm Sun and bank hols Mar–Nov, plus pm Weds July and Aug; (01928) 731781; £2.50. The White Lion at Alvanley is a popular nearby dining pub.

MOW COP SJ8557

❀ ⌂ Right on the Staffs border is a shaggy steep hill with a castellated folly on top, and a rock pinnacle left by former quarrying; rich views over Cheshire (the village just behind, which is in Staffs, is a reminder of the contrast with Cheshire's richness). Worth a look if passing.

NANTWICH SJ6552

✝ A pedestrian-only centre protects the splendid 14th-c **church**, with its exceptional carved choir stalls; look out for the devil forcing open a nun's mouth, and the wife threatening her husband with a ladle. Much of the town, destroyed by a firestorm in 1583, was rebuilt then in intricate black and white timbering, and with countless window-boxes in flower in spring and summer is a fine sight especially around the centre. Quite a few decent antique shops, and the central Crown has a good lunchtime carvery. As most of south Cheshire's roads seem to intersect at the town, traffic can be a problem.

⚘ **Firs Pottery** (Aston; A530 towards Whitchurch) Friendly place organising one-day pottery workshops (half-days for children). Booking essential; (01270) 780345; *£25 for a day course, inc lunch and tea and coffee (*£10 children, during school hols). A shop sells all sorts of useful pots; disabled access to ground floor only. The nearby Bhurtpore has enjoyable food and a good range of real ales. Readers enjoy

the vast array of different flavours of ice-cream available at **Snugbury's Ice-Cream Farm** (Hurleston, A51 N); cl 25–26 Dec, 1 Jan.

❗**Hack Green Secret Nuclear Bunker** 💷 (off A530 towards Whitchurch) Built in the 1950s, this concrete labyrinth is where civil servants and military commanders would have hidden in the event of a nuclear war. An ordinary utility building on the surface, inside it is crammed with gadgets and interactive displays conjuring up a picture of what life would be like during a nuclear fall-out – you can even view the original TV broadcasts that would have been transmitted before a strike; children's trail. Snacks, shop, disabled access; cl wkdys Mar and Nov, plus Sat Nov–Jan (exc school hols); (01270) 629219; £4.80.

❀ ♪ **Stapeley Watergardens** (A51, about a mile SE of Nantwich) The world's largest and best-regarded watergarden centre with display pools, fountains (the dancing ones are popular with younger visitors), waterfalls, gardens, coldwater and tropical fish, and a huge heated glasshouse full of over 350 waterlilies (at their best Jun–Sept), piranhas, sharks, palms and parrots. Plenty of other gifts (lots for fishermen) as well as plants, and frequent special events. Meals, snacks, shop, disabled access; cl 25 Dec; (01270) 623868; gardens free, palm house £3.50.

NESTON SJ3075

❀ **Ness Gardens** Liverpool University's extensive collection of specimen trees and shrubs, herbaceous plants, renowned heather, rock, rose and watergardens; visitor centre, good children's adventure playground, and picnic area. Meals, snacks, shop and plant sales, wheelchair route; cl 25 Dec (open till dusk in summer); (0151) 353 0123; £4.30. The Red Lion is the nicest place in nearby Parkgate for a light lunch.

NETHER ALDERLEY SJ8476

✗ ❀ ⌂ **Nether Alderley Mill** Lovely 15th-c watermill with carefully preserved atmosphere, and restored working water wheels. The Victorian machinery still grinds flour (water supplies permitting). Open pm Weds,

Sun and bank hols Apr–Oct, plus pm Tues, Thurs, Fri and Sat Jun–Sept; (01625) 523012; £2; NT. Nearby Alderley Edge SJ8677 (not to be confused with the straggling suburban settlement named after it), rises high out of the plain, with good walks through the woodland and fine views of the higher hills to the E. The local caving club members are working towards opening some of the former copper mines which honeycomb the area.

NORTHWICH SJ6674

⬆ ⋔ ⚓ **Salt Museum** (London Rd) Cheshire is the only British county to produce salt on a large scale, and much of it comes from this town. This interesting museum has the industry pretty well covered; microscopes let you see the intricacy of each crystal. Snacks, shop, limited disabled access; cl am wknds, all Mon (exc bank hols and in Aug), 24–26 Dec; (01606) 41331; £2. You can follow the Salt Heritage Trail around some of the other buildings. From the Quay there are cruises down the river. The Smoker at Plumley (A556 E) is a reliable dining pub.

PECKFORTON HILLS SJ5256

❄ ⛰ ⌂ These are tracked by a particularly fine section of the 30-mile **Sandstone Trail**, with splendid views of real and real-looking romantic castles, and good pubs usefully placed at Bulkeley and Higher Burwardsley. The Trail offers very varied scenery, following the romantically wooded sandstone ridges, crags and outcrops stretching from Overton in the N (the church here is pretty, and the Ring o' Bells is a most attractive pub, with Mersey views) to the Shropshire border S of Malpas (the ancient Bell o' the Hill pub nr Tushingham down there is a useful stop).

POYNTON SJ9283

🚉 ❀ ⚘ ♥ 🐦 **Brookside Garden Centre** (Macclesfield Rd) A splendid miniature railway chuffs its way through an authentically detailed circuit in a pretty garden setting to a replica West Country station, packed with railway memorabilia. Also pottery and birds of prey. Parking is not always easy. Meals, snacks, shop, disabled access (not train); railway runs wknds all year plus Weds Apr–Sept and daily mid-July and

Aug; (01625) 872919; train £1, garden centre free. A mile away at Higher Poynton, Coppice Fruit Farm has **pick-your-own**.

PRESTBURY SJ9077

★ ⌂ Very prosperous-feeling now, with leafy surroundings, good shops, and for refreshment the smart Legh Arms and homelier Admiral Rodney. There are pleasant riverside walks to the S, along the Bollin.

RAW HEAD SJ5154

⌂ ❄ 🏺 From the A534 nr Harthill a section of the 30-mile Sandstone Trail ascends Raw Head, the most spectacular natural feature of the central Cheshire ridge, with sandstone cliffs weathered into bizarre shapes, and a cave to explore.

ROSTHERNE SJ7483

★ ❄ ✝ As well as charming brick cottages along its quaint cobbled pavement, this picture-postcard village gives a lovely view over one of the county's broadest meres from the graveyard of its attractive timbered church.

RUNCORN SJ5182

🚉 ❄ 🏰 Apart from Norton Priory, this New Town has some enjoyable surprises – such as the Sunday-afternoon **miniature train rides** in the Park on Stockham Lane (Halton), popular with children. There are views from the nearby ruins of **Halton Castle** up on its grassy hill.

🏛 ⛲ ⚘ 🏵 **Norton Priory Museum & Gardens** (Tudor Rd, Manor Park) Lovely 12th-c priory that developed into a Georgian stately home, with exhibitions on medieval monastic life, and demonstrations of tile-making, carving and sculpture inc a 12-ft sandstone statue of St Christopher, said to be carved by a member of the priory 600 years ago. Outside is an enchanting 18th-c walled garden, and beautiful woodland gardens. Snacks, shop, disabled access; cl am, 24–26 Dec, 1 Jan, walled garden cl Nov–Feb; (01928) 569895; £3.30.

SANDIWAY SJ6171

⚘ **Blakemere Craft Centre** (Chester Rd) Much better than average craft centre based around a restored Edwardian stable block, with interesting range of goods in the 18 shops, aquatic centre, and good food hall. Wknd craft fairs, meals, snacks, disabled access; cl Mon (exc bank hols); (01606) 883261; free.

STRETTON SJ4453

⚒ △ **Stretton Watermill** Working watermill set in lovely countryside which still produces corn, powered by two ancient wheels. Shop, some disabled access; cl am, all Mon and Oct–Mar (open wknds only Apr and Sept); (01606) 41331; £1.75. The Cock o' Barton up on the A534 is quite useful for lunch (and a good base for walks – as is the Farndon Arms in the attractive Dee-side village of Farndon).

STYAL SJ8383

↓↑ 🏢 🕸 🐣 △ **Quarry Bank Mill & Country Park** One of the best and most extensive places in the country to get to grips with the Industrial Revolution – you can easily spend the best part of a day here. The 18th-c cotton mill that's the centrepiece still produces cloth (you can buy it in the shop), and as well as demonstrations of spinning and weaving has lively exhibitions looking at factory conditions for the millworkers and their bosses. A hands-on exhibition explains how the 1840 beam engine in the original engine house was restored, whilst the 50-ton working water wheel remains an impressive sight. The surrounding village has carefully preserved workers' cottages, chapels and shop; at the apprentice house enthusiastic guides in period dress explain the lifestyle and 12-hour working days faced by young pauper children; you can even try out their beds. They grow rare types of fruit and vegetables in the garden (timed tickets in operation here, so it makes sense to see this bit at the start of your visit). Good woodland and riverside walks in the park, lots of events throughout the year. Meals, snacks, shop, disabled access; cl winter Mons, apprentice house cl am wkdys and Mon during school terms; (01625) 527468; all-in ticket £5.80, mill only £4.40, apprentice house only £3.60; NT. The Ship is pleasant for lunch.

SWETTENHAM SJ8067

★ One of Cheshire's tucked-away comfortable villages – rich paddocks with wrought-iron fences, daffodils in spring in a dell by an old mill, a good dining pub (the Swettenham Arms) behind the partly 13th-c church.

TABLEY SJ7277

⏰ ! **Cuckoo Clock Collection** (Old School House, Nether Tabley) A unique collection of these and other mechanical timepieces from all over the world. They currently have over 500 rare and beautiful clocks, most of them working, but the number constantly increases as the owners nip off to Europe to track down more. Four working historic fairground organs are among the other mechanisms on show. By appointment (phone to order snacks). Shop, disabled access; (01565) 633039; *£5.

🏛 🖼 **Tabley House** (off A5033) Probably the finest Palladian House in the North-West, with a splendid collection of paintings. Sir John Fleming Leicester (whose family lived here for over 800 years) was the first great collector of British art, and though plans to turn his home into a National Gallery came to nothing, most of the works he assembled are still here, inc pictures by Turner (the one of a pineapple shows why he is remembered for his landscapes), Reynolds, Henry Thompson and James Ward. Snacks, shop, very good disabled access (though they prefer notice); open Apr–Oct, pm Thurs–Sun and bank hols; (01565) 750151; *£4. The Smoker at Plumley is good for lunch.

TARPORLEY SJ5562

★ Largely bypassed and quietly attractive, with very individual shops inc antique shops; the Rising Sun is a fine pub, the Swan a well restored old coaching inn.

TATTENHALL SJ4858

🐄 🏢 **Cheshire Ice-Cream Farm** (Drumlan Hall Farm) Watch the cows being milked then sample the delicious end product. Snacks, shop, disabled access; cl two wks mid-Jan; (01829) 770995; free. The Egerton Arms down the A41 at Broxton is a good lunch stop.

TEGGS NOSE COUNTRY PARK SJ9472

☀ △ 🐣 Cheshire's hilly eastern edge forms part of the Peak District, and offers some grand views westwards towards North Wales. This country park has a useful summer information centre, and good walks with far views, punctuated by relics of the former quarrying here. By the turn off the A537, the Setter Dog is a nice pub. From the park, a well marked track heads off into the **Macclesfield Forest**, with steep green pine plantations around neatly walled small reservoirs; on the far side of this the isolated Leathers Smithy E of Langley is a welcoming moorside refuge with superb views, and the Stanley Arms tucked away at Bottom of the Oven is also good. This track is actually part of the long-distance Gritstone Trail, which is well marked and offers a few days' walking of the highest quality.

WARRINGTON SJ6087

☺ **Gulliver's World** Theme park very similar to its sister parks in Milton Keynes and Matlock Bath (see *Buckinghamshire and Derbyshire chapters*), with rides and entertainment aimed at the under-12s. Meals, snacks, shop, disabled access; open wknds Apr–Oct, daily Jun–mid-Sept and during school hols; (01925) 444888; £6.

♿▣! **Warrington Museum & Gallery** (Bold St) The newly refurbished geology and botany galleries contain hands-on displays and a 'breathing' model dinosaur. Other weird and wonderful exhibits include decorated skulls and shrunken heads, an Egyptian mummy, a toy-packed nursery, and a number of beetles and other creepy-crawlies. Snacks, shop, disabled access; cl Sun and bank hols; free. The Ferry at Fiddlers Ferry down by the Mersey off the A562 at Penketh is prettily placed for lunch.

WHARTONS LOCK SJ5360

⌂ With a handy family dining pub nearby, this is a good place for walks along the **Shropshire Union Canal**; this is a charming section, winding through the richly wooded farming country below Beeston Castle.

WHITEGATE SJ6168

★ 🏛 ⌂ An interesting village, with thatched houses around the village green, fragmentary remains of what was once the biggest Cistercian monastery in the whole of England opposite its church, and a lakeside walk along a nearby derelict railway.

WIDNES SJ5185

⬇↑! ❀ **Catalyst** (Mersey Rd) Award-winning centre exploring the chemical industry and how it affects our lives. Put like that it doesn't sound too gripping, but children who enjoy museums where you poke, press and push things will really get a lot out of it. It's all presented in a splendidly enjoyable and entertaining way, with interactive games and displays such as Apples and Maggots, where you battle against maggots, gales and floods to grow a successful crop of apples, or the Game of Health, which involves travelling from the past to the present without falling victim to any deadly diseases. A glass lift whisks you up to a roof-top observatory with splendid views. There's an adjacent waterside park, with wildlife and brightly coloured fishing boats. Meals, snacks, shop, disabled access; cl Mon exc bank and school hols, 24–26 Dec, 1 Jan; (0151) 420 1121; £4.65.

WRENBURY SJ5947

⌂ **Canal walks** The pretty **Llangollen Branch** is a relaxing canal for gentle waterside walks, with access, for example, at Wrenbury; the good Dusty Miller dining pub here has an interesting lifting bridge by it.

Where to eat

ALDFORD SJ4159 **Grosvenor Arms** *(01244) 620228* Sizeable but friendly Victorian pub, attractively decorated, with huge panelled library and several quieter rooms, and an airy conservatory; good interesting food from a daily changing menu, well kept real ales, lots of New World wines (and malt whiskies), and a large elegant sun-trap terrace and neat lawn; best to get there early; children allowed until 6pm; disabled access. £22|£5.95.

ALTRINCHAM SJ7788 **Juniper** *21 The Downs (0161) 929 4008* Smart but informal-feeling restaurant with a huge Italian mural, lots of plants, and wooden floor and ceiling; beautifully presented modern cooking (super fish), lovely puddings, good cheeses, a carefully chosen and interesting wine list, and efficient service; downstairs bar, too; cl am Sat, all Sun, and am Mon. **£40**.

BOLLINGTON SJ9377 **Mauro's** *88 Palmerston St (01625) 573898* Friendly Italian restaurant with lots of good pasta, excellent fresh fish and lovely puddings; cl am Sat and Sun, Mon; disabled access. **£30|£4.90**.

BUNBURY SJ5758 **Dysart Arms** *Bowes Gate Rd (01829) 260183* By the village church, this neat former farmhouse has a civilised, old-fashioned atmosphere, log fires, lots of antique furniture, and cosy alcoves; well kept ales and house wines, interesting food, friendly service, and tables in the lovely elevated big garden; no children evenings; disabled access. **£19|£6.50**.

CHESTER SJ4166 **Francs** *14 Cuppin St (01244) 317952* Cheerful timbered brasserie on two floors of an old converted warehouse, with very good French country food; partial disabled access. **£20|£6.95** – children free if adults eat set meal.

CHESTER SJ4166 **Old Harkers Arms** *1 Russell St, under Mike Melody Antiques, off City Rd (01244) 344525* Attractive conversion of an early Victorian canal warehouse with lofty ceiling, tall windows and well spaced tables and chairs, lots to look at, a comfortably busy atmosphere, friendly and efficient staff; a changing choice of nicely presented, sometimes unusual food (inc interesting sandwiches), well kept real ales, and New World wines; disabled access. **£16.85|£5**.

HASSALL GREEN SJ7858 **Canal Centre and Tearoom** *(01270) 762266* 200-year-old house with tearoom offering breakfasts, snacks, lunches, cream teas, and evening restaurant; you can sit on the lawn and watch the narrow boats going through the locks; gift shop and towpath walks; bdrms; cl 25–26 Dec, 1 Jan; disabled access. **£17|£4.95**.

KNUTSFORD SJ7578 **Belle Epoque Brasserie** *60 King St (01565) 633060* Popular restaurant with rooms decorated in Art Nouveau style with lavish drapes, marbled pillared alcoves, and smartly set tables; enthusiastic friendly staff and lovely modern cooking; cl Sun, bank hols; children over 12. **£25|£4.95**.

PEOVER HEATH SJ7973 **Dog** *(01625) 861421* Set on a quiet lane, this bustling pub has two big no smoking areas, a cosy, comfortable tap room with darts and pool, open fires, well kept real ales, a good choice of whiskies, a comprehensive wine list, and well liked, often interesting food using local produce; bdrms; cl pm 25 Dec; disabled access. **£23.95|£3.50**.

PLUMLEY SJ7175 **Smoker** *(01565) 722338* Popular thatched 16th-c pub with open fires and comfortable sofas in three well decorated connecting rooms; good, swiftly served food, a wide choice of whiskies, well kept real ales, and friendly service; big garden; disabled access. **£19.50|£6.95**.

POTT SHRIGLEY SJ9478 **Cheshire Hunt** *(01625) 573185* Isolated stone pub with several rambling small rooms (one is no smoking), solid furnishings, beams, flowers and roaring log fires; good popular bar and restaurant food, and no noisy games machines or piped music; seats outside with country views; cl am Mon except bank hols; disabled access. **£15|£5**.

SWETTENHAM SJ8067 **Swettenham Arms** *(01477) 571284* Tucked-away country dining pub with three spacious beamed bar areas, winter log fires, nice furnishings, real ales, a no smoking restaurant, and huge range of very popular food; cl pms 25 and 26 Dec; partial disabled access. **£23.95|£3.50**.

WHITELEY GREEN SJ9278 **Windmill** *(01625) 574222* Close to the canal and other walks and with plenty of seats in the attractive 4-acre garden, this large slate-roofed white house has a 16th-c heart with wooden-floored, open-plan extensions; country kitchen-style furnishings, a welcoming atmosphere, very good, well prepared interesting food, well kept ales, and friendly service. **£21.50|£7.50**.

Special thanks to Mr and Mrs McKay, P Dobson, E G Parish, Michael and Jenny Back.

Cheshire Calendar

Some of these dates were provisional as we went to press. Please check information with the telephone numbers provided.

Chester Public Proclamations by the Town Crier, 12 noon at the Cross – every *Tues–Sat, April–October* (01244) 402445
Chester Band Concerts by the river *2pm* and *3.30pm* and *4pm* and *6pm* at the Edwardian bandstand in the Groves – *every Sat and Sun and bank hol Mon, May–Sept* (01244) 402445
Chester Guided Walk of Roman Chester, *1.45pm* from Chester Visitor Centre and *2pm* from the Tourist Information Centre – *till 3 June* (01244) 402445
Chester Ghost Walk *at 7.30pm*, from Chester Town Hall Tourist Information Centre – *till 3 June* (01244) 402445

JANUARY

 1 **Frodsham** Plant a Millennium Tree at Foxhill Arboretum – *till 1 June* (01928) 739189
16 **Knutsford** Dolls, Dolls Houses and Teddy Bear Fair at Tatton Park (01270) 878519
22 **Nantwich** Holly Holy Day: re-enactment of the Battle of Namptwyche 1643 (01270) 610983

MARCH

10 **Great Budworth** Cheshire County Antiques Fair at Arley Hall – *till 12 March* (01565) 777284
13 **Warrington** Fleadh: Irish Festival at Parr Hall – *till 19 March* (01925) 442362

APRIL

 1 **Macclesfield** Model Railway Club Annual Show – *till 2 April* (01625) 610276
 2 **Chester** Dolls, Dolls Houses and Teddy Bear Fair at Tatton Park (01270) 878519
 8 **Macclesfield** Rainbow Craft Fair: over 200 stands at Capesthorne Hall – *till 9 April* (01625) 861221
 9 **Great Budworth** Rare and Unusual Plant Fair at Arley Hall (01565) 777284
16 **Sandbach** Transport Festival (01270) 764499
21 **Ellesmere Port** Traditional Boat Gathering at the Boat Museum – *till 24 April* (0151) 355 5017; **Nantwich** Jazz and Blues Festival – *till 24 April* (01270) 625283
22 **Knutsford** Easter Festival at Tatton Park: circus, fair, fun-on-the-farm, living history; incorporating a flower festival in the Mansion and Spring Craft Fair in the Tenants Hall – *till 24 April* (01565) 534403

MAY

 1 **Macclesfield** Children's Garden Party at Capesthorne Hall (01625) 861221; **Sandbach** May Day Fair (01270) 763231

Cheshire Calendar (cont.)

 6 **Knutsford** Royal May Day Festival: pavements are carpeted with elaborate sand patterns, and there is a procession, horse-drawn tableaux, Morris dancers, maypole dancers, fireworks (01565) 633074; **Marbury** Merry Days: falconry, raft racing – *till 7 May* (01948) 663758

 9 **Chester** May Festival (racing) at the racecourse – *till 11 May* (01244) 323170

13 **Chester** Lord Mayor's Parade (01244) 375283; also carnival and vintage car rally at the racecourse – *till 14 May* (01244) 375283

14 **Knutsford** Dolls, Dolls Houses and Teddy Bear Fair at Tatton Park (01270) 878519

18 **Alderley Edge** Music Festival – *till 20 May* (01625) 524535

20 **Chester** Regatta – *till 21 May* (01244) 335593

21 **Macclesfield** Kit Car Show at Capesthorne Hall (01625) 861221; **Nantwich** Reaseheath College Open Weekend: nature trails, gardening, tractor rides, animals and pets, sheepdog displays (01270) 625131

26 **Kelsall** Chester Folk Festival at the Morris Dancer Pub – *till 29 May* (01244) 320424

28 **Macclesfield** Classic Car Show at Capesthorne Hall – *till 29 May* (01625) 861221; **Runcorn** Town Park Show (01928) 576246

29 **Audlem** Carnival (01270) 811467; **Knutsford** Street Market and Fair (01565) 632611; **Northwich** Regatta (01606) 862862

JUNE

 1 **Neston** Ladies Day: afternoon procession in period costume (0151) 3363104

 3 **Chester** Mystery Plays: Free open-air productions performed on a cart, as in medieval times – *every Sat June–July* on Town Hall Sq, *every Sun June–July* at The Cross (01244) 402111

 4 **Knutsford** Orchid Show at Tatton Park (01565) 654822

 9 **Great Budworth** Cheshire County Antiques Fair – *till 11 June* (015665) 777284; **Ness** Garden Festival at Ness Botanic Gardens – *till 11 June* (0151) 353 0123

10 **Woodford** Air Show (0161) 439500

11 **Knutsford** Fireworks Concert at Tatton Park (01625) 575681

17 **Appleton Thorn** Bawming the Thorn: traditional procession and festivities during which children *bawm* (dance round) a hawthorn tree, originated when a knight went on the Crusades with an offshoot of the Glastonbury Thorn (01925) 266764

20 **Tabley** Cheshire Show at the Showground – *till 21 June* (01829) 760020

24 **Chester** Midsummer Watch Parade: re-creation of medieval procession inc family of four Chester giants, ship of fools, angels, devils and mythical beasts – *till 25 June* (01244) 348365; **Great Budworth** Garden Festival at Arley Hall – *till 25 June* (01565) 777353; **Ness** Open-air Concert at Ness Botanic Gardens (0151) 353 0123

30 **Warrington** Walking Day: long processions wind round the town originally to draw people away from the races (01925) 442180

JULY

 1 **Great Budworth** Fireworks Concert at Arley Hall (01565) 777284

 2 **Chester** River Carnival and Raft Race (01244) 324888

 3 **Runcorn** Carnival (01928) 580366

Cheshire Calendar (cont.)

8 Warrington Steam Fair at Grappen Hall – *till 9 July* (01751) 473780

9 Great Budworth Summer Concert at Arley Hall (01565) 777284; **Wilmslow** Wilmslow and Bollin Valley Show at the Carnival Field (01625) 251126

14 Chester Summer Music Festival with international performers – *till 29 July* (01244) 320722

15 Widnes Halton Show at Spike Island – *till 16 July* (0151) 424 2061

20 Knutsford RHS Flower Show at Tatton Park – *till 23 July* (020) 7821 3042

26 Nantwich Nantwich & South Cheshire Agricultural Show at Dorfold Hall Park (01270) 780306

29 Knutsford Firework Concert at Tatton Park (01565) 534403

AUGUST

6 Macclesfield Fireworks Concert at Capesthorne Hall (01625) 575681

12 Chelford Astle Park Traction Rally – *till 13 August* (01751) 473780

13 Knutsford Dolls, Dolls Houses and Teddy Bear Fair at Tatton Park (01270) 878519

13 Macclesfield Forest Chapel, Rushbearing Ceremony (01625) 572013; also Firework and Laser Symphony Concert at Capesthorne Hall (01625) 861221; **Rainow** Rushbearing Ceremony at the parish church (01625) 572013

20 Macclesfield Family Fun Day: free day, two arenas, parachute drop, 250 stalls at West Park (01625) 504114; **Over Peover** Game and Angling Fair at Peover Hall: gun dogs, parade of hounds, fly-fishing demonstration, birds of prey (01565) 733847

26 Crewe Crewe & Nantwich Carnival at Queen's Park – *till 28 August* (01270) 610983; **Poynton** Show at Poynton Park (01625) 504114

27 Macclesfield Sports Car Show at Capesthorne Hall – *till 28 August* (01625) 861221

SEPTEMBER

3 Knutsford Fireworks Concert at Tatton Park (01625) 575681

16 Macclesfield Rainbow Craft Fair: over 200 stands at Capesthorne Hall – *till 17 September* (01625) 861221; **Winsford** Vale Royal Show at the Civic Hall (01606) 862862

17 Norton Horticultural Show at Norton Priory (01928) 569895

OCTOBER

6 Great Budworth Cheshire County Antiques Fair (01565) 777284

7 Chester Literature Festival: famous guest authors, readings and workshops – *till 22 October* (01244) 319985

22 Chester Dolls, Dolls Houses and Teddy Bear Fair at Tatton Park (01270) 878519

28 Great Budworth Crafts at Arley Hall with 70 exhibitors from across the country – *till 29 October* (01565) 777284; **Wilmslow** Chrysanthemum Show at the Wilmslow Royal British Legion – *till 29 October* (01625) 585678

Cheshire Calendar (cont.)

NOVEMBER

5 Knutsford Dolls, Dolls Houses and Teddy Bear Fair at Tatton Park (01270) 878519

DECEMBER

7 Chester Lantern Parade; *also on Dec 14* (01244) 348365

We welcome reports from readers

This *Guide* depends on readers' reports. Do help us if you can – in return, we offer a discount on the next edition to people who've helped us with reports for it. Tell us what you think about places already in it, and anything extra you think we should say about them. And send us your ideas for inclusion in the next edition: places to visit, eat at or stay in, attractive drives or walks, maybe even unusual interesting shops you know of. Use the card in the middle, the report forms at the end, or just write – no stamp needed: *The Good Britain Guide*, FREEPOST TN1569, Wadhurst, E Sussex TN5 7BR.

CORNWALL

Seaside Britain at its best, from sandy family resorts through picturesque creeks, coves and quaint fishing villages to wild majestic cliffs; masses of family attractions, some spectacular gardens, a fine choice of places to stay in.

Cornwall's great gardens, at their best in late spring but gorgeous at almost any time, are quite unlike those elsewhere in England – altogether more exotic, almost subtropical. Among many splendid gardens, the Lost Gardens of Heligan (Mevagissey), Lanhydrock (the house too is special), Trelissick and Trebah (Mawnan Smith) are outstanding. The Eden Project at Pentewan, bringing a corner of paradise to Cornwall, won't be opening properly until 2001, but can be visited from 2000 to see the remarkable work in progress.

A great range of enjoyable family outings is topped by Paradise Park in Hayle (HQ of the World Parrot Trust), the Dobwalls family adventure park, Flambards theme park near Helston (entertaining for all ages), and Dairyland near Newquay. Animal-lovers have plenty to enjoy at Newquay Zoo (good conservation projects), the monkey sanctuary near Looe, and the seal sanctuary at Gweek. Readers particularly like the expanding animal centre at Trecangate for its friendly and uncommercial atmosphere.

The fairytale castle on St Michael's Mount, off Marazion, is a most enjoyable outing, and other places to note particularly include the Minack open-air theatre at Porthcurno, the odd collection of stuffed animals at Bolventor, the Goonhilly Earth Station, and two newcomers to the *Guide*, the Pilchard Works in Newlyn (much more interesting than that sounds) and the pre-industrial tin workings at Trevallas Coombe. Cotehele, near Calstock, is Cornwall's most lovely house, and Trerice, and Antony House at Torpoint, are also well worth visiting.

There are many delightful seaside villages and towns, keeping their charm even in summer, as the strolling crowds never quite override their friendly local character. Readers like the gently picturesque south coast best – very sheltered, with wonderful places to stay in. East of the Lizard Point are plenty of interesting little coves, winding estuaries and creeks rich in bird life, and boat and fishing trips from virtually every harbour. There are some dramatic cliffy stretches too, interspersed with fine sandy beaches, especially west of the Lizard.

The north coast scores for uncomplicated family beach holidays, around the attractive town of St Ives, and between Padstow (appealing combination of fishing port and resort) and lively Newquay (Cornwall's biggest resort, increasingly a surfing centre despite the 1999 sighting of a great white shark). This stretch is an almost continuous line of resort developments, with plenty of family attractions nearby.

West of St Ives are rugged stretches of windswept empty clifftop moorland, with a hinterland exceptionally rich in well preserved, visible archaeology – Bronze Age burial chambers and standing stones, Iron Age hill forts and village sites, ancient stone crosses. Small rather withdrawn-looking granite villages and farmsteads among wind-beaten pastures give this western part a rather clannish feel, almost like the more nationalistic parts of Wales; but though visitors are clearly seen as outsiders, the locals are far from unfriendly. Another stretch of wild grandeur is up towards Devon, north of commercialised Tintagel – towering precipices, dramatic surfing beaches and much completely unspoilt seaboard, with no development, little car access, just wildlife, wind, waves and the occasional walker. Port Isaac and Boscastle are the pick of this part's few settlements.

Away from the sheltered south-east, the inland parts are largely treeless, with rolling pasture and moorland. Windswept Bodmin Moor is the county's most untouched inland area. In the more exposed spots the towering alloy propellers of the new windfarms are becoming a striking landscape feature.

In high summer Cornwall's better for long stay-put holidays than for short breaks or touring: with lots of traffic on the narrow roads (and some serious parking problems), getting there, back and around can overshadow a short summer visit. On a longer holiday, it's surprisingly easy to escape the crowds that go with the big family attractions, honey-pot fishing villages and famous beaches. With 500 miles of coastal walks here, much of the land owned and beautifully preserved by the National Trust, you can always quickly escape into solitude. Incidentally, few roads actually follow the coast – good for walkers, if disappointing for drivers (or cyclists). The relatively warm sea makes Cornwall popular bathing country in summer: we pick out reliably clean beaches in the text.

Out of high season, Cornwall comes into its own for those prepared to spend the time getting there: lots to do, a very relaxed pace of life, and attractive prices. Generally well sheltered, most of the coastal places can be pleasantly mild when other parts of the West Country are cold. Late May and early June is an ideal time for a short break here, with the scenery at its best, and relatively few other visitors. In spring and early summer, the tall roadside hedged banks, which block the view from many byroads, compensate by being virtual walls of wild flowers. September and October is seal-pup time. From London, you should allow about five hours' driving out of season to get well into the county; it's about three hours' from Bristol – across just a couple of counties. The A30 is now a good fast long-distance route (much better than the A390).

If you'd rather avoid the roads altogether, a Cornish Rail Rover ticket is good value for eight days (which don't have to be consecutive) unlimited train journeys throughout the county for around £35; you can also get a ticket for three days.

The Isles of Scilly are ideal for a really quiet and relaxing holiday, with Penzance the quickest jumping-off point.

Where to stay

BODINNICK SX1352 **Old Ferry** *Bodinnick, Fowey PL23 1LX (01726) 870237* **£60;** 12 comfortable and spacious rms, most with own bthrm and river views. 400-year-old inn in lovely situation overlooking Fowey estuary; with back flagstoned bar partly cut into the rock, real ales, comfortable lounge with French windows opening on to a terrace, and decent food in both the bar and little evening restaurant; pool in games room; quiet out of season.

BOTALLACK SW3633 **Botallack Manor Farm** *Botallack, St Just in Penwith, Penzance TR19 7QG (01736) 788525* ***£50;*** 3 rms. Blissfully quiet and friendly 17th-c local granite farmhouse on working farm, with a medley of furnishings in the comfortable lounge, good breakfasts with home-baked bread, and a safe walled garden; no pets; marvellous cliff walks, ruined mines and small coves.

BURYAS BRIDGE SW4429 **Rose Farm** *Chyanhal, Buryas Bridge, Penzance TR19 6AN (01736) 731808* ***£40,*** plus winter breaks; 3 delightfully furnished rms. Relaxed, informal, friendly farmhouse tucked away down a remote country lane; excellent breakfasts around a big table; can see animals (working farm), and children love it; cl 24–25 Dec; disabled access.

CARNE BEACH SW9038 **Nare** *Carne Beach, Veryan, Truro TR2 5PF (01872) 501279* **£184,** plus special breaks; 36 lovely rms to suit all tastes – some stylish ones overlook garden and out to sea. Attractively decorated and furnished hotel in magnificent clifftop position with secluded gardens, outdoor and indoor swimming pools; antiques, fresh flowers and log fires in the airy, spacious day rooms, very good food inc wonderful breakfasts, and run by staff who really care; ideal for quiet family hols, with a safe sandy beach below; cl Jan; disabled access.

CONSTANTINE BAY SW8574 **Treglos** *Constantine Bay, Padstow PL28 8JH (01841) 520727* ***£96,*** plus special breaks; 44 light rms, some with balcony. Quiet and relaxed hotel close to good sandy beach, and in the same family for 30 years; comfortable traditional furnishings, log fires, decent food, friendly and helpful staff; sheltered garden, indoor swimming pool, pool and snooker, and children's playroom; lovely nearby walks; self-catering apartments; cl end Oct–mid-Mar; children over 7 in restaurant; disabled access.

CRACKINGTON HAVEN SX1396 **Manor Farm** *Crackington Haven, Bude EX23 0JW (01840) 230304* ***£60;*** 4 pretty rms. Lovely, Domesday-listed, no smoking manor surrounded by 25 acres of farmland and carefully landscaped gardens; with antiques in the lounges, a log fire, a house-party atmosphere, games room, big breakfasts, and a delicious 4-course dinner at 7pm; cl 25 Dec; no children.

CRANTOCK SW7960 **Highfield Lodge** *Halwyn Rd, Crantock, Newquay TR8 5TR (01637) 830744* ***£42,*** plus special breaks; 11 rms, most with en suite shower. Close to a super beach, this neatly kept, no smoking sea-view house offers a friendly welcome, a hearty breakfast, a licensed bar serving snacks, and plenty to do nearby; no pets.

FALMOUTH SW8032 **Penmere Manor** *Mongleath Rd, Falmouth TR11 4PN (01326) 211411* **£93,** plus special breaks; 37 spacious rms. Run by the same owners for 28 years, this quietly set Georgian manor has 5 acres of subtropical gardens and woodland, heated outdoor swimming pool, giant chess, croquet, and leisure centre with indoor swimming pool, mini-gym and sauna, and woodland fitness trail; particularly helpful and friendly staff, peaceful connecting rooms, an evening pianist, and enjoyable food in the restaurant and informal bar; cl 24–27 Dec.

FOWEY SX1252 **Carnethic House** *Lambs Barn, Fowey PL23 1HQ (01726) 833336* ***£60,*** plus special breaks; 8 rms. Warm, friendly Regency house in lovely gardens with heated swimming pool, badminton and putting; a relaxed and informal atmosphere, very helpful owners, attractive lounge, and good home-made food (local fish is popular); cl Dec and Jan; limited disabled access.

FOWEY SX1252 **Marina** *The Esplanade, PL23 1HY (01726) 833315* **£82,** plus special breaks; 11 rms, several with lovely views (some with balcony). Homely, friendly hotel in fine position overlooking River Fowey and open sea (private access from secluded walled garden); comfortable lounge, attractive dining room overlooking the water, good food, and helpful service; cl mid-Dec–end Feb; children over 12.

GERRANS BAY SW8937 **Pendower Beach House** *Gerrans Bay, Ruan High Lanes, Truro TR2 5LW* (01872) 501241 **£134 inc dinner,** plus special breaks; 15 rms. Family-run hotel dating back to the 16th c in 8 acres by a lovely beach, with superb sea and coastal views, and plenty of seats on sunny terrace; a relaxed, friendly atmosphere in attractive and comfortable rooms, good food in the cosy restaurant (super fresh local fish and shellfish), and tennis court; cl Nov–Feb; disabled access.

GILLAN SW6527 **Tregildry** *Gillan, Helston TR12 6HG* (01326) 231378 ***£130 inc dinner,** plus special breaks; 10 good rms with fine views over Falmouth Bay. Elegantly furnished hotel in 4 acres of grounds with private access to the cove below; spacious comfortable lounges, fresh flowers and books, a restful atmosphere, very good food in the attractive restaurant, and kind, courteous service; cl Nov–end Feb; no children.

GUNWALLOE SW6522 **Halzephron** *Gunwalloe, Helston TR12 7QB* (01326) 240406 **£64;** 2 cosy rms. 500-year-old former smugglers' inn run by knowledgeable and friendly Cornish couple, good food in bar areas and bistro-style restaurant, open fire, and fine views of Mount's Bay; lots of walks, nearby beaches, golf, and boating; no accommodation 24–25 Dec; no children.

LAMORNA COVE SW4524 **Lamorna Cove** *Lamorna Cove, Penzance TR19 6XH* (01736) 731411 **£69;** 12 well furnished rms, most with cove views. Beautifully placed hotel overlooking gardens to the sea; with comfortable homely rooms, a light, airy restaurant using fresh local food (especially seafood), warmly welcoming owners, and an outdoor heated swimming pool; marvellous walks; cl Nov–end Feb, but open at Christmas and New Year; no children.

LISKEARD SX2564 **Well House** *St Keyne, Liskeard PL14 4RN* (01579) 342001 **£115,** plus special breaks; 9 good rms with fine views. Light and airy Victorian country house with friendly owner, and courteous staff; comfortable drawing room, cosy little bar, and particularly good food and fine wines in the dining room overlooking terrace and lawns; 3 acres of gardens with hard tennis court, swimming pool and croquet lawn; children over 8 in evening restaurant.

LITTLE PETHERICK SW9172 **Old Mill Country House** *Little Petherick, Wadebridge, Cornwall PL27 7QT* (01841) 540388 ***£65;** 7 rms. 16th-c corn mill in lovely riverside gardens with waterwheel and other original features; enjoyable breakfasts in beamed dining room, lounges, and attentive service; plenty of places nearby for evening meals; cl Nov–Feb; no children.

LOOE SX2652 **Talland Bay** *Talland, Looe PL13 2JB* (01503) 272667 **£112,** plus special breaks; 19 charming rms with sea or country views. Down a little lane between Looe and Polperro, this restful partly 16th-c country house has lovely sub-tropical gardens just above the sea; comfortable drawing room with log fire, smaller lounge with library, fresh flowers, courteous service, good food in the pretty oak-panelled dining room, and pleasant afternoon teas; heated outdoor swimming pool, putting, croquet; cl Jan and Feb; children over 5 in evening restaurant (high tea for younger ones); dogs by prior arrangement.

MAWNAN SMITH SW7728 **Meudon** *Mawnan Smith, Falmouth TR11 5HT* (01326) 250541 **£150,** plus special breaks; 29 well equipped comfortable rms in separate wing. Run by the same caring family for over 30 years, this is an old stone mansion with a newer wing set in beautiful subtropical garden laid out by Capability Brown; fine views from the dining room, comfortable lounge with log fire and fresh flowers, good English cooking, and old-fashioned standards of service; cl Jan; dogs by arrangement (not in public rooms); limited disabled access.

MAWNAN SMITH SW7728 **Nansidwell Country House** *Mawnan Smith, Falmouth TR11 5HU* (01326) 250340 **£135,** plus special breaks; 12 individually decorated rms. Comfortable, creeper-covered granite house in wonderful woodland garden with sea views and direct access to good beach; comfortably elegant rooms with log fires, fresh flowers, and books; fine food inc home-grown produce and home-made jams and breads in the excellent restaurant, and hard-working, enthusiastic owners; cl Jan; children over 7 in evening restaurant (high tea available); disabled access.

MAXWORTHY SX2592 **Wheatley Farm** *Maxworthy, Launceston PL15 8LY (01566) 781232* ***£42,** plus special breaks; 5 attractive rms with showers. In the same family for five generations, this working sheep and dairy farm has comfortable, pretty furnishings, log fires, good 4-course evening meals using local produce in the spacious dining room and hearty breakfasts; games room with table tennis and toys, animals to visit, pony rides, and safe play area for children; cl Nov–Feb; self-catering cottages, too.

MITHIAN SW7450 **Rose-in-Vale Country House** *Mithian, St Agnes TR5 0QD (01872) 552202* **£80,** plus special breaks; 18 pretty rms. Secluded and quietly set Georgian house in 4 acres of neatly kept gardens; with spacious day rooms, a friendly atmosphere, helpful, long-standing local staff, and good food in enlarged dining room; also, ducks in ponds, a trout steam, outdoor swimming pool, badminton and croquet; children over 7 in evening in public rooms and restaurant (high tea for smaller ones); well behaved dogs welcome; cl Jan–Feb; disabled access.

MULLION SW6719 **Polurrian** *Mullion, Helston TR12 7EN (01326) 240421* ***£162 inc dinner,** plus special breaks; 39 rms (plus 5 new family rms), some with memorable sea views. White clifftop hotel in lovely gardens with path down to sheltered private cove below; a restful atmosphere in the comfortable lounges and bright cocktail bar, fresh flowers, good food using fresh local ingredients (pianist plus sea views in the dining room), enjoyable breakfasts; leisure club with heated swimming pool, and heated outdoor pool, badminton, tennis, mini-golf, squash and croquet; good with children (hotel nanny for babies and toddlers); disabled access.

NEWLYN SW4628 **Higher Faugan** *Newlyn, Penzance TR18 5NS (01736) 362076* ***£94,** plus special breaks; 11 attractive rms with garden and sea views. Country house in 10 quiet acres, with outdoor swimming pool, tennis and putting green; pleasantly old-fashioned restful sitting rooms, helpful owners, and good home-made food using fresh local produce in the cosy dining room (incorporating an original Edwardian conservatory); cl mid-Oct–mid-Mar; disabled access.

PADSTOW SW9175 **Treverbyn House** *Station Rd, Padstow PL28 8AD (01841) 532855* **£60;** 5 rms with lovely views over the Camel estuary. Carefully restored Edwardian house opposite the famous Seafood Restaurant, with friendly owners, open fires in the comfortable public rooms, and good breakfasts; cl Christmas.

PELYNT SX2055 **Jubilee** *Pelynt, Looe PL13 2JZ (01503) 220312* **£65,** plus special breaks; 12 rms. Neat 16th-c inn with Queen Victoria mementos, oak tables and a mix of nice seats under the beams in the relaxed lounge bar, log fire, gleaming brass and fresh flowers, and good waitress-served bar food; a well equipped play area.

PENDEEN SW3834 **Trewellard Manor Farm** *Pendeen, Penzance TR19 7SU (01736) 788526* **£42;** 3 rms, 2 with own bthrm. Victorian house in a lovely coastal spot; with log fire in the guests' lounge, outdoor summer swimming pool, and fine walks all round; self-catering also.

PENZANCE SW4730 **Abbey Hotel** *Abbey St, Penzance TR18 4AR (01736) 366906* **£100,** plus winter breaks; 7 charming rms. Stylish little 17th-c house close to the harbour, with marvellous views; a relaxed atmosphere in comfortable drawing room full of flowers, fine paintings and antiques, a good set menu in the small restaurant, and pretty garden; cl 20–27 Dec; children over 7.

PILLATON SX3664 **Weary Friar** *Pillaton, Saltash PL12 6QS (01579) 350238* ***£55,** plus special breaks; 12 rms. Pretty 12th-c inn by the church in a pleasantly remote village; with lots of character in its four knocked-together rooms (one no smoking), attractive furnishings, well kept real ales, and good food in both the bar and restaurant; children over 10.

POLPERRO SX2051 **Landaviddy Manor** *Landaviddy Lane, Polperro, Looe PL13 2RT (01503) 272210* **£48,** plus special breaks; 7 pretty rms. Attractive and carefully furnished, no smoking 18th-c manor house with fine views over the 2 acres of peaceful gardens and over the bay beyond; comfortably furnished lounges, an open fire, a relaxed atmosphere and Aga-cooked breakfasts in the beamed dining room; cl mid-Oct–mid-Mar; no children and no pets.

POLPERRO SX2051 **Old Mill House** *Mill Hill, Polperro, Looe PL13 2RP* (01503) 272362 **£55,** plus special breaks. 8 attractive rms. Pretty, white cottagey pub with a nice civilised feel; solid stripped pine furniture on polished boards, log fire in big fireplace, fishing boat pictures; well kept real ales, enjoyable food inc fresh fish (no food winter lunchtimes), in the cosy little bistro, and friendly service; fishing trips/boating outings arranged.

PORT ISAAC SX0080 **Port Gaverne** *PL29 3SQ* (01208) 8802441 ***£102,** plus special breaks; 17 comfortable rms. Lovely place to stay and an excellent base for area (dramatic coves, good clifftop walks, and lots of birds); big log fires in well kept bars, relaxed lounges, decent bar food, good restaurant food, and fine wines; also, restored 18th-c self-catering cottages; children over 7 in restaurant; cl early Jan–mid Feb; dogs allowed.

PORT ISAAC SX0080 **Valancia House** *Trewetha Lane, Port Isaac PL29 3RL* (01208) 880677 **£40;** 3 rms with thoughtful extras. Carefully renovated Victorian house up on a hill overlooking the harbour; with warmly welcoming, helpful hosts and good hearty breakfasts in the homely dining room; lots of walks; cl Dec–Feb.

QUINTRELL DOWNS SW8560 **Manuels Farm** *Quintrell Downs, Newquay TR8 4NY* (01637) 873577 ***£44;** 3 rms. Comfortable and relaxed 17th-c farmhouse with log fires, candlelit dinners, and a pretty garden; good for children – they can bottle-feed calves, collect eggs and so forth (free babysitting); cl Christmas and New Year; limited disabled access.

RUAN HIGH LANES SW9039 **Crugsillick Manor** *Ruan High Lanes, St Mawes TR2 5LJ* (01872) 501214 **£80,** plus special breaks; 3 rms. One of the loveliest houses in Cornwall, this Queen Anne manor is extended from a pre-Elizabethan farmhouse and surrounded by a big quiet garden with wooded valley views; log fire in drawing room with Napoleonic ceiling, candlelit dinners in 17th-c dining room using home-grown produce where possible, fine breakfasts, and charming owners; self-catering cottages in grounds – excellent disabled access, and children welcome (but must be over 12 in main house); cl Christmas and New Year.

ST AUSTELL SX0553 **Boscundle Manor** *Tregrehan, St Austell PL25 3RL* (01726) 813557 ***£170 inc dinner,** plus special breaks; 10 rms. Mainly 18th-c rambling manor run by the same caring owners for over 20 years – with country-house atmosphere in its low-beamed and carefully furnished rooms, enjoyable food, a good wine list, and breakfasts in the pretty conservatory; 14 acres of grounds inc 2 acres of terraced gardens, croquet, badminton, outdoor heated swimming pool, indoor swimming pool, golf practice area with 2 greens and 2 all-weather teeing positions, and barn with gym, snooker, table tennis, and darts; woodland walks, too; self-catering cottage; cl Nov–end Mar.

ST BLAZEY SX0654 **Nanscawen House** *Prideaux, St Blazey, Par PL24 2SR* (01726) 814488 ***£60;** 3 spacious, pretty rms overlooking the garden. Attractive creeper-covered, no smoking Georgian house in 5 acres of quiet grounds; helpful owners, big drawing room with small bar, and plenty of places to eat nearby in the evening; heated outdoor swimming pool and outdoor whirlpool bath; cl 25–26 Dec; children over 12.

ST IVES SW5140 **Blue Hayes** *Trelyon Ave, St Ives TR26 2AD* (01736) 797129 **£84,** plus special breaks; 9 rms, most with own bthrm. Long-standing and friendly guesthouse in wonderful clifftop position overlooking the sea; quiet flower-filled garden leading to beach, comfortable rooms, and enjoyable food; cl mid-Oct–mid-Mar; children over 5.

ST IVES SW5140 **Countryman** *Old Coach Rd, St Ives TR26 3JQ* (01736) 797571 ***£60,** plus special winter breaks; 6 rms. Small, friendly, no smoking hotel in 2 acres of gardens; with log fire in comfortable lounge, bright flower-filled breakfast room, and a cosy little restaurant; walks, golf and Tate Gallery nearby; children over 9.

ST IVES SW5441 **Garrack** *Burthallan Lane, St Ives TR26 3AA* (01736) 796199

***£116,** plus wknd breaks; 18 rms, some in more modern wing. Friendly, no smoking hotel in 2 acres of gardens with wonderful sea views; cosy lounges with antiques, books and open fires, a fine collection of paintings by Newlyn artists, a family room, restaurant with good food inc fresh shellfish, helpful staff, and indoor leisure centre (heated outdoor swimming pool, too); disabled access.

ST IVES SW5140 **Kandahar** *11 The Warren, St Ives TR26 2EA (01736) 796183* **£48;** 5 rms with sea views. No smoking B & B in splendid water's-edge position overlooking the harbour and up the coast to Newquay, with comfortable old-fashioned lounge and good breakfasts in the small dining room overlooking the sea; cl Nov–Mar; children over 6; no pets.

ST KEYNE SX2564 **Old Rectory** *St Keyne, Liskeard PL14 4RL (01579) 342617* ***£65,** plus special breaks; 8 comfortable rms. Friendly, family-run hotel in 3 acres; an open fire in the comfortably furnished lounge, cosy bar, good homely atmosphere, and enjoyable food; cl Christmas and New Year; children over 12; pets by prior arrangement; disabled access.

ST MARTIN SX2655 **Bucklawren Farm** *St Martin, Looe PL13 1NZ (01503) 240738* ***£46,** plus special breaks; 6 rms. Spacious farmhouse on 500-acre dairy and arable working farm with coastal and sea views, croquet and putting in the big garden; large homely lounge, south-facing sun lounge, and farmhouse cooking using home-grown and local produce; cl Nov–mid-Mar; children over 5; disabled access.

ST MAWES SW8433 **Rising Sun** *St Mawes, Truro TR2 5DJ (01326) 270233* **£99,** plus special breaks; 9 rms. Small attractive hotel in popular, picturesque waterside village, with harbour views; large, comfortable, newly refurbished lounge bar area, airy conservatory, charming terrace; partial disabled access.

ST MAWES SW8433 **Tresanton** *St Mawes, Truro TR2 5DR (01326) 270055* ***£180,** 26 rms all with individual furnishings and sea views. Hidden away behind a discreet entrance, with elegant terraces (heating for cool weather); a little bottom bar, steps up to the main building and its stylish lounge with deeply comfortable sofas and armchairs, big bowls of flowers, log fire, daily papers, and sophisticated but relaxed atmosphere; excellent food, a fine (if rather pricey) wine list, and friendly informal service; several boats for hire inc the beautiful 48-ft yacht, *Pinuccia*; plenty of cliff walks (and smart wellington boots of all sizes to borrow); cl 4 Jan–11 Feb.

ST WENN SW9665 **Wenn Manor** *St Wenn, Bodmin PL30 5PS (01726) 890240* ***£70,** plus special breaks; 3 rms. Carefully restored and friendly restaurant with rooms, tucked away among rolling hills in 4 acres of wooded grounds; panelled bar with inglenook fireplace and deep well, candlelit dining room with 2 open log fires, a garden room for light lunches, and good, fresh food; croquet; cl 1 wk Christmas; children over 10.

SALTASH SX4258 **Erth Barton** *Saltash PL12 4QY (01752) 842127* **£64;** 3 rms. Lovely old manor house with its own chapel, peaceful rooms with lots of books, pictures and big fireplaces, good enjoyable food; birdwatching in the surrounding estuaries, and riding (you can bring your own horse); no children.

SENNEN SW3425 **Land's End Hotel** *Sennen, Land's End, Penzance TR19 7AA (01736) 871844* **£114,** plus special breaks; 33 elegant airy rms, many with splendid sea views. Comfortable hotel right on the clifftop with fine sea views; good food in the attractive conservatory-style restaurant, elegant seating areas, informal bar with lots of malt whiskies, and helpful staff.

TREGADILLETT SX2983 **Eliot Arms** *Tregadillett, Launceston TL15 7EU (01566) 772051* ***£50,** plus special breaks; 3 rms, 2 with own bthrm. Friendly, creeper-covered old house with fascinating collections (72 antique clocks inc 7 grandfathers, 400 snuffs, hundreds of horse brasses and so forth), and very good food with plenty of fish and interesting daily specials; dogs by arrangement; cl 25 Dec.

TREGASWITH SW8963 **Tregaswith Farmhouse** *Tregaswith, Newquay TR8 4HY (01637) 881181* **£44,** plus special breaks; 3 pretty, homely rms. 18th-c house with beams and antiques, on smallholding breeding horses (pony rides as well) and rare poultry; good breakfasts and proper country cooking; dogs welcome by arrangement.

TREGONY SW9245 **Tregony House** *Tregony, Truro TR2 5RN (01872) 530671*
***£45,** plus winter breaks; 5 individually furnished rms, some with own bthrm. Partly
17th-c, no smoking house with very friendly and helpful owners; big breakfasts and
good evening meals in the low-beamed dining room, a cosy sitting room with open
fire, and a pretty cottagey garden; cl Nov–Feb; children over 7.

TRENALE SX0688 **Trebrea Lodge** *Trenale, Tintagel PL34 0HR (01840) 770410*
***£84,** plus special breaks; 7 pretty rms with views across fields to the sea.
Handsome manor house with log fire and honesty bar in the comfortable smoking
room, elegant first-floor drawing room, and good set dinner in the oak-panelled
dining room; lots of walks; cl Jan–mid-Feb; children over 12; dogs welcome by prior
arrangement.

WIDEGATES SX2858 **Coombe Farm** *Widegates, Looe PL13 1QN (01503)*
240223 **£60,** plus special breaks; 10 comfortable rms. Warmly welcoming and
relaxed, no smoking country house in 10 acres of garden, meadows, woods and
streams, with distant sea views, outdoor swimming pool, and a stone barn with
table tennis and snooker; plants, log fires and antiques in the sitting room, hearty
English breakfasts, enjoyable set evening meals, and honesty drinks tray; cl Nov–end
Feb; children over 10; disabled access.

To see and do

CORNWALL Family Attraction of the Year

🐾 🏠 🐾 🦉 **HAYLE** SW5537 **Paradise Park** Plenty for families at this
colourful place, the headquarters of the World Parrot Trust. Since the park
first opened in 1973 they've successfully bred over 200 species of birds from all
over the world. Some of the beautiful current residents are showcased to
spectacular effect in the huge Parrot Jungle, a splendid mix of waterfalls,
swamps and streams, and in their daily free-flying bird show (usually at
12.30pm). Star of the show is Sam the cockatoo, who's been trained to collect
coins from volunteers and pop them into a collecting box for the charity. For
another splendid show, try feeding some parrots in the new Australian aviary –
40 rainbow lorikeets swoop down for the nectar that you can buy for 50p at
the shop. As well as rare and exotic birds they have lots of animals, including
their own otter sanctuary with entertaining feeding times twice a day; they
usually pick out volunteers to help, and if it's your child's birthday you can
usually fix it in advance so their name will be called out. Other highlights include
penguin feeding shows, and a daily display of eagles, owls and falcons (not Sat,
except July and Aug). Times for these are displayed at the entrance, or you can
find them in advance on the park's information line. More animals to feed at the
Fun Farm, though they limit sales of feed so that the animals don't stuff their
faces all day. There's a big adventure play area decked out as a mock fort, with
an adjacent picnic area, and quiz trails with badges as a prize at the end. Adults
may prefer the Victorian walled garden (lovely clematis arches in May) or the
pub that brews its own real ale, and there's a narrow-gauge railway rattling
gently through the grounds. Though there's a good deal of shelter, this isn't
really somewhere to come on a wet day. Meals, snacks, shop (and plant sales),
mostly disabled access; open every day; (01736) 757407; £5.99 (£3.99 children
4–14). You can usually get good-value return tickets.

Please let us know what you think of places in the *Guide*. Use the report forms
at the back of the book or simply write us a letter.

ALTARNUN SX2281

✝ 🏛 **Altarnun church** The church has
an enchanting set of 16th-c carved
bench ends, much humanity and
humour. The unpretentious Rising Sun
just N does decent simple food. Nearby
Wesley's Cottage, just off A30 at
Trewint, the world's smallest Methodist
place of worship, has a primitive time-
warp room used by Wesley in 1744.

BEDRUTHAN STEPS SW8469

⌂ (off B3276 Newquay–Padstow)
Really special, with their dramatic rock
pinnacles, cliffs and lovely sandy coves.
A splendid place for walks.

BODMIN SX0360

🚂⌂ **Bodmin & Wenford Railway**
(General Station, St Nicholas St)
Restored steam locomotives take you
back to the glory days of the Great
Western Railway when hordes of
holiday-makers travelled this route to
the sun. As well as enjoying the view,
you can stop off for pleasant woodland
walks. Regular trains connect with
Bodmin Parkway station. Snacks, shop,
disabled access; cl Jan–late Mar, and
Nov, with a limited service in May, Oct
and Dec – best to phone for train times;
(01208) 73666; from *£5.

🏛 **Bodmin Gaol** (Berrycombe Rd)
The former county prison, built in 1778,
with spooky underground dungeons;
the Crown Jewels were stored here in
the First World War. Meals and snacks
(pub on site), shop; (01208) 76292;
£3.50. There's a sacred well in the
churchyard of St Petroc's Church. The
Borough Arms (A389 NW) is good
value for lunch.

🏛 ⌷ 🐾 **Pencarrow** (Washaway,
3m N of Bodmin off A389) Notable
18th-c house with fine paintings and
furniture, rococo ceiling in the music
room, and, perhaps the highlight, 50
acres of lovely formal and woodland
gardens with over 600 different
rhododendrons and an acclaimed
conifer collection. Also marked trails,
children's play area, peacocks, chickens
and other birds, craft centre and
ancient British encampment. Snacks,
shop, disabled access; house open all
day (exc Fri, Sat) Jun–mid-Sept, pm
Easter–May and mid-Sept–mid-Oct;
gardens open daily; (01208) 841369;
£4.50.

BODMIN MOOR SX1875

⌂ This windswept expanse is not as
richly endowed as Dartmoor for
walking, and much is boggy and rough. It
does have its own bleak character, with
strange tors, prehistoric traces, wind-
bent trees, granite walls, lonely lakes,
and, despite official denials, continuing
tales of black panthers. The main A30
actually gives more striking views of the
moor than the small side roads, which
tend to burrow along wooded
coombes or between rather high dykes
or walls. Riding is popular on the moor,
and quite a few stables on or around it
cater for all levels of riding ability.

⌂ **The Cheesewring** (Bodmin
Moor) A striking megalithic tomb, the
massive stones now left high and dry by
a fall in the soil level over thousands of
years, its several improbably
overhanging granite slabs making an
appealing camera subject with Bodmin
Moor stretching into the distance.
There is a clear track to the nearby
Hurlers stone circles.

BOLVENTOR SX1876

✦ ✦ 🐑 ⌂ **Colliford Lake Park
Complex** (off A30 just S of Bolventor)

Days Out

Island escapade: St Michael's Mount; Penzance – lunch at the Turks Head;
Flambards, nr Helston.

Lost gardens and a remote coast: Mevagissey; Charlestown; lunch at the
Crown, St Ewe; the Lost Gardens of Heligan; Portloe and Veryan villages.

Animal magic and a look at the past: Looe; Monkey Sanctuary; Polperro
(walk in from Talland Bay), lunch at the Old Mill House or Crumplehorn Mill;
Lanreath folk museum and church.

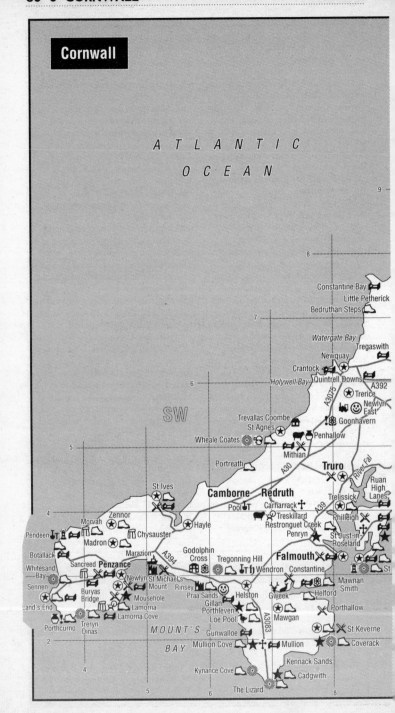

Cornwall

A T L A N T I C

O C E A N

9

8

Constantine Bay
Little Petherick
Bedruthan Steps

7

Watergate Bay
Tregaswith
Newquay
Crantock
Quintrell Downs
A392
Holywell Bay
Trerice
Newlyn East

6

A3075

Trevallas Coombe
St Agnes
Goonhavern
Wheale Coates
Penhallow
Mithian
Portreath
Truro
River Fal

SW

5

St Ives
Camborne   **Redruth**
Ruan High Lanes
Pool
Carharrack
Trelissick
A30
A39
A392
Zennor
Morvah
Chysauster
Hayle
Treskillard
Phillleigh
Pendeen
Madron
Restronguet Creek
Penryn
St Just-in-Roseland
Botallack
Marazion
Godolphin Cross
Tregonning Hill
Falmouth
Whitesand Bay
Sancreed
Penzance
A394
Constantine
Sennen
Newlyn
St Michael's Mount
Rinsey
Wendron
Mawnan Smith
Land's End
Buryas Bridge
Mousehole
Praa Sands
Gweek
Helford
Porthcurno
Treryn Dinas
Lamorna
Lamorna Cove
Gillan
Porthleven
Loe Pool
Mawgan
Porthallow
M O U N T ' S
Gunwalloe
St Keverce
B A Y
Mullion Cove
Mullion
Coverack

4

Kennack Sands
Kynance Cove
Cadgwith
The Lizard

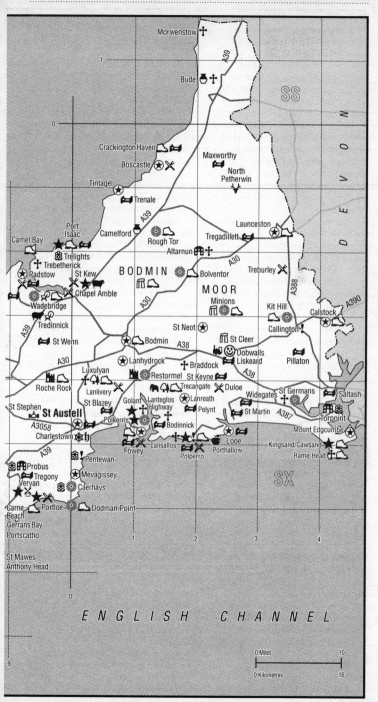

ENGLISH CHANNEL

0 Miles 10
0 Kilometres 16

Barn owls and red squirrels are among the animals being reintroduced at this family-orientated place; also rare breeds of birds, cattle, poultry and sheep, indoor and outdoor pets, adventure play areas, undercover assault course, museum, and lakeside walks. Meals, snacks, shop, some disabled access; cl Oct–Easter (exc wknds); (01208) 821469; £3.95. About a mile away, Dozmary Pool is one of two Cornish lakes that claim to be where a legendary arm rose from the depths and reclaimed Excalibur (the other is Loe Pool nr Porthleven), and it's an easy starting-point for Bodmin Moor.

⌂! **Potter's Museum of Curiosity** Set in the little complex that's sprung up around Jamaica Inn, the pub immortalised by Daphne du Maurier, this is a bizarre Victorian collection of stuffed animals and other assorted oddities. Rather than simply displaying them in cases, Mr Potter constructed elaborate tableaux around the bodies brought to him by local farmers, with the animals positioned as if they were tiny humans. Guinea-pigs play cricket, rabbits sit in a classroom, and squirrels carouse in a pub in this weird little world – while the Kittens' Wedding has to be seen to be believed. Meals, snacks, shop, disabled access; cl Jan; (01566) 86838; £2.50. The pub itself is still atmospheric despite the developments. The A30, incidentally, has better views of the moor than any of the byroads.

BOSCASTLE SX0991
★ ⌂ ※ † Pretty harbour with 16th-c pier squeezed into a rocky creek, cottages converted from warehouses, gift shops, a witchcraft museum; the Cobweb and (a stiff climb) Napoleon are useful for lunch. The cliffs nearby afford some fascinating views. Not far from here at Trevalga, Tredole Farm will arrange coastal or country **horse and pony trekking**; non-riders welcome; (01840) 250495. Nearby **St Juliot Church** was restored by Thomas Hardy in his career as an architect; he described the area later in *A Pair of Blue Eyes*.

BOTALLACK SW3632
⌂ On a wild day this rugged corner of West Cornwall, with its ruined engine

house right down by the sea, is very dramatic, and there are fine steep walks all around.

BRADDOCK SX1662
† **Braddock church** Hardly striking as a building, but well worth visiting for its handsome wood carvings.

BUDE SS2106
⌂† A popular area for surfing, with great beaches beyond the dunes; Sandy Mouth slightly N has clean water for bathing, and there's a nature trail close to surfers' favourite Duckpool. Otherwise it's an unremarkable resort, though the **Bude & Stratton Museum** (The Wharf) is a decent rainy-day retreat (shop, disabled access; cl Oct–Easter; 50p). The Falcon Hotel does good-value quick food. The carved bench ends up at **Poughill church** (pronounced 'Poffle') are entertaining; the Preston Gate is a decent pub here.

CADGWITH SW7214
★ ⌂ This picturesque village on its pretty cove has photogenic fish stores, thatched cottages, and a decent pub. A rewarding short stroll on the coast path leads S to Chynhalls Point past the aptly named Devil's Frying Pan, where the waves foam into a spectacular collapsed cavern.

CAERHAYS SW9741
❀ ※ **Caerhays Castle Gardens** Relatively undiscovered, these magnificent spring gardens are beautifully set around the back of a striking castle, with lovely coastal views. Renowned especially for their rhododendrons, magnolias and camellias, they're easily combined with a visit to the now better known Lost Gardens of Heligan (they do a map showing how to get between the two). Good afternoon teas, shop, some disabled access; open wkdys from mid-Mar to around the end of May; (01872) 501144; £3.50. The Crown over at St Ewe does good lunches, but depending on where you're coming from, the King's Arms at Tregony up on the main road might be handier.

CALLINGTON SX3769
! **Dupath Holy Well** (off A388 S) The best-preserved of Cornwall's many holy wells, its unappetising water said to cure whooping cough. The town is not in itself remarkable.

CALSTOCK SX4268

🏛️ ⛪ ✕ 🍴 △ ✿ **Cotehele** (1m W by footpath, 6m by road) Tucked away in a network of twisting roads high above the Tamar, this rambling granite house has hardly changed since built in the late 15th c; there's no electricity, so the dark and atmospheric rooms – with fine furniture, armour and tapestries – have an authentically medieval feel. Outside are lovely terraced gardens, a medieval dovecot, restored watermill, and miles of woodland walks. Down at Cotehele Quay a National Maritime Museum outpost shows the quay's history, and the last of the Tamar ketch-rigged barges has been restored here. One of the most rewarding places to visit in Cornwall, but now so over-visited that to protect it the National Trust have had to limit entrance to 600 people a day. Best to come mid-week out of high season, or at least early in the morning; at other times you'll have to wait, and may not get in at all. Meals, snacks (tearoom in pleasant riverside setting with good cream teas), shop, limited disabled access; house cl Fri and Nov–Mar, mill as house (but cl am and open Fri July–Aug), garden open daily all year; (01579) 351346; *£6, *£3.20 garden and mill only; NT. Pleasant walks along the Tamar from the village. The Carpenters Arms at Lower Metherell and the unusual Who'd Have Thought It at St Dominick are good for lunch.

CAMEL BAY SW9280

△ On the E side, sand dunes suddenly give way to a rocky headland, Rumps Point, which can be walked round in an hour or so; or at low tide there's a pleasant sandy walk between Rock and Polzeath (which has one of Cornwall's best beaches, popular with surfers).

CAMELFORD SX1083

Locals will tell you this is the site of Camelot, and send you a mile N to the otherwise unremarkable Slaughter Bridge, where Arthur supposedly fell at his last battle. The Masons Arms has good-value food.

🎡 **British Cycling Museum** (The Old Station – B3266 N of Camelford) Comprehensive (and still growing) collection of over 400 bicycles, tricycles and even a five-wheeled Hen and Chickens bike, ranging from an original 1819 hobby-horse through boneshakers and penny-farthings to the hi-tech bikes of today. The couple who run it met through cycling, and really know their stuff. Outside is a sculpture made up of old bicycles. Shop, disabled access; usually cl Fri and Sat; (01840) 212811; *£2. 40.

🎡 **North Cornwall Museum & Gallery** (The Clease) Good exploration of regional life over the past century, with displays of cider-making and farming, and collections of pottery and even early vacuum cleaners. Shop; cl Sun and Oct–Mar; (01840) 212954; £1.50.

CARHARRACK SW7341

† **Carharrack church** Has an exhibition on Cornish Methodism and John Wesley, who preached at the chapel that used to stand here. Disabled access; open by appointment; (01209) 820381; free. Wesley preached more regularly at nearby **Gwennap Pit**, which still has services (2.30pm Suns in July and Aug), and a visitor centre. Shop, snacks, disabled access; centre cl Oct–Apr and pm Sat, the peaceful grass amphitheatre itself is open all the time; free. The Fox & Hounds at Lanner is useful for lunch.

CHARLESTOWN SX0351

✿ ⚓ A picturesque working china-clay port, with sailing ships as well as modern cargo boats; it's much used as a film/TV setting, featuring in *Poldark* and ITV's *Moll Flanders*. Two square-rigged sailing ships, stars of many films inc *1492: Conquest of Paradise* maybe in the harbour. The **Shipwreck & Heritage Centre** (Quay Rd) has an exhibition about the *Titanic* and is good for local history (cl Nov–Feb; £4.45). The waterside Harbour Inn is useful for lunch.

CHYSAUSTER SW4734

🏛️ **Chysauster Ancient Village** (off B3311 N of Gulval) On a windy hillside overlooking the coast, these stunted remains of eight courtyard houses give some impression of village life 2,000 years ago. The site is also notable for its large untreated meadow, popular with wild birds, and, depending on the season, bright with bluebells, heather or unusual orchids. Snacks, shop; cl Nov–Mar; (01831) 757934; £1.60.

COVERACK SW7818
★ ❋ ⌂ An attractive coastal village, with a decent pub. A rewarding walk takes you down to Black Head and maybe beyond, or to Lowland Point, for dramatic views of The Manacles – striking offshore rocks.

CRACKINGTON HAVEN SX1496
⌂ With a superbly sited dining pub, the Coombe Barton, to set you up (or reward you afterwards), this has a good walk to **High Cliff**, Cornwall's highest.

DOBWALLS SX2165
☺😊🏚 **Dobwalls Family Adventure Park** (off A38) Good theme park with lively attractions inc steam and diesel train rides along a two-mile stretch of miniature American-style railroads, aerial cableways, and lots of excellent play areas (outdoors and under cover), with their Skydome – a complex climbing frame of latticed ropework – particularly unusual. Also weekly sheepdog trials in the summer hols, and an interesting wildlife gallery. Meals, snacks, shop, disabled access; cl Oct (exc half-term)–Easter; (01579) 320325; £6.50. The Highway is useful for lunch.

DODMAN POINT SX0039
❋ ⌂ Reached from Gorran Haven, or one of the closer car parks – for instance, at Hemmick Beach, this allows a round walk mainly along clifftops.

FALMOUTH SW8132
★ ⚓ The county's biggest town has a huge natural harbour full of sailing boats of every description, big sea-going ships, little passenger ferries (to St Mawes and Truro – great fun) and boat trips (2-hour trip £5.50; (01326) 374241); it's also a busy but pleasant shopping centre with some nice old-fashioned streets, ships' chandlers and a good bustling atmosphere, though surprisingly few sea views. Broad avenues of spiky-leaved dracaena trees away from the centre give it a quite foreign feel. The Quayside and Chain Locker by the inner harbour do useful food, and the Warehouse is an enjoyable waterside restaurant. The A39 here from Truro can be tiresomely slow.

⚜ **Cornwall Maritime Museum** 🖼 (Bells Court, opposite Marks & Spencer on Market St) Crammed with seafaring history (Shop; cl Sun; £2).

🏛 ❋ **Pendennis Castle** (1m SE of Falmouth) Superb views from this well preserved fort, one of Henry VIII's chain of coastal defences. Snacks, shop, some disabled access; cl 24–26 Dec, 1 Jan; £3.80.

FOWEY SX1251
★ ❋ 🏛 ⌂ (pronounced 'Foy') Steep, lively and bustling, in an exceptional riverside position, with pretty views from up the hill on either side, some interesting shops in its maze of quaint alleys and tiny lanes, and a choice of good-value food pubs – King of Prussia, Ship and Galleon. The harbour has yachts to ocean-going ships, also car ferry to Bodinnick, and foot ferry to Polruan, the similarly steep little harbourside hamlet opposite – less interesting, but with lovely views of Fowey (both have decent pubs). **St Catherine's Castle** is a ruined stronghold built by Henry VIII, restored mid-19th c; free. The NT owns most of the coastline in these parts, so count on clean beaches; just around from the harbour, the secluded cove at Lantic Bay (reached by a steep coastal path) is particularly nice. A popular circular route takes walkers across on the Bodinnick car ferry, then takes the path through the steep creekside woods round to Polruan, and comes back on the other foot ferry.

GODOLPHIN CROSS SW6031
🏠 🏵 **Godolphin House** Over the next year you'll be able to watch the restoration work at this 15th-c house of the Earls of Godolphin, well known for its colonnaded front, and gardens dating back to Tudor times. Open pm Thurs and bank hols May–Sept (all day Thurs in Aug, with a break for lunch) as well as pm Tues July–Sept; to confirm opening times, tel (01736) 762409; £3. The Queen's Arms down at Breage does decent food.

GOLANT SX1254
★ ✝ This waterside village has its attractions – particularly the **church**, unusual for its complete 15th-c fittings.

GOONHAVERN SW7953
❗ 🏵 **World in Miniature** The world's landmarks at a fraction of the normal cost – and size, and some much larger dinosaurs. Beautiful gardens with

thousands of plants, and children's fairground rides. Meals, snacks, shop, disabled access; cl Nov–Mar; (01872) 572828; £5.

GWEEK SW7027
✛♪ **National Seal Sanctuary** The biggest seal sanctuary in Europe, the National Seal Sanctuary provides a home for dozens of injured or orphaned seals that they hope to be able to release back into the wild, all with their own names and character traits. Underwater observatories, feeding time fun, guided woodland walks, play area, as well as donkeys, ponies and goats, an audio-visual display and a nature trail. Snacks, shop, disabled access; cl 25 Dec; (01326) 221361; £5.95. The Gweek Inn, with home-made food, is handy, and the Trengilly Wartha at Nancenoy is excellent for lunch, with a nice walk down to Scotts Quay on the creek.

HAYLE SW5537
✿🏠🐒🦜 **Paradise Park** See *separate family panel on p.84.*

HELFORD SW7526
⌂ There's an undemanding coast path E to **Dennis Head** and beyond. This NE part of the Lizard is appreciably leafier, with some intricate coves.

HELSTON SW6626
☺♨!✝🐒 **Flambards Village Theme Park** (off A394, S edge of village) Beautifully kept leisure park, a clear cut above the average theme park. A few new attractions in recent years include a weather station with live satellite pictures from space. One of the best parts is the very good reconstructed Victorian village; once just three period rooms, it now has over 50 authentically furnished and stocked houses, shops and settings, complete with cobbled streets, carriages and other period pieces. Also a state-of-the-art time travel exhibition from the Big Bang to the present day, a life-size 'Britain in the Blitz' street, a collection of aircraft, adventure playground and play areas, award-winning gardens, displays on topics as varied as wedding fashions and antique prams, and rides to suit all ages. A place which lets adults get at least as much out of as children, you could quite easily spend a day here. Meals, snacks, shop,

disabled access; cl Nov–Easter, and Mon and Fri at the start and end of season; (01326) 564093; £7.50 (less off-season or from mid-afternoon).
♨🏛 **Helston Folk Museum** World-famous for its annual Furry Dance, it has a popular Sat market and a little **folk museum** in the Old Butter Market; shop, disabled access; £2. The simple Blue Anchor pub has a 15th-c working brewhouse which you can usually look around at lunchtime; the best food nearby is at the Halzephron at Gunwalloe, off the A3083 S – a good road with views, and usually signs of action from the Culdrose helicopter base.

KENNACK SANDS SW7316
(just E of Kuggar) One of the cleanest beaches in Britain, with beautifully clear water; it can get crowded.

KINGSAND/CAWSAND SX4350
★⌂ Appealing seaside village with higgledy-piggledy charm, nr great cliff walks; the Halfway House and Rising Sun both have good local fish.

KIT HILL SX3771
⌂🌼 (off A390 N of Callington) With a huge chimney stack and mine shafts, this gives breezy walks, and impressive views across to Dartmoor.

KYNANCE COVE SW6813
⌂🌼 A particularly fine beach below the spectacular cliffs – a long walk down from the car park, but well worth it for the strange rock formations, caves and sandy coves. There are lovely views from the cliff walk S.

LAMORNA SW4424
⌂🏛 The cove is pretty, with good walks along the coast path. There's a good view of the **Merry Maidens** stone circle from the B3315. The Lamorna Wink is useful for lunch.
🎨 **Lamorna Pottery** As well as the pottery there's a garden with acclaimed cream teas. Meals, snacks, shop, disabled access; cl mid-Jan; (01736) 810330; free.

LAND'S END SW3425
⌂🌼🎨☺ **Land's End** The most westerly point of England, with wild and blustery walks along dramatic clifftops, and on a clear day views out as far even as the Isles of Scilly. You may not be able to stand and contemplate it on your own – the 200-acre site has been

extensively developed for families in the last few years, and it's become almost like a theme park, with 'multi-sensory experiences', gift shops, craft centres, farm animals and burger bars. It's not as bad as it sounds – the exhibitions and hi-tech displays are a useful enough introduction to the folklore of the area, and there's plenty to amuse children. An RSPB observation hide has information on the coastline's wildlife. Meals, snacks, neat shopping arcade, good disabled access; cl 25 Dec; (01736) 871501; £7.95 for all attractions, less off-season. A public right of way goes through here to Land's End itself, so you're not obliged to buy a ticket if you just want to walk to the end of England. The same goes for the fine cliff walks in both directions – the one to Sennen is lovely, and the cove there is worth looking around. Some of the wildest and most formidable cliffs in Britain are between here and Treen.

LANHYDROCK SX0863

🏠 🏵 🐾 **Lanhydrock House** A staggering 49 rooms to visit in this splendid old house, well liked by readers; the highlight is the Long Gallery, with its magnificently illustrated Old Testament scenes – it's one of the few original 16th-c parts left, as a disastrous fire in the 19th c resulted in major changes and refurbishments. Do leave time to explore the pretty formal **gardens** (glorious around May) and grounds, where they've recently re-opened the Victorian coach house stables; it's a lovely walk down to the river and back through the woods. Good meals and snacks, shop and plant sales, disabled access; house cl Mon (exc bank hols) and Nov–Mar, grounds cl Nov–Feb; (01208) 73320; £6.40, £3.20 grounds only; NT. The Crown down at Lanlivery is most enjoyable for lunch, in a Jane Austen village setting.

LANREATH SX1856

★ † Pretty village with some remarkable woodwork in its exceptional medieval **church**. The Punch Bowl has a fascinating old bar.

👃 **Folk Museum** Most fun for its summer demonstrations and workshops – corn dolly making (Mon), Cornish pasty crimping (Weds) and egg

decorating (Fri); all activities 2–4pm. Snacks, shop, disabled access; cl Nov–Easter; (01503) 220321; *£2.50.

LANSALLOS SX1751

† **Lansallos church** The attraction here is the ancient carved bench ends, each individual but all sharing a style.

LANTEGLOS HIGHWAY SX1453

† **Lanteglos Highway church** A curiosity, Perpendicular but not – subsidence has left the arches at drunken angles.

LAUNCESTON SX3285

★ The most attractive inland town in Cornwall, with winding old hillside streets and an untouristy feel; it was once Cornwall's capital. The White Hart does popular food.

🏰 **Launceston Castle** Set on a Norman motte, the ruined 12th- and 13th-c hilltop castle is substantial and commanding – it was captured four times during the Civil War. Shop, some disabled access; cl Nov–Mar; £1.60.

🚂 🏠 △ **Launceston Steam Railway** Two-ft gauge line on the trackbed of the old North Cornwall Railway, running through 2½ miles of scenic valley – on sunny days in an open carriage; also engine displays, model railway, and transport museum. An extension provides access to the region's network of footpaths. Snacks, shop, disabled access; open Easter, then Sun and Tues until May spring bank hol, after which daily (exc Sat) to end of Sept, Sun and Tues only in Oct, and some trains Dec wknds; (01566) 775665 for times; £5.20.

👃 **Lawrence House** (Castle St) Set in a Georgian house with useful displays on the town's past; cl wknds and mid-Oct–Mar; free.

🍴 ☺ 🐑 **Trethorne Leisure Farm** 🅰 (Kennards House, off A30 3m W of Launceston) 140-acre working dairy farm good for children, who can milk Daisy the cow, walk the miniature ponies, play with the rabbits, take a pony ride or bottle-feed the lambs. Also birds of prey, ten pin bowling, good 18-hole golf course, and big indoor and outdoor play areas. Meals, snacks, shop, disabled access; cl Sun (exc golf); (01566) 86324; £4.50, golf £19 round.

THE LIZARD SW7012

❋ △ This peninsula S of Helston is

famous as the most southerly part of mainland Britain, and though the inland parts can be rather flat and dull and not really worth extended walks, the coastline is altogether more attractive. The National Trust have improved the area around Lizard Point, the southern tip, in recent years, and it's a good start for bracing cliff walks in either direction, with good views. Readers very much enjoy exploring the Lizard's dramatic western and eastern edges. The W side has mighty cliffs, with roads down to beautiful Mullion Cove and Kynance Cove. The E side is more sheltered and lusher, with wooded creeks. **Lizard village** itself is pretty uninspiring (there's a very civilised pub, and they sell interesting local serpentine rock carvings), but is well placed for longer walks encompassing Church Cove to the E and Kynance Cove to the W. On top and inland the Lizard is disappointing, a big flat peninsula; although the Goonhilly satellite station is a remarkable landmark.

LOE POOL SW6424

Cornwall's largest lake, a haven for waterfowl, is blocked from the sea by an NT shingle bank called Loe Bar (only breeding place of the rare sandhill rust moth – and favourite place of worship of a German evangelical sect); a path leads round the lake. There's a coast walk from here to Gunwalloe fishing cove.

LOOE SX2553

Seaside resort packed with tourist shops, teashops and pubs, but with a nice easy-going atmosphere even in high season. The old fishing village with its picturesque harbour and narrow little back streets is now immersed in tourism, and is the main shark-fishing place (on 'shark-fishing' trips you watch others doing the catching). In summer, you may see a locally caught shark displayed in ice at the **Living from the Sea** exhibition (Buller Quay); also local lobsters and shellfish in an aquarium. Disabled access; cl 12.30–1pm, all Sat in low season, and all Nov–end May; £1.50. From the quay there are summer **boat trips**, the easiest out to nearby St George's Island. The Olde Salutation has plenty of atmosphere and decent,

simple food; the Smugglers is a friendly restaurant, and the quayside Trawlers has very good unusual seafood.

Monkey Sanctuary (signed off B3253 at No Man's Land, just E of Looe) One of the most fascinating places to visit in the entire county; established in 1964, its wooded grounds are home to the world's first colony of Amazon woolly monkeys to breed successfully outside their natural habitat. You can get right up to the animals, all of which were born here, and talks by staff give an intriguing insight into the dynamics and politics of the monkey community. Meals, snacks, shop, disabled access; cl Fri, Sat, and Oct–mid-Apr; (01503) 262532; £4.

LUXULYAN SX0558

The village has an attractive **church**, and from the village you can walk along the lush wooded valley to the S, strewn with huge granite boulders and crossed by an impressive viaduct; if you feel adventurous you can climb up the valley to the top of the viaduct.

MADRON SW4431

Trengwainton Garden (B3312) The name in Cornish means 'Farm of the Spring' and it does always seems to be spring at this lovely place, the climate favouring plants not usually found outside in England. Magnolias, azaleas, rhododendrons, unusual southern hemisphere trees and shrubs inc a delightful tree-fern grotto, walled gardens, good views to Mount's Bay and the Lizard. Cream teas, shop, interesting plant sales; open Sun–Thurs (and Good Fri) Mar–Oct, (01736) 362297; £3.50; NT. The King William IV has imaginative local food. The road to Morvah passes a very photogenic prehistoric burial chamber at Lanyon Quoit; a bit further along by a phone box a signed path on the right takes you to a great Bronze Age stone hoop at Men-An-Tol, and the lane opposite leads to **Chun Castle**, an Iron Age fort with great views.

MARAZION SW5130

St Michael's Mount There's something particularly awe-inspiring about this medieval castle, rising majestically from the sea. On gloomy or stormy days the picturesque silhouette seems even more dramatic. The little island is reached by ferry (it doesn't go in bad weather), or at low tide on foot along a causeway; the walk up to the castle, still the home of the family which acquired it in 1660, is quite steep. Fine Chippendale furniture, plaster reliefs, armour and paintings, audio-visual show. Summer meals, snacks, shop; open wkdys and most wknds Apr–Oct, best to ring for winter opening; (01736) 710507; £4.40; NT (members may have to pay some wknds). The Cutty Sark has decent food.

MAWGAN SW7125

🏠 🍴 △ ✿ **Trelowarren** This manor house is worth a look for its elaborate Strawberry Hill 'gothick' chapel (open pm Weds and bank hols only), and the surrounding estate (open all the time) has plenty going on, inc woodland walks, craft shops and pottery, a campsite, summer Thurs evening concerts, and good meals and snacks in the Yard Bistro; (01326) 221224; £1.50.

MAWNAN SMITH SW7728

★ △ This sheltered coastal village is pretty, and the Red Lion is good for lunch. From nearby Mawnan, a fine if blowy stretch of the coast path takes you around Rosemullion Head and on N to Maenporth, where there's a sheltered sandy cove with a decent modern pub/restaurant.

🌻 **Glendurgan Garden** Lovely subtropical garden in valley above Helford River, started by Alfred Fox in 1820; fine shrubs from all over the world, mature trees, walled garden and restored laurel maze. Shop, snacks; cl Sun, Mon (exc bank hols), Good Fri, all Nov–Feb; (01326) 250906; £3.40; NT.

🌻 △ **Trebah Garden** This steeply wooded ravine garden is well liked by readers and widely reckoned to be one of the finest in the world. At times it really feels as if you've strayed into a benign, exclusive jungle. Huge subtropical tree ferns and palms, giant gunnera, lots of blue and white hydrangeas, 100-year-old rhododendrons, some fine rare trees. Several activities for children, and at the bottom end a private beach on the Helford River – good for a picnic or secluded swim. Snacks, shop (plants for sale), disabled access; (01326) 250448;

£3.50.

MEVAGISSEY SX0144

★ This bustling place is a picturesque fishing village much expanded into quite a commercialised resort, but fun, with hillside cottages, narrow streets, gift shops, a busy working harbour. The Ship, Fountain and Harbour Lights are all worthwhile pubs, and the harbourside Mr Bistro does mainly fresh fish.

👃 **Folk Museum** This decent local museum in an 18th-c boat-builder's shed on East Quay includes a comprehensive wartime exhibition; shop, disabled access to ground floor; cl am Sat and Sun and Oct–Easter; *60p.

🌻 **Lost Gardens of Heligan** (off B2373, just NW of Mevagissey) Forgotten and neglected between 1914 and 1991, these highly acclaimed gardens have now been fully restored. Some very fine mature trees, Victorian walled gardens, lots of rhododendrons, lakes, and a big collection of tree ferns, bamboos and palms. It's a friendly place, and they're more than happy to talk about their work. Snacks, shop/nursery, disabled access; cl 24–25 Dec; (01726) 844157; £5. The Crown at St Ewe is good for lunch.

🚂 **World of Model Railways** 🔲 (Meadow St) Over 50 model trains trundling through a realistic little world that takes in Cornish china-clay pits, ski resorts, fairgrounds, towns and country. Shop, some disabled access; cl Mon–Sat Nov–early Mar; (01726) 842457; £2.75.

MINIONS SX2571

🏛 △ ✺ **Prehistoric Monuments** Above Minions, the highest village in Cornwall, the **Hurlers** are three Bronze Age stone circles – the central one still has 14 stones standing. Close by is the **Rillaton Barrow** where the lovely Rillaton gold cup (now in the British Museum) was found, along with other interesting relics. There is a clear track to the nearby Cheesewring; not far off, the track between Sharptor and Kilmar Tor affords fine views.

MORVAH SW4035

△ 🏛 The moors nearly reach the sea around here, and in a few miles walkers can take in the cliff path, the moors close to the ruin of Ding Dong Mine, the prehistoric stone hoop of Men-an-Tol and the Iron Age hillfort of Chun Castle (close by Chun Quoit, a Bronze Age burial chamber).

MORWENSTOW SS2015

† The **church**, in an idyllic setting, has Norman arches and 16th-c bench ends, with shipwrecked sailors' headstones in the graveyard. A driftwood shack, built for contemplation by a Victorian parson over the impressive cliffs, is preserved by the NT. The Bush is an interesting old pub, and the rectory tearoom is delightful.

MOUSEHOLE SW4626

★ Attractive working fishing village with steep little roads – too many summer visitors, but lovely out of season, with spectacular Christmas lights in the little harbour; the harbourside Ship (with good-value bedrooms) is fun for lunch, though the Old Coastguard has more interesting food and a lovely garden.

MULLION SW6719

★ † This attractive village has an enjoyable family pub (the Old Inn) and a possibly unique feature in its church – a dog flap. You can hire bicycles at Atlantic Forge (£5 half-day, £7 day); (01326) 240294 – open all year, but check first out of season. This is a good way to explore the Lizard.

MULLION COVE SW6617

⌂ This dramatic fusion of rock, sand and sea is most rewardingly reached by a there-and-back walk along the cliff from Porth Mellin; for the energetic, the extension S to Kynance Cove is outstanding.

NEWLYN SW4628

⌂ ▣ ❄ Cornwall's busiest working fishing port – it's great fun watching the boats come in – and home to the last working **Salt Pilchard Works**, a tour of which passes a surprisingly entertaining hour or so; shop; cl Sun and Nov–Mar; (01736) 332112; £2.95. There's an unusual Art Deco swimming pool, and an excellent and occasionally rather avant-garde **art gallery** (New Rd) in a lovely coastal setting with fine views (cl Sun, 25–26 Dec and 1 Jan; (01736) 363715; donations). At Christmas the fishermen decorate the harbour and its boats with spectacular lights. The Dolphin and Fisherman's Arms are useful for lunch.

NEWLYN EAST SW8356

▥ ☺ **Lappa Valley Steam Railway and Leisure Park** ▣ 15-in gauge steamtrain trips through pretty countryside to an old lead mine. It's surrounded by parkland with lakes, woodland walk, a maze, and play areas; a section of the old branch line leads to a soft ball golf course. Meals, snacks, shop, some disabled access; cl Nov–Easter, with limited opening in Oct – best to check train times; (01872) 510317; £5.90, covers fare and all attractions exc golf. The backstreet Pheasant has good home cooking.

NEWQUAY SW8261

Now famed as England's surfing capital, a thorough-going seaside resort with excellent safe golden beaches below fine cliffs; Crantock Beach is the best and least crowded, with great views from the Bowgie family pub on West Pentire headland. There's no shortage of souvenir shops, an alcohol-free zone declared on the streets, theme parks on the edge, and older houses around the harbour; there's decent food all day at the Fort Hotel (Fore St). Thanks in part to the surfers, the town has quite a cheery young feel these days. Fistral Beach is reckoned by some to be the best surfing beach in Europe; a couple of surfing schools here can get beginners started.

🐖 ☺ **Dairyland** (A3508 4m SE) Much expanded since it first opened 20 years ago, this bustling dairy farm is a huge favourite with families. Its showpiece remains the daily milking sessions, when cows step aboard a bizarre merry-go-round milking machine and are milked to the strains of classical music. Also well labelled nature trails, farm park, rural bygones, brass rubbing centre and plenty of activities for children. Meals, snacks, shop, disabled access; cl Nov–Mar (exc around Christmas); (01872) 510246; £4.95.

☺ **Holywell Bay Fun Park** (off A3075 SW of town) Active children should enjoy the go-karts, bumper boats, rides, indoor play area, golf; cl Nov–Mar; (01637) 830095; separate charges for various attractions.

🐾 **Newquay Zoo** (Trenance Leisure Park, off A3075 Edgcumbe Ave) The emphasis is very much on conservation here, with carefully designed enclosures for monkeys, penguins, lions and tortoises, as well as gardens, and summer activities. Feeding displays are well timetabled so there's something to see throughout the day. Also children's farm, play areas, and a maze. Meals, snacks, shop, disabled access; (01637) 873342; £4.80. You can get a joint ticket to **Water World**, a lively fun pool on the same site.

♪ **Sea Life Centre** (Towan Promenade) Another in the reliable chain – a see-through tunnel creates the illusion of walking along the seabed, and bubble windows bring you face to face with fish, sea horses and sharks. Meals, snacks, shop, some disabled access; cl 25 Dec; (01637) 872822; *£5.75.

NORTH PETHERWIN SX2889

ᴠ **Tamar Otter Park** Friendly place breeding otters then releasing them back into the wild; it's fun to watch the attractive Asian short-clawed otters playing. Three species of deer roam free, and there are waterfowl lakes, wallabies, and nature trails. The otters are fed at noon and 3.30pm. Snacks, shop, some disabled access; cl Nov–Mar; (01566) 785646; £4.50.

PADSTOW SW9175

★ ♨ ❄ Quaint streets, old buildings clustered around the working fishing harbour, and attractive slate houses; Rick Stein's restaurants are currently drawing the crowds (you'll need to book well in advance). The Golden Lion, London Inn and Old Custom House are useful for lunch. The Camel estuary is popular for sailing: gentle dreamy scenery with lots of little boats. Plenty of good clean beaches nr here; Constantine Bay is the best, and popular with surfers. The B3276 has the best roadside coastal views in this part of Cornwall.

🏠 **Prideaux Place** Still a lived-in family home, this fine old house has changed little since it was built in the late 16th c. Highlights include the elegant ceilings, atmospheric library and the intricate biblical tableaux in the Great Chamber. Notable concerts and special events in the grounds. Snacks, shop, disabled access to ground floor only; open pm Sun–Thurs Jun–Sept (may be subject to

change, best to phone); (01841) 532411; £4, gardens only £2.

⚓ **Shipwreck Museum** (South Quay) Not far from the town's little harbour, a collection of relics and tales of the plentiful shipwrecks along this coast. Shop, disabled access; usually open Mar–Oct; (01726) 69897; £4.45.

PENDEEN SW3834

⛏ ⚒ **Levant Mine** (B3306, 1m W of Pendeen) Unusual mine beneath the sea, powered by the oldest steam engine in Cornwall, all explained by knowledgeable staff. Shop; open every Fri (weather permitting), plus Easter and May bank hols, Weds, Thurs and Sun in Jun, and daily exc Sat July–Sept; (01736) 786156; £3; NT. The nearby **Pendeen Watch lighthouse** is worth a look, and the Radjel is handy for something to eat.

PENHALLOW SW7651

🍺 ♨ **Callestock Cider Farm** Traditional working cider farm producing scrumpy, country wines and jam, with seasonal demonstrations, and friendly horses, rabbits, goats, pigs and donkeys. Also cider museum with ancient presses, and hives of the bees needed for pollination; guided tours. Summer snacks, shop (with samples of everything they make), disabled access; cl Jan, plus all Sat (exc Sept–Oct) and winter Sun; (01872) 573356; free, £2 for museum and tractor ride. The Miners Arms at Mithian is useful for lunch.

PENRYN SW7834

★ Appealing waterside village, quite sizeable, with pretty houses dropping down to the estuary.

PENTEWAN SX0147

🏵 ! **Eden Project** (Water Inn Lane Nursery, Pentewan) One of the most exciting and innovative millennium projects, this (when completed in 2001) will see the transformation of a china-clay pit into a dramatic garden the size of 30 football pitches. The 60-metre-deep crater will contain thousands of plants from all over the planet inc the humid tropics and the warm temperate regions of the world; the latter to be housed in giant conservatories (big enough to accommodate full-size teak and mahogany trees), known as biomes. Outside, 12 acres of landscaped grounds will contain plants from temperate climates, as well as a central lake. The whole project has been developed with the environment and education in mind – even the construction of the site was designed so that run-off rainwater from the roof will be used for humidification in the hot houses – and experts will be on hand in the classrooms and exhibitions within the site. A few visitors will be able to see how the project is developing from spring; tel (01726) 222900 for details.

PENZANCE SW4730

✿ 🏠 ⚓ ❗ The area's main shopping centre, a pleasantly relaxed town by the sea. The prettiest part is Chapel St, where there's a decent **maritime museum** (cl Sun; £2); the extravagantly designed early 19th-c Egyptian House deserves a passing look, and the Turk's Head is a good pub. Harris's restaurant on New St has good local fish. In summer you can take **boat trips** around the coastline or across to the Isles of Scilly, and there are regular **helicopter flights** to the islands.

🏮 **National Lighthouse Centre** (Old Buoy Store, Wharf Rd) Easy to spot thanks to the big buoys outside, this has an excellent collection of lighthouse equipment, and a good audio-visual display on what it was like to live in one; a typical room is reconstructed, with original curved furniture. Many of the staff are former lighthouse personnel, so a good source of information and anecdote – and there is a lighthouse opposite. Shop, disabled access; cl Nov–Easter; (01736) 360077; £2.50.

🏛 **Penzance & District Museum** (Morrab Rd) Recently extended, with paintings that are certainly worth a look – mainly by the Newlyn school. Snacks, shop, disabled access; cl Sun exc July and Aug; £2 (free Sat).

POLKERRIS SX0952

★ ❄ Little seaside hamlet – scarcely more than the waterside inn – with a terrific view, almost even better in winter, across St Austell bay from the well restored ancient quay.

POLPERRO SX2150

★ ⌂ Almost unbelievably pretty, tiny streets around a very quaint sheltered fishing harbour, with little cottages perched on rocks. It was once a busy

smuggling place, and now has some enjoyable craft shops tucked away, one or two tourist attractions, oddities like the shell-encrusted Shell House, and unspoilt harbourside fishermen's locals (the Blue Peter and Three Pilchards); the Crumplehorn Mill does decent food, and the Old Mill House is good. The beaches around here are some of England's cleanest. It gets very busy in summer, with little electric buses (or horse and cart) shuttling in from the out-of-village car park. A sensible alternative to sweating out summer traffic jams in the village itself is to park instead in Talland Bay, for an easy one-mile walk along the coast to enter this harbour feeling you've earned it.

❗ **Land of Legend & Model Village** (The Old Forge, Mill Hill) With a model railway and scaled-down version of Polperro, this is a useful enough distraction for children, with improvements planned for next year; cl Nov–Easter; (01503) 272378; £2.50.

POOL SW6641

↓T **Cornish Engines** (A3047) Developing site based around two big beam engines, originally used for pumping water from tin and copper mines. Shop, visitor centre (open all year), some disabled access; cl Oct–Mar; (01209) 315027; £3.50; NT. The Cornish Choughs (at Treswithian, just off the far end of the Camborne bypass) has interesting food inc good fresh fish.

PORT ISAAC SX0080

★ ⌂ Delightful steep fishing village, a favourite with many: tiny streets, and houses hanging high over the pretty harbour – the Golden Lion's terrace overlooks it. Park at the top and walk down (at low tide you can park on the beach). There are some particularly fine stretches of cliffs for walking around here, and just up the coast Port Gaverne is a beautiful NT cove.

PORTHALLOW SX2251

🍎 This is snugly set above a little fishing harbour with a beautifully set pub, the Five Pilchards; the beach is notoriously polluted, and swimming in the sea is not recommended. A friendly little **vineyard** here has self-guided tours, free samples of their wines and cider, and a particularly tasty birch country wine; cl 1–2pm, all Sun, and Nov–Easter; (01326) 280050; 50p.

PORTHCURNO SW3822

⌂ Porthcurno's lovely silver sands – among Cornwall's best beaches – are now the property of the National Trust, in common with so much of the coastline round here. If you walk their length, be careful not to get cut off by high tide. The Logan Rock at Treen is good for lunch and ideal for cliff walkers.

! ♨ Minack Theatre & Exhibition Centre There are few better backdrops for plays than the one at this famous little open-air theatre – dramatic cliffs and blue sea stretching into the distance make this a magical setting. Varied summer season, and an exhibition on the life of Rowena Cade, the remarkable woman who built the theatre, cut into these steep cliffs, with her own hands. Tickets go on sale in May, but aren't for particular seats – if you've booked you'll still need to get there early to bag the best. Evening shows are more atmospheric. Shows are cancelled only in extreme conditions, so take a waterproof. Snacks, shop, disabled access to café and exhibition; performances May–Sept, exhibition cl during matinees; (01736) 810181; shows £6.50, exhibition £2.

♨ Museum of Submarine Telegraphy Don't let the name put you off – this museum housed in the secret wartime communications centre in underground tunnels is a good deal more interesting than you'd think. Meals, snacks, shop, disabled access, cl Sat (exc July–Aug) and Nov–Mar (exc Mon); (01209) 612142; £3.50.

PORTHLEVEN SW6225

★ ⌂ Pretty working fishing village; the Ship built into the cliffs is a good pub, and the long stretch of rocky beach S is a pleasant walk if the surf's not beating in too fiercely.

PORTLOE SW9339

★ ⌂ Tiny unspoilt village wedged into a precipitous cove, with splendid cliff walks in rugged scenery, and stiffish climbs on to Nare Head; good teashop/small restaurant.

PORTREATH SW6545

⌂ A good base for long bracing clifftop walks, with a decent pub; along this whole section of coast, between St Ives Bay and Trevose Head (nr Padstow), the coast path is rich in rugged views, and very rewarding to those with sturdy legs.

PORTSCATHO SW8735

★ ⌂ Very sheltered fishing village with a picturesque little harbour, and some fine nearby beaches – excellent for families. The Plume of Feathers is popular for lunch. Virtually the whole of Gerrans Bay around here is good easy walking, with some lovely clifftop stretches; there's a good sandy stretch at Pendower Beach.

PRAA SANDS SW5828

☺ A popular summer family beach.

PROBUS SW9147

❀ 🏠 Trewithen (off A390 between Probus and Grampound, where the Dolphin has good-value food) Justly famous landscaped gardens, with many rare trees and shrubs. The early 18th-c house is a little unfairly overshadowed by what's outside, and is an interesting, obviously lived-in family home. Snacks, rare plants for sale, disabled access; gardens open Mar–Sept (cl Sun exc Apr and May), walled garden open Mon and Tues in Jun, plus 3 and 4 July, house open only pm Mon and pm Tues Apr–July (and pm Aug bank hol); (01726) 883647; gardens *£3.50, house another *£3.50, joint ticket *£6.

RAME HEAD SX4248

✝ ⌂ Jutting far out at the E end of Whitsand Bay, this is capped by a primitive **hermitage chapel** – a worthwhile walk from the pretty village of Kingsand.

RESTORMEL SX1060

🏰 ❀ Restormel Castle Very well preserved Norman castle with notable round keep and fine views over Fowey Valley. Lots of flowers in spring. Snacks, shop limited disabled access; cl Nov–Mar; (01208) 872687; £1.60. The Royal Oak in Lostwithiel is good for lunch.

RESTRONGUET CREEK SW8137

⌂ Though the waterside village is mainly of no great age, its pub the Pandora has a lovely location – you can park in Mylor Bridge for a leisurely two-mile waterside walk there and back, or drive all the way.

RINSEY SW5927

⌂ ▥ The coast path passes two magnificently sited **ruined tin and copper mine** buildings, Wheal Prosper and Wheal Trewavas, both now maintained by the NT.

ROCHE ROCK SW9959

⌂ ▥ This small but picturesque crag is worth the short walk from the B3274, with a 14th-c, ruined, ivy-covered chapel built into it, and a ladder up (decent pub nearby, past the station).

ROUGH TOR SX1284

✸ ⌂ (pronounced 'Roe Tor') The summit, reached from a signed car park off the A39 nr Camelford, gives views of Brown Willy, the highest point in Cornwall.

ST AGNES SW7150

★ ✸ A former mining town, now with a holiday role; attractive steeply terraced cottages, fine cliff scenery nearby, and great views from the top of 630-ft St Agnes Beacon, just W of town. The Railway Inn has some interesting collections.

⚑ **Presingoll Barns** (Penwinnick Rd) Craft centre with demonstrations of glass-painting, candle- and fudge-making, good picnic areas. Snacks, some disabled access; cl Dec 25–26; (01872) 553007; free (a small charge for candle-dipping).

ST ANTHONY HEAD SW8431

⚑ ✸ ⌂ On the E side of the Fal estuary, by the **Zone Head lighthouse**, this has superb views, and easy walks along low, level cliffs; parking at the head itself, or just nr Porth Farm on the way down.

ST AUSTELL SX0352

✝ ⬜ The centre of the china-clay industry and a busy modern shopping town. **Holy Trinity Church** has a fine tower and interesting font, and you can tour the **St Austell Brewery** on Trevarthian Rd (booking recommended – 01726 66022; £4, inc samples of beer). The area N is a strange bleak moonscape of whitish spoil heaps with metallic blue lakes dotted among them; the B3279 St Stephen–Nanpean gives some of the best views over this.

↓⇂ ✸ **Wheal Martyn Museum** (B3274 N of St Austell – you don't have to go into the town) Interestingly restored 19th-c clayworks showing the 200-year history of china-clay production. Working waterwheels and other equipment, steam locomotives, nature trails with a spectacular viewpoint over a huge clay pit, and children's adventure trail. Meals, snacks, shop; cl Nov–Mar; (01726) 850362; £4.50 (a good-value family ticket gets 2 adults and up to 4 children in for £11.50).

ST CLEER SX2568

🪨 **Trevethy Quoit** This is a very photogenic megalithic tomb, its massive stones now left high and dry by a fall in the soil level over thousands of years. The Crows Nest down nr Darite is handy for lunch.

ST GERMANS SX3657

✝ ✸ **St Germans church** Wonderful Norman doorway and particularly fine east window; worth a look if you're passing this waterside village. There's a good view towards Port Eliot, a stately home designed by John Soane (not open).

ST IVES SW5039

★ ⚐ ✸ ⌂ A pretty place, despite the summer crowds, with its attractive working harbour and narrow streets and alleys (the cobbled Fore St is the prettiest). It has good wide beaches, and plenty of bird life along the Lelant Saltings (RSPB reserve). Besides the Pig 'n' Fish, the waterside Sloop (interesting pictures for sale) does reliable food. The best beach for surfers is Porthmeor slightly N, while in the other direction the B3306 to Land's End has great coast and moorland views. Out of season, when the caravan and camp sites are empty, the magnificent sands around St Ives Bay are well worth walking, with good cliff walks to the west.

🖼 ❀ **Barbara Hepworth Museum & Sculpture Garden** (Porthmeor Beach) This tranquil escape from the holiday hordes, devoted to the artist's work and life, has sculptures in the house, studio and subtropical garden, as well as photographs and letters. Shop; cl Mon (exc July–Aug, and bank hols); (01736) 796226; *£3.50. Other works by Hepworth are dotted about town.

🖼 ✸ **Tate Gallery St Ives** (Porthmeor Beach) St Ives's famous popularity with artists is best explored at this gallery, which can take a lot of the credit for the town's increasing number of satisfied visitors in recent years. Works by the familiar St Ives School names are regularly joined by new displays of 20th-c art with a Cornish connection. It's an impressive building, outside and in, fully exploiting its spectacular cliffside setting – views are best from the café. Meals, snacks, shop, disabled access; (01736) 796226; £3.50.

ST JUST-IN-ROSELAND SW8435

✝ An unspoilt spot, its **church** is in an idyllic creekside setting; the steep graveyard is like a lost subtropical garden – well worth a visit on a quiet sunny day, or in spring with the baby rooks blethering and the smell of wild garlic. The words on the inscribed stones by the path seem quite fitting.

ST KEVERNE SW7921

★ 🛏 △ ※ Set around a little square, this is a pleasant village with a good dining pub, the White Hart – and a lovely little **working farm** just S at Tregellast Barton, undeveloped and tranquil, with pleasant walks through woods and meadows, afternoon milking (4.30pm), and a good farm shop with samples of their unusually flavoured ice-cream; phone for opening times; (01326) 280479; free. There's a nice walk to Lowland Point, for dramatic views of The Manacles – striking offshore rocks.

ST KEW SX0276

★ 🛏 Delightful, quiet, leafy village with an old-fashioned feel, and agreeably low-key **Donkey and Pony Sanctuary**. Shop and visitor centre cl Nov–Easter; (01208) 841710; £3.95). The St Kew Inn is a pleasant place for a meal.

ST MAWES SW8533

※ ⚓ 🏰 △ Very pretty harbourside and estuary views, a long waterfront to stroll along, clean bathing waters, a foot-passenger ferry to Falmouth and other boat trips (full of yachtsmen and others in summer, lots of guesthouses). The 16th-c **castle** is remarkably well preserved (cl winter Weds and Thurs; £2.50). The Victory does good-value lunches. Readers recommend taking the ferry across to St Anthony-in-

Roseland for some remote and unspoilt views and walks. The King Harry chain-drawn car ferry, on the B3269 N of St Mawes, is a favourite family crossing, and on the way the Roseland at Philleigh is one of Cornwall's nicest pubs.

ST NEOT SX1866

✝ 🏛 ✪ The village **church** is well known for its early stained glass, and also has an unusual stone vault in the south porch. Nearby ancient remains include the five impressive **Brown Gelly Barrows** and some hut circles. **Carnglaze Slate Caverns** are big, long-abandoned mining chambers, with a lake at the far end of one; guided tours (cl Sat; (01579) 320251; £3). The London Inn is good for lunch.

ST STEPHEN SW9453

🚗 **Automobilia** (A3058 about 4m W of St Austell) Over 50 cars, motorcycles and other vehicles from 1904 to the 1960s, inc a vintage Bentley and Aston Martin, with a permanent auto-jumble that vintage-car owners may find useful. Snacks, shop, disabled access; cl Sats in Apr, May and Oct, and all Nov–Mar; (01726) 823092; £3.50.

SANCREED SW4129

🏛 **Carn Euny Ancient Village** Dating from the 1st c, substantial traces of a little village of stone courtyard houses, and a 66-ft underground passage leading to a circular chamber (some very minor rds to get here).

TINTAGEL SX0588

♿ **King Arthur's Great Halls** (Fore St) Arthurian legends are taken as fact here, and while there's no denying the impressive craftsmanship (especially in the 72 stained-glass scenes), it's done too seriously to be anything more than a time-filler on a rainy day. Decent shop, disabled access; cl 25 Dec; (01840) 770526; £2.50.

🏚 **Old Post Office** Small saggy-roofed 14th-c manor used in the 19th c as a post office; shop; cl Nov–Mar; (01840) 770024; £2.20; NT.

🏰 ※ ✝ **Tintagel Castle** Forgetting the myths and legends, these dramatic 12th- and 13th-c ruins have a spectacular setting and unrivalled views. A good start is from Rocky Valley, a craggy valley leading from the B3263 to the sea. Try and come out of season, when the crowds are fewer and the mist and crashing waves add a touch of mystery. There's quite a lot of climbing involved, and the often steep steps among the crags can be slippery in wet weather. As for King Arthur, latest theories suggest he was a Shropshire lad, but a small exhibition makes the most of the Cornish case. Shop; cl 24–26 Dec and 1 Jan; (01840) 770328; £2.80; EH. A Land-Rover service can ferry you to the site from the village (a tourist trap since the 19th c) at regular intervals throughout the day. The Cornishman is useful for lunch, and the parish church worth a look.

TORPOINT SX4355
🏚 🐾 **Antony House** (2m NW) A pleasant ferry ride from Devonport in Plymouth (it's a lot harder to get to by road), this is the finest Classical house in Cornwall, little changed since the early 18th c, with interesting contents and paintings in its panelled rooms; also riverside gardens redesigned by Humphrey Repton, and a dovecote. Snacks, shop, some disabled access to ground floor only; open pm Tues–Thurs and bank hols Apr–Oct, plus Sun Jun–Aug; (01752) 812191; £4, woodland garden £3; NT.

🏚 🐾 ❄ **Mount Edgcumbe** (B3247 E of Kingsand) A short walk up from the Cremyll pedestrian ferry from Plymouth, this mansion was reconstructed after World War II bombing, with period furniture and (the main attraction) acres of lovely gardens and parkland, divided into English, French and Italian sections. Great views to Plymouth. Meals, snacks, shop, disabled access; house cl Mon (exc bank hols), Tues, and Oct–Mar (but park and gardens open then, free); (01752) 822236; £4.50. The charmingly furnished Edgcumbe Arms, by the ferry, has good-value food.

TREBETHERICK SW9277
✝ **St Enodoc Church** Tucked well away from the roads under a seaside hill off the Rock road, looking out to Padstow Bay. A nice stroll from the village, it's the burial place of John Betjeman. Daymer Bay nr here is a very clean and attractive beach, and as it's so shallow ideal for families wanting to paddle. The Carpenters Arms is useful for lunch, and down on the water at

Rock, the Mariners Hotel has lovely views over to Padstow.

TRECANGATE SX1757
🐖 🐾 🗁 **Porfell Animal Land** Delightfully unspoilt and friendly, this expanding centre has deer, wallabies, racoons, meerkats, a capybara called Bart and a new enclosure for lemurs, as well as rabbits, guinea-pigs, goats, ducks and chickens in 15 acres of sloping fields and woodland. Readers very much enjoy the peaceful and remote feel. Snacks, shop, disabled access; cl Nov–Easter; (01503) 220211; £3.75. The Ship over at Lerryn is handy for lunch and often has good watercolours for sale; the stepping stones over the river there are a hit with children, and pleasant circular walks are signposted from the car park.

TREDINNICK SW9270
🐖 🐎 **Shire Horse Adventure Park** 🎫 Far more to this busy complex than just the magnificent horses: there's a children's farm, an exhibition of rural antiquities, nature trails, watermill and working craftsmen, and very big indoor and outdoor adventure playgrounds inc animated animal shows. The horses are displayed in an indoor arena, and you can see them being groomed in their stables – along with Shetland ponies. Lots for all ages, but ideal for children. Meals, snacks, shop, disabled access; cl Nov–Easter and Sat in Oct; (01841) 540276; £5.95. The Ring o' Bells at St Issey is useful for lunch.

TREGONNING HILL SW6029
🗁 ❄ Takes only a few minutes to climb but has an impressive view; here in 1746 William Cookworthy made the first discovery of china clay in England, and went on to make porcelain.

TRELIGHTS SW9979
🐾 **Long Cross Victorian Gardens** Slightly inland at Trelights (but with good views down to the sea) the prettily restored gardens by the Long Cross Hotel, intricately hedged against the sea winds, have interesting granite and water features, a maze, and playground and pets corner for children. Meals, snacks, plant sales (not Nov–Easter); (01208) 880243; *£1.50.

TRELISSICK SW8339
🐾 🐾 ❄ 🍂 🗁 **Trelissick Garden** (B3289) Woodland park with

beautifully kept gardens of camellias, magnolias and hydrangeas, also subtropical garden and other unusual plants; wonderful views of the King Harry Passage and over to Pendennis Castle. There's a pretty orchard, and good walks in the surrounding woodland. Meals, snacks, shop, disabled access; cl am Sun, and all Jan and Feb; (01872) 862090; £4.20; NT. The NT have four holiday cottages on the estate. The Punch Bowl & Ladle at Penelewey, on the King Harry Ferry road, is popular for lunch.

TRERICE SW8458

🏠🖼🏵 **Trerice House** Pretty Elizabethan house with unusual gables, and elaborate plasterwork ceilings in the magnificent Hall and Great Chamber. Fine furnishings from the 17th and 18th c, notable paintings, early embroideries, Oriental and English porcelain, and in the grounds an unusual collection of lawnmowers; lovely colourful gardens with Cornish fruit trees. Snacks (in a barn with activities for toddlers), shop, very good disabled access; cl Sat and Tues (exc Aug), and all Nov–Mar; (01637) 875404; £4; NT. The Two Clomes at Quintrell Downs is quite handy for lunch.

TRERYN DINAS SW4022

❋ ⌂ The most stunning of Cornwall's headlands, capped by the precariously balanced Logan Rock; it's a fairly easy walk from the Logan Rock pub (good food) in Treen.

TRESKILLARD SW6739

🐎 ⌘ **Shire Horse Farm & Carriage Museum** 🖼 An uncommercialised shire horse farm; most displays are indoors, and there are working blacksmith's and wheelwright's shops. Meals, snacks, shop, disabled access; open Sun–Fri, Easter–Sept, and Sun and Tues in Oct; (01209) 713606; £3.50.

TREVALLAS COOMBE SW7452

♨ **Blue Hills Tin Streams** Tours of this family-run outfit include demonstrations of vanning, panning and jigging. Snacks, shop, disabled access; cl Sun (bookings only Nov–Mar); (01872) 553341; £2.50.

TRURO SW8244

✝👑🏵 A busy but civilised town with good shops; Lemon St is a particularly fine Georgian street, and Boscawen St

is cobbled. The **cathedral** is one of the newer Anglican ones, designed in 1880 in Early English style and finished in 1910; the twin spires of the west front are handsome, and pop up dramatically from behind shops and houses; meals, snacks, shop. The **Royal Cornwall Museum** (River St) tells tales of local characters such as Black John of Tetcott, an 18th-c dwarf whose party piece was apparently tying mice together by their tails, swallowing them whole, and then pulling them up again; also natural history and textile galleries. Meals, snacks, shop, disabled access; cl Sun, bank hols; (01872) 272205; £2.50. Just outside the centre, **Bosvigo** (Bosvigo Lane) is a charming plantsman's garden, with most colour Jun–Sept; small nursery; open Thurs–Sat Mar–Sept; (01872) 275774; *£3. The Old Ale House and Wig & Pen are good for lunch.

VERYAN SW9139

★ ❋ Lovely village famous for its five devil-proof thatched round houses; also a watergarden sheltered by holm oaks. Nearby, 16th-c **Melinsey Mill** is a nicely restored watermill in a lovely setting, with good afternoon teas. The prettiest approach is to walk along the streamside 'Secret Valley' from Pendower Beach (off A3078 S) rather than go from the village itself.

WADEBRIDGE SW9673

⌂ ❋ ⌘ The disused railway track between Wadebridge and Padstow is a level six miles along the edge of the Camel estuary, with banks of wild flowers, birds, and lovely views between cuttings – you can walk or cycle (bike hire at either end), or picnic on the small beaches at low tide. Those with less energy could park at Wadebridge, walk to Padstow, have lunch and get the bus back (2.30pm from the old station). You might then walk on through scenic countryside beyond Bodmin (worth stopping at Helland pottery, just by the path at Helland Bridge).

WENDRON SW6731

⛏ 🏠 **Poldark Mine & Heritage Centre** A fun feature of this old tin mine is its underground post box, the deepest in Britain. More serious attractions include a tour of the mine, an 18th-c village, a film on Cornish mining, old cottages, a collection of working beam engines, and plenty of children's amusements. Varied enough to interest most members of the family. Meals, snacks, shop, limited disabled access; cl Nov–Mar; (01326) 563166; £5.25.

WHEALE COATES SW6949
△ ✳ One of the most photogenic mine ruins on the Cornish coast; for walkers, the diversion up St Agnes Beacon is well worth it for the commanding views.

WHITESAND BAY SW3526
△ ✳ Long expanses of wonderfully clean sands below the cliffs here give good walks, stretching away N of Sennen Cove (very popular with surfers; the Old Success here has a great view).

ZENNOR SW4537
✝ △ The **church** here is best seen in its granite landscape from the hills above. The Tinners Arms is useful for lunch. Around here you can walk for miles without seeing another soul. **Gurnards Head** juts dramatically into the Atlantic, and the hotel there is a good base for cliff walks (with unusual bar snacks).

✪ ⚔ **Wayside Folk Museum** Readers enjoy this decent little local history museum which has chatty descriptions and information scattered through the exhibits; you should be able to see the wheel of the adjacent watermill gently turning. Teas, shop (specialising in Cornish books and crafts); cl Nov–Mar and Sat in Oct; (01736) 796945; £2.20.

Where to eat

Many places in the **Where to stay** section, above, also have very good food.

BOSCASTLE SX0990 **Carpenter's Kitchen** *The Harbour (01840) 250595* In a picturesque village and actually built on the site of an old carpenter's workshop, this is a super (no smoking) place for morning coffee, light lunches, and cream teas, with everything made on the premises; polished tables, matching china, neatly uniformed staff, hard-working friendly owners, delicious local crab in sandwiches, a daily changing winter soup, and plenty of cakes, gateaux, scones, Cornish splits, and so forth; cl Oct–beginning Apr but open wknds Mar and Nov and open 27 Dec–1 Jan; disabled access. £3.

CHAPEL AMBLE SW9975 **Maltsters Arms** *(01208) 812473* Popular family-run pub with attractively knocked-together rooms (one is no smoking), flagstones, beams and a big stone fireplace; good interesting food inc lots of fish, afternoon summer cream teas, 20 wines by the glass, well kept real ales, a no smoking main restaurant, and helpful friendly staff; cl pm 25 Dec; children in family room or over 8 in restaurant; disabled access. £28|£6.

CONSTANTINE SW7229 **Trengilly Wartha** *Nancenoy (01326) 340332* Extremely well run, tucked away inn with a woodburner in the relaxed and civilised bar, a bright no smoking family conservatory, very good imaginative food, a fine range of changing real ales, a thoughtful wine list with 20 by the glass (they also operate a retail business), 40 malt whiskies, and a pretty, landscaped garden; nice bdrms. £19|£6.50.

DULOE SX2358 **Olde Plough House** *(01503) 262050* Very neatly kept pub with lovely slate floor in both communicating bar rooms, three woodburners, a mix of pews and chairs; good interesting food inc fishy specials, real ales, sensibly priced wines, and attentive service; disabled access. £16|£5.25.

FALMOUTH SW8032 **HMS Ganges** *Mylor Yacht Harbour (01326) 374320* Not actually a ship (though obviously named after one), this friendly little restaurant looks across the River Fal and specialises in fresh fish and seafood – they also serve breakfast for the many yachtsmen who sail into the harbour; good choice of wines from around the world at reasonable prices, and helpful service; cl pm Sun, Mon and Tues Oct–Feb, all Feb–mid-Mar; disabled access. **£26.60**|£6.

FALMOUTH SW8032 **Pennypots** *Maenporth Beach (01326) 250251* Attractively decorated and airy evening restaurant with fine views across Falmouth Bay, a strong emphasis on beautifully presented, really fresh local fish and shellfish dishes (lovely non-fishy things too), delicious puddings, an extensive wine list, and deft attentive service; cl Sun, Mon, 4 wks winter; disabled access. **£38**.

FOWEY SX1252 **Food for Thought** *Town Quay* (01726) 832221 Carefully run quayside evening restaurant with generous helpings of attractively presented food, fine fish and some simple as well as other elaborate dishes, and lovely puddings; cl Sun, Jan and Feb; children must be well behaved. **£26**.

LANLIVERY SX0759 **Crown** (01208) 872707 Pretty 12th-c inn with friendly licensees, a rambling series of rooms with open fires, a chatty atmosphere, good food using home-grown and local produce, well kept real ales, and a nice garden; disabled access. **£15.50|£5**.

MITHIAN SW7450 **Miners Arms** (01872) 552375 Secluded Tudor pub with lots of character, fine old furnishings and warm winter fires, popular food, a no smoking dining room, real ales, and friendly service. **£17|£6**.

MOUSEHOLE SW4726 **Cornish Range** (01736) 731488 Friendly and neatly kept restaurant with a friendly atmosphere and carefully cooked food inc plenty of good local fish dishes and enjoyable puddings; cl winter Mon–Weds; disabled access. **£25**.

NEWLYN SW4628 **Smugglers** *12–14 Fore St* (01736) 331501 In a fine setting on the edge of the fishing-boat harbour, this simply furnished little restaurant has candles on pine tables, a friendly atmosphere, and an interesting menu inc delicious fresh fish and super puddings; cl 25–26 Dec, 1 Jan; partial disabled access. **£17**.

PADSTOW SW9175 **St Petroc's** *4 New St* (01841) 532700 Attractive little hotel (under the same ownership as the Seafood Restaurant) with good, quickly served food from a short bistro-type menu (plenty of fish), a sensible wine list, and friendly atmosphere; cl Mon, Christmas. **£21.95|£11**.

PADSTOW SW9175 **Seafood** *Riverside* (01841) 532700 Wonderfully fresh seafood straight from the boats in busy (and famous – hence having to book so far in advance) airy quayside restaurant; good puddings, nice cheeses, a long, interesting and fairly priced wine list, and friendly service; conservatory for aperitifs; bdrms; cl Sun, 19–27 Dec; children over 3; limited disabled access. **£36 lunch, £39 dinner**.

PENZANCE SW4730 **Harris's** *46 New St* (01736) 364408 Long-standing and boldly decorated cosy restaurant in a narrow cobbled street, with good enjoyable food using local produce (popular fish and shellfish), well liked puddings, and a decent wine list; cl Mon, 3 wks in winter. **£28|£7.50**.

PHILLEIGH SW8639 **Roseland** (01872) 580254 Friendly little 17th-c pub just up the hill from the King Harry ferry, with lots of rugby and rowing prints, a relaxed atmosphere, a good winter fire, well kept real ales, and popular home-made food; disabled access. **£18|£5.50**.

POLPERRO SX2051 **Kitchen** *The Coombes* (01503) 272780 Cottagey, informal, no smoking evening restaurant with really enjoyable interesting food inc vegetarian and daily-changing fresh fish dishes (lovely fresh lobster and crab), and good-value wines; cl Sun, Oct–Easter; children over 12. **£25**.

POLPERRO SX2051 **Plantation Café** *The Coombes* (01503) 272223 Popular beamed teashop with good cream teas, a wide choice of interesting teas inc herbal and fruit, lunchtime sandwiches, and evening meals; cl Sat, Nov–Apr; disabled access. **£13.75|£2.95**.

PORTHALLOW SW7923 **Taranaki Tea Rooms** (01326) 280671 Lovely flower-filled tropical gardens with seats under covered pergola or in conservatory; home-baked scones and cakes, cream teas and light lunches (super crab sandwiches) all prepared by the friendly owner; no licence but can bring drinks from nearby pub; cl end Sept–Good Fri; partial disabled access. **£6.50|£3**.

PORTLOE SW9339 **Tregain** *The Post Office* (01872) 501252 Small, friendly, no smoking restaurant serving interesting, well cooked food using local produce; daily specials (fresh fish in the evening and lovely home-made crab soup at lunchtime), light lunches and super cream teas, a decent wine list, and local cider; 2 bdrms; cl pm Sun exc bank hol wknds, Nov–Mar. **£25|£6**.

ST IVES SW5140 **Porthminster Beach Café** (01736) 795352 Bustling, popular café open all day for morning coffee with home-baked pastries, cream teas, light lunches and more substantial evening meals offering good Mediterranean cooking (nice daily specials) using local produce, and a wide choice of coffees and teas; kind to children; cl Oct–Easter; disabled access. **£20|£5.50.**

ST KEVERNE SW7921 **White Hart** *The Square (01326) 280325* Well liked inn with beams, an open fire, a mix of simple furniture on the bare boards, a relaxed chatty atmosphere, enjoyable food inc good fresh fish, and well kept real ales; seats outside in the garden, too; disabled access. **£25|£5.95.**

ST KEW SX0276 **St Kew** *(01208) 841259* Rather grand-looking stone pub with a friendly welcome, nice old-fashioned furnishings in the neatly kept bar, good popular food, and a peaceful garden; lovely church next door. **£18|£6.95.**

ST MICHAEL'S MOUNT SW5130 **Sail Loft** *The Harbour (01736) 710748* Converted boat house, with enjoyable home-made cakes, Cornish cream teas, more substantial meals, and friendly service; no smoking; cl Nov–Mar; disabled access. **£16.95|£4.50.**

TRURO SW8244 **Old Ale House** *7 Quay St (01872) 271122* Appealing, bustling and friendly back-to-basics pub, popular with a good cross-section of people; interesting bric-à-brac and engaging old furnishings, up to 24 real ales, and enterprising, freshly prepared and very cheap food from a spotless kitchen. **£13|£4.50.**

TREBURLEY SX3477 **Springer Spaniel** *(01579) 370424* Lovely relaxed atmosphere in main-road pub, with totally home-made interesting food inc delicious puddings (some home-grown produce), very friendly service, simply furnished bars, well kept real ales, 7 good wines by the glass, and an attractive, no smoking restaurant; cl 4 days over Christmas. **£24|£4.50.**

Isles of Scilly

The islands, about 30 miles west of Land's End, are charmingly unspoilt and a great place for utter relaxation. They have beautiful scenery, an almost subtropical climate, and a variety of shorelines giving excellent coastal walks. In a lazy day you can comfortably walk round the largest, St Mary's, which is just six square miles. Tresco and St Agnes are the other main populated ones, though that means small undeveloped communities rather than any towns or big settlements. There are over 100 islands in all, some just strange-shaped rocks jutting out of the sea, their only visitors seals, dolphins and puffins.

You can get there from Penzance by ferry (around £30 day return) or more spectacularly by helicopter, a 20-minute ride with really beautiful views of the Cornish coast and of the islands (return fares start at around £60). The islands also have their own little airline Skybus which leaves from Land's End, Newquay or Exeter several times a day. The trip from Land's End is quickest and cheapest (from £40 return; no flights Sun). They also do packages in conjunction with InterCity – (01736) 787017 for details.

Where to stay

TRESCO SV8915 **Island** *Tresco, Isles of Scilly TR24 0PU (01720) 422883* **£260 inc dinner;** 48 rms, many with balconies and terrace overlooking gardens or sea. Tiny private island, renowned for its wonderful subtropical Abbey Gardens and reached by helicopter or boat – hotel's tractor-drawn bus (no cars allowed though bike hire available) takes you to spacious, very friendly modern hotel with colonial-style bar, library, fine food and wine, panoramic views, swimming pool, and private beach; no dogs; cl Nov–Feb.

HUGH TOWN SV9010 **Tregarthens** *Hugh Town, St Mary's, Isles of Scilly TR21 0PP (01720) 422540* **£148 inc dinner;** 33 rms, most with sea views. Magnificent views over the harbour and outer islands of Samson, Bryher and Tresco from this extended and modernised hotel, first opened in 1848; neatly kept rooms, good

food and pleasant service; cl mid-Oct–end Mar; no dogs.
PELISTRY BAY SV9311 **Carnwethers Country House** *Pelistry Bay, St Mary's, Isles of Scilly TR21 0NX (01720) 422415 *£106 inc dinner* – good-value weekly terms, too; 9 rms. Well run, no smoking country guesthouse nr very fine beach, with an acre of lovely gardens, heated swimming pool, and croquet; lounge with helpful books about the islands, well stocked bar, good, freshly cooked set 4-course dinner using local produce served at 6.30pm, sound wine list, and games room with pool table and table tennis; sauna; lots of coastal walks; cl Oct–Apr; children over 8.

To see and do

As each of the islands is so small, few apart from Tresco have many specific attractions – visitors come mainly to 'get away from it all', and there can be a refreshing feeling of complete isolation. By far the best activity is walking – there are plenty of white sandy beaches to stroll along (the sea is clean but cold), or unusual plants and birds to track down. Hiring bikes is another good way of exploring and enjoying the scenery. Thanks to the climate – the name means Sun Isles – flowers come out early, and spring and autumn sunsets can be particularly beautiful. A good plan is to island-hop – there are regular ferries between the larger islands, though it can prove expensive. Every Fri evening and some Weds in summer you can watch the racing of the traditional six-oar gigs that used to dash out to shipwrecks.

BRYHER SV8715
❀ A tiny quiet place, even by Scilly standards. The south bay has lots of wild flowers, and Watch Hill has wonderful views. The Hell Bay Hotel is good value.

ST AGNES SV8708
⚔❀ The most south-westerly community in the British Isles, joined to a smaller island called Gugh by a sandbar, awash at high tide. The sheltered cove here is especially popular. The 17th-c **lighthouse** is the second oldest in Britain. The views from here out to the rocks and islets are very atmospheric especially when you remember more ships have been wrecked here than anywhere comparable in the world.

ST MARTIN'S SV9315
❀ A narrow rocky ridge with flowers stretching down to the main attraction – the extensive beaches, very popular for picnics. There's a diving school, and the St Martin's Hotel has lovely sunset views.

ST MARY'S SV9010
⚓⛵⚓🏛❀⚔ The hub of Scilly Isles life, though its centre, Hugh Town, is little more than a village by mainland standards. Most ferries and planes arrive here, and you can get **pleasure cruises** from the Old Quay out to the bird and seal colonies on the outer islets and islands; there are fishing trips from here too. There's a **museum**, and 9-hole putting green with fine views. The **Longstone Papers Past Exhibition** has a huge collection of archive newspapers; snacks, shop; cl am Sat, am Sun and mid-Sept–mid-May; 99p. The Bishop & Wolf is a pleasant pub, and the Atlantic Holt has a good pub part. Up in the north at Bant's Carn there's a burial chamber and ancient village. Back down south, walk out to Penninis Head for good views of the Wolf and Bishop's Rock **lighthouses**. Just along the coast is **Star Castle**.

TRESCO SV8915
🌸🐚⛲⚓⛵ The highlight here is the amazing **subtropical garden** around the grounds of the abbey, begun in 1834, which, despite storms, contains a magnificent collection of exotic plants, bananas even. Also in these grounds is **Valhalla**, a collection of carved figureheads from wrecked ships, many dating back to the 17th-c. Helicopters from Penzance land just outside the garden gate, so it's possible (though not cheap) to come here just for a day. The southern parts of the

island are mainly sandy, but in the north it's more wild and rugged, with the remains of the castles of both Charles I and Oliver Cromwell, and a cave known as the Piper's Hole. Cycling and walking are real pleasures – not least because there aren't any cars. The New Inn, embellished with a mystery cargo of pine planking which washed ashore a while back, has good food inc seafood embellished with a mystery cargo of pine planking which washed ashore recently, has good food inc seafood.

Where to eat

ST AGNES SV8807 **Turks Head** *The Quay, Isles of Scilly* (01720) *422434* Idyllically placed pub (a pleasant place to stay) with outstanding views over the sweeping bay, enjoyable food in the simple pine-panelled bar inc legendary, huge, locally made pasties; also, afternoon teas, evening barbecues, real ales, and decent wines; you can walk down to the slipway and sit right on the shore – or enjoy the wonderful views from seats on the lawn; cl winter exc pm Weds and Sat and am Sun. **£14.75**|£5.50.

We welcome reports from readers

This *Guide* depends on readers' reports. Do help us if you can – in return, we offer a discount on the next edition to people who've helped us with reports for it. Tell us what you think about places already in it, and anything extra you think we should say about them. And send us your ideas for inclusion in the next edition: places to visit, eat at or stay in, attractive drives or walks, maybe even unusual interesting shops you know of. Use the card in the middle, the report forms at the end, or just write – no stamp needed: *The Good Britain Guide*, FREEPOST TN1569, Wadhurst, E Sussex TN5 7BR.

Cornwall Calendar

Some of these dates were provisional as we went to press. Please check information with the telephone numbers provided.

JANUARY

1 Bodmin Brown Willy Run (01326) 317534; **Mawnan Smith** Trebah Icicle: Charity Swim at Trebah Garden (01326) 250448
31 Saltash Music and Speech Festival – *till 12 February* (01752) 843073

FEBRUARY

7 St Ives Hurling the Silver Ball: the town and its people are divided in two and a ball is thrown *at midday* from the town hall by the mayor into the crowd below who carry, fight or secrete the ball to their town half (01736) 797840
27 Wadebridge Music and Speech Festival (01208) 863731

MARCH

5 St Piran's Day: various processions and church services in honour of the patron saint of Cornish tinners throughout Cornwall
6 Truro County Music Festival – *till 11 March* (01872) 573338
7 St Columb Major Hurling the Silver Ball: town and country residents battle in the streets with shop windows boarded up; the town goal is a small stone trough and the country goal is one mile north on the road to Wadebridge – *also 18 March* (01208) 841329
11 Perranporth Land Yachting Regatta – *till 12 March* (01326) 376191
17 Festival of Spring Gardens: over 70 gardens (in various locations) open – *till 31 May* (01872) 863300
25 Falmouth Spring Flower Show – *till 26 March* (01326) 311277
26 Wadebridge Music and Speech Festival (01208) 841329

APRIL

16 St Endellion Easter Music Festival – *till 23 April* (01208) 850463
28 Boscastle Beer Festival and Duck Race – *till 1 May* (01840) 250202
29 Camborne Trevithick Day: traction engine rally, traditional Cornish dancing, street parades (01209) 712941; **St Mary's** Isles of Scilly World Pilot Gig Championships – *till 30 April* (01720) 422536

MAY

1 Calstock Revels (01822) 834418; **Padstow** Obby Oss Celebrations: May song, man in large full-skirted horse costume with other strangely dressed characters (01841) 533449
2 Bugle Festival of Music and Speech – *till 6 May* (01726) 850535
5 Fowey and **St Austell** Daphne du Maurier Festival of Arts and Literature – *till 14 May* (01726) 274324
6 Helston Flora Day: from early morning dance *at 8.20am*, with Hal-an-Tow and Ancient Furry Dance later (01326) 565431; **Newquay** Great Cornwall Balloon Festival – *till 7 May* (01637) 872211
7 Bodmin Moor Ten Tors Walk (01208) 72793

Cornwall Calendar (cont.)

13 **Bude** March at *10.30am* preceding re-enactment of the Battle of Stamford Hill at Stratton – *till 14 May* (01288) 354886; **Stratton** Re-enactment of the Battle of Stamford Hill (1643) – *till 14 May* (01288) 354886
15 **Betjeman** Week (at various venues) – *till 19 May* (01726) 66232
26 **Calstock** Festival – *till 3 June* (01822) 832653
27 **Newquay** Surfing Festival – *till 29 May* (01736) 360250
28 **Launceston** Steam Engine Rally – *till 29 May* (01566) 772333

JUNE

3 **Point** and **Penpool** Regatta (01872) 864226
8 **Wadebridge** Royal Cornwall Show – *till 10 June* (01208) 812183
16 **Penzance** Golowan Festival: traditional sea and land festival, with theatre, street theatre, Celtic arts, carnival and fireworks – *till 25 June* (01736) 332211
17 **Redruth** Murdoch Day: street entertainment – *till 18 June* (01209) 210038
19 **Liskeard** Carnival Week – *till 24 June* (01579) 341343
24 **Bodmin** Cornwall Theatre and Heritage Festival – *till 30 June* (01208) 74159
25 **Mevagissey** Feast Week – *till 1 July* (01726) 74014

JULY

1 **Bodmin** Riding and Heritage Day (01208) 74159
2 **Newquay** 1900 Week: Victorian entertainments inc processions, flora dance, fireworks – *till 7 July* (01637) 878735
3 **St Day** Feast Day Celebrations (01209) 820639
7 **Penzance** West Cornwall Maritime Festival – *till 10 July* (01736) 362341
8 **Merrymeet** Liskeard Country Show at Trengrove Farm (01579) 343125
9 **Liskeard** Country Show (01579) 343125
15 **Camborne** Show (01209) 842228; **Looe** Beach Regatta (01872) 862286
17 **Stithians** Show (01872) 240113
20 **Launceston** Agricultural Show at Kennards House (01566) 772333
22 **Bodmin** Country Fair (01208) 72793; **Flushing** Regatta (01326) 372941
30 **Falmouth** Carnival Week – *till 6 August* (01326) 319126; **Mylor** Regatta (01326) 373663
31 **St Mawes** Regatta (01326) 270953

AUGUST

1 **St Endellion** Summer Music Festival – *till 11 August* (01208) 850463
2 **St Keverne** Ox Roast inc torchlight procession (01326) 280487
4 **Tintagel** Re-enactment of the Arthurian Battle of Camlann – *till 6 August* (01840) 770028
5 **Falmouth** Regatta Week inc parade of old wooden sailing boats – *till 12 August* (01326) 211555
9 **Camelford** Agricultural Show (01840) 213761
10 **Calstock** Carnival – *till 12 August* (01822) 834418
12 **Penryn** Carnival (01326) 372461
13 **Percuil** Regatta (01872) 580999
19 **Bude** Carnival Week – *till 26 August* (01288) 355100

Cornwall Calendar (cont.)

24 Newquay British National Surfing Championships – *till 28 August* (01736) 360250

25 Helston Harvest Fair – *till 28 August* (01326) 563167; **Wadebridge** Folk Festival – *till 28 August* (01208) 831123

26 Bude Jazz Festival: over 150 events, mostly trad jazz with street parades – *till 2 September* (01633) 211368; **Looe** Vintage Steam Rally at Bray Farm, Normansland – *till 27 August* (01503) 240520; **Newquay** Surfers Against Sewage Ocean Festival – *till 28 August* (01872) 553001; **Penryn** Town Fair (01326) 374763; **Portscatho** Regatta (01872) 580681

27 Stithians Cornish Game and Country Fair (01872) 273366

28 Bude Lifeboat Day (01288) 355100; **Newlyn** Fish Festival (01736) 363499

SEPTEMBER

2 Falmouth Cornish Gorsedd: celebration of the Cornish language inc traditional dancing and bards (01208) 79115

8 Truro Flower Festival at the Cathedral – *till 11 September* (01872) 276782

9 St Ives Festival: folk, jazz and poetry – *till 23 September* (01736) 796888

25 Newquay Summercourt Fair (01872) 510807

27 Lanlivery Vintage Rally and Country Fair – *till 28 September* (01208) 873798

OCTOBER

6 Callington Honey Fair; ancient street fair (01579) 350230

NOVEMBER

13 Camborne Music Festival – *till 18 November* (01209) 711455

22 St Austell Music and Speech Festival – *till 25 November* (01726) 75840

27 St Austell Music and Speech Festival – *till 2 December* (01726) 75840

DECEMBER

23 Mousehole Tom Bawcock's Eve: traditional event with lamplit boats and star-gazey pie to celebrate the man who saved the town from starving by going out in a storm to catch fish (01326) 312300

We welcome reports from readers

This *Guide* depends on readers' reports. Do help us if you can – in return, we offer a discount on the next edition to people who've helped us with reports for it. Tell us what you think about places already in it, and anything extra you think we should say about them. And send us your ideas for inclusion in the next edition: places to visit, eat at or stay in, attractive drives or walks, maybe even unusual interesting shops you know of. Use the card in the middle, the report forms at the end, or just write – no stamp needed: *The Good Britain Guide*, FREEPOST TN1569, Wadhurst, E Sussex TN5 7BR.

CUMBRIA

The glorious scenery, with outstanding access to open country, is the main draw, but there are also lots of interesting places to visit – and excellent places to stay in.

Each lake has its own character, and the landscape around them varies greatly too. Lake Windermere, the longest and busiest, has always been a general favourite; it's picturesquely dotted with villas built by Victorian magnates, and has masses of accommodation on its east side. Ullswater approaches the grandeur of Scottish lochs, and has some excellent (if not cheap) places to stay right by the lake shore. Buttermere and Crummock Water also have scenery on the grand scale, perhaps without quite matching Ullswater's scenic perfection. Derwent Water wavers charmingly between highland and lowland in flavour, and its islands and manageable proportions make it a favourite for idle boating as well as for bankside strolls. Coniston Water, quite well wooded, also appeals to both boaters and walkers, with some fine views – in some ways it's a junior version of Windermere, smaller and quieter. Wastwater, England's deepest lake, is austere, surrounded by towering screes. Bassenthwaite is altogether gentler, lowland in feel. Some much smaller lakes, notably Grasmere, Rydal Water and Elterwater, are idyllic.

The most beautiful scenery is concentrated thickly around the central area, especially around the towns of Ambleside and Windermere. Both places are quite intensively developed for visitors and very busy indeed in summer; Keswick, too, has lots going on for all ages. These parts really come into their own at quieter times of the year – you need a degree of peace and quiet to enjoy the beauty of the delicious central area between Windermere and Grasmere.

The best coastal scenery is around Morecambe Bay in the south. The west coast is untouristy, with miles of unfrequented beaches (as well as some run-down looking places, and the big nuclear power plant at Seascale, which has an excellent visitor centre).

There are lots of interesting places to visit, including many good craft shops – the Brougham Hall Craft Centre is perhaps the best. We'd recommend a look at the villages of Hawkshead, Troutbeck and Cartmel. Some outstanding attractions include the exotic creatures at Amazonia in Windermere, a refreshing break from all the boat cruises; Appleby Castle with its gardens, waterfowl, falconry and so on; Grizedale Forest Park, for an interesting 'outdoors' day out; Holker Hall at Cark-in-Cartmel – a great house with impressive gardens. A good point is that the stately homes up here tend to have a degree of intimacy and personal contact that's missing from many places further south – and this is particularly true of smaller houses, such as Mirehouse near Bassenthwaite, Townend at Troutbeck, or those connected with literary figures.

The literary trail is heavily trodden in summer, and though very well managed is specially rewarding at quieter times. The main Wordsworth focus is on Grasmere, Rydal and Cockermouth. Beatrix Potter is well served at her home at Near Sawrey, and in Ambleside (the Armitt Museum – a newcomer to the *Guide*) and Hawkshead, and for young children in Windermere. Ruskin has his admirers of course, but his house across the water from Coniston, and in Coniston itself the newly improved and very varied Ruskin Museum (another new entry for the *Guide*) have a more general appeal.

Other new entries this year include the unique alpaca farm at Stainton, the lovingly restored Swarthmoor Hall near Ulverston, and a big candlemaker's in Lindal-in-Furness.

The area's local history museums tend to be much more interesting than you might expect; we'd particularly pick out the one in Millom, and Abbot Hall in Kendal – Kendal has a good-value inclusive-price ticket for its museums. The bobbin mill at Finsthwaite is surprisingly interesting, and Ravenglass has a fine steam railway.

Cumbria is very good territory for children who get a kick out of doing outdoor things. Families who need more in the way of amusements laid on have tended to enjoy other areas more, but the growing list of enjoyable family attractions here is now reaching a level where there's really plenty to keep most children entertained. Among plenty of farm, animal and wildlife centres, the one at Dalton-in-Furness stands out. The Lowther Leisure Park at Hackthorpe will keep most younger kids amused for the best part of a full day.

Among the wealth of what one might call 'classic' visitor attractions, the few odd ones out such as the Seascale nuclear visitor centre and the Buddhist temple at Ulverston stand out all the more strikingly; and Whitehaven's friendly heritage centre, the Beacon, is fascinating for anyone with a weather obsession – all too easy to acquire in Lakeland.

The National Trust controls over a quarter of the land in the Lake District National Park. So preservation of and access to the countryside here is first class (and it's an area where membership of the Trust really pays off in terms of free admission). You could stay here for weeks every year of your life and never walk the same path twice – so our walks suggestions are really just initial pointers. Also, many of the recommended places to stay here have been chosen for the grand walks right from their doorsteps. There's an excellent choice of places to stay, many of which serve really good food. We have gone out of our way to recommend places that are strong on peace and quiet; there's a splendid range of styles and prices.

For a quiet break with plenty of walking on your doorstep, the Langdales, particularly Great Langdale, and Borrowdale are outstanding. The west is even quieter, separated from the central Lake District by high ridges with tortuous roads over the few passes. British rock-climbing was born over here, with England's highest mountain, Scafell Pike, surrounded by other awesome peaks – serious walking country.

Another area where you can reckon on peace and quiet even in summer is the part east of the M6. This is one of England's least-known areas, and though overshadowed by the Lake District proper has a lot of charm, and some excellent-value places to stay in. Quiet river valleys shelter below more awesome open country and high moors, and there are some attractive and untouristy places to visit. Much of the high country is too bleak and boggy for most walkers, but moorland roads give drivers good views (e.g. the A683 Kirkby Lonsdale–Kirkby Stephen, B6260 Tebay–Appleby, B6413 Lazonby–Brampton, A689 Brampton–Alston). The railway crossing the moors between Carlisle and Settle is perhaps the best way of all for seeing this unusual part of England. Carlisle itself is becoming more and more interesting for visitors, with a good millennium project coming to fruition now.

Lakeland generally is at its best out of season. May (sheets of wild flowers on the hills) and June are ideal: more sun, no crowds. The views are often clearest (and the ground firm and dry for walkers) in October and November, though afternoons are short then. In the summer holidays and at other peak times crowds make the best places less enjoyable, and indeed put a real strain on the environment. If you're determined to go at that time of year, you've more chance of finding peace in the west, or over by the Pennines east of the M6. For all but the hardiest expert outdoorsmen, winter up here is too bleak for pleasure – unless you plan to stay indoors. Whenever you come bring something waterproof – the Lake District has more annual rainfall than any other part of the country.

Public transport in the Lakes is good and useful for round-trip long walks; information service (01228) 812812. Local information leaflets offer plenty of choice of well guided walks; information too from National Park visitor services (01539) 446601, and from the flourishing Cumbria Wildlife Trust (01539) 432476, which controls many reserves. Bicycles can be hired by the day in the main towns (considering the scenic grandeur, you can cycle for a surprisingly long way, at least in the central area, without having to struggle up steep hills). Many places offer riding: around £10 an hour for adults, £8 for children.

Where to stay

ALSTON NY7246 **Lovelady Shield** Nenthead Rd, Alston CA9 3LF (01434) 381203 **£163 inc dinner,** plus special breaks; 12 rms. In a lovely setting with the River Nent running along bottom of the garden (tennis and croquet), this handsome country house has a tranquil atmosphere, courteous staff, and log fires in comfortable rooms (no smoking in sitting room or restaurant); very good food inc fine breakfasts; cl Jan; dogs by prior arrangement.
AMBLESIDE NY3804 **Rothay Manor** Rothay Bridge (Coniston Rd), Ambleside LA22 0EH (015394) 33605 **£170 inc dinner,** plus special breaks; 18 attractive rms, many overlooking garden. Family-run Regency-style country house in neatly kept mature grounds, with log fires and fresh flowers in the quietly civilised comfortable day rooms, very good English food in no smoking dining room, a thoughtful wine

list, super big breakfasts, and helpful friendly service; windsurfing/waterskiing, etc, close by, free use of nearby leisure club; cl Jan; good disabled access.

AMBLESIDE NY3804 **Rowanfield Country House** *Kirkstone Rd, Ambleside LA22 9ET (015394) 33686* ***£60,** plus special breaks. 7 rms. Charming, carefully restored Lakeland house looking across Lake Windermere to distant hills, with a woodburner in the comfortable and attractively furnished sitting room, enjoyable interesting food at 7pm in the flagstoned and candlelit dining room (bring your own wine), super breakfasts, and friendly owners; cl mid-Nov–Mar but open Christmas and New Year; children over 8.

AMBLESIDE NY3804 **Wateredge** *Borrans Rd LA22 0EP (015394) 32332* ***£104,** plus special breaks; 22 good, comfortable rms. Beautifully placed, warmly welcoming hotel with neat gardens running down to Lake Windermere (embarkation point for cruising the lake), light airy lounges, good meals in cosy, beamed, no smoking dining room, and excellent service; cl mid-Dec–mid-Jan; children over 7; dogs by prior arrangement.

APPLEBY NY6921 **Appleby Manor** *Roman Rd, Appleby CA16 6JB (01768) 351571* ***£122,** plus special breaks; 30 well equipped rms in original house (the nicest), coach house annexe or modern wing. Very friendly, family-run hotel with fine views over Appleby Castle and Eden Valley, log fire in one of the 3 comfortable lounges, relaxed bar with wide range of whiskies, excellent service, good, interesting food in the panelled restaurant; also, a leisure centre; cl 25–26 Dec; disabled access.

BARBON SD6282 **Barbon Inn** *Barbon, Carnforth LA6 2LJ (015242) 76233* **£60;** 10 simple but comfortable rms, some with own bthrm. Small, friendly village inn in a quiet spot below the fells; relaxing bar, traditional lounge, good meals in candlelit dining room, and helpful service.

BASSENTHWAITE LAKE NY1930 **Pheasant** *Bassenthwaite Lake, Cockermouth CA13 9YE (017687) 76234* **£90,** plus special breaks; 20 rms. Civilised hotel with delightfully old-fashioned pubby bar, restful lounges with open fires, antiques, fresh flowers and comfortable armchairs, and interesting gardens merging into surrounding fellside woodlands; cl pm 24 Dec, 25 Dec; disabled access.

BORROWDALE NY2413 **Seatoller House** *Borrowdale, Keswick CA12 5XN (017687) 77218* ***£58;** 9 spotless, comfortable rms. Friendly house-party atmosphere in this 17th-c house that has been a guesthouse for over 100 years, with self-service drinks and board games in the comfortable lounges (no TV), and good no-choice fixed-time hearty dinner (not Tues) served at two big oak tables; packed lunches; 2 acres of grounds and many walks from the doorstep as the house is at the foot of Honister Pass; cl Nov–Mar; children over 5.

BOWNESS SD4097 **Linthwaite House** *Crook Rd, Bowness-on-Windermere, Windermere LA23 3JA (015394) 88600* **£130,** plus special breaks; 18 individually decorated rms, some with lake views. Stunningly set Lakeland house in 14 acres of immaculate gardens overlooking Lake Windermere, and with their own tarn fishing; comfortable, stylish furnishings in engaging day rooms, an easy-going atmosphere, very good service, and most enjoyable, modern British cooking in the cosy candlelit restaurant; croquet, putting, golf practice hole; children over 7 in evening restaurant; disabled access.

BRAMPTON NY5361 **Farlam Hall** *Hallbankgate, Brampton (A689 S) CA8 2NG (016977) 46234* ***£220 inc dinner,** plus special breaks; 12 comfortable rms. Charmingly Victorian (though parts are much older) and very civilised country house with log fires in the spacious lounges, excellent attentive service, good 4-course dinner, marvellous breakfasts, and peaceful spacious grounds with a croquet lawn and a small pretty lake; cl Christmas–New Year; children over 5; dogs by prior arrangement.

BRANDLINGILL NY1626 **Low Hall** *Brandlingill, Cockermouth CA11 0RE (01900) 826654* **£60;** 3 pleasant rms. Beautifully sited, partly 17th-c farmhouse below Whinlatter Pass and close to Cockermouth, with a big peaceful garden, log fires and books in lounges, and super farmhouse breakfasts inc 20 different teas, home-made oatcakes, muesli, and preserves; no smoking; children over 10.

BUTTERMERE NY1817 **Bridge Hotel** *Buttermere, Cockermouth, CA13 9UZ (017687)* 70252 ***£96,*** plus special breaks; 22 rms. Comfortable hotel surrounded by some of the best steep countryside in the county, with a beamed bar (the flagstoned part is popular with walkers), log fire and deep armchairs in the sitting room, good food in the bar and no smoking restaurant, real ales, decent malt whiskies, and friendly atmosphere; self-catering also.

CARLISLE NY4056 **Number Thirty One Howard Place** *31 Howard Pl, Carlisle CA1 1HR (01228)* 597080 ***£60;*** 3 well equipped individually decorated rms. Carefully restored, no smoking Victorian townhouse with a relaxed informal atmosphere, open fire and plenty of books in the cosy lounge, delicious interesting food using the best local products, breakfast with home-baked bread, home-made preserves and home-made Cumbrian sausages, and helpful courteous owners; cl Dec–Mar; no children.

CARTMEL SD3879 **Uplands** *Haggs Lane, Cartmel, Grange-over-Sands LA11 6HD (015395)* 36248 **£142** inc dinner, plus special breaks; 5 pretty rms. Comfortable Edwardian house in 2 acres of garden with views over to the Morecambe Bay estuary, attractively decorated rooms, and helpful service; the main draw is undoubtedly the richly imaginative food in the no smoking dining room; cl 1 Jan–1 Mar; children over 8; well behaved dogs welcome.

CASTERTON SD6379 **Pheasant** *Casterton, Carnforth LA6 2RX (015242)* 71230 **£68,** plus special breaks; 10 comfortable rms, most with countryside views. Small civilised inn with a pleasant atmosphere, cosy residents' lounge, no smoking garden lounge, and cheerful staff; good food in the panelled dining room, and small but sound wine list; dogs allowed; disabled access.

CATLOWDY NY4677 **Bessiestown Farm** *Catlowdy, Longtown, Carlisle CA6 5QP (01228)* 577219 **£47;** 4 rms. Friendly farmhouse (mainly no smoking) on a small beef and sheep rearing farm close to the Scottish borders, with 2 comfortable lounges, good home-made food and big breakfasts in the attractive dining room, indoor heated swimming pool, and a games room; self-catering also; well behaved children.

CROOK SD4695 **Wild Boar** *Crook, Windermere LA23 3NF (015394)* 45225 ***£82;*** 36 rms. Comfortable, well run, extended hotel with period furnishings and log fires in its ancient core, attentive service, and good food in no smoking dining room; free access to nearby leisure club and discounts on watersports.

CROSBY ON EDEN NY4559 **Crosby Lodge** *High Crosby, Crosby on Eden, Carlisle CA6 4QZ (01228)* 573618 ***£100,*** plus wknd breaks; 11 spacious rms (2 in stable conversion). Imposing and carefully converted country house in attractive mature grounds in nice countryside, with comfortable and appealing individual furnishings, a good choice of tasty food in the bar and no smoking restaurant, and friendly long-established owners; cl 24 Dec–mid-Jan; limited disabled access.

DENT SD7187 **Sportsmans** *Cowgill, Dent, Sedbergh LA10 5RG (01539)* 625282 **£44;** 6 rms with shared bthrm. Unassuming, comfortable pub notable for its wonderful position in Dentdale by the River Dee with the viaduct of the Settle–Carlisle railway close by, and walks in all directions; open log fires and good value home-made food; well behaved dogs allowed.

DOCKRAY NY3921 **Royal** *Dockray, Matterdale, Penrith CA11 0TT (017684)* 82356 **£58,** plus special breaks; 10 rms. Friendly family-run hotel with open fires in the big, modernised open-plan bar, good-value hearty meals, and well kept beers; in a fine spot between hills and lake with walks from the doorstep; children must be well behaved; partial disabled access.

ELTERWATER NY3305 **Britannia Inn** *Elterwater, Ambleside LA22 9HP (015394)* 37210 ***£70,*** plus winter breaks; 13 rms, most with shower, some in quiet annexe opposite. Simple, charmingly traditional pub in fine surroundings opposite the village green, happy friendly atmosphere, hearty home cooking inc superb breakfast, comfortable no smoking lounge and a bustling bar, real ales; fine walks; cl 25 Dec, pm 26 Dec; well behaved dogs allowed.

ESKDALE GREEN NY1400 **Bower House** *Eskdale Green, Holmbrook CA19 1TD (019467) 23244* **£64,** plus wknd breaks; 24 comfortable rms, some in annexe. Relaxed and pleasantly isolated old stone inn with a nicely tended, sheltered garden, lounge bar with log fire and a comfortable separate one with sofas and easy chairs, several bar rooms, popular good-value food inc wonderful puddings, no smoking restaurant, and friendly staff; disabled access.

FAR SAWREY SD3893 **Sawrey** *Far Sawrey, Ambleside LA22 0LQ (015394) 43425* ***£58;** 18 rms. Friendly hotel well placed at the foot of Claife Heights, with simple pubby and smarter bars, friendly staff, good straightforward food, and seats on pleasant lawn with good views of Lake Windermere; cl Christmas; kind to children; dogs allowed; partial disabled access.

GARRIGILL NY7441 **Crossgill Farmhouse** *Garrigill, Alston CA9 3HE (01434) 381383* **£40;** 3 rms, 2 with own bthrm. 18th-c ex-shooting lodge on a hill overlooking River Tyne, with open fire in the lounge, good home cooking, and friendly owners; no evening meal Weds; no smoking; cl Apr, Christmas.

GARRIGILL NY7441 **George & Dragon** *Garrigill, Alston CA9 3DS (01434) 381293* **£37;** 4 small rms, shared bthrm but clean and comfortable. Friendly 17th-c pub on a dead-end road in beautiful countryside, with an informal flagstone bar, stone and panelled dining room, log fire in smashing fireplace, and good service; children over 10.

GRANGE-OVER-SANDS SD4077 **Graythwaite Manor** *Fernhill Rd, Grange-over-Sands LA11 7JE (015395) 32001* ***£85,** plus special breaks; 21 individually furnished rms, many with fine views. Set in flower-filled landscaped gardens with views over Morecambe Bay, this comfortable hotel (run by the same family since 1937) has a particularly relaxed, friendly atmosphere, elegantly furnished lounges with flowers and antiques, open fires, and good, carefully prepared food in the attractive, no smoking dining room; cl 4–22 Jan; no dogs; disabled access.

GRASMERE NY3406 **Michael's Nook** *Grasmere, Ambleside LA22 9RP (015394) 35496* **£170 inc dinner,** plus winter breaks; 14 lovely rms. Beautifully furnished hotel with fine antiques, paintings and rugs (the owner is a former antique dealer), lovely flowers, comfortable sofas by open fires in the cosy bar or elegant drawing room, excellent food, landscaped garden with specimen rhododendrons, and good walks; also, Great Danes and exotic cats; free use of indoor pool and health facilities at the nearby Wordsworth Hotel (under the same ownership, and listed below); children by arrangement but no under-7s in evening restaurant.

GRASMERE NY3406 **Swan** *Grasmere, Ambleside LA22 9RF (015394) 35551* **£78;** 36 rms, most with fine views. Smart and friendly 17th-c hotel in beautiful fell-foot surroundings, with beams and inglenooks, an elegant no smoking dining room, and attractive garden; lovely walks; partial disabled access.

GRASMERE NY3406 **Wordsworth** *Grasmere, Ambleside LA22 9SW (015394) 35592* **£179,** plus special breaks; 37 comfortable, pretty rms. Well run hotel, right in village next to the churchyard where Wordsworth is buried; stylish lounges and airy restaurant overlooking landscaped gardens, a relaxed conservatory and popular pubby bar, friendly service, enjoyable food, and heated indoor pool, mini-gym, and sauna; good disabled access.

GRIZEDALE SD3494 **Grizedale Lodge** *Hawkshead Hill, Grizedale, Ambleside LA22 0QL (015394) 36532* ***£75,** plus special breaks; 9 no smoking rms. Friendly, comfortable hotel in the middle of the magnificent Grizedale Forest, with lots of walks from the front door, a log fire in the lounge bar, imaginative fresh food in the attractive restaurant, and big breakfasts; children under 5 provided with high tea at 5.30pm; disabled access.

HAWKSHEAD SD3598 **Drunken Duck** *Barngates, Hawkshead, Ambleside LA22 0NG (015394) 36347* **£75,** plus specials breaks; 9 rms. Very friendly popular inn alone in 60 hillside acres, with several cosy rooms, open fires, views of Lake Windermere in distance, home-brewed ales, good interesting food, and a no smoking restaurant; fishing in private tarn; cl pm 25 Dec; limited disabled access.

HAWKSHEAD SD3598 **Highfield House** *Hawkshead Hill, Hawkshead,*

Ambleside LA22 0PN (015394) 36344 **£76,** plus winter breaks; 11 good rms. Welcoming Victorian country house in a spacious woodland garden with fine views (good walks from the door), open fire in the comfortable lounge, a cosy bar, and generous food inc packed lunches and children's high tea; cl Jan.

IREBY *NY2439* **Overwater Hall** *Ireby, Carlisle CA5 1HH (017687)* 76566 **£84,** plus special breaks; 12 rms. Relaxed and friendly family-run hotel in 18 acres of gardens and woodland, with a log fire in the elegant, comfortable drawing room, good imaginative food in the cosy dining room, and lots of walks; children over 7 in restaurant (high tea 5pm); well behaved dogs welcome; cl first 2 wks Jan.

KENDAL *SD5293* **Low Jock Scar** *Selside (6m from Kendal), Kendal LA8 9LE (01539)* 823259 *****£55;** 5 rms, most with own bthrm. Relaxed and friendly little country guesthouse in 6 acres of garden and woodland, with a residents' lounge, and good home cooking (picnic lunches on request); no smoking; cl Nov–end Feb; children over 12.

KESWICK *NY2618* **Shu-le-Crow** *7 Penrith Rd, Keswick CA12 4HF (017687)* 75253 *****£38;** 3 attractive rms. Pink-washed, no smoking 18th-c cottage with plenty of original features, cheerful owners who can advise on local walks, and super breakfasts (vegetarian options); plenty of places to eat nearby; no children.

KESWICK *NY2521* **Stakis Lodore** *Derwent Water, Keswick CA12 5UX (017687)* 77285 *****£116,** plus special breaks; 75 well equipped rms. Long-standing but well updated big holiday hotel with lots of facilities in 40 acres of lakeside gardens and woodlands, open fires in the comfortable day rooms, and an elegant restaurant; leisure club, tennis and squash, outdoor swimming pool, games room and lots for children such as nursery with NNEB nannies, remote control cars, Sega computer games, babysitting, baby-listening service, high tea; spacious self-catering house too.

KESWICK *NY2624* **Swinside Lodge** *Newlands, Keswick CA12 5UE (017687)* 72948 **£88,** plus special breaks; 7 comfortable rms. Victorian hotel in own grounds surrounded by wonderful unspoilt scenery at the foot of Cat Bells, and a few minutes from the shore of Derwent Water, with hearty breakfasts and super home-made evening meals in the candelit dining room, helpful friendly service, and 2 relaxing sitting rooms; cl Dec–Jan; children over 12.

KIRKCAMBECK *NY5269* **Cracrop Farm** *Kirkcambeck, Brampton CA8 2BW (016977)* 48245 **£50;** 3 rms overlooking garden and open fields. Friendly Victorian farmhouse on 425 acres with stock animals and very good marked farm trails (they are keen on conservation), comfortable and homely rooms, good traditional breakfasts (other food arranged in advance), games room and sauna; no smoking; cl Christmas; children over 12.

LANERCOST *NY5664* **Abbey Bridge** *Lanercost, Brampton CA8 2HG (016977)* 2224 **£60;** 7 simple rms, most with own bthrm. Beautifully placed small country inn in quiet spot nr the ancient priory, decent food in the informal converted forge which also houses a cheerful bar; pleasant staff; cl 25 Dec; disabled access.

LANGDALE *NY2906* **Old Dungeon Ghyll** *Great Langdale, Ambleside LA22 9JY (015394)* 37272 **£66,** plus special breaks; 15 rms, some with shared bthrm. Friendly, simple and cosy walkers' and climbers' inn dramatically surrounded by fells, wonderful views and terrific walks; cosy residents' lounge and popular food – best to book for dinner if not a resident; cl 3 days over Christmas.

LINDALE *SD4280* **Greenacres** *Lindale, Grange-over-Sands LA11 6LP (015395)* 34578 *****£52,** plus special breaks; 5 appealing rms. Charming 19th-c cottage with friendly atmosphere, pretty sitting room, conservatory, log fire, good home-made food and big breakfasts in the cosy dining room, and packed lunches on request; cl Christmas–New Year.

LITTLE LANGDALE *NY3204* **Three Shires** *Little Langdale, Ambleside LA22 9NZ (015394)* 37215 **£72,** plus special breaks; 10 rms. Family-run stone-built country inn with beautiful views, comfortably old-fashioned residents' part, separate walkers' bar with real ales, decent food, and pretty gardens; cl Jan.

LORTON *NY1525* **New House Farm** *Lorton, Cockermouth CA13 9UU (01900)* 85404 **£70,** plus special breaks; 4 rms with wonderful hillside views. Friendly no smoking 17th-c house (not a working farm) in 15 acres of grounds, with beams and rafters, flagstones, open fires, and 2 residents' lounges, very good food inc game and fish caught by the owner, home-made scones and preserves, a thoughtful wine list; lots of nearby walks; children over 12.

MUNGRISDALE NY3731 **Mill Hotel** *Mungrisdale, Penrith CA11 0XR* (017687) 79659 **£120 inc dinner;** 9 rms, most with own bthrm. Very friendly, small streamside hotel beautifully placed in lovely valley hamlet hidden away below Blencathra, with open fire in the cosy and comfortable sitting room, good imaginative 5-course evening meals, and a small, carefully chosen wine list; cl Nov–Feb; dogs welcome by arrangement; disabled access.

POOLEY BRIDGE NY4724 **Sharrow Bay** *Pooley Bridge, Penrith CA10 2LZ* (017684) 86301 **£290 inc dinner;** 26 lovely rms with antiques, books, and games, mostly with own bthrm. Country-house hotel in a quiet idyllic spot by Ullswater with lovely views of the lake and mountains, showing the years of loving care the owners have put into the distinctive style, furnishings and décor; unobtrusively attentive service and excellent English cooking in the 2 contrasting dining rooms; cl Dec–late Feb; no children.

RAVENSTONEDALE NY7204 **Fat Lamb** *Cross Bank, Ravenstonedale, Kirkby Stephen CA17 4LL* (015396) 23242 **£60,** plus special breaks; 12 comfortable rms. Welcoming moorland inn set in beautiful open countryside; a log fire and good local photographs in the cheerfully modernised 2-room bar, decent food, and 17 acres of land, 7 of which are nature reserve; very good disabled access.

RYDAL WATER NY3606 **White Moss House** *Rydal Water, Grasmere, Ambleside LA22 9SE* (015394) 35295 **£150 inc dinner,** plus special breaks; 7 thoughtfully furnished and comfortable little rms in main house plus separate cottage let as one unit with 2 rms. Bought by Wordsworth for his son, this attractive stripped-stone country house, set in charming, mature grounds overlooking the lake, is a marvellously relaxing place to stay, with a comfortable lounge, excellent fixed price 5-course meals in the pretty no smoking dining room, a fine wine list, and exemplary service; free use of hotel rowing boat, free fishing and free use of local leisure club; cl Dec–Feb.

ST BEES NX9712 **Queens** *Main St, St Bees CA27 0DE* (01946) 822287 **£45;** 15 rms. Set in an attractive village with a marvellous beach, this 17th-c hotel has 2 bars with real ales and over 100 whiskies, beams and log fires, generous helpings of good food in the dining room or no smoking conservatory, a garden with fine views, and friendly staff.

TALKIN NY5557 **Hullerbank** *Talkin, Brampton CA8 1LB* (016977) 46668 **£42;** 3 rms. Comfortable and very friendly, no smoking, Georgian farmhouse in unspoilt countryside with a relaxed atmosphere in the homely lounge, and good food using home-grown and local produce inc home-produced lamb (packed lunches on request); cl Christmas–New Year; children over 12.

THIRLMERE NY3116 **Dale Head Hall** *Thirlmere, Keswick CA12 4TN* (017687) 72478 *****£80,** plus special breaks; 9 pretty rms, most with lake views. Peaceful, partly 16th-c country house in lovely lakeside grounds, with comfortable lounges, log fire, friendly owners, and home-cooked food using produce grown in own walled garden; children over 10 for evening meals; cl Jan.

TIRRIL NY5126 **Queens Head** *Tirril, Penrith CA10 2JF* (01768) 863219 **£45,** plus special breaks; 7 lovely rms, most with own bthrm. Bustling inn with flagstones and exposed floorboards in the bar, spacious back restaurant (mostly no smoking), low beams, black panelling, inglenook fireplace and old-fashioned settles in the older part, good interesting food inc snacks and OAP specials, and well kept real ales.

TROUTBECK NY4103 **Mortal Man** *Troutbeck, Windermere LA22 3PL* (015394) 33193 **£122 inc dinner;** 14 rms. Spotlessly kept, relaxing inn surrounded by marvellous scenery, with a partly panelled bustling bar, big open fire, dark beams, picture windows in the restaurant, well kept real ales, good food, lovely breakfasts, and friendly staff; cl mid-Nov–mid-Feb; children over 5.

WASDALE HEAD NY1808 **Wasdale Head** *Wasdale Head, Seascale CA20 1EX*

(019467) 26229 *£78; 9 simple, but warmly comfortable, pine-clad rms. Old flagstoned and gabled walkers' and climbers' inn, in a magnificent setting surrounded by steep fells, with civilised day rooms, popular home cooking for 7.30pm dinner, good wine list, huge breakfasts, and cheerfully busy public bar; self-catering cottages; disabled access.

WATER YEAT SD2989 **Water Yeat** *Water Yeat, Ulverston LA12 8DJ (01229) 885306 £57;* 5 pretty rms. Attractively converted and neatly kept 17th-c farmhouse by Coniston Water, set in 3 acres of garden and woodland; an especially relaxing atmosphere, a log fire in the lounge, enjoyable breakfasts, particularly good food in the heavily beamed dining room, and friendly new owners; cl mid-Dec–mid-Feb; children over 4.

WATERMILLOCK NY4522 **Leeming House** *Watermillock, Ullswater, Penrith CA11 0JJ (017684) 86622 £160,* plus special breaks; 40 cosseting rms, many with beautiful views. Well run, extended hotel in 20 acres of quiet lakeside grounds, with log fires in the comfortable lounges, a cosy panelled bar, fine food in the lovely no smoking dining room, and good courteous service; boating and fishing; high teas for young children; good provision for disabled.

WATERMILLOCK NY4522 **Old Church** *Watermillock, Penrith CA11 0JN (017684) 86204 £85,* plus special breaks; 10 rms, some with lovely Ullswater views. Attractive 18th-c Lakeland house peacefully situated in waterside gardens, with log fires and individual furnishings in civilised day rooms, kind service, and excellent English dinners at 8pm in the no smoking dining room; rowing/windsurfing boats; cl Dec–Feb.

WATERMILLOCK NY4522 **Rampsbeck Country House** *Watermillock, Ullswater, Penrith CA11 0LP (017684) 86442 £116;* 21 rms. Run by friendly helpful people, this 18th-c hotel is set in 18 acres by Lake Ullswater, and has an open fire in the cosy sitting room, French windows into the garden from the plush, comfortable lounge, and carefully prepared food in the attractive dining room; croquet; lots to do nearby; cl Jan–mid-Feb; children over 8 in evening restaurant.

WINDERMERE SD4199 **Fir Trees** *Lake Rd, Windermere LA23 2EQ (015394) 42272 *£56;* 8 attractive spotless rms inc 2 big family ones. Well run and comfortable, no smoking, Victorian house with an informal relaxed atmosphere, antiques, fine prints and fresh flowers, warmly helpful service (detailed suggestions of what to do), and good hearty breakfasts.

WINDERMERE SD4199 **Holbeck Ghyll Country House** *Holbeck Lane, Windermere LA23 1LU (015394) 32375 £170 inc dinner,* plus special breaks; 20 individual rms with fresh flowers and complimentary sherry and many with fine views – 6 in new building (could be self-catering). Charming, warm and friendly country house in mature landscaped gardens and 5 acres of woodland overlooking Lake Windermere, with tennis court, putting green, and croquet – their Labradors like to walk with you; immaculate comfortable lounges with antiques and panelling, log fires, billiard room, and very good food (vegetarian too) and wine in the oak-panelled restaurant; health spa; children over 8 in evening restaurant; disabled access.

WINDERMERE SD4199 **Langdale Chase** *Windermere LA23 1LW (015394) 32201 £130;* 29 rms, many with marvellous lake view. Welcoming, family-run hotel in a lovely position on the edge of Lake Windermere, with waterskiing and bathing from the hotel jetty; tennis, croquet, putting and rowing; afternoon tea on the terraces, gracious oak-panelled rooms with antiques, paintings, fresh flowers, open fires, very good food (huge breakfasts, too), and friendly service; disabled access.

WINDERMERE SD4199 **Miller Howe** *Rayrigg Rd, Windermere LA23 1EY (015394) 42536 from £160 inc dinner,* plus special breaks; 12 comfortable, well equipped rms, many with fine views. Splendid, immaculately kept, Edwardian country house set high over the lake, with unbeatable views from the day rooms, conservatory and sloping garden, excellent evening meals, a remarkably wide-ranging New World wine list with helpful tasting notes, and super breakfasts; children over 8; cl Jan.

WINTON NY7810 **Bay Horse** *Winton, Kirkby Stephen CA17 4HS (017683) 71451* **£35;** 3 clean, good-value rms. Well kept, unpretentious moorland pub in lovely setting, with welcoming low-ceilinged rooms, friendly owners, and good generous home cooking; well behaved children over 5.

WITHERSLACK SD4384 **Old Vicarage** *Witherslack, Grange-over-Sands LA11 6RS (015395) 52381* **£130 inc dinner,** plus special breaks; 15 individually decorated rms – some in the modern Orchard House are more spacious and have their own woodland terraces. Late Georgian vicarage in 5 acres of peaceful gardens and woodland, with 2 comfortable lounges, a log fire, good interesting food in the cosy restaurant inc home-made bread, cakes and preserves, and hearty breakfasts; tennis and lots of surrounding walks; dogs welcome by arrangement.

To see and do

CUMBRIA Family Attraction of the Year

🐾 🏇 ❀ DALTON-IN-FURNESS SD2374 **South Lakes Wild Animal Park** (Crossgates) One of the area's most visited attractions, this very committed and rapidly expanding wildlife centre has a number of unique features that well reward a special trip. Perhaps most dramatic is watching their Sumatran and Amur tigers clamber up a 20ft vertical pole to hunt their meat (daily at 2.30pm); quite a spectacle, it leads you to suspect that should you ever find yourself pursued by a hungry wild tiger, hiding up a tree might not be terribly effective. Also fun is the chance to handfeed their big collection of kangaroos, the only place you can do this outside Australia. You may also be able to join in feeding the lemurs. The animals are gathered together according to the continents they hail from – among the most popular residents, you'll find rhinos, zebra, cheetah, and wolves, with spider monkeys swinging high above on their canopy of ropes and branches, and lots of smaller creatures like meerkats, racoons, coatis and porcupines. There's a 4-acre section with pheasants and ducks waiting to be fed, as well as a nature trail, lakeside walks, and pets corner. Some of the picnic areas are indoors, but as lots of the animals wander free in natural surroundings you'll be better off visiting on a dry day. With a play area, and a miniature railway (summer only), there's lots to keep most age groups happy for a good chunk of the day. It's well placed for fine views of the entire Furness peninsula. Meals, snacks, shop, disabled access; cl 25 Dec; (01229) 466086; *£6.50 (*£3.50 children 3–15). The family ticket is better value than usual at *£17. Admission is half price Nov–Feb.

ABBEY TOWN NY1751
✝ **Holme Cultram** (B5302 Wigtown–Silloth) Remains of formidably rich Cistercian abbey – extraordinarily grand for this quiet village. The New Inn at Blencogo has good food – must book (016973) 61091.

ALSTON NY7146
★ This interesting, little well weathered Pennine market town is the highest of its kind in England, with a surprising number of pubs up and down its very steep cobbled main street (the Angel is best), and a couple of craft shops. *Oliver Twist* was recently filmed here.
📷 🎨 **Gossipgate Gallery** (The Butts)

Local art and crafts, with changing exhibitions and a good big shop. Tea garden, disabled access (though no facilities); cl Jan–mid-Feb, wkdys mid-Feb–Easter and am wkdys Nov–Dec; (01434) 381806; free.
🌸 **Hartside Nursery** (A686 W of Alston) Beautifully placed alpine nursery with small streamside garden and rare plants for sale; it's quite a draw for birds and wildlife. Shop, some disabled access with notice; cl Nov–Feb (exc by appointment); (01434) 381372; free.
🚂 **South Tynedale Railway** The chief attraction around here, with diesel and occasionally steam vintage

narrow-gauge train trips along a lovely winding valley. They now also run a service up to Kirkhaugh in Northumberland. Teas, shop, disabled access by arrangement; open wknds and bank hols Apr–Oct, daily Jun–Sept (exc most Mons and Fris Jun and Sept), and some wknds in Dec – best to ring for timetable; (01434) 381696; fares from £2.50.

AMBLESIDE NY3704

🏌 🕸 A busy holiday-oriented shopping centre inc excellent outdoor equipment shops strung along its central one-way system, with the quaintest information centre in the Lakes – the little NT shop in the tiny stone Bridge House over Stock Ghyll by the main car park. In the side lanes above here are one or two attractive older buildings. Traditional **glass blowing** at Adrian Sankey, Rydal Rd; good demonstrations and shop, but no pressure to buy; (015394) 33039. **Hayes Garden World** (Lake Rd) is a big garden centre in landscaped gardens; café, disabled access. The Queen's Hotel is good value for lunch.

🖼 ♿ **Armitt Ambleside Museum** Decent local history museum with the largest collection of Beatrix Potter's watercolours, plus works by local artists, photographers, several original manuscripts by local writers and numerous archeological remains. Shop, disabled access; cl Christmas wk; (015394) 31212; £2.50.

🕸 **Brockhole** (A591 S of Ambleside, or launch from town pier) National Park information centre in a country house with well landscaped gardens and attractive lakeshore grounds; also audio-visual show, exhibitions, and an adventure play area. Special talks and events throughout the year. Meals, snacks, shop, disabled access; visitor centre cl Nov–mid-Apr, gardens and grounds open all year; (015394) 46601; free, but charge for parking (£4 all day).

🕸 🏛 **Stagshaw Garden** (Waterhead, just S) Hillside woodland garden with lovely lake views, mature camellias, rhododendrons, magnolias and heathers; best in spring. Open daily Apr–Jun then by appointment July–Oct; (015394) 35599; £1.30; NT. Parking is very limited. There's little left of the

Roman fort in nearby Borrans Park.

APPLEBY NY6820

★ An attractive riverside village; the main street, rising from the harmonious 12th-c church to the castle, is still a grand sight despite the cars, with a good few handsome buildings inc a lovely courtyard of almshouses. Pleasant strolls by the River Eden. The Royal Oak is most enjoyable for lunch.

🏰 🏠 🕸 🐾 🐄 **Appleby Castle Conservation Centre** One of the best-preserved Norman keeps in the country, the rest of the buildings are later additions; terrific views from the ramparts. The Clifford family lived here for nearly 700 years, though they moved later to the grander house next door, the great hall of which has antiques, paintings and Chinese porcelain on display. The main feature of the attractive grounds is the big collection of birds, waterfowl and farm animals, in a lovely setting above the river; also brass rubbing, exhibitions and falconry displays. Meals, snacks, shop, limited disabled access; cl Oct–Easter (exc wknds); (017683) 51402; *£4.

ARNSIDE SD4578

🚂 ❄ A good start for the 20-minute train trip along the N shore of Morecambe Bay to Ulverston: long viaducts, stupendous views. The Ship at nearby Sandside also has glorious views.

ARNSIDE KNOTT SD4577

❄ ⌂ Nr Arnside, this looks across Morecambe Bay to the southern Lakeland fells – very rewarding views for walkers.

ASKHAM NY5123

★ An attractive village in fine scenery, with not one but two village greens – each with a good pub.

BARBON SD6282

★ An unpretentious village given appeal by its fine setting, just below the fells; the road up to Dent, Dent Head and Deepdale reaches deep into the hills. The Barbon Inn is good.

BARROW SD1875

♈ **Sandscale Haws** These dunes are protected as a **nature reserve**.

BARROW-IN-FURNESS SD1969

🚂 ❄ The town shows the effects of the virtual collapse of shipbuilding in this country, on which it depended. The main line **railway** from here to Whitehaven hugs the coast and has good views, missed by the road, though in the other direction the A5087 to Ulverston has fine views across Morecambe Bay. The Anchor out at Lindal has decent food.

❋ **Dock Museum** (North Rd) Futuristic-looking museum exploring how Barrow developed from a tiny hamlet to the biggest iron and steel centre in the world, before becoming renowned for shipbuilding; displays range from simple fishing boats to Trident submarines; also interactive displays and an adventure playground. A recent Lottery grant has enabled the museum to purchase the rare Vickers Shipmodel and Photography collection, and the new galleries are scheduled to open at Easter (ring to check). Snacks, shop, good disabled access; cl Mon (exc bank hols), Tues; (01229) 894444; free.

🏛 **Furness Abbey** (slightly NE of Barrow, towards Dalton) Impressive warm sandstone Norman remains of the one-time second richest monastery in England, with lovely arched cloisters, peaceful lawns, and views of a pretty valley. Small museum, disabled access; cl winter Mon and Tues, 24–26 Dec; (01229) 823420; £2.60; EH.

BASSENTHWAITE NY2332

★ † ⚓ Attractive close-set little village – the 12th-c parish church is 3m S; the Sun is an enjoyable pub. Escorted woodland **horse-riding** can be arranged from £12 an hour; (017687) 76949 for details. You can also hire rowing boats on Bassenthwaite Water. Readers tell us they know of few nicer sites for a caravan than the one at Englethwaite Hall nr here.

🏠 ❋ † ♘ **Mirehouse** (off A591 S of Bassenthwaite) The family that still live in this modest 17th-c house once had excellent literary connections, so the fine rooms have mementos of Wordsworth, Carlyle and Tennyson among others. There may be piano recitals in the music room, and on Weds in Jun, July and Sept they usually have displays of lace-making. Interesting garden (bee/butterfly plants), as well as peaceful lakeshore grounds, a lakeside church, and woods with well thought-out adventure play areas. Lots to do,

with a surprising number of activities for children – they may even let them ring the gong in the house. Good home cooking in the tearoom – converted from its former use as a mill, shop, disabled access; open Easter–Oct, house pm Sun and Weds, plus pm Fri in Aug, garden daily; phone for winter opening; (017687) 72287; £3.75, garden only £1.50.

BASSENTHWAITE LAKE NY2324

🐗 ⚥ ⚘ **Trotters & Friends Animal Farm** (Coalbeck Farm) Excellent for families; children can join in feeding and milking, and there are plenty of other opportunities to get close to the animals. The 23-acre deer park is good for a picnic, and there are birds of prey and a reptile house. Indoor areas make it a good bet on drizzly days. Meals, snacks, shop, disabled access; cl wkdys Nov–Mar; (017687) 76239; £3.60.

BEETHAM SD5079

✗ 🏠 ★† **Heron Cornmill & Papermaking** Well organised working watermill, dates back to 1096, though the current building is 18th c; baking exhibition. The big paperworks next door has displays of papermaking. Snacks, shop; cl Mon (exc bank hols), and Oct–Easter; (015395) 65027; £1.50. Beetham itself is attractive, with an interesting **church**, and the Wheatsheaf is good for lunch.

BINSEY NY2235

⌂ ❀ A pathless lump of a hill, but it rewards walkers with splendid views of the Lakes and Solway Firth (and into southern Scotland).

BOOT NY1801

🚂 The steam railway from Ravenglass ends here, at Dalegarth station, and Dalegarth Falls here are lovely. The Burnmoor Inn, very well placed for walkers, has extremely good-value food; the Bower House and King George IV further down Eskdale at Eskdale Green are also good.

✗ **Eskdale Watermill** Guided tours of attractively set 16th-c working two-wheeled mill, with a picnic area nr woodland waterfalls. Snacks, shop; cl Mon (exc bank hols), all Oct–Mar; (019467) 23335; £1.25.

BORROWDALE NY2517

⌂ ❀ Many people's favourite Lakeland

base for walks, with good paths along or just above the River Derwent, especially from Grange (useful teashop). For lazier souls, the drive along the B5289 gives glorious views. Other prized walks giving or leading to fine views include mossy Johnny Wood (from Rosthwaite or Seatoller, where there's an NT centre exc in winter), and the two famous waterfalls, both best after rain, Taylorgill Force and Lodore Falls (behind the Lodore Hotel).

BRAMPTON NY5361

✝ **Lanercost Priory** (signed away from Brampton) Impressive and extensive remains of Norman priory, built with stone recycled from Hadrian's Wall. Shop, some disabled access; cl Nov–Apr; £2; EH. The nave, picturesquely framed by an arch, was restored in the 18th c as a red sandstone church, and now has stained glass by William Morris and Burne-Jones. The Abbey Bridge Inn by the priory has good food.

BROUGH NY7914

🏰 ✳ **Brough Castle** Classic ruined Norman fortress, in a romantic setting on moors above the village, with great views; free. The Golden Fleece is useful for lunch.

BROUGHAM NY5328

🏰 ✳ 🏛 **Brougham Castle** (off A6 S of Penrith) A sturdy Norman ruin on steep lawns above riverside sheep pastures; climb to the top of the keep for the best view. Traces of Roman remains too, with a small exhibition of

tombstones. Snacks, shop, disabled access; cl Nov–Mar; (01768) 862488; £2; EH.

🌳 🏛 ✝ **Brougham Hall Craft Centre** 13 different craft workshops inc metal workers, furniture restoration and home-made chocolates, in the attractive stone courtyard of a 15th-c Hall. Plenty to see around the house and grounds inc a Cromwellian chapel and a collection of dolls and dolls' houses. Meals and snacks (in summer), shop, disabled access; cl 25 Dec; (01768) 862488; £2 suggested donation.

BUTTERMERE NY1815

⌂ ✳ ⛵ A splendid varied flat walk circles the lake, with glorious views, plenty of safe opportunities for children aged 6 or more to let off steam, and even a tunnel; weather has to be really savage to spoil it. Parking at Gatescarth. The Bridge Hotel in the little village is good for lunch, and you can hire **rowing boats**.

⌂ ✳ **Hay Stacks** To the south of Buttermere and high above it, this is a challenging walk, but a rewarding one for the changing views, continuing on to Fleetwith Pike.

⌂ ✳ **The ceiling of the Lakes** The green slatey fells N of Buttermere offer keen walkers superlative routes along high ridges: Whiteless Pike, Causey Pike, Crag Hill and Grasmoor are among the most exciting points.

CALDBECK NY3239

⌂ John Peel's grave can be found in the

Days Out

Industrial time-warp by Windermere: Sculpture trail in Grizedale Forest; Hawkshead, lunch up at the Drunken Duck, Barngates; Stott Park Bobbin Mill; steamer trip on Windermere from Lakeside; Lakeside & Haverthwaite Railway; Aquarium of the Lakes, Newby Bridge.

A Cumbrian farmhouse and Ullswater's landscapes: Ambleside; Townend, Troutbeck – lunch at the Queen's Head; steamer from Glenridding to Howtown, and walk back along shore of Ullswater; Aira Force (with children, afternoon could include Lowther Leisure Park at Hackthorpe instead of the walk, after lunch at the Punch Bowl, Askham).

Rainy day options: Levens Hall or Sizergh Castle; lunch at the Strickland Arms or the Hare & Hounds, Levens; Kendal – especially Abbot Hall Art Gallery or Museum of Lakeland Life, and walk up to the castle.

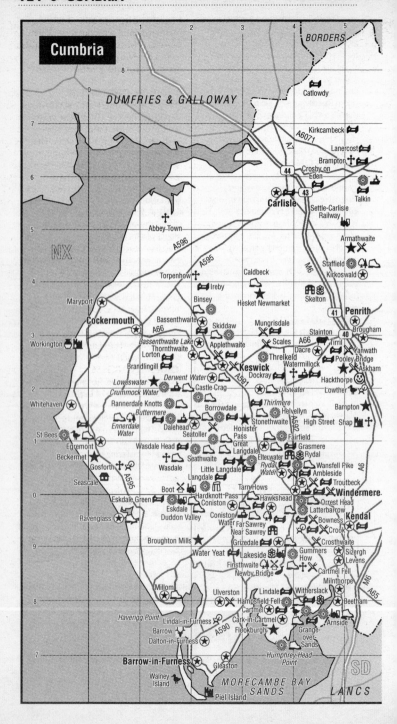

Cumbria

DUMFRIES & GALLOWAY

BORDERS

Catlowdy

Kirkcambeck

Lanercost

Brampton

Crosby on Eden

Carlisle

Settle-Carlisle Railway

Talkin

Abbey Town

Armathwaite

Staffield

Kirkoswald

Torpenhow

Caldbeck

Binsey

Hesket Newmarket

Skelton

Maryport

Ireby

Penrith

Cockermouth

Bassenthwaite

Skiddaw

Mungrisdale

Brougham

Workington

Bassenthwaite Lake

Thornthwaite

Applethwaite

Scales

Stainton

Dacre

Tirril

Yanwath

Lorton

Threlkeld

Watermillock

Pooley Bridge

Brandlingill

Keswick

Dockray

Askham

Loweswater

Derwent Water

Castle-Crag

Ullswater

Hackthorpe

Lowther

Whitehaven

Crummock Water

Rannerdale Knotts

Borrowdale

Thirlmere

Helvellyn

Bampton

Buttermere

Dalehead

Stonethwaite

High Street

Shap

St Bees

Ennerdale Water

Seatoller

Honister Pass

Fairfield

Egremont

Wasdale Head

Great Langdale

Grasmere

Beckermet

Seathwaite

Elterwater

Rydal

Gosforth

Wasdale

Little Langdale

Rydal Water

Wansfell Pike

Ambleside

Seascale

Langdale

Troutbeck

Boot

Tarn Hows

Windermere

Hardknott Pass

Hawkshead

Orrest Head

Eskdale Green

Coniston

Latterbarrow

Kendal

Eskdale

Duddon Valley

Coniston Water

Bowness

Crook

Ravenglass

Far Sawrey

Near Sawrey

Crosthwaite

Broughton Mills

Grizedale

Sizergh

Water Yeat

Lakeside

Gummers How

Levens

Finsthwaite

Cartmel Fell

Newby Bridge

Milnthorpe

Millom

Ulverston

Lindale

Witherslack

Hampsfield Fell

Beetham

Haverigg Point

Cartmel

Lindal-in-Furness

Cark-in-Cartmel

Arnside

Barrow

Flookburgh

Grange-over-Sands

Dalton-in-Furness

Humphrey Head Point

SD

Barrow-in-Furness

Gleaston

Walney Island

MORECAMBE BAY SANDS

LANCS

Piel Island

A6071

A7

A595

A596

A66

A591

A593

A590

A65

A6

M6

NX

churchyard here, and the Oddfellows Arms has good generous food. There's a pretty drive to attractive Mungrisdale; alternatively, a pleasant stroll to a peaceful spot with a waterfall called the Howk.

CARK-IN-CARTMEL SD3577

Holker Hall & Gardens Opulently built and furnished, mainly Victorian mansion with appealingly unstuffy feel despite the beauty. The glorious 25-acre formal and woodland gardens are among the best in the country, with spectacular water features, a rose garden, rhododendron and azalea arboretum and rare plants and shrubs. Also a deer park, entertaining motor museum, falconry displays, an adventure playground, plus the new Victorian arcade, a collection of old tools and gardening implements, and an audio-visual display – enough to take up most of the day. Meals, snacks, shop, disabled access; cl Sat, and Nov–Easter; (015395) 58328; £3.35 gardens, grounds and exhibitions; Hall, motor museum and birds of prey centre extra. The nearby Engine is useful for lunch.

CARLISLE NY3956

✝ A sizeable town, not an obvious holiday destination, but plenty to interest the visitor, with several quietly attractive old buildings (and a very helpful visitor centre in one of them, the Old Town Hall). Plans are under way for a new crossing over the River Eden as part of the National Cycleway, and a new riverside walkway along the West Wall. **St Cuthbert's Church** is remarkable for its mobile pulpit. The Crown & Mitre (English St) has a good-value lunchtime buffet, and there's good home cooking in the Black Lion out at Durdar, where the attractively placed racecourse has meetings every month exc July; (01228) 522973 for dates.

Carlisle Castle This extensive medieval fortress, rather gaunt and forbidding, is surprisingly well kept considering its violent history. Interesting period furnished rooms, a portcullised gatehouse, lots of staircases and passages, and centuries of prisoners' carved graffiti in the dungeons; good views from the ramparts. Snacks, shop; cl 24–26 Dec,

1 Jan; (01228) 591922; £3; EH.

† **Carlisle Cathedral** This unpretentious abbey church, founded in 1122 and severely damaged in the Civil War, has fine stained glass; try to go on a bright morning when the sunlight comes streaming colourfully through the east window. Also medieval carvings inc the Brougham Triptych, painted panels and stonework, and crypt treasury. Meals, snacks, good shop (some tasty local foods), disabled access (exc to restaurant); free but donations encouraged.

Guildhall Museum (Green Market) A handsomely restored medieval timbered hall; worth a look inside if passing – some displays inc interesting Guild silver (open, Easter–Oct, pm Thurs–Sun; 50p).

Settle–Carlisle railway Running up Ribbledale and into the Cumbrian Pennines, stopping at Dent Station, Garsdale Head, Kirkby Stephen, Appleby, Langwathby and other Eden Valley villages, this is a memorable 70 miles of grand scenery, best from Appleby to Settle; (0345) 484950 for times and fares.

Tullie House (Castle St) Great fun: dramatic displays of Border history, using state-of-the-art techniques of sight, sound and smell. Children especially find lots to do, from exploring mine tunnels to trying out a Roman crossbow. The ground floor has a more conventional art gallery/museum, and a new gallery housing various millennial exhibits will open under Castle Way. Meals, snacks, shop, disabled access; cl am Sun, 25 Dec; (01228) 534781; £3.75 (get there between 10 and 11am Mon–Sat and it's half-price).

CARTMEL SD3778

★† Picturesque little alleys lead off the delightfully harmonious central square – especially the one out through the former **Priory Gatehouse**. The **Priory Church**, which towers massively over the village, is a mix of architectural grandeur from 12th to 16th c, inc fine carving. Lots of arts and crafts in the village. The Cavendish Arms is good for lunch.

CARTMEL FELL SD4189

† In a wonderful tucked-away country location, the **church** here has interesting early pews and a fine triple-decker pulpit. The Masons Arms is deservedly popular for lunch. The road here from Winster is very pretty and makes a pleasant drive.

CASTERTON SD6279

★† Brontë fans will want to see **Casterton School**; attractive Pre-Raphaelite stained glass and paintings in the **church** result from enthusiastic Brotherhood holidays here. The Pheasant is good.

CASTLE CRAG NY2416

☁ ❋ This impregnable-looking pinnacle can be reached by a path winding up the back, from Grange. It's a challenging hike, but gives terrific lake views.

COCKERMOUTH NY1130

★ Quietly attractive riverside town, increasingly worth a holiday visit, with a wide range of places to visit. The comfortable Trout does good food.

Castlegate House (Castlegate) Friendly lived-in Georgian house opposite the castle, with a walled garden, Adam ceiling and sales of paintings and crafts. Disabled access; cl Thurs, Sun, and all Jan and Feb; (01900) 822149; free.

Cockermouth Motor Museum A family-run motor museum next to the Brewery, with a good changing range of vehicles, audio-visual displays, and a model race track for children. Snacks, shop, disabled access; cl Jan and wkdys Nov–mid-Mar (exc Feb half-term); (01900) 824448; £3.

Jennings Brewery Tours of traditional Castle Brewery, where the water for brewing is still drawn from the well that supplied the castle at the time of the Norman Conquest. Shop; tours 11am and 2pm wkdys Mar–Oct (plus maybe 12.30pm in summer hols), and 11am and 2pm Sat Apr–Sept – booking advisable; (01900) 823214; £3. No children under 12.

Lakeland Sheep & Wool Centre (off the A5086 slightly S) Entertaining live show starring 19 different species of sheep and maybe a few geese; they demonstrate shearing and sheepdog trials, and an adjacent exhibition is a worthwhile introduction to the area. Show times 10.30am, noon,

2pm, and 3.30pm; no shows Mon or Tues from Easter–mid-Nov; meals, snacks, shop, disabled access; cl 25 Dec; (01900) 822673; show *£3, exhibitions free.

🖶 **Printing House** (next to Wordsworth House) This working print museum has a good range of historic presses and equipment; you can try out various printing methods. Shop, disabled access; cl Sun, 24–26 Dec and 1 Jan; (01900) 824984; £2.50. The Norham opposite is a worthwhile teashop.

🖙 **Toy & Model Museum** (Market Pl) Good expanding collection of mainly British toys from the 20th c; shop, limited disabled access; cl Dec and Jan exc by appointment; (01900) 827606; £2.60.

🏠 **Wordsworth House** (Main St) The poet's happy childhood home, a handsome restored 18th-c town house with fine furniture, pictures by friends and contemporaries, good original panelling, and walled garden above river. Well worth a visit in its own right as well as for its Wordsworth associations, and interesting to see how different it is from the places he lived in later on. Snacks, shop; cl wknds (exc Sats from Jun–Aug or before bank hols), and Nov–Apr; (01900) 824805; £3; NT.

CONISTON SD2997
Unpretentious village at the foot of its mountain, the Old Man. From Spoon Hall there's **pony trekking** on the fells above; cl Nov–Easter; (015394) 41391; from £12 an hour.

🏠 🕷 ⚘ ◠ ❄ **Brantwood** Ruskin's rambling Victorian house, with lots of his furniture, books and paintings. It's appealingly unstuffy, but the real attraction is the surroundings and setting, especially the very extensive informal hillside woodland gardens (best in late May/Jun). Good hour's walk on nature trail, and wonderful views of lake and fells. Meals, snacks, good shop, disabled access (grounds steep in places); cl winter Mon and Tues and 25–26 Dec; (015394) 41396; £4.

◠ ❄ **Coniston Water walks** There's a lovely path on the W side, S of Coniston; you can combine this walk with one on a higher-level route along the Walna Scar 'road' (an ancient hard track closed to through traffic) beneath the **Old Man of Coniston**, the outstanding viewpoint of the vicinity. Climb the Old Man from Coniston, go up past the remains of copper mines, and return down the Walna Scar road.

♂ **Ruskin Museum** The mix of displays at this recently improved museum is truly catholic, ranging from local architecture and lace-making to a video of Donald Campbell's land speed record attempts, and of course, a comprehensive look at the life of the Victorian philosopher, with artefacts as diverse as his watercolours and essays and funeral pall. Shop, disabled access; cl mid-Nov–Mar (tel for winter opening); (015394) 41164; £3. The nearby Black Bull is good for lunch.

CONISTON WATER SD3197
⚓ An opulent Victorian **steam yacht** sails daily end Mar–Oct, from Coniston Pier, Brantwood and Park-a-Moor; (015394) 41288 for times – best to ring between 9 and 10.30am or you're likely to get the answerphone; £4.75. Or hire **rowing boats** (or other boats) from the boating centre run by the National Parks, 15 minutes' walk from the village; cl Nov–Mar; (015394) 41366; rowing boats from £5 an hour (£1 each extra person), motorboats from £10, electric boats £14.50.

CRUMMOCK WATER NY1518
🎣 ◠ ❄ ⚓ The scenery is less rewarding than around Buttermere, but it's not to be sniffed at. A good start for a walk is the car park by **Lanthwaite Wood**, off the B5289 towards Loweswater at the N end; there's a pretty view from the hill above the wood. You can hire **rowing boats** on this lake, and if you're keen to swim in one of the lakes this is probably the best.

DACRE NY4626
🏠 🕷 † **Dalemain House** Largely Elizabethan despite the Georgian façade, and with a number of even older features, so an appealing variety of periods and styles. Some rooms are grand, others are charming, with splendid furnishings and paintings and a good deal for children to enjoy. Particularly interesting is the Chinese Room with hand-painted wallpaper. There's an adventure playground, and deer in the carefully landscaped **park**

with lake and mountain views. Atmospheric restaurant, shop, plant centre, limited disabled access; cl Fri and Sat, and 2nd wk in Oct–Mar; (017684) 86450; *£5, *£3 grounds. The village **church** has pre-Norman sculpture, and quaint medieval stone bears in the graveyard. The King's Arms in Stainton is good for lunch.

DALEHEAD NY2215

☖ † ✠ ✺ From Howtown there's a good walk up Martindale (where the **church** has attractive primitive stonework), then up over the fells to Bedafell Knott and down into Patterdale; hard work, but gorgeous views, Herdwick sheep, buzzards and ring ouzels.

DALTON-IN-FURNESS SD2374

🏰 The village has a rather austere square castle; the Black Dog (Broughton Rd) has decent food.

🐘 🐾 ✺ **South Lakes Wild Animal Park** See separate family panel on p.120.

DENT SD7087

★ † ℘ ☖ Inside the modern outskirts is a delightful steep cobbled village (thought by some readers to be the prettiest in Lakeland), a rewarding end to an attractive drive – though now on the tourist trail, so busy in summer. The welcoming Sun brews its own beer, and the church is well worth a look. E of the village, towards Denthead, Colin Gardner (Stone House, Cowgill; cl wknds) makes traditional furniture. Dentdale has easy to middling walks, in the shadow of Whernside.

DERWENT WATER NY2523

✺ ⚓ ☖ With all its inlets and little islets, a pleasant place for pottering about in boats. It has gorgeous lakeside scenery, romantic little islets, ancient woodland, and a variety of mountain backdrops. You can hire **rowing boats** and launches in Keswick (not Nov–Easter); from around £6 per hour. Regular launches run all year from Keswick to half a dozen points around the lake. Walks along the lake's western shore, best reached from car parks off the back road between Grange and Swinside, can be combined with the more demanding walk up Cat Bells for the best views of the lake.

★ ☖ **Watendlath** This lovely 'lost village' is little more than a tarn, a farm

and a very modest café. There is narrow road up from the B5289 by Derwent Water, but the village makes a very rewarding destination for a walk over the hills – for instance from Rosthwaite, where the Scafell is a fine walkers' local.

DUDDON VALLEY SD2296

☖ This is known to be a favourite starting point for rather more demanding walks, either by the river or up into the heights, with the Newfield Inn at Seathwaite a good base.

DUFTON NY6926

☖ **The High Pennines** To the E of the Lakes, these have few walking routes and are extremely bleak: this is the reserve of the dedicated peat-bog enthusiast. An easy way to get an idea of the remoteness of these hills is to walk along paths encircling **Dufton Pike** from Dufton (the Stag has good food).

EGREMONT NY0110

🏰 🖼 ℘ Dominated by its very ruined Norman **castle**; as so often, the gatehouse is the best preserved part. **Lowes Court Gallery** Georgian house with local arts and crafts for sale, disabled access; cl Sun, pm Weds and pm wkdys Jan–Feb; (01946) 820693; free.

⌂ ♪ **Florence Mine Heritage Centre** (A595 just SE of Egremont) Based around what was the last working iron ore mine in Europe. Tours of the pit (wknds at 10.30am and 1.30pm – tel for wkdy times), and visitor centre with reconstructions of pit life at the turn of the century. Snacks, shop, disabled access to visitor centre; cl Nov–Mar; (01946) 820683; £6.50 pit tour, £1 visitor centre.

ELTERWATER NY3204

★ ✺ Idyllically placed village, with lake views. The Britannia is very popular for lunch. The B5343 past here gives awesome mountain views; you can keep on a poorer, steeper road, passing near pretty Blea Tarn, and coming back down through the gentler Little Langdale.

ENNERDALE WATER NY1016

☖ 🐾 Gentle walks by the lake (no boating) and through forestry, with high peaks above; the Fox & Hounds at Ennerdale Bridge is a good pub.

ESKDALE NY1700

☖ ✺ 🐾 Excellent for walks, especially

around Boot. Here, a prime objective is the **Stanley Ghyll Force** waterfall, approached by a series of bridges and visible from a dizzying view-platform high above. From Trough House Bridge car park near the waterfall you can walk along one side of the river to Doctor Bridge, then return the other side, for an easy route – with delectable views throughout. Other walks take you up towards the open fells (the landlord of the Burnmoor Inn is helpful with route suggestions). You can use the Ravenglass & Eskdale railway as part of a round trip.

FAIRFIELD NY3511

⌂ ❀ Rewarding for determined fell-walkers, climbed by a horseshoe layout of ridges from Rydal.

FAR SAWREY SD3895

⌂ ❀ Between the ferry here and the Wray Castle estate to the north can be found the cream of Windermere's waterside strolls, along the lake's western shore. The estate is a large NT tract with general public access. The forested slope rising from this shore has several well signposted routes, with Far Sawrey and Near Sawrey villages and Latterbarrow worthwhile objectives for circular walks.

FINTHSWAITE SD3788

❀ ✕ **Stott Park Bobbin Mill** (just N of Finsthwaite) Set in coppiced woodland, this former water-and-steam mill made wooden cotton reels from 1835 right up to 1971; enthusiastic guides give excellent demonstrations of 19th-c industrial techniques. The mill is still powered by steam Tues–Thurs: the lathes look lethal. Snacks, shop, disabled access; cl Nov–Mar; (015395) 31087; £2.90; EH. The Swan at Newby Bridge is attractively set for lunch.

FLOOKBURGH SD3675

★ This peaceful village has excellent potted local shrimps, and a decent craft shop.

GLEASTON SD2671

✕ ❀ 🏭 **Watermill** Well restored working watermill in peaceful surroundings, with a working corn mill, and leather-making demonstrations. Meals, snacks, shop, some disabled access; cl all Mons (exc bank hols), plus Tues in winter; (01229) 869244; £1.50. The ruins of a partly built medieval

castle are nearby.

GOSFORTH NY0603

✝ 🐾 The churchyard has a 10th-c carved **cross**, one of Britain's finest; there are more ancient carved hogback tombstones in the church. The working **pottery** may let you try making a pot (only in school hols); good shop. Cl Mon Oct–May, plus Tues and Weds Jan–Feb, 25–26 Dec; (01946) 725296.

GRANGE-OVER-SANDS SD4077

⌂ ❦ ❀ This sedately old-fashioned resort is the start for summer guided walks over **Morecambe Bay Sands**, oddly other-worldly; glistening tidal flats, quick-stepping patrols of wading birds, distant hills, grisly tales of people and horses sucked under – a guide really is essential; phone Cedric Robinson, the official guide appointed by the Queen, on (015395) 32165 for times.

GRASMERE NY3406

★ 🏠 ☕ ✝ ⌂ ❀ The pretty village swarms with visitors in summer, most of them here to see **Dove Cottage** – still much as Wordsworth had it in his most creative years (he completed *The Prelude* here), with sister Dorothy's journals and his extensive cottage garden. Informative guided tours cope well with the bustle, but in early morning (opens 9.30am) out of season you may get some space to yourself. The place always was crowded; barely big enough for two, with the poet's children and friends it often had a dozen or more people living here. The adjoining **Wordsworth Museum**, included in the price, has changing exhibitions and possessions of the poet and his family and friends, as well as a reconstructed Lakeland kitchen. Meals, snacks, shop, limited disabled access; cl last 3 wks Jan and first wk Feb, 24–26 Dec; (015394) 35544; £4.80. Wordsworth is buried in the graveyard of the robust old church, which has quite an unusual interior. Sarah Nelson's gingerbread shop by the church is wonderfully old fashioned. The Traveller's Rest (A591) is our current pick for lunch. The lake itself, with Rydal Water and Elter Water, is the very heart of picturesque Lakeland. All three are famous for their lovely settings, and there are pleasant walks all around; you can even link all three together in a long afternoon's walk filled with glorious views. The walk up the good track to Easedale Tarn from Grasmere quickly gets you away from the crowds, into a fine valley; the lake itself is romantically set below rocks.

GREAT LANGDALE NY2806

⌂ Dominated by the awesome Langdale Pikes, this is the area's main centre for more serious fell-walking in grand scenery. One very popular shorter walk here is up the good track to Stickle Tarn, from the car park by the Stickle Barn (useful for refreshments), and Bow Fell and Crinkle Crags are two longer fell walks. Wainwright's, in the not specially graceful settlement of Chapel Stile off the B5343, another useful refreshment place, is particularly popular with many of our contributors as a base for walks along here.

GRIZEDALE SD3494

⌂ 🏞 🏠 🐾 ✛ ! **Grizedale Forest Park Visitor Centre** Woodland trails from short strolls to half-day walks, punctuated by often hard-to-spot timber and rock sculptures. These trails are good when rain cuts off more open views; the sculptures are set in various sites throughout the plantations (map from visitor centre). Lots of other activities too: craft centre, good information centre, bookable deer observation hides, orienteering, bike hire (it's an ideal area for cycling), and adventure play area. In all, six or seven square miles of mainly coniferous hillside timber to get lost in. Meals, snacks, shop, some disabled access; cl 25–26 Dec and 1 Jan; (01229) 860373; parking charge, £2 for 4 hours. A highlight is the Theatre in the Forest; (01229) 860291 for what's on. The Eagle's Head at Satterthwaite (some winter closures) is good value for lunch, and the back roads through this area are quiet and pleasant.

GUMMERS HOW SD3988

⌂ 🌼 An easy 20-minute climb from the road, for a fine lake view.

HACKTHORPE NY5423

☺ **Lowther Leisure Park** 🎦 (signed off A6 S of Penrith) Plenty to keep children up to around 11 amused for most of the day (the pace is too sedate for teenagers). Some features have a

refreshingly old-fashioned appeal: there's a circus with trapeze and clown acts, and the rides are more along the lines of a traditional funfair than gravity-busting rollercoasters. The attractive parkland has a developing wildlife area, as well as puppet shows, boating, miniature train rides, challenging play areas, and an archery range. Meals, snacks, shop, disabled access; open wknds Easter–spring bank hol (plus Easter hols) then daily till early Sept; £7.45. The Punch Bowl at Askham does interesting food.

HADRIAN'S WALL NY5664

🏛 ⌂ 🐄 Surviving traces of this far less known western section of the Roman wall can be reached on well signed paths from the lanes between the A69 and B6318 N of Brampton. For the Birdoswald Roman fort at Gilsland, *see Northumbria chapter* (the **goat farm** at Holme View nearby sells prize-winning traditional cheeses).

HAMPSFIELD FELL SD3979

⌂ 🌼 A pleasant walk up through the woods from Grange-over-Sands, giving terrific views over the Bay from its limestone pavements and summit 'hospice' inscribed with 19th-c words of wisdom.

HARDKNOTT PASS NY2101

🏛 🌼 **Hardknott Roman Fort** Quite well preserved and interestingly restored, but most notable for its staggering lonely position high in the mountains; magnificent views to sea and even the Isle of Man. The drive up here is not for the faint-hearted – it's very steep and twisting, through this pass and Wrynose Pass, but the scenery makes it worthwhile; the Woolpack Inn at Bleabeck just W is good value.

HAWKSHEAD SD3598

★✛ 🎵 🛶 Don't miss this virtually unchanged Elizabethan Lakeland village, with sturdy outside walls, and sheltered flower-filled inner courtyards. Though very popular with summer visitors, even at its busiest it has a pleasantly foreign 'different' feel, and the fact that cars are kept out helps a lot. The church has some eye-catching early 18th-c murals. The best nearby pub for lunch is the Drunken Duck up at Barngates. Trout **fishing** and **boat hire** on nearby Esthwaite Water, the largest stocked lake in the region.

▣ **Beatrix Potter Gallery** 🖼 (Main St) A generous annually changing selection of the original illustrations of *Peter Rabbit* and other favourites, as well as rather different more acutely observed drawings. A timed ticket system keeps it uncrowded – during holiday periods you may have to wait to get in. Shop; cl Fri, Sat, and Nov–Mar; (015394) 36355; £2.90; NT.

👃 **Old Grammar School** Now a museum, this is worth poking your nose into, if only to see where Wordsworth carved his name on a desk (he attended 1779–83); limited disabled access; cl 12.30–1.30pm, am Sun, and Nov–Easter; £2.

HELVELLYN NY3415

⌂ ☀ This famous Lakeland landmark is most easily (and crowdedly) tackled from Thirlmere, but much more exciting when reached from Glenridding and **Striding Edge**, where the path follows a narrow rocky edge (mild scrambling needed – best ascended rather than descended) above a great post-glacial corrie; it's a day's severe walking, for perhaps the grandest and certainly the most popular of all Lakeland panoramas, with dramatic ridges leading off for miles.

HIGH CUP NICK NY7426

⌂ ☀ A great scoop in the ridge of the Pennines, this is one of the most dramatic features in the whole of the range, well worth the long (but easily followed) walk from Dufton.

HIGH STREET NY4515

⌂ One of Lakeland's great fell walks, this is a Roman ridge road, reached best from Hawes Water reservoir (the hotel here, under newish management, is a good stop).

HONISTER PASS NY2213

⌂ ☀ From the top of the pass stout-hearted and well equipped walkers can tackle Brandreth, and perhaps head on via Windy Gap for the least taxing ascent of **Great Gable**. Even if you decide not to go the whole way, the views in clear weather are spectacular.

HOWGILL FELLS SD6897

⌂ ☀ Bold 2,000-footers, empty and tough going even for hardened walkers; the easiest walks into them are up Winder from Sedbergh, and from the A683 N of Sedbergh to majestic **Cautley Spout** waterfall.

HUMPHREY HEAD POINT SD3874

☀ ⌂ This ¾-mile-long headland protruding into the sea gives walkers stunning views of Morecambe Bay.

KENDAL SD5192

▣ ✿ 🏛 A real town as opposed to a tourist centre, busy, with hectic traffic, but lots of small closes leading off the main street, some of them attractively restored to give a feel of what the place was like in the 18th-c heyday of the wool-weaving industry. The mint cake that takes its name comes in a surprising number of varieties. The Gateway (Crook Rd) is a good pub/restaurant.

Brewery Arts Centre (Highgate) Good changing events and exhibitions, café, bar, and landscaped garden; (01539) 725133 for what's on. K Shoes have a **factory shopping centre** at Netherfield (cl 25 Dec). Lakeland Canoes (Hollins Lane, Burneside) hire canoes by the day, and will take them to and fro for you. **Webbs Garden Centre** (Burneside Rd) is big, with lots of plants; decent café, disabled access.

🎭👃▣ **Abbot Hall Art Gallery & Museum** (Kirkland) Beautifully restored Georgian house with period furniture, silver, china and glass, and an art collection that reflects Kendal's importance in the 18th c as the centre of an artists' school – includes works by Ruskin, Turner, Constable, and especially George Romney. Meals, snacks, good craft shop, disabled access; cl 25 Dec–9 Feb; (01539) 722464; *£3 (or £1 if you have visited one of Kendal's other three museums).

🏰 ☀ 🎭 **Kendal Castle** Ruin on a small hill on the E edge of town, the birthplace of Henry VIII's wife Catherine Parr. There's little more now than parts of the outer wall with some towers – but children enjoy it, and there are fine views. A humble building associated with it is the **Castle Dairy** (Wildman St), an unspoiled Tudor house with some period furniture, inc the oldest bed the V & A have ever recorded. It's a restaurant but they are happy to let people look around.

👃 **Kendal Museum** (Station Rd) Less immediately appealing than the town's other museums, comprehensive but mostly traditional; lots of realistically mounted stuffed animals, and a gallery devoted to the work of Alfred Wainwright, the walkers' guru. Shop, disabled access to ground floor only; (01539) 721374; cl Sun and Jan–mid-Feb; *£3 (or £1 if you have visited one of Kendal's other three museums).

Museum of Lakeland Life (behind Abbot Hall, Kirkland) Lovingly re-created period rooms, shops and workshops, and an almost palpable feel of the past. Subjects as diverse as shoemaking, Arthur Ransome and Postman Pat. Some disabled access; *£3 (or £1 if you have visited one of Kendal's other three museums).

Quaker Tapestry Exhibition (Friends Meeting House, Stramongate) Bayeux-style tapestry history of the Quaker movement, also embroidery demonstrations. Shop, disabled access; cl Sun and all Nov–Easter; (01539) 722975; £2.85.

KESWICK NY2623

▣ ✿ The tourist centre of the northern Lakes, handy for Derwent Water, with lots of Victorian villas (many of them now guesthouses and small hotels) outside quite a traditional centre, with small cobbled closes running off the main streets. It's full of breeches, boots and backpacks in high season, with good outdoor equipment shops, and is a routine stop on coach tours. The Dog & Gun and the older-fashioned George Hotel are very popular for lunch, with the Pheasant out towards Crosthwaite also good. The **Wild Strawberry** is a quaint tearoom with an upstairs gallery; cl Tues and Weds. **Lakeside Tea Gardens** (Lake Rd) have home baking, lots for children, pleasant modern furniture and crockery and a garden with trees and chaffinches; cl about 5pm. George Fisher (Borrowdale Rd) is a good big outdoors shop. The new Theatre by the Lake seats 400 people; cl Sun; box office (017687) 74411. The back road around Swinside is pretty, and in clear weather is worth following up the gauntly formidable Keskadale Pass.

Cars of the Stars Motor Museum 🄴 (Standish St) Unusual

collection of cars from film and TV dating back to Laurel & Hardy's Model T Ford, taking in Chitty Chitty Bang Bang, the Batmobile and cars used by James Bond and Postman Pat along the way. Shop, disabled access; open Easter–New Year (wknds only in Dec) plus Feb half-term; (017687) 73757; £3.

Castlerigg Stone Circle (just E of Keswick) This Neolithic monument is well preserved, and gives photogenic perspectives of the mountains (the best times for pictures are morning and evening); take a map to identify the peaks it aligns with. The site is owned by the National Trust, and there's a brief explanation of the stones' history.

Dodd Wood (off A591 N of Keswick) Marked walks through the woods, or on open hillside, with Bassenthwaite views.

Friar's Crag An easy walk S from Keswick, this gives exquisite views of Derwent Water, with more prospects unfolding as you walk up to Castlehead Wood (there's more direct access to this from a car park on the B5289 S of Keswick).

Keswick Museum & Art Gallery (Fitzpark, Station Rd) Thoroughly traditional; the Poets Corner stands out. Shop, disabled access; cl Nov–Mar; (017687) 73263; £1.

Pencil Museum (Southey Works) Alongside the Derwent pencil factory, this surprisingly interesting musuem has some unexpected exhibits inc, at 7ft, the world's tallest pencil. Shop, disabled access; cl 25–26 Dec, 1 Jan; (017687) 73626; £2.50.

Teapottery (Central Car Park Rd) The only shape you won't see among the often ludicrous examples here is the traditional one we all have in our kitchens; shop, some disabled access; cl 25–26 Dec, 1 Jan; (017687) 73983; free.

Walla Crag S of Keswick and a steep walk up above Great Wood (often teeming with red squirrels), this gives fairly high views over Derwent Water; a moorland path heads to the photogenic Ashness Bridge, from where a rewarding return walk is one down to the shore and back again.

KIRKBY LONSDALE SD6178

★†✿⌂ Small and usually quiet town of considerable character, with interesting old yards and ginnels and good country shops; it's more lively on Thurs country-market day. Behind the fine **Church of St Mary** is a pretty stretch of the River Lune, good for walking or just lazing about – even swimming if it's hot. Along here 87 steps lead up to Ruskin's View, a beautiful panorama over the Lune Valley, appealing countryside little visited by tourists. The Snooty Fox has a range of good food.

KIRKOSWALD NY5541

★🏰✿ This attractive village has the ruins of a 13th-c **castle**, views towards the Pennines, and a useful pub.

LAKE WINDERMERE SD4096

⛴ The most popular boating lake, so the easiest place to hire **rowing boats** and other vessels. Lots of launches, of all sorts of shapes and sizes, run cruises of varying lengths from Bowness Bay, Ambleside, Waterhead and (not Nov–Mar) Newby Bridge. The pick of the sightseeing boat trips is the 50-minute tour on the silent steam launch *Osprey* or *Swallow* – available only to visitors to the Steamboat Museum (*see Windermere entry*). The pier at the S end of the lake is the terminus for the Haverthwaite steam railway. Rowing boats can be hired from the Bowness Bay Boating Company; from £2.50 per hour, £2 per extra person. They also have motorboats, and a number of launches – at least one of which is equipped to take disabled people; (015394) 43360 to check. Lake Holidays Afloat do motorboats too; (015394) 43415; around £20 an hour. A pleasant place to hire rowing boats (not Nov–Easter) is **Fell Foot Park** nr Newby Bridge, an 18-acre park with plenty of room for lakeside picnics; café and shop (cl Nov–Easter), some disabled access; (015395) 31273; parking charges (around £2), rowing boats £5 per hour for two people; NT. They can provide details of boating and fishing on other NT waters. Maples (Marina Village, Bowness) do day, weekend or longer cruises and courses on large sailing yachts; from £135 a day. Windsurfing or waterskiing can be arranged at Low Wood Water Sports Centre, Windermere; windsurfing, canoeing or dinghy sailing Mar–Oct at Windermere Sailing Centre, Rayrigg Rd, Windermere. The chain ferry linking the ferry road below Bowness with the Hawkshead road below Far Sawrey is a utilitarian way of taking to the water; but though it runs every 20 minutes and saves miles of driving, queues mean that it saves time only out of season.

LAKESIDE SD3791

✿ **Graythwaite Hall Gardens** (2m N of Lakeside) Well kept, late Victorian garden, strong on rhododendrons and a variety of other late-spring-flowering shrubs. Open Apr–Jun only; (015395) 31248; *£2.

🚂 **Lakeside & Haverthwaite Railway** A short steam trip running up to Haverthwaite. There's a small collection of steam and diesel locomotives. Meals, snacks, shop, disabled access; trains daily Apr–Oct; (015395) 31594 for times; £3.50 return. The White Hart at Bouth does good food.

LANGWATHBY NY5633

🐖 **Eden Ostrich World** (Langwathby Hall Farm) Pigs, shire horses, ducks, geese and, of course, ostriches at this friendly farm. Meals, snacks, shop, disabled access; cl Nov–Mar; (01768) 881661; £3.75.

LATTERBARROW SD3699

⌂✿ A dwarf in comparison to the great Lakeland fells, but elevated enough above a relatively low-lying area to give views over Windermere and Langdale.

LEVENS SD4985

🏛✿🚂 **Levens Hall** (A6) Impressive Elizabethan mansion based around an older core, with fine carved oak chimney-pieces, ceiling plasterwork, Spanish leather panelling, period furnishings and interesting paintings. The magnificent **topiary gardens** in their original layout of 1692 are perhaps the highlight, the fantastic shapes really standing out against the ancient grey stone of the house. Also model and other **steam engines** (pm only; in steam, some bank hols and some summer Suns), play area, grand beech trees, and deer park. Snacks, plant sales,

shop, disabled access to grounds only;
open Sun–Thurs, Apr–mid-Oct (plus
gardens open wkdys till end Oct);
(015395) 60321; £5.30, £3.90 grounds
only. The Hare & Hounds is good for
lunch.

LINDAL-IN-FURNESS SD2576
⚲ **Colony Country Store** View the
candlemakers at work then browse
among the vast array of candles and
other craftware in the shop; disabled
access; cl am Sun, 25–26 Dec and 1 Jan;
(01229) 461102. Chandlers Café next
door is a useful place that has good-
value home-made food.

LONG MEG AND HER DAUGHTERS NY5737
🏛 There's access off the lane N of Little
Salkeld to this **stone circle**.

LOWTHER NY5323
🐦⚲ **Lakeland Bird of Prey Centre**
Set in the huge Victorian walled garden
at Lowther Castle, hawks, eagles, owls,
buzzards and falcons, with flying
displays at 11am, 2pm and 4pm. Also
crafts. Teas, shop, disabled access; cl
Nov–Feb; (01931) 712746; £5.

MAIDEN WAY NY6433
🏛⌂ The back road from Langwathby
on the A686 through Skirwith to
Kirkland leads to a **Roman road**, still
sound for walkers, which plunges
northwards into the bleak high
Pennines, giving a great feeling of
solitude. There are other walks from
the sheep farms along the foot of the
Pennines between here and Appleby.

MALLERSTANG NY7800
This area, which the B6259 S of Kirkby
Stephen runs through, is reckoned by
some readers to be one of the best
places to stay for a short break.

MARYPORT NY0337
❋🛥 There's a straightforward
maritime museum on Senhouse St
(cl Sun exc summer pms, and Fri and Sat
lunchtimes; donations) and an
aquarium on South Quay (snacks,
shop, disabled access; cl 25–26 Dec;
£4.25). Elizabeth Dock is home to two
fully restored **steamships**, bought
from the council for £1 by local
volunteers; best to check opening times
on (01900) 815954; £1.50. The B5300
N has good views across to Scotland.
🛥 **Senhouse Museum** (The Battery,
Sea Brows) Impressive collection of

Roman military altar stones and
inscriptions, dug from the former fort
next door from the 1570s onwards,
making it one of the oldest collections
of antiquities in the country; also other
artefacts inc a Celtic serpent stone.
Snacks, shop, disabled access; open
Fri–Sun all year, plus Tues and Thurs
Apr–Jun, bank hols, and daily July–Oct;
(01900) 816168; *£2.

MILLOM SD1779
✝🏛🛥⌂ Not much of a town, but
there's an interesting **church**, and
ruined castle around what's now a
farm (A5093 N: ask at the house for
permission to look round the ruins). As
we went to press, there were plans to
move the decent **folk museum** on St
Georges Rd to another site in town;
they hope to include a café on the new
premises – tel (01229) 772555 for
details. S of the town a broad lagoon
built to protect former mineworks is
now a bird reserve (also home to
natterjack toads), the loneliness
exaggerated out of season when the
nearby unsmart but enjoyable little
resort of Haverigg SD1678 (great
beaches, good sailing and fishing) has
closed down; the Harbour Inn has good
cheap food, good walks in the wild
flower dunes.
⌂ **Haverigg Point** (nr Millom) This
huge stretch of impressive **dunes** is a
high point on this section of coast, but
virtually the whole length from
Ravenglass down to Hodbarrow Point
is good for breezy, seaside walks – lots
of long beaches, deserted except in high
season.

MILNTHORPE (HALE) SD5078
🐘❗❋ **Lakeland Wildlife Oasis** (A6
S of Milnthorpe) Millions of years of
evolution flash before your eyes at this
lively jungle house, a fascinating cross
between zoo and museum. Interactive
displays alongside the brightly coloured
and unusual fish, birds, insects and
animals, and woodland where children
can crawl along tunnels overlooking the
meerkat enclosure. Activities include
fossil rubbing and an animal rubber-
stamping trail. Snacks, shop, disabled
access; cl 25–26 Dec; (015395) 63027;
£4.50. A good-value family ticket
covering entry for 2 adults and 3
children is around £12.50. The B5282

to Arnside has quiet estuary and mountain views.

MORLAND NY6022

🐂 🦃 **Highgate Farm** 🖼 Cheerful farm with plenty of fun activities from cuddling bunnies and egg collecting to pony rides and pig feeding and sheep racing; falconry displays and an indoor play barn with go-karts and a sandpit. Snacks, shop, disabled access; cl Nov–Easter; (01931) 714347; £5.50.

NEAR SAWREY SD3796

🏚 **Hill Top** Small, remote 17th-c farmhouse, kept exactly as it was when owned by Beatrix Potter, who wrote many of her stories here. Or at least as it was apart from the tourists; the NT (great beneficiaries of Potter's generosity) feel the place is over-visited, and are keen to reduce visitor numbers – there's a daily limit of 800. It's so small they don't allow many people in at once, so if you do decide to visit be prepared to queue. Shop (the turnover is higher than at any other NT shop), disabled access to ground floor by prior arrangement; cl Thurs, Fri, and all Nov–Mar; (015394) 36269; £3.90; NT. The old-fashioned NT-owned Tower Bank Arms (with nicely furnished bedrooms) is pictured in *The Tale of Jemima Puddle-Duck*.

NEWBY BRIDGE SD3787

🐟 **Aquarium of the Lakes** By the steamer stop is this imaginatively laid out aquarium-style centre which vividly demonstrates the story of a local river. You can walk in see-through tunnels along a re-created lake bed, with the area's animal (inc otters), insect, bird and plant life all around, and there's a water lab with microscopes for close-up examinations of tadpoles, plankton and larvae. Snacks, shop, disabled access; cl 25 Dec; (015395) 30153; £4.95.

ORREST HEAD SD4199

⌂ 🌼 A short, steep walk (half-hour each way) from Windermere (opposite station), this gives spectacular views over the lake and the Pennines, lovely at sunset.

PENRITH NY5130

🌡 A real locals' rather than tourists' town, and the biggest in Lakeland. It's very much a northern country town, with solid stone streets, farmers from far and wide descending on its Skirsgill

agricultural market (Tues, sometimes Fri too in late summer/autumn), and genuinely traditional Lakeland shops selling real fudge and toffee, rich cakes (Birketts), local cheeses (Grahams), prize Cumberland sausages (Cranstons), local antiquarian books, and cheap and sturdy country clothes. John Norris (21 Victoria Rd) is the outstanding fishing/outdoor wear shop, with something for everyone; good prices. A **museum** on Middlegate is a useful introduction to the area, and the George does decent lunches.

Oasis Holiday Village Six miles out of Penrith in Whinfell Forest is the Rank Organisation's Center Parcs-style holiday village. It's been very well thought out as far as visitors are concerned, and for small groups the lodges are pretty good value; (01990) 086000.

🏰 **Penrith Castle** Built in the 14th c as a defence against Scottish raids, and the home of Richard III when he was Duke of Gloucester. The ruins are surrounded by a park; free.

❗ **Rhedig Discovery Centre** (Redhills) Opening at Easter, the centrepiece of this vast new development set right into the hillside, will be a colossal six-storey cinema showing the history of the county. The huge glass atrium will give views across to the High Pennines, and there'll also be sound and light shows, and specialist shops and restaurants offering local produce. Disabled access; (01768) 868000; cinema and shows around £4.95.

✝ **St Wilfred's Church** (B6262 E of Eamont Bridge) A striking exception to the usual Lakeland rule of simplicity in churches, filled with magnificent furnishings inc Continental treasures; candlelit.

🎨 🦃 🐷 **Wetheriggs Pottery** (Clifton Dykes, signed off A6 S of Keswick) Interesting and very smart working pottery – one of the oldest in the country – with 19th-c steam engine and equipment; children can try their hands at the wheel, and there's a play area, birds of prey and rare breeds of pig. Restaurant, shop, disabled access; cl 25–26 Dec, 1 Jan, Mon and Tues from Nov–Mar; (01768) 892733; free.

PIEL ISLAND SD2363

Small island shared by a basic inn and a grand 14th-c ruined fortress commanding Barrow Harbour and Morecambe Bay. It's reached by ferry (by arrangement only in winter) from Roa Island nr Barrow.

RANNERDALE KNOTTS NY1618

Best reached by a walk via Low Bank from Buttermere village, this vantage point gives good views of Crummock Water and the hills surrounding it. The green slatey fells N offer walkers superlative routes along high ridges: Whiteless Pike, Causey Pike, Crag Hill and Grasmoor are among the most exciting points.

RAVENGLASS SD0896

Pretty sailing harbour by the well sheltered Esk estuary; in summer a local fishing boat sells freshly caught fish on the shore. The so-called **Walls Castle** just outside the village is actually a Roman bath-house; its walls stand taller than any other building of its age so far north.

Muncaster Castle & Owl Centre (A595 1m E of Ravenglass) The same family have lived in this grand old house since 1208 – and will continue to do so as long as a magical glass drinking bowl remains intact. Extended over the centuries (especially 19th) from its original tower, its elegant rooms have rich furnishings and décor, inc fine Elizabethan furniture and embroidery. Entertaining Walkman tour, and glorious Esk and mountain views from the terrace. The lovely 77-acre grounds are particularly rich in species rhododendrons, and also have unusual trees, nature trails, adventure play area and lots of rescued birds of prey. The Owl Interpretation Centre has closed-circuit TV of nesting owls, along with talks and flying displays every afternoon at 2.30pm (Apr–Oct), weather permitting. The house and gardens have been fully renovated and a new underground interactive maze (where you can only advance by answering questions about the environment) will open this year. Meals, snacks, shop and plant centre, good disabled access; house open pm daily (exc Sat), garden and owl centre open all year; (01229) 717614; £5.50, just garden and owl centre £3.80. The fell above has good views.

Muncaster Mill (A595 NE of Ravenglass) A well restored working **watermill** with Victorian machinery, and flour for sale. Cl Nov–Easter (exc some wknds); (01229) 717232; £1.60. They also do good-value B & B.

Ravenglass & Eskdale Railway England's oldest narrow-gauge steam trains, lovingly preserved, with open carriages chugging up seven miles of unspoilt valley to Dalegarth; admirers say it's the most beautiful train journey in England. Cafés each end, and a small museum at Ravenglass. Shop, disabled access (with notice); cl most wkdys Dec–mid-Feb, but best to phone for train times and dates; (01229) 717171; £6.50 return. Good 3-hour summer walk back from Boot (walks' booklets from stations).

RAVENSTONEDALE NY7203

✝ The village is notable more for its pleasant riverside scenery than for its buildings – apart from the unspoilt **church** which escaped Victorian refitting; longitudinal pews, three-decker pulpit, steeply pitched gallery (steep stairs up), and a fine east window memorial to the Fothergill family (one was the last female Protestant martyr to be burned at the stake). Choose a bright day for the best light. The Black Swan and King's Head both have decent food.

RYDAL NY3706

Rydal Mount (A591) Wordsworth's sister Dorothy described Rydal as 'a paradise' when the family moved here from Grasmere in 1813; they stayed for the rest of their lives. The house itself is rather modest, with family portraits and period furniture, and it's what's outside that really stands out – the good-sized garden is still much as the poet laid it out, consciously picturesque, with original ideas that people are still rediscovering today. The setting is lovely, overlooking mountains and lakes, and they often have readings of the poetry it inspired. Shop, limited disabled access; cl Tues Nov–Feb, and the last 3 wks of Jan; (015394) 33002; £3.50. Decent campsites nearby. The Glen Rothay Hotel does respectable lunches.

ST BEES NX9511

☁ ☘ ❄ **Cliffs and birds** The Cumbrian coast has one particular lure for walkers and birdwatchers: the cliff path between Whitehaven and St Bees – each town has a railway station. From the beach car park NW of St Bees an easy walk takes you up the nature-reserve sandstone headland, famous for its bird life, and with magnificent sea and hill views.

SEASCALE NY0401

🏛 **Sellafield Visitor Centre** (off A595) Not everyone approves of the pro-nuclear PR, but children certainly enjoy the hands-on Disney-style approach to the industry at this nuclear power visitor centre with imaginative exhibitions and displays. Meals, snacks, shop, disabled access; cl 25 Dec; (019467) 27027; free. Seascale itself has a pleasant beach, and a singularly scenic golf course, where every hole offers views of the sea or the mountains; the third tee ironically puts Sellafield into the same frame as a ring of prehistoric stones.

SEATHWAITE NY2109

❄ ☁ **Packhorse track** Determined fell-walkers enjoy the unspoilt packhorse track from Seathwaite over **Styhead Pass** down into Wasdale. The summit of the pass is a start point for a fiercely dramatic route up Scafell Pike.

SEDBERGH SD6390

Hardy small town at the foot of the Howgill Fells, with a helpful Yorkshire Dales National Park Centre on Main St (cl Dec–Easter). A while ago it replaced its picturesque cobbles with an ordinary surface – much to the chagrin of the National Parks and English Heritage, who only a few years previously paid for new cobbles. The Dalesman is good for lunch.

🐗 **Holme Farm** 🖼 (Middleton, just SW of Sedbergh) 2pm tours of traditional hill farm, with plenty of young animals and nature trail. They do occasional evening tours with a badger watch. Disabled access; cl Oct–Feb exc by arrangement; (015396) 20654; £2. You may be able to camp here.

SHAP NY5415

🏚 ✝ **Shap Abbey** (left towards Keld off A6 going N out of village) The best feature is the unspoilt and undeveloped riverside seclusion; the abbey itself is very ruined, but you can trace the 13th-c layout in some detail. Nearby **Keld Chapel** is a lonely untouched shepherds' church in a riverside hamlet, and the gated Swindale road signed off the Bampton road nr Rosgill is pretty. The Greyhound is good value for lunch.

SIZERGH SD4987

🐄 ☙ **Low Sizergh Barn** Plenty of fresh farm foods (cheese, meat, ice-cream, sausage and bread), and other local produce inc Morecambe Bay shrimps. Also craft shop and **pick-your-own** strawberries (late Jun–July). The tearoom overlooks the milking parlour and they now bottle and sell milk themselves. Meals, snacks, shop; cl 25–26 Dec and 1 Jan; (015395) 60426; free.

🏠 ❁ ☙ **Sizergh Castle** Lovely lakeside house, over the centuries harmoniously extended from its original sturdy 14th-c tower by the family who have lived here for generations. Fine Tudor and Elizabethan carving, panelling and furniture, Jacobite relics, and terraced gardens surrounding a grand flight of steps to water. Lots to interest a gardener, inc an enormous rock garden, Japanese maples, watergarden, wild flowers, and daffodils in the crab-apple orchard; the autumn colours are lovely. Snacks, shop, disabled access to garden; open pm Sun–Thurs Apr–Oct; (015395) 60070; £4.50, £2.20 garden only; NT. The Strickland Arms, owned by the NT, is good for lunch.

SKELTON NY4435

🏠 ❁ **Hutton-in-the-Forest** (B5305) Some say this formidable mansion was the castle of the Green Knight of Arthurian legend. Grandly extended in the 17th c from its 14th-c peel tower core, then castellated more recently, it has a magnificent panelled gallery. A terraced garden runs down to the lake; there's an 18th-c walled formal garden, and a more romantic Victorian garden with grand trees, dovecot and woodland nature walk. Snacks, shop; garden open daily (exc Sat), house open pm Thurs, Fri and Sun Apr–Sept, plus Easter wknd and all bank hols; (017684) 84449; £4, £2.50 garden only.

SKIDDAW NY2629

⌂ ☀ One of Cumbria's great peaks, but more accessible than many – quite an easy haul up from Applethwaite, for far views.

STAFFIELD NY5342

⌂ ⚘ ☀ **Nunnery Walks** These are private paths through old woodland, taking you through a lovely **Eden Valley** river gorge with waterfalls and quiet pools; teas; 50p. There are other good free walks in this delightfully wooded sheltered valley, for instance from Armathwaite and Wetheral. The Eden Valley has the reputation of staying dry when it's pouring over in Lakeland.

STAINTON NY4827

🐂 **Alpaca Centre** The only centre for this Andean animal (a kind of fluffy llama) in Britain, you can view them in their paddocks, from the tearoom, or get up close on a field tour (£1.50). Shop, disabled access; cl all Mons and wkdys Nov–Mar; talks by prior arrangement; (01768) 891440; free. The King's Arms is good for lunch.

TALKIN TARN NY5457

☀ ⌂ ⛵ Lovely lake with partly wooded shores, peaceful mountain views, plenty of space for strolling; nature trail, orienteering and **rowing boats**; disabled access, teas. The village is pretty; the Blacksmith's Arms is popular for food.

TARN HOWS SD3299

⌂ An easy hour's walk from Hawkshead, this is a gorgeously photogenic small lake; particularly beautiful on a still clear autumn day.

TEMPLE SOWERBY NY6127

🌸 ✗ ☀ **Acorn Bank Garden** Richly planted terraced and walled garden with 250 varieties of medicinal and culinary herbs, clematis, unusual old fruit trees, and herbaceous borders; the steep wild garden drops down to the stream. A **mill** down here has been restored, and the wheel turns at wknds. This is a lovely spot at daffodil time. Shop, tearoom opening this year, disabled access; cl Nov–Mar; (017683) 61893; £2.20; NT. The B6412 to Lazenby and then the back road through the Eden Valley to Armathwaite and on up to Wetheral gives quiet views.

THORNTHWAITE NY2225

📖 ✍ **Thornthwaite Galleries** Fine art, pottery and other crafts, as well as teas, summer try-your-hand-at-it demonstrations, and a play area. Snacks, shop, disabled access (but no facilities); cl Tues and Dec–Feb; (017687) 78248; free. The Coledale Inn at Braithwaite is good for lunch (and walkers).

THORNTHWAITE FOREST NY2124

⚘ ⌂ ☀ The first-ever Forestry Commission plantation: walks through it, and up to the fells above (with lake and mountain views), are best started with a visit to the Whinlatter Visitor Centre (B5292 above Braithwaite). This has good explanatory forestry displays, shop, forest maps, and teas.

THRELKELD NY3123

☀ **Scenic road** The B5322 Threlkeld–Thirlmere is pretty, with a very photogenic view of Clough Head from the Brigham/Keswick side road turning off just past Yew Tree Farm.

TORPENHOW NY2039

✝ **Torpenhow church** A formidably Norman building, striking in itself, but worth looking at closely for the even older Roman masonry.

TROUTBECK NY4100

🏵 ☀ **Holehird Garden** (off A592 S of Troutbeck) The Lakeland Horticultural Society's hillside garden – 5 acres of well grown plants in wide variety, inc National Collections of hydrangeas and some other families; lovely views. Open all year (exc 25 Dec, 1 Jan), but manned in summer only; (015394) 46008; donations (they rely on these to maintain the gardens). Rookin House Farm has accompanied **horse-riding**, beginners welcome; (017684) 83561; £10 an hour. The quaint Queen's Head is an excellent place for refreshment.

🏠 ★ **Townend** The perfectly preserved home of a comfortably off, very traditional farming family who lived here for 300 years till the 1940s, the house showing little change over all that time. Solid, simple, unshowy comfort, and a sensible, down-to-earth and entirely self-sufficient layout. This is one of several such beautifully placed 'statesmen's' farms making up this lovely village strung along the steep valley below high fells. Braille guide; cl am, all day Mon (exc bank hols) and Sat, and Nov–Mar; (015394) 32628; £3; NT.

ULLSWATER NY4421

⚓ Here elegant Victorian steamers converted to diesel run between Pooley Bridge, Howtown and Glenridding; disabled access, cl Dec–Mar. **Sailing dinghies** can be hired by competent sailors from Ullswater Marina at Watermillock, (017684) 86415, or the sailing school at Glenridding (017684) 82541; cl winter. Rowing and other **boats** can be hired from Tindals in Glenridding; (017684) 82393; around £8 per hour, motorboats around £14.

❉ ⌂ **Aira Force waterfall** This is the best-known walk on Ullswater's west side – a pleasant if rather populated stroll of a mile or so from the car park on the A592 just NE of the A5091 junction through NT lakeshore woods to the waterfalls themselves, and the 'gothick' folly of Lyulphs Tower, with Wordsworth's daffodils a bonus in spring; above here, Gowbarrow Park has the best lake views on this side. Aira Force is a 20-metre (65-ft) waterfall, at its best after rain or on a misty morning; restaurant and shop, £1.60 parking charge. The Royal Hotel at Dockray is handy for lunch.

⌂ ❉ **Ullswater walks** The eastern shore is outstanding; there are many different views, with a rewarding combination of waterside stretches and higher ground – from which to see more sweeping vistas. On the best and most popular stretch, Howtown–Patterdale–Glenridding, you will meet quite a few other people in summer (when it can be combined with the steamer for a round trip; best to take the steamer on the way out in case the service is cancelled). The charmingly old-fashioned Howtown Hotel is a good place for a break in a stunning setting, and Hallin Fell nearby gives an aerial view of the lake.

ULVERSTON SD2978

🎋 ⛶ This town holds the bizarre double claim of being the birthplace of both pole-vaulting and the Quaker movement. The Pork Pie Shop at the N end of Market Pl is very good indeed,

while the Dolls' House Man (Furness Galleries, Theatre St) makes dolls' houses, farms, wooden animals and so on, and usually has examples on display. The **Heritage Centre** on Lower Brook St has local history displays (cl Sun, and Weds Christmas–Whit; £2). The Rose & Crown (King St) has decent food, and the Bay Horse out at Canal Foot is very good for lunch.

✝ **Conishead Priory** (Priory Rd) There's a newish Buddhist temple in the grounds here; guided tours of the priory around £2; open pm most summer wknds.

🏭 **Lakes Glass Centre** (Oubas Hill) Watch the craftsmen blowing, cutting and engraving. The factory shop is good value, with cheap seconds. Meals, snacks, shop, disabled access; cl 25–26 Dec; (01229) 584400; £2.

🎭 **Laurel & Hardy Museum** (Upper Brook St) The owner of this unique exhibition (a former mayor) really knows his subject, and it's his obvious enthusiasm that makes this one of Lakeland's best-loved attractions. Fittingly in Stan Laurel's home town, with delightfully presented mementos and all-day films. Shop, disabled access; cl Jan; (01229) 582292; £2.

🏛 **Swarthmoor Hall** This Elizabethan manor is known as the actual birthplace of Quakerism after George Fox was sheltered here in 1652. The interior has been lovingly restored with period furnishings, and they've rebuilt an old barn within the grounds. Guided tours (£2.50) are planned for three pms a week from Mar onwards; tel (01229) 583204 for details.

WALNEY ISLAND SD1869

🐦 Over the bridge from Barrow, this has some long roads of low houses but is mostly a windswept sweep of duney grass, very offshore-feeling; nature reserves at both ends, with excellent birdwatching and interesting plants. The George has decent food.

WANSFELL PIKE NY3904

⌂ ❉ Reached by a path from Ambleside, this is toylike in size compared with the bigger fells, but the view is as good as from many more imposing peaks.

WASDALE NY1808

⌂ ✝ The start for many magnificent fell

walks, inc the ascents of Great Gable and Scafell Pike; one less taxing walk is straight up the head of the valley to the summit of Black Sail Pass and back. Apart from around the interesting churchyard, it's not so good for gentle strolls, and parking at Wasdale Head can be a problem in summer or at holiday times. Besides the Wasdale Head Hotel, the Strands lower down is a useful stop for food.

WATERMILLOCK NY4422
✝ ♨ The **church** is worth stopping at for its evocative photographs of all its 1930s parishioners. **Sailing dinghies** can be hired by competent sailors from Ullswater Marina here.

WHITEHAVEN NX9718
★ Planned as an 18th-c industrial town and major port, the restoration of this interesting place continues after its decline. The harbour is attractive at high tide (a bit dirty at low tide). Michael Moon's **bookshop** (Lowther St) has a vast and rewarding secondhand stock, the best in the Lakes; cl Sun, bank hols, and Weds Jan–Easter. There are some other interesting shops in side streets, and the Richmond (Hensingham) is useful for lunch. Just S at Sandwith, the Lowther Arms is recommended by readers for good, homely food and accommodation, handy for the coast-to-coast walk.

♫ ❇ **The Beacon** (West Strand) Whitehaven's history is excellently covered here, but what really makes this friendly heritage centre worth a look is the Met Office Weather Gallery on the top floor, full of hi-tech monitoring and recording equipment, and excellent hands-on displays explaining how weather forecasts are put together. The building itself is striking, with good views over the town and harbour from the top floor. Shop, snacks, disabled access; cl Mon (exc bank hols) and 25 Dec; (01946) 592302; £4.

WINDERMERE SD4199
🐾 🐦 **Amazonia** Fascinating changing collection of reptiles – all shapes and sizes including snakes, crocodiles and brightly coloured lizards. All housed among koi and turtle ponds, waterfalls and free-nesting tropical birds. Meals, snacks, shop, disabled access; cl 25 Dec,

1 Jan; (015394) 48002; £3.75.
❇ ⛴ **Steamboat Museum** (Rayrigg Rd) Nearly three dozen gleamingly restored graceful antique steamboats, inc the 1850 SL Dolly, the oldest mechanically powered steamboat in the world, and the record-breaker Miss Windermere IV. Also a few boats that comfortably predate steam, and events like vintage boat rallies and model boat regattas. Snacks, shop, disabled access; cl Nov–Mar; (015394) 45565; £3.25. For an extra £4.75, there are stately 50-minute tours of the lake on the silent steam launch Osprey or Swallow, weather permitting.

❗ **World of Beatrix Potter** (Old Laundry, Crag Brow, Bowness) Much enjoyed by young children, delightfully detailed re-creations of characters and scenes from Peter Rabbit and other tales. Some bits have smells, so you can get more of the atmosphere of Mrs Tiggy-Winkle's laundry or nasty old Mr McGregor's potting shed. Meals and snacks (in the Tailor of Gloucester's kitchen), shop, disabled access; cl 25 Dec, and last 3 wks Jan; £3.25.

WINDERMERE/BOWNESS SD4096
🐾 An extensive, largely Victorian development of guesthouses and small hotels spreads up between the older village of Bowness and the hillside station. It has a touristy feel right through the year, especially around the main street down to the steamer piers. In Bowness itself there is an inner core of narrower, much older streets and buildings – one of the most ancient is the engaging Hole in t' Wall pub, with its characterful décor. **Horse-riding** can be arranged from Wynlass Beck Stables (bottom of Patterdale Rd). The tourist information centre on Victoria St has a useful range of locally produced crafts if you haven't time to look properly, and the Birdcage (College Rd) is a good antique shop – mostly lamps and small things.

WITHERSLACK SD4384
❀ **Halecat Garden** (A590) Good example of modern landscaping with fine views from the mainly herbaceous garden; plants for sale (inc hydrangeas). Some disabled access with notice; cl am Sat and all Sun; (015395) 52229; free.

WORKINGTON NX9928

ठ **Helena Thompson Museum** (Park End Rd) Some antique and Georgian costumes, as well as pottery, silver, furniture and local history, in period surroundings. Disabled access to ground floor only; cl Sun; (01900) 62598; free. Cobbled Portland Sq is pretty, and the Alamin Indian restaurant (Jane St) is good.

🏚 **Workington Hall** 🖭 (Curwen Pk, NE edge of town) Former mansion, now a ruinous hulk around a Norman tower, in a public park – an odd conjunction. A famous letter by Mary, Queen of Scots to her cousin Elizabeth I was written here. Shop; cl 1–2 pm, am wknds, all day Mon (exc bank hols), and Nov–Easter; (01900) 735408; £1.

★ **Other attractive villages** in fine scenery, all with good pubs, include Armathwaite NY5146, Bampton NY5118, Beckermet NY0207, Broughton Mills SD2290, Crosby Ravensworth NY6215 (Maulds Meaburn is also pretty), Garrigill NY7441, Hesket Newmarket NY3438 and Stonethwaite NY2613. The comfortable Kirkstile Inn at Loweswater NY1222 deserves a mention for its glorious setting.

Where to eat

AMBLESIDE NY3804 **Sheila's Cottage** *The Slack (015394) 33079* 250-year-old cottage and converted barn run by the same owners for over 30 years, with very good and enjoyable food served all day inc popular afternoon teas; **£25|£6**.

APPLEBY NY6921 **Royal Oak** *(017683) 51463* Friendly, very popular, partly 14th-c coaching inn with good and enjoyable food, huge breakfasts, a fine range of beers, and carefully chosen wines; comfortable bdrms. **£23|£7**.

APPLETHWAITE NY2726 **Underscar Manor** *(01768) 775000* Italianate Victorian house in a wonderful position with panoramic views, a comfortable sitting room, 2 pretty restaurants with ornate drapes and lovely fresh flowers, beautifully presented, very good classical cooking, and a mainly French wine list; smart dress; no smoking; children over 12. **£45**.

ARMATHWAITE NY5146 **Dukes Head** *(016974) 72226* In an attractive village, this is a comfortable and friendly inn with a civilised lounge bar, a warm coal fire, good home cooking, well kept real ales, and decent wines; bdrms; disabled access. **£18.80|£6**.

ASKHAM NY5123 **Punch Bowl** *(01931) 712443* Attractively set by a village green, this bustling pub has an interestingly furnished rambling bar, an open log fire, friendly atmosphere, generous helpings of good bar food, and well kept beers; cl pm 25 Dec; disabled access. **£16.80|£6.50**.

BOWNESS SD4097 **Hole in t' Wall** *(015394) 43488* Bustling, interesting and ancient Lakeland pub with a friendly welcome for all, lots to look at, a fine log fire, good home-made food, well kept real ales and home-made lemonade; can be busy in summer; no food pm Sun. **£16|£6**.

BOWNESS SD4097 **Porthole** *3 Ash St (015394) 42793* Long-established, bustling bistro with consistently good meals (mainly Italian), a genuine personal touch to service, simple furnishings, and decent wine – a reliably enjoyable evening out; cl am Sat, Tues, mid-Dec–mid-Feb; limited disabled access. **£28|£7.50**.

CARTMEL FELL SD4288 **Masons Arms** *(015395) 68486* Old-fashioned building in a unrivalled setting with wonderful views, a superb range of beers inc summer own-brew and interesting Continental real ales, and very popular food, many vegetarian dishes; self-catering accommodation; cl 25 Dec. **£22|£7.95**.

CROOK SD4795 **Sun** *(01539) 821351* Friendly and relaxed pub away from the Windermere bustle, with 2 opened up rooms (1 no smoking) and a wide range of imaginative food inc proper puddings; cheerful, efficient staff, well kept ales, and interesting, good-value wines. **£20.90|£8.50**.

CROSTHWAITE SD4491 **Punch Bowl** *(015395) 68237* Prettily set, Lakeland inn concentrating very much on excellent food in an interesting series of nicely furnished rooms, with a good pubby atmosphere, well kept real ales, and friendly service; bdrms; may cl winter Mon. **£22|2-course lunch £6.95**.

DENT SD7187 **Stone Close** *Main St (015396) 25231* Cottagey, 17th-c teashop with pine furniture on the flagstones, cast-iron ranges, beams, and local crafts, home-made meals served from mid-morning until early evening inc delicious cakes and pastries, and a relaxed friendly atmosphere; bdrms, plus self-catering cottage next door; cl Jan. **£15.95|£4.85.**

KESWICK NY2618 **Maysons** *33 Lake Rd (017687) 74104* Busy restaurant with an interesting range of highly enjoyable food inc good vegetarian dishes, nice salads, and yummy cakes; cl evenings Nov–May (exc Easter). **£15|£5.**

KESWICK NY2618 **Wild Strawberry** *54 Main Street (017687) 74399* Cheerfully run tearoom in beamed and flagstoned, no smoking, 17th-c cottage with strawberry-themed furnishings, enjoyable home-made light meals, cakes, lovely scones, and pies, and a good choice of teas; cl winter Fri, cl Jan; no pushchairs. £4.10.

KIRKBY LONSDALE SD6278 **Snooty Fox** *(015242) 71308* Rambling inn with plenty of interest in the various relaxed pubby rooms, good interesting food, a no smoking dining annexe, well kept beers, and pretty garden; cl pm 25 Dec; children must be well behaved; disabled access. **£22.50|£5.75.**

MELMERBY NY6237 **Shepherds** *(01768) 881217* Friendly place in an unspoilt sandstone village with popular home-made food inc a marvellous range of cheeses, delicious puddings, and lots of daily specials using only local produce; quick friendly table service; cl 25 Dec; fair disabled access. **£17|£6.50.**

MELMERBY NY6237 **Village Bakery** *(01768) 881515* Converted stone barn selling wonderful organic bread and cakes for cream teas, super breakfasts (until 11am) and good home-made restaurant food using produce grown organically behind the bakery; craft gallery upstairs; cl 25–26 Dec, 1 Jan; and 2pm wkdys in Jan and Feb. **£17.40|£5.50.**

MUNGRISDALE NY3630 **Mill Inn** *(017687) 79632* Friendly inn in a high secluded valley with a warm fire in the simply furnished main bar, separate restaurant, enjoyable home-made food inc home-baked bread, vegetarian and vegan dishes, and a good choice of cheeses, well kept real ales, 10 wines by the glass, and really friendly helpful service; there is a separate Mill Hotel in the same hamlet. **£17.95|£6.95.**

SCALES NY3427 **White Horse** *(017687) 79241* Cosy and isolated farmhouse inn in a dramatic setting under Blencathra, a perfect haven after walks; best to book as the generously served food, using fresh local produce, is very popular; cl Mon, and Nov–Apr. **£20|£5.90.**

SEATOLLER NY2414 **Yew Tree** *(017687) 77634* Set at the foot of a lovely valley, this restaurant was originally 2 17th-c miners' cottages and has fine oak beams, a slate floor, an open range and brick bread oven, lots of interesting old photographs and memorabilia, a super atmosphere, and good, interesting food using local produce; cl 9 Jan–13 Feb; disabled access. **£24|£5.65.**

TROUTBECK NY4103 **Queens Head** *(015394) 32174* Popular, gabled 17th-c coaching inn with a rambling bar, some fine antique carving, 2 roaring log fires, helpful friendly staff, particularly good first-class bar food, and well kept real ales; bdrms; cl 25 Dec. **£30|£5.50.**

ULVERSTON SD2978 **Bay Horse Hotel and Restaurant** *Canal Foot, past Glaxo (01229) 583972* Civilised and nicely placed inn overlooking Morecambe Bay, with beautifully presented innovative food, well kept real ales and good wine list; bdrms; children over 12; cl am Mon. **£35|£8.50.**

WINDERMERE SD4199 **High Street Restaurant** *4 High St (015394) 44954* Intimate, well liked little evening restaurant with good French-influenced English cooking, candlelit tables on wooden floors, a relaxed bistro-type atmosphere, and helpful service; good-value set menus; cl Sun. **£20.**

YANWATH NY5128 **Gate** *(01768) 862386* Unpretentious village local with really good inventive food, well kept real ales, obliging service, a log fire in the simple chatty bar, and a no smoking dining room; cl 25 Dec. **£20|£5.90.**

Special thanks to Mr and Mrs D J Elleanor.

Cumbria Calendar

Some of these dates were provisional as we went to press. Please check information with the telephone numbers provided.

Medieval rushbearing ceremonies mark the time when earthen church floors were covered with straw and sweet-smelling herbs for warmth and cleanliness. Rushes are carried into the church in a colourful procession, followed by children (bearing flowers and garlands) and the town or village band with merry-making and thanksgiving.

JANUARY

 I **Kirkby Stephen** Nine Standards Fell Race (017683) 71199
21 **Grasmere** Book Collectors' Festival at Dove Cottage – *till 23 January* (015394) 35544

FEBRUARY

 6 **Grasmere** Wordsworth Winter School at Dove Cottage: residential course of lectures, seminars and poetry – *till 11 February* (015394) 35544

MARCH

18 **Ambleside** Daffodil and Spring Flower Show – *till 19 March* (015394) 32252
20 **Sedbergh** Mystery Plays – *till 26 March* (015396) 50852

APRIL

15 **Crosthwaite** Damson Day (015395) 68246
21 **Barrow-in-Furness** Model Railway and Transport Exhibition at Forum 28 Main Hall – *till 23 April* (01229) 588082; **Ravenglass** Steam Gala at Ravenglass and Eskdale Railway – *till 1 May* (01229) 717171
23 **Whittington** Point to Point (015242) 21175
30 **Carlisle** Spring Show at Victoria Park – *till 1 May* (01228) 810208; also Spring Flower Show – *till 1 May* (01228) 625444

MAY

 6 **Windermere** Model Boat Rally at Windermere Steamboat Museum – *till 7 May* (015394) 45565; **Carlisle** Spring Orchid Show at Carlisle College (016977) 2476
12 **Kirkby Stephen** Walking and Countryside Festival inc tutored walks, guided routes and 3-day trek – *till 15 May* (017683) 71199
13 **Barbon** National Speed Hill Climb for racing, sports and vintage cars at Barbon Manor (01539) 740777; **Gleaston** National Mills Day at Gleaston Water Mill: blacksmith, clog dancers – *till 14 May* (01229) 869244
19 **Keswick** Jazz Festival – *till 21 May* (01900) 602122
26 **Ulverston** Festival of Furness Tradition – *till 27 May* (01229) 582704
27 **Coniston** Water Festival – *till 4 June* (015394) 41707; **Workington** Fair at Workington Hall (01900) 602122
29 **Kendal** Medieval Market (015395) 63595

Cumbria Calendar (cont.)

JUNE

1 **Windermere** Electric Boat Association Rally inc lake tours (015394) 45565
2 **Cark-in-Cartmel** Garden and Countryside Festival at Holker Hall and Gardens: festival gardens, lectures and demonstrations, steel band, children's play area – *till 4 June* (015395) 58838; **Keswick** Beer Festival: over 100 beers, bands and sideshows – *till 3 June* (017687) 73591/78277
3 **Ulverston** Complementary Medicines Festival (01229) 582298
5 **Bowber Head** Fell-walking Festival
7 **Appleby-in-Westmorland** Horse Fair at Fair Hill: gypsies from all over Europe gather on Fair Hill for this 300-year-old event with fortune telling, racing and spectacular horse, carriage and van sales on the last 2 days – *till 14 June* (017683) 51177
10 **Grange-over-Sands** Carnival (015395) 325529
11 **Carlisle** Carnival (01228) 625444
18 **Barrow-in-Furness** Gala: dancing, vintage vehicles, stunt cars (01229) 835123; **Brough** Hound and Terrier Show: classes for working dogs, gun dogs, children's pets, dry-stone walling competition at Castle Garth (017683) 51921; **Flookburgh** Charter Fair (015395) 58421; **Keswick** Carnival (017687) 73189; **Kirkby Lonsdale** Brass Bands Gathering (015242) 71115
25 **Endmoor** Country Fayre: ring events, wrestling (015395) 67858; **Patterdale** Ullswater Country Fair (01539) 723531
29 **Warcop** Rushbearing (017683) 41774

JULY

1 **Cockermouth** Festival – *till 31 July* (01900) 823608; **Musgrave** Rushbearing (017683) 41355; **Ulverston** Carnival and Parade (01229) 580640; **Whitehaven** Carnival (01946) 66307
2 **Distington** West Cumbria Vintage Vehicle and Machinery Rally at Hayes Farm (01900) 871637
8 **Appleby** Town Carnival and Sports – *till 9 July* (017683) 53056; **Grange-over-Sands** Lakeland Rose Show (015395) 34026; **Maryport** Carnival (01900) 813171
15 **Carlisle** Cumberland County Show at Rickerby Park: music, children's entertainment, vintage vehicles, air and animal displays (01228) 560364; **Cleator Moor** Sports (01946) 811656
17 **Appleby** Jazz Festival at Appleby Castle – *till 18 July* (017683) 51052
20 **Carlisle** Carlisle and Cumbria Artists' Exhibition: work by 70 artists (01228) 710261
22 **Penrith** Agricultural Show at Brougham Hall Farm (01931) 713325
26 **Ulverston** North Lonsdale Show at Bardsey Park (01229) 585140
29 **Grasmere** Wordsworth Summer Conference at Dove Cottage: residential course of lectures, seminars and poetry – *till 12 August* (015394) 35544
30 **Coniston** Country Fair (015395) 52314

AUGUST

2 **Cartmel** Agricultural Show (01539) 722777

Cumbria Calendar (cont.)

3 Ambleside Sports: traditional Lakeland sports (015394) 45531; **Ings** Lake District Sheepdog Trials at Hill Farm (015394) 33721 or (017684) 82260

5 Cockermouth Agricultural Show (01946) 692798

6 Grasmere Rushbearing (015394) 35326

8 Kirkby Lonsdale Lunesdale Show (015396) 20471

10 Appleby Agricultural Show (01931) 714571

11 Ambleside Garden Festival and Craft Fair: three marquees – *till 13 August* (015394) 32904; **Lowther** Horse Driving Trials and Country Fair at Lowther Castle – *till 13 August* (01931) 712378

12 Dalston Agricultural Show (01228) 523034

16 Gosforth Agricultural Show (019467) 24652

19 Hutton-in-the-Forest Skelton Horticultural and Agricultural Show at Old Park: vintage vehicle parade, equestrian and driving events, 140 stands, music (017684) 83032

20 Langdale Country Fair (01229) 837680

25 Kendal Folk Festival at the Brewery Arts Centre – *till 27 August* (01539) 725133; **Kendal** Gathering: music, theatre, vintage vehicles, torchlight procession – *till 9 September* (01539) 720040

26 Dufton Agricultural Show and Sheepdog Trials (017683) 62015

27 Broughton-in-Furness Millom and Broughton Agricultural Show (01229) 772556; **Eskdale Green** Fête (019467) 23319; **Grasmere** Traditional Sports inc Lakeland wrestling, hound trails, mountain bike and fell races inc English Hill Championship (015394) 32127; **Kentmere** Sheepdog Trials (01539) 821550

28 Keswick Agricultural Show (016973) 23418; **Ravenglass** Country Fair and Sheepdog Trials at Muncaster Castle (01229) 717608; **Silloth** Carnival (016973) 31257

30 Kirkland Ennerdale and Kinniside Show at Leaps Field (01946) 861391

31 Crosby Ravensworth Agricultural Show (01931) 715382

SEPTEMBER

2 Caldbeck Hesket Newmarket Agricultural Show; **Kirkby Lonsdale** Victorian Fair: vintage vehicles, street entertainers, fair, dancing – *till 3 September* (015242) 71237; **Lowick** Show (01229) 861420; **Ulverston** Market Charter Festival – *till 16 September* (01229) 462334; also Lowick and District Agricultural Show (01229) 885230

7 Crooklands Westmorland County Show: around 240 trade stands (015395) 67804

8 Kendal Weekend of Traditional Dance – *till 12 September* (01524) 388978

9 Kendal Torchlight Procession: 2-mile long procession with over 100 illuminated floats, 20 marching bands and classic cars (015395) 63018

16 Egremont Crab Fair inc world gurning (pulling a face) championships, greasy pole, pipe-smoking contest (01946) 821554

17 Rosthwaite Borrowdale Shepherds' Meet and Show (017687) 77678

21 Loweswater Loweswater & Brackenthwaite Agricultural Show (01900) 85294

24 Urswick Rushbearing (01229) 587913

30 Boot Eskdale Show (019467) 23170

OCTOBER

14 Wasdale Head Show and Shepherds' Meet (019467) 25340

Cumbria Calendar (cont.)

15 **Kendal** Mountain Film Festival at the Brewery Arms Centre – *till 17 October* (01539) 725758

29 **Whitehaven** Cumbria Brass Band Association Annual Open Contest in the Civic Hall (01946) 61955

NOVEMBER

5 **Cockermouth** Firework Display (01900) 823608

6 **Carlisle** Fireworks and Music in Bitts Park (01228) 817359

16 **Santon Bridge** Biggest Liar in the World Competition at the Bridge Inn (01946) 67575

18 **Hensingham** Chrysanthemum Show (01946) 592302

DECEMBER

3 **Keswick** Victorian Fair (017687) 71337

We welcome reports from readers

This *Guide* depends on readers' reports. Do help us if you can – in return, we offer a discount on the next edition to people who've helped us with reports for it. Tell us what you think about places already in it, and anything extra you think we should say about them. And send us your ideas for inclusion in the next edition: places to visit, eat at or stay in, attractive drives or walks, maybe even unusual interesting shops you know of. Use the card in the middle, the report forms at the end, or just write – no stamp needed: *The Good Britain Guide*, FREEPOST TN1569, Wadhurst, E Sussex TN5 7BR.

DERBYSHIRE

Great days out and glorious landscapes – plenty to fill a holiday at any age; very good places to stay in.

One of Britain's richest pre-industrial areas, this has some splendid stately homes. Magnificent Chatsworth (an excellent family day out), Hardwick Hall (some impressive restoration with heritage funding), Calke Abbey, charming Haddon Hall, Sudbury Hall, Kedleston Hall, Bolsover Castle and – less lofty but no less enjoyable – Eyam Hall are all well worth a visit, and each quite distinctive. Ruined Wingfield Manor at South Wingfield puts an ironic twist on past glories.

Underground Derbyshire is also quite special, laced with remarkable underground caverns. The Heights of Abraham in Matlock Bath is a great family draw. Poole's Cavern in Buxton is the most striking of all, Treak Cliff Cavern the best of several good ones around Castleton.

Other highlights include the tramway museum at Crich (much more than just trams), the National Stone Centre in Wirksworth (surprisingly interesting), Derby's industrial museum, the Chestnut nature park in Chapel-en-le-Frith, the enjoyable Peak Rail at Darley Dale, and Lea Gardens (especially in late spring). Proto-industrial Cromford is quite an eye-opener. There is plenty of family entertainment around Matlock, where the Riber Castle wildlife park is a strong draw. The American Adventure theme park at Ilkeston is another reliable family outing.

The best of the scenery is in the central area, more or less south of the A625, known as the White Peak. This limestone country, picturesquely cut by the intricate channels of the dales, has an abundance of generally gentle walking – and is very rewarding for drivers too. High, flat pastures have small fields of rich grassland enclosed by silvery stone walls, clusters of often very photogenic pale stone farm buildings, and small old-fashioned villages. In summer the loveliest dales do have almost a crocodile of walkers snaking along them, though even then you can find quiet areas. Further north, up in the High Peak, the scenery becomes bleaker and more forbidding – daunting for all but the most committed walker, though exhilarating for drivers – the A6024, A628 (rather slow), A57, A5002, A624 and A625 all have outstanding views.

Where to stay

ASHBOURNE SK1846 **Callow Hall** *Mappleton Rd, Ashbourne DE6 2AA (01335) 343403* **£120,** plus special breaks; 16 lovely well furnished rms, excellent bthrms. Quietly smart and friendly Victorian mansion up a long drive through grounds with fine trees and surrounded by marvellous countryside; comfortable drawing room with open fire, fresh flowers and plants, and period furniture; very good traditional food using home-grown produce, excellent breakfasts, and kind hosts; good private fishing; cl Christmas; disabled access.

ASHFORD IN THE WATER SK1969 **Riverside House** *Fennel St, Ashford in the*

Water, Bakewell DE4 1QF (01629) 814275 **£135,** plus special breaks; 15 individually decorated pretty rms. Creeper-covered Georgian house in delightful village with attractive riverside gardens, a relaxed house-party atmosphere, antiques and log fires in cosy sitting rooms, fine modern English cooking, and good service; children over 8; disabled access.

BAKEWELL SK2272 **Hassop Hall** *Hassop, Bakewell DE45 1NS (01629) 640488* **£92.90,** plus winter breaks; 13 gracious rms. Mentioned in the Domesday Book, in lovely parkland surrounded by fine scenery, this handsome hotel has antiques and oil paintings, an elegant drawing room, oak-panelled bar, good food and friendly service; tennis and croquet; no acommodation 3 nights over Christmas; partial disabled access.

BASLOW SK2572 **Cavendish** *Baslow, Bakewell DE45 1SP (01246) 582311* **£146.20,** plus winter wknd breaks; 24 spotless, comfortable and individually furnished rms (varying in size). Charming hotel with magnificent views over Chatsworth estate, most attractive, well furnished day rooms (some furnishings come from Chatsworth), an eclectic collection of the owner's pictures, open fires and fresh flowers, fine food in the two restaurants, very courteous staff.

BASLOW SK2572 **Fischer's** *Baslow Hall, Calver Rd, Baslow, Bakewell DE4 1RR (01246) 583259* ***£100,** plus special breaks; 6 comfortable, pretty rms. Handsome Edwardian manor house with individually chosen furnishings and pictures, open fires, fresh flowers and plants; beautifully presented food using the best ingredients (some home-grown and lots of game and fish) in the airy dining room or in the lunchtime Café Max (both no smoking), and courteous attentive service; cl 25–26 Dec; children over 12 in evening restaurant.

BIGGIN-BY-HARTINGTON SK0673 **Biggin Hall** *Biggin-by-Hartington, Buxton SK17 0DH (01298) 84451* **£59,** plus special breaks; 17 spacious rms with antiques, some in converted 18th-c stone building and in bothy. Cheerfully run 17th-c house in quiet grounds; with a very relaxed atmosphere, two comfortable sitting rooms, log fires, freshly cooked straightforward food, with an emphasis on free-range wholefoods served at 7pm in the attractive dining room, and packed lunches if wanted; children over 12; disabled access.

BIRCH VALE SK0286 **Waltzing Weasel** *New Mills Rd, Birch Vale, Stockport SK12 5BT (01663) 743402* **£68,** plus special breaks; 8 lovely rms. Attractive traditional inn with open fire, some handsome furnishings, daily newspapers and plants in the civilised bar, very good food using the best seasonal produce in the charming back restaurant (fine views), excellent puddings and cheeses, obliging service; children over 7; disabled access.

CASTLETON SK1583 **Bargate Cottage** *Market Pl, Castleton, Sheffield S30 2WG (01433) 620201* ***£44;** 3 well equipped rms. Lovely, beautifully restored old cottage with beams, an inglenook fireplace, delicious breakfasts, enjoyable evening meals, and super packed lunches; also, a pretty terraced garden; no smoking; cl 25 Dec; children over 12.

DOVE DALE SK1452 **Peveril of the Peak** *Dove Dale, Ashbourne DE6 2AW (01335) 350333* **£106,** plus special breaks; 47 rms. Relaxing hotel in pretty village with comfortable sofas and log fire in lounge, modern bar and attractive restaurant overlooking the garden, and good English cooking; tennis; wonderful walking nearby; disabled access.

DOVERIDGE SK1134 **Beeches** *Doveridge, Ashbourne DE6 5LR (01889) 590288* ***£62;** 10 rms with home-made biscuits, fruit and flowers. 18th-c farmhouse with an open fire in the rustic beamed bar, several cosy beamed eating areas with original brickwork, good English food, and hearty breakfasts; cl Christmas; partial disabled access.

GLOSSOP SK0394 **Wind in the Willows** *Derbyshire Level, Sheffield Rd, Glossop SK13 9PT (01457) 868001* **£87;** 12 individual rms with thoughtful extras. Set in 5 acres of grounds on the edge of the Pennines, this early Victorian house has a restful atmosphere in its tranquil, traditionally furnished sitting rooms, log fires and antiques, enjoyable set dinners (the restaurant is not open to the general public), particularly good breakfasts, and charming, helpful service; adjoining golf course; cl Christmas and New Year; children over 10.

GRINDLEFORD SK2478 **Maynard Arms** *Main Rd, Grindleford, Sheffield S30 1HP (01433) 630321 *£77,* plus special breaks; 10 rms. Comfortable hotel with log fire and Peak District views from the first-floor lounge, a smart welcoming bar, fine choice of food, particularly attentive service; good walks nearby.

HATHERSAGE SK2381 **George** *Hathersage, Sheffield S30 1BB (01433) 650436* **£99.50,** plus special breaks; 19 pretty rms (the back ones are quietest). Substantial and comfortably modernised old inn with an attractive airy lounge, beamed friendly bar, popular food, and a neat flagstoned back terrace by the rose garden; good walks all around.

HOPE SK1783 **Underleigh House** *Edale Rd, Hope, Castleton S30 2RF (01433) 621372 *£68,* plus special breaks; 6 thoughtfully decorated rms with own teddy bears. In unspoilt countryside, this spotlessly kept converted barn has fine views from the comfortable sitting room, hearty breakfasts and very good home-made evening meals enjoyed around a communal table in the flagstoned dining room, friendly cheerful owners (who used to run a successful restaurant), and neat gardens; children over 12.

KIRK IRETON SK2650 **Barley Mow** *Kirk Ireton, Ashbourne DE6 3JP (01335) 370306 £45;* 5 rms. Tall, Jacobean, walkers' inn with lots of woodwork in a straightforward series of interconnecting bar rooms, a solid fuel stove in the beamed residents' sitting room, and well kept real ales; close to Carsington Reservoir; cl Christmas wk.

MATLOCK SK3060 **Riber Hall** *Matlock DE4 5JU (01629) 582795* **£118.50,** plus special breaks; 14 lovely beamed rms with antiques, chocolates and baskets of fruit. Elizabethan manor house in pretty grounds surrounded by peaceful countryside, with antiques-filled heavily beamed rooms, fresh flowers, and two elegant dining rooms with reliable food and fine wines; tennis and clay-pigeon shooting; children over 10.

MONSAL HEAD SK1871 **Monsal Head Hotel** *Monsal Head, Bakewell DE4 1NL (01629) 640250* **£60,** plus special breaks; 8 very good rms. Comfortable and enjoyable small hotel in marvellous setting high above the River Wye; with horsey theme in the bar (converted from old stables), a Victorian-style restaurant, well prepared decent food, and good service; cl 25 Dec; dogs by prior arrangement.

ROWLAND SK2072 **Holly Cottage** *Rowland, Bakewell DE45 1NR (01629) 640624* **£44,** plus special breaks; 2 rms, shared bthrm; 200-year-old, no smoking cottage on a quiet lane, surrounded by peaceful rolling countryside, with an open fire in large lounge, woodburner in panelled hall, attractive dining room, excellent breakfasts with home-made rolls, bread and preserves; lovely gardens, and a friendly black Labrador; lots of walks; cl Nov–Dec.

ROWSLEY SK2566 **Peacock** *Rowsley, Matlock DE4 2EB (01629) 733518* **£110,** plus special breaks; 17 comfortable rms. Handsome, early 17th-c hotel by lovely trout river (private fishing in season), with well kept gardens, friendly staff, an interesting old-fashioned inner bar, spacious comfortable lounges, and a very popular restaurant.

SHIRLEY SK2141 **Shirley Hall Farm** *Shirley, Ashbourne DE6 3AS (01335) 360346* **£44;** 3 rms. Timbered and part-moated farmhouse on family-run dairy/sheep/arable farm, with homely sitting room, and fine breakfasts using home-made bread, jam and marmalade and local organic sausages; private coarse fishing and lots of walks; self-catering cottages; nearby pub for evening meals; cl Christmas; children over 8.

SHOTTLE SK3149 **Dannah Farm** *Bowmans Lane, Shottle, Belper DE56 3DR (01773) 550273 *£70,* plus special breaks; 8 rms with old pine and antiques, and some with private sitting rooms, four-posters and whirlpool baths. Carefully restored and friendly Georgian farmhouse with two comfortable sitting rooms, and popular, imaginative cooking in the attractive, no smoking dining room; calves, ducks, hens, lambs in spring, Vietnamese pot-bellied pigs, farm dogs and cats; cl 25 Dec; children over 10.

To see and do

DERBYSHIRE Family Attraction of the Year

✲ ❀ ⚄ MATLOCK BATH SK2958 **Heights of Abraham Country Park** Derbyshire is full of stunning show caverns, and though some might excite geologists more than this well organised place, few are as good for families, and none can boast as thrilling an introduction as the one here: cable cars whisk you up from the Derwent Valley to a 60-acre country park, with dramatic views over the ancient limestone gorge (not to mention a railway and the busy A6). At the end of the 5-minute trip a multi-media show explains how the rock was formed 325 million years ago, then guides escort you into the two show caverns themselves. Displays are well thought out and instructive, and the caves atmospherically lit to create a suitably mysterious feel. One cavern used to be a lead mine, so has models and tableaux illustrating how 16th-c miners struggled to work by candlelight. Outside are nature trails, the Prospect Tower to climb, dinosaur displays, and a few play areas (including a maze), as well as great views and nicely laid out woodland walks. They usually have Punch and Judy shows or similar entertainments, and there's a choice of places to eat – though the picnic areas fit in better with the natural tone. Most people spend around 2½ hours here before taking the cable car back down (check the times on the last one if you're visiting in the afternoon), though it's quite possible to stretch it out longer. Children might not take in all the information, but enjoy the combination of cable car, caves, and space to run around; the very young probably won't get as much out of it. You can visit the caverns without going on the cable car – though it really does add to the overall appeal. Don't forget it's never as warm underground as it is on the surface, so even on sunny days you may be glad of a jumper. Meals, snacks, shop, some disabled access; open most wknds from mid-Feb–Easter (best to check first as dates can depend on the weather), then daily Easter–Oct; (01629) 582365; £6.20 (£4.10 children).

ALKMONTON SK1838

☛ Bentley Fields Open Farm Unspoilt traditional livestock farm stretching over 245 acres; they milk their cows at 1pm and 4pm. In spring you may see calving or lambing – or chicks pecking their way out of their eggs. Teas, shop, some disabled access; open daily Easter wk and May half-term, bank hol Suns and Mons, but best to phone to check (01335) 330240; £2. The Holly Bush over at Church Broughton is quite handy for lunch.

ASHBOURNE SK1846

✝ 🏛 A good few interesting Georgian buildings in the streets off the hillside market place, especially leading to its elegantly proportioned **church**, which has a famous white marble statue of a sleeping child. The Gingerbread Shop sells the town's long-standing speciality. Smiths Tavern and the White Lion are good for lunch. The B5056 towards Bakewell and B5053 to Wirksworth have characteristic views. You can hire

bicycles by the half-day or day from Ashbourne Cycle Hire, Mapleton Lane, Ashbourne.

⌂ Carsington Water Britain's newest reservoir is beginning to tone into the landscape; good visitor centre, water sports, walks, cycling, etc. New café, shop, disabled access; cl 25 Dec; (01629) 540696; car park charge, £1.50 all day.

🏛 Derwent Crystal Centre (Shaw Croft) Quality glassworks and engravers, with demonstrations (am wkdys) and factory shop. Disabled access; cl winter Suns, 25–26 Dec, 1 Jan; (01335) 345219; free.

⌂ Tissington Trail This path for walkers and cyclists follows a disused railway track from Ashbourne up to Parsley Hay on the A515, where it joins the similar High Peak Trail from Buxton to near Cromford. You can hire cycles in Ashbourne, or from Parsley Hay Cycle Hire, Parsley Hay. This has a particularly interesting finale from

Middleton Top engine house (cycle hire here, too) to High Peak Junction, dipping down a great incline past old engine houses to reach the Cromford Canal.

ASHFORD IN THE WATER
SK1969

★ One of the area's more appealing villages.

BAKEWELL SK2168

Away from the traffic this is a civilised small town, especially around the church. You can still get those raspberry tarts here, though there has been some dispute over the original recipe – two shops have claimed rights to the authentic Bakewell Pudding, and the case even went to court. The Castle Hotel and Aitch's are useful for lunch.

🏠 🎱 ❄ **Haddon Hall** One of the most perfectly preserved medieval manor houses in England, still with its 12th-c painted chapel, 14th-c kitchen, and banqueting hall with minstrels' gallery. Some rooms can seem rather bare (there aren't many furnishings or pictures), but a bright spot is Rex Whistler's painting of the house in the silver-panelled long gallery. It's a particularly pretty location in summer when the long, terraced rose gardens are in full bloom. Several films and TV adaptations have had scenes shot here in recent years. Meals, snacks, shop; cl Fri–Sun in Oct, and Nov–Mar; (01629) 812855; £5.50. The Lathkil Hotel up in Over Haddon is good for lunch, and nearby roads have attractive views.

⛏T **Magpie Mine** (3m W of Bakewell) Surface remains of a mine last worked in 1958 and stabilised in the 1970s give a good idea of a 19th-c lead mine; free.

⛏ **Old House Museum** (Cunningham Pl) The future of this folk collection in the 16th-c former home of pioneer industrialist Richard Arkwright (still with its original wattle-and-daub interior walls and open-timbered chambers) was in jeopardy as we went to press. Tel (01629) 813165 for details.

BERESFORD DALE SK1259

⛰ Not so popular as the downstream parts of Dove Dale (of which this is an upstream continuation), this wooded section rewards walkers with a real sense of peace, even though it's easily reached from the B5054 between

Hulme End and Hartington.

BIRCHOVER SK2362

⛰ 🏠 ❄ The starting-point for an extraordinary walk over **Stanton Moor**, where among quarry workings and prehistoric burial mounds are the Nine Ladies stone circle, a folly tower and a huge boulder known as the Cork Stone, equipped with metal steps for the courageous and adorned with at least four centuries' worth of graffiti (the earliest we found was 1613); there are good views into Darley Dale from the edge of the escarpment. Behind the Druid Inn in Birchover are **Rowtor Rocks**, a gritstone outcrop into which one Rev Eyre cut steps, benches and a stone armchair for contemplation.

BOLSOVER SK4770

🏰 **Bolsover Castle** 📷 The original ruined castle dates back to the 12th c, but was rebuilt in 1613 as a spectacular mock castle – about 200 years ahead of this fashion. Battlements and turrets outside, and inside allegorical frescoes, fine panelling and ornate fireplaces; new visitor centre. Snacks, shop, some disabled access; cl winter Mon and Tues, 24–26 Dec; (01246) 823349; £4, inc Walkman tour. Just on the other side of the M1 at Sutton Scarsdale (and in fact looking down on the motorway), the ruins of a once-grand 17th-c hall are quite evocative.

BRADBOURNE SK2152

★ ✝ Appealing Dales village, with an ancient Saxon cross outside its Norman church.

BUXTON SK0572

Much changed, but it still has some handsome buildings dating from its days as a flourishing spa, with Georgian terraces (the Crescent is a noble Georgian streetscape) and a restored Edwardian opera house. St Ann's Well is the only direct reminder of its water-based heyday – you can take the water for free here (it's naturally warm). Many of the grander buildings come back to life during the town's excellent annual festival. The Columbine (Hall Bank) is good for lunch.

⛏ 🖼 **Buxton Museum & Art Gallery** (Terrace Rd) A useful introduction to the area; shop, disabled access; cl Mon (exc bank hols) and winter Sun, 25 Dec and 1 Jan; £1.

△ ❋ **Grin Low Woods** (just S of Buxton) Well landscaped, with mature woodland and the Victorian folly of Solomon's Temple (good views from the top), though it's not always open.

🕏 △ **Poole's Cavern** (Buxton Country Park, Green Lane) The best show cave in the Peak District and the longest in Britain, a spectacular natural limestone cavern in 100 acres of woodland, with well lit stalactites and stalagmites, and exhibitions on caves, woodland and the Romans. As in other caverns, wrap up well. Snacks, shop, limited disabled access; cl Nov–Feb; (01298) 26978; £4.20.

CALKE SK3722

🏠 ❀ **Calke Abbey** One of the most rewarding NT properties in Britain, an unusual baroque mansion still in pretty much the same state as when the last baronet died here in 1924. You might expect the splendidly decorated rooms with their fascinating displays (inc an extensive natural history collection), but it's quite a surprise to find the more dilapidated corridors and areas where family possessions were just bundled together in heaps. This gives you a better appreciation of how the abbey was a much-loved family home – and of how things forgotten in the attic can quickly become social history. Also extensive wooded parkland and walled gardens. Meals, snacks, shop, disabled access; cl Thurs, Fri, and Nov–Mar, house cl am; (01332) 863822; £5, garden only £2.30 – there's a £2.50 vehicle charge on entering the park, refundable on entry to the house (which has a timed ticket system); NT. The Hardinge Arms at Kings Newton is

quite handy for lunch.

CASTLETON SK1582

★ 🏚 ❋ ⌂ Very much geared to visitors, and filled with walkers and cavers in summer; plenty of cafés, and shops selling expensive worked pieces of the Blue John fluorspar that's found only in the nearby mine workings. The village's attractive dark stone buildings (one of the most impressive now a youth hostel) are dominated by the ruins of **Peveril Castle**, built high above in the 11th c – magnificent views. Shop, snacks; cl Mon and Tues from Nov–Mar, 24–26 Dec and 1 Jan; (01433) 620613; £2; EH. The Rose Cottage, Castle, Olde Nags Head and Peak all do decent food, and in the pretty nearby village of Hope the Cheshire Cheese is good. The B6061 to Sparrowpit (where the Wanted Inn has good-value home cooking) has fine views. The most varied **walks** in the High Peak are found around Castleton and Hope. The great walk here takes in Castleton, the Lose Hill/Mam Tor ridge, the caves, and Winnats Pass; Mam Tor is so shaly and prone to landslips that it's dubbed the Shivering Mountain – the abandoned section of the A625 is a testament to the victory of the mountain over man. Cave Dale is an optional side trip from the back of Castleton. Quarrying has had an unfortunate effect on the local landscape in the area, and limits walks further afield, though there are some pleasant walks to be had in the gentler high pastures of the limestone country to the south.

🕏 **Blue John Cavern & Mine** (Buxton Rd) Containing 8 of the 14

Days Out

Tram treat: Cromford village (or in spring/early summer Lea Gardens); lunch at the Boat, Cromford; Crich Tramway Museum.

Heights and depths: Matlock Bath, for Riber Castle Wildlife Park and Heights of Abraham (inc cable car); riverside lunch at the Midland, Matlock Bath; Peak District Mining Museum, Temple Mine, Peak Rail (see *Darley Dale*).

Aristocratic eye-catcher: Chatsworth House and Gardens; lunch at the Devonshire Arms, Beeley; Edensor village; stroll by the River Derwent in Chatsworth estate.

known veins of Blue John, this has been the main source of the precious stone for nearly 300 years. It's an impressive example of a water-worn cave, over a third of a mile long, with chambers 150ft high. Snacks, shop; cl 25 Dec, 1 Jan; (01433) 620638; £5.

☺ **Peak Cavern** Right in the village, this is the biggest natural cavern in the county and really does seem huge – the entrance hall is so large it used to house an entire village. From there it's a half-mile walk along lighted subterranean passageways to the Great Cave, 45 by 27 metres (150ft wide, 90ft long). By the time you reach the Devil's Dining Room you'll be nearly 140 metres (450ft) underground. Snacks, shop; cl wkdys Nov–Easter (exc school hols); (01433) 620285; £4.75.

☺ ⛴ **Speedwell Cavern** (Winnats Pass – former A625 W of Castleton) Very atmospheric former lead mine, with 105 steps down to a half-mile underground boat trip along floodlit passages, finishing up in a cathedral of a cavern with an impressive 'bottomless pit'. Good fun, though you may have to queue. Shop, snacks; (01433) 620512; cl 25 Dec; £5.25.

☺ **Treak Cliff Cavern** (off former A625 W) Informative tours of the first Blue John mine, worked since 1750, with rich veins of the mineral and quite staggering stalactites and stalagmites. Well placed lights create spooky shapes and atmospheric shadows. The entrance is narrow, and it's quite steep, but readers prefer this to many of the other caverns nearby. They're developing a visitor centre and workshop. Snacks, shop; cl 25 Dec, but worth checking for other times; (01433) 620571; £4.99.

CHAPEL-EN-LE-FRITH SK0580
✦ ✤ **Chestnut Centre** 🖾 (A625) Warmly recommended conservation park, concerned especially with breeding otters and barn owls, but other animals and birds of prey too. Good observation platforms. Snacks, shop; cl wkdys Jan and Feb; (01298) 814099; £4.50. The Cross Keys has decent food (all day Sun).

CHATSWORTH SK2669
🏠🖾🌸❗🐾 **Chatsworth House & Gardens** (off B6012) Splendidly grand home of the Duke and Duchess of Devonshire, prettily set on the banks of the River Derwent. Sumptuously furnished, the 17 rooms on display show off a superb collection of fine arts, inc paintings by Rembrandt and Van Dyck, and all sorts of intriguing decorative details. The gardens cover over 100 acres and are full of surprises, with a maze, and brass bands playing on summer Sunday afternoons. The surrounding park was landscaped by Capability Brown. Also a farmyard (milking at 3.30pm) and elaborate adventure playground. Meals, snacks, shops, garden centre; disabled access to garden only; cl Nov–mid-Mar; (01246) 582204; £6.50 house and garden, £3.75 garden only, and £3.20 for just the farmyard and adventure playground. Also in the grounds, at Stud Farm, 1½m from the house towards Pilsley, is one of England's best farm shops, and the estate village of Edensor opposite the main gate is a marvellous mix of styles, with fine views from the lane leading up out of it. Around Chatsworth, two more most attractive small estate villages are Baslow and Beeley (the former has a good food pub). The B6012 (busy in summer) has pleasant views.

CHESTERFIELD SK3871
✝🛏🕸 ◠ ⚓ Not a tourist town, but its largely 14th-c **church** has a really striking leaning spire, and is a rich building inside; the **town museum** (Corporation St) has the full angle on it; cl Weds and Sun. The Victorian market hall has flourishing indoor and outdoor markets every day exc Sun (junk Thurs, street entertainment summer Sats). Nearby **Grassmoor Country Park** is a pleasant place to stroll; also has fishing lake. The Derby Tup (Sheffield Rd) is an enjoyable ale house with good-value simple food.

CRESWELL CRAGS SK5374
◠ 🐦 Beside Crags Pond, these form the basis of a short but attractive there-and-back walk through woodland.

CRICH SK3554
🚋 **National Tramway Museum** 🖾 A favourite of many correspondents: lovingly restored vintage trams from all over the British Isles and beyond, many of them in working order and running

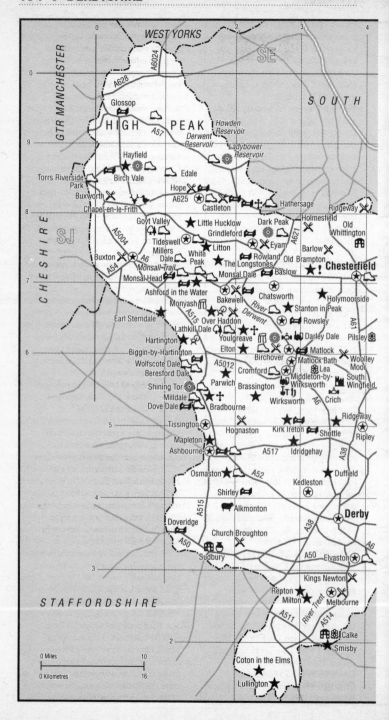

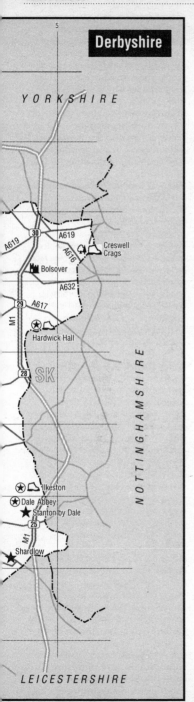

along a one-mile period street overlooking the Derwent Valley. Unlimited rides on the vehicles, and very good indoor exhibitions and an indoor play area. They have a guide book in Braille. Meals, snacks, shop, some disabled access; open daily Apr–Oct, and Sun only Nov–Mar; (01773) 852565; £6.50. The Derwent over at Whatstandwell on the A6 has good-value food. The village is pronounced 'Cry', not 'Critch', and is the setting for TV's *Peak Practice*.

CROMFORD SK2956

🏛️ 🛶 ⚓ ❄️ Good example of an 18th-c cotton-milling village, little developed after its original building, and rewarding to stroll through. Carefully preserved North St is the first true industrial street in the world (built in 1777). The restored **canal** is a quiet and attractive early Industrial Revolution setting, with a restored steam-powered pumping house and a fine aqueduct over the river; pleasant walks along here, and horse-drawn barge trips in summer; branching off at Roystone Grange is an archaeological trail. The Boat has well priced food. The A5012 to Grangemill gives evocative views.

🚂 🐾 **Cromford Mill** (Mill Lane) Richard Arkwright established the world's first successful water-powered cotton mill here in 1771 – the true beginning of the factory age; several craft shops. Wholefood restaurant, shop, limited disabled access; cl 25 Dec; (01629) 825776; site free, tours £2.

🚂 **High Peak Junction Workshops** Oldest surviving railway workshops in the world. The visitor centre includes exhibitions and a film. Snacks, shop, disabled access; cl winter wkdys; 50p.

DALE ABBEY SK4338

🏰 ✝️ ★ Abbey ruins, Hermit's Cave and the remarkable All Saints Church, part of which was formerly the village inn; the Carpenters Arms has good-value food, and the village is attractive.

DARK PEAK SK2575

❄️ 🛶 The eastern edges include the abrupt ramparts of Curbar Edge and Froggatt Edge, popular with rock-climbers and easily accessible from the road. Birchen Edge and Wellington's Monument are obvious objectives for walkers from the Robin Hood at Curbar.

DARLEY DALE SK2663

🐴 **Carriage Museum** 🖼 (Red House Stables) Collection of vehicles and equipment, some of which you can ride in. Also horse and pony rides – booking essential. Teas, disabled access; cl 25 Dec; (01629) 733583; £2.50.

🚂 **Peak Rail** 🖼 Blooming private railway, very popular with readers. Trains run between here and Matlock, then on to Rowsley. The eventual aim is to run as far as Buxton. Wknd restaurant car, shop, disabled access; usually open wknds all year (not Sat in depths of winter), plus most days in summer hols, but best to check times; (01629) 580381; £5. The Grouse (A6 N) is handy for a snack.

DERBY SK3536

A big busy city, but not too daunting for a visitor to penetrate, and has several things worth visiting; it's got far more open spaces than you'd expect, and a pedestrianised centre.

✝ ❋ **Derby Cathedral** The 16th-c tower is the second highest in the country; the rest of the building was replaced in the 18th c. Bess of Hardwick is buried in the vaults, and there's a delightful early Georgian screen. Shop, disabled access; £2 suggested donation. The quaint nearby Olde Dolphin (Queen St) has bargain food all day.

🍴 🖼 **Derby Museum & Art Gallery** (The Strand) Stands out for its collections of porcelain and the paintings of local artist Joseph Wright; shop, disabled access; cl Sun, Christmas period; free.

🏛 ☁ **Heritage Centre** (St Peter's churchyard) Once a Tudor grammar school, ghost walks through the city's tunnels and other themed tours leave here (and from the Old Gaol, Friargate) 7pm in summer; booking essential on (01332) 299321. Centre cl Sun and bank hols; free.

⚙ **Industrial Museum** (Full St) Warmly praised by some readers, this restored early 18th-c silk mill and adjacent flour mill has probably the world's finest collection of Rolls-Royce aero engines, and a Power Gallery with lots of hands-on displays. Shop, disabled access; cl am Sun and bank hols, 25–28 Dec, 1 Jan; (01332) 255308; free. The nearby Old Silk Mill is a decent pub,

open all day.

🏠 **Pickfords House Museum** (Friargate) Gives a very good idea of 18th-c domestic life, with period furnished rooms and Georgian garden. Shop, some disabled access; cl 25 Dec and maybe Sun; phone (01332) 255363 to check; free.

🖼 **Queen Street Gallery** (Queen St) City centre gallery showing contemporary visual art, photography and new media; shop, disabled access; open pm Weds–Fri and all Sat; (01332) 385601; free.

🏺 **Royal Crown Derby** (Osmaston Rd) Cheerfully informative tours of a bone-china factory, celebrating 250 years of porcelain production with a series of events and activities throughout the year. A visitor centre traces the industry's development from its origins. Snacks, shop (lots of bargain seconds); visitor centre open daily, but no tours wknds, bank hols or during factory shut-down weeks; (01332) 712800; £5.50 (£2.50 without tour) – no children under 10 on tours.

DOVE DALE SK1452

☁ Shared between Derbyshire and Staffordshire, with the River Dove as the boundary, this is the most popular of all the dales. Partly wooded, it has a beautifully varied mixture of water, trees and pastures, and is lined with crags and curiously shaped outcrops of rock. To see fewer people, head further upstream. Handy nearby refreshment places are the Okeover Arms at Mapleton (with a domed church, and a nice riverside walk to Thorpe), the Coach & Horses at Fenny Bentley and (to be found on the Staffordshire side) the Izaak Walton Hotel nr Ilam (cosier inside than it looks from out).

EDALE SK1285

☁ Famous as the start of the 256-mile Pennine Way to the Scottish border, with a good information centre and a couple of hikers' pubs. It tends to be packed with expectant long-distance walkers on Sun mornings. For a taste of the Dark Peak proper, this can be the start for half-day walks that quite quickly take you up through the stone-walled pastures of the valley on to the edge of the dark plateau above. The track signed as the alternative Pennine

Way route up Jacob's Ladder is easier to find, and has more to see, than the official Pennine Way plod across a huge blanket bog.

ELVASTON SK4032

✿ ⌂ 🗀 🐾 **Elvaston Castle Country Park** (B5010) 200 acres of lovely 19th-c landscaped parkland, with formal and old English gardens, wooded walks, and wildfowl on the ornamental lake. Also a museum with traditional craft workshops, and nature trails. Meals, snacks, shop, disabled access; open all year, but museum cl Mon, Tues, am Weds–Sat and Nov–Apr; (01332) 571342; museum £1.30, car park 70p wkdys, £1.30 wknds. Shardlow is convenient for lunch.

EYAM SK2276

★ † Attractive secluded village with a dark past: in the Great Plague sick villagers confined themselves here for fear of infecting people outside – plaques record who died where, and stones on the village edge mark where money was disinfected. The Miners Arms is very good for lunch. Just up the B6521 at Upper Padley, **Padley Chapel** is an interesting 15th-c revival, effectively restored in 1933.

🏠 🐾 **Eyam Hall** 🖭 Sturdy-looking 17th-c manor house, still very much a family home, with furniture, portraits and tapestries, fine Jacobean staircase and an impressive stone-flagged hall. Small craft centre in the stables. Meals, snacks, shop, some disabled access; house open Weds, Thurs, Sun and bank hols Jun–Aug, craft centre open daily exc Mon; (01433) 631976; *£4 – timed ticket system.

GOYT VALLEY SK1077

⛲ ⌂ The well wooded valley with its three miles of reservoirs is a man-made landscape, but nonetheless charming for walks or picnics; reached off the A54 W of Buxton.

HARDWICK HALL SK4463

🏠 ✿ 🏛 ✕ ⌂ The marriages of the redoubtable Bess of Hardwick couldn't necessarily be described as happy but she certainly did very well out of them, the fourth leaving her enough money to build this triumphant Elizabethan prodigy house. The beautifully symmetrical towers are crowned with the monogram ES, and there's an amazing expanse of glass (her sight was dimming). Also fine tapestries and needlework, a large park, and gardens laid out in a walled courtyard. Heritage-funding will pay for restoration of the huge and ancient Gideon tapestries (which run the length of the 167-ft Long Gallery), a silk canopy and the garden wall, as well as a garden history exhibition in the gazebo; guided walks to stone mason's yard (Weds, Thurs at 1, 2 and 3.30pm). Meals, snacks, shop, disabled access; open pm Apr–Oct, house cl all Mon (exc bank hols), Tues and Fri; (01246) 850430; £1.50 vehicle charge to enter the grounds; £6 house and garden, £3 garden only, operating on a timed ticket; NT. Not far from this 'new' house is the shell of Hardwick Old Hall, the first house that Bess built; (01246) 850431; £2.50 (NT members free). A joint ticket is available for both houses (£7.90). Also on the estate is a restored watermill (another £1.60, NT). The park is attractive for walks, and at the end of it the Hardwick Inn, also NT-owned, is useful for lunch.

HARTINGTON SK1260

★ 🐾 This attractive village has a good cheese shop selling local Stilton, and a pottery on Mill Lane.

HATHERSAGE SK2281

† ⌂ Charlotte Brontë wrote *Jane Eyre* here. The **church** is the legendary site of Little John's grave. It's a good village for walkers and climbers, with fine walks inc the attractive moorland, pastures and woodland making up Longshaw, nr the Fox House Inn up on the Sheffield road; or, closer and gentler, down along the River Derwent towards Grindleford. Besides the George, the Plough (A622) is useful for lunch. The B6001 S is a pleasant drive.

HAYFIELD SK0387

★ ⌂ ❀ This moorland village and its attractive nearby smaller sister Little Hayfield have good walks around them, both up towards Kinder Scout and to the Lantern Pike viewpoint in the opposite direction. There's also a popular walk or cycle ride – the **Sett Valley Trail** – along a hillside former railway to New Mills, looking down on the mill buildings by the River Sett. There's a handy bike shop in Hayfield itself, and an information centre for the trail. The Lantern Pike Inn in Little Hayfield could hardly be more welcoming.

HIGH PEAK SK1092

⌂ These dark moors are one of England's great wildernesses. But they have few easy circular routes, are largely very bleak indeed, and often consist of private grouse moor with no right of public access. The car park at the top of Snake Pass (A57 Glossop–Hathersage) is nr the centre of the biggest of the National Trust's moorland holdings here, giving free access to the miles of Hope Woodlands (there aren't actually many trees).

ILKESTON SK4642

☺ **American Adventure Theme Park** (Pit Lane) Excellent theme park with around 100 rides and attractions; all supposedly have an American theme, though this can be rather tenuous – ever so English Sooty stars in a Wild West show. Highlights include dropping 13 metres (42ft) at 62mph on the Nightmare Niagara triple log flume, and the Missile, a stomach-churning roller-coaster that twists and turns at unfeasible angles, before going the whole route again backwards. Live shows include a Wild West saloon and a Mexican fiesta, and there's a huge indoor play area for younger children; some extra charges for go-karts, crazy golf and so on. Meals, snacks, shops, good disabled access; cl Nov–Mar; (01773) 531521; £12.99.

❀ ⚲ ⌂ **Shipley Country Park** (off A6007) Medieval estate landscaped in the 18th c, with 600 acres of woodland, lakes and fields. A pleasant place to wander, with railway lines transformed into leafy walkways; you can hire bikes (daily July–Aug, wknds Easter–Nov, £4 for 2 hours). Snacks, shop, disabled access; visitor centre cl 25 Dec; (01773) 719961; free.

KEDLESTON SK3041

🏠 🖼 ♿ ❀ **Kedleston Hall** 🆔 This 18th-c Palladian mansion is thought by many to be the finest example of Robert Adam's work – it's certainly the least altered. Interesting objets d'art, original furnishings, good collection of paintings, and a museum of items collected by Lord Curzon when he was Viceroy of India. Adam designed a

charming boathouse and bridge in the park outside, which also has extensive formal gardens with marvellous rhododendrons, and long woodland walks. Meals, snacks, shop, disabled access (best to phone in advance); open Apr–Oct, house pm Sat–Weds, grounds daily plus wknds Nov–Dec; (01332) 842191; £4.90, £2.10 grounds only; NT. We've had no suggestion of a closer place for lunch than the Black Cow at Lees, beyond the A52.

LADYBOWER RESERVOIR SK1788

⌂ ❄ Pretty enough to drive past; also the lane up to the car park by the Derwent Reservoir (with a summer minibus service beyond to Howden Reservoir) gives plenty of easy waterside-forest **walking** on the relatively sheltered stone-walled slopes of the upper parts of Derwent Dale, with access to the higher moors for better views – for example, up on to Win Hill, or on a kind day on to the formidable Derwent Moors to the E. The Ladybower pub down on the main road is useful.

LATHKILL DALE SK1865

⚲ ⌂ Charming combination of woods, steep pastures and well weathered signs of old mines; its short tributary Bradford Dale is also very attractive for walks.

LEA SK3257

❀ **Lea Gardens** Beautiful woodland gardens with rhododendrons inc rare species and cultivars, azaleas and rock plants. Home-baked snacks, shop and garden centre, some disabled access; open 20 Mar–4 July; (01629) 534380; £3.

THE LONGSTONES SK1871

★ Little Longstone and nearby Great Longstone are charming, steep, stone-built villages, and the back road from Baslow through here to Tideswell is a pretty drive.

MATLOCK SK3060

⚘ 🏰 ❄ **Riber Castle Wildlife Park** (off A615 at Tansley) Specialising in rare breeds and endangered species of birds and animals (it's renowned for its lynx), a 25-acre park set high up on Riber Hill in the grounds of ruined Riber Castle. Excellent views; you find yourself looking down on the Heights of

Abraham. Wrap up well – even in summer the wind can make it feel rather chilly. Café, shop, disabled access; cl 25 Dec; (01629) 582073; £5. The Boat House is good value for lunch, with interesting walks. The A615 E and B5056 and B5057 W are nice drives.

MATLOCK BATH SK2958

🐧 ❄ Pleasantly busy place, with lots to do. A spectacular wooded cliff looks across the lower roadside town to pastures by the Derwent; up the side of the gorge, quiet lanes climb steeply past 18th- and 19th-c villas. The Temple Hotel (Temple Walk) has great views and decent food.

☺ **Gulliver's Kingdom & Royal Cave** (1m S of Matlock Bath, off A6) Family theme park with chair lift and hectic rides, cave tour, and cowboy and ghost towns; it's aimed at the under-12s so don't expect white knuckles. Meals, snacks, shops; open wknds and school hols Easter–Oct; (01629) 580540; £5.80.

🐧 ❄ 🐧 **Heights of Abraham Country Park** See separate family panel on p.150.

♪ **Matlock Bath Aquarium & Hologram** A useful family attraction if you're staying in the area; cl winter wkdys; £1.80.

⛏ **Peak District Mining Museum** (Temple Rd) Lively exploration of mining, with a unique early 19th-c water-pressure pumping engine, and interactive display on the pitfalls of working in a mine. Also tours of the old Temple Mine workings, and the chance to pan for minerals – in the past they've even found a tiny amount of gold. Snacks, shop, disabled access; cl 25 Dec; (01629) 583834; £2.50, joint ticket inc mine tours £4.

MELBOURNE SK3825

★ † This pleasant small town has a good, relaxed feel and villagey lanes; the White Swan and Railway Hotel are good for lunch. The **Church of St Michael and St Mary** is impressive, more like a cathedral than an ordinary parish church.

🏛 🐝 ✿ **Melbourne Hall** Behind its 18th-c façade, this grandly extended house dates back in part to the 13th c, and has twice been the home of British prime ministers; fine pictures and

furnishings. Glorious formal gardens with fountains, pools, and famous yew tunnel; interesting craft centre (open all year). Meals, snacks, shop, disabled access; Hall open pm daily in Aug (exc first 3 Mons), plus gardens open pm Weds, Sat, Sun and bank hol Mons Apr–Sept; (01332) 862502; £2.50 (with gardens, £4.50).

MIDDLETON-BY-WIRKSWORTH SK2756

🚂 **Middleton Top Engine House** Home to a beam engine built in 1829 to haul waggons up a steep incline on the Cromford & High Peak Railway. Snacks, shop, disabled access; engine in motion first wknd of month and bank hol wknds; cl wkdys Oct–Mar; (01629) 823204; £1. The Knockerdown Inn out on the B5035 is pleasant for lunch.

MILLDALE SK1354

⛰ This section of Dove Dale has barer pastures and steeper hillsides than the lower sections – but fewer other walkers to keep you company. Handy refreshment places on the Staffordshire side of the river are the Watts Russell Arms at Hopedale and the George at Alstonefield.

MILLERS DALE SK1573

⛰ The B6049 N off the A6 SE of Buxton gives access to Millers Dale, just past the little village of that name (the Anglers Rest is a decent pub); upstream of Monsal Dale, this is rather less visited but also a lovely spot for walks – as is its continuation, Chee Dale.

MONSAL DALE SK1771

⛰ This winding valley is the outstanding place for walks in this central part of the White Peak area, its pastoral quality emphasised by the disused limestone cotton mills along the way. It's especially lovely in May and June with wild flowers enriching the pastures along the broader stretches. Don't expect to have it to yourself. There's good access from the A6, a couple of miles towards Buxton from Ashford in the Water; and from Monsal Head (handy hotel), where a disused railway viaduct adds interest. This viaduct forms part of the Monsal Trail.

MONSAL TRAIL SK1172

⛰ This outshines the other former railway-track walks in the Peak District, though like them is in parts more exposed to the winds than walks down in the dales. It runs from Wye Dale E of Buxton to Coombs Road viaduct S of Bakewell. W of Millers Dale Station, the trail leaves the old railway and takes a stepping-stone route along the river beneath the towering cliffs of Chee Tor, before rejoining the railway track.

MONYASH SK1566
🏠 Quiet village with good-value home cooking at the Bull's Head, and (2m S) the mysterious **Arbor Low stone circle**.

OLD BRAMPTON SK3371
★ ! The village itself is attractive, and has one special curiosity: count the minutes between one and two o'clock on its church clock.

OLD WHITTINGTON SK3874
🏠 **Revolution House** (High St) Innocuous-looking thatched cottage, 300 years ago the birthplace of what came to be known as the Glorious Revolution. Good audio-visual display, period rooms and furniture. Shop, disabled access to ground floor only; open Good Fri–Oct and last 2 wks in Dec (exc 25–26); (01246) 453554; free. The White Horse is useful for lunch.

OSMASTON SK2043
★ 🖎 This village of pretty thatched cottages has a pleasant path through a lakeside park.

OVER HADDON SK2066
★ 🌿 **Lathkill Dale Craft Centre** (Manor Farm) Set in a pretty village, this has plenty of craft shops and demonstrations. Café, disabled access; cl 25 Dec; (01629) 813589; free.

PILSLEY SK4264
❀ **Herb Garden** Big main garden with lots of herbs and old English roses, smaller gardens specialising in rare medicinal herbs, pot-pourri or lavender. Meals, snacks, shop, disabled access; cl Tues and mid-Sept–mid-Mar; (01246) 854268; £1. Pilsley itself is a charming village.

RIPLEY SK3947
🏭 **Denby Pottery Visitor Centre** (B6179 S of Ripley) Guided factory tours (10.30am and 1pm – not Fri or wknds; booking essential) show the intricate skills of potters and craftsmen. Big factory shop, and children's play area. Meals, snacks, shop, disabled access; cl 25–26 Dec; (01773) 743644;

full tours £3.75, otherwise £2.75.

🚂🚆 **Midland Railway Centre** 🖼 (Butterley Station) Regular steam-train passenger service through country park, and a developing railway museum. Meals, snacks, shop, disabled access; cl 25 Dec; best to ring for train timetable, (01773) 570140; £7.95 (£8.95 bank hols). It's good for families – not only are there a few farm animals on the adjacent farm (you can visit here free without having to go on the railway), but two children are admitted free with every adult ticket during special events. The Excavator on the A610 out at Buckland Hollow is a good-value family dining pub.

RIVER DERWENT SK2666
🖎 You can walk along pleasant stretches where Izaak Walton fished, either upstream from Rowsley, or from the B6012 N of there at the Calton Lees car park – there's open access to Chatsworth Park on this W side of the river, which is particularly lovely.

RIVER TRENT SK3427
This impresses with its silent power – perhaps Britain's most formidable river. Ingleby is one good access point – for example, from the big garden of the John Thompson pub, which brews its own beer.

ROWSLEY SK2566
✕ 🌿 🏠 **Caudwell's Mill & Craft Centre** Working 19th-c flour mill, powered by water turbines, with crafts such as glass-blowing and wood-turning. Meals, snacks, shop; cl wkdys Jan; (01629) 734374; mill *£3, craft centre free. Rowsley also has an interesting **stone circle** called the Nine Ladies. The Grouse & Claret does decent food (all day wknds).

SHARDLOW SK4430
★ **Shardlow Canal Basin** Attractive, with some handsome former wharf buildings – one now an antique warehouse, another, the Malt Shovel, a good pub.

SHINING TOR SK1454
🖎 ❀ A breezy but undemanding moorland walk from the summit of a minor road.

SOUTH WINGFIELD SK3754
🏰 **Wingfield Manor** (B5035) Substantial ruin with virtually complete banqueting hall, tower and undercroft.

The 16th-c Babington Plot is thought to have been hatched here, leading to the final downfall of Mary, Queen of Scots. Used as a filming location for Zeffirelli's *Jane Eyre*. Shop, some disabled access; cl Mon and Tues, winter wkdys, 1–2pm winter, 24–26 Dec and 1 Jan; (01773) 832060; £2.95, inc Walkman tour. The White Hart at Moorwood Moor has reasonably priced food.

SUDBURY SK1632

🏛️🐚 Sudbury Hall Individual but attractive Stuart mansion with elaborate carving, frescoes, murals and plasterwork in splendidly elegant rooms; the interiors featured in the BBC's *Pride and Prejudice* as the home of Mr Darcy. It's worth a visit just for the excellent **National Trust Museum of Childhood**, which has a chimney climb for sweep-sized children. You can play with some exhibits, and at weekends the schoolroom is staffed by an Edwardian teacher. Meals, snacks, shop, disabled access (bear in mind, new car park is 400 yds from Hall); open pm Weds–Sun (and bank hol Mons) Apr–Oct, plus museum open pm wknds till Christmas; (01283) 585305; £5.70 for everything, or £3.60 house and grounds or museum only; NT. The Boar's Head Hotel is useful for lunch.

TIDESWELL SK1575

✝ ★ 🐚 ❀ The spacious 14th-c **church** is known as the Cathedral of the Peak; the village is attractive with an excellent butcher, and this is good walking country. The B6049 across Millers Dale has nice views.

TISSINGTON SK1752

★ 🏛️ ✝ The Peak District's most beautiful village, its broad main street wonderfully harmonious, with wide grass verges, handsome stone houses inc a Jacobean hall (guided tours pm Mon–Weds Jun and July; best to book (01335) 350501; £7) and interesting church. The grey stone gardener's cottage is familiar from many calendars; garden centre, decent homely café.

TORRS RIVERSIDE PARK SJ9984

🐚 This deep gorge below New Mills is a good place to potter among the ivy-covered remains of former mills and other industrial relics; the canal basin restoration has been completed over at Buxworth – the Navigation here is a

very enjoyable pub. The **Goyt Way** is a track heading N towards and beyond Marple, partly following the Peak Forest Canal – a pretty walk.

WHITE PEAK SK1572

🐚 This area, picturesquely cut by the intricate channels of the dales, has high, flat pastures with small fields of rich grassland enclosed by silvery stone walls, clusters of often very photogenic farm buildings, and small old-fashioned villages. It gives an abundance of generally gentle walking.

WIRKSWORTH SK2854

⬇️ **National Stone Centre** (Porter Lane, Middleton) Readers have been impressed by this centre, featuring 330-million-year-old tropical lagoons and limestone fossil reefs, as well as an exhibition, guided fossil trails, and, for an extra charge, activities like gem-panning or fossil-rubbing. Snacks, shop, some disabled access; cl 25 Dec; (01629) 824833; £1.80.

ⓘ **Wirksworth Heritage Centre** (Crown Yard, Market Pl) Attractive old silk and velvet mill, with displays on quarrying and local customs like well-dressing and clypping the church, and a few children's activities. Meals, snacks, shop; cl Mon (exc bank hols and mid-July–mid-Sept), Tues (exc Apr–mid-Sept), and all Dec–mid-Feb; (01629) 825225; *£2. The town boasts a lot of recently restored old buildings; the Blacks Head (Market Pl) is a useful local pub.

WOLFSCOTE DALE SK1357

🐚 One of the quieter sections of Dove Dale, its dramatic rocky gorge and still trout pools are best reached on foot from Hartington, where the Devonshire Arms and Minton House are both reliable hotels.

YOULGREAVE SK2164

★✝ A charming dales village, with an interesting church.

★ **Other attractive villages** include Brassington SK2354, Coton in the Elms SK2415, Duffield SK3443, Earl Sterndale SK0967, Elton SK2261, Holymoorside SK3469, Idridgehay SK2849, Kirk Ireton SK2650, Little Hucklow SK1678, Litton SK1675, Lullington SK2513, Mapleton SK1648 (domed church, nice riverside walk to Thorpe), Milton SK3126, Parwich

SK1854, Repton SK3026, Ridgeway SK3551, Smisby SK3419, Stanton by Dale SK4638 and Stanton in Peak SK2464.

Decent country pubs perfectly placed for walkers include the Miners Arms at Milltown, Ashover SK3561 (despite quarrying), Peacock at Barlow SK3474, Robin Hood at Baslow SK2572 (handy for the ridge of Baslow Edge), King's Head at Bonsall SK2858 (very child-friendly, by the Limestone Way), Bowling Green at Bradwell SK1781 in Smalldale, Barrel on the ridge at Bretton SK2077, Church at Chelmorton SK1170, Beehive at Combs SK0478 (lovely valley), Bridge at Ford SK4080, Chequers just below Froggatt Edge SK2476, Queen Anne at Great Hucklow SK1878, Royal Oak at Millthorpe SK3276, Bull's Head at Monyash SK1566, Grouse at Nether Padley SK2577, New Napoleon by Ogston Reservoir SK3761, Little Mill nr Rowarth SK0189 (particularly for Lantern Pike), Queen's Arms at Taddington SK1472 and Bull's Head at Wardlow SK1874 (for well wooded Cressbrook Dale).

Where to eat

BAKEWELL SK2168 **Byways** *Water Lane (01629)* 812807 Olde-worlde tea-room with several separate areas, roaring log fire, well presented, good-value food from snacks to meals, and friendly staff. £3.

BAKEWELL SK2168 **Renaissance** *Bath St (01629)* 812687 Overlooking a little walled garden where fresh herbs are grown, this beamed restaurant serves imaginative French dishes inc gourmet specials and a fresh fish of the day, and delicious puddings; friendly service; cl pm Sun, Mon, first 2 wks Jan, first 2 wks Aug; disabled access. **£24.90|£5.99.**

BARLOW SK3474 **Trout** *(01742)* 890893 Refurbished dining pub with plenty of brocaded banquettes and neat tables, beamery and old-world prints, a proper pubby part and a second dining room; good, genuinely home-made food inc delicious puddings, no smoking restaurant, well kept real ales, and quick competent service. **£19.50|£5.50.**

BIRCHOVER SK2462 **Druid** *(01629)* 650302 Pleasantly remote, creeper-covered dining pub with a huge choice of very popular interesting food (best to book), well kept real ales, and friendly service; bustling little bar with big coal fire, no smoking garden room, and a spacious and airy two-storey dining extension; children under 5 must leave by 8pm; cl 25 Dec. **£25|£8.50.**

BUXTON SK0673 **Coffee Bean Café** *50 Spring Gardens (01298)* 27345 Small bustling café, long and narrow, with old tea and coffee advertisements, 15 types of coffee, all-day breakfasts, savouries and light lunches, and delicious cakes; cl evenings; disabled access. £3.95.

BUXTON SK0673 **Old Sun** *High St (01298)* 23452 Refurbished old coaching inn with several small cosy rooms leading off the central bar, open fires, low beams, comfortable leather armchairs and chesterfields, fresh flowers and carefully chosen bric-à-brac; a good choice of real ales, a dozen wines by the glass, adventurous food inc excellent puddings, and friendly staff; children until 8pm; disabled access. **£16|£6.50.**

BUXWORTH SK0282 **Navigation** *(01663)* 732072 Very welcoming extended pub by restored canal basin, with low-ceilinged rooms, plenty to look at, good fires, well kept real ales, good-value generous food, and cheerful staff; also, tables on the sunken flagstone terrace; disabled access. **£15|£5.50.**

CASTLETON SK1583 **Rose Cottage** *Cross St (01433)* 620472 Friendly village cottage with lots of summer flowering baskets, pretty garden, lunchtime home-made snacks, meals and afternoon cream teas; cl Fri, Jan; disabled access. £3.50.

CHURCH BROUGHTON SK2033 **Holly Bush** *(01283)* 585345 Neat brick village pub, nicely refurbished, with well kept real ale and good-value, home-made food in both the bar and separate dining room; disabled access. **£13|£4.**

EYAM SK2276 **Eyam Tearooms** *The Square (01433) 631274* Family-run tea-shop with sandwiches, salads and good cream teas, and lots of speciality teas; cl Mon, Dec, wkdys Nov, Jan and Feb; partial disabled access. £3.50.

EYAM SK2276 **Miners Arms** *Water Lane (01433) 630853* Carefully refurbished pub with a restful atmosphere in its three little plush beamed rooms, and interesting lunchtime food served by attentive staff, well kept ales, and decent nearby walks; bdrms; cl pm Sun, am Mon, first 2 wks Jan; disabled access. £22.90|£6.95.

HOGNASTON SK2350 **Red Lion** *(01335) 370396* Carefully renovated, open-plan, oak-beamed dining pub with a friendly welcome and relaxed atmosphere, attractive mix of candlelit tables on ancient flagstones, three open fires, a collection of teddy bears, well presented imaginative food (book at wknds), well kept real ales, and attentive staff; bdrms; cl am Mon; children over 12; disabled access. £28|£5.50.

HOLMESFIELD SK3277 **Robin Hood** *(01742) 890360* Rambling former farmhouse with open fires, a neat, extended, comfortable lounge, generous helpings of good food inc interesting daily specials, real ales, and friendly staff; enjoyable Cordwell Valley walks. £18.50|2-course lunch £4.95.

HOPE SK1783 **Cheshire Cheese** *Edale Rd (01433) 620381* 16th-c village pub with three cosy beamed rooms, each with its own coal fire, well kept real ales, a decent choice of house wines, good food (especially evenings), obliging service, and two small no smoking dining rooms; cl winter pm Sun and am Mon. £21.50|£4.95.

KINGS NEWTON SK3826 **Hardinge Arms** *(01332) 813808* Civilised friendly pub with beams, open fires and comfortable rambling rooms, popular lunchtime carvery and other enjoyable bar food, and well kept real ales; disabled access. £16|£5.95.

MELBOURNE SK3825 **Bay Tree** *4 Potter St (01332) 863358* Small, family-run cottagey restaurant, with beams and simple furnishings, carefully presented popular food (Sun lunch is booked up weeks ahead), and thoughtful relaxed service; cl am Sat, pm Sun, Mon. £40|£7.

OVER HADDON SK2066 **Lathkil** *(01629) 812501* Busy civilised pub in lovely walking spot; with open fires, beams and comfortable furnishings, good food and well kept real ales, and helpful service; cl 25 Dec; children lunchtime only. £22|£6.

RIDGEWAY SK4081 **Old Vicarage** *(0114) 247 5814* Big Victorian house in lovely gardens, with a marvellously relaxing atmosphere, cosy sitting room for pre-dinner drinks, and beautifully presented, quite exceptional cooking using home-grown produce in candlelit dining room or the light and airy less formal conservatory; cl am Sat, pm Sun, Mon; disabled access. £49|3-course Sun lunch £37.

WOOLLEY MOOR SK3661 **White Horse** *(01246) 590319* Popular old pub run by very friendly people – and much liked by locals; very good food using the best local produce, lots of daily specials, decent wines and beers, new conservatory, lovely view from garden (pleasant Ashover Valley walks), nice play area; disabled access. £15|£6.50.

Special thanks to H S Wilson, Dave and Deborah Irving, Michael and Jenny Back.

Please let us know what you think of places in the *Guide*. Use the report forms at the back of the book or simply write us a letter.

Derbyshire Calendar

Some of these dates were provisional as we went to press. Please check information with the telephone numbers provided.

Many villages here decorate their wells and springs with flower-petal pictures in annual festival well-dressings. Originally a pagan water-worshipping ceremony, this is now part of the Christian calendar. A procession led by the clergy and a blessing of the wells initiates a week of village celebrations. To avoid the crowds, go a day or two before the actual ceremony for a good close view of the elaborate flower pictures which should stay fresh for almost a week. Some of the best are at Chesterfield, Eyam, Tissington, Wirksworth and Youlgreave.

FEBRUARY

5 Ripley Diesel Gala at Midland Railway Centre – *till 6 February* (01773) 570140

19 Ripley Children's Weekend at Midland Railway Centre – *till 27 February* (01773) 570140

MARCH

7 Ashbourne Shrovetide Football Game: free-for-all between unlimited number of Up'ards and Down'ards (from above and below Henmore Brook) who compete to get the ball to goals 3 miles apart along the brook – *till 8 March* (01335) 343666

APRIL

1 Derby Celebration of the Georgian Period at Royal Crown Derby Visitors' Centre: talks, demonstrations and activities – *till 30 April* (01332) 712841

24 Chesterfield Easter Market and Entertainment inc street organ festival (01246) 207777

MAY

1 Chesterfield May Day Market and Rally (01246) 345777; **Derby** Discover the Victorian Period at Royal Crown Derby Visitors' Centre: Victorian characters, talk and demonstrations – *till 31 May* (01332) 712841

8 Chatsworth Angling Fair at Chatsworth House – *till 9 May* (01246) 565300

12 Derby Flower Festival at the Cathedral – *till 17 May* (01332) 341201

13 Chatsworth Horse Trials at Chatsworth House – *till 14 May* (01328) 830367

14 Elvaston Derbyshire County Show at Elvaston Castle Country Park (01332) 571342

27 Ashbourne Derbyshire Steam Fair at Hartington Moor Showground – *till 28 May* (01663) 732750; **Brackenfield** Well-dressings: five displays (01629) 534767; **Chester Green** Well-dressing (01332) 673210; **Middleton-by-Youlgreave** Well-dressing (one of the best) – *till 4 June* (01246) 345777; **Wirksworth** Well-dressing (one of the best) – *till 4 June* (01246) 345777

Derbyshire Calendar (cont.)

29 Bamford Sheepdog Trials (01433) 651588; **Castleton** Ancient Garland Ceremony: ancient pagan fertility ceremony with Celtic origins now encompassing Oak Apple Day – the procession stops and dances outside the six village inns (01433) 620571; **Chesterfield** Spring Bank Holiday Market and Street Entertainment (01246) 345777

JUNE

1 Derby Festival of Tea-drinking at the Royal Crown Derby Visitors' Centre – *till 30 June* (01332) 712841; **Tissington** Well-dressing (one of the best) – *till 6 June* (01283) 732200
17 Ashford in the Water Well-dressing – *till 21 June* (01629) 813005

JULY

1 Derby Festival of Floral Art: displays, talks and demonstrations – *till 31 July* (01332) 712841; **Elvaston** Steam Rally at Elvaston Castle Country Park – *till 2 July* (01332) 773548; **Glossop** Carnival and Country Fair at Manor Park – *till 2 July* (01457) 868996
5 Derby Beer Festival – *till 9 July* (01332) 729128
12 Buxton Festival and Fringe – *till 23 July* (01298) 70395; **Buxton** Well-dressing – *till 17 July* (01298) 25106
25 Chesterfield Medieval Market and Street Entertainment (01246) 345777
28 Buxton Gilbert and Sullivan Festival: competition, masterclasses, costumed parade – *till 20 August* (01298) 72190
29 Buxton Jazz Festival inc parade – *till 30 July* (01625) 528336

AUGUST

1 Derby Discover or Revisit Post-War Britain inc street party and big bands – *till 31 August* (01332) 712841
2 Bakewell Show: biggest show in the county – *till 3 August* (01629) 812736
5 Tansley Cromford Steam Rally at Highacres Farm – *till 6 August* (01629) 824263
9 Ashover Agricultural and Horticultural Show (01629) 581082
12 Ripley Garden Railway Festival at Midland Railway Centre – *till 13 August* (01773) 570140
26 Eyam Well-dressing (one of the best) with carnival (01433) 631328; **Foolow** Well-dressing – *till 2 September* (01433) 630602
27 Crich Festival of Transport at the National Tramway Museum – *till 28 August* (01773) 852565; **Eyam** Plague Commemoration Service in Cucklet Dell (01433) 630935
28 Chesterfield August Bank Holiday Market and Street Entertainment, plus evening fireworks (01246) 345777; **Hope** Show and Sheepdog Trials (01433) 620905

SEPTEMBER

2 Chatsworth Country Fair at Chatsworth House – *till 3 September* (01246) 565300; **Glossop** Victorian Weekend – *till 3 September* (01457) 855920

Derbyshire Calendar (cont.)

4 **Chesterfield** Well-dressing Demonstration at Peacock Centre Courtyard – *till 9 September* (01246) 345777

9 **Chesterfield** Well-dressing (among the best) at several locations inc Crooked Spire Church – *till 16 September* (01246) 345777

16 **Little Hayfield** Sheepdog Trials and Country Show at Spray House Farm – *till 17 September* (01663) 733644

OCTOBER

7 **Elvaston** Garden, Leisure and Craft Fair at Elvaston Castle Country Park – *till 8 October* (01332) 571342

NOVEMBER

5 **Chesterfield** Fireworks at Whittington Moor (01246) 345777/8

We welcome reports from readers

This *Guide* depends on readers' reports. Do help us if you can – in return, we offer a discount on the next edition to people who've helped us with reports for it. Tell us what you think about places already in it, and anything extra you think we should say about them. And send us your ideas for inclusion in the next edition: places to visit, eat at or stay in, attractive drives or walks, maybe even unusual interesting shops you know of. Use the card in the middle, the report forms at the end, or just write – no stamp needed: *The Good Britain Guide*, FREEPOST TN1569, Wadhurst, E Sussex TN5 7BR.

DEVON

Devon has an outstanding range of places to stay in, great scenic variety, masses of things to do and see, and some very good food. There are glorious vistas of coast and moor, lovely gardens, delightful thatched villages clustered around ancient church and equally ancient pub, some lively museums, and lots of country life. We have divided these riches into three areas: East Devon (classic family holiday country, with Exeter a charming small city); South Devon and Dartmoor (glorious scenery, the widest range of interesting places to visit – good all year); and North Devon and Exmoor (a quieter appeal than other parts, less touristy but plenty of interest).

Splendid day-out treats for children are Crealy Country at Clyst St Mary (East Devon), and in South Devon the new National Maritime Aquarium in Plymouth (where the Dome too is good), Paignton Zoo and Morwellham Quay. Moreover, even 'adult' places generally have a lot to entertain children as well – Powderham Castle and Buckland Abbey in South Devon are fine examples. And vice versa – many family places can keep adults smiling too, such as the Big Sheep near Bideford or the Gnome Reserve near Bradworthy (North Devon), with its unexpectedly appealing plantings. Devon also boasts the country's most enjoyable 'attraction shop' – the one attached to Buckfast Abbey at Buckfastleigh (South Devon).

Some of the best views here are from trains; besides vintage steam trains puffing through gorgeous river valleys, the standard railway Devon Rover is a good deal, with unlimited train journeys in the area at a reduced rate for either a week or any three days out of seven.

East Devon

Appealing seaside resorts, interesting places to visit; we include Exeter here – a most attractive small city with a very distinctive atmosphere.

The coast has four main beach resorts, each quite different from the others. Exmouth is the liveliest and biggest, and doubles as a working port. Seaton, quieter, is a more typical family resort, with much less of a beach. Budleigh Salterton, the quietest, is rather retiring and genteel. Sidmouth is slightly busier, with a good deal of character as well as plenty for families – the broadest all-round appeal. Branscombe is the prettiest coastal village.

Exeter is civilised and gently attractive, with a decidedly relaxed and easy-going West Country feel. It has a lot to see, with good free guided walks. Its museums are interesting and particularly well organised: the Royal Albert Memorial Museum, with several fine new galleries, is now one of the best in the country. The new Bill Douglas Centre is intriguing for film buffs. Served by fast trains and the M5, Exeter can be reached quickly from far away – and good roads bring the other parts of Devon within comfortable reach for a day out.

Besides Crealy Park, the World of Country Life in Exmouth is a good children's day out, and the Escot Aquatic Centre and Gardens (animals and birds too) near Ottery St Mary has wide appeal. Killerton, Bicton Park gardens at East Budleigh, the working-mill museum at Uffculme, and the aptly named Music Fun based in Seaton are all favourites here. Praise to the Otterton Mill Centre for cutting its admission price by 25% this year. Another value point: the Cullompton farmers' market is a front-runner in the current revival of the direct farmer-to-customer markets which used to be the norm a century ago, and have such a refreshing appeal in this supermarket age.

Inland, coastal downs give a gently varied landscape of charming wooded valleys with views and high pastures between, and several attractive villages. North of the A30/A35 is more self-contained farmland, mainly well hedged traditional stock and dairy farms.

Where to stay

CHARDSTOCK ST3004 **George** *Chardstock, Axminster EX13 7BX* (01460) 220241 **£50;** 4 rms. Neatly thatched old village inn with character furnishings, beams and old gas lamps, a quietly chatty feel, good food in the bar and restaurant; nr good walks.

EXETER SX9292 **Edwardian** *30–32 Heavitree Rd, Exeter EX1 2LQ* (01392) 276102 **£48,** plus special breaks; 12 individually furnished rms, some with four-posters. Popular guesthouse close to the cathedral and city centre, with a pretty lounge, enjoyable breakfasts in attractive dining rooms, and warmly friendly and knowledgeable resident owners; plenty of places nearby for evening meals; cl 25–26 Dec.

EXETER SX9292 **St Olave's Court** *Mary Arches St, Exeter EX4 3AZ* (01392) 217736 **£90,** plus special breaks; 15 well equipped rms. Handsome Georgian-style house, just 400 yards from the cathedral, in its own walled garden, with a warm welcome from helpful friendly staff, comfortable rooms, enjoyable evening meals in the candlelit restaurant, and good breakfasts.

EXETER SX9292 **White Hart** *66 South St, Exeter EX1 1EE* (01392) 279897 **£94,** plus special breaks; 54 modern but slightly dated rms. Rather splendid 14th-c inn with lots of different eating areas (wine-bar-type as well as a proper restaurant), marvellous atmospheric bar, open fires, beams, antiques, a good range of wines, friendly service, an attractive courtyard with proper barbecues, and enjoyable breakfasts; no accommodation 3 days Christmas.

GITTISHAM SY1398 **Combe House** *Gittisham, Honiton EX14 0AD* (01404) 540400 **£102,** plus winter breaks; 15 individually decorated, pretty rms with lovely views. Peaceful Elizabethan country hotel in gardens with lawns and shrubbery, and walks around the 3,000-acre estate; elegant day rooms with antiques, pictures and fresh flowers, a happy relaxed atmosphere, very good food using some home-grown produce, and fine wines; can use the house for a private house party; young children have their own supper; well behaved dogs by prior arrangement.

HIGHER BULSTONE SY1988 **Bulstone** *Higher Bulstone, Branscombe, Sidmouth EX12 3BL* (01297) 680446 **£75,** plus special breaks; 20 rms, most with own bthrm. In over 3 acres and surrounded by fields, this is a super place for family holidays – with both parents' and children's needs catered for – out of season, it is much enjoyed by those without children, too; completely no smoking; lots of facilities and friendly staff.

LYMPSTONE SX9984 **River House** *The Strand, Lympstone, Exmouth EX8 5EY*

(01395) 265147 **£86,** plus special breaks; 3 pretty rms. Warmly welcoming restaurant-with-rooms with marvellous river views from big picture windows, good imaginative food (wonderful fresh fish and interesting vegetable dishes) in the first-floor restaurant using some home-grown produce, thoughtfully chosen wines, and kind service; practical cookery courses, too; cl 25–27 Dec, 1–2 Jan, restaurant cl pm Sun–Mon (though open if residents want to eat and open for private parties of 6 or more); children over 6; limited disabled access.

MEMBURY ST2703 **Lea Hill Hotel** *Membury, Axminster EX13 7AQ (01404) 881881* **£106,** plus special breaks; 11 rms, inc 2 suites, in carefully converted barns, mostly with private garden areas or terraces. Set in 8 acres in lovely countryside, this thatched 14th-c longhouse has comfortable beamed rooms, a convivial bar, relaxed and friendly owners, good evening meals, and nice breakfasts; well behaved dogs by special arrangement.

SIDFORD SY1390 **Blue Ball** *Sidford, Sidmouth EX10 9QL (01395) 514062* **£42;** 3 rms with nice touches like free papers, fruit and fresh flowers, shared bthrm – they hope to add private bthrms and another 2 rms. Welcoming thatched 14th-c inn run by the same family since 1912, with a lovely winter log fire in the low partly panelled lounge bar, heavy beams, lots of bric-à-brac, no smoking snug, very friendly service, and decent food inc hearty breakfasts; dogs by arrangement.

STOCKLAND ST2404 **King's Arms** *Stockland, Honiton EX14 9BS (01404) 881361* **£40;** 3 rms. Cream-faced thatched pub with elegant rooms, open fires, first-class food in the bar and evening restaurant (especially fish), and an interesting wine list; skittle alley, live music pm Sun; no accommodation 24 Dec–1 Jan; well behaved children only.

WHIMPLE SY0497 **Woodhayes** *Whimple, Exeter EX5 2TD (01404) 822237* **£90;** 6 lovely spacious rms. Big Georgian country house in neat grounds, with comfortable, quietly decorated lounges, a small library, open fires, flagstoned bar and pretty dining room, fine food, afternoon teas, and excellent breakfasts; tennis, croquet; cl 2 wks over Christmas/New Year; children over 12.

To see and do

BEER SY2289

★ ♣ ⊕ 🏛 Rather cottagey resort village, still with fishing boats pulled up on the shingle beach (summer boat hire, too), and a stream channelled down the main street. The village was famous from Roman times for its cavernous whitestone quarries, which can be visited, and the B3174 inland passes lots of Bronze Age burial mounds. The Anchor Hotel has good fresh local fish, and readers have also praised the good-value bedrooms and breakfasts at the Dolphin.

🏨 ❄ **Pecorama Pleasure Gardens** Fun for railway lovers, with models and train collections in the house, and outside a miniature steam and diesel passenger line with stunning views of the bay. Also crazy golf, aviary, children's maze and assault course, a big garden (with a new multi-themed garden to open in summer), live entertainment and maybe children's pony rides. Meals, snacks, shop, mostly disabled access; cl pm Sat, Sun (exc Jun–Aug), and outdoor features cl Oct–Easter (exc Oct half-term); (01297) 21542; £3.75 (less for just outside features).

BRANSCOMBE SY1988

✝ ★ The **church** has a magnificently carved oak gallery, and a Norman tower with distinctive stair-turret. The village is notably pretty – a series of largely unspoilt thatched hamlets strung along a lovely seaside valley. Branscombe, lying just inland, is linked to the coast path by other paths and has the good Masons Arms in the main part of the village as well as the NT Old Bakery tearoom opposite the unique NT thatched smithy.

BROADCLYST SX9897

★ ✝ ! Pretty thatch-and-cob village, with a marvellous old **church**, photogenic outside, interesting in. The Red Lion has good food – and the post office has a unique computer information kiosk.

CLYST ST MARY SX9790

☺ 🍴 **Crealy Park** 🅿 (Sidmouth Rd) There's plenty to amuse children of all ages at this bustling family complex, which celebrated its 10th birthday last year. The Magical Kingdom, a delightfully constructed area aimed mostly at under-7s, has play areas and a High-gliding Honey Swing, while amongst the attractions to occupy older children are bumper boats, go-karts and a farm where you can milk the cows (and always meet baby animals). Many of the attractions are indoors, including some of the animals, and a very good and varied adventure playground with lots of slides (one has a practically vertical drop) and things to swing on. Other features include pony rides and lakeside walks, and they have a particularly wide range of special events and activities (usually on summer Suns) from pirates' treasure hunts to conker championships. Meals, snacks, shop, disabled access; (01395) 233200; cl 24–26 Dec; £4.95; several family tickets available. They have an adjacent paintball site. If you don't want to eat in the park, the Half Moon has decent food.

CULLOMPTON ST0207

✝ ★ The **church** is notable for its remarkable painted screen; the busy little town has an attractive feel, and a farmers' market (the first of its kind in the West Country) is held in Station Rd on the second Sat of every month (exc Jan and Feb).

CULMSTOCK ST1013

✝ ☂ The village has a handsome **church**, a prettily placed old pub, and a pleasant riverside walk to Uffculme.

DALWOOD SY2499

🈁 ❀ ★ **Burrow Farm Gardens** (½m or so off the A35, turn off at signs for Taunton Cross) Part of this 5-acre site has been created from an ancient Roman clay pit, and there are spacious lawns, borders and unusual shrubs and trees as well as a woodland garden, pergola walk with old-fashioned roses, and super views. A new rill garden will open later this year. Cream teas, snacks, nursery, disabled access; cl Oct–Mar; (01404) 831285; *£3. The pretty Tuckers Arms in the attractive village is good for lunch.

DOWLANDS CLIFFS SY2889

🦅 The steeply tumbled brambly wooded wilderness of this undercliff 3m E of Axmouth has numerous small birds.

EAST BUDLEIGH SY0684

★ ✝ Attractive and quietly placed cob-and-thatch village; the pleasant **church** has fascinating Jacobean carved pew ends – some grotesque, some hilarious, some frankly rude. The Sir Walter Raleigh has good food.

🈁 ♿ **Bicton College of Agriculture** The gardens here are of great if rather specialised appeal: long monkey-puzzle avenue through parkland, a rich collection of magnolias, camellias and flowering cherries, national pittosporum and agapanthus collections, and there's also a 17-acre arboretum with woodland garden. Snacks, plant centre; cl winter wknds, 25 Dec and Good Fri; (01395) 568353; £2.

🈁 ♿ 🚂 **Bicton Park** 50 acres of lovely gardens, shrubs, lakes and woodland. A futuristic-looking glass Palm House turns out to be early Victorian, and has a fine collection of

---

Days Out

Sheltered combes and dramatic undercliff: Sidmouth, inc Donkey Sanctuary; Branscombe, lunch at the Masons Arms, look at the church, smithy, NT bakery/tearoom; Branscombe Mouth – walk along Hooken Cliffs and through the undercliff.

Otter potter and Exe exploits: Bicton Park, or (at Ottery St Mary) Cadhay; Otterton Mill Centre; Topsham – lunch at Denleys, the Globe, the Lighter or Passage House; A la Ronde, Exmouth.

tropical trees and plants; also fuchsia, geranium and orchid houses, bird garden, pinetum, magnificent Italian gardens and miniature train rides. Snacks, shop and plant centre, disabled access; cl Nov–Easter; (01395) 568465; *£4.75. The Salterton Arms is handy, in nearby Budleigh Salterton – a peaceful seaside resort, perked up a few summers back when another guide book boobed by suggesting the entire beach was a haven for nudists (it's actually just the bottom end).

EXETER SX9292

★ ⛴ Though large parts of the centre were devastated by World War II bombing, some choice streets and buildings survive, with partly Tudor narrow lanes leading from the mainly pedestrianised High Street into the serene tree-shaded cathedral close. The atmosphere is distinctive – relaxed and liberal yet responsible, buoyed up by the thriving university. In the centre, modern shops are integrated into the old layout very discreetly indeed. With many smaller churches, decent book and other shops, pubs and so forth nearby, this is a very pleasant part for browsing around. Particularly attractive streets include Southernhay at the end of the close, and Stepcote Hill, a picturesque detour from Fore Street. The Quay, beyond the streams of fast traffic on the ring road (there are quiet underpasses), has become lively and entertaining, with handsomely restored buildings, resurgent cafés and pubs (the Prospect and Port Royal are worth knowing), and a growing number of craft shops and the like; the Old Quay House has a visitor centre with audio-visual show. Apart from the White Hart, civilised pubs and wine bars with decent food include the sumptuous Imperial (New North Rd), Chaucers (High St, under C&A), Ship (14th-c, Martins Lane), Well House (The Close – cathedral view and Roman well) and Papermakers (Exe St). There are **boat trips** down the ship canal to Exminster; or you can walk down, passing the Double Locks (a favourite pub) and ending at the Turf Hotel looking out over the estuary. Daily free guided tours leave the Royal Clarence Hotel (Cathedral Close) throughout the day

(tel (01392) 265203 for details, or pick up a programme from the Tourist Information Centre, Paris St). The quickest way into the city from either the M5 or the A38 is to keep on round to the westbound A30 and go into the city from the Alphington roundabout.

🏛 **Bill Douglas Centre** (Old Library, Exeter University, Prince of Wales Road) Collection of almost 1,000 cinema-related objects amassed by the late film-maker Bill Douglas; items inc film star dolls, 19th-c optical toys and oriental shadow puppets. Disabled access; cl all wknds (inc bank hols), Easter and Christmas wks; (01392) 264321; free (guided tours £2).

✝ **Exeter Cathedral** England's finest example of decorated Gothic architecture, with its magnificent nave soaring to the fan-vaulted roof, and intricately carved choir stalls; the misericords are thought to be the longest in the country. It also boasts the longest Gothic vault in Europe, superbly atmospheric. Lots of colourfully embroidered cushions, chronologically illustrating English and local history. The façade has three tiers of sculpted figures, inc Kings Alfred, Canute and William I. Meals, snacks, shop, disabled access; guided tours 11am and 2.30pm wkdys, just 11am Sat; £2.50 suggested donation.

🏛 **Guildhall** This medieval municipal building with its colonnaded Elizabethan façade is one of the oldest still in use; it has displays of civic regalia. Disabled access to ground floor only; cl 1–2pm, pm Sat (and all Sats in winter), all Sun and bank hols, during civic functions and over Christmas; free.

🏛 **Royal Albert Memorial Museum** (Queen St) Wonderful Gothic exterior, and inside notable displays of regional silver, African carvings, archaeology, paintings and natural history. This year, World Cultures: three new galleries with touch-screen computer displays and intriguing exhibits such as materials collected during Captain Cook's voyages. Snacks, shop, disabled access; cl Sun, Good Fri, 25–26 Dec and 1 Jan; (01392) 265858; free.

🏛 **St Nicholas's Priory** (Mint Lane) 11th-c Benedictine monastery with

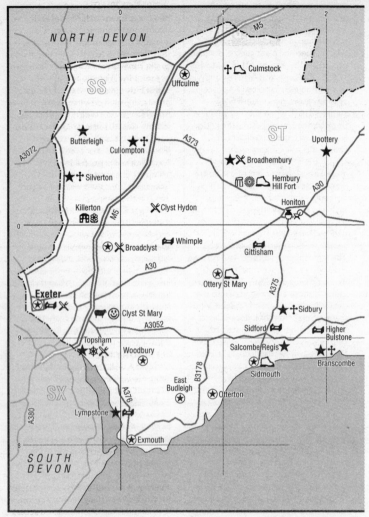

unusual Norman undercroft, Tudor room and 15th-c kitchen. Shop, disabled access to ground floor only; open 2.30–4.30pm Mon, Weds and Sat Easter–Oct, occasionally cl for private functions; (01392) 665858; free.

! Underground Passages (entrance via Boots Arcade in High St) An unusual medieval attraction is this atmospheric network, built in the 13th c to bring water into the city; there's an introductory exhibition and video, then a guided tour of the tunnels themselves, still much as they were centuries ago.

The guides can be very entertaining, and clearly enjoy their work. Flat shoes are recommended. Shop; cl am wkdys (exc July–Sept and school hols), all day Mon (exc school hols) and Sun; (01392) 265887; £2.50 (£3.50 July and Aug).

EXMOUTH SY0080

☺ ✝ ⚓ 🦈 Good family seaside holiday town, worth a visit for its lively harbour and marina, its long sandy beach and its stately **church**. Summer **cruise trips** go from the harbour up to Topsham, and there are **sea fishing trips** from the clock tower (they supply rod

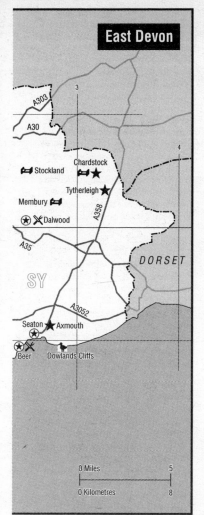

East Devon

A303
A30
3
4
🦴 Stockland
Chardstock ★★
Tytherleigh ★
Membury 🦴
A358
⊛ ✕ Dalwood
A35
DORSET
SY
A3052
Seaton ★ Axmouth
⊛
⊛✕
Beer Dowlands Cliffs

0 Miles   5
0 Kilometres   8

and bait); (01395) 222144 for both. The Seafood Restaurant (Tower St) has nothing but the freshest fish and shellfish; the Grove (with an attractive seafront garden) and the seafront Deer Leap are useful too.

🏠 ! **A la Ronde** (A376 2m N of Exmouth) Extraordinary 16-sided house, built around 1795 and decorated in part with feathers, seashells, seaweed and sand. A charmingly whimsical place, the outside looking not entirely unlike a giant biscuit barrel. Meals, snacks, shop; cl Fri, Sat, and all Nov–Easter; (01395)

265514; £3.20; NT.

🚂 **Great Exmouth Model Railway** (Sea Front) Home to the world's biggest 00 gauge model railway, nearly 1½ miles of track indoors with outside trains running round a pond of koi carp. It took 14 years to build and is constantly updated; some of the detail is amazing, right down to the birds in the trees. Shop, some disabled access; cl Nov–Feb; (01395) 278383; £2.25.

△ ☀ **High Land of Orcombe** Reached by the shore road E out of Exmouth and protected against campsite encroachment by its NT ownership, this gives walkers a short stroll with sea views.

☺ 🍴 🛏 🐾 🚂 🦅 **World of Country Life** (Sandy Bay) 40 acres of decent family-based activities, with friendly animals, adventure playground and undercover play areas, safari rides through deer and llama paddocks, reconstructed Victorian street, classic motorcycle collection, crafts, steam engines, and falconry centre (no displays Sat, exc July and Aug). Meals, snacks, shop, disabled access; cl Nov–Easter; (01395) 274533; £5.25.

HEMBURY HILL FORT ST1103 △ 🏛 ☀ A walk up from the A373 NW of Honiton, for good views.

HONITON ST1600 Some handsome Georgian buildings along this country town's long high street, and some interesting shops. The Red Cow (High St) is good value for lunch. Fine views from the A375 S.

👑 🐾 **Allhallows Museum** (High St) This recently redecorated 13th-c building has useful displays of Honiton lace, and lace-making demonstrations in Jun, July and Aug. Shop, disabled access to ground floor only (but there are plans for a lift this year); cl Sun, and Nov–Easter; (01404) 44966; £2.

KILLERTON SX9897 🌼 🏠 Best of all in spring, 15 acres of beautiful hillside gardens, shrub borders and planted beds, with an impressive avenue of beech trees. The 18th-c house has an annually changing costume exhibition in period furnished rooms, but it's the gardens that really give the place its special appeal. Meals, snacks, shop and plant centre, good disabled access (with buggies round the grounds); house cl Tues, and all Nov–mid-Mar; (01392) 881345; £5, £3.50 garden only; NT. The Three Tuns in Silverton has decent food, especially vegetarian, and readers recommend the antique centre at nearby Hele (towards Bradninch).

OTTERTON SY0684
✖ ✗ ★ **Otterton Mill Centre**
Working watermill still grinding flour for the bread, cakes and pies sold on the premises. Also craft workshops, display of East Devon lace, and interesting evening events. Meals and snacks (restaurant cl winter wkdys), shop and garden centre; cl 24–27 Dec; (01395) 568521; £1.50. The village is pretty, and the King's Arms has good food (with a lovely evening view from the back garden).

OTTERY ST MARY SY1095
★ ✝ Restrained small town – or extended village – with some attractive old buildings around its interesting twin-towered **church**. The circular **tumbling weir** by an 18th-c mill signed off Mill St is unusual, and photogenic. The London Inn is useful, and the Otter Nurseries (award-winning lavatories) have good plants.

🏠 **Cadhay** (just NW of Ottery St Mary) Beautiful Tudor and Georgian manor house, with fine timbered 15th-c roof in its Great Hall, and unusual Court of Sovereigns – a pretty courtyard with statues of various monarchs. Disabled access to garden and downstairs; open pm Tues–Thurs July and Aug, plus Sun and Mon spring and Aug bank hols; (01404) 812432; *£4.

♪ 🐴 🐟 △ 🌿 **Escot Aquatic Centre & Gardens** 🔣 (Parklands Farm, Escot) Tropical and coldwater fish from koi carp to piranhas, as well as rabbits and other pets, otters (fed at 11am and 3pm), Victorian walled rose garden, wild boar enclosures, walks, views and parkland. Also wetlands and waterfowl park, birds of prey, play area and pet centre with all you'll need for any kind of pet, inc the animals themselves. Meals, snacks, shop, disabled access; cl Mon Jan–Mar and 25–26 Dec; (01404) 822188; £2.95.

SEATON SY2391
🐴 🍎 **Lyme Bay Cider** (Manor Farm; A3052 just N) Vintage equipment and free tastings; cl winter wknds and some

summer Suns; (01297) 22887; free. Open-top trams run from Seaton to Colyton, where the Kingfisher is a good pub; back in town, the Fisherman's (Marine Crescent) has decent cheap food all day.

! Music Fun An opportunity to try your hand at playing any kind of musical instrument – you don't even have to have picked it up before. Woodwind, brass, percussion, keyboards, they've got the lot – though in the past they've told us that bagpipes are what most people want to have a go at. As we went to press, the owner was trying to find a new location. In the meantime, individuals can visit the music room at the owner's home or groups can be visited by arrangement; (01297) 445803; from £3.

SIDBURY SY1391
★ ✝ A pretty village, with a charming **church**, and a very good pub nearby at Sidford.

SIDMOUTH SY1287
★ 🐴 🍺 Attractive old streets, very 18th c, running back from the seafront, and grander Regency buildings facing the sea. It was a fashionable upper-class resort in the early 19th c, and many of the town's buildings show undoubted architectural verve – there's very little seaside tat. The pebbly beach has fishing boats pulled up on it, and the town is protected by warm red sandstone cliffs; it stretches back along the river valley, though away from the sea the buildings are less interesting. The partly 14th-c Old Ship is the best pub here, and Sue's Pantry (High St) has tasty cakes and pastries. The dedicated **Donkey Sanctuary** is a useful free attraction for families – readers report an unbelievable number of donkeys; meals, snacks, disabled access. The **Heritage Centre** (in a fine Regency house on Church St, cl am Sun and Mon and all Nov–Easter; 75p) organises summer walking tours round the town, Tues and Thurs at 10.15am.

△ **Cliff walks** The long stretch of red sandstone cliff between Sidmouth and Branscombe can be reached from either place (or, steeply but very prettily, from Salcombe Regis).

SILVERTON SS9502
★ ✝ An attractive village, with a

particularly handsome **church**.
TOPSHAM SX9688
★ ❀ Old-world seaside village, well
worth a quiet potter, its buildings
showing its past importance as a port –
as do its large number of good pubs and
inns. The Passage House is currently
the best for food, and readers like the
fresh fish at the Galley restaurant.
There's a small maritime museum.
UFFCULME ST0612
★ † A large pleasant village above the
River Culm, with a magnificent carved
screen in the attractive **church**. The
B3397 to Culmstock and then the turn
to Hemyock is a pretty drive; beyond at
Clayhidon the Half Moon has good
food, by a footpath to the Blackdown
Hills visitor centre.
⬥T **Coldharbour Mill Working
Museum** 🖼 Every stage in the
production of wool, in a well restored
18th-c mill building. Also restoration of
a steam engine, and the New World
Tapestry, one of the largest tapestries
in the world – for a donation you can

add your own stitch. Meals, snacks,
shop, limited disabled access; cl winter
wknds, and at least 1 wk at Christmas;
(01884) 840960; £5.50.
WOODBURY SY0387
❀ �🏠 ★ **Lonely heathland, fine
views** Off the B3180 E of Woodbury,
miles of heath with some pinewoods
are a place to get away from people
even in high summer (red flags warn if
there's firing on one section which is a
shooting range). From the highest
points, near the road, there are far
views along the coast and to Dartmoor.
The wooded **hill fort** right by the road
is worth a look, and it's a bit eerie
tracing the ramparts through the beech
trees. The village of Woodbury itself is
attractive, with a decent pub.
★ **Other attractive villages**, all with
decent pubs, include seaside Axmouth
SY2591, Broadhembury ST1004,
Butterleigh SS9708, Chardstock
ST3004, Lympstone SX9984, Salcombe
Regis SY1488, Tytherleigh ST3103 and
Uppottery ST2007.

Where to eat

BROADCLYST SX9897 **Red Lion** *(01392) 461271* Ochre-washed pub in a
quiet village setting, with popular food, very good wines, heavy-beamed long bar,
and skittle alley. **£15|£4.50.**
BROADHEMBURY ST1004 **Drewe Arms** *(01404) 841267* Charming 15th-c
pub in an attractive village, with carved beams and handsome stone-mullioned windows
in the bar, several other interesting rooms; excellent fresh fish dishes, lovely puddings,
well kept beers, fine wines, and a lovely garden; disabled access. **£25.50|£8.50.**
CLYST HYDON ST0301 **Five Bells** *(01884) 277288* Charming, spotless,
thatched pub, very good food inc fresh fish in a long bar divided by standing timbers,
warmly friendly service, and lovely cottagey gardens; cl pm 25–26 Dec; children
over 8 in evening restaurant; partial disabled access. **£30|£7.**
DALWOOD ST2400 **Tuckers Arms** *(01404) 881342* Delightful, thatched,
medieval longhouse with a fine flagstoned bar, lots of beams, a log fire in inglenook,
woodburner, a good mix of dining chairs, window seats and wall settles, a huge
collection of miniature bottles, well prepared enterprising bar food and lots of
colourful hanging baskets; bdrms; disabled access. **£19|£6.50.**
EXETER SX9190 **Double Locks** *Canal Banks, Alphington (01392) 56947* Friendly
and very relaxed lock-side country pub, popular with students, with good simple
bar food (all day), summer barbecues, and up to 10 real ales on handpump; no
children; disabled access. £5.40.
EXETER SX9292 **Lambs** *15 Lower North St (under the iron bridge) – car access via
Exe St (01392) 254269* 18th-c house close to the cathedral and cheerfully run by
knowledgeable staff, with a thoughtful wine list and well balanced menu using fresh
seasonal local produce – everything from nibbles to breads, yoghurt, pasta, cheese
and puddings is totally home-made; cl am Sat, all Sun and Mon. **£24|£12.**
EXETER SX9292 **St Martin's Café Bar** *Cathedral Close (01392) 310130*
Attached to the Royal Clarence Hotel and overlooking the cathedral precinct,
attractive, light and airy with lots of pine, helpful young service, a relaxed

atmosphere, and enjoyable food usefully served all day (from breakfast until last orders 11pm). **£20|£4.95.**

TOPSHAM SX9688 **Georgian Tearoom** *Broadway House, 35 High St (01392) 873465* 18th-c house with pretty embroidered tablecloths and fresh flowers, and good food all day – breakfasts, morning coffee, snacks, lunchtime meals inc a popular roast on Tues, Thurs and Sun, cream teas with home-made cakes and cookies, and a wide range of teas and coffees, plus home-made lemonade. **£14.50|£4.20.**

South Devon and Dartmoor

Lovely coast, magnificent Dartmoor, charming villages, plenty of interest; beautiful places to stay in.

Dartmoor is a powerful brooding wilderness, with complete walking freedom in most parts (you're not confined to footpaths), and all sorts of points of interest – especially its strange-shaped tors and its prehistoric remains. Around its edges are intimate and picturesque valleys and villages, delightful to explore. There's a similar intimate appeal in the small coves, stretches of cliff, sheltered boating creeks and estuaries cut deeply into the hills of the south and west coast. Here, relaxed and welcoming small towns such as Dartmouth and Totnes offer plenty to see and do. Some of England's best and cleanest beaches are to be found here, too, such as Slapton Sands.

Torbay and its English Riviera offer a complete contrast: spacious promenades, low cliffs, bright gardens and palm trees. Plymouth is also another world: a big busy city, yet with a great deal to interest both children and adults, including its magnificent new marine aquarium, the Plymouth Dome heritage centre, and the well restored Crownhill Fort.

Other particularly enjoyable family days out here include Morwellham Quay, Powderham Castle with its ancient tortoise, the friendly Pennywell Farm Centre near Buckfastleigh, the steam railway between there and Totnes (perhaps combined with a river trip), and the Dunstone shire horse centre. Readers enjoy the butterfly park at Buckfastleigh (particularly for its otters). Some special places for adults include Overbecks near Salcombe with its lush seaside gardens and bizarre inventions; the remarkable Benedictine craft shop at Buckfast Abbey; magnificent Saltram near Plympton; the exotic gardens at Plant World near Newton Abbot; romantic Coleton Fishacre garden at Kingswear; and Castle Drogo at Drewsteignton, Lydford Gorge, Buckland Abbey and the Garden House at Buckland Monachorum, and the friendly medieval farmhouse at Malborough. The new Goss Visitor Centre in Totnes is an intriguing place to catch up on Britain's fastest ocean-racing yacht's progress – wherever it is. If you then need to catch your breath, what better place than under the oak tree in Meavy – planted near the end of the first millennium.

Away from Dartmoor, the inland landscape is made up largely of well hedged hilly pastures, steeply wooded valleys and occasional vivid red-earth fields.

Where to stay

ASHBURTON SX7569 **Holne Chase** *Ashburton, Newton Abbot TQ13 7NS* (01364) 631471 ***£130,** plus winter breaks; 17 comfortable and individually furnished rms, many with views over the Dart Valley, some split-level suites in converted stables. Marvellously peaceful ex-hunting lodge to Buckfast Abbey, in 70 acres with sweeping lawns and plenty of woodland walks, a mile of Dart fishing, shooting and riding on Dartmoor; cheerful welcoming owners, comfortable public rooms with log fires, very good modern English cooking using home-grown vegetables, and enjoyable breakfasts and afternoon teas (home-made breads, marmalades and so forth); children over 10 in evening restaurant; disabled access.

AVETON GIFFORD SX6947 **Court Barton Farmhouse** *Aveton Gifford, Kingsbridge TQ7 4LE* (01548) 550312 ***£44;** 7 rms, 6 with own bthrm. Pretty, creeper-clad, 16th-c farmhouse on 300 acres of arable land, with a cosy, homely lounge, log fires, a warm welcome, farmhouse breakfasts, and a flower-filled garden; cl Christmas.

BANTHAM SX6643 **Widcombe House** *Bantham, Kingsbridge TQ7 3AA* (01548) 561084 ***£60;** 3 well equipped neat rms. In lovely countryside with fine views down to the sea, this modern no smoking house is spotlessly kept and very relaxing, with a log fire in chilly weather, very good breakfasts and delicious evening meals in the dining room using home-grown produce (bring your own wine); cl Nov–Jan; no children.

BLACKAWTON SX8050 **Normandy Arms** *Blackawton, Totnes TQ9 7BN* (01803) 712316 ***£52,** plus special breaks; 5 pretty rms. Quaint, friendly pub in quiet village, with a cosy main bar, log fire, some interesting displays of World War II battle gear, generous food in the bar and restaurant, real ales, and seats in the garden.

BOVEY TRACEY SX8178 **Edgemoor Hotel** *Haytor Rd, Bovey Tracey, Newton Abbot TQ13 9LE* (01626) 832466 ***£92.50,** plus special breaks; 17 charming rms. Ivy-covered country house in neatly kept gardens on the edge of Dartmoor, with a comfortable lounge and bar, log fires, good food in elegant restaurant, and high tea for children under 8; dogs welcome; cl 6 days over New Year; children over 8 in restaurant.

BURGH ISLAND SX6443 **Burgh Island Hotel** *Burgh Island, Bigbury-on-Sea TQ7 4BG* (01548) 810514 **£218 inc dinner;** 14 Art Deco seaview suites, most with balconies. Extravagantly decorated and restored 1929 hotel on a cut-off small island – access by the hotel Land Rover (or foot) at low tide, and on a seagoing summer tractor-on-stilts at high tide; domed palm court, sun lounge, classic cocktail bar, Art Deco furniture, kind helpful hosts, good food, and super breakfasts; tennis, mini gym, snooker, water sports, natural pool and private beach, walks, and sea fishing. Island has a 14th-c pub – and summer day crowds. No dogs; cl Jan and wkdys Feb; disabled access.

CHAGFORD SX7087 **Easton Court** *Sandy Park, Chagford, Newton Abbot TQ13 8JN* (01647) 433469 **£90,** plus special breaks; 8 rms. Creeper-clad, thatched 15th-c house with beams, inglenook fireplace, granite walls, and a big library (literary connections include Evelyn Waugh writing *Brideshead Revisited* here), cosy bar, and a charming sitting room; good breakfasts, delicious evening meals in the candlelit restaurant; cl Jan; children over 12; disabled access.

CHAGFORD SX7087 **Gidleigh Park** *Chagford, Newton Abbot TQ13 8HH* (01647) 432367 **£375 inc dinner,** plus winter breaks; 15 opulent and individual rms with fruit and flowers. Exceptional, luxurious, Dartmoor-edge, mock Tudor hotel with a deeply comfortable panelled drawing room, wonderful flowers, a conservatory overlooking the fine grounds (40 acres, with walks straight up on to the moor), log fires, particularly fine cooking and a fine wine list, and caring staff.

DARTINGTON SX7762 **Cott** *Dartington, Totnes TQ9 6HE* (01803) 863777 **£65,** plus special breaks; 6 character rms. Pretty and very warmly friendly ancient inn with a fine thatched roof (the longest in southern England), heavy-beamed communicating rooms with open fires and flagstones; fine lunchtime buffet and interesting evening food (lots of fresh fish), real ales and quite a few wines by the glass; no smoking restaurant, seats on terrace, friendly cats; fine nearby walks.

DARTMOUTH SX8751 **Ford House** *44 Victoria Rd, Dartmouth TQ6 9DX (01803)* 834047 *£75,* plus special breaks; 4 individually decorated rms. Nr the harbour, this Regency town house has a log fire in the comfortable drawing room, antiques, good interesting food using fresh local produce eaten around a big table, delicious breakfasts, helpful service, and a sheltered garden; you can take over the whole house for a wknd party; cl Oct–Mar; no children.

DARTMOUTH SX8751 **Royal Castle** *11 The Quay, Dartmouth TQ6 9PS (01803)* 833033 *£103.90,* plus special breaks; 25 individually furnished rms. Well restored mainly Georgian hotel (part 16th c) overlooking the inner harbour – great views from most rooms; lively and interesting public bar with open fires and beams, a quiet library/lounge with antiques, and a drawing room overlooking the quayside; winter spit-roasts in the lounge bar, elegant upstairs seafood restaurant, decent bar food, and friendly staff.

DODDISCOMBSLEIGH SX8586 **Nobody** *Doddiscombsleigh, Exeter EX6 7PS (01647)* 252394 *£64;* 7 rms, some in a Georgian manor house 150 yards down the road, and most with their own bthrm. Friendly, atmospheric 16th-c pub with beams, heavy wooden furniture, and an inglenook fireplace in the attractively furnished 2-roomed lounge bar; an outstanding cellar running to 800 wines and 250 malts, and popular food in the bar and restaurant inc a huge range of Devon cheeses; good views from the garden, and the church is worth visiting for its fine stained glass; cl 25–26 Dec; no children.

GALMPTON SX6840 **Burton Farm** *Galmpton, Kingsbridge TQ7 3EY (01548)* 561210 *£52;* 12 rms, most with own bthrm. Welcoming working farm in lovely countryside with dairy herd and pedigree sheep (guests welcome to look around and help); traditional farmhouse cooking using home-produced ingredients; no smoking; cl Christmas; disabled access.

GOVETON (just E) SX7546 **Buckland-Tout-Saints** *Goveton, Kingsbridge TQ7 2DS (01548)* 853055 *£195,* plus special winter breaks; 10 luxuriously period rms. Handsome Queen Anne mansion (carefully refurbished this year) in 6 well kept acres of gardens with croquet/putting; relaxing rooms with antiques, fine panelling and plasterwork, chintzy furniture and a roaring log fire; imaginative food using good local produce in a lovely no smoking restaurant, notable wines, and excellent personal service; dogs by arrangement; children over 6 in restaurant.

HAYTOR SX7677 **Bel Alp House** *Haytor, Newton Abbot TQ13 9XX (01364)* 661217 *£120,* plus special breaks; 8 spacious rms. Handsome Edwardian country house with an elegant drawing room, comfortable sitting room, log fires, friendly atmosphere, and fine careful cooking in the pretty restaurant; wonderful views and peaceful garden; disabled access.

HAYTOR VALE SX7677 **Rock** *Haytor Vale, Newton Abbot TQ13 9XP (01364)* 661305 *£75.95,* plus special breaks; 9 rms. Civilised old inn on the edge of Dartmoor National Park, with good food (inc fresh fish), a nice mix of visitors and locals in the 2 rooms of the panelled bar, open fires, no smoking restaurant, courteous service, and a big garden; walking, fishing, riding and golf nearby; cl 24–25 Dec.

HAZELWOOD SX7148 **Crannacombe Farm** *Hazelwood, Loddiswell, Kingsbridge TQ7 4DX (01548)* 550256 *£38;* 2 rms. Quietly set and comfortable Georgian farmhouse on a working stock farm in a lovely unspoilt valley, with prize-winning cider, and hearty food; no smoking; babysitting; cl Christmas.

HOLNE SX7069 **Church House** *Holne, Newton Abbot TQ13 7SJ (01364)* 631208 *£50,* plus special breaks; 6 rms, most with own bthrm. Medieval Dartmoor-edge inn with a comfortable and interesting pine-panelled lounge bar, freshly prepared food using local produce, restaurant, decent wine list, pleasant service, and lots of good walks close by.

HOLNE SX7069 **Wellpritton Farm** *Holne, Ashburton TQ13 7RX (01364)*

631273 **£38;** 4 pretty rms, 3 with own bthrm. Small friendly Dartmoor farm with lots of animals, a comfortable sitting room, good food (packed lunches if you want), and a small swimming pool.

HOPE COVE SX6739 **Hope Cove** *Hope Cove, Kingsbridge TQ7 3HH* (01548) *561233* **£47,** plus special breaks; 7 rms with fine sea views. Neatly kept and welcoming little hotel in a tranquil spot with sandy beaches and plenty of walks, lovely views from the lounge or dining room, helpful owners and staff, and enjoyable food; cl Oct–Easter; children from 6; no dogs.

KINGSTON SX6347 **Dolphin** *Kingston, Kingsbridge TQ7 4QE* (01548) *810314* **£49.50;** 3 rms. Peaceful 16th-c inn with several knocked-through beamed rooms, a warmly welcoming atmosphere, a small no smoking area, very good home-made food, and real ales; tracks down to the sea.

LEWDOWN SX4486 **Lewtrenchard Manor** *Lewdown, Okehampton EX20 4PN* (01566) *783256* **£155,** plus special breaks; 9 well equipped rms with fresh flowers and period furniture. Lovely Elizabethan manor house in a garden with fine dovecot and surrounded by a peaceful estate with shooting, fishing and croquet; dark panelling, ornate ceilings, antiques, fresh flowers, and log fires, a friendly welcome, relaxed atmosphere, and a candlelit restaurant with very good food; children under 8 by arrangement; partial disabled access.

LIFTON SX3885 **Arundell Arms** *Lifton PL16 0AA* (01566) *784666* **£110,** plus special breaks; 28 well equipped rms, 5 in annexe over the road. Carefully renovated old coaching inn with 20 miles of its own waters – salmon and trout fishing and a long-established fly fishing school; comfortable sitting room, log fires, very good food in the smart restaurant, decent wines, and kind service from local staff; dogs welcome away from the restaurant and river bank; cl 4 days over Christmas.

LYDFORD SX5184 **Castle** *Lydford, Okehampton EX20 4BH* (01822) *820242* **£65;** 9 individually decorated rms, most with own bthrm. Very well run, charming Tudor inn with particularly friendly staff, lots of interesting antiques and furnishings in lounge areas (one overlooks a nice garden with covered terrace), log fires, beams and flagstones, lovely food, well kept real ales and decent wines; pets corner; next to the castle and near a gorge.

MALBOROUGH (2m S) SX7037 **Soar Mill Cove** *Malborough, Salcombe TQ7 3DS* (01548) *561566* **£164 inc dinner,** plus special breaks; 21 comfortable rms, some opening on to the garden. Neatly kept single-storey building in an idyllic spot by a peaceful and very beautiful cove on NT coast (excellent walks), with lovely views, extensive private grounds, tennis/putting, and a warm indoor pool; outstanding service, log fires, very good food (marvellous fish), and thoughtful early-evening children's meal; cl Nov–Feb (open Christmas and New Year); small, mature, well behaved dogs by arrangement; disabled access.

MORETONHAMPSTEAD SX7585 **White Hart** *Moretonhampstead, Newton Abbot TQ13 8NF* (01647) *440406* **£60,** plus special breaks; 18 rms. Comfortable former Georgian posting house, interesting furnishings in the civilised lounge bar and hall; lively back bar, good bar food, and no smoking restaurant; well placed for Dartmoor.

MORETONHAMPSTEAD SX7586 **Great Sloncombe Farm** *Moretonhampstead, Newton Abbot TQ13 8QF* (01647) *440595* ***£44;** 3 rms – the big double is the favourite. Lovely 13th-c farmhouse on a working dairy and stock farm, with friendly owners, carefully polished old-fashioned furniture, decent food, log fires, a relaxed atmosphere, and good nearby walking and birdwatching; no smoking; children over 8; dogs by arrangement.

NORTH BOVEY SX7483 **Gate House** *North Bovey, Newton Abbot TQ13 8RB* (01647) *440479* **£54;** 3 charming rms. 15th-c thatched cottage in picturesque village, with a huge granite fireplace in an attractive beamed sitting room; breakfasts and candlelit evening meals served in the beamed dining room, tea with home-made cakes, friendly owners; outdoor swimming pool in peaceful garden; plenty to do nearby; no children.

PRESTON SX8574 **Sampsons Farm** *Preston, Newton Abbot TQ12 3PP* (01626) 54913 **£55,** plus special breaks; 10 rms, most with own bthrms. Thatched 14th-c longhouse with beams, panelling and big open fires in cosy sitting rooms, a very relaxed welcoming atmosphere, most enjoyable food in the popular restaurant, and lots of nearby walks; children over 3; disabled access; self-catering too.

SALCOMBE SX7337 **Tides Reach** *South Sands, Salcombe TQ8 8LJ* (01548) 843466 **£162,** plus special breaks; 38 rms, many with estuary views. Unusually individual resort hotel run by long-serving owners, in a pretty wooded cove by the sea, with airy luxury day rooms, a big sea aquarium in the cocktail bar, good restaurant food using fresh local produce, friendly efficient service; squash, snooker, leisure complex, health area, and a big heated pool; windsurfing etc, beach over the lane, and lots of coast walks; cl Dec and Jan; children over 8.

SANDY PARK SX7189 **Mill End** *Sandy Park, Chagford, Newton Abbot TQ13 8JN* (01647) 432282 ***£75,** plus special breaks; 17 neat rms, most with views. Quietly set former flour mill with waterwheel in neatly kept grounds below Dartmoor; comfortable lounges, carefully prepared, interesting food and fine breakfasts, and good service; well behaved dogs welcome away from public rooms; cl Jan; partial disabled access.

SOUTH ZEAL SX6593 **Oxenham Arms** *South Zeal, Okehampton EX20 2JT* (01837) 840244 ***£70,** plus special breaks; 8 rms, 7 with own bthrm. Grandly atmospheric old inn dating back to the 12th c and first licensed in 1477 (a Neolithic standing stone still forms part of the wall in the TV room); elegant beamed and panelled bar with chatty, relaxed atmosphere and open fire, decent food and wines, and a charming, former monastery small garden; well behaved dogs welcome.

STAVERTON SX7964 **Sea Trout** *Staverton, Totnes TQ9 6PA* (01803) 762274 **£70;** 10 cottagey rms. Comfortable pub in quiet hamlet nr the River Dart, with 2 relaxed beamed bars, log fires, popular food in the bar and airy dining conservatory; terraced garden with fountains and waterfalls; cl Christmas.

STOKE GABRIEL SX8457 **Gabriel Court** *Stoke Gabriel, Totnes TQ9 6SF* (01803) 782206 **£77,** plus special breaks; 19 rms, some in former hay lofts. In a walled Elizabethan garden, this attractive family-run manor has quiet relaxing lounges (winter log fire), enjoyable traditional English food, and courteous helpful staff; outdoor heated swimming pool and grass tennis court; dogs welcome.

TEIGNMOUTH SX9473 **Thomas Luny House** *Teign St, Teignmouth TQ14 8EG* (01626) 772976 ***£70,** plus special breaks; 4 pretty rms with flowers and books. Lovely no smoking Georgian house nr the fish quay; open fires in the spacious, comfortable drawing room and elegant dining room, a relaxed friendly atmosphere, enjoyable food around a big dining table; sunny walled garden; children over 12.

TWO BRIDGES SX6175 **Prince Hall** *Two Bridges, Yelverton PL20 6SA* (01822) 890403 **£85;** 9 attractive, spacious rms. Surrounded by Dartmoor National Park, this tranquil 18th-c country house is run by caring friendly owners and their helpful staff; lovely views from the convivial bar, a comfortable sitting room, and cosy dining room, open fires, very good evening meals, enjoyable breakfasts, and lots of fine walks; cl mid-Dec–mid-Feb; children over 10.

We welcome reports from readers

This *Guide* depends on readers' reports. Do help us if you can – in return, we offer a discount on the next edition to people who've helped us with reports for it. Tell us what you think about places already in it, and anything extra you think we should say about them. And send us your ideas for inclusion in the next edition: places to visit, eat at or stay in, attractive drives or walks, maybe even unusual interesting shops you know of. Use the card in the middle, the report forms at the end, or just write – no stamp needed: *The Good Britain Guide*, FREEPOST TN1569, Wadhurst, E Sussex TN5 7BR.

To see and do

DEVON Family Attraction of the Year

♪ **PLYMOUTH** SX4753 **National Maritime Aquarium** (The Barbican) Quite a contrast to some of the older buildings nearby, this splendid looking building is an enthralling world-class aquarium, still relatively new, but already adding new exhibitions and residents. The fish are shown in elaborate indoor reconstructions of their natural habitats, starting with a moorland stream and bog, and progressing over the three floors through an estuary, seashore, and coral reef. The range of marine life is fantastic, with some splendidly coloured and curiously shaped individuals, and they've worked hard to make the environments as authentic as possible, with plenty of sound and other effects – there's even a moorland mist rolling down the tor side. The most spectacular display is the huge deep reef tank, straddling two of the floors, and containing over half a million litres of water. Designed to represent the deeper offshore waters around the British Isles, it's well worth studying carefully – some of the camouflaged things hidden under rocks turn out to be alive if you watch them for long enough. Divers descend into the depths to feed the fish by hand every now and again; best to check times for this when you arrive. In the shore section are discovery pools for children to gently touch starfish and the like, and there's a new exhibition showing off Europe's largest collection of seahorse species. Of course, no aquarium would be complete without a few sharks, and this is no exception; the Shark Theatre has spooky lighting to create an appropriate air of menace. They usually feed the sharks Mon, Weds and Fri – check in advance to make sure. Some people can stare at fish all day, and even the most casual visitor will find this a rewarding place to spend a couple of hours, whatever the weather. Meals and snacks (the café has nice views over Plymouth Sound), shop, disabled access; cl 1 Jan, 25 Dec; (01752) 229984; £6.50 (£4 children 4–15). The family ticket, at £18, offers better than usual savings. Tickets usually allow same-day re-entry.

ASHBURTON SX7370
★ 🦋 ♪ ⌂ Probably the best of the small towns around Dartmoor, with distinct character. The **River Dart Country Park** (Holne Park) is pleasant for walking or fishing, with adventure playgrounds. Snacks, shop; cl Oct–Mar; (01364) 652511; £4.50. The London Hotel is good.

BANTHAM SANDS SX6643
⌂ 🌼 A gentle walk from Bantham through dunes (good picnic spots) to the broad stretch of rivermouth sand facing Burgh Island. You can go on above the rocks S, for views of Bolt Tail and the coves between.

BERRY HEAD SX9356
🌼 ♟ ☙ Tremendous coast, sea and shipping views from ex-quarry country park; squat lighthouse, formidable Napoleonic War battlements with cannon (and guardhouse café), a nature trail takes in kittiwakes and guillemots on the cliffs, and uncommon plants.

BERRY POMEROY SX8261
🏚 † **Berry Pomeroy Castle** (off A385 just E of Totnes; keep on past the village) Reputedly Devon's most haunted castle, hidden away on a crag over a quiet wooded valley. Appropriately spooky Norman gatehouse and walls around the ruins of an imposing and unexpected Tudor mansion, with an interesting 15th-c fresco inside. The lawns in front are ideal for a picnic. Snacks, shop, disabled access; cl Nov–Mar; (01803) 866618; £2.20; EH. The red sandstone 15th-c village **church** is worth a look on the way; there's an odd monument in Seymour Chapel. The road through here from Ashburton via Littlehempston and on to Stoke Gabriel is a pleasant drive.

BICKINGTON SX7972
🚂 🎡 **Gorse Blossom Railway Adventure Park** Rides on 7¼-in gauge steam railway through acres of woodland; also nature trails, play areas,

and an indoor model railway. Meals, snacks, shop, some disabled access; cl Nov–Easter, phone (01626) 821361 to check times; £4.50. The Toby Jug is useful for lunch.

BLACKAWTON SX8050

☺ 🐘 ⬆ **Woodland Leisure Park** off A3122) One of the best family days out in Devon. A highlight is the Twister, an exhilarating spiralling and plunging water-coaster – be prepared to get wet. There are several other rides and lots of well thought out play areas (inc several for younger children), as well as a honey farm with millions of bees behind glass, daily falconry displays, and a small zoo with wallabies, llamas and foreign birds. There are boats on the lake and plenty of quieter areas for woodland walks. Meals, snacks, shop, disabled access; open wknds and school hols and daily mid-Mar–mid-Nov; (01803) 712598; £5.40.

BOVEY TRACEY SX8078

🎨 🏛 An unassuming small Dartmoor-edge town; the Devon Guild of Craftsmen have a good varied **craft centre** at Riverside Mill (cl winter bank hols; £1.25 for exhibitions). **House of Marbles & Teign Valley Glass** (Pottery Rd) Demonstrations of glass-blowing at a factory specialising in marbles, with a fantastic array of these and some interesting marble runs in its museum. It will reopen in mid-Jan after refurbishment. Meals, snacks, shop, disabled access; no glass-blowing Sat and winter Suns; (01626) 835358; free. The **Lowerdown Pottery** (off B3344) does fine decorated pottery; it's open by appointment only, (01626) 833408; free. The Cromwell Arms does

generous food.

BRIXHAM SX9256

★ ⛴ ✿ Busy fishing port, perhaps the prettiest of the Riviera resorts, with some attractive narrow streets on the hill above. Lots of activity (and summer seaside shops and cafés) in the harbour, inc (for no apparent reason) a full-size reconstruction of Drake's *Golden Hind*, and summer boats around Torbay. The local history **museum** (Bolton Cross) has something of a maritime emphasis (shop; cl Sun, and Oct–Feb; £1.20). The quaint Quayside Inn is handy for lunch, and Shoalstone beach nr here has some of the cleanest bathing water in the UK. ⌂ **Scabbacombe Head** A blowy but rewarding day's walk from Brixham to Kingswear, 12 miles of stunning wild scenery (and some steep climbs), passing the oasis of Coleton Fishacre gardens.

BUCKFASTLEIGH SX7367

✝ 🎨 **Buckfast Abbey** Originally established in 1018, but after the Dissolution of the Monasteries left abandoned until 1882, when it was refounded by 4 remarkable monks, who then did most of the rebuilding work themselves over a period of 32 years. It's now one of the most visited religious sites in Britain, with an interesting exhibition, and several services each day. An excellent shop sells not just their own famous honey, but goods produced at other Benedictine monasteries around Europe, inc Bavarian beer, French cakes, and Irish linen; many people feel this alone is worth a special journey. Good meals and snacks, disabled access; cl Good Fri and 25 Dec; guided

---

Days Out

The Dart's changing moods: Totnes; South Devon Railway to Buckfastleigh (via the Butterfly Park & Otter Sanctuary, after lunch at the Kingsbridge Inn, Totnes); or a river trip to Dartmouth, lunch there at the Carved Angel, Billy Budds, the Cherub or the Royal Castle, then walk along the coast path S from the castle to Bolt Tail and Bolt Head.

Dartmoor ponies, Uncle Tom Cobbleigh and all: Miniature Pony Centre, North Bovey; Widecombe in the Moor; lunch at the Rock, Haytor Vale; strolls from the road to Hound Tor and Haytor; North Bovey and Lustleigh villages – cream tea at Primrose Cottage, Lustleigh.

tours (01364) 642519; free.

✻ ⚘ Butterfly Park & Otter Sanctuary (Dart Bridge Rd) You can watch otters swimming and playing from an underwater viewing tunnel, or see them on land in the 6 big landscaped enclosures; summer feeding times (readers enjoy this part most) 11.30am, 2pm and 4.30pm. Also an undercover tropical garden with free-flying butterflies and moths. Meals, snacks, shop, disabled access; cl Nov–Feb; (01364) 642916; £4.75. Combined with a trip on the South Devon Railway (the trains stop here), this makes for a very pleasant day out.

🐷 ⚘ Pennywell Farm Centre (Lower Dean, off A38 just S of Buckfastleigh) Friendly and unfussy, with over 750 animals in 80 acres, as well as lovely scenery, wildlife viewing hides, and falconry demonstrations. Different events every half-hour, from milking and feeding to ferret racing and worm charming, so always something for children to get involved in; also play areas, an assault course, pony and donkey rides and an area where children can try out crafts like basket weaving. Meals, snacks, shop, disabled access; open most winter wknds (tel for Christmas opening), Feb half-term, then daily from late Mar–Oct; (01364) 642023; *£6.25.

🚂 South Devon Railway (Buckfastleigh) GWR steamtrain trips through lovely unspoilt scenery along the wooded River Dart (some of which is hard to see any other way). It now stops just outside Totnes as well as at Staverton, and they do tickets combining it with a Dartmouth–Totnes river trip; also a small museum, play area and a chance to see the ongoing restoration of rolling stock. Shop, disabled access; trains usually run every 1¼ hrs summer, less often other times; best to check dates; (01364) 642338 for timetable (or pick one up from local tourist information centres); £6.50. The Dartbridge opposite is a popular family dining pub.

BUCKLAND MONACHORUM
SX4868

🏠 ⚘ ☗ ⌂ Buckland Abbey The home of Francis Drake until his death in 1596, and of his family until 1946. They still have the famous drum said to sound whenever England is in danger, as well as craft workshops, a new brass-rubbing centre, herb knot garden, thyme garden (they've recently started work on an Elizabethan garden), good walks, and entertaining summer activities for children. In Aug for a small extra charge, you can play bowls on the lawn. Meals, snacks, shop, disabled access to ground floor only; cl Thurs, and Nov–Mar exc pm wknds; (01822) 853607; £4.40, £2.30 grounds only; NT.

☗ 🏚 Garden House Profusion of unusual plants beautifully laid out in a warm garden sheltered by picturesque, partly ruined walls of former abbey buildings; also a spring garden, quarry garden, rhododendron walk and wild flower meadow. Interesting plant sales, teas Apr–Sept; cl Nov–Feb; (01822) 854769; £3.50. The Drake Manor is good for lunch.

BURGH ISLAND SX6544
! Connected at low tide by a causeway to Bigbury-on-Sea (undistinguished for much save its clean sandy beaches); spectacular cliffs on the seaward side, a true island and quite remote-seeming when the tide's in. At high tide an odd giant tractor-on-stilts wades back and forth with passengers. The Pilchard is a quaint seaview pub, and you can windsurf or fish nearby.

CHAGFORD SX7087
★ ☗ A large village, quite busy, and an attractive jumping-off point for the moor; even the bank is thatched, and the two old-fashioned general stores are fun. The Ring o' Bells is good for lunch, and the Bullers Arms is useful too. If you eat at the luxury country-house hotel **Gidleigh Park**, you can stroll around their lovely grounds, with colourful woodland walks and water garden, and immaculate more formal gardens.

CHUDLEIGH SX8678
★ Despite the 1807 fire which destroyed lots of the buildings, this is a pleasant old wool town with pretty cottages in narrow, winding lanes.

☗ ☗ ⌂ ❋ Rock Garden & Cave 3 acres of wild gardens, populated by a good range of birds and wildlife. The cave has some interesting calcite formations and they are still digging in

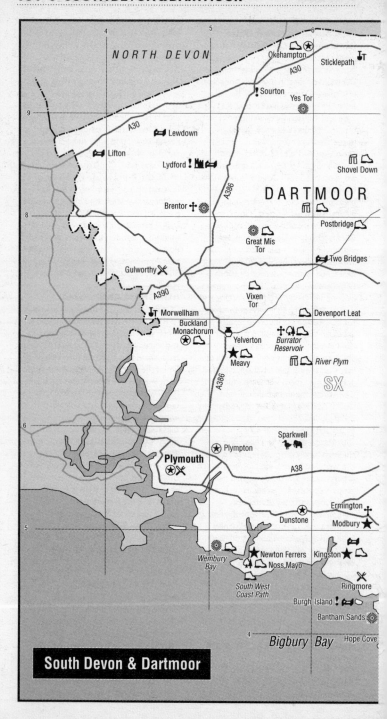

NORTH DEVON

Okehampton

Sticklepath

A30

Sourton

Yes Tor

Lewdown

Lifton

Lydford

Shovel Down

Brentor

D A R T M O O R

Great Mis Tor

Postbridge

Gulworthy

A390

Two Bridges

Vixen Tor

Devonport Leat

Morwellham

Buckland Monachorum

Yelverton

Burrator Reservoir

River Plym

Meavy

A386

SX

Sparkwell

Plympton

Plymouth

A38

Dunstone

Ermington

Modbury

Wembury Bay

Newton Ferrers

Noss Mayo

Kingston

Ringmore

South West Coast Path

Burgh Island

Bantham Sands

Bigbury Bay

Hope Cove

South Devon & Dartmoor

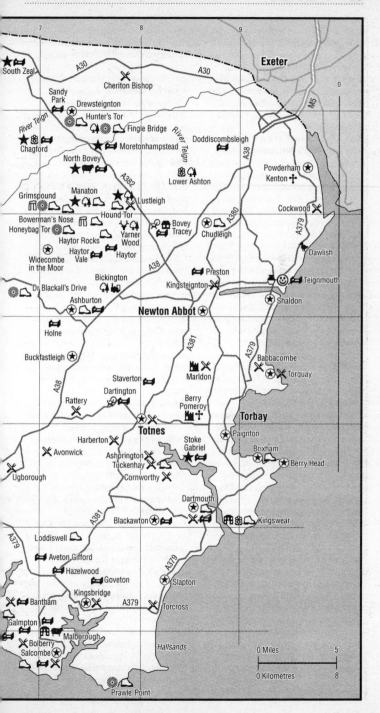

South Zeal

Cheriton Bishop

Sandy Park

Drewsteignton

Hunter's Tor

Fingle Bridge

River Teign

Chagford

Moretonhampstead

North Bovey

Doddiscombsleigh

Powderham

Kenton

Grimspound

Manaton

Lustleigh

Cockwood

Bowerman's Nose

Honeybag Tor

Hound Tor

Yarner Wood

Bovey Tracey

Chudleigh

Dawlish

Haytor Rocks

Haytor Vale

Haytor

Widecombe in the Moor

Dr Blackall's Drive

Bickington

Preston

Kingsteignton

Teignmouth

Ashburton

Newton Abbot

Shaldon

Holne

Buckfastleigh

Babbacombe

Torquay

Staverton

Marldon

Dartington

Rattery

Berry Pomeroy

Torbay

Totnes

Paignton

Harberton

Stoke Gabriel

Avonwick

Brixham

Ashprington

Tuckenhay

Berry Head

Cornworthy

Ugborough

Dartmouth

Loddiswell

Blackawton

Kingswear

Aveton Gifford

Hazelwood

Goveton

Slapton

Bantham

Kingsbridge

Galmpton

Torcross

Bolberry

Malborough

Salcombe

Hallsands

Prawle Point

| 0 Miles | | 5 |
| 0 Kilometres | | 8 |

Exeter

M5

A30

A382

A38

A380

A379

A381

search of legendary larger caverns. From the pretty neighbouring waterfall, it's a short walk up Chudleigh Rock for dramatic vistas of the surrounding countryside and moors. Snacks, nursery, craft shop, limited disabled access; cl Christmas, and possibly some parts in winter; (01626) 852134; *£2. You can arrange abseiling or caving on (01626) 852717.

🏠 ⊛ **Ugbrooke Park** (off A380 just SE of Chudleigh) An interesting early example of the work of Robert Adam, in lovely Capability Brown parkland. Delightfully informal guided tours (2pm and 3.45pm). Teas, disabled access; open pm Sun, Tues, Weds, Thurs and bank hols mid-July—early Sept; (01626) 852179; £4.80.

DARTINGTON SX8062

🎗 **Dartington Cider Press Centre** (Shinners Bridge) Cluster of 16th- and 17th-c buildings with craft shops, farm foods, herbs and such, and restaurants, inc a good vegetarian one. The surroundings add a lot to the attraction, with a nearby medieval great hall on a photogenic lawned courtyard, sculpture gardens, and streamside nature trail. Disabled access; cl Sun Jan—Easter; (01803) 864171; free. The Cott, excellent for lunch, is close by.

DARTMOOR SX5880

🏠 ⌂ Classic moorland, where distant vistas of changing greens and browns fade into the austere grey-blues of far shoulders and edges. The moor is punctuated with all sorts of interesting focal points and features: numerous easily traceable prehistoric remains; strange wind-sculpted, eroded granite tors which crown many of the slopes; the little streams that thread over boulders; tamed watercourses where leats or miniature canals (dating back to the 16th-c one cut by Drake to supply Plymouth) curl carefully around the contours; sheltered valleys cut into the moors, where white houses crouch among sycamores and oaks; occasional higher clusters of much more stunted oaks mark abandoned tin-mine workings with ruined wheelhouses, and shaggy ponies hope for a hand-out. Good roads over the moor are the B3212 and B3357, and the back road towards Ashburton off the B3344 just

NW of Manaton. The villages around it are well worth exploring: typically thatched white-plastered stone cottages clustered around an ancient stone church beside its church-house inn. The towns ringing the moor have useful facilities. A big chunk of NW Dartmoor is used by the Ministry of Defence for firing practice; it's marked out by red and white posts, and you can go in when there are no red lights or red flags. Dartmoor is outstanding for walking, but mist can come down very suddenly, so on the open moor you must carry a compass. A lot of the moor is a long way from the road, hence rather inaccessible. There are more paths for walkers than the right-of-way network suggests, but don't assume a right of way marked on the OS map will be visible on the ground (the black dashed lines on these maps are generally more reliable). Old mineral railways and cart tracks make for some good walkers' routes. There are plenty of things to head for, to give a moorland walk a sense of purpose – most obviously, one of the many tors of naked rock rising out of the moor (beware: the rounded rocks can be a good deal more slippery than they look).

🏛 **Ancient sites** The upper valley of the River Plym has numerous visible hut circles, stone rows and cairns.

⌂ **Bowerman's Nose** This quaint tor, looking snootily out over a patchwork of pastures, makes a pleasant objective for a Dartmoor walk.

✝ ❊ **Brentor church** (above back road Lydford—Tavistock, just S of North Brentor) 12th-c, one of England's smallest churches, notable for its lonely hilltop position with remarkable coast and Dartmoor views.

⌂ ⚲ ✝ **Burrator Reservoir** This gives a 5-mile walk in beautiful woodland and moorland surroundings. **Sheepstor church** on the way has interesting memorials to the Brookes family, former rajahs of Sarawak.

⌂ **Devonport leat** This watercourse, still largely complete, was first engineered 200 years ago to give Devonport a water supply. A path along the gently graded channel takes in some remote scenery in Dartmoor's western moors, and makes getting lost quite difficult; it's easily reached off the B3212 NE of Yelverton.

✳ △ **Dr Blackall's Drive** This specially created carriage drive from Bel Tor Corner to New Bridge gives splendid views of the Dart Valley, and is among Dartmoor's finest paths for walkers.

✳ △ **Great Mis Tor** In the lonely terrain N of Dartmoor Prison, this gives walkers panoramic views over much of the moor – though access may be barred by army firing practice (red flags give warning).

🏛 ✳ △ **Grimspound** By a stream, this is one of the most impressive of Dartmoor's **ancient sites**, with a fine old lichened granite cross nearby to mark the way for later medieval travellers; great views from the round walk to Widecombe.

△ **Haytor Rocks** This fortress-like collection of rocks makes a striking and popular objective for walks; nearby is an **abandoned quarry** served by an unusual 19th-c tramway with grooved-granite rails.

✳ △ **Honeybag Tor** Marvellous views over Widecombe – and though the OS map doesn't show this, there's a path over to Hound Tor to the E, along the spine of the ridge.

🏛 △ **Hound Tor** Majestically monumental and a good destination for a walk, with an interesting excavated abandoned **medieval village** nearby.

✳ △ **Hunter's Tor** The ridge path to this landmark gives panoramic views of Lustleigh Cleave and the Bovey valley.

△ **Postbridge clapper bridge** By the road at Postbridge, this ancient stone packhorse bridge is an attractive – and in summer very popular – focus for Dartmoor strolls, often complete with hopeful ponies.

🏛 △ **Shovel Down** These open moorland expanses harbour some of Dartmoor's richest concentrations of antiquities. You'll need a map just to find the car park at Scorhill, SW of Gidleigh and W of Chagford; from there, a path brings you out on to the moor within sight of Scorhill stone circle. Close by are stone slab bridges over clear brooks; among the litter of rocks by one river is the Teign Tolmen,

a natural boulder through which the water has gouged a perfectly circular hole. You can walk over to nearby Kes Tor, close to which is the Long Stone and a fine stone row of about 2500–1500BC.

△ **Vixen Tor** Towering up from the bracken, this looks unclimbable, but is quite easily reached from behind. This area of the Walkham valley is relatively lush and green, and walkers can explore the old railway tracks which once served local quarries.

✟ 🐾 **Yarner Wood** (nr Bovey Tracey) This National Nature Reserve still has a good nature trail, despite the fact that hundreds of acres nearby were torched by arsonists 3 years ago – the continuing strong re-growth is very heartening.

✳ **Yes Tor** Up in the lonelier northern part of the moor, this landmark gives great views over Dartmoor. This area of Okehampton Common is the highest terrain in southern England, though (as throughout this northern area) access is often barred by army firing practice – look out for red flags on approach roads.

DARTMOUTH SX8751

★ 🏛 Charming waterside small town with many exceptional buildings, especially around the inner harbour. Though so popular, it's kept its own strong character, and stays very much alive through the winter. Cobbled Bayards Cove, with an old fort and steep wooded hills behind, is particularly photogenic, as is pedestrianised Foss St. Markets are on Tues and Fri: Old Market is picturesque. The Royal Naval College is a striking building. Interesting shops, plenty of waterside seats, lots of action on the river. Parking in summer can be trying: best to use the good Park & Ride on the B3207 Halwell road.

🏰 ✳ ⚓ △ **Dartmouth Castle** (slightly SE of town, off B3205) Classic late 15th-c battlemented fortress, virtually intact, with cannon and later gun batteries (a new video shows it firing), and great views out into the Channel. Snacks; shop; cl winter lunchtimes, and Mon and Tues; (01803) 833588; £2.60; EH. In summer a little ferry leaves the South Embankment for

here every 15 minutes or so.
Otherwise it's an enjoyable and fairly
gentle 20-minute walk from Dartmouth
itself, though the immediate hinterland
is unremarkable.

✿ ♿ **Dartmouth Museum** (Duke St)
Well restored 17th-c timbered house,
with mainly nautical displays; shop; cl
Sun, 25–26 Dec, and 1 Jan; £1. **Henley
Museum** (Anzac St) Smaller but
interesting, this should reopen later this
year after major refurbishment to
increase its appeal to children; tel
(01803) 832281 for details.

↓⏳ **Newcomen Engine House** (Royal
Ave Gardens) Huge steam-powered
atmospheric beam-engine pump,
thought to be the world's oldest,
worked 1720–1913. Shop, disabled
access; cl Sun Nov–Mar and Christmas;
(01803) 834224; 50p.

⏳🚂 **River trips to Totnes** Pass
some of Devon's prettiest scenery,
much of which can't be seen on foot or
by car; you can combine this with
steamtrains or a connecting bus back
– which saves hearing the commentary
a second time. You can also go on
circular tours of the surrounding area.
There may still be boats in winter –
(01803) 832109 to check; £6.20 return
to Totnes. Also quaint car and
pedestrian ferries to Kingswear and the
A379 (can be a 2-hour car wait at peak
summer times).

✝ **St Saviour's** Lots of charming detail,
well worth a close look, inc altar, pulpit,
painted rood screen, brasses on the
chancel floor, and elaborate 14th-c
hinges on the south door.

DAWLISH SX9576
Old-fashioned small resort with
modern developments and camps
outside; red sandstone cliffs, a good
beach, waterside parks with black
swans, a small summer museum, and
pier; the main line railway cut through
the cliffs right by the water is striking.

🐦 **Dawlish Warren** Sandy grassy spit
(with golf course) largely blocking in the
Exe estuary, with glistening tidal flats full
of wading birds, and dunes with some
rare plants. In summer get well out to
the point, to avoid the crowds and
caravan parks at the station end; in
winter it's splendidly wild and blowy,
with thousands of ducks, brent geese

and waders (even avocets)
congregating at high tide to wait till the
mudflats show again. Visitor centre cl
winter wkdys; free, guided nature walks
£2; (01626) 863980 for times. The
Mount Pleasant out here has decent
food.

DREWSTEIGNTON SX7390
★ 🏰 ⛲ ♿ ✿ 🏛 **Castle Drogo**
Above the charming village of
Drewsteignton is this impressive
granite castle, designed by Sir Edwin
Lutyens and built as a bizarre and
brilliantly inventive mixture of medieval
style and 20th-c luxury, with cunningly
disguised radiators and amazing details
even in the kitchen and lavatory. Lovely
grounds with yew hedges form an outer
barbican. There are good guided walks
through the surrounding woodland,
and super views – it's 275 metres
(900ft) up overlooking the gorge of the
River Teign. Meals, snacks, shop; cl
Nov–Mar, plus castle cl Fri (though
garden, shop and tearoom still open);
(01647) 433306; £5.30, garden and
grounds only £2.50; NT. A well
signposted minor road W of the village
takes you to **Spinster's Rock**, a well
preserved Neolithic burial chamber and
the most easily accessible prehistoric
feature in the area.

DUNSTONE SX5951
🐖 🦋 🐦 ♔ **National Shire Horse
Centre** Shire horses and foals, waggon
rides, smithy and saddlery, butterfly
house, falconry displays (pm only),
adventure playground and pets corner.
Meals, snacks, shop and craft centre,
disabled access; tel (01752) 880268 for
winter opening; £3.95; reduced rates
and displays in winter. The Dartmoor
Union in Holbeton is quite handy for
lunch, and the road from there to Noss
Mayo has good views.

ERMINGTON SX6353
✝ **Ermington church** Notable for the
crooked 14th-c stone spire above its
tower – Victorian rebuilding kept the
tilt. The B3210 from Totnes is pretty,
and the First & Last an attractive pub.

FINGLE BRIDGE SX7489
⛵ ♿ ✿ From the Anglers Rest a
lovely 'Fisherman's Path' winds along a
wooded stretch of the River Teign; you
can return at high level on the 'Hunter's
Path', passing nr Castle Drogo at

Drewsteignton, (*see above*) and gaining tremendous views.

KENTON SX9583

✝ **Kenton church** A delightful church, its harmonious medieval sandstone masonry photographing well against blue sky; fine carving inside.

KINGSBRIDGE SX7344

★ ✝ Small town of character, with pretty cobbled lanes diving off steep Fore St, arcaded shops, pillared market house (market day Weds), interesting monuments in the church, boats on the tidal estuary (and ferry to Salcombe); the waterfront Crabshell is very popular for seafood. At the head of the nearby creek, pretty South Pool has a fairly interesting **church**, with a delightfully ghoulish story attached, and a good pub.

♖ **Cookworthy Museum of Rural Life** (Fore St) Collection of rural artefacts from Victorian kitchen implements to modern farming equipment, housed in a 17th-c grammar school. Shop; cl Sun, and all Nov–Mar; (01548) 853235; £1.80.

KINGSTON SX6347

◺ ★ There are several walks from the village down to an unspoilt beach.

KINGSWEAR SX9051

✿ 🏠 ★ ◺ **Coleton Fishacre** (3m E of Kingswear, off Lower Ferry Rd at Tollhouse) D'Oyly Carte's romantic and lush subtropical garden, with 20 colourful acres dropping down to a pretty cove; formal terraces, walled garden with stream-fed ponds, unusual trees and shrubs, grassy woodland paths. Snacks, shop, limited disabled access; open Weds–Sun Apr–Nov, plus bank hols, and pm Sun in Mar; (01803) 752466; £3.70 (house £1 extra); NT. More ambitious marked paths beyond the gardens take you along the cliffs, showing how wild this part was before the garden was planted. The Royal Dart in the pretty waterside village of Kingswear has good seafood upstairs, and the Dart Valley Railway runs between the village and Paignton.

LODDISWELL SX7248

◺ If you cross the river by the lane towards Woodsleigh, there's a quiet walk upstream by riverside pastures and woods towards Topsham Bridge.

LOWER ASHTON SX8484

✿ 🎗 **Canonteign Falls & Country Park** Pleasant country park covering 80 acres of ancient woodland, with a spectacularly high waterfall; also lakes, wildfowl, and a children's commando course. Meals, snacks, shop; cl mid-Nov–Mar (exc most Suns and Feb half-term); (01647) 252434; £3.75. The Manor pub in the village is useful for lunch (no children inside).

LUSTLEIGH SX7881

★ ◺ 🎗 One of the most attractive villages in the whole of England, with charming riverside walks in utterly unspoilt woodland around it, or up to Hunter's Tor on Dartmoor. Primrose Cottage is hotly tipped for cream teas, and the Cleave Inn is good.

LYDFORD SX5184

! 🏔 **Lydford Gorge** Spectacular gorge formed by the River Lyd cutting into the rock, causing boulders to scoop out potholes in the bed of the stream. Walks along the ravine take you to dramatic sights such as the White Lady waterfall and the Devil's Cauldron whirlpool (summer crowds around this bit). Children like it but need to be watched carefully, and paths can be narrow and slippery. Snacks (in an ingeniously designed tearoom), shop; most parts cl Nov–Mar; (01822) 820441; £3.40; NT. The forbidding ruined **castle** has a daunting 12th-c stone keep, its upper floor once used as a court, and the lower as a prison; free. The Castle Inn is excellent, and the Dartmoor Inn now has good food.

MALBOROUGH SX7039

🏠 🐄 **Yarde Medieval Farmhouse** (just outside Malborough, towards Salcombe) Although somewhat delapidated – a programme of restoration proceeds as finances allow – readers enjoy visiting this attractive old farmhouse complete with brewhouse and stables; also shetland ponies, goats, hens, ducks and a pets corner. Tea and cakes; open pm Sun, Weds and Fri, Easter–Sept; (01548) 842367; £2.

MANATON SX7581

★ 🎗 ◺ A pretty village, with the private riverside woodland around **Becky Falls Woodland Estate** (B3344 to Bovey Tracey) useful enough for undemanding family walks if you don't plan to take advantage of the countryside proper. Meals, snacks, shop, some disabled access; cl Nov–late-Mar (exc wknds, weather permitting); (01647) 221259; £3.80. The Kestor has decent food.

MARLDON SX8663

🏰 **Compton Castle** (1m N, off A3022; or off A381 at Ipplepen turnoff) Formidably fortified and rather picturesque 14th- and 16th-c manor around a courtyard with portcullised entrance, particularly interesting for its completeness. The exterior was used as Willoughby's house in the recent film of *Sense and Sensibility*. Shop, very limited disabled access; open Mon, Weds and Thurs Apr–Oct, cl 12.15–2pm; (01803) 827112; £2.80; NT. The Church House Inn is handy for lunch.

MEAVY SX5367

🏕 ⌂ ★ This clear wooded river has some pleasant spots for strolling. Meavy itself (pronounced 'Mewy' locally) is an attractive village with one of the oldest oak trees in Britain, and where the parish still owns the (good) pub (whose locals dance around the tree on New Year's Eve). Another useful pub for people walking in this valley is the Skylark at Clearbrook.

MODBURY SX6551

★ Attractive buildings especially in steep Church St, with the quite photogenic church at the top and pretty Exeter Inn at the bottom. Brownston St is quite interesting too, with an ornate water conduit at top.

MORWELLHAM SX4469

⬇T **Morwellham Quay** Thriving and meticulously researched open-air museum in lovely countryside, with costumed guides convincingly re-creating the boom years when Morwellham was the greatest copper port in the British Empire. The restored cottages come complete with pigs in the backyard, and you can watch the work of a blacksmith, a cooper, coachmen and quay workers. Also rides into the mines, horse-drawn carriages, and lovely walks. Very popular in school hols – a visit can easily last all day. Meals, snacks, shop, some disabled access; cl Christmas wk; (01822) 832766; £8.50 (reduced price and operations in winter). The Ship (part of the centre) is good, with period waitresses and drinks.

NEWTON ABBOT SX8670

A working town rather than a holiday centre, but several interesting places here or nearby.

🏰 ✾ **Bradley Manor** (off A381 S of Newton Abbot) Peaceful 15th-c house nr a stream through extensive wood-fringed grounds, quiet walks. Open pm Weds Apr–Sept, plus some Thurs at start and end of season – best to phone; (01626) 354513; £2.60; NT.

✾ **Orchid Paradise** (Forches Cross, A382 N of Newton Abbot) Colourful place, with lots of rare and endangered species in elaborate indoor reconstructions of their natural habitats. Snacks, nursery and shop, disabled access (but no facilities); cl winter bank hols; (01626) 52233; £1.50.

✾ ✿ **Plant World** (St Marychurch Rd, Coffinswell) Unusual 4-acre garden built and planted as a giant map of the world, with the countries containing their correct native plants, trees and flowers – many of them quite rare in this country, but flourishing in the mild Devon climate. Also plant centre (with seeds of some of the rarest plants), old-fashioned English garden and fine views from the picnic area. Snacks; cl Weds and Oct–Easter; (01803) 872939; £1. The Linny in the village is a charming old thatched pub.

🍺 **Tuckers Maltings** (Teign Rd, Newton Abbot) One of the few remaining working malthouses in the country, and the only one open to the public – every year they produce enough malt for 15 million pints of beer. Tours show all aspects of malting (you can touch the grain and taste the malt); they also have their own brewery. There's a hands-on section for children. Snacks, shop with over 145 speciality bottled beers; last guided tour starts 3pm (3.45pm July–Sept and bank hols), cl Nov–Easter; (01626) 334734; £4.35 (inc sample of beer).

NEWTON FERRERS SX5548

★ Picturesque village on a very sheltered rocky wooded creek of the Yealm estuary; besides modern development, there are some attractive whitewashed cottages. Lots of yachting in summer. The Dolphin, overlooking the harbour, is a pleasant place for lunch.

NORTH BOVEY SX7483

★ 🐄 A delightful, peaceful spot, not usually invaded by tourists: oak-shaded green with mounting block, stone cross, pump, ancient cottages and an attractive pub. **Miniature Pony Centre** (Wormhill Farm) Lots of friendly and engaging tiny ponies, happy to give children steady rides. Also bigger horses, pigs, donkeys, and pigmy goats, bird garden, and a good adventure playground. The setting is lovely. Meals, snacks, shop, good disabled access; cl Nov–Easter; (01647) 432400; £4.95.

NOSS MAYO SX5449

△ 𝒬 **Yealm estuary** There are attractive walks by this wooded estuary from Noss Mayo (the Old Ship and the Dolphin are good pubs), then beyond to Gara Point and exposed cliff; largely NT. This can be reached in sections via the Noss Mayo–Holbeton coastal ridge road.

OKEHAMPTON SX5895

This Dartmoor-edge working town has a couple of things worth stopping for.

👣 ℘ **Museum of Dartmoor Life** (West St) Well converted old watermill with interactive displays on local life, tourist information centre and working craft studios next door. Tea-room, shop, some disabled access; cl Sun (exc Jun–Sept) and all Nov–Easter; (01837) 52295; £1.90.

🏰 𝒬 △ **Okehampton Castle** The tower on a steep grassy mound above the river is remarkable above all for the way it stays standing – a balancing act of ruined masonry zigzagging up into the sky. It's the biggest medieval castle in Devon, with sections dating from 11th to the 14th c; good woodland walks. Snacks, shop; cl all Nov–Mar; (01837) 52844; £2.30.

PAIGNTON SX8861

🏨 🎡 Largely a typical resort, with a long promenade between the good sandy beach and green; the little harbour is pretty, with working fishing boats as well as yachts. The original inland core has an attractive red sandstone church with some interesting buildings nearby, especially **Kirkham House**, a handsome, sandstone, Tudor merchant's house with a lofty hall. The formal and subtropical lakeside gardens at **Oldway** are colourful; on summer weekday mornings there are guided tours of the Versailles-style colonnaded mansion at their centre (tel (01803) 201201 and ask for Oldway House details). Attractive Elberry Cove between Paignton and Brixham is altogether quieter. Decent places for lunch include the Blagdon Inn (off A385) and the Ship (Totnes road).

🚂 **Paignton & Dartmouth Steam Railway** (Queen's Park Station, Torbay road) One of the nicest such trips we know of – GWR steamtrains run from here right by the sea along Tor Bay (halts at Goodrington Beach, which has closer parking, and Churston), then along the Dart estuary to Kingswear. The front Pullman coach is less crowded, and there's a model railway at the Paignton end. You can combine this with a boat Dartmouth–Totnes, and bus Totnes–Paignton. Snacks, shop, disabled access; cl Nov–Feb (exc parts of Dec), and some wkdays and wknds out of season, (01803) 555872 for timetable; £6.10 return.

🐾 **Paignton Zoo** (St Michael's) Well run and shown, with over 1,300 animals and birds (many of them breeding) in 75 acres of beautifully planted surroundings; it's perhaps the country's most visually appealing zoo, and lays a decent emphasis on conservation. The latest addition was a tropical reptile exhibition. Also a lakeside miniature railway, and a splendid hands-on animal education centre for children. Lots of events and feeding displays. Meals, snacks, shop, good disabled access; cl 25 Dec; (01803) 557479; £7.

PLYMOUTH SX4753

⚓ Apart from the area round the Barbican, most of the old areas of the city were destroyed in the war, and in parts it is like lots of other busy modern towns. There are some interesting escapes from the bustle, and in places the Hoe has something of the feel of smaller seaside promenades, with great views out over the Sound; decent food from the Yard Arm (looking out in suitably nautical style) and the Waterfront bar/restaurant. A statue of Drake is a reminder that he's supposed to have played his famous game of bowls here; there's still a bowling green close by. A tour bus can take you to the main attractions, though it's perhaps more fun on one of the **boat trips** run by Tamar Cruises from Mayflower Steps, off Madeira Rd, Barbican; (01752) 822105. There are also boats from here to the **Mountbatten Peninsula**, a former Ministry of Defence area now open to the public; you can walk along the breakwater, which goes right out into the Sound with views back towards the city. The ferries over to Torpoint in Cornwall put Antony House and Mt Edgcumbe in very easy reach. The Bank (behind Theatre Royal) does good-value food all day, and the tourist information centre is one of the most efficient we've come across.

🏚 **Barbican** Carefully restored since the war, a series of narrow twisty streets of old buildings W of working Sutton Harbour; photogenic – and evocative even in wet weather. New St is its oldest core. The Dolphin pub has original Beryl Cook paintings.

🎨 **Barbican Glassworks** The old fishmarket (the Barbican) has been redeveloped as a visitor centre. You can watch glass-blowing demonstrations by Dartington Crystal, and there are exhibitions on the local area. Large shop, disabled access; cl 25–26 Dec, 1 Jan and Easter Sun; free.

🍸 **Black Friars Distillery** (60 Southside St) Photogenic home of Plymouth Dry Gin, now the only English gin still made in its original distillery, founded in 1793. The building itself dates back much further, and has had periods as a monastery and a prison; tours include demonstrations of production, a film of the town's history and, of course, a sample of the gin itself. Shop; cl Sun Sept–May, and all Jan–Easter; (01752) 665292; £2.75.

👁 🖼 **City Museum & Art Gallery** (Drake Circus) Well shown collections of mostly West Country interest. Snacks, shop, good disabled access; cl Sun, Mon (exc bank hols); free.

🏰 **Crownhill Fort** 🖸 (Crownhill Rd) Just N of town, the biggest and least altered of Plymouth's Victorian forts, though from the road it looks little more than a wooded hill. Used by the army right up to 1986, it's been well restored by the Landmark Trust, with barrack rooms, underground tunnels, secret passageways, and lookout towers to explore; children can run around quite freely, and there's an adventure playground. You can stay here in a Victorian officer's flat (all year), and have the run of the place after dark. Snacks, shop, limited disabled access (lots of steep steps); cl Nov–Mar; (01752) 793754; £3.50.

🏚 🪟 **Elizabethan House** (32 New St) The future of this splendid timber-framed Tudor sea-captain's house with period furniture was looking dubious as we went to press; phone (01752) 304774 for details. There's an Elizabethan garden just down the road at number 39.

👁 **Merchant's House** (St Andrew St) Well restored 16th-c jettied house, telling the city's day-to-day history in displays themed on tinker, tailor, soldier, sailor; also an early Victorian apothecary's shop and schoolroom. Shop; cl 1–2pm, Sun, Mon (exc bank hols), and Nov–Mar; (01752) 304774; £1.

🎵 **National Maritime Aquarium** *See separate family panel on p.181.*

🏛 **Plymouth Dome** 🖸 (The Hoe) State-of-the-art evocation of Plymouth's past and present using feel-part-of-it technology – you can stroll along lively Elizabethan streets, dodge press gangs, meet Drake and the Pilgrim Fathers, and come bang up to date with satellite and radar monitoring of current harbour action and weather. Good fun as well as interesting, and well worth 2 hours (you may have trouble parking nearby for longer than that). Particularly good for families – children don't mind learning about a place's heritage when it's presented like this. Snacks, shop, good disabled access; cl 25 Dec; (01752) 603300; £3.95 (includes admission to Smeaton's Tower).

🏚 **Prysten House** 🖸 (Finewell St) The city's oldest house, an austere late 15th-c granite building with galleried courtyard. Unpretentious but quite atmospheric restored rooms feature a model of 17th-c Plymouth, and several yards of an ambitious tapestry showing American colonisation; cl Sun, and

Nov–Mar; (01752) 661414; 70p.

❄ ⛴ **Royal Citadel** (The Hoe)
Unrivalled views of the city and sea
from the ramparts of this magnificent
17th-c battlemented fortress. The
gateway is striking, and the barracked
parade-ground is still in use. Shop,
disabled access (though no facilities);
admission by guided tour only, at
2.30pm May–Sept, starting from the
main gate – get tickets at least 15
minutes earlier from the Dome or the
tourist information centre; (01752)
775841; £3.

🏛 ❄ **Smeaton's Tower** (The Hoe)
Colourfully striped 18th-c former
Eddystone Rocks lighthouse, moved
here 110 years ago, with a good view
from the top if you like steps; cl
Nov–Mar, and maybe in bad weather;
(01752) 600608; 75p.

✝ **St Andrew's Church** (St Andrew
St) Bombed but lovingly restored, with
stained glass by John Piper illustrating
the city's history.

PLYMPTON SX5255

🏠🖼❄✗★ **Saltram** (2m W of
Plympton, off A38/A379 at Marsh Mills
roundabout) Magnificent, mostly 18th-c
mansion still with pretty much all the
original contents, especially notable for
its unaltered Robert Adam rooms.
George II furnishings, decoration and
paintings (strong on Reynolds, who as a
regular guest advised on which other
pictures to buy), interesting period
kitchen, stately garden with orangery,
and parkland by wooded Plym estuary.
The house has attracted lots of extra
visitors since starring as Norland Park
in *Sense and Sensibility*. Meals, snacks,
shop, local art/crafts gallery, disabled
access; cl Fri, Sat, and all Nov–Mar
(house cl am); (01752) 336546; £5.70,
garden only £2.70; NT. The old town
around St Maurice Church is worth a
look if you're here: attractive partly
arcaded streets, very ruined motte and
bailey castle, decent food at the
George.

POWDERHAM SX9683

⛴❄🐎 **Powderham Castle** The
ancestral home of the Earls of Devon,
badly damaged in the Civil War but
elaborately restored in the 18th and
19th c. The richly decorated state
rooms were used in the film The
Remains of the Day. Spectacular rose
garden, home to Timothy the 157-year-
old tortoise, spring woodland garden, a
secret garden especially designed for
children (with ducks, rabbits, guinea-
pigs and chinchillas), and a broad deer
park with views over the Exe estuary.
Good guided tours, lots of special
events, and a new farm shop. Meals,
snacks, some disabled access; cl Sat, and
Nov–Mar; (01626) 890243; *£5.95. The
ancient waterside Anchor has good
seafood.

PRAWLE POINT SX7735

❄ ⌂ Impressive scenery: wind-blasted
gorse, grass and thrift above low but
fierce cliffs, lending itself to a round
walk, with a useful network of green
lanes leading inland to the village of East
Prawle (good food at the Freebooters
Arms).

SALCOMBE SX7438

★ ⚓ Steep narrow-streeted fishing
village, full of enjoyable holiday bustle in
summer, with lots of souvenirs, bric-à-
brac, boating shops, teashops and pubs
overlooking the sea, nearby beaches
and coves, **boat trips** and boat hire.
Besides the Spinnaker and the Foot in
the Plate restaurants, the Ferry,
Victoria and Fortescue are all popular
for food.

⌂ ❄ 🏛 **Bolt Head/Bolt Tail** SX6937
6 miles of one of the best coast-path
sections, with remote exposed clifftops,
glorious coves, far views, well preserved
Iron Age earth ramparts on Bolt Tail; all
NT. Best access is via Overbecks, Soar
Mill Cove or Hope Cove.

🏠❄❄ **Overbecks** (South Sands;
signed from Salcombe and Malborough)
Named after the eccentric research
chemist who lived here until 1937;
among his possessions and inventions
you can still see the Rejuvenator which
he claimed 'practically renewed' his
youth. For most people the chief
attraction is the luscious subtropical
gardens, with terraced plantings among
woodland, many rarities and plenty of
palms and citrus fruits; the place is
outstanding late May–Jun for the
magnolias, but worth a trip any time of
year. Glorious views out to sea, also a
colourful statue garden, picnic
belvedere and collections of dolls and
lead soldiers. Snacks, shop; cl Sat (exc

Aug), Fri in Oct, and all Nov–Mar; (01548) 842893; £4, £2.80 garden only; NT. Mill Bay nr here has one of the area's safest bathing beaches.

SHALDON SX9372

★ ※ Interesting and colourful mix of seaside houses spanning 200 years of architectural fancy; some lovely corners especially down by the water away from the centre, also much older cottages in Crown Sq. The Clifford Arms has good local fish. High grassy sandstone Ness overlooks the sea and Teignmouth, with a tunnel cut by the 19th-c landowner to a sheltered beach; the beautifully set Ness House up here is useful for food. The A379 to Maidencombe has sea views.

🐾 🐒 **Wildlife Trust** (Ness Drive) Nicely low-key breeding collection of rare and endangered foreign birds, and small mammals inc monkeys. Shop; cl 25 Dec; (01626) 872234; £3.

SLAPTON SANDS SX8343

🏖 ✔ 🐾 One of the finest beaches in the country, 6 miles of almost straight shingle N of the lighthouse at Start Point, backed by hills in the S and by road, shingle bank, lake (Slapton Ley nature reserve, marked nature trail) and marsh, then low cliffs, in the N. Good for out-of-season desolation, sheltered from winds, with a storm-ruined village at Hallsands, and salvaged tank memorial to a US Normandy landings practice disaster at Torcross.

SOURTON SX5390

❗ **Highwayman** An extraordinary pub, one bar recalling a galleon, the other a sort of fairytale fantasy, and the garden demonstrates yet more exuberant imagination – all meticulously done by the owners, not some brewery theme pub.

SOUTH-WEST COAST PATH SX5446

⌣ The finest part of Devon's south coast for walkers is between Plymouth and Brixham – much of it quite unspoilt. In summer, ferries cross the rivers (except the River Erme S of Ermington, which you have to cross at low tide).

SPARKWELL SX5858

🐾 🦅 **Dartmoor Wildlife Park & Westcountry Falconry Centre** 📷 Various animals inc big cats (feeding time 3.30pm) in 30 acres of

countryside. Also a falconry centre with displays at 12pm and 4pm (Easter–Oct exc Fri), adventure playground and picnic area. Meals, snacks, shop, disabled access; (01752) 837209; £5.95.

STICKLEPATH SX6494

⬇️ **Finch Foundry** 📷 No longer producing the sickles, shovels and tools for which it was known in the 19th c, but the waterwheels and machinery are all still working. Snacks, shop, limited disabled access; cl Tues, and Nov–Mar; (01837) 840046; £2.70; NT. The thatched Devonshire Inn in the village is good value.

STOKE GABRIEL SX8457

★ Steep village above a sheltered side-pool of the Dart estuary, with 14th-c church (with ancient yew) and Church House (pleasant for lunch) perched prettily on a high cobbled terrace.

TEIGNMOUTH SX9473

☺ 🍵 (French St) A popular resort for family holidays, with good beaches, windsurfing and so on, some handsome 19th-c streets and active docks, and a decent local history **museum** (cl am Sun, and Oct–Apr; £1). The beach-side Ship has enjoyable food all day in summer.

TORQUAY SX9163

⚓ 🚤 🎡 The busiest of the area's resorts, good for evening strolling, with palm trees and rocks, promenades, colourful gardens, decorous guesthouses and huge hotels, broad Victorian streets and expensive shops. The sheltered beaches around here are cleaner than many along this coast. Summer bustle centres around the attractive harbour, with lots of shops, boat trips, and an aquarium. In summer a **cliff railway** takes care of a dizzy swoop from Oddicombe Beach to the high wooded clifftop (around 80p each way). The quaint Hole in the Wall (Park Lane) and smart new London (Strand) do good-value food.

🎭 **Bygones** (Fore St, St Marychurch) Enthusiastically reconstructed life-sized Victorian street, with well stocked period shops and rooms, model railway, and re-created World War I trench, replete with sound effects and cooking smells. Open till 10pm (6pm Fri and Sat) in summer. Café, shop; cl 25 Dec; (01803) 326108; *£3.50.

★ ❀ **Cockington** Winding lanes of olde-worlde thatched cottages and bric-à-brac/craft shops in a sheltered village with millpond etc, well preserved by Torbay Council; adjoining a 500-acre park. The Drum pub (a useful stop) was designed to match by Lutyens in 1934. Terribly pretty, and very touristy in season, with open horse-drawn carriages.

🏛 ☗ **Kents Cavern Showcaves** (Ilsham Rd, Wellswood) The oldest directly dated archaeological site in Britain; continuing excavations often make scientists reconsider their theories about prehistoric life. Good guided tours really bring out the mystery of the caves, and colourful stalagmites and stalactites add to the eerie atmosphere. In summer they do spooky evening tours (booking essential). Very well presented, and definitely worth an hour or so if you're in the area. Special visits at Christmas. Summer meals, snacks, shop, disabled access (with prior notice); cl 25 Dec, and maybe 1 Jan (tel to check); (01803) 215136; £4.40 (£4.90 evening tours).

! **Model Village** (Hampton Ave, Babbacombe) Hundreds of 1:12 scale buildings in 4 acres of miniaturised landscape, beautifully done. Try coming at dusk between Easter and Oct, when the scenes are prettily floodlit. Snacks, shop, good disabled access; cl 25 Dec; (01803) 328669; £4.60 – a little pricey, but it's probably the best of its type (you may also have to pay for parking). The beach here has safe bathing water, and the Cary Arms (Beach Rd) is good.

☗ **Torquay Museum** (529 Babbacombe Rd) Finds from ancient local caves, local history, Victoriana and a cannon that turns out to be a clock, designed to fire its charge at midday. Shop; cl am Sun, winter wknds and 25 Dec; (01803) 293975; £2.

🏛 🖼 ❀ **Torre Abbey** (King's Drive) Some of the earlier parts of the abbey remain, inc the medieval sandstone gatehouse and ruined Norman tower, but they've been eclipsed by the later house with its 17th-, 18th- and 19th-c period rooms. The main feature now is the art gallery, along with a showy garden and palm house and an Agatha Christie room, full of possessions of the locally born author. Snacks, shop; cl Nov–Mar; (01803) 293593; £3.

TOTNES SX8060

★ 🏛 ✝ 🏚 Busy in summer, but still keeping most of its charm even then, particularly early in the morning. The picturesque Elizabethan area known as **The Narrows** is very atmospheric, especially along the High St down to the arch at the top of Fore St, with quaint pillared arcades. On Tues ams May–Sept many traders wear Elizabethan costume, and the main streets are closed to traffic then, delighting visitors but infuriating some local traders. There's a working harbour (see *Dartmouth for river trips*), and you can walk some way downstream on either side of the River Dart. Behind the Church of St Mary's (which has a super rood screen), several rooms in the 11th-c **guildhall** may be open; it was once part of a Benedictine priory. Perhaps unexpectedly, Totnes has quite a New Age flavour; there's even a flotation tank to wash away city stresses. The Kingsbridge Inn (Leechwell St), Royal Seven Stars Hotel (Fore St) and the Albert (Bridgetown) have decent food, though the Cott at nearby Dartington easily merits the extra distance. The **South Devon Railway**, which stops here, is described under Buckfastleigh.

🏛 ☗ **Bowden House** (Ashprington Rd, S of town) Tours by costumed guides of handsomely restored grand Tudor and baroque rooms (plenty of weaponry, and well documented tales of ghosts), and separate **photography museum** with still and moving pictures (inc cartoons) in attractive grounds. Meals, snacks, shop, disabled access to museum only; open pm Mon–Thurs and bank hol Suns from May–Oct; (01803) 863664; £4.95.

☗ **Devonshire Collection of Costume** (43 High St) Period costumes and accessories from the 18th c to the present, from high fashion to ordinary work clothes, with changing annual exhibitions. Shop; cl wknds, and Nov–Apr; £1.50.

✻ ! **Goss Visitor Centre** (Building A, Baltic Wharf Boatyard, St Peter's Quay) Chance to watch the progress of

Britain's fastest ocean-racing yacht to date, as it endeavours to complete the quickest circumnavigation of the world. Live linkages with the crew, captained by Pete Goss (who famously saved a French yachtsman's life a few years ago), plus video theatre and interactive displays which explain the details of the project. Snacks, shop, disabled access; tel (01803) 865592 to arrange guided tours; free.

🏰 ❋ **Totnes Castle** Part Norman, part 14th c, these classic circular remains were lucky enough to escape any battles, so the keep is pretty much intact. There's a tree-shaded inner lawn, and lovely views of the town and down to the river. Shop, snacks; cl winter Mon and Tues (and maybe lunchtimes then); (01803) 864406; £1.60.

👑 **Totnes Museum** (70 Fore St) Stately Elizabethan merchant's house with a galleried courtyard, herb garden, and a display on the inventions of Totnes boy Charles Babbage, who was the creator of one of the earliest computers. Shop, disabled access with prior arrangement; cl wknds, and Nov–Mar; (01803) 863821; £1.50.

TUCKENHAY SX8156
⛵ This gives a pretty one-mile stroll E along wooded Bow Creek, from the Maltsters Arms – good food here.

WEMBURY BAY SX5148
⛵❋ A walk here gives good views, starting from Wembury past the church

at the start of NT clifftops; woods and pastures on the opposite shore, Plymouth shipping in the distance.
WIDECOMBE IN THE MOOR
SX7176
★ ✝ 🏚 One of the most visited villages on Dartmoor, immortalised by the trip of Uncle Tom Cobbleigh and all to Widecombe Fair. The granite-carved village sign shows them all crowded on to their old grey mare. The **church**, known as the Cathedral of the Moors, has a distinctive, disproportionately high tower. The adjoining 16th-c **church house**, now the church hall, is worth a look. Next door, the **Sexton's Cottage** is a NT and Dartmoor National Park information centre and gift shop; cl 24 Dec–mid-Feb. The Post Office Stores has good ice-cream and local honey. The reconstructed Olde Inne in the village is very popular with tourists, but for more of a Tom Cobbleigh flavour try the Rugglestone Inn just S. The **Shilstone Rocks Riding Centre** organises horse-riding over Dartmoor, beginners welcome. Disabled access; (01364) 621281; from £14 an hour.
YELVERTON SX5267
👑 **Paperweight Centre** (Buckland Terrace) Odd collection of hundreds of glass paperweights, all sizes and designs, inc collector's pieces. Shop, disabled access; open wknds and daily Apr–Oct and Dec; (01822) 854250; free. The Rock (A386) is a good family pub.

Where to eat

ASHPRINGTON SX8156 **Durant Arms** (01803) 732240 Friendly gable-ended dining pub with 2 attractive bar rooms, several open fires, good bar food, well kept beers, and friendly service; cl pm 25 Dec; disabled access. **£20.55|£7**.

AVONWICK SX7157 **Avon Inn** (01364) 73475 Popular dining pub with comfortable, fairly modern furnishings, a wide range of good food inc lots of interesting pasta dishes, plenty of fish, and lovely puddings, fine Italian wines, well kept real ales, and a pleasant riverside garden; cl Sun, am Mon, 1 wk Jan; disabled access. **£22|£5.25**.

BABBACOMBE SX9365 **Tea Rose Tearooms** Babbacombe Downs Rd (01803) 324477 Charming small tearoom with inside and outside tables set in a garden opposite the sea, with waitresses in period dress, and generous cream teas, and snacks; disabled access. **£3.25**.

BANTHAM SX6643 **Sloop** (01548) 560489 Nr sandy beach (good for surfing), this 16th-c nautical village inn has good bar food inc lots of fish, hearty breakfasts, and decent beers and wines; bdrms and self-catering cottages. **£22|£5**.

BOLBERRY SX6939 **Port Light** (01548) 561384 Popular even on dismal winter weekdays, this clifftop former RAF radar station (easy walk from Hope Cove) is warm and friendly with good home-made food in an attractive bar and restaurant, super sea views, woodburner, and a good outdoor children's play area; bdrms; cl Jan. **£16.75|£5.95.**

CHERITON BISHOP SX7793 **Old Thatch** *(01647) 24204* Welcoming 16th-c inn with good bar food from a big menu, interesting puddings, beamed bar and big open stone fireplace, and friendly service; bdrms; cl 25 Dec. **£17.95|£5.**

COCKWOOD SX9780 **Anchor** *(01626) 890203* Friendly pub by the harbour, with small low-ceilinged rambling rooms and lots of good fresh fish dishes – 30 ways of serving mussels, 12 of serving scallops, 10 of oysters, and so forth, no smoking restaurant, well kept real ales, 10 wines by the glass, and 50 malt whiskies; disabled access. **£25|£5.95.**

CORNWORTHY SX8255 **Hunters Lodge** *(01803) 732204* Welcoming and popular country local with a 2-roomed low-ceilinged bar, cottagey restaurant with 17th-c fireplace, well liked food from an extensive menu, well kept real ales, and plenty of seats outside; partial disabled access. **£19.50|£4.95.**

DARTMOUTH SX8751 **Café Alf Resco** *Lower Rd (no telephone)* On 3 levels (partly open-air at street level), this is a bustling café offering hearty breakfasts, morning coffee and lunchtime snacks; bdrms; cl Mon, Tues; disabled access. **£10|£4.**

DARTMOUTH SX8751 **Carved Angel** *2 South Embankment (01803) 832465* Black and white timbered restaurant, airy and attractive, overlooking the quay, with wonderful meals using carefully chosen absolutely fresh produce – superb fish, delicious puddings and lovely cheeses – fine wines in every price range, and a smart yet friendly atmosphere; no smoking; cl pm Sun, Mon, 5 days Christmas, 6 wks from 1 Jan; children under 5 free; partial disabled access. **£48.75|£21.**

DARTMOUTH SX8751 **Cherub** *10 Higher St (01804) 832571* Dartmouth's oldest building (already 300 years old when Sir Francis Drake used it), this has a bustling bar, liked by locals, an upstairs dining room, decent food, and well kept ales; children in upstairs restaurant only. **£19|£5.**

GULWORTHY SX4472 **Horn of Plenty** *A390 just W of Tavistock (01822) 832528* On the edge of Dartmoor in flower-filled gardens, this relaxed, Georgian, no smoking restaurant-with-rooms has carefully cooked food using top quality local produce inc lovely puddings and cheeses (wonderful breakfasts, too), a good wine list, and a vine-covered terrace for aperitifs; comfortable bdrms; cl am Mon, 25–26 Dec; disabled access. **£21 lunch, £35 dinner**.

HARBERTON SX7758 **Church House** *(01803) 863707* Ancient village pub with magnificent medieval panelling, attractive old furnishings, generous helpings of interesting daily specials, well kept beers, and decent wines; bdrms; children in family room; cl pm 25–26 Dec, 1 Jan. **£18.75|£4.75.**

KINGSBRIDGE SX7344 **Crabshell** *The Quay, Embankment Rd (01548) 852345* Famous old dining pub, very popular for its lovely waterside position and fresh local fish – they also do picnics and take-aways; quick, friendly staff, well kept real ales, decent wines, warm winter fire, and live music Thurs; disabled access. **£22|£5.**

KINGSTEIGNTON SX8773 **Old Rydon** *(01626) 54626* Cosy old pub with wide choice of constantly changing imaginative bar food, big winter log fire, well kept real ales, helpful service, and a prettily planted dining conservatory. **£23.50|£6.50.**

LUSTLEIGH SX7881 **Primrose Cottage** *(01647) 277365* Thatched 15th-c cottage by the old village church, with seats in a riverside garden, clotted cream teas, lovely home-made cakes and pastries, and tasty all-day light meals; cl Tues, and mid-Oct–mid-Mar. **£14|£7.**

MARLDON SX8663 **Church House** *(01803) 558279* Well run bustling pub with several different attractive bar areas, candles on tables, bare boards, hops and dried flowers; characterful restaurant, good popular food inc nice daily specials and themed food evenings, well kept real ales, and seats outside; bdrms; children over 10 in evening. **£20|£5.**

PLYMOUTH SX4755 **Chez Nous** *13 Frankfort Gate (01752) 266793* Informal and friendly French bistro with careful cooking of fresh local produce, especially fresh fish and fine puddings, some distinguished wines, and friendly atmosphere; cl

Sun–Mon, am Sat, bank hols, 3 wks Feb, 3 wks Sept; partial disabled access. **£42**.

RATTERY SX7461 **Church House** *(01364) 642220* One of Britain's oldest pubs, with big open fires, friendly customers and staff, good bar food, decent wines and beers, fine malt whiskies, and a nice dog and cats; peaceful setting; disabled access. **£15.95|£3.95**.

RINGMORE SX6545 **Journey's End** *(01548) 810205* Partly medieval inn in a pretty setting with thatched servery in panelled bar, open fire, a warm welcome, well kept beer, and nice fresh food; good-value bdrms; cl pm 25 Dec. **£19.95|£5**.

SALCOMBE SX7338 **Foot in the Plate** *Russell Ct (01548) 842189* Bustling and enjoyable evening restaurant with a relaxed atmosphere, a good choice of pasta and Greek dishes, and music from around the world; cl Sun, and Nov–Easter; children must be well behaved. **£18.50**.

SALCOMBE SX7338 **Spinnaker** *(01548) 843408* Relaxed waterside restaurant with good fresh local fish and shellfish (some meat also), lunchtime bar snacks, and nice puddings; cl Mon, all Dec and Jan (open Christmas wk). **£21|£6**.

TORCROSS SX8241 **Start Bay** *(01548) 580553* Notable and very popular fresh seafood generously served in a busy thatched pub overlooking a 3-mile pebble beach; farm cider; family room; cl pm 25 Dec; partial disabled access. **£16.85|£5**.

TORQUAY SX9264 **Mulberry Room** *1 Scarborough Rd (01803) 213639* Popular no smoking restaurant-with-rooms, with good, interesting food using local produce, and very enjoyable home-made cakes and scones for afternoon tea; cookery demonstrations; bdrms; cl Mon, Tues; disabled access. **£25|£7.50**.

TORQUAY SX9264 **The Table** *135 Babbacombe Rd (01803) 324292* Pretty little restaurant in a white terraced house with excellent modern cooking (lots of local fish and shellfish), a relaxed atmosphere, super bread, and good-value wines; cl Sat/Sun/Mon lunch and all lunches May–Sept, first 2 wks Feb, last 2 wks Mar; children over 10; disabled access. **£37**.

TOTNES SX8060 **Greys Dining Room** *96 High St (01803) 866369* No smoking Georgian house with pretty china on a handsome dresser and partly panelled walls; lots of teas plus herb and fruit ones, sandwiches, salads and omelettes as well as various cakes and set teas; cl Weds; no pushchairs; partial disabled access. **£6**.

TUCKENHAY SX8156 **Maltsters Arms** *(01803) 732350* Very well run creekside pub with enthusiastic friendly owners, particularly good interesting food – though they are keen to keep it as a pub where people also feel comfortable dropping in for a drink – well kept real ales, 12 wines by the glass, and relaxed, airy bars; seats by the water; super bdrms; open all day Sat–Sun and all day during summer hols. **£21.65|£5**.

UGBOROUGH SX6755 **Anchor** *(01752) 892283* Friendly pub, oak beams and log fire, a wide choice of very good food inc unusual things such as ostrich, alligator, emu and bison, lots of fresh fish, courteous service, and well kept real ales; disabled access. **£25.50|£6**.

North Devon and Exmoor

Outstanding coastal scenery, particularly below Exmoor; easy to find peace and quiet even in summer.

Much of this area is largely untouched by tourism, with long stretches of coast which are empty even in summer – and a magnificent coast path. Even Ilfracombe, the main resort, is not too trippery; it's pleasant and distinctive, with plenty for families, and stays active all year. The lower-key beach resorts such as Woolacombe and Westward Ho! virtually shut down when the season's over, their marvellous beaches then ideal for lonely walks; elsewhere there are fine bracing cliff walks. Lundy Island is a relaxing windswept wilderness.

Exmoor itself is full of interest for walkers (and drivers), and quieter in summer than Dartmoor. Though part lies in Somerset, we've covered the whole of the moor area in this chapter (some places such as Dunster within the boundary of the National Park but outside the moor itself are described in the Somerset chapter). Some of the best parts of the Tarka Trail, a growing destination for walkers and cyclists, are on and around the moor. Other inland parts are largely secluded farmland. The twisty wooded Taw Valley is pretty; the A377 gives drivers some good views here, though not quite so outstanding as the Exeter–Barnstaple rail journey, one of England's finest.

Despite the area's relative quietness, there is plenty to do – indeed, more and more each year. Interesting additions to the *Guide* this year include a good new heritage centre in Barnstaple and the unusual Art Hotel just outside the town, and an excellent Civil War centre in Torrington. Clovelly, and Combe Martin with its odd Pack of Cards pub, are legendarily pretty (and do draw the summer crowds). Arlington Court is an interesting day out for any age, and children really enjoy the Big Sheep near Bideford and the quirky Gnome Reserve near Bradworthy. Other favourite places here are Bickleigh Castle, the woodland gardens at Rosemoor near Torrington, Knighthayes Court at Bolham (great garden here too), Lynton, Lynmouth (good boat trips) and Hartland Quay. Value point: entry prices have been cut significantly this year at Clovelly Court Gardens, and the friendly Exmoor Falconry and Animal Centre near Allerford.

Where to stay

ASHWATER SX3895 **Blagdon Manor** *Ashwater, Beaworthy EX21 5DF (01409) 211224* ***£115;** 7 pretty rms. Standing in rolling countryside, this carefully restored and tranquil 17th-c manor has 8 acres of grounds (croquet and 4-hole practice golf course); beams and flagstones, log fires, fresh flowers, lovely food in a dinner-party atmosphere, and kind staff; cl Christmas; no children.

BISHOPS TAWTON SS5630 **Halmpstone Manor** *Bishops Tawton, Barnstaple EX32 0EA (01271) 830321* ***£110,** plus special breaks; 5 pretty rms. Quietly relaxing small country hotel with a log fire in the comfortable sitting room, enjoyable food in the panelled dining room, good breakfasts, caring service, an attractive garden, and nice views; cl Christmas and New Year; children over 12.

BUCKLAND BREWER SS4220 **Coach & Horses** *Buckland Brewer, Bideford EX39 5LU (01237) 451395* ***£50;** 2 rms above bar (so could be noisy for children until 11.30pm). Welcoming well preserved 13th-c thatched village pub with a cosy beamed bar, log fires in inglenook fireplaces, enjoyable food, dining room, and a pleasant garden; children over 8; no dogs; partial disabled access.

CADBURY SS9005 **Beers Farm** *Cadbury, Exeter EX5 5PY (01884) 855426* **£36;** 2 rms. Set in several acres with lovely views across to the Raddon Hills, this non-working farm is quiet and comfortable (and no smoking) with friendly, helpful owners and good breakfasts; packed lunches on request; lots to do nearby.

CHITTLEHAMHOLT SS6420 **Highbullen** *Chittlehamholt, Umberleigh EX37*

9HD (01769) 540561 ***£100,** plus special breaks; 40 comfortable and elegant, often spacious rms in main building and various attractively converted outbuildings. Victorian Gothic mansion set in huge wooded parkland and gardens with lots of wildlife, fishing (several beats), 9-hole golf course, indoor tennis court and swimming pool, table tennis, and squash court; consistently good food in an intimate restaurant overlooking the valley, busy little bar, library, and relaxed informal service (no reception, you ring a bell and wait); children over 8; no dogs.

CLAWTON SX3599 **Court Barn** *Clawton, Holsworthy EX22 6PS (01409) 271219* **£80,** plus special breaks; 8 individually furnished rms. Charming country house in 5 pretty acres with croquet, 9-hole putting green, small chip-and-putt course, and tennis and badminton courts; comfortable lounges, log fires, a library/TV room, good service, imaginative food and award-winning wines (and teas), and a quiet relaxed atmosphere; dogs allowed away from public rooms; cl 2–12 Jan.

DULVERTON SS9127 **Ashwick House** *Dulverton TA22 9QD (01398) 323969* ***£96,** plus special breaks; 6 peaceful rms with thoughtful extras. Quietly set Edwardian house in 6 lovely acres overlooking the Barle Valley, with personal service from caring owner, comfortable old-fashioned furnishings, fresh flowers, log fires, and candlelight; enjoyable food, hearty breakfasts (which can be taken on the south-facing terrace), and a really relaxing atmosphere; children over 8.

EAST BUCKLAND SS6731 **Lower Pitt** *East Buckland, Barnstaple EX32 0TD (01598) 760243* ***£70;** 3 comfortable rms. Quiet, pretty stone farmhouse with a log fire in the cosy lounge, good, well presented food using herbs and veg from own garden, simply furnished dining room and attractive conservatory, and friendly service; good cycling/walking from the door; children over 12; cl Jan; disabled access.

HATHERLEIGH SS5404 **Pressland House** *Hatherleigh, Okehampton EX20 3LW (01837) 810871* **£56,** plus special breaks; 6 rms overlooking the gardens or open countryside. Relaxed and friendly, no smoking Victorian house in neat grounds with views to Dartmoor; 2 attractive lounges, good homely food, and a small wine list; lots to do nearby; cl mid-Nov–mid-Mar; children over 12.

HATHERLEIGH SS5404 **Tally Ho** *Market St, Hatherleigh, Okehampton EX20 3JN (01837) 810306* **£50,** plus wknd breaks; 3 rms. Friendly and interesting old inn with genuinely old-fashioned fittings in opened-up beamed rooms, good food and own-brew beers.

HAWKRIDGE SS8530 **Tarr Steps** *Hawkridge, Dulverton TA22 9PY; off B3223 towards Hawkridge, N of Dulverton; (01643) 851293* **£140 inc dinner,** plus special breaks; 11 rms, most with own bthrm. Former Georgian rectory in 11 acres of gardens, surrounded by 500 acres of land with rough shooting and trout-filled river, riding, and clay-pigeon shooting; carefully refurbished, comfortable drawing room with log fires and flowers, oak-panelled bar, good food in an attractive dining room (popular locally) using own organic vegetables, a relaxed happy atmosphere, and friendly staff; self-catering cottage also; cl 12 days beginning Feb; disabled access; well behaved dogs.

HEDDON'S MOUTH SS6549 **Heddon's Gate** *Heddon's Mouth, Parracombe, Barnstaple EX31 4PZ (01598) 763313* ***£84,** plus special breaks; 14 comfortable rms named for their original use and many with views. Victorian country house hotel in interesting large gardens on the edge of Exmoor, with marvellously relaxed and friendly atmosphere, a comfortable sitting room with lovely views, a good library/Victorian morning room, attractive dining room, very good home cooking inc 6-course dinners and proper afternoon tea, and friendly helpful service; cl 1 Nov–31 Mar; children welcome if able to eat at 8pm (no special meals for them); dogs by prior arrangement; disabled access in annexe cottage.

HORNS CROSS SS3823 **Lower Waytown** *Horns Cross, Bideford EX39 5DN (01237) 451787* ***£49;** 3 rms. Beautifully converted barn and roundhouse in 5 acres of grounds with ornamental waterfowl on stream-fed ponds; round sitting room with beams and inglenook fireplaces, and lovely breakfasts in a big dining room; no smoking; self-catering cottages; cl Christmas and New Year; children over 12; partial disabled access.

KNOWSTONE SS8223 **Masons Arms** *Knowstone, South Molton EX36 4RY (01398) 341231* **£55;** 4 rms. Delightfully unspoilt 13th-c thatched pub with very individual character, relaxed friendly service, good homely bar food, restaurant, decent wines, and a nice garden; nearby walks; dogs welcome.

LYNMOUTH SS7249 **Rising Sun** *Mars Hill, Lynmouth EX35 6EQ (01598) 753223* **£98;** 16 comfortable and cosy rms. Historic thatched 14th-c inn with lovely views over the little harbour and out to sea; oak-panelled dining room, beamed and panelled bar with uneven oak floors, good food and wines, a charming terraced garden, and lots of nearby walks; children over 12.

LYNTON SS7149 **Highcliffe House** *Sinai Hill, Lynton EX35 6AR (01598) 752235* ***£70,** plus special breaks; 6 well equipped attractive rms. Carefully refurbished, no smoking Victorian house with wonderful views over Lynton, the sea, and wooded countryside; comfortable sitting room with log fire, conservatory, good food in the candlelit dining room, and kind staff; cl Dec–Jan; no children.

MORCHARD BISHOP SS7707 **Wigham** *Morchard Bishop, Crediton EX17 6RJ (01363) 877350* **£70,** plus special breaks; 5 rms. Picturesque thatched longhouse on 30-acre farm with a house-party atmosphere; 2 sitting rooms, big log fires, a snooker room, a dining room with an honesty bar, and a good set dinner and breakfasts using home-grown organic fruit and veg, home-made butter, breads and jams, and their own free-range eggs; no smoking and no pets (they have their own); outdoor heated swimming pool; children over 8.

NORTHAM SS4429 **Yeoldon House** *Durrant Lane, Northam, Bideford EX39 2RL (01237) 474400* **£90,** plus special breaks; 10 cosy rms. At the end of a long private drive, this quietly set hotel by the River Torridge has a warmly friendly and relaxed atmosphere, a comfortable lounge where you can enjoy a complimentary sherry before dinner, good food using local produce in the attractive dining room, and helpful service; lots to do nearby; cl Christmas.

OAKFORD SS9121 **Newhouse Farm** *Oakford, Tiverton EX16 9JE (01398) 351347* ***£42,** plus special breaks; 2 rms. 17th-c longhouse on the edge of Exmoor, part of a farm with beef suckler cows and a small flock of friendly sheep; cottagey sitting room, inglenook fireplace, beams, and a country dining room serving home-made food inc good bread, pâtés and puddings; cl Christmas; no children or pets.

PORLOCK SS8846 **Oaks** *Doverhay, Porlock, Minehead, Somerset TA24 8ES (01643) 862265* ***£95,** plus special breaks; 9 airy and pretty rms. Particularly welcoming and spotless Edwardian country house looking down from Exmoor to Porlock Bay, with surrounding lawns and oak trees, a relaxed atmosphere and log fire in the lounge, and good unpretentious cooking in the attractive no smoking restaurant; cl Nov–Mar; children over 8.

PORLOCK SS8846 **West Porlock House** *Porlock, Minehead, Somerset TA24 8NX (01643) 862880* **£51;** 5 rms. Nicely proportioned, no smoking, former manor house in 4 acres, with spacious carefully furnished rooms, and kind personal service; cl Dec–Jan; children over 6; no pets.

SELWORTHY SS9346 **Hindon Farm** *Selworthy, Minehead TA24 8SH (01643) 705244* ***£40;** 3 rms, 1 with own bthrm. Relaxed and friendly working farm with sheep, pigs, calves, goats and horses (you can help if you want), lots of lovely walks around the farm or further afield, and a large lawn with stream and ducks; attractive sitting room and dining room, log fires, fine breakfasts, and a games barn with snooker, table tennis, darts and fancy dress; can arrange riding or bring your own horse; dogs welcome; self-catering wing also; cl Christmas; no children in B & B.

SHEEPWASH SS4806 **Half Moon** *Sheepwash, Beaworthy EX21 5NE (01409) 231376* ***£62.50,** plus special breaks; 14 rms. Civilised heart-of-Devon hideaway in colourful village square, with 10 miles of private salmon, sea trout and brown trout fishing on the Torridge; a neatly kept friendly bar, solid old furnishings and a big log fire; good wines, lovely evening restaurant, lunchtime bar snacks; dogs welcome; disabled access.

SOUTH MOLTON SS7527 **Whitechapel Manor** *Whitechapel, South Molton EX36 3EG (01769) 573377* **£110,** plus special breaks; 10 pretty rms. Carefully restored Grade I listed Elizabethan manor in large grounds with a magnificent Jacobean carved oak screen in the entrance hall, fine panelling, beams and log fires, relaxed atmosphere in the cosy bar and comfortable lounge, excellent thoughtful service, fine modern cooking as well as home-made breads, jams and marmalade, and carefully chosen wines; handy for Exmoor.

WEST BUCKLAND SS6531 **Huxtable Farm** *West Buckland, Barnstaple EX32 0SR (01598) 760254* ***£50,*** plus special breaks; 6 rms. 16th-c farmhouse surrounded by carefully converted listed stone buildings, open fields, fine views, sheep, chickens, and rabbits; candlelit dinner with wholesome home-made food using home-grown produce, home-made wine and bread, a relaxing sitting room, and beams, open fireplaces with bread ovens, and uneven floors; sauna, fitness room, tennis court, games room, and outside children's play area with swings, sandpit and Wendy house; cl Dec–Jan (but open New Year); disabled access.

WEST PORLOCK SS8746 **Bales Mead** *West Porlock, Somerset TA24 8NX (01643) 862565* ***£64;*** 3 comfortable rms with sherry, fresh flowers, and thoughtful little extras. This quiet and relaxing, no smoking Edwardian house has lovely Exmoor views towards the sea, a particularly pretty little garden, a charmingly decorated sitting room with log fire and baby grand piano, super breakfasts (no evening meals), and helpful owners; cl Christmas and New Year; no children.

WITHYPOOL SS8435 **Westerclose Country House** *Withypool, Minehead TA24 7QR (01643) 831302* **£69,** plus special walking breaks; 10 rms. Family-run 1920s hunting lodge with moorland views and 9 acres of gardens and paddocks; comfortable lounges, a relaxed atmosphere, and good, interesting food using local produce; cl Jan–Feb; dogs welcome.

To see and do

ALLERFORD SS9047
★ ☺ ☂ Pretty stone-built village with lovely packhorse bridge, and enthusiastic **West Somerset Museum of Rural Life** (cl Sun exc school hols and Nov–Easter, £1) with summer craft demonstrations.

🐖 🐦 **Exmoor Falconry & Animal Centre** 🔠 Friendly place with rare breeds, pony rides, baby animals for children to feed, and birds of prey. They also do summer evening hawk walks up on Exmoor, when you may be able to fly the birds yourself (£30 for 2 hours inc light supper). B & B in the 15th-c farmhouse. Snacks, shop, disabled access; cl Nov–Feb; (01643) 862816; £3.95.

APPLEDORE SS4630
★ A pretty centre of narrow cottagey streets off the quayside road which looks out over the Taw estuary, and ship- and boat-building in the yard just upstream. There's a pedestrian ferry over to Instow. The Royal George has lovely views and decent food and the Beaver is also good for lunch.

✤ **North Devon Maritime Museum** (Odun House, Odun Rd) Good museum exploring a different topic in each room. Shop, disabled access to ground floor only; cl 11–12.30pm, and Nov–Easter; (01237) 422064; £1.

ARLINGTON SS6140
🏠 ✿ **Arlington Court** (A39) From its Victorian heyday up to 1949, Rosalie Chichester filled this early 19th-c house with model ships, stuffed birds, holiday souvenirs – in fact anything she could get her hands on; her assemblages have been watered down since, but there's still quite a fascinating medley. Covering 3,500 acres, the grounds have attractive landscaped gardens and a number of Shetland ponies and sheep, along with a Victorian garden and conservatory, woodland and lakeside nature trails, and an unusual collection of carriages and horse-drawn vehicles (rides available). Meals, snacks, shop, disabled access; cl Sat (exc bank hol wknds), and Nov–Mar; (01271) 850296; £5.30, garden only £3.30; NT. The Pyne Arms

at East Down is useful for lunch.

ASHFORD SS5335

🦋 ❀ **Butterfly House & Gardens**
Well looked after collection of tropical
butterflies, with plenty of plants and
birds, and 2 acres of landscaped gardens
outside. Meals, snacks, shop, disabled
access; cl Nov–Easter; (01271) 342880;
£2.50, gardens free. The Ring of Bells at
Pilton is useful for lunch.

BARNSTAPLE SS5533

★ 🏛 🏚 The main regional shopping
centre, with a good deal of unforced
charm in the older parts. Interesting
buildings include an imposing 18th-c
colonnaded arcade on the Great Quay,
a lofty Victorian market hall (market
days Tues and Fri), almshouses behind
the church, more off the square by the
long old stone bridge, and some
interesting shops. It's still a working
port, though in a very small way now.
The best nearby pub is the Chichester
Arms up in Bishops Tawton. On Pilston
Causeway there's a good **sheepskin
shop**; you can tour the adjacent
factory. In summer you can hire bikes at
the main railway station – a good ride is
the one along the disused rail track up
to Torrington. The surviving main line
Exeter–Barnstaple line (known as the
Tarka Line), mostly tracking along
closer to the River Taw than the road
does, is one of the finest of all train rides
for scenery.

🖼 **Art Hotel** (off B3230, from
Barnstaple towards Ilfracombe) There's
an appealing blend of old and new at this
friendly late Victorian hotel surrounded
by woodland. Inside, the house is
decorated with antiques and
contemporary art, while new works are
continually added to the evolving
sculpture garden; they also run a
programme of lectures, music recitals
and poetry readings. Meals, snacks,
shop; garden and gallery cl Mon and
Tues; (01271) 850262; £3. The hotel
has a tennis court and heated outdoor
swimming pool; B & B £25 (wknd
£28.50).

ƌ **Barnstaple Heritage Centre** 📷
(Queen Anne's Walk) You pass
through an ornate Georgian colonnade
to reach this new centre which tells the
1,000-year history of the town with the
help of computer interactive and hands-

on displays; occasional historical re-
enactments. Shop, disabled access; cl
Mon and winter Suns; (01271) 373003;
*£3.50.

🏚 **Brannam's Pot Factory**
(Roundswell Industrial Estate) Guided
tours of big pottery (their terracotta
pots are indispensable to many
gardeners) with a chance to throw your
own pot. Meals, snacks, shop, disabled
access; no tours wknds, but shop open
Sat and summer Sun; (01271) 343035;
£3.50.

⌂ 🌾 **Disused railway paths** Down at
sea level, sections of the former track
from Barnstaple and Bideford can be
walked or cycled (local bicycle hire
around £5 a day, more for mountain
bikes). The best section is the one from
Barnstaple through Instow and
Bideford up to the Puffing Billy at the
former Torrington Station. In autumn
and winter particularly, this gives close
views of the wading birds massed on the
tidal sands of the estuary, and year-
round the section up to Torrington is
very attractive.

❀ **Marwood Hill Gardens**
(Marwood; off A361 towards
Braunton) 18 well kept and colourful
acres inc rare trees and shrubs, small
lakes, extensive bog garden, clematis,
camellias, alpines and eucalyptus, and
national collections of astilbes (best in
July) and tulbaghia. Cream teas on Sun
and bank hols, plant centre, some
disabled access; cl 25 Dec; £3. The New
Ring o' Bells at Prixford is very handy
for lunch.

ƌ **Museum of North Devon** (The
Square) Some interactive displays, and
an exhibition on the local environment.
Snacks, shop, disabled access; cl Sun,
Mon, 25–26 Dec and bank hols; (01271)
346747; £1 (free am Sat).

BICKLEIGH SS9407

🏰 ✝ ƌ ❀ **Bickleigh Castle** Charming
moated and fortified manor house, still
very much a family home; the 11th-c
chapel is said to be Devon's oldest
complete building. Also a medieval hall,
armoury and guard room, Tudor
bedroom, 17th-c farmhouse, and
exhibitions on maritime history and the
Civil War. All done with great
enthusiasm, and with a fair bit to amuse
children. Good cream teas, plant sales

in the Victorian walled garden, shop, limited disabled access; open pm Weds, Sun and bank hols Easter–May then pm daily (exc Sat) till early Oct; (01884) 855363; £4. The Fisherman's Cot is a beautifully placed riverside dining pub with good food inc a reasonably priced carvery.

BIDEFORD SS4526

★ ♨ Quiet hillside town now bypassed, with a notable medieval bridge and some pleasant old streets, partly pedestrianised, behind the Quay. The day-trip boat for Lundy (a good long day) sails from here year-round, though not every day, and only rarely in Mar. One of the oldest streets is Bridgeland St, and up towards the top of Bridge St there are quite a few antique or antiqueish shops. The Joiners Arms (Market Sq) has decent food, and readers recommend the Vagabond Cavalier (Cooper St) for good-value Italian meals.

♥ ! **The Big Sheep** 🎟 (A39, 2m W of Bideford) Exuberant sheep centre, best known for its splendidly entertaining sheep steeplechasing (usually around 3.20pm), when sheep with knitted jockeys on their back race 200 yards from their field towards the prize of extra food. Even better are the duck trials half an hour later, miniature sheepdog trials with the sheep replaced by ducks; there are more traditional sheepdog demonstrations too. Other events and displays take in everything from shearing and bottle-feeding to milking, with plenty of opportunities to get close to the animals (lambs are born throughout the year, so there are always some to cuddle). Decent adventure play area, and a couple of puppet shows. Lots under cover, and it's particularly good value – tickets are valid for unlimited return visits for a week. Home-made meals and snacks (good teas), shop, disabled access; reduced winter opening times (01237) 477916; £4.50. The Thatched House family dining pub at Abbotsham is handy for lunch.

BOLHAM SS9514

※ ⁂ 🏠 **Knightshayes Court** Lovely woodland garden with acres of unusual, even unique plants, especially lovely in spring but a glory at any time of year. Alpine and more formal gardens, an ancient yew topiary, attractive walks, and good Exe Valley views. The spooky-looking house itself is extravagantly ornate Victorian Gothic, with elaborate painted ceilings and décor and a restored minstrels' gallery. The original plans were even more over-the-top, but when the horrified owner saw them he sent the architect packing. Meals, snacks, shop and plant centre, disabled access; cl Nov–Mar, plus house cl Fri (exc Good Fri); (01884) 254665; £5.20, garden only £3.60; NT. The Rose & Crown at Calverleigh is pleasant for lunch.

BRADWORTHY SS3213

⌂ A pleasant jumping-off point for walks, with some quiet local strolls on the common, or over by the Tamar Lake a couple of miles SW.

※ ! **Gnome Reserve** (West Putford, 2¼m E of Bradworthy) One of the most delightfully silly places in the area, woodland and wild-flower meadows populated by hand-painted and individually modelled pixies. They lend you gnome hats and fishing rods so that resident gnomes will think you're one of them. The setting is pretty (flowers and plants are labelled), and small children love it. Shop, snacks, limited disabled access; cl Nov–mid-Mar (exc shop); (01409) 241435; £1.75. Coming from the N you could stop for something to eat at the thatched Farmers Arms at Woolfardisworthy.

BRATTON FLEMING SS6437

🚂 **Exmoor Steam Railway** (Cape of Good Hope Farm) Enthusiastically run, family-owned narrow-gauge railway with half-sized steamtrains winding through a mile of countryside, and a small display of traction engines. Meals, snacks, shop, disabled access; cl Mon, Thurs, Fri in low season, all Sats, and Nov–mid-Mar (exc Dec specials); (01598) 710711; £3.50. The White Hart is useful for lunch.

BRAUNTON BURROWS SS4532

Ѵ This vast nature reserve expanse of great swelling dunes is easily reached from the B3231 W of Braunton (red flags warn if there's shooting on the range here). The Mariners Arms in South St in Braunton itself is a useful pleasantly untouristy pub, and the Coffee Shoppe (Copperfields) has good local seafood).

THE BROWNSHAMS SS2825

⌂ These isolated farmhouses, now NT property, give walkers good quiet access to the woods, cliffs and clifftop farmland W of Clovelly.

BULL POINT SS4646

🏛 ⌂ ✝ There's a lighthouse here, and dramatic cliff walks between here and Morte Point; the Ship Aground public house by the interesting **church** in Mortehoe is a useful break, or a starting point.

CALVERLEIGH SS9214

★ ✝ An attractive village with a fine **church** and decent pub.

CHITTLEHAMPTON SS6325

🏨 **Cobbaton Combat Collection**
🔲 (off A377) Growing private collection of British and Canadian World War II vehicles, quite tightly packed under cover but looking ready for action; also mock-ups of wartime scenes, wartime memorabilia, and a play area with a Sherman tank. Summer snacks, shop, some disabled access; open daily Apr–Oct, best to ring for winter opening; (01769) 540740; *£4.25. The Exeter Inn at Chittlehamholt has good food.

CHULMLEIGH SS6814

★ Lovely unspoilt village with a decent pub, the Old Court House. It's a good base for touring the coast and Taw Valley.

CLOVELLY SS3124

🌼 ★ ⚓ 🎏 🐾 ⌂ One of Devon's most famous views, down the very steep old cobbled street, free from traffic and with flower-covered cottages either side, to the tiny harbour below. It's a delightful village, best appreciated out of season. At any time of year you'll have to park up at the top, outside the village, then pay £2.50 to pass through a turnstile, and walk down. The Red Lion down by the quay is pleasant; if you can't face the climb back up a Land Rover can drive you back from behind here (summer only, £1.60). You may be able to get boats to Lundy in summer. Up towards the A39 is a big Iron Age hill fort, Clovelly Dykes, and along the coast the beachside hamlet of Bucks Mills is well worth a visit. The woods, cliffs and clifftops farmland W of Clovelly is attractive walking country.

The moorland road down from Stibb Cross on the A388 via Woolfardisworthy is good, and the woodland Hobby Drive toll road is the area's best coast drive.

🏵 ❄ **Clovelly Court** These parkland gardens have tranquil sea views, and a fine walled garden and restored Victorian greenhouse. Open Apr–Sept; (01237) 431200; £1.

🐖 🌱 **Milky Way** (Downland Farm) One of the biggest covered attractions in the region, losing a bit of its original character as it grows, but still friendly, and very good for families. They guarantee all children will be able to feed a lamb or kid, and there's also cow-milking, a working pottery, golf driving nets, laser clay-pigeon shooting, birds of prey (twice-daily displays), sheepdog training centre (no demonstrations Sun) and a little railway. Good indoor and outdoor play areas and a Clone Zone interactive ride game. Snacks, shop, disabled access; cl wkdys Nov–Easter (exc during school hols); (01237) 431255; £5.50.

COMBE MARTIN SS5846

A string of former smallholdings and cottages scattered down a lovely sheltered valley, with an odd pub, the Pack of Cards, built to celebrate a cards win – 4 floors, 13 doors, 52 windows. There's a little fishing harbour in the shingly cove between the cliffs, and the Dolphin and Fo'c'sle are useful for lunch.

🏨 **Combe Martin Motorcycle Collection** 🔲 (Cross St) British bikes displayed against old petrol pumps, signs, garage equipment and other motoring nostalgia. Shop, disabled access; cl Nov–mid-May; (01271) 882346; *£3.

🐖 ! 🎏 🏵 **Combe Martin Wildlife & Dinosaur Park** (A399) Good range of animals and birds in over 20 acres of woodland inc a pair of rare snow leopards, and meerkats in a huge desert enclosure. Also meticulously researched life-size dinosaurs, some of which move and roar – like the towering *Tyrannosaurus rex*. A themed train ride (they assure us that you don't actually get wet) runs through the gardens which have rare and tropical plants, and there's a petting zoo for

children. Meals, snacks, shop; cl
Nov–Easter; (01271) 882486; £6.95.
CROYDE SS4439
⌒ A magnet for surfers, this clean-sand
village has a good family pub, the
Thatch. Baggy Point W of here has a
path good enough for wheelchairs.
EGGESFORD SS6811
✝ ❀ ♤ ⌒ ❊ This quiet Taw Valley
village has a 14th-c **church**, and a
garden centre prettily set in the walled
garden of a ruined house; refreshments
on a terrace with lovely views. A good
base for inland walks (and a stop on the
Barnstaple–Exeter rail line): in
Flashdown Wood, up wooded Hayne
Valley to Wembworthy (the Odd
Wheel is a decent family pub), or
through Heywood Wood, where the
mound of the former castle gives good
views (and there are picnic sets).
EXMOOR SS7739
⌒ ❊ Excellent walking, less busy than
Dartmoor in summer. In some places
it's been more tamed than Dartmoor –
drained and resown with richer-
growing grasses for better pasture. But
it's still a wild place, with hawthorns and
low oak trees bent and gnarled by the
winds, and (unlike Dartmoor) wild
deer. Where it drops away sharply to
the sea, fast streams and rivers cut
deeply into beautiful wooded valleys.
Note that some of Exmoor's moorland
paths have a disconcerting habit of
fizzling out without warning. It's
rewarding territory for drivers, with
plenty of good views; the B roads are
generally less congested.
⌒ **Badgworthy Water** This Exmoor
stream is the focus of a walkers' path
from Malmsmead which takes you into
the very heart of Lorna Doone country
– it gets wilder and more remote with

every step southwards (the
surrounding moors provide a handful of
return routes).
★ **Dulverton** The main town for
Exmoor is a civilised place, with a
handsome old stone market house, and
a fine bridge over the river which has
cut this steeply wooded valley. The Lion
Hotel is useful for lunch, and the area's
main information centre is at the S end
of Fore St, (01398) 323841.
⌒ ❊ **Dunkery Hill** Exmoor's great
ridge walk, with Dunkery Beacon as its
high point surveying a huge chunk of
south-west England and south Wales
(as tramping boots have worn 3ft off the
top of the Beacon, walkers are now
asked to take a bag of stones and earth
up to deposit there). It is easily walked
from the nearby road; a splendid place
to leave the car is Webbers Post (which
is also good for local pottering). It can
also be incorporated into longer walks
from Horner Woods or Luccombe.
★ ✝ ⌒ **Exford** Prettily set in a
sheltered valley by a small streamside
green; the **church** up the hill a bit is
well worth a look. The White Horse
and Crown are useful for lunch. The
peace of inland Exmoor is perhaps best
appreciated from along paths by the
rivers. A notable stretch of the Exe is
between Exford and Winsford.
Ⓥ **Malmsmead Natural History
Centre** The Exmoor Natural History
Society run leisurely 2-hour strolls
through the striking scenery around
their **Natural History Centre** every
Weds (plus Thurs in Aug) from mid-
May–early Sept at 2pm. Very
enthusiastically done, and especially
worth knowing about as they're free
(inc a cup of tea afterwards for a small
donation); Mrs Waite has full details on

Days Out

Village Exmoor: Allerford and Selworthy villages; stroll from the road up
Dunkery Beacon; Exford; lunch at the Royal Oak, Withypool; Winsford; Tarr
Steps for a stroll by the river (good picnic spot); Dulverton.

Picture-book scenes on a wild coast: Rosemoor Garden, Torrington;
Clovelly–Hobby Drive toll road, Bucks Mills village, Milky Way, lunch at the
Red Lion; Hartland Quay, and walk along cliffs in either direction; Hartland
Abbey.

(01643) 703470. The best way of finding the centre is from the County Gate National Park centre on the A39. Jan Ridd brought his bride Lorna around here in *Lorna Doone*. The Exmoor Sandpiper at Countisbury up towards Lynton has decent food.

★ † **Parracombe** A lovely little village worth visiting in its own right, but particularly interesting is **St Petroc's Church**, one of the few churches to have a completely unspoilt medieval fabric with Georgian interior; locked Nov–Easter, but key available from the custodian then. The Fox & Goose is useful for lunch.

★ † **Selworthy** Gloriously unspoilt village, rated by a number of our contributors as the most attractive they've ever seen, with groups of white thatched cottages around a prettily planted hillside green looking out over Exmoor, and trees behind. The **church** is a gem, with a fine waggon-ceiling with roof bosses.

◻ **Tarka Trail** This long-distance figure-of-eight signed path runs nearly 200 miles linking Exmoor, Dartmoor and the north Devon coast, following the route of Henry Williamson's *Tarka the Otter* – and is most enjoyable with a copy of the book. One beautiful section is the route around **Pinkworthy Pond** and the Chains, reached from the car park a couple of miles along the B3358 E of Challacombe (where the Black Venus is good). It's even more popular with cyclists than walkers.

◻ **Tarr Steps** The River Barle's most famous feature, the finest of all the stone-and-slab clapper bridges for packhorses. The path along the river, which runs between Simonsbath and Dulverton, is uneven and surprisingly slow going in places.

◻ ⌇ **Watersmeet** Paths run eastward out of Lynton along the River Lyn to Watersmeet (1½m E), where the Farley Waters tumble down to meet the East Lyn in a series of rocky cascades among steeply picturesque oak woods (there's a discreet NT refreshment pavilion here).

🏠 ⌇ ◻ ❋ **Watersmeet House** The 19th-c fishing lodge itself is not particularly remarkable (though has interesting local wildlife displays), but

the estate that surrounds it really is attractive – a perfectly relaxing wooded valley, with the house at the meeting point of the rivers. Just right for an afternoon's pottering (and forming one of the best parts of the Tarka Trail long-distance walk), though some of the walks can be steep. Meals, snacks, shop, disabled access with notice; cl Nov–Mar; (01598) 753348; free; NT. Another scenic path leads high above the same valley along its S side, and riverside paths head on further upstream, to the prettily set Rockford Inn (a good base for walks – food finishes at 2pm). Just N of Watersmeet, the **Foreland Cliffs** are the highest in the country – a good walk with dramatic views.

★ **Winsford** A quiet and attractive village below high hills, with the River Exe lacing through its countless bridges. The carefully restored Royal Oak is good for lunch.

HARTLAND SS2524

🏠 🖼 ❀ ⚘ **Hartland Abbey** Fine old house on the site of an Augustinian abbey, with elegant rooms (the drawing room is modelled on the House of Lords), paintings by Gainsborough and Joshua Reynolds, several interesting historic documents, an exhibition of old photography, and woodland walks in peacock-filled parkland. Along with the walled gardens, they're currently restoring a Victorian fernery, recently uncovered whilst clearing undergrowth. Snacks, shop; open pm Easter Sun and Mon, and Weds, Thurs, Sun and bank hols May–Sept, plus Tues July and Aug; (01237) 441264; £4.50, grounds only £2.75. The village has **craft shops** inc a working pottery and a Windsor-chair maker (children's sizes too).

HARTLAND QUAY SS2224

❋ ❀ ◻ ! Grand isolated spot at the foot of a toll road, on jagged coast which looks a dramatic cross between illustrations for geology textbooks and ones for a shipwreckers' manual. Down by the sea is a wonderfully maritime old inn, and the **museum** covers 4 centuries of shipwrecks – even big ships still go down here – and smuggling; cl Oct–Whit (exc Easter); £1. For walkers, the cliffs around here are much more dramatic than those at nearby Hartland

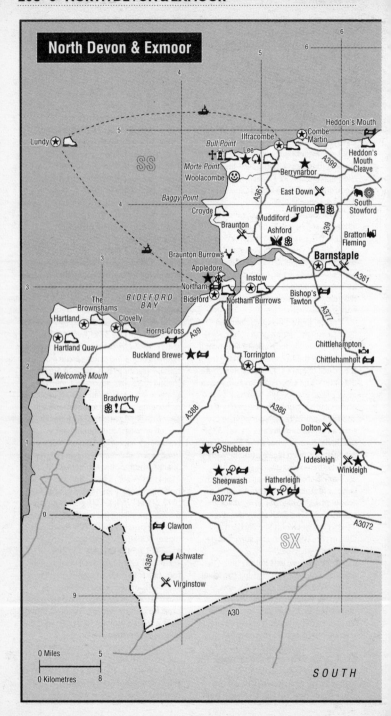

North Devon & Exmoor

Heddon's Mouth

Combe Martin

Heddon's Mouth Cleave

Ilfracombe

Lee

Bull Point

Morte Point

Woolacombe

Berrynarbor

East Down

South Stowford

Baggy Point

Croyde

Arlington

Bratton Fleming

Braunton

Muddiford

Ashford

Barnstaple

Braunton Burrows

Appledore

Instow

Northam

Bishop's Tawton

BIDEFORD BAY

Bideford

Northam Burrows

The Brownshams

Hartland

Clovelly

Horns Cross

Chittlehampton

Chittlehamholt

Hartland Quay

Buckland Brewer

Torrington

Welcombe Mouth

Dolton

Bradworthy

Shebbear

Iddesleigh

Winkleigh

Sheepwash

Hatherleigh

Clawton

Ashwater

Virginstow

SS

SX

Lundy

| 0 Miles | 5 |
| 0 Kilometres | 8 |

SOUTH

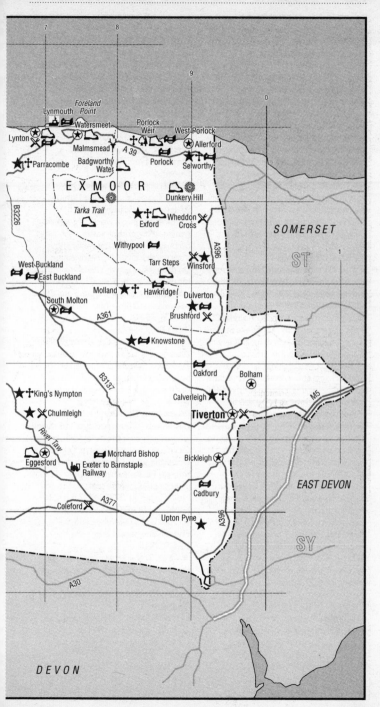

DEVON

Point (which also has a toll gate). Just S at Spekes Mill Mouth the sea-eroded valley leaves the river spewing down the cliff in a **seaside waterfall**.

❋ ✕ **Docton Mill** (Milford) They've recently planted a magnolia collection at this extensive and interesting sheltered streamside garden, largely naturalised, beside an ancient restored watermill. It's especially attractive in spring. Snacks (good cream teas), plant sales; cl Nov–Feb; (01237) 441369; £3. They have a couple of bedrooms you can stay in.

HATHERLEIGH SS5404

★ ⚘ An attractive hillside village – even the church slopes – with fine inns (the Tally Ho, brewing its own beer, and the George) and a good **pottery** (20 Market St).

ILFRACOMBE SS5147

★ ✝ ⚓ ✕ ⌂ Picturesque resort around a busy harbour sheltered by high cliffs, with terraces of late Victorian boarding houses and small hotels looking out over it from their perches among the trees of the steep bay. There are period resort buildings and gardens, and even tunnels cut through the rock to a former Victorian bathing place. The 14th-c chapel above the harbour mouth has doubled as a lighthouse for over 450 years; the **lifeboat station** can be visited (donation requested). **Holy Trinity Church** (Church St) is worth a look for its richly carved 15th-c waggon roof, one of the most striking in the area. The Royal Britannia (harbour) has good-value food, and we can also recommend the George & Dragon. In summer the paddle-steamer *Waverley* or the traditional cruise ship *Balmoral* run cruises from the pier to Lundy, Minehead, and other places – even as far as Swansea. Bicclescombe Park (A361 just S) has a restored 18th-c **cornmill**; the Coach House nearby has decent food. The best cliff walks are to the W of the town, towards Lee Bay.

✕ ⚘ **Hele Mill** (A399 just E of Ilfracombe) Well restored early 16th-c mill still producing wholemeal flour. Pottery demonstrations and the chance to throw your own pot. Snacks, shop; cl Nov–Mar; (01271) 863185; £2.50.

○ **Ilfracombe Museum** (Runnymede Gardens) Cheerful and enthusiastic town museum, if unsurprising (cl wknds winter; £1).

⌂ ❋ **Old Railway** This disused railway trail above Ilfracombe is popular with walkers and cyclists, with a tunnel, interesting plants, and attractive scenery inc the lakes of Slade Reservoirs. For a one-way walk it's best to do it in reverse, for better views – and it's downhill all the way; Red Bus 31 or Filers 303 up from the town to Lee Bridge or Lee Cross (or to the Fortescue Hotel for a preliminary bracer).

☺ **Watermouth Castle** 'Devon's Happy Castle', this is a fine 19th-c structure overlooking the bay, transformed into a world of gnomes, goblins, trolls and fairytales, with slides, carousels and a musical water show. Very much for families, with young children the ones who'll enjoy it most. Meals, snacks, shop, disabled access; cl Sat, plus Fri at the start and end of the season, and all Nov–Mar; (01271) 867474; £5.50.

INSTOW SS4728

❋ At the mouth of the Torridge estuary, this has an expanse of tidal sands, with dozens of moored boats beached on them at low tide. The Boathouse has good food and views.

❋ ⚘ ⌂ ❋ **Tapeley Park** (Westleigh) The very pretty Italianate garden with rococo features and walled kitchen garden is the main draw, though there's also a pets corner, play area, and woodland walk. Lovely views down to the sea. Teas and snacks in period dairy, plant sales, disabled access; cl Sat, and Nov–Easter; (01271) 342371; £3.50.

KING'S NYMPTON SS6819

★ ✝ An attractive village with a fine **church** and decent pub.

LEE SS4846

★ ⚘ ⌂ This pretty village in a sheltered woody valley has an attractive ancient pub, the Grampus. There are good cliff walks between Lee Bay and Ilfracombe.

LUNDY DAY TRIPS SS1344

⚓ ⚘ ⌂ (boat from Bideford or, in summer Ilfracombe) Well worth considering if you're in Devon for more than just a few days. The island's best known for the migrant birds that come here in spring and autumn, but the remoteness and loneliness is also a powerful draw – the permanent population is around a dozen. Lovely walks along its 7 miles of formidably high cliffs, windswept rough pastures, small church, evocative castle ruins, two lighthouses (one the highest in Britain), wandering goats, small Soay sheep and ponies, and the chance of seeing seals (especially in autumn), the introduced small sika deer, and, in Apr and May, the island's trademark puffins. Accommodation can be arranged through the Landmark Trust (01628) 825925. The Marisco Tavern is a good place to eat. The return boat trip (about 2¼ hours each way) is about £25; (01237) 423365 for sailing times.

LYNMOUTH SS7249

⚓ **Exmoor Boat Cruises** Informative boat trips, inc talks about sea birds and coastal geography, leave from the harbour from 11am daily, Apr–Oct; (01598) 753207; around £4.

LYNTON SS7249

★ ⚐ 🐾 ⌂ Merging into its harbourside extension, Lynmouth, down at the bottom of the cliff railway track, this delightfully situated steep village tucks into the wooded seaside gorge where the East and West Lyn tumble down to the sea. The most delightful walks in north Devon are around here. Lynton clearly shows its origins as a Victorian resort in one of the many areas then known as Little Switzerland, with hillside villas now quiet boarding houses, photogenic corners and some older cottages. Pretty cottages down by the little tidal harbour, as well as craft shops and so forth (there's a friendly hands-on pottery); lots of trippers during the day in summer. The Olde Cottage Inne (B3234 – lovely walk up The Lynway from Sinai Hill) is useful for lunch, and the Rising Sun down by the harbour has a good restaurant. The Valley of Rocks (*see below*) is an easy walk from the village, and Watersmeet (*see Exmoor entry*) is also within reach.

⌂ **Glen Lyn Gorge** Carefully restored after the tragic flood of 1952, with pretty walks and an exhibition on water power. Exhibition cl Nov–Mar, gorge cl 26 Dec, third Weds in Jan, and possibly in bad weather; (01598)

753207; £2. They have decent holiday flats and cottages in a peaceful setting.

⌂ **Heddon's Mouth Cleave** This secretive wooded combe runs up through the rugged seaside moorland hills by the sea W of Lynton. This and others like it are prime territory for walkers. There's a good walk down from the beautifully placed Hunters Inn W of Martinhoe, and another fine one in this area is the terraced walkway known as the Ladies Mile which runs along a charming valley near Trentishoe.

🕭 **Lyn & Exmoor Museum** (Market St, Lynton) In the old part of the upper village, this engagingly simple museum is in an 18th-c cottage with a scale model of the former Lynton–Barnstaple narrow-gauge railway (you can still walk much of its track bed). Shop; cl 12.30–2pm, Sat, and Nov–Easter; (01598) 752205; £1.

⌂ **Valley of Rocks** A great valley bowl with steep crags and pinnacles of rock dividing it from the sea (and a dreadful unscreened car park smack in the middle). It's reached by an easy coast path from Lynton, or by paths over Hollerday Hill (wooded, but opens out dramatically on top).

MOLLAND SS8028

★ ✝ An attractive village with a fine **church** and decent pub.

MUDDIFORD SS5540

🐟 **Blakewell Trout Farm** Good for experts and beginners, with a little pool where you're practically guaranteed a bite; cl 25 Dec; (01271) 344533; *85p. More serious trout fishing in the carefully landscaped reservoir at **Roadford Lake** 🅿 (cl Nov–Mar; £12.50 day permit; voucher applies only to the fishing).

NORTHAM BURROWS SS4430

⌂ Dunes, sand slacks and meres behind a pebble ridge, with the Atlantic rollers swinging in along the rock-strewn Saunton Sands beyond – deserted out of season for lonely walks; in summer a popular family beach.

PORLOCK SS8846

A lot of traffic, but some attractive cottages with distinctive lighthouse-like chimneys and thatched roofs.

PORLOCK WEIR SS8647

⌂ ⚐ ✝ This harbour tucked below

wooded cliffs is much quieter than nearby Porlock, though it does get a lot of summer visitors; decent food at the thatched Ship. There are long walks along the coast: heading W along the shore at the foot of the wooded cliffs, even the most avid pebble-hunters would find all they wanted. Another good walk is through the woods up to the tiny and quite isolated **Culbone church**.

SHEBBEAR SS4409

★ ✕ An interesting and attractive tucked-away village, with the odd Devil's Stone by the green (and a decent pub named after it), and a working wood-fired **pottery**.

SHEEPWASH SS4806

★ ✕ Quiet village with cob-and-thatch houses around the green; the Half Moon is good for lunch. A mile N is Duckpool Cottage, a traditional wood-fired **pottery**.

SOUTH MOLTON SS7125

★ ⚲ An attractive central square and imposing church – and its farming roots show in the Thurs cattle market. The 18th-c Guildhall has a local history **museum** (cl 1–2pm, Fri, Sun, and Dec–Feb; free), and monthly art-and-craft shows. The Castle at George Nympton has generous home cooking.

🏠 🖣 **Hancock's Devon Cider** (Clapworthy Mill, 3m SW of South Molton) Exhibition and film showing how they produce their good scrumpy. It's a nice spot for a picnic. Snacks, shop, good disabled access; cl 1–2, all day Sun, and Oct–Easter; (01769) 572678; £2.30.

❗ **Quince Honey Farm** (North Rd) The biggest wild-bee farm in the world, with observation hives looking right into the centre of the colonies. Snacks, shop (lots of honey and their own beeswax skin and hair care products); cl Nov–Easter (though shop stays open); (01769) 572401; £3.

SOUTH STOWFORD SS6541

🐘 🌼 **Exmoor Zoological Park** 🈺 (off B3226 N of Bratton Fleming) Good-sized collection of rare and endangered creatures, many of which breed successfully throughout the year. Children can feed the smaller animals or play on the assault course, and there are good views from the well

landscaped grounds. Snacks, shop, disabled access; cl 25–26 Dec; (01598) 763352; £4.25. The Old Station House at Blackmoor Gate is a pleasant dining pub.

TIVERTON SS9512

✝ ✕ ⚓ Formerly prosperous wool town, well worth wandering round; **St Peter's Church** is magnificently decorated with rich carving, and other grand buildings include the Jacobean council offices. The 4 showrooms of the **Tiverton Craft Centre** showcase the work of over 170 local craftsmen (cl Sun). In summer there are 2½-hour **horse-drawn boat trips** along the attractively restored canal from the wharf; booking advisable, (01884) 253345; £6.35. They hire out **rowing boats** and do motor-boat trips too, and can sort out fishing permits.

🏰 👑 **Tiverton Castle** The handsome castle was built in 1106 as a royal fortress dominating the River Exe, and still has its Norman tower and gatehouse, as well as an interesting clock collection and one of the best assemblages of Civil War armour and arms. You can stay in apartments in the oldest parts of the building. Shop, limited disabled access; open pm Sun, Thurs and bank hol Mon Easter–Sept, plus pm Mon–Weds July and Aug; (01884) 253200; £3.

👑 **Tiverton Museum** (St Andrew St) A 19th-c school houses this local history **museum**, with 2 waterwheels, an excellent railway gallery and a display about the work of the wheelwright (shop, disabled access; cl Sun, and Christmas–Jan; £2).

TORRINGTON SS4919

✝ 🌼 ⌂ Quiet dairy-farming town on a ridge above the River Torridge, with some attractive buildings inc 14th-c Taddiport Chapel (for a former leper colony), the imposing Palmer House, and a rather grand church built to replace the original which was blown up in the Civil War. There are good views from the neatly mown hill above the river, and other nearby strolls on the preserved commons surrounding the town. The Black Horse is useful for lunch.

🏠 **Dartington Crystal** (Linden Close) On weekdays you can tour the factory (last tour 3.15pm); there's a useful visitor centre, and shop with well priced goblets and decanters. They get very busy on wet days in summer – best to phone and check tour availability. No tours bank hols or 2 wks at Christmas, shop cl 25–26 Dec, Easter Sun; meals, snacks, disabled access (prior arrangement); (01805) 626242; £3.50.

🕸 **The Downes** (A386 Torrington–Bideford, nr Monkleigh) Fine big woodland garden with interesting flowering trees and shrubs and lovely landscaped lawns. Wknd teas, plant sales; open early Apr–mid-Jun, then by appointment till Sept; (01805) 622244; *£2. You can stay in a self-contained wing of the Georgian house.

🕸 **RHS Garden Rosemoor** (off B3220 just S of Torrington) A wonderful place, constantly being developed and updated by the Royal Horticultural Society; marvellous rare trees, shrubs, and other plants in a charmingly landscaped sheltered woodland setting, rose, stream and bog gardens, foliage and plantsman's garden, and trails for children. Meals, snacks, picnic area, smart shop, disabled access; cl 25 Dec; (01805) 624067; £4.

♭ **! Torrington 1646** (by South St car park) One of the more innovative redevelopments of a run-down building, this heritage centre commemorating the Civil War (the Battle of Torrington, one of the last of the conflict, broke out on 16 Feb 1646) is great fun. A time tunnel leading back to the start of the war takes you into the museum where numerous hands-on activities keep children occupied, including a touch-screen computer quiz to help you decide whether you're a Roundhead or Cavalier. However, the fun really begins in the back room: your guide disappears and is replaced with a wartime counterpart, who takes you on a tour around 17th-c Torrington, passing dead bodies and even an exploding church as you go. Out in the safety of the garden, more staff in period costume (they really enjoy the part) hawk their goods, and you can try your hand with a pike, or see how you suit Civil War armour; there's also a replica period herb garden. Snacks, shop, disabled access; cl Tues and Weds Oct–mid-Dec, and from then till mid-Jan; (01805) 622442; £3.50.

UPTON PYNE SX9197
★ Readers particularly enjoy this unspoilt village, the basis of Barton in *Sense and Sensibility*.

WELCOMBE MOUTH SS2118
⌂ Rather a rough drive down, but an attractive spot, and the cliffs around have possibilities for wild coast walks.

WOOLACOMBE SS4843
The beach here is particularly nice, and its Atlantic breakers now draw quite a few surfers. The Rock at Georgeham and Mill at Ossaborough are pleasant for lunch, and the back road to Mortehoe is scenic.

☺ **Once Upon a Time** (Old Station, B3343 inland) Run by the same people as Watermouth Castle at Ilfracombe, this is a super place for children up to about 11, with lots of rides and other activities; there's a driving school that even offers tests. Meals, snacks, shop, disabled access; cl Sat, plus Fri at start and end of season, and all Oct–Mar; (01271) 867474; £2.55 (£4.95 children).

★ **Other attractive villages** with decent pubs include Berrynarbor SS5646, Buckland Brewer SS4220, Iddesleigh SS5708, Knowstone SS8223 and Winkleigh SS6308.

Where to eat

BARNSTAPLE SS5533 **Lynwood House** *Bishops Tawton Rd (01271) 343695* The same family have run this no smoking restaurant-with-rooms for 29 years and the elegant Victorian dining room specialises in popular fresh local seafood (though meaty and vegetarian dishes are covered, and there's also a lighter menu); bdrms; cl Sun, 26 Dec, 1 Jan. **£28|£6.**

BRAUNTON SS4836 **Squires** *Exeter Rd (01271) 815533* First-class fish and chip take-away and restaurant with really excellent fish, good wines, friendly service and attractive airy surroundings; cl Sun (but open school summer hols then), 25–26 Dec, 1 Jan; disabled access. £4.

BRUSHFORD SS9225 **Carnarvon Arms** *Brushford (01398) 323302* Good English bar and restaurant food and friendly staff in this comfortable and individual sporting hotel with its own stabling, fishing and shooting; bdrms; disabled access. **£35|£7.50.**

CHULMLEIGH SS6814 **Old Bakehouse** *South Molton St (01769) 580137/580074* Thatched 16th-c merchant's house with lots of beams, a flower-filled courtyard, and a dining room serving morning coffee, light lunches and afternoon teas (plus breakfast and dinner for residents); bdrms. cl Mon, 2 wks Feb; disabled access. **£16 lunch, £21 dinner|£5.**

COLEFORD SS7701 **New Inn** *(01363) 84242* Comfortable thatched 14th-c inn with good interesting food, an extensive wine list, well kept real ales, 4 nicely furnished areas, a winter log fire, and an attractive garden with stream; bdrms; cl 25–26 Dec; disabled access. **£25|£6.95.**

DOLTON SS5712 **Union** *(01805) 804633* Relaxed and friendly old pub with good, interesting, genuinely home-made food using first-class produce, well kept real ales, and decent wines; comfortable little lounge, characterful lower bar with chatty drinking area and tables for eating, and charming owners; bdrms; cl first 2 wks Feb. **£19|£4.95.**

EAST DOWN SS5941 **Pyne Arms** *(01271) 850207* Popular pub with lots of nooks and crannies in a low-beamed bar, small no smoking galleried loft, games area, good food, and well kept real ales; cl 25 Dec; no children. **£17.60|£5.95.**

EXEBRIDGE SS9224 **Starlight Express** *Lakeside Caravan Park (01398) 324028* Bustling little restaurant (you can't actually see the caravans) with enjoyable home-made food (good local steaks and trout), decent wines, and friendly service; cl Mon. **£20|£7.50.**

LYNTON SS6549 **Lee Cottage** *Lee Abbey (01598) 752621* Charming cottage run by the Christian community from Lee Abbey, in pretty, terraced, streamside gardens with coast views; a few seats inside but plenty on the lawns and verandah; all the scones, bread and cakes used in the snacks and cream teas are home-made; no smoking; cl Sun (Mon in Jun); cl mid-Sept–late-May. **£1.90.**

TIVERTON SS9512 **Four & Twenty Blackbirds** *43 Gold St (01884) 257055* Friendly tea shop with beams, a mix of old tables and chairs, lots of interesting things to look at, delicious food (everything is home-made), and an upstairs antique shop. **£4.**

VIRGINSTOW SX3792 **Percy's at Coombeshead** *(01409) 211236* Carefully renovated 16th-c longhouse in 40 acres which provide some of the organic produce used in the no smoking evening restaurant; good, imaginative, modern cooking (super bread and puddings) and a well chosen wine list; comfortable, spacious bdrms; children over 12; disabled access. **£32|£12.**

WHEDDON CROSS SS9238 **Rest & Be Thankful** *(01643) 841222* Helpful staff and varied bar food in a comfortably modern 2-room bar with 2 nice log fires, a big jug collection, and an aquarium; restaurant; good bdrms; cl 25 Dec; disabled access. **£17.50|£5.95.**

WINKLEIGH SS6308 **Pophams** *Castle St (01837) 83767* Tiny bustling place for morning coffee and lunch – bring your own wine – with particularly good, freshly cooked food, and a relaxed happy atmosphere; cl Sun, Mon, Tues, Feb; no children. **£25.**

WINSFORD SS9034 **Royal Oak** *(01643) 851455* Beautiful thatched inn in a quiet spot with attractively furnished cosy bars, a smartly civilised atmosphere, log fire, good home-made bar and restaurant food, well kept real ales, and friendly staff; lots of surrounding walks; bdrms; disabled access. **£25|£7.65.**

Special thanks to Mrs Julia Rees, Mrs Y Champion, Mr and Mrs Hulme, Jeff Hall.

Devon Calendar

Some of these dates were provisional as we went to press. Please check information with the telephone numbers provided.

JANUARY

1 **Bideford** Millennium Celebrations – *till 6 January* (01392) 425426
2 **Clyst St Mary** Baby Pets and Animal Day at Crealy Park (01395) 233200
6 **Clyst St Mary** Antiques Fair at Westpoint: about 500 stands – *till 9 January* (01392) 446000
9 **Exeter** Epiphany Pageant at Exeter Cathedral (01392) 214219
29 **Bovey Tracey** Quilter's Guild of the British Isles Exhibition – *till 19 March* (01626) 832223

FEBRUARY

5 **Exeter** Antiques Fair at the Exeter Livestock Centre: about 430 stands (01363) 82571; **Exmouth** RSPB Cruise on the River Exe to view the wintering avocets – *till 6 February* (01392) 432691
19 **Exmouth** RSPB Cruise on the River Exe to view the wintering avocets – *till 20 February* (01392) 432691

MARCH

4 **Clyst St Mary** Antiques Fair at Westpoint: about 500 stands – *till 5 March* (01392) 446000; **Exmouth** RSPB Cruise on the River Exe to view the wintering avocets – *till 5 March* (01392) 432691

APRIL

1 **Exeter** Antiques Fair at the Exeter Livestock Centre: about 430 stands (01363) 82571
13 **Newton Abbot** Beer Festival at Tuckers Maltings: over 120 West Country real ales – *till 16 April* (01626) 334734
15 **Exeter** 'Icons of Pop' Photographic Exhibition at the Royal Albert Memorial Museum – *till 10 June* (01392) 265104
19 **Exeter** Walking Festival – *till 23 April* (01392) 265104
21 **Torquay** Spring Crafts Festival inc street entertainers – *till 8 May* (01803) 327822
22 **St Thomas** South-West Alpine Show at St Thomas High School (01395) 273636
23 **Clyst St Mary** Easter Egg Hunt at Crealy Park – *till 24 April* (01395) 233200
28 **Clyst St Mary** Lippizaner Stallion Show at Westpoint – *till 30 April* (01392) 444777; **Yettington** Horse Trials at Bicton Arena – *till 30 April* (01404) 871296
30 **Exeter** Great West Run (01392) 265118; **Tiverton** Plant Market with over 30 nurseries at the Pannier Market (01395) 273636

MAY

1 **Kingsteignton** Old World Street Market (01626) 351119; **Uffculme** Sheep Show: coloured and rare breeds at Coldharbour Mill Working Wool Museum (01884) 840960

Devon Calendar (cont.)

4 Torrington May Fair and Carnival – *till 6 May* (01805) 622441

5 Dartmouth Music Festival – *till 7 May* (01803) 834224

7 Blackawton International Festival of Worm Charming (01803) 712316

11 Holsworthy Agricultural Show (01409) 253979

13 Exeter Antiques Fair at the Exeter Livestock Centre: about 430 stands (01363) 82571; **Tiverton** Spring Festival – *till 21 May* (01884) 258952

18 Clyst St Mary County Show at Westpoint – *till 20 May* (01392) 444777

20 Babbacombe Devon Art Society Exhibition and Sale at St Anne's Institute Hall – *till 4 June* (01803) 328141

26 Combe Martin Hunting of the Earl of Rone *at 6pm*: effigy is captured, seated backwards on a donkey and after procession with fool and hobby horse is thrown into the sea – *till 29 May* (01271) 882524

27 Brixham Heritage Festival: live music, dance displays, fireworks – *till 4 June* (01803) 296296; **Budleigh Salterton** Gala Week – *till 4 June* (01395) 445275; **Clyst St Mary** Fun Days at Crealy Park – *till 29 May* (01395) 233200; **Exeter** Blues Festival – *till 29 May* (01392) 265118; **Seaton** 30th Anniversary Fortnight at Seaton Electric Tramway Company Riverside Depot – *till 11 June* (01297) 20375

29 Stockland Country Fair and Donkey Derby (01404) 881447; **Tavistock** Festival – *till 4 June* (01822) 615526; **Torquay** Millennium Celebrations (01803) 296296; **Totnes** Glamorous Nights: one hundred years of evening dress at the Totnes Costume Museum – *till 30 September* (01803) 862857

JUNE

1 Bovey Tracey Devon Guild of Craftsmen Exhibition at Riverside Mill – *till 10 September* (01626) 832223

3 Exeter Antiques Fair at the Exeter Livestock Centre: about 430 stands (01363) 82571; **Tavistock** Steam Fair – *till 4 June* (01822) 615526; **Topsham** Maritime Weekend and Armada Celebrations – *till 4 June* (01392) 265104

4 Salcombe Festival – *till 11 June* (01548) 843927

10 Beer Steam and Model Festival at Pecorama Pleasure Gardens – *till 11 June* (01297) 21542

17 Topsham Civil War Re-enactment – *till 18 June* (01392) 265104

18 Ivybridge Vintage Rally at Challonsleigh Farm (01752) 896253

21 Exeter Gardens Festival – *till 25 June* (01392) 265104

24 Ashburton Carnival Week – *till 1 July* (01364) 652142; **Buckland Monachorum** Craft Fair at Buckland Abbey – *till 25 June* (01822) 853607

30 Exeter Festival – *till 16 July* (01392) 265118

JULY

1 Clyst St Mary Antiques Fair at Westpoint: about 500 stands – *till 3 July* (01392) 446000

2 Ilfracombe National Youth Arts Festival – *till 7 July* (01271) 862419

7 Dartington Literature Festival at Dartington Hall – *till 17 July* (01803) 867311

8 Tavistock Carnival – *till 9 July* (01822) 615526

9 Topsham Battle of Agincourt Re-enactment (01392) 265104

11 Exeter Open-air Shakespeare at Rougemont Gardens – *till 8 August* (01392) 265118

Devon Calendar (cont.)

13 Topsham Patronal Flower Festival – *till 15 July* (01392) 265104
15 Tavistock European Town Criers' Competition (01822) 615526
22 Tiverton Mid-Devon Show at Hartnoll Farm (01884) 821815; **Torbay**
Carnival – *till 30 July* (01803) 296296; **Torquay** South Devon Fuchsia and
Pelargonium Society Annual Show – *till 23 July* (01803) 312267
24 Dartmouth Town Week – *till 30 July* (01803) 835200
25 Chulmleigh Old Fair inc street parade, sheep fair, flower show – *till 30
July* (01769) 580276; **Honiton** Hot Penny Ceremony and Fair (01404)
43716
27 Berry Pomeroy Totnes and District Show (01803) 863168
30 Stoke Gabriel Carnival Week with procession on 5 August – *till 6 August*
(01803) 782483

AUGUST

2 Huntshaw Cross North Devon Show at Belle Vue Aerodrome (01769)
560205
3 Honiton Agricultural Show (01404) 891763
4 Exeter Heritage Weekend: Exeter through the ages – *till 6 August* (01392)
265118; **Sidmouth** International Folk Festival: one of Europe's largest
with dance, concerts and carnival – *till 11 August* (01296) 393293
5 Exeter Antiques Fair at the Exeter Livestock Centre: about 430 stands
(01363) 82571
6 Kingston Maurward Teddy Bear Fair at Kingston Maurward College
(01305) 269741
7 Paignton Regatta – *till 13 August* (01803) 296296; **South Zeal** Dartmoor
Folk Festival – *till 13 August* (01837) 840162
11 Plymouth Street Fair: festival of arts and crafts and street entertainers –
till 26 August (01803) 327822
12 Babbacombe Devon Art Society Exhibition and Sale at St Anne's
Institute Hall – *till 27 August* (01803) 328141; **Beer** Regatta Week – *till 18
August* (01297) 22815; **Kingsbridge** Vintage Machinery Show at Sorley
Cross – *till 13 August* (01548) 852939
18 Torbay Regatta – *till 27 August* (01803) 296296
19 Topsham Medieval Week inc town fair and carnival – *till 20 August*
(01392) 265104; **Torquay** Royal Regatta – *till 23 August* (01803) 299772
22 Totnes Orange Races in the Main St (01803) 863714
24 Dartmouth Royal Regatta: Red Arrows, fireworks, barrel rolling – *till 26
August* (01803) 832435; **Mortonhampstead** Carnival (01647) 440145
25 Tavistock West Country Hot-air Balloon Fiesta – *till 29 August* (01822)
615526
26 Topsham Carnival Day and International Town Criers' Competition
(01392) 265104
27 Clyst St Mary Adventure Sports Special at Crealy Park: free canoeing,
abseiling and archery (01395) 233200
28 Brixham Fish Market Open Day (01803) 859123

SEPTEMBER

2 Clyst St Mary Antiques Fair at Westpoint: about 500 stands – *till 3
September* (01392) 446000
16 Exeter Antiques Fair at the Exeter Livestock Centre: about 430 stands
(01363) 82571

Devon Calendar (cont.)

OCTOBER

1 Winkleigh West of England Vintage Transport Collection (01769) 580811

7 Buckland Monachorum Tudor Living History at Buckland Abbey – *till 8 October* (01822) 853607

11 Tavistock Goose Fair (01822) 615526

14 Exeter Antiques Fair at the Exeter Livestock Centre: about 430 stands (01363) 82571

22 Clyst St Mary Halloween Magic Lantern Days at Crealy Park – *till 29 October* (01395) 233200; **Kingston Maurward** Teddy Bear Fair at Kingston Maurward College (01305) 269741

26 Bampton Fair (01884) 255255

NOVEMBER

4 Clyst St Mary Antiques Fair at Westpoint: up to 500 stands – *till 5 November* (01392) 446000; **Ottery St Mary** Rolling of the Tar Barrels: since 1688 (01404) 813964

23 Plymouth Christmas Crafts Festival at the Sundial – *till 3 December* (01803) 327822

25 Exeter Antiques Fair at the Exeter Livestock Centre: about 430 stands (01363) 82571

We welcome reports from readers

This *Guide* depends on readers' reports. Do help us if you can – in return, we offer a discount on the next edition to people who've helped us with reports for it. Tell us what you think about places already in it, and anything extra you think we should say about them. And send us your ideas for inclusion in the next edition: places to visit, eat at or stay in, attractive drives or walks, maybe even unusual interesting shops you know of. Use the card in the middle, the report forms at the end, or just write – no stamp needed: *The Good Britain Guide*, FREEPOST TN1569, Wadhurst, E Sussex TN5 7BR.

DORSET

Great coastal variety, from Bournemouth through character family resorts to striking unspoilt stretches; interesting days out, some untouched countryside.

Dorset has some lovely scenery. Striking coastal features include Lulworth Cove, the rugged Isle of Purbeck, Portland Bill (its lighthouse has a new visitor centre), and the tremendous sweep of Chesil Beach with its great lagoon near East Fleet. A coastal path, often with magnificent views, runs the length of the county. Inland, the countryside has a subtle understated appeal, with secluded valleys, narrow lanes threading through peaceful farmland and tucked-away villages (Milton Abbas best of all – a good day out). The central area's chalk uplands cut by intricate valleys give some splendid high viewpoints – not to mention the prehistoric giant cut into the hillside north of Cerne Abbas. In May, the bluebell woods at Bere and Delcombe make lovely walks. The west's intimate farming country feels very untouched by passing time, with ancient monuments such as the impressive earth ramparts of Eggardon Hill. The heathland west of Poole Harbour, partly planted with conifers, has a quite different character – largely flat tank-training ground west of Weymouth; a more interesting roaming ground for nature-lovers towards Studland Bay with its fine beach. Brownsea Island off Poole is also particularly good for nature.

Bournemouth has miles of good beaches, with plenty to see and do, and a civilised and spacious spread of comfortably sedate resort areas and leafy suburbs. It does have its lively side, including a new IMAX cinema among quite a few other changes here this year. Other smaller places – nearby Poole and Christchurch, and particularly Weymouth and Lyme Regis – have a lot to offer families who want something a bit different.

Dorchester is an interesting country town with lots to see, including its dinosaur and Tutankhamun museums. The dinosaur museum has gained good material moved from Bournemouth, with the Expo Centre there changing emphasis from tourism to conferences; another Dorchester beneficiary of this change is the new Teddy Bear House. Elsewhere in the town you will soon be able to walk the mosaic floors of Britain's most complete Roman town house. The county museum has a good new writer's gallery, and there's plenty for Thomas Hardy fans here and elsewhere; his books (and films of them) are vividly conjured up by particular Dorset villages and tracts of countryside. Sherborne, Shaftesbury and Blandford Forum are smaller towns well worth visiting.

Forde Abbey at Thorncombe, and Abbotsbury with its gardens, swannery and more, are outstanding places to visit, and other rewarding places include Kingston Maurwood Park, Corfe Castle, Horne Park and Mapperton Gardens (both near Beaminster), Kingston Lacy near Wimborne, Athelhampton House, and Compton Acres gardens in Poole.

Poole Pottery have cut their admission price by £1. Among new places, the farm centre at Langton Matravers is fun (daily ferret-racing), and the electricity museum in Christchurch is a good deal livelier than you might imagine. A particularly enjoyable family outing is Monkey World at Wool – a good conservation record, too. Children also like the costume museum in Blandford Forum, while the tank museum at Bovington Camp appeals to many.

An Explorer ticket is a worthwhile buy here if you're going to be doing much travelling on buses.

Where to stay

ABBOTSBURY SY5785 **Ilchester Arms** *Abbotsbury, Weymouth DT3 4JR (01305) 871243* **£57.40;** 10 comfortable rms. Handsome old stone inn nr the abbey, with log fire and hundreds of swan pictures in the rambling beamed bar, breakfasts in the attractive, no smoking conservatory, restaurant, and pleasant staff; plenty of walks; no accommodation Christmas; disabled access.

BOURNEMOUTH SZ0991 **Langtry Manor** *26 Derby Rd, Eastcliff, Bournemouth BH1 3QB (01202) 553887* ***£99.50,** plus special breaks; 28 pretty rms, some in the manor, some in the lodge. Built by Edward VII for Lily Langtry with lots of memorabilia, relaxed public rooms, and helpful, friendly staff; good food inc an Edwardian dinner every Sat evening; disabled access.

BRIDPORT SY4692 **Britmead House** *West Bay Rd, Bridport DT6 4EG (01308) 422941* **£62,** plus special breaks; 7 rms. Extended Victorian hotel with lots to do nearby, comfortable lounge overlooking the garden, attractive dining room, good food using fresh local produce, and kind, helpful service; self-catering bungalow; dogs by prior arrangement.

CORFE CASTLE SY9681 **Knitson Old Farmhouse** *Corfe Castle, Wareham BH20 5JB (01929) 422836* ***£40;** 3 rms, shared bthrm. Big ancient cottage on working farm with sheep and Jersey cows, large garden with hens, pigs and horses; comfortable sitting room with flagstones and woodburner, and good evening food, by arrangement, using home-reared pork and lamb served in the spacious kitchen; no smoking and free babysitting.

CRANBORNE SU0513 **Fleur-de-Lys** *Cranborne, Wimborne BH21 5PP (01725) 517282* **£55,** plus special breaks; 8 rms. Nicely placed, old creeper-clad pub with oak-panelled lounge bar, simply furnished beamed public bar, lots of historical documents and mementos of past customers such as Thomas Hardy, and decent food.

DORCHESTER SY6890 **Casterbridge** *49 High East St, Dorchester DT1 1HU (01305) 264043* ***£70,** plus wknd breaks; 14 rms. Small Georgian hotel in town centre, with modern annexe across a little courtyard; elegant drawing room, cosy library, attractive dining room and conservatory, and good breakfasts; no evening meals (lots of nearby restaurants); cl 25–26 Dec; disabled access.

DORCHESTER SY6890 **Kings Arms** *High East St, Dorchester DT1 1HF (01305) 265353* **£59.40,** plus special breaks; 31 rms – the Lawrence of Arabia and the Tutenkhamun suites are extraordinary. Smart, thriving coaching inn made famous by Hardy; different menus in restaurant, coffee shop and bar, old-fashioned public bar with real ales, live music twice a week; disabled access.

DORCHESTER SY6789 **Maiden Castle Farm** *Dorchester DT2 9PR (01305) 262356* **£48;** 4 rms. Victorian farmhouse on a big working farm beneath the prehistoric earthworks from which it takes its name; views of the castle and countryside, and comfortable, traditionally furnished sitting room which overlooks the garden.

EAST KNIGHTON SY8185 **Countryman** *East Knighton, Dorchester DT2 8LL*

(01305) 852666 **£55;** 6 rms. Attractively converted pair of old cottages with open fires and plenty of character in the main bar, no smoking family room, generous food in the carvery restaurant, and courteous staff; cl 25 Dec.

EVERSHOT ST5403 **Summer Lodge** *Evershot, Dorchester DT2 0JR (01935) 83424* **£175,** plus special breaks; 17 big, individually decorated rms. Beautifully kept, peacefully set former dower house with lovely flowers in the comfortable and elegantly furnished day rooms, excellent food using the best local produce in a most attractive restaurant overlooking the pretty garden, delicious breakfasts and afternoon tea, and personal, caring service; outdoor swimming pool, tennis and croquet; dogs by prior arrangement and away from public rooms; children over 7 in evening restaurant; partial disabled access.

FARNHAM ST9515 **Museum** *Farnham, Blandford Forum DT11 8DE (01725) 516261* **£55;** 4 rms in converted stables. Traditional, civilised old country inn in a thatch and stone village, with inglenook fireplace and classical music in the lounge bar, attractive conservatory, good food inc excellent breakfasts, and sheltered terrace and garden; cl 25 Dec; disabled access.

FLEET SY6280 **Moonfleet Manor** *Fleet, Weymouth DT3 4ED (01305) 786948* **£135;** 40 rms. Handsome stuccoed Georgian manor with a very relaxed atmosphere, helpful staff, Edwardian furnishings, log fires and plants, enjoyable food in the restaurant and Verandah Bar; lots to do for adults and children, residents' nightclub in Georgian cellars, and lovely countryside; disabled access.

GILLINGHAM ST8026 **Stock Hill** *Wyke, Gillingham SP8 5NR (01747) 823626* **£240 inc dinner,** plus special breaks; 9 lovely very comfortable rms. Marvellously relaxing, carefully run Victorian manor house in 11 acres of wooded grounds, with antiques and paintings in opulent day rooms, particularly welcoming service, and excellent food in the no smoking restaurant using home-grown herbs and vegetables, local meat and fish; all-weather tennis court, croquet; children over 7.

HALSTOCK ST5407 **Halstock Mill** *Halstock, Yeovil BA22 9SJ (01935) 891278* ****£50;** 4 rms. Attractive 17th-c house quietly set in 10 acres with lots of surrounding walks; log fire in the cosy beamed lounge, pleasant little dining room, and good food using home-grown fruit and vegetables, local fish and cheese; stabling; cl Christmas; children over 5.

LODERS SY4994 **Loders Arms** *Loders, Bridport DT6 3SA (01308) 422431* **£45;** 2 rms. Carefully refurbished pub in pretty village, friendly and unspoilt atmosphere, interesting food in the small restaurant, comfortable bar with log fire and a nice mix of customers, good beers and wines, and skittle alley.

LOWER BOCKHAMPTON SY8290 **Yalbury Cottage** *Lower Bockhampton, Dorchester DT2 8PZ (01305) 262382* **£74,** plus special breaks; 8 rms overlooking garden or fields. Very attractive, family-run, 16th-c thatched house with a relaxed atmosphere, low beams and inglenook fireplaces in the comfortable lounge and dining room; carefully cooked often imaginative food, and good wines.

MELBURY ABBAS ST8819 **Melbury Mill** *Melbury Abbas, Shaftesbury SP7 0DB (01747) 852163* ****£50;** 3 rms, 1 in the main house and 2 in beautifully converted mill building. Quietly set and welcoming 18th-c stone farmhouse with an open fire and flagstones in the dining room, a comfortable sitting room with windows looking on to the garden and mill pond (lots of waterfowl), and imaginative evening meals by arrangement – bring your own wine; cl Christmas; partial disabled access.

MILTON ABBAS ST8001 **Hambro Arms** *Milton Abbas, Blandford Forum DT11 0BP (01258) 880233* **£60;** 2 rms. Pretty and popular old inn in beautiful village, with beamed front lounge, log fire, popular food, and prompt, friendly service.

POOLE SZ0190 **Mansion House** *Thames St, Poole BH15 1JN (01202) 685666* **£98,** plus special breaks; 32 cosy rms with lots of little extras. Close to waterfront, this civilised old merchant's town house has a lovely sweeping staircase, antiques in the pretty residents' lounge, a cosy cocktail bar, good food in the attractive restaurant, and courteous, old-fashioned service.

SHAFTESBURY ST8622 **Old Rectory** *St James, Shaftesbury SP7 8HG (01747) 853658* ****£66;** 3 rms. Elegant 18th-c house with a friendly, informal atmosphere, comfortable sitting room with log fire, very good food and an interesting wine list; also, a sunny conservatory and quiet walled garden; cl Christmas.

STURMINSTER NEWTON ST7814 **Plumber Manor** *Hazelbury Bryan Rd, Sturminster Newton DT10 2AF (01258) 472507* **£95,** plus special breaks; 16 very comfortable rms. Handsome 17th-c house in quiet countryside, with tennis and trout stream; warm fires, resident Labradors, good uncomplicated food, a relaxed atmosphere, and friendly, helpful service; dogs allowed away from public rooms; children welcome by prior arrangement; cl Feb; disabled access.

SYDLING ST NICHOLAS SY6399 **Lamperts Cottage** *Sydling St Nicholas, Dorchester DT2 9NU (01300) 341659* **£40;** 3 little attic rms, shared bthrm. Charming, mainly no smoking, 16th-c thatched cottage in unspoilt village, with friendly welcome from helpful owner, and good breakfasts in the beamed dining room with huge inglenook fireplace and bread oven; pretty garden; children over 8.

UPLYME SY3293 **Amherst Lodge Farm** *Uplyme, Lyme Regis DT7 3XH (01297) 442773* ***£70,** plus special breaks. 4 rms. Comfortable long house surrounded by 140 acres of gardens, woodlands, fields and 8 lakes – coarse and trout fishing; friendly country-house atmosphere, oak-panelled lounge with fire, books and magazines, and enjoyable evening meals; self-catering also; no children.

WAREHAM SY9287 **Bradle Farmhouse** *Bradle, Wareham BH20 5NU (01929) 480712* **£42,** plus special breaks; 3 rms. Fine Victorian stone house on 550 acres of working farmland with fine views, good breakfasts in the homely dining room with its wood-burning stove, unlimited tea with home-made cake, welcoming owners, and suppers on request – decent nearby pub; cl 25–26 Dec; children over 8.

WAREHAM SY9287 **Priory** *Church Green, Wareham BH20 4ND (01929) 551666* **£160,** plus special breaks; 19 very comfortable rms – the best being in the converted boathouse with its own landscaped gardens. Beautifully converted medieval buildings in 4 acres of carefully kept riverside gardens; elegant lounges with antiques, delicious English cooking served in the converted abbot's cellar (exceptional English cheese board), and genuinely welcoming service; disabled access.

WEST BEXINGTON SY5387 **Manor** *West Bexington, Dorchester DT2 9DF (01308) 897616* **£95,** plus special breaks; 13 cottagey rms. Handsome and civilised old stone building mentioned in Domesday Book, in a pleasant setting not far from beach; relaxed and informal atmosphere, comfortable lounge, popular pubby cellar bar, log fires, good bar food, excellent restaurant, and friendly service.

WIMBORNE MINSTER SZ0199 **Beechleas** *Poole Rd, Wimborne Minster BH21 1QA (01202) 841684* **£89,** plus special breaks; 9 attractive, comfortable rms. Carefully renovated Georgian house with open fires in the cosy sitting room and charming dining room, airy conservatory, enjoyable Aga-cooked food using organic produce, nice breakfasts, and friendly, helpful owners; cl Christmas–New Year; disabled access.

YETMINSTER ST5910 **Manor Farmhouse** *High St, Yetminster, Sherborne DT9 6LF (01935) 872247* ***£55;** 4 rms. Fine, carefully modernised, no smoking, 17th-c building with beams and oak panelling, inglenook fireplaces, helpful owners, and good traditional cooking; no children or dogs; partial disabled access.

We welcome reports from readers

This *Guide* depends on readers' reports. Do help us if you can – in return, we offer a discount on the next edition to people who've helped us with reports for it. Tell us what you think about places already in it, and anything extra you think we should say about them. And send us your ideas for inclusion in the next edition: places to visit, eat at or stay in, attractive drives or walks, maybe even unusual interesting shops you know of. Use the card in the middle, the report forms at the end, or just write – no stamp needed: *The Good Britain Guide*, FREEPOST TN1569, Wadhurst, E Sussex TN5 7BR.

To see and do

DORSET Family Attraction of the Year

✚ 🐾 **WOOL** SY8486 **Monkey World** (off A35 towards Bere Regis) As enjoyable as it is worthwhile, this enthusiastic rescue centre for apes and chimps delights visitors of all ages. Founded in 1987 to rehabilitate abused or injured chimpanzees, the centre now looks after all kinds of primates that are gradually reintroduced to natural surroundings; there are usually ring-tailed and ruffed lemurs, Barbary macaques, capuchins and vervets, orangutans and gibbons, all roaming and climbing freely in decent-sized open enclosures. The experiences some of the rescued chimps have been through are heartbreaking. You can usually go into the lemur enclosure – though don't try to feed or pet them. Keepers give useful talks, and you can see baby chimps playing in their nursery. They put as much care into looking after visitors as they do the animals, and with added attractions such as a pets corner, mini-motor bikes, and jet boats, it's a very satisfying fine weather half-day out for families. There may be a clown some afternoons in summer. Pretty woodland walks through the surrounding countryside, and a very good range of play areas (some indoors) including a 15-stage obstacle course. Parents aren't slow to see the irony in placing this so close to the main chimp enclosure; child and chimp seem to be clambering over not entirely dissimilar equipment. So much for evolution. Snacks (and picnic area), shop, disabled access (a few steep paths); cl 25 Dec; freephone (0800) 456600; £5.25 (£3 children). A family ticket is £15, and they do a good-value ticket for a single adult with two children, at £10.50.

ABBOTSBURY SY5982

★ ✝ 🐾 🐄 ⌂ ❄ Delightful Dorset village with several worthwhile places to visit – most famous are the swannery and sub-tropical gardens (see separate entries). The 14th-c hilltop **chapel** (not always open), with a bare earth floor, belonged to the abbey, of which there are a few medieval fragments around the church. A huge medieval thatched **tithe barn** now houses a friendly children's farm and a display of Chinese terracotta warriors. Shop, disabled access; (01305) 871817; £3.75. After visiting one of Abbotsbury's attractions you get discounts on the others. The village also has an **oyster farm** (cl am winter), and the Ilchester Arms is good for lunch. Abbotsbury is the start for strolls around Chapel Hill and on to the massive shingle bank of Chesil Beach (exhausting to walk any distance along – see, too, East Fleet on p.231). Paths leading N from the village get lovely views from the chalk downs. The B3157 W also has fine views.

🐚 🌷 **Abbotsbury Subtropical Gardens** 20 acres of beautiful woodland with very mild coastal climate letting rare and record-breaking plants and trees flourish; they claim the tallest cultivated rose in the world. The central walled garden in spring is a mass of azaleas, camellias and rhododendrons. Also woodland trail, aviary and play area. Meals, snacks, shop and plant centre, some disabled access; cl 25–26 Dec; (01305) 871387; £4.40 summer, less in winter.

🐦 ! ⌂ **Abbotsbury Swannery** (Newbarn Rd) Home to the only sizeable colony of swans in the world that can be seen during nesting time. The swan families quite happily come right up to visitors, and during the cygnet season (late May–Jun) you might see some of the hundreds of eggs hatching right next to you. All year there are mass feedings of the flock at noon and 4pm; they sometimes choose a visitor to help, and it can be rather dramatic – certainly a far cry from the average trip to feed the swans. An ugly duckling trail keeps younger children amused, and there are interesting reed-bed walks; also the country's oldest duck decoy, and an audio-visual show. No dogs. Restaurant (reached by a little bridge), shop, good disabled access; cl Nov–mid-Mar; (01305) 871684; £4.80. A joint ticket with the subtropical garden is £7.

ARNE SY9788

♂ � This relatively undiscovered little village has a good toy museum (Arne House); cl Oct–Mar, plus am Mon and Sat in Apr and Sept; 📷 *£2.50). There's also a beach and a nature trail.

ASHLEY HEATH SU1006

♨ ⌂ ♪ ✸ ㎞ **Moors Valley Country Park** Good for families, nearly 400 hectares of forest, with river and lakeside walks, fishing, nature trails, plenty of wildlife, narrow-gauge steam railway, unusual treetop walkway, and 18-hole golf course. Meals, snacks, shop, disabled access; cl 25 Dec; (01425) 470721; £3.50 car parking charge (£1.50 after 4pm), free winter wkdys (£1.50 wknds then).

ATHELHAMPTON SY7794

🏠 ❀ **Athelhampton House** (A35) Readers enjoy coming to this magnificent 15th-c house, built on the legendary site of King Athelstan's palace. The great hall has a fantastic roof. You'd never know now there was a disastrous fire here in 1993 – most of the beautiful furnishings and contents (even much of the panelling) were saved, and are back in their original positions. An added bonus is the acres of wonderful formal and landscaped gardens with rare plants, topiary and fountain pools. Meals, snacks, shop, disabled access; open daily (exc Sat) Mar–Oct, Sun only Nov–Feb; (01305) 848363; £5.25 house and gardens, £3.75 garden only. The Martyrs at Tolpuddle has good home cooking.

BEAMINSTER ST4602

❀ ♨ ✻ **Horn Park** 📷 (A3066 N of Beaminster) Unusual plants in a series of gardens with bluebell woods, ponds, wild flowers and good views. Teas, plant sales, some disabled access; open pm Sun–Thurs Apr–Oct; (01308) 862212; £3.

❀ 🏠 ⌂ ✻ **Mapperton Gardens** 📷 (off B3163 E of Beaminster) Several delightful acres of terraced hillside gardens in the grounds of a 16th-c manor house; specimen trees and shrubs, fountains, grottoes, fishponds, orangery, good walks and views.

Occasional musical events in summer. Snacks, shop, some disabled access; cl am, and all Nov–Feb; (01308) 862645; *£3.50.

❀ 🏠 ♿ ♨ ⌂ **Parnham** (A3066 Beaminster–Bridport) Surrounded by 14 acres of lovely gardens, a fine Tudor mansion famous as the home of John Makepeace the furniture-maker. His workshop is open, with completed pieces shown around the house, along with exhibitions by other craftsmen. The mix of modern furniture with period rooms is refreshingly different. Also formal gardens and play area. Meals, snacks, shop, mostly disabled access; open Apr–Oct, Sun, Tues–Thurs, and bank hols; (01308) 862204; *£5. The nearby woods of Hooke Park are pleasant for a stroll; you can get a combined ticket with the house. In Beaminster, Pickwicks and the Greyhound are good bets for food.

BERE REGIS SY8494

✝ **Bere Regis church** This boasts the finest timbered roof in Dorset, with extraordinary carved figures; 20p in a slot lights these up to remarkable effect. It also contains the Turberville tomb and window mentioned in *Tess of the D'Urbervilles*. The Royal Oak is good value for lunch.

BERE WOOD SY8794

♨ ⌂ At the W end of Bloxworth, this is a fine bluebell wood, at its best in May; the track can be followed right through to Bere Regis.

BLANDFORD FORUM ST8806

★ Georgian market town, rebuilt in 1731 after the older buildings were destroyed by fire – very interesting to walk round. The Dolphin and Nelsons have decent food.

♂ **Mrs Penny's Cavalcade of Costume** (The Plocks) Wide-ranging collection of clothes in Georgian Lime Tree House; children can try on copies of some of the exhibits. Snacks, shop, limited disabled access; cl Tues, Weds and 3 wks from mid-Dec; (01258) 450388; £3.

♂ **Royal Signals Museum** (Blandford Camp) A lively look at the history of army communications, with an exhibition for children on codes and code-breaking. Cl wknds exc May–Oct; (01258) 482248; £4.

BOURNEMOUTH SZ0890

☺ Still has something of the 'very salubrious air' that Queen Victoria recommended to Disraeli. Neatly kept streamside gardens in the centre, a pier that's one of the few to look as fresh as when it was built, long promenades below the low cliff, and miles of well organised sandy beach (no dogs in summer, and children's activities then). The best beaches, with water safe for swimming and good wrist-band schemes to prevent children from getting lost, are at Durley Chine and Southbourne. All this, along with the mild climate and a good local orchestra, has made the town expansively popular both as a civilised place to retire to and as a centre for regular development. Over the last year new additions have included a seafront IMAX cinema (Pier Approach), Bournemouth Square (a new town-centre forum replete with palm trees, Edwardian furniture, and a camera obscura), and the erection of what must be one of England's cheekiest monuments – a statue depicting on one side Bournemouth's founder Captain Tregonwell, and perched on a lavatory facing the other direction, Christopher Crabbe Creeke, the town's first sanitation inspector (outside the International Centre, Exeter Rd). It's a big, busy town surrounded by suburbs, with tall modern buildings and monumental traffic schemes. But down by the sea you're well insulated from all of that. And the western residential suburbs of Westbourne and particularly Branksome Park (it's virtually impossible to tell here when Bournemouth becomes Poole) are quiet, with pinetree valleys winding down to the sea. Butlers Crab & Ale House (Old Christchurch Rd) is useful, the Moon on the Square (Exeter Rd) is good value, and the Durley (Durley Chine) is a very well run beachside pub.

◌ ❀ **Hengistbury Head** By far the best place close to Bournemouth for a stroll: not a long walk, but the feeling of space and views are outstanding.

♪ **Oceanarium** (Pier Approach, West Beach) An impressive range of fish from all around the world, with an emphasis on the environment and conservation. Snacks, shop, disabled access; cl 25 Dec; (01202) 311993; £5.25.

▣ ♨ **Russell-Cotes Art Gallery & Museum** Due to reopen in spring, this refurbished Victorian mansion houses a good collection of 17th- to 20th-c paintings, ceramics and furnishings. A new extension will have exhibitions on Japanese art, and a story-telling gallery aimed at children. New café, shop, disabled access; cl Mon, 25 Dec, and Good Fri; (01202) 451800; free.

♨ **Shelley Rooms** (Boscombe Manor, Beechwood Ave) Small museum devoted to the life and work of the poet, especially the later part of his life. Disabled access; cl am, all Mon, 25–26 Dec, Good Fri; (01202) 303571; free. Shelley's heart is buried beneath the impressive tombstone of Mary Shelley in St Peter's churchyard.

BOVINGTON CAMP SY8388

🏠 **Clouds Hill** A mile or so up the road from Bovington Camp is the cottage Lawrence of Arabia lived in as a private in the tank corps, and his sleeping bag, furniture and other memorabilia can be seen in the three ascetic little rooms on display. Open pm Weds, Thurs, Fri, Sun and bank hols mid-Apr–Oct; (01929) 405616; £2.30; NT.

📷 ! **Tank Museum** Over 260 armoured fighting vehicles from 23 countries, some of which you can go inside, as well as a tank simulator (the screen can be a bit fuzzy), costumes, medals, weapons and videos. Many of the tanks are now put through their paces, complete with gunfire (Thurs July–Sept, plus Fri in Aug), there are armoured vehicle rides on summer wkdys, and their Battle Day, the last Sun in July, is quite a spectacle. There's an exhibition on Lawrence of Arabia, and an assault course for children. Meals, snacks, shop, disabled access; cl Christmas wk; (01929) 405096; £6.50. The very child-friendly Countryman at East Knighton has good food.

BRADFORD PEVERELL SY6593

🏚 ⚘ ❖ **New Barn Field Centre** Authentic re-creation of Iron Age homestead, complete with animals and so on; also working potter, wild flower reserve and nature trails. Summer meals and snacks, shop, some disabled access; cl Oct–Easter; (01305) 268865; £3.50.

BRIDPORT SY4692

Still the country's main rope producer, and its old harbour is now the busy fishing port of nearby West Bay, a restrained small resort (where the West Bay Hotel has good local seafood). The Harbour Life Exhibition (Salt House) tells the story of the area with the aid of pictures, photographs and videos. Shop, disabled access; cl Nov–May; £1.25.

Bridport Museum (South St) Opening in early Apr, this will offer rope and net-making displays (with free activity sheets for children), plus a study of local history, and an upstairs art gallery. Shop, disabled access to ground floor only; cl Sun, and Nov–mid-May; (01308) 422116; £2.

BROADWINDSOR ST4302

Craft & Design Centre Good centre in former farm buildings; woodworkers, hatters, painters and so forth. Meals, snacks, shop, disabled access; cl 23 Dec–1 Mar; (01308) 868362; free. The B3164 W to Birdsmoorgate and then the B3165 through Marshwood (where there is a worthwhile country pub) is an unspoilt scenic drive through a little-known valley.

BULBARROW HILL ST7705

Memorable viewpoint on the narrow lanes just S of Woolland, especially on a summer evening with the sun going down over Somerset. Around here, a scenic drive runs from Piddletrenthide through Plush (the Brace of Pheasants is a very good lunchtime stop) and Mappowder to Hazelbury Bryan, then through Ansty and Melcombe Bingham, to turn right at Cheselbourne for Piddletrenthide again.

CERNE ABBAS ST6701

★ ✝ 🏛 🞂 Attractive village with a fine church, fragments of the old abbey, a remarkable collection of good pubs (the Red Lion and Royal Oak are the best), and its famously indelicate prehistoric giant cut into the chalk above, best seen from the main road N. The National Trust took a dim view when he acquired a £40,000 pair of plastic blue jeans one night in May 1998

as a publicity stunt for a new range of jeans. There's a working **pottery** (cl winter Mons) on the way up the giant; above it, the old Dorchester–Middlemarsh ridge road has some bracing views.

CHARMOUTH SY3693

The beach here is famous for fossil-hunting. A small museum exhibits locally found relics; good shop, hammers for hire £3.

CHETTLE ST9413

🏠 🞲 🞂 🞄 **Chettle House** Fine baroque country house, with beautifully laid out gardens, vineyard and gallery; various craft weekends and special events. Snacks, disabled access to garden; cl Tues, Sat, and Oct–Easter; (01258) 830209; *£2.50. The Bugle Horn at Tarrant Gunville is handy for lunch.

CHICKERELL SY6480

🞲 🞂 **Bennetts Watergardens** (Putton Lane) Eight acres of landscaped lakes renowned for their summer waterlilies – over 100 varieties. As we went to press, there were plans to construct a bridge akin to the one Monet painted at his gardens in Givenchy; also a museum covering local history and the gardens and Chickerell brickworks. Home-made teas, shop, disabled access; open Tues–Fri Apr–Oct, plus Sats Sept, and Suns Apr–Aug; (01305) 785150; £3.95.

CHRISTCHURCH SZ1592

★ 🞾 🏛 ⌂ At the 'Hampshire' end of the Bournemouth complex, with attractive Georgian brick buildings in its old centre, a restored watermill, and a quay looking out over the yachting harbour, busy in summer. Hengistbury Head overlooking the harbour and reached from the Bournemouth side is a popular place for strollers, with traces of an Iron Age hill fort (good beach here too). On the other side of the harbour mouth, long beaches stretch way into Hampshire from the vast Mudeford car park (the Haven House by the sea here is well worth knowing for its unrivalled position, and there's an excellent fishmonger nearby). Pleasant walking out of season.

! Big Top Jousting A good distraction for children (especially in poor weather), a lively two-hour spectacle under cover, with mock jousting displays. As we went to press, they hadn't yet decided whether or not to move site; best to ring (01202) 483777 for details; £6. Shows run from May–Sept.

🏰 **Christchurch Castle & Norman House** All that remains is a ruined keep, and the ruins of the Norman house probably used by the castle constable. It's quite well preserved, with one of the earliest chimneys in the country, and an ancient midden by a millstream; free.

✝ ♿ ❋ **Christchurch Priory** Magnificent medieval monastic church, at well over 90 metres (300ft) the longest parish church in the country; very striking inside, with remarkable carving. The 'Miraculous Beam', apparently fitted in the roof only with divine assistance, prompted the renaming of the borough to Christchurch (it used to be called Twynham). Free recitals most Thurs lunchtimes. Shop, snacks on recital days; disabled access; £1 suggested donation. The church has a small museum open in the summer, and good views from the tower (50p) – though with 176 spiral steps you have to earn them.

🐾 ♿ **Red House Museum & Gardens** (Quay Rd) Georgian house with local history, dolls and costumes, and walled herb garden. Shop, disabled access to ground floor only; cl am Sun, Mon (exc bank hols), Christmas wk; (01202) 482860; £1.

♿ 🏛 **Southern Electric Museum** (opp Castle's Ironmongers, Bargates) Housed in an Edwardian power station, this has a range of electrical exhibits from antique washing machines to power generators. A transport gallery houses vehicles as diverse as the fully restored no 85 tram (which ran in Bournemouth from 1914–35), a 1970s electric car, and Sir Clive Sinclair's much ridiculed Sinclair C5; interactive displays, and occasional demonstrations of early electrical experiments. Shop, some disabled access; cl wknds, and Oct–Easter; (01202) 480467; £1.50.

CORFE CASTLE SY9681

🏰 ❋ 🐾 ♿ ★ The **castle** is the most spectacular ruin in the area, and gives superb views from its dramatic hilltop position. The site is remarkably atmospheric considering how little of the castle is left, and it's great fun clambering over the ancient stones. Meals, snacks, shop; cl 25–26 Dec; (01929) 481294; £4; NT. The Swanage Railway now runs to here; a joint ticket is available. A Tudor building on West St has a decent local history **museum**, with dinosaur footprints; cl wkdys Nov–Apr; free. Parking can be a problem in the attractive, ancient small town in summer. The Halfway at Norden Heath (A351 towards Wareham) has good food. The road W through Church Knowle is pretty.

! 🐾 **Corfe Castle Model Village** Set in attractive gardens, with a faithful reconstruction of what the Norman castle looked like before the Parliamentarians destroyed it in 1646. Meals, snacks, shop, disabled access; cl Oct–Easter; (01929) 481234; £2.

CRANBORNE SU0513

A peaceful place, with the Fleur-de-Lys a good pub well known to Hardy and the subject of an entertaining poem by Rupert Brooke (framed inside).

Days Out

Monkey business: Monkey World, Wool; lunch at the Countryman, East Knighton; Bovington Camp Tank Museum – or walk from Lulworth Cove.

Fossils and Forde Abbey: Boat trip from Lyme Regis; lunch at the Pilot Boat there; Forde Abbey, Thorncombe.

Poole and its unique island: Poole, Compton Acres Gardens; lunch at the Inn in the Park (Pinewood Rd, Branksome Park) or Shah of Persia (A35); boat trip to Brownsea Island; Sandbanks beach.

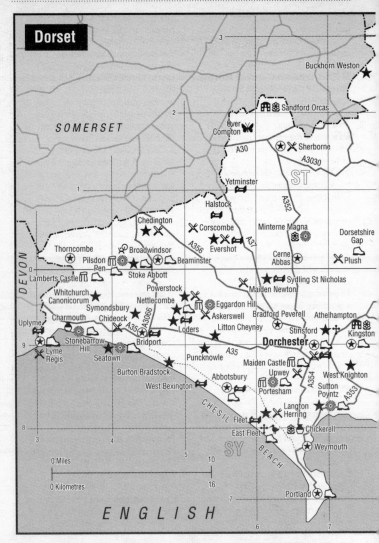

Dorset

SOMERSET

DEVON

Buckhorn Weston ★

Sandford Orcas

Over Compton

Sherborne

Yetminster

ST

A30

A3030

A352

Halstock

Chedington ★

Corscombe

Minterne Magna

Dorsetshire Gap

Thorncombe

Broadwindsor

Evershot

Plush

Pilsdon Pen

Beaminster

Cerne Abbas

Lamberts Castle

Stoke Abbott

A356

A37

Whitchurch Canonicorum

Powerstock

Maiden Newton

Sydling St Nicholas

Symondsbury

Nettlecombe

Eggardon Hill

Bradford Peverell

Athelhampton

Charmouth

Chideock

Askerswell

Kingston

Uplyme

Loders

Litton Cheyney

Stinsford

A30066

A35

Dorchester

Lyme Regis

Stonebarrow Hill

Bridport

Maiden Castle

West Knighton

Seatown

Puncknowle

Maiden Castle

Upwey

Sutton Poyntz

A354

A353

Burton Bradstock

Abbotsbury

Portesham

West Bexington

CHESIL BEACH

Langton Herring

Fleet

Chickerell

East Fleet

SY

Weymouth

ENGLISH

Portland

| 0 Miles | | 10 |
| 0 Kilometres | | 16 |

❀ Cranborne Manor Gardens
Splendid 17th-c gardens originally laid out by Tradescant; Jacobean mount garden, herb garden, lovely river garden and avenues of beech and lime. Particularly attractive in spring. Snacks, shop and garden centre, disabled access; gardens open Weds only Mar–Sept, garden centre daily all year; (01725) 517248; £3. The B3078 has good country views, as does the minor road crossing it to Three Legged Cross and the Gussages.

CRANBORNE CHASE ST9116
◠ ❀ Shared between Dorset and Wiltshire, this offers good walking with some fine views, especially around Ashmore.

DELCOMBE WOOD ST7805
◔ ◠ A lovely bluebell wood, sheets of colour in May; but the only public track just skirts the W edge of the wood.

DORCHESTER SY6990
⌂ ⌂ ☎ Thriving country town, with busy shopping streets and Weds market, and several worthwhile antique

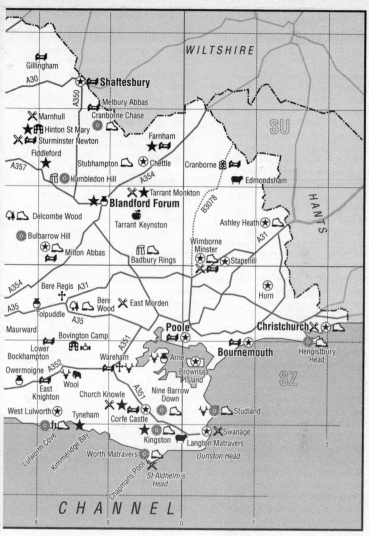

and print shops. Though most of the more attractive Georgian buildings are just out of the bustle, there are a few distinguished buildings on the main streets, inc the timbered building of **Judge Jeffreys' Lodgings** in High West St; he stayed here during his notorious Bloody Assizes. The trial of the Tolpuddle Martyrs also took place on High West St, in the **Shire Hall**; the room is preserved as a memorial, and is open wkdys in summer hols, as are some of the cells. There are one or two

traces of the Romans' occupation, inc the fragmentary remains of a town house behind the County Hall (you'll soon be able to walk on its intricate mosaic floors; tel (01305) 251000 for details), and of an amphitheatre on Weymouth Ave. Not far from here **Eldridge Pope's Victorian Brewery** has tours at 11am and 1pm on summer Weds, or you may be able to squeeze in on a pre-booked tour at other times, (01305) 251251 to check. The Napper's Mite restaurant (South

St), a former almshouse, has good-value food.

! ☉ Dinosaur Museum (Icen Way) The best of Dorset's dinosaur-related exhibitions, a well displayed and entertaining collection very much designed with younger visitors in mind. Although it is quite small there are full-size skeletons and reconstructions, lots of opportunities to handle bones, fossils and the like (not many exhibits have barriers), and fun activities like Dinosaurs and You, where you put in your height and weight and the computer works out how you compare with a couple of dinosaurs. Look out for the intriguing Dinosaurid – a Canadian expert's idea of what dinosaurs would have evolved into if they hadn't become extinct. Shop, some disabled access; cl 24–26 Dec; (01305) 269880; £4.25 (£2.95 children).

☉ Dorset County Museum (High West St) Hardy's study from Max Gate has been reconstructed at this comprehensive museum, and there's a display on his namesake, Nelson's flag-captain at the Battle of Trafalgar. A new writer's gallery looking at the lives of Hardy and other Dorset novelists such as Sylvia Townsend Warner, has touch-screen computer displays. Shop, disabled access to ground floor only; cl Sun (exc July and Aug), 25–26 Dec, Good Fri; (01305) 262735; £3. Along in High East St the King's Arms Hotel, full of Hardy associations, is a good place for lunch.

🏛 ⌖ ⌂ ✔ Hardy's Cottage (Higher Bockhampton, just off A35 3m E of Dorchester) The writer's 1840 birthplace is just outside town; the thatched house hasn't changed much since. Cl Fri and Sat and all Nov–Mar; (01305) 262366; £2.60; NT. The surrounding heath is now largely forested. You can walk into the plantations, and just SE of the cottage are stretches of open heathland, much as Thomas Hardy knew it, on Black Heath and Duddle Heath, parts of the 'untamed and untameable' Egdon Heath that he described in his novels. A path from the river at Lower Bockhampton leads to the village, and a nature trail leads through Thorncombe Wood to Hardy's cottage.

☉ ❀ Keep Military Museum (Bridport Rd) More interesting than most military museums, in handsome Victorian barracks gatehouse; splendid views from the battlements. Shop, disabled access; cl Sun (exc July–Aug), plus 2 wks at Christmas; (01305) 264066; £2.50.

🏛 ⌂ Maiden Castle (off A354 S of Dorchester) One of the best examples of an Iron Age fort, a massive series of grassy ridges covering 47 acres. It's so vast that the tour of its grassy ramparts almost qualifies as a fully fledged walk.

🏛 ❀ Max Gate (Alington Ave, A351 1m E) Among the places still associated with Thomas Hardy (who lived in Dorchester for most of his life, using the town as the centre of events in *The Mayor of Casterbridge*), this is the house he designed and lived in from 1885 to his death in 1928, and where he wrote *Tess* and *Jude the Obscure*. You can see only the dining and drawing rooms (the study has been moved to the County Museum), but the gardens are fascinating, not least because they inspired so much of Hardy's poetry. Shop, disabled access; open pm Sun, Mon and Weds Apr–Sept; (01305) 262538; £2.10; NT. The Trumpet Major food pub is very handy.

! ☉ Teddy Bear House (Antelope House) Tucked away in an old coaching house behind a good teddy shop, a family of human-sized bears dwell in blissful oblivion to the outside world. You can snuggle up next to a dozing grandpa on the sofa, go upstairs to see mother and her ever-increasing brood of baby bears, or head downstairs to the cellar, where the Dorset Teddy Bear Museum collection (recently moved from Bournemouth) includes all kinds of teddy; enthusiastically run, this is a must for all teddy-lovers. Shop; cl 24–26 Dec, ring for winter hours; (01305) 263200; £2.95.

☉ ! Tutankhamun Exhibition (High West St) Readers are impressed by the exhibits here, which re-create the discovery of ancient treasures using a mix of sights, sounds and smells. Shop, some disabled access; cl 24–26 Dec; (01305) 269880; £4.25 (£2.95 children).

DORSETSHIRE GAP ST7403 ⌂ The downland W of Binghams

Melcombe is attractive for walkers; the dry ground of the Gap comes as a pleasant surprise on those days when it seems as if all Dorset is turning to chalky mud. Despite the ultra-English charm of much of inland Dorset – chalk downs, sleepy thatched villages, clumps of beechwoods and fine views – the area is surprisingly little walked, so field routes are often not obvious, careful map-reading is necessary, and even then, sometimes the longer paths can be difficult to follow.

EAST FLEET SY6380

✝ ⚘ ⌂ Interesting, particularly for the tiny ruined church which was wrecked by a legendary 1824 storm. Nearby Chesil Beach, its pebbles and boulders immaculately graded by millennia of storms, is emphatically not for swimmers – the undertow will suck you straight down – but with its long lagoon behind is very interesting for beach-combers and nature-lovers. Swans nest on the great lagoon, which was used for trying out the World War II dam-busting bouncing bomb; now a peaceful spot, with lots of other birds too. The vicinity's walks are especially interesting if you've read J M Faulkner's *Moonfleet*. The Elm Tree at Langton Herring is useful for lunch.

EDMONDSHAM SU0611

🐖 **Dorset Heavy Horse Centre** (well signed from Verwood) Cheery place with five different breeds of huge heavy horse, and miniature Shetland ponies at the other extreme as well as llamas, miniature donkeys and pygmy goats. Snacks, shop, disabled access; cl Nov–Feb; (01202) 824040; £3.95, maybe less out of season. The Albion is handy for lunch.

EGGARDON HILL SY5494

❀ ⋒ On the summit this has wonderful views and – still after thousands of years – impressive earthen ramparts.

HAMBLEDON HILL ST8412

⋒ ❀ Iron Age hill fort in a commanding position just above Child Okeford; has a winning view, and still gives a strong sense of how formidable it must have been.

HINTON ST MARY ST7816

★ 🏛 One of Dorset's many attractive villages, this has a superb manor house and a striking medieval tithe barn.

HURN SZ1296

‼ 🐑 🐓 🐖 **Alice in Wonderland Family Park** (opposite Bournemouth Airport) This is home to the biggest maze in the south of England, made up of 5,200 bushes cut into the shape of Alice characters; also play areas, croquet lawns, herb gardens, theatre, a few rides, farmyard with rare breeds, and pick-your-own fields with berries, beans, potatoes, courgettes and sweetcorn. Lots of thought and effort have been put into the site. Meals, snacks, shop, some disabled access; open Easter–Oct (wknds only from mid-Sept, exc half-term); (01202) 483444; £4.25. The Avon Causeway Hotel does decent food.

KIMMERIDGE BAY SY9179

A lovely spot with intriguing rock strata, kept quieter than it might be by the toll. The New Inn up at Church Knowle is good for lunch.

KINGSTON SY9579

⌂ ❀ From here there's an easy level path to **Hounstout Cliff**; fortify yourself beforehand at the Scott Arms, a good family pub with superb views of Corfe Castle. Turn left at the end and you are into Dorset fossil country, presided over by the primitive hermitage chapel on St Aldhelm's Head; the path here is of the switchback sort, and the chalk mud can make it tough going in wet seasons.

KINGSTON MAURWARD SY7290

🐑 ♘ 🐖 ⌂ **Kingston Maurward Park** Very close to Dorchester, but feeling like the heart of the countryside, with peaceful woodland and lakeside walks, visitor centre, farm park (children can feed the animals), and plenty of garden variety inc Elizabethan and Edwardian gardens, penstemon and salvia national collections. Snacks, shop, some disabled access; cl Nov–mid-Mar; (01305) 215000; *£3.75.

LAMBERTS CASTLE SY3799

⋒ ⌂ This unspoiled hill fort is charming for strolls, especially in late summer when the heather is out; it's quite hard to spot the turning from the road.

LANGTON MATRAVERS SZ0078

🐖 **Putlake Country Farm** Ferret-racing is one of the daily highlights at this lively place with lots to keep children occupied; pony rides, milking demonstrations (daily at 4pm), and lots of animals under cover if it's raining. It's worth taking the trailer ride round the farm if only to appreciate the good views over the Isle of Purbeck. Animals include Highland cattle, sheep, goats, poultry, two barn owls, and a variety of pigs. There's a collection of farming implements, playground and mini-tractors for children to clamber over, and a land trail. Meals, snacks, farm shop, good disabled access; cl Nov–Easter; (01929) 422917; £3.70.

LULWORTH COVE SY8279

◠ ✿ ♮ This beauty-spot, a magnet for summer visitors and really best appreciated out of season, has a classic mini-walk W along the cliffs to Durdle Door, a natural arch eroded by the sea; the unusually shaped rocks are surrounded by particularly good beaches. Inland is prairie-like monotony, and it is best to return the same way. Exhibitions on smuggling and country wines in the **Lulworth Cove Heritage Centre** (cl 25 Dec; nearby parking 50p half-hour). E of Lulworth Cove is army training land, which means high-security fences and dire warning notices, but you are allowed in most wknds and daily in Aug and during Easter (keep to the paths; firing times are published in local papers). Information boards by road junctions off the A351 and A352 nr Wareham give opening times; or ring (01929) 462721 ext 4824 and ask for the guardroom. The coast walk between Lulworth Cove and Kimmeridge Bay is very strenuous but excellent, heading past the surreal 'fossil forest' (formed of petrified algae that once clung to tree-trunks) to Mupe Bay. Another path ascends Bindon Hill, looking down over the semi-circular cove.

LYME REGIS SY3492

★ ✛ ◠ ✿ Enchanting old seaside town, well liked by readers, with rather an elegant, steep main street and interesting side streets; the esplanade is pretty, and there's a lively little fishing and yacht harbour. The sea has been cleaned up by a sewage treatment plant, tempting some quite varied animals to make the occasional visit. A coast path snakes W through an intriguing nature-reserve undercliff, still subject to

landfalls; this is a celebrated area for fossils and flora (several shops sell fossils, with show collections too). There are pleasant walks in the valley. The Pilot Boat on the front is the best place for lunch; the enjoyable old Royal Standard has a terrace leading to the beach. The town gets very busy in summer, but it is worth braving the crowds. The Jane Austen cliffside gardens have peaceful sea views.

♨ ◠ **Dinosaurland** (Coombe St) An excellent collection of fossils, and they can tell you about any you may have at home. They do two-hour fossil walks along the beach. Shop; cl 25–26 Dec; (01297) 443541; £3.20, guided walks £4.50 (booking recommended).

♪ **Lyme Regis Marine Aquarium** (The Cobb) Right on the historic harbour wall, this decent family-run aquarium has some exhibits about local history too. Shop, some disabled access; cl Nov–Easter; (01297) 443678; £1.40.

MILTON ABBAS ST8001

★ ✿ ✛ ◠ ✟ ✿ Lovely thatched village built in the 18th c to replace an earlier one which had spoilt the view from the big house; the 17th-c almshouses were moved here at the same time. Pleasant stroll past the lake through the Capability Brown park to the fine 15th-c **abbey church** of a former Benedictine monastery (it now serves the public school in the nearby house). There's an attractive signed walk over the lane to a former chapel in the wood. Another pleasant walk through the abbey estate leads into **Green Hill Down Nature Reserve**, and a longer walk continues NW to **Bulbarrow Hill**, which looks far into Somerset and Wiltshire.

MINTERNE MAGNA ST6504

✿ ✿ **Minterne Gardens** (Minterne House, A352) Beautiful landscaped gardens, with lakes, cascades, streams, rare trees and impressive spring shows of azaleas, rhododendrons and spring bulbs; the autumn colours can be quite spectacular. Open April–mid-Nov; (01300) 341370; *£3. The road W up Gore Hill and Batcombe Hill to Holywell has memorable views.

NETTLECOMBE SY5295

★ ◠ This sleepy village is in charming walking country, little touched by agricultural improvement – delectable downland and valley landscapes, with a reasonably good path network. There's a decent pub here too.

NINE BARROW DOWN SY9982
❋ ⌂ The main Purbeck ridge, this has far-ranging two-way views – good from a car, and also a pleasing goal for walks from Corfe Castle.

OVER COMPTON ST5817
🦋 **Worldlife & Lullingstone Silk Farm** Superb collection of butterflies, flying free in reconstructions of their natural habitat inside Elizabethan Compton Hall. The silk farm demonstrates production of English silk used for coronations and royal weddings. Snacks, shop, some disabled access; cl Sat and all Oct–Easter; (01935) 474608; £3.95.

OWERMOIGNE SY7685
🗝 **Mill House Cider Museum & Dorset Clock Collection** 🖼 Cider museum with fully restored 18th- and 19th-c equipment, and a video demonstrating the process. Also collection of locally made 18th- and 19th-c clocks. Shop with local ciders, some disabled access; cl Dec 25–mid-Jan; (01305) 852220; £1.50 cider museum, £2 clocks, £2.90 both. The beautifully placed Sailors Return at East Chaldon is good value for lunch.

PILSDON PEN ST4101
❋ ⌂ 🏰 Not a place for long walks, but ideal for those who want a rewarding view in a very short stroll – Dorset's highest point, capped by a hill fort, and looking over Lyme Bay and N towards the Mendips. It is reached within minutes from the layby.

POOLE SZ0190
⛴ 🏰 Merging indistinguishably into Bournemouth on the edges, its centre is wholly distinct, with a more lively feel, especially around The Quay. The broad natural harbour is still busy with the comings and goings of boats and small ships (several decent pubs to watch them from – the nautical Portsmouth Hoy is best for lunch); launch ferries around the harbour, and out to Brownsea Island. There are interesting old buildings along here; the streets behind, some pedestrianised, are well worth strolling through. The Old Harry (High St) has good local fish and the Custom House (The Quay) has a marvellous quayside location.

🎵 🐚 ! **Aquarium Complex** (Hennings Wharf, The Quay) Busy indoor centre with an enormous 00 gauge model railway as well as the aquarium, also smuggling and space exhibitions, and insectarium. Good for families on rainy days. Meals, snacks, shop; cl 25 Dec; (01202) 686712; £4.95.

🕊 🦋 🐚 ❋ **Brownsea Island** Unspoilt 500-acre island in the middle of the huge natural harbour, famous as the site of the first scout camp in 1907. Lots of birds (inc peacocks), animals and butterflies in heath and woodland (you may spot red squirrels), large heronry, nature reserve, and fine views back towards the coast from its beaches. It's a really splendid place to explore. Guided walks 2.45pm daily in July and Aug, and from mid-July to mid-Aug maybe open-air Shakespeare or opera. Snacks, shop, disabled access; cl Nov–Mar; (01202) 707870; £2.50; NT. Ferries to the island run every half-hour from Poole Harbour (£4 return, takes half an hour) or Sandbanks (£2.80 return, only takes six minutes); don't forget to check the time of the last one back.

⛴ **Chain ferry** This runs from Sandbanks, by the harbour mouth, to the Studland side – a spectacular entrance to Dorset proper; it's quickest to go as a foot passenger or by bus (they have priority; around 90p each way). The beach at Sandbanks is regularly lauded as one of the best in Britain.

🎋 ❋ **Compton Acres Gardens** (Canford Cliffs) Perhaps Poole's outstanding attraction, with lovely statuary among fine plants landscaped in an eclectic variety of styles – the Japanese garden is the foremost in Europe. Good views of the hills and Poole harbour. Sat is the least busy day to visit. Snacks (nice crêperie), shop and plant sales, disabled access; cl Nov–Feb; (01202) 700778; £4.95. The Nightjar has decent food.

🏺 ⚗ **Poole Pottery** 🖼 (The Quay) Distinctive china has been produced here since 1873. Good factory tours (exc wknds and pm Fri), and a museum and film; you can have a go at throwing and decorating your own pot, and even smash up a few plates. Other craft demonstrations too. Restaurant with harbour views (open evenings), shop, disabled access; cl 12.30–1.30pm, 25 Dec, and some winter wknds, phone to check; (01202) 666200; £2.50.

☺ **Splashdown** (Tower Park, 2m NE on A3049) Good for children, a water park with 11 rides and slides (indoor and out), inc a near-vertical drop in total darkness. Snacks; cl am wkdys outside school hols (in peak periods they may have limits on how long you can stay), also 25, 31 Dec, 1 Jan, and for 3 or 4 wks at the start of Jan – best to ring; (01202) 716123; £5.50.

♨🏛 **Waterfront Museum** (High St) Two floors of well laid out local history; disabled access; (01202) 683138; cl am Sun (reduced hours in winter); £2). For around £2 extra in July and Aug, you can go next door to **Scaplen's Court**, a well restored medieval merchant's home, with exhibitions upstairs.

PORTESHAM SY6086

△ ☀ The high heathland above here is good walking territory, with a view covering the entire sweep of the West Dorset coast.

☀ △ 🏛 **Hardy Monument** As hideous as it is prominent, this commemorates Nelson's flag-captain, not the Dorset author; it has tremendous views. A track along Bronkham Hill SE from the car park feels truly ancient, with prehistoric burial mounds flanking it. If you don't feel like leaving the car, the Black Down road passing the monument towards Martinstown also gives fine views.

PORTLAND SY6973

☀ △ 🛡 This odd, much-quarried promontory with its narrow neck and long naval connections gives tremendous views from its peak. Nearer at hand, the remarkable sea defences of Portland Harbour laid out below are a fine sight – and you may glimpse Britain's first prison ship for generations moored off here. The Pulpit and the Lobster Pot are both handy pubs for a stroll to the **lighthouse** (new visitor centre; maybe cl winter wknds; (01305) 861233) and cliffs.

🏰 **Portland Castle** Built under Henry VIII to defend the south coast. Audio tour, snacks, shop, limited disabled

access; cl Nov–Mar; (01305) 820539; £2.30; EH. From the car park you may see helicopters landing and taking off from the naval base next door.

♨ **Portland Museum** (Wakeham St) A cottage used by Hardy in *The Well-Beloved* is now a local history museum which was founded by Dr Marie Stopes, the birth-control pioneer. Shop, some disabled access; cl 1–1.30pm, all Weds and Thurs, and all Nov–Mar; (01305) 821804; £1.70.

SANDFORD ORCAS ST6220

🏚 🏵 **Manor House** Interesting lived-in Tudor manor house, largely unaltered since the 16th c, with fine furnishings and family portraits, and pleasant gardens, at their best May and Jun. Open Easter Mon, then pm Sun and all Mon May–Sept; (01963) 220206; *£2.50. The Queen's Arms at Corton Denham has decent food.

SEATOWN SY4291

★ △ ☀ This seaside hamlet has some charming stone cottages and a perfectly placed seaside pub. There's a steep walk up to the **Golden Cap**, the highest point on the county's coast, and another good walk along to the New Inn at Eype. Just inland, the village of Chideock is pretty – or would be, if it weren't sadly ripped in half by the busy A35.

SHAFTESBURY ST8623

★ ☀ 🐾 Hilltop town with good views from Castle Hill and Park Walk; there are several craft shops and workshops. The most famous street is Gold Hill – thatched cottages stepped down a steep cobbled street, familiar from those yesteryear Hovis TV advertisments. At the bottom, St James (where the Two Brewers is the town's best family food pub) is attractive.

🏚 ♨ 🏵 **Shaftesbury Abbey Museum & Garden** You can still see the ancient gravestones at this abbey set up by Alfred the Great; excavated remains from the site can be seen at an adjacent museum, along with an Anglo-Saxon herb garden. A new gallery houses more stonework, which children can touch; new audio tour of site. Shop, disabled access; cl Nov–Apr; (01747) 852910; £1.

♨ **Shaftesbury Town Museum** At the top of Gold Hill the local history museum includes a mummified cat found during the rethatching of a local cottage, an 18th-c fire engine and a collection of old farm implements. Shop, disabled access to ground floor only; cl Oct–Easter; (01747) 852157; £1.

SHERBORNE ST6316

★ † ⚲ An attractive town to wander through, given a feeling of unchanging solidity by the handsome stone medieval abbey buildings that mix in with later ones of the public school here, and by many other fine old buildings in and near the main street. The **abbey** itself is a glorious golden stone building with a beautifully vaulted nave; at the Dissolution the townspeople raised the money to buy it, and it's been the parish church ever since. Locals remain very much involved in its fortunes: a while ago they won their campaign to rid the church of a 19th-c stained-glass window by Pugin, in which Old Testament prophets were said to resemble Mr Blobby. The unspoilt Digby Tap (handy for the abbey but no food Sun) and Skippers (Horsecastles) are useful for lunch. The town has several antique and craft shops inc a working saddlery in the main street.

🏛 ⚘ **Sherborne Castle** (just E of town) Striking old house built by Sir Walter Raleigh in 1594, standing out particularly for its wonderful period furnishings, though there are also interesting paintings and porcelain. Outside are gardens designed by Capability Brown, and beautiful parkland with an enormous lake. Snacks, shop; open pms Apr–Oct, grounds cl Weds, house same, plus Mon and Fri; (01935) 813182; £4.80 house and gardens, £2.40 grounds only.

♿ **Sherborne Museum** (Abbeygate House, Church Ave) An eclectic collection includes a reconstruction of the old castle in its heyday, as well as a Victorian dolls' house and Roman remains. Shop, disabled access to ground floor only; cl am Sun, Mon (exc bank hols), and Nov–Easter; (01935) 812252; £1.

🏰 **Sherborne Old Castle** (Castleton) Facing Sherborne Castle across the lake is the original 12th-c

castle, now a beautifully evocative ruin. Good for a picnic, and especially appealing in Apr when the dry ditch is full of wild primroses. Shop, disabled access (but no facilities); cl 1–2pm, winter Mon and Tues, 24–26 Dec; (01935) 812730; £1.60.

STAPEHILL SU0500

† ⚲ 🕸 ⚘ 🐄 **Stapehill Abbey** Just right for a relaxed, unhurried afternoon, a 19th-c Cistercian abbey (the nuns moved out in 1989, although the chapel has been preserved) now houses craft workshops and exhibitions on monastic life; acres of park and landscaped gardens with waterfalls and woodland walk, and play area and farm animals for children. Meals, snacks, shop, limited disabled access; cl Mon and Tues Oct–Easter, Christmas hols and all Jan; (01202) 873060; £5 (less in winter). The Barley Mow at Colehill is a good food pub.

STINSFORD SY7191

★ † On the Thomas Hardy trail: he featured the village as Mellstock, and at the church his heart is buried beside the body of his first wife.

STOKE ABBOTT ST4500

★ ⌂ With thatched houses, a good deal of charm, and a pleasant pub, this offers walkers attractive undisturbed surrounding countryside, with a reasonably good path network.

STONEBARROW HILL SY3893

⌂ ❈ Reached by a steep narrow road just E of Charmouth, this has good easy walking, fine sea and inland views, a disabled WC, and NT shop in season.

STUBHAMPTON ST9214

⌂ In decent weather the bridleway from here along Ashmore Bottom to Ashmore is well worth exploring; but it can be muddy in a wet spring.

STUDLAND SZ0482

⌂ ❈ ✚ The most remarkably varied short walk in Dorset. In a couple of hours you can take in Ballard Down (huge views over Poole Harbour), Old Harry Rocks (tooth-like chalk pinnacles detached from the cliff) and the Agglestone (a rock standing solitary on Dorset's largest surviving heath). The beach is lovely – there's a charge to go on it in summer (less after 2pm), two areas are set aside for dog-owners in summer and car parking is expensive exc for NT members; behind is a nature reserve, with an NT visitor centre with snacks and shop nearby, and decent food at the Manor House Hotel (where Churchill and Eisenhower watched D-Day rehearsals).

SUTTON POYNTZ SY7083

★ ☀ ⌂ This attractive thatched village, with a decent pub, has a good path to the nearby village of Osmington (also thatched, pretty and with a nice pub). The path gives views of the **White Horse** – an equestrian portrait of George III etched into the hillside. You can walk back along the Dorset coastal path, which here leads along the top of the downs rather than along the coast itself.

SWANAGE SZ0278

Fairly quiet 19th-c resort which, for reasons hotly disputed by locals, seems to be losing much of the sand from the northern end of its beaches. The seaview Mowlem Theatre restaurant (Shire Rd) is good.

☷ ☀ ⅄ **Durlston Country Park** On the edge of Swanage, this has spectacular clifftop scenery and unspoilt countryside, with fine views from the headland, the **Great Globe** (a 40-ton global representation in Purbeck marble), and good spots to watch seabirds, butterflies or deer (let them know if you see dolphins, seals or whales). Snacks, shop, good disabled access (they have a little buggy for bumpy ground); information centre cl wkdys Nov–Mar; (01929) 424443; free, though there's a parking charge of around £2.50 in summer (less in winter).

🚂 **Swanage Railway** Steamtrains now run along six miles of track to Corfe Castle (a joint ticket is available): a nice way of approaching the ruins – or you could walk there and ride back. The Swanage station has an exhibition of old railway memorabilia, and, more unusually, a travel agency where the commission goes to the railway's upkeep. (Parking is easier at the Norden end of the line) Snacks, shop, disabled access; cl 25 Dec, and winter wkdys exc school hols, best to ring for timetable; (01929) 425800 for train times; £6.

TARRANT KEYNSTON ST9204

🍇 **Keynston Mill Fruit Farm** Interesting vineyard and farm shop, with 21 different kinds of pick-your-own. Meals, snacks, disabled access; open daily (exc Mon) Apr–Sept, plus wknds Jan–Mar; (01258) 452596; free. The True Lovers Knot has decent food and a big garden.

THORNCOMBE ST3504

☷ 🏠 ⅄ **Forde Abbey** The extensive gardens here really are special, with glorious trees and shrubs, a fine collection of Asiatic primulas, many interesting plants, and sweeping lawns; they've recently added a visitor centre and Ionic-style temple. The striking abbey buildings still retain some of the features of the original 12th-c Cistercian monastery, but it was modernised in 1500 by Abbot Chard, and it's his great hall and tower that remain. Cromwell's Attorney-General later turned the abbey into a house, and the interior has changed little since, with magnificently furnished rooms, unusual plaster ceilings and a set of Raphael tapestries. Meals and snacks (in 12th-c undercroft), shop, disabled access to gardens only; house open pm Weds, Sun and bank hols Apr–Oct, garden and nursery all year; (01460) 220231; £5, £3.75 garden only. Thorncombe Wood is is awash with bluebells in spring. The George over at Chardstock is the closest good place for lunch.

TOLPUDDLE SY7994

♦ Famous for the agricultural workers who were transported to Australia after they united to improve their working conditions and terms of employment. The Martyrs' Tree under which they supposedly met still remains, but the little museum, between the six cottages built by the TUC as a memorial, will be closed for refurbishment over the winter; ring for details (01305) 848237. The Martyrs pub is useful for lunch.

TYNEHAM SY8880

★ **Abandoned village** On the army's Purbeck firing ranges (open holidays and most wknds), this is quite poignant; there's an explanatory exhibition in the former church.

WAREHAM SY9287

✝ This largely modern town has a few striking old buildings, inc the Church of St Martin's, with a finely carved memorial to Lawrence of Arabia. The

Church of Lady St Mary not far from the quay has the coffin of Edward the Martyr, murdered at nearby Corfe Castle in 978. Two very traditional old inns, the Black Bear and King's Arms; another, the Quay, is in a fine position. The attractive road over the West Creech Hills may sometimes be closed for army firing practice.

✦ Blue Pool 🔲 (Furzebrook, 3m S of Wareham) Peaceful beauty-spot with curious colour changes in the water whenever the weather alters, from light green to blue to suddenly a rich turquoise; it's bluest on an overcast day. Also 25 acres of heathland with rare plants and animals. Snacks, shop, some disabled access; facilities and museum cl Oct–Easter, site cl Dec–Feb; (01929) 551408; £2.80.

WEST LULWORTH SY8280

❋ A lovely spot, though hardly undiscovered (parking can be a nightmare), just above a very beautiful cove with extraordinary nearby rock formations; the thatched Castle Inn is useful for lunch. The Lulworth Equestrian Centre can arrange **horse-riding**; (01929) 400396; around £12 an hour.

🏛❋⚜✝🐂 Lulworth Castle Fully restored 17th-c castle with splendid views over the park from its south-east tower; the formal gardens are a nice spot for a picnic. The Catholic chapel was the first to be built in England after the Reformation, and an Anglican church was built in part by Thomas Hardy, about whom there's an exhibition inside; also children's summer farm and play area. Meals, teas, shop, some disabled access; cl 25–26 Dec; (01929) 400352; £4.

WEYMOUTH SY6878

★ 🏠♿☺ Elegant 18th- and 19th-c terraces along its curving esplanade, and some older buildings in the narrower partly pedestrianised streets behind. The harbour is lively, with big ferries leaving from the outer quay, and the town's inner ring road running one-way around the inner harbour. The Old Rooms has good-value food and interesting harbour views. On the far side of the harbour, the narrow streets of the old town are worth exploring; there's a **Tudor house** on Trinity St.

The resort has a good beach, and lots of lively family attractions.

🍴♿! Brewers Quay In the heart of the Old Harbour, this is a skilful conversion of a harbourside Victorian brewery into shopping and leisure complex, with plenty of good year-round activities: the **Timewalk** imaginatively re-creates scenes from the town's history (limited disabled access; £3.95), there's a craft market, ten-pin bowling, microbrewery, and lively hands-on science centre. Several places to eat, and good specialist shops; cl 25–27 Dec, and a couple of wks late Jan; (01305) 777622; centre free, charges for some attractions.

❋! Deep Sea Adventure & Titanic Story (Custom House Quay) Fascinating look at underwater exploration, shipwrecks, and the search for buried treasure, with lots of interactive displays. There's an exemplary exhibition on the *Titanic*, and a first-class indoor play area taking up most of the second floor (extra charge). Meals, snacks, shop, disabled access; cl 24–26 Dec; (01305) 760690; *£3.50.

! 🏠 Model World 🔲 (Lodmoor Country Park, Preston Rd) Set in landscaped gardens, this miniature world includes a model airport, funfair, space centre, zoo and 0-gauge railway (runs daily, weather permitting); also plenty of models to operate yourself, and an aviary. Snacks, shop, disabled access; cl Oct–May; (01305) 781797; £2.50.

🏛❋⚜ Nothe Fort (Barrack Rd) Interesting armed Victorian fort on three levels, spread over a staggering 70 rooms. Children can clamber over some of the vehicles and guns, and there are fine views of the harbour and coast. Snacks, shop, some disabled access; open daily mid-May–mid-Sept, Easter hols and Oct half-term, plus pm Sun and bank hols rest of year; (01305) 787243; £3. Good views too from the garden of the Nothe Tavern (with tasty fresh fish), and from the pleasant nearby Nothe Gardens.

🐟 Sea Life Park (Lodmoor Country Park) One of the most elaborate in the excellent Sea Life Centres chain. As well as the stunning marine displays and touch pools, features include a Shark

Academy, with fun interactive games and quizzes leading to a scholarship, and a splendid outdoor play area. Meals, snacks, shop, disabled access; cl 25 Dec; (01305) 788255; £5.95.

WIMBORNE MINSTER SZ0199

✝ ! ⌂ Georgian houses (and decent antique shops and auctions) in the narrow central streets around the **Minster** – a fine, well preserved, largely Norman church with contrasting red and grey masonry, twin towers, and a brightly coloured jack striking the clock bell every quarter. Inside, an interesting Norman crypt, a distinctive astronomical clock and the original chained library. Further along King St is an entertaining model town (cl Oct–Easter; £2.50). Dormers (Hanham Rd) and the Cross Keys (Victoria Rd, W) are best for lunch. Just W of town at Pamphill is a good big farm shop, and just E there are pleasant country walks around the Fox & Hounds at Little Canford.

⛰⌂ **Badbury Rings** This once formidable Iron Age hill fort, just off B3082 NW of Wimborne, is associated by some with King Arthur. It's a good strolling ground with an impressive range of wild flowers – and if you feel more energetic, a **Roman road** lets you strike out for miles N.

⛪▣🌺 **Kingston Lacy House** (B3082 NW of Wimborne) Impressive 17th-c mansion later remodelled by Charles Barry, with a grand Italian marble staircase and superb Venetian ceiling; outstanding paintings such as the *Judgement of Solomon* by Sebastiano del Piamtino, and others by Titian, Rubens and Van Dyck. The enormous grounds have landscaped gardens, a herd of Red Devon cattle in the park, and summer concerts and plays. Lovely snowdrops in Feb and early Mar. Meals, snacks, shop, disabled access to park and gardens; open Apr–Oct, house cl am and Thurs, Fri; (01202) 883402; £6, £2.50 grounds only; NT.

🌺 **Knoll Gardens** (Stapehill Rd) Rare and exotic plants in various colourfully

themed, well developed gardens, with over 4,000 different named species, many of which can be bought in the expanding nursery. Meals, snacks, shop and garden centre, disabled access; cl Jan, Feb, Mon and Tues in Mar and Oct, plus Sats Nov–Dec; (01202) 873931; £3.50. Adjacent Trehane Nurseries have a great range of camellias.

⛪👑🌺 **Priest's House Museum** (High St) Historic town house with carefully researched period rooms; regular cooking displays in the Victorian kitchen, and a charming walled garden. Summer teas, shop, disabled access to ground floor and garden; cl Sun (exc pm Jun–Sept and bank hol wknds), and Nov–Mar (exc special exhibition 2 wks after Christmas – best to tel); (01202) 882533; £2.

✂ ⚘ **Walford Mill** (Stone Lane) Former 18th-c flour mill with exhibitions and local crafts. Meals, snacks, shop, disabled access; cl 25–26 Dec, 1 Jan, and Mons Jan–Mar; (01202) 841400; free.

WOOL SY8486

🐵 **Monkey World** See separate family panel on p.223.

WORTH MATRAVERS SY9677

❇ ⌂ In this prettily set coastal hamlet, the unpretentious Square & Compass has lovely views, and is a good base for coastal walks. Nr here, the rock pool at Dancing Ledge is said to have been cut by a local schoolmaster.

★ **Other attractive villages** with decent pubs include Buckhorn Weston ST7524, Burton Bradstock SY4889, Chedington ST4805, Church Knowle SY9481, Evershot ST5704, Farnham ST9515, Fiddleford ST8013, Kingston SY9579, Langton Herring SY6182, Litton Cheyney SY5590, Loders SY4994, Powerstock SY5196, Puncknowle SY5388 (pronounced 'Punnel'), Sydling St Nicholas SY6399, Symondsbury SY4493, Tarrant Monkton ST9408, West Knighton SY7387 and Whitchurch Canonicorum SY3995 (fine church).

Please let us know what you think of places in the *Guide*. Use the report forms at the back of the book or simply write us a letter.

Where to eat

ASKERSWELL SY5292 **Spyway** *(01308) 485250* Former smugglers' look-out with exceptional-value, very popular bar food, lots of salads, and cheesecake; good views, big garden, walks nearby; no children under 14 inside; cl Mon exc bank hols. **£15**|£4.95.

CHEDINGTON ST4805 **Winyards Gap** *(01935) 891244* Tastefully modernised pub with marvellous views and nearby walks; a wide choice of good bar food especially pies and fish, well kept real ales, a no smoking area, and skittle alley. **£15.50**|£5.95.

CHIDEOCK SY4292 **Betchworth House** *(01297) 489478* Welcoming, no smoking, 17th-c house with attractive tearoom and pretty cottagey garden, and offering morning coffee and home-made clotted cream teas; bdrms; cl Mon–Thurs Nov–Feb. £3.

CHRISTCHURCH SZ1593 **Splinters** *12 Church St (01202) 483454* Fine old building nr the priory, with three attractively decorated rooms, imaginative modern cooking, lovely puddings, a fine British cheese choice, good-value wines, and friendly, helpful owners; also run Pommery's (next door) with delicatessen and lively upstairs café bar; cl Sun, Mon. **£38**|£6.50.

CHURCH KNOWLE SY9481 **New Inn** *(01929) 480357* Very attractive, partly thatched old pub with two nicely furnished main bar areas, lots of bric-à-brac, log fires, and a relaxing dining lounge; very good fresh fish (and other food), well kept ales, decent wines, and skittle alley; camping in field behind (need to book). **£18.75**|£7.50.

CORSCOMBE ST5105 **Fox** *(01935) 891330* Cosy thatched pub, very much a traditional family-run place, with lovely polished copper pots and pans, scrubbed pine tables, candles in champagne bottles, open fires in one room and woodburner in another; particularly good food (especially daily specials), well kept real ales, local cider, and a decent wine list; nice surrounding walks; well behaved children welcome; bdrms. **£22**|£5.50.

DORCHESTER SY6890 **Potter In** *19 Durngate St (01305) 260312* All-day food inc English breakfast, enjoyable lunchtime meals and snacks, and afternoon teas; walled garden for summer, open fire and fresh flowers, and a friendly welcome; disabled access. £3.10.

EAST MORDEN SY9195 **Cock & Bottle** *(01929) 459238* Popular dining pub with several beamed communicating areas, a nice mix of old furnishings, good log fire, enjoyable food inc interesting daily specials with plenty of fish and seasonal game, well kept beers and fine wines; disabled access. **£23.50**|£5.55.

EVERSHOT ST5704 **Acorn** *(01935) 83228* Carefully improved recently, this well run old coaching inn has a comfortable L-shaped bar with two fine old fireplaces and copies of the inn's deeds going back to the 17th c; imaginative daily specials, well kept ales, home-made damson vodka and sloe gin, and a thoughtful wine list; nice village and good nearby walks. **£19.70**|£6.25.

LANGTON HERRING SY6182 **Elm Tree** *(01305) 871257* Busy pub in pretty thatched village; with copper, brass and bellows on the walls of the beamed main rooms, a traditionally furnished dining extension, interesting daily specials, and real ales; flower-filled garden, and nearby walks. **£18.95**|£6.95.

LYME REGIS SY3492 **Pilot Boat** *(01297) 443157* Welcoming place across from the beaches; with a bustling atmosphere, light comfortable dining bar decorated with fishing and nautical memorabilia, good food, no smoking restaurant, and decent wines and liqueurs; disabled access. **£17.50**|£6.50.

LYME REGIS SY3492 **Victoria Hotel** *Uplyme Rd (01297) 444801* Friendly family-run Edwardian hotel, with a relaxed dining area in the open-plan bar, a stylish restaurant, particularly good imaginative food, real ales, and a terraced garden; cl pm Mon; children must be over 12 in restaurant; bdrms. **£25**|£5.50.

MAIDEN NEWTON SY5997 **Petit Canard** *Dorchester Rd (01300) 320536* Welcoming little restaurant (they prefer you not to smoke) with simple furnishings, very interesting food inc fine puddings, and a well chosen wine list; cl am, Sun, Mon, 1 wk Jan, 1 wk May; children over 6. **£30**.

MARNHULL ST7718 **Blackmore Vale** *(01258) 820701* Relaxed and friendly old pub with good home-made bar food, decent beer and wine, and a log fire and interesting furnishings in the comfortably modernised bar; can also eat in garden where one of the tables is thatched; no children. **£19|£6**.

PLUSH ST7102 **Brace of Pheasants** *(01300) 348357* Long, low, 16th-c thatched cottage with a civilised but relaxed atmosphere, good solid furnishings, fresh flowers and a nice log fire in the airy beamed bar; interesting food, well kept real ales; swings and an aviary in the garden; children in the family room. **£20|£5.75**.

POWERSTOCK SY5196 **Three Horseshoes** *(01308) 485328* Popular, stone- and thatch pub with comfortable L-shaped bar, warm fires, lovely sea views, well kept ales, 20 wines by the glass, and (depending what the local fishermen bring in) a very good choice of well prepared, interesting fish dishes. **£21.25|£6**.

SHERBORNE ST6316 **Pheasants** *24 Greenhill (01935) 815252* Georgian restaurant-with-rooms in an attractive town; with friendly staff, enjoyable modern English cooking, good breakfasts; cl pm Sun, Mon, 2 wks mid-Jan; well behaved children welcome; disabled access. **£30|£15** 3 courses Sat/Sun only.

STURMINSTER NEWTON ST7814 **Red Rose** *Market Cross (01258) 472460* Long-standing, family-run lunchtime restaurant with proper English cooking using their own lamb and local produce, and with a very relaxed and happy atmosphere; popular locally; cl evenings and Sun; disabled access. **£8.45**.

SWANAGE SZ0278 **Galley** *9 High St (01929) 427299* Enjoyable little evening restaurant not far from the seafront, with an emphasis on fresh local fish and game, good, reasonably priced wines, and helpful service; cl Nov–Mar; no children. **£25.75**.

TARRANT MONKTON ST9408 **Langton Arms** *(01258) 830225* Thatched 17th-c pub in a pretty village; wide choice of fresh home-made food (inc popular children's menu), bistro restaurant, well kept beers, decent wines, comfortable bar, open fire, and skittle alley; pleasant bdrms; children in family room; disabled access. **£25|£7.50**.

UPWEY SY6684 **Old Ship** *7 Ridgeway (01305) 812522* Pretty and friendly, whitewashed cottagey pub with several interconnected beamed rooms; fresh flowers and an open fire, very good bar food, well kept beer, a fine range of wines, attentive service, and seats in the garden; cl 24 Dec. **£15.50|£6.50**.

UPWEY SY6684 **Wishing Well** *(01305) 814470* Nice little restaurant, popular locally, with interesting lunchtime food and afternoon teas, friendly service; bring your own wine; cl Mon and Tues Mar–Easter and Oct–Dec, plus Jan and Feb; disabled access. **£10|£5.50**.

WIMBORNE MINSTER SZ0199 **Cloisters** *40 East St (01202) 880593* Friendly restaurant with pleasant décor and enjoyable food inc breakfast with home-made marmalade, lunchtime snacks and meals, and afternoon teas; cl 25–30 Dec; disabled access. **£15|£3.50**.

WORTH MATRAVERS SY9777 **Worth Café & Craft Centre** *(01929) 439360* Welcoming converted barn with enthusiastic staff, good home-made lunches (lots for vegetarians) and cakes, and locally made crafts; walkers welcome; disabled access. **£5.50**.

Special thanks to Paul Kennedy, Michel Hooper-Immins, Mrs A K Davies, B and K Hypher, James B Graham.

Please let us know what you think of places in the *Guide*. Use the report forms at the back of the book or simply write us a letter.

Dorset Calendar

Some of these dates were provisional as we went to press. Please check information with the telephone numbers provided.

JANUARY

1 **Poole** Bath Races in Poole Quay (01202) 253253

FEBRUARY

4 **Dorchester** Real Ale Festival – *till 5 February* (01305) 267992

MARCH

4 **Weymouth** Music Festival (01305) 765265
7 **Corfe Castle** Marblers' and Stonecutters' Day: to enforce rules laid down in 1651. *At noon* the church's pancake bell summons the company from the Fox Inn to the Town Hall. After the meeting a football is kicked along the old road to Ower Quay (each participant carrying a pint of beer and loaf of bread) to preserve an ancient right of way used in the shipping of marble (01929) 422885
18 **Kingston Maurward** Spring Lambing at Kingston Maurward College – *till 19 March* (01305) 215000
25 **Kingston Maurward** Spring Lambing at Kingston Maurward College – *till 26 March* (01305) 215000

APRIL

21 **Weymouth** Easter Festival at Brewers Quay – *till 24 April* (01305) 785747; **Weymouth** Easter Egg Hunt at Abbotsbury Gardens – *till 24 April* (01305) 206449
22 **Kingston Maurward** Easter Egg Hunt at Kingston Maurward College – *till 24 April* (01305) 215000
23 **West Lulworth** Easter Bunny Hunt at the Castle (01929) 552740
24 **Kingston Maurward** Teddy Bear Fair at Kingston Maurward College (01305) 269741
28 **Dorchester** Festival of Music and Arts (01305) 267992
30 **Weymouth** International Beach Kite Festival: 175-ft kites, stunt kite teams and children's workshop, plus fireworks and night kite-flying display – *till 1 May* (01305) 765211

MAY

1 **Cerne Abbas** Wessex Morris Men dance on Giant Hill *at 7am* (01305) 251481
7 **Bovington** Dorset Children's Show at the Tank Museum: rare breeds, arena events (01929) 405096
13 **West Lulworth** Country Gardening Festival at the Castle – *till 14 May* (01929) 552740
14 **Kingston Maurward** Garden Show and Plant Sale at Kingston Maurward College (01305) 215000
21 **Weymouth** Vintage Motorcycle Display on the Pavilion forecourt (01305) 206449

Dorset Calendar (cont.)

28 Athelhampton Flower Festival at Athelhampton House – *till 1 June* (01305) 848363; **Weymouth** Oyster Festival at the Old Harbour: live music and side shows (01305) 785747; also, Dorset Tour: vintage and classic vehicle rally (01305) 785747

29 Abbotsbury Music Festival – *till 3 June* (01305) 267992; **Blandford Forum** Georgian Fayre and Town Criers' Competition (01258) 480808; **Weymouth** Trawler Race and Water Carnival (01305) 765211

31 Abbotsbury Baby swans hatching: hundreds of baby swans smother the pathways – *till 30 June* (01305) 871684

JUNE

1 Sherborne Ascension Day: abbey choir sing from the roof of the abbey tower *at 7am* (01935) 815341

8 Weymouth Jazz Festival at Brewers Quay; free music inc open-air performances – *till 11 June* (01305) 785747

10 Netherbury Open Gardens – *till 11 June* (01308) 488270; **West Bay** Traction Engine Rally – *till 11 June* (01308) 424901

17 Abbotsbury Garden Festival at Abbotsbury Subtropical Gardens – *till 18 June* (01305) 206449; **Cerne Abbas** 20 Gardens Open – *till 18 June* (01300) 341311; **Dorchester** Carnival (01305) 785747; **Weymouth** International Military and Veterans' Festival inc Remembrance Parade with over 90 military and historic vehicles – *till 23 June* (01305) 785747

24 Bournemouth Music-makers'- Festival: free amateur events, parades, tattoo – *till 8 July* (01202) 451718

25 Beaminster 18 Open Gardens (01308) 862675; **Cattistock** 20 Open Gardens, plus vintage cars and aeroplanes at Chalmington Manor (01300) 320226; **Poole** Carnival (01202) 686931; **West Lulworth** Classic Car Event at the Castle (01929) 552740

30 Lyme Regis Jazz Festival – *till 2 July* (01297) 442138

JULY

1 Christchurch Festival – *till 2 July* (01202) 471780; **Shaftesbury** Gold Hill Fair – *till 2 July* (01308) 424901

2 Athelhampton MG Owners Rally at Athelhampton House (01305) 848363; **Frampton** Village Fête (01300) 320394

6 Bovington Firepower Mobility: tank battles *from noon* in the arena, and also *every Thurs till September* (01929) 405096

8 Puddletown Carnival (01305) 848625; **Yetminster** Fair: Yetties concert, art exhibition, street market, dancing (01935) 872123

15 Weymouth International Maritime Modelling Festival – *till 16 July* (01305) 765211

16 Tolpuddle Rally: trade union banners, speeches (0117) 950 6425

22 Dorchester Thomas Hardy Conference – *till 29 July* (01305) 267992; **Lyme Regis** Lifeboat Week: Red Arrows, opera and fireworks – *till 30 July* (01297) 442951

26 Bournemouth Flowers by Candlelight: 15,000 candles in the Lower Gardens – *till 30 August* (01202) 451718

29 Abbotsbury Colombian Festival of Music and Dance at Abbotsbury Subtropical Gardens (01305) 206449; **Bournemouth** Carnival – *till 6 August* (01202) 451718; also, Fireworks *every Fri evening* – *till 1 September* (01202) 451718; **Chedington** Street Fair (01305) 267992; **Portland** Festival –

Dorset Calendar (cont.)

till 5 August (01305) 267992; **West Lulworth** Horse Trials and Country Fair at the Castle – *till 30 July* (01929) 552740

31 Weymouth International Fireworks Festival: live bands and music, street entertainers (01305) 206449

AUGUST

2 Portesham Possum Fez Wik: traditional fair week (appears in Hardy's *Under the Greenwood Tree*) – *till 6 August* (01305) 871316

3 Bovington Firepower Mobility: tank battles *from noon* in the arena – also *every Thurs and Fri in August* (01929) 405096

4 Bovington Camp Dorset County Arts and Crafts Exhibition at Bovington County Middle School – *till 8 August* (01305) 267992; **Sidmouth** International Folk Festival (01305) 267992

7 Weymouth International Fireworks Festival: live bands and music, street entertainers (01305) 206449

11 Weymouth Sailing Regatta – *till 13 August* (01305) 206449

12 Chickerell Carnival (01305) 267992

14 Weymouth International Fireworks Festival: live bands and music, street entertainers (01305) 206449

16 Motcombe Gillingham and Shaftesbury Agricultural Show (01747) 823955; **Weymouth** Carnival: Red Arrows, procession, fireworks (01305) 765211

18 Broadwindsor Flower Show – *till 28 August* (01305) 267992; **Weymouth** Real Ale and Cider Festival at the Rugby Club – *till 19 August* (01305) 785747

19 Bridport Carnival Procession (01308) 422884

20 Poole Powerboat racing (01202) 707227

21 Weymouth International Fireworks Festival: live bands and music, street entertainers (01305) 206449

24 Bridport Melplash Agricultural Show (01308) 423337

25 Milton Abbas Milton Abbey Music Festival – *till 28 August* (01305) 267992

26 Abbotsbury Open-air Opera at the Subtropical Gardens (01305) 871387

28 Weymouth International Fireworks Festival: live bands and music, street entertainers (01305) 206449

29 Bournemouth Festival of Lights: light show set to music – *till 1 September* (01202) 451700

30 Tarrant Hinton Great Dorset Steam Fair: 30th anniversary on 500-acre site, with steam funfair – *till 3 September* (01258) 860361

SEPTEMBER

2 Dorchester Agricultural Show at Cokers Frome – *till 3 September* (01305) 264249

7 Bovington Firepower Mobility: tank battles *from noon* in the arena – *also every Thurs in September* (01929) 405096

9 Bradford Peverell Cooking and Garden Show (01305) 267992

11 Weymouth European Boat Championships – *till 15 September* (01305) 206449

17 Weymouth Vintage and Classic Car Rally at Weymouth Pavilion (01305) 765265

30 Shaftesbury Carnival (01747) 854327

Dorset Calendar (cont.)

OCTOBER

2 **Weymouth** Speed Sailing Week – *till 8 October* (01305) 206449
7 **Gillingham** Carnival (01747) 853514
16 **Sherborne** Pack Monday Fair (01935) 813343

NOVEMBER

4 **Mudeford** Fireworks (01202) 471780
13 **Weymouth** Christmas Festival at Brewers Quay – *till 24 December* (01305) 785747
26 **Christchurch** Winter Carnival: Snow Queen procession (01202) 471780

DECEMBER

9 **Weymouth** Victorian Show Night (01305) 267992
31 **Weymouth** Fancy Dress Street Party: one of Britain's biggest (01305) 206449

We welcome reports from readers

This *Guide* depends on readers' reports. Do help us if you can – in return, we offer a discount on the next edition to people who've helped us with reports for it. Tell us what you think about places already in it, and anything extra you think we should say about them. And send us your ideas for inclusion in the next edition: places to visit, eat at or stay in, attractive drives or walks, maybe even unusual interesting shops you know of. Use the card in the middle, the report forms at the end, or just write – no stamp needed: *The Good Britain Guide*, FREEPOST TN1569, Wadhurst, E Sussex TN5 7BR.

ESSEX

Gentle charm, some good days out, traditional seaside resorts.

Colchester, the liveliest town here, is well worth a visit, with an excellent zoo (good value too) and the enjoyable Castle Museum among several other interesting places to visit in the town. Magnificent Audley End makes for a good family day out, though the pleasant old town of Saffron Walden nearby has a more adult appeal. Other worthwhile family outings include the toy museum and reconstructed Norman castle at Stansted, the wildlife park at Widdington and several well organised farm parks and private railway centres. Southend-on-Sea, the main seaside resort, has plenty to do and a buoyant charm in summer; Brightlingsea has the best beach. Castle Hedingham passes a pleasant afternoon.

There are fascinating gardens at Elmstead Market (Beth Chatto), Lamarsh (plenty to keep children occupied here), and Rettendon, with the Gibberd Garden in Harlow (a newcomer to the *Guide*) one of that town's several surprises for visitors. Among other new entries this year we'd mention the Munnings galleries in charming Dedham (a reminder that Constable was not the only artist to have found inspiration around here), East Anglia's largest vineyards at Purleigh, and the giant summer maize maze at Great Leighs.

Essex has many beautiful villages, especially Finchingfield, Thaxted and Great Bardfield (all of which have windmills). Other appealing places include Layer Marney Tower, Coggeshall and Burnham-on-Crouch. Many of the churches are well worth a look. North Essex has a real East Anglian flavour. Driving through, you pass lots of attractive houses right by the road, often with fine old timbering and distinctive colourwashed plasterwork – the intricate patterning is known as pargeting. Constable's Stour Valley still enchants, though the unspoilt character which makes its landscapes so attractive is under growing threat from the sheer number of visitors. In stark contrast, the two nuclear war command bunkers at Kelvedon Hatch and Mistley have a chilling fascination.

The Blackwater/Crouch coast has a surprisingly remote feel, given the closeness of densely urban South Essex. Further north, there are good coastal walks at Walton on the Naze.

Where to stay

BROXTED TL5827 **Whitehall** *Church End, Broxted CM6 2BZ (01279) 850603* **£115,** plus special breaks; 26 pretty rms. Fine Elizabethan manor house in lovely walled gardens, with outdoor swimming pool and tennis court; restful, spacious lounge, a smaller cosier one with log fire, pleasant bar, good food in the big timbered restaurant, and friendly service; cl 25–31 Dec; disabled access.
BURNHAM-ON-CROUCH TQ9595 **White Harte** *Burnham-on-Crouch CM0 8AS (01621) 782106* **£55;** 19 rms, 11 with own bthrm. Old-fashioned, 17th-c yachting inn on quay overlooking the River Crouch, with its own jetty; high ceilings,

oak tables, polished parquet, sea pictures, panelling, residents' lounge, decent bar food, and restaurant; cl Christmas.

COGGESHALL TL8422 **White Hart** *Market End, Coggeshall, Colchester CO6 1NH (01376) 561654* **£75w,** plus wknd breaks; 18 attractive rms. Family-run, 15th-c hotel with a beamed lounge bar and residents' bar, log fires, friendly staff, and good food in both the bar and restaurant; cl 25–26 Dec.

DEDHAM TM0432 **Maison Talbooth** *Dedham, Colchester CO7 6HN (01206) 322367* **£150,** plus special breaks; 10 luxuriously furnished rms. Tranquil Victorian country house in fine Constable country; comfortable seating and fresh flowers in the elegant lounge, very good imaginative food in the lovely timber-framed restaurant overlooking river and gardens, and marvellous breakfasts; partial disabled access.

DEDHAM TM0533 **Marlborough Head** *Dedham, Colchester CO7 6DH (01206) 323250* ***£55;** 3 rms. Comfortable, old-fashioned, early 18th-c inn in the heart of Constable's home village; unusual carved woodwork in the central lounge, wide choice of interesting food; cl 25 Dec.

MALDON TL8407 **Blue Boar** *Silver St, Maldon CM9 4QE (01621) 852681* **£80,** plus wknd breaks; 28 comfortable rms. Fine 14th-c coaching inn with cosy little beamed and oak-panelled rooms, roaring log fires, good food (nice breakfasts), and friendly staff; limited disabled access.

RICKLING GREEN TL5029 **Cricketers Arms** *Rickling Green, Saffron Walden CB11 3YG (01799) 543210* ***£70;** 10 rms, some in modern block behind. Cheerful family-run pub by the village green with cricketing mementos; beamed bar with open fires, home-made food in the bar and attractive restaurant; handy for Stansted Airport; partial disabled access.

THAXTED TL6031 **Swan** *Thaxted, Dunmow CM6 2PL (01371) 830321* **£60;** 20 comfortably modernised rms. Four-gabled late 15th-c inn with views towards the church and almshouses; pleasantly pubby big bar area with a warm atmosphere, well kept real ales, and good food.

WEST MERSEA TM0012 **Blackwater** *West Mersea, Colchester CO5 8QH (01206) 383338* **£60,** plus special breaks; 8 pretty rms. Creeper-covered hotel with neat little sitting room, fresh flowers, attractive beamed restaurant with mainly French food (emphasis on fresh fish), the relaxed and informal Mussel Pan Bistro which specialises in mussels; big breakfasts, and friendly service; cl start Jan.

To see and do

ESSEX Family Attraction of the Year

🐾 🦋 **WIDDINGTON** 🖼 TL5331 **Mole Hall Wildlife Park** Run by the same family for over 40 years, this unspoilt, friendly place was a favourite with our research officer when he was a child. It's a very pretty spot, set around a moated manor house, with willows hanging over the water, and plenty of free-roaming ducks and geese. It's much less sophisticated than the county's main animal attraction, Colchester Zoo, but it's precisely that low-key appeal that brings people back over and over again. One couple we know have been coming here for over 20 years; they reckon the park is currently smarter and neater than it has been for some time. Spread over 20 acres, the wide range of animals takes in two species of otter (they were the first regular UK breeders of the North American otter), the South American llama, wallabies, chimpanzees, flamingoes, and big paddocks of various types of deer, including the Formosa sika, now extinct in the wild. Plenty of domestic animals such as ponies, rabbits, goats and pigs, and small play areas. A Butterfly Pavilion has free-flying butterflies in a re-created jungle environment, and a variety of snakes, spiders and other creepy crawlies; there's usually an insect expert on hand to answer questions. There may be a bouncy castle some days in summer. Summer snacks and shop, disabled access; park cl only 25 Dec, but butterfly house cl Nov–mid-Mar; (01799) 540400; £4.50 (£3.20 children) – less in winter.

ABRIDGE TQ4897

🎇 ☛ **Crowther Nurseries** (Ongar Road) Working florist garden with decorative shrub beds, flower borders inc a good dahlia area, vegetable plot and greenhouses; also pets corner inc sheep, goats, a donkey and a tortoise, and a Lego corner to keep children occupied. Plant sales, teas, disabled access; cl 25–26 Dec; (01708) 688581; free.

BATTLESBRIDGE TQ7894

★ 🐾 △ Attractive village, with popular antique and crafts centre, walks to the head of Crouch estuary, and a good pub.

BILLERICAY TQ6794

🐖 🐾 🏭 **Barleylands Farm Museum & Visitor Centre** 🖼 (A129 SE of Billericay) Expanding series of attractions, from farm animals and rural life displays to working glassworks, craft studios and miniature railway (summer Sun only). Meals, snacks, shop, disabled access; cl Nov–Feb; (01268) 282090; £3.25. The nearby Duke of York (South Green) has decent food.

BLACKWATER ESTUARY TL9610

△ Vast skies, with boats and bird life punctuating the flat sea and landscapes; the pick of local walks include paths along the dykes from Tollesbury, and towards isolated St Peter's Chapel from Bradwell-on-Sea. The Chequers at Goldhanger is another good start point. Like other parts of this low-lying much indented coast, the immediate hinterland is generally too dull to make circular walks worthwhile – usually best to come back the way you went.

BOCKING TL7523

🎇 **Windmills** As well as the one here in Churchstreet, good examples can be found in Aythorpe Roding TL5815, and Mountnessing TQ6397.

BRADWELL-ON-SEA TL9907

★ △ † Worth the long drive for the sense of being right out on the edge of things – the timeless emptiness if anything exaggerated by distant views of vast industrial installations (there are free tours of the nuclear power station; cl Nov–Feb; (01621) 873395). The walk E down the old Roman road across the marshes takes you to a little restored **Saxon chapel** right on the sea wall,

the scene of an annual pilgrimage in July. The Green Man is a good traditional pub.

BRAINTREE TL7622

⬇T 🐾 **Working Silk Museum** (South St) Silk production demonstrated from start to finish, in a well restored old mill building; the hand looms they use are over 150 years old. Shop, disabled access; cl 12.30–1.30pm, wknds, bank hols, and Christmas–New Year; (01376) 553393; £3.20. The Green Dragon just S at Young's End has good food.

BURNHAM-ON-CROUCH TQ9595

★ △ 🐾 Attractively old-fashioned yachting station, lively in summer (packed around the Aug bank hol for its regatta), but nice in winter too with rigging clacking forlornly against the masts of those yachts left to ride at anchor off shore. There are pleasant walks along the banks of the River Crouch. The White Harte on the quay is good for lunch and there is a decent little **craft centre** (where they filmed some episodes of *Lovejoy*) at Blake End, a little W on the A120.

🏭 🚂 **Mangapps Farm Railway Museum** (B1021 Burnham-on-Crouch–Southminster) Friendly and growing collection of vintage rolling stock and railway memorabilia. They have a station formed from railway buildings from sites all over East Anglia and steam rides along 1½ miles of track. Mostly under cover; open pm wknds, daily in summer and Easter school hols – best to ring for winter opening; (01621) 784898; £4. Further along, The Limes is a decent farm shop, with nature trails and **pick-your-own**.

CASTLE HEDINGHAM TL7835

★ 🏰 † 🐾 The town, which has some attractive buildings, is named for the Norman **castle** which dominates it, the magnificent four-storey keep towering above the surrounding trees. Exceptionally well preserved, it still has its roof, banqueting hall and minstrels' gallery. Teas, shop; cl Oct–Easter; (01787) 460261; £3.50. The **church** has grand Norman masonry and interestingly carved choir seats. There's a good working pottery in St James St, and the Bell is good for lunch. The

B1058 towards Sudbury, then left through Gestingthorpe and the Belchamps is a pleasant excursion.

🚂🐄 Colne Valley Railway & Museum (Yeldham Rd; A1017 N of Castle Hedingham) Lovingly restored Victorian railway buildings with a collection of vintage engines and carriages; short steamtrain trips pm Sun mid-Mar–mid-Oct, and pm Weds and Thurs in hols; diesel rides pm Tues, Fri and Sat in school hols – best to ring for a timetable. Admission price now includes entry to rare breeds farm park. Meals on Pullman coaches, snacks, shop, limited disabled access; cl 23 Dec–Feb; (01787) 461174; £6, £3 when trains not running.

CHAPPEL TL8927

🌿🚂 **Knights Farm** (Swan St) has everything for the dried, flower enthusiast, plus other local crafts. The prettily sited Swan has good food, in sight of the Chappel Viaduct (reputedly the biggest brick structure in Europe), and there's a decent **railway museum** 🎟 – maybe rides on a short demonstration line – best to ring for timetable. Wknd snacks, shop, disabled access; cl 25–26 Dec; (01206) 242524; £5 (£3 non-steam days).

CHELMSFORD TL7006

✝ A big busy city with little for visitors, but its 15th-c **cathedral**, consecrated as such only in 1914, has particularly harmonious Perpendicular architecture.

CLACTON TM1714

☺🎣 Spacious, family seaside resort, with long stretches of gently shelving sandy beach and all the usual amusements. Readers enjoy watching the fishing off the end of the pier, which has an aquarium, reptile house and various rides (cl winter). The Robin Hood (London Rd) is the best family dining pub in the area.

COGGESHALL TL8422

★🌿🏠 Attractive small town with a good few antique shops, and a working **pottery** along West St. The Woolpack out by the church is a magnificent timbered building.

🏠 Grange Barn (Grange Hill; B1024 S edge of Coggeshall) 12th-c, the oldest surviving timber-framed barn in Europe, originally part of a Cistercian monastery. Disabled access; hours as Paycocke's – see below; (01376) 562226; £1.60, or joint ticket with Paycocke's £3; NT.

🌳🌿 **Marks Hall** (B1024 N of Coggeshall) Gradually being restored, this estate is recommended by readers for an undemanding stroll. There's a massive 13th-c oak, and a developing arboretum. Tea shop, shop, disabled access; cl Mon, and wkdys Nov–Easter; (01376) 563796; £3 per car.

🏠❀ Paycocke's (West St) A fine timber-framed, medieval merchant's home with unusual panelling and carvings, and pretty garden behind. Open pm Tues, Thurs, Sun and bank hols Apr–mid-Oct; (01376) 561305; £2 (joint ticket with Grange Barn £3); NT. The Fleece next door has decent food.

COLCHESTER TL9925

🏛🏠✝📷🌳 Britain's oldest recorded town, the capital of Roman Britain. You can trace the Roman wall (the Hole in the Wall, Balkerne Gardens, is a decent pub built into the one surviving fragmentary gatehouse). The High St has handsome buildings, some extravagantly timbered, and plenty more historical buildings inc **St Botolph's**, the oldest Augustinian priory in the country; readers have enjoyed the contemporary **art gallery**

Days Out

Pargeting extravaganza: Audley End; Saffron Walden – lunch at the Eight Bells there; Arkesden and Clavering villages.

Inland from the Blackwater: Beth Chatto Gardens, Elmstead Market; Layer Marney Tower; Abberton Wildfowl Centre, Layer de la Haye; lunch at the Sun, Feering; Feeringbury Manor garden there; Thames barges at Maldon; Wivenhoe, Rowhedge and Wickham Bishops villages.

at No 74. Town tours leave the tourist information centre (Queen St) at 11am (Jun–Sept; £3). The Rose & Crown (East St) is popular for lunch.

✗ **Bourne Mill** (just off B1025 S of Colchester) Delightfully quaint restored watermill by pretty millpond, worth a look from the outside even when it's not open. Open pm Sun and Mon bank hol wknds, plus pm Sun and Tues Jun–Aug; (01206) 572422; £1.50; NT.

🏰 ♨ 🏚 † **Colchester Castle & Museum** (Castle Park, off High St) Ideal for families, at the museum they let you try on Roman togas and helmets, or touch 2,000-year-old pottery excavated nearby; also splendid collection of Roman relics from jewellery to military tombstones. The castle itself has the biggest Norman keep in Europe, and stands on the site of a colossal Roman temple (you can still see the vaults). They've made a valiant attempt to bring grisly moments in its history to life: you can hear dramatisation of one of the forced confessions of the suspect witches incarcerated here. For £1 extra, a guided tour of the castle takes you up on the roof as well to the vaults and chapel. Good shop, mostly disabled access (not to the castle itself); cl am Sun; (01206) 282931; £3.70.

🐾 **Colchester Zoo** (Maldon Rd, Stanway, 2m E of Colchester by B1002) Not only is this one of the country's most satisfying zoos as far as animals are concerned, it also stands out in the value for money stakes; even extra activities such as face-painting and brass rubbing are included in the price, as well as Punch and Judy and magic shows. Over 170 rare and endangered species housed in glass-panelled enclosures as close to their natural habitats as possible, with a particularly good timetable of events and demonstrations. New attractions include the Wilds of Asia (with red pandas and an aquarium), and Spirit of Africa (soon to be home to cheetah, hyena and African primates). Children can join in feeding the seals and elephants, and there are good play areas (best is the splendid Kalahari Capers undercover complex). Meals,

snacks, shop, some disabled access (a few steep hills); cl 25 Dec; (01206) 330253; £7.95 (good-value annual tickets).

♨ **Hollytrees Museum** (High St) Georgian town house with a collection of toys, costumes and curios from the last two centuries. Shop; cl 12–1pm, all Mon and Sun; (01206) 282940; free.

♨ **Natural History Museum** (All Saints Church, High St) Lots of hands-on displays, with an emphasis on man's impact on the environment. Shop, disabled access; cl 1–2pm, am Sun and all Mon; (01206) 282941; free.

❗ **Rollerworld** (Eastgates) Children like this place, the only international-standard roller-skating rink in Britain; evenings only during the week, cl Mon; (01206) 868868; from £3.50; also Quasar and ten pin bowling.

♨ 🕰 **Tymperleys Clock Museum** (Trinity St) A particularly unusual selection in a lovely 15th-c house; there's something very special about coming here and hearing all the ticking; also reconstructed Tudor herb garden. Shop, disabled access; cl 1–2pm, all Sun and Mon, and Nov–Mar; (01206) 282931; free.

COPFORD TL9222

† **Copford church** Worth a visit, particularly for its well restored 12th-c wall paintings.

CRESSING TL7918

🏚 🕰 **Cressing Temple** (Witham Road) Medieval barns with exhibitions on medieval husbandry, surrounded by a 16th-c-style garden. Snacks, shop, disabled access; cl Sat and all Nov–Easter; (01376) 584903; £3.

DEDHAM TM0533

★ † ⌂ Several fine old buildings, especially the 15th-c flint church, its pinnacled tower familiar from so many Constable paintings. There's also the school Constable went to, and good walks through the protected riverside meadows to his father's mill at Flatford (across the river lock, so in Suffolk, and described in that chapter). Worries about the hordes of visitors the Constable connection attracts have led local tourist boards to cut down on the publicity they give the village in their literature. The handsome Marlborough Head, a wool merchant's house dating

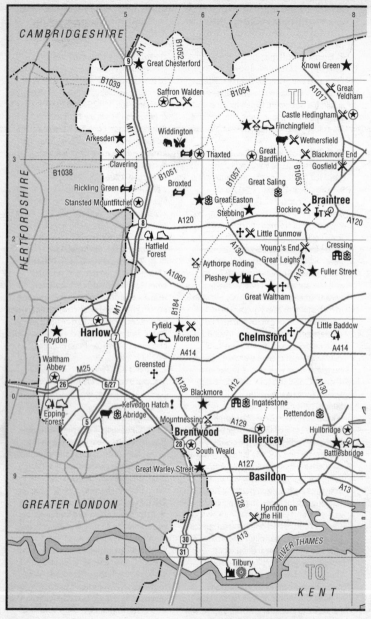

CAMBRIDGESHIRE

★ Great Chesterford
Knowl Green ★
Saffron Walden
⚔ Great Yeldham
Widdington
Castle Hedingham
Finchingfield
Arkesden ★
Wethersfield
Clavering
✦ Blackmore End
✦ Thaxted
Great Bardfield
Gosfield
Rickling Green
Broxted
Great Saling
Stansted Mountfitchet
Braintree
Great Easton
Bocking
Stebbing
A120
HERTFORDSHIRE
Hatfield Forest
Little Dunmow
Young's End
Cressing
Aythorpe Roding
Great Leighs
Fuller Street
Pleshey
Great Waltham
Fyfield
Little Baddow
Roydon
Moreton
Chelmsford
Harlow
A414
Waltham Abbey
Greensted
Blackmore
Ingatestone
Rettendon
Epping Forest
Kelvedon Hatch
Hullbridge
Abridge
Mountnessing
Brentwood
Billericay
Battlesbridge
South Weald
Great Warley Street
Basildon
GREATER LONDON
Horndon on the Hill
RIVER THAMES
Tilbury
KENT
TQ

from 1475, has good food, and the partly medieval Sun here is a useful place for refreshment too.

🎨 **Dedham Art & Craft Centre** 🖼 (High St) A number of crafts, growing collection of dolls' houses, stained-glass

workshop and candle-making. Wholefood café; cl 25 Dec, and Mon Jan–Mar; (01206) 322666; 50p.

🐄 **Dedham Vale Family Farm** (Mill St) Nicely undeveloped 16-acre farm, where children can feed the animals

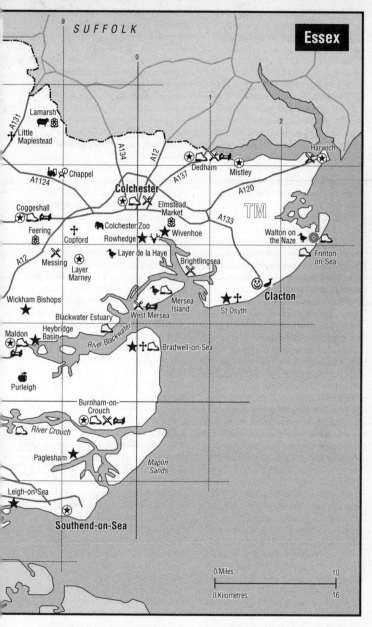

(bags of feed provided); pony rides at wknds and during school hols. Snacks, shop, some disabled access; cl mid-Sept–mid-Mar; (01206) 323111; £3. **Sir Alfred Munnings Art Museum** (Castle House, Castle

Hill) The house itself is a mix of Tudor and Georgian styles, and inside the artist's own furniture gives a real sense of how it would have looked when he and his wife lived here. His paintings are hung throughout the house, and you can also view his studios and stroll through the pleasant gardens. Shop, disabled access to ground floor only; open pms Sun, Weds and bank hol Mons Easter–Sept, plus pm Thurs and Sat in Aug; (01206) 322127; £3.

ELMSTEAD MARKET TM0624

❀ **Beth Chatto Gardens** A riot of colour in summer, it's hard to believe that in 1960 these attractive gardens were four acres of wasteland. Lots of gardening ideas, and unusual varieties of plants for sale. Cl Sun, bank hols and winter Sats, 2 wks over Christmas; (01206) 822007; £3. Over at Great Bromley the Old Black Boy has good-value food.

EPPING FOREST TQ4197

🐟 ⌂ A magnificent survival, an expansive tract of ancient hornbeam coppice, mainly tucked between the M25 and outer London. There are miles of leafy walks (and rides – you can hire horses locally), with some rough grazing and occasional distant views. There are so many woodland paths that getting lost is part of the experience; the long-distance Forest Way is, however, well marked. On the W side there's a pleasant diversion to High Beach, from where a few field paths lead SW.

FEERING TL8621

❀ **Feeringbury Manor** (Coggeshall Rd) Fine big riverside garden with ponds, streams, a little waterwheel, old-fashioned plants and bog gardens. Disabled access; open Thurs and Fri May–Jul; (01376) 561946; £2. The Sun towards Kelvedon has interesting food.

FINCHINGFIELD TL6734

★ ✗ ⌂ The county's prettiest village, with charming houses spread generously around a sloping green that dips to a stream and pond; just off stands a pristine-looking small windmill. The Fox (one of the most attractive buildings) is useful for lunch. There's a pleasant, easily followed path along the Finchingfield Brook to nearby Great Bardfield.

FRINTON-ON-SEA TM2419

⌂ A pleasant family seaside resort, with long stretches of gently shelving sandy beach; it's a quieter place than its neighbour Clacton. Beyond, the blowy open space of The Naze is pleasant for strolling, especially out of season when you're likely to have its 150 acres virtually to yourself.

GREAT BARDFIELD TL6730

★ ✝ ✗ 🛆 Known as the 'Montmartre of Essex' due to the group of artists who once lived here, this has several attractive pargeted houses, a village green, a church with a rare 14th-c carved stone screen and a windmill. The tiny Cottage Museum (Dunmow Rd) has a collection of rural bygones; open wknds Apr–Sept.

GREAT EASTON TL6125

★ ❀ This is an attractive village, worth strolling through. Nearby there are pleasant gardens at **Little Easton Manor**; open pm Thurs Jun–Sept; (01371) 872857; £2.

GREAT LEIGHS TL7217

! **Great Maize** 🖼 (Rochester Farm, 2m S of Braintree) As well as adding traditional children's swings and slides to the site, they hope to outgrow last year's record-breaking crop labyrinth this summer. Open daily mid-July–mid-Sept; (01245) 361411; £4.

GREAT SALING TL7025

❀ **Saling Hall Gardens** 12 acres of tranquil gardens created over the last 50 years. There is a fine walled garden and water features, but the aboretum is the main draw here. Disabled access; open pm Weds May–July; (01371) 850243; *£2.50.

GREAT WALTHAM TL6913

★ ✝ Pleasant village, with an attractive and interesting church.

GREENSTED TL5302

✝ **St Andrew's church** Tests have established that it was probably built around the time of the Norman Conquest – the oldest wooden church in the world; shop, disabled access. The nearby Green Man at Toot Hill has decent food in its plush dining lounge (and many fine wines).

HARLOW TL4611

A New Town, and not perhaps top of most itineraries, but has a couple of surprisingly good museums.

🖼 **Gibberd Collection** Housed on the first floor of the town hall, this surprisingly fine collection of British modern art includes works by Graham Sutherland, Elizabeth Blackadder and John Nash, to name but a few. Some disabled access; open wkdys; (01279) 446611; free.

❀ Gibberd Garden (Marsh Lane, Gilden Way) The master planner of Harlow New Town designed these gardens in the late 1950s and continued to develop them until his death in 1984. Planned as a series of individual 'rooms', the glades, groves, pools and alleys provide settings for sculpture, architectural salvage, a gazebo and even a moated castle. Snacks, disabled access – a shop is planned for later this year; open wknd pms Easter–Sept; (01279) 446611; £3.

♻ ✿ Harlow Museum (Third Ave) This has an important Roman collection, and a butterfly garden. Shop; cl Sun, Mon and Sat lunchtime; (01279) 454959; free.

HARWICH TM2632

🏰 ♻ ⚓ ⚜ ♨ ✕ The Redoubt here is a circular fort built in 1808 in case of invasion by Napoleon, with three small museums. Shop; cl Sept–Apr; (01255) 503429; £1. Harwich's two lighthouses both have small museums, one a **maritime museum** (times as above; 50p), the other a collection of vintage radios and televisions (times as above; £1). Also a little lifeboat museum (times as above, 50p), and **summer cruises** around the harbour. From the A120 W there's an unusual sight for this part of Essex – a tall narrow **windmill** (actually an interloper, as it was brought from Suffolk).

HATFIELD FOREST TL5320

♻ ⌂ (just S of Stansted Airport) An unexpected survivor, ancient mainly hornbeam woodland, not on quite the same scale as Epping Forest but still extensive enough, with a nature trail and boating lake.

HULLBRIDGE TQ8194

🐖 ♪ ♻ Jakapeni Rare Breeds Farm Small rare breeds park, specialising in pigs and sheep; you can fish on the lake (£3 a day). Snacks, shop, disabled access; open Sun and bank hols Easter–Oct; (01702) 232394; £1.75. The Bull nearby at Hockley has decent food, and is handy for walks in Hockley Woods.

INGATESTONE TQ6598

🏠 ❀ Ingatestone Hall 🖼 Interesting old house, nothing too remarkable but

with enthusiastic tours by the family that live here, and lovely grounds. Teas, shop; open pm wknds, bank hols and Weds–Fri in school hols Easter–Sept; (01277) 353010; £3.50. The Cricketers Arms out at Mill Green is a handy food pub.

KELVEDON HATCH TQ5798

! Secret Nuclear Bunker 🖼 (off A128) Who'd have thought that a three-storey Cold War underground complex lay beneath this innocuous 1950s bungalow? Knowledgeable tours take you through all parts of this clinically self-sufficient little world, and are done with real relish, but you can't help feeling relieved when you're back in the surrounding woodland. Wknd meals, snacks, shop; cl Mon–Weds Nov–Feb; (01277) 364883; *£5. The Black Horse in Pilgrim's Hatch is a good dining pub.

LAMARSH TL8835

❀ 🐐 Paradise Centre (Twinstead Rd) Fascinating for gardeners, with a very wide variety of unusual plants beautifully laid out and for sale, particularly woodland ones; also miniature goats, bantams and play area. Open wknds and bank hols Easter–Oct, or by appointment; (01787) 269449; £1.50. The Lion is good for lunch, and the Bures–Henny Street road is a pretty drive.

LAYER DE LA HAYE TL9619

🦆 Abberton Reservoir Wildfowl Centre (B1026, Layer de la Haye) Popular wetland stop for wildfowl; observation room and hides, nature trails, and events for families in summer. Snacks, shop, disabled access; cl Mon; (01206) 738172; £1 suggested donation (more for special events). The Donkey & Buskins (B1026) is handy for a meal.

LAYER MARNEY TL9317

🏠 ❀ 🐐 Layer Marney Tower The mansion here was never completed, but its eight-storey Tudor gatehouse is very impressive – one of the most striking examples of 16th-c architecture in Britain. Around it are formal gardens, a rare breeds farm, medieval barn, farm shop and deer park. Tearoom, shop, disabled access to grounds; cl am, all Sat, and Oct–Mar; (01206) 330784; £3.50.

LITTLE BADDOW TL7707

♻ Blakes Wood Ancient woodland of hornbeam and chestnut coppice, with lovely bluebells in spring. The Generals Arms is useful for lunch.

LITTLE DUNMOW TL6521

✝ **Little Dunmow church** Unusually stately for such a relatively small village – it's the surviving part of a priory founded in 1106. The Flitch of Bacon is a good pub.

LITTLE MAPLESTEAD TL8234

✝ **Little Maplestead church** Very different from most in the area – an unusual round building modelled on the Holy Sepulchre in Jerusalem.

MALDON TL8507

⛃ ▓ ✝ ⌂ The old Moot Hall is no longer open to the public and the ambitious tapestry commemorating the 1,000th anniversary of the crucial Battle of Maldon is now housed in the **Maeldune Centre** (junction of Market Hill and High St); shop, (01621) 851628; £1.50. The **Millennium Gardens** are named for the same event, and re-create what a garden might have looked like at the time of the battle. Also a **church** with an unusual triangular tower, some decent shops, a couple of small museums, and a riverside stroll past the golf course to the pretty weir by Beeleigh Abbey. **Hythe Quay** is full of life, and the best place to see one of the classic Thames barges with its ox-blood sails in action.

MERSEA ISLAND TM0012

🖖 ⌂ Linked to the mainland by a little causeway, which can get covered by the tide; much of its coast is a National Nature Reserve for its shore life, and there's a bracing coastal walk from East Mersea along the sea dyke overlooking the Colne estuary. It does feel very much an island, and away from the extended village of West Mersea, popular for retirement homes, there are few people about out of season (in summer the caravan parks bring in lots of families). The Willow Lodge has decent food; the Blackwater and Fox are good value too.

MISTLEY TM1231

🐖 ✝ **Environmental & Animal Centre** 🏠 (New Rd) Very friendly animal rescue centre: Ping and Pong, the Vietnamese pot-bellied pigs, may come to greet you as you go in. Snacks (not summer Mons, wknds only in winter), shop, disabled access; (01206)

396483; £2.50. The village has the remains of a Robert Adam church (known locally as the Mistley Towers). If you come by train, don't miss the splendid station buffet at Manningtree.

! **Essex Secret Bunker** (B1352) Much of its original equipment has been returned by the government and other groups, so the operations centre at this nuclear war command centre looks especially authentic. Odd seeing something so contemporary consigned to history, especially when similar establishments are still in operation. Snacks, shop, disabled access; cl all Dec–Jan and wkdys Oct–Mar; (01206) 392271; *£4.95.

MORETON TL5306

★ ⌂ This is an attractive village, and helpfully the pubs here usually have a leaflet detailing an interesting walk through and around it.

PLESHEY TL6614

★ 🏰 ⌂ This attractive village has a ruined castle, charming churchyard, country walks – and a good pub.

PURLEIGH TL8302

🍇 **New Hall Vineyards** Covering 85 acres, this 30-year-old vineyard is reputedly the largest in East Anglia; free tastings, guided group tours (by arrangement). They host the annual English wine festival (craft fair, live music, art exhibitions) on the wknd before Aug bank hol. Shop, disabled access; cl wknd pms; (01621) 828343; free.

RETTENDON TQ7698

🌸 **RHS Garden** (Hyde Hall) Eight acres of year-round hillside colour, with woodland garden, big rose garden, ornamental ponds, shrubs, trees, and national collections of malus and viburnum. Meals and snacks in thatched barn, plant sales, limited disabled access; cl Nov–Mar; (01245) 400256; £3. The Barge at Battlesbridge is quite handy for lunch.

RIVER CROUCH TQ8596

⌂ The Ferryboat Inn, down nr the River Crouch at the end of the lane through North Fambridge, is a good base for lonely waterside **walks**.

ROWHEDGE TM0221

★ ⚶ The village itself is well worth a visit; and nearby is a nature reserve among former gravel workings at

Fingringhoe.

SAFFRON WALDEN TL5438

★ † ⚲ ⌂ ⛴ The finest small town in the region, with prime examples of warmly colourwashed pargeting throughout. Walking around looking at buildings, you'll find it difficult to avoid being tempted into one of the many antique shops (or David Prue, the fine cabinet-maker in Radwinter Rd; cl wknds). The grand airy **church** has a magnificent spire, the very ruined **castle** up on a grassy mound is worth prowling around and children will enjoy the maze on the common. The Crown just N at Little Walden is nice for lunch, and in town the Eight Bells is good. The town has a goodish network of tracks for walks around it, extending into the parkland of nearby Audley End House. Longer rambles can take in Newport, where the houses have characteristic pargeted plaster walls, and Wendens Ambo. The B184 to Chipping Ongar is a pleasant country drive; about 4m along, Grace's Farm Shop at Wimbish is good, with **pick-your-own** in summer. Another enjoyable drive is the B1053 to Braintree.

🏛 ⚘ ▣ **Audley End House** (B1383, 1m W of Saffron Walden) Spectacular Jacobean mansion and former royal palace remodelled by Robert Adam, serenely surrounded by splendid gardens landscaped by Capability Brown – from the town you can walk straight into the park. Nothing inside can compete with the quite breathtaking façade, but it's not for want of trying – there are around 30 rooms to see, crammed with fine furnishings inc a magnificent dolls' house, and art. Suitably grand concerts and other events in the grounds. Meals, snacks, shop, disabled access to gardens and ground floor; cl Mon (exc bank hols), Tues, and Oct–Mar; (01799) 522842; £6, £4 grounds only.

⚘ **Bridge End Gardens** (Bridge St) Pleasant early Victorian gardens spread over 3½ acres, with rose garden, formal Dutch garden, kitchen garden and an atmospheric wilderness leading to a little grotto. You'll need to get a key from the tourist information centre (Market Pl) to explore the yew tree maze. Disabled access; cl 25 Dec; free.

⚲ **Saffron Walden Museum** Notable natural history section in the town museum as well as social history and toys and dolls. Shop, good disabled access; cl am Sun and bank hols, 24–25 Dec; (01799) 510333; £1.

ST OSYTH TM1215

★ † This pretty village is distinguished by the remarkable crenellated flint gateway leading to **St Osyth Priory**. The buildings and grounds behind are lovely, but as we went to press, there were no plans to re-open them to the public. The White Hart towards Point Clear has decent food, and not too far away, the beach at Brightlingsea is probably the county's best.

SOUTH WEALD TQ5793

★ 🍖 ⚘ ☘ Attractive village; the Tower Arms is a decent food pub. **Old Macdonald's Farm Park** (Weald Rd) Very extensive range of animals, with 30 breeds of sheep alone. Also, demonstrations, nature trails and craft displays, and plenty of opportunities to stroke the animals. Meals, snacks, shop, disabled access; cl 25–26 Dec; (01277) 375177; £2.75. Nearby is a **country park** with deer enclosure, lakes, woods, and visitor centre.

SOUTHEND-ON-SEA TQ8885

☺ ⚓ ⛴ 🏨 ▣ ⚲ Traditional seaside resort long favoured by East Londoners, with many of the attractions you'd expect to find. Most famous is the pier, the longest in the world, excellent for fishing, with a museum and, happily, a restored train service – it's a long walk there and back. Like many resorts, Southend in winter has a special appeal for people who wouldn't like it in summer – seafront shops by the endless promenade looking closed for ever, the sea a doleful muddy grey. Readers enjoy the Westcliff part of town, with its decent **art gallery** (cl 1–2pm; Sun and Mon, free). Summer **boat trips** include occasional runs on a vintage paddle-steamer; (01634) 827648 for dates. There are year-round ferries to Felixstowe.

⚲ **Central Museum & Planetarium** (Victoria Ave) The only planetarium in the South-East outside London, with a local history museum too. Shop; cl Sun, Mon, inc bank hols (planetarium also cl Tues); (01702) 330214; planetarium £2.25, museum free.

★ **Leigh-on-Sea** Though attached to Southend, this has a quite distinct character, altogether more intimate, with wood-clad buildings and shrimp boats in the working harbour; Ivy Osborne's cockle stall here is justly famous, and the Crooked Billet overlooking the water has real old-fashioned character.

✝ ⊛ ♨ **Prittlewell Priory Museum** (Priory Park, slightly N of Southend centre) 12th-c Cluniac priory in nice grounds, with eclectic collections of local and religious history. Shop; cl 1–2pm, all Sun and Mon; free.

♪ **Sea Life Centre** (Eastern Esplanade) Fun way of exploring underwater life, with bubble-windows to make it seem as if you're in there with the sea creatures, and walk-through tunnel along reconstructed sea bed. Children like the shark exhibition. Snacks, shop, disabled access; cl 25 Dec; (01702) 462400; £5.25.

🏭 ⊛ ♨ **Southchurch Hall Museum** (Park Lane) An unexpected find, a medieval moated manor house in an attractive park, with period room settings, and fun talks on Tudor life; occasional lute demonstrations. Shop, limited disabled access; cl 1–2pm, all Sun and Mon (and Tues after bank hols), 25 Dec, 1 Jan and Easter; (01702) 467671; free, talks £1.50.

STANSTED MOUNTFITCHET TL5222

♨ ! **House on the Hill Toy Museum** Home to what we think is the biggest privately owned toy collection in the world, with over 30,000 toys, games and playthings from Victorian times to the 1970s. Quite a few toy museums attract parents more than children (which might explain why so many have unfortunately closed over the last couple of years), but this one avoids that by making its very well thought out displays entertaining to look at; lots of them are animated, and it's great fun watching the soldiers, trains and Meccano in action. There are a few coin-operated slot machines and puppet shows, a new collection of celebrity memorabilia, and a decent collectors' shop. All indoors, so good in any weather. Cl mid-Dec–mid-Jan; (01279) 813237; £3 (£2.50 children).

🏯 ↓т **Mountfitchet Castle & 1066 Village** Intriguing, an authentically reconstructed Norman castle and village, complete with thatched houses, and deer, sheep, goats and chickens wandering around between them. The castle includes a small chunk of the original, and there are dummies displaying gruesome examples of torture and punishment. Cheerful and enthusiastic rather than particularly sophisticated, it's a good introduction to life a thousand years ago, though you will need to visit on a dry day. Snacks (and space for picnics), shop, some disabled access; cl mid-Nov–mid-Mar; £4.50 (£3.50 children). It's under the same management as the toy museum five minutes' walk up the hill, but there's no joint ticket available. Though prices overall compare favourably with other places in the county, it's a little annoying when visiting both to have to fork out twice.

✗ **Stansted Mountfitchet Windmill** The well preserved 18th-c windmill still has much of its original equipment (though not working). Shop; open pm first Sun of month Apr–Oct, plus pm every Sun in Aug, and pm bank hol Suns and Mons; 50p. The Cricketers Arms at nearby Rickling Green is good for lunch.

THAXTED TL6131

★ ✝ 🏭 ♨ ✗ ⚙ This engaging small town has a graceful, airy **church** (where Holst was organist) with a tremendous spire, several handsome buildings inc nearby almshouses, a fine **guildhall** (small local museum), and a restored **windmill**. The **Raven Armoury** (B184 towards Dunmow) does hand-forged steel and weaponry. The 15th-c Swan has decent food.

TILBURY TQ6476

🏯 ❄ ◠ **Tilbury Fort** Well preserved 17th-c fort with unusual double moat; good views of the Thames estuary. The most violent episode in its history was a 1776 cricket match that left three dead. Snacks, shop, some disabled access; cl Mon and Tues Oct–Mar, 24–26 Dec; (01375) 858489; £2.30. For an extra £1 you can fire a 1943 3.7 anti-aircraft gun – irresistible for several children of our acquaintance. There is a pleasant 3-mile walk along the Thames to **Coalhouse Fort** (off A1013, Orsett–Stanford-le-Hope; open last Sun of month and bank hols Nov–Feb; £2).

WALTHAM ABBEY TL3800

✝ ♿ ⛪ Despite the surrounding housing developments, the centre has some handsome buildings – especially the **Abbey Church** with its famous peal of 13 bells (and a museum in the crypt; shop, some disabled access; cl Good Fri and 25 Dec). Associated ruins include part of a Norman cloister, and the bridge dates back to the abbey's time.

♿ **Epping Forest District Museum** (Sun St) Lively holiday activities for children, and archeological displays, in two timber-framed old houses. Shop, limited disabled access; open pm Fri–Tues; (01992) 716882; free.

🐖 **Lee Valley Park Farms** 🖼 (B194, 2m N of Waltham Abbey) Takes in Hayes Hill children's farm with plenty of traditional animals, and a pet centre and play area, and Holyfield Hall working farm and dairy, with 150 cows milked every afternoon around 3pm, and seasonal events like sheep-shearing and harvesting. Meals, snacks, shop, disabled access; (01992) 892781; £2.95.

WALTON ON THE NAZE TM2623

⌂ ❋ 🦜 There's a pleasant walk northwards from this quiet seaside town, along the coast to a **nature reserve** harbouring migrant birds; there is a nature trail here.

WETHERSFIELD TL7131

🐖 **Boydells Dairy Farm** 🖼 Working dairy farm where you may be able to join in milking the goats and cows – or even the sheep. Also working beehive, various other animals, and ice lollies made from their own sheep yogurt. Snacks, shop, disabled access; open pm Fri–Sun Easter Sun–Sept, plus pm daily in May half-term and summer hols; (01371) 850481; £2.50.

WIDDINGTON TL5331

🐗 🦋 **Mole Hall Wildlife Park** See separate family panel on p.246.

★ **Other attractive villages**, all with decent pubs, include Arkesden TL4834, Blackmore TL6001, Fuller Street TL7416, Fyfield TL5606, Great Chesterford TL5143, Great Warley Street TQ5890, waterside Heybridge Basin TL8707, Knowl Green TL7841, Paglesham TQ9293, Roydon TL4109, Stebbing TL6624, Wickham Bishops TL8412 and Wivenhoe TM0321.

Where to eat

BLACKMORE END TL7430 **Bull** *(01371) 851037* Comfortable, tucked-away dining pub with pretty, cottagey, restaurant area, good snacks, excellent meals, and fine choice of wines; cl Mon exc bank hols; children in restaurant only. **£15|£5**.

BRIGHTLINGSEA TM0816 **Coffee Pot** *Victoria Pl (01206) 305738* Spotlessly clean place with very good breakfast, lunch and tea – everything freshly made daily; helpful and friendly staff; cl pm, Sun; disabled access. **£3.25**.

BURNHAM-ON-CROUCH TQ9596 **Contented Sole** *80 High St (01621) 782139* Long-standing, family-run evening restaurant (though they do Sun lunch), very popular for consistently imaginative food with an emphasis on fine seafood; popular wine tastings all year; cl pm Sun, 4 wks from 24 Dec, 2 wks July; disabled access. **£30|2 courses £12.95**.

CASTLE HEDINGHAM TL7835 **Bell** *St James's St (01787) 460350* Interesting old coaching inn with a log fire in the beamed lounge bar, traditionally furnished public bar, no smoking area, well liked bar food, and a lovely big walled garden behind; disabled access. **£15|£4**.

CLAVERING TL4731 **Cricketers** *Wicken Rd (01799) 550442* Attractive and cosy L-shaped dining pub with low beams, two open fires, and a wide choice of imaginative, well presented food in both the bar and restaurant; pretty bedrooms; cl 25–26 Dec; disabled access. **£24.50|£6**.

COLCHESTER TM0025 **Clowns** *61 High St (01206) 578631* Huge helpings of good, straightforward food in clean spacious restaurant; nice children's menu, too; cl 25–26 Dec; disabled access. **£18|£4.95.**

COLCHESTER TM0025 **Warehouse Brasserie** *12 Chapel St N (01206) 765656* Bustling brasserie on several levels, with really enjoyable food using organic produce, a relaxed chatty atmosphere, good service, and an eclectic wine list; very good-value set meals; cl pm Sun; disabled access. **£20|£4.**

DEDHAM TM0533 **Millstream Riverside Cottage** *Mill Lane (01206) 322066* Little, no smoking, riverside restaurant with a homely, relaxed atmosphere and a good choice of popular food; also, morning coffee and cream teas; cl Mon and Tues, part of Jan; children over 7 in evening. **£22|£5.70.**

FYFIELD TL5606 **Black Bull** *(01277) 899225* Prettily lit, vine-covered dining pub with interesting food (the daily specials are very good value) in low-beamed communicating rooms, well kept real ales, and a welcoming atmosphere; seats and an aviary in the garden. **£16|£4.15.**

GOSFIELD TL7829 **Green Man** *(01787) 472746* Smart dining pub with a relaxed, chatty atmosphere, two little bars and no smoking dining room, enjoyable food inc marvellous lunchtime cold buffet and delicious puddings; well kept real ales and decent wines, many by the glass; no food pm Sun; partial disabled access. **£20|£7.**

GREAT YELDHAM TL7638 **White Hart** *Poole St (01787) 237250* Striking Tudor inn with attractive garden; beams and oak panelling in the refurbished rooms (one no smoking), exceptionally good, inventive food inc home-made pasta, ice-cream and wafer biscuits (very good-value set 3-course menu), and a fine wine list; cl pm Sun, Mon; disabled access. **£26|**2-course lunch £8.50.

HARWICH TM2632 **Pier at Harwich** *The Quay (01255) 241212* Delicious fish and chips and smarter fish dishes in an attractive building overlooking the Stour and Orwell estuaries; cl pm 24–26 Dec. **£31.50|£7.50.**

HORNDON ON THE HILL TQ6683 **Bell** *(01375) 673154* Flower-decked medieval inn with welcoming licensees, open-plan beamed bar with polished oak floorboards and flagstones, carefully prepared, imaginative food that changes twice daily, 5 real ales, good choice of wines; restaurant cl pm 25–26 Dec. **£25|£6.**

LITTLE DUNMOW TL6521 **Flitch of Bacon** *(01371) 820323* Friendly pub with a small, attractively furnished, timbered bar, a sensibly small range of good unpretentious bar food, popular Sun buffet, and real ales; comfortable bdrms; children away from bar area; disabled access. **£16.50|£4.50.**

MESSING TL8918 **Crispin's** *The Street (01621) 815868* Friendly Elizabethan restaurant with an open fire in the beamed lounge, candles on the walls and tables; enjoyable food inc fish and vegetarian choices, monthly themed evenings, a growing wine list, helpful service, and quiet back garden; bdrms; cl pm Sun and Mon. **£24.**

SAFFRON WALDEN TL5438 **Eight Bells** *Bridge St (01799) 522790* Handsome Tudor inn with a neatly kept and friendly open-plan bar; lots of daily specials in the splendidly timbered and partly no smoking restaurant, well kept real ales, a good choice of wines by the glass, and friendly service. **£18|£6.50.**

WEST MERSEA TM0112 **Willow Lodge** *108 Coast Rd (01206) 383568* Large, busy restaurant with a wide range of very good food inc lots of fresh fish; cl pm Sun, Mon; well behaved children welcome; disabled access. **£20|£6.**

WETHERSFIELD TL7131 **Dickens** *The Green (01371) 850723* Mainly 17th-c, very popular restaurant in a quiet country spot; lovely modern cooking, fine wines, very good service; cl pm Sun, Mon, Tues; disabled access. **£25.**

YOUNG'S END TL7319 **Green Dragon** *(01245) 361030* Well run dining pub, restaurant area with an attractive understated barn theme (no smoking part); an extensive range of very good, interesting bar food, well kept real ales, plenty of seats in back garden. **£17.50|£5.50.**

Special thanks to David Johns.

Essex Calendar

Some of these dates were provisional as we went to press. Please check information with the telephone numbers provided.

JANUARY

9 Lee Valley Park Bird Race: competition to spot the most birds in one day; starts at information centre (01992) 702200

MARCH

24 Harwich Film Festival – *till 26 March* (01255) 553333

APRIL

1 Braintree Home Leisure and Gift Fair – *till 2 April* (01376) 326802
2 Chappel Mother's Day Special at East Anglian Railway Museum (01206) 242524
15 Southend-on-Sea Easter Fair (01702) 215166
21 Chappel Thomas the Tank Engine at East Anglian Railway Museum – *till 24 April* (01206) 242524
22 Higham Essex and Suffolk Hunt: a day of point-to-point races at the Racecourse (01787) 228575
23 Billericay Barleylands Farm Easter Weekend – *till 24 April* (01268) 532032
24 Southend-on-Sea Motorcycle Run (01702) 215166
28 Billericay May Family Weekend at Barleylands Farm – *till 29 April* (01268) 532032

MAY

14 Colchester Classic Vehicle Rally at the Colchester Institute, Sheepen Rd (01206) 718000; **Dovercourt** Tour de Tendring: cycle rally (01255) 256168; **Epping** Air Show at North Weald Airfield (01992) 524225
19 Manningtree Festival of Arts 2000 – *till 5 June* (01206) 393171
27 Wormingford Flower Festival – *till 29 May* (01787) 227187
28 Chappel Whitsun Steamings at East Anglian Railway Museum – *till 29 May* (01206) 242524; **Southend-on-Sea** Air Show: free event – *till 29 May* (01702) 215465

JUNE

3 Chappel Model Railway Exhibition at East Anglian Railway Museum – *till 4 June* (01206) 242524; **Thaxted** Morris Ring: annual meeting of over 200 Morris Men, massed dancing in the morning – *till 4 June* (01245) 420742
4 Southend-on-Sea Brass Band Competition (01702) 215120
10 Maldon Blackwater Barge Match: historic boat race on River Blackwater, best at Maldon Quay in the afternoon (01621) 851147
11 Aldham Open gardens (01206) 240425; **Cressing** Essex History Fair: re-enactments, plays and music (01206) 868015
12 Castle Hedingham Thomas the Tank Engine at the Colne Valley Railway – *till 25 June* (01787) 461174

Essex Calendar (cont.)

16 Great Leighs Essex County Show at the Essex Showground – *till 18 June* (01245) 362412

17 Harwich Festival: inc special openings of historic buildings, concerts – *till 25 June* (01255) 880590

18 Southend-on-Sea Clifftop Open-air Concerts (01702) 215120

23 Southend-on-Sea Folk Festival: more than 350 free music and dance events, also at Leigh-on-Sea – *till 25 June* (01702) 215465; **Thaxted** Festival: classical and jazz concerts, workshops (weekends only) – *till 16 July* (01371) 831421

25 Southend-on-Sea Concert in the Park at Priory Park (01702) 215166

JULY

2 Southend-on-Sea Clifftop Open-air Concerts (01702) 215166

8 Great Dunmow Flitch Trials: ancient event, a trial is held to find a couple who haven't quarrelled for a year and a day (01371) 874255; **Lawford** Tendring Hundred Show at House Park (01206) 571517; **North Weald** Wings and Wheels Model Spectacular at the Airfield Museum – *till 9 July* (01684) 562038

9 Clacton Classic Vehicle Show 2000 (01255) 253124

14 Coggeshall Women's Institute Show at Marks Hall Estate and Arboretum – *till 15 July* (01245) 261771

16 Southend-on-Sea Clifftop Open-air Concerts (01702) 215166

29 Pitsea Basildon Zoo Festival at Wat Tyler Country Park – *till 30 July* (01268) 550088; **West Bergholt** Historic Vehicle Show: about 500 entries – *till 30 July* (01206) 271253

30 Southend-on-Sea Classic Car Run from London to Southend (01702) 215166

AUGUST

1 Southend-on-Sea Jazz Festival – *till 6 August* (01702) 215166

2 Chappel Summer Mid-week Steamings at the East Anglian Railway Museum (01206) 242524

5 Maldon Carnival (01621) 852147

6 Chappel Summer Sunday Steamings at the East Anglian Railway Museum (01206) 242524

12 Southend-on-Sea Carnival Week – *till 19 August* (01702) 215118

19 Southend-on-Sea Illuminated Carnival Procession, plus Illuminations Switch-on and Fireworks Spectacular (01702) 215118

24 Clacton Air Show: Red Arrows – *till 25 August* (01255) 253208

25 Clacton Jazz Festival – *till 28 August* (01245) 253208

26 Chelmsford Spectacular at Hylands Farm: open-air concerts, street entertainment, fringe tents – *till 28 August* (01245) 606977; **Clacton** CAMRA Real Ale Festival – *till 28 August* (01255) 253124; **Southend-on-Sea** Sailing Barge Race (01702) 215465

SEPTEMBER

2 Burnham-on-Crouch Town Show (01621) 784097; **Orsett** Horticultural and Agricultural Show at Orsett Showground (01375) 481900; **Southend-on-Sea** Water Festival – *till 3 September* (01702) 215465

Essex Calendar (cont.)

9 Billericay Essex Steam Rally and Craft Fair at Barleylands Farm: over 300 stands – *till 10 September* (01268) 532253; **Essex** Heritage Open Days: a number of listed buildings not normally accessible to the public will be open – *till 10 September* (01206) 282934

16 Leigh-on-Sea Regatta – *till 17 September* (01702) 215166

19 Purleigh English Wine Festival and Country Craft Fair at New Hall Vineyards: country skills fair and family events – *till 20 September* (01621) 828343

30 Burnham-on-Crouch Carnival (01621) 784097

OCTOBER

1 Colchester Countryside Open Day at High Woods Country Park: historic re-enactments, rare breeds, activities (01206) 853588

27 Saffron Walden Folk Festival – *till 29 October* (01799) 528046

NOVEMBER

9 Southend-on-Sea Christmas Lights switched on (01702) 215465

25 Southend-on-Sea Victorian Christmas in the High St – *till 26 November* (01702) 215120

DECEMBER

7 Maldon Victorian Christmas (01621) 856125

14 Maldon Victorian Evening – *till 21 December* (01621) 856125

We welcome reports from readers

This *Guide* depends on readers' reports. Do help us if you can – in return, we offer a discount on the next edition to people who've helped us with reports for it. Tell us what you think about places already in it, and anything extra you think we should say about them. And send us your ideas for inclusion in the next edition: places to visit, eat at or stay in, attractive drives or walks, maybe even unusual interesting shops you know of. Use the card in the middle, the report forms at the end, or just write – no stamp needed: *The Good Britain Guide*, FREEPOST TN1569, Wadhurst, E Sussex TN5 7BR.

GLOUCESTERSHIRE

Idyllic Cotswold villages and countryside, lots of interesting places to visit.

This is one of the best parts of Britain for a relaxing short break. It has plenty of marvellous outings for adults, with fine food and lovely places to stay in, but although its strongest appeal is to them it does have good family days out, too. Among the best things for children are the farm park at Kineton, Berkeley Castle, the country park at Tockington, and steam railways at Lydney and Toddington. The bird of prey centres at Batsford and near Newent have a wide appeal, and the Slimbridge wildfowl centre is outstanding for all ages. Bourton-on-the-Water, despite the crowds, is well worth a visit by old and young alike, with several appealing places in charming surroundings; Folly Farm there is an unusual spot for a family picnic. The labyrinthine Clearwell caverns are quite an adventure.

Gloucester – a busy modern city – has a great deal to reward a day visit. Nearby Cheltenham still has a considerable degree of Regency elegance (and good events – see *Calendar*). It's a useful base for exploring the area; the tourism office does a decent leaflet detailing how to get to most Cotswold attractions by public transport. The county's speciality is its fine range of handsome, stone-built Cotswold towns of real individuality. Chipping Campden, Cirencester, Northleach, Painswick and Stow-on-the-Wold all bulge with sightseeing possibilities – and antique shops; Tewkesbury too is attractive.

When people think of Gloucestershire, they usually think 'Cotswolds': broad landscapes of rolling hills, traditional dry stone-walled fields, occasional beechwoods, meandering streams, beautiful villages of warm golden-tinted stone, picturesquely roofed in heavy stone slabs. Many villages have handsome medieval churches, and their cottages and houses don't hide away behind gardens and high walls, but tend to be right by the road. Often, there's a strip of daffodil-planted grass between pavement and road (the area is particularly attractive in spring), and sometimes a little stream. The one snag is that the Cotswolds tend to be expensive – particularly in the north. In the summer they do attract a great many visitors, though even then you can find delightful villages that have escaped the crowds – especially in the south.

Favourite places to visit include Snowshill Manor, Stanway House, Sudeley Castle near Winchcombe, the Chedworth Roman villa, and the never-finished Gothic mansion at Nympsfield. Some of the county's gardens and parks are unforgettable, especially Kiftsgate near Mickleton, the arboretums at Westonbirt and Batsford near Moreton-in-Marsh, and, particularly in late May, the gardens of Lydney Park. The Nature in Art collection at Twigworth is very special.

For cyclists, the Cotswolds are great – quiet village-to-village lanes with ever-changing views. Campus Holidays hire bikes and can arrange your route and accommodation too; (01242) 250642. Extended walks over the Cotswold plateau are not always rewarding, with unchanging views of arable fields often the rule; however, there are plenty of really enjoyable walks through choice scenery, with the long-distance Cotswold Way between Chipping Campden and Bath tracing through much of the best.

Away from the Cotswolds, some less well known parts are delightful (and generally cheaper): the tortuously steep hills and valleys around Stroud, the quiet watermeadows of the upper Thames, the unspoilt orchard and farming countryside around the Severn Valley (so few river crossings that the little villages down by the west bank, with few people passing through, have a very secluded and unchanging feel). The Forest of Dean has a unique landscape: hilly woodland, much of it ancient, that shows many traces of the way it has provided a livelihood for the people living around it (the Hopewell free-miner colliery is particularly interesting). The forest is flanked by a spectacular stretch of the Wye Valley, and its woodland colours are at their best in late May and autumn.

Where to stay

ASHLEWORTH SO8125 **Ashleworth Court** Ashleworth, Gloucester GL19 4JA (01452) 700241 *£40; 3 rms, shared bthrm. Set by a small elegant church and NT tithe barn, this striking ancient house is part of a working farm and has a homely kitchen with an Aga and dogs; comfortable sitting room, enjoyable breakfasts served in what was originally part of the Great Hall, and chickens in the back garden; two good pubs in the village; cl Christmas.

BERKELEY ST6899 **Old Schoolhouse Hotel** Canonbury St, Berkeley GL13 9BG (01453) 811711 *£60; 8 rms. Carefully converted former schoolhouse and chapel, with fine views and surrounded by the grounds of Berkeley Castle; friendly and relaxed atmosphere, log fire in the comfortable lounge, imaginative food in the popular restaurant, and seats on the terrace; disabled access.

BIBURY SP1106 **Bibury Court** SP1106 Bibury, Cirencester GL7 5NT (01285) 740337 £99, plus special breaks; 19 individual rms. Lovely peaceful mansion dating from Tudor times and set in beautiful gardens, with an informal, friendly atmosphere, panelled rooms, antiques, huge log fires, conservatory, a fine choice of breakfasts, and good interesting food; cl Christmas and New Year.

BIBURY SP1106 **Swan** Bibury, Cirencester GL7 5NW (01285) 740695 £165, plus special breaks; 18 very pretty individually decorated rms. Handsome creeper-covered hotel on the River Coln, with private fishing and attractive formal gardens; lovely flowers and log fires in carefully furnished comfortable lounges, a cosy no smoking parlour, good food in the opulent dining room, nice breakfasts, and attentive staff; disabled access.

BLEDINGTON SP2422 **Kings Head** The Green, Bledington, Chipping Norton OX7 6XQ (01608) 658365 *£65; 12 rms (2 over the kitchen can be noisy). Very nicely placed 15th-c Cotswold inn by a duck-filled stream; cheery log fire in the atmospheric bar, lounge overlooking garden, good food in both the bar and partly no smoking restaurant, friendly service; cl 24–25 Dec; limited disabled access.

BROADWELL SP2027 **College House** Chapel St, Broadwell, Moreton-in-Marsh GL56 0TW (01451) 832351 £60; 3 lovely big rms, 2 with own bthrm. 17th-c house with large inglenook fireplace in flagstoned sitting room, good breakfasts, and delicious evening meals – which can be eaten on the terrace in summer; no children.

BROOKTHORPE SO8312 **Gilberts** Gilberts Lane, Brookthorpe, Gloucester GL4

0UH (01452) 812364 **£53;** 4 rms. 400-year-old house with woodburner and games in the sitting room, organic produce from the surrounding smallholding used for delicious breakfasts (own honey and eggs), and a relaxed atmosphere; non smokers preferred.

BUCKLAND SP0836 **Buckland Manor** *Buckland, Broadway, Worcs WR12 7LY (01386) 852626* ***£205,*** plus special breaks; 13 sumptuous rms. Really lovely 13th-c building in 10 acres of beautifully kept gardens, comfortable lounges with magnificent oak panelling, flowers and antiques, and elegant restaurant with fine food using home-grown produce; outdoor swimming pool, riding, tennis, croquet, putting; children over 12.

CHARINGWORTH SP2039 **Charingworth Manor** *Charingworth, Chipping Campden GL55 6NS (01386) 593555* **£140,** plus special breaks; 26 lovely rms with thoughtful extras. Early 14th-c manor with Jacobean additions, set in fine grounds; with mullioned windows, antiques, log fires and heavy oak beams in the relaxing sitting room, good modern cooking in the charming restaurant, excellent breakfasts, and friendly staff; billiards, leisure spa with indoor swimming pool, and all-weather tennis court; dogs by arrangement; disabled access.

CHELTENHAM SO9522 **Hotel on the Park** *Evesham Rd, Cheltenham GL52 2AH (01242) 518898* **£121,** plus special breaks; 12 lovely rms. Warmly welcoming and handsome Regency house with elegantly furnished drawing room and dining room, pretty flowers and antiques, and imaginative food in the stylish restaurant – good breakfasts, too; children over 8.

CHELTENHAM SO9421 **Lypiatt House** *Lypiatt Rd, Cheltenham GL50 2QW (01242) 224994* **£65,** plus wknd breaks; 10 attractive rms. Carefully restored Victorian house in its own grounds; with open fire, books and plants in the light comfortable drawing room, a little conservatory bar, and friendly, personal service.

CHELTENHAM SO9422 **Wyastone Hotel** *Parabola Rd, Montpellier, Cheltenham GL50 3BG (01242) 245549* ***£75,*** plus special breaks; 13 pretty rms. Run by particularly welcoming, helpful people, this quietly set Victorian house has a panelled bar and cosy, pink-coloured lounge, plenty of period features, a charming little terraced garden, enjoyable breakfasts, and French-flavoured evening meals; cl Christmas and New Year.

CHIPPING CAMPDEN SP1539 **Eight Bells** *Chipping Campden GL55 6JG (01386) 840371* **£50;** 6 rms. Neatly restored, heavy-beamed, 14th-c pub by the church; three log fires, interesting food with fresh local produce, friendly staff, decent wines and beers, and a pleasant courtyard; cl 25 Dec; disabled access.

CHIPPING CAMPDEN SP1539 **Noel Arms** *High St, Chipping Campden GL55 6AT (01386) 840317* **£105,** plus special breaks; 26 comfortable rms. Bustling 14th-c inn with comfortable, traditionally furnished small lounge areas, open fire, armour and antiques, conservatory, restaurant, and decent wines; dogs by prior arrangement; disabled access.

CLAPTON SP1617 **Clapton Manor** *Clapton, Cheltenham GL54 2LG (01451) 810202* **£60;** 2 charming rms. Fine, 16th-c Cotswold stone house set in lovely, interestingly planted gardens with marvellous views across the Windrush Valley; large inglenook fireplaces, heavy beams, mullioned windows, antiques, and a relaxed, informal family atmosphere; log fire and television in residents' sitting room, and good breakfasts with home-made jams and their own eggs served in the dining room or on the terrace; no smoking; several restaurants and pubs nearby for dinner; cl Christmas.

CLEARWELL SO5708 **Tudor Farmhouse** *Clearwell, Coleford GL16 8JS (01594) 833046* **£60,** plus special breaks; 20 cottagey rms. Carefully restored Tudor farmhouse and stone cottages with landscaped gardens and surrounding fields; lots of beams, sloping floors and oak doors, delicious food in the candlelit restaurant, and friendly staff; cl 23 Dec–30 Jan; disabled access.

CLEARWELL SO5708 **Wyndham Arms** *Clearwell, Coleford GL16 8JT (01594) 833666* ***£80,*** plus special winter and wknd breaks; 17 well equipped rms. Smart and neatly kept old country inn with a comfortable beamed bar, open fire, particularly good food (much home-grown), nice service, and friendly dogs – you stay free on Sun if you eat in the restaurant; good disabled access.

CORSE LAWN SO8330 **Corse Lawn House** *Corse Lawn, Gloucester GL19 4LZ* *(01452) 780771* **£100,** plus special breaks; 19 pretty, individually furnished rms. Magnificent Queen Anne building with comfortable and attractive day rooms, a distinguished restaurant with interesting food and excellent wines (there's a less pricey bistro-style operation too), warm, friendly staff, and a relaxed atmosphere; 12 acres of surrounding gardens and fields; dogs welcome; cl 24–26 Dec; disabled access.

GREAT RISSINGTON SP1917 **Lamb** *Great Rissington, Cheltenham GL54 2LP* *(01451) 820388* **£60,** plus special breaks; 14 pretty rms – several are suites with own lounge. Civilised 17th-c inn with a sheltered hillside garden, cosy two-roomed bar, residents' lounge with log fire, good nearby walks; cl 25–26 Dec; dogs by prior arrangement.

GREET SP0230 **Manor Farm** *Greet, Cheltenham GL54 5BJ (01242) 602423* ***£50;** 3 rms. Carefully restored, 16th-c manor house on a mixed farm; with fine views, big garden and croquet; also, self-catering cottages; cl Christmas.

HAZLETON SP0818 **Windrush House** *Hazleton, Cheltenham GL54 4EB* *(01451) 860364* ***£48;** 4 rms, 2 with own bthrm. Warm, friendly and neatly kept, no smoking guesthouse with exceptionally imaginative food, lovely breakfasts, and traditional furnishings; cl mid-Dec–mid-Feb; no children, no dogs.

KINETON SP0926 **Halfway House** *Kineton, nr Guiting Power, Cheltenham GL54 5UG (01451) 850344* **£50,** 3 rms. Friendly little stone pub with a good mix of customers, a warm fire, farm tools and pictures in the unpretentious bar, tasty food inc themed nights, and well kept real ales.

LEONARD STANLEY SO8003 **Grey Cottage** *Leonard Stanley, Stonehouse GG10 3LU (01453) 822515* ***£55;** 3 rms overlooking garden or countryside with chocolates, fruit and biscuits. Carefully restored, 170-year-old cottage with a pretty garden, really kind and thoughtful owners who cosset you, interesting furnishings and fresh flowers, comfortable sitting room, marvellous breakfasts, and enjoyable evening meals by prior arrangement (bring your own wine); children over 7.

LITTLE BARRINGTON SP2012 **Inn For All Seasons** *Little Barrington, Burford, Oxon OX18 4TN (01451) 844324* ***£85;** 10 rms. Handsome old inn with low beams, stripped stone and flagstones, a big log fire, old prints, particularly good fresh fish and other food, well kept real ales and wines, lots of malt whiskies; a pleasant garden surrounded by nice walks; children over 10.

LITTLE RISSINGTON SP1819 **Touchstone** *Little Rissington, Cheltenham GL54 2ND (01451) 822481* ***£40;** 3 rms with thoughtful extras. Attractive, traditional Cotswold stone house with very friendly owners, good breakfasts in the dining room with doors on to terrace, lots of nearby walks; no children; cl Jan and Feb.

LOWER SLAUGHTER SP1622 **Lower Slaughter Manor** *Lower Slaughter, Cheltenham GL54 2HP (01451) 820456* **£175;** 16 luxurious rms with thoughtful extras. Grand 17th-c manor house with 4 acres of neatly kept grounds, a 15th-c dovecot, all-weather tennis court, croquet, and indoor pool; lovely flower arrangements, log fires, fine plaster ceilings, antiques and paintings, excellent modern cooking and award-winning wines in the elegant restaurant, and attentive welcoming staff; children over 8; disabled access.

LOWER SWELL SP1725 **Old Farmhouse** *Lower Swell, Cheltenham GL54 1LF* *(01451) 830232* ***£73,** plus special breaks; 13 rms, some in main building but most in various barns, stables and outbuildings, and most with own bthrm. Peaceful and unpretentious 16th-c manor farm, with a log fire in the cosy beamed lounge bar, interesting food using fresh local produce, a thoughtful wine list, friendly staff, and a walled rose garden; they are very kind to children.

MORETON-IN-MARSH SP2032 **White Hart Royal** *GL56 0BA (01608)* *650731* **£68;** 19 good rms. Busy and comfortable, partly 15th-c inn with interesting Civil War history; oak beams and stripped stone, a big inglenook fire in the lounge area just off the main bar, helpful staff, well kept real ales, and decent food in both the bar and pleasant restaurant; attractive courtyard; disabled access.

NAILSWORTH ST8599 **Egypt Mill** *Nailsworth, Stroud GL6 0AE (01453) 833449* *£75,* plus special breaks; 18 comfortable airy rms. Carefully converted 16th-c watermill with original millstones and lifting equipment in the spacious lounge, a split-level restaurant, ground floor bar where two waterwheels can be seen, good, freshly made food, friendly service, and seats in the waterside gardens.

NORTH CERNEY SP0208 **Bathurst Arms** *North Cerney, Cirencester GL1 9XX (01285) 831281* **£50;** 5 pleasant rms. Civilised and handsome old inn with lots of atmosphere, notably friendly staff, a nice mix of polished old furniture, warm fires, very good food, fine wines, and an attractive garden running down to river.

NORTH NIBLEY ST7596 **New Inn** *Waterley Bottom, North Nibley, Dursley GL11 6EF (01453) 543659* **£40;** 2 rms, shared bthrm. Simple inn with new Anglo-French owners, wholesome home-made food, plentiful breakfasts, and several interesting ales; neatly kept garden, small orchard, good nearby walks; cl Christmas–New Year; no children.

NORTHLEACH SP1114 **Market House** *The Square, Northleach, Cheltenham GL54 3EJ (01451) 860557* **£48,** plus special breaks; 4 rms, mostly shared bthrm. Pretty 400-year-old stone house with flagstones, beams and inglenook fireplace, and good breakfasts; cl Dec and Jan; children over 12.

ODDINGTON SP2225 **Horse & Groom** *Oddington, Moreton-in-Marsh GL56 0XH (01451) 830584* **£55,** plus special breaks; 6 quaint and comfortable rms. Attractive, well run inn in pretty Cotswold village, with handsome old furnishings, big log fire, candlelit dining room, and lovely garden with watergarden and large play area; small well behaved dogs by arrangement.

PAINSWICK SO8609 **Painswick Hotel** *Kemps Lane, Painswick, Stroud GL6 6YB (01452) 812160* **£135,** plus special breaks; 19 well equipped comfortable rms. 18th-c Palladian mansion – once a grand rectory – with fine views, antiques and paintings in the elegant rooms, open fires, good food using the best local produce, a thoughtful wine list, and a relaxed friendly atmosphere; garden with croquet lawn.

PARKEND SO6108 **Edale House** *Folly Rd, Parkend, Lydney GL15 4JF (01594) 562835* **£45,** plus wknd breaks; 5 rms. Georgian house opposite the cricket green and backing on to Nagshead Nature Reserve; with homely sitting room, very good food in the attractive dining room (overlooking garden), and a relaxed atmosphere; self-catering cottages; cl Christmas–New Year; children over 12.

PUCKRUP SO8836 **Puckrup Hall** *Puckrup, Tewkesbury GL20 6EL (01684) 296200* **£130,** plus special breaks; 112 comfortably spacious rms. Handsome Regency mansion in over 140 acres of parkland with its own par 71, 18-hole golf course, and leisure club inc indoor swimming pool, crèche, gym and so forth; elegant lounge with fine plasterwork, a relaxed, newly enlarged bar overlooking croquet lawn, and good food in four different dining areas; disabled access.

ST BRIAVELS SO5605 **George** *St Briavels, Lydney GL15 6TA (01594) 530228* **£45;** 4 rms, plus special breaks. Pleasant old pub in a particularly interesting village overlooking the 12th-c castle; with three rambling rooms, big stone fireplace, a Celtic coffin lid dating from 1070 (found in a fireplace here and now mounted next to the bar counter), cosy dining room, and good food; outdoor chessboard.

SHURDINGTON SO9218 **Greenway** *Shurdington, Cheltenham GL51 5UG (01242) 862352* **£180,** plus special breaks; 19 well equipped, spacious and pretty rms. Very well run, lovely 16th-c manor house with antiques, fresh flowers and comfortable seats in the attractive drawing room, cosy cocktail bar, particularly good modern British cooking, excellent wine list, attentive service, and neatly kept gardens; children over 7; limited disabled access.

STOW-ON-THE-WOLD SP1925 **Grapevine** *Sheep St, Stow-on-the-Wold, Cheltenham GL54 1AU (01451) 830344* **£122,** plus special breaks; 22 well furnished, no smoking rms. Warm, friendly and very well run hotel with antiques, comfortable chairs and a relaxed atmosphere in the lounge, a beamed bar, and good food in the sunny restaurant with its 70-year-old trailing vine; cl 31 Jan; disabled access.

STOW-ON-THE-WOLD SP1925 **Old Stocks** *The Square, Stow-on-the-Wold, Cheltenham GL54 1AF* (01451) 830666 **£80,** plus special breaks; 18 rms. Well run 16th/17th-c Cotswold stone hotel with cosy welcoming small bar, beams and open fire, good food, friendly staff, and a sheltered garden; cl Christmas; disabled access.

STOW-ON-THE-WOLD SP1925 **Royalist** *Digbeth St, Stow-on-the-Wold, Cheltenham GL54 1BN* (01451) 830670 *****£70,** plus special breaks; 12 rms. Ancient, family-run hotel with good claims to origins in the 10th c; friendly and full of character, with log fire in the charming lounge, cosy beamed bar, all-day coffee shop, and good home-made bar food; disabled access.

UPPER SLAUGHTER SP1523 **Lords of the Manor** *Upper Slaughter, Cheltenham GL54 2JD* (01451) 820243 **£138,** plus special breaks; 27 rms carefully furnished with antiques, Victorian sketches and paintings. Warm, friendly hotel with mid-17th-c core (though it's been carefully extended many times); lovely views over 8 acres of grounds from the very comfortable library and drawing room, log fires, fresh flowers, fine modern English cooking in the attractive candlelit restaurant overlooking the original rectory gardens, good breakfasts, and kind service; cl New Year; children over 7.

VINEY HILL SO6506 **Viney Hill Country Guest House** *Viney Hill, Blakeney GL15 4LT* (01594) 516000 *****£52,** plus special breaks; 6 well furnished comfortable rms. Delightful, old, no smoking farmhouse in lovely countryside, with very pretty garden, two cosy lounges (one with TV), lots of books and local information, decent evening meal and good breakfast, and friendly efficient service; very fine walking all around.

WESTONBIRT ST8589 **Hare & Hounds** *Westonbirt, Tetbury GL8 8QL* (01666) 880233 **£106,** plus special breaks; 31 comfortable rms. Cotswold stone hotel in 10 acres of grounds with two tennis courts, squash and croquet; pleasant old-fashioned bars, relaxed, spacious and comfortable lounges, open fires, good food, friendly service; table tennis, and snooker; limited disabled access.

WILLERSEY SP1039 **Old Rectory** *Church St, Willersey, Broadway WR12 7PN* (01386) 853729 **£65,** plus special breaks; 8 attractive, well equipped rms. Quietly set and friendly 17th-c house opposite the church (nice walks from the churchyard), with a log fire in dining/sitting room and pretty, flower-filled walled gardens with an ancient mulberry tree; good breakfasts, but no evening meals – though several places nearby; self-catering also; cl 22–28 Dec; children over 8; disabled access.

WINCHCOMBE SP0327 **Sudeley Hill Farm** *Winchcombe, Cheltenham GL54 5JB* (01242) 602344 *****£48;** 3 no smoking rms. Friendly 15th-c farmhouse on a working mixed farm, with log fires, guests' sitting room, and dining room overlooking the large garden; no dogs; cl Christmas.

WINCHCOMBE SP0228 **Wesley House** *High St, Winchcombe, Cheltenham GL54 5LJ* (01242) 602366 **£75,** plus special breaks; 5 pleasantly furnished rms with antiques and showers. Pretty, half-timbered, 15th-c town house with quiet friendly atmosphere, log fire in the comfortable front lounge, prettily presented, very good food (inc lovely puddings) in the attractive beamed restaurant, enjoyable breakfasts, and friendly informal service; old-fashioned garden furniture on small back terrace with pretty view; cl 14 Jan–9 Feb.

WINSTONE SO9509 **Winstone Glebe** *Winstone, Cirencester GL7 7JU* (01285) 821451 **£58;** 3 rms. Small Georgian rectory in quiet countryside, with 5 acres of gardens and paddocks, tennis, lots of surrounding walks; friendly hosts, traditional furnishings, and delicious food (by arrangement); dogs welcome; cl Christmas.

WITHINGTON SP0315 **Halewell Close** *Withington, Cheltenham GL54 4BN* (01242) 890238 *****£95;** 6 beamed and comfortable rms. Lovely old Cotswold stone house, dating back to the 15th c, with relaxed house-party atmosphere, beamed sitting room, late breakfasts, and good English food in the panelled dining room; 50 acres of grounds inc big garden with stone terraces, heated outdoor swimming pool, and fish in trout lake and on River Coln; riding can be arranged; children and dogs by arrangement; good provision for the disabled.

To see and do

GLOUCESTERSHIRE Family Attraction of the Year

🐃 **KINETON** SP0924 **Cotswold Farm Park** (off B4077) A huge site covering 1,000 acres of some of the highest ground in the area, this was the first rare breeds park to open to the public, nearly 30 years ago (the owners started collecting stock as a hobby). Full of delightfully odd-looking species of sheep, cattle, pigs, goats, horses and poultry, it's very much a working farm rather than a more developed leisure attraction, but is particularly well organised as far as children are concerned; it's excellent value too. The touch barn and pets corner have smaller animals like piglets and rabbits to cuddle or feed (you'll probably see eggs hatching in here too), and even the bigger ones come to the gates of their paddocks to be stroked. The feed they sell is specially made (£1.80) so that the animals can safely keep eating it all day. Tractor and trailer rides are popular with children, and there are good safe rustic-themed play areas, with climbing frames, slides, aerial walkways, and tractors to clamber over. There's a designated children's shop, with items arranged in price order, from 5p to around £2 at the most. Try to visit close to the start of the season (up to the end of Apr), when the lambs are being born. You can easily spend most or all of a day here; nature trails and woodland walks are ideal for a break from the animals, and there are 19 acres where you can have a picnic, kick a ball around, or relax on the grass. Lots under cover, so still good when the weather isn't perfect (best to wear wellies then). They have a camping and caravan site. Meals, snacks, shop, disabled access; open mid-Mar–Oct; (01451) 850307; £3.50 (children £1.80). A family ticket is £9.50.

ARLINGHAM SO7010
🐃 **St Augustine's Working Farm** (B4071) They're currently rebuilding this friendly working dairy farm, and hope to be open again by late summer. Phone to check; (01452) 740277. The Ship at Upper Framilode nearby is a good family dining pub in an attractive setting.

ASHLEWORTH SO8125
🏚 There is a **tithe barn** of some note, a good dining pub, the Queen's Arms, and a splendidly traditional pub, the Boat, right on the River Severn – in the same family for centuries.

BARNSLEY SP0705
🌺 **Barnsley House Garden** (B4425) Lovely little herb, vegetable and knot gardens, fruit trees and decorative plants, laburnum and lime walks and 18th-c summerhouses; attractive spring blossom and autumn colours. Plant sales, some disabled access; cl Tues, Fri, Sun, and Christmas–Jan; (01285) 740561; £3.75. The Village Pub is good.

BELAS KNAP SP0125
❄ ⌂ 🏚 🪏 There's a pleasant walk up to Belas Knap and its steep grassy slopes – and great views – from the

Craven Arms in Brockhampton (a decent pub, with a nice garden in a lovely setting; this could be tied in with a walk past some very surprising ruins of a Roman villa tucked away in the woods.

BERKELEY ST6899
🏰 🖼 🌺 🦋 **Berkeley Castle** (off A38) Excellently preserved castle, very much a family home, but still keeping a flavour of its days as a Norman fortress. Impressive paintings, furnishings and silver, fine old keep and Great Hall, terraced gardens, park, extensive butterfly farm – and the dungeon where Edward II was murdered in 1327. Snacks, shop, limited disabled access; open Tues–Sun Apr–Sept (cl am Sun, and am daily in Apr and May), plus Mons July and Aug, and pm Sun in Oct; (01453) 810332; £5.20, £2 butterfly farm. The Pickwick at Lower Wick is a popular dining pub.

🐃 **Cattle Country Adventure Park** 🖼 (off B4066 E) Various cattle including American bison, yaks, and you can feed the wild boar; also a farm trail and large adventure playground. Snacks, shop, disabled access; open wknds and school hols Easter–Christmas; (01453) 810220; £4.25.

🏛🖐 **Jenner Museum** (High St) Largely unchanged Georgian home of Edward Jenner, who discovered the vaccine against smallpox here. He gave free vaccinations from the thatched hut in the attractive grounds. Shop, some disabled access; cl am, all Mon exc bank hols, Oct exc Sun, and all Nov–Mar; (01453) 810631; £2.20.

BIBURY SP1106

★ ⌂ One of the most popular villages in the area, with lovely golden streamside houses; summer crowds can rather blunt its appeal. The **River Coln** lets you approach Bibury more quietly and prettily, along the path from the toll-house just S of Coln St Aldwyns. This route takes you in by the mill and bridge over the Coln itself. Besides Bibury Court, the Catherine Wheel is the best place here for lunch.

✗ 🏵 **Arlington Mill Museum** The 18th-c machinery of this well restored watermill is demonstrated every day, with guided tours by arrangement; at the back, a developing herb garden overlooks the river. Meals, snacks, shop, disabled access to tearoom; cl 25 Dec; (01285) 740368; £2.50.

♪ **Bibury Trout Farm** 🔲 Long-established working farm breeding rainbow trout in 20 ponds. You can feed the fish, or try to catch your own. Snacks, good shop; cl 25 Dec; (01285) 740215; £2.

★ **River Coln villages** By the same trout stream as over-visited Bibury, a pleasant drive links other villages that are just as engaging, but bypassed by most visitors, particularly Coln St Aldwyns (the New Inn is excellent) and Quenington (a decent village pub). On the far side of Bibury, the back road tracking along the river passes through a string of pleasant little villages such as Coln Rogers, Coln St Dennis and Yanworth, eventually reaching the pretty village of Withington (delightful pub right on the stream).

BIRDSWOOD SO7418

🐖 **Old Ley Court** 🔲 (Chapel Lane) Working farm producing double and single Gloucester cheese – you can watch them make it on Tues and Thurs, 9.30–11.30am and 12.30–4pm. Some

disabled access (but no facilities); (01452) 750225; £2. The Apple Tree at nearby Minsterworth is a pleasant dining pub, and the lane past it leads to a good quiet spot for watching the Severn Bore.

BLOCKLEY SP2032

Sleepy Hollow Farm Park Planning restraints have forced this nicely unspoilt farm park to close down and relocate their premises. Phone Tim Spittle on (01386) 701264 for more details.

BOURTON-ON-THE-HILL SP1732

🏵 **Bourton House** Unusual plants in an attractive garden around a fine old house (not open). Teas in 16th-c tithe barn, shop; open pm Thurs and Fri late May–3rd wk in Oct; £3. The Horse & Groom does decent food.

🏛 🏵 **Sezincote House and Garden** (off A424 about 1m S) Exotic onion-domed forerunner of Brighton Pavilion, stunning from the outside, less interesting inside. Also classic early 19th-c watergarden, and a more recent Indian-style garden to match the building. Garden open pm Thurs, Fri and bank hols (cl Dec), house pm Thurs and Fri May–July and Sept; £4.50, £3 garden only. Children are not allowed in the house.

BOURTON-ON-THE-WATER SP1620

★ ⌂ One of the best-known Cotswold villages, but disfigured by sprawly crowds in summer unless you get there very early in the morning – when it's enchanting. There is a wealth of attractions aimed at visitors. The Old Manse has decent food and garden tables overlooking the Windrush; the Mousetrap and riverside Kingsbridge Arms are useful, too. The best walk out of Bourton-on-the-Water is the exit by the church, heading out W past the school and over the old railway line, then following the lanes and tracks S of Upper Slaughter to rejoin the River Windrush and back to Bourton.

🦜 **Birdland** 🔲 (Rissington Rd) Rare and exotic birds on the banks of meandering River Windrush, inc one of the biggest colonies of penguins outside America. Meals, snacks, shop, disabled access; cl 25 Dec; (01451) 820480; £4.

Cotswold Motor Museum & Toy Collection (Sherborne St) As we went to press, they had just sold this motor collection housed in an old watermill, but told us that the new owners would be running it along similar lines. Cars and motorcycles from vintage years to 1950s, along with advertising signs, automobilia, and toy collection. It's the home of Brum the children's TV character. Shop, disabled access; best to phone for opening times; (01451) 821255; £2. The adjacent **Village Life Exhibition** (re-created Edwardian rooms, village shop, and blacksmith's forge) did not know whether they would be affected by the change in ownership – as we were writing this entry, the admission price covered both attractions.

! Dragonfly Maze (Rissington Rd) Follow clues on engraved flagstones to find your way through a yew tree maze to an ornate central pavilion filled with charming animated sculptures. Shop, disabled access; open daily in summer, best to check in winter; (01451) 822251; £2.

Folly Farm Waterfowl (A436 3m W) Lakes and pools with 160 species of waterfowl, as well as friendly ducks, geese and poultry, and hand-reared animals. Good for children, and a nice spot for a picnic (or to camp). Their lavender fields are in full bloom in July. Shop, disabled access; cl 25 Dec; (01451) 820285; £3.50.

! Model Village (High St) Charming replica of the village, modelled from Cotswold stone in the 1930s to a scale of one-ninth, complete with working waterwheel and music in the church. Good home-made food (and lovely river view) in adjacent Old New Inn, snacks, shop, limited disabled access; cl 25 Dec; (01451) 820467; £2.

! Perfumery Exhibition (Victoria St) Aromatic displays and demonstrations of perfume-making and scent extraction, with scented garden. Shop, disabled access; cl 25–26 Dec; (01451) 820698; £2.

BROOKTHORPE SO8412
Guided horse-riding is organised at Ongers Farm; (01452) 813344; from £9.

CHELTENHAM SO9523
★ Beautiful spa town, useful for exploring the Cotswolds, shopping, or admiring the elegant Regency architecture of its tree-lined avenues. These days Cheltenham is best known for its races, and the racecourse at Prestbury Park (N on A435) has an exhibition on Gold Cup winners; (01242) 513014; cl wknds; free. Lots of antique shops, especially around the Montpellier area. Taylors wine bar (Cambray Pl), the Restoration (Grosvenor St), Beehive (Montpellier Villas) and Beaufort Arms (London Rd) have decent food, and the well run café in the beautiful Imperial Gardens is suitable for families.

Art Gallery & Museum (Clarence St) Excellent Arts and Crafts collection inspired by William Morris, fine paintings inc 17th-c Dutch works, and rare porcelain and ceramics. Meals, snacks, shop, disabled access; cl Sun and bank hols; (01242) 837431; free.

Holst Birthplace Museum (Clarence Rd) Nr the Pump Room, this interesting Regency house is where the composer was born in 1874; you can see his first piano. Worthwhile even if you're not mad about Holst, as the rooms are all carefully furnished in period style. Shop; cl Sun, Mon and bank hols; (01242) 237431; £2.

Pittville Pump Room (Pittville Park) A short walk from the centre, this is generally regarded as the town's finest building, 19th-c Greek Revival with a colonnaded façade and balconied hall. It's easy to imagine the place's Regency heyday, especially strolling round the super park and gardens, or during concerts in the July music festival; on summer Suns they may have teas accompanied by live music. You can still sample the spa water – rather salty. Shop, disabled access to ground floor only; cl Tues, and maybe Jan–Feb – best to phone to check opening times; (01242) 523852; *£1.50.

CHIPPING CAMPDEN SP1539
★ † ⌂ Extremely attractive town, with interesting old buildings inc an ancient covered open-sided market hall, a grand Perpendicular church typical of the area's rich 'wool churches', enjoyable shops, and fine old inns. Many of our contributors would put it among the country's most delightful small

towns, though until they get the cars out of the centre not all would agree. The Eight Bells, Volunteer, Noel Arms and Red Lion are all good for lunch. The **Cotswold Way**, a 100-mile path from here all the way to Bath, carefully picks out some of the choicest Cotswold scenery – a worthwhile aid for those planning a shorter stroll.

CIRENCESTER SP0201

★ 🏛 ✝ ☙ A busy country town, particularly on its Mon and Fri market days, with a succession of fine Cotswold stone streets off the long market place. It has many attractive buildings, and interesting antique and other shops inc traditional country saddlers, etc. Though one of the most handsome of all the Cotswold towns, it isn't too touristy. The **Church of St John the Baptist** (Market Pl) is wonderfully grand, and has a striking late Gothic tower. **Brewery Court** 16 independent craft businesses and shops in a former brewery (cl Sun and some bank hols), along with theatre, gallery and café. Also worth a look are the 12th-c remains of **St John's Hospital**, the **Norman arch**, and the various well preserved wool merchants' houses. Cecily Hill, one of the town's most attractive streets, gives on to the pleasant strolling-ground of Cirencester Park. Decent places for lunch include the Slug & Lettuce, Corinium Court, Tatyans (Chinese) and (very local, but good value) Golden Cross.

🏛 ☙ **Corinium Museum** (Park St) Cirencester was one of the most important cities in Roman Britain, and this spacious museum has one of the finest collections of antiquities from the period (all clearly displayed and labelled). Reconstructed period dining room and kitchen (complete with menus), with Saxon and medieval galleries too. Meals, snacks, shop, excellent disabled access; cl am Sun, Mon Nov–Mar, Christmas; (01285) 655611; *£2.50.

CLEARWELL SO5608

☙ **Clearwell Caves** (off B4228) Tours of huge caverns, a source of ore from the Iron Age right up to 1945; deeper trips for the more adventurous. It's quite a labyrinth, with many miles of passageways, so stout shoes recommended. Lively themed displays down here at Christmas. Meals, snacks, shop; open Mar–24 Dec, and wknds Jan–Feb; (01594) 832535; *£3.50. The Wyndham Arms is handy for lunch, and though the village is not in itself particularly pretty it's a very good centre for the lovely surrounding countryside.

CLEEVE COMMON SO9924

⌂ ❀ The steep grassy slopes of the W escarpment of the Cotswolds make for some of the area's best walking. This, the highest point of the Cotswolds, has breezy, unkempt grassland on its open expanses and can either be reached from the nearby village of Cleeve Hill on the A46, or integrated into a circular walk past Belas Knap long barrow and through the Sudeley Castle estate into Winchcombe.

DEERHURST SO8729

✝ Ancient remains here include **Odda's Chapel**, a restored 11th-c

---

Days Out

Meet the animals and ride the train: Stroll up Cleeve Hill from Cleeve Common (good for kite-flying); lunch at the Hollow Bottom, Guiting Power; Cotswold Farm Park at Kineton; steamtrain trip from Toddington or Winchcombe.

The ancient forest: Forest of Dean Sculpture Trail; lunch at the Wyndham Arms, Clearwell; Clearwell Caves; Symonds Yat Rock, walk along Wye gorge southwards to Biblins suspension bridge.

Sanctuaries along the Severn Estuary: Frampton Court; lunch at the Bell, Frampton on Severn; Wildfowl and Wetlands Trust, Slimbridge.

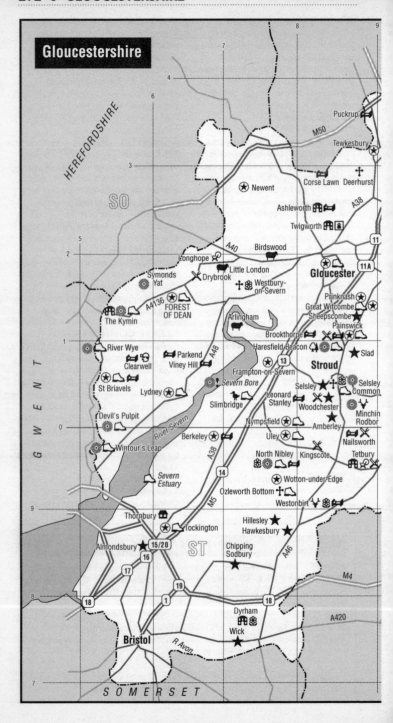

Gloucestershire

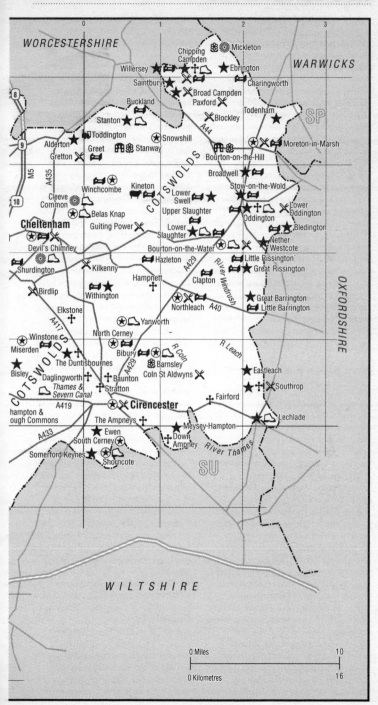

WORCESTERSHIRE

WARWICKS

Mickleton
Chipping Campden
Willersey
Saintbury
Broad Campden
Paxford
Buckland
Stanton
Toddington
Snowshill
Alderton
Greet
Gretton
Stanway
Winchcombe
Kineton
Cleeve Common
Belas Knap
Cheltenham
Devil's Chimney
Guiting Power
Lower Slaughter
Upper Slaughter
Lower Slaughter
Shurdington
Kilkenny
Hampnett
Birdlip
Withington
Clapton
Elkstone
Northleach
Winstone
Yanworth
Miserden
North Cerney
The Duntisbournes
Bibury
Bisley
Daglingworth
Barnsley
Coln St Aldwyns
Thames & Severn Canal
Baunton
Stratton
Fairford
hampton & ough Commons
Cirencester
The Ampneys
Ewen
Meysey-Hampton
South Cerney
Down Ampney
Somerford Keynes
Shorncote

Ebrington
Charingworth
Blockley
Todenham
Bourton-on-the-Hill
Moreton-in-Marsh
Broadwell
Stow-on-the-Wold
Lower Oddington
Oddington
Bledington
Nether Westcote
Bourton-on-the-Water
Hazleton
Little Rissington
Great Rissington
Great Barrington
Little Barrington
Eastleach
Southrop
Lechlade

COTSWOLDS

SP

OXFORDSHIRE

River Windrush
R Coln
R Leach
River Thames

SU

WILTSHIRE

0 Miles 10
0 Kilometres 16

chapel discovered as part of a farmhouse, and the **Priory Church of St Mary**, a mainly Saxon church with a lovely atmosphere and some intriguing original carvings and features. The Farmers Arms at Apperley is a good dining pub (brewing its own beers).

DEVIL'S CHIMNEY SO9418

❋ ⌂ On the Cotswold Way, a viewpoint rock pinnacle amid old quarries on Leckhampton Hill, perched above Cheltenham.

DYRHAM ST7475

🏚 🐾 **Dyrham Park** Set in an ancient park grazed by fallow deer, this fine William and Mary house has hardly changed since the late 17th c. The interiors have Dutch-style furnishings, Delft ware, Dutch bird paintings and a remarkable *trompe l'oeil* by Hoogstraten. Meals, snacks, shop, disabled access to ground floor; house cl am, all day Weds and Thurs, and all Nov–Mar, park open all year; (0117) 937 2501; £7.50; garden and deer park only £2.60; deer park only £1.80; NT. The Bull at Hinton Dyrham and Crown at Tolldown (A46) are handy for lunch.

EASTLEACH SP2005

★ Delightful Cotswold village; a lovely ancient clapper bridge links the two Norman churches, very photogenic when the daffodils are out.

FAIRFORD SP1501

✝ Pleasant riverside meadows, and a wonderful 15th-c Perpendicular **church**, well known for its remarkable medieval stained glass (inc a fascinating depiction of hell), and comical misericords. The Bull has decent food.

FOREST OF DEAN SO6212

🦆 ❋ ♓ 🖼 ⌂ The Forest of Dean has a unique landscape: hilly woodland that shows many traces of the way it has provided a livelihood for the people living around it. It's flanked by a spectacular stretch of the Wye Valley, and its woodland colours are at their best in late May and autumn. Still largely ancient oak woodland despite encroaching pine plantations, the forest rolls over many miles of hilly countryside, giving plenty of space – even in summer you can often have much of the woods to yourself. There are ponds, streams with stepping stones, cattle and maybe fallow deer,

sudden distant views, the humps and gouges that mark ancient iron workings, the tracks of abandoned railways and tramways, and still one or two of the freeminers, who've been digging coal by hand from surface seams for hundreds of years. The forest scenery has most impact on those prepared to delve into its past a bit – a good start is the **Heritage Centre** at Upper Soudley; the forest is well equipped with car parks, picnic sites and forest trails. The **Sculpture Trail takes** a four-mile route passing nearly 20 specially commissioned sculptures hidden deep in the forest (from picnic site nr the comfortable Speech House Hotel). The **Kidnalls Forest Trail** is a good way of tracking down some early industrial sites. The **Foundry Wood Trail** passes Soudley fish ponds and gains some fine views. The **Wench Ford Forest Walk** leads past a series of quite interesting rock outcrops. Signed paths ensure easy route-finding up to the open summit of May Hill, where on a clear day you can see the Cotswolds, Malverns, Welsh Marches and Severn Estuary. Around the edges of the forest, the scenery changes to a patchwork of steep pastures – also very attractive. It's well worth getting a forest map, either from the Dean Heritage Centre or direct from the Forestry Commission in Coleford (01594) 833057; these outline walks (inc the sculpture trail), and mark the best spots for views or picnics. The information centres can also provide details of canoeing, caving, cycling or fishing in the forest. The B4432 to Symonds Yat does give some good views, the B4228 down past St Briavels is a pleasant country road, and the little lanes around the edges of the forest are rewarding drives – but need a large-scale map.

🦆 **Conifer arboretum** This makes an interesting change from the forest's predominantly broad-leaved trees; nr Speech House Hotel.

♓ ⬇T 🌳 **Dean Heritage Centre** (Camp Mill, Upper Soudley) Useful introduction to the Forest of Dean, set around an old watermill in a pretty wooded valley. Plenty going on, inc a working beam engine, a collection of clocks, craft displays, adventure playground, and occasional traditional charcoal-burning. Meals, snacks, shop, disabled access; cl 24–26 Dec; (01594) 822170; £3.30.

⚓ **Hopewell Colliery** (B4226 E of Broadwell) 45-minute underground tours of the 'free' mine guided by ex-miners, and display of mining tools and equipment. You'll need sturdy shoes and warm clothing. Snacks, shop; cl Nov–Mar; (01594) 810706; £3.

♥ ⚘ **Nagshead RSPB Nature Reserve** (W of Parkend, off B4431 to Coleford) A good place to see deer and other wildlife.

⌂ 🏚 ♨ ♞ ! **Puzzle Wood** (just off B4228 S of Coleford) Wooded paths arranged as a stroll-along puzzle, landscaped in the 19th c nr remains of Roman iron mines. Snacks, shop; cl Mon (exc bank hols), and Nov–Mar; (01594) 833187; £2.50. Across the road is the **Treasure Train**; steamtrains run along a ¾-mile stretch of narrow-gauge track, with children solving clues that lead to treasure along the way. There are four stops, with footpaths through the woods nearby. Snacks, disabled access; open wknds and bank hols Easter–Oct, maybe Tues–Thurs and Sat too in summer hols; (01594) 834991; £2.95 for unlimited train journeys, plus £1.50 for the treasure trail. The Dog & Muffler at Joyford is a pretty place for lunch; good walks nearby.

🏚 **Roman road** You can track the remarkably durable paving of this just off the B4431 at Blackpool Bridge.

❄ **Symonds Yat Rock** Perhaps the Forest of Dean's most distinctive feature, where the River Wye rolls around a monumental wooded cliff barrier, a favourite spot with peregrine falcons; tremendous views in all directions from the top, and at the bottom a ferry runs between two inns.

FRAMPTON ON SEVERN SO7407

🏚 🖼 ❀ **Frampton Court** Elegant lived-in Georgian house, with original furniture, porcelain and paintings, and fascinating gardens. The 18th-c orangery has been converted into self-catering holiday flats. Snacks (by prior arrangement), shop, disabled access to gardens; personal tours all year by appointment, (01452) 740267; £4.50.

The village green is said to be the largest in the country, with the orangery on one side, and the civilised Bell (good range of food) on another. Just outside the village, the Gloucester & Sharpness Canal passes grand colonnaded lock keepers' houses by pretty swing bridges.

GLOUCESTER SO8318

🏚 A busy modern city despite its long history – you have to search out the old buildings among today's big shops (for instance the splendid timber-framed house tucked down a passageway off 26 Westgate St). The tourist office at St Michael's Tower (itself a fine ancient building at the central Cross) is particularly good at sending you off well equipped for the hunt. The Waterfront (Llanthony Rd, S end of docks), and – all handy for the cathedral – Fountain, New Inn and Tailor's House (Westgate St) are useful for a quick lunch.

🖼 🖼 **City Museum & Art Gallery** (Brunswick Rd) Local history (inc the oldest known backgammon set), and paintings by Gainsborough and Turner. Shop, disabled access; cl Sun (exc July–Sept); (01452) 524131; £2.50. Guided tours of the ancient **City East Gate** leave here every hour on Sats May–Sept; £1.20.

♨ 🖼 🚂 **Docks** The revitalised waterfront deserves much of the credit for the city's tourism renaissance; guided walks, summer boat trips along the canal or up the river as far as Tewkesbury (contact National Waterways Museum (01452) 318054). Attractions here include the unusually interesting **Soldiers of Gloucester Museum** (cl Mon exc Jun–Sept and bank hols; (01452) 522682; £4), and a big **antiques centre**, with 110 varied antique shops in Dickensian arcades (limited disabled access; cl am Sun; free wkdys, 50p wknds and bank hols).

🖼 🏚 **Folk Museum** (Westgate St) Social history in a group of Tudor and Jacobean timber-framed houses; Victorian classroom, reconstructed ironmonger's shop and a toy gallery. In summer there may be Gloucestershire Old Spot pigs in the yard. Shop, limited disabled access; cl Sun exc July–Sept; (01452) 526467; £2 (children and Gloucester residents free).

✝ ⛪ **Gloucester Cathedral** A drunken daredevil trying to scale the cathedral walls recently came unstuck along with the statue he was clambering on, when the head of St Osric (the cathedral's founder) came away in his hands, sending them both crashing to the floor. Towering majestically over the city's more recent buildings, it has lovely fan-vaulted cloisters, the second largest medieval stained-glass window in the country, and a fine collection of church plate in the Treasury. In 1330, the abbot astutely purchased the remains of murdered Edward II, and the resulting stream of pilgrims paid for elaborate rebuilding, an early example of Perpendicular style. Meals, snacks, shop, some disabled access; (01452) 528095; donations. Not far from here are the remains of 9th-c **St Oswald's Priory**, the city's oldest structure, and other ecclesiastical remains inc **Greyfriars** and **Blackfriars**, the latter pretty much unchanged since the 13th-c, with a rare scissor-braced roof.

🏛 **Gloucester Prison Museum** (Barrack Sq) Because of a lack of volunteers, this museum in the old Gate Lodge – the only one of its type attached to a fully operational prison – was closed as we went to press. They hope to re-open around spring – best to phone to check; (01452) 529551.

🏛 **House of the Tailor of Gloucester** (College Court) Inspiration for Beatrix Potter's story; exhibition and shop. Disabled access to shop only; cl Sun, bank hols and 25 Dec; £1.

✝ **Jet Age Museum** 🆓 (Airport, Cheltenham Rd E) The working surroundings make this collection seem more ready for action than some; children can climb into some of the cockpits. Shop, disabled access; open daily Easter–Sept, plus Weds and wknds in winter; (01452) 330761; £3.

🏛 **Museum of Advertising & Packaging** (Albert Warehouse, Docks) Great for nostalgia-lovers, an enormous and quite fascinating assembly of packets, tins, bottles, posters, street signs and more from Victorian days onwards. Also continuous showing of vintage TV commercials. Snacks, shop, disabled access; cl winter Mons, 25–26 Dec; (01452) 302309; £3.50.

✹ **National Waterways Museum** The story of Britain's inland waterways, and the first heyday of these docks after the opening of the Gloucester & Berkeley Canal. It's a lively place, with a good deal to amuse children, who can even try their hand at steering a narrow boat. A new painted boats' gallery covers trends from ancient mythology to Victorian art (interactive screens let you create your own design), and a few more will be added by the summer. Snacks, shop, good disabled access; cl 25 Dec; (01452) 318054; £4.75.

🐟 **Over farm shop** (1m W of Gloucester) A good one, with local produce and pick-your-own in summer (plus a PYO pumpkin festival in Oct half-term); disabled access; cl 25–26 Dec.

◠ ✹ **Robinswood Hill Country Park** (2m S) A little outcrop of the Cotswolds, with 250 acres of walks and trails, a wildlife information centre (fun talks and events), and wonderful views of the city from the summit. Snacks, shop, disabled access; (01452) 303206; free. Not far away is a dry ski slope.

GREAT WITCOMBE SO9114

🏛 ◠ 🏕 ✹ **Crickley Hill Country Park** (just N of village) Has a few ancient sites, as well as nature trails, lovely clearly marked woodland walks, and fine views. Some disabled access; visitor centre cl winter; (01452) 863170; free.

🏛 **Roman villa** The outlines of a substantial Roman villa can still be traced here, around a courtyard, with several mosaics and evidence of an underfloor heating system. The Royal George Hotel at Birdlip has decent food, and the Golden Heart at Brimpsfield is good.

HARESFIELD BEACON SO8108

🏕 ◠ ✹ (3m NW of Stroud), 450 acres of NT woodland and grassland on the Cotswold escarpment, with spectacular views; free, and just a short ascent from the road.

KINETON SP0924

☛ **Cotswold Farm Park** See separate family panel on p.268.

LECHLADE SU2199

★ ◠ Graceful village with one or two decent antique shops, good traditional toy shop, pleasant walks, and access to the quiet reed-fringed Thames for footpath walks – especially along to Kelmscot in Oxfordshire. The Trout along the A417 at St John's Bridge has lovely riverside tables.

LITTLE LONDON SO7019

🐐 **Angora Goat & Mohair Centre** (Blakemore Farm) Unusual goat farm with shop selling clothes made from their fleeces; other animals too. Snacks, shop, disabled access; cl Mon (exc bank hols) and Tues, 24 Dec–Jan; (01452) 830630; £1. The Red Hart at Blaisdon is attractive for lunch.

LONGHOPE SO6818

✿ **Harts Barn Flower & Craft Centre** Smart craft workshops, including dried flowers, jewellery and ceramics, set in an attractive Norman hunting lodge. Courtyard tearoom, disabled access; cl Mon exc bank hols; (01452) 830954; free.

LOWER SLAUGHTER SP1622

★◁ With its sister village Upper Slaughter, this is perhaps the prettiest village in Britain – a perfect harmony of stone, water, grass and trees. It's not as overwhelmed by summer visitors as its nearby rival Bourton-on-the-Water, though it certainly gets its fair share. The riverside stroll from Lower to Upper Slaughter is a leisurely mile or so; to make a longer walk for a circuit of a couple of hours, you can follow the signposted Warden's Way.

LYDNEY SO6304

🚂◁ **Dean Forest Railway** (New Mills, slightly N of Lydney) Lots of locomotives, wagons and equipment at the station, and steam trips through the forest (mainly just wknds, best to ring for dates). Snacks, shop, disabled access; static displays open Easter–Dec; (01594) 843423; £4. The Woodman at Parkend, handy for the stop there, has decent food and good nearby walks.

❀ 🏛 ☕ **Lydney Park** Extensive sheltered spring garden, rich with flowering shrubs, rhododendrons, azaleas and magnolias; also lakes and deer park. Tucked away among the trees are the remains of a Roman temple, and a museum with finds from the site, inc the astonishingly intricate Lydney dog. Snacks, shop, plant sales; open Sun, Weds and bank hols

Easter–early Jun; (01594) 842844; £2.50 (£1.50 Weds).

MICKLETON SP1742

❀ **Hidcote Manor Garden** (off B4081) Series of small gardens separated by walls and hedges of different species, with rare shrubs, trees and roses. Very popular even mid-week, despite the price. Meals, snacks, good shop, some disabled access; as we went to press, opening times for this year had not yet been decided – best to phone; (01684) 855370; £5.60; NT. The King's Arms is good value for lunch.

❀ ✾ **Kiftsgate Court Garden** (off B4081) Renowned for its old-fashioned roses (best Jun and July), inc reputedly the largest rose in England, this has many other rare plants, shrubs and trees, good views across the Vale of Evesham, and that special feel that comes from generations of care by a gifted gardening family. Snacks, rare plant sales; open pm Weds, Thurs, Sun and bank hols, Apr–Sept, plus pm Sat Jun and July; (01386) 438777; £3.50.

MINCHINHAMPTON & RODBOROUGH COMMON ST8699

❀ ✚ 900 acres of open land with fine views and a wide range of wildlife; NT, free. The Old Lodge on Minchinhampton Common has good food, and the steep lanes all around make interesting drives.

MISERDEN SO9308

❀ ❀ ❀ ⌖ ★ **Miserden Park** Views over the wooded Golden Valley from the handsome gardens of a 17th-c manor house (not open), with Lutyens topiary, mature shrubs and trees, and colourful walled garden. Meals, snacks, nursery, some disabled access; open Tues–Thurs Apr–Sept; (01285) 821303; *£3. Also a woodland trail down by the river. The quiet village is charming, with decent food in the Carpenters Arms.

MORETON-IN-MARSH SP2032

★ Attractively bustling old place, once an important linen weaving centre and coaching town, now with popular Tues market. For food, besides the good Marsh Goose, the Inn on the Marsh is useful – and the Farriers Arms (by the church in the quiet village of Todenham) is worth the trip.

❀ **Batsford Arboretum** (Batsford Park, just NW of Moreton) Well grown private collection of over 1,000 rare and beautiful species of tree spread over 50 acres; hundreds of maples, 90 different magnolias, flowering cherries. Best in May and autumn, but relaxing any time. Meals, snacks, garden centre, disabled access; cl mid-Nov–mid-Feb; (01608) 650722; £3.50. The park is home to plenty of deer.

🦅 **Cotswold Falconry Centre** £ (Batsford Park, just NW of Moreton) Flying demonstrations throughout the day, with a chance to handle some of the birds. Close-circuit TVs give a bird's-eye view of life in the nest. Snacks, shop, disabled access (but no facilities); open Mar–Nov; (01386) 701043; *£3.50.

▣ **Wellington Aviation Museum** (Broadway Rd) World War II aircraft pictures, sculpture and related material. Shop, disabled access; cl 12.30–2pm, all day Mon, 25 Dec, and Jan–Feb; (01608) 650323; £1.50.

NEWENT SO7225
Small country town with some timbered buildings which have a bit of a Worcestershire or Herefordshire look.

🦅 **National Birds of Prey Centre** £ (Great Boulsdon, just S of Newent) Exceptional collection of birds of prey, with flying displays and breeding aviaries. Meals, snacks, shop, some disabled access; cl Dec, Jan (exc for special events); (01531) 820286; £4.95. (Discount voucher is not valid for special events.) The Yew Tree at Cliffords Mesne, a bit further on this road, has decent food, and is handy for May Hill.

�🏠 **Shambles Museum of Victorian Life** Enthusiastic re-creation of Victorian cobbled square, with shops and furnished tradesman's house. Summer snacks, shop, limited disabled access; cl Mon (exc bank hols), Jan–mid-Mar; (01531) 822144; £3.45. The George opposite is useful.

🍇 **St Anne's Vineyard** (Oxenhall, off B4221) Grow and sell 100 varieties of vine, and make wines; cl some winter wkdys, best to check on (01989) 720313; free.

🍇 **Three Choirs Vineyard** (off B4215 towards Dymock) Now one of the six largest vineyards in the country. Meals, snacks, shop, disabled access; cl 25, 31 Dec and 1 Jan; tastings free, tour and exhibitions £2.75.

NORTH CERNEY SP0107

❀ 🐄 ★ **Cerney House Gardens** Expansive old garden behind 13th-c church, with old roses, trees, shrubs, walled and herb gardens, a few animals (they make tasty goat's cheese), and a watergarden. The surrounding woods are lovely at bluebell time. Teas, shop, some disabled access; open Tues, Weds and Fri Easter–Sept; (01285) 831300; £3. The village is attractive, and the Bathurst Arms is good for lunch.

NORTH NIBLEY ST7495

❀ ☀ ⌂ **Hunts Court** Informal gardens with over 400 varieties of old roses, plus unusual shrubs and other plants; fine views. Plant sales, disabled access; open Tues–Sat (though cl Aug), plus spring bank hols and usually last 3 Sun pms in Jun and first 2 in July; (01453) 547440; £1.50. The walk up to the Tyndale Monument gives even better views, and the Black Horse is handy for lunch.

NORTHLEACH SP1114

★† Fine example of an unspoilt small wool town, with a particularly interesting **church**, renowned for its collection of brasses. A while ago they installed an automatic winder to the church clock, allowing retirement for the man who'd faithfully wound it for the last 65 years. The Red Lion is useful for lunch.

🏠 **Cotswold Heritage Centre** (Fosseway) Decent collection of rural bygones. Snacks, shop, mostly disabled access; cl am Sun, and all Nov–Mar; £2.50.

! **World of Mechanical Music** (Oak House, High St) Quite captivating collection of clocks, musical boxes and automata in an old wool merchant's house, displayed and played in period settings. It's quite spooky watching the instruments work themselves. Shop, good disabled and blind access; cl 25–26 Dec; (01451) 860181; £5.

NYMPSFIELD SO8101

🏛! ⌂ ★ ☀ **Woodchester Mansion** (B4066, Nympsfield) Construction of this splendid unfinished Gothic mansion was inexplicably abandoned virtually overnight in 1870. It's being repaired but not finished, and you can usually see traditional building techniques like stonemasonry. Five species of bat add to the atmosphere. Readers report excellent guided tours. No children inside, for safety reasons. Snacks, shop, disabled access to ground floor only; open first wknd of month Easter–Oct, plus bank hol wknds, and Sun July–Aug; (01453) 860661; £4. You should be able to explore the surrounding valley, recently purchased by the NT. The Rose & Crown in the attractive village has good-value food (and comfortable bedrooms), and the walk up Coaley Peak gives tremendous views over the Severn Valley.

ODDINGTON SP2325

★ † ◠ Charming Cotswold village; the 11th-c **church** has an interesting mural, and there are pleasant walks, especially from the Fox at Lower Oddington – very good food there, too.

OZLEWORTH BOTTOM ST7992

◠ † This valley, not far from Wotton-under-Edge, has a nostalgically forgotten quality about it, providing an interesting walk between Lasborough Manor and Ozleworth Park, with its unusual Norman **church** endowed with a hexagonal tower.

PAINSWICK SO8609

★ ⚏ ◠ ❊ ♞ ♘ † Readers really enjoy this delightful little town sometimes referred to as 'Queen of the Cotswolds'. There's been a settlement here since Celtic times, and **Painswick Beacon** has the remains of the earliest structures; it's a short ascent from the road, with great views towards the Malvern hills. Plenty of old buildings to look at, such as the 15th-c **post office**, and several antique shops and craft workshops. The **Church of St Mary** has fine interesting tombs and a fascinating churchyard where 99 immaculately clipped yews form gateways and canopies. The Falcon opposite is popular for lunch.

❀ **Rococo Garden** (The Stables, Painswick House) Careful restoration of sizeable 18th-c garden to match a 1748 painting showing its fanciful mix of precisely trimmed hedging, paths and shrubs, unrestrained trees; also a maze and slightly zany garden buildings.

Pleasant vistas, children's walks – a cheery-feeling place. Snacks, shop, plant sales, some disabled access; cl Mon, Tues, and Dec; (01452) 813204; £3.

PRINKNASH SO8614

† ♞ ❀ ❊ **Prinknash Abbey & Pottery** ⌂ (off A46) Unusual 20th-c Benedictine monastery and earlier house, now home to the world-famous pottery; you can watch production from the viewing gallery. Snacks, shop, disabled access; cl 25–26 Dec, Good Fri; (01452) 812239; £1.50 for pottery tours. The abbey buildings aren't to everyone's taste but the grounds are attractive, with good views over the Severn Vale. The Black Horse in the very steep village of Cranham has enjoyable food.

♞ ♥ **Prinknash Bird Park** (Prinknash Abbey) Exotic pheasants, peacocks and other birds, as well as deer, goats and waterfowl; most animals feed from your hand (the fallow deer are particularly friendly). Snacks, shop; cl 25–26 Dec, 1 Jan, Good Fri; (01452) 812727; £3.40.

ST BRIAVELS SO5504

★ ⛰ ❊ ◠ ♞ Attractive and unusual small village focused on the ruins of its 13th-c castle (the inhabited part is a youth hostel), with a steeply grassy former moat and views from the ramparts of the curtain wall. The George is good for lunch, and there are various circular walks around the parish, devised by Mr McGubbin in the **craft shop**.

SELSLEY SO8203

★ † Strung-out Cotswold village in the steep country just S of Stroud; William Morris, Maddox-Brown, Burne-Jones and Rossetti all worked on the **church windows**.

SELSLEY COMMON SO8304

❀ ◠ ❊ **Selsley Herb Farm** Besides the herb garden this sizeable place has cream teas on Sun and bank hols, and a good nursery. Limited disabled access; cl Mon, am Sun and bank hols, and all Oct–Mar (exc by appointment); (01453) 766682; £1. They also have a herb shop just up the A46 in Nailsworth (which also has plenty of trails around its old mills). The grassland common itself is quite high, with good views and pleasant walks; the Bell is a handy refreshment stop.

SEVERN BORE SO6904

! ※ Tidal wave surging upstream at high tide, which can sometimes reach up to six feet in height around the spring and autumn equinox. The Environment Agency produce a calendar listing the best times and places to catch the phenomenon, with a rating of how spectacular it's likely to be; (01684) 850951. A good quiet spot to get down to the river is from Purton, where the Berkeley Arms has a wonderful estuary view.

SEVERN ESTUARY ST6196

▱ This makes for some lonely walks along the sea wall, with power station cooling towers and the vast Severn bridges emphasising the emptiness of the tidal flats. The White Hart in Littleton-upon-Severn, the Anchor in Oldbury-on-Severn and right by the embankment the Windbound at Shepperdine and Berkeley Arms at Purton are useful starting-points. Further upstream, Arlingham is locked within a big bend of the Severn, about a mile from the river, with the river path looking across to the Forest of Dean.

SHEEPSCOMBE SO8910

★ Delightful Cotswold village, clinging to picturesque hillsides; the cricket ground's so steep that fielders can scarcely see the bowler.

SHORNCOTE SU0296

♪ ▱ ✦ ⍦ **Cotswold Water Park** 2,000 acres of lakes with facilities for angling, windsurfing, sailing and other water sports, country parks and walks, birdwatching and nature reserves. Snacks at some lakes, shop, disabled access; some activities cl winter; (01285) 861459; £5 (£3 wkdys) car parking, £1 in winter.

SLIMBRIDGE SO7703

✦ ▱ **Wildfowl & Wetlands Trust** (off A38) The first of the Wildfowl and Wetlands Trust's eight centres, and still the best, this enormous place is a lot more than just a bird and nature reserve. Thoughtfully upgraded in recent years (with more to come thanks to a hefty grant from the Millennium Commission), it shows off probably the world's most comprehensive collection of geese, swans and ducks, as well as six species of flamingo (you won't see so many anywhere else in Europe), rare and wild birds, and a tropical house that re-creates the sights, sounds and smells of a rainforest. In the Pond Zone section, children are encouraged to learn about wetland environments by taking part in pond-dipping and seeing what they help fish out of the water magnified on to TV screens. Also quite a few computer and video displays and games, and extra events and talks in the school holidays. It's unusual in being somewhere that you might get more out of visiting in the winter, when up to 8,000 wild birds fly in; several of the excellent hides and viewing facilities are heated then. Some birds can be fed by hand. There aren't any play areas or anything like that, but it's one of the most visitor-friendly bird reserves in the country, with plenty of activities specifically aimed at primary school children. They'll hire out binoculars if you've left your own at home. Meals and snacks, shop, disabled access; cl 25 Dec; (01453) 890065; £5.25 (£3.25 children over 4, free to WWT members). A family ticket for two adults and two children is £13.50. The Tudor Arms by the swing bridge across the canal is useful for food, and the village post office has details of pleasant little walks.

SNOWSHILL SP0933

🏰 ⌂ ❀ **Snowshill Manor** It looks like an ordinary Cotswold manor house, but inside is one of those extraordinary collections of ephemera great eccentrics somehow amass. Each room is carefully themed, full of maybe toys, musical instruments, bikes hanging from the ceiling – and even suits of Japanese samurai armour, spookily arranged to look like a group of warriors meeting in the gloom. There's a charming cottage garden, and you can stay in one of three cottages. Meals, snacks, shop and secondhand books by the entrance, disabled access to garden only; open Weds–Sun and bank hols Apr–Oct; (01386) 852410; *£6; NT. This is one of the Trust's busier properties, and there's a timed ticket system; try and come mid-week or out of season. The nearby Snowshill Arms is popular for lunch (busiest 12–1.15pm), and the drive along the River Windrush to

Ford, Kineton and Naunton is delightful.

SOUTH CERNEY SU0497

🐄 ⚘ ★ **Butts Farm** 🏠 (1m NE of S Cerney, on A419) Notably friendly, with a good range of animals for children to feed, and daily pony or cart rides and goat-milking. New dairy and wartime farming exhibitions, along with spinning demonstrations, and a straw tunnel to play in. Snacks, shop, disabled access; cl Mon and Tues outside school hols, phone for winter opening; (01285) 862205; £3. The Eliot Arms in the prettily preserved 16th-c village has good food.

SOUTHROP SP2003

★ † Charming Cotswold village that really comes into its own when the daffodils appear, with a delightful riverside **church**.

STANTON SP0734

★ ⌂ One of the prettiest Cotswold villages, very small – and rarely overrun with visitors. The best views over it are from the Mount pub, up the steep no through road beyond the village centre. This is the start of a trio of timeless villages on the **Cotswold Way**, a well marked track that conveniently picks out some of the best scenery for walkers. The next two are Stanway and Buckland; field paths and farm track let you detour to Snowshill, and from there it's a pleasant three-mile walk to Broadway just over the Worcs border.

STANWAY SP0632

🏛 ❀ **Stanway House** One of the most beautiful 16th-c manor houses in the country, a cluster of gabled buildings popping up unexpectedly from the countryside, with charming and clearly lived-in rooms. The early 18th-c grounds have fine trees and interesting buildings, inc a folly pyramid on a steeply wooded hill. Open pm Tues and Thurs Aug–Sept; (01386) 584469; £3.

STOW-ON-THE-WOLD SP1925

★ Handsome market town with fine stone buildings around its square and in the narrow lanes around, and a good few antique shops, book shops and so forth. It's something of an antidote to the more sweetly pretty Cotswold villages, on quite a high plateau and altogether more austere in style – not for nothing was it known as 'Stow-on-

the-Wold, where the wind blows cold', and the ancient stocks on the village green add a touch of quaint severity. The Queen's Head is the best pub for lunch.

TETBURY ST8993

🏛 ⚘ A splendid raised **market house**, some interesting little lanes, quite a few antique shops and craft workshops, and decent food in the Crown.

🏛 **Chavenage** 🏠 (2m NW of Tetbury) Friendly, unspoilt, 16th-c manor house with entertaining tours by the owner. It's a popular location for TV programmes, providing a backdrop for characters from *Poirot* to *Casualty*. Shop, disabled access to ground floor only; open pm Easter Sun and Mon, then pm Thurs, Sun and bank hols May–Sept; (01666) 502329; *£4. Out this way the Gumstool (A46/A4135) has very good food.

TEWKESBURY SO8832

★ 🏛 ♖ † Severn-side town, site of the last battle in the Wars of the Roses in 1471, still full of attractive half-timbered medieval buildings in a maze of little alleyways. Two of these old places now house **museums**. Most impressive is the **abbey**, its massively confident Norman tower one of the finest in existence. Also splendid vaulting, some 14th-c stained glass, and regular concerts. The historic Bell Hotel and (simpler) ancient Black Bear are good for lunch.

THAMES & SEVERN CANAL
SO9303

⌂ The rich, steeply sheltered valleys around Stroud make up a complicated landscape, seen to best advantage for example between Chalford and Sapperton. The derelict canal here is atmospherically overgrown, although its towpath survives as an attractive wooded walkway; the Crown at Frampton Mansell, Butchers Arms at Oakridge Lynch or Daneway at Sapperton are useful jumping-off points.

THORNBURY ST6390

⚛ **Oldbury Power Station** Tours of nuclear power station, with hands-on displays, multi-media show, and nature trail. Shop, disabled access (not on tour); cl Nov–Feb (01454) 419899; free. The Anchor at Oldbury-on-Severn has good food.

TOCKINGTON ST6187

🕸 🍴 🍺 ★ **Oldown** (B4461) Lively country park with good adventure play areas for older children – lots of rope bridges, tube slides and climbing nets. Play area for younger children too, though they'll probably get more out of the animals and demonstrations at the farm. Several picnic areas, pleasant walks, summer pick-your-own, and excellent farm shop – organic meat, local cheeses, home-made honey and so on. Meals, snacks, shop, disabled access; cl Mon (exc bank hols), and winter (exc shop and restaurant); (01454) 413605; £4. The quiet village itself is attractive, with good-value food in the Swan.

TODDINGTON SP0432

🚂 **Gloucestershire–Warwickshire Railway** Steam and diesel train trips through around six miles of quiet countryside, departing from restored GWR stations either here or at Winchcombe. Snacks, shop, good disabled access (though watch out for the potholes in the car park); phone for timetable (01242) 621405; around £6.50. They stop nr the Harvest Home at Greet and the Royal Oak at Gretton, both doing good food.

TWIGWORTH SO8422

🏠 🔲 **Nature in Art** (Wallsworth Hall, A38) In an imposing Georgian mansion, a growing collection of well displayed paintings, sculpture and mosaics inspired by nature – more interesting than you'd expect – artists represented include Picasso, Henry Moore and Graham Sutherland. Readers very much enjoy coming here. Good meals and snacks, shop, disabled access; cl Mon (exc bank hols), 24–26 Dec; (01452) 731422; £3.10.

ULEY ST7898

★ ⌂ 🏚 Attractive former weaving village with some 18th-c or older stone houses; the Old Crown is good value (ditto its bedrooms), and a good base for walkers. **Uley Tumulus** (off B4066 N) Quite daunting 55-metre (180-ft) long burial mound known as Hetty Pegler's Tump, with stone central passage and three burial chambers; key from nearby house.

🏠 🕸 🐸 **Owlpen Manor** (B4066, just E) Charming Tudor manor house, with

lovely formal gardens and peaceful woodland. Restaurant; open pm daily (exc Mon) Apr–Oct; (01453) 860261; £4.50. Good views from this B-road.

WESTBURY-ON-SEVERN SO7114

✝ 🕸 **Westbury Court** Formal Dutch garden with canals, yew topiary, etc, restored to its 1700s layout using pre-1700 cultivars inc old fruit varieties. Disabled access; cl Mon (exc bank hols), Tues, Good Fri, and all Nov–Mar; (01452) 760461; £2.80; NT. The Red Lion has good generous food, by the **church** with its unusual detached tower. The village is a good spot for catching the Severn Bore.

WESTONBIRT ST8589

🕸 ⅄ **Westonbirt Arboretum** 🔲 Over 18,000 numbered trees and shrubs fill the 17 miles of pathways at this magnificent collection, begun in 1829. Outstanding in spring and autumn, but worth a stop any time, with lots of wildlife hidden away amongst the trees. Meals, snacks, shop, disabled access; open all year, though visitor centre cl late Dec–Feb; (01666) 880220; £4. The Hare & Hounds is handy for food.

WINCHCOMBE SP0228

★ ✝ ❋ Very peaceful and photogenic – once the capital of Mercia, now worth a stop for a look at the **church** with its grotesque and sometimes rather rude gargoyles, or just to soak up the tranquil atmosphere. The Plaisterers Arms (High St) has good food, and there are interesting craft and other shops here. Splendid views of the area from Belas Knap.

🛢 **Folk & Police Museum** In the old town hall, this has a sometimes surprising collection of British and international police uniforms. Shop; cl Sun, and Nov–Mar; 80p.

🏚 ✝ 🍺 **Hailes Abbey** (Hailes, off B4632) Graceful ruins of a 13th-c Cistercian abbey, once a centre for pilgrims who flocked to see a phial containing what they believed to be Christ's blood. Walkman tour, shop, some disabled access; cl winter wkdys; (01242) 602398; £2.60; NT. The Harvest Home at Greet has the best food nearby, but Hayles Fruit Farm down the road is good for snacks, and has **pick-your-own**.

✤ ⚑ **Railway Museum & Garden** (Gloucester St) Victorian garden full of lovingly rescued railway memorabilia inc booking office, working signals and signal box. Snacks, shop, disabled access; usually open wknd pms Easter–Oct and daily in Aug, plus Weds–Fri in between, and second Sun of month in winter; (01242) 620641; £2.25.

🏰 ▣ ✤ ⚘ **Sudeley Castle & Gardens** (off B4632) The owners of this delightful old house recently ran into controversy with their plans to convert an old farm on the estate into a new visitor centre, which villagers argue, would make local facilities redundant. As we went to press, a decision had not yet been made. Once home to Catherine Parr, the luckiest of Henry VIII's wives, the remains of the original medieval castle were skilfully blended into a 19th-c reconstruction. Rich furnishings, porcelain and tapestries, and notable paintings by Turner, Van Dyck and Rubens. The eight gardens are splendid, and include a knot garden constructed using flowers shown on a 16th-c tapestry on view in the library; a former workshop adjacent to the castle houses an exhibition on lace. Meals, snacks, shop and specialist plant centre, disabled access to garden; house open Apr–Oct (gardens from Mar); (01242) 604357; £6, £4.50 grounds and exhibition only. There's a working pottery nearby (cl winter Suns).

WOTTON-UNDER-EDGE
ST7693

★ ✝ ♪ More small town than village, and full of charm, with a fine Schreider organ in its church, a little **heritage centre**, and some handsome old buildings; the B4058 is a good drive.

WYE VALLEY SO5309

❈ ◠ The lower Wye Valley on the W side of the Forest of Dean cuts through a gorge giving some very picturesque views. As there are few crossing points, and the scenery away from the gorge is relatively unspectacular, walks along it are generally of the there-and-back sort. On the Gloucestershire side the valley is tracked by the Offa's Dyke Path; the Wye Valley Walk takes in the western bank. S of Monmouth, the A466 tracks through the valley below the paths.

❈ ◠ **Devil's Pulpit** A great viewpoint on the Offa's Dyke Path, where trees frame a perfect vista of Tintern Abbey far below on the opposite bank of the Wye.

❈ ◠ 🏛 **The Kymin** Can be climbed from May Hill just across the river border opposite Monmouth; at the summit is the Naval Temple, a quaint rustic conceit put up in 1800 to commemorate admirals of the Napoleonic Wars.

◠ ❈ **Wintour's Leap** A highlight of the Offa's Dyke Path: a sheer cliff over the Wye N of Chepstow, with dizzy views downwards.

YANWORTH SP0713

★ An attractive village, especially at daffodil time.

🏛 ⚐ ◷ ◠ **Chedworth Roman Villa** The best example of a 2nd-c Roman house in Britain, excavated in 1864 and nicely set in secluded woodland. Well preserved rooms, bath-houses and 4th-c mosaics, with smaller remains in museum. Shop, some disabled access; cl Mon (exc bank hols), and Dec–Feb (exc first wknd in Dec); (01242) 890256; £3.40; NT. The Mill at Withington and Seven Tuns in Upper Chedworth are quite handy for lunch – and the walk from each is very picturesque and unspoilt, with Chedworth Woods providing further scope for short walks.

★ **Other attractive villages**, all with decent pubs, include Alderton SP0033, Almondsbury ST6084, Amberley SO8401, Bisley SO9005, Bledington SP2422, Broad Campden SP1637, Broadwell SP2027, the Duntisbournes SO9709, Ebrington SP1840, Ewen SU0097, Great Barrington SP2013 (good cheap bedrooms at the Fox, lovely walks), Great Rissington SP1917, Lower Swell SP1725, Meysey Hampton SU1199, Nether Westcote SP2120, Slad SO8707 (the setting for Laurie Lee's *Cider With Rosie*), Somerford Keynes SU0195, South Woodchester (particularly for the views) SO8302, Todenham SP2436, Wick ST7072 (pleasant walks) and Willersey SP1039. Though there's no pub to recommend there, Saintbury SP1139 is a winner when the daffodils are out. The B4060 N of Chipping Sodbury ST7282 and the side roads through Hawkesbury ST7786 and Hillesley ST7689 take you through attractive Cotswoldy scenery. † Many villages have most **attractive churches**, few of them as yet locked. Cirencester is a good base for planning circuits of these. One such group E of the town consists of Ampney Crucis SP0602, Ampney St Peter SP0801, Ampney St Mary SP0802, Down Ampney SP1097 (Vaughan Williams was the vicar's son) and Hampnett SP1015. Another group, NW of Cirencester, has Elkstone SO9612, Duntisbourne Abbots SO9707, Duntisbourne Rouse SO9806, Daglingworth SO9905 (with its finely preserved Saxon carving of Christ on the cross), Stratton SP0103 and Baunton SP0204.

Where to eat

BIRDLIP SO9214 **Kingshead House** *(01452) 862299* 17th-c former coaching inn, with lovely English/French cooking using the best fresh produce (home-grown herbs), impeccable service, and good wines; cl pm Sun, Mon; disabled access. **£33|£8**.

BLOCKLEY SP1634 **Crown** *(01386) 700245* Smart and civilised Elizabethan stone inn with very good food in the bar or one of two restaurants (marvellous fresh fish), lots of good wines; comfortable lounge bar, attractive split-level hotel bar; children allowed if well behaved; pretty bdrms. **£40|£6.95**.

BOURTON-ON-THE-WATER SP1620 **Vernes Restaurant** *Riverside (01451) 822005* Pretty 17th-c cottage in a charming village, with enjoyable light breakfast, lunch and early evening meals, all-day savouries, and cream teas; disabled access. **£16|£5**.

BROAD CAMPDEN SP1637 **Bakers Arms** *(01386) 840515* Atmospheric ex-granary in a tranquil village; good-value bar food (inc children's menu), a fine range of real ales, cosy, beamed bar, log fires, friendly cats, pleasant service, and a nice garden; cl pm, pm 26 Dec. **£4.95**.

CHELTENHAM SO9421 **Champignon Sauvage** *24–26 Suffolk Rd (01242) 573449* Classic French cooking in quietly and simply decorated restaurant, with helpful service and good thoughtful wine list; cl Sun, Mon, 2 wks Christmas, 2 wks Jun; partial disabled access. **£23.75 lunch, £40.25 dinner**.

CHIPPING CAMPDEN SP1539 **Forbes Brasserie** *High St (01386) 840330* Fine 17th-c hotel, with stylish and attractive brasserie offering good interesting meals and light snacks, plus morning coffee and afternoon tea – more formal restaurant, too; pretty bdrms; cl 3 days Christmas; partial disabled access. **£16|£6.50**.

CIRENCESTER SP0201 **Swan Yard Café** *6 Swan Yard (01285) 641300* Popular with shoppers, this small simple family-run café has friendly service, and tasty, very good-value, totally home-made food (inc vegetarian choices); cl Sun in Jan and Feb; disabled access. **£13|£4.95**.

COLN ST ALDWYNS SP1405 **New Inn** *(01285) 750651* Civilised, ivy-covered inn, with beautifully presented restaurant-standard food served in a relaxed pubby atmosphere; attractively decorated rooms, a central log fire, well kept real ales and good wines, a no smoking restaurant, and split-level garden; nice surrounding countryside and walks; comfortable bdrms; children over 10. **£32.25|£10**.

DRYBROOK SO6518 **Cider Press** *(01594) 544472* Enjoyable little country restaurant specialising in delicious, interestingly cooked fresh fish, often using home-grown herbs; free-range meat dishes, too, plus lovely puddings and cheeses, and reasonably priced wines; cl Tues, and early Jan; disabled access. **£25**.

GRETTON SP0131 **Royal Oak** *(01242) 602477* Enjoyable pub with bare-boarded and flagstoned rooms, beams, old prints and a mix of pews and various chairs; a no smoking dining conservatory, friendly young service, well kept real ales, and good food; seats on a flower-filled terrace and more on a lawn; cl 25–26 Dec; disabled access. **£18.50|£5.95**.

GUITING POWER SP0924 **Hollow Bottom** *(01451) 850392* Beamed pub run by licensees with racing connections, log fire in main bar, flagstoned public bar, friendly staff, decent bar food, afternoon teas, well kept beer, and separate restaurant; good nearby walks. **£18|£5.50.**

KILKENNY SP0018 **Kilkeney Inn** *(01242) 820341* Comfortable dining pub, airy and spacious, with extended and modernised bar (drinking area at one end), lovely food that changes twice daily (best to book), well kept ales, excellent range of wines, and no smoking dining conservatory; cl pm Sun Jan–Mar, 25–26 Dec; children must be well behaved; disabled access. **£21.75|£6.25.**

KINGSCOTE ST8196 **Hunters Hall** *(01453) 860393* Civilised, creeper-covered old inn with some fine old furniture and big log fires in high-beamed connecting rooms, good bar and restaurant food, excellent breakfasts, and quite a few wines by the glass; big garden with play area; bdrms; disabled access. **£20|£5.**

LOWER ODDINGTON SP2325 **Fox** *(01451) 870555* Carefully restored and elegant inn with well presented, imaginative food, a superb wine list, well kept real ales, fresh flowers and open fire in neat rooms, a lovely dining room, and a relaxed atmosphere; cl 25 Dec, 31 Dec; disabled access. **£19.50|£6.50.**

MORETON-IN-MARSH SP2032 **Marsh Goose** *(01608) 652111* Cotswold stone house with local artists' work on the walls in the several eating areas, good inventive cooking inc lovely puddings, a thoughtful wine list, and quick, young staff; weekly cookery lessons; cl pm Sun, Mon; disabled access. **£35.50|£10.**

NAILSWORTH ST8599 **William's Bistro** *3 Fountain St (01453) 835507* Marvellous delicatessen with good-value bistro in a back extension; cheerful and informal atmosphere and décor, delicious interesting fish dishes (a few non-fishy things too), efficient service even when really busy, and fairly priced wines; cl Sun, Mon, Tues after bank hols, Good Fri, 2 wks over Christmas. **£25.**

NORTHLEACH SP1114 **Red Lion** *Market Pl (01451) 860251* Good-value, well presented, generous food in comfortable and friendly pub, with a straightforward bar, open fire, well kept ales, and friendly service; no food pm Mon; disabled access. **£16|£5.**

PAINSWICK SO8609 **Country Elephant** *New St (01452) 813564* Popular little restaurant open for morning coffee and summer afternoon tea as well as lunch and dinner; delicious interesting food, good wines, and friendly service; no smoking in restaurant, but can do so in bar/lounge; big summer garden; cl pm Sun, Mon, 1 wk Christmas; disabled access. **£25|£7.**

PAXFORD SP1837 **Churchill** *(01386) 594000* Under the same ownership as the Marsh Goose, Moreton-in-Marsh, this quaint Cotswold-stone pub has a restaurant extension, small side drinking bar with a proper pubby feel, good log fire, assorted tables and chairs on flagstones, particularly interesting modern cooking, well kept real ales, and fine wines. **£20.50|£9.50.**

SOUTHROP SP1903 **Swan** *(01367) 850205* Civilised, creeper-covered, old stone-tiled pub in a pretty village, with good interesting food inc delicious ice-creams, a respectable wine list, no smoking restaurant, friendly service, and log fires; cl pm Sun. **£20|£4.75.**

TETBURY ST8494 **Gumstool** *(01666) 890391* Bustling pubby bistro (actually part of rambling Calcot Manor) with stripped pine, flagstones, and hop bines, neatly modern furnishings, a relaxed but civilised atmosphere, particularly interesting food, well kept real ales, a thoughtful choice of wines by the glass, and good service; comfortable bdrms. **£22|£7.95.**

WOODCHESTER SO8302 **Ram** *(01453) 873329* Bustling cheerful pub with spectacular valley views from the terrace, attractive beamed bar, good bar food inc interesting daily specials, prompt friendly service, and lots of real ales; partial disabled access. **£13.60|£5.45.**

Special thanks to B and K Hypher.

Gloucestershire Calendar

Some of these dates were provisional as we went to press. Please check information with the telephone numbers provided.

FEBRUARY

4 **Cheltenham** Folk Festival – *till 6 February* (01242) 227979

MARCH

14 **Cheltenham** National Hunt Racing Festival – *till 16 March* (01242) 513014

APRIL

8 **Gotherington** Midland Hill-climb Championship at Prescott Hill – *till 9 April* (01242) 673136; **Tewkesbury** Cheltenham Bach Choir at the Abbey (01684) 850959

27 **Cheltenham** Jazz Festival – *till 30 April* (01242) 227979

29 **Tewkesbury** Cheltenham Choral Society at the Abbey (01684) 850959

MAY

6 **Gotherington** British Hill-climb Championship at Prescott Hill – *till 7 May* (01242) 673136

7 **Randwick** Cheese Rolling – after church service *at 10.30am* three cheeses are blessed and rolled anticlockwise round the church three times. One cheese is cut and distributed, the other two are kept *till the following Sat* when they are rolled down a slope to open the Randwick Wap (01453) 766782

13 **Randwick** Randwick Wap (see above): carnival, maypole and Morris dancing (01453) 766782; **Tewkesbury** Tewkesbury Choral Society at the Abbey (01684) 850959

28 **Gloucester** Town and Country Show at the Showground – *till 29 May* (01242) 256446

29 **Brockworth** Coopers Hill Cheese Rolling: locals chase cheeses down steep hill *from 6pm* (01452) 421188; **Tetbury** Woolsack Races: teams of men and women race up and down steep Gumstool Hill carrying 65lb woolsacks, plus medieval market and street entertainers (01452) 425673; **Tewkesbury** Fête at the Abbey (01684) 850959

JUNE

1 **Bisley** Blessing of the Wells at the Parish Church (01452) 770056

2 **Chipping Campden** Robert Dovers Cotswold Olimpick Games at Dovers Hill: traditional sports, bands, dancing, torchlight procession (01384) 274041

3 **Chipping Campden** Scuttlebrook Wake with street entertainment, Morris dancing and procession (01384) 274041; **Gotherington** Classic Car Hill-climb at Prescott Hill – *till 4 June* (01242) 673136

24 **Gotherington** Midland Hill-climb Championship at Prescott Hill – *till 25 June* (01242) 673136

30 **Newent** Flower Festival – *till 2 July* (01594) 812389

Gloucestershire Calendar (cont.)

JULY

1 **Cheltenham** International Festival of Music and Fringe Festival – *till 16 July* (01242) 521621; **Stroud** Show at Stratford Park – *till 2 July* (01453) 751191
4 **Hailes** Music Festival – *till 30 July* (01242) 602379
8 **Tewkesbury** Medieval Fayre – *till 9 July* (01684) 294939
15 **Tewkesbury** Herb Day at the Abbey (01684) 850959
21 **Tewkesbury** Musica Deo Sacra at the Abbey – *till 6 August* (01684) 850959
22 **Fairford** International Air Tattoo – *till 23 July* (01285) 713456

AUGUST

5 **Gotherington** Vintage Sports Car Club Hill-climb at Prescott Hill – *till 6 August* (01242) 673136; **Minchinhampton** Horse Trials at Gatcombe Park – *till 6 August* (01937) 844265
26 **Westonbirt** Festival of Wood: 100 stands, demonstrations and attractions – *till 28 August* (01666) 880220

SEPTEMBER

2 **Gotherington** British and Midland Hill-climb Championship at Prescott Hill – *till 3 September* (01242) 673136; **Moreton-in-Marsh** Agricultural and Horse Show (01608) 650881
9 **Stow-on-the-Wold** Day of Dance: Morris dancing around the town *from 11am* (01451) 831082
16 **Painswick** Ancient Clypping Ceremony at St Mary's Church (01452) 812334
23 **Cirencester** Cotswold Country Fair – *till 24 September* (01285) 652007

OCTOBER

9 **Cheltenham** International Festival of Literature: 50th anniversary – *till 25 October* (01242) 227979; **Tewkesbury** Mop Fair: mainly a funfair – *till 10 October* (01684) 295027

DECEMBER

9 **Tewkesbury** Tewkesbury Choral Society Concert at the Abbey (01684) 850959
26 **Gloucester** Mummers and Morris dancers in the Cathedral precincts and New Inn courtyard *at midday* (01453) 759921

Please let us know what you think of places in the *Guide*. Use the report forms at the back of the book or simply write us a letter.

HAMPSHIRE

Attractive countryside, especially the New Forest; plenty of interesting places to visit, for all ages.

The New Forest countryside, mainly rolling heathland, is great for free-form wandering among ponies and deer. Its coast has sheltered yachting harbours, the pleasant waterside town of Lymington with warm Georgian buildings (the rest of Hampshire's coastline is largely built up), and the interesting Bucklers Hard. Excellent places to visit in and around it include Beaulieu with its great range of subsidiary attractions, the farm and nature centres at Ashurst, the grounds of waterside Exbury (irresistible in late spring), the newer gardens of Spinners at Boldre (exciting for plantsmen), and Breamore House.

Portsmouth has a splendid range of interesting places to visit, especially connected with ships and warfare, ancient and modern. A vast programme of harbour rejuvenation is now under way in the city. Top of its list of other attractions must be its good Sea Life Centre – especially since this year's price cut. Winchester is a lovely city, with a charming old quarter around its cathedral, and plenty of opportunities for strolls nearby; a possibility for a quiet city break. Though Southampton is big and busy, it has some surprisingly fine medieval heritage (including a new entry this year, the splendidly refurbished Medieval Merchant's House).

Elsewhere, there are some magnificent houses and gardens. Broadlands near Romsey, Hinton Ampner, the Vyne at Sherborne St John (they've now opened the bedrooms and domestic areas), Stratfield Saye and the tranquil ruins of Basing House are all very rewarding. Mottisfont Abbey has wonderful old-fashioned roses, Houghton Lodge, just upriver towards Stockbridge, is a peaceful spot, and the gardens and arboretum at Ampfield are very fine. The Sandham Memorial Chapel at Burghclere is thought by some to be the greatest masterpiece of 20th-c British art.

First-class family outings include Marwell Zoo at Colden Common, one of Britain's finest (there are new owl aviaries and a nocturnal house); the lovely Watercress Line from Alresford (they now do steam trips to other parts of the country); the cheerful Hollycombe Steam Collection near Liphook; and the working Iron Age farm at Chalton, the imaginative Hawk Conservancy at Weyhill, and the farm park near Andover. Paultons Park at Ower is a treat for younger children.

Inland, a broad belt of gentle countryside stretches from Andover, Stockbridge and Romsey along the Test Valley in the west through Winchester and Alresford, to Alton and Petersfield in the east. This is a quietly charming mix of rolling, blowy, chalk downland, a patchwork of hedged fields and clumps of steep beechwood, the rich valleys of the clear chalk streams, and attractive small villages often of brick and flint, with plenty of peaceful walking opportunities.

Where to stay

BEAULIEU SU3902 **Montagu Arms** *Palace Lane, Beaulieu SO42 7ZL* (01590) 612324 **£125**, plus special breaks; 24 individually decorated rms. Attractive creeper-clad hotel with a lovely terraced garden; comfortable sitting room, conservatory lounge, very good food in the beamed restaurant, and attentive staff; their health club is in the village; they also run the village shop, post office and bakery; children over 5 in evening restaurant (high tea for little ones).

CHERITON SU5828 **Flower Pots** *Cheriton, Alresford SO24 0QQ* (01962) 771318 *£52.50; 5 rms. Unspoilt and quietly comfortable village local run by a very friendly family, with 2 pleasant little bars, a log fire, decent bar food, own-brew beers, and old-fashioned seats on the pretty lawns; no accommodation 24–26 Dec, 31 Dec, 1 Jan; children over 12.

DROXFORD SU6018 **White Horse** *Droxford, Southampton SO3 1PB* (01489) 877490 **£50**; 3 rms, 1 with own bthrm. Rambling 16th-c inn with a relaxed atmosphere, small cosy lounge bars, log fires, a sizeable public bar, good, reasonably priced bar food, no smoking restaurant areas, well kept real ales, and seats in a flower-filled courtyard; no accommodation 25–26 Dec, 31 Dec; no dogs.

EASTLEIGH SU4317 **Park Farm** *Stoneham Lane SO50 9HS* (023) 8061 2960 *£35; 3 rms, shared bthrm. Lots of country walks around these converted coaching stables, coarse fishing in their own lake, and evening meals by arrangement.

HURSTBOURNE TARRANT SU3954 **Esseborne Manor** *Hurstbourne Tarrant, Andover SP11 0ER* (01264) 736444 *£120, plus special breaks; 15 individually decorated rms. Small, stylish Victorian manor with a calm and relaxed atmosphere, comfortable lounge and snug little bar, good modern cooking, and friendly staff; neat gardens with tennis, croquet and golf; disabled access.

LYMINGTON SZ3094 **Efford Cottage** *Everton, Lymington SO41 0JD* (01590) 642315 *£46, plus special breaks; 3 comfortable rms. Spacious family home nr the New Forest, with marvellous breakfasts inc freshly baked bread and home-made jams, optional evening meal (jacket and tie for men), and good parking; no children; well behaved dogs welcome by arrangement.

LYMINGTON SZ3097 **Passford House** *Mount Pleasant Lane, Lymington SO41 8LS* (01590) 682398 **£100**, plus special breaks; 55 neatly kept, pretty rms. Attractive hotel by the New Forest, with a comfortable panelled lounge (3 others, too), cocktail bar, open fires, and excellent service; 9 acres of gardens and parkland with indoor and outdoor swimming pools, tennis, croquet, and putting.

LYMINGTON SZ3295 **Stanwell House** *High St, Lymington SO41 9AA* (01590) 677123 **£95**; 30 pretty rms. Handsome town house with a comfortable, attractively furnished lounge, cosy little bar, and good imaginative food; also a pretty walled back garden; 50-ft yacht for charter.

LYNDHURST SU3107 **Parkhill** *Beaulieu Rd, Lyndhurst SO43 7FZ* (023) 8028 2944 **£115**, plus special breaks; 20 carefully furnished rms, some overlooking the lawns. 13th-c hunting lodge rebuilt by the Duke of Clarence in the 18th c, in parkland with fine views; comfortable lounges, antiques, flowers, and a civilised atmosphere; good food in the attractive dining room, and friendly, professional staff.

MIDDLE WALLOP SU2837 **Fifehead Manor** *Middle Wallop, Stockbridge SO20 8EG* (01264) 781565 **£125**, plus special breaks; 17 spacious rms. Friendly and comfortable old brick manor house in several acres of lovely gardens, with a restful atmosphere, pleasant small lounge and bar, fine food in the candlelit restaurant, enjoyable breakfasts, and friendly staff; croquet; disabled access.

MOCKBEGGAR SU1609 **Plantation Cottage** *Mockbeggar, Ringwood BH24 3NL* (01425) 477443 *£55; 3 rms. Charming 200-year-old cottage with 3 acres of gardens and paddocks and nice breakfasts; no smoking; lots of pubs and restaurants nearby; self-catering cottage; no children.

NEW MILTON SZ2293 **Chewton Glen** *Christchurch Rd, New Milton BH25 6QS* (01425) 275341 **£350 inc dinner;** 53 really beautiful rms. Luxurious hotel in lovely grounds with fine antiques in sumptuous day rooms, excellent modern French cooking, and very good service; gardens inc 9-hole golf course, swimming pool, tennis (2 indoor courts as well) and croquet; also health club with indoor swimming pool, gym, saunas, treatment rooms; children over 7; disabled access.

NEW MILTON SZ2497 **Yew Tree Farm** *Bashley Common Rd, New Milton BH25 5SH* (01425) 611041 **£60**; 2 lovely spacious rms. Marvellously comfortable and well run traditional thatched smallholding on the edge of the New Forest; small cosy hall, friendly welcome, extensive breakfasts (taken in bedroom), and good home-made dinners (if required) using top quality produce; riding nearby; no smoking, children or dogs.

PORTSMOUTH SZ6299 **Fortitude Cottage** *51 Broad St, Old Town, Portsmouth PO1 2JD* (023) 9282 3748 **£46**; 3 neat and attractive rms. Comfortable B & B in a cottage named after an old ship, with a pretty, beamed breakfast room overlooking fishing boats; no evening meals but places nearby; cl 25–26 Dec; children over 9.

PORTSMOUTH SU6399 **Sally Port** *High St, Old Town, Portsmouth PO1 2LU* (023) 9282 1860 **£65**, plus special breaks; 10 rms. Beautifully kept 16th-c inn in a quiet spot, with good food and very friendly, efficient service; said to have been a favourite of Nelson; disabled access.

ROCKBOURNE SU1117 **Shearings** *Rockbourne, Fordingbridge SP6 3NA* (01725) 518256 **£52**; 3 rms plus garden annexe. Beside a winter stream, this warmly welcoming and pretty 16th-c thatched cottage has inglenook fireplaces, ancient beams (some nearly 1,000 years old), and a comfortable sitting room; good pub just up the road; cl mid-Dec–end Jan; children over 12; no dogs.

ROMSEY SU3321 **Spursholt House** *Salisbury Rd, Romsey SO51 6DJ* (01794) 512229 **£50**; 3 rms with antiques, fireplaces, and sofas. Lovely welcoming house with beautiful garden and a view of Romsey Abbey; an open fire in the characterful sitting room, no evening meals, and warmly friendly owners; cl Christmas–New Year.

ROTHERWICK SU7155 **Tylney Hall** *Rotherwick, Basingstoke RG27 9AZ* (01256) 764881 **£155**, plus special breaks; 110 comfortable, well equipped rms. Grand Victorian mansion in 66 acres of gardens and parkland, with gracious day rooms, ornate plasterwork, oak panelling, oil paintings, log fires in big ornate fireplaces; interesting food in the candlelit restaurant, and good, attentive service; tennis, golf, indoor and outdoor swimming pools; gym and sauna; disabled access.

SPARSHOLT SU4431 **Lainston House** *Sparsholt, Winchester SO21 2LT* (01962) 863588 **£171**, plus wknd breaks; 37 spacious, individually decorated rms. Close to Winchester, this elegant William and Mary hotel has 63 acres of fine parkland, a relaxing, elegant lounge, panelled bar and restaurant, flowers and paintings, a fine wine list and good British cooking; disabled access.

SWAY SZ2798 **Nurses Cottage** *Station Rd, Sway, Lymington SO41 6BA* (01590) 683402 **£90 inc dinner**, plus special breaks; 3 rms. Small immaculately kept cottage with a comfortable lounge and dining room, enjoyable evening food using seasonal produce, a thoughtful wine list, hearty breakfasts; very helpful owner, and a neat garden; cl mid-Nov–mid-Dec; children over 10.

THRUXTON SU2945 **May Cottage** *Thruxton, Andover SP11 8LZ* (01264) 771241 *£50*; 4 rms. Early Georgian house in a quiet village, with friendly owners, residents' sitting room, good breakfasts, afternoon tea with home-made cake in a pretty garden, and dinner by arrangement; no smoking; cl Christmas; children over 6.

WICKHAM SU5711 **Old House** *The Square, Wickham, Fareham PO17 5JG* (01329) 833049 **£80**, plus special breaks; 8 rms. Lovely early Georgian house under the same charming owners for 27 years, with beamed and panelled rooms, antiques, fresh flowers, and open fires; reliably good French cooking in the restaurant (once the timber-framed outhouse and stables), and a pretty back garden; cl 2 wks Christmas.

WINCHESTER SU4729 **Hotel du Vin & Bistro** *14 Southgate St, Winchester SO23 9EF* (01962) 841414 **£118**; 23 rms, real quality, and each sponsored by a well known wine company with relevant paintings, labels and old photographs. An engaging early 18th-c town house with enthusiastic owners and hard-working staff, a deeply comfortable sitting room, 2 relaxed and pretty eating areas with good bistro-style cooking and an exceptional wine list, and a lovely walled garden for summer dining; disabled access.

WINCHESTER SU4828 **Wykeham Arms** *75 Kingsgate St, Winchester SO23 9PE (01962) 853834* **£79.50;** 13 well equipped attractive rms. Very well run, smart old town inn, close to the cathedral, with very interestingly furnished buoyant bars, 2 small dining rooms serving an excellent daily changing menu (very good breakfasts, too), fine wines (lots by the glass), and prompt, friendly service; several no smoking areas; cl 25 Dec; no children.

To see and do

HAMPSHIRE Family Attraction of the Year

🐎 ♨ ❉ **FAREHAM** SU6007 **Fort Nelson** (Downend Rd) Children can get a surprising amount of pleasure from this big restored 19th-c fort, built in response to fears of an attack from France. And though it's part of the Royal Armouries Museum, housing the national collections of guns and artillery, you don't have to be massively interested in military history to enjoy it. They used to call it the noisiest museum in the world, thanks mainly to the roar of the 2 huge cannon fired twice a day, usually at noon and 3pm; there may be other bangs, booms and crashes throughout the day, with the lingering smell of gunpowder adding to the atmosphere. Children aren't discouraged from clambering over the building and even some of the exhibits, so for energetic youngsters it's not unlike an enormous adventure playground. Plenty of underground tunnels to investigate, long enough and dark enough to be spooky, but light enough to be safe. Running round the ramparts is ideal for letting off steam as well – altogether the site has 19 acres to explore. The place really comes to life on their frequent re-enactment days, usually twice a month in summer (best to ring for dates); depending when you come, you might encounter Roman legionaries or World War II troops, armed with appropriate period weapons. Perhaps the biggest draw for families is the fort's exceptional good value: as part of the national scheme to encourage wider access to museums, children are admitted free (as are OAPs from the start of the 2000 season). Families often spend around 3 hours here, but even if you pop in for only an hour or so it's an interesting place to visit without spending too much money. Guided tours at regular intervals; children may prefer to be accompanied by a hand-held acoustiguide (neither option has any extra charge). Good views of Portsmouth Harbour from the ramparts. Meals, snacks, shop, disabled access; cl Mon–Weds Nov–Mar; (01329) 233734; £4.25 (children free). The Osborne View (Hill Head) is a comfortable modern dining pub with superb views – and also handy for the beach and walks in Titchfield Haven nature reserve.

ALDERSHOT SU8651
✝ **Airborne Forces Museum** (Browning Barracks) The best of Aldershot's profusion of military museums (most of which are of rather specialist appeal), looking at the parachute forces. Lots to take in, with very traditional displays. Snacks, shop, some disabled access; cl Christmas and 1 Jan; (01252) 349619; £2.50.
♨ **Military Museum** (Queen's Ave) Quite well done, exploring the development of the local military camps and their impact on civilian and military

life. Shop, disabled access; cl Christmas–New Year; (01252) 314598; £2. The Swan out at Ash Vale is a decent dining pub.
ALRESFORD SU5832
🚂 🚃 ★ 🌾 **Watercress Line** One of the nicest steam railways in the country, with 10-mile trips between Alresford and Alton through wonderful countryside and its watercress beds. They try to create a pre-war feel, with stations decked out accordingly. Their Thomas the Tank Engine weeks around Easter and in Aug are extraordinarily

popular; several railways organise something similar, but the Thomas here is unusual in being built to the design and proportions in the books, and there may also be other characters such as James the Red Engine, Diesel and the Fat Controller. Properly called the Mid-Hants Railway, it has connections to Waterloo, and now runs special main line monthly trips to places as far away as Worcester and Canterbury. Meals, snacks, shop, disabled access; phone for timetable, (01962) 734866, no trains Nov–Jan (exc Dec Santa specials); £8. On some wkdys you can combine it with a visit to the modern Bass brewery at the Alton end, usually open only to groups (01420) 541177. Alresford itself is a charming little town, from the Roman ponds teeming with wildfowl in Old Alresford to the so-called New Alresford founded around 1200; good antiquarian bookshop here. The Globe overlooking the ponds does decent lunches, and the Café Cressdon is good. The Itchen road W through Ovington and Easton is pretty, the B3046 N shows high Hampshire farmland well, and the old road E past Ropley and Monkwood to Steep gives a fine downland impression.

ALTON SU7139

♔ ⚑ ✝ **Allen Gallery** (Church St) Superb collection of pottery, and a little herb garden. Snacks, shop, some disabled access; cl Sun, Mon; (01420) 82802; free. The town is the other terminus of the Watercress steam line (see Alresford). Bass Brewery (Turk St) offers wkdy tours (inc snacks) 11.30am–3pm and 7–10pm (not pm Fri); (01420) 541177; £8.50. A church bears scars from one of the last battles of the Civil War. The French Horn (The Butts) is a friendly food pub.

AMPFIELD SU3824

⚑ ⚙ ◠ **Sir Harold Hillier Gardens** (Jermyns Lane, off A31) Impressive collection of trees and shrubs, the biggest of its kind in Britain, covering 160 beautifully landscaped acres. Full of colour and surprises all year, and good walks and events (especially first Sun of month). Summer meals, snacks, nursery, disabled access; cl Christmas bank hols; (01794) 368787; £4.50 (£3.50 Nov–Mar). The White Horse nearby is a comfortable lunch break.

ANDOVER SU3847

🐖 🎣 **Finkley Down Farm Park** (just NE of Andover) Well laid out working farm with a wide range of animals and poultry inc rare breeds; they encourage you to touch the tamer animals, and there are varied activities every half hour. Also a countryside museum, adventure playground and picnic site. Readers rate this very highly, and it has lots for children (inc space for them to run around). Meals, snacks, shop, disabled access; cl Nov–mid-Mar; (01264) 352195; £4.50. There are well stocked **trout fishing** lakes around Andover including Rooksbury Mill. Poplar Farm (on A343 at Abbotts Ann) is a useful food stop.

⚱ **Museum of the Iron Age** Nr the church at the top of the impressive High St of this very extended country town, the museum looks particularly at finds from nearby Danebury Ring, giving a vivid impression of life for the pre-Roman Celts. Snacks, shop, limited disabled access; cl Sun (exc pm summer), and Mon (exc pm summer bank hols), and Christmas; (01264) 366283; *£1.50. There's an adjacent more general **museum** (open same hours, free).

! **Test Valley Tapestry** (Weyhill Rd – B3402) The local authority's conference room houses this remarkable textile, each of its many panels embroidered by a different village to show a scene relating to that community. Disabled access; generally open Mon lunchtimes and pm last Thurs each month – best to phone (01264) 368000 to check; free.

ASHMANSWORTH SU3758

❄ ◠ **Hampshire's high country** There are fine views from many of the lanes around Ashmansworth and Linkenholt – best explored by car, though there are good walks too. The Plough does simple home cooking.

ASHURST SU3310

🐖 **Longdown Dairy Farm** (Deerleap Lane) This friendly place has plenty of animals to feed; their herd of Jersey cows is milked from 2.30pm every day. There's a small play area. Snacks, shop, disabled access; cl Nov–Apr; (023) 8029 3326; £4.

✤ ♭ ♘ **New Forest Otter & Owl Park** (Longdown; off A326 nr Marchwood) Large collection of otters, owls and other indigenous wildlife; woodland nature trails. Meals, snacks, shop, disabled access; cl 25 Dec; (023) 8029 2408; £4.95. The Pilgrim is an attractive thatched dining pub.

AVINGTON SU5332

🏛 ❀ **Avington Park** Georgian mansion with Tudor origins, set in lovely parkland. Teas in the orangery, disabled access; open pm Sun and bank hols May–Sept; (01962) 779260; £3.50. The Bush at Ovington is a nicely placed nearby pub.

BASING SU6652

🏚 ❀ ◠ **Basing House Ruins** 🔲 Peaceful ruins of what was once the country's largest house, destroyed during a 2-year siege during the Civil War. Also remnants of a Norman castle, a 16th-c barn, dovecots, an exhibition explaining the eventful history of the site and a re-created 17th-c garden. Nice walks from here along the River Loddon. Shop, disabled access; open pm Weds–Sun and bank hols Apr–Sept; (01256) 467294; £1.50.

BASINGSTOKE SU6250

🎨 **Viables Craft Centre** Fourteen craft workshops housed in the grounds of an 18th-c timber granary; ceramics studio, craft gallery, miniature railway, and various courses and events throughout the year (ring for details). Meals, snacks, shop, disabled access; cl am, all Mon, and Jan–Easter; (01256) 473634; free.

BEAULIEU SU3802

🏰 ❗🏛 ❀ **Beaulieu Abbey** Justifiably popular family day out, its centrepiece is still the **National Motor Museum**, a collection that from humble beginnings has grown to become one of the most comprehensive in the world. Other features have a motoring theme too, inc a hands-on gallery about how cars work, and Wheels, probably the highlight for children – you sit in a pod-like vehicle and trundle through 100 years of motoring. For an extra £2 a simulator ride gives you a more robust driving experience. A monorail whizzes round the grounds, and in summer they usually have a daily Disneyland-style parade of vintage vehicles. Also go-kart-

style mini-bikes, radio-controlled cars, and some hi-tech arcade-style driving games. Meanwhile the Palace House is a fine old mansion based around the gatehouse of the huge Cistercian Abbey that stood here until the Reformation (still with what are thought to be the original monastic fan-vaulted ceilings). The surrounding lakeside parkland and gardens are rewarding to explore, with ruins of other abbey buildings, and an exhibition on the monks who lived here. Meals, snacks, shops, disabled access; cl 25 Dec; (01590) 612123; £9. In the village facing the Palace House gates, the Wine Press is popular for lunch, and a marked trail leads from it down to Bucklers Hard.

BEAULIEU ROAD STATION SU3506

◠ **New Forest walks** A good starting point, for its surrounding remote-feeling heaths.

BEDLAM BOTTOM SU6246

♘ ◠ Pleasant, partly wooded valley walks, particularly pretty in spring, just W of Ellisfield SU6345 (where the Fox has good food), with more downland walks above.

BEECH SU6838

✝ ♘ ◠ ❀ **Alton Abbey** (signed off the A339) The home of a community of Benedictine monks, in peaceful woodland, so a relaxing place for a stroll. The grounds have mature specimen trees and shrubs, especially rhododendrons and azaleas. The Sun at Bentworth does good food.

BINSTED SU7740

✝ **Binsted church** Where Field Marshal Montgomery is buried; after the war he lived a mile away at Islington Mill – a pretty spot. The Cedars has decent food.

BISHOP'S WALTHAM SU5517

🏚 🏛 **Bishop's Waltham Palace** Impressive ruins of the Bishop of Winchester's majestic 12th-c palace, with the remains of state apartments round a cloister court, and William of Wykeham's great hall and tower. Shop, snacks, disabled access to ground floor; cl Nov–Mar; (01489) 892460; £2. The Barleycorn (Basingwell St) has decent food, and the downs N of here between Owslebury, Beauworth and Warnford give scenic drives.

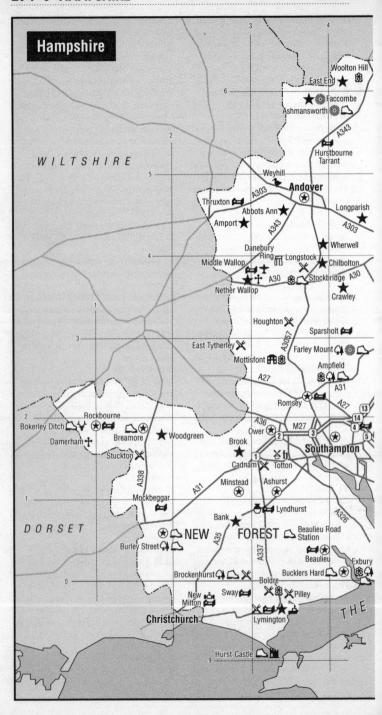

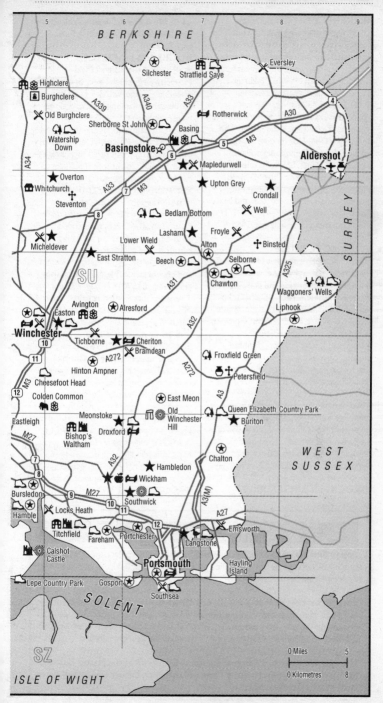

BERKSHIRE

Highclere
Burghclere
Old Burghclere
Watership Down

Silchester

Stratfield Saye

Rotherwick

Sherborne St John
Basing
Basingstoke

Mapledurwell

Upton Grey

Crondall

Overton
Whitchurch
Steventon

Well

Micheldever

Bedlam Bottom

Lasham
Lower Wield
Froyle
Alton
Binsted

East Stratton

Beech
Selborne
Chawton

Waggoners' Wells

Liphook

Avington
Easton
Alresford

Winchester
Tichborne
Cheriton
Bramdean

Hinton Ampner

Froxfield Green

Petersfield

Cheesefoot Head
Colden Common

Eastleigh

East Meon

Old Winchester Hill

Queen Elizabeth Country Park
Buriton

Meonstoke
Droxford
Bishop's Waltham

Chalton

WEST SUSSEX

Burseldon
Hamble

Hambledon
Wickham

Locks Heath
Southwick

Titchfield
Fareham
Portchester

Emsworth
Langstone

Calshot Castle

Portsmouth

Hayling Island

Lepe Country Park
Gosport
Southsea

SOLENT

SZ

ISLE OF WIGHT

ALDERSHOT

SURREY

0 Miles 5
0 Kilometres 8

BOKERLEY DITCH SU0419

⌂ ⚥ This dyke acted as a bulwark from raiders into Dorset in the 4th c; still impressive to walk along, it marks the county boundary and can be reached by walking up from Martin. Towards Pentridge Hill is a nature reserve.

BOLDRE SZ3298

🏵 **Spinners** (School Lane) Wonderful gardens created since the 1960s. The nursery is famed for its rare trees (especially maples and magnolias), shrubs and plants. Some disabled access; gardens open Tues–Sat mid-Apr–mid-Sept, or by appointment, nursery open all year exc Sun and Mon Sept–Apr; (01590) 673347; £1.50. The Red Lion (no children) is good for lunch.

BREAMORE SU1519

🏠🖼👶★⌂ **Breamore House** Late Elizabethan manor house, with fine furnishings, tapestries and paintings (mainly 17th- and 18th-c Dutch school), and a better than average countryside museum where children aren't left out – there's a maze and adventure playground. Snacks, shop, disabled access; open pm Tues, Weds, Sun and bank hols Apr–Sept, plus Thurs and Sat May–Sept, and daily in Aug; (01725) 512468; £5. The village has many thatched houses, and is within a pleasant walk of Breamore House – and the mysterious Mizmaze, cut in the turf at Breamore Woods. The home cooking at the Horse & Groom at Woodgreen is good, with more lovely wood and riverside walks.

BROCKENHURST SU2902

🐾 ⌂ **New Forest walks** Well placed for forest walks; you can also hire bicycles here.

BUCKLERS HARD SZ4099

★ 🏵 ⓗ ⚓ ⌂ **Bucklers Hard Maritime Museum** Very pretty little waterside village, with long red-roofed cottage rows flanking a wide, grassed waterside street. It was once an important centre for shipbuilding, and the **Maritime Museum** tells the story of the industry, right up to the voyages of Sir Francis Chichester. You have to pay to come into the village, though admission includes entry to the museum and the various other exhibitions and reconstructions dotted around, inc the carefully restored 18th-c homes of a shipwright and labourer, and a typical inn scene complete with costumed figures, smells and conversation. Meals, snacks, shop; cl 25 Dec; (01590) 616203; £3.20. There are summer **boat trips**, and the Master Builder's House is useful for lunch. A pleasant 2½-mile riverside walk takes you to Beaulieu.

BURGHCLERE SU4761

🖼 **Sandham Memorial Chapel** Stanley Spencer's moving masterpiece, built in memory of H W Sandham, killed in the World War I. The final resurrection scene is especially dramatic, best on a bright day as the room is quite dark. Open Weds–Sun Apr–Oct, wknds only Nov–Mar, and bank hols (cl following Weds); (01635) 278394; *£2; NT. The Carpenters Arms opposite is pleasant for lunch, with superb views.

Days Out

Army and Navy: D-Day Museum and Sea Life Centre, Portsmouth; lunch at the Still & West (Bath Sq); boat trip to Spitbank Fort; HMS *Victory* or *Mary Rose*; or spend a full day at Portsmouth's Historic Dockyard.

Escape to the Forest: New Forest Otter & Owl Park, Ashurst; Furzey Gardens, Minstead; picnic in the New Forest, or lunch at the Trusty Servant, Minstead; stroll or mountain bike ride in the New Forest, or Bolderwood/Rhinefield Ornamental Drives; Spinners garden, Boldre.

Hampshire's watery fringes: Bucklers Hard; lunch at the Master Builder's House there; Beaulieu National Motor Museum, or Exbury Gardens; if time, stroll in Lepe Country Park.

BURLEY STREET SU1904

🎏 🌥 **New Forest walks** A good
starting point for New Forest walks; the
White Buck, and the Queen's Head in
busier nearby Burley, are both handy
pubs.

BURSLEDON SU4911

🌥 🐖 🐷 ♟ ✗ **Manor Farm Country
Park** (Pylands Lane) Woodland and
riverside walks based around a
traditional working farm, with lots of
animals, crafts and activities, inc a forge
and a wheelwright. Meals, snacks, shop,
mostly disabled access; park open all
year, farm cl Nov–Easter exc Sun and
Feb half-term; (01489) 787055; £3.70.
There may be **boat trips** on some
summer Sats from here along the
Hamble. Bursledon also has a
windmill; open Sun and summer Sats.
The Jolly Sailor is a beautifully placed
food pub.

CALSHOT CASTLE SU4802

🏰 ✳ Down past the oil refineries and
power stations, this Tudor fort stands
on the end of the spit of land beyond
the tidal mudflats at the end of
Southampton Water; splendid views of
the shipping and the Isle of Wight. The
Jolly Sailor at Ashlett Creek nr Fawley is
a pleasant waterside food pub.

CHALTON SU7117

🎞 🐄 🐷 **Butser Ancient Farm**
(Bascombe Copse) Reconstructed Iron
Age farm, with crops, animals, crafts
and demonstrations. You can try your
hand at grinding corn on a stone, and
there's a Celtic maze (planted with
period herbs). Shop, disabled access; cl
Nov–Apr; (023) 9259 8838; £3. The
ancient Red Lion is good for lunch.

CHAWTON SU7037

🏛 🎎 🏵 🌥 **Jane Austen's House**
Readers really enjoy this unpretentious
17th-c house where the author lived
and worked between 1809 and 1817,
still with some of her letters and
possessions. Rooms are furnished in
period style, and the pleasant garden is
good for picnics. Good bookshop,
disabled access to ground floor and
garden; cl wkdys Jan and Feb, 25–26
Dec; (01420) 83262; £3. The Greyfriar
opposite has reasonably priced food,
and there are good walks here. Just up
the road, Chawton House, the former
home of Jane Austen's brother Edward,

will soon become a centre for the study
of early English women's writing.

CHEESEFOOT HEAD SU5327

🌥 (locally pronounced 'Chesford')
Good for walks; a natural amphitheatre
where Eisenhower and Montgomery
addressed the troops before the
Normandy invasion.

CHILBOLTON SU3940

★ An attractive village where the
common is being carefully preserved.
The Abbots Mitre (open all day Sun) is a
good pub.

COLDEN COMMON SU5121

🐘 🐦 🏵 **Marwell Zoological Park**
(Colden Common, off the A333
towards Bishop's Waltham) Too many
supposedly conservation-minded
animal attractions still shove their
animals into overcrowded cages or
enclosures, so it's particularly nice to
find one like this where – at least in
places – the tables are turned; visit the
lemurs for instance and they'll be
enjoying plenty of space and freedom
while you watch from covered
walkways. Other well conceived
viewing areas include a glass wall at the
end of the tiger enclosure (so they can
jump up at you in perfect safety) and
underwater windows into the Penguin
World. The Tropical House may be
familiar to dedicated zoo-watchers; it
used to be at the Windsor Safari Park,
and was reconstructed here. It takes 2
hours each day to water the plants in
here. Last year they added owl aviaries
and the Night Life nocturnal house.
Children can join in Animal Encounters
during the summer holidays, maybe
handling a snake or riding a camel, and
touch tables allow you to feel things you
wouldn't normally be able to get close
to – lion and tiger skins for example.
The thousand acres of parkland are
attractively laid out, with particularly
pleasant picnic areas; the old hall at the
centre is the HQ of their successful
breeding programme. There's a good
adventure playground, and road and rail
trains whisk you between the different
enclosures, home to a good range of
animals, many of which no longer exist
in the wild. *Fierce Creatures*, the less
successful follow-up to *A Fish Called
Wanda*, was filmed here. Meals and
snacks, shop, good disabled access;

cl 25 Dec; (01962) 777406; £8.50 (£6 children aged 3–14). A family ticket for 2 adults and 2 children costs £27. On the downs above, the Ship at Owslebury is popular with walkers and good for a family lunch – quieter than the big nearby Fishers Pond.

DAMERHAM SU1016

✝ **Damerham churchyard** Well worth a Feb visit, to see the carpet of snowdrops. The Compasses has good food inc vegetarian.

DANEBURY RING SU3237

▥ Iron Age hill fort rich in (excavated) remains. The Peat Spade at Longstock to the E is a useful dining pub.

EAST MEON SU6822

★ ✝ This appealing village has a splendid Norman church; the George is a rambling country pub (children welcome).

🍂 **Snowdrop woods** Many of the woodlands in this part of Hampshire fill with snowdrops in Feb.

EASTON SU5031

★ ⌂ This attractive village is well placed for pleasant Itchen Valley walks; we can recommend both the Cricketers and the Chestnut Horse.

EXBURY SU4200

❀ 🍂 ⌂ **Exbury Gardens** Wonderful 200-acre landscaped woodland gardens on E bank of the River Beaulieu, with a splendid rock garden, heather garden and river walk, and above all the Rothschild collection of rhododendrons, azaleas, magnolias and camellias – one of the world's finest, at its best May and early Jun. Meals, snacks, shop, disabled access; cl Nov–Feb; (023) 8089 1203; price varies with the season, from £3.30 in summer, to £4.80 in spring. The Jolly Sailor at Ashlett Creek nr Fawley is quite handy.

FACCOMBE SU3957

★ ❈ Bright with daffodils in spring, this attractive village has a decent pub, and great views from Pilot Hill.

FAREHAM SU6007

🏰 🌣 ❈ **Fort Nelson** See separate family panel on p.291.

FARLEY MOUNT SU4229

🍂 ❈ ⌂ An attractive area of downland and woodland, with good views – a pleasant spot for walks.

FROXFIELD GREEN SU7124

🍂 **Bluebells** In May much of the woodland around Froxfield Green is carpeted with bluebells, as are woods elsewhere in the area – for example at East Tisted and Ropley.

GOSPORT SU6199

♿ ❗ Like its larger neighbour (Portsmouth) across the water, this is benefiting from huge millennium grants seeking to exploit the town's historic naval roots. Among the attractions under construction are Explosion! – a museum looking at the history of armaments, a giant 15-metre sundial by the harbour, and a waterfront International Maritime Event Centre which will provide a forum for yachtsmen during international boating events. A heritage trail (a trans-harbour extension of the one in Portsmouth) will link the town's historic sites.

🏰 🌣 **Fort Brockhurst** A good overview exhibition of how the various forts protected Portsmouth; the Dolphin (Fort Rd) has popular food.

❋ ⚓ **Royal Navy Submarine Museum** (Haslar Jetty Rd) The highlight here is the tour of beached World War II submarine HMS *Alliance*, still in full working order, and fascinating inside to children of any age. More conventional features include an audio-visual show giving the flavour of diving into the depths. Snacks, shop, some disabled access; cl 24 Dec–1 Jan; (023) 9252 9217; £3.75. You can get a Waterbus across to Portsmouth (Apr–Oct), and the sea at Stokes Bay is probably Hampshire's cleanest for swimming in. The Clarence (A32) is a good new pub brewing its own beer.

HAMBLE SU4806

★ ⌂ ⚓ ⛵ ❀ 🏰 This pleasant village in *Howards Way* country has interesting views of the yachts, and you can walk a long way upriver or towards the Solent; the simple Olde Whyte Harte has decent food. There's a friendly little ferry to Warsash taking about 10 people at a time, where the riverside Rising Sun has good food, and there's a wildfowl nature reserve just N. Nearby Netley has a coastal **country park** and the extensive ruins of a 13th-c abbey.

HAYLING ISLAND SU7201

Readers enjoy this holiday resort, popular for water sports and particularly busy in summer.

HIGHCLERE SU4360

🏠 ❀ **Highclere Castle** (best approached from the A34 rather than Highclere itself) Magnificent pastiche of a medieval castle, impressively grand inside and out. Elaborate saloon and main staircase, a desk that belonged to Napoleon, and a Van Dyck of Charles I. Exhibitions of Egyptian relics (the 5th earl discovered Tutankhamun's tomb with Howard Carter), and horse-racing (the current earl is the Queen's racing manager). The lovely gardens and grounds include a Victorian tropical conservatory and walled garden. Meals, snacks, shop and plant centre, disabled access; open daily July–early Sept, plus bank hol wknds; (01635) 253210; £6, £3 gardens only. The Yew Tree (A343 S of village) is a good-value dining pub.

HINTON AMPNER SU5927

🏠 ❀ ❄ Attractive Georgian house, but it's the impressive grounds that impress most, with tranquil 20th-c shrub gardens. Teas, disabled access; gardens may be open last 2 Suns in Mar (good for daffodils), then pm Tues, Weds, wknds and bank hols Apr–Sept, house open only pm Tues and Weds, plus Sat and Sun in Aug; (01962) 771305; £4 house and garden, £3.20 garden only; NT. The Fox at Bramdean nearby is good for lunch.

HURST CASTLE SZ3189

🏰 ⌂ One of the most sophisticated fortresses around when built by Henry VIII, on a little spit commanding the Solent, and best reached on foot or by summer ferry from Keyhaven (there's a pleasant walk from the 17th-c Gun pub – good-value food). Fortified again in the 19th c, it still has two huge 38-ton guns. Summer snacks, shop; cl wkdys Nov–Mar, 24–26 Dec, 1 Jan; (01590) 642344; £2.50.

LANGSTONE SU7104

★ ⌖ ⌂ Thatched cottages, an old tidal mill, and a couple of decent pubs looking out over the thousands of acres of silted harbour – winter sunsets are memorable. Swans float up at high tide, with oystercatchers and droves of darting dunlins on the low-tide mudflats. Interesting walks along the old sea wall.

LEPE COUNTRY PARK SZ4598

⌂ A pleasant spot for mild saunters along the coast.

LIPHOOK SU8330

❀ 🌱 **Bohunt Manor** Lovely woodland gardens owned by the Worldwide Fund for Nature, with a watergarden, roses and herbaceous borders, lakeside walk, and unusual trees and shrubs. Disabled access; (01428) 722208; suggested donation of around £1.

⚙ 🎡 **Hollycombe Steam Collection** (Midhurst Road) Huge collection of steam-driven equipment, from paddle-steamers to an entire Edwardian fairground, including the big wheel. Sometimes open in the evening when the fairground is delightfully lit. Traction engine rides, and woodland steamtrain trips. Snacks, shop; open pm Sun and bank hols Easter–mid-Oct, and usually daily last wk in July–Aug; (01428) 724900; £6.50. The nearest place for a good lunch is the Red Lion over at Fernhurst.

LYMINGTON SZ3295

★ ⛵ Handsome and relaxed waterside town, very popular in summer with yachting people; it has quite a number of attractive Georgian buildings and some good shops. The Chequers down Ridgeway Lane, S of Pennington, has good food; the Angel (High St) and Toll House (A337) are also useful. You can get **ferries** to the Isle of Wight from here, and the B3054 to Dibden Purlieu is a pretty road.

LYNDHURST SU2908

The tourist centre of the New Forest, as well as the main shopping town for people living here, so lots of tea shops, cafés etc. In the car park there's a good information centre for the area. The Royal Oak in the pretty village of Bank just outside has a good choice of food.

🎞 **New Forest Museum** (High St) From outside it looks like a modern supermarket but inside there are very good themed displays and audio-visual exploration of the forest's history and wildlife, and a 7½-metre (25ft) embroidery. Decent children's features too. Shop, disabled access; cl 25 Dec; (023) 8028 3914; £2.75.

MEONSTOKE SU6119

★ ⌂ An attractive village, with a decent pub. The road from here down through Soberton runs by the River Meon, and is quiet enough to suit walkers; the old Meon Valley railway line nearby is now open as a walkway.

MIDDLE WALLOP SU3038

✝ **Museum of Army Flying** One of the country's best military museums, exploring man's efforts to fly. Kites, balloons, vintage aircraft, World War II gliders, and interactive displays. Some exhibits still soar occasional weekends. Meals, snacks, shop, disabled access; cl Christmas wk; (01980) 674421; £4.50.

MINSTEAD SU2711

❀ ✿ ★ ✝ **Furzey Gardens** Eight peaceful heather-filled acres, with a developing young arboretum, around a charming 16th-c thatched cottage and local craft gallery. Snacks, plant sales, limited disabled access; cl 25–26 Dec; (023) 8081 2464; *£3 (£1.50 winter). The village is quiet and pretty, with a fine old church at the top of the hill; the Trusty Servant by the green has good food.

MOTTISFONT SU3227

🏛 ❀ **Mottisfont Abbey** 12th-c priory salvaged from the Reformation as a delightful family house, in wonderful, peaceful surroundings. The gardens are a delight, housing a national collection of old roses (largely scented). You can usually see a few of the rooms, inc one richly decorated by Rex Whistler. Meals, snacks, shop, good disabled access; open pm Sat–Weds late Mar–Oct, and daily during the rose season (usually mid to end of Jun); (01794) 340757; £4.50, £5.50 rose season; NT. The Bear & Ragged Staff up on the A3057 does good-value food all day, and the road along the Test through Houghton and on to the attractive village of Wherwell is pretty.

NETHER WALLOP SU2936

★ ✝ An attractive sleepy village with an interesting Saxon church; surprisingly Leopold Stokowski died here, not in Hollywood. The Five Bells is a pleasantly modest place for lunch.

NEW FOREST SU2605

⚘ ⚘ ⌂ ☗ The New Forest countryside has great charm. Only parts of it are in fact wooded; the rest is unspoilt rolling heathland. Walkers can head off in virtually any direction without worrying about trespassing. Once away from the roads, it does give

a great feeling of untrammelled space. Children like it: there are free-running ponies and deer, and plenty of scope for generally running riot without coming to grief. This unchanging blend of woodland and heath covers nearly 150 square miles, designated a royal hunting preserve by William the Conqueror not long after the Battle of Hastings. The 2 best drives are the slow back road from Brockenhurst N through Bolderwood and then round past Linwood to Rockford, and the road from Brockenhurst to Burley; main roads can get very busy around the more popular areas, especially on summer weekends. Still with quite a medieval feel, the ancient woodlands are very atmospheric to stroll through, especially when you come across an unexpected sunlit leafy glade. It's most fun just to potter around, but you'll also get a lot out of a guided tour with people who've lived or worked in the forest all their lives; (023) 8028 2269 for details. Many of them have ancient forest rights and privileges, such as letting their pigs forage for acorns. The path network in the New Forest is remarkably comprehensive, and in most places there's no obligation to stick to rights of way (of which there are very few). The lack of major objectives can be a problem for purists: there are no obviously defined hills, and long walks in the eastern woodlands, many of which are coniferous, can become monotonous. Further W, the scenery is more intricate and a touch more varied. It is often a good idea to use routes which have plenty of landmarks to guide the way; the heath and forest can be fiendishly disorienting. Besides the ponies, you may see fallow deer, especially at the Bolderwood Deer Sanctuary (and in the woods, very occasionally, the smaller, shyer roe deer; even in some places red deer). The best walks alternate mixed forest with heathland; isolated ponds and country pubs provide focal points. In summer you can usually go on guided badger watch evenings; (01425) 403412. The **Museum and Visitor Centre** at Lyndhurst is a good place to start, and has details of water sports, riding and campsites. Handy pubs include the Royal Oak at Bank, Red Lion at Boldre (nr Raydon Woods nature reserve), Royal Oak at Fritham, Foresters Arms at Frogham, High Corner Inn or Red Shoot nr Linwood, Royal Oak at North Gorley, Alice Lisle at Rockford, Sir Walter Tyrell at Upper Canterton, and perhaps Turf Cutters Arms at East Boldre and Filly at Setley.

NEW MILTON SZ2394

Sammy Miller Museum (Bashley Manor) Well regarded changing collection of fully restored motor cycles, many the only surviving examples of their type in the world. Snacks, shop, disabled access; cl 25–26 Dec; (01425) 620777; £3.50. There's an adjacent craft shop.

OLD WINCHESTER HILL SU6420

This hill fort gives wide views of Hampshire, the Solent and Isle of Wight, with nature trails through natural downland that's never been ploughed and resown; fairly busy on fine weekends, wonderfully remote on a blustery spring or autumn weekday. The George & Falcon at Warnford is popular for food.

OVERTON SU5149

★ There's a charming drive along the B3400 to Hurstbourne Priors and B3048 to Wherwell; Overton though quite large is an attractive stop along the way, with a decent pub.

OWER SU3116

Paultons Park Agreeable family theme park with 140 acres of rides, gardens, animals, birds and wildfowl, as well as moving dinosaurs, a 10-acre lake with working waterwheel, hedge maze, animated scenes from *The Wind in the Willows*, and a unique Romany Experience with the sights, sounds and smells of traditional gypsy life. A new log flume joins rides such as the Runaway Train rollercoaster, tea-cups, go-karts (the only thing with an extra charge), bumper boats and several good play areas, many ideal for toddlers. A few years ago mirrors were installed to help the modest flamingos breed – they only do so when surrounded by large numbers. Meals, snacks, shop, disabled access; cl wkdys Nov and Dec (exc Christmas specials), and all Jan–mid-Mar; (023) 8081 4455; £9 adults (£8 children under 14;

children under 1 metre tall are free – though they can't go on everything). There's a range of family tickets, starting at £24 for 2 adults and 1 child.

PETERSFIELD SU7423

Bear Museum (Dragon St) Teddies, dolls and toys in a nursery setting. Children (or anyone else for that matter) can cuddle the exhibits; shop; cl Mon and Sun; (01730) 265108; free. There's an interesting **church** on Market Sq, and the Good Intent does good lunches.

PORTCHESTER SU6204

Portchester Castle The imposing high walls and towers stretching right down to the waterfront were originally part of a 3rd-c Roman fort – they're the best example of their type in Europe. Other remains include a 12th-c church and 14th-c great tower, and what's left of a palace built by Richard II. Snacks, shop, disabled access; cl 25–26 Dec; (023) 9237 8291; £2.70. The nearby Cormorant has good-value food.

PORTSMOUTH SZ6299

A massive £85 million harbour redevelopment project is nearing completion in this island town, with just 2 roads and the motorway bridging it and its residential/resort part Southsea to the mainland – traffic can be very slow indeed on the main approaches. Its great claim on the imagination is its place at the heart of English naval history, and it is this heritage that forms the focus of the city's rejuvenation. Six miles of new promenade will form part of a trail linking the 2 parts that are interesting to visitors: the Old Town and the Historic Dockyard, on either side of the ferry berths and well away from the traffic. Overlooking the narrow harbour neck, Georgian buildings on an old-fashioned cobbled hard give a good feel of the old days, and the little inner Camber Harbour still has fishing boats. Part of the trail is already open, and the rest should be ready by the end of the year. The naval base is also being revitalised, with its centrepiece, the 165-metre Spinnaker Tower due for completion this year (you won't be able to go up it till Easter 2001), and Guns Wharf – a huge waterfront shopping and leisure complex designed by the same company that constructed Cape Town's Alfred Docks – will include an outdoor ice-rink, arts theatre and multiplex cinema. A lot of development is also happening across the harbour in Gosport (see separate entry) and a new **Waterbus** service will link the 2 towns from the start of the year (an existing service already runs from Apr–Oct). An all-in-one ticket (inc ferry fare) will cover all the new attractions. By the harbour, the Still & West is a beautifully positioned food pub, and the Dolphin's a cosy place in the old High St behind. The **cathedral**, dating from the 13th c to the present, is a delightful departure from the traditional layout.

☉🏛 **City Museum** (Museum Rd) Very good displays on the city's history, in an astonishing former barracks that looks rather like a French château. Also decorative art and crafts. Meals, snacks, shop, disabled access; cl 24–26 Dec; (023) 9282 7261; free.

☉🦋 **Cumberland House Natural History Museum** (Eastern Parade, Southsea) Interesting collections, with a splendid butterfly enclosure in summer, and full-size dinosaur reconstructions. Shop, very limited disabled access; cl 24–26 Dec; (023) 9282 7261; £2 summer (butterfly season), less rest of year.

☉ **D-Day Museum** (Clarence Esplanade, Southsea) The most notable of the museums devoted to Portsmouth's fighting history; it vividly recalls and explains the Normandy landings from the point of view of both sides. Very realistic in places – you almost panic when the sirens sound. There's a remarkable 84-metre (272ft) D-Day embroidery inspired by the Bayeux Tapestry. Snacks, shop, disabled access; cl am Mon Nov–Mar, 24–26 Dec; (023) 9282 7261; £4.75.

🏚☉ **Dickens' Birthplace Museum** (Old Commercial Rd, in the main town) Restored to the modest middle-class style it had when the author was born here in 1812. Still various Dickens-related objects such as the couch on which he died. Shop; cl Nov–Mar (exc three wks before Christmas); (023) 9282 7261; £2.

🏚 **Guildhall** (Guildhall Sq) Contains

what's said to be the world's biggest glass mural. Snacks, disabled access; free tours, usually 10am and 11.30am Mon, Weds and Fri, May–Sept; (023) 9283 4092.

❋☉ **HM Naval Base** The main stop for most visitors, with lots to see. It houses **HMS Victory**, the **Mary Rose**, **HMS Warrior**, and the **Royal Naval Museum**. The flagship is of course HMS Victory, still in commission, and manned by regular serving officers. Guided tours bring those Trafalgar days very close, and include the spot where Nelson died. The raising of the Mary Rose from the Solent silt where it had sat for 437 years provided a wealth of material and information about the Tudor period. The discoveries are well shown in an airy hall, while the great oak hull itself is in a separate shed, sprayed almost constantly to prevent the timbers from drying out (they plan to build a new hall as part of the harbour redevelopment). HMS Warrior, when launched 140 years ago, was the most fearsome battleship in the world; she's been immaculately restored, and is manned by tars in period uniform. Again, tours are very vivid. New galleries are being added to the **Royal Naval Museum**, in handsome 18th-c dockside buildings, with lively displays on the development and history of the Navy up to and beyond the Falklands War (or as it's called here the South Atlantic Campaign). Lots of Nelson memorabilia, and a very jolly gallery looking at popular images of the sailor. Action Stations, a new attraction looking at the modern Navy through an IMAX film and interactive displays is planned for late summer. Each ship costs £5.95 to visit individually (though the HMS Victory ticket also includes entry to the museum, which on its own costs £3), but if you want to see more than one it's well worth getting the all-in ticket at £14.90, which covers all 3 ships and the museum. The site – which itself costs nothing to enter, after a security check – has a restaurant and shop, and there's disabled access to all the ships; (023) 9287 0999.

☉ **Royal Marines Museum** (Royal Marines Eastney, Southsea) This vigorous place couldn't be more different from the usual military exhibitions – lively re-creations of major amphibious actions, a junior commando assault course, and a jungle room with real snakes and scorpions. Meals, snacks, shop, disabled access; cl Christmas; (023) 9281 9385; £3.75.

✝ **Royal Garrison Church** (French St) Roofless now, this once-grand place was where Charles II was married in 1662; usually open Mon–Weds, but best to make an appointment (023) 9252 7667.

♪ ♨ **Sea Life Centre** (Clarence Esplanade, Southsea) Excellent for families, this is one of the most hi-tech of these centres, with all sorts of multi-sensory experiences and displays, and an exciting shark encounter. Children complete a scratchcard trail as they go round, and there's an indoor soft play area. Snacks, shop, disabled access; cl 25 Dec; (023) 9273 4461; £4.95 (they'll stamp your hand and let you come back later in the day). **Boat trips** round the harbour from nearby.

🏰 ☕ ❄ △ **Southsea Castle** The fortifications in defence of Portsmouth Harbour, here, around Gosport, and up on Portsdown, give a remarkably complete picture of the development of defensive strategy from Tudor times to the fears of French invasion in the 1860s, though they have more appeal to people interested in warfare than to those who like the romantic idea of a regular 'castle'. Southsea Castle and Museum is the best place to start, built in 1545 as part of Henry VIII's coastal defences. Good displays on Portsmouth's military history, and some splendid fish-bone model ships made by Napoleonic prisoners-of-war; special events (especially in summer). Snacks, shop; cl wkdys Nov–Mar, 24–26 Dec; (023) 9282 7261; £2. On the seaward side of Southsea are sturdy Tudor and later towers, bastions and batteries, alongside the resort's gardens and entertainments, giving interesting sea views. Good guided walks around the Tudor fortifications and the best parts of the Old Town leave the Square Fort at 2.30pm on Sun (not late Sept–mid-Apr).

🏰 ♨ **Spitbank Fort** Wind up an exploration of Portsmouth's naval past with the boat trip from the Naval Base to this granite, iron and brick fortress a mile out to sea. Its 2 floors are linked by a maze of passages, and there's a 130-metre (420ft) deep well which still draws fresh water. The inner courtyard is now a sheltered terrace for summer refreshments from the café. Cl Mon (exc bank hols), and mid-Sept–Apr; (01329) 664286; £6.50 inc boat trip. Ferries leave the pontoon beside HMS *Warrior*, but as we went to press they were changing their timetable – best to ring (01983) 564602. You can stay overnight out on the fort if you really do want to get away from it all (great views from comfortable rooms).

QUEEN ELIZABETH COUNTRY PARK SU7117

🐾 △ Lots going on all year, with woodland walks and rides (stables at the park), open downland, an adventure play trail, and events like Easter egg rolling. You can hire bikes or arrange horse riding (023) 9259 9699. Shop and café (cl wkdys Nov–Mar), disabled access; (023) 9259 5040; £2 parking charge Sun and bank hols, £1.50 rest of wk. Nearby is the excellent Five Bells at Buriton, a pretty village with a duck-pond.

ROCKBOURNE SU1117

🏛 ☕ ★ **Rockbourne Roman Villa** (off B3078, Rockbourne) Remains of the largest known Roman villa in the area, found by chance 50 years ago by a farmer digging out a ferret. Interesting mosaics in the museum. Snacks, shop, disabled access; cl am wkdys exc July and Aug and all Oct–Mar; (01725) 518541; £1.75. In the charming thatched village, the Rose & Thistle is useful for lunch.

ROMSEY SU3520

🏠 ❀ ♪ ✝ **Broadlands** (just S of Romsey) Elegant Palladian mansion on the banks of the River Test, surrounded by beautiful landscaped grounds. Fine furnishings and paintings, and a good exhibition on former resident Earl Mountbatten. You can fish on an adjacent stretch of the River Test. Snacks, shop, mostly disabled access; open pm mid-Jun–mid-Sept; (01794) 516878; £5. The nearby Old Horse & Jockey and (afternoon teas too) Three Tuns have enjoyable food. Mountbatten is buried in the interesting 13th-c **abbey**, bought by the townspeople for their parish church at the Dissolution. There are some notable Saxon crosses and a 16th-c panel painting.

SELBORNE SU7433

🏠 ⛫ ♨ ♈ ⌂ **Gilbert White's House** (The Wakes) Impressive 18th-c home of naturalist Gilbert White, furnished in period style. The extensive gardens are being restored to their original form, and separate galleries commemorate the explorers Captain Oates and Frank Oates. Impressive teas and 18th-c style snacks, good shop, plant sales, disabled access to ground floor and garden; cl Christmas wk; (01420) 511275; *£4. The Queen's Hotel is handy for lunch. There are good pockets of scenery nearby – the countryside White recorded in such detail. The zigzag path he created with his brother in 1753 still climbs Selborne Hanger. The hangers hereabouts are beechwoods which cling to the abrupt escarpments; Noar Hill close by has been designated a nature reserve for its chalkland flora. From Selborne churchyard, a path leads into The Lythe, a wooded hillside that was another favourite haunt of White's.

SHERBORNE ST JOHN SU6356

🏠 ⛫ ♈ ⌂ **The Vyne** Tudor mansion with splendid 17th- and 18th-c embellishments: a stonemason's error led to a parrot's beak being carved onto the statue of an eagle. You can now see the bedrooms and domestic areas. The gardens include a 19th-c walled garden and a summerhouse garden; there are pleasant woodland walks. Meals, snacks, shop, disabled access; cl am, Mon (exc bank hols), Tues, and all Nov–Mar, (grounds open wknds in Mar); (01256) 881337; £5, grounds only £2.50; NT.

SILCHESTER SU6262

🏛 ✝ ♨ **Calleva Museum** The site of the Roman town Calleva Atrebatum has been excavated nearby; 1½ miles of city wall to walk along (tricky in places), as well as a 9,000-seat amphitheatre, 12th-c church on the site of the Roman temples, and a **museum** with a small collection of finds from the site. The Calleva Arms (with a family dining conservatory) does cheap lunches, and sells good guides to the site; the Red

Lion at Mortimer West End is a good dining pub.

SOUTHAMPTON SU4111

🏠 ⌂ Known early in the 20th c (through its shipping importance) as the Gateway to the World, this huge bustling town rather unexpectedly has one of the 3 best-preserved medieval town walls in the country. The best stretch is along the western side of the old core, around from the magnificent partly Norman **Bargate** (which has a small local museum); there are usually guided walks along here on Sun mornings, or you can walk it yourself at any time. Lots of other old buildings dotted around the less appetising modern townscape, though if you're short of time it's best to concentrate your efforts on the area around St Michael's Sq, Bugle St and perhaps the old High St. Parking around the centre is metered. The quayside nearest here has been cleaned up, with modern café-bars overlooking yachting berths.

🖼 **City Art Gallery** (Civic Centre, Commercial Rd) Extensive and distinguished collection of British and European paintings and sculptures from the last 600 years, particular emphasis on the 20th c; highly praised by readers. Snacks, shop, disabled access; cl Mon, 25–26 Dec and Good Fri; (023) 8063 2601; free.

🏰 ♨ **God's House Tower** (Winkle St) An early 15th-c prototype gun battery, now housing an archaeology museum with displays on the city's Saxon forebear, Hamwic. Shop, cl 12–1pm, all Mon, and Christmas–New Year; free. The nearby bowling green is said to be the oldest in the world.

✈ **Hall of Aviation** (Albert Rd S) Various aircraft of local interest – inc prototype helicopters and the Spitfire. Shop, disabled access; cl am Sun, all day Mon (exc bank and school hols), Christmas; (023) 8063 5830; *£3.

✳ 🏠 **Maritime Museum** (Bugle St) A fine 14th-c warehouse with an impressive timber ceiling, and useful displays on the history of the port. Especially good on the great liners. Shop, disabled access to ground floor only; cl 1–2pm, am Sun, Mon, Christmas–New Year; (023) 8063 5904; free. The pretty 15th-c **Tudor house** on the same road has been restored (disabled access to ground floor and garden; same opening hours as Maritime Museum; free). The ancient nearby Duke of Wellington has decent food.

🏠 Medieval Merchant's House (French St) Timbered building, quarter of a mile from the city centre, splendidly refurbished with period furnishings which vividly re-create what life must have been like for a wealthy merchant's family; free audio tour. Shop; cl Nov–Mar; (023) 8022 1503; £2.10; EH.

SOUTHWICK SU6208

★ ⌂ ✿ This attractive village, with a decent pub, is well placed for good walks on Portsdown Hill – fine views.

STEVENTON SU5447

✝ **Steventon church** 12th c, with a memorial to Jane Austen, who was born in the village.

STOCKBRIDGE SU3433

🌼 **Houghton Lodge Gardens** (just SW of Stockbridge) Pretty and very peaceful gardens running down to the River Test, with fine trees and lawns, topiary peacocks and a topiary dragon that breathes 'steam'. An intriguing hydroponicum demonstrates how to grow plants without soil, and one garden is made from recycled car metal; there are plans to restore the 18th-c shrubbery. Wknd snacks, plant sales (especially good on fuchsias), disabled access; open Mar–Sept, all day wknds and bank hols, plus pm wkdys (exc Weds); (01264) 810177; £5. In the pleasant nearby town of Stockbridge, the Grosvenor, Vine and White Hart are all useful for lunch.

STRATFIELD SAYE SU6962

🏠 ⌂ **Stratfield Saye House** (off the A33) A grateful nation granted the Duke of Wellington the money to buy this 17th-c house after Waterloo. Perhaps surprisingly, the Duke had a taste for French furniture, lots of which is still here – as is his splendid funeral carriage, and his hearing aid (needed after prolonged exposure to cannon). His beloved horse Copenhagen is buried in the grounds. Snacks, shop, disabled access; as we went to press, they were changing their opening times and prices – best to ring; (01256) 882882. The elegant Wellington Arms has good food. There are pleasant

walks on Heckfield Heath E of the estate, and Wellington Country Park in Berkshire is nearby.

TITCHFIELD SU5305

🏛 🏠 ⌂ **Titchfield Abbey** Ruined 13th-c abbey, almost overshadowed by the grand Tudor gatehouse built after the Dissolution. Some of Shakespeare's plays were reputedly first performed here. Disabled access; cl 25 Dec; free; EH. The riverside Fisherman's Rest opposite does food all day, and there's a fine walk by the old canal to the coast at Meon Shore nr Hill Head.

TOTTON SU3612

✗ ⫯ **Eling Tide Mill** (Eling Toll Bridge) There's been a mill on this causeway for over 900 years, and the present one still uses tidal energy to produce flour. Heritage centre, snacks, shop, disabled access to ground floor only; cl Mon, Tues, and 25 Dec – ring for milling times, which of course depend on the tide; (023) 8086 9575; £1.60. In unpromising surroundings, the Anchor on Eling Quay is a good, cheap place for something to eat.

WAGGONERS' WELLS SU8534

⚐ ⌂ ✝ A series of hammer ponds, a legacy of the medieval Wealden iron industry, set in charming, heathy woodlands in a valley, and perfect for a picnic. Paths skirt these NT-owned ponds, which are a haven for wildlife.

WATERSHIP DOWN SU4957

⚐ ⌂ (just S of Kingsclere) The home of the rabbits in the novel by Richard Adams – their final adventure was down at Freefolk, where the eponymous pub often has live rabbits. Pleasant wooded walks through this area.

WEYHILL SU3046

🦅 **Hawk Conservancy** One of the best birds of prey centres we've come across; you can handle some of the birds, and there are regular flying displays (the best at 2pm). Wild flower meadow, ferret racing in school hols and toddlers' play area. Snacks, shop, disabled access; cl Nov–mid-Feb; (01264) 772252; £5.75. The Weyhill Fair is handy for lunch, and the lanes N take you into a particularly unspoilt corner of Hampshire.

WHITCHURCH SU4648

🏭 **Whitchurch Silk Mill** (Winchester St) Working mill

producing fabric for theatrical costumes, interior designers and historic houses using Victorian machinery and traditional processes. Prettily set on an island in the River Test, where you can watch the trout or feed ducks. Snacks, shop; cl Mon exc bank hols, 24 Dec–2 Jan; (01256) 892065; £2.50 (guidebook is a little pricey). The Red House (London St) is the best pub here, and you can get a good cup of coffee at the White Hart Hotel (The Square).

WICKHAM SU5711

★ 🐦 An attractive village despite the traffic, notable for its huge village square; at nearby Droxford there's a good farm shop with pick-your-own.

WINCHESTER SU4829

★ 🏛 △ ⛪ The compact and fascinating medieval centre still has 2 city gates intact; it was capital of England in Saxon times. Guided walks around the sights from the tourist information centre at 11am and 2.30pm Mon–Sat, 11.30am Sun May–Sept (2.30pm only in Apr and Oct), and 11am Sat in winter; £2.50. There's a multi-storey car park at the top of the High St, or a Park & Ride nr the junction with the M3. The most attractive part of the city is the glorious and peaceful **Cathedral Close**, surrounded by a very harmonious and distinguished collection of buildings; the handsome old Eclipse Inn, nr the NE edge, is a useful refreshment break. The Brooks Shopping Centre has a few jolly dioramas and displays on the city's history (cl Sun; free), with the chance for children to make their own Roman mosaic. There are pleasant walks up rounded **St Catherine's Hill**, which has a small medieval turf maze and traces of a hill fort.

✗ **City Mill** (Bridge St) Restored 18th-c working watermill, with timbered and raftered ceilings and a pretty little island garden. Cl Mon (exc bank hols) and Tues, wkdys in Mar, and all Nov–Feb; (01962) 870057; £1; NT.

👁 **City Museum** (The Square) This well organised local history and archaeology museum should reopen around Jan following refurbishment. Exhibits include a telling Roman mosaic. Shop, limited disabled access; cl 1–2pm

Sat, am Sun, Mon Oct–Mar, 25–26 Dec; (01962) 863064; free.

🏰 **Great Hall of Winchester Castle** All that remains of the castle is its huge 13th-c great hall, where Raleigh was tried and condemned to death; hanging off one wall is a round table they call King Arthur's (actually made the same date as the castle, and painted with its Arthurian scenes later). You should be able to see the restored roof, stone parapets and stained-glass windows by Jan. A small but interesting garden is laid out on the lines of what might have been there in the 13th c. Shop, disabled access; cl 25–26 Dec; (01962) 846476; free.

🖼 **Guildhall Gallery** (Broadway) 19th-c building with changing exhibitions of fine art, crafts and photography. Snacks, shop, disabled access; cl am Sun and Mon (all Mon Oct–Mar), Good Fri, 25–26 Dec, 1 Jan; (01962) 848269; free.

👁 **Gurkha Museum** Anyone interested in military history will enjoy the 3 Light Infantry museums in Winchester, but of these only the Gurkha Museum (Romsey Rd) could be said to have a wider appeal. Disabled access; cl am Sun, Christmas wk; (01962) 842832; £1.50.

🏛 △ **Hospital of St Cross** 🔞 A short stroll along the watermeadows by the River Itchen. Very attractively set around 2 quadrangles, the quaint 15th-c almshouses still provide bread and ale to travellers who ask at the massive gate (you have to ask for 'wayfarer's dole'). 19th-c scandals here inspired Trollope's *The Warden*. Summer snacks, shop, disabled access; cl winter 12.30–2pm, Sun, 25 Dec; £2. The Bell out here is useful for lunch.

👁 ❄ **Westgate Museum** (High St) Local history above a formidable medieval city gate – the panorama of the city and surrounding countryside is rewarding. Shop; cl 1–2pm Sat, am Sun, Mons in Oct, Feb and Mar, and all Nov–Jan; (01962) 869864; 30p.

✝ 🏰 △ **Winchester Cathedral** Awesome and full of interest – one of Europe's finest, with the longest of all Gothic naves, and quite a mixture of architectural styles. Among many rare books and manuscripts in its library is a wonderful 12th-c illuminated Bible, while the sculpture gallery contains some outstanding late Gothic work. William of Wykeham paid for much of the rebuilding, so his tomb is appropriately the finest; also memorials and monuments to Jane Austen, King Canute and St Swithin. Good guided tours, and a first-rate visitor centre in the 16th-c coach house, with very good meals and snacks (not cheap) and a distinguished shop; disabled access; £2.50 suggested donation. Close by are the appreciable remains of Wolvesey Castle, the original Bishop's Palace begun in the 12th c, and beside it (not open, but a handsome sight), the present Bishop's Palace of 1684. The best way out of the cloisters is through the medieval King's Gate, which includes the upper-floor church of St Swithin. This takes you into Kingsgate St, calm and old-fashioned, with an excellent dining pub, the Wykeham Arms. Down on the left, a lovely riverside path takes you along to the City Mill and a mighty statue of King Alfred.

🏛 Winchester College All along Kingsgate St are buildings connected with this, the oldest school in the country. Most of the original school buildings remain intact, especially around the grand 14th-c chapel and its calm, tilting cloisters with a delightful 2-storey chantry in their centre, and a glimpse of the warden's garden through one gate. Good shop in the former tuck shop, some disabled access; guided tours Apr–Sept, cl 1–2pm, am Sun (winter tours by appointment only); (01962) 621217; £2.50.

WOOLTON HILL SU4261

🏵 Hollington Herb Garden Tranquil and relaxed walled gardens; snacks, shop; open Mar–Sept, Weds–Sat, pm Sun and bank hols; £1.

★ Other attractive villages with decent pubs include Abbots Ann SU3243, Amport SU2944, Bank SU2807, Brook SU2714, Buriton SU7320, Cheriton SU5828, Crawley SU4234, Crondall SU7948, East End SU4161 (the one nr Highclere), East Stratton SU5439, Hambledon SU6414, Lasham SU6742, Longparish SU4344, Mapledurwell SU6851, Micheldever SU5142, Upton Grey SU6948, Wherwell SU3840 and Woodgreen SU1717.

Where to eat

BOLDRE SZ3198 **Red Lion** *(01590) 673177* Very busy, friendly, refurbished pub with 4 black-beamed rooms, interesting bric-à-brac and bygones, impressive bar food, a fine choice of wines by the glass, and well kept beer; prompt service; worth getting there early; cl 25 Dec, pm 26 Dec; no children; disabled access. **£24.50**|£5.20.

BRAMDEAN SU6127 **Fox** *(01962) 771363* Welcoming 17th-c dining pub with famous fox masks in a modernised and neatly cared for open-plan bar; lots of good fish (other food, too), extensive wine list, well kept real ales, and obliging service; no children; cl 25 Dec. **£25**|£8.95.

BROCKENHURST SU2902 **Poussin** *The Courtyard, Brookley Rd (01590) 623063* Popular little restaurant with carefully cooked, interesting food using the best local produce, good cheeses and puddings, friendly service, and chicken-themed decorations; cl Mon, Tues; disabled access. **£35**.

BROCKENHURST SU2902 **Thatched Cottage** *16 Brookley Rd (01590) 623090* Charming 400-year-old thatched cottage, with a cosy beamed lounge, good dried and fresh flower arrangements, pretty restaurant, and enjoyable, well presented, imaginative food served by friendly staff; super cream teas in the neat garden, morning coffee too; cl Mon, Jan; children over 12. **£43.78**.

CADNAM SU2913 **White Hart** *(023) 8081 2277* Big, multi-level dining lounge with good solid furnishings, a wide choice of interesting food inc fine daily specials and tempting puddings, well kept real ales and decent wines; goat, horses and dogs; cl 25–26 Dec; disabled access. **£20.50**|£7.25.

EAST TYTHERLEY SU2928 **Star** *(01794) 340225* Friendly country local by the village cricket field, with homely furnishings, log fires, and a no smoking lower lounge bar; pretty no smoking restaurant, pleasantly informal atmosphere, enjoyable home-made food inc good daily specials, well kept real ales, and smart, efficient staff; garden and skittle alley; bdrms; disabled access. **£24**|**£5.95**.

EMSWORTH SU7405 **36 On The Quay** *South St* (01243) 375592 Charming, cheerfully decorated quayside restaurant with extremely good modern cooking, friendly and helpful service and a sound wine list; cl am Sat, Sun, am Mon, first 2 wks Jan, last wk Oct; disabled access. **£39.45**|**£16.50 for 2-course lunch**.

EVERSLEY SU7662 **New Mill** *New Mill Rd* (0118) 973 2277 16th-c watermill by the Blackwater River with working waterwheel and grinding equipment; big windows overlooking the river and its wildlife, open fires and candlelit tables, a good range of interesting, carefully cooked food, and a thoughtful wine list with many by the glass; the beamed Grill Room is more informal and cheaper; cl am Sat, 26 Dec, 1 Jan; partial disabled access. **£30**|**£9.50**.

FROYLE SU7542 **Hen & Chicken** (01420) 22115 Old coaching inn with interconnecting rooms, hops on beams, candles on tables, and daily papers; neat staff serving imaginative food, a partly no smoking restaurant, well kept real ales, and a big garden with children's play equipment. **£22**|**£8.50**.

HOUGHTON SU3432 **Boot** (01794) 388310 Friendly, well run dining pub with simple décor; popular bar and restaurant food, well kept real ales, and pleasant service; cl Mon, no food pm Sun; disabled access. **£16.20**|**£6.25**.

LOCKS HEATH SU5006 **Jolly Farmer** *Fleet End Rd* (01489) 572500 Thriving old inn with lots of character, small rooms with plenty of country bric-à-brac, a wide choice of quickly served food, well kept real ales, and neat, friendly staff; disabled access. **£16**|**£5.95**.

LONGSTOCK SU3536 **Peat Spade** (01264) 810612 Lively popular dining pub with an airy, attractive bar, Toby jugs around the fire, and an elegant little dining room with a no smoking area; imaginative, enjoyable food, well kept real ales, and decent wines; bdrms; disabled access. **£20.50**|**£6.50**.

LOWER WIELD SU6339 **Yew Tree** (01256) 389224 Welcoming country dining pub with fresh flowers, central open fire, and dresser with pretty china in the small, cosy, flagstoned bar; a civilised atmosphere, beautifully presented, really good food, helpful service, and decent wines; nice nearby walks. **£19.90**|**£6.95**.

LYMINGTON SZ2996 **Gordleton Mill** *Silver St* (01590) 682219 300-year-old converted watermill with lovely romantic gardens (you can sit on the terrace and enjoy an aperitif by the water); comfortable, attractive interior, exquisitely presented, exceptional modern cooking, and a marvellous wine list; comfortable bdrms; cl pm Sun, Mon, Jan; **£32.50**.

MAPLEDURWELL SU6851 **Gamekeepers** (01256) 322038 Interesting old pub in a lovely thatched village, with enterprising food, good-value wines, friendly service, and a separate more upmarket restaurant; disabled access. **£24.50**|**£5.50**.

MICHELDEVER SU5138 **Dever Arms** (01962) 774339 Attractive country pub with a simply decorated beamed bar, woodburners at each end, solid furniture; generous helpings of interesting food inc lots of good daily specials, well kept real ales, and decent wines; seats on the terrace and by the cricket green; disabled access. **£17.50**|**£6.95**.

OLD BURGHCLERE SU4658 **Dew Pond** (01635) 278408 Beautiful 16th-c country house with log fires, friendly atmosphere, and imaginative food using fresh local produce on a frequently changing small menu – good game, fish and lovely puddings; no smoking; cl Sun, Mon, 2 wks Jan, 2 wks Aug; children over 5; disabled access. **£32**.

PILLEY SZ3298 **Fleur de Lys** (01590) 672158 The oldest pub in the New Forest (an inn since 1096); plenty of atmosphere, huge inglenook fireplace, well kept real ales, good wines and farm cider, a wide range of carefully prepared food inc vegetarian and fish, and a thoughtful children's menu; also a pretty garden. **£19**|**£7**.

SOUTHSEA SZ6499 **A Fistful of Tacos** *Albert Rd* (023) 9229 3474 Evening restaurant with good Californian/Mexican food; cl 25–26 Dec, 1 Jan; partial disabled access. **£17**.

SOUTHSEA SZ6698 **Tenth Hole** *Eastern Parade (023) 9283 0009* Bustling café by the pitch-and-putt, with snacks, light lunches and generous teas served by friendly staff; cl Jan; no very young children; disabled access. £4.25.

STUCKTON SU1613 **Three Lions** *(01425) 652489* Warmly welcoming restaurant with an informal atmosphere, a neat airy bar and fresh flowers; very imaginative food inc forest fungi and lovely puddings, a fine wine list, superb breakfasts, and charming owners; good atmosphere and efficient service; cl 2 wks Jan, 2 wks Feb; disabled access; comfortable bdrms. **£35**|£13.50 for 2-course lunch.

TICHBORNE SU5730 **Tichborne Arms** *(01962) 733760* Attractive thatched country pub in rolling countryside, with very good imaginative bar food, delicious puddings; big garden; cl pm 25 and 26 Dec; no children; disabled access. **£16.50**|£5.95.

WELL SU7646 **Chequers** *(01256) 862605* Neatly kept and rather smart country pub with relaxed atmosphere, snug rooms, beams, lots of 18th-c country-life prints, and very good bar food; partial disabled access. **£18.25**|£6.50.

WINCHESTER SU4829 **Cathedral Refectory** *Visitors' Centre, Inner Close (01962) 853224* Excellent, totally home-made food in a bright, airy, modern conservatory; lovely breads and soups, afternoon cream teas, good children's menu, a friendly informal atmosphere, and nice staff; cl 25–26 Dec, 1 Jan, Good Fri; disabled access. **£14**|£3.25.

Special thanks to Phyl and Jack Street, B and K Hypher, Mrs C Dewell, Paul Kennedy, Mrs V Pinn.

Hampshire Calendar

Some of these dates were provisional as we went to press. Please check information with the telephone numbers provided.

JANUARY

1 **Eastleigh** Friends of Thomas the Tank Engine at Lakeside Railway – *till 2 January* (023) 8063 6612; **Southampton** Millennium Trust Celebration in Mayflower Park (023) 8083 2691

APRIL

12 **Southampton** Tall Ships inc parade of sail, fireworks and daily entertainments – *till 16 April* (023) 8083 2525

16 **Beaulieu** Boat Jumble at the National Motor Museum (01590) 612345

20 **Fareham** and **Gosport** Easter Folk Festival – *till 24 April* (023) 9254 5294

22 **New Forest** and **Beaulieu** Rufus Weekend: 900th anniversary of the death of this important character in New Forest history inc jousting, archery and re-enactments – *till 23 April* (01590) 612345

28 **Alton** Millennium Festival at various venues inc 17th-c market, living history camp, re-enactment of Civil War battle at Alton etc – *till 1 May* (01420) 88448

29 **Alton** Heritage Festival – *till 1 May* (01962) 846008; **Farnborough** and **Aldershot** Arts and Local History Festival – *till 20 May* (01962) 846008; **Portsmouth** Heavy Horse Show – *till 1 May* (023) 8028 2269

Hampshire Calendar (cont.)

MAY

6 Beaulieu Auto Jumble and Classic Car Show at the National Motor Museum – *till 7 May* (01590) 612345; **Highclere** Country Homes and Gardens Show at the castle – *till 7 May* (01635) 253210

13 Christchurch Food and Drink Festival – *till 20 May* (01962) 846008; **Winchester** and **Romsey** Winchester and County Music Festival at the cathedral and Romsey Abbey – *till 20 May* (01962) 846008

14 Basingstoke Festival of Transport at War Memorial Park (01256) 845682

28 Highclere Southern Counties Game and Country Fair at the castle – *till 29 May* (01635) 253210

29 Southsea Heavy Horse Parade at Castlefield Arena – *till 1 June* (023) 9283 4146

JUNE

3 Basingstoke Kite Festival at War Memorial Park – *till 4 June* (01256) 845682; **Highcliffe Castle to Beaulieu** Historic Vehicle Rally – *till 4 June* (01590) 612345

4 Southampton 'Seawings 2000' Airshow inc Spitfire and Seaplane static and flying displays (02380) 832691

17 Basingstoke Outdoor Pop Concert at War Memorial Park – *till 18 June* (01256) 845682; **Netley** Art in the Park at Royal Victoria Country Park – *till 1 July* (01962) 846008; **Southampton** Street Festival – *till 18 June* (023) 8083 2525; **Southsea** Carnival – *till 18 June* (023) 9283 4118

21 Bucklers Hard Millennium Celebrations (01590) 612345

25 Odiham Re-enactment of Magna Carta (01962) 846008

30 Southampton Balloon and Flower Festival – *till 2 July* (023) 8083 2755

JULY

1 Portsmouth and **Southsea** Regatta – *till 31 July* (023) 9283 4118

7 Southampton Millennium Festival – *till 16 July* (01962) 846008

8 Aldershot Summer Evening Walk at the Rowhill Nature Reserve (01962) 846008; **Catisfield** Flowers and Fun Day at the Memorial Hall (01962) 846008; **Portsmouth** Festival of Dance (023) 9283 4118

9 Southampton Power in the Park: free pop concert (023) 8083 2525; **Winchester** Bus Rally at Royal Victoria Park (023) 8045 5157

11 Highclere Castle Theatre Company at the castle (01635) 253210

15 Winchester Show – *till 16 July* (01962) 866556

17 Southampton Multicultural Carnival in Mayflower Park (023) 8083 2151

19 Mottisfont Open-air Theatre at the abbey – *till 29 July* (01794) 340757

23 Highclere Porsche Rally at the castle (castle closed) (01635) 253210; **Southsea** Post-1940s car rally arrives from Oxford (023) 9283 4118

25 Brockenhurst New Forest and County Show at New Park – *till 27 July* (01590) 622400

28 Southampton Festival of the Ocean inc light and music show at Mayflower Park and World Carnival – *till 30 July* (023) 8083 2525

29 Beaulieu Fireworks Concert at the National Motor Museum (01590) 612345

Hampshire Calendar (cont.)

AUGUST

4 Basingstoke Balloon Festival at War Memorial Park – *till 6 August* (01256) 845682; **Portsmouth** Portsmouth and Southsea Show on Southsea Common inc arena events, circus and farm trail – *till 6 August* (023) 9283 4146

8 Portsmouth Bonfire and Fireworks Display (023) 8028 2269

19 Netley Abbey Hobbies Fair at Royal Victoria Park – *till 20 August* (023) 8045 5157

26 Southsea International Kite Festival – *till 28 August* (023) 9283 4553

28 Highclere Horse Trials at the castle (01635) 253210

SEPTEMBER

2 Alresford Agricultural Show at Tichborne Park (01962) 732023

9 Basingstoke Fabulous Forties Weekend: taking the whole town back to the 1940s – *till 10 September* (01256) 844844; **Beaulieu** Auto Jumble at the National Motor Museum – *till 10 September* (01590) 612345

15 Southampton International Boat Show at Western Esplanade – *till 24 September* (01784) 473377

OCTOBER

7 Portsmouth Opening of Portsmouth Harbour (023) 9283 4118

17 Kingsworthy Millennium *Son et Lumière* at St Mary's Church – *till 20 October* (01962) 846008

NOVEMBER

4 Alton Fireworks and Bonfire (01420) 561460; **Netley Abbey** Fireworks at Royal Victoria Park (023) 8045 5157

6 Aldershot Bonfire, fireworks and laser show (01962) 846008

DECEMBER

2 Winchester Victorian Christmas Fair at Royal Victoria Park – *till 3 December* (023) 8045 5157

26 Crookham Mummers Plays: *from midday* outside the Black Prince, Chequers and Queen's Head (01252) 811151

Please let us know what you think of places in the *Guide*. Use the report forms at the back of the book or simply write us a letter.

HEREFORDSHIRE

Unchanging truly rural England, with quiet countryside, lovely black and white villages, appealing small towns, great gardens.

The classic unspoilt scenery and sheer sense of peace makes this is a splendid area for restorative short breaks. As you head west the countryside becomes almost bewitchingly untouched – not at all showy, but the sort of peaceful world that elsewhere tends to survive only in people's memories. Not many tourists or second-homers have penetrated here, even at the height of summer, yet there's an abundance of art galleries and bookshops (Hay-on-Wye, that town-sized bookshop, is an attractive drive just over the Welsh border), and excellent natural cooking using local produce.

The main appeal is decidedly adult – beautiful black and white villages, civilised and attractive small towns, quiet scenic drives, good craft centres, inspiring walks with long gentle views, and an exceptional number of fine gardens, from attainably small ones such as Kingstone Cottages near Ross-on-Wye or relatively young ones such as the one at Kimbolton to products of several generations such as Hergest Croft near Kington. Eastnor Castle, Berrington Hall at Ashton, Lower Brockhampton House, Croft Castle and Goodrich Castle make pleasant outings, and there are several enjoyable cider farms.

The pig centre at Linley Green is a hit with many children, and the expanding farm park at Kington is another family favourite.

Hereford is engaging and relaxing, with plenty of varied attractions – the cathedral has a splendid display of its great treasures. Ledbury is attractive, with several appealing places to visit. Kington, Leominster and Ross-on-Wye are also agreeable to wander around.

In winter, big log fires and generous central heating are the rule – people here really seem to appreciate their warmth. By contrast, summers are relatively hot here.

Where to stay

BRIMFIELD SO5267 **Roebuck** *Brimfield, Ludlow SY8 4NE (01584) 711230* ***£60;** 3 rms. Civilised dining pub with good stylish food in the elegant, modern, no smoking restaurant and panelled bar; open fires, caring staff, well kept real ales, and fine wine list.

BROMSBERROW HEATH SO7333 **Grove House** *Bromsberrow Heath, Ledbury HR8 1PE (01531) 650584* ***£69.50;** 3 spacious rms, 2 with four-posters. Wisteria-clad 15th-c manor house with dark panelling, open fires, beams, fresh flowers and polished antiques, and good evening meals served at a huge dining table, using home-grown produce; 13 acres, hard tennis court, and neighbour's outdoor swimming pool; cl Christmas and New Year.

CAREY SO5631 **Cottage of Content** *Carey, Hereford HR2 6NG (01432) 840242* **£48;** 3 rms. Very pretty medieval country cottage in a peaceful setting, with flagstoned and timbered bars, enjoyable food, well kept real ales, a good wine list, and seats on the flower-filled front and back terraces; cl 25 Dec.

FOWNHOPE SO5734 **Green Man** *Fownhope, Hereford HR1 4PE (01432)
860243* *£57.50,* plus special breaks; 20 rms. Attractive Tudor inn with an
impressive oak-beamed lounge (the residents' lounges are no smoking), log fire, and
generously served, popular bar food; disabled access.

GRAFTON SO4936 **Grafton Villa Farm** *Grafton, Hereford HR2 8ED (01432)
268689* *£42;* 3 rms. Characterful, early 18th-c farmhouse with panoramic views,
friendly dogs, open fire in lounge, and enjoyable breakfasts using their own free-
range eggs; cl Christmas; disabled access (and self-catering cottage suitable also).

KINGTON SO3156 **Penrhos Court** *Kington, Hereford HR5 3LH (01544) 230720*
£95, plus special breaks; 19 elegant rms. Beautifully restored 13th-c Hall in 6 acres,
with fine beams and flagstones, and very good, carefully cooked food using home-
grown herbs and vegetables; medieval banquets, too; cl Jan; disabled access.

KINNERSLEY SO3349 **Upper Newton Farmhouse** *Kinnersley, Hereford HR3
6QB (01544) 327727* *£40,* plus special breaks; 3 prettily decorated rms with hand-
crafted items. 17th-c farmhouse in the middle of a working farm, with log fires,
beams, sloping floors, good food (inc vegetarian) using fresh farm veg; colourful
garden, and lots of walks; no smoking or pets; self-catering cottage.

LEDBURY SO7137 **Feathers** *High St, Ledbury HR8 1DS (01531) 635266* *£89.50,*
plus special breaks; 19 carefully decorated rms making the most of the old beams
and timbers. Very striking, mainly 16th-c, black and white hotel with a relaxed
atmosphere, log fires, and comfortable lounge hall with country antiques, beams
and timbers; particularly enjoyable food and friendly service in Fuggles bar, good
wine list, and a fine mix of locals and visitors.

LEYSTERS SO5762 **Old Vicarage** *Leysters, Leominster HR6 0HS (01568) 750208*
£64; 2 rms. 17th-c farmhouse with Victorian additions, comfortable and friendly, in
18 acres with a sizeable garden and all-weather tennis court, surrounded by the
unspoilt north Herefordshire hills; antiques, good food with home-baked bread eaten
around a big dining table; cl Christmas and New Year; children over 12; no dogs.

ROSS-ON-WYE SO6024 **Brookfield House** *Ledbury Rd, Ross-on-Wye HR9 7AT
(01989) 562188* *£45,* plus special breaks; 8 rms, some with own bthrm. Part Queen
Anne and part Georgian house with sunny terrace and little garden with a view over
the town; very friendly and welcoming owners, log fire in the lounge, and super
breakfasts in the big airy breakfast room; children over 8; pets allowed.

RUCKHALL COMMON SO4539 **Ancient Camp** *Ruckhall Common, Hereford
HR2 9QX (01981) 250449* *£65;* 5 rms, 2 with river views. Smart country inn in a
pleasantly remote spot with good views of River Wye and beyond from the terrace;
beamed and flagstoned bar, good bar and restaurant food (not pm Sun or Mon); cl
first 2 wks Jan; no children.

ULLINGSWICK SO5849 **Steppes** *Ullingswick, Hereford HR1 3JG (01432)
820424* *£80,* plus special breaks; 6 spacious, pretty rms in barn and restored stone
stable. Attractive 17th-c country-house hotel with heavy beams, flagstones and
inglenook fireplaces in the cellar bar, lounge and dining room; very good food, fine
breakfasts, and hospitable owners; cl Dec and Jan; children over 12.

WEOBLEY SO4051 **Salutation** *Market Pitch, Weobley, Hereford HR4 8SJ (01544)
318443* *£67;* 4 rms. Friendly, 500-year-old inn with a good bar and elaborate
restaurant food, quiet lounge with standing timbers and log fires, and small public
bar; also, self-catering cottage; children in cottage only.

WOOLHOPE SO6135 **Butchers Arms** *Woolhope, Hereford HR1 4RF (01432)
860281* *£39;* 2 neat, attractive rms with fruit and chocolates (shared bthrm). Family-
run, 14th-c timbered building with low oak beams and log fires in bars, friendly staff,
lots of flowers, and decent food (good breakfasts); lovely surrounding walks.

Please let us know what you think of places in the *Guide*. Use the report forms
at the back of the book or simply write us a letter.

To see and do

HEREFORDSHIRE Family Attraction of the Year

🐗 **LINLEY GREEN** SO6953 **Pig Pen** 🖾 (Hareley Farm) A bit different from most farms open to the public, this is very much a working pig farm rather than a cutesy tourist attraction, so although small children still get the same excitement from seeing and meeting the animals, older visitors enjoy an intriguing introduction to the realities of the pig business. They've been opening to visitors for only a few years, and there's a genuine enthusiasm in the owner's approach – they can be as interested in the visitors as the visitors are in the pigs. They do conducted tours of the piggery, where visitors can generally hold a piglet in the pens or yards. Pigs are fascinating enough at the best of times, but hearing about farming them is a real eye-opener; who'd have thought that, according to regulations, the lighting level in the pens should be bright enough to read standard newsprint without difficulty? Fair enough – the pigs need something to do in the evenings. As well as the pigs, you might come across lambs in early spring. Wear wellies in wet weather. All the equipment in the play area is made on the farm. For a small extra charge there are quiz trails around the attractive surrounding woodlands, and there's plenty of space for picnics (they open an hour early for picnickers). Staff are friendly and knowledgeable. Though you might spend less time here than at more developed attractions, you really do go away feeling you've not only had fun, but learned something as well. Pig fans should visit their rather jolly website (www.btinternet.com/~pigpen) for downloadable oinks and snuffling noises. Snacks, shop, some disabled access; open pm May–Sept, plus in Easter and October school hols; (01886) 884362; £2.50 (£1.50 children 3–12).

ABBEY DORE SO3830
🏛 🕸 ❋ Primarily the impressive surviving part of a once-huge 12th/13th-c Cistercian abbey church, with Early English features and an awesome stone altar. **Abbey Dore Court Garden** Attractive riverside lawns and gardens, with good views across to the ruins. Snacks (in 17th-c stables), disabled access; cl Weds, and mid-Oct–Feb; (01981) 240419; *£2.50.

ALMELEY SO3351
🕮 Early 18th-c half-timbered Quaker Meeting House, contemplative feel; key in porch.

ASHTON SO5164
🕮 🕸 **Berrington Hall** (A49) Elegant late 18th-c neo-classical house, very elaborate inside, with beautiful décor and furnishings (mostly French), charming nursery, and interesting examples of 'downstairs' life in a Georgian dairy and laundry. The grounds were landscaped by Capability Brown – and in fact the house was built by his son-in-law. Pleasant circular walk through the park (July–Oct only); new play area and children's orienteering course. Meals, tearoom, shop, disabled access; open pm daily except Thurs and Fri and Good Fri Apr–Oct; (01568) 615721; £4.20, £2 garden only; NT. The Stockton Cross Inn (A4112 NE of Leominster) is good.

BISHOP'S FROME SO6647
🐗 🕸 ⚘ **Hop Pocket Hop Farm** Traditional hop farm, its hundred acres a hive of activity in the harvest season. Tours of kilns by arrangement, pretty gardens. They were moving the craft centre into a larger building as we went to press, and a plant centre should be open by the summer. Tearoom/restaurant – you can buy hop bines, and their hop pillows for poor sleepers are particularly popular. Disabled access; cl am Sun, Mon (exc bank hols), and Mon–Thurs Jan–Feb – best to phone for craft centre times; (01531) 640323; tours £2.50. The Green Dragon is a good pub.

BODENHAM SO5151
🕸 ♘ ❦ ❋ **Queenswood Country Park** 170 acres of woodland and

arboretum with over 500 tree varieties; also wildlife displays and good views. Meals, snacks, shop and information centre, disabled access; café cl 25–26 Dec; (01568) 797052; free, though car park 50p. The Three Crowns between Ullingswick and unspoilt Little Cowarne has very good food.

BROBURY SO3344

❀ ❀ 🖼 **Brobury House Gallery** Eight acres of semi-formal gardens with fine views; also watercolours and prints for sale. Disabled access (but no facilities); cl Sun, 25 Dec and 1 Jan; (01981) 500595; gardens £3, gallery free. They do B & B in the smart Victorian house, with fishing permits available. The Portway nr Monnington on Wye is a useful food stop.

BROCKHAMPTON SO5931

✝ Extraordinary turn-of-the-century Arts and Crafts church designed by Lethaby; note that this is in the little village between Hereford and Ross-on-Wye.

CAREY SO5630

★ Delightful tucked-away village, with a charming pub.

CREDENHILL SO4443

! **Escargot Anglais** (A480) Part of the National Snail Farming Centre, with snail trails showing various species (even hairy ones) and exhibitions. Shop, open summer wknds and Mon, Thurs and Fri by appointment only; (01432) 760218; £2.80. The Bell at Tillington does more orthodox food.

CROFT SO4565

⛪ ❀ ⌂ 🏚 ❀ **Croft Castle** The walls and turrets date from the 14th and 15th c, but the inside is mostly 18th-c, with an interesting staircase and plastered ceilings. Attractive parklands with avenue of 350-year-old chestnuts. New tearoom, shop, disabled access; open

pm Weds–Sun and bank hols May–Sept, plus wknds Apr and Oct; (01568) 780246; *£3.80; NT. The picturesque Bell at Yarpole is handy for lunch. The brackeny expanse of Leinthall Common, scattered with cottages, is a quiet corner of Herefordshire where you can walk around the castle's estate, and scale the modest heights of Croft Ambrey, an Iron Age hill fort with a view into Shropshire.

DINMORE SO4850

🍏 Near to the now closed Dinmore Manor, Green Acres has organically grown pick-your-own fruit and veg; Dinmore Fruit Farm has a very wide choice of apple varieties, as well as more conventional pick-your-own.

EARDISLAND SO4158

★ A gorgeous riverside black and white village; the spectacularly wonky weather-vane on one ivy-clad dovecot has been at that angle for years. The friendly Cross Inn has decent food.

🏠 ⌂ 🍏 **Burton Court** (A44 just S of Eardisland) Interesting old house with 14th-c great hall, and collections of ship models, costumes and natural history specimens, and a railway room with working model railway. Also working model fairground, and pick-your-own. Teas, shops, disabled access; open pm Weds, Thurs, wknds and bank hols May–end Sept, or evenings by arrangement; (01544) 388231; £2.50.

EARDISLEY SO3149

✝ **Eardisley church** 12th-c font with wonderfully vivid carvings of sinner being wrested from clutches of evil.

EASTNOR SO7336

⛪ ❀ ⚦ ♕ **Eastnor Castle** (just E of Ledbury) Splendid neo-Gothic castle, especially dramatic in autumn, when the virginia creeper that all but envelops the stirring battlements turns a fierce red.

Days Out

Black and white villages: Weobley, Pembridge and Eardisland villages; lunch at the Riverside, Aymestrey; Croft Castle; walk over Leinthall Common to Croft Ambrey.

Wye cornucopia: Ross-on-Wye; Hoarwithy church; lunch at the Cottage of Content, Carey; Brockhampton church; Weston's Cider Farm, Much Marcle; Goodrich Castle.

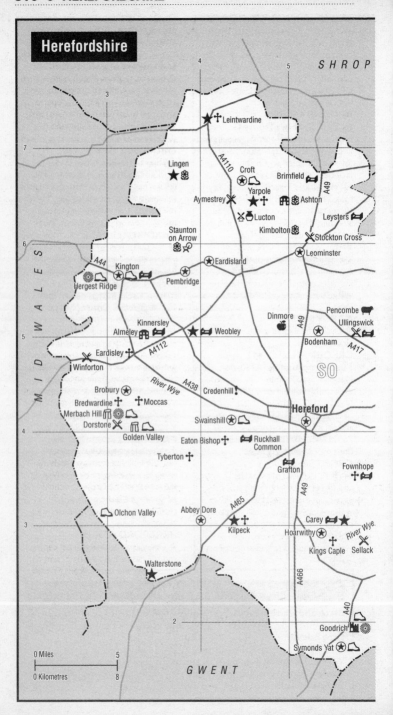

Herefordshire

S H R O P

Leintwardine

A4110

Lingen

Croft

Brimfield

Aymestrey

Yarpole

Ashton

A49

Lucton

Leysters

Staunton
on Arrow

Kimbolton

Stockton Cross

Leominster

A44

Kington

Eardisland

M
I
D

Hergest Ridge

Pembridge

W
A
L
E
S

Kinnersley

Dinmore

Pencombe

Ullingswick

Almeley

Weobley

A49

Bodenham

A417

Eardisley

A4112

SO

Winforton

A438

Credenhill

Brobury

River Wye

Bredwardine

Moccas

Merbach Hill

Swainshill

Hereford

Dorstone

Golden Valley

Eaton Bishop

Ruckhall
Common

Tyberton

Grafton

Fownhope

A49

Olchon Valley

Abbey Dore

A465

Carey

River Wye

Kilpeck

Hoarwithy

Sellack

Kings Caple

Walterstone

A466

2

A40

Goodrich

Symonds Yat

0 Miles   5

0 Kilometres   8

G W E N T

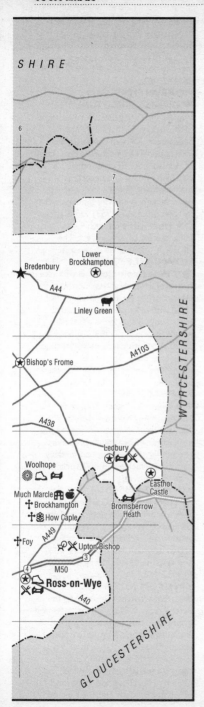

Designed by Pugin, the richly decorated rooms are breathtaking, with fine collections of armour, tapestries, furniture and paintings. The attractive grounds have an arboretum, 300-acre deer park, woodland walks, adventure playground, children's maze and garden centre. Meals, snacks, shop; open Sun and bank hols Easter–early Oct, and every day except Sat in July and Aug; (01531) 633160; £4.75. Eastnor village's thatched post office is lovely.

GOLDEN VALLEY SO3141

△ 🏛 The B4348/B4347 Golden Valley road is a pretty drive, with particularly satisfying walks in the surrounding hills; the tucked-away village of Dorstone has an impressive prehistoric burial mound nearby (and Herefordshire's oldest pub). The remoter roads parallel to this, to the W, are also well worth the drive, through Clodock (delightful church) and Michaelchurch Escley (another good pub down by the river), or passing Craswall.

GOODRICH SO5719

🏰 ❋ △ **Goodrich Castle** Readers are very fond of this proper-looking 12th-c castle, built using the same red sandstone rock it stands on so that it seems almost to grow out of the ground. Still plenty to see, with towers, passageways, dungeon and marvellous views of the surrounding countryside. Shop; cl 24–26 Dec, 1 Jan; (01600) 890538; £3.10. These formidable ruins are a feasible objective for stout-hearted walkers from Symonds Yat – or could be a starting-point for Wye Valley gorge walks. The Crown off the B4228 at Howle Hill is the nearest recommended place for lunch (not Mon).

HEREFORD SO5039

★ Grew as a regional market centre, and still has its busy livestock and general market every Weds. For the rest of the week it feels very quiet-paced and old-fashioned, its streets (some pedestrianised now) lined with handsome Georgian and other buildings (Church St is almost wholly medieval). Guided walks leave the tourist information centre every day from May–mid-Sept at 10.30am (2.30pm Sun). Wye-side walks give a pleasing view of the city, its spires and towers.

Saxtys, the Green Dragon Hotel and Imperial Hotel are all useful for lunch.

🐂 **Bulmer's Cider Mill** (Plough Lane) This enormous modern plant has tours and tastings. Shop, cl wknds, bank hols, and mid-Dec–Feb, tours (10.30am, 2.15pm, 7.30pm) by appointment; (01432) 352000; £2.95, joint ticket with cider museum below £3.95.

🏛 ⚘ ♿ **Churchill House Museum** (Venns Lane, northern outskirts) Regency house in fine grounds, with good local history, room settings, and 18th- and 19th-c furniture, costumes and paintings. Shop, some disabled access; open pm Weds–Sat; cl Oct–Mar; (01432) 267409; free.

♿ 🐂 **Cider Museum** Cider-making through the ages, with huge 17th-c French press, original cellars, and a working cider-brandy distillery – the first licensed for over 250 years. Shop, limited disabled access; cl winter Mon, 25–26 Dec and 1 Jan; (01432) 354207; *£2.30.

♿ 🖼 **City Museum & Art Gallery** Natural history and archaeology, interesting bee-keeping display, and changing art exhibitions. Shop, disabled access; cl 25–26 Dec and winter Suns; (01432) 260692; free.

✝ **Hereford Cathedral** Nicely placed on the banks of the Wye, this largely Norman building has a lovely 13th- and 15th-c chapel, as well as the country's biggest chained library (the second biggest is at All Saints Church, at the opposite end of the main street) and the famous Mappa Mundi, the largest surviving 13th-c world map. There's a splendid interpretative exhibition, with computer displays; the map is shown in a specially dimmed room to preserve it. Meals, snacks, shop, disabled access; some parts cl Sun, occasional lunchtimes, Good Fri, 25 Dec; (01432) 359880; cathedral free, exhibition £4. Guided tours at 11am, 1pm and 2.30pm (£1.50) summer to end Sept.

🏛 **Old House** (High Town) Glorious Jacobean house with period furnishings and paintings. Shop, limited disabled access; cl Sun (exc Apr–Sept), Mon (exc bank hols), 25–26 Dec, 1 Jan and Good Fri; (01432) 260694; free.

⛲ **Waterworks Museum** Restored Victorian pumping station, with giant steam pumping engines, and smaller handpumps; you can try working some. Snacks, shop, disabled access; open pm last Sun of month, Apr–Sept, second Sun July–Sept, plus bank hols; (01432) 361147; *£2.

HOARWITHY SO5429

🐎 **Glenda Spooner Farm** This friendly and caring place, former home of the jockeys Michael and Peter Scudamore, is now a centre for the International League for the Protection of Horses, offering care and rehabilitation for equine victims of maltreatment. Some disabled access; open Sat and Weds 11–4pm or anytime by appointment; (01953) 498682; free.

✝ ★ **Hoarwithy church** Remarkably Italianate, full of mosaics, etc. The village, nr the River Wye, is attractive.

HOW CAPLE SO6130

⚘ ✝ **How Caple Court** Eleven acres of peaceful formal and woodland Edwardian gardens overlooking the river, with old roses and unusual herbaceous plants for sale. Snacks; cl wknds Oct–Feb; (01989) 740626; £2.50. Also interesting medieval church and fabrics shop. The Green Man at Fownhope serves generous, popular bar food.

KILPECK SO4430

✝ ★ **Kilpeck church** This small Norman church in a delightful little hamlet has amazing sandstone carving inside and out, beautifully preserved (except for the more uncomfortably pagan bits which prudish Victorians tried to remove).

KIMBOLTON SO5161

⚘ **Stockton Bury Gardens** (A4112 S) Attractive and developing garden complex covering 4 acres, good for a gentle wander. Plant sales, disabled access; cl am, all Mon (exc bank hols) and Tues, plus Nov–Mar; (01568) 613432; *£3.

KINGTON SO2956

★ ⌂ Attractive border town by the River Arrow, well placed for walks (for example up the Hergest Ridge). Antiques and bric-à-brac are noticeably cheaper here than – say – in Gloucestershire; one shop specialises in cigarette cards, by the thousand. The Queen's Head has good-value food. NE of town at Bradnor Hill, the Kington

Golf Club (set in 240 acres of NT-owned land) is the highest in the country, and has good views.

⚜ 🏵 **Hergest Croft Gardens** (just W, off A44) The splendid result of inspired work by several generations of keen gardeners; some of the centenarian rhododendrons in the woods are of almost incredible size. Famous kitchen garden with colourful flowerbeds, and the national collections of birches and maples. Snacks, shop, some disabled access; cl am, and all Nov–Apr; (01544) 230160; *£3.50.

◠ ☀ **Hergest Ridge** Reached via a cul-de-sac from Kington, this is NW Herefordshire's answer to the Malvern Hills – and like them (allegedly) triggered Elgar, in this case to write his *Introduction and Allegro for Strings*, as well as Mike Oldfield with his album *Hergest Ridge*; the less-known composer Moeran also walked here frequently, and his *Sinfonietta* was inspired by the area. It's another of those ridges for walkers who can't decide whether they prefer the gentle lowland textures of England or the more rugged offerings of Wales. The walk gets better with every step, as the wide ridge tapers into horseback width at the far end, above Gladestry in Powys.

🐄 🐤 ⚜ **Small Breeds Farm Park** (off A4111 S) Friendly little farm with rare and unusual miniature horses, goats, poultry, pheasants and waterfowl, as well as a family of playful chipmunks. New this year are a pair of Kune Kune pigs. A particular favourite is Dorrie, the miniature Dexter cow, who even on tiptoe is just 81cm (32in) high; she has a strapping daughter, Delores. All the animals can be displayed under cover if it's raining, and there's a heated barn for picnics. The views and setting are a bonus, and the extensive collections of owls and waterfowl are set in an attractively landscaped garden. They plan to make a play pen for the under-5s. Snacks, shop, disabled access; cl Nov, and Jan–Easter; (01544) 231109; *£3 (£2 children).

LEDBURY SO7137

★ 🏯 ✝ 🏠 ⚘ The spaciously leisured High St has some fine buildings: the old Market House, the Feathers Hotel and Ledbury Park House are famous for

their well balanced 15th- and 16th-c timbering, and there are plenty of similar structures. From the Market House an exceptional alley of ancient jettied buildings leads to the partly Norman church of St Michael and All Angels, with an unusual spire tower detached from the main building, and its carillon ringing out a well known hymn every third hour. The Old Grammar School along here has been restored as a heritage centre (cl Nov–Easter). The council offices must be the only ones in the country decorated with medieval wall paintings; you can see these any weekday between 11am and 2pm; free. There are craft workshops, antique shops, a national Playmobile specialist and a decent book shop, and the Feathers has good food. The road N towards Mathon through Wellington Heath (where the Farmers Arms is a good dining pub) has some nice views.

LEINTWARDINE SO4074

★ ✝ This appealing riverside village is notable partly for its church – much bigger than usual for this county.

LEOMINSTER SO4958

★ ✝ An attractive centre, the medieval streets almost lined with black and white timbered houses. The red priory church still has many of its original Norman features, and the handsome old Talbot has decent food.

🏛 **Herefordshire Cheese-making** (A44, 2m W) You can watch cheese being made by hand using traditional methods. Snacks (inc ploughman's with their own cheese), shop, disabled access; shop and café cl winter Sun and Mon (cheese-making only Mon, Weds and Fri 10–2.30pm); (01568) 720307; *£1.75.

LINGEN SO3667

★ ⚜ Attractive village prettily set among hills, with Kim Davis's renowned alpine nursery and garden.

LINLEY GREEN SO6953

🐖 **Pig Pen** See *separate family panel on p.314*.

LOWER BROCKHAMPTON SO7055

🏯 ☀ ⚜ 🏠 **Lower Brockhampton House** Idyllic timber-framed and moated 14th-c manor house in attractive secluded countryside. Particularly interesting 15th-c gatehouse, and the ruins of a 12th-c chapel. Shop, some disabled access; cl Mon exc bank hols, Tues, and Nov–end Mar; (01885) 488099; £2; NT. The Trust also own the adjacent 1,720-acre Brockhampton Estate, with splendid views from its park and woodlands, marked trails and a sculpture trail. The Talbot at Knightwick is nice for lunch.

LUCTON SO4263

✗ ☗ **Mortimer's Cross Mill** Charming watermill on banks of River Ludd, still in working order, with an exhibition on the decisive Wars of the Roses battle fought here in 1461. Open pm Thurs, Sun and bank hols Apr–Sept; (01568) 708820; *£2. The Riverside at Aymestrey has good food.

MERBACH HILL SO3143

△ ❋ ⬚ Reached by driving up from Bredwardine, and then walking from the top of the lane, this gives a view right over the Black Mountains, Herefordshire and Radnorshire. A short stroll along the lane SE brings you to Arthur's Stone, a prehistoric burial chamber.

MUCH MARCLE SO6433

⬚ **Hellens** Unspoilt manor house dating from the 13th c; you can see the portrait of Catherine of Braganza that convinced Charles II to marry her. Teas; open pm Sat, Sun, Weds and bank hols Easter–Sept; (01531) 660668; £3.50.

☗ **Weston's Cider Farm** ▣ Still alongside the family house, this has an engaging combination of modern equipment and old-fashioned atmosphere. Enthusiastic guided tours, liberal tastings, interesting ciders and perries. Meals, snacks, good shop with wide range of ciders, tours by appointment; cl Sun and pm Sat and Christmas wk; (01531) 660233; *£3. The nearby Slip has good dishes of the day and outstanding gardens; the memorial monuments in the village church are unrivalled in the area.

OLCHON VALLEY SO3029

△ Perhaps the remotest place in Herefordshire, a magnificent dead-end valley beneath the E flank of the Black Mountains. From the well signed picnic site nr Longtown, a path heads up the Black Hill, an exciting knife-edge ridge, its end-on aspect strikingly triangular – this bit is known as the Cat's Back; after

the trig point you can make a circuit by dropping down from the very head of the Olchon Valley, or carrying on over peaty terrain to join the Offa's Dyke path.

PEMBRIDGE SO3958

★ ✝ One of Herefordshire's most striking black and white villages, full of fine timbered buildings inc a medieval market hall, the ancient New Inn, and a lovely church with an unusual detached belfry where you can watch the clock mechanism.

☗ **Dunkerton's Cider Farm** (Luntley) Uses ancient, traditional, local cider-apple and pear cultivars, for distinctive ciders and perries; welcoming atmosphere. Free tastings, and good restaurant; cider mill cl Sun; restaurant cl Jan–Feb.

PENCOMBE SO5951

🐄 **Shortwood Dairy Farm** Working farm ideal for children, with hands-on afternoon activities like milking Daisy or feeding the pigs and calves; sheep-shearing May bank hol. Good play area. Snacks, shop; cl Oct–Easter (though open Oct half-term for cider-making); (01885) 400205; £3. The Three Crowns at Ullingswick has very good food.

ROSS-ON-WYE SO5924

★ ⬚ △ ⚲ Picturesquely perched on a sandstone cliff by the river, with twice-weekly markets at the striking 17th-c market hall. The lower riverside part has attractive waterside walks; the Hope & Anchor here has decent food and Oat Cuisine on Broad Street has substantial vegetarian food. There are pleasant woodland walks in Penyard Park, SE of the town.

❀ ❋ **Kingstone Cottages** (Bury Hill, Kingstone; off A40 E) Charming, exuberant cottage garden, not to be missed at midsummer for its profusion of old-fashioned pinks and border carnations. Also fine views, and a tucked-away little grotto – looking out it seems as though you're waist-high in water. Unusual plants for sale; open wkdys early May–early July, or by appointment; (01989) 565267; *£1.

STAUNTON ON ARROW SO3560

❀ ⚘ **Horseway Herbs** (Horsewayhead Cottage) Friendly little place; you can wander around the gardens, and the herb plants are sold as both plants and crafts; they also sell home-made pickles and jams. Snacks, disabled access; cl Weds, all Nov–Mar; (01544) 388212; free. The New Inn at Pembridge has good food.

SWAINSHILL SO4341

❀ ♨ ◠ ❋ **Weir Gardens** Delightful riverside gardens at their best in spring, with displays of bulbs set in woodland trails, and fine views from clifftop walks. Paths can be steep in places. Open Weds–Sun (and bank hols) mid-Feb–Oct; £2; NT. The Ancient Camp at Ruckhall is quite handy.

SYMONDS YAT SO5517

♥ ❋ ◠ ⚓ Shared with Gloucestershire on the other side of the river, this is a spectacular bend of the River Wye through a steep wooded rock gorge, where peregrine falcons nest (the RSPB have a demonstration area); splendid Wye views, nature trails; two inns on either side of the river are linked by a hand-pulled ferry, and there's ample (walkers would say over-generous) parking. It's a big tourist draw. There's potential for more ambitious walks in the gorge, where an old railway line follows the river; to the SW an entertainingly rickety wire-mesh suspension bridge at the Biblins gives access to the W bank, in addition to the chain ferry at Symonds Yat village.

❀ ! ☺ **Jubilee Park** Centres on a hedge maze created for the Queen's Silver Jubilee; a lively maze museum tells the history of similar labyrinthine creations. Meals, snacks, shop, disabled access; open Good Fri–end Sept; (01600) 890360; £3.50.

❀ **Splendour of the Orient** On the same site as Jubilee Park this has

oriental watergardens; £1. For an extra £2, an indoor tropical garden area has an adventure playground with scenes from fairytales. Maybe weekend events such as martial arts displays or talks on feng shui. Snacks, shop (specialising in cane furniture), disabled access; cl Dec 25–26; (01600) 890668.

UPTON BISHOP SO6327

⚒ **Wobage Farm Craft Workshops** Several potters, a furniture-maker, wood-carver and jeweller; open wknds only; (01989) 780233; free. The Moody Cow is a good individual lunch stop.

WEOBLEY SO4051

★ In the very top rank of Herefordshire's black and white villages, with its long sloping green, and idyllic stroll out past the bowling green to the church; the Olde Salutation is good for lunch.

WOOLHOPE SO6135

◠ ❋ The elevated country around here has a good variety of scenery for walkers; the views from Ridge Hill east and the more densely wooded hills nr Mordiford are among the highlights.

YARPOLE SO4765

★ ✝ The church of this attractive streamside village has an uncommon free-standing medieval bell tower.

★ **Other attractive villages**, all with decent pubs, include Bredenbury SO6056 (despite the main road) and Walterstone SO3425 (peaceful walks). ✝ Quiet country drives can link several **attractive churches**, such as Bredwardine SO3344, Moccas SO3543, Tyberton SO3839 and Eaton Bishop SO4439; or perhaps Fownhope SO5834, Kings Caple SO5528 and even Foy SO5928 with Brockhampton and Hoarwithy.

Please let us know what you think of places in the *Guide*. Use the report forms at the back of the book or simply write us a letter.

Where to eat

AYMESTREY SO4265 **Riverside** *(01568) 708440* Black and white timbered riverside inn with a rambling beamed bar, some fine furniture, log fires and a relaxed atmosphere; good ambitious food, well kept own-brewed beers, decent wines, and obliging service; pleasant bdrms. **£19.50|£5.95.**

DORSTONE SO3141 **Pandy** *(01981) 550273* Cosy half-timbered ancient pub, very relaxed and friendly, with imaginative food (lots of fresh fish and game), beamed and flagstoned rooms, a woodburning stove, and well kept beers; partial disabled access. **£18|£5.95.**

LEDBURY SO7137 **Market Place** *(01531) 634250* Pleasant bustling restaurant open all day for morning coffee, lunch and afternoon tea with home-made cakes, flans and puddings; cl pm, 25–26 Dec, 1 Jan. **£9.40|£3.**

ROSS-ON-WYE SO5924 **Faisan d'Or Brasserie** 52 *Edde Cross St (01989) 565751* Attractively refurbished little restaurant with an Art Nouveau feel, an expanded menu offering good, interesting food (inc nice cheeses), and a relaxed atmosphere; cl Sun–Mon, 25 Dec–2 Jan; well behaved children welcome. **£24.50.**

SELLACK SO5526 **Lough Pool** *(01989) 730236* Attractive black and white timbered cottage in lovely countryside, with a log fire at each end of the beamed central room, flagstones and bunches of dried flowers, plus other individually decorated rooms leading off; well liked, interesting food, well kept real ales, several malt whiskies, local farm ciders, and a well chosen wine list; cl pm 25 Dec; well behaved children in snug or restaurant only; disabled access. **£19.95|£3.25.**

STOCKTON CROSS SO5261 **Stockton Cross Inn** *(01568) 612509* Heavy-beamed long bar with old-fashioned feel, a huge log fire and woodburner, solid furnishings, a wide choice of enjoyable food, well kept beer, and good, welcoming service; seats in garden; cl pm Mon (exc bank hols); children over 6. **£21.25|£6.50.**

ULLINGSWICK SO5949 **Three Crowns** *(01432) 820279* As well as a place for local farmers to enjoy their well kept ales, this bustling place is very popular for its very good, imaginative food from an extensive, seasonally changing menu (the choice is smaller at lunchtime); charming, cosy, traditional rooms with hops on low beams, open fires, some no smoking areas, and fine wines; tables outside. **£25|£8.**

UPTON BISHOP SO6326 **Moody Cow** *(01989) 780470* In a quiet village, this friendly pub has several snug separate areas, a pleasant medley of stripped country furniture, a big log fire, no smoking, rustic candlelit restaurant and a second small dining room; good choice of enjoyable food, and well kept beers; cl Mon; children must be well behaved. **£22|£7.**

WINFORTON SO2946 **Sun** *(01544) 327677* Very friendly and neatly kept little pub with beamed rooms, woodburners, particularly interesting food, real ales, and a sheltered garden; good bdrms; cl Tues; children over 10. **£25.50|£7.50.**

Special thanks to Dirk Eachus.

We welcome reports from readers

This *Guide* depends on readers' reports. Do help us if you can – in return, we offer a discount on the next edition to people who've helped us with reports for it. Tell us what you think about places already in it, and anything extra you think we should say about them. And send us your ideas for inclusion in the next edition: places to visit, eat at or stay in, attractive drives or walks, maybe even unusual interesting shops you know of. Use the card in the middle, the report forms at the end, or just write – no stamp needed: *The Good Britain Guide*, FREEPOST TN1569, Wadhurst, E Sussex TN5 7BR.

Herefordshire Calendar

Some of these dates were provisional as we went to press. Please check information with the telephone numbers provided.

MARCH

25 Herefordshire Music, Speech, Drama and Dance Festival – *till 31 March* (01432) 275072

APRIL

1 Hereford Hereford Choral Society Concert in the Cathedral (01981) 250106
16 Leominster Easter Parade (01568) 616460
20 Ross-on-Wye Real Ale Festival at the Crown & Sceptre – *till 23 April* (01989) 562765
30 Eastnor Spring Country Craft Fair at the Castle – *till 1 May* (01531) 633160

MAY

1 Kington Spring Plant Fair at Hergest Croft Gardens (01544) 230160
2 Hereford May Fair – *till 4 May* (01432) 268430
6 Bromyard Spring Festival – *till 13 May* (01885) 482429
11 Abbey Dore Medieval Mystery Play at Dore Abbey – *till 27 May* (01981) 570251
27 Kingsland Show (01568) 612118
29 Eastnor Steam Fair and Country Show with Fred Dibnah at Eastnor Castle (01531) 633160

JUNE

3 Leominster Festival – *till 11 June* (01568) 612874
10 Goodrich Castle Welsh Male Voice Choir Open-air Concert and Stained-glass Window Dedication (01600) 890135; **Ross-on-Wye** Millennium Weekend: Herefordshire Life Through the Ages – *till 11 June* (01989) 564641
16 Credenhill Traherne Festival – *till 18 June* (01432) 760512; **Pembridge** St Mary's Church Flower Festival – *till 18 June* (01544) 388292
23 Abbey Dore Music Festival at Dore Abbey – *till 25 June* (01873) 821456
30 Ledbury Poetry Festival – *till 9 July* (01531) 634156

JULY

1 Bromyard Gala at Birchyfields Showground – *till 2 July* (01885) 483378
15 Eastnor Malvern Classic Mountain Bike Rally at the Castle – *till 16 July* (01531) 633160; **Madley** Festival of Classical Music – *till 22 July* (01981) 250309; **Much Marcle** Steam Rally – *till 16 July* (01531) 660464
23 Eastnor Classical Concert at the Castle (01531) 633160
29 Eastnor Hot-air Balloon Festival – *till 30 July* (01531) 633160

Herefordshire Calendar (cont.)

AUGUST

5 Ross-on-Wye Carnival (01989) 564651
13 Hereford Show – *till 14 August* (01432) 350338
14 Eastnor Children's Fun Week at the Castle (01531) 633160
17 Ross-on-Wye International Festival – *till 28 August* (01989) 562768
19 Hereford Three Choirs Festival at the Cathedral – *till 25 August* (01432) 359880; **Leominster** Millennium Family Fun Weekend – *till 20 August* (01568) 616348
20 Hereford Three Choirs Festival Fringe – *till 25 August* (01432) 268430; **Kington** Vintage Club Annual Rally (01544) 231568
25 Hereford Beer Festival at the Barrels – *till 28 August* (01432) 274968
27 Ross-on-Wye Regatta – *till 28 August* (01989) 564100
28 Ledbury Carnival (01531) 636147; **Leominster** Horse Show (01568) 612118

SEPTEMBER

15 Bromyard Folk Festival – *till 17 September* (01531) 670593
30 Eastnor Christmas Craft Fair at the Castle – *till 1 October* (01531) 633160

OCTOBER

14 Much Marcle Big Apple Weekend – *till 15 October* (01531) 670544
21 Hereford Photographic Festival – *till 18 November* (01432) 351964

DECEMBER

9 Leominster Victorian Street Fair (01568) 616348

HERTFORDSHIRE

Some interesting outings, and well protected areas of quiet countryside.

Though much of the county is built up, there are attractive villages and good escapes into protected countryside. Highlights for most adults are the Henry Moore sculpture garden at Much Hadham and in summer the rose gardens just outside St Albans – which itself is rewarding to visit, especially for its Roman remains. The zoological museum at Tring is remarkably intriguing. Knebworth House is a very good family outing; Standalone Farm on the edge of Letchworth and the friendly wildlife park at Broxbourne are also enjoyable for children. Three subterranean curiosities are the carved, medieval cavern under the pavements of Royston (new to the *Guide* this year), the shell-encrusted 'gothick' caverns under Ware, and the Roman bath hiding under the A1(M) near Welwyn.

Large areas of this county are taken up by the northward spread of London with continuous swathes of development, and also by the first early 20th-c New Towns, the garden cities of Letchworth and Welwyn, and their more modern successors Hatfield, Hemel Hempstead and Stevenage. But between and beyond these are green windows of carefully preserved farmland and some more wooded countryside. These yield pockets of pleasant walking terrain, though there is little that is really outstanding. A good point is that even in the prairie-like arable farmland that characterises large chunks of the county, the field paths are often in remarkably good condition and very adequately waymarked.

Where to stay

CHIPPERFIELD TL0401 **Two Brewers** *The Common, Chipperfield, Kings Langley WD4 9BS (01923) 265266* **£98.90;** 20 comfortable rms. Comfortable and very neatly kept country hotel with relaxing views of the pretty village green, a dark-beamed main bar with cushioned antique settles, bow-windowed lounge with sofas and easy chairs, open fires, and good bar and restaurant food; pleasant nearby walks; disabled access.

ST ALBANS TL1407 **The Manor St Michael's Village** *Fishpool St, St Albans AL3 4RY (01727) 864444* **£135;** 23 rms, with plenty of extras. Part 16th-c, part William and Mary house, this is a fine hotel in 5 acres of lakeside gardens, with comfortable lounges, a convivial bar, imaginative food in the attractive restaurant, and friendly staff.

ST ALBANS TL1407 **Sopwell House** *Cottonmill Lane, St Albans AL1 2HQ (01727) 864477* **£132.75;** 138 attractive rms. Cream-coloured Georgian house, much extended over the years, with a conservatory and traditional lounges, a cosy bar, good food in the smart Magnolia restaurant with fine trees that disappear up through the glass roof, a corridor with framed and signed shirts from FA Cup-winners and other international stars, and plenty of leisure facilities.

ST ALBANS TL1407 **White Hart** *Holywell Hill, St Albans AL1 1EZ (01727) 853624* **£67;** 11 rms, most with own bthrm. Civilised former coaching inn with 2 bar areas, antique panelling, handsome fireplaces and furnishings, a residents' lounge reached by barleytwist staircase, courteous friendly service, and a good restaurant.

To see and do

HERTFORDSHIRE Family Attraction of the Year

⌂ ❀ ! KNEBWORTH TL2221 **Knebworth House** (Old Knebworth)
The splendid house and its grounds are a huge draw for adults, but what gives the 250-acre park its main appeal to families is the really excellent extensive adventure playground. There's plenty to keep active boys and girls busy for quite some time, and as there's no extra charge on top of what it costs to see the rest of the estate you can keep coming back during the day. In addition to the usual wooden climbing equipment and so forth, there are quite a few exciting slides, including the monorail suspension slide (you hang on to a rope then slide back down to the ground), and the twisting corkscrew. Younger children get their own enclosure, Fort Knebworth. The house was originally a straightforward Tudor mansion, but was spectacularly embellished by Victorian author Sir Edward Bulwer Lytton; he wanted it to be a castle fit for the romantic characters in his novels. Still a lived-in home (the same family has been here for over 500 years), the grand rooms include a splendid Jacobean great hall, an exhibition on the great days of the Raj, and mementos of former guests like Dickens and Churchill. The well restored gardens were designed by Lutyens, and include a herb garden laid out to plans by Gertrude Jekyll; there's also a deer park, a Victorian maze, and a miniature railway (extra). Lots of special events throughout the year. With plenty of space for a picnic, to run around or kick a ball about, there's enough here to occupy families for a good lump of the day. Meals, snacks, shop, limited disabled access; open wknds Easter–Sept, and daily from Jun–early Sept and in the Easter hols – the house is only open in the afternoons; (01438) 812661; £6 for everything (£5.50 children 5–16) – £5 grounds only. A family ticket for the grounds only (which includes all the play areas) is £17.50 for 2 adults and 2 children. Along the outer edge of the park is the pretty little hamlet of Old Knebworth; the Lytton Arms here is a very good pub with a play area in the back garden.

ALDBURY SP9612
★ ⌂ A perfect village green, stocks, etc, attractive houses, teas and 2 friendly pubs; good walks nearby.

ALDENHAM COUNTRY PARK TQ1695
❀ ✇ Plenty of space for children to run around in, with an adventure play area, nature trails and a herd of longhorn cattle.

ARDELEY TL3027
★ ⌂ Attractive thatched village with good food at the Jolly Waggoner, and a pleasant quiet drive along the lane down through Wood End, Haultwick and Dane End. This rolling countryside is very rural, with quite an East Anglian flavour; some of Hertfordshire's best walking territory.
✗ **Cromer Windmill** (just NW) Partly 13th c, lovingly restored, the last remaining post-mill in the county, its sails turning again after standing idle for nearly 80 years. Open pm Sun, bank

hols and alternate Sats mid-May–Aug; (01992) 504331; £1.25.

ASHWELL TL2639
★ Attractive village with some fine houses and an unusually tall church tower; the Bushel & Strike just beside it and the Three Tuns are both useful for lunch.

AYOT ST LAWRENCE TL1916
★ ✝ ⌂ Delightful little backwater, with a very picturesque 12th-c ivy-covered ruined church near its old-fashioned inn; the existing church is an incongruously grand neo-Grecian affair. The village is conveniently close to link to a walk along the River Lea, which has been dammed at Brocket Hall to form a lake (in view from the public right of way). Shorter walks can start from Ayot Green, where an abandoned railway line is open to walkers and forms a useful link.
⌂ ⏛ **Shaw's Corner** Much as it was when GBS lived here, 1906–1950; Shaw

devotees will enjoy seeing his exercise machine, pen, spectacles, and even the soft Homburg he wore for 60 years. The tiny writing shed at the bottom of the garden was designed to revolve and so maximise sunlight. Open pm Weds–Sun and bank hols, Apr–Oct; (01438) 820307; £3.30; NT.

BENINGTON TL2923

🐝 ★ ◠ **Benington Lordship** Seven acres of Edwardian terraced gardens with many unusual plants, fine herbaceous borders, roses and a rock garden, and a particularly lovely splash of snowdrops in spring. The grounds include a very picturesque early 19th-c 'Norman' ruined gatehouse, actually put together from stones of the genuinely Norman ruined moated keep. Snacks, open pm Weds Apr–Sept and Sun Apr–Aug, plus pm bank hols, 3rd Sun in Oct for plant sales, and some dates Feb/Mar for snowdrops – ring for details; (01438) 869668; *£2.80. The village is one of the county's prettiest and most interesting, its church lovely when the snowdrops are out in late Feb. The handsome old Bell has generous food. The countryside around offers some of Hertfordshire's better walking, with quite an East Anglian flavour.

BRAUGHING TL3924

★ † Attractive village (pronounced 'Braffing') with a pretty 14th-c riverside church; the Axe & Compass is a decent pub with a restaurant.

BROXBOURNE TL3306

🐾 ⏚ 🐒 **Paradise Wildlife Park** (White Stubbs Lane) Friendly little zoo and leisure park with lions, monkeys, camels and zebras, and events from meeting the python to feeding the lions; also falconry displays; adventure playground, crazy golf, woodland walk and paddling pool. Meals, snacks, shop, disabled access; cl 25 Dec; (01992) 468001; £6.50.

ESSENDON TL2708

◠ The mildly hilly, partly wooded country around here is popular with weekend walkers, with pleasantly varied village-to-village paths.

GREAT AMWELL TL3612

★ † Pretty conjunction of a church, the pre-Norman Emma's Well and a pool with islets.

🐝 **Van Hage Garden Co** (A1170) This popular garden centre is an unusually lively place, good for an afternoon out, with a children's farm, and plenty to look at in addition to the excellent range of plants. Miniature railway some summer wknds. Meals, snacks, shops, disabled access; cl Easter Sun; (01920) 870811; free.

GREAT HORMEAD TL4029

★ An attractive village, with plenty of thatch and timbering.

GREAT WOOD TL2704

◠ 🐾 (Off the B157 N of Northaw; the Two Brewers is a useful stop) Pretty walks in ancient woodland.

HATFIELD TL2308

🏠 🐝 † **Hatfield House** Set in an extensive park, this great Jacobean house was built in 1611 on the site of a childhood home of Elizabeth I; the splendid State Rooms include portraits of the queen, and even her silk stockings, perhaps among the earliest worn in this country. Also the National Collection of Model Soldiers, with over 3,000 exhibits. The scented garden and knot garden contain plants that were typical between the 15th and 17th c. Meals, snacks, shop, disabled access; open Apr–Sept, park and gardens every day, house cl am and all day Mon exc bank hols and Fri. No guided tours pm Sat, Sun or bank hols; (01707) 262823; £6, park and garden only £1.50. The nearby church has a window by Burne-Jones, and the attractive village of Old Hatfield has a fine old pub (the Eight Bells). Beyond is the extensive built-up area that has now subsumed the Hatfield name.

HERTFORD TL3212

🏠 Some quiet older parts include the old main Fore St, which has handsomely pargeted buildings – one of them the relaxing old Salisbury Arms Hotel. There are several antique shops in St Andrew St (one in a fine 15th-c house).

🏰 🐝 **Hertford Castle** This so-called castle is in fact the 15th-c gatehouse for Edward IV's original moated castle, carefully restored and now occupied by the council; open pm first Sun in month May–Sept, for guided tours ring (01992) 584322; free. The extensive riverside grounds (with the massive flint walls of Henry II's castle) are always open.

McMullens Brewery is a striking Victorian building on the river. The Old Barge by the Lee Navigation Canal has a wide choice of vegetarian food among other dishes, and the Silver Fox (B1197, Hertford Heath) is very popular for lunch. Nearby Hertingfordbury is an attractive village, between river and beechwoods.

ð ✿ **Hertford Museum** (Bull Plain) Cheery local history museum, in an elegant 17th-c building; it has a graceful Jacobean knot garden. Shop, disabled access to ground floor and garden; cl Sun, Mon (exc bank hols), 25–26 Dec and Good Fri; (01992) 582686; free.

KING'S WALDEN TL1623
◠ This quiet village and the rolling farmland around it is pleasant walking territory.

KNEBWORTH TL2221
🏠 ✿ ! **Knebworth House** See *separate family panel on p.326.*

LETCHWORTH TL2232
The country's first garden city, begun in 1903.

ð ♭ **First Garden City Heritage Museum** (Norton Way S) Set in the architects' charming Arts and Crafts-style thatched cottages, the exhibits here illustrate the thinking behind this uniquely 20th-c idea. Shop, limited disabled access; cl Sun, 25–26 Dec; (01462) 482710; *£1. The nearby Three Magnets (Leys Ave) is a good new pub.

🐄 **Standalone Farm** (Wilbury Rd) Simple and unfussy working show farm, best for younger children with a genuine interest in animals. Milking demonstrations every day at 2.30pm, and in Mar and Apr (definitely the best time to come) you can bottle-feed new-born lambs (usually at noon and 4pm). Also pigs, free-range chickens and rare breeds of poultry wandering round the farmyard, exhibition barn with working beehive, model dinosaurs and various creepy-crawlies, outdoor play area, and 170 acres of farmland, with walks and arboretum. Shire horse wagon rides wknds and school hols. Teas, shop, disabled access; cl Oct–Feb (exc autumn half-term); (01462) 686775; £2.70.

LONDON COLNEY TL1604
✿ **Aylett Nurseries** (A414 N) Enthusiastically run garden centre specialising in geraniums, fuchsias and especially their award-winning dahlias. Meals, snacks, disabled access; cl 25–27 Dec, Easter Sun; (01727) 822255. The trial grounds for the dahlias are at Bowmans Farm, 5 minutes away by car – you can walk round free from Aug to the first frost of autumn. The farm itself has become quite a draw, not least because of its huge **farm shop**, practically a supermarket (though cheaper for most things), with an enormous range of produce. Also animals, tractor rides, lakeside walks, and play areas. Meals, snacks, disabled access; cl 25–26 Dec; (01727) 821253; shop free, farm £3.75.

✚ **De Havilland Heritage Museum** 📧 (adjacent to Salisbury Hall, off B556) The Mosquito bombers were developed here in secret from 1939, and the site now houses a collection of 20 different De Havilland aircraft, as well as engines and other memorabilia; a new education centre is opening this year with the history of De Havilland and engine exhibits. Snacks in the new verandah-style area in main hangar. Shop, disabled access; open Mar–Oct, pm Tues, Thurs and Sat, all day Sun and bank hols; (01727) 826400; *£4. There are pretty riverside gardens down by

---

Days Out

Distinctly East Anglian: Braughing; Westmill – lunch at the Sword in Hand there, or the Jolly Waggoner, Ardeley; Cromer windmill (limited opening) NW of Ardeley; Benington village and Benington Lordship (limited opening).

Romans and roses: St Albans Abbey; Verulamium Roman town, amphitheatre and museum; lunch at the watermill's Waffle House (St Michael's St), St Albans; Gardens of the Rose.

the bridge; the Green Dragon here is useful for lunch.

MILL GREEN TL2309

✕ ✧ **Mill Green Museum & Mill** Well restored working watermill with craft demonstrations most Suns Apr–Sept and Sats July and Aug, from paper-quilling to lovespoon carving. Shop, disabled access to ground floor only; cl am wknds, all day Mon, milling Sun pm, Tues and Weds; (01707) 271362; free.

MUCH HADHAM TL4219

★ An attractive village, with fine Tudor and Georgian houses, and a good specialist nursery (Hopleys).

✧ ✧ ✿ **Forge Museum & Cottage Garden** (High St) Based around a working blacksmith, the story of such craftsmen through the ages, with an unusual bee shelter in the Victorian-style garden. Snacks, shop, some disabled access; open Fri–Sun and bank hols in summer, in winter by appointment on wkdys only; (01279) 843301; 80p.

▣ ✿ **The Henry Moore Foundation** (Dane Tree House, Perry Green) This excellent sculpture garden is much enjoyed by readers. Several works are displayed in the studios where they were made, while the larger ones are shown off against a backdrop of woodland, pasture and hedgerows. Open wkdys only for 90-minute guided tour at 2.30pm, must book; (01279) 843333; *£3. The Hoops opposite has decent food.

NORTHCHURCH SP9609

✝ Largely swallowed up in Berkhamsted, but notable for the ancient church where Peter the Wild Boy is buried; the George & Dragon is handy for lunch.

PIRTON TL1431

★ ᠁ This is an attractive village; the green is actually the remains of a Norman motte and bailey.

RAVENSBURGH CASTLE TL1029

᠁ ⌂ Up in the woods above Hexton, this is an easily traced Iron Age hill fort – a pleasant stroll.

RINGSHALL SP9912

✿ ⚘ ⚘ ⌂ **Ashridge Estate** (Ringshall) Right on the county border and nr Whipsnade Zoo in Beds, 4,000 acres of unspoilt woodlands and open spaces. Plenty of deer and other wildlife (inc the dormouse, though you won't see it in daylight), and a monument erected for the Duke of Bridgewater. Teas summer wknds, shop and information centre, disabled access; monument and facilities cl am, Fri, and Nov–Mar; (01442) 851227; monument £1; NT. The Greyhound and the Valiant Trooper both at nearby Aldbury are good for lunch.

ROYSTON TL3540

⚑ ! **Royston Cave** (Melbourn St) Tucked beneath the pavement, this cave is thought to have been cut into the 60-metre layer of chalk, which underlies the town, by the Knights Templar in the 13th c; fascinating figures of saints and kings are carved into the walls. Open wknds and bank hols Easter–Sept (otherwise by appointment); (01763) 242223; £1.

ST ALBANS TL1407

✧ ⚐ Though modern shops dominate your first impressions, corners of real antiquity are tucked away between and behind them. This was one of the most important Roman towns in northern Europe, and has some fine, well excavated remains in peaceful surroundings. A stroll through the town in search of other notable buildings (the tourist information office in the Town Hall, Market Pl, has helpful guide maps) is rewarded by the surprisingly large number of decent pubs here. Down between abbey gate and park, the Fighting Cocks is based on an ancient building which had some connection with the abbey, and its interesting layout includes the clearly discernible shape of a cockpit. In the quietly attractive, largely Georgian St Michael's St, the Rose & Crown is very civilised, and the Six Bells is on the site of a Roman bath-house, though not visibly so. The Cock (Hatfield Rd) is worth looking out for because of its bizarre history; its floors were found to rest on thick foundations of human bones. Worth a look if you're nearby are the **museum** (Hatfield Rd), covering the town's post-Roman history (shop, disabled access to ground floor; cl am Sun, 25 Dec; free), and **Grebe House** in the park nr Verulamium, a regional wildlife trust HQ with a woodland

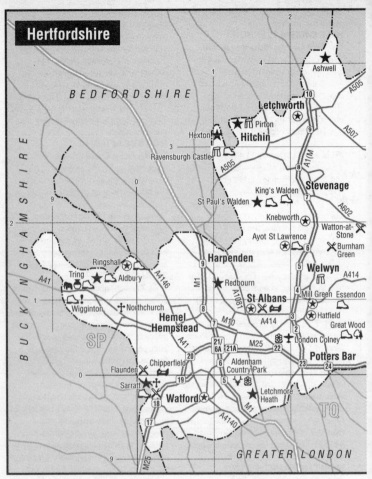

Hertfordshire

garden (cl wknds and bank hols; free). The B651 N towards Hitchin is quite a scenic country drive.

🏛 ❋ **Clock Tower** This medieval free-standing stone building has a bell, striking on the hour, even older than the tower itself. Exhibitions on the way up and fine views from the top; open wknds and bank hols Easter–mid-Sept; 25p. Nearby, French Row is a narrow alley of striking timbered buildings jettied out over the street, right by a modern shopping centre. The Fleur de Lys pub here is a remarkable medieval building.

🎇 **Gardens of the Rose** (B4630 S) The showgrounds of the Royal National Rose Society, with over 1,600 cultivars, many in mass plantings. Plenty of interesting cultivation trials going on, new roses from all over the world, lots of clematis, and a new iris garden. Snacks, shop, disabled access; open Sun and bank hols Apr–May and all Jun–Sept; (01727) 850461; *£4. The Holly Bush at nearby Potters Crouch has decent food (not Sun).

🏛 **Gorhambury** Two miles out of St Albans (the other side of Verulamium's park) but peaceful enough to make you think it's the heart of the country, an 18th-c house with a collection of 17th-c family portraits, and some 16th-c enamelled glass. Open pm Thurs

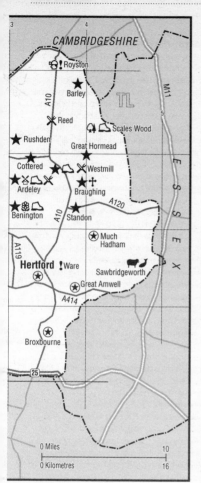

May–Sept; (01727) 855000; £4.50.
✕ ⏿ **Kingsbury Watermill** 16th-c
watermill half a mile from the city on
the banks of the River Ver, still with one
working waterwheel and a museum.
Meals, snacks, shop, disabled access;
cl 25 Dec; (01727) 853502; £1.25.
⏿ **Organ Museum** (Camp Rd, 2m
from the centre) Tuneful collection of
automatically operated organs and
other musical instruments. Recitals
every Sun 2–4.30pm, and concerts once
a month. Shop, disabled access (but no
facilities); open pm Sun only; (01727)
869693; £2.50.
† ❋ ⏿ **St Albans Cathedral** Up on a
mound, this has good views; its 11th-c

reddish exterior uses flint recycled
from the Roman remains. Once the
country's premier abbey, it suffered a
little after the Reformation, and its
fortunes didn't revive until Victorian
times. It was touched up a lot then, but
the majestic interior does have some
earlier features, inc 13th- and 14th-c
paintings in the long nave, and some
Saxon transept pillars. Meals, snacks,
shop, disabled access; cl pm 25 Dec,
cathedral free, £1.50 for audio-visual
show. The great 14th-c **abbey
gatehouse** beyond leads down to a
neat park, its lake and willow-edged
stream packed with ducks – a pleasant
place for a gentle stroll.
⏿ **Verulamium** This was the name of
the Roman city; its remains are down in
the SW corner of town, past the
cathedral and the attractive park
(coming from outside, most easily
reached by the A4147 off the Hemel
Hempstead exit from M1, junction 7).
⏿ **Verulamium Museum** (St
Michael's) This excellent museum, with
its lively interpretation of everyday
Roman life, as well as jewellery, wall
paintings and domestic items found
nearby, is undoubtedly the best place to
start a visit to the Verulamium site.
Shop, disabled access; cl am Sun, 25–26
Dec; (01727) 751810; £1.70. Follow
signs from here into the adjacent playing
fields: an unassuming brick building
looking like a garage or changing rooms
houses the carefully restored mosaic
floor and hypocaust underfloor heating
system of an excavated Roman villa;
free. Further on is a well preserved
section of the Roman town wall.
⏿ **Verulamium Roman Theatre**
Most impressive; not large by the
standards of some others in England
(room for 1,600), but taking into
account its good state of preservation
it's unique. Shop, limited disabled
access; cl 25–26 Dec, 1 Jan; (01727)
835035; £1.50.
ST PAUL'S WALDEN TL1922
★ ⌂ Birthplace of the Queen Mother,
a quiet village which, with the rolling,
rather East Anglian-feeling surrounding
countryside, offers some of
Hertfordshire's most pleasant walking.
SARRATT TQ0498
★ † ⌂ Long and attractive village

green; the church is partly Saxon, and the Cock nearby is good. There are pleasant unspoilt walks from here into the Chess Valley in Bucks.

SAWBRIDGEWORTH TL4815

🐷 🎵 **Kecksy's Farm** (off A1184) Working farm with sheep, cattle, poultry, rabbits and rare breeds of pig; coarse fishing is available on the river, and they have a campsite. Disabled access; cl Oct–Easter; (01279) 600896; £2. The George IV (nr the station) has a good restaurant, and the Coach & Horses up at Thorley Street is a good-value family food pub.

SCALES WOOD TL4133

🌂 ⌂ (nr Anstey) A useful strolling ground for gentle walks.

STANDON TL3822

★ Has some good timbered buildings in its curving High St.

TRING SP9211

🐘 👃 ⌂ **The Walter Rothschild Zoological Museum** (Akeman St, off High St) Part of the national Natural History Museum, this is made up primarily of the remarkably eclectic collections of the second Lord Rothschild, started when he was a little boy; thousands of preserved mammals, insects, birds, fish and reptiles. Snacks, shop, limited disabled access; cl am Sun, and 23–26 Dec; (01442) 824181; £3, children free (under-5s might find the displays slightly startling). Entry is free after 4pm wkdys, and 4.30pm wknds and bank hols, though as it shuts at 5pm you'd have to dash round a bit to see everything then. The Cow Roast (A4521 towards Berkhamsted) has good food (and popular family barbecues). Tring has a choice of canal towpath walks from nr the Grand Junction Arms pub (B488 at Bulbourne), where the Grand Union Canal has a part-abandoned offshoot, the Wendover Arm, and the still-operational Aylesbury Arm. (There's also canal access from the Boat down Ravens Lane in Berkhamsted and the Fisheries at Boxmoor.) For more ambitious walkers, the Royal Hotel on Station Rd stands by the Ridgeway long-distance path, which heads off W right across southern England.

WARE TL3513

! **Scott's Grotto** (Scotts Rd) Built in the 1760s by the poet John Scott, this is one of the finest bits of romantic 'gothickry' in the world, extending 20 metres (67ft) into the hillside under a modern housing development, with underground passages and chambers decorated with flints, shells, stones and minerals. Wear flat shoes and bring a torch. Open pm Sat and bank hols Apr–Sept, or by appointment; (01920) 464131; donation £1 requested. Several private gardens running down to the quiet River Lee have antique gazebos over the water, neatly restored with crisp white paintwork. The A10 N of here is quite a pleasant road, with decent food at the Sow & Pigs.

WATFORD TQ1097

🌂 🕸 🍴 ♨ ⌂ **Cheslyn Gardens** An unexpected pleasure in this largely modern urban area, with 3½ acres of woodland and formal gardens, and an aviary; cl 25 Dec; free. From Cassiobury Park there are **canal boat trips** along the Grand Union Canal on bank hols and pm Sun Easter–Sept, plus Tues and Thurs in Aug; (01438) 714528; around £5. The local **museum** (High St) has a display on the Watford Home Guard, the basis for the TV series *Dad's Army*. Shop, disabled access; cl pm Sat, all day Sun, bank hols; free.

WELWYN TL2315

🏛 **Welwyn Roman Baths** (just off A1(M), junction 6 – towards Welwyn on A1000, and counting M-way slip roundabout as the first roundabout go nearly all way round the second roundabout – car park through two 5-barred gates) Excavated before the construction of the A1 and since then rather ingeniously preserved within the motorway embankment, this Roman bath-house is all that remains of a 3rd-c villa. Very good condition, with explanatory displays. Shop, disabled access; cl am wkdys Jan–Nov (exc bank and school hols), all Dec, and occasional other dates; (01707) 271362; £1.

WESTMILL TL3627

★ ⌂ A happy combination of neat green, tiled cottages and a fine old church; the Sword in Hand, well restored after fire damage, has decent food. Pleasant walks nearby.

WIGGINTON SP9310

⌂ ! The landlord of the Greyhound

here is very helpful with suggestions for walks; the 18th-c summerhouse in the woods is an odd find.

★ **Other attractive villages**, all with decent pubs, include partly thatched Barley TL3938, Cottered TL3129, Hexton TL1230, Letchmore Heath TQ1597, Redbourn TL1012 (despite motorway noise, Church End with its workhouse and Norman church is pretty) and Rushden TL3031.

Pubs handy for walks include the Clarendon Arms at Chandlers Cross TQ0698, Two Brewers on Chipperfield Common TL0401, the Stag at Chorleywood TQ0295, Fish & Eels at Dobbs Weir TL3808 nr Hoddesdon, Three Blackbirds at Flamstead TL0714, Bricklayers Arms and Green Dragon at Flaunden TL0100, Alford Arms at Frithsden TL0110, the Huntsman at Goose Green TL3509 (for Hertford Heath), Cross Keys at Gustard Wood nr Wheathampstead TL1716, Five Horseshoes at Little Berkamstead TL2908, Bridgewater Arms at Little Gaddesden SP9913, the Cabinet at Reed TL3636, Harvest Moon at Thorley TL4718 and the White Lion at Walkern TL2826.

Where to eat

ARDELEY TL3026 **Jolly Waggoner** *(01438) 861350* Friendly and pretty little pub with lots of woodwork, civilised relaxed atmosphere, carefully prepared food in the bars and restaurant, a good range of wines, well kept Greene King ales, and an attractive garden; cl Mon; children over 7. **£30|£8.**

BURNHAM GREEN TL2616 **White Horse** *(01438) 798416* Thriving dining pub with attractive original black-beamed part by the bar counter, a big 2-floored extension (no smoking downstairs), good-value food, friendly service from uniformed staff, and well kept real ales. **£16.45|£4.95.**

FLAUNDEN TL0101 **Bricklayers Arms** *(01442) 833322* Cottagey pub with roaring log fires, snug low-beamed rooms, good-value bar snacks and a more elaborate restaurant menu (which can be eaten anywhere in the pub), a good range of real ales and wines, and friendly efficient service; it does get busy at weekends. **£19|£6.95.**

REED TL3636 **Cabinet** *(01763) 848366* Tiled and weatherboarded village house, now a civilised dining pub with a small cosy main bar and snug, no smoking restaurant with stripped floors, winter log fire and simple mix of wooden tables and chairs; good food with an emphasis on fresh fish dishes − lovely home-made puddings and cheeses, too − and real ales and fine wines. **£19.25|£6.**

ST ALBANS TL1307 **Waffle House** *Kingsbury Watermill, St Michael's St (01727) 853502* Little restaurant attached to mill (*see* **To see and do** *section, above*), serving delicious sweet and savoury waffles, and a good choice of drinks inc fresh milk shakes and pure fruit juices; riverside terrace; disabled access. **£10.**

SARRATT TQ0499 **Cock** *(01923) 282908* Cosy, white, 17th-c country pub with a carpeted snug, oak panelled lounge, inglenook fireplaces, a restaurant in a nicely restored thatched barn, generous helpings of well liked food (especially the daily specials), real ales, and benches in front as well as seats on a pretty back lawn with country views. **£19.70|£5.95.**

WATTON-AT-STONE TL2919 **George & Dragon** *High St (01920) 830285* Civilised pub first licensed in 1603, with antiques, open fires and daily newspapers, friendly efficient service, first-class, imaginative food in both the bar (good-value daily specials) and no smoking restaurant, and decent house wines; cl pm Sun; children must be well behaved. **£24|£6.**

WESTMILL TL3627 **Sword in Hand** *(01763) 271356* In a very attractive village, this 14th-c colour-washed pub is full of character with exposed beams, log fires and traditional-style furniture; the partly no smoking dining room has nice views over the garden and church, food is well presented and very good, ales are well kept, wines are decent, and there are plenty of seats on the terrace and in the garden, with a play area for children. **£21.95|£7.50.**

Hertfordshire Calendar

Some of these dates were provisional as we went to press. Please check information with the telephone numbers provided.

JANUARY

1 **St Albans** Wildlife Photographer of the Year at the Museum of St Albans – *till 30 January* (01727) 819340

8 **St Albans** Living History: Roman Legionaries at the Verulamium Museum – *till 9 January* (01727) 751810

22 **St Albans** New Year 2000 Concert (01727) 851557

FEBRUARY

12 **St Albans** Living Roman History at the Verulamium Museum – *till 13 February* (01727) 751810

13 **Hatfield** Snowdrop Sunday: gardens open at Hatfield House – *also on February 20* (01707) 262823

MARCH

4 **Hatfield** Listed Building Show at Hatfield House – *till 5 March* (01707) 262823

11 **St Albans** Living Roman History at the Verulamium Museum – *till 12 March* (01727) 751810

APRIL

8 **St Albans** Living Roman History at the Verulamium Museum – *till 9 April* (01727) 751810

23 **Knebworth** Jousting at Knebworth House – *till 24 April* (01438) 812661

30 **Knebworth** Country Show at Knebworth House – *till 1 May* (01438) 812661

MAY

1 **Hertford** Theatre Week at Hertford Castle – *till 6 May* (01992) 581993; also, Music Festival – *till 31 May* (01992) 503129

4 **Hatfield** Living Crafts: over 500 craftspeople at Hatfield House – *till 7 May* (01705) 426523

13 **Knebworth** Garden Show at Knebworth House – *till 14 May* (01438) 812661; **Rickmansworth** Festival Week – *till 21 May* (01923) 772325; **St Albans** Living Roman History at the Verulamium Museum – *till 14 May* (01727) 751810

20 **Rickmansworth** Canal Festival – *till 21 May* (01923) 778382

27 **Redbourn** County Show – *till 28 May* (01582) 792626

28 **New Mill** Canal Festival at Tring Wharf – *till 29 May* (01525) 381614

JUNE

10 **St Albans** Living Roman History at the Verulamium Museum – *till 11 June* (01727) 751810

11 **Knebworth** Heavy Horse Show at Knebworth House (01438) 812661

Hertfordshire Calendar (cont.)

17 Borehamwood Carnival Parade (020) 8207 1382
24 Hatfield Festival of Gardening: lectures, guided tours, flower marquee, arena events at Hatfield House – *till 25 June* (01707) 262823

JULY

1 Hatfield English Folk Dance Festival at Hatfield House (01707) 262823; **Knebworth** Concert at Knebworth House – *till 2 July* (01438) 812661; **St Albans** Festival – *till 16 July* (01727) 864511
8 St Albans Living Roman History at the Verulamium Museum – *till 9 July* (01727) 751810
15 Knebworth Pre-50 American Auto Club Rally at Knebworth House – *till 16 July* (01438) 812661
22 Knebworth Classic Corvettes Rally at Knebworth House – *till 23 July* (01438) 812661
29 St Albans National Show of Miniature Roses at the Gardens of the Rose, Chiswell Green – *till 30 July* (01727) 850461
30 Knebworth Fireworks Concert at Knebworth House (01438) 812661

AUGUST

4 Hatfield Pottery and Ceramics Festival at Hatfield House – *till 6 August* (01707) 262823
5 Knebworth NSRA Hot Rod Supernationals at Knebworth House – *till 6 August* (01438) 812661
12 St Albans Living Roman History at the Verulamium Museum – *till 13 August* (01727) 751810
19 Knebworth Craft Fair at Knebworth House – *till 20 August* (01438) 812661
26 Hatfield Fireworks Concert at Hatfield House – *till 27 August* (01707) 262823
27 Knebworth Classic Car Show at Knebworth House – *till 28 August* (01438) 812661

SEPTEMBER

8 Hatfield Country Homes and Gardens Show at Hatfield House – *till 10 September* (01707) 262823
9 St Albans Living Roman History at the Verulamium Museum – *till 10 September* (01727) 751810

OCTOBER

3 St Albans *Son et Lumière* at the Cathedral – *till 12 October* (01727) 864511
7 St Albans Living Roman History at the Verulamium Museum – *till 8 October* (01727) 751810
28 Hatfield Witches, Pumpkins and Fireworks at Hatfield House (01707) 262823

NOVEMBER

4 St Albans Gala and Fireworks Celebration at Verulamium Park (01727) 860780

Hertfordshire Calendar (cont.)

5 Hatfield Autumn Colours: gardens open at Hatfield House (01707) 262823

11 St Albans Living Roman History at the Verulamium Museum – *till 12 November* (01727) 751810

DECEMBER

9 St Albans Living Roman History at the Verulamium Museum – *till 10 December* (01727) 751810

We welcome reports from readers

This *Guide* depends on readers' reports. Do help us if you can – in return, we offer a discount on the next edition to people who've helped us with reports for it. Tell us what you think about places already in it, and anything extra you think we should say about them. And send us your ideas for inclusion in the next edition: places to visit, eat at or stay in, attractive drives or walks, maybe even unusual interesting shops you know of. Use the card in the middle, the report forms at the end, or just write – no stamp needed: *The Good Britain Guide*, FREEPOST TN1569, Wadhurst, E Sussex TN5 7BR.

ISLE OF WIGHT

Great for old-fashioned family seaside holidays – good beaches, better weather than most places in Britain, interesting events and places to visit; also under-rated coast and countryside, quiet off-season breaks.

The main family attractions here, Blackgang Chine and its Robin Hill stablemate at Downend, and Brickfields Horse Centre (other animals put through their paces here too) at Binstead, are firmly traditional. Quite a few other enjoyable visits centre on animals or birds, particularly Amazon World at Newchurch and the bird and animal attractions at St Lawrence. Many of the more child-oriented places close for six months over winter.

Osborne House at East Cowes is a highlight for many older people, Haseley Manor at Arreton is an enjoyable day out for young and old, the dinosaur museum near Brighstone brings interesting real-life authenticity to fossil hunting, and the newly opened Dimbola Lodge (Freshwater Bay) has interesting Victorian associations.

In high summer the main resorts and places to visit get very busy, yet even then, away from the main tourist haunts, much of the island is surprisingly unspoilt and little visited. The most attractive scenery is in the west, the largest concentration of things to do in the east.

At other times the island feels fresh, uncrowded and leisurely. The coastal walks are the finest in south-east England – worth coming just for these. Inland are long curving chalk ridges (tracks often follow the crests) and forestry plantations with many signposted woodland trails. The crossing takes about 30 minutes – half that for the Portsmouth–Ryde catamaran, even less for the Southsea Hovercraft.

Readers like the Lymington–Yarmouth trip best (you'll need to book in summer). Foot fares start at around £8, cars from around £35 – though the very cheapest fares are usually at pretty antisocial times: (0990) 827744 for bookings from Portsmouth to Fishbourne or Ryde, and Lymington to Yarmouth; (023) 8033 4010 for Southampton–Cowes; (023) 9281 1000 for Hovercraft Southsea–Ryde. Once you're there, prices are rather on the low side compared with the mainland, and for longer stays some hotels do good-value package deals that include the ferry fare.

The island bus service is excellent, especially between May and September; a week's bus pass is good value, as is a daily Rover road/rail ticket.

Where to stay

BONCHURCH SZ5777 **Lake Hotel** *Shore Rd, Bonchurch, Ventnor PO38 1RF (01983) 852613* ***£56,*** plus special breaks; 20 rms. Early 19th-c country house in 2 acres of pretty gardens with lots of flowers and plants in 3 light and airy lounges (one is an attractive conservatory), bar, restaurant and enjoyable food; cl Nov–Feb; children over 3; dogs by prior arrangement.
BONCHURCH SZ5778 **Winterbourne** *Bonchurch, Ventnor PO38 1RQ (01983) 852535* **£146 inc dinner;** 15 rms, most with own bthrm and many with sea views

and some in the coach house. Charming creeper-covered house with 4 acres of pretty grounds inc waterfalls, a stream, a small heated swimming pool, and restful day rooms, good food in attractive restaurant, and friendly staff and resident owners; Charles Dickens wrote *David Copperfield* here; cl Nov–Mar (though open wknds in Nov and Dec, and open Christmas and New Year); dogs welcome.

CHALE SZ4877 **Clarendon** *Chale, Ventnor PO38 2HA* (01983) 730431 ***£78;** 15 rms inc 3 suites, plus 10 more rms at Chale Bay Farm; winter special breaks. Warmly friendly hotel (and very well run Wight Mouse family pub, attached) with engaging helpful owners, lots of charm and character, a comfortable sun lounge and cocktail bar, good food, wines and real ales, and an extraordinary collection of whiskies; excellent for families; disabled access.

RYDE SZ6092 **Ryde Castle** *Esplanade, Ryde PO33 1JA* (01983) 563755 **£60;** 20 rms, many with sea views, and some quite modern. 16th-c castle with comfortable lounge, tapestries, a good bar, friendly helpful staff, enjoyable food in galleon-look restaurant, and excellent breakfasts.

ST LAWRENCE SZ5476 **Lisle Combe** *Bank End Farm, Undercliffe Drive, St Lawrence, Ventnor PO38 1UW* (01983) 852582 ***£38;** 3 rms, shared bthrm. Elizabethan-style farmhouse in 5-acre coastal garden with great sea views, friendly courteous staff, and lovely paintings and furniture – it was once the home of poet Alfred Noyes and is still owned by the family; they keep their own rare breeds and waterfowl park, and are close to coves and beaches; must book months ahead (so popular with return customers); self-catering cottage; cl Christmas–New Year; no dogs.

SEAVIEW SZ6291 **Seaview Hotel** *High St, Seaview PO34 5EX* (01983) 612711 ***£90,** plus special breaks; 16 attractively decorated rms, some with sea views and private drawing rooms. Small, friendly and spotlessly kept hotel with fine ship photographs in the chatty and relaxed front dining bar, an old-fashioned characterful back bar, good imaginative bar food, and a highly regarded evening restaurant; proper high tea for children (must be over 5 in evening restaurant); cl Christmas for 3 days.

SHANKLIN SZ5779 **Luccombe Chine House** *Luccombe PO37 6RH* (01983) 862037 **£80,** plus special breaks; 6 rms, all with four-posters and sea or garden views. Very friendly small hotel at the end of a long drive and surrounded by large wooded grounds – you can watch foxes and badgers at night taking food left for them on the lawn; a homely lounge with help-yourself drinks tray, beams and inglenook fireplaces, and very good food in the cosy dining room; good walks; cl Dec and Jan; no children or dogs.

SHORWELL SZ4582 **Westcourt Farm** *Shorwell, Newport PO30 3LA* (01983) 740233 ***£36;** 3 rms. Fine Elizabethan manor connected to a farm of 250 acres, with a comfortable lounge/dining room, and a restful atmosphere; no smoking; lots of surrounding walks; cl Nov–Apr; children over 12 – though may take younger ones out of season.

VENTNOR SZ5577 **Royal** *Belgrave Rd, Ventnor PO38 1JJ* (01983) 852186 **£120;** 55 well equipped rms. Friendly Victorian hotel with fine sea views, neat gardens with a heated outdoor pool, spacious and comfortable day rooms, good food in the attractive restaurant, and helpful service; disabled access.

YARMOUTH SZ3589 **Bugle** *The Square, Yarmouth PO41 0NS* (01983) 760272 **£66;** 9 rms, most with own bthrm (best to have one not above the lively bar). Bustling inn with bar decorated like a galleon stern, other panelled rooms, a friendly atmosphere, good bar and restaurant food (restaurant closed Sun and Mon), children's room, and sizeable garden.

YARMOUTH SZ3589 **George** *Quay St, Yarmouth PO41 0PE* (01983) 760331 **£130;** 17 comfortable rms. 17th-c house by the harbour with a marvellously relaxing atmosphere, a fine flagstoned hall, fresh flowers and open fires, a convivial bar and an attractive residents' sitting room, imaginative and enjoyable food in the informal brasserie and smart restaurant, hearty breakfasts, prompt, courteous service, and gardens leading to little private beach; children over 8.

To see and do

ISLE OF WIGHT Family Attraction of the Year

🐄 🐓 🦔 🦉 ST LAWRENCE SZ5276 **Rare Breeds & Waterfowl Park**
(Undercliff Drive) This good-sized collection of rare farm animals boasts a
really lovely setting, covering 30 secluded coastal acres, with fine views out to
sea. They recently added a meerkat enclosure, while the range of other animals
takes in miniature horses, deer, pigs, otters, llamas, cattle, owls, and delightful
pygmy goats. There are a hundred or so species of waterfowl and poultry, and
an undercover temperate waterfall house with free-flying birds. Younger
children have plenty of opportunities to get close to the animals: the highlight
for them is likely to be the Guinea-pig Village (which also has plenty of rabbits)
or the Chipmunk Mansion. Other animals to pet are located near to a simple
enough play area. Relaxed and undemanding, it's a charming spot to stroll
around, with natural ponds and streams amongst the appealing countryside.
You won't want to come in wet weather, but when it's dry it's possible to
spend anything from a couple of hours to most of a lazy day here. There's
plenty of space for picnics. Meals, snacks, shop, some disabled access; open
Mar–Oct; (01983) 852582; £3.70 (£2.20 children over 5). They do B & B in the
attractive old house, and there's a bus stop just outside (numbers 7, 7A and 31
all come here).

ALUM BAY SZ3085
The beach here is famous for its multicoloured sands from the different rock
strata in the cliff that runs down to it;
20 shades of pinks, greys and ochres,
showing up brightest after rain. The
High Down Hotel towards Totland has
decent food.
🏰 ❄ **Needles Old Battery** From
Needles Pleasure Park it's a ¾ mile walk
to this 19th-c Palmerstonian fortress
(you can't go by car); the parade-
ground shows off 2 12-ton gun barrels
salvaged from the sea and there is a
exhibition about World War I. A
longish underground tunnel leads to a
look-out spot that gives stunning views
of the Needles themselves, a group of
wave-battered chalk pinnacles, and
their lighthouse. Snacks; cl Fri and Sat
(exc July and Aug), and Nov–Mar;
(01983) 754772; £2.50; NT.
☺ ❄ 🐾 🏠 **Needles Pleasure Park**
Otherwise unremarkable clifftop
pleasure park which stands out for its
spectacular chairlift down to the beach,
with wonderful views along the way.
They sell little glass tubes with the sands
carefully layered inside. Meals, snacks,
shop, disabled access; cl Nov–Mar;
(01983) 752401; park entry free
(though car parking is £3), then
individual charges for attractions

(return trip on the chairlift is £2.50).
Glass-blowing demonstrations at
adjacent Alum Bay Glass (not Sat or
winter Sun; 80p); there's also a good
factory shop.
ARRETON SZ5386
✝ A pleasant place with a delightful
13th-c **church** (which has a brass-
rubbing centre). The White Lion is
good for lunch, and the cross-island
Wootton Bridge–Niton back road
through here has quietly attractive
views.
🐾 The lovely Elizabethan mellow stone
manor house here is no longer open to
the public, but nearby, the **Country
Craft Village** has craft workshops,
pub, and restaurant with home baking.
🏛 🐄 🐾 **Haseley Manor** 🔲 The
largest and oldest manor house open
on the island, some parts dating from
1310. The enthusiastic owners have put
a lot of effort into restoring the place,
and the 20 or so rooms are carefully
decorated in period style. The
reconstructed 18th-c farm here has
been greatly expanded over the last
year, with many crafts displays and
archeological exhibits housed in 2
barns; also animals, herb gardens, a
pottery and an adventure playground,
and so a useful family day out. Snacks,
shop, disabled access; cl Sat, Sun and

Oct–Apr; (01983) 865420; £5.

BEMBRIDGE SZ6488

⚓ ❄ Even in summer this is quiet for a coastal place, though with plenty going on in its yachting harbour, and a lifeboat station nearby. Though most of Wight's E coast is heavily developed, with the coastal path sometimes following roads and skirting large residential areas, Bembridge has the best opportunities for walks. Out on the Foreland the magnificent rock pools would keep any beachcomber happy for hours. The clifftop Crab & Lobster (Forelands), an easy walk up from the beach, has fabulous views. There's also a good walk S to Culver Cliff, for more views – the isolated clifftop Culver Haven pub nr the Yarborough Monument there commands a great panorama.

❋ **Maritime Museum & Shipwreck Centre** (Sherbourne St) Six galleries of salvage and shipwreck items, and tales of pirates and mermen. Shop, disabled access ground floor only; cl Nov–Mar; (01983) 872223; £2.50.

✗ **Windmill** The only surviving windmill on the island, built in 1700 and used until 1913. Shop; cl Sat (exc Easter Sat and July–Aug) and Nov–Mar; £1.40; NT.

BINSTEAD SZ5792

🐎 **Brickfields Horse Country** 🈸 Two daily parades of horses in the indoor arena (noon and 3.30pm), livened up by the appearance of a medieval knight, and a cowboy and indian, who chase each other around firing pistols and flinging tomahawks.

Also tours of stables, wagon rides, rabbits and guinea-pigs, and a collection of shetland ponies. This year they have branched out into pigs and there are pig races 3 times every day. Show-jumping displays from 7pm on summer Weds evenings (car boot sales Mon evenings), and on 3 evenings in mid-Dec they put on a spectacular Christmas show, which might include a pantomime and shetland pony Grand National. Meals, snacks, shop, disabled access; cl 25–26 Dec; (01983) 566801; £4.50. The old White Hart at Havenstreet is handy for lunch.

BLACKGANG SZ4876

☺ ❋ ↥ **Blackgang Chine Fantasy Park** This 40-acre family leisure park has an excellent policy on return visits: each ticket allows free entry for a second visit within 7 days. The liveliest attraction is an enjoyable high speed water chute, and there are plenty more gentle rides to suit younger children. The most interesting parts are the maritime museum at the restored quayside, and the complete replica of a Victorian sawmill, inc working steam and oil engines. The plentiful models of dinosaurs, goblins, and nursery rhyme scenes dotted around the gardens have been done with a fair bit of flair and panache, and the gardens are well illuminated on summer evenings. Also fossils and gemstones, a hedge maze, and several play areas, including one for toddlers. Meals, snacks, shop, some disabled acess; open late Mar–Oct; (01983) 730330; £5.50 (children 3–13

Days Out

Tennyson's strolling ground: Yarmouth; Newtown Old Town Hall and nature reserve; lunch at the Blacksmiths Arms W of Carisbrooke; Carisbrooke Castle; Calbourne; walk on Tennyson Down from Alum Bay, or visit Needles Old Battery – or dinosaur museum nr Brighstone.

Thatched cottages and a ruined mansion: Godshill; Appuldurcombe House, Wroxall; lunch at the Spyglass, Ventnor; Rare Breeds and Waterfowl Park, St Lawrence; Shorwell.

Queen Victoria's retreat: either Brickfields Horse Country, Binstead and Isle of Wight Steam Railway (described under Havenstreet) or Bembridge windmill and stroll on Culver Cliff; lunch at the Seaview Hotel, Seaview; Osborne House.

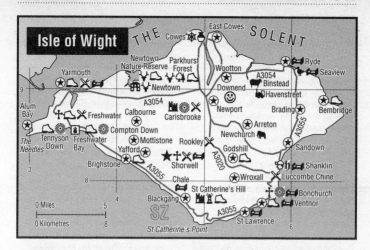

£4.50). The Wight Mouse at Chale is an excellent family pub, and the A3055 in both directions gives fine sea and coast views.

BONCHURCH SZ5778

✝ ✺ Much quieter than nearby Ventnor, with leafy lanes hugging the steep slopes and passing an unexpected tree-shaded pond; steep steps connect the different levels, and there's a quiet cove down below the cliff. The small 13th-c **church** has a lovely peaceful graveyard, and above the cliff St Boniface Down has tremendous views. The Bonchurch Inn is rather unusual, with its Italian landlord and food. For several miles along this section of coast, the cliffs have been and to some extent still are subject to massive landslides.

BRADING SZ6087

★ ✝ 🏛 ö ✺ Busy and attractive with interesting monuments in its Norman **church**, and a pretty graveyard. The Bugle is a useful family food pub. The remains of a **Roman villa** have good mosaics (cl Nov–Mar; £2.50). The road out over Bembridge Down to Culver Cliff gives fine views, especially from the Culver Haven pub at the end.

🏛 ö ! **Isle of Wight Waxworks** Set in the partly 11th-c Ancient Rectory Mansion, this is largely what you'd expect from a wax museum, with an adjacent collection of stuffed animals and birds. In the summer there are candle carving demonstrations. Shop, mostly disabled access; cl 25–26 Dec; (01983) 407286; £4.50.

ö **Lilliput Doll and Toy Museum** Excellent private collection, with over 2,000 exhibits dating from as far back as 2000 BC, and examples of almost every seriously collectable doll in Britain. Shop, disabled access (though there are 2 steps); cl 25 Dec; (01983) 407231; £1.55.

🏛 ⚙ 🌳 **Morton Manor** (off A3055 S) Friendly partly 13th-c manor house, set in lovely landscaped gardens with ornamental ponds and Elizabethan turf maze. The little vineyard has an exhibition of winemaking relics. Meals and snacks in new tearooms, shop, some disabled access; cl Sat, and Nov–Mar; (01983) 406168; £3.75.

🏛 ⚙ **Nunwell House and Gardens** (West Rd, off A3055 NW of Brading) Lovely lived-in 16th-c house with 5 acres of charming gardens, and interesting furniture and family memorabilia. Charles I spent his last night of freedom here. Snacks, shop; cl am, all Thurs–Sun, and all Oct–Jun; (01983) 407240; *£4 (inc guide book), £2.50 garden only.

BRIGHSTONE SZ4282

! ö **Dinosaur Farm** (A3055 SE) One of most important dinosaur skeletons to be found in the UK was discovered here in 1992. There's an enthusiastic museum dedicated to the find and you can watch the experts at work, preparing the bones for scientific research and display. Snacks, shop, disabled access; open Easter–Sept Thurs and Sun, plus Tues and Fri July and Aug; (01983) 740401; £2.

⌂ 🏕 ☀ **Inland walks** Inland, the island is characterised by long curving chalk ridges (tracks often follow the crests) and forestry plantations (with many signposted woodland trails). The hills N of Brighstone represent some of the pick of the scenery. The Countryman on Limerstone Rd is a good refreshment break, with fine views down to the sea.

CALBOURNE SZ4186

★ ✝ ♞ Attractive village with photogenic streamside thatched cottages, 13th-c **church**, and the enjoyable working **Chessell Pottery** (cl Sun Jan–Easter and two wks at Christmas, but shop open summer Sun; 50p). It's worth getting here early to avoid the coach tours. Fine views from the Blacksmiths Arms, a good family pub on the Carisbrooke road.

✂ **Watermill & Rural Museum** (on the B3401) A 6-metre (20ft) waterwheel still powers this 17th-c mill, and the grounds have tame peacocks. Home-baked snacks, shop with stoneground flour, etc, some disabled access; cl Nov–Easter; (01983) 531227; £3.

CARISBROOKE SZ4888

🏰 ☀ **Carisbrooke Castle** Ruins of the only medieval castle on the island, between 1647 and 1648 home to the imprisoned Charles I (his daughter died here in 1650). Some later buildings behind the imposing gatehouse and walls, and entertaining demonstrations of how donkeys traditionally drew water from one of the medieval wells. Snacks, shop, summer café, disabled access to ground floor; cl 24–26 Dec; (01983) 522107; £4.50. The Eight Bells above the waterfowl lake has decent food, welcomes children and provides good Solent views.

COMPTON DOWN SZ3785

⌂ ☀ Another good place for walks on this S coast, a hogsback grassy hill E of Freshwater Bay; circular walks can take in the coast path along Compton Bay – one of the island's best beaches, not touristy, with impressive cliff views (NT car park).

COWES SZ4995

⚓ ⛵ Stylish and lively, very much centred on its yachting connections, with interesting buildings and shops inc fascinating ships' chandlers in the long narrow High St, and the battery of over 20 brass cannons used to start the yacht races down by the harbour. The Union (Watchhouse Lane) has good-value food. Seafaring collections at the small **maritime museum** in the public library on Beckford Rd (cl Thurs and Sun, Christmas and 1 Jan; free), and at the pretty **Sir Max Aitken Museum** (open Tues–Sat May–Sept; £1).

DOWNEND SZ5387

☺ **Robin Hill Country Park** By mainland standards this 88-acre site is a little tame, but it's a very useful retreat for families, particularly those with younger children who want to run around. And it's especially good value if you then feel like coming again within the next week: a return ticket costs only 50p. Like its stablemate Blackgang Chine it has a few rather dated-looking representations of trolls and the like, but scores more highly for activities and play areas, inc quite a few new slides, underground tunnels and assault course-style equipment. Paths and trails wind through the woodland, and there's a pitch and putt course, along with look-out tower, wooden maze (like walking round lots of high garden fences), and plenty of space for football, basketball or just wandering round. Children between around 5 and 11 will probably be kept interested longest, though the toboggan run is fun for older children (and parents); it's £1 extra a ride. Best in fine weather (most features are outdoors); easy to spend an undemanding half day here. Meals, snacks, shop, disabled access but rather hilly; cl Nov–Mar; (01983) 527352; £3.95 (£2.95 children 3–13). The nearby Hare & Hounds is a good family dining pub, open all day.

EAST COWES SZ5194

🏛 🎖 **Osborne House** (1m SE) Queen Victoria's favourite residence, where she died in 1901; the state and private apartments haven't changed much since. Designed to resemble an Italian villa, by Prince Albert with professional help from Thomas Cubitt, it's a striking place. Albert and his wife were also responsible for the original layout of the fine gardens. A horse-drawn carriage conveys you in style to the Swiss cottage, where the royal children learnt cooking and gardening. The house featured in the film *Mrs Brown*. Snacks, shop, disabled access to ground floor only; open daily Apr–Oct, phone for winter opening; (01983) 200022; £6.90. Down on the River Medina, the beautifully placed Folly Inn has an appropriately nautical atmosphere.

✝ **Whippingham church** Said to have been another of Prince Albert's designs, this is a good deal more eccentric than Osborne House: a bizarre mix of different styles.

FRESHWATER SZ3386

✝ ⌂ A very extended, rather sprawling village, with a charming quiet core. The picturesque thatched 20th-c **church** includes quite a few Tennyson family memorials, and beyond it a causeway crosses the head of the Yar estuary. The Red Lion has good food, and the Vine has a pleasant terrace for warm days. There are fine walks nearby, and Hill Farm has riding.

FRESHWATER BAY SZ3485

▣ **Dimbola Lodge** (Terrace Lane) When the photography pioneer Julia Cameron lived here in the 1860s and 70s regular guests (and sitters) included Edward Lear, Lewis Carroll, Ellen Terry and her next-door neighbour Alfred Lord Tennyson. Vacant for years (and very nearly demolished), the restored house now proudly displays her famous portraits, plus changing exhibitions by today's artists; summer music recitals. Restaurant (good vegetarian meals), shop, disabled access; cl Mon, 24–26, 31 Dec and 1 Jan; (01983) 827005; £2.50.

GODSHILL SZ5281

★ ✝ ⌂ ❊ Best appreciated in winter, when there are fewer coach parties. Plenty of famously pretty thatched cottages, and a good 15th-c **church**, with interesting 15th-c wall painting. The Taverners has good food. Godshill is an inland starting point for a walk via the Worsley Trail on to Stenbury Down (radio masts, but redeemed by wide views), then back via Appuldurcombe House and passing through a huge estate gateway.

❗ **Model Village** Painstakingly recreates Shanklin, its Chine valley, and Godshill in miniature (there's even a model model village), and is nicely floodlit on summer evenings. Shop, disabled access; cl Nov–Feb; (01983) 840270; £2.50.

🜁 **Natural History Centre** (High St) Decent collection of fossils and minerals and some tropical fish and sea shells; shop, disabled access; cl Jan and first 2 wks Feb; *£1.50.

🜁 **Nostalgia Toy Museum** (High St) Lots of post-war toys and die-cast model cars; cl Nov–Easter; £1.25.

🐦 ❀ ❗ **Old Smithy Tourist Centre** Based around a former blacksmith's forge, this has an aviary of exotic birds, and a garden in the shape of the island itself. Snacks, shop (with local crafts), disabled access; cl 25–26 Dec, gardens cl Oct–Mar; (01983) 840364; 80p.

HAVENSTREET SZ5589

🚂 **Isle of Wight Steam Railway** Well restored railway with very pleasant 10-mile trip from Wootton to Smallbrook Junction nr Ryde (where you can change directly on to main line trains). Vintage engines and rolling stock, and related memorabilia displayed in the old gasworks at Havenstreet Station. Meals, snacks, shop, disabled access if accompanied; open Apr–Oct and over Christmas/New Year, phone for timetable, (01983) 884343; £6.50. The Island Line day ticket (around £7) includes the steam railway with travel on all regular trains on the island. The White Hart does good generous food.

MOTTISTONE SZ4083

★ ♘ Charming old village with a well in the centre of the green. The **bluebell wood** opposite the church is lovely in spring.

🏛 ⚜ **Mottistone Manor** The fine gardens are open pm Sun, Tues and bank hols Apr–Sept; on fine days there are teas; (01983) 740552; £2; NT. The medieval and Elizabethan manor house itself is open Aug bank hol only.

NEWCHURCH SZ5685

🐾 **Amazon World** (Watery Lane) Expanding collection of the kind of animals you'd find in an Amazon rain forest, with lively jungle and village settings; an effective mix of entertainment with environmental awareness. Also animal petting area and adventure playground. Meals, snacks, shop, disabled access; cl 25 Dec; (01983) 867122; £4.50. The village is quiet, with a photogenic church; the Pointer beside it has decent home cooking.

NEWPORT SZ5089

★ ✝ ⚲ The island's capital, with a good deal of character, some fine old Georgian houses, and warm red brick 18th-c buildings down by the quay. It's the main place on the island for antique shops. The parish **Church of St Thomas** is worth a look – it has an interestingly carved Jacobean pulpit and a 19th-c memorial to Charles I's daughter. The 17th-c Wheatsheaf nearby is good for lunch. The Quay Arts Centre (Sea St) has craft fairs some Sats. The back road to Brading has pleasant views.

✽ **Classic Boat Museum** (The Quay) Collection of vintage motor boats inc the oldest lifeboat in the country, and a 1910 wooden launch used for Thames cruises. Meals, snacks, disabled access; open daily Apr–Oct; (01983) 533493; £2.50.

🏛 **Roman Villa** (Clatterford Rd) Well preserved baths and reconstructed rooms on the site of a 3rd-c Roman villa, with an informative museum; also a Roman garden. Shop; cl Sun and all Nov–Mar; (01983) 529720; £1.75.

NEWTOWN SZ4290

🏚 ❦ For a while this was the island's capital, but it began a slow decline after a disastrous fire in 1377, and eventually faded out altogether – what used to be rich merchants' streets are now just grassy tracks. The **Old Town Hall**, rebuilt in 1699 but now left stranded and unusually isolated from any houses, is all that's left to mark the once thriving town; open pm Mon, Weds and Sun Apr–Oct, plus pm Tues and Thurs in July and Aug, Good Fri and Easter Sat; £1.30; NT. Rewarding walks for bird-watchers at the nearby nature reserve. The New Inn at Shalfleet, open all day in summer, has good seafood.

NEWTOWN NATURE RESERVE SZ4291

❦ ◠ On the N coast, this has walks around the tranquil Norfolk-like creeks of the Newtown/Clamerkin estuaries, but there are few circular routes; from Newtown village a boardwalk leads out into the heart of the reserve within a few minutes.

PARKHURST FOREST SZ4891

⚘ ◠ Just W of the prison, this is a couple of miles across, with plenty of signposted paths and a good chance of seeing red squirrels.

RYDE SZ5992

☺ ⚲ Now the biggest town here, with a long triple pier, good sandy beaches, and a full set of holiday-resort amusements – just right for a straightforward family holiday. Free tours and tastings at the **Rosemary Vineyard** on Smallbrook Lane; (01983) 811084.

⚲ **National Wireless Museum** (Puckpool Hill, off Seaview toll rd) Moved from Arreton Manor, this tells the story of broadcasting from 1922 onwards, inc demonstrations of how the first radio sets sounded; open all Suns, most wkdys exc Sat, best to phone for winter opening; (01983) 567665; free.

ST CATHERINE'S HILL SZ4978

🏔 ◠ ⚲ Capped by the ruins of a 14th-c oratory, a short walk up from the coast path further E; you can walk on along a ridge to the prominent **Hoy's Monument** at the far end of St Catherine's Down. The coast path meanwhile skirts the undercliff of St Catherine's Point, the isle's southern tip, which has a modern working **lighthouse**; there are several other paths through the undercliff here.

ST LAWRENCE SZ5276

🏛 **Isle of Wight Glass** Offers demonstrations (not wknds), lovely displays, and shop. Disabled access (but no facilities); cl winter wknds and for 3 wks at Christmas; (01983) 853526; 60p. The St Lawrence Inn is a popular dining pub with superb Channel views.

🐑 ❧ ✿ **Rare Breeds & Waterfowl Park** See separate family panel on p. 339.

SANDOWN SZ6084

⚓ ⚲ All the usual things for a family beach holiday – pier, boat trips, canoeing lake, discos – and a fine beach. You can usually tour the partly underground winery of **Adgestone Vineyard** on Upper Rd, but you'll need to book on (01983) 402503; free.

⚲ **Museum of Isle of Wight Geology** (High St) Small but interesting collection of local fossils and rocks, with recently excavated dinosaur fossils. Shop, some disabled access; cl Sun, 25–26 Dec and 1 Jan; (01983) 404344; free.

🐘 **! Sandown Zoo** Rare and endangered animals like tigers, panthers and leopards, as well as a notable collection of poisonous snakes and primates. A new dinosaur attraction complete with static and animatronic models will be open from the first May bank hol. Summer meals and snacks, shop, disabled access; cl Nov–mid-Feb (exc wknds); (01983) 403883; each attraction £4.95, or £7 joint ticket.

SEAVIEW SZ6291

A timelessly quiet retreat, with sedate streets of unassuming villas; the Seaview Hotel does very good lunches.

🦩 **Flamingo Park** 📷 Hundreds of birds in spacious landscaped grounds; some can be fed by hand. Meals, snacks, shop, disabled access; cl Nov–Easter; (01983) 612153; £4.50.

SHANKLIN SZ5881

🏛 ⅊ **Shanklin Chine** Quite glorious natural gorge with a magnificent 14-metre (45ft) waterfall. A heritage centre gives details of rare flora, nature trails and life in Victorian Shanklin. Snacks, shop, some disabled access; cl mid-Oct–Easter; (01983) 866432; *£2.50. Down on the beach, the thatched Fisherman's Cottage is charmingly placed for lunch (cl Nov–Mar), and up at the top the Chine Inn is a good-value family pub (no food Sun evening, Tues or Sat).

SHORWELL SZ4583

★ † One of the few really pretty villages on the island to have escaped a flood of tourist interest, with charming streamside thatched cottages and a fine **church**; the attractive Crown is very good for lunch.

TENNYSON DOWN SZ3285

☁ ❋ On Wight's western tip, the best place of all for walkers here: a friendly grassy ridge and cliff walk rolled into one, with views over most of the island and across to the mainland. You pass the monument to Alfred Lord Tennyson (who lived nearby and loved this place), and the walk culminates in spectacular fashion above the Needles. You can walk the entire ridge from Freshwater Bay (summer bus service

from Alum Bay to bring you back), or make a round walk from Alum Bay car park, past the Needles Old Battery and along to the monument, then up on to Headon Warren before going down to Alum Bay. The High Down Hotel (B3322) is another start point.

VENTNOR SZ5476

🕸 ♻ Relatively untouristy little town up on the cliff, the fairly restrained and decorous seafront down below is linked to it by a tortuously steep loop of road; between them perched on ledges among the trees is quite a number of Victorian villas – many of them still private houses rather than guesthouses. Its great pride is the **Botanic Garden**, where an exceptional collection of subtropical plants make the most of the mild climate; a new visitor centre should be ready by Easter (gardens free, 50p for temperate house); the Garden Tavern here has decent food and sea views. There are 2 decent local history museums: the **Heritage Museum** on Spring Hill (limited disabled access; cl 12.30–2pm, pm Weds and Sat, all Sun, and Nov–mid-May; 75p), and the **Longshoreman's Museum** on the Esplanade (shop, disabled access; cl Feb–end Mar; *50p). The Spyglass is an interesting pub with superb sea views, and the seafront Mill Bay is useful.

☁ ❋ **Bonchurch Down** Above Ventnor, this has unsightly radar installations but gives walkers fine views.

♻ **Museum of Smuggling History** In the Botanic Garden (or more correctly under it) this demonstrates the tricks smugglers past and present have used to sneak in wool, brandy, tobacco or drugs. Meals, snacks, shop; cl Oct–Easter; (01983) 853677; *£2.20.

⅄ **Undercliff** Formed from the irregular masses of earth which have come to rest below, with often rocky chasms between each other and the cliff itself. Sometimes planted and sometimes with profuse natural vegetation, the resulting scenery is unlike anything else on the island, with quite a subtropical aspect. Some of the attractions along here we've listed under St Lawrence.

WOOTTON SZ5290

🚂 † A terminus for the steam railway

(see *Havenstreet* entry). It has an attractive partly Norman **church**. The Sloop down overlooking the creek is a reliable food pub.

✗ ✿ Butterfly World & Fountain World 🔲 (Staplers Rd) A tropical butterfly house, next to a 5-acre garden centre with watergardens and fountains; snacks, shop, disabled access (but no facilities) cl Nov–Easter; £3.75.

WROXALL SZ5480

✿ ✿ ✦ Appuldurcombe House (off B3327 W of Wroxall) Intriguing shell of a Palladian house, nestling among grounds beautifully landscaped by Capability Brown. You can still catch something of the atmosphere of the days when this was one of the grandest houses on the island. The stables have been converted into holiday cottages, and the old laundry and brewhouse into a new owl and falconry centre (daily flying displays) – Henry VIII is said to have stayed here with his falconers. Snacks, shop, some disabled access; cl Nov–Mar; (01983) 840188; £3.75 for house, grounds and falconry centre, £2 house, grounds only.

YAFFORD SZ4481

✗ ✦ ✦ Yafford Water Mill Farm Park Fun: a seal lives in a special enclosure beside the millpond of the working 18th-c watermill, various species of waterfowl fill the pools of the stream, and rare breeds of sheep and cattle graze along its banks. Also nature trails, wagons and traction engines (sometimes in steam), an adventure playground across the lane and a recently constructed 2ft 6in gauge railway. Meals and snacks, shop, disabled access; cl 25 Dec; (01983) 740610; £3.70.

YARMOUTH SZ3489

✿ ✿ ✦ ✦ ✦ ✦ Fort Victoria Country Park Surrounding a 19th-c fortress, this has good views down over the Solent, as well as 50 acres of woodland and a mile or so of pebbly beach. In the grounds are a maritime heritage centre (£1), excellent aquarium (£1.90) and planetarium (£2). Snacks, shop, disabled access (exc planetarium); not all parts open winter – best to check first; (01983) 760860; park free. The adjacent Fort Victoria model railway is reckoned to be the biggest model railway in the country, and the only one completely controlled by computer. Good shop; open Easter–Sept; (01983) 761553; £3.30.

⌂ ✦ Yar Estuary The unspoilt reed-fringed estuary is skirted by a footpath along the former railway line S from Yarmouth.

✿ ✿ Yarmouth Castle A lively place, its old harbour busy with yachts in summer. The castle was built as part of Henry VIII's coastal defences; it's in an excellent state, and you can see the Master Gunner's surprisingly homely parlour and kitchen. Outside, the open gun platform has good views of the harbour. Shop, snacks, disabled access to ground floor; cl Nov–Mar; (01983) 760678; £2.10. The Wheatsheaf serves popular food all day.

Where to eat

CARISBROOKE SZ4687 **Blacksmiths Arms** *(01983) 529263* Very neatly kept pub with fine views over the Solent from the simply built and furnished dining extension, and from tables in the smallish back garden; several bars, 4 real ales, varied and imaginative food cooked by the welcoming Bavarian landlord (Bavarian-sized helpings, too) inc enjoyable platters and various German dishes, and polite, helpful service. **£19|£6.**

FRESHWATER SZ3487 **Red Lion** *(01983) 754925* Carefully run, civilised pub with comfortably furnished open-plan bar, lots of local pictures and photographs, open fires, an interesting and extensive range of food, real ales, nice little wine list, and seats outside; children over 10; disabled access. **£18.50|£6.95.**

LUCCOMBE CHINE SZ5880 **Dunnose Cottage Tearooms** *(01983) 862585* 16th-c thatched cottage in 3 landscaped acres, all-day breakfasts, cream teas, snacks, good-value 3-course meal, and lots of different teas; cl pm and Oct–Easter. **£13|£5.**

ROOKLEY SZ5083 **Chequers** *(01983) 840314* Comfortable lounge with easy chairs and settees by the end fire, a lively public bar, a large, no smoking family room with exceptionally good facilities for children, and an extensive choice of consistently good bar food. **£15.50|£5.45.**

SHORWELL SZ4583 **Crown** *(01983) 740293* The big back garden with its trout-filled stream, ducks, doves and lilies is nice in summer, and there's an extended beamed lounge with a log fire, good food, and friendly staff; disabled access. **£14.50|£5.95.**

YARMOUTH SZ3589 **Jireh House** *St James's Sq (01983) 760513* 17th-c guest house with friendly owners, a relaxed atmosphere, and a range of home-made meals, snacks and afternoon tea inc daily specials and fresh fish; cl Nov–Easter; disabled access (restaurant only). **£9.50|**special afternoon tea £5.50.

YARMOUTH SZ3589 **Wheatsheaf** *Bridge Rd (01983) 760456* Handy for the ferry, this inn has 4 comfortable and spacious eating areas inc an airy conservatory with a wide choice of good food served all day (daily specials are the best choice), well kept beers and quick, friendly service; cl 25 Dec, pm 26 Dec; children in harbour lounge and conservatory. **£19|£7.**

Isle of Wight Calendar

Some of these dates were provisional as we went to press. Please check information with the telephone numbers provided.

APRIL

7 Shanklin A Century of Solent and Sea – *till 29 October* (01983) 866432

22 Yarmouth Easter Parade (01983) 760108

24 Brook Easter Steam-up and Vintage Ploughing Match at Compton Farm (01983) 740215

30 Isle of Wight Bicycle Island Randonnee: cycle round the island from any of 6 starting points (01983) 526774

MAY

1 Mottistone Morris Men dance at dawn at the Longstone, *5am* (01983) 882143

26 Bembridge Festival with street fair on last day – *till 29 May* (01983) 872175

29 Whitwell Crab Fair at the rugby club: stalls, fresh crabs (01983) 855794

JUNE

3 Shorwell Open Gardens: up to 17 gardens – *till 4 June* (01983) 551304

9 Binstead Heavy Horse and Rural Life Festival at Brickfields Horse Country – *till 12 June* (01983) 566801

10 Cowes Round the Island Yacht Race: over 1,000 yachts (01983) 296621

24 Niton Mackerel Fair (01983) 730502

JULY

8 East Cowes Victorian Festival (01983) 281524

Isle of Wight Calendar (cont.)

22 Northwood County Show at the Showground – *till 23 July* (01983) 526851

26 Sandown Carnival (01983) 402024

28 Mottistone Open-air Jazz at Mottistone Manor Gardens – *till 29 July* (01983) 741020

29 Cowes Cowes Week – *till 5 August* (01983) 813800

AUGUST

5 Yarmouth Carnival Week and Procession – *till 12 August* (01983) 760108

6 Shanklin Carnival Week with procession *on Weds*, Fireworks *on Thurs* and floodlit carnival *on Sat – till 13 August* (01983) 862117

16 Shanklin Regatta (01983) 862422

19 Newchurch Garlic Festival at the Fighting Cocks Crossroads: biggest festival on the island with arena events, arts and crafts, circus, live bands – *till 20 August* (01983) 853411

24 Newport Carnival Procession (01983) 526595

25 Havenstreet Island Steam Show inc live bands at Isle of Wight Steam Railway – *till 28 August* (01983) 882204

26 Newport Carnival Procession (01983) 526595

28 St Helens Carnival (01983) 873240

30 Sandown Illuminated Carnival (01983) 402024

SEPTEMBER

16 Ryde Garden Show – *till 17 September* (01983) 568867

NOVEMBER

4 St Helens Bonfire (01983) 872948

DECEMBER

21 East Cowes Christmas in the Square: evening charity stalls and entertainments (01983) 281524

Please let us know what you think of places in the *Guide*. Use the report forms at the back of the book or simply write us a letter.

KENT

Excellent choice of things to see and do, for days out or longer holidays; good seaside resorts, some attractive countryside.

Dover is excellent for a family day out, with its splendid castle and well done White Cliffs Experience. The zoos at Bekesbourne and Lympne are also outstanding family attractions, and there's lots more in the county to entertain children, including several friendly animal and rare breeds places; the Beltring hop farm is a good varied day out. The historic Chatham dockyard is fun (adding a brewery exhibition of beer's naval role). There are several enjoyable steam railways – the Romney Hythe & Dymchurch is delightfully quaint.

This is perfect country for the *aficionado* of stately homes, with Leeds Castle, Knole near Sevenoaks, Penshurst Place, Squerryes Court and Chartwell near Westerham, Ightham Mote and Hever Castle all very satisfying, and Darwin's Down House near Westerham adding a touch of cerebral appeal. Many fine gardens are headed by grand Groombridge Place (lots for families here) and Hever, romantic Sissinghurst and (near Lamberhurst) Scotney Castle. The comprehensive Brogdale fruit tree collection near Faversham and the unusual organic gardens at Yalding are quite eye-opening.

Canterbury has many fine buildings besides the cathedral itself, including two interesting heritage centres, and well shown Roman remains. Rochester makes the most of its Dickens connections, and has a dramatic castle and cathedral. Tunbridge Wells has some interesting places to see – and a good round-trip bus service linking some excellent attractions outside.

Among less conventional places, the bizarre *memento mori* in Hythe church, the extraordinary collections at Birchington, the Finchcocks collection of keyboard instruments at Goudhurst, the bird park at Wingham, and the ruined houses and birds of prey centre at Eynsford all stand out – and most have plenty to entertain children. Newcomers to the *Guide* include interesting Higham Park at Bridge, and a butterfly centre at Swingfield.

The north-east seaside resorts date from pre-railway Victorian days, when well-to-do Londoners came by boat. When the early coast-bound railways took people further afield, these forerunners – most notably Broadstairs – rather escaped the new train-borne crowds. So they have kept a certain dignified charm that gives them an unusual appeal.

Inland, the Weald (roughly west of the M20) has peaceful and intimate landscapes of little hills and valleys, small pasture fields and oak woods, and villages with attractive tile-hung and weatherboarded houses, early medieval stone-built churches, and a good smattering of antique shops, teashops and so forth – pleasant territory for pottering about by car. The North Downs between the M20 and the M2, also north of the M25/M26, are more open; the best parts are above Wye. The flatlands of Romney Marsh have a certain bypassed-by-time appeal.

Where to stay

BIDDENDEN TQ8435 **Bishopsdale Oast** *Biddenden, Ashford TN27 8DR* (01580) 292321 **£50;** 3 large, homely rms with king-size beds and country views. Large double-kiln oast house in 4 acres of wild and cultivated gardens, with beams and original features, good breakfasts and imaginative dinner (excellent cheeseboard and home-grown vegtables) eaten on the terrace or in the dining room, and friendly owners; cl Christmas; children over 12; disabled access.

BOUGHTON LEES TR0147 **Eastwell Manor** *Eastwell Park, Boughton Lees, Ashford TN25 4HR* (01233) 219955 **£180,** plus special breaks; 23 prettily decorated, spacious rms and 19 apartments in recently converted mews. Fine Jacobean-style manor (actually built in the 1920s) in 62 acres, with grand oak-panelled rooms, open fires, comfortable leather seating, antiques and fresh flowers, excellent service and extremely good food in atmospheric restaurant; snooker, croquet, pitch-and-putt, riding, tennis and lots of walks; disabled access.

BOUGHTON MONCHELSEA TQ7849 **Tanyard** *Wierton Hill, Boughton Monchelsea, Maidstone ME17 4JT* (01622) 744705 **£115;** 6 lovely beamed rms. Appealing medieval yeoman's house with fine views, beams and log fires in the cosy day rooms, a restaurant in the 13th-c part of the building (open to non-residents, too), and 10 acres of landscaped gardens; cl 2 wks end Oct/early Nov, 4 wks late Dec–early Jan; children over 6.

CANTERBURY TR1457 **Cathedral Gate** *36 Burgate, Canterbury CT1 2HA* (01227) 464381 *****£79,** plus special breaks; 26 rms, 12 with own bthrm and some overlooking the cathedral. 15th-c hotel with bow windows, massive oak beams, sloping floors, antiques and fresh flowers, and a quiet restful atmosphere.

CANTERBURY TR1457 **Thanington** *140 Wincheap, Canterbury CT1 3RY* (01227) 453227 *****£68,** plus special breaks; 15 rms linked to the main building by a Georgian-style conservatory. Thoughtfully run and warmly welcoming hotel with elegant little rooms, games room, walled garden, and indoor swimming pool; cl 25–26 Dec.

CHARING HEATH TQ9247 **Barnfield** *Charing Heath, Ashford TN27 0BN* (01233) 712421 **£40;** 5 beamed rms, shared big bthrm. Delightful early 15th-c farmhouse with fine beams, big open fires, comfortable sitting rooms, lots of books, antiques and homely knick-knacks, good breakfasts, friendly owners, and big garden; cl Christmas.

CHIDDINGSTONE HOATH TQ4842 **Hoath House** *Penshurst Rd, Chiddingstone Hoath, Edenbridge TN8 7DB* (01342) 850362 **£45;** 3 rms, 1 with own bthrm. Wonderful medieval house – added to over the years – with huge beams and plastered walls in the sitting room, family portraits, an open fire in the library, heaps of interest and atmosphere, homely suppers, kind, welcoming owners, and a big garden with fine views; cl Christmas.

DOVER TR3141 **Churchill** *Dover Waterfront, Dover CT17 9BP* (01304) 203633 **£99,** plus special breaks; 68 comfortable rms, several with balconies. Overlooking the harbour, this Regency terrace hotel has a congenial bar, sun lounge and terrace, friendly staff, and enjoyable food; disabled access.

EAST PECKHAM TQ6651 **Roydon Hall** *East Peckham, Tonbridge TN12 5NH* (01622) 812121 **£42;** 15 rms, some with own bthrm. Fine Tudor manor offering vegetarian B & B (vegetarian lunch and light supper by arrangement); 10 acres of woodlands and garden, original oak panelling in the public rooms, and regular meditation courses; no smoking.

FRITTENDEN TQ8041 **Maplehurst Mill** *Mill Lane, Frittenden, Cranbrook TN17 2DT* (01580) 852203 **£60;** 3 rms with views over the water and surrounding countryside. Carefully restored 18th-c watermill attached to a 15th-c mill house, with original machinery, millstones and waterwheel, a big comfortable drawing room, and delicious imaginative food using home-grown organic produce in beamed and candlelit dining room; 11 acres of gardens and grounds and heated outdoor swimming pool; no smoking, no dogs; children over 12; disabled access.

GOUDHURST TQ7237 **Star & Eagle** *High St, Goudhurst TN17 1AL (01580)* 211512 *£55;* 10 character rms, 9 with own bthrm. Striking medieval inn with comfortable Jacobean-style furnishings in heavy-beamed day rooms, pretty views, polite staff, good food, and well kept ales; cl 24–25 Dec.

GROOMBRIDGE TQ5337 **Crown** *Groombridge, Tunbridge Wells TN3 9QH (01892)* 864742 *£40;* 4 rms, shared bthrm. Carefully preserved Elizabethan inn on the village green, with snug atmospheric timbered bar rooms, a log fire in the big brick inglenook, traditional furnishings, good popular food, well kept beers, good-value house wines, and quick service; children over 4.

LITTLESTONE TR0825 **Romney Bay House** *Coast Rd, Littlestone, New Romney TN28 8QY (01797)* 364747 *£75,* plus winter breaks; 10 rms. 1920s house on a private road facing the sea with a log fire in the comfortable drawing room, first-floor 'look-out' with telescope, games and library, charming friendly owners and a relaxed atmosphere, enjoyable set evening meal, afternoon teas, and garden with tennis court and croquet; golf close by; cl 1 wk Christmas; no children.

MARDEN TQ7341 **Tanner House** *Goudhurst Rd, Marden, Tonbridge TN12 9ND (01622)* 831214 *£40;* 3 rms (showers). Quietly set Tudor farmhouse on a small family mixed farm with a residents' lounge, an inglenook in the dining room, a large garden, and walks and picnic areas around the farm; they breed shire horses; cl Christmas; children over 5; no pets.

PENSHURST TQ5342 **Swale Cottage** *Old Swaylands Lane, Penshurst, Tonbridge TN11 8AH (01892)* 870738 *£66,* plus winter breaks; 3 beamed rms. Careful conversion of a 13th-c Grade II listed barn and hayloft, with beams and an inglenook fireplace in the sitting room, good breakfasts, and cottage garden; not far from Hever; no smoking; dogs by arrangement; children over 10.

PLAXTOL TQ6054 **Jordans** *Sheet Hill, Plaxtol, Sevenoaks TN15 0PU (01732)* 810379 *£69;* 3 rms, 2 with own bthrm. 15th-c no smoking house with leaded windows and beams, a warm fire in the inglenook fireplace, good breakfasts, and a pretty garden; lots to see nearby; cl mid-Dec–mid-Jan; children over 12.

PLUCKLEY TQ9243 **Dering Arms** *Pluckley, Ashford TN27 0RR (01233)* 840371 *£40;* 3 rms, shared bthrm – 2 extra en suite rms shortly. Dutch-gabled old inn with friendly and relaxed attractive bars, and super food with an emphasis on excellent fresh fish; monthly vintage-car rally; cl 26–29 Dec.

PLUCKLEY TQ9145 **Elvey Farm** *Pluckley, Ashford TN27 0SU (01233)* 840442 *£59.50,* plus special breaks; 9 rms, some in the oast house roundel, some in original barn and stable block. 15th-c farmhouse in secluded spot on 75-acre working family farm with timbered rooms, inglenook fireplace, and French windows from lounge on to sun terrace; ample play areas for children; well behaved pets welcome; disabled access.

ST MARGARET'S AT CLIFFE TR3444 **Wallett's Court** *St Margaret's at Cliffe, Dover CT15 6EW (01304)* 852424 *£100,* plus special breaks; 15 rms, some in converted stable block with gentle views. Fine old manor house with 13th-c cellars, beams, antiques, comfortable seating and open fires, helpful service, charming owners, marvellous food, and swimming pool; very close to ferries; cl Christmas.

SANDGATE TR1934 **Sandgate Hotel** *The Esplanade, Sandgate, Folkestone CT20 3DY (01303)* 220444 *£56;* 15 restful, elegant rms. Smart, impeccably kept Victorian hotel overlooking the beach, with huge picture windows, open fires, fresh flowers, and antique mirrors, exceptional French cooking in the pretty restaurant, enjoyable breakfasts, and friendly, mainly French staff; cl 4 wks Jan, 1 wk Oct.

SHIPBOURNE TQ5952 **Chaser** *Stumble Hill, Shipbourne TN11 9PE (01732)* 810360 *£65;* 15 rms. Colonial-style building with porticoed front in a lovely spot by the village church and green; comfortable and homely atmosphere in the well kept bar, and a wide range of attractively presented good food in both the bar and the beamed restaurant.

SISSINGHURST TQ8037 **Sissinghurst Castle Farm** *Sissinghurst, Cranbrook TN17 2AB (01580)* 712885 *£58,* plus special breaks; 5 rms, some with own bthrm. Gabled Victorian farmhouse in the grounds of Sissinghurst Castle, with spacious rooms, a pretty garden, and a farm shop; farm is mostly arable with cattle and sheep;

cl Christmas; children over 8.

SMARDEN TQ8742 **Chequers** *Smarden, Ashford TN27 8QA (01233) 770217*
***£50;** 6 rms, 3 with own bthrm. Comfortable olde-worlde pub full of character,
with beams and a log fire, a varied choice of good, reasonably priced food, and nice
breakfasts; cl 25 Dec.

TENTERDEN TQ8733 **Brattle House** *Watermill Bridges, Tenterden TN30 6UL
(01580) 763565* ***£63,** plus special breaks; 3 rms. Partly 17th-c tile-hung house, said
to have been the home of Horatia, illegitimate daughter of Nelson and Lady
Hamilton, in 11 acres of garden, meadow and woodland; charming owners, low-
beamed residents' sitting room, good breakfasts in conservatory, and delicious
imaginative dinners in candlelit dining room; no smoking; cl Nov–Mar; no children.

TUNBRIDGE WELLS TQ5839 **Hotel du Vin & Bistro** *Crescent Rd, Tunbridge Wells
TN1 2LY (01892) 526455* from ***£85;** 32 very attractive individually decorated rms with
CD players, satellite TV and power showers. Handsome sandstone building, extended in
the 19th c, with a relaxed atmosphere in the 2 rooms of the bar, comfortable sofas and
chairs in the lounge rooms, good modern cooking in the airy high-ceilinged informally
French-feeling restaurant, and particularly good wines; disabled access.

TUNBRIDGE WELLS TQ5739 **Spa** *Mount Ephraim, Tunbridge Wells TN4 8XJ
(01892) 520331* ***£112,** plus wknd breaks; 71 comfortable rms. Run by the same
family for 3 generations, this Georgian hotel, in 14 acres of landscaped gardens, has
a comfortable and quietly decorated, partly no smoking lounge, a popular and
attractive bar, good food in the Regency-style restaurant, a nice old-fashioned
atmosphere and friendly long-serving staff; leisure centre with indoor heated
swimming pool, gym, beauty salon, sauna, Jacuzzi, and solarium, and floodlit hard
tennis court; disabled access.

WEST MALLING TQ6757 **Scott House** *High St, West Malling ME19 6QH
(01732) 841380* ***£69;** 3 pretty little rms. No smoking, Georgian town house (from
which the family also run an antique business) with a big comfortable lounge, good
breakfasts in the dining room, a friendly atmosphere, and helpful owners; cl
Christmas; children over 10.

To see and do

KENT Family Attraction of the Year

🐾 **BEKESBOURNE** TR1956 **Howletts Zoo** (signed off A2) Howletts and
its bigger sister park at Lympne are well known for their genuinely dedicated
approach to looking after the rare or endangered animals in their care; animals
are kept in enclosures as close to their natural habitats as possible (they aim to
return them to the wild if they can), and, more controversially, they try to
develop a real bond between the keepers and the animals. Each of the parks is
as rewarding to visit as the other, but this one, the first, is a more manageable
size, and the animals are spread over lovely grounds. A highlight is the world's
largest collection of gorillas in human care, with which they've had important
breeding successes – over 60 gorillas have been born here since 1975.
Less well known are their successes at breeding other species; they have a
unique herd of breeding elephants. Other animals include deer, antelope,
leopards, tigers, bison, bongos, gibbons, and snakes; you'll need around 3 hours
to see everything, and it can repay an even longer visit. Unlike at Port Lympne,
the house here isn't open to the public, but the walk up to it, along a tree-lined
avenue, is very attractive. As seen on a recent fly-on-the-wall ITV series,
Howletts is very much the kind of place where the residents come first: you
won't find play areas or elaborate family facilities here, just the animals, and a
sincere conservation message. Meals, snacks, shop, disabled access; cl 25–26
Dec; (01227) 721286; £8.90 (£6.90 children 4–14). A family ticket for 2 adults
and 2 children offers a good saving at £26; an even better deal covering 3
children is £29.

ASH TR2858

✝ A handsome partly 12th-c **church** can be found on the Street.

AYLESFORD TQ7258

✝ 🖼 🔆 🌼 **Aylesford Priory** Often referred to as the Friars, these carefully restored 13th/14th-c buildings are once again the home of a group of Carmelite monks. Fine cloisters and chapels, sculptures and ceramics by modern artists, working pottery, and beautiful grounds. Snacks, shop, disabled access; cl Good Fri; (01622) 717272; free. The Little Gem pub is very quaint and ancient.

🏛 **Kits Coty House** (towards A229) A massive Stone Age tomb chamber which 'mightily impressed' Pepys when he saw it; free.

BARHAM TR1947

🍎 **Elham Valley Vineyards** Friendly little vineyard in pretty sheltered valley; guided tours and tastings around £2.50; snacks, wine sales, good craft shop, disabled access; cl am Sun, Christmas wk; (01227) 831266. The Duke of Cumberland has decent food, and the B2065 through this valley is a pretty drive.

BEDGEBURY TQ7233

🔆 🍃 **Bedgebury Pinetum** Lakeside landscaped valley full of magnificent conifers, with walks up through forest plots designed to try out the commercial possibilities of all sorts of little-known species. Meals, snacks, shop; visitor centre cl wkdys Jan and Feb; (01580) 211044; £2.50.

BEKESBOURNE TR1956

🐾 **Howletts Zoo** *See separate family panel on p.352.*

BELTRING TQ6746

🐷 🐄 🍃 🌼 **Hop Farm Country Park** (off A228) A popular and very well organised family outing, based around the largest surviving group of Victorian oast houses and galleried barns. Clearly laid out exhibitions on hop-farming, rural bygones and, somewhat incongruously, the water industry, easy nature trails, animals (they have more than you'll find in quite a few farm parks), falconry displays, shire horses, pottery, and special events most summer wknds. Snacks, shop, some disabled access (not into oast houses); cl 25–26 Dec; (01622) 872068; £5.50.

Brookers next door has decent food in a smart conversion of another oast house. Traditionally used for drying hops (though usually now converted into homes), oast houses with their tall white cowls turning with the wind are a trademark of the Weald of Kent and E Sussex.

BEWL WATER TQ6733

🚣 🎣 🍃 Boating and fishing, picnic areas, and cycle hire (and a great adventure play area); summer events; can be very busy on bank hols. A new extension to the visitor centre includes interactive displays and videos about the reservoir, and their extensive new dry garden is interesting. Meals, snacks, shop, disabled access; £4 parking charge summer wknds and bank hols, less at other times. The reservoir, dissected by the Kent/Sussex boundary, is skirted by a 14-mile path around its banks.

BIDDENDEN TQ8538

★ ✝ Attractive village with several interesting old houses on the S side of the High St, and a handsome 13th-c **church** with a bold tower. The picturesque old Three Chimneys just W has enjoyable food.

🍎 **Biddenden Vineyards** (Benenden rd) Thriving wine- and cider-producing vineyard. All-year tastings, harvesting in Oct and bottling in Mar. Snacks, shop, disabled access (but no facilities); cl Sat, Sun Jan–Feb, and 24 Dec–2 Jan; (01580) 291726; free, guided tour £2.85.

BIRCHINGTON TR3068

🏺 🏛 🌼 **Powell-Cotton Museum & Quex House** (off A28) Fascinating museum attached to a fine Regency house with furnished period rooms. Nine galleries display the collections of Victorian explorer and naturalist Major Powell-Cotton, with hundreds of well mounted animals, ethnic artefacts and oriental art. The walled gardens have been restored, and the grounds have an odd early 19th-c bell tower with bizarre wrought-iron spire (open some Suns in summer). Summer snacks, shop, disabled access; open Tues–Thurs, Sun and bank hols Apr–Oct (house open pm only), plus gardens and museum open first 3 Suns in Mar, Nov and Dec; (01843) 842168; £3.50, £2.50 in winter. The Mortons Fork Hotel inland at Minster does worthwhile lunches, and the Minnis Bay beach is good.

BLEAN TR1161

🐗 ✙ ⌂ **Druidstone Wildlife Park**
🎫 (A290) Farmyard animals, parrots
and other animals and birds, with
woodland trails, and a couple of
adventure playgrounds (one for under
5s). Snacks, shop, disabled access; cl
wknds Nov and Mar, and all Dec–Feb;
(01227) 765168; *£3.50. Nearby Blean
Woods are protected as a nature
reserve, with well signed walks in the
RSPB area.

BOROUGH GREEN TQ6356

🐝 **Great Comp Garden** (St Mary's
Platt, 2 miles E of Borough Green)
Interesting collection of trees, shrubs,
herbaceous plants and heathers with
fine lawns and paths. Snacks, plant shop,
disabled access; cl Nov–Feb; (01732)
886154; £3. The Plough at Ivy Hatch a
few miles S is a good restaurant.

BOUGH BEECH TQ4846

✙ ⌂ **Bough Beech Nature Reserve**
At the N end of the reservoir, with
wildlife exhibitions in a 19th-c oast
house. Open Weds, wknds and
bank hols Apr–Oct; (01732) 750624;
free. The Wheatsheaf has good food,
and there are pleasant walks around
here.

BOUGHTON TR0459

🐗 🍴 **Farming World** (Nash Court)
Friendly farm with traditional and rare
breeds and heavy horses, tractor and
wagon rides, nature trails, adventure
playground, walled garden, and pick-
your-own fruit and veg (Jun–Oct).
Meals, snacks, farm shop, disabled
access; cl Nov–Feb; (01227) 751144;
£3.50. The White Horse at Boughton
Street has decent food all day.

BRASTED TQ4852

🐝 ❋ ⌂ **Emmetts Garden** (Toys
Hill, 3m S) Charming hillside shrub
garden with magnificent views – it's the
highest garden in Kent. Full of bluebells
in spring and a riot of colour in autumn.
Teas, shop, some disabled access; open
wknds, Weds and bank hols Apr–Sept
(Weds–Sun Apr–May); (01732)
868381; £3; NT. The quaint Fox &
Hounds out here has good cheap
snacks, and there are pleasant walks
around here; back in the attractive
village there are quite a few antique
shops.

BRENCHLEY TQ6840

🐝 ★ **Marle Place** Pretty garden
around a fine 17th-c house (not open),
with interesting scented plants in the
walled garden, new artists' studios and a
mosaic terrace, woodland walk, and
showy bantams. Teas, some disabled
access; cl Nov–Mar; (01892) 722304;
£3. The village has some attractive old
houses and a venerable inn.

BRIDGE TR1953

🏛 🐝 **Higham Park** 🎫 It is claimed
that this restored Palladian manor was
the first house in the world to have a
wireless radio. The friendly owners are
more than willing to pore through
albums celebrating the house's
colourful history with their visitors.
Although the gardens are being
restored, the grounds are pleasant to
stroll around: a highlight is the yew-
lined Italian watergarden with waterlilies, a secret garden, and an extensive
terraced rose garden. Meals, snacks,
shop, some disabled access; cl Fri and
Sat, and all Oct–Mar; (01227) 830830;
£2.50. The White Horse is a good-value
dining pub, and the Plough & Harrow
(open all day Sat) is useful.

BROADSTAIRS TR3967

★ ⌂ Broadstairs is still appealingly
unspoilt, attractively meandering up
among the trees on the low hill behind,
with pleasant gardens, old-fashioned
bathing-huts on its central beach, and a
good relaxed atmosphere. There are
fishing boats and yachts in the lively little
harbour (where the Tartar Frigate has
good views from its upstairs
restaurant), 7 sandy bays (Joss Bay,
slightly E from the centre, is excellent
for families), refreshing clifftop walks
(even to Ramsgate if you're feeling
energetic), and lots of Dickens
connections ('Our watering place', he
called the town). Bandstand concerts at
2.30pm on summer Suns.
🍴 **Bleak House Dickens Museum**
(Fort Rd) Dickens's favourite seaside
residence, where he wrote *David
Copperfield*, and which he used as the
title for another novel. Lots of his
belongings and related memorabilia,
plus displays on local wrecks and
smuggling. Shop, some disabled access;
cl Dec–Feb exc wknds in Jan; (01843)
862224; £3.

⚱ **Dickens House Museum** (Victoria Parade) Former home of Miss Mary Strong, the basis for Betsey Trotwood in *David Copperfield* – the parlour is furnished as in the book. Also more of Dickens's letters and possessions. Shop; open pm all Apr–mid-Oct; (01843) 862853; £1.50.

BROOKLAND TQ9626

✝ **Fairfield Church** Standing quite alone in the Walland Marsh NW of Brookland, this is a tent-roofed brick-and-timber building, remarkable for its utterly lonely surroundings – and attractive inside.

⚘ **Philippine Village Craft Centre** (A259 SW of Brookland) Unique centre selling crafts from the Philippines, with occasional special events. Snacks, limited disabled access; open wknds Easter–first May bank hol, then daily till end Sept, other times by arrangement; (01797) 344616; free. The Walland Marsh here is an extension of Romney Marsh; the sign off the A259 to the Woolpack leads you to a particularly good pub with the right sort of atmosphere for the area.

CANTERBURY TR1457

🏛 One of Britain's most satisfying places to visit – but as around 100,000 visitors arrive each day in summer, you'll find it much more pleasant out of season. Redevelopment after World War II air-raid damage has been rather unsympathetic, but there's still a wealth of historic buildings tucked away in surviving narrow medieval streets. Much of the centre is pedestrianised, with good car parks on the fringes of the old centre (and a reliable Park & Ride). Interesting guided walks leave from the very helpful Visitor Information Centre, 34 St Margaret's St (11.30am and 2pm, 2pm only in winter); if you're making your own way, don't miss Palace St, Burgate with the Buttermarket Sq, and St Peter's St, all of which have fine buildings, and you can follow quite a lot of the ancient city wall on a walk passing the remains of the **Norman castle** (some information panels, not always open). The city's Roman and ecclesiastical heritage is well known, but there are other remains here too, notably a **prehistoric tumulus** in Dane John

Garden. The Canterbury Tales (just off St Peter's St) is the best pub here for lunch.

✝ **Canterbury Cathedral** Dramatically floodlit in summer, this spectacularly lives up to expectations – for the most overwhelming first impression, it's best approached from Queningate. The earliest parts are Norman, with much added in the 15th c. Rewarding features are everywhere – an airily impressive nave, fascinating stained glass, the Bell Harry Tower, lovely cloisters, and the shrine of Thomas à Becket, murdered here in the 12th c. In the crypt are some wonderfully grotesque carvings, full of strange animals and fantastic fighting monsters. Snacks, shop, disabled access; may be closed for services at certain times, limited opening Sun; £3 – note this isn't a donation, you'll be charged this just to enter the precincts, and there are additional charges for everything from guided tours to visiting the lavatory. This is intended to reduce the sheer pressure of numbers visiting, sometimes disruptive and according to the cathedral authorities even dangerous. It even charges on Sun – the first British cathedral to do so. In the precincts are fine buildings connected to the cathedral, inc the ruins of the former monastery in Green Court, and the impressive Norman Staircase. Not far outside is the medieval King's School (The Borough).

♿⚱ **Canterbury Heritage Museum** (Stour St) Housed in the medieval Poor Priests Hospital (look out for the magnificent oak roof), a splendid interpretation of the city's history, told with deft use of lavishly up-to-date display technology inc holograms, leaving many vivid visual impressions – one of the most rewarding places in SE England. There's a gallery devoted to Rupert Bear. Shop, disabled access to ground floor only; cl Sun Nov–May, Good Fri and Christmas wk; (01227) 452747; £2.30. Hidden away through an arch beside the building is the charming Greyfriars, above the River Stour.

♿ ! **Canterbury Tales** (St Margaret's St) Well put together, Chaucer's characters brought enthusiastically to life with smells, sound effects and lively

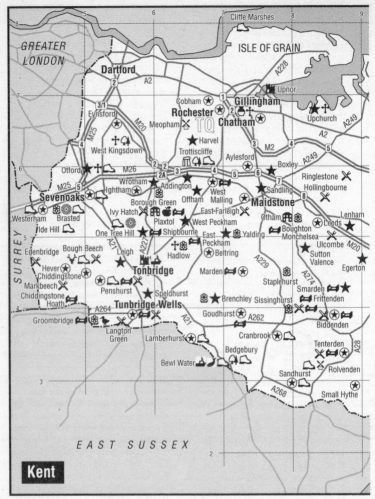

Kent

celebrity voices. Meals, snacks, very good unusual shop, disabled access (prior notice preferred); cl 25 Dec; (01227) 454888; £5.20. They also organise evening ghost tours (phone for details). The **Chaucer Centre** on St Peter's St also has an interesting shop, and maybe displays (cl all Suns, Mon Oct–Mar, and 25 Dec; free).

Roman Museum (Longmarket) Splendid underground museum, by the remains of a Roman town house; lively reconstructions of a market and aromatic kitchen, as well as lots of hands-on and hi-tech displays. The house's mosaic floor is very well displayed. Shop, disabled access; cl Sun (exc Jun–Oct), Good Fri and Christmas wk; (01227) 785575; £2.30.

Royal Museum & Art Gallery Fine porcelain, glass, clocks and watches, Roman and Anglo-Saxon jewellery, and Victorian animal paintings by T S Cooper. Shop; cl Sun, Good Fri and Christmas wk; (01227) 452747; free.

St Augustine's Abbey (Longport) Founded at the end of the 6th c, but most of the remaining ruins date from the Benedictine rebuilding in the 11th c. A free audio tour takes you around the ruins and adjacent museum.

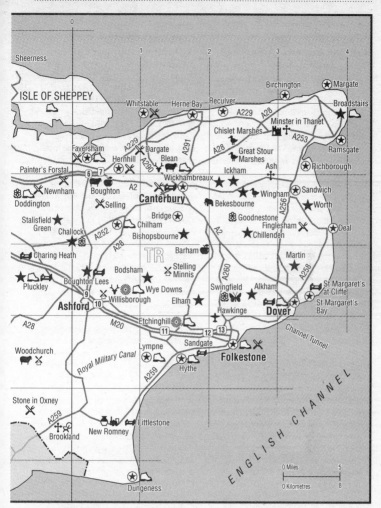

Shop, disabled access; cl 24–26 Dec, 1 Jan; (01850) 293822; £2.50; EH.
† St Martin's Church (North Holmes Rd) The country's oldest church in continual use; the Venerable Bede says it was built by the Romans, and there are certainly Roman bricks in the walls. The Roman road S to the coast (B2068) is a good drive.
West Gate Museum (where St Peter's St meets St Dunstan's St) The city's last remaining fortified gatehouse, built in the late 14th c, with interesting cells, and excellent views from the battlements. Children can do brass rubbing or try on replica armour. Shop; cl 12.30–1.30pm, all day Sun, Good Fri, Christmas wk; (01227) 452747; £1.
CHALLOCK TR0152
Beech Court Gardens Peaceful gardens surrounding a medieval farmhouse; and lots of spring and autumn colour; the firs and pines reflect the designer's admiration for Inverewe in Scotland. They hold the national record for the biggest prunus. Teas in oast house, picnic areas, plant sales and craft shop, disabled access; cl am Fri and wknds, and mid-Nov–Easter; (01233) 740735; *£2.50. The 17th-c Chequers

by the village green has good-value food.

CHATHAM TQ7568

🏰 🎫 **Fort Amherst** 🎫 (Dock Rd) Perhaps the finest surviving 18th-c fort in the country, with massive ditches, gun emplacements, a warren of tunnels and a firing gun battery. 18 acres of parkland, and live re-enactments the first 3 Suns of each month. Meals, snacks, shop; cl 25–26 Dec, 1 Jan; (01634) 847747; £4. The Command House below by the water does limited but decent food.

🏛️ ❋ 🔎 ⚓ **Historic Dockyard** Excellent 80-acre working museum set in the most complete Georgian dockyard in the world. Lots to see and do: the Wooden Walls exhibition uses sights, sounds and smells to show how 18th-c warships such as HMS *Victory* were built here, and there's an exhibition on the RNLI, with 15 lifeboats. An exhibition centre in the Flagship Brewery (Building 64) explores the role of beer in the navy (disabled access; open Mon, Weds, Fri; free). Also restorations, rope-making demonstrations, craft workshops, and lively events. A visit here can easily fill most of the day. Meals, snacks, shop, disabled access; open daily Apr–Oct, plus wknds and Weds in Nov, Feb and Mar; (01634) 812551; £8.50. You can get a ticket that includes **boat trips** on the paddle steamer *Kingswear Castle*, and may be able to tour the submarine *Ocelot* moored in Chatham Maritime.

CHIDDINGSTONE TQ5045

★ A favourite Kentish village, an unspoilt cluster of Tudor houses and buildings owned by the NT, in lovely countryside. The church and the mysterious stone which one story claims gives the village its name are worth a look. The Kentish Horse over at Markbeech has good food.

🏛️ 🖼️ 🎫 🎣 **Chiddingstone Castle** 17th-c house rebuilt in castle style at the start of the 19th c; renowned paintings and antiquities from England, Egypt and the Orient, inc fine collections of Japanese swords and Buddhist art. Attractively restored landscaped grounds, and you can fish in the lake (£8 a day). Snacks, shop; open pm Weds–Fri Jun–Sept, Sun and bank hols only in Apr, May and Oct; (01892) 870347; £4.

CHILHAM TR0653

★ The lovely village square is the prettiest in Kent, and several antique shops reflect its popularity with visitors – in summer, get there early to catch it at its most photogenic. The Woolpack just down the hill is useful for lunch.

🍴 🔎 🐄 🔄 **Badgers Hill Farm** (New Cut Rd – towards Selling) Cheerily unspoilt spot, with cider-making, local crafts, a barrel merchant, free-roaming pigs (you may find them in the shop) and other animals, a play area, and **pick-your-own** apples (10 types, Aug–Oct). Snacks, farm shop, disabled access; cl 24 Dec–early Mar; (01227) 730573; free. Further towards Selling, the Rose & Crown at Perry Wood is a nice pub, with woodland walks nearby.

CHISLET MARSHES TR2366

🦆 Thousands of geese and ducks; duck food by the bag from the nice little Gate Inn at Boyden Gate.

CLIFFE MARSHES TQ7279

🔄 N of Rochester, these are bounded by a long sea wall cum footpath which feels (and is) extraordinarily remote and not a little surreal – perhaps the best Thames estuary walk in N Kent.

COBHAM TQ6668

★ ✝ 🏛️ Another attractive village, with a good mix of unspoilt buildings from various centuries – an excellent place to walk round (as Dickens liked to do). The partly 13th-c **church** is worth examining, with its magnificent brasses and tombs, as is the 14th-c **New College**, like a miniature Oxford college but far less known to visitors (disabled access; free). The Leather Bottle has decent food, interesting Dickens memorabilia and a good garden.

🏛️ 🎫 **Cobham Hall** The Earls of Darnley once lived in this impressive place, now a girls' school. The décor is quite splendid in parts (some notable marble fireplaces), and the lovely grounds are being restored. Snacks, shop; open pm selected dates Mar, Apr, July and Aug; (01474) 824319; £3.50.

🏛️ **Owletts** At the S end of Cobham, this modest 17th-c yeoman's house has an interesting staircase – and in the garden the grandest bird bath we've ever seen. Open pm Weds and Thurs Apr–Oct; (01892) 890651; *£2; NT.

CRANBROOK TQ7736

✗ ★ ♨ ⌂ **Cranbrook Union Mill**
This very good working **windmill**, picturesquely set almost in the centre, still grinds corn. The restored workshop behind should soon be open, with displays on the mill's history; shop; open pm Sat and bank hols Apr–Sept, plus pm Sun mid-July–Aug; (01580) 712824; donations. The attractive miniature town, with largely unspoilt lanes of tile-hung buildings, also has a friendly local-history **museum**, and for picnics Perfect Partners (Stone St) is the best delicatessen for many miles. The walk to Sissinghurst and back is a pleasant way of joining 2 very interesting places.

DEAL TR3752

★ Once the busiest harbour in SE England, and Caesar's landing point in 55BC; now pleasantly understated seaside resort, full of pretty little streets and alleys – but beware of vigilant traffic wardens. The seaview King's Head (Beach St) has good-value food (and bedrooms).

🏰 **Deal Castle** The biggest in Henry VIII's chain of coastal defences, uniquely shaped like a Tudor rose with every wall rounded to deflect shot. Snacks, good audio tour, shop; cl Mon and Tues Apr–Nov, 24–26 Dec; (01304) 372762; £3; EH.

♨ **Time-Ball Tower** (Victoria Parade) Museum of time, telegraphy and maritime communication, with time-ball dropping on the hour. Shop; open July and Aug (not Mon); (01304) 360897; £1.25.

🏰 ❀ **Walmer Castle** (just S of Deal) Another of Henry VIII's coastal defence fortresses, later the official residence of the Lord Warden of the Cinque Ports (one was the Duke of Wellington, who left behind his famous boot). It became more stately home than fortress, with rooms furnished in 18th-c style, and pretty gardens laid out mainly by a niece of William Pitt (a more recent one is dedicated to the Queen Mother). Snacks, shop, some disabled access; cl Mon and Tues Nov–Dec and Mar, wkdys Jan and Feb, and whenever the Lord Warden is in residence (usually

over Christmas); (01304) 364288; £4.50; EH.

DODDINGTON TQ9357

❀ ⌂ **Doddington Place Gardens**
Grand garden with formal plantings, some massive topiary, an old-fashioned rock garden, rhododendrons in woodland, broad views, and delightfully peaceful atmosphere. Plant sales, café, disabled access; open Weds, bank hols, and pm Sun May–Sept; (01795) 886101; *£3. The George at Newnham is nice for lunch, with good walks nearby.

DOVER TR3241

The busiest ferry port in Europe, Dover is not in itself an attractive town but has several extremely interesting places to visit, reflecting the fascinating history it owes to its strategic importance. Blakes (Castle St) is useful for lunch and there is fast and helpful service at Valentino's on Townland Street.

✗ **Crabble Corn Mill** (Lower Rd) Beautifully restored working 19th-c watermill. Fairs held year round. Snacks (made with their own flour), shop, limited disabled access; open Apr–Dec; (01304) 823292; tours £2.

🏰 �📷 ❀ † **Dover Castle** Not to be missed, a magnificent and excellently preserved Norman fortress with its original keep, 74-metre (242ft) well and massive walls and towers. There's a lot to see inc a lively collection of secret-agent gadgetry, a children's activity area, Hellfire Corner, the atmospheric complex of underground tunnels that played a vital role in World War II, and an exhibition which dramatically recreates an early 13th-c siege. Also included are the Pharos Tower, a Roman lighthouse using a 4th-floor flaring brazier as a guide-light, and a restored Saxon church. A walk round the battlements gives interesting views of the comings and goings down in the harbour (something which captivates small children); you can get an audioguide to listen to as you stroll. Meals, snacks, shop, disabled access; cl 24–26 Dec; (01304) 211067; £6.90 (£3.50 children), family ticket (2 adults and up to 3 children) £17.30; EH.

! **Grand Shaft** An unusual spiral stone staircase which links top and bottom of Dover's famous cliffs; open Tues–Sun July–Aug; £1.25.

♄ **Old Town Gaol** 🖼 (High St) Hi-tech effects recreate courtroom scenes and life in a Victorian prison; they'll even lock you (albeit briefly) in a tiny cell. Shop, disabled access; cl Mon and Tues; (01304) 242766; *£3.50.

🏛 **Roman Painted House** (New St) Well preserved remains of a Roman hotel with unique wall paintings and panels, and an elaborate underfloor heating system. Brass rubbing, shop, disabled access; cl Mon, and Oct–Mar; (01304) 203279; *£2.

👶♄ **White Cliffs Experience** (Market Sq) Refreshingly lively museum where children can press, poke and push things, and inadvertently learn about Dover's history while they're doing it. Splendid Roman Encounter and World War II section, as well as a 20-minute animatronic show bringing the town's history to life. In summer there may be outdoor activities like archery. Snacks (and picnic site), shop, disabled access (they prefer notice); cl 25–26 Dec; (01304) 214566; £5.75. The same site also has a more conventional museum and a gallery based around the Dover Bronze Age boat (discovered during roadworks in 1992).

⌂ ❀ 🏛 ✗ **White Cliffs of Dover** These provide an exhilarating walk (and interesting views of the harbour – you can even see France on a clear day) from Dover Castle to St Margaret's at Cliffe, passing the Roman lighthouse above Dover, and a curious scaled-down windmill at St Margaret's at Cliffe. There's a bus back to Dover (no point making a circuit, as the inland scenery here is not worth while), or you can press on to Kingsdown (the Rising Sun is a handy stop) or to Deal.

DUNGENESS TR0817

❗🚃 Fascinatingly odd, a real curiosity and quite foreign-feeling, its acres of shingle colonised by fishing shacks and railway carriages converted into homes (Derek Jarman used to live here). It's a terminus for the little steam railway described under New Romney. And there are more pebbles than you could ever imagine.

🏛 **Dungeness Information Centre & Power Stations** Tours of either the A or the B nuclear power station, with interactive displays, videos, and nature trail. Snacks, shop, disabled access to visitor centre only; cl Nov–Mar; no children under 5, as everyone has to wear a hard hat; (01797) 321815; free.

✣ ➤ **Dungeness Nature Reserve** RSPB, on the shingle headland, interesting for its unusual plants and in late spring for the nesting terns. Snacks, shop, disabled access; cl 25–26 Dec; (01797) 320588; £2.50, RSPB members free.

❀ ⌂ **Old Lighthouse** Fine views from the top of its 167 steps; shop; cl wkdys Mar–May and Oct, and all Nov–Easter; (01794) 321300; £2.20. The friendly Britannia nearby has fresh local fish.

ETCHINGHILL TR1638

❀ ⌂ **Saxon Shore Way** This long-distance path gives some good views and interesting walks. A section starting at Etchinghill crosses under an old railway line, heads up an unspoilt dry valley, and leads along the top of the slope for sightings of Dungeness and the French coast (Cap Gris Nez in Picardy).

EYNSFORD TQ5365

➤ **Eagle Heights** Readers enjoy this informative birds of prey centre, good in any weather as many displays are indoors (outdoor ones at 12 noon and 3.30pm). You can handle snakes and reptiles (1.45pm) and meet the owls (2.15pm). Snacks, shop, disabled access; cl wkdys Dec–Feb; (01332) 866466; £4.50.

🏰 **Eynsford Castle** Norman knight's fortress with impressive 9-metre (30ft) walls, and remains of the hall and ditch; free. There are organised trails from the nearby countryside centre along the River Darent and into woods above the golf course. The Malt Shovel has good seafood.

🏠 ❀ **Lullingstone Castle** Historic family mansion with fine state rooms, great hall, staircase and library, and beautiful grounds. The 15th-c gate tower was one of the first buildings to be made entirely of brick. Snacks, shop, disabled access; open pm wknds and bank hols July–Sept plus Sun Apr–Jun; (01322) 862114; *£4.

🏛 ✝ **Lullingstone Roman Villa** (just SE of Eynsford, off A225) Remains of rather well-to-do 1st- and 2nd-c family's villa, with exceptionally well preserved floor mosaics and an extensive bath complex. Also an early Christian chapel – the only one so far found in a private house. Snacks, shop, some disabled access; cl 24–26 Dec; (01322) 863467; £2.50.

FAVERSHAM TR0161

★ Delightfully photogenic small town ideal for a stroll: plenty of colour-washed timbered old buildings such as the Elizabethan grammar school and the Guildhall (one of the few raised market halls still to shelter stallholders in the pillared market court beneath it – Tues/Fri/Sat). The Albion (Front Brents) has good food, and just N of the town, a track off the road to Oare leads to a remote waterside pub, the Shipwrights Arms: a charming setting on summer evenings.

🏠 ❀ **Belmont** (Throwley, 4m SW of Faversham) A pleasant 18th-c mansion in well placed parkland, with a walled garden, and a collection of unusual clocks – one looks like a church steeple. Snacks, shop, disabled access; open pm wknds and bank hols Easter–Sept; (01795) 890202; £5.25, £2.75 garden only.

🍎 **Brogdale Orchard** (Brogdale Rd, S of A2 nr Faversham) As we went to press, this mammoth fruit farm, inc the National Fruit Collection, was awaiting the outcome of a deal with a construction company which would lead to the addition of new laboratories and a visitor centre over the next few years. Beautiful but baffling to stroll through (guided walks available), its 30 acres of orchards produce hundreds of distinct varieties of every hardy fruit

imaginable; there are 2,500 types of apple alone. The shop sells trees, bushes and flowering plants, as well as crops from pears, plums and cherries to cobnuts, quinces and medlars. Meals, snacks, disabled access; orchards cl Nov–Apr, though shop and tearoom open then; (01795) 535286; £2.50.

⛏ **Chart Gunpowder Mills** (Westbrook Walk) Well restored old gunpowder mills, reputedly the last left in the country. Small shop; open pm wknds and bank hols Apr–Sept, by appointment at other times (01795) 534915; donations.

🏠 **Fleur de Lis Heritage Centre** 🏛 (Preston St) A generous heritage fund has helped this enthusiastically run centre (housed in a 15th-c building) towards extending its premises into adjacent houses. Colourful displays, reconstructions and a working vintage-telephone exchange. Shop (good for books on Kent), disabled access to ground floor only; cl Sun, Oct–Mar; (01795) 534542; £1.50 for museum. Walking tours of Faversham leave here at 10.30am every Sat Apr–Sept (£1).

FOLKESTONE TR2335

✝ 🏛 ❀ 🏠 ☺ 🏠 Despite much development of this major cross-Channel port, there is an intact pre-19th-c area called the Bayle around the interesting old **church** – very pretty and Kentish. The part around the harbour, previously a picturesque warren, was badly bombed in World War II, but the fish stalls there contribute authentic local colour, the Old High St has a Cornish-type quaintness, and Carpenters (The Stade) has good fresh fish. The remains known

---

Days Out

Weatherboarding and pantiles: Tenterden, and steamtrain trip; lunch aboard (Sun only), or at the Three Chimneys, Biddenden; Biddenden Vineyards; Sissinghurst; Cranbrook.

Journey to the end of the Earth: Folkestone harbour and The Leas; lunch at the Clarendon, Sandgate; perhaps stroll from Hythe town centre to Saltwood Castle; Romney Hythe & Dymchurch Railway from Hythe to Dungeness.

The White Cliffs: Dover Castle; lunch at the harbourside Churchill Hotel; White Cliffs Experience, or walk along the cliffs to St Margaret's Bay.

as **Caesar's Camp** in fact long pre-date the Roman invasion. Particularly pleasant is a walk along **The Leas**, a clifftop expanse of lawns and flower gardens with good views. A water-balanced cliff lift operates between here and the seafront. You can watch sweet-and-rock making in the afternoons (exc Weds and Sun) at **Rowlands Confectionery** on the Old High St; free. The **Rotunda Amusement Park** 🎡 has traditional fairground rides, crazy golf and rollercoasters, with lots under cover.

! **Battle of Britain Memorial** Just W on the B2011, this is worth a look. The huge stone figure looking out in contemplation across the Channel gives this place an extraordinary air of calm solemnity. There's a new conservatory and memorial wall engraved with Churchill's unforgettable tribute to the airmen. Snacks, shop, disabled access; cl Nov–Apr; (01303) 276697; free (parking £1).

⛰ **Warren** This intriguingly jungly tumbledown undercliff is reached from the East Cliff at Folkestone by a walk out past the Martello Tower; once there you can cross a railway footbridge and reach the shore, or go up a flight of steps and on to the clifftop, to return along the cliffs past the Battle of Britain Memorial. The cliff path also makes for a good bracing walk from Folkestone all the way to Dover for the train or bus back.

GILLINGHAM TQ7669

♂ ✝ **Royal Engineers Museum** (Brompton Barracks, Prince Arthur Rd) More appealing than you might think, with sound effects, and art and oddities brought back from various countries, including a Harrier jump jet and displays relating to mine clearance. Snacks, shop, disabled access; cl Fri, 25–26 Dec, 1 Jan; (01634) 406397; £3. The town has a partly Norman **church**. Off the A2 between here and Boughton Street village, any of the little lanes take you deep into orchard country, with foody pubs at Dargate, Selling and Eastling; blossom-time Apr and early May; farm shops with local apples Sept onwards.

GOODNESTONE TR2653

🌺 **Goodnestone Park** Old-fashioned roses in traditional walled garden recalling Jane Austen's stays in the fine 18th-c house (not open). Also a woodland garden with good trees. Teas Weds and Sun May–Aug, nursery, disabled access; cl Tues, Sat, and Nov–Mar; (01304) 840107; £3. The Fitzwalter Arms has good-value food.

GOUDHURST TQ7237

★ ❀ Charming Wealden village, with quite a few antique shops and so forth, and spectacular views from the graveyard of the 14th-c hilltop church (but during the day too much traffic for comfort). The Spread Eagle up by the church, one of the village's most handsome old buildings, is useful for lunch.

🏠 🌺 ♨ **Finchcocks** (off A262 W of Goudhurst) The early Georgian house and its lovely gardens are attractive, but the main draw is the big collection of working keyboard instruments from the 17th c onwards. Some of these are played whenever the house is open, the well organised recitals really adding to the atmosphere. Meals (by arrangement), snacks, shop, some disabled access; open pm Weds and Thurs in Aug, as well as pm Sun and some bank hols Easter–Sept – phone to check; (01580) 211702; £6. The Green Cross Inn up by the main road has good home cooking.

GREAT STOUR MARSHES TR2462

🦅 Interesting for their thousands of geese and ducks; access from the good Grove Ferry pub just off the A28 near Upstreet.

GROOMBRIDGE TQ5337

🌺 🦅 **Groombridge Place Gardens** (B2110) Beautiful walled gardens, among the country's most spectacular, around a 17th-c moated mansion, the parkland and forest inspiring generations of artists and writers. Drunken topiary garden, oriental garden, rose garden, sculpture garden (the flower-pot men are in a different league to Bill and Ben), paths patrolled by peacocks and the moat guarded by black swans. The developing fantasy wilderness is best for children, complete with magic pools, teepees, gypsy caravans and atmospheric wind chimes. Families are in general better provided for than at most gardens, with play areas, birds of prey (daily displays 11.30am, 1pm and 3.30pm), lots of animals, a new snake and spider house, and canal boat and tractor rides. Snacks, gift shop; cl Nov–Mar; (01892) 863999; *£7.50. Nr the entrance, up the hill on the village green, the prettily placed Crown does good food.

HADLOW TQ6249

⚜ ✝ Broadview Gardens A good mix of traditional and imaginatively themed gardens put together by horticulturists at neighbouring Hadlow College; the atmospheric Heaven and Hell Garden is one of our favourites. National collections of hellebores and Japanese anemones, and a well stocked plant centre. Meals, snacks, shop, disabled access; cl Nov–Mar; (01732) 850551; £2; free car parking. Hadlow's **church** has the interesting Hop Pickers Memorial, dedicated to the 30 hop pickers who one wet day in 1853 drowned on their way back from the fields; the enormously tall folly of Hadlow Tower is worth a look, and the Artichoke has decent food.

HAWKINGE TR2039

✝ Kent Battle of Britain Museum Plenty of aeroplanes, and an extensive collection of relics and memorabilia of British and German aircraft involved in the fighting, inc relics of more than 600 crashed aircraft. Snacks, shop, some disabled access; cl Nov–Easter; (01303) 893140; £3. The Valiant Sailor at Capel le Ferne (A20) saves you going into Folkestone for lunch.

HERNE BAY TR1868

⛆ ▣ ✗ Not terribly exciting, but a decorous and spaciously laid-out 19th-c resort. Mike Turner runs **boat trips** around the bay and out to see seals from May–Oct; best to book for the seal trip, (01227) 366712. There's a decent art gallery on William St; shop, disabled access; cl Sun exc pm July–Aug; free. The Ship and Richmond, on or just off the front, both have decent food. The **windmill** may be open by the time this book is published; shop; open pm Sun and bank hols Easter–Sept, plus Thurs July–Aug; £1.50.

HERNHILL TR0659

⚜ 🍴 ⚘ ★ Mount Ephraim Gardens Seven acres of pleasant gardens, with a Japanese rock garden, topiary garden,

watergarden, woodland walk and small vineyard; good views. Teas (not Tues), craft shop; cl am, Tues, Fri, and Oct–Easter; (01227) 751496; *£3. There's a craft centre on Sun. By the church and small green of this charming village, the ancient Red Lion has decent food.

HEVER TQ4745

🏰 ⚜ ▣ ! Hever Castle & Gardens In 30 acres of beautiful gardens, this double-moated 13th-c castle has hardly changed externally since Anne Boleyn lived here as a child. Inside it's a different story, as the rooms were magnificently restored by the Astor family at the start of the 20th c. Antiques, furnishings and art from all over Europe, plus a new room dedicated to Henry VIII's wives. Another building is home to an exceptional collection of astonishingly detailed miniature houses, furnished and decorated in authentic period styles. The grounds are a draw in their own right, with lakes, an Italianate garden with antique sculptures, a walled rose garden and a maze; also a summer splashing water maze and adventure playground. Meals, snacks, shop, good disabled access to gardens; cl Dec–Feb, castle cl am; (01732) 865224; £7.30, £5.80 gardens only. The Henry VIII is popular for lunch.

HYTHE TR1634

🚣 This hillside town, served by the classic Romney Hythe & Dymchurch Railway (see New Romney entry), is well worth a look, with attractive old houses in its narrow High St and the pretty lanes around the church. Its beach stretches to Sandgate, also pleasant to stroll through; the Clarendon up a steep cobbled lane on the way, has enjoyable food.

✝ ! St Leonard's Church The crypt houses an amazing collection of 2,000 skulls and 8,000 thigh bones, dating from before 1500 and all neatly arranged on shelves or carefully stacked in a large heap (cl lunchtime, wknds, and Oct–Apr; 50p).

⌂ 🏰 West Hythe walk From West Hythe the towpath of the Royal Military Canal takes you up into Hythe itself, where a path from the junction of Station Rd (B2065) and Mill Lane enters

parkland and continues up to
Saltwood Castle (not open to the
public), which still has its impressive
medieval curtain wall.

IDE HILL TQ4851

⌂ With its pubs and picture-book
green, this is on the scarp slope of the
lower greensand escarpment, and on the
Greensand Way: a good walking area.

IGHTHAM TQ5853

🏠 🏵 ♿ **Ightham Mote** (off A227, 2m
S) Lovely medieval manor house, still
with its surrounding moat, a unique
survival that looks especially beautiful
on a sunny day. Fascinating great hall,
Tudor chapel and 14th-c crypt, while
the drawing room has a striking
Jacobean fireplace, frieze and windows.
Pretty courtyard, garden and woodland
walks. Snacks, shop, some disabled
access; cl am Tues, Sat, and all
Nov–Mar; (01732) 810378; £5; NT.
The George & Dragon in the village is a
good dining pub, popular with families
at weekends.

ISLE OF SHEPPEY TR0469

⌂ Walkers may enjoy the E end, with a
path along the sea dyke S from
Leysdown-on-Sea to Shell Ness, at the
mouth of the Swale.

LAMBERHURST TQ6436

✝ **Bayham Abbey** (2m W, just over
the Sussex border) Impressive ruins of
a 13th-c Premonstratensian abbey and
gatehouse in a pretty wooded valley.
Occasional outdoor theatre. Snacks,
shop, disabled access; cl 25 Dec and
wkdys Nov–Mar; (01892) 890381;
£2.10. The Elephant's Head at Hook
Green is a useful nearby pub, popular
with families at weekends.

🍷 ★ **Lamberhurst Vineyard** (Ridge
Farm) One of the biggest vineyards in
SE England, no tours but you can
wander round; disabled access; cl
Christmas wk; (01892) 890286; free.
Also, a useful if short public path skirts
the vineyard. The attractive village still
awaits its bypass.

🏵 **Owl House Gardens** (off A21 NE
of Lamberhurst) 16 acres of sweeping
lawns, flowers, shrubs and fruit trees
around a timber-framed 16th-c wool
smugglers' house; sunken watergardens
and woodlands. Teas, shop, disabled
access; cl 25 Dec, 1 Jan; (01892)
890230; £4.

🏵 🏰 ⌂ **Scotney Castle Garden**
(A21 just S) Beautiful 19th-c gardens
surrounding the ruins of a small 14th-c
moated castle, with impressive
rhododendrons, azaleas and roses – a
really romantic place. Shop, some
disabled access (they recommend a
strong pusher); open Weds–Fri and pm
wknds and bank hols Apr–Oct (exc
Good Fri); castle open same hours
May–mid-Sept; (01892) 891081; £4;
NT. A public footpath strides through
the estate's woods and pastures, which
can provide walks from Kilndown to
Lamberhurst and back. The Brown
Trout, on the B2169 nearly opposite
the main entrance, has good fish.

LEEDS TQ8353

🏰 🏵 ♨ 🖼 ♥ ! **Leeds Castle** Long
renowned as one of the loveliest castles
in the country, perfectly placed on 2
little islands in the middle of a lake in
500 acres of landscaped parkland. It
dates from the 9th c, and was converted
into a royal residence by Henry VIII.
Lots of paintings, furniture and
tapestries, and a unique dog-collar
museum in the gatehouse. The
enormous grounds have gardens (inc a
new Mediterranean one), a maze and
grotto, duck enclosure and aviary (well
liked by readers), golf course; as this
suggests, it's a busy place, not quite as
idyllic as it appears from a distance, but
very satisfying for a day out. Special
events from wine festivals to open-air
concerts. Meals, snacks, shop, good
disabled access; cl 25 Dec, and the day
prior to evening ticketed events (3 days
a year, usually the last wknd in Jun, the
first in July and the one nearest 5 Nov
but best to check first); (01622)
765400; £9.30, £7.30 park and gardens
only. The Pepper Box nr Ulcombe is the
best nearby place for lunch.

LYMPNE TR0935

🐘 🏵 🏠 **Port Lympne Wild Animal
Park** Set in wonderful ornamental
parkland around a well restored house,
Port Lympne and its sister park
Howletts (see separate family panel on p.
352) are well known for their dedicated
approach to caring for their rare or
endangered animals. There's a lot to
see, paths can be steep and there are
300 acres altogether so the free Safari
Shuttle trailers between enclosures is a

welcome improvement. Particular highlights include the 2-acre moated gorilla enclosure, and the country's largest breeding herd of black rhino. Also tigers, elephants, lions and wolves, and occasional special talks and events. The house has a number of unusual features, including the Hexagonal Library where the Treaty of Paris was signed after World War I, but most remarkable must be the incredible Tent Room by Rex Whistler; there's also a room entirely covered by a mural showing south-east Asian animals and birds. Meals, snacks, shop; cl 25 Dec; (01303) 264646; £8.90.

⛴ ⌂ Royal Military Canal Built along the N fringe of Romney Marsh as a defence against Napoleon, this forms a section of the Saxon Shore Way long-distance path. You can combine it with a path along the escarpment at Lympne Castle; the Botolphs Bridge Inn just S has decent home cooking.

MAIDSTONE TQ7555

⛴ Busy modern town, but worth penetrating for its good museums. The Muggleton (King St) is an exemplary pub converted from a very grand Victorian building in conjunction with English Heritage, and the White Lion just out at East Farleigh has good food. You may be able to go on a **boat trip** along to Allington.

🏛 Archbishop's Palace (Mill St) Striking edifice used by the Archbishops of Canterbury as a stopping-place on their way from London. If there are no functions occurring, you can visit the Great Hall and other rooms; cl 25–26 Dec; (01622) 663006; free.

🏛 ⛴ 🖼 Maidstone Museum & Art Gallery (St Faith's St) Handsome Elizabethan manor house with period original room settings. Snacks, shop, some disabled access; cl am Sun, 25–26 Dec; (01622) 754497; free.

⛴ ⽊ 🐎 ⸙ Museum of Kent Life (Sandling) The story of the Kent countryside, entertainingly told over 27 acres, taking in farming tools, crafts, gardens, animals, and a working oast house. A fair bit for children, and special events at least every other wknd. Snacks, shop, disabled access; cl Nov–Mar; (01622) 763936; £4.20. Nearby, the well restored 17th-c

Tyland Barn on Bluebell Hill is the HQ of the Kent Wildlife Trust, with information on the area's nature reserves; cl Jan; (01622) 662012; free. The King's Arms in the pretty neighbouring village of Boxley does decent lunches, with pleasant walks nearby.

✝ ⛴ Tyrwhitt Drake Museum of Carriages Notable collection of horse-drawn vehicles housed in the palace stables. Shop, disabled access to ground floor only; cl am winter, 25–26 Dec; (01622) 754497; £1.50. The site also includes the old parish **church** of All Saints.

MARDEN TQ7444

★ ✝ ⸙ This attractive village has a 12th/14th-c ragstone **church** with a unique white weatherboarded tower, and other buildings going back to the 14th c. **Marden Meadow** (Staplehurst Rd) A lovely unimproved hay meadow, with wild flowers and butterflies in late spring and early summer. The Wild Duck just S (Pagehurst Lane) has good food.

MARGATE TR3571

⛴ 🏛 ⽊ Often rather brash seaside resort, past its best, though huge grants from the European Union are having a noticeable effect, and there's plenty for families, inc excellent sandy beaches. The Old Town Hall (Market Pl) has a local history **museum** (cl winter wknds; 🖼, £1.50), and nearby is a well preserved **Tudor house**, open only on special occasions, but worth a look from the outside. The Spread Eagle (Victoria Rd) has popular food. To the E of town on College Rd there's a working **windmill** (open pm Easter Sun, pm Sun May–Sept and Thurs evening July and Aug, 80p).

☺ Dreamland Theme Park Once through the inauspicious entrance, this is a very satisfactory and well laid out fairground with rides from dodgems to rollercoasters and a log flume; meals, snacks, shop; cl Nov–Mar; (01843) 227011; £9.99.

⸙ Margate Caves These huge caverns are atmospheric – with wall-paintings and spooky shapes and shadows; shop; open Easter–Oct; (01843) 220139; £1.50.

⸙ ! Shell Grotto (Grotto Hill) An unexpected puzzle is this 185 sq metres

(2,000 sq ft) of winding underground passages and exquisitely decorated tunnels leading to a mysterious ancient shell temple, thought to be the only one in the world. No one really knows its origins or what it was for. Shop; cl Nov–Easter; (01843) 220008; £1.50.

MEOPHAM TQ6365

✗ **Meopham Windmill** Unusual both for its 6 sides and for the fact that its base is a meeting place for the parish council. Shop; open pm Sun and bank hols May–Sept; 70p. The Cricketers, prettily set on the green, is a useful chain-food pub.

MINSTER IN THANET TR3164

🏰 † **Minster Abbey** Site of one of the earliest nunneries in the country, with ruins and cloisters of the 7th-c building. The current house is still run by Benedictine nuns. Shop; some disabled access; open 11am–noon, then 2–4.30pm, am only Oct–Apr, cl Sun and pm Sat; (01843) 821254; free. The Mortons Fork hotel does interesting bar food.

NEW ROMNEY TR0724

🚂🚃 **Romney Hythe & Dymchurch Railway** The world's smallest-scale public railway, with 13½ miles of 15in-gauge track between Hythe and Dungeness. The station has a toy and model museum with 2 magnificent model railways. Engines are often changed *en route*, and the carriages are comfortable. Well run and friendly, it's quite a favourite with readers. Snacks, shop, disabled access (they prefer notice); trains daily Apr–Sept, wknds Oct and Mar – ring for timetable; (01797) 362353; £8.90 full fare (but there's a wide range of lower ones available).

ONE TREE HILL TQ5653

⌂❋ Reached from an NT car park S of Godden Green, this gives walkers a grand view over the Weald. From here the Greensand Way (look for GW markers) follows the very edge of the lower greensand escarpment which dips gently down to Ightham Mote, 2m E; Ivy Hatch and Stone Street have handily placed pubs to make this into a circuit.

OTFORD TQ5159

★ ⌂ † This charming village has a ruined archbishop's palace, and pleasant walks along an easy track to the attractive nearby village of **Shoreham**, which has a lovely church. There are decent pubs in both villages. The downlands to the E give scope for longer walks across Magpie Bottom and past Romney Street.

OTHAM TQ7953

🏰 🏚 **Stoneacre** Lovely half-timbered 15th-c manor house, restored in 1920s, with a charming cottage garden. Open pm Weds and Sat Apr–Oct; (01622) 862871; £2.50; NT.

PENSHURST TQ5244

★ 🏰 🏚 🍴 ♨ 🌸 ⌂ A pretty village, with antique shops, teas and so forth, and, above all, **Penshurst Place**, a great medieval manor house, unchanged since the Sidney family first came here centuries ago. Interesting combination of architectural styles, a huge chestnut-beamed baronial hall, extensive collections of portraits and furnishings, a toy museum, and marvellous formal gardens with nature trails and an adventure playground. Meals, snacks, shop, disabled access to the grounds (inc a garden for the blind); house cl am, wkdys in Mar, all Nov–Feb; (01892) 870307; £5.70, grounds only £4.20. The Leicester Arms in the village is good for lunch, and above it up on Smarts Hill the Spotted Dog has lovely views down over Penshurst Place. The Bottle House and the Rock out in this direction are also both well worth tracking down if you're walking in this attractive area, which has some of the Weald's most luscious lowlands, predominantly pasture, the cottages characteristically tile-hung, and the paths just elevated enough to gain charming views. As with much of the rest of the area, route-finding for walks is fiddly and patient map-reading is in order. One of the best circular routes, passing several good pubs, is Penshurst–Chiddingstone Hoath–Chiddingstone.

🍇 🐑 **Penshurst Vineyards** (Grove Rd) Self-guided tours, tastings and various animals inc rare breeds of sheep. Cl 25 Dec–2 Jan, and wknds Jan and Feb; (01892) 870255; *£1.50 to see the animals.

PLAXTOL TQ6154

🏰 🏚 **Old Soar Manor** An ancient oak door at this 13th-c knight's dwelling has graffiti spanning the ages, and there's also a very well preserved chapel and barrel-vaulted undercroft; cl Fri, Oct–Mar; free; NT. This general area is attractive orchard country, not too hedged, with good-value apples from the farm shops, from Sept onwards; many here also have fresh cobnuts in Sept. The old Kentish Rifleman (Silver Hill, Dunks Green) has enjoyable food and a good garden.

PLUCKLEY TQ9245
★ ⌂ This attractive village has had quite a flood of visitors since *The Darling Buds of May* was filmed here; well marked walks, good pubs for refreshment.

RAMSGATE TR3864
★ Quietly civilised seaside resort, with some elegantly colonnaded Georgian buildings and other fine houses up on the cliffs (Pugin, the architect of the Houses of Parliament, designed the church – where he's buried – and the house next door), and a historic harbour (bustling now with its yacht marina and Hoverport). Churchills (The Paragon) has harbour views and good-value food.

✿ **Maritime Museum** (Pier Yard) Good collection of historic ships and boats in a handsome early 19th-c clock-house in the harbour; shop, limited disabled access; cl wknds Oct–Mar; (01843) 587765; £1.50.

🚗 **Motor Museum** (West Cliff Hall, The Paragon) Vintage cars, motorbikes and bicycles in cheerful period settings; shop, disabled access; cl Nov–Mar exc Sun; £2.50.

RECULVER TR2269
🏛 † ✿ **Reculver Towers & Roman Fort** Built in the 3rd c, this was well preserved until the 18th c, when cliff erosion collapsed some of it into the sea; some parts remain, though it's the proud pair of tall Saxon towers of the former church on the mound above the beach that stay in the memory. Surrounding these remains is a **country park**, with a visitor centre (cl all Mon exc bank hols, plus Tues Sept–Mar and Mon–Sat Oct–Mar); (01227) 740676; free.

RICHBOROUGH TR3260
🏛🏚👣 **Richborough Castle** Another evocative ruined Roman castle – lots of walls and foundations, and a small

museum. Snacks, shop, disabled access; cl Mon and Tues Nov and Mar and all wkdys Dec–Feb; (01304) 612013; £2.50 (inc Walkman tour).

ROCHESTER TQ7468
🏚 A busy town, but well worth walking round, with several attractive buildings besides those we mention; one of the quaintest is Kent's oldest pub, the Coopers Arms (St Margaret's St; cheap lunches) and many of those on the High Street are featured in Dickens's novels.

ⓘ **Charles Dickens Centre** 🖼 (High St) Late Tudor house used in both *Pickwick Papers* and *Edwin Drood*, with scenes and characters from the author's books brought vividly to life using impressive hi-tech effects. Shop; cl Christmas; (01634) 844176; £3.50.

🏚 **Gad's Hill School** (Higham, A226 NW) Dickens fans should also try to visit this, the only house the writer ever owned. He wrote many of his novels here, and his first sight of the house, many years before he lived here, is described in *A Christmas Carol*. Meals, snacks, shop; open pm first Sun of month Easter–Oct, plus bank hol Suns, during Broadstairs' summer and Christmas Dickens festivals, and other times – out of school hours – by arrangement; (01474) 822366; £2.50.

👣 **Guildhall Museum** (High St) Impressive decorated plaster ceilings, and some hands-on exhibits for children. Shop, disabled access to ground floor only; cl 24–26 Dec; free.

🏰 **Rochester Castle** One of the best examples of 11th-c military architecture – dramatic too; the great square keep looks a little like the Tower of London, only more forbidding. Shop; cl Christmas wk; £3.50.

† **Rochester Cathedral** Spectacularly Norman, with original richly carved door, vaulted crypt, St Gundolph's tower, tombs and effigies and a huge 15th-c window. The choir sings Evensong at 5.30pm wkdys, 3.15pm wknds. Snacks, shop, good disabled access; (01634) 401301; £2 suggested donation.

ROLVENDEN TQ8331
⌂ ✗ Good walking territory, with consistently appealing Wealden scenery, a **windmill** and oast houses gracing the landscape.

ST MARGARET'S BAY TR3844

※ ⧖ **Pines Garden** (Beach Rd) Six acres of trees, shrubs, flowers and an ornamental lake, with a small local-history museum. Summer snacks, shop, disabled access; museum cl am, Mon and Tues and all Sept–May, garden cl 25 Dec; (01304) 852764; *£1.50. The spectacularly sited Coastguard is useful for refreshments.

🏛 ⧖ ※ **South Foreland Lighthouse** Clifftop exhibition on Guglielmo Marconi, who used the lighthouse in his early radio experiments, plus a new visitor centre and excellent views from the top. Shop; open pm wknds and bank hols, plus daily in school hols Apr–Oct; £1.50; NT.

SANDHURST TQ7828

⧖ † **Sandhurst Vineyard** (Hoads Farm, Crouch Lane) Tours of the vineyard and hop gardens (£2); hop-picking in Sept. Tastings and shop; cl am, and Jan–Easter exc by arrangement; (01580) 850296; free. They do B & B in a 16th-c farmhouse. The village has a fine 14th-c **church** with good views from the graveyard.

※ **Tile Barn Nursery** (Standen Street, Iden Green) The only nursery in the world to specialise in wild cyclamen, with 4 greenhouses filled with over 24 miniature species, most of them hardy, in flower Sept–Apr. Usually cl Sun–Tues, best to ring first to check; (01580) 240221. The 17th-c Woodcock signed nearby has decent food.

† ⌂ **Wealden Walk** E of Sandhurst, an attractive round walk runs from Burnt House Farm on the A268, via Cledge Wood and Marsh Quarter Farm to the Kent Ditch and the River Rother, to take you round to Bodiam Castle in Sussex, and back via Northlands Farm and Silverden.

SANDWICH TR3358

★ 🏰 † Pleasant quiet town with a surprising number of medieval remains, inc some sections of the old town wall and 3 handsome medieval churches, one part-Norman. In its day it was one of England's main commercial ports; the sea's now left it far behind. The best timbered buildings are in Strand St, with some by the attractive former quay on the River Stour (the old Bargate is very photogenic). The Red Cow (Moat Sole) is a decent pub with a friendly atmosphere and good-value food, and the St Crispin in the pretty village of Worth just S, not far from the sands, is pleasant for lunch.

⧖ ✗ **White Mill** (A257 just outside) A cheerful place with a little folk museum; shop; open all year am Fri and Sun, plus daily pm Easter–mid-Sept; (01304) 612076; *£2.

SEVENOAKS TQ5453

⌂ This commuters' town has little to see apart from the handsome old buildings of Sevenoaks School. However, the area around it has more walk potential than a glance at the OS map might suggest. The terrain is complicated, the Wealden villages unspoilt to a remarkable degree, and the path network dense and very well kept. Orchards, hop gardens, tile-clad timber-framed cottages and oast houses set the Kentish theme. Newcomers may be surprised to find such attractive and deeply rural countryside so close to London.

🏰 ※ **Knole** (just E) Originally a simple medieval manor house, this was transformed into a palace by a 15th-c archbishop, Henry VIII, and several generations of the Sackville family. It's now a magnificent set piece, the largest – some would say the grandest – still lived-in private house in the country. It's a calendar house, with 365 rooms, 52 staircases and 7 courtyards. Wrap up well: some of the beautifully furnished rooms can get a little chilly. Outside are 26 acres of attractive grounds and a 1,000-acre deer park. Meals, snacks, shop, some disabled access; open pm Weds–Sun and bank hol Mon Apr–Oct; the garden is open only on the first Weds of each month May–Sept; (01732) 450608; £5, £2.50 car park; NT. The Park is criss-crossed with public paths and tracks encompassing the deer park, as well as the great house itself; free. The Bucks Head at nearby Godden Green has decent food.

※ ⌂ ⧖ ※ **Riverhill House Gardens** (A225 S of Sevenoaks) Hillside gardens with rose and shrub terraces, woodland walks among fine trees, rhododendrons, bluebells in spring, and fine views. Teas, plant sales; open pm Weds, Sun and bank hol wknds Apr–Jun; (01732) 458802; £2.50.

🦢 🕊 Sevenoaks Wildfowl Reserve (Bradbourne Vale Rd) 135 acres of lakes, ponds, woodland and reedbeds, several viewing hides and a satisfying nature trail. Snacks, shop, disabled access; open Weds, Sat, Sun and bank hols; (01732) 456407; £4.

SISSINGHURST TQ8037

✿ Sissinghurst Garden Several charming gardens themed according to season or colour and cared for by obviously loving hands, all offset by the lovely tall-towered Elizabethan gatehouse (not open). Get there early – a timed ticket sytem is in operation, and they may close once capacity has been reached. Meals, snacks, shop, disabled access; cl am wkdys, all day Mon, and mid-Oct–Mar; (01580) 712850; £6; NT. The Three Chimneys on the way to Biddenden is good for lunch.

SMALL HYTHE TQ8930

🏠🍷✿ Smallhythe Place (B2082) Handsome half-timbered house, now a museum of the life of former resident, the actress Dame Ellen Terry. Charming rose garden. Open pm Sat-Weds Apr–Oct; (01580) 762334; £3; NT.

🍷🍶 Tenterden Vineyard (Spots Farm) Acres of vines, attractive lakes ideal for picnics, winery, herb garden, agricultural museum and children's adventure trail; group guided tours £3. Meals, snacks, shop, some disabled access; cl 25 Dec–1 Jan; (01580) 763033; free.

✕ ❀ Wittersham Windmill (B2082 S) The tallest post mill in Kent with good views over Romney Marsh and the Isle of Oxney; shop; open pm Easter, and Sun and bank hols May–Sept, other times by appointment £1. The nearby Crown at Stone has good food.

STAPLEHURST TQ7842

✿ Iden Croft Herbs (Frittenden Rd) Peaceful walled herb gardens, thyme rockery, and gardens designed for the blind or disabled. Snacks, plant sales; cl winter Suns; (01580) 891432; £1.50 gardens. The Lord Raglan (Chart Hill Rd) has good-value food and reasonable wheelchair access.

STELLING MINNIS TR1446

✕ Stelling Minnis Windmill Working mill with small museum; open pm Sun and bank hols Easter–Sept; 50p.

SWINGFIELD TR2142

❀ 🦋 Butterfly Centre (MacFarlane's Garden Centre) Family-run garden centre and butterfly house; snacks, plant sales, shop; open 21 Apr–early Oct (exc Easter Sun); (01303) 844244; £2.

TENTERDEN TQ8833

★ Busy but attractive small town with lots of charming old buildings, especially 17th- and 18th-c character cottages on the N side of the very broad High St. A few antique shops, and the striking 15th-c Woolpack has good food.

🚂🍴🍶 Kent & East Sussex Railway (A28 W) Steamtrains should be running from here as far as Bodiam Castle in Sussex by Easter, following a grant of nearly £1m from the Millennium Commission and a great deal of work by volunteers; lovely Wealden views. Meals, snacks, shop, disabled access; phone (01580) 765155 for timetable; £6.80. There's a small local history **museum** further up the road (open pm wknds Mar–Oct, pm Mon–Thurs Apr–Oct, plus Fri late July–Aug; 75p).

TONBRIDGE TQ5946

🏰⚓ Tonbridge Castle (just off High St) This splendid Norman castle is closed for refurbishment until Sept, so best to phone for opening times and prices; (01732) 770929. The commuter town is perked up a bit by the distinguished buildings of Tonbridge School, and the swimming pool, with an outdoor area, is a cut above the average municipal baths. In summer you can hire **rowing boats** on the river.

TROTTISCLIFFE TQ6561

⛰🏚🕊 (pronounced Trosley) There's a good walk E to the **Coldrum Stones**, a 4,000-year-old burial chamber, with an extension on to the North Downs (Trosley Country Park), densely wooded except on the steep slope itself. A problem for walkers elsewhere around here is that as you head E the farmland soon gets arable, with tedious slogs over ploughed fields.

TUNBRIDGE WELLS TQ5838

🏠✝ Very much a busy commuters' shopping centre nowadays, but parts still show its former character as a genteel spa town. The allegedly health-restoring water still trickles through the Pantiles, the former centre of the town, full of elegant buildings and interesting shops. You can try the water at the Chalybeate Spring here, 25p a glass; cl Nov–Mar. The **Church of King Charles the Martyr** is an interesting chapel built in the late 17th c for the gentry visiting the Pantiles; it has a remarkable plaster ceiling. Above the Pantiles the hillside Common is pleasant for strolls among trees and rocks.

♪ **A Day at The Wells** 🖼 (The Pantiles) The town's Georgian heyday elaborately recreated using very up-to-date display technology. Meals, snacks, shop, disabled access (prior notice preferred); cl 25 Dec; (01892) 546545; £4.95.

🏛 ◑ **High Rocks** (off A264 just W) On the edge of town, this former Stone Age camp has impressive sandstone formations in scenic woodland; take care when wet. Cl 26 Dec; (01892) 515532; *£2.

🚂 **Spa Valley Railway** 🖼 (Old West Station, by Sainsburys off A26 just S of the centre) Developing railway running steamtrain trips as far as Groombridge. Snacks, shop, disabled access; best to ring (01892) 537715 for timetable; £3.50 return.

♨ 🖼 **Tunbridge Wells Museum & Gallery** (Civic Centre, Mount Pleasant Rd) Examples of Tunbridge ware, the area's speciality small-scale woodware. Shop, disabled access; cl Sun and bank hols; (01892) 526121; free.

UPCHURCH TQ8467
✝ ★ **Upchurch church** 13th c, with a unique 'candle snuffer' tower. An attractive village, with a decent pub.

UPNOR TQ7570
🏰 **Upnor Castle** Well preserved Elizabethan castle famous for failing to protect the Medway from the Dutch in 1667; attractive turrets, gatehouse and windows. Snacks, shop; open Apr–Sept; (01634) 718742; £3.50. Up towards the Thames marshes, the Black Bull at Cliffe has authentic Malaysian food.

WEST KINGSDOWN TQ5763
✝ ◑ The **church** here is largely Saxon, and is given great appeal by its unique tranquil setting, secluded in the middle

of a wood. The yew tree by the west door looks very old indeed.

WEST MALLING TQ6857
★ ✝ 🏰 Attractive village, most of which is a conservation area thanks to its many old timbered houses and wells; lots of nice alleyways to explore. Particularly worth a look are the **abbey**, one of the country's oldest ecclesiastical buildings, and **St Leonard's Tower**, a fine Norman tower from an 11th-c castle. The Five Pointed Star has a good choice of food.

❀ **Manor Park Country Park** Lots of wildlife in its lake and the surrounding copses, a children's play area and plenty of space to run round. Cl 25 Dec; £1 parking Sun and bank hols, 50p other days.

WESTERHAM TQ4454
⌂ This pleasant country town is perhaps best known to visitors for Chartwell nearby; there are pleasant walks in the surrounding countryside.

🏠 ❀ ⌂ **Chartwell** (off B2026 S) The home of Winston Churchill until his death. Still much as he left them, the rooms are full of his possessions and reminders of his career, and the gardens are very attractive, with the famous black swans on the lakes. Though this is one of the NT's most popular houses (entry is by timed ticket), you need at least a passing interest in the statesman really to enjoy it. Meals, snacks, shop, disabled access; house and garden cl Nov–Mar, all Mon and Tues (exc bank hols and Tues July and Aug); (01732) 866368; £5.50 house and garden, gardens and studio only £2.75; NT. This is good walking country.

🏠 ♨ **Down House** (Luxted Rd, towards Downe) Attractive restored house, former home of Charles Darwin who lived here with his family for 40 years during which he wrote most of his major works including *On the Origin of Species*. Filled with his personal belongings, notes and journals, the ground floor is much as it was when the Darwins were in residence, while upstairs there is an exhibition on Darwin's life and work; the gardens have also been restored. Snacks, shop, disabled access; cl Mon, Tues, all Feb and 24–26 Dec; essential to pre-book on (0870) 6030145; £5; EH. The

Queen's Head up the road in Downe is good.

⌂ ♨ Quebec House Gabled boyhood home of General Wolfe with exhibitions on his life and the battle that made his name. Disabled access to ground floor (new lavatories); open pm Tues and Sun Apr–Oct; (01892) 890651; £2.50; NT.

⌂ ❀ 🖼 Squerryes Court Overshadowed by its more famous neighbour Chartwell but for some people more satisfying, this fine 17th-c manor house overlooks attractive grounds and has excellent collections of paintings, china and furniture. The garden was first laid out in 1689 and is being painstakingly restored; some of the magnificent lime trees are as old as the house. Teas, shop; open pm Weds, wknds and bank hols Apr–Sept; (01959) 562345; £4, grounds only £2.40.

WHITSTABLE TR1066
The focus here is still very much the busy working harbour.

♪ Oyster Fishery Exhibition (East Quay) Looks at the traditional Kentish industry of oyster fishing, with live shellfish, and a hands-on seashore exhibit for children. Snacks, shop, disabled access (though no facilities); cl wkdys Apr and Sept–Oct, and all Nov–Mar; (01227) 272003; £1.50. They sell fresh oysters (which you can order by mail), and a recipe book with ideas for cooking them.

♨ 🖼 Whitstable Museum & Art Gallery (Oxford St) This explores the town's maritime history and traditions. Shop, disabled access; cl 1–2pm, Weds and Sun, Good Fri, Christmas wk; free. Pearsons fish restaurant is good value.

WILLESBOROUGH TR0342
✗ Willesborough Windmill Working mill, open pm wknds and bank hols Apr–Sept; snacks, shop; £1.

WINGHAM TR2558
★ ❦ Wingham Bird Park Endangered birds from all over the world, with the emphasis very much on breeding and conservation; they have a large walk-through aviary. Also racoons, wallabies and other animals, and a good adventure playground (made from recycled materials). Snacks, shop, disabled access; cl 25–26 Dec; (01227) 720836; £3.50. The village is

attractive, with decent food in two medieval inns, the Dog and Red Lion.

WOODCHURCH TQ9534
🐖 South of England Rare Breeds Centre 🖼 Covering acres of Kentish farmland some readers really enjoy this, one of the largest collections of rare farm animals in Europe; lots of pigs (including the runaway Tamworth Two), cattle, horses, goats and poultry. All nicely undeveloped and friendly, with plenty for children to touch and fuss (and a paddling pool and play area for letting off steam). In summer there are lots of special events. Meals, snacks, shop, disabled access; cl Mons Oct–Mar, 24–25 Dec; (01233) 861493; £3.25. The Bonny Cravat has good-value food.

✗ Woodchurch Windmill Well restored, still grinding corn for demonstrations, and its sails turning whenever it's open. Shop; open pm Sun and bank hols Easter–Sept, other times by appointment; (01233) 860043; *£1.

WYE DOWNS TR0746
△ ❀ ❦ Some of Kent's nicest walks are on the North Downs – not that high, but steep enough along the escarpment to give some great views. The Wye Downs, designated a nature reserve for their chalkland flora that includes a variety of orchids, look across the orchards below to both the Thames estuary and the Channel. The road above Wye through Hastingleigh, Bodsham Green, Sole Street (where the Compasses is a pleasant stop-off) and along the Crundale Downs is a pleasant drive.

YALDING TQ6949
❀ Yalding Gardens (B2162 just S of Yalding) Interesting series of gardens maintained by the Henry Doubleday Research Association, the organic farming and gardening organisation (see also Ryton Gardens in Warwickshire); each looks at how people have cultivated land in a given period, from medieval physick gardens to modern organic vegetable plots. Snacks, shop, disabled access; open wknds Apr and Oct, Weds–Sun May–Sept, and Easter and bank hols; (01622) 814650; £2.50. In the attractive village, the Walnut Tree has good-value food inc weekday OAP bargains.

★ **Other attractive villages**, all with decent pubs, include Addington TQ6559, Alkham TR2542, Bishopsbourne TR1852, Bodsham TR1045, Boughton Lees TR0247, Boxley TQ7758, Bridge TR1854, Challock TR0050, Chillenden TR2653, Egerton TQ9047, Elham TR1743, Harvel TQ6563, Ickham TR2257, Leigh TQ5446, Lenham TQ8952, Martin TR3346, Offham TQ6557, Sandling (despite the M20) TQ7558, Shipbourne TQ5952, Smarden TQ8842, Speldhurst TQ5541, Stalisfield Green TQ9553, Sutton Valence TQ8149, West Peckham TQ6452, Wickhambreaux TR2158, Worth TR3356 and Wrotham TQ6159.

◠ **Pubs useful for walkers** include the Bald Faced Stag at Ashurst TQ5038, Woolpack at Benover TQ7048, Pepper Box at Fairbourne Heath above Ulcombe TQ8550, Woodman on Goathurst Common TQ4952, Bucks Head at Godden Green TQ5555, Ringlestone Inn TQ8755 N of Harrietsham, Rock at Hoath Corner TQ4943, Cock at Ide Hill TQ4851, Cock at Henley St nr Luddesdown TQ6667, Kentish Horse at Markbeech TQ4742, Horns and Bull at Otford TQ5359, Fox & Hounds at Toys Hill TQ4751, Harrow at Warren Street TQ9253 and Rising Sun at Woodlands TQ5560.

Where to eat

BIDDENDEN TQ8438 **Claris's** *High St (01580) 291025* Charming no smoking 15th-c tearoom and gift shop with beams and inglenook fireplaces, lace tablecloths, a little garden, and home-made cakes and savouries all day; cl Mon, 3 wks Jan. £3.90.

BIDDENDEN TQ8238 **Three Chimneys** *A262 W (01580) 291472* Atmospheric country pub with small beamed rooms, log fires, and imaginative food; children in garden dining room only. **£19**|£5.50.

BOUGH BEECH TQ4846 **Wheatsheaf** *(01732) 700254* Lovely old pub – thought to have started life as a hunting lodge belonging to Henry V – with oak timbers in unusually high ceilings, several bars and some interesting decorations, a massive stone fireplace, piles of smart magazines to read; nice nibbles, chestnuts to roast in winter, summer Pimms and mulled wine in winter, and popular, interesting bar food (served all day); real ales, decent wines, and lovely gardens. **£22.40**|£7.

CANTERBURY TR1556 **La Bonne Cuisine** *Canterbury Hotel, 71 New Dover Rd (01227) 450551* Run by the same family for over 20 years, this neat little hotel is warmly friendly and comfortable and serves beautifully presented, very good French food in the cheerfully yellow dining room; attractive bdrms. **£23**.

CANTERBURY TR1457 **Sully's** *High St (01227) 766266* Part of the County Hotel, this slightly old-fashioned-looking restaurant has good imaginative seasonally changing cooking inc 2 and 3-course set menus (plenty of choice), and a generous lunchtime roast; disabled access. **£31**|£13.

DARGATE TR0861 **Dove** *(01227) 751360* Well liked pub with popular imaginative food and well kept real ales in rambling rooms with good winter fires, plenty of seats on the bare boards, and a sheltered pretty garden. **£22.75**|£5.

EAST FARLEIGH TQ7353 **White Lion** *(01622) 727395* Charming little white cottage with country pictures, a growing collection of jugs hanging from beams, an inglenook fireplace, and plenty of tables set for dining; imaginative food (simpler at lunchtime), real ales, several wines by the glass, and very pretty flowering tubs and baskets; cl am Sat, pm Sun, Mon. **£18**|£5.25.

EDENBRIDGE TQ4445 **Honours Mill** *87 High St (01732) 866757* Charmingly converted watermill with lots of beams in the downstairs bar and upstairs restaurant, good interesting food (the weekday set menus are popular and good value), and a mainly French wine list; cl am Sat, pm Sun, Mon, 2 wks Christmas. **£25 dinner, £20.50 lunch**.

FAVERSHAM TR0161 **Albion** *(01795) 591411* Creekside pub (nice walks) with a pleasant chatty atmosphere in airy open-plan bar, perfectly kept beer and a sensible choice of very imaginative food from the French chef; lots of outside seats for summer evenings; disabled access. **£18|£6.50.**

FINGLESHAM TR3353 **Crown** *(01304) 612555* Pleasant 16th-c country pub, attractively refurbished, with a wide choice of reasonably priced bar food, popular old-world restaurant with an inglenook fireplace and flagstones, and good, friendly service; cl pm 25–26 Dec. **£15|£5.**

FOLKESTONE TR2335 **Paul's** *2a Bouverie Rd W (01303) 259697* Popular, enjoyable restaurant run by the same owners for well over 20 years, with very imaginative food inc good fish, game and vegetarian options, and a decent wine list; cl 1 wk after Christmas; disabled access. **£22.20|£4.95.**

HERNHILL TR0660 **Red Lion** *(01227) 751207* Pretty Tudor inn next to the church, with long narrow, beamed and flagstoned interior, good interesting bar food, well kept real ales, and an upstairs restaurant. **£19.50|£8.**

HOLLINGBOURNE TQ8455 **Dirty Habit** *(01622) 880880* Early 15th-c inn with quite a bit of character in the various rooms, a panelled and candlelit dining room with an interesting mix of seats, good enjoyable bar food, well kept real ales, a relaxed atmosphere, and friendly staff. **£22|£9.**

IVY HATCH TQ5854 **Plough** *(01732) 810268* Relaxed and friendly tile-hung house with good, imaginative and constantly changing French food (using French produce), carefully chosen wines and well kept beers, and efficient service; front dining bar with dark panelled walls, an old brick fireplace, and dining chairs and settles, separate little room to left of door, and popular conservatory restaurant; nearby walks; best to book; disabled access; cl pm Sun. **£23|£6.95.**

LANGTON GREEN TQ5439 **Hare** *(01892) 862419* Popular, civilised dining pub with light, airy knocked-through rooms, a chatty atmosphere, imaginative generously served food from a menu that changes twice daily, attentive waitress service, and decent wines and beers; outside terrace; children in restaurant (not in bar); cl pm 25 Dec, pm 1 Jan; partial disabled access. **£24|£6.95.**

MARKBEECH TQ4742 **Kentish Horse** *(01342) 850493* Partly white weatherboarded country pub with particularly good, interesting food from a modern menu, well kept ales, a simply furnished bar, a woodburning stove in the restaurant with French windows to the terrace and garden with a safe children's play area. **£18.95|£5.90.**

NEWNHAM TQ9557 **George** *(01795) 890237* Distinctive 16th-c pub with a spreading series of atmospheric rooms, open fires, friendly staff, imaginative food using fresh local produce, well kept beers, and good wines; cl 25 Dec. **£25|£6.75.**

PAINTER'S FORSTAL TQ9958 **Read's** *(01795) 535344* Excellent restaurant with a comfortable bar and airy dining room, and lovely views from the back terrace; exceptionally good innovative English cooking using the best local ingredients, wonderful puddings, a marvellous wine list, and neat young staff; cl Sun, Mon; disabled access. **£30.50** wkdys, **£43.50** wknds.

PENSHURST TQ5142 **Bottle House** *Coldharbour Rd (01892) 870306* Relaxed and friendly 15th-c pub with huge beams, stone pillars, and big windows in the unpretentious bars, lots of old sewing machines, excellent popular food, efficient service, and well kept local ales; cl 25 Dec. **£24|£6.95.**

PENSHURST TQ5242 **Spotted Dog** *Smarts Hill (01892)870253* Quaint tiled house with fantastic views over Penshurst Place from the terrace, particularly good food from a constantly changing menu, very good wines and real ales, popular restaurant, and a fine inglenook and a bustling atmosphere in the neatly kept beamed and timbered bar; cl pm Mon, 25–26 Dec. **£22|£8.**

RINGLESTONE TQ8755 **Ringlestone** *(01622) 859900* Welcoming atmosphere in interestingly decorated, deservedly popular country pub, with very good interesting food, especially the hot and cold lunchtime buffet (no chips or fried food), and lots of real ales and country wines; cl 25 Dec; bdrms. **£20|£6.65.**

SELLING TR0455 **Rose & Crown** *Perry Wood (01227) 752214* Quietly civilised tucked-away woodland pub (good walks) with a relaxed atmosphere, lots of beams, hops and interesting corn-dolly work, a huge fireplace, comfortably cushioned seats, friendly helpful service, good generously served food, well kept real ales, and decent wines; children in restaurant/family room; limited disabled access. **£18|£6.**

SISSINGHURST TQ7937 **Rankins** *The Street (01580) 713964* Interesting enjoyable food from a fixed evening and Sun lunch menu in pretty white clapboarded cottage inc lovely puddings and vegetarian choices; no smoking until food service has finished; cl Mon, Tues; children by prior arrangement; partial disabled access. **£29.50.**

STONE IN OXNEY TQ9427 **Crown** *(01233) 758789* Friendly, tucked-away pub which manages to strike a good balance between drinking and dining, with dark wooden pews and a big inglenook fireplace in the bar, a longish lounge with 2 big bay windows looking over country views, a relaxed atmosphere, and tasty, imaginative food; cl pm Sun, Mon. **£20|£6.95.**

TENTERDEN TQ8833 **Kent & East Sussex Railway** *Tenterden Town Station (01580) 765155* Steam-hauled and ornately decorated Pullman dining car with good English food served by authentically dressed stewards – most Sat evenings, some Weds evenings, Sun roast lunches and afternoon teas, and Christmas dinners; great fun; open Apr–Sept daily and wknds Mar/Oct/Dec; children on selected services; disabled access. **£28|£4.50.**

TUNBRIDGE WELLS TQ5839 **Sankeys** *39 Mount Ephraim (01892) 511422* Excellent fresh fish and seafood cooked in all sorts of ways in several cosy and relaxed restaurant rooms, very good wines, real ales, and friendly service; cheaper lively downstairs cellar wine bar too (get there early for a seat), and seats in the walled garden; cl Sun. **£25|£6.50.**

TUNBRIDGE WELLS TQ5839 **Thackeray's House** *85 London Rd (01892) 511921* Civilised detached house with 2 beamed upstairs rooms, pretty paintings, a mix of tables with crisp white cloths, very relaxed comfortable atmosphere, friendly but carefully professional service, interesting and enjoyable food, and very good house wines; downstairs, the small wine bar does simpler food; cl pm Sun, Mon, Christmas. **£35|£10.**

ULCOMBE TQ8550 **Pepper Box** *Fairbourne Heath (01622) 842558* Cosy old country pub with low beams and standing timbers in the friendly homely bar, comfortable sofa and armchairs by a splendid inglenook fireplace; very good imaginative food, well kept real ales, and efficient courteous service; nice views from the garden. **£23.50|£8.**

WHITSTABLE TR1066 **Pearsons** *(01227) 272005* Consistently good very fresh seafood in homely upstairs restaurant; kind and quick service – even when very busy; bustling traditional pub downstairs; cl 25 Dec. **£21|£7.**

Special thanks to Michael and Jenny Back.

Please let us know what you think of places in the *Guide*. Use the report forms at the back of the book or simply write us a letter.

Kent Calendar

Some of these dates were provisional as we went to press. Please check information with the telephone numbers provided.

JANUARY

I Dover Carnival of Planets and the Third Millennium Clock: Mardi Gras along the seafront with sculptural costumes, music, dance, fireworks and animation of a huge clock (01304) 821199; **Leeds** New Year's Day Treasure Trail at the Castle – *till 3 January* (01622) 765400

FEBRUARY

12 Rochester Organ and Three Cathedral Choirs Concert with Carlo Curley (01634) 849683

19 Tenterden Thomas the Tank Engine at the Kent & East Sussex Railway – *till 27 February* (01580) 765155

21 Leeds Historical Story-telling at the Castle – *till 25 February* (01622) 765400

APRIL

2 Tenterden Re-opening of 3.5 miles of track between Northiam and Bodiam and 100th anniversary of the line – *till 9 April* (01580) 756155

8 Leeds Greenhouse Weekend: meet the groundsmen at the Castle – *till 9 April* (01622) 765400

17 Folkestone Children's Fun Festival – *till 22 April* (01303) 255070

21 Sandling Easter Chicken Hunt at the Museum of Kent Life – *till 24 April* (01622) 763936

22 Leeds Celebration of Easter at the Castle – *till 24 April* (01622) 765400

23 Beltring Easter Fun at the Hop Farm – *till 24 April* (01622) 872068; **Penshurst** Easter at Penshurst Place: trailer rides, stories and eggs – *till 24 April* (01892) 870307

29 Rochester Sweeps Festival: processions, Morris dancers, ceilidhs, street entertainment – *till 1 May* (01634) 843666; **Tonbridge** Garden Show and Craft Fair – *till 1 May* (01732) 357872

30 Detling Smallholders' Show – *till 1 May* (01306) 741302; **Sandling** May Day Celebrations at the Museum of Kent Life – *till 1 May* (01622) 763936

MAY

I Ramsgate Classic Tall Ships Race – *till 19 May* (01843) 592277; **Whitstable** May Day Celebrations (01227) 275959

13 Leeds Festival of English Food and Wine at the Castle – *till 14 May* (01622) 765400

14 Faversham Classic Car Rally (01795) 539658

21 Ramsgate Spring Festival: classical, jazz and popular concerts, street entertainment, children's events – *till 3 June* (01843) 580994

26 Whitstable Festival of Arts – *till 4 June* (01227) 862066

27 Deal East Kent Garden Show at Castle Community School – *till 29 May* (01304) 201644; **Dover** Festival: street entertainment, dance – *till 29 May* (01304) 872074; **Leeds** Family Maze and Garden Week at the Castle – *till 4 June* (01622) 765400; **Sellindge** Steam Special at Hope Farm – *till 29 May* (01303) 813000; **Woodchurch** Beer Festival at the South of England Rare Breeds Centre (01233) 861493

Kent Calendar (cont.)

28 Detling Kent Garden Show – *till 29 May* (01795) 474660; **Goudhurst** Spring Garden Fair at Finchcocks – *till 29 May* (01580) 211702; **Woodchurch** Piggy Picnics: pig obstacle course, races, puppet shows at the Rare Breeds Centre – *till 29 May* (01233) 861493

29 Aylesford Spring Fair at Aylesford Priory (01622) 717272

JUNE

3 Biggin Hill International Air Fair – *till 4 June* (01959) 572277; **Faversham** Open Gardens – *till 4 June* (01795) 534542; **Folkestone** Roman re-enactment at the Martello Tower, East Cliff – *till 4 June* (01303) 852321

4 Herne Bay Heavy Horse Parade (01227) 742690

10 Wrotham Vintage and Veteran Steam and Transport Rally – *till 11 June* (01732) 883773

15 County-wide Kent Week Festival 2000 – *till 25 June* (01622) 694045

17 Broadstairs Dickens Festival – *till 24 June* (01843) 601364; **Gravesend** Regatta – *till 18 June* (01474) 337302

18 Beltring Garden of England Motorcycle Show at the Hop Farm (01622) 872068

22 Faversham Open Gardens – *till 23 June* (01795) 534542

24 Eythorne Steam and Vintage Vehicle Weekend at Waldershare Park – *till 25 June* (01227) 362755; **Leeds** Open-air Concert at the Castle (01622) 765400

25 Sittingbourne Carnival (01795) 479796

28 Leeds Children's Promenade Concert at the Castle (01622) 765400

30 East Farleigh Flower Festival – *till 2 July* (01622) 726919; **Hythe** Festival Week – *till 9 July* (01303) 268715

JULY

1 Beltring World of Steam and Fred Dibnah at the Hop Farm – *till 2 July* (01622) 872068; **Dover** Carnival (01304) 872074; **Faversham** Open House Day: properties not normally open to the public (01795) 534542; **Ightham** Songs from the Shows: open-air concert at Ightham Mote (01732) 810378; **Leeds** Open-air Concert at the Castle (01622) 765400; **Ramsgate** Ships Open Days at Ramsgate Royal Harbour – *till 2 July* (01843) 587765; **Swale** Festival – *till 31 July* (01795) 580068

2 Herne Bay Punch and Judy Day (01227) 742690

6 Lamberhurst Open-air Opera at Scotney Castle – *till 9 July* (01892) 891081

8 Faversham Open House Day: properties not normally open to the public (01795) 534542; **Tonbridge** Arts Festival – *till 9 July* (01732) 876333

13 Detling Kent County Show – *till 15 July* (01622) 630975

15 Lamberhurst Firework and Laser Concert at Bewl Water (01892) 890661

16 Faversham Open House Day: properties not normally open to the public (01795) 534542

19 Beltring Invicta Military War and Peace Show at the Hop Farm – *till 23 July* (01622) 872068

20 Canterbury Kent Beer Festival: over 80 real ales and ciders, live bands – *till 22 July* (01227) 463478; **Leeds** Flower Festival at the Castle – *till 23 July* (01622) 765400; **Whitstable** Regatta and Oyster Festival: landing of oysters and parade – *till 30 July* (01227) 265666

Kent Calendar (cont.)

21 **Ashford** Music Extravaganza – *till 23 July* (01233) 629165
24 **Woodchurch** Millennium Festival at the South of England Rare Breeds Centre – *till 6 August* (01233) 861493
26 **Tunbridge Wells** Scandals at the Spa: re-creation of Georgian life – *till 30 July* (01892) 515675
27 **Smallhythe** Open-air Theatre at Smallhythe Place – *till 30 July* (01580) 762334
30 **Beltring** Classic Car Show at the Hop Farm (01622) 872068

AUGUST

1 **Ramsgate** Royal Harbour Heritage Festival – *till 31 August* (01843) 591008
3 **Smallhythe** Open-air Theatre at Smallhythe Place – *till 5 August* (01580) 762334
5 **Beltring** Mini Rally at the Hop Farm – *till 6 August* (01622) 872068; **Herne Bay** Festival – *till 20 August* (01227) 742690; **Sandling** Woodland and Traditional Crafts at the Museum of Kent Life – *till 6 August* (01622) 763936; **Whitstable** Carnival (01227) 273436
6 **Margate** Carnival Procession (01843) 293733
9 **Broadstairs** Water Gala (01843) 863225
11 **Broadstairs** Folk Week: international shows, torchlight procession – *till 19 August* (01843) 604080
12 **Brasted** The Blues Band at Emmetts Garden (01892) 890651; **Detling** Transport and Country Fair: over 1,000 exhibits – *till 14 August* (01622) 630975; **Herne Bay** Carnival and Regatta – *till 13 August* (01227) 742690; **Isle of Sheppey** Pirates Festival – *till 13 August* (01795) 585601
16 **Ramsgate** International Sailing Week – *till 19 August* (01843) 591766
19 **Beltring** Heavy Horse Show at the Hop Farm – *till 20 August* (01622) 872068; **Folkestone** Carnival (01303) 220889
25 **Margate** Festival of Fun – *till 28 August* (01843) 225511
26 **Goudhurst** 18th-century Gala: concerts and dancing at Finchcocks – *till 28 August* (01580) 211702
27 **Beltring** Garden Show at the Hop Farm – *till 28 August* (01622) 872068
28 **Sandling** Family Fun Day at the Museum of Kent Life (01622) 763936; **Tunbridge Wells** Sedan Chair Race on the Pantiles (01892) 515675

SEPTEMBER

2 **Detling** Kent Country Music Festival at the County Showground – *till 3 September* (01795) 843764; **Faversham** Hop Festival – *till 3 September* (01795) 585601; **Folkestone** Shepway Festival: airshow, fireworks and motoring pageant – *till 3 September* (01303) 852321
3 **Beltring** Historic Hop Festival (01622) 872068
8 **Deal** Sea Shanty Festival – *till 10 September* (01304) 872058
9 **Goudhurst** Finchcocks Festival: opera and chamber music played on period instruments – *till 10 September* (01580) 211702; **Leeds** Balloon and Vintage Car Weekend at the Castle – *till 10 September* (01622) 765400; **Sandling** Hop Picking and Beer Festival at the Museum of Kent Life – *till 10 September* (01622) 763936
11 **Tunbridge Wells** Food and Drink Festival – *till 17 September* (01892) 515675

Kent Calendar (cont.)

16 **Goudhurst** Finchcocks Festival: opera and chamber music played on period instruments – *till 17 September* (01580) 211702; **Tenterden** Thomas the Tank Engine at the Kent & East Sussex Railway – *till 17 September* (01580) 765155; **Whitstable** Harbour Day (01227) 274086

17 **Biggin Hill** Battle of Britain 60th Anniversary Open Day (01959) 572277; **Boughton** Farming Festival at Farming World – *till 18 September* (01227) 751144

20 **Folkestone** Kent Literature Festival at the Metropole Arts Centre – *till 25 September* (01303) 255070

23 **Folkestone** Euromilitaire: one of the world's largest military modelling displays inc bands, war gaming and re-enactments at Leas Cliff Hall – *till 24 September* (01303) 253193; **Goudhurst** Finchcocks Festival: opera and chamber music played on period instruments – *till 24 September* (01580) 211702

30 **Goudhurst** Finchcocks Festival: opera and chamber music played on period instruments – *till 1 October* (01580) 211702

OCTOBER

6 **Folkestone** Model Railway Exhibition at Leas Cliff Hall – *till 8 October* (01303) 253193; **Goudhurst** Autumn Fair at Finchcocks – *till 8 October* (01580) 211702; **Tenterden** Folk Festival – *till 8 October* (01892) 540766

7 **Sandling** Apple and Cider Festival at the Museum of Kent Life – *till 8 October* (01622) 763936

14 **Canterbury** Festival: classical, jazz, folk, blues, street entertainment, children's events, fireworks – *till 28 October* (01227) 452853; **Faversham** Carnival (01795) 534542; **Folkestone** Southern Counties Brass Band Competition at Leas Cliff Hall – *till 15 October* (01303) 253193

18 **Leeds** Festival of Autumn Flowers and Produce at the Castle – *till 22 October* (01622) 765400

20 **Broadstairs** Celebrity Connections: concerts, films, dance and exhibitions – *till 27 October* (01843) 868718

23 **Leeds** Halloween Events at the Castle – *till 27 October* (01622) 765400

28 **Beltring** Fireworks and Live Music at the Hop Farm (01622) 872068

NOVEMBER

4 **Leeds** Fireworks at the Castle (01622) 765400; **Sandling** Fireworks at the Museum of Kent Life (01622) 763936

5 **Broadstairs** Fireworks and Illuminated Vessels in Ramsgate Royal Harbour (01843) 587765

DECEMBER

11 **Leeds** Christmas Carols at the Castle – *till 24 December* (01622) 765400

27 **Tunbridge Wells** Street Festival – *till 30 December* (01892) 515675

Please let us know what you think of places in the *Guide*. Use the report forms at the back of the book or simply write us a letter.

LANCASHIRE

Lots of new places to visit, and scope for surprisingly varied holiday breaks.

Manchester and Liverpool are both great for day visits, with grand Victorian buildings as well as lively redevelopment areas, and all sorts of attractions. Both have very good public transport. Liverpool in particular has several very interesting new places for visitors to see this year – and a bargain joint admissions ticket, as well as a particularly helpful tourist office. Manchester has the major new Lowry centre in Salford, as well as its established favourites such as the vast and exhilarating Museum of Science and Industry and the Granada studios (both of these are real treats for children). A good range of days out elsewhere includes as highlights the engrossing re-creation of 1900s life at Wigan Pier, the Birkenhead warships, the Camelot theme park at Charnock Richard, the safari park at Prescot, Bury's steam railway, and, in a quieter vein, Hoghton Tower, Leighton Hall, Rufford Old Hall and the Martin Mere wildfowl centre. Two good new places are the animal centre in Fleetwood, and the air raid shelters with surprisingly interesting tours in Stockport.

There's glorious countryside even just outside the big cities, where the moors have plenty of scope for exhilarating drives and walks, and bewitched Pendle Hill still holds the imagination. Other areas of fine countryside include the great whaleback of Longridge Fell, the wooded Beacon Fell country park, the magnificent Pennine moorland of the Forest of Bowland (as yet very little known to visitors, though right-to-roam legislation may change that), and the equally peaceful Silverdale/Arndale area up beyond the attractive town of Lancaster.

The area's vast stretches of sand have, of course, spawned household-name traditional seaside resorts. Blackpool, with more visitors each year than the whole of Spain, has lots of discos, fun pubs and so forth as well as its vivid array of entertainments – more a place for young adults to have summer fun than for family beach holidays. Out of season, Lancashire's long stretches of beach and dune are empty, with a lonely charm for walkers; year-round, there's an element of fascination about the treacherous tidal sands of Morecambe Bay.

Where to stay

ASHWORTH VALLEY SD8512 **Leaches Farm** *Ashworth Valley, Rochdale OL11 5UN* (01706) 41117 *£38; 3 rms, shared bthrm. 17th-c hill farm with really wonderful views, massive stone walls, beams and log fires; cl 22 Dec–2 Jan; children over 7 and dogs by arrangement.

BILSBORROW SD5039 **Guy's Thatched Hamlet** *Bilsborrow, Preston PR3 0RS* (01995) 640010 *£49, plus wknd breaks; 53 smartly modern rms. Bustling complex by the canal; thatched tavern, restaurant and pizzeria, outside terrace, play area and craft shops; good base for exploring the area; open all day; cl 25 Dec; disabled access.

BLACKPOOL SD3037 **Imperial** *North Promenade, Blackpool FY1 2HB* (01253) 623971 **£150,** plus special breaks; 181 well equipped rms. Fine Victorian hotel overlooking the sea, with spacious and comfortable day rooms, lots of period features, and a full health and fitness club with indoor swimming pool, gym, Jacuzzi, steam and sauna room and solarium free to residents; disabled access.

BROMLEY CROSS SD7213 **Drop Inn** *Hospital Rd, Last Drop, Bromley Cross BL7 9PZ* (01204) 591131 **£75;** 128 rms. Big, well equipped Rank hotel complex cleverly integrated into an olde-worlde pastiche village complete with stone-and-cobbles street of gift and tea shops, bakery, etc, even a spacious creeper-covered pub with lots of beamery and timbering, popular one-price hot and cold buffet, and heavy tables out on the attractive flagstoned terrace; disabled access.

BURY SD8313 **Normandie** *Elbut Lane, Birtle, Bury BL9 6UT* (0161) 764 3869 ***£69;** 23 attractive rms. Unpretentious hotel high on the Pennines with fine views, homely lounge and snug bar, excellent French and English restaurant food, fine wine list, and friendly professional service; cl 26 Dec–4 Jan, 1 wk over Easter; disabled access.

CAPERNWRAY SD5371 **New Capernwray Farmhouse** *Capernwray, Carnforth LA6 1AD* (01524) 734284 ***£60;** 3 comfortable rms. Pretty, 300-year-old former farmhouse with helpful friendly owners, cosy lounge, stone walls and beams, and candlelit dinner in what was the dairy; they offer personally conducted tours; cl Nov–Feb; children over 10.

CHIPPING SD6343 **Gibbon Bridge** *Chipping, Preston PR3 2TQ* (01995) 61456 **£100,** plus special breaks; 29 rms, inc 22 split-level suites overlooking gardens. Family-owned country hotel with beautiful landscaped gardens (plus popular bandstand with local bands), attractively presented food in spacious, airy restaurant and adjoining conservatory, a quiet relaxing atmosphere, fine wines, and helpful service; health and gym area; a good base for walking and short driving trips; licensed for marriages, they have a thriving weddings trade; good disabled access.

COLNE SD8741 **Higher Wanless Farm** *Red Lane, Colne BB8 7JP* (01282) 865301 ***£44;** 2 rms, one with own bthrm. Warmly welcoming farmhouse with beams, log fires and lovely surrounding farmland used mainly for breeding of shire horses, as well as sheep; cl Christmas and New Year; children over 3.

COWAN BRIDGE SD6475 **Hipping Hall** *Cowan Bridge, Kirkby Lonsdale, Carnforth LA6 2JJ* (01524) 271187 **£88,** plus special breaks; 7 pretty rms, 5 in main hotel, 2 cottage suites across courtyard (can be self-catering). Relaxed country-house atmosphere and delicious food in this handsome small hotel with help-yourself drinks in the conservatory, open fire, lovely beamed Great Hall with minstrels' gallery where guests dine together, and 4 acres of walled gardens; fine walks from the front door; cl Nov–Mar; children over 12; disabled access.

DARWEN SD7222 **Old Rosins** *Pickup Bank, Hoddlesden, Darwen BB3 3QD* (01254) 771264 **£65,** plus wknd breaks; 15 well equipped rms. Friendly old pub tucked below the moors, ideal as a base for exploring the area; good views from the cosy open-plan bar, interesting bar and restaurant food, and seats on the terrace also with fine views; partial disabled access.

HURST GREEN SD6937 **Shireburn Arms** *Hurst Green, Blackburn BB7 9QJ* (01254) 826518 **£60,** plus special breaks; 18 rms. Lovely 17th-c country hotel with a refined but friendly atmosphere, airy and neatly modernised bar, comfortable lounge, open fires, well presented, enjoyable food in the restaurant, good service, and fine view of the Ribble Valley from the conservatory; disabled access.

LANGHO SD7034 **Northcote Manor** *Northcote Rd, Langho, Blackburn BB6 8BE* (01254) 240555 **£110;** 14 attractive rms with antiques, bric-à-brac and board games, reached up a fine staircase. In pretty countryside, this neatly kept red brick Victorian house is more of a restaurant-with-rooms, with beams and oak panelling, big log fires, and two comfortable lounges; wonderful breakfasts, and delicious food in the civilised dining room; cl 25 Dec, 1–7 Jan; partial disabled access.

MANCHESTER SJ8397 **Malmaison** *Piccadilly, Manchester M1 3AQ* (0161) 278 1000 **£96w;** 112 chic rms with CD player, in-house movies, smart bthrms, and really good beds. Stylishly modern hotel with comfortable, contemporary furniture, exotic flower arrangements, bright paintings, very efficient service, French brasserie, generous breakfasts, and free gym; other hotels in the same small chain in Edinburgh, Glasgow and Newcastle; good disabled access.

MANCHESTER SJ8397 **Victoria & Albert** *Water St, Manchester M3 4JQ (0161) 832 1188 £115w,* plus special breaks; 156 rms, individually styled and named after TV programmes. Carefully converted Victorian warehouse opposite Granada TV studios (free entry if staying here), with original iron pillars, oak beams and exposed brickwork; particularly good service, comfortable bar overlooking the river, and imaginative food in the restaurant and all-day brasserie; disabled access.

WADDINGTON SD7243 **Backfold Cottage** *The Square, Waddington, Clitheroe BB7 3JA (01200) 422367 £42;* 3 rms. Tiny 17th-c cottage in a cobbled street; beautifully furnished with antiques, very good service, all-day snacks, candlelit evening meals (bring your own wines), and nice walks; children at owner's discretion.

WADDINGTON SD7144 **Peter Barn** *Cross Lane, Waddington, Clitheroe BB7 3JH (01200) 428585 *£44,* plus special breaks; 3 lovely rms. Converted old stone tithe barn with beamed sitting room, antiques, lovely home cooking, warmly welcoming owners and gentle atmosphere; surrounded by a delightful garden, fine walking country; cl Christmas; children over 12.

WHITEWELL SD6546 **Inn at Whitewell** *Whitewell, Clitheroe BB7 3AT (01200) 448222 *£82;* 15 rms, some with open peat fires. Civilised stone inn in the Forest of Bowland, attractive setting and grounds with views down the valley; interesting period furnishings, plenty of room, highly praised food (they also serve coffee and cream teas all day), fine wines (they house a wine merchant), courteous service, and unusual facilities such as an art gallery and 6 miles of trout, salmon and sea trout fishing; friendly dogs welcome; partial disabled access.

YEALAND CONYERS SD5074 **Bower** *Yealand Conyers, Carnforth LA5 9SF (01524) 734585 *£54;* 2 attractive rms. Charming little, no smoking, Georgian house in a big garden with views of Ingleborough and the surrounding hills; friendly owners (keen bridge players), open fire and piano in the comfortable sitting room, and enjoyable food served around a large table in the dining room; children over 12; dogs by prior arrangement.

We welcome reports from readers

To see and do

LANCASHIRE Family Attraction of the Year

⬆T ! MANCHESTER SJ8398 **Museum of Science & Industry** (Castlefield)
On the site of the oldest passenger railway station in the world, this is one of the most impressive and imaginative museums you're ever likely to visit. Everything is done with real verve, using the most up-to-date technology – there's plenty to touch and fiddle with, and more than enough to keep most families intrigued and entertained for the bulk of the day. It's worth planning what you want to see – the place is so overwhelming you might not have time for everything; the electricity gallery alone covers four storeys. The main galleries take a broad and accessible look at power, industry, and transport (going right up to space travel), with highlights including an exciting simulator in the air and space gallery, a big hands-on interactive science area, and a fascinating exhibition on sanitation (its reconstructed sewer is replete with appropriate sounds and, er, smells). The vast power hall has working engines and railway locomotives – plus a glimpse on to the cobbles of Coronation Street at adjacent Granada Studios. There's a fascinating exhibition on the history of photography, from the earliest efforts to the latest TV cameras, and a comprehensive look at the development of Manchester. Quite a draw are their changing exhibitions, the kind of major shows that are worth a visit in their own right; until 4 June they're offering an exhaustive look at the Science of Sport, covering everything from how athletes train and what they eat to the design of football strips. Interactive displays here are designed to challenge your speed and test your reactions under pressure – you can see how you'd fare in a penalty shoot-out. The museum is in the middle of an ongoing development programme; this year they'll open new restaurant and exhibition areas, and from July a new entrance on Lower Byrom St. Even if you're not planning a visit, their remarkable website (www.msism.org.uk) is well worth a look. Meals, snacks, shop, disabled access; cl 24–25 Dec; (0161) 832 1830; *£6.50 (children are free to the main galleries, and *£2 for the Science of Sport). Good value considering how much there is to do, and a real bargain compared to some higher-priced attractions nearby.

ACCRINGTON SD7627
📖 🏵 **Haworth Art Gallery** (Haworth Park, Manchester Rd) Notable for its collection of Tiffany glass, said to be the biggest in Europe (an Accrington man used to manage the Tiffany studios). Nice setting, with nature trail through grounds. Snacks, shop; cl am, all Mon and Tues, 25–26 Dec, 1 Jan and Good Fri; (01254) 233782; free.

ALTRINCHAM SJ7587
🏠 🏵 **Dunham Massey Hall** 16th-c moated manor house extensively remodelled in the 18th c, with impressive silverware, paintings and furnishings, and restored kitchen, pantry and laundry. The largely unaltered grounds have plenty of deer, formal avenues of trees, and a working Elizabethan saw mill (usually Weds and Sun only). Concerts and events even in winter when the house is closed. Meals, snacks, shop, some disabled access; open Sat–Weds Apr–Oct, house cl am; (0161) 941 1025; £5 house and garden, £3 garden only; NT. In town the Old Packet House (Navigation Rd, Broadheath) by the canal does decent food.

BARNOLDSWICK SD9046
⬆T **Bancroft Mill Engine Museum** 📷 The last working steam mill in the area – not that long ago Barnoldswick had 13. Snacks, shop, disabled access; open most Sats for static viewing, (01282) 813932 for dates of steam days; *£2. The Fanny Grey (B651 towards Colne) has decent food.

BARROWFORD SD8639
🍺 🏵 🍴 † **Pendle Heritage Centre** Growing local history centre, with

18th-c walled gardens, small farm, country trails, 14th-c barn with pot-bellied pig, and an exhibition on the Pendle witches – the house itself looks appropriately witchy. Snacks, shop, disabled access; cl 25 Dec; (01282) 661701; £1.50. This is picturesque, evocative countryside; the **church** at nearby unspoilt Newchurch has the witches' grave, and there's good food at the Forest Inn at Fence and the Bay Horse at Roughlee – a stone's throw from Alice Nutter's home.

BIRKENHEAD SJ3288

✝ ❀ ⚘ 🐾 Waterfront views over to Liverpool, of course, but a surprise in **Birkenhead Priory** (Priory St), a ruined 12th-c Benedictine priory with notable visitor centre. Shop, some disabled access; open pm wknds all yr, plus pm daily (exc Mon) in school hols; (0151) 666 4010; free. There are good views from the tower of the neighbouring church. A regeneration project in the Hamilton Quarter continues, with various craft and art galleries. Birkenhead Park laid out in 1853 was the world's first public park. The Shrewsbury Arms out in Claughton Firs is the best place for lunch.

❋ **Historic Warships** 🖼 (Birkenhead Docks) HMS *Plymouth* and the submarine *Onyx* both took part in the Falklands War. You can peep up the periscope on the *Onyx*, and there's plenty for children to fiddle with. A few ladders to negotiate, but don't be put off – readers find this a very satisfying afternoon out. Snacks, shop; cl 24–26 Dec; (0151) 650 1573; *£5 for both ships. The German U-boat displayed alongside spent the last 50 years on the seabed.

⥮ 🏠 **Shore Road Pumping Station** (Woodside, nr ferry terminal) This unusual **steam pumping station** has an adjacent small transport museum with a working tram. Open pm wknds, and daily (exc Mon) in school hols; (0151) 650 1182; *£1.

🖼 🏠 **Williamson Art Gallery & Museum** (Slatey Rd) English watercolours and art by the Liverpool school, sculpture and ceramics, model ships, and a collection of cars and motorcycles in a period garage setting. Shop, disabled access; cl am, all Mon,

Good Fri, 25 Dec and 1 Jan; (0151) 652 4177; free. On summer Suns in Aug there are generally free concerts at either the museum or the priory.

BLACKBURN SD6828

🏛 ✝ Put firmly on the map by the Industrial Revolution, this has bustling shops and market, some fine buildings, and lots of beautiful unspoilt countryside around. The parish **church** (actually now a cathedral) is very handsome – grand yet elegant; there are plans to incorporate a window commemorating Diana, Princess of Wales, in one of the towers.

⛀ 🖼 **Blackburn Museum & Art Gallery** (Museum St) Quite a mixture – English watercolours, Japanese woodblock prints, Greek and Russian Orthodox icons, and a fantastic collection of beetles, some pretty scary. Shop, disabled access; cl Sun, Mon, 25–26 Dec, 1 Jan, Good Fri; (01254) 667130; free.

🐾 **Witton Country Park** (off A674 W) 480 acres of attractive countryside to explore. Snacks, shop; (01254) 55423; visitor centre cl am Mon–Sat, plus all Mon–Weds Oct–Mar, and 25–26 Dec, 1 Jan; free.

BLACKPOOL SD3036

☺ Britain's most loved and loathed seaside resort, in summer offering more bed spaces than the whole of Portugal. The atmosphere then is unashamedly boisterous (it's pretty dreary in winter), and though it's now more geared to young adults, most children love it, with plenty for them to do from donkey rides along the beaches to days at the **Sandcastle** leisure complex. The tram to Fleetwood is a must for tram freaks. The civilised Bispham Hotel (Red Bank Rd) has good-value bedrooms.

☺ **Blackpool Pleasure Beach** These days this dominates the town more than ever, thanks to its monster roller-coaster – at 72 metres (235ft) high quite reasonably called the Big One, its coaches running at up to 85mph. Crowded and noisy, with a sprawling mass of over 145 other breathtaking rides inc a new haunted house and its very own millennium dome, the amusement park is year after year Britain's most visited attraction. Meals, snacks, shops, disabled access; open daily Easter–Oct and wknds Mar; (01253) 341033; individual prices for rides, or books of tickets (around £20).

☺ ♪ **Blackpool Tower** The outstanding landmark has several lively attractions geared towards families, inc a circus, laser shows, aquarium (rare giant sea turtles), science gallery, dinosaur ride, a lift to the top, replica Crown Jewels and the Walk of Faith – a 5-cm-thick glass floor 385ft above the ground. Perhaps most fun at night (they're open till 11pm in summer). Meals, snacks, shop, limited disabled access; cl winter wkdys; (01253) 622242; £7.50, more during the Illuminations. These famous autumn light displays are the best of their kind – if you don't mind travelling at a snail's pace along the Golden Five Hundred Yards (or Mile as they call it here).

🐘 ❀ ♥ **Blackpool Zoo Park** (East Park Dr) Over 400 animals in 32 acres of landscaped gardens inc a walk-through lemur wood, and free-flying bird hall. The big cats are usually fed at 11.45am (not Fri), the sealions at 11am and 3pm, and the penguins at 2.30pm. Meals, snacks, shop, disabled access; cl 25 Dec; (01253) 765027; £6.

▣ **Grundy Art Gallery** (Queen St) This decent gallery away from the crowds is proof that there's more to Blackpool than ice-creams and eyesores. Shop, disabled access but no facilities; cl Sun and bank hols; free.

♪ **Sea Life Centre** (Golden Mile Centre) Broadly similar to others in the chain, but with a bonus: one of the biggest displays of tropical sharks in Europe, with a walk-through tunnel underneath so you feel you're in there with them. Meals, snacks, shop, disabled access; cl 25 Dec; (01253) 622445; £5.50 (they stamp your hand so you can come back later that day).

BOLTON SD7109

🏭 Quite a few places to visit here, and you can tour **Warburtons Bakery** (Hereford St) by arrangement, Tues–Thurs only; (01204) 523551; free. The King's Head (Junction Rd, Deane), with a bowling green behind, is useful for lunch, as is the restaurant of the Queen's Moat House – an interesting church conversion.

🕭 ▣ **Bolton Museum & Art Gallery** (Le Mans Crescent) Quite good, with Egyptian mummies, lots of watercolours and 20th-c sculpture. Shop, disabled access; cl Sun and bank hols; free.

🏠 **Hall i' th' Wood** (Crompton Way) 15th-c, where Samuel Crompton developed his Spinning Mule in 1779; it was refurnished by the first Lord Leverhulme in 1902. Shop, disabled access to ground floor; cl am Sun, all Mon (exc bank hols), all Oct–Mar; £2.

🏠🕭 **Smithills Hall Museum** (Smithills, Dean Rd) Interesting (though much restored) old manor house with 14th-c Great Hall and splendid panelled drawing room. Shop, disabled access to ground floor only; cl am Sun, all Mon (exc bank hols), all Oct–Easter; (01204) 841265; £2 (£3 joint ticket with Hall i' th' Wood).

BOLTON BY BOWLAND SD7849 ★ ✝ Attractive, streamside Forest of Bowland village, with a fine **church**. The Coach & Horses has good fresh food.

BRAMHALL SJ8886

🏠 ▣ ❀ **Bramall Hall** One of the finest houses in the area (particularly from the outside), a splendid timber-framed 14th-c hall with rare 16th-c wall paintings and furniture, and extensive parkland; there was a fair bit of prettifying restoration in the last century. Meals, snacks, shop, disabled access to ground floor; cl am Mon–Sat Good Fri–Sept, plus Mon Oct–Dec, then every day exc pm wknds; (0161) 485 3708; £3.50, park free. The Davenport Arms at Woodford does decent lunches.

BROMLEY CROSS SD7213 ★ 🏘 **Last Drop Village** (N of Bolton) Pastiche of an 18th-c village, very rustic and quaint, with cottages, shops, decent pub and craft centre. The B6391 and old Roman road through Edgworth N of here are fine moorland roads, as are the A675 N of Bolton itself (good detours off at Belmont), and A666 to Darwen.

BURNLEY SD8530

🕭 ⌂ The **canal wharf** (Manchester Rd), which has a small museum, allows short towpath walks along the Leeds & Liverpool Canal, giving a vivid impression of the towering old weaving mills; the raised canal embankment across the valley is a remarkable sight.

⚘ ⚘ ⌂ Rockwater Bird Conservation Centre (Foxstones Lane, Cliviger – above Mereclough) Expanding collection taking in pheasants, bantams, foreign birds and owls as well as rabbits, chipmunks and miniature sheep. Children can feed some animals. Snacks, disabled access (but no facilities); cl Mon (exc bank hols), wkdys Mar and Oct, all Nov–Feb; (01282) 415016; £2.50. Nearby **Cliviger Gorge** has pleasant walks, with stream, woodland and farmland; moors above. The Kettledrum at Mereclough has good home cooking, and the moorland roads around it are attractive – especially the old packhorse road from Mereclough up Stansfield Moor; nice views from the back road angling off SE from the A52 to the junction of the A671 and B6238.

🏠 ⦿ Towneley Hall A646 S of Burnley) A striking 14th-c building housing a decent museum (summer snacks, shop, disabled access; cl am Sat, Sun, Christmas; free).

BURY SD8010

🚂 East Lancs Railway (Bolton St Station) Well regarded by enthusiasts, a scenic 17-mile steam journey along the pretty Irwell Valley; you can get on or off along the way. Meals, snacks, shop, disabled access; open wknds, bank hols, and other dates July and Aug; (0161) 764 7790 for timetable; £6 full return. The Lord Raglan up at Nangreaves (off A56/A666 N) has great moorland views and hearty food.

CARNFORTH SD4970

🏠 🏭 ✳ ⌂ The dilapidated station at this otherwise unremarkable little town starred in *Brief Encounter* in 1945; Railtrack have been developing the site to capitalise on the connection. A mile or so N are the ruins of a 14th-c manor house, Warton Old Rectory. At **Warton Crag** (just N) there are fine views over Morecambe Bay and the coast, and enjoyable walking.

🏠 ⚘ ✿ Leighton Hall (off A6, 3m N) A notably friendly welcome at this neo-Gothic mansion (more restrained inside), still the home of the Gillow family and with early examples of their furniture. The grounds have a collection of birds of prey, nature trails, and beautifully kept gardens. The setting is lovely, with Lakeland hills rising up behind. Snacks, shop, disabled access; cl am, all Sat and Mon (exc bank hols), Sept–Apr; (01524) 734474; £3.70. The nearby New Inn at Yealand Conyers has good food.

CATFORTH SD4735

⚓ ⌂ Lancaster Canal Between Preston and Carnforth, this is ideal for boating – 40 miles without a single lock; often through quiet countryside, with herons and even occasional kingfishers – best in spring or early summer, with ducklings and cygnets bobbing about, and lambs in the fields alongside. From Easter–Oct (and wknds out of season) boats can be hired by the day at Catforth, (01772) 690232, where there's a decent teashop. This is also a good departure point for pleasant towpath walks, largely through quiet countryside.

CHARNOCK RICHARD SD5415

☺ ⚘ 🐄 Camelot Adventure Theme Park 130-acre park themed around the mythical world of Camelot and Arthurian legend – the rides and shows have on the whole been carefully thought out to fit in with this; one of the rollercoasters hurtles around a pseudo-medieval castle, and a dizzying swing-boat ride is in the shape of Excalibur. In Pendragon's Plunge, you sit in an inflatable boat and drop 9 metres through a series of twists and turns at speeds of up to 25mph; there are three different routes; also a driving school for younger children. As well as the rides, there are displays of falconry and jousting in a full-sized arena, a very good rare breeds farm, and dozens of other attractions. Meals, snacks, shop, disabled access; open daily Easter–Aug, plus wknds and half-term Sept–Oct – best to check; (01257) 453044; £7.99 (though frequent discounts).

CHORLEY SD5718

🏠 🖼 ✿ ♿ Astley Hall (Astley Park) Unusual-looking, timber-framed, 16th-c house with particularly elaborate carvings and plasterwork, interesting pottery and paintings, and extensive gardens and woodland. It was used in the TV adaptation of *Moll Flanders*. Shop, disabled access to ground floor

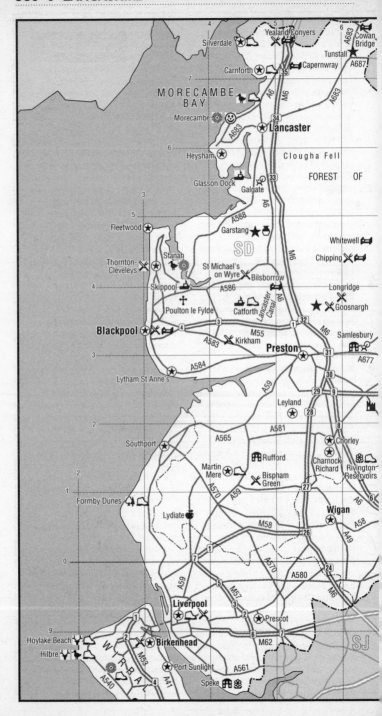

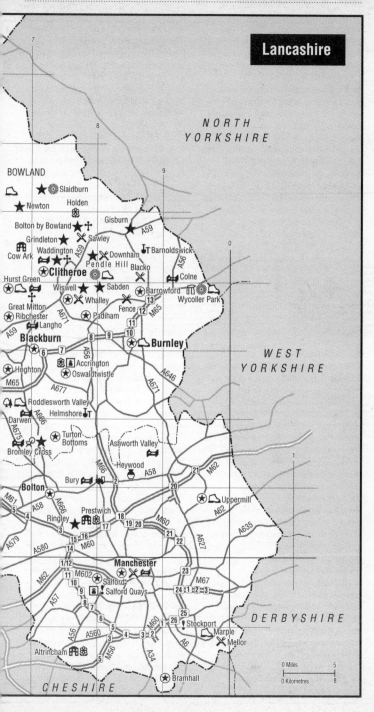

Lancashire

NORTH YORKSHIRE

WEST YORKSHIRE

DERBYSHIRE

CHESHIRE

BOWLAND

Slaidburn
Newton
Holden
Bolton by Bowland
Gisburn
Grindleton
Sawley
Cow Ark
Waddington
Downham
Barnoldswick
Hurst Green
Clitheroe
Pendle Hill
Blacko
Colne
Wiswell
Sabden
Barrowford
Great Mitton
Whalley
Fence
Wycoller Park
Ribchester
Padiham
Langho
Blackburn
Burnley
Hoghton
Accrington
Oswaldtwistle
Roddlesworth Valley
Helmshore
Darwen
Turton Bottoms
Ashworth Valley
Bromley Cross
Heywood
Bury
Uppermill
Bolton
Prestwich
Ringley
Manchester
Salford
Salford Quays
Stockport
Marple
Mellor
Altrincham
Bramhall

0 Miles 5
0 Kilometres 8

only; cl am, Mon (exc bank hols, and
wkdys Nov–Mar; (01257) 262166;
£2.80, free for Chorley residents. The
Malt 'n' Hops behind the station in the
town itself is useful for a bite to eat.

CLITHEROE SD7441

🏚🍖❄ 🖼 Bustling old market town:
every Weds evening hundreds of
poultry and small livestock enthusiasts
come to the auctions, some from as far
away as Scotland. The High St is
dominated by the **castle** perched on its
limestone rock. One of the oldest
buildings in Lancashire, it has one of the
smallest Norman keeps in the country.
The **castle museum** has an extensive
geology exhibition, and good views of
the Ribble Valley. Shop, limited disabled
access; cl Thurs and Fri Oct–Mar, and
all Jan; (01200) 424635; £1.45.
Cowmans on Castle St has an incredibly
wide range of traditional and speciality
sausages. The Starkie Arms below is
handy for lunch, and readers enjoy the
sculpture trail in Bungerley Park.
There's a lovely drive through Bashall
Eaves, the Trough of Bowland and
Quernmore.

COW ARK SD6845

🏛 **Browsholme Hall** Unpretentious-
looking Tudor house on the edge of the
Forest of Bowland, with a surprisingly
rich range of contents. Good guided
tours by members of the family. Snacks,
shop; open pm Easter and spring bank
hol wknds, plus pm Fri–Sun in Aug;
(01254) 826719; £3.50. The Inn at
Whitewell in one direction and Red
Pump at Bashall Eaves in the other offer
a choice of good places to eat.

DOWNHAM SD7844

★ Below Pendle Hill, carefully
preserved and outstandingly pretty, on
the side of a steep pasture valley with a
stream winding along the bottom; the
Assheton Arms is useful.

FLEETWOOD SD3448

⚓🛳🍖❄ Developed as a rather
elegant 19th-c resort, with landscaping
by Decimus Burton, plenty of smart
buildings, lively harbour (summer boat
trips), excellent market, two elegant if
not entirely practical lighthouses (one's
in the middle of the street), decent
summer museum (cl am exc Tues, Fri,
Sat July–Aug, all day Weds exc
July–Sept, and all Nov–Good Fri; £2),

factory shopping centre, and trams
from Blackpool right through the town.
The architecturally interesting North
Euston Hotel by the terminus is a safe
bet for food. The Marine Hall exhibition
centre on the front has a decent bar
(the Wyre) with excellent views of the
harbour and Morecambe Bay.

🐖🍖 Farmer Parr's Animal World

🖼 (Wyrefield Farm, Rossall Lane)
Children can feed the lambs at this 20-
acre farm with over 200 animals inc
rare breeds, llamas, wild boar, emu and
owls; pony and tractor rides; also small
country life heritage centre. Snacks,
shop, disabled access; cl 25–26 Dec;
(01253) 874 389; *£3.25.

FOREST OF BOWLAND SD6650

☁ Magnificent Pennine moorland, less
visited than most areas of comparable
scenery, as much of the moorland,
privately owned, is closed to walkers.
Only a few paths cross the impressive
massif that forms some of the county's
most significant scenery; the Ramblers
Association has often organised mass
trespasses as demonstrations against
denial of access, and hopes for big
changes here from right-to-roam
legislation. Development in some of the
villages (also in private hands) is
controlled too strictly for any
significant expansion of holiday
accommodation – let alone a
proliferation of camp sites and so forth.
These restrictions make the area
particularly appealing for people who
want peace and quiet, and it's not
impossible to find good walks. There
are some fine ones on rights of way –
for instance, up Clougha Fell from
Quernmore; above Tarnbrook Wyre;
up Dunsop Fell from Slaidburn or
Dunsop Bridge; up Fairsnape and Wolf
Fell from Chipping or Bleasdale. Beacon
Fell Country Park is an atmospheric
place to wander through, and there are
some pleasant walks around the
Coronation Arms at Horton.

FORMBY DUNES SD2808

☁ 🦉 Reached from the NW edge of
Formby, a large tract of sweeping sandy
dunes which in some areas is being
stabilised by pine plantations; broad
beaches and good walks through the
adjacent pinewoods, made interesting
by the chance of seeing and even

feeding red squirrels (you can buy nuts here). Best in spring and autumn – can be busy in summer; parking in some places may cost £1.50, but keep looking – a number of other spots are free.

GALGATE SD4855

🐾 **Canalside Craft Centre**
Converted farm buildings with various crafts inc a woodturner producing unusual clocks, barometers and bowls; seating by canalside. Meals, snacks, shops, disabled access; (01524) 752223; free. The Plough has good food.

GARSTANG SD4945

★ 🐚 Quite an attractive small market town, with a good deal of canal activity (and a fine aqueduct crossing the River Wyre). The entertaining, creeper-covered waterside Owd Tithebarn (with waitresses in period costume, and a canal museum upstairs) is fun for lunch, and the **Discovery Centre** (High St) is a useful introduction to the area's natural history.

GLASSON DOCK SD4456

⚓ Once an important port for Lancaster, this still has the occasional coaster berthing, but is mainly a lively summer boating place now, in pleasant countryside. The Victoria on the dock is a popular dining pub, as is the 17th-c Stork up on the A588.

GREAT MITTON SD7139

✝ **Great Mitton church** Attractive, with an outstanding range of memorial tombs.

HELMSHORE SD7821

⚒ **Helmshore Textile Museums** (Holcombe Rd) Two stone mills with comprehensive collections of textile machinery, much still in working order. Easily one of the best textile museums in the country, but if social history and machinery aren't your things it's unlikely to convert you. Snacks, shop, disabled access; cl am, Sat, and Nov–Mar; (01706) 226459; £3. The Duke of Wellington on the B6232 W of Haslingden is a reliable family dining pub in fine surroundings, with more views further on that road.

HEYSHAM SD4160

⚒ ✝ ✝ **Heysham Power Stations** Hi-tech interactive exhibition on electricity generation, with tours of power station and nuclear reactor, and 25-acre nature reserve. This is the most elaborate of Nuclear Electric's visitor centres. Tours by arrangement (ring for details); it may be worth booking in summer. Snacks, shop, disabled access; cl Sat, and Nov–Mar; (01524) 855624; free. A tremendous contrast is the quaint squint-walled little village **church**, partly Saxon, with Norse-carved hogback tombstone inside. The unusual waterside Golden Ball at Heaton with Oxcliffe, off the Lancaster road (may be cut off by very high tides) is fun for lunch.

HEYWOOD SD8510

🛞 **Corgi Heritage Centre** (53 York St) Hundreds of die-cast model vehicles from pre-war cars to James Bond's Aston Martin – even a turning Magic Roundabout; of course it's all a huge plug for the company that makes them, but fascinating for collectors. Shop, disabled access; cl Tues and Sun, bank hols; (01706) 365812; free. The Egerton Arms off the B6222 Bury road is a good moorland dining pub.

HILBRE SJ1887

☁ ✌ 🐦 The biggest of three tidal islands which you can reach on foot at low tide from West Kirby; Hilbre is a **nature reserve**, once popular with sunbathers, now visited mainly by birds and occasional seals. Make sure you know the tide times – (0151) 648 4371 – as it's easy to be stranded out here.

HOGHTON SD6226

🏚 ⚜ ❋ **Hoghton Tower** (A675) Splendid, 16th-c, fortified hilltop mansion, with grand state rooms and royal bedchamber, and a collection of dolls and dolls' houses. The gardens are lovely (particularly the rose garden) and the surrounding grounds offer wonderful views of the sea, moors, Lakeland hills and Welsh mountains. Meals, snacks, shop; open pm Sun and Mon bank hol wknds, plus Mon–Thurs and pm Sun July–Sept; (01254) 852986; £1 parking and grounds, £2.50 house. The Royal Oak at Riley Green has decent food.

HOLDEN SD7749

⚜ **Holden Clough Nursery** Old-fashioned nursery with thoroughly up-to-date approach to raising interesting plants in Victorian kitchen garden of Holden Clough Hall; beds of alpines, trough gardens, herbaceous perennials, shrubs and rhododendrons and maybe RHS special events. Shop, disabled access; cl 12–1pm, all Suns, 25 Dec–1 Jan; (01200) 447615; free. The Copy Nook has good food, and is a useful stop for walkers.

HOYLAKE BEACH SJ2088
¥ ⌂ These sweeping sands are beautiful, with an unusual partly tidal **nature reserve** at Red Rocks, N of the golf links.

HURST GREEN SD6939
🏠 🏵 ⌂ **Stonyhurst College** Magnificent 16th-c manor house, now home to the famous Roman Catholic boarding school. You can see the library, chapel, other historic rooms and the extensive grounds. Snacks, shop, limited disabled access; open pm Aug exc Fri, gardens usually open July–Aug – phone to check; (01254) 826345; £4, £1 garden only. The Punch Bowl and the Bayley Arms both have good food, with pleasant Ribble Valley walks nearby.

LANCASTER SD4761
⚓ Friendly and relaxed despite the grandeur of many of its stone buildings; ambling down the cobbled streets and alleyways (much is pedestrianised), it's hard to believe this was once a major West Indies shipping port. These days the water traffic is more sedate, with punts for hire and canal cruises in summer. A millennium project hopes to create a circular riverside path as well as a new bridge over the Lune. The Lancastrian (Scale Hall Farm, A589 Morecambe rd) has good food, and other places worth knowing for lunch include the George & Dragon (nr River Lune) and canalside White Cross.

🏠 🏵 ❀ 🦋 **Ashton Memorial & Butterfly Park** (Williamson Park) A magnificent folly clearly visible from the motorway, set in 38 acres of lovely landscaped parkland; splendid views from upper galleries. Displays on Edwardian life, and a butterfly house with good collection of plants and lepidoptera, as well as free-flying birds and various creepy-crawlies. Snacks, shop, disabled access; cl 25–26 Dec, 1 Jan; (01524) 33318; £2.95.

🏠 ☕ **Judge's Lodging** (Church St) 17th-c house with well restored period rooms, plenty of Gillow furniture, and a museum of childhood. Shop; open pm Mon–Sat Good Fri–Oct, plus all day Mon–Sat July–Sept, and pm Sun on bank hol wknds; (01524) 32808; £2. Other decent collections at the firmly traditional **City Museum** on Market Sq, in a very grand Georgian former town hall (shop, disabled access; cl Sun, 24 Dec–1 Jan; free), and at the **Cottage Museum** opposite the castle, furnished in the style of an early 19th-c artisan's house (open pm Easter–Sept; 75p).

🏛 **Lancaster Castle** Dramatic 12th-c Norman fortress famous for hangings and witch trials, owned by the Queen as Duke of Lancaster. Part of it is still used as a prison, but the cells, tower and 18th-c Gothic Revival Shire Hall can all be visited. Shop; open wknds Apr–Oct, and wkdys when Court not in session – usually around school hols but best to check; (01524) 64998; £3.50.

Days Out

Liverpool walkabout: Museums in William Brown St; Roman Catholic cathedral; lunch at the Philharmonic (Hope St); Anglican cathedral; walk via Rodney St and Hanover St to Albert Dock; Tate Gallery or Merseyside Maritime Museum; walk to Royal Liver Building for Mersey ferry to Birkenhead and back; walk back to William Brown St via Water St and Dale St.

Industrious Manchester: Town Hall; walk Rochdale Canal towpath from Princess St to junction with Bridgewater Canal in Castlefield area; lunch at Dukes 92, Castle St; Museum of Science and Industry, or Granada Studios Tour.

Pennine heritage: East Lancs Railway, Bury; lunch at the Lord Raglan, Nangreaves; Helmshore Textile Museums (not Sat).

✳ **Lancaster Maritime Museum** 🏛
(St George's Quay) Up-to-date look at
the local maritime trade and fishing
industry; the audio-visual show is fun.
Snacks, shop, disabled access; cl am
Nov–Easter, 25 Dec and 1 Jan; (01524)
64637; £2 (free to local residents).
✝ 🏛 **Lancaster Priory** Dates back to
before the Conquest, though the
present hilltop building is mainly 14th
and 15th-c; very interesting medieval
choir stalls, needlework and Anglo-
Saxon cross fragments. Snacks, shop,
some disabled access; cl winter
lunchtimes; free. Nearby are the
remains of a Roman bath-house.
LEYLAND SD5422
🚗 **British Commercial Vehicle
Museum** (King St) Jazzed up with
sound effects, this has over 90 perfectly
restored British wagons, buses, trucks,
vans, fire engines and even a
Popemobile, shining so much you'd
think they were new. Snacks, shop,
disabled access; open Sun, Tues, Weds
and bank hols Apr–Sept, Sun only Oct;
(01772) 451011; £4.
🍺 🦋 🏛 🐾 ✝ **Old Grammar School**
(Church Rd) This sturdy 16th-c building
has changing local history displays; open
pm Thurs, all day Tues and Fri, am
Sat; (01772) 422041; free. **Worden
Park** has art displays and nine varied
craft workshops, as well as walks,
gardens, a maze, and miniature golf.
Leyland also has a pleasant little town
trail, and the 15th-c church has some
fine stained glass. The friendly little
Rose & Crown (A581 S) has decent
basic food.
LIVERPOOL SJ3590
🏛 🍺 ⚓ The fine 19th-c buildings which
mark Liverpool's past as one of the
world's great ports have in the last few
years taken on a cleaner and prouder
look. At the same time a good few
varied family attractions have opened.
You can visit many of them without
straining your pocket with the
excellent-value National Museums and
Galleries on Merseyside Eight Pass:
admission to any one of the eight
attractions in the scheme (£3, £1.50
concessions), allows unlimited visits for
a year to that and the other seven
attractions. The Philharmonic (Hope
St) is probably the country's grandest

late Victorian pub; nearby, the
Everyman Bistro has good-value food.
You can tour the city's trademark Liver
Building on wkdys Apr–Sept by
arrangement, (0151) 236 2748, though
it's best viewed from one of the famous
ferries across the Mersey, which leave
regularly from Pier Head. The real
commuter ferries operate half-hourly
during rush-hours (£1.80 return); the
rest of the day the boats are hourly and
aimed at visitors, with a commentary
(£3.40 return).
🏛 ⚓ **Albert Dock** Spectacular
restoration of previously redundant
warehouse buildings by the river, now a
lively complex of shops, cafés and
exhibitions, with regular entertainers,
performers, events, boat trips and of
course Fred's weather map. The Baltic
Fleet, a majestically restored Victorian
dockside pub, is handy for lunch, and
the Hope on the Waterfront cybercafé
is different for a drink. Some of the
listed attractions are housed in the
complex – you can easily base a whole
day around a visit here.
❗ **Beatles Story** (Albert Dock)
Bouncy (and pricey) tribute to the local
boys made good and the sights and
sounds of the 60s, including a
reconstruction of the Cavern Club.
Shop, disabled access; cl 25–26 Dec;
(0151) 709 1963; £6.95. Beatles' fans
(considering the price you need to have
been really devoted) can also go on a
two-hour tour in a Magical Mystery
Tourbus around related city sites – it
leaves the Albert Dock daily at 2.20pm,
calling at the Clayton Sq shopping
centre at 2.30pm; best to book in
advance: (0151) 709 3285; £9.50.
🏛 🐾 **Bluecoat Arts Centre** (School
Lane) Changing exhibitions, plus art and
craft shops and occasional recitals in an
attractive Georgian building. Meals,
snacks, shop, disabled access to ground
floor only; cl Mon, 25–26 Dec, 1 Jan and
all bank hols; (0151) 7072390; free (exc
for events).
🍺 ❗ **Conservation Centre**
(Whitechapel) Fascinating new glimpse
at the world of museum and gallery
conservation; interactive displays and
demonstrations explain how various
objects are preserved, and exhibits
range from a mummified Egyptian

crocodile to two of the Beatles' gold discs; good programme of events. Café, shop, disabled access; cl am Sun, 23–26 Dec, 1 Jan; (0151) 478 4999; £3 Eight Pass – see *Liverpool above* (children free).

🎔 🐖 🏵 ⌂ **Croxteth Hall & Country Park** (5m NE) Period displays in Edwardian house, and a working farm, Victorian walled garden, miniature railway, and country walks in the grounds – a pleasant family trip out. Meals, snacks, shop, some disabled access; house cl Oct–Easter, farm cl 25 Dec–1 Jan, park open all year; (0151) 228 5311; park free, house, farm and garden £3.60, house or farm only £1.80.

⬧ ! **Grand National Visitor Centre** (Aintree Race Course) This excellent new attraction takes you behind the scenes of the world's most famous steeplechase. A visitor centre within the County Stand has memorabilia charting the history of the race from its origins in 1839, while in the weighing room you can try on the silks of past winners, test out the scales and experience a steward's enquiry. Perhaps the highlight, though, is the simulator ride – find out what it's like to jump a National fence; guided tours of the racecourse (11am, 1pm, 3.30pm) include a look around the stables. Meals, snacks, shop, disabled access; cl Mon, Oct–Apr, and all race days; (0151) 522 2922; visitor centre £3 (with simulator ride £5, plus tour £7).

⬧ ! **Liverpool Football Club Museum** (Anfield Rd) The visitor centre and Anfield tours are a must for the faithful. There are cups, trophies, programmes and other treasured memorabilia as well as films of the club's finest hours. The tour takes in the grounds, dressing room and pitch – you can even sit on the manager's bench. Snacks, shop, disabled access; visitor centre cl 25 Dec, no tours on match days and booking essential (0151) 260 6677. Shop, some disabled access; £8 (visitor centre only £5).

⬧ ♪ ! **Liverpool Museum** (William Brown St) You could spend hours at this excellent museum and still not see everything. There's an aquarium, a particularly good planetarium (shows 3.15pm, plus 1.15pm, 2.15pm and 4.15pm wknds; cl Mon), and a hands-on

natural history centre (pm only, cl Mon). Snacks, shop, disabled access; cl am Sun, 23–26 Dec, 1 Jan; (0151) 207 0001; £3 – Eight Pass (see *Liverpool above*), children free. Just along the road you can tour one of the biggest public libraries in Europe (not Sun or bank hols); (0151) 225 5445 to book; free.

🏵 ⬧ **Merseyside Maritime Museum** (Albert Dock) Huge museum spread over six floors, with boats, ships, craft demonstrations and a lively interpretation of what it was like for the millions who travelled from here to the New World. It takes in the **Museum of Liverpool Life**, vividly re-creating social history from the last century or so, and the **Customs and Excise Museum, Anything to Declare** – a lot more fun than it sounds, with an intriguing look at concealment techniques, and even demonstrations by sniffer dogs. A gallery on transatlantic slavery has bitterly divided local historians, who disagree on Liverpool's true role in the slave trade. Meals, snacks, shop, disabled access; cl 24–26 Dec, 1 Jan; (0151) 478 4499; £3 – Eight Pass (see *Liverpool above*).

✿ 🏵 **National Wildflower Centre** As we went to press, work on this £3.4 million Millennium Commission-backed venture was still under way. When it opens around Aug, it will act as a conservation centre for British wildflowers under threat. Former wastelands have been transformed by the charity Landlife into natural havens inc a therapeutic forget-me-not garden, and a new purpose-built visitor centre will have hands-on activities, exhibitions about conservation, a small shop and a café (the centre will have disabled access); (0151) 737 1819 for further information.

🖾 **Open Eye Gallery** (Wood St) Good changing photography exhibitions; disabled access; cl Sun and Mon; (0151) 709 9460; free.

🎔 **Paul McCartney's home** (20 Forthlin Road, Allerton) 1950s terraced council house, the former home of the McCartney family. John, Paul and George met, rehearsed and wrote many of their earliest songs here, inc *Love Me Do* and *I Saw Her Standing There*. Open Weds–Sat Apr–Oct, then Sats only till mid-Dec; essential to book on (0151) 486 4006; access is by minibus from Speke Hall (see entry on p.399) only; £4.20 (NT members free).

🏛 **Robert Cain & Co Ltd** (Stanhope St) Evening tours of red brick brewery inc buffet and tastings; shop; cl Fri–Sun; (0151) 709 8734; £3.75. The splendidly restored Brewery Tap pub is good.

🏛 🕸 🖼 **Sudley House** (Mossley Hill Rd) Interestingly unspoilt private Victorian house with good gardens, attractive furniture, and paintings by Turner and the Pre-Raphaelites. Wknd snacks, disabled access to ground floor only; cl am Sun, 23–26 Dec, 1 Jan; (0151) 207 0001; £3, Eight Pass (see Liverpool above).

🖼 **Tate Gallery** (Albert Dock) Plenty of sculptures, paintings and various special events. All very well presented with especially good use of natural light, though not really for traditionalists. Meals, snacks, shop, disabled access; cl Mon (exc bank hols), Good Fri, 24–26 Dec, 1 Jan; (0151) 709 3223; free, though £3 for special exhibitions.

🖼 **Walker Art Gallery** (William Brown St) One of the finest art collections outside London, with especially notable Italian, Dutch and Pre-Raphaelite works. Meals, snacks, shop, disabled access; cl am Sun, 23–26 Dec, 1 Jan; (0151) 478 4199; £3 Eight Pass (see Liverpool above).

🏛 👁 ! **Western Approaches** (Rumford St) Evocatively restored underground command centre for the World War II Battle of the Atlantic; a labyrinth of rooms covering 50,000 sq ft under the city's streets. Snacks, shop; cl Fri, Sun, and Nov–Mar; (0151) 227 2008; £4.75.

LIVERPOOL CATHEDRALS SJ3589

✝ Unusually, both Liverpool's cathedrals were built this century, in widely differing styles. Walk along Hope St (the heart of the city's 18th-c area, with many Georgian brick terraces) to the impressive and more obviously modern Metropolitan Roman Catholic cathedral, designed by Frederick Gibberd after a vast earlier scheme by Lutyens ran out of money; blue light from the 16-sided glass tower reflects evocatively on the marble inside. The Anglican cathedral looks much older, but was completed only in 1978. Britain's biggest, it's undeniably powerful, though its soaring proportions and cavernous scale make it impersonal. Both have good concerts.

LYDIATE SD3604

🍎 **Pick-your-own** Popular around here, with lots of places on the flat ground – soft fruit the speciality, late Jun to Aug; **Lydiate Fruit Farm** (Pilling Lane) has a good farm shop in attractive, 18th-c former stable buildings.

LYTHAM ST ANNE'S SD3228

✗ ❀ Decorous seaside town that seems a world away from nearby Blackpool. It has a splendidly restored **windmill** by the promenade in the centre of Lytham green (cl 1–2pm, Mon and Fri, and all Sept–Apr exc Easter; donations), and a small **lifeboat museum** next door (open Tues, Thurs and wknds, plus pm Weds July–Aug; free). The Taps is a good real ale pub here.

👁 ❤ **Toy & Teddy Bear Museum** (Clifton Drive N, St Anne's) Porritt-built Victorian building with big collection of nostalgic children's items; good shop, some disabled access; open wknds, school hols, and bank hols all year, plus Weds–Fri first May bank hol–Oct; (01253) 713705; £2.75. A sand dune **nature reserve** stretches opposite.

MANCHESTER SJ8398

🏛 ✝ 🕸 Ambitious works on the redevelopment of the city centre, backed by huge government grants, are greatly enhancing Manchester's already significant appeal. It's packed with interesting places to visit; no fewer than four of the city's impressive museums were among the first two dozen places outside London on the Heritage Secretary's new shortlist of nationally important museums. Last year the construction of the grand canalside Imperial War Museum of the North was finally given the go-ahead – it should be open by the end of 2001. On a fine weekend or summer evening, strolling around the very impressive buildings is already a real pleasure; Albert Sq is one of the finest areas, with the great Albert Memorial (predating London's), several key cultural centres, and some lively café-bars. The town hall is a massively impressive piece of Victoriana, facing colourful summer gardens; there may be guided tours in summer. The **cathedral** is a very wide 15th-c church, with notable choir stalls; the small medieval centre around it, and Shambles Sq (not far from the bomb-blasted Arndale Centre, but sustaining only superficial damage itself), deserve a look, as do Exchange St and St Ann's Sq. Sinclairs Oyster Bar in Shambles Sq is good value (not just oysters), while Mash & Air (Chorlton St) is currently drawing in the young and fashionable, thanks to its unusual own-brew beers and equally distinctive food. The Castlefield area by the basin where the Bridgewater and Rochdale canals meet is interesting: restored warehouses, viaducts and the like, lots of lively redevelopment inc a tramway and wonderfully light and airy footbridge, also the good Dukes 92 pub (maybe street theatre outside) – and not far off, on the other side of the GMEX exhibition centre, the very smart Bridgewater concert hall (box office (0161) 907 9000). By contrast, the Rochdale canal towpath is a fascinating seamy-side walk. Chinatown here, incidentally, is the second-largest Chinese community in England: lots of authentic restaurants and a Chinese Arts Centre. The city has the nation's largest Marks & Spencer's, while young trendies head to Afflecks Palace on Church St for four floors of antique clothing, records, etc, and there's a huge shopping centre with a 20-screen cinema at Trafford Park to the N. It's surprisingly easy and quick getting across the city, and the useful Metrolink trams quickly cover much of Greater Manchester.

🏛 **Chetham's Library** (Long Millgate) Founded in 1653, this is the oldest public library in Britain. The attractive building itself dates from the 15th c and was originally a college for priests. Many of the original features remain inc fellows' dormitories, and 17th-c reading tables (still used). Recent heritage grants are funding more restoration projects. Cl 12.30–1.30pm, wknds, 25 Dec, 1 Jan; (0161) 8347961; free.

🍴🏛 **Gallery of Costume** (Platt Hall, Rusholme) The best museum of its kind, a Georgian mansion with displays of fashion over the last 400 years. Displays change regularly – though like the styles themselves eventually come back. Shop, disabled access to ground floor only; open daily 10am–5.30pm; (0161) 224 5217; free.

☺ **Granada Studios Tour** (Water St) The behind-the-scenes studio tour at this lively place has quickly become eclipsed by the other attractions, and it's now practically a theme park. Most features are based on TV programmes that Granada produce, though there are exceptions: the Alien motion-master ride for example. Other highlights include a replica of the House of Commons, an interactive mystery based on *Cracker*, and the exterior sets for the *Sherlock Holmes* series, *Moll Flanders* and, of course, *Coronation Street*. You'll find plenty of people peering through the letterboxes of the latter, and there's usually an appearance by a member of the cast. The main shows and exhibitions each last around half an hour, so check the times of what's on as you arrive – some bits overlap, and you'll need to do a bit of planning (seeing everything once takes seven and a half hours). Meals, snacks, shop, disabled access; open daily July–Aug, cl Mon in Sept, plus Tues Nov–Jun, best to check; (0161) 833 0880; £14.99.

🏛 ❀ **Heaton Hall** (Prestwich) Splendidly decorated, 18th-c neo-classical house in extensive, well used public parkland; fine paintings, plasterwork and furniture, unusual circular Pompeiian room, and various recitals and temporary exhibitions. Disabled access; probably cl 12–1pm, all Mon and Tues, and Oct–Easter, phone to check; (0161) 773 1231; free. The Victorian Woodthorpe by the main gate has decent food.

🏛 **John Rylands Library** (Deansgate) One of the city's most remarkable buildings – magnificently neo-Gothic. Small exhibitions and tours (Weds noon, £1); shop, cl pm Sat, all Sun, and 24 Dec–1 Jan; (0161) 834 5343; free.

🍴 **Manchester Jewish Museum** (Cheetham Hill Rd, A665 1m N) In a former synagogue, the story of Manchester's Jewish community over the last 200 years, with fascinating recorded recollections of life earlier this century. Shop, some disabled access; cl Fri, Sat and Jewish holidays; (0161) 834 9879; £2.95. The nearby Derby Brewery Arms is a classic Mancunian pub, good-value snacks.

🜨 **Manchester Museum** (Oxford Rd) Good Japanese collection, as well as Egyptian relics, and beehive. Shop, limited disabled access; cl Sun, Good Fri, 25–26 Dec and 1 Jan; (0161) 275 2634; free.

🜨! **Manchester United Museum** (Old Trafford) Purpose-built football museum, covering the club's history from its foundation in 1878 to the more recent glory days. Hundreds of exhibits (changing almost as frequently as their strip) and tours of the ground (not match days, and limited on the days before). Meals, snacks, shop (not unjustifiably they call it a megastore), disabled access; cl 25 Dec; (0161) 877 4002; £7.50 tour and museum, £5 museum only.

⬆! **Museum of Science & Industry** *See separate family panel on p.382.*

🏛 **Museum of Transport** 🎫 (Boyle St, Cheetham) Around 80 vintage local buses and other vehicles, as well as photographs, tickets and memorabilia – even historic bus stops. Snacks (Sat and Weds only), shop, disabled access; open Weds, Sat, Sun and bank hols; (0161) 205 2122; £2.50.

🜨 ✿ **Pankhurst Centre** (62 Nelson St, Chorlton on Medlock) Emmeline Pankhurst launched the Suffragette movement from this Georgian semi, now with period-furnished parlour and interestingly planted garden. Meals, snacks, shop, disabled access; cl wknds and bank hols; (0161) 273 5673; free.

Royal Northern College of Music (Oxford Rd) Regular concerts, recitals and exhibitions; meals, snacks, shop; box office (0161) 907 5278/9.

🖼 **Whitworth Art Gallery** (Oxford Rd) British watercolours from Sandby to Turner, plus modern paintings and sculpture, and unusual collections of textiles and wallpaper. Meals, snacks, shop, disabled access; cl am Sun, Good Fri, Christmas wk; (0161) 275 7450; free.

MARPLE SJ9688
⌓ **Peak Forest Canal** Reached from Marple, the towpath soon leaves suburbia for green countryside; N is the famous set of Marple locks and aqueduct over the River Etherow. To the S, you can leave the canal at Strines and climb on to Mellor Moor.

MARTIN MERE SD4214
🐦⌓ **Wildfowl & Wetlands Trust** (off A59) Thousands of wild geese, swans, ducks and flamingos regularly visit the re-created natural open water habitats at this important 376-acre centre. Some birds will feed straight from your hand. Good visitor centre, well organised walks, lively activities for children and adventure playground, and plenty of instructive and entertaining events. Meals, snacks, shop, disabled access; cl 25 Dec; (01704) 895181; *£5. The canalside Ship at Lathom is very popular for lunch.

🐖🐇 **Windmill Animal Farm** (Fish Lane, Holmeswood) Just N of Martin Mere, this friendly 40-acre place has animals and their babies to feed (inc rare breeds), tractor rides, miniature railway, and an adventure playground. Snacks, shop, disabled access; cl wkdys mid-Sept–Easter; (01704) 892282; £3.

MORECAMBE SD4264
Five miles of promenade and more of beaches to stroll along at this cheery resort, with pretty sunsets over the bay (beware of colour clashes during their July Punk Festival). A lovely new seafront statue commemorates the town's funniest son, Eric Morecambe, who so loved the place, he adopted its name. The Dog & Partridge (Bare) has decent fresh food.

❉ ☺ **Frontierland** Wild West theme park with 30 family rides and attractions (inc circus), and spectacular views across the bay from the top of the bizarre Polo Tower, designed to look like end-to-end tubes of sweets. Meals, snacks, shop, disabled access; cl Nov–Easter and some other days outside high season; (01524) 410024; £8.95 (less in low season).

MORECAMBE BAY SD4666
🐦⌓ Vast mudflats and sands, home to 200,000 wading birds. Walks over them are easiest from the Cumbrian side, though guided walks are also available

from Hest Bank (details from local tourist information centres; the galloping tides and quicksand do make a guide essential).

OSWALDTWISTLE SD7428

🏛️ ✈️ 🐝 🐦 ⛲ **Oswaldtwistle Mills** (Moscow Mill, Colliers St) Shopping village set around a working mill with various craft workshops inc a sweet factory; also garden, wildfowl reserve, textile museum (£1), and summer events. Meals, snacks, disabled access; cl 25–26 Dec; (01254) 871025; free.

PADIHAM SD8034

🏛️ 🐝 ⛲ 🖼️ **Gawthorpe Hall** Early 17th-c manor house with fine panelling and moulded ceilings, minstrels' gallery, and Jacobean long gallery. Important collections of costume, embroidery and lace, and paintings from the National Portrait Gallery. Snacks, limited disabled access; house cl am, Mon (exc bank hols), Fri, and Nov–Mar, grounds open all year; (01282) 771004; £3; NT. The hilly cobbled alleys in the town's centre are now a conservation area.

PENDLE HILL SD8240

⛰️ ❄️ An excellent network of paths lets you walk round and almost all over it. Although Pendle's witch-persecuting days are happily over, the place still has a haunting elemental appeal. The view that enraptured George Fox, the founder of the Quakers, is as good as ever. The quickest way up is from Barley village.

PORT SUNLIGHT SJ3384

🖼️ **Lady Lever Art Gallery** Lord Leverhulme, who had built his Sunlight Soap factory here, donated the village its outstanding gallery. It has interesting Victorian paintings inc Turners and Pre-Raphaelites – many adapted for use in soap ads, to the fury of the artists. Meals, snacks, shop, disabled access; cl am Sun, 23–26 Dec, 1 Jan; (0151) 645 3623; £3 for an Eight Pass ticket, covering seven other galleries in the area (see Liverpool entry).

🏃 ★ **Port Sunlight Heritage Centre** Sets the scene for this most famous of the garden villages built by 19th-c philanthropists, contriving something better than the appalling squalor of northern England's factory towns. Historically important as the precursor of garden cities, garden suburbs and

New Towns, it's perfectly preserved, with groups of mock-Tudor cottages, swathes of greenery and parkland: no two groups of houses are alike. Useful village trail leaflets; also period soap packaging (you can buy soap in replica wrappings). Shop, improved disabled access; cl wknds Nov–Easter, Christmas and New Year; (0151) 644 6466; £1. Nearby Thornton Hough was also built by Lord Leverhulme, as a mock-Tudor estate village – Port Sunlight on a much smaller scale; the Seven Stars there is useful for lunch.

POULTON LE FYLDE SD3439

✝️ Quite an attractive pedestrianised market square, with a lovely church (as others in Lancashire, looking a good deal older than in fact it is), and several useful places to eat – the Old Town Hall is particularly good value.

PRESCOT SJ4793

🐘 🐄 ⛲ **Knowsley Safari Park** Five-mile drive through very natural-looking reserves of lions, tigers, rhinos, monkeys and other animals; they have the biggest herd of African elephants in Europe. Also pets corner and miniature railway. Meals, snacks, shop, disabled access; cl wkdys Nov–Feb; (0151) 430 9009; £12 per car – load in all your friends and it's very good value indeed. If you have to pass through the town, the **museum** (Church St) has an interesting collection relating to the area's former clock-making industry; cl 1–2pm, am Sun, Mon (exc bank hols), Tues, Good Fri, 25–26 Dec, 1 Jan; (0151) 430 7787; free. The Clock Face is a pleasant old mansion-house pub here.

PRESTON SD5329

⛲ 🖼️ 🐄 The town has two decent museums: the impressive if rather dour Greek revival **Harris Museum & Art Gallery** on Market Sq (cl Sun and bank hols; free), and the **Museum of Lancashire** on Stanley St (cl Thurs, Sun and bank hols; £1). There's a good big market (the space is used for car-boot sales instead on Tues and Thurs); Wall Street (Fishergate) has decent food. After delays, the **Railway Centre** from Southport is due to re-open as **the Ribble Steam Railway** in Preston Marina this year. **Moor Park Observatory** is open most Thurs evenings (exc the second of the month)

Sept–Mar (not Dec); (01772) 257181 to check this.

† Church of St Mary (Penwortham) 14th-c chancel, and the scant remains of a motte and bailey castle in the churchyard; nearby the Fleece (Liverpool Rd) is useful for lunch.

RIBCHESTER SD6535

★ ⋔ † Attractive little town, many of its buildings incorporating masonry plundered from the former Roman town here: the White Bull pub, with decent food, has a couple of Tuscan pillars for its porch and an excavated Roman bath-house behind. The 15th-c **church** stands on the site of the Roman fort, and looks as if it uses much salvaged material from it.

♂ Ribchester Roman Museum On the site of a fort occupied between the 1st and 4th c, with lots of coins, pottery and the famous Ribchester helmet. Shop, disabled access; cl 25 Dec; (01254) 878261; £1.50.

⋔ ❀ Stydd Nursery (Stoneygate Lane) There are excavated Roman granaries behind this nursery specialising in old-fashioned roses and hardy perennials; some disabled access; open pm Tues–Fri, best to check; (01254) 878797; free.

RINGLEY SD7605

★ Unexpected corner so close to urban areas – village stocks and an ancient bridge over the Irwell (and a decent pub).

RIVINGTON RESERVOIRS SD6215

◠ ❀ These attractive waters just outside Horwich make good walking territory. Lower Rivington Reservoir has a waterside path along its eastern edge, and a curious mock-up of Liverpool castle (built in 1912) as an adornment to the vast and atmospherically decayed gardens of Lever Park, which cover the hillside. A trail guides you around the undergrowth and up to the Pigeon Tower, within a few minutes of Rivington Pike, the summit. The Great House Barn is the place to start, with a good information centre, maps and guides.

RODDLESWORTH VALLEY SD6622

⛺ ◠ ⛰ Good woodland walks from

the Royal Arms at Tockholes, and maybe on to the ruins of Hollinshead Hall and its restored curative well.

RUFFORD SD4616

⋔ Rufford Old Hall ⊞ Lovely timber-framed Tudor house built by the Hesketh family in the 16th c, with an intricate hammerbeam roof in the Great Hall, and impressive collections of 17th-c Lancashire oak furniture, and 16th-c arms, armour and tapestries. Some later rooms too; new audio tour. Snacks, shop, limited disabled access (no facilities); cl am, all Thurs and Fri, and Nov–Mar; (01704) 821254; £3.80, £1.70 garden only; NT. The Robin Hood just the other side of Mawdesley has good home cooking.

SABDEN SD7737

★ Attractive village, with a decent antique centre, on the slopes of Pendle Hill; linked by a scenic drive to another charming Pendle Hill village, Pendleton.

SALFORD SJ8198

Merging almost imperceptibly into Manchester, this owes its distinct place in the popular consciousness mainly to the works of L S Lowry – a giant arts centre dedicated to the artist opens in Apr (*see below*). The waterside Mark Addy (Stanley St) has a great choice of cheeses and pâtés.

♦T Mining Museum (Eccles Old Rd) Georgian building with two reconstructed mines, and displays showing the history and development of coal-mining. Snacks, shop; cl 12.30–1.30pm, am Sun, Sat; (0161) 736 1832; free.

⋔♂ Ordsall Hall Museum (Ordsall Lane) Timbered Tudor manor house with local history exhibits and Victorian farmhouse kitchen. Shop, some disabled access; cl 12.30–1.30pm, am Sun, Sat, Good Fri, 25–26 Dec; (0161) 872 0251; free.

♂ ▣ Salford Museum & Art Gallery (Peel Park) A fine showing of L S Lowry paintings, also a nostalgic reconstructed industrial street scene, with some wonderfully over-the-top period advertisements. Snacks, shop, disabled access; cl 25–26 Dec, 1 Jan, Good Fri; free.

SALFORD QUAYS SJ7998

▣ ! Lowry ⊞ Due to open at the end of Apr, this £96 million waterfront complex will include a huge theatre, a gallery presenting works by the eponymous artist, a children's interactive gallery and the National Industrial Centre for Virtual Reality; also a new footbridge and public plaza. Phone (0161) 955 2032 for more details.

SAMLESBURY SD6130

🏠 🐾 **Samlesbury Hall** 🖼 Well restored, half-timbered 14th-c manor house, with changing exhibitions and craft demonstrations, and sales of antiques. Meals, snacks, disabled access to ground floor only; cl Mon exc bank hols, and mid-Dec–mid-Jan; (01254) 812010; £2.50. The Myerscough Hotel (A59) is good for lunch.

SILVERDALE SD4875

★ 🐦 † 🐾 ⌒ A little-visited peaceful oasis, up beyond the attractive town of Lancaster: hilly countryside well suited both to walkers and to drivers, and a coastline that's particularly interesting to birdwatchers and naturalists. The small town looks out over the tidal sands to the Cumbrian hills, with streets of quiet houses and a church that looks 14th-c but was built barely a century ago. Various crafts are sold at the Georgian buildings of the **Wolf House Gallery** (Gibraltar), which also has an adventure playground and a courtyard garden. Snacks, some disabled access (with notice); cl 1–2pm, Mon; (01524) 701405; free. There are good woodland walks behind the town, and the Silverdale Hotel on Shore Rd is worth knowing.

🐦 ⌒ ※ **Leighton Moss Nature Reserve** (off Yealand Redmayne Rd) RSPB reserve with several roomy hides looking out on to reedbeds where bitterns, bearded tits and marsh harriers breed; good walks and views. Guided wildlife outings on Tues and Thurs evenings in August. Meals, snacks, shop, disabled access; cl 25 Dec; (01524) 701601; *£4 (RSPB members free). The Moss is also crossed by a (free) public footpath.

🏠 **Yealand Conyers Friends' Meeting House** Unobtrusively charming, in a quiet and pleasant village; the New Inn here is a popular pub.

SKIPPOOL SD3540

⚓ Lots of yachting activity in an attractive boating area, with a decent small café.

SLAIDBURN SD7152

★ ※ A perfectly preserved Forest of Bowland village: charming stone cottages, a green with the River Hodder running by, and at the opposite end an early 18th-c schoolhouse and a church with a very 18th-c feel inside. Readers enjoy the Whiteholme Victorian tearooms and the Hark to Bounty is good for lunch and has comfortable bedrooms. The B6478, and the narrow road N past Stocks Reservoir, have appealing views.

SOUTHPORT SD3217

☺ Smartish Victorian seaside resort, long famed as the most pleasant shopping town in the area, and as the place where the sea doesn't come in. In fact it comes in as often as anywhere else, but doesn't stay quite as long; this could be due to the famously mucky beach – for cleaner shores try slightly S at Formby. The promenade is set back quite a way from the sea, and looks over a man-made lake with boats. From here there are bracing trips down the **pier**, either on foot or on the little train, and there are plenty of good summer activities inc pleasure flights over the sands. Lord St is the elegant main shopping street; there's an excellent antiquarian bookshop down the Wayfarers Arcade just off it.

Pleasureland is a typical fairground, its wooden rollercoaster and new gut-wrenching Traumatiser ride well regarded by connoisseurs (£13 wristband for all rides, £8 low season).

🖼 **Atkinson Art Gallery** (Lord St) Specialises in 19th- and 20th-c watercolours, oil paintings, prints and sculpture. Shop, disabled access; cl pm Thurs and Sat, all Sun, plus bank hols; (01704) 533133; free.

👁 **British Lawnmower Museum** (Shakespeare St) Fully restored and often bizarre machines from the 1830s to the present, inc one of the first racing lawnmowers – the curator used to be a champion. Shop; cl Sun and bank hols; (01704) 535369; £1.

★ 🏵 👁 🖼 **Churchtown** Southport's villagey oldest part, with a number of pretty thatched cottages, and the lakeside **botanic gardens**, which are very attractive as well as being interesting to plantsmen; boats to hire, fernery, pets corner, and local history **museum** (open 11–3pm Tues–Fri and am wknds and bank hols; free). Just opposite, **Meols Hall** is worth a look for its paintings, inc works by Ramsey, Reynolds, Romney and Poussin. Disabled access; open pm mid-Aug–mid-Sept; (01704) 28326; £3. The Hesketh Arms across from the main gate is good for lunch.

🐾 🐦 **Southport Zoo** (Princes Park) Has one of the few snow leopards to be bred in captivity in the West, a tropical wader aviary, and a small endangered cat enclosure is due to open soon. Snacks, shop, some disabled access; cl 25 Dec; £3.

SPEKE SJ4282

🏠 ✿ **Speke Hall** Built around a square courtyard, this is one of the most beautiful and richly timbered black and white houses in the country; the inside is mainly Victorian, though there's a vast Tudor Great Hall. Restored Victorian garden. Hard to believe the centre of Liverpool is just six miles away. Meals, snacks, shop, disabled access; house open pm exc Mon Apr–Oct, plus wknds Nov–mid-Dec, garden open pm exc Mon all year; (0151) 427 7231; £4, £1.50 grounds only; NT. They do occasional roof tours to show how the timbers were put together.

STANAH SD3542

🐦 ✺ Out on the Wyre estuary, this has a stretch of waterside country with reedbeds, birds and views, attractive despite the chemical works in the background. On the opposite bank, over the toll bridge past Poulton, the Shard Bridge Inn at Hambleton is nicely placed for lunch.

STOCKPORT SJ8990

❗ **Air Raid Shelter Tours** (Chestergate) Displays include a reconstructed canteen, tool stores and first aid post, re-creating a wartime atmosphere in this labyrinth of tunnels designed to protect thousands of people during World War II; guided tours around the more remote tunnels first Weds of month at 7pm. Shop, disabled access; cl am Sun, 25–26 Dec and 1 Jan; (0161) 474 1940; £3.25. The

Arden Arms (Millgate St) has good-value food – and a great collection of working grandfather clocks.

THORNTON-CLEVELEYS SD3342

✗ 🐾 🐦 **Thornton Windmill** (B5412) This working windmill has a good range of craft shops alongside: excellent tea shop, summer wknd entertainments, even a little clog museum.

TURTON BOTTOMS SD7315

🏠 🐦 ✿ **Turton Tower** 15th-c Renaissance house with Elizabethan buildings and earlier peel tower; mostly a museum inside, but there are a couple of period rooms, and a major collection of carved wood furniture. It was interestingly extended by followers of the Romantic and later Arts and Crafts movements. Formal Victorian gardens. Snacks, shop; open daily (exc Fri) May–Sept (cl 12–1pm for lunch, and am wknds), pm Sat–Weds in Mar, Apr and Oct, and just pm Sun Nov and Feb; (01204) 852203; £3. The Strawbury Duck just N at Entwistle is prettily placed for lunch.

UPPERMILL SD9905

★ ⌂ This whole area of mill settlements in steep valleys cut through the moors is full of interest, and Uppermill itself is one of the most attractive places. Up above the town is a lonely moorland church, with good walks around it and an ancient pub opposite. Fine drives around here include the A635 over Saddleworth Moor, and B6197 Delph–Grains Bar then A672 or A640 over the moors.

🐦 🖼 **Saddleworth Museum & Art Gallery** (High St) Based around an old mill, and volunteers occasionally dress up in appropriate garb. Shop, limited disabled access; (01457) 874093; *£1.25.

WADDINGTON SD7243

★ ✝ Forest of Bowland village, with a fine **church**, and a lovely drive from Longridge. The Waddington Arms has imaginative fresh food.

WHALLEY SD7336

🏛 🏠 ✝ **Whalley Abbey** Striking remains of a 14th-c Cistercian abbey – the monks' quarters, rather than the church which has virtually disappeared – in the grounds of a 16th-c manor house used as a religious retreat (they do B & B). Two gatehouses are intact, and there's a visitor centre. Snacks, shop, disabled access; cl Christmas and New Year; (01254) 822268; £1.50. The separate 13th-c parish **church** has interesting woodwork and three ancient Celtic-Scandinavian crosses. The Freemasons Arms at Wiswell does good food.

WIGAN SD5908

✿ ⚲ ✿ ▥ **Haigh Hall Country Park** (N of Wigan) 250-acre country park with guided walks, nature trails, beautifully set golf course, craft centre, walled gardens and miniature railway. Occasional tours of house – phone for dates. Meals, snacks, shops (one excellent for golfers), some disabled access; cl 25–26 Dec; (01942) 832985; park free, charges for parking and attractions.

⌅ ♭ ! **Wigan Pier** (Wallgate) Rather different from when Orwell knew it, this is now a dynamic and entertaining wharfside centre demonstrating local life in the early 1900s, with actors performing in a reconstructed mine, pub, school, music hall, houses and even seaside. An ingenious mix of museum and theatre, it's an enormously enjoyable family day out, and you really do get a tangible impression of what life was really like at the turn of the century. Readers love it. Meals, snacks, shop, disabled access; cl Fri (exc Good Fri), 25 Dec; (01942) 323666; £6.95.

WIRRAL SJ2484

✿ ⌂ Its Merseyside parts aren't on the whole that appealing to visitors, especially on the built-up E side (with the notable exception of Port Sunlight). The NW corner can be rather more attractive, particularly along the edges of the Dee, looking across to the mountains of North Wales. The more interesting bits, inc unusual National Trust heathland, are linked by a 12-mile footpath, best joined at the **Wirral Country Park** at Thurstaston, and running down to the Cheshire parts of

the Wirral. The Irby Mill at nearby Irby has decent food.

WYCOLLER PARK SD9339

⌂ ▥ ✿ Lancashire Brontë country (the ruined hall at Wycoller features in *Jane Eyre*), with walks along a beck to Clam Bridge, an Iron Age slab, and up to Foster's Leap, a finely placed crag.

★ **Other attractive villages**, all with decent pubs and great surrounding scenery, include Goosnargh SD5537, Hurst Green SD6838, Tunstall SD6173 (Brontë church) and Wiswell SD7437. Particularly pretty ones in or on the edges of the Forest of Bowland are Gisburn SD8248, Grindleton SD7545 and Newton SD6950.

⌂ **Pubs well placed for walks** include the Hare & Hounds at Abbey Village SD6422, Pack Horse at Affetside SD7513, Bay Horse at Arkholme SD5872, Black Dog at Belmont SD6716, the Dog at Belthorn SD7224, White House on Blackstone Edge SD9716, Owd Betts at Cheesden on Ashworth Moor SD8316, Edisford Bridge on the B6243 W of Clitheroe SD7241, Ram's Head nr Denshaw SD9710, Diggle Hotel at Diglea Hamlet above Diggle itself SE0008, Wright Arms at Egerton SD7114, Strawbury Duck by Entwistle Station SD7217, Bull's Head on Grains Bar SD9608, Duke of Wellington on the B6232 west of Haslingden SD7522, Egerton Arms off the narrow Ashworth Rd above Heywood SD8513, Green Man at Inglewhite (nr Beacon Fell) SD5440, New Drop on Longridge Fell SD6439, the Romper at Ridge End above Marple SJ9686, the Kettledrum at Mereclough SD8632, the Highwayman at Nether Burrow SD6275 (pretty stretch of the Lune Valley), Old Rosins at Pickup Bank, Old Hoddlesden SD6922, the Roebuck on Roebuck Low SD9606 and the Railway at White Coppice SD6118. Up on the moors, many of these are closed during lunchtime Mon–Thurs.

Where to eat

Manchester and Liverpool both have plenty of good ethnic restaurants.

BIRKENHEAD SJ3288 **Pastime Restaurant & Premier Etage Tearooms** 42 *Hamilton Sq* (0151) 647 8095 Popular restaurant in handsome Victorian building with good food (the fixed price menu is good value), a relaxed atmosphere, and friendly helpful service; the newly opened tearooms overlook the square; cl Mon. **£25|£5.**

BISPHAM GREEN SD4813 **Eagle & Child** (01257) 462297 Striking 3-storey dark brick pub with civilised, mainly open-plan bar, fine old stone fireplaces, oriental rugs and some coir on the flagstones, handsome oak settles, imaginative food, well kept real ales, and friendly service; bowling green and croquet behind. **£20|£8.**

BLACKO SD8542 **Moorcock** (01282) 614186 Isolated old stone inn with wonderful views from big picture windows in the spaciously comfortable lounge bar, tasty generous food (inc some Austrian specialities), and efficient friendly service; cl 25 Dec; disabled access. **£15|£5.**

BLACKPOOL SD3036 **September Brasserie** 15-17 Queen St (01253) 623282 Not far from the seafront and set above a hairdresser's, this busy little airy restaurant's open-view kitchen does particularly good inventive food from a short menu, with ideas from all over the world (inc lovely puddings), and a thoughtful wine list; cl Sun, Mon. **£28|£5.90.**

CHIPPING SD6243 **Dog & Partridge** *Hesketh Lane* (01995) 61201 Spotlessly kept and relaxed dining pub with comfortable main lounge, winter log fire, good choice of enjoyable food (inc fine home-made chips), real ales, and quite a few wines and malt whiskies. **£20|3-course lunch** £11.75.

DOWNHAM SD7844 **Assheton Arms** (01200) 441227 Charmingly set dining pub in prettily preserved village; with rambling beamed bar, a massive stone fireplace, no smoking area, popular bar food (lots of good fresh fish dishes), well kept real ales, and decent wines; disabled access. **£19|£6.50.**

FENCE SD8237 **Forest** (01282) 613641 Comfortable pub with heavy panelling, lots of paintings, vases, plates, books and a big open fire, no smoking restaurant, inventive food, decent choice of wines, and friendly, helpful service; hoping to have disabled access soon. **£23.75|£6.95.**

GOOSNARGH SD5537 **Bushells Arms** *Church Lane* (01772) 865235 Friendly modernised pub close to Chingle Hall, with excellent choice of imaginative food from a constantly changing menu, and a range of wines; cl occasional Mon, 25 Dec; well behaved children only; partial disabled access. **£16|£5.**

KIRKHAM SD4232 **Cromwellian** 16 Poulton St (01772) 685680 Tiny evening restaurant in 17th-c house; with consistently good, interesting food from a fixed-price menu – thoughtful wine list, too; cl Sun, Mon, 2 wks Jun, 1 wk Oct. **£23.25.**

LIVERPOOL SJ4395 **Bechers Brook** 29a Hope St (0151) 707 0006 Popular Georgian restaurant, close to theatres, with downstairs bar, restaurant decorated with Canadian ethnic art, interesting modern cooking (pre-theatre suppers also), a carefully chosen wine list, and friendly staff; cl am Sat, Sun, Christmas, bank hols; children over 7; disabled access. **£32|£8.**

LONGRIDGE SD6137 **Paul Heathcotes** 104 Higher Rd (01772) 784969 Pretty restaurant with flowers, beams and candlelit tables in little interconnected rooms, exceptional modern British cooking, marvellous puddings, and exemplary service; cl Mon, and lunchtimes on Tues, Weds, Thurs, Sat. **£61.75 dinner, £29.25 lunch.**

MANCHESTER SJ8497 **Little Yang Sing** 17 George St (0161) 228 7722 Very busy and popular basement restaurant with super Chinese food (very good casseroles, vegetarian dishes, and dim-sum), a children's fixed menu, decent wines, and friendly service; cl 25 Dec; disabled access. **£23.50|£10.**

MANCHESTER SJ8499 **Mark Addy** Stanley St Salford (0161) 832 4080 Smart pub in converted boat waiting-rooms with a good range of food – though its choice of 50 different cheeses is the main feature; extremely big helpings, doggy-bags provided; bread and cheese £3.40.

MANCHESTER SJ8497 **Mash & Air** *40 Chorlton St (0161) 661 6161/1111* In a converted canalside mill are two restaurants on four floors with a microbrewery in the middle and three real ales to sample; Mash is informal and serves 'smart' pizzas from wood-fired ovens, grilled sandwiches, salads and so forth; cl 25–26 Dec; disabled access. **£22|£8**. Air (evenings only) is more formal and decorated in stylish blues with lots of modern art; imaginative modern cooking with influences from all over the world, plenty of New World wines, and good service; cl Sun, bank hols; disabled access. **£32**.

MANCHESTER SJ8491 **Royal Oak** *729 Wilmslow Rd, Didsbury (0161) 445 3152* Busy pub with exceptional choice of cheeses from around the world – rare to be given less than a pound; bread, cheese or pâté and salad £3.40 (not wknds); no children.

MANCHESTER SJ8398 **Simply Heathcotes** *Jackson Row, Deansgate (0161) 835 3536* Stylish modern restaurant with high ceilings, polished wood floors, bright paintings on coloured walls, and contemporary furniture; up-to-the-minute brasserie-style cooking inc very good-value set lunches, thoughtful wine list, and efficient service; cl 25 Dec, 1 Jan, bank hol Mons; disabled access. **£29.75**.

MANCHESTER SJ8497 **Yang Sing** *34 Princess St (0161) 236 2200* Exceptionally good Chinese food using the best fresh ingredients (tanks of live fish, too), wonderful dim-sum, some unusual dishes among traditional Cantonese specialities, good-value set meals, a bustling atmosphere, and efficient service; must book ahead; cl 25 Dec; disabled access. **£25**.

MELLOR SJ9888 **Oddfellows Arms** *73 Moor End Rd (0161) 449 7826* Fine old building with low ceilings, open fires and a chatty atmosphere in two flagstoned rooms, no smoking restaurant, and a wide range of interesting food inc lots of different types of fresh fish; cl 4 days over Christmas; children must be well behaved; disabled access. **£17.50|£6**.

ST MICHAEL'S ON WYRE SD4641 **Mallards** *Garstang Rd (01995) 679661* Well run and busy little restaurant in former village smithy, with reliably good straightforward food, good-value wines, and helpful service; cl lunchtimes except Sun, plus 1 wk Jan, July, Oct; disabled access. **£24.50**.

SAWLEY SD7746 **Spread Eagle** *(01220) 441202* Attractive 16th-c hotel, with fine views over the River Ribble and valley from big picture windows, a bustling bar, thoughtful wine list, and particularly good, interesting modern food in comfortable dining area; may cl Sun evening; cl 2 wks Nov; partial disabled access. **£22**/wkdy 2 courses £7.95.

THORNTON-CLEVELEYS SD3541 **River House** *Wyre Rd, Skippool Creek (01253) 883497* Delightful restaurant with long-serving owners, very good honest cooking using the freshest local ingredients, a decent wine list, fresh flowers and log fires, and fine views; bdrms; cl Sun; children over 7, must be well behaved. **£40**.

WHALLEY SD7336 **Toby Jug Tea Shop** *(01254) 823298* 300-year-old listed building with oak beams, old stone fireplaces, and wooden panelling on the upstairs walls; afternoon tea with cream and scones, cakes and cucumber sandwiches (all home-made), lots of teas and coffees, and light lunches with a fine choice of filled sandwiches and rolls; cl Sun, Mon, Christmas; children over 6. £3.85.

YEALAND CONYERS SD5074 **New Inn** *(01524) 732938* Ivy-covered stone dining pub with a log fire in the little beamed bar, and two communicating cottage dining rooms; novel daily specials, fine salads served with meals, friendly professional service, decent wines, well kept ales, and a sheltered side lawn. **£22|£8**.

Special thanks to Dave and Deborah Irving.

Lancashire Calendar

Some of these dates were provisional as we went to press. Please check information with the telephone numbers provided.

JANUARY

I **Salford** Millennium Waterfronts Festival with activities linking many new tourism and cultural venues throughout the area – *till 31 December* (0161) 7932486

11 **Lancaster** New Year's Eve Old Calendar Walk: torchlit walk with re-enactments, *starts 7pm* from John o'Gaunt Gateway (01524) 32878

FEBRUARY

6 **Manchester** Chinese New Year Street Celebration in Chinatown (01625) 618333

25 **Lancaster** Valentine's Day Old Calendar Walk: torchlit walk with re-enactments, *starts 7pm* from John o'Gaunt Gateway (01524) 32878

MARCH

2 **Accrington** Lancashire Food Festival (01254) 380298

28 **Upton** Countryside Fair at Arrowe Country Park – *till 29 March* (0151) 678 4200

APRIL

6 **Aintree** Grand National – *till 8 April* (0151) 532 2600

21 **Lancaster** Maritime Festival at the Maritime Museum and St George's Quay: sea songsters, shanty men and entertainments – *till 24 April* (01524) 582394

22 **Bacup** Britannia Coconut Dancers: thought to be pirate dances brought with miners moving north from Cornwall (01706) 226590

28 **Manchester** Millennium Festival: free outdoor festival of street entertainment, fireworks and special events – *till 4 June* (0161) 224 0020

MAY

4 **Lancaster** St George's Day Old Calendar Walk: torchlit walk with re-enactments, *starts 7pm* from John o'Gaunt Gateway (01524) 32878

13 **Lancaster** May Day Old Calendar Walk: torchlit walk with re-enactments, *starts 7pm* from John o'Gaunt Gateway (01524) 32878

19 **Accrington** Clog Dancing Festival and Competition – *till 21 May* (01254) 380298

26 **Blackpool** British Open Dance Championships – *till 2 June* (01253) 625252

JUNE

15 **Manchester** Jazz Festival – *till 30 June* (0161) 237 1010

16 **Liverpool** Mersey River Festival – *till 19 June* (0151) 233 6351

18 **Manchester to Blackpool** Veteran and Vintage and Classic Car Run (01253) 478203

Lancashire Calendar (cont.)

22 **Liverpool** The Grand Turk: replica of Horatio Hornblower's first ship – *till 28 June* (0151) 708 8838
23 **Blackpool** Championship Dog Show – *till 25 June* (01253) 478203
24 **Fulwood** Armed Forces 2000: Open day at The Queen's Lancashire Regiment with static military displays, arena displays, bands and beating the retreat (01772) 260219
30 **Carnforth** Fireworks Concert at Leighton Hall (01625) 575681

JULY

1 **Partington** Waterfront Arts Festival – *till 31 July* (0161) 237 1010
8 **Lancaster** and **Morecambe** One-man Band Shebang – *till 9 July* (01524) 582828; **Wigan** Wirral Show: free arena displays, attractions and funfair – *till 9 July* (0151) 647 2366
9 **Whalley Abbey** Open Day – *till 15 July* (01254) 822268
15 **Blackpool** Kids Megafest – *till 28 August* (01253) 625212; **Morecambe** Summerbreeze 99: jazz and soul music festival – *till 16 July* (01524) 582828
17 **Fleetwood** Tram Sunday: large transport festival, bands and side shows (01253) 876525
21 **Morecambe** Holidays in the Sun: punk festival – *till 23 July* (01524) 401552
22 **Morecambe** Peripatetic Promenaders – *till 23 July* (01524) 582828
25 **Manchester** XVII Commonwealth Games – *till 4 August* (0161) 228 2002
29 **Morecambe** Streetband Festival – *till 30 July* (01524) 582828; **St Helens** Show in Sherdley Park inc circus, live bands, craft stalls, flower show, funfair and more – *till 31 July* (01744) 456991
30 **Blackpool** Carnival Parade (01253) 693661

AUGUST

5 **Garstang** Agricultural Show (01772) 717418; **Morecambe** Festival of Light and Water – *till 6 August* (01524) 582801
6 **Blackpool** Carnival Spectacular (01253) 478203
11 **Accrington** Festival: live music in the town centre – *till 13 August* (01282) 421986
12 **Lancaster** and **Morecambe** Folklore Festival and Carnival – *till 15 August* (01524) 582828; **Rochdale** Rushbearing Ceremony – *till 13 August* (01706) 356592
17 **Saddleworth** Flower Show at Victoria Park inc live music and craft stalls – *till 19 August* (01704) 547147; **Southport** Flower Show inc live music, arena events and fireworks – *till 19 August* (01704) 547147
23 **Liverpool** International Beatles Festival – *till 29 August* (0151) 236 9091
25 **Morecambe** Worldbeat Weekend – *till 27 August* (01524) 582828
26 **Liverpool** Matthew Street Festival – *till 28 August* (0151) 236 9091
28 **Hoylake** Lifeboat Open Day with air displays, stalls and sideshows (0151) 6472366; **Lancaster** Georgian Festival Fair: inc historic re-creations and national sedan chair-carrying championships (01524) 582394

SEPTEMBER

1 **Blackpool** Illuminations – *till 5 November* (01253) 478203; **Fleetwood** Fylde Folk Festival: over 130 events – *till 3 September* (01253) 872317; **Manchester** Castlefield Carnival – *till 30 September* (0161) 237 1010

Lancashire Calendar (cont.)

2 Preston Lancashire Vintage and Country Show at Hamilton House Farm – *till 3 September* (01772) 687259

OCTOBER

5 Manchester Food and Drink Festival – *till 28 October* (0161) 832 9000

10 Lancaster Michaelmas Day Old Calendar Walk: torchlit walk with re-enactments, *starts 7pm* from John o'Gaunt Gateway (01524) 32878

22 Blackpool British Freestyle Dance Championships (01253) 478203

23 Blackpool Sequence Dance Championships – *till 26 October* (01253) 478203

24 New Brighton Classic Car Show at Fort Perch Rock Car Park: gathering of vintage, veteran and classic cars (0151) 647 2366

NOVEMBER

4 Lancaster Fireworks and Beacon Lighting (01524) 32878

10 Lancaster Halloween Old Calendar Walk: torchlit walk with re-enactments, *starts 7pm* from John o'Gaunt Gateway (01524) 32878

16 Blackpool British National Dance Championships – *till 18 November* (01253) 478203

24 Lancaster Jacobite Day: events commemorating the arrival of Bonnie Prince Charlie in 1745

DECEMBER

17 Lancaster St Nicholas Day Old Calendar Walk: torchlit walk with re-enactments, *starts 7pm* from John o'Gaunt Gateway (01524) 32878

We welcome reports from readers

This *Guide* depends on readers' reports. Do help us if you can – in return, we offer a discount on the next edition to people who've helped us with reports for it. Tell us what you think about places already in it, and anything extra you think we should say about them. And send us your ideas for inclusion in the next edition: places to visit, eat at or stay in, attractive drives or walks, maybe even unusual interesting shops you know of. Use the card in the middle, the report forms at the end, or just write – no stamp needed: *The Good Britain Guide*, FREEPOST TN1569, Wadhurst, E Sussex TN5 7BR.

LEICESTERSHIRE AND RUTLAND

Sweeping country views, grand houses and castles, some unusual places to visit – and not too many tourists.

Great houses and castles in attractive parkland and fine scenery make this a good area for a civilised break. The sweeping countryside particularly suits scenic drives or cycle rides, especially in the east: graceful patches of woodland, plenty of charming stone-built villages to potter through, delightful churches. Many of the less busy roads stride along old coach routes, with broad views. There are quite a few good walks, too – and you get out into unspoilt countryside very quickly from the built-up areas.

Rutland Water has the look of a huge natural lake, pleasant to walk around, with quite a lot of varied things to see and do around it. Elsewhere, favourite family outings include Twycross Zoo (good for apes), the Coalville discovery park and the steam railway near Market Bosworth. Among several enjoyable farm parks, the friendly, well organised one at Oadby stands out, and people also very much like the one near Oakham (though it may be changing its format this year). Some unusual visits include the Loughborough bell foundry, and Moira Furnace, emerging from major restoration this year; the Ashby Canal alongside has also been restored and re-opened.

Leicester is a good place for day visits, with lots to see – often out of the ordinary. It sets a splendid example, with its free museums policy.

Information centres here are very helpful, and bus services excellent.

Where to stay

EMPINGHAM SK9508 **White Horse** *Main St, Empingham LE15 8PS* (01780) 460221 *£63,* plus special breaks; 13 pretty rms, some in a delightfully converted stable block. Popular refurbished old pub handy for Rutland Water, with a relaxed and friendly atmosphere, big helpings of excellent food inc fine breakfasts, coffee and croissants from 8am, and cream teas all year; log fire, an attractive restaurant and efficient friendly service; cots/high chairs; good disabled access.

GLOOSTON SP7394 **Old Barn** *Main St, Glooston, Market Harborough LE16 7ST* (01858) 545215 **£49.50;** 2 rms. Attractively restored 16th-c pub with civilised décor and an open fire in the beamed main bar; charming little restaurant, super inventive food (some produce from their kitchen garden), good breakfasts, and decent real ales; pleasant walks nearby; well behaved children and dogs allowed.

HAMBLETON SK9107 **Hambleton Hall** *Hambleton, Oakham LE15 8TH* (01572) 756991 **£209;** 15 luxurious rms. In beautiful grounds by Rutland Water, this grandly restored Victorian manor house has elegant day rooms with fine views, antiques, open fires and exceptional flower arrangements; professional friendly staff, wonderful food in the no smoking restaurant, a stimulating wine list, and a marvellously pampering atmosphere; no babies in restaurant (exc for breakfast); disabled access.

KINGS MILLS SK4127 **Priest House** *Kings Mills, Castle Donington DE74 2RR* (01332) 810649 **£120w,** plus special breaks; 45 good rms, some in annexe. At the end of a country lane in a pretty spot by the River Trent, this extended, partly

11th-c hotel has a Gothic tower and arched windows and doors, a huge Adam fireplace in the comfortable library, cheerful bar, and a restaurant looking over the river; cl 27–30 Dec.

MARKET HARBOROUGH SP7387 **Three Swans** *21 High St LE16 7NJ* *(01858) 466644* **£85,** plus special breaks; 49 rms. Fine old coaching inn with a plush lounge bar, attractive conservatory and glorious courtyard; very friendly helpful staff, and good food; cl 1–3 Jan; disabled access.

MEDBOURNE SP7992 **Nevill Arms** *Medbourne, Market Harborough LE16 8EE* *(01858) 565288* **£50;** 8 rms, 6 in separate cottage and barn conversion. Bright and busy, old mullion-windowed inn just across a footbridge over the stream; excellent food, lots of bar games, friendly prompt service, and an inglenook log fire; cl 25 Dec; disabled access.

OAKHAM SK8608 **Whipper-In** *Market Pl, Oakham LE15 6DT* *(01572) 756971* ***£75,** plus special breaks; 24 rms. Attractive and well run 17th-c stone coaching inn with oak-beamed and panelled lounge opening into a cosy eating area, log fires, good food in the neat restaurant, and well kept ales; disabled access.

PACKINGTON SK3512 **Springs Hydro** *Packington, Ashby-de-la-Zouch LE65 1TG* *(01530) 273873* **£89.95** inc full use of all facilities, plus special breaks; 57 rms. Britain's first purpose-built health hydro with all the amenities, good healthy food, and friendly staff; cl 20–27 Dec; no children; disabled access.

ROTHLEY SK5712 **Rothley Court** *LE7 7LG* *(0116) 237 4141* **£95;** 32 rms (the ones in the main house have more character). Mentioned in the Domesday Book, this carefully run manor house, with its beautifully preserved 13th-c chapel, has some fine oak panelling, open fires, a comfortable bar, conservatory, a terrace and garden, and courteous staff; disabled access.

SAXELBYE SK7020 **Saxelbye Manor House** *Church Lane, Saxelbye, Melton Mowbray LE14 3PA* *(01664) 812269* ***£42;** 3 rms, 1 with own bthrm. Attractive old house (parts several hundred years old) with marvellous Victoriana, and a long passage leading to a fine Elizabethan oak stairway built in the old stone stairwell; helpful and friendly owner, and very good traditional evening meals and breakfasts; cl Dec–Mar.

STAPLEFORD SK8118 **Stapleford Park** *Stapleford, Melton Mowbray LE14 2EF* *(01572) 787522* **£235;** 51 lavishly decorated rms, plus cottage. Luxurious country house, extravagantly restored, in lovely large grounds, with lots of mahogany, opulent furnishings, fine oil paintings and impressive library, good restaurant food, enthusiastic American owner, and warmly welcoming staff; health spa, indoor swimming pool, riding, stabling, tennis, croquet, miniature golf (and newly opened golf academy), coarse fishing, clay-pigeon shooting, hunting; cots/babysitting; dogs welcome; disabled access.

STRETTON SK9416 **Ram Jam Inn** *Great North Rd, Stretton LE15 7QY* *(01780) 410776* ***£64.90;** 7 comfortable and well equipped rms. Actually on the A1, this civilised place has a comfortable, airy, modern lounge bar blending into a wine-bar-like eating area, a good choice of food quickly served all day, and a useful small wine list; cl 25 Dec.

UPPINGHAM SP8699 **Lake Isle** *16 High St E, Uppingham, Oakham LE15 9PZ* *(01572) 822951* ***£74,** plus special breaks; 12 rms with home-made biscuits, sherry and fresh fruit, and two cottage suites. In a charming market town, this 18th-c restaurant-with-rooms has an open fire in the attractive pink-walled lounge, a little bar (once a barber's where the schoolboys had their hair cut), excellent food in the pine-walled country restaurant (delicious breakfasts, too), a fine, carefully chosen wine list, and a small, pretty garden.

Please let us know what you think of places in the *Guide*. Use the report forms at the back of the book or simply write us a letter.

To see and do

LEICESTERSHIRE Family Attraction of the Year

🐏 **OADBY** SK6102 **Farmworld** 🖼 Nicely set in charming countryside, this is one of the best of its kind, a particularly well organised working farm with a good range of traditional farm animals and rare breeds. As with most farms, it's children between around 3 and 10 who'll appreciate it best, but we know of plenty of adults who've visited without children and enjoyed it immensely. You can feed most of the inhabitants (they sell food, but don't mind you bringing sensible offerings from home), and they usually have some kind of baby or young animals all year round. Small children enjoy the rabbit warren, while at the opposite end of the scale are some magnificent shire horses. Milking displays most days, and good play areas for younger children, including an indoor sandpit and toy tractor park. Though some areas are under cover, it's better in fine weather. The pub is an unusual feature – it's an enjoyable pastiche of an Edwardian alehouse, with plenty of period memorabilia. Meals, snacks, shop, disabled access; cl Christmas–New Year; (0116) 271 0355; £4 (£2.50 children 3–16) – the price has remained unchanged for some years now.

ARNESBY SP6192
✕ **Arnesby windmill** Handsomely preserved, well worth a look.

ASHBY CANAL SK3707
⌂ The towpath has good countryside walking, with green fields and stone-arched bridges, as well as coots, moorhens, herons and maybe even the flash of a kingfisher. The best parts run from the tunnel under Snarestone past Gopsall Park, and then on through Shackerstone and Congerstone to pass Shenton Park on an embankment, before heading into Warwickshire and its junction with the Coventry Canal. It also makes an ideal walking link between Bosworth battlefield and the steam railway to the N.

ASHBY-DE-LA-ZOUCH SK3516
🏛 ⛓ **Ashby-de-la-Zouch Castle** The Norman core and its 15th-c extension were largely destroyed in the Civil War, but the ruins are impressive, and the adjoining fields were the setting for Sir Walter Scott's *Ivanhoe*. Bring a torch for the underground passage. Shop, limited disabled access; cl 24–26 Dec, 1 Jan, and Mon and Tues Nov–Mar; (01530) 413343; £2.50; EH. There's a little **museum** (open Easter–Oct) next to the tourist information centre on North St, and the Royal Hotel has a good-value carvery.

BELVOIR SK8133
🏛 ❀ **Belvoir Castle** Pronounced 'Beaver', this is best from the outside, a glorious fantasy of turrets and battlements, pinnacles and towers, surrounded by terraced gardens peopled with sculptures. Inside, only a couple of rooms are grand enough to impress, and some of the contents are starting to look a little shabby. Meals, snacks, shop, limited disabled access – it's quite a walk up the hill; cl Mon (exc bank hols), Fri, and Oct–Mar; (01476) 870262; £5. The Peacock at Redmile not far off is excellent for lunch. Good drives on fine old coach roads centre on Belvoir: for instance, from Long Benington (Lincs) through Bottesford, Harby and Hose, or via Knipton down through Eastwell and past Grimston all the way to Barrow upon Soar, where the Navigation is a useful pub.

BOTTESFORD SK8139
† **Bottesford church** Full of elaborate tombs and monuments; they had to raise the roof to fit them all in.

BREEDON ON THE HILL SK4023
† 🏛 **Breedon on the Hill church** On an interesting, partly quarried Iron Age hill fort, this has some unique Anglo-Saxon carvings.

BURROUGH ON THE HILL SK7510
⌂ ❋ 🏛 **Burrough Hill** has an enjoyable path along its escarpment. The summit has splendid views, and an imposing Iron Age hill fort, its high ramparts still largely intact (50p parking charge).

CHARNWOOD FOREST SK4515

✳ ◠ **Charnwood Forest views** The friendly Bull's Head (on the former B587 Whitwick–Copt Oak road), with a big garden and lots of animals, has fine views over surviving remnants of this former hunting park, popular for walks; the Copt Oak pub itself, over on the B591, is also a useful base for walks.

CLIPSHAM SK9716

🐾 ! **Yew Tree Avenue** (just E, off Castle Bytham Rd) Readers are fascinated by this delightfully quirky avenue of 150 yew trees, clipped in sometimes bizarre shapes to represent animals, characters and events; free. The surrounding woods are full of deer (not to mention bluebells in spring).

COALVILLE SK4114

🚂 ! 🎴 ✌ 🎵 **Snibston Discovery Park** (Ashby Rd) Busy 100-acre centre based around a former colliery (the first shaft was sunk by George and Robert Stephenson), with fun exhibitions and interactive displays on a hugely varied range of topics connected to science and industry. Children like the Science Alive gallery best, with plenty of hands-on experiments and activities (inc the illusion of cycling with a skeleton), while similarly organised galleries look at transport, mining, and fashion. The landscaped grounds include a huge play area and nature reserve, with extra charges for golf, fishing, and tours of the mine workings by former pitmen. Snacks, shop, disabled access; cl 25–26 Dec and 1 wk in Jan – phone to check; (01530) 510851; £4.75. The Birch Tree (A50) has good-value food.

COTTESMORE SK8913

🚂 🚃 ◠ ★ **Rutland Railway Museum** Nearly 40 industrial steam and diesel locomotives, and 60 other wagons and vehicles used in the ironstone quarries and industry. Occasional steam rides, and quite a nice lineside walk to the old Oakham Canal. Snacks, shop, disabled access; open wknds and bank hols – best to tel (01572) 813203 for dates of steam days; *£3. The Sun in the pretty village is good for lunch.

DESFORD SK4704

🐦 🎴 **Tropical Bird Gardens** (Lindridge Lane) This pleasant five-acre woodland garden is a favourite of some of our readers, with over 50 different species, many in walk-through aviaries; the free-flying macaws are particularly spectacular – they may even perch on your shoulder. There are plans for a penguin pool. Snacks, shop, disabled access; cl Oct–Easter (01455) 824603; £3.

DONINGTON LE HEATH SK4212

🏚 🎴 **Donington le Heath Manor House** One of the very rare examples of an almost untouched medieval manor house, pretty much unaltered since it was built in 1280. Developing 17th-c style gardens inc a decorative maze. Snacks, shop; disabled access to ground floor only, cl 25–26 Dec, 1 Jan; (01530) 831259; free.

DONINGTON PARK SK4225

🏎 **Donington Collection** Largest private collection of single-seat racing cars in the world, with vehicles driven by all the greats, and related memorabilia. The price means you really have to be a racing fan to appreciate it. Meals, snacks, shop, some disabled access; cl 25–26 Dec, 1 Jan; (01332) 811027; £7. The Nag's Head is a good dining pub.

EXTON SK9110

🎴 ★ † **Barnsdale Gardens** (The Avenue) Familiar to viewers of *Gardeners' World*; they were developed on the programme by the late Geoff Hamilton. The interesting plants are grown organically using peat-free compost, and there are plenty of useful ideas and techniques. Coffee shop, nursery, disabled access; gardens cl Nov–Feb (nursery only cl Christmas week); (01572) 813200; *£5, ticket required for wknds and bank hols, best to phone. S of here towards the A606, the Barnsdale Lodge Hotel has good food, comfortable bedrooms and a neighbouring antique centre. In the opposite direction, Exton village is a handsome collection of thatched houses surrounding a tree-studded green, with pleasant walks around; the attractive **church** is beautifully placed in a park, and the Fox & Hounds has decent home cooking.

EYEBROOK RESERVOIR SP8595

🐦 🎣 Rewarding for birdspotters and fishermen, though as it has no hides or facilities appeals mainly to true enthusiasts.

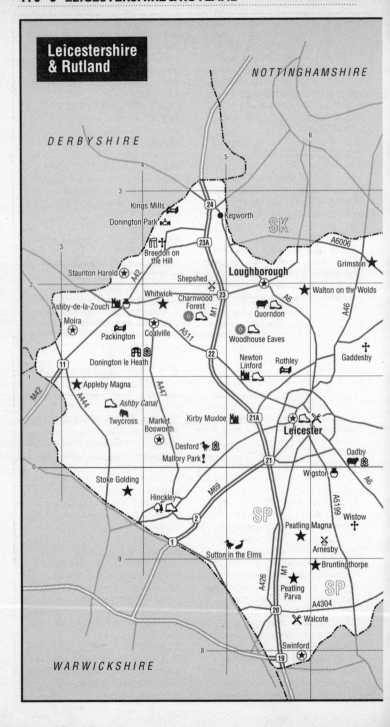

Leicestershire & Rutland

NOTTINGHAMSHIRE

DERBYSHIRE

SK

Kings Mills
Donington Park
Kegworth

Breedon on
the Hill

Staunton Harold
Shepshed
Loughborough
Grimston

Whitwick
Charnwood
Forest
Walton on the Wolds

Ashby-de-la-Zouch
Quorndon

Moira
Coalville
Woodhouse Eaves

Packington
Gaddesby

Donington le Heath
Newton
Linford
Rothley

Appleby Magna

Ashby Canal

Twycross
Market
Bosworth
Kirby Muxloe
Leicester

Desford
Oadby

Mallory Park

Wigston

Stoke Golding

Hinckley
Wistow

Peatling Magna

Sutton in the Elms
Arnesby

Bruntingthorpe

Peatling
Parva

Walcote

Swinford

WARWICKSHIRE

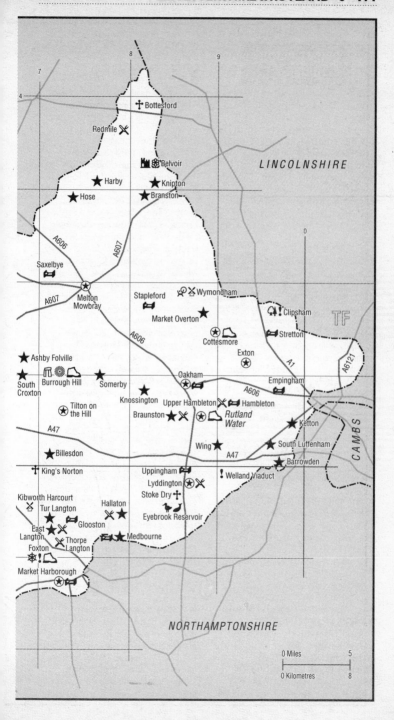

LINCOLNSHIRE

✝ Bottesford

Redmile ✕

🏰⚜ Belvoir

★ Harby
★ Knipton

★ Hose
★ Branston

A606
A607

Saxelbye 🛏

A607
★ Melton Mowbray

★ Stapleford
⚜✕ Wymondham

🛏 Market Overton
★

⚐✕ Clipsham
TF

Cottesmore ⚐🏕

🛏 Stretton

Exton
⚐

A1

★ Ashby Folville

🏛⚜🏕 Burrough Hill
★ Somerby

A6121

South Croxton
★

⚐ Tilton on the Hill

★ Knossington
Oakham ⚐🛏

A606
Empingham

★ Braunston
Upper Hambleton ✕
⚐🏕 Hambleton

✕ *Rutland Water*

★ Ketton

A47

Wing ★
A47
★ South Luffenham

★ Billesdon

★ Barrowden

CAMBS

✝ King's Norton

Uppingham 🛏
! Welland Viaduct

Kibworth Harcourt
✕

Lyddington ⚐✕

Tur Langton
★

Hallaton
✕ ★

Stoke Dry ✝

⚐ Eyebrook Reservoir

East Langton
★

✕ Glooston
★

Foxton
⚐!

🛏 ★ Medbourne

✝ Thorpe Langton

Market Harborough
⚐🛏

NORTHAMPTONSHIRE

0 Miles   5
0 Kilometres   8

FOXTON SP6989

❋ ! ⌂ **Foxton Canal Museum** Next to an interesting staircase flight of locks, and based around the extraordinary Victorian steam-powered boat lift built to avoid using the lock and so save water – now being restored, they hope to have it up and running by 2011! Meals, snacks, shop, some disabled access; cl winter Mon and Tues; (0116) 279 2657; site free, museum £2. Bridge 61 at the bottom of the locks has basic food and welcomes children (lots of ducks – take plenty of bread). The locks are a good focus for Grand Union Canal towpath walks. The reservoir over at Saddington is a pretty spot, and the Queen's Head there is a popular dining pub.

GADDESBY SK6812

✝ **Gaddesby church** Notable for its elaborate 13th-c workmanship.

HINCKLEY SP4594

🐾 ⌂ **Burbage Common & Woods** (off A47, just E) Ancient forest with lots of footpaths (some accessible by wheelchair), observation hides, and spectacular ground flora. Visitor centre open Sun, pm Sat, Tues and Thurs Apr–Nov, plus Mon and Fri Jun–Aug; (01455) 633712; free.

KEGWORTH SK4826

Country drive The Cap & Stocking in Kegworth is an interesting old tavern, at the start of a pleasant drive through the Leakes, Wysall, Widmerpool, Kinoulton, Colston Bassett (just over the Notts border – the Martins Arms is the best lunch stop of all), Granby and Orston.

KIBWORTH HARCOURT SP6894

✖ **Kibworth Harcourt windmill** The county's only remaining post mill, a fine example from the early 18th c. The Three Horseshoes is good for lunch. The old coach road through Kibworth from Uppingham (another nice little town with well known school and old church) and on to Kilby, Countesthorpe and Cosby is a fine long-striding drive.

KING'S NORTON SK6800

✝ **King's Norton church** A graceful Gothic Revival building.

KIRBY MUXLOE SK5204

🏰 **Kirby Muxloe Castle** Peaceful 15th-c ruins, barely used by their original owner before he was executed.

Shop, disabled access; open wknds and bank hols (exc 1–2pm) Apr–Nov; (0116) 238 6886; £1.85. The Royal Oak is useful for lunch.

LEICESTER SK5804

🏛 🐾 👶 🖼 ⌂ In this busy city's mix of ancient and modern, it's the modern which makes the most immediate impression. But a bit of digging around among the shops, office blocks and traffic schemes does turn up reminders of its long and varied past – most notable among some fine old buildings is the 14th-c Guildhall. In stark contrast and hurtling full pelt into the future, the strikingly modern building of the National Space Science Centre (Abbey Meadows) will house an exhibition centre with collections of space artefacts, a planetarium, and a learning centre with simulated space missions, when it opens next spring. The city's staunch defence of free entrance to museums, etc, while places elsewhere are increasingly demanding a fee, is most attractive. Besides those described individually, good ones include **Newarke Houses** (The Newarke), where there's a quiet period garden, and the **Leicestershire Museum & Art Gallery** (New Walk), which has a collection of German Expressionist art that for this country must be unique and a Discovery Room with interactive displays for children; both open as Jewry Wall (see p.413). The **Jain Centre** (Oxford St) has some fantastic examples of traditional Indian architecture (disabled access; open pm wkdys; (0116) 254 3091; donations, maybe introducing a charge). The Hindu temple on Narborough Rd is reckoned to be one of the finest outside India. Towpath walks along both the Grand Union Canal and the River Soar give a relatively tranquil back view of the city's industrial life. The Welford Place (on Welford Pl) serves good food all day.

↓T **Abbey Pumping Station** (Corporation Rd) Redeveloped as a museum of public health with some bizarre displays inc the Flush With Pride exhibition, where you flush imitation faeces down a see-through loo to follow their movements through the drains. Shop, disabled access to ground floor only; cl am Sun and Christmas; (0116) 299 5111; free (maybe small charge on days when beam engines in steam).

Belgrave Hall (Church Rd, Leicester's N edge) A fine example of 18th-c architecture, furnished with period pieces. Charming gardens. Shop, disabled access to ground floor and gardens; cl am Sun, 24–26 Dec, 1 Jan; (0116) 266 6590; free.

Eco House (Western Park, Hinckley Rd) From the outside, this 1930s former park-keeper's lodge resembles any other ordinary house, but inside it's a showcase for energy-efficient and environment-friendly living. Recent heritage grants have allowed them to add solar panels, a lift and toilets for disabled people, and a new café and shop. When it re-opens around Feb, there'll even be a family in residence; organic garden. Cl Mon, Tues and am Weds–Fri; (0116) 222 0239; donations.

Gas Museum (Aylestone Rd) Comprehensive study of the industry and its application, from cookers and washing machines to hairdryers and magic lanterns. Shop, disabled access to ground floor only; open pm Tues–Fri (though cl Tues after bank hols and 24 Dec–1 Jan); (0116) 250 3190; free.

Gorse Hill City Farm (Anstey Lane) Friendly little community farm with the usual animals and activities, and developing organic garden. Meals, snacks, disabled access; (0116) 253 7582; donations.

Jewry Wall Museum & Site (St Nicholas Circle) Site of 2nd-c Roman baths, the courtyard now excavated to reveal porticoes and shops sheltered by the remains of a massive stone wall. Excellent collections of mosaic pavements and painted wall plaster. Shop, disabled access with prior arrangement; cl am Sun, 24–26 Dec; (0116) 247 3021; free.

Wygston's House Museum of Costume (Applegate) Reconstructed 1920s draper's shop and entertainingly displayed English costume from the 17th c to the present; you may be able to try some on. Shop, disabled access to ground floor only; cl am Sun, 24–26 Dec and 1 Jan; (0116) 247 3056; free.

LOUGHBOROUGH SK5419

Bell Foundry Museum (Freehold St) Part of the largest working bell foundry in the world, with a quite remarkable array of bells in the tuning room. Shop, disabled access; cl 12.30–1.30pm, Mon (exc bank hols), wknds and winter exc by arrangement; (01509) 233414; £1.50 (£3.80 for tour of the works).

Great Central Railway (Great Central Rd) Main line steam railway to Leicester, with a museum this end. Meals, snacks, shop, disabled access; no trains wkdys Oct–May (exc Easter hols) – best to phone; (01509) 230726; £8.50. The Swan in the Rushes (A6) has good home cooking.

LYDDINGTON SP8796

★ **Bede House** An attractive stone-built village. Handsome 15th-c **Bede House** was a residence of the Bishops of Lincoln until the Reformation. Notable carved ceilings, 15th-c glass, and tranquil garden. Shop, disabled access to ground floor only; cl Nov–Mar; (01572) 822438; £2.50. The Old White Hart is a pleasant place for lunch.

MALLORY PARK SK4500

Mallory Park Circuit Motor sport meetings every wknd Mar–Oct, a splendid spectacle if your idea of a day at the races doesn't involve horses – only horsepower. Meals, snacks, shop, disabled access; (01455) 842931; from £7. The Royal Arms at Sutton Cheney is the nearest good eating place.

MARKET BOSWORTH SK3706

Battlefield Steam Railway Line Runs from Shackerstone through Market Bosworth to Shenton by Bosworth Battlefield, a rather nice return trip of just over 9 miles. There's a Victorian tearoom at the Shackerstone end (open Tues–Sun), and some displays. Trains usually run wknds and bank hols Mar–Oct, plus Weds and Fri Jul–Aug; (01827) 880754 for timetable; £5 return.

★ **Bosworth Battlefield Visitor Centre & Country Park** Site of the deciding action in the War of the Roses, when Richard III's defeat led to the Tudors' seizing the English throne. The centre has explanatory films and exhibitions, as well as a detailed trail following the sites of the fighting (now thought to be ever so slightly out). Also an exhibition of armory from the *Mary Rose*. Meals, snacks, shop, disabled access; cl Nov–Mar; (01455) 290429; £2.80. The Royal Arms at nearby Sutton Cheney has good food. Market Bosworth village itself is interesting to walk through, and the Black Horse (by the market square alms houses) has worthwhile food.

MARKET HARBOROUGH SP7387
★ ☗ ✝ An attractive market town which used to specialise in the production of corsets; bizarre, florid and even agonising examples can be seen in the **town museum** (shop, disabled access with notice; cl am Sun, Good Fri and 24–26 Dec; free). The centre has some fine old Georgian buildings, and above them the gracefully soaring 14th-c spire of the church. The Three Swans Hotel is a nice old coaching inn and does decent lunches.
✝ **Little Bowden church** (outskirts, nr Sainsburys) Handsome 12th-c church, set off charmingly by its fine old rectory. The adjacent Cherry Tree has good-value food.

MELTON MOWBRAY SK7519
✝ Stilton cheese, pork pies and the Quorn hunt all originate in this little town, which also has a particularly distinguished church, **St Mary's** (Burton St). Beside it the attractive Anne of Cleves has good-value food. Dickinson & Morris (Nottingham St) still make the pies to a traditional recipe.
☗ **Melton Carnegie Museum** (Thorpe End) Celebrates Melton Mowbray's fashionable 19th-c days. Shop, disabled access; cl am Sun, Good Fri and 25–26 Dec; free.
🏚 **Websters' Dairy** (Saxelbye SK6921) This is a good place to buy Stilton. In the next village of Grimston, the Black Horse has decent food and a remarkable collection of cricket memorabilia.

MOIRA SK3115
🗘 **Heart of the National Forest Visitor Centre** Along the same road as Moira Furnace (see below), this shows progress on the ambitious plan for vast new tracts of traditional broadleafed woodland (restaurant, shop, disabled access; (01283) 216633;

£2.95). The Rawdon Arms out here is useful for lunch.
🗘 T ⚘ **Moira Furnace & Craft Workshops** (B5003 W of Ashby) As we went to press, this 19th-c blast furnace was undergoing major restoration. New developments include interactive displays explaining the operation of the furnace, the first stretch of the Ashby Canal to be reopened in the county, and improved tearoom and playground facilities. There are also a few craft workshops in the grounds. Snacks, shop, disabled access; cl Mon, Tues, best to check opening times; (01283) 224667; £3. The canal towpath links the furnace to the attractions listed under Market Bosworth.

NEWTOWN LINFORD SK5210
🏛 ◠ **Bradgate Country Park** This extensive tract of the former Charnwood Forest hunting park is little changed over the last 750 years. At its heart are the ruins of the 15th-c home of Lady Jane Grey, and a visitor centre tells her sad story. Shop, limited disabled access; visitor centre cl am, Mon, and wkdys Nov–Mar; (0116) 234 1850; pay and display parking, visitor centre £1.20. The entrance off the B5328 N of Cropston has better lavatories than the main entrance on the B5327. Fallow deer still roam these heathy slopes among the rock outcrops, and there's general access, plenty of waymarked paths, and lots of opportunities for picnics. Nearby Cropston Reservoir has waterfowl. The Pear Tree in Woodhouse Eaves has good food.

OADBY SK6102
🐖 **Farmworld** See separate family panel on p.408.
❀ **University Botanic Gardens** (Stoughton Drive South) Set around student halls of residence, these university gardens are 16 acres filled with a wide variety of plants in different and delightful settings, inc a hardy fuchsia collection. Plant sales, some disabled access; cl wknds and bank hols; (0116) 271 7725; free. The Grange Farm (Florence Wragg Way) has imaginative food.

OAKHAM SK8608
★ Now that Rutland has won its battle

for independence from Leicestershire, this is a county town again. It's an attractive small town with a good sense of country bustle about it and one or two interesting antique shops. By the church, the 17th-c Wheatsheaf has decent food, and Barnsdale Lodge (just off A606 E) does good lunches. There's a fine drive through Ashwell, Wymondham and Waltham on the Wolds to Harby.

🏛️🖼️ **Oakham Castle** The magnificent Norman banqueting hall is all that's left of the building, but earthworks and walls give a good idea of what it must have been like. The hall itself is decorated with a droll collection of extraordinary horseshoes, some grossly opulent, some simply enormously oversized. Shop, disabled access; cl am Sun, am Nov–Mar, Good Fri, 25–26 Dec; (01572) 723654; free.

🖼️ **Rutland County Museum** (Catmose St) The emphasis is on rural life, though there are some Roman and Saxon finds. Snacks, shop, disabled access; cl am Sun, 25–26 Dec and Good Fri; (01572) 723654; free.

🐃 **Rutland Farm Park** (Uppingham Rd) This well liked place may change its format and opening hours this year – phone for details (01572) 756789.

QUORNDON SK5415

🐃 ⌂ **Whatoff Lodge** (Woodhouse, then E towards Quorn) There's a decent nature trail around this working farm; cl Mon (exc bank hols), and mid-Oct–mid-Mar; (01509) 412127; £2. The Pear Tree at Woodhouse Eaves is the best nearby place for lunch.

RUTLAND WATER SK9308

🦋 **Butterfly & Aquatic Centre** 🖼️ off A606 Empingham–Whitwell) Next to the main Rutland Water information centre, there's a butterfly house with a good water feature, and various other insects and reptiles; also a video on the reservoir's construction in the 1970s. Snacks, shop, disabled access; cl Nov–Mar; (01780) 460515; *£3.

⛴️ 🎣 ✝️ 🖼️ **Rutland Water** Europe's biggest man-made lake, oddly shaped, with a number of attractions. On the N side of the lake are nature trails, an unusual drought garden created by the late Geoff Hamilton, places to hire bikes, and hourly **boat trips**. The White Horse at Empingham is good for lunch, and other handy dining places are the Finches Arms at Upper Hambleton (the best views over the water), and the Noel Arms at Whitwell. You can fish in various parts of the water, and there's a fishing centre down at Normanton, as well as a small **museum** in a church modelled on London's St John's, Smith Sq. The refreshingly informal Normanton Park Hotel here has decent food.

🦅 ⌂ **Rutland Water Egleton Reserve** 🖼️ This nine-mile reserve is divided into two parts. The part at Egleton is aimed at the more serious birdwatcher (with a comfortable purpose-built observation centre – several breeding pairs of ospreys have now been settled here, the first in England for generations). Varied talks, walks and events; (01572) 770651; open usually every day (shop, excellent

---

Days Out

Leicester city freebies: Jewry Wall Museum; Wygston's House Costume Museum; lunch at Welford Place (Welford Pl); Leicestershire Museum & Art Gallery; Belgrave Hall.

Apes, steamtrains and battleground: Twycross Zoo; lunch at the Cock at Sibson; steamtrain from Shackerstone to Bosworth Battlefield.

The miniature county: Oakham, inc Rutland Farm Park; Rutland Railway Museum at Cottesmore; lunch at Barnsdale Lodge at Barnsdale; antique centre there; Barnsdale Gardens towards Exton, then Exton village – or Rutland Water for a boat trip and/or walk along the water's edge and a visit to the Butterfly & Aquatic Centre there.

disabled access; cl 25 Dec; £3, £2 after 1pm).

△ ⚲ **Rutland Water Lyndon Reserve** The Lyndon part of this nine-miled tract (off the Lyndon–Manton rd) is for the general public (with a useful visitor centre, and maybe summer Sun crafts). Varied talks, walks and events; (01572) 737378; reserve usually open all year, visitor centre open all wknds, plus wkdys exc Mon in summer (£1.20).

SHEPSHED SK4618

✗ **Shepshed windmill** Handsomely preserved, well worth a look.

STAUNTON HAROLD SK3720

★ ⚲ † (off B587 N of Ashby) In this pretty village the **Ferrers Centre** has enjoyable craft shops around a striking Georgian courtyard and special events most summer Suns (cl Mon exc bank hols, plus 25–26 Dec, 1 Jan; free). The **church** out here (owned by the NT) was one of the few built during the Commonwealth; open pm Sat–Weds and bank hols Apr–Sept, plus pm wknds in Oct.

SUTTON IN THE ELMS SP5093

☌ ♪ **Falconry Centre** (Mill on the Soar, Coventry Rd) Flying demonstrations of owls, hawks, falcons and buzzards; they really try to get the audience involved. On the same site are a fishing lake and thriving family dining pub. Shop, disabled access; cl Mon, 25–26 Dec; (01455) 285924; £2.

SWINFORD SP5879

🏛 ⌂ † ⚲ **Stanford Hall & Motorcycle Museum** 5,000 books line the library of this handsome 17th-c house, an elegant place that still keeps a cosy lived-in atmosphere. Highlights are the painted ceiling in the ballroom, the portraits that accompany the winding grand staircase, and a good costume collection. The excellent motorcycle museum is in the grounds, which also have a lovely 14th-c church with splendid stained glass, walled rose garden, Sun craft centre, and a replica of the first successful flying machine in the country. Snacks, shop, limited disabled access; open pm wknds, bank hols and Tues after bank hols, Easter–Sept; (01788) 860250; house and grounds £4, grounds only £2.20, motorcycle museum £1 extra. The Cherry Tree at Catthorpe (cl Mon, Tues lunchtime) has

good-value food.

TILTON ON THE HILL SK7505

🐄 ♪ 🐾 † **Halstead House Farm & British Pony Centre** (Oakham Rd) Farm animals including some rare breeds, and every breed of British pony (rides at wknds). Also nature trail along a disused railway, fishing lake, gardens, and they also do tractor rides. Meals, snacks, well stocked farm shop (game and other fresh meats), disabled access; cl Mon, and all Oct–Mar; (0116) 259 7239; £3. The village **church** is notable, and the Rose & Crown is handy for lunch.

TWYCROSS SK3305

🐒 **Twycross Zoo Park** 🅿 (A444) Specialises in primates, with an enormous range of apes, gibbons, orang-utans, and chimpanzees – every shape, size and species. Plenty of other animals too, inc giraffes, sealions, elephants and penguins; the reptile house is 20p extra. Can get crowded on summer afternoons. Meals, snacks, shop, disabled access; cl 25 Dec; (01827) 880250; £6 (£4 children).

WELLAND VIADUCT SP9197

❗ (nr Seaton) One of the county's most striking sights: nearly a mile long, swooping across the pastures of the valley, it is the country's longest viaduct.

WIGSTON SP6099

⌘ **Framework Knitters' Museum** (Bushloe End) A restored 18th-c knitters' house and workshop, with original hand frames. Open pm Sun and first Sat of month, plus most bank hols (also by appointment); (0116) 288 3396; £1. The Royal Oak has cheap food.

WOODHOUSE EAVES SK5114

❊ △ **Beacon Hill Country Park** This is a good surviving chunk of the former vast Charnwood Forest hunting park. The hill itself (above Woodhouse Eaves) is one of the best viewpoints in the area – an intriguing mix of the industrial and the very rural; it's a popular local beauty-spot, rising almost like a volcano above its lower woodland slopes. From the 245-metre (800-ft) summit, the Jubilee Walk heads N and E through partly wooded country. A trail S makes a small circuit around Broombriggs Farm with boards explaining farming methods by the path (£1 car park charge). The Wheatsheaf is handy for lunch.

WYMONDHAM SK8518

✗ ♫ **Wymondham windmill** One of only four six-sailed mills in the country, with tearoom, craft shops and disabled access; cl Mon exc bank hols, and wkdys Nov–Mar; free.

★ **Other attractive villages**, all with decent pubs, include Appleby Magna SK3109, Ashby Folville SK7011, Barrowden SK9400, Billesdon SK7202, Branston SK8129, Braunston SK8306, Bruntingthorpe SP6089, East Langton SP7292, Grimston SK6821, Hallaton SP7896, Harby SK7531, Hose SK7329, Ketton SK9704 (good walks), Knipton SK8231, Knossington SK8008, Market Overton SK8816, Medbourne SP7993 (interesting church too), Peatling Magna SP5992 and Peatling Parva SP5889,

Somerby SK7710, South Croxton SK6810, South Luffenham SK9402, Stoke Golding SP3997, Tur Langton SP7194, Walton on the Wolds SK5919, Whitwick SK4316, and Wing SK8902, notable for its small medieval turf maze. Stoke Dry SP8596 and Wistow SP6496 have fine churches.

◠ **Pubs useful for walks** here include the Pear Tree and Bull's Head in Woodhouse Eaves SK5214; and, all handy for canals, the George & Dragon at Stoke Golding SP3997, Soar Bridge in Barrow upon Soar SK5717, the Griffin at Congerstone SK3605, and the Navigation at Kilby Bridge SP6097. The Cove Inn spectacularly overlooking the Stoney Cove diving centre nr Stoney Stanton SP4894 is an attractive spot for something to eat.

Where to eat

BRAUNSTON SK8306 **Old Plough** *(01572) 722714* Flower-decked stone inn with a pubby atmosphere, traditional bar with heavy beams, stylishly modern, no smoking conservatory, seasonally changing and well presented, imaginative food, good beers and a well noted wine list; seats out under the fruit trees; boules; disabled access. **£20**|**£6.95**.

COTTESMORE SK9013 **Sun** *(01572) 812321* This 17th-c stone-built thatched village pub has a few tables in the rooms off the bar (best to get there early, or even book), a warm fire in the stone inglenook, sunny yellow walls with some nice sporting prints and other pictures, stripped pine furnishings, imaginative food, real ales, decent wines, and friendly, helpful service; tables and boules in garden. **£19.70**|**£5.95**.

EAST LANGTON SP7292 **Bell** *(01858) 545278* Pretty creeper-covered inn with an inviting atmosphere, a warming log fire and plain wooden tables in the long stripped stone bar, imaginative food from a seasonally changing menu, OAP weekday lunches, a no smoking dining room, well kept real ales, and friendly, efficient service; cl 25 Dec; partial disabled access. **£22**|**£5.50**.

HALLATON SP7896 **Bewicke Arms** *(01858) 555217* Thatched cottage by the village green, with a warm welcome and traditional feel in its two beamed bar rooms, generous helpings of popular food inc fine puddings, well kept real ales, and friendly service; they've now opened a tearoom and gift shop in the converted stables, and a small farm park walk; cl 25 Dec; bdrms; no dogs. **£18**|**£6.80**.

LEICESTER SK5804 **Welford Place** 9 Welford Pl *(0116) 247 0758* Once a Victorian gentlemen's club, this friendly place offers full meals in the civilised high-ceilinged restaurant, as well as a spacious bar with enjoyable food served all day – breakfast, snacks and light meals, morning coffee and afternoon tea; efficient service; cl Sun; disabled access. **£20.50**|**£6.50**.

LYDDINGTON SP8797 **Old White Hart** *(01572) 821703* Warm and welcoming 17th-c village inn with just three tables in front of the log fire, heavy bowed beams, and dried flowers in the cosy softly lit bar; an attractive, no smoking restaurant with corn dollies and a big oak dresser, and a tiled-floor room with some stripped stone, cushioned wall seats and shipmates' chairs, and woodburning stove; very popular, imaginative bar food, well kept ales, and picnic sets and boules in the pretty walled garden; good nearby walks, and handy for 15th-c Bede House. **£21.45**|**£5.25**.

REDMILE SK7935 **Peacock** *(01949)* *842554* Atmospheric little village house below Belvoir Castle, with extremely popular, imaginative and enjoyable food in the bar or pretty no smoking restaurant, well kept real ales, thoughtful wines, and courteous, friendly service; open fires, attractive conservatory. **£22.45**|£7.95.

THORPE LANGTON SP7492 **Bakers Arms** *(01858)* *545201* Extended thatched pub with a warm and friendly welcome, simple furnishings, well presented, interesting food (need to book well ahead), helpful service, well kept beer, an extensive wine list, and no smoking snug; cl Mon, am wkdys, pm Sun; children over 12. **£24**.

UPPER HAMBLETON SK9007 **Finches Arms** *(01572)* *756575* Delightfully placed pub looking over Rutland Water, with stylish cane furniture and paintings (for sale) in both the bar and more modern no smoking restaurant, interesting upmarket food with a Mediterranean slant, and real ales; bdrms. **£22**|£7.

WALCOTE SP5683 **Black Horse** *(01455)* *552684* Big helpings of authentic Thai food cooked by Thai landlady, unusual drinks, chatty unpretentious atmosphere, big open fire, no smoking restaurant, and outside seats for summer; must book; cl am Mon, Tues and Sat, and open all Sun; children in dining area only; disabled access. **£17.50** for 5-course meal|£6.25.

Special thanks to Michael and Jenny Back.

Leicestershire Calendar

Some of these dates were provisional as we went to press. Please check information with the telephone numbers provided.

JANUARY

8 **Castle Donington** Antiques Fair: about 200 stands at the International Exhibition Centre (IEC) – *till 9 January* (01332) 810048

22 **Castle Donington** Classic Bike Show at the IEC – *till 23 January* (01332) 810048

FEBRUARY

5 **Castle Donington** Antiques Fair *(for details see 8 Jan) – till 6 February*

11 **Leicester** Comedy Festival – *till 20 February* (0116) 291 5511

12 **Loughborough** Friends of Thomas the Tank Engine at Great Central Railway – *till 13 February* (01509) 230726

MARCH

4 **Castle Donington** Antiques Fair *(for details see 8 Jan) – till 5 March*

17 **Leicester** Jazz Festival – *till 25 March* (0116) 247 3014

22 **Leicester** Short Film and Video Festival – *till 24 March* (0116) 255 4854

APRIL

1 **Castle Donington** Antiques Fair *(for details see 8 Jan) – till 2 April*

7 **Loughborough** National Folk Music Festival – *till 9 April* (01296) 415333

22 **Hallaton** Bottle Kicking and Hare Pie Scrambling: teams compete to get 3 small kegs of beer across 2 streams a mile apart (01858) 821270

Leicestershire Calendar (cont.)

23 Cottesmore Steam Open Day at the Rutland Railway Museum – *till 24 April* (01572) 813203

30 Cottesmore Steam Open Day at the Rutland Railway Museum – *till 1 May* (01572) 813203; **Loughborough** County Show at Dishley Grange Farm – *till 1 May* (01509) 646786

MAY

1 Castle Donington Medieval Street Market (01332) 810432

6 Castle Donington Antiques Fair (*for details see 8 Jan*) – *till 7 May*; **Loughborough** Friends of Thomas the Tank Engine at Great Central Railway – *till 7 May* (01509) 230726

12 Donington Park World Superbikes – *till 14 May* (01332) 810048

20 Leicester Motor Show and Transport Pageant at Abbey Park – *till 21 May* (0116) 222 4041; also, Early Music Festival – *till 10 June* (0116) 247 3043

28 Belvoir Re-enactment of Civil War Siege at the Castle – *till 29 May* (01476) 870262; **Burley on the Hill** Rutland County Show (01162) 597466; **Cottesmore** Steam Open Day at the Rutland Railway Museum – *till 29 May* (01572) 813203

29 Exton Street Market (01572) 812594; **Loughborough** Carnival (01509) 218113; **Melton Mowbray** Show: arena events, Royal Air Force and bands (01788) 573062

JUNE

3 Castle Donington Antiques Fair (*for details see 8 Jan*) – *till 4 June*

4 Brooksby Open Day and One Day Horse Event at Brooksby College (01664) 434291

7 Little Casterton Stamford Shakespeare Company Summer Season at Rutland Open-air Theatre – *till 2 September* (01780) 754381

10 Market Harborough Carnival (01858) 462626

15 Leicester International Music Festival – *till 25 June* (0116) 247 3043

JULY

2 Market Bosworth Show (01530) 411767

7 Donington Park British Motorcycle Grand Prix – *till 9 July* (01332) 810048

8 Breedon on the Hill Open Gardens: 20 gardens – *till 9 July* (01332) 862099; **Wymeswold** Rempstone Steam and Country Show – *till 9 July* (01509) 890063

16 Measham Ashby Show (01283) 704801

23 Belvoir Medieval Jousting at the Castle (01476) 870262

26 Belvoir Medieval Jousting at the Castle (01476) 870262

29 Leicester Mardi Gras (07899) 676460

AUGUST

5 Leicester Caribbean Carnival (0116) 253 0491

11 Ashby-de-la-Zouch Fireworks Concert at Calke Abbey – *till 12 August* (01332) 863822

Leicestershire Calendar (cont.)

12 Leicester Abbey Park Music Festival (0116) 247 3013
18 Egleton British Birdwatching Fair at Rutland Water – *till 20 August* (01780) 460321
19 Leicester Castle Park Festival – *till 28 August* (0116) 299 8888; **Loughborough** Friends of Thomas the Tank Engine at Great Central Railway – *till 28 August* (01509) 230726; **Market Bosworth** Re-enactment of 1485 Battle of Bosworth at Bosworth Battlefield – *till 20 August* (01455) 290429
27 Belvoir Medieval Jousting at the Castle (01476) 870262; **Cottesmore** Steam Open Day at the Rutland Railway Museum – *till 28 August* (01572) 813203

SEPTEMBER

8 Leicester Festival of Wind and Sun at Western Park – *till 10 September* (0116) 222 0254
9 Castle Donington Antiques Fair (*for details see 8 Jan*) – *till 10 September*
16 Castle Donington Kit Car Show at the IEC – *till 17 September* (01332) 810048

OCTOBER

7 Castle Donington Antiques Fair (*for details see 8 Jan*) – *till 8 October*
14 Loughborough Friends of Thomas the Tank Engine at Great Central Railway – *till 15 October* (01509) 230726

NOVEMBER

4 Coalville Fireworks at Snibston Discovery Park (01530) 510851; **Leicester** Bonfire Night at Abbey Park (0116) 299 8888
11 Castle Donington Antiques Fair (*for details see 8 Jan*) – *till 12 November*

DECEMBER

9 Castle Donington Antiques Fair (*for details see 8 Jan*) – *till 10 December*

We welcome reports from readers

This *Guide* depends on readers' reports. Do help us if you can – in return, we offer a discount on the next edition to people who've helped us with reports for it. Tell us what you think about places already in it, and anything extra you think we should say about them. And send us your ideas for inclusion in the next edition: places to visit, eat at or stay in, attractive drives or walks, maybe even unusual interesting shops you know of. Use the card in the middle, the report forms at the end, or just write – no stamp needed: *The Good Britain Guide*, FREEPOST TN1569, Wadhurst, E Sussex TN5 7BR.

LINCOLNSHIRE

Away from the famous traditional beach resorts, this largely undiscovered county has a lot to offer a touring holiday or get-away-from-it-all break – at generally low prices.

Outstanding places to visit here include Grimsby's National Fishing Heritage Centre, the seal sanctuary at Skegness, and magnificent houses and castles, led by Burghley House at Stamford, Belton House, and Tattershall and Grimsthorpe castles, with less-known delights such as Doddington Hall, Gunby Hall gardens and the vast classical gardens at Harlaxton. The cheerful entertainment museum at Whaplode St Catherine's is fun, the ruined abbey at Thornton Curtis is a little-known romantic gem, and there are interesting plans for Isaac Newton's home at Woolsthorpe. There's RAF nostalgia at Coningsby and East Kirkby.

Families have plenty to do, with well arranged and lively country parks at Elsham Hall and Normanby Hall, heavy horses at Great Steeping, and seals at Mablethorpe and Skegness. Both Skegness and Cleethorpes have lots to fill seaside summer days. Warm escapes on those days when east winds blow from the North Sea include the butterfly park at Long Sutton, and the largely under-cover amusement park at Ingoldmells – which has Europe's longest rollercoaster and quite a few additions this year.

Lincoln is an interesting city with plenty to see and a glorious cathedral; Stamford and Boston too have a good deal of character. North and east of Lincoln, the rolling Wolds countryside makes for enjoyable drives on uncrowded roads, punctuated by attractive villages and charming small towns, and by soaring church spires.

Around The Wash and up the coast towards Wainfleet and Coningsby, the land is very flat, reclaimed from the sea: in springtime the endless bulbfields around Spalding burst into spectacular bloom, and we have included an interesting waterside fenland drive south of here. Throughout the county's farmland, huge fields of arable crops can be rather tedious for walkers; speeding past more quickly in a car, bus or train, you're more aware of the shape of the countryside, giving it more appeal, though we have picked out some interesting walks.

In winter, Lincolnshire can be very chilly.

Where to stay

BOURNE TF0919 **Bourne Eau House** *30 South St, Bourne PE10 9LY (01335) 350287* **£60;** 3 rms. Handsome house, partly Elizabethan, partly Georgian, with beams and inglenook fireplaces, good dinner in the elegant dining room, enjoyable breakfasts, and friendly owners; cl Christmas and Easter.

BUSLINGTHORPE TF0985 **East Farm House** *Middle Rasen Rd, Buslingthorpe, Lincoln LN3 5AQ (01673) 842283* ***£44,** plus special breaks; 2 rms. 18th-c farmhouse surrounded by family farm; with beams, log fires, relaxed atmosphere, and good breakfasts; tennis and lots of walks; self-catering cottage; cl Christmas.

DYKE TF1022 **Wishing Well** *Dyke, Bourne PE10 0AF (01778) 422970* **£50;** 14 rms. The wishing well is at the dining end of the long rambling bar – heavy beams, dark stone, brasswork, candlelight and a big fireplace; good popular food, helpful service, friendly atmosphere; disabled access.

EAST BARKWITH TF1581 **Bodkin Lodge** *Grange Farm, Torrington Lane, East Barkwith, Market Rasen LN8 5RY (01673) 858249* ***£48;** 2 pretty ground-floor rms. Run by the same friendly family as the farm, this carefully extended bungalow has a comfortable sitting room with books, fresh flowers, open fire and a baby grand piano; good breakfasts in the big dining room (evening meals by arrangement), award-winning wildlife farmland trails from the door, and marvellous country views; cl Christmas and New Year; children over 10.

HOLBEACH TF3426 **Pipwell Manor** *Washway Rd, Saracen's Head, Holbeach, Spalding, PE12 8AL (01406) 423119* ***£40;** 3 rms. Handsome 18th-c farmhouse, welcoming and spotless, with a log fire in the comfortable sitting room, pretty panelled dining room, afternoon tea with home-made cakes on arrival, good breakfasts with their own eggs and home-made preserves, and a conservatory; free bikes, no children, no smoking and no pets; cl Christmas and New Year.

LINCOLN SK9771 **Carline** *1–3 Carline Rd, Lincoln LN1 1HL (01522) 530422* ***£42;** 12 well equipped rms. Spotlessly kept and comfortable, double-fronted, no smoking Edwardian guesthouse 5 minutes from the cathedral, with helpful and cheerful long-serving owners, quiet sitting rooms, and fine breakfasts; cl Christmas and New Year; no baby facilities.

LINCOLN SK9871 **D'Isney Place** *Eastgate, Lincoln LN2 4AA (01522) 538881* **£76,** plus special breaks; 17 charming rms. Friendly 18th-c hotel with lovely gardens (one wall of the cathedral close forms its southern boundary); a relaxed and homely atmosphere, good breakfasts served in the rooms (there are no public rooms), and friendly owners; partial disabled access.

MARKET DEEPING TF1309 **Caudle House** *High St, Market Deeping, Peterborough PE6 8ED (01778) 347595* **£52**; 2 rms. Georgian house with comfortable sitting room, carefully cooked three-course evening meals for residents, a thoughtful wine list, helpful staff, and enjoyable breakfasts (served in the walled garden, weather permitting).

STAMFORD TF0306 **George** *71 St Martin's, Stamford PE9 2LB (01780) 750700* **£109,** plus special breaks; 47 rms. Historic, ancient, former coaching inn with quietly civilised atmosphere, sturdy timbers, broad flagstones, heavy beams and massive stonework; open log fires, wonderful food in the garden lounge (tempting help-yourself buffet), restaurant and courtyard (in summer), excellent range of drinks – very good-value Italian wines, and welcoming staff; well kept walled garden and sunken lawn where croquet is played; disabled access.

WHAPLODE TF3323 **Guy Wells** *Eastgate, Whaplode, Spalding PE12 6TZ (01406) 422239* ***£44;** 3 rms. In a country garden, this Queen Anne house is surrounded by the friendly owners' daffodil and tulip fields and glasshouses (cultivated spring flowers) – you can buy bulbs; low beams, woodburner, pretty furnishings in the sitting room, and very good food using their own vegetables and free-range eggs; no smoking; cl 25 Dec; children over 5.

WINTERINGHAM SE9322 **Winteringham Fields** *Winteringham, Scunthorpe DN15 9PF (01724) 733096* ***£90;** 10 pretty, chintzy rms with period furniture (3 off courtyard). Thoughtfully run restaurant-with-rooms in a 16th-c manor house; comfortable and very attractive Victorian furnishings, beams and open fires, really excellent inventive food (beautifully presented) in the no smoking dining room, fine breakfasts, and warm, friendly service; cl 2 wks Christmas; children over 7 (babies allowed).

Please let us know what you think of places in the *Guide*. Use the report forms at the back of the book or simply write us a letter.

To see and do

LINCOLNSHIRE Family Attraction of the Year

✔ 🐾 🦭 **SKEGNESS** TF5663 **Natureland Seal Sanctuary** 🆔 (North Parade) Opposite the beach, this rewarding place is renowned for its success in rescuing baby seal pups found stranded on beaches around The Wash, and then returning them to their natural environment. Sick seals are treated in their seal hospital, then moved to the rearing pool outside. Friendly staff explain their work during the entertaining feeding displays at various times during the day (announced over the public address system); it's clear from the way they talk about each animal that they're treated very much as individuals. Watching the seals perform tricks is fascinating – they aren't trained in any way, they just like showing off. A new pool has underwater viewing areas. As well as the seals, they have quite a range of other things to see, including penguins, a colourful aquarium, and tropical house with crocodiles, snakes, a tarantula, and insects. A 170-ft-long greenhouse shows off birds, flamingos and a splendid range of flowers and plants, with butterflies between May and Sept. And there's a pets corner for children, who can feed the farmyard animals with food from the gift shop. Though fine days are best for a visit, a series of covered walkways means that if it does rain, you can see almost everything without needing to venture into the open. Dogs are allowed, if kept on a lead. Each year's intake of baby seals is named according to a specific theme, from pop stars and tennis players to characters from *Coronation Street* and *The Archers*; they're always keen to hear new suggestions, but forget footballers – that wouldn't be suitable for the female seals. Snacks, shop, disabled access; cl 25–26 Dec, 1 Jan; (01754) 764345; £3.90 (£2.60 children over 3). The family ticket is good value at £11.70 for two adults and two children.

ABY TF4179

🍴 ❀ ✔ 🦆 **Claythorpe Watermill & Wildfowl Gardens** Pretty spot around a 18th-c watermill (where they've reconstructed an early 1900s bakery), the grounds full of ornamental wildfowl and poultry, and animals such as rabbits and a miniature pony. Fun to wander through the woods. Meals, snacks, shop, mostly disabled access; cl Nov–Feb; (01507) 450687; £3. The Vine at South Thoresby is a civilised place for lunch.

ALFORD TF4575

★ 🐂 Pleasant town with some attractive brick and thatch buildings, and a summer craft market (Fri). The White Horse Hotel is useful for lunch. W of here, just N of the A16/A1104 junction, the Bluestone Heath hill road past South Ormsby and on to the A157 W of Louth is a splendid scenic drive.

ALKBOROUGH SE8821

⌂ Overlooks the confluence of the Trent and Humber from a high (for this area) scarp called The Cliff; walks along it on a path leading S to the attractive village of Burton upon Stather.

ASWARBY TF0639

✝ **Aswarby church** Delightfully set in a well tended park.

BARTON-UPON-HUMBER TA0222

❀ ✔ ⌂ 🛶 **Barton Clay Pits Country Park** Informative country park based around former clay pits, with nature reserves, walks, fishing (extensive reed beds), sailing – and good views of the Humber Bridge. Limited disabled access; visitor centre open wknds and bank hols Easter–Sept; (01652) 633283; free.

🏛 🍵 **Baysgarth House Museum** (Caistor Rd) This handsome 18th-c house has well displayed local history exhibits, especially good on rural crafts. Shop, disabled access to ground floor only; cl Mon (exc bank hols)–Weds, 25–26 Dec, 1 Jan; (01652) 632318; free.

BELTON SK8844

🏛 🖼 ❀ **Belton House** Splendid Restoration-period mansion with wonderful carvings, ornate plasterwork, and sumptuous furnishings, paintings and ceramics – they've redecorated the Queen's bedroom and Staircase Hall. The thousand-acre deer park has an orangery and formal Italian garden. They now run behind-the-scenes tours. Meals, snacks, shop, limited disabled access; open pm Weds–Sun and bank hols Apr–Oct, grounds open 11am; (01476) 566116; £5.20; NT. The relaxing Brownlow Arms in picturesque Hough on the Hill has good-value food.

BOSTON TF3243

✝ ✾ ✕ Once the country's second-largest seaport, this little town has a number of pretty spots and handsome historic buildings. Most famous is the **Boston Stump**, the graceful tower of the magnificent 14th-c church St Botolph's. Climb to the top for far views over this flat landscape – it's the second-tallest parish church in the country (the tallest is in Louth); the inside is spectacular too. Another prominent feature of the skyline is the **Maud Foster Mill**, the tallest working windmill in the country, and surely one of the most photogenic. The King's Arms opposite has lovely views of it, and cheap food; Goodbarns Yard (Wormgate) is a popular central pub/restaurant. The surroundings (and the Lincolnshire coast generally) are too flat for driving to be very interesting around here, and side roads which look clear on a map can turn out to be tryingly slow in practice, with agricultural vehicles trundling along slowly and muddily; the B1183 and B1192 aren't bad.

🏛☕ **Boston Guildhall Museum** (South St) In 1607 this was the prison of the Pilgrim Fathers after their unsuccessful attempt to flee to Holland (they did, of course, eventually escape further afield, taking this town's name with them). Displays cover this and the rest of the town's history. Shop, disabled access to ground floor only; cl Sun exc pm Apr–Sept, Christmas and New Year; (01205) 365954; £1.25.

BOURNE WOOD TF0721

⚘ ⌂ (A151, just outside Bourne) Sheltered woodland good for a gentle stroll, especially welcome as so much of the country is flat, treeless fens. Plenty of bird life, busy at weekends with locals exercising their dogs; parking charge. In the town's market place, there's decent food in the Angel Hotel, opposite an interesting antique shop.

BRANDY WHARF TF0197

🍺☕ **Cider Centre** (B1205 SE of Scunthorpe) Pleasingly zany 18th-c riverside cider house with up to 60 different varieties; also orchard and small museum. The enthusiastic owner really knows his stuff. Meals and snacks (not Mon), shop, disabled access; open licensing hours, though cl Mon lunchtimes Nov–Easter and over Christmas; no children under 14; (01652) 678364; free.

BRANT BROUGHTON SK9154

✝ **Brant Broughton church spire** Elegant and very tall, a landmark for miles around.

BURGH LE MARSH TF4965

✝ ✕ Has a notable **church**, and a **windmill** nearby has unusual left-handed sails.

CANDLESBY TF4567

✿ **Candlesby Herbs** (Cross Keys Cottage) Good range of herb plants for sale and on display in the garden; cl Mon; (01754) 890211; free. There's a specialist cactus grower at nearby Candlesby House.

CLEETHORPES TA3108

✝ Big traditional seaside resort with extensive gently shelving tidal sands, and a surprisingly ancient **church** among some attractive older houses in its original core. The new road in from the A16 is a big help. Willys (which brews its own beer) is useful for lunch.

🚂 **Cleethorpes Coast Light Railway** 📷 (Kings Rd) Gentle trip around local scenery (not wkdys mid-Sept–Easter; for information on special events tel (01472) 604657; £1.80).

☘ ! **Cleethorpes Discovery Centre** 📷 (Kings Rd) Hands-on look at local wildlife; its unusual spiral shape was inspired by a seashell. An interactive exhibition about time (Cleethorpes lies on the prime meridian) begins Jan. Teas, shop, disabled access; cl 25–26 Dec, 1 Jan; (01472) 323232; £1.85.

✿ **Fuchsia Fantasy** (Kings Rd) Hundreds of varieties of fuchsia, and other plants according to season; disabled access; open daily Easter–Sept,

best to check other times on (01472)
883075; free.

☺ **Pleasure Island** (Kings Rd) Family
theme park with all the usual rides, plus
a circus and various animal shows.
Meals, snacks, shop, disabled access;
open all Apr–Oct, plus wknds and
school hols Sept–Oct and Mar; (01472)
211511; £9.

CONINGSBY TF2257

✚ ✝ **Battle of Britain Visitor
Centre** (A153) Subject to operational
commitments you can see the aircraft
of the Battle of Britain Memorial Flight –
inc the only flying Lancaster in Europe.
A visitor centre has exhibitions.
Summer snacks, shop, disabled access;
cl Sun, some Sats, bank hols, and 2 wks
over Christmas; (01526) 344041 –
check first if you hope to see a
particular aircraft; £3.50. The **church**
has what's said to be the biggest dial of
any clock with just a single hand. Just
out of town, the interesting old Leagate
Inn is useful for lunch.

CROWLAND TF2410

✝ **Crowland church** The imposing
remains of a once-great abbey, part still
used as the parish church – the village
also has a three-legged bridge.

DODDINGTON SK9070

🏠 🐝 **Doddington Hall** (B1190)
Striking lived-in Elizabethan mansion,
unchanged externally since it was built,
and still with its original walled gardens,
gatehouse and family church. The
elegant rooms are mostly Georgian.
Regular concerts in the Long Gallery.
Teas, shop, disabled access to gardens;
open pm Weds, Sun and bank hols
May–Sept, plus garden also open Sun
Mar and Apr – maybe open extra days
July–Sept, phone to check; (01522)
694308; £4.20, garden only £2.10. The
Stones Arms, prettily placed in nearby
Skellingthorpe, has good-value food.

EAST KIRKBY TF3563

✝ **Lincolnshire Aviation Heritage
Centre** (A155) Enthusiastic World
War II collection on a wartime airfield.
The highlight is *Just Jane*, the famous
Avro Lancaster NX611, lovingly
restored by two brothers as a memorial
to their brother who died during the
Nuremberg Raid in 1944. They hope
that one day it will fly again but for the
moment are content with taxiing it

around the airfield in summer. Snacks,
shop, disabled access; cl Sun and
Christmas; (01790) 763207; £3.90.

ELSHAM TA0311

🐖 🐝 ☺ ⚘ 🦅 **Elsham Hall Country
Park** Lots for families – farmyard
animals, arboretum, adventure
playground, puppet shows, craft and
garden centres, and falconry with
regular flying displays. Carp will feed
from your hand at the jetty. Meals,
snacks, shop, disabled access; cl mid-
Sept–Easter; (01652) 688698; *£4.

EPWORTH SE7803

★ 🏛 Pleasant village, the centre of the
Isle of Axholme, with Georgian houses
around the market place. **Old Rectory**
🖼 (Rectory St) The childhood home of
John and Charles Wesley, built in 1709
by their father. Restored in 1957, with
rooms furnished in period style. Shop,
some disabled access; cl 12–2 pm, am
Sun, Nov–Feb; (01427) 872268; *£2.50.
They do B & B. Thanks to the Wesley
connection, the whole village has
become something of a Methodist
centre; the friendly Red Lion has decent
food, especially vegetarian.

FOLKINGHAM TF0733

★ Picturesque village with a fine market
place. The Greyhound Inn, crammed
with antiques, is good for lunch.

FRAMPTON TF3239

★ Perhaps the prettiest Fenland village.

FREISTON SHORE TF3942

⌒ 🦅 (off A52 via Freiston) Good paths
to the sea wall, with desolate views of
myriad birds and even seals on the
marshes and banks beyond – don't be
tempted out among them, the tides are
lethal.

GAINSBOROUGH SK8189

🏛 ☀ **Old Hall** 🖼 (Parnell St)
Restored medieval manor house with
interesting Great Hall and original
kitchen. Good Walkman tour. Snacks,
shop, disabled access to ground floor
only; cl Sun exc pm Easter–Oct, 25–26
Dec, 1 Jan, Good Fri; (01427) 612669;
£2.50. The Trent Port is useful for
lunch, and the lane N along the Trent
embankment gives views of the flood
plain of this powerful brooding river;
the Jenny Wren at Susworth is another
good stop.

GEDNEY DROVE END TF4828

⌒ 🎋 **Sea walk** An enjoyable way of

seeing The Wash is by following the dyke forming the sea wall; access is from a car park nr Gedney Drove End, from which you can follow the dyke to the mouth of the Nene, with its twin lighthouses either side.

GRANTHAM SK9136

✝ ! **Two rarities** The unusually tall church spire here is commemorated in an early 19th-c jingle: 'Grantham, now two rarities are thine, A lofty steeple and a living sign'. The living sign is the hive with living bees – descended from those of that time – still used as an inn sign by the good Beehive pub on Castlegate here.

GREAT STEEPING TF4364

🐎 **Northcote Heavy Horse Centre** 📷 Magnificent horses showcased from 11am, with harnessing demonstrations, grooming and wagon rides. Snacks, shop, disabled access; open Sun and Weds Apr–Sept, and daily (exc Sat) July–Aug; (01754) 830286; £4. The Bell at Halton Holegate has nice home cooking.

GRIMSBY TA2609

🎣 Still important as a fishing port, this is making considerable strides towards attracting visitors. A new road makes access from the A16 much easier. The Abbeygate Centre has reasonably priced antique shops, also upstairs craft workshops inc lace-making; café. Alfred Enderby's smoked-fish house (Fish Docks Rd) demonstrates traditional methods of smoking salmon, haddock and cod; cl Sun, most Sats and 2 wks at Christmas; (01472) 342984 to check. Cyclists should note that there are plenty of new cycleways here and in adjoining Cleethorpes.

❋ ⑁ **National Fishing Heritage Centre** 📷 (Alexandra Dock) Fascinating displays provide the full experience of a trawlerman of the mid-1950s, taking you from the back streets of Grimsby to the fishing grounds of the Arctic Circle and back, complete with smells and sensations as well as sights and sounds. Everything in the main centre is under cover, but outside there are guided tours of a real trawler, the *Ross Tiger*, led by a former trawlerman. Plenty of special events and extra activities in the summer, from craft exhibitions to pirate days. Snacks, shop,

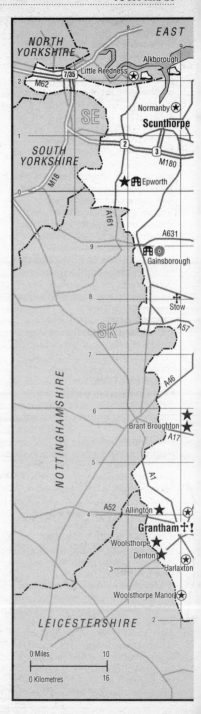

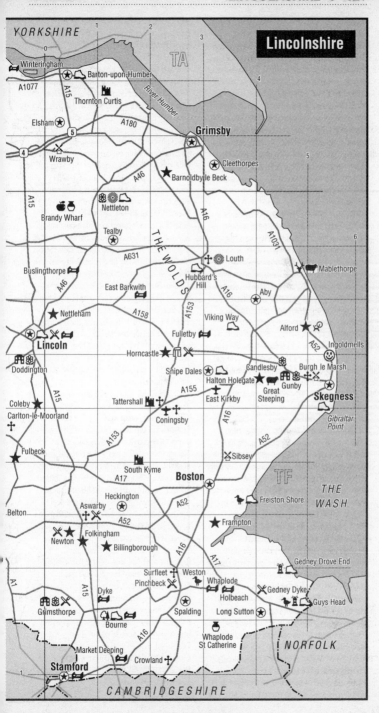

Lincolnshire

YORKSHIRE

TA

Winteringham
A1077
A15
Barton-upon-Humber
Thornton Curtis
River Humber
Elsham
5
Wrawby
A180
Grimsby
4
A46
Cleethorpes
Barnoldby le Beck
5
A15
Brandy Wharf
Nettleton
Tealby
A16
THE WOLDS
A631
Louth
A1031
Mablethorpe
6
Buslingthorpe
A46
East Barkwith
Hubbard's Hill
A16
Aby
Nettleham
A158
A153
Viking Way
Alford
A52
Ingoldmells
Fulletby
Lincoln
Horncastle
Snipe Dales
Candlesby
Burgh le Marsh
A15
Doddington
Halton Holegate
Great Steeping
Gunby
Skegness
Coleby
A155
Tattershall
East Kirkby
Carlton-le-Moorland
A16
A52
Gibraltar Point
Fulbeck
A153
Coningsby
Sibsey
TF
South Kyme
A17
Boston
THE WASH
Heckington
A52
Aswarby
Freiston Shore
Belton
A52
Frampton
Newton
Folkingham
Billingborough
A16
A1
Grimsthorpe
A15
Dyke
Surfleet
Weston
Pinchbeck
Whaplode
Gedney Drove End
Bourne
Holbeach
Gedney Dyke
Guys Head
Spalding
Long Sutton
A16
Whaplode St Catherine
NORFOLK
Market Deeping
Crowland
Stamford
CAMBRIDGESHIRE

disabled access (not to *Ross Tiger*); cl Fri, 25–26 Dec, 1 Jan; (01472) 323345; £4.95.

🏠 **Time Trap** In the prison cells of the town hall the town's social history gets a lively treatment. Interactive games and rather jolly displays cover the building of the docks and the struggle for women's suffrage – and you can see what it's like to be locked in a prison cell. As we went to press, the town hall had just taken it over, and they open when requested Mon–Thurs, best to phone; (01472) 324109; free.

GRIMSTHORPE TF0422

🏛️ 🦌 **Grimsthorpe Castle** A patchwork of styles from its medieval tower and Tudor quadrangle to the baroque north front by Vanbrugh; the state rooms and galleries have especially fine furnishings. Outside are formal gardens and parkland with lake (you can take a tour with the ranger in his Land Rover), and red deer tame enough for children to feed. Meals, snacks (inc the bizarrely popular courgette cake), shop, some disabled access; open Sun, Thurs and bank hols Easter–Sept, plus Mon–Weds in Aug, house cl am; (01778) 591205; £6 all-in, £3 just castle or garden. The Five Bells at Edenham is a good dining pub (and handy for walkers).

GUNBY TF4666

🏛️ 🦌 **Gunby Hall** (the Gunby nr Spilsby; off A158) Interesting neat red brick William III house, with fine oak staircase and clock collection; especially worth visiting for the nine acres of splendid gardens, said to be Tennyson's 'haunt of ancient peace'. Open pm Weds (plus garden only pm Thurs) Apr–Sept; (01909) 486411; £3.50, £2.50 garden only. The Blacksmiths Arms at Skendleby does good-value simple lunches.

GUYS HEAD TF4925

⌂ 🎣 🐦 **Peter Scott Walk** A 10-mile walk E from the mouth of the Nene, with its twin lighthouses either side. Scott used to come here to study and paint wildfowl. It leads along the dyke into Norfolk, with access from a car park on the Nene's E bank.

HARLAXTON SK8832

🏛️ 🦌 🌳 **Harlaxton Manor Gardens** (A607) The stunning mansion at the heart of this estate features as the eponymous house in the forthcoming horror film *The Haunting of Hill House*. Rather contrary to its new-found spooky status, it takes on a gorgeous golden glow in the late afternoon sun. The 45 acres of surrounding classical gardens were built in the early 19th c to rival the finest in Europe, and are currently being restored. Rose and herb gardens in six-acre walled garden, and nature trails through surrounding woodland. Snacks, shop; cl Mon (exc bank hols), and Nov–Mar; (01476) 592101; £3. The Red House over at Knipton is a good dining pub.

HECKINGTON TF1443

🍴 🐦 ✝ Understated but pleasant small town, its well restored **windmill** is the only one in Britain with eight sails. Shop (selling their flour and locally made bread and ginger cake); open pm Thurs–Sun and bank hols Easter–mid-July, then daily until mid-Sept, and then pm Sun only until Easter; (01529) 461919; £1.50. Nearby the Pearoom is a decent **craft centre**, and the 17th-c, white-painted Nags Head has consistently good, homely bar food for lunch. The **church** still has many of its original 14th-c fittings.

HORNCASTLE TF2569

★ 🏛️ Attractive market town popular for antiques, with 30 shops in the Bridge St Antique Centre. You can still see parts of the town's **Roman wall**. Old Nicks (North St) has a decent carvery, and the Fighting Cocks (West St) is also good value. Some 3 miles N, the 'High Street' forking off the A158 is a good drive, following an Iron Age trackway up to Caistor. The A153 to Louth gives some good rolling Wolds views. Another pleasant drive here includes Scrivelsby and its vast deer park, Belchford (Blue Bell useful for lunch), Fulletby (perhaps a stroll on the footpaths here), Somersby (Tennyson's birthplace – his bust is in the church), Old Bolingbroke (castle ruins), Spilsby (nice delicatessen in the quiet market place with its statue of Sir John Franklin), and, if you've made good time, Wainfleet and Boston.

INGOLDMELLS TF5666

☺ **Fantasy Island** (Sea Lane) Just opposite the beach, this is more elaborate than your average fairground and ideal in any weather – 95% of the rides and other features are inside, with thatched buildings and palm trees nestling under a giant pyramid. Europe's longest rollercoaster opened here last year, and other highlights include a volcano theme ride, the IMAX simulator's three rollercoaster type experiences (the screen is all around you, and your seat slides towards it as well as shaking about all over the place), the Balloon Flight, with authentically created computer-controlled balloons soaring around the pyramid, a sail-through aquarium, and two water rides – one quite long, the other rather wet. Meals, snacks, shop, disabled access; open wknds Mar–Apr, and daily in Easter hols and May–Oct; (01754) 872030; free admission to park, then rides separately charged.

LINCOLN SK9771

⌂ The cathedral and castle, both very striking, share the central hilltop, with enough old buildings around them to keep a sense of unity. There's a lot to appeal up here, and in the steep streets (Steep Hill, and Strait St) of ancient buildings running down from them to the 15th-c Stonebow Gate at the top of the High St below. This lower part of the town is much more of a normal bustling shopping and working centre, though even here there are a good few interesting old buildings – inc several Saxon churches and the Norman guildhall. The **Greyfriars Exhibition Centre** (Broadgate) – formerly the County Museum – is in a lovely 13th-c Franciscan building (open Weds–Sat; free). The Wig & Mitre and Brown's Pie Shop, both on Steep Hill, and Lincolnshire Poacher (Bunkers Hill) are good for lunch, and behind the cathedral and castle the Adam & Eve is a nice old pub. There are some fine views from the A607 to Grantham.

! Incredibly Fantastic Old Toy Show (Westgate) Growing collection of old toys and end-of-pier amusements, close to both the cathedral and castle, so a good treat for unwilling culture buffs. Shop, disabled access; from Easter–Sept open Tues–Sat and pm Sun and bank hols, then Oct–Dec wknds plus Tues–Fri in

school hols; (01522) 520534; £1.90.

▥ ※ Lincoln Castle In beautiful surroundings on a formidable earthwork, this was originally built in 1068 for William the Conqueror, but only two towers and two impressive gateways date back to that. One of only four remaining originals of Magna Carta is on display, and there are super views from the ramparts. A 19th-c prison has suitably gruesome exhibits; its chapel is unusually designed so that none of the congregation could see each other. Snacks, shop, mostly disabled access; cl 25–26 Dec, 1 Jan; (01522) 511068; £2.50.

† Lincoln Cathedral Many people reckon that this is England's finest. The original building was largely destroyed in an 1185 earthquake, but the magnificent west front survived, and after nearly a century of rebuilding it was complete by 1280. The triple towers rise spectacularly above the nearby rooftops, and are beautifully lit at night. Inside, the carvings and stained glass are stupendous, and the architecture gracefully harmonious. Snacks, shop, disabled access; £4 suggested donation. The ruins of the once formidable Bishop's Palace are close by.

♂ ♒ Museum of Lincolnshire Life (Burton Rd) County life over the last couple of centuries, well illustrated in big former barracks. A recent lottery grant is paying for the refurbishment of the regimental galleries – should be open by Apr. Snacks, shop, disabled access; cl am Suns Nov–Apr, 24–27 Dec, 1 Jan, Good Fri; (01522) 528448; *£2. A lawn in the courtyard makes a good picnic area.

▥ ◠ Roman remains These include the high wall along Westgate, and the largely reconstructed Newport Arch north of the cathedral (it had survived intact until a 1964 disagreement with a lorry); the Fossdyke canal between Lincoln and the River Trent is also Roman – you can walk out into the country along it from the city, and the Pyewipe Inn out by the Saxilby road there makes a good destination.

♂ Royal Lincolnshire Regiment Museum (Burton Rd) Refurbished and due to re-open in Mar; snacks, shop, disabled access; *£2.

⚒ 🎭 🎵 **The Lawn** In 1820 this was the county's first lunatic asylum; now its landscaped grounds include hands-on history and archaeology exhibits, an aquarium and exotic glasshouse, and a restaurant, coffee shop and bar. Shop, disabled access; cl 25–26 Dec; (01522) 560330; free.

🖼 **Usher Gallery** (Lindum Rd) Attractive gallery with fine watches, porcelain and miniatures, Tennyson memorabilia, and Peter de Wint watercolours. Snacks, shop, improved disabled access; cl am Sun, 25–26 Dec, 1 Jan, Good Fri; (01522) 527980; £2 (free Fri).

LITTLE REEDNESS SE8022
★ ✝ ⌂ 🐦 Attractive village with 14th-c **church** and Ouse walks. There's an **RSPB** nature reserve just E at Blacktoft Sands marshes.

LONG SUTTON TF4324
🦋 🐦 ✝ **Butterfly & Wildlife Park** One of Britain's biggest walk-through tropical houses, with hundreds of butterflies flying free. Also creepy-crawly little insectarium, reptiles, snakes, wild flower meadows, and twice-daily falconry displays – a 9-hole mini-golf course opens this year. A well organised place. Snacks, shop, disabled access; cl Nov–Mar; (01406) 363833; £4.80. The village **church spire** is unusual for the hundreds of tons of lead sheathing it. The 17th-c Olde Ship has good home cooking.

LOUTH TF3186
⌂ **Hubbard's Hill** A walk SW from Louth; not in fact a hill, but a river valley – surprisingly deep for the Wolds.
✝ 🌼 **Louth church** A very elegant 16th-c building with the tallest spire of any parish church in Britain. The tower can be climbed on summer afternoons; hundreds of steps for a fabulous view.

MABLETHORPE TF4987
🌱 🐾 **Animal Gardens & Seal Trust** (North End) Rescued seals unable to return to the wild find a permanent home here, along with monkeys, parrots, porcupines, llamas, emus, wild cats and many other animals. It's right by the beach. Snacks, shop, mostly disabled access; cl Nov–Easter; (01507) 473346; £3.50.

NETTLETON TA0900
🎭 ✹ ⌂ **Potterton & Martin Cottage Nursery** (Moortown Rd) This has unusual and interesting plants – mainly alpines and small bulbs; disabled access; (01472) 851714. Just S towards Normanby le Wold, Caistor Top is the highest point on the Wolds, at 550 metres (1,805ft), with bracing walks. The Nickerson Arms over at Rothwell has decent food.

NORMANBY SE8816
🎭 ⚒ 🏠 **Normanby Hall Country Park** (B1430) Pleasant spot with grazing deer, lots of wildfowl, nature trails, some interesting sculptures, a restored Victorian kitchen garden and a farm museum in its 350 busy acres. Period rooms in the Regency mansion. Meals, snacks, shop, disabled access to ground floor only; house and museum cl am and all Oct–Mar, park open all year; (01724) 720588; £2.50 (North Lincs residents half-price). The Sheffield Arms at Burton upon Stather has reliable food.

SIBSEY TF3551
❌ **Trader Mill** (A16 N of Boston) The village has a couple of **windmills**, one of them splendidly restored six-sailed

---

Days Out

The best of Lincoln: Lincoln Cathedral; Castle; explore Steep Hill area – lunch at the Wig & Mitre or Brown's Pie Shop there; Usher Gallery; Museum of Lincolnshire Life; Incredibly Fantastic Old Toy Show.

Those in peril: Fishing heritage centre, Grimsby; fish lunch at Leons there; trawler visit, and Time Trap.

Showpiece stone-built town: Stamford; lunch at the George there; Burghley House, or Grimsthorpe Castle.

model with fine views from the top.
SKEGNESS TF5663
Built as a late 19th-c resort, this has been an archetypal one, with the first Butlin's Holiday Camp just up the coast; the beach has clean bathing water. The comfortable old Vine Hotel on the southern edge of the town was here long before the resort, welcoming Tennyson among others; it's pleasant for lunch.

🐖👶♿ **Church Farm Museum** 🖼 (Church Rd South) Good re-creation of daily farm life at the end of the 19th c, with craft demonstrations, and quite a few Lincoln longwool sheep. Snacks, shop, disabled access; cl Nov–Apr; (01754) 766658; £1.

🦌🐦☁ **Gibraltar Point Nature Reserve** (Gibraltar Rd) 1000 acres of sandy and muddy seashore stretching 3m S from Skegness to the entrance of The Wash. The impressive complex of sand dunes and saltmarsh is good for birdwatching, and home to a wide variety of wildlife; guided walks daily in summer. Shop, disabled access to visitor centre; reserve open all year, centre cl wkdys Nov–May; (01754) 762677; free (small parking charge).

🦌🐾🦭 **Natureland Seal Sanctuary** *See separate family panel on p.423.*

SNIPE DALES TF3368
⛲🦌❄☁ Country park and nature reserve, managed by the county council, covering 210 acres rich in bird and plant life; the country park is a 90-acre area of pinewoods, while the adjacent nature reserve has a trail leading through two valleys and to a viewpoint over the Wolds.

SOUTH KYME TF1650
🗼 A fine 14th-c battlemented tower stands alone in a meadow quite nr the road.

SPALDING TF2624
All around this area, the flat fields by the roadside are a mass of colour in spring, first daffodils and then a multicoloured sea of tulips – very Dutch. The riverside Lincolnshire Poacher is useful for lunch.

🏰👶🌸 **Ayscoughfee Hall Museum** (Church Gate) Spooky-looking medieval manor house, with social history museum, and five acres of gardens and ancient yew hedges –

readers tell us they're particularly nice in spring. Meals, summer snacks, shop, disabled access to ground floor only; museum cl wknds Nov–Feb, gardens open all year; (01775) 725468; free.

🌸 **Tropical Forest** (Rose Cottage Watergarden Centre, Pinchbeck, just N) One of the biggest displays of tropical and subtropical plants in the country. Snacks (summer only and not Mon), shop, watergarden centre, disabled access; cl 25–26 Dec; (01775) 710882; £2.45.

🦆 **Waterside drive** A remarkable Fenland drive runs S from Spalding: turn left off the B1172 in Little London, keeping alongside the Welland New River. Lagoons and reclaimed land on the right have water birds, with more on the river – maybe even a seal, and on the pastures maybe great percheron horses. At the B1116, a short diversion left takes you to Crowland, with a remarkable landlocked triangular medieval bridge and what's left of a great abbey. Back towards Deeping the road has more river views, and passes the Exotic Pet Refuge (occasional open days).

STAMFORD TF0307
★ 🏰✝ John Betjeman considered this England's most attractive town. Within the medieval walls are no fewer than 500 listed buildings, inc a good number of attractive medieval **churches** – particularly All Saints in the centre, St George's with excellent 15th-c stained glass, and St Mary's nearby. The George, one of the town's grandest buildings with some parts going back to Saxon times, is excellent for lunch.

🏰🌸 **Burghley House** A 20-minute walk from Stamford's centre leads to this splendid mansion, built by William Cecil and still the home of his family. The exterior is Tudor at its most solidly showy, but the state rooms inside are largely baroque, with wonderful frescoes by Antonio Verrio – the Heaven Room is astonishing. The peaceful grounds, where the Burghley Horse Trials are held, were landscaped by Capability Brown. Meals, snacks, shop, limited disabled access; cl early Oct–Mar (though gardens may open some dates in Apr for spring flowers display); (01780) 52451; £6.10.

⚲ **Stamford Museum** (Broad St) Includes life-size figures dressed in the clothes of Tom Thumb (only 1 metre – 3ft 4in – tall) and Daniel Lambert, a portly fellow who weighed 218 kg (50 stone) when he died on a racing outing here. Shop, disabled access to ground floor only; cl Sun exc pm Apr–Sept, 25–26 Dec; (01780) 66317; free.

🎭 **Tolethorpe Hall** (off A6121 N of Stamford) This has Europe's biggest **open-air theatre** in its grounds, with a covered auditorium and a good Shakespeare season; box office (01780) 756133.

STOW SK8881

† **Stow church** Notable for its fantastic Saxon arches.

SURFLEET TF2528

† **Leaning spire** The tower and spire of Surfleet church lean alarmingly.

TATTERSHALL TF2056

🏰 † ⚔ **Tattershall Castle** The 15th-c castle has a magnificent 30-metre (100ft) turreted keep, with fine heraldic chimneypieces on each of the four storeys; there's a double moat with peacocks and waterfowl. Snacks, shop (with food for the birds), some disabled access; open Sat–Weds Apr–Oct, and pm wknds Nov–Dec; (01526) 342543; £3; NT. The airy 15th-c **church** is also attractive, and just off the A153 towards Sleaford, on the left before you reach Tattershall Bridge, is a preserved **steam engine** which worked at keeping this area of fens drained for nearly a century. The Abbey Lodge Hotel (B1192 towards Woodhall) has good food.

TEALBY TF1590

⚜ † ✗ The best example of that Lincolnshire speciality – colourful **village cottage gardens**, easily seen from the road. Here, a great variety of neat and charmingly planted gardens front the stone-built cottages, some thatched, on the main street, running down from the 12th-c **church** to a watersplash near a watermill, and there is more colour in the quaintly named side lanes. The 14th-c King's Head has decent food.

THORNTON CURTIS TA1118

🏰 **Thornton Abbey** (East Halton rd) Ruins of a 12th-c Augustinian abbey, very atmospheric with its worn spiral

stone stairs and dark corridors, well worth a visit. Also a small exhibition in the magnificent 14th-c gatehouse. Disabled access (not into gatehouse); grounds open daily, gatehouse open only pm third Sun in month, plus pm first Sun Apr–Sept; free.

VIKING WAY TF3072

⌂ Long-distance path helping village-to-village walks, with 'Tennyson country' a popular focus (Tennyson was born at the rectory in Somersby, when his father was rector at Bag Enderby); the Black Horse at Donington on Bain TF2382, the Bell at Coleby SK9760 and the two Tealby pubs are handy stops.

WESTON TF2924

🦉 **Baytree Owl Centre** (A151) Expanding collection of owls and other birds, with displays in a big arena (12pm and 3pm Mar–Oct); some birds can be handled. They also have a creepy crawly house, and may be adding red squirrels. Good meals and snacks, shop, disabled access; cl 25–26 Dec, 1 Jan; (01406) 371907; *£2.50. It's part of a busy little complex, with ducks and rabbits in a landscaped glasshouse, nice garden centre, and play area; also donkeys and a mule in a paddock by the car park – regular visitors tell us the latter can't resist carrots.

WHAPLODE ST CATHERINE'S TF3219

⚲ **Museum of Entertainment** (Millgate, off B1165) Unusual and quirky collection tracing the development of entertainment from barrel and church organs to puppets and phonographs, taking in a history of the fairground along the way. Many exhibits are working (there are organ concerts throughout the summer), and the owner clearly loves her subject. Snacks, shop, disabled access; open pm Sun–Thurs July–Sept, plus Easter wknd and pm Sun Easter–Jun; (01406) 540379; *£2.50.

WOOLSTHORPE SK9224

🎭 ⚲ ⚜ **Woolsthorpe Manor** (nr Colsterworth) This is the birthplace of Isaac Newton, and in Apr an interactive discovery centre exhibiting his work will be opening. He conducted some of his more important experiments here: geometry workings said to be in his handwriting are scratched into the plasterwork – and of course the garden has a venerable apple tree. As we went to press, opening times were pm Weds–Sun Apr–Oct, but in light of the new developments, these (and prices) were under review – best to phone; (01476) 860338; £2.70; NT.

WRAWBY TA0208

✗ **Wrawby Post Mill** Working windmill with snacks and a shop; open bank hols and some Suns Apr–Aug – ring Mrs Day to check; (01652) 653699; £1.

★ **Other attractive villages**, all with decent pubs, include Allington SK8540 (despite the nearby A1), Barnoldby le Beck TA2303, Billingborough TF1134, Brant Broughton SK9154, Carlton-le-Moorland SK9058, Coleby SK9760, Denton SK8632, Fulbeck SK9450, Halton Holegate TF4165, Nettleham TF0075, Newton TF0436 and Woolsthorpe SK8435 (the one nr Belvoir). Readers recommend the woods at Stapleford SK8857 for picnics (especially when the rhododendrons are in bloom). Castle Bytham SK9819 has decent views and a duckpond, with nature trails in nearby woods. Langton by Partney TF3970 has an attractive church.

Where to eat

ASWARBY TF0639 **Tally Ho** *(01529) 455205* Handsome 17th-c stone inn with beams and an open fire in the country-style bar, a gently civilised atmosphere, papers to read, good enjoyable food inc fine puddings, well kept real ales, decent house wines, and an attractive pine-panelled restaurant (best to book); bdrms; disabled access. **£19|£6.95**.

GEDNEY DYKE TF4126 **Chequers** *(01406) 362666* Warmly welcoming and neatly kept small pub with lots of fresh fish and seafood and a wide choice of other interesting dishes, an open fire, elegant dining conservatory, well kept beer, decent wines, and helpful service. **£25|£8.50**.

GRIMSTHORPE TF0423 **Black Horse** *(01778) 591247* 18th-c coaching inn with log fires, beams, exposed stone and plenty of brass, excellent food with an emphasis on fish and game (all beautifully presented), an intimate candlelit dining room, real ales, an impressive wine list with helpful notes, and friendly staff; pretty bdrms; no children; disabled access. **£22|£6.25**.

HORNCASTLE TF2669 **Magpies** *73–75 East St (01507) 527004* Popular, well run restaurant with a relaxed atmosphere and very good French cooking using top quality, fresh local ingredients; cl Mon, 2 wks Aug; disabled access. **£30|£6**.

LINCOLN SK9771 **Brown's Pie Shop** *33 Steep Hill (01522) 527330* Spectacular, really interesting pies (and lots of other food), helpful staff, comfortable seats and pleasant traditional atmosphere; cl 25 Dec and 1 Jan. **£24|£5.95**.

LINCOLN SK9771 **Jews House** *15 The Strait (01522) 524851* Small, intimate and elegantly furnished restaurant in one of the oldest buildings in the city, with very good imaginative food, well schooled friendly service, and upstairs coffee lounge for those who want to smoke after the meal; cl Sun. **£30|£7.95** 3-course lunch.

LINCOLN SK9771 **Wig & Mitre** *30 Steep Hill (01522) 535190* Attractively restored 14th-c building with imaginative food served all day (breakfast too), excellent puddings, an elaborate restaurant menu, interesting wine list, and consistently efficient, prompt service; disabled access. **£24.50|£6.95**.

NEWTON TF0436 **Red Lion** *(01529) 497256* Full of charm and character, this civilised pub specialises in an imaginative hot and cold buffet (which comes in small, medium or large helpings) plus other hot dishes, four roasts on Sat evening and Sun lunchtime, well kept real ales, friendly service; also, a neat, well sheltered garden with a good play area; cl 25 Dec; disabled access. **£18.95|£8.95**.

PINCHBECK TF2225 **Ship** *Northgate (01775) 723792* Friendly pub with comfortable small lounge and dining area, helpful service, good-value bar food, smarter restaurant, and real ales; cl pms 25–26 Dec; disabled access. **£19.75|£4.95**.

Special thanks to Mrs H Hawthorn, Michael and Jenny Back, Mrs A K Davies.

Lincolnshire Calendar

Some of these dates were provisional as we went to press. Please check information with the telephone numbers provided.

JANUARY

6 Haxey Haxey Hood Game: created in the 13th c by Lady de Mowbray whose hood was blown away and retrieved by labourers, the game resembles rugby played with leather hoods. Procession of players, colourfully dressed Boggons, king and fool. (01302) 735385

22 Spalding Motorbike 2000 at Springfields Exhibition Centre – *till 23 January* (01775) 724843

FEBRUARY

3 Spalding Horticultural Exhibition at Springfields Exhibition Centre – *till 6 February* (01775) 724843

20 Belton Snowdrop Day at Belton House (01476) 566116

MARCH

11 Spalding Craft Fair at Springfields Exhibition Centre – *till 12 March* (01775) 724843

13 Spalding Show Gardens: World of Flowers at Springfields Exhibition Centre – *till 7 May* (01775) 724843

26 Spalding Toy and Train Collectors' Fair at the Lincolnshire Showground (01526) 398198

APRIL

8 Belton Horse Trials at Belton House – *till 9 April* (01476) 566116

22 Alford Easter Gala Weekend: vintage cars, military vehicles, town criers, carnival – *till 24 April* (01507) 462541

23 Belton Easter Egg Trail at Belton House (01476) 566116

26 Belton Guided Tour of the Garden at Belton House (01476) 566116

28 Lincoln Folk Festival – *till 30 April* (01522) 569434

29 Spalding Flower Festival and Country Fair: famous flower-float parade through the town, and entertainment at Springfields Exhibition Centre – *till 1 May* (01775) 713253

MAY

1 Alford Morris Men dance *at dawn* at the Windmill (01507) 462136

7 Belton Specialist Plant Fair at Belton House (01476) 566116

18 Tallington Beer Festival at Barholm Road Showfield – *till 21 May* (01780) 763063

21 Tallington Steam and Country Festival – *till 22 May* (01780) 763063

27 Alford Working Crafts at Manor House Museum – *till 29 May* (01754) 890211

28 Carrington Steam and Vintage Rally – *till 29 May* (01507) 568796; **Lincoln** Classic Car Rally at Castle Square (01522) 873561

29 Woodhall Spa Agricultural Show (01526) 352825

Lincolnshire Calendar (cont.)

JUNE

4 Belton Family Day at Belton House (01476) 566116; **Bransby** Gala Open Day at Bransby Home of Rest for Horses (01702) 215120; **Messingham** Show (01724) 763004

8 Belton Backstairs Tour: parts of Belton House not usually open to the public (01476) 566116

17 Grantham Carnival – *till 18 June* (01476) 574484; **Lincoln** Search for Adventure at Lincoln Castle (01777) 702913; **Old Bolingbroke** Open-air Concert at Bolingbroke Castle (01529) 461499; **Stamford** Fireworks Concert at Burghley House (01625) 575681

18 Appleby Country Fair: jousting, falconry (01724) 732666

21 Grange de Lings Lincolnshire Show at the Showground – *till 22 June* (01522) 524240

24 Waddington RAF Waddington Air Show: foreign aircraft and display teams, Red Arrows, Service displays, crafts, funfair – *till 25 June* (01522) 726100

25 Burgh le Marsh Carnival – *till 2 July* (01754) 810474; **Horncastle** Gala Day (01507) 527520

JULY

1 Wrangle Show (01205) 270401

8 Lincoln Water Carnival at Brayford Pool – *till 9 July* (01522) 881188

9 Spilsby Show (01790) 752319

13 Belton Backstairs Tour: parts of Belton House not usually open to the public (01476) 566116

14 Belton International Dance and Music Festival at Belton House – *till 16 July* (01476) 591591

15 Barton Carnival – *till 16 July* (01652) 635330

17 Lincoln Lincoln Mystery Plays – *till 29 July* (01522) 510800

21 Wainfleete Family Fun Weekend – *till 23 July* (01754) 765746

22 Lincoln Street Festival (01522) 873561; **Mablethorpe** District Show and Illuminations Switch-on (01507) 472496; **North Somercotes** Carnival (01507) 358474; **Sutton on Sea** Horticultural Society Annual Show (01507) 441284

23 North Somercotes Horticultural Show (01507) 358474

24 Belton Fireworks Concert at Belton House (01476) 566116

29 Skegness Illuminations Switch-on (01754) 764821; **Stamford** Fireworks Concert at Burghley House (01625) 575681; **Sutton on Sea** Carnival and Parade – *till 2 August* (01507) 472496

AUGUST

1 Partney Sheep Fair – *till 2 August* (01754) 810477

5 Mablethorpe Carnival Week – *till 12 August* (01507) 441364

6 Revesby Country Fair (01205) 365213; **Skegness** Carnival Week – *till 13 August* (01754) 610614

9 Lincoln Early Music Festival – *till 13 August* (01522) 873561

16 Chapel St Leonards Carnival – *till 20 August* (01754) 873812

19 Grange de Lings Steam and Vintage Rally at the Showground – *till 20 August* (01507) 605937

Lincolnshire Calendar (cont.)

26 Alford Craft Market – *till 28 August* (01507) 480342; **Boston** Show at Central Park – *till 27 August* (01205) 368966; **Horncastle** Gardens and Allotments Association Annual Show – *till 27 August* (01507) 526474

28 Epworth Agricultural Show (01427) 872571

SEPTEMBER

6 Belton Guided Tour of the Garden at Belton House (01476) 566116

10 Epworth Festival of the Plough: horse-ploughing competitions, steam roundabouts, vintage cars, sheepdog trials (01427) 872659

15 Lincoln World Ploughing Contest and British Ploughing Championship at the Showground – *till 16 September* (01302) 852469

21 Lincoln International Clowns Festival – *till 26 September* (01522) 873561

23 Belton Bat Weekend at Belton House – *till 24 September* (01476) 566116

OCTOBER

7 Corby Glen Sheep Fair – *till 9 October* (01476) 550502

26 Belton Ghost Tour at Belton House (01476) 566116

NOVEMBER

4 Lincoln Fireworks at City Football Ground (01522) 881188

25 Alford Christmas Craft Market – *till 26 November* (01507) 480342

DECEMBER

7 Belton Backstairs Tour: parts of Belton House not usually open to the public (01476) 566116

10 Louth Craft Market (01507) 606574

We welcome reports from readers

This *Guide* depends on readers' reports. Do help us if you can – in return, we offer a discount on the next edition to people who've helped us with reports for it. Tell us what you think about places already in it, and anything extra you think we should say about them. And send us your ideas for inclusion in the next edition: places to visit, eat at or stay in, attractive drives or walks, maybe even unusual interesting shops you know of. Use the card in the middle, the report forms at the end, or just write – no stamp needed: *The Good Britain Guide*, FREEPOST TN1569, Wadhurst, E Sussex TN5 7BR.

NORFOLK

Timeless unspoilt north coast, civilised cathedral city, interesting outings; Broads boating, good range of beach resorts.

North Norfolk is charmingly untouristy and traditional-feeling, with a real sense of place from its Dutch-gabled buildings, flint walls, broad sweeps of sea, saltings and sky, and the odd windmill. A path runs the length of the coast, with often hundreds of sizeable and colourful birds in sight at a time. There's a real get-away-from-it-all feel, and inland too, this part has the same sort of appeal (though the weather is often kinder on the coast). Hunstanton and Cromer are civilised seaside resorts, and there are many attractive smaller places. Driving along the twisty coastal A149 is pleasant out of season, and Norfolk Buses run coastal tours; (0845) 300 6116. Further down, the coast is dotted with beach resorts, some large and lively (most obviously, Great Yarmouth), some relaxed and more individual.

Many of the most enjoyable places to visit appeal to children as well as adults: seal boat trips from Blakeney, the Village at Burgh St Margaret, the tropical centre in Great Yarmouth (Amazonia which drops its price this year), and Bressingham's steam museum and gardens. There are several other steam centres (we like the Thursford Green one best), lots of wildlife, zoo and farm parks, unusual outings such as the Fairhaven Garden Trust's watergardens at South Walsham (*under the Broads entry*), the dinosaur park at Lenwade, the ancient sites at Cockley Cley and Grimes Graves, and the retired fighting vehicles at Weybourne. Castle Acre and Castle Rising make an interesting outing, and readers are very fond of Blickling Hall, Holkham Hall, Houghton Hall, Felbrigg Hall (lots of summer events), and Sandringham, less grand than other royal residences.

Norwich is distinguished yet lively, not overly touristy, with plenty to see.

Much of the countryside is flat and repetitive – better for cyclists than walkers, with quiet lanes, attractive villages and country churches, and fair views. The best parts – the winding rivers and reed-fringed meres of the Broads – are best seen from a boat, but we've also found some good bits for landlubbers.

Where to stay

BANNINGHAM TG2129 **Wheelers Meadow** *Colby Rd, Banningham, Norwich NR11 7DY (01263) 733325* **£40;** 3 rms, 1 with own bthrm. Attractive country house in pretty, recently landscaped gardens with a newly furnished residents' sitting room, open fires, tasty evening meals, good breakfasts with their own eggs and home-made preserves, real ales (brewed on the premises), and friendly owners; plenty to do nearby.
BLAKENEY TG0243 **Blakeney Hotel** *Blakeney, Holt NR25 7NE (01263) 740797* **£176,** plus special breaks; 60 very comfortable rms, many with views over

the salt marshes and some with their own little terrace. Overlooking the harbour with fine views, this friendly hotel has appealing public rooms, good food, very pleasant staff, indoor swimming pool, saunas, spa bath, billiard room, and garden; good disabled access.

BLICKLING TG1728 **Buckinghamshire Arms** *Blickling, Norwich NR11 6NF (01263) 732133* **£50,** plus special breaks; 3 rms with four-posters, one with own shower. Handsome Jacobean inn in the grounds of Blickling Hall, with a civilised atmosphere, helpful staff, interesting food in the bar and restaurant (best to book), nice breakfasts, well kept ales and good wines.

BURNHAM MARKET TF8342 **Hoste Arms** *The Green, Burnham Market, King's Lynn PE31 8HD (01328) 738777* **£76,** plus special breaks; 28 comfortable rms. Handsome inn on the green of a lovely Georgian village, with a smartly civilised atmosphere, attractive bars, some interesting period features, stylish food in the conservatory and restaurant, inc morning coffee and afternoon tea, well kept real ales and good wines, and professional friendly staff; disabled access.

CAISTOR ST EDMUND TG2303 **Old Rectory** *Caistor St Edmund, Norwich NR14 8QS (01508) 492490* *£58;* 3 rms. Handsome Georgian former rectory in a country village just a couple of miles from Norwich; friendly owners, fine antiques and paintings, residents' own drawing and dining rooms with winter log fires, super 4-course evening meals using much home-grown produce, and enjoyable breakfasts; croquet in the quiet garden, ponies in surrounding paddocks, and 2 big welcoming lurchers; children over 8.

DOWNHAM MARKET TF6103 **Crown** *Bridge St, Downham Market, Norfolk PE38 9DH (01366) 382322* **£55,** plus special breaks; 9 rms. 17th-c coaching inn with an interesting history, low beams, flagstones and a roaring log fire, restaurant in the former stables, and a welcoming cheerful landlord.

GREAT BIRCHAM TF7632 **King's Head** *Great Bircham, King's Lynn PE31 6RJ (01485) 578265* **£59;** 5 rms. Old-fashioned and rather grand-looking Victorian country inn with an unassuming lounge, a quiet pleasant atmosphere and good log fire, cheerful Italian landlord, reliable generous bar food (quite a few Italian specialities and tempting puddings), no smoking dining area, decent wines and well kept beers, and a big side lawn with seats and playthings.

GRIMSTON TF7022 **Congham Hall** *Grimston, King's Lynn PE32 1AH (01485) 600250* **£145,** plus special breaks; 14 individually decorated rms. Warmly welcoming and handsome Georgian manor in 40 acres inc herb, vegetable and flower gardens (herbs for sale and garden open to the public), outdoor swimming pool, tennis court, paddock, orchards, and cricket pitch – also, walks leaflets; lovely drawing room, a pretty orangery formal restaurant with excellent modern cooking (lighter lunches in the bar), and exemplary service; children over 12.

KING'S LYNN TF6120 **Tudor Rose** *St Nicholas St, King's Lynn PE30 1LR (01553) 762824* **£50,** plus special breaks; 14 refurbished rms. Attractive half-timbered 15th-c inn with interesting medieval door, friendly chatty atmosphere, decent food in the bar and no smoking raftered restaurant, and good breakfasts; disabled access.

MORSTON TG0043 **Morston Hall** *Morston, Holt NR25 7AA (01263) 741041* *£110,* plus special breaks; 6 comfortable rms with country views. Attractive 17th-c flint-walled house in a tidal village; lovely quiet gardens, beams and open fires in 2 small lounges, hard-working friendly owners, very good modern English cooking (they also run cookery demonstrations and hold wine and food events), thoughtful small wine list, and super breakfasts; croquet; cl Jan.

MUNDFORD TL8093 **Crown** *Crown St, Mundford, Thetford IP26 5HQ (01842) 878233* *£55;* 14 good rms. Friendly small village pub, originally a hunting inn and rebuilt in the 18th c, with an attractive choice of reasonably priced, straightforward food, very welcoming staff, happy atmosphere, and well kept real ales; dogs welcome; disabled access.

NORWICH TG2208 **Beeches** *2–6 Earlham Rd, Norwich NR2 3DB (01603) 621167* **£76,** plus special breaks; 35 quiet rms. Three listed Victorian mansions and an extension only 10 minutes' stroll from the city centre but standing in 4 acres of

English Heritage Victorian gardens, with a relaxed informal atmosphere, friendly resident owners, enjoyable food in the bistro-style restaurant, and good breakfasts; cl Christmas; no children; disabled access.

PULHAM MARKET TM1986 **Old Bakery** *Church Walk, Pulham Market, Diss IP21 4SJ (01379) 676492* **£50**; 3 rms. 16th-c no smoking house with lots of beams and timbers, an inglenook with a fine log fire in the lounge, good breakfasts, enjoyable evening meals, and a friendly atmosphere; cl Christmas/New Year; no children.

SOUTH LOPHAM TM0381 **Malting Farm** *Blo'Norton Rd, South Lopham, Diss IP22 2HT (01379) 687201* ***£44**, plus special breaks; 3 well furnished rms, 1 with own bthrm. Welcoming, no smoking Elizabethan farmhouse on a working dairy farm, with woodburners in the inglenook fireplaces in both the sitting and dining rooms, big breakfasts with home-baked bread and preserves around a large table, and small play area with toys; the owner's passion is embroidery, patchwork, spinning and quilting; cl Christmas/New Year.

SPROWSTON TG2512 **Sprowston Manor** *Wroxham Rd, Sprowston, Norwich NR7 8RP (01603) 410871* **£130**, plus special breaks; 94 individually decorated, spacious rms. Extended 16th-c manor house in 10 acres of parkland surrounded by Sprowston Park golf course; comfortable day rooms, fine food in the elegant orangery and attractive restaurant, leisure club with palms and stone balustrades, poolside bar, health spa; disabled access.

STARSTON TM2384 **Starston Hall** *Starston, Harleston IP20 9PU (01379) 854252* **£70**; 3 rms. Of Elizabethan origin and partly surrounded by the original moat, this attractive house stands in landscaped gardens within a large farm estate; carefully restored and with many original features, there is a spacious and elegant drawing room with beams and an open fire, a candlelit dining room, enjoyable food using organic produce (available to non-residents also), and helpful owners; cl Christmas/New Year; children over 12; disabled access.

STOKE HOLY CROSS TG2302 **Salamanca Farm** *Stoke Holy Cross, Norwich NR14 8QJ (01508) 492322* ***£36**; 4 rms. Mainly Victorian farmhouse (parts are much older) just a short stroll from the River Tas, with a guests' lounge, a spacious dining room, a big garden, and a farm shop; cl 15 Dec–15 Jan; disabled access.

SWAFFHAM TF8109 **Strattons** *Ash Close, Swaffham PE37 7NH (01760) 723845* ***£90**, plus special breaks; 7 interesting, pretty rms. Warmly welcoming, elegant Queen Anne house (no smoking throughout) with delicious English food using home-grown herbs and vegetables from a family smallholding, a carefully chosen wine list illustrated with Mrs Scott's own watercolours, and comfortable drawing rooms with open fires and lots of china cats, dried flowers, and books; big cupboard full of toys and games for children; cl 24–26 Dec; dogs welcome.

THORNHAM TF7343 **Lifeboat** *Thornham, Hunstanton PE36 6LT (01485) 512236* **£74**, plus special breaks; 13 pretty rms, most with sea view. Well placed by coastal flats, with a very cosy atmosphere – especially in winter, when there are 5 fires and antique paraffin lamps; good food in both the bar and elegant restaurant; partial disabled access.

THORPE MARKET TG2434 **Elderton Lodge** *Thorpe Market, North Walsham NR11 8TZ (01263) 833547* ***£90**, plus special breaks; 11 rms. 18th-c shooting lodge and dower house for adjacent Gunton Hall estate, lots of original features such as old gun cabinets and fine panelling, a comfortable lounge bar, dining conservatory for less formal meals, restaurant with good food using fresh fish and game from the estate, and 6 acres of mature grounds overlooking herds of deer on the 1,000 acres of Gunton Park; cl 2 wks Jan; children over 10; disabled access.

TITCHWELL TF7543 **Titchwell Manor** *Titchwell, King's Lynn PE31 8BB (01485) 210221* ***£110**, plus special breaks; 16 rms. Comfortable hotel, handy for the nearby RSPB reserve, with an open fire, magazines and good naturalists' records of the wildlife, a cheerful bar, a pretty no smoking restaurant with French windows on to the sheltered neatly kept walled garden, very good food (especially fish), and particularly helpful licensees and staff; lots of good walks and footpaths nearby; dogs welcome (bdrms only, £2.50); cl last 2 wks Jan; disabled access.

WARHAM TF9441 **Three Horseshoes** *Warham, Wells-next-the-Sea NR23 1NL (01328) 710547* **£52;** 5 rms, 1 with own bthrm. Basic but cheerful local with marvellously unspoilt traditional atmosphere in its 3 friendly gaslit rooms, simple furnishings, a log fire, very tasty generous helpings of bar food, decent wines, home-made lemonade, and very well kept real ales; bdrms are in the Old Post Office adjoining the pub, with lots of beams and a residents' lounge dominated by an inglenook fireplace; cl 24–26 Dec; no children.

WINTERTON-ON-SEA TG4919 **Fisherman's Return** *The Lane, Winterton-on-Sea, Great Yarmouth NR29 4BN (01493) 393305* ***£50;** 3 characterful rms, shared bthrm. Traditional 300-year-old pub in a quiet village, close to the beach, with warmly welcoming owners, a relaxed lounge bar, open fire, good home-made food inc fresh fish (fine crabs), enjoyable breakfasts, and sheltered garden.

To see and do

NORFOLK Family Attraction of the Year

☺ ! 🐾 **LENWADE** TG1017 **Dinosaur Park** (Weston Park, off A1067) Splendidly silly, but put together with some style, this is a fun treat for small children mad about dinosaurs. Hidden in 300 acres of nicely kept woodland are life-size reconstructions of the fearsome creatures, lying in wait around each corner. Young children can have great fun running round between them, and it's interesting seeing how big some of these beasts really were. There are various themed play areas (one specially for under-5s), with the most ingenious the Climb-a-Saurus, a 75ft brontosaurus replica with slides, ladders, and so on tucked away inside. A woodland maze is also included in the price, but other activities, including a deer 'safari' and crazy golf, have a small extra charge. It's not the best value trip out in the area, and visitors over 9 or 10 are less likely to be enthralled, but for some reason dinosaurs never lose their appeal to the very small, who'll enjoy this more than you might expect or understand. The picnic area has barbecues. Meals, snacks, shop; open daily May–Aug, plus wknds and school hols from Easter–Oct; (01603) 870245; £4.50 (£3.50 children 3–14).

ACLE TG3910
✗ The **windmill** is a fine example.
ATTLEBOROUGH TM0292
🐝 † **Peter Beales Rose Nursery** A specialist in old-fashioned roses that you won't find for sale elsewhere; you can wander around the 3 acres of gardens; cl Sun in Jan; (01953 454707). The 15th-c **church** is interesting, with an unusual round tower and a screen decorated with the arms of the 24 bishoprics in England when it was built. The White Lodge has decent food.
AYLSHAM TG1926
🚂 ♿ **Bure Valley Railway** 🔳 Steamtrain trips along 9 miles of narrow-gauge track between here and Wroxham; you can combine the journey with a 1½-hour Broads cruise. The stock isn't very old, but the people are friendly and the journey is good value. Snacks, shop, disabled access;

trains Apr–Oct, best to ring for timetable; (01263) 733858; £6.90 full return (£10.75 inc Broads cruise).
BACONSTHORPE TG1336
🏰 **Baconsthorpe Castle** The gatehouses, curtain walls and towers are all that's left of this moated and semi-fortified 15th-c house, but displays show what it must have looked like in its glory. A very pretty peaceful spot, with swans on the lake adding to its charm; free. You can find information booklets at the nearby post office. The Hare & Hounds on the way to Hempstead is useful for lunch.
BANHAM TM0587
🐘 🐝 ❀ **Banham Zoo** (The Grove) Over 20 acres of parkland and garden with rare and endangered species, particularly monkeys and apes. Also an indoor activity centre, ice-cream parlour, play area and putting green.

Across the road is **Appleyard Craft Court** around a cobbled courtyard. Helpful explanatory notes beside enclosures, and feeding times are spread throughout the day. Regular visitors tell us it gets better with every visit. Meals, snacks, shop, disabled access; cl 25–26 Dec; (01953) 887771 ext 217; £6.95 (crafts free). The King's Head opposite the medieval market hall in New Buckenham has inexpensive home cooking.

BLAKENEY TG0443

☐ Crabbing is fun from here, and surprisingly successful. Also a (free) collection of waterfowl down by the harbour, long breezy walks, unspoilt flint cottages, broad sky and sea vistas. There's a good dyke walk to Cley-next-the-Sea, with the birds on the mudflats for company. Blakeney has a very good tea shop; besides the Blakeney Hotel, the Manor, White Horse and King's Arms are all good.

🐦 ☐ **Blakeney Point** This NT-owned **nature reserve** is edged by a good stretch of the North Norfolk Coast Path, which gets better as you walk along it, although the shingle bank needs patience and is hard on the ankles; pleasant dunes await at the far end for walkers who persevere.

⛴ **Seal boat trips**
(Morston/Blakeney) Boats leave from Morston Quay slightly W of Blakeney on the A149 coast road once or twice a day from Mar–Oct (times depend on the tide), and on most winter wknds; when the tide allows you'll also find trips wending their way down the creek from the little harbour at Blakeney itself. Most last 2 hours, which takes in an hour or so exploring the bird reserve at Blakeney Point (see *above*). The highlight comes just before that, when the boat goes past the sandbanks at the end of the Point, where dozens of grey and common seals lie basking happily in the sun. Several different operators run boats, with the smaller ones owned by the Beans, our favourites. Booking is recommended (especially in summer, when there are crowds of visitors waiting on the quay), on (01263) 740038. £4.50. Local information centres have full details of operators and times.

BLICKLING TG1728

🏫🖼⚙ ☐ **Blickling Hall** (B1354)
Magnificent house dating mainly from early 17th c, though the hedges that flank it may be older. Dramatic carved oak staircase and splendid paintings (inc a famous Canaletto), but best of all is the 38-metre (125ft) Long Gallery with its ornate Jacobean plaster ceiling, and the Chinese bedroom, still lined with 18th-c hand-painted wallpaper. The gardens and grounds are lovely, with several miles of footpaths. Meals, snacks, shop, plant centre, good disabled access (a lift in the house); house open pm Thurs–Sun and bank hols Apr–Oct, plus Tues in Aug, garden also open am, daily in Aug and winter Sun; (01263) 733084; £6, £3.50 garden only; NT. There's a pleasant walk from the Buckinghamshire Arms (good for lunch), and free public access to the parkland on the W side of the pike-filled lake with its water birds. Here there are large tracts of woodland and pasture, as well as a disused railway line, and perhaps even kingfishers on the River Bure. There are circular walks within the park.

BRANCASTER TF7944

🐦⛴ **Scolt Head** Miles of dunes, flat coastal saltings, broad tidal beaches: a fine lonely place, largely National Trust and full of birds – Scolt Head island is an important breeding ground, and in good weather a boat takes people across from Brancaster Staithe. Incidentally all along this coast the wading birds are best seen on a falling tide. The Jolly Sailors is useful for lunch.

BRECKLAND TL9188

☐ ✤ **East Wretham Heath Nature Reserve** Around Thetford, this is a region of poor, flat, sandy heathland with scattered shallow meres and originally scrubby mixed woodland, extensively planted now with pines instead; there are forest walks, for example from car parks on the A134 NW of Thetford, where you may disturb roe deer. A good place to see it as it was is East Wretham Heath off the A1075 NE of Thetford: limited visitor facilities but plenty of wild flowers, nature trails, and hides for watching the birds and deer; free.

✤ **Pingo Trail** Starting from Stow

Bedon, this is an 8-mile path through the unforested part of the adjacent Breckland grasslands, largely army training ground. It passes through 3 Sites of Special Scientific Interest (inc Cranberry Rough, an alder swampland), taking you along a disused railway line before joining the Peddars Way at Hockham Heath.

BRESSINGHAM TM0880

⊛ ⚑⛊ **Bressingham Steam Museum & Gardens** (A1066) The founder, Alan Bloom, has effectively combined his two interests at this rewarding site. The 6 acres of informal gardens are planted with 5,000 species and cultivars of alpines and perennials in island beds, with lots of the dwarf conifers Bloom has done so much to popularise. Then there's the excellent steam collection, inc 50 road and rail engines, mostly restored to working order, and a charming fairground carousel. Four steam-hauled trains run through the charming countryside and parts of the garden (all may not be in steam out of high season). Meals, snacks, shop, disabled access; cl Nov–Mar; (01379) 687382; £4.50. The Garden House is handy for lunch.

THE BROADS TG3017

Norfolk's network of linking waterways is not easy to visit on foot or by car; few paths get close enough to the Broads themselves, often tantalisingly out of sight, and once away from the waterside and fenny woodlands you are immediately into the flat, humdrum agricultural landscapes found in much of the rest of the area. There is some scope for strolling along rivers, with pumping-mills, birdlife and the boating scene being the principal features. The best way to see the Broads is undoubtedly by boat.

✗ ⌂ **Berney Arms Windmill** Across the water from Burgh Castle and amazingly remote, this and its nearby pub can be reached not by road but either by boat or train from Great Yarmouth, or as a worthwhile objective for a long walk with a real sense of adventure, across the marshes from Wickhampton or Halvergate, passing other former windpumps. The 7-storey mill dates from the 19th c when it was used to drain water from the marshes.

Cl 1–2pm, and Oct–Mar; (01493) 700605; *£1.50. There's also scope for walking by reedy Breydon Water, the estuarine channel of the River Yare between here and Great Yarmouth.

⛴ **Boat cruising** Broads cruising is generally a week-long affair, but could be worked into a short-stay holiday; the boats nowadays have every mod con and are easy for even a novice to handle, but it's a chilly pastime until summer's well established. Wroxham is the main centre for this, with several boat hire firms (though one of the quieter bases in the N might make a better choice for just a day on the water). So it's a good place to watch the boating activities from dry land, or to use as the start of a longer cruising holiday. It can be very congested in summer. The Bell has kept more character than many places around.

⛴ ⚑ **Day boating** The quieter reaches of the more northern Broads are probably more suited to this than the busier parts around Wroxham and Horning. Stalham TG3724, Barton Turf TG3522 and Wayford Bridge TG3424 are possible bases. For a quick taste of the Broads, you can combine a boat trip with the trains on the **Bure Valley Railway** at Aylsham.

⊛ ⚐ ⛴ **Fairhaven Garden Trust** Charming wooded watergardens set beside the private South Walsham Inner Broad, the waterways linked by little bridges. Rare plants, masses of rhododendrons among the flowers and a tree – the King Oak – said to be 900 years old. It's an extensive place, running to some 230 acres, inc a big **bird sanctuary** – to visit this part you need permission from the warden. **Boat trips** every half-hour. Snacks, shop, disabled access – but the paths are quite uneven; open all year exc 25 Dec; (01603) 270449; £3. The Ship has good home cooking.

⛴ ⌂ **Hickling** It's normally possible to hire a boat for just the day or maybe an even shorter period here. And walkers have a pleasant path along the north shore.

⛴ ⌂ **Horning** One of the main centres for Broads boat hire, chiefly for longer spells afloat. So it's a good place to watch the boating activity, perhaps from the Swan or the Ferry, both busy Chef & Brewer pubs. There's also some scope for walking along the canalised parts of the River Bure.

★ ˅ **Neatishead** This attractive village, with a decent pub, gives access to the **Barton Broad** nature reserve.

˅ † **Ranworth Broad** One of the few broads the cruise boats can't get to. A **conservation centre** here has nature trails and displays of local and natural history; snacks, shop, disabled access; cl Nov–Mar; free. There may be guided tours of the local wildlife on summer Suns; best to book, on (01603) 270479. The village **church** has the best painted rood screen in the county.

◠ **River Thurne** The towpath by the canalised parts gives one of the relatively few opportunities for Broadland waterside walks.

˙ **Strumpshaw Marsh** (off Low Rd, Brundall) Partly drained water meadows and fen between woodland and the River Yare, with RSPB hides for watching marsh birds inc harriers and bearded tits, winter geese, and maybe swallowtail butterflies in June; *£2.50 (RSPB members free). The Yare Inn in Brundall is popular for food.

Watching the boats At **Surlingham** by the Ferry House pub there's still a rowing-boat ferry. And nearby Coldham Hall is a pub with lovely riverside gardens. **Geldeston** is at the navigable head of the River Waveney; down a long track from the road, the Lock, a remote candlelit pub, gives a flavour of how the Broads were 40 years ago – at least out of high season. **Dilham** is one of the few places where by car you can get down to the Norfolk Broads waterside; the Crown pub here is useful. At **Stokesby**, the Ferry House pub is well placed for quite a busy stretch of the River Bure. **Sutton Staithe** is a lovely quiet waterside spot; the Sutton Staithe Hotel here is useful. **Bramerton** gives car access to the waterside; the Woods End pub here is handy. In the pretty village of **Coltishall**, the Rising Sun pub is on a bend of the River Bure; you can hire bikes from nearby Just Pedalling. **Ormesby St Michael** gives views from the attractive waterside lawns of the Eel's Foot pub.

BURGH CASTLE TG4705

🏛 You can still see sections of the massive walls of this coastal Roman fortress, built in the 3rd c to protect the coast from Saxon marauders; free. The Church Farm Inn overlooking the Yare and Waveney has decent food.

BURGH ST MARGARET TG4513

♫ ☺ ♣ 🐄 ⌂ **The Village** (A1064) Delightful pastiche of a 19th-c village, but an idealised one rather than an authentic set-up along the lines of somewhere like Beamish (in Northumbria). Old-fashioned fairground rides (inc traditional Victorian gallopers), candle-making and other crafts, and amusing live shows – the puppet show effectively blends marionettes with people. Also silent comedy films in 1920s concert hall, miniature railway, steam-hauled trailer rides, working sawmill, collections of vintage motorbikes and other vehicles, woodland walks, and decent adventure play area. Meals, snacks, shops, disabled access; cl Nov–Mar; (01493) 369770; *£5.95 (*£2.75 Sat, when less going on: no crafts or live shows).

BURNHAM MARKET TF8342

★ Handsome and opulent village with a fine green, and gatehouse and 13th-c priory remains; the Hoste Arms is a good dining pub.

BURNHAM THORPE TF8541

† This hamlet's strong Lord Nelson connections include a pub named after him, with interesting related memorabilia. The lectern in the village church uses wood from HMS *Victory*, and the church has other Nelson mementos.

CAISTER-ON-SEA TG5012

🏛 Like the other settlements down this coast, Caister plays host to a good many summer visitors, with all the usual attractions, inc long sandy beaches. It's also got a lifeboat station, right by the beach. The town has various remains of an excavated **Roman fort** inc one gateway and a town wall. The Ship pub (Victoria St) has amazing summer floral displays.

🏰 🐄 **Caister Castle** This moated ruin is set back from the town, a little way inland. Falstaff (the original behind Shakespeare's creation) built it on returning from Agincourt; its walls surround a 30-metre (98ft) tower. The grounds contain a **motor museum** with a good collection of vehicles from 1893 onwards. Snacks, some disabled access; open daily exc Sat mid-May–Sept; (01572) 787251; £5.

CASTLE ACRE TF8115

★ ▥ ❧ A delightful village, with an 18th-c feel along the tree-shaded walk of Stocks Green (the Ostrich here is handy for lunch). The sparse ruins of a great **Norman castle** are still awe-inspiring. The site is on the Peddars Way, a Roman road following the track of an earlier herding way. West Acre, 2 or 3 miles W, has a few further priory remains, and (like Castle Acre itself) picturesque fords over the River Nar. A few miles N, some private woodland opens for 3 wks in late spring for its magnificent azaleas.

▥ **Castle Acre Priory** Extensive ruins of a Cluniac building by William the Conqueror's son-in-law include the fine arcaded W front of the 11th/12th-c church, and a chapel and 15th-c gatehouse; good Walkman tour, some special events. Well laid out, and very picturesque. Snacks, shop, some disabled access; cl winter Mon and Tues, 24–26 Dec, and 1–2pm for lunch; (01760) 755394; £3.10; EH.

CASTLE RISING TF6624

▥ **Castle Rising Castle** 🖼 Massive earthworks surround this fine Norman keep, a marvellous setting for the summer jousting they occasionally stage here. Shop; cl winter Mon and Tues, 24–26 Dec; (01553) 631330; £2.75. In the attractive village the Black Horse is a popular dining pub.

CLEY-NEXT-THE-SEA TG0443

✝ ✗ ❀ Handy for the bird-sanctuary marshes towards the Blakeney Point sandspit, a pleasant village with a magnificent **church**. The neatly restored **windmill** is a more obvious landmark, and has great views from the top (open pm Easter–Oct; (01263) 740209; £1.50), as well as very good accommodation. The George & Dragon and the Three Swallows are decent food stops, and there's a long pebbly beach.

COCKLEY CLEY TF8004

♨ ❧ ✝ ⌂ ! Lots of interesting historical things to see around this village

(pronounced to rhyme with 'fry'). There's a **museum** in a 17th-c cottage, nature reserve, carriage collection, and 7th-c Saxon church, but most unusual is the **Iceni village**, built as and where it was believed to exist 2,000 years ago. Snacks, some disabled access; cl Nov–Easter; (01760) 724588; £3.30 covers all attractions. The Twenty Churchwardens is handy for lunch.

CROMER TG2242

✝ ❀ ♨ ❀ Popular seaside resort since Victorian times, with lovely sandy beaches, more sun than average, bustling markets, golf courses, interesting shops and galleries and lots of entertainments. The pier is one of the last in the country to present an end-of-pier show – very popular, so worth booking early. The tower of the imposing **church** on Church St – Norfolk's tallest – gives spectacular views of the surrounding countryside. A good local-history **museum** next door is spread over 5 19th-c fishermen's cottages (shop; cl Mon lunch, am Sun, Good Fri, 23–26 Dec, 1 Jan; £1.80), and on the prom a small **lifeboat museum** looks at local lifeboatman Henry Blogg, who over 53 years saved 873 lives (shop, disabled access; cl Oct–Apr; free). Nearby you often find dressed crabs for sale; the crab boats still work from here, and Cromer crabs are the best on England's E coast. The clifftop Dolphin has decent food.

△ ❧ **Beacon Hill** The only place of any height (a humble 90-metre, 300ft) on the North Norfolk coast; the coast path here detours over the sandy heath and through woodlands.

DENVER SLUICE TF5800

! These towering hydraulic sluice gates control water levels in these parts – quite a sight. The Jenyns Arms, with peacocks in its riverside gardens, is a pleasant lunch stop nearby.

DOWNHAM MARKET TF5903

✝ ♨ ⌂ ✙ **Hermitage Hall** (Bridge Farm, A1122 just W) Based around an old chapel used by pilgrims on the way to Walsingham, now with mementos of local boy Nelson (inc letters, birth certificate and death mask), small collection of cars, Victorian street, and gentle walks down to the Ouse. Snacks, shop, disabled access; normally open pm Fri and Sun and bank hols, Easter–Dec; (01366) 383185; *£1, guided tour extra *£3. There's an adjacent animal sanctuary. In town, the Crown has good-value food Thurs–Sun.

EARSHAM TM3188

ᵛ **Otter Trust** (off A143) This charitable trust works towards reintroducing otters to rivers from which they've disappeared; they're displayed here in a natural environment. They're obviously cheerful and intelligent, but don't perform on demand and you may have to wait a while to see anything. Snacks, shop, disabled access; cl Nov–Mar; (01986) 893470; £4.50. The Green Dragon in Bungay is a heartening retreat if they don't show.

ERPINGHAM TG2032

❀ ☗ ⌖ **Alby Crafts & Gardens** Four acres of interesting shrubs, plants and bulbs, with a museum devoted to lace, another concentrating on bottles (over 2,000 of them, mainly from regional brewers), a bee observation hive, and crafts inc woodturning and stained glass. Very good roses and lilies in July. Meals, snacks, shop, mostly disabled access; cl Mon (exc bank hols), all wkdys mid-Dec–mid-Mar (lace museum also cl Sat); (01263) 761226; crafts and lace museum free, gardens *£2, bottle museum *50p. The Ark, and the Saracen's Head out at Wolterton (at the start of a pleasant 2- or 3-hour circular walk), are both very good for lunch.

FAKENHAM TF9429

★ A pleasant market town; the comfortable Wensum Lodge Hotel has good food (as does the prettily set Sculthorpe Mill off the A148 just W), and the roads N pass through attractive villages.

FELBRIGG TG1939

❀ ❀ ⌖ **Felbrigg Hall** Magnificent 17th-c house in splendid grounds, inc an orangery with a fine collection of camellias, and a colourfully restored walled garden overlooked by a dovecot. The house is decorated with paintings and furnishings from the 18th c, and has a wonderful Gothic library. Lots of events, with something going on at the stable block most Sun pms. Meals,

snacks, shop, disabled access; hall and gardens cl Thurs, Fri, and Nov–Mar, hall also cl am; (01263) 837444; £5.50, garden only £2.20; NT. There's public access to the 1,700-acre wooded grounds (cl 25 Dec only), landscaped by Repton, with their fine mature trees and lake.

FILBY TG4612

❀ ⌖ **Thrigby Hall Wildlife Gardens** 18th-c park filled with Asian animals and birds, with tropical and bird houses, a tree walk, a willow pattern garden, and ornamental wildfowl on the lake. Also a huge jungly swamp hall where crocodiles doze under water. Readers enjoy coming here – though warn of queues on summer wknds. Summer snacks, shop, disabled access; (01493) 369477; *£5.50.

FORNCETT ST MARY TM1694

⌖ **Industrial Steam Museum** Unusual collection of 8 giant stationary steam engines rescued from all over the country, inc one that used to open Tower Bridge, and another, the Dover engine, which after 20 years' restoration is finally back to working order. Snacks, shop, disabled access; open first Sun of month, May–Nov, when the engines are in steam; (01508) 488277; *£3.50 (2 children free with every adult). The Bird in Hand over at Wreningham is a good-value dining pub.

FOXLEY WOOD TG0522

⌖ A big block of ancient woodland, mainly deciduous and grown naturally for many centuries; lovely woodland spring flowers.

GLANDFORD TG0441

☗ **Shell Museum** Curious little museum housing the often very beautiful seashells and other interesting objects collected by Sir Alfred Jodrell, who lived in nearby Bayfield Hall. Some disabled access; cl lunchtimes, all day Sun and Mon (exc bank hols), and Nov–Feb; (01263) 740081; £1.50. The King's Head at Letheringsett is quite handy for lunch.

GOODERSTONE TF7602

★ † ❀ Attractive village, with decent pub, an ancient **church** and nearby **watergardens**.

GREAT BIRCHAM TF7632

✕ ✿ ★ ▣ **Windmill** Not far from Houghton Hall, this striking mill is on

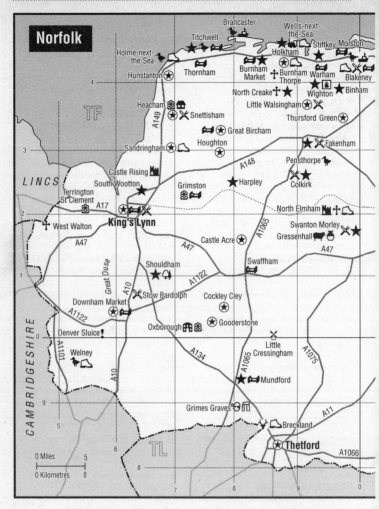

Norfolk

that Norfolk rarity, a hill – so one of the few places with views. They sell bread baked at the mill's own bakery. Tearooms, shop, some disabled access; open daily in school hols, plus Weds–Sun Easter–Sept; (01485) 578393; £2.50. You can hire bikes. The village is attractive, with an **art gallery**, and the King's Head Hotel (unpretentious despite being a favourite with Sandringham shooting parties) is good for lunch.
GREAT WITCHINGHAM TG0818
♥ ❦ **Norfolk Wildlife Park** (A1067)
40 acres of attractive parkland filled with a good range of British and

European wildlife. In spring they have around 500 heron nests up in the trees – an unusual feature is a tower you can climb up to be on their level. The 2 big play areas appeal most to slightly older children, with tyres, rope swings and the like. Meals, snacks, shop; cl Nov–Mar; (01603) 872274; £4 (£2.50 children 4–15). The Old Brewery House in Reepham is the nearest good place for lunch.
GREAT YARMOUTH TG5307
☺ ✝ A cross between working town and resort, this still has a busy fishing harbour – also used as a port of call by the Broads cruising boats. There are

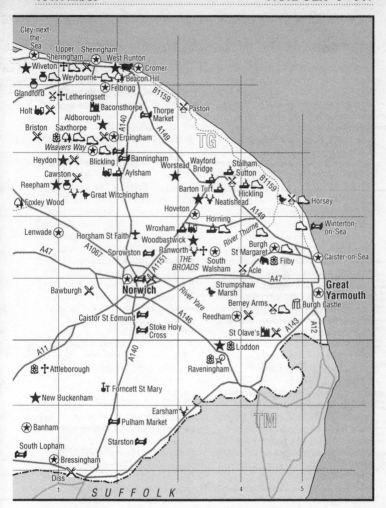

Cley-next-the-Sea
Upper Sheringham
Sheringham
West Runton
Wiveton
Weybourne
Cromer
Beacon Hill
Glandford
Felbrigg
Letheringsett
Holt
Baconsthorpe
Thorpe Market
Paston
Briston
Aldborough
Saxthorpe
Erpingham
B1159
Heydon
Blickling
Banningham
Wayford Bridge
Stalham
Cawston
Aylsham
Worstead
Sutton
Reepham
Barton Turf
Hickling
Great Witchingham
Neatishead
Horsey
Foxley Wood
Hoveton
Horning
Lenwade
Wroxham
River Thurne
Winterton-on-Sea
Horsham St Faith
Woodbastwick
Burgh St Margaret
Sprowston
Ranworth
THE BROADS
South Walsham
Caister-on-Sea
Acle
Bawburgh
Norwich
Strumpshaw Marsh
River Yare
Berney Arms
Great Yarmouth
Burgh Castle
Caistor St Edmund
Reedham
Stoke Holy Cross
St Olave's
Attleborough
Loddon
Raveningham
New Buckenham
Forncett St Mary
Earsham
Banham
Pulham Market
South Lopham
Starston
Bressingham
Diss
SUFFOLK
TG
TM
A140 A149 A1151 A47 A146 A143 A12 A11 A1067 A47

lots of holiday entertainments, particularly good for families (there's a decent fairground too) and some attractions that might well tempt older visitors into the town if they were nearby. The last surviving steam drifter, the *Lydia Eva*, divides her time between here and Lowestoft – if she's in South Quay then she can usually be visited Easter–Oct; donations. The 14th-c **Church of St Nicholas** at the top end of the market place has an exceptionally wide nave, and an impressive west front. The smart quay-view Star Hotel has good-value bar food.

Amazonia (Sea Front) Indoor tropical paradise with reptiles, insects, butterflies and birds; they have a 4-metre (13ft) alligator, a python well over 7 metres (24ft) long, and an iguana named Levi. Snacks, shop, disabled access; cl 25–26 Dec; (01493) 842202; *£2.50.

Elizabethan House Museum (South Quay) Recently refurbished, this is a patchwork of historical detail – built in 1596, it has a Georgian façade, 16th-c panelled rooms and, among features from later periods, some rooms decorated and furnished in 19th-c style, and a functional Victorian kitchen. Shop, disabled access to ground floor only; open 2 wks at Easter, then daily exc Sat Jun–Sept; (01493) 745526; £2. The **Maritime Museum of East Anglia** (Marine Parade) looks at the local fishing industry, with some more incongruous features inc a mummified hand and an Indian scalp; times as Elizabethan house; £1; (01493) 745526. The 13th-c **Tolhouse Museum** (Tolhouse St) used to be the town's gaol and courthouse (you can still see the dungeons). It now has local history, and a brass rubbing centre; times as Elizabethan House; (01493) 745526; £1.

❀ ! **Merrivale Model Village** (Wellington Pier Gardens) Attractive landscaped gardens with children's rides and remote-controlled cars, and the exceptionally detailed village – featuring a railway, radio-controlled boats and over 200 models. Meals, snacks, shop, disabled access; cl Nov–Easter; (01493) 842097; £2.50.

🏚 **Old Merchant's House** (Row 117) 17th-c house standing among the narrow lanes or Rows nr the waterfront, with some well restored rooms. Shop; cl 1–2pm, and all Nov–Mar; (01493) 857900; £1.85.

🐟 **Sea Life Centre** (Marine Parade) Displays of the kinds of marine life found on the Norfolk coast, as well as underwater tunnels through shark-infested oceans and tropical fish. Meals, snacks, shop, disabled access; cl 25 Dec; (01493) 330631; *£5.50.

GRESSENHALL TF9716
🐄🐷 **Norfolk Rural Life Museum** Re-creation of a typical 1920s farm, with rare breeds of sheep, pigs, cattle and poultry, and working reconstructions of agricultural life. Meals, snacks, shop, disabled access; cl am Sun, Nov–Easter; (01362) 860563; £3.90. The White Horse at Longham has good-value food.

GRIMES GRAVES TL8189
⚒🏚 Bring a torch to this Breckland site, as you can climb into one of the 300 pits and vertical shafts which lead down into the galleries – some around 10 metres (33ft) deep – where the Neolithic people mined their flint; the landscape around is pitted by their efforts. No lavatories at the site, but there are

some within a mile. Shop; cl 1–2pm, all day Mon and Tues Nov–Mar, Christmas; (01842) 810656; £1.95.
GRIMSTON TF7022
❀ **Congham Hall Herb Garden** In summer this has around 500 different herbs, in traditional layouts, with many unusual varieties for sale; open 2–4pm Apr–Sept (cl Sat); free.
HEACHAM TF6837
❀🏚 **Norfolk Lavender** (Caley Mill) The largest lavender-growing and distilling operation in the country, along with a national collection of lavender species and cultivars. The guided tour (daily spring bank hol–Sept) really adds interest, and at harvest time they may drive visitors out to the fields. Also rose and herb gardens. Snacks (inc their lavender and lemon scones), shop, disabled access; cl 25–26 Dec, 1 Jan; (01485) 570384; tours (mid-July–mid-Aug) £1.50, £3.95 by minibus. The Gin Trap at Ringstead (with a decent nearby art gallery) and the Rose & Crown at Snettisham both have good food.
HEYDON TG1127
★ Delightfully unspoilt tucked-away village, with a green that time seems to have passed by, and good food at the Earle Arms.
HOLKHAM TF9143
🏚❀🖼🐦⌂ **Holkham Hall** Splendid Palladian mansion in delightful and very extensive tree-filled grounds with an ornamental lake and an 18th-c walled garden. Sumptuously furnished state rooms, with fine paintings by Claude, Rubens, Van Dyck and Gainsborough. An ancestor of the present owner was Thomas Coke, whose revolutionary farming techniques are described in an exhibition in the porter's lodge; there's also a pottery. Snacks, shop, limited disabled access; open pm Sun–Thurs, and bank hols Easter–Oct; (01328) 710227; £6 for everything, £4 hall only. Walkers have free access to this coastal estate's driveways; the parkland is a bit sombre, but impressively landscaped with the lake, a temple and an obelisk. The Victoria Hotel is handy for lunch. The beach has a bird reserve (and a nudist section). There is a car park quite close to the beach, where pine trees meet the sands; this coastal section of the **North Norfolk Coast Path** is

good for lonely walks – westwards any summer crowds rapidly thin out. From **Overy Staithe** a particularly fine stretch of the path follows a zigzagging dyke – saltmarsh on one side, neat farmland on the other – to the dunes and sandy beach, which never quite looks the same from one day to the next.

HOLME-NEXT-THE-SEA TF6943
🌿 ⌒ From the sandy beach there's a 2-mile walk past a rewarding **bird sanctuary** and saltings to Thornham – another good birdwatching place. Another more serious walking possibility is the **Peddars Way** which starts here – an inland link from the Coast Path, running from Holme down through Castle Acre and then in a strikingly straight bee-line right across the county to Knettishall Heath nr Thetford, following ancient-feeling green ways and quiet lanes. Earnest walkers may find there is a little too much road-walking to sustain interest.

HOLT TG0738
🚂 Pleasant little town with some handsome Georgian buildings; Nicholsons in the High St sells anything from clothes to antiques, and has a useful continental-style licensed café; the market-place Feathers has good-value food. Holt is the terminus of the **North Norfolk Steam Railway** from Sheringham.

HORSEY TG4622
✕ ⌒ 🌿 A quiet corner of the coast, below sea level – among the places most at risk of flooding if the sea defences are breached. There's a good path to the dunes and the sea from the lane past the Nelson Head (good food). On the other side of the main road, **Horsey Windpump** is a restored drainage windmill, now in full working order. Teas, small shop; cl Oct–Mar; £1.20; NT. This is a good area for a varied round walk: a path along quiet reed-fringed Horsey Mere (NT, with wildfowl and otters) and the New Cut to another former drainage windmill – the marshes on the far side of the cut seem alive with birds. Then you can either walk straight back to the village, or for a total contrast join the beach for sea views nr Horsey Corner.

HORSHAM ST FAITH TG2114
✈ **Norwich Aviation Museum** 🖼 (Old Norwich Rd) Enthusiastic displays of local aeronautical history, with aircraft (there's a Vulcan bomber), engines, and other paraphernalia; on the edge of Norwich Airport, so a good view of the live article too. Snacks, shop; cl Mon and winter wkdys; (01603) 625309; *£2.50. The thatched Chequers, prettily placed at Hainford, has good food.

HOUGHTON TF7928
🏠 ⚅ ♨ **Houghton Hall** Built for Robert Walpole and obviously designed to impress, this is a spectacularly grand Palladian mansion set in charming parkland. The state rooms were decorated and furnished by William Kent, and house an important collection of 20,000 model soldiers and other militaria. Heavy horses, Shetland ponies and llamas in the stables. Snacks, shop, disabled access; open pm Thurs, Sun and bank hols Easter–Sept; (01485) 528569; £6.

Days Out

Tanks, shells and fairground organs: Muckleburgh Collection, Weybourne; lunch at the White Horse, Blakeney; Glandford shell museum; Thursford Collection; Letheringsett watermill (if open).

The Broads: Fairhaven Garden Trust, South Walsham, or rent a boat from Wroxham; lunch at the Ferry, Reedham; walk along the River Yare, or take a boat or train from Great Yarmouth to Berney Arms windmill.

Norfolk's mansions: Walk in Mannington Hall/Wolterton Park estates, Saxthorpe; visit Mannington Hall Gardens if open; lunch at the Saracen's Head, Wolterton, or the Buckinghamshire Arms, Blickling; Blickling Hall.

Driving along the C road nr North Pole farm you may spot unusual herds of white deer. The 17th-c Duke's Head at West Rudham has good home cooking.

HOVETON TG3120

❁ **Hoveton Hall Garden** Large and attractive spring woodland garden with daffodils and rhododendrons, lakeside walk and a kitchen garden. The walled old-fashioned herbaceous 'spider garden' has been recently redesigned. You can stay in a wing of the house. Teas, plant sales, disabled access; open Weds, Fri, Sun and bank hols Easter–mid-Sept; (01603) 782798; £3. The Black Horse is useful for lunch.

⚘ 🐄 **Wroxham Barns Craft Centre** 🅳 (Tunstead Rd) Good for families, with several craft workshops in 18th-c restored farm buildings, as well as a children's farm and traditional fair. Meals, snacks, shop, play area, disabled access; cl 25–26 Dec; (01603) 783762; £2 for farm, otherwise free.

HUNSTANTON TF6740

⚓ 🐦 Clean, fresh and well kept resort with gently shelving tidal sands (donkey rides still), summer **boat trips**, and pleasant dune walks past the golf course up to the **bird reserve** on Gore Point. On a clear day you can see Boston's Stump across The Wash. The low cliffs around the town are quite colourful, with different rock strata. The Ancient Mariner (part of Le Strange Hotel, Old Hunstanton) is good value, opposite an interesting craft gallery, and the Marine Bar (St Edmund's Terrace) has decent food all day.

☺ **Oasis** 🅳 Standing out among the typical resort entertainments is this giant leisure park on the prom with tropically heated indoor and outdoor pools and both towering and toddler aquaslides; cl Dec–Feb; £3.35.

🐟 **Sea Life Aquarium** (Southern Promenade) An ocean tunnel at this excellent place brings you face to face with deep-water creatures as well as octopuses and toothy conger eels. Snacks, shop, disabled access; cl 25 Dec, Jan; (01485) 533576; £5.35.

KING'S LYNN TF6120

✝ 🏛 ⚘ Once England's fourth-largest town, it's quieter now, with pleasant corners, some attractive Georgian brick buildings and a few much older

places such as the 17th-c Custom House on the quay by the River Purfleet, the 15th-c **Church of St Nicholas** (Chapel Lane; attractive for festival concerts), the South Gates, Red Mount Chapel and the 2 medieval guildhalls. The first of these, the 15th-c **St George's Guildhall** (King St), is now the town's theatre, and home of the King's Lynn Festival (cl Sun); the tourist information centre has details of tours, (01553) 763044. On Tues the main market place has some good craft stalls. The Tudor Rose between there and St Nicholas is good for lunch, and the Globe Hotel on the market place itself is good value.

◉ **Lynn Museum** (Old Market Sq) Includes the skeleton of a Saxon warrior, and a surprisingly interesting collection of medieval pilgrim badges; cl Sun and Mon; £1.

🏛 🐦 **Old Gaol House** 🅳 (Saturday Market Pl) Lively journey through the town's rich history; with spirited models, and spooky sights, sounds and smells, this is particularly good for children. Shop, disabled access; cl Weds and Thurs from Nov–Easter, 25–26 Dec and 1 Jan; (01553) 763044; £2.30 (inc audio tour). The tour includes the 14th-c King John Cup and other fabulous examples of civic paraphernalia housed in the Undercroft of the handsome medieval Trinity Guildhall (not open to the public).

◉ **Town House Museum** (Queen St) More social history. Shop, limited disabled access; cl Sun exc pm May–Sept, and bank hols; £1.80.

🐦 **Trues Yard** 🅳 (North St) Restored old fishermen's cottages giving a good picture of life here in the 19th century, when families of up to 11 were often squeezed into 2 little rooms. Snacks, shop, mostly disabled access; cl 24 Dec–first Mon in Jan; (01553) 770479; £1.90.

LENWADE TG1017

☺ ! 🦕 **Dinosaur Park** See separate family panel on p.440.

LETHERINGSETT TG0638

✕ ✝ The **church** has an unusual round tower. A restored **watermill** in a pretty setting still mills flour from local wheat. Cl 1–2pm, Sun (exc school and bank hols), Mon, and in winter pm Sat, with demonstrations pm every day; (01263) 713153; £3 during demonstrations, otherwise £2. The King's Head is pleasant for lunch.

LITTLE CRESSINGHAM TF8600
✕ The **windmill** is a fine example. The White Horse does fresh snacks.

LITTLE WALSINGHAM TF9336
🚻 Once as popular a centre of pilgrimage as Canterbury, thanks to a replica of the Virgin Mary's home in Nazareth. Things tailed off when Henry VIII destroyed the priory and its shrine in 1538, but picked up again earlier this century. The Bull Inn is a good place, with plenty of pilgrimage customers. The terminus of the **steam railway** from Wells-next-the-Sea.
🏛🍴 **Shirehall Museum** Emphasis on the pilgrimage to Walsingham; displays are in an almost perfect Georgian courtroom complete with original fittings. Shop, limited disabled access; cl Oct–Easter; (01328) 820510; 75p, joint ticket with abbey £2.50.
🏛 🌿 **Walsingham Abbey Grounds** Plenty of remains of the 12th-c building, inc the Abbey Gates, Great Arch, part of the refectory and the Holy Wells. Pleasant gardens and woodland walks, with masses of snowdrops in early spring. Open via the Shirehall Museum and Tourist Information Centre in summer (joint tickets available), or the estate office in winter (office hours only), cl Christmas wk and wknds Nov–Jan; (01328) 820259; £2.50.

LODDON TM3695
★ 🌸 **Reads Nursery** (Hales Hall, off A146 SE of Loddon) Specialising for the last century in unusual conservatory plants, inc a good range of lemon, orange and other citrus fruits, also nut trees, etc. Disabled access; cl Mon (exc bank hols), Sun exc pm Jun–Sept, 24 Dec–5 Jan; (01508) 548395; nursery free, barn and garden £1.50. The village is attractive, and the 17th-c Swan has home-made food.

NEW BUCKENHAM TM0890
★ A fine village, largely medieval, with a decent pub.

NORTH CREAKE TF8539
✝ ★ **Creake Abbey** All that remains of this early 13th-c Augustinian priory is the crossing and east arm, but it's still worth a passing look, and the village is

charming. Cartwrights at South Creake has good food.

NORTH ELMHAM TF9821
✝ 🏛 ☁ **North Elmham church** An attractive 13th-c building, odd in that there's a step down into it; a little further N are the interesting ruins of a **Saxon cathedral**, and there are pleasant walks. The King's Head is useful for lunch.

NORWICH TG2308
Busy but civilised, the old centre has quite a concentration of attractive streets and buildings, with all sorts of surprises in the narrow streets and lanes that still follow its medieval layout; Elm St is especially handsome, and there are plenty of antique shops and so forth. Even the more commercial/industrial centre N of the River Wensum has fine patches (such as Colegate), and the main shopping areas are closed to traffic. Fortunately the visually disappointing university is hidden away out on the W edge, though in term-time its students do bring a good bit of life into the centre. Norwich is the home of Colmans mustard, and the Mustard Shop (Bridewell Alley) has some varieties you may not have come across before. The ancient Adam & Eve (Bishopgate) is good for lunch, and other pubs useful for a bite to eat include the Unthank Arms (Newmarket St) and the riverside Ribs of Beef (Wensum St).
🏛 **Assembly House** (Theatre St) Founded as a hospice in 1248, this veritable chameleon of buildings has served as priest's college, family home, 18th-c cards house, girls' school and wartime camouflage school in its time. Although the chapel was completely destroyed in 1548, and more recently, a fire ravaged the building in 1995, some of the original buildings remain and the brick-vaulted medieval cellar still lies beneath the restaurant. Meals, snacks, shop, disabled access; cl Sun; (01603) 626402; free.
⛵ **Boat trips** From the River Wensum you can clearly see how some of the city's older buildings were designed for water-borne traffic, rather than road transport.
🏛🍴 **Bridewell Museum** (Bridewell Alley) 14th-c building used as a prison

from 1583 to 1828, now with exhibits on the town's trade and industries, and reconstructed late 19th- and early 20th-c shops. Cl Mon, and Oct–Mar; (01603) 667228; £1.80.

🏛 **Castle Museum** (Castle Meadow) This impressive four-square Norman fortress, which dominates the city from its hill, is currently closed for refurbishment, and will not reopen until 2001. Linked to its museum via an underground passage is a former courtroom in the historic Shirehall, now a regimental museum; any enquiries, best to phone (01603) 223624.

🏛 **Dragon Hall** (King St) Well preserved medieval merchant's hall, with splendid timber-framed roof, intricate carvings, cellars, vaulted undercroft, and some finely painted roundels. Shop, limited disabled access; cl wknds exc summer Sats, 21 Dec–2 Jan, bank hols; (01603) 663922; *£1.50.

✝🏛 **Inspire Hands-on Science Centre** Popular with readers, in medieval St Michael's Church (Coslany St, Norwich) – hence the witty name. Snacks, shop, disabled access; cl Mon, Christmas wk; £3.

✝🏛 **Norwich Cathedral** Basically medieval, the church has some fine features from later periods – the flying buttresses for example, and the late 15th-c vaulted roof, spire and west window with Victorian glass. The Norman cloisters are the largest in the country, rebuilt after a serious riot between city and cathedral in 1272, and remarkable for the 400 bosses carved with scenes of medieval life (there are hundreds more in the cathedral itself, though less easy to see). Snacks and shop (not Sun), disabled access. Free guided tours leave the Information Desk at 11am wkdys and Sat, and 2.15pm wkdys only. The extensive precincts make an awe-inspiring impression: great medieval gateways firmly exclude the modern city from these closes, medieval alleys and secluded gardens, with all sorts of varied buildings from the cottages of Hooks Walk through the finer houses in the Upper Close to the buildings of Norwich School. The best view of the cathedral is from the river by Pulls Ferry; it's not easy to see from other parts of the town.

❗ **Puppet Theatre** 🎭 (St James's Church, Whitefriars) Another useful diversion for children. Shop, snacks, disabled access; open only on performance days; (01603) 629921; £5, children £3.75.

🏛 **Sainsbury Centre for Visual Arts** (University of East Anglia, off B1108 W) Striking Norman Foster building with notable 19th- and 20th-c European art, and a fascinating range of ethnographic art, inc African tribal sculpture, and Egyptian and Asian antiquities. Meals, snacks, shop, disabled access; cl Mon, 23 Dec–2 Jan; (01603) 592467; £2.

✝ **St Peter Hungate** Literally dozens of churches, in great variety, are one of the city's joys. Perhaps the finest of all is this one on Princes St, an impressive 15th-c church with a grand hammer-beam roof, museum of church art and brass rubbing centre.

OXBOROUGH TF7401

🏛 🌸 **Oxburgh Hall** Henry VIII stayed in this pretty moated manor house in 1487, and the room is now decorated with wall hangings worked by Mary Queen of Scots. Unfortunately, most of the house was thoroughly refurbished during Victorian times, but the gatehouse remains as an awe-inspiring example of 15th-c building work, 24 metres (80ft) high. The garden has a colourfully restored French parterre. Meals, snacks, shop, disabled access to ground floor only; cl am, Thurs, Fri, and Nov–Mar, garden also open some wknds Mar; (01366) 328258; £5, £2.40 garden only; NT. The Bedingfeld Arms opposite has decent food.

PASTON TG3135

⚒ The **windmill** is a fine example.

PENSTHORPE TF9429

🦢 **Pensthorpe Waterfowl Trust** (A1067) Good-sized collection of wild and exotic waterfowl, many of them rare, and now also red squirrels. The visitor centre has displays of wildlife art and photography. Also woodland, meadow, lakeside and riverside nature trails, adventure playground, and very good talks and events. Meals, snacks, shop, disabled access; cl wkdys Jan–Mar,

25 Dec, 1 Jan; (01328) 851465; £4.50.

RAVENINGHAM TM3996

❀ **Raveningham Hall Gardens**
Interesting collection of rare shrubs, shrub roses, a traditional kitchen garden, an arboretum, and a Victorian conservatory. Teas; open pm Sun and bank hols Apr–July; (01508) 548222; £2.

❀ **Raveningham Craft Workshops** (Beccles Rd) Victorian farm buildings with furniture-making, piano workshop, antiques and other workshops; teas; free. Loddon's the best nearby place for a meal.

REEDHAM TG4202

❀ ✿ ☺ **Pettitts Animal Adventure Park** You can still watch the demonstrations of feather craft, though they've become a little swamped by the other attractions here, inc aviaries, gnome village, American-style locomotive ride around the grounds, big adventure playground, miniature horse stud, deer-petting park and crazy golf. Meals, snacks, shop, some disabled access; cl Sat, and Nov–Easter (exc bank hols); (01493) 701094; £6.50. The Railway Tavern (open all day wknds) has good food and brews its own fine beers, and the little car ferry here is fun.

REEPHAM TG0922

★ ☻ This attractive large village or small town has some worthwhile shops, a fine old inn (the Old Brewery House) and a **nostalgia collection** in the station.

ST OLAVE'S TM4599

⚰ **St Olave's Priory** Ruins of a 13th-c Augustinian priory; you can still see the fine brick undercroft in the cloister – a remarkable early use of this material; free. The riverside Bell is very old indeed, though much modernised.

SANDRINGHAM TF6928

🏠 ❀ ✝ ♣ 🐴 ☺ Many people come to this part of the county for its connection with the Royal Family. **Sandringham House** was bought by Queen Victoria for her son Edward in 1862 and has become famous as the royal Christmas residence; the 19th-c building is filled with their portraits and those of their European counterparts, and has various gifts presented to the family over the years. Unlike at their other homes, you can see most of the rooms the family use, so there's a much more intimate feel than you'd get at

Windsor or Buckingham Palace; expect queues though. The grounds and surrounding country park are lovely, with nature trails, adventure playground, and the parish Church of St Mary Magdalene. Lovely rhododendrons in the woods May/Jun. Meals, snacks, shop, disabled access (a train runs between the grounds entrance and the house); open Easter–Sept, exc during summer royal visit – best to check for dates; (01553) 772675; £5.50, £4.50 grounds and museum only. In summer pick-your-own lets you sample fruit that might otherwise have graced the royal table. There's free access to **Sandringham Country Park** with its majestic trees and glades, a notable parkland walking area. The Feathers towards Dersingham is useful for lunch.

SAXTHORPE TG1332

❀ 🐴 ☁ **Mannington Gardens** The most beautiful feature of these gardens is the summer rose display, but 20 miles of footpaths around the hall and woodland are open all year (£1 parking). Snacks, shop, disabled access; gardens open pm Sun May–Sept plus Weds–Fri Jun–Aug; (01263) 874175; £3. Paths lead to the pleasant grounds of Wolterton Park. The Walpole Arms in the pretty nearby village of Itteringham has good food.

SHERINGHAM TG1543
The working fishing harbour has some old buildings around it, though there's a lot of more modern building up behind. The beach is nice, and the Two Lifeboats has good sea views (as well as decent food inc fresh fish).

🚂 **North Norfolk Railway** 🎫 Full-size steam railway, chugging through over 5 miles of lovely coastal scenery to Holt. Plenty of railway memorabilia at the Sheringham station, and a collection of steam engines and vintage rolling stock. Meals, snacks, shop, disabled access; steamtrains Mar–Dec; (01263) 822045 for timetable; £6.50 full return journey.

❀ ❄ ☁ **Sheringham Park** This extensive parkland, gloriously landscaped by Humphrey Repton (it was his favourite work), gives excellent coastal views from its waymarked walks and viewing towers. Also mature trees and fine azaleas and rhododendrons (best late May/Jun), with good walks to the coast. A restored steam-powered sawmill operates some wknds; Snacks, disabled access; (01263) 823778; free, but parking £2.60; NT.

† **Upper Sheringham** The 14th-c **church** in this quiet flintstone village is very attractive, and the Red Lion is a pleasant stop. Footpaths from here lead to Sheringham Park.

SHOULDHAM TF6709

★ ♘ Just outside this attractive village, with a decent pub, are **nature trails** in pleasant woods just N.

SNETTISHAM TF6833

🐄 ♙ △ **Park Farm** Working farm offering good insight into seasonal farming operations – lambing, shearing, and red deer calving. Lots of animals, plus impressive adventure playground, craft centre and mini golf. Meals, snacks, shop, disabled access; cl some days in winter, so best to check first out of season; (01485) 542425; £3.95 for either farm or 45-minute guided ride around deer park, £7 for both. Pretty walks nearby, as well as a nature reserve along the beach. The Rose & Crown is a good dining pub.

SUTTON TG3923

✖ The most striking **windmill** in Norfolk and the tallest in Britain, 9 floors high; shop, limited disabled access; cl Oct–Mar; (01692) 581195; £3.

TERRINGTON ST CLEMENT TF5519

✿ **African Violet Centre** Wide range of plants besides the African violets it's developed so successfully as house plants; the owner is also a priest, and runs services in a former packing shed here. Good tearoom; cl 22 Dec–mid-Jan; (01553) 828374. The Woolpack at Walpole Cross Keys has decent food.

THETFORD TL8683

🏠🚽👶🏛 **Ancient House Museum** Early Tudor house with fine oak ceilings, now a local history museum with a small period herb garden behind. Shop; cl 12.30–1pm, Sun (exc pm in summer); (01842) 752599; free exc July and Aug, when £1. **Thetford Priory** Ruins of 12th-c Cluniac monastery; you can easily make out the full ground plan

of the cloisters, and the 14th-c gatehouse still stands; disabled access; free. **Warren Lodge** 15th-c flint former hunting lodge, worth a look. The Bell and Thomas Paine are both civilised places for lunch.

THURSFORD GREEN TF9734

🚽👶☺ **Thursford Collection** Bouncy collection of musical organs, whether barrel, street or fairground. Most are demonstrated every day, and the Wurlitzer cinema organ also stars in daily concerts. Showmen's steam engines too, plus 2ft gauge steam railway, adventure playground, and Venetian gondola switchback ride. Meals, snacks, shop, disabled access; cl am and Jan–Easter; (01328) 878477; £4.60.

TITCHWELL TF7544

★ ♙ This is a pleasant coastal village with good **RSPB reserve** nearby; besides the Manor Hotel, the Three Horseshoes has good-value food and bedrooms.

WEAVERS WAY TG1531

△ This long-distance path can be used as part of a link from the parkland of Blickling Hall to take in walks through and around the **Wolterton Park** and **Mannington Hall** estates, both owned by the Walpoles, who have opened up a network of paths in the area extending NW to **Holt Country Park**. The Saracen's Head on the edge of Wolterton Park is a very civilised dining pub.

WELLS-NEXT-THE-SEA TF9142

★ △ Pleasant and rather gracious little village-sized town; don't be fooled by the name – the sea is a mile away these days, though there's a particularly good stretch of the North Norfolk Coast Path from here to Overy Staithe. The Crown is good for lunch.

🚂 **Wells & Walsingham Light Railway** Passing through quietly attractive scenery, this railway is remarkable for being the longest in Britain to use a 10¼in gauge track, with a steam locomotive built specially for it not long ago. Snacks, shop; cl end Oct–Easter; (01328) 856506 for times; £5 return.

WELNEY TL5393

♙ △ **Wildfowl & Wetlands Trust** (Hundred Foot Bank) Excellent 1,000-

acre wild bird reserve, with numerous hides, a spacious observatory, and a floodlit lagoon. In winter the sights include up to 4,000 migratory Bewick's swans and all sorts of duck; it can be busy then, and you'll need to wrap up well. In spring the emphasis switches to waders and other birds. There's a summer nature trail, and interesting conducted summer evening walks. Snacks, shop, disabled access; cl 24–25 Dec; (01353) 860711; *£3.50. In winter some local roads can be flooded, and then you can only approach the reserve from the E.

WEST RUNTON TG2042

★ 🐎 **Norfolk Shire Horse Centre** Extensive collection of draught horses and moorland and mountain ponies (they have 9 breeds). You can hire riding horses by the hour, and there's a children's farm (though some readers feel the aviaries and hutches are a little crowded). Meals, snacks, shop, disabled access; cl Sat (exc maybe July and Aug), and Nov–Easter; (01263) 837339; £4.50. The seaside village itself is attractive, and the Village Inn is useful for lunch.

WEST WALTON TF4713

† **West Walton church** A textbook example of early Gothic architecture; just about all of it dates from the mid-13th c, and there's a cool elegance throughout. The King of Hearts (good for lunch) holds the key.

WEYBOURNE TG1043

♨ △ **Muckleburgh Collection** (A149) World War II fighting vehicles and other soldierly relics on the site of a former military camp, once the lynch-pin of defences on this coast. Tank demonstrations every Sun, bank hols and wkdys during summer school hols. Meals and snacks (in NAAFI-style café), shop, disabled access; cl Nov–mid-Feb;

(01263) 588210; *£4. The Dun Cow overlooking the Salthouse marshes has decent food, with a nearby shack selling very fresh shellfish and samphire. Salthouse and Kelling back heathy hinterlands, allowing walkers a mix between this and the unvaryingly straight coast.

WIGHTON TF9439

★ 🖼 Pleasant village in an attractive coastal area, where the sculptor Henry Moore lived for a while; the Sandpiper is a decent pub, and there's a good **art gallery**. A stop on the steam railway between Wells and Walsingham.

WINTERTON-ON-SEA TG4919

△ One of the quieter seaside resorts on this coast, with a gentle villagey feel, and a particularly good beach over the dunes – nice for a wander by the sea; the 17th-c Fisherman's Return is very pleasant for lunch.

WOODBASTWICK TG3215

★ 🏚 This picturesque thatched estate village includes Woodfordes Brewery, one of Britain's best microbreweries; the Fur & Feather dining pub is the brewery tap.

WROXHAM TG3017

🚂 🏚 **Barton House Railway** (Hartwell Rd) Miniature railway through a big riverside garden; open pm third Sun of month in summer, 40p. Boats leave for here from Wroxham Bridge (80p).

★ **Other attractive villages** here, all with decent pubs, include Aldborough TG1834, Binham TF9839, Colkirk TF9126, Harpley TF7825, Mundford TL8093, South Wootton TF6422, Stiffkey (pronounced 'Stukey') TF9743, Swanton Morley TG0116, Wiveton TG0342 and Worstead TG3025. **Decent pubs** in attractive coastal areas include the Red Lion at Stiffkey TF9743 and the Three Horseshoes at Warham TF9441.

Please let us know what you think of places in the *Guide*. Use the report forms at the back of the book or simply write us a letter.

BAWBURGH TG1508 **Kings Head** *Harts Lane (01603)* 744977 Bustling old pub with friendly licensees, 4 linked rooms with low beams and standing timbers, a big log fire and a woodburner, generous attractively presented food (the weekly specials are much liked), a no smoking restaurant, and well kept real ales; cl pm 25 Dec. **£25|£6.25.**

BLAKENEY TG0243 **White Horse** *4 High St (01263)* 740574 Small hotel nr harbour (if that's not too grand a word), with a long cosy bar, a good mix of customers, efficient friendly service, good, well presented food inc local fish, reasonably priced wines, and attractive evening restaurant; bdrms. **£24.50|£6.50.**

BRISTON TG0632 **John H Stracey** *(01263) 860891* Neatly kept and well run country dining pub with a wide choice of well cooked and fairly priced bar food, popular restaurant, speciality evenings, comfortable seats and a log fire, well kept real ales, and friendly licensees; comfortable bdrms; partial disabled access. **£20|£7.**

CAWSTON TG1422 **Ratcatchers** *Eastgate (01603)* 871430 Popular dining pub with a huge choice of good, freshly prepared food (so there may be a wait) inc interesting fresh fish dishes; open fires, real ales, country wines, an L-shaped beamed bar, and a cosy candlelit dining room, too; cl 25–26 Dec; disabled access. **£25|£5.95.**

COLKIRK TF9126 **Crown** *(01328) 862172* Unpretentious, friendly village pub with open fires, solid country furniture, pleasantly informal, no smoking, dining room, good promptly served food (nice daily specials inc vegetarian choices), well kept real ales, decent wine list, and helpful landlord; own bowling green behind. **£17.50|£6.50.**

DISS TM1279 **Salisbury House** *Victoria Rd (01379)* 644738 Victorian country house in pleasant gardens, with fresh flowers and period décor, a good choice of interesting food on the monthly changing menu in the relaxed bistro, a set menu in the more formal restaurant, a good choice of mainly French wines, and friendly helpful service; bdrms; open Tues–Sat evenings only; cl 2 wks summer, 1 wk Christmas; disabled access. **£30** restaurant, **£22** bistro.

ERPINGHAM TG1631 **Ark** *The Street (01263)* 761535 Lovely individual food inc home-made bread and home-grown vegetables in a simple relaxed cottage with log fire and courteous service; bdrms; cl 25–26 Dec, pm Sun and Mon; disabled access. **£32|£21** 3-course Sun lunch.

ERPINGHAM TG1631 **Saracen's Head** *Wolterton (01263)* 768909 Comfortably civilised inn with simple, stylish 2-room bar, a nice mix of seats, log fires and fresh flowers, excellent inventive food inc good-value 2-course Sun supper and 3-course monthly feasts, very well kept real ales, interesting wines, and a charming old-fashioned gravel stableyard; good bdrms; cl 25 Dec; limited disabled access. **£20|£4.75.**

FAKENHAM TF9129 **Wensum Lodge** *Bridge St (01328)* 862100 Brick-built former grain store by the river with a very roomy, relaxed and civilised bar, 2 beamed dining rooms (one no smoking), interesting food inc sandwiches and filled baked potatoes served all day, real ales, and attentive service; bdrms; disabled access. **£28|£6.50.**

HEYDON TG1127 **Earle Arms** *(01263) 587376* 17th-c inn (Norfolk's only fully licensed pub theatre) in a lovely village with 2 individually furnished rooms opening off the small lobby, interesting bric-à-brac, tiny homely dining room, no smoking simple conservatory, very good interesting food (lunchtime dishes all £4.95), well kept real ales, decent wine list, and friendly enthusiastic licensee. **£17.75|£6.25.**

HOLT TG0738 **Owl Tea Rooms** *White Lion St (01263)* 713232 Georgian building with bakery and tearooms behind serving home-made bread, scones, quiches and pies served on plates made by the owners, organic local vegetables, daily specials and vegetarian choices, home-made preserves, and good cream teas; cl Sun, bank hols; disabled access. **£12.25|£3.75.**

KING'S LYNN TF6119 **Rococo** *11 Saturday Market Pl (01553)* 771483 Delicious imaginative modern cooking using fresh local produce in a pretty dining room with lots of fresh flowers and paintings; also a cosy lounge area, relaxed atmosphere, good informal service, and decent wines; cl Sun, am Mon, Christmas–New Year; disabled access. **£33.50 dinner, £19.50 lunch**|£3.

LITTLE WALSINGHAM TF9336 **Old Bakehouse** *33 High St* (01328) 820454 In an attractive medieval village, this Georgian-fronted house has high beams in the main restaurant, a smaller dining room with a brick oven dating from 1550, and downstairs bar; sound cooking (evenings only) with plenty of choice, and a reasonably priced French wines; bdrms; cl Sun, Mon and Tues (but for residents, no food only on Mon), 2 wks Jan–Feb, 1 wk Jun, 2 wks Nov. **£27.50**.

NORWICH TG2208 **Adlards** *79 Upper St Giles St* (01603) 633522 Warmly friendly, quietly decorated restaurant serving delicious carefully thought-out food from a menu that changes daily, lovely puddings, fine service, and good wine list; cl Sun, am Mon; disabled access. **£40 dinner, £26 lunch**.

REEDHAM TG4001 **Ferry** *(01493)* 700429 Perfectly placed pub beside River Yare, with plenty of tables to watch boats or swans (good moorings), a secluded back bar with a fine log fire, a long front bar with big picture windows, a no smoking restaurant, and very popular good food; disabled access. **£17**|£4.25.

ST OLAVE'S TM4599 **Priory Farm** *(01493)* 488432 Good interesting food inc fresh fish and children's menu; right by St Olave's Priory; open all day Jun–Sept (normal hours the rest of the year), cl 26 Dec; disabled access. **£20**|£4.95.

SNETTISHAM TF6834 **Rose & Crown** *Old Church St* (01485) 541382 Pretty white cottage with a nice traditional layout to the 4 bustling bars, log fires, 5 real ales, 20 wines by the glass, good daily specials as well as the standard menu, afternoon teas, colourful garden, and an adventure playground; disabled access. **£25**|£4.50.

STOW BARDOLPH TF6205 **Hare Arms** *(01366)* 382229 Good-value quickly served interesting lunchtime bar food in a pleasantly refurbished country pub with cheerful licensees, prompt courteous service even when busy, fresh flowers, a separate, elegant evening restaurant, and a big conservatory for children (not allowed in main bar; must be over 10 in restaurant); cl 25–26 Dec. **£23**|£7.

SWANTON MORLEY TG0117 **Darbys** *Elsing Rd* (01362) 637647 Cosy beamed country pub decorated with lots of farm tools and so forth, very well kept real ales, good generously served and often interesting bar food (their beef comes from their own farm), log fire, friendly staff, a children's room and an adventure playground; also bdrms, self-catering, camping, caravan site, horse facilities, country trails; disabled access. **£17.50**|£5.50.

UPPER SHERINGHAM TG1542 **Red Lion** *(01263)* 825408 Relaxing little flint cottage with 2 quiet small bars, simple furnishings, a big woodburner, newspapers to read, very good food inc quite a few fish dishes, well kept real ales and over 60 whiskies. **£17.50**|£6.95.

Special thanks to Michael and Jenny Back.

We welcome reports from readers

This *Guide* depends on readers' reports. Do help us if you can – in return, we offer a discount on the next edition to people who've helped us with reports for it. Tell us what you think about places already in it, and anything extra you think we should say about them. And send us your ideas for inclusion in the next edition: places to visit, eat at or stay in, attractive drives or walks, maybe even unusual interesting shops you know of. Use the card in the middle, the report forms at the end, or just write – no stamp needed: *The Good Britain Guide*, FREEPOST TN1569, Wadhurst, E Sussex TN5 7BR.

Norfolk Calendar

Some of these dates were provisional as we went to press. Please check information with the telephone numbers provided.

JANUARY

1 **Norwich** Festival of Lights – *till 9 January* (01603) 622237; **South Walsham** New Year's Day Walk at Fairhaven Garden Trust (01603) 270449

APRIL

15 **South Walsham** Primrose Weeks at Fairhaven Garden Trust – *till 30 April* (01603) 270449
21 **Blickling** Country Skills and Working Crafts Show at Blickling Hall – *till 24 April* (01263) 738049
24 **Hunstanton** Morris Dancing at various venues (01553) 768930

MAY

8 **Norwich** LEAP: Festival of Contemporary and World Dance – *till 14 May* (01603) 766400
13 **South Walsham** Candelabra Primulas at Fairhaven Garden Trust: the largest collection in England – *till 31 May* (01603) 270449
28 **Downham Market** Festival – *till 4 June* (01366) 387440

JUNE

10 **Hunstanton** Festival of Arts – *till 1 July* (01485) 540950
28 **Norwich** Royal Norfolk Show 2000 – *till 29 June* (01603) 748931

JULY

1 **Norwich** Open-air Theatre Festival: over 30 performances in parks and open spaces – *till 31 August* (01603) 666071; **Sandringham** Country Show and Horse Driving Trials at Sandringham House – *till 2 July* (01553) 772675
2 **Hunstanton** Carnival (01485) 526510
7 **Norwich** Lord Mayor's Weekend Celebrations: carnival floats, music, fireworks – *till 9 July* (01603) 666071
8 **Sandringham** Fireworks Concert at Sandringham House (01553) 772675
14 **Wheeting** Steam Rally – *till 16 July* (01842) 810317
15 **Hunstanton** Street Organ Festival – *till 16 July* (01485) 533165
20 **King's Lynn** Festival of Music and the Arts – *till 29 July* (01553) 773578
22 **Blickling** Concert at Blickling Hall – *till 29 July* (01263) 738049
26 **Sandringham** Flower Show inc arena events at Sandringham House (01485) 540860
28 **Worstead** Festival – *till 30 July* (01603) 666071

AUGUST

5 **Blickling** Hot-air Balloon Rally at Blickling Hall – *till 6 August* (01263) 738049

Norfolk Calendar (cont.)

6 Blickling Kite Flying Day at Blickling Hall (01263) 738049; **Norwich** Free Music Festival at Waterloo Park: two stages, entertainers, dance, children's area (01603) 212137

16 Cromer Carnival (01263) 512497

18 Blickling Firework and Laser Concert at Blickling Hall – *till 19 August* (01263) 738049

28 Blickling Aylsham Agricultural Show at Blickling Hall (01263) 733903

SEPTEMBER

3 Hemsby Herring Festival: helicopter rides, Morris Men at Hemsby Beach (01493) 731606

10 Hunstanton Kite Festival (01485) 572032

27 Norfolk and **Norwich** Festival – *till 15 October* (01603) 766400

NOVEMBER

6 Great Yarmouth Historic Re-creation: Nelson's return to Great Yarmouth (01502) 580670

18 Thursford Christmas Spectacular at the Thursford Collection: two performances daily – *till 23 December* (01328) 878477

We welcome reports from readers

This *Guide* depends on readers' reports. Do help us if you can – in return, we offer a discount on the next edition to people who've helped us with reports for it. Tell us what you think about places already in it, and anything extra you think we should say about them. And send us your ideas for inclusion in the next edition: places to visit, eat at or stay in, attractive drives or walks, maybe even unusual interesting shops you know of. Use the card in the middle, the report forms at the end, or just write – no stamp needed: *The Good Britain Guide*, FREEPOST TN1569, Wadhurst, E Sussex TN5 7BR.

NORTHAMPTONSHIRE

Little-known charming countryside with fine houses and grounds; not so much family interest.

This archetypal shire county has gently appealing, partly wooded landscapes, villages built of red or honey-coloured stone, the fine churches of the Nene Valley – very relaxing. It also has an unrivalled concentration of great houses in grand surroundings – Rockingham Castle, delightfully restored Canons Ashby, Deene Park, Cottesbrooke Hall, Boughton House and Althorp, with more lovely grounds to wander through at Coton Manor, Castle Ashby, Cottesbrooke and Holdenby House.

Wicksteed Park on the edge of Kettering is a good treat for children, Sulgrave Manor has very enjoyable living history events, the canal museum at Stoke Bruerne has wide appeal, and the dragonfly centre at Oundle adds a touch of the unusual.

Where to stay

ASHBY ST LEDGERS SP5768 **Olde Coach House** *Ashby St Ledgers, Rugby CV23 8UN (01788) 890349* **£65**, plus special breaks; 6 rms. In an attractive thatched stone village, this handsome creeper-covered inn has several comfortable, rambling atmospheric rooms, a winter log fire, straightforward bar food, well kept beer, and big gardens with children's activity centre.

BADBY SP5559 **Windmill** *Badby, Daventry NN11 3AN (01327) 702363* **£69**, plus special breaks; 8 rms. Traditional, carefully modernised, thatched stone inn with beams, flagstones and a huge inglenook fireplace in the front bar, cosy comfortable lounge, good, generously served bar and restaurant food, and decent wines; fine views of the pretty village from the car park.

CASTLE ASHBY SP8659 **Falcon** *Castle Ashby, Northampton NN7 1LF (01604) 696200* **£92.50**; 17 nicely decorated rms. Smart hotel in attractive, preserved village, with stone walls and hops on dark beams in the 16th-c cellar bar, open fire, real ales, restaurant overlooking the pretty garden, good breakfasts, and a welcoming landlord; children over 10 in evening restaurant; disabled access.

EAST HADDON SP6668 **Red Lion** *East Haddon, Northampton NN6 8BU (01604) 770223* **£75**; 5 rms. Welcoming and popular golden stone inn with pretty gardens, a neat white-panelled lounge, small public bar, pretty restaurant, high quality daily-changing food, and nice breakfasts; disabled access.

OLD SP7873 **Wold Farm** *Old, Northampton NN6 9RJ (01604) 781258* **£52**; 5 rms. No smoking, 18th-c house at the heart of a beef and arable farm, with spacious interesting rooms, hearty breakfasts in the beamed dining room, attentive and welcoming owners, log fire, snooker table, and two pretty gardens.

OUNDLE TL0488 **Talbot** *New St, Oundle, Peterborough PE8 4EA (01832) 273621* **£85**, plus special breaks; 39 most attractive big rms. Mary, Queen of Scots walked to her execution down one of the staircases in this carefully refurbished 17th-c hotel; attractive lounges, big log fires, good food in timbered restaurant, and a garden.

PAULERSPURY SP7245 **Vine House** *100 High St, Paulerspury, Towcester NN12 7NA (01327) 811267* ***£69**; 6 individually decorated rms. 300-year-old building with carefully preserved original features, a relaxed welcoming atmosphere, cosy bar with open fire, and very good modern English cooking (inc home-made bread

and petits fours) in attractive restaurant; pretty cottage garden; disabled access.
SUDBOROUGH SP9682 **Vane Arms** High St, Sudborough, Kettering NN14 3BX (01832) 733223 ***£45;** 3 rms. Cheerful, relaxed thatched pub on a picturesque village street; with comfortable main bar, inglenook fireplaces, friendly helpful staff, no smoking upstairs restaurant, and a marvellous range of real ales; disabled access.

To see and do

NORTHAMPTONSHIRE Family Attraction of the Year

☺ **KETTERING** SP8678 **Wicksteed Park** (off A6, S outskirts) Our continued recommendation of this big amusement park owes a lot to the real scarcity of other places for families to visit in the area; it's definitely a part of the world that looks after adults rather better than it does children. That said, children up to around 12 will have great fun at Wicksteed, and there's easily enough to amuse them for quite some time. The park was one of the first of its type, set up in 1921 when they introduced boating facilities on the lake. Some older features still remain (an antique roundabout for example), though in the last few years they've been joined by more modern attractions, such as a monorail, rollercoaster and films in the Cine 2000 dome. It's still relatively low-key compared to other leisure parks – thrill rides here are mainly of the dodgems, ferris wheel and pirate ship school – but for many visitors that's precisely the appeal. You can still row on the lake, and the grounds are very pleasant for a stroll or a picnic, with a pitch-and-putt course, various well laid out gardens, an aviary, paddling pools, and free play areas for younger children. Dogs are welcome on a lead. Their home-made ice-creams are very tasty. Meals, snacks, shop, disabled access, open daily Easter–early Sept, then wknds and school hols in Oct; (01536) 512475; £5 parking charge (less out of season, or after 3pm), then you buy vouchers for the rides (not all of which have to be used on the same day), or a wristband with a day's unlimited rides for £11 children and £7 for the over-18s.

ALTHORP SP6864
🏛️🛎️🖼️🐾✝️⚕️⌂★ The home of the Spencer family since 1508, remodelled several times, especially in the 17th and 18th c, and now firmly on the map as the resting place of Diana, Princess of Wales. You can't see the grave itself (it's on an islet in the Oval Lake in a small arboretum just NE of the house), but you can view the lake, and the former stable block is now a museum/memorial filled with her personal possessions, favourite clothes, video footage of her life and some of the thousands of books of condolences sent to Kensington Palace on her death. The house itself has a splendid collection of furnishings and porcelain, and paintings by Rubens, Van Dyck and Lely. Snacks, shop, some disabled access; open pm daily July and Aug but only by advance booking; (01604) 7702097/592020; £9.50. The attractive **church** is on the edge of the park; its graveyard has fine views. On

the far side of the estate there's public access to a sandy-floored area of wildlife-filled pine woods and heathland known as Harlestone Firs, pleasant for walking. The village, Great Brington, is charming, and the Fox & Hounds here has good food, and lots of character.
ASHBY ST LEDGERS SP5768
★🏛️✝️ This village is quite a gem: fine manor house, Lutyens almshouses, and a remarkable church with wall paintings, pre-Reformation pews and triple-decker pulpit (few signs of interference by the Reformers, Cromwell or even the Victorians). The Olde Coach House has decent food.
BADBY SP5559
⌂★⚕️ **Knightley Way** This path takes a pleasant 12-mile course from the attractive village of Badby, through an area where gorgeous orange-coloured stone adds to the charm of the buildings; it's well waymarked to Greens Norton. The finest part is

between Badby Wood and Fawsley Park, where the path drops to landscaped lakes by the hall and estate church. In May, the Badby Wood bluebells are lovely.

BOROUGH HILL SP5962

❋ ▥ Ths gives the best views in the region, from above the golf course; an Iron Age hill fort shares the top with a formidable array of television and telecommunications masts, but on a clear day the views are tremendous.

BRIGSTOCK SP9485

✝ ⚘ ◠ The **church** has a Saxon tower, and a bell that used to be rung three times a day to help anyone lost in the woods; the Olde Three Cocks is useful for food. **Brigstock Country Park** is a good place for a wander, especially around wildlife-filled Fermyn Woods on the edge; it can be muddy.

🏠 ❀ **Lyveden New Bield** Unfinished 'new building' started in 1595 but abandoned after the owner Sir Thomas Tresham's son died in the Tower. Intriguing and unusual, it was intended to celebrate the Passion of Christ, and is shaped like a Greek cross; the Elizabethan watergardens are still being restored – open selected days, best to phone; (01832) 205358; £1.70; NT. It's a half-mile walk from the car park.

BRIXWORTH SP7471

✝ **Brixworth church** Particularly fine Anglo-Saxon church, one of England's oldest – mostly 7th-c with much reused Roman material. The George has decent food.

CANONS ASHBY SP5750

🏠 ❀ ✝ **Canons Ashby House** (B4525) Exceptional little manor house, more northern-looking than Midlands, beautifully restored with Elizabethan wall paintings and glorious Jacobean plasterwork. The formal gardens have also been carefully restored over the last 20 years, and now closely reflect the layout of the early 18th c. A reasonably sized park has a hilltop 12th–14th-c priory church. Brewhouse café, shop, disabled access; open pm Sat–Weds and bank hols Apr–Oct; (01327) 860044; £3.70; NT – it's one of their busier properties. The Olde House at Home at Moreton Pinkney is handy for lunch.

CASTLE ASHBY SP8659

🏠 ❀ ✝ ⚘ **Castle Ashby House** Only the gardens can be visited, but the house is well worth seeing from outside – a splendidly palatial Elizabethan building at the end of a magnificent mile-long avenue planted nearly 300 years ago. The gardens include grand Victorian terraces, sweeping lawns, Italianate gardens with an orangery, and lakeside parkland that may well be the prolific Capability Brown's most enduring achievement. Disabled access; cl 25 Dec; (01604) 696696; £3.50. The **church**, within the park, is very attractive; there's a public path to it. Restored farm buildings nearby house a **Craft Centre & Rural Shopping Yard** (cl Mon). The Falcon in the handsomely preserved estate village has good food (and attractive bedrooms), and the drive through Cogenhoe, Whiston, Grendon and Easton Maudit is pleasant.

CHAPEL BRAMPTON SP7366

🚂 ◠ **Northampton & Lamport Railway** (Pitsford Rd) Enthusiastic little railway, with short train rides some wknds and all bank hols mid-Mar–Dec, best to phone (01604) 820327. Snacks, shop, and they're working on improving disabled access; £2.80. Its name is a proud commitment to growth northwards, but for the time being the 14-mile walk and cycle way through pretty countryside by the line is a very pleasant foretaste. The Brampton Halt here has decent food.

COTON SP6771

❀ ❦ ⚘ **Coton Manor** (off A428) Attractive views from charming gardens around a 17th-c stone-built manor house (not open); interesting plantings, and watergardens with flamingos, cranes and ornamental waterfowl wandering freely. The wood is lovely at bluebell time. Meals, snacks, interesting plant sales, disabled access; open pm Weds–Sun and bank hols Easter–Sept; (01604) 740219; *£3.50. Besides Grooms Cottage in the stables, the Red Lion at East Haddon is good for lunch.

COTTESBROOKE SP7174

🏠 ▣ ❀ **Cottesbrooke Hall** Very attractive Queen Anne house, reputedly the model for Jane Austen's *Mansfield Park*, with a renowned collection of mainly sporting and equestrian paintings. The lovely garden has formal borders, venerable cedars, greenhouses, extensive wild garden, and a separate cottage garden. Teas, unusual plant sales, disabled access to gardens only; open pm Thurs and bank hols Easter–Sept, plus pm wknds in Sept, garden also open pm Tues, Weds and Fri Easter–Sept; (01604) 505808; £4, garden only £2.50. The George in nearby Brixworth has decent food.

CROUGHTON SP5433

† **Croughton church** Handsome church well worth a visit for its unusual murals, dating from the 14th and 15th centuries.

DEENE SP9592

🏛 ✿ ★ **Deene Park** (off A43) Lord Cardigan who led the Charge of the Light Brigade used to live in this beautifully presented partly Tudor house; there's a high-spirited contemporary portrait of him in full attack gallop. Extensive parklands with woodside and lakeside walks, and gardens reflecting continuing interest by the owners over the generations. Cream teas, shop, some disabled access; open pm Sun Jun–Aug, plus Sun and Mon of bank hol wknds Easter–Aug; (01780) 450223; £4.50 (gardens only, 2.50). The Queen's Head opposite the church in the pretty village of Bulwick has good-value food.

🏛 ⛪ ✿ **Kirby Hall** (W) Splendidly ruined Elizabethan mansion with a bizarre mixture of styles and design; from some angles it still looks intact – even close up. The 17th-c gardens are being restored, and it's a tranquil spot for a picnic. Shop, disabled access; cl 1–2pm and wkdys Nov–Mar, 24–26 Dec, 1 Jan; (01536) 203230; £2.50 (inc Walkman tour); EH.

DENFORD SP9976

† ✿ ⌂ **Denford church** Attractive in any event (like so many other churches along this river valley); doubly worth a visit for its nature-reserve churchyard by the River Nene, with waterside walks from here.

FOTHERINGHAY TL0793

★ † 🏛 Lovely village with interesting historical displays in the charming if slightly out-of-proportion 14th-c **church** across a watermeadow from the River Nene. It was part of a small pre-Reformation college and doubles as a memorial to the House of York, with some interesting heraldry. There's only a fragment left of the **castle** where Mary, Queen of Scots was imprisoned, beside the castle mound. The Falcon is excellent for lunch.

GEDDINGTON SP8982

★ † The very well preserved, elaborate 13th-c cross was erected by Edward I where Queen Eleanor's funeral cortège rested on its way to Westminster. The photogenic packhorse bridge is even older, and there's a 12th-c church. The Star has decent food.

HARRINGWORTH SP9197

★ This attractive village is famous for its 82-arch **railway viaduct**. The White Swan has decent food.

HOLDENBY SP6967

🏛 🐾 🐑 ✿ ⌂ **Holdenby House Gardens** In Elizabethan times this was one of the biggest houses in the country and the extensive gardens and grounds have been restored in the original style. Also a reconstructed 17th-c farmstead, play area and children's farm. The BBC's *The Woman in White* was filmed here. Sun meals, snacks, shop, some disabled access; open pm daily exc Sat Apr–Sept; (01604) 770074; £3. An adjacent falconry centre is open the same times. The house itself (with its unique piano collection) is open only Easter, spring and Aug bank hol Mons; £4.

IRCHESTER SP9265

✿ 🐦 ⌂ **Irchester Country Park** (Gypsy Lane, Little Irchester) 200 acres of lovely woodland with nature trails, picnic sites, children's play area and even a railway museum; shop (pm Sun only), disabled access; cl 25 Dec; (01933) 276866; small parking charge.

KETTERING SP8678

🏛 🖼 ✿ **Boughton House** 📷 (SE of Geddington) Impressively grand old place often compared to Versailles (some of its treasures were in fact made for there). Richly furnished and decorated, with gorgeous mythical scenes painted on the ceilings, and works by El Greco, Murillo and Caracci lining the walls. Excellent armoury, beautiful parklands, and adventure playground and garden shop. Snacks,

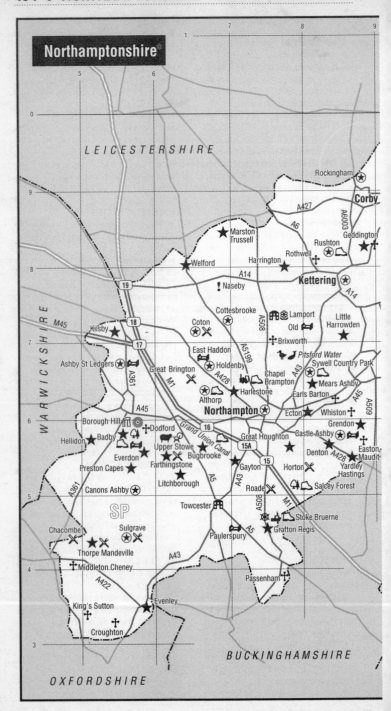

The Good Britain Guide

The Good Britain Guide
FREEPOST TN1569
WADHURST
E. SUSSEX
TN5 7BR

2

Please use this card to tell us about anything which *you* think should or should not be included in the next edition of *The Good Britain Guide*. Just fill it in and return it to us – no stamp or envelope needed. You can also use the report forms at the end of the book

ALISDAIR AIRD

YOUR NAME AND ADDRESS (BLOCK CAPITALS PLEASE)

☐ *Please tick this box if you would like extra report forms*

REPORT ON *(its name)*

Its address/location

Postcode: Telephone:

What is this? *(hotel, restaurant, garden, village, drive, walk etc)*

Description/why it appeals

REPORT ON *(its name)*

Its address

Postcode: Telephone:

What is this? *(hotel, restaurant, garden, village, drive, walk etc)*

Description/why it appeals

Code GBG

THE GOOD BRITAIN GUIDE 2000

Hand in this Discount Voucher to claim *free admission for one child* when you buy admission at full price for two adults at attractions with a £ sign after their name.

Please see overleaf for further details and conditions.

Code GBG

THE GOOD BRITAIN GUIDE 2000

Hand in this Discount Voucher to claim *free admission for one child* when you buy admission at full price for two adults at attractions with a £ sign after their name.

Please see overleaf for further details and conditions.

Code GBG

THE GOOD BRITAIN GUIDE 2000

Hand in this Discount Voucher to claim *free admission for one child* when you buy admission at full price for two adults at attractions with a £ sign after their name.

Please see overleaf for further details and conditions.

Code GBG

THE GOOD BRITAIN GUIDE 2000

Hand in this Discount Voucher to claim *free admission for one child* when you buy admission at full price for two adults at attractions with a £ sign after their name.

Please see overleaf for further details and conditions.

Code GBG

THE GOOD BRITAIN GUIDE 2000

Hand in this Discount Voucher to claim *free admission for one child* when you buy admission at full price for two adults at attractions with a £ sign after their name.

Please see overleaf for further details and conditions.

Code GBG

THE GOOD BRITAIN GUIDE 2000

Hand in this Discount Voucher to claim *free admission for one child* when you buy admission at full price for two adults at attractions with a £ sign after their name.

Please see overleaf for further details and conditions.

CONDITIONS

1. This discount offer cannot be used in conjunction with any other offer, and is not available as part of a group booking or for more than one child. The voucher is not transferable.
2. Free admission for one child is available only if two adults are paying the full normal tariff.
3. The offer may not be available on bank holidays, or on special event days – in this case our entry for that attraction notes this fact in brackets immediately after the 🎟 sign.
4. A very few attractions are offering some special variation on this offer – their entries spell this out in brackets immediately after the 🎟 sign.
5. This offer expires on 31 December 2000 (or at the close of the attraction's season if that is earlier).

✂ -

CONDITIONS

1. This discount offer cannot be used in conjunction with any other offer, and is not available as part of a group booking or for more than one child. The voucher is not transferable.
2. Free admission for one child is available only if two adults are paying the full normal tariff.
3. The offer may not be available on bank holidays, or on special event days – in this case our entry for that attraction notes this fact in brackets immediately after the 🎟 sign.
4. A very few attractions are offering some special variation on this offer – their entries spell this out in brackets immediately after the 🎟 sign.
5. This offer expires on 31 December 2000 (or at the close of the attraction's season if that is earlier).

✂ -

CONDITIONS

1. This discount offer cannot be used in conjunction with any other offer, and is not available as part of a group booking or for more than one child. The voucher is not transferable.
2. Free admission for one child is available only if two adults are paying the full normal tariff.
3. The offer may not be available on bank holidays, or on special event days – in this case our entry for that attraction notes this fact in brackets immediately after the 🎟 sign.
4. A very few attractions are offering some special variation on this offer – their entries spell this out in brackets immediately after the 🎟 sign.
5. This offer expires on 31 December 2000 (or at the close of the attraction's season if that is earlier).

✂ -

CONDITIONS

1. This discount offer cannot be used in conjunction with any other offer, and is not available as part of a group booking or for more than one child. The voucher is not transferable.
2. Free admission for one child is available only if two adults are paying the full normal tariff.
3. The offer may not be available on bank holidays, or on special event days – in this case our entry for that attraction notes this fact in brackets immediately after the 🎟 sign.
4. A very few attractions are offering some special variation on this offer – their entries spell this out in brackets immediately after the 🎟 sign.
5. This offer expires on 31 December 2000 (or at the close of the attraction's season if that is earlier).

✂ -

CONDITIONS

1. This discount offer cannot be used in conjunction with any other offer, and is not available as part of a group booking or for more than one child. The voucher is not transferable.
2. Free admission for one child is available only if two adults are paying the full normal tariff.
3. The offer may not be available on bank holidays, or on special event days – in this case our entry for that attraction notes this fact in brackets immediately after the 🎟 sign.
4. A very few attractions are offering some special variation on this offer – their entries spell this out in brackets immediately after the 🎟 sign.
5. This offer expires on 31 December 2000 (or at the close of the attraction's season if that is earlier).

✂ -

CONDITIONS

1. This discount offer cannot be used in conjunction with any other offer, and is not available as part of a group booking or for more than one child. The voucher is not transferable.
2. Free admission for one child is available only if two adults are paying the full normal tariff.
3. The offer may not be available on bank holidays, or on special event days – in this case our entry for that attraction notes this fact in brackets immediately after the 🎟 sign.
4. A very few attractions are offering some special variation on this offer – their entries spell this out in brackets immediately after the 🎟 sign.
5. This offer expires on 31 December 2000 (or at the close of the attraction's season if that is earlier).

✂ -

CONDITIONS

1. This discount offer cannot be used in conjunction with any other offer, and is not available as part of a group booking or for more than one child. The voucher is not transferable.
2. Free admission for one child is available only if two adults are paying the full normal tariff.
3. The offer may not be available on bank holidays, or on special event days – in this case our entry for that attraction notes this fact in brackets immediately after the 🎟 sign.
4. A very few attractions are offering some special variation on this offer – their entries spell this out in brackets immediately after the 🎟 sign.
5. This offer expires on 31 December 2000 (or at the close of the attraction's season if that is earlier).

✂ -

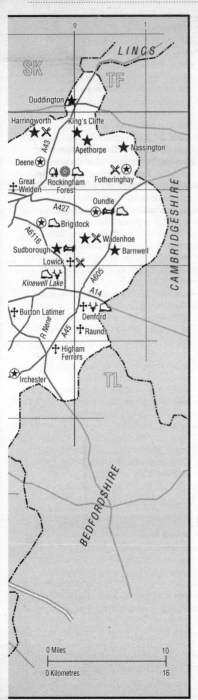

shop, disabled access; grounds open pm May–Sept (exc Fri), house pm Aug only; (01536) 515731; £6, grounds only £1.50.

🚻 🖻 **Manor House Museum** (Sheep St) This and the adjacent **Alfred East Gallery** are worth a look if passing; the former has free children's activities in school hols (and a famous mummified cat). Both have shop and disabled access, and are cl Sun and bank hols; free.

☺ **Wicksteed Park** *See separate family panel on p.461.*

KINEWELL LAKE SP9979

Ⅴ ⌂ Well managed local **nature reserve** around former gravel-pit lakes by the River Nene; pleasant walks.

LAMPORT SP7574

🏠 🐝 **Lamport Hall** (A14) Mainly 17th- and 18th-c house in spacious park, with tranquil gardens containing a remarkable alpine rockery – the home of the first garden gnomes, only one of which now survives. Frequent antique fairs, concerts and other events. Snacks, shop, disabled access to ground floor only; open pm Sun and bank hols Easter–Oct, plus daily guided tours at 3.30pm in Aug (exc Sun); (01604) 686272; £4. The Swan, with great views, has good-value food.

NASEBY SP6877

! **Battle of Naseby Model** Model of the crucial Civil War battle set out by the owner of Purlieu Farm, using many hundreds of model soldiers, with a 10-minute commentary; open pm bank hol Sun and Mon and by appointment, (01604) 740241; £1.50. The nearby Fitzgerald Arms is a good dining pub. One battle monument (Sibbertoft Rd) marks the position of Cromwell's New Model Army before his devastating counter-attack; there's another on the B4036 towards Clipston (this road from West Haddon and on to Market Harborough in Leics gives a good feel of rural Northants).

NORTHAMPTON SP7560

🏠 † ♨ Daniel Defoe would no longer describe this prosperous shoe-making town as one of the most handsome in the country, but it has a few interesting buildings. There are several fine **churches**, most notably the 12th-c Holy Sepulchre (one of only four remaining round churches in the country), the very grand central All Saints, and the ornate Norman St Peter's in Marefair right by the dual carriageway. The Welsh House (now a china shop) and Hazelrigg House are also very handsome. A social history museum in Abington Park is set in the 15th-c home of Shakespeare's granddaughter; cl am, Mon exc bank hols, 25–26 Dec; free.

☉ Central Museum (Guildhall Rd) Home to a remarkable collection of boots and shoes, which includes an elephant's boot, Margot Fonteyn's ballet shoes, Roman sandals, and Queen Victoria's wedding slippers. Shop, disabled access; cl am Sun, 25–26 Dec; (01604) 639415; free.

OUNDLE TL0488

★ Charming and elegant stone-built town with a graceful church, several antique shops and a fine old public school. The ancient Ship does decent food.

☷ ☐ ❦ Barnwell Country Park (just S) A good spot for a walk, with a variety of birds; the waterside Mill is a pleasant place for lunch.

! ★ National Dragonfly Museum (just SE – coming from town take a right at the A605 Oundle roundabout) At pretty Ashton Mill, this unique place has dramatic feeding sessions, several different habitats, and a TV microscope link to the larvae under the water. Fully grown dragonflies put on their best shows on sunny days, though it's a rewarding place in any weather. Teas, shop, disabled access; open wknds and bank hols mid-Jun–late Sept; (01832) 272427; around £3. Ashton itself is attractive.

PITSFORD WATER SP7669

❦ ❧ Praised for birdwatching, especially in winter when wildfowl flock to the northern part of the lake; the southern part is popular for fishing. The White Swan at Holcot has decent food.

ROCKINGHAM SP8691

⌂ ⚒ ▣ Rockingham Castle (A6003) Lovely old house still tucked away behind the curtain wall of the original Norman fortress – obviously quite an effective defence, as the castle was able to resist repeated assaults in the Civil War. The site of the original keep is now a rose garden, but the outline of the two baileys and the drum towers survive, and the later Elizabethan building has a good range of furnishings and art. Meals, snacks, shop, limited disabled access; open pm Sun, Thurs, and bank hols Easter–Sept, as well as Tues in Aug or after bank hols; (01536) 770240; £4.20, garden only £2.70.

ROCKINGHAM FOREST SP9892

⚘ ❋ ☐ Pleasant back roads through the former Forest of Rockingham give quiet views of a particularly attractive part of the county. This area is good for walks, too, with enough country houses scattered around it to spice interest, and grey-stone cottages are a local feature; on its NW edge the Exeter Arms at Wakerley, a former hunting lodge, gives access to both Wakerley Woods and the Welland Valley.

RUSHTON SP8388

☷ ☐ ⚘ East Carlton Country Park

Days Out

Canals and canons: Walk the towpath and/or take a canal boat trip from Stoke Bruerne; canal museum, and lunch at the Boat Inn there; Canons Ashby; walk Knightley Way from Eversden, through Badby Wood and to Fawsley Park.

Gardens after lunch: Lunch at Grooms Cottage, Coton; Coton Manor gardens; then (depending on day) choice of Cottesbrooke Hall gardens, Lamport gardens, Holdenby House gardens or (half-hour drive) Boughton House gardens.

Around the Nene: Stroll in Barnwell Country Park; Oundle (and National Dragonfly Museum if open); lunch at the Falcon, Fotheringhay; Fotheringhay; Elton Hall (see Cambridgeshire chapter).

A pleasant spot for strolls, with a few **craft workshops** nr the entrance.
🏚 **! Triangular Lodge** (1m W) Late 16th-c oddity designed by same man as Lyveden New Bield nr Brigstock: three walls, three windows and three gables on three levels, and a three-sided chimney, to represent the Holy Trinity. Shop; cl Nov–Mar; (01536) 710761; £1.40.

SALCEY FOREST SP8051
🐾 ⌂ A couple of miles of ancient forest, largely oak, now managed for nature conservation, with well marked trails inc one good for wheelchairs.

STOKE BRUERNE SP7449
❄ ⚓ ⌂ **Canal Museum** Close to a flight of locks on the Grand Union Canal, with fine old canal buildings (inc a popular pub, the Boat), and lots happening on the water, this is a handsome former corn warehouse housing a good collection of canal memorabilia, inc a reconstructed traditional narrow boat complete with immaculately packed-in colourful furniture and crockery. Also boat trips through nearby tunnel. An extension is planned. Shop, limited disabled access (though they plan to improve facilities); cl winter Mon, 25–26 Dec; (01604) 862229; £3. Good towpath walks from here.

SULGRAVE SP5545
🏚 ⚑ 🕸 **Sulgrave Manor** (off B4525) The ancestral home of George Washington's family, a modest manor with exceptionally good special events when the whole place returns to how it would have been during a particular period. People in period costume go about their daily business, and children can take part in a wide range of activities from wassailing or helping in the kitchen at Christmas, to joining in the harvest during the Apple Day Festival. Still worth a visit on non-event days, several relics of Washington (he never lived here – it was his great-great-grandfather who emigrated to America), as well as elegant rooms and well kept gardens. A new conference centre with café and shop opened last year. Meals, snacks, shop, disabled access; open wknds Mar–Dec, and pm wkdys (exc Weds) Apr–Oct, maybe cl 1–2pm; (01295) 760205; £3.75 (special

events £4.50). Just down the road, the Star is enjoyable for lunch.

SYWELL COUNTRY PARK SP8365
🕸 🐾 ⌂ 🎣 (off A4500) Woodland and lakeside walks, play areas, and a little wildlife display; you can fish on the lake (in fact a reservoir).

TOWCESTER SP6948
🏚 This small town (pronounced 'toaster'), despite some light industry on the edge, has quite a pleasantly villagey feel, and some attractive Georgian and Victorian buildings.

UPPER STOWE SP6456
🐑 🦚 **Old Dairy Farm Centre** Sheep, pigs, peacocks, ducks and donkeys, as well as craft workshops, antiques, classic clothes, farm shop and wool collection. Well organised, and decent views – though be prepared for it to be muddy. Restaurant, snacks, shop, disabled access; cl two wks from 25 Dec; (01327) 340525; free, exc special wknds. The Narrow Boat (with towpath walks on the Grand Union Canal) and the Globe at Weedon are good for lunch.

✝ The county is notable for its lovely stone-built **churches**, many with elegant spires visible a long way off and a memorable feature of the county's landscape – particularly along the valley of the River Nene. Besides those mentioned above we'd suggest Burton Latimer SP9075, Dodford SP6160 (striking memorials), Earls Barton SP8563 (fine Saxon tower), Easton Maudit SP8858, Great Weldon SP9289, Higham Ferrers SP9669, King's Sutton SP4936, Lowick SP9780, Middleton Cheney SP4941, Passenham SP7739 (17th-c murals), Raunds SP9972, Rothwell SP8181 and Whiston SP8460. With many of these, the village is well worth seeing, too.

★ **Other attractive villages**, all with decent pubs, include Apethorpe TL0295, Barnwell TL0484, canalside Bugbrooke SP6757, Denton SP8358, Duddington SK9800, Ecton SP8263, Evenley SP5834, Farthingstone SP6155 (Knightley Way walks), Gayton SP7054, thatched Grafton Regis SP7546, Great Houghton SP7958, Grendon SP8760, Harlestone SP7064, Harrington SP7779, Hellidon SP5158 (pleasant walks nearby), Kilsby SP5671, Litchborough SP6353, Little Harrowden SP8771, Marston Trussell SP6985, Mears Ashby SP8466 (narrow lanes of thatched cottages), Nassington TL0696, Sudborough SP9682, Thorpe Mandeville SP5344, riverside Wadenhoe TL0383, Welford SP6480 and Yardley Hastings SP8656. We'd also recommend rather Cotswoldy King's Cliffe TL0097, and two lovely, mellow, orange ironstone villages, Preston Capes SP5754 and Everdon

SP5957.

⌂ **Grand Union Canal** The towpath is popular for country walks, with access among other places from the Royal Oak at Blisworth SP7253, Admiral Nelson (Dark Lane) at Braunston SP5466, New Inn at Buckby Wharf SP6065, Navigation Inn at Thrupp Wharf SP7843 nr Cosgrove, and Wharf Inn in Welford SP6481.

Where to eat

CHACOMBE SP4943 **George & Dragon** *(01295) 711500* Handy for the M40, this charming village pub has a tidy spacious bar with comfortable seats, beams, flagstones, and logs burning in a massive fireplace, real ales, a wide range of good imaginative food from a changing blackboard (also, afternoon snacks and teas), and friendly, attentive service; bdrms. **£19.20**|£7.25.

COTON SP6771 **Grooms Cottage** *(01604) 740219* Attractively converted stable block, serving good English food, in the lovely gardens of Coton Manor; open Easter–Oct for light lunches Weds–Sun, and from Sept–Easter, evening meals on last Fri and Sat of month; disabled access. **£15**|£6.

FARTHINGSTONE SP6155 **Kings Arms** *(01327) 361604* In a pretty village, this handsome 18th-c stone building has homely comfortable sofas and armchairs, a huge log fire in the small atmospheric bar, lots of decorative plates and pictures, a spacious dining area, a wide choice of good imaginative food, well kept real ales, decent wines and friendly licensees; nearby walks; cl wkdy lunchtimes; disabled access. **£17**|£6.

FOTHERINGHAY TL0593 **Falcon** *(01832) 226254* Stylish but relaxed old country pub with a good mix of customers, comfortable lounge with fresh flowers and fireplaces at each end, no smoking conservatory and dining room, little tap bar for locals, excellent food from a varied interesting menu, well kept real ales, and a fine wine list; neat garden; cl Mon. **£24**|£9.50 2-course lunch Tues–Sat.

GREAT BRINGTON SP6664 **Fox & Hounds** *(01604) 770651* Golden stone, thatched village inn with lots of old beams, big flagstones and bare boards, attractive mix of country tables and chairs, two fine log fires, lots of bric-à-brac, a decent range of real ales, country wines, a sensibly short choice of good freshly cooked food (especially the game); sheltered tables in paved courtyard and side garden. **£20**|£7.

HARRINGWORTH SP9197 **White Swan** *Seaton Rd (01572) 747543* Neatly kept, stone-built Tudor pub with generous helpings of enjoyable food, a comfortable lounge/dining area, quieter dining room, and friendly staff; bdrms. **£18.50**|£6.60.

HORTON SP8154 **French Partridge** *Newport Pagnell Rd (01604) 870033* Lovely little evening restaurant run by the Partridges for over 30 years, consistently excellent food (marvellous puddings), a relaxed atmosphere, and fine wines; cl Sun, Mon, 2 wks Christmas, 2 wks Easter, 3 wks summer; well behaved children only; disabled access. **£35** for 4 courses.

LOWICK SP9780 **Snooty Fox** *(01832) 733434* Imposing 17th-c inn with a roaring log fire, dark oak beams and neat, attractive dining chairs around well spaced tables in the atmospheric two-roomed lounge, very good food from a changing blackboard menu, well kept real ales, and plenty of picnic-sets on the grass. **£18**|£7.

ROADE SP7551 **Roadhouse** *16 High St (01604) 863372* Smart and popular restaurant-with-rooms, with long-standing owners, comfortable surroundings, courteous service, reliably enjoyable food, and reasonably priced wines; cl pm Sun, am Mon, am Sat; disabled access. **£30**|3-course lunch £16.

SULGRAVE SP5545 **Star** *Manor Rd (01295) 760389* Hospitable, small, creeper-covered pub with good seasonal food, friendly staff, lots to look at, well kept real ales, and no smoking restaurant; bdrms; cl winter pm Sun; no children. **£25**/£7.50.

THORPE MANDEVILLE SP5344 **Three Conies** *(01295) 711025* This friendly, stone-built, 17th-c dining pub (with a fine wall-mounted sundial) places much emphasis on fresh fish, with more than 10 specials available every day – other bar food too; real ales, a mix of old and new tables on flagstones, modern art and sculpture on the striking blue walls of the open-plan bar, and on the red and yellow walls of the dining room, and seats on the spacious back lawn. **£20.20**|£7.95.

WADENHOE TL0183 **Kings Head** *Church St (01832) 720024* In an attractive village of thatched stone houses, this welcoming pub has seats among willows by the River Nene, a bar with woodburner and pale pine furniture, a little beamed dining room, particularly good imaginative evening and winter lunchtime food (summer lunchtime is limited to soup and sandwiches or ploughman's), well kept real ales, an extensive wine list, pleasant service, and magazines to read; cl am Mon and winter pm Sun; disabled access. **£20**|£5.

Special thanks to Mrs M Coffer, Michael and Jenny Back, Mrs Thompson, Ian Grafton.

Northamptonshire Calendar

Some of these dates were provisional as we went to press. Please check information with the telephone numbers provided.

FEBRUARY

5 **Sulgrave** Chamber Music Concert in the Grand Hall at Sulgrave Manor (01295) 760205

MARCH

4 **Sulgrave** Concert in the Grand Hall at Sulgrave Manor (01295) 760205

APRIL

1 **Sulgrave** Chamber Music Concert in the Grand Hall at Sulgrave Manor (01295) 760205

8 **Sulgrave** Herbs, Hives and Honey at Sulgrave Manor – *till 9 April* (01295) 760205

21 **Sulgrave** Festival of Easter Customs and Traditions at Sulgrave Manor – *till 24 April* (01295) 760205

30 **Lamport** Craft Festival and Garden Show at Lamport Hall (01604) 686272

MAY

1 **Sulgrave** May Day Festival at Sulgrave Manor (01295) 760205

Northamptonshire Calendar (cont.)

7 Daventry Country Day: demonstrations of country crafts at Daventry Country Park (01327) 871100

14 Rockingham Kite Festival at the Castle (01536) 770240

19 Moulton Village Festival – *till 20 May* (01905) 673436

27 Braunston Boat Show: historic boats, parade and fireworks – *till 29 May* (01788) 891555; **Sulgrave** American Living History at Sulgrave Manor – *till 29 May* (01295) 760205

28 Lamport Country Festival at Lamport Hall: field events, steam engines, vintage cars (01604) 686272; **Rockingham** Antiques Fair at the Castle – *till 29 May* (01536) 770240

JUNE

9 Northampton Arts and Music Festival – *till 18 June* (01604) 238791

17 Corby Carnival (01536) 402551; **Northampton** American Auto Club: thousands of American cars, bands, sideshows at Billing Aquadrome – *till 18 June* (01948) 830754

24 Flore Flower Festival: about seven open gardens, over 60 flower displays in the church – *till 25 June* (01327) 341264

JULY

1 Sulgrave Tudor Living History at Sulgrave Manor – *till 9 July* (01295) 760205

14 Northampton Town Show (01604) 238791; **Oundle** International Festival of Music – *till 23 July* (01832) 272026

15 Corby Highland Gathering at West Glebe Park: UK's longest-running games (01536) 402551 ext 8006

16 Rockingham Open-air Theatre: *The Tempest* at the Castle (01536) 770240; **Silverstone** British Grand Prix (01327) 857271

22 Rockingham Craft Fair at the Castle – *till 23 July* (01536) 770240

28 Sulgrave Open-air Theatre at Sulgrave Manor – *till 30 July* (01295) 760205

29 Rockingham Outdoor Opera: *The Barber of Seville* at the Castle (01536) 770240

AUGUST

12 Blakesley Agricultural Show at Seawell Grounds (01327) 359821; **Sulgrave** Festival of Needlework at Sulgrave Manor – *till 20 August* (01295) 760205

18 Northampton Hot-air Balloon Festival (01604) 238791

26 Sulgrave Seven Years War: living history at Sulgrave Manor – *till 28 August* (01295) 760205

SEPTEMBER

16 Northampton Heritage Open Day: free classic bus tour and admission to several places not normally open – *till 17 September* (01604) 238775; **Rockingham** Antiques and Collectors' Fair at the Castle – *till 17 September* (01536) 770240; **Sulgrave** Siege of Sulgrave 1644: re-enactment of an actual event that took place at Sulgrave Manor during the Civil War – *till 17 September* (01295) 760205

Northamptonshire Calendar (cont.)

30 **Sulgrave** Chamber Concert at Sulgrave Manor (01295) 760205; also, Tudor Living History at Sulgrave Manor – *till 8 October* (01295) 760205

OCTOBER

8 **Oundle** World Conker Championships at Chequered Skipper, Ashton (01832) 272735
21 **Sulgrave** Apple Day Festival at Sulgrave Manor – *till 22 October* (01295) 760205

NOVEMBER

4 **Sulgrave** Chamber Concert at Sulgrave Manor (01295) 760205
11 **Sulgrave** Embroidery Day: displays based on the Elizabethan embroideries project at Sulgrave Manor – *till 12 November* (01295) 760205

DECEMBER

2 **Sulgrave** Traditional Christmas Customs at Sulgrave Manor – *till 3 December* also *9–10 Dec, 16–17 Dec, 27–30 Dec* (01295) 760205; **Sulgrave** Chamber Concert at Sulgrave Manor (01295) 760205
26 **Moulton** Mummers Play and Morris Dancing on Stocks Hill (01604) 646818

We welcome reports from readers

This *Guide* depends on readers' reports. Do help us if you can – in return, we offer a discount on the next edition to people who've helped us with reports for it. Tell us what you think about places already in it, and anything extra you think we should say about them. And send us your ideas for inclusion in the next edition: places to visit, eat at or stay in, attractive drives or walks, maybe even unusual interesting shops you know of. Use the card in the middle, the report forms at the end, or just write – no stamp needed: *The Good Britain Guide*, FREEPOST TN1569, Wadhurst, E Sussex TN5 7BR.

NORTHUMBRIA

Grand unspoilt scenery, outstanding places to visit; very good value.

People up here are among Britain's friendliest, and prices are low. There are great sweeps of largely unspoilt scenery, quiet and uncrowded even in summer – including majestic stretches of coast, with a path along the finest sections. Peaceful lower landscapes are enlivened by streams and woodland, solid stone country buildings, and unhurried small market towns. The area is very good both for walking and for driving, with little traffic (outside the Tyneside/Teesside industrial areas).

Newcastle and now Gateshead are rapidly developing into really lively and interesting places to visit, with good free museums and galleries. Here and elsewhere are plenty of historic highlights, carefully thought through so as to be great fun for children as well as full of interest for older people. Many are outstanding, but if you have time for only two don't miss either the remarkable reconstruction of North of England life a century ago, at Beamish, or Hadrian's Wall, striding indomitably across England for nearly 2,000 years – an amazing sight, with Roman forts and engrossing reconstructions and interpretations. This is classic castle country, and there's a fine range of other places to visit. The new Life Centre in Newcastle is quite a break-through, and other interesting new places include Crook Hall in Durham (a great town for a short break, with its fiercely beautiful cathedral), the Allenheads heritage centre, the Endeavour in Stockton and the Roman world now emerging in Wallsend.

This year is the 175th anniversary of Stephenson's first steam locomotive, and quite a few events will commemorate the momentous event, in this area where rail transport was pioneered.

May and June are the best months here, with long evenings (stay away from inland waters in later summer, unless you're midge-proof). September can be delightful, but autumn tends to set in quite fiercely in October, and winter is bleak.

Where to stay

ALNMOUTH NU2411 **Marine House** *1 Marine Rd, Alnmouth, Alnwick NE66 2RW (01665) 830349* **£84 inc dinner,** plus special breaks; 10 rms. 17th-c stone hotel by golf links, with fine sea views, a log fire and plenty of books in the traditional upstairs residents' lounge, cosy bar, and enjoyable freshly prepared food in the cheerfully decorated, no smoking dining room; self-catering also; well behaved dogs welcome; cl Jan; children over 7.

CAMBO NZ0383 **Shieldhall** *Cambo, Wallington, Morpeth NE61 4AQ (01830) 540387* **£47;** 4 well equipped suites, each with its own entrance. 18th-c stone house and carefully converted farm buildings around a courtyard, with antiques and other interesting furnishings (Mr Robinson-Gay is a fine cabinet-maker), a library, bar, and cosy lounge with French windows opening on to the neatly kept big garden; enjoyable freshly produced food in the candlelit, beamed dining room; cl Christmas; children over 11.

CHOLLERFORD NY9170 **George** *Chollerford, Hexham NE46 4EW (01434) 681611* **£110,** plus special breaks; 47 well equipped rms. Quiet hotel with fine gardens sloping down to the river, 17th-c bridge over North Tyne visible from the candlelit restaurant, and thoughtful attentive service; swimming pool and leisure club; disabled access.

CORNHILL-ON-TWEED NT8742 **Tillmouth Park** *(just NE) Cornhill-on-Tweed TD12 4UU (01890) 882255* **£120,** plus special breaks; 14 spacious, pretty rms with period furniture. Solid stone-built country house in 15 acres of parkland (fishing on the River Till, rod and drying room), with comfortable relaxing lounges, open fires, a galleried hall, and good food in either the bistro or restaurant; lots to do nearby; dogs welcome.

COTHERSTONE NZ0119 **Fox & Hounds** *Cotherstone, Barnard Castle DL12 9PF (01833) 650241* ***£55;** 3 no smoking rms. Attractive building in lovely setting overlooking Teesdale village green, with alcoves, local photographs, and an open fire in the comfortably furnished, cosy beamed bar, good food in the no smoking dining room, and courteous friendly service; handy for walks; cl 25 Dec.

CROOKHAM NT9138 **Coach House** *Crookham, Cornhill-on-Tweed TD12 4TD (01890) 820293* ***£72;** 9 individual rms with fresh flowers and nice views, 7 with own bthrm. 17th-c farm buildings around a sunny courtyard, airy beamed lounge with comfortable sofas and big arched windows, good breakfasts, enjoyable dinners, and very warm, friendly, long-standing and helpful owner; lots to do nearby; cl Nov–Easter; good disabled access.

DURHAM NZ2742 **Royal County** *Old Elvet, Durham DH1 3JN (0191) 386 6821* **£145,** plus special breaks; 151 attractive well equipped rms. Close to the city centre with views of the castle and cathedral, this extended hotel has pleasant furnishings, original Tudor beams, panelling and an unusual stained-glass ceiling, several restaurants, and lots of leisure facilities; disabled access.

GATESHEAD NZ2560 **Eslington Villa** *8 Station Rd, Low Fell, Gateshead NE9 6DR (0191) 487 6017* **£74.50,** plus wknd breaks; 12 rms – by the time this book is published, there should be 8 more. Newly extended and comfortable Edwardian house in quiet residential area; with some original features, a lounge with comfortably modern furniture and bay windows overlooking the garden, good food in the conservatory restaurant, and a friendly atmosphere; cl 25 Dec; disabled access.

GREENHEAD NY6667 **Holmhead** *Hadrian's Wall, Greenhead, Carlisle CA6 7HY (01697) 747402* ***£55,** plus special breaks; 4 cosy rms with showers. Family home, built of Wall stones, once a farmhouse but now a comfortable B & B with moorland, wildlife, Hadrian's Wall and Roman castles all nearby; airy lounge with TV at one end, small bar at the other, games and children's toys, good, freshly prepared food using organic farm and local produce eaten family-style around a candlelit oak table, and pretty garden with a stream and games (table tennis and snooker in garage); also self-catering; cl mid-Dec–mid-Jan; disabled access.

GRETA BRIDGE NZ0813 **Morritt Arms** *Greta Bridge, Barnard Castle DL12 9SE (01833) 627232* **£75,** plus special breaks; 23 rms. Smartly old-fashioned coaching inn where Dickens stayed in 1838 to research for *Nicholas Nickleby* – one of the interesting bars has a colourful Dickensian mural; comfortable lounges, fresh flowers, good open fires, and pleasant garden; coarse fishing; no children in evening dining room; pets allowed; disabled access.

HALTWHISTLE NY7366 **Ald White Craig** *Shield Hill, Haltwhistle NE49 9NW (01434) 320565* **£48;** 2 rms. Homely and neatly kept, no smoking, 17th-c croft overlooking South Tyne valley, with prize-winning sheep, rare cattle, dogs, cats and poultry; coal fire and local information in the beamed sitting room, good breakfasts around a central table in the dining room; plenty of walks; self-catering cottages; cl Nov–Mar; no children; disabled access.

HAYDON BRIDGE NY8366 **Hadrian Lodge** *(just N) Haydon Bridge, Hexham NE47 6NF (01434) 688688* ***£49.50;** 10 comfortable rms, most with own bthrm. Attractive, modern, stone-built lodge in 18 acres of pasture close to Hadrian's

Wall, with summer residents' bar, family tearoom, a self-catering kitchen, small launderette, and two trout lakes with rods for hire; self-catering cottages, bunkrooms, and caravan/camp site; disabled access.

HEADLAM NZ1818 **Headlam Hall** *Headlam, Darlington DL2 3HA* (01325) 730238 **£80,** plus wknd breaks; 36 pretty rms, in the main house and adjacent coach house, plus 2-bdrm cottage in village. Peaceful Jacobean mansion in four acres of carefully kept gardens with little trout lake, tennis court, small golf practice area, and croquet lawn; elegant rooms, a fine carved oak fireplace in the main hall, good traditional food in the four individually decorated rooms of the restaurant, and courteous staff; indoor swimming pool, snooker and sauna, and new gym; cl 25 Dec; disabled access.

HIGH FORCE NY8828 **High Force Hotel** *High Force, Barnard Castle DL12 0XH* (01833) 622222 ***£50;** 6 rms. Close to England's highest waterfall (for which it's named), this is a cheerful and friendly place with log fires in relaxing bars, good service, straightforward food, a microbrewery, and lots of malt whiskies; it includes a mountain rescue post; no pets.

KIRKWHELPINGTON NY9684 **Cornhills** *Kirkwhelpington, Newcastle upon Tyne NE19 2RE* (01830) 540232 ***£45;** 3 rms, some with own bthrm. Big no smoking, Victorian farmhouse on a large stock-rearing farm with marvellous views towards the coast and Tyne Valley, lots of original features, a comfortable lounge, good breakfasts (local pubs for evening meals), and indoor and outdoor games for children; self-catering also; cl Apr.

LONGFRAMLINGTON NU1301 **Embleton Hall** *Longframlington, Morpeth NE65 8DT* (01665) 570249 **£85;** 13 comfortable, pretty and individually decorated rms. Charming hotel in lovely grounds surrounded by fine countryside, with a particularly friendly, relaxed atmosphere and courteous staff; neat little bar, elegant lounge, log fires, excellent-value bar meals, and very good food in the attractive dining room; disabled access.

LONGHORSLEY NZ1496 **Linden Hall** *Longhorsley, Morpeth NE65 8XF* (01670) 516611 **£125,** plus special breaks; 50 individually decorated rms. Georgian hotel in 450 acres of landscaped park, with coarse fishing, clay-pigeon shooting, mountain biking (bike hire available), 18-hole golf course, pitch and putt, croquet, jogging routes, giant chess, and lots of leisure facilities inc a big swimming pool; pubby bar, elegant drawing room, and good food in the attractive restaurant; children in main restaurant early evening only; disabled access.

NEWCASTLE UPON TYNE NZ2563 **Malmaison** *The Quayside, Newcastle upon Tyne NE1 3DX* (0191) 245 5000 **£96;** 116 individually decorated and well equipped rms. In a former Co-operative Society warehouse and overlooking the river, this stylish hotel (part of a small chain with other hotels in Edinburgh, Glasgow and Manchester) is boldly decorated throughout with contemporary furniture and artwork, genuinely friendly staff, modern cooking in the fashionable brasserie, and decent breakfasts.

ROMALDKIRK NY9922 **Rose & Crown** *Romaldkirk, Barnard Castle DL12 9EB* (01833) 650213 **£84,** plus special breaks; 12 rms – those in the main house have lots of character. Smart and interesting old coaching inn by the green of this delightful Teesdale village, with Jacobean oak settle, log fire, old black and white photographs, and lots of brass in the beamed traditional bar, a cosy residents' lounge, very good popular food in both the bar and fine oak-panelled restaurant, and well kept real ales and wines; cl Christmas; disabled access.

SEAHOUSES NU2232 **Olde Ship** *Main St, Seahouses NE68 7RD* (01665) 720200 **£64,** plus special breaks; 16 rms, inc 4 apartments. Thriving harbourside inn with small rooms full of nautical items and fishing memorabilia, windows looking out towards the Farne Islands, comfortable residents' lounge and new sun lounge, popular bar food, five real ales, and good service; ideal for coastal walks; cl Dec and Jan; children over 10.

SLALEY NY9757 **Rose & Crown** *Slaley, Hexham NE47 0AA* (01434) 673263 ***£45;** 3 attractively modernised rms. Traditional village inn with mugs hanging from

the beams, popular food in bar and restaurant, and friendly service; lots to do nearby.
STANNERSBURN NY7286 **Pheasant** *Stannersburn, Hexham NE48 1DD
(01434) 240382* ***£60,** plus special breaks; 8 rms. Beautifully located,
unpretentious, 17th-c stone inn close to Kielder Water and its quiet forests, with a
traditional comfortable lounge, simple public bar, a happy mix of customers, good
food inc excellent fresh vegetables and enjoyable Sun lunch, well kept real ales, a
fine choice of malts, welcoming service, nice breakfasts, and picnic sets in
streamside garden; cl 25–26 Dec; disabled access.
WOLSINGHAM NZ1037 **Greenwell Farm** *Wolsingham, Tow Low, Bishop
Auckland DL13 4PH (01388) 527248* ***£45,** plus special breaks; 6 rms in comfortably
converted stone barn. 300-year-old farmhouse with fine views, sitting and dining
rooms, and good food using naturally reared meats and locally grown produce; also,
and spring lambs, calves and chicks, nature trail and conservation areas; can bring
your own horse or mountain bike; self-catering cottage; cl Christmas and New
Year; disabled access.

To see and do

NORTHUMBRIA Family Attraction of the Year

👤! **NEWCASTLE UPON TYNE** NZ2163 **International Centre for
Life** (Times Sq) It's not often we stick our neck out and recommend
somewhere before it's even opened, but this major new development sounds
so intriguing we couldn't resist. Set to open in spring 2000, it's one of the
Millennium Commission's landmark projects, a £58 million centre taking in
science and research labs, offices for biotechnology companies, and, our main
concern, an innovative visitor attraction exploring the origins of life. You'd
think anywhere setting out to explain DNA in an accessible way would be on to
a loser, but the four main exhibition areas here sound like they'll be a lot of fun,
putting across some serious science far more entertainingly than you might
expect. A visit will start with the River of Life, a trip back through billions of
years of evolution, tracing how mankind has got to where we are today. Most
obviously enjoyable will be Life on the Edge, a motion simulator film designed
to make you feel you're skateboarding, windsurfing or even bungee-jumping
without leaving your seat (which will move along with the action). A live show
in the Secret of Life will explain what we have in common with everything from
dinosaurs to daffodils, while an ambitious multi-media experience in a theatre
designed to look like a giant brain aims to illustrate the range of emotions and
activities going on in our heads, as seen through the minds of a typical local
family. In between will be more than 50 state-of-the-art interactive exhibits
offering the chance to hang-glide over Newcastle or score against a virtual
goalie. A number of respected scientists are backing this project, housed in a
dramatic new building beside the city's main railway station; the site has
previously enjoyed periods as a bowling green, market, army barracks and
hospital. They say a typical visit will last between two and three hours – maybe
longer if they really can live up to the hype. We're looking forward to finding
out. Meals, snacks, shop, disabled access; best to ring for the opening date, after
which they'll open daily exc 25 Dec and 1 Jan; (0191) 261 6006; admission was
still to be confirmed as we went to press, but should be around £7 (less for
children, and there will be a family ticket).

Please let us know what you think of places in the *Guide*. Use the report forms
at the back of the book or simply write us a letter.

ALLENDALE NY8352

❁ △ The B6305/B6295 is a great scenic drive; lots of walks up there, and the King's Head in Allendale village is a good stop.

ⓗ **Allenheads Heritage Centre** (Allenheads) The history of this former lead-mining village, the highest in England, is told in its heritage centre, blacksmith's shop and engine house; also nature trails. Meals and snacks in the Hemmel café, shop, disabled access; (01434) 685326; £1. The Allenheads Inn is an entertaining stop.

ALNMOUTH NU2410

★ △ This pleasant town has attractive beaches, good coastal walks, and a lot for summer visitors; the Saddle has good food.

ALNWICK NU1813

✝ Busy town at the heart of prosperous farming country, with some attractive old streets nr the market square – it was recently used in the film *Elizabeth*. The hillside **church** of St Michael and All Angels above the river is a perfect example of a complete Late Gothic building. The Market Tavern has bargain food.

🏛🖼👁❁ **Alnwick Castle** The 'Windsor of the North' dates back to the 11th c, and is the second-largest inhabited castle in the country. Stone soldiers stand guard on the battlements, and inside all is Italian Renaissance grandeur, with a magnificent art collection taking in works by Titian, Van Dyck and Canaletto, and an outstanding Claude. Also famous collection of Meissen china, Roman remains, children's playground. Landscaped grounds by Capability Brown: restoration of the 12-acre walled garden starts this summer and should be completed by the end of 2001. Meals, snacks, shop; cl Oct–Easter; (01665) 510777; £5.95.

❁ **Hulne Park** Excellent for gentle parkland walks; dogs not allowed. Don't miss the whimsical Brizlee Tower and hermit's cave.

AMBLE NU2604

★ ⚓ ⚑ This attractive small town has a solid old fishing harbour, and modern yacht marina; RSPB **boat trips** around nearby Coquet Island, with its colourful eider ducks and puffins.

AYDON NZ0066

🏛 **Aydon Castle** 13th-c, and remarkably well preserved, in a lovely setting. Snacks, shop, some disabled access; cl Nov–Mar; (01434) 632450; £2; EH.

BAMBURGH NU1835

🏛 ★ ✝ **Bamburgh Castle** Stunning huge square Norman castle on a cliff above the sea, its clock serving as time-keeper for the cricket green in the attractive village below. Despite the forbidding exterior, the inside is very much a lived-in stately home, with armour from the Tower of London. Snacks, shop; cl Nov–Mar; (01668) 214515; *£4. There's a neo-Gothic shrine to Grace Darling in the yard of the interesting 13th-c **church**. The Lord Crewe Arms is well placed for lunch.

👁 **Grace Darling Museum** (Radcliffe Rd) Pictures and mementos of the local heroine, inc the boat in which Grace and her father rescued nine survivors from the wrecked SS *Forfarshire*. Shop, disabled access; cl am Sun and all Nov–Easter; (01668) 214465; free (donations to RNLI).

BARNARD CASTLE NZ0416

★ ♘ △ Pleasant market town, still coming to life on Weds market day, with several attractive buildings. In the centre, the Old Well, with a terrace over the town walls, has good-value food. There's charming gorge scenery nearby, wooded, romantic and unmistakably lowland in character – making for good walks. The valley path W eventually climbs above the river and follows field routes as it leads towards Cotherstone.

🏰👁🖼❁ **Bowes Museum** A beautiful French-style château in 20 acres of meticulously kept formal grounds. The 40 rooms are filled with sumptuous fine arts and an outstanding display of paintings by Canaletto, Goya, El Greco and others; also children's room and local history section. Relatively few people find their way to this treasure-house, though it's one of the most worthwhile places to visit in the entire country – those readers who have visited, certainly enjoyed it. Meals and snacks (summer only), shop, disabled access; cl 25–26 Dec, 1 Jan;

(01833) 690606; £3.90.

Castle These dramatically set 12th-c ruins include the original keep and the 14th-c hall. Shop, disabled facilities; cl Mon and Tues Nov–Mar, and maybe lunchtimes, 24–26 Dec, 1 Jan; (01833) 638212; £2.30 (inc audio tour).

✝ ◠ **Egglestone Abbey** Downstream from Barnard Castle, this is reached by a couple of miles of enjoyable riverside walk – or by car. Substantial remains include gracefully arched windows, and some remnants of the monastic buildings; disabled access; free.

Rokeby Park (just SE) Elegant 18th-c villa in a fine setting, most famous for its *Rokeby Venus* by Velasquez (though the original is now in the National Gallery). The best of the other pictures is probably Pellegrini's *Venus disarming Cupid*. Open May bank hols and the following Tues, then pm Mon and Tues Jun–2nd Tues in Sept; (01833) 637334; £5.00. The Morritt Arms nearby does good meals. The B6278 to Stanhope and Edmundbyers is a fine drive.

BEADNALL NU2329
★ On Northumberland's underpopulated coast, this attractive village has boats on the beach, and an interestingly restored waterside limekiln; nearby Benthall is also a pleasant place to visit.

BEAMISH NZ2154
North of England Open-air Museum Perhaps the most rewarding paid attraction in Britain, an amazingly ambitious 300-acre museum exhaustively re-creating life in the North of England at the turn of the century. No detail is overlooked, and there's something for everyone in the five main sections: a town with streets, shops, houses and businesses, colliery village with mine, chapel, cottages and school, manor house with formal gardens and orchard, railway station, and home farm with animals and craft demonstrations. A re-created engine shed, the centrepiece of which is a magnificent 1822 locomotive, opened last year, and a full-scale replica of Stephenson's *Locomotion No. 1* carries visitors down a ¼-mile track. Costumed interpreters really bring the place to life. Children can wander round this authentic little world at their leisure, touching everything, and joining in most of the activities, from learning to play hoops and hopscotch to taking part in lessons in the schoolroom (bad handwriting is rewarded by a light rap on the knuckles). A Victorian fairground has rides including a Hall of Mirrors (small extra charge), and working trams and buses join up the different areas. Meals and snacks (inc period pub), good shops, some disabled access; cl Mon and Fri Nov–Mar, and 3 wks over Christmas; (01207) 231811; £10, or £3 late Oct–Mar when only the town and tramway are open. The Shepherd & Shepherdess not far from the gate is useful for lunch, as is the more individual Beamish Mary (follow sign from A693 to No Place & Cooperative Villas).

BELLINGHAM NY8383
✝ ◠ (pronounced 'Bellingjum') A small country town with an attractive 13th-c **church**, stone-roofed to protect it against arson-minded Border raiders; Black Middens Bastle House, a 16th-c stone-built farmhouse is usually open to the public. There's a pretty walk just N of the town, to the 9-metre (30ft) cascade of Hareshaw Linn. The Cheviot Hotel does decent food. This is the main town in North Tynedale, one of the least-known and most unspoilt parts of Northumberland, with good scenic drives. Between the Pennines and the Cheviots, it's a peaceful river valley surrounded by wild moorland, with fine scenery and a particularly unrushed atmosphere – very relaxing.

BELSAY NZ1078
Belsay Hall & Gardens (A696) The same family have lived here for nearly 600 years, first in a medieval castle, then a Jacobean manor house and finally a grand mansion designed to look like a Greek classical temple – all can still be seen, but the mansion is strangely eerie, there's no furniture and in some rooms no floors either. The 30 acres of landscaped parkland are especially agreeable, with rhododendron garden, formal terraces and woodland walks. Snacks, shop, disabled access; cl 24–26 Dec; (01661) 881636; £3.80. The Highlander has

good food.

BERWICK-UPON-TWEED
NT9953

★ 🏰 ✝ ⌂ ❋ Largely unspoilt, this has some handsome 18th-c buildings and a fine 17th-c church; most people who come here seem to while away at least a bit of time watching the swans on the River Tweed. Alternatively, look out over the sea from the Rob Roy (Spittal Rd), which has good local fish. The town has an extraordinary trio of bridges, and deserves to be approached by walking along the Tweed: there are paths on both banks, starting from the East Ord picnic site by the A1 road bridge. The **town ramparts**, impressively intact, were a masterpiece of 16th-c military planning. Partly grassed over and easy to walk, they give good views.

🍴 🖼 **Berwick Barracks** (The Parade) Britain's oldest surviving purpose-built barracks, now a local history museum and gallery, with an interesting exhibition on the British soldier, another on early local maps, and a new contemporary art gallery. Snacks, shop, disabled access; cl winter Mon and Tues and maybe lunchtimes, 24–26 Dec, 1 Jan; (01289) 304493; £2.60.

🍴 🌿 **Wine & Spirit Museum and Chemist** (Palace Green) The mainland base of Lindisfarne mead and country wine-makers, with a collection of objects from the wine and spirits industries, working potter, home-made pot-pourri, and Victorian chemist shop. Snacks, shop, disabled access; cl Sun Nov–Easter, and Christmas wk; (01289) 305153; free.

BINCHESTER NZ2332

🏛 ✝ **Binchester Roman Fort** Quite a lot left of this 1st-c 10-acre fort, inc the best-preserved military baths in the country, with an exceptional hypocaust system. Interesting events include days when you can sample Roman food. Shop, disabled access; open Easter wknd, then May–Oct; (01388) 663089; £1.50. Nearby **Escomb church** is interesting, built in the 7th c from stone from the fort. A 3rd-c fort can be seen a few miles S at Piercebridge (where the riverside George, with its famous grandfather clock which stopped when the old man died, is useful for lunch); finds from both sites are shown at the Bowes Museum in Barnard Castle.

BISHOP AUCKLAND NZ2130

🏛 🏵 **Auckland Castle** The main country residence of the Bishops of Durham, a grand series of buildings entered through a splendid Gothic gatehouse in the town's market place. Some rooms are relatively stark, but a highlight is the chapel, splendidly transformed from a 12th-c banqueting hall by John Cosin from 1660. The attractive grounds have an unusual 18th-c deercot. Snacks, shop, limited disabled access; open pm Fri and Sun May–Sept, and daily exc Sat mid-July–Aug; (01388) 601627; £3.

BLANCHLAND NY9650

★ The archetypal border village, every house looking a stronghold, alone in a great bowl of magnificent scenery; the Lord Crewe Arms here is an interesting hotel, in parts very ancient indeed.

BOULMER NU2613

★ One of several attractive villages and small towns dotted down Northumberland's scenic and underpopulated coast, this has active fishing boats.

BOWES NY9913

🏰 **Bowes Castle** Within the earthworks of a Roman fort, these remains include the great Norman keep, three storeys high; free. A few miles W, the Bowes Moor Hotel, one of England's highest, is a welcoming moorland oasis.

BURNOPFIELD NZ1857

🏛 🏰 🏵 ⌂ **Gibside Chapel & Grounds** Marvellous Palladian mausoleum for the Bowes family in an 18th-c landscaped park, with the rather sad ruins of a hall and other estate buildings dotted around. Miles of pleasant walks. Snacks, shop, disabled access; cl Mon (exc bank hols) and Mon–Sat Nov–Mar; (01207) 542255; *£3; NT. The Highlander at White le Head has decent food.

BYRNESS NT7702

🏛 🐟 ⌂ ❋ **Chew Green Roman Camps** Little-visited spectacular earthworks alone in wild country, well repaying the stiff walk up the Pennine Way through the Redesdale Forest. The Pennines up here contain a great many more unspoilt prehistoric and other archaeological remains – useful goals for walkers in these magnificent hills, often yielding remarkable views. Some areas N of the A68 (which as it approaches the Scottish border is a remarkably dramatic drive) and W of the B6341 may temporarily be put out of bounds by Army training; current proposals to extend the Army area are being resisted by conservationists.

CAMBO NZ0283

🏠 🕸 ♿ 🏛 **Wallington House** Built in 1688 and altered in the 1740s, with fine plasterwork and porcelain, and works by the Pre-Raphaelite circle which often congregated here in the house's 19th-c cultural glory days. Showpiece fuchsias in the conservatory, and 100 acres of lawns, terraces, lakes and woodland landscaped by Capability Brown. Meals, snacks, shop, plant centre, adventure playground, disabled facilities; house cl am, all Tues, and Nov–Mar, grounds and garden open all year; (01670) 774283; £5.20, grounds only £3.80; NT. There is free access to the huge surrounding estate, which is laced with footpaths and includes prehistoric sites and more parkland.

CAULDRON SNOUT NY8128

⌂ ❄ Beyond High Force, The Pennine Way rewards walkers with some truly wild landscape as the Tees rushes along a gorge beneath Cronkley Scar and tumbles down Cauldron Snout, a 60-metre (200-ft) cascade which can be reached from the dam at Cow Green Reservoir (where there is also a nature trail). The pleasant Langdon Beck Inn is a short drive or walk below the dam.

CHEVIOT HILLS NT9716

⌂ Part of the Northumberland National Park, the Cheviots are strikingly empty and solitary, with only the characteristic local breed of hardy sheep for company in most places – an area that suits walkers who really want to get away from other people.

CHILLINGHAM NU0525

🏰 🕸 ♿ ❄ **Chillingham Castle** Striking old castle dating back to the 12th c, full of antiques, tapestries, arms and armour. Formal gardens, woodland walks, lake, and splendid views of the surrounding countryside; occasional concerts and special events. Brave souls can rent one of their haunted rooms. Snacks, shop; cl am, Tues (exc July and

Aug), and Oct–late Apr; (01668) 215359; £4.30. The Percy Arms at Chatton is good for lunch.

✙ 🏛 🕸 **Chillingham Wild Cattle Park** The famous large-horned white cattle have been here for the last 700 years, the only animals of their kind still pure and uncrossed with domestic breeds. As they're potentially aggressive, tours are led by a warden. Bring binoculars for a closer view. Shop, limited disabled access; cl 12–2 pm, am Sun, all Tues, and Nov–Mar; (01668) 215250; £3. Above the park, Ross Castle **hill fort** has great views.

CHOLLERFORD NY9070

🕸 ♿ ⌂ **Hexham Herbs** (B6318, nr Chesters) Over 800 varieties of herbs beautifully laid out in attractive walled gardens; also old-fashioned roses, many other plants, and woodland walk. Shop, some disabled access, plant sales; telephone for winter opening; (01434) 681483; £1.50.

CLENNEL STREET NT9207

⌂ This ancient drove road leading from Coquetdale is a good walking route into the Cheviots – lonely grassy moors (boggy in parts when it's wet), drystone walls, sheep, dark conifer plantations. You can pick up the route nr Alwinton, and there's a pretty way back, along a track by the River Alwin.

CRASTER NU2519

★ ⌂ A pleasant place to visit, with its tidal fishing harbour, good kippering factory, excellent pub, and magnificent clifftop walk to Dunstanburgh Castle.

DARLINGTON NZ2815

🏭 🍺 ! ✝ **Railway Centre & Museum** Interesting museum in carefully restored North Rd Station, part of which is still used for train services. Exhibits include the *Locomotion* built by Robert Stephenson in 1825, which pulled the first passenger steamtrain on a public railway. Steam rides some summer wknds. Snacks, shop, disabled access; cl 25–26 Dec and all Jan; (01325) 460532; £2.10. An extraordinary £760,000 **brickwork locomotive**, a 40-metre (130ft) approximation of the pre-war record-breaking *Mallard*, complete with clouds of bricky steam, lies beside Morrisons supermarket. St Cuthbert's (Church Row) is an interesting Early English **church**.

DURHAM NZ2742

★ 🏚 ⛳ The ancient core of the town stands on a crag defended by an almost complete loop of the River Wear, with a rewarding riverside path going from Prebends Bridge up to South St (with some of the best views of the cathedral's magnificent pinnacled towers), recrossing the river by Silver St bridge. The old part of town is largely pedestrianised, with attractive cobbled alleys and narrow medieval lanes, and fine medieval buildings among the Georgian and later ones, particularly around the 12th-c pedestrians-only Elvet Bridge (where the Regatta tea rooms have decent food). There are several medieval churches, and interesting little shops. You can hire rowing boats nr Elvet Bridge, which is also the departure point for launches. The Court (Court Lane) has cheap food all day exc Sun; the best-value food is out at the Seven Stars at Shincliffe.

🏚 ❀ **Crook Hall & Gardens** 🔲 (Frankland Lane, Sidegate) Medieval manor surrounded by delightful gardens, currently being restored. Snacks; open Easter wknd, May bank hols, all Suns May–mid-Sept, and daily (exc Sat) late July–early Sept; (0191) 384 8028; *£3.75.

🔲 ❧ **Durham Art Gallery** (Aykley Heads) When we went to press, this good gallery, with unusual temporary exhibitions and adjacent regimental museum, had closed for refurbishment – it should re-open some time in the summer; phone then for opening times and prices; (0191) 384 2214.

🏰 **Durham Castle** Developed from an early Norman motte and bailey. Still a proud building, with original chapel and 13th-c great hall, which is now used for university accommodation, and you can stay here. Shop; guided tours Mon, Weds and wknds 2–4 pm in term-time, usually every day in hols – best to check first; (0191) 374 3800; £3.

✝ **Durham Cathedral** Huge, and probably England's finest, a fiercely beautiful and unusually well preserved Norman building, breathtaking and very masculine inside; it was the first in Britain to use pointed arches. St Cuthbert's shrine is here, and they say that the Lady Chapel owes its odd

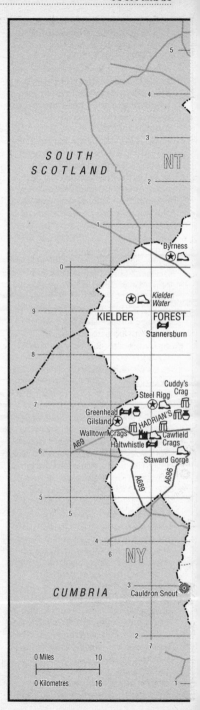

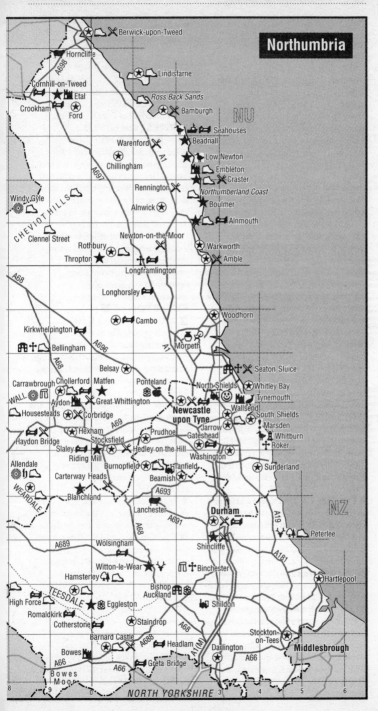

Northumbria

Berwick-upon-Tweed
Horncliffe
Cornhill-on-Tweed
Etal
Crookham
Ford
Lindisfarne
Ross Back Sands
Bamburgh
NU
Warenford
Seahouses
Beadnall
Chillingham
Low Newton
Embleton
Craster
Rennington
Northumberland Coast
Windy Gyle
Boulmer
Alnwick
CHEVIOT HILLS
Alnmouth
Clennel Street
Newton-on-the-Moor
Rothbury
Thropton
Warkworth
Longframlington
Amble
Longhorsley
Kirkwhelpington
Cambo
Woodhorn
Bellingham
Morpeth
Belsay
Carrawbrough
Chollerford
Matfen
Ponteland
Seaton Sluice
WALL
Aydon
Great Whittington
North Shields
Whitley Bay
Housesteads
Corbridge
Newcastle upon Tyne
Tynemouth
Haydon Bridge
Hexham
Stocksfield
Prudhoe
Wallsend
South Shields
Slaley
Riding Mill
Hedley-on-the-Hill
Jarrow
Gateshead
Marsden
Whitburn
Allendale
Burnopfield
Tanfield
Washington
Roker
Carterway Heads
Beamish
WEARDALE
Blanchland
Lanchester
Sunderland
A693
Durham
NZ
A689
Wolsingham
Shincliffe
Peterlee
Witton-le-Wear
Binchester
Hamsterley
High Force
Bishop Auckland
Shildon
Hartlepool
TEESDALE
Eggleston
Romaldkirk
Staindrop
Cotherstone
Barnard Castle
Stockton-on-Tees
Bowes
Headlam
Darlington
Middlesbrough
BOWES MOOR
Greta Bridge
A66
NORTH YORKSHIRE

position at the west end to his hatred of women; every time they tried to build it in the right place his spirit apparently caused the foundations to collapse. Try and spot the unique bronze knocker that seems to have a cheery grin. Rare books and manuscripts in the 15th-c monks' dormitory. Meals, snacks, shop, disabled access; monks' dormitory open 10am–3.30pm Mon–Sat, 12.30–3pm Sun (80p), Treasury cl am Sun (£2), tower cl Sun, during services and inclement weather (£2). The close behind the cathedral has some handsome old houses.

▥ Finchale Priory (3m NE, minor rd off A167) St Godric chose this site in 1110 as a place to meditate, and it's still a pleasant spot for contemplation, beside the graceful ruins of the 13th-c church.

❀ ♧ Houghall College Gardens (Shincliffe Rd) The county's main horticultural training centre, with 10 acres of hardy plants, a watergarden, woodland garden, Alpine rock garden, parterre and arboretum. This area records some of the lowest temperatures in the country, so if it grows here, it'll grow anywhere. Snacks, plant sales, disabled access; best to phone for opening hours (0191) 386 1351; free.

♂ Oriental Museum (Elvet Hill) Unrivalled collections include displays of everything from plates, carvings and paintings to costumes and mummies. Shop; cl 1–2pm, am wknds, Christmas–New Year; (0191) 374 7911; £1.50.

✝ ♄ St Mary le Bow Church 🖼 (The Bailey) The heritage centre here has exhibitions on the city's history. Shop, disabled access; cl am (exc July–Aug), wkdys in Apr and May, and all Oct–Mar; £1.

❀ ▤ University Botanic Garden (Hollingside Lane) Hugely enjoyable 18-acre garden in mature woodland with exotic trees from America and the Himalayas, tropical house, cactus house and visitor centre, and an unusual sculpture garden. Snacks, shop, disabled access; cl Christmas–New Year; (0191) 374 2671; around £1.

♂ University Museum of Archaeology On the river bank below the cathedral's south-west corner, a former fulling mill with finds from the city and surrounding area. Shop, some disabled access; cl am and all Tues and Weds Nov–Mar, plus 24–25 Dec; (0191) 374 3623; *£1. Also along these banks is a sculpture of the Last Supper, carved by Colin Wilbourn from 13 trees that died of Dutch elm disease.

EGGLESTON NY9923

❀ ★ Eggleston Hall Gardens A good example of an updated 19th-c country-house garden, with rare and unusual trees, shrubs, perennials and other plants. Plans are afoot to open the ruined early 17th-c chapel (in which they hope to plant specialised trees). They sell plants, organically grown herbs, and fruit and vegetables from the walled kitchen garden. Snacks, some disabled access; (01833) 650403; 50p, or £1 for a season ticket (money refunded if you buy a plant). The moorside village is attractive.

EMBLETON NU2521

▥ ⌂ Dunstanburgh Castle Screeching gulls add to the atmosphere at these huge ruins, standing imposingly on the cliff above the North Sea. Turner painted the scene three times. Snacks, small shop; cl winter Mon and Tues, 24–26 Dec, 1 Jan; (01665) 576231; £1.80; EH (NT members also free). The Sportsman, with stunning views of the castle, does decent food. The NT owns much of this stretch of coastline, inc the pleasantly bracing walk to Craster – one of the finest sections of the Northumbrian coast path.

ETAL NT9239

★ Pretty row of white cottages running down to a ford across the river, with a working forge and nice thatched pub.

▥ Etal Castle Good Walkman tours guide you round these evocative 14th-c ruins; also an exhibition on Border history. Shop, disabled access to exhibition area; cl Nov–Mar; (01890) 820332; £2.60; EH.

FORD NT9338

★ ✿ ✕ Built as an estate-workers' model village, for Ford Castle; very attractive, with one or two craft workshops, a well restored working corn mill (cl Nov–Mar; (01890) 820338; £2.50), and the friendly Heatherslaw Bakery making good use of the resulting corn. You can also hire bikes from here.

🚉 Heatherslaw Light Railway
Steam or diesel journeys on a narrow-gauge railway to Etal, along pretty valley of the River Till. Snacks, shop, disabled access; cl Nov–Easter, exc some wknds before Christmas, (01890) 820317 for times; £3.70.

🏠 Lady Waterford Hall Well worth a look: used till 1957 as the village school, with murals showing the village children and their families as characters from well known Bible stories; cl 12.30–1.30pm and all Nov–Mar; around £2.

GATESHEAD NZ2162
☺ ! 🖼 Not yet the area's most appealing stop for visitors, though work is well under way on the multi-million Baltic Centre for Contemporary Arts (they're currently seeking funds to build an adjacent concert hall) – if you can wait till 2001. Meantime, the **Metro Centre** (A1 just W) is a useful rainy-day outing from Newcastle, a vast modern shopping and leisure complex with several different themed undercover areas, all sorts of fairground attractions (better for younger children than teenage thrill seekers), even a Roman Catholic church. Do remember exactly where you put your car – there are 12,000 parking spaces. If you're in Gateshead, the **Shipley Art Gallery** on Prince Consort Rd is worth a look (cl am Sun; free), the Keelmans riverside walk (off South Shore Rd) is quite pleasant, and you'll find it difficult to miss the Angel of the North, towering over the A1.

HADRIAN'S WALL NY7868
🏛 ❋ ⌂ An amazing sight, if you've never seen it before. It's extraordinary to imagine those Roman military engineers, so far from their warm homeland, building this remarkable construction through such inhospitable surroundings. Many of its 73½ miles run along the natural crag of the great Whin Sill, making it that much more formidable; the overall sense of grandeur is a definite part of the appeal. The stone wall itself, with its turret watchtowers, milecastles and more sporadic forts, defines the north side of a narrow frontier zone, bounded on its south side by an equally remarkable

ditch between turf ramparts; a military road runs between wall and ditch. It was this whole installation rather than just the wall itself which the Romans used to control trade and cross-border travel. The B6318 following the military road is a fine drive, with some of the best views of the wall. This road also gives walkers easy access to the line of the Wall, with numerous car parks on the way. There's not a lot of point trying to make walks into circuits: all the interest is along the Wall itself, although in places you may prefer to drop down beneath the switchback Whin Sill (the ridge of hard rock on which the Wall stands), which itself can be quite tiring. The views are bleak and exhilarating. Even in fine summer weather the wind can be chilly on the Wall, so go well wrapped up. English Heritage are cutting back on the publicity for some sites – thousands of marauding tourists have caused more damage than centuries of harsh weather and unstable politics ever managed. In summer a tourist bus runs between Hexham and several of the main sites (and even as far as Carlisle), and you can get on or off at any of the stages along the way; check with the information centre on (01434) 605225 for times. The best place to eat nr the main sites is the Milecastle Inn on the B6318 NE of Haltwhistle.

🏛 ❋ 🐄 Birdoswald Roman Fort (Gilsland) Overlooking the Irthing Gorge (and in fact just over the Cumbrian border), this is one of the most impressive sites on Hadrian's Wall, partly because it has so many features in such a small area, and partly for its grand views. Good visitor centre; snacks, shop, some disabled access; visitor centre cl Dec–late Mar; (01697) 747602; £2.50. The **goat farm** at Holme View nearby sells prize-winning traditional cheeses.

🏛 Carrawbrough Mithraic Temple Three 3rd-c altars to Mithras were found here, on the line of the Roman wall near the fort of Brocolitia. They're now in Newcastle's Museum of Antiquities, but you can see replicas in their original setting.

🏛 Cawfield Crags One of the best-preserved sections of the Wall.

🏛 ⛰ Chesters Roman Fort (B6318,

slightly W of Chollerford) The best-preserved example of a Roman cavalry fort in Britain, in an attractive riverside setting. In the bath-house you can see exactly how the underfloor heating system worked, and a museum has sculptures and inscriptions from here and other sites. Summer snacks, shop, disabled access; cl 24–26 Dec, 1 Jan; (01434) 681379; £2.80; EH. The Hadrian Hotel at Wall (A6076 S) has good-value food.

🏠🗑★🗑 **Corbridge Roman Site** (slightly NW) Granaries, portico columns and what may be the legionary HQ survive among these 3rd-c remains. The adjacent museum has the magnificent Corbridge Lion. Shop, limited disabled access; cl Mon and Tues, and maybe lunchtimes Nov–Mar; (01434) 632349; £2.80; EH. The village, above the Tyne, is attractive; the Black Bull is good for lunch, and Brocksbushes Farm (2m E) has **pick-your-own** fruit and a farm shop; (01434) 633400.

🏠🗑 **Cuddys Crag** Perhaps the most beautiful section of the Wall, very photogenic and giving glorious views.

🗑 **Greenhead Roman Army Museum** (Carvoran) Entertaining and informative intrepretation of what it was like to be a Roman soldier, with everything you could possibly want to know about his training, pay, and off-duty hobbies. Snacks, shop, disabled access; cl mid-Nov–mid-Feb; (01697) 747485; £3.

🏠🗑🗑 **Housesteads Roman Fort & Museum** (B6318) The best-known and most visited section of the Wall (and also one of the best-preserved), pretty much slap bang in the middle. It owes its fine state of preservation partly to the fact that while other stretches were being used as a handy source of free recycled quality masonry, this fort was base camp for a powerful group of border bandits; woe betide anyone who tried to use their fortifications as material for cowsheds or churches. A museum has altars, inscriptions and models, and there are good walks in either direction. Snacks, shop; cl 24–26 Dec, 1 Jan; (01434) 344363; £2.80; EH.

🗑🗑🗑 **Once Brewed National Park Centre** (Steel Rigg) Very useful National Park Information Centre, handy for Housesteads and Vindolanda, with exhibitions and audio-visual presentations. Guided walks leave from here (though not every day). Snacks, shop, disabled access; cl Nov–mid-Mar; (01434) 344396; free; EH. The walk from here to Housesteads offers some of the best views of the Wall; it's only three miles, but is up and down so can take up to two and a half hours.

🏠🗑 **Vindolanda** Started well before the Wall itself, this Roman fort and frontier town soon became a base for 500 soldiers. Full-scale reconstructions, lots of well preserved remains and possibly further excavations in progress. The adjacent museum has a fascinating selection of hand-written letters and documents found on the site, inc party invitations, shopping lists and a note that could have been written by many a modern mother: 'I have sent

---

Days Out

The Roman Wall: Birdoswald Roman Fort; Greenhead Roman Army Museum; lunch at the Milecastle Inn, B6318 NE of Haltwhistle; Vindolanda frontier town; Housesteads Roman Fort, and walk along Hadrian's Wall; or skip the walk and look at Chesters Roman Fort.

Teesdale gems: Barnard Castle and Bowes Museum; lunch at the Rose & Crown, Romaldkirk; nature trail from Bowlees Visitor Centre to Gibson's Cave; High Force; walk from Cow Green Reservoir to Cauldron Snout.

Island eye-openers: Boat trip to Farne Islands from Seahouses; lunch at the Olde Ship, Seahouses; Bamburgh Castle; Holy Island (time visit to catch low tide).

you socks and two pairs of underpants.'
Shop, snacks, disabled access to
museum but not site; cl late Nov–mid-
Feb; (01434) 344277; £3.80.
🏛 **Walltown Crags** One of the best-
preserved sections of the Wall.

HALTWHISTLE NY7063
🏰⌂ **Bellister** This NT estate has a
ruined castle and peel tower; good
for gentle walks, with year-round
access to the paths.

HAMSTERLEY NZ1231
🐟⌂ **Hamsterley Forest** 5,000-
acre fellside forest with good walks,
cycle routes, four-mile forest drive, and
visitor centre with local wildlife
exhibitions and a new tearoom. Meals,
snacks, shop, disabled access; cl
Nov–Mar; (01388) 488312; forest drive
£1.50 a car. The Cross Keys at
Hamsterley is a useful base.

HARTLEPOOL NZ5132
Developing several lively attractions
likely to put it firmly on the tourist map.
The town has remains of its medieval
wall, and a factory shopping mall.
↓T ✺ **Hartlepool Historic Quay &
Museum** 📷 At the old docks, this is a
vivid open-air re-creation of an 18th-c
port, complete with painstakingly
reconstructed furnished houses,
market, prison, and fully stocked shops.
Also a couple of film shows, and
dramatic (and noisy) exhibition on
fighting ships. Lots to see, exceptionally
well done. At the **museum** (The
Marina) there are more
reconstructions – excellent, again
something of a maritime emphasis; the
well restored paddle steamer *Wingfield
Castle* is used in part as a café. Meals,
snacks, shop, disabled access; cl 25–26
Dec, 1 Jan; (01429) 860888/222255;
£4.95; entrance to maritime museum is
free. The next-door Jackson's Wharf
has decent food.
🔌 **Hartlepool Nuclear Power
Station** (3m S) The visitor centre has
lively displays and tours (best to book
48 hours before). Shop, disabled access;
cl wknds, 25–26 Dec, 1 Jan; (01429)
853888; free.
✺ **HMS** *Trincomalee* (Jackson Dock)
The world's second-oldest floating
warship – there are plans for a visitor
centre; cl 25, 26 Dec, 1 Jan; (01429)
223193; £2.50.

HEXHAM NY9364
★ A pleasant market town, not too big,
with some attractive stone buildings.
The County Hotel is a standby for
lunch.
☗ **Border History Museum**
Formerly the country's first purpose-
built prison; colourfully charts the
chequered contacts between the
English and Scots. Shop; cl Sun and
Weds–Fri Nov and Feb–Easter, and
every day Dec–Jan; (01434) 652351;
£1.80.
✝ **Hexham Abbey** Founded around
674 by St Wilfrid, once the largest
church north of the Alps. The bulk of
what is seen today dates from the 12th
c, though there are two splendid Saxon
survivals – the superbly atmospheric
crypt, and the throne of the Bishop (St
Wilfrid's Chair or Frith stool). The
choir still descend the unique Night
Stairs for services. Summer snacks,
shop, disabled access; free, but
donations welcome.
✝ **Warden church** (just N) Down a
lane by the Tyne, this is a fine example
of the sturdy northern churches that
had to do double duty as holy places
and watchtowers to warn of Border
raiders.

HIGH FORCE NY8828
⌂ **High Force waterfall** England's
most powerful waterfall, this drops into
a craggy cauldron at the end of a striking
wooded gorge – though you'll have to
pay around 50p (on top of parking) for
the short path from the B6277 for the
best view. From Bowlees Visitor
Centre you can make more of a walk of
it, first detouring N to Gibson's Cave, a
pretty waterfall at the top of a gorge,
and then heading S to cross the Tees for
an easy two miles upriver, passing Low
Force on the way. The nearby High
Force Hotel has decent food (and the
highest brewery in England).

HORNCLIFFE NT9450
🐝 **Chain Bridge Honey Farm** Over
1,000 colonies of bees, a good visitor
centre, and honey-based products for
sale. Limited disabled access; cl am Sun,
and wknds Nov–Mar; (01289) 386362;
free.

JARROW NZ3365
✝ ☗ 🐝 **Bede's World** The Venerable
Bede lived here at St Paul's monastery

for most of his 7th/8th-c life, producing the 37 books that encompass much of what is known of life in early Christian England. Along with the other half of the monastery, St Peter's, at nearby Monkwearmouth, the site is still a major Christian shrine. Very little remains of the original monastery, but there's Saxon stained glass in the church, and the chancel incorporates one of the earlier chapels. A museum in adjacent Jarrow Hall has finely carved Anglo-Saxon stones, more stained glass, and excavated relics. There's an authentically re-created 11-acre period farm and a visitor reception centre. Meals, snacks, shop, some disabled access; cl am Sun, all Mon (exc bank hols), Christmas wk; (0191) 489 2106; £3.

KIELDER WATER NY6293

⛵ 🏊 This huge reservoir has done a lot to open up a remote part of the Borders; an attractive drive from Bellingham. It's an interesting shape, modelled by the steep folds of the land, and is already beginning to look as if it's always been tucked away in these pine-blanketed hills. You can hire out rowing boats for around £8 an hour (01434) 250217. Visitor centres can supply fishing permits for the lake. You can rent log cabins around the lake by the week; (01502) 500500.

Ꝟ Bakethin Conservation Area Up at the top of Kielder Water, this is particularly rewarding for wildlife.

Ꝟ 🌲 🏰 🏞 Kielder Castle Visitor Centre This 18th-c hunting lodge built for the Duke of Northumberland is now a very good Forest Enterprise visitor centre with exhibitions, closed-circuit TV birdwatching and a sculpture trail. Shop, meals and a play area, disabled access; (01434) 250209; cl wkdys Nov–Christmas and all Christmas–Easter; free. Regular guided walks from here into the great surrounding tract of Kielder Forest – miles of pine trees with a good chance of seeing red squirrels, as well as deer. There are also self-guided forest walks (easy to follow) from half a dozen or more points along the road through; and a 12-mile forest drive. The Pheasant at Stannersburn has good food.

Kielder cycling The shores of Kielder Water and the surrounding forests have been well developed for cycling – the very friendly Kielder Bikes Company hire bikes from Hawkhope car park (they're good for repairs too), (01434) 250392, and from Kielder village itself; a decent mountain bike costs around £8 for three hours.

🚣 Leaplish Waterside Park (slightly round to the W) Another good starting point for Kielder Water, with lots to do in summer, inc plenty of water sports, trails, and canoe and other **boat hire**; (01434) 250312.

🚣 Tower Knowe Visitor Centre Down at the foot of Kielder Water, with an exhibition and useful information about the area and its wildlife. Meals, snacks, shop, disabled access; cl 25–26 Dec, maybe half of Jan; (01434) 240398; centre free, exhibition £1. **Cruises** start from here too, and call all around the lake (takes about an hour and a half).

LANCHESTER NZ1243

🐄 Hall Hill Farm (B6296 SW) Friendly working farm with lots of animals, nature trails, riverside walk and trailer rides. Snacks, shop; cl most Sats (exc Aug), and Christmas–mid-Feb – best to check; (01388) 730300; £3.20. The Queen's Head is good for food.

LINDISFARNE NU1242

Ꝟ ❁ ☁ Otherwise known as Holy Island, this important centre for Christian pilgrims is linked to the mainland by a causeway which you can drive (or walk) over at low tide. Tide tables are posted at each end, or tel (01289) 389200; it really is worth checking these carefully – the causeway is impassable for two hours before high tide and four hours after. If you want to visit a particular attraction, make sure that the tide and the opening times match on the day you want to go. There are nature-reserve dunes, fishermen's huts made of upturned former boats, old limekilns, a small extended village with tourist cafés and pubs (the Ship has good-value food), and nice views from the close-grazed grassy crags. The three-mile walk around the island's shores is easy but fascinating.

🏰 🕸 Lindisfarne Castle The rather lonely and austere exterior belies what's within; the 16th-c fortress was restored by Lutyens for the editor of *Country Life* in a suitably monolithic quasi-medieval style. Sumptuous furnishings inc a fine collection of antique oak furniture, and there's a walled garden designed by Gertrude Jekyll to protect against the North Sea winds. Cl am, Fri (exc Good Fri), and Nov–Mar – phone to check daily opening times; (01289) 389244; £4; NT. It's a mile's walk from the car park.

🏰 † **Lindisfarne Priory** From here St Aidan and monks from Iona replanted the seeds of Christianity in 7th-c England. These early monks were driven out by Vikings, so it's the extensive remains of a later 12th-c church you can see today; a very peaceful and romantic spot, with graceful red sandstone arches bordered by incongruously neat lawns. Shop, disabled access to visitor centre; cl 24–26 Dec; (01289) 389200; £2.70.

🍴 ℘ **St Aidan's Winery** Home of Lindisfarne Mead, a fortified wine made from grapes, honey, herbs and water from an island well. They make honey too, and the shop has British beers, ciders and cheeses, as well as local pottery and jewellery. Shop; cl Christmas, and other times according to tide – best to phone; (01289) 389230; free.

LONGFRAMLINGTON NZ1199
† **Brinkburn Priory** Well preserved 12th-c church (thanks to some Victorian restoration), still with medieval grave slabs, font and double piscina. Occasional services and concerts. Shop, some disabled access; open pm Apr–Oct; (01665) 570628; £1.60; EH. The Granby is useful for lunch.

LOW NEWTON NU2325
★ ℘ A charming seaside village on a fine stretch of little-visited coast, with a **bird reserve** nearby. The Joiners Arms in High Newton is famous for its fish and chips.

MARSDEN NZ3964
! **Grotto** (A183) The Grotto here is unique: a lift (or a hundred or so steps) down to a pub cut into the seaside cliffs.

MATFEN NZ0370
★ One of the prettiest inland villages in Northumbria, with a riverside village green – and a good pub.

MORPETH NZ2086
The clock tower here is one of only eight non-church bell towers in Britain; it has only one hand, but still rings the curfew every night. The Tap & Spile, open all day, has good-value food.

🍴 ℘ **Morpeth Chantry Bagpipe Museum** (Bridge St) Harmonious collection of small pipes and bagpipes from around the world. Headphones explain the difference between a rant and a reel. Shop; cl Sun, 25 Dec; (01670) 519466; £1.50. Good **craft centre** next door (cl Sun).

NEWCASTLE UPON TYNE NZ2563
This big industrial conurbation is far from being conventionally pretty, but has a strong vibrant atmosphere, and several excellent free museums. Its best parts are grouped very compactly high above the River Tyne with its three great bridges – particularly what has become almost the city's trademark, the two-decker High Level Bridge for road and rail designed by Robert Stephenson in the 1840s. The Metro system makes it quick and straightforward to get around, and to the attractions noted under North and South Shields, Tynemouth and Whitley Bay; a one-day Day Rover ticket (available from stations or the tourist information centre) costs around £3.50 and is good for all Metro trips and stations (and the ferry between North and South Shields). You can still trace some stretches of the medieval city wall, especially from St Andrew's Church along the cobbled lane west of Stowell St – Chinese restaurants around here – and past the Heber Tower along Bath Lane. Grey's Monument is now closed to the public – people were throwing pennies and stones from the top and causing damage below. Fitzgeralds down the street is useful for a bite to eat. Steep alleys and steps lead from the centre down to The Quay, the oldest part of town, with several unexpected and quaintly attractive timber-framed medieval buildings; one of the oldest, the Cooperage, is a good pub. Downstream, east of the 1920s Tyne Bridge, an area of refurbished 19th-c wharf buildings is enjoyable to walk

through, with crafts and bric-à-brac on Sun, and a useful pub for food – the Baltic Tavern. This whole quayside area is gradually being redeveloped on a most impressive scale. Another stylish quayside warehouse conversion, the Waterline (by the new law courts) has good food, as does the Fog on the Tyne overlooking St Peter's Basin marina. Besides the pubs mentioned above, the handsome Crown Posada (The Side, off Dean St) and the Duke of Wellington (High Bridge) are pleasantly civilised.

🏠 **Bessie Surtees House** (Sandhill) Well renovated, timbered Jacobean house, with elaborate plaster ceilings and carved panelling. Cl wknds, bank hols and Christmas; (0191) 261 1585; free.

ठ **Hancock Museum** (Barras Bridge) Very good natural history museum, with magnificent collections of stuffed birds and mammals. Lively temporary exhibitions, and plenty for children. Meals, snacks, shop, disabled access; cl am Sun, 25, 26, 31 Dec, 1 Jan, Good Fri; (0191) 222 7418; £2.75–£3.95 (price varies according to exhibitions).

ठ ! **International Centre for Life** *See separate family panel on p.475.*

🖼 **Laing Art Gallery** (New Bridge St) Notable temporary exhibitions, and excellent children's gallery, the activities well designed to encourage young children to think about shapes, texture and patterns. Free guided tours of the main galleries 11.30am Sat. Cl am Sun, 25–26 Dec, 1 Jan, Good Fri; (0191) 232 7734; free.

ठ **Museum of Antiquities** (The University) Particularly good on Roman remains, with reconstructions of various points along Hadrian's Wall. The displays have been organised in a very user-friendly fashion. Shop, disabled access by arrangement; cl Sun, Good Fri, 24–26 Dec, 1 Jan; (0191) 222 7846; free.

🏰 **Newcastle Castle** This Norman building gave the city its name; a lot still remains. It's a little spoiled by the main railway line which cuts the gatehouse off from the keep, but as much of the fortress was rediscovered only during the railway's construction it seems a little churlish to complain. Shop; cl Mon, 25 Dec, 1 Jan, Good Fri; (0191) 232 7938; £1.50.

✝ **Newcastle Cathedral** The 14th/15th-c Anglican cathedral is worth a look; a dramatic stone sculpture occupies the Chapel of the Incarnation. Refectory wkdys only, shop (cl Sun), disabled access; cl 12–4pm Sun; free.

ठ ✺ ☺ **Newcastle Discovery** (Blandford Sq) Thriving complex with galleries and interactive features on subjects likely to appeal to the whole family – it's the biggest and busiest museum in the area. Pride of place goes to the 30-metre (100ft) *Turbinia*, once the fastest ship on the seas, shown off in a splendid multi-media gallery, and the interactive Science Factory with plenty to push, press and poke: TV effects create the illusion of flying down the Tyne, there's a soft play area for very young children, and lots of mirrors, magnets and microscopes to fiddle with. Other galleries offer a similarly hands-on look at the history of the city (inc the early days of Newcastle United), fashion, shipbuilding, army life, and local inventors. Snacks, shop, disabled access; cl am Sun, Good Fri, 25–26 Dec, 1 Jan; (0191) 232 6789; free.

NORTH SHIELDS NZ3568

🚂 **Stephenson Railway Museum** (Middle Engine Lane) Excellent, with steamtrain trips along a short section of the North Tyneside Railway, as well as displays on the development of steam and a collection of rolling stock, inc George Stephenson's *Billy*. As we went to press they hadn't yet confirmed this year's opening times: last year they were open wknds from May–Sept, but best to ring (0191) 200 7146 for details; site free, £2 steam trips. The Magnesia Bank (Camden St) has good-value food.

☺ **Wet 'n' Wild** (Royal Quays) Children like this well heated, indoor water park with exciting flumes and slides (one has a very steep drop). Meals, snacks, disabled access; cl some days in Nov and Dec; (0191) 296 1333; £6.75 wknds and school hols, less at other times.

NORTHUMBERLAND COAST NU2615

⌒ This has much to interest walkers along its sandy and rocky shores, but the hinterland is rather dull, so it's better for pottering and for there-and-back walks than for round ones. A coast path covers the finest sections, which we pick out individually on the map.

PETERLEE NZ4338

✤ ⚘ ◠ **Castle Eden Dene Nature Reserve** The biggest of Durham's wooded coastal ravines, now a picturesque nature reserve with 12 miles of footpaths over 550 acres; free.

PONTELAND NZ1577

❀ ◑ **Kirkley Hall Gardens** (2m NW towards Morpeth) Attractive and thoughtfully maintained, with a big collection of herbaceous perennials, Victorian walled garden, pretty sunken garden, woodland garden and unusual trees and shrubs. Plant sales, disabled access; cl Oct–Mar; (01661) 860808; £1.50. Nearby Milbourne has a good farm shop with **pick-your-own**.

PRUDHOE NZ0963

⛫ ⌂ **Prudhoe Castle** 12th/14th-c ruined castle on an impressive mound (the name means 'proud hill') overlooking the Tyne, once the stronghold of the powerful Percy family. Remarkable restored gatehouse, and exhibition in nearby 19th-c manor house. Snacks, shop, disabled access; (01661) 833459; cl Oct–Mar; £1.80; EH. The Feathers at Hedley on the Hill does good weekend food.

⚭ **Stephenson's Birthplace** (Wylam) The single room open here is the NT's least visited property, some days attracting nobody at all (open pm Thurs, Sat, Sun and bank hol Mon, Apr–Oct; 80p); the Fox & Hounds (a short walk along the old railway track) and the Boathouse have good-value food.

ROKER NZ4058

✝ **Roker church** The interesting church was designed by leading members of the Arts and Crafts movement.

ROSS BACK SANDS NU1339

◠ One of the finest sections of the Northumbrian coast path – splendid windswept solitude, looking out to Holy Island.

ROTHBURY NY9799

◠ **Coquetdale** Northumberland's most scenic drive is the B6344 following the river past Brinkburn Priory to Rothbury, then W on the B6341 past Hepple, then turning right on the unclassified road past Holystone and Alwinton. Picturesque walks around Holystone (where the Salmon is a useful stop), increasingly desolate up towards Blindburn.

⌂ ❀ ◠ ♪ **Cragside** Opulent Victorian mansion of Lord Armstrong, the armaments king, with spectacular rooms and some of the amazing gadgets he designed. Best of all are the miles of well wooded landscaped grounds, with lakes, glorious rhododendrons, showy formal garden, and a walk illustrating the various elements of the hydro-electric scheme he devised to light the house. Meals, snacks, shop, disabled access (inc fishing pier on trout lake); cl Mon exc bank hols, and Nov–Mar (house cl am, garden, grounds and visitor centre open selected days in winter); (01669) 620333; £6.20, £3.95 grounds only; NT. The Newcastle Hotel (open all day) has good-value food inc (not winter) high teas. Nearby the **Rothbury Terraces** are excellent for gentle parkland walks.

SEAHOUSES NU2232

An unpretentious seaside resort, with amusement arcades and so forth – and a busy fishing harbour, overlooked by a good interesting pub, the Olde Ship.

⚓ ↟ **Farne Islands** From Apr to Sept, weather permitting, **boat trips** from Seahouses let you see the eider ducks, thousands of other seabirds, and grey seals. Breeding season for the birds is usually around May–July, though perhaps a little later for the seals, whose plaintive-voiced pups stay on shore for only a few weeks. Most boats cost around £7. Landing on the NT-owned islands is extra (from £3, £4 breeding times). The NT has a shop with information about the islands on Main St, cl winter Mon and Tues; (01665) 721099.

SEATON SLUICE NZ3276

⌂ ✝ **Seaton Delaval** Vanbrugh's Palladian masterpiece, a splendid design of central porticoed main block and massive outer wings. Not all the interior has survived unscathed, and much of the original park and grounds has been submerged by surrounding developments. Snacks, shop; open pm May bank hols, Weds and Sun Jun, plus Thurs and bank hol in Aug; (0191) 237

3040; £3. The buildings around the Norman **church** are attractive, and the Waterford Arms, nr the low-key seafront, does generous fresh fish.

SHILDON NZ2326

🚂 **Timothy Hackworth Railway Museum** (Hackworth Close, just SE) Restored home of early railway pioneer, with working replica of *Sans Pareil* in goods yard, and occasional passenger rides along 400 yds of original Stockton & Darlington track bed. To mark the 175th anniversary of Stephenson's *Locomotion 1*, they're holding a steam cavalcade in summer (phone for details). Snacks, shop, limited disabled access; cl Mon (exc bank hols), Tues, and Nov–Easter; (01388) 777999; £1.50. The nearby Flag & Whistle has good-value food.

SOUTH SHIELDS NZ3667

🏛️👶 **Arbeia Roman Fort** (Baring St) Huge variety of remains, as well as re-created scenes of camp life, museum with excellently displayed finds, and plenty for children to enjoy. Snacks, shop, some disabled access; cl Sun exc pm Easter–Sept; (0191) 456 1369; free, £1.50 for Time Quest (splendid hands-on archaeology exhibition). Kirkpatricks (Ocean Rd) is a comfortable dining pub, and the Marsden Rattler (South Foreshore) is an enjoyable seafront bar complete with two original railway carriages.

🌿 **Marsden Bay** (nr South Shields) The **nature reserve** here gives one of the few reasonable coastal walks in industrial Tyneside.

👶🖼️ **South Shields Museum & Art Gallery** (Ocean Rd) Good displays, incl some hands-on exhibitions; (0191) 456 8740; free.

STAINDROP NZ1221

🏰⚜️★ **Raby Castle** Imposing fortress with Saxon origins; vast medieval hall, 14th-c kitchen, and dazzling Victorian octagonal drawing room – restored to its original splendour. From the outside – where there are walled gardens and a deer park – it looks just as a castle ought to. Snacks, shop (selling oven-ready game from the estate); open bank hol wknds from Easter, Weds and Sun May–Jun, and Sun–Fri July–Sept, castle pm only; (01833) 660202; £4, £1.50 park and

gardens only. The village is pretty. Up at Butterknowle, the Malt Shovel has good-value food, evenings and wknd lunchtimes.

STAWARD GORGE NY8063

🌿 Part of the Allen Banks estate (NT, with year-round access to the paths along the wooded River Allen – frequented by roe deer – and a ruined peel tower.

STOCKSFIELD NZ0762

🏚️🐄⚜️❄️ **Cherryburn** (slightly E at Mickley) Well preserved 18th-c farm, the birthplace of artist and naturalist Thomas Bewick, with an exhibition on his life. A nice spot, with farm animals running about the yard, craft demonstrations, and good valley views. Annual special event on first May bank hol. Shop, some disabled access; cl am, all day Tues and Weds, and Nov–Mar; (01661) 843276; £2.80; NT. The Highlander at Ovington has good-value food.

STOCKTON-ON-TEES NZ4419

👶 **Green Dragon Museum** (Theatre Yard) Local history inc a good audio-visual presentation on the birth of the railways here in 1825. Shop, some disabled access (prior notice preferred); cl Sun, bank hols and Christmas wk; (01642) 674308; free. There's a railway heritage trail around town. Slightly E along the river, the surprisingly graceful Tees Barrage keeps polluted tidal water from mixing with water from the hills, moors and valleys, which it's hoped will stimulate water sports in the area.

❄️⚓ HM *Bark Endeavour* (Castlegate Quay) Full-size replica of Captain Cook's famous vessel with re-created cabins and exhibits from surgeons' knives to telescopes; trips on a smaller boat to the Tees Barrage or Preston Park (Weds and wknds, best to phone before). Shop, disabled access to main exhibition area; cl Oct–Mar, 24–26, 31 Dec and 1 Jan; (01642) 676844; £3.

👶⚜️🕊️🦋 **Preston Hall Museum** (A135 Stockton–Yarm) Very well constructed Victorian high street and other period rooms, plus working craftsmen, aviary, and woodland and riverside walks. Snacks, shop, disabled access to ground floor only; cl am Sun Oct–Mar, 1 Jan, Good Fri, 25–26 Dec;

(01642) 781184; £1. On the same site **Butterfly World** has a re-created jungle environment with hundreds of exotic butterflies flitting between the trees, rocks and waterfalls. Shop, disabled access; cl Nov–Jan; (01642) 791414; £2.90.

SUNDERLAND NZ3959

🚌 **Monkwearmouth Station Museum** (Monkwearmouth Station) As well as trains, the chance to learn to drive a bus. Cl am Sun; (0191) 567 7075; free.

👶 🏛 ! **National Glass Centre** (Liberty Way) This dazzling exhibition is a fascinating cross between gallery, museum, and factory visit. Housed in a striking glass structure on a sloping site alongside the River Wear (you can walk along the glass roof, looking down on the exhibitions below), it focuses on how glass is made and used all around the world. You can even have a go at glass-making yourself, with a range of classes and workshops (around £5 extra, must be over 9). The Kaleidoscope Gallery explores the more imaginative ways glass is used, from time-lapse photography to a hall of mirrors. Several exhibits are interactive, with computer displays and activities, and trails and quizzes keep younger children amused. They occasionally have extra activities for children such as painting and story-telling. Meals, snacks, good shop, disabled access; cl 25 Dec; (0191) 515 5555; £5 (children £2.50).

† **St Peter's Church** Sister church of St Paul's at Jarrow, its early years equally well documented by the Venerable Bede. Much of the original Saxon church still remains, inc the west wall and tower. A striking Colin Wilbourn sculpture outside commemorates the church's 7th-c founder Benedict Biscop.

TANFIELD NZ2057

🚌 **Tanfield Railway** (A6076) The world's oldest surviving railway, built in 1725 to carry coal to the Tyne, and set in a picturesque wooded valley. Steam trains still chuff along the route, and you can get off by a wooden gorge spanned by **Causey Arch**, the earliest railway bridge. There's a collection of locomotives, and they often have a blacksmith forging new parts for restoration work. Summer snacks, shop, disabled access; trains usually run every Sun, plus Weds and Thurs in summer hols, and bank hols; (0191) 274 2002 for timetable; fares from £3.50.

TEESDALE NY9425

⌂ ❦ ★ † ♪ The best of County Durham's scenery; the B6277 below its moors and on to Alston in Cumbria is one of the finest drives in England. Upper Teesdale has much of the best walking in the Durham Pennines, and is famous for its limestone flora, inc rare arctic alpine species and the unique Teesdale violet; Widdybank Fell is a National Nature Reserve. The attractive villages of Middleton in Teesdale, Romaldkirk (there's an especially distinguished church here), Eggleston and Cotherstone all have good pubs and inns. A side track with a reward at its end is the cosy Strathmore Arms in Holwick. There's good fishing on the river or the reservoirs above it, and fine landscapes all the way along.

TYNEMOUTH NZ3769

🏰 **Castle & Priory** Evocative clifftop ruins, high above the Tyne estuary. Little remains of the once-rich 11th-c Benedictine priory beyond its stirring nave and chancel, and the spooky gravestones outside. Even less is left of the 11th–14th-c castle, but it's unusual to find two such ruins next to each other, and it's a great spot for picnics. Shop, disabled access; cl Mon and Tues Nov–Mar, 24–26 Dec, 1 Jan; (0191) 257 1090; £1.80; EH. The Salutation (Front St) is comfortable for lunch.

♪ **Sea Life Centre** (Grand Parade, Beaconsfield) The same reliable mixture as at their other centres, with a spectacular underwater tunnel surrounded by shark-infested water, and the unique Jelly Lab, demonstrating the life cycle of a jelly fish. Meals, snacks, shop, disabled access; cl 25 Dec; (0191) 257 6100; £4.50.

WALLSEND NZ3066

🏛 👶 ! **Segedunum** (Buddle St) This ambitious £7.5 million project, opening around May, involves the reconstruction of a Roman bath-house on the original site of Segedunum (meaning strong fort), the remains of which were covered by 18th- and

19th-c industrial developments. Computer displays in an interactive museum aim to capture the atmosphere of a Roman camp, and from the top of an 18-metre tower you'll be able to watch the continuing excavation work. Café, shop, disabled access. As we went to press, admission prices had not been decided, so phone before visiting; (0191) 200 7100.

WARKWORTH NU2305

! Hermitage Prettily placed a short way upstream, this 14th-c cell of retreat is cut into the sandstone cliff, with some crude wall carvings and a tiny vaulted chapel; on Weds, Sun and bank hols Apr–Sept a boat can take you, £1.60.

★ † 🏰 **Warkworth Castle** The main street of this quietly picturesque **small town** rises attractively from the riverside 12th-c Norman **church**, with its finely vaulted chancel, to the striking **castle** on its hill above the River Coquet. It's virtually complete, so wandering round the crooked passageways and dark staircases is wonderfully atmospheric. Events here were immortalised in Shakespeare's *Henry IV*. Shop, limited disabled access; cl 1–2pm winter, 24–26 Dec, 1 Jan; (01665) 711423; £2.40; EH. The Hermitage Hotel is good for lunch, there are one or two antique shops, and this stretch of coast has some lovely beaches.

WASHINGTON NZ3156

🏠 ★ ⬇T **Washington Old Hall** 🖼 (The Avenue) Well restored, stone-built 13th-c manor, for several hundred years the home of George Washington's family, though his ancestors had been established elsewhere (notably Sulgrave Manor in Northants) for quite a while by the time he was born. Snacks, shop, disabled access to ground floor only; open Sun–Weds Mar–Oct; (0191) 416 6879; £2.80; NT. The unspoilt old village comes as a real surprise when you've penetrated the surrounding New Town. The Washington Arms is good value for lunch, and there's a small **mining museum** down Albany Way (free).

🦆 **Wildfowl & Wetlands Trust** 🖼 (District 15, off A1231 E) 100 acres with hides, well laid out walks, adventure play area, and very good

visitor centre. Some birds will feed from your hand (you can buy birdseed – worth it to see the flamingos squabbling over every mouthful). Meals, snacks, shop, disabled access; cl 25 Dec; (0191) 416 5454; £4.50. In summer the River Wear ferry from Sunderland stops here.

WEARDALE NY8242

★ ⌂ This gave much of County Durham's wealth, with lead and iron mining along its length and in the moors above. There's little reminder of those days now, but the A689 is a memorable drive. A **riding centre** at Low Cornriggs Farm has lessons, guided rides along scenic former packhorse routes, and farmhouse B & B; cl Weds and Jan–Feb; (01388) 537600. Along the dale is a string of attractive villages such as Wolsingham (good-value food at the Black Bull), as well as pleasant waterside and moorland walks. The Golden Lion at St John's Chapel, open all day in summer, is another useful stop.

⬇T **Killhope Lead Mining Centre** Probably the best-preserved lead mining site in Britain, and unmissable if you're at all interested in industrial history. Equipped with hard hat and lamps, you're led through the mine's dark, chilly passageways to a huge underground waterwheel. Snacks, shop; cl Nov–Mar; (01388) 537505; £3.40 for surface exhibitions, £5 inc mine trip.

🌸 ⚘ ⌂ **Rookhope** This diversion is worthwhile: fine alpine plants nursery, small craft centre, decent pub, more good walks.

🍵 **Weardale Museum** (Ireshopeburn) Near the source of the river, this re-creates life in this high valley's heady lead-mining days, and has an exhibition on John Wesley, who often preached in the adjacent chapel. Shop; cl am, all Mon and Tues (exc in Aug), and Oct–Easter; (01388) 537417; £1.

WHITBURN NZ4064

🏛 🕯 **Souter Lighthouse** 🖼 When built in 1870 this was the most advanced lighthouse of the day, and the first to be powered by electricity; it still has period rooms and equipment. Meals, snacks, shop, disabled access (but not to tower); cl Fri, all Nov–Mar;

(0191) 529 3161; £2.80; NT. The Trust also own the Leas, the spectacular stretch of coastline around here, leading to Marsden Rock with its colony of kittiwakes, cormorants and fulmars. The Jolly Sailor has decent food.

WHITLEY BAY NZ3575

🏛️ ☀️ ⚓ **St Mary's Lighthouse** Out on St Mary's Island, reached by a causeway at low tide. Good views from the top – for those unable to climb the 137 steps, a camera at the top relays the image to a colour TV at the bottom. Shop; cl wkdys Nov–Mar (exc school hols), and poss other times depending on the tide; (0191) 200 8650; £2. When the lighthouse is closed the island is worth a visit for the rock pools alone, and is visited all through the year by a wide range of birds. The Shiremoor House Farm up on Middle Engine Lane, New York (handy too for North Shields and Tynemouth) has some of the best food in this area – good value.

WINDY GYLE NT8515

⛰️ ☀️ The high summit by a fine ridge section of the Pennine Way, along the English/Scottish border – the best of the Way's long, lonely plod over the Cheviots' grassy moors. You have to walk some way from the road to reach this main ridge: start from Coquetdale and walk along The Street, an ancient drovers' track. Gradients are mild but the peaty ground can get boggy after rain; not all routes are defined on the ground, but stone boundary walls and forest plantations are useful guides.

WITTON-LE-WEAR NZ1631

✤ ★ **Low Barns Nature Reserve** 100-acre reserve with nature trails, woodland, grassland, lake and lots of interesting wildlife. Meals, snacks, shop, good disabled access; cl 25–26 Dec, 1 Jan; (01388) 488728; free. The village is attractive, with a tree-lined sloping green; the Victoria is useful for lunch.

WOODHORN NZ2988

✝ ☗ ♫ **Woodhorn Church** Partly Saxon and Norman, said to be the oldest on this coast; it has a local history museum and wknd craft demonstrations. Shop, disabled access; cl Mon (exc bank hols), Tues, all Nov–Mar; (01670) 817371; free.

⚒ 🚂 ♫ **Woodhorn Colliery Museum** (Queen Elizabeth II Country Park) Former colliery buildings re-creating life in the pit and the communities around it. Also short trips on narrow-gauge railway, displays of art by local miners, craft workshops and woodland walks. Meals, snacks, shop, some disabled access; cl Mon (exc bank hols) and Tues; (01670) 856968; free, though charge for railway.

★ Apart from those already mentioned, the **villages** of Riding Mill NZ0262, Shincliffe NZ2941 and Thropton NU0302 are all worth a look – and each has a decent pub.

Where to eat

AMBLE NU2604 **Charlie's Chip Shop** *Albert St (01665) 710206* Popular family-run restaurant serving chips with fish, chicken, and pies, vegetarian options and children's dishes, plus a take-away service; disabled access. £4.55.

BAMBURGH NU1835 **Copper Kettle Tearooms** *21 Front St (01668) 214315* 18th-c cottage nr the castle, with beams, panelling, and copper implements, light lunches, home-made scones and cakes, more substantial suppers, a fine range of teas inc many fruit and herb ones, and a good choice of other drinks; no smoking; cl Dec and Jan; limited disabled access. £18|£4.50.

BARNARD CASTLE NZ0617 **Market Place Teashop** *29 Market Pl (01833) 690110* Long-standing tearoom in 17th-c building, with flagstones and an open fire, smart uniformed waitresses, home-made cakes, light lunches, a good choice of teas, and a friendly, relaxed atmosphere; cl Sun, 24 Dec, 5 Jan; disabled access. £3.

BERWICK-UPON-TWEED NU0052 **Foxtons** *26 Hide Hill (01289) 303939* Lively bistro with good, imaginative and varied food that changes daily, decent wine list, and friendly service; cl Sun, bank hols. £22|£4.80.

CARTERWAY HEADS NZ0452 **Manor House** *(01207) 255268* Popular, slate-roofed stone house with fine southerly views over moorland pastures, interesting, well liked food from a wide, changing menu, partly no smoking restaurant (with a huge collection of jugs), and a friendly atmosphere; comfortable bdrms, nice breakfasts. **£21.25|£8.**

CORBRIDGE NY9864 **Valley** *Old Station House, Station Rd* (01434) 633434 Extremely friendly Indian restaurant in an attractively converted sandstone station house, with a wide choice of very good Indian food and kind service; also, a special train service for parties from Tyneside, with uniformed escort and free travel, and your order is phoned ahead to be ready on arrival – good fun; cl lunchtimes, cl Sun. **£17.50.**

CRASTER NU2519 **Craster Restaurant** (01665) 576230 Upstairs restaurant overlooking the harbour, with candles on tables, exceedingly welcoming staff, and huge helpings of fairly priced really fresh fish from the owners' fish factory – they have their own smoking yard, too; cl end Sept–end Apr; well behaved children. £13.

DURHAM NZ2643 **Bistro 21** *Aykley Heads House, Aykley Heads* (0191) 384 4354 Former 17th-c farmhouse, now a light and airy Mediterranean-style restaurant with pine dining chairs on wooden or flagstoned floors, a good choice of very enjoyable, interesting modern cooking, a thoughtful wine list, and professional but relaxed service; cl Sun; disabled access. **£28.50|£8.50.**

GREAT WHITTINGTON NZ0071 **Queens Head** (01434) 672267 Simple stone inn with two beamed, comfortable and neatly furnished rooms, a wide choice of good interesting food, no smoking restaurant, log fires, well kept real ales, decent wines, and quite a few malt whiskies; cl Mon exc bank hols; disabled access. **£20|2-course special £7.95.**

HAYDON BRIDGE NY8464 **General Havelock** (01434) 684283 Very civilised old stone terraced house with stripped-stone back dining room overlooking the Tyne, good if limited lunchtime food and interesting evening meals, well kept real ales, fine wines by the glass, pleasant service, and friendly local atmosphere; cl Mon and Tues; disabled access. **£25** for 4 courses|**£6.**

HEDLEY ON THE HILL NZ0759 **Feathers** (01661) 843607 Little stone local with three neatly kept traditional bars, woodburning stoves, straightforward furnishings, a charming, relaxed and welcoming atmosphere, imaginative meals (not wkdy lunchtimes exc bank hols), and well kept real ales; disabled access. **£13|£5.**

NEWCASTLE UPON TYNE NZ2563 **Courtney's** *5–7 The Side, Quayside* (0191) 232 5537 Popular little quayside restaurant with very enjoyable, international modern cooking, nice puddings, good service, and a decent wine list; cl Sun. **£35|£7.50.**

NEWCASTLE UPON TYNE NZ2666 **Fisherman's Lodge** *Jesmond Dene* (0191) 281 3281 Once the town residence of Lord Armstrong and in a quiet spot down a long drive, this popular restaurant has an attractive bar and elegant dining room, and specialises in delicious fresh seafood – though the local meat and lovely puddings are quite a draw too; professional service and reasonably priced wines; cl am Sat, Sun, bank hols; children over 9 in evening; disabled access. **£36 dinner, £24 lunch**.

NEWTON-ON-THE-MOOR NU1605 **Cook & Barker Arms** (01665) 575234 Bustling stone pub with an unfussy, long beamed bar with partly panelled walls, paintings by local artists, and a coal fire and coal-effect gas one (one area is no smoking); beautifully prepared, imaginative food, two other bars, changing real ales, decent whiskies and 12 wines by the glass. **£19.45|£7.50.**

RENNINGTON NU2119 **Masons Arms** (01665) 577275 Friendly, well run old coaching inn with good-value and quickly served bar food inc nice daily specials, a modernised beamed lounge bar, friendly and helpful staff, real ales, and decent breakfasts; comfortable bdrms; children over 5 in evening. **£17|£6.50.**

SEATON SLUICE NZ3477 **Waterford Arms** (0191) 237 0450 Popular dining pub with comfortable homely bar, separate restaurant, a no smoking area, very good enjoyable food with a strong emphasis on fresh fish, real ales, and friendly service; bdrms. **£20.35|£7.25.**

SHINCLIFFE NZ2941 **Seven Stars** (0191) 384 8454 Just 10 minutes' or so drive from central Durham, this early 18th-c village inn, with its pretty window-boxes and creepers, is comfortable and welcoming; coal fire in a handsome Victorian fireplace, copper kettles hanging from the beams, enjoyable and imaginative bar food from a changing menu (the candlelit dining room is no smoking), real ales, quite a few malt whiskies; parking can be tricky. **£19.25**|£6.50.

WARENFORD NU1328 **Warenford Lodge** *(01668) 213453* Very individual, old, though rather modern-feeling, dining pub with stripped stonework, big stone fireplace, comfortable extension with woodburner, really good, attractively presented, imaginative food, and decent wines; children in evening dining room only; cl Mon, am Tues–Fri; limited disabled access. **£19**|£4.20.

Special thanks to Christine and Ken Perry, Mr and Mrs D Pilgrim, Mrs K Taphouse, Louise Stephenson, Mrs Glennys Sanders.

Northumbria Calendar

Some of these dates were provisional as we went to press. Please check information with the telephone numbers provided.

MARCH

7 **Alnwick** Shrovetide Football at the Castle: ball is thrown from battlements and piped in procession to the pastures where the game is played (01665) 510665

APRIL

3 **Newcastle** Music Festival – *till 7 April* (0191) 211 5699

8 **Gateshead** Spring Flower Show at Gateshead Central Nurseries – *till 9 April* (0191) 477 1011

23 **Rothbury** Easter Egg Hunt at Cragside (01669) 620150

28 **Barnard Castle** Teesdale Thrash at Witham Hall – *till 30 April* (01833) 638288; **Morpeth** Northumbrian Gathering: festival of Northumbrian traditions – *till 30 April* (01670) 513308

MAY

1 **Berwick-upon-Tweed** Earth Day (01289) 330044

27 **North Shields** Fish Quay Festival: international street theatre, world music stage, Irish stage, children's village, parade, fireworks – *till 29 May* (0191) 200 5415

29 **Bishop Middleham** Countryside Fair at Island Farm (01388) 424200; **Corbridge** Northumberland County Show inc arena events at Tynedale Park (01434) 344443; **Rothbury** Street Fair (01669) 620574

JUNE

3 **Walker** East End Riverside Millennium Festival (0191) 375 3004

4 **Bedlington** Environment Fair (01670) 821000

10 **Durham** Regatta – *till 11 June* (0191) 384 0615

15 **North Pennines** Arts Festival at different venues – *till 25 June* (0191) 383 3611

Northumbria Calendar (cont.)

16 Newcastle Hoppings: funfair at Town Moor – *till 25 June* (0191) 454 6239

17 Meadowfield Vintage Rally – *till 18 June* (01429) 880673

18 Stockton-on-Tees Music Festival at Preston Hall Museum (01642) 393904

23 Holy Island Time Day – *till 25 June* (01289) 330044

24 Alnwick Unique Northumberland: millennium festival at Alnwick Castle – *till 25 June* (01670) 533923; **Darlington** Carnival – *till 25 June* (01325) 253686; **Hartlepool** Maritime Festival – *till 26 June* (01429) 523445

25 Alnwick Medieval Fair: costumed re-enactment, duckings, courts – *till 1 July* (01665) 602552

JULY

1 Durham Summer Festival – *till 2 July* (0191) 386 3050; **Lanchester** Show at Newhouses Farm – *till 2 July* (0191) 373 4565; **South Shields** Cookson Country Festival: free family festival – *till 6 August* (0191) 427 1717; **Sunderland** International Kite Festival – *till 2 July* (0191) 514 1235

7 Whitley Bay Jazz Festival – *till 9 July* (0191) 281 2935

8 Durham Miners' Gala: colourful march culminating in Trade Union rally on racecourse (0191) 384 3515

14 Whitley Bay North of England Motorshow – *till 16 July* (0191) 516 0085

15 Durham County Show at Lambton Park – *till 16 July* (0191) 388 5459; **Wooler** Air Day – *till 16 July* (01289) 330044

16 Middlesbrough Mela: Asian festival (01642) 263839

21 Burnopfield Open-air Pop, Fireworks and Songs at Gibside – *till 23 July* (01670) 774691; **Rothbury** Traditional Music Festival – *till 23 July* (01669) 620718

22 Beamish Festival of the Horse at the North of England Open-air Museum – *till 23 July* (01207) 231811; **Middlesbrough** Cleveland Show at Stewart Park (01642) 312231

28 Chester-le-Street Traction Engine Rally – *till 30 July* (0191) 492 3912; **Stockton-on-Tees** International Riverside Festival – *till 8 August* (01642) 666000

29 Gateshead Summer Flower Show at Gateshead Central Nurseries – *till 30 July* (0191) 477 1011; **Sunderland** International Airshow: largest airshow in the country – *till 30 July* (0191) 510 9317

AUGUST

4 Saltburn-by-the-Sea International Festival of Folk Music, Dance and Song – *till 6 August* (01947) 840928

5 Alnwick International Music and Dance Festival – *till 12 August* (01665) 602682

11 Alnwick Horse Driving Trials at the Castle – *till 13 August* (01668) 217329

12 Billingham International Folklore Festival: up to 10 countries represented – *till 19 August* (01642) 553220; **Hartlepool** Headland Carnival (01429) 523445; **Slaley** Show: traditional agricultural show at Townhead Field (01434) 673530

19 Falstone Shepherds' Show (01434) 240228; **Hartlepool** Show at Grayfield Recreation Ground: arena events, vintage vehicles – *till 20 August* (01429) 523445; **Whittingham** Show (01665) 574353

25 Cambo Pop and Fireworks Concerts at Wallington House – *till 26 August* (01670) 774691

Northumbria Calendar (cont.)

26 **Darlington** and **Shildon** Millennium Cavalcade of Steam: up to 40 of Britain's most famous steam locomotives can be viewed from field sites and grandstand in a sealed corridor along the Bishop Auckland Branch Line – *till 28 August* (0191) 261 7155; **St John's Chapel** Weardale Show – *till 28 August* (01388) 537398

27 **Durham** Military Vehicle Rally at Durham Light Infantry Museum – *till 28 August* (0191) 384 2214; **Newcastle** Mela – *till 28 August* (0191) 211 6232

28 **Bedlington** Street Fair (01670) 862721; **Seahouses** Lifeboat Fête (01668) 214256; **Wooler** Glendale Agricultural Show (01665) 578361

SEPTEMBER

2 **Alnwick** Show at the Castle (01665) 602596; **Berwick-upon-Tweed** Military Tattoo – *till 3 September* (01289) 307426; **Wolsingham** Agricultural Show and Country Fair at Scotch Isle Farm – *till 4 September* (01388) 527862

9 **Bowes** Agricultural Show (01833) 637059; **Seahouses** Sea Shanty Festival – *till 10 September* (01289) 330044; **Stanhope** Agricultural Show at Unthank Park – *till 11 September* (01388) 528642

16 **Darlington** Championship Dog Show at South Park – *till 17 September* (01325) 312484; **Eggleston** Agricultural Show at High Shipley Farm (01833) 638749; **Hexham** Hexham Abbey Festival – *till 24 September* (01661) 843347

17 **Darlington** Rhythm and Blues Day: live bands in Market Sq (01325) 388584

24 **Beamish** Classic Car Day: over 200 pre-war cars at the North of England Open-air Museum (01207) 231811

OCTOBER

7 **Northumberland** Traditional Music Festival at different venues – *till 22 October* (01670) 533923

14 **Alwinton** Border Shepherds' Show (01669) 630246

NOVEMBER

1 **Gateshead** Rugby League World Cup: Fiji v Australia (0191) 477 1011

16 **Darlington** Lantern Parade (01325) 388584

DECEMBER

2 **Durham** Christmas Festival – *till 3 December* (0191) 386 3050

Please let us know what you think of places in the *Guide*. Use the report forms at the back of the book or simply write us a letter.

NOTTINGHAMSHIRE

Good family outings, some fine landscapes, low prices.

Nottingham itself is lively and interesting – well worth a visit, with the newly rehoused Museum of Nottingham Lace one highlight. Elsewhere are some charming and interesting villages, and one or two attractive old towns such as Newark and Southwell. The mansions and families which gave the name of the Dukeries to the countryside in the north are long gone, but broad tracts of landscaped wooded parkland remain, such as Clumber Park.

Parts of Robin Hood's Sherwood Forest still survive, with good family days out at Edwinstowe and Haughton; there are also treats for young children at Rampton and Farnsfield. The Creswell Crag cave tours are intriguing.

Where to stay

GRINGLEY ON THE HILL SK7391 **Old Vicarage** *Gringley-on-the-Hill, Doncaster, Yorkshire DN10 4RF (01777) 817248* ***£56,** plus special breaks; 3 rms. Pretty cottage in 3 acres with fine views, a comfortable sitting room, delicious food using some home-grown produce, friendly owners, a flower-filled garden, tennis court and super views; cl 23 Dec–3 Jan; dogs by prior arrangement.

LANGAR SK7234 **Langar Hall** *Langar, Nottingham NG13 9HG (01949) 860559* ***£95,** plus special breaks; 10 lovely rms, some in wing and courtyard as well. Fine country house in spacious grounds with beautifully furnished elegant rooms, a pillared dining hall with paintings for sale, antiques and fresh flowers, a relaxed informal atmosphere, a lively and friendly owner, and very good food; regular theatricals and murder wknds; dogs by arrangement.

NOTTINGHAM SK5640 **H & H Narrowboat Hotels** *(020) 7272 0033* **£255** per person, full board; 7 oak panelled cabins. Hotel boat cruises in narrowboats painted in traditional canal colours, with oak and ash panelling, dining lounge, little bar, library and observation saloon, enjoyable food inc breakfast, morning coffee, light lunch, afternoon tea, and 4-course dinner, and helpful informative staff – great fun, plenty of time to explore, themed tours, too. Nottingham departures (set dates only) pass the famous Foxton locks; departures on other dates from other key canal localities throughout England and Wales.

SOUTHWELL SK6953 **Old Forge** *Burgage La, Southwell NG25 OER (01636) 812809* ***£58,** plus special breaks; 5 rms. 200-year-old former blacksmith's house with a welcoming owner, interesting furnishings, super breakfasts in conservatory overlooking the Minster, light suppers on request, and a pretty terrace; well behaved dogs welcome.

SOUTHWELL SK7053 **Saracens Head** *Market Pl, Southwell BG25 OHE (01636) 812701* **£75;** 26 well kept rms. Interesting old hotel (Charles I spent his last free night here) with ancient-feeling beamed main bar, pleasant staff, straightforward bar lunches, and restaurant.

Please let us know what you think of places in the *Guide*. Use the report forms at the back of the book or simply write us a letter.

To see and do

NOTTINGHAMSHIRE Family Attraction of the Year

🐂 ✦ **EDWINSTOWE** SK5865 **Sherwood Forest Farm Park** 🏛
(Lamb Pens Farm, off A6075) Readers say it's one of the few farm parks they know of where they can spend half the day without any trouble at all. A friendly, family-run place, it's very pleasant to stroll around, with pens and enclosures nicely spaced out over a fairly sizeable area, and pretty watergardens and waterfowl lakes offering tranquil corners to relax. Among the rare breeds here are endangered and protected varieties of cattle, sheep, pigs, goats, horses, turkeys and chickens; they also have water buffalo, and a small group of wallabies. They've recently added an owl garden, and children particularly like the purpose-built guinea-piggery and the miniature Kune Kune pigs – they can go right up to the animals in the pets corner. You'll generally find newly hatched chicks in the hatchery, and there might be tractor and trailer rides around the farm on busier days (small extra charge). Sensibly arranged play areas include an adventure playground and a separate section for under-5s. They usually have some undercover activities in a barn, but the further you get from the entrance the less shelter there is, so it's very much a place for fine weather. It's an ideal spot for a picnic. Special events typically include an Easter treasure hunt, and their Woolly Sheep Days, usually around the second May bank holiday, with demonstrations of sheep shearing and spinning, and a barbecue (best to check exact dates). They don't allow dogs (except guide dogs) on to the farm, but have kennels so you won't have to leave them in the car. Home-baked teas and snacks, shop, mostly disabled access (can be tricky around the lakes); open daily Easter–Sept, plus wknds till mid-Oct; (01623) 823558; £4, children £2.50.

BEACON HILL SK7490
☀ Above the Chesterfield Canal at Gringley on the Hill, this gives magnificent views in all directions; you can make out the towers of Lincoln Cathedral on a clear day.

BLYTH SK6185
★ ✝ An attractive small town, with interesting wall paintings in the **church**; the White Swan's good for lunch.

CHESTERFIELD CANAL SK7284
⌂ This has scope for towpath walks; one quiet stretch is by the Boat at Hayton.

CLUMBER PARK SK6375
🏵 ⚘ ⌂ **Clumber Park** One of the great former Dukeries estates, nearly 4,000 acres of farmland, parks, lake and woodland, with an interesting walled garden, and the longest lime avenue in Europe, almost 2 miles long. The estate is outstanding for its walks, enough for a full-day excursion. You can also hire bikes. Meals, snacks, shop, disabled access; park open all year, some parts cl winter; (01909) 476592; £3 per car; NT.

COSSALL SK4743
★ Attractive village in D H Lawrence country: he was once engaged to the girl who lived in Church Cottage.

CRESWELL SK5474
🏛 🐛 **Creswell Crags Visitor Centre**
Stone Age man lived in the caves and rock shelters of this limestone gorge right by the Derbyshire border (the village is actually over in Derbys). Even on days when there aren't cave tours it's an intriguing prehistoric site, with a good visitor centre, reconstructions of Ice Age family life, and other displays and activities. They sometimes have children's stories in one of the caves (booking required). Picnic area, shop, disabled access; cl Nov–Jan exc Sun – best to check for cave tour dates (usually every wknd at least); (01909) 720378; site free, cave tours £2.25. Take a torch. The Greendale Oak at Cuckney has good-value food.

CROMWELL SK7961
🎎 **Vina Cooke Museum of Dolls**
(Old Rectory) Thousands of toys and objects related to childhood, in an

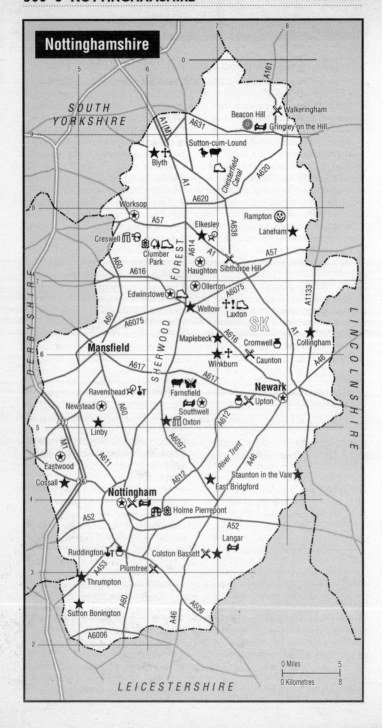

Nottinghamshire

SOUTH YORKSHIRE

DERBYSHIRE

LINCOLNSHIRE

LEICESTERSHIRE

Walkeringham
Beacon Hill
Gringley on the Hill
Sutton-cum-Lound
Chesterfield Canal
Blyth
Worksop
Rampton
Elkesley
Laneham
Creswell
Clumber Park
Haughton
Sibthorpe Hill
Ollerton
Edwinstowe
Wellow
Laxton
Maplebeck
Cromwell
Collingham
Mansfield
Winkburn
Caunton
Newark
Ravenshead
Farnsfield
Newstead
Southwell
Upton
Oxton
Linby
Eastwood
Cossall
Nottingham
Staunton in the Vale
East Bridgford
Holme Pierrepont
Langar
Ruddington
Colston Bassett
Plumtree
Thrumpton
Sutton Bonington

SHERWOOD FOREST

River Trent

A1(M) A631 A161 A620 A1 A620 A57 A638 A614 A1 A57 A616 A60 A6075 A1133 A616 A1 A46 A617 A617 A612 A60 A6097 A46 A611 A612 A52 A453 A60 A6006 A606 A46 A52 M1 27 26

0 Miles 5
0 Kilometres 8

imposing 17th-c rectory. Very lively on Easter Mon, with Morris dancers, crafts and the like. Teas, shop, limited disabled access; cl 12–2pm, all day Fri; (01636) 821364; *£2.50. The Great Northern at Carlton-on-Trent has decent food.

EASTWOOD SK4647

🏠👁🐾 **D H Lawrence Birthplace Museum** (8a Victoria St) The writer was born in this typical working-class house in 1885; it's been carefully restored to how he knew it. Shop, limited disabled access; cl 24 Dec–1 Jan; (01773) 763312; £1.75. Craft workshops next door (not Weds, or pm Sats). Another home of Lawrence's, on Garden Rd, is furnished as he described it in *Sons and Lovers*; open by appointment with Mr Roberts on (0151) 653 8710. The chatty Foresters Arms (Newthorpe) is appealing.

EDWINSTOWE SK5865

🐾🌿 **Sherwood Forest Farm Park** *See separate family panel on p.499.*

🏞☁🐾 **Sherwood Forest Visitor Centre** With an exhibition on Robin Hood, the visitor centre is a good springboard for the forest itself, only a fraction of what it once was (it used to cover a fifth of the county) but still miles across, though the heathland that Robin himself would have known has largely been swallowed up either by farmland or by forestry plantation. Good waymarked paths and footpaths, the most popular being to the Major Oak (a huge tree in the heart of the forest). Meals, snacks, shop, disabled access; park free, car park £1.50 wknds, bank hols and all Aug. **Sherwood Forest Art & Craft Centre** nearby has 17 craft studios housed in a mid-18th-c coach house and stables; cl Mon and Tues Oct–Mar. Nr the village church (supposedly where Robin Hood and Maid Marian were married), the Black Swan is handy for something to eat. The best drive is the B6034 N towards Worksop, then the right turn to Carburton and Clumber Park. Sherwood Forest has one of England's three **Center Parcs**, a rewarding place to stay with excellent leisure facilities; (0990) 200300.

ELKESLEY SK6875

★ 🐾 Attractive village, with a working potter nr the church. The Robin Hood is useful for lunch.

FARNSFIELD SK6257

🐄 **White Post Modern Farm Centre** 🖼 (1m W) Great for children, a bustling, modern, working farm with exhibits ranging from a mouse town to llamas, quails, snakes and fish. The pig breeding unit is fun, and you may be able to watch eggs hatching in the huge incubator. The Farm Show in the barn is a highlight. Good play areas, heated picnic barn, snacks, farm shop, disabled access; (01623) 882977; £4.50. Their well stocked pet centre sells mice, gerbils, hamsters and rats, along with everything you'd need to look after them. The Waggon & Horses at Halam is a popular dining pub.

🦋 **White Post Wonderland** (1m W) Useful enough for families, with free-flying butterflies, a maze, indoor play area, junior rollercoaster and train rides. Meals, snacks, shop, disabled access; cl 24–26 Dec; (01623) 882773; £3.60. Combs Farm Shop nearby is a good one (cl Sun and Mon).

HAUGHTON SK6872

🏰!🌿 **World of Robin Hood** With an emphasis on fun that may put off historical purists, this is a splendidly enjoyable re-creation of medieval life, placing the Robin Hood stories in their historical context. They've

---

Days Out

Robin Hood country: Creswell Crags; Sherwood Forest, Edwinstowe; picnic there, or lunch at the Black Swan; walk or hire a boat or bike in Clumber Park; or Sherwood Forest Farm Park, Edwinstowe; or Mr Straw's House, Worksop (timed ticket needed).

Byron and the Minster: Southwell Minster; lunch at the Burnstump, Papplewick or the French Horn, Upton; Newstead Abbey or Upton Hall.

meticulously constructed an entire medieval village, with moated drawbridge, cobbled streets and authentic shops and houses. There are costumed guides and plenty for children, inc a Disneyish version of the legends inside the castle for younger children, a small animal farm, and play area. Outside is a deer park and owl sanctuary, with summer activities such as archery. Meals, snacks, shop, some disabled access; cl Nov–Feb; (01623) 860210; £3.95. The Robin Hood at Elkesley has good-value food.

HOLME PIERREPONT SK6339

🏛 ⚜ **Holme Pierrepont Hall** Early Tudor manor house with interesting early 15th-c timbers, and an elaborate parterre in the formal courtyard garden. Several rooms inc the ball room and billiard room have been restored and are now open to the public. Teas, shop, disabled access to gardens only; phone for opening; (0115) 933 2371; £3.50, £1.50 garden only. The Round Oak in Radcliffe-on-Trent has decent food.

LAXTON SK7267

! ⌂ ✝ Unique for having kept the pattern of its **medieval farming**, with different villagers each owning strips of the 3 great fields. You can walk the grass paths or sykes which divide groups of these strips, and the Dovecote, a good village pub, has an exhibition in the yard explaining the system. It's worth popping into the **church** to see its fine 15th-c screen.

MAPLEBECK SK6961

★ Delightfully rustic village; the Beehive's a classic country tavern, and nearby Woodborough and Lambley are also worth a look.

NEWARK SK7953

★ ✝ ⚓ ⏱ Attractive old market town with some interesting buildings in its side streets, a fine **church**, and walks by the River Trent with summer **boat trips**. The Old Kings Arms (Kirkgate) is handy for lunch. Useful museums include the **Museum of Social and Folk Life** on Millgate (cl am wknds, bank hols and 25–26 Dec; free), and the local history collection on Appletongate (cl 1–2pm, Thurs, and Sun exc summer pms; free).

✝ **Newark Air Museum**

(Winthorpe, NE of Newark) Over 40 assorted aircraft inc rare jet fighters and bombers; half the exhibits are under cover so fine all year round (and the Willow Tree over at Barnby in the Willows is handy for lunch). Snacks, shop, disabled access; cl 24–26 Dec; (01636) 707170; *£3.75.

🏰 ⅼ **Newark Castle** The ruins date from the 11th c, and there's still a fair bit to see; it was destroyed during the Civil War then had periods as a cattle market and a bowling green. The gardens have been re-laid as they were in Victorian times. Good explanatory displays at the **Gilstrap Heritage Centre** in the grounds; cl 25–26 Dec, 1 Jan, Easter; (01636) 655765; free.

NEWSTEAD SK5454

🏛 🏰 ⚜ **Newstead Abbey** (off A60) Splendid former home of Lord Byron, in gorgeously romantic grounds; many of his possessions can still be seen. Rooms are decorated in a variety of styles from medieval through to Victorian, and there are substantial remains of the original abbey. Meals, snacks, shop, limited disabled access; cl am and Oct–Mar; (01623) 793557; house and gardens £4, gardens only £2. The Horse & Groom in the attractive nearby village of Linby is a useful stop.

NOTTINGHAM SK5739

⏱ At weekends and on summer evenings it quickly loses its big-city character, and is then easy to park in and stroll through, without the rush of traffic that otherwise swarms along its inner ring road. The parts around the parish church (which has some interesting carvings) and the Lace Market are particularly attractive. The tourist information centre on Smithy Row has a useful ½ hour introduction to the town (Mon, Fri and Sat only), which has an amazing number of decent pubs – handy for the thirsty work of serious sightseeing. You can buy an Explorer Pass covering entry to the main attractions, valid for a year. Besides the museums described below the **Museum of Costume and Textiles** (43–51 Castle Gate, cl Mon (exc bank hols), Tues, 24 Dec–1 Jan; free) is well worth a look. Useful lunch places are Fellows Morton & Clayton (Canal Rd; brews its own beer), the quaint old Bell (Angel Row), Limelight (attached to the Playhouse) and the Lincolnshire Poacher (Mansfield Rd).

♥ Attenborough Nature Reserve Unusual reserve with birdwatching down by Beeston at the extensive, partly wooded Attenborough lakes; on the far side a path takes you along the narrow spit of land dividing them from the mighty River Trent. The Manor at Toton is a good nearby dining pub.

🏠♨❀ Brewhouse Yard Museum (Castle Boulevard) Spread over 5 17th-c houses with period rooms and reconstructions, this has very good interactive displays on local life, and several features designed with children in mind (the Feely Boxes are fun). Award-winning historic roses in the cottage garden. Shop, some disabled access; cl winter Fri, 25 Dec, 1 Jan; (0115) 948 3504; *£1.50 wknds and bank hols, otherwise free.

🏛♨🖼 Castle Museum & Art Gallery Up on the summit, this dates from the 17th c, but the gateway is from an earlier 13th-c fortress. It now houses an appealing museum, with a history of the site and the subterranean passageways. Meals, snacks, shop, disabled access; cl 24–25 Dec, 1 Jan; (0115) 915 5555; *£2 wknds and bank hols.

♻ Caves of Nottingham (Drury Walk) This is a tour with taped commentary of 700-year-old caverns beneath a busy modern shopping centre, through an underground tannery, Victorian slum, air raid shelters, and pub cellars. Shop; cl 25–26 Dec, 1–2 Jan; (0115) 924 1424; *£3.25.

♻ Cave tours The rock on which old Nottingham stood is honeycombed with hundreds of galleries, cellars and passageways (one attractive old pub, the Olde Trip to Jerusalem, has a fascinating bar tunnelled right into the rock face). Tours usually leave the Castle every ½ hour 1.30–3.30pm Mon–Thurs and Sat, and at 2pm and 3pm Fri (and 4pm in summer) – in case of occasional rock falls it's always best to call (0115) 915 3700 first. They're quite strenuous; £2.

🖼 Djanogly Art Gallery (University Arts Centre, University Park, SW of the centre) Good temporary exhibitions;

cl am Sun, am bank hols, 24–26 Dec, 1 Jan; (0115) 951 3189; free.

♪ Galleries of Justice (Shire Hall, High Pavement) The grim realities of a 19th-c trial and prison life are re-enacted with real verve at this growing centre, set around 2 Victorian courtrooms in use right through to 1986. The award-winning centrepiece – designed very much to entertain children – is called Condemned, and begins with visitors being given a criminal identity number before being sent to trial in the Criminal Court. It's hardly giving the game away to say that the verdict is always guilty – 'prisoners' are then taken down to the cells, where costumed interpreters posing as prison warders lead them to their fate. Nicked is a similar new police station experience where visitors can help to solve a murder. Meals, snacks, shop, some disabled access; cl Mon (exc bank hols) and 24–26 Dec, 1 Jan; (0115) 952 0555; Condemned *£7.95.

✗ ! Green's Mill and Science Centre (Windmill Lane, Sneinton) Good for families: the restored tower mill still produces flour, and you can try grinding corn on part of an old millstone. Among the exhibits at the hands-on Science Centre next door is a weather satellite receiver showing pictures live from space. Shop, disabled access; cl Mon (exc bank hols), Tues, and Christmas – best to tel (0115) 915 6878 to check if the mill is working; free.

♗ Lace Centre 🖼 (Castle Rd) This pretty 15th-c house has lace hanging from almost every beam, much of it for sale. Lace-making demonstrations pm summer Thurs. Some disabled access; cl 25–26 Dec; (0115) 941 3539; free.

♨ Museum of Nottingham Lace 🖼 (High Pavement) Across the road from its former premises in Lace Hall, this tells the story of the city's lace industry, with demonstrations and interesting displays touching on social conditions; their visitor centre arranges self-guided audio tours of the lace market. Shop, limited disabled access; cl 25–26 Dec, 1 Jan; (0115) 989 7365; £2.95.

♪ Tales of Robin Hood 🖼 (Maid Marian Way) Cars carry you through the sights, sounds and smells of a re-created medieval Sherwood Forest, and a film looks at the truth behind the stories. Pretty much for insistent children only – otherwise you might be better going out to Haughton (see *entry above*). Meals, snacks, shop, disabled access; cl 25–26 Dec; (0115) 948 3284; £4.75.

🏠🕐🎡⬆ᴛ **Wollaton Hall** (Wollaton Park, 3m W) Splendidly ornate Tudor house with the city's natural history collection. The 500-acre grounds are a delight. Shop, some disabled access; cl 25 Dec; (0115) 915 3900; free wkdys, £2 wknds and bank hols, small car parking charge. The adjacent **Industrial Museum** (Courtyard Buildings) looks once again at lace-making, along with other local industries (cl Nov–Mar; phone for steam days (0115) 915 3910; £1.50 wknds, also free wkdys). As we went to press, they were refurbishing a gallery at the Hall, and so for the early part of the year admission to both attractions will be £1.

OLLERTON SK6567

✖ **Ollerton Mill** 🖼 (Market Pl) The only working watermill in the county, still producing flour as it did in the early 18th c, in a pleasant setting on the edge of Sherwood Forest. Award-winning teas (teashop often open when mill isn't), shop; mill working pm Sun and bank hols Apr–Sept; (01623) 822469; £1.50. The Hop Pole in the pretty market place has good-value food.

🏞🦌 **Rufford Country Park** (off A614 S) Pleasant lakeside spot on the edge of Sherwood Forest, with the ruins of a 12th-c abbey, a craft centre and family activities most summer wknds (£1.50 car park charge).

OXTON SK6251

★ 🏛 Attractive village; the lane up the hill N below the power lines leads to an Iron Age hill fort.

RAMPTON SK7978

☺ **Sundown Adventureland** (Treswell Rd; N of A57) Cheerful little leisure park best for children between around 4 and 8. It's full of life-size representations and tableaux of stories and fairytales, from the Wild West to the Three Little Pigs. There are gentle rides – readers tell us that the Boozy Barrel Boats are a must – as well as a

few animals, and several themed play areas, one under cover (height restrictions apply in here). Good Christmas displays, when every child gets a present from Santa (not everything else is working then). Snacks (mostly fast food), shop, some disabled access; cl 25–26 Dec and all Jan wkdys; (01777) 248274; *£4.75 everyone over 2.

RAVENSHEAD SK5654

🎨 **Longdale Craft Centre** (Longdale Lane) Very good craft centre, partly set out as a Victorian village street, with rows of period workshops and a small museum. Decent restaurant, snacks, shop, disabled access; (01623) 794858; cl 25–26 Dec; free. The Little John (B6020) has decent food.

⬆ᴛ **Papplewick Pumping Station** 🖼 (Longdale Lane) A working Victorian waterworks with 2 beam engines; best to ring for steam days, though open for static displays pm most wknds and Weds Easter–Oct; (0115) 963 2938; £1.50 (*£3 steam days). The Burnstump in the Country Park is a good-value family dining pub.

RUDDINGTON SK5732

⬆ᴛ **Framework Knitters Museum** Housed in restored 19th-c workshops, cottages and a frameshop, this museum explores the industry for which Nottinghamshire was once famous. Besides reconstructed cottages you can see the machinery working, incl the bizarre circular sock-knitting machines. Snacks, shop; open Weds–Sat Mar–Dec, plus Sun Jun–July; (0115) 984 6914; £1.50.

🕐 **Village Museum** (Church St) Reconstructed Edwardian shops; usually open pm Weds, Thurs and bank hols Apr–Jun, then all wkdys till Aug, and Weds only Sept–Oct – best to phone; (0115) 914 6645; £1.

SOUTHWELL SK7053

★ ✝ 🎡 🕐 An attractive town around a magnificent 12th-c **Minster**, a fine sight from miles around (especially at night when it's floodlit), and glorious to walk through. Fine leaf carvings and a lovely choir screen; it's worth catching one of the regular concerts. There's a smart visitor centre. This attractive old town, small and quiet, is the home of the Bramley apple, developed by Henry

Merryweather in the 19th century. One of the original trees still prospers at his descendant's garden centre on Halam Rd, where there's a small exhibition on the subject. The Bramley Apple next door is good for lunch. There's a **fruit farm** in the grounds of nearby Norwood Park.

SUTTON BONINGTON SK5025
★ A pleasant village to saunter through.

SUTTON-CUM-LOUND SK6985
🐦 🐾 **Wetlands Waterfowl Reserve** (off Loundlow Rd) Lagoons full of birds from ducks and swans to flamingos, and many more wild birds inc parrots in the surrounding countryside. Also owls, foxes, llamas, wallabies, hopefully prairie dogs by the time this book reaches the shops and a children's farm. Meals, snacks, shop, disabled access; cl 25 Dec; (01777) 818099; £2. The canalside Boat at Hayton has decent food.

UPTON SK7254
👃 **Upton Hall** The HQ of the British Horological Institute includes a museum of clocks and time pieces from marine chronometers to the first telephone speaking clock. Some exhibits are over 300 years old, so don't expect them to keep perfect time. Snacks, shop, disabled access; open pm (exc Sat) Apr–Oct; (01636) 813795; *£2.50. The French Horn and the Cross Keys have good food.

WELLOW SK6665
★ An attractive village, unusual for its permanent maypole – which used to be the trunk of a Sherwood Forest tree, but is now metal. It stands on the only genuine village green in the county, kept that way since the village was founded in the 12th c (all the others were just open spaces used by the villagers and itinerant traders for buying and selling, which have been grassed over since all that stopped). The Olde Red Lion is good for lunch.

WINKBURN SK7158
★ † Attractive village; unusually, its

simple 12th-c village **church** was formerly a temple of the Knights Hospitaller.

WORKSOP SK5880
🏠 👃 † 🖼 **Mr Straw's House** (7 Blyth Grove) One of the NT's most unusual properties, an ordinary 1920s semi, left untouched by 2 brothers who inherited it when their parents died. Even the calendar remains unturned. A fascinating time-capsule, it's open by pre-booked timed ticket only (Tues–Sat Apr–Oct), but it really is worth taking the trouble to get one and by limiting numbers the Trust ensures that you can get a really good feeling of what it was like to live here; (01909) 482380; £4. The town museum has a display on the Pilgrim Fathers (cl Sun and pm Thurs and Sat; free), and the **priory church** is worth a look for the elaborate scrollwork on its 12th-c yew door; there's an art gallery and tearoom in the gatehouse. The Newcastle Arms (Carlton Rd) is a useful place for good-value food.

★ **Other attractive villages** include Collingham SK8663, East Bridgford SK6943 (the Reindeer has good fresh fish), and, with their more 'Leicestershire-ish' character, Colston Bassett SK7033 (the Haby Lane dairy makes good Stilton), Linby SK5351 and Staunton in the Vale SK8043.

The River Trent gives a tremendous sense of power even when it's on its best behaviour, sliding swiftly and massively along; its occasional floods are devastating, and most years it claims lives. Villages giving pleasant river access include Laneham SK8076 and Thrumpton SK5031.

Decent pubs and inns in good riverside spots include the Hazleford Ferry at Bleasby SK7149, Lazy Otter in Wyke Lane, Farndon SK7651, Bromley Arms at Fiskerton SK7351, Unicorn Hotel at Gunthorpe SK6844 and Ferry at Wilford SK5637.

Please let us know what you think of places in the *Guide*. Use the report forms at the back of the book or simply write us a letter.

Where to eat

CAUNTON SK7459 **Caunton Beck** *Main St (01636) 636793* Built in 1820, this roomy and welcoming place was carefully restored using reclaimed oak and Elizabethan timbers, and has an open fire and a wide choice of food ranging from breakfasts to sandwiches and traditional and imaginative modern dishes, served right through the day; friendly staff, a good wine list, and real ales; disabled access. **£20.50|£6.95.**

COLSTON BASSETT SK7033 **Martins Arms** *School Lane (01949) 81361* Civilised, rather smart pub with particularly good imaginative food in the bar and restaurant (lovely puddings), well kept real ales, a fine choice of malt whiskies, quite a few wines by the glass, an open fire, and smart uniformed staff; cl pm Sun; no children; disabled access. **£28|£7.95.**

NOTTINGHAM SK5740 **Lincolnshire Poacher** *Mansfield Rd (0115) 941 1584* Cheerful town pub with really tasty home-made food using fresh local produce (inc lots of vegetarian dishes), interesting real ales, good ciders, lots of whiskies, and a wine of the week, pleasant service, a big wood-floored bar with breweriana, a lively smaller bar, and a chatty back snug; popular with young people in the evening. **£16.50|£4.95.**

PLUMTREE SK6132 **Perkins Restaurant and Bar** *Station Rd (0115) 937 3695* Delightfully converted old railway station with very popular fresh and delicious food (strong French influence), excellent friendly service, and good wines; cl pm Sun, Mon, 1 wk Christmas; children over 7. **£25|£9.75 wkdy 2-course lunch.**

SIBTHORPE HILL SK7273 **Mussel & Crab** *(01777) 870491* Friendly, well run dining pub with a spacious lounge bar, a Mediterranean-style restaurant leading off, most enjoyable food with a strong emphasis on fish, a thoughtful wine list (quite a few, inc champagne by the glass) with helpful notes, and 2 outside terraces; good disabled access. **£21.80 dinner, £14.75 lunch.**

UPTON SK7354 **French Horn** *(01636) 812394* Friendly and bustling dining pub with a neat and comfortable open-plan bar, a nice relaxed atmosphere, imaginative food inc very good daily specials and lots of puddings, well kept real ales, several wines by the glass, friendly and efficient service, and a big sloping back paddock. **£23.35|£7.**

WALKERINGHAM SK7792 **Three Horseshoes** *(01427) 890959* Warmly welcoming distinctive pub, rather like a French *logis*, with quite amazing flowers and hanging baskets (using 9,000 plants); a wide choice of often inventive food, and well kept real ales. **£17|£65.50.**

Special thanks to Michael and Jenny Back, Mrs S Downs.

We welcome reports from readers

This *Guide* depends on readers' reports. Do help us if you can – in return, we offer a discount on the next edition to people who've helped us with reports for it. Tell us what you think about places already in it, and anything extra you think we should say about them. And send us your ideas for inclusion in the next edition: places to visit, eat at or stay in, attractive drives or walks, maybe even unusual interesting shops you know of. Use the card in the middle, the report forms at the end, or just write – no stamp needed: *The Good Britain Guide*, FREEPOST TN1569, Wadhurst, E Sussex TN5 7BR.

Nottinghamshire Calendar

Some of these dates were provisional as we went to press. Please check information with the telephone numbers provided.

JANUARY

1 Nottingham Millennium Festival – *till 3 January* (0125) 915 9232

FEBRUARY

7 Winthorpe Antiques Fair: largest in Europe at Newark Showground – *till 8 February* (01636) 702627

APRIL

3 Winthorpe Antiques Fair *(see 7 Feb for details)* – *till 4 April* (01636) 702627

7 Sutton Bonington National Folk Music Festival – *till 9 April* (01296) 415333

21 Nottingham Easter Treasure Hunt at Tales of Robin Hood – *till 24 April* (0125) 915 9232

29 Nottingham May Day Festivities at Tales of Robin Hood – *till 1 May* (0125) 915 9232

MAY

1 Mansfield May Day Market (01623) 656656; **Nottingham** May Day Celebrations at Brewhouse Yard Museum (0115) 948 3504

6 Winthorpe Nottingham County Show at Newark Showground – *till 7 May* (01636) 702627

28 Nottingham Pop Concert at Wollaton Park – *till 29 May* (0115) 915 5555

29 Wellow Maypole Dancing: one of only 3 permanent maypoles in the country (01623) 824545

JUNE

2 Nottingham Shots in the Dark Film Festival at Broadway Media Centre – *till 12 June* (0115) 915 9232

4 Nottingham Motor Show at Wollaton Park (0115) 915 5555; **Southwell** Countryside Festival at Brackenhurst College (01636) 817034

5 Winthorpe Antiques Fair *(see 7 Feb for details)* – *till 6 June* (01636) 702627

15 Calverton Annual Art and Craft Convention: over 150 artists and craft designers demonstate, exhibit and sell their work – *till 18 June* (0115) 965 3479

17 Winthorpe Kit Car Show at Newark Showground – *till 18 June* (01636) 702627

23 Upton Annual Clock and Watch Fair at Upton Hall, the British Horological Institute HQ: inc clock and watchmaking demonstrations, wood turning, dial painting and the Institute's collection open to the public – *till 25 June* (01636) 813795

Nottinghamshire Calendar (cont.)

JULY

1 **Nottingham** Community Festival at Wollaton Park (0115) 915 5555
7 **Winthorpe** Americana: American show with cars, music at Newark Showground – *till 9 July* (01636) 702627
8 **Mansfield** Mardi Gras – *till 9 July* (01623) 656656
31 **Edwinstowe** Robin Hood Festival at Sherwood Forest Visitor Centre – *till 6 August* (01623) 823202

AUGUST

5 **Nottingham** Riverside Festival: free event with street theatre, carnival, fireworks, world music, steam organs at Victoria Embankment – *till 6 August* (0115) 915 5555
10 **Nottingham** Pop Concert at Wollaton Park – *till 20 August* (0115) 915 5555
12 **Nottingham** Millennium Mela at Victorian Embankment – *till 13 August* (0115) 915 9232
14 **Winthorpe** Antiques Fair *(see 7 Feb for details)* – *till 15 August* (01636) 702627
26 **Nottingham** Pop Concert at Wollaton Park – *till 27 August* (0115) 915 5555
27 **Watnall** Moorgreen Country Show: classic cars, shire horses, heritage marquee – *till 28 August* (01773) 711767

SEPTEMBER

1 **West Bridgford** Rushcliffe Festival – *till 14 September* (0115) 915 5555
9 **Winthorpe** Autumn Exhibition and Balloon Festival at Newark Showground – *till 10 September* (01636) 702627
16 **Winthorpe** Gardening Exhibition Newark Showground – *till 17 September* (01636) 702627

OCTOBER

5 **Nottingham** Goose Fair: largest funfair in the country – *till 7 October* (0115) 915 5555
16 **Winthorpe** Antiques Fair *(see 7 Feb for details)* – *till 17 October* (01636) 702627
26 **Nottingham** Robin Hood Pageant at the Castle – *till 29 October* (0115) 915 5555

DECEMBER

4 **Winthorpe** Antiques Fair *(see 7 Feb for details)* – *till 5 December* (01636) 702627

OXFORDSHIRE

Lots of interest for adults, with richly varied scenery too; some good family days out.

Excellent news for visitors is the new ban on traffic in much of Oxford's centre. It has masses of striking buildings, fascinating collections, and lots more; the university's botanic garden is the oldest in the world. The tourist office is particularly helpful (though one of the hardest to get through to on the phone).

Blenheim Palace by the attractive small town of Woodstock just north of Oxford is the county's great showpiece, with memorable lakeside grounds, and all sorts of things going on to entertain families. Elsewhere, there's a long list of impressive old houses, other interesting buildings, and attractive places such as Burford and Henley. Many other villages and small towns are very rewarding, with picturesque stone houses (up in the north-west corner many glow with a glorious golden stone), and plenty of antique and craft shops.

Treats for children include the Cotswold Wildlife Park near Burford, lively Cogges Farm Museum in Witney, the animals and birds at Ipsden, and the charming model landscape at Long Wittenham.

The scenery has considerable variety, from the edge of the Cotswolds in the west and some sweeping downland in the south to the lush fringes of the Chilterns in the east, with some of the finest Thames scenery.

There are very good hotels and places to eat in – at a price.

Where to stay

ASTHALL SP2811 **Maytime** *Asthall, Burford OX18 4HW (01993) 822068* **£62.50,** plus bargain breaks; 6 quiet rms. Attractive 16th-c Cotswold stone inn with a comfortable and relaxing dining bar, good food, decent wines, and huge breakfasts; worth an early spring-morning walk through the pretty village, across the fields to Swinbrook and back along the river; disabled access.

BAMPTON SP3102 **Morar** *Weald, Weald St, Bampton OX18 2HL (01993) 850162* ***£45,** plus special breaks; 3 rms. Warm, friendly and neatly kept modern stone house (no smoking) with helpful knowledgeable owners (keen gardeners, barn dancers, Morris dancers and church bell ringers), separate lounge and dining room, lovely English cooking in winter using home-grown produce (home-made bread and preserves, too), a pretty flower-filled big garden, and pet sheep, goat and cats; cl Jan and Feb; children over 6.

BURFORD SP2512 **Burford House** *High St, Burford, OX18 4QA (01993) 823151* ***£80,** plus winter breaks; 7 cosy individually decorated rms. Attractive 14th-c Cotswold stone beamed building, with 2 comfortable lounges (1 for residents only), log fires, super breakfasts, and lots of plants in the pretty stone courtyard; children over 10.

BURFORD SP2412 **Lamb** *Sheep St, Burford OX18 4LR (01993) 823155* **£105,** plus special breaks; 15 rms. Very attractive 500-year-old Cotswold inn with a lovely restful atmosphere, a spacious beamed, flagstoned and elegantly furnished lounge, a civilised public bar, bunches of flowers on good oak and elm tables, 3 winter log fires, antiques, very good food in the airy restaurant, and a pretty little walled garden; cl 25–26 Dec.

CHARLBURY SP3519 **Bell** *Church St, Charlbury, Chipping Norton OX7 3PP* (01608) 810278 **£75,** plus special breaks; 11 comfortable rms. Small, neatly kept 17th-c hotel with a warm and friendly atmosphere, a quiet and civilised flagstoned bar, a huge open fire, short choice of interesting bar lunches, a decent restaurant, well kept real ales, and good breakfasts.

CHURCH ENSTONE SP3724 **Crown** *Mill Lane, Church Enstone, Chipping Norton OX7 4NN* (01608) 677262 **£45;** 4 well appointed rms, 3 with own bthrm. Cotswold stone inn in a pretty village, with attractive horseshoe bar, conservatory, friendly atmosphere and staff, good food in the bar and restaurant, and decent breakfasts; Heritage barn nearby can be viewed by appointment.

CLANFIELD SP2802 **Plough** *Bourton Rd, Clanfield, Bampton OX18 2RB* (01367) 810222 **£95,** plus special breaks; 6 lovely rms – they hope to have 12 rms soon. Rose-clad 16th-c Cotswold stone manor house with armchairs and sofas in the relaxed, beamed lounge bar, open fire, friendly helpful staff and very good food in the elegant restaurant; cl 26–30 Dec; children over 12.

CLIFTON SP4831 **Duke of Cumberlands Head** *Clifton, Banbury OX15 0PE* (01869) 338534 **£60;** 6 rms in sympathetic extension. Pretty thatched 17th-c stone inn with friendly atmosphere, very good food in the bar and the back restaurant, enjoyable breakfasts, a log fire, well kept beers and wines, and helpful service; tables in garden.

CLIFTON HAMPDEN SU5495 **Plough** *Clifton Hampden, Abingdon OX14 3EG* (01865) 407811 **£82.50;** 10 rms with four-posters. Quaint little no smoking village pub close to the Thames, run by obliging and idiosyncratic Turkish couple, with a marvellously relaxed, friendly atmosphere, cosy bar with beams and panelling, 2 civilised lounge areas, and good fresh food in the bar and restaurant.

CROPREDY SP4646 **Old Manor** *Cropredy, Banbury OX17 1PS* (01295) 750235 **£54;** 2 rms. In a historic village, this lovely old place has 2 acres of garden and orchard, a moat with ducks and geese, and Gloucester old spot pigs in the fields bordering the Oxford Canal; guests' sitting room with games and books, breakfast in the 15th-c dining room with antiques, clocks and more books, and several dogs and cats; self-catering barn; private motor museum; cl Christmas–New Year; disabled access.

DORCHESTER SU5794 *George High St, Dorchester, Wallingford OX10 7HH* (01865) 340404 **£80,** plus special breaks; 18 characterful rms. Lovely 500-year-old building with a medieval dining room, a comfortably old-fashioned and civilised bar, ancient beams, a big fireplace, good wines, interesting food, and pleasant service; first used as a brewhouse for the Norman abbey opposite; disabled access.

GREAT MILTON SP6202 **Manoir aux Quat' Saisons** *Great Milton, Oxford OX44 7PD* (01844) 278881 ***£230,** plus winter breaks; 32 opulent rms. Luxurious Jacobean manor in 27 acres of parkland and lovely gardens with a heated pool and kitchen garden (providing many of the cooking ingredients), sumptuous lounges with fine furniture, beautiful flowers and open fires, conservatory, exemplary service, and exquisitely presented superb food (at a price); residential cookery courses; disabled access.

HENLEY-ON-THAMES SU7481 **Hernes** (out towards Rotherfield Greys), *Henley-on-Thames RG9 4NT* (01491) 573245 **£75,** plus special breaks; 3 rms. In big gardens and grounds surrounded by farmland, this peaceful no smoking family house has a 16th-c heart, comfortable sitting room with panelled ceiling, family portraits, and good breakfasts – dinner by arrangement; cl Christmas–New Year; no children.

HENLEY-ON-THAMES SU7682 **Red Lion** *Hart St, Henley-on-Thames RG9 2AR* (01491) 572161 **£137,** plus special breaks; 26 rms, some with river views. Handsome, family-run and recently refurbished 16th-c riverside hotel with comfortable public rooms, very good, interesting food in the elegant Regency-style restaurant, and particularly helpful, warmly friendly staff.

HORTON-CUM-STUDLEY SP5912 **Studley Priory** *Horton-cum-Studley, Oxford OX33 1AZ (01865) 351203* **£146,** plus special breaks; 18 rms. Once a Benedictine nunnery, this lovely 12th-c Elizabethan manor stands in 13 wooded acres; fine panelling, 16th- and 17th-c stained-glass windows, antiques and open fires in the elegant drawing room and cosy bar, and seasonally changing menus in the attractive restaurant; grass tennis court and croquet.

KELMSCOT SU2599 **Plough** *Kelmscot, Lechlade, Gloucs GL7 3HG (01367) 253543* *****£60,** plus special breaks; 8 comfortable rms. Pretty little inn nr the Thames with an attractively traditional small bar, ancient flagstones, stripped stone walls, and a relaxed chatty atmosphere; a larger, cheerfully carpeted back bar, log fires, a wide choice of food, and well kept real ales; boats for hire, and fishing (both nearby), and lots of surrounding walks – on the Oxfordshire cycleway, too; no rooms 24–30 Dec; children over 10.

KINGHAM SP2523 **Mill House** *Station Rd, Kingham, Chipping Norton OX7 6UH (01608) 658188* **£110,** plus special breaks; 23 good rms with country views. Carefully renovated 17th-c flour mill in 7 acres with a trout stream, a comfortable and spacious lounge, an open log fire in the lounge bar, original features such as 2 bread ovens, a cosy popular restaurant, and very good, interesting food; disabled access.

KINGSTON BAGPUIZE SU3997 **Fallowfields** *Southmoor, Kingston Bagpuize, Abingdon OX13 5BH (01865) 820416* *****£120;** 10 rms. Delightful Gothic-style manor house with elegant, relaxing sitting rooms, open fires, good Aga-cooked food (using home-grown produce) in the attractive dining room, and 2 acres of pretty gardens with outdoor heated swimming pool and tennis court; no smoking; children over 10.

LITTLE WITTENHAM SU5692 **Rooks Orchard** *Little Wittenham, Abingdon OX14 4QY (01865) 407765* *****£48;** 2 rms. Comfortable 17th-c house in lovely gardens by a nature reserve and Wittenham Clumps, with beams, inglenook fireplaces, good breakfasts (evening meals by arrangement), welcoming owners, and baby-sitting service; dogs by arrangement; cl Christmas; children over 8.

LONG HANBOROUGH SP4214 **Old Farmhouse** *Station Hill, Long Hanborough, Witney OX8 8JZ (01993) 882097* *****£45;** 2 rms, 1 with own bthrm. Welcoming no smoking 17th-c house with lots of charm, stone walls and beams, homely sitting rooms with inglenook fires, a conservatory, good breakfasts with home-made preserves, and enjoyable meals using home-grown produce, and a pretty, cottagey garden; Oxford only a 10-minute train ride away, and plenty to do nearby; cl Christmas; children over 12.

MINSTER LOVELL SP3211 **Hill Grove Farm** *Crawley Dry Lane, Minster Lovell, Witney OX8 5NA (01993) 703120* *****£42;** 2 rms. Friendly B & B on a family-run 300-acre mixed working farm with a homely lounge and sun room, good breakfasts, and nice views and walks; no smoking; cl Christmas.

MOULSFORD SU5983 **Beetle & Wedge** *Ferry Lane, Moulsford, Wallingford OX10 9JF (01491) 651381* *****£150,** plus special breaks; 10 pretty rms, most with lovely river view. Civilised riverside hotel where Jerome K Jerome wrote *Three Men in a Boat* and where H G Wells lived for a time (it was the Potwell in *The History of Mr Polly*); informal old beamed Boathouse bar and a lovely conservatory dining room (both with wonderful food – but must book), a carefully chosen wine list, open fires, fresh flowers, a riverside terrace and waterside lawn with moorings, and a warmly welcoming atmosphere; nice walks; disabled access.

OXFORD SP5009 **Cotswold House** *363 Banbury Rd OX2 7PL (01865) 310558* **£65;** 7 comfortable rms with showers. Beautifully kept, modern, no smoking Cotswold stone house with particularly helpful owners, a residents' lounge, very good breakfasts, pretty flowers throughout, and a neat back garden; cl 10 days at Christmas; children over 6.

OXFORD SP5106 **Old Parsonage** *1 Banbury Rd OX2 6NN (01865) 310210* **£160;** 30 lovely rms. Handsome and civilised 17th-c parsonage, fairly central, with very courteous staff, good breakfasts and excellent light meals in the cosy bar/restaurant, a small lounge, open fires and fine paintings, and a pretty little garden; they have their own punt and provide picnics; the luxurious Old Bank Hotel has just opened under the same ownership; cl 25–26 Dec.

OXFORD SP5204 **Pine Castle** *290/292 Iffley Rd OX4 4AE (01865)* 241497 **£67,** plus wknd breaks; 8 rms. Small family-run Edwardian hotel with a comfortable, cosy lounge, and good breakfasts in the small restaurant; cl Christmas wk.

OXFORD SP5106 **Randolph** *Beaumont St OX1 2LN (01865)* 247481 **£187.50,** plus special breaks; 119 rms. Fine neo-Gothic Victorian hotel facing the Ashmolean Museum, with elegant and comfortable day rooms, a grand foyer, a graceful restaurant with lovely plasterwork ceiling, and a cellar wine bar; disabled access.

SHENINGTON SP3642 **Top Farm House** *Shenington, Banbury OX15 6LZ (01295)* 670226 **£45;** 2 rms, shared bthrm. 18th-c farmhouse by the village green, with oak beams, inglenook fireplaces, a residents' sitting room, and good breakfasts.

SHILLINGFORD SU5991 **Shillingford Bridge** *Ferry Rd, Shillingford, Wallingford OX10 8LZ (01865)* 858567 **£95,** plus special breaks; 42 rms. Riverside hotel with its own river frontage, fishing and moorings, spacious comfortable bars and an attractive, airy restaurant (all with fine views), squash, outdoor heated swimming pool, and Sat dinner-dance; disabled access.

SHIPTON-UNDER-WYCHWOOD SP2717 **Lamb** *Shipton-under-Wychwood, Chipping Norton OX7 6DQ (01993)* 830465 **£75;** 5 comfortable rms. Ancient Cotswold stone pub with a relaxed and civilised atmosphere, an open log fire, highly polished furniture and newspapers to read in the beamed bar, good food in the no smoking restaurant, and enjoyable breakfasts.

SHIPTON-UNDER-WYCHWOOD SP2717 **Shaven Crown** *Shipton-under-Wychwood, Chipping Norton, OX7 6BA (01993)* 830330 **£85,** plus special breaks; 9 comfortable rms. Densely beamed ancient stone hospice built around a striking medieval courtyard with old-fashioned seats on cobbles, lily pool and roses. Impressive medieval hall with a magnificent lofty ceiling, sweeping stairway and old stone walls, a log fire in the comfortable bar, intimate candlelit restaurant, well chosen wine list, good friendly service, a warm and relaxed atmosphere; also a bowling green; children over 5 in evening dining room; disabled access.

SHIPTON-UNDER-WYCHWOOD SP2717 **Shipton Grange House** *Shipton-under-Wychwood, Chipping Norton, OX7 6DG (01993)* 831298 ***£62;** 3 rms. Carefully converted, no smoking Georgian coach house and stabling with elegantly furnished sitting rooms, good breakfasts, a friendly welcome, and attractive walled garden; cl Christmas; children over 12.

STONOR SU7388 **Stonor Arms** *Stonor, Henley-on-Thames RG9 6HE (01491)* 638345 ***£115,** plus special breaks; 10 pretty rms. Carefully restored 18th-c hotel with fine, imaginative food in 2 elegant restaurants, each with a pretty conservatory; a relaxed flagstoned bar, and friendly staff; disabled access.

UFFINGTON SU3089 **Craven** *Fernham Rd, Uffington, Faringdon SN7 7RD (01367)* 820449 ***£70,** plus special breaks; 5 pretty rms, some with own bthrm. Most attractive 17th-c thatched house with a beamed sitting room, a log fire in the inglenook, antiques, a friendly relaxed atmosphere, good food in the beamed farmhouse kitchen, and lots of nearby walks; disabled access.

WOODSTOCK SP4416 **Feathers** *Market St, Woodstock OX20 1SX (01993)* 812291 **£105,** plus special breaks; 22 individually decorated rms. Lovely old building with a fine relaxing drawing room and study, open fires, first-class friendly staff, a gentle atmosphere, daily-changing imaginative food inc lovely puddings, and a sunny courtyard with attractive tables and chairs.

WOODSTOCK SP4416 **Holmwood** *6 High St, Woodstock OX20 1TF (01993)* 812266 ***£80;** 2 pretty rms, both with their own sitting room. Early 18th-c Cotswold stone house with oak beams and antiques, an attractive dining room, and friendly, helpful owners; no smoking; cl Jan; children over 12.

To see and do

OXFORDSHIRE Family Attraction of the Year

🐘 ♪ **BURFORD** SP2512 **Cotswold Wildlife Park** 🏞 (Bradwell Grove, A361, 2m S of junction with A40) Plenty for children at this big place, well liked by readers and a thoroughly reliable family day out. Spread around acres of gardens and parkland, with a 'gothick' manor house at the centre, it has hundreds of different creatures from all over the world in spacious re-creations of their natural environment. Everything's well signposted and labelled, so you always have a good idea of where you're going and what you're looking at. They have an excellent track record with breeding (a family of baby meerkats and a striking baby Brazilian tapir among the latest additions as we went to press), and have high hopes for their newly acquired pair of rare Asiatic lions; there are only 300 of these left in the wild. All the animals you'd hope to see are here, and they have various animal encounters and feeding displays throughout the day; penguin feeding times are always popular. A children's farmyard has the usual petting opportunities, and there's a good adventure playground; more unusually, there's animal-themed brass rubbing in the house. A narrow-gauge railway operates Apr–Oct. As well as the animals outside, there's a tropical house, reptile house, aquarium, insect and butterfly house, and a new 49-metre (160ft) walk-through aviary, so no problem in keeping children entertained for most of the day. Meals and snacks (and plenty of space for picnics), shops (one specially for children), disabled access; cl 25 Dec; (01993) 823006; £6 (£4 children 3–16).

ABINGDON SU4997

★ ✝ 🕭 🏛 Attractive Thames-side town, until 1974 the county town of Berkshire. Much expanded around its old partly pedestrianised core, which still has a fine old gatehouse, several attractive old buildings and almshouses around the impressive 15th/16th-c Wren-style **Church of St Helen** off Thames St, and the unusual **Church of St Mary**, wider than it's long. The good museum in the 17th-c former county hall (free) is creating a new exhibition, funded by a recent heritage grant, focusing on the town's claim to be England's oldest continuously inhabited settlement. The remains of the partly Norman Benedictine **abbey**, once the second most powerful in England, have been restored, with part now housing a local theatre. The riverside Old Anchor is prettily placed for lunch, and there's decent food at the Mill House, built into the medieval town bridge.

ARDINGTON SU4388

★ ✿ This is an attractive small village, with a good dining pub, and several craft workshops in the Home Farm buildings.

BANBURY SP4540

🕭 🍴 The busy shopping town was actually without its famous cross for 250 years, between the Puritans' destroying it in 1602 and the construction of its replacement in 1859. In the church graveyard is the tomb from which Jonathan Swift borrowed the name Gulliver for his traveller. There's a decent local history **museum** (cl winter Sun and Mon; free), and the Reindeer and the Wine Vaults, both in Parsons St, are useful for lunch. The B4035 towards Sibford Ferris runs through attractive hilly farmland, with summer **pick-your-own**; the loop N through North Newington, Shutford and Epwell is good too.

BENSON SU6292

🕭 ⛴ **Benson Veteran Cycle Museum** Private collection of over 500 bicycles from between 1818 and 1930; shop; open mornings Easter–Sept by appointment with Mr Passey, on (01491) 838414; free. Down by the river at the Cruiser station you can hire boats by the day or the hour; (01491) 838304. The footpath beyond the weir bridge leads to Wallingford. The Home Sweet Home at Roke is a nice pub.

BIX BOTTOM SU7285

⌂ **Oxfordshire Way** This long-distance path gives one short walk with a palpable sense of peace, from the lane out past Bix Hall to Valley End Farm.

❦ ❧ ⌂ **Warburg Reserve** Extensive wildflower-rich rough grassland and ancient beech wood, good for wild orchids and butterflies, besides birds and maybe deer.

BROUGHTON SP4138

🏛 ☗ **Broughton Castle** (B4035 SW of Banbury) Striking early 14th–16th-c house with proper moat and gatehouse, originally owned by William of Wykeham. Exceptional oak panelling, period furniture, and Civil War relics. Some rooms have bare stone walls under elaborately plastered ceilings, an unusual combination that works rather well. *Shakespeare in Love* was partly filmed here. Snacks, shop, disabled access to ground floor only; open Easter, then mid-May–mid-Sept pm Weds, Sun and bank hols, plus Thurs July and Aug; (01295) 262624; £4. There's a decent village **museum**, and the Roebuck at North Newington is a good pub for food.

BURFORD SP2512

★ ✝ ☗ ⌂ Lovely little Cotswold town with interesting shops and teashops along its pretty main street. The **church** is particularly intriguing, with a super graveyard, and 17th-c graffiti by some of the 400 Leveller mutineers imprisoned here by Cromwell. The town also has an interesting little museum (open pm Apr–Nov; 50p), and is full of attractive pubs: the best for food and atmosphere is the Lamb, and the Mermaid serves food all day in summer. Burford does get very busy indeed with visitors, and it's worth noting that several smaller and altogether quieter nearby villages are, in their way, as pretty: Taynton, the Barringtons (just over the Gloucs border), Fulbrook, Swinbrook and Asthall. All except the first have a decent pub. There are attractive walks between these, along the River Windrush for much of the way – the back roads along the Windrush Valley give pleasant drives, too.

🐦 ♪ **Cotswold Wildlife Park** See separate family panel on p.513.

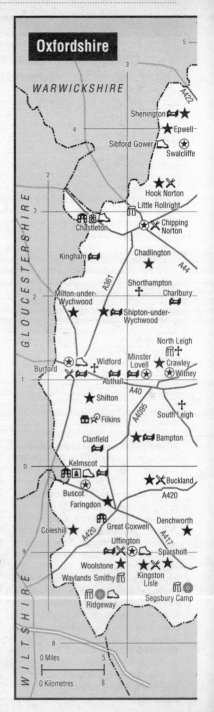

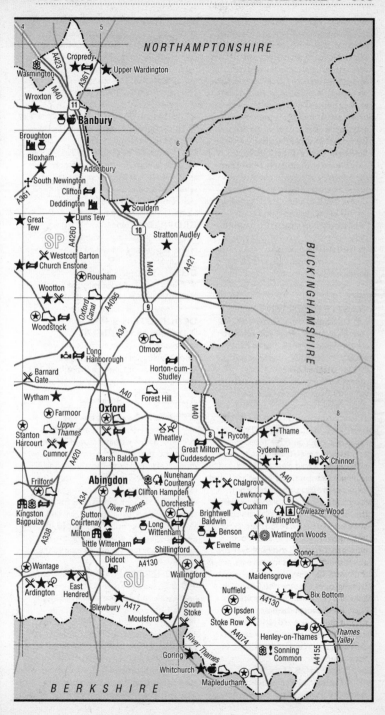

NORTHAMPTONSHIRE

Cropredy
Warmington
Upper Wardington
Wroxton
11
Banbury
Broughton
Bloxham
Adderbury
South Newington
Clifton
Deddington
Souldern
Great Tew
Duns Tew
Stratton Audley
10
SP
Westcott Barton
Church Enstone
Rousham
Wootton
Oxford Canal
9
Woodstock
Otmoor
Long Hanborough
Horton-cum-Studley
Barnard Gate
Wytham
Forest Hill
Farmoor
Oxford
Upper Thames
Wheatley
8
Rycote
Thame
Stanton Harcourt
Sydenham
Cumnor
Marsh Baldon
Great Milton
Cuddesdon
Chinnor
Frilford
Abingdon
Nuneham Courtenay
Chalgrove
Clifton Hampden
Lewknor
Cuxham
Cowleaze Wood
Kingston Bagpuize
Sutton Courtenay
Dorchester
Brightwell Baldwin
Watlington
Milton
Long Wittenham
Benson
Watlington Woods
Little Wittenham
Shillingford
Ewelme
Stonor
Didcot
Wantage
Wallingford
Maidensgrove
Ardington
East Hendred
Nuffield
Bix Bottom
Blewbury
Moulsford
South Stoke
Ipsden
Stoke Row
Henley-on-Thames
Thames Valley
Goring
Whitchurch
Sonning Common
Mapledurham

BERKSHIRE

BUCKINGHAMSHIRE

BUSCOT SU2496

🏠🖼️🎟️🚤 **Buscot Park** (A417) What makes this 18th-c house really special is the amazing collection of art and furnishings amassed by its owners; paintings by Reynolds, Gainsborough, Rembrandt, Murillo and several of the Pre-Raphaelites (inc a splendid series by Burne-Jones), with some more recent pictures too. The attractive grounds have formal watergardens and a mouth-watering kitchen garden, and maybe pick-your-own in summer. Teas; open Apr–Sept, pm Weds–Fri and every second and fourth wknd in the month; (01367) 240786; £4.40, £3.30 grounds only; NT. The Thames-side Trout (A417 towards Lechlade) is popular for lunch.

CHALGROVE SU6396

★ ✝ Attractive small village, with notable medieval wall paintings in the 11th-c **church** – which owns the village pub.

CHASTLETON SP2429

🏠🎟️🌥️ **Chastleton House** (off A44 NW of Chipping Norton) Opened in autumn 1997 after 6 years and £3 million of restoration, this handsome Jacobean manor house was little changed by the family who owned it 1605–1991, really feeling like a well lived-in family house of that period, and not oversmartened despite the lovely plasterwork, beautiful oak and walnut furnishings, embroideries, Jacobite glassware, and even the Bible Charles I took to the scaffold. Peaceful Jacobean gardens inc a topiary and first-class croquet lawn. Car park up hill from house. Open Apr–Oct pm Weds–Sat; (01608) 674284; £4.80, must have pre-booked timed ticket; NT. There's pleasant walking in the area between this village, Cornwell and (just over the Gloucs border) Adlestrop.

CHINNOR SP7500

🚂 **Chinnor & Princes Risborough Railway** Four-mile train trips up into Bucks; trains most wknds Apr–Sept, some steam-hauled – (01844) 353535 for timetable and prices (they can get busy so you may need to book for special events).

CHIPPING NORTON SP3127

★🏠🔔 Pleasant old stone-built wool town with an unusually wide market place, pretty church, some fine 17th-c almshouses, a good few antique shops, and a local history **museum** in the Co-op Hall; cl am, all day Mon exc bank hols, Oct–Easter; *£1. The Chequers has decent food. The roads to Hook Norton, or B4026/B4022 to Witney, are good Cotswoldy drives.

COLESHILL SU2393

★ This attractive village is owned by the NT; lots of good walks nearby.

COWLEAZE WOOD SU7295

🌳🖼️ Between Christmas Common and the M40, this has forest art exhibits scattered around as part of a sculpture trail. The Fox & Hounds on Christmas Common is useful for walkers.

CROPREDY SP4646

★ An attractive village, where you may find sheep grazing the raised churchyard.

CUXHAM SU6695

★ Pretty thatched houses by the stream which runs along beside the road – and a good village pub.

DEDDINGTON SP4631

🏰 **Deddington Castle** 12th-c fortress remains; there are attractive stone buildings around the village square, inc several antique shops, and the Deddington Arms and the Unicorn (good for lunch).

DIDCOT SU5290

🚂 **Didcot Railway Centre** The biggest collection anywhere of Great Western Railway stock, housed under cover, inc 20 steam locomotives, a diesel railcar and lots of passenger and freight rolling stock. Snacks, shop, disabled access; open wknds all year and wkdys Easter–Sept, best to ring for steamday dates, usually every Sun and Weds in summer hols; (01235) 817200; £4–£8 depending on event. The town itself more or less sprang up around the railway sheds.

DORCHESTER SU5894

✝🍺★🌥️ **Dorchester Abbey** Impressive and well preserved abbey, with a 12th-c nave and rare lead font. The tower was rebuilt in 1605 and has a 14th-c spiral staircase, as well as an exceptional Jesse window from the same period, and some mosaic-like 12th-c glass in other windows. The adjacent former guesthouse now houses a little **museum**. In summer they do very individual ever-so-English teas (Weds–Sun (exc Fri) pm), all home-made and quite addictive. Shop, disabled access; museum cl Mon, wkdys in Oct and all Nov–Apr; free. The whole Thames-side village is a lovely place to explore, with interesting antique shops. The River Thames has pleasant walks starting and finishing here; you can cross at Day's Lock, and a short walk brings you to Wittenham Clumps (alternative access from the adjacent car park), a pair of hillocks which look across the Chilterns and Berkshire Downs. The George and Fleur de Lys do good lunches.

EWELME SU6491

★ One of Oxfordshire's prettiest and most unspoilt villages. The Shepherds Hut has good-value food.

FARMOOR SP4405

🎣 ⛵ 🐦 **Farmoor Reservoir** Trout fishing, sailing, birdwatching, and other activities, though you'll need a permit; (01865) 863033 for details and prices.

FILKINS SP2207

🏠 🐑 **Cotswold Woollen Weavers** Friendly working woollen mill with demonstrations of traditional production methods in 18th-c buildings. Snacks, well stocked shop, some disabled access; (01367) 860491; cl am Sun, 25–31 Dec; free. The Five Alls and Lamb are useful for lunch.

FOREST HILL SP5807

⌂ Above Oxford, this gives several pleasant walks from the White Horse pub.

FRILFORD SU4397

🍎 🐄 ⌂ 🐾 **Millets Farm Centre** Pick-your-own fruit, animals, walks, and an unusually extensive farm shop which takes in a bakery, delicatessen, garden centre, and wine merchant; cl 25 Dec; (01865) 391625.

GREAT COXWELL SU2693

🏠 **Great Coxwell Barn** As noble as a cathedral according to William Morris, a 13th-c stone-built tithe barn 46 by 13 metres (152ft long and 44ft wide), with beautifully crafted timbers supporting the roof; free (donations).

GREAT TEW SP3929

★ The most charming village in the area (some would say in all England). It's an outstanding series of golden stone 17th- and 18th-c cottages, some

thatched and others with stone-slabbed roofs, around an attractive sloping green and among ancient trees, with wooded slopes above.

HENLEY-ON-THAMES SU7781

★ ⛵ Pleasant, well heeled Thames-side town famed for its summer regatta. You can usually see other rowing races or practices on the river throughout the year, or hire your own boat on (01491) 572035. The informal Anchor (Friday St) and comfortable, beamed Old White Horse (Northfield End) are good-value riverside pubs, and the Three Tuns (Market Pl) does food all day.

🏠 ⚜ ✝ **Greys Court** (Rotherfield Greys, 3m W) An attractive gabled Jacobean house with interesting ruins of its medieval predecessor; the gardens are even more alluring, with white and rose gardens, ancient wisterias, a kitchen garden, wheelhouse, icehouse and brick maze. Teas, bookstall, some disabled access; open Apr–Sept, house pm Mon, Weds and Fri, garden pm daily exc Thurs and Sun; (01491) 628529; £4.50, £3.20 gardens only; NT. The village **church** is delightful, and the Maltsters Arms dining pub has lovely country views, and good nearby walks. The B480 to Watlington is a pleasant Chilterns drive.

⚜ **Museum of Rowing** (in a stunning new building by Mill Meadows) As well as comprehensive displays on the sport, the museum focuses on the Regatta and the history and life of the river itself. Meals, snacks, shop, disabled access; cl 25–26 Dec, 1 Jan; (01491) 415600; £4.95.

IPSDEN SU6386

🐦 🐄 ! **Wellplace Zoo** Mainly a bird park, but also animals such as lambs, goats, otters, donkeys and monkeys. You can feed several of them, so good for children. Snacks, shop, disabled access; cl wkdys Oct–Easter; (01491) 680473; £2. The King William IV at Hailey is handy for something to eat. Ian Smith can arrange **horse-drawn wagon rides** through these pretty Chilterns fringes; most fine summer days he runs 2-horse wagons from Darkwood Farm, Park Corner on a local pub tour; (01491) 641324. Even by car, these are pleasant Chilterns drives

– for instance the loop S of Nettlebed through Highmoor Cross, Stoke Row and Nuffield.

KELMSCOT SU2599

🏠 🖼 ◠ **Kelmscott Manor** The summer home of William Morris until his death in 1896, now with one of the best assemblages of Morris memorabilia, standing out all the more for its domestic setting. Works by other Pre-Raphaelite artists include splendid paintings by Rossetti, who initially shared the lease. Snacks, shop, disabled access to ground floor only; open Weds (exc 1–2pm) and pm third Sat of month Apr–Sept; (01367) 252486; £6. The Plough in the peaceful little Thames-side village is good, and there's a waterside walk of a mile and a half E to the Swan at Radcot Bridge.

KINGSTON BAGPUIZE SU4098

🏠 🏵 **Kingston House** (off A415) Charming 17th-c manor house, remodelled in the early 18th c, with lovely panelling, attractive furnishings and a friendly unstuffy feel; peaceful garden with mature flowering shrubs, woodland walks, and a Georgian gazebo. Shop; usually open pm bank hol wknds, and occasional other summer pms – best to ring for exact dates; (01865) 820259; *£3.50, *£1.50 garden only. The Hinds Head has good-value food.

LITTLE ROLLRIGHT SP2931

🏛 **Rollright Stones** Dramatic and mysterious Bronze Age stones, chiefly in a circle about 30 metres (100ft) across, now thought to date from between 1500 and 2000 BC; legend has it that the stones are a king and his men tricked by a witch into falling under her spell, and petrified. It's supposed to be impossible to count them as you can never tell where you started – which must have been frustrating for the estate agent when the stones were put on the market a couple of years ago. The Gate Hangs High nr here is useful for lunch.

LONG HANBOROUGH SP4314

🏛 **Oxford Bus Museum** 🖼 Around 40 vehicles, from Oxford horse trams to more modern machines up to the 1960s, some roadworthy, others being restored. Disabled access; open Sat and Sun; (01993) 883617; *£3. The Hand &

Shears at Church Hanborough is a very good dining pub.

LONG WITTENHAM SU5493

🕰 **Pendon Museum Miniature Landscape** Charming exhibition showing a highly detailed model railway and meticulously researched model 1930s village scenes; you can often see modellers working on the exhibits, and they're always happy to chat. Snacks, shop; open pm wknds and bank hols Jan–Nov, plus pm Weds Jun–Aug; (01865) 407365; *£3. The Machine Man has good fresh food.

MAPLEDURHAM SU6776

★ 🐎 ⚓ Very attractive little community with lovely beechwoods full of birds; the nicest way to reach it is by boat from the Caversham Promenade at Reading (summer wknds only).

🏠 🏵 🖼 ╳ ◠ **Mapledurham House** Impressive Elizabethan mansion in pretty Thames-side parkland, with paintings and family portraits, great oak staircases, and moulded Elizabethan ceilings. In the grounds is the last **watermill** on the Thames to use wooden machinery; dating from 1423, it still produces flour, bran and semolina. Also riverside walks and an island with picnic area. Teas, shop, disabled access to ground floor only; open pm Sat, Sun and bank hols Easter–Sept; (0118) 972 3350; £6 house and watermill, £4 house only, £3 watermill only. You can stay in a number of lovely cottages on the estate (some thatched).

MILTON SU4892

🏠 🐎 **Milton Manor** Elegant 17th-c manor house with a splendid Strawberry Hill 'gothic' library, an interesting chapel, walled garden, and unusual collections of teapots and fine china. Open bank hol wknds and daily in August; (01235) 831287; £4. The Admiral Benbow has decent food. The cherry orchards around Milton Hill are a fine sight when the white blossom is out in spring, and around July roadside stalls sell plump red-black fresh cherries – the Grove Farm Shop (A4130) is especially friendly.

MINSTER LOVELL SP3211

★ † One of the prettiest and most unspoilt old villages in the area; there's an attractive 15th-c **church** and village green, and a 15th-c bridge over the

River Windrush narrow enough for the Welsh drovers to use for counting the sheep in the flocks they brought this way each year. The smart Old Swan does good light lunches.

🏛 **Minster Lovell Hall** Imposing and attractively set, this was being used as ramshackle farm buildings until its 'restoration' as neat ruins in the 1930s. Macabre stories about the 15th-c Hall usually involve people being shut up in various places and forgotten about until their skeletons are discovered much later. Open every day, free. There's a well restored medieval dovecot nearby.

NORTH LEIGH SP3813

🏚 ✝ **Roman villa** Occupied between the 2nd and 4th c, when it was a very grand place with several dozen rooms, it's now just a few neat but poignant traces, in a very pleasant wooded setting; free. The medieval village **church**, with a Saxon tower, is lovely inside, and the Woodman is popular for lunch.

NUFFIELD SU6787

🏠 ❀ 🏚 **Nuffield Place** The home of Lord and Lady Nuffield 1933–1963, with the original 1930s furnishings. Very good gardens with mature trees and shrubs inc rhododendrons, lawns, a pond and rockery, as well as Lady Nuffield's own Wolseley and a display of vintage cars. Teas, small shop, limited disabled access; open pm second and fourth Sun each month May–Sept; (01491) 641224; £3. The Crown pub here has decent food – from sandwiches to fresh fish.

NUNEHAM COURTENAY SU5599

🏞 ❀ **Oxford University Arboretum** (A4074) Fine conifers and other trees over 55 acres, as well as plants like rhododendrons that won't grow in the soil of Oxford itself. Some disabled access; cl wknds Oct–Apr, and 2 wks at Christmas; free. About half a mile away, the roses at Notcutts Garden Centre are a blaze of summer colour easily seen from the road; decent meals here.

OTMOOR SP5614

🌿 🍂 🍎 🌼 Several square miles of flatland, so poorly drained that in very wet weather its river actually flows backwards, and interesting to walk through. Because serious farming is virtually out of the question, it does have more natural wildlife than most places in the county; there are several paths through it. The Abingdon Arms at Beckley, with enjoyable food, is one starting point (and there's a good farm shop there on the B4027 from Stanton St John); the Nut Tree at Murcott does excellent steaks. On one edge, the pick-your-own fruit farm at Elsfield has nice views over the wilderness, as well as an unusually wide range of varieties.

OXFORD SP5105

🏚 On first impression this can seem quite a frenetic city: the ancient university buildings with their medieval lanes and scholarly corners are surrounded by a bustling, largely industrialised town, with a formidable amount of traffic. Last year, some of the

---

Days Out

Stroll round Oxford: Christ Church quads and Meadow; Botanic Garden; Magdalen College; walk past the Bodleian Library; lunch at the Turf Tavern; walk down Holywell St and Broad St; Ashmolean Museum – or spend the afternoon punting along the river from Magdalen Bridge or Folly Bridge, or walking out along the Oxford Canal to Port Meadow, for an early evening drink at the Trout, Godstow.

Cotswolds tones: Walk in the park of Blenheim Palace, Woodstock, or hire a boat; lunch at the Feathers there; Roman villa, North Leigh; Minster Lovell; Burford.

Victorian farming, world wildlife: Cogges Farm Museum, Witney; lunch at the Lamb, Burford; Cotswold Wildlife Park.

major city centre thoroughfares were pedestrianised in a bid to relieve the nightmarish congestion problems; if you don't come by train or coach, it's certainly a good idea to leave your car at one of the Park & Rides around the ring road. Otherwise, the tourist information centre does a useful car park map, with times and prices. For first-time visitors, hop-on-and-off **tour buses** from St Aldates, High St, Gloucester Green or Pembroke College take in all the best sites and last about 1½ hours (£7–£10). Many of the city's oldest or most interesting buildings are grouped around the Bodleian Library, the Sheldonian Theatre and the splendid domed Radcliffe Camera (also a library). This partly cobbled central university area is most attractive, but does sometimes overfill with visitors – recently students have been complaining that the noise of tourists puts them off their exams. In the streets and lanes leading off, the honey-coloured stone makes for a harmony that unites different styles and different centuries. There are a few good shops dotted about; Blackwells is the main bookseller, with several branches around the Broad St area (the secondhand section in the main branch is well used by students, and their music shop on Holywell St is rewarding). Nr the station, the **Oxford Antique Trading Co** has 80 dealers.

🏚 🏵 **Colleges** Most allow visitors into at least some of their quads, and do have a wonderful, timeless appeal. One of the few they failed to impress was William Cobbett, who wrote in his *Rural Rides* that he 'could not help reflecting on the drones that they contain, and the wasps they send forth'. Newcomers are often surprised to discover that the colleges are all separate bodies with little in common, each firmly maintaining its own dons, rules and traditions; the university itself is little more than an administrative umbrella. Several now charge admission, notably Christ Church, New, Magdalen, Trinity and Brasenose. Access may be more limited in term-time. A few may let you in only with a guide, so a good way of making sure you see a cross-section is to join one of the

walking tours that leave the tourist information centre (Old School, Gloucester Green) every day at 10.30am, 11am, 1pm and 2pm; £4. Afternoon tours are the best, but get there early – places are limited. Guided walks may also leave from the Catte St/High St corner and your guide might turn out to be an enterprising student. Ideally though, it's worth trying to explore at your own pace away from the crowds – again, afternoons are best, with more colleges open then. Besides colleges we pick out individually, more are tucked down some of the town's prettiest streets, such as charming **Exeter**, **Jesus** and **Lincoln** down Turl St, and **Corpus Christi** and **Oriel** around Merton Lane and Oriel Sq. This last college has a very attractive and unusual entrance to its dining hall. **Trinity** on Broad St though not large is very grand. Around Radcliffe Sq **Brasenose** is quaint (and has good views of the surrounding skyline from its quads), and **Hertford** has its Bridge of Sighs over New College St, in itself worth exploring for some more unusual and less busy views and a good look at the gargoyles on the backs of some of the buildings. **Worcester** has particularly nice **gardens**, and many of the other colleges' private Fellows' gardens not usually open to visitors can be seen under the National Gardens Scheme.

♨ 🖼 **Ashmolean Museum** (Beaumont St) The country's first museum, and still one of its finest, opened in 1683 and rehoused in this imposing building from 1845. The well arranged galleries include marvellous European paintings, an extensive collection of Pre-Raphaelite pictures, a representative range of work by French Impressionists, and antiquities from ancient Egypt, Greece and Rome. Meals, snacks, shop, disabled access; cl am Sun, Mon (exc pm bank hols), first wk of Sept (St Giles Fair), Christmas wk, Easter; (01865) 278000; free.

♨ **Bate Collection of Instruments** (St Aldates) Outstanding, constantly developing, collection of early keyboards, woodwind, brass, percussion and other instruments inc a complete Javanese gamelan. Shop, mostly disabled access; cl am, wknds (exc am Sat during term-time), and a few days at Christmas and Easter; (01865) 276139; free.

Bodleian Library (Broad St) One of the oldest in Europe, its splendidly grand quad dominated by the Tower of the Five Orders. Most of it is closed to the public, but guided tours take in the beautifully vaulted 15th-c Divinity School, which shows some of the library's treasures and for the first time this year the Chancellor's Court and Convocation House. Tours every 10 minutes, and additional tours of Duke Humfrey's Library, the oldest reading room, usually at 10.30am, 11.30am, 2pm and 3pm; (01865) 277000; no children under 14, excellent shop, limited disabled access (notice preferred); cl some bank hols and maybe last wk of Aug; £3.50. Altogether the library houses over 5,500,000 books, going down 6 storeys under the centre of the city.

Carfax Tower Right at the traditional centre of Oxford, all that remains of a 14th-c church; good views, and the bells in the tower are interestingly designed. Shop; cl 25 Dec–1 Jan; £1.20.

Castle Mound There isn't much of the Norman castle left save a tower and crypt of the castle church, and an underground well chamber, but the mound gives quite good views over the city and its surroundings.

Christ Church The best-known college, a magnificently stately place begun by Cardinal Wolsey in the 16th c, but soon taken over by Henry VIII. The main entrance is through Tom Tower, designed by Christopher Wren and named after its famous bell that rings out 101 times at 9 o'clock every night – in less liberal times the hour when students were due back in their rooms. The Hall is worth a look, with its remarkable hammerbeam roof, paintings of alumni and benefactors by all the most expensive portrait-painters of the period, and the long tables laid out with silver for meals; there may be teas here some afternoons. The elaborate little **cathedral** is England's smallest, and doubles as the college chapel. It has some excellent stained glass by Burne-Jones, fantastic pendant vaulting in the choir, and some of the original Norman priory work. Entry into the college may be limited on Suns. A hidden treasure unnoticed by most visitors is the college's **picture gallery** (Canterbury Quad), with an important collection of Old Master paintings and drawings, and various temporary exhibitions. Shop; cl 1–2pm, am Sun, and Christmas and Easter wks; guided tours Thurs at 2.15pm; (01865) 276172; *£1.

Christchurch Meadow An unspoilt expanse of green astonishingly close to the busy city streets. You can gaze across the fields of grazing longhorn cattle to the spires in the distance, or walk under overhanging trees along the banks of the river to the boathouses; college eights row from here all year, in just about any weather.

! Covered market (High St) A maze of stalls with something different at every turn; chic boutiques, speciality shops, cafés and old-fashioned butchers and poultry merchants. The Oxford Sandwich Co do excellent take-away sandwiches here, and Ben's Cookies are a favourite with students.

! Curioxity (Gloucester Green) The Old Fire Station complex houses a theatre and this **interactive science gallery**, where visitors can experiment with the exhibits. The staff are helpful, and several sets of parents have told us it kept their children captivated for a full hour. Meals, snacks, shop; open wknds and daily during school hols; (01865) 794494; *£2.10. This area, interestingly rejuvenated with trendy shops, cafés and a bustling Weds market, was once one of the less desirable parts of town. Not far from here among the fashionable shops and boutiques of Little Clarendon St, George & Davies is a good ice-cream parlour.

History of Science Museum (Broad St) Excellent collection of national importance, in one of the city's nicest old buildings (cl am, Sun, Mon, and 1 wk at Christmas and Easter; free). It has been rather scholarly, but they are emerging from an extensive refurbishment programme and will reopen in April.

Iffley Meadows These are

conserved for wildlife, and in late spring are a sea of purple snake's-head fritillaries.

🏛️ **Keble College** (Parks Rd) Brightly Victorian and very red-brick, with perhaps the most famous Pre-Raphaelite painting of all, Holman Hunt's *Light of the World*, in its chapel.

🏛️ ✠ 🐝 **Magdalen College** The most beautiful college, its tower a dramatic sight for visitors entering the city from the S. The quads and cloisters are very pleasant to stroll through, but the chief attraction is the **deer park**, an unexpected haven in the heart of the bustling city. There's a circular path around this meadow (you can't go in) called Addison's Walk; in spring it's a mass of snowdrops and daffodils, then has hundreds of thousands of fritillaries in later spring, and after that the deer. Over a small bridge is the Fellows' Garden with a small ornamental lake – a very peaceful, sheltered spot.

🏛️ **Merton College** The most ancient buildings, with the country's oldest library (tours available).

🖼️ **Museum of Modern Art** (Pembroke St) Modern art museum with the sort of exhibitions and displays not often found in galleries outside London. They open till 9pm on Thurs. Meals, snacks, good bookshop, disabled access; cl Mon, and 2 wks between exhibitions – worth checking; (01865) 722733; *£2.50.

👑 **Museum of Oxford** (St Aldates) Interesting little local history museum, with re-created rooms, maps, and period music. Shop; cl Sun (exc July–Oct) and Mon, Good Fri, 25–26 Dec; (01865) 815559; £2, free for county residents.

🏛️ ✝ **New College** Impressive chapel, atmospheric wisteria-covered cloisters, and remains of the city wall.

🎢 **Oxford Story** (Broad St) Europe's longest dark ride, with cars designed as desks taking you through a cheerful and well researched re-creation of university history, complete with sights, sounds and smells. A useful introduction to the city (especially for families), though no substitute for the real thing. Good shop (you can just visit here using the entrance on Ship St), disabled access; cl 25 Dec; (01865)

790055; £5.50. In summer you can get a ticket which also includes entry to Magdalen and New College (£7.75).

👑 **Oxford University Museum of Natural History** (Parks Rd) Victorian Gothic structure specialising in natural history – outstanding if solidly earnest collection, enlivened by a working beehive in summer; cl am, some days over Easter and Christmas; free.

👑 **Pitt Rivers Museum** (Banbury Rd) This fascinating close-packed ethnological museum off the tourist track hopes to reopen (following refurbishment) by Jan. Shrunken heads, totem poles and fertility rites, along with art and ingenuity from all cultures and periods. The million or so exhibits range from Captain Cook's Pacific Islands collection and 18th-c ship models to severed fingertips and an eskimo coat made from seal intestines. Everything has been displayed in firmly traditional cases or drawers, with neatly handwritten labels, and we trust it'll still keep something of the Victorian atmosphere that's been part of its charm. Shop, limited disabled access; cl am, Sun, a few days over Christmas and Easter; (01865) 270927; free. The adjacent Balfour Building has a gallery of archaeology and a large collection of musical instruments.

🏞️ **Port Meadow** This is the best outlying area for Oxford walks, an expanse of waterside common land with grazing horses and flocks of geese, which extends N from Jericho and can be reached on the far side of the Oxford canal via Walton Well Rd, crossing the Thames and turning right along the W bank. Just beyond the far end of Port Meadow is the ruin of 12th-c Godstow Nunnery, where Fair Rosamund, the mistress of Henry II, is buried; nearby, the riverside medieval Trout pub is touristy but very attractive, and there are often peacocks around here. A second well sited riverside pub, the thatched Perch at Binsey, is another popular walking objective in this direction.

🚣 **Punting and boat trips** Good fun in sunny weather; once you've got the knack it's a very nice way of spending a lazy afternoon. You can hire boats from Magdalen Bridge or Folly Bridge; usually

£8–£10 an hour – you'll have to put down a big deposit. Salters run steamer trips from Folly Bridge to Abingdon.

⌂ **Ruskin walk** From the big garden of the Fishes pub at North Hinksey, a footpath towards Oxford partly follows a causeway built originally by John Ruskin to give students experience of healthy outdoor labour.

🏛 **St Edmund Hall** The only surviving medieval college, complete with Norman crypt.

† ✹ **St Mary's** (High St) Interesting university church with fine views from the tower, and a nice – if busy – café in the crypt; cl am Sun; £1.50.

† ✹ **St Michael at the North Gate** (Cornmarket St) Oxford's oldest building, a Saxon church with displays of silver, clocks and bells; great views from the tower. Cl 1–2pm and during services, 25 Dec and Good Fri; £1.50.

🏛 **Sheldonian Theatre** (Broad St) A grand classical building, with a lovely painted ceiling. In its time it's been used for parliaments, and nowadays university ceremonies are held here; you may see gowned students heading for these on some weekends, though the theatre is closed to the public then.

❀ **University Botanic Garden** (High St) Britain's oldest botanic garden, founded in 1621, with 8,000 species of plant from all over the world. It's a lovely place to sit for a while, or wander through on the way to the river. Disabled access; cl Good Fri and 25 Dec; (01865) 276920; £2. They also administer the University Arboretum at Nuneham Courtenay.

🏛 **University College** Harmonious buildings – and an interesting monument to Shelley despite having thrown him out.

⌂ **University Parks** There are countrified walks almost from Oxford's city centre. The Parks (primarily playing fields) are the closest place for a good stroll – and in summer you can watch first-class cricket matches for free.

⌂ **Waterside walks** The rivers Thames and Cherwell cut strikingly rural corridors through the city, though walks along the Cherwell may be impeded by closed college gates. They are most likely to be open in mid-afternoon.

OXFORD CANAL SP4816

⌂ The towpath is shadowed by the railway, so you can walk by the canal from one village to another, for example from Lower Heyford to Nethercott, and return by train. There's access from the Jolly Boatman pub at Thrupp.

RIDGEWAY SU2885

⌂ ✹ 🏛 Nr the N crest of the downs, the Ridgeway tracks right across from Wilts to Berks. This broad grassy trackway was used as a herding highway for some 2,000 years before the Romans came, and after the break-up of the Roman Empire came back into use for the same purpose, well into medieval times. It's now part of the long-distance path network, and gives good walking with fine views. This particularly atmospheric short stretch nr Compton Beauchamp takes in the ancient sites of Waylands Smithy, the White Horse and Uffington Castle.

ROUSHAM SP4824

🏛 ❀ † **Rousham House** Nicely unspoilt 17th-c house embellished by court artists and architects, and remodelled in the 18th c by William Kent to give the external appearance of a Gothic Tudor mansion. It still has Civil War shooting holes in the door. Excellent 18th-c classically landscaped garden with buildings, cascades, statues and vistas in 30 acres of hanging woods above the River Cherwell, and walled flower and vegetable gardens. No children under 15. Some disabled access to grounds; house open pm Weds, Sun and bank hols Apr–Sept, gardens open daily all year; (01869) 347110; £3 house, £3 garden. There's a 12th-c church. The Red Lion at Steeple Aston is very good for lunch (no children here, either).

RYCOTE SP6604

† **Rycote Chapel** (off A329) Peaceful little 15th-c private chapel, later visited by both Elizabeth I and Charles I. The wedding scene in the TV production of *Jane Eyre* was filmed here. Shop, disabled access; open pm Fri–Sun and bank hols Apr–Sept; £1.60. The picturesque King's Heads at Great Milton has decent food.

SEGSBURY CAMP SU3883

🏛 ✹ Extensive Iron Age hill fort, later

used by the Romans, with good views; reached by the dead-end lane up past the Sparrow in Letcombe Regis.

SHIPTON-UNDER-WYCHWOOD SP2717
★ Old houses around a lovely big sloping green, 2 good inns (one very ancient), and an interesting bookshop.

SHORTHAMPTON SP3220
✝ The **church** here is notable for its fine wall paintings.

SIBFORD GOWER SP3537
◠ There are pleasant walks in the countryside around the quiet village of Sibford Gower, where the thatched Wykham Arms is good for lunch.

SONNING COMMON SU7079
❀ ! **Herb Farm** 💷 (Peppard Rd) Extensive range of herb plants and products, with over 3,200 different species in the display garden. There's an impressive maze (summer only), and agricultural displays in a restored granary. Summer snacks, shop, disabled access; cl Mon; (0118) 972 4220; free, *£1 for maze. The Greyhound (Gallowstree Common Rd) has good food.

SOUTH LEIGH SP3908
✝ **South Leigh church** Notable for its fine wall paintings.

SOUTH NEWINGTON SP4033
✝ Another **church** notable for its fine wall paintings; College Farmhouse next door keeps the key.

STANTON HARCOURT SP4105
🏠 ❀ ★ **Manor House** The medieval Great Kitchen has no chimney – the smoke from ovens and fireplaces collected in the cone of the roof and drifted out through wooden louvres. The gardens too are striking, with neat lawns and topiary, and a wilder wooded area. Teas, shop, disabled access; usually open pm Thurs and Sun fortnightly from mid-Apr–Sept, plus bank hols – best to check first; (01865) 881928; *£5, garden only £3. The village is attractive, and the Harcourt Arms nearby does good meals.

STONOR SU7489
🏠 ❀ 📺 ⚥ ◠ **Stonor House** Even older than the stately Tudor façade suggests, with beautiful furnishings, paintings, sculptures and tapestries, and mementos of Jesuit scholar Edward Campion, one of the many Catholic recusants who found refuge here during the Reformation. The lovely gardens have an unusual exhibition of sculpture from Zimbabwe, and there's a wooded deer park. Snacks, shop; usually open pm Sun and bank hols Apr–Sept, plus pm Weds July–Aug, and pm second May bank hol and Aug bank hol Sat – best to phone; (01491) 638587; £4.50, chapel and garden only £2.50. The smart Stonor Arms is useful for lunch. The deer park is skirted by an attractive right of way from the village, and you can link this with the famous and unusual Maharajah's Well in the charming village of Stoke Row; or for a longer Chilterns walk you can continue E to Turville in Bucks.

SUTTON COURTENAY SU5093
★ An attractive village to stroll through, with things to look out for – like Asquith and Orwell, unlikely bedfellows in their final rest in the graveyard. The George & Dragon has fair-priced food.

SWALCLIFFE SP3737
🏠 ⛪ ★ **Swalcliffe Barn** (B4035) Another well preserved tithe barn, with much of its medieval half-cruck timber roof intact. There's a display of agricultural and trade vehicles. Disabled access; open pm Sun and bank hols Apr–Oct; free. The village is pretty, and the Stag's Head has good food.

SYDENHAM SP7301
★ ✝ A charming village, with a lovely church.

THAME SP7006
★ ✝ Well worth a look for its splendid range of unspoilt architecture. The very wide main street has escaped any significant 20th-c development, and has medieval timber-framed buildings next to stately Georgian houses; the 13th-c **church** is attractive. The 15th-c Birdcage Inn used to be the town lock-up; the Rising Sun has decent food – though the best nearby place for lunch is the Mole & Chicken at Easington out past Long Crendon.

THAMES VALLEY SU7678
◠ Shared with Berks and Bucks, this has a classic, very English sort of beauty, with boating scenes, superb trees and riverside architecture. Riverside walks on the Oxfon side are possible only in places, notably between Henley and

Sonning – for instance to Shiplake Lock from the Plowden Arms at Shiplake; you can also get down to the Thames from the attractive Perch & Pike at South Stoke SU5983.

UFFINGTON SU3089
★ † Charming village, with decent food at the Fox & Hounds. Opposite here is John Betjeman's former home Garrard Farm, which you can rent in summer, (01328) 851155; as warden of **St Mary's Church**, he made sure its oil lamps were preserved.

ö Tom Brown's School Museum (Broad St) Young Mr Brown's schooldays were based on those the author Thomas Hughes passed here; there's an exhibition on his life and work. Shop; open pm wknds May–Oct; 60p.

🏛 ❀ ◠ ! **Uffington Castle** High above the village, this Iron Age fort covered 8 acres but had only one gateway; great views over the vale below. On the hillside a 115-metre (375ft) **white horse** carved into the chalk is now thought to be around 3,000 years old; it's a striking design, very Celtic. If you stand in the centre of the eye and turn around 3 times with your eyes closed, any reasonable wish will be granted. This is one good setting-off point for the Ridgeway. The flat-topped little hill below is said to be where George killed the dragon. A bit over a mile E, off the B4507, the turning off up towards the downs opposite the Kingston Lisle road almost immediately passes a cottage on the left which has outside a huge pitted flint rock, locally known as the blowing stone: if you blow in the right hole and in the right way you can produce a splendid deep blast of sound.

UPPER THAMES SP4304
◠ W of Oxford, the Thames flows through low-lying country, giving the sort of walk you enjoy more for the people you're with than the scenery itself. The Trout pub on the Bampton–Buckland road at Tadpole Bridge SP3300 is a useful focus for pleasant if undramatic riverside strolls, as are the Ferryman pub off the B4449 at Bablock Hythe SP4304, the Talbot on the B4044 nr the Swinford toll bridge SP4408, and the Maybush pub on the A415 at Newbridge SP4001. The Rose Revived there is worth knowing for its big Thames-side lawn.

WALLINGFORD SU6089
ö 🏛 ♪ ◠ **Wallingford Museum** (High St) Very good sight-and-sound history of the area, complete with reconstructed Victorian street. Shop; cl am (exc Sat), all Mon (exc bank hols), winter Suns, and all Dec–Feb; (01491) 835065; £2. There are the ruins of a 13th-c **castle** on a hill, and plenty of places to hire boats or fish around here.

WANTAGE SU3987
† ❀ Historic town where King Alfred was reputedly born; recently much expanded, though there's an attractive quiet corner by the 13th/15th-c **church** with its raised graveyard, and in Newbury St 17th-c almshouses have a courtyard cobbled with bones. The downland roads S into Berks have fine views.

ö Vale and Downland Museum Centre (Church St) Well displayed local history and geology in a recently restored gallery; the tourist information centre is also situated here. Snacks, shop, limited disabled access; cl Mon, Good Fri, a few days at Christmas; £1.50.

🗙 **Venn Mill** (A338 N) Still the area's regularly used working corn mill; open second Sun in month Apr–Oct; *£1.

WARMINGTON SP4047
❀ **National Herb Centre** (Banbury Rd) Wide range of herbs in display gardens set in an attractive valley; also walks, nature trails and a small exhibition on local wildlife and the history of herbs. Bistro, herb and plant sales, disabled access; (01295) 690999; free (maybe small charge for exhibition).

WATLINGTON WOODS SU7093
◑ ❀ A mass of bluebells in spring, these give great views from the steep edge of the Chiltern Hills.

WAYLANDS SMITHY SU2885
🏛 Midway along the Ridgeway between the Uffington White Horse and the B4000 above Ashbury (where the Rose & Crown is ideally placed for walkers), this was even in Saxon times reputed to be the forge of a magic blacksmith, who would invisibly shoe your horse overnight if you left it there with a silver

coin – and exact horrid penalties if you tried to slip by without paying. It's an impressive place, alone on the downs, an excavated **Neolithic burial chamber** rather over 5,000 years old, made with massive sarsen stones each weighing several tons; free.

WHEATLEY SP5805

⚒ 🎋 A place of bizarre-shaped buildings: the unusual octagonal **windmill** is open by appointment (maybe at other times, (01865) 874610; free), while the village lock-up is shaped like a pyramid. Just S at Garsington Jennings Farm Shop has a wide range of produce as well as craft workshops and a working blacksmith's forge. Garsington has decidely smart open-air operas (and good food at the Three Horseshoes).

WHITCHURCH SU6377

★ ⌂ An attractive little village, with nice walks nearby; the Greyhound does good-value food.

🍇 **Boze Down Vineyard** (B471 N) Free tastings pm wknds, and guided tours by appointment, cl Jan, Feb; (0118) 984 4031. Path Hill Farm on Goring Heath nearby has a shop selling organic products.

WIDFORD SP2712

† **Widford church & lost village** (just outside Burford) The church is very simple, but notable for 3 things – its medieval wall paintings, the remains of a Roman pavement at the west end of the chancel, and its surroundings, a former village that save one solitary house has now virtually disappeared.

WITNEY SP3609

★ 🏚 † Saxon kings used to hold their meetings, or witans, here – hence the name. It was a prosperous town in the Middle Ages, and is well known for its blankets, made here ever since. Quiet and relaxed, with picturesque stone buildings, the market square still with its ancient butter cross and 17th-c clock, and quite a few interesting old buildings such as the 13th-c church and 18th-c blanket hall. Just off Church Green you can see the excavated foundations of a 12th-c palace of the Bishops of Winchester (pm wknds only, free), and the nearby Angel has good-value food.

🍼🏚🐄🎋 **Cogges Farm Museum** (Church Lane) Entertaining and informative Victorian working farm museum, with period farmhouse, kitchens and dairy, walled gardens, and local breeds of farm animals. Daily feeding, agricultural and craft demonstrations. Snacks, shop, mostly disabled access; cl am wknds, Mon(exc bank hols) and Nov–Mar (exc various events near Christmas); (01993) 772602; £3.50.

WOODSTOCK SP4416

★ † Civilised and prosperous small town, with good antique shops and fine stone buildings. The Feathers Hotel, Bear Hotel and homelier Queen's Own (food all day wknds) are all good. The graveyard of nearby **Bladon church**, where Churchill is buried, has views over Blenheim Park.

🏚 🌺 🦋 🚂 ♨ ⌂ **Blenheim Palace** Undoubtedly one of England's most impressive stately homes: given to the Duke of Marlborough by Queen Anne as a reward for his military achievements, the house itself covers 14 acres, and the grounds stretch for well over 2,000. Churchill was born here and there's a straightforward exhibition on his life. Highlights within the palace include the sumptuous State Rooms and 56-metre (183ft) Long Library, along with plenty of opulent furnishings and sculpture; tours leave every 5–10 minutes. The very extensive grounds, landscaped by Capability Brown, are full of interesting paths and tracks; you can picnic. Also butterfly house, miniature railway and play areas with swings, ropes and slides. An extra £1 adds a hedge maze, putting green, and model village based on Woodstock and surroundings. You can hire **rowing boats** (£1 per person per half hour) or arrange coarse fishing on the lake, and at weekends they have a bouncy castle. There's enough space to absorb the crowds (Sun is busiest, and Weds is popular with overseas students); the house usually gets quieter after about 3pm. You can avoid having to wait for tickets by arriving early; though most parts are closed till 10.30am, the gates and ticket office open at 9am. Meals and snacks (3 restaurants), several shops and a plant centre, some disabled access; house cl Nov–mid-Mar, grounds open all year; (01993) 811325; £8.50,

£5 per car grounds only. There is also a public right of way through the huge estate, with pleasant walks in, for example from the attractive village of Combe.

☺ **Oxfordshire County Museum** (Fletcher's House) Elegant town house with pleasant gardens and good displays, although much will be closed for refurbishment until this summer. Snacks, shop, disabled access; cl am Sun, Mon; (01993) 811456; £1.

WOOLSTONE SU2987
★ An attractive village in the Vale of the White Horse; Thomas Hughes reputedly wrote *Tom Brown's Schooldays* in the bar here.

WYTHAM SP4708
★ Charming unspoilt village, all houses owned and preserved by Oxford University; the White Hart here is a good dining pub.

★ **Other charming small towns and villages**, all with decent pubs, include Adderbury SP4635, Bampton SP3103, Blewbury SU5385, Bloxham SP4235, Brightwell Baldwin SU6595, Buckland SU3497, Chadlington SP3222, Church Enstone SP3724, Clifton Hampden SU5495, Crawley SP3412, Cuddesdon SP5903, Cumnor SP4603, Denchworth SU3791, Duns Tew SP4528, East Hendred SU4588 (interesting church), Epwell SP3540, Faringdon SP2895, Goring SU6080, Hook Norton SP3533, Kingston Lisle SU3287, Lewknor SU7198, Marsh Baldon SU5699, Milton-under-Wychwood SP2618, Shenington SP3742, Shilton SP2608, Souldern SP5131, Sparsholt SU3487, Stratton Audley SP6026, Upper Wardington SP4945, Wootton SP4320 and Wroxton SP4142.

Where to eat

ARDINGTON SU4388 **Boars Head** *(01235) 833254* Civilised and upmarket dining pub with 3 simply furnished but smart rooms, low beams, bare boards, fresh flowers, and lots of pictures, particularly good wines, well kept real ales, imaginative, ambitious food under the new chef, and no smoking restaurant; good nearby walks; no food pm Sun, cl Mon; disabled access. **£26|£8.**

BARNARD GATE SP4010 **Boot** *(01865) 881231* Friendly dining pub with an interesting collection of celebrities' boots, good, interesting food under the new licensee, a partly no smoking restaurant, prompt and friendly service, decent wine, well kept beers, and a big log fire. **£24|£10.**

BUCKLAND SU3498 **Lamb** *Lamb Lane (01367) 870484* Extended 18th-c stone dining pub in a tiny village, with very popular and imaginative food changing seasonally, good-value house wines from a strongly French wine list, real ales, and smart, helpful service; comfortable bdrms; good walks nearby. **£29.50|£5.25.**

BURFORD SP2512 **Mermaid** *High St (01993) 822193* Busy pub with handsome Tudor frontage, an attractive, long narrow bar with flagstones, stonework and some panelling, pretty dried flowers, a no smoking dining conservatory and upstairs restaurant, good food inc cream teas usefully served all day, well kept real ales, and courteous, efficient staff; no children in the bars. **£23|£5.95.**

CHALGROVE SU6396 **Red Lion** *(01865) 890625* Delightful pub owned by the local church since the 17th c, with a traditional atmosphere, stylish simple furnishings, a log fire and old woodburner, carefully collected prints and period cartoons, well kept real ales, decent wines, imaginative very well presented food, a helpful landlord, and no smoking back dining room; no food pm Sun; cl pm 25 Dec; disabled access. **£20|£12.50** 2-course set meal.

CHINNOR SU7598 **Sir Charles Napier** *Spriggs Alley (up on the escarpment) (01494) 483011* Decidedly civilised place with excellent food in the stylish back restaurant, champagne on draught, a huge wine list, and freshly squeezed juice; smartly relaxed little bar with homely furnishings, a log fire, delicious food from a short bar menu, and real ales; croquet lawn; cl pm Sun, Mon; children over 7; partial disabled access. **£36.50|£9.50.**

CHIPPING NORTON SP3127 **Chavignol** *7 Horsefair (01608) 644490* Pretty Cotswold stone cottage with open fires, beams, and Mediterranean colours, really excellent, beautifully presented meals, a careful wine list with helpful notes, and a friendly, relaxed atmosphere; cl Sun, Mon, 3 wks Jan. **£48**.

CUMNOR SP4604 **Bear & Ragged Staff** *(01865)* 862329 Refurbished under the new licensees, this smart old pub has roaring log fires in the comfortably rambling, softly lit bar, a civilised atmosphere, well presented food, well kept real ales, and several wines by the glass; cl Christmas and New Year; disabled access. **£25|£10**.

EAST HENDRED SU4688 **Wheatsheaf** *(01235)* 833229 Attractive black and white timbered 16th-c village pub with a good mix of locals and visitors, high-backed settles, some panelling and an inglenook fireplace, well liked often interesting food, well kept real ales, and decent wines. **£17|£6.50**.

HOOK NORTON SP3533 **Sun** *High St (01608)* 737570 In a pretty village and facing the church, this bustling, friendly pub has a flagstoned front bar with a huge log fire and hop-strung beams, a snug carpeted room with comfortable banquettes, an attractive partly no smoking green-walled restaurant, a wide choice of imaginative, popular food (inc a good range of excellent triple-decker sandwiches), real ales, good-value wines, and efficient service; bdrms; good disabled facilities. **£19.95|£6.95**.

KINGSTON LISLE SU3287 **Blowing Stone** *(01367)* 820288 Comfortable brick-built dining pub under new licensees, with a brightly modernised bar, simple furnishings, fresh flowers and newspapers, a comfortable lounge, restaurant and conservatory, imaginative carefully prepared food, real ales and a fine choice of wines. **£22|£8.50**.

MAIDENSGROVE SU7288 **Five Horseshoes** *(01491)* 641282 High up in the Chilterns beechwoods, this little 17th-c brick house has fine views from several tables in the newly extended restaurant, and from the sheltered back garden; rambling bar with a log fire and lots of banknotes from around the world, good, imaginative food, a decent wine list, well kept real ales, and separate walkers' bar; cl 25 Dec; children must be well behaved; partial disabled access. **£27.45|£5.95**.

OXFORD SP5106 **Café Moma** *Museum of Modern Art, Pembroke St (01865)* 722733 Clean, light and very popular self-service café in the basement, simple modern furnishings, exhibitions on walls, largely vegetarian food from a blackboard, excellent cakes, and efficient, friendly service; open till 5pm (till 9pm Thurs only); cl Mon, bank hols; disabled access. **£10.30|£4.95**.

OXFORD SP5107 **Gees** *61a Banbury Rd (01865)* 553540 Relaxed, airy atmosphere, fresh herbs and spices to enliven interesting vegetarian pastas, wild mushrooms and so forth as well as good meat and fish dishes, decent, unusual wines; in genuine old conservatory; cl 25–26 Dec. **£25.50|£9.75** 3-course lunch.

OXFORD SP5007 **Petit Blanc** *71–72 Walton St (01865)* 510999 Very popular, stylish and airy 2-room brasserie open all day for breakfast, lunch, afternoon tea and dinner; from the smarter room you can see into the kitchen and watch the preparation of the extremely good Mediterranean food; friendly service and helpful notes against each wine listed; children very welcome; cl 25 Dec; disabled access. **£30|£7.75**.

As well as these, the city is full of useful stop-offs. The King's Arms (Holywell St) and venerable Turf Tavern (Bath Pl, between Holywell St and New College Lane) are the most interesting pubs, and other decent ones include the ancient Bear (Alfred St), the unspoilt old Rose & Crown (North Parade) and the handily central White Horse (Broad St). The Victoria Arms at Old Marston, with a big garden on the Cherwell, is a popular punters' destination. The Pizza Express (Golden Cross) is in a surprisingly interesting medieval building.

SOUTH STOKE SU5983 **Perch & Pike** *(01491)* 872415 Attractive little brick and flint pub, under new licensees this year, with a relaxed atmosphere, comfortable seats, open fires, a nice assortment of tables, a good wine list, real ales, and imaginative, modern cooking; they plan to open bdrms and a restaurant; cl 25 Dec. **£26|£6.25**.

STOKE ROW SU6884 **Crooked Billet** *(01491)* 681048 Open-plan beamed dining pub with a relaxed, homely atmosphere (rather like a French country restaurant), log fires, a wide choice of good, interesting food inc vegetarian menu, decent wines and real ales, and a big garden by Chilterns beechwoods. **£19.95|£5.95**.

UFFINGTON SU3087 **Britchcombe Farm** *(01367) 820667* Working farm in a lovely spot below White Horse Hill; afternoon cream teas on Sat, Sun and bank hol Mon with home-made scones, cakes and so forth; very friendly service, a log fire in winter, tables outside among the geese and sheep in summer; some fruit and vegetables, home-made mohair knitwear and crafts, caravan for hire, and certified camping/caravan site; disabled access. **£2.80**.

WALLINGFORD SU6089 **Annie's Tearooms** *79 High St (01491) 836308* Prettily decorated and friendly no smoking 17th-c house serving morning coffee, lunches with a home-made daily dish, and afternoon tea inc a fine choice of home-made cakes and quite a few teas; cl Weds, Sun (Oct–June); disabled access. **£3.90**.

WATLINGTON SU6894 **Chequers** *Love Lane (01491) 612874* Cheerful, cosy old pub with low beams, candlelight, nice old chairs and antique tables, conservatory, wide choice of good popular food, real ales, and a pretty garden; no food pm Sun, cl 26 Dec; no children. **£20|£6**.

WESTCOTT BARTON SP4325 **Fox** *(01869) 340338* Lovely stone-built village pub with enjoyable authentic Italian food cooked by the Italian landlord and his brother, a relaxed little bar with hops on low beams, open fires, high-backed settles and pews on the flagstones, an elegant restaurant, well kept ales, and espresso and cappuccino coffee; pleasant garden with wooden play fort. **£18.50|£5.25**.

WOOTTON SP4319 **King's Head** *(01993) 811340* Pretty 17th-c Cotswold stone pub with civilised and beamed no smoking lounge, a nice mix of furniture, an open log fire, very good, imaginative food inc lovely puddings, well kept real ales, and decent wines; children over 12. **£26 dinner, £16.80 lunch|£7.95**.

Special thanks to Mrs McFadyen, M G Hart, Mrs M Skudder.

Oxfordshire Calendar

Some of these dates were provisional as we went to press. Please check information with the telephone numbers provided.

JANUARY

1 **Chinnor** Mince Pie Specials on the Chinnor and Princes Risborough Railway from Chinnor Station – *till 3 January* (0181) 386 2783; **Didcot** New Year Steamings at Didcot Railway Centre – *till 3 January* (01235) 817200

30 **Oxford** Chinese New Year Celebrations at the Town Hall (01865) 204188

MARCH

1 **Oxford** Torpids: college rowing races – *till 3 March* (01865) 726871

3 **Didcot** Thomas the Tank Engine at the Railway Centre – *till 5 March* (01235) 817200

5 **Woodstock** Winston Churchill Memorial Concert at Blenheim Palace (01993) 811325

Oxfordshire Calendar (cont.)

APRIL

24 **Steeple Aston** Spring Flower Show (01869) 340512
29 **Woodstock** Craft Fair at Blenheim Palace – *till 1 May* (01283) 820548

MAY

1 **Oxford** May Morning: Magdalen College choir sings from Magdalen Tower, Morris dancing in Radcliffe Sq and Broad St (01865) 726871
6 **Wallingford** Regatta (01491) 836517
22 **Henley-on-Thames** Artspace 2000 – *till 11 June* (01491) 577786
27 **Didcot** Didcot 2000: Steam Event to celebrate the millennium with visiting steam locomotives – *till 4 June* (01235) 817200

JUNE

1 **Oxford** Beating the Bounds: starts at the Church of St Michael at the North Gate (01865) 726871
3 **Woodstock** Fireworks Concert at Blenheim Palace (01993) 811325
17 **Abingdon** Election of the Mayor of Ock Street (since fight over an ox in 1700), new mayor is chaired down Ock St, Morris dancing into evening (01235) 522711; **Wallingford** Carnival (01491) 836594; **Woodstock** Carnival at Quarry Park (01993) 811495
18 **Banbury** Banbury and District Show (01295) 252535
24 **Banbury** Steam and Vintage Vehicle Rally – *till 26 June* (01295) 730272
25 **Thame** Civil War Re-enactment (01865) 810191
28 **Henley-on-Thames** Royal Regatta – *till 2 July* (01491) 572153

JULY

1 **Whitchurch** Weekend of Dance inc Morris Men – *till 2 July* (01865) 766191
2 **Hook Norton** Rural Fair (01608) 737617
15 **Hook Norton** Beer Festival at the Pear Tree Inn (01608) 737482
17 **River Thames** Swan Upping on the river between Sunbury and Abingdon: colourful traditional ceremony – *till 21 July* (01628) 523030
20 **Waterperry** Arts and Crafts in Action at Waterperry Gardens: over 300 craftsmen and artists from around the world – *till 23 July* (0171) 381 3192

AUGUST

26 **Woodstock** Craft Fair at Blenheim Palace – *till 28 August* (01993) 811325
28 **Steeple Aston** Summer Flower Show (01869) 340512; **Uffington** White Horse Show (01367) 820393

SEPTEMBER

7 **Woodstock** Blenheim International Horse Trials at Blenheim Palace – *till 10 September* (01993) 813335
21 **Thame** Agricultural Show at the Showground (01844) 212737

Oxfordshire Calendar (cont.)

OCTOBER

6 Didcot Thomas the Tank Engine at the Railway Centre – *till 8 October* (01235) 817200

DECEMBER

15 Didcot Thomas and Santa Steamings at the Railway Centre – *till 17 December* (01235) 817200

23 Didcot Thomas and Santa Steamings at the Railway Centre – *till 24 December* (01235) 817200

We welcome reports from readers

This *Guide* depends on readers' reports. Do help us if you can – in return, we offer a discount on the next edition to people who've helped us with reports for it. Tell us what you think about places already in it, and anything extra you think we should say about them. And send us your ideas for inclusion in the next edition: places to visit, eat at or stay in, attractive drives or walks, maybe even unusual interesting shops you know of. Use the card in the middle, the report forms at the end, or just write – no stamp needed: *The Good Britain Guide*, FREEPOST TN1569, Wadhurst, E Sussex TN5 7BR.

SHROPSHIRE

Largely unspoilt countryside, yet with plenty of interesting and unusual outings.

Shropshire, particularly in its southern parts, has very attractive unspoilt countryside, with charming places to stay in. Drives and walks pass attractive buildings in stone or black and white timbering, and a set of uncommonly distinctive hills give sleepy views. Yet this county saw the birth of modern industry: the Ironbridge museums are among Britain's most interesting days out, with enough variety to hold anyone's attention – and plenty to entertain children at lively open-air Blists Hill.

Shrewsbury, too, has a lot to see (with free museums), and elsewhere there's a good mix of outings, from the peace of Boscobel House, Stokesay Castle, Much Wenlock Priory, Benthall Hall at Broseley and unusual Hawkstone Park, to the lively Severn Valley steam railway out of Bridgnorth, and Cosford Royal Air Force Museum. Ludlow Castle has an invigorating mix of ancient fortress with modern holograms. Among new places here this year, the Shopshire Hills Discovery Centre near Craven Arms is particularly interesting. There are quite a few appealing open farms, especially Rays Farm at Billingsley.

Where to stay

ALL STRETTON SO4595 **Jinlye** *Castle Hill, All Stretton, Church Stretton SY6 6JP (01694) 723243* **£60,** plus special breaks; 8 spacious comfortable rms with lovely views. Charming 16th-c house in large grounds surrounded by National Trust land, with log fires in the comfortable lounges (one has an inglenook fireplace, lots of heavy beams, and a mix of interesting furniture), good home cooking in the big no smoking dining room, enjoyable breakfasts, and friendly owners; self-catering also; children over 12; disabled access.

BISHOP'S CASTLE SO3288 **Castle** *Market Sq, Bishop's Castle SY9 5BN (01588) 638403* ***£60;*** 6 spacious rms with fine views, some with own bathrm. Standing on the site of the old castle keep, this enjoyable 18th-c hotel has good fires, a relaxed and friendly atmosphere, lovely home-made food, well kept beers, and welcoming owners.

BOURTON SO5996 **Bourton Manor** *Bourton, Much Wenlock TF13 6QE (01746) 785531* ***£130,*** plus special breaks; 8 rms. In landscaped grounds surrounded by pretty countryside, this extended 16th-c manor house has comfortably old-fashioned rooms with lots of panelling, a convivial bar, open fires, very good service from friendly staff, and most enjoyable food; partial disabled access.

CLUN SO2881 **New House Farm** *Clun, Craven Arms SY7 8NJ (01588) 638314* **£46;** 2 rms. Remote 18th-c farmhouse nr the Welsh border with plenty of surrounding hillside walks, homely rooms with copper pans and decorative plates on the walls, enjoyable home-cooked evening meals, packed lunches, good breakfasts, plenty of books, a country garden, and helpful, friendly owner; cl end Oct–Easter; children over 5.

CRESSAGE SJ5604 **Cholmondeley Riverside** *Cound, Cressage, Shrewsbury SY5 6AF (01952) 510900* **£65;** 6 rms. Neatly converted 17th-c inn overlooking an exceptionally pretty stretch of the River Severn, with church pews, cushioned settles and oak tables in the civilised, roomy bar, wicker chairs in the conservatory with more out on the terrace, good imaginative food, well kept beers, a fine choice of wines, and a relaxed, friendly atmosphere; coarse fishing.

DIDDLEBURY SO5085 **Delbury Hall** *Diddlebury, Craven Arms SY7 9DH (01584) 841267* **£90**; 3 rms. Beautiful stately Georgian house in 80 acres of landscaped parkland with ornamental duck on the lake, trout fishing, flower-filled gardens, and a hard tennis court; large hall with fine oak staircase, spacious drawing room, sitting room and snooker room, enjoyable food using their own vegetables, milk, eggs, hand-churned Jersey butter, a good wine list, and hearty breakfasts; cl Christmas.

GRETTON SO5195 **Court Farm** *Gretton, Cardington, Church Stretton SY6 7HU (01694) 771219* ***£48**; 3 rms. Large, comfortable no smoking stone-built farmhouse on 325-acre mixed farm with a warm welcome, big woodburner in the inglenook fireplace and good food using home-grown and local produce; self-catering also in adjacent stables; cl Nov–Feb; no children or pets.

HANWOOD SJ4409 **White House** *Hanwood, Shrewsbury SY5 8LP (01743) 860414* ***£60**, plus special breaks; 6 rms, 3 with own bthrm. Charming 16th-c black and white half-timbered house with 2 sitting rooms, breakfasts using their own eggs, enjoyable evening meals with some home-grown produce (must pre-book), and 2 acres of garden; children over 12.

HOPESAY SO3883 **Old Rectory** *Hopesay, Craven Arms SY7 8HD (01588) 660245* ***£70**; 3 comfortable rms, one with own sitting room. 17th-c rectory with lovely 2-acre garden overlooking Hopesay Hill (NT), comfortable drawing room with a log fire and a baby grand piano, attractive dining room with excellent home cooking, and hearty breakfasts with home-baked bread; no smoking; super walks from the house; cl Christmas; children over 12.

HOPTON WAFERS SO6376 **Crown** *Hopton Wafers, Kidderminster, Worcs DY14 0NB (01299) 270372* **£75**, plus special breaks; 7 rms. Attractive creeper-covered stone inn in pleasant countryside, with an interestingly furnished bar, inglenook fireplace, enjoyable food, decent house wines, beers and malt whiskies, friendly efficient service, and a streamside garden.

KNOCKIN SJ3321 **Top Farmhouse** *Knockin, Oswestry SY10 8HN (01691) 682582* **£42**; 3 pretty rms. Most attractive Grade I listed black and white timbered house dating back to the 16th c, with friendly owners, lots of timbers and beams, a log fire in the restful, comfortable drawing room, good breakfasts in the large dining room, and an appealing garden; snooker; children over 12.

LONGVILLE SO5393 **Longville Arms** *Longville, Much Wenlock TF13 6DT (01694) 771206* ***£44**, plus special breaks; 5 comfortable rms in converted stables with fresh flowers, home-made biscuits, and showers. Warmly friendly inn with 2 spacious bars, well kept real ales, a wide range of enjoyable food, superb breakfasts, and a neat terraced side garden; cl 25 Dec; partial disabled access.

LUDLOW SO5174 **Feathers** *Bull Ring, Ludlow SY8 1AA (01584) 875261* **£108.50**, plus special breaks; 40 comfortable rms. Striking hotel with exquisitely proportioned and intricately carved timbered frontage, Jacobean panelling and carving, period furnishings, artistically presented restaurant dishes, decent food in the bar, and efficient, pleasant service; partial disabled access.

LUDLOW SO5174 **Unicorn** *Lower Corve St, Ludlow SY8 1DU (01584) 873555* **£50**; 5 beamed and timbered, recently refurbished rms. Enjoyable 17th-c inn with a warmly atmospheric beamed and partly panelled bar, a huge log fire in the big stone fireplace, a good mix of locals and visitors, a timbered, candlelit no smoking restaurant, tasty home-made food, real ales, cheerful service, and a pretty little terrace by the modest River Corve.

LUDLOW SO5174 **Wheatsheaf** *Lower Broad St, Ludlow SY8 1PQ (01584) 872980* ***£42.50**, plus special breaks; 5 comfortable oak-beamed rms with showers. Attractively furnished small 17th-c pub spectacularly built into the medieval town gate; traditional atmosphere, 2 log fires, lots of hops, timbers, and exposed stone walls, a wide range of good food in the bar and no smoking restaurant (super steaks), real ales and farm ciders, and friendly owners.

MUCH WENLOCK SO6299 **Talbot** *High St, Much Wenlock TF13 6AA (01952)*

727077 **£90,** plus special breaks; 6 rms. Dating from 1360 and once part of Wenlock Abbey, this converted 18th-c malthouse is very civilised, with pretty flowers, log fires, prints, pleasant staff, good food in the no smoking restaurant and bar, and well kept real ales.

NORTON SJ7200 **Hundred House** *Bridgnorth Rd, Norton, Shifnal TF11 9EE (01952) 730353* **£100,** plus special breaks; 10 cottagey rms (some with a swing and lavender-scented sheets). Carefully refurbished mainly Georgian inn with quite a sophisticated feel, neatly kept bar with old quarry-tiled floors, beamed ceilings and oak panelling, handsome fireplaces, elaborate evening meals using inn's own herbs, friendly service, good bar food, excellent breakfast and afternoon tea; delightful garden, no dogs.

RHYDYCROESAU SJ2430 **Pen-y-Dyffryn** *Rhydycroesau, Oswestry SY10 7JD (01691) 653700* ***£74,** plus special breaks; 10 rms. Handsome Georgian stone-built rectory in 5 acres with lovely views of the Welsh hills, log fires in both comfortable lounges, good food using the best local ingredients, trout fishing, hill-walking and riding (shooting can be arranged), and a relaxed, friendly atmosphere; well behaved dogs welcome; cl 20 Dec–20 Jan; partial disabled access.

SHREWSBURY SJ4917 **Albright Hussey** *(off A528 N) Ellesmere Rd, Broad Oak, Shrewsbury SY4 3AF (01939) 290571* **£95,** plus special breaks; 14 lovely rms. Fine moated medieval manor house, partly timber-framed and partly stone and brick, in 4-acre garden, with particularly good food in the timbered and panelled restaurant, and excellent service; children over 3; disabled access.

SHREWSBURY SJ4417 **Fitz Manor** *(off B5067 NW) Bowmere Heath, Shrewsbury SY4 3AS (01743) 850295* **£50;** 3 rms, shared bthrm. Lovely black and white timbered 15th-c manor house with oak panelling and a log fire in the comfortable sitting room, a big dining room with antiques, paintings and parquet flooring, good enjoyable evening meals, big breakfasts, friendly owners, and outdoor heated swimming pool.

STREFFORD SO4485 **Strefford Hall Farm** *Strefford, Craven Arms SY7 8DE (01588) 672383* ***£42;** 3 rms. No smoking Victorian stone-built farmhouse surrounded by 360 acres of working farm, with a woodburner in the sitting room, good breakfasts (evening meals by arrangement), and lots of walks; cl Christmas–New Year; disabled access.

WENLOCK EDGE SO5796 **Wenlock Edge Inn** *Hilltop, Wenlock Edge, Much Wenlock TF13 6DJ (01746) 785678* ***£70,** plus special breaks; 3 rms, showers only (served by 190ft well). Popular and cheerfully welcoming family-run inn by the Ippikins Rock viewpoint, with lots of walks through NT land that runs along the Edge, chatty and relaxed atmosphere, good fresh home-made bar food inc old-fashioned puddings, fine breakfasts, and wide range of drinks; second Mon evening of month is story-telling night; cl 24–26 Dec; children over 8; disabled access.

WESTON SJ5729 **Citadel** *Weston, Shrewsbury SY4 5JY (01630) 685204* **£80;** 3 rms in 2 turrets. Fine castellated house overlooking Hawkstone Park, with country-house atmosphere, a baby grand piano and unusual strapwork ceiling in the elegant sitting room, full-sized table in the snooker room, enjoyable food (bring your own wine) in the no smoking dining room, and welcoming owners; cl Nov–Mar; no children.

WORFIELD SO7595 **Old Vicarage** *Worfield, Bridgnorth WV15 5JZ (01746) 716497* ***£107.50,** plus special breaks; 14 pretty rms. Restful and carefully restored Edwardian rectory in 2 acres, with 2 airy conservatory-style lounges, very good interesting food in the no smoking restaurant, a fine wine list, and warmly friendly helpful service; good disabled access.

WROCKWARDINE SJ6212 **Church Farm** *Wrockwardine, Telford TF6 5DG (01952) 244917* ***£50;** 6 individual well equipped rms, most with own bthrm. Friendly Georgian farmhouse on a very ancient site overlooking the attractive garden and church, with a relaxed atmosphere, particularly good caring service, beams and log fire in the lounge, and good daily changing food in the traditionally furnished dining room; cl Christmas; children over 10.

To see and do

SHROPSHIRE Family Attraction of the Year

🐂 🐑 ▦ 🦅 **BILLINGSLEY** SO7183 **Rays Farm Country Matters** A lovely new feature at this traditional farm is a short woodland walk through half a mile or so of ancient trees and fast-flowing streams. Along the way are various works by a North Wales sculptor, representing the Spirit of the Woods and the creatures you'll find there – both real and imagined. Some are spookily crafted into dead or damaged trees and stumps. With picnic sites and seats along the trail, it's a nice addition to the more established attractions at the farm, all of which share the same appealing backdrop of truly unspoilt countryside. The mix of animals is delightfully diverse – as well as sheep, horses and cattle you'll meet the odd llama, lots of rabbits and pigs, and plenty of red and fallow deer (you may meet wild deer while exploring the woods, along with other local residents like buzzards and kingfishers). They're particularly strong on goats and owls (over 40 species of each), and hope to introduce otters soon. There are quite a few undercover areas and barns, but like most farms you'll get more out of a visit when it's dry. It's rather relaxed and low-key compared to many animal attractions, so you won't find elaborate play areas or anything like that – though there's plenty of open space for letting off steam. They have atmospheric activities in the run-up to Christmas; Father Christmas is usually here then. For longer walks, you can try a section of bridleway starting at the farm, meandering eventually into Wales. Snacks, shop (some well priced things for children to buy), disabled access; cl Jan and Feb, exc school hols and some wknds; (01299) 841255; £3.50 (£2.25 children over 2).

ACTON BURNELL SJ5301

🏛 **Acton Burnell Castle** Ruined red sandstone manor house built in the 13th c, but almost abandoned by 1420; disabled access; free. The Plume of Feathers at Harley is fairly handy for lunch.

ACTON SCOTT SO4589

🐂 🐾 **Acton Scott Historic Working Farm** (off A49) Vivid introduction to traditional rural life, with plenty of rare breeds, and crops cultivated using old rotation methods; all the work is done by hand or horse power, with period farm machinery. Lots of craft demonstrations, and daily butter-making. Unusually, this is a farm aimed just as much at adults (maybe more) as at children. Meals, snacks, shop, disabled access; cl Mon (exc bank hols), and Nov–Mar; (01694) 781306; £3.50. The handiest place for lunch is Little Stretton – the Green Dragon or the Ragleth.

ASTLEY ABBOTS SO7096

🐝 **Astley Abbots Lavender Farm** ▦ (off B4373 N of Bridgnorth) You can pick your own lavender at this friendly farm; also 5 acres of attractive gardens, and an intriguing look (through an infra-red viewing screen) at bumble-bees, busy at work. They were building a tearoom as we went to press; open mid-July–mid-Aug; farm free, gardens £1.50. Mrs Hodgson has kindly offered our readers a small discount on lavender purchases.

ATCHAM SJ5409

🏠 ▦ 🐝 **Attingham Park** Splendidly grand late 18th-c house on the site of an old Roman town, with an imposing 3-storey colonnaded portico. The extensive picture gallery was designed by Nash, who made imaginative use of early curved cast iron and glass for the ceiling; attractive mature gardens and deer park outside. Snacks, shop, disabled access by prior arrangement; grounds open daily, house open pm and bank hol Mon Apr–Oct, cl Weds, Thurs; (01743) 708123; house and grounds £4, £1.50 grounds only; NT. The Cholmondeley Riverside towards Cressage has good food.

🐂 **Home Farm** ▦ Rare breeds and traditional farm machinery; you can watch the milking of the Jersey cows (3.30pm), and play with the pets. Farmhouse teas, shop, limited disabled access; cl am, all day Thurs and Fri (exc school hols), and Oct–Easter; (01743) 709243; £2.50.

BILLINGSLEY SO7183

🐖 🐄 🖼 🐐 **Rays Farm Country Matters** *See separate family panel on p.535.*

BISHOP'S CASTLE SO3288

🏰 🐄 Historic little market town with some fine Elizabethan and Georgian buildings, railway and local history museums, good shops, and the curious House on Crutches. It's handy for exploring Offa's Dyke.

🍺 **Hobbs History of Beer & Brewing** The Three Tuns has a unique Victorian tower brewhouse, still in use – you can usually arrange a tour, (01588) 638797.

BOSCOBEL SJ8308

🏰 🏵 **Boscobel House** Interesting old house renowned for sheltering Charles II after the Battle of Worcester, with an unusually well preserved 17th-c garden and cobbled courtyard, and 19th-c décor giving a romanticised view of the king's drama. Good guided tour. Meals, snacks, shop, disabled access to gardens only; cl winter Mon and Tues, 24–26 Dec, all Jan; (01902) 850244; £4. The **Royal oak** here is said by some to have been the hiding place of the king, by others to be a descendant, and by still others to be just a fine old tree. The Bell in Tong is good for lunch, and Weston Park at Weston under Lizard (Staffs) is nearby.

🏛 **White Ladies Priory** (just SW of Boscobel) The ruins of an Augustinian nunnery destroyed in the Civil War; free.

BRIDGES SO3996

★ Pleasant quiet village, with a good pub and nearby walks.

BRIDGNORTH SO7193

★ 🏛 ✝ On the Severn, this old market town is picturesque without being touristy. It's divided into the High Town and Low Town, with steps between the two – though it's easier (and more fun) to take the hair-raising **Cliff Railway**. On the way down you pass some small caves that people lived in till 1856 (they're not open, but labelled). As well

as some handsome red brick, High Town has lots of fine timbered buildings, such as the odd town hall built on a sandstone-arched base that straddles the road in the high street. The **castle** was largely destroyed in the Civil War, but part of the keep remains, left at a scary tilt by the constant bombardment; the grounds are now a park with good views – the best are from Castle Esplanade. The unusual **church** on nearby East Castle St was designed by Thomas Telford. The best pubs for food here are the Bear (Northgate) and the Punch Bowl (B4364; good carvery, great views).

🐄 **Costume & Childhood Museum** (Newmarket Building) Lots of old costumes, dolls, and a Victorian nursery. Not open every day (usually cl Tues), but if you find them shut, next door Beryl's Pantry has a key and can let you in; £1.25.

✂ **Daniels Mill** (B4555, 1m S) Working cornmill still powered by its big waterwheel; a picturesque old place, run by the same family for 200 years. Snacks, shop; open pm wknds, Weds and bank hols Easter–Sept; (01746) 762753; £2.50.

🚗 **Midland Motor Museum** (off A458 SE) Over 100 well restored sports cars, racing cars and motorcycles, in converted stables in the beautiful grounds of Stanmore Hall. Snacks, shop, disabled access; cl 25 Dec; (01746) 762992; around £4. The grounds also have a caravan site.

🚂 **Severn Valley Railway** 🚉 The leading standard-gauge steam railway, with a great collection of locomotives, a splendidly lively atmosphere, and trips through beautiful scenery; for details *see entry under Bewdley, in Worcs*. The Railwayman's Arms in the station is an atmospheric place for a snack.

BROSELEY SJ6701

🏰 🏵 ✝ **Benthall Hall** (just NW of Broseley) Well liked by readers, an Elizabethan sandstone house with fine oak woodwork and panelling, decorative plasterwork, an interesting garden, and a 17th-c **church** (services 3.15pm most Suns). Some disabled access; open pm Weds, Sun and bank hols Apr–Sept; (01952) 882159; £3, £2 garden only; NT. The Foresters Arms is useful for lunch.

⚲ Broseley Clay Tobacco Pipe Museum (Duke St) Recently opened, part of the Ironbridge Gorge Museum (and included in its Passport Ticket); see how they made those long clay pipes that are a trademark of olde-worlde pictures.

BROWN CLEE HILL SO5986

⌂ Aptly named, this is Shropshire's highest point at nearly 550 metres (1,800ft). It has a disappointingly flat top but offers walkers a certain solitary grandeur.

BUILDWAS SJ6404

⛪ Buildwas Abbey (B4378) Beautiful remains of a 12th-c Cistercian abbey – apart from the roof it's practically all still here. Snacks, shop, reasonable disabled access; cl Nov–Mar; £1.85. It's right next to the gigantic cooling towers of a power station, which this close seem to have a geometrical beauty of their own. The Meadow coming out from Ironbridge has decent food.

BURY DITCHES SO3283

⛰ ❋ Iron Age ring fort, high on a hill, with superb views of South Shropshire and North Herefordshire.

CAER CARADOC SO4794

❋ ⌂ (NE of Church Stretton) This hill has a pleasingly compact summit, and the pick of the local views. The best start for walks is Hope Bowdler, not far from Shropshire's oldest pub, the Royal Oak at Cardington.

CHIRBURY SO2698

★ An attractive village, with a famously haunted graveyard.

CLAVERLEY SO7993

★ ✝ An attractive village of black and white timbered houses. The **church** has impressive medieval wall paintings.

CLEOBURY MORTIMER SO6775

✝ ⚔ Civilised small town, most notable perhaps for its church's **crooked spire**, though timbered Tudor buildings among its more elegant Georgian ones are picturesque. A restored **watermill** produces its own stoneground flour. The 16th-c King's Arms has good-value food (and comfortable bedrooms).

CLUN SO3080

★ ⚐ ⛪ ❋ Attractive stone-built village on the edge of the **Clun Forest**, a peaceful pastoral area of rolling partly wooded hills. The ruined Norman

castle gives fine views from the castle mound; free. Down by the River Clun, the 16th-c stone bridge is very picturesque. The Sun and the White Horse are useful for lunch.

COSFORD SJ7805

✝ ▣ **Royal Air Force Museum** (A41) One of the country's best aviation museums, a spectacular collection of carefully arranged aircraft inc the Victor and Vulcan bombers, Hastings, York and British Airways airliners, and the last airworthy Britannia, as well as lots of missiles and a display of engines. Large new extension, including an art gallery. Snacks, shop, disabled access; cl 24–26 Dec, 1 Jan; (01902) 376200; £5. There's a decent farm shop on Holyhead Rd, and the Bell at Tong is a reliable family dining pub.

CRAVEN ARMS SO4282

⚲ ! ⚷ **Shropshire Hills Discovery Centre** ▣ (A 49 just S of Craven Arms) Another innovative Millennium Commission-funded project, this grass-roofed structure built into the hillside and set in 25 acres of meadows takes a look at the natural and cultural history of the surrounding countryside. Various viewing rooms will house interactive exhibitions on topics as diverse as the geology of landscape, and the art and music it's inspired. A simulated balloon ride over the hills should amuse children, and other attractions will include a full-size model of a mammoth skeleton, and craft workshops. Restaurant, shop, good disabled access; the centre should open around Easter, and admission for an adult will be around £4 (café, crafts and meadows free); for more details phone (01743) 252593.

ELLESMERE WALKS SJ4035

⌂ There are several meres or lakes around here – the mere by Ellesmere itself, Blake Mere, and Cole Mere, which has a country park around it. This is close enough to the Shropshire Union Canal to include a walk along the towpath, with Colemere village a suitable starting place.

GRINSHILL HILL SJ5223

⌂ ❋ ⚐ (between Grinshill and Clive) This gives walkers much wider views than you'd expect from its modest height, and quite an atmospheric summit, where woods open out by sheer quarried rock-faces.

HARMER HILL SJ4921

🐗 **Pim Hill Farm** (Lea Hall; A528 S) Organic farm with rare breeds, a picnic site, a friendly donkey called Jenny, a shire horse called Blossom, a farm trail and well priced produce shop. Snacks from their own bakery; cl 25 Dec; (01939) 290342; free. The Bridgewater Arms is a useful family dining pub.

HAUGHMOND ABBEY SJ5214

🏚 (off B5062 E of Shrewsbury) Extensive ruins of an Augustinian abbey, inc a fine Norman doorway in the chapter house, some interesting sculpture, and well preserved lodgings and kitchens. Good for picnics. In the grounds are some plants unique to the area. Shop, some disabled access; open Apr–Mar; (01743) 709661; £1.85; EH.

HAWKSTONE PARK SJ5628

🐾 🏚 ! **Hawkstone Park Follies** Created in the 18th c, this remarkable, steeply wooded parkland has been restored after a period of neglect; spectacular views from the monuments dotted around its 100 acres. Highlights include the ruins of a medieval red castle, intricate arches and pathways, and a fantastic underground grotto with tales told by an eerily convincing laser-powered animatron. The full circuit can easily take up to 3 hours and the path isn't always easy going, so sensible shoes are recommended (and you may need a torch for some of the caves and tunnels). The BBC filmed their *Chronicles of Narnia* here. Meals, snacks, shop, limited disabled access; cl wkdys Nov–Mar; (01939) 200611; £4.50. The Caspian Bar of the Hawkstone Park Hotel has good-value food.

HODNET SJ6128

★ Several attractive half-timbered houses here, and some interesting old books in the church.

🐾 **Hodnet Hall Gardens** Sixty acres of lovely landscaped gardens with spacious lawns, lush pools, plants and trees; the astonishingly decorated tearoom is full of big-game trophies. Snacks, shop, disabled access (prior notice preferred); cl am, Mon, and Oct–Mar; (01630) 685202; £3. The Bear Hotel opposite is good for lunch (children welcome).

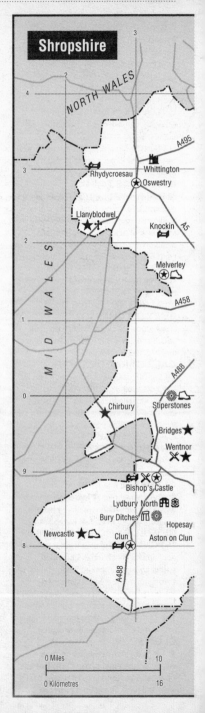

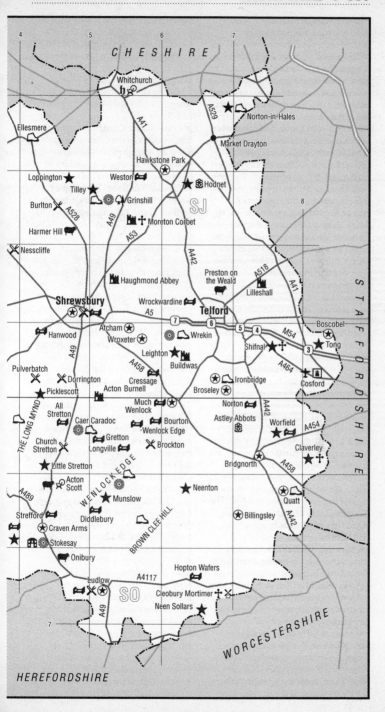

CHESHIRE

Whitchurch

A41

A529

Norton-in-Hales

Ellesmere

Market Drayton

Hawkstone Park

Loppington

Weston

Hodnet

Tilley

Grinshill

SJ

Burlton

Moreton Corbet

A528

A49

A53

Harmer Hill

Nesscliffe

A442

Preston on
the Weald

A518

Lilleshall

A41

Haughmond Abbey

STAFFORDSHIRE

Shrewsbury

Wrockwardine

Telford

A5

7

6

5

4

M54

Boscobel

Hanwood

Atcham

Wroxeter

Wrekin

3

Tong

A49

Leighton

Shifnal

Cosford

Pulverbatch

Buildwas

A464

A458

Dorrington

Cressage

Picklescott

Acton Burnell

Ironbridge

Broseley

THE LONG MYND

All
Stretton

Much
Wenlock

Norton

Astley Abbots

Worfield

A442

A454

Caer Caradoc

Bourton
Wenlock Edge

Claverley

Church
Stretton

Gretton

Longville

Brockton

Little Stretton

Bridgnorth

A458

A442

WENLOCK EDGE

Acton
Scott

A489

Munslow

Neenton

Quatt

Strefford

Diddlebury

Billingsley

Craven Arms

BROWN CLEE HILL

Stokesay

Onibury

Hopton Wafers

Ludlow

A4117

SO

Cleobury Mortimer

A49

Neen Sollars

WORCESTERSHIRE

HEREFORDSHIRE

IRONBRIDGE SJ6703

★ This steep town, with intriguing hillside paths and narrow lanes, was the birthplace of the Industrial Revolution: it was Abraham Darby's use here of coke instead of charcoal for smelting which made mass-production of iron possible. Well set among the woods and grassy slopes of the Severn Gorge, it was known as Coalbrookdale until the Darbys built the **iron bridge** across the river that today gives the town its name. As their industry took off they produced the world's first iron rails, boats, trains, and wheels, and for quite some while the valley was the biggest iron-making area in the world. Attractively placed by the riverside, the Meadow, Woodbridge and Olde Robin Hood, and (all handy for Maws craft centre and the Coalport Museum) the Boat and Half Moon at Jackfield and the Shakespeare at Coalport are all useful for lunch; there's a pleasant terraced walk between the river and the Golden Ball (Wesley Rd, off Madeley Hill). For a fuller restaurant meal, the Coracle in the village square is nice.

↓ ☖ **Ironbridge Gorge Museum** Many of the former industrial sites now make up this outstanding network, one of the most satisfying places to visit in the whole country, scattered over 6 miles along the gorge. 50-acre **Blists Hill** is the highlight, and the part children like best – a complete reconstructed Victorian village, showing everything from the offices, houses and machinery to the school, pubs, pigsties and swingboats; it's the biggest open-air museum of its kind. Costumed staff add authenticity, and there are extra activities in the school hols. The other main sections include museums devoted to the river, and the iron, china and tile-making industries, with some beautifully restored houses (and wonderful echoes in the brick kilns at Coalport) and a former clay tobacco pipe factory in Broseley. You need only buy tickets for the parts you're interested in (useful leaflets suggest a variety of itineraries, from 3 hours to a whole day), but a special offer Passport Ticket covering everything is good value – and remains valid indefinitely until you've seen all the bits you want.

On bank hols the sites are linked by a bus, otherwise it's best to drive (or walk). Meals, snacks, shops, disabled access; cl 24–25 Dec, 1 Jan and some parts cl Nov–Mar – best to ring first then; (01952) 432166; £9.50 Passport Ticket, or individual tickets to each museum available – Blists Hill is around £6.50.

🐾 **Maws Craft Centre** Across a footbridge from the Coalport tile museum, big centre with 26 workshops selling things as diverse as pottery, puzzles and pictures (cl 25 Dec; free).

🗿 **Museum of Steel Sculpture** 🖼 (Cherry Tree Hill) Dramatic sculptures inspired by the industrial heritage in 10 attractive acres. Cl Mon exc bank hols and all Dec–Feb; *£2.

⌒ **Severn Gorge** This has such fascinating and picturesque (though not always exactly pretty) scenery that its industrial monuments cry out for a tour on foot. Steep lanes and paths connect Ironbridge and Coalbrookdale, and an old railway track and a path along the base of Benthall Edge Wood assist walking routes along the gorge. A fine linear walk can be taken from Broseley, descending NW into the gorge via Corbett's Dingle to Coalport. From Coalport, you could even follow the river all the way S to Bridgnorth.

🧸 **Teddy Bear Museum** Next to the Museum of the River, with bears and other furry animals made here by the long-established Merrythought Co; cl 25 and 31 Dec, 1 Jan; free.

LILLESHALL SJ7314

🏛 **Lilleshall Abbey** Impressive ruins of a 12th-c abbey in a pleasant setting surrounded by yew trees – it's a nice spot for a picnic, peaceful and undisturbed; usually open; free; EH.

LLANYBLODWEL SJ2422

★ † This attractive village, with a charming ancient riverside pub, has an exuberantly decorated **church**.

LONG MYND SO4294

⌒ The partly heather-covered Long Mynd, England's southernmost grouse moor, has great character, with the much smaller but very striking Caer Caradoc just across the valley. For walks, it's best reached from Church Stretton. The bracken-and-bilberry-clad massif has a flat plateau-like top, crossed by the Port Way, an ancient track dating from Neolithic times. Its sides are cut into by a series of narrow, remote-feeling valleys, of which Cardingmill Valley (NT) is best known because of its relative accessibility.

LUDLOW SO5174

★ ⌂ Beautiful 12th-c town, its original grid plan still obvious today. The best road in is via Wigmore and Leinthall Starkes – lovely views as you approach. Dotted around are 500 listed buildings, with particularly good examples down Broad St, a charming mixture of Tudor and Georgian architecture. Book well in advance if you're planning to visit during the festival in early July. The most famous building is the lavishly carved and timbered Feathers Hotel on the Bull Ring; some parts inside are almost as striking. The Broadgate, the only one of the town's 13th-c gates to have survived, is interesting. Quite a few antique shops; the Unicorn is the nicest pub for lunch. The town is overlooked by the rather volcanic-looking Titterstone Clee to the NE.

▟ ※ ! **Ludlow Castle** Dating from around 1086, this splendid fortress has lots of original parts inc the Norman keep, and the chapel with its unusual circular nave. The towers and battlements on their wooded crag over the River Teme have wonderful views, and a properly 'castle-ish' feel. An unusual hologram exhibition in the dungeon has a good-sized collection of laser-generated images and illusions forming a dramatic contrast to the ancient Norman walls. Shakespeare plays are performed here during the festival, and there are lots of events throughout the year; cl 25 Dec, Jan

wkdys; (01584) 873355; *£3, hologram show £1.50 (children 50p).

♨ **Ludlow Museum** (Castle St) Good local history museum; cl 1–2pm, all day Sun exc Jun–Aug, and all Nov–Mar; *£1.

† **Ludlow Parish Church** (off King St) Dominating the town almost as much as the castle, with its magnificent pinnacled tower; it's in an attractive tranquil enclave behind the old buttermarket, and has a wonderful sense of timeless peace inside. Magnificently intricate carvings, especially on the ceiling and the choir stalls. In winter it's open 12.30–3pm on Sun only, but in summer you can visit all day (exc am Sun).

LYDBURY NORTH SO3485

⌂ ❀ **Walcot Hall** Fine Georgian house built for Clive of India; free-standing ballroom, stable yard with matching clock towers, a big walled garden, and an arboretum with good rhododendrons, azaleas and specimen trees. Disabled access; usually open pm bank hol Mon and the preceding Sun, and by appointment; (020) 7581 2782; *£3. You can stay in various wings of the house, and they can arrange fishing and riding.

MARKET DRAYTON SJ6734

The traditional home of gingerbread; the unique local recipe is locked in a bank, but you can still find plenty of toothsome samples in the shops. The big new Gingerbread Man (northern outskirts) is a decent family dining pub.

MELVERLEY SJ3316

⚲ † ⌖ ⌂ The stables of the Old Rectory have a **craft centre** (open Sun–Tues). The beautiful black and white **St Peter's Church** was rebuilt in 1406 after Owain Glyndwr burned

---

Days Out

Follies and other surprises: Hawkstone Park; bar lunch at the Hawkstone Park Hotel, or the Bear Hotel, Hodnet; Hodnet Hall Gardens; Moreton Corbet Castle; walk up Grinshill Hill.

Planes and trains: RAF Museum, Cosford; lunch at the Bell, Tong; Bridgnorth – Severn Valley Railway there.

The Welsh Marches: Stokesay Castle; Ludlow; lunch at the Unicorn, the Olive Branch or the Merchant House there; Clun; Bishop's Castle.

the previous one; it has a fine Jacobean pulpit and chain Bible. The Old Three Pigeons over at Nesscliffe has good food and all-day coffee, with **Kynaston Cave** and good cliff walks nearby.

MORETON CORBET SJ5623

☖ † Moreton Corbet Castle Destroyed by Parliament in 1644, but you can still see a small 13th-c keep and the substantial ruins of the once-grand Elizabethan house; free. There are some elaborate tombs in the adjacent **church**; the 18th-c Raven at Tilley up towards Wem is a good dining pub.

MUCH WENLOCK SJ6200

★ Lovely little medieval market town, with lots of timbered and jettied buildings. The Talbot is good for lunch.

☖ Much Wenlock Museum Local history in the Old Market Hall with displays on geology, natural history and local doctor William Penny Brookes, founder of the modern Olympic Games – the town still holds its own version of the games every summer. Cl 1–2pm, Sun exc Jun–Aug, and all Oct–Mar; 50p.

☖ Much Wenlock Priory Has its origins in the 7th c, but it's the magnificent remains of the 11th-c building and later additions you can see today. The chapter house has remarkably patterned interlaced arches. Shop; disabled access; sometimes cl 1–2pm, and cl Mon and Tues Nov–Mar, 24–26 Dec, 1 Jan; £2.50 (inc Walkman tour); EH.

△ ❋ Wenlock Edge This very long smooth hill is wooded (and much quarried) along its flanks, but has possibilities for walks. The B4371 along Wenlock Edge has good views.

NEWCASTLE SO2482

★ △ An attractive village, with pleasant local walks, and a decent pub, the Crown, with good-value food.

NORTON-IN-HALES SJ7038

★ △ Attractive village with a 13th-c church and a mysterious brading stone on its green. The Hinds Head has above-average food and attentive service; good nearby walks.

ONIBURY SO4378

☛ Wernlas Collection of Rare Poultry (Green Lane, W of A49) Readers report that they have never seen so many chickens and bantams. Also rare breeds of pheasant, unusual European species, as well as pigs, donkeys and goats. About 6,000 chicks are hatched each year, so there are usually some for children to handle or feed. Snacks, shop; cl Mon (exc mid-July–mid-Sept and bank hols), 25 Dec; (01584) 856318; £3. The Hollybush is handy for lunch.

OSWESTRY SJ2929

☖ ☝ Cambrian Railway Museum (Oswald Rd) Joint museum with the Oswestry Cycle Museum, so lots of old bicycles and a history of cycling (esp good on Dunlop), as well as steam engines and railway memorabilia; one locomotive may be in steam bank hols last Sun of month. Snacks, shop, some disabled access; cl 25 Dec; (01691) 671749; £1. The Butchers Arms has good-value food, and the Wynnstay Hotel is a comfortable refuge.

🏛 Old Oswestry (just N) Impressive Iron Age hill fort covering 68 acres. The elaborate western defensive entrance and 5 ramparts remain; free.

PICKLESCOTT SO4399

★ Attractive tucked-away village, with a delightfully placed ancient pub (the welcoming Bottle & Glass), and good walking nearby.

PRESTON ON THE WEALD SJ6814

☛ Hoo Farm Animal Kingdom 🔲 Exceptionally good-value traditional working farm, with enough to keep families with very young children happy for a sizeable chunk of the day. All the ingredients you'd expect, from bottle feeding the lambs and milking demonstrations to a petting corner, egg collecting and nature trails, as well as several more unusual features, such as ostriches, pheasant-rearing, and a big walk-in beehive, where a glass window lets you watch the bees at work. Also sheep-racing (summer afternoons at 3pm, not Fri), they have a tiny Tote to put your bets on before the race. There's a Christmas tree plantation and a Christmas tree maze, with a story for toddlers to follow as they go round; Father Christmas is here in Dec. Picnic and play areas, and occasional spinning demonstrations. Snacks, shop, disabled access; cl Mon Sept–mid-Nov and 25 Dec–20 Mar; (01952) 677917; £3.95. The Tayleur Arms over at Longdon upon Tern is a decent family dining pub.

QUATT SO7487

🏠🖼️🎴🍴🌳 **Dudmaston** (off A442) 17th-c house with the old flower-painting collection of Francis Darby of Coalbrookdale, modern art, and lakeside and woodland walks in the extensive parkland. Meals, snacks, shop, disabled access; open pm Weds and Sun Apr–Sept; (01746) 780866; £3.50 house and garden, £2.50 garden only; NT. There's usually free pedestrian access to the woods. Nearby the Lion at Hampton Loade is a good start-point for walks by the River Severn.

SHIFNAL SJ7407

★ ✝ Much expanded under the influence of nearby Telford, but still with a villagey heart and attractive buildings, inc an interesting **church** and some good food pubs such as the Star (Market Pl) and Jaspers (Victoria Rd).

SHREWSBURY SJ4912

★ ✝ The central street layout is still largely medieval, with oddly named streets (Shoplatch, Murivance, Wyle Cop), and plenty of quiet corners up narrow alleys and courtyards among its more modern shops and offices. It's rich in striking architecture, both Tudor timbering and Georgian brick. There's a signposted trail between some of the more interesting buildings. Around The Square numerous buildings reflect the medieval wool fortunes, inc the old market hall; in the adjacent High St, Owens Mansion and Irelands Mansion are fine half-timbered houses worth looking at from outside. Even McDonald's is in a medieval building. The walk up Castle St is worth while, passing the original Grammar School building and the half-timbered Council House Court. Nearby the **Church of St Mary** has one of the tallest spires in England. The original town is almost entirely ringed by a loop of the Severn (quiet waterside paths and parks, and you can hire boats along some stretches). Places to mention for food include the Three Fishes (Fish St), Armoury (Victoria Ave), riverside Boat House (New St/Quarry Park), Coach & Horses (Swan Hill/Cross Hill; brews its own beer), cheery Dun Cow Pie Shop (Abbey Foregate), Cromwells (Dogpole) and Shrewsbury (Old Welsh Bridge; food all day). Heading SW from

Shrewsbury, the old coach road through Longden and Pulverbatch is an attractive drive – great views the further you go.

🏠🖐️ **Rowley's House Museum** (Barker St) Impressive timber-framed building with social and natural history, and some interesting Roman remains. Shop, disabled access to ground floor only; cl Sun Oct–Easter, all Mons (exc bank hols), and 24–25 Dec, 1 Jan; (01743) 361196; free.

🎴 **St Julian's Craft Centre** (St Alkmunds Sq) Among other interesting shops in this part of town is an excellent craft centre in a 12th-c church, with several cheery workshops, a bustling craft fair every Sat, and a good restaurant (especially useful for vegetarians). Some disabled access; cl Sun; (01743) 353516; free. The Old Post Office nearby (Milk St) does decent pub lunches.

🏰🖐️ **Shrewsbury Castle** 12th-c, guarding the narrow neck of land between the river's loop. It was refurbished by Thomas Telford in 1790, though still has parts of the earlier building; cl Mon and varying times in winter. The **Shropshire Regimental Museum** has recently reopened here after a terrorist attack in 1992. The grounds are attractive. Shop, some disabled access; cl Mon (exc bank hols) and Sun Sept–Easter; (01743) 358516; free.

🏚️🎴✝ **Shrewsbury Quest** (Abbey Foregate) Delightful reconstruction of medieval monastic life, loosely based around the Brother Cadfael books by Ellis Peters (set in medieval Shrewsbury). You can create your own decorated manuscript or try your hand at ancient games and crafts. The carefully researched period herb garden is a draw in its own right – quite a few poisonous plants despite the lovely smell. Meals and snacks (some inspired by medieval recipes), shop, disabled access; cl 25 Dec, 1 Jan; (01743) 243324; £4.50. Just opposite, the impressive 14th-c **abbey** includes a statue of Edward III, and a memorial to Wilfrid Owen.

STIPERSTONES SO3799

❄️🌳 The rather eery Stiperstones are outcrops of harder quartzy rock leaving strange-shaped boulders, tors and crests on the skyline – and strange tales among the people living nearby. The ridge is crowned with dramatic rocks and has a splendid view; a short walk from a nearby car park (you can make an interesting 8½-mile circuit with a stop at the More Arms at Hope), or you can take the longish walk up from the former lead-mining village of Snailbeach.

STOKESAY SO4381

🏠 ※ **Stokesay Castle** (off A49) One of the finest examples of a medieval manor house in existence, 13th-c, in a notably charming setting. The hall with its cruck-framed roof and early English windows is just as it was 700 years ago, and there's a timbered Tudor gatehouse. Good views from the top of the tower, and excellent Walkman tour. Summer snacks, shop; Nov–Mar cl 1–2pm and all day Mon and Tues, plus 24–26 Dec; (01588) 672544; £3.20. The hotel of the same name in Craven Arms now has good food.

WHITCHURCH SJ5440

🐎 ♭ **Rocking Horse Workshop** (Cottage Farm, B5476 S) Here you can watch the production and restoration of traditional rocking horses; cl Sun, 25 Dec; (01948) 666777; free. In town, there's a lively heritage centre on St Mary's St (cl Sun; free), and the Horse & Jockey (Church St) has good-value food.

WHITTINGTON SJ3131

🏰 **Whittington Castle** (off A5) Handsome remains of a 13th-c castle, with good-value food at the Olde Boot alongside.

WREKIN SJ6108

※ ⌒ (just W of Telford – and towering boldly over it) The Wrekin is no Everest (an easily attained 407 metres, 1,334ft), but because it's so isolated on the edge of the Shropshire uplands it offers walkers a huge panorama, spanning places over 100 miles apart; just below, the Huntsman in Little Wenlock is handy for refreshment.

WROXETER SJ5608

👍 🍴 🏠 **Roman Vineyard** Friendly little place producing several wines; Also lavender farm, rare breeds, and some interesting glacial stones – not to mention a Roman wall. Teas, shop (with various lavender-based products), disabled access; cl Sun Jan–Mar, 25 Dec; (01743) 761888; free.

🏠 👍 **Wroxeter Roman City** One of the country's most important Roman sites, though the majority of the remains are buried under fields. There's a well preserved colonnade and municipal bath, with useful explanatory boards, and the museum has a good range of finds from the town (then Britain's fourth biggest) and the earlier fortress. Snacks, shop; some disabled access; cl Mon and Tues Nov–Mar, 25 Dec, 1 Jan; (01743) 761330; £3.10; EH. The Horseshoes at Uckington is a decent family dining pub.

★ **Other attractive villages**, with decent pubs, include Aston on Clun SO3982, Leighton SJ6105, Little Stretton SO4392, Loppington SJ4729, Lydbury North SO3586, Munslow SO5287, Neen Sollars SO6672, Neenton SO6488, Tilley SJ5027, Tong SJ7907, Wentnor SO3893 and Worfield SO7696.

Local tourist information centres have details of **imaginative trails** around the region, centring on the work of Thomas Telford, haunted villages, the novels of Ellis Peters, and sites connected with King Arthur (recent theories suggest the mythical king was a 5th-c warlord ruling from a post-Roman city here – possibly Wroxeter). They also have **balloon trip** details.

Where to eat

BISHOP'S CASTLE SO3288 **Three Tuns** (01588) 638797 Bustling lively atmosphere in simply furnished, beamed bar rooms, own-brewed beer from the handsome Victorian brewhouse, newspapers to read, a good mix of customers, and tasty home-made bar food. **£17.25|£6.50.**
BROCKTON SO5793 **Feathers** (01746) 785202 Stylish stone pub with charming atmospheric beamed rooms (2 are no smoking), a restaurary feel, conservatory, very good interesting food using fresh seasonal produce, efficient,

friendly waitress service, and well kept real ales. **£23.65**|£9.50.

BURLTON SJ4526 **Burlton Inn** (01939) 270284 Attractively restored pub with 3 cottagey connecting rooms, fresh flowers, magazines to read, winter open fires, very attractively presented interesting food from a seasonal menu, well kept real ales, and neatly uniformed helpful staff. **£20.45**|£8.50.

CHURCH STRETTON SO4593 **Acorn Wholefood** 26 Sandford Ave (01694) 722495 Simple, unpretentious family-run restaurant with friendly service in several no smoking rooms, good filling and daily-changing food (mostly vegetarian), delicious puddings and soups, and cream teas with a choice of 25 teas; cl Tues, Weds (but open Weds during school hols), 2 wks Feb. 2 wks Nov–Dec. **£10**|£2.95.

DORRINGTON SJ4702 **Country Friends** (01743) 718707 Cosy half-timbered no smoking restaurant with consistently enjoyable, interesting food inc lovely puddings and British cheeses with home-made bread; super breakfasts; bdrms; cl Sun, Mon, 2 wks beginning of July. **£36**|£8.

LUDLOW SO5174 **Merchant House** Lower Corve St (01584) 875438 Two simply furnished, decorated rooms in friendly and relaxed Jacobean house with exceptionally good food (wonderful fish and fine game) from a set 3-course menu, good-value interesting wines, and competent service; cl Sun, Mon, 1 wk Christmas, 2 wks spring; no children. **£34**.

LUDLOW SO5174 **Olive Branch** Old St (01584) 874314 Cheery wholefood restaurant in 17th-c former inn with a changing range of tasty lunchtime meals and snacks inc often inventive vegetarian meals, and teas with home-made cakes and scones; cl pm. **£13**|£6.

NESSCLIFFE SJ3818 **Old Three Pigeons** (01743) 741279 Bustling dining pub in 2 acres with ducks and swans on the new lake, a well stocked bird garden, and a Russian tank and other military hardware (which they often lend to museums or shows); 2 traditional bar areas with log fires and cushioned wall sofas, separate restaurant, particularly good meat and fish dishes, friendly service and well kept real ales; cl Mon in winter. **£21.20**|£9.

PULVERBATCH SJ4202 **White Horse** (01743) 718247 Bustling, welcoming country pub with beams and heavy timbering in several rambling areas, plates, pewter mugs and a collection of antique insurance plaques, well kept beers, decent wines by the glass, over 100 malt whiskies, and good, homely food served by friendly efficient staff; disabled access. **£14**|£4.95.

SHREWSBURY SJ4912 **Armoury** Victoria Quay (01743) 340525 Smartly converted warehouse with big arched windows overlooking river, lots of old prints and documents, cabinets with shells and explosives, corks and bottle openers, a good range of well kept real ales, 25 wines by the glass, 70 malt whiskies, and interesting bistro-style food. **£21**|£8.95.

SHREWSBURY SJ4912 **Poppy's Restaurant and Tearooms** 8 Milk St (01743) 232307 Lovely 17th-c building with really fine timbers in an upstairs room, plenty of space for shoppers on the ground floor and in the courtyard, a little room for smokers, enjoyable lunches with interesting daily-changing salad garnish, and popular morning coffee and afternoon tea; cl Sun; good disabled access. **£13.75**|£4.55.

WENTNOR SO3892 **Crown** (01588) 650613 16th-c inn in a quiet village with beams, standing timbers, a good log fire, a collection of china and glass, and a mix of tables set for eating in the main area, and a snug end with comfortable sofas; a good choice of enjoyable food, and a cosy beamed no smoking restaurant; well kept real ales, decent wines, helpful friendly staff, and fine views of the Long Mynd from seats on the neat back lawn. **£19**|£6.

Special thanks to E G Parish.

Shropshire Calendar

Some of these dates were provisional as we went to press. Please check information with the telephone numbers provided.

APRIL

25 Ironbridge Fred Dibnah at Blists Hill Ironworks (01952) 433522
28 Shrewsbury Children's Book Festival – *till 1 May* (01743) 350761
29 South-west Shropshire Georgian Arts Festival in Bishop's Castle and surrounding areas – *till 7 May* (01588) 680312

MAY

1 Newport Shropshire Game Fair at Chetwynd Park (01588) 672708
2 Clun Green Man Day and May Fair (01588) 640042
5 Bishop's Castle May Fair – *till 6 May* (01588) 638467; **Bridgnorth** Diesel Gala at Severn Valley Railway – *till 7 May* (01299) 403816; **Church Stretton** Mary Webb Weekend: local folklore, talks and walks at the Thresholds Centre – *till 7 May* (01694) 751411
13 Bridgnorth Friends of Thomas the Tank Engine at the Severn Valley Railway – *till 14 May* (01299) 403816
19 Shrewsbury Shropshire and West Midlands Show at Shropshire and West Midlands Showground – *till 20 May* (01743) 362824
27 Ludlow Festival of Crafts at the Castle – *till 29 May* (01588) 650307
29 Acton Scott Plant Sale at Acton Scott Working Farm (01694) 781306

JUNE

3 Acton Scott Sheep Shearing at Acton Scott Working Farm – *till 4 June* (01694) 781306; **Shrewsbury** Vintage Rally at Shropshire and West Midlands Showground – *till 4 June* (01743) 350761
10 Bridgnorth Heavy Horse Weekend at the Severn Valley Railway – *till 11 June* (01299) 403816
17 Bishop's Castle Rushbearing festival with Morris dancing and procession – *till 18 June* (01588) 638467; **Shrewsbury** Carnival and Show (01743) 350761
18 Cosford Royal Air Force Open Day at Aviation Museum (01902) 374112
20 Much Wenlock Festival inc Open-air Shakespeare at the Abbey – *till 25 June* (01952) 727858
23 Shrewsbury St Mary's Flower Festival – *till 29 June* (01743) 350761; also, International Music Festival – *till 29 June* (01743) 244255
24 Ludlow Festival – *till 9 July* (01584) 872350; **Shrewsbury** International Kite and Boomerang Festival – *till 26 June* (01743) 350761; **Wem** Millennium Festival (01948) 664577

JULY

1 Bridgnorth 1940s Weekend at Severn Valley Railway – *till 2 July* (01299) 403816
2 Bishop's Castle Carnival (01588) 638462
7 Bishop's Castle Real Ale and Food Festival – *till 8 July* (01588) 638467; **Much Wenlock** Olympiad – *till 8 July* (01952) 727679
8 Oswestry Festival of the Arts – *till 16 July* (01691) 662488
9 Much Wenlock Open Gardens (01952) 727858
15 Ratlinghope Music at Leasowes Bank – *till 29 July* (01743) 790769

Shropshire Calendar (cont.)

21 **Much Wenlock** International Story-telling Festival – *till 23 July* (01952) 883936

22 **Church Stretton** South Shropshire Arts Festival, with events and shows planned elsewhere in the area – *till 5 August* (01694) 723402; **Ludlow** Open-air Theatre at Ludlow Castle – *till 23 July* (01584) 873355; **Wem** National Sweet Pea Society and Wem Sweet Pea Festival: celebration of 300 years of the sweet pea – *till 23 July* (01952) 727679

29 **Bishop's Castle** Agricultural Show (01588) 638467; **Ironbridge** Victorian Wedding Day at Ironbridge Gorge Museum, Blists Hill – *till 30 July* (01952) 433522

30 **Acton Scott** Falconry at Acton Scott Working Farm (01694) 781306

AUGUST

3 **Burwarton** Show (01746) 787535

5 **Acton Scott** Herb Weekend at Acton Scott Working Farm – *till 6 August* (01694) 781306; **Oswestry** Show (01691) 654875

11 **Shrewsbury** Flower Show at Quarry Park: one of England's largest – *till 12 August* (01743) 364051

19 **Minsterley** Show (01743) 790767

25 **Bridgnorth** Folk Festival – *till 27 August* (01746) 768813

27 **Bicton** County Steam Engine Rally at Onslow Park – *till 28 August* (01694) 723799

28 **Ellesmere** Carnival (01691) 622981; **Whitchurch** Carnival (01948) 664577

29 **Ellesmere** Regatta (01691) 622417

SEPTEMBER

2 **Bridgnorth** Thomas the Tank Engine at Severn Valley Railway – *till 3 September* (01299) 403816

8 **Ellesmere** Festival – *till 10 September* (01691) 622097

9 **Bridgnorth** Thomas the Tank Engine at Severn Valley Railway – *till 10 September* (01299) 403816; **Ludlow** Ludlow and Marches Food and Drink Festival – *till 10 September* (01588) 650307

10 **Shrewsbury** Real Ale Festival at the Music Hall – *till 11 September* (01743) 244255

16 **Bishop's Castle** Michaelmas Fair: vintage vehicles, Morris dancing – *till 17 September* (01588) 638462

17 **Acton Scott** Traditional Harvest Festival at Acton Scott Working Farm (01694) 781306

22 **Bridgnorth** Autumn Steam Gala at Severn Valley Railway – *till 24 September* (01299) 403816

24 **Acton Scott** Crafts in Action at Acton Scott Working Farm (01694) 781306

OCTOBER

8 **Bridgnorth** Classic Vehicle Day at Severn Valley Railway (01299) 403816

21 **Acton Scott** Cider Weekend at Acton Scott Working Farm – *till 22 October* (01694) 781306

28 **Ironbridge** Ghostly Gaslight at Ironbridge Gorge Museum, Blists Hill (01952) 433522

NOVEMBER

4 **Ironbridge** Traditional Bonfire Night at Ironbridge Gorge Museum, Blists Hill (01952) 433522

SOMERSET

All sorts of places to visit, two fascinating cities, charming smaller towns and villages, unspoilt countryside; good value.

Bath is sophisticated, mellow, graceful and elegant, with a profusion of worthwhile museums – great for a short break. Bristol has masses of things to pack a day visit with interest, including the excellent zoo with its new seal and penguin coasts, the exciting new @Bristol development, and a lively harbour-based industrial museum – its good museums are now free.

Elsewhere, there's a wide range of things to see, for all ages, including some fine gardens, friendly animal centres and cider mills, steam railways, the charming miniature city of Wells, and the brooding Mendips' great limestone gorges (including Wookey Hole). On the coast, Minehead is a pleasant traditional resort, and Weston-super-Mare and Clevedon have their attractions.

Over in the west the countryside feels very secluded and self-contained, with each small valley of the Quantocks seeming a private world, and the Blackdown Hills charmingly untouristy, too – classic quiet English countryside with some lovely villages. (Exmoor is discussed separately, in the Devon chapter.) The Somerset Levels are an interesting contrast – vivid green marshy pastures, rewarding for wildlife and for traditional crafts such as basket-making. Towards the east, richer, more rolling farmland with small valleys and wooded hillsides offers some gentle country drives.

The countryside is dotted with landmark church towers, pinnacled, turreted and gargoyled. Many churches, particularly in the west, have intriguingly carved 15th- and 16th-c bench ends, also fine oak waggon roofs, brass candelabras and carved screens. In the hillier parts, buildings are generally of stone, varying in colour and character from the Cotswold style of the north-east, through the pale limestones of the Mendips and the golden warmth of south Somerset's Ham stone, to the rugged and stolid greys of the hamlets tucked into the green folds of the Quantocks.

Tourist information centres here have a great deal of helpful material.

Where to stay

BARWICK ST5613 **Little Barwick House** *Barwick, Yeovil BA22 9TD (01935) 423902* **£93,** plus special breaks; 6 rms. Carefully run, listed Georgian dower house in 3½ acres, with a lovely relaxed atmosphere, log fire in the cosy lounge, excellent food using local produce, a thoughtful wine list, super breakfasts, nice afternoon tea with crumpets, and particularly good service; 2m S of Yeovil; cl Christmas and New Year; dogs by arrangement.

BATH ST7464 **Badminton Villa** *10 Upper Oldfield Park, Bath BA2 3JZ (01225) 426347* ***£60,** plus special breaks; 5 rms. Big, no smoking, Victorian house with marvellous city views, comfortable lounge, good breakfasts, and helpful, friendly owners; cl 24 Dec–2 Jan; children over 8.

BATH ST7465 **Brocks** *32 Brock St, Bath BA1 2LN (01225) 338374* ***£65,** plus special breaks; 6 rms. Georgian house with fine breakfasts in a big dining room, lounge area, helpful staff, and good central position; cl Christmas and New Year.

BATH ST7463 **Haydon House** *9 Bloomfield Park, Bath BA2 2BY (01225) 427351* **£75,** plus special breaks; 5 good rms with sherry and home-made shortbread. Deceptively unassuming-looking Edwardian house with comfortable, elegant and restful rooms, antiques, excellent breakfasts (no evening meals), warmly welcoming owners, and a pretty garden; no smoking; children by arrangement.

BATH ST7565 **Old Boathouse** *Bath Boating Station, Forester Rd, Bath BA2 6QE (01225) 466407* ***£50;** 4 rms. Edwardian boating station with black and white timbered verandah overlooking the river, free launch to Bath centre, punting and rowing boats for hire, sitting room with river views, and a separate restaurant; partial disabled access.

BATH ST7464 **Paradise House** *86–88 Holloway, Bath BA2 4PX (01225) 317723* ***£65,** plus special breaks; 10 rms (room 6 has a super view). Classically elegant early 18th-c hotel, lovingly restored and recently refurbished, with marvellous views over the city, pretty breakfast room, restful drawing room, log fire, spacious walled gardens; peaceful, though only 7 minutes' walk to centre; cl Christmas.

BATH ST7465 **Queensberry** *Russel St, Bath BA1 2QF (01225) 447928* **£135,** plus special breaks; 29 lovely rms. Three beautifully decorated Georgian town houses in a quiet residential street, with a comfortable, restful drawing room, open fire, attractive modern restaurant (Olive Tree, *see* **Where to eat**) and professional service; cl Christmas and New Year

BATH ST7465 **Royal Crescent** *16 Royal Crescent, Bath BA1 2LS (01225) 739955* **£222,** plus special breaks; 45 luxurious rms. Elegant Georgian hotel in glorious curved terrace, with comfortable antiques-filled lounges, very attractive garden room (with own menu), open fires and lovely flowers; excellently presented, very well prepared fine food in the Dower House Restaurant, impeccable service; outdoor pool and croquet; children over 7 in restaurant in the evening; disabled access.

BATH ST7565 **Villa Magdala** *Henrietta Rd, Bath BA2 6LX (01225) 466329* **£85,** plus winter breaks; 18 comfortable rms. Overlooking Henrietta Park, this elegant Victorian house is close to the centre and has good breakfasts in the attractive dining room, a spacious comfortable lounge, and friendly, helpful staff; cl Nov, Jan, Feb; children over 6.

BEERCROCOMBE ST3120 **Frog Street Farm** *Frog St, Beercrocombe, Taunton TA3 6AF (01823) 480430* **£60,** plus special breaks; 3 rms. Peaceful 15th-c listed farmhouse deep in the countryside on a big working farm, with beams, fine Jacobean panelling, inglenook fireplaces, warmly friendly owner, delicious food (much produce from the farm, local game and fish; bring your own wine), and good breakfasts; cl Nov–Mar; no children.

CANNINGTON ST2538 **Blackmore Farm** *Cannington, Bridgwater TA5 2NE (01278) 653442* ***£42;** 4 rms. Grade I listed manor house dating from 15th c, with garderobes, beams and stone archways, good breakfasts around a huge table in the Great Hall, and a log fire in the comfortable sitting room; no evening meals; disabled access.

HATCH BEAUCHAMP ST3020 **Farthings** *Hatch Beauchamp, Taunton TA3 6SG (01823) 480664* **£87,** plus special breaks; 9 rms with thoughtful extras. Charming little Georgian house in 3 acres of gardens, with open fires in quiet lounges, and good food using fresh local produce; can arrange golf, etc.

HINTON CHARTERHOUSE ST7759 **Homewood Park** *Freshford, Bath BA3 6BB (01225) 723731* **£139;** 19 lovely rms. Charming Victorian hotel on the edge of Hinton Priory ruins, with flowers, oil paintings and fine furniture in graceful relaxing day rooms, elegant restaurant with very good imaginative food (honey from their own bees – you can help them collect it), and 10 acres of gardens and woodlands; tennis, croquet; disabled access.

HOLFORD ST1541 **Combe House** *Holford, Bridgwater TA5 1RZ (01278) 741382* **£76,** plus special breaks; 16 rms. Warmly friendly former tannery (still has waterwheel) in a pretty spot, with comfortable rooms, log fires, good home-made food, and relaxed atmosphere; heated indoor swimming pool, sauna, croquet and tennis court.

HOLFORD ST1541 **Quantock House** *Holford, Bridgwater TA5 1RY (01278) 741439* ***£42;** 3 rms. Thatched 17th-c house with large cottagey garden, big inglenook fireplace in residents' lounge, nice breakfasts, and a friendly welcome; well behaved pets allowed; cl 25 Dec; disabled access.

HUNSTRETE ST6461 **Hunstrete House** *Hunstrete, Pensford, Bristol BS18 4NS (01761) 490490* **£220 inc dinner,** plus special breaks; 23 individually decorated rms. Classically handsome, mainly 18th-c country-house hotel on the edge of the Mendips, in 92 acres inc walled garden and deer park; comfortable and elegantly furnished day rooms with antiques, paintings, log fires, fresh flowers from the garden, a tranquil atmosphere, excellent service, and very good enjoyable food using produce from the garden when possible; lovely gardens, croquet lawn, heated swimming pool, all-weather tennis court, and nearby riding; disabled access.

LANGPORT ST4226 **White House** *The Hill, Langport TA10 9QZ (01458) 250892* **£40;** 2 rooms (one with lovely view). Attractive house with charming owners, drawing room with open fire in Ham stone fireplace, fine rugs on the polished wooden floor, and lots of pictures and antiques; a snug study with TV, good full breakfasts with home-made marmalade taken in a dining room with French windows leading to conservatory, and marvellous views over the Somerset Levels.

LOWER VELLOW ST0938 **Curdon Mill** *Lower Vellow, Williton, Taunton TA4 4LS (01984) 56522* **£60,** plus special breaks; 8 smallish but pretty and individually furnished rms. Charming, beautifully furnished, no smoking hotel between the Quantocks and Brendon Hills, with 200 acres of working farm to wander over, a lovely garden, very good evening meal in the antique-filled dining room, substantial breakfasts, and friendly staff; the waterwheel and mill shaft have been carefully preserved and still work; outdoor heated swimming pool; civil marriage licence; children over 8.

LUXBOROUGH SS9737 **Royal Oak** *Kingsbridge, Luxborough, Watchet TA23 0SH (01984) 640319* **£55;** 12 simple rms, most with own bthrm. Unspoilt and interesting old pub in an idyllic spot, a chatty and friendly, beamed bar with log fire, decent choice of well kept real ales, good food in both the bar and restaurant (plenty of game), and well liked breakfasts; disabled access.

MIDDLECOMBE SS9545 **Periton Park** *Middlecombe, Minehead TA24 8SW (01643) 706885* **£99,** plus special breaks; 8 rms (3 no smoking) with views of surrounding countryside. Fine Exmoor-edge Victorian country house with a comfortable lounge, books, log fire, a relaxed atmosphere, friendly service, and good food in the panelled, no smoking dining room; pleasant walks nearby, and they can arrange shooting, fishing or riding at adjacent riding centre; dogs in one rm only; cl Jan; children over 12; disabled access.

NORTH PERROTT ST4709 **Manor Arms** *North Perrott, Crewkerne TA18 7SG (01460) 72901* ***£48,** plus special breaks; 9 rms in restored coach house inc a fine panelled and beamed one. Comfortable and attractive 16th-c inn with friendly, helpful licensees, beams, exposed stone and inglenook fireplace, good home-made food in the small restaurant and bar, and a garden with play area; free coarse fishing, free entry to some South Somerset gardens; disabled access.

NORTON ST PHILIP ST7755 **George** *High St, Norton St Philip, Bath BA3 6LH (01373) 834224* **£110;** 8 comfortable rms of real character in galleried wing. Carefully restored, exceptional building that has been offering hospitality to travellers for nearly 700 years; individual bars with trusses and timbering, fine old stone fireplaces, really heavy beams, 18th-c pictures, oak dressers and settles and so forth, a marvellous restaurant, good food, real ales, decent wines, and organised, friendly service; a stroll over the meadow behind the pub (past the picnic sets on the narrow grass pub garden) leads to an attractive churchyard around the medieval church whose bells struck Pepys (here on 12 June 1668) as 'mighty tuneable'.

POLSHAM ST5142 **Southway Farm** *Polsham, Wells BA5 1RW (01749) 673396* ***£38;** 3 rms. Friendly Georgian farmhouse between Wells and Glastonbury, with an open fire in the comfortable lounge, an attractive dining room, good breakfasts and pretty garden; cl Dec and Jan.

PORLOCK SS8846 **Seapoint** *Redway, Porlock, Minehead TA24 8QE (01643) 862289* **£48,** plus winter breaks; 3 rms. Surrounded by the Exmoor hills and with views of Porlock Bay, this Edwardian guesthouse has a comfortable sitting room with winter log fire, a friendly and relaxing atmosphere, enjoyable home-made food in the candlelit dining room, and fine breakfasts; cl Dec–Jan.

ROADWATER ST0337 **Wood Advent Farm** *Roadwater, Watchet TA23 0RR (01984) 640920* ***£50;** 4 rms. Relaxed, spacious farmhouse on 340 acres of working farm within Exmoor National Park; log fire in the comfortable lounge, good country cooking using their own produce in an attractive dining room with woodburner; grass tennis court, outdoor heated swimming pool, and fishing, clay pigeon and pheasant shooting; children over 10.

SEAVINGTON ST MARY ST4014 **Pheasant** *Seavington St Mary, Ilminster TA19 0QH (01460) 240502* **£90,** plus special breaks; 8 comfortable, pretty rms. Carefully converted and spotlessly kept, thatched 17th-c former farmhouse with an open fire in the low-beamed bar, enjoyable food in the attractive candlelit restaurant, and a quiet landscaped garden.

SOMERTON ST4828 **Lynch Country House** *4 Behind Berry, Somerton TA11 7PD (01458) 272316* **£49;** 5 prettily decorated rms. Carefully restored, homely Georgian house with books in the comfortable lounge, and good breakfasts (no evening meals) in an airy room overlooking tranquil grounds and lake with black swans and exotic ducks; also self-catering cottages; cl Christmas and New Year.

STANTON WICK ST6161 **Carpenters Arms** *Stanton Wick, Pensford, Bristol BS18 4BX (01761) 490202* **£69.50;** 12 rms. Warm and attractively furnished, tile-roofed inn converted from a row of miners' cottages, with big log fire, woodburner, wide choice of good food inc generous breakfasts, well kept beers, and friendly, efficient staff.

STOGUMBER ST1037 **Hall Farm** *Stogumber, Taunton TA4 3TQ (01984) 656321* **£37;** 6 rms. Old-fashioned B & B with optional evening meals (bring your own wine) – wonderfully unpretentious, with warmly friendly staff; cl Christmas and New Year; well behaved dogs welcome; disabled access.

STOKE ST GREGORY ST3527 **Rose & Crown** *Woodhill, Stoke St Gregory, Taunton TA3 6EW (01823) 490296* ***£50;** 5 rms, shared bthrm, plus 2 rms in annexe. Very friendly 17th-c cottagey inn with a cosy and pleasantly romanticised stable theme, generous helpings of particularly good-value food in the no smoking dining room, excellent breakfasts, decent wine list, efficient service from hard-working family in charge, and popular skittle alley; self-catering nearby; disabled access.

STON EASTON ST6254 **Ston Easton Park** *Ston Easton, Bath BA3 4DF (01761) 241631* **£220,** plus special breaks; 21 really lovely rms. Majestic Palladian mansion of Bath stone with beautifully landscaped 18th-c gardens and 26 acres of parkland; elegant day rooms with antiques and flowers, attractive no smoking restaurant with good food (much grown in the kitchen garden), fine afternoon teas, library and billiard room, and extremely helpful, friendly and unstuffy service; no dogs in rooms (though have kennels), babies and children over 7 welcome by prior arrangement.

TAUNTON ST2224 **Castle** *Castle Green, Taunton TA1 1NF (01823) 272671* **£139,** plus special breaks; 44 lovely rms. Appealingly modernised, partly Norman castle (its west front almost smothered in wisteria), with fine old oak furniture, tapestries and paintings in comfortably elegant lounges, really excellent modern English cooking, good breakfasts, and good-value wines from a thoughtful list, efficient, friendly service, and pretty garden; dogs by arrangement; disabled access.

WELLS ST5445 **Infield House** *36 Portway, Wells BA5 2BN (01749) 670989* **£49,** plus special breaks; 3 comfortable rms (best view from back rm). Carefully restored, no smoking, Victorian town house with period furnishings, an unusual paperweight collection, elegant lounge (with lots of local guidebooks), good breakfasts in the dining room with Adam-style fireplace, evening meals by arrangement, and friendly personal service; cl 1 wk Jan; no pets (they have a cheery Labrador); children over 12.

WOOKEY HOLE ST5347 **Glencot House** *Glencot Lane, Wookey Hole, Wells BA5 1BH (01749) 677160* **£85**, 13 rms, many with four-posters or half-testers. In 18 acres of gardens and parkland (and with its own cricket pitch), this Jacobean-style Victorian mansion has some fine wood panelling, carved ceilings, antiques and flowers in the public rooms and hallways, a relaxed friendly atmosphere, and good food in the restaurant; fishing, table tennis, and snooker; lots to do nearby; cl first wk Jan.

To see and do

SOMERSET Family Attraction of the Year

🐾 ☺ 🦋 **BRISTOL** ST5873 **Bristol Zoo Gardens** (Clifton Downs; several buses run to here from the city centre, inc the 8, 9, 508 and 509 – you may be able to get joint bus/zoo tickets) One of the most enjoyable zoos in the country, excellent value, lots to see, and plenty of well thought out children's activities. Lots of time and effort has been spent on improvements in recent years, with the most exciting new feature undoubtedly the breathtaking Seal and Penguin Coasts, a £2 million development opened by David Bellamy in July 1999. Transparent underwater walkways offer an unrivalled view of the penguins and seals in their natural environment – you can see them swimming through water all around you, and from almost every conceivable angle (there's an elevated boardwalk to look down on them from above). Imaginatively landscaped with a shipwreck and other features, this new addition is well worth a visit in its own right, even if you've visited the zoo fairly recently. Other highlights include the big Gorilla Island, Bug World, showing creatures like desert scorpions and a giant octopus in careful re-creations of their natural environment, and Twilight World, its showcase of wide-awake nocturnal creatures including a walk-through bat enclosure. Also lions, tigers, reptiles, tropical birds, and a good aquarium, and an activity centre with face-painting and maybe the chance to handle a snake or snail. Animal encounters are spread throughout the day (more of them in summer, when they have bird displays too). There's a good adventure playground, with separate areas for toddlers and younger children, but standing out amongst the activities for younger visitors is the Zoolympics, a trail around the enclosures that lets them measure their skills and strength against some of the animals – seeing how their speed compares with a cheetah for example, or whether they can flap their arms as much as a humming bird does its wings. Lots of themed weeks and events, with an enjoyable Christmas festival. A bonus is that everything is spread over beautifully laid out gardens, with spacious lawns and colourful borders. You'll need most of a day to stand a chance of seeing everything, and several parts are under cover (inc some of the picnic areas). Meals, snacks, shop, good disabled access; cl 25 Dec; (0117) 973 8951; £7.95 (£4.50 children 3–13).

Please let us know what you think of places in the *Guide*. Use the report forms at the back of the book or simply write us a letter.

AXBRIDGE ST4354

★ Pleasant small town with an appealing, largely medieval square and narrow winding high street, unusual in this part of the world for its jettied timber-framed buildings. The rambling old Lamb, on the corner of the tranquil market square, is good for lunch.

🏠 ⊙ **King John's Hunting Lodge** (High St) Actually built around 1500, so having no connection with King John (nor in fact with hunting) – but no less attractive for that. It houses a local history museum. Shop, disabled access to grounds; open pm Apr–Sept; (01934) 732012; donations; NT.

BARRINGTON ST3918

🏠 ❀ ★ **Barrington Court** In the grounds of a splendid 16th-c house, a magnificent series of gardens influenced by Gertrude Jekyll, inc a rose garden, and traditional walled kitchen garden, the produce from which is on sale in the shop. The house shows off the reproduction furniture of Stuart Interiors. Meals, snacks, plant centre, disabled access; open Apr–Oct exc Fri; (01460) 241938; *£4.50; NT. The village itself is attractive, and the Royal Oak does good lunches.

BATH ST7564

★ 🏠 ⊙ ⌂ For many this is England's most rewarding old town, though its throngs of summer visitors tend to mask its charms a bit then. Many places enjoyably recall the days of Beau Nash and the building of Bath as a fashionable resort; other draws go back to the Roman Baths, and come right up to date with the city's interesting and unusual shops. If ambitious plans come off, taking the spa waters won't just be something out of Jane Austen: the architect of Waterloo's Eurostar terminal has been commissioned to design a new spa building, likely to be ready in time for the Millennium. In the meantime our favourite places to visit are the Roman Baths, Pump Room, Museum of Costume at the Assembly Rooms, Building of Bath Museum, Industrial Heritage Centre, No 1 Royal Crescent, and Bath Abbey. The American Museum on the edge of the city at Claverton is very special (*see* Claverton *entry*). Parts not to be missed include the great showpieces of 18th-c town planning, Queen Sq, The Circus and the Royal Crescent; the quieter Abbey Green and cobbled Abbey St and Queen St; and the great Pulteney Bridge (there's a fine view of it from the bridge at the end of North Parade, or the riverside Parade Gardens, where brass bands play in summer). The narrow little lanes between the main streets can be fascinating. In summer lots of informal eating places have tables outside. Good pubs with decent food include the Old Green Tree (Green St), Crystal Palace (Abbey Green) and Saracen's Head (Broad St). Good street markets are in Bartlett St (daily), junk to top-drawer antiques, often buzzing with dealers from elsewhere; Guinea Lane (very early am Weds), antiques changing hands quickly; and Walcot St (Sat, occasional Sun) flea market, good bargains. On the first Sat of the month there is a farmers' market with lots of fresh fruit and vegetables adjacent to Green Park Station. The beautifully restored historic Theatre Royal presents more pre-West End productions than anywhere else in the country. Don't try to drive around the city: Bath's streets were laid out for travel by sedan chair, not car, and a tortuous one-way system seems designed to deter drivers rather than to make traffic flow more easily. Inadvertently park your car in the wrong place and it may be quickly towed away, despite a lack of proper warnings. Walking around Bath is anyway a delight; there are flat parts, though to make the most of it you have to be prepared to slog up some of the steeper streets. Readers particularly enjoy the somewhat irreverent **Bizarre Bath** walking tours that leave the Huntsman Inn on North Parade Passage at 8pm daily, Apr–Sept (£3.50) – more street theatre than a typical tour. The rush of a day trip doesn't do justice to the host of things worth seeing; it is best to stay, preferably out of season. On summer days, crowds of trippers and school parties tend to spoil the best-known parts, and if you want to visit during Bath's early summer festival, book accommodation well ahead.

! Balloon trips Hot-air balloons give a good view of the city as it's shown in the great architectural drawings. They take off, subject to weather, from the Royal Victoria Park; (01225) 466888; from £115.

† Bath Abbey & Abbey Heritage Vaults Particularly renowned for its fan vaulting, the current building is the third great church to be built on this site, begun in 1499. The Elizabethans called it the Lantern of the West because of its profusion of stained glass. Most impressive is the great east window, depicting 56 scenes from the life of Christ. On one side of this is a finely carved memorial to Bartholomew Barnes (1608), and on the other the beautiful medieval carving of the Prior Birde chantry. Restoration work has been returning the interior's gradually blackened Bath stone to its more appealing honey colour. Shop, disabled access; cl Good Fri, 24–26 Dec, 1 Jan, and during private services; £2 suggested donation. A very good exhibition on the abbey's history is in the adjacent carefully restored 18th-c vaults. Disabled access; cl Sun; (01225) 422462; £2. In summer there may be walking tours from the abbey churchyard (usually around 10.30am and 2pm).

☉ Bath Postal Museum (Broad St) First-class exploration of the development of the postal system since the 16th c, inc a full-scale replica Victorian post office; it was from here that the world's first postage stamp was sent in 1840. Snacks, shop, disabled access to ground floor only; cl am Sun; (01225) 460333; £2.50.

✻☉ Beckford's Tower (Lansdown Rd) Italianate tower with fine views from the top, and a little museum commemorating the well travelled collector William Beckford. It's due to re-open after restoration later this year, phone for opening details; (01225) 460705.

⚓ ⛵ Boating Cruises leave Pulteney Bridge landing stage at a quarter to and a quarter past the hour (not Oct–Easter). Boats and punts can be hired in summer from the Boating Station on the River Avon, Forester Rd, Bathwick; (01225) 466407. The revivified **Kennet & Avon Canal** is one of Bath's pleasures, with quiet towpath walks along to Bathampton (where the George I is popular for lunch); it has quite a few colourful narrow boats in summer. You can cycle right into the centre along the Avon Cycleway, cycle tracks converted from the old Bath and Bristol railway.

☉ 📖 Book Museum (Manvers St) First and early editions of authors who lived or worked in Bath, especially Jane Austen and Charles Dickens; there's a reconstruction of Dickens's study at Gads Hill on the other side of England. A good chunk of the exhibition is devoted to the history and art of bookbinding, and adjoining this is the shop of **George Bayntun**, who has been binding and selling antiquarian books for 50 years. Cl 1–2 pm, pm Sat, all Sun and bank hols; (01225) 466000; bookshop customers free, others *£2.

☉ Building of Bath Museum (The Vineyard, Paragon) Fascinating displays on how John Wood and others transformed the town and its architecture, with full-scale reconstructions, original tools, and a fabulous model of the entire city, lighting up when you press the buttons. Shop, disabled access but no facilities – and those who have difficulty walking might notice the floor's slight unevenness; cl Mon (exc bank hols), and Dec–mid-Feb; (01225) 333895; *£3.50.

❀ Georgian Garden (Gravel Walk) Nr Queen Sq, another striking reminder of the period, this re-creates the original layout and the kind of plants that would have been used in a small town garden in the 1760s. Given the high ratio of walking-space to plants, the emphasis back then was clearly on strolling and chatting rather than horticulture itself. Cl wknds and bank hols, and all Nov–Apr; free.

♜☉ Herschel House & Museum (New King St) Interesting Georgian home and workplace of William Herschel, the astronomer (and composer), with period rooms, models of his telescopes, and other scientific equipment. He discovered the planet Uranus from the back garden. Book shop; cl am, and wkdys Nov–Feb; (01225) 311342; *£2.50.

🖾 **Holburne Museum** (Gt Pulteney St) Fine old building displaying the decorative and fine-art collection of Sir Thomas William Holburne (1793–1874), as well as lots of 20th-c art and crafts. Meals, snacks, shop, disabled access; cl am Sun, Mon Nov–Easter, and all mid-Dec–mid-Feb; (01225) 466669; £3.50.

🏗 **Industrial Heritage Centre** (Julian Rd) The highlight is the engaging **Mr Bowler's Business**, an elaborate re-creation of a factory first established in 1872, providing various services from plumbing and engineering to gas-fitting and bell-hanging. Everything is just as it was then, inc the antique soda fountain that turned out such intriguingly named drinks as Hot Tom and that distant harbinger of today's alcopops, Cherry Ciderette. Snacks, shop, some disabled access by arrangement; cl wkdys Nov–Easter; (01225) 318348; *£3.50.

👶 **Jane Austen Centre** 🖾 (Gay St) A look at the life of the novelist, who lived in the city (indeed in this street) 1801–6. Displays on Austen's contemporary Bath include re-creations of a Georgian shop-front and town garden, exhibitions on places mentioned in her novels, and costumes from the BBC's adaptation of *Persuasion*; also walking tours of Austen's Bath (£3.50 extra). Shop, disabled access; (01225) 443000; £4.

👶🏛 **Museum of Costume & Assembly Rooms** (Bennett St) Dazzling – over 200 figures dressed in original costumes from the late 16th c to the present, one of the most impressive displays of fashion and fashion accessories in the world. It's housed in the Assembly Rooms built in 1771 by John Wood the Younger, where the audio-guide has a particularly entertaining commentary – listen out for the bun fight. Summer coffee, shop, disabled access; cl 25–26, 31 Dec, and Assembly Rooms may be cl other dates for functions; (01225) 477752; £3.80. Along the same street is a small **museum of East Asian art**.

🏛 **No 1 Royal Crescent** The most splendid example of the architecture that sprang up in the town's Georgian heyday. In 1768 it was the first house built in Bath's most regal terrace, and now has two floors restored and beautifully furnished in the style of that time. Shop; cl Mon (exc bank hols), and Dec–mid-Feb; (01225) 428126; £4. The Crescent is now closed to traffic at one end, with the hope of reducing damage inflicted by tour buses.

🌸🌼🏡 **Prior Park Landscape Garden** (Ralph Allen Drive, off A3062 S of Bath) In a sweeping valley, these striking 18th-c landscaped gardens are being comprehensively restored by the National Trust after a period of neglect. Capability Brown and Alexander Pope helped local entrepreneur Ralph Allen with the original design, and there are plenty of unique ornamental features (inc 18th-c graffiti on the Palladian bridge). Woodland walks offer unusual views over Bath (they hope to start guided walks later this year). Note you can't drive all the way here: there's no car parking on site or nearby. You can walk from town, but the hill is very steep, so best to take the number 2 or 4 bus. Cl am, all Tues, 25–26 Dec, 1 Jan; (01225) 833977; £3.80 (£1 off if show bus or train ticket); NT. There's decent food at the Cross Keys over on Midford Rd.

🏛 **Pump Room** This stylish 18th-c mecca for the fashionable was built directly above the Roman temple courtyard; you can catch a glimpse of the baths next door. It now houses a restaurant serving morning coffee, lunches and teas to the gay strains of the Pump Room trio. You can sample the hot spa water, which always comes out at 46.5°C (116°F).

🏛👶 **Roman Baths** Founded by AD 75, and undoubtedly one of Britain's most remarkable Roman sites. They were built to service pilgrims visiting a temple to Sulis Minerva, which had been constructed around a sacred hot spring. After this the spring played a dual role – as both a focus for worship, and a reservoir supplying the baths with spa water. The baths were all but forgotten until the 18th c, when workmen chanced upon a bust of Minerva, and it was not until 1878 that most of what you see today was uncovered. The main baths are pretty much intact, though some of the columns are 18th- and 19th-c reconstructions; in August

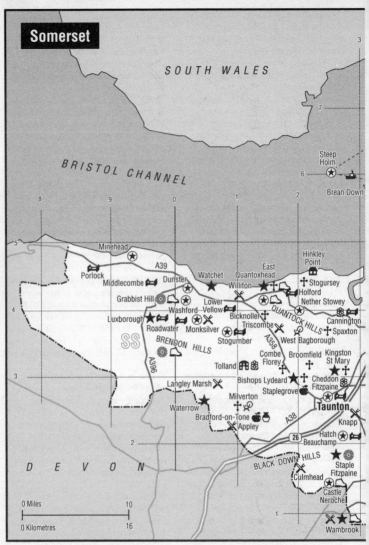

Somerset

SOUTH WALES

BRISTOL CHANNEL

Steep Holm

Brean Down

Minehead

Porlock

Middlecombe

Grabbist Hill

Dunster

Watchet

Williton

East Quantoxhead

Hinkley Point

Stogursey

Holford

Nether Stowey

Cannington

Spaxton

Lower Vellow

Washford

Bicknoller

Triscombe

West Bagborough

Broomfield

Kingston St Mary

Luxborough

Roadwater

Monksilver

QUANTOCK HILLS

SS

BRENDON HILLS

Stogumber

Combe Florey

A358

Tolland

Cheddon Fitzpaine

Bishops Lydeard

Staplegrove

Taunton

Langley Marsh

Milverton

Waterrow

A396

Bradford-on-Tone

Appley

A38

Knapp

Hatch Beauchamp

26

D   E   V   O   N

BLACK DOWN HILLS

Culmhead

Staple Fitzpaine

Castle Neroche

Wambrook

0 Miles   10

0 Kilometres   16

they're open at night and quite beautifully floodlit. Work is under way on a new spa complex, 100 metres away, due to open in summer 2001. A **museum** shows finds made during excavations, inc the bust of Minerva and a remarkable gorgon's head pediment (thought by some authorities to depict not a gorgon at all but King Bladud, father of Lear and aeronaut extraordinaire), and a model of the site as it would have appeared in the 4th c.

Meals, snacks, shop, some disabled access (though not to baths themselves); cl 25–26 Dec; (01225) 477785; £6.70, inc an audio-guide.

🖼 **Royal Photographic Society** (The Octagon, Milsom St) Five galleries with major international exhibitions and useful displays on photographic history, inc the first picture ever taken. Meals, snacks, shop, disabled access (not to restaurant); cl 25–26 Dec; (01225) 462841; £2.50 (free to

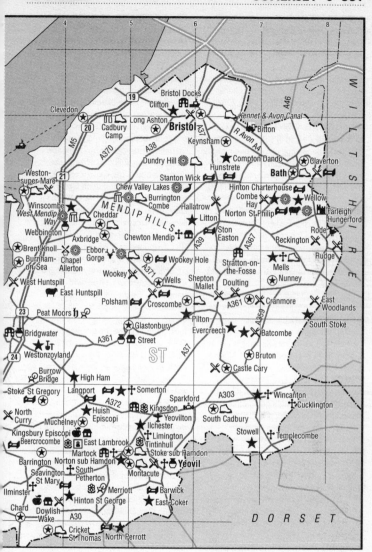

members).

🏠🍽 Sally Lunn's Kitchen Museum (North Parade Passage) Reputedly the oldest house in Bath, a charming partly timbered medieval structure, still preserving in its cellars the original kitchen of the legendary Sally Lunn, who in the 17th c created her famous brioche bread buns here. Meals and snacks (inc of course the buns, made to a secret recipe), shop; cl 25–26 Dec; (01225) 461634; 30p. They now have a sister shop in Windsor.

🖼🍽 Victoria Art Gallery (Bridge St) European Old Masters and 18th- to 20th-c British paintings and drawings, as well as decorative arts inc porcelain, glass and watches. Disabled access to ground floor only; cl am Sun, all Mon, 25–26 Dec and most bank hols; (01225) 477233; free.

BISHOPS LYDEARD ST1729
★ † Attractive village; interesting church with handsome carving.

BITTON ST6769

🚂 **Avon Valley Railway** 🔢 (Bitton Station) Friendly little railway extending lines along the old Midland Railway towards Bath. Snacks, shop, disabled access; open wknds and bank hols, steamtrains Sun May–Sept plus bank hols and Christmas; (0117) 932 7296 for timetable; £3.

BRADFORD-ON-TONE ST1722

🍎🍺 **Sheppy's Cider** 🔢 (Three Bridges) The Sheppys have been making cider here since the early 19th c, and you can follow the entire process over the 370-acre farm. Tastings in the shop, and a little museum. Snacks, shop, disabled access to shop and museum; cl Sun (exc 12–2pm Easter–Christmas); (01823) 461233; farm free, museum £1.75. The White Horse has good food.

BREAN DOWN ST2958

⛰ Protruding into the Bristol Channel between Weston-super-Mare and acres of holiday camps, this gives the best coastal walk in east Somerset.

BRENDON HILLS SS9738

⛰❋ These give breezy walks with long views; the Royal Oak at Luxborough is a good base.

BRENT KNOLL ST3450

★✝❋ The attractive village has a church with remarkable carved bench ends; the Red Cow is a good dining pub. A path leads up to the prominent summit giving the village its name.

BRIDGWATER ST3036

Once you're through the industrial outskirts, some central bits are worth seeing: Castle St is the finest early 18th-c street in the county.

🏛🍺 **Admiral Blake Museum** (Blake St) Now the local history museum, this picturesque house was the birthplace of the admiral in 1598, and shows his personal possessions (inc his sea chest) and a diorama of his great victory over the Spaniards at Santa Cruz. Shop; cl Sun, Mon, Christmas and New Year; (01278) 456127; free.

BRISTOL ST5873

🏛🍺 A busy industrial city with the usual big-city problems, this is not the best base for an enjoyable stay, but has all sorts of things to fill a lively day visit. One excellent new initiative here is free entry to five of the city's best museums: City Museum & Art Gallery, Industrial Museum, Georgian House, Red Lodge and Blaise Castle Museum (see separate entries). It's easily reached from Bath – or from one of the cosseting nearby country-house hotels we list, and day visits are made easy by good rail connections, and the motorway that plunges right into the city's heart. The city's prosperity still stems from its port, though aerospace now predominates among many other manufacturing interests. There are some striking buildings around the centre, notably the Corn Exchange and the Old Council House on Corn St, and on Broad St the Grand Hotel (1869), the Guildhall (1843) and the Art Nouveau façade of the former Edward Everard printing house. The Theatre Royal, opened in 1766, is one of the oldest working theatres in the country. The best part for leisurely strolls is the elegant suburb of Clifton, with handsome Georgian terraces and its famous suspension bridge. (see Clifton entry). Central places for a cheapish lunchtime bite are the Bridge (Passage St), Commercial Rooms (Corn St) and Le Chateau (Park St). In 1997 a 250-mile cycleway was opened from here to Padstow in Cornwall, keeping off roads as much as possible.

❗ **@Bristol** (Harbourside) Opening in the spring, this £97 million waterfront development promises to be one of the most exciting urban millennium projects. Two main visitor attractions, Explore @Bristol and Wildscreen @Bristol, will be linked by a new tree-lined central square, surrounded by sculpture-filled avenues, shops and restaurants. Building on the work of the Bristol Exploratory (now closed), Explore will be an interactive science centre inc a planetarium, studio-theatre – where children can make their own programmes or join in science debates and experiments via the internet – and a series of touch-screen displays. Wildscreen will take a closer look at nature: walk through a hot-house with free-flying birds and butterflies, face an advancing herd of elephants in the giant IMAX cinema, or pore through ARKive, an electronic library of wildlife films and sound recordings. With different IMAX films and special events planned for the evening, this truly 21st-c development should have more than enough to keep a family entertained all day. Separate charges for individual places, with the two main attractions around £7 each; for details phone (0117) 909 2000 or check their website: www.at-bristol.org.uk

Blaise Castle House Museum (Henbury, 4m NW of city, off B4047) A spacious and locally popular undulating park with some woodland and refreshments. The late 18th-c house is now a branch of the City Museum, with lots of carefully explained farming equipment, and collections of costume and dolls. The castle itself is a Gothic folly built in 1766 within the now scarcely discernible ramparts of an Iron Age hill fort. Shop; museum cl Thurs and Fri, and all Nov–Feb, park open daily; (0117) 950 6789; free. Nearby Blaise Hamlet is a NT-owned estate village designed by John Nash.

† **Bristol Cathedral** This was originally an Augustinian monastery, founded on what's supposedly the spot where St Augustine met the Celtic Christians in the early 7th c. It's a real mix of architectural styles, and perhaps the country's most splendid example of a hall church, where the nave, choir and aisles are all the same height. Highlights include the Chapter House (one of the finest Norman rooms in Britain), and the candlesticks given in thanks by the privateers who rescued Alexander Selkirk (whose adventures inspired Daniel Defoe to write *Robinson Crusoe*). Snacks, shop, some disabled access; (0117) 925 3678; free.

Bristol Industrial Museum (Princes Wharf) Housed in a converted dockside transit shed, and especially good on transport, with locally built steam locomotives and aircraft (inc a mock-up of Concorde's flight deck), and a good look at the development of the port. Shop, disabled access; open Sat–Weds Apr–Oct, wknds only Nov–Mar; (0117) 925 1470; free. Steamtrains run along the docks between here and the SS *Great Britain* every ¼ hr 12–5pm on selected days Mar–Oct; £1.

Bristol Zoo Gardens See separate family panel on p.552.

Cabot Tower The attractive park at the end of Great George St is an urban nature reserve, and its tower rewards those willing to climb the hundreds of steps with probably the best views of the city. Snacks, cl 25 Dec; free. Nearby **St George's** has good Fri lunchtime concerts, usually with seats available on the day, but best to check on (0117) 923 0359.

† **Christmas Steps** This famously old-fashioned alley is quaintly lined by steep buildings. At the top is the tiny late 15th-c **Chapel of the Three Kings of Cologne** (the 'three kings' are the three wise men whose shrines are in Cologne Cathedral); the warden of the nearby almshouses can let you in. And at the bottom is the lodge of **St Bartholomew's** – all that remains of the 13th-c hospital and almshouse which once stood on this site. This is a good area for shops selling antiques, stamps and old books.

City Museum & Art Gallery (Queens Rd) Good collections of fine and applied art, archaeology, geology, and history – well worth a look. Meals, snacks, shop, disabled access; cl 25 Dec; (0117) 922 3571; free. The neo-Gothic Wills Memorial tower next door is a distinctive landmark.

Harveys Wine Museum (Denmark St) Unique collection of antique corkscrews, decanters, glasses, bottles, furniture and other items associated with the production and serving of wine, housed in the medieval cellars of this wine company. There's a very good shop, and you may occasionally be able to join one of the guided tours with tutored tastings. Restaurant, wine shop; cl Sun and bank hols and occasionally at other times; (0117) 927 5036; £4 (inc a glass of sherry).

Historic Boat Trips (from Princesss Wharf) Moored here is the 1860s steam-tug *Mayflower*, which has interesting trips round the docks every hour pm alternate wknds in summer. It only takes 12 passengers, so best to book with the Industrial Museum; £3. From Apr to Oct the **pleasure steamers** *Waverley* and *Balmoral* run fairly frequent day cruises from here, along the Avon and Severn or to Devon, Wales or Lundy; (0117) 926 0767 for programme. The *Balmoral* has surprisingly well kept real ale in its bar.

✝ **John Wesley's Chapel** (Horsefair) Incongruously set in a shopping centre, but much as it was when Wesley preached here (from the famous double-decked pulpit upstairs); the oldest Methodist chapel in the world, built in 1739 and rebuilt in 1748. Guided tours by arrangement. Snacks (not Jan–Easter), shop, disabled access to ground floor only; cl Sun; (0117) 926 4740; free (£2.50 tour).

✝ **Lord Mayor's Chapel** (Park St) Rare civic church, with glorious 16th-c stained-glass windows, floor tiles and fan-vaulted ceiling; guided tours 11am and 2pm.

🏠 **Red Lodge** (Park St) The house was altered in the 18th c, but on its first floor still has the last surviving suite of 16th-c rooms in Bristol, as well as a wonderful carved stone chimney-piece, plasterwork ceilings and fine oak panelling. They occasionally open the reconstructed Tudor-style garden. Open Sat–Weds and most bank hols Mar–Oct; (0117) 921 1360; free. There are several elegant Georgian streets round here, notably Great George St, where the **Georgian House**, built in 1790 for a wealthy sugar merchant, is a fine illustration of a typical town house of the day. Three floors are decorated in period style, inc the below-stairs area with kitchen, laundry and housekeeper's room. Times as for Red Lodge; (0117) 921 1362; free.

✝ **St Mary Redcliffe** (Redcliffe Hill) Elizabeth I described this as 'the goodliest, fairest and most famous parish church in England'. Most of the current building dates from the late 13th c, inc the wonderful hexagonal outer porch. Notable features include the tomb of Admiral Sir William Penn, the father of the man who founded Pennsylvania, and the Handel Window, where eight passages of the *Messiah* commemorate the great composer's ties with this church. Wkdy snacks, disabled access (through south door). Maybe free organ recitals Thurs lunchtimes during term-time.

🚢 ❀ **SS Great Britain** On the dockside a small steam railway on summer wknds will whisk you along the old cargo route to and from this ship, designed by Isambard Kingdom Brunel as the first iron, screw-propelled, ocean-going vessel, and a real departure from what had gone before. It's being restored, after a half-century or so lying neglected in the Falkland Islands and you can see various curiosities including the captain's bath. Snacks, shop; cl 24–25 Dec; (0117) 926 0680; £6. This includes entry to the **Maritime Heritage Centre**, with reconstructions and original machinery illustrating the city's long history of ship-building. The nearby diesel-powered firefloat *Pyronaut* (1934) and Fairbairn steam-crane (1876) operate occasional summer wknds.

🌸 **University Botanic Gardens** (Leigh Woods) Attractive gardens with several rock and water features, set around students' halls of residence. All the plants are excellently labelled, and the grounds include BBC *Gardener's World* micro-climate gardens; some disabled access; cl wknds and bank hols; (0117) 973 3682; free.

BRISTOL DOCKS ST5872
🏠 ⛴ Being attractively restored, with distinctive blue and yellow ferries (Apr–Sept) linking several points. The old part around King St, between the waterfront and the Bristol Old Vic, has quiet cobbled streets of Georgian buildings, pleasant to wander through, and elsewhere some of the bigger warehouses (and even the boats) are being pressed into service as museums, café-bars and the like. The Arnolfini, a big former tea warehouse, is now a contemporary arts complex with bar, restaurant, exhibitions, cinema, theatre and so forth.

BRUTON ST6834
★ ✝ ❀ Fascinating little town; worth looking out for are the Bartons, narrow alleys leading down from the High St to the river (which you can cross either by footbridge or by using stepping stones). **St Mary's Church** is on the site of a medieval Augustinian priory and abbey – the old abbey wall with its buttresses still stands in Silver St. The church has a spectacular altarpiece, and in the chancel is a fine effigy of Sir Maurice

Berkely, a great survivor who was standard-bearer to Henry VIII, Edward VI and Queen Elizabeth I. Interesting and individual shops – antiques, books and prints. The Castle Inn is good for lunch. The drive up towards Alfred's Tower gives some open views, and below it the Old Red Lion at North Brewham has decent food.

BURNHAM-ON-SEA ST3050
☺ ✝ In summer a bustling inexpensive family seaside resort, with wide beaches, sandy dunes, and the usual holiday facilities. Its plain-looking **church** surprises with its collection of Grinling Gibbons carvings from the long-demolished Palace of Whitehall in London.

🐄 ⚥ **Animal Farm Country Park** 📷 (Red Rd, N of Berrow) Good fun for children, with animals and conservation trails, trampolines and play areas. Meals, snacks, shop, disabled access; cl 25–26 Dec (maybe other dates too in winter); (01278) 751628; *£3.75. There's a small **nature reserve** in the nearby sand dunes. The Red Cow at Brent Knoll has good food.

BURRINGTON COMBE ST4858
⌂ ☀ 🏛 An easy walk by the B3134 (the best drive through the Mendips), this great steeply wooded limestone gorge on the N flank of the Mendips can be combined with walks up on to Black Down for memorable views in all directions, and over the heather and cranberry tops to Dolebury Warren, where the site of an Iron Age hill fort marks a splendid Mendip viewpoint. Other useful starting-points for Mendips walks include the Crown at Churchill, Swan at Rowberrow and Ring o' Bells at Compton Martin.

BURROW BRIDGE ST3428
✾ **Somerset Levels Basket Centre** (Lyng Rd) Sells baskets made from local materials cut on the surrounding Levels; there may be demonstrations, and they have other crafts too. Shop, disabled access; cl Sun, 25 Dec–1 Jan; (01823) 698688; free. The Rose & Crown at East Lyng has good food.

CADBURY CAMP ST4572
🏛 ⌂ This Iron Age hill fort makes a good destination for a walk from the engaging Black Horse in Clapton in Gordano, by a lane past the church,

which leads to a footbridge high over the M5. This should not be confused with the more famous Cadbury Castle down towards Yeovil.

CANNINGTON ST2539
🏵 **Cannington College Heritage Gardens** Extensive gardens inc over 10,000 different types of plant, with eight national collections, display and ornamental beds, tropical and sub-tropical glasshouses, and gardens of bees and butterflies. Cl am, and Nov–Easter Mon; (01278) 655000; £2.25. The Malt Shovel at Bradley Green has decent food, and there's a nice drive to Nether Stowey via Combwich and Stogursey.

CASTLE CARY ST6432
★ 🏠 ⛪ Very attractive – basically a medieval market town, now with a useful range of traditional family-run shops and crafts and antique shops. The 18th-c **Roundhouse** is Britain's smallest prison, and the local museum is worth a look if you've time. The George, a comfortable old thatched coaching inn in the village square, has enjoyable food.

🏵 🏠 **Hadspen Gardens** (off A371, 2m SE of Castle Cary) Beautiful eight-acre gardens surrounding a fine 18th-c house; many old favourite plants, but also lots of exotics. A delightful 17th-c walled garden has all sorts of herbaceous plants and old-fashioned roses, and there's a lily-pond and ancient flower meadow. Teas (Sun only), nursery, some disabled access; open Thurs–Sun and bank hols Mar–Sept; (01749) 813707; *£3.

CASTLE NEROCHE ST2715
🏰 � ⌂ ☀ This isolated ruined Norman fortification, with more the aspect now of a hill fort than a castle, is the central feature of well marked woodland walks down towards the Blackdown Hills S of Taunton; fine views at the top.

CHAPEL ALLERTON ST4150
✗ ☀ **Ashton Windmill** The only complete mill left in Somerset, built in the 18th c, with splendid views over the Cheddar Gorge and Somerset Levels. Open pm Sun and bank hols Easter–Sept, plus pm Weds July–Aug (and by appointment in Sept); (01934) 712694; free.

CHARD ST3108

☗ ✿ **Chard Museum** The local history museum (High St) has good displays on local industries such as lace-making, and a bizarre collection of artificial limbs. Shop, disabled access; cl Sun (exc July and Aug), Nov–Apr; (01460) 65091; £2. There are a couple of places to hire bikes; the local tourist board do good cycle routes. **Forde Abbey**, just over the border in Dorset, is particularly worth visiting.

✗ ✿ **Hornsbury Mill** (just N of Chard) 200-year-old watermill, with landscaped watergarden, trout lake, and play area; you can stay here. Meals, snacks, shop, disabled access; cl Jan; (01460) 63317; *£2. Past here at Combe St Nicholas the Green Dragon has good-value food.

CHEDDAR ST4553

✝ ✿ In its older part, this extended village has a very fine market cross, with some interesting shops and a tall-towered 14th/15th-c **church**. The Galleries is quite useful for lunch, and outside are roadside strawberry stalls and **pick-your-own** in summer. Cheddar gets astonishingly busy in summer, when every building seems to be either a tearoom or a shop selling cheese or cider.

△ ✿ ✿ **Cheddar Gorge** The area's big attraction, a magnificent limestone gorge with picturesque cliffs, formed when a cavern roof collapsed. Further up the dramatic B3135 road through the gorge, it rapidly loses its commercialised trappings. When you reach the far end two worthwhile paths leave the road. On the E side is a quiet dale with two nature reserves, Black Rock and Velvet Bottom. On the W side, the West Mendip Way climbs through woods and gives access to another path which skirts the top of the gorge (the views into it are hair-raising). You can also get up to this viewpoint via the 274 steps of Jacob's Ladder from the road at the W entrance to the gorge; a £2 million cable-car system should open within the next 5 years.

✿ ✿ **Cheddar Gorge Cheese Co Village** (The Cliffs) Shops and traditional crafts based around a factory that thanks to its location claims to make the only genuine Cheddar cheese in the world. You can watch each stage of the seven-hour process, and of course taste the matured product. Also fudge-making, scrumpy sampling, and less flavoursome crafts inc lace- and candle-making. Meals, snacks, shops, disabled access; cl Nov–late Mar; (01934) 742810; £1.50.

✿ △ **Cheddar Showcaves** Two beautiful caves beneath the gorge; quite cathedral-like with spectacular stalagmites and stalactites joining to form columns. Also an exhibition devoted to 'Cheddar Man', Britain's oldest complete skeleton, with a re-creation of his world of 9,000 years ago. Good clifftop walks, and plenty of activities for children, inc the lively Crystal Quest. Meals, snacks, shop; cl 24–25 Dec; (01934) 742343; £7.50. The more daring can don hard hats and boiler suits for what they call Adventure Caving Expeditions; £10 (no under-12s).

CHEDDON FITZPAINE ST2428

✿ **Hestercombe Gardens** Raised walks, sunken lawns and a watergarden are all part of the grand design which Lutyens and Gertrude Jekyll created for this beautifully restored garden set around the Somerset Fire Brigade HQ; also intriguing landscaped earlier gardens. Snacks, shop (inc plant sales), limited disabled access; cl 25 Dec; (01823) 413923; £3.50. If you don't want to go into Taunton, the Bathpool Inn at Bathpool (A38) is a handy family dining pub.

CHEW VALLEY LAKES ST5760

♪ ✿ The Chew Valley Lake itself and Blagdon Lake are more popular as breathing places for people living nearby than as places for visitors from afar; both are pleasant large stretches of water, with managed fishing, and the B3130 and B3114 have pleasant views. The New Inn at Blagdon is nicely set for lunch.

CHEWTON MENDIP ST5952

✿ ✝ **Chewton Cheese Dairy** (Priory Farm) Another traditional cheese dairy, one of the few to mature their cheeses properly, so producing not just the characteristic rind but also the true depth of flavour. They start at 7.30am and go on till 3pm, with the best time to watch between 11.30am and

2.30pm. A video shows the stages you may have missed. Meals and snacks (they're building a new restaurant), farm shop, disabled access; no cheese-making Thurs or Sun, cl 25–26 Dec, 1 Jan; (01761) 241666; free (£2.50 guided tour, 11.30am–1.45pm not Thurs or Sun). The 15th-c **church tower** is perhaps the most magnificent in any village in the area. The Waldegrave Arms has decent food.

CLAVERTON ST7864

🏠🕘❀ **American Museum in Britain** (Claverton Manor, just SE of Bath) Quite a contrast to the rest of Bath's attractions, a fascinating illustration of American history and life, in lovely gracious surroundings. Eighteen rooms are fully furnished and decorated to re-create the style of American homes from the 17th to the 19th c, while the grounds include a replica of part of George Washington's garden at Mount Vernon, and an American arboretum. Collections of folk art and patchwork quilts (an exhibition on the Indiana Amish and their quilts runs from Apr–Sept this year), with sections on Native Americans and Shakers, and good special events. Well liked by readers, it's the only museum in the country completely devoted to our colonial cousins. Snacks, shop, some disabled access; cl am, all day Mon (exc Aug and bank hols), and Nov–Mar; (01225) 460503; £5.

CLEVEDON ST4071

📷⚓🎣♪♫ After partly collapsing in 1970, the Victorian **pier** was lovingly restored, and finally reopened in 1998.

It is pleasant for a stroll (shop, disabled access; cl Oct–Mar (exc Weds); *75p). Upstairs, above the tollhouse, a gallery sells paintings, and there are sailings and fishing from the pier itself; shop, disabled access; cl Weds Oct–Mar, and 25 Dec; (01275) 878846; *75p. Round the corner in Waterloo House is a **heritage centre**; donations. Good views from Church Hill, and in Moor Lane the **Clevedon Craft Centre** has 15 varied workshops and a tearoom; some parts cl Mon. The Little Harp and Moon & Sixpence are seafront family dining pubs with views to Wales.

🏠❀ **Clevedon Court** (B3130 just E of Clevedon) Most of the original structure of this manor house, built in 1320, is still intact, though there are interesting additions from other periods inc a charming 18th-c garden. Thackeray wrote part of *Vanity Fair* here. Snacks, some disabled access to ground floor; open pm Sun, Weds, Thurs and bank hols Apr–Sept; (01275) 872257; £4; NT.

CLIFTON ST5673

★ The quiet side of Bristol, with some fine late 18th- and 19th-c terraces, an antique market (Mall, cl Sun, Mon), a big park right on the spectacular Avon gorge facing the NT woodlands on the crags opposite, and the remarkably modern-looking suspension bridge, based on an 1836 design by Brunel and finished in 1864; a Victorian girl leapt off here after a tiff with her boyfriend, but was saved when her huge skirts acted as a parachute. The Somerset House (Princess Victoria St) is useful for something to eat.

Days Out

Uniquely Bath: Building of Bath Museum; Museum of Costume; No 1 Royal Crescent; lunch at the Beaujolais (Queen Sq) or Old Green Tree (Green St); Roman Baths; tea in the Pump Room.

Bristol-fashion: SS *Great Britain* and Maritime Heritage Centre; @Bristol; Bristol Zoo – picnic here; Clifton suspension bridge.

Wonders of the Mendips: Burrington Combe (walk on to Dolebury Warren if time); Cheddar Gorge (take Jacob's Ladder steps up the south side, hold on to something, and look down into the gorge); lunch at the Lamb, Axbridge or Burcott Inn, Wookey; Wookey Hole Caves; Ebbor Gorge.

COMBE FLOREY ST1531
† **Combe Florey church** Charming church with attractive carvings; Evelyn Waugh lies buried outside.

COMBE HAY ST7359
★ ※ This charming steep village has a good pub, and the road to Monkton Combe gives good views.

CRANMORE ST6745
🏰 ※ **Cranmore Tower** Good views from the top of this folly; cl Oct–Mar; around £1.

🚂 ▣ **East Somerset Railway** Steam trips along what's known as the Strawberry Line, as well as engine shed and workshops, with nine steam locomotives and rolling stock, and an art gallery with wildlife paintings by David Shepherd who founded the railway. Meals and snacks (on steamdays), shop, disabled access; open daily, though trains don't run every day – best to ring for timetable; (01749) 880417; £5.50, less when no trains running. The Strode Arms in this quiet and pleasant village is very good for lunch.

CRICKET ST THOMAS ST3708
🏰 ▼ 🦢 △ **Cricket St Thomas Park** Wildlife centre within the lovely parkland of a great estate, familiar from *To The Manor Born*. The theme park attractions have gone, and all of the emphasis is now laid on the conservation of the 600 animals, inc many endangered species. A highlight is a walk through the lemur woods, where you can see the primates swinging happily from the trees above. There's plenty more to amuse children inc a pets corner and miniature railway. Meals, snacks, shop; (01460) 30111; £4.95 (under-3s free).

CROSCOMBE ST5844
★ † ※ △ Croscombe is an attractive village, with great 17th-c woodwork in its 15th-c church. The walk from here to Wells gives unforgettable views of the cathedral.

CUCKLINGTON ST7527
† **Cucklington church** 13th-c, with small side chapel dedicated to St Barbara, whose sacred well lies further down in the village.

DOWLISH WAKE ST3712
🍎 🏠 **Perry's Cider Mills** They've been making cider here for centuries, and between Oct and Nov you can watch it being produced. The cider mill is in a group of thatched 16th-c buildings around a yard with brightly painted old farm wagons and so forth. Enthusiastically run, with a video on cider-making, liberal tastings and half a dozen different ciders for sale, in old-fashioned earthenware flagons if you want. Shop, disabled access; cl 25–26 Dec, 1 Jan; (01460) 5268; free. The nearby New Inn is very good for lunch (and has Perry's cider).

DUNDRY HILL ST5666
※ △ Just S of Bristol's suburbs, this gives walkers views over the city, Chew Magna and Blagdon lakes and the Mendips.

DUNSTER SS9943
★ † ♨ Well worth a day of anybody's time, with fine medieval houses along the wide main street below the wooded castle hill, as well as a handsome octagonal former yarn market and market cross, a lovely 15th-c priory **church** with particularly tuneful bells, and a well established **doll museum** in the Memorial Hall (cl Oct–Mar; 50p). If you plan to visit Exmoor, the National Park Information Centre is a useful first stop. The handsome old Luttrell Arms Hotel is good for lunch, and there's a wealth of tearooms.

🏰 ❀ ※ **Dunster Castle** Dramatically set in a 28-acre park rich with exotic flora and even subtropical plants, the castle was largely rebuilt in the 19th c, but has older features inside such as the 17th-c oak staircase and gallery with its brightly painted wall hangings. Excellent views. Shop in 17th-c stables, limited disabled access (a buggy avoids the steep climb up the hill); castle cl Thurs, Fri, and all Nov–Mar (gardens open all year); (01643) 821314; £5.40, £2.90 garden and park only; NT.

! **Old Dovecot** (St Georges' St) In summer you can go right up this 12th-c dovecot, special for still having its potence or revolving ladder, used for harvesting the plump squabs from the nesting boxes.

⚒ **Watermill** Well restored 18th-c mill still grinding and selling flour; teas in a pleasant riverside garden. Cl Thurs (exc July–Aug), and all Nov–Easter; (01643) 821759; £2.

EAST COKER ST5412
★ Charming quiet village; T S Eliot's ashes are buried here.

EAST HUNTSPILL ST3345
🐄 **Secret World** 🔟 (New Rd Farm) Very friendly family-run working farm, with an emphasis on wildlife rescue (especially badgers). The best feature is the unique observation badger sett in the Nocturnal House, with glass viewing panels to watch the creatures' life underground. Also farm trail, barn owls, lots of other animals, adventure playground, and special events. Meals, snacks, shop, disabled access; cl Jan; (01278) 783250; £4.95. You can hire bikes here too (without having to go into the farm). The Crossways Inn over at West Huntspill is a popular lunch place.

EAST LAMBROOK ST4318
🕸 🖼 **East Lambrook Manor Garden** This well loved cottagey garden around a 15th-c house (not open) is now Grade I listed and is under new ownership. It was started by Walter and Margery Fish in 1937, and Mrs Fish described the process in her book *We Made A Garden*, which became immensely popular; a national collection of geraniums is here. The new owners plan to re-establish the greater use of herbs in the garden (Mrs Fish was interested in their remedial qualities), and have converted the malthouse, in which they hope to house occasional art exhibitions. Snacks, plant sales, shop; cl Sun, Mon, and all Oct–Feb; (01460) 240328; £2.50. The Rose & Crown opposite does good-value food.

EAST QUANTOXHEAD ST1343
★ ✝ ⌂ Delightful village with archetypal duckpond, tiny church with fine oak carvings, and walks to the coast.

EBBOR GORGE ST5248
🌿 ⌂ ❋ If you like Cheddar Gorge but don't like the souvenir stalls, coach parties and all, then Ebbor Gorge is for you. It's the same sort of thing, above Wookey Hole, but altogether quieter and more unspoilt. It has an attractive nature trail, and a good walk runs from Wookey Hole through the Gorge to Pen Hill for panoramic views. The Hunters Lodge and New Inn up around Priddy have sensibly priced food.

FARLEIGH HUNGERFORD ST8057
🏰 **Farleigh Hungerford Castle** Extensive ruins of a 14th-c castle, with monuments in the chapel to the Hungerford family, who once owned the land from here to Salisbury. Picnics welcome, shop, limited disabled access; cl Mon and Tues Nov–Mar, 24–26 Dec; (01225) 754026; £2.30 inc audio tour; EH. The Hungerford Arms overlooking it has decent food.

GLASTONBURY ST4938
★ Tales of King Arthur can be found all over the country, but are especially prominent here; they like to say that bones reinterred in the abbey in 1191 were those of Arthur and Guinevere. The best approach is by the B3151, showing the town below the famous Tor. Glastonbury has quite a New Age feel, probably due to all the legends and the famous annual rock festival. The George & Pilgrims, its medieval carved façade one of the sights of the town, is quite useful for lunch, and the Who'd A Thought It has good-value food. The bypass has made the town much more pleasurable.
🕸 ! **Chalice Well** (Chilkwell St) Legend has it that the Holy Grail was hidden here, now set in a colourful 2½-acre garden; the spring has apparently possessed healing powers ever since. True or not, it's a nice peaceful spot. Shop, disabled access; (01458) 831154; *£2.
🏰 **Glastonbury Abbey** These noble ruins are said to mark the location of the birth of Christianity in this country. The story goes that Joseph of Arimathaea struck his staff into Wearyall Hill, where it took root. (Offshoots of the tree, the famous Glastonbury Thorn, have flourished to this day and there's a fine specimen in the parish churchyard.) He is also said to have brought with him the Holy Grail (Jesus's Last Supper platter, used by Joseph to receive his blood at the cross), which Arthur's knights heroically sought through so many famous stories. The remains of the church date mainly from 1524, though the Lady Chapel is much older, and massive roof timbers and richly decorated gable ends and porches

testify to the enormous wealth of the order who ran it. An interpretation area has a good range of stories connected with the site. Snacks (July–Aug), shop, disabled access; cl 25 Dec; (01458) 832267; £3, maybe more in winter.

🏛🏠👶 **Glastonbury Tribunal** (High St) Glastonbury was formerly an island rising from a vast inland lake, and you can almost see this from the top of the Tor, the highest point of the hills and ridges among which the little town nestles, with fantastic views. Excavations here have revealed a prehistoric **lake village** covering three or four acres below it, consisting of nearly a hundred mounds surrounded by a wooden palisade. Lots of items and timbers from the village have been unusually well preserved thanks to the waterlogged state of the site; and some of the finds, providing a fascinating insight into the life of the settlement, are displayed in this fine 15th-c town house. The tourist information centre is here too, and there's some notable plasterwork in the lower back room. Shop, limited disabled access; cl 25–26 Dec; (01458) 832954; £1.50; EH.

🐄👶🐑 **Somerset Rural Life Museum** (Chilkwell St) Housed in the Abbey Barn and outbuildings, with displays of traditional regional skills such as cider-making, peat-cutting and basket-weaving. Also orchard, rare breeds, and bee garden with hives. Summer snacks, shop, some disabled access; cl Sun, Mon, Good Fri and Christmas; (01458) 831197; £2.50.

GRABBIST HILL SS9843
⌂ ❈ Not as famous as Dunkery Hill (and less frequented even in summer), but recommended to walkers in search of rewarding views; it can be climbed from nearby Dunster.

HATCH BEAUCHAMP ST3021
🏠🐝👶 **Hatch Court** Fine Palladian mansion with impressive hall, walled kitchen garden, deer park, plenty of china and a small military museum. It's one of those places where the family take real care showing you round, enlivening the tour with lots of anecdotes. Teas (Thurs only), disabled access to garden; house open pm Thurs mid-Jun–mid-Sept, garden open daily

Easter Mon–Sept; (01823) 480120; £3.50, £2.50 garden only. The Hatch Inn is good value.

HINKLEY POINT ST2146
🏭 **Hinkley Point Power Station** The visitor centre has displays and interactive videos explaining how electricity is generated, with information on local ecology and wildlife (several nature trails nearby); tours by arrangement, (01278) 652461. Snacks, shop, disabled access; cl Sat Oct–Mar, Christmas wk; free.

ILCHESTER ST5222
★ Charming, with a useful range of well stocked little shops. Used to be a Roman town, and one of the houses has a piece of Roman paving. The whole of the green fronting the town hall is said to be the burial ground of plague victims. The comfortable Ilchester Arms has good food.

ILMINSTER ST3614
✝ **Ilminster church** Magnificent 15th-c tower, all turrets, pinnacles and gargoyles.

KENNET & AVON CANAL ST6470
⌂ Attractively restored, with a good footpath alongside, it runs from Bristol through Hanham (where the Lock & Weir is a charmingly placed pub), Saltford and Bath to the spectacular aqueduct at Avoncliff (and beyond, across Wiltshire and into Berkshire).

KEYNSHAM ST6768
🐖🎣🐝 **Avon Valley Country Park** (Pixash Lane) Lots of animals from rare breed pigs to wallabies, deer park, riverside trails (inc plenty of places to fish), an excellent adventure playground, and free boating on the pond. Snacks, shop, disabled access; cl Mon (exc Aug), and Nov–Easter; (0117) 986 4929; £3.50. The river-view New Inn (Bath Hill) has decent food.

KINGSBURY EPISCOPI ST4321
🏭👶 **Somerset Cider Brandy Co** England's first fully licensed cider distillery, with huge copper stills, oak vats and wooden presses, and traditional cider orchards to stroll through. Maybe tastings of their cider brandy. Shop, limited disabled access; cl Sun, 25–26 Dec; (01460) 240782; free. The village green has an ancient lock-up, and the Wyndham Arms is useful for lunch.

KINGSDON ST5226

🏠 ❀ **Lytes Cary Manor** Most of the surviving building dates from the 16th c, though there are interesting earlier features inc the 14th-c chapel, and the Great Hall with its 15th-c stained glass. The gardens were designed and stocked by Henry Lyte, a notable Elizabethan horticulturist, and are being brought back to their original state – they are hoping that otters will return to the grounds, following improvements to the river banks. Plant sales, disabled access to garden only; open pm Mon, Weds and Sat Apr–Oct; (01985) 843600; £4, £2 garden only; NT. The Kingsdon Inn does good home cooking.

KINGSTON ST MARY ST2229

★ † Pretty village, with attractive church.

LIMINGTON ST5422

† **Limington church** Interesting for its effigies of the Giverney family, dating back to the 1300s.

LONG ASHTON ST5571

🐾 ⋎ ❉ 🏠 **Ashton Court Estate** 850 acres of woods and grassland with deer enclosures, pitch-and-putt golf, and views across Clifton and Bristol to the hills beyond. The large manor house (not open) is mostly 19th-c, although some parts date from medieval times. Part of the stables is now a visitor centre (open wknds and some summer wkdys, phone to check; (0117) 963 9174). Café, shop, disabled access; park open all year; free. The Angel has reasonably priced food.

MARTOCK ST4619

† 🏠 The magnificent **church** has a splendid roof; also look out for the old Court House turned into a Grammar School by William Strode in 1661, with the inscription above the door 'Martock neglect not your opportunities' in English, Latin, Hebrew and Greek. The Fleur de Lis in Stoke sub Hamdon is useful for lunch.

MELLS ST7249

★ † ⌂ Delightful and venerable stone-built village, with marvellous church and graveyard, charming ancient inn, pleasant walks nearby.

MERRIOTT ST4412

❀ 🌾 **Scotts of Merriott** Perhaps the last of the big general retail nurseries to raise and grow most of their own trees and shrubs, on 90 acres – a sea of colour when the 500 varieties of roses are in flower in July. Shop; cl 25 Dec, Easter Sun, (01460) 72306; free. In the village **D B Pottery** (Highway Cottage, Church St) make attractive teapots and other stoneware; (01460) 75655; free. The Lord Poulett on the attractive main street of nearby Hinton St George is good for lunch.

MILVERTON ST1225

† 🌾 The parish church has some fine carving, and there's a little pottery on the charming High St.

MINEHEAD SS9646

🌾 🚂 ⚓ There's an easily missed area of sloping streets and thatched cottages around the church, with Church Steps a quaint steep back lane. Around this original fishing village is a spacious resort, its beach and promenade sheltered by the wooded hills to the NE. It has the usual attractions, a lively harbour, a sizeable holiday camp recently re-designed to be more family-friendly, and a modern shopping area; plans to build England's first new pier for many years were still on hold as we went to press. The Old Ship Aground has good-value food and pleasant harbour views. There's an unusual **pottery shop** (cl 12–1.30pm) on Park St, and a little **shoe factory** you can visit on North Rd (cl 1–2pm and wknds exc am Sat). From the harbour you may be able to catch the *Waverley* (paddle steamer) or *Balmoral*, along the Bristol Channel or to Lundy Island. The clifftop Blue Anchor at the end of the B3191 has decent food and great views.

🚂 **West Somerset Railway** Steam trains run from the Minehead terminus along the coast to Watchet and then inland to Bishops Lydeard – a splendid long run stopping at several little stations. Meals, snacks, shop, very good disabled access, with a specially adapted coach; station open daily but no trains Mon (exc bank hols) and Fri in Apr, May and Oct, and none except Santa specials Nov–Feb, best to ring (01643) 707650 for timetable; £8.90 full return fare.

MONKSILVER ST0737

❀ 🐾 ✗ 🏠 **Combe Sydenham Country Park** (B3188) Just over half-way through a 40-year restoration plan,

580 acres of Exmoor-edge woodland, with walks and trails, corn mill, and play areas. On summer wkdy pms they sometimes do tours of the 16th-c house. Cl Sat, and Nov–Mar; (01643) 702259, £3 car park, charges for some features (pm house tour £5, not Sun). As we went to press, prices were being reviewed so best to check beforehand. The Notley Arms is excellent for lunch.

MONTACUTE ST4917

🏠🖼️🐌 ⌂ ★ **Montacute House** Magnificent 16th-c honeyed stone house in beautiful little village, with a wealth of interesting tapestries, furniture, paintings and ceramics, set in rooms with decorated ceilings, ornate fireplaces and fine wood panelling. A highlight is the collection of Tudor and Jacobean paintings from the National Portrait Gallery. Impressive formal gardens. Meals, snacks, shop, disabled access to grounds only; cl am, Tues and Nov–Mar; (01935) 823289; £5.40, £3 garden only; NT. The park is open to walkers. In the village, features worth seeing include the Borough (a quite charming square of two-storey houses), and Abbey Farm and the Monk's House – all that remains of the Norman priory destroyed during the Dissolution. The Phelips Arms is good for lunch.

MUCHELNEY ST4224

🏛️🏠🐾 **Muchelney Abbey** The abbey was founded in the 9th c (perhaps earlier), but the well preserved ruins date from the 15th, inc part of the cloister, and the abbot's lodging with its splendidly carved fireplace. Shop, limited disabled access; cl Oct–Mar; (01458) 250664; £1.70. The tiny 14th-c priest's house opposite is worth a quick look; open pm Sun and Mon Apr–Sept; £1.70; NT. The **John Leach Pottery** has a few items on display in the abbey, with the main showroom a couple of minutes' drive S (cl lunchtime, pm Sat, and Sun).

NETHER STOWEY ST1939

🏠 **Coleridge Cottage** (Lime St) Little changed since the poet moved here in 1796; he lived here with a pig or two, and his friends the Wordsworths resided in considerably more style not far away – the two families were regarded with suspicion by the local population. Open pm Tues–Thurs and Sun, Apr–Sept; (01278) 732662; £2.50; NT.

★ 🌼 **Quantock Hills Visitor Centre** In this appealing large village with winding streets, handy for both Exmoor and the Quantocks, with good views over the Levels from the mound of the former Norman castle, the visitor centre in Castle St is a valuable source of information. The road up wooded Cockercombe gives a lovely sense of the Quantocks' feeling of peace and timelessness; it's generally the roads on the W side of the hills that give the best views. The Cottage Inn at Keenthorne just E of the village is a useful lunch stop.

NORTON ST PHILIP ST7756

🐂 🌼 **Norwood Rare Breeds Farm** (B3110) Friendly organic farm on high open land with plenty of traditional and rare breeds, nature trails, and good views. You can go right up to the animals, and watch the pigs being fed. Meals, snacks, good farm shop, disabled access; cl Sept–Mar; (01373) 834356; *£4. Refurbishments in the George, one of the most interesting ancient inn buildings in Britain, have uncovered some rare medieval wall paintings. The B3110 has some steep intricate views.

NUNNEY ST7345

🏛️ ★ † **Nunney Castle** This 14th-c fort was reduced to ruins in the Civil War, but has one of the deepest moats in the country; it and its feeder stream running through the green of this quaint and quiet village are jostling with ducks. The castle's layout and round towers were supposedly modelled on France's Bastille; free. There's a small covered market place just above the stream, and nearby are 18th-c weavers' cottages. The **church**, as usual in so many Somerset villages, is well worth a look.

PEAT MOORS ST4241

🏠 🐾 **Peat Moors Visitor Centre** (Shapwick Rd, Westhay) In the heart of the peat-cutting area of the Somerset Levels, with an excellent exhibition on the topic, and a reconstructed Iron Age village. Craft demonstrations most summer wknds. Snacks, shop, disabled access (but no facilities); cl Nov–Feb; (01458) 860697; £2.25. The Olde Burtle Inn, over past Catcott Burtle, has good fresh fish.

QUANTOCK TOPS ST1537

🏛 ⌂ ❄ The moorland tops of these hills are quite a different world, where ancient trackways lead past prehistoric cairns and burial mounds; Exmoor, the Bristol Channel, South Wales and the Mendips are in sight. The tiny road crossing the ridge between Nether Stowey and Crowcombe (which has a delightful church) gives walkers easy access to the moor.

QUANTOCK WALKS ST1540

⌂ 🏑 🏛 ❄ The Quantock Hills have the most for walkers in west Somerset (short of Exmoor). Their secretive quality is illustrated by the dense broad-leafed woodlands on the N side, where shady combes display splendid spring and autumn colours. The village of Holford is a good starting-point: the paths begin with helpful signposts, though you may soon get bemused by the complexity of the path junctions. Holford Combe is reasonably easy to find, and a map will get you to the ancient hill fort site capping Dowsborough, from where a moorland track leads gently north to Holford. Another good approach is from Kilve, from where you can take a path to and along the coast, then through East Quantoxhead to the north Quantock slopes for a remarkably varied circuit.

QUANTOCKS – WESTERN SLOPES ST1139

⌂ ✝ The W slopes of the Quantock Hills, less wooded than the NE side, have some attractive valleys enclosed by plunging slopes, with tracks along the bottom: Bicknoller with its fine church (good carvings) is an attractive start for walks, the Blue Ball at Triscombe another useful port of call.

RODE ST8053

🐦 **Tropical Bird Gardens** 🔳 Huge collection of around 200 species of colourful and exotic birds flying through 17 acres of grounds, with ornamental lakes, ponds and masses of trees and shrubs. Also pets corner and woodland miniature railway (Easter–mid-Sept). Summer meals, snacks, shop (inc sales of clematis, of which they have a notable collection), disabled access; cl 25 Dec; (01373) 830326; £5.50. The Woolpack at Beckington is a popular pub that has good food.

SOMERTON ST4928

★ ✝ Built in light grey stone, this market town has a 17th-c market cross and fine old Georgian buildings in the quiet main square, where the Globe has decent food. **St Michael's Church** is stupendous, its roof supposedly created by monks of Muchelney from 7,000 fetter pieces, among which is a beer barrel – apparently a reference to Abbot Bere.

SOUTH CADBURY ST6325

★ ✝ An attractive scatter of golden cottages huddle around the church with its striking gargoyled tower; Waterloo Crescent is a distinctive row of farm workers' cottages built in 1815. 🏛 ⌂ **Cadbury Castle** Its Arthurian connection is the main draw. The legendary king and his knights are still said to sleep below the turf of this huge hill fort, waking on Christmas Eve to ride down the hill, along what's long been known as King Arthur's Hunting Causeway, and through the village on their pilgrimage to Glastonbury. The castle, covering about 18 acres, is in fact a massive Iron Age camp: many relics have been found there – especially Roman artefacts. It's quite a steep climb, and can be muddy. The nearby Sparkford Inn is a nice place for lunch. Compton Pauncefoot just E is pretty.

SOUTH PETHERTON ST4317

✝ The **church** has the second-highest octagonal tower in the country.

SPARKFORD ST6127

🚗 **Haynes Sparkford Motor Museum** (A359) Huge collection of gleamingly restored vintage and classic cars and motorcycles; you should be able to see some being test-driven outside. Meals, snacks, shop, disabled access; cl 25 Dec, 1 Jan; (01963) 440804; £4.95. The Sparkford Inn has a good carvery.

STAPLE FITZPAINE ST2618

★ ❄ Pretty village with a fine pub; a quiet drive with good views loops along the S edge of Staple Hill then crosses the B3170 to run over Culmhead (where the Holman Clavel is a good stop), along the Blackdown Hills and past the Wellington Monument.

STAPLEGROVE ST2027

🍇 **Staplecombe Vineyards** Friendly little vineyard, with self-guided tours of the fields, then back at the house a cheery couple happy to chat. Open pm exc Sun Apr–Oct, or by appointment; (01823) 451217; free. Avoiding Taunton, the Lethbridge Arms at Bishops Lydeard does decent lunches.

STEEP HOLM ST2260

✓ ❋ ⚓ A small island a few miles offshore, its 50 acres a nature reserve teeming with rare plants, wildlife and historic remains. Terrific views from the rugged cliffs. You can get snacks out here, and there's a shop in former Victorian barracks, but it's not really suitable for the disabled. Boat trips to the island run from Knightstone Causeway, Weston, Apr–Oct – Mrs Rendell has dates and times on (01934) 632307; all-day trip £13.

STOGUMBER ST0937

★ ✝ Charming village with cottage gardens, an unblemished main street, and an interesting **church**; the White Horse has good food.

🐷 **Bee World & Animal Centre** (just S of Stogumber Stn) Rather jolly bee farm with observation hives, useful enough exhibition, and plenty of rare breeds and farm animals, some of which children can stroke. Also play area, a crazy golf course, nature trails, and children's pony rides. Staff are helpful and friendly, and you can see trains go past on the West Somerset Railway (combined tickets available). Good meals and snacks, shop, disabled access; cl Nov–Mar; (01984) 656545; £3.15.

STOGURSEY ST2042

✝ **Stogursey church** Exceptional Norman church with charming carved 15th- and 16th-c pew ends – fascinating figures, faces and grotesques.

STOKE ST GREGORY ST3427

🌿 **English Basket Centre** (Curload, between Stoke St Gregory and Athelney) Produces baskets from its own willow plantations, as well as art charcoal. Also a working blacksmith and a display of willow sculptures. Shop, disabled access; cl pm Sat, Sun, bank hols; (01823) 698418; free. The Rose & Crown at Woodhill, on the edge of Stoke St Gregory, is popular for lunch.

✓ 🌿 **Willow & Wetlands Visitor Centre** (Meare Green Court, between Stoke St Gregory and North Curry) Shows how this area – the most

important area of wetland in England – developed from marsh and swamp, and looks at its wildlife and industries, especially willow-growing and basket-making (of which there may be demonstrations). Shop, some disabled access; cl Sun; (01823) 490249; free.

STOKE SUB HAMDON ST4716

🐝 ♘ ❋ ⌂ **Ham Hill Country Park** 140 acres of grassland and woodland, full of wildlife and plants. The hill has provided the stone for many of the villages in the area, producing that distinctive warm honey-coloured look. The elevated area of old stone quarries gives walkers splendid views; you can go E from here on paths past St Michael's Hill to Montacute.

🏛 ★ **Stoke sub Hamdon Priory** The former 14th- and 15th-c priory manor house has long since vanished, but its fine thatched barn and the screens, passage and Great Hall of the chantry can still be seen; free. The **village** is charming, and the Fleur de Lis is good for lunch. Between here and Montacute is a striking folly, St Michael's Tower; it's one of three, all built by neighbouring friends in the 18th c – whenever one had a flag up it was an invitation for the others to go round for a hearty evening.

STRATTON-ON-THE-FOSSE ST6550

🏛 Notable for the spectacular modern (though not modern-looking) Downside Abbey.

STREET ST4836

👞 🏭 **Shoe Museum** Clarks Shoes have been made in Street for quite some while now, and their museum on the High St has examples of footwear from Roman times to the present, along with machinery and advertising material. Shop, disabled access; cl Christmas week; (01458) 443131; free. Behind here **Clarks Village** is an attractively laid out factory shopping centre, with well known names from Jaeger to Black & Decker; some real bargains, plenty of snacks.

TAUNTON ST2224

✝ 🏛 🌿 Busy and prosperous shopping country town with a lively Sat cattle market. It's not of great visual distinction; the best bit is Hammet St, a short street of 18th-c red brick terraces leading to the county's biggest

church, which has an exceptionally ornate roof, lovely pinnacled tower and lofty Perpendicular chancel. The **Tudor House** on Fore St is attractive. Just behind Riverside Pl the **Shakespeare Glassworks** may have demonstrations of glass-blowing, and in Bath Pl **Makers** is a decent craft shop selling local hand-made crafts (cl Sun). The Masons Arms in Magdalene St is good for lunch (not Sun).

☗ **Somerset County Museum** Fine museum, housed in part of the former castle (whose 13th-c portcullised gate-tower is absorbed into the County Hotel). Shop, disabled access to ground floor only; cl Sun, Mon (exc bank hols), Good Fri, 25–26 Dec; (01823) 355455; £2.50.

☗ **Somerset Cricket Museum** (Priory Bridge Rd) Old building, thought to have been the gatehouse for the priory that once stood on the cricket ground: bats, balls and blazers, cards, cuttings and caps, and a cricketing reference library too. Some disabled access; open wkdys Apr–Oct, plus wknds when there's a match on; (01823) 275893; £1.

TEMPLECOMBE ST7022
✝ Ancient village with stocks still in place; the name comes from the medieval order of Knights Templar, dedicated to the protection of the Holy Sepulchre and pilgrims to it. The church, supposedly founded by King Alfred's daughter, houses a 13th-c painting of Christ, found by accident in an outhouse 30 years ago; possibly an early copy of the Turin Shroud, which the Knights Templar may have had in their possession for a while.

TINTINHULL ST5020
❀ **Tintinhull House Garden** Colourful and attractive 1930s formal garden sheltered by walls and hedges, around a 17th-c house with Queen Anne façade (not open). Teas, some disabled access; open pm Weds–Sun Apr–Sept; (01935) 822545; £3.70; NT. The Lamb has good-value food.

TOLLAND ST1131
⌂ ❀ **Gaulden Manor** (B3224) Nicely tucked-away medieval manor house distinguished for its early plasterwork. The gardens are pleasant too, with a rose garden and bog garden. Teas,

shop, plant sales, disabled access; open pm Sun, Thurs and bank hols early Jun–Aug; (01984) 667213; £3.80, gardens only £2. The Fitzhead Inn at Fitzhead has good food.

WAMBROOK ST2908
★ ⌂ Attractive village, in quiet countryside suiting both walkers and cyclists; the Cotley Inn here is pleasant.

WASHFORD ST0440
✝ **Cleeve Abbey** (signed S of Washford) Remarkably well preserved 12th-c Cistercian abbey, the gatehouse, dormitory and refectory all in good condition. Fine timbered roof, detailed wall paintings and traceried windows, and an exhibition on monastic life. Snacks, shop, some disabled access; cl winter lunchtimes, 24–26 Dec, 1 Jan – best to phone for winter opening; (01984) 640377; £2.60; EH. The Notley Arms at Monksilver is the closest good place for a meal.

🐟 🦜 ✈ 🐛 ☗ 🐒 **Tropiquaria** (A39 – easy to spot by tall radio masts) This enjoyable place is an amazing transformation of a 1930s BBC transmitting station into an indoor jungle with high waterfall, tropical plants, free-flying birds and weird and wonderful animals. You can touch all sorts of creatures: plenty of snakes and lizards, maybe a millipede if you're lucky. There's an aquarium beneath the hall, while out in the landscaped gardens are birds, lemurs, chipmunks, guinea pigs and wallabies, as well as a couple of good play areas. A delightful puppet theatre (for many, the highlight) below the café has 20-minute marionette and shadow puppet shows (usually hourly in summer, but at other times much less frequent – so worth checking first). Also an intriguing collection of vintage radios and televisions. Meals, snacks, shop, disabled access (not to aquarium); open daily Easter–Oct, then wknds and school hols Nov, Feb and Mar, and a wk after Christmas; (01984) 640688; £4.40. The nearby station on the steamline from Minehead has a little **railway museum** devoted to the old Somerset & Dorset Railway; cl Nov–Feb; (01984) 640869; £1.

WATCHET ST0743
★ This small working port has fishing boats and coasters using its tidal

harbour, and enough industry to keep it from being too touristy – though it's by no means unattractive. The West Somerset Hotel has good cheap food.

WEBBINGTON ST3855

☷ **Forgotten World** Romany museum and working wheelwright's shop, with brightly coloured carriages and caravans, and an Edwardian fairground. Snacks, shop, disabled access; open daily Easter–Sept; (01934) 750841; £2.

WELLS ST5546

★ With a population of only 9,500 this delightful place wouldn't normally even qualify as a big town, but in fact it's England's smallest city. The **Vicars Close** is said to be one of the oldest complete medieval streets in Europe; the cathedral's Vicars Choral still live here, passing the 15th-c Chain Gate to the cathedral itself. There are a good few other attractive old buildings, many now used as offices and shops (inc several antique shops), and several grouped around the Market Pl; the City Arms is a charming place for lunch, and there's a big cheese shop not far away. From Wells, the B3139 through to Wedmore and side roads off it give a good feel of the dead flatness of the Somerset Levels.

🏰 ❀ **Bishop's Palace** Moated and fortified, approached through a 14th-c gatehouse; it's quite dramatic going across the drawbridge. The beautiful series of buildings still has some original 13th-c parts, notably the banqueting hall and undercroft, as well as several state rooms and a long gallery hung with portraits of former bishops. The grounds are the site of the wells that give the town its name, producing on average 150 litres (40 gallons) of water a second. Also lovely gardens, decent arboretum and a rather clever pair of swans, trained to ring a little bell under the gatehouse window when they're hungry (so many people feed them in summer that this isn't terribly often). Snacks, disabled access to ground floor; open Tues–Fri plus bank hols and pm Sun Easter–Oct, daily in Aug; (01749) 678691; £3, maybe more for special exhibitions.

✝ **Wells Cathedral** Stunning structure right in the centre, its three towers stretching up against the Mendip foothills. The spectacular west front is reckoned by many to be the finest cathedral façade in the country; dating from the 13th c, it carries 293 pieces of medieval sculpture. Unmissable oddities inside include the wonderful scissor-shaped inverted arches, the north transept's 14th-c clock where horsemen still joust every quarter of an hour, and the fine carvings in the south transept, inc various victims of toothache and four graphic scenes of an old man stealing fruit and getting what for. The embroidered stallbacks in the choir (1937–1948) are a riot of colour, and the library, with documents dating back to the 10th c, is at 51 metres (168ft) the longest medieval library building in England. Evensong is at 5.15pm wkdys (not Weds), 3pm Sun. Meals, snacks, shop, disabled access; £4 suggested donation.

☷ **Wells Museum** (Cathedral Green) Tudor building with good local history museum inc notable embroidery samplers, and stone figures originally on the west front of the cathedral, but now too fragile to be returned there. Disabled access to ground floor only; cl Tues Nov–Easter; (01749) 673477; *£2.

WEST BAGBOROUGH ST1733

❀ Tiny village well placed below the Quantocks, with a traditional working **pottery**, and fresh generous food (and comfortable bedrooms) at the Rising Sun.

WEST MENDIP WAY ST3956

⌂ 🏰 ❀ This long-distance footpath, all the way between Wells and Weston-super-Mare, crosses the Mendip plateau, poor windswept sheep pasture on top, pocked with unseen caverns used by potholers, and more visible Bronze Age funeral barrows; there are some stunning views from this section along Crook Peak, Compton Hill and Wavering Down. A path up from Compton Bishop ST3955 gives good access.

WESTON-SUPER-MARE ST3161

☺ ⌂ 🏰 Friendly family seaside resort, its Latin epithet added in the 19th c in an attempt to be one up on the fashionable French resorts. The seafront Pavilion (Knightstone Parade) is a rather stylish new family dining place, and there are pleasant walks (and a toll road) through the woods around the Iron Age fort above the town. The quietest beaches are to the N, around Sand Bay.

✠ **Helicopter Museum** 🏛 (B3146, was A370) An unexpected find with over 50 helicopters and autogyros on display, and a realistic simulator. Usually on the second Sun each month (Mar–Oct), they have an Open Cockpit Day, when some helicopters are opened up for visitors to inspect, and others even offer flights. Snacks, shop, disabled access; cl Mon, Tues Nov–Mar, and 25–26 Dec, 1 Jan; (01934) 635227; *£3.50.

♪ **Sea Life Centre** (Marine Parade) Another in the reliable chain, right by the beach, with walk-through underwater tunnel, and plenty of sharks. Meals, snacks, shop, disabled access; cl 25 Dec; (01934) 641603; £4.50.

♨ **Time Machine** (Burlington St) Actually a fairly unsurprising local history museum, focusing mainly on Victorian domestic life, with reconstructed shops and lots of seaside displays; it includes adjacent Clara's Cottage, a typical Westonian home of the 1900s with period kitchen, parlour and bedroom. Snacks, shop, disabled access on ground floor only; cl 25–26 Dec, 1 Jan; (01934) 621028; £3.

WESTONZOYLAND ST3534
★ ⚒T Pretty village with a **steam pumping station**.

WINCANTON ST7128
★ ✠ Fine Georgian houses and many of the multitude of inns and hotels survive from the coaching era; many still have old coach-entry gates. The **church porch** has a medieval relief of St Eligius. The cheerful Nog (South St) has decent food.

WOOKEY HOLE ST5347
♨ ✗ ☺ **Wookey Hole Caves & Papermill** Guided tours of half a mile of dramatic subterranean tunnels and caverns, using remote-controlled lighting and special effects to spotlight the geological features and bring to life associated history and myths. Just along the river the papermill demonstrates paper production, and also houses an authentic Edwardian fairground, Magical Mirror Maze and an Old Penny Arcade. A bustling place, all under cover, so ideal when the sun's not shining. Meals and snacks (readers find them a little pricey), shop, disabled access exc to caves; cl 17–25 Dec; (01749) 672243; £7. The Burcott Inn nearby is good for lunch.

YEOVIL ST5515
♨ ✠ Little to interest visitors, but the **Museum of South Somerset** (Hendford) is worth a look if passing, with a good range of local history exhibits and reconstructed Roman and Georgian rooms (shop, disabled access; cl Sun and Mon, plus Sat Sept–Mar; free); there's also a dry-ski centre and partly 14th-c **church**.

YEOVILTON ST5423
✠ **Fleet Air Arm Museum** (Royal Naval Air Station, off A359) Big place concentrating on the story of aviation at sea from 1908, and the history of the Royal Naval Air Service. Lively displays on the WRENS, the Falklands and Gulf Wars, jets and helicopters, as well as nearly 50 historic aircraft, and lots of models, paintings, weapons and photographs, plus a new exhibition on supersonic flight. Viewing galleries look out over the aircraft using this busy base. Also adventure playground, and hi-tech flight simulator. You could easily spend a good few hours here. Meals, snacks, shop, disabled access; cl 24–26 Dec; (01935) 840565; £7. The Kingsdon Inn is the best nearby place for lunch.

✠ **Other interesting churches** with fine carvings include Bicknoller ST1139, Broomfield ST2231 and Spaxton ST2237.

★ **Particularly attractive villages**, all with decent pubs, include Batcombe ST6838, Compton Dando ST6464, Evercreech ST6438, Hinton St George ST4212, Huish Episcopi ST4226, Litton ST5954, Luxborough SS9837, North Perrott ST4709, Norton sub Hamdon ST4615, South Stoke ST7641 (picturesque views from the steep nearby lanes), Waterrow ST0425 and Wellow ST7458. High Ham ST4330, Pilton ST5940, Stowell ST6822 and Winscombe ST4157 are also well worth a visit.

Where to eat

APPLEY ST0621 **Globe** *(01823) 672327* Cheerfully run, unspoilt 15th-c pub with a relaxed, chatty atmosphere, generous helpings of good interesting food inc adventurous specials and vegetarian meals, and super puddings; no smoking dining room; cl Mon lunch exc bank hols. **£20|£7.**

BATCOMBE ST6838 **Three Horseshoes** *(01749) 850359* Honey stone, slate-roofed pub serving very popular food in the bustling main room decorated with pretty ivy stencils and artificial ivy, fruit and flower decorations, and a few naive farm animal paintings on the lightly ragged dark pink walls; a woodburning stove and big open fire, attractive stripped stone dining room, well kept real ales, a good choice of wines, and a big, well equipped play area in the garden. **£18.70|£6.95.**

BATH ST7464 **Beaujolais** *5 Chapel Row, Queen Sq (01225) 423417* Bustling wine bar with naughty postcards and so forth on the walls, a conservatory area, enjoyable French food, cheerful staff, and small summer courtyard; cl Sun, 2 wks Jan. **£25.50 supper, £13.80 lunch.**

BATH ST7464 **Lettonie** *35 Kelston Rd (01225) 446676* Super restaurant with rooms in a lovely Georgian house set in gardens with fine views; spacious reception area, convivial bar, elegant restaurant with paintings by Mr Blunos's Latvian uncle, beautifully presented, exceptional food (French with Latvian touches), a relaxed atmosphere, and helpful, keen French staff; comfortable, pretty bdrms; cl Sun and Mon, 2 wks Aug, 2 wks after Christmas; disabled access. **£53 dinner, £33.90 lunch|2 courses £15.**

BATH ST7464 **Moody Goose** *7A Kingsmead Sq (01225) 466688* Stylish basement restaurant with large namesake pottery goose, paintings on whitewashed walls, fresh flowers on crisp white tablecloths, deft modern English cooking, and a thoughtful wine list; cl Sun, Mon, 2 wks Jan, between Christmas and New Year; children over 7. **£29|2 courses £10.**

BATH ST7464 **Old Green Tree** *12 Green St (01225) 448259* Genuinely unspoilt pub with bustling, cheerful atmosphere in its three oak-panelled little rooms, a no smoking back bar, several well kept real ales, lots of malt whiskies, a nice little wine list with a dozen by the glass, and good home-made lunchtime bar food; cl am Sun, 25–26 Dec, 1 Jan; no children. **£4.80.**

BATH ST7465 **Olive Tree** *Russel St (01225) 447928* Light and airy, no smoking basement restaurant in the Queensberry Hotel; stylishly simple modern décor, friendly helpful service, super Mediterranean cooking (delicious fish and tempting puddings), and good-value wines; cl am Sun, 1 wk at Christmas. **£24 dinner, £14.50 lunch.**

BATH ST7564 **Rajpoot** *4 Argyle St (01225) 466833* Exceptionally good, carefully cooked Indian food in an attractively decorated restaurant, particularly good service (you are met at the door by a colourfully uniformed doorman), and used by stars of screen and stage; cl 25–26 Dec; disabled access (by arrangement). **£20|£6.95.**

BECKINGTON ST8051 **Woolpack** *(01373) 831244* This old inn has a spacious, light and modern interior with an attractive no smoking lounge, antique furnishings, a lively flagstoned public bar with a good log fire, cosy, candlelit, no smoking dining room, imaginative daily specials, and real ales and decent wines; comfortable bdrms. **£25.45|£10.**

BRISTOL ST5872 **Harveys** *12 Denmark St (0117) 927 5034* Attractive restaurant in 13th-c wine cellars with lots of interesting memorabilia (old sherry casks, wine bottles, and old silver and glassware), very good imaginative food, an exceptional cheese board, friendly knowledgeable staff, and a wonderful wine list; cl am Sat, Sun, 1 wk Feb, 2 wks Aug. **£47.50.**

BRISTOL ST5873 **Markwicks** *43 Corn St (0117) 926 2658* Elegant restaurant in the vaults of an old bank building, delicious, daily-changing French and English cooking (first-class fish, lovely puddings), a carefully chosen wine list, and good friendly service; cl am Sat, Sun, 1 wk Christmas, 1 wk Easter, 2 wks Aug. **£32 dinner, £24 lunch.**

BRISTOL ST5873 **Naranjas Fusion Brasserie** *59 Apsley Rd, Clifton (0117) 973 4892* Bustling brasserie with interesting modern cooking inc popular weekend breakfasts, a relaxed atmosphere, helpful staff, and year-round outside dining on the retractable covered, heated terrace. cl 24–25 Dec. **£22.50**.

BRISTOL ST5672 **Neil's** *112 Princess Victoria St, Clifton (0117) 973 3669* Cosy and brightly decorated family-run restaurant with friendly owner and a good choice of imaginative French/English food; cl Sun, Mon, 3 wks Christmas. **£21.95**.

BRISTOL ST5672 **River Station** *The Grove (0117) 914 4434* Converted ex-River Police HQ on the waterfront with informal ground-floor bistro, airy first-floor restaurant, modern furnishings, enjoyable, popular modern British cooking with Mediterranean slant, and a marvellous choice of wines by the glass; cl am Sat, 25–28 Dec; disabled access downstairs only. **£27.50**|2-course lunch £10.50.

CASTLE CARY ST6432 **George** *(01963) 350761* Lovely thatched coaching inn with a huge black elm mantlebeam said to be over a thousand years old over the log fire in beamed front bar, a civilised relaxed atmosphere, no smoking restaurant and inner no smoking bar, well kept ales, decent wines by the glass, enjoyable, and pleasant staff; bdrms. **£21.65**|£7.95.

COMBE HAY ST7359 **Wheatsheaf** *(01225) 833504* Popular country pub in a pretty setting, with pleasantly old-fashioned rooms, a big log fire, shuttered windows, reliably good food (plenty of game and fish), well kept real ales, decent wines, and friendly staff; cl 25–26 Dec; disabled access. **£25**|£4.75.

CRANMORE ST6743 **Strode Arms** *(01749) 880450* Neatly kept former farmhouse with charming country furnishings, newspapers to read, log fires in handsome fireplaces, generous helpings of good interesting food in both the bar and restaurant, well kept real ales, and decent wines; cl winter pm Sun; children in restaurant only; disabled access. **£17.50**|£4.50.

CULMHEAD ST2016 **Holman Clavel** *(01823) 421432* Friendly free house high up in the middle of the Blackdown Hills, with a relaxed atmosphere, roaring log fire, ancient skittle alley, simple furnishings, imaginative and enjoyable daily-changing food using organic produce and free-range eggs, real ales, and 15 wines by the glass. **£25**|£4.95.

DOULTING ST6445 **Waggon & Horses** *(01749) 880302* 18th-c inn with stone-mullioned latticed windows, rambling bar with interesting pictures for sale, two no smoking rooms, a wide choice of enjoyable, robustly flavoured food (good fresh seafood Thurs and Fri), decent house wines, cocktails, real ales, and a lovely big walled garden with some remarkable fancy fowl (they sell the eggs), a goat and horses; big raftered gallery for art shows and classical music; children must be well behaved. **£22**|£6.90.

DOWLISH WAKE ST3712 **New Inn** *(01460) 52413* 17th-c stone pub with hops and old-fashioned furnishings in the spotlessly kept, dark-beamed bar, woodburner in inglenook, a no smoking family room, good enjoyable bar food, well kept real ales and Perry's ciders, pleasant back garden; no food winter pm Sun; children in family room only. **£20**|£4.85.

EAST WOODLANDS ST7944 **Horse & Groom** *(01373) 462802* Small civilised pub on the edge of Longleat estate with a pleasant little bar, comfortable lounge, sizeable no smoking dining conservatory, good, well presented food, well kept real ales, decent wines by the glass, helpful service, and seats in the attractive garden; no food pm Sun, Mon; children in restaurant only. **£25**|£7.50.

HALLATROW ST6356 **Old Station** *(01761) 452228* Extraordinary pub packed with a formidable collection of bric-à-brac in its dimly lit bars, a handsome beer counter with well kept real ales, a mix of furniture, surprisingly good, enjoyable food (given the style of the place), and a no smoking railway carriage restaurant in a garden with a well equipped play area; bdrms; disabled access. **£20**|£5.95.

KNAPP ST3025 **Rising Sun** *(01823) 490436* Rather smart 15th-c longhouse with genteel landlord, a friendly atmosphere, stripped beams and stonework, two inglenook fireplaces, good food with a strong emphasis on fish, a partly no smoking restaurant, well kept real ales, farm ciders, a decent wine list, and welcoming staff (and dogs); bdrms; some disabled access. **£23.25**|**£8**.

LANGLEY MARSH ST0729 **Three Horseshoes** *(01984) 623763* Unpretentious red sandstone pub with a short, changing choice of imaginative food (inc vegetarian dishes and always a game casserole), veg from their own garden, no chips or fried food, a wide choice of often unusual real ales, farm ciders, no fruit machines or pool tables; skittle alley, beer garden, and a sloping back garden with play area and farmland views; good nearby walks; cl winter Mon; children must be well behaved. **£18**|**£6.50**.

MONKSILVER ST0737 **Notley Arms** *(01984) 656217* Immensely well liked, friendly pub with a characterful, beamed L-shaped bar, candles and fresh flowers, woodburners, reasonably priced, very good food, well kept beers, and neatly kept cottagey garden running down to a swift clear stream; cl last wk Jan, first wk Feb; disabled access. **£16**|**£5**.

MONTACUTE ST4916 **Milk House** *The Borough (01935) 823823* Lovely old golden stone evening restaurant with antiques, a big open fire, and friendly welcome, very good interesting food (using home-grown produce), and a reasonably priced wine list; bdrms; cl Sun, Mon, Tues, and all Nov–Apr; well behaved children only. **£25**.

NORTH CURRY ST3125 **Bird in Hand** *(01823) 490248* Friendly village pub with flagstones, beams, timbers and log fires, a proper public bar, interesting enjoyable food using organic vegetables (à la carte meals in winter only served Fri and Sat evenings), free hors d'oeuvres Sun lunchtime, separate restaurant with conservatory, good choice of real ales (festival May and Oct), and a thoughtful choice of wines; cl Mon, Tues and Thurs lunchtimes; children must be gone by 9pm. **£19**|**£5**.

RUDGE ST8251 **Full Moon** *(01373) 830936* Attractive rustic pub with friendly licensees, a lot of character in the different rooms, a gently upmarket atmosphere, small flagstoned dining room (and separate plush restaurant), generous helpings of good bar food inc a bargain 3-course set lunchtime and early evening meal, and well kept real ales; comfortable bdrms. **£22.50**|**£5.50**.

SHEPTON MALLET ST6143 **Blostins** *29 Waterloo Rd (01749) 343648* Friendly little candlelit evening bistro with consistently good, interesting food inc lovely puddings, and fairly priced wines; cl Sun, Mon, 1 wk Jan, 1 wk Easter, 2 wks Aug. **£23**.

TRISCOMBE ST1535 **Blue Ball** *(01984) 618242* Snug little unspoilt pub tucked away into the Quantocks, with quite a reputation for its popular, imaginative food with an emphasis on fresh fish dishes; friendly, cheerful landlord, a carefully improved beamed bar with panelling and rough-sawn oak partitions, attractive sporting prints, memorabilia, and woodburner, real ales, a marvellous wine list, and woodside terraced garden with peaceful views; self-catering also. **£19.90**|**£5.50**.

WAMBROOK ST2907 **Cotley** *(01460) 62348* Bustling country pub with a relaxed, happy yet rather smart atmosphere, two-room no smoking dining area, a no smoking separate restaurant, open fires, really enjoyable food (especially daily specials for large and smaller helpings), well kept real ales, a good choice of wines, a children's play area in the garden, and lots of nearby walks; nice bdrms; disabled access. **£19**|**£7.95**.

WELLS ST5545 **City Arms** *High St (01749) 673916* Characterful 16th-c pub reached through a charming cobbled courtyard with white metal seats and tables, Virginia-creepered walls, and attractive side verandah; cellar-like bar with double ballaster-shaped pillars in arched doorways, homely sofas and other seats, a really relaxed, friendly atmosphere, a fine open-beamed upstairs restaurant, good, interesting food, real ales, and neat, cheerful staff. **£13**|**£4.70**.

WEST HUNTSPILL ST3145 **Crossways** *(01278) 783756* Popular dining pub with a buoyant atmosphere and plenty of space, enjoyable food (especially daily specials), well kept real ales, and decent wines; comfortable bdrms; cl 25 Dec; disabled access. **£14.50**|**£5**.

WESTON-SUPER-MARE ST3261 **Reflections** *22 Boulevard (01934) 622454* Informal family-run restaurant, a good but ordinary café at lunchtimes (exc Sun, when

decent set lunch), but transformed Thurs, Fri and Sat evenings with elaborate and well presented high-quality meals; cl pm Sun–Weds, 1 Jan for 12 days. **£23.75|£4.50**.
WILLITON ST0741 **White House** *Long St (01984)* 632777 Charming shuttered Georgian hotel under the same owners for over 30 years, with antiques and more modern furnishings, paintings and ceramics, very good, enjoyable, carefully cooked food using the best local produce, and a fine choice of reasonably priced wines; nice breakfasts; bdrms; cl Nov–mid-May; disabled access. **£39.50**.
WOOKEY ST5145 **Burcott** *(01749)* 673874 Little roadside pub, close to Wells, neatly kept and friendly with two simply furnished small front bars, an open fire, a roomy, attractive back restaurant, nice bar food, well kept real ales, and a sizeable garden; no food pm Sun; cl 25 Dec, 1 Jan; disabled access. **£22|£5.25**.

Special thanks to B and K Hypher, Michael and Lorna Helyar, H Knight, Mr and Mrs G Selvester, Dave Braisted.

Somerset Calendar

Some of these dates were provisional as we went to press. Please check information with the telephone numbers provided.

JANUARY

14　**Shepton Mallet** Outdoor Leisure: camping and caravanning show at the Royal Bath & West Showground – *till 16 January* (01775) 768661
22　**Shepton Mallet** Antiques Fair: up to 500 stands at the Royal Bath & West Showground – *till 23 January* (01775) 768661

FEBRUARY

5　**Shepton Mallet** Bristol Classic Car Show at the Royal Bath & West Showground – *till 6 February* (0117) 907 1000
12　**Shepton Mallet** Classic Motorcycle Show at the Royal Bath & West Showground – *till 13 February* (0117) 907 1000
20　**Shepton Mallet** Toy and Train Collectors' Fair: up to 350 stands at the Royal Bath & West Showground (01373) 452857
25　**Bath** International Literature Festival – *till 5 March* (01225) 463362

MARCH

18　**Shepton Mallet** West Country Game Fair at the Royal Bath & West Showground – *till 19 March* (01775) 768661

APRIL

9　**Shepton Mallet** Toy and Train Collectors' Fair: up to 350 stands at the Royal Bath & West Showground (01373) 452857
21　**Shepton Mallet** County Home, Garden and Leisure Show at the Royal Bath & West Showground – *till 24 April* (01775) 768661
24　**Mells** Daffodil Fair: inc Civil War battle, egg rolling, street fair (01373) 812898

Somerset Calendar (cont.)

29 Bath Spring Flower Show at Royal Victoria Park – *till 1 May* (01225) 482624; **Minehead** Hobby Horse Celebrations: old May Day custom, hobby horse dances around the streets – *till 3 May* (01643) 702624; **Shepton Mallet** South-West Custom and Classic Bike Show at the Royal Bath & West Showground – *till 30 April* (01749) 823260; **Yeovil** Abbey Hill Steam Rally at the Showground – *till 1 May* (01935) 863603

30 Long Ashton North Somerset Show at Ashton Court – *till 1 May* (0117) 964 3498

MAY

4 Badminton Horse Trials at Badminton House – *till 7 May* (01454) 218375

6 Shepton Mallet Antiques Fair: up to 500 stands at the Royal Bath & West Showground – *till 7 May* (01775) 768661

13 Bristol Natural House and Ecology Show at Watershed Media Court – *till 14 May* (01934) 813407; **Claverton** US Civil War Camp Life at the American Museum – *till 14 May* (01225) 460503

19 Bath International Music Festival – *till 4 June* (01225) 463362

26 Bath Festival Fringe – *till 11 June* (01225) 480079; **Bath** Jazz Weekend – *till 29 May* (01225) 462231

31 Shepton Mallet Royal Bath & West Show at the Royal Bath & West Showground – *till 3 June* (01749) 822200

JUNE

10 Long Ashton Bristol Motor and Classic Car Show at Ashton Court Estate – *till 11 June* (0117) 934 3542

11 Shepton Mallet Collectors' Toy Fair: up to 350 stands at the Royal Bath & West Showground (01373) 452857

17 Claverton Native American Weekend at the American Museum – *till 18 June* (01225) 460503

22 Glastonbury Millennium Celebrations at Glastonbury Abbey – *till 24 June* (01458) 832267

23 Glastonbury Festival – *till 25 June* (01749) 890470

JULY

1 Claverton Independence Day Celebrations at the American Museum – *till 2 July* (01225) 460503

7 Banwell Wild West Week: over 2,000 cowboys and Indians, live bands at Court Farm Country Park – *till 23 July* (01934) 822383

8 Shepton Mallet Antiques Fair: up to 500 stands at the Royal Bath & West Showground – *till 9 July* (01775) 768661; **Weston-super-Mare** Children's Festival at the Winter Gardens – *till 9 July* (01934) 813407

15 Long Ashton Bristol Community Festival at Ashton Court – *till 16 July* (0117) 904 2275; **Shepton Mallet** Countryside Cavalcade: country show at the Royal Bath & West Showground – *till 16 July* (01458) 274086; **Yeovilton** International Air Day (01935) 456751

28 Weston-super-Mare Helicopter Fly-in: static displays, flights, variety show, fair – *till 30 July* (01934) 822524

29 Claverton French/Indian War Re-enactment at the American Museum – *till 30 July* (01225) 460503

Somerset Calendar (cont.)

AUGUST

 5 **Nunney** Street Fair (01373) 836322
10 **Long Ashton** Bristol Balloon Fiesta and Night Glow at Ashton Court Estate – *till 12 August* (0117) 953 5884
11 **Cricket St Thomas** Fireworks Concert (01625) 575681
12 **Yeovil** Festival of Transport – *till 13 August* (01963) 34532
16 **Priddy** Sheep Fair: colourful event (01249) 445599
18 **Dunster** Show (01398) 341490
19 **Glastonbury** Open-air Fireworks Concert at Glastonbury Abbey (01749) 890470
26 **Bristol** Jazz on King Street – *till 28 August* (0117) 938 2567

SEPTEMBER

 1 **Shepton Mallet** National Amateur Gardening Show at the Royal Bath & West Showground – *till 3 September* (01460) 66616
16 **Frome** Carnival (01373) 464278
21 **Frome** Cheese Show (01373) 463600

OCTOBER

 8 **Shepton Mallet** Toy and Train Collectors' Fair: up to 350 stands at the Royal Bath & West Showground (01373) 452857
16 **Taunton** Illuminated Carnival and Cider Barrel Rolling Race (01823) 286137
20 **Shepton Mallet** Festival of Food and Drink at the Royal Bath & West Showground – *till 22 October* (01775) 768661
21 **Bath** Bach Festival: 250th anniversary of the composer's death – *till 28 October* (01225) 477101
27 **Wells** Festival of Literature – *till 29 October* (01749) 673385
28 **Shepton Mallet** County Home, Garden and Leisure Show at the Royal Bath & West Showground – *till 29 October* (01775) 768661

NOVEMBER

 2 **Bridgwater** Guy Fawkes Illuminated Carnival: visited by one of Europe's most spectacular parades with floats up to 30 metres or 100ft long with thousands of lights (01278) 429288
 4 **North Petherton** Guy Fawkes Illuminated Carnival (see *Bridgwater above*)
 6 **Burnham-on-Sea** Guy Fawkes Illuminated Carnival (see *Bridgwater above*)
 8 **Shepton Mallet** Guy Fawkes Illuminated Carnival (see *Bridgwater above*)
10 **Bath** Mozart Festival – *till 19 November* (01225) 477101; **Wells** Guy Fawkes Illuminated Carnival (see *Bridgwater above*)
11 **Glastonbury** Guy Fawkes Illuminated Carnival (see *Bridgwater above*)
13 **Weston-super-Mare** Guy Fawkes Illuminated Carnival (see *Bridgwater above*)
18 **Shepton Mallet** Antiques Fair: up to 500 stands at the Royal Bath & West Showground – *till 20 November* (01775) 768661
30 **Shepton Mallet** Winter Fair at the Royal Bath & West Showground (01775) 768661

DECEMBER

 8 **Shepton Mallet** Crafts for Christmas at the Royal Bath & West Showground – *till 10 December* (01775) 768661

STAFFORDSHIRE

Good-value family outings, some lovely countryside.

Alton Towers stands out as an exceptional theme park, and there are a good few other family days out – even a working farm that's free, at Stowe by Chartley. There's all-round appeal at Tamworth Castle, and those splendid great houses in equally splendid grounds, Shugborough and Weston Park at Weston under Lizard. For adults, the county's unique facet is the Potteries around Stoke-on-Trent – full of industrial museums and show-places that fascinate anyone even remotely interested in china.

The north-east gives beautiful walks and drives in glorious Peak District limestone country. In the more industrial south, Cannock Chase has miles of fine landscape, and the canal network allows some unusually attractive walks.

Where to stay

BETLEY SJ7847 **Adderley Green Farm** *Heighley Castle Lane, Betley, Crewe CW3 9BA (01270) 820203* ***£40;** 3 rms. Georgian farmhouse on a big dairy farm with good breakfasts in the homely dining room, and a large garden; fishing on an adjoining farm; cl Christmas/New Year; children over 5.

BLACKSHAW MOOR SK0161 **Three Horseshoes** *Buxton Rd, Blackshaw Moor, Leek ST13 8TW (01538) 300296* ***£60,** plus special breaks; 6 rms. Large, well appointed family-run pub with lots of nooks and crannies, open fire, no smoking area, good atmosphere, generous food served by young friendly staff in a separate candlelit restaurant, well kept real ales, and a decent wine list; cl Christmas.

CAVERSWALL SJ9542 **Caverswall Castle** *Caverswall, Stoke-on-Trent ST11 9EA (01782) 393239* **£75;** 6 oak-panelled rms with four-posters. Castle dating from 1270 with turrets, dungeon, portcullis and moat; lots of atmosphere, fine panelling and paintings, comfortable, restful day rooms, a grand dining room, and a big billiard room; indoor swimming pool and two lakes for fishing; self-catering in restored stone turrets; cl Dec–Jan; disabled access.

CHEADLE SK0044 **Ley Fields Farm** *Leek Rd, Cheadle, Stoke-on-Trent ST10 2EF (01538) 752875* **£36;** 3 rms. Listed Georgian farmhouse on working dairy farm in lovely countryside with lots of walks; traditional furnishings in lounge and dining room, good home cooking, and friendly welcome; cl Christmas/New Year; partial disabled access.

CHEDDLETON SJ9651 **Choir Cottage** *Ostlers Lane, Cheddleton, Leek ST13 7HS (01538) 360561* ***£53;** 2 pretty rms in an adjacent cottage. 17th-c no smoking cottage with comfortable lounges, attractive dining room with country views, nice breakfasts, and evening meals by prior arrangement; cl Christmas; children over 5.

ECCLESHALL SJ8329 **George** *Castle St, Eccleshall, Stafford ST21 6DF (01785) 850300* **£80,** plus special breaks; 9 rooms. Friendly 18th-c hotel with an open fire in big brick inglenook in a cosy, beamed bar, ales from their own microbrewery, and good food in the bistro.

OAKAMOOR SK0544 **Bank House** *Farley Lane, Oakamoor, Stoke-on-Trent ST10 3BD (01538) 702810* **£68;** 3 lovely big rms. Carefully restored country home in neat gardens on the edge of the Peak National Park and with lovely views; log fire in comfortable drawing room, library, piano in the inner hall, and most enjoyable food using home-grown and local produce – super home-made breads, brioches, pastries and jams and marmalade at marvellous breakfast; friendly dog and cats; lots to do nearby; cl Christmas wk.

OAKAMOOR SK0747 **Tenement Farm** *Three Lows, Ribden, Oakamoor, Stoke-on-Trent ST10 3BW (01538) 702333* ***£50;** 8 rms with showers. Comfortable, no smoking house on traditional farm surrounded by fine countryside, with airy, homely lounge, licensed bar, and sunny conservatory; also self-catering cottage; cl Nov–Mar.

ROLLESTON ON DOVE SK2327 **Brookhouse** *Brookside, Rolleston on Dove, Burton on Trent DE13 9AA (01283) 814188* ***£99,** plus wknd breaks; 19 comfortable rms with Victorian brass or four-poster beds. Handsome ivy-covered William & Mary brick building in 5 acres of lovely gardens with comfortable antique-filled rooms, and good food in elegant little dining room; children over 12; disabled access.

WARSLOW SK0858 **Greyhound** *Warslow, Buxton SK17 0JN (01298) 84249* ***£33;** 4 clean and comfortable rms with shared bthrms. Warm, welcoming atmosphere in comfortably refurbished slated stone inn handy for Peak district, with generous helpings of home-made food inc hearty breakfasts, live Sat evening entertainment; cl Christmas; children over 12.

WETTON SK1055 **Olde Royal Oak** *Wetton, Ashbourne DE6 2AF (01335) 310287* **£38,** plus wknd breaks; 4 rms. Shuttered old stone village inn in lovely NT walking country, with a warm cheerful welcome, an attractive older part that leads into a more modern-feeling area, open fires, country furniture, sun lounge overlooking small garden, decent food, and nice breakfasts; children by arrangement.

To see and do

STAFFORDSHIRE Family Attraction of the Year

☺ ❀ **ALTON** SK0743 **Alton Towers** (off B5032) This 200-acre giant is consistently Britain's top paid attraction, and it's not really any wonder – there isn't anywhere that compares with it. They're never content to rest on their laurels, each year adding new rides and features; latest additions include Ug Land, a Stone Age theme park with its own Corkscrew, and the Riverbank Eye Spy for younger visitors. The most notorious ride is the fearsome rollercoaster Oblivion, a £12 million 3-minute horror that climaxes with a 70mph vertical drop; it's unsuitable for anyone under 1.37 metres (4ft 6in). Other highlights (if you like that sort of thing) are a ride that spins you round 3 complete loops before leaving you dangling 50ft above ground (while being attacked by jets of water from handily placed fountains), and Nemesis, which whisks you through unfeasible angles at a greater G-force than that faced by astronauts during a space shuttle launch. Though it's these rides that draw the crowds, they've deliberately set out to appeal to whole families rather than just daredevil teenagers: Storybook Land, for example, has quite a range of gentle rides aimed at children up to around 7 (toddlers love the singing barn). Dozens of other distractions, from log flumes and rowing boats to live shows, and lovely extensive gardens that anywhere else would probably be worth a visit in their own right. There's even a splendidly zany (but thoroughly comfortable) hotel, with a bizarre cross between a galleon and a hot-air balloon in the lobby, and a room which keeps dishing out chocolate; you'll need to book well in advance for themed rooms, such as the Peter Rabbit burrows. Though you can expect queues at the most popular rides, they're working hard to get waiting times down; during busy periods in summer 1999 they introduced timed tickets for Oblivion and Nemesis, so you wouldn't have to wait more than 20 minutes. And they experimented with letting people who'd booked in advance ride Oblivion before the park opened its gates to most visitors. Other rides have an average wait of around 10 minutes. It's not cheap (though see below for ways of getting the best value), and you'll need the whole day and some fairly organised planning to get the most out of it, but the presentation and facilities are excellent – if you don't normally like theme parks you may be pleasantly surprised. They usually end the season with a spectacular firework display. Meals, snacks, shops, disabled access (on most rides too); open mid-Mar–early Nov; (01538) 702200; £19.50 (£15.50 children). The family ticket – covering 2 adults and 2 children, or 1 adult and 3 children – costs £59, an unusually good deal offering savings of up to £59. You can usually buy a good-value ticket for a second day's entry from any of the information booths or ticket offices.

ABBOTS BROMLEY SK0824

★ Quite a lot of attractive buildings, with pleasant countryside around.

ALTON SK0743

☺ ❀ **Alton Towers** See separate family panel on p.581.

BIDDULPH SJ8858

❀ **Biddulph Grange Garden** (Grange Rd) Notable and really quite charming high Victorian garden, extensively restored; divided by its founder into a number of smaller themed gardens to house specimens from all over world. Also a display by Spode on the history of the Willow Pattern plate and how the design was used to create the Chinese garden. Snacks, shop; cl am wkdys, all day Mon (exc bank hols), Tues, and Nov–Mar (exc wknds Nov–mid-Dec); (01782) 517999; £4 (£2 Nov and Dec); NT. You can get a joint ticket with Little Moreton Hall, 6 miles away in Cheshire.

BLYTHE BRIDGE SJ9441

🚂 **Foxfield Steam Railway** Five miles through scenic countryside; a return ticket gives unlimited travel for the whole day (exc during special events). Staff are particularly friendly, and there's a collection of locomotives and rolling stock. Open wknds and bank hols Apr–Oct; (01782) 396210; £3.90. The Ship at Teanford has decent food.

BREWOOD SJ8808

★ Charming small town, with many attractive Georgian and older buildings.

BURTON UPON TRENT SK2523

🍺T The town is dominated by its connections with the brewing industry, and the **Bass Museum** (Horninglow St) explores this topic in some detail – with an emphasis on Bass and the company's shire horses. You can tour the brewery (no under-13s); also indoor and outdoor play areas. Summer special events and occasional lunchtime brass-band concerts. Meals, snacks, shop, disabled access; cl 25–26 Dec, 1 Jan; (01283) 511000; *£4.50.

🍺 **Burton Bridge Brewery** A complete contrast to the giant breweries that dominate the town, this shows brewing at the very opposite end of the scale. There's an attached pub; or the Queen's Hotel is a comfortable place for lunch, as is the Marquis Suite carvery at the New Talbot Hotel on Anglesey Rd.

🚣 ❀ 🚌 **River Trent boat trips** The Boat House at Stapenhill has river and wetland views (boat trips leave on the hour from the ferry bridge from midday onwards in summer). Nearby Rangemore has a good **garden centre**, with farm animals for children.

CALDON CANAL SK0348

🛶 ⚓ The towpath gives many miles of good interesting walks. There's usually something happening at the Froghall Wharf canal terminus (maybe inc horse-drawn barge trips – (01538) 266486), with an interesting walk along the canal to Consallforge (unusual remote pub here). The nearby **nature park** continues this strange lost-valley scenery. There's also good access to this, the most attractive of Staffordshire's canals, from the good Boat pub at Cheddleton, and from Denford nr Leek.

CANNOCK CHASE SK0215

🏕 🏛 ⚓ ❄ 🛶 Miles of lovely woodland and rolling heath, threaded with quiet side roads – the breathing space for the more industrial part of Staffordshire. Dotted around the 17,000 acres are Iron Age hill forts, nature trails, streams, pools and springs, and nice spots for picnics or dramatic views; fallow deer are often seen. There's an information centre at Marquis Drive, and decent campsites. The canalside Moat House at Acton Trussell does good food.

🏛 ❄ **Castle Ring** This large hill fort has fine views over the forests of Cannock Chase to the Trent Valley.

CAULDON SK0749

! Notable for its pub, the **Yew Tree**; a very unpretentious place packed with an extraordinary and delightfully higgledy-piggledy collection of remarkable bygones, especially mechanical music.

CHARTLEY SK0228

🏰 ❄ **Chartley Castle** (just over 6 miles W of Uttoxeter) A fine old ruin, with good views.

CHEDDLETON SJ9752

✂ 👁 🛶 **Cheddleton Flint Mill** (Cheadle Rd) Fully preserved 17th- and 18th-c watermills, with a little museum. Shop, disabled access to ground floor; cl am most wkdys, 25–26 Dec, 1 Jan;

(01782) 502907; free. The Boat does decent lunches, with pleasant canal walks from it.

🚂 **Churnet Valley Railway** 💷 (Station Rd) Small steam locomotive museum in Victorian station building, complete with signal box and engine sheds. Short steam and diesel runs in attractive surroundings. Snacks, shop; open wknds Easter–mid-Oct, plus Weds in Aug and for various special events (inc in Dec); trains running Sun Apr–Oct, plus Sat July and Aug and Weds in Aug; (01538) 360522; £3.90 (less when no trains running).

🎨 **Old School Craft Centre** Readers like this well set out craft centre, with its pleasant tearoom.

CHURNET VALLEY SK0545 ☁ ✝ Very pretty walks from Alton or Oakamoor; the best goes through Hawksmoor and Greendale to pass the broad fishponds in wooded Dimmings Dale and comes back down to the river past an old smelting mill – and a good café called the Ramblers Retreat (cl Mon). Hawksmoor Wood is itself an attractive nature reserve, and the Talbot in Alton is useful for lunch.

CLIFTON CAMPVILLE SK2510 ✝ **Clifton Campville church** One of those rare country churches that seems practically perfect in every way.

CODSALL SJ8604 ★ Notable in summer for its profusion of lupins. Moors Farm has a good farm shop and a small country restaurant.

CROXDEN ABBEY SK0639 🏚 Ruins in quiet surroundings, with some towering arches surviving. The Raddle at Hollington is a good family country pub.

ECCLESHALL SJ8329 🐷 🐓 🚂 **Fletchers Garden Centre** (Bridge Farm, Stone Rd) Plenty to amuse children, inc an adventure playground, falconry displays, aquatic centre, animals, crazy golf and (summer wknds and bank hols) a miniature railway; (01785) 851057. The St George (Castle St) has good home cooking, and on the other side of town the Star out at Copmere End is prettily set overlooking the lake.

ENVILLE SO8287 ☁ **Staffordshire Way** This way-marked footpath offers scope for

walking; the Cat at Enville is a useful place to join it.

FRADLEY JUNCTION SK1513 ☁ **Trent & Mersey Canal** Generally less opportunity for towpath walks than with other Staffordshire canals, but Fradley Junction, with a waterside pub and lots happening on the water, is an attractive place for a stroll.

GREAT HAYWOOD SJ9923 ☁ There are interesting **canal walks** from here, and the longest **pack-horse bridge** in the country is nearby.

ILAM SK1350 ★ 🏕 Attractive estate village, in lovely countryside. Wooded Ilam Park shows the Manifold Valley at its most sheltered.

INGESTRE SJ9824 ✝ **Ingestre church** Designed by Christopher Wren, and reckoned by some to be the finest small 17th-c church outside London.

KINVER SO8582 ❄ 🏚 (the one right over in the W of Staffordshire) Interesting village, with some of Britain's only rock houses nearby, still lived in 30 years ago; there are good views from the Iron Age fort on the ridge above.

LEEK SJ9856 🐦 **Coombe Valley Bird Reserve** This RSPB reserve has a shop, and disabled access; (01538) 384017; free. The A53 high moorland road N has good views, and E of here the B5053 gives an excellent impression of the dales country (the Jervis Arms at Onecote is a good family stop).

LICHFIELD SK1109 ★ The attractive centre is largely pedestrianised, with many 18th-c and older buildings among the more modern shops (and antique shops). On Sats from May–Sept you can see the remains of a 16th-c gaol behind the Guildhall (Bore St); 30p. The Queen's Head (Queen St) has an amazing choice of cheeses.

🏛 ❄ **Heritage Exhibition & Treasury** (Market Sq) Worth a look, in a sympathetically restored chapel site; cl 25–26 Dec, 1 Jan; £2. You may be able to go up to the viewing platform in the spire, which has splendid views of the surrounding countryside (£1).

✝ **Lichfield Cathedral** with its 3

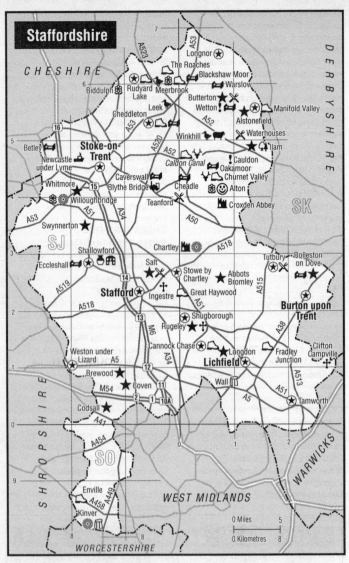

graceful spires and close with lovely buildings around it, this is magnificent inside, and its west front is memorable, especially at dusk or in the dark when shadows seem to bring the profusion of statues to life. There are wonderful illuminated gospels in the chapter house.

☙ **Samuel Johnson Birthplace Museum** (Breadmarket St) Dr Johnson was born here in 1709; the house is now furnished in period, with many mementos of him. Shop; cl Sun Nov–Jan; (01543) 264972; £2, free entry on Sat nearest to Dr Johnson's birthday, 16 Sept.

LONGNOR SK0865

★ ✝ ✿ This attractive small town, despite its grand church, has a pleasantly villagey feel (and a good craft centre). The interesting Olde Cheshire Cheese has good-value food.

MANIFOLD VALLEY SK1350

△ ⌂ ☺ ❋ This has many good walks, with fewer of the sensational rock features that abound in Dove Dale, but plenty of charm – more or less steep riverside pastures, ancient woodland in the narrower steeper gorges, and waterside caves; there's good access to the hills above it, such as Wetton Hill, which have attractive views. The best viewpoint of all, not to be missed, is Thor's Cave, high above the dale. The branch off up Hamps Dale is extremely pretty. There are good pubs nearby at Warslow, Wetton and Hulme End.

MEERBROOK SJ9959

△ ❦ ❀ **Tittesworth Reservoir** Large reservoir with visitor centre and restaurant, nature trails and bird hides, adventure playground and a sensory garden for the partially sighted; cl 25 Dec (restaurant cl Mon, Tues Nov–Feb); (01538) 300224; parking 50p.

NEWCASTLE UNDER LYME SJ8349

⚓ **Heritage Narrow Boats** Electric narrow boats to hire by the day; cl Nov–Easter; (01782) 785700; £50–£75 wkdys for up to 12 people, (£65–£90 wknds) – very satisfying, gliding along in silence.

THE ROACHES SJ9963

△ These form an impressive western barrier at the edge of the Dark Peak; this is perhaps the most exhilarating of several moorland walks from the side roads off the A53 N of Leek. A walk here can be combined with the path through the unspoilt Dane Valley to Danebridge on the Cheshire border;

hidden in the woods above the Dane is Lud's Church – not a church, but a miniature chasm reputed to have been a hiding place for religious dissenters.

RUDYARD LAKE SJ9459

⚓ 🐕 ❦ △ Though man-made it's perhaps one of Staffordshire's prettiest sights (a certain Mr Kipling liked it so much he named his son after it); you can hire a boat, there's a miniature railway (Mar–Oct), and the muddy marshland provides a haven for wading birds. The meadows and forested slopes above are pleasant for walks and picnics.

RUGELEY SK0418

★ ✝ Quite a few attractive old buildings, including a beautiful 12th-c **church**.

SHALLOWFORD SJ8729

☗ 🏠 **Izaak Walton Cottage** (Worston Lane) Smartly re-thatched home of the author of *The Compleat Angler*, with displays on the development of angling, period herb garden and picnic orchard. Shop, limited disabled access; cl Mon (exc bank hols), and Nov–Mar; (01785) 760278; £1.75. The Worston Mill at Little Bridgeford is attractive for lunch.

SHUGBOROUGH SJ9921

🏠 ☗ ❀ ☎ **Shugborough Hall & County Museum** (A513) Imposing ancestral home of the Earls of Lichfield, begun in the late 17th c and enlarged in the 18th; magnificent state rooms, restored working kitchens, interesting marionette collection, and exhibition of the present Earl's photography. The park has a variety of unusual neo-classical monuments, a working rare-breeds farm, and a restored corn mill.

Days Out

Strolling in Dovedale: Walk into Dovedale from Alstonefield; lunch at the George, Alstonefield; 11am; drink at the Yew Tree, Cauldon.

The Potteries: Gladstone Pottery Museum, Longton (*see Stoke-on-Trent*); lunch at the Plough, Etruria; Etruria Industrial Museum; visitor centre at Spode (factory tour most days), Royal Doulton or Wedgwood.

Transports of delight: Caldon Canal (Froghall Wharf) for a walk or horse-drawn barge trip; or a trip on the Foxfield steam railway, Blythe Bridge; lunch at the Ship, Teanford; Chartley Castle (for the view); Amerton working farm, Stowe by Chartley.

Meals, snacks, shop, disabled access; open Easter–Sept, plus Sun in Oct; (01889) 881388; entry to estate £2 (payable by NT members), museum and servants' quarters £4 (NT members £3), house £4, farm £4 (NT members £3); NT. An all-in ticket is quite expensive at £8 – better value on one of their special event days, when there are more activities (such as hands-on Victorian cookery displays) for no extra cost. The ancient Holly Bush up in the pretty village of Salt (off A51 N) is a charming place for lunch.

STAFFORD SJ9223

Greengate St has what's said to be the biggest timber-framed house in the country, built with local oak in 1595; period room settings and an information centre. The Malt & Hops (A34/A449 roundabout) and the Stafford Arms (near the station) are useful for something to eat.

Shire Hall Gallery (Market Sq) Handsome former county hall complete with courtrooms that were used until 1992; exhibitions of art, craft and photography, and a good craft shop. A series of disabled artists' workshops throughout the summer will culminate in an exhibition of their work in the autumn. Cl Sun and bank hols; (01785) 278345; free.

Stafford Castle Visitor Centre (A518 SW) Norman remains, rebuilt in the Gothic Revival style in the early 19th c, then allowed to fall into disrepair. Good visitor centre, and a medieval herb garden. Teas Sun only, shop, disabled access to visitor centre; cl Mon (exc bank hols), 25–26 Dec, 1 Jan; (01785) 57698; *£2.

STOKE-ON-TRENT SJ8646

The Potteries The five linked towns within the Stoke-on-Trent conurbation still produce some of the finest china and pottery in the country. You can tour several of the factories, and most have museums or a visitor centre; a good local bus service connects them all, taking you through a memorable urban landscape, the buildings clinging to small steep hills.

Etruria Industrial Museum (Lower Bedford St, Etruria) Based around the only surviving steam-powered potter's mill in the country,

grinding materials right up to 1972. It's been well restored, and there's a working blacksmith. Museum open Weds–Sun all year (exc Christmas), engine in steam one wknd each month Apr–Dec, usually the first, but best to check; (01782) 287557; £1.50. The Plough (off A53 opposite Festival site in Etruria) is our current lunch recommendation for the Potteries.

Ford Green Hall (Smallthorne) An interesting little 17th-c house with occasional informal performances of period music. Limited disabled access, cl am, Fri, Sat and 25 Dec–1 Jan; (01782) 233195; £1.50.

Gladstone Pottery Museum Uttoxeter Rd, Longton) Particularly engrossing, a complete Victorian pottery made much more appealing to families over the last few years, with lively demonstrations and interpretation. It's very much hands-on, and even hands-in – they're quite keen to get your fingers round the clay. It's quite possible to spend up to half a day here. Meals, snacks, shop, mostly disabled access; cl Christmas wk; (01782) 319232; £3.95.

Penkhull SJ8644 Despite the development of the Potteries on the slopes below and all around, this hilltop enclave somehow preserves an undisturbed village feel.

Potteries Museum & Art Gallery (Bethesda St, Hanley) Excellent: more pottery and porcelain, plus other local history. Meals, snacks, shop, disabled access; cl am Sun, 25 Dec–1 Jan; (01782) 232323; free.

Royal Doulton Visitor Centre (Nile St, Burslem) Potted history of the famous fine china company, with craft demonstrations, and a well displayed collection of Royal Doulton figures. Factory tours wkdys at 10.30am, 1.15pm and 2.45pm (no 2.45pm tour Fri), booking recommended; no under-10s. Good shop, disabled access to visitor centre only; cl Christmas, and no tours on factory and bank hols – best to check first; (01782) 292434; visitor centre and tour £5.75, visitor centre only £3.

Spode (Church St) The birthplace of fine bone china, this is the oldest manufacturing ceramic factory in the Potteries. A museum has rare and precious pieces, especially in the beautifully laid-out Blue Room, and you can have a go at making a piece yourself. Meals, snacks, factory shop, disabled access; no tours Fri pm or wknds, though shop and visitor centre open wknds, cl 25–26 Dec, 1 Jan; tours by appointment, (01782) 744011; £4.75 inc factory tour, or £2.75 just visitor centre and museum.

🏠 ♿ 🐾 **Wedgwood Visitor Centre** (Barlaston) The story of that favourite item on wedding lists; as we went to press, they had just started refurbishing the visitor centre, which when it re-opens around spring, will have more of an emphasis on hands-on activities and throwing demonstrations. Full factory tours by arrangement. Meals, snacks, shop, disabled access; cl 24 Dec–2 Jan; (01782) 204141; £3.25 (tours £7.25). A bus service to here and Spode leaves from the Stoke-on-Trent Tourist Information Centre; £4 day pass.

STOWE BY CHARTLEY SJ9927
🐃 🐾 ✡ 🚂 **Amerton Farm** Working dairy farm with milking at 4pm, farm shop, trails, garden centre, craft workshops, pottery, wildlife rescue centre and little steam railway (Sun and bank hols Apr–Oct, diesel summer Sats). Meals and snacks (with cream and ice-cream made on the premises), shop, disabled access; cl 25–26 Dec, 1 Jan; (01889) 270294. This busy place stands out all the more because admission is free (£1.50 for wildlife centre, £1 train). The Plough opposite is handy for lunch.

TAMWORTH SK2003
🏠 ❗ ✝ A decent town trail links a number of historic buildings; there's also a unique indoor ski slope with real snow. **St Editha's Church** has windows by William Morris.

😊 🏮 **Drayton Manor Park & Zoo** (off A4091 S of Tamworth) Popular theme park, with 50 rides and attractions inc small zoo, and Europe's only stand-up rollercoaster. Meals, snacks, shop, disabled access; cl Nov–Mar, zoo open all year; (01827) 287979; £3 entry to park, rides extra, or £11 for a wristband giving unlimited rides. The good Twycross Zoo is a few miles E, just over the Leics border.

🏠 🚂 ♿ **Tamworth Castle** (off Market St) Glorious mixture of architectural styles from the original Norman motte and bailey walls through the Elizabethan timbered hall to the fine Jacobean state apartments. Perhaps more museum than historic home, but plenty to see, with a fair amount to please children, inc high tech talking heads. Shop, disabled access to ground floor; cl am Sun, 24–6 Dec, 1 Jan; (01827) 709626; £4.

TUTBURY SK2129
★ ✝ 🐾 🏯 Pleasant village: the Norman **church** has a notable west doorway and elaborate carvings; there are 2 crystal works, craft shops, an attractive ruined castle with good views, and the Olde Dog & Partridge does decent food.

WALL SK0806
🏛 **Wall Roman Site** (Watling St) An important military base from around AD 50; excavations began in the 19th c and revealed one of the most complete Roman bath-houses in the country. Good audio-tour, and finds from the area. Snacks, shop; cl 1–2 pm, and all Nov–Mar; (01543) 480768; £2.25. The Black Bull at Shenstone is useful for lunch.

WESTON UNDER LIZARD SJ8010
🏠 🖼 🐝 **Weston Park** (A5) Striking, richly decorated 17th-c house, with a fine collection of paintings inc works by Van Dyck, Rubens, Gainsborough and Constable, and Disraeli letters that still somehow catch the imagination. The deer park and grounds, landscaped by Capability Brown, feature a restored 18th-c terrace garden, brightly planted broderie garden, and interesting trees and shrubs; in the 19th century it took 37 gardeners to look after it all. Also play area, pets corner, and miniature railway through the woodland. Meals, snacks, shop, some disabled access; open Easter, then wknds and bank hols mid-Apr–mid-Sept, and daily in summer hols; (01952) 850207; £5.50, £3.80 park and gardens only. The Bell at Tong is a reliable food pub; there are several interesting places close by, just over the Shrops border.

WETTON SK1055
❗ **Peak District School of Hang Gliding** Adventurous souls can learn

to hang glide here; (01335) 310257; 2-day courses start at around £85.

WILLOUGHBRIDGE SJ7539

⚘ ✺ **Dorothy Clive Garden** (A51) Woodland gardens created by the late Col Harry Clive in memory of his wife; at their best perhaps in spring and early summer, but lovely all year. Rhododendrons, azaleas, old roses, watergarden, rock garden and stunning views of the surrounding countryside. Tearoom with good home-made cakes, disabled access; cl Nov–Mar; (01630) 647237; £3. The Falcon in Woore does good food.

WINKHILL SK0551

🐾 🐖 **Blackbrook Zoological Park** 🅿 Unusual species and aviaries, as well as waterfowl, insects and reptiles, and children's farm – all much enjoyed by readers. Tearooms, shop, disabled access (although paths are steep); cl wkdys Nov–Mar; (01538) 308293;

£4.50. At pretty Waterhouses nearby you can hire bikes from the Old Station Car Park, (01538) 308609; around £6 for 3 hours. The attractively set Cross there has decent food – or treat yourself at the Old Beams.

★ **Other attractive villages**, with decent pubs, include Alstonefield SK1355, Butterton SK0756, Coven SJ9006, Longdon SK0714, Rolleston on Dove SK2427, Salt SJ9527, Swynnerton SJ8535 and Whitmore SJ8141.

◠ **Decent pubs** with good canal access can be found at Amington SK2304 (the Gate), Armitage SK0816, Gnosall Heath SJ8220, Norbury Junction SJ7922, Filiance Bridge in Penkridge SJ9214, Shebden SJ7626 (great echoes under the aqueduct) and Wheaton Aston SJ8412.

Moseley Old Hall nr Wolverhampton is listed in the *Warwickshire* chapter.

Where to eat

BUTTERTON SK0756 **Black Lion** (*01538*) *304232* Homely 18th-c stone inn with neat rambling rooms, plenty of interesting things to look at, a good log fire, well liked changing food, real ales, weekend evening cocktail bar, games room, seats on terrace, and pleasant views over the Peak National Park; bdrms; cl Mon. **£16.15|£5.50.**

SALT SJ9627 **Holly Bush** (*01889*) *508234* Thatched house dating in part from the 14th c, with pretty hanging baskets and a big back lawn, some ancient beams in several cosy spreading areas, a more modern back extension, coal fires, extremely good popular food (go for the daily specials), Sunday roasts, well kept ales, and friendly, efficient service; children in eating area until 8.30pm. **£17.55|£7.**

TEANFORD SK0040 **Ship** Cheadle Rd (*01538*) *722253* Busy little local with generous choice of good home-made food (especially bread and puddings), changing daily specials, good-value Sun lunch, and friendly staff; cl Mon; disabled access. **£16.95|£5.95.**

TUTBURY SK2128 **Olde Dog & Partridge** (*01283*) *813030* Popular carvery in half-timbered dining inn with stylish layout, well kept beers, good wines, and friendly helpful service; nice bdrms; cl pm 25–26 Dec, pm 1 Jan; disabled access. **£18.50|£5.75.**

WATERHOUSES SK0850 **Old Beams** Leek Rd (*01538*) *308254* Very pretty cottage surrounded by flowers and creepers, with oak beams, antique furniture, a cosy friendly atmosphere, excellent, carefully cooked food, and good service; bdrms; cl am Sat, pm Sun, Mon and pm Tues, all Jan; disabled access. **£45.50 dinner, £31.50 lunch|£16.95 2-courses.**

Special thanks to Gillian E Scarisbrick, Michael and Jenny Back.

Staffordshire Calendar

Some of these dates were provisional as we went to press. Please check information with the telephone numbers provided.

JANUARY

 I **Lichfield** Millennium Firework Display at Stone Fields (01543) 252109

FEBRUARY

 8 **Lichfield** Garrick Drama Festival – *till 12 February* (01543) 254021
11 **Stafford** Antiques Fair at Bingley Hall – *till 13 February* (01785) 240204

MARCH

 7 **Lichfield** Shrovetide Fair and Pancake Race inc colourful procession in Market Sq (01543) 250011
17 **Stafford** Antiques Fair at Bingley Hall – *till 19 March* (01785) 240204
18 **Uttoxeter** The Other Grand National at the Racecourse (01889) 562561

APRIL

15 **Milford** Gamekeepers Fair at Shugborough – *till 16 April* (01889) 881388
21 **Tamworth** Folk Moot – *till 24 April* (01827) 286001
22 **Lichfield** St George's Day Court: light-hearted gathering at the Guildhall – *till 23 April* (01543) 250011

MAY

 I **Newborough** Well Dressing (01283) 575430
 3 **Leek** Arts Festival – *till 20 May* (01538) 300492
14 **Biddulph** Plant Sale at Biddulph Grange Garden (01782) 517999
27 **Endon** Well Dressing – *till 29 May* (01785) 277397; **Milford** Spring Craft Show at Shugborough – *till 29 May* (01889) 881388
29 **Lichfield** Court of Arraye at the Guildhall: traditional ceremony to start Bower Day, with a carnival and displays (01543) 250011
30 **Milford** Classic Car Show at Shugborough – *till 31 May* (01889) 881388
31 **Stafford** County Show at the County Showground – *till 1 June* (01785) 258060

JUNE

 3 **Stoke-on-Trent** Canal Festival at Etruria Industrial Museum – *till 4 June* (01782) 233144; **Wetton** World Toe Wrestling Championships at Ye Olde Royal Oak (01538) 483741
 4 **Uttoxeter** Midland Counties Show at the Racecourse (01889) 564085
 9 **Stafford** Antiques Fair at Bingley Hall – *till 11 June* (01785) 240204
16 **Lichfield** Folk Festival – *till 18 June* (01889) 582908; **Tutbury** Arts Festival – *till 18 June* (01530) 564414
29 **Stafford** Festival inc open-air Shakespeare at the Castle – *till 16 July* (01785) 277397

Staffordshire Calendar

JULY

1 **Milford** Gardeners Show at Shugborough – *till 2 July* (01889) 881388
2 **Uttoxeter** Family Day at the Racecourse (01889) 562561
7 **Lichfield** International Arts Festival – *till 16 July* (01543) 257298
8 **Burton upon Trent** Regatta and Riverside Show – *till 9 July* (01283) 221333
9 **Lichfield** Medieval Market – *till 10 July* (01543) 418413
16 **Milford** Goose Fair at Shugborough (01889) 881388
22 **Milford** Fireworks Concert at Shugborough (01889) 881388
29 **Leek** Show (01538) 372006

AUGUST

6 **Milford** Victorian Circus and Street Market at Shugborough (01889) 881388
20 **Milford** Fireworks Concert at Shugborough (01889) 881388
26 **Milford** Craft Show at Shugborough – *till 28 August* (01889) 881388

SEPTEMBER

9 **Lichfield** Sheriff's Ride: riding the bounds (01543) 250011
11 **Abbots Bromley** Horn Dance: ancient ritual dance (01283) 840224
18 **Lichfield** Open Day at Dr Johnson Birthplace Museum and Dr Johnson birthday celebrations (01543) 250011
21 **Burton upon Trent** Beer Festival at the Town Hall – *till 1 October* (01283) 569310

DECEMBER

5 **Milford** Christmas at Shugborough – *till 8 December* (01889) 881388

Please let us know what you think of places in the *Guide*. Use the report forms at the back of the book or simply write us a letter.

SUFFOLK

Charming villages and unspoilt coast; good for a peaceful break.

Southwold, Walberswick, Aldeburgh and Orford are ideal for a seaside stay in understated civilised surroundings. Even in summer you can walk for miles along fairly empty beaches and long stretches of coastal bird country here and elsewhere, for instance near the attractive drowning village of Dunwich, or on the Shotley peninsula: these wide sea- and skyscapes are very restorative.

Inland there are delightful villages with colour-washed timbered buildings, glorious churches, attractively restored windmills — and lots of antique shops. Long Melford, Lavenham, Clare and Cavendish stand out. There are lots of rewarding great houses, often with wide family appeal — particularly Ickworth at Horringer, Kentwell Hall in Long Melford and Somerleyton Hall.

The area's importance to the Battle of Britain leaves it with several air museums, including free ones at Flixton and Great Bricett. The collection of music machines at Cotton is great fun. The open-air museum at Stowmarket is very good for families, children also enjoy West Stow, and Kessingland wildlife park, particularly strong on African animals, is another favourite. There are several good farm and country centres (we've added one at Baylham this year).

Bury St Edmunds has a good range of interesting places to visit, and anyone who is keen on racehorses could spend a very enjoyable weekend based at Newmarket.

Constable country, around East Bergholt by the border with Essex, has had more than a comfortable share of summer visitors, but it is very pretty, and people interested in traditional British painting can easily combine visits to Flatford Mill, Christchurch Mansion in Ipswich (free) and Gainsborough's House in Sudbury.

Suffolk is excellent for cycling — quiet back roads, lots of villages, gentle gradients, and a very low accident rate.

Where to stay

ALDEBURGH TM4656 **White Lion** *Market Cross, Aldeburgh IP15 5BJ (01728) 452720* **£98**, plus special breaks; 38 rms, some with sea view. Popular, rather smart 16th-c family-run seafront hotel with comfortable lounges, 2 bars, log fires, good food in the panelled and beamed restaurant, and cheerful friendly staff.

BEYTON TL9363 **Manorhouse** *The Green, Beyton, Bury St Edmunds IP30 9AF (01359) 270960* **£33**; 4 pretty rms, 2 in house, 2 in barn conversion. Overlooking the village green, this charming long-house has lots of beams and panelling in the sitting/dining room, fine china figurines and paintings by the friendly owner's mother, super breakfasts, enjoyable dinners (by arrangement), and a big garden; no smoking, no children, and no dogs.

BILDESTON TL9949 **Crown** *Bildeston, Ipswich IP7 7EB (01449) 740510* **£59**, plus special breaks; 15 individually furnished rms. Lovely timber-framed Tudor inn with a comfortable, well furnished beamed lounge, open fires, good food in the popular restaurant, welcoming courteous service, attractive 2-acre informal garden – and a resident ghost; disabled access.

BURSTALL TM0944 **Mulberry Hall** *Burstall, Ipswich IP8 3DP* (01473) 652348 ***£45;** 2 comfortable rms with showers. Once owned by Cardinal Wolsey, a lovely old farmhouse with a fine garden, an inglenook fireplace in the big beamed sitting room, excellent food (ordered in advance) in the pretty little dining room, very good breakfasts with home-baked bread, helpful friendly owners; cl Christmas.

BURY ST EDMUNDS TL8564 **Angel** *Angel Hill, Bury St Edmunds IP33 1LT* (01284) 753926 **£106w,** plus special breaks; 42 individually decorated rms. Thriving creeper-clad 15th-c country-town hotel with particularly friendly staff, a comfortable lounge and relaxed bar, log fires and fresh flowers, and good food in the elegant newly refurbished restaurant and downstairs medieval vaulted room (Mr Pickwick enjoyed a roast dinner here).

BURY ST EDMUNDS TL8564 **Twelve Angel Hill** *12 Angel Hill, Bury St Edmunds IP33 1UZ* (01284) 704088 **£80,** plus wknd breaks; 6 individually decorated rms. Warmly welcoming, mainly early 19th-c house (no smoking) with a cosy oak-panelled bar, a comfortable sitting room, good breakfasts in the separate dining room, period furniture, and a pretty little walled garden; cl Jan; no children.

CAMPSEA ASHE TM3255 **Old Rectory** *Campsea Ashe, Woodbridge IP3 0PU* (01728) 746524 **£58,** plus special breaks; 8 comfortable and pretty rms. Very relaxed and welcoming no smoking Georgian house by the church, with a log fire in the comfortable restful drawing room, lovely food from a set menu in the summer conservatory or the more formal dining rooms with more log fires, good wine list, and peaceful gardens; dogs allowed (not in dining rooms); cl Christmas.

FRAMLINGHAM TM2863 **Crown** *Market Sq, Framlingham, Woodbridge IP13 9AN* (01728) 723521 **£65,** plus special breaks; 12 comfortable rms. Bustling and friendly little black and white Tudor coaching inn with a pleasantly old-fashioned feel, a comfortable lounge and open fire, a cosy bar with heavy beams and another log fire, good food in the bar and restaurant, friendly helpful staff, and attractive small courtyard.

HADLEIGH TM0242 **Edgehill** *2 High St, Hadleigh, Ipswich IP7 5AP* (01473) 822458 **£60,** plus special breaks; 9 pretty rms. Friendly family-run Tudor house with Georgian façade, comfortable carefully restored rooms, personal service, traditional English cooking in the no smoking dining room, and an attractive walled garden with croquet.

HARTEST TL8353 **Hatch** *Pilgrims Lane, Cross Green, Hartest, Bury St Edmunds IP29 4ED* (01284) 830226 **£56;** 2 pretty rms. Pretty 15th-c thatched cottage, Grade II listed, on the pilgrims' way to Bury; charming owners, lovely beamed drawing room with antiques, separate dining room for enjoyable breakfasts, a conservatory, seats out on the terrace and a pretty garden; occasional evening meals, and the nearby Crown does good food; cl Christmas; children over 9 (though babies welcome); disabled access.

HIGHAM TM0335 **Old Vicarage** *Higham, Colchester, Essex CO7 6JY* (01206) 337248 **£58,** plus special breaks; 4 rms. Charming Tudor house nr quiet village with very friendly owners, a pretty sitting room with fresh flowers, log fire and antiques, enjoyable breakfasts in the attractive breakfast room, and neatly kept grounds with river views, tennis court and swimming pool (unheated).

HINTLESHAM TM0743 **College Farm** *Hintlesham, Ipswich IP8 3NT* (01473) 652253 ***£42;** 3 rms, 1 with own bthrm and 2 with TV. Late 15th-c no smoking house on a 600-acre mixed farm with neat garden, a guests' lounge with TV and log fire in the inglenook fireplace, hearty Aga-cooked breakfasts in separate dining room, and friendly owners; walks around the farm, and riding and golf nearby; cl mid-Dec–mid-Jan; no pets; children over 12.

HINTLESHAM TM0843 **Hintlesham Hall** *Hintlesham, Ipswich IP8 3NS* (01473) 652334 **£115,** plus special breaks; 33 lovely rms. Magnificent mansion, mainly Georgian but dating from Elizabethan times, in 175 acres with big walled gardens,

18-hole golf course, outdoor heated swimming pool, tennis, trout fishing, snooker, croquet, sauna and steam room; restful and comfortable day rooms with books, antiques and open fires, fine modern cooking in several restaurants, a marvellous wine list, and exemplary service; well behaved children over 10 in evening restaurant.

HITCHAM TL9751 **Hill Farmhouse** *Bury Rd, Hitcham, Ipswich IP7 7PT* (01449) 740651 £46; 3 rms. Georgian/Victorian farmhouse with adjoining 15th-c timbered cottage in 3 acres with ducks on 2 ponds, croquet and badminton; a residents' sitting room and separate dining room, dried flowers in the inglenook fireplace, home-grown veg (where possible) and eggs used in the imaginative dinners (on Tues and Thurs, set meals only), bring your own wine, and good breakfasts; cl end Oct–Mar.

LAVENHAM TL9149 **Angel** *Market Pl, Lavenham, Sudbury CO10 9QZ* (01787) 247388 £69, plus special breaks; 8 comfortable rms. 15th-c inn with original cellar and pargeted ceiling, several Tudor features such as a rare shuttered shop window front, a civilised atmosphere, good food in the bar and restaurant (they smoke their own meat and fish), lots of decent wines, several malt whiskies, well kept real ales, thoughtful friendly service, and maybe live classical piano pm Fri; cl 25–26 Dec; disabled access.

LAVENHAM TL9149 **Swan** *High St, Lavenham, Sudbury CO10 9QA* (01787) 247477 £130; 46 rms. Handsome and comfortable Elizabethan hotel with lots of cosy seating areas, interesting historic prints and alcoves with beams, timbers, armchairs and settees, good food in the lavishly timbered restaurant (actually built only in 1965), afternoon teas, an intriguing little bar, and friendly helpful staff; disabled access.

LONG MELFORD TL8645 **Bull** *Hall St, Long Melford, Sudbury CO10 9JG* (01787) 378494 £100, plus special breaks; 25 rms, ancient or comfortably modern. An inn since 1580, this fine black and white hotel was originally a medieval manorial hall, and has handsome and interesting carved woodwork and timbering, a large log fire, an old weavers' gallery overlooking the courtyard, old-fashioned and antique furnishings, a lovely calm atmosphere, good food, and pleasant friendly service; beautiful village.

MILDENHALL TL7074 **Riverside** *Mill St, Mildenhall, Bury St Edmunds IP28 7DP* (01638) 717274 £82, plus special breaks; 24 rms. 18th-c country house by the River Lark with a relaxed restaurant overlooking lawns, a comfortable bar, welcoming staff, enjoyable food, real ales, croquet, and boats to hire; bridge wknds.

NEEDHAM MARKET TM1053 **Pipps Ford** *Norwich Rd, Needham Market, Ipswich IP6 8LJ* (01449) 760208 *£67, plus winter breaks; 7 pretty rms with antiques and fine old beds, 4 in converted Stables Cottage. Lovely 16th-c farmhouse in a quiet garden surrounded by farmland alongside an attractive river, with log fires in big inglenook fireplaces, good imaginative food in the conservatory with subtropical plants (some meals can be communal); home-baked bread, home-produced ham and pork and own honey, eggs, and preserves with organically home-grown veg and herbs; cl Christmas–New Year; children over 5; disabled access.

NEWMARKET TL6463 **White Hart** *Newmarket CB8 8JP* (01638) 663051 £55.95; 19 rms. Comfortable hotel with racing pictures and an open fire in the spacious lounge, traditional restaurant, reliable bar food, friendly staff, front bar where the trainers meet, and a solid back cocktail bar where they take their more important owners.

ROUGHAM TL9063 **Ravenwood Hall** *Rougham, Bury St Edmunds IP30 9JA* (01359) 270345 £87, plus special breaks; 14 comfortable rms with antiques, some rms in mews. Tranquil Tudor country house in 7 acres of carefully tended gardens and woodland, with a log fire in the comfortable lounge, cosy bar, good food in the timbered restaurant with big inglenook fireplace (home-preserved fruits and veg and home-smoked meats and fish), a good wine list, and helpful service; croquet, heated swimming pool and hard tennis court; disabled access.

SOUTHWOLD TM5076 **Crown** *High St, Southwold IP18 6DP* (01502) 722275

£72; 12 rms. Outstanding old inn with excellent imaginative food in the no smoking restaurant and smart but relaxed main bar, inventive breakfasts, lots of interesting properly kept wines by the glass, well kept real ales, and friendly helpful staff; cl first wk Jan.

SOUTHWOLD TM5076 **Swan** Market Pl, Southwold IP18 6EG (01502) 722186 *£103.95, plus special breaks; 43 rms. 17th-c hotel with a comfortable and restful drawing room, upstairs reading room, convivial bar, interesting, enjoyable food in the elegant no smoking dining room, fine wines, well kept real ales (the hotel backs on to Adnams Brewery), and polite helpful staff; no dogs in main hotel; children must be over 5 in evening dining room; limited disabled access.

STOKE-BY-NAYLAND TL9836 **Angel** *Stoke-by-Nayland, Colchester CO6 4SA* (01206) 263245 **£61;** 6 comfortable rms. Civilised and elegant dining pub in the Stour Valley with Tudor beams in the cosy bar, stripped brickwork and timbers, fine furniture, a huge log fire and a woodburner, decent wines, and particularly good imaginative and reasonably priced bar food; cl 25–26 Dec; children over 8.

WANGFORD TM4679 **Angel** *Wangford, Beccles NR34 8RL* (01502) 578636 *£56; 6 rms. Neatly kept and handsome Georgian-faced 17th-c inn with a light and airy bar, no smoking restaurant, good-value dishes of the day and Sun lunch, well kept real ales, decent house wines, pleasant staff, and a garden.

WESTLETON TM4469 **Crown** *The Street, Westleton, Saxmundham IP17 3AD* (01728) 648777 *plus freephone (0800) 328 6001* **£94.50;** 19 quiet, comfortable rms. Smart extended country inn in a lovely setting with good nearby walks, comfortable bar, no smoking dining conservatory, restaurant, a wide range of good food (nice breakfasts, too), log fires, several well kept real ales, decent wines, and a pretty garden with aviary and floodlit terrace; cl Christmas; disabled access.

WOODBRIDGE TM2548 **Seckford Hall** *Woodbridge IP13 6NU* (01394) *385678* **£110,** plus special breaks; 32 comfortable rms. Handsome Tudor mansion in 34 acres of gardens and parkland with a trout-filled lake, putting, and a leisure club with indoor heated pool and gym; fine linenfold panelling, huge fireplaces, heavy beams, plush furnishings and antiques in the comfortable day rooms, and good food (inc lovely teas with home-made cakes) and service; cl 25 Dec; well behaved dogs welcome; disabled access.

WORLINGTON TL6973 **Worlington Hall** *Worlington, Bury St Edmunds IP28 8RX* (01638) 712237 **£55,** plus special breaks; 9 comfortable rms with decanter of sherry, fruit and fresh flowers. 16th-c former manor house in 5 acres of grounds with a 9-hole pitch and putt course, a comfortable panelled lounge bar with a log fire, good food in the relaxed candlelit bistro, and friendly staff; pets welcome.

We welcome reports from readers

This *Guide* depends on readers' reports. Do help us if you can – in return, we offer a discount on the next edition to people who've helped us with reports for it. Tell us what you think about places already in it, and anything extra you think we should say about them. And send us your ideas for inclusion in the next edition: places to visit, eat at or stay in, attractive drives or walks, maybe even unusual interesting shops you know of. Use the card in the middle, the report forms at the end, or just write – no stamp needed: *The Good Britain Guide*, FREEPOST TN1569, Wadhurst, E Sussex TN5 7BR.

To see and do

SUFFOLK Family Attraction of the Year

🏛 🖼 🐝 **HORRINGER** TL8261 **Ickworth House, Park & Gardens** In an area with more perhaps for grown-ups than for children, this very untypical stately home tries really hard to make sure younger callers enjoy their visit. A particularly good idea is their handling boxes: families pay a £5 returnable deposit for a box full of pieces of chandelier, stucco, or candles, which you carry round with you as a sort of superior I-Spy trail. It's a useful way of engaging children's attention as they tour the house. Other quizzes and trails are available: children can do the free touch tour, introduced primarily for partially-sighted visitors. Children who've been dragged round other historic properties will quickly spot that this is quite different from your average stately home: it's an oval rotunda 30 metres (100ft) high — rather like an over-sized biscuit barrel. The curved corridors are filled with a fascinating art collection, with pictures by Gainsbrough, Titian and Velasquez; there's also an exceptional array of Georgian silver, and some fine Regency furniture. Outside are some formal Italianate gardens, and 1,800 acres of attractive parkland and grounds, with variously lengthed woodland walks, cycle routes, and plenty of space for ball games or running around. Bring a picnic and you could spend a good part of the day here. There's a decent sized play area, with rope swings, tyres and the like, and on some days during school holidays you may find special events and activities for children (perhaps a small extra charge for some of these). They have nice themed events in the run up to Christmas (best to ring for dates). Meals, snacks, shop, plant centre, good disabled access (there's a stair-lift); house open late Mar to Oct, pm daily exc Mon (though open bank hols) and Thurs; garden cl winter wknds; park open all year; (01284) 735270; £5.20 house, park and garden (£2.20 children); £2.20 park and gardens only (70p children); NT. Dogs are allowed in the park, but must be on a lead near any livestock. Just as we went to press, it was reported in some newspapers that the National Trust are to convert some of the site into a luxury hotel; when we asked them, they wouldn't comment on their plans, but told us nothing would change for ordinary visitors.

ALDEBURGH TM4656
★ 🐟 Fishing village with quaint little streets running down to the shingle beach where the fishermen still haul in and sell their catch, and a much loved boating pond; touristy, but in a quiet way. Benjamin Britten, founder of the town's annual music festival, and his companion the singer Peter Pears are now buried side by side in the churchyard. The attractively placed Cross Keys and the Mill are both good for lunch. There's an **RSPB reserve** just N at North Warren.
🏛👤 **Moot Hall Museum** 16th-c brick and timber, with outside staircase; scene of the trial in Britten's *Peter Grimes*. It has displays on maritime history and coastal erosion, and finds from the Anglo-Saxon ship burial at

Snape. Shop; open pm wknds Apr–May, Sept–Oct, plus daily pm Jun–Aug (cl 12.30–2.30pm July–Aug); (01728) 452730 *60p.
ALDRINGHAM TM4461
🎨 **Craft Market** Three extensively stocked galleries of local crafts and fine art. Teas, disabled access; cl 12–2pm Sun (all am winter Suns), 25–28 Dec, 1 Jan; (01728) 830397; free. The Parrot & Punchbowl has decent food.
BARDWELL TL9473
🪟 ★ Carefully restored, the windmill is an attractive sight; open, at least summer Suns. The village green, with an ancient church and 16th-c pub, is attractive, too.
BAYLHAM TM1152
🐖 🏚 🐄 **Baylham House Rare Breeds Farm** (Mill Lane) Friendly farm

park with rare breeds, pets corner and picnic area; a visitor centre has information about the Roman site on which the farm is situated. Snacks, shop, disabled access; cl Mon (exc bank hols), and Nov–Easter; (01473) 830264; £3, children £1.50. The Sorrel Horse over at Barham has decent food, and walks nearby.

BECCLES TM4290
⬥ ⬥ **William Clowes Print Museum** (Newgate) Interesting look at the development of printing from 1800 onwards, with a wide range of machinery, woodcuts and books. Shop; open 2–4.30pm wkdys Jun–Sept, or by appointment; (01502) 712884; free. There's also a decent local history **museum** in Ballygate, housed in a 17th-c school; cl am, Mon (exc bank hols), Nov–Mar. The Swan House is a comfortable dining pub with unusual bottled beers from around the world.

BLYTHBURGH TM4575
✝ ⬥ **Blythburgh church** Magnificent building in a lovely setting above the marshes; there's a little working pottery nearby, and the White Hart is a good family dining pub.

BRAMFIELD TM4073
✝ **Bramfield church** Interesting building, with an unusual detached round tower. The Queen's Head has good food.

BRANDON TL7884
⬥ ⬡ **Brandon Country Park** Largely pine woods, and pleasant to stroll around; for a car-borne impression of Thetford Heath, the best road is the B1106.

⬥ **Brandon Heritage Centre** (George St) Brandon used to be the centre of the Stone Age flint industry, so among the local history here is a reconstructed flint-knappers' workshop; also displays on the fur industry and Thetford Forest. Shop, disabled access; open Sat, pm Sun, and bank hols, Apr–Oct, plus Thurs Jun–Aug; (01842) 813707; *50p.

BRUISYARD TM3266
⬥ **Bruisyard Vineyard** ⬚ (signed off B1119 Framlingham rd) Picturesque 10-acre vineyard producing decent English wine, with herb garden, watergardens and woodland picnic area. Meals, snacks, shop, some disabled access;

cl 25 Dec–mid-Jan; (01728) 638281; free, tours £3.50.

BUNGAY TM3389
⬥ Right in the centre of this historic little market town are the ruins of its Norman **castle**, with twin towers and massive flint walls. Bungay straddles the county border, with the Otter Trust at Earsham close by in Norfolk. The Green Dragon has decent food and brews its own beers.

BURY ST EDMUNDS TL8464
★ ✝ This busy shopping town has a good deal of character, with quite a few attractive Georgian and earlier houses, and several antique shops. The **cathedral** gained that status only in 1913; parts are 15th c, but the hammer-beamed ceiling is 19th c, and work still goes on. The nearby Queen's Head (Churchgate St) has good food. Another fine old church, **St Mary's** (Crown St), contains the tomb of Mary Tudor. The Linden Tree (Out Northgate St), Masons Arms (Whiting St) and Cupola House (Traverse) do decent food.

⬥ ⬚ **Art Gallery** (Market Cross) A fine Robert Adam building with changing exhibitions and a decent craft shop. Shop; cl Sun, Mon, and between exhibitions, Christmas; (01284) 762081; 50p.

⬥ ⬥ **Manor House Museum** (Honey Hill) Georgian mansion with a marvellous collection of watches, clocks and other timepieces, as well as period costumes and quite a few hands-on displays. A seemingly innocuous pair of breeches fell into this category not so long ago; they'd been worn by Mr Darcy in the TV adaptation of *Pride and Prejudice* and had to be put under guard when female visitors wouldn't stop stroking them. Snacks, shop, disabled access; cl Mon (exc bank hols), Good Fri, 25 Dec–Jan; (01284) 757072; *£2.95, less for locals.

⬥ **Moyses House Museum** ⬚ (Cornhill) Unusual 12th-c flint and stone house with a good range of Suffolk history, inc gruesome relics of the 'Murder in the Red Barn' – the murderer's account of his trial is bound in his own skin. Displays are firmly traditional, but there's lots to grab the attention. Shop, disabled access to ground floor only; cl am Sun, Good Fri, 25–26 Dec; (01284) 757488; £1.50.

🏛️🏚️🏵️ **Samsons Tower Museum** Little remains of the former medieval abbey beyond the 12th- and 14th-c gatehouses, but the tranquil gardens are very pleasant, and a visitor centre in Samson's Tower has a history of the site. Shop, disabled access; cl Nov–Easter; (01284) 763110; free. An oddity nearby is the pretty little Nutshell (Traverse), probably the country's smallest pub, with long church connections (cl Sun and holy days).

🏛️❗ **Theatre Royal** (Westgate St) Britain's third oldest working theatre, and very handsome – built in 1819 by William Wilkins, the designer of London's National Gallery. It's owned by the NT, and you can look round when productions or rehearsals are not in progress (not Sun or bank hols); (01284) 769505. Walking tours usually leave the tourist information centre at 2.30pm every day Jun–Sept (more varied ones Sat).

BUTLEY TM3751

🏵️ **Butley Pottery** (Butley Barns, Mill Lane) Working pottery, with tearoom, restaurant and disabled access; cl Mon and Tues (exc July–Aug), best to phone for winter opening; (01394) 450785; free. The Oyster pub is good for lunch. The B1084 Woodbridge–Orford is a quietly attractive drive, and the even quieter back road S to Capel St Andrew passes the remains of a medieval abbey gatehouse.

CAVENDISH TL8046

★🏛️† A lovely sight, its green framed by colourfully plastered timbered houses, with the tower of the attractive medieval **church** behind. The 16th-c Bull has good-value food. The A1092 from Clare goes on to Long Melford with a back road on to Lavenham – 3 lovely villages. The back roads N of here are also pleasant drives, with plenty of colour-washed old houses.

CHEDBURGH TL8058

🐑 **Rede Hall Farm Park** 🖼️ (A143 just E) Working farm based around agricultural life in the 1930–50s, with rare breeds, huge working horses and seasonal activities. Snacks, shop, disabled access; cl Oct–Mar; (01284)

850695; £3. A little further E, the Plough at Rede has good food.

CLARE TL7645

★†🏛️🏚️ Another of the area's very special timber-and-plaster villages, with a huge and beautiful **church**, the sketchy ruins of a **castle** on an Iron Age earthwork above the River Stour, some remains of a 13th-c Augustinian priory, and little modern intrusion; nature trails around the castle. There's a 3-storey antiques warehouse, and the Clare Hotel and the Swan have decent food.

🏛️👹 **Clare Ancient House Museum** 🖼️ (High Street) Local history in an attractive listed 15th-c building, which re-opened last year after lottery-funded restoration. Shop; open pm Thurs–Sun (plus am Sat) Easter–Sept; £1.

CODDENHAM TM1252

🏵️ **Shrubland Hall Gardens** Stunning Victorian gardens including a formal terrace and a wild woodland garden. There's a magnificent conservatory and enchanting follies inc a Swiss chalet. Limited disabled access; open pm Sun and bank hols Apr–Sept; (01473) 830221; £2.50.

COTTON TM0667

👹 **Mechanical Music Museum** Big collection of instruments and musical items taking in not just the expected organs, street pianos, polyphons and gramophones, but dolls, fruit bowls and even a musical chair. Their pride and joy is the Wurlitzer theatre pipe organ in the reconstructed cinema. Teas, shop, disabled access (but no facilities); open pm Sun Jun–Sept, plus usually the first Sun in Oct, a Fair Organ enthusiasts' day; (01449) 613876; £3. The Trowel & Hammer is good for lunch.

COVEHITHE TM5281

†⌂ **Covehithe church** Attractive building; just down the lane this stretch of coast is good for nature walks, especially out of season.

DEBENHAM TM1763

★† This attractive village has a fine partly Saxon **church**.

🏵️ **Carters Ceramics** (Low Rd) Pottery specialising in unusual teapots. Snacks, shop; cl Sun (exc pm Easter–Christmas), and they don't make pots at wknds; (01728) 860475; free.

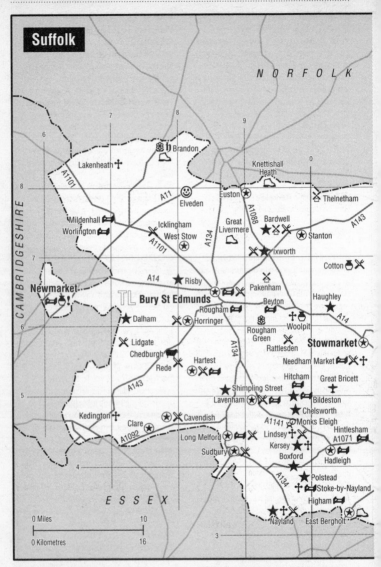

Suffolk

NORFOLK

CAMBRIDGESHIRE

Brandon

Lakenheath †

Euston

Knettishall
Heath

Thelnetham

Elveden

Mildenhall

Icklingham

West Stow

Great
Livermere

Bardwell

Stanton

Worlington

Ixworth

Cotton

Risby

Pakenham

Haughley

Newmarket

Bury St Edmunds

Beyton

Dalham

Rougham

Horringer

Woolpit

Stowmarket

Rougham
Green

Rattlesden

Lidgate

Chedburgh

Hartest

Needham Market

Rede

Hitcham

Great Bricett

Shimpling Street

Kedington

Lavenham

Bildeston

Chelsworth

Cavendish

Monks Eleigh

Clare

Hintlesham

Long Melford

Lindsey

Kersey

Boxford

Hadleigh

Sudbury

Polstead

Stoke-by-Nayland

ESSEX

Higham

0 Miles ————— 10

0 Kilometres ————— 16

Nayland

East Bergholt

DENNINGTON TM2866

† Dennington church Interesting and attractive – with excellent sermons – in pleasant surroundings. The Queen's Head next door is good.

DUNWICH TM4770

Once quite a sizeable town, but it's slipping slowly under the sea – most is now submerged. Some say that on quiet nights, when there's a swell running after a storm, they can hear the bells of a submerged church tolling. There are some fragmentary ruins of a friary up on the cliffs. Excellent coastal walks along the cliffs, beaches and heathland of Dunwich Heath, which has a NT tearoom (£1.60 parking charge).

Dunwich Museum (St James St) Small but very interesting, with exhibitions on the village's gradual erosion; shop, disabled access; cl Nov–Feb; free.

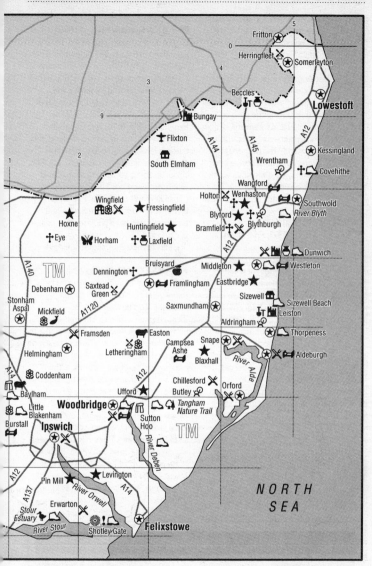

EAST BERGHOLT TM0733

🏠🪑⛵†⌂ **Bridge Cottage, Flatford** 17th-c cottage nr the mill immortalised by Constable, with a good interpretative centre for his paintings. Teas (highly recommended by readers), shop, disabled access; cl Mon and Tues (exc May–Sept), and Jan–Feb, limited opening in Dec, best to phone; (01206) 298260; free; NT. Guided walks through areas that inspired his work

leave here several times a day May–Sept, but fill up quickly (£2.80). You can hire **rowing boats** for trips along the River Stour. The mill itself and its famous partner **Willy Lott's Cottage** are both owned by the NT and leased by them to the Field Studies Council. You can see inside only by taking part in their arts courses or popular wildlife watching wknds; (01206) 298283. The **church** with its uncompleted tower has a unique 16th-c timber-framed bell cage, and the King's Head (with a haywain out in front!) has good-value food. From the village the walk along the watermeadows by the Stour is East Anglia's most famous walk – picturesque views immortalised by Constable, and well worth while. There is no real point in leaving the path to make a circular route. Elsewhere, the Stour Valley's attractive villages don't quite compensate for the humdrum scenery in between, and although you can find field paths, it's difficult to work these into circular walks. This Constable country is shared with Essex, around Dedham.

EASTON TM2758

🐄 **Easton Farm Park** Friendly farm with milking demonstrations in the Victorian dairy and its more modern counterpart alongside; also, rare breeds, a working blacksmith, adventure playground, and nature trails. Readers with very small children have found the gravel paths tricky with pushchairs. Meals, snacks, shop, disabled access; open Mon–Sat Easter–Sept; (01728) 746475; £4.25. The quaint White Horse has decent food, and the Wickham Market–Debenham back road through here via Brandeston and Cretingham has some attractive views.

ELVEDEN TL8080

☺ **Center Parcs** A relaxing place to stay on the edge of – indeed, virtually part of – Thetford Forest, with the same excellent leisure facilities as the other two Center Parcs (at Longleat and Edwinstowe); (0870) 520 0300.

EUSTON TL8978

🏠 ✝ 🐾 🖼 **Euston Hall** (A1088) Elegant old house built by Charles II's Secretary of State Lord Arlington. The highlight is probably the excellent art collection, with several portraits of the Merry Monarch and his family and court, inc works by Lely and Van Dyck. The grounds were laid out by John Evelyn, William Kent and Capability Brown, with stately terraced lawns, fine trees, a lake, lovely rose garden and classical temple. Teas in former kitchen, shop, disabled access to grounds and tearoom; open pm Thurs Jun–Sept; (01842) 766366; £3. The Pykkerel down at Ixworth and the Six Bells at Bardwell both have good food.

EYE TM1473

✝ **Eye church** Beautiful stonework and rood screen.

FELIXSTOWE TM2832

⚓ 🏠 Quite a busy port, with a ferry (passengers, not cars) across to Harwich, and further afield to Zeebrugge. Thanks to its beaches and relatively dry climate it's developed into a popular low-price family resort. Along the coast N, past a Martello Tower, golf course and quiet sand dunes, is the gently attractive and altogether quieter little settlement of Felixstowe Ferry, with another foot-ferry across the estuary of the River Deben, and good local seafood in the waterside Victoria.

🏰 ⏱ **Landguard Fort** 18th c, and well worth a look (open Sun and bank hols May–early Oct; £2); displays on local history in adjacent museum (open pm Weds and Sun May–Sept; (01394) 276800; £1).

Days Out

Stour Valley gems: Clare, Cavendish and Long Melford villages; lunch at the Bull, Long Melford; Gainsborough's House, Sudbury; Stoke-by-Nayland and Nayland churches; Kersey and Lavenham villages.

Sole Bay: Southwold (walk along the shore and river, and across to Walberswick if time); lunch at the Crown, Southwold; Blythburgh church; Kessingland Wildlife Park.

Anglo-Saxon chronicle: Bury St Edmunds; lunch at the Beehive, Horringer or the Red Lion, Icklingham; Ickworth at Horringer, or West Stow Country Park and Anglo-Saxon Village.

FLIXTON TM3288

✝ Norfolk & Suffolk Aviation Museum (Homersfield Rd) Aircraft and related items from the Wright Brothers to the present day, with aeroplanes displayed outside and in the Blister Hangar. Shop, disabled access; cl Fri and Sat Easter–Oct, plus Mon and Thurs Nov–Mar, and all mid-Dec–mid-Jan; (01986) 896644; donations. The Green Dragon in Bungay is a useful nearby pub.

FRAMLINGHAM TM2863

✝ The sloping market square is attractive, and the Crown at its head is useful for lunch. The **church** has an excellent hammerbeam roof. The B1116 to Fressingfield is quite a pleasant drive.

▦ ❊ ☵ Framlingham Castle (B1116) 12th c, this is where Mary I heard that she had become Queen. Unusually the entire curtain wall has survived (you can walk all the way along it), and there are 13 towers, some 17th-c almshouses, and an array of Tudor chimneys. Good views, interesting museum. Snacks, shop, disabled access to ground floor only; cl 25–26 Dec; (01728) 724189; £3.10; EH.

FRITTON TG4700

⌂ ➹ ✍ ▥ ✦ ⚘ Country World (Church Lane) Good for families, with woodland walks, children's farm, fishing, heavy horse stables, miniature railway, birds of prey (displays 11.30am and 3pm, not Fri), golf, rowing, boat trips, craft demonstrations and plenty of space for pottering. Snacks, shop, disabled access; open daily Apr–Sept, then wknds and half-term hol in Oct; (01493) 488208; £5.

GREAT BRICETT TM0351

✝ Wattisham Airfield Museum (off B1078) Small exhibition related to the adjacent airfield which is now one of the largest helicopter bases in Europe. Disabled access; open pm Sun Apr–Oct; (01449) 728933; free.

GREAT LIVERMERE TL8871

⌂ There's a charming shortish walk from the church here, past the Ampton Water lake, to Ampton church. A longer path leads through farmland from Great Livermere to Ixworth.

HADLEIGH TM0242

▦ ✝ ⚘ Old market town with some striking buildings (including the **church**, famously painted by Gainsborough); there's a nearby woodland **RSPB reserve**. The Ram has good-value food.

HARTEST TL8352

★ The village green is attractive; at the end, the Crown is pleasant for lunch.

⚘ ☷ ❀ Giffords Hall (Shimpling, just SE) 33 acres with vineyard and winery, wild-flower meadows, rare breeds of sheep, pigs and domestic fowl, and a rose garden. It's perhaps best known among gardeners for its sweet peas, and they have a Rose and Sweet Pea Festival the last wknd in June. Meals, snacks, shop, disabled access; cl Nov–Easter; (01284) 830464; £3.25. They do B & B.

HELMINGHAM TM1857

❀ ▥ ⚘ Helmingham Hall Gardens (B1077) Beautiful gardens pretty much as they were in Tudor times. The grand battlemented house they stand around (not open) is ringed by a moat, over which the drawbridge is still raised each night. Extensive deer park with hundreds of red and fallow deer, as well as Highland cattle and Soay sheep, and magnificent old oak trees. Constable painted a number of views of the woodlands. Teas, shop (inc Helmingham produce), disabled access; open pm Sun May–early Sept (summer pm Weds by appointment); (01473) 890363; *£3.75. The welcoming Dobermann at Framsden has good food.

HERRINGFLEET TM4797

✗ Carefully restored **windmill**, and an attractive sight above the river if you're passing (though rarely open).

HOLTON TM4077

✗ Another **windmill**, carefully restored and picturesque (though it's rarely open for visits).

HORHAM TM2172

✹ **St Mary's churchyard** The churchyard here has for generations been conserved as natural grassland around its older graves, just scythed for hay in the first week of July; so from spring onwards it's a mass of wild flowers, with plenty of butterflies (and beehives). The Ivy House in the quiet village of Stradbroke does good-value lunches.

HORRINGER TL8261

★ ⚘ A serenely attractive village with

well spaced colour-washed buildings. On Suns Mar–Dec you'll usually find various crafts in the Community Centre.

🏠🖼🌳 Ickworth House, Park & Gardens See separate family panel on p.595.

IPSWICH TM1644

🏠✝ After King John granted it a charter in the 13th c, it flourished as a port sending cloth to the continent; the port is still quite active. Too busy now to consider as a place to stay in, it has quite a few things to look at on briefer visits (traffic schemes make getting in and out by car rather slow). Cardinal Wolsey set up a college here, but all that remains is the 16th-c gatehouse in College St. The Ancient House in the Butter Market (now a kitchenware shop) has some 15th-c carvings, exceptionally neat pargeting (decoratively patterned external plasterwork) and even a priest's hiding hole – ask staff to show you. Dotted about the town are several attractive **medieval churches**, especially the 15th-c St Margaret's (Soane St); St Mary at the Elms (Elm Rd) has the town's oldest cottages behind it. If you're there on a winter's night, 5 medieval churches are nicely floodlit. In the central pedestrian area the Great White Horse, a former coaching inn, is useful for snacks; the County (opposite County Hall), Old Rep (Tower St) and the Greyhound (Henley Rd) have decent food.

🏠♨🖼🌳🌿 Christchurch Mansion (Soane St) Perhaps the town's highlight; the original 16th-c house was altered in the following century after a fire, but since then it's escaped any further redevelopment. The rooms are furnished in period style, with a Victorian wing inc servants' quarters, and the Suffolk Artists' Gallery has the best collection of works by Constable and Gainsborough outside London. Shop, disabled access to ground floor only; cl am Sun, Mon (exc most bank hols), 24–26 Dec, 1 Jan, Good Fri; (01473) 253246; free. Another gallery is next door, and the surrounding park has play areas and a bird reserve.

♨ Ipswich Museum (High St) The natural history section has been

painstakingly restored to how it was in its Victorian heyday, and includes the first gorillas brought to Europe in the mid-19th c. Other parts have quite an emphasis on Roman Suffolk. Shop, disabled access to ground floor only; cl Sun, Mon, 24–26 Dec, 1 Jan, Good Fri; (01473) 213761; free.

🎪 Peter's Ice Cream Factory Tours (Grimwade St) A small museum and tours of the factory, and of course a café where you can sample the finished product. Restaurant, shop, disabled access; tours Mon–Fri, 10am, 12noon, 2pm and 4pm, but best to ring; (01473) 253265; £3.50.

↧T Tolly Cobbold Brewery (Cliff Rd) Striking waterside Victorian brewery, with tours. Some particularly interesting old equipment, inc a Victorian steam engine, and tastings in the Brewery Tap (which functions as a separate pub). Shop; tours daily May–Sept at noon, best to check winter times; (01473) 231723; £3.90 (inc drink).

🚍 Transport Museum (Lupin Rd) In an old trolley-bus depot, a developing collection of around 100 ancient commercial vehicles built or used in the area, from fire engines to buses and milk floats. Snacks, shop, disabled access; open Sun and bank hols Easter–Oct, and maybe pm wkdys school hols; (01473) 715666; £2.25.

KEDINGTON TL7046

✝ Kedington church One of Suffolk's many attractive churches, this is unusual for its Saxon crucifix.

KERSEY TM0044

★✝ A very pretty one-street village, full of timbering and attractive and colourful plasterwork – though one or two buildings look ready for some attention. It runs from the fine 14th-c **church** down to a ford with ducks, and up the other side; several craft and antique shops, and the Tudor Bell has decent food.

KESSINGLAND TM5286

🐾🌿☺ Suffolk Wildlife Park (A12) Quite an emphasis on African wildlife at this 100-acre park; some of the animals are the only examples of their type in the country, inc the wonderfully strange bonteboks (they look like a cross between a horse and a goat with a bit of cow thrown in). Lots for families in summer, with a bouncy castle beside the play areas, animal demonstrations, birds of prey displays (selected days only), crazy golf, and games and activities in summer hols. Feeding times are spread throughout the day. The same people run Banham Zoo in Norfolk. Meals, snacks, shop, disabled access; cl 25–26 Dec; (01502) 740291; £6.50. Kessingland's beach is good, though busy in summer, and it's only 3 or 4 miles to Lowestoft.

KNETTISHALL HEATH TL9480
⌂ This country park has some pleasant strolls – and if you're overflowing with energy (and several days' supplies), you may even be tempted northwards on the Peddars Way, waymarked from here all the way to Norfolk's north coast.

LAKENHEATH TL7182
✝ **Lakenheath church** One of Suffolk's elegant and charming churches, though now a bit hidden away among the sprawl edging the nearby huge air base.

LAVENHAM TL9149
★ 🏚 One of the finest surviving examples of a small medieval town, this lovely little place has delightful rickety-looking 14th- and 15th-c timbered buildings wherever you look; many now house teashops, banks or antique shops. The old wool hall has been incorporated into the Swan Hotel, itself well worth seeing. Both it (at a price) and the Angel are good for lunch. The A1141 through Monks Eleigh and then the B1115 through Chelsworth to Hitcham is a pretty drive.

🏚⛾ **Guildhall** (Market Pl) Picturesque 16th-c timbered building, at various stages in its career a town hall, prison, workhouse and wool store; its beamed and oak-filled interior has interesting local history displays. Disabled access to tearoom and shop; cl Good Fri, and all Nov–Mar; (01787) 247646; £2.80; NT.

🏚⛾📷❀ **Little Hall** (Market Pl) Delightful 15th-c house, attractively repainted, showcasing the Gayer-Anderson collection of books, pictures and antiques, with a pleasant enclosed garden. Open pm Weds, Thurs, Sat, Sun and bank hols Apr–Oct; (01787)

247179; *£1.50. There's a good small commercial art gallery nearby.

LAXFIELD TM2972
✝⛾ **Laxfield church** Well worth a visit, in tucked-away quiet surroundings; nearby is a charmingly preserved very old-fashioned pub, and a small **museum** (open pm wknds May–Sept; free).

LEISTON TM4462
⬇ᴛ 🏭 **Long Shop Museum** (Main St) Big industrial museum in preserved buildings of Garrett Engineering Co, with steam engines, steam rollers, traction engines, and memorabilia from the nearby World War II air base. Shop, disabled access; cl Nov–Mar; (01728) 832189; £2.50. The Engineers Arms opposite has so much memorabilia it seems almost an extension. The sizeable shopping town has the fragmentary remains of a 14th-c abbey off the B1122 just N.

LETHERINGHAM TM2858
✗ ❀ **Letheringham watermill** Pretty, and surrounded by nice gardens, maybe open in summer.

LEVINGTON TM2338
★ A pleasant spot, with ancient almshouses, a marina below, and the Ship, a good pub (no children) with estuary views.

LINDSEY TL9744
✝ **St James's Chapel** A charming little thatched flint and stone chapel, built during the 13th c but inc some earlier work too.

LITTLE BLAKENHAM TM1048
❀ ⌂ **Blakenham Woodland Garden** Woodland garden richly planted with camellias, rhododendrons, magnolias and the like; lovely in May when the bluebells are out. Lots of rare trees and shrubs. Open pm Sun–Fri Mar–Jun; *£1. The Sorrel Horse over at Barham has decent food (and pleasant walks nearby).

LONG MELFORD TL8645
★ ✝ A very nice old place to stroll around: the fine green and exceptionally long main street (Hall St) are lined with buildings from varied eras, many with lovely timbering, and around 20 of them now antique shops (not cheap, but interesting). The **Church of Holy Trinity** is glorious, with ornate carvings and dozens of

spectacular windows; especially attractive when floodlit at night. The Bull Hotel, one of the finer old buildings here, does good light lunches, as does the comfortable Black Lion Hotel; the Hare, George & Dragon and Crown are also useful for food.

🏃🏠🍺 ⚜ **Kentwell Hall** Beautiful Tudor mansion with genuinely friendly lived-in feel, best during their enthusiastic re-creations of Elizabethan life (several wknds Apr–Sept), when everything is done as closely as possible to the way it would have been then – even the speech. It's surrounded by a broad moat, and there's a rare breeds farm within the grounds. Snacks, shop, disabled access; house open pm Sun Mar–Oct, and daily Easter wk and mid-July–Sept; (01787) 310207; most re-creations cost around £8 (£5.20 children 5–15), though the Great Annual one is £11.60 (£8.25 children). On non-event days entry is £5.50, or £3.50 garden and farm only.

🏠 ⚜ **Melford Hall** Turreted Tudor house mostly unchanged since Elizabeth I stayed here with hundreds of servants and courtiers in 1578; it still has the original panelled banqueting hall. Fine collection of Chinese porcelain; the gardens have a Tudor pavilion. Some disabled access; open pm wknds and bank hols Apr–Oct, plus pm bank hols, Weds–Fri May–Sept; (01787) 880286; £4.20; NT.

LOWESTOFT TM5492

✝ ⚓ Britain's most easterly town, this is the area's main fishing port, so the harbour always has lots to see. It's developed as a resort thanks to its beaches (South Beach has the best bathing water) and proximity to the Broads. Cobbled streets of old buildings survive in the part known as The Scores, and the early medieval parish **church** is imposing and attractive. In the High St, the Bayfields Hotel and Volunteer are useful for lunch, as is the seafront Jolly Sailors near the quaint Pakefield church. There are regular summer sea **boat trips**, (01502) 523000 for details.

☺ **Discoverig** (East Point Pavilion, Esplanade) Children's play area themed as a North Sea rig. Meals, snacks, shop, disabled access; cl 25–26 Dec and 1 Jan;

adults free, children £2.20 per hour. It shares the rather grand old pavilion with the tourist information office and good local history displays.

🚋 **East Anglia Transport Museum** (Carlton Colville; B1384 SW of Lowestoft) Lots of lovingly restored vehicles around 3 acres of woodland. The best part is the reconstructed 1930s street scene used as a setting for working trams, trains and trolley-buses. Snacks, shop, some disabled access; open Easter, then Suns May–Sept, plus pm Weds and Sat Jun–Sept, and pm wkdys in summer hols; (01502) 518459; £4. The nearby Crown (A146) does good cheap lunches.

⚓ **Lydia Eva Steam Drifter** (Harbour) Last surviving herring drifter, with an exhibition on life aboard. Usually open July–mid-Oct (moored in Great Yarmouth Apr–Jun, when maybe a sidewinder diesel trawler is here instead); free.

⚓ ⚔ **Maritime Museum** (Whapload Rd) Housed under the lighthouse on Whapload Rd; cl mid-Oct–Easter; *50p. There's a small **Royal Naval Museum** nearby (cl 1–2pm, am Sun, all day Sat, mid-Oct–mid-Apr; free).

☺ **Pleasurewood Hills Theme Park** (Corton Rd) Lots of rides and family attractions; trains and chairlifts speed up travel round the grounds. Meals, snacks, shop, disabled access; open daily mid-May–Aug, and wknds and school hols Apr–Oct; (01502) 508200; £10.95.

MICKFIELD TM1461

⚜ 🌿 **Mickfield Watergarden Centre** Two acres of ornamental watergardens and working nursery, with displays of marine and freshwater fish. Wknd teas in summer, garden centre, disabled access; cl 25 Dec; (01449) 711336; free.

MONKS ELEIGH TL9747

🌾 **Corn Craft** (A1141) Traditional corn dollies and their production (demonstrations by appointment). In Aug and Sept you can walk through the fields and pick the flowers. Snacks, big shop, disabled access; cl 25–26 Dec, 1 Jan; (01449) 740456; free. The Swan Hotel is handy.

NAYLAND TL9734

★ ✝ Well rewards a stroll – its fine **church** has an altar painting by

Constable; the old White Hart is now a smart restaurant.

NEEDHAM MARKET TM0854
† The **church** has a marvellous hammerbeam roof that has been described as 'a whole church seemingly in the air'.

NEWMARKET TL6463
Newmarket has been the centre of horseracing since James I used to slope off here from 1605, and in the early morning people driving through are quite likely to have to give way to a string of racehorses. The Rutland Arms (across the road from the Jockey Club) and the Bedford Lodge Hotel are useful for lunch.

🐾! **National Horseracing Museum** (High St) The stories and scandals of the sport's development through the centuries, with trophies, videos of classic races, a display on the history of betting, and racing relics from saddles to skeletons. You don't have to be interested in racing to get something out of it. Meals, snacks, shop, disabled access; cl Mon (exc bank hols and July–Aug), and Nov–Mar; (01638) 667333; £3.50. They also organise informative tours of the local breeding and racing scene, with a look at horses at work on the gallops, and visits to a training yard, stud and to the handsome Georgian Jockey Club itself; booking essential on (01638) 560622; prices start at around £20.

! **National Stud** (A1304 W) Tours of this Mecca of horse breeding by arrangement, (01638) 663464. Snacks, shop, disabled access; guided tours are at 11.15am and 2.30pm wkdys, 11.15am Sat, and 2.30pm Sun, cl Oct–Feb (exc race days); £4. The King's Head at Dullingham is a good nearby lunch spot.

ORFORD TM4249
🐾 **Dunwich Underwater Exhibition** (Front St) The process of coastal erosion is well illustrated at The Craft Shop; snacks; shop; cl 25–26 Dec; 50p.

🐦⚓ **Havergate Island** Bird watchers can arrange whole day trips to this marshy **RSPB reserve** by writing to the warden, Mr Partridge, at 30 Mundays Lane, Orford, Woodbridge IP12 2LX (with SAE); permits usually available every Thurs and alternate

wknds Apr–Aug, then in winter just the first Sat of the month; around £5 inc boat trip from Orford quay.

🏰❋† **Orford Castle** When Henry II commissioned this castle it was right on the shore, but since then the river has silted so much that it's now slightly inland. It has an amazing 18-sided keep rising to 27 metres (90ft), supported by 3 extra towers. Good views from the top (as usual, at the end of a spiral staircase). Shop; cl 1–2pm Nov–Mar, 24–26 Dec, 1 Jan; (01394) 450472; £2.50; EH. The **church** has the ruined chancel arches of a Norman predecessor in the graveyard. There's a long lane down to the shore with its quay and old smugglers' inn, the Jolly Sailor. The road through Iken Heath to Snape is a pleasant drive through quiet pinewoods.

🐦⚓ **Orford Ness** After years of belonging to the Ministry of Defence (who barred access to anyone who wasn't in uniform), this magnificently desolate shingle spit just opposite the quay is now owned by the NT and open to the public, though it's more for serious wildlife fans than day-trippers. Ferries leave the quay every 20 minutes from 10am till 2pm Thurs–Sat Easter–Oct – you can book if you want; (01394) 450057; £5.20.

PAKENHAM TL9369
✕ **Pakenham Watermill** (Mill Rd) 18th-c watermill restored to working order by preservation society, pretty mill pond. Snacks, shop, disabled access; open pm Easter–Sept Weds, wknds and bank hols; or party bookings (01359) 270570; £2. The village also has an attractively restored **windmill**, open for visits at least summer Sun.

PIN MILL TM2037
★ A nice spot below the wooded slopes by the River Orwell, with Thames barges on tidal moorings, and much favoured by artists; the Butt & Oyster here is attractively placed for a bite to eat.

RIVER DEBEN TM3041
☁ Broad winding river close to the coast, best reached from side roads off the B1083 S of Shottisham: good walks.

ROUGHAM GREEN TL9261
🌸 **Netherfield Cottage Herb Garden** (Nether St, towards Hessett)

Proof that you don't have to have a massive garden to make it very special indeed: hundreds of different herbs, beautifully yet sensibly grouped by how you'd use them, with 2 small knot gardens. They've recently re-shaped the hedge to include a window. Best May–Oct, but a peaceful haven at any time. The cheery owner is happy to chat. Cl Nov–Mar; (01359) 270452; free, guided tours by appointment. The Gardeners Arms over at Tostock is an appropriate place for lunch.

SAXMUNDHAM TM3863
★ ✝ ℘ This attractive bypassed village has yet another fine **church**. The Poachers Pocket at Carlton just N has decent food, and nearby Yoxford has a couple of good craft workshops.

SAXTEAD GREEN TM2564
✗ **Saxtead Green Post Mill** (A1120) Traditional Suffolk windmill dating from 1854, meticulously brought back into perfect working order, but it's a steep climb up the staircase; audio tour; cl 1–2 pm, Sun, and all Nov–Mar; (01728) 685789; *£2; EH. Attractive surroundings; the Old Mill House over the green has good home-made food.

SHOTLEY GATE TM2434
❊ ◠ ! At the meeting of the Stour and Orwell estuaries, this is at the hub of a rewarding walk with good views across to Harwich and its shipping. Start inland at Shotley and cross the fields either N to the Orwell or S to the Stour, then follow the waterside. The Bristol Arms has good fresh fish, and up the hill, the colossal mast of HMS *Ganges* (now a police training centre) is worth a look.

SIZEWELL TM4763
🏢 **Sizewell Visitor Centre** (B1353) Interactive displays and exhibitions on energy and nuclear power, with tours of both the Sizewell A and B power stations (booking essential); snacks, shop, disabled access; cl Nov–Easter; (01728) 642139; free. The Vulcan Arms opposite has good-value food.

SIZEWELL BEACH TL4761
◠ Generally virtually deserted out of season, and pleasurable walking ground despite the rather graceless Sizewell nuclear power plant in the distance. Agate and other semi-precious stones are common among the pebbles, sometimes even amber after stormy

east winds; heathland, an old railway track walk and The Meare (Thorpeness's lake) justify detours inland.

SNAPE TM3957
🏢 🖼 ♿ The converted 19th-c **maltings** are home of the Aldeburgh Music Festival begun by Benjamin Britten, with other concerts throughout the year. The centre is pleasant to wander around, with unusual shops and galleries, and in summer there are one-hour **boat trips** down the River Alde. The Plough & Sail just outside is good for lunch; up in the village, the Crown (with a bar re-created in Peter Grimes) and Golden Key are both good, too.

SOMERLEYTON TM4997
🏢 ❀ ♣ **Somerleyton Hall** (B1074) Popular with readers, this interesting Jacobean house was rebuilt in the Anglo-Italian style in 1840, and today is still very much lived in, with period furnishings and paintings. The lovely gardens have a maze and miniature railway; live music in the gardens on bank hol afternoons. Good-value snacks, shop, disabled access; open pm Sun, Thurs and bank hols Easter–Sept, plus Tues and Weds July–Aug; (01502) 730244; £4.80. The Plough at Blundeston, home of Barkis ('is willing') in *David Copperfield*, is useful for lunch. N of here, with access from the Hall, is wooded **Fritton Lake**, which attracts numerous wildfowl, particularly in the autumn and winter.

SOUTH ELMHAM TM3385
🏢 **St Peter's Brewery** Medieval St Peter's Hall has in its outhouses this more modern small brewery, whose excellent bitters, porters and fruit beers (all highly praised by readers) are made with water from their own source. Tours take in the whole brewing process, as well as parts of the hall; a visitor centre is planned for later this year. Good meals and snacks, shop, some disabled access; open Fri–Sun, ring for tour times; (01986) 782322; free entry to site, £4 tour.

SOUTHWOLD TM5076
★ ♜ ✝ ♿ Once an important fishing port, now a quite enchanting and civilised little resort with a distinctive lighthouse as its main landmark, an attractive unspoilt green by the sea, and

no end of good pubs and inns supplied by the local Adnams brewery (their wholesale wine shop has interesting stock). For food, the Crown is outstanding, and though more straightforward the King's Head is good, as is the smart Swan Hotel; the Sole Bay and Lord Nelson have the most atmosphere. The Denes is the best beach. Southwold Jack on the tower of the interesting **church** is worth a look; he's an automaton that rings the bell for services. Across the golf course or along the breezy sea wall you come to the harbour, a tidal inlet, with its cheerful mix of beached fishing boats, multitudes of sailing boats, and tall black fishing shacks; the Harbour Inn here is full of character. There's a rowing-boat ferry over to **Walberswick** on the other side of the water – an attractively decorous seaside village, popular with artists ever since Wilson Steer's days here in the 1890s. The Bell is a striking old inn, and the 15th-c church, parts now destroyed and other bits looking shaky, is attractive. (The drive round by car between Southwold and Walberswick is several miles.)

✷ **Lifeboat Museum** (Gun Hill) Always worth a look; open pm daily Jun–Sept; (01502) 722422; free.

◠ **River Blyth** Broad winding river close to the coast nr Southwold, with delightful waterside paths, and marshy and heathy expanses to explore around Walberswick at its mouth (where the waterside scenery has drawn generations of artists).

♂ **Southwold Museum** (Bartholomew Green) Decent town collections, housed in a 17th-c Dutch gabled cottage; open pm Easter–Oct; free.

STANTON TL9671

❀ ♧ ♛ **Wyken Hall Gardens** Formal herb, knot and woodland gardens, walled old-fashioned rose garden, copper beech maze, new pond, and woodland walk to 7-acre vineyard. A very nice unspoilt estate, just right for exploring. Meals and snacks in medieval barn, unusual country shop, disabled access; open Weds–Fri, Sun and bank hols, and some evenings by appointment Easter–Oct; (01359)

250240; *£2.50. The Six Bells at Bardwell has decent food.

STOKE-BY-NAYLAND TL9836

✝ The lovely 15th-c **church** has a tower familiar from several Constable paintings, and a few handsome Tudor buildings among more ordinary ones; the Angel is excellent for lunch, but get there early.

STONHAM ASPAL TM1459

🐦🐗 ♞ ❀ **British Birds of Prey and Conservation Centre** ▣ (Stonham Barns, A1120) Flying displays Apr–Oct, and every species of British owl; also pony rides, pond-dipping, ostriches, lots of goats, rabbits, chickens and guinea-pigs; (01449) 711425; cl 25 Dec; £4.95 (inc nature centre). Around 30 small businesses share the site, inc various craft workshops, a bonsai shop, and a garden centre.

STOUR ESTUARY WALKS TM1534

◠ ♞ Stutton gives access to a fine stretch of the broad Stour estuary just S; on its N side, Alton Water is a reservoir recreation area, with a bird reserve and cycle track.

STOWMARKET TM0458

♟ ♞ ♞ **Museum of East Anglian Life** (Iliffe Way) Excellent 70-acre open-air museum. Children look at the reconstructed buildings with a genuine sense of astonishment: did people really live like that? Even the room settings from the 1950s seem prehistoric to fresher eyes. The main buildings (which include a watermill, chapel, smithy and wind pump) are quite spread out, so there's a fair bit of walking involved, inc a nice stroll down by the river. Also a few animals including Remus the Suffolk punch horse and his friend Blackberry the Shetland pony; adventure playground. Often wood-turning or basket-making demonstrations on Sun. Snacks, shop, disabled access; cl Nov–Mar – phone for occasional winter opening; (01449) 612229; £4. The Magpie (Combs Ford) has decent food.

SUDBURY TL8741

🏛 ▣ ★ **Gainsborough's House** (Gainsborough St) The famous painter was born here in 1727, and the house has an excellent collection of his work; unexpected finds include his efforts at sculpture. Plenty of period furniture and china too, and contemporary arts and crafts. Shop, disabled access to ground floor only; cl am Sun, all day Mon (exc pm bank hols), Christmas wk, Good Fri; (01787) 372958; £3. This market town is pleasant, with useful market stalls on Sat; the Waggon & Horses (Acton Sq) has good plain food.

SUTTON HOO TM2849

🏛️⌂ **Sutton Hoo Archaeological Site** One of the most famous archaeological sites in the country, where in 1939 the discovery of an Anglo-Saxon ship burial made historians completely reinterpret the Dark Ages. Most of the finds from here are in the British Museum, but you can see the burial mounds, and an exhibition explains the site's importance. At the moment tours are at 2pm and 3pm wknds and bank hols, Easter Sat–Oct; £2 (arrive in good time, there is a 20-minute walk from the car park to the site). The NT, who took over the site in 1997, are developing a £3.6 million Lottery-supported upgrade which by 2001 should include a new visitor and study centre with a reconstruction of the ship itself. A turn off the B1083 S takes you to the Ramsholt Arms at Ramsholt for lunch among waterside pinewoods, with quiet walks along the Deben estuary.

TANGHAM NATURE TRAIL TM3548

⌂ 🐦 A short walk among the plantations off the B1084 towards Woodbridge specially designed for disabled people; there are also longer walks through the pinewoods here, where red squirrels often show themselves.

THELNETHAM TM0078

✗ Carefully restored **windmill** and now an attractive sight; open for visits at least summer Suns.

THORPENESS TM4759

! ✗ At the S end of Sizewell beach, this curious place was built as a holiday village in a deliberately fanciful olde-worlde style, with quite a few attractive mock-Tudor houses (one even masking a water-tower); it has a sizeable artificial but now thoroughly natural-looking picturesque lake, and the **windmill** here was brought over from

Aldringham. The newly reopened Dolphin has good food.

🐦⌂ **North Warren** Miles of **RSPB nature reserves** stretching along the coast between Thorpeness and Aldeburgh; nature trails, many different birds (especially waders in winter), butterflies and dragonflies; free.

WENHASTON TM4275

✝ ★ **Wenhaston church** Attractive building, with a 15th-c wall painting (in excellent condition) full of lovely devils; it's a nice peaceful village, too.

WEST STOW TL7971

🕸️ 🐦 🐦 ♈ 🌲 **West Stow Country Park** Attractive, with 125 acres of heath and woodlands bordered by the River Lark. Over 120 different species of bird have been sighted here, and 25 species of animal; the visitor centre often has art exhibitions. The most interesting feature is the reconstructed **Anglo-Saxon Village**, its buildings erected using the same methods and tools as in the 5th c. A new visitor centre houses original finds from the Anglo-Saxon site. Occasional costumed days, and special events such as their Easter Sun market. Meals, snacks, shop, disabled access; cl 25–26 Dec; (01284) 728718; park free, village £4.50 (very good Walkman guide £1.50 extra). The Red Lion at Icklingham has decent food.

WESTLETON TM4369

★ 🕸️ A pleasant village with an attractive green. The White Horse has good-value food, and just past it **Fisks Clematis Nursery** has many varieties of clematis on show and for sale; cl winter wknds.

🐦 🐦 ⌂ **Minsmere Reserve** Big **RSPB reserve** with lots of different species among the heath, woods, marshes and lagoons – good observation hides, and enjoyable walks at any time of year. Meals, snacks, shop, disabled access; cl Tues, and 25–26 Dec; (01728) 648281; *£5 for non-RSPB members. The reserve is skirted by public paths, and one hide is available free for public use, but you need a permit to enter the rest of the reserve. Approach points are Dunwich and Eastbridge. Outside the reserve, much of the flat formerly heathy land nr the coast in this area is now covered with pine plantations: also pleasant for undisturbed walks, with the chance of seeing red squirrels, and in summer with that lovely, fresh, foreign, pinewood smell.

WINGFIELD TM2276

🏠 🎗 **Wingfield College** Quite a surprise to find a splendid medieval timber-framed building behind the Georgian façade. One of its 18th-c owners constructed the Palladian exterior to make his home more fashionable, using false ceilings, floors and windows so skilfully that for 200 years the house's earlier parts were forgotten. Striking great hall, and topiary and kitchen gardens. Snacks; open pm wknds and bank hols Easter–Sept; (01379) 384888; £3.60. They also organise Wingfield Arts, a varied programme of events in churches, halls and other everyday buildings all over the region; phone for programme. The De La Pole Arms has good food.

WOODBRIDGE TM2749

★ † Quietly attractive and rather dignified market town, with many fine buildings and interesting book and antique shops, and a **church** of great style and interest. The Cherry Tree and Seckford Hall Hotel (both off A12 N) do nice lunches, and in the town the Seckford Arms (Seckford St) is good. The B1079 and then B1077 up to Eye is a pleasant drive on an old coach road.

※ **Buttrums Mill** (Burkitt Rd) Six-storey tower mill, now fully restored, with displays of its history; open pm wknds and bank hols May–Oct; *£1.

※ ⌂ **Tide Mill** Restored 18th-c mill on a busy quayside, its wheel usually working when tides allow. Shop, disabled access to ground floor only; open Easter, then daily May–Sept and wknds in Oct; *£1. The Wilford Bridge Hotel nearby at Melton is a good lunch stop – and well placed for river walks.

ŏ **Woodbridge Museum** (Market Hill) Looks at the ship burial at nearby Sutton Hoo, as well as the recent Anglo-Saxon finds at Burrow Hill. Shop, disabled access (but no facilities); cl Sun am, all day Mon and Tues (exc bank and school hols), Weds, and all Nov–Easter; (01394) 380502; £1 (inc free activity sheets for children).

WOOLPIT TL9762

† The **church** here has a hammer-beam roof, and a translation of the village tale that in the 12th c two slightly strange-looking green-skinned children were found by a pit that was suddenly blasted in the earth one night; the boy soon died, but the girl lived, and grew up to marry a local lad and have children. She never said more about her origins than that she'd come from a land far away. The drive to Buxhall is pretty.

ŏ **Woolpit & District Museum** (The Institute) Small but interesting, with annually changing local history displays (and more on the 12th-c children). Shop, disabled access; open pm wknds and bank hols Easter–Sept; donations.

WRENTHAM TM4982

🧺 **Wrentham Basketware** (London Rd) They make and sell traditional willow baskets and hampers, with up to 320 styles. Cl pm Sun, 25 Dec; (01502) 675628; free.

★ **Other attractive villages**, all with decent pubs, include Bildeston TL9949, Blaxhall TM3657, Blyford TM4277, Boxford TL9640, Chelsworth TL9848, Dalham TL7261, Eastbridge TM4566, Fressingfield TM2677, Haughley TM0262 (its Jacobean manor house in lovely grounds), Hoxne TM1777, Huntingfield TM3374, Ixworth TL9370, Middleton TM4367, Polstead TL9938, Risby TL8066 (with a decent antique centre), Ufford TM2953 and Shimpling Street TL8752.

Please let us know what you think of places in the *Guide*. Use the report forms at the back of the book or simply write us a letter.

Where to eat

ALDEBURGH TM4656 **Regatta** *171–173 High St (01728) 452011* Bustling seaside restaurant decorated with pennants and seaside murals, and specialising in fresh local seafood – though they also offer interesting meat dishes and fine puddings; a relaxed atmosphere, friendly service, and no smoking area; may cl some winter wkdys; disabled access. **£25|£6.**

BARDWELL TL9473 **Six Bells** *(01359) 250820* Quietly placed 16th-c pub with heavy beams and timbering, attractive decorations, a snug dining room and a bigger restaurant with conservatory, wide range of good interesting evening food (light lunches, too), polite service, real ales, good wines, and seats out in front and on back lawn; bdrms; cl 25–26 Dec; disabled access. **£17.50|£6.95.**

BRAMFIELD TM3973 **Queens Head** *(01986) 784214* Popular pub with pleasantly relaxed high-raftered lounge bar, good log fire in the impressive fireplace, no smoking side bar, family room, wide choice of very good interesting food (super puddings), well kept real ales, good wines, maybe home-made elderflower cordial; cl 26 Dec. **£19.70|£6.95.**

BURY ST EDMUNDS TL8564 **Maison Bleue** *31 Churchgate St (01284) 760623* Airy French seafood restaurant with a big seaside mural, super fish dishes (and some meaty ones too), a thoughtful wine list, and helpful, friendly staff; cl Sun, 27 Dec for 3 wks; disabled access. **£22|£6.95.**

CAVENDISH TL8046 **Bull** *(01787) 280245* Cheerful pub hiding an attractive 16th-c beamed interior behind a Victorian frontage, big standing timbers and attractive fireplaces in the open-plan rooms, thriving atmosphere, wide range of enjoyable good food (fresh fish is delivered daily), well kept real ales, and a decent choice of wines by the glass; cl Mon; disabled access. **£20|£6.95.**

CHILLESFORD TM3852 **Froize** *(01394) 450282* Heavy beams and lots of interesting things to look at in the big, comfortable, open-plan dining bar and no smoking restaurant, very generous helpings of excellent food, especially wide choice of particularly good fresh fish, super schoolboy puddings, a fine choice of real ales and good range of wines by the glass, courteous service, hard-working owners, and seats in the garden; bdrms; cl Mon (open bank hols), 5 wks Feb/Mar, 1 wk Sept; disabled access. **£25|£8.**

COTTON TM0667 **Trowel & Hammer** *Mill Rd (01449) 781234* Big, friendly, partly thatched and partly tiled white pub with a sprawling lounge, lots of dark beamery and timber baulks, a big log fire, good interesting food, and a large pretty back garden with swimming pool; cl 25 Dec; no small children in Cotton Club restaurant; disabled access. **£18|£5.**

DUNWICH TM4770 **Flora Tearooms** *(01728) 648433* Extended former fisherman's hut right on the beach, with great views of the sea and fishing boats, famous for very good fish and chips but also other snacks, teas and home-made cakes; cl Dec–Feb; disabled access. **£5.**

DUNWICH TM4770 **Ship** *(01728) 648219* Delightful old pub by the sea with a good bustling atmosphere, friendly helpful staff who cope cheerfully with the crowds, wonderfully fresh fish off the boats on the beach, traditionally furnished bar, conservatory, sunny back terrace, and well kept garden; bdrms; the RSPB reserve at Minsmere is close by; cl 25 Dec; disabled access. **£18|£5.45.**

ERWARTON TM2134 **Queens Head** *(01473) 787550* Remote and unspoilt little pub with lovely views, welcoming unpretentious atmosphere, a cosy coal fire in the beamed bar, good well priced bar food inc fresh fish and game in season and decent value Sun lunch, well kept real ales, and friendly service; cl 25 Dec; children in restaurant only; disabled access. **£18|£6.50.**

FRAMSDEN TM1959 **Dobermann** *(01473) 890461* Charmingly restored thatched pub with a twin-facing fireplace separating the friendly, spotlessly kept bars, good popular food, and a decent choice of beers and spirits; disabled access; no children. **£19|£7.50.**

HARTEST TL8352 **Crown** *(01284) 830250* Comfortably modernised and brightly lit pink-washed pub by village green and church (bell ringing practice pm Thurs), lots of space in 2 no smoking dining areas and large conservatory restaurant, reliably good reasonably priced food inc take-away fish and chips and really good-value Mon, Weds and Fri 2-course lunches; quick friendly black-tie staff, a chatty local atmosphere, well kept real ales, and a big back lawn and side courtyard; disabled access. **£20|£6.95** 2 course Fri fish lunch.

HORRINGER TL8261 **Beehive** *The Street (01284) 735260* Particularly well run and pretty ivy-covered pub with extremely helpful service, friendly atmosphere, attractively furnished little rambling rooms, a woodburner, excellent imaginative food with lots of daily specials and a pudding board, well kept real ales, and decent wines; no food pm Sun; disabled access. **£21.50|£6.95**.

ICKLINGHAM TL7772 **Red Lion** *(01638) 717802* Civilised and rather smart thatched pub with a nice mix of wooden chairs, candlelit tables, fresh flowers, fishing rods and various stuffed animals, an inglenook fireplace and heavy beams, very good food, well kept real ales, and country wines; disabled access. **£25|£8.95**.

IPSWICH TM1644 **Mortimers on the Quay** *Wherry Quay (01473) 230225* This is the place for really fresh daily-changing fish, simply cooked; a thoughtful French wine list and relaxed atmosphere; cl am Sat, Sun, 24 Dec–5 Jan. **£24.75|£4.50**.

IXWORTH TL9370 **Theobalds** *68 High St (01359) 231707* Consistently good imaginative food (inc vegetarian choice) in 17th-c restaurant with log fires, beams and standing timbers in cosy rooms, very good wine list, and kind service; cl am Sat, pm Sun, Mon, 2 wks Aug; children in evening over 8 only. **£35|£8.75**.

LAVENHAM TL9149 **Great House** *Market Pl (01787) 247431* Restaurant-with-rooms in ancient house behind an handsome Georgian façade, bare boards, antiques, open fires (inc an inglenook in the restaurant itself), very good French cooking plus lighter lunches and a super French cheeseboard, friendly staff, mainly French wines, and attractive flower-filled courtyard for outside eating; charming beamed bdrms; cl pm Sun, Mon, 3 wks Jan. **£23.95|£7**.

LIDGATE TL7257 **Star** *(01638) 500275* Quaint old place with an interesting small bar, a big log fire, handsomely moulded heavy beams and polished oak and pine tables, chatty Spanish landlady, big helpings of hugely enjoyable food with Mediterranean hints, good wines and ales, a cosy simple dining room, and tables in front and in the little rustic back garden; cl pm Sun. **£24|£5.50**.

LINDSEY TL9744 **White Rose** *Rose Green (01787) 210664* Civilised thatched and timbered dining pub with a long beamed main bar, a log fire in the inglenook, country chairs and pine tables, a second cosy bar opening into a restaurant in former raftered barn, a no smoking area, attractively presented, imaginative bar food from a changing menu, well kept real ales, good wines, and welcoming service. **£19.95|£6.75**.

LONG MELFORD TL8645 **Chimneys** *Hall St (01787) 379806* Lovely beamed 16th-c building with very good carefully prepared interesting food and thoughtful wine list; paintings for sale; cl pm Sun; disabled access. **£33 dinner, £18 lunch**.

NAYLAND TL9734 **White Hart** *(01206) 263382* Smart 15th-c pub/restaurant with 18th-c coaching frontage, polished tables on wooden floors, comfortable sofa by the log fire, and a glass-floored section over wine cellar, good well presented cooking, a wide choice of wines, real ales in straight glasses, and a relaxed atmosphere; popular with businessmen and retired folk; cl 26 Dec, 1 Jan; disabled access. **£22.50|£7.50**.

NEEDHAM MARKET TM0855 **Bonds** *Bridge St (01449) 720265* Excellent fish and chip shop with enviable local reputation; can buy fresh fish here too; cl Sun, Mon. **£2.50**.

ORFORD TM4249 **Butley Orford Oysterage** *(01394) 450277* Simple restaurant with its own oyster beds, fishing boat and smoke house; very popular locally and with yachtsmen for its wonderfully fresh fish, decent wines, and brisk friendly service; cl 25–26 Dec; disabled access. **£23|£5.50**.

RATTLESDEN TL9758 **Brewers Arms** *(01449) 736377* 16th-c pub with a pleasantly simple beamed lounge and small lively public bar, very welcoming friendly service, imaginative food, decent wines, well kept ales, and magnificent old bread oven in the main eating area; children must be well behaved; disabled access. **£20.90|£7.95.**

REDE TL8055 **Plough** *The Green* *(01284)* *789208* Welcoming, partly thatched cottage in a lovely spot, with particularly helpful owners, lots of well presented fresh fish and game in season, imaginative daily specials, good evening restaurant, decent wine, and pretty sheltered cottagey garden; disabled access. **£19.40|£7.95.**

SNAPE TM3958 **Crown** *(01728)* *688324* Unspoilt smugglers' inn with a relaxed and warmly friendly atmosphere, old brick floors, beams, a big brick inglenook and nice old furnishings, particularly good interesting well presented food served by smiling staff, pre- and post-concert suppers, a thoughtful wine list (12 by the glass inc champagne), well kept real ales, and tables in pretty garden; bdrms; cl 25 Dec, pm 26 Dec; no children; partial disabled access. **£20.70|£7.95.**

SNAPE TM3957 **Plough & Sail** *The Maltings* *(01728)* *688302* Part of the Snape Maltings centre with a relaxed and friendly series of attractively furnished rooms, busy little restaurant, delicious food, well kept real ales, and a fine wine list; cl Sun, pm Mon Christmas–Easter; disabled access. **£19|£7.50.**

SUDBURY TL8640 **Red Onion Bistro** *57 Ballingdon St* *(01787)* *376777* Bustling, friendly bistro serving good fairly priced honest food with dishes from all over the world (usually some French and English choices), helpful service, a select-your-own-wine room, and sunny garden; cl Sun, 1 wk Christmas; disabled access. **£14.50 dinner, £12 lunch|£4.75.**

WINGFIELD TM2276 **De La Pole Arms** *(01379)* *384545* Carefully converted village pub with interesting bric-à-brac, comfortable traditional seats, a pleasantly civilised feel, good enjoyable bar food, well kept ales, and prompt welcoming service. **£20.80|£8.50.**

WOODBRIDGE TM2749 **Captain's Table** *3 Quay St* *(01394)* *383145* 16th-c cottage with 3 beamed inter-connecting rooms, cheerful décor, enjoyable, interesting food inc plenty of fresh fish, helpful service, and a thoughtful wine list; cl pm Sun, Mon (open bank hols); disabled access. **£19.45|£5.**

Special thanks to Lucie Miell, Karen Ford, Mark Baynham and Rachael Ward, C M Draycott, Tom Gondris.

Suffolk Calendar

Some of these dates were provisional as we went to press. Please check information with the telephone numbers provided.

JANUARY

1 **Bury St Edmunds** Millennium New Year's Day Celebrations (01284) 764667

FEBRUARY

19 **Capel St Mary** Primrose and Spring Plant Festival at By-Pass Nurseries – *till 27 February* (01473) 311690

MARCH

5 **Long Melford** Lambing Sunday and Spring Bulb Days at Kentwell Hall – *till 2 April* (01787) 310207

APRIL

2 **Rede** Lamb and Spring Working Day at Rede Hall Farm Park (01284) 850695
6 **Bury St Edmunds** Beer Festival – *till 8 April* (01842) 860063
8 **Long Melford** Land Girls and War Time Farm at Kentwell Hall – *till 9 April* (01787) 310207; **Otley** Open Weekend at Otley College of Agriculture and Horticulture – *till 9 April* (01473) 785543
20 **Needham Market** East Anglian Art and Crafts Exhibition and Sale – *till 24 April* (01449) 722202
21 **Long Melford** Easter Egg Hunt Quiz and Re-creation of Tudor Life at Easter at Kentwell Hall – *till 1 May* (01787) 310207; **West Stow** Saxon Activity Days: demonstrations, costumed Saxons at West Stow Anglo-Saxon Village – *till 24 April* (01284) 728718
30 **Mendlesham** Street Fair and Art Exhibition – *till 1 May* (01449) 766563; **Rede** Heavy Horse Working Day and Vintage Tractor Day at Rede Hall Farm Park (01284) 850695

MAY

1 **Ipswich** Woodbridge Horse Show at the Showground (01728) 723067; **West Stow** Archaeology Day at West Stow Anglo-Saxon Village (01284) 728718
5 **Newmarket** Guineas Festival at the Racecourse – *till 7 May* (01638) 663482
7 **Ipswich** Historic Vehicle Run from Christchurch Park to Felixstowe (01394) 276770
12 **Bury St Edmunds** Festival – *till 28 May* (01284) 757080
14 **Ingham** South Suffolk Show at Ampton Park (01638) 750879
20 **Hadleigh** Agricultural Show (01473) 827920
21 **Stoke-by-Nayland** Open Garden at The Priory (01206) 262216
27 **Felixstowe** Drama Festival – *till 3 June* (01394) 282126; **Long Melford** Tudor Living History at Kentwell Hall – *till 29 May* (01787) 310207; **Mildenhall** RAF Air Fête 2000 – *till 28 May* (01638) 543341; **West Stow** Englisc Ham: at home with an Anglo-Saxon family at West Stow Anglo-Saxon Village – *till 29 May* (01284) 728718

Suffolk Calendar (cont.)

28 Bury St Edmunds Bury in Bloom Spring Flower Market (01284) 764667
29 Framlingham Gala (01728) 723857; **Woolpit** Street Fair (01359) 240297
31 Ipswich Suffolk Show at Suffolk Showground – *till 1 June* (01473) 726847

JUNE

3 Bury St Edmunds Carnival (01284) 701215; **Wetherden** Woolpit
Steam Rally at Warren Farm – *till 4 June* (01359) 241886
9 Aldeburgh Festival of Music and the Arts at the Snape Maltings – *till 25
June* (01728) 453543; **Ipswich** Music Festival – *till 11 June* (01473) 258070
10 Long Melford Country Fair at Melford Hall – *till 11 June* (01787) 280941
18 Bury St Edmunds Nowton Park Country Fair (01284) 757092; also,
Open Gardens at various venues (01284) 754993; **Lavenham** Open
Gardens at various venues (01787) 248235; **Long Melford** Re-creation
of Tudor Life at Kentwell Hall – *till 9 July* (01787) 310207
23 Ipswich Maritime Festival – *till 25 June* (01473) 262053
24 Eye 20 Open Gardens – *till 25 June* (01379) 870703; **Ipswich** Flower
Show at the Showground – *till 25 June* (01473) 401733; **Lowestoft** Fish
Fair (01502) 523004
25 Chelsworth Open Gardens at various venues (01449) 740438;
Lowestoft Classic Vehicle Event (01502) 523004; **Stoke-by-Nayland**
Open Garden at The Priory (01206) 262216
29 Ipswich Charter Celebrations inc jousting and medieval siege – *till 1 July*
(01473) 258070

JULY

2 Ipswich Music Day in Christchurch Park (01473) 255851; **Lowestoft**
Armada Special: family fun day, fireworks (01502) 523004
9 Ipswich Music Day: free music festival (01473) 258070
14 Hacheston Rose Festival – *till 16 July* (01728) 747440; **Weeting** Steam
Engine Rally at Fengate Farm – *till 16 July* (01842) 810317
15 Lowestoft East Point Musical Explosion: rock and folk festival – *till 16 July*
(01502) 523004
16 Needham Market Summer Festival (01449) 676800
22 Cowlinge Suffolk Craft Society Exhibition at Peter Pears Gallery – *till 28
August* (01440) 820204; **West Stow** Anglo-Saxon Family: Living History
at West Stow Anglo-Saxon Village – *till 28 July* (01284) 728718
23 Lowestoft Motorcycle Rally on the Seafront (01502) 523004
28 Bury St Edmunds Fireworks Concert at Ickworth House (01625)
575681
29 Ipswich Carnival (01473) 743861

AUGUST

1 Snape Proms: folk, jazz, classical, opera, dance at the Maltings – *till 31
August* (01728) 453543
3 Lowestoft Seafront Airshow – *till 4 August* (01502) 523004
4 Beccles Carnival – *till 7 August* (01502) 712627
5 Haverhill Thurlow Steam Rally and Show – *till 6 August* (01440) 783457;
West Stow Living House: living history at West Stow Anglo-Saxon
Village – *till 7 August* (01284) 728718
13 Lowestoft Carnival (01502) 523002

Suffolk Calendar (cont.)

19 Felixstowe Fuchsia Festival and BFS Show – *till 20 August* (01394) 272839; **West Stow** Meet the Saxons at West Stow Anglo-Saxon Village – *till 27 August* (01284) 728718

21 Aldeburgh Carnival (01394) 383422

25 Long Melford Re-creation of Tudor Life at Kentwell Hall – *till 28 August* (01787) 310207

27 Eye Show – *till 28 August* (01379) 870224; **Walsham-le-Willows** Gardens Weekend: about 25 gardens – *till 28 August* (01359) 259450

28 Lowestoft Gala Day (01502) 523004; **West Stow** Saxon Activity Day at West Stow Anglo-Saxon Village (01284) 728718

SEPTEMBER

16 Henham Steam Rally – *till 17 September* (01502) 523004; **Somerleyton** Horse Trials at Somerleyton Hall – *till 17 September* (01502) 523004

23 Long Melford Re-creation of Tudor Life at Michaelmas at Kentwell Hall – *till 24 September* (01787) 310207

OCTOBER

14 Long Melford World War II Event at Kentwell Hall – *till 17 October* (01787) 310207

NOVEMBER

3 Long Melford Fireworks at Melford Hall (01787) 379783

4 Ipswich Fireworks at Christchurch Park (01473) 258070

11 Ipswich Model Railway Exhibition at Northgate Sports Centre – *till 12 November* (01473) 711718

DECEMBER

22 Rede Lantern Light Christmas Celebrations with the animals at Rede Hall Farm Park – *till 23 December* (01284) 850695

SURREY

Surprisingly unspoilt scenery, with very good walking; good days out.

Forget its commuter-belt image: Surrey is in fact England's most wooded county, and away from the urban corridors much of the countryside is beautifully preserved, and quite hilly. The National Trust owns vast tracts of the finest scenery, and walkers have an excellent choice, with relatively free access. There are some beautiful villages, too.

The county's open-air appeal extends to the grounds around its enjoyable great houses such as those at East and West Clandon (good-value joint ticket) and Great Bookham, and to the wonderful Claremont landscape garden in Esher, the gardens at Wisley, and Winkworth Arboretum. Unexpected finds include the intimate sculpture garden at Ockley, the Watts picture gallery at Compton, and even a network of tunnels hidden under Reigate.

There's no shortage of family outings, from the action-packed theme parks at Thorpe Park and Chessington to quieter animal and bird places and well organised open farms. Days out here are headed by Chessington World of Adventures and Thorpe Park. Brooklands in Weybridge has strongly nostalgic motor-racing appeal (historic aircraft, too), and Derby Day Experience in Epsom delights even people who aren't horse-racing enthusiasts.

Where to stay

BAGSHOT SU9062 **Pennyhill Park** *College Ride, Bagshot GU19 5ET (01276) 471774* **£218,** plus special breaks; 114 charming, spacious rms. Impressive Victorian country house in 120 acres of well kept gardens and parkland, with and friendly and courteous staff, comfortable two-level lounge with panelling and beams, little bar, tapestries and fine paintings, and very good, imaginative cooking; outdoor swimming pool, tennis, 9-hole golf course, stabling, game fishing, and clay-pigeon shooting – they can arrange riding too; disabled access.

CHERTSEY TQ0466 **Crown** *7 London St, Chertsey KT16 8AP (01932) 564657* **£58w;** 30 comfortable, modern rms. Bustling, friendly place with some original features and an open fire in the large bar, conservatory extension, good food, attractive restaurant, and lovely big garden; disabled access.

CHOBHAM SU9760 **Knap Hill Manor** *Carthouse Lane, Chobham, Woking GU21 4XT (01276) 857962* **£70;** 3 spacious rms with garden views. Really welcoming and relaxing, late 18th-c family home with lovely peaceful gardens (tennis and croquet), big comfortable sitting room, delicious breakfasts with home-made preserves, and helpful, knowledgeable owners; golf nearby; cl Christmas–Easter; children over 8.

EWHURST TQ0840 **High Edser** *Shere Rd, Ewhurst, Cranleigh GU6 7PQ (01483) 278214* **£50;* 3 charming rms, shared bthrm. 16th-c timber-framed farmhouse in lovely countryside, with a comfortable residents' lounge, friendly owners, enjoyable food (by arrangement) and an open fire in the dining room, and tennis court in the grounds; cl Christmas.

FARNHAM SU8145 **Farnham House** *Alton Rd, Farnham GU10 5ER (01252) 716908* **£65w,** plus special breaks; 25 comfortable rms. Attractive Victorian 'gothick' manor house with oak panelling and open fires in the comfortable public rooms, split-level restaurant, and a tennis court and outdoor heated swimming pool in the five-acre gardens.

GODSTONE TQ3551 **Godstone Hotel** *The Green, Godstone RG9 8DT* (01833) 742461 *£55; 8 rms. Well run, late 16th-c hotel with an open fire in the comfortable residents' lounge, good popular food in the attractive beamed restaurant, summer cream teas, and helpful service from very welcoming owners.

HASLEMERE SU8931 **Deerfell** *Blackdown Park, Fernden Lane, Haslemere GU27 3LA* (01428) 653409 *£44; 2 rms with showers. Comfortable, no smoking, stone coach house with wonderful views and nice nearby walks; generous meals in handsome dining room (if ordered in advance), open fire in the sitting room, pictures, antiques and old rugs, a sun room, good breakfasts, and friendly owners; cl mid-Dec–mid-Jan; children over 6.

HASLEMERE SU9232 **Lythe Hill Hotel** *Petworth Rd, Haslemere GU27 3BQ* (01428) 651251 £142, plus special breaks; 41 individually styled rms, a few in the original house. Lovely partly 15th-c building in 20 acres of parkland and bluebell woods (adjoining the NT hillside), with floodlit tennis court, croquet lawn and jogging track; plush, comfortable and elegant lounges, a relaxed bar, two no smoking restaurants (one with French cooking, the other with traditional English), and good, attentive service; disabled access.

HOLMBURY ST MARY TQ1144 **Bulmer Farm** *Holmbury St Mary, Dorking RH5 6LG* (01306) 730210 *£46; 8 big comfortable rms, 5 in no smoking barn conversion with own showers. Attractive and welcoming 17th-c farmhouse on a 30-acre beef farm in lovely countryside, with oak beams and an inglenook fireplace in the attractive sitting room, breakfasts with home-made preserves in the neatly kept dining room, and a large garden; self-catering also; children over 12; disabled access.

HORLEY TQ2842 **Langshott Manor** *Horley RH6 9LN* (01293) 786680 £155, plus special breaks; 15 individually furnished rms. Elizabethan house in fine 3-acre garden with roses and lakes; beams, oak panelling, fresh flowers and open fires in the elegant rooms, and enjoyable traditional cooking in the no smoking restaurant; well behaved dogs in their kennels; disabled access.

NUTFIELD TQ2950 **Nutfield Priory** *Nutfield, Redhill RH1 4EL* (01737) 822066 *£132, plus special breaks; 60 rms. Impressive Victorian 'gothick' hotel in 40 acres of parkland; with lovely elaborate carvings, stained-glass windows, gracious day rooms, a fine panelled library, cloistered restaurant, and even an organ in the galleried grand hall; extensive leisure club with indoor heated swimming pool.

We welcome reports from readers

This *Guide* depends on readers' reports. Do help us if you can – in return, we offer a discount on the next edition to people who've helped us with reports for it. Tell us what you think about places already in it, and anything extra you think we should say about them. And send us your ideas for inclusion in the next edition: places to visit, eat at or stay in, attractive drives or walks, maybe even unusual interesting shops you know of. Use the card in the middle, the report forms at the end, or just write – no stamp needed: *The Good Britain Guide*, FREEPOST TN1569, Wadhurst, E Sussex TN5 7BR.

To see and do

SURREY Family Attraction of the Year

☺ ☛ ⚘ **CHERTSEY** TQ0467 **Thorpe Park** (A320 N of Chertsey) There isn't too much to choose between this 500-acre leisure park and its local rival Chessington, though this is perhaps less manic, with gentler rides and lots of activities for younger children. That's not to say there's nothing for thrill-seekers – star attraction is still the oddly named rollercoaster X:\No Way Out, hidden in an enormous pyramid, which not only soars up and down in total darkness, but does it all backwards. A popular new feature is the 4-D pirate experience – you put on 3-D glasses for a very well put together multi-sensory film, during which you not only see and hear exciting attacks from pirates and giant hornets, but, thanks to special effects built into the seats, at various stages you'll feel water, wind and the occasional mild shock. Other highlights include lively rides like Thunder River and Calgary Stampede, Loggers Leap (the highest log flume in the country), more sedate play areas, and a man-made beach and pools. Quite a few activities are water based, and you'll need swimming things for the slides around Wet! Wet! Wet! Across the lake (reached either by a train or waterbus) is a decent-sized traditional working farm with animals and a craft centre. Staff are helpful, and the visitor facilities excellent. In summer 1999 we were pleased to see the park opening till midnight on Saturdays in August, which not only gave the place a different atmosphere but also meant there weren't quite so many people waiting for some of the rides; on busy summer days it doesn't escape the crowds and queues that theme parks invariably attract. They also have later opening on several dates in October for their rather spectacular firework displays. Meals, snacks, shop, disabled access; cl Nov–mid-Mar; (01932) 562633; £17.50 (£14 children over one metre tall and under 14). The family ticket, covering admission for 2 adults and 2 children or 1 adult and 3 children, is good value at £56 – you can get it even cheaper if you book in advance (which you can do up to 5pm the day before you plan to visit).

ABINGER COMMON TQ1245
★ † ⚘ ◠ Charmingly set village, with pretty church, ancient pub and duckpond surrounded by woodland – popular for walks.

ALBURY TQ0547
★ Attractive village, with glimpses of the Victorian mansion Albury Park – or at least its famous chimneys.

BANSTEAD WOOD TQ2657
⚘ ◠ Popular strolling-ground, surprisingly peaceful despite the proximity of Surrey's northern suburbia and heavily used trunk roads.

BETCHWORTH TQ2149
★ ◠ Attractive village, pleasant for strolls along an annotated trail from a church where *Four Weddings and A Funeral* was filmed, passing a working blacksmith. The Dolphin is a decent pub, and there's a nice drive via Brockham and Newdigate to Rusper in Sussex.

BOX HILL TQ1751
❀ ◠ Surrey's most popular viewpoint, with a summit car park and walks on its steep juniper and boxwood slopes: great views, wild orchids and butterflies in early summer, maybe field mushrooms in early autumn; the attractively placed King William IV at Mickleham is excellent for lunch.

CHALDON TQ3155
† Attractive **church**, particularly worth a visit for its unique wall painting of the Ladder of Salvation.

CHARLWOOD TQ2341
🐾 🐦 ✸ **Gatwick Zoo & Aviaries** £ (Russ Hill) Readers are surprised by the hundreds of mammals and birds here, many in big naturalistic settings – some of which you can walk through, inc the two big tropical houses with plants and butterflies from around the world. Meals, snacks, shop, disabled access; cl 25–26 Dec; (01293) 862312; £4.95. The

Greyhound has good-value food.
CHERTSEY TQ0467
🏠 ⌂ A good few Georgian buildings in its main streets, and pleasant walks by the Thames.
🏛 **Chertsey Abbey** Medieval remains standing in Abbeyfields Park.
🗿 🏛 **Chertsey Museum** (Windsor St) Late Georgian building, displays on the abbey, a good costume collection, a hands-on gallery, and a pleasant little garden. Shop, disabled access to ground floor only; cl am wkdys, all day Sun, Mon, and bank hols; (01932) 565764; free.
🚂 **Great Cockcrow Railway** (Hardwick Lane, Lyne, slightly NW) A notable miniature steam railway, with a unique signalling system. Snacks, some disabled access; open pm Sun May–Oct; (01932) 565474; £1.50. The Golden Grove on St Ann's Hill out towards here is a nice spot for lunch.
☺ 🐄 🎡 **Thorpe Park** See separate family panel on p.618.
CHESSINGTON TQ1762
☺ 🎡 **Chessington World of Adventures** (A243) Surrey's other superior theme park, excellently put together, with around 100 rides and amusements. The big ride is Rameses Revenge, which spins you round 360 degrees at speeds of up to 60mph while plummeting towards a rock-lined pit and water fountains, but there's also plenty to amuse younger children, from the Dragon River log flume to a circus show. Over on the quieter, greener side of the park, the once famous zoo (perhaps a little lost now among the other attractions) is popular with children, and there are sealion and penguin displays at set times throughout the day. It's worth taking advantage of their later opening hours in the summer hols (till 9pm) as the park isn't so busy later in the day. Meals, snacks, shop, some disabled access but best to phone in advance; open late Mar–Oct; (01372) 727227; £19 (£15 children 4–13). Some of their leaflets have coupons that can save up to £20 off the total admission. The North Star (Hook Rd) is a popular family dining pub.
CHIDDINGFOLD SU9635
★ ✝ Exceptional village in fine

surroundings, with one window of its church made up from locally excavated fragments of 13th-c glass made here. The old Crown is a handsome place for lunch or afternoon tea.
🏵 **Ramster** (A283 S) Splendid Edwardian woodland spring garden. Teas (May only), plant sales, disabled access; open mid-Apr–mid-July; (01428) 654167; *£3.
COBHAM TQ1159
Quite a busy shopping town, with some fine older buildings around the church and in Church St; just SW, Downside Common is a classic cricket green, with cottages scattered around it and an attractive pub – the Cricketers.
✗ **Cobham Mill** (Mill Rd) Prettily set working watermill, authentically restored by enthusiastic locals. Open pm 2nd Sun of month Apr–Oct; free.
🏵 **Painshill Park** (A425 slightly W) These beautifully restored 18th-c landscape gardens are a continual surprise, with Gothic temples, Chinese bridges, even a Turkish tent and other follies at every turn, and a lake with seemingly endless bays and inlets. Lots of unusual trees and shrubs. Snacks, shop, limited disabled access; cl Mon (exc bank hols), and Fri Nov–Mar; (01932) 868113; £3.80. Almost opposite the gates, the Snail brasserie has decent food.
COMPTON SU9547
🖼 ✝ **Watts Picture Gallery** (Down Lane) Memorial gallery to Victorian painter and sculptor G F Watts, in his time one of the most celebrated artists in the world. Good tearoom (readers report 24 different teas and not a microwave in sight), shop, disabled access; cl all Thurs, am Mon, Tues, Fri and Sun; (01483) 810235; free. Just down the road the Art Nouveau tomb built by his widow is worth a look, and the village church is attractive. The Harrow and Withies have good but pricey food.
DEVIL'S PUNCHBOWL SU8936
🐿 ⌂ ❋ A spectacular fold of the Downs, with nature trails through mixed woodlands, quiet valleys and sandy heaths with scattered ponds. The area is quite developed but the woods and intricacy of the landscape give it a wholesome rurality, and the footpath

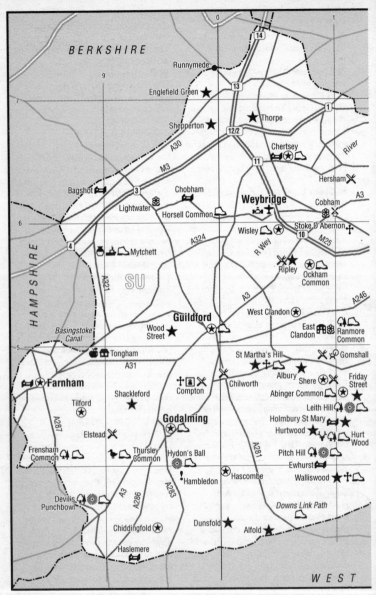

network is dense. Gibbet Hill above the A3 gets a view over most of it.

DORKING TQ1649

★ ♂ A pleasant market town with a lot of antique shops, and a local museum (West St, where the 16th-c King's Arms has decent food); the roads S of the A25, W of here, are the county's most pleasant drives, and the steep road up Box Hill N opens a great panorama.

♣ ! **Denbies Wine Estate** (London Rd) Britain's biggest vineyard – at 250 acres, bigger than most in France. The tour is unique, with road-train rides round the winery, and a 3-D film, where four months of vine growth is

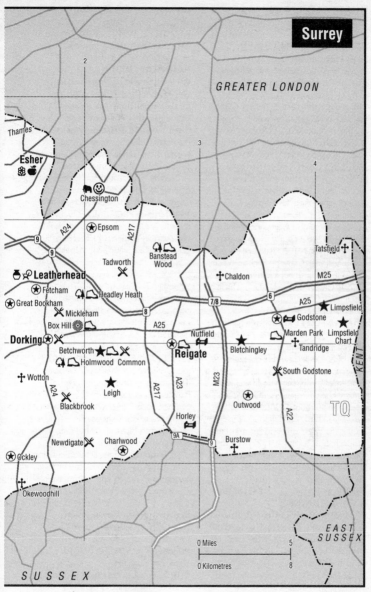

Surrey

GREATER LONDON

Thames

Esher

Chessington

Epsom

Tatsfield

Tadworth

Banstead Wood

Chaldon

M25

Leatherhead

Fetcham

Headley Heath

Great Bookham

Godstone

Limpsfield

Mickleham

Box Hill

Dorking

Nutfield

Marden Park

Limpsfield Chart

Betchworth

Reigate

Bletchingley

Tandridge

Holmwood Common

Wotton

South Godstone

Leigh

Blackbrook

Outwood

TQ

Horley

Newdigate

Charlwood

Burstow

Ockley

Okewoodhill

0 Miles 5

0 Kilometres 8

EAST SUSSEX

SUSSEX

condensed into four minutes, and grapes seem to fly out of the screen. You don't have to be a wine buff to enjoy it. Meals and snacks (in unusually designed restaurant), big shop, good disabled access; cl am Sun, 25–26 Dec; (01306) 876616; £5 (inc tastings). Fine views and walks nearby.

DOWNS LINK PATH TQ0735

⌂ This follows a disused railway track through pleasant countryside, and is increasingly popular for walks and family cycling. The Thurlow Arms, at Baynards Station Yard nr Cox Green, is handy for access and does reasonably priced food.

DUNSFOLD TQ0036

★ One of Surrey's most picturesque village greens; the Sun is a pleasant pub.

EAST CLANDON TQ0651

🏠 🌸 **Hatchlands** 💷 Handsome 18th-c brick house with more floors than are visible from the outside, thanks to an ingenious use of false windows. The grand rooms are especially notable for their ceilings and fireplaces, early examples of the work of Robert Adam. A fine collection of keyboard instruments includes a piano once played by Mozart. The garden has a parterre by Gertrude Jekyll. Meals, snacks, shop, disabled access (with notice); open Apr–Oct, house and garden pm Sun, Tues–Thurs and bank hols, plus pm Fri in Aug, park walk daily; (01483) 222482; £4.30, £1.75 garden and park walk; NT. A visit here is easily combined with Clandon Park at West Clandon (you can get a joint ticket £6.20). The Queen's Head is useful for lunch.

EPSOM TQ2158

❗👹 **Derby Day Experience** (Queen's Stand) The Derby (first run in 1780) is still the most prestigious race for three-year-olds – and a grand social event. At its home racecourse, this re-creates the excitement, with the help of archive film, interactive displays and various relics and mementos. Worth a look even if you're not a racegoer – though it's usually open only one Sun and Tues a month; best to ring (01372) 726311 for dates; £4. Other racecourses in this area include Sandown Park, (01372) 463072; Kempton Park, (01932) 782292; and Lingfield, (01342) 834800; all have good facilities.

🐦 **Horton Park Children's Farm** (B280 W) Plenty of animals to feed and cuddle, tractor rides (a little extra), and an adventure playground. Meals, snacks, shop, disabled access; cl 25–26 Dec; (01372) 743984; £3.45 per child (one accompanying adult free).

ESHER TQ1464

🌸 🌳 **Claremont Landscape Garden** (off A307) The oldest surviving landscaped garden in the country, laid out by Vanbrugh and Bridgeman before 1720 and extended and naturalised by Kent; 50 colourful acres to lose yourself in. Meals, snacks,

shop, disabled access; cl Mon Nov–Mar, 25 Dec, 1 Jan, and maybe some days in July; (01372) 469421; £3; NT. There's a farm shop with **pick-your-own** fruit on Winterdown Rd just N.

FARNHAM SU8346

★ Handsome town that owed its Georgian heyday to the importance of local corn and hops. Many elegant buildings from this period remain, and there are some even older ones such as the early 17th-c Spinning Wheel. The area around Castle St is especially nice to stroll round, and the Spotted Cow and newly refurbished Fox (both Lower Bourne) are pleasant lunch spots.

🐦 🌸 🎣 **Birdworld & Underwater World** (Holt Pound, off A325 3m SW – actually just over the Hants border) A wide variety of birds in 18 acres of garden and parkland – all shapes and sizes from the tiny tanagers to the huge ostrich, with many rare species. Woodland walks and trails. The adjacent **Underwater World** has tropical and other freshwater and marine fish. Meals, snacks, shop, disabled access; usually cl wkdys Nov and Jan–mid-Feb, phone to check; (01420) 22838; £6 just Birdworld, £2 just Underwater World, £7.50 both. The nearby 16th-c Cherry Tree at Rowledge has good food.

🏰 **Farnham Castle** For 800 years a residence of the Bishops of Winchester. Most of the buildings have been adapted to suit the briefing organisation based here, but the major rooms, inc the Great Hall, can be seen on a guided tour Weds 2–4pm; shop; cl Christmas–New Year; (01252) 721194; £1.50.

🏰 **Castle Keep** Administered separately; includes the massive foundations of a Norman tower. Open daily Apr–Oct; (01252) 713393; £2, inc Walkman tour; EH.

👹 🌸 **Farnham Museum** (West St) Excellent local history museum; some William Cobbett memorabilia (his birthplace in Bridge Sq is now a pub named after him), and a pleasant walled garden. Shop, disabled access to ground floor; cl Sun and Mon; free.

🎨 **Maltings Gallery** (Bridge Sq) Diverse arts and crafts. Meals, snacks, shop, disabled access; cl Mon; (01252)

713637; free, although maybe £1 for national exhibitions.

FETCHAM TQ1555

🐄 🐖 ⚘ **Bocketts Farm Park** 🅰🅳 Working farm in a pretty historic setting, with traditional and rare breeds, cart rides, falconry, craft demonstrations and their latest attraction – pig racing (wknds and school hols). Meals, snacks, shop, disabled access; cl 25–26 Dec; (01372) 363764; £3.25.

FRENSHAM COMMON SU8540

☁ 🌣 Popular for walks, with heather and woodland around a lake formed in the 13th c for fish-breeding.

GODALMING SU9643

★ 🏛 Attractive town with a good few interesting buildings and, because of its narrow streets (part cobbled and pedestrianised), a more old-fashioned feel than most in Surrey. The Inn on the Lake (A3100 S) is good for lunch, and the Star (Church St) has decent snacks.

🐖 ✹ **Busbridge Lakes** (Hambledon Rd, off B2130) Very pretty spot with three lakes in fine parkland – exotic waterfowl, peacocks, ornamental pheasants and many other kinds of bird, as well as follies and grottoes throughout the grounds. Snacks, shop; only open 16–24, 30 Apr, 1, 28–29 May, and 20–28 Aug; (01483) 421955; £3.50.

🍶 ✹ **Godalming Museum** (High St) 15th-c house with local history, and Gertrude Jekyll-style walled garden. Some disabled access; cl Mon, Sun, bank hols; free. The town hall opposite is known affectionately by the locals as the Pepper Pot.

🏛 ⚓ ☁ **River Wey & Godalming Navigation** This 17th-c canal, passing through some fine scenery, was extended here in 1763, to link Godalming with the Thames. The wharf has some fine Georgian buildings, and the locks and towpath have been restored by the NT – a visitor centre has exhibitions on Surrey's barge-building history. A river bus runs to and from the town centre, and guided nature walks along the canal take place throughout the year – best to ring for dates. Snacks, shop, disabled access; open Thurs, wknds and bank hols Apr–Oct; (01483) 561389; £2.50; NT. You can walk all the way to Weybridge,

some 20 miles, or hire boats from Farncombe Boat House (01483) 421306.

GODSTONE TQ3551

★ ✝ Attractive despite its main roads, spread around a broad green with a duckpond, and a pretty group of houses around the imposing **church**, 14th/15th-c with a Norman tower. The Bell is an enjoyable dining pub.

🍎 **Flower Farm** (Quarry Rd, just off A22 W of Oxted) Looking up to the Downs, this has organically grown **pick-your-own** produce and a vineyard. Meals, snacks, shop, disabled access; cl Oct–Apr (exc vineyard, open all year); (01883) 744590; free.

GOMSHALL TQ0846

⚘ **Gomshall Gallery** (A25) Contemporary arts and crafts; also French wine wholesaler, and house plants for sale. Cl Sun and bank hols.

GREAT BOOKHAM TQ1352

🏛 🖼 ✹ 🌣 **Polesden Lacey** (off A246 S) Attractive Regency house once at the centre of Edwardian high society, now with photographs of some of the notable guests, as well as splendid tapestries, porcelain, Old Masters and other art. The spacious grounds have a walled rose garden and open-air theatre. Meals, snacks, shop, disabled access; house open pm Weds–Sun and bank hols Apr–Oct, grounds open all year; (01372) 458203; £6, £3 grounds only; NT. On the other side of the extended commuter village, the Bookham Commons, with a mixture of thorny scrub (full of birds), small lakes, marshy bits and oakwoods, are attractive. In Effingham nearby, the Plough and Sir Douglas Haig are both reliable food pubs.

GUILDFORD SU9949

🏛 ☁ The biggest town in the area, Guildford is older than you might at first think; although many of the buildings are Georgian-fronted, what's behind often dates back much further. The sloping High St has attractive parts as well as its briskly modern shops, with interesting buildings inc the **Abbots Hospital** and the **Grammar School** with its notable chained library; Tunsgate Arch is the start for free guided walks of the city – 2.30pm every Sun, Mon and Weds May–Sept (plus

7.30pm Thurs till end Aug).
🏠⛵ Guildford Boat House
(Millmead) Handsome and impressive
building; you can hire boats here for the
Wey Navigation (01483) 504494.
Nearby, the Jolly Farmer does decent
food in a lovely riverside setting.
🏰 ❄ 🏛 Guildford Castle 🖼 The hill
of the ruined 12th-c castle has fine
views of the town, and a garden in the
former castle ditch. Shop; open
Easter–Sept; (01483) 444702; keep 40p,
grounds free.
✝ Guildford Cathedral The
cathedral, begun in 1936, is one of the
only two entirely 20th-c Anglican
cathedrals in the country; it's quite
austere, but has a cool elegance inside.
⛲ Guildford Museum (Quarry St)
Local history, with a display on Lewis
Carroll, who died here in 1898 (shop; cl
Sun; free). He's buried in the cemetery
on the Mount, the continuation of the
High St.
🏠 Guildhall (High St) Mainly Tudor,
with one of the few existing sets of
Elizabethan standard measures. Free
guided tours at 2pm and 3pm Tues and
Thurs and 3.30pm Weds when you can
have tea with the mayor; (01483)
444035; (free but you need a ticket
from the tourist information centre for
Weds).
🏠 🍴 🏛 Loseley House 🖼 (off
B3000, 3m SW) Most people are
familiar with the name from the
yoghurts and ice-cream produced here
(try the white chocolate and
butterscotch versions). The stately
Elizabethan country house was built in
1562, and has fine panelling, ceilings,
paintings and tapestries. The gardens
include a fountain garden. Trailer rides

across the estate on Sats. Meals, snacks,
shop, limited disabled access; house and
farm open pm Weds–Sat and bank hols
May–Aug, plus Sun in Aug, gardens
open from 11am; (01483) 304440; £5
house and gardens, £2.50 gardens only,
£3 trailer rides.
HAMBLEDON SU9639
❗ You can climb inside what's said to be
a witch's tree in front of the church
here; walk round the tree three times
and the witch may well appear.
HASCOMBE SU9940
★ ✝ A lovely village with an interesting
church; Dirk Bogarde's old local the
White Horse is good for lunch (with a
great garden), and the B2130 S and then
the Dunsfold–Chiddingfold back road is
a pleasant drive.
🍃 ❄ Winkworth Arboretum
(B2130 just NW) Nearly 100 acres of
lovely hillside woodland, with fine views
over the North Downs – especially nice
in spring, and with unusual flaring
colours in the autumn. Summer snacks
and shop, some disabled access;
(01483) 208477; £3; NT.
HEADLEY HEATH TQ2053
⌂ 🍃 Sandy walks and rides through
heather, birchwoods and, as summer
wears on, rather too much bracken.
HOLMWOOD COMMON
TQ1845
🍃 ⌂ Popular for walks, with
undulating oak and birchwoods, lots of
good paths; the Plough at Blackbrook is
useful for lunch.
HORSELL COMMON TQ0060
⌂ A touch of interest for walkers in the
sandpits which inspired and saw the
start of H G Wells's *The War of the
Worlds*; the Bleak House at the
Anthonys and Red Lion in Horsell have

Days Out

Surrey's greensand country: Ockley sculpture garden; lunch at the
Cricketers there, or Stephan Langton, Friday Street; walk up to Leith Hill
tower; Shere.

Exploring the North Downs: Stroll on Box Hill or Ranmore Common;
Denbies vineyard; lunch at the King William IV, Mickleham; Polesden Lacey.

A house and garden theme: Clandon Park, West Clandon; lunch at the
Onslow Arms there, or at Michels in Ripley; Wisley Garden.

decent food.
HURT WOOD TQ0943
🐾 ᗇ ⍓ Large areas of private
broadleafed forest around here are
open to walkers; relatively
unfrequented, so it's a good place to
spot birds and wild animals.
HYDON'S BALL SU9739
❀ ᗇ There's unspoilt walking terrain
off the road between Loxhill and
Hydestile S of Godalming, with Hydon's
Ball a fine viewpoint, though rather hard
to find.
LEATHERHEAD TQ1658
⚒ **Fire and Iron Gallery** (Oxshott
Rd, A244 N) Unusual exhibitions of
ornamental metalwork; limited disabled
access; cl Sun and some bank hols;
(01372) 386453; free.
🕯 **Museum of Local History**
(Church St) In a pretty 17th-c timber-
framed building, and well worth a visit;
shop, open Sat, pm Thurs and am Fri
Apr–Christmas; (01372) 386348; free.
The Duke's Head in the pedestrianised
High St is pleasant for lunch, and there
are riverside walks nearby.
LEITH HILL TQ1343
ᗇ 🐾 ❀ Perhaps the best stretch of
country for walkers in Surrey – which
surprises by being England's most
wooded county. It has heather, sandy
walks, steep pinewoods and
tremendous views. An 18th-c tower on
top of the hill, the highest point in
south-east England, is the best
viewpoint of all, with a surprising view
of South London – which feels 100
miles away. It's open with teas on pm
Weds and Sat, Sun and bank hols, but cl
Oct–Mar exc fine wknds – 80p. Friday
Street, with a fine pub and a lake, is one
starting-point for switchback routes S
through a series of brackeny summits to
the tower. Leith Hill can also be
approached through farmland from the
S, from Ockley or from the Parrot at
Forest Green.
LIGHTWATER SU9262
✿ **Lightwater Country Park** A new
visitor centre, to replace the one which
burnt down, opened here last year, and
there are plenty of nature trails. Snacks,
shop, disabled access; park open all
year, visitor centre open Sun, bank hols
and pm Tues–Fri in school hols
Mar–Dec; (01276) 479582; free.

MARDEN PARK TQ3653
ᗇ Popular strolling-ground,
surprisingly peaceful despite the
proximity of Surrey's northern
suburbia and even the M25.
MYTCHETT SU8955
🛁 ⚓ ᗇ **Basingstoke Canal** Formerly
derelict, this has been undergoing a
tremendous programme of
rehabilitation over the last 15 years or
so. In its Surrey section it does not pass
through such fine scenery as the Wey
Navigation, but its towpath has been
well restored. **Basingstoke Canal
Visitor Centre** (Place Rd) Displays on
the canal, and good access to its
towpath, with boat trips (wknds, bank
hols and daily in school hols,
Easter–Nov); you can hire rowing
boats. Teas, shop, disabled access; cl
Mon (exc bank hols), wknds Oct–Mar;
(01252) 370073; information centre
and play areas free, exhibition £1.50.
OCKHAM COMMON TQ0858
🏰 ❀ 🐾 ᗇ **Chatley Heath
Semaphore Tower** (Old Lane, off A3
to Effingham) Unique tower rather like
a lighthouse, the only surviving member
of a chain that once sent messages
between the Admiralty in London and
Portsmouth; excellent views from the
top of the 88 steps. Surrounding it are
700 acres of heath and woodland, with
a nature trail and good walks (inc the
20-minute trek from the car park to the
tower). Shop; open pm wknds and bank
hols Apr–Sept, plus Weds in school
hols; (01932) 862762; £2. The
extraordinary 'gothick' Hautboy
(Ockham Lane) has a good brasserie.
OCKLEY TQ1439
★ Some attractive old houses along the
Roman road here, with the 15th-c
Cricketers Arms doing good-value
food; the Scarlett Arms out at
Walliswood is a delightful old place with
a pretty garden.
✿ 🖼 🌿 **Hannah Peschar Gallery &
Garden** (Black and White Cottage,
Standon Lane) Lush garden filled with
contemporary sculpture: the water
garden is now more like a tropical
rainforest than the cottage garden it
started as, and the atmospheric
sculptures and ceramics blend perfectly
with its unusual design. Some disabled
access but no facilities; open Fri, Sat and

pm Sun and bank hols May–Oct, other times (exc Mon) by arrangement; (01306) 627269; £7. There's a good big farm shop with **pick-your-own** fruit nearby.

OUTWOOD TQ3245

★ 🐿 Spread around an attractive common, with an antique shop, and adjacent NT woodlands ideal for a picnic. The Bell nr the common and Dog & Duck out towards Coopers Hill are good for lunch.

✗ 🐿 **Outwood Post Mill** Very well preserved, England's oldest working windmill, built in 1665. It's a lovely spot, 120 metres (400ft) above sea level, with ducks, goats and horses all wandering freely about its grounds. In Apr they do tours of the adjacent woods to see the bluebells. Shop, disabled access to ground floor only; open pm Sun and bank hols Easter–Oct; (01342) 843644; £2.

PITCH HILL TQ0842

🐿 ◠ ❀ Though this is largely wooded, it's good heathy country for walkers, with pleasant views on the relatively open approach from Ewhurst; above the village, the Windmill pub has glorious views from its garden.

RANMORE COMMON TQ1551

🐿 ◠ Chalk downland with sheep, wild orchids and dense woodlands, within close range of Polesden Lacey. You can walk on the well marked North Downs Way.

REIGATE TQ2548

🏰 **Barons Cave tours** Below the peaceful castle grounds is a network of old tunnels, notably this splendidly atmospheric passageway with all sorts of myths and stories attached. The tours are enthusiastic and entertaining; open on selected days, best to ring the Wealden Cave and Mine Society (who plan to open even more caves soon) on (01737) 823456, for full details and dates; £1. Among the few surviving original buildings in this mainly modern town are one or two timber-framed houses around the High St, where the Market pub (open all day) has decent food.

✗ ✝ ◠ **Windmill church** (off A25 W) The 220-year-old former windmill on Reigate Heath was converted into a church in 1882. They still have services at 3pm on the 3rd Sun each month in summer. Disabled access; open all year – if cl, key at golf club clubhouse. There are pleasant walks out here, and the Skimmington Castle is a nice country pub.

RUNNYMEDE TQ0071

A field by a main road; not worth visiting unless you are quite fascinated by Magna Carta, though up the hill beyond the trees, the nearby memorials to John F Kennedy and, with their names, to the aircrew who died during World War II, are dignified and touching.

ST MARTHA'S HILL TQ0348

✝ ◠ ★ (E of Guildford) The church on its summit can be reached only on foot, and by starting from the attractive village of Chilworth, where the prettily set pub the Villagers at Blackheath has maps for walkers, you can see the long-abandoned gunpowder mills by the Tilling Bourne.

SHEPPERTON TQ0766

★ One of the best places to watch the comings and goings on the **River Thames**, with the Wey Navigation joining the river here; the Red Lion (Russell Rd), Warren Lodge Hotel (Church Sq) and handsomely refurbished Thames Court Hotel (Ferry Lane) all have riverside gardens, and there's a quiet and attractive 18th-c village square with a pleasant church.

SHERE TQ0747

★ ✝ 🐎 Very picturesque village, with 17th-c timber-framed cottages, a grassy-banked stream with ducks and ford, and lots of interesting corners. In the partly Norman **church** a quatrefoil blocked hole in the chancel wall marks the spot where a 14th-c anchorite had herself walled in, being fed through another hole outside. The Malt House is a decent local history museum, and the ancient White Horse is a good place for lunch. The village is within reach of both the North Downs around Ranmore Common and the greensand hills to the S; the view from the Ewhurst road is particularly memorable.

STOKE D'ABERNON TQ1259

✝ **Stoke d'Abernon church** Notable for the earliest surviving memorial brass in Britain, dating from the 13th c; set in the floor of the chancel, it's very well preserved.

THURSLEY COMMON SU9040

◠ ✦ Mainly pleasant sandy walking country, with heather and quite often unusual birds, also boggy patches with shallow ponds where dragonflies breed; the Three Horseshoes at Thursley is useful for lunch).

TILFORD SU8543

⬌т ◔ 🏚 **Rural Life Centre** (Reeds Rd, just W) Carefully displayed private collection of farm implements and machinery, spread over 10 acres of field and woodland, with an arboretum, children's playground, and miniature railway on Suns. This year, they're re-constructing a 19th-c cricket pavilion. Snacks, shop, disabled access; cl Mon (exc bank hols), Tues, all Oct–Mar; (01252) 795571; £3.50. The village has a massive oak tree, thought to be 800 years old; the Barley Mow between the river and the goose-cropped cricket green is a pleasant spot for lunch, and it's not far from here to the remains of Waverley Abbey.

TONGHAM SU8848

🏠 ☕ **Hogs Back Brewery** 💷 (Manor Farm, the Street) Tours of friendly little brewery, using traditional methods to produce its six distinctive ales. The shop has over 500 different English, Belgian and German beers (as well as their own), alongside English wines and farm ciders. Tours 6.30pm Weds Thurs and Fri, 11am and 2.30pm Sat, 2.30pm Sun, other times by arrangement, shop open daily (exc 25 Dec); (01252) 783000; tour £5.75 (inc tastings and commemorative glass). Manor Farm also has **pick-your-own** fruit on the same site Jun–Sept.

WALLISWOOD TQ1138

★ ◠ ✝ Attractive village, with a delightful woodland walk from the pub to the 13th-c church.

WEST CLANDON TQ0451

🏚 ☕ 🌼 **Clandon Park** 💷 (A247) Grand 18th-c house with unusual collection of porcelain birds, and fine furnishings and paintings. Regular concerts in the grand two-storeyed Marble Hall. Also a regimental museum. The gardens have a Maori house brought over from New Zealand in 1892, and they planted a Dutch garden last year. Meals, snacks, shop, disabled access to ground floor; open Apr–Oct,

house from 11.30am Sun, Tues–Thurs and bank hols, gardens every day; (01483) 222482; £4.30 NT. The smart Onslow Arms is good for lunch, and the 16th-c Bull's Head is popular too.

WEYBRIDGE TQ0862

🏎 ✝ **Brooklands Museum** (B374) Exhaustive museum re-creating the racing circuit's 1920s and 30s heyday, with plenty of racing cars, motorbikes and bicycles displayed in the restored clubhouse. Also a restored Wellington bomber and a comprehensive collection of vintage Vickers and Hawker planes. This was the site of the first British Grand Prix (a new exhibition telling the history of the race opens in the converted motoring sheds this year), and the first 100mph motor ride. Demonstrations and events most wknds. Snacks, shop, good disabled access; cl Mon (exc bank hols), Good Fri, Christmas wk; (01932) 857381; *£6. In the town the waterside Old Crown (Thames St) does good-value food.

WISLEY TQ0658

🌸 🍽 ☕ ◠ **Wisley Garden** (A3) These 300-acre gardens have come a long way since they were set up in 1904 as experimental gardens for the Royal Horticultural Society; half the area is devoted to garden, inc vegetables, and the rest to farm, orchard and woodland, with lots of unusual plants, shrubs and trees, exemplary glasshouses. The gardens get very busy (especially at weekends) but are big enough to cope. Meals, snacks, shop (lots of hard-to-get gardening/plant books), garden centre (good plants from a wide range of nurseries, but expensive), disabled access; cl Sun (exc to RHS members), 25 Dec; (01483) 224234; £5. The nearby Anchor at Pyrford Lock (turn left down exit road) is well placed for walks along the prettiest section of the **Wey Navigation Canal**, whose towpath gives Surrey's best waterside walks.

★ **Other attractive villages**, all with decent pubs, include Alfold TQ0334, Bletchingley TQ3250 (Norman church), Englefield Green SU9970 (handy for Savill Garden in Berks), Friday Street TQ1245 (good walks), Holmbury St Mary TQ1144, Hurtwood

TQ0845, Leigh TQ2246, Limpsfield TQ4152 (church where Delius is buried), Limpsfield Chart TQ4251 (good walks), Ripley TQ0556, Shackleford SU9345, Thorpe TQ0268 and Wood Street SU9550.

✝ Besides those mentioned, other **churches** worth a look include Burstow TQ3140, Okewoodhill TQ1337, Tandridge TQ3750, Tatsfield TQ4156 and Wotton TQ1247. You'll usually have to get the key from a local keyholder.

⌂ Popular starts or finishes for **walks** include the William IV at Little London TQ0646, the Sportsman at Mogador TQ2452, the Donkey at Charleshill SU8944, the Plough high on its hill at Coldharbour TQ1543 and Surrey Oaks at Newdigate TQ1942.

Besides places already mentioned for the **River Thames**, the Swan in Staines TQ0471 (The Hythe), the Magpie in Sunbury TQ1068 (Thames St), and the Anglers Tavern (off Manor Rd) and the Weir (Sunbury Lane) in Walton-on-Thames TQ1066 all have good views and access to the river. The county council has guided walks all year, exploring historical or more usually natural history themes; a typical Sun might have eight or more to choose from. For the current programme ring the Planning Dept, (020) 8541 9463.

❗ You can book **balloon trips** on (01252) 844222.

Where to eat

BETCHWORTH TQ2149 **Dolphin** *The Street* (01737) 842288 Bustling village local with homely front room, panelled back bar, three open fires, real ales and 18 wines by the glass, very popular, good-value food, and seats on the front courtyard and on the lawn; no children inside. **£14.60|£5.45.**

BLACKBROOK TQ1846 **Plough** (01306) 886603 Popular pub with award-winning hanging baskets and window-boxes, generous helpings of good, imaginative food, very friendly service from smart staff, marvellous choice of wines by the glass, well kept real ales, and a pretty cottagey garden with Swiss playhouse for children – they are not allowed inside; cl 25–26 Dec, 1 Jan; limited disabled access. **£18.35|£6.45.**

CHILWORTH TQ0346 **Villagers** *Blackheath* (01483) 893152 Surrounded by quiet woodland and walks, this pub has a pretty terrace and garden, and a path through trees to the cricket green (where Monty addressed thousands of Canadian troups before D-Day – a shame there isn't a commemorative plaque); rambling beamed main bar, small flagstoned room with big fireplace, decent food, real ales, and pleasant staff; bdrms; disabled access. **£17|£5.50.**

COMPTON SU9547 **Tea Shop** *Down Lane* (01483) 811030 Well liked tea shop doing morning coffee, light lunches and afternoon tea; home-made cakes, scones and jams, free-range eggs, a wide range of drinks inc interesting juices, seltzers, and fruity mineral waters, lots of Indian, China, herbal, and fruit teas, and different coffees; cl 24 Dec–7 Jan; partial disabled access. **£3.70.**

DORKING TQ1649 **Partners & Sons** *2–4 West St* (01306) 882826 Heavily beamed 16th-c building with dining rooms on two floors, very good, imaginative modern cooking, and a thoughtful wine list; cl Sun, pm 25 Dec–11 Jan; disabled access. **£24.50.**

ELSTEAD SU9043 **Woolpack** (01252) 703106 Cheerfully old-fashioned pub, bustling and friendly, with generous helpings of good, interesting bar food inc vegetarian choices and lovely home-made puddings, a fair amount of wool trade memorabilia, open fires, well kept real ales, and play area in the garden; cl pm 25–26 Dec; children in family room or dining room only. **£20|£6.**

GOMSHALL TQ0847 **Mulligans** *Station Rd (A25)* (01483) 202242 Friendly staff in this attractively decorated and relaxed fish restaurant, with live French café music on Thurs; cl pm 25 Dec, pm 1 Jan; disabled access. **£18|£6.95.**

HERSHAM TQ1164 **Dining Room** *Village Green* (01932) 231686 Five little rooms with log fires, very good food (half English, half the rest of the world) inc huge puddings, a relaxed atmosphere, and cheerful friendly staff; shaded terrace garden; cl am Sat, pm Sun, 1 wk at Christmas, bank hol Mons; disabled access by arrangement. **£23|£6.95.**

MICKLEHAM TQ1753 **King William IV** *(01372)* 372590 Relaxed and unpretentious pub cut into the hillside, with fine views from the snug front bar, a spacious back bar with log fires and fresh flowers, wide range of interesting daily specials inc good vegetarian choice, well kept ales, lovely terraced garden, and nice walks; no food pm Mon; cl 25 Dec, 1 Jan; children over 12. **£18.75|£6.95.**

NEWDIGATE TQ2042 **Surrey Oaks** *Parkgate Rd (01306)* 631200 Cheerful little country pub with a small snug beamed room in the older part, a woodburning stove and a coal-effect gas fire, an airy main lounge, games room, very well liked food (especially the daily specials), real ales (small beer festival over Aug bank hol), friendly service, and an elaborate garden with rockery and fountains, a goat, doves, and aviary. **£17.40|£5.95.**

RIPLEY TQ0556 **Michels** *13 High St (01483)* 224777 Charming Georgian house with carefully cooked seasonal food (inc some unusual dishes), a decent range of wines, and good service; cl am Sat, pm Sun, Mon; children over 5. **£50|**2-course weekday lunch £14.

SHERE TQ0747 **Kinghams** *Gomshall Lane (01483)* 202168 Beamed 17th-c cottage with a relaxed atmosphere, unpretentious surroundings, cheerful service, good sound cooking from a shortish menu inc daily fish dishes and vegetarian choices, and nice puddings; cl pm Sun, Mon, 25–31 Dec; disabled access. **£30|£11.95.**

SOUTH GODSTONE TQ3549 **Fox & Hounds** *(01342)* 893474 Pretty, old-fashioned inn in a pleasant spot, with lots of little nooks and crannies, cosy low-beamed bar with a good mix of seats and woodburner, popular imaginative food, restaurant with more elaborate dishes, well kept ales, and an extensive wine list; cl pm Sun–Tues; children lunchtime only; partial disabled access. **£20|£6.**

TADWORTH TQ2356 **Gemini** *28 Station Approach (01737)* 812179 Bustling and popular local restaurant with very good modern cooking using influences from all over the world, super puddings, a mainly French wine list, and courteous service; cl am Sat, pm Sun, Mon, 2 wks Christmas, 2 wks July; children lunchtime only; disabled access. **£30.25|£6.50.**

Special thanks to R L Martin, R E Perry, Michael and Jenny Back, Mrs Danielle McFarland, S Nelkin.

Surrey Calendar

Some of these dates were provisional as we went to press. Please check information with the telephone numbers provided.

JANUARY

6 Guildford Wassailing: Twelfth Night pub tour by Morris Men who perform a mummers' play and drink spiced beer from the wassail bowl (01483) 444751

15 Wisley Orchids for All: displays, lectures and demonstrations at RHS Garden – *till 23 January* (01483) 212387

FEBRUARY

15 Esher Antiques Fair at Sandown Park (020) 7249 4050

MARCH

3 Wisley Garden Crafts: practising craftsmen around the RHS Garden – *till 14 March* (01483) 212387

APRIL

11 Esher Antiques Fair at Sandown Park (020) 7249 4050

13 Farnham Beer Festival at the Maltings (limited tickets available well in advance only) – *till 15 April* (01252) 726234

MAY

1 Guildford May Day Ceremony: *at 5.30am* Pilgrim Morris Men dance to greet the sunrise on St Martha's Hill; later procession carries maypole up High St to Castle Green, folk dancing around the pole and elsewhere throughout the day (01483) 444751

6 Guildford Motor Show at Loseley Park – *till 7 May* (01483) 578003

14 Esher Spring Plant Fair at Claremont (01372) 467806; **Mytchett** Surrey Association of Woodturners Exhibition (01483) 444333

18 Tilford Bach Festival – *till 20 May* (01252) 782167

20 Farnham Craft Festival at the Maltings – *till 21 May* (01252) 726234

29 Guildford County Show at Stoke Park (01483) 414651

JUNE

10 Abinger Old Fair: Medieval fair with maypole dancing, knights, traditional competitions (01306) 731083; **Caterham** Carnival (01883) 342008; **Epsom** Derby Day at Epsom Racecourse (01372) 470047

16 Great Bookham Open-air Theatre at Polesden Lacey Open-air Theatre – *till 2 July* (01372) 451596

20 Esher Antiques Fair at Sandown Park: over 550 stands (020) 7249 4050

JULY

7 East Clandon Open-air Concerts at Hatchlands – *till 9 July* (01372) 451596

Surrey Calendar (cont.)

8 Chertsey Black Cherry Fair Day at the Chertsey Museum (01932) 565764; **Redhill** Motor Show at Redhill Memorial Park – *till 9 July* (01737) 732005

13 Esher Fête Champêtre at Claremont: music, dance, storytelling, street theatre, fireworks, themed costume – *till 16 July* (01372) 451596

21 Guildford Garden Festival at Loseley House and Park – *till 23 July* (01483) 797332

29 Wisley Family Fortnight at RHS Garden – *till 13 August* (01483) 212387

30 Tilford Rustic Day: traditional crafts and entertainments at Old Kiln Rural Life Centre (01252) 792300

AUGUST

5 Lingfield Steam and Country Show – *till 6 August* (01293) 771980; **Wisley** Flower Show at RHS Garden – *till 6 August* (01483) 224234

13 Guildford Fireworks Concert at Loseley Park (01625) 575681

27 Lingfield Edenbridge and Oxted Agricultural Show at Ardenrun Showground – *till 28 August* (01737) 645843

28 Bramley The Life of Christ: a dramatic production with a cast of hundreds (01483) 444333; **Woking** Classic Car Rally (01483) 743487

OCTOBER

3 Esher Antiques Fair at Sandown Park: over 550 stands (020) 7249 4050

15 Guildford Book Festival – *till 29 October* (01483) 259767

19 Wisley Apple Days at RHS Garden – *till 22 October* (01483) 212387

21 Farnham Craft Festival at the Maltings – *till 22 October* (01252) 726234

NOVEMBER

18 Wisley Christmas at RHS Garden – *till 26 November* (01483) 212387

26 Farnham Blues Festival at the Maltings (01252) 726234

28 Esher Antiques Fair at Sandown Park: over 500 stands (020) 7249 4050

SUSSEX

Lots to see and do, sunny resorts, attractively varied scenery – a favourite with many readers.

The great Sussex gardens are spectacular – Leonardslee at Lower Beeding, Wakehurst Place at Ardingly, Nymans at Handcross, Sheffield Park (with the charming Bluebell steam railway nearby) and (under restoration) Borde Hill near Haywards Heath. There are glorious grand houses, too, particularly in West Sussex.

Brighton has elegant Regency architecture, the remarkable Royal Pavilion, good free museums, endless antiques, and also a more raffish and studenty side that gives it a real buzz. By contrast, Eastbourne, sandy Bognor and Worthing are relatively sedate seaside resorts. Rye is an enchanting small town.

Special favourites for children include Bodiam Castle, Drusillas zoo near the delightful village of Alfriston, Bentley at Halland, and the Bluebell steam line near Sheffield Park. Herstmonceux Castle has quite a bit to hold the attention, and seaside Hastings has plenty for a family day out. In high summer the huge maize-field maze at Turners Hill (one of our new entries here this year) is fun – though parents may be exasperated by the way their children seem quicker-witted about it than they are themselves. Even the splendid Roman villas at Bignor and Fishbourne, appealing primarily to adults, are enjoyed by many children.

The Sussex countryside has very varied yet very characteristic scenery: the South Downs with their attractive flint buildings and expansive views, culminating in Beachy Head and its nearby cliffs (good, well organised walks from the visitor centre); the sparsely wooded high sandy heathland of the Ashdown Forest; and the intricate landscapes of the Weald. Much of the coast is developed, but the great sea inlet of Chichester Harbour has some very attractive places along its shore. Chichester itself has plenty to see in and around it.

Quite a few of the places we recommend to stay in here are fine buildings in their own right.

Where to stay

ALFRISTON TQ5103 **Star** *High St, Alfriston, Polegate BN26 5TA (01323) 870495* **£112,** plus special breaks; 37 rms. Fine hotel with fascinating atmospheric front part, built in the 15th c as the guesthouse for pilgrims; lots of medieval carvings, sanctuary post in bar, decent food and drinks, and excellent service; disabled access.

AMBERLEY TQ0213 **Amberley Castle** *Amberley, Arundel BN18 9ND (01798) 831992* **£170;** 20 very well equipped charming rms. Magnificent 900-year-old castle with day rooms filled with suits of armour and weapons as well as antiques, roaring fires and panelling; friendly service, imaginative food in the no smoking 13th-c dining room, and exceptionally pretty gardens; children over 12.

ARLINGTON TQ5507 **Bates Green** *Tye Hill Rd, Arlington, Polegate BN26 6SH*

*(01323) 482039 *£50;* 3 rms. Originally an 18th-c gamekeeper's cottage, now a no smoking farmhouse on a 130-acre turkey and sheep farm, with beams and a log fire in the oak-panelled sitting room, home-made cake and tea on arrival, big breakfasts with home-made preserves, and good Aga-cooked evening meals; sizeable garden (open under the National Garden Scheme), and a fine wood with lovely May bluebells; cl Christmas; children over 10; no pets.

BATTLE TQ7714 **Little Hemingfold Farmhouse** *Hastings Rd, Battle TN33 0TT (01424) 774338 *£76,* plus special breaks; 12 rms. Partly 17th-c, partly early Victorian farmhouse in 40 acres of woodland, with trout lake, tennis, gardens, and lots of walks (the 2 Labradors may come with you); comfortable sitting rooms, open fires, restful atmosphere and very good food using home-grown produce – either in the style of a dinner party or at your own candlelit table; children can feed farm animals; tennis court; cl 3 Jan–11 Feb; dogs welcome.

BATTLE TQ7217 **Netherfield Place** *Netherfield, Battle TN33 9PP (01424) 774455 £130;* 13 lovely rms. Handsome Georgian-style hotel in 30 acres of gardens and parkland, with light attractive day rooms, a log fire, lovely flowers, a relaxed and friendly atmosphere, and imaginative food using garden's produce; 2 hard tennis courts, croquet and putting green; cl 2 wks Christmas–New Year.

BATTLE TQ7414 **Powder Mills** *Powdermill Lane, Battle TN33 0SP (01424) 775511 £85,* plus special breaks; 35 rms, some in annexe. Attractive 18th-c creeper-clad manor house in 150 acres of park and woodland with 4 lakes (trout fishing) and outdoor swimming pool; country-house atmosphere, log fires and antiques in elegant day rooms, attentive service, and good modern cooking in the Orangery restaurant; children over 10 in evening restaurant; well behaved dogs by prior arrangement; disabled access.

BEPTON SU8618 **Park House** *Bepton, Midhurst GU29 0JB (01730) 812880 *£130,* plus special breaks; 14 rms. Quietly set country house nr Goodwood and Cowdray Park, with heated swimming pool, grass tennis courts, croquet and putting, comfortable drawing room, convivial small bar, and good homely cooking in the elegant dining room; disabled access.

BOSHAM SU8005 **Kenwood** *Bosham, Chichester PO18 8PH (01243) 572727 £50;* 3 large rms. Comfortable and well kept Victorian house with harbour views, a plushly furnished lounge, pleasant dining room (with useful fridge for your own picnic things), lots of old sporting bats, hockey sticks and tennis rackets, super breakfasts, games room with pool, heated swimming pool, croquet, and free-range poultry; disabled access.

BOSHAM SU8004 **Millstream** *Bosham Lane, Bosham, Chichester PO18 8HL (01243) 573234 *£115,* plus special breaks; 33 rms. Warmly friendly small hotel in a charming waterside village, with an attractive bar and sitting room, open fire and fresh flowers, very good food using fresh local produce, good wine list, and a streamside garden; disabled access.

BRIGHTON TQ3004 **Dove** *18 Regency Sq, Brighton, BN1 2FG (01273) 779222 *£69,* plus special breaks; 10 rms, 4 with sea view. Lovely, neatly kept and recently refurbished bow-windowed Regency house, with warmly welcoming helpful owners, and very good breakfasts in the light and airy dining room (enjoyable evening meals by prior arrangement); they are kind to families, with toys and babysitting available.

BRIGHTON TQ3004 **Grand** *King's Rd, Brighton, BN1 2FW (01273) 321188 £195,* plus special breaks; 200 handsome rms, many with sea view. Famous Victorian hotel with marble columns and floors and fine moulded plasterwork in the luxurious and elegant day rooms, exemplary service, very good food and fine wines, popular afternoon tea in the sunny conservatory, a bustling nightclub, and health spa with indoor swimming pool; disabled access.

BRIGHTON TQ3004 **Topps** *17 Regency Sq, Brighton BN1 2FG (01273) 729334 £84;* 15 lovely comfortable rms, 11 with gas-effect coal fires and many with sea views. Carefully furnished and well kept Regency town house nr seafront with particularly helpful and genuinely friendly owners, really good breakfasts and unpretentious dinners in the attractive basement restaurant, and a library/reception room.

BURWASH TQ6724 **Ashlands Cottage** *Burwash, Etchingham TN19 7HS* *(01435) 882207* **£40;** 2 rms, shared bthrm. In a lovely spot nr Batemans, this pretty cottage has marvellous views, a homely sitting room, attractive dining room (no full suppers but pubs nearby), charming owner, and appealing garden; children over 12.

CHICHESTER SU8604 **Bedford** *Southgate, Chichester PO19 1DP (01243)* *785766* **£85,** plus special breaks; 20 attractive rms, most with own bthrm. Family-run Georgian hotel in the centre, with a friendly atmosphere, and comfortable no smoking lounge and restaurant opening on to a quiet terrace; cl Christmas.

CHICHESTER SU8604 **Suffolk House** *3 East Row, Chichester PO19 1PD (01243)* *778899* ***£89,** plus winter breaks; 11 rms, some overlooking the garden. Friendly Georgian house in the centre with a homely comfortable lounge, a little bar, traditional cooking in the dining room, and a small walled garden; disabled access.

CHIDHAM SU7804 **Old Rectory** *Chidham Lane, Chidham, Chichester PO18 8TA* *(01243) 572088* **£48;** 3 rms. Handsome country house with an elegant sitting room, friendly owners, good breakfasts (nice pub nearby for evening meals), and croquet and a summer swimming pool in the big garden.

CLIMPING TQ0000 **Bailiffscourt** *Climping, Littlehampton BN17 5RW (01903)* *723511* **£140,** plus special breaks; 32 rms, many with four-poster beds and winter log fires, and with super views. Mock 13th-c manor built only 60 years ago but with tremendous character – fine old iron-studded doors, huge fireplaces, heavy beams and so forth – in 22 acres of coastal pastures and walled gardens: elegant furnishings, enjoyable modern English and French food, fine wines, a relaxed atmosphere, and outdoor swimming pool, tennis and croquet; children over 8.

CUCKFIELD TQ3024 **Ockenden Manor** *Ockenden Lane, Cuckfield RH17 5LD* *(01444) 416111* **£125,** plus special breaks; 22 pretty rms. Dating from 1520, this carefully extended manor house has antiques, fresh flowers and an open fire in the comfortable sitting room, good modern cooking in the fine panelled restaurant, a cosy bar, and lovely views from the neatly kept garden (surrounded by 23 acres of parkland).

EAST GRINSTEAD TQ3634 **Gravetye Manor** *Vowels Lane (off B2110 SW),* *East Grinstead RH19 4LJ (01342) 810567* **£232;** 18 lovely rms. Elizabethan manor house in magnificent grounds and gardens – over 400 years old, and also over 40 years with the Herbert family at the helm; antiques, fine paintings, and lovely flower arrangements in spacious panelled public rooms, an excellent restaurant using home-grown produce (inc spring water and free-range eggs) and their own home-smoked fish and meats, an exceptional wine list, exemplary service, and a relaxed, almost old-fashioned atmosphere; children over 7 (but babies welcome).

EAST HOATHLY TQ5116 **Old Whyly** *Halland Rd, East Hoathly, Lewes BN8 6EL* *(01825) 840216* **£90;** 3 rms. Handsome and historic 17th-c manor house in a lovely garden with tennis court and swimming pool and very close to Glyndebourne (hampers can be provided); fine antiques and paintings, and delicious food; plenty of walks; no children.

EASTBOURNE TV6097 **Grand Hotel** *King Edward's Parade, Eastbourne BN21* *4EQ* **£145,** plus special breaks; 152 rms, many with sea views. Gracious and very well run Victorian hotel, recently refurbished, with spacious, comfortable lounges, lots of fine original features, lovely flower arrangements, imaginative food in elegant restaurants, courteous, helpful service, leisure club, and outdoor pool and terraces; disabled access.

EASTBOURNE TV6097 **Hydro** *Mount Rd, Eastbourne BN20 7HZ (01323)* *720643* **£98,** plus special breaks; 85 rms, many with fine sea views. Long-standing hotel with a loyal following, quiet gardens with croquet, putting, heated outdoor pool, and sea views, comfortable, spacious lounges, tranquil library, courteous helpful staff, and good reliable food in the elegant restaurant; disabled access.

ETCHINGHAM TQ7126 **King John's Lodge** *Sheepstreet Lane, Etchingham* *TN19 7AZ (01580) 819232* **£70;** 4 rms. The gardens surrounding this historic

Jacobean house are lovely – wonderful views, romantic and secret gardens, a wild garden with rose walk, white garden, and lily pond – plants and statuary for sale; guests' private sitting room, stone mullioned windows, heavy beams and inglenook fireplaces, breakfasts served in Elizabethan dining room (on the terrace in fine weather), and evening meals by arrangement; swimming pool, tennis court and croquet; cl Christmas; children over 7.

FAIRLIGHT TQ8611 **Fairlight Cottage** *Fairlight, Hastings TN35 4AG (01424) 812545* ***£40,** plus winter breaks; 3 rms, one with four-poster. Comfortable and very friendly house in fine countryside with views over Rye Bay and plenty of rural and clifftop walks; big, comfortable lounge (nice views), good breakfasts in the elegant dining room, and generous, carefully prepared food (by prior arrangement, but not at Christmas); well behaved pets welcome.

FITTLEWORTH TQ0018 **Swan** *Fittleworth, Pulborough RH20 1EN (01798) 865429* ***£60;** 11 rms. Attractive 15th-c inn with a big inglenook log fire in the comfortable lounge, friendly service, enjoyable food in the beamed restaurant, attractive panelled side room, and sheltered back lawn; good nearby walks; cl Christmas; disabled access.

FRANT TQ5935 **Old Parsonage** *Church Lane, Frant, Tunbridge Wells, Kent TN3 9DX (01892) 750773* ***£74,** plus special breaks; 3 very pretty rms, 2 with four-posters. Just 2 miles from Tunbridge Wells, this carefully restored, imposing former Georgian rectory has antiques, watercolours and plants in elegant sitting rooms, a spacious Victorian conservatory, good food in the candlelit dining room, and a balustraded terrace overlooking the quiet 3-acre garden; several nearby walks; children over 7.

HARTFIELD TQ4737 **Bolebroke Mill** *Perry Hill, Edenbridge Rd, Hartfield TN7 4JP (01892) 770425* **£62;** 5 rms, some in the mill and some in the adjoining Elizabethan miller's barn. A working mill until 1948, this ancient place was mentioned in the Domesday Book, and is surrounded by mill streams and woodland; the internal machinery has been kept intact and steep narrow stairs lead to bedrooms that were once big corn bins; both this and the barn have their own sitting room, breakfasts are marvellous, light suppers enjoyable, and the owners very friendly; no smoking; cl mid-Dec–end Jan; children over 8.

HELLINGLY TQ5914 **Grove Hill House** *Hellingly BN27 4HG (01435) 812440* **£40;** 2 spacious, pretty rooms. Lovely, heavily beamed 17th-c farmhouse in quiet countryside, with charming, friendly owners, a relaxed and restful atmosphere, traditional furnishings inc antiques and family photographs, fresh flowers and an open fire, good hearty breakfasts in the separate dining room, enjoyable evening meals (by arrangement) using home-grown produce, and an attractive flower-filled garden; cl Christmas.

MAYFIELD TQ5826 **Middle House** *Mayfield, TN20 6AB (01435) 872146* **£55,** plus special breaks; 6 spacious rms, most with own bthrm. Old-world Elizabethan hotel nr the church, with the lovely panelled restaurant, red leather chesterfields and armchairs by a cosy log fire, chatty locals' bar with a big open fire (maybe spit roasts), a wide choice of good, interesting bar food, an attractive back garden, and pleasant views.

OFFHAM TQ4011 **Ousedale House** *Offham, Lewes BN7 3QF (01273) 478680* **£52,** plus special breaks; 3 pretty rms with shower or bthrm. Victorian country house with good views, 3½ acres of garden and woodland, friendly owners, a spacious lounge, and traditional cooking using home-grown seasonal produce; no children.

PETWORTH SU9721 **Old Railway Station** *Petworth GU28 0JF (01798) 342346* **£30;** 6 rms, some in Pullman railway cars. Petworth's former railway station, carefully restored, with a large lounge and dining area (the former waiting room with original ticket office windows), fine breakfasts, friendly owners, and a terrace (once the platform) and garden; children over 10; disabled access.

ROGATE SU8022 **Mizzards** *Rogate, Petersfield GU31 5HS (01730) 821656* **£56;** 3 rms. 16th-c house in quiet country setting, with a comfortable and elegant sitting room, vaulted dining room, outside swimming pool, landscaped gardens and lake, and fine farmland views; no evening meals, no smoking; cl Christmas; children over 8.

RUSHLAKE GREEN TQ6218 **Stone House** *Rushlake Green, Heathfield TN21 9QJ* (01435) 830553 ***£127,** plus winter breaks; 7 rms, some with four-posters. In a thousand acres of pretty countryside (with plenty of walks and country sports) and surrounded by an 18th-c walled garden, this lovely house was built at the end of the 15th c and extended in Georgian times; there are open log fires, antiques and family heirlooms in the drawing room, a quiet library, an antique full-sized table in the mahogany-panelled billiard room, wonderful food in the panelled dining room, fine breakfasts, and a cosseting atmosphere; cl 24 Dec–1 Jan; children over 9.

RYE TQ9120 **Cadborough Farm** *Udimore Rd, Rye TN31 6AA* (01797) 225426 **£55;** 5 rms, 3 large ones in main house, 2 in converted dairy. Fine country house in 24 acres of grounds with views to the sea over Camber Castle – you can walk across the private fields to the town centre; a comfortable drawing room, super breakfasts with home-made preserves, freshly baked breads, their own eggs, and fresh seasonal fruits taken in the dining room, log fires, and attractive gardens; self-catering in restored stables; no smoking; children over 8; dogs welcome by arrangement.

RYE TQ9120 **Jeakes House** *Mermaid St, Rye TN31 7ET* (01797) 222828 **£65,** plus special breaks; 12 rms overlooking the rooftops of this medieval town or across the marsh to the sea, 10 with own bthrm. Fine 16th-c building, well run and friendly, with good breakfasts, lots of well worn books, comfortable furnishings, linen and lace, a warm fire, and lovely peaceful atmosphere.

RYE TQ9220 **Little Orchard House** *West St, Rye TN31 7ES* (01797) 223831 **£64;** 3 rms. Beautifully furnished fine old house with antiques and personal prints and paintings, Georgian panelling, a big open fireplace in the study, good generous breakfasts (the friendly owners will make evening reservations at any of the many nearby restaurants), and a wonderful secluded garden; children over 12.

RYE TQ9220 **Old Vicarage** *66 Church Sq, Rye TN31 7HF* (01797) 222119 **£64,** plus bargain breaks; 5 pretty rms with complimentary newspaper and glass of sherry. Charming, quietly placed mainly 18th-c house with helpful friendly owners, comfortable sitting room or small library, a log fire in the elegant dining room, and marvellous breakfasts with freshly baked breads, free-range eggs, and home-made jams, jellies and ketchups; cl Christmas; children over 8.

SHIPLEY TQ1523 **Goffsland Farm** *Shipley, Horsham RH13 7BQ* (01403) 730434 **£40;** 1 family rm. 17th-c Wealden farmhouse on a 260-acre family farm with good breakfasts, afternoon tea and evening meals by arrangement, and a friendly welcome; good walks.

SLINFOLD TQ1131 **Random Hall** *Stane St, Slinfold, Horsham RH13 7QX* (01403) 790558 **£87.50,** plus special breaks; 15 comfortable rms. Restored 16th-c farmhouse with lots of beams, flagstones, copper and brass and a fine inglenook fireplace in the lounge, a friendly relaxed atmosphere, good breakfasts, and enjoyable modern cooking in candlelit restaurant (or on terrace); cl first wk Jan.

STORRINGTON TQ1015 **Little Thakeham** *Merrywood Lane, Storrington, Pulborough, RH20 3HE* (01903) 744416 **£176.25,** plus special breaks; 9 individually decorated rms with stylish fabrics and early antiques. Splendid combination of magnificent Lutyens house, delightfully restored Gertrude Jekyll garden, antiques and Arts and Crafts furniture and objets d'art; log fires, traditional English and French food using local produce, good French wines; outdoor swimming pool, tennis court, croquet; cl Christmas/New Year; children by arrangement.

TILLINGTON SU9622 **Horse Guards** *Tillington, Petworth, GU28 9AF* (01798) 342332 ***£66;** 3 spacious, clean rms. Neat, friendly and civilised 17th-c pub in a lovely village setting with a beamed front bar, very good imaginative food (fresh fish delivered 5 times a week, and excellent puddings), up to a dozen wines by the glass; no children.

UCKFIELD TQ4718 **Horsted Place** *Little Horsted, Uckfield TN22 5TS* (01825)

750581 **£199;** 20 individually decorated spacious rms. Stately Victorian country house on an extensive estate, with antiques, flowers and log fires in luxurious lounges, delicious food and good wine list in the no smoking dining room, and croquet, tennis, indoor heated swimming pool, and reduced green fees at East Sussex National Golf Club; babies or children over 8 in restaurant; disabled access.

WADHURST TQ6632 **Newbarn** Wards Lane, Wadhurst TN5 6HP (01892) 782042 **£50;** 3 pretty rms, some with own bthrm. Carefully renovated 18th-c tile-hung farmhouse in marvellous position by Bewl Water (walks, bike hire, boating, etc); very friendly, helpful owners, an inglenook fireplace in the attractive and comfortable sitting room, good breakfasts with home-made preserves, lakeside gardens; self-catering cottages also; cl Christmas.

WARTLING TQ6509 **Wartling Place** Wartling, Hailsham BN27 1RY (01323) 832590 **£60;** 3 individually furnished rms. Handsome Georgian house in lovely gardens with antiques in residents' drawing room, good breakfasts in the elegant dining area (they will arrange a hamper service for picnics), fresh flowers, and helpful owners.

WESTDEAN TV5299 **Old Parsonage** Westdean, Seaford BN25 4AL (01323) 870432 **£60;** 3 rms, 2 reached by narrow spiral staircases, with fresh flowers. In a conservation village by a 12th-c church, this beautifully preserved and spotlessly kept medieval house (with carefully Victorian extension) has mullioned windows and big stone walls, old beams and antiques, and friendly and helpful owners; nearby places for evening meals; the sea is a walk away; cl Christmas/New Year; children over 12.

WINCHELSEA TQ9017 **Cleveland House** Winchelsea TN36 4EE (01797) 226256 *£60; 2 pretty rms – 1 overlooking the sea, and 1 overlooking a rose garden. Peacefully set 18th-c house set in a fine walled garden with heated swimming pool and views to the sea, carefully furnished rooms, and good breakfasts served in the dining room; nearby inns for evening meals; cl Christmas.

WISBOROUGH GREEN TQ0625 **Old Wharf** Wharf Farm, Wisborough Green, Billingshurst RH14 0JG (01403) 784096 **£60;** 3 rms with views over farmland and canal. Carefully restored no smoking canal warehouse with fine old hoist wheel, comfortable sitting room with a log fire, breakfasts using free-range eggs from the farm, a walled canalside garden, and a friendly atmosphere; cl Christmas/New Year; children over 12; no pets.

To see and do

SUSSEX Family Attraction of the Year

🏠 ✝ 🐾 ⚓ HALLAND TQ4815 **Bentley Wildfowl & Motor Museum**
There's plenty of variety on this busy estate. The lakes and ponds have more varieties of waterfowl than you could imagine – many hundreds of colourful ducks and geese (including most of those that are threatened with extinction in the wild), and every variety of swan in the world. Woodland trails get children thinking about how the wildlife and woodland management interact – specially pretty in May, with the bluebells. Besides a good adventure playground, miniature trains steam through the grounds (wknds Easter–Sept, bank hols, also Weds in Aug). Under cover, a motor museum has a gleaming collection of cars and motorcycles, from antique veterans to racy more recent classic sports models. You can watch on-site craftsmen and artists. The house has been grandiosely extended to make a sort of reproduction Palladian palace around its Tudor core, and has a splendid collection of wildlife paintings by Philip Rickman, and a striking Chinese room, as well as other fine furnishings. Special events (no extra price) run from veteran and vintage car and other transport rallies to woodcraft, fire brigade and birds-of-prey displays. Meals, snacks, shop, disabled access; open daily mid-Mar–Oct (house cl am and Mar), and all exc house also open wknds in Nov, Feb and early Mar; (01825) 840573; £4.50, less in winter. The Forge is useful for lunch.

ALFRISTON TQ5102

★ † In a sheltered spot below the downs, this is one of Britain's most charming villages – at quieter times of year (in high summer the ice-cream eaters, teashops and curio shops somewhat blunt its appeal). Thatched, tiled and timbered houses, and a fine **church** built on a Saxon funeral barrow, by a large green just off the single main street. One of the most engaging buildings in the village is the Star Inn, with its Old Bill, a bright red figurehead lion on one corner taken as a trophy from a 17th-c Dutch ship, and some intricate painted 15th-c carvings among its handsome timbering. Besides the Star, the Market Cross is good for lunch.

🏚 🏵 **Clergy House** (The Tye) 14th-c, the first building to be taken over by the National Trust. Carefully restored, it now gives a faithful impression of medieval life; charming cottage garden. Shop; cl Tues, Fri and all Nov–Mar; (01323) 870001; £2.50; NT.

🐘 🏵 🐾 **Drusillas Park** (up towards A27) One of the best organised places for children in the entire country, a small zoo keeping only animals that they can provide with everything they'd have in the wild, so no lions, tigers or elephants, but plenty of smaller and arguably more entertaining creatures like meerkats, otters, beavers, and parrots, in thoughtfully designed enclosures. You watch the meerkats through a little dome in the floor of their spacious enclosure, and underwater vantage points in Penguin Bay make it look as if the birds are flying above you. The new pet world has animals as diverse as snakes and chinchillas. Excellent play areas (one especially for toddlers), and lots of opportunities for hands-on fun. Nearly half is under cover, and there's also a railway and pottery, with special events like birds of prey or knights, jesters, and jugglers in school hols. Shops and eating areas are just outside in Drusillas Village (along with some delightful gardens); you can visit here free without having to go in the zoo. Good meals and snacks, shops, disabled access; cl 24–26 Dec; (01323) 870234; £6.95.

† **Litlington** On the other side of the Cuckmere valley from Alfriston, notable for its **church** down a footpath – so small there can scarcely be room in it for a congregation of more than about 15. The Plough & Harrow here is useful.

AMBERLEY TQ0212

★ 🐦 ❄ A delightful thatched village; from the churchyard you can peer into the castle (now a good hotel), and there is public access to the Wild Brooks, a large expanse of watermeadows which form an important habitat for wetland plants and birds; there's also a way up to the downs here. The unspoilt Black Horse has good food, and there are lovely downs views from the Sportsman's conservatory, balcony and garden.

⬇T 🐾 **Amberley Museum** (by Amberley Station) A carefully thought-out open-air museum covering 36 acres of former chalk quarry and limeworks, with plenty of traditional crafts and re-created workshops. Lots going on, from pottery and cobbling to a working village telephone exchange. Meals, snacks, shop, disabled access; cl Mon and Tues (exc school or bank hols), and Nov–mid-Mar; (01798) 831370; £6. Nearby the riverside Bridge Inn at Houghton Bridge is great in summer; the B2139 is a pleasant drive.

ARDINGLY TQ3431

🏵 🔔 ⌂ **Wakehurst Place Garden** (B2028) The 'Southern Kew', administered by the Royal Botanic Gardens, with a tremendous variety of interesting trees and shrubs inc many tender rarities. Lakes and watergardens, steep Himalayan glade, woodland walks and fine rhododendron species. Plenty to see throughout the year, and all very peaceful. When it is finally completed in autumn, the millennium seed bank will store over 25,000 seeds from all over the world. Meals, snacks, plant and book sales, disabled access; cl 25 Dec, 1 Jan; (01444) 894066; £5 (free to NT members). Wknd guided walks usually start in front of the mansion at 11.30am and 2.30pm (2pm in winter); (020) 8332 5585 to check. The Gardeners Arms (children in garden only), Ardingly Inn and the Oak all do good lunches.

Nearby **Ardingly Reservoir** offers pleasant strolls by its shores, or you can plan a longer walk around the elevated farmland and woodlands surrounding Wakehurst Place and Balcombe.

ARUNDEL TQ0107

★ ✝ Dating from pre-Roman days, this is dominated by the magnificent walls and towers of the castle on a mound high over the River Arun. Attractive buildings, inc antique shops and so forth, cluster along the sides of the steep main street climbing up from the bridge to the castle. The 19th-c Roman Catholic **cathedral** complements the castle well, giving rather a French feel to the whole small town. The Swan and St Mary's Gate Hotel have decent food. There are public paths along the canalised River Arun and into Arundel Park, with its lakes and woodlands beneath the slopes of the downs.

🏰 🖼 **Arundel Castle** Seat of the Dukes of Norfolk for over 700 years – a magnificent sight, a great spread of well kept towers and battlements soaring above the village and the trees around it. The keep is the oldest part; the rest dates mainly from the 19th c. Excellent art collection, inc portraits by Van Dyck, Reynolds, Lely and Gainsborough, as well as 16th-c furniture, and personal possessions of Mary Queen of Scots. Meals, snacks, shop; cl am, Sat, Good Fri and all Nov–Mar; (01903) 883136; £6.70.

👑 **Arundel Museum** (High St) Local history and heritage; cl am Sun, and all Oct–Mar; £1.

🦢 ⚓ **Wildfowl & Wetlands Trust** (Mill Rd) 55 acres of well landscaped pens, lakes, and paddocks, home to over 1,000 ducks, geese and swans from all over the world. Hides overlook the various habitats, and there are children's activities in school hols. Meals, snacks, shop, disabled access; cl 25 Dec; (01903) 883355; £4.75. The lane past the Trust ends at a little cluster of houses by an isolated church and former watermill. On the way to the Trust, the Black Rabbit has a superb location and does food, and in summer there are **boat trips** from it.

ASHDOWN FOREST TQ4832

⌂ 🌳 ❋ A major inland attraction for walkers, part forest, part heathland – sandy tracks, clumps of Scots pines, secretive glades and exhilarating views.

Traffic restrictions introduced 3 years ago have made it even more peaceful – you may meet sheep on the road. Don't be put off by the OS map: there are far more walking routes than it suggests (there's a useful 1:30,000 scale walkers' map issued by the Ashdown Forest Centre showing all the paths and rides as well as naming the car parks – an extremely useful idea given the Forest's lack of other landmarks). The Forest still looks just like the E H Sheppard drawings for A A Milne's Winnie the Pooh stories, which were set here. Five Hundred Acre Wood is the Hundred Acre Wood of Pooh's world, and with a little searching you can find, SE of Hartfield, the Poohsticks Bridge and, by the B2026, Gills Lap (the 'enchanted place' at the top of the Forest, nr Piglet's house), where a memorial to Milne has been placed nr the triangulation point. Handy pubs for Forest walks include the Foresters Arms at Fairwarp, Half Moon at Lye Green and Hatch at Colemans Hatch.

ASHINGTON TQ1317

🌵 **Holly Gate Cactus Garden** (Billingshurst Lane) Over 30,000 succulents and cactus plants from both tropical and arid habitats all over the world – a cactus enthusiast's prickly paradise. Ice-creams, cheap plant sales, disabled access; cl 25–26 Dec; (01903) 892930; £1.50. The Franklands Arms at Washington is a useful lunch stop.

BARCOMBE MILLS TQ4316

⌂ ⚓ One of Sussex's secrets, with lazy riverside walks (or **boat trips**) from the tucked-away Anchor pub here.

BATTLE TQ7515

🏛 ✝ Takes its name from certainly the most celebrated and perhaps the most disorganised skirmish in English history, thrashed out here in 1066. The main streets (carrying a fair bit of traffic, so not exactly peaceful) have a lot of attractive old buildings, some now antique shops and cafés; beyond them the town extends into spreading new estates. The friendly Olde King's Head has decent food, and the **church** of St Mary has some 13th-c wall paintings.

🏛 **Almonry** (High St/Virgins Lane) Ancient building with town model, teas, and a pretty little garden (cl Sun and bank hol Mons, 25–26 Dec; *£1).

☖ † Battle Abbey The battlefield has a mile-long walk around it with a good audio tour explaining what happened. Four years after the bloodshed William built an abbey on the site as penance, the altar reputedly on the very spot where Harold fell. Not much is left of the original building, but later remains include the monks' dormitory and common room, and the great 14th-c gatehouse which looms over the small market square. Snacks, shop, mostly disabled access; cl 24–26 Dec, 1 Jan; (01424) 773792; £4; EH.

☖ Battle Museum of Local History (High St) Good local history inc diorama of the Battle of Hastings and a reproduction of the Bayeux Tapestry (cl am Sun and all Oct–Easter; £1).

♪ Buckleys Yesterday's World 🖭 (High St) Carefully reconstructed period shops, railway station and the like; lots of hands-on activities, and nostalgic film show. Snacks, shop; cl 25–26 Dec, 1 Jan; (01424) 775378; £4.25.

❀ ♖ Weald views The B2096 Heathfield road gives views S to Beachy Head from its highest points, nr Netherfield and just before Dallington. Off this road any of the narrow side roads N into the countryside between Burwash and Dallington take you into the most unspoilt part of the steep Wealden woods and pastures.

BEACHY HEAD TV5997

❀ ⌂ This towering, abruptly cliffy end of the downs is a landmark for miles around, and the giant of this stretch of cliffy headlands: an unspoilt spot with terrific views, inc the lighthouse dwarfed far below. It's easily reached from Eastbourne, and the eponymous hotel, open all day, has decent food.

♪ ⌂ Beachy Head Countryside Centre Surprisingly enjoyable hands-on exhibitions, as well as indoor and outdoor play areas, and a full programme of guided walks (best to book for these) around cliffs, beaches and wildflower meadows. Meals, snacks, shop, disabled access; usually open daily late Mar–Oct, plus wknds Nov–Christmas (may close lunchtime), with walks wknds and school hols – ring for exact dates; (01323) 737273; free, walks around £2.

BEXHILL TQ7407

♜ A low-key seaside town with a pebble beach interrupted by cumbersome groynes – an unlikely setting for a gem of Bauhaus architecture, the shoreside De La Warr Pavilion designed by Mendelsohn and Chermayeff. The Italian-run café opposite is good value.

☖ Bexhill Museum of Costume Set in the delightful grounds of the Old Manor House up towards the tiny 'Old Town', a good look at 18th- to 20th-c fashions, with accessories and other domestic items as well as the clothes. Shop, disabled access; cl Weds (exc Jun–Sept), am wknds, and all Nov–Easter; (01424) 210045; *£1.50.

BIGNOR SU9814

♜ ☖ Roman Villa & Museum One of the largest villas discovered so far, with marvellous mosaics inc the longest in Britain – 25 metres (82ft) long, and still in its original position. Snacks, shop, some disabled access, and largely under cover; cl Mon (exc bank hols and Jun–Sept), and all Nov–Feb; (01798) 869259; £3.35. The White Horse at nearby Sutton has fine food (and good-value bedrooms).

BIGNOR HILL SU9813

⌂ ♖ Up here the trees that obscure views for much of the way in this part of the South Downs give way to open ground; Stane St, a Roman road here relegated to a path, takes a strikingly straight course SW over a woodland and pasture landscape.

BIRDHAM SU8401

🦅 Sussex Falconry Centre (Lockacre Aquatic Nursery, Wophams Lane) Originally set up as a breeding and rescue centre, then opened to the public with birds such as falcons, hawks, eagles and owls flown throughout the day. Shop, disabled access; cl Mon (exc bank hols), and Nov–Mar; (01243) 512472; £3. This area S of Chichester is flat country, full of nurseries and huge glasshouses; the Lamb towards West Wittering is a popular dining pub.

BODIAM TQ7825

☖ ⚓ ♜ Bodiam Castle The perfect picture-book castle, a classic example of 14th-c fortification at its peak, with massive walls rising sheer and virtually complete from the romantic moat, and round drum towers steadfastly guarding each corner. Built to withstand attack from the French, it was only ever besieged by other Englishmen, and on both occasions was rather weedily handed over without a fight. The interior was destroyed around the Civil War, and wasn't repaired until Lord Curzon bought it in 1916; he left the castle to the NT in 1925. Plenty of space for picnics. They have several enjoyable special events, inc a fun day with donkey rides and Punch and Judy, a Christmas cracker hunt, and children's story-telling. It's worth reading the leaflet they give you on arriving at the car park – most people fail to spot that the lavatories are at this end rather than at the castle itself. Meals, snacks, shop, limited disabled access; cl Mon Nov–Dec, 24–26 Dec; (01580) 830436; £1.50 for parking, then £3.60 for castle; NT. Next to the castle, Knollys is a good teashop, and the Salehurst Halt at Salehurst just W does good lunches. In summer you can put together a very enjoyable full day out by taking the 45-minute **boat trip** to the castle through peaceful countryside from Newenden (they don't run in bad weather); (01797) 280363 for times; £6.50 return. This can then link with a **steamtrain** on the Kent & East Sussex Railway, from the Tenterden terminus (Bodiam's station has been recently restored) over the Kent border. Up the hill in Ewhurst Green, the White Dog has interesting food, and **Bodiam Bonsai** grow, show and sell these miniature trees.

BOGNOR REGIS SZ9398

⛱ An old-fashioned seaside family resort, popular above all for its sandy beaches. A wireless museum on the High St displays 40 years of valve radio, and the Alex (London Rd) has good-value food.

BOSHAM SU8004

✝ ★ The Saxon **church** here figures in the Bayeux Tapestry, and the village is a lovely cluster of old cottages around it, the green, and a broad, almost landlocked, inlet of Chichester harbour, busy with boating in the summer. Don't be tempted to park on the shore – the incoming tide is well known for its trick of lapping around parked cars. Very

pleasant to stroll around, with antique shops and craft galleries, especially on Bosham Lane. The Anchor Bleu, by the water, is popular for lunch.

BOXGROVE SU9007

✝ 🏛 **Boxgrove Priory** Now the parish church, this 12th-c building is one of the most outstanding Early English churches in the region, with a surprising 16th-c painted ceiling, free-standing chantry chapel, and the remains of various monastic buildings outside.

BRAMBER TQ1810

🏠 ✤ **St Mary's House** Striking medieval house, with fine panelling, a pretty garden with topiary, and unusual Elizabethan painted room. Concerts in spring and autumn. Teas, shop; open pm Sun, Thurs and bank hols Easter–Sept; (01903) 816205; *£4. The Bramber Castle has decent food. Adjacent Steyning has some attractive timber-framed and Georgian buildings (and a good Tudor pub, the Chequer).

BRIGHTON TQ3104

★ ✝ Despite its many more modern blocks, huge shopping centre and vast modern sports halls, Brighton still has plenty of glistening white Regency buildings dating from its fashionable days in the 18th c, when the idea that sea-bathing was good for you sent London's finest scurrying to the coast. Still a thriving resort, its atmosphere gets a real kick from its vigorous young university and from its several language schools for foreign students; there's also a booming gay scene. The most lively part is the Lanes – 17th-c fishermen's cottages squeezed together in narrow twisting byways, now crammed with jewellery and antique shops, restaurants and bars; they're mostly closed to traffic. English's here is entertaining for lunch. The North Laine area is slightly more trendy, with good buskers and cool cafés. Throughout, there's no shortage of simple places to eat, inc the Cricketers (Black Lion St), Greys (Southover St, Kemp Town), Mary Packs Cliftonville (good local fish; Hove Pl) and, if you like sausages, the Sussex Yeoman (Guildford Rd). On Sun mornings there's a good **market** by the station approach; you do have to get there well before breakfast for the bargains, as it's become a major source

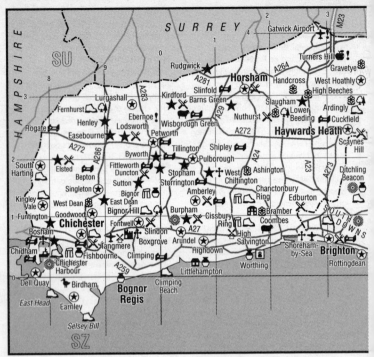

of supply for the countless Brighton antique dealers. Nr here **St Bartholomew's Church** (Anne St) is an odd building, like a huge brick barn. Film buffs will be well satisfied with the Duke of York's cinema at nearby Preston Circus, which shows the kind of movies not always found outside London.

Barlow Collection (Brighton University, Falmer; off A27 N) Reckoned to be Europe's finest collection of Chinese ceramics. It's usually open 11.30am–2.30pm Tues and Thurs; (01273) 606755; free.

Booth Museum of Natural History (Dyke Rd) Superb and well presented collection of animal skeletons (inc some dinosaur bones), as well as the Victorian collection of birds the museum was first built to house. Shop, disabled access; cl am Sun, Thurs; (01273) 292777; free.

Brighton Fishing Museum (King's Rd) The seafront Arches across from the Old Ship Hotel used to be occupied by local fishermen, and a couple still are, the rest given over to

little craftshops and artists. One houses this collection of local boats, nets, models and pictures. New shellfish stall and fish smokery, shop, disabled access; cl 25–26 Dec, and any day Nov–Apr when the weather is poor; (01273) 723064; free.

Brighton Marina (E of centre) This modern place is lively in summer, with lots of boutiques, bars, tables out by the water and so forth. A new waterfront entertainment centre opens around spring, and will be home to a celebrity walk of fame. An electric train runs to here along the beach from the pier.

Brighton Museum & Art Gallery (Church St) As we went to press, they were about to start a 2-year refurbishment programme at this outstanding collection of Art Nouveau and Art Deco, housed in the Prince Regent's stables and riding school. Every gallery will be redisplayed, and they hope to keep certain areas open throughout the renovations; usually cl am Sun, all day Weds, 24–26 Dec, 1 Jan, Good Fri, but best to phone

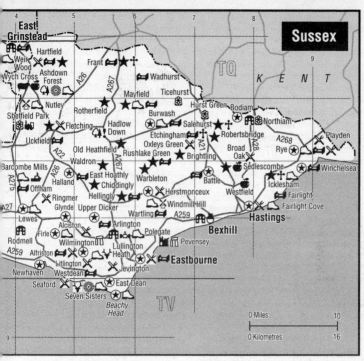

beforehand; (01273) 290900; free.

♿ ⬥ British Engineerium (Nevill Rd, Hove) All sorts of road, locomotive and marine steam engines, as well as tools, models, and a restored Victorian water pumping station. Shop, limited disabled access; cl wk before Christmas, engines in steam first Sun in month and bank hols; (01273) 559583; £3.50.

! ※ ⬥ Foredown Tower (Foredown Rd, Portslade) Very well done, with a **camera obscura** (best on bright days) as well as a weather station with satellite images, astronomy displays, and splendid views. They can arrange visits to Portslade Old Manor, a ruined medieval house a short stroll away. Snacks, shop; cl Mon–Weds, and Christmas; (01273) 292092; £2.

♿ ⬛ Hove Museum & Art Gallery (New Church Rd) This grand Victorian villa houses a fine collection of British painting; cl am Sun, all day Mon, and Christmas wk; (01273) 290200; free.

♿ ✕ Hove Windmill Museum (Holmes Ave, Hove) With local history displays; open pm Sun and bank hols May–Sept; 70p.

Palace Pier Brighton was one of the earliest resorts to have a pier – that rusting original is now being restored; in the meantime the Palace Pier is a more than satisfactory replacement, and looks magnificent at night.

🏛 ⬥ Preston Manor (A23) Entertaining and vivid illustration of life in Edwardian times, with fully furnished period rooms, and pleasant walled gardens. Shop; cl am Sun and Mon, 25–26 Dec, Good Fri; (01273) 292770; £3.10.

🏛 † Regency Town House Hove, the quieter half of the resort, is just W of Brighton proper. On the way you may be able to visit this Regency house in Brunswick Sq – still being restored so you'll need to make an appointment on (01273) 206306; £3; if not, at least pass **St Andrew's Church** (Waterloo St), designed by Sir Charles Barry – quite dull from the outside, but inside rather elaborate in places.

🏛 ! Royal Pavilion Nash's flamboyant Indianesque confection should be top of anyone's itinerary: the most eccentric of all royal palaces, a riot of chinoiserie inside. Queen Victoria was the last monarch to own it, but was hardly its greatest fan; if the town council hadn't bought it from her she might well have demolished it. She would no doubt not have been amused to see her apartments restored to their full overblown glory. The gardens have also been returned to the original Regency plan. The whole building is beautifully floodlit at night. It's less busy after 3pm – and better still out of season, when you may find more going on. Meals, snacks, shop, disabled access to ground floor only; cl 25–26 Dec; (01273) 290900; *£4.50.

🗡 **Sea Life Centre** (Marine Parade) Lively displays of creatures found off the British coast, with seahorses, touch pools and a new undersea soft play area. Meals, snacks, shop, disabled access; cl 25 Dec; (01273) 604234; £5.50.

🌸 ⌂ **South Downs** In this area the downs are open country; arable farming and the presence of pylons rather detract from the pleasure of walking, but the steep N slopes are still impressive, as at Devil's Dyke (with its tremendous view over Brighton, even more startling at night than by day), Wolstonbury Hill and the Jack and Jill windmills nr Clayton.

🍵 **Sussex Toy & Model Museum** (Trafalgar St) Over 10,000 objects from Victorian dolls to Meccano; shop, disabled access; cl am, Sun, and 25–26 Dec; (01273) 749494; £3.

BURPHAM TQ0309
🌸 ★ Great views from this attractive coastal hill village; maybe even bison.

BURWASH TQ6724
★ 🌸 The single main street of this ridge village has many attractively restored tile-hung cottages, inc a good antique centre and teashop, with lime trees along its brick pavement. The graveyard of the Norman-towered church gives fine views over the Dudwell Valley, and the Bell is useful for lunch. Around here the intricate landscapes of the Sussex Weald show steep slopes and valleys, ancient woods and hedgerows punctuated by great oaks, pretty villages, tile-hung or weatherboarded oast houses and wood-and-tile barns with their long 'cats'-slide' roofs.

🏠 🌸 🍴 ⌂ **Batemans** (off A265) Handsome early 17th-c stone-built ironmaster's house, home to Rudyard Kipling from 1902 to 1936. His study is preserved much as it was then, as is the hefty pipework he installed for a pioneer hydro-electric lighting plant. The attractive gardens have a quaint operating **watermill**, grinding flour every Sat at 2pm. A couple of friendly donkeys are paddocked opposite. Dog crèche, snacks, shop, disabled access to ground floor only; cl Thurs, Fri (exc Good Fri), and Nov–Mar; (01435) 882302; £5; NT. Good little-used walks up the wholly unspoilt valley from here, where you can look for Kipling landmarks such as Pook's Hill.

CHANCTONBURY RING
TQ1312
🏛 ⌂ One of the great South Downs landmarks, an Iron Age fort, now a prominent hilltop clump of trees, a bracing walk, best reached from Steyning or Washington.

CHICHESTER SU8504
★ Partly pedestrianised and easy to get around, this handsome former Roman city is one of the country's finest examples of Georgian town planning and architecture. Useful central pubs for food are the Bell (Broyle Rd) and the Coach & Horses (St Pancras).
⌂ **Centurion Way** This short stretch of disused railway track has been converted to an easy route for cyclists (and walkers) W of Chichester to Mid Lavant.
✝ 🌸 **Chichester Cathedral** Mostly Norman, and unusual for rising straight out of the town's streets rather than a secluded close. The spire collapsed in the 1860s (the latest in a long line of structural problems), and was rebuilt, but even now the scaffolding always seems to be up. Highlights include the 14th-c choir stalls, John Piper's Aubusson tapestry, and the window by Chagall. Guided tours (not Sun) at 11am and 2.15pm Easter–Oct. Snacks, shop in the medieval bell tower (23 South St – unusual for being separated from the main building), disabled access; £2 suggested donation. The Bishop's Palace gardens are very pleasant.
🏠 🍵 **Guildhall Museum** (Priory Park) Began life as a medieval Grey Friars

church, now houses the city's archaeological collections; shop, disabled access; usually open pm Sat Jun–Sept, (01243) 784683 to check; free. The Park Hotel opposite has decent food.

⛨ Mechanical Music & Doll Collection (Church Rd, Portfield) A multitude of barrel, fair and Dutch street organs, music boxes and phonographs – all restored and ready to play. Shop, disabled access; open pm Weds Jun–Sept; (01243) 785421; £2.50.

⚑ Pagham Harbour (off B2145 S) Peaceful nature reserve, largely silted marshy tidal flats, full of wading birds and wildfowl, particularly in spring and autumn; on the way the Blacksmiths Arms at Donnington, packed with bric-à-brac, has a good children's play area.

🏠🖼 Pallant House (North Pallant) Interesting Queen Anne town house with an Edwardian kitchen and fine furnishings. The gallery has fine Bow porcelain, and an excellent range of carefully chosen 20th-c art – Sutherland, Klee, Leger, Ben Nicholson and the like. Shop; cl am Sun, all day Mon, bank hols, 25–26 Dec; (01243) 774557; £4.

🏠✤ St Mary's Hospital (St Martin's Sq) 13th-c almshouse with some unique misericords in its chapel, and a pretty walled garden; disabled access; usually open wkdys (not 12.30–2.30pm), but best to check first, (01243) 783377; free.

CHICHESTER HARBOUR SU7702 ✺ ⌂ The most attractive views for walkers are from the shoreside path which skirts the quiet unspoilt peninsulas of Thorney Island and Chidham.

⛵ Boat trips Peter Adams runs these around Chichester Harbour, full of yachts and dinghies in summer. They leave from Itchenor and are best at high tide; (01243) 786418; £5. There's also an hourly passenger ferry between here and the landing at the end of the lane S from Bosham (daily Jun–Aug, wknds only Apr, May and Sept).

⌂ **East Head** A NT-owned promontory on the E entrance of Chichester Harbour, a sandy spit with dunes overlooking the marshes and mudflats of the estuary.

CISSBURY RING TQ1308 🏛 ⌂ This huge ramparted Iron Age hill fort, one of the great downland landmarks, is quite close to Findon, where the Gun and Village House are both good lunch places. Readers recommend the walk from here to Chanctonbury Ring.

CLIMPING BEACH TQ0000 ⌂ This allows an attractive few miles' walk; this bit of coast between Middleton-on-Sea and Littlehampton is the only appreciable undeveloped seaside stretch in W Sussex, apart from Chichester Harbour.

COOMBES TQ1908 **🐄 Church Farm** 🈐 Trailer rides over farmland and through conservation areas – you have to book, but it's great fun, especially in the lambing season (Mar–mid-Apr). Snacks, shop, disabled access; cl mid-Oct–Feb; (01273) 452028; *£3. They also have a coarse fishing lake.

DELL QUAY SU8303 ★ 🏛 Attractive waterside hamlet with remains of a Roman quay, harbour views (and fresh fish) from the Crown & Anchor.

✿ Apuldram Roses (Apuldram Lane S) Over 300 kinds of old-fashioned and new roses in harbourside field and gardens made from former orchards. The field is at its best from Jun to Sept, after which they have a good end-of-season sale. Snacks, plant sales, some disabled access; cl 24 Dec–8 Jan; (01243) 785769; free.

DITCHLING TQ3313 ✺ ⌂ ⛨ **Ditchling Beacon** 🈐 Right by the road, with superb views all around, especially out over the villages and towns to the N; a nice walking area of preserved sheep-cropped unimproved downland, with chalk hill blue butterflies in summer. The village below is pleasant, with a decent **museum** (shop, disabled access; cl Mon and Nov–Mar; *£2.50). The B2116 to Offham has views of the South Downs, and off it the Jolly Sportsman at East Chiltington has good food.

EARNLEY SZ8197 ✿ 🦋 🐾 ⛨ ! **Earnley Gardens** (Almodington Lane) This 5-acre site is these days quite a busy day out; as well as the long-established 17 themed gardens, exotic birds and free-flying butterflies, they now have a shipwreck display, small animal farm, and a refreshingly informal nostalgia museum, Rejectamenta. This takes in thousands of everyday objects from the last hundred years, collected over nearly a quarter of a century by a former art student who says she just can't stop. Meals, snacks, shop, disabled access; open mid-Mar to end of Oct; (01243) 512637; £5.50 everything, £3.50 just gardens and butterflies or just nostalgia museum, £1.50 crazy golf.

EAST DEAN TV5597

🐑 ❀ 〇 🗿 **Seven Sisters Sheep Centre** (Gilberts Drive) Very enjoyable family-run downland sheep farm with compact visitor centre, and paved paths between pens of many breeds of sheep. Lambing (mid-Mar–early May), demonstrations of shearing (Jun–mid-July), spinning, milking and cheese-making, and plenty of young animals to cuddle or bottle-feed. The farm shop sells sheep cheeses and yoghurts. Snacks, disabled access; cl am wkdys (exc school hols), all mid-Sept–mid-Mar, and maybe part of May, best to phone; (01323) 423302; £3. The village itself is prettily set around a sloping green, with an attractive pub, the Tiger. A lane past the farm continues to the **Birling Gap**, a cleft in the coastal cliffs famous since smuggling days, with a lighthouse (moved back 17 metres (55ft) last Mar to save it from coastal erosion) and a coastguard station; and on to Beachy Head. The Birling Gap Hotel is nicely set just above the shore.

EAST GRINSTEAD TQ3835

🏠 **Standen** (off B2110 W) A fine example of the many talents of the 19th-c Arts and Crafts Movement. Designed by Philip Webb (even down to the unusual light fittings), a friend of William Morris, and little changed since; the interior of the house is decorated with several different William Morris wallpapers, and many of the furnishings are of the period. Snacks, shop, limited disabled access; open pm Weds–Sun mid-Mar–Oct; (01342) 323029; £5, £3 garden only; NT.

EASTBOURNE TV6198

★ ✝ The Duke of Devonshire still owns much of this civilised and restrained seaside resort; as he prohibits seaside tat the place has a more dignified and solid feel than many of its livelier rivals – fun seekers should head elsewhere, but it's perfect for gentle seafront strolling, and a new promenade links the recently snazzed-up marina with the beach. The **church** in the Old Town is lavish; next to it the Lamb is a nice old pub.

❋ **Lifeboat Museum** (Grand Parade) Makes up in enthusiasm what it lacks in size; cl Jan–Easter; free.

🏛 **Museum of Shops** (Cornfield Terr) One of the most comprehensive collections of its type, 20 reconstructed and very well filled shops and rooms, inc an old seafarers' tavern. Shop, disabled access to ground floor only; cl 24–6 Dec; (01323) 737143; £2.50.

🏰 🏛 **Redoubt Fortress** (Royal Parade) A splendid tower, housing a more interesting than average military museum. Open-air concerts (usually every Weds and Fri Jun–Aug) always end in a firework display. Snacks, shop; cl early Nov–Easter; (01323) 410300; £2.10.

ⵌ **Sovereign Park Shingle Nature Reserve** Nature trails around an attractive stretch of shingle coastline, best between Easter and June, when most plants are in flower; from Easter to autumn, a train connects this with the rest of the seafront. Some disabled access; open all year; free. They try to discourage people from walking across the shingle, as it damages the plantlife.

🏠 🖼 🏛 **Towner Art Gallery & Museum** (High St, Old Town) Handsome building, with good temporary exhibitions; shop, disabled access; cl am, and all day Mon (exc bank hols), 25–27 Dec, 1 Jan and Good Fri; charges for some exhibitions.

🏛 **Wish Tower** (King Edward's Parade) Another of the 103 Martello Towers built in case of French invasion; there's a fascinating collection of puppets, some centuries old. Shop; cl Nov–Easter (exc school hols); (01323) 411620; £1.80.

EBERNOE SU9627

❗ **British School of Ballooning** (just N of Petworth) Organised champagne balloon trips over the Sussex countryside; not pm Sat or all day Sun;

(01428) 707307; *£135.

ETCHINGHAM TQ7126

† **Etchingham church** Lovely sturdy and ancient semi-fortified building in honey-coloured stone – quaintly, the station is built to match.

FERNHURST SU8928

△ ⚐ Nicely varied surrounding countryside for walkers; much is densely wooded, but there are some chances to get out on to the open hillsides as on Woolbeding Common and the S tip of Black Down. The pretty Red Lion has good-value food.

FIRLE TQ4707

★ △ ❊ An attractive quiet village, with a decent pub. **Firle Beacon**, a South Downs landmark, is a lovely walk above the village, with good views.

† **Berwick church** 1940s murals by the Bloomsbury Group; the Cricketers Arms here is a good lunch place.

🏠 **Charleston Farmhouse** (A27 Firle–Selmeston) Delightful 17th/18th-c house which was the home of Duncan Grant and Clive and Vanessa Bell; decorated by them, it and its magical garden still evoke the atmosphere of those Bloomsbury days. Teas Sat, shop; open pm Weds–Sun and bank hols Apr–Oct (am too in summer hols), no guided tours Sun and bank hols; (01323) 811265; £5.50. Longer tours on Fri (when children under 8 aren't admitted). Nr here at Alciston, the Rose Cottage has very good home cooking.

🏠 **Firle Place** 🖼 (off A27) Beautiful house, essentially Tudor but remodelled in the 18th c, with some real treasures of European and English painting, and wonderful furnishings.

Meals, snacks, shop, some disabled access; open pm Weds, Thurs and Sun mid-May–Sept, as well as Easter, spring and summer bank hols; (01273) 858335; *£4. There are longer unguided tours the first Weds in the month, when more rooms are open (and the price is higher).

🍺 **Middle Farm Cider Centre** (A27 E) Best known for its excellent farm shop, with a huge range of English ciders and perries, farmhouse cheeses, English wines, good sausages, organic meats, and other produce. Also children's farmyard, and always lots going on at apple harvest time; restaurant, disabled access; cl 25–26 Dec; (01323) 811411; site free, around £1 for farmyard.

FISHBOURNE SU8304

🏛👤 **Roman Palace** (Salthill Rd) This magnificent villa with its 100 or so rooms was occupied from the 1st to the 3rd c, and is the largest known residence from the period in Britain. You can see 25 superb mosaic floors (a bigger collection than anywhere else in Europe), and a garden has been laid out according to its 1st-c plan. One theory about the site is that it was a high-class brothel. Snacks, shop, disabled access; cl mid-Dec to mid-Feb; (01243) 785859; £4.20. The comfortable Woolpack has good food.

FLETCHING TQ4223

★ Attractive village – often Sussex's Best-Kept Village.

FONTWELL SU9406

🦋 ★ † **Denmans Garden** (off A27) Colourful series of vistas over 3½ acres, inc exuberantly oriental-feeling areas with a gravel stream, ornamental grasses, bamboos and flowering

---

Days Out

1066 and all that: Bodiam Castle; lunch at the Salehurst Halt, Salehurst; Battle Abbey and battlefield – and/or Buckleys Yesterday's World.

Bloomsbury Group mementos: Berwick church paintings; Charleston Farmhouse and Middle Farm, Firle; lunch at the Juggs, Kingston nr Lewes; Monks House, Rodmell (limited opening); Lewes.

Gardens, Arts and Crafts: Leonardslee, Lower Beeding, or Wakehurst Place, Ardingly or Nymans, Handcross; lunch at the Crabtree, Lower Beeding, or the Gardeners Arms, Ardingly; Standen, East Grinstead.

cherries, as well as a beautiful richly planted walled garden. Meals, snacks, plant sales, disabled access; cl Nov–Feb; (01243) 542808; £2.80. In the pretty nearby village of Eartham there is a small but charming **church**; the George here is a good place to eat.

FRANT TQ5935

★ † Despite the main road this is a charming and rather elegant village, with an ancient **church** and handsome green. The George has decent food,

GATWICK AIRPORT TQ2740

† ! Skyview ⌨ (S Terminal) Entertaining visitor gallery, with a multi-media show demonstrating a typical airport day, good explanation of cockpit controls, and excellent simulator rides. Splendid runway views. Shop, disabled access; (01293) 502244; £4.50.

GLYNDE TQ4509

🏠 🐝 † **Glynde Place** Elizabethan manor house in the beautiful setting, extensively remodelled inside in the 18th c, but outside left pretty much unchanged. Portraits and mementos give a good grounding in the family history, while outside are pleasantly wild parklands and lawns. Snacks, shop; open pm Sun and bank hols in May, then pm Weds, Sun and bank hols Jun–Sept, plus Thurs July–Aug; (01273) 858224; £4. There's a neat neo-Palladian **church** nearby, and the Trevor Arms has decent food. The Glyndebourne Festival, with its decidedly smart operas and marvellous new auditorium designed by Sir Michael Hopkins, takes place May–Aug.

GOODWOOD SU8808

🏠 🐝 ▣ **Goodwood House** Unusual-looking house in beautiful downland countryside, especially renowned for its paintings, inc works by Canaletto and Stubbs. There's quite a riding feel – it was acquired by the first Duke of Richmond in 1697 so that he could ride with the local hunt, and the stables added during 18th-c alterations seem grander even than the house. Snacks, shop, disabled access; open pm Sun and Mon Apr–Sept, plus maybe Tues–Thurs in Aug; (01243) 755040; £6. The adjacent **racecourse** is the setting for Glorious Goodwood, and as well as around 19 race days a year has monthly

antique markets; (01243) 774107 for dates.

▣ **Sculpture at Goodwood** (Hat Hill Copse, towards East Dean) Excellent changing exhibitions of sculpture in 20 acres of beautiful wooded parkland; it's established an excellent reputation in the few years it's been open, so it's a shame the high admission price limits it to people with more than just a passing interest in the subject. Some disabled access; open Thurs, Fri and Sat Mar–Nov; (01243) 538449; £10. This is a good area for a country drive; the Anglesey Arms at Halnaker is the best nearby place for a meal.

GRAVETYE TQ3534

🐝 **Ingwersens** (Birch Farm) Very long-established alpine plants specialist nursery; cl 1–1.30pm, wknds Oct–Feb, 2 wks at Christmas; (01342)810236. Out this way, the White Hart at Selsfield (B2028) and the Red Lion at Turners Hill are useful for lunch.

HADLOW DOWN TQ5424

🐿 ! **Wilderness Wood** ⌨ (A272) Acres of working woodland, good for learning about forests and their wildlife, or for a pleasant stroll. Several picnic areas and a play area, occasional demonstrations of heavy horses and other traditional woodland working methods, and a new discovery trail for children. Teas, shop (they make chestnut furniture and other goods), improved disabled access; (01825) 830509; *£1.90. Nearby Buxted has one of the oldest trees in Britain, a yew thought to be 2,480 years old.

HALLAND TQ4815

🏠 🕊 🐝 🏛 **Bentley Wildfowl & Motor Museum** *See separate family panel on p.637.*

HANDCROSS TQ2629

🐝 **Nymans Garden** (B2114) Some very impressive rare trees here, inc magnificent southern beeches and eucryphias, as well as fine camellias, rhododendrons and magnolias, countless other interesting flowering shrubs, a secluded sunken garden, and an extensive, artfully composed wilderness. Meals, snacks, plant sales, shop, disabled access; cl Mon (exc bank hols), Tues, and wkdys Nov–Feb; (01444) 400321; £5; NT. The Chequers at Slaugham is a good nearby dining pub.

HARTFIELD TQ4735

★ Pleasant village with some attractive houses. The well stocked shop at Pooh Corner reflects the fact that surrounding Ashdown Forest was the inspiration for A A Milne's tales of Winnie the Pooh. Perryhill Nursery (B2026 N) has many unusual plants, and past it at Blackham (A264) the Sussex Oak does very good fish.

HASTINGS TQ8209

★ † The Old Town below the cliff at the E end is very attractive – 2 medieval churches, a couple of streets with raised pavements, lots of medieval buildings, and relatively unobtrusive more recent infilling. Down below, the fishermen still haul their boats up on to the beach and sell excellent fresh fish by the unusual tall, black, wooden net huts. At each end of the cliffs is an unusual sloping tracked lift down to sea level (80p). The First In Last Out in the Old Town has interesting food and brews its own beer. The rest of the town is a busy shopping town, rather run-down in parts, with 19th-c resort buildings nearer the seafront, seaside hotels and B & Bs, a good prom, and shingle beach. As we went to press, the future of the facilities on the **pier** was in doubt.

◠ **Fairlight Cove** A good destination for walks from Hastings Old Town, by a path climbing on to the sandstone cliffs for a rugged couple of miles. The tumbled appearance of the coast here bears witness to the occasional cliff-falls.

✺ **Fisherman's Museum** (Rock-a-Nore Rd) Interestingly housed in a former fishermen's chapel; cl Good Fri and 25 Dec; free.

▥ **Hastings Castle** Bracingly set above crumbling cliffs (and the tracked lift), the evocative Norman ruins are close to the site of William the Conqueror's first English motte and bailey castle. There's a lively audio-visual exhibition on the Battle of Hastings. Shop, some disabled access; (01424) 422964; £3.

♨ ▣ **Hastings Museum & Art Gallery** (Johns Pl, Cambridge Rd) A little way out of the centre, but worth a look for its American Indian displays; children may prefer the dinosaur gallery. Shop, disabled access; cl 1–2pm Sat, am Sun, 25 Dec and Good Fri, although times may change, so best to check; (01424) 781155; free.

▣ **Hastings Tapestry** This ambitious 73 metres (240ft) tapestry depicting great events in British history, created by the Royal School of Needlework, can now be seen at the White Rock Theatre; meals, snacks, shop, disabled access; cl Mon, Christmas and all Mar; *£2.

➴ **Sea Life Centre** (Rock-a-Nore Rd) Another in the lively chain, with a walk-through underwater tunnel. Snacks, shop, disabled access; usually only cl 25 Dec, but best to check first in winter; (01424) 718776; £5.50.

ƒ **Smugglers Adventure** (Cobourg Pl) A labyrinth of deep caverns and passages, with models, museum and well done life-size tableaux illustrating life for an 18th-c smuggler. Spooky lighting and sound effects in places. Shop, limited disabled access; cl 25–26 Dec; (01424) 422964; £4.50, joint ticket with castle £6.45.

HAYWARDS HEATH TQ3226

❀ ♧ ➴ **Borde Hill Garden** (Balcombe Rd, N) Lovely 40-acre gardens with woodland walks through rare maples, oaks, conifers and many other fine trees, as well as a lake, herbaceous borders and magnificent rhododendrons. Last year they restored 3 Victorian greenhouses, and they're currently working on a new Mediterranean garden. You can fish on the lake, and there's an adventure playground. Meals, snacks, plant sales (Blooms of Bressingham), disabled access; cl 25 Dec; (01444) 450326; *£4.50. The White Harte at Cuckfield does good-value simple lunches.

HERSTMONCEUX TQ6410

❀ ▥ ♨ ! **Herstmonceux Castle** ▣ (SE of village) Extensive gardens around handsome 15th-c brick-built castle, with nature trails, a hands-on science centre, and astronomy displays in former buildings of the Greenwich Royal Observatory. You can tour the castle itself by arrangement (£2.50). Children's play area; snacks, shop, disabled access; cl Nov–Mar; (01323) 834444; grounds and gardens £3, science centre £3.50, all-in ticket £5.70. The Ash Tree over at Brownbread

Street has good old-fashioned home cooking.

⚘ **Sussex Trug demonstrations** (Hailsham Rd) Thomas Smith demonstrates the local art of trug basket-making; disabled access; not wknds (though shop open Sat); (01323) 832137.

◠ ✖ ✵ **Windmill Hill** From here you can follow paths and tracks for an absorbing walk of about 4 miles past Herstmonceux Castle and the former observatory (now the Science Centre). And yes, there is a windmill.

HIGH BEECHES TQ2730

✵ **High Beeches Gardens** (B2110, Handcross) Well worth a look, 20 acres of landscaped woodland, lots of rare plants, watergardens, and wildflower meadows. Snacks, plant sales; usually open pm daily exc Weds Apr–Jun and Sept–Oct, and Mon and Tues July–Aug; (01444) 400589; £3.50. The Chequers at Slaugham is a good nearby dining pub.

HIGH SALVINGTON TQ1206

✖ **High Salvington Windmill** An 18th-c post-mill; open pm first and third Sun Apr–Sept, £1.

HIGHDOWN TQ0903

✵ ✵ ⋔ **Highdown Hill** (A259, Highdown) Excellent views from this famous garden, which differs from most of the other great Sussex gardens in that it's on very uncompromising chalk – laid out in and around a chalk pit high on the downs above Angmering; many rarities, inc unusual Chinese plants. Some disabled access; cl wknds Oct–Mar; (01903) 501054; free. There is a nearby Iron Age hill fort, and the Spotted Cow at the foot of the hill does good-value food.

HORSHAM TQ1428

⋔ ▣ **Christ's Hospital** (just SW) You may be able to join tours of the refreshingly egalitarian public school, where a remarkable painting by Verrio fills an entire wall of the Dining Hall. Meals, snacks, shop, disabled access; tours from £3.50 – booking essential; (01403) 211293 for dates.

♨ ✵ **Horsham Museum** Timber-framed Tudor house with well organised local history, and an extraordinary collection of early bicycles. The small but pretty garden has some unusual wild cyclamen. Shop,

some disabled access; cl Sun and bank hols; (01403) 254959; free. The town's much developed, but a particularly attractive quiet corner is The Causeway, by the church. The Black Jug (North St) has good food.

❦ **Huxley Experience** ▣ (Brighton Road) Large collection of birds of prey inc falcons, vultures and even a laughing jackass. Informative and friendly staff give flying demonstrations from 2.30pm, and you can handle the creatures at 12 noon and 2pm. Shop; disabled access; cl Tues and Nov–Mar exc Sun; (01403) 273458; £2.95.

HURST GREEN TQ7327

✵ **Merriments Garden** (Hawkhurst Rd) Developing 4-acre demonstration garden with lots of planting ideas, some unusual plants, and comprehensive nursery inc rare hardy plants. Tearoom, disabled access; garden open Easter–Oct, nursery all year; (01580) 860666; £2.50.

ICKLESHAM TQ8616

★ † ◠ Attractive village despite the main road, with a Norman **church** and country walks.

KINGLEY VALE SU8210

◠ ꩜ ✵ ⋔ An interesting walk though needing some stamina, whether you approach via the nature trail on the S side or from Stoughton to the N (the Hare & Hounds will fuel you well). This nature reserve is Europe's largest yew forest, a magical place where the trees create some eerie pools of darkness on the S slopes of the downs; above, you can look over Chichester Harbour from a prehistoric burial mound.

LEWES TQ4110

★ ⋔ ⚘ ✵ ◠ ⋔ The administrative capital of East Sussex, this is a pleasantly unrushed country town below the quarried white edge of the South Downs. It has some attractive old buildings, mainly Georgian though with a few older stone-built or timber-framed specimens, particularly along its steep main street and in the little narrow alleys and other streets alongside. This is where you'll see Sussex tile-hanging at its best; there's also quite a lot of 'mathematical tiling' – sham bricks over timbered buildings to make them look more progressive. There are several decent antique shops, and an attractive complex of **craft shops** in a former candlemaker's factory in Market Lane; café, cl Sun. The Dorset Arms (Malling St) and the more bohemian Snowdrop (South St) are useful for lunch. Local brewers Harveys have opened a new brewery tap on Cliffe High St. From Bell Lane on the SW edge you can follow the old Juggs Road track, used by the Brighton fishwives, up past Kingston and the downland nature reserve by Newmarket Hill to the outskirts of Brighton itself. There are more public paths than the OS map suggests; from the town centre you can walk up Chapel Hill, through the golf course and on via an unspoilt dry valley to **Mount Caburn**, rather grandiosely named for its size but capped by an Iron Age fort and with views towards the coast; it's also popular with paragliders. A fine 3-mile circuit from Lewes is had by following the Ouse N, then heading under the railway line, through the woods to cross the A275 at Offham, then keeping left to follow a path (not on OS) above some spectacularly deep chalk pits; another unmapped path leads along a downland crest past the site of the Battle of Lewes and past the prison to re-enter the town.

🏠⛪🏛 **Anne of Cleves House** 🖼 (Southover High St) Henry VIII's wife number four received this fine 16th-c house as part of her divorce settlement. She probably never came here, but its rooms give a good idea of regional life over the following 2 centuries. Shop; cl am Sun, and all Nov–Feb exc Tues, Thurs and Sat; (01273) 474610; £2.30 (combined ticket with castle £4.80). Guided tours of the ruined Norman **priory** leave here in summer, phone (01273) 486290 for details.

🏛✳ **Lewes Castle** 🖼 Norman, unusual for being built on not one but two artificial mounds (Lincoln is the only other such place we know of). The best view of the town is obtained from the roof of the keep, and there's a good archaeological museum. Shop; cl 25–26 Dec; (01273) 486290; £3.50.

🏵 **Southover Grange Gardens** (Southover Rd) Diarist John Evelyn's handsome boyhood home is now the District Registry Office, but you can visit the attractive gardens free.

LITTLEHAMPTON TQ0202 Little sign here of its age (it was an important port up to the 1500s), but its long sandy beaches make it a popular, simple family resort. Towards the W, beyond the River Arun, there's quite an extensive area of unspoilt dunes between beach and golf course. The 18th-c Arun View right on the river does decent lunches.

🏭 **Body Shop Tour** (Watersmead, A259 N) You can book to visit – the 90-minute tours are interesting and informative; snacks, shop, disabled access; (01903) 844044; no tours Sun; £3.95.

🏛 **Littlehampton Museum** (Church St) In an early 19th-c manor house, this will reopen in Aug, following refurbishment.

LOWER BEEDING TQ2225 🏵 🌳 **Leonardslee Gardens** Enormous Grade I listed garden set in a 240-acre valley with 6 beautiful lakes; marvellous rhododendrons, magnolias, oaks and unusual conifers, delightful rock garden, extensive greenhouse and Japanese garden, bonsai exhibition, and wallaby and deer. The gardens are on the edge of the ancient St Leonards Forest, and there's a summer wildflower walk. Readers get a great deal of pleasure from coming here. Meals, snacks, plant sales, limited disabled access; cl Nov–Mar; (01403) 891212; May £5, other times £4. The Crabtree does good food.

LULLINGTON HEATH TQ5401 ☁ 🌿 A rare survival of downland untampered with by modern farming practices, and managed as a National Nature Reserve for its chalkland and heathland flora; a good spot for walks, which can be spun out with a diversion to Wilmington for a view of the enigmatic Long Man.

LURGASHALL SU9327 ★ ✝ Attractive small village, with an unusual loggia outside the largely Saxon **church** where parishioners walking in from a distance could eat their sandwiches. The Noah's Ark here is prettily placed for lunch.

🍷 **Lurgashall Winery** Produces a wide range of traditional country wines, meads and cordials. Tastings, shop,

limited disabled access; cl 25–26 Dec,
1 Jan; (01428) 707292; self-guided
tours wknds; free.

MAYFIELD TQ5826
★ ⌂ One of Sussex's prettiest villages,
with interesting shops, and pleasant
hilly terrain around it. A reasonable
network of paths includes a short
waymarked circular walk.

NEWHAVEN TQ4400
🏰 ✳ ⚓ **Newhaven Fort** (Fort Rd)
Built 120 years ago in case of French
attack, this is a big place to explore,
with underground installations, period
reconstructions and tunnels burrowing
into the cliffs, super views from its
ramparts, and an assault course for
children. Snacks, shop; cl wkdys in Mar,
and all Nov–Feb; (01273) 517622;
£3.95. You can take the ferry to Dieppe
in France from here. The harbourside
Hope has decent food.

🎡 ⛲ **Paradise Park & Planet Earth**
(Avis Rd) Garden centre with an
exhibition on the last few million years
of evolution, complete with earthquake
experience and life-size moving
dinosaurs. Also model village with
miniaturised Sussex landmarks, and a
new indoor oriental garden. Meals,
snacks, shops, disabled access, cl 25–26
Dec; (01273) 512123; *£4.25.

NORTHIAM TQ8225
🏛 🎡 **Great Dixter** (turn off A28 at
post office) Timbered 15th-c house,
carefully restored and added to by
Lutyens in the early part of this century.
He designed the attractive gardens too;
originally arranged as a series of distinct
areas, they were later stocked more
informally with interesting plants by the
gardening writer Christopher Lloyd
who lives here. Snacks, plant sales,
limited disabled access; cl am, all day
Mon (exc bank hols) and all Nov–Apr;
(01797) 252878; £5, £4 gardens only.
The Hayes Arms has decent food.

NUTLEY TQ4428
✗ ⌂ **Nutley Windmill** 17th-c mill
saved by enthusiastic locals before such
action became more common; open pm
last Sun of month Apr–Sept; free.
Nearby Camp Hill is one of the best
walking areas in the Ashdown Forest.

OLD HEATHFIELD TQ5920
★ Charming peaceful hamlet – so
different from the sprawly small town

of Heathfield nearby which sprang up
around the now-defunct railway (the
town does surprise with an excellent
delicatessen specialising in unusual
cheeses, a top-class genuinely French
patissier, and a first-rate
farmer/butcher – Pomfrets).

PETWORTH SU9721
⚱ **Doll House Museum** (Station Rd)
Over 100 dolls' houses, with 2,000
miniature inhabitants; shop, disabled
access; open Sun Jan–Oct, plus
Thurs–Sat Mar–Oct; (01798) 344044;
£3.50.

⚱ **Petworth Cottage Museum** 📷
(High St) Interesting reconstruction of
an estate worker's cottage; open pm
Weds–Sun and bank hols Apr–Oct,
*£2.

🏛 📷 ★ **Petworth House** Splendid, its
magnificent rooms filled with one of the
most impressive art collections in the
country, inc Dutch Old Masters and 20
pictures by Turner, a frequent visitor.
Other highlights include the 13th-c
chapel, grand staircase with frescoes,
and the carved room, elegantly
decorated by Grinling Gibbons. You
can see extra rooms on Tues and
Weds, and there may be conservation
demonstrations on Mon. Meals, snacks,
shop, disabled access; cl am, all day
Thurs and Fri, and all Nov–Mar; (01798)
342207; £5.50; NT. The deer park, with
stately trees and prospects still
recognisable as those glorified by
Turner, is open all year; free. The village
has narrow streets of attractive old
houses, inc a good few antique shops.
The Angel Hotel fits in well, and has a
good wknd carvery; the Well Diggers
(A283 E) has decent food too.

PEVENSEY TQ6505
🏰 🏛 **Pevensey Castle** Formidable
castle based around a huge 4th-c
Roman fort, with massive bastions and
walls of Roman masonry still up to 9
metres (30ft) high in places. The
Norman keep was built by William the
Conqueror, and you can see interesting
interior details inc fireplaces, dungeons
and an oubliette. Shop, some disabled
access; cl Mon and Tues Nov–Easter,
24–26 Dec; (01323) 762604; £2.50; EH.
The Castle Cottage restaurant does
decent food, inc light summer lunches
in the castle garden.

POLEGATE TQ5804

△ **Cuckoo Trail** Following the route of a former railway Polegate–Heathfield (with plans for extension beyond), good for traffic-free walking or family cycling; the mileposts, sculpted by local artists, each have a cuckoo hidden in their design.

△ **Filching Manor Motor Museum** (Jevington Rd, Wannock) Gleamingly restored vintage cars, shown to great effect in the grounds of a striking manor house. Unique panelling in the minstrels' gallery, acres of woodland, and Donald Campbell connections. They now also have a go-kart track (extra). Snacks, disabled access; open Thurs–Sun, plus bank hols Easter–Oct; (01323) 487838; £3.50.

PULBOROUGH TQ0518

➤ The town has some attractive buildings down towards the river; the Waters Edge, with lake views, has a good choice of food. There's an **RSPB reserve** just S, and the Citrus Centre (off A283 E, just past the White Horse pub; cl Mon, Tues) has all sorts of orange, lemon and related trees. The charmingly placed White Hart at Stopham is another nearby place with good food.

● **Nutbourne Vineyards** (Nutbourne Manor) 18-acre vineyard with tours and tastings, and visitor centre in a former windmill; shop; no tours am wkdys and all mid-Oct–May; (01798) 815196; free.

△ **Parham House** Charming Elizabethan house, still a family home, its panelled rooms full of notable portraits, furniture, oriental carpets and rare needlework. The surrounding grounds are really very special – popular with birds, they include a rose garden and a vegetable garden, the produce from which is sold in the shop. Also a deer park, and a maze designed with children in mind. Lunches in 15th-c kitchen, shop, plant sales; open pm Weds, Thurs, Sun and bank hols Apr–Oct; (01903) 744888; £5, £3 garden only.

RODMELL TQ4206

△ **Monks House** A quiet lived-in house, in a pleasant village, that is a beautifully kept place of pilgrimage for followers of the Bloomsbury Group, as Leonard and Virginia Woolf lived here from 1919 until Leonard's death in 1969. Open pm Weds and Sat Apr–Oct; (01892) 890651; £2.50; NT. The Juggs at Kingston on the way from Lewes is good for lunch.

ROTTINGDEAN TQ3602

△ **✿ † Grange Museum & Kipling Gardens** A pretty place, worth a stop. Enthusiastic local volunteers are responsible for preserving both the handsome Georgian grange, now a **museum** (cl Weds and Christmas), and the pleasant 2-acre **Kipling Gardens**, well restored Victorian gardens named after the author who lived here for 5 years from 1897. Burne-Jones was a resident for a while too, designing the windows built by William Morris for the Early English **church**.

RYE TQ9321

★ † ✿ ❉ Enchanting, and still relatively unspoilt despite its many charms. Before the wind and sea currents did their work, the little town was virtually surrounded by sea, and as one of the Cinque Ports played an important part in providing men and ships for coastal defence. It's built on a hill crowned by the partly Norman **St Mary's Church** (with a notable churchyard, and very early turret-clock, 2 quarter-jacks by it striking the quarter-hours); up here the largely cobbled streets still follow a 12th/13th-c narrow layout, with most of the houses lining them dating from the 16th c. The town is full of antique shops, book shops, craft shops and an exceptional kitchenware shop; Rye Art Gallery (107 High St) is a non-profit trust with several floors selling the best of local art and craft. The views are lovely, and steep Mermaid St in particular is famously photogenic (the Mermaid itself is a handsome old inn).

△ **Camber Castle** This massive Tudor fort had the sea lapping up to it when it was built, but is now stranded a mile or so inshore by the encroaching shingle (open wknds July–Sept; £2). Beyond it the Ship on Winchelsea Beach is a welcoming refuge. On the other side of the river **Camber Sands** is a splendid beach, with plenty of room for walking.

✿ **Heritage Centre** (Strand Quay)

A useful introduction, with a sound-and-light show based around an intricate town model. Shop, disabled access; cl 25 Dec; *£2.

🏠 **Lamb House** (West St) Built in 1723 for former mayor James Lamb, and chiefly devoted to mementos of the author Henry James, who lived here from 1898 to 1916; after his death E F Benson, who also became mayor, moved here. Open pm Weds and Sat Apr–Oct; (01892) 890651; £2.50; NT.

👃 **Rye Castle Museum** (just below Church Sq) A lottery grant has allowed this lively local history museum to share its exhibitions between 2 sites. The main gallery is in East St, while other displays are housed in the striking 13th-c Ypres Tower (as in Wipers). Shop, disabled access to East St museum; cl Tues, Weds and wkdys Nov–Mar; (01797) 226728; £2 per site or £3 joint ticket. The Ypres Castle pub just below has good food in a nice setting.

♨♪🚣 **Rye Harbour** Because of the build-up of shingle along this coast, the harbour is now a mile or two from the town, though yachts and fishing boats do still come right up the river to the pretty quay. The Inkerman Arms has good fresh fish (as does the Hope & Anchor up in the town). Tony Easton will take you **sea fishing** for the day; (01797) 252104; from £25. The expanse of shingle stretching around the river mouth is now preserved as a **nature reserve**, with hides to watch the shore birds.

👃 **Treasury of Mechanical Music** (Cinque Ports St) An entertaining collection of music boxes, barrel organs and pianolas, and you can hear them all. Shop, disabled access; cl Tues Nov–Feb; (01797) 223345; £3.

SALEHURST TQ7424
★ ✝ Attractive tucked-away village with a 14th-c **church** and good pub.

SEDLESCOMBE TQ7719
★ 🍎 Attractive village, with an unusual organic vineyard.

SELSEY BILL SZ8592
⌂ One of the nicest and cleanest **beaches** along the south coast.

SEVEN SISTERS COUNTRY PARK TV5199
✛ ❈ ⌂ (A259, Exceat) Runs down to

the sea by the River Cuckmere – protected meadow, saltings, shingle and the flanking chalk headlands; you can hire bikes from the Cuckmere Cycle Co at Granary Barn, (01323) 870310. The chalk cliffs, together with Beachy Head, form the spectacular finale of the South Downs; the South Downs Way long-distance path angles up over them above the flats and the sea at Cuckmere Haven. For an interesting circular walk you can head inland by Friston Forest, West Dean and East Dean. The roomy Golden Galleon at Exceat does good food.

SHEFFIELD PARK TQ4124
🕸 Wonderful 120-acre garden partly landscaped by Capability Brown, since then imaginatively planted with many varieties of tree unknown to him, especially chosen for their autumn colours. Also marvellous rhododendrons, azaleas and waterlilies on the lakes. Snacks, shop, disabled access; cl Mon (exc bank hols), and all wkdys Jan–Feb; (01825) 790231; £4.20; NT. The Griffin at Fletching nearby is very good for lunch.

SHEFFIELD PARK STATION TQ4023
🚂 **Bluebell Line** (A275) Earliest preserved steam railway in Britain, and one of the best; 9-mile trips through Horsted Keynes to Kingscote (where there are period bus connections to main line East Grinstead), with splendid stations decked out with period advertisements and genuine period carriages. The journey passes woodlands that are a mass of bluebells in late spring, usually at their best in mid-May – hence the name of the line. Part of the station is a museum housing the region's largest railway collection, inc some 30 locomotives. Pullman dining specials, Santa specials, shop, café, disabled access (with notice); trains wknds all year, daily May–Sept and school hols – (01825) 722370 for timetable; £7.40. The Sloop at Scaynes Hill not far off is good for lunch.

SHOREHAM-BY-SEA TQ2106
✝ Though not one of England's more famous ports, this is quite a busy one, with several attractive old buildings around the harbour. Inland, in Old Shoreham, the early Norman **church** is

accompanied by some handsome old houses (among them the good 16th-c Red Lion). Just W is striking **Lancing College Chapel**, begun in 1868, with a soaringly handsome nave, and elaborate stained-glass rose window.

✝ **Museum of D-Day Aviation** 🖼 (Shoreham Airport) Uniforms, engines, artefacts and a replica Spitfire. Meals, snacks, shop, disabled access; cl wkdys in Mar and Nov, all Dec–Easter; (01374) 971971; £3. Housed in England's oldest airport, with an appealing 1930s Art Deco terminal; tours available (£2), good-value restaurant with uninterrupted views.

SINGLETON SU8713

↓T 🏛 🚃 🏘 **Weald & Downland Open-air Museum** (A286) Fascinating collection of over 40 historic buildings rescued from all over the SE, dismantled and re-erected here. They're arranged to form an authentic-looking village, with outlying farm and agricultural buildings, a Tudor market hall, blacksmith's forge, tollhouse and Victorian schoolroom. You can buy flour from the medieval farmstead's working watermill. Well organised children's activities might include brick-laying or basket-making. A futuristic timber-built 'gridshell' should open in the summer, inside which visitors will be able to watch timber frames being restored. Snacks, shop, some disabled access, but the site is rather steep; open daily Mar–Oct, then Weds and wknds, plus Christmas wk Nov–Feb; (01243) 811348; £5.20. The handy Fox & Hounds is a friendly stop.

SOUTH HARTING SU7819

★ 🏠 A pretty downland village, with good-value food in the nicely set Ship. The chalk Harting Downs involve no more than a level stroll from the road above the village; the Coach & Horses at nearby Compton is another good base for walks in this area.

Downland drive The roads round here give attractive drives – the B2141 and B2146 S of South Harting, the Walderton–East Mardon back road between them, and the downs-foot road E through East Harting, Elsted, Treyford and Cocking.

🏛 🏵 ⚘ 🏠 **Uppark** (B2146 S) Splendid 17th-c house, extensively

restored after a disastrous fire in 1989. Incredibly, most of the house's public treasures were rescued, even the wallpaper, but behind the scenes it's a different story: the family that live here lost almost everything, and one wonders how they feel about the way the Trust has left a few charred floorboards in place – and recycled others into fruit bowls sold in the shop. The grounds, designed by Humphrey Repton, have a woodland walk and fine views towards the Solent. Meals, snacks, shop, disabled access; open pm Sun–Thurs Apr–Oct; (01730) 825857; £5.50; NT. Entrance is by timed ticket, a few of which can be booked in advance – otherwise get there between 11.30am and 1.30pm. The White Hart has good home cooking.

TANGMERE SU9106

✝ ✗ **Military Aviation Museum** (off A27) Good collection of flying memorabilia based around the former RAF base where H E Bates finished writing *Fair Stood the Wind for France*. Meals, snacks, shop, disabled access; cl Dec–Jan; (01243) 775223; *£3. The nearby Bader Arms has more memorabilia; and there's good food at the Anglesey Arms at Halnaker (with the shell of an 18th-c windmill nearby).

TICEHURST TQ7029

🏵 **Pashley Manor Gardens** (B2099) Eight acres of beautifully restored, mainly Victorian, formal gardens around a handsome house once owned by the Boleyn family. Magnificent old trees, delightfully placed moat and walled garden, views, folly, fine shrubs, roses, herbaceous beds, and clever focal points; very relaxed, charming and peaceful. Tulip festival in May, and a festival of old-fashioned roses in June. Snacks, plant sales, limited disabled access; open Tues–Thurs, Sat and bank hols, early Apr–Sept; (01580) 200692; £5. The village is attractive; up a side road at Three Legged Cross, Maynards has good pick-your-own.

TURNERS HILL TQ3335

🌶 ! **Amazing Maize Maze** 🖼 Huge range of pick-your-own from rhubarb in Apr to beetroot in Oct, as well as a tearoom, good farm shop and, of course, the annual crop labyrinth – don't worry if you get stuck, from a watchtower an eagle-eyed guide will lead you to the centre via walkie-talkie communication; July–mid-Sept (£4, £3 child). Pick-your-own Apr–Oct, shop open all year; (01342) 718472. The Red Lion has good-value food.

UPPER DICKER TQ5509

🏠✝⌖✕ **Michelham Priory**
Charming 16th-c house based around 13th-c Augustinian priory, with 15th-c gatehouse by the moat (which has plenty of waterfowl). Interesting furniture, tapestries and local ironwork, as well as crafts, working watermill, and rope-making museum. Meals, snacks, shop, disabled access to ground floor only; open Weds–Sun and bank hols mid-Mar–Oct, daily in Aug; (01323) 844224; £4.40; EH. The Plough is useful for lunch.

WARBLETON TQ6018

★ Right off the beaten track and as a result very unspoilt – the village has more pre-1750 Sussex barns than anywhere else in the county.

WEIR WOOD RESERVOIR TQ3935

⌂ There's a pleasant waterside walk along its N shore, with paths leading up to Standen House.

WEST CHILTINGTON TQ0918

✝ ★ **West Chiltington church**
Beautiful building in a pretty village in lovely downland countryside – this is windmill country, too.

WEST DEAN SU8612

❀ **West Dean Gardens** Old roses, 100-yard pergola, wild garden, walled kitchen garden and interesting collection of stately mature conifers in park and arboretum; a splendid downland setting, notably peaceful and relaxed. Meals, snacks, shop, some disabled access, plant sales; cl Nov–Feb; (01243) 811303; £3.50. The smart White Horse at Chilgrove or Royal Oak a little N of it would be our choice for lunch.

WEST HOATHLY TQ3632

★ ❀ Attractive village tucked quietly away from the road, with tremendous views from the lane down past the ancient Cat pub. On a clear day you can see the whole sweep of the South Downs between Chanctonbury Ring and the Long Man of Wilmington.

🕯 **Priest House** Nr the 13th-c church,

this 15th-c timbered house is now a folk museum with a little cottage garden. Shop; cl am Sun, and Nov–Feb; (01342) 810479; £2.30. They can arrange guided tours of the village.

WESTFIELD TQ8115

🍇 **Carr Taylor Vineyard** One of England's most successful commercial vineyards, producing sparkling wine as well as still (shop, disabled access; cl Christmas wk, and Sun Jan–Feb; (01424) 752501; trails £1.50).

WILMINGTON TQ5403

🏛 **Long Man of Wilmington**
Gigantic chalk-cut figure so far impossible to date – guesses hover anywhere between the early 18th c and the Bronze Age. The Giant's Rest in the village below has good home cooking.

WINCHELSEA TQ9017

★ ♪ ✝ ❀ Storms and French raids pretty much put paid to this once-flourishing port's importance; today it's a quiet and pleasant little place, dwarfed by the distances between the 3 surviving town gates around it. The **Royal Military Canal** runs from here to Hythe in Kent, a never-used Napoleonic defence that was meant as a sort of glorified coastal moat – now a peaceful spot for coarse fishermen. The New Inn is popular for lunch, and the tranquil **church** of St Thomas is elaborately decorated, with some fine old stained glass and medieval tombs. The Fairlight road has clifftop views.

WISBOROUGH GREEN TQ0526

🐄 **Fishers Farm Park** 🎫 Friendly farm, well equipped for families, with animal shows and petting areas, good indoor and outdoor play areas, paddling pool and a go-kart track. Meals, snacks, shop, disabled access; cl 25–26 Dec; (01403) 700063; £6, less in winter; also holiday cottages and campsite. The Cricketers Arms on the green has good food.

WORTHING TQ1402

🕯 Restrained but rather charming town, with a pleasant seafront; in the same mould as Brighton but altogether quieter and less gaudy. There's an excellent **herb shop** on Field Row, opposite M&S. The formerly separate village of West Tarring has a 250-year-old fig garden by the 14th-c parish hall, a folklore **museum** in a row of 15th-c cottages,

and a welcoming old pub, the Vine.
♿ 🏛 **Worthing Museum & Art Gallery** (Chapel Rd) Extremely rich archaeological collection, and a sculpture garden. Shop, disabled access; cl Sun, 25–26 Dec, Good Fri; (01903) 239999; free.
WYCH CROSS TQ4235
🐖 🐐 **Ashdown Llama Farm** Unusual working llama farm, with big breeding herds of alpacas; sheep and goats too. Snacks, shop, disabled access (but no facilities); cl Mon (exc bank hols), and wkdys Nov–Mar; (01825) 712040; *£2.50. The same people run Barnsgate Manor Vineyard a few miles down the road at Herons Ghyll, which has great views from its attractive restaurant.

★ **Other attractive villages**, all with civilised pubs doing decent food, include Barns Green TQ1227, Brightling TQ6921 (the pub is at nearby Oxleys Green), Byworth SU9820, Chiddingly TQ5414, Easebourne SU8922, East Dean SU9013, Elsted SU8119, Fittleworth TQ0118, Funtington SU7908, Hellingly TQ5812, Henley SU8925, Kirdford TQ0126, Lodsworth SU9223, Robertsbridge TQ7323, Rotherfield TQ5529, Rudgwick TQ0833, Rushlake Green TQ6218, Slaugham TQ2528, Stopham TQ0218, Sutton SU9715, Waldron TQ5419 (ancient church) and West Chiltington TQ0918.

Where to eat

ALCISTON TQ5005 **Rose Cottage** *(01323) 870377* In the same family for over 30 years, small, charming wisteria-covered cottage full of harness, traps, ironware and bric-à-brac, as well as Jasper the talking parrot (mornings only); very good promptly served food (especially the simply cooked fresh fish) using organic vegetables and their own eggs, well kept real ales, decent wines and a good range of other drinks like kir and Pimms, a small no smoking evening restaurant, and seats outside; cl 25–26 Dec; children over 6 in evening. **£19|£6.50.**

ALFRISTON TQ5202 **Moonrakers** *(01323) 870472* Reliably enjoyable evening food (Sun lunch, too) in this cosy little cottage with a log fire, a good wine list and friendly staff; cl pm Sun, 2 wks early Jan; children over 8. **£17.90** set 3-course meal.

AMBERLEY TQ0211 **Bridge** *Houghton Bridge (01798) 831619* Nice old white-painted pub by a pretty stretch of the River Arun; relaxed and friendly bar, attractively furnished 2-room dining room, interesting modern portraits and Impressionist-style paintings, generous helpings of good home-made bar food (lots of fresh fish), proper puddings, 4 Sunday roasts, well kept real ales, and friendly, helpful service. **£18.75|£6.50.**

BRIGHTON TQ3103 **Black Chapati** *12 Circus Parade, New England Road (01273) 699011* Particularly good Eastern cooking with Anglo-Indian influences in starkly furnished restaurant with white walls and black tables and chairs, and Breton cider – wine does not always compliment the style of food; cl Sun, Mon; disabled access. **£27.75.**

BRIGHTON TQ3103 **Browns** *Duke Street (01273) 323501* Relaxed and chatty restaurant with an airy, spacious feel, lots of greenery, and enjoyable, reasonably priced English food with European influences; cl 25–26 Dec; disabled access. **£19|£7.55.**

BRIGHTON TQ3103 **Mock Turtle** *4 Pool Valley (01273) 327380* Delightful, no smoking, traditional English teashop with enjoyable snacks and light lunches (local fish and local sausages), lovely home-made cakes, bread, and so forth, and popular cream teas; cl Sun, Mon, Good Fri, 2 wks spring, a few days over Christmas. £3.99.

BRIGHTON TQ3203 **One Paston Place** *1 Paston Pl (01273) 606933* Just off the seafront, this airy, enjoyable restaurant has a big mural, very good modern British food inc super fish and game dishes, nice puddings, decent house wines, and a friendly atmosphere; cl Sun, Mon, first 2 weeks Jan, first 2 wks Aug; children welcome lunchtimes only. **£40.**

BRIGHTON TQ3004 **Whytes** *33 Western St (01273) 776618* Popular and attractive cottagey restaurant just off the seafront with a relaxed and friendly atmosphere, enjoyable food using fresh local produce, and a decent wine list; cl Sun, Mon, end Feb–early Mar; children over 10. **£25.83**.

BROAD OAK TQ8219 **Rainbow Trout** *Chitcombe Rd (01424) 882436* Pleasant pub with an attractive bustling old bar, big restaurant extension, wide range of well cooked food (especially fish) served by friendly waitresses, and well kept real ales; disabled access. **£20|£4.95**.

BURPHAM TQ0308 **George & Dragon** *(01903) 883131* Smartly comfortable dining pub with splendid views down to Arundel Castle and the river; good promptly served food with unusual specials inc nice vegetarian dishes; elegant restaurant – worth booking; cl pm Sun winter, 25 Dec. **£21|£6.20**.

CHICHESTER SU8605 **Comme Ça** *67 Broyle Rd (01243) 788724* Busy little restaurant close to Festival Theatre with good classic French cooking, popular Sun lunches and children's menu; cl pm Sun, Mon, Christmas; partial disabled access. **£26.75|£11.45**.

CHICHESTER SU8604 **St Martin's Tearooms** *3 St Martin's St (01243) 786715* Handsome brick Georgian-fronted house with a pretty garden for summer eating, good lunchtime snacks and meals (mainly vegetarian but with some fish dishes) and afternoon teas using organic produce; cl Sun, bank hols; disabled access. **£16|£5**.

DUNCTON SU9517 **Cricketers** *(01798) 342473* Pretty little white house with welcoming staff and a jovial landlord, an inglenook fireplace, standing timbers and country furniture in the small bar, and a dining room decorated with farm tools; good popular food, well kept real ales, and a charming back garden with proper barbecue; skittle alley; no food pm Sun/Mon; no children. **£19.40|£7.25**.

EAST CHILTINGTON TQ3715 **Jolly Sportsman** *(01273) 890400* Tucked away Victorian dining pub with stripped wooden floors, groups of mixed tables and chairs, a fireplace in the chatty little bar, and contemporary light wood furniture and modern landscapes on pale yellow painted brick walls in the informally civilised restaurant; well kept real ales, a remarkably good wine list, and imaginative cooking from a changing menu; rustic tables and benches under gnarled trees in a pretty cottagey front garden. **£23.50|£8**.

EASTBOURNE TV6098 **Downland** *37 Lewes Rd (01323) 732689* Pretty candlelit evening restaurant in a well run small hotel with carefully prepared innovative food, good vegetables and lovely puddings, a relaxed atmosphere, and friendly service; bdrms; children over 10. **£23**.

EDBURTON TQ2211 **Tottington Manor** *(01903) 815757* Cosy country house with particularly good food using fresh seasonal produce in both the bar and restaurant, winter log fire, friendly service and a relaxed atmosphere; bdrms; cl pm Sun, first 2 wks Jan; children over 5. **£30.50|£13** 2-course lunch.

ELSTED SU8320 **Elsted Inn** *(01730) 813662* Victorian roadside pub with a warmly friendly welcome, unpretentious bars with open log fires, lots of original wood, a candlelit dining room, extremely good interesting cooking using fresh local ingredients (Weds theme night), very well kept real ales, 2 dogs, and a large garden (with dog-free zone); bdrms; partial disabled access. **£21.50|£5**.

ELSTED SU8119 **Three Horseshoes** *(01730) 825746* Cosy Tudor pub in a lovely setting, with fine views of the South Downs from the garden (and good walks), snug rustic rooms with huge log fires, ancient beams and venerable furnishings, very good English country cooking inc lovely puddings, well kept real ales, decent wines by the glass; cl pm Sun Oct–May; well behaved children welcome. **£25|£6**.

FLETCHING TQ4223 **Griffin** *(01825) 722890* Civilised old country inn with blazing log fires in quaintly panelled rooms, old photographs and hunting prints, very good innovative food, well kept beers, a good wine list with lots (inc champagne) by the glass, a relaxed, friendly atmosphere, and a lovely garden; bdrms; cl 25 Dec; disabled access. **£27|£7.50**.

HARTFIELD TQ4735 **Anchor** *Church St (01892) 770424* Relaxed and friendly pub on the edge of Ashdown Forest, with good bar food, quick service, a chatty heavily beamed bar, dining area, well kept real ales, and popular front verandah; cl pm 25 Dec; disabled access. **£20|£5.**

HASTINGS TQ8209 **Harris** *58 High St (01424) 437221* Relaxed, informal and chatty, reasonably priced mainly Spanish food (enjoyable tapas), friendly staff in long white aprons, and decent wine; cl Sun (but open all day Sat). **£19.50|£5.50.**

HASTINGS TQ8009 **Rosers** *64 Eversfield Pl, St Leonards (01424) 712218* Extremely rewarding and generous, imaginative food using top-quality produce inc home-cured, smoked and pickled ingredients in a straightforward-looking little restaurant opposite the pier; fine wines, too; cl am Sat, Sun, Mon; disabled access. **£22.95 set dinner, £19.95 set lunch.**

HERSTMONCEUX TQ6312 **Sundial** *Gardner St (01323) 832217* Pretty and plush 17th-c cottage with excellent, carefully cooked food inc lovely vegetables and delicious puddings, a praiseworthy wine list, relaxed atmosphere, formal but warmly friendly service, and terrace and garden for summer eating; cl pm Sun, Mon, Christmas–20 Jan, 3 wks Aug; disabled access. **£30|£15.50.**

HORSHAM TQ1730 **Black Jug** *31 North St (01403) 253526* Most attractively refurbished Edwardian town pub with a relaxed atmosphere, big airy bar around the central servery, lots of old prints and photographs, a plant-filled conservatory, very popular interesting bar food, chilled flavoured vodkas, well kept real ales, decent wines, and a small back terrace; no children pm Sat/Sun; cl pm Sun. **£20|£5.95.**

JEVINGTON TQ5601 **Hungry Monk** *The Street (01323) 482178* Long-standing popular candlelit evening restaurant (also Sun lunch) with 3 beamed sitting rooms, bar, little dining room, open fires, a friendly dinner-partyish atmosphere, and good interesting food; cl am Mon–Sat, pm 25 Dec, 26 Dec, bank hols; children over 4. **£40.**

KIRDFORD TQ0126 **Half Moon** *(01403) 820223* Family-run inn with marvellous fresh fish (the family have had Billingsgate links for 130 years) inc some really unusual ones, well kept real ales, local wine and cider, friendly service, simple neat bars, and a big garden; cl pm 25 Dec; disabled access. **£25|£5.75.**

LITLINGTON TQ5201 **Litlington Tea Gardens** *(01323) 870222* Established 150 years ago, these tearooms still keep their quaint Victorian elegance, with seating on an attractive sheltered lawn under a copper beech or ginkgo, in renovated beach huts with open fronts, or the tearoom/restaurant; colourful hanging baskets and flowering tubs, quick efficient service; morning coffee, light lunches, and cream teas; handy for Alfriston; cl end Oct–1 wk before Easter; disabled access. **£5.**

LODSWORTH SU9321 **Halfway Bridge** *A272 (01798) 861281* Stylish and civilised but warmly friendly family-run pub with big helpings of delicious inventive home cooking in the no smoking restaurant or attractively decorated comfortable bar rooms; log fires, well kept real ales, ciders and wines; cl pm Sun in winter; children welcome over 10. **£20.95|£7.25.**

NUTHURST TQ1926 **Black Horse** *(01403) 891272* Warmly welcoming black-beamed pub in lovely walking country with a log fire in the inglenook fireplace, good, promptly served bar food, very well kept real ales and country wines, friendly service; cl pm 25 Dec. **£20|£6.95.**

OXLEYS GREEN TQ6921 **Jack Fullers** *(01424) 838212* Cosy and softly lit dining pub with enjoyable pies and steamed puddings, good side dishes, and some vegetarian choices – all in big helpings; excellent wines (English ones, too), and seats in the pretty flower-filled garden with fine views; cl Mon, Tues; disabled access. **£18.50|£6.**

PLAYDEN TQ9122 **Peace & Plenty** *(01797) 280342* Cottagey dining pub with lots of little pictures, china and lamps and a big inglenook with comfortable armchairs on either side in the cosy bar, 2 intimate dining areas, very well prepared traditional food, well kept ales, and a pretty garden. **£19|£7.95.**

RINGMER TQ4313 **Cock** *Uckfield Rd (01273) 812040* Civilised heavily beamed country pub with a log fire in the big inglenook, a fine range of good food, decent wines, 2 lounges (one no smoking), and seats on the terrace and in the attractive fairy-lit garden; cl 25 Dec, pm 26 Dec. **£20|£6**.

RYE TQ9220 **Flushing** *4 Market St (01797)* 223292 Run by the same family for 38 years, this fine old timber-framed inn serves particularly good local fish and seafood (local meat dishes, too) and holds various gastronomic occasions; note the fine 16th-c wall painting; bdrms; cl pm Mon, Tues, first 2 wks Jan. **£30|£6.50**.

RYE TQ9220 **Landgate Bistro** *5–6 Landgate (01797)* 222829 Simply furnished beamed bistro (evenings only) with good accomplished cooking, nice puddings, relaxed service, and a carefully chosen little wine list; cl Sun, Mon, Christmas–New Year, 2 wks June, 1 wk Oct. **£25**.

RYE TQ9321 **Ypres Castle** *Gun Garden (steps down from Church Sq) (01797)* 223248 Popular pub in fine setting nr 13th-c Ypres Tower with unassuming décor, warm and friendly atmosphere, enjoyable interesting food inc fresh local fish and seafood, good fresh veg, well kept changing ales, good-value wine with 20 by the glass, and seats on a sizeable lawn with fine views out over the coastal flats; cl pm 25 Dec. **£18.95|£5.85**.

SCAYNES HILL TQ3824 **Sloop** *Sloop Lane, Freshfield Lock (01444)* 831219 Country pub tucked away in this lovely spot with a sheltered garden nr the Bluebell Line; long saloon bar with pine furniture and comfortable old seats, a simple public bar, good bar food (especially the daily specials), well kept real ales, and decent wines; cl pm 25–26 Dec; children must be well behaved; partial disabled access. **£21|£4.95**.

SEAFORD TV5199 **Golden Galleon** *Exceat, A259 E (01323)* 892247 Huge, bustling popular pub with high, trussed and pitched rafters in the airy bar and dining area, an open fire in a nice little side area, conservatory, up to a dozen real ales inc some from their own microbrewery, good food inc lots of Italian dishes (the chatty landlord is from Italy), and good views from tables in the sloping garden; bdrms; cl pm Sun Sept–May. **£18.80|£6.80**.

SEAFORD TV4898 **Quincy's** *4 High St (01323)* 895490 Enjoyable little cottagey restaurant with homely décor, really friendly service, very good soundly based interesting food (fresh fish from Newhaven and lovely puddings), and a thoughtful wine list; cl pm Sun, Mon, am Tues–Sat, first wk Jan. **£30.50**.

SLINDON COMMON SU9608 **Spur** *London Rd (01243)* 814216 Attractive little 17th-c pub with 2 big log fires, a good choice of daily changing food, a sizeable restaurant, well kept ales, friendly dogs, and a pleasant garden; bdrms. **£25|£7**.

Special thanks to Paul Kennedy, N Ellis, E G Parish.

Sussex Calendar

Some of these dates were provisional as we went to press. Please check information with the telephone numbers provided.

JANUARY

11 **Ardingly** Antiques Fair: up to 4,000 stands at the South of England Showground – *till 12 January* (01636) 702326

FEBRUARY

11 **Chichester** Festival of Music, Dance and Speech – *till 18 March* (01243) 785715
15 **Brighton** CAMRA Beer Festival – *till 21 February* (01903) 692370

Sussex Calendar (cont.)

18 Brighton International Model Festival at Brighton Centre – *till 20 February* (01273) 290131; also, Icons of Pop: 50 years of pop photography at the Brighton Museum and Art Gallery – *till 9 April* (01273) 290900

21 Fishbourne Family Fun Days at Fishbourne Roman Palace – *till 24 February* (01243) 785858

MARCH

1 Ardingly Antiques Fair (*see 11 Jan for details*)

19 Brighton Motorcycle Run, Madeira Drive (01273) 292606; **Hadlow Down** Heavy Horses at Work in Wilderness Wood (01825) 830509

21 Brighton Horse Show at the Brighton Centre – *till 22 March* (01273) 292589

APRIL

15 Brighton UK Coach Rally, Madeira Drive – *till 16 April* (01273) 292606; **Chichester** Tudor Living History Day at the Chichester District Museum (01243) 784683; **Haywards Heath** Garden Festival at Borde Hill Garden – *till 16 April* (01444) 450326

18 Ardingly Antiques Fair (*see 11 Jan for details*)

21 Tinsley Green British and World Marble Championships at the Greyhound (01403) 730602; **Upper Dicker** Garden Festival at Michelham Priory – *till 24 April* (01323) 844224

23 Hadlow Down Easter Bunny Hunt in Wilderness Wood – *till 24 April* (01825) 830509; **Haywards Heath** Easter Trail for Children at Borde Hill Garden – *till 24 April* (01444) 450326; **Singleton** Traditional Food Fair at the Weald & Downland Open-air Museum – *till 24 April* (01243) 811348

27 Ticehurst Tulip Festival at Pashley Manor Gardens – *till 1 May* (01580) 200888

28 Brighton Horse Driving Trials at Stanmer Park – *till 30 April* (01323) 841641; **Hastings** Jack in the Green Morris Dance Festival: procession, concerts, street entertainment – *till 1 May* (01424) 716576

29 Bexhill Festival of Motoring: hundreds of military and vintage vehicles and air displays – *till 1 May* (01424) 730564

MAY

1 Upper Dicker May Day Festival at Michelham Priory (01323) 844224

6 Brighton Festival: over 450 events – *till 28 May* (01273) 700747; **Eastbourne** International Folk Festival (01323) 415442; **Haywards Heath** Children's Animal Fair at Borde Hill Garden – *till 7 May* (01444) 450326; **Lower Beeding** Bonsai Weekend at Leonardslee Gardens – *till 7 May* (01403) 891212

7 Brighton Historic Commercial Vehicle Run, Madeira Drive (01273) 292606

11 Brighton International Street Theatre Weekend – *till 14 May* (01273) 292589

13 Brighton Family Fun Day: inc country and western bands, re-enactments, shoot-outs, steam engines and fair at Wild Park (01273) 701152

14 Laughton Young Farmers Country Fair (01323) 840332

Sussex Calendar (cont.)

15 Hadlow Down Bluebell Walk at Wilderness Wood (01825) 830509
16 Brighton Dieppe Market in Bartholomew Square (01273) 292589; also, Mackerel Fayre at the Fishing Museum (01273) 292606
20 Brighton Brighton Philharmonic Orchestra 75th Birthday Festival Weekend – *till 21 May* (01273) 622900; **Chichester** Celtic Living History Day at the District Museum (01243) 784683; **Rye** Plant Fair (01797) 222876
21 Ticehurst Spring Plant Fair at Pashley Manor Gardens (01580) 200888
25 Chichester Chartres 2000: events to celebrate 200 years of twinning between Chichester and Chartres – *till 28 May* (01243) 788502; **Firle** Charleston Festival at Charleston Farmhouse – *till 29 May* (01323) 811265
26 Brighton Old Ship Royal Escape Race: yacht race from beach in front of the Old Ship, King's Rd (01273) 329001; **Upper Dicker** Weavers, Potters and Woodturners at Michelham Priory – *till 29 May* (01323) 844224
27 Broad Oak Heathfield Agricultural Show (01435) 830977; **Chichester** Folk Festival – *till 29 May* (01705) 471929; **Eastbourne** Millennium Parade (01323) 415442
28 Battle Medieval Fair – *till 29 May* (01424) 774447; **Crawley** Spring Carnival – *till 29 May* (01293) 553636
29 Upper Dicker Teddy Bears Picnic at Michelham Priory – *till 31 May* (01323) 844224

JUNE

1 Chichester Flower Festival in the Cathedral: half a million flowers and country fair – *till 3 June* (01243) 776922
3 Durrington Festival – *till 11 June* (01903) 600516; **Hadlow Down** Tinkers Park Traction Engine Rally – *till 4 June*
4 Brighton Classic Car Show, Madeira Drive (01273) 292606; **Singleton** Heavy Horses at the Weald & Downland Open-air Museum (01243) 811348
10 Ardingly South of England Show – *till 12 June* (0891) 884513
17 Eastbourne International Ladies Tennis Championship – *till 24 June* (01323) 415442; **Haywards Heath** Days of Crafts and Roses at the National Rose Society at Borde Hill Garden – *till 30 June* (01444) 450326; **Pulborough** Parham Park Steam Rally and Country Show – *till 18 June* (01903) 744888
19 Fishbourne Shakespeare Production at Fishbourne Roman Palace – *till 30 June* (01243) 785858
21 Arundel Corpus Christi Carpet of Flowers and Floral Festival at the Cathedral – *till 22 June* (01903) 882297
23 Goodwood Festival of Speed at Goodwood House: historic motor sport event – *till 25 June* (01243) 755000; **Petworth** Open-air Concerts at Petworth House – *till 25 June* (01798) 342207
24 Lower Beeding Country Craft Fair at Leonardslee Gardens – *till 25 June* (01403) 891212
30 Crawley Folk Festival at the Hawth – *till 2 July* (01293) 553636

JULY

1 Littlehampton Carnival (01903) 716634
5 Pulborough Outdoor Theatre: *Romeo and Juliet* at Parham House – *till 8 July* (01903) 744888

Sussex Calendar (cont.)

6 Hastings Beer and Music Festival – *till 9 July* (01424) 781066

7 Chichester Festival – *till 23 July* (01243) 785718; **Crowborough** Sherlock Holmes Festival – *till 9 July* (01892) 665464

8 Crawley Fireworks Concert at Tilgate Park (01293) 553636

9 Upper Dicker Open-air Shakespeare at Michelham Priory (01323) 844224

14 Petworth Festival – *till 23 July* (01798) 343523

15 Eastbourne Friends of Thomas the Tank Engine at the Miniature Steam Railway Park – *till 16 July* (01323) 520229; **Pulborough** Garden Weekend at Parham House – *till 16 July* (01903) 744888

18 Ardingly Antiques Fair (see *11 Jan for details*)

22 Bodiam Fireworks Concert at the Castle (01892) 890651; **Brighton** Carnival at Preston Park (01273) 543615; **Eastbourne** Emergency Services Display at Western Lawns – *till 23 July* (01323) 415442

23 Crawley Children's Festival: an afternoon of free events (01293) 553636; **Singleton** Rare and Traditional Breeds at the Weald & Downland Open-air Museum (01243) 811348

24 Eastbourne County Cup Tennis at Devonshire Park – *till 28 July* (01323) 415442

25 Ebernoe Horn Fair (01428) 707587

AUGUST

1 Goodwood Glorious Goodwood – *till 5 August* (01243) 755022

4 Crawley Music, Arts and Dance International Festival – *till 6 August* (01293) 553636

5 Burwash Fireworks Concert at Batemans – *till 6 August* (01892) 891001

6 Arundel Art and Craft exhibition inc have-a-go days – *till 29 August* (01903) 730602

7 Eastbourne Family Festival of Tennis at Devonshire Park – *till 12 August* (01323) 415442

10 Upper Dicker Guild of Sussex Craftsmen in Action at Michelham Priory – *till 13 August* (01323) 844224

12 Crawley Juggling Convention – *till 31 August* (01293) 553636; **Eastbourne** Horse Show at Gildredge Park (01323) 415442; **Pulborough** Open-air Theatre: *The Rivals* at Parham House (01903) 744888; **Singleton** Children's Activities at the Weald & Downland Open-air Museum – *till 13 August* (01243) 811348

17 Eastbourne Airborne 2000 and RAF Show – *till 20 August* (01323) 415442

18 Pulborough Live Crafts Show at Parham House – *till 20 August* (01903) 744888

24 Singleton Rural History Re-enactment at the Weald & Downland Open-air Museum – *till 29 August* (01243) 811348

26 Arundel Festival Fringe – *till 3 September* (01903) 882904; **Hellingly** Festival of Transport at Broad Farm – *till 28 August* (01323) 843202; **Rotherfield** Torchlight Procession (01273) 515451

28 Eastbourne South of England Tennis Championship at Devonshire Park – *till 2 September* (01323) 415442

SEPTEMBER

2 Uckfield Torchlight Procession and Fireworks (01273) 515451

Sussex Calendar (cont.)

3 Bognor Regis Birdman Competition (01903) 716133; **Haywards Heath** Rare Plants Fair at Borde Hill Garden (01444) 450326

9 Brighton National Speed Trials (0860) 730349; **Crowborough** Torchlight Procession and Fireworks (01273) 515451; **Findon** Sheep Fair at Nepcote Farm (01435) 873999

10 Eastbourne Vintage Bus Rally (01323) 520229

16 Mayfield Torchlight Procession and Fireworks (01273) 515451

18 Ardingly Antiques Fair (see 11 Jan for details)

23 Burgess Hill Torchlight Procession and Fireworks (01273) 515451

OCTOBER

7 Brighton Festival of Animated Theatre – till 29 October (01273) 643010

14 Newhaven Torchlight Procession and Fireworks (01273) 515451

20 Chichester Sloe Fair (01243) 775888

21 Singleton Autumn Countryside Cavalcade at the Weald & Downland Open-air Museum – till 22 October (01243) 811348

28 Littlehampton Torchlight Procession and Fireworks (01273) 515451

31 Ardingly Antiques Fair (see 11 Jan for details)

NOVEMBER

4 Lewes Torchlight Procession and Fireworks: best of Britain's bonfire celebrations, town closed to traffic 5.30pm, spectacular celebrations with bands, effigies and burning tar barrel race (01273) 515451

5 Brighton RAC London–Brighton Veteran Car Run arrives (01273) 290000

11 East Hoathly Torchlight Procession and Fireworks (01273) 515451

DECEMBER

3 Singleton Tree Dressing at the Weald & Downland Open-air Museum (01243) 811348

We welcome reports from readers

This *Guide* depends on readers' reports. Do help us if you can – in return, we offer a discount on the next edition to people who've helped us with reports for it. Tell us what you think about places already in it, and anything extra you think we should say about them. And send us your ideas for inclusion in the next edition: places to visit, eat at or stay in, attractive drives or walks, maybe even unusual interesting shops you know of. Use the card in the middle, the report forms at the end, or just write – no stamp needed: *The Good Britain Guide*, FREEPOST TN1569, Wadhurst, E Sussex TN5 7BR.

WARWICKSHIRE
(with Birmingham and the West Midlands)

Some great days out; good places for enjoyable holiday breaks, too.

This is an excellent area for family outings, topped by the lively re-creation of a turn-of-the-century working Black Country village in Dudley (good-value family tickets), spectacular Warwick Castle (enjoyable summer events), and Cadbury World in Bournville. There are a few good farms. The historic car collection at Gaydon is outstanding.

Birmingham has great scope for day visits, with top-class art collections, lively museums, good botanic gardens, a fine sea life centre, and interesting period houses; many places are free. The new art gallery out in Walsall is a stunner. Warwick has the character and atmosphere to make a short stay enjoyable; its neighbour Leamington Spa still has some of the elegance of its spa-resort heyday. Stratford is the obvious focus for people on the Shakespeare trail. Elsewhere, striking historic houses include Moseley Old Hall (good guided tours) and charmingly different Wightwick Manor (both near Wolverhampton), Arbury Hall, Coughton Court, imposing Ragley Hall at Alcester, and the atmospheric ruins of Kenilworth Castle. The Kingswinford glass museum is an unexpected dazzler, and the Nickelodeon at Ashorne has a fine nostalgic appeal. People get a lot out of the organic gardening centre at Ryton-on-Dunsmore.

The countryside (which edges into the Cotswolds in the south) is quietly attractive, laced with canals and dotted with charming villages and appealing places to stay in.

Where to stay

AVON DASSETT SP4150 **Crandon House** *Avon Dassett, Leamington Spa CV33 0AA (01295) 770652* ***£40,** plus winter breaks; 5 no smoking rms, 2 in converted dairy. Welcoming farmhouse on a small working farm with various livestock, fine views, a big garden, comfortable sitting rooms (one with a woodburning stove), and extensive breakfasts with home-made marmalade and preserves and free-range eggs; cl Christmas; children over 10.

BINTON SP1454 **Gravelside Barn** *Binton, Stratford-upon-Avon CV37 9TU (01789) 750502* **£60;** 3 well equipped rms. Carefully restored old barn with marvellous views, residents' lounge and dining room, interesting furnishings, tennis court and garden, and nearby pubs and restaurants for evening meals; plenty to do nearby; children over 12; disabled access.

BISHOP'S TACHBROOK SP3262 **Mallory Court** *Harbury Lane, Bishop's Tachbrook, Leamington Spa CV33 9QB (01926) 330214* **£312,** plus special breaks; 18 wonderfully comfortable and luxurious rms. Fine ancient-looking house – actually built around 1910 – with elegant antique and flower-filled day rooms (carefully refurbished this year), attentive staff, excellent food using home-grown produce in the panelled restaurant, and 10 acres of lovely gardens with outdoor swimming pool, tennis, squash, croquet; cl 2–9 Jan; children over 9 (they take babes in arms).

BLACKWELL SP2343 **Blackwell Grange** *Blackwell, Shipston on Stour CV36 4PF* (01608) 682357 ***£60;** 3 pretty rms. 17th-c Cotswold farmhouse with a log fire in the comfortable beamed sitting room, a large inglenook fireplace in the flagstoned dining room, good home cooking using own free-range eggs (evening meal by arrangement; bring your own wine), a pretty garden, and nice country views; cl Jan; children over 12, but parents with younger children stay in annexe; good disabled access.

ILMINGTON SP2143 **Howard Arms** *Ilmington, Shipston on Stour CV36 4LT* (01608) 682226 **£55;** 2 rms. Neatly kept golden stone 17th/18th-c inn opposite the village green with a pleasant sheltered garden, a beamed and flagstoned bar, open fires, friendly service, very good food, and decent wines.

LEAMINGTON SPA SP3265 **Lansdowne House** *Clarendon St, Leamington Spa CV32 4PF* (01926) 450505 **£65,** plus special breaks; 14 rms. Enjoyable Regency town house with particularly good service, very attractive public rooms, a tranquil atmosphere, good daily-changing dinners, fine-value wine list, and a small prize-winning garden; cl 25 Dec, 1 Jan; children over 5.

LITTLE COMPTON SP2630 **Red Lion** *Little Compton, Moreton-in-Marsh GL56 0RT* (01608) 674397 **£40;** 3 rms, shared bthrm. Attractive 16th-c stone inn with low beams, log fires, separate dining area, an extensive menu and tasty food, no smoking area, real ales, a large wine list, and seats in the sizeable, attractive garden; no dogs; children over 8.

LOXLEY SP2755 **Loxley Farm** *Loxley, Warwick CV35 9JN* (01789) 840265 **£55;** 2 suites with their own sitting rooms in attractive barn conversion. Not far from Stratford, this tucked-away, thatched and half-timbered partly 14th-c house has low beams, wonky walls and floors, antiques and dried flowers, an open fire, helpful and friendly owners, and good Aga-cooked breakfasts; peaceful garden, and a fine old village church; cl Christmas/New Year.

SHERBOURNE SP2562 **Old Rectory** *Vicarage Lane, Sherbourne, Warwick CV35 8AB* (01926) 624562 ***£62,** plus special breaks; 14 rms, all with antique brass or brass and iron beds, and some in converted stables. Georgian house not far from Warwick, with a cosy sitting room, a big log fire, beams, flagstones, honesty bar, hearty breakfasts and enjoyable evening meals, and pretty walled gardens; no children.

STRATFORD-UPON-AVON SP1954 **Carlton** *22 Evesham Pl CV37 6HT* (01789) 293548 ***£48;** 8 homely rms, some with own bthrm. Neatly kept and very welcoming no smoking Victorian house, close to theatre and restaurants, with helpful owners, very good breakfasts in the airy dining room, and a little garden.

STRATFORD-UPON-AVON SP2054 **Melita** *37 Shipston Rd, Stratford-upon-Avon CV37 7LN* (01789) 292432 ***£66,** plus special breaks; 12 well equipped rms. Friendly family-run Victorian hotel with a pretty, carefully laid-out garden, a comfortable lounge with an open fire, extensive breakfasts, and some provision for non-smokers; close to town centre and theatre; cl Christmas; pets by arrangement; partial disabled access.

STRATFORD-UPON-AVON SP2055 **Payton** *6 John St, Stratford-upon-Avon CV37 6UB* (01789) 266442 ***£64;** 5 charming rms with showers. Quietly set no smoking Georgian house, handy for theatre, with caring owners, very good breakfasts in pretty dining room, and seats in flower-filled courtyard; no children.

STRATFORD-UPON-AVON SP2054 **Shakespeare** *Chapel St, Stratford-upon-Avon CV37 6ER* (0870) 400 8182 **£173.90,** plus wknd breaks; 74 comfortable, well equipped rms. Smart ex-Forte hotel based on handsome lavishly modernised Tudor merchants' houses, with a comfortable bar, good food, quick friendly service, tables in the back courtyard, and civilised tea or coffee in peaceful chintzy armchairs by blazing log fires; 3 minutes' walk from theatre.

STRATFORD-UPON-AVON SP2056 **Welcombe** *Warwick Rd, Stratford-upon-Avon CV37 0NR* (01789) 295252 **£175,** plus special breaks; 64 rms with antiques and luxurious bthrms. Jacobean-style mansion in a parkland estate with an 18-hole golf course and 2 all-weather floodlit tennis courts, deeply comfortable day rooms inc fine panelled lounge, open fires and fresh flowers, an elegant restaurant, and good service; disabled access.

SUTTON COLDFIELD SP1394 **New Hall** *Walmley Rd, Sutton Coldfield B76 1QX* (0121) 378 2442 **£136,** plus wknd breaks; 60 lovely rms (the ones in the manor house are the best). England's oldest moated manor house, in 26 beautiful acres, with luxurious day rooms, a graceful panelled restaurant with carefully cooked imaginative food using very fresh (often home-grown) produce, and excellent service; they can hold wedding ceremonies, and are planning a leisure club; children over 8; disabled access.

WALCOTE SP1258 **Walcote Farm** *Walcote, Alcester B49 6LY* (01789) 488264 *****£38;** 3 rms, 2 with fine views, one with an early 16th-c window. Attractive 16th-c farmhouse on a 75-acre working sheep farm with plenty of surrounding walks, a warm welcome from the friendly owners, log fires in inglenook fireplaces, beams and flagstones, good breakfasts (several local pubs for evening meals), and a pretty garden; no smoking; cl Christmas and New Year.

WARWICK SP2864 **Forth House** *44 High St, Warwick CV34 4AX* (01926) 401512 *****£60;** 2 appealing and spacious suites – one is almost a garden flat with its own kitchen. Prettily decorated no smoking house with a lovely, surprisingly big garden, and good breakfasts (supper trays by prior arrangement); self-catering flat; disabled access.

WILMCOTE SP1658 **Pear Tree Cottage** *7 Church Rd, Wilmcote, Stratford-upon-Avon CV37 9UX* (01789) 205889 *****£48;** 7 rms. Charming half-timbered Elizabethan house owned by the same family for 3 generations, with beams, flagstones, country antiques, a cosy atmosphere, good breakfasts, and a sizeable shady garden; self-catering also; cl 24 Dec–2 Jan; children over 3.

To see and do

WARWICKSHIRE Family Attraction of the Year

⬆🚶☺ **DUDLEY** SO9591 **Black Country Living Museum** (Tipton Rd, 1m N of town centre) Great value, and with enough to fill a whole day without any trouble, this well thought out open-air museum gives a good feel of how things used to be in the Black Country, the heavily industrialised and proudly individual areas in the west part of the Birmingham conurbation. Period trams and trolley-buses take you from the entrance in a re-created factory to an authentically reconstructed turn-of-the-century village, the historic cottages and other buildings all moved from their original locations and rebuilt here by the canal basin. There's a full programme of informative and knowledgeable demonstrations and shows, with staff in period costumes illustrating traditional crafts, test-driving old vehicles, and leading trips down the mine; it's worth checking in advance what's going on when. The shops are fully stocked with fascinating period wares, and there's an authentic pub and fish and chip shop (be prepared for queues here, especially on a cold day). Black and white comedies from Laurel and Hardy or Harold Lloyd flicker back to life in the old cinema, and there's an old-fashioned working fairground just outside the village (Mar–Nov; extra charges for some rides). Though there'll be something happening whenever you visit (you can usually count on taking lessons in the school hall, for example), the village and houses are perhaps at their most lively on their Living History weekends, or in school holidays when plenty of extra activities are laid on for children. In summer for a small extra charge they do boat trips through the canal tunnel. Services in the chapel can be atmospheric – you can get tickets in advance for things like their Dec carol service and autumn harvest festival. Plans are well under way for a new exhibition area near the entrance. Many of the attractions are under cover, so though it's a better bet when it's dry, you can still enjoy most parts on a drizzly day. Meals and snacks (and space for picnics), shop, mostly disabled access (it may be worth calling first); open daily, exc Mon and Tues Nov–Feb, and several days over Christmas; (0121) 557 9643; £7.50 (£4.50 children). The family ticket is outstanding value – £20 for 2 adults and up to 4 children.

ALCESTER SP0755

🏠🖼️🕷️ ★ 🛶 **Ragley Hall** (A435) Perfectly symmetrical Palladian house in 400 acres of parkland and gardens; excellent baroque plasterwork in Great Hall, fine paintings (inc some modern art), and adventure playground, maze and woodland walks in the grounds. Good outdoor concerts. Snacks, shop, disabled access; open Thurs–Sun and bank hols, Easter–Sept; (01789) 762090; £5, £4 grounds only. The village itself is attractive, and the Roebuck has good-value food; the nearby village of Arrow is interesting to stroll around (despite some development) – as is the pretty stream that divides the two. Fruit farming around here is much rarer than it used to be, but you can still find delicious fresh dessert plums for sale in Sept. The county's best drive (partly in Gloucs) circles Alcester via Walcote, Aston Cantlow, Wilmcote, Temple Grafton, Wixford, Radford, Inkberrow, Holberrow Green, New End and King's Coughton.

ARBURY SP3388

🏠🕷️ **Arbury Hall** (off B4102 just S of Nuneaton) Splendid-looking place, the original Elizabethan house elaborately spruced up in the 19th c to make it one of the best examples of the Gothic Revival style. The writer George Eliot was born on the estate, and her *Mr Gifgil's Love Story* describes some of the rooms – not unreasonably comparing the dining room to a cathedral. Some work by Wren in the stables (now housing a collection of vintage cycles), and the gardens are a pleasure. Meals, snacks, shop, limited disabled access; open pm Sun and bank hols Easter–Sept; (024) 76382804; £4.50, £2.50 gardens only.

ARDENS GRAFTON SP1253

! **Doll & Toy Collection** (Golden Cross Inn) Unusually decorated with over 250 antique dolls, teddies and toys. Small shop, decent food; open licensing hours (cl 3–6pm), cl 25–26 Dec.

ARMSCOTE SP2444

★ Picturesque Cotswold stone village with a nice pub.

ASHBY CANAL SP3688

🛶 Canal towpaths offer some of Warwickshire's nicest walks, and heading off into the Leics countryside from its junction with the Coventry Canal at Marston Junction, on the edge of Bedworth, this canal has perhaps the prettiest of them.

ASHORNE SP3057

🕷️ 👃 ! 🚂 **Nickelodeon** (Ashorne Hall, off B4100) Unique collection of mechanically played musical instruments inc self-playing harps, drums and violins, and a vintage theatre, complete with organ rising from the floor (demonstrated daily at 4.15pm). They show silent comedies and 1950s Pathé newsreels, and have various nostalgic tea concerts and events. There's a miniature railway in the grounds (£1.80 extra). Meals, snacks, shop, disabled access; open pm Sun Mar–Nov, plus Fri July–Aug, and maybe other days too – worth checking; (01926) 651444; *£6.80. The Cottage has good-value food (may cl wkdy lunchtime).

ASTON CANTLOW SP1461

★ † Charming timbered houses and guildhall, lovely **church** where Shakespeare's parents married, and a fine old pub.

AUSTREY SK2906

★ Attractive village with black and white timbered houses and cottages, some thatched.

BADDESLEY CLINTON SP2072

🏠🕷️ † **Baddesley Clinton House** Romantic 13th-c moated manor house, mostly unchanged since the 17th c. Interesting portraits, priest's holes and garden with chapel and pretty walks. The family history is intriguing. Meals, snacks, shop, some disabled access; house open pm Weds–Sun and bank hols Mar–Oct (shop and restaurant open till Christmas), grounds open same days mid-Feb–mid-Dec; (01564) 783294; £5 (timed ticket system), grounds only £2.50; NT. The nearby **church** has a lovely east window, and the canalside Navigation at Lapworth and prettily set Cock Horse at Rowington do decent food.

BICKENHILL SP2083

🏍️ **National Motorcycle Museum** 🅿️ (Coventry Rd) Handy for the NEC, 5 halls displaying over 650 gleamingly restored motorcycles, all British.

Incongruously, they also have the biggest theatre organ in Europe. Meals, snacks, shop, disabled access (not to restaurant); cl 24–26 Dec; (01675) 443311; £4.50. The White Lion at Hampton in Arden has good-value food.

BIRMINGHAM SP0786

The city has masses of things to see and do. It has a long heritage despite its mainly modern centre, and a rich and varied industrial history taking in everything from guns to chocolate buttons. Reputedly there are more canals here than in Venice, and redevelopment of old canal buildings is bringing a lively new focus to the Gas St/Brindley Pl area. However, the city centre doesn't really have the overall appeal which would encourage long stays. So Birmingham's strength is as a place for enjoyable day trips, particularly at weekends – the formidably efficient traffic system which ploughs through its heart makes it easy to penetrate from outside. The city has had a dearth of decent pubs, but now has enough to keep visitors happy, especially around the canal area: Flapper & Firkin (Cambrian Wharf), Tap & Spile (Brindley Wharf), James Brindley (Gas St Basin) and Malt House (Brindley Pl), with the newish Fiddle & Bone (Sheepcote St), owned by 2 members of the City of Birmingham Symphony Orchestra, the current favourite.

Aston Hall Aston, 2m NE of centre) Strikingly grand Jacobean mansion with a panelled long gallery, balustraded staircase and magnificent plaster friezes and ceilings. Snacks, shop, disabled access to ground floor; cl am, and all Nov–Easter; (0121) 327 0062; free (and more satisfying than a good many houses you'd have to pay for).

Barber Institute of Fine Arts (Birmingham University) Excellent collection of paintings and sculptures, well housed in a very attractive gallery; just the right size to be enjoyable without being overwhelming. Quite a lot of Impressionist works as well as European masters. Shop, disabled access; cl am Sun, 24–26 Dec, 1 Jan, Good Fri; (0121) 472 0962; free. The university (marked out by its huge clock tower) is on the outer fringes of Edgbaston, a couple of miles S of the city centre. This area developed as a smart residential part of town, where industry and commerce gave way to parks and greenery, much of which still remains.

Birmingham Museum & Art Gallery (Chamberlain Sq) Perhaps the best collection of Pre-Raphaelite paintings anywhere, plenty still looking as brilliantly, almost shockingly, fresh and detailed as when they were first painted. Other notable paintings too, and lots of coins and archaeology – one of the first two dozen museums to make the Heritage Secretary's new shortlist of excellence and national importance. Meals, snacks, shop, disabled access; cl am Sun, 5 days over Christmas; (0121) 303 2834; free. Local boy Burne-Jones, a leading light in the Pre-Raphaelite movement, was responsible for 4 stunning windows in **St Philip's Church** on Colmore Row nearby, since 1905 the city's cathedral. The Old Contemptibles (Edmund St) is a useful nearby Edwardian pub, quite striking in its own right.

Birmingham Nature Centre (Pershore Rd) British and European animals in indoor and outdoor enclosures designed to resemble natural habitats. Snacks, shop, disabled access; cl wkdys Nov–Mar; (0121) 472 7775; *£1.50.

Birmingham Railway Museum (Warwick Rd, Tyseley; A41 3m SE) Working railway museum with fully equipped workshop, steam locomotives, and several historic carriages and wagons. Trains run along a short track, but you can ride on them only in summer, usually first Sun of the month. Meals and snacks, shop, limited disabled access; cl wkdys exc bank hols, and 25–26 Dec and 1 Jan; (0121) 707 4696; £2.50.

Botanical Gardens (Westbourne Rd, Edgbaston) Outstanding: 15 acres featuring a tropical house (with lily pool, bananas and cocoa), palm house, orangery, a national collection of bonsai, cactus house and the gardens themselves, filled with rhododendrons and azaleas and a goodly collection of trees. Bands play on summer Sun and bank hol pms. Meals, snacks, shop, disabled access; cl 25 Dec; (0121) 454 1860; £4.20, £4.50 summer Suns.

🏛☺! **Cadbury World** (Bournville) Attached to the Cadbury factory, this hugely enjoyable place is ideal for anyone who's ever had a taste for chocolate, with all you could ever want to know about how it's made and marketed. Obviously there's something of a corporate bias (you could be forgiven for thinking nobody else has ever made chocolate apart from the Aztecs and the Cadburys), but the displays and exhibitions have been put together with great verve. You visit a production area, with demonstrators hand-making and decorating luxury chocolates, and the packaging plant where the more standard bars are wrapped and packed. Children enjoy the alternative view of chocolate-making offered by Mr Cadbury's Parrot at the Fantasy Factory, as well as Cadabra, a jolly ride through an imaginative chocolate-themed world in a car shaped like a cocoa bean. Older visitors get nostalgic watching TV adverts for Cadbury's products from the last 40 years (some from overseas), and there's a collection of period wrappers displayed in a 1930s-style sweet shop. Elsewhere cars and climbing frames are disguised as Creme Eggs (and a slide as a box of Roses), and there are plenty of samples to satisfy the cravings created by the sumptuous smells. You'll need to book in advance to be sure of getting in; on popular days tickets can be sold out well in advance. Restaurant and picnic areas, good shop (some bargains and unusual varieties), mostly disabled access; open daily Mar–Oct, and usually wknds and at least a couple of other days Nov–Feb, so best to phone; (0121) 451 4180; £6.50.

🖼 **Ikon Gallery** (Oozells Sq) Vibrant modern art in a stunningly converted school building. Meals, snacks, shop, disabled access; cl Mon and bank hols; free.

🏛 **Museum of the Jewellery Quarter** (Vyse St) Birmingham is still Britain's biggest producer of gold jewellery, if not as important to the jewellery trade as it used to be. This excellent centre is built around the perfectly preserved workshops of the Smith & Pepper company, still much as they were at the start of the 20th century. There's a good overview of the industry, as well as tours of the factory and demonstrations of jewellery-making techniques. Snacks, shop, disabled access; cl Sun; (0121) 554 3598; £2.50. Around 100 jewellery shops nearby, so useful for browsing or repairs. The Rosevilla has decent food.

♪ **National Sea Life Centre** (Water's Edge, Brindley Pl) Very much the flagship of the excellent Sea Life Centre chain that we recommend in quite a few resorts around the country. The hi-tech displays are both fun and instructive, with around 3,000 native British marine and freshwater creatures shown off in careful re-creations of their natural habitats; also a themed soft play area and a reconstructed *Titanic* wreck. The highlight is a walk-through tube designed to create the impression of walking along the sea bed, with sharks, rays and other creatures swimming above, alongside and beneath you. Norman Foster designed the building. Meals, snacks, shop, disabled access; cl 25 Dec; (0121) 633 4700; £7.50.

✗ **Sarehole Mill** (Hall Green, 3m SE of city centre) Working 18th-c watermill, with several displays explaining the milling process. Tolkien often came here as a child. Limited disabled access; cl am, and Nov–Mar; (0121) 777 6612; free. Other local sites that influenced Tolkien are listed on a leaflet available at information centres.

🏛👶🧺♿ **Selly Manor Museum** (Maple Rd, A441 4m S) When the Cadbury family moved their factory out of the city centre in 1879, part of their plans for this new garden suburb involved uprooting timber-framed manor houses from elsewhere and re-erecting them here; 2 survive as this museum, with a herb garden, crafts and various exhibitions. Snacks, shop, disabled access to ground floor only; open Tues–Fri, plus bank hols and wknds Apr–Sept, best to phone for winter opening; (0121) 472 0199; £1.50.

🏛👶 **Soho House** Elegant former home of Matthew Boulton, famous for his development of the steam engine with James Watt, and possibly the first centrally heated house in England since Roman times. Furnished in 18th-c style with Boulton-related displays. Snacks, shop, disabled access; cl am Sun, and all day Mon (exc bank hols); (0121) 554 3598; *£2.50.

CASTLE BROMWICH SP1489

🏵 **Castle Bromwich Hall Garden** (Chester Rd) Carefully restored 18th-c formal gardens, with authentic collection of period plants, inc ancient vegetables as well as herbs and shrubs. Snacks, plant sales, disabled access; cl am, all day Mon and Fri, and Nov–Mar, plus wkdys in Apr; (0121) 749 4100; *£3.

CHARLECOTE SP2656

🏠 🏵 **Charlecote Park** 250 acres of parkland, full of deer (Shakespeare is said to have poached them from here), along with the descendants of reputedly the country's first flock of Jacob sheep. Well furnished Great Hall and Victorian kitchen, and an impressive Tudor gatehouse. Two bedrooms and a dressing room in the North Wing should be open by June, and new gardens, designed by Sir Edmund Fairfax Lucy, should be ready by April. Meals, snacks, shop, disabled access; open Fri–Tues Apr–Oct (cl Good Fri); (01789) 470277; £4.90; NT. By the park is a charming little 19th-c village of timbered cottages, and a show Victorian church. The Boar's Head in pretty Hampton Lucy has decent food.

CLIFFORD CHAMBERS SP1952

★ Pretty black and white timbered houses and cottages, and a Tudor former rectory which has some claim to being the true birthplace of Shakespeare.

COUGHTON SP0860

🏠 🏵 **Coughton Court** (A435) Several priest's holes are hidden in this mainly Elizabethan house, renowned for its imposing gatehouse and beautiful courtyard; the Throckmortons have lived here since 1409. Notable furniture and porcelain, and an exhibition on the Gunpowder Plot, with a lake, 2 churches, pleasant walks, formal gardens and play area in the grounds. Meals, snacks, shop, plant sales, limited disabled access; open wknds mid-

Mar–mid-Oct, plus Weds–Fri Apr–Sept, bank hols (exc Good Fri), and Tues in Aug, also closed some summer Sats, best to phone; (01789) 462435; £6.25, £4.50 grounds only; NT. The Green Dragon on the fine old green at nearby Sambourne and the interesting Old Washford Mill at Studley are good for lunch.

COVENTRY SP3379

Like Birmingham, more a place to dip into than to fix on as your base for a short holiday. Its most interesting street is Spon St, with one or two ancient buildings that started their lives here and others that have been rescued from elsewhere and rebuilt here (the picturesque Old Windmill does cheap basic lunches). One of the town's most famous inhabitants was Lady Godiva, commemorated best by the Coventry Clock – where she pops out in the pink every hour. The Royal Court Hotel, Greyhound out at Sutton Stop (Alderman's Green/Hawkesbury) and Prince William Henry and William IV (both Foleshill Rd – authentic Indian) are popular for lunch.

✝ **Coventry Cathedral** (Priory Row) Bombed during the war, the old cathedral ruins have been carefully preserved, and parts of it such as the 14th-c tower remain intact. These have been joined by the new cathedral designed by Sir Basil Spence. It is, perhaps quite rightly, in no way an orthodox church building, but is worth a look for its unusual modern art (inc windows by John Piper, tapestry by Graham Sutherland, even holograms); the visitor centre (cl Sun) has more, as well as a full history of its development. Meals, snacks, shop, disabled access; cl 4 days in July and Nov for degree ceremonies; £2 suggested donation, £1.25 for visitor centre.

♨ 🖼 **Herbert Art Gallery & Museum** (Jordan Well) Fine silver and furniture, Chinese art, and a lively interactive history of the city. Meals, snacks, shop, disabled access; cl am Sun, and Christmas wk; (024) 76832381; free. Browns café-bar nearby serves good food all day.

🏠 **Lunt Roman Fort** (Coventry Rd) Fun reconstruction of 1st-c Roman fort, interesting to see such a site in all

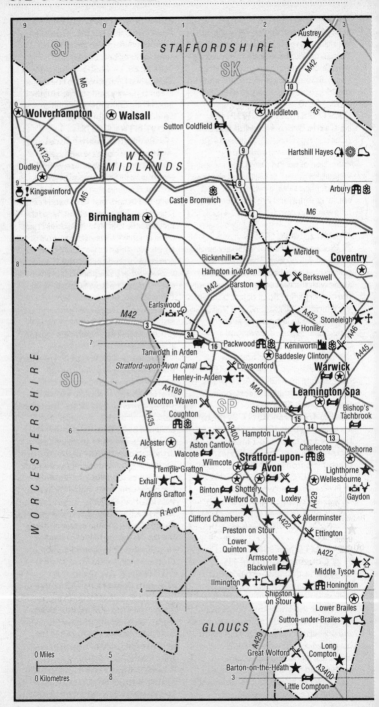

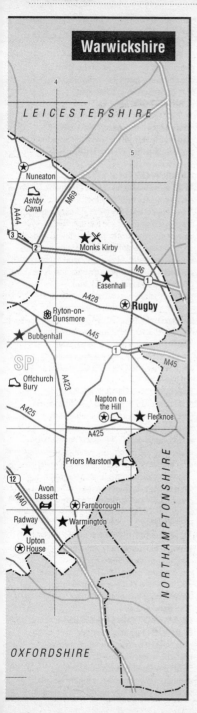

its glory. Good interpretive displays. Shop, some disabled access; open wknds and bank hols Easter–Oct, plus daily May half-term and late July–mid-Sept; (024) 76832381; £1.80.

✝ **Midland Air Museum** (Coventry Airport) Displays of civil and military aircraft spanning more than 70 years. Snacks, shop, disabled access; cl 25–26 Dec; (024) 76301033; £3.25.

🏛 **Museum of British Road Transport** (St Agnes Lane) Big collection of motor cars (the industry developed here as an offshoot of sewing-machine production), as well as commercial vehicles and bicycles, and die-cast models. Snacks, shop, disabled access; cl Christmas wk; (024) 76832425; free.

🏛 **St Mary's Guildhall** (Bayley Lane) Very well preserved medieval building, with its minstrels' gallery still, and some Flemish tapestries; it's usually open Easter–Sept (exc Fri and Sat), provided there aren't any civic functions, but best to check; (024) 76832381.

🧸 **Toy Museum** (Much Park St) Toys from 1740 to 1990, housed in a 14th-c monastery gatehouse. Shop; cl am, and 25 Dec; (024) 76227560; £1.50.

DUDLEY SO9591

🛥 ☺ ♨ **Black Country Living Museum** See *separate family panel on p.667.*

🧸 🖼 **Dudley Museum & Art Gallery** (St James's Rd) Some fine paintings, well displayed geology, and appealing temporary exhibitions. Shop, disabled access but no facilities; cl Sun and bank hol Mon, Christmas and New Year; (01384) 815575; free.

🐾 🐘 **Dudley Zoo** 🖼 (The Broadway) Based around an impressive **ruined castle**, so the animals enjoy rather special views. Meals, snacks, shop, disabled access; cl 25 Dec; (01384) 215300; £6.50.

⛴ **Tunnel boat trips** The Dudley Canal Trust do boat trips along part of a unique network of canal tunnels and limestone mines. Trips Mar–Nov, and some days in Dec – best to ring for times; (01384) 236275; £2.70.

EARLSWOOD SP1074

🌳 🏛 **Manor Farm Craft Workshops** (Wood Lane) Furniture restoration, stained glass, print-making, needlework, a vintage car display, and farm shop with home-made ice-cream. Meals, snacks, shop, disabled access; cl Mon, Christmas wk; (01564) 702729; free. The canalside Bluebell and the Red Lion (past the lakes) are useful dining pubs.

EXHALL SP1055

★ ⌂ Pretty black and white timbering, and some pleasant gently hilly walks nearby; very quiet, as no through road.

FARNBOROUGH SP4349

🏛☗▣ ❀ **Farnborough Hall** Palladian villa filled with splendid sculptures, paintings and fine rococo plasterwork; the staircase, hall and 2 main rooms are on show. The 18th-c landscaped gardens have a couple of ornamental temples, and views from the terrace walk – less impressive than they were thanks to the arrival of the M40. Disabled access to ground floor only; open pm Weds and Sat Apr–Sept, terrace also open pm Thurs and Fri; (01295) 690002; £3, £1.50 terrace walk only; NT. The Butchers Arms nearby is useful.

GAYDON SP3354

🏯 ⅄ **Heritage Motor Centre** ▣ (Banbury Rd) Busy centre with the world's biggest collection of historic British cars – 300 in all, starting with an 1895 Wolseley. Also hundreds of drawings, photographs, trophies and models, hi-tech displays and video shows, and a nature reserve. The design of the building is incredible, especially inside. Meals, snacks, shop, disabled access; cl 24–26 Dec, 1 Jan; (01926) 641188; £5.50. The Malt Shovel is handy for lunch.

HARTSHILL HAYES SP3194

🐸 ❊ ⌂ Country park with mixed woodland, opening out at the top for broad views towards the Peak District. The Coventry Canal below allows more extended rambles.

HENLEY-IN-ARDEN SP1565

★ ✝ More small town than village, but a pretty conservation area, with good churches. The Blue Bell and the White Swan, both handsome, have decent food.

HONILEY SP2472

★ The village has virtually gone now, and there are only vestiges of the big house, but you can still sense the

vanished settlement around the surviving 18th-c church.

HONINGTON SP2642

★ 🏛 Attractive village, its church prettily set on the edge of the lawn of the charming late 17th-c Honington Hall (open pm Weds Jun–Aug).

ILMINGTON SP2143

★ ✝ ⌂ Quietly attractive village, with a peaceful path to a partly Norman church, lovely inside; pleasant walks on the hills above; the Howard Arms is good for lunch.

KENILWORTH SP2772

🏰 ❀ **Kenilworth Castle** Dramatic castle transformed by John of Gaunt into a spectacular fortress. These are among the finest castle ruins in the country, with a still impressive keep and several other buildings within the sandstone walls. Also a restored Tudor garden, various re-enactments and open-air plays and operas, and children's activities most summer hol wknds. Shop, disabled access (but no facilities); cl 24–26 Dec, 1 Jan; (01926) 852078; £3.10; EH. The town itself has a Norman church and some pleasant strolls, especially around the castle area, where the Queen & Castle has decent food.

KINGSWINFORD SO8888

☗ **Broadfield House Glass Museum** (Barnett Lane) Excellent collection of glass from nearby Stourbridge, displayed to dazzling effect. Clever use of lighting shows off the exhibits quite spectacularly, and even the audio-visual shows create a sense of excitement. One of the area's least expected treasures. Teas, shop; cl Mon (exc bank hols), 24–28 Dec, 1 Jan; (01384) 812745; free.

❗ **Crooked House** (off B4176 E of Himley) Extraordinary pub bent by mining subsidence into a three-dimensional optical illusion that'll have you imagining things roll uphill here, instead of down; perhaps surprisingly, it's a good pub too.

LEAMINGTON SPA SP2864

🏛 ❀ ▣ ☗ Elegant spa resort popularised by the rich who came to take the waters in the 18th and 19th c. Still many fine Regency buildings, though today the town is better seen as a civilised shopping centre, and perhaps as a base for sallies into the surrounding countryside – or into Warwick, across the River Avon. Beautifully laid-out **Jephson Gardens** (The Parade) are worth a look, with wild ducks on the lake. The adjoining **Royal Pump Rooms** have been restored and now house an art gallery, museum and café. The Carpenters Arms (Chandos St) is a decent well restored early Victorian pub.

LONG COMPTON SP2932

★ This pleasant Cotswoldy village of thatched stone houses has some antique shops; the Red Lion has good food.

LOWER BRAILES SP3139

★ † ✷ Attractive Cotswold-edge village with lovely slender-spired **church**, pretty stone houses, good views, and a nice old inn.

MERIDEN SP2482

★ A cross on the green marks what the village feels is the centre of England – one of the streams rising in the village pond ends up in the Severn and the other over in the Humber. The Bull's Head does good-value food.

MIDDLE TYSOE SP3344

★ ⌂ ✗ Charming village – with a very traditional cottage bakery. The walk S from Upper Tysoe over Windmill Hill (which does have a windmill) takes you to the church on the edge of Compton Wynyates park, giving views of the attractive Tudor manor – a refreshing bit of brick building in this Cotswold-edge stone country.

MIDDLETON SP1797

🐖 **Ash End House Farm** (off A4091) Friendly farm set up specifically for children; animals from shire horses to baby chicks and fluffy ducklings, as well as rare breeds of goats, pigs and sheep. A pony ride is included in the price, and there's plenty under cover for wet days. Snacks, shop, disabled access; cl 25–27 Dec, 1 Jan; (0121) 329 3240; £3.60 children (adults half price).

🏰 ✿ ✿ ❧ ⚘ **Middleton Hall** (A4091) Varied architecture in the house, also a nature reserve, walled gardens, orchards and woodland, and a new play area later this year. There's a good craft centre in the stables. Snacks, shop, some disabled access; house open pm Sun and bank hols Apr–Sept, craft

centre open all year exc Mon and Tues; (01827) 283095; £2. The Green Man is a decent family dining pub.

NAPTON ON THE HILL SP4661

★ ⌂ ✷ Attractive village on a rounded hill above a curve in the Oxford Canal – perhaps the prettiest canal in this part of the world, with pleasant towpath walks. Great views of seven counties from the hill.

🐖 ⌂ **Church Leyes Farm** ▣ Friendly 40-acre family-run organic farm with animals, walks and wild-flower conservation headlands by the hedges. Meals, snacks, shop, disabled access with prior notice; cl Sat, and Jewish holy days; (01926) 812143; *£1.

NUNEATON SP3691

🖼️▣⚘ **Nuneaton Museum & Art Gallery** (Coton Rd) Nicely set in colourful Riversley Park, with display on George Eliot; cl am Sun, all day Mon (exc bank hols), and Christmas; (024) 76350720; free. Good craft centre nearby. The central Felix Holt has decent food all day.

OFFCHURCH BURY SP3565

⌂ Attractive riverside parkland, with a pleasant walk winding through from the Stag's Head.

PACKWOOD SP1772

🏰 ✿ **Packwood House** ▣ (off A34) Friendly old house with origins as a 16th-c farmhouse, carefully restored and not at all commercialised; interesting panelling, furniture and needlework, and in the garden unusual yew trees clipped to represent the Sermon on the Mount. Snacks, shop, some disabled access; open pm Weds–Sun and bank hols Apr–Oct, gardens open from Mar; (01564) 782024; £4.60, garden only £2.20; NT. The Navigation by the canal at Lapworth has good-value food.

PRIORS MARSTON SP4857

★ ⌂ Attractive old houses around the village green, and unusual blue brick paths; the ancient Holly Bush is a decent pub. There's a walk up Marston Hill behind, and quite a good network of paths around nearby Priors Hardwick taking you down to the Oxford Canal. The old drovers' Welsh Road through here via Southam to Cubbington is a pleasant drive; just before Offchurch it crosses the remarkable Fosse Way, a quiet Roman road running dead straight from Brinklow through Stretton-on-Dunsmore and Princethorpe down to Halford.

RUGBY SP5074

🏛️⛲ **Rugby School** Founded in 1567, moving to its current site nearly 200 years later. A **museum** on Little Church St looks at its history and former pupils, such as Rupert Brooke and Lewis Carroll. Shop, disabled access; cl am, all day Sun and Mon, and 2 wks at Christmas; (01788) 574117; £1.50. Guided tours of the school buildings leave here at 2.30pm (not Sun or Mon), and other times by arrangement; (01788) 573959; £3, or £4 combined ticket with museum.

🎫 **Gilberts** (St Matthew's St) The game the school invented is commemorated at this shop, that's been making the standard rugby ball since 1842. You can watch them do it, and there are related displays and collections. Shop, some disabled access; cl Sun and a few days over Christmas; (01788) 333888; free. The Three Horseshoes Hotel not far off in Sheep St is useful for lunch.

RYTON-ON-DUNSMORE SP3874

🏵️ **Ryton Gardens** (Wolston Rd, off A45) Home of the Henry Doubleday Research Association, the organic farming and gardening organisation, landscaped with thousands of organically grown plants and trees; herb garden, rose garden, garden for the blind, and shrub borders among the displays, as well as some free-range farm animals and a cook's garden where all of the plants are edible. A garden dedicated to the late Geoff Hamilton opened last year. Very good meals and snacks in the wholefood café, shop, disabled access; cl Christmas wk; (024) 76303517; £2.50 (usually less in winter).

SHIPSTON ON STOUR SP2540

★ Small town with quite a busy shopping centre, but also rewarding to stroll through, with a good church and a good few handsome old stone buildings, antique shops among them. The Black Horse (Station Rd) has interesting food.

SHOTTERY SP2055

🏛️🕸️🌿 **Anne Hathaway's Cottage** A substantial thatched Tudor farmhouse, the home of Anne Hathaway until her marriage to William Shakespeare. Displays of domestic life during the period, and colourful cottage garden. Snacks, shop; cl 23–26 Dec; (01789) 292100; £3.90. There's a craft centre next door, and the Bell is handy for something to eat away from the tourists.

STONELEIGH SP3271

★ ✝ Though primarily known as the showground for the Royal Show, with an increasing number of permanent displays, the village itself has an attractive sandstone Norman **church**, timber-framed houses, and Stoneleigh Abbey which should be restored by the end of the year.

STRATFORD-UPON-AVON SP2055

Visitors who look at the town just as a town can be disappointed, but if you have a grounding in Shakespeare's plays the interesting buildings seem that bit more interesting – and not so outnumbered by the workaday ones, the overpriced antique shops and the gift shops. The gardens by the River Avon make a memorable setting for the Memorial Theatre. If you're looking

---

Days Out

Black Country heritage: Broadfield House Glass Museum, Kingswinford; lunch at the Crooked House, Himley; Black Country Living Museum, Dudley.

Birmingham gems: Birmingham Railway Museum; Museum of the Jewellery Quarter; lunch at the Rosevilla (Vyse St); Cadbury World.

Machine aesthetics: Heritage Motor Centre, Gaydon; lunch at the King's Head, Wellesbourne; watermill there (limited opening); Nickelodeon, Ashorne.

forward to a good production at the theatre that evening, or, better still, able to run through much of the verse in your head, then you'll love Stratford. But if you've always thought Shakespeare overrated, then you'll think the same about Stratford, too. The pub with the most theatrical Shakespeare connections is the Mucky Duck, or more properly White Swan (Southern Way) – traditionally where the RSC actors and actresses drink; the Arden Hotel has the closest bar to the Memorial Theatre, with good snacks. Useful places for lunch include the Brasserie (Henley St), quaint old Garrick (High St), Vintner Wine Bar (Sheep St) and Slug & Lettuce (Guild St/Union St). Tea in the smart Shakespeare Hotel (Chapel St) is relaxing. Ghost tours around Stratford's more chilling historic places depart from the Country Artist's Fountain (in front of the Royal Shakespeare Theatre) at 3.30pm, 5.50pm and 7.30pm Apr–Sept, other times by appointment; £4.

꙳ ! Butterfly Farm & Jungle Safari (Tramway Walk) Cascading waterfalls and tropical forests, with up to 1,500 exotic butterflies flying free in a re-created jungle habitat. There's an incredible collection of spiders and insects. Shop, disabled access; cl 25 Dec; (01789) 299288; *£3.75.

🏠 🏵 Hall's Croft (Old Town) Lovely gabled Tudor home of Dr John Hall, who married Shakespeare's daughter; good displays on the medicine of the time, Elizabethan and Jacobean furniture, and a walled garden. Teas, shop, disabled access to ground floor; cl 23–26 Dec; (01789) 292107; £3.30.

🏠 Harvard House (High St) Late 16th-c home of the mother of the man who founded Harvard University – no direct connection with Shakespeare, but a striking example of houses of his day. Shop; the house may be closed throughout the year due to restoration work, so best to phone; (01789) 204507; free.

† Holy Trinity Church (Waterside) 15th c, where Shakespeare was baptised and buried; cl am Sun and for services; 70p to enter the chancel where the grave is.

♨ ! National Teddy Bear Museum (Greenhill St) Delightfully displayed, furry friends of all shapes and sizes – mechanical and musical ones, ones that belonged to famous people, and some that are famous themselves. Shop; cl 25–26 Dec; (01789) 293160; £2.25.

🏠 🏵 New Place/Nash's House (Chapel St) Shakespeare died here in 1616; the house was destroyed in the 18th c, but the Elizabethan knot garden remains, and the adjacent house, former home of the writer's granddaughter, has a good collection of furniture and local history. Shop, disabled access to ground floor and gardens only; cl 23–26 Dec; (01789) 292325; £3.30.

☺ Ragdoll (Chapel St) They make children's TV programmes like *Teletubbies* and *Tots TV*; the ground floor of their HQ has a shop, play areas and plenty to amuse small children, they can even talk to their favourite Teletubby on the phone. Disabled access; cl am Sun, 25–26 Dec, 1 Jan; free.

♨ ! Royal Shakespeare Theatre (Waterside) Shakespeare's plays are of course still performed here by the Royal Shakespeare Company. You can sometimes book guided tours of their main theatre (usually at 1.30pm, 5.30pm, and after evening performances; best to phone as they quickly get booked up); the gallery with temporary exhibitions is likely to close soon. Meals, snacks, shop, disabled access; cl am Sun, 24–25 Dec; (01789) 296655; £2 for gallery, tours £4. The RSC productions themselves are performed in repertory, so if you're in the area a few days it's quite possible to see several. Advance booking is recommended – (01789) 295623 – though 100 tickets are kept back for each performance and sold on the day from 9.30am; don't leave it much later, they go pretty fast.

🏠 Shakespeare's Birthplace (Henley St) Though there's no guarantee the playwright really was born here, there are interesting period features, and good interpretative displays. Shop; cl 23–26 Dec; (01789) 204016; £4.90. If you want to see all the Shakespearian properties it makes sense to buy a joint ticket which costs

£11, and covers this, New Place, Hall's Croft, and the Shottery and Wilmcote sites (which all open the same hours). You can also buy tickets covering just the 3 in-town sites for £7.50. A tour bus with commentary links the sites but costs another £8.

☛ ♦ Shire Horse Centre & Farm Park (Clifford Rd – B4632 S) Parades and demonstrations of the huge horses, as well as goats, pigs, rare breeds, owl sanctuary with falconry displays, adventure playground, and a new theatre with cinema and displays about the horses. Readers rate this very highly. Good meals and snacks, shop, disabled access (can be a bit bumpy); cl Thurs and Fri Nov–Feb, and 25 Dec; (01789) 415274; £4.95.

STRATFORD-UPON-AVON CANAL SP1867
◩ This gives some pleasant towpath walks; the Fleur de Lys at Lowsonford is a good start.

SUTTON-UNDER-BRAILES SP3037
★ ◩ Attractive stone-built village, with some pleasing Cotswold countryside around it – good walks.

TANWORTH IN ARDEN SP1270
☛ Umberslade Children's Farm
Friendly family-run farm with animals to stroke and feed, and play areas for letting off steam. Also nature trails and walks, and a goat-milking area. Snacks, shop, disabled access; cl Nov–mid-Mar and usually some wkdys Oct; (01564) 742251; £3.

UPTON HOUSE SP3745
◪ ▦ ★ The exceptional art collection is the main draw here, an enormous range of paintings inc works by Bosch, El Greco, Bruegel and Hogarth, all sensibly arranged and displayed. Also Brussels tapestries, Sèvres porcelain, and woodland and terrace walks. The late 17th-c house was remodelled in the the 20th c. Teas, shop, disabled access; open pm Sat–Weds Apr–Oct (cl Good Fri); (01295) 670266; £5.20, garden only £2.60; NT. There's a timed ticket system at peak periods. Nearby, Ratley itself is a pretty village, with a lovely church and good home cooking in the Rose & Crown; and the Castle on Edge Hill is a very interesting place for lunch, with terrific views.

WALSALL SP0099
✿ ⚓ **Birchills Canal Museum** (Top Lock, Old Birchills) Small museum with a replica boat cabin, and maybe **boat trips**; shop; open pm Thurs–Sun, and am Tues and Weds, 25–26 Dec and 1 Jan; (01922) 645778; free.

◔ **Jerome K Jerome Birthplace Museum** (Bradford St) Dedicated to the life and work of the author of *Three Men in a Boat*, with a reconstructed 1850s parlour; phone for opening times; (01922) 653116; free.

▣ **Walsall Art Gallery** (Lichfield St) This imaginative £21 million building is a landmark West Midlands millennium project, already being referred to as a classic piece of modern architecture by some critics. It houses an impressive collection of 20th-c European art inc Epstein drawings and paintings, and lots of effort has been put in to make it appealing to all ages and tastes. There's a children's interactive gallery, temporary exhibitions of contemporary art and a street-level artist's workshop, so that passers-by can watch work in progress. Meals, snacks, shop, disabled access; cl Mon; (01922) 653116; free.

▩ **Walsall Leather Museum** (Wisenmore) Well restored 19th-c leather goods factory with tours of aromatic workshops and leather-making demonstrations (not Sun). Meals, snacks, shop (lots of local leather goods), disabled access; cl am Sun, all day Mon (exc bank hols), Easter Sun, 24–26 Dec, 1 Jan; (01922) 721153; free. The Hammakers Arms (Shaw St/Blue Lane) does good-value food.

WARWICK SP2864
★ Though many older buildings survived a major fire in 1694, today's centre is dominated by elegant Queen Anne rebuilding. Some of the oldest structures are to be found around Mill St, which is very attractive to stroll along; there are a good few antique and other interesting shops. The Rose & Crown (Market Pl) is the best pub here; the Saxon Mill (Guys Cliffe) is a prettily placed waterside family dining pub, and the Warwick Arms Hotel does good-value teas.

◔ **Doll Museum** (Castle St) Half-timbered Elizabethan house with comprehensive collection of antique dolls and toys. A fun video shows the exhibits come to life. Shop, limited disabled access; cl all Nov–Easter exc Sat; (01926) 412500; £1.

🏛 **Lord Leycester Hospital** (High St) Delightfully wonky half-timbered building built in 1383, still used as a home of rest for retired servicemen. Fine old guildhall, candlelit chapel, gatehouse and courtyard, and garden with Norman arch and a 2,000-year-old urn from the Nile. Snacks (summer only), shop, disabled access to ground floor only; cl Mon, Good Fri, 25 Dec; (01926) 491422; *£2.95.

🏵 **Mill Garden** Delightful series of plantings in a super setting on the river beside the castle – very nice to stroll through, with plenty of old things to look at along the way. Disabled access; open Easter–mid-Oct; (01926) 492877; *£1.

🏛 **St John's House** (St John's) 17th-c house with exhibits from the county museum, and several room reconstructions. They plan considerable refurbishment over the next year so best to check opening times. Shop, disabled access to ground floor only; cl 12.30–1.30pm, all day Sun (exc pm Apr–Sept), and Mon (exc bank hols) and Christmas wk; (01926) 410410; free.

✝ 🏵 **St Mary's Church** (Old Sq) Splendid medieval church on the town's highest point, with a Norman crypt, chapter house and magnificent 15th-c Beauchamp chapel; in summer you can go up the tower which has excellent views – small admission charge.

🏛 🏵 🏵 **Warwick Castle** (Castle Hill) One of the country's most splendid castles and certainly the most visited. It's a lively place, with plenty for children to enjoy (especially in summer). Several displays showing the influence of the Tussaud's group who own the site, but purists shouldn't be put off by the gloss or waxwork figures; the rooms are excellently preserved, and their fine furnishings and art well worth braving the crowds for. The marvellous grounds were designed by Capability Brown, and as well as delightful gardens have pleasant strolls along the banks of the River Avon; the

views from the parklands are dramatic, stirring stuff. Meals, snacks, shop, disabled access to grounds only; cl 25 Dec; (01926) 406600; £10.50 (£6.25 children). A family ticket (2 adults and 2 children) is £28. All prices are slightly reduced out of high season.

🏛 **Warwickshire County Museum** (Market Pl) In the 17th-c Market Hall, with lots of fossils, and a Sheldon tapestry map of the county. Shop, disabled access to ground floor; cl Sun exc May–Sept, 25–26 Dec; (01926) 410410; £1.

WELLESBOURNE SP2653

✚ **Wartime Museum** Housed in the underground HQ of a former RAF base, a collection of aeronautical archaeology and wartime memorabilia, with a restored Vampire. Shop, some disabled access (not underground); open Suns only; £1.50. The King's Head is a decent pub.

✗ 🌣 **Wellesbourne Watermill** (B4086) Historic watermill still producing flour in secluded rural setting, with striking wooden wheel. Helpful staff, nature trails and traditional crafts. Snacks, shop, some disabled access (there are steep steps); open Fri–Sun Apr–Sept, maybe other times outside summer, best to phone; (01789) 470237; £3.

WILMCOTE SP1658

🏛 🐓 🐎 **Mary Arden's House** The picturesque home of Shakespeare's mother, with the barns given over to countryside memorabilia. Daily falconry displays, and rare breeds. Snacks, shop, some disabled access; cl 23–26 Dec; (01789) 293455; £4.40. The Masons Arms has decent food.

WOLVERHAMPTON SJ9400

🏛 Not really a town for visitors, though its **museum** (Lichfield Rd) is a good one. Wightwick Manor and Moseley Old Hall right out on the outskirts are splendid.

🏛 🏵 **Moseley Old Hall** 🖼 (Featherstone, off A460/A449 4m N) Tudor house famed as a hiding place for Charles II after the Battle of Worcester. The façade has altered since, but the furnishings and atmosphere in its panelled rooms don't seem to have changed much, and there's a 17th-c knot garden. Readers particularly enjoy the guided tours. Teas, shop, limited disabled access; open pm wknds and all day bank hol Mons Apr–Oct, plus pm Weds from Jun, pm Tues July–Aug, and pm Suns Nov–Christmas; (01902) 782808; £3.90; NT.

🏛️ 🖼️ ❀ **Wightwick Manor** (just off A454, 3m W) Only a century old, but beautifully and unusually designed by followers of William Morris, and a fine testimonial to the enduring qualities of his design principles. Flamboyant tiles, fittings, furnishings and glass, and lots of Pre-Raphaelite art, cannily acquired while it was unfashionable. Also period garden with yew hedges and topiary. Snacks, shop, some disabled access; open pm Thurs, Sat and bank hol wknds, Mar–Dec, garden also open Weds; (01902) 761108; *£5.40, £2.40 garden only.

★ **Other attractive villages**, almost all with decent pubs, include Barston SP2078, Barton-on-the-Heath SP2532 (no pub), Berkswell SP2479 (pretty Norman church), Bubbenhall SP3672, Easenhall SP4679, Flecknoe SP5164, Hampton in Arden SP2081, Hampton Lucy SP2557, upmarket Lighthorne SP3355, Lower Quinton SP1847, Monks Kirby SP4683 (huge church), Preston on Stour SP2049, Radway SP3748 (we've had no pub recommendation here yet), Temple Grafton SP1255 (Shakespeare's 'Hungry Grafton'), Warmington SP4147 and Welford on Avon SP1452.

🛶 **Canals** give some of the county's best walking opportunities. Besides places already mentioned, useful canalside pubs include the Black Boy and Herons Nest at Knowle SP1876, the Waterman at Hatton SP2467 (by a flight of locks), the Navigation at Lapworth SP1670, the Anchor at Leek Wootton SP2868, Two Boats at Long Itchington SP4164 (the flight of Stockton Locks just E usually has plenty going on), Wharf Inn SP4352 (A423 Banbury–Southam), Bull's Head at Wootton Wawen SP1563, and Dog & Doublet at Bodymoor Heath SP2096 (useful for the Kingsbury Water Park too). There are pleasant walks by the **River Avon** from the Cottage of Content at Barton SP0950, which has day fishing tickets.

Where to eat

ALDERMINSTER SP2348 **Bell** *(01789) 450414* Popular and rather civilised dining pub nr Stratford, with excellent imaginative food using fresh local produce (no fried food), several communicating areas with flagstones and wooden floors, fresh flowers, good wines, real ales, obliging service, and no smoking restaurant; cl evenings 24 Dec–2 Jan; disabled access. **£21|£6.95.**

ASTON CANTLOW SP1359 **King's Head** *(01789) 488242* Carefully restored and beautifully timbered Tudor pub with a massive inglenook fireplace and flagstones in the comfortable village bar, an old-fashioned snug, a gently upmarket atmosphere, good often inventive food in the carpeted main room, cheerful service, well kept ales, and decent wines; close to Mary Arden's house in Wilmcote. **£23.15|£8.**

BERKSWELL SP2479 **Bear** *(01676) 533202* Handsomely refurbished 16th-c timbered pub with a relaxed atmosphere, comfortable snug low-beamed areas, nooks and crannies, beams and panelling, bric-à-brac, well kept ales, decent house wines, and a wide choice of food inc interesting daily specials; seats on the back lawn. **£18|£6.25.**

ETTINGTON SP2749 **Chequers** *(01789) 740387* Welcoming restaurant with comic hunting scenes in the carpeted lounge, spacious conservatory, imaginative Mediterranean-style food served by charmingly attentive bow-tied waiters, real ales on handpump, an extensive wine list, no smoking area, and seats in the neat back garden. **£19.50|£6.**

GREAT WOLFORD SP2434 **Fox & Hounds** *(01608) 674220* Inviting 16th-c inn with a good mix of locals and visitors in the cosy low-beamed old-fashioned bar, candlelit tables, flagstones and a roaring log fire, really enjoyable imaginative daily specials, over 200 malt whiskies, and a little tap room with several changing real ales; cl Sun evening, Mon. **£17.50|£6.50.**

KENILWORTH SP2871 **Time for Tea** *40 Castle Hill* (01926) 512765 Charming and very popular tearoom with pine furnishings and a collection of teapots and tea caddies, a conservatory, delicious home-made cakes and scones, a choice of teas, and a cheerful atmosphere; cl Mon and Tues (open Tues during school summer hols); disabled access. £2.20.

LOWSONFORD SP1867 **Fleur de Lys** *(01564)* 782431 Bustling canalside pub with a comfortable civilised atmosphere, smart spreading bar with lots of low black beams, open fires, good food, well kept real ales, and decent wines by the glass; cl 25 Dec; children in dining room only. **£19|£7.**

MONKS KIRBY SP4682 **Bell** *Bells Lane* (01788) 832352 Busy pub with warmly chatty Spanish landlord, timbered and flagstoned rambling rooms, cheerful locals, marvellous tapas (Spanish hors d'oeuvres) as well as more usual bar food, an extensive wine list, well kept real ales, and quite a few whiskies; cl am Mon, 26 Dec, 1 Jan; disabled access. **£25|£4.50.**

STRATFORD-UPON-AVON SP2054 **Benson's** *4 Bards Walk* (01789) 261116 Close to Shakespeare's birthplace, this light and airy tearoom has lots of plants and flowers, neatly dressed staff, papers and magazines to read, a wonderful patisserie, a marvellous choice of teas and coffees (plus Pimms, buck's fizz and kir), and breakfasts, morning coffee, lunches, and afternoon tea; no smoking; disabled access. **£15|£4.50.**

STRATFORD-UPON-AVON SP2054 **Opposition** *13 Sheep St* (01789) 269980 Small bustling restaurant with a friendly atmosphere, generous helpings of very good interesting food – handy for theatres and open for after-show meals; cl 25 Dec, evening 26 Dec. **£20|£5.95.**

STRATFORD-UPON-AVON SP2054 **Russons** *8 Church St* (01789) 268822 Cheerful and popular bistro in 17th-c malt house with very good imaginative food (plenty of fresh fish) and good-value simple wine list; pre-theatre meals, too; cl Sun, Mon, 1 wk Christmas–New Year, 1 wk May, 2 wks Aug; **£24.50|£5.95.**

STRATFORD-UPON-AVON SP2055 **Slug & Lettuce** *38 Guild St* (01789) 299700 Cheerfully friendly and popular, with good food, helpful staff, well kept real ales, decent wine, an attractive bar with open fire and newspapers, and a pretty back terrace. **£24|£8.50.**

WOOTTON WAWEN SP1563 **Bull's Head** *(01564)* 792511 Charming old black and white timbered building with a heavy-beamed bar, low-ceilinged lounge with huge upright timbers, handsome restaurant, generous helpings of good often unusual food from a sensibly short menu, notably friendly young staff, several wines by the glass, well kept beer; handy for walks by the Stratford Canal; cl 25 Dec; children over 8. **£22.50|£8.**

Special thanks to Joseph P Stachura, A Fairgrieve, Mrs M Coffer, Judith Benney.

Warwickshire Calendar

Some of these dates were provisional as we went to press. Please check information with the telephone numbers provided.

JANUARY

18 **Kenilworth** Antiques Fair at National Agricultural College, Stoneleigh Park (01636) 702326

MARCH

7 **Atherstone** Shrovetide Football: hundreds of locals gather for the game in the Main St (01827) 716410
9 **Alcester** Crufts Dog Show at the NEC – *till 12 March* (01625) 573477
14 **Kenilworth** Antiques Fair at National Agricultural College, Stoneleigh Park (01636) 702326
25 **Alcester** Craft Fair at Ragley Hall – *till 26 March* (01789) 762090

APRIL

15 **Alcester** Gardeners' Weekend at Ragley Hall – *till 16 April* (01789) 762090
23 **Stratford-upon-Avon** Shakespeare Birthday Celebrations: procession and birthday lunch – *till 30 April* (01789) 204016
30 **Kenilworth** National Kit Car Show at National Agricultural College, Stoneleigh Park – *till 1 May* (01775) 712100

MAY

6 **Solihull** Festival – *till 13 May* (0121) 7046130
13 **Kenilworth** Amateur Spring Gardening Show at National Agricultural College, Stoneleigh Park – *till 14 May* (024) 7669 6969
20 **Kenilworth** Antiques Fair at National Agricultural College, Stoneleigh Park (01636) 702326
27 **Coventry** Godiva Festival – *till 6 June* (024) 76832303

JUNE

1 **Charlecote Park** Family Day (01789) 470277; **Coventry** Mystery Plays (024) 76832303
4 **Solihull** Carnival (0121) 7046130
17 **Gaydon** Thirty Years of the Range Rover at Heritage Motor Centre – *till 18 June* (01926) 645042; **Leamington Spa** Peace Festival – *till 18 June* (01787) 281855; **Ryton-on-Dunsmore** Organic Gardening Weekend at Ryton Gardens – *till 18 June* (024) 76303517
21 **Coventry** International Church Music Festival – *till 24 June* (0121) 7046130
24 **Warwick** Carnival (01926) 411020
25 **Alcester** Music from the Movies at Ragley Hall (01789) 762090

JULY

1 **Kenilworth** Carnival (01926) 852595; **Warwick** Warwick and Leamington Festival – *till 15 July* (01926) 410747

Warwickshire Calendar (cont.)

3 Kenilworth Royal Show at National Agricultural College, Stoneleigh Park – *till 6 July* (024) 76696969

AUGUST

5 Alcester Fireworks Concert at Ragley Hall (01789) 762090; **Himley** Dudley Show at Himley Park – *till 6 August* (01905) 763436
19 Alcester Warwicks and West Midlands Game Fair inc arena events, military bands at Ragley Hall – *till 20 August* (01588) 672708
26 Kenilworth Town and Country Festival at National Agricultural College, Stoneleigh Park – *till 28 August* (024) 76696969

SEPTEMBER

1 Alcester Firework Concert at Ragley Hall (01789) 762090

OCTOBER

13 Stratford-upon-Avon English Music Festival – *till 22 October* (01789) 261561

We welcome reports from readers

This *Guide* depends on readers' reports. Do help us if you can – in return, we offer a discount on the next edition to people who've helped us with reports for it. Tell us what you think about places already in it, and anything extra you think we should say about them. And send us your ideas for inclusion in the next edition: places to visit, eat at or stay in, attractive drives or walks, maybe even unusual interesting shops you know of. Use the card in the middle, the report forms at the end, or just write – no stamp needed: *The Good Britain Guide*, FREEPOST TN1569, Wadhurst, E Sussex TN5 7BR.

WILTSHIRE

Great appeal to older people, but plenty for children too.

Salisbury is a splendid small city for a short civilised break, with a lovely cathedral precinct and interesting places to visit tucked quite closely around it. Other major draws here are beautifully landscaped Stourhead, Wilton House and Lacock. Castle Combe is exceptionally pretty, and Bradford-on-Avon, Devizes, Marlborough and Malmesbury are attractive small towns with a good deal of character. Prehistoric sites abound here. The great stone circles of Stonehenge and Avebury are best appreciated at quiet times of day, out of season.

Longleat is a superb family day out. Children also like the farms at Cholderton and Teffont Magna, and the story-book ruins of Old Wardour Castle near Tisbury.

The steam museum in Swindon has some striking improvements for the new century.

The most appealing countryside is along the valleys of the southern chalk streams – intimate scenery with stone or flint houses and sparkling rivers now recovering after recent dry summers. The northern part of the county has some quietly attractive drives and walks, especially around Marlborough.

Where to stay

BRADFORD-ON-AVON ST8261 **Bradford Old Windmill** *4 Masons Lane, Bradford-on-Avon BA15 1QN (01225) 866842* ***£69;** 3 rms, one with a giant waterbed, another with a round bed. Interesting and carefully converted windmill with a log fire in the attractive circular lounge (former grain store), lots of books, a friendly atmosphere; good evening meals inc vegetarian dishes from Thailand, Nepal, Mexico and so forth, and fine breakfasts eaten around a communal refectory table; pretty cottagey garden; no smoking; cl Jan and Feb; children over 6.

BRADFORD-ON-AVON ST8359 **Widbrook Grange** *Trowbridge Rd, Widbrook, Bradford-on-Avon BA15 1UH (01225) 864750* **£105;** 19 pretty rms, many in carefully converted courtyard cottages. Handsome stone former farmhouse in 11 acres, with comfortable drawing rooms, good food in the elegant dining room, a sunny conservatory, and an indoor swimming pool and exercise machines; cl New Year; disabled access.

BRADFORD-ON-AVON ST8361 **Woolley Grange** *Woolley Green, Bradford-on-Avon BA15 1TX (01225) 864705* ***£105,** plus winter breaks; 23 rms, with fruit and home-made biscuits. Civilised Jacobean manor house with a relaxed and informal atmosphere, lovely flowers, log fires and antiques in the comfortable and beautifully decorated day rooms, and a pretty conservatory; delicious food using local (or home-grown) produce, often organic, inc home-baked breads and muffins and home-made jams and marmalades for breakfast, marvellous staff, and very good for children – nursery with full-time nanny, games room, their own sort of food, and outdoor toys; swimming pool, tennis and croquet.

CALNE ST9871 **Chilvester Hill House** *Chilvester Hill, Calne SN11 0LP (01249) 813981* **£80;** 3 charming spacious rms. Big Victorian house with neat gardens and grounds, particularly helpful friendly owners, comfortable sitting rooms with antiques, good breakfasts and honest no-choice dinners around a large table in the separate dining room (using home-grown produce), and plenty of local sights; children over 12 (babies allowed).

CASTLE COMBE ST8477 **Manor House** *Castle Combe, Chippenham SN14 7HR (01249) 782206* **£231,** plus special breaks; 45 lovely rms, some in mews cottage. 26 acres of garden and parkland, inc an Italian garden, around a 14th-c manor house with gracious day rooms, panelling, antiques, log fires and fresh flowers; a warm friendly atmosphere, and very good innovative food; 18-hole golf course, croquet, boules, and all-weather tennis court; disabled access.

CHICKSGROVE ST9729 **Compasses** *Lower Chicksgrove, Tisbury, Salisbury SP3 6NB (01722) 714318* **£45;** 2 rms with showers. Lovely thatched house in delightful hamlet, with old bottles and jugs hanging from the beams, home-made food, well kept real ales, and a peaceful farm courtyard and garden.

COLERNE ST8272 **Lucknam Park** *Colerne, Chippenham SN14 8AZ (01225) 742777* **£180,** plus special breaks; 41 luxurious rms. Noble Georgian house reached by a long beech-lined drive through extensive grounds, with elegant carefully furnished day rooms, a panelled library, lovely flowers, antiques and paintings, and excellent food and extremely good service in the charming restaurant; leisure spa with an indoor swimming pool, gym, beauty salon, hairdresser, snooker and floodlit tennis courts; croquet; equestrian centre; children over 12 in evening restaurant; disabled access.

CORSHAM ST8770 **Methuen Arms** *High St, Corsham SN13 0HB (01249) 714867* **£65,** plus special breaks; 24 rms. Georgian inn (former nunnery) with mullioned windows and heavy oak beams in 14th-c part, comfortable seats in the neatly kept bar, good food and friendly staff; pretty walled garden and fine skittle alley; disabled access.

CROCKERTON ST8642 **Springfield House** *Crockerton, Warminster BA12 8AU (01985) 213696* ***£54,** 3 rms with garden views. 17th-c house on the edge of Longleat Estate, with tennis in the garden, beams, flowers and open fires, dinner by the inglenook fireplace in candlelit dining room, and lots to do nearby; cl Christmas.

CRUDWELL ST9592 **Crudwell Court** *Crudwell, Malmesbury SN16 9EP (01666) 577194* **£88;** 15 big, homely rms. 17th-c former rectory in grounds with walled garden, swimming pool and pond, airy drawing room, relaxed reading room, enjoyable dinner-party style food in the panelled restaurant, afternoon tea, and friendly staff.

DEVIZES SU0061 **Bear** *Market Pl, Devizes SN10 1HS (01380) 722444* **£80,** plus special breaks; 24 rms. Very much at the town's heart, this 16th-c inn has an old-fashioned feel, a wide choice of food from snacks to more elaborate meals served in the oak-panelled Lawrence room, 2 more formal restaurants, beams and fresh flowers, and prompt service; cl 25–26 Dec.

DOWNTON SU1821 **Warren** *15 High St, Downton, Salisbury SP5 3PG (01725) 510263* ***£48;** 5 rms with fresh flowers, 2 with own bthrm. Friendly 15th-c house with lots of beams and antique furnishings, a lounge with open fire, helpful staff, and enjoyable breakfasts in a lovely oak-panelled room with French windows on to a big walled garden; cl Christmas; children over 5.

EASTON GREY ST8987 **Whatley Manor** *Easton Grey, Malmesbury SN16 0RB (01666) 822888* **£132,** plus special breaks; 29 rms with antique furniture, 18 in main house, 11 in Court House across courtyard (which are cheaper). Lovely Cotswold manor house in quiet gardens with riverside paddocks, and tennis court, swimming pool, croquet lawn, putting green, billiards, sauna, solarium and Jacuzzi; spacious and rather fine oak-panelled drawing room, a pine-panelled lounge, log fires, a relaxed atmosphere, lots of books in the library-bar, and an attractive dining room overlooking the garden; partial disabled access.

EBBESBOURNE WAKE ST9924 **Horseshoe** *Ebbesbourne Wake, Salisbury SP5 5JG (01722) 780474* **£50;** 2 rms. Particularly welcoming pub with a beautifully kept little bar, an open fire, fresh flowers and interesting bric-à-brac on beams, popular home-made food in the bar or no smoking restaurant, big breakfasts and nice Sun lunches, well kept real ales, pretty little garden, and pets corner in paddock; cl 25 Dec.

FORD ST8374 **White Hart** *Ford, Chippenham SN14 8RP (01249) 782213* **£79;** 11 rms. Very well run, popular and attractive ivy-covered inn in a lovely spot by a trout stream, with old-fashioned atmosphere, heavy black beams, a big woodburner in the ancient fireplace, particularly good imaginative food, well kept real ales, malt whiskies and fine wines, attentive cheerful service, and secluded small swimming pool.

GASTARD ST8867 **Boyds Farm** *Gastard, Corsham SN13 9PT (01249) 713146* **£42,** plus special breaks; 3 rms, 1 with own bthrm. Friendly and handsome 16th-c house on family-run working farm with pedigree Herefords; homely lounge, woodburner, traditional breakfasts; no evening meals (local pubs nearby); cl Christmas.

GRITTLETON ST8679 **Church House** *Grittleton, Chippenham SN14 6AP (01249) 782562* *****£58.50,** plus winter breaks; 4 big comfortable rms. Large Georgian rectory on the edge of a lovely village, in 11 acres of gardens and pasture with a heated indoor swimming pool and croquet; a relaxed and friendly house-party atmosphere, open fire, antiques and paintings in the drawing room, very good imaginative food using organic home-grown vegetables and fruit (advance notice required), and breakfasts with their own eggs; children under 1 and over 12; lots to do nearby.

HEYTESBURY ST9242 **Angel** *High St, Heytesbury BA12 0ED (01985) 840330* **£49;** 3 comfortable rms. Beautiful little 16th-c coaching inn with armchairs, sofas, and a good fire in the cosy homely lounge, a long beamed bar with a woodburner, quite a few prints, good service from friendly staff, well kept real ales, decent wines, and a wide choice of consistently good food in the charming back dining room opening on to a secluded garden.

HINDON ST9132 **Lamb** *High St, Hindon, Salisbury SP3 6DP (01747) 820573* **£70,** plus special breaks; 13 rms. Solidly built, welcoming and civilised old inn (once a smugglers' haunt) with log fires in the fine old bar, attractive lounges, imaginative food, friendly helpful service, and a no smoking restaurant.

LACOCK ST9168 **At the Sign of the Angel** *Church St, Lacock, Chippenham SN15 2LB (01249) 730230* **£90,** plus special breaks; 10 charming rms. This fine 15th-c house in a lovely NT village is full of character, with heavy oak furniture, beams and big fireplaces, a restful oak-panelled lounge, and good English cooking in 2 candlelit restaurants; cl Christmas; disabled access.

MALMESBURY ST9387 **Old Bell** *Abbey Row, Malmesbury SN16 0AG (01666) 822344* **£95,** plus special breaks; 32 rms. With some claim to being one of England's oldest hotels and standing in the shadow of the Norman abbey, this fine wisteria-clad building has traditionally furnished rooms with Edwardian pictures, an early 13th-c hooded stone fireplace, 2 good fires, cheerful helpful service, and an attractively old-fashioned garden; very good for families – they have a children's den supervised by nursemaids, baby-sitting/listening service, and thoughtful food.

MILDENHALL SU2168 **Fisherman's House** *Mildenhall, Marlborough SN8 2LZ (01672) 515390* *****£50;** 4 lovely rms, 1 with own bthrm. Extremely pretty house with lawns running down to the River Kennet, fresh flowers and stylish furniture, friendly owners, and good breakfasts in the airy conservatory; cl Christmas; children over 12.

NETTLETON ST8377 **Fosse Farmhouse** *Nettleton Shrub, Nettleton, Chippenham SN14 7NJ (01249) 782286* *****£125,** plus special breaks (inc some interesting craft wknds); 5 rms. 18th-c Cotswold stone house extensively restored with decorative French antique furniture and pretty English chintzes; morning coffee, lunch and afternoon cream teas served on the lawns or in the very attractive dining room; antique shop with dried flowers and decorative items in the former dairy behind the house.

PURTON SU0987 **Pear Tree** *Church End, Purton, Swindon SN5 9ED (01793) 772100* *****£95;** 18 very comfortable, pretty rms. Impeccably run, former vicarage with elegant comfortable day rooms, fresh flowers, a fine conservatory restaurant with good modern English cooking using home-grown herbs, and 7½ acres of grounds inc a traditional Victorian garden; cl 26–30 Dec; disabled access.

SALISBURY SU1430 **Farthings** *9 Swaynes Close, Salisbury SP1 3AE (01722) 330749 *£44;* 4 rms, some with own bthrm. Spotlessly kept no smoking house with friendly owners, good breakfasts, and a pretty garden; nr cathedral; no children.

SALISBURY SU1329 **Old Mill** *Town Path, Salisbury SP2 8EU (01722) 322364* **£80,** plus special breaks; 11 comfortably converted rms. Based on Wiltshire's first paper mill and warehouse – there's been a mill here since 1135, terrace out by the mill pool, and meadow walks with classic cathedral views; good honest English cooking in evening restaurant, where the mill race rushes through, and beamed bar.

SALISBURY SU1428 **Rose & Crown** *Harnham Rd, Salisbury SP2 8JQ (01722) 399955 *£130,* plus special breaks; 28 rms in the original building or smart, modern extension. It's almost worth a visit just for the view – well-nigh identical to that in the most famous Constable painting of Salisbury Cathedral; elegantly restored inn with a friendly beamed and timbered bar, log fire, good bar and restaurant food, and a charming Avonside garden; disabled access.

SALISBURY SU1431 **Stratford Lodge** *4 Park Lane, Salisbury SP1 3NP (01722) 325177 *£60,* plus special breaks; 8 rms. Warmly friendly and relaxed Victorian house with antique furnishings, fresh flowers, generous helpings of very good carefully prepared evening food, super breakfasts in conservatory, and quiet garden; cl 25 Dec–1 Jan; children over 5; limited disabled access.

SUTTON VENY ST9041 **Old House** *Sutton Veny, Warminster BA12 7AQ (01985) 840344* **£68;** 3 rms. Carefully modernised 17th-c thatched house in 4 quiet acres, winter log fires, nice food using home-grown vegetables, and good breakfasts; cl Christmas/New Year; children by arrangement.

TEFFONT EVIAS ST9931 **Howards House** *Teffont Evias, Salisbury SP3 5RJ (01722) 716392 *£125,* plus special breaks; 9 rms. Very well run, welcoming and comfortable little hotel in 2 acres of gardens surrounded by quiet countryside; log fire and lots of fresh flowers from the garden in a restful sitting room, delicious food (using their own vegetables and herbs), fine breakfasts, particularly good wines, and extremely good service; cl Christmas.

UPPER MINETY SU0091 **Flisteridge Cottage** *Flisteridge Rd, Upper Minety, Malmesbury SN16 9PS (01666) 860343 *£45;* 3 rms, 1 with own bthrm. Warmly welcoming and homely cottage with a pretty garden, and a woodburner in the sitting room, good breakfasts with home-made preserves (evening meals by arrangement), and friendly helpful owners; children over 11; well behaved pets by arrangement.

WARMINSTER ST8943 **Bishopstrow House** *Borham Rd, Bishopstrow, Warminster BA12 9HH (01985) 212312* **£175,** plus special breaks; 32 sumptuous rms, some with Jacuzzi. Charming ivy-clad Georgian house in 27 acres with heated indoor and outdoor swimming pools, indoor and outdoor tennis courts, fitness centre and beauty treatment rooms, and own fishing on River Wylye; very relaxed friendly atmosphere, log fires, lovely fresh flowers, antiques and fine paintings in boldly decorated day rooms, and really impressive food; disabled access.

WARMINSTER ST8744 **Old Bell** *Market Pl, Warminster BA12 9AN (01985) 216611* **£58,** plus special breaks; 20 refurbished rms. Old-world country-town hotel with traditional bar food, bistro and restaurant, good choice of wines, pretty central courtyard, and friendly service; lots to do nearby.

WEST GRAFTON SU2459 **Rosegarth** *West Grafton, Marlborough SN8 3BY (01672) 810288 *£40;* 2 rms. Charming 16th-c thatched and half-timbered cottage in 3-acre garden, with a comfortable lounge, good breakfasts, friendly owners, and a big garden; cl Christmas/New Year; no children.

WINSLEY ST7960 **Burghope Manor** *Winsley, Bradford-on-Avon BA15 2LA (01225) 723557* **£80;** 6 rms. Lovely 13th-c manor house in attractive countryside, with carefully preserved old rooms and an interesting fireplace engraved with Elizabethan writing, antiques in the big drawing room, welcoming caring owners, nice breakfasts, and evening meals by arrangement; wknd self-catering in Dower House in grounds; cl Christmas/New Year; children over 10.

WOOTTON BASSETT SU0783 **Marsh Farm Hotel** *Wootton Bassett, Swindon SN4 8ER (01793) 848044* **£50w;** 38 rms. Handsome Victorian farmhouse in landscaped grounds with particularly warm and friendly atmosphere, comfortable lounge, convivial bar, and enjoyable food in the relaxed restaurant; disabled access.

To see and do

WILTSHIRE Family Attraction of the Year

🐖 🐝 🐇 **CHOLDERTON** SU2042 **Cholderton Rare Breeds Farm** 🏫
(Amesbury Rd, just off the A338) Though Longleat draws the crowds, this rather smaller animal attraction is just as good a bet for families with young children: it's a fun place, friendly and well laid out, with plenty of opportunities to get close to the animals. A long-standing favourite with visitors is their pig racing (or National Grunt Racing as they call it), twice a day at wknds and in school hols, usually around 12.30pm and 3.30pm). They're also particularly strong on rabbits, with nearly 60 breeds on show in spacious undercover pens; there are always younger rabbits for children to stroke, and it's fascinating seeing all the different varieties. Other animals to pet include pygmy goats and sheep, and wandering around you'll come across friendly residents, Hannah the shire horse, Coco the donkey, and Ebenezer the goat (actually Ebenezer II). They do tractor and trailer rides, and pony rides for children. The grounds are attractive, with tranquil carp-filled watergardens, and nature trails through orchards and woodland; on a clear day you can see the spire of Salisbury Cathedral 10 miles away. Plenty of pretty picnic spots. Rare breeds include a herd of Exmoor ponies, and there are a couple of play areas, one specifically for under-7s. They recently added a small aviary, and have plans to extend the watergardens. Lots under cover (inc the sheep unit) and always plenty going on – families stay here for anything between 2 hours and a whole day. They don't like you to feed the animals with anything other than their own feed; it's on sale in the gift shop. Meals and snacks (good cream teas), shop, disabled access; cl Nov–Mar; (01980) 629438; *£4.25 (£2.75 children). A family ticket is *£13.

ALTON BARNES SU1061
△ ¥ ⋔ **Kennet & Avon Canal** Here the canal lies close enough to **Pewsey Down nature reserve** for an afternoon's walk to incorporate both features; the spine of the downs here is followed by the Wansdyke, an ancient earthwork which runs across the downs for miles from Morgan's Hill nr Calne nearly as far as the Savernake Forest.

ANSTY ST9526
★ Pleasant village, notable for England's tallest maypole.

AVEBURY SU1070
♂ **Alexander Keiller Museum** Interesting, with an important collection of archaeological finds from the area. Shop, disabled access; cl 24–26 Dec, 1 Jan; (01672) 539250; £1.70; NT.
⋔ ★ **Avebury Stone Circle** This spectacular ancient site shares its setting with the pretty village – where Stones does good vegetarian food, and the Red Lion's position within the circle makes it special too. It's the largest stone circle in Europe, the 200 stones enclosed in a massive earthen rampart nearly a mile in circumference. One of Avebury's main draws has always been the free and open access to the stones, but the number of visitors is beginning to take its toll – it would be a tragedy if this ultimately proved the site's downfall.
⋔ **West Kennett Avenue** Leading away from the circle is this imposing 1½-mile avenue of stones – a good stretch has been restored.
⋔ 🕈 **West Kennett Long Barrow** The prehistoric remains of a 5,000-year-old chambered tomb and barrow,

where several dozen people were buried – take a torch if you want to venture in behind the massive entrance stone: the chamber with 2 side chapels runs some 9 metres (30ft) or more into the barrow. The Waggon & Horses at Beckhampton (of *Pickwick Papers* fame) is quite handy.

🏛 **Windmill Hill** Neolithic enclosure on a slight rise a mile or so N of the stone circle.

BARBURY CASTLE SU1476

🏛 △ One of Wiltshire's 4,500 recorded ancient sites. Many are scarcely a lump in the ground, but this Iron Age camp at the northernmost point of the Marlborough Downs, splendidly remote and atmospheric, still has formidable ramparts. There is a car park nearby, but you can also walk up to it from Ogbourne St George along Smeathe's Ridge, a preserved stretch of downland (gorse and all). The Castle is on the long-distance Ridgeway Path.

BISHOPS CANNINGS SU0364

★ † Attractive village, with an outstanding **church**. The Crown has good-value food.

BOX ST8268

★ An attractive up-and-down village, its interesting parts hidden down the steep valley below the A4, with cottages and houses using the same stone that's been quarried nearby since Roman times. There's a story that on 9 Apr, Brunel's birthday, the rising sun shines right through the great railway tunnel he quarried through the hill above here (you can see the restored grand entrance from the A4).

🌺 † **Hazelbury Manor** (off B3109 just E) Richly varied landscaped gardens, recently restored, with a medieval archery alley, stone and yew circles, fountain, waterfall, pond, large rockery, formal areas and laburnum walk, all laid out as a sort of giant maze. Open by appointment, (01225) 812952; £2.80. In Chapel Plaister on the way, look out for the 15th-c chapel for Glastonbury pilgrims on the little hilltop green. The Quarryman's Arms tucked away on Box Hill is good for lunch.

BRADFORD-ON-AVON ST8260

★ † 🏛 Attractive hillside town given a distinguished air by the same sort of golden stone as was used in Bath; it's very steep, and has some handsome buildings reflecting its past wealth as a wool town – and quite a few serious antique shops. Nr the Norman parish church is a tall narrow late **Saxon church**, unusual for having virtually no later additions. The Dandy Lion (Market St) is good for lunch. A medieval **tithe barn** can be seen at nearby Barton Farm down by the river and canal, its massive stone-slab roof supported by an impressive network of great beams and rafters.

△ **Avoncliff** A short walk along the canal, this quite steep gorge is shared by canal, river and railway, the canal disdainfully stepping over the river by way of an aqueduct. The Cross Guns has remarkable views over it, and is a good place for lunch.

🌺 **Iford Manor** (just past Westwood) Notable for its stylish Edwardian Italianate riverside terraced garden, well liked by readers, with romantic cloisters, colonnade and statues; house not open. Teas wknds and bank hols, May–Aug; open pm Sun and bank hols Apr–Oct, and pm daily (exc Mon and Fri) May–Sept; (01225) 863146; £2.50.

🏠 🌺 **Westwood Manor** (above Avoncliff, just SE) Fully furnished 15th-c stone manor house with its original Gothic and Jacobean windows, fine 17th-c plasterwork, and modern topiary garden. Open pm Sun, Tues and Weds Apr–Sept; (01225) 863374; £3.60; NT. The New Inn in Westwood village has decent food, and the church has some interesting late medieval stained glass.

BROKERSWOOD ST8352

🍴 🌳 🚂 **Woodland Heritage Museum** 80 acres of woodland, with lakes, campsites, conservation displays, summer guided walks, an adventure playground, and a little railway. Snacks, shop; park open daily; (01373) 823800; £2.50. The Woolpack at Beckington has good food.

BROMHAM ST9464

🐷 **Sandridge Farm** They cure bacon and Wiltshire ham using traditional recipes; also summer nature trail through woodland and pig paddocks (wellies recommended). Shop (good bacon and sausages), disabled access; cl Sun; (01380) 850304; free. The

Greyhound in the village has good food, especially fish.

CALNE ST9770

❀ ⌂▣⌂ **Bowood** (off A4) The extensive Capability Brown parkland and colourful pleasure gardens are the glory of Bowood, with their temples, cascades and hermit's cave shielded from the outside world by further miles of partly wooded grounds; in May and Jun a woodland garden is open for rhododendron walks. Much of the main building was demolished in 1955, but there's plenty left, inc the impressive library designed by Robert Adam. There's an excellent collection of English watercolours, and an outstanding adventure playground. Joseph Priestley discovered oxygen here in 1772. Meals, snacks, shop, garden centre, limited disabled access; cl Nov–Mar; (01249) 812102; £5.50. The Lansdowne Arms at Derry Hill, nr the house, is popular for lunch, and Calne also has a **motor museum**.

CASTLE COMBE ST8477

★ † ⌂ For many the prettiest village in Britain, this has a classic group of stone-tiled Cotswoldy cottages by the turreted **church** at the bottom of a tree-clad hill running down to a trout stream and its ancient stone bridge. Preservation of the village is taken so seriously that you won't even see television aerials on the houses. Several villagers open their beautifully kept gardens for charity the last wknd of June. Best of all during the week out of season; at other times it does get a great many visitors, even though the car park is sited some way up the hill. The charming old Castle Inn has good food. The village has surroundings that are equally appealing, and attractive paths along deep peaceful valleys.

CASTLE EATON SU1495

★ ⌂ Attractive village, by a quiet stretch of the upper Thames, pleasant for strolling.

CHERHILL DOWN SU0469

⌂ ⌂ This large NT area of ancient downland has free access for walkers. A range of man-made features of various periods adorn its slopes, inc a figure of a white horse, an Iron Age hillfort (Oldbury Castle), the mid-19th-c Lansdowne Monument, and an assortment of long barrows, tumuli and ancient field systems; the site is rich in chalkland flora such as orchids, and associated butterfly and bird life.

CHICKSGROVE ST9730

★ ⌂ Charming tucked-away hamlet; peaceful walk to Sutton Mandeville church, and back by the Nadder Valley.

CHILMARK ST9732

★ † Attractive village, with a decent partly 13th-c **church**. The Black Dog does interesting food.

CHOLDERTON SU2042

🐖 ❀ ⌂ **Cholderton Rare Breeds Farm** See separate family panel on p.688.

CLEY HILL ST8344

⌂ ⌂ ❀ This steep-sided hill just W of Warminster involves a short, puffy stroll to the Iron Age hill fort at its summit, looking across Longleat Park.

CORSHAM ST8770

⌂▣ ❀ † **Corsham Court** Fine house and park begun in 1582 but subsequently added to and developed by these busy masters Capability Brown, John Nash, Robert Adam and Humphrey Repton. The paintings are among the best at any stately home in the country, inc works by Caravaggio, Reynolds, Rubens and Van Dyck. In the gardens, the peaceful lake and a Georgian bath-house are patrolled by a number of peacocks – if they haven't decided to wander off into the village. Shop, disabled access; cl am, Mon (exc bank hols), wkdys mid-Oct–late Mar and all Dec; (01249) 701610; £4.50. Nearby there are some attractive former weavers' cottages; the **church**, on the edge of the park, is largely 12th c, partly Saxon. The town has a surprising number of antique shops, some very fine, and the Methuen Arms is good for lunch.

CRANBORNE CHASE ST9319

⌂ In the S of Wiltshire, some of the finest walking is to be found here close to the Dorset border, where the county's abundant chalk downland shows at its best. A good example is **Ashcombe Bottom** N of Tollard Royal, a deep remote valley which plunges into the heart of the Chase.

CRICKLADE SU1093

† ⌄ Small town quietly separated from the busy A419, with some attractive

buildings and a glorious tower crowning the fine parish **church**. At the end of the High St, just N of the Thames, a path on the left off the slip road heading back towards the A419 leads to a broad **riverside meadow** kept unimproved for decades, and mown only in July after the numerous wild flowers have seeded. The Vale and White Hart have popular food.

CROFTON SU2662

⚙★✕ **Crofton Beam Engines** 🖼 Still pumping water into the Kennet & Avon Canal, the oldest working beam engines in the world, an 1812 Boulton & Watt, and an 1845 Harveys of Hayle. Snacks, shop; open Easter–Sept, engines usually static, but in steam bank hols and last wknds of June and July; (01672) 870300; static £2, steam wknds £3.50. Nearby Wilton village is picturesque, with a windmill; the Swan here is good for family lunches, and the Harrow at Little Bedwyn has good food.

DEVIZES SU0061

⚱ Lots of grand old buildings in this interesting and friendly town, and a good town trail takes most of them in. The 29 locks of the Kennet & Avon Canal coming up Caen Hill from the W form one of the longest flights of locks in the country. The headquarters of the Canal Trust on the Wharf has a **museum** and information centre; (01380) 729489; £1.50. The Bear Hotel, Elm Tree and Castle, all tied to Wadworths the local brewery, are all friendly places and good for lunch with reasonably priced food.

🌼 **Broadleas** (Potterne Rd) Rare plants in secluded dell among rhododendrons and other fine flowering shrubs, unusual trees, spring and autumn colour too. Teas Sun, unusual plant sales; open pm Sun, Weds and Thurs, Apr–Oct; (01380) 722035; £3.

⚱🖼 **Devizes Museum** (Long St) First-class local history, particularly good on finds from the area's ancient sites (the Bronze Age gallery is especially interesting); art gallery with John Piper window. Shop, some disabled access (to be improved soon); cl Sun, bank hols, Christmas; (01380) 727369; £2 (free on Mons).

DINTON SU0031

🏚🌼⌂ **Philipps House & Dinton Park** Fine early 19th-c mansion recently restored and opened by the National Trust, with an interesting Portland stone staircase and underfloor heating system. The surrounding parkland offers plenty of scope for a stroll. Some disabled access; house open Apr–Oct, Sat and pm Mon; park open all year; (01985) 843600; house *£2, park free.

EBBLE VALLEY SU0024

The valley of the Ebble chalk-stream winds prettily through a sleepy stream of villages from Odstock to Alvediston – a delightful drive.

FIGSBURY RING SU1833

🏛❈ Iron Age hill fort with good views over Salisbury.

FOVANT SU0128

❗ **Regimental Badges** Huge chalk carvings on the escarpment (visible from the road), cut by regiments stationed here in World War I – a sight to rival England's various white horses. The Pembroke Arms, with interesting war memorabilia, has good-value food.

FYFIELD DOWN SU1470

🏛⌂ Primeval-feeling and unkempt, scattered with outcrops known as sarsen stones, the raw material of Avebury stone circle and of part of Stonehenge; a good spot for walks.

GREAT BEDWYN SU2764

⚙ **Bedwyn Stone Museum** Fascinating little open-air museum demonstrating the ancient art of stonemasonry (the nearby church has fine examples of the finished product). Disabled access but a bit bumpy in places; (01672) 870234; free.

HAYDOWN HILL SU3156

🏛⌂ Reached from the E by a walk up from Vernham Dean in Hants, this has the ramparts of a hill fort bounded by steep gradients on its S side; the 3 counties of Berks, Hants and Wilts meet close by at SU350590.

HOLT ST8661

🌼 **The Courts** (B3107) Weavers used to come here to settle their disputes; the 15th-c house isn't open, but there are lovely and extensive formal gardens full of yew hedges, pools and borders, with the other half of the grounds given over to wild flowers

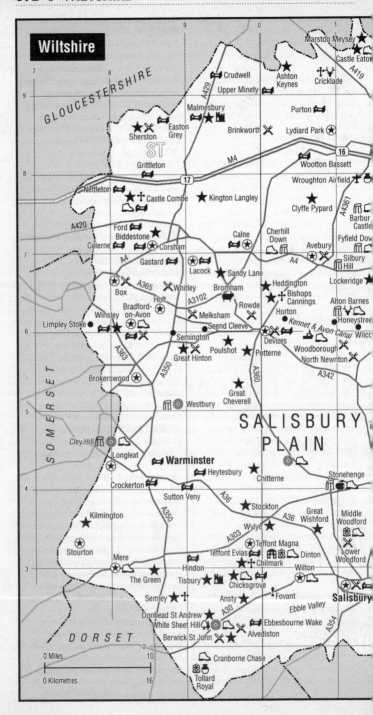

Wiltshire

Marston Meysey ★
Castle Eaton ★
Crudwell ★
Ashton Keynes ★
Cricklade ✝✝
Upper Minety
A429
A419
Purton 🚂
Malmesbury 🚂 ★ 🏰
Lydiard Park ⊛
Brinkworth ✕
Easton Grey 🚂
Sherston ★ ✕
ST
Grittleton 🚂
Wootton Bassett 🚂
M4
Wroughton Airfield ✕ ✝
17
Nettleton 🚂
Kington Langley ★
Clyffe Pypard ★
A4361
Castle Combe ★ ✝
🏠🚂
Barbur Castle 🏛🚂
A420
Ford 🚂
Biddestone ★
Cherhill Down
Avebury 🏠
Fyfield Dov
Colerne 🚂 🚂⊛ Corsham
Calne 🚂⊛
🏠🚂 🏛
Silbury Hill
A4
Gastard 🚂
A4
Lacock ⊛🚂
Sandy Lane ★
Lockeridge ·
Box ⊛✕
A365
Whitley ✕
Bromham 🐄
Heddington ★
Bishops ✝
Cannings
Alton Barnes
A3102
Holt
Bradford-on-Avon ⊛
Melksham ✕
Rowde
Horton ·
🏛🗙🚂
Honeystre
Winsley ⊛★🚂
Kennet & Avon Canal
Wilcc
Limpley Stoke ●
Seend Cleeve
Devizes ⊛🚂
Woodborough 🚂
North Newnton
A363
Semington ●
Poulshot ★
Potterne ★
A350
Great Hinton
A360
A342
Brokerswood ⊛
Westbury 🏛🌟
Great Cheverell ★
SALISBURY
PLAIN
Cley Hill 🏛🌟
🌟🏠
Longleat ⊛
Warminster 🚂
Heytesbury 🚂
Chitterne ★
Stonehenge 🏛🍎
Crockerton 🚂
Sutton Veny 🚂
A36
Stockton ★
Great Wishford ★
Middle Woodford
🐄🗙
Kilmington ★
A350
Wylye ★
A36
Lower Woodford
Stourton ⊛
A303
Teffont Magna ⊛
Mere ⊛
Teffont Evias 🚂
🏛🚂 Dinton
Wilton
Hindon 🚂
Chilmark ★✝
⊛🚂
Salisbury ⊛🗙🚂
The Green ★
Tisbury ★ 🏰
Chicksgrove
Semley ★ ✝
Ansty ★
Fovant ·
Ebble Valley
Donhead St Andrew 🚂🌟
White Sheet Hill 🏛🌟🏠
Ebbesbourne Wake 🚂
Berwick St John 🗙★
Alvediston
A354
A30
DORSET
Cranborne Chase 🏠
0 Miles 10
Tollard Royal 🍎🚂
0 Kilometres 16
GLOUCESTERSHIRE
SOMERSET

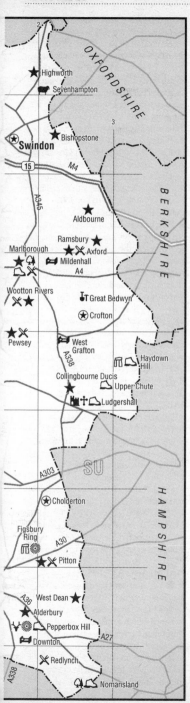

among interesting trees. Some disabled access; cl am, Sat, and Nov–Mar; (01225) 782340; £3; NT. The Old Bear at Staverton has good food.

🏠 † **Great Chalfield Manor** (N of Holt) Beautiful moated manor house, restored in 1920 and still with its original Great Hall. Open Tues–Thurs Apr–Oct, guided tours only, at 12.15pm, 2.15pm, 3pm, 3.45pm and 4.30pm; (01249) 730141 to book; £3.60; NT. Next door is a small 13th-c **church**.

KENNET & AVON CANAL

⛴ 🛶 Recently restored, this runs right across the county, and there are pleasant **boat trips** from several places; Devizes SU0061 or Wootton Rivers SU1962 for example, or the notably friendly hire companies at Hilperton ST8559 and Bradford-on-Avon. In the canal's restoration, a great deal of attention has been paid to the natural environment, so it's attractive for walks alongside; in winter you may even see a kingfisher flashing along it. For a more sedentary view, try the Beehive in Bradford-on-Avon (Trowbridge Rd), Barge Inn at Seend Cleeve ST9361, French Horn at Pewsey Wharf SU1560, Barge at Honeystreet SU1061 or Bridge Inn at Horton SU0563. The Golden Swan at Wilcot SU1461, Crown at Bishops Cannings SU0363, Somerset Arms at Semington ST8960 and Hop Pole at Limpley Stoke ST7861 are also near the canal.

LACOCK ST9168

★ † A favourite village of both visitors and film-makers, its grid of quiet and narrow streets a delightful harmony of mellow brickwork, lichened stone and timber-and-plaster. The **church** is 15th c, and nothing in the village looks more recent than 18th c. It's remained so remarkably unspoilt because most of its buildings were owned for centuries by the Talbot family, until they left them to the NT in 1944. It gets very busy in summer, but the Trust has preserved it against a surfeit of antique shops (you'll find all you want in the nearby old market town of Melksham). However, the village has a splendid collection of pubs – the George is the best.

🏠 ▒ ☖ **Lacock Abbey** Tranquil

spread of mellow stone buildings, around a central timber-gabled courtyard, based on the little-altered 13th-c abbey. Tudor additions include a romantic octagonal tower, and there was a successful 18th-c 'Gothicisation'. Surrounded by quiet meadows and trees, this was the setting for Fox Talbot's experiments which in 1835 led to the creation of the world's first photographic negative – a picture of part of the abbey itself. There's a museum devoted to this in a 16th-c barn at the gates, and the gardens are evidence of Fox Talbot's skills in other fields. Limited disabled access; open daily Apr–Oct (plus grounds and museum only in Mar), abbey cl am and all day Tues; (01249) 730227; £5.70, £3.60 museum, grounds and cloisters only; NT. The photography museum may also open some winter wknds.

LONGLEAT ST8043

🐎🎠☺🦡🎡❗**Longleat** (off A362 4m W of Warminster) Easily a full day's activities on this well organised estate, which has been open to the public for over 50 years. Children will probably get most excited about the safari park, which as well as the famous lions has rhinos, camels, elephants and a rare white tiger; unusually, you can walk through some parts. Among what seem like hundreds of other attractions are displays of parrots, butterflies, and sea lions, a narrow-gauge railway, a collection of dolls' houses, and exhibitions based around the worlds of Postman Pat and Dr Who. A splendid big play area is themed around a mock castle, and there's a simulator ride and children's petting zoo. Older visitors may prefer the formal gardens laid out by Capability Brown, and of course the handsome 16th-c house itself, much restored inside, but still with impressively grand formal rooms, and the individual murals of the colourful current Marquis of Bath. He has had several mazes and labyrinths built around the grounds; one is still Britain's longest, another has a slightly saucy shape that can be appreciated only from the Marquis's private roof terrace, and the most bizarre is a bewildering knot of mirrors, with animatronic effects adding to the confusion. Meals, snacks,

shop, disabled access; most attractions, inc safari park, are cl Nov–Apr, but the house is open all year (exc 25 Dec); (01985) 844400; you can get individual tickets to each of the attractions (the house on its own is £5, the safari park £6, and grounds only £2), but it works out much cheaper to buy the all-in Passport ticket for £13 (£10 for children). The Bath Arms at Horningsham at the S entrance to the park, and the White Hart at Corsley on the N side, are good for lunch. One of England's 3 **Center Parcs** is nearby, a rewarding place to stay with excellent leisure facilities; (0990) 200300.

LUDGERSHALL SU2651

🏚✝⌂**Ludgershall Castle** The ruins of a royal **castle** and hunting palace, still with some of the original large Norman earthworks, as well as the later flint walling; free. The **church** is also Norman; the Bull & Butcher has reasonably priced food. The nearby area is very pretty and unspoilt, the little villages of the Chutes, Tangley and Vernham Dean straddling the Hants border all worth a look (with the pubs over that way worth exploring too).

LYDIARD PARK SU1084

🏛🦡✝Painstakingly restored grand Georgian house (nr M4 junction 16, or A3102), with interesting early wallpaper, rare painted glass window, and elegant furnishings much as they would have been when first installed. Extensive lawns, lakes and well wooded parkland, with nature walks and adventure playgrounds. Snacks, shop, disabled access; cl 1–2 pm (exc school hols), am Sun, Good Fri, 25–26 Dec; (01793) 770401; car parking £1, house £1.20 – quite a bargain. The adjacent parish **church** has interesting monuments to the St John family, who lived in the house for 500 years.

MALMESBURY ST9387

★🏚Yet another charming old town, especially around the green facing its serene Norman **abbey**, from the tower of which a medieval monk called Elmer made one of the earliest semi-successful attempts at flight – he covered a couple of hundred yards, but did break both legs when he crash-landed. The picturesque Old Bell is almost as old as the abbey beside it. The

B roads radiating from here are all quite pleasant drives.

MARLBOROUGH SU1868

★ △ 🛶 One of the area's most attractive towns; its very pleasing wide High St has a market each Weds and Sat. Its annual autumn Mop Fair (as in most market towns, formerly for the hiring of servants) has been revived here as a general celebration. Even the more modern additions don't look obtrusively out of place among the harmonious mix of Georgian and Tudor buildings. The Sun (by St Peter's church where Cardinal Wolsey was inducted as a priest) and Bear are useful for lunch. The Broad Hinton road N gives a good feel of the downs' great open spaces, as does the Manton–Alton Priors road to the SW, passing one of the area's several white horses cut into the chalk, and leading into a pleasant valley drive through Allington and Horton to Devizes. To the E, the quiet road along the Kennet Valley has some attractive views, with good food stops at the Red Lion in Axford and Bell in Ramsbury, and pleasant walks; there are also walks through the surviving miles of Savernake Forest woodland.

MERE ST8132

★ † ❋ Attractive village, dominated by its 30-metre (100ft) church tower, and views from Castle Hill.

△ �🏛 ⚔ **White Sheet Hill** Easily reached from Mere (via a road bridge over the busy A303) or from Stourton, this lofty chalk downland is studded with antiquities – among them a Neolithic causewayed camp and Bronze Age barrows. It's a good site for cowslips, orchids and such butterflies as adonis and chalkhill blues.

MIDDLE WOODFORD SU1236

❋ △ **Heale Gardens** Eight acres of lovely formal gardens beside the Avon chalk stream, with lots of varied plants; the watergarden is especially nice in spring and autumn. Snacks, shop, specialist plant sales with many rare types propagated from the main gardens, disabled access; cl Christmas; (01722) 782504; £3. The Wheatsheaf in nearby Lower Woodford is popular for lunch, and this Salisbury road along the Avon's quieter bank is a pretty drive (as is the continuation N of Amesbury, through Fittleworth and East Chisenbury).

NOMANSLAND SU2517

🛶 △ There are some pleasant walks, in countryside that's unusual for Wiltshire, near the Lamb down on the edge of the New Forest.

PEPPERBOX HILL SU2125

❋ △ (5m SE of Salisbury) Named after the strangely shaped 17th-c tower on its summit. You can't get into the tower, but the site commands fine views over Salisbury itself, and S as far as Southampton. The Hook & Glove at Farley has decent food.

❦ △ **Bentley Wood** Beyond East Grimstead N of here, there's a **nature reserve** with good walks.

SALISBURY SU1429

★ 🏤 ❋ ☕ A beautiful and gently relaxed city, with a good many fine old buildings, particularly around the lovely cathedral close. The most extensive in

---

Days Out

Prehistoric enigmas: Avebury Stone Circle and stone avenue; a look at Silbury Hill; West Kennett Long Barrow; lunch at Stones or the Red Lion, Avebury; walk up on to Fyfield Down to see sarsen stones.

Grandeur and charm: Bowood House; drive to Lacock via Sandy Lane; lunch at At the Sign of the Angel there, or in one of the pubs; look round Lacock.

Eye-catchers beneath the downs: A30 drive from Wilton past Regimental Badges nr Fovant; Ansty's maypole; Old Wardour Castle nr Tisbury; lunch at the Beckford Arms, Fonthill Gifford; drive through Fonthill park; Wilton House.

the country, it's always been a distinct area of town, and the gates to it are still locked each night. The buildings cover a variety of architectural styles from the 13th c to the present, and while of course its great glory is the elegant cathedral itself, you can't help being struck by how impeccably mown the lawns are. Outside the close, there are some interesting antique and other shops, and the broad Market Sq still has a traditional market each Tues and Sat; parking in town can be tricky then. The Haunch of Venison (Minster St) is a delightful old town tavern, while the no smoking New Inn (New St) is good for lunch, as is the waterside Old Mill out at West Harnham. Besides places we describe individually below, the cathedral close also includes the striking St Anne's Gate, a regimental **museum**, handsome **Malmesbury House** (open bank hols) and the peaceful riverside **North Canonry Gardens** (occasionally open in summer – check with the friendly tourist information centre, (01722) 334956).

Mompesson House (The Close) Exquisite Queen Anne building, probably the most interesting in the close, with period furnishings, china and paintings, a remarkable collection of 18th-c drinking glasses, and an interestingly carved oak staircase. Teas, some disabled access; cl am, all day Thurs and Fri, and Nov–Mar; (01722) 335659; £3.40; NT. The NT shop is a couple of minutes' walk away on the High St.

Old Sarum (off A345 2m N) This substantial and easily defended Iron Age hill fort continued as a town right through the Roman occupation and Dark Ages into Norman times. In the early 13th c there was a general move to the much more fertile site of the present city, and the fort gradually fell into decline, becoming a quarry for the new centre; consequently there's not much left, but the views are splendid, and the foundations give interesting clues to ancient architecture. Snacks, shop, limited disabled access; cl 24–26 Dec, 1 Jan; (01722) 335398; £2; EH.

Salisbury & South Wiltshire Museum (Kings House, The Close) Local history and archaeology in lovely building, with an excellent Stonehenge gallery, collections of Wedgwood, costume, lace and embroidery, and some beautiful local watercolours by Turner. Its most recent acquisition is an aestel, an Anglo-Saxon jewel with links to King Alfred, found by a metal-detector enthusiast in a Wiltshire field. Meals, snacks, shop, disabled access to ground floor; cl Sun exc pm July and Aug, and Christmas; (01722) 332151; £3.

† Salisbury Cathedral Begun in 1220 and completed in only 38 years – giving a rare uniformity of style. The magnificent spire (added in 1334 along with the tower) is at 123 metres (404ft) the tallest in the country, and many would say the finest in the world; Christopher Wren discovered it was leaning, and managed to put it right. Also notable are the 14th-c clock (the oldest working mechanical clock in the world), and the tomb of the first Earl of Salisbury, who gave the church one of only 4 surviving copies of the Magna Carta; it's still on display (exc in Dec). The cloisters stand out too. Snacks, shop, disabled access; cl during services, and on Good Fri; (01722) 555120; £3 suggested donation. The guides are entertaining and knowledgeable. There's a good view of the cathedral from outside the 13th-c Bishop's Palace, though the one immortalised by Constable, and still much as then, is from across the meadows by the River Avon over by West Harnham.

St Thomas's Church (off The Close) Built for cathedral workers and in part slightly older than the cathedral itself; it has a scary medieval Doom painting.

SALISBURY PLAIN ST9648 Better for driving over than walking – an almost unbroken expanse of rolling high ground, a mixture of pasture and broad unhedged arable fields intersected by tank-training tracks. The A360 gives a good feel of its emptiness. The county council has a leaflet mapping out clearly various way-marked walks around the edges of the army's Imber firing range, totalling some 30 miles for the complete circuit: generally peaceful countryside with large-scale arable farming, but some wide views and maybe the sight of tank and infantry training.

SANDY LANE ST9668

★ Attractive village; the road from here through Bowden Hill is the prettiest approach to Lacock.

SEMLEY ST8926

★ † Attractive village, with an interesting **church**.

SEVENHAMPTON SU2188

🐏 **Roves Farm** The 8-week spring lambing season is the time to come to this friendly sheep farm; trailer rides and shearing in summer. Snacks, shop, disabled access; open Weds–Sun Mar–Sept; (01793) 763939; *£4. The Saracens Head in Highworth has good-value food.

SILBURY HILL SU1068

🏛 This towering prehistoric mound, purpose unknown, is the largest man-made mound in Europe – it would have taken a thousand men about 10 years to build. Don't follow the example of the people you'll see clambering all over it – that's how monuments like this are gradually worn away. It's anyway more impressive from down at normal ground level.

STONEHENGE SU1142

🏛 ⌂ 🍎 Definitely one of the most famous prehistoric monuments in the world (just off the A344); everyone knows what it looks like, and how they got the stones here has been pretty much sorted out (the larger ones local, the smaller ones all the way from Wales), but no one's really sure exactly what Stonehenge with its careful astronomical alignments was for. Some experts now reckon it could even have been built by the French. In the interests of conservation, you can't go right up to the stones, but you can get pretty close and the fact that people are kept back means that your photos won't be cluttered by the crowds. The best views are very early in the morning from the track from Larkhill, on the other side of the A344, or on a cold clear winter evening looking W past the monument towards the sunset; the ancient stones look very impressive silhouetted against the sky. Even in the crowded light of day the place never quite loses its power to inspire awe,

although the car park area would definitely benefit from some investment. The busy main roads nearby detract too; although improvements here are at last in the pipeline. Snacks, shop, disabled access; (01980) 624715; cl 24–26 Dec; £4 (inc very good Walkman tour); NT. On a handful of dates through the year you can still wander among the stones by joining one of the coach tours of mysterious sites organised by Astral Travels, (01628) 488413; these cost around £60 for a whole day and currently leave only from London, but it's worth it just for the moment when they set you loose at Stonehenge with dowsing rods. Good walks from here around associated ancient monuments (leaflet from the car park). There's good pick-your-own fruit late Jun–late July at Rolleston Manor Farm on the B3086 NW of Stonehenge.

🏛 **Woodhenge** The scant traces of another prehistoric monument which consisted of 6 rings of timber posts in a ditch; the positions are now marked by concrete posts, and a cairn marks the central spot where the tomb of a little girl ceremoniously axed to death was found.

STOURTON ST7835

🎗 ❋ 🏛 **Stourhead** (off B3092) Marvellous 18th-c gardens, gradually laid out in Italian style by the banker Henry Hoare II following his return from an Italian tour; a beautifully harmonious landscape of temples, lakes, bridges and splendid trees and other plants. Remarkable views into Somerset from Alfred's Tower, the very tall 18th-c folly at the far end, though there are 221 steps (cl Mon and Fri, and winter). The early Georgian Palladian house has some good Chippendale furniture, and the church in the grounds is in a lovely hillside setting. Meals, snacks, shop, disabled access; garden open all year, house pm daily exc Thurs and Fri, Apr–Oct; (01747) 840348; £8 for gardens and house, £4.60 for one or the other (£1 less for gardens Nov–Feb) – if you can do only one, make it the gardens; NT. The Red Lion at Kilmington, and the Spread Eagle at Stourhead's entrance, are useful for lunch.

SWINDON SU1484

Much older than you might think, this bustling market town and business centre was caught up with a vengeance in the railway age, and in the Railway Village had one of the earliest examples of a planned workers' estate. The excellent Great Western Railway Museum closed last year and will be reincarnated in the form of Steam (see below).

Railway Village House & Museum (Faringdon Rd) Restored foreman's house next to the former railway museum, furnished in typical turn-of-the-20th-century working-class style; around £1. Not far from here, the Garden Restaurant has good Thai dishes among other food; the Gluepot (Emlyn Sq) has decent food in a more down-to-earth atmosphere.

Steam (next to Great Western Designer Outlet Village) Opening around May as a jazzier version of the old museum, with lots of locomotives and related train memorabilia celebrating this most highly regarded railway. There'll be a greater emphasis on hands-on activities, and visitors will be able to watch the restoration of the trains. Meals, snacks, shop, disabled access; cl 25–26 Dec; (01793) 466646; although they had not confirmed prices when we went to press, adult admission will be around £5.

Swindon & Cricklade Railway (Blunsdon, off B4553 N) One of the only live steam projects in the area, gradually being restored, with occasional trips through the countryside, and small museum. Snacks, shop, disabled access; cl wkdys; (01793) 771615 for train times; around £3.

Swindon Museum & Art Gallery (Bath Rd) Includes works by important 20th-c artists such as Moore and Sutherland. Shop, limited disabled access; cl am Sun, bank hols; (01793) 466556; free.

TEFFONT MAGNA ST9832

★ Farmer Giles Farmstead Friendly working dairy farm, with 150 cows milked every afternoon; children can feed lambs and other animals, or simply sit and stroke them. Also tractor rides, play areas, old farming equipment, and small vineyard. Meals,

snacks, shop, disabled access; cl wkdys Nov–Mar; (01722) 716338; £3.95. The village is very attractive, full of charming stone-built cottages with neatly banked stone-walled gardens; the Black Horse has good food.

TISBURY ST9429

★ Charming small town, left behind by the main roads so largely unspoilt, with some fine old buildings, riverside church, and just outside to the E an immensely long medieval tithe barn. The lovely old Crown does decent food.

Old Wardour Castle (a couple of miles S) Remains of a substantial 14th-c lakeside castle. Though badly damaged in the Civil War, its walls still stand to their original 18 metres (60ft), and you can walk almost to the top. It's a lovely peaceful setting, landscaped in the 18th c (and used for Kevin Costner's *Robin Hood* in the 20th). Snacks, shop, disabled access to grounds only; cl 1–2pm and all Mon and Tues Nov–Mar, 24–26 Dec, 1 Jan; (01747) 870487; £1.90; EH.

TOLLARD ROYAL ST9517

Larmer Tree Pleasure Grounds (off A354) Attractive Victorian pleasure gardens in the heart of Cranborne Chase. Laid out by General Pitt Rivers, they were the first privately owned gardens open to the public but then closed for almost a century, opening again just a couple of years ago. Pheasants, macaws and peacocks wander merrily about, you can play croquet, and the temples and grottos are an appealing backdrop to the band concerts they have most Suns; also adventure playground and a small museum. Teas, disabled access; open daily exc Sat and special events Easter–Oct; (01725) 516228; £3.

UPPER CHUTE SU2953

There are some pleasant walks around the Cross Keys here.

WESTBURY ST8951

To the E you can see the huge Westbury **white horse** cut into the chalk of the downs; late 18th-c, it was an 'improvement' on an altogether older one which may have been Saxon, and which faced in the opposite direction. Above the white horse is an extensive Iron Age hill fort, with good views right down to the Mendips in Somerset.

WHITE SHEET HILL ST9424
◁ ❀ ⛿ The Harepath here is a high track giving sweeping views; you can branch off into a forest plantation. Confusingly, Wiltshire has a second hill with the same name, above Mere.

WILTON SU0931
🏠 🖼 ❦ ✝ ◁ **Wilton House** One of the most satisfying historic houses we know, well organised and friendly, with lots to see. The original house was damaged by a fire in 1647, and superbly redesigned by John Webb and Inigo Jones, the latter responsible for the magnificent double cube room. There's an outstanding art collection inc works by Rubens, Van Dyck and Brueghel, as well as fine furnishings, Tudor kitchen, Victorian laundry, and the Wareham Bears, a collection of 200 dressed teddies. Outside are 21 acres of landscaped parkland, with water and rose gardens, cloister garden, woodland walk, and huge adventure playground. Meals, snacks, shop, disabled access; cl Nov–early Apr; (01722) 743115; £6.75. The ornately Italianate 19th-c **church** incorporates all sorts of more ancient treasures, especially its magnificent medieval Continental stained glass and 2,000-year-old marble pillars. Wiltons (Market Pl) is good for lunch, the Pembroke Arms has a good Sunday carvery, and the charming Victoria & Albert in nearby Netherhampton is nicely off the tourist track, with a pleasant riverside walk into Salisbury.

🎠 **Wilton Royal Carpet Factory** (King St) Surprisingly interesting demonstrations of how they make Wilton weaves and Axminster carpets. Tours 4 times a day between 10.15am and 3.30pm, best to book, on (01772) 742733; disabled access; cl 2 wks at Christmas; £4. There's now a shopping village next door.

✄ ★ **Wilton Windmill** (off A338 E of Burbage) Wiltshire's only working windmill, built in 1821 after the construction of the Kennet & Avon Canal had diverted the water previously used to power mills. Now restored, it's beautifully floodlit most evenings. Shop (sells flour milled on site); open pm Sun Easter–Sept, plus Mon and Sat bank hol wknds; (01672) 870427; £1. The little village of Wilton (not to be confused with the larger town nr Salisbury) is attractive; the Swan has decent food.

WROUGHTON AIRFIELD SU1379
⛽ ✝ A branch of London's **Science Museum**, with national collections of aircraft, rockets, hovercraft, and road transport vehicles. Not really aimed at entertaining the general public, it's usually open around 10 times a year, with lively special events or air displays; disabled access; (01793) 814466 for 2000 dates.

WYLYE SU0037
★ Attractive village in delightful valley; one lane is called Teapot St.

★ **Other attractive villages**, all with decent pubs, include Aldbourne ST2675, Alderbury SU1827, waterside Ashton Keynes SU0494, Axford SU2370, Berwick St John ST9323 (steep walks nearby), Biddestone ST8773, Bishopstone SU2483, Chitterne ST9843 (good walks), Collingbourne Ducis SU2453, Clyffe Pypard SU0777, Great Cheverell ST9754, Donhead St Andrew ST9124, Great Hinton ST9059, Great Wishford SU0735, Heddington ST9966, Highworth SU2092, Kilmington ST7736, Kington Langley ST9277, Lockeridge SU1467 (good walks), Marston Meysey SU1297, Pewsey SU1560, Pitton SU2131 (wood and downland walks), Potterne ST9958, Poulshot ST9559, Ramsbury ST2771, Sherston ST8585, Stockton ST9738, The Green ST8731 (nr East Knoyle), West Dean SU2527, Winsley ST7961 and Wootton Rivers SU1963.

Where to eat

ALVEDISTON ST9723 **Crown** *(01772)* 780335 Lovely old thatched inn with 3 charming low-beamed panelled rooms, 2 inglenook fireplaces, lots of bric-à-brac, very good imaginative bar food, well kept ales, and an attractive garden; bdrms. **£20.25**|£7.50.

AVEBURY SU1070 **Stones Restaurant** *(01672) 539514* Excellent vegetarian restaurant in converted farm building opposite the stone circle; local, organic and home-grown produce used in the delicious cooking (lovely cakes and soups), afternoon teas, and friendly service; they sell country wines and organic wines; open all day (not evenings; and during Nov–Mar open only Fri–Sun); cl Jan; disabled access. **£17**|£2.95.

AXFORD SU2370 **Red Lion** *(01672) 520271* Welcoming brick and flint pub with fine views over valley from sheltered garden or bustling beamed and pine-panelled bar, good popular food in the bar and no smoking restaurant (enjoyable daily specials and fresh fish and game), decent wines, and well kept real ales; bdrms and self-catering; cl 25 Dec; disabled access. **£23.50**|£5.

BERWICK ST JOHN ST9422 **Talbot** *(01747) 828222* Well run and friendly village pub with simply furnished heavily beamed bar, a huge inglenook fireplace and freshly prepared food in the bar and restaurant; cl pm Sun; children over 7 in evening. **£19**|£6.

BOX ST8369 **Quarryman's Arms** *Box Hill (01225) 743569* Tucked-away unspoilt hillside pub with fine views, 2 small interesting knocked-together rooms with quarrying memorabilia, a wide choice of good home-cooked food, well kept real ales, and very friendly staff; bdrms. **£18.75**|£5.75.

BRADFORD-ON-AVON ST8260 **Bridge Tearooms** *24a Bridge St (01225) 865537* Old-fashioned no smoking 17th-c tearooms with a large choice of teas, lots of coffees, sandwiches and snacks, lovely home-made cakes and pastries, cream teas; waitresses in mob caps and aprons; cl 25–26 Dec. £4.95.

BRADFORD-ON-AVON ST8260 **Dandy Lion** *35 Market St (01225) 863433* Particularly relaxed and friendly place with an interesting and varied mix of people, big windows on either side of the door with a table and chairs in each, high-backed farmhouse chairs and old-fashioned dining chairs on the stripped wood floor, newspapers to read, nostalgic pop, a snug little back room, very well liked and reasonably priced food, real ales, good coffee, and a candlelit upstairs restaurant. **£18.60**|£6.50.

BRINKWORTH SU0184 **Three Crowns** *The Street (01666) 510366* Friendly atmosphere in villagey pub with imaginative food from a changing menu that covers an entire wall, many wines by the glass, well kept real ales, elegant no smoking conservatory, and garden looking out towards church and rolling country; get there early as they don't take bookings and it is very busy; disabled access. **£25**|£9.45.

DEVIZES SU0061 **Wiltshire Kitchen** *11 St John's St (01380) 724840* Bustling little no smoking self-service coffee house (open all day) just off the market sq, serving breakfast, lunch, and afternoon tea inc good-value OAP 2-course lunches; quite a few coffees, lots of sandwiches, and home-made scones and cakes; evening cellar restaurant, too – cl pm Sun; cl Christmas. £4.95.

GREAT HINTON ST9059 **Linnet** *(01380) 870354* Attractive old brick pub with pretty summer flowering tubs and window boxes, little right-hand bar with lots of interest on the green walls, comfortable wall banquettes, a biggish rather smart dining room with pink ragged walls, bric-à-brac, plenty of dining chairs and tables, good, popular food, friendly licensees, real ales, quite a few malts, and nice summer Pimms; cl Mon exc bank hols. **£17.15**|£5.95.

LOWER WOODFORD SU1235 **Wheatsheaf** *(01722) 782203* Friendly pub with indoor goldfish pond (crossed by a miniature footbridge), wide choice of popular food, partly no smoking dining room, well kept real ales, helpful staff, and a big walled garden; cl 25 Dec; good disabled access. **£18.50**|£4.95.

MARLBOROUGH SU1969 **Munchies** *8 The Parade (01672) 512649* Lovely beamed building with a marvellous range of really interesting and delicious sandwiches with daily changing home-made fillings using the freshest ingredients; cl Sat and Sun; disabled access. £1.80.

MARLBOROUGH SU1868 **Polly Tearooms** *26–27 High St (01672) 512146* In the centre of the pretty High St, well known for very good cream teas, with home-made bread, scones, jams and cakes; also light lunches and cooked breakfasts;

cl evenings, and 25–26 Dec; disabled access. Teas £4.45.

MELKSHAM ST9164 **Toxique** *187 Woodrow Rd (01225) 702129* Former farmhouse with unusual artwork in colourfully and eccentrically decorated rms, comfortable armchairs in lounge, excellent really adventurous meals, thoughtfully planned and prepared, and a good wine list with helpful notes; nice atmosphere, popular themed evenings – and booking essential; open Weds–Sat and am Sun, but will open at other times by appointment; bdrms; disabled access. **£40**.

NORTH NEWNTON SU1357 **Woodbridge** *A345 (01980) 630266* Bustling pub with large garden by the River Avon (boules, play area and space for a few tents/caravans), cheerfully decorated bars, a huge choice of dishes from all over the world inc quite a few Mexican dishes and super puddings, afternoon teas and Sun lunch, real ales, two dozen enjoyable wines by the glass, and friendly service from enthusiastic licensees. **£20.65|£7.95**.

PEWSEY SU1660 **London House** *Market Pl (01672) 564775* Elegant, popular restaurant with a relaxed bar, open fire in the cosy sitting room, particularly good interesting well prepared food, a thoughtful wine list, and professional service; cl Sun, am Mon, first wk Jan, first wk Aug, 16–18 Sept; children over 8; disabled access. **£29|£10**.

PITTON SU2131 **Silver Plough** *(01722) 712266* Stylish village inn with lots to look at in the beamed and comfortable front bar, good bar snacks and more elaborate meals with emphasis on fresh fish and seafood, well kept real ales, country wines, and efficient service. **£24.75|£4.50**.

REDLYNCH SU2120 **Langley Wood** *(01794) 390348* Very good innovative food and decent wines in homely creeper-covered restaurant-with-rooms set in its own grounds; cl Mon, Tues, pm Sun; children must behave (small helpings but no special menu); disabled access. **£26|£8**.

ROWDE ST9762 **George & Dragon** *(01380) 723053* Interesting old pub with log fire and plenty of dark wood, a simple dining room, exceptional imaginative food (especially delicious fresh fish and lovely puddings), good-value set lunches, a relaxed atmosphere, friendly efficient service, and well kept real ales; cl Mon, no food Sun, 25 Dec, 1 Jan. **£25|£6**.

SALISBURY SU1429 **New Inn** *(01722) 327679* Very attractive pub, no smoking throughout, with ancient heavy beams, timbered walls, an inglenook fire, panelled dining room, an unpretentious relaxed atmosphere, good range of well presented home-made food with nice daily specials and good hearty puddings, well kept beer, decent wines, friendly helpful licensees and staff, and a pleasant walled garden looking up to the nearby cathedral. **£19.65|£6.95**.

SHERSTON ST8586 **Rattlebone** *Church St (01666) 840871* 16th-c pub with low beams, country furnishings, big dried-flower arrangements, pleasant relaxed atmosphere in several rambling rooms, wide choice of good interesting food, partly no smoking restaurant, decent wines, well kept real ales, lots of malt whiskies, 20 rums, and pretty little garden; cl am 25 Dec; good disabled access. **£20|£5**.

WHITLEY ST8866 **Pear Tree** *(01225) 709131* Attractive honey-coloured stone farmhouse with a civilised, friendly and chatty atmosphere, a good mix of locals and visitors, front bar with cushioned window seats, some stripped shutters, a mix of dining chairs around good solid tables, a variety of country pictures, a little fireplace on the left, and a lovely old stripped stone one on the right, a popular big back restaurant, enticing and delicious food served by first-class staff, well kept real ales, a good wine list with 10 by the glass, and seats on the terrace; boules; cl pms 25, 26, 31 Dec, and all Jan. **£24.70|£8.95** 2-course lunch.

WOODBOROUGH SU1159 **Seven Stars** *Bottlesford (01672) 851325* Civilised pub in 7 acres of riverside gardens, with attractively moulded panelling in the main bar, a hot coal fire in a range at one end and a big log fire at the other, a pleasant mix of seats and tables, cosy nooks, retired wine bottles on Delft shelves, attractive back dining area, exceptionally good, daily changing Anglo/French cooking (inc marvellous veg, winter game and summer seafood), an exemplary wine list with a dozen by the glass, and very friendly owners; cl pm Sun, Mon (open bank hols);

children must be well behaved. **£25|£7.95.**
WOOTTON RIVERS SU1962 **Royal Oak** *(01672) 810322* Prettily thatched
16th-c pub with relaxed atmosphere, an L-shaped dining lounge with a
woodburning stove, comfortably furnished timbered bar, very popular food from a
huge menu, well kept beer, decent wines and some interesting whiskies, and
friendly service; bdrms with help-yourself breakfasts. **£17.50|£7.**

Special thanks to I and L Cook, B and K Hypher, Paul Kennedy.

Wiltshire Calendar

Some of these dates were provisional as we went to press. Please check
information with the telephone numbers provided.

APRIL

2   **Wilton** Easter Children's Quiz at Wilton House (01722) 746720
12 **Amesbury** Beating the Retreat (01980) 623283
15 **Wilton** Celebration of Shakespeare at Wilton House – *till 16 April*
    (01722) 743115
24 **Salisbury** St George's Spring Festival: traditional medieval events and
    pageantry (01722) 434359
29 **Downton** Cuckoo Fair (01725) 510646
30 **Amesbury** Sarsen Trail Walk and Marathon starting at Avebury (*from
    7pm*), crossing Salisbury Plain (normally closed to the public), and ending
    at Stonehenge (01380) 725670

MAY

20 **Wilton** Beating the Bounds (01722) 742185
26 **Chippenham** Folk Festival – *till 29 May* (01249) 657190
27 **Corsham** Festival: concerts, open gardens – *till 9 June* (01249) 701628

JUNE

8   **Chalke Valley** Festival – *till 11 June* (01722) 780367
17 **Chippenham** Carnival – *till 24 June* (01249) 706333; **Downton Mill**
    Fireworks Concert (01725) 511221
18 **Salisbury** Choral Festival (01722) 782329
24 **Wilton** Horse Trials at Wilton House – *till 25 June* (01722) 743115

JULY

1   **Amesbury** Carnival (01980) 622173; **Heddington** Steam Rally at Home
    Farm: rural crafts and shire horses – *till 2 July* (01380) 850885
8   **Swindon** Old Town Festival – *till 9 July* (01793) 641033; **Wilton** Carnival
    (01722) 742667
15 **Wilton** Fireworks Concert at Wilton House (01722) 743115
19 **Salisbury** Southern Cathedrals Festival – *till 22 July* (01722) 555121
20 **Chippenham** North Wiltshire Festival at Monkton Park inc 4 arenas and
    fireworks concerts – *till 22 July* (01249) 706534; **Stourton** Fête
    Champêtre at Stourhead – *till 22 July* (01985) 843600

Wiltshire Calendar (cont.)

AUGUST

5 Salisbury Country Festival – *till 6 August* (01722) 323564
12 Bowood Fireworks Concert at Bowood House (01625) 575681
20 Edington Music Festival – *till 3 September* (01373) 827158
28 Corsley Show (01373) 832643

SEPTEMBER

2 Bradford-on-Avon Wharf Show and Boat Parade – *till 3 September* (01225) 864378
9 Westbury Medieval Fayre (01373) 827158
16 Pewsey Illuminated Carnival Procession (01672) 563378

OCTOBER

7 Marlborough Mop Fair: fun fair (01672) 513989
14 Marlborough Mop Fair: fun fair (01672) 513989
28 Warminster Carnival – *till 29 October* (01985) 218548

We welcome reports from readers

This *Guide* depends on readers' reports. Do help us if you can – in return, we offer a discount on the next edition to people who've helped us with reports for it. Tell us what you think about places already in it, and anything extra you think we should say about them. And send us your ideas for inclusion in the next edition: places to visit, eat at or stay in, attractive drives or walks, maybe even unusual interesting shops you know of. Use the card in the middle, the report forms at the end, or just write – no stamp needed: *The Good Britain Guide*, FREEPOST TN1569, Wadhurst, E Sussex TN5 7BR.

WORCESTERSHIRE

Classic English countryside, some interesting places to visit.

The Malvern Hills, dominating the view from much of the county, stand as a symbol of Englishness, for many people almost inseparable from thoughts of Elgar's music (Lower Broadheath is the place to start the Elgar trail). On their flanks the sober town of Great Malvern is attractive, as are Evesham and Cotswolds-edge Broadway. Worcester is a busy city, but has interesting finds and good museums; the Commandery, with unusual special events and re-enactments, is exceptional.

The buildings' museum at Bromsgrove is a much more interesting outing than you might guess, the extraordinary ruin and splendid church at Great Witley are striking, and Hanbury Hall is very handsome. There are quite a few good family outings; Bewdley in particular has plenty for children to enjoy, and nearer Evesham the Domestic Fowl Trust at Ullington is friendly for children too.

The orchards make blossom-time (usually April through early May) and harvest time (September) attractive: local tourist board trails make it easy to see the best of this, especially in the Vale of Evesham – rich farmland and orchard country, full of farm shops. There's an abundance of fresh local asparagus in May. In winter, big log fires and generous central heating are the rule – people here really seem to appreciate their warmth.

Where to stay

ABBERLEY SO7367 **Elms** *Stockton Rd, Abberley, Worcs WR6 6AT (01299) 896666* **£140;** 16 comfortable rms. Lovely Queen Anne mansion with fine views from the well kept grounds, an elegant, restful drawing room with antiques, log fires and flowers, very good food and wines in the airy restaurant, and friendly, efficient staff.

BROADWAY SP0937 **Broadway Hotel** *The Green, Broadway, Worcs WR12 7AA (01386) 852401* **£110,** plus special breaks; 20 well kept rms. Lovely 16th-c building, once a monastic guesthouse, with a galleried and timbered lounge, cosy beamed bar, attractively presented food served by attentive staff in the airy comfortable restaurant, and seats outside on a terrace; dogs by prior arrangement; disabled access.

BROADWAY SP0839 **Collin House** *Collin Lane, Broadway, Worcs WR12 7PB (01386) 858354* **£92,** plus special breaks; 7 warm, comfortable and quiet rms. Golden-stone 16th-c Cotswold house in 3 acres of gardens, orchard and meadow; with restful and refurbished public rooms, oak beams, log fires, very good English food and carefully chosen wines in the candlelit beamed restaurant with mullioned windows, and friendly, helpful service; cl 5 days at Christmas.

BROADWAY SP0937 **Lygon Arms** *High St, Broadway WR12 7DU (01386) 852255* **£214.82,** plus special breaks; 65 lovely period rms (some more modern, too). Handsome hotel where Oliver Cromwell and King Charles I once stayed, with interesting old beamed rooms, oak panelling, antiques, log fires, fine traditional food in the Great Hall with minstrels' gallery and heraldic frieze, excellent service, and a charming garden; health spa; disabled access.

CHADDESLEY CORBETT SO8873 **Brockencote Hall** *Chaddesley Corbett, Kidderminster, Worcs DY10 4PY (01562) 777876* ***£125,** plus special breaks; 17

individually decorated rms. Grand country-house hotel in 70 acres, with half-timbered dovecot and lake; large, airy and attractively furnished rooms, conservatory lounge with garden views, elegant restaurant with modern French and English cooking, and very good service; no dogs; disabled access.

EVESHAM SP0443 **Evesham Hotel** *Coopers Lane, off Waterside, Evesham, Worcs WR11 6DA (01386)* 765566 ***£96,*** plus special breaks; 39 spacious rms. Comfortably modernised and cheerfully run hotel with warm, friendly and relaxed atmosphere, lots of facilities for children, very good food (especially the lunchtime buffet) from jokey menu, a huge range of spirits, indoor swimming pool, and croquet; cl 25–26 Dec; pets welcome (not in public rooms); children must be well behaved; partial disabled access.

HARVINGTON SP0548 **Mill** *Anchor Lane, Harvington, Evesham, Worcs WR11 5NR (01386)* 870688 **£99;** 21 comfortable rms overlooking grounds. Handsome Georgian hotel in eight acres of parkland with 180 metres (600ft) of river, mooring for guests' boats, fishing, hard tennis court, and heated outdoor swimming pool; carefully refurbished airy lounges with open fires, courteous helpful staff, fine, imaginative food using fresh local produce, thoughtful wine list with helpful notes, and good breakfasts; cl Christmas; children over 10.

HIMBLETON SO9459 **Phepson Farm** *Himbleton, Droitwich, Worcs WR9 7JZ (01905)* 391205 **£40;** 4 rms. Relaxed and friendly 17th-c farmhouse on 170-acre working farm with beef and sheep; comfortable lounge, good breakfasts in separate dining room; self-catering apartment; cl Christmas and New Year; pets by arrangement; partial disabled access.

KEMERTON SO9437 **Upper Court** *Kemerton, Tewkesbury, Glos GL20 7HY (01386)* 725351 **£90,** plus special breaks; 6 rms, plus others in cottages. Lovely Georgian Cotswold manor with Domesday watermill, lake (lots of wildfowl and free fly-fishing in season), and dovecot in 15 acres of fine gardens; outdoor heated swimming pool, tennis court, croquet, and boating; relaxed atmosphere and many antiques (the owners run an antiques business and there is always something for sale) in the elegant rooms, very good food using home-grown produce, and nice breakfasts; cl Christmas; dogs by arrangement; good disabled access.

MALVERN SO7647 **Cowleigh Park Farm** *Cowleigh Rd, Malvern, Worcs WR13 5HJ (01684)* 566750 ***£49;*** 3 rms. Carefully restored and furnished black and white timbered 13th-c farmhouse in own grounds, surrounded by lovely countryside, with good breakfasts and light suppers or full evening meals (prior booking); self-catering also; cl Christmas; children over 7.

MALVERN WELLS SO7845 **Cottage in the Wood** *Holywell Rd, Malvern Wells, Worcs WR14 4LG (01684)* 575859 ***£89.50,*** plus special breaks; 20 compact but pretty rms, some in separate nearby cottages. Family-run, Georgian dower house with quite splendid views across the Severn Valley (marvellous walks from the grounds); antiques, log fires, comfortable seats and magazines in the public rooms, and modern English cooking and an extensive wine list in the attractive, no smoking restaurant.

OMBERSLEY SO8463 **Crown & Sandys Arms** *Ombersley, Droitwich, Worcs WR9 0EW (01905)* 620252 **£48;** 6 no smoking rms, most with own bthrm. Civilised and pretty, Dutch-gabled inn with good views from the garden; comfortable lounge bar with beams, timbers, log fires and maybe daily newspapers, and good popular food inc lots of fish; no dogs; cl 24–30 Dec.

WICKHAMFORD SP0642 **Wickhamford Manor** *Wickhamford, Evesham, Worcs WR11 6SA (01386)* 830296 ***£65;*** 3 rms. Striking timbered manor, first mentioned in the Domesday Book, in 20 acres with 12th-c dovecot and lake; a big log fire in beamed drawing room, good breakfasts in the flagstoned kitchen, dinner by arrangement, and a really warm welcome from the owners; tennis and fishing; self-catering cottage; cl Christmas and New Year; children occasionally allowed.

To see and do

WORCESTERSHIRE Family Attraction of the Year

🐾 ☺ **BEWDLEY** SO7874 **West Midlands Safari Park** (Spring Grove, just E on A456) Good fun for children, this busy place doesn't just have plenty of animals, it also has around 30 rides in an adjacent leisure park. Both bits are kept sensibly separate, so you don't have to go into the leisure park if you don't want to. The main attraction is the drive-round animal reserves, home to over 40 species of rare and exotic animals. Lions, tigers, monkeys, elephants, camels, giraffes and wolves have the run of the park while you sit in your car – you'll envy them their freedom if you come on a bank holiday, when the usual hour-long circuit takes much longer thanks to traffic jams. Bear in mind that though some animals may come right up to your car, others will watch nonchalantly from a distance; luckily you can go round as often as you like, so if you don't see what you want it's easy enough to give it another go. You may be able to feed the deer through the car window, with special feed available at the ticket office. Admission also covers the entertaining sealion show, a seal aquarium with well positioned viewing platforms, hippo feeding displays, reptile house, and the pets corner, which as well as smaller animals for children to touch has a different Animal Encounter session every day, showcasing anything from a sheep to an iguana. It's worth checking timings for these when you arrive, so you can plan your safari around them. The leisure park is hardly Alton Towers, but there's a good mix of rides, from gentle carousels and dodgems to a log flume and a couple of decent rollercoasters. The rides cost extra (see below), with the wristband best value. Lots of differently themed shops and places to eat, and if you need a break, the undercover Dome shows cartoons all day. Dogs aren't allowed in the animal enclosures, but they have free kennels. Meals, snacks, shop, mostly disabled access; open daily Mar–Oct; (01299) 402114; the safari park is £5.25 for adults and children over 4; this entitles you to a return visit any time during the rest of the season. At the leisure park, rides are priced individually, or an all-day wristband is £6.50.

ABBERLEY HILLS SO7567
🏔 🐔 ❄ (nr Stourport) Little visited by walkers but rewarding for them: partly wooded, with good views and close to the extraordinary ruins of Witley Court.

ABBOTS MORTON SP0255
★ ✝ Charming village, with a lovely church and decent pub.

ASHTON UNDER HILL SO9938
★ ✝ Charming black and white timbered houses and a good Norman church; made all the more attractive by the brooding backdrop of Bredon Hill.

BEWDLEY SO7874
★ 🏔 Attractive small town, with riverside walks and interesting side streets. The Little Pack Horse (old High St) is full of character.
🔥 **Bewdley Museum** (Load St) An 18th-c row of butchers' shops houses this local history museum; shop, disabled access; cl Nov–Apr; £2.

🚂 **Severn Valley Railway** 🖼
Splendid steamtrain trips through the Wyre Forest and the Severn Valley between Kidderminster and Bridgnorth in Shrops, with lots going on – this railway is run with great verve. The station has a fine model railway. Meals, snacks, shop; trains daily May–Sept and most other wknds – (01299) 403816 for timetable; £9.20 for full trip.
🐾 ☺ **West Midlands Safari Park**
See separate family panel above.

BREDON SO9236
★ 🏚 Attractive village above the River Avon, with magnificent medieval tithe barn and good pub.
🏔 **Bredon Hill** The Vale of Evesham's one notable feature for walkers. It's an outlier of the Cotswolds, distinctively rounded and on cloudy days rather ominous. It's easily reached from Overbury, but the best walk over it is from Bredon's Norton to Elmley Castle.

BRETFORTON SP0944

★ ✝ 🏠 One of the prettiest black and white thatched villages, with an interesting church and a splendid medieval pub, the Fleece, left to the National Trust after being in the same family for several centuries; a proper pub, it's kept just as it was, with a magnificent collection of Jacobean oak furniture and pewter.

BROADWAY SP0937

★ Exceptionally harmonious stone-built Cotswold village, with the golden stone and uneven stone-tiled roofs perfectly blending the grand houses and the humbler cottages together, in a long, grass-lined main street. It's decidedly on the coach-tour trail, very busy indeed in summer (though the recent bypass helps). Fine things for sale in extraordinarily expensive antique shops, and a very grand old inn, the Lygon Arms, with a useful side wine bar. Our other recommendations in the **Where to stay** section do good bar lunches; a good escape from the tourists is the Crown & Trumpet in Church St, an archetypal Cotswold pub, and the Buckland Manor does decent teas.

🏠 ✳ 🐄 **Broadway Tower** (off A44 SE) Above the village, this late 18th-c folly has marvellous views that on a clear day – with the help of the telescope – are said to stretch over 12 counties. There are exhibitions on the history of the tower and regular visitor William Morris, while the country park around it has farm animals and nature trails. Meals, snacks, shops, some disabled access; cl wkdys Nov–Mar; (01386) 852390; £2.20 tower only, £3.20 tower and park.

🐻 **Teddy Bear Museum** (High St) Decent collection of old bears and toys. Shop; cl 25–26 Dec; (01386) 858323; £1.50.

🏠 🐄 **Vale of Evesham farm shops** Good for all manner of local produce inc eggs, jams, pickles and trout as well as fruit and veg, but the highlights of the year are asparagus in May and apples and particularly plums in Sept. The A44 W almost always has good pickings.

BROMSGROVE SO9468

⛟ 🚂 ⌂ 🐄 🐎 **Avoncroft Museum of Buildings** (Stoke Prior; B4091 S) Threatened buildings of historical interest are carefully re-erected and restored here – anything from a 14th-c monastic roof through an 18th-c dovecot and ice-house to a 1946 prefab, not to mention the National Collection of Telephone Kiosks. Demonstrations of traditional building techniques, maybe wknd miniature train rides. Meals, snacks, shop, disabled access; cl Mon (exc July–Aug and bank hols), Fri in Mar and Nov, all Dec–Feb; (01527) 831363; £4.50. The Country Girl here does generous food and is handy for walks on Dodderhill Common; the parish council have mapped out other walks too. Bromsgrove proper has a thoroughly traditional local history museum (cl 12.30–1pm, Sun and Christmas; £1.20) and Daub & Wattle's Pottery, a largely unchanged pottery building with displays and shop (cl Sun, Mon).

BURFORD SO5968

🐝 🖼 **Burford House Gardens** (off A456, W of Tenbury Wells) Delightfully set by the River Teme, these tranquil gardens are the home of a national collection of clematis. The ground floor of the Georgian house is open as a contemporary art gallery. Meals, snacks, plant sales, disabled access; cl 25–26 Dec and 1 Jan; (01584) 810777; £2.50.

CHADDESLEY CORBETT SO8973

★ ✝ Despite the trunk road an attractive village, with a decent pub and a fine partly Norman church.

CHILDSWICKHAM SP0738

★ This streamside village has some delightful timbered stone cottages.

CLENT SO9380

✳ ⌂ **Clent Hills Country Park** A fine high hillscape for walkers, open and exhilarating, with waymarked routes. The Holly Bush at Clent is a good lunch break.

CLIFTON UPON TEME SO7161

★ ⌂ A pleasant village, with lots of quiet strolls above the orchards.

DROITWICH SO8963

❗ 🏠 ✝ **Droitwich Spa Brine Baths** (St Andrew's Rd) Just the thing after an exhausting day's sightseeing – you don't drink the water of this famous spa town, but float in it; cl Easter Sun, 25–26

Dec, 1 Jan; (01905) 794894; £6.50 (includes sauna). Interesting buildings include the timbered houses around the High St, and the Sacred Heart church with its fine stained-glass mosaics. The Firs out at Dunhampstead (just SE) is a pleasant dining pub.

ꬵ **Heritage Centre** (Victoria Sq) Unusual exhibition on radios and broadcasting, and brass rubbing. Shop, disabled access; cl Sun and bank hols; (01905) 774312; free.

ELMLEY CASTLE SO9841
★ ✝ Very old-fashioned village below Bredon Hill, with attractive houses strung out between its lovely church and the millpond.

EVESHAM SP0343
★ 🏠✝☕🎿 🏵 The pedestrianised market square has some fine buildings around it incl a 12th-c abbey gateway; the church's striking 16th-c bell tower is well preserved, and some altogether more ruined remnants in the town park beyond lead to riverside meadows. The tourist information centre is in another attractive abbey building, the Almonry, a Tudor timbered house with craft shows, small museum, and nice gardens. The Royal Oak (Vine St) is useful for lunch, and the Green Dragon (Oat St) visibly brews its own ales. In Apr or early May, the orchard drive through Harvington, the Lenches, Badgers Hill, Fladbury Cross, Wood Norton and Chadbury is pretty.

🐦🐖 **Domestic Fowl Trust** (Ullington, just N of Honeybourne) Friendly place with rare breeds of sheep, hens, ducks, geese and turkeys, plus chicks for children to handle (all year), adventure playground and an indoor play area planned. You'll need wellies on wet days. Summer snacks, shop, limited disabled access; (01386) 833083; £2.50.

FECKENHAM SP0061
★ Attractive green and some fine Georgian red brick.

FLADBURY SO9946
★ ⌂ This appealing village offers walks by the River Avon, a 9th-c Saxon cross, and a handsome Georgian village green. The Chequers is a good dining pub.

GREAT MALVERN SO7745
★ ❋ 🎿 Elegant hillside spa town with easy access to inspiring hill scenery; the

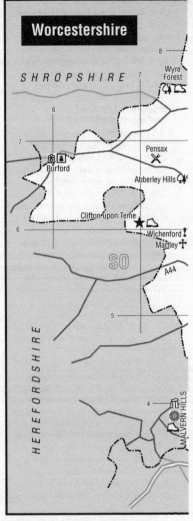

B4232 from Upper Colwall to Wynds Point has some of the best high views, while the B4218 on the E side gives several good views of the hills themselves. A good few craft workshops include musical instrument-makers such as Hibernian Violins, Players Ave; cl wknds. The Foley Arms and Mount Pleasant Hotel have decent food, good views.

🏵 **Barnard's Green House** On the E side of the Malvern Hills, this has an attractive garden with a wide range of

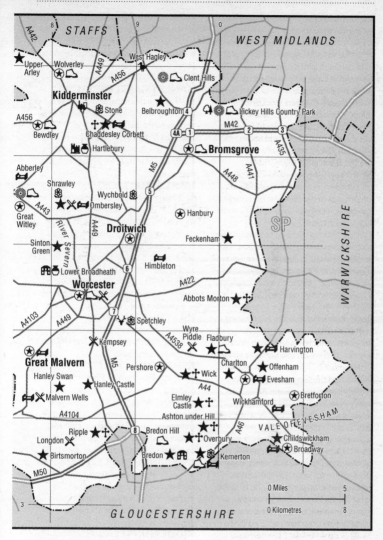

gardening ideas around a gracious 17th-c house (not open). The owner is an authority on dried flowers. Teas, plant sales, disabled access; open pm Thurs mid-Mar–Sept, a couple of Suns in Apr, Jun and Aug, and other times by appointment; (01684) 574446; *£2. The nearby Bluebell is useful for lunch.

△ ※ 🏛 **Malvern Hills** Forming a splendid backdrop to the Vale of Evesham, these offer good walking. From a distance they look a formidable mountain range, but seem to get milder and more welcoming as you approach. The gentle up-and-down path along their spine makes one of England's great ridge walks, with the Cotswolds and Midland plain on one side and wilder Wales on the other. The Herefordshire Beacon, capped by ramparts of an Iron Age hill fort, is easily reached from the car park on the A449 nr Little Malvern. Great Malvern is well placed for the Worcestershire Beacon, the highest point of the range (425 metres, 1,395ft), and for long circular walks. The Chase at

Upper Colwall and Malvern Hills Hotel by the British Camp car park on Wynds Point are also useful start or finish points.

♨†**Malvern Museum** (Abbey Rd) This splendid former gateway of a Benedictine monastery houses a museum with displays on local history, Malvern spring water, and Elgar's life. Shop; cl Weds in term-time, all Nov–Mar; (01684) 567811; *£1. The beautifully symmetrical priory just along the road has a notable collection of medieval wall tiles.

❀ **Picton Garden** (Old Court Nurseries, Walwyn Rd, Colwall) On the W side of the Malvern Hills, this has a nicely laid out cottagey collection of hardy plants and shrubs, best in summer, with a national collection of asters (late summer/autumn) and rock garden. Plant sales, disabled access; cl all day Mon and Tues, and Nov–July; (01684) 540416); £2. The Chase Inn at Upper Colwall is handy for lunch.

GREAT WITLEY SO7765

🏛❀†**Witley Court** Astonishing ruined shell of a Jacobean house transformed into an Italianate palace by the Earl of Dudley, and partly destroyed by fire in 1937. It's an elaborate place, with an enormous Perseus fountain, and balustraded garden – very atmospheric to wander through. Overlooking the lake beside it, a gloriously baroque church is no less dramatic, and one of the county's great finds; it has splendid paintings and stained glass around the largely papier-mâché interior. Snacks, shop, some disabled access; cl 24–26 Dec; (01299) 896636; £3.50; EH. The Hundred House is handy for lunch.

HANBURY SO9463

🏛❀†✻**Hanbury Hall** 18th-c country house with outstanding painted ceilings and staircase, fine porcelain, and contemporary ice-house and orangery in grounds. The formal gardens are being carefully restored. You can book rooms in the Lodge on the edge of the estate. Snacks, shop, some disabled access; open pm Sun–Weds Apr–Oct; (01527) 821214; £4.40, £2.50 garden only; NT. The church, high on a hill, has superb views over the countryside. The Gate Hangs Well (Woodgate) has a good carvery.

✿ **Jinney Ring Craft Centre** (B4091

Droitwich Rd) Various craft workshops in beautiful timbered barns, from pottery to violin-making; some weekend courses. Meals, snacks, shop, some disabled access; cl Mon exc bank hols; (01527) 821272; free.

HANLEY CASTLE SO8342

★ Well worth a stop, a rustic little place around a great cedar tree, with an unusually unspoilt pub.

HANLEY SWAN SO8142

★ An attractive village, with a pleasant traditional pub by the village green and duck pond.

HARTLEBURY SO8371

🏛♨**Hartlebury Castle State Rooms** The official residence of the Bishops of Worcester since 850, now part of the County Museum. You can visit some of the state rooms; snacks, shop, some disabled access; museum cl am Fri and Sun, all Sat, Good Fri, and all Dec–Jan; (01299) 250416; £2.20 (inc state rooms). The elegant state rooms are usually open Tues–Thurs.

HARVINGTON SP0549

★ One of the area's oldest villages, brilliantly black and white. The Golden Cross has nice food.

KEMERTON SO9437

❀★⌂ **The Priory** Big garden richly planted with colourful borders; also cool streamside plantings, handsome trees and shrubs. They've recently re-designed the walled kitchen garden. Plant sales; open pm Thurs May–Sept plus half a dozen Suns (when they do teas); (01386) 725258; £2 (£1.50 in May and Jun). There are other pretty stone-built houses among the trees of this attractively leafy village, handy for Bredon Hill walks. The Crown is popular for lunch.

KIDDERMINSTER SO8376

🚂 Not an alluring place to visit, but a terminus of the excellent Severn Valley steam railway (see Bewdley), with a cheerful replica of Edwardian station refreshment rooms.

LICKEY HILLS COUNTRY PARK SO9975

⌂ ⚘ ✻ A good example of the interesting topography W of Birmingham: high (rising to over 300 metres – 1,000ft), and densely wooded, a fragment of primeval forest, with the views suddenly opening out over the sprawling city;

waymarking makes the maze of paths and tracks less confusing. The Peacock at Forhill has good-value food all day.

LOWER BROADHEATH SO8157

🏛️♿ **Elgar's Birthplace Museum** (Crown East Lane) Modest cottage where the composer was born in 1857; now, as he wanted, a museum of his life and work, with displays of musical scores and letters, and the desk where he did his writing. Shop, disabled access to ground floor; cl am winter, all Weds, and mid-Jan–mid-Feb; (01905) 333224; £3. You can pick up routes and information here about the Elgar Trail around the area, and the Bear & Ragged Staff over at Bransford is a very suitable place for lunch with pleasing views of the countryside.

MARTLEY SO7559

✝ **Martley church** Notable for its 13th-c wall paintings.

OFFENHAM SP0546

★ Still has its original gaily striped maypole in its wide black and white main street; a nice village.

OMBERSLEY SO8463

★ Attractive mix of handsome black and white timbered houses with elegant Georgian brick; there's a choice of good pubs, too.

OVERBURY SO9537

★ ✝ Immaculate stone-built estate village, with older buildings and a fine church.

PERSHORE SO9445

★ ✝ ! Very much a working town, the 'capital' of the fruit- and vegetable-growing area around it. It's a pleasant place, largely Georgian, with an impressive abbey, and River Avon walks. The Brandy Cask (Bridge St) has good value food and brews its own beer. Heading out along the A4104 SW, when you've passed the Oak in Defford keep your eyes skinned for a group of cottages on your right; the last,

surrounded by farm animals and without an inn sign, is the Monkey House, a uniquely old-fashioned cider tavern (cl Mon evening, Tues).

RIPPLE SO8737

★ ✝ Appealing village, with finely carved choir seats in its imposing, largely 13th-c church.

SHRAWLEY SO7964

🌸 **Eastgrove Cottage Garden** (Sankyns Green, off A443 E of Great Witley) Interesting and unusual hardy and tender perennial plants in a cottage-garden setting by ancient timbered house (not open). Good plants for sale, disabled access; open pm Thurs–Mon Apr–July, then pm Thurs–Sat Sept–mid-Oct; (01299) 896389; *£2.

SPETCHLEY SO8953

🌸 ✾ **Spetchley Park Gardens** (A422) Thirty acres of lovely gardens, with sweeping lawns and herbaceous borders, rose lawn, and interesting trees and shrubs; usually a special plants fair in Apr. The adjacent park has both red and fallow deer. Snacks, disabled access (but no facilities); cl am Sun, all Sat, Mon (exc bank hols), and Oct–Mar; (01905) 345213; *£3.20. The Berkeley Knot is handy for lunch.

STONE SO8675

🌸 **Stone House Gardens** Unusual walled garden with colourful plants, especially climbers and tender flowering shrubs; plant sales. Disabled access; open Weds–Sat Mar–Oct; (01562) 69902; *£2. The Fox at Chaddesley Corbett has a popular carvery.

WEST HAGLEY SO8979

🦅 **Falconry Centre** 💶 (Hurrans Garden Centre, Kidderminster Rd S) Frequent flying displays of hawks, owls and other birds of prey; short falconry courses. Shop, some disabled access; cl 25–26 Dec; (01562) 700014; £2.50. The Holly Bush (A491 towards

---

Days Out

The great train ride: Trip on Severn Valley Railway, Bewdley; lunch at the Little Pack Horse there; stroll around Bewdley; Witley Court.

A day in Worcester: Commandery; lunch at Browns (Quay St) or King Charles II (New St), or a snack at the Cardinal's Hat (Friar St); Greyfriars, Tudor House; Worcester Cathedral.

Bromsgrove) has popular fresh food.
WICHENFORD SO7759
!Wichenford dovecot Unusually
constructed, timber-framed, wattle and
daub 17th-c dovecot with nearly 600
nesting boxes. Open daily Apr–Oct,
winter by appointment; (01684)
850051; 60p; NT.
WICK SO9645
★ † This riverside village has attractive
houses and a good church.
WOLVERLEY SO8279
★ Steeply gabled cottages below a
brick-built hilltop church, and the
decent cliffside Lock Inn by the quaint
Staffs & Worcs Canal.
⚙ 🦋 △ **Kingsford Country Park**
(Blakeshall) 200-acre park with pine
forests, birch groves and plenty of walks
and trails (inc one for the disabled).
Very nice unspoilt feel – even the
signposts and picnic sets are made at
the saw mill here.
WORCESTER SO8554
🏠 Though it's a busy commercial
centre, this has some splendid medieval
buildings dotted about, with lots of half-
timbered houses, particularly around
Friar St, where the Lemon Tree has
good food, and New St. Plenty of shops,
inc some nice specialist ones and cafés in
Hopmarket Yard, a former coaching inn;
the King Charles I (New St) does good
meals. You can tour the handsome
Georgian Guildhall (not Sun).
🐄 △ 🎵 **Bennetts Farm Park**
(Lower Wick) Working dairy farm with
animals, weekend milking parlour and
vintage machinery museum in pretty
16th-c farm buildings. Walks and fishing
in season. Snacks (inc their own ice-
cream), shop, disabled access; (01905)
748345; *£3.
🍵 🖼 **City Museum & Art Gallery**
(Foregate St) Local and natural history,
with River Severn gallery and several
children's activities. Meals, snacks, shop,
disabled access; cl Thurs, Sun, 25 Dec,
Good Fri and around other public holidays
– best to check; (01905) 25371; free.
🏠🍵 **Commandery** (Sidbury) The
only museum in the country wholly
devoted to the English Civil War, in a
striking, timber-framed 15th-c building.
Lots of weaponry, spectacular audio-
visual shows and life-size talking figures
re-creating events from the war.

Unusual special events and military
displays, and brass-rubbing centre.
Meals, snacks, shop; cl am Sun, 25–26
Dec, 1 Jan; (01905) 361821; £3.60.
🏠 ⚙ **Greyfriars** (Friar St) Beautiful
and carefully restored, medieval timber-
framed town house (still lived in), with
delightful walled garden. Open pm
Weds, Thurs and bank hols, Easter–Oct;
(01905) 23571; £2.60; NT. The nearby
Cardinal's Hat is the town's oldest
tavern – lovely panelled back room.
🍵 🏛 **Museum of Worcester
Porcelain** (Severn St) The country's
oldest continuous producer of
porcelain, with weekday factory tours
(no children under 11), and rare 18th-c
porcelain in the excellent developing
museum. Meals, snacks, shop, disabled
access to museum only; cl 25–26 Dec
and Easter Sun; (01905) 23221; tour £5,
museum £3. The Potters Wheel
opposite has decent food.
🍵 **Tudor House** (Friar St) This 15th-c
building houses a museum of local life,
with events such as children's
workshops. Shop with interesting
reproduction nostalgiamenta, some
disabled access; cl Thurs, Sun, 25–26
Dec, 1 Jan, Good Fri, Easter Sun;
(01905) 722349; free.
† **Worcester Cathedral** Founded
on the site of a Saxon monastery, in a
calm and peaceful setting overlooking
the river. It took from 1084 to 1375 to
build, and has an attractive 14th-c
tower, Norman crypt, and the tombs of
Prince Arthur and King John, the latter
topped by the oldest royal effigy in the
country. Lots of Victorian stained glass,
and some monastic buildings. Guided
tours in summer. Snacks, shop, some
disabled access; £2 suggested donation.
🦋 △ **Worcester Woods
Countryside Centre** (just E off A442)
140 acres of ancient woodland on the
edge of the city; not as interesting as
woodlands elsewhere, but useful for
strolling if you don't want to leave the
city. Snacks, shop, disabled access; cl
25–26 Dec, 1 Jan; (01905) 766492; free.
WYCHBOLD SO9165
⚙ **Webbs Garden Centre** (A38
towards Bromsgrove) One of the best
in the country, attractively laid out, with
a massive choice of things to buy, fine
amusements for children and good

disabled access. The thatched café is exemplary; cl 25–26 Dec; (01527) 861777; free.

WYRE FOREST SO7574

🍺 🛏 This major broadleaved woodland, on the Shropshire border, has numerous ready-made Forestry Commission trails (leaflets available from the visitor centre; the Royal Forester

nearby, if open, is useful for lunch).

★ **Other attractive villages**, all with decent pubs, include Belbroughton SO9277, Birtsmorton SO7936, thatched Charlton SP0145, Sinton Green SO8160 and Upper Arley SO7680 (the Severn Valley Railway from Bewdley stops at a station over the River Severn footbridge).

Where to eat

KEMPSEY SO8548 **Walter de Cantelupe** *(01905) 820572* Popular roadside pub with a friendly, relaxed bar, quite a mix of furniture, flowers and candles on tables, a good big fireplace, well kept real ales, a decent choice of wines by the glass, and hard-working young landlord; cl Mon exc bank hols, no food 1 wk in Jan; children over 3 until 8.15pm; disabled access. **£21|£5.**

LONGDON SO8433 **Hunters** *(01684) 833388* Friendly, rather civilised place, with good imaginative food in the smart heavy-beamed restaurant and small dining room, two comfortable bars with flagstones and a woodburning stove, well kept beer and nice wines; and 6 acres with dogs, rabbits and ponies. **£19.90|£5.**

MALVERN WELLS SO7742 **Croque-en-Bouche** *221 Wells Rd (01684) 565612* Boldly decorated Victorian house with delicious, carefully cooked, evening food from a shortish menu, with marvellous puddings and cheeses, and an exceptional wine list – must book; open pm Thurs–Sat only; cl 1 wk May, 1 wk Sept, Christmas. **£29.**

OMBERSLEY SO8463 **Kings Arms** *(01905) 620142* Big, black-beamed and timbered Tudor pub with comfortably informal rambling rooms, various nooks and crannies full of stuffed animals and birds, rustic bric-à-brac and four open fires; excellent varied bar food, well kept real ales, and seats in the sheltered courtyard and terrace; children over 8. **£22.50|£4.25.**

PENSAX SO7468 **Bell** *(01299) 896677* Welcoming and unpretentious mock Tudor pub with a woodburning stove and traditional décor, an airy no smoking dining room with a log fire, enjoyable straightforward food, four quickly changing real ales on handpump, and seats in the back garden with fine views over the hills to the Wyre Forest; cl am Mon except bank hols and summer holiday period; disabled access. **£17|£5.95.**

WORCESTER SO8454 **Browns** *24 Quay St (01905) 26263* Most attractive and spacious warehouse conversion with big windows overlooking the river, excellent modern cooking inc fish and vegetarian dishes, and good wines; cl am Sat, pm Sun, Mon, 1 wk Christmas; well behaved children over 8; disabled access. **£18.50 lunch, £34.50 dinner.**

WORCESTER SO8554 **King Charles II** *29 New St (01905) 22449* Inn from which King Charles II made his escape through the back door, closely pursued by Cromwell's forces; enjoyable food, open fires, and a relaxed atmosphere in the downstairs restaurant and upstairs bar; cl Sun, 25 Dec, 1 Jan. **£30|£7.95.**

WYRE PIDDLE SO9647 **Anchor** *(01386) 552799* Relaxing 17th-c pub with lovely views over lawn, river and on over the Vale of Evesham; friendly little lounge with log fire, comfortable bar, and good popular food. **£15.50|£4.50.**

Special thanks to Jacqui and Ian Ross.

Worcestershire Calendar

Some of these dates were provisional as we went to press. Please check information with the telephone numbers provided.

MARCH

25 Redditch French Street Market (01527) 60806

APRIL

14 Redditch Medieval Street Market – *till 15 April* (01527) 60806
 7 Worcester Medieval Money-maker at the Commandery (01905) 361821
27 Upton upon Severn Oak Apple Day Celebrations (01684) 594200;
    Worcester Oak Apple Day at the Commandery: celebration of the Restoration of Charles II (01905) 361821
29 Pershore Carnival (01386) 554677

JUNE

23 Redditch Folk Festival – *till 25 June* (01527) 60806; **Upton upon Severn** Jazz Festival – *till 25 June* (01684) 593254

JULY

 8 Worcester Arts Festival – *till 15 July* (01905) 722322
14 Redditch French Street Market – *till 16 July* (01527) 60806
22 Bretforton Silver Band Fireworks Concert (01386) 834326
23 Welland Steam Rally (01684) 890417
29 Badsey Flower Show and Fête (01386) 423771

AUGUST

12 Pershore Flower and Craft Show (01386) 554235
26 Great Comberton Flower Show (01386) 710252

SEPTEMBER

16 Redditch Carnival (01527) 60806

OCTOBER

28 Worcester One World Fair at Worcester Woods Country Park – *till 29 October* (01905) 766493

NOVEMBER

16 Martley Music Festival – *till 19 November* (01886) 821570
25 Worcester Green Fair at Worcester Woods Country Park – *till 26 November* (01905) 766493

DECEMBER

 3 Redditch Christmas Craft Fair at Forge Mill Museum (01527) 60806
 8 Redditch Victorian Street Market – *till 9 December* (01527) 60806

YORKSHIRE

Very friendly, with attractive prices – very rewarding for holidays. The city of York itself is excellent for a short break. We have separate sections on the other three main areas, each of which has a great choice of places to visit. With the Dales, first-class walking country, we include Ripon, civilised Harrogate, and their surroundings (virtually all North Yorkshire west of the A19). The Moors and East Yorkshire (North Yorkshire east of the A19 along with the administrative county of East Yorkshire) also include memorable walks and drives, with plenty to keep children amused on the coast. West and South Yorkshire (particularly West Yorkshire) have an outstanding range of unusual visitor attractions, especially for families, often free.

York

Masses to see and do in delightful surroundings.

York is unique: a walled medieval city with a virtually traffic-free centre, full of lovely medieval buildings and twisting alleys, tempting shops and lots of lively cafés, pubs and bars. An extraordinary variety of things to interest all ages includes the magnificent Minster (one of Britain's great sights), the outstanding Castle Museum and National Railway Museum, and the Jorvik Centre, Britain's first modern heritage centre and still one of the best. Though it's undeniably a tourist city, with summer queues and crowds at the main attractions, all the other visitors actually seem to add to the atmosphere, rather than detracting from it.

You can do the circuit of the 13th-c city walls and their many towers in a couple of hours or so, mostly on top. One of the best stretches, with fine views of the Minster, is between the Monk Bar and Bootham Bar. If you plan on doing the whole circuit it's well worth using one of the Walkman guides rented by the helpful tourist office (Exhibition Sq).

Where to stay

SHIPTON BY BENINGBROUGH SE5458 **Sidings** *Shipton by Beningbrough, York YO6 1BS (01904) 470221* **£106,** plus special breaks; 8 rms with showers in 2 converted coaches. A railway enthusiast's paradise, based on restored former railway carriages with good food served at Pullman-style tables, and a decent wine list; railway viewing platform, models, videos, and paintings and artefacts; disabled access.

YORK SE5952 **Arnot House** *17 Grosvenor Terrace, York YO3 7AG (01904) 641966* **£50,** plus winter breaks; 4 rms with brass beds. Friendly no smoking Victorian terraced house with lots of original features, antiques and paintings, good breakfasts in the neat dining room (evening meals on request), and a pleasant, relaxed atmosphere; children over 12.

YORK SE5849 **Curzon Lodge** *23 Tadcaster Rd, Dringhouses, York YO2 2QG (01904) 703157* **£70,** plus winter breaks; 10 rms, some in former old coach house and stables. Charming early 17th-c house in a marvellous spot just S of the city overlooking Knavesmire racecourse with an attractive, comfortable drawing room, sunny farmhouse dining room (good breakfasts), and a secluded walled garden; cl Christmas; children over 7.

YORK SE6050 **Dairy Guesthouse** *3 Scarcroft Rd YO23 1ND (01904) 639367* ***£50;** 5 attractive rms (with thoughtful extras), some with own bthrm. Carefully restored no smoking Victorian house with lots of original features and attention to detail, enjoyable breakfasts with vegetarian choices, a warmly hospitable atmosphere, and a flower-filled courtyard; cl mid-Dec–end Jan; disabled access.

YORK SE6052 **Dean Court** *Duncombe Pl, York YO1 2EF (01904) 625082* **£120,** plus special breaks; 39 rms. Next to the Minster, this comfortable and neatly kept hotel has fresh flowers and plants in airy rooms, very helpful, efficient staff, enjoyable food in the elegant restaurant, and a tearoom/conservatory serving late breakfasts, light lunches and so forth; good for families, with thoughtful extras; children over 5 in evening restaurant.

YORK SE5952 **Grange** *Clifton, York YO3 6AA (01904) 644744* **£120,** plus special breaks; 30 individually decorated rms with antiques and chintz. Close to the Minster, this Regency town house has elegant public rooms, an open fire, newspapers, good breakfasts, excellent restaurant food (there's also a brasserie), and warmly friendly staff; car park; disabled access.

YORK SE6052 **Hazlewood** *24–25 Portland St, Gillygate, York YO3 7EH (01904) 626548* ***£59,** plus winter breaks; 14 recently refurbished, individually decorated rms. Just 4 minutes from the Minster, this no smoking, neatly kept Victorian house has quite a few original features, a cosy lounge, an attractive dining room, helpful owners, and a pretty little garden; off-street parking; children over 8.

YORK SE5951 **Holmwood House** *114 Holgate Rd, York YO2 4BB (01904) 626183* **£70,** plus special breaks; 14 pretty rms. Built as two 19th-c houses, this no smoking hotel is 5 minutes from the city walls, with books in the comfortable sitting room, and very good breakfasts; children over 8.

YORK SE5948 **Middlethorpe Hall** *Bishopthorpe Rd, Middlethorpe, York YO23 2GB (01904) 641241* **£190,** plus special breaks; 30 elegant rms, most in the converted stables. Lovely immaculately restored William III country house just S of the city, with fine gardens and parkland, antiques, paintings and fresh flowers in comfortable, quiet day rooms, and excellent food and service; children over 8.

YORK SE6052 **Palm Court** *17 Huntington Rd, York YO3 7RB (01904) 639387* ***£44;** 8 rms. Quiet and spotlessly kept Victorian house 5 minutes from the Minster, with a pleasant sitting room, very good breakfasts, particularly helpful and friendly owners, and evening meals on request; cl Christmas.

To see and do

YORKSHIRE Family Attraction of the Year

⛟ 🎫 **National Railway Museum** (Leeman Rd) You don't have to be a train buff to enjoy coming here (though if you are you'll be in heaven); in recent years they've spent a lot of time developing the museum as somewhere for the whole family, a process that's been given a real boost by the abolition of entrance charges for children. It's a big place, spread over a 17-acre site not far from the city's main railway station, and to see it properly you'll need to allow a fair amount of time (and energy). Best for children is the Interactive Learning Centre, much more fun than it sounds, with plenty of hands-on exhibits and activities vividly explaining how trains and railways work. Also at this end of the site is a miniature railway operating most weekends and school holidays, with steamtrain rides on certain dates too, and an outdoor play area with appropriately themed slides and so on. It's worth calling to check when the trains are running, and for dates when you'll find performances by their perky theatre company; as not everything happens every day, it's very much the sort of place where advance planning pays off. The museum's centrepiece is still the spectacular great hall, in which 2 sets of tracks and platforms radiate from central turntables, one with a changing display of two dozen great locomotives from the museum's huge collection, the other with all sorts of carriages and wagons, from the humblest and most utilitarian to Queen Victoria's sumptuous royal coach. You can clamber aboard most of them, and there are all sorts of noises and smells to make it feel like a proper railway station. Other displays show how railways changed the world, with as much on the social side of things as the technical. Highlights include the excellent exhibition on the story of the mail, which has lots of push-button games and displays (not to mention a karaoke machine) to engage children's attention, and the major new galleries The Works, and The Workshop. These have a story for younger visitors to follow as they go round, but it's often one of the simpler features that children find most fun: they can see from the equipment when trains are approaching on the adjacent GNER line, then dash on to a terrace to watch them roar past. You can usually get a road train from York Minster to the museum – every half-hour in summer, less often in winter (when it may be wknds only). Meals and snacks (and picnic areas), shop, disabled access; cl 24–26 Dec; (01904) 621261; £5.90. Their all-day car park costs £3.

♿🏭✝🐜 **ARC** (St Saviourgate) Refreshingly accessible archaeology centre; with the help of hands-on interactive displays you can decipher Viking-age writing, sort bones, tiles and pottery, or learn to make a Roman shoe, all with professional archaeologists on hand to give advice. During the summer you may even be able to watch a dig on Walmgate. Very much on the school-trips circuit, so best out of term-time. It's set in a beautifully restored medieval church, with an interesting old-fashioned garden. Shop, disabled access; cl am Sat, Sun, Good Fri, last 2 wks Dec; (01904) 643211; £3.60.

🏛 **Barley Hall** 🏷 (Swinegate) The Archaeological Trust that runs the ARC (and the Jorvik Centre) has restored this medieval family home, complete with audio tour. Shop, disabled access to ground floor only; cl am winter; (01904) 610275; *£3.50. The nearby Punch Bowl has good-value food.

♿✖ **Castle Museum** (Tower St) Housed in 18th-c prison buildings on the site of the former castle (part of the outer wall still stands), this is one of the best social history museums in the country, with a huge range of everyday objects from the past 4 centuries shown in convincingly reconstructed real-life settings, from Edwardian streets to prison cells and more contemporary living rooms. There's even a **watermill**, by the river outside. They have one of only 3 Anglo-Saxon helmets in the world, found here in York in the 1980s. Again, best out of term-time. Shop, disabled access ground floor only; cl Christmas and New Year; (01904) 613161; £4.95.

⬛ **City Art Gallery** (Exhibition Sq) Well displayed collections running from Old Masters to the lusciously romantic nudes of William Etty, with some very handsome stoneware pottery. Shop, disabled access; cl am Sun, 25–26 Dec, maybe other dates for civic events; (01904) 551861; free.

🏰 ❄ **Clifford's Tower** (Tower St) This former castle keep is perhaps York's most interesting building after the Minster. You can walk around the top of the walls, which enclose a garden, and there are good views of the city. It gets its name from Roger Clifford, who was hanged from the tower in chains. There's an unusual Lowry painting of the tower in the City Art Gallery (see entry above). Shop; cl 24–26 Dec, 1 Jan; (01904) 646940; £1.80. The Tudor Masons Arms is a handy stop.

🏛 ➰ **Fairfax House** (Castlegate) Magnificently restored mid-18th-c townhouse, probably one of the finest in England, its richly decorated rooms fully furnished in period style. Much of the impressive collection of paintings, pottery, clocks and Georgian furniture was donated by the great-grandson of the confectionary baron Joseph Terry, and there's a re-created mid-18th-c meal. Shop, some disabled access by arrangement (steps at front); cl Fri, am Sun, and Twelfth Night–mid-Feb; (01904) 655543; *£4.

🏛 **Guildhall** (St Helen's Sq) Exact replica of the original building of 1446, destroyed in a 1940 air raid. The stone walls of the earlier building form the framework of the new one. Disabled access; cl Nov–April wknds (and am Sun in summer), and bank hols; (01904) 613161; free.

🏠 **Jorvik Viking Centre** (below Coppergate Shopping Centre) The first place in the country to utilise the sights-sounds-and-smells technology that's gradually revolutionised the heritage industry, and still one of the best. Time-cars whisk you through an exact reconstruction of the Viking street, market and quayside that used to stand here, with quite astonishing detail: some of the faces were painstakingly constructed from actual Viking skulls. At the end are excavated finds from the site. Queues can be horrifically long, but almost everyone finds the wait well worth while (you can book tickets 7 days in advance (01904) 543403). Snacks, shop, disabled access; cl 25 Dec; (01904) 643211; £5.35.

🏛 **Merchant Adventurers' Hall** ⓔ (Piccadilly) The largest timber-framed building in the city, and one of the finest in Europe. Built for the powerful Merchant Adventurers' Company in the 1350s and hung with banners of medieval guilds, it has a chapel and undercroft as well as the Great Hall itself. Cl Sun Nov–Mar, and Christmas wk; (01904) 654818; *£1.90.

🏛 ➰ **Micklegate Bar Exhibition** Another of York's medieval gateways, now housing social history displays. Cl 25–26 Dec, 1 Jan, mid-Jan–mid-Feb and maybe other times in winter; (01904) 634436; £1.50.

🏛 ➰ **Monk Bar** The most striking and best preserved of York's 4 turreted medieval gateways. It now houses the **Richard III Museum**, where displays on the much-maligned monarch (or evil hunchbacked murderer depending on your point of view) are themed as if he were on trial – you put your verdict in the appropriate Guilty or Innocent book on the way out. Shop; cl 25–26 Dec; (01904) 634191; £1.50.

🎡 🚂 🐾 **Murton Park** (Murton, just E) Busy 8-acre park, excellent for children and best known for its **Museum of Farming**, with exhibitions of agricultural equipment, some animals and a Land Army display (museum cl 25 Dec). Also here the **Derwent Valley Light Railway** has trips along what was once known as the Blackberry Line, and a reconstructed Dark Age settlement (aimed mostly at children). Snacks, shop, disabled access; limited facilities Nov–Mar; (01904) 489966; £3.

🐾 ➰ **National Railway Museum** See separate family panel on p.717.

★ **The Shambles** SE6052 Jettied medieval buildings lean towards each other across these alleys, perked up by witty details such as the red figure of the printer's devil almost opposite the courtyard entry to the Olde Starre (a touristy pub, but genuinely old, with a view of the Minster from seats in its yard). This area has some of the city's most interesting shops, inc good bookshops, all sorts of unusual specialist shops, and, especially in Stonegate, nearer the Minster, and in elegant Micklegate, some serious silver and antique shops.

🏛 **Treasurer's House** 🖂 (Chapter House St; next to the Minster) There's been a house here since Roman times – this one dates from the 17th c, and the basement has an exhibition on its history. The timbered hall is very fine, as is the period furniture, and there is a newly restored period kitchen. Meals and snacks; cl Fri, all Nov–Mar; (01904) 624247; £3.50; NT.

🎪 👃 **York Brewery** (Toft Green) Tours and tastings (not am Sun; £3.75 – includes a pint of their beer). Just along the road from here the **Bar Convent** has a museum looking at early Christianity (and decent accommodation).

! **York Dungeon** (Clifford St) Carefully researched exploration of 2,000 years of superstition, torture and various forms of death, full of grue and gore. There's an extensive Guy Fawkes Experience and Dick Turpin Story; also an exhibition on the Plague. Snacks, shop, some disabled access; cl 25 Dec; (01904) 632599; £5.95.

✝ 👃 ❈ **York Minster** A glorious example of Gothic architecture, in soft-coloured York stone, this is Britain's largest medieval building, begun in 1220 and taking a staggering 250 years to build. The richly detailed interior contains more original medieval glass than any other church in England – and indeed is reckoned to house half of all that's known in the country. Look out for the great east window which shows Genesis and Revelations in 27 panels, the splendid 5 sisters window in the north transept, and the beautiful ceilings of the central tower and chapter house. The choir screen has 15 niches containing statues of the kings of England from William the Conqueror to Henry VI. There's a display on the church's turbulent history in the Foundations Museum and Treasury. Shop, disabled access and facilities (touch and hearing centre, Braille guides, guide dogs welcome); cl am Sun, and occasionally for major services; £2 for museum and treasury, also small charges for chapter house and crypt. You can climb the tower for good views of the city (£3). Largely traffic-free, the Close outside is fairly quiet, but not enclosed, and without the tranquil serenity of say Exeter, Salisbury or Winchester. Evening walking tours start from various points around it.

🏛 **York Minster Information Centre** (College St, opposite the Minster) 15th-c, with an exhibition, three finely timbered rooms – and a good restaurant. Shop; cl 25–26 Dec, Good Fri, and if they have conferences, so best to phone and check; (01904) 557233; 60p. Another useful nearby food stop is Peels in High Petergate.

✝ 👃 Besides the Minster, the city has a good few other fine medieval churches, though many are no longer used for services. Most were built during the prosperous 15th and 16th c, and among the finest are Holy Trinity (Goodramgate, which also contains in Our Lady's Row the oldest houses in the city) and St Helen's (St Helen's Sq). All Saints (North St) has some fascinating windows illustrating the world's last 15 days. In 15th-c St Mary's (Castlegate), the church has lively exhibitions on the city's history in the **York Story**; cl 25–26 Dec, 1 Jan; (01904) 628632; £1.90. The spire is York's tallest, at 46 metres (152ft).

🚂 **York Model Railway** (York Station, Tearoom Sq) Painstakingly re-created miniature town and country landscape, running as many as 20 trains at a time; a second much smaller model shows a typical German town at night. Shop, disabled access; cl 25–26 Dec; (01904) 630169; *£2.95.

👃 🏛 ❀ 🏛 **Yorkshire Museum** (Museum Gardens) A real treasure-trove, crammed with a myriad archaeological finds and riches from Roman, Anglo-Saxon, Viking and medieval times, inc the fabulous medieval Middleham Jewel. All set out very sensibly, with the displays effectively put into context. Shop, disabled access; cl 25–26 Dec, and am Sun Nov–Mar; (01904) 629745; £3.75, less for York residents. Outside are 10 acres of botanical gardens by the wall: peaceful and attractive, around a shapely group of ruins inc the Benedictine St Mary's abbey and the Multangular Tower (medieval, on a Roman base), as well as a working observatory.

Where to eat

YORK SE6051 **Bettys** *6 St Helen's Sq (01904) 659142* Famous tearooms opened in 1937 with fine teas and coffees (they import their own), good sandwiches, salads and hot specialities, delicious scones, tea breads, and patisseries, home-made milk shakes, Alsace wines from family vineyards, and evening pianist; cl 25–26 Dec. £6.50.

YORK SE6050 **Meltons** *7 Scarcroft Rd (01904) 634341* Smart little restaurant with paintings for sale, a cheerful mural and collection of cookery books, very good imaginative modern cooking using tip-top ingredients (plenty of vegetarian choice), lovely puddings, fair-value wines, and a relaxed, friendly atmosphere; cl pm Sun, am Mon, 3 wks Christmas, 1 wk end Aug. **£26.50|£6.40.**

YORK SE6052 **St William's College Restaurant** *College St (01904) 634830* Lovely 15th-c buildings with enclosed courtyard for outside summer eating next to York Minster, enjoyable varied food, and evening jazz and candlelight; cl Good Fri, 25–26 Dec. **£19.75|£7.**

YORK SE6052 **Treasurer's House** *Minster Yard (01904) 624247* Lovely National Trust property, once home to the medieval treasures of York Minster, with a tearoom in the converted cellars: traditional and herbal teas, good coffee, fruit wines, home-baked cakes and scones, savoury dishes and good puddings, all served by friendly staff; no smoking; cl Fri, Nov–Mar. **£4.95.**

The Yorkshire Dales, Harrogate and Ripon

Glorious countryside, and really interesting places to visit.

This area has some of Britain's most invigorating countryside and interesting scenery. The Dales' steep stone-walled pastures, majestic moors, wind-carved limestone crags and rushing streams give drivers and particularly walkers a succession of mouth-watering, quickly varying views, and of appealing villages and small towns. Each of the main dales or valleys has its own distinct character (which we describe in the text). The most rewarding places to visit here are Skipton Castle and Bolton Abbey. The train trip over the Pennines from Settle to Carlisle is memorable – on a clear day.

Harrogate is a civilised former spa resort with some of Yorkshire's smartest shops – a comfortable base, in easy reach of both Dales and Moors, with fine gardens at nearby Harlow Carr. Ripon (with one of Britain's largest cathedrals) and Richmond are appealing. Towards the east, Fountains Abbey, Ripley Castle, Newby Hall and Beningborough Hall are splendid outings. Among treats for children, the theme park at North Stainley stands out.

Where to stay

ALDBOROUGH SE4066 **Ship** *Aldborough, Boroughbridge, York YO5 9ER* (01423) 322749 **£45**; 5 rms, showers. Friendly and neatly kept 14th-c pub nr an ancient church and Roman town, with a coal fire in the stone inglenook fireplace and old-fashioned seats in the heavily beamed bar, ample food, good breakfasts, well kept real ales, and seats on spacious lawn; no children.

ARNCLIFFE SD9371 **Falcon** *Arncliffe, Skipton BD23 5QE* (01756) 770205 **£60**; 6 rms, some with own bthrm. Friendly, delightfully basic Georgian inn ideal for walkers, with functional little rooms and a fire, homely front lounge, an airy conservatory, no smoking dining room, generous plain lunchtime snacks; no B & B Nov–Mar, but self-catering cottage available then.

BAINBRIDGE SD9390 **Rose & Crown** *Bainbridge, Leyburn DL8 3EE* (01969) 650225 **£52**, plus special breaks; 11 comfortable rms. 15th-c coaching inn overlooking a lovely green, with antique settles and other old furniture in the beamed and panelled front bar, open log fires, cosy residents' lounge, big wine list, and home-made traditional food in both the bar and restaurant; pets welcome by prior arrangement.

BOLTON ABBEY SE0753 **Devonshire Arms** *Bolton Abbey, Skipton BD23 6AJ* (01756) 710441 **£155** plus special breaks; 41 individually furnished rms with thoughtful extras. Close to the priory itself and in lovely countryside, this civilised former coaching inn owned by the Duke of Devonshire has been carefully furnished with fine antiques and paintings from Chatsworth; log fires, impeccable service, beautifully presented imaginative food in the elegant restaurant, super breakfasts; health centre; children over 12 in restaurant; disabled access.

BUCKDEN SD9477 **Buck** *Buckden, Skipton BD23 5JA* (01756) 760228 *****£72,** plus special breaks; 14 comfortable rms. Busy pub surrounded by moorland views (lots of walkers) with snug original area and bustling extended open-plan bar, popular food served by smartly uniformed staff in the attractive no smoking dining room, decent wines, and well kept real ales; children over 6 in restaurant; disabled access.

BURNSALL SE0361 **Red Lion** *Burnsall, Skipton BD23 6BU* (01756) 720204 *****£95,** plus special winter breaks; 11 rms. Pretty 16th-c family-run ferryman's inn overlooking the river and village green with its tall maypole; an attractively panelled bar with beams and log fires, good food in both the bar and no smoking restaurant, decent wine list, big gardens and a riverside terrace; 75 yards of private fishing, permits for a further 7 miles; disabled access.

CARPERBY SE0089 **Old Stables** *Carperby, Leyburn DL8 4DA* (01969) 663590 *****£46,** plus special breaks; 3 rms, showers. Carefully converted stables with lots of original features (inc a manger in the dining room) in unspoilt moorland country with warmly welcoming, helpful owners, pleasantly furnished and neatly kept lounge and dining room (glass door to a terrace with fine views), log fire in the inglenook fireplace, and marvellous breakfasts with home-made marmalade; no smoking; cl Nov–Feb; no children or pets.

CRAY SD9479 **White Lion** *Cray, Skipton BD23 5JB* (01756) 760262 **£50,** plus special breaks; 8 comfortable rms with showers in adjoining barn. Welcoming little pub spectacularly isolated 335 metres (1,100ft) up with super views, lots of walks, traditional feel with flagstones, beams and log fires, good bar food, and decent wines.

DANBY WISKE SE3398 **White Swan** *Danby Wiske, Northallerton DL7 0NQ* (01609) 770122 *****£36**; 3 comfortable rms, shared bthrm. Cosy little pub in the middle of nowhere, handy for walkers on the coast-to-coast footpath, with very friendly licensees, and a decent choice of good-value food inc free-range eggs from their chickens.

FEIZOR SD7967 **Scar Close Farm** *Feizor, Austwick, Lancaster LA2 8DF* (01729) 823496 **£46,** plus special breaks; 4 clean, well appointed rms. Friendly converted barn on a working farm with large guest lounge, books, magazines and TV, and big breakfasts and homely evening meals – packed lunches, too; lovely quiet countryside; cl 25–26 Dec; disabled access.

GRASSINGTON SE0064 **Black Horse** *Garrs Lane, Grassington, BD23 5AT* *(01756) 752770* **£56,** plus special breaks; 15 rms. On the edge of the cobbled square, this is a bustling place with open fires and beams in the comfortable bar, friendly service, and enjoyable food in the attractive little restaurant; sheltered terrace.

HARROGATE SE2955 **Alexa House** *26 Ripon Rd, Harrogate HG1 2JJ (01423)* *501988* *£65,* plus special breaks; 13 rms, some in a former stable block. Attractive Georgian house with friendly staff, a comfortable lounge, good home cooking in the no smoking dining room, and marvellous breakfasts; you can use the local health club; good disabled access.

HARROGATE SE3055 **Balmoral** *16–18 Franklin Mount, Harrogate HG1 5EJ* *(01423) 508208* **£94,** plus special breaks; 20 lovely rms, many with four-posters. In quiet gardens but nr the centre, this popular hotel has a restful drawing room (lots of cat decorations), cosy snug, an interesting Oriental bar, fine food in the elegant restaurant, and helpful, friendly staff; you can use the nearby leisure club; cl Christmas–New Year; disabled access.

HAWES SD8789 **Cocketts** *Market Pl, Hawes DL8 3RD (01969) 667312* ***£59,** plus special breaks; 8 warm rms. Friendly, hard-working owners make this a most attractive and enjoyable place to stay, with a candlelit restaurant, woodburner in the small bar, and a residents' lounge with books; cl Christmas, 2 wks beginning of Feb; children over 10; disabled access.

KILNSEY SD9767 **Tennant Arms** *Kilnsey, Skipton BD23 5PS (01756) 752301* **£50,** plus special breaks; 10 rms. In a nice spot nr the River Wharfe, this spacious beamed and flagstoned inn has open fires (one fireplace made from an ornate carved four-poster), friendly service, good-value food, and views of spectacular overhanging Kilnsey Crag from the restaurant; pets welcome by prior arrangement; cl 25 Dec.

KNARESBOROUGH SE3457 **Dower House** *Bond End, Knaresborough HG5 9AL* *(01423) 863302* *£99,* plus special breaks; 31 clean, comfortable rms. Creeper-clad former dower house with attractively furnished public rooms of some character, good food in the Terrace Restaurant, super breakfasts, helpful service, and a leisure and health club.

LEYBURN SE1190 **Golden Lion** *Market Pl, Leyburn DL8 5AS (01969) 622161* **£64,** plus special breaks; 15 good-value rms. Homely inn with comfortable and quietly friendly bay-window 2-room bar with light squared panelling, good home-cooked traditional food in both the bar and evening restaurant, well kept real ales (inc one brewed to their own recipe), and helpful service; self-catering in nearby Hawnby; cl 25–26 Dec; disabled access.

LONG PRESTON SD8358 **Maypole** *Long Preston, Skipton BD23 4PH (01729)* *840219* **£46,** plus special breaks; 6 comfortable rms. Neatly kept 17th-c pub with generous helpings of enjoyable traditional food in the spacious, beamed dining room, open fire in the lounge bar, real ales, and helpful service; plenty of outside pursuits in the Dales National Park; disabled access.

MALHAM SD9062 **Miresfield Farm** *Malham, Skipton BD23 4DA (01729)* *830414* ***£52,** plus winter breaks; 14 rms. Spacious old farmhouse with good, freshly prepared food in the beamed dining room, a pleasant conservatory, 2 lounges and a lovely garden by the stream and village green; disabled access.

MARKINGTON SE2764 **Hob Green** *Markington, Harrogate HG3 3PJ (01423)* *770031* ***£105,** plus special breaks; 12 well equipped, pretty rms. Lovely gardens and over 800 acres of rolling countryside surround this charming 18th-c stone hotel with its comfortable lounge and garden room, log fires, antique furniture, fresh flowers, relaxed atmosphere, good food and friendly service.

MASHAM SE2280 **King's Head** *Market Sq, Masham, Ripon HG4 4EF (01765)* *689295* **£73.90;** 10 rms. Tall and handsome Georgian stone inn on the market square of this attractive small town, with lovely hanging baskets, 2 opened-up rooms of the neatly kept lounge bar, home-made food from an extensive menu, a separate restaurant, well kept real ales, helpful service, and good breakfasts.

MIDDLEHAM SE1287 **Greystones** *Market Pl, Middleham DL8 4NR* (01969) 622016 **£60** plus special breaks; 4 rms. Friendly family-run Georgian house with a log fire, books, magazines and TV in the restful lounge, generous helpings of good home-made food using home-grown vegetables; also, home-made bread, cakes and sweet and savoury biscuits, and enjoyable breakfasts; cl Jan–Feb.

MIDDLEHAM SE1287 **Millers House** *Market Pl, Middleham DL8 4NR* (01969) 622630 **£80,** plus special breaks; 7 pretty rms. Neatly furnished Georgian house with fine views, an open fire in the pleasant lounge, and an attractive restaurant with good, interesting, home-cooked food using vegetables and herbs grown in their garden; lunchtime picnic hampers, and helpful service; cl Jan; children over 10.

NEWTON-LE-WILLOWS SE2189 **The Hall** *Newton-le-Willows, Bedale DL8 1SW* (01677) 450210 **£80;** 3 spacious rms. Handsome Georgian house with quiet gardens and acres of paddocks, lots of fine antiques, paintings and wall hangings, a tranquil drawing room with an open fire and French windows into the garden, a cosy, homely snug with another fire, an honesty bar, good breakfasts in the light breakfast room (home-made fruitcake, tea and coffee always available), enjoyable food in the elegant dining room (by prior arrangement), and a helpful and hospitable owner; children over 13.

RAMSGILL SE1171 **Yorke Arms** *Ramsgill, Harrogate HG3 5RL* (01423) 755243 **£130 inc dinner,** plus special breaks; 13 attractive rms, many refurbished this year. Enjoyable small former shooting lodge with antique furnishings, log fires, particularly good and imaginative cooking in both the brasserie and comfortable dining room, fine wines, real ales, courteous service, and lovely surrounding walks; open all day for tea and coffee.

RICHMOND NZ1700 **Millgate House** *Richmond DL10 4JN* (01748) 823571 ***£50;** 3 rms overlooking the garden. Georgian townhouse with lots of interesting antiques and lovely plants, a peaceful drawing room, warm and friendly hosts offering meticulous attention to detail, and good breakfasts in the charming dining room which also overlooks the garden; it is this award-winning small garden, with views over the River Swale and the Cleveland hills beyond, that is so special, filled with wonderful roses, ferns, clematis and hostas – they have a booklet listing the plants; children over 10.

RICHMOND NZ1600 **Old Brewery** *29 The Green, Richmond DL10 4RG* (01748) 822460 ***£43;** 5 rms. In a pretty corner overlooking the village green and castle ruins is this delightful former inn with Victorian-style renovations and furnishings, a hospitable atmosphere, and nice garden; dinner by arrangement; cl Dec–Jan; no children.

RICHMOND NZ1404 **Whashton Springs Farm** *Whashton Springs, Richmond DL11 7JS* (01748) 822884 ***£46;** 8 comfortable rms. Attractive stone-built Georgian farmhouse on a 600-acre working mixed farm with a log fire in the comfortable sitting room, good country breakfasts in the attractive dining room (no evening meals), lovely countryside; cl Christmas–Jan; children over 5.

RIPLEY SE2860 **Boars Head** *Ripley, Harrogate HG3 1AY* (01423) 771888 ***£120,** plus special breaks; 25 charmingly decorated rms. In a delightful estate village, this fine old coaching inn has a relaxed, welcoming atmosphere, with comfortable sofas in attractively decorated lounges, a long flagstoned bar, notable wines by the glass, fine food in the bar and restful dining room, and unobtrusive service; disabled access.

RIPON SE3071 **Ripon Spa** *Park St HG4 2BU* (01765) 602172 ***£84,** plus special breaks; 40 individually furnished rms, many overlooking the grounds. Neatly kept, friendly and comfortable Edwardian hotel with 7 acres of charming gardens, yet only a short walk from the centre; attractive public rooms, and good food in both the bar and restaurant; disabled access.

SEDBUSK SD8790 **Stone House** *Sedbusk, Hawes DL8 3PT* (01969) 667571 **£70** plus special breaks; 22 rms, 2 with own conservatories. Small, warmly friendly Edwardian hotel with a country-house feel and appropriate furnishings, stunning setting with magnificent views, an attractive oak-panelled drawing room, billiard room, log fires, exemplary service, good local information; pleasant extended dining room with excellent wholesome food (special needs catered for) inc super breakfasts, and a reasonable choice of wines; tennis lawn in the grounds, wonderful walks; P G Wodehouse stayed here as a guest of the original owner who employed a butler called Jeeves – it was on him that Wodehouse based his famous character; cl Jan; dogs welcome; good disabled access

SETTLE SD8162 **Falcon Manor** *Skipton Rd, Settle BD24 9BD (01729) 823814* **£80,** plus special breaks; 19 rms. Quietly set, imposing Victorian hotel in its own grounds with original features in the spacious public rooms, log fires, fine food and lovely views in the elegant restaurant, and obliging service; a well placed touring base; disabled access.

SHIPTON BY BENINGBROUGH SE5458 **Sidings** *See under York, p.715.*

STARBOTTON SD9574 **Fox & Hounds** *Starbotton, Skipton BD23 5HY (01756) 760269* **£55;* 2 rms with showers. Prettily placed and rather smart little Upper Wharfedale village inn, warmly welcoming, with flagstones, beams and a big log fire, imaginative food and well kept real ales; cl Jan–mid-Feb.

STUDLEY ROGER SE2970 **Lawrence House** *Studley Roger, Ripon HG4 3AY (01765) 600947* **£80;** 2 spacious, lovely rms. Attractive Georgian house with 2 acres of garden on the edge of Studley Royal deer park and Fountains Abbey; lovely antiques and fine pictures, log fires, good breakfasts, and delicious evening meals; cl Christmas–New Year; children by arrangement.

THORALBY SE0086 **Scarr House** *Thoralby, Leyburn DL8 3SU (01969) 663654* **£64,** plus special breaks; 3 rms with showers. Relaxed and friendly no smoking 18th-c former farmhouse with lovely views, lots of books (no TV), comfortable lounge in a converted hayloft with beams, exposed stones and an open fire, carefully cooked, imaginative food (bring your own wine) at candlelit tables, and nice breakfasts; no children.

THORNTON WATLASS SE2385 **Buck** *Thornton Watlass, Ripon HG4 4AH (01677) 422461* **£55,** plus fishing and racing breaks; 7 rms, most with own bthrm. Warmly friendly country pub overlooking the cricket green in a very attractive village; interesting beamed and panelled rooms, open fire, live music weekends in the function room, excellent food inc summer barbecues, and lots of nearby walks (the arboretum is very popular); the inn offers guided walking holidays; limited disabled access.

WATH IN NIDDERDALE SE1467 **Sportsmans Arms** *Wath in Nidderdale, Harrogate HG3 5PP (01423) 711306* **£70,** plus special breaks; 13 refurbished rms – most with own bthrm; more rms to be added in a converted barn and stables. Friendly, quietly placed 17th-c hotel with lovely views, an elegant bar, a good range of wines, excellent food (especially fish) in the no smoking evening restaurant, super lunchtime bar food, and attentive service; particularly good Sun lunch, and lots of fine cheeses; cl 25 Dec; disabled access.

WEST WITTON SE0688 **Wensleydale Heifer** *West Witton, Leyburn DL8 4LS (01969) 622322* **£72* plus special breaks; 15 rms in 2 adjacent old buildings. Friendly 17th-c stone coaching inn with comfortable furnishings, log fires and oak beams, a cosy bar, and good local game and fresh seafood in the bistro or spacious restaurant; well behaved dogs allowed.

WIGGLESWORTH SD8056 **Plough** *Wigglesworth, Skipton BD23 4RJ (01729) 840243* **£60,** plus special breaks; 12 well equipped rms, some in newer extension. Friendly and well run country inn with popular food in the conservatory restaurant and bar, lots of little rooms surrounding the bar area – some smart and plush, others spartan yet cosy – friendly service, big breakfasts, packed lunches, and views of the Three Peaks; disabled access.

To see and do

AISKEW SE2787
🐑 Big Sheep & Little Cow Farm
Small-scale dairy farm, with friendly sheep and dexter cows (Britain's smallest), and pigs and chicks – the family in charge love talking to visitors. A new undercover animal display should be ready this year. Don't come when it's wet. Snacks, shop selling sheep's milk and home-made sheep's milk ice-cream, some disabled access; cl Sept–Mar; (01677) 422125; £2.95.

ALDBOROUGH SE4066
🏛☗✝★ Aldborough Roman Town
The northernmost civilian Roman town was here, its houses, courts, forum and temple surrounded by a massive 6 metres (9ft) wall. All that remain are 2 pavements, the position of the wall and, in the museum, some finds from the site. Shop; open pm Apr–Oct (cl 1–2pm); (01423) 322768; £1.70, free admission to site only in winter. It's a pleasant village with an impressive church (check out the sundial); the Ship opposite is good for lunch.

ARKENDALE SE3861
! Balloon trips You can book these from the Flight Centre, (01423) 340664 (£125); they also have an authentic Boeing 737 **flight simulator**, though you may experience some turbulence paying for the £125 session.

ARNCLIFFE SD9371
★ ⌂ Charming tucked-away Dales village, well placed for walks. The road up Littondale is pretty, and that to Langcliffe in Ribblesdale runs through dramatic scenery. The Falcon, in the same family for many generations, is an archetypal Dales inn, very simple but warmly welcoming.

ASKRIGG SD9491
★ ✝ ⌂ Delightful collection of elegant stone houses around neat streamside greens, walks to nearby waterfalls, a fine 15th-c church, and 2 decent pubs in this lovely village.

AYSGARTH SE0188
★ ⌂ Aysgarth waterfalls The Lower Fall is the most spectacular of this famously romantic series of waterfalls, via a path over the road from the car park. The falls are the National Park's chief visitor honeypot and do get crowded, particularly through Aug (when even parking can be a problem here). They're better in late spring or early autumn, when there tends to be more water in the river and therefore a better show. In severely cold weather they can be stunning, with wonderful ice sculptures building up. There's generally a small charge to see the Upper Fall (it's on private land), but you can see it almost as well without paying, from the bridge on the road. The main car park (around £1 for 3 hours, more at wknds) has a **National Park Centre**, with displays on the Dales, and useful walks, maps, and guides. Café, shop, disabled facilities; cl Mon–Thurs Nov–Mar; (01969) 663424; free. For more of a walk, you can contrive longer routes along the S bank of the Ure from the delightful village of West Burton.

☗ Yorkshire Carriage Museum (Yore Mill) A collection of Victorian coaches and carriages. Meals, snacks; cl Christmas; (01969) 663399; *£2. The George & Dragon is a good place for lunch.

BAINBRIDGE SD9390
★ Delightful, its broad sloping green still with the village stocks, and still ringing with the blowing of a buffalo-horn to guide shepherds down through the mists each night at 9pm from the end of Sept till late Feb, as it has done for centuries.

✗ 🏭 Low Mill Restored 18th-c **corn mill** with a collection of fully furnished hand-made dolls' houses, all produced on the premises. Good shop (sells plans to make your own). Open pm Weds July–mid-Sept, maybe bank hols, and by appointment; (01969) 650416; *75p.

BEDALE SE2685
🌸 Thorpe Perrow (off B6268 S) Well laid-out 60-acre landscaped lakeside collection of rare trees and shrubs among some splendid mature specimens that have been growing here for over 400 years. Particularly strong on oaks, ornamental cherries, willows and hazels, and lovely in spring when the bulbs are out. Snacks, shop, disabled access; (01677) 425323; £3.50. In the town the convivial Olde Black Swan does good-value lunches.

BENINGBROUGH SE5358

🏠🖼️🐝 **Beningbrough Hall** Stately early 18th-c baroque mansion, with a good collection from the National Portrait Gallery, also a marvellous staircase with balusters carved in imitation of wrought iron, fine carvings, and a big restored Victorian dairy. Regular events for families, and lovely formal gardens. Meals, snacks, shop, disabled access to ground floor only; cl Thurs, Fri (exc July–Aug), and all Nov–Mar; (01904) 470666; £5, garden only £3.50; NT. The riverside Dawnay Arms at Newton-on-Ouse is useful for lunch.

BISHOPDALE SD9885

⌂ One of Wensleydale's tributary dales, broader than the others but still quite dramatic for walkers.

BOLTON ABBEY SE0754

🏰✝️🐦⌂🌼 Beautiful spot in lovely rolling wooded parkland on a knoll above the River Wharfe. Most of the priory buildings, dating from the 12th to the 16th c, are in ruins, but the central core of the main church is still used for Sunday services. 19th-c additions such as stained glass (some by Pugin) and murals oddly don't strike a false note. The car park gets rather full in summer (£3 charge). The Devonshire Arms is very fine for lunch. Attractive walks lead off in most directions: the landscape has a lowland beauty, with the ruined abbey, the turf banks of the Wharfe and the oaks of the Strid Wood, where a leaflet detailing nature trails is available. A steep ascent from Howgill is rewarded by views from Simon's Seat, on the edge of moors.

BRIMHAM ROCKS SE2065

🐦 **Brimham Rocks** (off B6265) Spectacular and extraordinarily weathered gritstone pinnacles, tors and boulders facing the winds at a height of 290 metres (950ft), conjuring up people, animal heads and other strange figures – a Victorian guidebook declared that they were 'grim and hideous forms defying all description and definition'. Children like them a lot – Henry Moore said that when he was a boy they strongly moulded his imagination. Information centre, shop and tearoom open wknds and bank hols Easter–Oct, daily Jun–Sept and school hols – weather permitting, the site is open all year; (01423) 780688; parking £2.30; NT. The Half Moon on the B6265 is handy for lunch.

CASTLE BOLTON SE0095

⌂🌼 **Apedale Head** This spectacular viewpoint is reached by a 3-mile plod up tracks NW of Castle Bolton; on fine days it feels like the top of the world, with views encompassing both Wensleydale and Swaledale.

🏰🌼 **Bolton Castle** 🏯 (off A684) A massive 14th-c structure towering over the tiny single-street village built for it. Considering it was partly dismantled in 1645 and has been empty ever since, it's still in fine shape; great views from the 30-metre 100ft towers. Meals, snacks, shop; cl Dec–Feb; (01969) 623981; £4. The King's Arms at Redmire has good food.

CLAPHAM SD7469

★🐦⌂ Attractive village that has turned walking and caving into something of an industry. The riverside New Inn is useful for lunch (and a good place for walkers to stay in).

🌼⌂ **Ingleborough** (721 metres – 2,376ft) Best approached from Clapham, along the Reginald Farrer Trail, past Ingleborough Cave (see below) and Gaping Gill (a vast pothole); the panorama extends far across Lancashire and into Cumbria.

🐦 **Ingleborough Cave** One of the most easily visited of the vast network of caverns plunging into the limestone hills around here – and probably the only one that wheelchairs can go all the way through. It's set in the grounds of the outdoors centre at Ingleborough Hall – formerly the family home of the great plantsman Reginald Farrer, who in his short life introduced and eulogised many notable plants from the Himalayas and China. A **nature trail** leads past Farrer's woods and small lake to the cave; unusually, it's a place that looks better in wet weather. Snacks, shop, some disabled access; cl wkdys Nov–Feb; (01524) 251242; £4.

National Park Centre Good introductory centre; best to check winter opening, usually wknds only; (01524) 251419; parking around £1 for 3 hours (more at wknds).

COVERDALE SE0481

Wensleydale's major tributary valley, relatively very quiet; fairly gentle in its lower reaches, climbing high into a wild and untamed-feeling world of lonely sheep farms.

CRAKEHALL SE2490

Crakehall Watermill 17th c, on the site of a still earlier one; restored in 1980, it now produces flour again. Even when they're not milling, the wheel should still be turning. Snacks, shop; cl Mon, Tues and Oct–Mar; (01677) 423240; £1. The Bay Horse in a nice spot on Little Crakehall green has good-value food.

CROFT NZ2809

† Right on the border with County Durham is a pleasant **church** where Lewis Carroll's father was parson; there's a plaque in memory of the writer, complete with an enamelled White Rabbit, and an unusual family pew reached by a staircase. If the church is closed, the key is kept at the hotel across the road. Nice river views.

DENTDALE SD7586

Just on the Cumbrian side of the Yorkshire border, this offers walks along a lonely green track above the S side of the dale.

DENTON MOOR SE1450

Above the reservoirs S of Blubberhouses, this offers scope for fairly stretching walks (though nothing to compare with the Dales themselves).

DRUIDS TEMPLE SE1879

! Nr the hamlet of Ilton, a no-through road leads up to woodlands where you can walk to this scaled-down Stonehenge, built by a landowner in the 1820s as work for local unemployed people.

EMBSAY SE0053

Embsay Steam Railway Steam trips along a couple of miles of railway, prettily set beneath limestone crags. There's a ticket office from Ilkley, and a collection of old locomotives and carriages. They have now extended the track to Bolton Abbey. Snacks, shop (remarkable range of books), disabled access (notice preferred); usually open Sun all year, and other days in summer – best to ring (01756) 795189 for timetable; £5. The well run Elm Tree has fine food, and the Wayside Café in nearby Draughton does good scones.

FOUNTAINS ABBEY SE2769

† **Fountains Abbey & Studley Royal Watergarden** (off B6265) The largest monastic ruin in the country, this romantic place was founded in 1132 by Cistercian monks, in a delightful riverside setting. Said to be haunted by a full choir of ghostly monks, most of the remains are 12th c, but the proud main tower is 15th c. Opposite are the lovely landscaped gardens begun by William Aislabie in 1768, which include ornamental temples and follies, formal watergardens, lakes aflutter with waterfowl, and 400 acres of deer park. The most beautiful approach is through the extraordinarily ornate Victorian **church** at the far end (maybe restoration in progress, best to phone for opening), and this 'back-door' entrance is the most tranquil too. A helpful modern visitor centre has been skilfully constructed so that it blends in and doesn't spoil the view. Free guided tours of abbey 11am, 2.30pm and 3.30pm Apr–Oct. Meals, snacks, shop, good disabled access; cl Fri Nov–Jan, and 24–25 Dec; (01765) 608888; £4.30, deer park – an excellent strolling ground – free; NT. The very civilised Sawley Arms in Sawley just W does good food.

GIGGLESWICK SD7867

★ **Falconry & Conservation Centre** (top of Crows Nest, off A65 N of Settle) Well organised, with lots of vultures, eagles, hawks, falcons and owls, and regular flying displays (from noon). Meals, snacks, shop, disabled access; cl 25 Dec, maybe other days too in winter; (01729) 825164; £4.95. The village is attractive.

GLASSHOUSES SE1764

Yorkshire Country Wines (The Mill) Traditional country wines produced in a 19th-c flax mill, with free tastings, antiques, and a tearoom overlooking the River Nidd; they prefer notice for disabled access. Cl Mon and Tues and wkdys Nov–Easter, winery tours (£2.50) Fri and Sat at 11.45am; (01423) 711947.

GRASSINGTON SE0063

★ Pleasant small town or large village around a sloping cobbled square, depending a lot on walkers and other

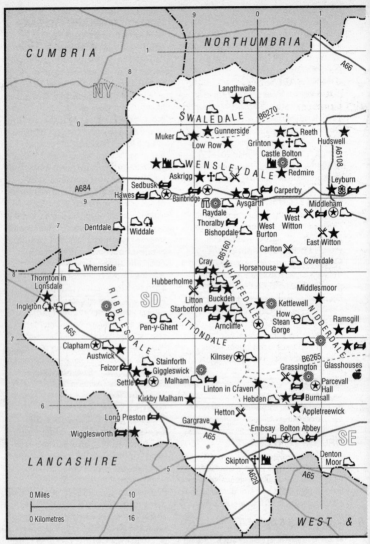

visitors, with some attractive shops and a few interesting old buildings; there's a National Park information centre. The Black Horse has decent food and comfortable bedrooms. The B6160 gives lovely Wharfedale views, and the B6265 to Pateley Bridge also has memorable views (and passes the colourfully lit underground Stump Cross Caverns, well worth a look.

GRINTON SE0498

★ † ⌂ Attractive riverside village with a charming church known as the 'cathedral of the Dales', and pleasant walks nearby. The waterside Bridge Inn, opposite the church, is open all day and has decent food.

HARROGATE SE3054

★ 🏰 🏵 This elegant and self-confident inland resort has kept its Victorian spa-town atmosphere despite now filling many of its handsome hotels with up-to-date conferences and so forth. The layout of the town is very gracious, and

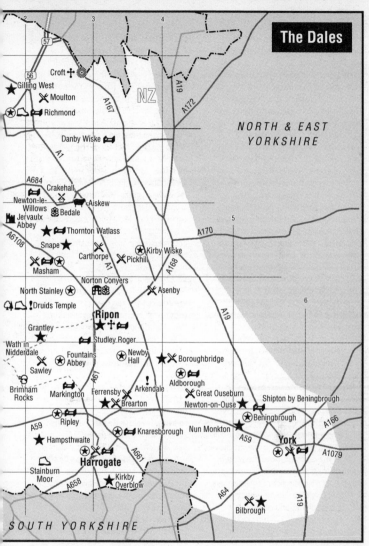

The Dales

NZ

NORTH & EAST YORKSHIRE

Croft †
Gilling West
Moulton
Richmond
Danby Wiske
A1
A684
Crakehall
Newton-le-Willows
Bedale · Aiskew
Jervaulx Abbey
Thornton Watlass
Snape
Carthorpe · Pickhill
Kirby Wiske
Masham
Norton Conyers
North Stainley
Asenby
Druids Temple
Ripon
Grantley
Studley Roger
Wath in Nidderdale
Fountains Abbey
Newby Hall
Boroughbridge
Sawley
Aldborough
Brimham Rocks
Markington
Ferrensby
Arkendale
Great Ouseburn
Shipton by Beningbrough
Brearton
Newton-on-Ouse
Ripley
Beningbrough
York
Hampsthwaite
Knaresborough
Nun Monkton
A166
Stainburn Moor
Harrogate
A1079
Kirkby Overblow
A64
Bilbrough
A19

SOUTH YORKSHIRE

you couldn't ask for better shops (interesting antiques and some top-notch specialist shops). Almost every available space is filled with colourful plant displays, as if to shake off the gloom of the dark stone buildings. The first thing a visitor notices is the great sweep of The Stray, open parkland which runs right along and through the S side of the centre. The original sulphur well was discovered in the 16th c and named the **Tewit Well**, after the local word for the lapwings which led a local sporting gent to ride into what was then a smelly bog. It's up on The Stray, grandly encased in what looks like an Italianate mausoleum. The elegant buildings of the compact central area run down from here to the pleasantly laid-out Valley Gardens, very Victorian, their curlicued central tea house run by a friendly Italian family. The relaxed tempo of the place, and the clean bracing climate (it's quite high on the moors), have made it a popular retirement area. Besides the places mentioned in **Where to eat**, the Drum & Monkey (fish restaurant/wine bar, Montpellier Gardens), Hedleys (wine bar, Montpellier Parade) and the Regency (off East Parade) are all good for lunch or a snack; the café of the Theatre Royal is also pleasant, as is the Lascelles Arms out in Follifoot.

Harlow Carr Botanical Gardens (Crag Lane, off B6162 W) Ornamental and woodland gardens over 68 acres, with streams, pools, rockeries, rhododendrons, spring bulbs and many interesting plants. Also a museum of gardening, model village, scented garden, and developing rose garden. A place of real peace and fresh moorland air, the finest strolling ground near Harrogate, and virtually deserted out of season, when the excellent collection of heathers comes into its own. Meals, snacks, plant centre, limited disabled access; (01423) 565418; £3.60. The adjacent Harrogate Arms has good-value food.

Mercer Art Gallery (Swan Rd) Another early spa building, with an excellent collection (cl am Sun, and Mon exc bank hols; free).

Royal Pump Room Museum (Royal Parade) The central sulphur wells (there are other outlets all over the town) are housed here, enclosed by glass to contain the reek. You can still order a free glass of the water at the original spa counter, now the ticket counter for the museum. The octagonal pump room building contains displays of 19th-c fine china and jewellery, as well as bath chairs and other impedimenta of the golden spa days. Shop, disabled access; cl Oct–Mar; (01423) 503340; £2.

HAWES SD8789

★ Busy in summer with hikers and coach parties, but pretty, and a proper market town, its Tuesday mart full of livestock in late summer. The Crown and White Hart are useful for lunch.

Dales Countryside Museum (Station Yard) Developing centre with interesting displays of local crafts and domestic and industrial life as well as hands-on exhibits, a steam locomotive and displays on transport. Shop, disabled access; maybe cl Mon, Tues and Thurs Nov–Mar, so best to phone; (01969) 667450; £3.

Hardraw Force (just N of Hawes) England's tallest waterfall cascading over a 30-metre (100ft) lip; it's best after rain (though the paths can be muddy then), and at dry times you may see barely a trickle; small fee at the Green Dragon pub. A longer excursion follows the Pennine Way from Hawes and over the River Ure. The valley above the falls is attractive, and this can be a start for the long day's walk to Great Shunner Fell. The B6255 S to Ribblehead gives fine mountain views, and the Buttertubs Pass northwards through High Shaw over into Swaledale is a spectacular drive (the Buttertubs are deep ferny holes near the summit where carriers used to cool their butter in hot weather).

Outhwaites Ropemakers (A684, Town Foot) They've been making rope for 200 years – see how it's done. Shop (not just great hawsers, useful things too like dog-leads), disabled access; cl wknds (exc Sat July–Oct, Easter and spring bank hol), 10 days at Christmas; (01969) 667487; free, guided tours £1.60.

Wensleydale Creamery (Gayle Lane) Saved from closure by a timely management buy-out a few years ago, this has developed a fascinating visitor centre, with a well set-out dairying/cheese museum; you can watch the cheese being made by the traditional method, all by hand. The shop (busy in summer) has samples of their variously flavoured cheeses – our favourite was one with blueberries. Very good café, disabled facilities; cl 25 Dec; (01969) 667664; £2.

HEBDEN SE0263

Hebden lead mines There's a rewarding walk from Hebden up Hebden Beck with its legacy of old lead-mine workings; the route can be extended to take in Grassington and the path along the River Wharfe.

HUBBERHOLME SD9377

★ ✝ Beautifully placed riverside Dales hamlet with a good 13th-c **church**, built on an ancient burial site, with a Norman tower, unusual rood loft and pews by Thompson of Kilburn –

with their little carved mouse trademark. The charmingly set George, J B Priestley's favourite pub, has good food and bedrooms. A walk not to be missed is up to Scar House and along a level turfy terrace, which commands magnificent views down the dale, to Cray (another good inn there). The walk can be expanded to include Buckden – in fact there are good walks between all the Wharfedale/Littondale places flagged on our map, with good pub food available in each of them.

INGLETON SD7174

🐾 🍴 ⌂ **White Scar Cave** (B6255 towards Hawes) The country's biggest show cavern and one of the most spectacular, with underground waterfalls and streams, and an Ice Age cavern. Some amazing sights and atmospheric formations, and stunning stalactites and stalagmites that have been here for 100,000 years. Wrap up well – the guided tour takes about 80 minutes and gets chilly. Snacks, shop, disabled access by arrangement; cl 25 Dec (and sometimes after heavy rain); (01524) 241244; £6.20. The Wheatsheaf and Bridge are useful, and the B6255/B6479 is a very scenic long way round to Settle. Ingleton Glen is a lovely wooded walk up the River Twiss, over the moor and back down the River Doe, past a series of picturesque waterfalls; not too strenuous, with very varied scenery, it takes 2 or 3 hours – the admission fee for this is amply justified by the delightful gorge and waterfalls.

JERVAULX ABBEY SE1785

🏰 Less imposing than Fountains, Rievaulx and Bolton, but in some ways even more appealing – perhaps because the rough-cropped grass and wild flowers around the shattered walls emphasise the slightly melancholy atmosphere of a place of great worldly wealth and power that's come to nothing. Teas, shop, disabled access; abbey open all year, visitor centre cl am Nov–Dec, and all Jan–Feb; (01677) 460391; £2. The Blue Lion at East Witton nearby has superb food.

KETTLEWELL SD9672

★ ❀ Popular village for walkers, with 3 decent pubs; there are exhilarating views from the back roads from here up into Coverdale, and to Hawes via Hubberholme.

KILNSEY SD9767

🎣 ⊛ ✟ **Kilnsey Park & Trout Farm** (B6160) Two lakes for fly-fishing, plus a fun-fishing area for children, adventure playground, and good estate shop with fish, oven-ready game and other local produce. There's an aquarium in the visitor centre and a sizeable collection of orchids. You have an even better chance of spotting a red squirrel now (this is a conservation area for these shy creatures), as 4 babies were born last year. Good meals and snacks (inc tasty trout from their new smokery, and local cheeses), disabled access; cl 25 Dec; (01756) 752150; £2 for visitor centre, £4.20 for children's fishery (only open wknds and school hols), and proper fishing from around £15 per half-day. The Tennant Arms has decent food.

KIRBY WISKE SE3684

🏛 ✟ ♻ **Sion Hill Hall** Splendid Georgian mansion, one of the last country houses to be built before World War I, with period furnishings and an enormous collection of antiques, porcelain, paintings and clocks. Also costume and doll collections and birds-of-prey centre. Snacks, shop (inc antiques), some disabled access; cl am, all day Mon and Tues; all Nov–Mar; (01845) 587206; £4.

KNARESBOROUGH SE3557

★ ⚓ The little town above the steeply picturesque river gorge, with its spectacular railway viaduct, is pleasant and colourful (especially on Weds market day), with some attractive buildings. The chemist's shop on the square is said to be the oldest in the country; established in 1720, it still has all its original fittings. You can hire **rowing boats** down on the river, and there are pleasant riverside paths and walks: from Abbey Rd for example you should be able to see the intriguing **House in the Rock**, and a 15-minute walk down here brings you to St Robert's Cave, the riverside home of a 12th-c hermit. The Mother Shipton and Yorkshire Lass both have good-value food.

🏰 ♻ **Knaresborough Castle** All that remains are the 14th-c keep (with a museum and suitably dank dungeon), gatehouse and some of the curtain wall, but it's easy to imagine what an imposing sight it must have made, glowering over the gorge of the River Nidd – a suitable spot for Thomas à Becket's murderers to hide in. Shop, limited disabled access; cl Oct–Easter; (01423) 503340; £2, also includes entrance to the 14th-c **Old Court**, now a local history museum.

! Mother Shipton's Cave & Well
In the 19th c quite a little tourist industry was concocted for the toffs from Harrogate around the alleged 16th-c prophecies of Mother Shipton. The cave she lived in is pleasantly set in 12 acres of riverside parkland, along with this limestone spring, which quickly coats teddy-bears and other unlikely objects in rock so that they can be sold as souvenirs. There are guided tours, and a local history museum, but admission to the site is £4.55 and not everyone comes away feeling it was worth it. Snacks, shop; (01423) 864600; cl 25 Dec.

LANGTHWAITE NZ0002
★ ◩ Idyllic Dales hamlet, with good circular walks from the pub – and the Arkengarthdale road up to the remote but very popular Tan Hill Inn is a very fine drive.

LEYBURN SE1190
★ Bustling little agricultural town with a proper country atmosphere and lively Friday market: the Sandpiper's the nicest pub, and Tennants is Europe's largest auction room for house clearances and antiques. Off the A684 W there are fine drives: up Coverdale

to Kettlewell; up Bishopdale on the B6160 and on down past Cray into Wharfedale; up into the Eden Valley's Cumbrian headwaters on the B6269; and the Carperby–Castle Bolton–Reeth road.

⊗ Constable Burton Gardens
(A684 E) A series of fine terraced gardens around a handsome Georgian house (not open); the cyclamen at the end of the short lime avenue flower beautifully in early Aug. Some disabled access but no facilities; open late Mar–mid-Oct; (01677) 450428; £2.50.

LINTON IN CRAVEN SD9962
★ A gem of a Dales village, with lovely stone buildings, set off by lawns running down to a duck-filled stream. The Fountaine is a nice pub

MALHAM SD9062
◩ This has a good National Parks information centre, and the Lister Arms is a good refuge. A fine if popular walk leads along the beck to Janet's Foss waterfall, and to the romantic severity of dramatic Gordale Scar, Malhamdale's most memorable natural feature, where a beck makes a spectacular leap from the rocks. The Pennine Way N of Malham waterfall ascends the side of Malham Cove, a great cliff, then crosses a natural rock pavement and heads over a landscape of limestone scars, disappearing streams and green turf to Malham Tarn, a lovely mountain lake skirted on its E side by a nature trail.

◩ ✿ **Malhamdale** One of the smaller dales, its upper stretches cut tortuously and deeply out of the limestone by the River Aire and its steep tributaries, leaving spectacular cliffs, extensive bare

---

Days Out

Southern gateway to the Dales: Embsay Steam Railway; Skipton Castle; lunch at the Royal Shepherd, Skipton, or the Angel, Hetton, or the Old Hall, Threshfield; Grassington; walk through Strid Woods; Bolton Abbey.

Drive through Wensleydale and Swaledale: Hawes; Bainbridge; lunch at King's Arm's, Askrigg, or the George & Dragon, Aysgarth; Aysgarth Falls; Castle Bolton; Reeth and Muker (optional walk along Swale to Keld and return on the Pennine Way); cross Buttertubs Pass to return to Hawes.

Monastic mementos and Georgian follies: Ripon Cathedral; lunch at the Sawley Arms, Sawley; Fountains Abbey and Studley Royal.

upland limestone 'pavements', craggy bowls carved out of the overhanging hillsides, and sparkling waterfalls. This area is understandably a magnet for visitors.

MASHAM SE2280

★ † (pronounced 'Mazzum') Civilised small market town, with an interesting **church**, and dignified Georgian houses around its broad market square – which comes to life on Weds. The King's Head does good food.

🍺 **Black Sheep Brewery** Set up by a breakaway member of the Theakston family a few years back, its beers since proving very popular. Readers enjoy the fun and imaginative tours: best to book, (01765) 689227 – evening tours are best, with more time to enjoy samples at the end; disabled access; £3.75. Good place for refreshments, too.

🍺 **Theakston Brewery Centre** Next to the brewery, this explains the brewing process behind Theakstons beer, inc their Old Peculier. Shop, disabled access; open daily Easter–Oct, and wknds and Weds Nov–mid-Dec; £2. Enthusiastic tours of the brewery itself (£3), best to book on (01765) 689057; you see more in the mornings; no under 10s.

🔮 **Uredale Glass** (42 Market Pl) Hand-made glassware, with glass-blowing demonstrations (not Sun or Mon); cl Christmas wk; (01765) 689780; free.

MIDDLEHAM SE1287

★ 🛆 Attractive and civilised, basically Georgian stone-built village, still with the style that came from its days as the country's top racehorse-training centre in the 18th and early 19th c. Even now there are times when it seems to have more horses than people: pick up breeding and gallops gossip in the bar of the good Black Swan. This is a useful area for self-catering accommodation – and fine walking country.

🏰 ❊ **Middleham Castle** This 12th-c structure dwarfs the village. For a time it was the home of young King Richard III. Only the huge keep and some later buildings remain, but there are marvellous views from the top and an informative exhibition centre. Snacks, shop, disabled access; cl 1–2pm and all

Mon and Tues Nov–Mar, 24–26 Dec; (01969) 623899; £2.20; EH.

MUKER SD9197

★ 🛆 Attractive Dales hamlet, with very good woollens shop and well liked tearooms. Between here and Keld, the River Swale enters a deeply cut valley and tumbles over waterfalls; there are paths on both sides of the river, or you can take a more upland route over neighbouring Kisdon.

NEWBY HALL SE3568

🏠 ❊ 🖼 🕹 🚂 This late 17th-c mansion (off B6265 E of Ripon) is set in beautiful formal gardens covering 25 acres. Redesigned inside and out by Robert Adam, it has an important collection of classical sculpture and Gobelins tapestries, as well as a good range of Chippendale furniture. In the grounds are a miniature railway, children's adventure garden, paddling pool and woodland discovery walk. Meals, snacks, shop, some disabled access; house cl am, all day Mon (exc bank hols), and Oct–Mar; (01423) 322583; £6.30, £4.50 gardens only. The Ship over in Aldborough is the nearest good place for food.

NIDDERDALE SE1073

🛆 ❊ This quiet yet beautiful valley has an impressive solitary grandeur. Just outside the National Park, it and the hills above are less liberally laced with footpaths and open-access moorland than the other dales here, and attract far fewer visitors – but there are plenty of relatively unfrequented walks, often on good paved but untarred tracks. The Nidderdale Way allows a fine, fairly gentle walk of a couple of hours or so, up on to the high pastures (see lambs being born in spring) and moorland at Glasshouses and back, with spectacular views almost all the way. It's well signed; start from Dacre Banks and take the lane a couple of hundred yards past the church. The stretch between the attractive small town of Pateley Bridge and the little village of Lofthouse is dominated by the sheltered 2-mile waters of Gouthwaite Reservoir, serenely set below the hills with some tall trees alongside. From Lofthouse a path runs beside the River Nidd, with picturesque tracks among small woods and ruined farmhouses, to Scar House

Reservoir, quite exposed at the valley head (there's also a toll road up to it); high, exposed routes line the N side of the dale up here.

⊕ ⌂ How Stean Gorge To the W of Lofthouse, this is a spectacular ravine pocked with potholes and caverns; a footpath snakes between miniature cliffs, with bridges giving views into the gorge; there's also a visitor centre.

NORTH STAINLEY SE2876

⊠ ☺ ⊞ Lightwater Valley Theme Park Family fun from the nostalgic pleasure of a steam train to the white-knuckle, green-faced thrills of one of the world's biggest rollercoasters; another rollercoaster is entirely underground. Meals, snacks, shop, disabled access; open wknds and school hols (not Christmas) Easter–Oct, and daily Jun–early Sept; (01765) 635321; £11.95. There's an adjacent factory shopping village, open all year. The Staveley Arms does decent food.

NORTON CONYERS SE3076

⊞ ⊛ The same family have lived in this late medieval house (3½m N of Ripon) for 370 years, and the furniture and pictures reflect the fact that it's still very much a family home. Charlotte Brontë used the building as one of her models for Thornfield Hall. Look out for the hoofprint on the stairs. Attractively planted 18th-c walled garden. Shop (with unusual plants and, in season, garden fruits), limited disabled access; open pm bank hol Suns and Mons, then pm Sun early Jun–mid-Sept, plus pm daily mid-July, phone for dates; (01765) 640333; £3. The Freemasons Arms at Nosterfield is useful for lunch.

NUN MONKTON SE5057

★ This attractive village is in appearance almost more like France than Yorkshire, with its broad avenue, and the stately meeting of the rivers Nidd and Ouse.

PARCEVALL HALL SE0660

⊛ ⊞ ※ Parcevall Hall Gardens Surrounding an Elizabethan house, 16 acres of woodland gardens charmingly set on a hillside E of the main Wharfedale Valley; superb views from the cliff walk. Tea garden, plant sales; cl Nov–Easter exc by appointment; (01756) 720311; £2. The Craven Arms at nearby Appletreewick is good for lunch, with lovely views.

PEN-Y-GHENT SD8473

⌂ ⊕ (694 metres; 2,277ft) Reached from Horton in Ribblesdale; its satisfyingly compact summit is the craggiest feature on the Pennine Way, which near here passes some potholes inc Hull Pot.

RAYDALE SD9187

⌂ ⊞ ※ (nr Bainbridge) The most interesting of Wensleydale's subsidiary valleys for walkers. Its lower neck is quite narrow, but it broadens out into a sheltered bowl of valley, with Semer Water, a sizeable glacial lake which legend has it was conjured up by a wandering beggar to drown a village which had spurned him. It's Yorkshire's third-largest natural lake, and has a path along its half-mile-long S side, but to make up circular routes you have to do some road walking. The walled track (a Roman road) just N has wide-ranging views as it descends to Bainbridge.

REETH SE0399

★ ⌂ Attractive Dales village with a high, wide, sloping green; the King's Arms is a popular dining pub. The village is a centre for rambles ranging from pottering along the meadows by the Swale to walks over moors into adjacent Arkengarthdale (where the ascent on to Fremington Edge is memorable).

RIBBLESDALE SD7776

⌂ ※ Climbing above Settle into severe and grand mountain scenery, this is craggy and remote: a major magnet for walkers on the Three Peaks Walk, 24 miles taking in the summits of Ingleborough, Pen-y-ghent and Whernside. This is a tough undertaking in its entirety, but each of the peaks on its own is a manageable half-day excursion: choose a clear day – not just for the magnificent views but for your own safety. Below Settle, the valley is less interesting for walkers, and marred by some quarrying.

⌂ ⊕ **Upper Ribblesdale** This high walking country is riddled with impressive potholes, some of them gaping chasms of sensational size that can be admired from the surface, as well as the intricate underground passages that make the area so popular with cavers. Up in the loneliest parts, useful refuges are the cheerful cavers' inn the Old Hill at Chapel le Dale, and the isolated Station Inn at Ribblehead.

RICHMOND NZ1600

★ 🏠 ⌂ A most attractive riverside country town, with steep and pretty streets of old stone buildings, and a splendid, broad, sloping market square (still cobbled, and perhaps the biggest in the country; market day is Sat). Scollards Hall, built in 1080, is possibly the oldest domestic building in Britain. An attractive riverside walk beneath the towering bulk of its castle heads W through Hudswell Woods, with an extension to Whitcliffe Scar, a cliff above the Swale with an exciting path along its top. The army connection with the town is still strong; nearby Catterick Camp is the biggest in the north. The Black Lion in Finkle St is good value for lunch.

🏯 ⌂ **Easby Abbey** Extensive remains of a 12th-c Premonstratensian abbey, a pretty riverside walk SE.

🛡 **Green Howards Museum** (Market Sq) In a converted 12th-c church, this includes amongst duller regimental history the blood-stained pistol holsters of the Grand Old Duke of York. Shop, some disabled access; cl wknds in Feb–Apr and Oct–Nov, am Sun mid-May–Oct, and all Dec–Jan; (01748) 822133; *£2.

🏯 **Richmond Castle** These austere and intricate ruins dominate the town, and overlook the River Swale from a high rocky outcrop. Shop, some disabled access; cl 1–2pm in winter, 24–26 Dec; (01748) 822493; £2.30; EH.

🎭 **Theatre Royal** (Victoria Rd) The country's oldest and most authentic working theatre still in its original form, complete with gallery, boxes and pit. Built in 1788, it doesn't look much from the outside but the immaculately restored interior is really special. Snacks, shop, limited disabled access; guided tours and museum open Easter–Oct, other times by appointment; (01748) 823021; £1.50.

RIPLEY SE2860

🏯 ❀ 🦅 ★ **Ripley Castle** (off A61) Beautifully picturesque castle, in the same family for an amazing 26 generations. Most of the current building dates from the 16th c, inc the

tower housing a collection of Royalist armour. For some the main attraction is the splendid gardens, the setting for a national collection of hyacinths and (under glass) a fine tropical plant collection. Also birds-of-prey centre. Meals, snacks, shop, some disabled access; open Tues, Thurs, Sat and Sun Jan–Mar and Nov–Dec, Thurs–Sun Apr–Jun and Sept–Oct, and daily July–Aug; (01423) 770152; £5, gardens only £2.50. The attractive village, rebuilt in the 1820s, has a superb delicatessen, and the Boar's Head Hotel is a fine old place for lunch.

RIPON SE3171

★ On Thurs, colourful stalls fill the attractive and ancient market square (quite a few stalls too on Sat, inc bric-à-brac); it's largely unspoilt, lined with specialist shops and old inns and hotels. At 9pm each night the Wakeman, a red-coated bugler, blows a buffalo horn here, as one has done for centuries. Going from here down one of the town's engagingly narrow old streets, you're rewarded by a magnificent view of the elegant Early English west front of the cathedral. The Golden Lion just off the market square is useful for a bite to eat. Fountains Abbey is within a walk from here, and Newby Hall and Norton Conyers are also quite close.

✝ **Ripon Cathedral** Spectacularly floodlit at night, this is one of the largest half-dozen in the country, and has plenty to see, inc very fine carving indeed in both stone and wood, and a 7th-c crypt – the oldest surviving part of any British cathedral building (and probably the oldest surviving crypt outside Italy). Shop, disabled access; £2 suggested donation.

SETTLE SD8163

★ 🎭 Market day (Tues) around the Shambles is particularly attractive; look out to the right of here for the Folly, an extraordinary 17th-c town house. Mary Milnthorpe & Daughter is a good antique jewellery and silver shop, and the Golden Lion has decent food. Just across the Ribble, Giggleswick is a peaceful contrast to the hectic little town.

🚂 **Settle–Carlisle Railway** A magnificent 70-mile route carved up through Ribblesdale across the wild moors between here and Cumbria, and then dropping down through the lovely Eden Valley; (0345) 484950 for times and fares, £15.80 for day return. All year on Sats and some Suns and Weds there's a programme of walks connecting with the moorland stops; they start quite early, (8.45am Sat), with dates and times listed on the timetable. Aside from the setting, it's an ordinary railway line: steamtrains do run most Sats in summer, but only from cities in the south – (01543) 419472 for routes and times – resulting in the bizarre situation that you can travel by steam if you're coming from Norwich or London, but not if you're in the immediate vicinity. The B6479 is not quite comparable to the train, but a good drive.

SKIPTON SD9851

✝ On Sat the main street has a colourful market (at least some stalls here most other days too, exc Sun, Tues and Thurs). The 14th-c **church** has a 16th-c rood screen and interesting stained glass. A canal runs through the town, and the Royal Shepherd in an attractive spot has good-value, quick food.

🏰 **Skipton Castle** ⬜ 12th c, and properly romantic, with sturdy round towers, broad stone steps, and a lovely central flagstoned and cobbled courtyard with a seat around its venerable central yew tree. One of the best-preserved medieval castles in Europe, it really is remarkable how much is left, interior and all – very few other castles have kept their roofs and stayed habitable. The original Norman arched gateway still stands – the word 'Desormais' carved above it is the motto of the family who lived here 1310–1676. Snacks, shop; cl am Sun, 25 Dec; (01756) 792442; £4.

STAINBURN MOOR SE2452

⌂ The area E of the Dales really has nothing to compare with the Dales themselves for serious walking, but this moorland W of Harrogate has some possibilities for fairly stretching walks, for instance from the car park by the woods along the side road W from Beckwithshaw.

STAINFORTH SD8167

⌂ Pleasant and gentle Ribblesdale walk from Stainforth Force to Langcliffe.

STARBOTTON SD9574

★ ⌂ Tiny but delightful Wharfedale village; a good base for walks, for example along the river to Kettlewell, then back up over the high land; or follow less obvious paths W to Arncliffe in Littondale – which is very similar to the Wharfedale parent valley, though with a flatter damper valley floor.

SWALEDALE SE0098

⌂ The northernmost of all the Dales, and one of the least visited – giving more chance of getting away from it all at even peak times. Its bold hills, abundant stone barns and extreme tranquillity make it a walkers' favourite. It's grandly austere for the most part, though quite heavily wooded as it drops down towards Richmond. In the steeper parts there are some fine waterfalls. The upper slopes, especially towards the Durham and Cumbrian borders, are wild and empty, except for the huge scattered flocks of hardy clean-limbed Swaledale sheep with their dark faces, grey muzzles, thick fleeces, and curly-horned rams. The meadowland down in the valleys of this dale and its broad tributary Arkengarthdale is largely unimproved, with slow-growing natural grasses and lots of wild flowers. Many of the area's 1,200 traditional stone hay barns, which are such a distinctive feature here, have been rehabilitated in the last few years, with generous National Parks grant aid. Gunnerside still has around it many of the 'rushes' where lead-miners dammed streams to form torrents that could break up the lead-bearing rock strata below; this whole area was an important lead centre until Victorian times, and other visible mementos are ruined mill buildings, tunnel entrances and spoil heaps. Between Muker and Keld the Swale enters a deeply cut valley and tumbles over waterfalls; there are paths on both sides of the river, or you can take a more upland route over neighbouring Kisdon.

WATH SE1467

★ ⌂ Attractive Dales hamlet spreading up the valley, with pleasant walks along past the reservoir to Ramsgill – beyond there's a splendid moorland drive over to Masham, where the King's Head is a useful pub for lunch.

WENSLEYDALE SD9889

△ ★ 🏚 More expansive in character and not quite as dramatic as Swaledale, but richly picturesque; its unspoilt villages and numerous waterfalls make for pleasurable walking. It used to be one of the richest dales, its broad pastures and countless sheep supporting the wealthy abbeys and castles whose ruins now add so much interest to its scenery. Wensleydale sheep are very distinctive, with long fleecy dreadlock curls. Upper Wensleydale (around and W of Hawes) is steep and wild; E of here the valley starts broadening out, with richer lower pastures, and more regular farmland below Middleham.

WHARFEDALE SE0361

△ 🐾 ✿ ★ With its tributary valley Littondale and its headwaters up in the steep conifer plantations at the top of Langstrothdale, this is one of England's most popular areas for walkers, and very beautiful indeed in parts. The Dales Way follows the River Wharfe for the length of the dale, except between Kettlewell and Grassington. **Upper Wharfedale** above Grassington has a level floor of sheltered, well drained pastures with the river winding through, a few grey stone barns, and steep sides laced with dry-stone walls, gnarled woodland and occasional austere crags, climbing up to high, fairly level tops some 365 metres (1,200ft) above the valley floor. The smaller villages are delightfully private and unspoilt, their grey or whitewashed stonework blending perfectly with the long scars of the limestone terraces above them. Away from the valley floor, stone-walled grassy tracks are the easiest ways of gaining height. Below Grassington there's an extremely pretty stretch where the valley winds more sinuously past Burnsall, Appletreewick and Bolton Abbey, below hills which though less grand are more varied in shape, with rather sensitively laid-out conifer plantations adding a slightly subalpine feel to some of the views.

WHERNSIDE SD7381

△ Sometimes criticised by keen walkers as the boring one of the Three Peaks, this is Yorkshire's highest point (736 metres – 2,415ft), and has an exhilarating ridge section; start from the magnificent Ribblehead Viaduct carrying the Settle–Carlisle railway over the head of the dale (the Station Hotel here is a comfortable halt).

WIDDALE SD8287

△ 🐾 Widdale is a tributary of Wensleydale, steep-sided and dramatic, with extensive conifer plantations above it.

★ **Other attractive villages** include Appletreewick SE0560, Austwick SD7768, Bilbrough SE5346, Boroughbridge SE3967, Brearton SE3261, Buckden SD9477, Burnsall SE0361, Carlton in Coverdale SE0684, Cray SD9379, East Witton SE1586 (ancient houses, long wide green), Gargrave SD9354 (on the Pennine Way), Gilling West NZ1804, Grantley SE2369, Gunnerside SD9598, Hampsthwaite SE2659, Horsehouse SE0481, Hudswell NZ1400, Kirkby Malham SD8961, Kirkby Overblow SE3249, Low Row SD9897 (popular with potholers), Middlesmoor SE0874, Newton-on-Ouse SE5160, Ramsgill SE1271, Redmire SE0591, Snape SE2784, Thornton in Lonsdale SD6873 (Conan Doyle was married in the charming church), Thornton Watlass SE2486, West Burton SE0186 and Wigglesworth SD8157.

Where to eat

ASENBY SE3975 **Crab & Lobster** (01845) 577286 Old, thatched pub/restaurant, relaxed, informal but civilised, interestingly furnished cosy rooms with lots of bric-à-brac, delicious food, and good wines by the glass; bdrms. **£20|£9.50.**

ASKRIGG SD9490 **Rowan Tree** (01969) 650536 Cosy little candlelit stone barn run by an Irish husband and German wife team; just a few tables so booking advisable, good imaginative evening meals and reasonably priced wine list; cl Sun, Mon, and winter Sun–Weds (best to phone for winter opening times); children over 10. **£22** for 5 courses.

BILBROUGH SE5346 **Three Hares** *(01937) 832128* Smartly refurbished dining pub with a welcoming landlord and staff, traditional bar with lots of polished copper and brass, no smoking restaurant, very good modern cooking using the freshest local produce, interesting wine list and well kept real ales; children must be well behaved and be gone by 8.30pm; cl Mon; disabled access. **£20.40|£7.95.**

BOROUGHBRIDGE SE3966 **Black Bull** *St James Sq (01432) 322413* Lovely old inn said to date from the 13th c, with a big stone fireplace in the main bar area (served from an old-fashioned hatch), a cosy traditional snug, an extended dining room, well presented food – even the bread, pasta, sorbets and ice-creams are home-made – fresh daily fish and lovely puddings, well kept real ales, enjoyable wines with 10 by the glass, afternoon teas (not Sun), friendly and attentive service, a plump ginger cat, and classical piped music; bdrms; disabled access. **£22.50|£5.95.**

BREARTON SE3260 **Malt Shovel** *(01423) 862929* Unspoilt village pub with hard-working licensees, heavily beamed rooms with open fires and lively hunting prints, very good bar food (super fresh fish and lovely puddings), 5 well kept real ales, and a good choice of malt whiskies and wines; cl Mon, first 2 wks Jan; disabled access. **£14.50|£6.**

CARLTON SE0684 **Foresters Arms** *(01969) 640272* Friendly, carefully restored inn with log fires, low beams and a nice atmosphere, well kept real ales, a good choice of whiskies, imaginative food in both the bar and restaurant, and friendly, helpful service; good bdrms; cl Mon, pm Sun, am Tues, Jan; children over 12 in restaurant in evening. **£30|£7.95.**

CARTHORPE SE3083 **Fox & Hounds** *(01845) 567433* Pretty little extended village house with 2 log fires and some evocative Victorian photographs of Whitby, attractive high-raftered no smoking restaurant with lots of farm and smithy tools, enjoyable, interesting food (fine daily specials and puddings inc yummy home-made ice-creams), decent wines, and helpful service; cl Mon, first wk Jan; disabled access. **£15|£7.95.**

EAST WITTON SE1485 **Blue Lion** *(01969) 624273* Stylish and civilised dining pub with a log fire, daily papers, bric-à-brac and rugs on flagstones in the distinctive old rooms, exceptionally good imaginative food, nice breakfasts, decent wines, real ales, and a pretty garden; bdrms; disabled access. **£25|£6.75.**

FERRENSBY SE3660 **General Tarleton** *Boroughbridge Rd (01423) 340284* Bustling 18th-c dining pub with beams and open fires, a relaxed atmosphere, delicious food inc super puddings, polite service, and plenty of wines by the glass from a good list; cl 25 Dec; disabled access. **£29.95|£7.25.**

GRASSINGTON SE0064 **Dales Kitchen Tearooms & Brasserie** *51 Main St (01756) 753208* Former apothecary's house (no smoking) with lovely cakes, scones and so forth, very good and imaginative light lunches, delicious puddings, and a children's menu; cl Christmas wk; disabled access. **£11|£4.95.**

GREAT OUSEBURN SE4461 **Crown** *(01423) 330430* Cheery and notably friendly village pub (where Ambrose Tiller started his Tiller Girls dancing troupe) with plenty of interest in the warmly welcoming bar, 2 no smoking eating areas opening off, serving excellent well presented food using home-grown herbs and salad, and well kept real ales; cl am Mon–Fri exc bank hols; disabled access. **£21|£5.95.**

HARROGATE SE3055 **La Bergerie** *11–13 Mount Parade (01423) 500089* Delightful, unassuming French evening restaurant with freshly prepared and interesting food and very good French staff; cl Sun, 25–26 Dec; disabled access. **£22.**

HARROGATE SE3055 **Bettys** *1 Parliament St (01423) 502746* Famous cake shop run by the same Swiss family that started this small chain in 1919, with special blends of teas and coffees, Alsace wines, wonderful light home-cooked meals, traditional afternoon tea, over 75 different delicious cakes and pastries; they also have 2 tearooms in York, one in Ilkley and one in Northallerton – same details apply to each; cl 25–26 Dec, 1 Jan. **£20|£4.55.**

HARROGATE SE3055 **Bistro** *1 Montpellier Mews (01423) 530708* Relaxed and attractively decorated little mews restaurant with enjoyable, interesting

Mediterranean-style food, and French wines; cl Sun, Mon, 1 wk Christmas. **£30|£5**.

HARROGATE SE3055 **Tannin Level** *5 Raglan St (01423) 560595* Very good basement wine bar with brick walls and country dining chairs, imaginative food inc lovely puddings, a fine wine list, and early evening tapas; children lunchtime only; cl Sun. **£25.45|£5**.

HARROGATE SE2954 **William & Victoria** *Cold Bath Rd (01423) 521510* Busy wine bar with an upstairs evening restaurant and hearty helpings of decent country cooking; cl Sun; first wk Jan; children over 11. **£22|£13.95** 3 course early bird menu.

HETTON SD9658 **Angel** *(01756) 730263* Extremely popular dining pub with old-fashioned rambling rooms, consistently excellent imaginative food, very good service from hard-working, friendly staff, well kept real ales, and over 300 wines; cl 2 wks Jan; disabled access. **£35|£8**.

LITTON SD9073 **Queens Arms** *(01756) 770208* Welcoming, quietly placed 17th-c inn with good popular food, a big collection of cigarette lighters in the main bar, another room with more of a family atmosphere, and 2 coal fires; cl Mon exc bank hols, second wk Jan for 4 wks; pretty bdrms. **£15|£6.50**.

MASHAM SE2280 **Floodlite** *7 Silver St (01765) 689000* Bustling little candlelit restaurant with lots of bric-à-brac, particularly good, sound cooking using top local ingredients with emphasis on fish and game, lovely puddings, and a sizeable, fairly priced wine list; cl Mon, am Tues–Thurs. **£22|** £10.50 2-course lunch.

MIDDLEHAM SE1287 **Waterford House** *Kirkgate (01969) 622090* This most enjoyable restaurant-with-rooms, close to the market square, is filled with all sorts of antiques, has a friendly atmosphere, a superb wine list (they will offer you a glass from any of their 900 bottles), and delicious food using tip-top produce; bdrms (lovely breakfasts); **£34**.

MOULTON NZ2303 **Black Bull** *(01325) 377289* Decidedly civilised, well run pub with old-fashioned style and standards of service, memorable bar snacks (excellent smoked salmon), conservatory restaurant or one in the Brighton Belle Pullman dining car, and good wines; cl Sun, 24–26 Dec; children over 7. **£30|£6**.

PICKHILL SE3483 **Nags Head** *(01845) 567391* Deservedly popular old inn with a nice mix of customers, a busy tap room, smarter lounge, no smoking restaurant, particularly good food inc interesting daily specials and lovely puddings, friendly, efficient staff, a fine wine list and well kept real ales; bdrms; cl 25 Dec; disabled access. **£22|£5.50**.

SAWLEY SE2467 **Sawley Arms** SE2568 *(01765) 620642* Rather smart pub with absolutely stunning flowering tubs and baskets, several small rooms with log fires and comfortable furniture, daily papers, a no smoking restaurant, good, enjoyable bar food (inc interesting soups and fishy starters), and nice house wines; bdrms; cl pm Sun in winter; children over 9. **£18.50|£6.50**.

North York Moors and East Yorkshire

Unusual places to visit, expansive countryside, interesting coast.

The North York Moors National Park is less visited than the Dales, but gives walkers (and drivers) broad and inspiring landscapes. The cliffy coast is full of character north of the attractive resort of Scarborough (lots to see and do here), with some delightful little fishing villages. Bridlington is another attractive seaside resort, with a restrained charm and plenty of family amusements. Whitby is a working fishing port of real individuality; Hull is a bigger port, but again has a lot to interest visitors. Inland, Helmsley and Beverley are attractive small towns.

Several very imposing mansions in splendid grounds are led by magnificent Castle Howard. The ruins of Rievaulx Abbey have a powerful appeal, and unusual experiences include Eden Camp just outside Malton, Beverley's surprisingly enjoyable army transport museum, the Hutton le Hole folk museum, the Skinningrove mining museum, and even llama trekking in Staintondale. The Burnby Hall waterlilies (at Pocklington) are rather special in summer. Children have several good open farms and the Pickering steam railway, as well as the seaside resort amusements.

Where to stay

AMPLEFORTH SE5678 **Carr House Farm** *Shallowdale, Ampleforth, York YO6 4ED* (01347) 868526 **£35;** 3 rms. In peaceful undulating farmland and with an acre of garden, this no smoking 16th-c stone farmhouse has beams and oak panelling, a flagstoned dining room with woodburner in the inglenook, separate lounge, and good breakfasts using home-made butter and preserves and fresh farm eggs; cl 25 Dec; children over 7; no dogs.

BLAKEY RIDGE SE6799 **Lion** *Blakey Ridge, Pickering YO6 6LQ* (01751) 417320 ***£59,** plus winter breaks; 10 clean rms, most with own bthrm. The fourth-highest inn in England, this has spectacular moorland views, characterful rambling bars, blazing fires, generous helpings of decent food served all day, good breakfasts, a candlelit restaurant, quite a few real ales, and genuinely friendly licensees and staff; fine walking country; disabled access.

CHOP GATE SE5796 **Hillend Farm** *Chop Gate, Bilsdale, Middlesbrough TS9 7JR* (01439) 798278 ***£42;** 2 rms. Friendly 17th-c farmhouse with good home cooking, a comfortable lounge and dining room, and fine walks; on the farm is part of one of the last remaining ancient oak forests; cl Nov–Easter.

COXWOLD SE5377 **Fauconberg Arms** *Coxwold, York YO6 4AD* (01347) 868214 **£55;** 4 rms. Civilised old stone inn in a lovely setting; big log fire, some handsome settles and gleaming copper in the 2 cosy and comfortably furnished rooms of the lounge bar, good food in both the restaurant and bar, an extensive wine list, and decent breakfasts.

EGTON BRIDGE NZ8004 **Horse Shoe** *Egton Bridge, Whitby YO21 1XE* (01947) 895245 **£48,** plus special breaks; 6 simple rms, most with own bthrm. Beautifully placed inn by the River Esk (stepping stones big enough for children to sit on), lots of friendly wild birds, a pleasant sheltered lawn, open fires, attractive traditionally furnished bars, well cooked food inc excellent breakfasts in the cottagey dining room, and decent wines; no accommodation 25 Dec.

ESCRICK SE6343 **Church Cottage** *Escrick, York YO19 6EX* (01904) 728462 **£55,** 7 comfortable, individually furnished rms. Friendly extended house next to the church with a spacious, no smoking dining room overlooking the landscaped gardens (spit-roast barbecues), a comfortable lounge, and enjoyable breakfasts.

FLAMBOROUGH TA2270 **Manor House** *Flamborough, Bridlington YO15 1PD* (01262) 850943 **£62;** 2 rms, the more expensive room has a 17th-c four-poster. Beautifully restored Georgian house with a log fire and books in the guest sitting room, lots of antiques (Mrs Berry is an antiques dealer), good breakfasts, and a friendly atmosphere; the old stable block has antiques and intricate hand-knitted fishermen's sweaters called ganseys for sale; cl Christmas; children over 8.

HAROME SE6481 **Pheasant** *Harome, Helmsley, YO6 5JG* (01439) 771241 ***£128 inc dinner,** plus special breaks; 12 rms. Family-run hotel with a relaxed homely lounge and a traditional bar with beams, inglenook fireplace and flagstones; good, very popular food, efficient service, and an indoor heated swimming pool; cl Dec–Feb; children over 8; disabled access.

HARTOFT END SE7592 **Blacksmiths Arms** *Hartoft End, Rosedale Abbey,*

Pickering YO18 8EN (01751) 417331 ***£59,** plus special breaks; 15 rms. Carefully extended and modernised former farmhouse in lovely surroundings at the foot of Rosedale, with a friendly, traditionally furnished bar, open fires in cosy and comfortable lounges, and enjoyable food in the spacious and attractive restaurant; lovely walks all round.

HAWNBY SE5690 **Laskill Farm** *Easterside, Hawnby, York YO6 5NB (01439) 798268* **£52;** 6 rms, some in a beamy converted outside building. Attractive and welcoming creeper-covered stone house on a big sheep and cattle farm nr Rievaulx Abbey; open fire and books in the comfortable lounge, good food using home-grown produce, and their own natural spring water; self-catering also; cl 25 Dec; partial disabled access.

HELMSLEY SE6183 **Black Swan** *Market Pl, Helmsley YO6 5BJ (01439) 770466* **£140,** plus special breaks; 45 well equipped and comfortable rms. Striking Georgian house and adjoining Tudor rectory with a beamed and panelled hotel bar, attractive carved oak settles and Windsor armchairs, cosy and comfortable lounges with lots of character, and a charming sheltered garden.

HOVINGHAM SE6675 **Worsley Arms** *Hovingham, York YO6 4LA (01653) 628234* **£80,** plus special breaks; 18 individually decorated bedrooms. Stone-built Georgian inn with comfortable and pretty sitting rooms, fresh flowers and open fires, very good modern cooking in the elegant restaurant and more informal Cricketers Bistro, and seats out by the stream; disabled access.

KILBURN SE5179 **Forresters Arms** *Kilburn, York YO6 4AH (01347) 868386* ***£58,** plus special breaks; 10 clean, bright rms. Friendly old coaching inn opposite the pretty village gardens, with sturdy but elegant furnishings made next door at the Thompson furniture workshop, a big log fire, and decent food in both the restaurant and beamed bar; disabled access.

LASTINGHAM SE7390 **Lastingham Grange** *Lastingham, York YO6 6TH (01751) 417345* **£155,** plus special breaks; 11 rms. Attractive stone-walled country house in 10 acres of neatly kept gardens and fields – with the moors beyond; relaxed homely atmosphere in the spacious lounge, an open fire, decent food, extremely helpful service, and marvellous walks; good for children, with ponies and playground; cl Dec–Feb.

MIDDLETON SE7887 **Cottage Leas Country Hotel** *Nova Lane, Middleton, Pickering YO18 8PN (01751) 472129* ***£80,** plus special breaks; 12 comfortable rms. Delightful 18th-c farmhouse with extensive gardens, comfortable informal rooms, beamed ceilings, an open log fire in the cosy lounge, and a snug bar; pets by prior arrangement; partial disabled access.

PICKERING SE7983 **White Swan** *Market Pl, Pickering YO18 7AA (01751) 472288* **£80,** plus special breaks; 12 comfortable rms. 16th-c coaching inn with inviting small and quiet plush hotel bar, friendly staff and locals, log fires, antiques in the comfortable beamed residents' lounge, good traditional bar food, an attractive restaurant with fine clarets and daily-changing food using the best local produce, and breakfasts with home-made marmalade; pets welcome; partial disabled access.

ROBIN HOOD'S BAY NZ9504 **Coble** *Covet Hill, Robin Hood's Bay YO22 4SN (01947) 880042* ***£40** plus special breaks; 3 rms, 1 with own shower. 17th-c former-coastguard's cottage by the beach with views over the bay from the lounge and sun terrace, warmly friendly caring owners and huge first-class breakfasts (8 courses); good nearby walks; cl Christmas–New Year.

ROSEDALE ABBEY SE7296 **Milburn Arms** *Rosedale Abbey, Pickering YO18 8RA (01751) 417312* **£80,** plus special breaks; 11 rms. Friendly 18th-c inn in a village surrounded by fine steep moorland; log fire and books in the comfortable drawing room, traditionally furnished beamed bar, very good English cooking in the attractive restaurant, decent wine list, excellent breakfasts, and helpful staff; cl 24–27 Dec; pets by prior arrangement.

ROSEDALE ABBEY SE7294 **White Horse Farm Hotel** *Rosedale Abbey, Pickering YO18 8SE (01751) 417239* **£75,** plus special breaks; 15 rms. Friendly country hotel above the village in 11 acres, with marvellous views, a cosy beamed bar and log fire, comfortable lounge, generously served food, and a decent range of wines and malt whiskies; excellent walks; cl 24–25 Dec; dogs by prior arrangement.

SCARBOROUGH TA0191 **Wrea Head** Scalby, Scarborough YO13 0PP (01723) 378211 **£90,** plus special breaks; 20 individually decorated rms. Victorian country house in 14 acres of parkland and gardens, with friendly staff, minstrels' gallery in the oak-panelled hall and lounge, open fires, a bow-windowed library, pretty flowers, and good food in the airy restaurant; disabled access.

WASS SE5579 **Wombwell Arms** Wass, York YO6 4BE (01347) 868280 **£49,** plus special breaks; 2 individually furnished rms. Attractive, warmly welcoming small inn with a cosy rambling bar, good, imaginative food and decent wines in comfortable dining rooms (2 are no smoking), and enjoyable breakfasts; cl 2 wks Jan; children over 8.

WHARRAM LE STREET SE8666 **Red House** Wharram le Street, Malton YO17 9TL (01944) 768455 ***£52,** plus special breaks; 3 rms. Spacious and comfortable no smoking country house with friendly owners, log fires in sitting rooms, good home cooking in the dining room (using home-grown organic produce where possible), and a lovely garden with grass tennis court; cl Christmas wk; pets welcome.

WILLERBY TA0230 **Willerby Manor** Well Lane, Willerby, Hull HU10 6ER (01482) 652616 **£67w;** 51 individually decorated rms. Family-owned Victorian house in 3 acres of gardens with an airy and attractive conservatory dining bar and more formal restaurant, good food, helpful service, and a health club.

To see and do

ACKLAM NZ4915
❀ ⱱ **Nature's World** (Ladgate Lane) Thriving environmental demonstration centre, developing all the time, with organic gardens, nature trails, and a number of re-created natural habitats (moorland, wetlands, etc) under construction. Splendid home-cooked meals and snacks, shop, good disabled access; cl 25–26 Dec, 1 Jan; (01642) 594895; £3.50.

BECK HOLE NZ8202
★ ⌂ Charming tucked-away village; Birch Hall here is a unique cross between country tavern and village store. The most rewarding way to get here is walking along the **historic rail trail** along the abandoned line that preceded the current North Yorkshire Moors Railway route, between Grosmont and Goathland.

BEMPTON TA1973
⚓ ⚒ **Bempton Cliffs** The **RSPB bird reserve** here has the biggest colony of seabirds in the country, with up to a quarter of a million of them nesting in the cliffs. Best views of puffins Jun–July, but plenty of skuas and shearwaters later in summer, with weekend **boat trips** from Flamborough (North Landing) or Bridlington, though what you'll see depends on the weather.

Snacks, shop, some disabled access; visitor centre cl all Jan, wknds Dec and Feb; (01262) 851179 – book well ahead for the boats; *£2.50 car parking charge. Local fishermen run early summer weekend boats to the cliffs too.

BEVERLEY TA0339
★ Attractive country town, in a way like a small-scale York, with much the same sort of appeal. It's partly pedestrianised, with many fine Georgian buildings, several antique shops and so on, but unlike York is still very much an honest market town rather than a tourist place. Up to 1,000 animals, mainly pigs, are still sold at the Tues and Thurs market, and the racecourse is central to local life. For meals, the comfortably traditional Beverley Arms and cheap Tiger are good. The B1248 N has rolling Wolds views.

▣ ⌘ **Art Gallery & Museum** (Champney Rd) Includes lots of pieces by Fred Elwell the woodcarver, most famous for his work in the Minster (cl 12.30–1.30pm wknds, all Mon and Tues, 25–26 Dec, 1 Jan, bank hols; free).

✝ **Beverley Minster** Wonderful 12th/14th-c building, with elegant buttressing and elaborately pinnacled towers. The west front is richly carved yet extraordinarily harmonious. Inside are several delights, inc the intricately carved Percy tomb canopy, the unusual Saxon *fridstol* (one of only two such seats in the country), and the biggest collection of misericords in Britain. Shop, disabled access; guided tours summer only; £2 suggested donation.

🏛 **Guildhall** (Register Sq) Parts of this mainly Georgian building are open to view, although changes are afoot and they were unable to give us specific opening times as we went to press. Best to phone (01482) 884471.

🏯 ✝ **Museum of Army Transport** (Flamingate) Huge hangar with all sorts of military vehicles inc planes, tanks and cars, many displayed in realistic settings – down to farm-building camouflage for the Second World War and scratchy sand for the Gulf War. Children can climb into the jeeps and so on. Some vehicles may be demonstrated on summer Suns. Meals, snacks, shop, disabled access; cl 24–26 Dec; (01482) 860445; £4.

✝ **St Mary's Church** (Hengate) The former wealth of the town can be guessed at from the magnificence of another subsidiary church not far from the Minster; the weather-vane on the SW turret is said to have been the last design by Pugin, who sketched it on the back of an envelope. Opposite is the White Horse, a quaint old gaslit bare-boarded tavern.

BLACKTOFT SE8424

★ 🐦 Attractive Humberside village; its pub the Hope & Anchor, with tables out by the waterside, is great for bird watchers, right by the **RSPB marsh reserve**.

BOLTON PERCY SE5341

✝ ✿ Behind its medieval gatehouse the 15th-c church has perhaps the most unusual **churchyard** in the country: 15 years ago local lecturer Roger Brook set about tackling its profusion of weeds, and since then has transformed it into a splendidly colourful garden, with more than a thousand different types of plant creeping around and over the headstones. Rather like a semi-wild cottage garden, it houses part of the National Collection of dicentras. Open all the time, with regular open days to

find out more; (01904) 744213 for dates. The Crown has generous simple food (not Mon or Tues).

BRIDLINGTON TA1767

★ ✝ 🛁 Famous for its bracing image in the heyday of the traditional seaside resort, and the way the country rolls down to the long sands of the shore still gives that feeling. The centre is a quay and small harbour, with the usual summer attractions, but the original core of the town is half a mile in from the sea, with some charming old houses among the more modern ones around the heavily restored **priory church**. A 14th-c gateway (the Baylegate) gives some idea of how imposing the priory must have been before the Dissolution, and houses a local history museum; open Mon–Fri (inc maybe Tues and Thurs evenings) Jun–mid-Sept; £1. Broadacres (A165) has reliable family food inc a carvery. The coast to the S is generally much flatter.

△ 🏛 **Bondville Model Village** (Riviera Drive, Sewerby) Readers enjoy this; disabled access; cl Oct–Apr; (01262) 401736; *£2.50. A walk along the low cliff from here towards Flamborough Head soon brings you to a strip of woodland by a stream; if you follow the lane up from here past the car park and along the wood, you come to Iron Age earthworks which cut right across the head – making it a pretty impressive defensive position.

🛁 ✒ **Harbour Museum & Aquarium** (Harbour Rd) The best place to find out about the town's seafaring heritage; shop, disabled access; cl Nov–Mar; (01262) 670148; 50p.

🎪 **John Bull's World of Rock** (Carnaby Industrial Estate, off A614 SW) See how they squeeze the words into the candy, and maybe even personalise your own stick of the seaside favourite. Usually cl winter wknds, Christmas, best to check; (01262) 678525; £1 factory and exhibition.

🎪 🐦 **Park Rose Pottery** (Carnaby Covert Lane, off A614 SW) Factory visits and a seconds shop, as well as 12 acres of strollable parkland with play areas, owl sanctuary and bee exhibition. Meals, snacks, shop, disabled access; cl

25–26 Dec; (01262) 602823; site entry free, £1.75 owl sanctuary; they are building a new play area for children, so entrance to the old one is free.

🐾 🕸 🏠 **Sewerby Hall** (NE edge) In spacious parkland right on the coast, with a miniature zoo and aviary (good for children), and a charming garden. The elegant early 18th-c house includes some Amy Johnson memorabilia – the pioneer aviator lived nearby. Snacks, shop, disabled access (but not to the hall); grounds open daily all year, house open Mar–mid-Jan, though only Sat–Tues out of season; (01262) 673769; £2.90.

BROMPTON SE9582

🖼 ☕ ★ **Wordsworth Gallery** (Gallows Hill) The former home of Mary Hutchinson, who married William Wordsworth at Brompton Church in 1802. The medieval barn has an exhibition on the poet and Samuel Coleridge, as well as an exhibition of paintings and prints. Meals, snacks, shop; cl Mon exc bank hols; (01723) 863298; free. The village is pretty, and the Cayley Arms does good food.

BUGTHORPE SE7757

★ † Attractive village, especially in spring, with an interesting **church**.

BURTON AGNES TA1063

🏠 🖼 🕸 † **Burton Agnes Hall** Marvellous richly decorated Elizabethan house, with a fantastically carved Great Hall, 16th-c antiques, and some splendid Impressionist paintings. A fine woodland garden has colourful borders, pets corner and a topiary walk to an orangery. Meals, snacks, shop, disabled access to ground floor only; cl Nov–Mar; (01262) 490324; £4.50. The earlier Norman manor house stands between here and the church. Nearby Kilham's attractive church has a memorable Norman door; the 18th-c Bell in Driffield is pleasant for lunch.

BYLAND ABBEY SE5478

🏚 The jagged ruins of this abbey, built for Cistercian monks, date from the 12th and 13th c. Enough detail survives to show how fine it must have been: look out for the well preserved floor tiles and carved stone. Good for picnics. Snacks, shop, some disabled access; cl 1–2pm, Nov–Mar; (01347) 868614; £1.60. The nearby Abbey Inn is

most enjoyable for lunch. The drive past here from Bagby (SE of Thirsk), Kilburn and Coxwold, and on via Wass and Ampleforth to Oswaldkirk is very attractive.

COXWOLD SE5377

★ Neat and very attractive little stone-built village, very harmonious. The Fauconberg Arms does good food.

🏠 🕸 **Newburgh Priory** (just S) Charming old house, partly Norman with Tudor and Georgian additions. One of the family married Oliver Cromwell's daughter, who is supposed to have rescued her father's headless corpse and had it reburied here; the room with the tomb is on the tour. Outside is a 40-acre lakeside and riverside garden with a fine collection of dogwoods, splendid formal borders and lots of unusual plants. Snacks; open pm Weds and Sun Apr–Jun and Sun and Mon Aug bank hol wknds; (01347) 868435; £3.50, grounds only £1.50.

🏠 🕸 † **Shandy Hall** Laurence Sterne's quaint house has been well restored, the little study much as it must have been when he wrote *Tristram Shandy* here. Outside is a lovely walled garden. Shop with unusual plant sales; open Jun–Sept, house pm Weds and Sun, gardens daily exc Sat; (01347) 868465; £3.50. Close by is the attractive 15th-c **church** of which Sterne was curate – it still has the box pews it had in his day.

CROPTON SE7588

🍺 **Cropton Brewery** The small family-run brewery has guided tours on the hour 10am–4pm summer (best to phone for winter times), and samples of their robustly flavoured beers, as well as a children's treasure hunt, and good adjacent pub, the New Inn; disabled access to ground floor; (01751) 417330; *£2.75.

DALBY FOREST SE8789

🦢 🌲 The E part of the National Park has large forest plantations; this part has colour-coded trails.

DANBY NZ7108

🌲 🦢 **Moors Centre** (Lodge Lane) Helpful National Park information centre, with exhibitions, guided walks and events, and adventure playground; terraced riverside and woodland grounds. Meals, snacks, shop, disabled access to ground floor only; cl wkdys Jan and Feb, Christmas; (01287) 660540; free. This area has decent **horse riding** centres, good for experts and beginners alike; the Moors Centre has the full list, and can also provide numbers for the various **cycle hire** firms dotted about the region. The Duke of Wellington has good-value food.

EAST AYTON SE9985
🐑 🐾 **Honey Farm** (Betton Farm Centre) Exhaustive exhibition on bees and honey-making, with sales of wax and honey-based products. Also animals, craft shops, farm shop and play area. Meals, snacks, shop, disabled access; (01723) 864001; £2.95. The Londesborough Arms at Seamer has decent food, and the Forge Valley drive to Hackness runs through ancient woodlands.

EGTON BRIDGE NZ8005
★ ❀ Charming Eskdale village, pleasantly eccentric, twinned with a fictional French one; lovely Esk views, plus a good riverside pub.

ELVINGTON SE6748
✈ **Yorkshire Air Museum** Part of a World War II airfield and base preserved as it was then, with fine aircraft, an old control tower and plenty of other memorabilia inc a Halifax Mk III, engines, models and photographs. Meals, snacks, shop, disabled access; open daily in summer, best to check in winter; (01904) 608595; £4. The St Vincent Arms at Sutton upon Derwent is good for lunch.

ESTON NAB NZ5618
❀ ◠ Outside the National Park, this gives walkers a massive view over industrial Teesside.

FADMOOR SE6789
★ Attractive village with a good pub, on a charming drive from Kirkbymoorside, on over Rudland Slack and past Cockayne to Helmsley. The graveyard of nearby **Gillamoor church** gives a classic view of interlocking moor and valley landscapes.

FANGFOSS SE7653
🐾 **Rocking Horse Shop** Splendid collection of antique rocking horses; you can watch replicas being constructed, and buy either a finished horse or plans for doing it yourself.

Open by appointment (not Sun), (01759) 368737.

FARNDALE SE6697
◠ ❀ The largest dale in the National Park, with characteristic North York Moors scenery – lush green fields and red-roofed yellow-stone houses beneath the brooding moorland plateau. It's famous for its miles of wild daffodils in April, introduced and naturalised here many centuries ago. They're at their best around Low Mill, and any walk to enjoy them gives the chance of coming back down the ancient green lane of Rudland Rigg, for spectacular views. The friendly Feversham Arms at Church Houses, right next to the daffodil reserve, does very good-value food.

FELIXKIRK SE4684
★ Attractive village, with a pleasant drive to Kepwith and Nether Silton; the Carpenters Arms is a good-value dining pub.

FILEY TA1180
❀ Much quieter resort than Scarborough, its neighbour up the coast, with the main road dropping down a steep little valley between the church and the old town (and under a footbridge linking the two) to the beach, where fishermen still haul up their boats. The rock reef N of the town beyond the sands is interesting; to the S are holiday camps, and the seafront Coble Landing Bar has decent food and great views.
🐚 **Filey Museum** (Queen St) Small and attractively homely summer local museum in former medieval fishermen's cottages; cl 12.30–2pm, am Sat, 31 Oct–Easter; £1.25.

FLAMBOROUGH TA2270
† ❀ ◠ 🦅 A blowy place, high on the headland, with some old houses in the core around the 15th-c **church**; down below past the holiday camp the natural rock harbour is well sheltered, with a lifeboat station, and there are fine views of coast and sea from the point of the headland, by the lighthouse. Flamborough Marine sell a local version of guernseys, weatherproof 'ganseys', hand-knitted in the round. The Seabirds is good for lunch, and the B1259 and B1229 are the most interesting coast roads. There is some quite exciting

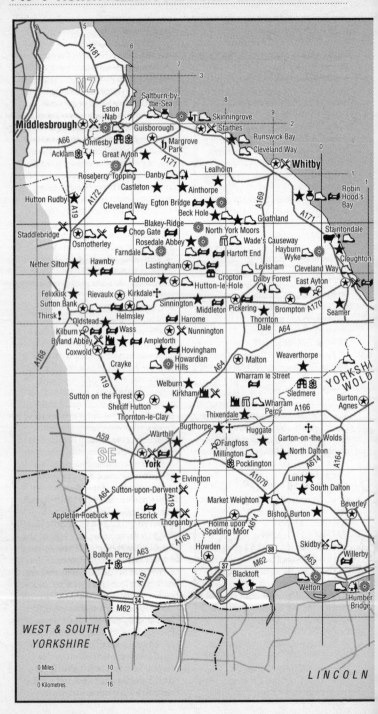

North York Moors & East Yorkshire

*N O R T H
S E A*

0

Newlands 2

9

Scarborough

3

8

Filey

Bempton

RE
S
A165
A614

Flamborough

*Flamborough
Head*

Bridlington

6

Foston on
the Wolds

TA
A165

5

Hornsea

4

Sproatley

4

Hull

Holderness

3

Withernsea

A1033

Patrington

2

River Humber

Spurn Head

SHIRE

walking, particularly around the N side of Flamborough Head, with the cacophony of thousands of kittiwakes sounding within the inlets; puffins can sometimes be seen on rock ledges. A level mile and a half from the lighthouse along clifftops leads to North Landing (café and car park). A longer walk making the Head the midway point starts from the village, skirting fields to join the coast path; to avoid anticlimax, walk the southern cliffs first and keep the real drama for later on. To the N the path follows the coast closely nearly all the way, and hilly country coming right to the coast makes for interest.

FOSTON ON THE WOLDS
TA0855

🐐 **Cruckley Farm** 💷 Friendly working farm, with lots of animals to fuss over – inc some very strange-looking rare breeds. Daily milking displays (usually around 10.45am). Snacks, shop, disabled access; cl Oct–Apr; (01262) 488337; *£3. The Trout at Wansford has decent food.

GARTON-ON-THE-WOLDS
SE9859

✝ The **church** here dates from the 12th c, and is very High Church inside, with 19th-c mosaics and frescos.

GOATHLAND NZ8301
★ ⌂ In the heart of the moors, the picturesque setting for TV's *Heartbeat*; filming can be rather intrusive, and some villagers have started to wonder how they can cope with the coachloads of tourists, but there are interesting walks from here, inc the short one from opposite the church to **Mallyan Spout**, a waterfall which tumbles into the side of a fine wooded smooth-rocked gorge. The Mallyan Spout Hotel does popular food.

GUISBOROUGH NZ6116
🏛 ★ ❊ **Gisborough Priory** 14th-c ruined church, one huge window rising dramatically from the rest of the more or less foundation-level ruins. The gatehouse is fairly well preserved, and it's an atmospheric spot for a picnic. Shop; cl Mon Oct–Mar, 24 Dec–1 Jan; 95p. The Fox nearby has decent food, and the market town has attractive corners. Out at Newton (A173) the King's Head is a popular dining pub by Roseberry Topping viewpoint.

HAWNBY SE5489

★ Attractive village, on the very scenic Rievaulx Abbey–Osmotherley road; there's a good pub.

HAYBURN WYKE TA0096

⌂ ❈ From the very well sited hotel here (good-value Sun carvery) steep Victorian woodland paths wind down to the cliff-sheltered cove; a clifftop path to the S gives fine views.

HELMSLEY SE6184

★ Lanes run straight up on to the moors from this attractive small market town (the B1257 is one of the best moorland roads, and the lane at SE6188, a bit more than a mile N of Carlton, gives a fine view of the contrasting moor and valley landscapes). There's a large cobbled square (busy Fri market), and enough antique shops and craft shops to please a visitor without seeming too touristy. A lively and bustling place, with a lot of class. A rewarding and very varied drive is past Rievaulx Abbey, Old Byland and Cold Kirby to Sutton Bank, left along the A170 then next right turn to Kilburn, Coxwold, Byland Abbey and back via Ampleforth and Oswaldkirk.

⌂ **Cleveland Way** Meticulously waymarked and signposted, this is a great help to there-and-back walks here, following the W, N and E margins of the Moors National Park. Starting from Helmsley, it passes Rievaulx Abbey.

🏛 ❀ ⚘ **Duncombe Park** Beautifully restored early 18th-c house, rebuilt after a fire at the turn of the 20th century. The landscaped gardens, with grand terracing, are magnificent, covering around a tenth of the 300 acres of memorable parkland. Meals, snacks, shop, some disabled access; cl Nov–Mar, best to phone for opening times; (01439) 770213; *£5.75, £3.75 gardens only. You can wander through the estate (which has been granted nature reserve status) for £2.

🏰 **Helmsley Castle** This 12th-c pile, ruined in 1644, stands within enormous earthworks and dominates the town; good for picnics. Shop; cl 1–2pm, winter Mon and Tues, 24–26 Dec; (01439) 770442; £2.30.

HOLDERNESS TA3029

⌂ ✝ The area between the Wolds, Humber and coast is flat: rich farming country with huge fields and not many buildings, though the fine village churches often with soaring towers or spires reflect the wealth that this fertile land has put into them in the past. The long southern stretch of coast is flat country too, without a great deal of appeal for walkers – except for long, lonely off-season walks by the edge of the North Sea.

HOLME UPON SPALDING MOOR SE7838

↧ 🐄 ☺ **Major Bridge Park** (Selby Rd) Private collection of working rural equipment, small rare breeds farm and vintage fairground rides (you can go on these), with nature trails through surrounding countryside. Snacks, disabled access; open Thurs and Sun May–Sept, daily (exc Sat) in Aug; (01430) 860992; *£2. The Red Lion has good food.

HORNSEA TA2145

🐦 Sizeable resort; behind the town, Hornsea Mere, 2 miles long, is the biggest natural lake in this region, with herons and other birds.

🦋 🐦 ☺ ⚘ **Hornsea Freeport** (Rolston Rd) One of the area's most visited attractions, a developing leisure centre based around a factory shopping village. Several well known brands and stores (some good bargains), and family features such as butterflies, a model village, a birds-of-prey centre and an adventure playground. Meals, snacks, shop, disabled access; cl 25–26 Dec; (01964) 534222; site free, £1 (50p children) for family attractions. Next door is the well established working **Hornsea Pottery**.

HOVINGHAM SE6675

★ Attractive village, with a good pub and a pleasant drive S to Sheriff Hutton and Flaxton.

HOWARDIAN HILLS SE6575

⌂ ❈ These gentle generously wooded hills have a path along their N flanks, giving intermittent rather patrician views across the plain to the North York Moors.

HOWDEN SE7428

★ ✝ ❀ Unpretentiously attractive, with cobbled alleys, a fine market hall, a majestic **minster** with a tall tower, the ruins of a charming medieval chapter house, and a small marshland country park down the lane opposite the minster, with ponds and raised walkways. The White Horse is useful for lunch.

HUGGATE SE8855

★ Attractive Wolds village, with a good pub and easy walks nearby.

HULL TA1028

🏠 Kingston-upon-Hull is the full name of this big port, surprisingly pleasant for visitors now that the former docks have been so well tidied up. The landing stage for the former Humber ferry has become an attractive pedestrian enclave with some solid well restored Georgian buildings, and Humber views from the waterfront Minerva (which brews its own beer). Nearby, the original dock has become a yacht marina, with quite cheerfully buoyant modern buildings around it. Away from the water, some of the most ancient buildings in the narrow streets of the old town have survived, notably on the High St. One of the most delightful old buildings is the Olde Whyte Harte just off Silver St; it was in its heavily panelled upper room that the town's governor made the fateful decision to lock the town's gate against King Charles in 1642, depriving him of the arsenal that might otherwise have swung the Civil War in his favour. These 2 enclaves, the old town and former docks, are separated from each other by good main roads through to the modern container and ferry docks; the traffic just sweeps by, leaving them as self-contained islands – very quiet at weekends. Hull's enjoyable museums are mostly concentrated in the old town, so it's easy to walk from one to another. A free copy of the city's ale trail (a self-guided tour around the best pubs) is available from the tourist information centre.

🖼 **Ferens Art Gallery** (Queen Victoria Sq) Enterprisingly run general collection, with lots of maritime paintings and Dutch Old Masters; particularly strong on Frank Brangwyn. Snacks, shop, disabled access; cl am Sun, 25 Dec, Good Fri; (01482) 613902; free.

👃 **Hull & East Riding Museum** (High St) Fine mosaics and a new medieval section; cl 25 Dec, 1 Jan; (01482) 613902; free.

✷ **Hull Maritime Museum** (Queen Victoria Sq) This massive yet solidly stylish 3-domed Victorian building has good displays on Hull's maritime history. There's a long-established section on whales and whaling, and the huge skeletons on display were mentioned in *Moby Dick*. Shop, disabled access; cl 25 Dec, 1 Jan and Good Fri; (01482) 613902; free.

🚂 **Hull Museum of Transport** (High St) Recently doubled in size, this expanding collection is devoted mainly to local public transport and bicycles, some weird and wonderful, with a few interactive displays inc the new Streetlife exhibition. Shop, disabled access; cl 24–26 Dec, 1 Jan; (01482) 613902; free.

🏠 **Maister House** (High St) Only the staircase and entrance hall are open in this mid 18th-c rebuilding (the rest is still used as offices), but the Palladian staircase is splendid, and the doors ornate and finely carved. Cl wknds and bank hols; 80p; NT.

🏠👃 **Wilberforce House** (High St) William Wilberforce was born in this 17th-c house, and its Jacobean and Georgian rooms have a good exploration of the horrors of the slave trade and the struggle for its abolition; also a notable collection of dolls. Shop, limited disabled access; cl am Sun, 25 Dec, 1 Jan, Good Fri; (01482) 613921; free. The Olde Black Boy nearby was the site of slave auctions.

⚓ **Yorkshire Water Museum** (Springhead Ave) Its main feature is a beam engine that in its day could raise about a million litres of water an hour from the well below. Shop, limited disabled access; open pm Fri–Sun, cl Dec; (01482) 652283; free.

HUMBER BRIDGE TA0224

⚐ ✻ ◠ The longest single-span suspension bridge in the world, nearly a mile between the towers, and a very impressive sweep of engineering (there's a footway across as well as the road). At the N end, the **Humber Bridge Country Park** has woodland and clifftop walks, and an old mill. Meals, snacks, shop, good disabled access; (01482) 640852; free.

HUTTON-LE-HOLE SE7090

★ ⬆️ ⌂ 🎣 ❄️ Neat and pretty streamside village at the mouth of Farndale; sheep wander the streets – though they won't be alone in the summer months. Its excellent **folk museum** is practically a village itself, made up of various old buildings from the area re-erected in the 2-acre grounds, inc an Elizabethan manor house, gipsy caravan, and an Edwardian photographic studio; craft demonstrations most Sat–Weds. Shop, disabled access; cl Nov–Mar; (01751) 417367; £3.25. The Crown here is useful for lunch. There's a pleasant walk (an hour or so) over to Lastingham, and the Blakey Ridge road to Castleton is a great drive with classic moorland views.

KILBURN SE5179

🎣 **Robert Thompson Furniture Workshop** 🖵 The quiet village is almost a place of pilgrimage to this workshop, famous for the unobtrusive little mouse carved as a trademark that you'll see all over North Yorkshire, on church pews and in the better inns and pubs. A visitor centre traces the company history, and you can watch the craftsmen at work. Shop; cl Mon (exc bank hols and Jun–Sept), and Nov–Mar; (01347) 868218; £1.50. They make lovely, simple furniture – though not cheap (for a wider choice you might try the Old Mill at nearby Balk, where the craftsmen include a former Thompson employee and prices seem lower). The oak they use can be seen all around. Nr the church (with a memorial to Thompson carved by his own craftsmen) the Singing Bird does refreshments, as does the Forresters Arms – full of Thompson work. Up above the village on Roulston Scar is a **white horse** cut in the turf in 1857 and unique in this part of the country.

KIRKDALE SE6686

✝ **Kirkdale church** Saxon, with a rare original sundial, and 7th-c Celtic crosses and carved stones.

KIRKHAM SE7366

🏛 **Kirkham Priory** Remains of an Augustinian priory in an attractive quiet spot by the River Derwent; finely sculpted lavatorium, graceful arcaded cloister, and handsome 13th-c gatehouse with some finely carved

sculptures and shields. Snacks, shop, disabled access; open Easter–Oct; (01653) 618768; £1.60. The Stone Trough overlooking the ruins is good for lunch, and a pleasant path meanders S by a placid stretch of the River Derwent, to Howsham Bridge and beyond.

LASTINGHAM SE7290

★ ✝ ❄️ ⌂ Attractive village, with a former **monastery**, once one of the area's most sacred spots of pilgrimage, with an outstanding 11th-c crypt; good pub. The hillside just S gives a classic North York Moors view, and there's a pleasant hour's walk over to Hutton-le-Hole.

LEVISHAM SE8390

⌂ A good spot for walkers, with open scenery around it, a track across the blustery moors, and an attractive valley giving separate routes to and from the Hole of Horcum, just below the A169.

MALTON SE7871

Comfortable market town with some interesting side streets, in prosperous farming and racehorse-training country. Sat is a busy market day (the lively livestock mart is on Tues and Fri). The Royal Oak and King's Head do good, generous food. A scenic road towards York is the old coach road parallel to the A64, from Norton to Buttercrambe and Gate Helmsley.

🏰 🖼 ✿ 🍴 **Castle Howard** (off A64 W) Magnificent 18th-c palace designed by Sir John Vanbrugh, who up to then had no architectural experience whatsoever, but went on to create Blenheim Palace. The striking 90-metre (300ft) long façade is topped with a marvellous painted and gilded dome, an unforgettable sight beyond the lake as you approach from the N. Splendid apartments, sculpture gallery and long gallery (58 metres 192ft) long to be exact), magnificent chapel with stained glass by Burne-Jones, and beautiful paintings inc a Holbein portrait of Henry VIII. The grounds are impressive but inviting, inc the domed Temple of the Four Winds by Vanbrugh, a beautiful rose garden and the family mausoleum designed by Hawksmoor. Also, a fantastic collection of period costume, and a good, unobtrusive adventure playground. The palace celebrated its tercentenary in 1999. Meals, snacks, shop, disabled access; cl Nov–mid-Mar; (01653) 648333; £7. A grand public road runs through the grounds, from Slingsby on the B1257; the vast estate is also threaded by a few public footpaths which gain glimpses of the great house and the landscaped parts of its grounds. There's good food at the Bay Horse at Terrington.

! Eden Camp (A64/A169 N) Elaborately re-created wartime scenes in buildings of former prisoner-of-war camp, very well done with sound, smells and even smoke effects. Covers a wide range of World War II experiences, from the rise of the Nazis to the Blitz and Bomber Command ops room. There's a children's commando assault course, but it's perhaps the wartime generation that will get most out of the place. Meals and snacks in NAAFI, shop, disabled access; cl 24 Dec–10 Jan; (01653) 697777; £3.50.

MARGROVE PARK NZ6515
ℏ South Cleveland Heritage Centre (Margrove Park) Right on the edge of the moors, with natural history and wildlife exhibitions; can organise walks and nature trails. Meals, snacks, shop, disabled access; cl Fri, Sat and all Oct–Mar; (01287) 610368; free.

MARKET WEIGHTON SE8741
★ ◠ Neat and pleasant old market town with one or two useful antique shops. Here the well signposted Wolds Way long-distance path briefly divides in two, allowing walkers a circuit taking in the old railway line, now the Hudson Way, and the villages of Goodmanham and Londesborough, with its fine parkland.

MIDDLESBROUGH NZ5116
◔ ✿ **Captain Cook Birthplace Museum** (Stewart Park, Marton, 3m S) The sound of creaking ship's timbers accompanies some of the displays, and the impressive grounds have a conservatory with tropical plants, animals and birds. Meals, snacks, shop, disabled access; cl Mon exc bank hols, 25–26 Dec, 1 Jan; (01642) 311211; £2.40. The nearby Apple Tree has good food.

🐄 Newham Grange Leisure Farm (Coulby Newham, off A174) Rare breeds and other animals and poultry, an agricultural museum, and a reconstructed vet's surgery and saddler's shop. Snacks, shop, disabled access; cl wkdys Oct–Mar; (01642) 300202; £1.65.

! Transporter Bridge (A178) Unique, with the central section serving as a ferry, every 15 minutes shuttling cars and pedestrians across the Tees; cl am Sun, am bank hols, 25–26 Dec, 1 Jan; 80p cars, 30p pedestrians.

MILLINGTON SE8351
◠ Good base for round walks based on the well signed Wolds Way, with the landscape here rolling most attractively.

NORTH YORK MOORS NATIONAL PARK SE7199
❄ This has fewer visitors than the Dales: rich valley pastures, with red-tiled stone farmhouses, twisting rivers, quiet roads, and few villages. The higher moorland is generally very grand and empty, mile after mile of heather scoured by breath-snatching winds, where the few walkers have for company scatterings of hardy sheep and

---

Days Out

Grit and grace: Eden Camp, nr Malton; lunch at the Cornucopia there; Castle Howard.

Seabird city: Cliff stroll at Flamborough Head; lunch at the Seabirds, Flamborough; boat trip or walk to see Bempton Cliffs.

Byways of the Wolds: Burnby Hall waterlily gardens; Londesborough, with a stroll into parkland on the Wolds Way; South Dalton and Lund villages; lunch at the Star, North Dalton; Sledmere House (limited opening); Wharram Percy medieval village site.

the occasional harsh cry of a grouse.

NUNNINGTON SE6779

🏛 ★ ✝ **Nunnington Hall** Big 16th/17th-c house nicely set on the banks of the River Rye, with fine panelling and a magnificent staircase. A family home for nearly 400 years, with the intriguing Carlisle Collection of miniature rooms, each of them ⅛ life-size. Snacks, shop, limited disabled access; cl am, all day Mon (exc bank hols) and Tues (exc Jun–Aug), and all Nov–Mar; (01439) 748283; £4, garden only £1; NT. In the attractive village the Royal Oak is good for lunch, and the church has a fine effigy of a knight said to have rid the district of a Loathly Worm.

ORMESBY NZ5317

🏛 ✿ **Ormesby Hall** Elegant 18th-c house with elaborate plasterwork, Victorian laundry and kitchen, model railway, and pleasant gardens and grounds. Snacks, shop, disabled access to ground floor only; cl am, all day Mon (exc bank hols), Fri, Sat, and Nov–Mar; (01642) 324188; £3.50, garden and railway only £2.20; NT.

OSMOTHERLEY SE4597

★ ⌂ Perhaps more small town than village, but quietly attractive; the Three Tuns has good food (and comfortable bedrooms). A lonely stretch of the Cleveland Way well signed long-distance path runs up over the Hambleton Hills from here, with some road access along the way; and the 44-mile Wyke Way path starts here.

🏰 🏛 **Mount Grace Priory** (A19 NW) Carthusian monks not only took a vow of silence but rarely emerged from their own individual cells. One of those cells at this ruined 14th-c priory has been fully restored, giving a good illustration of how the monks must have worked and lived. The ruins are better preserved than those of any other Carthusian establishment in England, and in spring an impressive display of daffodils makes it especially attractive. An adjacent 17th-c manor house has an exhibition, and interesting Arts and Crafts connections. Snacks, shop; cl winter 1–2pm, maybe Mon and Tues, 24–26 Dec, 1 Jan; (01609) 883494; £2.80; EH.

❗ **North York Moors Adventure Centre** (Ingleby Cross) Organised climbing, caving and canoeing by arrangement, (01609) 882571.

PATRINGTON TA3122

✝ The **church** is glorious, with lovely carving inside – its graceful spire beckoning you from a long way off.

PICKERING SE7984

★ ✝ Another attractive small town, usually very quiet (busier Mon market day), with vividly restored medieval murals in the splendid tall-spired **church**. The White Swan has good food; the A169 N has sweeping moorland views (up there the Saltergate Inn is a useful stop).

♨ **Beck Isle Museum** Charmingly set 17th-c riverside house with a wonderful collection of local bygones and period shops. Shop, disabled access; cl Nov–Mar; (01751) 473653; *£2.50.

🚂 **North Yorkshire Moors Railway** (Pickering Station) Steamtrain trips through some lovely countryside and nostalgically restored stations, a distance of 18 miles; the line was originally built by George Stephenson. The Grosmont end has various locomotives and antique carriages, and you can stop off at Goathland. Meals, snacks, shop, disabled access; cl Jan–Apr (exc Nov and Dec wknds); (01751) 472508 for timetable; £8.90 full return journey. The nearby Station Hotel has decent food.

🏰 **Pickering Castle** Ruins of a 12th-c keep and later curtain walls and towers, with fine views from its imposing castle mound above the town. Snacks, shop, some disabled access; cl winter Mon and Tues; (01751) 474989; £2.30.

POCKLINGTON SE8048

An open-faced market town below the Wolds, with a good few handsome buildings; the Feathers is popular for lunch (and has decent bedrooms). The B1246 Driffield road runs through some quite picturesque hills.

✿ ♨ **Burnby Hall** (B1247 S) Famous for their waterlilies, with dozens of varieties in 2 lakes; also a splendid rose garden, and intriguing collection of all sorts of ethnic material and sporting trophies from across the world. Snacks, shop, disabled access; cl Oct–Mar; (01759) 302068; £2.40. From out here it's not far to the Plough at Allerthorpe (good for lunch).

RIEVAULX SE5785

🏰❋ Rievaulx Abbey Superbly atmospheric ruins of a magnificent and once highly prosperous abbey, among the wooded hills of Rye Dale (the most dramatic views are gained by walking down the dale from the N). The nave, dating from 1135, is one of the earliest built in England. Also among the spectacular 3-tiered remains is a fine 13th-c choir, and a new visitor centre, with hands-on displays about the history of the site, should be open by summer. The graceful colonnades, arches and lancet windows are especially evocative if you get there early or late on a weekday out of season (if they're not shrouded in scaffolding). Snacks, shop, some disabled access; cl 24–26 Dec, 1 Jan; (01439) 798228; £3; EH. Besides the many places in Helmsley not far off, the Hare over in Scawton (a pleasant drive) is good for lunch.

🎭❋🏛 Rievaulx Terrace & Temples This half-mile-long grass-covered 18th-c terrace overlooks the abbey, with dramatic views. Each end is adorned with a classical temple; one a small Tuscan rotunda built to while away the hours in peaceful contemplation, the other, an elaborate Ionic creation, for hunting parties. An ideal spot for a picnic, with good frescoes and an exhibition on landscape design. Snacks, shop; cl Nov–Apr; (01439) 798340; £2.80; NT.

ROBIN HOOD'S BAY NZ9505

★ 🏖 Picturesque fishing village, once popular with smugglers and still largely unspoilt (though there are quite a few shops and cafés for visitors now), its cottages clustered steeply above the rocky shore – a rich hunting-ground for fossil hunters at low tide, when a surprising expanse of sand is exposed beyond the fascinating rock pools. You can walk along a fine section of cliffs to Ravenscar, where a geological trail takes in old alum quarries; an abandoned railway provides an easy walkway back. The Laurel and Olde Dolphin are good value. The village car park is up at the top – quite a climb.

🎵 Music in Miniature Exhibition (Albion Rd church hall) Charming collection of painstakingly created models illustrating English musical history; among the 50 or so dolls' house-sized scenes are medieval minstrels, Victorian carol singers, and a 1920s palm court orchestra, all imaginatively put together by one dedicated woman. Shop, disabled access; cl Nov–Easter; (01947) 880512; £1.

ROSEBERRY TOPPING NZ5712

🏖❋ A memorable viewpoint on the extreme N edge of the moors, reached by a moorland walk from Gribdale Gate car park E of Great Ayton; a popular circuit goes by way of Airy Home Farm, the childhood home of Captain Cook.

ROSEDALE SE7296

❋🏖 With its lush fields and red-roofed yellow-stone houses sheltering warmly below the gaunt moorland, this now seems to typify the quiet pastoral countryside of the area. But until 60 or 70 years ago it was a busy iron-working site: the old railway track that once served the quarries loops around the moor above, and makes an easily followed stroll. The hillside at the top of the dreadfully steep Rosedale Chimney road, heading S over Spaunton Moor, gives motorists too a classic view.

RUNSWICK BAY NZ8016

★ 🏖 Very pretty, harbourless fishing village, good pubs; an attractive stretch of the well signed Cleveland Way long-distance path runs from here to Staithes (or you can begin closer from tiny Port Mulgrave).

SALTBURN-BY-THE-SEA NZ6621

🏖 Originally a superior Victorian seaside resort, with traces of those days still in the Italianate valley garden and the water-operated sloping tramway by the pier. The Ship Inn, a good pub right by the boats pulled up on the beach, is probably the most ancient building. The beach is sheltered by the great headland of Warsett Hill to the S, and a grand section of the well signed Cleveland Way long-distance path takes walkers over this and beyond.

🛢 Smugglers Heritage Centre 🏷 (Whitby Rd) Vivid interactive exhibition on the town's smuggling heritage, housed in old seaside cottages. Shop; cl Oct–Easter; (01642) 444318; £1.75.

SCARBOROUGH TA0488

⋔ † ❋ All the usual seaside attractions in a place of some style, its 2 great curves of firm sandy beach separated by the small harbour below a high, narrow headland. Between castle and cliff are the remains of a Roman signal station, one of 5 such structures built in the 4th c to warn of approaching raiders. To the S is the older part of the resort, with antique tracked cliff lifts between the promenade and the pleasant streets of the upper town; a house associated with Richard III is here (it now looks a little dilapidated), and there's a small craft centre in a former 14th-c inn. The train station has one of the longest benches in the world; 139 metres (456ft) long, it can seat 228 people. Interesting churches include medieval St Mary's, where Anne Brontë is buried, and 19th-c St Martin's with elaborate work by Burne-Jones, William Morris and other Pre-Raphaelites. One unique and entertainingly quaint tradition is the summer staging of miniaturised sea battles with all sorts of special effects among the ducks on the lake of Peasholm Park in the more seasidey N part of the town; 3.30pm Mon and Thurs, May–early Sept. Good views of the bay from the top of Olivers Mount (and harbour views from the Golden Ball on the front); good-value food all day in the very grand Lord Rosebery (Westborough).

ℌ **Millennium** (Harbour) Vivid journey across this last millennium, through Vikings, Normans and the Civil War to the town's early days of rail and Victorian sea bathing – very entertainingly done. Shop, limited disabled access; cl 25 Dec; (01723) 501000; £3.95.

⚱ **Rotunda Museum** (Vernon Rd) Georgian local history museum, with a Bronze Age skeleton and displays on the resort's Victorian heyday. Shop; cl Mon, and also cl Weds–Fri Nov–May; (01723) 374839; £2 (£3 joint ticket with Wood End and Art Gallery).

🏛 🖻 **Scarborough Art Gallery** (The Crescent) Striking Italianate villa with good temporary exhibitions; cl Mon; (01723) 374753; £2 (£3 joint ticket with Rotunda and Wood End museums).

🏯 ❋ **Scarborough Castle** Looking down over the town from the headland, this stands on the site of British and Roman encampments. It was a royal palace of some importance until the reign of James I. Remains include the 13th-c barbican, medieval chapels and house, and the shell of the original 12th-c keep; great coastal views from the walls. Shop, snacks; cl winter Mon and Tues, 24–26 Dec, 1 Jan; (01723) 372451; £2.30.

♪ **Sea Life Centre** 🖻 (Scalby Mills) The same lively mixture we've described in several other resorts. Snacks, shop, disabled access; cl 25 Dec; (01723) 376125; £5.50.

! **Terror Tower** 🖻 (Martin Marine, Foreshore Rd) A diversion for children on wet days, with ghoulish reconstructions of horror film sets and actors adding to the tension. Shop, cl winter wkdys; (01723) 501016; £2.50.

🏛 **Wood End Museum** (The Crescent) The Sitwells lived here for 60 years from 1870 (Edith was born here), and there are displays of their work and associated memorabilia. Also lots of fossils, and a Victorian conservatory with tropical plants – though not the free-flying birds that once mingled with party-goers. Shop; cl Mon, and also cl Tues, Thurs and Fri Nov–May; (01723) 374839; £2.

SHERIFF HUTTON SE6566

★ 🏰 † Attractive village, with a castle and 12th-c church; good pub.

SKIDBY TA0333

❌ ◁ **Windmill** Well restored; open wknds and bank hols plus Weds–Fri in summer hols, mill working Sun only; £1.50. There are gentle country walks nearby, and the Half Moon is useful for something to eat.

SKINNINGROVE NZ7119

⬇ ◁ ❋ **Tom Leonard Mining Museum** Good mining museum well demonstrating the reality of work underground. You can see how the stone is drilled, charged with explosives and fired. Snacks, shop; cl am, and all Nov–Mar; (01287) 642877; £3. The village is industrial, with a steel-rolling mill – far from picturesque, but it has strong local colour, with its odd shantytown of pigeon-fanciers' sheds spreading over the cliff. Walkers can join the well signed Cleveland Way southwards to ascend monumental Boulby Cliff, the highest point on the E coast, before re-entering the National Park.

SLEDMERE SE9365

🏛 ❀ **Sledmere House** Grand 18th-c mansion decorated and furnished in the style of the period, with one showpiece room done in Turkish tiling and a library bigger than many public ones. There's an 18th-c walled garden and the extensive park was landscaped by Capability Brown. They usually play their pipe organ pm Weds, Fri and Sun. Cl all day Mon (exc bank hols), Sat, and Oct–Easter; (01377) 236637; £4. The Triton nearby is a useful place for lunch.

SPROATLEY TA1836

🏛 ❀ 🎵 **Burton Constable Hall** The wonderful exterior gives away this delightful house's Elizabethan origins, but the inside was extravagantly remodelled in the 18th c. Around 30 beautifully preserved rooms to see, with a sweeping long gallery and some intriguing collections. Capability Brown landscaped the 200 acres here too, and there's a riding centre in the stables. Teas, shop, disabled access to ground floor only; cl am, all day Fri, and Nov–Easter; (01964) 562400; £4. Camping, caravanning and seasonal fishing are available. The Cock & Bell down at Preston does good-value lunches.

SPURN HEAD TA4010

🐦 ⌂ This spit which curls like a claw round the mouth of the Humber estuary has a rough track open to cars almost to its end: a bleak place to some but a paradise for birdwatchers, who often wait here in spring and autumn for glimpses of rare migrant species. Thanks to the vagaries of nature the peninsula is gradually becoming an island, so best to check tide times carefully. The estuary itself is usually grey, solemn and grim.

STAINTONDALE SE9998

! ⌂ **Llama trekking** Bruce Wright organises this, across the moors or along the coast; the llamas hump your bags while you walk beside them. They can do specialist treks with forest rangers or experts on wild flowers or archaeology. All treks include home-made food; (01723) 871234; from £20 for three hours.

🐄 ⌂ **Shire Horse Farm** (Staintondale) Friendly little farm with good demonstrations and talks; as well as horses there are various rabbits, small animals and poultry, nature trails, and bracing clifftop walks along part of the Cleveland Way. Snacks, shop, limited disabled access; open Sun, Tues, Weds, Fri and bank hols, spring bank hol–18 Sept; (01723) 870458; £3.50. The Bryherstones Hotel, off the Cloughton road, has good-value food.

STAITHES NZ7818

★ Steep fishing village, unspoilt down by the shore, where little cottages and the storm-battered Cod & Lobster pose fetchingly against the staggering background of a great red sandstone headland, a striking colour picture as the sun comes up.

🏚 ⏚ **Captain Cook & Staithes Heritage Centre** 🖼 (High Street) This converted Methodist chapel in the village where the great explorer worked as a young man in 1745 now houses a decent heritage centre, with a reconstructed street scene showing village life at the time; lots of Cook-related artefacts inc a collection of Webber's superb engravings from the voyages. Also displays looking at the importance of local industries such as fishing, mining and smuggling. Shop, disabled access to ground floor only; cl wkdys Jan; (01947) 841454; *£2.25.

SUTTON BANK SE5182

❀ ⚘ ⚘ ⌂ This steep escarpment gives an enthralling view, particularly from the very popular section of the Cleveland Way that runs S from the A170 along the level clifftop to the white horse cut into the hill. Immediately N of the A170 you can combine the path along the top of the slope with a venture down the nature trail into Garbutt Wood, a **nature reserve** abutting Gormire Lake, the only natural lake in the National Park.

SUTTON ON THE FOREST SE5864

🏛 ❀ ★ **Sutton Park** The friendly 1730s manor house itself is now open only Sat, Sun and Mon bank hol wknds, but the delightful grounds are open pm daily Easter–Sept, with terraced gardens, a Georgian ice house, lily pond, and pleasant woodland walks and nature trails. Tearoom; (01347) 810249; *£4, £2 gardens only. The village with its broad street is pretty, and the smart Rose & Crown has good food.

THIRSK SE4281

! World of James Herriot (23 Kirkgate) A lively look at the country's favourite vet as well as his profession, set in the Skeldale House of his novels; you can even take part in your own TV programme. Shop, disabled access; cl 25 Dec, 1 Jan; (01845) 524234; £4.

THORNTON DALE SE8383

★ Despite the main road, one of the most delightful villages in this part of Yorkshire – with an attractive forest toll road running NW to Langdale End.

WADE'S CAUSEWAY SE8097

⛪ ⌂ Also known as Wheeldale Roman road, this mile-long stretch of broad, paved, Roman road up over the moors is well restored and maintained. It's open to walkers only, but reached easily by the narrow moorland lane S from Egton Bridge (or a longish walk S from Goathland).

WELTON SE9627

⌂ ※ Good area for round walks based on the well signed Wolds Way, with fine views over the Humber in places.

WHARRAM PERCY SE8564

⛪ ⌂ The most famous of the medieval abandoned villages of the Wolds, with lots of grassy humps and an evocative ruined church; English Heritage site, free access. From Thixendale a stretch of the well signed Wolds Way gives walkers a view of the village, and takes in a stretch of classic dry valley.

WHITBY NZ8911

★ † ✿ Famous as the port at which Count Dracula came ashore; Bram Stoker got the idea for the book in the fishermen's graveyard of the partly Norman **church**, 199 steps up from the harbour, with lovely woodwork. Not too far from the abbey on Church Rd is a small but interesting workshop where you can watch jet being crafted into jewellery. Away from the bright waterfront the town is steep and quite attractive, with picturesque old buildings (now often rather smart shops) and some quaint cobbled alleys in its original core E of the busy

harbour, where excellent fresh fish is sold straight from the catch. Besides excellent fish and chips from the Magpie café, the Duke of York (Church St, at the bottom of the 199 steps) does decent food all day. In the 2 weeks around the summer solstice the sun both rises and sets above the sea.

♂ **Captain Cook Memorial Museum** (Grape Lane) In the house where the great explorer lived as an apprentice in the shipping trade from 1746; rooms are furnished in period style with models, letters and drawings from Cook's later voyages. Shop; cl Nov–Easter; (01947) 601900; £2.60.

! Dracula Experience ▣ (Marine Parade) Children probably won't be satisfied until they've visited this vividly spooky re-creation of scenes from the classic tale. Shop; cl winter wkdys, and maybe other times, so best to check; (01947) 601923; £1.95.

▮ **Whitby Abbey** Impressive set of 13th-c ruins dramatically overlooking the harbour from their windswept clifftop setting. You can see the skeletal remains of the magnificent 3-tiered choir and the north transept, and it's an evocative spot for a picnic (site of a famous scene in *Dracula*). An earlier building had been the site of the Synod of Whitby, where the dating of Easter was thrashed out in 664. Last year, archaeologists claimed to have discovered a Celtic Christian cemetery here; excavations will take 4 years to complete. Snacks, shop; cl 25–26 Dec; (01947) 603568; £1.70; EH.

♂ **Whitby Museum** (Pannett Park) Delightfully old-fashioned and crowded, with the only surviving part of Captain Cook's original journal, Queen Victoria's nightdress, some spectacular fossils and the hand of a murderer used as a candle-holder by superstitious burglars. Shop, some disabled access; cl am Sun, and in winter cl pm Tues and all day Mon, 25 Dec, 1 Jan; (01947) 602908; £2.

WITHERNSEA TA3428

※ ▮ **Withernsea Lighthouse** Towering above the houses of this little resort, with fantastic views for those keen enough to climb the 144 steps. Teas, shop, disabled access to ground floor only; open pm wknds and bank hols

Mar–Oct, daily mid-Jun–mid-Sept; (01964) 614834; *£1.80. The Commercial Hotel has very low-priced food.

YORKSHIRE WOLDS SE8461

◠ Quiet agricultural chalk country dissected by dry valleys, with extensive views over huge cornfields. The bulk of the off-road walking is found on the well signposted 79-mile Wolds Way from Hessle Haven down on the Humber to Filey Brigg on the coast, where it meets the Cleveland Way. Some of the lesser roads are a delight to walk on, with wide verges, good views and virtually no traffic.

◠ **Cleveland Way** NZ8215 Along the coast this well marked long-distance path is consistently interesting – and so much more rewarding than the immediate hinterland that there-and-back walks, keeping to the Way itself, are more fun than trying to work out circular walks heading inland. A bus service is useful for the section linking Whitby, Robin Hood's Bay and Scarborough. A fine section can be reached off the B1257 N of Chop Gate NZ5703 (where the Buck does good food). The path westwards on the N slopes of the moors takes in rock outcrops.

★ **Other attractive villages** here, all with decent pubs, include Ainthorpe NZ7008, Ampleforth SE5879 (with its famous school and partly wooded moors), Appleton Roebuck SE5542, Bishop Burton SE9939, Castleton NZ6908 (high above the Esk Valley), Cloughton Newlands TA0196, Crayke SE5670, Great Ayton NZ5611, Hutton Rudby NZ4706, Lealholm NZ7608, Lund SE9748, Nether Silton SE4692, North Dalton SE9352, Oldstead SE5380, Rosedale Abbey SE7395, Seamer TA0284, Sinnington SE7485, South Dalton SE9645, Thixendale SE8461, Thorganby SE6942, Thornton-le-Clay SE6865, Warthill SE6755, Weaverthorpe SE9771 and Welburn SE7268.

Where to eat

BYLAND ABBEY SE5478 **Abbey** (01347) 868204 Beautifully placed dining pub opposite the abbey ruins with an interesting series of rambling old rooms, big fireplaces, polished floorboards and flagstones, good enjoyable food, decent wines and well kept beers, and a big garden; cl pm Sun, am Mon (exc bank hols), 24–25 Dec; limited disabled access. **£25|£4.95.**

FLAMBOROUGH TA2270 **Seabirds** (01262) 850242 Friendly old pub full of shipping memorabilia, with excellent fresh fish and other home-made dishes, lots of wines, and cheerful hard-working staff; cl pm Mon in winter; partial disabled access. **£15|£5.95.**

KIRKHAM ABBEY SE7365 **Stone Trough** (01653) 618713 Quaint beamed inn with small, cosy and interesting bars, log fires, good lunchtime bar food, an old-fashioned no smoking restaurant with farmhouse atmosphere, seats outside with valley views; **£18.90|£6.95.**

MIDDLESBROUGH NZ4919 **Purple Onion** 80 Corporation Rd (01642) 222250 Bustling Victorian building filled with bric-à-brac, ornate mirrors, and house plants, an informal atmosphere, downstairs cellar bar with live music, particularly good, interesting food, friendly staff, and a decent wine list; cl pm Sun, 25 Dec; disabled access. **£21.90|£11.95** 2 courses.

NUNNINGTON SE6679 **Royal Oak** (01439) 788271 Attractive little dining pub nr Nunnington Hall with log fires, beams hung with copper jugs, antique keys, and earthenware flagons, carefully chosen furniture, and generous helpings of enjoyable home-made bar food – super daily specials; cl Mon; children over 8. **£20|£8.25.**

OSMOTHERLEY SE4597 **Three Tuns** South End (01609) 883301 Unassuming and popular front bar area, comfortable and stylish back restaurant with an emphasis on fish, good bar food inc interesting daily specials, well kept real ales, smart and courteous service, and tables in the garden with lovely views; bdrms; no food pm Sun. **£20|£5.95.**

SCARBOROUGH TA0488 **Golden Grid Fish Restaurant** 4 Sandside (01723)

360922 Very long-standing and famous fish restaurant overlooking the harbour serving snacks, lunches (super daily-fresh fish), vegetarian dishes, and afternoon teas; cl Dec; disabled access. **£12.50**|£3.75.

STADDLEBRIDGE SE4499 **McCoys Bistro** *Cleveland Tontine (01609) 882671* A rather special place – though the marvellous, rather eccentric restaurant is now open only on Fri/Sat evenings; downstairs bistro (open 7 days a week) has a friendly, bustling atmosphere and the same particularly good modern food, and a short but thoughtful wine list; bdrms. **£32.50**.

STAITHES NZ7818 **Endeavour** *I High St (01947) 840825* Popular little quayside restaurant at the bottom of a steep hill, with lovely fresh local fish dishes (delicious meat and game, and vegetarian dishes, too), super puddings, decent good-value wine list, and friendly service; bdrms; cl Sun, Mon, all Nov, mid-Jan–mid-Mar; well behaved children only. **£25**.

SUTTON-UPON-DERWENT SE7047 **St Vincent Arms** *(01904) 608349* Relaxed atmosphere in the traditional panelled front parlour with an open fire, high-backed old settles, good solid home-cooked food in the spacious dining room, friendly staff, well kept beers and a good choice of wines; big garden. **£16.20**|£6.50.

THORGANBY SE6942 **Jefferson Arms** *Main St (01904) 448316* Handsome old village inn run by two hard-working sisters, with a spotlessly kept, stylish and spacious main bar, delightful little beamed lounge with sofas and armchairs, open fire and fresh flowers, a narrow conservatory with grape vines and passion flowers, interesting Swiss rostis (grated and fried potatoes) with various toppings and other good food, real ales, and a careful wine list; quiet bdrms. **£20.50**|£4.90.

WHITBY NZ9011 **Duke of York** *Church St (01947) 600324* Bustling, welcoming pub with a fine outlook over the harbour entrance and western cliff from the comfortable beamed bar (lots of fishing memorabilia), a wide choice of good-value fresh local fish as well as other things, well kept real ales, decent wines, and quick, pleasant service; bdrms. **£15**|£4.95.

WHITBY NZ8911 **Magpie Café** *Pier Rd (01947) 602058* Overlooks the town and river, with lots of wonderfully evocative sepia photographs of old Whitby, and much liked for its delicious fresh haddock served by cheerful staff; cl Jan. **£15**|£5.

WHITBY NZ8910 **Trenchers** *Newquay Rd (01947) 603212* Neatly kept, big busy diner by the harbour with delicious fresh fish (and other food), friendly and helpful staff, and a good wine list; cl mid-Nov–mid-March; disabled access. **£16.25**|£6.35.

West and South Yorkshire

First-class outings, often free; lots for children.

This part of Yorkshire is increasingly attractive for a get-out-and-see-things holiday break. Leeds is full of life these days, with a great deal of appeal for a short stay or day visits, and masses to see and do. Lots of work (and lottery money) is going into the rejuvenation of Sheffield, making it altogether more interesting and attractive to visitors. Bradford's photography, film and TV museum has just emerged from an invigorating refit – superb, and free. Halifax is a striking cleaned-up mill town – great buildings put to interesting new uses; its Eureka! centre is excellent for children.

Elsewhere, Harewood House is a favourite, with wide appeal. There are particularly lively and interesting industrial heritage centres at Elsecar, Golcar and Middlestown, and the pioneering industrial village of Saltaire is well worth a visit. Other fine places include Brodsworth Hall, Bramham

Park, Conisbrough Castle and the Bagshaw Museum in Batley. Good family outings include the picturesque Keighley & Worth Valley Railway (based at Haworth) and the open farm at Cawthorne.

Ilkley on the edge of the moors is attractive, and Hebden Bridge is interesting, with good-value subsidised train links to Bradford, Halifax, Saltaire and Huddersfield (the Halifax–Huddersfield journey is through fascinating trouble-up-mill scenery).

In the west is a real Yorkshire mix of steep stone cottage terraces, remarkable mill buildings and some dramatic moorland coming right up to the towns, with plenty of exhilarating walking.

With the present counties of South and West Yorkshire, we have included the bottom corner of North Yorkshire, below York itself and the A64.

Where to stay

BRADFORD SE1632 **Victoria** *Bridge St, Bradford BD1 1JX (01274)* 728706 **£69w,** plus wknd breaks; 60 well equipped rms with CD and video (they have a library). Carefully renovated Victorian station hotel with many original features and lots of stylish character, a bustling bar, popular and informal brasserie serving good modern food, and marvellous breakfasts; disabled access.

FIRBECK SK5688 **Yews Farm** *Firbeck, Worksop S81 8JW (01909)* 731458 ***£52;** 2 rms. In an attractive village, this charming, carefully furnished country home dates from the 16th c and has views over woodland and fields, tasty home cooking, and friendly owners; cl Nov–Feb.

HALIFAX SE0828 **Holdsworth House** *Holdsworth, Halifax HX2 9TG (01422)* 240024 **£101,** plus wknd breaks; 40 pretty, individually decorated rms. Lovely 17th-c house a few miles outside Halifax, with antiques, fresh flowers and open fires in the comfortable lounges, friendly, helpful staff, a very fine oak-panelled dining room with imaginative food and carefully chosen wines, and a garden; dogs by prior arrangement; cl first wk after Christmas; disabled access.

HAWORTH SE0237 **Old White Lion** *Haworth, Keighley BD22 8DU (01535)* 642313 **£60,** plus special breaks; 14 rms, many with lovely views. Friendly, warm and comfortable 300-year-old inn with 3 bars, a cosy restaurant with enjoyable food, and an oak-panelled residents' lounge; nr the Brontë museum and church, and the Keighley & Worth Valley steam railway.

LEEDS SE3033 **42 The Calls** *Leeds LS2 7EW (0113)* 244 0099 **£85w,** plus special breaks; 41 attractive rms using original features, with lots of extras, CD stereo with disc library, satellite TV, and good views. Stylish modern hotel in a converted riverside grain mill with genuinely friendly staff, marvellous food in both the restaurant and next-door Brasserie Forty-Four, and fine breakfasts; cl 5 days over Christmas; limited disabled access.

LINTON SE3946 **Wood Hall** *Trip Lane, Linton, Wetherby LS22 4JA (01937)* 587271 **£130;** 42 spacious, well furnished rms. Grand Georgian mansion set in over a hundred acres of parkland overlooking the River Wharfe; comfortable reception rooms, log fire, antiques and fresh flowers, and imaginative cooking in the no smoking restaurant; indoor swimming pool and health centre; disabled access.

MONK FRYSTON SE5029 **Monk Fryston Hall** *Monk Fryston, Leeds LS25 5DU (01977)* 682369 **£99,** plus wknd breaks; 30 comfortable rms. Grand manor house in attractive grounds with antiques, log fires and fresh flowers in the oak-panelled bar and lounge, friendly staff, and good food in the original manor house dining room; disabled access.

OTLEY SE2143 **Chevin Lodge** *Yorkgate, Otley LS21 3NU (01943)* 467818 ***£105,**

plus special breaks; 50 rms. Built of Finnish logs with walks through the 50 private acres of birchwood (free mountain bike too), and good restaurant food; tennis, fishing, and free membership of the nearby leisure club: indoor swimming pool, gym and supervised crèche; disabled access.

ROYDHOUSE SE2112 **Three Acres** *Roydhouse, Shelley, Huddersfield HD8 8LR (01484) 602606* **£65,** plus special breaks; 20 pretty rms. In lovely countryside, this extended 18th-c hotel has a welcoming atmosphere in its traditional bars, good wines and well kept real ales, and excellent food in the 2 restaurants (one with an occasional pianist), using fresh local produce; cl 25 Dec.

SCISSETT SE2408 **Bagden Hall** *Wakefield Rd, Scissett, Huddersfield HD8 9LE (01484) 865330* ***£80;** 17 rms. Handsome hotel in 40 acres of parkland with its own 9-hole par 3 golf course, comfortable airy public rooms inc a conservatory bar, well prepared French and English food, and quietly efficient service; limited disabled access.

SHEFFIELD SK3485 **Charnwood** *10 Sharrow Lane, Sheffield S11 8AA (0114) 258 9411* ***£95,** plus special breaks; 22 comfortable, well equipped rms. Friendly extended Georgian house with peaceful lounges, a conservatory, and very good food in both the Brasserie and elegant little Henfreys restaurant; cl 24 Dec–3 Jan; disabled access.

To see and do

ANSTON BROOK SK5184
🐟 🏞 Reached on foot from South Anston, this flows through a wooded valley that interrupts the monotony of the flat farmlands SE of Rotherham. It can be combined with a walk along the towpath of the derelict Chesterfield Canal.

BATLEY SE2325
🏛 🎨 🍽 **Bagshaw Museum** (Wilton Park) Beautiful Victorian Gothic mansion in a pleasant lakeside park, with one of those excellent miscellaneous collections based on the curio-hunting of an individual enthusiast. Shop, some disabled access; cl wknds, Good Fri, Christmas; (01924) 472514; free. The Old Hall at Heckmondwike (B6117), once Joseph Priestley's home, is interesting for lunch.

BRADFIELD SK2692
★ ✝ 🏞 Attractive 2-part village, with interesting **church** and good walks in great scenery.

BRADFORD SE1632
🏛 ✝ Though horribly knocked-about by heavy-handed civic designers in the 1960s and 1970s, many buildings survive from what was one of Britain's finest Victorian cities. These, in a solidly unifying northern stone, are a staggering monument to the days when its wools, woollens and worsteds ruled

the world: gigantic and confidently Renaissance-style woollen and velvet mills, the imposing Wool Exchange, the opulent city-centre cliffs of heavily ornate merchants' warehouses in Little Germany behind the mostly 15th-c cathedral, and the florid exuberance of the municipal buildings such as the Gothic city hall, the neo-classical St George's concert hall, even the great Undercliffe cemetery with its sumptuous Victorian memorials (and sweeping Pennine views) – it's been called the most spectacular graveyard in Britain. The city's Asian immigrants have brought a vivid and visible dash of cultural diversity, and there's a feeling of underlying vigour and zest which makes it exciting to visit. Useful places for a pub lunch include the Fountain (Heaton Rd), the Office (off City St) and the Rams Revenge (Kirkgate), but you might prefer one of the multitude of Indian, Pakistani or Bangladeshi restaurants.

🏛 🍽 🖼 **Bolling Hall Museum** (off Brompton Ave, S) Classic mainly 17th-c Yorkshire manor house, now home to the city's collection of local furniture and pictures. Shop; cl Mon (exc bank hols) and Tues; (01274) 723057; free.

🎨 🖼 **Cartwright Hall Art Gallery** (Lister Park) Dramatic baroque-style building in attractive floral park, housing the *Brown Boy* by Reynolds and a good representative selection of late 19th- and early 20th-c paintings. Snacks, shop, disabled access; cl am Sun, and all day Mon (exc bank hols), and over Christmas; (01274) 493313; free.

⬙ **Industrial Museum** (Moorside Rd, Eccleshill) Former spinning mill well illustrating the growth of the woollen and worsted textile industry. Horse-drawn trams carry you up and down the Victorian street, which is complete with workers' cottages and working Victorian stables with shire horses. Meals, snacks, shop, disabled access; cl am Sun, and all day Mon (exc bank hols), 25–26 Dec, Good Fri; (01274) 631756; free.

⬙ **National Museum of Photography, Film and Television** (Princes View) Following a £13.25 million refurbishment, new galleries at this well loved museum look at, among other things, animation, news broadcasting and digital technology. It's a wonderfully lively place, with plenty of hands-on (and face-on) opportunities. Meals, snacks, shop, disabled access; cl Mon (exc bank hols); (01274) 727488; free, IMAX cinema £5.80.

BRAMHAM SE4041
🕸 🏠 🖼 **Bramham Park** The garden here is really quite beautiful, very much in the grand style – Versailles comes to Yorkshire. Long prospects of ornamental lakes, cascades, temples, statuary, grand hedges and stately trees and avenues surround a classical Queen Mary house of great distinction, with lovely period furnishings and paintings. House open by written appointment only (minimum group of 6 people), gardens open daily Feb–Sept (exc 5–11 Jun); (01937) 844265; grounds and gardens £2.50. The Red Lion has decent food.

BRODSWORTH SE5007
🏠 🕸 **Brodsworth Hall** Grand house vividly illustrating life in Victorian times; the family that lived here closed off parts of the house as their fortunes waned, inadvertently preserving the contents and décor exactly as they were (right down to the billiard score-book). Richly furnished rooms, lots of marble statues, and busily cluttered servants' wing. The family

commissioned some of the largest and fastest yachts of the Victorian era and an exhibition charts the history of these splendid vessels. The marvellous formal gardens and parkland are gradually being restored. Snacks, shop, some disabled access; cl Mon (exc bank hols), and all Nov–Mar; (01302) 722598; £4.70; EH.

CARL WARK SK2581
🏛 ⌒ On the edge of the Peak District, this hill fort is set handsomely in a great bowl fringed by gritstone outcrops, and offers a more interesting walk than most in South Yorkshire.

CAWTHORNE SE2708
🎒 ☕ 🕸 ★ **Cannon Hall Open Farm** Unusual animals like wallabies and llamas among the residents at this busy working farm; also baby animals throughout the year, with piglets born every 2 weeks. Good play areas, and mostly concreted so it doesn't get muddy. Meals, snacks, shop, disabled access; cl 25 Dec; (01226) 790427; £2.10. Cannon Hall itself is now a museum and the grounds have been turned into an attractive country park. The village is pleasant.

CONISBROUGH SK5198
🏰 **Conisbrough Castle** Mightily impressive 12th-c castle with uniquely designed 27-metre (90ft) keep – circular, with 6 buttresses and a curtain wall with solid round towers. An added roof and floors re-create something of the original feel, and there's a good audio-visual show. Tours by costumed guides in summer. Snacks, developing craft shop, some disabled access; cl Christmas; (01709) 863329; £2.80; EH. Sir Walter Scott set much of *Ivanhoe* here, writing the novel while staying at the Boat at Sprotbrough nearby; then a riverside farm, it's now a popular dining pub.

CUSWORTH SE5403
🏠 ⬙ **Cusworth Hall Museum** (Cusworth Lane, just W of Doncaster) Excellent museum of South Yorkshire life, in an elegant 18th-c house. Displays on mining, transport, costume and entertainment, and a popular gallery of toys and childhood. Snacks, shop, disabled access; cl am Sun; (01302) 782342; free. The Boat at Sprotbrough is a fairly handy waterside dining pub in a

quiet spot by the River Don.

DENABY MAIN SK4999

! ⬛ ⚥ **Earth Centre** A redevelopment of over 400 acres left derelict by the decline of the coal industry, this environmental centre was awarded one of the Millennium Commission's biggest grants, and by the time it's finished in 2001, it will have cost around £100 million. As we went to press, it was just about to start the second phase of its development, and so it's best to phone for opening times; (01709) 512000. The aim is to promote environmental issues in an enjoyable way.

DONCASTER SE5802

Not really a great deal to attract visitors apart from its race meetings, but there is some fine architecture, especially around the High St and Market Pl, and a good antiques and junk market on Weds.

⬛ **Doncaster Museum & Art Gallery** (Chequer Rd) A good deal of natural history (shop, good disabled access; cl am Sun; free).

ELSECAR SK3899

⬛⬛⚘🏛 **Elsecar Heritage Centre** (Wath Rd) Developing centre in restored industrial workshops. Lots to see including a **hands-on science centre**, a **history centre** where you can dress up and star in a Victorian melodrama, a beam engine and **craft workshops**. On summer Suns there's a **steamtrain** to the Hemingfield Basin. Meals, snacks, shop, disabled access; cl 25 Dec–2 Jan; (01226) 740203; £3.25 science centre, £1 history centre, £2.50 train, or £5.25 for all.

GOLCAR SE0915

⬛⚘🔺 **Colne Valley Museum** (Cliff Ash) Enthusiastic museum spread over 3 weavers' cottages, with hand weaving, spinning and clog-making in gaslit surroundings, and a re-created 1850s living room. Snacks, shop, occasional craft festivals, some disabled access; open pm wknds and bank hols; (01484) 659762; £1.10. The Sands House up on Crosland Moor is a decent dining pub. There's a good year-round walk along the Huddersfield Canal's restored towpath between here and Marsden in *Last of the Summer Wine* country. The Tunnel End pub here is useful for food,

as are the Carriage House and the Olive Branch just a little further away.

GOMERSHAL SE2026

⬛ 🏵 **Red House Museum** (Oxford Rd) Vividly re-creates the 1830s in its 9 carefully furnished period rooms. Charlotte Brontë often stayed at the house (which stands out from its stone neighbours for its unusual red brick), and used it as the basis for Briarmains in her novel *Shirley*. The gardens have been restored in 1830s style, and more galleries opened last year. Snacks, shop, disabled access; cl am wknds, Christmas wk, Good Fri; (01274) 335100; free.

GOOSE EYE SE0240

★ Interesting preserved village; there are good drives around here.

HALIFAX SE0925

✝ 🏚 ✹ Another town with an impressive show of former textiles wealth, interesting to drive through when it's quiet on a summer evening or a Sunday, and surrounded by a splendid ring of moorland. The centre's been cleaned up and partly pedestrianised, which makes it pleasant to potter through, and there are several first-class attractions, with the town now going through something of an artistic renaissance. The medieval **church** has an extremely grand spire and fine carving: look out for Old Tristram, the life-size painted carving of a beggar which was used to collect alms. The Shears (Paris Gates, Boys Lane) down steep lanes among the mill buildings is a pub that embraces much of Halifax's past and atmosphere; the Sportsman (Lee Lane, Shibden – off A647) has a good-value carvery and impressive views.

⬛ **Bankfield Museum** (Ackroyd Park, Boothtown Rd) Collection of textiles and costume, as well as a regimental museum and display of toys. Shop, disabled access to ground floor only; cl am Sun, all day Mon (exc bank hols), 25–26 Dec, 1 Jan; (01422) 354823; free.

⬛ **Calderdale Industrial Museum** (Central Works, Square Rd) Social and industrial heritage from textiles and steam engines to coal mining carpet manufacture and cat's-eyes. Closed for refurbishment until Easter; phone for opening details; (01422) 358087.

⬛ **Dean Clough** Enormous carpet

mill, faced with demolition when it closed down some years ago, but now well restored and home to a thriving complex of galleries and small businesses; best are the Crossley Gallery and Henry Moore Studio, the latter a good showcase for contemporary sculpture (cl am and all day Mon).

♨ ! **Eureka!** (Discovery Rd) Remarkable hands-on museum designed exclusively for children; few places are as likely to spellbind anyone aged between around 3 to 12. Each of the 4 main galleries ostensibly explores one subject, but in fact covers a multitude of topics and ideas. Particular highlights are the broad-based Things Gallery, full of bright colours and images, the communications gallery (you can put your picture on a front page, save a yacht in distress, or read the TV news), and Living and Working Together, where children try their hand at grown-up activities like filling a car with petrol at the garage, working in a shop or bank, or making a meal in the kitchen. Easy to see why in the 7 years it's been open Eureka! has won just about every award going, from Most Parent Friendly and Best Customer Care to several for Loo of the Year. Meals, snacks, shop, disabled access; cl 24–26 Dec; (01426) 983191; £5.75, children 3–12 £4.75, under-3s free.

🏛 🖻 **Piece Hall** (town centre) Magnificent Renaissance-looking galleried and arcaded building put up in 1775 by the merchants of Halifax as a market for their cloth. Now it's filled with specialist shops selling books, antiques and bric-à-brac, as well as an art gallery (cl Mon) and other exhibitions. Meals, snacks, shop, disabled access by prior arrangement; cl 25–26 Dec; (01422) 368725; free. The Italianate courtyard comes to life on Fri and Sat when there are 160 bustling stalls; a good few on Thurs too.

🏛 ♪ ✿ **Shibden Hall & Folk Museum** (Godley Lane, off A58 just E) Excellently refurbished 15th-c house in a 90-acre park, each room illustrating a different period from its history. In the barn a folk museum has an interesting collection of horse-drawn vehicles, while around it is a reconstructed

19th-c village, with workshops, cottage and even a pub. For many this is a real Halifax highlight. Snacks, shop, disabled access; cl am Sun, and usually all Dec–Feb, but best to check; (01422) 352246; £1.90.

🏛 ✿ **Wainhouse Tower** (off A646 just W) This 75-metre (250ft) folly offers good views if you can manage all those steps; shop; usually open only bank hols and a couple of other dates – best to check with the tourist information centre (01422) 368725; £1.30.

HAREWOOD SE3245

🏛 🖻 🐾 🕇 🚲 **Harewood House & Bird Garden** (A61) The area's most magnificent stately home, inside and out. The 18th-c exterior is splendidly palatial, and inside there's some glorious restored Robert Adam plasterwork. Fine Chippendale furnishings, exquisite Sèvres and Chinese porcelain, and paintings by Turner, El Greco, Bellini, Titian, and Gainsborough. Capability Brown designed the thousand-acre grounds, which have very pleasing lakeside and woodland walks, an outstanding collection of rhododendron species, and the famous landscaped bird gardens (you could spend half a day in just this part). Charles Berry's Terrace has an excellent gallery with contemporary art and crafts. Try to visit the 15th-c **church**, with a splendid array of tombs, and a curious tunnel under the wall of the churchyard, so that servants could arrive unseen by sensitive souls. There's a first-class adventure playground. Meals, snacks, shop, disabled access; cl Nov–mid-Mar; (0113) 288 6331; £6.95 everything, £5.75 bird garden and grounds only. TV's *Emmerdale* is filmed on a purpose-built set on the Harewood estate. The Harewood Arms opposite has good food, and just N Wharfedale Grange have **pick-your-own** fruit.

HAWORTH SE0237

✿ ✿ △ A touristy village with plenty of craft shops, antique shops and tea shoppes catering for all the people drawn here by the Brontës (spelt Brunty before father Patrick went posh). A visit out of season catches it at its best, though at any time the steep

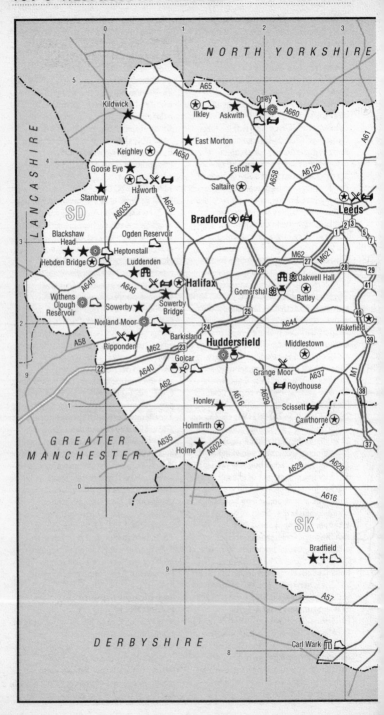

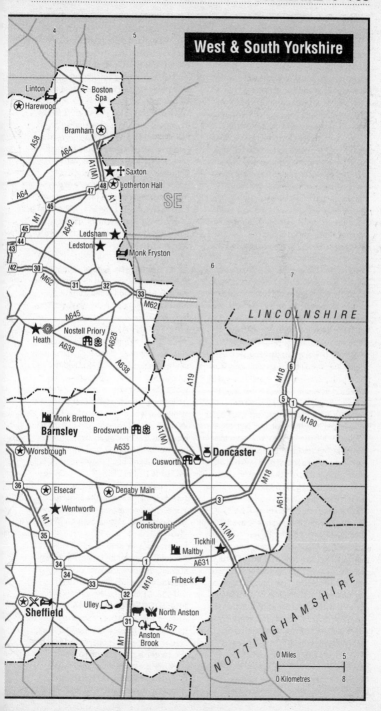

West & South Yorkshire

Linton
Harewood ★
Boston Spa ★
Bramham ★
★ ✝ Saxton
48 ★ Lotherton Hall
47
46
45
44
43
/42 30
Ledsham ★
Ledston ★
Monk Fryston
SE
Heath ★✳
Nostell Priory
Monk Bretton
Barnsley
Brodsworth
Worsbrough ★
Elsecar ★
Denaby Main ★
Wentworth ★
Conisbrough
Cusworth
★ Doncaster
Tickhill ★
Maltby
Firbeck
North Anston
Ulley
Sheffield
Anston Brook

L I N C O L N S H I R E

N O T T I N G H A M S H I R E

0 Miles 5
0 Kilometres 8

Roads: A1, A58, A64, A1(M), A642, M1, M62, A645, A638, A628, A635, A19, M18, M180, M62, A631, A57, A614 cobbled main street has quieter, more atmospheric side alleys. Most of the family are buried in the churchyard, except Anne, interred in Scarborough. For the most evocative views and atmosphere go up to the moors above town, very grand and not much different from when the Brontës knew them – despite the Japanese footpath signs. The Fleece and the Old White Lion are useful for lunch. The A6033 is an interesting drive to Hebden Bridge, and there's a fine old moors road via Stanbury over to the Colne Valley in Lancs. The Pennine moors around Haworth are a favourite stamping-ground for walkers, with a good walk W through Penistone Hill Country Park to the much-visited **Brontë Waterfalls**, and on through a remote valley to Withins, the original Wuthering Heights. There are plenty of paths, though finding the way across fields frequently entails searching for unprominent stone stiles over the dry-stone walls.

🚂🌂 Keighley & Worth Valley Railway Actually begins just N at Keighley (where you can connect with main line trains) but is based here. Run by enthusiastic volunteers, the line was built to serve the valley's mills, and passes through the heart of Brontë country. The Oxenhope terminus has a **museum**, but the prettiest station is Oakworth (familiar to many from the film *The Railway Children*). Snacks, shop, some disabled access; open wknds all year, daily Jun–early Sept, and most school hols; (01535) 645214 for timetable; £6 return.

🏠🌂 Parsonage Museum The Brontës' former home has some 120,000 visitors a year (it was something of a tourist attraction even while Charlotte still lived here). The house is very carefully preserved, with period furnishings, very good changing exhibitions, and displays of the siblings' books, manuscripts and possessions; also the original ink-stained manuscript of *Jane Eyre*, and the sisters' writing table. Shop; usually cl mid-Jan–early Feb, 24–27 Dec; (01535) 642323; £3.80.

HEATH SE3519
★ 🌼 Extraordinarily old-fashioned

common with gypsy ponies alongside 18th-c mansions (and contrasting views over Wakefield); the gaslit King's Arms here is good.

HEBDEN BRIDGE SD9927
★ 🌂🌂🌂 Engaging small town deep in a valley below the moors, and stepped very steeply up the hillsides, with quite a lively subculture of art and craft shops. There is a small museum; the Robin Hood (A6033 towards Keighley) has good-value food. At Hebble End are several working craftsmen, with demonstrations of skills inc glass-making, and in summer there are **horse-drawn barge trips** along the canal basin, (01422) 845557. The hold of one barge in the marina has been converted into a **visitor centre** with a traditional boatman's cabin (cl Nov–Easter; free).

🌂 🏔 **Hardcastle Crags** A beauty spot above the wooded river valley, ideal for walks or a picnic. The Nutclough House on the way up also has decent food.

HEPTONSTALL SD9828
★ 🏔 🌼 An interesting and ancient village, a crippling climb up a fearsomely steep cobbled lane above Hebden Bridge; Sylvia Plath is buried in the churchyard. There's a rewarding scenic path along Heptonstall Crags (the cliffs above the wooded valley of Colden Water). An exhilarating old high road leads out to Widdop and beyond (for fine views and walks), and another runs via Colden and Blackshaw Head.

HOLMFIRTH SE1408
★ † Instantly recognisable as the setting for TV's *Last of the Summer Wine*, with evocative little alleys, several good pubs, and a handsome Georgian **church**.

! **Compo's World** (Huddersfield Rd) An exhibition on the longest-running comedy series in the world. Meals, snacks, shop; cl 25 Dec; (01484) 681408; £1.50.

HUDDERSFIELD SE1416
There's a great sense of style in many of its buildings, especially around the station and central square, and much of the centre is now closed to traffic. The A640 W is a good moorland drive.

🌂 **Tolson Memorial Museum** (Ravensknowle Park) The myths and legends asssociated with Castle Hill are outlined in this former wool baron's mansion, which also has a look at the textile industry, and a collection of horse-drawn vehicles. Shop, disabled access; cl 25–26 Dec, 1 Jan, Good Fri; (01484) 223830; free.

✳ **Victoria Tower** (Almondbury) Castle Hill is 275 metres (900ft) high, overlooking the surrounding moors, even the Pennines and Peak District. This tower, with 165 steps, gives unrivalled views; open pm May–Sept, plus most bank hols; £1.20.

ILKLEY SE1147

★ ✝ ⌂ ◿ Owes its Victorian and Edwardian spaciousness and style to the mid-19th-c and later craze for hydropathic 'cures', which produced quite a rash of luxurious hydros using the town's pure moorland spring water. Their forerunner was the simple little bath-house built in the mid-18th c around the ice-cold spring up on the moor just S at **White Wells** – you can still follow the paths the infirm took by donkey. The group of quaintly shaped rocks known as the Cow & Calf up here also makes a pleasant short walk above the town. The church has 3 lovely Saxon crosses, and just beside it are more traces of the Roman fort. There are a good few prehistoric remains around the town, the best known of which is the Bronze Age **Swastika Stone**, a symbol of eternity carved on a flat rock by a moorland path SE of the town, above wooded Heber's Ghyll; the stone is marked on the Ordnance Survey 1:50,000 map, at SE095469. Heber's Ghyll itself is a picturesque ravine with steep Victorian walkways, and the town with its attractive gardens and interesting shops (you can see chocolate being made at Humphreys) makes a nice stop. Useful places for lunch include the Ilkley Moor Vaults (Stockel Rd/Stourton Rd) and Wheatley Arms (Ben Rhydding). Ilkley Moor S of the town has potential for satisfying high-level walks (without your hat).

🏛 ☕ **Manor House Gallery & Museum** (Castle Yard) One of the few buildings in town to predate the 19th c, an Elizabethan manor house built on the site of a Roman fort, with local history displays. Shop; cl am Sun, all day Mon (exc bank hols) and Tues; (01943) 600066; free.

KEIGHLEY SE0542 (pronounced Keithly) A busy working town with a pleasant centre. The Grinning Rat nr the 16th-c church is useful for lunch.

☕ ♿ **Cliffe Castle Museum & Gallery** (Spring Gardens Lane) 19th-c mansion with French furniture from the Victoria & Albert Museum, as well as various local ephemera. Though quite close to the centre, it's set in a park well above the main road, with an aviary and greenhouses. Shop, disabled access ground floor only; cl am Sun, all day Mon (exc bank hols), 25–26 Dec, Good Fri; (01535) 618238; free.

🏛 ✳ **East Riddlesden Hall** (Bradford Rd, just NE) Interesting early 17th-c oak-panelled stone manor house with attractive plasterwork, period textiles and furniture, and formal walled garden. There's a medieval monastic

---

Days Out

Bradford bounce: National Museum of Photography, Film and Television or Bradford's Industrial Museum; stroll through Little Germany, behind the cathedral; lunch at one of the city's Indian restaurants; Saltaire (easiest by train).

Last of the Summer Wine: Holmfirth; lunch at the Butchers Arms, Hepworth; Colne Valley Museum, Golcar; stroll along the Huddersfield Canal towpath.

Leading Leeds: Royal Armouries Museum; lunch at the Brasserie Forty-Four (The Calls); Temple Newsam House.

fishpond, and huge medieval tithe barn. Snacks, shop, some disabled access; open pm Sat–Weds Mar–Oct, plus Thurs July and Aug; (01535) 607075; £3.30; NT.

LEEDS SE2934

🏛 Leeds has become a really rewarding place to visit, with something for all ages: its Royal Armouries Museum is an outstanding family day out, Tropical World is very enjoyable (and free), and there's plenty more to fill a short stay. A great deal of effort has gone into developing a 24-hour café culture here, and behind the hype there really is a surprisingly cosmopolitan city, its compact centre increasingly popular with young people in the evenings (lots of bars and clubs), and ideal for exploring during the day – it's largely free of traffic. There are lots of splendid covered arcades (Victorian, Edwardian and modern), and all sorts of interesting and engaging Victorian architectural details to spot. Shoppers and theatre-goers are well catered for – the former in the exuberantly Venetian/Oriental glass-roofed **market**, the biggest in Yorkshire, and the latter by the West Yorkshire Playhouse (a useful meeting place with fine city views from its good café/bar) and The Grand (home of Opera North). The imposing **town hall** is perhaps the high point of Leeds' essentially Victorian centre; and there are good gardens and open spaces. Whitelocks (Turk's Head Yard, off Briggate) is a marvellous old city tavern, very much a Leeds institution. The historic Waterfront area has been well developed for visitors in recent years.

🖈🚂 **Armley Mills Museum** (Canal Rd) Once the largest woollen mill in the world, now a huge working museum, its floors given over to a massive display of textile machinery. Also a printing gallery, reconstructions of a turn-of-the-20th-century tailor's shop, clothing factory, and demonstrations of static engines, steam locomotives and underground haulage. Snacks, shop, disabled access; cl am Sun, Mon (exc bank hols), 25–26 Dec; (0113) 263 7861; *£2.

🏛 **Corn Exchange** (Call Lane) This impressive 1860s building is now filled with neat little specialist and designer shops, and has plenty of places for tea, coffee and so forth, as well as an excellent fresh continental bread stall; there's a stamp market here on Sun, and often a small jazz group at teatime.

🖼 **Henry Moore Institute** (The Headrow) Over a footbridge is this delightful place, with temporary exhibitions of sculpture from Roman times to the present, displayed in quite an unusual building (they don't actually show anything by Henry Moore). Shop, disabled access; (0113) 234 3158; free. Stays open late on Weds.

🖼 **Leeds City Art Gallery** (The Headrow) Excellent collection of 20th-c British art, as well as English watercolours and a sculpture gallery, inc carefully chosen works by Henry Moore (he had his first exhibition here in 1941). Meals, snacks, shop, limited disabled access; cl am Sun, bank hols; (0113) 247 8248; free.

🏺 **Leeds City Museum** (Claverley St) Deservedly on the Heritage Secretary's shortlist of excellent museums, of national importance (cl Sun, Mon, and Tues after bank hols; (0113) 247 8275; free).

🐄 **Meanwood Valley Urban Farm** (£) (Meanwood) Small working farm on regenerated waste land N of the centre, with rare breeds, organic garden, and a new environment centre. Meals and snacks (not Mon), shop, good disabled access; (0113) 262 9759; 50p.

🚂🔧 **Middleton Railway** Running from Turnstall Rd to Middleton Park, this is the oldest running railway in the world and was the first to be authorised by Parliament. Later it was the first to succeed with steam locomotives, and in 1960 became the first standard-gauge line to be operated by enthusiasts. With a picnic area, fishing, nature trail and playgrounds as well as the trains, there's plenty for families here. Snacks, shop, disabled access; diesel or steamtrains most wknds, plus some other days in summer; (0113) 271 0320 for timetable; *£2.

🏺 **Museum of the History of Education** (Parkinson Court, Leeds University) Small but interesting, inc text and exercise books going back to the 17th c – it's usually best to book with Dr Foster, (0113) 233 4665; open pm Mon–Fri (exc Tues); free.

❀ ♦ **Roundhay Park** (off A58) 700 acres of rolling parkland, well known for concerts and events. On Princes Ave here the Canal Gardens are a very pleasant and peaceful corner of the city, with several national flower collections (inc dahlias and violas), lots of roses, and ornamental wildfowl; free.

♨ ! **Royal Armouries Museum** (Clarence Dock, Waterfront) A far cry from the average military museum, this houses the National Museum of Arms and Armour, previously displayed at the Tower of London, but shown off here in a radically different way. It's almost completely interactive, with hi-tech effects and push-button displays, and plenty of costumed demonstrations showing not just how weapons were made and used, but how they affected everyday life; children can try on costumes and helmets, or even test their aim with a crossbow. The building's design is stunning (don't miss the breathtaking Hall of Steel, with 3,000 pieces of gleaming arms and armour on the walls), but the most spectacular feature is outside: the country's only full-size authentically re-created tiltyard, with dramatic exhibitions of jousting, fencing, duelling, and hunting dogs and birds of prey; phone for dates and times. An inside display area often has martial arts displays, and there are demonstrations of traditional skills in the Craft Court. Meals, snacks, shop, good disabled access; cl winter Mons, 24–25 Dec; (0990) 106666; £7.95 (£4.95 low season).

❀ ♨ ▣ ☞ **Temple Newsam House** (5m E, S of A63) That trusty old faithful Capability Brown designed the wonderful 1,200 acres of landscaped parkland and gardens in which this house stands, an extraordinary asset for any city. The house itself dates from Tudor and Jacobean times, and contains the city's very good collections of decorative and fine art, as well as an exceptional assemblage of Chippendale furniture. There are rare breeds in the grounds; picnic areas and a children's play area. Snacks, shop, disabled access to ground floor only; cl am Sun, all day Mon, and Jan–Feb; (0113) 264 7321; £2

(£1 car parking charge).

♨ ▦ **Tetleys Brewery Wharf** (Waterfront) Small museum, shire horses and tour of the Tetleys brewery itself (booking recommended – or at least reserve a place as soon as you arrive, not suitable for under 14s). Indoor and outdoor play areas for children. Meals, snacks, shop, disabled access to ground floor of museum; cl 24–26 Dec, 1 Jan; (0113) 242 0666; £3.95. Granary Wharf nr here on Nevill St has plenty of interesting shops and weekend events, festivals and entertainment.

♨ **Thackray Medical Museum** (Beckett St) Dynamic museum at St James's Hospital, well known from the TV series *Jimmy's*. The emphasis is more on social history than science, but there are interactive displays on how the body works, and good reconstructions showing the progress of medical care in Britain, inc some deliciously gruesome parts on surgery before the development of anaesthetics. Snacks, shop, disabled access; cl Mon (exc bank and school hols), 24–26, 31 Dec, 1 Jan; (0113) 244 4343; £4.40.

✕ ⚙ **Thwaite Mills** (Stourton, 2m S) This water-powered mill was the focus of a tiny island community perched between the River Calder – which drives the mill wheels – and the Aire & Calder Navigation. The Georgian mill-owner's house has been restored and has displays on the site's history; guided tours of the mill every hour. Snacks, shop, disabled access; cl am Sun, all day Mon (exc bank hols), Christmas, and Jan–Feb; (0113) 249 6453; £2.

❀ ♦ ❀ **Tropical World** (Roundhay Park) Huge conservatory with the biggest collection of tropical plants outside Kew, along with all sorts of exotic trees, reptiles, fish, birds, and butterflies, in careful re-creations of their natural settings. Meals, snacks, shop, disabled access; cl 25 Dec; (0113) 266 1850; £1.50.

LOTHERTON HALL SE4436

♨ ▣ ♦ ❀ Edwardian house (on the B1217 Garforth–Tadcaster) with displays ranging from Oriental art to British fashion, as well as collections of paintings, silver and ceramics and some lovely furnishings. There's a bird garden in the restored grounds. Meals, snacks, shop, some disabled access; cl Mon (exc bank hols), am Sun, Jan–Feb; (0113) 281 3259; £2 house, grounds free. The Swan at nearby Aberford is popular for lunch, with good-value food.

LUDDENDEN SE0426
★ ⌂ Interesting village with Brontë connections; the enormous Oats Royd Mill in the valley is a remarkable sight.

MALTBY SK5489
⛪ Roche Abbey (off A634 SE) A fine gatehouse to the NW and the still-standing walls of the south and north transepts are all that's left of this 12th-c Cistercian abbey, but they make an impressive sight. Snacks, shop, some disabled access; cl Nov–Mar; (01709) 812739; £1.60; EH.

MIDDLESTOWN SE2416
☺⛏ ! National Coal Mining Museum (Caphouse Colliery, New Rd) Well deserves its many awards for its exploration of life as a coal miner. No simple reconstruction this – they take you 140 metres (450ft) underground, down one of Britain's oldest working mine shafts, where models and machinery have been set up to show the methods and working conditions of miners from the 1800s to the present. For the faint-hearted (and under 5s), on the surface there are pit ponies, 'paddy train' rides, steam winder, nature trail, and an adventure playground. Dress sensibly if you're going underground. Meals, snacks, shop, disabled access and excellent facilities – helpful to arrange it in advance; cl 24–26, 31 Dec, 1 Jan; (01924) 848806; £5.75. The Kaye Arms at Grange Moor is a good, smart dining pub.

MONK BRETTON SE3706
⛪ Monk Bretton Priory The red sandstone remains of an important 12th-c priory, with gatehouse, church and other buildings, as well as some unusually well preserved drains. The ancient Mill of the Black Monks is pleasant at lunchtime (live music for young people most nights).

NORLAND MOOR SE0521
⌂ ☀ S of Sowerby Bridge, this gives walkers views from the Calderdale Way into adjacent Calderdale, with the Rochdale Canal along its foot.

NORTH ANSTON SK5284
🐖 🦋 Tropical Butterfly House ⊞ (Woodsetts Rd) Friendly place with insects, reptiles, snakes, birds of prey and farm animals besides the butterflies; they positively encourage you to touch as well as look. Meals, snacks, shop, disabled access; cl 25–26 Dec; (01909) 569416; £3.50.

NOSTELL PRIORY SE4017
⌂ ❀ This sumptuous Palladian mansion (off A638), with perhaps the best collection of Chippendale furniture anywhere, is likely to be closed throughout the year for essential maintenance work; best to phone for details; (01924) 863892; NT. The Spread Eagle has decent food.

OAKWELL HALL SE2127
⌂ ❀ Moated Elizabethan manor house (signed off A651/A652 S of Birkenshaw), altered in the 17th c, and still furnished to give something of the atmosphere then; look out for the unusual dog gates at the foot of the staircase. Also period formal gardens, extensive country park with an adventure playground, visitor centre and for children the Discovery Gallery – a hands-on exploration of the four elements. Snacks, shop, limited disabled access; cl am wknds (Discovery Gallery cl all am), Christmas wk; (01924) 326240; £1.20 house (free Nov–Feb), visitor centre and Discovery Gallery free. The Black Bull opposite the ancient Norman church in nearby Birstall has good-value home cooking.

OGDEN RESERVOIR SE0630
⌂ N of Halifax, this is well served with paths for walkers (including a stretch of Roman road).

OTLEY SE2045
★ Archetypal Yorkshire market town with a most attractive atmosphere (helped by its number of pubs?).
☀ ⌂ The Chevin Behind Otley, this is not a high hill, but gives walkers a grand view of Wharfedale.

RIPPONDEN SE0318
★ Rather austerely attractive village, with medieval pack-horse bridge; the B6113 and B6114 above here are interesting moors roads.

SALTAIRE SE1337
★ 🏭 The pioneering industrial village that Titus Salt developed in Shipley in

the 1850s. Salt's beautifully thought-out, classically designed village was so successful that even now it's a favoured place to live. It's well worth looking around, and you might want to try the antique **cable railway**. There's a splendid flight of locks on the Leeds–Liverpool Canal.

🏠🖼 **1853 Gallery** (Victoria Rd) Named after the date when the magnificent mill it's housed in was built, this is probably one of the largest private collections of art in the country, with around 300 works by David Hockney, inc some of his intriguing experiments with photography. Huge bookshop, disabled access; (01274) 531163; cl 25–26 Dec; free. Some good smart shops in the building too (inc one selling clothes made in the mill).

🖥 **Victorian Reed Organ Museum** (Victoria Hall, Victoria Rd) Unique, with some eye-opening exhibits, inc one organ no bigger than a family Bible. If you're an organ-player you may get the chance to try some of those on display. Limited disabled access (with notice); cl Fri, Sat, all Dec and first wk Jan; (01274) 585601; *£2.

SAXTON SE4736

★ ✝ Attractive village with a decent pub; don't miss the **church**, where Lord Dacre is buried sitting on his war horse.

SHEFFIELD SK3281

A vast industrial city, redeveloped extensively in post-war years – you really have to be a local to tap into the increasingly thriving and enjoyable cultural life of the city, but several places are rewarding to visit – though needing a street map and quite a bit of journeying. Best to use the comfortably modern tram to get about; it runs out to the giant indoor shopping mall at Meadowhall. Hefty millennium grants are set to revitalise the city centre over the next couple of years, with a winter garden, new public squares, new art gallery and museum, and redesigned botanic gardens all hopefully completed by 2001.

🏠🖥 **Bishop's House** (Meersbrook Park, S Sheffield) Striking 15th- and 16th-c yeoman's house, now a good museum of social history. Shop, limited disabled access; cl Mon (exc bank hols),

Tues; (0114) 255 7701; £1.

🖥🖼 **City Museum and Mappin Art Gallery** (Weston Park) Firmly traditional in its approach, but with some interesting collections, inc fine cutlery and a splendid display of antique Sheffield plate. The excellent gallery features works by Renoir, Cézanne, Turner and even Walt Disney. Meals, snacks, disabled access; cl Mon (exc bank hols), Tues Jan–Apr, Christmas; (0114) 276 8588; free.

🖼 **Graves Gallery** (Surrey St) Well worth a visit, with some fine decorative art; cl Sun; (0114) 273 5158; free.

⬇T **Kelham Island Industrial Museum** (around Alma St, signed from Sheffield centre) Lively exploration of Sheffield's industrial development, with all sorts of buildings, workshops and machinery collections (inc formidable working engines), and traditional cutlery craftsmen at work. Snacks, shop, disabled access; cl Fri, Sat; (0114) 272 2106; £3.50. The Fat Cat here has really good cheap food.

❗ **National Centre for Popular Music** Costing £15 million and set in a distinctive building shaped like a pair of drums, this new centre opened last year; exhibitions look at the development of popular music from classical to hip-hop, with an emphasis on post-1945 sounds. Also a surround-sound auditorium and you can try your hand at playing an instrument or mixing a record. Meals, snacks, shop, disabled access; (0114) 279 8941; £5.95.

🖼🎨 **Ruskin Gallery** (Norfolk St) The collection of Victorian artist and writer John Ruskin, with an adjacent craft gallery; cl Sun; free.

🚌 **Sheffield Bus Museum** (Tinsley) Diverse collection of buses and even pre-war milk floats, with related memorabilia and a big model railway. Shop, snacks, some disabled access; open pm wknds for restoration work, with special open days every couple of months when the displays are more lively; (0114) 255 3010; £1.

SOWERBY BRIDGE SE0623

★ Worth a stop if you're passing; turn down to the canal basin, which always has a lot going on.

ULLEY SK4687

⌂ ✒ Pleasant walks around a

reservoir, also good for fishing and watersports; the Royal Oak is in a lovely setting by the church.

WAKEFIELD SE3221

⌖✝ A number of handsome buildings, inc its **cathedral**, much restored in Victorian times but with some fine 15th-c masonry and carvings (and a marvellous spire – the tallest in Yorkshire), its rare 14th-c bridge chapel over the River Calder, some Georgian and Regency houses most notably around Wood St and St John's Sq, and its imposing civic buildings.

▣ **Wakefield Art Gallery** (Wentworth Terrace) Good collection of 20th-c painting and sculpture, internationally famous for its galleries devoted to 2 famous local sculptors – Barbara Hepworth and Henry Moore. Shop; cl am Sun, all Mon, 25 Dec, 1 Jan; (01924) 305796; free.

⌘ **Wakefield Museum** (Wood St) Opening in Feb after a £1.4 million lottery-funded refurbishment. Along with the unique collection of preserved animals and exotic birds, and an exhibition of 1940s women's costume, there will be new displays and full disabled access. Shop; (01924) 305351; free.

✿ ▣ **Yorkshire Sculpture Park** (Bretton Hall College, West Bretton; A637 SE) Carefully and imaginatively displayed series of major contemporary sculpture set in fine 18th-c landscaped parkland. There are 16 works by Henry Moore in the adjacent country park, often surrounded by grazing sheep. Café, shop, disabled access; cl Christmas wk; (01924) 830579; free (though £1.50 car parking charge).

WENTWORTH SK3898

★ Reckoned by some readers to be the prettiest village they've ever seen.

WITHENS CLOUGH RESERVOIR SD9822

◠ ✿ S of Hebden Bridge, this has a path for walkers – and the more energetic can climb up to the prominent monument on Stoodley Pike, for the views.

WORSBROUGH SE3503

✿ ✗⌘☛ **Worsbrough Mill Museum & Country Park** (A61) Hard to believe this peaceful country park was once a busy industrial area;

the only sign of those days is the working corn mill, now a museum but still producing stoneground flour. The 200 acres also include nature trails, traditional and rare breeds, and several beehives; lots of events throughout the year, especially on bank hols and summer Suns. Snacks, shop, some disabled access; cl Mon (exc bank hols), Tues, and mid-Dec–early Jan; (01226) 774527; *50p.

★ **Other attractive or attractively placed villages** with decent pubs include Askwith SD1648, Barkisland SE0420, Blackshaw Head SD9527, Boston Spa SE4345, East Morton SE1042, Esholt SE1840, Holme SE1006, Honley SE1312, canalside Kildwick SE0145, Ledsham SE4529 and nearby Ledston SE4328, Ogden SE0730, Saxton SE4736 (magnificent church), Sowerby SE0423, Stanbury SE0037 and Tickhill SK5993 (especially the church and the semi-ruined castle).

✺ **Other useful pubs in fine positions or with good views** include Dick Hudsons on the Otley road at High Eldwick above Bingley SE1240, the Castle overlooking the reservoirs nr Bolsterstone SK2796, the Brown Cow on open-access woods at Ireland Bridge (B6429) nearer Bingley, the Strines nr Strines Reservoir above Bradfield SK2692, the Stanhope Arms on Windle Edge Lane nr Winscar Reservoir by Dunford Bridge SE1502, the New Inn at Eccup SE2842, the Cow & Calf up Skew Hill Lane at Grenoside above Sheffield SK3293, the Malt Shovel at Harden SE0838, the Robin Hood at Pecket Well outside Hebden Bridge SD9928, the Cherry Tree on Bank End Lane at High Hoyland SE2710, the Fleece at Holme SE1006, the Buckstones on the A640 towards Denshaw high above Huddersfield SE1416, the Blacksmith's Arms on Heaton Moor Rd at Kirkheaton SE1818, the Shepherd's Rest and Top Brink on Mankinholes Rd at Lumbutts SD9523 (bracing walks to Stoodley Pike monument), the Hinchcliffe Arms at Cragg Vale, Mytholmroyd SE0126 (the B6188 S is a good moors road), the Hobbit up Hob Lane, Norland SE0723, the Grouse on Harehills Lane, Oldfield, nr Oakworth SE0038, the Causeway

Foot on the Keighley road by Ogden Reservoir SE0631, the Waggon & Horses (A6033) and Dog & Gun (off B6141 towards Denholme), both nr Oxenhope SE0335, the Pineberry on the A644 Keighley road out of Queensbury SE1030, the Brown Cow (A672) dramatically overlooking Scammonden Reservoir SE0215, the Clothiers Arms in Station Rd, Stocksmoor, nr Shepley SE1810, the White House on the B6107 or Rose & Crown up Cop Hill at Slaithwaite SE0813, the Blue Ball nr Soyland SE0120, the Sportsman's Arms at Hawks Stones, Kebcote on Stansfield Moor SD9227, the Ring o' Bells on Hill Top Rd at Thornton SE0933, the Freemason's Arms on Hopton Hall Lane at Upper Hopton SE1918, the Cross Keys overlooking the restored Rochdale Canal at Walsden SD9322, the Delvers on Cold Edge Rd and Withens on Warley Moor Rd at Wainstalls SE0428 and the Pack Horse at Widdop SD9333.

Where to eat

GRANGE MOOR SE2415 **Kaye Arms** *(01924) 848385* Civilised and busy family-run dining pub with a smart dining lounge, particularly good, imaginative food, exceptional-value house wines from a fine list, decent malt whiskies, and helpful, courteous service; cl Mon, 25–26 Dec; children allowed lunchtime only; disabled access. **£22.95|£5.95**.

HALIFAX SE0825 **Design House** *Dean Clough (01422) 383242* Stylish modern restaurant in a thriving, carefully restored carpet mill complex, with enjoyable modern cooking to match; relaxed and friendly atmosphere, good service, and a thoughtful wine list; cl pm Sun and Mon, 26 Dec, 1 Jan; disabled access. **£22**.

HAWORTH SE0237 **Weavers** *15 West Lane (01535) 643822* Charming evening restaurant made up of weavers' cottages, with lots of bric-à-brac, photographs, and spinning mementos, delicious food, cheerful service, and a good loyal following; bdrms; cl Sun, Mon, 1 wk after Christmas, last wk June. **£25**.

LEEDS SE3033 **Brasserie Forty-Four** *44 The Calls (0113) 234 3232* Originally a grain mill (below 42 The Calls, see **Where to stay**), this riverside restaurant is simply furnished with modern designs, and serves enjoyable British and Mediterranean food (very good-value early evening set menu), also a good-value wine list; cl am Sat, Sun, bank hols; partial disabled access. **£30|£9.75** 2-course lunch.

LEEDS SE3033 **Leodis** *Victoria Mill, Sovereign St (0113) 242 1010* Stylish modern restaurant on the ground floor of a former Victorian mill with carefully cooked popular brasserie food, decent wines, and a bustling buoyant atmosphere; cl am Sat, Sun, 25–26 Dec, 1 Jan; disabled access. **£30|£14.95** 3-course lunch.

LEEDS SE3033 **Pool Court at 42** *42 The Calls (0113) 244 4242* Cleverly converted quayside grain mill (also incorporating Brasserie Forty-Four and the stylish hotel, 42 The Calls), this is a smart modern restaurant with a calm atmosphere, very accomplished, enjoyable food with French leanings (the set meals are good value), lovely puddings, and an interesting wine list; cl am Sat, Sun, bank hols; no babies; disabled access. **£48.34**.

LEEDS SE2736 **Salvos** *115 Otley Rd, Headingley (0113) 275 5017* Welcoming Italian restaurant run by the same family for over 30 years, with good modern food (popular and interesting daily specials) and cheerful service; cl Sun, 31 Dec, bank hols; disabled access. **£21|£6**.

LEEDS SE2933 **Sous le Nez en Ville** *Basement, Quebec House, Quebec St (0113) 244 0108* Imaginative popular food in this fashionable basement restaurant with tiled floors and exposed brick walls, a very good wine list, and efficient service; cl Sun, bank hols. **£15.95 3-course set evening menu**.

RIPPONDEN SE0419 **Old Bridge** *(01422) 822595/823722* Well kept medieval inn by a pretty bridge over the River Ryburn with interesting rooms, good wines, and real ales, and a very popular cold buffet wkday lunchtimes (best to book);

charming evening restaurant just over the bridge; no bar food Sat, pm Sun; no children; disabled access. **£16|£4.75.**

SHEFFIELD SK3186 **Smith's of Sheffield** *34 Sandygate Rd (0114) 266 6096* Very popular restaurant, cheerfully decorated in cream and red with an unusual tented ceiling, a relaxed chatty atmosphere, stylish modern cooking using influences from all over the world, and a good wine list; upstairs is perhaps more serious, with an open-plan kitchen and 6 gourmet courses of the chef's choice; occasional cookery demonstrations, too. **£30.**

Special thanks to Derek and Sylvia Stephenson, Derek Stafford, E Warburton, Michael and Jenny Back.

Yorkshire Calendar

Some of these dates were provisional as we went to press. Please check information with the telephone numbers provided.

JANUARY

3 **Hubberholme** Land Letting at the George pub, *at 8pm* (01756) 760223

FEBRUARY

12 **Doncaster** Festival of Railway Modelling at the Exhibition Centre – *till 13 February* (01778) 391109

MARCH

3 **Bradford** Film Festival – *till 18 March* (01274) 394540
7 **Scarborough** Shrovetide Skipping Festival *at noon*: ¾ mile of Foreshore Rd closed to traffic *till 5pm* (01723) 373333
10 **York** Science Festival – *till 31 December* (01904) 554424
11 **Whitby** Eskdale Festival of the Arts: competitive event – *till 18 March* (01947) 601249

APRIL

2 **Sewerby** Craft Fair at Sewerby Hall and Gardens (01262) 673769
5 **York** Easter Festival at the National Centre for Popular Music – *till 9 April* (01904) 645738
12 **York** Jugglers Event – *till 16 April* (01904) 621756
17 **York** Early Music Festival – *till 23 April* (01904) 658338
20 **Doncaster** Easter Egg Rolling at Cusworth Hall Museum of South Yorkshire Life (01302) 782342
21 **Harrogate** International Youth Music Festival – *till 28 April* (01306) 744360; **Hebden Bridge** Pace Egg Plays: old custom (01422) 843831
22 **Hull** Easter Street Organ Festival in the city centre (01482) 615625; **York** Model Railway Show: up to 40 layouts – *till 25 April* (01653) 694319
23 **Beningbrough** Easter Egg Hunt at Beningbrough Hall and Gardens (01904) 470666
24 **Ossett** World Coal Carrying Championship (01924) 218990

Yorkshire Calendar (cont.)

27 Harrogate Spring Flower Show, one of Britain's best – *till 30 April* (01423) 536880

28 Cleethorpes Beer Festival at the Winter Gardens – *till 1 May* (01472) 692925; **Whitby** Gothic Weekend – *till 30 April* (0115) 949 7659

MAY

6 Gawthorpe Maypole Procession (01924) 305000

7 Great Ouseburn Festival of Springtime: open gardens, flower festival (01423) 330833; **Scarborough** Brass Band Contest (01430) 423451

13 Haworth 1940s Weekend: music, military vehicles – *till 14 May* (01535) 644407

14 Ilkley Music Festival – *till 21 May* (01943) 872067

20 Otley Show (01943) 462541

25 Beverley Beverley and East Riding Early Music Festival – *till 29 May* (01904) 645738; **Keld** Tan Hill Show at Tan Hill Inn (01833) 628246

27 Epworth Wesleyan Street Market and Pageant – *till 3 June* (01427) 873898

28 Stockton-on-Tees Regatta (01642) 393905

29 Helmsley Country Fair at Duncombe Park (01923) 788517

31 Whitby Planting of the Penny Hedge (corruption of penance hedge): a tradition since 1159 (01947) 602674

JUNE

4 York Millennium Tattoo (01904) 621756

10 Halifax Procession (01422) 341317; **Whitby** Festival – *till 18 June* (01947) 602674

16 Beverley Folk Festival – *till 18 June* (01377) 217662

17 Leeds Show at Roundhay Park – *till 18 June* (0113) 268 9973

18 Todmorden Agricultural Show (01706) 815648

19 Otley Carnival (01943) 873211

22 Fountains Abbey Open-air Shakespeare at Fountains Abbey – *till 24 June* (01765) 608888; **York** Millennium Mystery Plays – *till 22 July* (01904) 625444

24 Keighley Jazz in the Garden at East Riddlesden Hall (01535) 607075; **Linton** Fun Day and Feast inc fireworks (01937) 587451; **Pateley Bridge** Nidderdale Festival – *till 2 July* (01423) 711532; **South Otterington** North Yorkshire County Agricultural Show at Otterington Hall (01609) 773429; **Stockton-on-Tees** Transport Rally at Preston Park – *till 25 June* (01642) 393911

JULY

1 Harewood Fireworks Concert at Harewood House (01625) 575681; **Helmsley** Steam Fair at Duncombe Park – *till 2 July* (01439) 770213; **Thirsk** – *till 9 July* (01845) 522672; **Whitby** Angling Festival – *till 10 July* (01287) 660118

2 Oxenhope Straw Races: teams in fancy dress race between 5 pubs carrying a bale of straw (01535) 644298

7 Fountains Abbey Music by Moonlight at Fountains Abbey – *till 8 July* (01765) 608888; **York** Early Music Festival – *till 16 July* (01904) 645738

Yorkshire Calendar (cont.)

8 Hebden Bridge Riverside Music Festival – *till 9 July* (07801) 532931; **Kirkstall** Festival at the Abbey (0113) 243 2096

11 Harrogate Great Yorkshire Show at the Yorkshire Showground – *till 13 July* (01423) 541000

15 Barton Carnival – *till 16 July* (01652) 635330; **Leeds** Opera and Party in the Park – *till 16 July* (0113) 247 8397

21 Fountains Abbey Open-air Opera and Music Day at Fountains Abbey – *till 23 July* (01765) 608888

23 Skipton Fireworks Concert at Broughton Hall (01625) 575681

25 Rydale Show (01653) 697820

26 Whitby Sneaton and Hawsker Agricultural Show (01947) 602674

28 Stockton-on-Tees International Riverside Festival – *till 6 August* (01542) 393911

31 Leeds Rhythms of the City: largest street theatre festival in the north – *till 29 August* (0113) 213 7800

AUGUST

1 Egton Bridge Old Gooseberry Show at St Heddas School: since 1800, tastings *from 5pm*, music (01947) 810009; **Littlebeck** Garden Fête and Rose Queen Ceremony (01947) 810759

2 Hull Jazz Festival – *till 6 August* (01482) 615624

5 Fountains Abbey A Venetian Masquerade at Fountains Abbey (01765) 608888; **Leeds** Mela – *till 6 August* (0113) 249 2734

8 Halifax Agricultural Show at Savile Park (01422) 355056

12 Billingham Carnival – *till 19 August* (01642) 535424; **Kellythorpe** Driffield Steam and Vintage Rally at the Showground – *till 13 August* (01377) 256950

19 Whitby Folk Week – *till 25 August* (01757) 708424

23 Egton Show (01947) 895281

25 Fountains Abbey Fountains by Floodlight at Fountains Abbey – *till 14 October* (01765) 608888

26 Leeds Rock and Pop Festival – *till 28 August* (0113) 247 4477; **Leyburn** Wensleydale Agricultural Show (01969) 640261; **Stockton-on-Tees** Carnival – *till 28 August* (01642) 393911; **West Witton** Burning of the Bartle: effigy of legendary outlaw, and fun day (01969) 622034

27 Leeds Reggae Festival in Potternewton (0113) 247 8397

28 Burniston Horticultural and Agricultural Show (01723) 870049; **Epworth** Show (01427) 872571; **Leeds** West Indian Carnival (0113) 262 9496

SEPTEMBER

1 Hull International Sea Shanty Festival: music, classic boat regatta – *till 3 September* (01482) 615624

2 Filey Fishing Festival – *till 10 September* (01723) 515745; **Harewood** Fireworks Concert at Harewood House (01625) 575681; **Keighley** Keighley and District Agricultural Show (01535) 643206; **Sowerby Bridge** Rushbearing Festival – *till 3 September* (01422) 831896

7 Leeds International Piano Competition – *till 23 September* (0113) 244 6586

8 Leeds Ballet in the Park – *till 9 September* (0113) 247 4477

Yorkshire Calendar (cont.)

9 Billingham Carnival and Garden Show – *till 10 September* (01642) 393911; **Broughton** Carnival (01652) 654768; **Castleton** Castleton and Danby Agricultural Show (01287) 660409; **Hull** Show (01482) 327111; **Whitby** Heritage Week – *till 17 September* (01947) 602674

15 Harrogate Autumn Flower Show – *till 17 September* (01423) 561049

16 Ilkley British Society of Painters Exhibition at King's Hall and Winter Gardens – *till 24 September* (01943) 602319; **Leeds** Fireworks Concert at Kirkstall Abbey (0113) 247 4477

22 York National Book Fair at the Barbican Centre – *till 23 September* (01904) 656688; also, Festival of Food and Drink – *till 1 October* (01904) 653655

OCTOBER

1 Sewerby Craft Fair at Sewerby Hall and Gardens (01262) 675185

6 Hull Fair: huge funfair – *till 14 October* (01482) 615624

26 Leeds Diwali celebrations (0113) 247 4477

NOVEMBER

5 Stockton-on-Tees Fireworks Party (01642) 393911; **York** Bonfire Night (01904) 620557

8 Hull Literature Festival – *till 19 November* (01482) 615624

15 Huddersfield Contemporary Music Festival – *till 26 November* (01484) 425082

16 York St Nicholas Fayre and Festival (01904) 554425

DECEMBER

8 Broughton Victorian Christmas Fair and Millennium Carnival – *till 9 December* (01652) 654768; **Otley** Victorian Fair (01943) 46399

15 York Early Music Christmas Festival – *till 21 December* (01904) 658338

24 Dewsbury Tolling the Devil's Knell: old custom (01484) 223200

We welcome reports from readers

This *Guide* depends on readers' reports. Do help us if you can – in return, we offer a discount on the next edition to people who've helped us with reports for it. Tell us what you think about places already in it, and anything extra you think we should say about them. And send us your ideas for inclusion in the next edition: places to visit, eat at or stay in, attractive drives or walks, maybe even unusual interesting shops you know of. Use the card in the middle, the report forms at the end, or just write – no stamp needed: *The Good Britain Guide*, FREEPOST TN1569, Wadhurst, E Sussex TN5 7BR.

LONDON

Some spectacular new openings – as well as the old favourites that draw people from all over the world.

This year sees many millennium projects coming to fruition – not just the temporary ones such as the Dome and the Big Wheel (sorry, London Eye), but great places of permanent value, such as the new Tate Modern gallery on Bankside, the new pedestrian bridge linking St Paul's to Bankside, and the great refurbishment of the Greenwich Maritime Museum. We have grouped the main millennium openings together, at the start of this chapter – which is otherwise split into London's main areas for visitors. It's worth noting that much of the new and updated visitor developments are clustered around the South Bank, Bankside and Greenwich.

As almost everything worth visiting or looking at is concentrated in the relatively small centre, London is quite easy to explore on foot. There is no end of potential walks concentrating on particular interests – architecture, history, royalty or whatever. One of the best overviews of the capital is had by walking along the south bank of the Thames from Lambeth Bridge to Tower Bridge, giving mostly traffic-free panoramic views of the West End, St Paul's Cathedral, the City, the Tower of London and finally the Docklands. Quite a number of people lead guided walks. We have found Original London Walks ((020) 7624 3978) consistently good over the last few years, with a choice of nine or ten a day. Walks last about two hours, usually starting from a tube station; you don't need to book, and the cost is around £4.50.

A useful money-saver is the London White Card, covering entry to 15 of the top museums (including the Science Museum and the V & A) for £16, provided you can squeeze them all into three days. The *London for Less* guide gives discounts on some attractions including high-priced ones, restaurants, theatres and hotels: quite a bargain, it covers four people for eight days for £12.95, and is on sale at the tourist information centre at Victoria, the British Travel Centre in Regent St, and bookshops such as Waterstone's and WH Smith. Travel Cards are good-value cut-price tickets for the day, weekend or longer, valid on buses, tube and rail trains, for as many journeys as you want to make during the day (not the morning rush hour). You can add them to rail fares into London. London's Tube, the underground railway, is the most straightforward way of getting around. Pocket tube and bus route maps are free from ticket offices. In the text, we have grouped things to see and do under the heading of the most convenient tube station, using the ⊖ symbol – or the ⇌ symbol if it's surface rail instead.

Where to stay

BASIL STREET HOTEL *8 Basil St SW3 1AH (020) 7581 3311* **£232,** plus special breaks; 80 pretty, decent-sized rms, most with own bthrm. Handy for Harrods and Hyde Park, this very civilised privately owned Edwardian hotel has a relaxed atmosphere, antiques, fine carpets and paintings in the public rooms, a panelled restaurant with reliably good food, cellar wine bar, afternoon teas in lounge, and a ladies' club; helpful, courteous service – many of the staff have been here for years; children free in parents' rm.

CAPITAL *22–24 Basil St SW3 1AT (020) 7589 5171* **£276.13;** 48 luxury rms with lovely fabrics, fine paintings, marble bthrms, and complimentary extras. Exclusive little hotel nr Harrods, with a warm welcome and log fire in the reception, an intimate panelled bar with good nibbles, a small lounge, exemplary service, and exceptional French-inspired food in the chandelier-lit restaurant; disabled access.

CHESTERFIELD *35 Charles St W1X 8LX (020) 7491 2622* **£223.25;** 110 well equipped pretty rms. Charming hotel with particularly courteous helpful staff, afternoon tea in panelled library, relaxed club-style bar with resident pianist, and fine food in attractive restaurant or light and airy Terrace Room; disabled access.

CLARIDGES *Brook St W1A 2JQ (020) 7629 8860* **£252.62 inc champagne and chocolates,** plus luxury breaks; 197 excellent rms. Grand hotel long used by royalty and heads of state, with liveried footmen, lift attendants and valets, elegant and comfortable day rooms, civilised colonnaded foyer where the Hungarian Quartet plays; lovely formal restaurant with mirrored mural and terrace, and dinner-dance pm Fri and Sat; free golf at Wentworth (and tennis at Vanderbilt Racquet Club); disabled access.

CLAVERLEY *13–14 Beaufort Gardens SW3 1PS (020) 7589 8541* **£120,** plus special breaks; 30 individually decorated rms, most with own bthrm. Friendly, privately owned Edwardian house with a comfortable lounge, panelled reading room, and good breakfasts in the cheerful dining room; disabled access.

CONNAUGHT *Carlos Pl W1Y 6AL (020) 7499 7070;* 90 lovely, individually decorated rms inc 24 suites. A very special place with fine old-fashioned and dignified values – there's no brochure, no price list; elegant, restful day rooms filled with lovely flowers and antiques, fine panelling, exemplary service, and outstanding food in the two formal restaurants; disabled access.

CONRAD *Chelsea Harbour SW10 0XG (020) 7823 3000* **£270;** 160 suites with a light and spacious living room area (many have sofa-beds so two small children could stay with parents at no extra cost). American-owned, Europe's first purpose-built luxury 'suite hotel' is tucked away in the quiet modern enclave of the Chelsea Harbour development and overlooks its small marina; good food in the Brasserie (marina views) or the Long Gallery, friendly service, evening pianist, and health club; disabled access.

COVENT GARDEN HOTEL *10 Monmouth St WC2H 9HB (020) 7806 1000* **£268;** 50 big individual bdrms with smart bthrms. Stylish luxury hotel nr theatres; wrought-iron staircase from the foyer to the panelled upstairs drawing room and library filled with richly coloured, interesting furniture; small ground-floor brasserie.

DURRANTS *George St W1H 6BJ (020) 7935 8131* **£165.50;** 92 well equipped rms, with own bthrms; the quietest are at the back. Managed by the same family for over 70 years, this surprisingly quiet central hotel behind a delightful Georgian façade has fine paintings and antiques, a clubby bar, and relaxing lounges; cosy panelled restaurant with essentially English cooking, and helpful, pleasant staff.

GORING *15 Beeston Pl, Grosvenor Gardens SW1W 0JW (020) 7396 9000* **£229,** plus special breaks; 75 individually decorated rms, some with balconies overlooking a pretty garden. Built in 1910 by the grandfather of the present Mr Goring, this family-run, impeccably kept and very English hotel has a particularly welcoming atmosphere (many staff have been there for years), very good, enjoyable cooking in the elegant restaurant, a super wine list, comfortable lounge for afternoon tea, airy cocktail bar, and staunchly loyal customers; disabled access.

HALKIN 5 Halkin St SW1X 7DJ (020) 7333 1000 **£331.63,** plus special breaks; 41 stylish well equipped rms, with wonderful marble bthrms. Despite its Georgian exterior, the décor and furnishings here are ultra-modern but enjoyable; there's a particularly good Milanese restaurant overlooking the garden, fine breakfasts, and really charming staff; lots of facilities for businessmen; disabled access.

HAZLITTS 6 Frith St W1V 5TZ (020) 7434 1771 **£199.75;** 23 rms with 18th- or 19th-c beds and free-standing Victorian baths with early brass shower mixer units. Behind a typically Soho façade of listed early Georgian houses, this is a well kept and comfortably laid out little hotel which could scarcely be handier for the West End; good continental breakfasts served in your bedroom, snacks in the sitting room, lots of restaurants all around; kind, helpful service; disabled access.

L'HOTEL 28 Basil St SW3 1AS (020) 7589 6286 ***£170.37;** 12 well equipped rms. Small family-owned French-style city hotel, nr Harrods and above the neatly kept, well run Metro wine bar where English and continental breakfasts are served, as well as good modern French café food; friendly staff; disabled access.

22 JERMYN STREET SW1Y 6HL (020) 7734 2353 **£263.97;** 5 rms and 13 suites – spacious with deeply comfortable seats and sofas, flowers, plants, and antiques. Stylish little hotel owned by the same family for over 80 years and much loved by customers; with no public rooms, wonderful 24-hour service, helpful notes and suggestions from the friendly owners, in-room light meals, and a warm welcome for children; disabled access.

KNIGHTSBRIDGE GREEN 159 Knightsbridge SW1X 7PD (020) 7584 6274 **£161,** plus special breaks; 28 no smoking rms, most suites with sitting room. Friendly, family-owned hotel, carefully refurbished and neatly kept, with very good in-room breakfasts (no restaurant), bar service, free coffee and tea in lounge, and helpful efficient staff; cl 24–26 Dec.

LEONARD 15 Seymour St W1H 5AA (020) 7935 2010 **£263.20;** 31 rms – mainly luxury suites – with fine paintings, antiques, lovely fabrics, fresh flowers, videos, satellite TV, and hi-fi system. Smart 18th-c town house with marvellous staff, light modern meals all day in the café bar, and a compact exercise room.

LE MERIDIEN 21 Piccadilly W1V 0BH (020) 7734 8000 **£195w,** plus special breaks; 266 comfortable well equipped rms. The very best in modern French hotel-keeping; attractive and quiet public rooms with professional and friendly service, popular afternoon tea, marvellous food (one restaurant is the Oak Room of Marco Pierre White – see **Where to Eat**), and free membership of the good health club downstairs; one child under 12 free in parents' room; disabled access.

RUBENS 39–41 Buckingham Palace Rd SW1W 0PS (020) 7834 6600 **£238.50,** plus special breaks; 174 well equipped rms. Opposite Buckingham Palace and nr Victoria Station, this attractive hotel has comfortable day rooms inc a comfortable lounge with views of the Royal Mews, a restful library, open fire in the bar, and an attractive split-level restaurant with good food.

ST GEORGE'S Langham Pl W1N 8QS (020) 7580 0111 **£190,** plus special breaks; 86 light rms with marvellous views over London. Popular modern hotel next to the BBC headquarters and a stone's throw from Oxford Circus, with ground-floor reception lobby and all other public rooms on the 15th floor with super city views; good modern food in the new brasserie, with lighter meals in bar and lounge.

STAKIS ST ERMINS 2 Caxton St SW1H 0QW (020) 7222 7888 **£170;** 290 rms. Opulent Edwardian hotel with fine staircase, ornate plasterwork, antiques and elegant furniture in luxurious day rooms, fine food in two restaurants, and helpful staff; disabled access.

SWISS HOUSE 171 Old Brompton Rd SW5 0AN (020) 7373 2769 **£86;** 16 rms. Festooned with ivy and flower boxes, friendly and good-value, family-run hotel, relaxed and tidy inside, with very good buffet-style continental breakfast – English available, too; disabled access.

WINDERMERE 142–144 Warwick Way SW1 4JE (020) 7834 5163 **£93;** 22 recently refurbished individually decorated rms. Small, friendly private hotel with cosy lounge, decent breakfasts and evening meals in the pleasant no smoking dining room.

Millennium openings

LONDON Family Attraction of the Year

♄ ☺ ! ⊖ **NORTH GREENWICH Millennium Dome** (Greenwich Peninsula) Can there be anyone who hasn't heard about the Dome? Or who hasn't voiced an opinion on it? It's at once the most hyped and the most vilified attraction the country has ever seen. The papers have had a field day criticising almost every detail and stage of its conception, while the New Millennium Experience Company have hit back with reams of facts and figures: the Dome has the biggest roof in the world, and could contain more than 18,000 London buses. And yet other than what it looks like from the outside, few of us really know much about the Dome, or what it's going to be like to visit. They've tried to explain it to us: we know there will be 14 main exhibition zones, the most famous of which will contain a giant body, and that there'll be a specially filmed episode of *Blackadder*. It's supposed to be a year-long celebration of British ideas and technology, looking at how we learn, work, and play, and what our minds are capable of. The Body Zone will explain how we work, and the Mind Zone how we think; the Journey Zone will show us the transport of the future, and the Money Zone how our spending affects the economy. The Play Zone will have hundreds of interactive and digital games, while at the opposite extreme a Rest Zone will contain nothing but soothing sounds and images (probably very useful – they hope to welcome 35,000 visitors a day). A dramatic ride in the Home Planet section will take visitors across space and the landscapes of the world, and a live show repeated several times a day will feature hundreds of dancers, singers, performers. Living Island, an environmental exhibit, is entered through a giant sewer and contains its own beach and promenade. It's not simply a theme park, but with so many interactive elements and some astonishing designs and ideas it's clearly much more than just an exhibition. So will it be fun? And will it be worth it? We obviously won't know for sure until it opens on 1 January. One pessimistic way of looking at it is that for each visitor it's already cost about £50 of your money (in lottery 'taxes' and commercial sponsorship for which consumers have to foot the bill – the revenue from tickets is only a relatively small additional proportion). So if you don't go, that £50 of yours that they've already spent will be money down the drain. Buying a ticket is the only way of getting something for all that money. But we prefer to be gently optimistic. Given the names, talent and effort involved, it's hard to see how it can fail to be impressive. And let's be honest – after spending £758 million on the thing, they'd really have to mess up for the result to be not worth seeing. So we look forward to seeing a place that, for whatever reason, will undoubtedly be the most visited and the most talked about attraction in the country. Meals, snacks, shops, disabled access; open from 1 Jan for one year only; (0870) 606200; *£20 (*£16.50 children 5–15). A family ticket, covering two adults and three children or one adult and four children, is *£57 – quite a saving. When these prices were announced, the press quickly dubbed the Dome 'Britain's most expensive tourist attraction', which is hardly fair: it's true individual tickets are 50p more expensive than Alton Towers, but the family ticket is cheaper than the latest comparable prices we've been quoted for Alton Towers, Legoland or other attractions of that ilk. Tickets must be bought in advance, from the number above, from anywhere selling National Lottery tickets, or from train and bus stations (National Express offer a bargain flat-rate fare to London that includes entry to the Dome). There won't be car parks other than at nearby Park & Ride sites; the best way to get here will be by public transport – the new Jubilee Line station at North Greenwich is just alongside.

⇌ BARNES

♥ ⋎ ! ❋ Wetland Centre Four miles from the heart of the city, this Wildfowl & Wetlands Trust reserve is an incredible feat of environmental transformation. Forty hectares of reservoir have been broken up, and re-sculpted to create over 30 lakes linked by 27 bridges. With nearly 30,000 trees, and 200,000 aquatic plants, the centre will gradually provide a haven for a spectrum of wildlife, from herons and teals to newts and kingfishers; birds already spotted breeding here include little ringed plover, great crested grebe and lapwing. There are seven hides, and a three-storey viewing tower, but for those who like birdspotting in comfort, a glass-walled observatory, with views across the reserve, will relay live pictures via CCTV from the hides. A fun-looking discovery centre will provide lots of hands-on activities for children, with re-created wetland habitats. The visitor centre will house touch-screen displays on the wildlife seen at the reserve, as well as a café and shop. It's all been designed to accommodate wheelchair access, and there's even a lift in the observation tower. At peak times, the centre will provide riverbus services from Hammersmith, Barnes and maybe other stations, to prevent traffic from disturbing the wildlife. Opens from May (cl 25 Dec); as we went to press, they hadn't yet decided their admission prices, so best to phone, (020) 8409 4400.

⊖ NORTH GREENWICH

ⅰ ☺ ! Millennium Dome See separate family panel on p.781.

⊖ SOUTHWARK

▣ ❋ ! Tate Modern (Bankside) Standing proudly robust on the bank of the Thames opposite St Paul's Cathedral, this masterfully gentrified former power station is a salient landmark amid the cluster of new and exciting developments in this part of the city. Designed by Sir Giles Gilbert Scott in 1947 (the architect of Liverpool's Anglican Cathedral, Waterloo Bridge, and designer of the red telephone box), it stood derelict for nearly 15 years, until the Tate Gallery acquired it in 1994. Cathedral-like windows will give splendid views over central London,

and a series of stunning top-lit galleries will provide perfect lighting conditions in which to display artworks. When the gallery opens in May, the collection will cover every modern art movement from Pop Art to Surrealism, with works by all the great modern artists inc Dali, Picasso, Matisse and Duchamps, on permanent show for the first time. There will be around three major loan exhibitions a year, as well as an education centre, auditorium, café with outdoor terrace and a restaurant with river views. Very good disabled access; (020) 7887 8005; cl 24–26 Dec, 1 Jan. The gallery opens in May and will be free to enter (exc for special exhibitions); when the Jubilee Line is up and running, Southwark will be the nearest tube station, but until then, Blackfriars over the river is the most convenient. The building will also form the south bank anchor point of the new **Millennium Bridge**, an elegant teak-decked footbridge spanning the Thames in a single arch. The bridge, which will create a convenient short cut from the Tate to St Paul's, was designed by Sir Norman Foster in collaboration with the sculptor Sir Anthony Caro, and will be made from 360 tonnes of steel.

⊖ WESTMINSTER

❋ ! London Eye (County Hall) This gigantic ferris wheel designed, quite literally, to see in the new millennium, was successfully raised (after initial difficulties) as we went to press. The wheel stands nearly 140 metres (450ft) above the Thames – not as high as originally intended, but still the fourth tallest structure in London, three times the size of Tower Bridge. From its 32 glass capsules, passengers will be able to see up to 25 miles in each direction. If all goes well, the wheel should start turning at 8.30pm New Year's Eve, though nervous souls may at first be superstitious about trying it after breakages of simple key components halted the first attempt to get it upright. It's been given planning permission to stand for 5 years, but maybe (as with the Eiffel Tower), this millennial landmark will still be around to see in the next century. Admission will be £6.95 adults, £4.80 children.

The West End

World-famous for its shopping and window-shopping, from bustling Oxford St, through the bookshops around Charing Cross Rd, the specialist food and cookery shops of Soho, and the elegant stores of Regent St and Piccadilly, to the ultra-smart clothes shops of South Molton St and Bond St, and a wealth of fine art galleries and auction houses. The West End is synonymous with theatre; a half-price ticket booth on Leicester Sq sells off surplus tickets for that day's performances: open around 12–2pm for matinée tickets, then from about 2.30pm for evenings. Highlights here include the National Gallery and Trafalgar Square, Piccadilly with the Royal Academy, and Covent Garden. The BBC Experience up by Oxford Circus is great for anyone interested in what goes into TV or radio, not just what comes out. Chinatown is a vivid enclave, Neal St is a focus for vegetarian restaurants and rather alternative shops, and there are staunchly old-fashioned institutions of Englishness and English cooking like Rules or Simpsons – among an extraordinarily eclectic mix of other places to eat.

To see and do

⊖ BOND STREET

🏛 **Mayfair** W of Regent St and N of Piccadilly (and only the shortest of strolls from them; Bond St and Green Park tube stations are handy). This is mostly a quietly discreet area of elegant town houses, smart, well established hotels, and richly unobtrusive offices. Despite their famous names, Berkeley Sq and Grosvenor Sq don't have any special appeal for visitors – though you might want to stroll down Brook St to see the neighbouring blue plaques commemorating Handel and Jimi Hendrix living there (Handel House is being restored as a museum). Bond St with its continuation New Bond St is the area's main street for shopping, though unless you want to spend a great deal of money on top-notch designer clothes and shoes, jewellery or Oriental rugs this is likely to be confined to the window. Plenty of art and antique galleries, and a good indoor antique market (124 New Bond St). Asprey's is a remarkable place, famous for its opulent luxury goods and glittering with an awesome tonnage of gems and precious metals. Nearby is a charming

lifesize sculpture of Churchill chatting to Roosevelt on a bench – you can sit with them. Sothebys auction rooms are fascinating to wander around. Other small and prestigious art galleries are dotted throughout Mayfair, particularly in nearby Dover St and Cork St; Grays antique market off 58 Davies St has hundreds of indoor stalls. South Audley St has Hobbs of Mayfair, a delicious smart delicatessen, and Thomas Goode, a magnificent glass and china shop. Higgins in Duke St is the Queen's coffee-man. The best Mayfair pub is the Red Lion in Waverton St.

🏛 **Wallace Collection** (Hertford House, Manchester Sq – across Oxford St) Excellent art collection beautifully displayed in an elegant 18th-c house. It's visually very seductive, with probably the best collection of 18th-c French paintings in the world, inc luscious offerings from Watteau, Boucher and Fragonard. Also great Canalettos, fine works by Rembrandt, Rubens and Van Dyck, works by British painters, furniture (mostly 18th-c French), notable assemblage of Sèvres porcelain, and an amazing array of arms and armour, both Oriental and European. It's rarely busy, and in places feels more like a historic home than a museum. From May they will have a new gallery and public library in the basement, and a courtyard café. Meals, snacks, shop, disabled access with prior warning; cl am Sun, 24–26 Dec, Good Fri, 1 Jan, May Day bank hol; (020) 7935 0687; free.

✪ ⇄ CHARING CROSS

Trafalgar Square Many people think of this as the heart of central London (distances to and from central London used to be measured from the Cross on the Strand) and there are elaborate plans to pedestrianise at least part of it so as to make it more accessible. Named for the great naval victory of 1805, it was designed by Nash and completed in 1841; the fountains were added a century later. The centrepiece, **Nelson's Column**, stretches up 56 metres (185ft), its base guarded by four huge identical lions. Look out for the gifted roller-skaters who perform in the evenings around the base – and, of course, for the innumerable pigeons; Nelson has a special coating to protect him from their droppings.

▣ National Gallery This magnificent building right on the square houses the national collection of Western European painting, with around 2,000 pictures dating from the 13th c to the end of the 19th (some 20th-c works were recently swapped with the Tate, after a decision that 1900 is the date when modern art begins). You'll enjoy it most if you're firm and restrict yourself to just a few of the galleries, rather than trying to see everything. It's hard to pick out highlights (the whole collection is worth studying), but don't miss the Sainsbury Wing, which gives perfect lighting and viewing conditions for its treasure-trove of early Renaissance works. The gallery gets very busy, especially on a Sat, or at any time around the Impressionist works. The hi-tech audio tour, with a CD rather than a cassette (so you can skip to whichever bit you want), is well worth the cost, with a commentary on every single picture in the main gallery. Meals, snacks, shop, disabled access; cl 24–26 Dec, 1 Jan, Good Fri; (020) 7747 2885; free, charges for some exhibitions.

▣ National Portrait Gallery (St Martin's Pl, just round the corner) Grandly illustrates British history, with paintings of kings, queens and other notable characters arranged in chronological order from the top floor (medieval) to the present. Snacks, shop (where computer technology allows them to print you a poster of any painting in the gallery), disabled access; cl 24–26 Dec, 1 Jan, Good Fri, May Day hol; (020) 7306 0055; free, charge for some special exhibitions.

✝ ▣ ♪ St Martin-in-the-Fields This elegant church has frequent lunchtime and evening concerts; (020) 7930 0089 for programme. Unmistakeable for its blue clock-dial – the only clock in this part of London that seems always to keep the right time – the church has a busy but very well liked coffee bar in its crypt, with frequent art exhibitions; also brass-rubbing centre, shop (inc all the Academy of St Martin-in-the-Fields CDs) and good afternoon craft market, useful for bargains. Every night the church is used as a shelter for the homeless, but even so, as you make your way home from the theatre, you're likely to see plenty of bodies huddled in shop doorways in these streets – a sadly common sight all over London but especially obvious around here.

▥ Theatres Theatres abound off Trafalgar Sq, with a group based around this end of Charing Cross Rd, and another up along the Strand. Marked out by the globe on top of the building, the Coliseum (St Martin's Lane) is the home of the English National Opera, though they plan to move elsewhere in the next few years; in the meantime, you can usually get decently priced seats on the day, from 10am. (London's more famous Covent Garden Opera House is currently closed for restoration and extension.) Almost next door to the Coliseum, the Chandos is a good pub with food all day (upstairs is best), down past the Post Office the underground Tappit Hen is an atmospheric wine bar, and there's no end of smart little coffee shops and cafés near by – Gabys (30 Charing Cross Rd) does perfect hot salt beef sandwiches.

⊖ COVENT GARDEN

🎭 ✤ Partly pedestrianised, the former vegetable, fruit and flower market with its elegant buildings is now made over to smart café-bars, boutiques and stalls, such as those in the covered piazza, selling expensive hand-made clothes and craft items. There's a bustling cosmopolitan atmosphere and good street entertainers. There's also the Jubilee Market which specialises in different wares on different days. The many bars and restaurants are always lively at night, but again they're not cheap. One of the delights of this area is its range of unusual or specialist **shops**. In the streets around the Piazza, Knutz (Russell St) has everything for the practical joker, and Penhaligon's (Wellington St) sell lovely old-fashioned toiletries. On the other side of the market, N of the tube station, interesting and unusual shops are set in a labyrinthine network of attractively rejuvenated alleys and streets; you will get lost, but wandering around is great fun, and they all lead back to roughly the same area. Neal St is rewarding for its small craft and specialist shops, and Neal's Yard is full of healthy living. Floral St has elegant and expensive clothes and shoe shops (plus the Tintin shop – paradise for the Tintin fan). The Africa Centre on King St may have exhibitions of African art and culture. No shortage of places to eat around here, but useful pubs for lunch or refreshment include the Marquess of Anglesey on Bow Street, with a good-value upstairs restaurant, and the Lamb & Flag on Rose St, an attractive 300-year-old pub with decent snacks, its back room still much as Dickens described it.

ᗻ ! **Cabaret Mechanical Theatre** Tucked away in the heart of the former market buildings, an appealing collection of unique hand-made working automata, operated by the touch of a button or by inserting a coin. Great fun – though several exhibits are quite bizarre, notably the incredible Last Judgement by Paul Spooner. Shop, some disabled access; cl 25–26 Dec; (020) 7379 7961; £1.95.

🚋 **London Transport Museum** (The Piazza) On the site of the former Flower Market, this is a surprisingly fun attraction. You can race a tram and a bus, delve into feely boxes, design your own bus and see why a steamtrain doesn't suit the Underground. The main exhibition is quite traditional, but they don't mind if you climb aboard some of the buses, trams and tube trains, and the touch screens throughout are much more enticing for children than traditional information boards. Costumed actors tell nostalgic transport tales, and there might be story-telling, face-painting or craft workshops in school holidays. Snacks, interesting shop, disabled access; cl 24–26 Dec; (020) 7836 8557; £5.50.

✝ ! **St Paul's Church** The actors' church, full of interesting memorials to performers. Pepys watched the first-ever Punch and Judy show here in 1662. Outside its back gate, facing the covered market, the theatrical tradition continues, with jugglers, clowns, mountebanks and unusual musicians performing on the cobbles.

ᗻ **Theatre Museum** (Tavistock St) Exhaustive look at events and personalities on the stage over the last few hundred years. Posters, puppets and props are among the permanent collection, which although astonishingly comprehensive is arranged a little confusingly; it's easy to find yourself going round backwards. The very good temporary displays leave the deepest impression: they sometimes have free stage make-up demonstrations. Shop, disabled access; cl Mon, 25–26 Dec; (020) 7836 7891; *£4.50, children free.

🎭 **Theatre Royal** (Drury Lane) The oldest working theatre in the world, first opened in 1663 (Nell Gwynn was one of its earliest performers), but rebuilt several times over the next few centuries. Tours show backstage features inc the intriguing hydraulic lift beneath the stage, still in use. Meals, snacks, shop, disabled access; four tours a day (exc on Weds and Sat when only two because of matinée), 10.30am, 1pm (12.30pm Weds and Sat), 2.30pm and 5.30pm, (12pm, 2pm and 3.30pm Sun); (020) 7494 5091; around £5.

⊖ LEICESTER SQUARE

All central London's attractions are within easy walking distance of here, with several of the more interesting theatres little more than five minutes' stroll. The tube station's various exits are a favourite with Londoners stuck for a place to meet; hordes of them mill around anxiously looking for the friends they finally discover they've been standing next to for half an hour. Around the bustling edges of the pedestrian square, attractively cleaned up in recent years, are several huge cinemas, pricy but with excellent sound; you can see films more cheaply at the Prince Charles in Leicester Pl, leading off (where Notre Dame de France has an impressive Jean Cocteau mural). The well run Moon Under Water is much more reasonably priced than most pubs around here. Marked out by its dramatic ornamental gate, **Chinatown** has developed its own character, inviting despite the locals' cool indifference to outsiders; the supermarkets and shops along pedestrianised Gerrard St and in neighbouring streets are fascinating, with their weird and wonderful vegetables, strange squidgy things in little cellophane packets, and odd-smelling dried meats and fish. Plenty of authentic Chinese restaurants, as well as less convincingly adapted telephone boxes. Back by the tube station, this stretch of Charing Cross Rd is justifiably famous for its **bookshops**, specialist and general, new and secondhand. Foyle's is a London Landmark, with a huge stock, but trying to find what you want is time-consuming; Waterstone's is very friendly and relaxed, with informed staff. The side alleys between here and St Martin's Lane have good secondhand bookshops, several with specialisations such as the occult, antique children's books, or the theatre; Cecil Court is perhaps the best. Two distinctively designed pubs round here are the good-value Moon Under Water opposite Blackwells on Charing Cross Rd, and the Salisbury on St Martin's Lane, a splendid Victorian pub, all velvet and cut glass. Not far away on Long Acre is Stanfords, the best map and guidebook shop in Britain, with helpful, knowledgeable staff, and books and maps covering all corners of the globe. Leicester Sq is very handy for Soho,

described below under **Tottenham Court Rd**.

⊖ MARBLE ARCH

! 🖼 Striking in itself; originally a grand entrance for Buckingham Palace, moved here decades ago, and gleaming after its recent restoration. Over the road **Speakers Corner** on the edge of Hyde Park is where every Sun morning you can still hear impassioned diatribes on all sorts of causes. Traditional debating methods have practically disappeared, and disputes between rival fundamentalist groups have been known to become extremely heated, with the result that extra police armed with hidden cameras now patrol this famous bastion of free speech. Also on Sun you can see what's probably the longest free open-air art exhibition in the world, with the work of 300 artists and craftsmen laid out along the park railings on Bayswater Rd; the Swan opposite gives a pleasant break. The tube station – with so many exits it's a real initiative test finding your way out – is also handy for Oxford St.

Hyde Park Riding Stables (Bathurst Mews) Can organise horse-riding in the park; (020) 7262 3791; £25 an hour (not Mon).

⊖ OXFORD CIRCUS

The heart of the city's busiest shopping areas, congested and noisy Oxford St to the left and right, and altogether nicer Regent St to the S. **Oxford St** doesn't have a lot of character, but is full of good stores such as Selfridges, John Lewis (the self-service restaurant is good for lunch), Marks & Spencer (two major outlets), the two giant music shops HMV and Virgin Megastore, and the usual high street chains. South Molton St and St Christopher's Pl on either side of Oxford St are full of designer clothes shops and smart cafés; St Christopher's Pl also has quite an interesting antique market. **Regent St** is one of the grandest streets in the whole area, with a splendid curve as it reaches Piccadilly Circus. A harmonious street of considerable character, with the fine shops definitely enhancing its appeal, even if all you want to do is browse. Liberty's is a splendid Art Nouveau timbered building full of gorgeous soft furnishings and clothes,

Oriental and leather goods, jewellery and a good gift department. Other high points include Dickins & Jones for designer fashions and accessories; Mappin & Webb for fine china, glass, and jewellery; Hamleys, a marvellous toy shop (not cheap, though); Aquascutum, great for expensive English classic clothes; and Waterford/ Wedgwood, for lovely china and glass in quite a wide range of prices. The Old Coffee House in Beak St around the corner from here, and the Red Lion in Kingly St, are useful for lunch. Carnaby St, tucked away behind, has some rather florid men's shops and good street-fashion houses, but is mainly full of small boutiques with trendy accessories, leather goods and tacky souvenirs; not really worth seeking out.

♿! **BBC Experience** (Portland Pl) Below the imposing yet rather bullying bulk of Broadcasting House, this excellent visitor centre celebrates the work and programmes of the BBC over the last 75 years, with a mixture of multi-media exhibitions and hands-on displays. You can try your hand at directing *Eastenders*, or presenting the TV weather or sport, while the radio sections offer an interactive *Desert Island Discs*, and the chance to make a 3-minute play. Plenty for families, but also a great deal to please nostalgic-minded adults, and you'll come out with a much better idea of how programmes are put together. Meals, snacks, big shop, disabled access; cl 25 Dec; (0870) 603 0304; *£6.95.

⊖ **PICCADILLY CIRCUS** Another lively hub of London life, with famous streets radiating off in every direction, each quite different in character; handsome Piccadilly roughly to the W, the theatres of bustling Shaftesbury Ave to the E, with smarter ones on Haymarket to the S, Regent St coolly curving N towards Oxford Circus – and of course the famous statue of Eros, where all the foreign students sit to be photographed. The streets around here are excellent for shopping. On opposite sides of the traffic islands in Piccadilly Circus are Tower Records, three floors of pop, rock, classical and jazz (open till midnight), and Lillywhites, the long-established sports clothes and equipment store. On Piccadilly, the new Waterstone's is the biggest bookshop in Europe, while friendly Hatchards further down is a nicely old-fashioned bookshop where the staff can still sometimes turn vague requests into actual books. Almost next door, Fortnum's (Fortnum & Mason) has superior if expensive clothes, as well as the foods for which they're world-famous. Nearby, the Burlington Arcade is an elegant Regency covered arcade of expensive but good shops (excellent cashmere and knife/scissors shops, for instance), with a delightful set of rules, still enforced, that stop people whistling, singing or running in its confines. The Ritz hotel is gorgeously flamboyant inside: well worth the high price of having a frogged and liveried waiter bring you a cup of tea or a perfectly mixed whisky sour. Behind Piccadilly's S side is Jermyn St, where among other splendid but top-of-the-range shops you can buy fine cheeses at Paxton & Whitfield's, briar pipes at Astleys, hand-made shoes at Tricker's, hand-made shirts from Turnbull & Asser, flat hats at Bates, and old-fashioned toiletries at Floris. The Red Lion in Duke of York St, just off here, is a little gem of a pub, with decent snacks (but very busy on weekday lunchtimes). A landmark on Haymarket is one of the two branches of Burberrys the mac-makers (the other's in Regent St).

! **Rock Circus** (London Pavilion) Exuberant romp through the history of rock and roll, more fun than its stablemate Madame Tussaud's, but still alarmingly high-priced considering its comparative brevity. Wax figures from Elvis to Bono, some interesting archive film, and a finale with moving animatronic models. The headsets that provide musical accompaniment are ingeniously designed, though they don't always work properly. Snacks, shop; cl 25 Dec; it's open most nights till 9 or even 10pm; (020) 7734 7203; £8.25.

🖹 **Royal Academy of Arts** (Burlington House) Splendid building with excellent changing exhibitions for most of the year, then from early Jun–mid-Aug its famous (often notorious) Summer Exhibition of works by living artists great and small. Meals, snacks, shop, disabled access; cl 25 Dec, Good Fri; (020) 7439 7438; admission charge varies – usually between £5 and £8.

☺ **Segaworld** 🔞 Mammoth attraction as central redevelopment of the vast preserved Trocadero building; hasn't quite lived up to its promise, thanks mainly to a change in pricing policy; you now pay individually for all the rides and games, and though they insist the original cover-all charge had to go because it led to queues and overcrowding, the result is that this now seems little more than a glorified amusement arcade, which is a real shame. The best ride, Aqua Planet, has remarkable 3-D graphics, there's a 7-storey high IMAX cinema, and you can take part in your own winter Olympics in the only virtual reality bobsleigh outside Japan. Discount entitles you to 2 multi-ride passes for the price of 1 full-paying adult.

⊖ **TOTTENHAM COURT ROAD**
Soho Often heady mix of the tawdry and the fashionable, its coffee bars and cafés swarming with colourful young people in the evenings. Many of Soho's Georgian terraces are rather run-down, with peepshows and naughty video shops stuffed into basements and ground floors. But there are parts that have had much of their original quiet charm restored, like Soho Sq and Meard St, and it's still good for restaurants, and for shops connected with food or cooking. Old Compton St, central London's gayest street, has quite a few interesting shops – Italian delicatessens (I Camisa is the best, with fabulous salamis), the Algerian Coffee Store which also sells lots of fruit teas, and two cheap but good wines and spirits shops. Milroys in Greek St has a wonderful collection of hundreds of different malt whiskies. Berwick St has a daily fruit and veg market – the lower half is more expensive but has better produce; at Simply Sausages down here, you can watch them making some of their 43 different varieties of sausage, which include vegetarian and seafood flavours. The little Dog & Duck in Frith St and Coach & Horses in Poland St (the *Private Eye* pub) are two of the nicest Soho locals; in Romilly St another Coach & Horses is also on the well known Soho characters' circuit, and Kettners, now part of the Pizza Express chain, is a very entertaining old building. The area as a whole forms a sort of square, with the tube stations at Leicester Sq, Piccadilly Circus, Tottenham Court Rd and even Oxford Circus all just as handy.

Westminster

This centre of Court and Government is a pleasant area to walk around, much of it with only light traffic, and with few shops to add extra people to the wide pavements. Westminster Abbey and Buckingham Palace are divided by St James's Park – a fine walk between the two. The Tate Gallery, Westminster Cathedral and the RHS flower shows are also highlights here.

To see and do

⊖ **GREEN PARK**
❀ The park itself is the smallest of the parks in central London. It's not a formal garden but, watered by the Tyburn stream which runs below the park, stays genuinely green even in hot summers when London's other grassy spaces are dry and dusty. It's a short stroll to **Shepherd Market**, a colourful place where Mayfair lets its hair down, no longer a market but busy with cafés, good wine bars and pubs

(the Bunch of Grapes and King's Arms), and little lanes to wander down. **Clubland** The area around St James's St and Pall Mall seems to have more gentlemen's clubs than anything else, but there are a good number of interesting upmarket **shops** too: hand-made shoes at Lobb's, hats at Lock's, wonderful antiques and antiquities at Spink's, fishing equipment at Hardy's, and fine wines at Berry's, or Berry Bros & Rudd to give it its full name. This last is the only shop in London still to look both inside and out just as it did in the early 19th c (they've only just taken down the full-screen shutters), and they are very helpful even if you want just one humble bottle. Farlow's on Pall Mall have everything you might need for that expedition up the Limpopo or into the Gobi Desert. Christie's auction galleries are on King St (the friendly Red Lion off here in Crown Passage is useful for a snack), and there are some other top-of-the-market antique and book shops nearby, especially up Duke St.

🏛 **St James's Palace** Though comparatively domestic-looking, this is exceptionally harmonious and carries a real feel of old London. It's not open to the public (its apartments are used by members of the royal family and their officials), but does provide another good spot for the **Changing of the Guard**, with guardsmen leaving here at 11.15am to go the Palace, and coming back at around 12.10pm.

🏛 **Spencer House** (St James's Pl) Overlooking Green Park, this gleaming gilt-filled town house was built for the first Lord Spencer in the mid-18th c. Its sumptuous rooms, restored to their full glory, were among the first neo-classical interiors in Europe. Disabled access; open for guided tours every Sun (exc Jan and Aug), best to book on (020) 7499 8620; £6.

⊖ **PIMLICO**

🖼 **Tate Gallery** (Millbank) Designed in classical style to house the collection of Sir Henry Tate, the sugar refiner, and now containing the national collection of British art, this gallery is to be relaunched as **Tate Britain** from March; the opening of the **Tate Modern** in Bankside, will follow in May. Four new galleries are being created at Millbank (and existing ones refurbished), as well as a new visitor entrance, and the gardens are being re-designed to include sculpture courts. It is hoped a river bus service will link the gallery with its new counterpart a mile down river. When completed in 2001, Tate Britain will cover all important British artists for the past 450 years, with a large number of works by Turner and Constable, and plenty of contemporary sculpture. Building work will continue throughout the year, but the gallery will remain open; there's a good hi-tech audio guide. Meals, snacks, shop, disabled access; cl 24–26 Dec; (020) 7887 8000; free (exc for special exhibitions). Though the Tate Gallery restaurant is a particularly good one, you might find the Morpeth Arms nearby useful, with its views of the glossy MI6 ziggurat across the river.

⊖ **ST JAMES'S PARK**

✤ 🖼 This is the best approach to Buckingham Palace (you can get there more quickly, though less attractively, from Victoria). The oldest of London's royal parks, it was drained and converted into a deer park for Henry VIII, redesigned in the style of Versailles by order of Charles II (who often went for walks through it), and then re-created by Nash for George IV – this is the park which we see today, its relaxing lakeside environment particularly enjoyed by lunch-breaking office workers (and by hundreds of more or less exotic waterfowl), with a brass band in summer. It's beautifully floodlit at night, and on Sun traffic is barred from its roads. **The Mall** Running all the way along the top of the park, this 1,040-metre (3,412-ft) long ceremonial route was laid out from 1660 for Charles II, with the Palace at one end and the magnificent Admiralty Arch at the other. In between, as well as various grand buildings and government departments, are a couple of good contemporary art galleries, with various changing exhibitions at the **Mall Galleries** ((020) 7930 6844 for exhibition info; *£2), and a wonderfully informal little restaurant and bar at the **ICA**, which, with exhibitions and cinemas too, is an excellent place to spend an afternoon – and possibly the

evening as well (cl am; (020) 7930 0493;
£1.50 day membership).

🏛 **Buckingham Palace** A marvellous
position, surrounded by royal parks and
looking commandingly along the stately
Mall towards Admiralty Arch. At the
grand front palace gates the guards still
keep their unflinchingly solemn
positions: you can watch the **Changing
of the Guard** every day Apr–Aug
(every other day in winter) at 11.30am;
the ceremony may be late or even
cancelled in exceptionally wet weather.

🏛 🖼 **Buckingham Palace tour** Now
firmly established as one of London's
most visited attractions, usually
drawing around 400,000 visitors in the
eight weeks it's open. The main appeal
is that this is where the Queen actually
lives – her official London residence,
and where she meets other heads of
state; the royal standard flies above it
when she's home. But beyond that,
while perhaps not the most satisfying of
the royal palaces, it does pile a
magnificent series of opulent sights into
your walk through the state rooms.
Highlights include the beautiful Picture
Gallery, 46 metres (150ft) long and
filled with paintings from the royal
collection, the spectacular Grand
Staircase, and the throne room with its
predominant impression of gold, red
and splendour. Tours are unguided, and
there aren't many clues to help you, so
it's definitely worth buying the guide
book. Theoretically you see everything
at your own pace, but in practice you're
likely to be carried along in the stream
of other people, and you won't get
much of a chance to linger. Tickets are
sold from a little booth opposite the
palace by the entrance to Green Park,
though you can book in advance, on
(020) 7839 1377 – ask for the Visitor
Office. Busy shop, disabled access (with
notice); open Aug–Sept; £10.

♿🖼 **Royal Mews** (Buckingham Palace
Rd) Contains the state coaches, private
driving carriages and even sleighs of the
royal family, as well as the immaculately
turned out Windsor greys and
Cleveland bay carriage horses. The
longest painting in the royal collection is
here too, a 36-metre (120-ft) canvas
depicting William IV's Coronation
procession. Shop, disabled access; open

pm Tues–Thurs all year, all day
Mon–Thurs Aug–Oct; (020) 7839 1377;
£4.20.

⊖ ⇌ VICTORIA

🌼 **Royal Horticultural Society**
(Vincent Sq) Regular flower shows filled
with beautifully arranged displays by
specialist nurserymen; (020) 7828 1744
for information.

† 🌸 **Westminster Cathedral** (just
off Victoria St) Built in 1903, the red
brick Roman Catholic building is an
astonishing structure, very un-English,
with handsome mosaics and marble
work in its richly ornamental interior.
At night its black ceiling seems almost
to disappear in the darkness. Its
Byzantine splendour is a welcome relief
from the glassy governmental cliffs of
Victoria St. It offers great views over
Central London from its tall tower (lift;
cl Mon–Weds in winter; £2).

⊖ WESTMINSTER

🏛🖼 **Banqueting House** (Whitehall)
The only surviving part of the Palace of
Whitehall, designed by Inigo Jones and
built in 1619; it was a royal residence
until late that century. Charles I was
executed here, and it was also the site
of his son's restoration. The severely
classical hall is pretty much all there is
to see, but an entertaining Walkman
tour and good audio-visual exhibition
keep up your interest for quite some
time. The highlight is the wonderful
ceiling painted by Rubens,
commissioned by Charles I to glorify
the Stuart monarchy. They've put
mirrored tables underneath so you can
study the detail without straining your
neck; don't lean on these though –
they're on wheels and liable to speed off
like errant supermarket trolleys.
Snacks, shop; cl Sun, 24–26 Dec, 1 Jan,
Good Fri, bank hols, and for some
government functions; (020) 7839
7569; £3.60. The partly 13th-c Silver
Cross is an interesting old pub, the huge
and very ornate Lord Moon of the Mall
another good refuge.

♿ **Cabinet War Rooms** (King
Charles St, just off Whitehall) An
intriguing series of 21 rooms built to
provide Sir Winston Churchill, the War
Cabinet and his Chiefs of Staff with a
safe place from which to plan their
strategies during World War II. The

Cabinet Room, Map Room and Prime Minister's Room were preserved intact from the end of the war, and the other rooms have been authentically restored since. Quite basic, they're very evocative, with sound effects adding to the atmosphere. Shop, disabled access; cl 24–26 Dec; (020) 7930 6961; £5, children free.

Cenotaph (Whitehall) Designed by Lutyens, this is a sombre reminder of this century's two world wars, standing indomitably in the centre of the road. Initially planned as a temporary symbol, public opinion was such that the original wooden structure had to be replaced by the stone version you see today.

Downing Street Famous as the residence of the Prime Minister at No 10 and the Chancellor of the Exchequer at No 11. You can't get past the gates, but you can at least have a passing look at its surprisingly modest buildings.

Houses of Parliament These buildings are now of course the main seat of British government, but until Henry VIII moved to Whitehall Palace in 1529, the site was the main residence of the monarch – when they answer the phone today they still call it the Palace of Westminster. The present 19th-c building was designed by Charles Barry, though the 'gothick detail' which has given so much life to what would otherwise be rather a tiresomely deadpan classical façade is by Pugin. One end of the extraordinary 286-metre (940-ft) structure finishes in a lofty Victorian tower (which flies the Union Jack when Parliament is in session), and the other in the clock tower which contains **Big Ben**, the 3½-ton bell whose sonorous hourly rings are one of the best-known sounds in the world. Inside over two miles of passages link the central hall and two chambers – the Houses of Lords and Commons to the N and S of the building respectively. The Commons sits from 2.30pm Mon–Thurs, and from 9.30am on Fri; to gain entrance to the Strangers' Galleries, you'll need to queue by St Stephen's Gate (on the left for the Commons, right for the Lords – rather appropriate in a way) – or arrange it first with your MP. A letter from your MP can also give access to

what's called the Line of Route, going through both Houses and the Members' Lobby and Divisions Lobby, to Westminster Hall, from 1224–1882 the chief law court of the country. It witnessed such trials as those of Sir Thomas More and Charles I, and organising admission is worth the trouble even just to admire the magnificent hammerbeam roof, the earliest surviving example of its kind. The Westminster Arms in Storeys Gate across the square is a good pub, and you're likely to see politicians in the imposing Albert up Victoria St.

Jewel Tower (Parliament Sq) Across the road from the statue of Oliver Cromwell (whose attitude towards Parliaments when he was Lord Protector was not unlike that of Charles I – they were more trouble than they were worth), this 14th-c building has an exhibition on Parliament's history. It was originally a huge treasure chest for Edward III. Cl 24–26 Dec, 1 Jan; (020) 7222 2219; £1.50; EH.

Mounting the Guard (Whitehall) A survival of the kind of royal pageantry this area was once full of can be seen in this daily ceremony at Horse Guards Parade, 11am Mon–Sat and 10am Sun.

† St Margaret's Church (Parliament Sq) The official church of the House of Commons, worth a look particularly for its exceptional 16th-c Dutch stained glass; Sir Walter Raleigh is buried here.

† Westminster Abbey Surely one of the most impressive pieces of architecture to survive from the Middle Ages: Edward the Confessor transformed it into the crowning place of English kings, and his body now lies in the great shrine of the present building, erected in the 13th c on the site of his original. Recent restoration work has left the exterior looking almost as good as new (in fact, some bits are new), and a quite different colour from the one visitors had become used to, with monthly hawk patrols now deterring pigeon-nesting. Pretty much every king and queen up to George II is buried here; Henry VII's chapel is particularly impressive, and there are splendid tombs erected by James I for his mother Mary, Queen of Scots, and his predecessor Elizabeth I, under whose orders Mary had been executed. Perhaps it's in revenge for this that Elizabeth was lumped in with her sister Mary I, with whom she never got on. The loosely named Poets' Corner takes in a wide range of cultural figures. There's a brass-rubbing centre and a small medieval garden in the charming tranquil cloisters. Snacks, shop, disabled access (but not to Henry VII chapel);

royal chapels cl Sun, and between 2.45pm and 3.45pm Sat; £5. If you like history the **museum** in the Norman undercroft shouldn't be missed – it has effigies of many ancestors of the royal family made from their death masks, and often wearing their own clothes; £2.50 (which also includes entry to the Chapter House and Pyx Chamber); £7 inc audio tour and entry to all areas of the abbey.

Knightsbridge, Chelsea and Kensington

The three great South Kensington museums between them have something for everyone: the visually spectacular collections of the Victoria & Albert; and the lively Natural History and Science Museums, both favourites for children. There's grandeur in Kensington Palace, the less visited but free Leighton House, and across Hyde Park the excellent Apsley House. Harrods is irresistible to most visitors. Down towards the Thames, the Chelsea Physic Garden and the nearby free National Army Museum are both rather special. A placid grid of clean-cut, subdued Georgian terraced houses contrasts with the ostentatious bustle of the King's Rd in the south and the hubbub of the Portobello Rd market in the north.

To see and do

⊖ FULHAM BROADWAY
The best tube station for the clutch of good-value **antique shops** towards the bottom end of Fulham Rd. You can quickly cut through to the interesting series of more specialised antique shops on the New King's Rd, some of which yield unexpected treasures: lovely old clocks, imposing model ships, garden furniture, and ornaments going back to the 16th c. Two shops specialise expensively but magnificently in mirrors, and there's also Christopher Wray's enormous lighting shop which largely fuelled the vogue in Tiffany-style lamps and has almost any sort of lamp fitting you could possibly want. The tube station is also handy for the unfrequented, rather melancholy tranquillity of the somewhat overgrown **Brompton Cemetery**; and for

Chelsea Football Club, with the countrified Fox & Pheasant in Billing St just past it making a pleasant break. **Chelsea Harbour** (Lots Rd) This modern development includes a striking modern covered mall (mainly luxurious soft furnishings specialists), with popular Deals Restaurant, the stylish Canteen, the smart but relaxed Matts café, and an adjacent marina. Children like the glass-sided lifts which swoop up into the big dome, and on pm Suns, they often have jazz by the marina.
⊖ HIGH ST KENSINGTON
Albert Memorial (Kensington Gardens) Now restored to its former glory, a gleaming golden monument to Queen Victoria's beloved husband.
♂ Commonwealth Institute (Kensington High St) The refurbishments here continue, and new

galleries incorporating an interactive approach to each of the Commonwealth countries, should be ready in the next year or so; cl Sun; (020) 7603 4535 for details.

🐝 **Holland Park** One of London's lesser-known open spaces, a wooded park with peacocks, a summer open-air theatre and an airy restaurant.

🐝 **Kensington Gardens** Surrounding the palace, and well worth a wander, though less lush than neighbouring Hyde Park. There's a toy-boats lake, playground, a fetching statue of Peter Pan, and a tree trunk carved with all sorts of little painted animals. On a sunny day you could be forgiven for thinking you'd stumbled on a beach club, as the grass is covered with prone bodies soaking up the radiation.

🏛 **Kensington Palace State Apartments** (Kensington Gardens) Once-humble town house remodelled by Sir Christopher Wren and then enlarged by William Kent, the birthplace of Queen Victoria, and principal private royal residence until the death of George II. Diana Princess of Wales lived here until her death; people continue to leave flowers at the gates. It's still the home of Princess Margaret and Prince and Princess Michael of Kent. Some of the rooms are quite magnificent, with elaborate furnishings and décor, while others are interesting for their comparatively restrained understatement; a couple of the older ones could even be described as downright poky. Make sure you look up at the ceilings: some are exquisitely painted, inc an effective trompe l'oeil dome (a couple of the patterns transfer very nicely to stationery in the gift shop). Also pictures and furniture from the royal collection, and court dress collection. Snacks, shop, disabled access to ground floor only; cl Mon, Tues mid-Oct–mid-Mar; (020) 7937 9561; £9.50.

🐝 **Kensington shops** This is a good area for shopping, especially if you consider yourself young and fashionable. An unusual haven from the crowds is the **Roof Gardens** above BHS on the High St; these extraordinary gardens are usually open every day, but are often closed for private functions, so you'll need to check first on (020) 7937 7994; free. Their restaurant (open Thurs and Sat pms) does very good food.

🏛 ▣ **Leighton House** (12 Holland Park Rd) This splendid 19th-c house is a uniquely opulent monument to High Victorian art, its lavish décor and collections assembled by the first owner, Lord Leighton, former President of the Royal Academy. The centrepiece Arab Hall has a fountain and an almost dazzling assemblage of Islamic tiles, and there's a fine collection of paintings by Millais, Burne-Jones, and Leighton himself. Shop; cl Sun and bank hols; (020) 7602 3316; free.

🏛 **Linley Sambourne House** (18 Stafford Terrace) The 19th-c home of the celebrated *Punch* cartoonist, unchanged since – a fascinating example of a Victorian town house, with a fine collection of his work. Shop; open Weds and pm Sun, Mar–Oct; (020) 7937 0663; *£3.

▣ **Serpentine Gallery** (Kensington Gardens) Often has some of London's most interesting exhibitions, concentrating on younger contemporary artists; (020) 7402 6075 for what's on.

⊖ **HYDE PARK CORNER**

🏛 ▣ **Apsley House** The Duke of Wellington's elegant former home, designed by Robert Adam. It soon became known as Number One London, as it was the first house within a toll gate at the top of Knightsbridge. The magnificent building has been painstakingly restored; everything gleams and looks as good as new, and works by Correggio, Rubens and Velasquez amassed by Wellington as the spoils of war are back in their original positions (not always to their best advantage). Sumptuous furnishings, décor and sculpture – inc a statue of Napoleon by Canova that has him looking quite different from the usual image. Shop, limited disabled access; cl Mon (exc bank hols), 1 Jan, Good Fri, May Day bank hol, 24–26 Dec; (020) 7499 5676; *£4.50 inc audio guide, children free.

🐝 ▲ **Hyde Park** These 340 acres used to be a royal hunting park, and in 1851 were the site of the Great Exhibition. Now very much a city central park, complete with cycle lanes, roller-bladers, summer sunbathing and boating lake: you can hire boats (around £6 an hour), or even swim in parts. At the park's bottom corner is the relentless torrent of traffic around Hyde Park Corner; the subway can bring you up nr the glittering neo-baroque gates erected in honour of the Queen Mother.

⊖ KNIGHTSBRIDGE

Harrods (Brompton Rd) A wonderful place to browse, and has most things anyone could want – there's even a personal shopper available to help you choose. But it's the food halls that visitors to London really enjoy; they're divided into fruit and vegetables, an interesting delicatessen, grocery, meat, poultry, fish (the display of fresh fish at the end of the room is legendary), bread and cakes, flowers, and wines – and the downstairs pantry is not as expensive as you might think. The Scotch House, almost opposite, is not cheap but does have lovely cashmeres, fine woollens, kilts and so forth. Also along here is Harvey Nichols, a long-standing fashion store now split into numerous famous-brand boutiques; its 5th-floor food store is superb, alongside a very good bar/restaurant. **Sloane St** The street stretching down from here has had something of a renaissance recently, with international designers jostling to open very expensive new stores. In the handsome terraces beyond Sloane St can be found the charming Grenadier (Wilton Row; no food in the bar, but a snug little restaurant) and the surprisingly countryish Nag's Head (Kinnerton St).

⊖ NOTTING HILL GATE

Portobello Rd Famous for its market – fruit and veg during the week, antiques on Sat from 6am; with well over a thousand dealers you can still pick up a bargain. The quality and prices are higher at the Notting Hill end; it's more bric-à-brac as you get towards Ladbroke Grove. Damien Hirst's restaurant Pharmacy (150 Notting Hill Gate) has waiters dressed in surgical garb, and people eat surrounded by swabs and operating instruments. Besides the outstanding Ladbroke Arms (Ladbroke Rd), good food pubs in

this area include the Windsor Castle (Campden Hill Rd; excellent courtyard garden) and (a walk down Kensington Church St, which has some interesting antique shops) the Churchill Arms – surprisingly good Thai food.

⊖ SLOANE SQUARE

The heart of Chelsea, with Peter Jones, the mecca of the Sloanes, on the square itself (a sister department store of John Lewis, it's good value for money). Just around the corner, the Antelope in Eaton Terrace is a useful lunch stop. The bottom end of Sloane St has two interesting though expensive shops: Partridges, a fancy food shop, and the General Trading Company, with a fine collection of oddities, besides stylish kitchenware, soft furnishings, antiques, glass and so forth.

🏛 ✿ **Carlyle's House** (Cheyne Row) The home of the writer from 1834 till his death, with lots of letters and personal possessions, and an early piano played by Chopin. There's a charming little Victorian walled garden. Open Weds–Sun and bank hols Apr–Oct; (020) 7352 7087; £3.30; NT. The nearby King's Head & Eight Bells, across a green and a busy road from the Thames, is almost villagey, at the far end of the green, Old Church St past the elegant Chelsea Old Church takes you quickly to a good food pub, the Front Page.

✿ **Chelsea Physic Garden** (Royal Hospital Rd) If you're tired of the braying crowds of Chelsea, take refuge here. A real haven of peace, it was started in 1673 to study the plants used in medicine by the Society of Apothecaries. It's still used for botanical and medicinal research (there's a unique garden of medicinal plants), but is also full of lovely and unusual plants which thrive here in Thames-side London's warm microclimate. Snacks, shop, disabled access; open pm Weds and Sun Apr–Oct; (020) 7352 5646; *£4.

King's Rd Not what it used to be in the 60s and 70s, but you can still find some really individual clothes and shoe shops, and good antique markets. On your way along, refresh yourself at Henry J Beans (197 King's Rd; a rather stylish American-style bar with good quick snacks), La Bersagliera (a pleasantly clattery matriarchal pizza house just past Beaufort St) or the Sporting Page (Camera Pl/Limerston St). S from here, it's quite a short cut through to the Thames.

ᕼ **National Army Museum** (Royal Hospital Rd) Surprisingly little visited but well and honestly presented – the history of the men of the British, Indian and colonial armies from 1485, told with photographs, models, uniforms, prints and other mementos, and portraits by Gainsborough and Reynolds. Also the collections of the former Museum of the Women's Royal Army Corps. Snacks, shop, disabled access; cl 24–26 Dec, 1 Jan, Good Fri, May Day; (020) 7730 0717; free.

Pimlico Rd An interesting collection of antique and other small shops (and Peter's Restaurant, a very good-value all-day Italian-run café which has been a taxi-drivers' haunt for about 30 years). The Orange Brewery here is a pub brewing its own beers, with decent food. Keep on along to Ebury Bridge for a classic photographic view of partly dismantled Battersea Power Station, beyond a sinuous network of railway lines.

🏛 🏵 **Royal Hospital** (Royal Hospital Rd) Christopher Wren's most glorious secular building, which still houses some 400 Chelsea Pensioners. Cl 12–2pm, am Sun (though you can go to the full dress service in chapel at 11am on Sun); free. The spacious and calm adjacent riverside Ranelagh Gardens are the site of the Chelsea Flower Show.

⊖ **SOUTH KENSINGTON**
✝ **Brompton Oratory** Roman Catholic, and heavily magnificent – sombre despite the pallor of its marble.
✝ 🏵 **Holy Trinity Brompton** London's most fashionable and perhaps most lively church. Its gardens lead you into a very peaceful corner of residential London, with a decent pub in Ennismore Mews (the Ennismore Arms, which does Sun lunches).
🏛 ᕼ **Natural History Museum** (Cromwell Rd) This elaborate Romanesque building is a vast place covering four acres, with a huge range

of informative and entertaining displays and activities. It's been very successfully jazzed up in recent years; museum purists may feel some of the grandeur of the place has been lost, but families will find plenty to keep them busy for a good chunk of the day. It's long been a place where people have come to see the dinosaurs, but while that used to mean fossils and skeletons, it now involves a high-tech exhibition that even has robotic versions of the monsters. The revamped Earth Galleries are a highlight – an escalator whisks you up towards a revolving metal globe, and there's an earthquake simulator. Meals, snacks, shops, disabled access; cl 23–26 Dec; (020) 7938 9123; £6.50, children free (adults free after 4.30pm wkdys, 5pm wknds).

🏛 **Royal Albert Hall** (Kensington Gore) The home of the summer Promenade Concerts and many other concerts throughout the year; completed in 1871, this huge oval arena was built in honour of Prince Albert. Below its massive metal and glass dome, a terracotta frieze shows the progress of Man in the arts and sciences throughout the ages. Before modern technology (in the form of giant suspended mushrooms) got to grips with its acoustics, the hall used to be famous for its echo – it was said that this was the only hall where you could hear the works of modern composers twice.

ᕼ **Science Museum** (Exhibition Rd) The addition in June of the stunning new Wellcome wing, can only boost this amazing museum's popularity. Four new galleries cover as many floors, and look at subjects such as genetics, the Internet and the future role of science. The new area has been designed to capacitate fast-changing, interactive exhibitions, with plenty of hands-on displays, workshops and demonstrations, and a multi-sensory activity area aimed especially at the under-8s (and their parents!); also IMAX theatre, new café and shop and landscaped gardens outside. Elsewhere in the museum, exhibits range from Stephenson's *Rocket* to the Apollo 10 space capsule. They hold various special events such as the all-night camp-ins – which enthral children. Meals, snacks, shop, disabled access; cl 24–26 Dec; (020) 7938 8080; £6.50, children free (adults free after 4.30pm wkdys and 5pm wknds).

🕉 🖪 **Victoria & Albert Museum** (Cromwell Rd) Britain's national museum of art and design is one of the finest in the world; it was founded in 1851 by Prince Albert, and houses all manner of decorative arts, from all ages and countries. The galleries run to over seven miles, inc a spectacular glass gallery (with touch-screen computer displays), a dazzling silver gallery, and the world's greatest collection of Constables. In spite of all this, it's come under fire for being too dusty recently, and a new regime of directors have ambitious plans for extensions and improvements over the next few years. Meals and snacks (they do a good Sunday brunch with jazz), shop, disabled access; cl am Mon, 24–26 Dec; (020) 7938 8500; £5 though free after 4.30pm, and any time for the unwaged.

The City and East End

The City's most typical financial buildings are mainly Victorian and Edwardian, and its landmark churches are mostly elegant classical designs, but the ground-plan follows the narrow twisting streets and alleys of medieval times – though because of the Great Fire of 1666 only a handful of buildings are medieval or Tudor. Around St Paul's and the Tower of London (a winner with children), the layout is more open – and far less affected by the City's human tides: most of the rest of the area is packed with worried financial workers during weekdays, then when they leave goes completely quiet in the evening and at weekends. For every person who actually lives in the City, another 60 or 70 flood in each day to work there, then flood out again at night.

Besides the Tower, St Paul's and the host of glorious churches, highlights here include the Museum of London, Geffrye Museum and Museum of Childhood, and the highly individualistic 18 Folgate St. The Lothbury Gallery has a good art collection, and the Tower Bridge Experience is something that bit different. The new footbridge from St Paul's to Bankside will bring quite a new sense of direction.

Originally, particular streets came to be associated with particular crafts and trades, and this is reflected in street names throughout the City – Carter Lane, Hosier Lane, Cloth Fair, Ropemaker St, Milk St, Silk St, Coopers Lane and so forth. The great City Livery Companies representing the various trades have effectively run local government in the City for 800 years or more, and it's only now that the franchise is being widened to allow more modern financial institutions a share in local government here. Many guilds have only a tenuous connection with the original crafts involved in their trades. But in Billingsgate Market, still controlled by the ancient Fishmongers Company, you can still see the fish trade being carried on in much the same way as ever (West India Dock Rd, early morning Tues–Sat). Though the halls of the City Livery Companies may have been rebuilt since they were first established in the Middle Ages, they still house some remarkable treasures. Some are open to visit, but only by prior arrangement: you'll have to book well ahead, through the City of London Information Centre, St Paul's Churchyard, EC4; (020)

7332 1456. The liveliest glimpse of East End life nowadays is to be had on Sunday mornings in Brick Lane market.

To see and do

⊖ ALDGATE EAST
Brick Lane market London's biggest and most atmospheric street market, a riot of colour, smells and sound, inc some very entertaining market patter. There are plenty of bargains for early risers (and things to avoid – we've even seen someone specialising in secondhand felt-tip pens). The community is largely Asian, so much of the food and other wares are quite exotic; Sun 5am–2pm. Once the terror-stricken haunt of Jack the Ripper, Whitechapel, the area around here, is still one of London's poorest areas.
Columbia St market Entirely devoted to garden and house plants; has bargains as it closes around 1pm on Sun.

⊖ BANK
🏠 Some of the City's finest buildings are around here, though with most you'll have to content yourself with looking at just the outside. Besides the Bank of England itself, handsome or interesting buildings include the neo-classical Custom House on Lower Thames St, Lloyds of London on Lime St, and the Renaissance-style Royal Exchange on Cornhill, with several proud columns in front. **Mansion House**, the official residence of the Lord Mayor, now only offers tours to groups of fifteen or more people (no under-12s). If you apply in writing in advance, you should be able to see inside: there's a suite of sumptuous 18th-c rooms inc the fabulous Egyptian Hall.
🏠 👅 **Bank of England** (Bartholomew Lane) This neo-classical fortress does still contain oodles of gold – though you can't see it, let alone get your hands on it. There's a small but interesting **museum**, which even shows how computerised currency speculators work. Disabled access; cl wknds and bank hols; (020) 7601 5545; free.
Leadenhall market (Whittington Ave, off Gracechurch St) Victorian iron and glass covered market, vibrant with Cockney humour yet quite smart, and

filled with seafood, game, vegetables and fruit; cl afternoonish, and wknds. The Lamb's top-floor dining bar gives good views of the market activity.
🖼 **Lothbury Gallery** (Lothbury) The NatWest Bank's excellent collection of 17th- to 20th-c paintings, well worth tracking down (open wkdys; (020) 7726 1642; free).

⊖ BARBICAN
🖼 **Barbican Centre** Could be called the north bank's equivalent to the South Bank Centre – certainly its aesthetic equal. This complex includes theatres, exhibition and concert halls, galleries, and what some would say is the city's most comfortable cinema. The Barbican Theatre is the Royal Shakespeare Company's London home. There's often free entertainment in the foyers.
👅 **Museum of London** (London Wall) No other city museum in the world is quite as comprehensive as this; anyone with just a passing interest in history will find it compelling. London's development is told through chronological reconstructions and period clothes, music and various remains, from a medieval hen's egg to an early (and quite different) tube map – ever heard of the station called Post Office? – while the 18th-, 19th- and 20th-c sections have almost too much to take in. They're in the early part of a seven-year redevelopment programme, and are tackling each gallery in turn: first to be completed was the excellent Roman gallery (the building adjoins a stretch of original Roman wall). Also, a gallery called 'London Bodies' is based on research on 672 bodies from a 14th-c Black Death cemetery nr the Tower of London. Some of their archaeologists discovered a Tudor rubbish dump nr Tower Bridge last year. Meals, snacks, shop, disabled access; cl am Sun, all day Mon (exc bank hols), 24–26 Dec; (020) 7600 0807; £5 – ticket valid for three months, and it certainly is the sort of

place you want to come back to; children free.

⊖ BETHNAL GREEN

🖄 Museum of Childhood

(Cambridge Heath Rd) This very special little museum houses the V & A's collection of toys, dolls, dolls' houses, games, puppets and children's costumes. Excellent programme of events, theatre shows, and children's activities (most Sats and several school hols) – most completely free. Snacks, shop, disabled access with prior notice; cl am Sun, all Fri, 24–26 Dec, 1 Jan, May Day bank hol; (020) 8980 2415; free.

DOCKLANDS

Once the heartland of Britain's trade-based Empire, these 8½ square miles over the last decade became the largest redevelopment site in Europe, the old warehouses imaginatively converted into smart apartments and office blocks. 244-metre (800-ft) Canary Wharf is an all-too-obvious landmark, though as most of its floors are filled with offices the ground-level shops are the only parts you can visit inside. Many of the buildings around it were designed to give a taste of the 21st c. While they're undoubtedly striking there's sometimes a soullessness about the place that's positively eerie; on a weekend or holiday Docklands seems even more deserted than the rest of the City. Most parts are reached and seen best by the **Docklands Light Railway**; the best bit is between West India Quay and Island Gardens, where you can get off and walk through the foot tunnel under the Thames to Greenwich. The earliest docks to be redeveloped are the most visitor-friendly: St Katharine's Dock (Tower Hill tube station is quite handy), which has a lively marina, a quite cheerful pastiche of a Victorian pub, and lots going on, and Tobacco Dock, with an American-style factory shopping centre. Further E down the river is the gigantic closeable **Thames Flood Barrier**, built to protect the city from freak tides; a visitor centre is on Unity Way, Woolwich SE18; cl 24–26 Dec; (020) 8854 1373; £3.40. You can get boats down here from Westminster Pier (020) 7930 3373, £6.95 return), and these now stop at Canary Wharf too.

⊖ ≋ FARRINGDON

🖄 ! House of Detention Well put

together displays on crime and punishment in the underground cells of a former prison. Atmospheric without the sensationalised gore of other similar attractions. Cl 25 Dec; (020) 7253 9494; £4.

🏛🖄 Museum of the Order of St

John (St John's Lane) Housed in a 16th-c gatehouse and 12th-c crypt, silver, paintings and furniture belonging to the medieval Order, and displays relating to the history and work of its more modern offshoot, the St John Ambulance Brigade. Shop, some disabled access; cl Sun, Christmas, Easter, bank hol wknds; (020) 7253 6644; free, £4 guided tours of the gatehouse and priory church on Tues, Fri and Sat at 11am and 2.30pm. The Eagle in Farringdon Rd/Bakers Row has outstanding food, and there's an excellent secondhand bookshop opposite the station.

✝ St Bartholomew the Great

Church (West Smithfield) Partly Norman, with a 13th-c gateway into the market precincts.

⊖ ≋ LIVERPOOL STREET

🏛 ! 18 Folgate Street Guided tours

of a quite remarkable house – but be warned, this is no ordinary guided tour. It doesn't do the place justice to say that it's been furnished and decorated in period style – to all intents and purposes you really are back in the 18th c, with candles and firelight flickering away, food and drink laid out on the table, even urine in the chamber-pots. Dennis Severs the owner, who lives here, spends hours getting everything ready, and goes to extreme lengths to immerse people in the experience – it's not unusual to be locked in a cold dark cellar, and he's been known to throw people out if he doesn't like them. Open 2–5pm the first Sun of each month; (020) 7247 4013; £7. Elaborate candlelit tours the first Mon evening of the month (no children), £10. In Liverpool St station, Hamilton Hall is an extraordinarily grand former ballroom pub.

⊖ MONUMENT

❊ Monument (Monument St) A

fluted Doric column designed by Wren

and Hooke at an exact height of 202ft (62 metres) to mark the spot where the Great Fire of London began – in Pudding Lane 202ft from its base. The views of the city from the top are tremendous, though there are 311 spiral steps up. The viewpoint was designed as a cage to prevent people jumping off. Cl some bank hols, and occasional other dates; (020) 7626 2717; £1.50.

⊖ **OLD STREET**

🏛🗒🕸 **Geffrye Museum** (Kingsland Rd) One of London's most friendly and interesting museums, yet least known; 18th-c almshouses converted to show the changing style of the English domestic interior – a sort of historical *Through the Keyhole*. Displays go from lovely 17th-c oak panelling and furniture through elegant Georgian reconstructions and Victorian parlours to Art Deco fashions, though not all is as it seems – out of sight inside the shell of a vintage radio, for example, there's actually a distinctly modern CD player. Notable herb garden, and an excellent programme of exhibitions, special events, talks and activities. Well worth tracking down. Snacks, shop, disabled access; cl am Sun, all Mon (exc pm bank hols), 24–26 Dec, 1 Jan, Good Fri; (020) 7739 9893; free.

🏛† **Wesley's House** (49 City Rd) The father of Methodism had his house and chapel built here in 1778, and they're still much as they were then, with plenty of his personal possessions. You can see Wesley's tomb in the chapel, and the crypt has a museum on the history of Methodism. Snacks, shop, disabled access – limited in house, but good in museum; cl bank hols, Thurs 12.30–1.30pm, and limited opening Sun (when services); (020) 7253 2262; *£4.

⊖ **ST PAUL'S**

🏛🗒 **Guildhall** (off Gresham St) 15th-c, where the Court of Common Council, over which the Lord Mayor presides, administers the City of London. The Lord Mayor's Banquet is held in the Great Hall, hung with the banners and shields of the City's 90-odd livery companies. Underneath is the largest 15th-c crypt in the City, and there's also a clock museum, and library with unrivalled collection of City-related manuscripts and books. Disabled access; cl Sun Oct–Apr, and for civic occasions; guided tours, must book, (020) 7606 3030 ext 1460; free.

† **St Anne & St Agnes Church** (Gresham St) Particularly worth knowing for the Bach cantatas that may grace its Lutheran Sun services; (020) 7606 4986 for programme.

† **St Mary le Bow Church** (Cheapside) With the famous Bow Bells, and also Thurs lunchtime early music concerts; (020) 7248 5139.

† 🌼 **St Paul's Cathedral** Despite the attempts of brasher, taller modern buildings to take over, this masterpiece still asserts itself proudly as the area's real landmark, its unmistakeable shape repeatedly looming out above the crowded streets. Its huge dome is a pleasing shape after the stolid self-satisfaction of the Victorian and Edwardian masonry which dominates this area. Originally the cathedral was Gothic in style, with a towering spire. It fell into disrepair and Wren was assigned to work on its renovation. He didn't relish the job, and no doubt was delighted when the Great Fire of London swept the old church away, allowing him to construct something entirely new. His mainly classical design is unlike any other cathedral in Britain, and took just 35 years to build. The setting for various State occasions, it's full of interesting monuments – the one to John Donne was the only complete figure to be salvaged from the Great Fire. Look out for the wonderful carving on the exterior – some of which is by Grinling Gibbons, who also did the choir stalls. Other highlights include the dizzying Whispering Gallery, the panoramic views from the top (a very steep climb), and the crypt, full of tombs and memorials to notable figures from British history. Snacks, shop, disabled access; virtually cl Sun; (020) 7236 4128; £5. The City Pipe by the tube station is an enjoyable weekday wine bar.

⊖ **TOWER HILL**

🌼🗒 **Tower Bridge Experience** Inside the landmark bridge, with wonderful views from its glass-covered walkways, 43 metres (142ft) above the Thames; animatronic characters and hi-tech displays present the view at various other dates in the bridge's history, with lively multi-media shows designed to leave you feeling proud to be British. The bridge is unusual not just for its design, but because it's still fully operational, raising the roadway from each side drawbridge-style to allow ships to pass; you can see some of the Victorian machinery that does the work. Snacks, shop, disabled access; cl 24–26 Dec, 1 Jan, 19 Jan, 2 Oct; (020) 7403 3761; £6.15.

Tower of London Picturesque classic castle, the most notable building to survive the Great Fire of London. A lot of fun to look at even superficially, it dates back to the late 11th c, though the site had been used as a defensive position by the Romans much earlier. Almost every period of English history has witnessed gruesome goings-on here, with not even the highest or mightiest safe from imprisonment or even execution: Walter Raleigh, Lady Jane Grey and two of Henry VIII's wives spent their last days in the Tower. There's a mass of things to see, inc enough armour and medieval weaponry to glut the most bloodthirsty small boy's appetite, the Crown Jewels, the Beefeaters and the ravens. You can also walk along the elevated battlements. The Jewel House shows off the Crown Jewels to dazzling effect; on the busiest days those tempted to linger are gently drawn along by moving floorways. Two towers that were part of Edward I's medieval palace are furnished in period style, and peopled with appropriately costumed helpful guides; one room in this part has been left untouched to show what a difficult job the restoration was. A reorganisation of the oldest part, the White Tower, has revealed that the inside of the fortress when built was much less imposing than was suggested by the formidable exterior – they were clearly just trying to intimidate the locals. You need a fair bit of time to see everything properly. Snacks, shop, some disabled access; cl 24–26 Dec, 1 Jan; (020) 7709 0765; £10.50.

Bloomsbury, Holborn and Regent's Park

The British Museum with its stylish new plaza is the outstanding attraction in Bloomsbury and Holborn, a civilised if slightly faded area of Georgian squares, gardens and courts between the City and Westminster – legal and academic London. Much less well known, the Sir John Soane's Museum is also not to be missed, and the new British Library is at last open. Bloomsbury merges into a more genteel area to the West, over towards Marylebone (including Madame Tussaud's), with smart Regent's Park (and the zoo) on its northern border; away from the shopping streets of Marylebone High St and Baker St this is largely residential, and the capital of private medicine and dentistry.

Bloomsbury does have a large number of hotels, especially for the more budget-conscious visitor, though many are on the tawdry side. Ones which can be recommended include the Academy (17 Gower St WC1E 6HG (020) 7631 4115), the Morgan (24 Bloomsbury St WC1B 3QJ (020) 7636 3735) – both handy for the British Museum – and the George (60 Cartwright Gardens WC1H 9EL (020) 7387 6789).

To see and do

⊖ **BAKER ST**

♿ **! London Planetarium**
(Marylebone Rd) A satisfying place,
showing off one of the most advanced
star projectors in the world. Surround-
sound gives their enjoyable
presentations an added sense of
realism. Make sure you get to each
show on time – stragglers barely have a
moment to find a seat before the lights
are dimmed. Plenty of interactive
displays too – you can even see how
much you'd weigh on another planet.
Meals, snacks, shop, disabled access; cl
25 Dec; £6.35 (less in winter); joint
ticket with Madame Tussaud's available.
Opposite, the café of St Marylebone
Church has good-value simple
vegetarian meals.

! Madame Tussaud's (Marylebone
Rd) Almost half of overseas visitors
place this famous waxworks museum at
the top of their list of things to do in
London, which explains why the queues
can be so long and slow-moving (and
perhaps why German TV presenters
and Japanese sumo wrestlers now crop
up among more familiar simulacrums).
Some of the models are uncannily
realistic, others rather less so; several
members of the Royal Family spring to
mind. They've successfully reworked
the famous Chamber of Horrors (it no
longer has that rather unpleasant
emphasis on real-life crime), and the
Spirit of London finale is entertaining –
you sit in a black cab and are whisked
through a cheery interpretation of the
city's history. This part is excellently put
together, and in places rather witty, but
is over a little quickly – like the
waxworks as a whole. As you can be in
and out of the museum in little over an
hour, you're paying more per minute
here than practically anywhere else in
Britain. Meals, snacks, shop, disabled
access; cl 25 Dec; (020) 7935 6861; £10.

♿ **Sherlock Holmes Museum** (221b
Baker St) To many people the world
over, Baker St calls to mind only one
thing – Conan Doyle's great detective.
This famous address has various
Holmes paraphernalia, and something
of the atmosphere of the books re-
created – though 'The Case of Why

They Charge So Much To See It' might
have baffled even brother Mycroft.
Shop; cl 25 Dec; (020) 7935 8866; *£5.
A 9ft bronze statue of the super-sleuth
now stands outside Baker St station.

⊖ **GOODGE STREET**

♿ **Pollock's Toy Museum** (1 Scala St)
Housed in a rather charming setting, a
wide range of playthings from all over
the world and from all periods, almost
as if lots of enthusiastic children had just
left them scattered through these little
rooms. Mechanical and optical toys,
teddy bears, furniture, board games and
theatres, and a proper toy shop
downstairs. Shop, disabled access to
ground floor only; cl Sun and bank hols;
(020) 7636 3452; £3.

⊖ **HOLBORN**

🏛 🅿 **Legal London** A perfect
example of the tranquil architecture of
this area, **Lincoln's Inn Fields** is a
large open space with trees and lawns
surrounded by handsome houses, also
tennis courts and summer band
concerts; it's a pleasant place to spend a
summer afternoon. Nearby, the Gothic
Royal Courts of Justice are
impressive, and you can also stroll
through the gardens of **Gray's Inn**, said
to have been laid out by Francis Bacon
around 1600. This area really is legal
London, and you'll usually find a good
number of lawyers in the splendid Cittie
of York (22 High Holborn), an
enormous and very atmospheric
basement pub with little private booths
down one side. Other fine pubs in this
area are the opulent Victorian gin
palace, the Princess Louise (208 High
Holborn; good Thai food upstairs, not
wknds); and the classic Lamb in Lamb's
Conduit St. Dom Vitos Sandwich Bar on
Kingsway has superb sandwiches.

🏛 ♿ **Sir John Soane's Museum** (13
Lincoln's Inn Fields) One of London's
hidden highlights, built by the architect
for his splendid collection of pictures,
books and antiquities. It's most
eccentric, full of architectural tricks and
mirrors, which form a complex natural-
lighting system for the antiquities
covering most of the walls. There's a
lovely picture by Turner and an
Egyptian sarcophagus, but the highlight

is Hogarth's acid series on *The Rake's Progress* and *The Election*. When you've seen them the guide swings open the hinged 'walls' and further treasures emerge inc choice Piranesi drawings and a scale model of the Bank of England. The house is built around a central courtyard monument to Soane's dog ('Alas, poor Fanny!'); you ring the bell to get in, and sign a visitors' book. The guides are very friendly and helpful, the guidebook well worthwhile. Shop, limited disabled access; cl Sun, Mon and Christmas, open first Tues evening of every month; (020) 7405 0175; free (donations welcome). The breakfast room of Soane's first house, No 12 next door, can also be visited.

✪ ≋ KING'S CROSS

☝ **British Library** (Euston Rd) This vast modern library has good exhibition space for its national treasures such as the Lindisfarne Gospels and Magna Carta, and changes its displays frequently, as well as mounting special exhibitions; the entrance courtyard has a gigantic bronze of a crouching seated Sir Isaac Newton, by Paolozzi after William Blake, and impressive entrance gates. Open daily; (020) 7412 7111; free.

✪ REGENT'S PARK

🏛 ⚘ ⛵ (Great Portland St or Regent's Park tube station) Covering over 400 acres, this is the culmination of a glorious swathe of Regency terraces designed by John Nash, which can be seen almost all around it; the buildings of Park Crescent are among the finest. The park was originally intended to be the setting for a palace for the Prince Regent, after whom it was named: now it contains an open-air theatre where Shakespeare and other plays are performed in the summer, the lovely Queen Mary's Rose Garden, the spectacular Avenue Garden (now restored to its 1864 glory), a boating lake, bandstand concerts on summer Suns, and plenty of paths to stroll along.

🐾 **London Zoo** (Regent's Park or Camden Town tube station) The Web of Life centre, a £4 million live animal exhibition housed in a building inspired by an ant-heap, opened last year and has certainly given a much-needed breath of fresh air to the zoo. It's their first development since they opened the listed Mappin Terraces (a sort of animal playground shared by deer, peacocks, monkeys and bears) three years ago. All its animals have been chosen to demonstrate the variety of living organisms, and the range of ecosystems they inhabit; one intriguing exhibit is a geothermal cooling borehole, showing the ingenuity of the termite. Sadly other areas show only too well that the last few years haven't been the zoo's easiest, and despite the presence of lions, elephants and rhinos, it's with the smaller creatures that the zoo currently excels: there's a fascinating insect house, and other highlights are the irresistible children's zoo, where you can get right up to the animals (and maybe help feed the pigs at lunchtime), the biggest reptile house of any British zoo, and the spellbinding Moonlight World, where day and night are reversed so that you can watch nocturnal creatures such as vampire bats. The 1930s architecture of the penguin pool remains quite something. Meals, snacks, shop, disabled access; cl 25 Dec; (020) 7722 3333; £9.

⚘ ❄ **Primrose Hill** Once part of the same hunting park as Regent's Park, now a popular strolling ground for this sober residential area. The modest rounded summit gives eye-opening views of the city.

⛵ ⌂ **Regent's Canal** Offers an excellent walk from Little Venice to Camden Lock, passing by Regent's Park and Primrose Hill; boat cruises also operate along here – one-way tickets available. The London Waterbus Company – one of several companies who now run along the stretch of Regent's Canal between Little Venice and Camden Lock – make a stop for passengers who want to get off at the zoo; (020) 7482 2550 for timetable.

✪ RUSSELL SQUARE

☝ **British Museum** (Great Russell St) Monumental 19th-c building housing spectacular collections of priceless man-made objects from all over the world, some of them over 3,000 years old. The range is staggering, in which just a few highlights are the Elgin Marbles, the log-book of Nelson's *Victory*, the wonderful and intriguing

Egyptian galleries, the comprehensive galleries of Greek vases, the Oriental antiquities, and the Amaravati sculpture. Don't try to take it in all at once – decide what interests you most and stick to that, or your head will start reeling with the extent of this treasure-house before you've got even a tenth of the way through. Try to arrive early as it can get very busy. The inner courtyard, restored to its original 1857 splendour and now a covered public square, should be open by autumn. Meals, snacks, shop, disabled access; cl am Sun, 24–26 Dec, 1 Jan, May Day, 2 Apr; (020) 7636 1555; free exc for special exhibitions. Just up Gower St, the Waterstone's here is a first-class serious bookshop, and in Museum St the Museum Tavern does decent food all day.

Dickens' House (48 Doughty St) Dickens lived here during his 20s, and during that period wrote the *Pickwick Papers*, *Oliver Twist* and *Nicholas Nickleby*. The drawing room has been reconstructed to appear as it was then, and there are original manuscripts and first editions, pictures and personal possessions. His wife's sister died here in 1837, an event which the writer later used as the model for the death of Little Nell in *The Old Curiosity Shop*. Shop, some disabled access; cl Sun and some public hols; (020) 7405 2127; £3.50.

TEMPLE (not Sun)

Courtauld Institute Galleries (Somerset House, Strand) Outstanding collection of Impressionist and Post-Impressionist paintings inc works by Monet, Renoir, Degas and Cezanne, also Michelangelo, Rubens, Goya and other masters. Snacks, shop, disabled access; cl am Sun; (020) 7873 2526; *£4.

Dr Johnson's House (17 Gough Sq) A perfect example of early 18th-c architecture, just as Dr Johnson himself was a perfect example of 18th-c barbed, slightly flawed gentility. Between 1749 and 1759 he wrote his great *English Dictionary* here, and a first edition of this is on display, along with various memorabilia from his learned life. Shop; cl Sun and bank hols; (020) 7353 3745; *£3. The passages and walkways around here are a good reminder of how

London's streets used to be laid out; the 17th-c Olde Cheshire Cheese nearby is a splendid old tavern.

Gilbert Collection (South Building, Somerset House) Spectacular collection of over 800 pieces of silver made for the rich and famous over the past 500 years, from cups, bowls and soup tureens to a massive wine cistern weighing nearly 36kg and even a pair of silver chamber pots. Snacks, shop, disabled access; cl am Sun; (01787) 282288; £4.

Middle Temple Of all the Inns of Court, this is perhaps the most impressive, and it boasts many famous literary figures among its former members. Most of the buildings date from after the reign of Elizabeth I or the Great Fire, but the name points to an older history: the land was owned by the Knights Templar from about 1160. **Middle Temple Hall** is a fine example of Tudor architecture, with a double hammerbeam roof and beautiful stained glass. There is a table made from timber from Sir Francis Drake's ship the *Golden Hind* – he was a member of the Middle Temple – while a single oak tree from Windsor Forest supplied the wood for the 9-metre (29-ft) long High Table. Open 10am–noon Mon–Fri exc bank hols, during Aug, and over some vacations – best to check first, (020) 7427 4800; free. The **Inner Temple** has an unusual round church.

St Bride's Church (Fleet St) A Wren masterpiece, its splendid steeple the influence for today's traditional three-tiered wedding cake; good Sun choir and frequent short lunchtime recitals (020) 7353 1301 for programme). There's an interesting **museum** in the partly Roman crypt (cl bank hols; free). Caxton set up his first printing press alongside, and ever since St Bride's has been the parish church for anyone involved in the press. This was useful in the days when adjoining Fleet St was the hub of newspaperland; today it's really just a passage between the law courts and the City – but look out for relics of the newspaper kingdoms such as the black-glass former Daily Express Building. The opulent Old Bank of England is now a magnificent pub.

South of the River

South of the river, besides the new Tate Modern gallery, London Eye and, of course, the Dome (see **Millennium openings**), the strongest draws are the magnificent London Aquarium, the Imperial War Museum, Shakespeare's reconstructed Globe Theatre (performances all summer), Britain at War, and, for some, the Design Museum and IMAX cinema: children particularly like the expensive London Dungeon. (The very popular Museum of the Moving Image is being redeveloped this year.) The buildings of the South Bank Centre have been largely humanised inside (though not yet outside), with pleasant bars and so forth, and usually something going on in their foyers – including free entertainment. The walkways on this bank give marvellous views across the river – the best views of the Houses of Parliament are from the quiet riverside walk between Westminster Bridge and the ancient palace of the Archbishop of Canterbury by Lambeth Bridge.

To see and do

⊖ ELEPHANT & CASTLE
Bermondsey market (Bermondsey St/Long Lane) Get up very early on Fri for the bargains: when the antique-dealers start arriving around 5am, other dealers literally pounce on the choice items while they're being set out, and by 8am or 9am things are more ordinary. It's probably the biggest primary source of antiques and bric-à-brac in London, and can be the most exciting. Take a torch in winter.

⊖ LAMBETH NORTH
♨ Florence Nightingale Museum (St Thomas's Hospital, Lambeth Palace Rd) On the site of the first School of Nursing, a re-created hospital ward in the Crimea, and various artefacts and possessions of the Lady with the Lamp. Shop, disabled access; cl Mon (exc bank hols), Good Fri, Easter Sun, 24–25 and 31 Dec, 1 Jan; (020) 7620 0374; £3.50.
♨ Imperial War Museum (Lambeth Rd; Lambeth North tube station – or walk from Westminster) This top-notch museum uses very up-to-date presentation techniques to give a vibrant and sometimes even nerve-wracking exploration of aspects of all wars involving Britain and the Commonwealth since 1914. The Blitz Experience vividly re-creates London's darkest days, and a Trench Experience gives World War I the same treatment. Small boys of all ages love it, though the tone isn't all gung-ho: the interesting archive recordings of people's experiences of war can leave a deep impression, as do some of the harrowing paintings by official war artists. Excellent changing exhibitions. Meals, snacks, shop, disabled access; cl 24–26 Dec; (020) 7416 5000; £5.20, free after 4.30pm. It's housed in the former lunatic asylum known as Bedlam, the name a corruption of Bethlehem: the site was originally a hostel set up in the 13th c by the bishop of that town. There's a clutch of useful tapas bars and the like up past here, around the junction of Kennington Rd and Kennington Lane, and on Waterloo Rd the Fire Station does good food.
♔ ✝ ♨ Lambeth Palace (S end of Lambeth Bridge) The charming, late 15th-c, red brick official residence of the Archbishop of Canterbury, is open to the public this year only. Guided tours of the partly early medieval interior will take place every 15 minutes from 10.30am–3.15pm Tues–Sat, Apr–Nov (exc 16–24 Apr). A special exhibition will look at the Archbishop's role in contemporary life. You will need

to book, (020) 7898 1200; £6. The adjacent **Church of St Mary** has the tombs of several archbishops, and Captain Bligh of the *Bounty* is buried here too. Just by the S gateway is a little **Museum of Garden History** founded in memory of John Tradescant, Charles I's gardener (also buried in the church), with a small area planted with plants grown in his time. Snacks, shop, some disabled access; cl Sat, and early Dec–early Mar; (020) 7401 8865; free.

⊖ LONDON BRIDGE

❋ Bankside This area is very much on the up, with quite a bit of redevelopment going on in the old buildings (*see* **Millennium openings** *section for the new Tate Modern gallery and Millennium Bridge*) and plenty more to come. Riverside promenades offer good Thames and City views – Wren is said to have watched the building of St Paul's from here, and Pepys certainly did watch London burning down in the Great Fire, from nr the interesting old Anchor tavern. One of the best cross-river views of St Paul's is from the modern Founders Arms pub. For centuries this was London's entertainment centre, full of theatres, bars and licensed brothels. In Clink St are the medieval remains of the Bishop of Winchester's palace, once said to be the biggest building in Europe but now reduced to a single wall and an atmospheric rose window. A full-size replica of Francis Drake's *Golden Hind* is moored nearby (cl 25 Dec, but phone to check as it occasionally closes for functions; (020) 7403 0123; £2.30).

☗ Bramah Tea & Coffee Museum (Maguire Street, Butler's Wharf) Almost scholarly but surprisingly interesting, meticulously charting the history of these two favourite commodities, with around 1,000 teapots, and lots of ceramics, silver and prints. Teas (good stuff – they're not fans of the tea bag), snacks, shop, disabled access; cl 25–26 Dec; (020) 7378 0222; £4. Nearby the Anchor Tap (just off Shad Thames) is a handy refreshment stop.

☗ ♪ Britain at War ⊞ (Tooley St) A splendidly put-together re-creation of Blitz-hit London, from reconstructed streets and air-raid shelters to a BBC radio station and GI club. The special effects are suitably dramatic, with lots of smoke, smells and noise. Also authentic period newsreels and front pages, a fully stocked shop and bombed-out pub, and lots of fascinating little details. Shop, disabled access; cl 24–26 Dec; (020) 7403 3171; £5.95.

☗ Design Museum (Butler's Wharf) Intriguing museum showing how design is used in the mass production of everyday objects, from cars and furniture to graphics and ceramics. Snacks, interesting if pricey shop, disabled access; cl 25–26 Dec; (020) 7403 6933; £5.50.

! Globe Theatre (New Globe Walk) The most famous of Southwark's 1600s theatres, Shakespeare's Globe has been reconstructed on its original site, where it was open from 1599 to 1642 (when the Puritans closed it down). The late Sam Wanamaker's ambitious project was derided when first mooted, but the theatre has now enjoyed three very successful seasons. It couldn't be more different from the West End: shaped like an O, the three-tiered open-topped theatre is 30 metres (100ft) in diameter, seating audiences of 1,500 with a further 500 promenaders. Shakespeare's works are performed almost the way they were in the early 1600s – no spotlights, canned music or elaborate sets. Anyone who tells you the seats are uncomfortable has rather missed the point (and you can hire cushions). There are entertaining tours of the site during the day, and there's an exhibition on the Globes old and new – a good substitute if you can't make a performance. A new exhibition underneath the building will look at the life and works of Shakespeare, and will be the biggest of its kind in the world. Very good café and restaurant with river views, shop, disabled access; museum cl 24–25 Dec; (020) 7902 1500; tours £6, though prices may rise when new exhibition opens. The 17th-c galleried George pub in Borough High St, back past London Bridge station, gives another idea of how the area's buildings used to look back then; NT.

Hays Galleria (off Tooley St) An old dock attractively converted into a shopping arcade, with several places to eat inc a good river-view pub, and a fascinating whimsical pirate-ship working sculpture by David Kemp.

✵ **HMS** *Belfast* (E side of Southwark Bridge) Docked permanently in the Pool of London, this is the largest preserved Royal Navy cruiser. Its seven decks are now a floating naval museum, with sound and light displays and various exhibitions. Anyone with even a passing interest in naval life and history should get a lot out of this, and there's plenty to see, from the ship's gun decks to its dental surgery. Meals, snacks, shop, limited disabled access; cl 24–26 Dec; (020) 7407 6434; *£4.70, children free.

♨ **! London Dungeon** (Tooley St) A sensationalised look at London's seamy underside, so better for unsqueamish children, with witchcraft, torture, black magic and death all presented in ghoulishly life-like waxwork scenes. The Jack the Ripper Experience has a computer-controlled fireball blasting towards visitors as its climax, and there's an entertaining new water ride, Judgement Day. The whole place is very atmospheric and well laid out, though families may find the scariest thing about it is the rather high price. Snacks, shop, disabled access; cl 25 Dec; (0891) 600066; £9.50.

✝ **Southwark Cathedral** Off the busy main road and quite a contrast to the buildings cluttered all around it and well worth a passing look, with parts over 600 years older than the present late 19th-c nave; interesting memorials to William Shakespeare (whose brother is buried here) and John Harvard, the founder of the American university. They generally have free recitals Mon lunchtime, and sometimes Tues too. Restoration work on the cathedral continues.

♨ **! Vinopolis** (Bank End, Bankside) Cavernous vaulted arches housing a celebration of all things Bacchic. A self-guided audio tour takes you around displays on the world's wine-growing regions, and afterwards you can sample five wines from a choice of 200 (all of which feature in the exhibition). Restaurant, two shops, disabled access; (020) 7495 4909; £10.

⊖ ≷ **VAUXHALL**

! London Balloon Soar 500ft above London in 'Big Bob', the world's largest tethered balloon. A surprisingly affordable and truly unique view of the capital. Snacks, shop, disabled access; cl Nov–Mar and in bad weather; (020) 7587 1111; around £12.

⊖ ≷ **WATERLOO**

! BFI London IMAX (Charlie Chaplin Walk) Britain's largest 3D projection cinema (with a screen the height of 5 double-decker buses) housed in a stunning glass cylindrical building. Café, disabled access; daytime and evening screenings, phone (020) 7902 1234 for details; £6.50.

♨ **! FA Premier League Hall of Fame** 🅔 (County Hall) The country's largest attraction devoted to the beautiful game. Stroll through the hall of legends, come face to face with waxwork models of your favourite players (Alan Shearer was the first inductee), or test your footballing prowess in the interactive Virtual Stadium. Snacks, shop, disabled access; cl 25 Dec; (020) 7222 0282; £9.95.

♨ **! Museum of** (The Bargehouse, Oxo Tower Wharf) Series of temporary exhibitions, with a view to building a permanent Museum of the River Thames here in the future; subjects so far have included the Thames, emotions and the unknown. Ongoing programme of events and performances. Disabled access; cl am, Mon and Tues, and maybe other times, so best to phone; (020) 7401 2255; free.

🏵 ✿ ⌒ **South Bank** Quite a few projects have brightened up the area in recent years: relaxed **Gabriel's Wharf** on Upper Ground has a number of cheery designer and craft workshops, along with cafés, events, and Fri craft market, and new **Oxo Tower Wharf** offers great views over the city from the top of the lavishly restored Art Deco tower with its landmark logo (good food here too). Though the South Bank and its attractions are well signposted from Waterloo, if you have time to spare, the walk is more pleasant over Blackfriars Bridge, or from Westminster. Nr the Old Vic just S of Waterloo, La Barca (Lower Marsh St) is an enjoyably theatrical Italian restaurant, and Livebait (The Cut) is renowned for its fish. The café of the Young Vic (The Cut) does very good-value light lunches, but you'll feel centuries old if you're out of your 20s.

📖 ✐ **South Bank Centre** These theatres, concert halls, cinema and galleries contain multifarious cultural treasures – not for nothing do they boast that it's the biggest arts complex in the world. Externally, it's not appealing, but occasional open-air festivals, with stalls of books, clothes and jewellery going down to the river, create a buzzing atmosphere on a sunny day. Inside there are frequent free performances and interesting small exhibitions in the foyers of the various halls. The National Theatre, as well as the excellent productions in its three different-sized auditoria, has interesting artistic exhibitions, guided tours behind the scenes, and decent places to eat – often accompanied by live music in the foyer of the Olivier Theatre; (020) 7452 3400 to book a tour (£5; they don't do them on Sun). The National Film Theatre has good themed screenings and events as well as a riverside café. The Hayward Gallery specialises in world-class art exhibitions. The Royal Festival Hall has a full programme of music and dance; its People's Palace is a pleasant modern restaurant and bar. It's a short walk from here to the London Aquarium (a rather longer one to the Imperial War Museum).

➔ **WESTMINSTER**

♪ ❋ **London Aquarium** (County Hall, a pleasant walk across Westminster Bridge from Westminster tube station) This is one of Europe's biggest collections of underwater life, housed in around two million litres of water. The main Atlantic and Pacific tanks are spectacular in their sheer size, giving great views of the sharks, stingrays and conger eels swimming round the Easter Island-style giant heads. The creatures (and occasional divers – often more entertaining than the fish) have plenty of room to swim about, and if you come at a sensible time you'll get several chances to stare at the sharks close-up. The rest of the displays – arranged in different themed areas representing rivers, coral reefs and rainforests – are a more conventional size, so you may have to wait a couple of minutes to get right up to them (for example, on our summer holiday visit no-one left the seahorse tank until one of the shy little beasts had finally appeared). Some areas are fairly imaginative, making good use of sound and light effects, and of course the fish and sea life are quite spectacular, with breathtaking colours and patterns; some species haven't been seen in Britain before. Well sized touch tanks let you stroke a ray or gingerly handle a crab. To avoid the crowds at weekends and school holidays, try to come early or late in the day (they're open till 7.30pm in summer), otherwise you may end up having to queue. Meals, snacks, big shop, disabled access; cl 25 Dec; (020) 7967 8000; *£8. Great views of the Houses of Parliament and river from outside.

❋ ! **London Eye** (County Hall) *See entry under* **Millennium openings** *section.*

Further Afield

We include here only those places which, despite being away from the centre, appeal so much at least to some people that, for them, even a short stay in London would be incomplete without them. Greenwich now has the most to offer, with Kew also very appealing. Other highlights are the lively RAF Museum in Colindale, Kenwood in Hampstead, the unusual Horniman Museum in Forest Hill (a good family outing), and the Saatchi Gallery in St John's Wood.

Other parts of London do have many treasures tucked away, and though we don't list them, they are well worth Londoners themselves tracking down: prime among them are the Whitechapel Gallery in Whitechapel High St east of the City, and, out in west London, Osterley Park, Sion House, Chiswick Mall (18th-c Thames-side village), Chiswick Park (the first true example of English naturalistic landscaping, with Chiswick House, an early 18th-c partying pavilion), and perhaps Hogarth's House.

To see and do

⇌ BARNES
↟ ✦ ! ※ Wetland Centre *See entry under* **Millennium openings** *section.*
⊖ CAMDEN TOWN
✗ A bohemian's idyll, with a very wide variety of unusual shops from radical bookshops to fashion workshops, from comic shops to one of London's best brassware and ironmongery shops. Lots of restaurants and cafés too, and good delis serving the area's Italian and Greek communities; try the Parkway Deli for Italian, and Chris Milia (Pratt St) for Greek. The area's biggest draw is its weekend series of lively **markets**, particularly the interesting craft, hand-made fashion and other stalls around the attractively converted former warehouses of Camden Lock. There's also a covered market on Camden High St, the Inverness St market for fruit and veg, and the Stables, where the best food stalls are to be found. Go and browse, but be warned that you may never again see such huge crowds – the markets here draw 200,000 people every weekend.
♨ Jewish Museum (129 Albert St) Excellent look at Jewish life, history and religion, with a particularly fine collection of ceremonial art, portraits and antiques, and various audio-visual displays. Shop, disabled access; cl Fri, Sat, all bank and Jewish hols; (020) 7388 4525; £3. They have another branch on East End Rd, Finchley, (020) 8349 1143, which traces the history of Jewish immigration and has a moving exhibition on the Holocaust. The Princess of Wales up towards Primrose Hill (Chalcot Rd/Regent's Park Rd) does good bistro food.
⇌ ELTHAM
🏛 ❀ Eltham Palace (Court Yard) Situated on the site of an early 14th-c royal palace, this splendid 1930s country house, set in attractive grounds, was built around part of a medieval hall erected for Edward IV. Recently re-created by English Heritage, the Art Deco interior reflects the glamour of the age in which it was built. Teas; cl Mon (exc bank hols), Tues, and maybe other times, best to check; (020) 8294 2548; house and grounds £5.50, grounds only £3.30; EH.
⇌ GREENWICH
🏛 ♨ ✗ ⚓ The sort of place you can come back to time and time again, and now, with the addition of the Dome,

bound to be one of the visited places in Britain; some of our contributors rate Greenwich more highly than anywhere else in the country. Once a favoured residence of the Royal Family, Greenwich has a long and illustrious maritime heritage, still reflected in the museums, boats and grand old ships you can visit. A weekend market has some excellent antiques, junk and secondhand books, also arts and crafts. College Approach has a good weekend covered craft market. You should be able to get boat trips from the pier up to Westminster (around £5). The Cutty Sark pub (Lassell St) is an attractive old place for lunch; other reliable Thames-view pubs here are the Trafalgar (Park Row) and Yacht (Crane St). Three of the best attractions, the Queen's House, National Maritime Museum and Royal Observatory, can be visited on a joint ticket for £10.50. You'll still pay this even if you can visit only one of them, but you don't have to do them all the same day.

✵ *Cutty Sark* Moored not far from Greenwich Pier, this clipper built in 1896 was the fastest of her time – she once sailed 363 nautical miles in a single day. On board, you can watch a video telling her story, and there's an impressive collection of ships' figureheads. Shop; cl am Sun, 24–26 Dec; (020) 8858 3445; £3.50.

♀ **Fan Museum** (12 Crooms Hill) Unique collection of around 3,000 fans and related items from all over the world. They even do fan-making classes. Shop, disabled access (with notice); cl am Sun, and all Mon; (020) 8858 7879; £3.50.

✿ ✵ **Greenwich Park** Wonderful views from this carefully landscaped park sloping down towards the river; it's a great place for a picnic. A herd of deer graze in a smallish area of woodland and wild flowers known as the Wilderness, and there's the largest children's playground in any royal park (as well as the preserved trunk of a tree in which the young Elizabeth I is said to have played).

✵ ▣ **National Maritime Museum** (Romney Rd) After a £20 million expansion and redevelopment scheme, the new-look museum was opened by the Queen in May last year. Sixteen new galleries all under a spectacular glass canopy, house displays on topics as diverse as plant life, piracy and, of course, sea power. Hundreds of exhibits range from contemporary art and great masterpieces of naval battles, to hands-on activities and even hardy yachtsman Tony Bullimore's survival suit. It's all great fun and combines nicely with a visit to the Royal Observatory in Greenwich Park (a joint ticket is £9.50). Meals, snacks, shop, disabled access; cl 24–26 Dec; (020) 8312 6565; £7.50, children free.

🏠♀! **Queen's House** (Romney Rd) On the site of the original magnificent royal palace, this early 17th-c house was the first Palladian-style villa in the country, designed by Inigo Jones for Anne of Denmark. This year it houses one of the flagship millennium exhibitions, the Story of Time. Using myriad artefacts from museums the world over, such as Dali's *Watch* and early examples of clocks, it aims to explore the definitions of time, from biblical and religious contexts to the boundaries of science, nature and astronomy. Shop, disabled access; the exhibition runs from 1 Jan–24 Sept; (020) 8312 6608; £7.50, there may be a joint ticket with National Maritime Museum and Royal Observatory, phone to check.

🏠♀△ **Ranger's House** (Chesterfield Walk, Blackheath) Lovely stately home with fine furnishings, portraits and a collection of musical instruments. In the 19th c it was the official residence of the Greenwich Park ranger – and Blackheath, opposite, is a civilised place, for a pleasant stroll. Shop, disabled access; cl Mon and Tues, 24–26 Dec; (020) 8853 0035; £2.50.

🏠✵ **Royal Naval College** (Romney Road) With the Queen's House as its focal point, this glorious group of buildings was designed initially by Webb in the late 17th c, then augmented in succession by Wren, Vanbrugh, Hawksmoor and Ripley. It's a magnificently preserved part of old London. Visitors can see an interesting chapel and a notable painted hall. Meals, snacks, shop; cl am Sun, 25 Dec, 1 Jan; (020) 8858 2968; £5. The view from across the river (there's a pedestrian tunnel under the Thames here) looks like an 18th-c print come to life.

☉ ❋ **Royal Observatory** (Greenwich Park) The original home of Greenwich Mean Time – standing as it does on zero meridian longitude. The brass line marking the meridian is still there set in the ground: standing over it with one foot in the western hemisphere and one in the east is almost irresistible. The Wren-built observatory was founded by Charles II in 1675, and now houses a comprehensive collection of historic instruments for time-keeping, navigation and astronomy. Good views from the top. The Time Ball is rather confusing – it can go down and up so fast you barely notice it. Meals, snacks, shop; cl 24–26 Dec; (020) 8312 6565; £5, children free.

⊖ **NORTH GREENWICH**

ƕ ☺ ❗ **Millennium Dome** *See separate family panel on p.781.*

⊖ **HAMPSTEAD**

🏛 Prides itself on its villagey atmosphere, and off the main streets its maze of twisting lanes is very picturesque and seductively charming. It's home to artistes of all kinds, and well heeled bohemians in general; in some streets a commemorative blue plaque on the front of the house is almost compulsory. Particularly attractive parts include early Georgian Church Row, and Squires Mount (where the Regency-looking house at the end on the left, in fact built in the 1950s, belonged to Richard Burton and Elizabeth Taylor). The gaslit Holly Bush, prettily tucked away up Holly Mount, is a good pub, as is the Flask in Flask Walk (a favourite of local actors).

🏛 ❀ ☉ **Fenton House** (Windmill Hill) Fine William and Mary merchant's mansion, set in a walled garden, with Oriental, English and European china and an exceptional collection of early keyboard instruments. Their period-music concerts on some summer Weds evenings are well worth catching. Open pm Weds–Sun Apr–Oct, plus pm wknds in Mar; (020) 7435 3471; £4.10; NT.

❋ ❀ ◠ **Hampstead Heath** North London's best open space (good for walks and flying kites) with lakes, hilly prospects, and some wonderful views of the city skyline – Parliament Hill has a direction-finder pointing out various landmarks. On one edge the ancient Spaniards Inn, still as popular as when Dickens made it famous in the *Pickwick Papers*, faces an 18th-c toll booth notorious for the way its road-narrowing blocks the traffic here.

🏛 ▣ ❀ **Kenwood** (Hampstead Lane) Achieved its present splendid proportions in the 18th c at the hands of Robert Adam. The house contains a fine collection of paintings, inc old masters and 18th- and 19th-c portraits by Reynolds and Gainsborough, and efforts are being made to reacquire its original contents. The grounds are lovely, and in summer there are concerts out here, idyllic when it's fine, with the music drifting across the lake with its Japanese bridge, and sometimes a fireworks finale (virtually impossible to park anywhere near – but a free shuttle bus runs from East Finchley tube from 5pm then). Meals, snacks, shop, disabled access; cl 24–25 Dec, 1 Jan; (020) 8348 1286; free.

☉ **Sigmund Freud's House** (20 Maresfield Gardens) Extraordinary collection of antiques from various ancient cultures, as well as Freud's library, papers and indeed his desk and couch. Shop, some disabled access; open pm Weds–Sun; (020) 7435 2002; £4. The monumental seated statue of Freud by Oscar Nemon can be seen outside the Tavistock Clinic on nearby Belsize Lane.

🏛 ▣ **2 Willow Road** The first Modern Movement house acquired by the National Trust. Designed and built by the architect Erno Goldfinger, it has a good range of work by the artists and intellectuals who lived around Hampstead in the 1930s – as well as the only working TV on show in any NT property. Guided tours from noon Thurs–Sat Apr–Oct; (020) 7435 6166; £4.10; NT.

⇌ **HAMPTON COURT**

❀ **Bushy Park** Another royal park, formerly reserved for hunting. Wren laid out its famous double chestnut avenue, which runs from Teddington Gate to the great house.

🏠🖼 Hampton Court Palace An amazing place, just as a royal palace should be. Begun by Cardinal Wolsey in the early 16th c, the house's splendour soon so pricked Henry VIII's jealousy that Wolsey felt compelled to present it to his king in an attempt to appease him. Successive monarchs have left their architectural marks: the hammer-beamed hall and kitchens were Henry's addition, the Fountain Court was designed by Wren for William and Mary, and much comes from the work of the Victorians (the chimneys mostly date from then). The rooms have managed to keep their distinctive styles, from the starkly imposing Tudor kitchens (themselves taking up 50 rooms) to the elaborate grandeur of the Georgian chambers. The King's Staircase is wonderfully over the top, and the Picture Gallery has the finest Renaissance works from the royal collection, inc Brueghel the Elder's fascinating *Massacre of the Innocents*. Look out too for the carvings by Grinling Gibbons and the cartoons by Mantegna in the Lower Orangery. There are several audio guides you can pick up and listen to as you go along, with no extra charge. Tudor Christmas activities 27 Dec–3 Jan. Meals, snacks, shops, disabled access; cl 24–26 Dec; (020) 8781 9500; £10.

🏵 Hampton Court Gardens Worth a visit in their own right, especially since the restoration of William III's Privy Garden, damaged in the palace's 1986 fire. The last time these gardens looked as they do now was in 1702. The elaborately landscaped grounds also include the famous maze, and the annual flower show here is one of the world's biggest. Open as the palace; £3 gardens only. The King's Arms, next to the Lion Gate, is useful for something to eat.

☁🚶 River Thames There are pleasant Thames-side walks around Hampton Court, and summer cruise boats from here back down to Westminster, (020) 7930 4721; around £9.

⊖ HIGHGATE
🏠 An easy walk across the Heath from Hampstead, this dates largely from the Victorian period and still keeps a villagey atmosphere, centred as it is around the High St. The village is dominated by Highgate School (which Betjeman attended and where T S Eliot taught). There are lots of pubs in this area, and some smart little cafés. The Grove, a row of very elegant Victorian houses, has been home to such diverse musicians as Yehudi Menuhin and Sting.

🏵 ! Highgate Cemetery (Swains Lane) The most impressive of a series of landscaped and formal cemeteries started in the early decades of Victoria's reign on the outskirts of the city, very well restored over the last 20 years, and still in use. You'll find it hard to miss the tomb of Karl Marx – a monstrous head, frequently daubed with paint and slogans. It's more difficult to search out the graves of Christina Rossetti and George Eliot in the wonderfully atmospheric tangle of trees, shrubs and crumbling ivy-covered monuments. The east cemetery is open all year (exc 25–26 Dec), the west by guided tour only (not wkdys Dec–Feb), (020) 8340 1834 for times; east cemetery *£1, west cemetery *£3.

⊖⇄ KEW
↓T 🚂 Kew Bridge Steam Museum 🖼 (Green Dragon Lane) Over the bridge from the gardens, by the tube station, this is a splendid old pumping station housing five Cornish beam engines – one of which you can walk through while it's working. Also a miniature railway, and surprisingly interesting exhibition on the development of London's water supply: there are peepholes into the sewers. It won't appeal unless you've at least some interest in the subject – in which case you'll find the engines prime examples of their type. Wknd snacks, shop, some disabled access; cl Christmas, Good Fri; (020) 8568 4757; £3.80 wknds (when engines in steam), £2.80 wkdys.

🏵 ⚘ 🚶 Kew Gardens Started in 1759 by George III's mother as nine acres landscaped by Capability Brown. By 1904, they had grown to cover 300 acres, with the foundations of the present wonderful collection firmly laid. The glasshouses include the magnificent modern Princess of Wales range and the remarkable restored Victorian Palm

House, as well as an Evolution House displaying plants from up to 400 million years ago. The gardens nr the entrance are largely formally arranged, and drift into attractively landscaped woodland, glades and tree collections further out. The museum was extensively restored a few years ago, and there's also a gallery, and on some summer evenings jazz concerts with fireworks. A wonderful place you can come back to time and time again – always discovering something new. Meals, snacks, shop, disabled access; cl 25 Dec, 1 Jan; (020) 8332 5622; £5. The Flower & Firkin at Kew Gardens railway station does decent simple food. In summer you can come to Kew by cruise boat from Westminster – see the numbers we give for Hampton Court and Richmond.

🏠 🦋 **Queen Charlotte's Cottage** (Kew Gardens) This rusticated summerhouse was built for the Royal Family in the 18th c, its interior designed to look like a tent; it's usually open wknds and bank hols Apr–Sept; free with admission to the gardens.

⊖ ⇌ **RICHMOND**

🏠 ♨ △ Agreeable if much extended Thames village, with lots of fine 18th-c houses especially around the Green and up Richmond Hill. There are quite a few good dining pubs, inc the riverside White Cross, and the White Swan (Old Palace Lane), Orange Tree (Kew Rd) and Rose of York (Petersham Rd). The river here is really attractive for strolls, and there are summer cruise boats from here back down to Westminster, stopping at Kew and Putney (more fine riverside walks) on the way; (020) 7930 2062.

🏠 🦋 ♨ **Ham House** (Petersham) A pleasant two-mile walk W along the river from Richmond to this outstanding Stuart mansion. A ghost guide takes you on a tour of haunted rooms (3pm Mon). Meals, snacks, shop, disabled access; open pm Sat–Weds Apr–Oct; (020) 8940 1950; £5, £1.50 garden only; NT. If you happen to be in Twickenham you can get a ferry across.

🦋 ☘ ♪ △ **Richmond Park** The most country-like of all London's parks, with great rolling spaces and wildlife (inc herds of deer), model boats on Adam's Pond, and fishing in the 18-acre Pen Ponds. There's a good formal garden at Pembroke Lodge, and the Isabella Plantation's rhododendrons and azaleas are a must-see in season.

More Specialised Expeditions

To see and do

⊖ **ANGEL**
Camden Passage This and the surrounding streets have a great collection of **antique shops**, well worth the expedition if that interests you. The nearby Island Queen (Noel Rd) does good food in its bar and upstairs restaurant.

⇌ **CHISLEHURST**
🕯 **Chislehurst Caves** (entrance off Caveside Close nr Bickley Arms, B264; nr Chislehurst railway station) Atmospheric 45-minute lamplit tours of labyrinthine tunnels and passageways carved out of the rock over 8,000 years. They've been used by flint knappers, druids, and as an air-raid shelter during the war. Longer more adventurous tours on Suns and bank hols at 2.30pm. Snacks (wknds and school hols), shop; cl Mon and Tues (exc school hols); (020) 8467 3264; *£3 (£5 longer tour). The Olde Stationmaster nearby is a good-value family food pub.

⊖ **COLINDALE**
✈ **RAF Museum** 🎟 (Grahame Park Way) The story of flight from early times, with 80 full-size aeroplanes, dramatic simulators, films and hands-on exhibits (you can have a go at the controls of a modern jet trainer), lively Battle of Britain Experience, and an interesting examination of the impact of flight on history and politics. There's also an interactive Fun 'n' Flight gallery. Excellent for enthusiasts and flying-

minded children, and warmly recommended by several of our contributors. Meals, snacks, shop, disabled access; cl 24–26 Dec, 1 Jan; (020) 8205 9191; £6.50.

⇌ FOREST HILL

🖺 🎵 🐄 🐘 Horniman Museum

(London Rd) Art Nouveau building with eclectic mainly ethnographic collections inc fine group of mummies, religious artefacts, exotic folk art, also a remarkable musical instrument collection (interactive computers allow you to actually hear some of the extraordinary instruments), lots of stuffed animals, very well laid out aquarium/ecosystem; children love it, despite the old-fashioned feel. Friendly small farm animals in the gardens outside. Snacks, shop, some disabled access; cl am Sun, 24–26 Dec; free wknd talks/concerts; (020) 8699 1872; free.

⊖ HIGHBURY & ISLINGTON

🖺 Estorick Collection of Italian Art

(Northampton Lodge, 39A Canonbury Sq) This outstanding collection of modern Italian art includes fine futurist works by artists inc Balla and Boccioni, as well as later figurative works by Modigliani and Sironi. Meals, snacks, shop, disabled access; cl Mon, Tues and am Sun; (020) 7704 9522; £3.50.

⇌ KNOCKHOLT

❋ △ South London walks

The SE fringes of London give way to surprisingly rural North Downs countryside, still within the London borough of Bromley, around Knockholt, High Elms and Downe; paths are plentiful and well maintained. Only the view over South London from behind Knockholt church shows how close you are to the capital.

⊖ ST JOHN'S WOOD

🖺 Lord's Cricket Ground

(St John's Wood Rd) Tours of the famous club and grounds, and the excellent MCC Museum, with an exhaustive collection of cricket memorabilia, inc the Ashes urn and 18th-c paintings of the game. As this is a private club, visits are by appointment only, (020) 7432 1033 (usually at 12 and 2pm), though you can also see the museum if you're watching a cricket match during the season. Shop, disabled access by prior

arrangement; £5.80 (£2 for museum on match days). Down in Aberdeen Pl, Crockers is a remarkably opulent Victorian pub with decent food.

🖺 Saatchi Gallery

(98 Boundary Rd; nearest tube Swiss Cottage or St John's Wood) Challenging modern art inc works by Marcus Harvey, Richard Wilson and a shark in formaldehyde by Damien Hirst. Shop; cl am, Mon–Weds, and all August; *£4.

⊖ SOUTHFIELDS

🖺 ! Wimbledon Lawn Tennis Museum

(Church Rd) The only museum of its type, with trophies, pictures and other tennis memorabilia tracing the development of the game throughout this century. Also highlights of past Wimbledon Championships, and an interesting display on the changes in tennis fashions. You can see the famous Centre Court outside. Snacks, shop, disabled access; cl am Sun, all day Mon, and every day during the Championship fortnight (unless you've gone to watch the tennis); (020) 8946 6131; £4. If you're in London during the Wimbledon fortnight, it's always worth popping along to the club in the early evening around 5.30pm or 6pm – lots of people leave then and their seats are resold cheaply.

✗ 🎖 △ Wimbledon Windmill

There's an attractive old core around Wimbledon Common, and a striking windmill on Windmill Rd (open pm wknds and bank hols Mar–Oct; *£1). The common, with its ponds, is one of the best strolling grounds provided by South London's numerous commons and parks.

⇌ TWICKENHAM

🖺 ! Twickenham Experience

(Rugby Rd) Combines tours of the 75,000-seat home of rugby union with an excellent museum of related memorabilia under the East Stand; interactive displays and period reconstructions illustrate the game's history, and there's plenty of footage from classic matches. Snacks, shop, disabled access; cl Mon (exc bank hols), am Sun, 24–26 Dec, Good Fri and two days before and after match days; four tours a day (only two on Sun), best to book on (020) 8892 2000; £5, £3 for either the museum or tour only.

⊖ WALTHAMSTOW CENTRAL

▣ ✿ **William Morris Gallery** (Lloyd Park, Forest Rd) William Morris lived here 1846–1858, and the house has an excellent collection of his work: fabrics, furnishings and wallpaper, much of it still fashionable today. Pre-Raphaelite works upstairs include pictures by Burne-Jones and Rossetti. The attractive grounds are ideal for picnics. Shop, disabled access to ground floor only with prior notice – though this is where the main exhibition is; cl 1–2pm, all Mon, and Sun (exc first Sun in month); (020) 8527 3782; free.

⊖ WARWICK AVENUE

⚓ ! **Puppet Theatre Barge** (Little Venice) This wonderful floating puppet theatre is as entertaining for adults as it is for children. It seats 50, and is moored here from Nov–May, touring the Thames in the summer. Past productions have ranged from *The Three Little Pigs* to *Macbeth*. Snacks; they can accommodate up to 3 wheelchairs, so essential to phone in advance; box office (020) 7249 6876; £6.

⇌ WEST DULWICH

★ ⚑ ✯ △ **Dulwich** The village still is villagey, with imposing 18th-c houses, duckpond, a good pub, the Crown & Greyhound, and an almost rural feel (there's even a toll road). There are good walks, in Dulwich Park (best in rhododendron time), and through Dulwich Wood to adjacent Sydenham Hill Wood – the largest fragment of ancient woodland in inner London, and a most surprising place (just big enough to lose your way in), with woodpeckers among the oak and hornbeam trees. The best of the wood is a nature reserve jealously guarded against developers by the London Wildlife Trust; a trail starts from the Crescent Wood Rd entrance on the Sydenham side.

▣ **Dulwich Picture Gallery** (Dulwich College, Gallery Rd) This rather austere brick building designed by Sir John Soane in 1811, was England's first public gallery when it opened six years later. Recently refurbished to provide educational facilities and a new café, it's home to an impressive collection of 17th- and 18th-c works by artists including Rembrandt, Van Dyck and Canaletto. Shop, disabled access; cl Mon, and 25 Dec; (020) 8693 5254; *£3.

Where to eat

ALASTAIR LITTLE *49 Frith St W1 (020) 7734 5183* Uncluttered, almost starkly furnished restaurant, with very good, simple modern food from a sensibly short menu – plenty of strong flavours – enjoyable puddings, and an interesting small wine list; cl am Sat, Sun, bank hols. **£48 dinner, £40 lunch**|£7.

APPRENTICE *Butler's Wharf Chef School, Cardamon Building, 31 Shad Thames SE1 (020) 7234 0254* The school is a charitable organisation for hopeful chefs and front-of-house personnel; long, simple restaurant and good-value modern meals in an enjoyable atmosphere; weekend courses; cl Sat, Sun, Christmas, bank hols; disabled access. **£17.75**.

BANK *1 Kingsway WC2 (020) 7379 9797* Very modern restaurant with décor to match (the slanted glass decorations hanging from the ceiling are quite a sight), an open kitchen, and interesting food from a very varied menu (as well as lunch and dinner, they also serve breakfasts, from 7am, pre-theatre meals, and weekend brunches that includes a children's menu); cl bank hols; disabled access. **£35**.

BIBENDUM *81 Fulham Rd SW3 (020) 7581 5817* Magnificent Art Deco Michelin building housing a light and spacious restaurant, with exceptionally good French-style cooking (more elaborate in the evening), a marvellous wine list, and courteous, well trained staff; the unpretentious downstairs oyster bar is a fine place for a lighter (and cheaper) meal; cl 25–26 Dec; disabled access. **£45**.

BIRDCAGE *110 Whitfield St W1 (020) 7383 3346* Exotically decorated restaurant with antiques from all over the Far East, 18th-c birdcages from France, and so forth, beautifully prepared and presented food with influences from the Orient, India, and Europe, interesting puddings, and an eclectic wine list; cl am Sat, Sun. **£48**|£32.50 for 2 courses.

BISHOP'S FINGER *9–10 W Smithfield EC1 (020) 7248 2341* Swish little bar-cum-restaurant with fresh flowers on elegant tables set on polished bare boards, comfortably cushioned chairs under a wall lined with prints, distinctive food from an open kitchen, well kept real ales, a wide choice of wines, and friendly service; upstairs evening bar. **£18.50|£7.**

BLOOM'S *130 Golders Green Rd NW11 (020) 8455 3033* Strictly kosher Jewish restaurant with enjoyable food – most fun on Sun lunchtime when it's packed with Jewish families; cl Fri evening, am Sat, and Jewish hols (they are open bank hols); disabled access. **£20|£5.**

BLUEBIRD *350 King's Rd SW3 (020) 7559 1000* The Bluebird Garage, built in 1923, has been converted to house the King's Rd Gastrodrome with a food market offering all sorts of delicious specialist products (inc ready-made dishes), flower market, wine merchant, kitchenware shop, and private dining club, plus the huge, airy first-floor restaurant with its kite-like artwork hanging from the ceiling, dark green limestone floor, stainless steel bar at one end with a shellfish bar the other, open-plan kitchen with a big woodburning oven, and good modern British cooking served by friendly staff; pre-theatre meals and weekend brunches; cl 25 Dec; disabled access. **£35|£11.**

BLUE ELEPHANT *4–6 Fulham Broadway SW6 (020) 7385 6595* Luxurious Thai food among waterfalls and exotic jungle greenery, with produce flown in weekly from Thailand; the set meals are better value; cl am Sat, 24–26 Dec; disabled access. **£35|£10.**

BOMBAY BRASSERIE *Courtfield Close, Courtfield Rd SW7 (020) 7370 4040* Grand colonial-style furnishings in big restaurant and conservatory, with very good Indian food using recipes from all over India (lots of vegetarian dishes), and courteous, helpful staff; cheaper at lunchtime when there's a buffet; cl 25–26 Dec; children over 10; disabled access. **£31|£15.95 buffet lunch.**

CAFE FISH *36-40 Rupert St W1 (020) 7287 8989* This bustling, well run fish restaurant has become so popular that they have moved to bigger premises, and now have a brasserie with light meals and an upstairs restaurant; super fresh fish, fine French cheeses, and a fair wine list. **£24.25 in restaurant|£11.50 for 2-course lunch in brasserie.**

CAFE IN THE CRYPT *St Martin-in-the-Fields, Trafalgar Sq WC2 (020) 7930 0089* Popular place under the lovely arches of the church, with a relaxed atmosphere, good, freshly prepared, daily changing food; shop, free lunchtime concerts, candlelit evening concerts, brass rubbing; cl 25 Dec, am Good Fri. **£13.50|£5.50.**

CANTEEN *Chelsea Harbour SW10 (020) 7351 7330* Some tables overlook the marina in this smart modern restaurant with its excellent European food inc delicious puddings, and good service; cl am Sat, pm Sun, bank hols; disabled access. **£33|£8.50.**

LE CAPRICE *Arlington St SW1 (020) 7629 2239* For such an incredibly popular, sleek restaurant (must book some time ahead), the atmosphere is surprisingly friendly and welcoming; imaginative, eclectic, modern British and European food (plenty of fish), incredibly quick, efficient service, and a concise wine list; cl 25–26 Dec, 1 Jan, Aug bank hol; **£38|£13.**

CHAPEL *48 Chapel St NW1 (020) 7402 9220* Attractively refurbished pub with a civilised but relaxed feel, a light spacious main room dominated by the open kitchen, very good modern cooking, prompt efficient service, smart but simple furnishings, real ales, and a good range of interesting wines and teas; disabled access. **£23.50|£8.**

CHEZ NICO AT NINETY PARK LANE *90 Park Lane W1 (020) 7409 1290* Comfortable, elegant restaurant run by Nico Ladenis, one of the country's best-known chefs, serving impeccable food (the set lunch is marvellous value) and fine wines (at a price); cl am Sat, Sun, 10 days Christmas, 4 days Easter, bank hols; children over 12; disabled access. **£65 dinner not inc wine|£25 for 3-course set lunch.**

CHRISTOPHER'S *18 Wellington St WC2 (020) 7240 4222* Fashionable place in a Victorian building in Covent Garden, with high ceilings and rococo décor in the first--floor restaurant, ground-floor dining room, and basement Speakeasy Bar; highly enjoyable modern American cooking, cheery, speedy service, and lots of American wines; cl pm Sun. **£40**|£15.

CHUTNEY MARY *535 King's Rd SW10 (020) 7351 3113* Very good, interesting Anglo-Indian food in light conservatory and two dining rooms, plus a verandah bar, a good choice of drinks, and knowledgeable staff; only set lunch on Sun; cl pm 25 Dec, 26 Dec; some disabled access. **£35**|£12.50 for 2-course lunch.

CITY RHODES *1 New St Sq EC4 (020) 7583 1313* Airy light restaurant serving good, modern, inventive British food cooked by the well known TV chef, enjoyable puddings, helpful, efficient service, and an interesting if pricey wine list; cl wknds, Christmas, New Year, bank hols; disabled access. **£50**|£22.

CLARKE'S *124 Kensington Church St W8 (020) 7221 9225* Consistently excellent British and Mediterranean-style food (no choice at dinner, more informal at lunch) in two quietly decorated rooms, friendly staff, and a good choice of wines; cl Sat, Sun, bank hols, 2 wks Aug, 2 wks Christmas; disabled access. **£42** for 4-course set dinner|£29 for 3-course lunch.

CORK & BOTTLE *44–46 Cranbourn St WC2 (020) 7734 7807* Basement wine bar we've liked for over 25 years, nr West End theatres – good food inc interesting salads, cold buffet and unusual hot dishes, excellent wines, and cheerful service; cl 25 Dec, 1 Jan. **£19**|£5.95.

DEALS DINER *Chelsea Harbour SW10 (020) 7795 1001* Bustling café-restaurant with good food ranging from hamburgers to sizzle platters, generous glasses of decent house wine, good cocktails and very friendly service; best at lunchtime when it's less frenetic; good for children on Sun lunchtime (must book); cl pm Sun, 25, 31 Dec; disabled access; other branches. **£20**|£8.

EAGLE *159 Farringdon Rd EC1 (020) 7837 1353* Particularly good Mediterranean-style food in this popular, stylish pub where an open kitchen forms part of the bar; well kept real ales, lots of wine by the glass, properly made cocktails, a lively and chatty atmosphere (lots of young media folk), and simple furnishings; cl pm Sun, bank hols, Easter, 1½ wks Christmas. **£25**|£7.50.

EBURY WINE BAR *139 Ebury St SW1 (020) 7730 8206* Said to be London's first wine bar (established 1959) with a loyal following, excellent list of wines by the glass, and very good modern cooking; they have another bar restaurant called Carriages opposite the Royal Mews in Buckingham Palace Rd, and Joe's Brasserie at 130 Wandsworth Bridge Rd; cl 25–26 Dec, 1 Jan. **£33.50**|£6.50.

FIRE STATION *150 Waterloo Rd SE1 (020) 7401 3267* Remarkable conversion of a former fire station with two chatty front rooms, plenty of wooden pews, chairs and long tables, some brightly red painted doors, modern art on the walls, newspapers to read, very good imaginative food, a decent choice of wines, and well kept real ales. **£22**|£6.25.

FOOD FOR THOUGHT *31 Neal St WC2 (020) 7836 9072* Long-established and consistently good unlicensed vegetarian restaurant, with take-away service upstairs and communal eating at long tables downstairs – you can also eat at tables outside; no corkage; cl pm Sun, Christmas/New Year, and Easter Sun. **£9.30**|£3.50.

FOOTSTOOL *St John's, Smith Sq SW1 (020) 7222 2779* Partly no smoking restaurant in the church crypt below the concert hall, with plants, pictures and stripped brick, and good food from a monthly changing menu; lighter lunchtime buffet; cl am Sat and Sun; disabled access. **£20**|£5.95.

FORTNUM & MASON *181 Piccadilly W1 (020) 7734 8040* Famous store with elegant fourth-floor St James's Restaurant (must book), Fountain Restaurant (ground floor), Patio Restaurant and newly opened salmon and champagne bar (mezzanine) offering good breakfasts, morning coffee, lunches, fine afternoon tea and pre-theatre meals; cl Sun, bank hols; disabled access. **£32.45**|£16.95 for 2-course lunch.

LE GAVROCHE *43 Upper Broom St W1 (020 7408 0881* This put London on the eating map when it was opened by the Roux brothers 30 years ago; drinks and delicious canapés are served in the cosy lounge, and the quietly decorated, club-like restaurant with its pictures and table flowers is in the basement; cooking is exemplary classic French with modern touches (lovely puddings and perfect cheeses, too), service from French staff is attentive and professional, and the wine list is classy but expensive (some wines reach four figures); the set lunch is incredible value; cl Sat, Sun, 24 Dec–3 Jan. **£100|£38** set lunch.

GAY HUSSAR 2 Greek St W1 (020) 7437 0973 Very long-standing and happily unchanging Hungarian restaurant with bags of atmosphere (downstairs has the most), good, generous, authentic food, and friendly service; cl Sun, bank hols. **£23**.

GREENHOUSE 27A Hays Mews W1 (020) 7499 3331 In a mews hidden away in Mayfair, this upmarket, rather sedate restaurant is loved by long-standing customers, and serves very good-value and enjoyable English and Mediterranean food (lovely puddings); shortish wine list. **£15.50**.

HANOVER SQUARE WINE BAR 25 Hanover Sq (020) 7408 0935 Under the same enthusiastic ownership as the popular Cork & Bottle in Leicester Sq, this bustling wine bar offers a constantly changing cold buffet, plus daily hot dishes and charcoal grills, and a particularly good, interesting wine list; cl Sun, bank hols. **£21|£6.95**.

IVY 1 West St WC2 (020) 7836 4751 To be sure of a table you must book up ages ahead in this very fashionable, oak-panelled and stained-glass-windowed restaurant; a wide choice of really good, highly enjoyable food inc modern dishes as well as old-fashioned ones, a thoughtful short wine list, and friendly, most efficient service; cl 25–26 Dec, 1 Jan, Aug bank hol; **£34|£15.50** for 3-course weekend lunch.

KALAMARES MICRO 66 Inverness Mews W2 (020) 7727 5082 (Not to be confused with its larger sister restaurant at No 76.) Tiny, close-packed, authentically Greek restaurant with very good cheap food and friendly service; unlicensed, take your own wine; cl Sun, am, and bank hols; **£18|£6**.

MON PLAISIR 21 Monmouth St WC2 (020) 7836 7243 Bustling French bistro with super atmosphere, good-value, well prepared food, decent wines, and friendly staff; cl am Sat, all day Sun, bank hols, Christmas, New Year and Easter; disabled access. **£35**|popular 3-course pre-theatre meal £14.95.

MORO 34–36 Exmouth Mkt EC1 (020) 7833 8336 Simply decorated restaurant with smart bentwood chairs on bare boards, cream and green walls, side bar with high stools, and an open-plan kitchen; thriving atmosphere, interesting modern Spanish cooking with influences from North Africa and the Middle East, nice tapas, a short thoughtful wine list, and informal but punctilious service; cl wknds, Christmas, Easter; disabled access. **£30|£12.50**.

OAK ROOM MARCO PIERRE WHITE Le Meridien Hotel, 21 Piccadilly W1 (020) 7437 0202 Set in Le Meridien Hotel (but quite separate from it) this splendidly decorated restaurant has vast chandeliers, lots of gold, chiming wall clocks, and stunning flower arrangements, luxurious food with intense flavours (marvellous puddings and petits fours, and professional service; pricey wines; cl am Sat, Sun, 2 wks Christmas; disabled access. **£80|£37.50** for 3-course lunch.

L'ODEON 65 Regent St W1 (020) 7287 1400 Long restaurant reached by a rather fine staircase, with nine big semi-circular windows overlooking Piccadilly Circus, lots of tables and banquettes, a bustling atmosphere, classic French provincial cooking with modern additions, good puddings, a light menu in the bar, afternoon tea, and a well chosen wine list; pre-theatre meals; cl bank hols; disabled access. **£39|£16**.

ODETTE'S 130 Regent's Park Rd NW1 (020) 7586 5486 Smart front dining room with lots of gilded mirrors, airy back conservatory, and slightly cheaper downstairs wine bar with good modern English and more unusual dishes, friendly service, and thoughtful wine list; cl pm Sun, bank hols, 1 wk Christmas. **£35|£10** for 3-course set lunch.

OXO TOWER Barge House St SE1 (020) 7803 3888 Briskly modern brasserie and restaurant on the 8th floor of this South Bank redevelopment; light and airy, with busy open kitchen, lots of functional tables and chairs, and promptly served modern English food; what stands out, of course, is the panoramic view over the Thames and City – best in summer from tables on the outside terrace; cl 25–26 Dec. Restaurant – **£60**|£26.50 for 3-course lunch. Brasserie – **£35**|£13 for 3-course lunch.

POONS *27 Lisle St WC2* (020) 7437 4549 Atmospheric, unlicensed and unmodernised Chinese restaurant with extremely good-value, tasty barbecued and wind-dried food; cl Good Fri, 24–26 Dec; late opening Sun till 5.15pm. **£15**|£5.50. Other branches (more modern and expensive) at 4 Leicester St WC2 (020) 7437 1528, 50 Woburn Pl, Russell Sq WC1 (020) 7580 1188, and 2 Minster Court, Mincing Lane EC3 (020) 7626 0126.

QUAGLINO'S *16 Bury St SW1* (020) 7930 6767 Fashionable restaurant with big stone staircase to the antipasti bar overlooking the huge dining room with flamboyantly painted pillars, fine flowers, highly modern attractive furnishings, and a buoyant buzzing atmosphere; lovely fresh fish and other modern cooking, good wine list, and efficient service; cl pm 24 Dec, 25 Dec, am 26 and 31 Dec, am 1 Jan; no children in bar in evening; disabled access. **£24**|£12.50 for 2 courses.

RAINFOREST CAFE *20 Shaftesbury Ave W1* (020) 7434 3111 Exciting big restaurant on three floors with amazing special effects such as mist, wildlife noises, thunder and lightning storms, waterfalls, live tropical parrots and aquariums, animatronic trumpeting elephants, gorillas, fluttering butterflies, life-size splashing crocodile and so forth, and 'jungle-esque'-type food (burgers, pizzas, pasta, sandwiches, salad, and appetizers); cl Christmas. **£18.50**|£7.

REBATO'S *169 South Lambeth Rd SW8* (020) 7735 6388 Busy and attractive, high-ceilinged bar with friendly barman and waiters, a good choice of tapas (plenty of fresh fish), and lots of Spanish wines; also Spanish restaurant; cl am Sat, Sun, bank hols, Christmas. **£20.20**|£5.75.

RSJ *13a Coin St SE1* (020) 7928 4554 Handy for the South Bank, this relaxed and friendly restaurant serves fine modern British and Mediterranean cooking and exceptional Loire wines in simple surroundings; cl am Sat, Sun. **£22.40** for 3-course set lunch.

RULES *35 Maiden Lane WC2* (020) 7836 5314 One of London's oldest restaurants, smart and very British, with good English food inc fine seasonal game and oysters; interesting history; disabled access. **£39**|£14.95.

SIMPSONS IN THE STRAND *100 Strand WC2* (020) 7836 9112 Marvellously old-fashioned, with traditional English cooking inc nursery puddings, and roasts carved as you want them at your table on silver-domed trolleys – famous breakfasts, too; all very decorous – the surroundings and atmosphere are more memorable than the food; cl 25–26 Dec, 1 Jan; disabled access. **£40**.

SOTHEBY'S CAFE *34 New Bond St W1* (020) 7293 5077 Very small but very classy café with simple high-class food inc lovely puddings and good cheeses, a carefully chosen little wine list, and courteous staff; cl Sat, Sun, 2 wks Aug, Christmas and New Year; partial disabled access. **£32.50**|£9.95.

SQUARE *6–10 Bruton St W1* (020) 7495 7100 Elegant, slightly formal restaurant with bold modern drawings on the walls, well spaced tables on the parquet floor, superb English and French cooking with plenty of strong flavours and beautiful presentation, wonderful puddings, a fine wine list (plenty of Burgundies), and exemplary service; cl am Sat; children over 10; disabled access. **£90**|£20.

STEPHEN BULL *12 Upper St Martin's Lane WC2* (020) 7379 7811 Useful for pre-theatre meals, this simply decorated restaurant serves enjoyable innovative European food inc good puddings, and reasonably priced wines; service is efficient and friendly, and there are branches in Blandford St W1 and 71 St John St EC1; cl am Sat, Sun, Mon, Christmas and New Year, bank hols; partial disabled access. **£34.75 dinner**|/£15 for 2-course lunch.

TANTE CLAIRE *Wilton Pl, SW1* (020) 7823 2003 Fine restaurant in a wing of the Berkeley Hotel – exceptional and beautifully presented French cooking – more relaxed at lunchtime when the set menu is very good-value – courteous service, and some good-value French country wines; jacket and tie required; cl am Sat, Sun, 31 Dec; children over 10; disabled access. **£85 dinner**|£28 for 3-course set lunch.

TAPPIT HEN *5 William IV St WC2 (020) 7836 9839* Cosy and atmospheric little wine bar, very old-fashioned feeling, with good snacks and good-value wines – more for lunchtimes (when the smoked salmon sandwiches are lovely), though you can book for upstairs in the evening; cl Sat, Sun, bank hols. **£28**|£7.75.

TURNER'S *87–89 Walton St SW3 (020) 7584 6711* Most enjoyable, elegantly furnished restaurant run by the warm and friendly TV cook Brian Turner, with extremely good food based on sound, classic French techniques, lovely puddings, very good service, and a mainly French wine list; very good-value fixed price meals; cl Sun, Christmas, bank hols; no children in evening; disabled access. **£36 dinner, £22 lunch**|£14.50 for 2 courses.

WAGAMAMA *4 Streatham St WC1 (020) 7580 9365* You will have to queue to get into this trendy, simply furnished Japanese basement restaurant with its long tables and benches for communal eating; very friendly, cheerful service, noisy informal atmosphere, good healthy food – raw salads, ramens (huge bowls of noodles with meat, vegetables and Japanese additions), rice dishes, sake, grape and plum wines, beer, and free green tea; exceptionally good value; cl 25–26 Dec; several other branches too. £5.50.

Special thanks to Basil Cooper, Tony and Dorothy Eberts, Mrs C Dewell, R E Perry, Paul Kennedy, Mrs Marie Hyde.

London Calendar

Some of these dates were provisional as we went to press. Please check information with the telephone numbers provided.

JANUARY

1 **Central London** London Parade: Lord Mayor, marching bands from over 40 countries, vintage cars, from Westminster Bridge *at 12am* to Berkeley Sq (020) 8566 8586

6 **Earls Court** International Boat Show – *till 16 January* (01784) 473377

13 **Kensington Town Hall** West London Antiques and Fine Art Fair: 60 stands – *till 16 January* (01444) 482514

19 **Business Design Centre, N1** Art 2000: work by new young designers – *till 23 January* (020) 7359 3535

29 **Alexandra Palace** Road Racing and Superbike Show – *till 6 February* (01440) 707055

30 **Central London** Charles I Commemoration Ceremony: procession of members of the Society of King Charles and Royal Stuart Society in 17th-c costume, from St James's Palace to Banqueting House (020) 7730 3450

FEBRUARY

22 **Olympia** Fine Art and Antiques Fair – *till 27 February* (020) 7370 3188

MARCH

16 **Earls Court** Ideal Home Exhibition – *till 9 April* (020) 8515 2079

London Calendar (cont.)

18 Alexandra Palace London Classic Motor Show – *till 19 March* (01296) 631181; **River Thames** Head of the River Race, Mortlake to Putney (01932) 220401

19 London International Book Fair – *till 21 March* (020) 7371 3333

25 River Thames Oxford v Cambridge Boat Race, Putney to Mortlake (020) 7379 3234

APRIL

21 Greenwich Passion Play (020) 7639 4413

24 Battersea Park Harness Horse Parade: extensive display of horse-drawn vehicles (01733) 234451

MAY

13 Twickenham Rugby Union Cup Final (020) 8892 2000

14 Covent Garden Festival – *till 3 June* (020) 7379 8070

20 Wembley FA Challenge Cup Final (020) 7402 7151

23 Royal Hospital Chelsea Chelsea Flower Show – *till 26 May* (020) 7649 1885

26 Docklands Millennium Maritime Festival – *till 4 June* (020) 7932 2000

29 Piccadilly Royal Academy Summer Exhibition: large contemporary art exhibition – *till 7 August* (020) 7439 7438

JUNE

7 Horse Guards Parade Beating the Retreat: massed guards of the Household Division – *till 8 June* (020) 7839 5323

8 Olympia Fine Art and Antiques Fair – *till 18 June* (020) 7370 8234

10 Horse Guards Parade Queen's Birthday Parade: Trooping the Colour (tickets in advance only from The Brigade Major, Household Division, HQ London District, Horse Guards, Whitehall, London, SW1A 2AX) (020) 7414 2357

11 Battersea Park Christian Pageant (020) 7932 2000

18 Covent Garden Flower Festival – *till 25 June* (020) 7735 1518

20 City of London Festival – *till 13 July* (020) 7377 0540

24 Middlesex Showground Middlesex Show – *till 25 June* (01895) 252131

26 Wimbledon Lawn Tennis Championships – *till 9 July* (020) 8946 2244

30 Greenwich and **Docklands** Festival – *till 30 July* (020) 8305 1818

JULY

4 Hampton Court Palace Flower Show inc British Rose Festival – *till 9 July* (020) 7834 4333; **Horse Guards Parade** Royal Military Tattoo – *till 9 July* (020) 7932 2000

14 Royal Albert Hall Henry Wood Promenade Concerts – *till 9 September* (020) 7765 4296

AUGUST

5 Enfield Steam and Country Show – *till 6 August* (020) 8379 3784

London Calendar (cont.)

11 Kensington Town Hall Fine Art and Antiques Fair: 80 stands – *till 13 August* (01444) 482514

13 Oxford Street Street Festival (020) 7629 1234

26 Enfield Balloon Festival at Trent Country Park – *till 28 August* (020) 7222 1234

27 Notting Hill Carnival: largest carnival in Europe – *till 28 August* (020) 8964 0544

SEPTEMBER

15 Chelsea Old Town Hall Antiques Fair – *till 24 September* (01444) 482514

17 River Thames Thames Festival: between Westminster Bridge and Southwark Cathedral, and Putney Bridge and Hampton Court (020) 7928 0960

23 River Thames Great River Race: Chinese dragon boats and lots more between Richmond and Greenwich (020) 8398 9057

27 Wembley Horse of the Year Show – *till 1 October* (020) 8900 9282

OCTOBER

1 Trafalgar Square Pearly Kings' and Queens' Service at St Martin-in-the-Fields: since the 19th c, best occasion to see kings and queens in traditional button covered costumes (020) 7930 0089

12 Olympia Festival of Fine Wine and Food – *till 15 October* (020) 7453 5340

22 Trafalgar Square Trafalgar Day Parade: naval parade in memory of the Battle of Trafalgar (020) 7928 8978

NOVEMBER

5 Hyde Park London to Brighton Veteran Car Run sets off (01753) 681736

11 City of London Lord Mayor's Show: from Guildhall to Royal Courts of Justice (020) 7606 3030

12 Whitehall Remembrance Day Service and Parade at the Cenotaph (020) 7414 2357

16 Kensington Town Hall National Honey Show – *till 18 November* (01303) 254579

26 Earls Court Royal Smithfield Show – *till 29 November* (020) 7370 8226

DECEMBER

14 Olympia International Showjumping Championships – *till 18 December* (020) 7370 8206

31 Trafalgar Square New Year's Eve Celebrations (020) 7932 2041

Please let us know what you think of places in the *Guide*. Use the report forms at the back of the book or simply write us a letter.

LONDON INDEX

SCOTLAND

South Scotland includes Edinburgh (a great city for a short break) and Glasgow (lots to see here, too), and many of the most interesting places to visit. It has some charming and very peaceful countryside. A three-hour drive will get anyone living north of Manchester or York well into South Scotland. Beyond that, you really need a longer stay to make the driving worth while. Rail and air, of course, bring Scotland much closer. The fastest trains do the London–Edinburgh run in around four hours, and there are plans to improve the less reliable London–Glasgow service.

East Scotland has a marvellous variety of scenery, from Highland grandeur to placid lochs and rich valleys, from intimate fishing villages and sandy beaches to rugged cliffs. There's also a great variety of interesting places to visit, and the fastest roads run up this side.

West Scotland is on the whole less populated, with a glorious and intricate series of mountain and coastal landscapes, with magnificent gardens, at their best in May and June. There are interesting family outings, though not nearly so many as in the South and East. We've defined this area as north of the Clyde and south of the Great Glen, with Loch Lomond marking its eastern edge.

North Scotland, everything north of the Great Glen, has fewer places to visit (and fewer visitors – part of its charm for many); there is magnificent scenery on the west coast and on Skye, a quieter sandy east coast, and some wild and desolate places in the north.

Outside Edinburgh, Glasgow and areas within easy reach, many places close over winter – and others change to shorter winter opening hours in September, rather than October (the usual month for a change in England). For the scenery, the best time to visit is May and June, when the days are very long, the weather is generally at least as fine as in high summer, and the roads are not yet clogged by summer crowds.

The Scottish Tourist Board do a card that will save money on autumn flights, trains, accommodation and attractions, as well as getting two-for-one entry to the properties of the National Trust for Scotland (NTS) and Historic Scotland (HS). This second organisation looks after most of the castles and abbeys we list. A good-value Explorer ticket admits you free to all their properties, for £12.50 (one week) or £17 (two weeks); from tourist information centres, or in advance (0131) 668 8800. Accommodation is generally very good value here.

Direct flights connect London and some regional airports with Edinburgh, Glasgow, Inverness and Aberdeen, with some local connections from there.

Please let us know what you think of places in the *Guide*. Use the report forms at the back of the book or simply write us a letter.

South Scotland

Edinburgh is a winning city; lots going on elsewhere too.

Edinburgh looks great, and even repeated visits won't exhaust its store of treasures – including new places like the spectacular Our Dynamic Earth centre alongside its more historic side. Here, too, you can rediscover the pleasures of walking from place to place. The Festival is in August and September (when to go if that appeals, a time to avoid otherwise).

This part of Scotland has an abundance of ancient and evocative castles, romantic ruined abbeys, and some glorious gardens and grand houses such as Culzean Castle, Traquair, lavish Manderston at Duns and Mount Stuart on Bute. The new inventions discovery centre at Stevenston is an eye-opener. Glasgow may lack Edinburgh's easy charm, but has abundant vitality, and again masses of interesting places to visit – almost all free. And we're looking forward to the exciting new science centre there which looks like opening in 2001.

There are plenty of enjoyable family outings, most notably in New Lanark, Dalkeith, Largs – and Edinburgh's zoo.

The Borders hills are grand and relatively little-visited – peaceful get-away-from-it-all walking. A Freedom of the Fairways Tourist Board pass covers a round on the finest Borders golf courses. The gentler south-west corner is one of Britain's friendliest areas, with relatively few tourists.

Where to stay

AUCHENCAIRN NX8249 **Balcary Bay** *Auchencairn, Castle Douglas Kirkcudbrightshire DG7 1QZ (01556) 640217* **£106,** plus special breaks; 17 rms with fine views. Once a smugglers' haunt, this charming and much liked hotel has wonderful views over the bay, neat grounds running down to the water, comfortable public rooms (one with a log fire), a relaxed friendly atmosphere, good enjoyable food inc super breakfasts, and lots of walks; cl Dec–Feb.

BEATTOCK NT0603 **Auchen Castle** *Auchen, Beattock, Moffat, Dumfriesshire DG10 9SH (01683) 300407* *****£95,** plus special breaks; 25 pleasantly decorated rms, some in lodge. Smart but friendly country-house hotel in a lovely quiet spot with a trout loch and spectacular hill views, good food, and a peaceful, comfortable bar; disabled access.

CANONBIE NY3976 **Riverside** *Canonbie, Dumfriesshire DG14 0UX (013873) 71512/71295* **£80;** 7 chintzy rms, 2 in cottage. Civilised little inn with friendly owners, comfortable communicating bar rooms, open fire, attractive furnishings, good imaginative food with home-made breads and preserves and using top-quality produce, a fine wine list, and marvellous breakfasts; cl first 2 wks Nov, last 2 wks Feb.

CLARENCEFIELD NY0768 **Comlongon Castle** *Clarencefield, Dumfries, Dumfriesshire DG1 4NA (01387) 870283* **£90;** 12 rms. 15th-c castle keep with 18th-c mansion house adjoining – suits of armour and a huge fireplace in the oak-panelled great hall, good food in the Jacobean dining room, and a relaxing drawing room; dungeons, lofty battlements, archers' quarters and haunted long gallery – candlelit tour before dinner if you like; disabled access; cl part Jan.

EDINBURGH NT2573 **Balmoral** *Princes St, Edinburgh EH2 2EQ (0131) 556 2414* *****£258,** plus special breaks; 186 luxurious rms. Splendid Victorian hotel with wonderfully opulent entrance hall, elegant day rooms, lovely flowers, particularly friendly helpful staff, and very good food in several restaurants; excellent leisure facilities; good disabled access.

EDINBURGH NT2574 **Drummond House** 17 Drummond Pl, Edinburgh EH3 6PL (0131) 557 9189 *£110; 4 charming rms. Georgian town house in a handsome square with antiques and fine rugs in elegant rooms, a warmly welcoming atmosphere, and good Scottish breakfasts; cl Christmas; no children.

EDINBURGH NT2572 **Elmview** 15 Glengyle Terrace, Edinburgh EH3 9LN (0131) 228 1973 *£85; 3 large rms. Quietly placed in fine Victorian terrace overlooking a park 15 minutes' walk from the castle and centre; elegantly furnished, good breakfasts and welcome; no children.

EDINBURGH NT2674 **Greenside** 9 Royal Terrace, Edinburgh EH7 5AB (0131) 557 0022 *£60; 16 individually decorated rms. Family-run hotel in Georgian terrace with a friendly atmosphere, big lounge, hearty breakfasts, and a quiet terraced garden.

EDINBURGH NT2574 **Howard** 34 Great King St, Edinburgh EH3 6QH (0131) 315 2220 *£245, plus special breaks; 15 luxurious rms. Civilised little 18th-c hotel with comfortable, elegant public rooms, courteous, friendly service and good food in the fashionable modern basement restaurant; cl 24–28 Dec.

EDINBURGH NT2776 **Malmaison** 1 Tower Pl, Edinburgh EH6 7DB (0131) 555 6868 £120; 60 stylish rms with CD players and satellite TV. Converted baronial-style seamen's mission in the fashionable docks area of Leith with very good food in the downstairs French brasserie, a cheerful café bar, gym, and friendly service; free parking; pets by arrangement; disabled access.

EDINBURGH NT2574 **Sibbet House** 26 Northumberland St, Edinburgh EH3 6LS (0131) 556 1078 £100; 5 good rms. Lovely little Georgian house with warmly friendly owners, comfortable public rooms filled with antiques, delicious breakfasts, and evening suppers on request; self-catering flats also; cl Christmas; no children.

ETTRICK VALLEY NT3017 **Tushielaw** Ettrick Valley, Selkirk TD7 5HT (01750) 62205 *£44, plus special breaks; 3 small but well furnished rms. Friendly little inn in a lovely spot on Ettrick Water; good imaginative restaurant food, intimate bar, fine views, own loch, and shooting and fishing (as well as birdwatching and walking); cl Mon–Weds from Nov–Mar; disabled access.

GATEHOUSE OF FLEET NX5954 **Cally Palace** Gatehouse of Fleet, Castle Douglas, Kirkcudbrightshire DG7 2DL (01557) 814341 £104, plus special breaks; 56 rms. 18th-c country mansion with marble fireplaces and ornate ceilings in the public rooms, a relaxed cocktail bar, enjoyable food in the elegant dining room (smart dress required), evening pianist and Sat evening dinner dance, helpful friendly staff; 18-hole golf course, croquet and tennis, indoor leisure complex with heated swimming pool, private fishing/boating loch; cl Jan, and wkdys in Feb; disabled access.

GIFFORD NT5367 **Tweeddale Arms** Gifford, Haddington, East Lothian EH41 4QU (01620) 810240 *£65, plus special breaks; 16 rms. Civilised old inn in a quiet village with comfortable sofas and chairs in the tranquil lounge, gracious dining room, wide choice of good daily-changing food, and charming service; disabled access.

GLASGOW NS5965 **Babbity Bowster** 16–18 Blackfriars St, Glasgow G1 1PE (0141) 552 5055 £70; 7 clean simple rms, showers. Warmly welcoming, rather continental place with decent breakfasts (served till late), attractively decorated airy bar, and a cheery first-floor restaurant which hosts a gallery as well as a programme of musical and theatrical events; cl 25 Dec–1 Jan.

GLASGOW NS5865 **Malmaison** 278 West George St, Glasgow G2 4LL (0141) 572 1000 £120; 70 smart rms. Stylishly converted Nonconformist church with striking central wrought-iron staircase, friendly young staff, enjoyable food in the basement brasserie, café/bar with all-day snacks, gym, and a relaxed no-frills atmosphere; disabled access.

GLASGOW NS5567 **One Devonshire Gardens** Glasgow G12 0UX (0141) 339

2001 **£174;** 27 huge, opulent rms. Elegant cosseting hotel a little way out from the centre, with luxurious Victorian furnishings, fresh flowers, exemplary staff, and fine modern cooking in the stylish restaurant; disabled access.

GULLANE NT4983 **Greywalls** *Duncar Rd, Gullane, East Lothian EH31 2EG (01620) 842144* **£200;** 23 individually decorated rms. Overlooking Muirfield golf course, this beautiful family-run Lutyens house has antiques, open fires and flowers in its comfortable lounges and panelled library, very good food and fine wines in the restaurant, impeccable service, and a lovely garden; cl Nov–Mar; disabled access.

INNERLEITHEN NT3336 **Traquair Arms** *Innerleithen, Peeblesshire EH44 6PD (01896) 830229* **£70,** plus special breaks; 10 comfortable rms. Very friendly inn with an interesting choice of good food in the attractive dining room, a cosy lounge bar, friendly service, the superb local Traquair ale on handpump, and nice breakfasts; cl 25–26 Dec, 1–2 Jan.

LOCKERBIE NY1283 **Dryfesdale** *Lockerbie, Dumfriesshire DG11 2SF (01576) 202427* **£87,** plus wknd breaks; 15 rms, 6 on ground floor. Relaxed and comfortable former manse in 5 acres; open fire in the homely lounge, good food in the pleasant restaurant, and lovely surrounding countryside; cl 24–26 Dec; good disabled access.

MAYBOLE NS3103 **Ladyburn** *Kilkerran, Maybole, Ayrshire KA19 7SG (01655) 740585* **£145,** plus special breaks; 5 rms. Quietly set family home in lovely wooded countryside with antiques, books and open fires in comfortable day rooms, and friendly staff; shooting and fishing can be arranged; self-catering flat also; cl 2 wks Nov, 4 wks Jan–Mar; no children.

MELROSE NT5433 **Burts Hotel** *Melrose, Roxburghshire TD6 9PN (01896) 822285* **£88,** plus special breaks; 20 rms. Welcoming 18th-c family-run hotel in a delightfully quiet village, close to abbey ruins; a coal fire in the bustling bar, residents' lounge, consistently popular imaginative food, exceptional breakfasts, and a decent wine list; cl for accommodation 24–27 Dec.

MELROSE NT5434 **Dunfermline House** *Buccleuch St, Melrose, Roxburghshire TD6 9LB (01896) 822148* ***£50;** 5 rms. Neatly kept Victorian terraced house nr abbey ruins, with good breakfasts and friendly owners.

MINNIGAFF NX4165 **Creebridge House** *Minnigaff, Newton Stewart, Wigtownshire DG8 6NP (01671) 402121* **£98,** plus special breaks; 19 rms. Attractive country-house hotel in 3 acres of gardens with a relaxed friendly atmosphere, open fire in the comfortable drawing room, cheerful bar, and big choice of delicious food inc fine local fish and seafood; disabled access.

NENTHORN NT6938 **Whitehill Farm** *Nenthorn, Kelso, Roxburghshire TD5 7RZ (01573) 470203* **£46;** 4 rms, 3 with shared bthrm. Comfortable farmhouse on a mixed farm with fine views, a big garden, log fire in the sitting room, and good home cooking; cl Christmas and New Year.

PEEBLES NT2344 **Cringletie House** *Cringletie, Peebles EH45 8PL (01721) 730233* **£130,** plus special breaks; 13 pretty rms. Surrounded by 28 acres of garden and woodland and with fine views, this turreted baronial mansion, run by the same couple for over 20 years, is very welcoming and quiet, with delicious food using home-grown vegetables, extensive Scottish breakfasts, and excellent service.

PORTPATRICK NX0154 **Crown** *Portpatrick, Stranraer, Wigtownshire DG9 8SX (01776) 810261* **£72;** 12 attractive rms. Atmospheric harbourside inn with a rambling and interestingly furnished old-fashioned bar, airy Art Deco dining room, good food with an emphasis on local seafood, excellent breakfasts, and carefully chosen wines.

PORTPATRICK NX0252 **Knockinaam Lodge** *Portpatrick, Stranraer, Wigtownshire DG9 9AD (01776) 810471* **£170 inc dinner,** plus special breaks; 10 individual rms. Lovely very neatly kept little hotel with comfortable, pretty rooms, open fires, wonderful food, and friendly caring service; the surroundings are dramatic, with lots of fine cliff walks; children over 12 in evening restaurant (high tea at 6); disabled access to restaurant only.

QUOTHQUAN NT0040 **Shieldhill** *Quothquan, Biggar, Lanarkshire ML12 6NA*

(01899) 220035 **£114,** plus special breaks; 16 pretty rms. Partly 13th-c hotel in a fine setting with comfortable oak-panelled lounge, open fires, library, particularly good food in the no smoking restaurant, and warm, friendly service.

SWINTON NT8347 **Wheatsheaf** *Swinton, Duns, Berwickshire TD11 3JJ* *(01890) 860257* ***£78,** plus special breaks; 6 rms with showers. Warmly friendly inn with exceptionally good food, a pleasantly decorated and relaxed main lounge plus small pubby area, separate locals' bar, and a no smoking front conservatory; garden play area for children; cl Christmas and New Year, first 2 wks Jan, last wk Oct.

TURNBERRY NS2005 **Turnberry Hotel** *Ayrshire KA26 9LT* *(01655) 331000* **£318,** plus special breaks; 132 stylish and comfortable rms. Grand Edwardian country house in a spectacular 360-acre coastal setting with 2 championship golf courses that are ranked among the best in the world. Elegant reception rooms, quite a choice of places to eat inc a very good restaurant using tip-top local produce – and plenty of sporting activities: 12-hole pitch and putt (plus the 2 18-hole golf courses), indoor swimming pool, health spa, gym, sauna, solarium, squash, and tennis courts; disabled access.

UPHALL NT0571 **Houstoun House** *Uphall, Broxburn, West Lothian EH52 6JS* *(01506) 853831* **£116,** plus wknd breaks; 72 comfortable rms, 26 in new extension. 17th-c house divided into 3 distinct buildings: fine food in 3 wood-panelled dining rooms, vaulted bars (one with a fire that burns nearly all year), quiet lounge, lovely grounds, and a leisure complex with swimming pool, sauna, gym, tennis courts and bistro; disabled access.

We welcome reports from readers

This *Guide* depends on readers' reports. Do help us if you can – in return, we offer a discount on the next edition to people who've helped us with reports for it. Tell us what you think about places already in it, and anything extra you think we should say about them. And send us your ideas for inclusion in the next edition: places to visit, eat at or stay in, attractive drives or walks, maybe even unusual interesting shops you know of. Use the card in the middle, the report forms at the end, or just write – no stamp needed: *The Good Britain Guide*, FREEPOST TN1569, Wadhurst, E Sussex TN5 7BR.

To see and do

SCOTLAND Family Attraction of the Year

! ᴆ EDINBURGH NT2573 **Our Dynamic Earth** (Holyrood Rd) One of the most exciting attractions to open in Britain over the last few years, this exemplary new exhibition somewhat modestly sets out to show the story of the planet – and does so remarkably well, thanks to hi-tech effects and state-of-the-art displays. Housed in a tented (some might say Dome-like) structure opposite Holyrood Palace, it cost a whopping £34 million to create, opening its doors for the first time in July 1999. Perhaps better than anywhere else it.shows how much museums have benefited from new technology; not so long ago an exhibition looking at the evolution of the world would have been fairly static and a tad too worthy to tempt in children. Here the tale is vividly illustrated by giant screens, dramatic sounds and commentary, and evocative smells, spread over 11 hugely different and often quite spectacular display areas. The State of the Earth section sets the scene, its mix of continually updated footage and changing population data showing how the world is changing all the time. From here a lift representing a time machine takes you down to the observation deck of a futuristic spaceship, from which you watch the Big Bang, before venturing out into a world of earthquakes and volcanoes, where the floor shakes, and lava creeps towards you. After that there's an effectively filmed helicopter flight over the glaciers of Scandinavia, and a fun section exploring the evolution of life, with a giant pterodactyl and sabre-toothed tiger, and a dinosaur's foot crashing through the roof. Later on there's a miniature aquarium, and an elaborately re-created tropical rainforest, with insects underfoot and torrential rainstorms every 15 minutes; be prepared to feel the rain unless you move fast – though there's a bit of a warning as the sky slowly darkens. The finale is a colourful film taking in images of storms, hurricanes, and sunsets, with a serious environmental message of course – but hearing it has rarely been so much fun. A typical visit takes around an hour and a half to two hours, and as it's undercover it's a good bet in any weather; there's a play area for younger children. They have a well-illustrated website: www.dynamicearth.co.uk. Meals, snack, shop, disabled access; cl Mon and Tues between Nov and Mar, and 24–25 Dec; (0131) 550 7800; £5.95 (£3.50 children). The family ticket is good value, at £16.95 for 2 adults and 3 children.

ALLOWAY NS3318

ᕼ ⌂ **Burns National Heritage Park** A key stop on the Burns Trail: the poet was born here in 1759. The associated local sites are grouped together under the above name. The introductory visitor centre, the **Tam o'Shanter Experience** (Murdochs Lane) is a multi-media show bringing Burns's famous poem vividly to life. Up the road you can explore the tiny rooms of the poet's birthplace, thatched **Burns Cottage**, and there's an adjacent museum of his life, with a good collection of manuscripts and letters. In the other direction, S of the centre, **Burns Monument** was built in 1823 to a fine design by Thomas Hamilton Jr, and is adorned with characters from Burns's poems sculpted by James Thorn. Snacks, shop, disabled access; cl 25–26 Dec, 1 Jan; (01292) 443700; £4.50 for all 3 sites.

ARRAN NS0037

⛴ ⌂ This island is just under an hour by ferry from Ardrossan (2 ferries a day in winter, more in season; a popular public-transport day trip from Glasgow), with summer ferries from Claonaig on Kintyre too; (01475) 650100 for ferry enquiries. It has a marvellous variety of scenery from subtropical gardens to mountain deer forest – and highly regarded (and beautifully set) golf courses. Brodick, the main settlement, has several places to hire bikes. The Kingsley on Brodick esplanade has decent home cooking, and the Ormidale Hotel has good-value food. On the opposite side of the island nr Machrie are several intriguing Bronze Age stone circles. Arran has a good circular walk up and down Goatfell, prominent for miles around, and you can follow the shore right around the N tip, the Cock of Arran. Up nr the waterside Catacol Hotel has decent food. There's a good walk on the W coast, from Blackwaterfoot to the King's Cave, which supposedly sheltered Robert the Bruce.

🏰 🌸 **Brodick Castle & Garden** Fine old castle, in lovely surroundings between the sea, hills and majestic mountain of Goatfell. Partly 13th c, and extended in 1652 and 1844, it's very fierce-looking from the outside, but comfortably grand inside – even a little homely in places. There are almost a hundred antlered heads on the walls of the main staircase. It's surrounded by magnificent formal gardens, with the highlight the woodland garden started in 1923 by the Duchess of Montrose, inc many lovely rare and tender rhododendrons. Meals, snacks, shop, disabled access; castle cl Nov–Mar, garden and country park open all year; (01770) 302202; £5; NTS.

BALCARY POINT NX8149
⌂ ★ ☀ On the W side of sandy Auchencairn Bay, this makes for a good peaceful walk from the pretty village of Auchencairn. The Balcary Bay Hotel has good bar food, and lovely views from its terraces.

BALERNO NT1666
🌸 **Malleny House Garden** (off A70) Charming gardens that are home to a national collection of 19th-c shrub roses (best in late Jun), as well as 4 clipped old yew trees – the survivors of a dozen planted in 1603. Limited disabled access; (0131) 449 2283; around £1; NTS. The handsome Johnsburn House Hotel does good lunches.

BATHGATE NS9970
🏛 ☀ **Cairnpapple Hill** (just E of Torpichen, off B792) One of the most important prehistoric sites in the country, a stone circle and series of successive burial cairns that seems to have been used for around 3,000 years from Neolithic times to the first century BC, and especially during the second

millennium BC. Extraordinary views from this raw and atmospheric hilltop site, known locally as 'windy ways'.

BEARSDEN NS5472
🏛 **Roman Bath House** (Roman Rd) Probably the best surviving visible Roman building in Scotland, built in the 2nd c for the garrison at Bearsden Fort, part of the Antonine Wall defences; free. The appropriately named Fifty-Five BC (Drymen Rd) has decent food, as does the Beefeater (Station Rd).

BIGGAR NT0437
Several good museums here: with admission to one you get a 20% discount to all the others.

🜚 **Gasworks** (Gasworks Rd) This striking old building is now a museum on the coal-gas industry (open pm Jun–Sept; £1).

🜚 **Gladstone Court Museum** 🈸 (North Back Rd) Houses an entire reconstructed village street (cl am Sun, and all mid-Oct–Easter; £2).

🏚 🐄 **Greenhills Covenanters House** 🈸 (North Back Rd) 17th-c farmhouse originally at Wiston but moved piece by piece and reassembled here, with rare breeds of sheep and poultry; cl am, and all mid-Oct–mid-May; £1.

🜚 **Moat Park Heritage Centre** Good local history collections, and the centrepiece of the town's several worthwhile museums (cl am Sun, and all mid-Oct–Easter; £2).

❗ **Puppet Theatre** (just off A702) Very jolly; when they're not doing shows they sometimes do backstage tours. Teas, shop, disabled access (tel first – they have to remove some seats in the theatre); cl 25 Dec, 1 Jan, and maybe winter Sun; (01899) 220631 for programme and booking; shows £4.90.

BLANTYRE NS6958
🜚 **David Livingstone Centre** (Station Rd, off A724) The birthplace of the famous explorer, with a museum on his life and work. An African Pavilion looks at the continent today, with contemporary crafts, and there's an adventure playground in the landscaped grounds. Meals, snacks, shop, some disabled access; cl am Sun, and limited opening Nov–Mar – best to check first then; (01698) 823140; £2.95. The Cricklewood at Bothwell (B7071) is a good dining pub.

BUTE NS0864

♨ ☀ This popular Glasgow holiday island is a half-hour ferry trip from Wemyss Bay/Skelmorlie; it has a mix of fresh air and ebullient summer entertainments. In Rothesay, the island's main town, the seafront Black Bull has good food. There's lovely open country in the N, and its southern tip is rewarding too. There are grand sea views from the Kames Inn, which has food all day.

♨ **Bute Museum** (Stuart St, Rothesay) Decent museum, worth a visit (cl 24 Dec–4 Jan; £1.20). The gents' at the harbour, built in 1899, has ornate wall tiles and fine ceramic mosaic floors.

🏛 **Monastery of St Blane** Ruined Norman chapel in a delightful spot, a short way uphill from the road – just sheep and the occasional walker.

🏠 ❀ 🜨 **Mount Stuart House & Gardens** (off A844, just E of Upper Scoulag) Amidst this bracingly bleak landscape, the spectacular Victorian 'gothick' mansion is quite a shock; the elaborate rooms are splendidly over the top too. The 300 acres of landscaped grounds and woodland include several pretty gardens, as well as a pinetum of mature conifers and a nicely isolated stretch of sandy beach, reached via a lime tree avenue. Snacks, shop, disabled access; cl all day Tues and Thurs, and mid-Oct–beginning of May; (01700) 503877; £6, garden only £3.50. Scotrail do a special ticket (around £15) which includes entrance and train, ferry and bus travel from Glasgow Central or Strathclyde stations.

🏛 **Rothesay Castle** 13th-c; shop; cl am Sun, and in winter pm Thurs and all day Fri; £1.80.

CAERLAVEROCK NY0265

🏛 **Caerlaverock Castle** 13th-c, protected not just by its moat but by the wild swampy marshes around it, it has an unusual triangular inner courtyard, and elaborate projecting tops for dropping missiles on assailants. Snacks, shop, some disabled access; cl 12.30–1.30pm Nov–Mar, 25–26 Dec, 1–2 Jan; (01387) 770244; £2.50.

🦢 **Wildfowl & Wetlands Trust** The Caerlaverock salt marshes are a reserve with outstanding hide facilities and observation towers. Countless wildfowl flock here, especially barnacle geese; between Oct and Apr there are generally around 13,000 of them, very dramatic when they're all in flight. Snacks, shop, some disabled access; cl 25 Dec; (01387) 770200; £3.50 – discounts if you turn up by bike, foot or public transport. The Nith at Glencaple has good-value food.

CARDONESS NX5955

🏛 **Cardoness Castle** (A75) Well preserved 15th-c 4-storey tower house, overlooking the Water of Fleet; interesting fireplaces. Shop; cl winter wkdys; (01557) 814427; £1.80. A mile NE, Gatehouse of Fleet has places to eat.

CASTLE DOUGLAS NX7462

🏛 ♨ **Threave Castle** (off minor road Bridge of Dee–Townhead) The Black Douglas, Archibald the Grim, built this in the 14th c; 4 storeys high, it stands on an islet in the River Dee and you have to get a ferry across (ring the bell and the custodian will come to get you). Shop; cl Oct–Mar; (0131) 668 8800; £2, inc ferry; HS.

❀ **Threave Garden** (1m W off A75) The National Trust for Scotland's horticulture school, with plenty to see throughout the year in its walled garden and glasshouses. If you're there in spring, don't miss the massed display of over 200 varieties of daffodil. Meals, snacks, shop, some disabled access; visitor centre cl Nov–Mar; (01556) 502575; £4.40; NTS. The Royal Hotel has good-value food.

CLARENCEFIELD NY0669

🏛 **Comlongon Castle** (B725) 15th-c, unusually well preserved, with interesting original features inc dungeons, kitchen, great hall and even privies. Open am, but best to phone before visiting just to make sure; (01387) 870283; *£2.

COATBRIDGE NS7265

⬇ **Summerlee Heritage Trust** 🔲 (W Canal St) Ambitious centre looking at the local iron, steel and engineering industries. Lots going on, spread over 25 acres of a former iron works; the din from the working machines creates a real feeling of authenticity. Meals, snacks, shop, limited disabled access; cl 25–26 Dec and 1–2 Jan; (01236) 431261; free (tram 60p).

☺ **Time Capsule** (Buchanan St) Fun – swimming pools and leisure centre with a loose historic theme: water chutes whizz you through the origins of man, and a woolly mammoth holds court in the centre of the ice rink; (01236) 449572.

CRAMOND NT1877

★ Charming preserved former fishing village, the once-humble cottages now snapped up by Edinburgh's professionals.

🏚 **Lauriston Castle** Interesting, with mostly Edwardian décor and antiques; shop, disabled access; cl Fri, and wkdys Nov–Mar; (0131) 336 2060; £4.50.

⚓ **River Almond walk** W of Edinburgh, from the Cramond Brig Hotel on the A90, you can walk along the wooded valley to Cramond, cross the Almond by ferry, then go along the shore past Dalmeny House, and finish below the Forth Bridge at South Queensferry. There are frequent buses back to the start, and to Edinburgh.

CREETOWN NX4759

⚱ **Gem Rock Museum** (Chain Rd) Enormous private collection of gem stones and minerals, some displayed in an atmospheric crystal cave. Also an unusual fossilised dinosaur egg. Snacks, shop, disabled access; cl wkdys Dec–Feb (but worth phoning); (01671) 820357; £2.75.

CULZEAN NS2310

🏰 ❀ ♣ **Culzean Castle** (pronounced 'Cullane') A day here is one of the most popular outings in the region. The 18th-c mansion is one of great presence and brilliance, and the 563 acres of grounds are among the finest in Britain, lushly planted and richly ornamental, with woods, a lake, an abundance of paths, bracing clifftop and shoreline walks, and an 18th-c walled garden. The house was splendidly refashioned by Robert Adam, and has been well restored to show off his work to full effect. Meals, snacks, shop, disabled access; house cl Nov–Mar, park open all year; (01655) 760274; £7 park and castle, £3.50 park only; NTS. You can stay in rather smart self-contained apartments on the top floor; the harbourside Anchorage in the pleasant village of Dunure (off A719 N) does decent lunches.

DALKEITH NT3167

🦋 **Edinburgh Butterfly & Insect World** (Dobbies Nursery, off A720 at Gilmerton junction) Gloriously coloured exotic butterflies, as well as scorpions, tarantulas, a bee garden, and rainforest frogs. Handling sessions mean you can get even closer to some of the animals. Meals, snacks, shop, disabled access; cl 25–26 Dec, 1–2 Jan; (0131) 663 4932; £3.85. The Sun (Lothianbridge – A7 S) has good-value food.

DIRLETON NT5184

🏰 **Dirleton Castle** (A198) Grandly rebuilt after a siege in 1298, only to be destroyed again in 1650. It has a charming garden planted in the 16th c, with ancient yews and hedges around a bowling green. Cl 25–26 Dec, 1–2 Jan; (01620) 850330; £2.50. The Castle Hotel and Open Arms in this pleasant golfing village are both good for lunch.

DRYBURGH NT5932

🏰 ❀ **Dryburgh Abbey** Remarkably complete ruins of one of David I's monasteries, in a lovely setting among old cedars by the River Tweed – its graceful cloisters are very peaceful. Walter Scott is buried here (and on the B6356 N the signposted **Scott's View** is idyllic). Shop, some disabled access; cl am Sun, 25–26 Dec, 1–2 Jan; (01835) 822381; £2.50. The Buccleuch Arms at St Boswells is a civilised place for something to eat.

DUMBARTON NS4074

🏰 ❀ **Dumbarton Castle** (A82) Perched on a rock 73 metres (240ft) above the River Clyde, with dramatic views of the surrounding countryside. Most of what can be seen dates from the 18th and 19th c, though there are some earlier remains. Snacks, shop; open daily in summer, cl winter am Sun, pm Thurs and Fri; (01389) 732167; £1.80. The Ettrick in the picturesque Clydeside village of Old Kilpatrick has good-value food.

DUMFRIES NX9775

Another place with close Burns connections (you can get a ticket that covers all the related attractions). The **Globe Tavern** (off High St) has 2 rooms still very much as they were when this was his regular haunt (Anna Park, a barmaid here, bore his child).

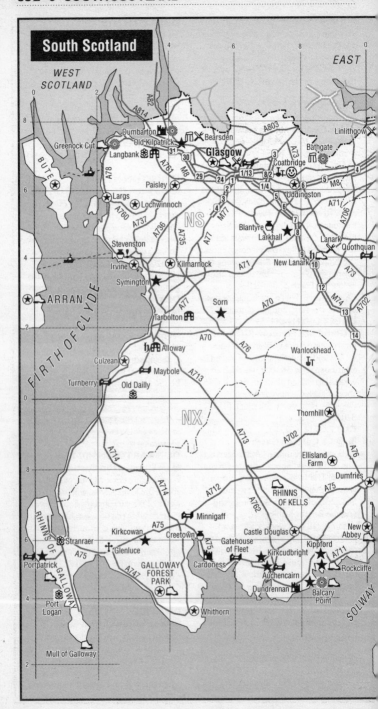

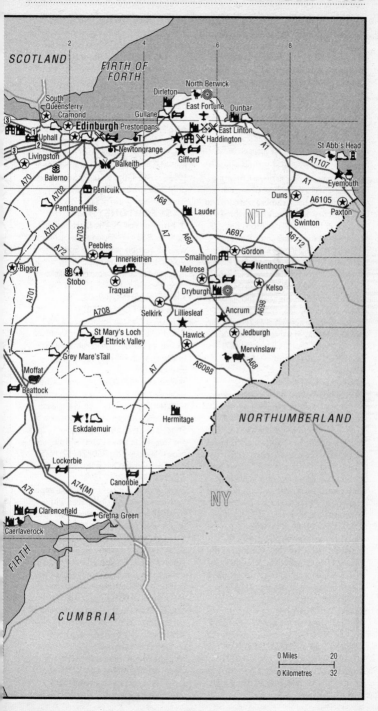

SCOTLAND

FIRTH OF FORTH

South Queensferry
Cramond
Uphall
Edinburgh Prestonpans
Livingston
Newtongrange
Balerno Dalkeith
Penicuik
Pentland Hills

Dirleton North Berwick
Gullane East Fortune Dunbar
East Linton
Haddington East Linton
Gifford

St Abb's Head
A1107
A1 Eyemouth

Duns A6105
Lauder Paxton
NT Swinton

A697

Biggar
Peebles
Innerleithen Smailholm Gordon
Stobo Melrose Nenthorn
Traquair Dryburgh Kelso
Selkirk Lilliesleaf Ancrum
St Mary's Loch Hawick Jedburgh
Ettrick Valley Mervinslaw
Grey Mare's Tail
Moffat
Beattock

Eskdalemuir Hermitage NORTHUMBERLAND

Lockerbie NY

Clarencefield Canonbie
Caerlaverock Gretna Green

FIRTH

CUMBRIA

0 Miles   20
0 Kilometres   32

🏠🍺 **Burns House** (Burns St) Where he lived for the 3 years before his death; has original letters and manuscripts along with the chair in which he wrote his last poems and songs. Shop; am Sun (all day in winter), winter lunchtimes and winter Mon, 25–26 Dec, 1–2 Jan; (01387) 255297; free. **Burns Mausoleum** (St Michael's churchyard) is the tomb of Robert Burns, his on-and-off wife Jean Armour, and their 5 sons; you can usually make an appointment to visit at Burns House.

✗🍺 **Museum & Camera Obscura** (Church St) In the tower of an 18th-c windmill, this has a camera obscura and local history. Shop, limited disabled access; cl 1–2pm, all day Mon, Sun Oct–Mar, plus am summer Sun, and 25–26 Dec, 1–2 Jan; (01387) 253374; museum free, camera obscura £1.50.

🍺 **Robert Burns Centre** (Mill Rd) Exhibition and audio-visual display, as well as an interesting scale model of the town at the time he wrote. Snacks, shop, disabled access; cl 1–2pm winter, am Sun (all day in winter), and winter Mons, 25–26 Dec, 1–2 Jan; (01387) 264808; £1.50 for audio-visual exhibition.

DUNBAR NT6779

🏰⌒ The harbour here is pretty, with some picturesquely jagged fragments of the medieval castle in the John Muir Country Park, and good walks nearby, along the cliffs and by the marshy inlets of Belhaven Bay; the harbourside Starfish has good seafood. Quite a few good clean beaches nr here, notably Belhaven, nearby Whitesands Bay, and the one at Thorntonloch a few miles down the coast.

DUNDRENNAN NX7547

🏰 **Dundrennan Abbey** (A711) Ruined Cistercian abbey famous as the place Mary, Queen of Scots is thought to have spent her last night in Scotland. Cl am Sun, winter wkdys; (01557) 500262; £1.50.

DUNS NT8054

🐄🏠 **Crumstane Farm Park** (2m E, off A6105) Children enjoy this cheerful place; cl Tues and all Oct–Easter; (01361) 883268; £2. Off the A6112 from Duns is **Edin's Hall Broch**, one of very few such Iron Age strongholds in the Lowlands.

🏠🕸🍺 **Manderston** (2m E, off A6105) Splendidly lavish house built for the plutocrat racecourse owner Sir James Miller; he told the architect to spare no expense, so ended up with the world's only silver staircase. Other gloriously extravagant parts are the painted ceilings, and a ballroom decorated in Miller's racing colours. Also fine formal gardens, and an unusual biscuit-tin museum. Teas, shop, limited disabled access; open pm Thurs and Sun mid-May–Sept, and pm bank hol Mon; (01361) 883450; £5.50, £3.50 grounds only. The Wheatsheaf at Swinton isn't far, for a very good meal.

EAST FORTUNE NT5578

✈ **Museum of Flight** (East Fortune Airfield, B1347) Good range of aircraft, with 35 aeroplanes from a Spitfire to a Vulcan bomber, and displays on famous flyers and air traffic control. Snacks, shop, disabled access; cl 25, 31 Dec, 1 Jan; (01620) 880308; £3.

EAST LINTON NT5875

🏰 **Hailes Castle** (minor road SW) Another brief stopping point for Mary, Queen of Scots, now in ruins, but lovely in spring, with wild flowers along the stream; free.

✗ **Preston Mill** (B1407) One of the oldest working water-driven oatmeal mills left. It's a pretty spot with geese and ducks, with an old dovecot nearby. Shop, limited disabled access; cl 1–2pm, am Sun, wknd ams in Oct, and all Nov–May; (01620) 860426; £2; NTS. The Drovers Inn has good food.

EDINBURGH NT2573

Edinburgh is a city of great visual appeal, with lots of interesting places within a pleasant walk of each other; the Festival is in August (when to go if that appeals, a time to avoid otherwise). This is one of Britain's most rewarding cities for visitors, whether you've been dozens of times before or are popping in for the first time. It's dominated by the ancient silhouettes of Edinburgh Castle on its castle cliff and of the long erratic line of tall, narrow Old Town buildings stretched along beside it. Up here narrow streets and alleys with steep steps between them and courtyard closes leading off have a real flavour of the distant past, with a good many interesting ancient buildings (and a lot of the city's antiquarian bookshops and other interesting specialist shops). When the authorities decided to redevelop the city in the 18th c, they did it not by knocking down the medieval buildings, but instead by creating an entirely new part of the city, working from scratch. The resulting New Town is a masterpiece of spacious Georgian town planning, stretching out handsomely below the steep crag of Castle Rock and its medieval skyline. As in most cities, there's a hop-on hop-off tour bus, and the ticket gives discounts to some of the places to visit. Walking tours in the evenings are often led by students. The regular bus services have good-value daily and weekly passes, and it is worth getting used to the public transport: the city council has come up with a radical road-pricing scheme to ease congestion and cut pollution, which they hope will be running this year. You can save money with the Edinburgh for Less scheme, which gives discounts at some restaurants and attractions (inc the castle) for up to 4 days; it's on sale in information centres. Edinburgh does put on its best clothes and best events for its Festival; it's easier to see, and truer to itself, at other times of year. If you do visit the Festival, make sure you've got accommodation sorted out well in advance. Edinburgh's pubs and bars are a special delight, chatty places often of great character. Among the best for atmosphere are the Bow Bar (Victoria St), Bannerman's Bar (Cowgate), Bennets Bar (Leven St), Café Royal and Guildford Arms (both West Register St), Cumberland (Cumberland St), Athletic Arms (Angle Park Terrace/Kilmarnock Rd), Kays Bar (Jamaica St W) and Milnes (Rose St); for food too, the Abbotsford, Kenilworth and Milnes (all Rose St), Starbank (Laverockbank Rd), Golf Tavern (Wrights Houses), Braidwoods (West Port) and Ship on the Shore (The Shore, Leith). The corner lobby bar of the Balmoral Hotel is a relaxing spot at the hub of the town. For a fuller meal, the city has a remarkable number of good-value bistro-style restaurants (as well as the places we mention in the **Where to eat** section). There are lots of good

shops dotted around town, especially on or near **Princes St** – its tall, mainly Georgian buildings lining just the one side, giving an expansive view across the sunken gardens to the castle. Parallel with here is George St, with some superior shops, while Rose St, an alley between the two, has plenty of pubs and cafés. More bars around the **Grassmarket** and **Lawnmarket**, a lively area of the Old Town; Victoria St here has interesting shops, notably that of Ian Mellis, who specialises in Scottish, Irish and English farm cheeses. Valvona & Crolla on Elm Row is a dazzling delicatessen.

✹ △ ⌂ **Arthur's Seat** Out beyond Holyrood in Holyrood Park is this saddleback mountain, a great volcanic mass giving a wonderful panorama over the city, and a pleasant place for wandering, with a hill fort on top and the largely unspoilt Duddingston village below it (the Sheep Heid here is a good pub).

△ ✹ **Blackford Hill** Virtually a mountain within the city, giving walkers great views of Edinburgh.

⚓ *Britannia* Displays about the yacht and its royal past on an onshore visitor centre, and a chance to explore 5 decks of the ship in which the Queen and Prince Philip have cruised the world. Snacks, shop, disabled access; cl 25 Dec, 1–2 Jan; (0131) 555 5566; £6.50.

✹ **Calton Hill** Dominating the E end of Princes St, with magnificent views over the city. An unusual sight up here is a romantic Doric colonnade, intended to be a full replica of the Parthenon (until the money ran out).

! **Camera Obscura** (Castlehill) Up at the top of the Royal Mile, these 19th-c revolving lenses and mirrors create unique panoramas of the city as soon as the lights go down, with a good commentary; best on a sunny day. Shop; cl 25 Dec, 1 Jan; (0131) 226 3709; £3.95.

🏛 ♭ **Canongate Tolbooth** (Canongate) This elaborate building houses an excellent social history exhibition, **The People's Story**, with reconstructions built very much around first-hand accounts of Edinburgh life. Shop, disabled access; cl Sun (exc pm during Festival), 25–26 Dec, 1 Jan; (0131) 529 4057; free.

⚙ 🏛 **Clan Tartan Centre** (Leith Mills, Bangor Rd) Displays of various clans and their costume, computers that allow you to trace your own Scottish heritage, and a factory shop with good-value Pringle knitwear and tweeds. Meals, snacks, shop, disabled access; cl 25 Dec, 1 Jan; (0131) 553 5161; free.

🏰 ⚙ **Edinburgh Castle** Perched on its hill above the city, this is a place of great magnetism; it's been a fortress since at least the 7th c, and excavations show there's been a settlement here for 4,000 years. The oldest building today is the beautiful St Margaret's Chapel, thought to have been built in the 12th c and little changed since. Other highlights include the apartments of Mary, Queen of Scots, Mons Meg (the 15th-c Belgian cannon with which James II cowed the Black Douglases), the Scottish Crown Jewels, and for romantics the Stone of Destiny or Scottish coronation stone, now returned by England which had seized it 700 years ago. Glorious views from the battlements, over the Firth of Forth to Fife beyond. You can wander around on your own, but the official guides are a great bonus – they leave from the drawbridge, several times a day. Meals, snacks, shop, disabled access; cl 25–26 Dec; (0131) 225 9846; £6.50 (inc audio tour). If you're around at lunchtime, look (and listen) for the firing of the One o'Clock Gun from the parapet.

🐧 **Edinburgh Zoo** (Corstorphine Rd; A8 W) Best known for its Penguin Parade every day at 2pm (Apr–Oct), but plenty of other rare and odd-looking animals around the attractive grounds. Children enjoy the yew-hedge maze loosely themed around Darwin's theory of evolution; it has several fountains along the way that periodically shoot out jets of water (summer only). Extra events and activities in summer hols. Meals, snacks, shops (special penguin and polar bear shops in summer), disabled access (though a little hilly); open every day (inc 25 Dec); (0131) 334 9171; £6.80.

🏛 **Georgian House** (Charlotte Sq) Archetypal period house, part of Robert Adam's magnificent terrace along the north side. The rooms and servants' quarters have been refurbished in the style of 1800. Shop, disabled access to ground floor only; cl am Sun, and Nov–Mar; (0131) 225 2160; £4.40; NTS. Close by, nr Queen St, beyond a further strip of gardens, is another Georgian area with some interesting shops. Hoggs, in the alley behind stately Great King St, has a wide choice of malt whiskies at low prices.

🏛 **Gladstone's Land** (Lawnmarket) Six-storeyed early 17th-c building, still with its arcaded front, and refurnished in period style. The walls and ceilings have remarkable tempera paintings. Shop; cl Nov–Mar; (0131) 226 5856; £3; NTS.

🏛 ⚙ **Huntly House** (Canongate) 16th-c, housing Edinburgh's main local history museum, with all the exhibits

---

Days Out

Edinburgh's Old Town: From Edinburgh Castle, walk down the Royal Mile past the Camera Obscura and Gladstone's Land; walk along Victoria St, Grassmarket and Candlemaker Row; snack at Bannerman's Bar (Cowgate); Royal Museum of Scotland; rejoin the Royal Mile, and continue past John Knox's House and Canongate Tolbooth to Holyrood Palace; Our Dynamic Earth; Arthur's Seat.

Glasgow's contrasts: Burrell Collection, and Pollok House; snack at the Willow Tearoom (Sauchiehall St); Tenement House; City Chambers, perhaps the Gallery of Modern Art; if you have time, the People's Palace, then walk along the Clyde Walkway.

Kidnapped country: Hopetoun House, South Queensferry; lunch at the Hawes Inn there, and look at the Forth bridges; boat to Inchcolm Abbey.

thoughtfully – even artistically – arranged. Shop; cl Sun (exc pm during Festival), cl 25–26 Dec, 1–2 Jan; (0131) 529 4143; free.

🏛 **John Knox House** (High St) The oldest house on the Royal Mile, where the great reformer is supposed to have died. Now looking every bit of its 500 years, it still has its original timber galleries, oak panelling and splendid painted ceiling. Snacks, shop; cl Sun, Christmas, New Year; (0131) 556 9579; £2.50.

🏛 👶 **Lady Stair's House** (Lady Stair's Close, off Lawnmarket) Named after its 18th-c occupant, this 17th-c building houses the **Writers' Museum**, a collection of manuscripts and objects associated with Robert Burns, Walter Scott and R L Stevenson. Shop; cl Sun exc Festival, 25–26 Dec, 1–3 Jan; (0131) 529 4901; free.

👶 **Museum of Childhood** (High St) The first of its type and still one of the best, an outstanding collection of games, toys and dolls from all over the globe. Shop, some disabled access; cl Sun (exc pm during Festival); (0131) 529 4142; free.

🖼 **National Gallery of Modern Art** (Belford Rd) Breathtaking collection inc outstanding recently acquired range of Surrealist works, and great works by Picasso, Barbara Hepworth and Lichtenstein. Meals, snacks, shop, disabled access; cl am Sun, 25–26 Dec, 1 Jan; (0131) 624 6200; free (maybe charges for temporary exhibitions).

🖼 **National Gallery of Scotland** (The Mound) Fine neo-classical building with particularly good examples of most European schools and periods. Plenty of Scottish paintings too, with many great works by Ramsay, Raeburn, Wilkie and McTaggart. Some art critics have objected to changes in the look of the gallery under its current director, but few would dispute that it's undoubtedly still one of the country's best. Look out for the rather incongruous portrait of one of the donor's dogs – it has to be hung here as a condition of the donation of other pictures. Shop, disabled access; cl 25–26 Dec; (0131) 624 6200; free (exc major exhibitions).

❄ **Nelson Monument** (Calton Hill) Best of all for the views of Edinburgh – if you can face the 31-metre (102ft) climb to the top. Every day at 1pm (exc Sun) the time ball drops as the gun at the castle goes off. Shop; cl am Mon; (0131) 556 2716; £2.

! 👶 **Our Dynamic Earth** See separate family panel on p.828.

🏛 🖼 🌸 **Palace of Holyroodhouse** (Canongate) Imposing yet human-scale palace with its origins in the Abbey of Holyrood, founded by David I. Later the court of Mary, Queen of Scots, it was used by Bonnie Prince Charlie during his occupation of Edinburgh, and is still a royal residence for part of the year. The oldest surviving part is James IV's tower, with Queen Mary's rooms on the second floor, where a plaque on the floor marks where her secretary Rizzio was murdered in front of her. The throne room and state rooms have period furniture, tapestries and paintings from the Royal Collection. Much more inviting than many English palaces, and in the last few years they've really improved visitor facilities. The palace gardens are open Apr–Oct. Shop, limited disabled access by prior arrangement; cl Good Fri, 25–26 Dec, and occasional other dates (if the Queen is in residence, for example) – best to check first on (0131) 556 1096; £5.50.

🏛 **Parliament House** (Parliament Sq) Just behind the cathedral, this was the seat of Scottish government until the Union of 1707, and now houses the supreme law courts of Scotland. Don't miss the fine hammerbeam roof in the Hall. Snacks, some disabled access; cl 1–2pm and wknds; (0131) 225 2595; free.

🌸 **Royal Botanic Garden** (Inverleith Row) Founded as a physic garden in 1670 at Holyrood and then transplanted here (just N of the centre) in the early 19th c. Covering 72 acres, it has various splendid themed areas, with a woodland garden, a peat garden, an arboretum and the Glasshouse Experience, inc palm houses, fern house and aquatic house. They keep the most comprehensive rhododendron collection in the country, and grow many other rare asiatic plants to perfection – particularly primulas and lilies and their more awkward relatives.

Guided tours leave from inside the West Gate at 11am and 2pm Apr–Sept. Meals, snacks, shop, disabled access; cl 25 Dec, 1 Jan; (0131) 552 7171; free (tours £2).

🏛 **Royal Mile** Between the castle and Holyrood Palace (for most people Edinburgh's 2 must-sees) is this largely medieval street, around which you'll find all sorts of interesting or historic houses and features, and quaint lanes leading off in all directions. Usefully, it's punctuated with cafés and bars in which to stop and work out your next move, starting with the old-world Ensign Ewart on the left as you leave the castle.

👹 **Royal Museum of Scotland** (Chambers St) A tremendous variety of collections, covering virtually anything you might care to poke around in, now shared between a gloriously light and spacious Victorian building, and its grand new counterpart next door. Children enjoy its intricate working scale models of early engines, but it has something for everyone . Meals, snacks, shop, disabled access; cl 25 Dec; (0131) 225 7534; £3.

❗ ❄ **Royal Observatory** (Blackford Hill) Good range of often lively astronomy displays, inc videos, computer games, and the biggest telescope in Scotland. In winter some telescopes are open till 9pm. Glorious views down over the city, and even as far as the Braid Hills. Shop, limited disabled access; cl am Sun, 24 Dec–2 Jan; (0131) 668 8405; £3.

🖼 🐝 **Royal Scottish Academy** (The Mound) Founded in 1826, in a second neo-classical temple alongside the National Gallery, with good changing exhibitions. Shop, disabled access; cl between exhibitions; (0131) 225 6671 for what's on; £2 for annual exhibition Apr–July. On either side, like a broad moat for the castle (this was a loch before the New Town was built), are well tended gardens.

✝ **St Giles Cathedral** (High St) The Royal Mile widens out briefly around Scotland's High Kirk, the city's most impressive ecclesiastical building, mainly 15th-c, but dating from around 1120. Topped with an ornate crown-like tower, it has monuments to famous Scots from Knox (minister here until

his death) to R L Stevenson.

🍸 **Scotch Whisky Heritage Centre** (Castlehill) Entertainingly illustrates the story of the national drink, starting off with a shortish journey in a barrel-shaped car through well put together sets and tableaux. The full tour is a useful introduction to the distilling process; if you haven't been to a real distillery it's a good substitute, and there's a decent sample and well stocked shop at the end. Meals, snacks, disabled access; cl 25 Dec; (0131) 220 0441; £4.95.

🏛 **Scott Memorial** (Princes St) After the castle, probably Edinburgh's most memorable building: remarkably ornate, with its handsome if mucky exterior. The historic crypt of St John's episcopal church on Princes St has interesting vegetarian and vegan food.

🖼 **Scottish National Portrait Gallery** (Queen St) The history of Scotland through a huge collection of portraits in a variety of media. Meals, snacks, shop, disabled access; cl 25–26 Dec; (0131) 624 6200; free. The **Museum of Scotland** is in the same building, with a fine collection of antiquities.

❄ ⌂ **Water of Leith** W of the centre and well worth exploring, often very picturesque and ravine-like. By its banks is the quaint little Dean Village, surprisingly close to the heart of the city, yet unaffected by all the New Town building above it. There's a fine series of Georgian crescents around Moray Pl. The river eventually winds down to Leith itself (a once prosperous and separate dockland area now swallowed up by the city, its waterfront reviving again with trendy bars). The Scottish Malt Whisky Society (Giles St), dedicated to cask strength top-quality malt whiskies, has a downstairs bar/restaurant.

ELLISLAND FARM NX9283
🏛 👹 🐎 This farm with Robert Burns connections is off the A76. The poet lived here from 1788 to 1791, trying unsuccessfully to introduce new farming methods. There are displays of material associated with Burns (who wrote *Tam o' Shanter* and *Auld Lang Syne* here), and cattle and sheep wander around much as they must have done

then. Lovely riverside walk. Shop, some disabled access; cl am Sun, and in winter all day Sun and Mon (though if you ring, you may find them open); (01387) 740426; £1.50.

ESKDALEMUIR NY2597

★ ! Beautifully set mountain village, famous for its cruel winter weather; it also has an unexpected Tibetan Buddhist temple and monastery.

⌂ **Borders hill walking** The Borders hills have plentiful solitary hill-walking. The Southern Upland Way (which makes a 212-mile coast-to-coast journey over the hills from Portpatrick to Cockburnspath) is a good basis for day walks, though large distances between places often make it hard to find focal points for walks.

EYEMOUTH NT9464

★ Understated family holiday seaside town around busy but pretty fishing harbour, with a decent beach. The Ship overlooking the harbour has reasonable food.

⚓ **Eyemouth Museum** 🔳 (Market Pl) Good local history museum in a former church, with magnificent tapestry commemorating the great fishing disaster of 1881 when 189 fishermen were lost at sea (cl Sun in Oct, all Nov–May; £1.75).

★ **St Abb's** A steep and pretty little seaside village nearby, with a sandy beach and old fishing harbour, little used now.

🐦 ⌂ 🏛 **St Abb's Head** The best of the E coast scenery for walkers; walk from Eyemouth or St Abb's, with a good path along the cliffs – noisily crowded with breeding seabirds in late spring, with high breezy walks, and a lighthouse. £1 parking, £1 visitor centre (cl Nov–Mar).

FIRTH OF FORTH NT4682

⌂ Excellent shoreside walks along the sands from Aberlady to North Berwick, with stop-off possibilities at Dirleton and Gullane; a good bus service connects the shoreside villages between North Berwick and Edinburgh, though the hinterland is dull.

GALLOWAY FOREST PARK NX3672

🐦 ❀ ⌂ Attractive and easily accessible, taking in around 100 lochs, 300 miles of river, great views, and thousands of hectares of forest,

mountain and moorland. Many of the trees are fairly recent replantings, the original woodland having from the 15th c onwards rapidly fallen victim to the demand for timber. Many of the lochs are ringed by waymarked walks and trails, and there are plenty of scenic drives and cycle routes. Visitor centres (open Apr–Sept only) at Kirroughtree, Glen Trool and Clatteringshaws all have exhibitions and information to help you make the most of the forests, inc details of where you can camp or fish, and the best places to spot wildlife. Stones mark 14th-c battles between Scotland and England, and the 1680s Killing Time, when Scottish covenanters were hunted down and killed in the government's attempts to impose bishops on the Scottish church.

⌂ **Loch Trool** There are particularly attractive trails around the loch, with a good informative summer visitor centre nearby. A memorial stone commemorates a 1307 battle between Robert the Bruce and the armies of Edward I.

❀ ⌂ **Merrick** The highest point in SW Scotland, a worthwhile but long and strenuous walk up from Glen Trool.

🐦 🐦 **Wood of Cree** One of the best surviving stretches of ancient forest, with an **RSPB reserve** among its trees and marshes.

GLASGOW NS5865

There's a real zing and vitality about this proud city, which is making great strides in its efforts to shake off its rather rough image. Besides the excellent art galleries and interesting museums, which the local director of museums has fought hard to keep free, it houses the Royal Scottish Orchestra (with a fine-sounding concert hall), the Scottish Opera and Scottish Ballet, and from next year, the exciting-sounding Glasgow Science Centre. Though there are many places to see and visit, a snag for visitors is that they are scattered around this sprawling city: the Burrell Collection, the most interesting place of all, is out in the suburbs. It's worth investing in a Day Tripper ticket, which allows virtually unlimited bus and train travel not just in the city but as far out as Ayr and Lanark. Besides the restaurants and bars mentioned in

Where to eat, Glasgow is full of places to eat out in, formal and informal; interesting and undaunting pubs and bars include the Auctioneers (St Vincent Pl), Cask & Still (Hope St), Counting House (George Sq) and Horseshoe (Drury St).

⚜ **Botanic Gardens** (730 Great Western Rd) Sloping gently down to the River Kibble, these are famous for their fantastic glasshouses, particularly the half-acre Kibble Palace, with its soaring tree ferns interspersed with Victorian sculpture. Disabled access; main glasshouse cl am wknds; (0141) 334 2422; free.

⚸🖼 **Burrell Collection** (Pollok Country Park) A couple of miles out in the suburbs, but not to be missed – and rarely gets too crowded. Splendidly and imaginatively housed in a modern building created to show its different parts to perfection, the huge collection – far too much to see at one go – includes Egyptian alabaster, Chinese jade, oriental rugs, remarkable tapestries, medieval metalwork and stained glass, even medieval doorways and windows set into the walls, as well as paintings by Degas, Manet and Rembrandt among others. Good meals and snacks, shop, disabled access; cl 25–26 Dec, 1–2 Jan; (0141) 287 2550; free, though you may have to pay for parking.

🏛 **Charles Rennie Mackintosh tours** 🚌 Sauchiehall St, a link between the museum/university quarter and the centre, is an ordinary shopping street, but well worth the walk for the ground-breaking designer and architect's most famous building, the **Glasgow School of Art** (Renfrew St, just off; the tours are highly recommended, (0141) 332 9797), and the decoratively mirrored **Willow Tearoom** (open till 5pm), furnished to his designs, too. Shop, disabled access; cl Sun; £5. As well as other places we mention with Mackintosh connections, you can buy works after him at the Glasgow Style Gallery on Gt Western Rd.

⌂ ⚓ **Clyde walks** A walkway tracks along the Clyde now that its waterfront has been cleaned up. The veteran pleasure steamer *Waverley* makes some runs from here Jun–Aug –

(0141) 221 8152 for times. Some Clydeside pubs well outside Glasgow with decent food and good sea views include the Cardwell at Cardwell Bay in Gourock and the Spinnaker there, and the Lookout down in Troon Marina.

🖼 **Gallery of Modern Art** (Queen St) Glasgow's latest big gallery, concentrating on art by living British artists – not just Scottish. Lively café-bar (open some evenings too), shop, good disabled access; cl 25–26 Dec, 1–2 Jan; (0141) 229 1996; free.

⚸🖼 **Glasgow Art Gallery & Museum** (Kelvingrove Park) Huge Victorian building with remarkably rich collection of paintings, especially strong in works by the French Impressionists, Post-Impressionists, and Scottish artists from the 17th c. Also sculpture, silver, porcelain, armour, ethnography and natural history. Meals, snacks, shop, disabled access; cl 25–26 Dec, 1–2 Jan; (0141) 287 2699; free.

✝ **Glasgow Cathedral** 12th-c, dedicated to St Mungo, the founder of the city. It's very well preserved, though most fittings date from the 19th c; best parts are the crypt, a gracefully vaulted affair built in the mid-13th c, and the Blackadder aisle; summer shop; cl 25–26 Dec, 1–2 Jan. The spectacular Necropolis graveyard is closed for restoration, but there's a fine overview from the cathedral. The area around here is the oldest part of Glasgow, though not the most interesting.

⚜ **Greenbank Garden** (Flenders Rd, Clarkston, off A726) Aims to encourage and help owners of small gardens, so has lots of different shrubs and flowers to spark ideas. Also garden and greenhouse designed to meet the needs of disabled gardeners, with advice on specially designed tools. Summer teas, shop, disabled access; cl 25–26 Dec, 1–2 Jan; house open pm Sun only Apr–Oct; (0141) 639 3281; £3.50; NTS.

🏛 ⚜ **House for an Art Lover** (Bellahouston Park) Built to 1901 designs by Charles Rennie Mackintosh, with an exhibition on him, and contemporary art exhibitions. Meals, snacks, shop, disabled access; cl winter Fri and best to phone for other winter wkdy opening times; (0141) 353 4449;

£3.50. The Empire Exhibition of 1938 was held on these 171 acres, which now comprise a walled garden, sunken garden and sweeping lawns.

🖼 **Hunterian Art Gallery** (Hillhead St) Dr William Hunter, the 18th-c physician, bequeathed the core of fine paintings which form the basis of this beautifully hung collection. A grand range of works by Whistler, interesting and well chosen contemporary British art and sculpture, and an amazing re-creation of the home of Charles Rennie Mackintosh (cl 12.30–1.30pm), the designer/architect whose exuberant yet very disciplined and clean-lined Art Nouveau buildings stand out among the more traditional solidity of much of Glasgow. Shop, disabled access with prior notice; cl Sun; (0141) 330 5431; free.

☋ **Hunterian Museum** (Hillhead St) Scotland's oldest museum, housing the University collections of ethnographic, palaeontological and anthropological material, along with lots of archaeology, and a coin display. Shop, disabled access; cl Sun and public hols; (0141) 330 4221; free. The exhibitions were also founded by Dr Hunter (*see above*).

🜨 ⚘ 🐾 **Linn Park** (Cathcart/Castlemilk) Lots to do – riverside walks, nature trails, children's zoo, golf course, and collections of British ponies and highland cattle, as well as a ruined 14th-c castle, and an adventure playground for the disabled (prior arrangement preferred). Visitor centre open pm wknds only; (0141) 637 1147; free.

🖼 **McLellan Galleries** (Sauchiehall St) Spacious and well lit, these have good changing art exhibitions; snacks, shop, disabled access; cl 25–26 Dec, 1–2 Jan; (0141) 332 7521; free.

🏛 ! **Merchant City** The area around George Sq and Buchanan St was built on a grid plan in the 19th c, and visually has something in common with New York City – Americans are said to feel at home here. With its proud Victorian buildings cleaned back to their warm sandstone, this smart shopping quarter is the city's most comfortable area to stroll around. The City Chambers (George Sq) is a spectacular monument to 1880s civic pride, marble everywhere; free tours. The Counting

House is a splendid new pub in an opulent converted bank nearby. There are café-bars and bistros off Princes Sq, and antique stalls in Victorian Village (West Regent St). On the SE edge of this area, between Gallowgate and London Rd past the Tolbooth, the **Barras** (barrows) is an entertaining weekend flea-market. With around 800 stalls it's one of the biggest covered markets in the world, great for bargains or just passing time; try the plump fresh clappie doos (mussels).

🎭 ✿ 🏰 ⌂ **Mugdock Country Park** (N Glasgow) Good strolling ground, with 2 castle ruins, a view over Glasgow, and an attractive loch.

🚋 **Museum of Transport** (Kelvin Hall, Bunhouse Rd) Comprehensive collection of vehicles, from trams to ships, very well displayed; the walk-through car showroom is arranged as if some were for sale, with original prices displayed on the windscreens. Meals, snacks, shop, disabled access; cl 25–26, 31 Dec, 1–2 Jan; (0141) 287 2720; free.

☋ 🎭 **Museum quarter** NW of the centre, the West End, Kelvingrove and the University quarter have some elegant streets, the main concentration of museums, and the botanic gardens.

☋ 🎭 **People's Palace** (Glasgow Green) Very enjoyable and recently refurbished social history museum looking at Glaswegians over the centuries, set in a park just SE of the centre; disabled access; cl 25–26 Dec, 1–2 Jan; (0141) 5540 223; free. The museum's café is in the adjacent **Winter Gardens**, a massive conservatory with huge tropical plants.

🎭 **Pollok Country Park** (SW Glasgow) One of the best of the several parks and gardens you'll find around Glasgow, with waterside and woodland trails, guided pm Sun walks, a rose garden, shire horses, and a herd of highland cattle. Shop, snacks, disabled access; cl 25–26 Dec, 1–2 Jan; (0141) 616 6410. £3.20 (free in winter).

🖼 **Pollok House** (Pollok Country Park, SW Glasgow) Treasures here include silver, ceramics and porcelain, but it's the paintings that stand out, with a collection of Spanish masters such as Goya and El Greco cannily acquired in the days when they were greatly undervalued. Snacks, shop; cl 25–26 Dec, 1–2 Jan; (0141) 616 6410; £3.20.

🌸 **Provan Hall** (Auchinlea Park, B806 E) Mansion house virtually unchanged since the 16th c, in a pleasant park with a variety of formal and informal gardens inc a herb garden. Disabled access; cl wknds and public hols, 25–26 Dec, 1–2 Jan; (0141) 771 4399; free; NTS.

🌸 ⛲ **Rouken Glen Park** (Thornliebank) A place of great tranquil beauty, with a walled garden, gorgeous lawns, and woodland walks to a waterfall at the head of the glen.

📖 🌸 **St Mungo Museum of Religious Life** (Cathedral Precinct) Unique collection of art from all the world's major religions – and some rather obscure ones too. Everything from an Egyptian mummy mask to Dali's *Christ of St John of the Cross*, and in the grounds Britain's only permanent Zen garden. Meals, snacks, shop, disabled access; cl 25–26 Dec, 1–2 Jan; (0141) 553 2557; free.

🏛 ⛄ **Scotland Street School Museum** Designed by Mackintosh, this spectacular building originally had a capacity of 1,250 pupils in 21 classrooms. It now houses a lively museum dedicated to education with reconstructed classrooms. You can be measured in the medical room and even peek into the headmaster's office. Snacks, shop; cl am Sun, 25–26 Dec, 1–2 Jan; (0141) 287 0500; free.

🏛 **Tenement House** (145 Buccleuch St) One-floor late 19th-c flat giving a vivid impression of life for many Glaswegians at the turn of the 20th century. The same woman lived here from 1911 to 1965 and in that time scarcely changed a thing; its time-capsule quality was preserved by a subsequent owner, and then the flat, still with its original furnishings and fittings, was left to the National Trust for Scotland. Open pm Mar–Oct, cl Nov–Mar; (0141) 333 0183; £3.20; NTS.

🏵 **University of Glasgow Visitor Centre** (University Ave) Interactive displays on the history and life of the university (founded in 1451), with tours around some of its grander features, such as the Lion and Unicorn Staircase, Bute and Randolph Halls and Memorial Chapel. Snacks, shop, disabled access; cl all day winter Sun, plus am summer Sun, 25–26 Dec, 1–2 Jan; (0141) 330 5511; visitor centre free, tours (11am and 2pm Weds, Fri and Sat May–Sept, Oct–Apr just 2pm Weds) £2. You can stay in some of the university buildings during vacations.

🌸 🏛 **Victoria Park** (Victoria Park Dr North) Tree-lined park where the fossil remains in the Fossil Grove, some of them 230 million years old, were discovered by workmen digging a path in the late 19th c.

⌂ 🌸 **West Highland Way** Level walks can take in the early stages of the West Highland Way, which starts at Milngavie. The determined can press on along glen routes all the way up to Fort William – the scenery getting better all the way.

GLENLUCE NX1858

✝ **Glenluce Abbey** Ruined Cistercian abbey founded in the late 12th c, in beautiful surroundings. Limited disabled access; cl wkdys Dec–Mar; (01581) 300541; £1.80.

GORDON NT6439

🏛 🌸 📖 🌸 **Mellerstain House** (just W, off A6089) William and Robert Adam both worked on this striking Georgian house, which has impressive plasterwork and furnishings, and paintings by Van Dyck and Gainsborough. Every house in Scotland seems to have something that belonged to Bonnie Prince Charlie – this one has his bagpipes. Very pleasant terraced gardens and parkland, with fine views towards the distant hills. Meals, snacks, shop, limited disabled access; cl am, all day Sat, and Oct–Apr; (01573) 410225; £4.50. The Gordon Arms has decent food.

GREENOCK CUT NS2472

⌂ 🌸 Part of an elaborate abandoned water scheme for Greenock below, this allows a level walk meandering around a hillside terrace giving views into the Highlands.

GRETNA GREEN NY3167

❗ **Old Blacksmith's Shop** It's now tourists rather than runaway couples that flock to the Old Blacksmith's Shop in this little Borders village. More people come here than to just about any other Scottish attraction outside Edinburgh, despite the fact that there's really very little to see. An exhibition centre looks at the once thriving marriage business. Cl 25 Dec, 1 Jan; (01461) 338224; £2

GREY MARE'S TAIL NT1814

⌂ Spectacular **waterfalls**, a pretty walk from the A708 car park NE of Moffat, up a narrow glen. You can continue beyond them along Tail Burn to Loch Skeen.

HADDINGTON NT5173

★ A pretty market town; the comfortable George and Maitlandfield House hotels, and the correctly named Waterside Inn, all have above-average food.

🏛 **Lennoxlove** £ (B6369 S) The Duchess of Lennox (La Belle Stuart) gave this old house its unusual name in memory of her dead husband. Among reminders of other members of her family are the casket and death mask of Mary, Queen of Scots. In the grounds the Cadzow herd of white park cattle are said to be descended from the sacrificial cattle of the Druids. Meals, snacks; cl am, Mon, Tues, and Nov–Easter; (01620) 823720; £4.

HAWICK NT5014

🏰 ♭ **Drumlanrig's Tower** (Towerknowe) Fearsome-looking 16th-c tower with state-of-the-art displays of Borders history, some quite gripping. Shop, disabled access; cl Sun; (01450) 377615; £2.

🏵 ⌚ 🖼 **Hawick Museum & Scott Art Gallery** (Wilton Lodge Park) Made considerably more appealing by its setting, a park with riverside walks and gardens. Cl 12.30–1.30pm, am Sat and Sun, winter Sat, 25–26 Dec, 1–2 Jan; (01450) 373457; *£1.25.

HERMITAGE NY4995

🏰 **Hermitage Castle** Almost perfect from the outside, the well restored but very forbidding remains of a 14th-c Borders stronghold reeking of dire deeds. Shop, limited disabled access; cl Fri and end Nov–Easter; (01387) 376222; £1.80.

INNERLEITHEN NT3336

🏰 **Robert Smail's Printing Works** (High St) Fully restored Victorian printer's shop, with water-powered press; you can try your hand at metal typesetting and hand-print your own bookmark. Shop, limited disabled

access; cl 1–2pm, am Sun, and all Oct–Apr (exc Oct wknds); (01896) 830206; £2.50; NTS. The Traquair Arms is the place to eat.

IRVINE NS3138

❀ **Scottish Maritime Museum** (Gottries Rd) Down by the harbour, very much a working museum, with lots of restoration work on the good range of historic vessels. Snacks, shop, some disabled access (not to boats); cl Nov–Mar; (01294) 278283; £2. The nearby Keys has decent food (all day wknds).

⌚ 🖼 **Vennel Art Gallery** Art gallery and museum, and behind, a reconstruction of the Heckling Shop where, as a young man, an unwilling Burns tried to learn the filthy trade of flax dressing. Happily for him, during a New Year's Eve party his aunt knocked over a candle and burnt the building to ashes. Shop, disabled access; cl 1–2pm, all day Sun and Weds; (01294) 275059; free.

JEDBURGH NT6420

⌚ **Castle Jail** (Castlegate) Now a local history museum (cl Oct–Mar; £1.25).

🏰 **Jedburgh Abbey** The most complete of ruined 12th-c Borders monasteries founded by David I, and an impressive sight, despite its town setting. Imposing 26-metre (86ft) tower, splendid west door, and audio-visual show in visitor centre. Snacks, shops, disabled access; cl am Sun, 25–26 Dec, 1–2 Jan; (01835) 863925; £3. The Pheasant has decent food (and makes a point of having good-value pheasant in season). Just off the A68 S of town are the ruins of **Ferniehurst Castle**.

🏛 ⌚ **Mary Queen of Scots House** (Queen St) Charming 16th-c fortified dwelling where Mary had to prolong her 1566 stay because of a near-mortal fever (she was later to say she wished she'd died here). There's a good interpretation of her life. Shop; cl Dec–Mar; (01835) 863331; £2.

KELSO NT7035

🏛 🏵 **Floors Castle** (1m NW) Magnificent building designed by William Adam in 1721, much embellished the next century. It's reputed to be Scotland's biggest inhabited house, with a window for every day of the year. Splendid collection of tapestries and French furniture, and wonderful walled garden (best July–Sept). Good home-made meals and snacks, shop, disabled access; cl Nov–Apr; (01573) 223333; *£5.

⚊ Kelso Abbey The greatest and wealthiest of the 4 famous Borders abbeys, though today not much of the building remains. Cobbles (Beaumont St) and the Queen's Head (Bridge St) have good-value food.

KILMARNOCK NS4339

⚊ �ృ ♨ Dean Castle (off Glasgow Rd) Very well restored family home, housing a wonderful collection of medieval arms and armour, musical instruments, tapestries, and a display of Burns's manuscripts. It's surrounded by 200 acres of woodland, with nature trails, deer park, riding and other activities. Snacks, shop; cl am, and wkdys Oct–Mar; (01563) 522702; £2.50. The 18th-c Wheatsheaf in the pretty village of Symington on the other side of town has good original food.

KIPPFORD NX8355

★ Charming yachting place, usually plenty to watch in summer. The Anchor here is good.

LANGBANK NS3673

❀ ⌂ Finlaystone (A8, 1m W) Some say the garden here is the finest in Scotland – formal and walled, with woodland walks and adventure playgrounds. They have recently renovated some of the greenhouses, making them more accessible to the disabled. The house has connections with Robert Burns and John Knox (unlikely partners), as well as displays of dolls, Victorian flower books and Celtic art. Snacks (summer only), shop, disabled access; gardens open all year, must book to see house; (01475) 540505; £2.50, house £1.20 extra. The modern Langbank Lodge nearby has sensibly priced food (inc afternoon tea and scones) and incredible Clyde views.

LARGS NS2059

★ ⌂ The pick of the traditional Clydeside resorts, with boats across the narrow strip of water to the island of Great Cumbrae. The pleasure steamer Waverley calls here in summer, and Nardinis (Esplanade) is a vintage tearoom – or rather tea palace, with acres of immaculate tables and smartly

aproned motherly waitresses.

♭ Vikingar! ⌨ (Barrfields Centre, Greenock Rd) Lively look at the Vikings in Scotland, from their arrival to their defeat at the Battle of Largs. Very much an 'experience', with lots of interactive displays, and a multi-media show as the centrepiece. There's an adjacent swimming pool. Meals, snacks, shop, disabled access; cl 25 Dec–3 Jan; (01475) 689777; £3.75.

LAUDER NT5347

⚊ Thirlestane Castle (off A697) Charming old castle with recently restored assemblage of pictures, interesting collection of old toys (some of which children can touch), and some outstanding plasterwork in the 17th-c state rooms. The bed chamber was opened for the first time last season. Snacks, shop; open 21 Apr–31 Oct but cl Sat; (01578) 722430; *£5, £1.50 grounds only. The Eagle and Lauderdale Hotel are useful for lunch.

LINLITHGOW NT0578

⌂ House of the Binns (3m E, off A904) The home of the Dalyell family since the 17th c, with some splendid plaster ceilings and a varied collection of furniture and porcelain. Limited disabled access; cl am, all day Fri, and Oct–Apr; (01506) 834255; £3.90; NTS.

⚊ Linlithgow Palace The birthplace of Mary, Queen of Scots, a magnificently sombre lochside ruin. You can still see the chapel, great hall and a quadrangle with fountain. Shop, limited disabled access; (01506) 842896; £2.50. In the town a pleasant old tavern, the Four Marys, is named for her maids-in-waiting Mary Livingstone, Mary Fleming, Mary Beaton and Mary Seton, with relevant memorabilia.

LIVINGSTON NT0366

♭ ⌨ ✗ ⊟ Almond Valley Heritage Centre ⌨ (off A705) Friendly 16-acre museum, with lots to see inc working farm, watermill, and underground shale mine. Also trailer rides (summer wknds and summer hols), adventure playground, and demonstrations of milking and other seasonal activities. Meals, snacks, shop, disabled access; cl 25–26 Dec, 1–2 Jan; (01506) 414957; £2.20.

LOCHWINNOCH NS3558

♥ ❀ ♨ Nature Centre (Largs Rd)

RSPB bird reserve with fine views, good woodland and marsh nature trails, and several observation hides – one specially for disabled visitors. Wknd snacks (wkdys too July and Aug), shop, disabled access; cl 25–26 Dec, 1 Jan; (01505) 842663; *£2. The Mossend is a useful dining pub.

MELROSE NT5034

🏛 **Abbotsford House** (B6360 3m W) Set grandly on the River Tweed, this was the home of Walter Scott until his death in 1832. You can still see his mammoth 9,000-volume library, and several of the historical oddities he liked to collect, like Rob Roy's sporran. Snacks, shop, disabled access; cl am Sun (Mar–May and Oct), plus all Nov–mid-Mar; (01896) 752043; £3.50.

⌂ **Eildon Hills** Above the town, these are splendidly compact, giving a very pleasing ridge walk along the top.

🏯 **Melrose Abbey** The ruins are among the finest in the country – best in moonlight, as Scott says (though he admitted he never saw them thus himself). Look out for the wonderful stonework on the 14th-c nave (and the pig playing the bagpipes). Archaeological investigations now leave little doubt that this was the burial place of Robert the Bruce's heart. Shop; limited disabled access; cl am Sun Oct–Mar, 25–26 Dec, 1–2 Jan; (01896) 822562; £3.

🏵 **Priorwood Garden** (Abbey St) Specialises in flowers suitable for drying, with a herb garden and display orchard illustrating apples through the ages. Shop, disabled access; cl am Sun, and 24 Dec–1 Apr; (01896) 822493; £1; NTS.

🧸! **Teddy Melrose** (The Wynd) Unusually comprehensive and informative teddy bear museum, with resident bear-maker, and bear fairs in May, Aug and Nov. Snacks (inc award-winning coffee), shop, disabled access; cl 1–2pm, Jan–Feb; (01896) 822464; *£1.50. Besides the Burts Hotel, the King's Arms is useful for lunch.

MERVINSLAW NT6713

🐗 🦌 **Jedforest Deer & Farm Park** (A68) Working hill farm with deer as well as other animals inc hawks and several rare breeds. Good for children, and peaceful walks and trails nearby.

Snacks, shop, some disabled access; cl mid-Oct–Apr; (01835) 840364; £3.50.

MOFFAT NT0804

🐕 **Tweedhope Sheepdog Centre** (Hamerlands Farm, Selkirk Rd) Friendly place with demonstrations of working sheepdogs (11am and 3pm), and an exhibition. Shop, some disabled access; open wkdys Apr–Oct (wknds by appointment); (01683) 221471; *£2.50. The small town nearby still has some of the poise of its former days as a spa; the Black Bull, the Star (Britain's narrowest hotel) and the Moffat House Hotel all do decent food.

MULL OF GALLOWAY NX1530

⌂ Beautifully unspoilt, Scotland's SW toe; good coastal walking.

NEW ABBEY NX9562

⌂ ☀ **Criffel** The summit gives walkers an astonishing view of the English Lake District over the Solway Firth.

✗ **New Abbey Corn Mill** The pretty village has a restored 18th-c corn mill; snacks, shop; cl 1–2pm Apr–Sept, 12–1pm Oct–Mar, pm Thurs, all Fri, am Sun Oct–Mar; (01387) 850260; £2.30.

👗 **Shambellie House of Costume** (A710) Much extended in recent years, often dazzling displays of costume, thoughtfully arranged in appropriately furnished rooms. Shop; cl Nov–Mar; (01387) 850375; £2.50.

🏯 **Sweetheart Abbey** (A710) One of the most romantic ruins in the area, with a lofty arched nave open to the sky, and a touching story attached. Shop; cl am Sun, winter pm Thurs and all day Fri; (01387) 850397, 25–26 Dec, 1–2 Jan; £1.20.

NEW LANARK NS8841

🏚 Founded in 1785 and now the subject of a major conservation programme, this is Scotland's best example of an industrial village (off A73), with plenty to keep families amused for a good chunk of the day. Many of the old millworkers' buildings have been interestingly converted to modern accommodation, so it's very much a living village rather than a museum. The village can be busy at wknds; try and visit during the week if you can. Meals, snacks, shop, disabled access; cl 25 Dec, 1 Jan; £3.75. In Lanark itself the Crown (Hope St) has a decent restaurant.

⌂ **Falls of Clyde** The countryside

here is spectacular, with a short walk snaking around river cliffs through a verdant gorge to these falls that used to power the mill; a visitor centre here has lots of information on badgers (open pm wknds Nov–Easter, then daily till Oct, cl all Jan). The falls are dramatic when the hydro-electric station upriver opens the sluices.

NEWTONGRANGE NT3363

⚒ Scottish Mining Museum (Lady Victoria Colliery, A7) Vivid re-creation of mining days, both at the well restored pithead and back home, even in the tearooms. Meals, home-baked snacks, shop, limited disabled access; cl Dec–Jan; (0131) 663 7519; *£4.

NORTH BERWICK NT5585

⚘ ※ Scottish Seabird Centre (North Berwick Harbour) Every year over 150,000 seabirds return to the islands off this town, and this new £3m centre will use remote camera technology to allow visitors to study the birds in extremely close detail. Shop; café with wonderful views across the Firth of Forth to Bass Rock; disabled access. When we went to press, they had not yet confirmed their times and prices, so best to phone to check; (01620) 890202.

OLD DAILLY NS2401

✿ Bargany Gardens Fine ornamental trees, woodland walks winding through springtime glades of snowdrops, bluebells and daffodils, and a lily pond enveloped by azaleas and rhododendrons in late spring and early summer. Disabled access; cl Oct–Mar; (01465) 871249; donations.

PAISLEY NS4863

! Coats Observatory (High St) Displays on astronomy, meteorology and space flight. Shop, cl 1–2pm, all Mon; (0141) 889 2013; free.

⚘ ▣ Paisley Museum & Art Gallery (High St) Paisley is not just a place but a pattern, so as well as a very wide range of 19th-c art, the appealing museum has a marvellous collection of antique and more modern paisley shawls, along with the looms on which they were made. Shop, some disabled access; cl am Sun and all Mon (exc bank hols), 25–26 Dec, 1–2 Jan; (0141) 889 3151; free. The Anchor (Glasgow Rd) does decent lunches.

PAXTON NT9352

⌂ ⛴ ♨ ♨ Paxton House (B6461) Built in 1758 by the love-struck Patrick Billie, who hoped to marry a daughter of Frederick the Great; the marriage never took place, but the result was a splendid neo-Palladian mansion, designed and later embellished by the Adam family, and furnished by the Chippendales; there's an 18th-c German/Prussian costume display this year. Also woodland and riverside walks, huge herd of highland cattle, and adventure playground designed by the Territorial Army. Meals, snacks, shop, disabled access; cl Nov–Apr; (01289) 386291; £5, £2.25 gardens only.

PEEBLES NT2540

★ Attractive if sedate Borders town, with quite a lot for visitors; the Green Tree (Innerleithen Rd) has good food.

✿ ▣ Kailzie (B7062, 2m SE) Extensive grounds with lovely old trees flanked by azaleas and rhododendrons, formal rose garden, walled garden, and small art gallery. Meals, snacks, shop, disabled access; restaurant and gallery cl Nov–Easter; (01721) 720007; *£2.50.

🏰 ※ Neidpath Castle (off A72 just W) Spectacularly set, converted from the original 14th-c tower in the late 16th and early 17th c. There's a rock-hewn well, small museum (children like the mummified rat), period kitchen, and a pit prison – not much chance of escape, as some of the walls are 3½ metres (11ft) thick. Super views from the parapets. The castle was used for the filming of the recent film version of *King Lear* with Brian Blessed. Shop; cl Oct–Mar; (01721) 720333; *£3.00.

PENICUIK NT2360

🏛 Edinburgh Crystal Visitor Centre (Eastfield) Demonstrations of glass-blowing, cutting and engraving, with an exhibition on the crystal's history. Meals, snacks, shop, disabled access; tours Mon–Fri all year and wknds Apr–Sept (last wknd tour 2.30pm, wkdys 3.30pm), cl 25–26 Dec, 1–2 Jan; (01968) 675128; £3. They run a free minibus service from Waverley Bridge in Edinburgh (on the hour, Apr–Sept only). The Horseshoe out on the Peebles road is a civilised dining pub.

PENTLAND HILLS NT1558

⌂ Within easy reach of Edinburgh,

genuine uplands with some good high-level walks and attractive reservoirs.

PORT LOGAN NX0942

🏵 Logan Botanic Garden (off B7065) A specialist garden of the Royal Botanic Garden of Edinburgh, containing a wide range of plants from the warm temperate regions of the southern hemisphere. Snacks, shop, plant sales; cl Nov–Feb; (01776) 860231; £3. The village itself has a natural sea pool where fat fish will eat from your fingers; the Inn does good food.

PORTPATRICK NX0154

★ Attractive harbour town, usually with something going on down by the water, and good food in waterside inn.

PRESTONPANS NT3874

⏚ Industrial Heritage Museum (B1348 Prestongrange Rd) Based around the oldest documented coal mining site in Britain. Reconstructed coalface and colliery workshop, as well as displays on other local industries, from brick and pipe making to brewing and weaving. Lots going on, especially at wknds. Snacks, shop, disabled access; cl late Oct–Mar (but open Christmas wk); (0131) 653 2904; free.

RHINNS OF GALLOWAY NX0650

⌂ This hammerhead of land in the extreme W of the area is largely empty even in high summer, a very peaceful place, with cliffs (especially on the southern point), rocks and small coves.

RHINNS OF KELLS NX7274

⌂ This ridge has energetic hill walking from Forrest Lodge NW of New Galloway.

ROCKCLIFFE NX8453

★ ⌂ Attractive yachting village, with a good peaceful walk to Castle Hill Point headland, and beyond by vast stretches of tidal sands.

ST MARY'S LOCH NT2320

⌂ A pretty spot for walks, tracked by the Southern Upland Way along its east shore; the Tibbie Shiels Inn is a handy stop.

SELKIRK NT4227

A decorous town, good for bargain-hunting for the tweeds, woollens and cashmeres which are woven and knitted here; the Queen's Head has freshly cooked food.

🏠 🏵 ⛪ ▣ Bowhill House (off A708, 3m W) Outstanding collection of paintings, inc works by Canaletto, Van Dyck, Gainsborough and Claude, as well as impressive furnishings and porcelain, and memorabilia relating to Scott and Queen Victoria. Also restored Victorian kitchen, adventure playground, very active little theatre, and surrounding country park. Snacks, shop, disabled access; grounds cl am, all Fri, and all Sept–late Apr; house open daily July only; (01750) 22204; £4.50.

🚌 Selkirk Glass (off A7 just N) Demonstrations of paperweight-making; meals, snacks, factory shop, disabled access; cl Christmas–New Year; (01750) 20954; free.

⛪ Sir Walter Scott's Courtroom (Market Pl) Low-key exhibition on Sir Walter Scott in the former courtroom where, as sheriff, he dispensed justice; shop, snacks, limited disabled access; cl am Sun and all Nov–Mar.

SMAILHOLM NT6334

🏠 Border Tower House (just S, signed off the B6404 NE of St Boswells) Classic 15th-c Borders tower house, very well preserved – all 17 metres (57ft) of it. Display based on Scott's book *Minstrels of the Borders*, and an exhibition of dolls. Shop, limited disabled access; cl pm Thurs, Fri Oct–Nov, wkdys Dec–Mar; (01573) 460365; £2.

SOUTH QUEENSFERRY NT1378

❋ Notable for its views of the 2 great Forth bridges on either side, with piers to potter on; the Hawes Inn, famous from *Kidnapped*, is still going strong.

🏠 Dalmeny House (B924, 3m E) Despite its Tudor Gothic appearance, this splendidly placed house dates only from the 19th c – there's a superb hammerbeamed roof, as well as fine furnishings, porcelain and portraits. Good walks in the grounds and on the shore. Snacks, disabled access; only open Mon, Tues and pm Sun in July–Aug; (0131) 331 1888; £3.80.

🏠 ▣ 🏵 ❋ Hopetoun House (off B904, 2m W) This huge place is probably Scotland's best example of the work of William and Robert Adam. The magnificent reception rooms have a wonderful art collection with works by

Canaletto and Gainsborough, while the superb grounds include a deer park and a flock of rare sheep. You can play croquet on the lawn, or climb to the rooftop for wonderful views. Meals, snacks, shop, some disabled access; cl Oct–Mar; (0131) 331 2451; £5.30.

STEVENSTON NS2740

♨! **Big Idea** (Ardeer Peninsula) Situated in a huge sand-dune shape building, this giant inventor's workshop will form a thoroughly unique attraction when it opens in spring. Entering the complex via an opening pedestrian bridge, visitors will be presented with a vast array of inventions from life-saving machines to utterly ridiculous contraptions. The centre aims to celebrate 100 years of Nobel Laureates as well as the inventions of the past millennium. The main emphasis, however, and what makes this development sound so much fun, is on visitor interaction – you're actively encouraged to create your own inventions, with kits capable of making devices from electric moon buggies to burglar alarms, and the best part of all, after testing them out, you get to take the end product home with you. The centre will also house an IMAX-style film, education facilities, café and gift shop. Disabled access; cl 25 Dec; (01294) 461999; *£7.

STOBO NT1534

❀ ⚘ **Dawyck Botanic Garden** (B712) Another specialist garden of the Royal Botanic Garden, particularly noted for its arboretum rich in mature conifers (inc a larch believed to have been planted in 1725), with notable Asiatic silver firs and many rarities. Snacks, shop, limited disabled access; cl Nov–Feb; (01721) 760254; £3.

STRANRAER NX0760

❀ **Castle Kennedy Gardens** (A75, 4m E) Prettily set between 2 lochs (with lots of good walks around), these gardens were first laid out in the early 18th c, then after years of neglect were restored and developed in the 19th. They're particularly admired for their walled garden and flowering shrubs. Snacks, shop, limited disabled access; cl Oct–Mar; (01776) 702024; £3.

TARBOLTON NS4327

🏠 **Bachelor's Club** (off A77 S of Kilmarnock, and off A76, 7½m NE of Ayr) 17th-c thatched house where Burns and his friends formed a debating club in 1780. Shop; open pm daily Good Fri–Sept, pm wknds only Oct; (01292) 541940; £2; NTS.

THORNHILL NX8599

🏰▣🐾 ♥ ⚘ **Drumlanrig Castle** (off A76) Spectacular and rather unusual pink sandstone castle built in the late 17th c, with a glory of fine panelling and furnishings (mainly Louis XIV), and splendid paintings by Leonardo, Holbein, Rembrandt and Murillo; you can see what's said to be Bonnie Prince Charlie's campaign kettle. Also craft workshops, adventure playground, peacocks wandering over the lawn, birds of prey, and extensive woodland walks. You can hire bikes. Snacks, shop, disabled access; cl Oct–Apr; (01848) 330248; £6.

TRAQUAIR NT3336

🏠 ❀ ▣ ⚘ **Traquair House** (B709) One of the longest-inhabited and most romantic houses in the country; no fewer than 27 English and Scottish kings have stayed here. The Bear Gates have remained closed since 1745 when Bonnie Prince Charlie passed through them for the last time – they won't open again unless the Stuarts regain their place on the throne. An 18th-c brewery still produces tasty beers; you can try them between 3pm and 4pm on Fri Jun–Sept. Traquair is particularly popular with our contributors, and with a maze, art gallery, and antique and craft shops (best on Weds and Thurs) as well as the house and gardens, there's plenty to see. Meals, snacks, shop, some disabled access; cl Mon–Thurs Oct–Apr but open 4–5 Dec; (01896) 830323; £5, grounds only £2.

UDDINGSTON NS6960

🏰 **Bothwell Castle** Picturesquely set by the river: now ruined, but once the finest stone castle in the country; shop; in winter cl pm Thurs, all day Fri, Sun; £1.80.

🦜 ♥ **Glasgow Zoo** (Calderpark) Growing open-plan zoo, specialising in cats and reptiles (snake-handling every day), with other rare mammals and birds, children's farm, orienteering course, and wknd car boot sales. Falconry and parrot flying displays in winter; Snacks, shop, disabled access; cl 25 Dec; (0141) 771 1185; £4.60 (less in winter).

WANLOCKHEAD NS8713

⚒ **Museum of Lead Mining** (B797) Guided tours of an 18th-c lead mine, heritage trail and miners' cottages furnished in the styles of 1740 and 1890. You can have a go at panning for gold. Meals, snacks, shop, limited disabled access; cl Nov–Mar; (01659) 74387; £3.95. This remote village is Scotland's highest.

WHITHORN NX4736

⚓ **Isle of Whithorn** Picturesque harbour with **boat trips** and lots of yachtsmen: the Steam Packet has good local fish.

🏛⚱⚙ **Whithorn Dig** Scotland's first-recorded Christian settlement was established here by St Ninian 1,500 years ago. There have been several churches on the site since, the last of the line the ruined 13th-c priory you can see today. Archaeologists have been hard at work here for some time, and you can generally watch the dig's progress during the summer. An excellent visitor centre and museum have plenty of the finds, with some fine

Celtic crosses. Shop, disabled access; museum and visitor centre cl Nov–Mar (though you may still be able to wander round the priory ruins then); (01988) 500508; £2.70.

★ **Other attractive villages** with decent pubs include Ancrum NT6325, Gifford NT5368, Kirkcowan NX3260, Kirkcudbright NX6851 (particularly enjoyable), Lilliesleaf NT5325, Larkhall NS7651, Old Kilpatrick NS4673, Sorn NS5526 and Symington NS3831.

✺ **Some Clydeside pubs** with decent food and good **sea views** include the Cardwell at Cardwell Bay in Gourock NS2477 and the Spinnaker there, and the Lookout in Troon Marina NS3230. Others with a decent bite to eat and particularly well placed for walkers, drivers or just strollers in these parts include the Murray Arms, Masons Arms and Angel at Gatehouse of Fleet NX5956, Golf Hotel and Old Clubhouse at Gullane NT4882, Breadalbane Hotel at Kildonan NS0231, Swan at Kingholm Quay NX9773, Border at Kirk Yetholm NT8328, Gordon Arms at Mountbenger NT3125 and Buccleuch Arms at St Boswells NT5931.

Where to eat

BEARSDEN NS5472 **Fifty-Five BC** *128 Drymen Rd* (0141) 942 7272 Friendly little bar with reliably good honest cooking, and pleasant staff – they also have a smarter evening restaurant; cl 1 Jan; disabled access. **£25|£5**.

EAST LINTON NT5977 **Drovers** *5 Bridge St* (01620) 860298 Comfortable 18th-c inn with an atmospheric and pubby main bar, prints and pictures for sale, cosy armchairs, a basket of logs by the woodburner, hops around the bar, very good interesting food (more elaborate in the evening), a good range of real ales, and partly no smoking upstairs restaurant; cl 25 Dec, 1 Jan. **£20|£6.95**.

EDINBURGH NT2473 **Atrium** *10 Cambridge St* (0131) 228 8882 Next to the Usher Hall and Traverse Theatre, unusually modern restaurant with wire sculptures, railway sleepers, dim lighting from glass torches, cheerful friendly staff, an interesting wine list, and very good and imaginative modern Scottish food – lunchtime snack menu, too; cl Sun, 10 days Christmas; disabled access. **£30|£6.50**.

EDINBURGH NT2672 **Kalpna** *2–3 St Patrick Sq* (0131) 667 9890 Extremely good Indian restaurant with carefully cooked very fresh Gujerati vegetarian food (super lunchtime buffets) and efficient service; cl Sun, 1 Jan; disabled access. **£13.50|£5**.

EDINBURGH NT2776 **Ship on the Shore** *26 The Shore, Leith* (0131) 555 0409 Lovely old pub with a charming ship model for its hotel sign, a bar with old painted company signs, ship lanterns and nautical equipment, popular food (especially the bargain 3-course lunches), plenty of fish and well liked Sun breakfasts; children over 8. **£27|£6.50** 3-course lunch.

EDINBURGH NT2676 **Vintners Rooms** *The Vaults, 87 Giles St, Leith* (0131) 554 6767 Bustling restaurant – former fine old sale room, above ancient wine vaults – with most enjoyable French provincial cooking plus more modern dishes, super puddings, and a good wine list; you can also choose to eat in the more informal bar; cl Sun, 2 wks from Christmas; partial disabled access. **£35|£11** 2-course lunch.

GLASGOW NS5667 **Di Maggios** *61 Ruthven Lane* (0141) 334 8560 A Glasgow institution with good Italian and other food, and a cheerful atmosphere; cl 25 Dec, 1–2 Jan; disabled access. **£16|£5.95**.

GLASGOW NS5965 **Rogano** *11 Exchange Pl* (0141) 248 4055 Long-standing restaurant in splendid 1930s ocean liner style with quite an emphasis on fish – vegetarian and meaty dishes, too; Café Rogano (downstairs) is open all day for lighter meals; cl 25 Dec, 1 Jan. **£40**.

GLASGOW NS5667 **Ubiquitous Chip** *12 Ashton Lane, Byres Rd* (0141) 334 5007 Friendly and informal restaurant (no chips, hence the name) in Victorian coach house with interesting modern Scottish cooking, outstanding wines, and no smoking areas; disabled access; cl 25 Dec, 31 Dec, 1 Jan. Upstairs is similar but cheaper. **£29 lunch, £37 dinner|£5.15**.

GLASGOW NS5865 **Willow Tearoom** *217 Sauchiehall St* (0141) 332 0521 Beautifully restored from the 1903 Art Deco original with careful reproductions of the stylish furniture, this tearoom (and the newly opened downstairs Gallery) has pastries and cakes, good sandwiches, toasties, filled croissants and bagels, salads, herbal, fruit and loose teas, quite a choice of coffees, and milk shakes; also at 97 Buchanan Street; cl 25 Dec, 1–2 Jan. **£4.50**.

GLASGOW NS5865 **Yes** *22 West Nile St* (0141) 221 8044 Stylish bustling restaurant with a relaxed, if fashionable, feel, very good modern cooking taking ideas from all over the world using first-class local produce, courteous service, and a short well chosen wine list; cl Sun, all public hols. **£40|£23.95** 2 courses.

HADDINGTON NT5173 **Waterside** *(01620) 825674* A really lovely spot on a sunny day with a fine view across the water, this long 2-storey white house has 2 plush rooms, a woodburner, a more formal stripped-stone conservatory, very good bistro-style food, real ales, and a good range of wines. **£21|£6.95**.

LANARK NS8843 **La Vigna** *40 Wellgate* (01555) 664320 Imaginative Italian menu with good basics, more imaginative dishes and lots of fresh fish; cl am Sun; disabled access. **£25|£9.95** 3-course lunch.

LINLITHGOW NT0378 **Champany** *(01506) 834532* Wonderful Aberdeen Angus beef as well as lovely fresh fish (they also have their own smoke-house), home-made ice-creams, and good wines; cheaper bistro-style meals in their Chop & Ale House next door; children over 8 in restaurant; disabled access. **£55** restaurant, **£23.75** Ale House|**£14.50**.

East Scotland

Plenty for families to see and do, and richly varied scenery.

The area has a splendid range of historic smaller towns and villages, glorious castles, palaces and great houses, and lots of entertaining family outings, such as the Blair Drummond safari park, the Kincraig wildlife park, the deep-sea centre at North Queensferry, the lively Romano-Pictish reconstructions at Oyne, Landmark Park at Carrbridge, the bouncy science and technology centre in Aberdeen, and a unique collection of emus, ostriches and so forth at Collessie. Dundee and Aberdeen both have plenty to see.

The best scenery here is in the north: both Highland, and the valleys – the well known Spey, Dee and Don, and lesser-known places such as the Angus glens of Glen Clova, Glen Esk and Glen Isla. Further south, the Trossachs are very pretty. The coast has appealing fishing villages in Fife's

East Neuk, and a little-known but charming stretch from Nairn to Aberdeen, with good sands, quaint little coves and awesome cliffy crags such as Slains Castle and the nearby Bullers of Buchan.

The relatively few roads through the best parts do tend to get crowded in high summer; to get a feeling of peace, June (when it's still light as midnight approaches) would be much better.

Where to stay

ABERDEEN NJ9305 **Ferryhill House** *169 Bon Accord St, Aberdeen AB11 6UA* *(01224) 590867* **£50w;** 9 rms. Well run small hotel with comfortable and spacious communicating bar areas, well over 100 malt whiskies, real ales, friendly staff, a wide choice of food in the bar and restaurant and lots of tables on neat, well sheltered lawns.

ABERFELDY NN8249 **Farleyer House** *Aberfeldy, Perthshire PH15 2JE (01887) 820332* ***£170,** plus winter breaks; 19 pretty rms. Charming country house with fine Tay Valley views, log fires, antiques and flowers in the library and drawing room, excellent food in the airy and elegant restaurant and Scottish bistro; use of nearby leisure club; disabled access.

ARDEONAIG NN6635 **Ardeonaig Hotel** *Ardeonaig, Killin, Perthshire FK21 8SU* *(01567) 820400* ***£97;** 12 rms. Extended 17th-c farmhouse on S shore of Loch Tay with log fire in snug and lounge, library with fine views, and tasty, honest food using plenty of fish and game; salmon fishing rights on the Loch – as well as fishing for trout and char – a drying and rod room, and boats and outboards; shooting and stalking can be arranged, lots of surrounding walks, and pony trekking; cl Nov–Mar.

AUCHTERARDER NN9211 *Gleneagles Auchterarder, Perthshire PH3 1NF* *(01764) 662231* **£270,** plus special breaks; 229 individually decorated rms. Grand hotel in lovely surroundings with attractive gardens and outstanding leisure facilities: golf courses (inc a championship one designed by Jack Nicklaus), shooting, riding, fishing, health spa, tennis, squash, bowling green, croquet and even falconry; comfortable, elegant high-ceilinged day rooms, a fine bar, exceptional service, pianists, enjoyable food (inc famous afternoon teas) using local produce (much is home-grown) in 4 restaurants; disabled access.

AVIEMORE NH8810 **Lynwilg House** *Lynwilg, Aviemore, Inverness-shire PH22 1PZ* *(01479) 811685* **£60;** 4 rms, 3 with shower. Attractive, quietly set 1930s-style house in 4 acres of landscaped gardens with an open fire in the spacious lounge, lovely breakfasts with their own free-range eggs and home-baked bread, super dinners using home-grown produce, and charming friendly owners; plenty to do nearby; cl beginning Nov–28 Dec.

BALLATER NO3696 **Auld Kirk** *Braemar Rd, Ballater, Aberdeenshire AB35 5RQ* *(013397) 55762* ***£52,** plus winter breaks; 6 attractive rms. 19th-c church converted to a hotel in 1990, still with bell tower (the bell is in the main entrance), stained glass and exposed rafters; original pillared pine ceiling in the lacy dining room, other public rooms with homely décor and lots of knick-knacks, and home cooking; cl Christmas–New Year.

BALLATER NO3696 **Balgonie Country House** *Braemar Pl, Ballater, Aberdeenshire AB35 5NQ (01339) 755482* ***£115,** plus special breaks. 9 pretty rms. Quietly set and spotless Edwardian house with fine views from 4 acres of mature gardens, particularly helpful friendly owners, fresh flowers, games and books in the lounges, and most enjoyable food using the best local produce in the charming dining room; cl Jan–Feb; dogs by arrangement (away from public rooms).

BALQUHIDDER NN4318 **Monachyle Mhor** *Balquhidder, Lochearnhead, Perthshire FK19 8PQ (01877) 384622* ***£70;** 11 rms with fine views overlooking Voil and Doine lochs. Remote 18th-c farmhouse/hotel several miles W of Balquhidder on 2,000-acre estate with prettily furnished rooms and good food using own game and herbs; private fishing and stalking for guests; no children.

BLAIRGOWRIE NO1345 **Kinloch House** *Blairgowrie, Perthshire PH10 6SG* (01250) 884237 ***£160 inc dinner,** plus special breaks; 21 individually decorated rms. Creeper-covered 19th-c country house in 25 acres of parkland with Highland cattle and fine views; relaxed lounges, a comfortable bar, pretty conservatory with lots of plants, and fine choice of carefully prepared food in an elegant dining room; popular sportsmen's room with own entrance, drying facilities, gun cupboard, freezer, game larder and so forth, and a new fitness suite; cl 17–29 Dec; no children under 7 in dining room; disabled access.

BRIDGE OF CALLY NO1451 **Bridge of Cally Hotel** *Bridge of Cally, Blairgowrie, Perthshire PH10 7JJ* (01250) 886231 **£55,** plus winter breaks; 9 rms. In an acre of grounds along the River Ardle, this former drovers' inn is a friendly family-run place with good-value home-made food using seasonal game in both the restaurant and comfortable bar; cl 25–26 Dec; pets welcome.

BRIDGE OF MARNOCH NJ5950 **Old Manse of Marnoch** *Bridge of Marnoch, Huntly, Aberdeenshire AB54 7RS* (01466) 780873 ***£94,** plus special breaks; 8 light, well equipped rms, some in new wing. Neat Georgian country house in 3 acres of gardens on the River Deveron, with antiques in the comfortable sitting room, a friendly and informal atmosphere, imaginative 4-course set dinner in the elegant dining room, a carefully chosen wine list, and superb breakfasts; liked by fishing people; cl 2 wks Nov, Christmas and New Year; children over 12; partial disabled access.

CALLANDER NN6208 **Poppies** *Leny Rd, Callander, Perthshire FK17 8AL* (01877) 330329 ***£44,** plus special breaks; 8 rms. Small private hotel with excellent food in the popular and attractive candlelit dining room, a convivial bar with RAF theme, comfortable lounge, helpful friendly owners, and seats in the garden; cl Oct–Apr; disabled access.

CALLANDER NN6208 **Roman Camp** *Main St, Callander, Perthshire FK17 8BG* (01877) 330003 **£110,** plus special breaks; 14 individually decorated pretty rms with garden views. Extended over the years since it was built as a hunting lodge in 1625, this pink-painted turreted house has warm open fires and lovely fresh flowers, an elegant drawing room, tranquil library, very good food in the candlelit dining room, and 20 acres of grounds; disabled access.

CRIANLARICH NN3726 **Allt-Chaorain Country House** *Crianlarich, Perthshire FK20 8RU* (01838) 300283 **£60,** plus special breaks; 7 rms. Comfortable small hotel with a homely atmosphere, log fire in the lounge, honesty bar, sunroom with marvellous views, and good home-cooked food in the panelled dining room; lots of fishing, golf and walks nearby; cl 1 Nov–1 May; children over 7; disabled access.

DALCROSS NH7451 **Easter Dalziel Farm** *Dalcross, Inverness IV1 2JL* (01667) 462213 ***£40,** plus special breaks; 3 rms with shared bthrm. Early Victorian farmhouse on 210 acres of a family-run mixed farm (beef cattle and grain) with friendly helpful owners, log fire in the lounge, good Scottish breakfasts in the big dining room and – when farm commitments allow – evening meal using own beef, lamb and vegetables; self-catering cottages, too; cl Christmas and New Year.

DUNBLANE NN7806 **Cromlix House** *Kinbuck, Dunblane, Perthshire FK15 9JT* (01786) 822125 **£215,** plus special breaks; 14 rms inc 8 spacious suites. Walking, loch and river fishing or shooting on 3,000 acres around this rather gracious country house; relaxing day rooms with fine antiques and family portraits, an informal atmosphere, very good food using estate game and local meats and fish in 2 dining rooms, and courteous service; cl 2 Jan–1 Feb.

DUNKELD NN9849 **Kinnaird House** *Kinnaird Estate, Dunkeld, Perthshire PH8 0LB* (01796) 482440 ***£255,** plus special breaks; 9 spacious, individually decorated rms. 18th-c country-house hotel on 9,000-acre estate with a very restful civilised atmosphere in deeply comfortable antiques-filled rooms, lovely flowers, family mementos and pictures, log fires, good creative food in the no smoking dining room with early 19th-c hand-painted frescoes, and a fine wine list; excellent fishing on the River Tay and 3 hill lochs, and shooting; cl Mon–Weds during Jan and Feb; children over 12.

EAST HAUGH NN9656 **East Haugh House** *East Haugh, Pitlochry, Perthshire PH16 5JS (01796) 473121 *£78,* plus special breaks; 12 rms, 4 in converted bothy. Turreted stone house with lots of character, a delightful conservatory bar, house-party atmosphere, helpful cheerful owners, and very good popular food inc local seafood and game in season; excellent shooting, stalking and salmon and trout fishing on surrounding local estates; cl 20–26 Dec; partial disabled access.

ELGIN NJ2163 **Mansion House** *The Haugh, Elgin, Moray IV30 1AW (01343) 548811 £120,* plus special breaks; 23 rms. Relaxed and friendly Scottish baronial mansion with prettily furnished public rooms, fresh flowers, lovely food inc fine breakfasts, and a good wine list; leisure club facilities; disabled access.

FINTRY NS6287 **Culcreuch Castle** *Fintry, Glasgow G63 0LW (01360) 860228 £76,* plus special breaks; 10 individually decorated rms with lovely views. Scotland's oldest inhabited castle, nearly 700 years old, in beautiful 1,600-acre parkland and surrounding hills and moors, with log fires and antiques in the public rooms, good freshly prepared food in the candlelit panelled dining room, and a friendly relaxed atmosphere; 8 modern Scandinavian holiday lodges, too; disabled access.

GLENDEVON NN9904 **Tormaukin** *Glendevon, Dollar, Clackmannanshire FK14 7JY (01259) 781252 £78,* plus special breaks; 10 refurbished rms, some in converted stable block. Comfortable neatly kept inn in good walking country, with loch and river fishing, lots of golf courses within reach, a beamed dining room and softly lit bar, very good food (soup and coffee all day), and fine breakfasts; cl 1 wk beginning Jan; disabled access.

GLENROTHES NO2803 **Balbirnie House** *Balbirnie Park, Markinch, Glenrothes, Fife KY7 6NE (01592) 610066 £180,* plus special breaks; 30 rms. Fine Georgian country house in 400-acre park landscaped in Capability Brown style, with fresh flowers, open fires and antiques in gracious public rooms, extremely good inventive food, and a big wine list; disabled access.

GRANTOWN-ON-SPEY NJ0227 **Culdearn House** *Woodlands Terrace, Grantown-on-Spey, Moray PH26 3JU (01479) 872106 *£130 inc dinner,* plus special breaks; 9 rms; Carefully run Victorian granite stone house with homely décor inc local watercolours, a friendly chatty atmosphere, helpful owners, and enjoyable Scottish food; packed lunches on request; self-catering, too; cl Nov–Feb; children over 10; disabled access.

INVERBOYNDIE NJ6764 **Links Cottage** *Inverboyndie, Banff AB45 2JJ (01261) 812223 £48;* 3 rms. Set in an acre of grounds and only a short walk to Banff's marvellous long, sandy beach, this neatly refurbished single-storey cottage is comfortable and homely with a friendly atmosphere, hearty breakfasts (places close by for evening meals), and plenty to do nearby; disabled access.

INVERNESS NH6245 **Bunchrew House** *Bunchrew, Inverness IV3 6TA (01463) 234917 *£140,* plus special breaks; 11 individually decorated rms. Friendly 17th-c mansion W of town by Beauly Firth with fine views and landscaped gardens, log fire in the elegant panelled drawing room, and traditional cooking using local produce and local game and venison.

KINCLAVEN BY STANLEY NO1336 **Ballathie House** *Kinclaven by Stanley, Perth, Perthshire PH1 4QN (01250) 883268 £160;* 27 pretty rms, some luxurious. On a vast estate with fine salmon fishing on the River Tay (special facilities for fishermen) and plenty of sporting opportunities, this turreted mansion has a comfortable and relaxed drawing room, separate lounge and bar, good enjoyable modern Scottish cooking, and tennis, croquet, and putting; limited disabled access.

KINGUSSIE NH7200 **Hermitage** *Spey St, Kingussie, Inverness-shire PH21 1HN (01540) 662137 £44,* plus special breaks; 5 rms. Welcoming house in a large garden with fine Cairngorm views, log fires in the comfortable lounge, enjoyable home-made set dinners, and hearty Scottish breakfasts; fishing, golf, walking, climbing and birdwatching close by; disabled access.

KINNESSWOOD NO1702 **Lomond Country Inn** *Main St, Kinnesswood, Kinross KY13 7HN (01592) 840253 *£65,* plus special breaks; 12 comfortable rms, 8 in an extension. Attractive little inn in the centre of the village with views across Loch

Leven (nice sunsets), open fires, an informal bustling bar, well kept real ales, and good reasonably priced bar and restaurant food using local produce; disabled access.

KIRKTON OF GLENISLA NO2160 **Glenisla** *Blairgowrie, Perthshire PH11 8PH (01575) 582223* **£85 inc dinner,** plus special breaks; 6 rms. Attractively placed peaceful 17th-c coaching inn, prettily restored with natural unpainted wood throughout, happily unmatched furniture, bar with open fire and 2 real ales, good food, very attentive owners and a cheerful warm atmosphere; nice garden; dogs welcome; cl 20–27 Dec.

MONYMUSK NJ6815 **Grant Arms** *Monymusk, Inverurie, Aberdeenshire AB51 7HJ (01467) 651226* **£65;** 17 rms, most with own bthrm. Smart old inn with a dark-panelled lounge bar divided in two by a log fire in the stub wall, simpler public bar, and exclusive right to 15 miles of good trout and salmon fishing on the River Don; ghillie available; disabled access.

NAIRN NH8756 **Clifton House** *Viewfield St, Nairn IV12 4HW (01667) 453119* ***£100,** plus special breaks; 12 individually decorated comfortable rms. Lovely, civilised, flower-filled old family hotel (the present owner has lived in this elegant Victorian house all his life and has been running it as a hotel since 1952), individually furnished with antiques, paintings and sculptures; extremely good food using local eggs, fish, meat and game, fine breakfasts with home-made jams, bread, and oatcakes, and an exceptional wine list; during the winter they stage some 20 concerts, plays and recitals; cl mid-Dec–mid-Jan; pets welcome.

PEAT INN NO4509 **Peat Inn** *Peat Inn, Cupar, Fife KY15 5LH (01334) 840206* ***£145,** plus special breaks; 8 luxurious suites. Famous restaurant with rooms: beams and white plaster walls, log fires and comfortable sofas, friendly service, fine interesting food using the best local produce inc plenty of game and seafood, and an excellent wine list; cl Sun–Mon, 25 Dec, 1 Jan; disabled access.

PITLOCHRY NN9162 **Killiecrankie** *Pitlochry, Perthshire PH16 5LG (01796) 473220* **£168 inc dinner,** plus special breaks; 10 spotless rms. Comfortable country hotel in spacious grounds with putting course and croquet lawn; splendid mountain views, mahogany-panelled bar with stuffed animals and fine wildlife paintings, spacious sitting room with books and games, a relaxed atmosphere, very friendly owners, and excellent well presented food in elegant restaurant; cl Jan–Feb.

ROTHES NJ2650 **Rothes Glen** *Rothes, Elgin, Moray NV38 7AH (01340) 831254* **£110;** 15 individually decorated, spacious rms. Fine baronial mansion in 10 acres with fishing, croquet and putting; lots of original features in the tranquil public rooms, good modern Scottish cooking using local game and fish in the attractive no smoking dining room, a fine wine list, and helpful friendly staff; children over 8.

SCONE NO1526 **Murrayshall House** *Scone, Perth, Perthshire PH2 7PH (01738) 551171* ***£120,** plus special breaks; 27 rms, plus lodge which sleeps 6. Handsome mansion in 300 acres of parkland, very popular with golfers (it has its own course): comfortable elegant public rooms, warm friendly staff, a relaxed atmosphere, imaginative food, and good wines; dogs welcome; disabled access.

SPEAN BRIDGE NN2281 **Letterfinlay Lodge** *Spean Bridge, Inverness-shire PH34 4DZ (01397) 712622* **£76,** plus special breaks; 13 rms, most with own bthrm. Secluded and genteel family-run country house with picture window in an extensive modern bar overlooking the loch; elegantly panelled small cocktail bar, good popular food, friendly attentive service; grounds run down through rhododendrons to the jetty and Loch Lochy; fishing can be arranged; cl Nov–Apr; disabled access.

SPITTAL OF GLENSHEE NO0971 **Dalmunzie House** *Glenshee, Blairgowrie, Perthshire PH10 7QG (01250) 885224* **£92;** 16 rms with own bthrm. Old-fashioned former Victorian shooting lodge, off the A93, peacefully set in a huge estate among spectacular mountains, plenty of walks within it, and own golf course; family-run atmosphere, enjoyable food using local produce, and tasty breakfasts; cl end Nov–28 Dec; disabled access.

STRATHKINNESS NO4616 **Fossil House & Cottage** *12–14 Main St, Strathkinness, St Andrews, Fife KY16 9RU (01334) 850639* **£44;** 4 well equipped, pretty rms with fresh flowers – particularly good family rm. Once a smallholding, the 2 stone buildings here have a comfortable little guest lounge and sunny conservatory, plenty of books, board games, videos, and lots of ornaments and fighter aircraft pictures, especially helpful, friendly owners, award-winning, really super breakfasts, and barbecue facilities in the garden; no smoking and no dogs.

STRATHYRE NN5617 **Rosebank House** *Strathyre, Callander, Perthshire FK18 8NA (01877) 384208* **£44;** 4 rms, most with own bthrm. Victorian house with open fires in comfortable lounge and dining rooms, wildlife paintings by the owner on the walls, enjoyable evening meals and breakfasts (lovely puddings), and a quiet, big garden; plenty to do nearby; cl Christmas.

WHITEBRIDGE NH4413 **Knockie Lodge** *Whitebridge, Inverness IV1 2UP (01456) 486276* **£110,** plus special breaks; 10 rms. In a wonderful setting by Loch Knockie above Loch Ness, this Georgian hunting lodge has plenty of outside pursuits, a warmly friendly and relaxed house-party atmosphere, lovely flower arrangements, log and peat fires, antiques, and comfortable day rooms, delicious evening meals, and super breakfasts; billiards; cl Nov–Mar; children over 10; dogs by prior arrangement.

To see and do

ABERDEEN NJ9305

★ Scotland's third-largest city, with a large active harbour, well worth pottering around (especially its early morning Fishmarket). The granite centre has wide, orderly streets not unlike Edinburgh's New Town in places, and parks. Leafy Seaton Park is famous for its 14th-c Brig (or bridge) o' Balgownie. The Ferryhill House Hotel (Bon Accord St), Royal Hotel (Bath St) and Athol (King's Gate, W of centre) are useful for lunch, and the Prince of Wales (St Nicholas Lane) is the best proper pub in this part of Scotland.

🖼 **Aberdeen Art Gallery** (Schoolhill) First-class collection of Scottish and English painting since the 16th c, especially strong on contemporary works (cl am Sun, 25–26 Dec, 1–2 Jan; free).

❀ **Aberdeen Maritime Museum** 🖼 (Provost Ross's House, Shiprow) In the town's third-oldest building (very striking), with very good displays on the city's nautical heritage. Meals, snacks, shop, disabled access; cl 25–26 Dec, 1–3 Jan; (01224) 337700; £3.50.

🏵 **Cruickshank Botanic Garden** (St Machar Drive) 11 acres first planted in the 19th c, and divided into various smaller gardens – rock, water, rose and herbaceous – as well as trees and shrubs and a small terrace garden; cl winter wknds; (01224) 272704; free.

🏛 **King's College** (High St) Founded in 1495; The chapel is one of the most complete examples of a medieval collegiate church in Britain. A visitor centre outlines the history. Snacks (in barrel-vaulted former library), shop, disabled access; cl 2 wks at Christmas; (01224) 273702; free.

🏛🖼 **Marischal Museum** (Broad St) The later Protestant rival to King's, though the two were joined to form Aberdeen University in the 19th century. A splendid neo-Gothic structure, it has a museum with interesting anthropological displays; cl am Sun, all day Sat; (01224) 274301; free.

🏛 **Old Town** N of the centre, really too far to walk, this part above the River Don seems quite separate. It has some charming old streets to explore, and attractive buildings; its pedestrianised villagey High St is dominated by the university, especially the very Oxbridge-like King's College.

🏛 **Provost Skene's House** 🖼 (Guestrow) Named after its most famous resident, a stately well restored 16th-c house with refurbished period rooms, and remarkable painted ceilings. Snacks; cl Sun, 25–26 Dec, 1–2 Jan; (01224) 641086; £2.50. The Illicit Still nearby has food all day.

✝ **St Machar's Cathedral** Austere mainly 15th-c church notable for its painted wooden heraldic ceiling. It's the only granite cathedral in the world.

! **Satrosphere** (Justice Mill Lane) Lively hands-on science and technology centre – everything is there to be touched, and they have lots of changing displays and exhibitions. Great fun. Snacks, shop, disabled access; cl Tues in winter (exc school hols); (01224) 213232; £4.50.

🌣 **Tolbooth Museum** (Castle St) Good civic history collection in a 17th-c building (cl Oct–Mar; £2).

ABERFELDY NN8549

★ △ ※ This quiet and pleasant small Highland shopping town has a fine 18th-c stone bridge designed by William Adam. Weem, for a good lunch at the Ailean Chraggan, is close by. There's a well restored **watermill** on Mill St (still mills oatmeal; all parts open to visit, cl mid-Oct–Easter; £2), and just S of town the delightful verdant 1½-mile walk along to the oak-lined Den and Falls of Moness inspired Burns's song *The Birks of Aberfeldy*.

ABERFOYLE NN5200

Lots of woollen shops, and in the heart of Queen Elizabeth Forest Park, so lovely scenery around; you can hire bikes. The Inverard has decent food.

🏫 **Scottish Wool Centre** The story of Scottish wool from sheep to shop, entertainingly told by a live sheep show in the amphitheatre (11am, 12, 2pm, 3pm). They have demonstrations of spinning and weaving. Meals, snacks, good shop, disabled access; cl 25 Dec, 1 Jan; (01877) 382850; *£3.

ALFORD NJ5815

🚂 **Alford Valley Railway** (A944) Narrow-gauge passenger railway with trips in 2 one-mile sections, and a good static display at the station. Shop, disabled access; trains in steam wknds Apr, May, Sept and daily pm Jun–Aug; (019755) 62326; £2.

🏛 **Grampian Transport Museum** (A944) Big collection of vintage vehicles, from horse-drawn sledges and carriages to motorcycles, cars and steamers; always plenty going on. Snacks, shop, disabled access; cl Nov–Mar; (01975) 562292; £3.50. There'a dry ski slope on Greystone Rd, and the Forbes Arms at Bridge of Alford has decent home cooking.

ANSTRUTHER NO5603

★ 🐦 ⚓ Pretty East Neuk fishing village; from May–Sept (weather permitting) you can get **boat trips** out to the nature reserve of the **Isle of May**,

home to countless puffins and seals in summer. The Craws Nest, Dreel and Smugglers all have good-value food.

🌣 **Scottish Fisheries Museum** 📷 Nicely evocative, in a little cobbled courtyard by the harbour; cl winter am Sun, 25–26 Dec, 1–2 Jan; £3.50.

ARBROATH NO6441

🏰 **Arbroath Abbey** Substantial remains of 12th-c abbey, connected with Thomas à Becket and Robert the Bruce. Shop, disabled access to ground floor only; cl 25–26 Dec, 1–2 Jan; (01241) 878756; £1.80.

AVIEMORE NH8912

Uncompromisingly modern ski-resort village. There are plenty of places to get something to eat in this sizeable tourist development (the Olde Bridge is our current recommendation).

△ ❀ **Cairngorms** A ski-lift from Glen More above the village gives an easy way up to the summits.

△ ♈ ❀ **Loch an Eilein** A draw for walkers, nestling beneath the Cairngorms; a forest track encircles this delightful little loch, with its castle romantically placed on an isle – great echoes here.

🚂 **Strathspey Steam Railway** 5 miles of great scenery between here and the Boat of Garten. Snacks, shop, limited disabled access; usually open daily Jun–Sept, plus other dates and wknds – best to ring for timetable; (01479) 810725; £5.

BALLINDALLOCH NJ1928

🏫 **Glenlivet Distillery** This was the first Highland malt whisky distillery to be licensed; (01542) 783220 for opening times; £2.50.

BALMEDIE COUNTRY PARK NJ9820

♈ Along a constantly shifting stretch of coast, this is splendidly bleak-feeling despite the closeness of Aberdeen. Visitor centre cl winter wknds. The beaches are clean and safe.

BALMORAL NO2693

🏰 ❀ ♈ **Balmoral Castle** (off A93) The royal family's Highland residence. Prince Albert bought the property 4 years after he and Queen Victoria had first rented it in 1848, and had a new castle built here by 1855. You can't go inside, but you can explore the wonderful gardens and woodlands, and there are various exhibitions in the ballroom. Also pony trekking and pony cart rides. Snacks, meals, shop, disabled access; open daily 17 Apr–31 July (exc Sun Apr and May); (013397) 42334; *£4.

BANFF NJ6963

🏛️🖼️❀ **Duff House** 🖼️ This magnificent example of 18th-c Baroque architecture has served as a ducal residence, hotel, sanitarium and prisoner-of-war camp in its time. It now houses a splendid collection of paintings and tapestries (some from the National Galleries of Scotland), hung in sumptuously furnished rooms including Chippendale furniture designed by Robert Adam. The extensive grounds laid out alongside the River Deveron are pleasant for strolling in, and include a mausoleum, vinery and, rather quaintly, the 19th-c headstones of various dogs. Tearoom with very good home-made food, shop, good disabled access including lifts to all floors; (01261) 818181; £3.

BEN VENUE NN4706

⌂✺ Allows some good mountain walks comparable in difficulty to some of the fells of the English Lake District.

BEN VORLICH NN6218

⌂✺ Good walking, for those used to pretty hearty fell walking.

BENNACHIE NJ6623

⌂✺ On the E edge of the Grampians nr Inverurie, this is not that high but gives walkers tremendous views over lowland Grampian; the gently rolling moorland top has several colour-coded Forestry Commission trails (the lower slopes are forested).

BLAIR ATHOLL NN8665

👣 **Atholl Country Collection** Friendly little **folk museum** beside the turn-in for the White Horse; open pm May–mid-Oct (am too wkdys July–Sept); *£2.

🏰❀ **Blair Castle** 🖼️ (off A9) Nestling among forests and heather-clad hills, this is Scotland's most visited privately owned house, dating back to the 13th c, though largely renovated in the 18th. You can see 32 of the rooms, and there's an 18th-c walled garden. A display charts the history of the Atholl Highlanders – the Duke of Atholl's unique private army that turns out here for its annual parade in May. A piper

outside every day in summer adds to the atmosphere. Meals, snacks, shop, disabled access to ground floor only; cl Nov–Mar; (01796) 481207; £5.50, plus grounds charge of £2 per car. The Atholl Arms has well priced food.

🏠 **House of Bruar** (Glen Atholl, A9) Country shopping complex with fine specialist foods and clothing; readers like it a lot.

BLAIR DRUMMOND NS7498

🐾 **Safari & Leisure Park** 🖼️ (A84) Wild animals in natural surroundings, with plenty of other activities included in the price, from gentle rides for younger children to the exhilarating Flying Fox slide over the lake. You can explore part of the water in pedal-boats, and boat trips circle Chimpanzee Island leaving the monkeys to enjoy their natural habitat undisturbed. Feeding times of lions, sealions, and penguins are posted up near the entrance. Meals, snacks, shop, disabled access; cl Oct–mid-Mar; (01786) 841456; £8.50 (£4.50 children 3–14) – not bad value if you bring a barbie and make a half-day of it. The Lion & Unicorn at Thornhill does good family lunches.

BO'NESS NS9981

🚂🚩 **Bo'ness & Kinneil Railway** 🖼️ Re-creation of the days of steam complete with relocated railway buildings and Scotland's largest collection of locomotives and rolling stock. The 7-mile round trip takes you to the woodlands of the Avon Gorge at Birkhill, for tours of an old clay mine. Snacks, shop, disabled access to railway only; trains usually run wknds Apr–mid-Oct, and daily (exc Mon) July and Aug, though you can see the locomotives all year; (01506) 822298; £7.30 mine and railway, £3.90 train only.

🏛️👣🔱 **Kinneil Estate** Includes the interesting if not extensive remains of a Roman fortlet, as well as a few later ruins and remains. The converted stables of adjacent Kinneil House have a museum on the site's history, with lots of local pottery. You can still see the workshop where James Watt developed the steam engine, and there are pleasant woodland walks. Shop, limited disabled access; cl am and all day Sun and bank hols; (01506) 778530; free.

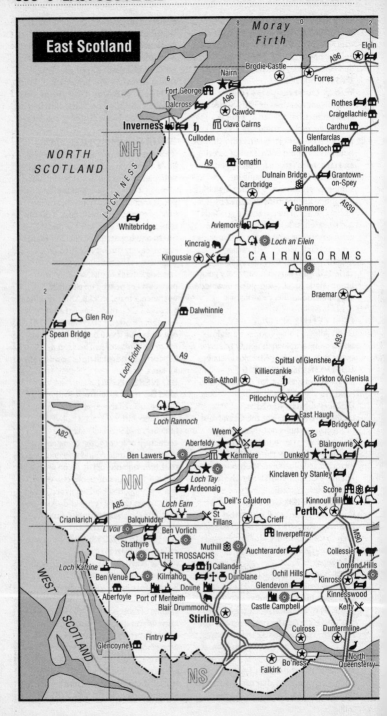

East Scotland

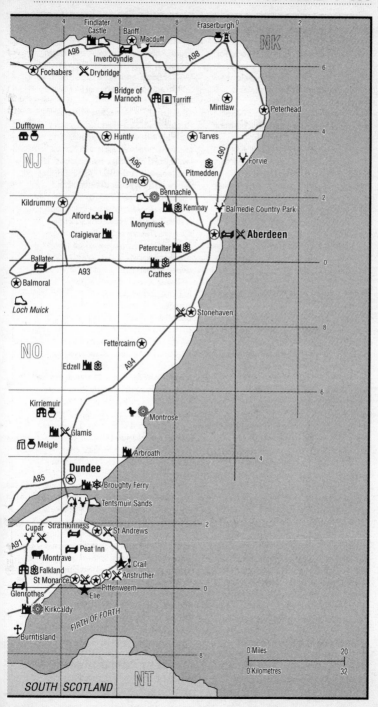

NK

Findlater Castle
Banff
Macduff
Fraserburgh
Inverboyndie
A98
A98
Fochabers
Drybridge
Bridge of Marnoch
Turriff
Mintlaw
Peterhead
Dufftown
Huntly
Tarves
NJ
A96
A90
Oyne
Pitmedden
Forvie
Bennachie
Kildrummy
Kemnay
Balmedie Country Park
Alford
Monymusk
Craigievar
Aberdeen
Peterculter
Ballater
Crathes
A93
Balmoral
Loch Muick
Stonehaven
NO
Fettercairn
Edzell
A94
Kirriemuir
Montrose
Glamis
Meigle
Arbroath
Dundee
A85
Broughty Ferry
Tentsmuir Sands
Cupar
Strathkinness
St Andrews
A91
Montrave
Peat Inn
Falkland
Crail
St Monance
Anstruther
Glenrothes
Pittenweem
Elie
Kirkcaldy
FIRTH OF FORTH
Burntisland
NT

0 Miles 20
0 Kilometres 32

SOUTH SCOTLAND

BRAEMAR NO1491

★ ⌂ One of the most beautifully set Highland villages; the Fife Arms (very much on the coach routes) is good for lunch. A steep path up Morrone takes the most determined walkers along a route used for a race in Braemar's famous Highland Gathering.

Braemar Castle ⊞ (A93 NE of Braemar) Highly unusual and charming exterior. Shop; cl Fri, and all Nov–Easter; (013397) 41219; £3.

ɪ) **Highland Heritage Centre** (Mar Rd) Shows useful films on the area's history and scenery (inc an interesting look at the building of Balmoral Castle), and on the Gathering. Shops, disabled access; cl 25 Dec, 1 Jan; (01339) 741944; free.

⌂ **Linn of Dee** Nr Braemar, gives glen walks into the Cairngorms along Glen Dee and the Lairig Ghru.

BRODIE CASTLE NH9757

Handsome gabled castle (off A96) with an extensive art collection featuring 17th-c paintings of the Dutch school, English watercolours and French Impressionists. Before the National Trust for Scotland took it over in 1980 it had been the seat of the same family since 1160. Outside are woodland walks and wildlife observation hides, and beautiful daffodils in spring. Snacks, shop, disabled access; cl am Sun, wkdys in Oct and all Nov–Mar; (01309) 641371; £4.20; NTS. Their occasional evenings of traditional Scottish music are enjoyed by readers. The nearest really good place for a meal is the Clifton Hotel in Nairn.

BROUGHTY FERRY NO4630

Broughty Castle Museum (off A930 4m E of Dundee) 15th-c seaside castle rebuilt in the 19th c to defend the estuary, now a maritime museum. Plenty of harpoons and whaling exhibits – whaling used to be one of Dundee's major industries. Shop; cl Mon from Oct–Mar; (01382) 436916; free. The Fisherman's Tavern and the Ship (fantastic view upstairs) are good.

BURNTISLAND NT2385

† Once famous for shipbuilding (and shipbreaking), now a popular little resort, with an unusual octagonal **church** where the decision was made to produce the Authorised Version of the Bible in 1601.

CALLANDER NN6207

Quite a busy tourist town, popular in Victorian times thanks to the works of Walter Scott, and more recently for its appearances in the original *Dr Finlay's Casebook*.

Kilmahog Woollen Mill (just N) Restored watermill with 250-year-old working wheel, selling tweeds, tartans and other woollen gifts; also maybe whisky tasting. Meals, snacks, shop; cl 25 Dec and 1 Jan; (01877) 330268; free. There is usually a piper outside and Highland dancing some days in summer. The Lade Inn out here has good food.

ɪ) **Rob Roy & Trossachs Visitor Centre** (Ancaster Sq) The story of Scotland's most whitewashed rascal (or brave supporter of the downtrodden, depending on your point of view), well told with hi-tech displays. Also information on the beautiful surrounding countryside. Shop, disabled access; cl wkdys Jan–Feb; (01877) 330342; £2.75.

The Trossachs The Highlands in microcosm, beloved by coach tours for their dense conifer forests, steep glens and beautifully framed lochs. Perhaps surprisingly, not brilliant for low-level walks unless you like forests; the route on to Callander Crags from Callander is one of the best. The Byre at Brig o' Turk is a good food stop.

CARRBRIDGE NH9022

☺ **Landmark Heritage & Adventure Park** Good family day out, with films on Highland life (inc one in 3-D), well signposted forest trails (one through the tree-tops), an elaborate adventure playground, water coaster, and Forestry Heritage Park with fully operational steam-powered sawmill (Apr–Oct). You can sometimes have a go at log-cutting or bark-stripping and Fred the giant Clydesdale horse may be hauling logs to the mill. Great views from the top of the viewing tower. Meals, snacks, shop, disabled access; cl 25 Dec; (01479) 841614; *£6.60. The Dalrachney Lodge Hotel does good lunches.

CASTLE CAMPBELL NS9699

Once known as Castle Gloom, this late 15th-c castle was burned by

Cromwell's troops in the 1650s, but still has its courtyard, great hall and barrel roof, as well as splendid views from the tower. Snacks, shop; cl am Sun, 25–26 Dec, 1–2 Jan, and in winter pm Thurs, all day Fri, am Sun; (01259) 742408; £2.30. The King's Seat in Dollar has good home-made food.

⌂ **Dollar Glen** An amazing short track takes you up through these spectacular 60 acres of Arthur Rackham-esque woodland – catwalks, rock overhangs, jungle-thick vegetation, and a swirling stream below. Take care, some paths are steep and narrow, and can be dangerous after rain. But this is a gripping approach to Castle Campbell.

CAWDOR NH8449

🏰 ⛲ ♔ **Cawdor Castle** (B9090) Home of the Thanes of Cawdor since the 14th c, this splendid old house is one of the most entertaining as well as interesting places to visit in the whole area. Look out especially for the tree inside a tower and the freshwater well inside the house, as well as the more usual fine tapestries, furnishings and paintings (inc Dali's odd interpretation of the Macbeth tale). The busy grounds have several pretty gardens, craft and wool shops, nature trails, and a little pitch-and-putt course. Meals, snacks, shop, disabled access to ground floor only; open May–mid-Oct; (01667) 404615; £5.40, grounds only £2.80. The nearby Cawdor Tavern is good for lunch.

CLAVA CAIRNS NH7544

🏛 A group of circular burial cairns from around 1600 BC surrounded by 3 concentric rings of great stones, on the banks of the River Nairn.

COLLESSIE NO2712

🐦 🐖 **Fife Animal Park** 🅿 (B937) Unique collection of ostriches, emus and rheas – they have birds of all ages (inc maybe newly hatched ones in the incubator house), as well as videos, play area, and animals like lambs, pigs, and wallabies. Meals, snacks, shop, good disabled access; (01337) 831830; £3.50.

CRAIGELLACHIE NJ2944

🍺 **Speyside Cooperage Visitor Centre** (Dufftown Rd) Working cooperage and visitor centre, with a viewing area to watch the craftsmen. There's a reconstructed Victorian cooperage where life-size models speak in the local dialect, and various improvements this year include an enlarged tasting area. Shop (wide range of wood goods), disabled access to exhibition only; cl Sun, winter Sats, 2 wks Christmas; (01340) 871108; £2.25. The little Fiddichside Inn (Keith Rd) is a charmingly old-fashioned fishing pub.

CRAIGIEVAR NJ5609

🏰 **Craigievar Castle** (A980) Perhaps the most fairytale-romantic of the area's castles, this picturesque early 17th-c multiple tower dotted with erratically shaped windows soars to a mushrooming of corbels, turrets and crow-stepped gables. Inside, a warren of narrow staircases climbs through a rich series of ornately beamed and plastered rooms. The National Trust for Scotland are worried that too many people come here, so if you do decide to visit (and it is worth while), try to avoid busy times – it's not a place to absorb coach parties comfortably. Castle open pm May–Sept, grounds open all year; (013398) 83635; £6, £1 grounds only; NTS.

CRAIL NO6107

★ One of the prettiest of the East Neuk fishing villages – the East Neuk being the local name for the east part of the Fife coast.

! **Secret Bunker** (B940 4m W) Beneath an innocuous-looking farmhouse is a network of underground rooms and corridors from where the government would have run the country in a nuclear attack (cl Oct–Easter; (01333) 310301; £6.45).

CRATHES NO7596

🏰 ⛲ **Crathes Castle** (A93) Beautiful 16th-c tower house with wonderful interiors – especially its ceiling paintings, filled with wise old sayings in a mixture of Scots and English. Best of all are the surrounding gardens, inc a 4-acre walled garden with a remarkable series of carefully toned colour borders. Meals, snacks, shop, some disabled access; open Apr–Oct; (01330) 844525; £5, garden only £2.10; NTS.

CRIEFF NN8621

♔ 🏠 ⌂ ❋ A pleasant airy town, perched on the edge of the Highlands. A modern visitor centre (A85) has a pottery, plant centre and demonstrations of paperweight making, and there's a Stuart Crystal factory shop on Muthill Rd. The Knock of Crieff, a wooded hill just above, gives walkers a good viewpoint.

Glenturret Distillery (off A85 NW) Scotland's oldest distillery, dating from 1775 and using the pure water of the Turret Burn. There's a statue of the distillery cat Towser, who died in 1987 but is still in the *Guinness Book of Records* as World Mousing Champion – challengers have 28,899 to beat. Good meals and snacks, shop, some disabled access; cl am Sun, all wknds Jan, 25–26 Dec, 1–2 Jan; (01764) 656565; *£3.50.

CULLODEN NH7445

Culloden Battlefield (B9006) The bleak site of the gruesome massacre in which the 25-year-old Duke of Cumberland destroyed the Highland army of Bonnie Prince Charlie. On the moor a cairn marks this last bloody battle fought on mainland Britain. You can see the Graves of the Clans and the Wells of the Dead, as well as the Old Leanach Cottage around which the battle was fought, now refurbished in period style. Meals, snacks, shop, disabled access; visitor centre cl Jan; (01463) 790607; £3.20; NTS. The Coach House (Stoneyfield, A96) does food.

CULROSS NS9885

★ Fascinating small town (off A985) on the Forth, virtually unchanged since the 16th and 17th c. Until the 1930s this was because no one could afford any improvements, and since then its red pantiled-roofed houses have been carefully restored and preserved by the National Trust for Scotland (they are still lived in). There are the remains of a 13th-c abbey.

Culross Palace The laird's house was the first building the Trust purchased here. It's fully furnished in 17th-c style, and they're creating a period garden. Guides are good at pointing out those small but fascinating details that make the difference between just another building and a real experience. Snacks, shop; cl wkdys in Oct, and all Nov–Mar; (01383) 880359; £4.40; NTS. The price includes admission to the Trust's 2 other main

properties here, the **Town House** (good visitor centre), and the **Study**, with a Norwegian painted ceiling in the drawing room.

CUPAR NO3313

Scottish Deer Centre (Bow of Fife; A91 just W) You can stroke the deer and feed the young fawns at this friendly place, and there are also nature and heritage trails, aerial walkways and observation platforms, and an adventure playground. There's an adjacent holiday shopping courtyard. Snacks, shop, disabled access; cl 25 Dec, 1 Jan; (01337) 810391; £3.95.

DEIL'S CAULDRON NN7624

Beauty spot reached by a signposted circular walk through Glen Lednock from Comrie (where the Earthquake House records tremors).

DOUNE NN6901

Doune Castle (A84) 14th-c stronghold with 2 fine restored towers on the banks of the River Teith. Strong associations with Bonnie Prince Charlie and Walter Scott, and the Knights of Ni – the castle was used in the filming of *Monty Python and the Holy Grail*. Shop; in winter cl pm Thurs and all Fri; (01786) 841742; £2.50. The village's bridge is said to have been built out of spite by James IV's tailor when the ferryman refused him passage.

DUFFTOWN NJ3240

Glenfiddich Distillery (A491, just N) The only Highland distillery where you can follow the entire whisky production process from barley to bottle; most other distilleries bottle elsewhere. Tastings, shop, disabled access; cl winter wknds, Christmas; (01340) 820373; free. Dufftown has a useful museum.

DULNAIN BRIDGE NH9823

Speyside Heather Centre (Skye of Curr, off A95) Over 300 different types of heather growing in ornamental landscaped garden, along with exhibition on its various uses, and shop with wide range of heather-based goods. Home-made meals and snacks, garden centre, disabled access; cl Jan (exc by appointment); (01479) 851359; *75p exhibition.

DUNBLANE NN7801

A small town of ancient origin, its name now tragically familiar all over the world. Plenty of old buildings in its narrow streets, especially around the close of its elegant 13th-c **cathedral**. This incorporates a much older tower, and has a beautiful oval window that you can see only from outside. There's a **museum** nearby (cl 12.30–2pm, all day Sun, some Sats, and Oct–May; free) and the Stirling Arms has good food.

DUNDEE NO3929

♿ ☎ Beneath the straightforward modern wrappings of this bustling city, you can uncover signs of its distinguished heritage in a number of museums. A new science centre should open later this year, and you can watch sweets being made at Shaws Factory (Mains Loan; phone for opening times, (01382) 461435; £1). The Chequers (South Tay St), Royal Oak (Brook St – Indian), Mercantile (Commercial St) and Number 1 (Constitution Rd) all do good-value food.

⚜ ✲ ♿ **Camperdown Country Park** (off A90) 400 acres of fine parkland with golf course, nature trails, woodland footpaths, and wildlife centre with indigenous animals from wolves to wildcats. Also adventure play area themed around the defeat of the Dutch at the 1797 Battle of Camperdown. Snacks, shop, disabled access; (01382) 432689; free, £1.80 wildlife centre.

✲ **Discovery Point** 🏛 (Docks) Excellent, lively visitor centre with hi-tech displays on the Royal Research Ship *Discovery*, moored here, which was the first British purpose-built research vessel, commissioned for Scott's ill-fated expedition to the Antarctic; displays too on him and others who used the ship. Snacks, shop, disabled access; cl 25 Dec, 1–2 Jan; (01382) 201245; £5.

✲ **Frigate *Unicorn*** 🏛 (Victoria Dock) This 1824 vessel is the oldest British-built warship still afloat, now with an audio-visual show and a museum of naval life in her days in commission. Snacks, shop; cl wknds Nov–Mar, 25–26 Dec, 1–2 Jan; (01382) 200900; £4.

🏛🖼 **McManus Museum & Art Galleries** (Albert Sq) Important works by 19th-c Scottish and English artists, and a splendid hall with vaulted ceiling and stained glass; cl am Sun, 25–27 Dec, 1–4 Jan; (01382) 434000; free.

! **Mills Observatory** (Balgay Park) Exhibits on space research and astronomy, as well as a small planetarium (by prior arrangement only), and a splendid 10-inch refracting telescope. Shop; best to ring for opening times, which vary depending on when the sun sets – in autumn and winter for example they're open 4pm–10pm (not wknds or Mon); (01382) 435846; free.

↓T **Verdant Works** 🏛 (West Hendersons Wynd) Lively look at the jute industry, once an important part of the local economy. Snacks, shop, disabled access; cl 25 Dec, 1–2 Jan; (01382) 225282; £5.

DUNFERMLINE NT0987

Quite a prosperous light-industry town with a distinguished distant past – it was once Scotland's capital.

♿ 🏛 **Abbot House** (Maygate) Exhibition on the life of St Margaret of Scotland, a key figure in the town's history; her shrine is outside the abbey nr the East Gate. Cl 25 Dec, 1 Jan; (01383) 733266; £3. The cave she used to pray in is 84 steps below the Glen Bridge car park (cl Oct–Easter; free).

♿ ♟ **Andrew Carnegie Museum** (Moodie St) Focuses on the man who from humble origins in this house made a fortune in Pittsburgh steel, then gave away over $350 million – all the while claiming he didn't believe in charity. There are handloom weaving demonstrations here on the first Fri of each month, May–Oct. Shop, disabled access; cl am Sun, am daily in winter, 24–26 Dec, 1 Jan; *£1.50.

🏛 † **Dunfermline Abbey** The remains of a Benedictine abbey and later church buildings are pleasantly set in quiet precincts away from the busy centre. The foundations of the original 11th-c church underlie the more elaborate Norman nave, and the grave of King Robert the Bruce is marked by a modern brass in the choir stalls. The Palace is the birthplace of Charles I. Shop, snacks; cl am Sun, plus in winter cl pm Thurs and all Fri; (01383) 739026; £1.80.

♿ **Pittencrieff House Museum** (Pittencrieff Park) Fine 17th-c mansion in lovely rugged glen, with costume displays (free).

DUNKELD NO0242

★ † ⌂ Charming small town by the River Tay. The **cathedral** has the tomb of the notorious Wolf of Badenoch, Alexander Stewart (the illegitimate son of English king Richard II). There are pretty preserved cottages (NTS), and riverside forest walks through National Trust land around the waterfalls nr the **Hermitage**, an 18th-c folly, and so-called Ossian's Cave; there may be bat tours and other ranger-led walks in summer.

EDZELL NO5969

▥ ❀ **Edzell Castle** (B966) Some unique features at this pretty old place – the walled garden planted here in 1604, and the charming series of heraldic and mythical sculptures that decorate the walls around it; these alternate with recesses for flowers and nests for birds. They claim to have captured on camera the castle's rather active ghost. Shop, snack, limited disabled access; in winter cl pm Thurs, all day Fri and am Sat; (01356) 648631; £2.50. The Ramsay Arms in Fettercairn has decent food, and just N there's a lovely drive up Glen Esk, passing a wayside folk museum.

ELGIN NJ2263

★ Shopping town of some poise, with some handsome ancient buildings and handy for the coast; Thunderton House has decent food.

▥ ❋ **Elgin Cathedral** Founded in 1224, and known as the Lantern of the North and the Glory of the Kingdom because of its extraordinary beauty and fine-traceried windows. There's still quite a lot to see of the ruins: the 15th-c nave has some ancient Celtic cross

slabs with Pictish symbols, and you can go inside the spires. There is a new viewing plaform in one of the towers with unrestricted views. Shop, some disabled access; cl winter pm Thurs and all Fri, 25–26 Dec, 1–2 Jan; (01343) 547171; *£2.50.

♿ **Elgin Museum** (High St) World-famous fossil collection (cl am Sun, all Nov–May; £2).

🚗 **Moray Motor Museum** (Bridge St) Decent little place, in a converted mill (cl Oct–Mar; *£2.50).

† **Pluscarden Abbey** (nr Barnhill, 5m SW) Fascinating; built in the 13th c, it gradually fell to ruin, but was rebuilt in the 20th c by monks from Prinknash Abbey in Gloucs – they now sing recently rediscovered chant which may well have been sung by St Columba himself; (01343) 890257; free.

▥ **Spynie Palace** (A941 2 m N) Former residence of the bishops of Moray, the biggest tower house in Scotland, with good views over Spynie Loch. Shop, disabled access; cl winter pm Thurs, Fri and am Sun; (01343) 546358; *£1.80.

ELIE NT4999

★ Attractive fishing village set around a broad bay – the beach is notably clean and safe (and has a good pub, the Ship, virtually on it).

FALKIRK NS8979

❀ ♿ ▥ ♿ **Callender House & Park** 🎫 (A803 just E) This huge park, with woodland walks and lots of summer activities, includes a striking old house used briefly as a HQ by Oliver Cromwell. Remodelled in the last century to look like a French chateau, it's now a museum, with costumed

---

Days Out

Villages of the East Neuk: St Andrews; Crail; lunch at the Cellar, Anstruther; Pittenweem; Kellie Castle, or Scotland's Secret Bunker nr Crail.

Cairngorm encounter: Strathspey Steam Railway, Aviemore; lunch at the Olde Bridge there; Highland Wildlife Park, Kincraig – or chairlift up to Cairngorm summit, and/or walk round Loch an Eilein.

Royal Deeside: Braemar Castle; lunch at the Fife Arms, Braemar; drive past Balmoral, then up Glen Muick for a walk round Loch Muick; Crathes Castle or Craigievar Castle.

guides interpreting its history. Part of the Antonine Wall, the Roman Empire's farthest frontier, runs through the grounds. Meals, snacks, shop, disabled access; house cl winter Suns; (01324) 503770; house *£3, park free.

▥ Rough Castle (6m W) One of the best-preserved sections of the Antonine Wall; not too much is left of the Roman fort that once stood here, but you can still see the ramparts and ditches; free.

FALKLAND NO2507

▥ ❀ Falkland Palace & Garden Lovely Renaissance palace of the Stuart kings and queens, set below the Lomond Hills on the main street. Not all is as old as it looks, but it doesn't really matter – accurate restoration work has created a comfortably cosy and genuinely lived-in feel. Pleasant gardens and grounds, with the 1539 tennis courts said to be the oldest in the country. Shop; cl am Sun, and Nov–Mar; (01337) 857397; *£5, £2.40 garden only; NTS. Parts of the village are delightful and were Scotland's first conservation area – the Hunters Lodge and the Stag both have decent food.

FETTERCAIRN NO6573

❀ The square has a magnificent archway erected to commemorate a visit by Queen Victoria, and the Ramsay Arms has decent food. The drive along the twisting and climbing B974 to Banchory is good, with spectacular views from Cairn o' Mount at the top – and when the water's high enough salmon jumping nr the Dee bridge as you enter Banchory.

▥ Fasque ▣ (just N) Prime Minister William Gladstone lived here 1830–1851, and it still belongs to his family. The main rooms look as if they've scarcely been changed (let alone modernised) since he moved to Wales, and it's quite cluttered with homely odds and ends. A couple of years ago a parcel of shooting targets turned up behind a chair posted from London in the 1920s and covered with 'Urgent' stickers – but not yet even opened. There's a touching gallery of servants' portraits and lots of Gladstone memorabilia. Shop, limited disabled access; open May–Sept; (01561) 340569; £3.50.

▥ Fettercairn Distillery (Distillery Rd) One of Scotland's oldest licensed distilleries, with tours, tastings, and a good audio-visual show. Shop, disabled access to visitor centre only; cl Sun, and Oct–Apr; (01561) 340205; free.

FINDLATER CASTLE NJ5467

▥ △ This windswept cliff-edge ruin makes a good destination for a walk; walkers can enjoy other stretches of this coast around Banff, with the bus service along the main road a useful method of return.

FOCHABERS NJ3359

▥ ❀ ⌖ Baxters Visitor Centre (A96 just W) Explores how the grocery shop set up by George and Margaret Baxter grew into a company whose food is now sold all over the world. Tours (not wknds), landscaped gardens and woodland walk. Meals, snacks, good shops, some disabled access; cl 24 Dec–7 Jan; (01343) 820393; free.

ŏ Folk Museum (High St) Very good; cl 1–2pm, free. The Gordon Arms is a reliable food stop in this pleasant town.

FORRES NJ0356

▥ Dallas Dhu Distillery (2m S) Perfectly preserved Victorian distillery, which you can wander around on your own. Animatronic models explain what's happening. Shop (nearly 200 different types of whisky), disabled access; cl winter pm Thurs, Fri, am Sun; (01309) 676548; £2.50.

ŏ Falconer Museum (Tolbooth St) Good fossil collection; cl Sun all year and Sat Oct–Apr; free.

▥ ❀ Sueno's Stone (E end of town) Mysterious 9th- or 10th-c stone that may have been erected to commemorate a forgotten battle. It's 6 metres (20ft) high, carved with a cross on one side and groups of warriors on the other. In summer you can usually climb the Nelson Tower in Grant Park for good views of the Moray Firth; free.

FORT GEORGE NH7656

▥ One of the finest examples of an 18th-c artillery building, one of 3 fortresses built after 1745, when the Hanoverians were taking no risks in keeping this area firmly under their thumb. Very big, with quite a bit to see. Snacks, shop, disabled access; cl Christmas and New Year; (01667) 462777; £4, £3.50 in winter. Just off from the fort in the Moray Firth you may be lucky enough to see one of the very few inshore schools of dolphins around the British coast.

FORVIE NK0029

ϔ Forvie Nature Reserve The fifth-largest sand dune system in Britain – and the one least disturbed by people, so lots of wildlife. You have to stick to the footpaths so as not to disturb the birds and other wildlife. Disabled access; visitor centre cl winter wknds; (01358) 751330; free.

FRASERBURGH NJ9967

Museum of Scottish Lighthouses (Quarry Rd) Based around a lighthouse working up to 1991; guided tours take you to the top and demonstrate how everything works. Snacks, shop, limited disabled access; cl 25–26 Dec and 1–2 Jan; (01346) 511022; *£2.75.

GLAMIS NO3847

Glamis Castle (A94) The family home of the Earls of Strathmore, and the childhood home of the Queen Mother; a splendid creation, utterly suitable as the setting for Shakespeare's murder of Duncan in *Macbeth*. Notable features include the chapel with its painted panels and ceiling, and of course there are those stories about what's locked away in one of the towers. Meals, snacks, shop, limited disabled access; cl Nov–Mar; (01307) 840393; £6. The Strathmore Arms is good for lunch.

GLEN ROY NN3088

ᗡ The glen and its curious Parallel Roads (not actually roads but the tubmarks of a former glacier) can be seen from an easily walked track along its bottom, a spectacular 4-mile route from Brae Roy Lodge (return the same way).

GLENMORE NH9809

ϔ Cairngorm Reindeer Centre (A951) Mingle with free-ranging reindeer in their natural surroundings, a pretty stretch of the Cairngorms; you can feed and stroke them too. Guided walks leave the visitor centre every day at 11am, weather permitting (maybe 2.30pm too in summer). Shop, disabled access to visitor centre only (though usually reindeer down here too); cl 25 Dec, 1 Jan; (01479) 861228; £4.

HUNTLY NJ5240

Huntly Castle The original medieval castle here was destroyed and rebuilt several times, once by Mary, Queen of Scots. Reconstructed for the last time in 1602, the ruins are worth a look for their ornate heraldic decorations. Shop, disabled access; in winter cl pm Thurs and Fri; (01466) 793191; *£2.50. In the square is a little local history **museum**, and a ski centre can teach you how to cross-country ski through the local forest.

ϔ North East Falconry Centre (Cairnie, off A96 N) Four flying displays a day in a richly meadowed glade, as well as a herd of red deer. Snacks, shop, disabled access; cl Nov–Feb; (01466) 760328; £3.75.

INNERPEFFRAY NN9018

Innerpeffray Library Founded in 1680 by the 3rd Lord Drummond, this is Scotland's oldest free-lending library; many rare and interesting books including a particularly fine collection of Bibles. Summer snacks; cl 12.45–2pm, all day Thurs (by appointment only Dec–Jan); (01764) 652819; *£2.

INVERNESS NH6645

The biggest town up here, and the main shopping town for the whole of the N of Scotland. It has an attractive riverside setting and is a handy centre without being at all touristy. James Thins is a good book shop, Nicky Tams (Ness Bank Rd) has decent food, and the Blackfriars (Academy St) is good for local colour. From here the train across to Kyle of Lochalsh gives good Highland views – 2½ hours, the last minutes of which are much the best.

KEMNAY NJ7212

Castle Fraser (off A944) Once one of the grandest castles of Mar, the z-shaped building incorporates the remains of an earlier one, and there are excellent formal gardens. Snacks, shop, meals; cl wkdys in Oct, and all Nov–Apr (exc Easter), grounds open all year; (01330) 833463; £4.20, grounds only £2; NTS.

KENMORE NN7644

★ Scottish Crannog Centre (Crossed-na-Caber) Interesting reconstruction of a prehistoric loch dwelling. Snacks, shop, disabled access; cl Nov–Mar; (01887) 830583; £3. The village itself is pleasant for a stroll.

KILDRUMMY NJ4516

🏰 **Kildrummy Castle** Now in ruins, though still with its original 13th-c round towers, hall and chapel, as well as some later remains. Cl am Sun, plus pm Thurs and all day Fri when quiet, and all Oct–Mar; (01975) 571331; *£2.

🌸 🌱 **Kildrummy Gardens** (A97) Very beautiful indeed and of some botanical interest. There's an alpine garden in an old quarry, a water garden, walks in the woods and a video showing the changes through the seasons. Shop, snacks, disabled access; cl Nov–Mar; (01975) 571203; £2. The ruins provide a spectacular backdrop.

KINCRAIG NH8305

🐘 **Highland Wildlife Park** (B9152) Owned by the same charity as Edinburgh Zoo, this 260-acre wildlife park somehow manages to seem a bit wilder than most animal attractions; perhaps it's because they specialise in species once native to the area, so you really get a feeling that the animals could have wandered out of the surrounding woods and mountains. You drive safari-style around enclosures of reindeer, bears, wildcats and enormous bison. The most exciting feature at the moment is the new wolf territory, where a walkway takes you to a safe vantage point right in the heart of the enclosure. Plenty of rare breeds, including the wild Przewalski's horses, one of the world's rarest mammals, and you may see red squirrels feeding in the forest; daily talks and wknd face painting. Snacks and shop in visitor centre (cl winter), disabled access; cl Nov–Mar in bad weather; (01540) 651270; £6.30.

KINGUSSIE NH7500

👗🎨 **Highland Folk Museum** (Duke St) The first folk museum in Britain, originally opened on Iona in the 1930s. Still a good range of exhibits, inc craft demonstrations and a reconstructed Isle of Lewis Black House. Disabled access; cl am Sun, wknds Sept–Oct and all Nov–Mar; (01540) 661307; £3 (inc admission to the Highland Folk Park below). The Royal is useful for lunch; the town's pronounced Kinoossie.

🚜 **Highland Folk Park** (A86 E) Demonstrates the life and work of crofters at the turn of the century; you may be able to help with some of the farming activities. Also a Museum of Highland Sport, which explains why so many of the area's golfers are left-handed. Usually open wkdys Apr–Oct; (01540) 673551; £3 (inc admission to the folk museum above).

KINNOULL HILL NO1423

⛰️ 🌱 🏰 Just outside Perth, this offers walkers forest tracks and paths, and two folly 'castles' above the River Tay.

KINROSS NO1202

🌸 **Kinross House Gardens** Rather fine and formal, with yew trees, roses and herbaceous borders. Disabled access; cl Oct–Apr; (01577) 863680; £2. The Muirs has good-value food, as does the Lomond Hotel at Kinnesswood with its quiet views over Loch Leven.

🏰 ⚓ **Loch Leven Castle** Reached by ferry from Kinross jetty, the islet fortress where Mary, Queen of Scots was imprisoned for a while; she was rowed to freedom by a page boy, but only after she had been persuaded to abdicate in favour of her infant son. Shop; limited disabled access; cl Oct–Mar; (0131) 668 8800; £3 (inc ferry).

🦅 **Loch Leven RSPB Visitor Centre** At the S end of the lake, with good facilities for watching the birds; in the winter the evening flights and sounds of the thousands of ducks and geese are very moving. Centre cl 25 Dec, 1 Jan; (01577) 862355; *£3. The lake itself is serene rather than dramatic.

KIRKCALDY NT3093

🏰 ❄️ This busy resort and shopping town is not too interesting to visitors, but has some charming old wynds and houses in the eastern suburb of Dysart, which has its own picturesque little harbour. Between here and the main town is 15th-c **Ravenscraig Castle**, perhaps most notable for its symmetrical shape. Great views over the Firth of Forth. Snacks, limited disabled access; free.

KIRRIEMUIR NO3854

🏠👗 **Barrie's Birthplace** (Brechin Rd) The birthplace of the writer of *Peter Pan* in 1860: the upper floors are furnished in the style of the period, and next door are displays relating to his work, both literary and theatrical. Teas, shop, disabled access; open Easter, daily May–Sept (exc am Sun), wknds in Oct; (01575) 572646; £2; NTS.

LOCH EARN NN5924
⌂ ✌ With a trunk road alongside, so not one of Scotland's quieter lochs – and largely given over to water-skiing and that sort of thing. Lochearnhead offers a round walk from along a nature trail into Glen Ogle and back via the trackbed of an abandoned railway.

LOCH ERICHT NN6284
⌂ Very peaceful but does involve foot-slogging to make the most of it. The road from Dalwhinnie on the A9 at the N end runs along the foot of a steep forested slope; the S end of the loch has more varied scenery, but no road once you reach the end of the little road off the B846 at Bridge of Ericht.

LOCH KATRINE NN4009
⚓ A lovely stretch of water that inspired Scott's *Lady of the Lake*, and has a Victorian steamer in summer. The main approach to the E end through the Trossachs does bring a fair bit of summer traffic, but the central part of the loch is served by just a narrow back road, so is fairly peaceful even then.

LOCH MUICK NO2984
⌂ Nestling below the summit of Lochnagar, this has paths around its shores, with a car park at the end of the Glen Muick road from Ballater.

LOCH RANNOCH NN6257
⚐ ⌂ Among the quieter and more beautiful lochs, wooded for much of its length. There are peaceful walks from the back road along the southern shore.

LOCH TAY NN7745
⌂ ★ ❀ Remarkably long, with the view seeming to change moment by moment as the clouds flit across the sky. It has a quiet road along its southern side. There are easy walks at the E end of the loch, from the attractive estate village of **Kenmore** (where the village inn has a poem in Burns's own handwriting on the wall of the lounge) along the banks of the River Tay, or into the adjacent forest to a viewpoint over the loch.

⌂ ❀ **Ben Lawers** This towering bulk, well over 1,200 metres (nearly 4,000ft), dominates Loch Tay, and is an interesting spot, with alpine wild

flowers not found elsewhere in Britain and a quite different feel from other Highland mountains; a steep road leads up the side.

LOCH VOIL NN5220
❀ Served by just a narrow back road, so fairly peaceful even in summer; it's famous for having Rob Roy's grave at Balquhidder. It's worth keeping on the road beyond the far end of the loch; there's some striking scenery around the picnic site at its end.

LOMOND HILLS NO2206
⌂ ❀ A level walk from the car park by the road above Falkland gives some pleasant rambles – not to be confused with Loch Lomond, this upland gives views over most of SE Scotland.

MACDUFF NJ7064
🐟 **Marine Aquarium** (High Shore) Huge central tank holding nearly half a million litres, open to the sky – a unique design. Emphasis on fish native to the Moray Firth, with touch pools and audio-visual presentation. Snacks, shop, disabled access; (01261) 833369; £2.75.

MEIGLE NO2844
🏛🍴 **Meigle Museum** Outstanding collection of Celtic Christian sculptured stones, all found in or around the churchyard. Shop, disabled access; cl 12.30–1.30pm, and all Nov–Mar; (01828) 640612; £1.80.

MINTLAW NJ9847
🐾 ⚐ ♿ **Aberdeenshire Farming Museum** More than 200 acres of lovely woodland and farmland, criss-crossed with nature trails and with plenty of wildlife. The museum here illustrates two centuries of farming history, with seasonal open-air demonstrations and tours. Meals, snacks, shop, disabled access; park open all year, heritage centre cl Oct–Apr; (01771) 622906; free.

MONTRAVE NO3806
🐷 **Praytis Farm Park** (A916) An indoor putting green and crazy golf in addition to the usual farm animals and walks; also deer park, play areas, and big farm shop with venison and smoked salmon. Home-made meals and snacks, some disabled access; cl Jan–Feb, 25–26 Dec; (01333) 350209; *£4.

MONTROSE NO6856
🐦 ❀ **Montrose Basin Wildlife Centre** 🅿 (A934) The enclosed

estuary is a rich feeding ground for thousands of native and migrant birds, including oystercatchers, curlews and eider ducks. This centre has great views, interactive displays and high-powered telescopes. Snacks, shop, disabled access; cl 25–26 Dec, 1 Jan; (01674) 676336); £2.50.

MUTHILL NN8616

❀ ✿ Drummond Castle Gardens (A822) Majestic formal gardens originally laid out in 1630 by the 2nd Earl of Perth. Lovely views from the upper terrace, splendid early Victorian parterre, and centrepiece sundial designed and built by the master mason of King Charles I. Open pm May–Oct; (01764) 681257; *£4.

NAIRN NH8856

★ A quiet, relaxed and rather discreet old-fashioned resort, with good clean sheltered beaches.

NORTH QUEENSFERRY NT1380

♪ **Deep-Sea World** 🖼 One of the most elaborate aquariums we know; moving walkways take you through an incredible transparent viewing tunnel as long as a football pitch, surrounded by a million gallons of water and sharks and exotic fish from all around the world. A new amphibian collection includes the world's most poisonous frog. You can go round and round as often as you like. Meals, snacks, shop, disabled access; cl 25 Dec; (01383) 411411; £6.25. The Ferrybridge Hotel has good-value food.

OCHIL HILLS NS9099

⌂ A range of green mountains which rise without preamble from the lowland plain – a striking textbook example of the Highland Fault. A path from Tillicoultry up Mill Glen takes you to Ben Cleuch, the highest point of the range.

OYNE NJ6725

♨ ▥ ⅄ **Archaeolink** This lively new centre is a fun exploration of the past. A remarkable turf-roofed building houses an audio-visual presentation, there's an exhibition on myths and legends and you can try out ancient crafts such as weaving, grinding and arrow-making. Outside are the remains of an Iron Age hill fort, a reconstructed Iron Age farm, a new Roman marching camp and a sandpit play area, where younger members of the family can dig for the past. Meals, snacks, shop, disabled

access; (01464) 851500; £3.90.

PERTH NO1223

★ ❀ Spaciously laid out along the broad River Tay, with an excellent specialist rhododendron nursery at Glendoick Gardens (A85). There are a couple of decent museums and galleries, and the Greyfriars and Timothy's are popular for lunch.

❀ **Branklyn Garden** (116 Dundee Rd) Only about 2 acres but seems much bigger, thanks to a remarkable planting of interesting rhododendrons, small trees, asiatic primulas, meconopsis, lilies and the like. Shop, disabled access; cl Nov–Mar; (01738) 625535; £2.50; NTS.

🏛 **Caithness Glass** (Inveralmond Industrial Estate, N edge) Displays of paperweight-making, with audio-visual theatre, collectors' museum and factory shop. Meals, snacks, shop, disabled access; cl am Sun Nov–Mar, 25–26 Dec, 1–2 Jan, no glass-making wknds (exc July and Aug); (01738) 637373; free.

🏰 **Huntingtower Castle** (just W) The main thing to see is its interesting painted ceiling; in winter cl pm Thurs and Fri, 25–26 Dec, 1–2 Jan; £2. The nearby Huntingtower House Hotel has good-value food.

PETERCULTER NJ7900

🏰 ❀ **Drum Castle** (off A93) Still looks out over what's left of the medieval forest granted the family by Robert the Bruce. Mainly a much-altered Jacobean mansion, the house is based around a 13th-c keep, one of the 3 oldest tower houses in Scotland. There's a historic rose garden. Snacks, shop, limited disabled access; cl am, wkdys in Oct, and all Nov–Easter; (01330) 811454; £4.40; NTS. The Lairhillock Inn at Netherley a few miles S is good for lunch.

PETERHEAD NK1246

♨ ♯ One of Europe's busiest fishing ports, with a bustling market and smartened up marina. There's a good local history **museum** on St Peter St (cl pm Weds, Sun and bank hols; free) and a **heritage centre** (South Rd) with interactive displays on the fishing industry. Shop, meals, snacks, disabled access; cl am Sun and winter wkdys; £2.50.

♪ **Ugie Fish House** (Golf Rd) Ancient place selling a good range of wild salmon and trout, caught from the adjacent river in season; cl pm Sat, all day Sun; (01779) 476209.

PITLOCHRY NN9458

🐟 An inland resort town for a good long time, beautifully set in fine countryside; a happy sort of place, with a comfortable feel. There's lovely woodland on the banks of man-made Loch Faskally, with walks and nature trails. The Westlands and the Moulin Inn (which brews its own beer) have decent food.

🏠 **Edradour Distillery** (A924 E) Scotland's smallest distillery, founded in 1825 and virtually unchanged since Victorian times. Guided tours, tastings, shop, some disabled access; cl am Sun, all Nov–Mar (exc shop); (01796) 472095; free.

🏛 **Killiecrankie Visitor Centre** (B8079 NW) Queen Victoria was just one of the people to have found this romantic spot beguiling, but it wasn't always so serene. In 1689 it was the site of a fierce battle when the Highlanders routed the troops of William IV, and this visitor centre tells the tale. Snacks, shop, disabled access; cl Nov–Apr; (01796) 473233; £1; NTS. The Killiecrankie Hotel, with good food, is an attractive place.

🏠 ♪ **Pitlochry Power Station** The visitor centre shows how the hydro-electric scheme works, and you may see salmon leaping up the fish ladder; cl Nov–Mar; £2.

PITMEDDEN NJ8828

✿ **Pitmedden Garden** (A920) Originally planted in the 17th c and pretty much unchanged since, with sundials, fountains and pavilions among the elaborate formal gardens. Snacks, shop, limited disabled access; cl Oct–Apr; (01651) 842352; £3.90; NTS. The Redgarth Hotel over at Oldmeldrum has decent food.

PITTENWEEM NO5402

★ Attractive East Neuk fishing village, with some attractive crow-gabled houses (the gables in steps which seagulls rather than crows sit on here).

🏛 ✿ **Kellie Castle & Gardens** (B9171) Fine example of 16th- and 17th-c domestic architecture, though

parts date from the 14th c, with good collections of plasterwork, panelling and furniture. Also 4 acres of gardens inc a Victorian walled garden. Snacks, shop; grounds open all year, house cl am, wkdys in Oct, and all Nov–May (exc Easter); (01333) 720271; £3.99, garden only £1; NTS.

PORT OF MENTEITH NN5700

🏛 ⛵ **Inchmahome Priory** Famous as the refuge of the infant Mary, Queen of Scots in 1543, this Augustinian priory was founded in 1238 on an island in the middle of the lake, and in spring and summer you can get a boat across. Robert the Bruce prayed here before the Battle of Bannockburn. Snacks, shop; cl Oct–Mar; (01877) 385294; £3 inc ferry.

ROTHES NJ2749

🏠 **Glen Grant Distillery** Founded in 1840 by the brothers Grant, whose malt whisky was one of the first to be bottled and sold as a single malt. Guided tours, tastings, shop, some disabled access; cl am Sun, all Nov–mid-Mar; (01542) 783318; *£2.50.

ST ANDREWS NO5116

🏌 ✝ ♪ This civilised university town doubles as rather a dignified seaside resort, with clean, safe beaches. It's outstanding for golfers, though to play on the hallowed greens of the Old Course, you'll need to ring the St Andrews Links Trust on (01334) 466666 before 2pm the day before you want to go, to enter a daily ballot; after that you'll have to tee up £70. There are a few interesting **museums** on the city's history, some quite lively, and a number of fine buildings belonging to Scotland's oldest university – especially St Leonard's and St Mary's colleges. South St is worth strolling along: attractive riggs or small courts and alleys off, the ancient West Port gateway at the end, and **Holy Trinity Church** where John Knox preached his first sermon in 1547. You can arrange **fishing trips** with Mr Thomas on (01334) 870957, rod and tackle provided. Ma Bells (pleasant seafront views outside), Ogstons, Westport and (1m S) Grange are all good eating places.

🏌 **British Golf Museum** (Bruce Embankment) Fascinates anyone keen on the game, with interactive and audio-visual displays going right through its 500-year history. Assorted memorabilia include lots of glamorous golfing gear, and the technology is some of the most up-to-date you'll find in any museum. Shop, disabled access; cl Tues and Weds mid-Oct–Easter; (01334) 478880; £3.75.

St Andrews Botanic Garden (just off Canongate) Around 18 pleasantly landscaped acres, with a good range of trees and shrubs, and several glasshouses. Disabled access; (01334) 477178; £2.

St Andrews Castle 13th-c, the scene of Bishop Beaton's murder during a wave of anti-Catholic feeling in 1546. It was largely demolished in the 17th c, but some substantial ruins remain. Shop, disabled access; cl 25–26 Dec, 1–2 Jan; (01334) 477196; £2.50.

St Andrews Cathedral Impressive twin-towered Norman remains; in its time this was the largest cathedral in Scotland, but angry locals sacked it in the 16th c. Shop, limited disabled access; cl 25–26 Dec, 1–2 Jan; (01334) 472563; £2. You can get a joint ticket with the castle. Beside it the very tall and narrow Romanesque **St Rules Tower** is part of the older church the cathedral was built to replace (perhaps pre-Conquest), and if you can face over 150 steps gives wonderful views from the top.

Sea Life Centre (The Scores) Three resident seals, and lots of other examples of British native marine life, well displayed in realistic re-creations of the sea bed. Meals, snacks, shop, limited disabled access; phone for winter opening, cl 25 Dec, 1 Jan; (01334) 74786; *£4.35.

ST MONANCE NO5201

★ † ✗ One of the most attractive East Neuk fishing villages, with an unusual fisherman's **church** and a restored 18th-c **windmill** (the Seafood Restaurant has good seafood and sea views).

SCONE NO1126

Scone Palace (off A93) The seat of government in Scotland from Pictish times, though the current building is largely 16th-c behind an 18th-c castellated façade. It was the site of the Stone of Destiny – the famous coronation stone – until it was seized by

the English in 1296 (it's at last returned to Scotland, though to Edinburgh Castle). Good displays of porcelain, furniture, clocks and needlework, and the grounds are pleasant. Meals, snacks, shop, some disabled access; cl mid-Oct–Good Fri; (01738) 552300; *£5.60. Pronounced 'Scoon', by the way.

STIRLING NS7994

† Strategically placed on the Firth of Forth, this is a very unstuffy place, with the university students putting quite a bit of buzz into the atmosphere. Dropping down the steep hill on which the castle stands is an attractive and interesting network of old streets, with a lot of character in their old-to-ancient buildings; Argyll Lodgings is an interesting ruined Renaissance-style mansion, and the Church of Holy Rude was where Mary, Queen of Scots and James VI were crowned as babies.

Bannockburn Heritage Centre (A872 S) Plenty of information on Robert the Bruce's finest hour, inc an audio-visual show on the battle itself. Shop, snacks, disabled access; cl Jan and Feb; (01786) 472140; £2.50.

Smith Art Gallery & Museum (Dumbarton Rd) Good changing exhibitions; cl am Sun, all day Mon; (01786) 471917; free.

Stirling Castle Provides magnificent views from its lofty hilltop site. It became very popular with the royal family in the 15th and 16th c, and most of the buildings date from that period. The finest features are the Chapel Royal built by James VI (and I of England), and the Renaissance palace built by James V. The Great Hall has been reopened to the public after restoration. Snacks, shop; cl 25–26 Dec, 1–2 Jan; (01786) 450000; *£6, parking £2.50. There's a good visitor centre in a restored building next door. Whistlebinkies (St Mary's Wynd), formerly part of the ancient castle stables, has decent food.

Wallace Monument (top of Abbey Craig, just NE) Perhaps Stirling's most satisfying attraction, a huge 67-metre (220ft) Victorian tower with dramatic views from the top of its 246 spiralling steps. Each floor has lively audio-visual displays, one looking at Sir William Wallace, another examining other Scottish heroes. There is a statue of Wallace as portrayed by Mel Gibson in *Braveheart* in the new car park. Snacks, shop; cl Christmas, New Year, and maybe for restoration work in Nov; (01786) 472140; £3.25.

STONEHAVEN NO8783
Dunnottar Castle (just S) On a precipitous sea-girt crag stands this bleak and battered but still extensive and well preserved 14th-c ruin, used for the filming of Mel Gibson's *Hamlet*. It sheltered the Scottish Crown Jewels during the Civil War, but has seen much darker episodes in its time. Shop; cl winter wknds, 25–26 Dec, 1 Jan; (01569) 62173; £3.

Tolbooth Museum (Old Pier) Good local history museum in ancient tolbooth; cl 12–2pm, am Weds and Sun, all day Tues, and Oct–May; (01779) 477778; free. This old fishing town has more seasidey but discreet Victorian streets in its upper part; the harbourside Marine has good, reasonably priced food.

TARVES NJ8634
Haddo House (off B999) Wonderfully grand yet still very much a family home; designed by William Adam, and refurbished in the 1880s in the Adam Revival style. The chapel has stained glass by Burne-Jones. Its Choral Society is renowned, holding concerts and operas in the adjacent hall; (01651) 851770 for what's on. Meals, snacks, shop, disabled access; house open Easter, then pm May–Sept and wknds in Oct, gardens open all year; (01651) 851440; £4.40; NTS. Surrounding the house is a 150-acre country park, with wildlife exhibition and guided walks, and a shop selling produce from the estate, and local salmon, venison, whisky and crafts. There's an interesting medieval tomb in Tarves churchyard.

Tolquhon Castle (off B999 S) Impressive remains of a 15th-c castle (cl winter wkdys; £1.80).

Tolquhon Gallery Decidedly unstuffy, with contemporary Scottish art and crafts; cl all day Thurs, and wkdys Jan and Feb; free.

TENTSMUIR SANDS NO5024
Five miles of shore walking from Kinshaldy car park on the Fife coast; you may see common and grey seals on the sandbanks, and there are good clean beaches – shorter routes back through the forest.

TURRIFF NJ7250
Fyvie Castle (off A947) Each of the 5 towers of this magnificent palace was built in a different century by the family that lived here throughout; the oldest parts date back to the 13th c, and the whole building is one of the most fantastic examples of Scottish baronial architecture. Collections of armour and tapestry, and paintings by Romney and Gainsborough. Snacks, shop; cl am (exc July/Aug), wkdys in Oct, and Nov–Easter; (01651) 891266; £4.40; NTS. The Towie Tavern does good food.

Working malt whisky distilleries open for tours and tastings include **Cardhu** NJ1943 (B9102 nr Knockando), cl wknds exc July–Sept; £2; **Dalwhinnie** NN6384 Scotland's highest, cl wknds; **Glencoyne** NS5086 (A81 nr Killearn); **Glenfarclas** NJ2138 (Marypark), cl wknds exc Jun–Sept; £3.50; and **Tomatin** NH7929, not wknds exc summer Sats.

Worthwhile inns in good spots for walkers, drivers or just strollers (besides those we've mentioned as places to eat at or stay in) include the lochside Achray at St Fillans NN6924, seaview Creel at Catterline NO8778, Loch Ericht Hotel at Dalwhinnie NN6384, Dores Hotel at Dores by Loch Ness NH5930, Clachan overlooking pretty Drymen's green square NS4788, Anchor at Dunipace NS8083, Old Smiddy in the pleasant village of Errol NO2523, Hungry Monk at Gartocharn NS4286, Clova Hotel in Glen Clova NO3373, Old Mill at Killearn NS5285, Cross Keys at Kippen NS6594 (pretty village), Trossachs Hotel nr Loch Achray NN5106, Corriegour Lodge nr Altrua on Loch Lochy NN2390, Loch Tummel Hotel above Loch Tummel NN8460, Meikleour Inn at Meikleour NO1539 (handy for the 30-metre (100ft) high beech hedge planted in 1746), Pennan Inn in the pretty seaside *Local Hero* village of Pennan NJ8465, Potarch Hotel at Potarch NO6097, Sheriffmuir Inn on wild Sheriff Muir NN8202 and Tomdoun Hotel at Tomdoun NH1501.

Where to eat

Many places in the **Where to stay** section, above, also have very good food.

ABERDEEN NJ9305 **Q Brasserie** *9 Alford Pl (01224) 595001* On the second floor of a former religious training college, this bustling place has bold modern paintings, simple contemporary furniture on bare boards, a bar in what was the altar, innovative brasserie-style cooking, super puddings, and a decent little wine list; cl am Sat, Sun. **£30|£6.**

ANSTRUTHER NO5603 **Cellar** *24 East Green (01333) 310378* Off a little courtyard nr the harbour, with beams, stone walls, and peat fires – and wonderful fresh fish, good wines; cl Sun, winter am Mon, am Tues, cl 25 Dec, 1 Jan. **£35|£8.50.**

BLAIRGOWRIE NO1845 **Cargill's** *Lower Mill St (01250) 876735* Busy bistro, part of a complex that includes a crafts gallery and coffee shop, antiques warehouse and upholstery business; good varied food inc nice puddings, and several teas and coffees; bright, helpful staff; cl Mon; disabled access. **£22|£6.50.**

CUPAR NO3714 **Ostlers Close** *25 Bonnygate (01334) 655574* Cosy unpretentious much liked restaurant with lovely food using the best local fresh produce, game and fish, and home-grown herbs, a reasonably priced wine list, and friendly owners; cl Sun, Mon, 2 wks Jun. **£33 dinner, £23 lunch|£9.50.**

DRYBRIDGE NJ4362 **Old Monastery** *(01542) 832660* Lovely views from former monastery – as well as very good fish, game and Aberdeen Angus beef, reasonably priced wines and friendly service; cl Sun, Mon, 2 wks Nov, 3 wks Jan; children over 8 in evening. **£30|£7.50 2-course lunch.**

GLAMIS NO3846 **Strathmore Arms** *(01307) 840248* Picturesque unspoilt village with a simply decorated old inn, well presented, popular food, roaring log fire in the lounge, and good caring service; disabled access. **£20|£7.50.**

KELTY NT1494 **Butterchurn** *Cocklaw Mains Farm (01383) 830169* Set in the courtyard of a farm, this popular restaurant has fine views over Loch Leven, and serves morning coffee, lunch, afternoon teas, snacks, and traditional high teas using fresh local ingredients; they also sell their own products to take away and have a craft and gift centre, farmyard pets for children, and walks and cycle trails; cl 25–26 Dec, 1–2 Jan; disabled access. **£20|£4.50.**

KILMAHOG NN6008 **Lade Inn** *(01877) 330152* Well run place in lovely wooded surroundings with a beamed and partly panelled main bar, Highland prints, no smoking room opening on to a terrace and attractive garden, a wide choice of interesting bar food, decent wine list and real ales; disabled access. **£20.25|£4.95.**

KINGUSSIE NH7500 **Cross** *(01540) 661166* Converted 19th-c stone tweed mill by a stream, now a no smoking restaurant-with-rooms, with a relaxed, friendly atmosphere, extremely good eclectic Scottish cooking (evenings only) using the best local produce, an excellent wine list, marvellous cheeses, and super breakfasts; bdrms; cl pm Tues, 1–26 Dec, 5 Jan–25 Feb; children over 12; disabled access. **£39.95 5 courses**.

PERTH NO1223 **Let's Eat** *77 Kinnoull St (01738) 643377* Very popular restaurant in what was the Theatre Royal with a relaxed friendly atmosphere, enjoyable modern cooking inc proper old-fashioned puddings, and a short selective wine list; cl Sun, Mon, 2 wks Jan, 2 wks July; disabled access. **£27|£6.50.**

ST ANDREWS NO5016 **Vine Leaf** *131 South St (01334) 477497* Warmly welcoming and attractively laid-out dining room overlooking walled herb garden, super food (inc seafood, game and vegetarian dishes), unobtrusive service and decent wines; evenings only; cl Sun, Mon and Jan; disabled access. **£25.**

ST FILLANS NN6924 **Four Seasons** *(01764) 685333* Long white family-run hotel with wonderful Loch Earn views, generous helpings of very good Scottish food inc super fish and game dishes; lunchtime snacks, too; you can eat in the Tarken Bar, on the terrace or in the smarter restaurant; comfortable bdrms and chalets; cl Jan–Mar. **£34.95 4 courses|£6.95.**

ST MONANCE NO5201 **Seafood Restaurant and Bar** *West End (01333)*

730327 Former Cabin, immaculate, snug and cosy inside, with seafaring models and mementos on illuminated shelves, plenty of well polished light wood panelling, plainer locals' bar, very good modern cooking inc excellent seafood in the no smoking back restaurant, and good enjoyable bar food; cl Mon, 3 wks Jan. **£27**|£13 2-course lunch.

STONEHAVEN NO8595 **Lairhillock** *Netherley, 6m N (01569) 730001* Relaxed and friendly extended 18th-c country pub with a wide choice of good, popular and imaginative food, well kept real ales, lots of malt whiskies and wines, nice views from the cheerfully atmospheric beamed bar, central fire in the spacious lounge, and an airy conservatory; cl 25–26 Dec, 1–2 Jan; disabled access. **£28**|£4.65.

WEEM NN8449 **Ailean Chraggan** *(01887) 820346* Small friendly inn with lovely views, very good food inc plenty of fresh fish and enjoyable puddings – you can eat in the bar or restaurant – and a very good wine list; comfortable bdrms; cl 25–26 Dec, 1–2 Jan. **£21.45**|£7.50.

West Scotland

Mainland Scotland's finest scenery; glorious coast.

Roads winding slowly along the intricate coast make driving here a succession of glorious sea-and-mountain views.

Oban is quite lively, Inveraray is interesting, and Dunoon has all you'd expect of a long-standing summer resort; all three have things to keep children entertained – as does Glencoe. Otherwise places to visit are mostly low-key, suiting the relaxed pace of life here – the great gardens are the high point for most people, and are at their peak in May and June. That's a glorious time to visit this part, with very long days and lots of wild flowers. In high summer the traffic on the twisting roads in the most scenic parts can make driving painfully slow, and the midges become a menace. In autumn the Highland heather's still gorgeous and the weather can be very kind, but the days are shortening dramatically. In winter most hotels here do stay open, and the coast stays very mild.

Where to stay

ARDUAINE NM7910 **Loch Melfort** *Arduaine, Oban, Argyll PA34 4XG (01852) 200233* **£106,** plus special breaks; 27 rms, gorgeous sea views. Comfortable hotel popular in summer with passing yachtsmen (hotel's own moorings), nautical charts and marine glasses in airy modern bar, own lobster pots and nets so emphasis on seafood, pleasant foreshore walks, outstanding springtime woodland gardens; cl mid-Jan–mid-Feb; disabled access.

BALLACHULISH NN0459 **Ballachulish House** *Ballachulish, Argyll PA39 4JX (01855) 811266* **£84;** 8 rms with views. Remote 18th-c house with a friendly atmosphere, spacious antique-furnished elegant rooms, log fires, an honesty bar, hearty helpings of good food using local fish and beef, and a billiard room; cl Oct–Mar; children over 8.

CRINAN NR7894 **Crinan Hotel** *Crinan, Lochgilphead, Strathclyde PA31 8SR (01546) 830261* **£105,** plus special breaks; 22 rms. Rather smart hotel by start of canal to Lochgilphead; marvellous views from the stylish formal top-floor restaurant, nautical decorations in the lounge bar, lots of local fish and a large wine list; disabled access.

DERVAIG NM4449 **Druimard Country House** *Dervaig, Tobermory, Isle of Mull*

PA75 6QW (01688) 400345 **£135 inc dinner,** plus special breaks; 7 rms. Peaceful Victorian country house with wonderful views across the glen and River Bellart, friendly helpful owners, a comfortable lounge and conservatory with lots of pictures, books and magazines, good breakfasts, and excellent food using the best local produce; the Mull Little Theatre is in the grounds; dogs welcome; cl Nov–end Mar; disabled access.

ELLANBEICH NM7417 **Inshaig Park** *Easdale, Oban, Argyll PA34 4RF (01852) 300256* **£62;** 7 rms. Solid family-run stone building on Seil island (bridge to mainland), a hotel since Victorian times, with stunning sea views, good food inc fresh local seafood, friendly bar, and a warm welcome.

ERISKA NM9042 **Isle of Eriska Hotel** *Ledaig, Eriska, Oban, Argyll PA37 1SD (01631) 720371* **£210,** plus winter breaks; 17 rms. In a wonderful position on a small island linked by bridge to the mainland, impressive baronial hotel with a very relaxed country-house atmosphere, log fires and a pretty drawing room; excellent really enjoyable food, exemplary service, and a comprehensive wine list; leisure complex with indoor swimming pool, sauna, gym and so forth, lovely surrounding walks, and 9-hole golf course, windsurfing or waterskiing, clay pigeon shooting, pony trekking, and golf – and plenty of wildlife inc tame badgers who come nightly to the library door for their bread and milk; cl Jan; children over 5 in evening restaurant (high tea provided); disabled access.

FORT WILLIAM NN0973 **Grange** *Grange Rd, Fort William, Inverness-shire PH33 6JF (01397) 705516* ***£78;** 4 rms. Charming Victorian house in quiet landscaped gardens with a log fire in the comfortable lounge, fine breakfasts in the dining room overlooking Loch Linnhe, and helpful hard-working owners; cl Dec–Feb; children over 12.

ISLE OF GIGHA NR6448 **Isle of Gigha Hotel** *Isle of Gigha, Argyll PA41 7AA (01583) 505254* **£84,** plus special breaks; 13 rms, most with own bthrm. Attractive traditional family-run small hotel with lots of charm, a bustling bar (popular with yachtsmen and locals), neatly kept and comfortable residents' lounge, and local seafood in the restaurant; self-catering cottages also; cl Nov–Feb.

KILBERRY NR7164 **Kilberry Inn** *Kilberry, Tarbert, Argyll PA29 6YD (01880) 770223* ***£67;** 3 ground floor, no smoking rms. Homely and warmly welcoming inn on W coast of Knapdale with fine sea views, old-fashioned character, entertaining owner, and outstanding country cooking – everything home-made, from soups and breads to chutney and marmalade; cl mid-Oct–Easter; well behaved children over 8.

KILCHRENAN NN0421 **Taychreggan** *Kilchrenan, Taynuilt, Argyll PA35 1HQ (01866) 833211* **£109,** plus special breaks; 19 rms. Civilised and extensively refurbished hotel with a fine garden running down to Loch Awe; comfortable airy bar with stuffed birds and fish, attractively served lunchtime bar food, polite, efficient staff, good freshly prepared food in the no smoking dining room, a careful wine list, dozens of malt whiskies, and a pretty inner courtyard; no children.

KILFINAN NR9279 **Kilfinan Hotel** *Kilfinan, Tighnabruaich, Argyll PA21 2EP (01700) 821201* **£88,** plus special breaks; 11 rms. Friendly former coaching inn, popular locally, in fine scenery with sporting activities such as shooting, fishing and stalking; very good restaurant food, decent bar food, and log fires; cl Feb; children over 12.

KILNINVER NM8724 **Knipoch** *Kilninver, Oban, Argyll PA34 4QT (01852) 316251* **£154;** 16 rms. Elegant and very well kept Georgian hotel in lovely countryside overlooking Loch Feochan; fine family portraits, log fires, fresh flowers and polished furniture in comfortable lounges and bars, carefully chosen wines and malt whiskies, and marvellous food inc their own smoked salmon; cl mid-Dec–Mar.

OBAN NM8529 **Dungallan House Hotel** *Gallanach Rd, Oban, Argyll PA34 4PD (01631) 563799* **£82,** plus special breaks; 13 rms, most with own bthrm. Victorian house in neat grounds with fine views over the bay to Mull and Lismore; marvellous food in the elegant no smoking dining room, a relaxed lounge bar and reading room, warm coal fires, and helpful friendly owners and staff; cl Nov and Feb; limited disabled access.

ONICH NN0461 **Allt-Nan-Ros** *Onich, Fort William, Inverness-shire PH33 6RY* (01855) 821210 **£110,** plus special breaks; 20 rms. Victorian shooting lodge with fine Scottish food, a friendly atmosphere, bright airy rooms, and magnificent views across Loch Linnhe and the gardens; cl mid-Nov–28 Dec; disabled access.

PENNYGHAEL NM5226 **Pennyghael Hotel** *Pennyghael, Isle of Mull, Argyll PA70 6HB (01681) 704288* **£98.90 inc dinner;** 6 rms. Beautifully placed converted byre by Loch Scridain with a comfortable little lounge, generous breakfasts, lovely (if limited in choice) evening food using local fish and venison, and really friendly owners and staff; cl end Oct–1 May.

PORT APPIN NM9045 **Airds Hotel** *Port Appin, Appin, Argyll PA38 4DF (01631) 730236* **£246 inc dinner,** plus winter breaks; 12 lovely rms – also, 4 cheaper rooms in Linnhe House 60 yards away. Instantly relaxing 18th-c inn with lovely views of Loch Linnhe and the islands of Lismore, blissfully comfortable day rooms, professional courteous staff, and charming owners; the food is exceptional (as is the wine list) and there are lots of surrounding walks, with more on Lismore (small boat every 2 hours); cl 18–27 Dec, 6–31 Jan; dogs by arrangement.

STRACHUR NN0802 **Creggans** *Strachur, Cairndow, Argyll PA27 8BX (01369) 860279* ***£95;** 19 rms. Smart inn in extensive grounds overlooking sea loch and hills (deer-stalking, fishing and pony-trekking can be arranged); attractive lounge, conservatory and cocktail bar, lively locals' bar, particularly fine cooking and carefully chosen wines, coffee bar, and gift shop.

TARBERT NR8768 **Columba** *East Pier Rd, Tarbert, Argyll PA29 6UF (01880) 820808* **£69.90,** plus special breaks; 10 rms. In a peaceful position on Loch Fyne with views of the surrounding hills, this family-run hotel has log fires in the friendly bar and lounge, an informal and relaxed atmosphere, enjoyable food using fresh local produce, and quite a few malt whiskies; cl 25–26 Dec.

TARBERT NR8671 **Stonefield Castle** *Tarbert, Argyll PA29 6YJ (01880) 820836* **£124 inc dinner,** plus special breaks; 33 rms. With wonderful views and surrounding wooded grounds, this Scottish Baronial mansion has comfortable public rooms and decent restaurant food; snooker room, sauna and solarium; heated swimming pool open in summer only; disabled access.

To see and do

ARDUAINE NM7910

✿ **Arduaine Gardens** (A816) The seaside gardens here, a very sheltered spot with lovely views of the islets and islands, are almost subtropical, with many rarities beside the rhododendrons, camellias and magnolias which flourish so in this part of the world. Disabled access, open all year; (01852) 200366; £2.50; NTS. The comfortable Loch Melfort Hotel, with great sea views, does good bar lunches.

AUCHINDRAIN NN0102

ⱦ **Auchindrain Township Museum** (A83) The only communal tenancy township to have remained on its ancient site much in its original form. All the buildings have been excellently restored and simply furnished in period style, so you get a real feeling of stepping back into the past. Snacks, shop; cl Oct–Mar; (01499) 500235; £3.

BARCALDINE NM9240

♪ **Sea Life Centre** 🅰 (A828) Lively underwater centre (part of a chain with several in England and one in St Andrews), with hi-tech face-to-fish-face displays of native marine life inc jelly fish, and playful seal puppies. Also nature trails and woodland adventure playground. Meals, snacks, shop, limited disabled access; cl Nov–Feb (open Christmas, New Year and all wknds); (01631) 720386; £5.95. The Lochnell Arms and Falls of Lora down at Connel are reliable lunch stops.

BEN NEVIS NN1671

⌂ ※ Though Britain's highest mountain, this is one of the more easily managed summits, with a long, safe path up: expect big crowds in season. Munro-baggers say it's far from being the best viewpoint mountain, though; a 'Munro' is any 3,000ft peak (914 metres),

named for Sir Hugh Munro, who first
tabulated them (in 1997 climbers
relaxing after a lifetime of gaining them
all were shocked by publication of a
new list adding several more).

BENMORE NS1391

❋ ❋ Younger Botanic Garden
(A815) An outstation of the Royal
Botanic Garden in Edinburgh, with
attractive woodland and glorious
rhododendrons. Some enormously tall
and magnificent conifers here, and a
good many rarities. Nice views too.
Meals, snacks, shop, disabled access;
cl Nov–Feb; (01369) 706261; £3.

CAIRNDOW NN1710

**❋ ❋ Ardkinglas Woodland
Garden** (off A83) On a hillside
overlooking Loch Fyne, the pinetum
here includes the tallest tree in Britain,
a grand fir well over 61 metres (200ft)
and still shooting upwards. Also
rhododendrons, azaleas and other
exotic plants, and daffodils in spring.
Open all year; disabled access; £2. The
same people run the **Tree Shop**
(about 2m N at the top of the loch),
which specialises in specimen trees,
indigenous Highland trees, and shrubs.
Also lots of well crafted woodware (inc
some lovely toys and puzzles); snacks,
shop, disabled access; cl 25 Dec–31 Jan;
(01499) 600263. Next door the Loch
Fyne Oyster Bar is renowned for its
fresh shellfish, which you can eat in the
restaurant or buy in the shop; the
Cairndow Hotel with a waterside
garden is also good.

COLINTRAIVE NS0374

**★ ❋ ⚓ This attractive village spreads
along the shore of the sea loch, with
lovely views (for example from the well
run Colintraive Hotel) across the
narrow Kyles of Bute. There's a short
ferry crossing to Rhubodach on Bute.

CORPACH NN1177

⌂ Caledonian Canal From Corpach
there are straightforward towpath
walks NE, up a flight of locks known as
Neptune's Staircase, with mountain
backdrops. There's good access to the
locks from the Moorings Hotel (good-
value basement wine bar) at Banavie.
⚒ Treasures of the Earth (Mallaig
Rd) Award-winning collection of
gemstones, crystals and minerals,
imaginatively displayed in carefully lit

rock cavities. Shop, disabled access; cl
25–26 Dec, 3–31 Jan; (01397) 772283;
£3.

CRINAN CANAL NR7894

**⌂ Cut through the 9 miles at the top of
the Kintyre peninsula at the end of the
18th c, to save coastal sailors many
miles of dangerous waters; the end at
Crinan is attractive, usually with one or
two yachts or even a rare fishing boat
waiting to enter the first lock, and the
Crinan Hotel is a comfortable lunch
stop. The canal towpath allows gentle
strolls.

DUNOON NS1878

**⚓ ❋ Brought in easy reach of Glasgow
by frequent ferries from Gourock, this
late Victorian resort has pleasant views
from its fine long promenade; very busy
in Aug.

FORT WILLIAM NN1276

**⌂ ⛟ ❋ A largely Victorian town,
partly pedestrianised, that manages to
combine its role as a regional centre
with its other life as a holiday base,
particularly for solid Ben Nevis which
rises above it, and for the Caledonian
Canal which leads on up into the Great
Glen and across eventually to the
North Sea. The Alexandra and Nevis
Bank hotels are useful for food, as is the
cheerful Grog & Gruel pub; the
Nevisport is the place for walking and
climbing chat. In summer you can take
steamtrain journeys on the **West
Highland Line** from here – it goes
right up into the Highlands and the
views are quite superb.
⛫ Inverlochy Castle (NE edge) Partly
13th-c ruins (usually under scaffolding),
site of the 1645 battle between
Montrose and the Campbells; free.
⚒ West Highland Museum
(Cameron Sq) Recently refurbished,
good on Jacobite relics: a secret
portrait of Prince Charlie needs a
curved mirror to decode it. Shop,
limited disabled access; cl Sun (exc July
and Aug), (01397) 702169; £2.

GIGHA NR6551

**⚓ ⛪ 3 miles offshore, linked by
frequent ferries from Tayinloan on the
A83 down the W coast of Kintyre; the
island is a perfect place for really getting
away from it all. Apart from the small
hotel, there are rooms at the post office
and other places, and you can hire

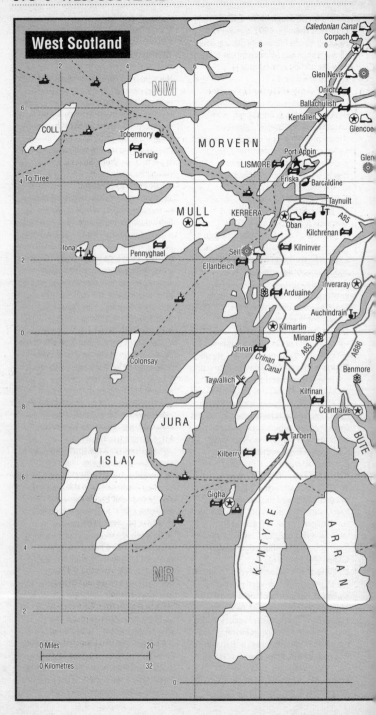

bicycles to explore it properly. Try to see the strange old stones, some of which are supposed to have mysterious powers. Tel (01583) 505254 for ferry times.

Achamore Gardens Created by Sir James Horlick, who bought the island in 1944; a garden of woodlands filled with rhododendrons and azaleas, many plants brought from his home in Berkshire in laundry baskets. Lots of subtropical plants – the climate and soil are perfect for them. Snacks, shop, limited disabled access; £2.

GLEN NEVIS NN1468

(nr Fort William) Probably the best-known Highland valley, with splendid gorge scenery for an easy long mile's walk to Steall Falls. The Pap of Glencoe and the succession of peaks in the largely unwooded Mamore Forest (access from the glen) are interesting viewpoint summits; they don't need rock-climbing expertise, just reasonable fitness, sensible walking boots and plenty of time.

GLENCOE NN1557

The scenery around here is some of Scotland's most beautiful and wild. It's understandably popular with walkers and climbers, who share it with deer, wildcats and golden eagles. The Clachaig and King's House do food. A forest walk runs from the hospital by Glencoe village past a lochan (small loch) above Loch Leven.

Altnafeadh Good start for walks from the top of the glen. The West Highland Way takes a zigzag route N up the Devil's Staircase and through the mountains to Kinlochleven; another hill walk from Altnafeadh heads E up Beinn a' Chrulaiste, one of Glencoe's more manageable peaks.

Glen Etive Reached from Glencoe by a squelchy walk along glens (or a long track from the A82 E of Glencoe), with close-ups of mighty peaks for reward.

Glencoe Visitor Centre (A82) Has the whole story of the massacre of 1692, when billeted troops tried to murder all their MacDonald hosts, as well as useful local information (and fishing permits). Snacks, shop, disabled access; cl 31 Oct–1 Apr; (01855) 811307; 50p, free parking all day; NTS.

! Highland Mysteryworld (Glencoe village) Children enjoy the spooky local myths and legends here. There may also be outdoor theatre productions. Meals, snacks, shop, disabled access; cl Nov–Apr; (01855) 811660; £4.95.

◠ Lost Valley This secret Glencoe pasture-ground was used by the MacDonalds for stolen cattle in times of clan warfare; the walk involves an ascent from the Meeting of the Three Waters.

HELENSBURGH NS2983

🏠 ⚜ Hill House (Upper Colquhoun St) In an area short of many great houses, this is a wonderful example of the work of Charles Rennie Mackintosh; there's an exhibition on his life, and the gardens are being restored. Snacks, shop; cl Nov–Mar; (01436) 673900; £6; NTS – it's one of their busier properties. The dignified resort town, attractively placed on the Clyde, has good views from its broad streets.

INVERARAY NN0908

★ Beautifully placed and rather self-consciously elegant, this was built as an estate village in the 18th c, and is now a magnet for visitors. The Loch Fyne Hotel is pleasant for lunch, with stunning views; the George is popular too.

✝ All Saints Church The bell tower has the world's second-heaviest ring of 10 bells, installed in 1931. Even if there's no one ringing them you should be able to hear a recording. Cl 1–2pm, all Oct–Apr; (01499) 302259; £2 for tower, exhibition free.

🐾 Argyll Wildlife Park 🏛 (Dalchenna; A83 SW) A collection of local or once-local animals (from wild boars to wildcats) plus chipmunks, wallabies, racoons and so forth – with some eminently tame wild creatures wandering around. Snacks, shop, disabled access; cl Nov–Mar; (01499) 302264; £3.75.

🏰 🚻 ✳ Inveraray Castle Built in 1743, and still the home of the Duke and Duchess of Argyll, it has particularly impressive state rooms, and a striking hall. Snacks, shop, ground floor disabled access; cl 1–2pm (exc July and Aug), am Sun, all day Fri (exc July and Aug), and mid-Oct–Mar; (01499) 302203; £4.50. Nearby woodland trails include a view over Loch Fyne from Dunchuach Tower.

♟ Inveraray Jail (Church Sq) Excellent prison museum, with costumed guides and Katie the Governor's cow (and other animated surprises) really bringing the place to life. You can watch a trial, try your hand at hard labour, and even experience being locked up in one of the sparse little cells. Shop; cl 25 Dec, 1 Jan; (01499) 302381; £4.75.

KILMARTIN NR8395

✝ 🏛 The church here is plain and Victorian, but it has a stunning 10th-c cross; the graveyard has interesting carved medieval tombstones. The simple Kilmartin Hotel is useful for lunch. A short walk away, tracks link the well signed North, Mid and South Cairns (impressive prehistoric burial mounds – you can climb into the north one via trapdoor and ladder, to see cup-and-ring carvings), and the Templewood stone circles.

🏛 Dunadd Fort (3m S) This

Days Out

Elegant Loch Fyne: Inveraray Jail and village; lunch at the Loch Fyne Hotel there; Inveraray Castle, or walk up to Dunchuach Tower; Auchindrain Township, or Crarae Gardens.

Island interlude: Dunstaffnage Castle; lunch at the Oban Inn, Oban (North Pier); boat to Kerrera, or visit Oban Rare Breeds Farm.

The grandeur of the glens: Stroll in Glen Nevis, or along the Caledonian Canal at Neptune's Staircase; Glencoe Visitor Centre; lunch at the Clachaig there; drive on the A82 through Glencoe to Rannoch Moor, with a walk up to the Lost Valley or up the Devil's Staircase.

prehistoric hill fort was one of the ancient capitals of Dalriada from which the Celtic kingdom of Scotland was formed. Look out for the carvings nearby of a boar and a footprint, which probably mark the spot where early kings were invested with royal power.

🗝 **Kilmartin House Museum** 🖼 Explains the rich and intriguing archaeology of the area. Meals, snacks, shop, disabled access; open daily; (01546) 510278; *£3.90.

KILMUN NS1781

🐾 △ **Kilmun forest walks** Rare conifers, an arboretum of great beauty, and some striking gum-trees.

LOCH LOMOND NS3884

❊ ♣ In spite of being so close to Glasgow and on every coach company's hit list, it does have a serene beauty that seems unspoilt by the visitors. Wee birdies sing and wild flowers spring – and the water is often calm enough to reflect the mountains. The best views are from the narrower north end. Surprisingly, there aren't many paths: the shoreline track, partly metalled, on the quieter east side, comes closest to the water. Cruises round the lake leave from Balloch, as well as from the pretty village of Luss, a good place to hire a boat for pottering about on the water (there's a visitor centre here too). Past the north end of the loch, the Inverarnan Drovers Inn is an entertaining and very idiosyncratic stop.

❁ ❊ **Balloch Castle Country Park** A useful introduction, with a visitor centre, woodland and meadow trails, walled garden, and fine views. Snacks, shop, limited disabled access; cl some lunchtimes, Oct–Easter; (01389) 758216; free. The Balloch Hotel has good-value bar food all day.

△ **Ben Lomond** The southernmost Munro (or peak over 3,000ft, 914 metres), with a good walk up from Rowardennan on the east shore.

△ **Conic Hill** Less than half Ben Lomond's height but more accessible, a straightforward but rewarding climb from Balmaha at Loch Lomond's south-east corner.

MINARD NR9799

❁ **Crarae Gardens** (A83) Lovely gardens noted for their rare ornamental shrubs and rhododendrons, azaleas and conifers, set in a beautiful gorge overlooking Loch Fyne. Snacks, shop, and interesting plant sales (all summer only), limited disabled access; visitor centre cl Oct–Easter; (01546) 886614; £2.50.

MULL NM5055

🗝 🐾 ♣ △ For most people this island takes a bit of getting to, but if you are within reach its unspoilt coasts are certainly a dramatic lure. There's a good ferry service from Oban and Lochaline (and in summer from Kilchoan). A couple of castellated mansions, one going back to the 13th c and another 19th-c, Torosay Castle, with attractive gardens (tearoom, shop, limited disabled access; open daily Easter–mid-Oct; £4.50 🖼), and a small museum in Tobermory, give some rainy-day scope. From May–Sept, the **Mull Experience** runs day trips from Oban to these attractions, including return ferry travel and a trip on Mull's unique railway (£16, call (01680) 812421 for details). The interior is less interesting than the coast, with brackeny moors and conifer plantations over much of it, though there is some mountainous hill walking in the S (as usual, not many defined paths).

🐇 **Angora Rabbit Farm** 🖼 (Bunessan) Children can cuddle some very fluffy bunnies here, and there is a new display system explaining all about the rabbits from the viewpoint of a rabbit; cl Sat and all Nov–Easter; snacks, shop; £2.

♣ ✝ **Iona** (off Mull) Lovely, filled with a sense of spirituality as well as its tangible remains of ancient shrines; Scotland's first kings were buried here (as is former Labour leader John Smith).

🗝 ♣ **St Columba Visitor Centre** (Fionnphort) Newish centre dedicated to the saint. The little west coast settlement overlooks Iona, and the boats go from here. The Keel Row has decent food.

OBAN NM8530

★ ♣ △ This bustling coastal town is a busy ferry port and a popular place for holidaymakers, with a good cheerful atmosphere; the Oban Inn is fun, and the Lorne has decent food inc fresh local fish. Besides the main ferries, there are boats to Lismore and (just a hop really) Kerrera, for shoreside walks with the odd ruined fort. A little way S at Cologin, the countrified Barn is useful for lunch, and often has evening folk music.

🏰 **Dunstaffnage Castle** (off A485 4m N) Beautifully set, this was once the prison of Flora MacDonald. It's now in ruins, but you can still see its gatehouse, round towers and massively thick walls. Shop, disabled access to visitor centre only; cl Thurs and Fri in winter; (01631) 562465; £1.80.

🐷 **Oban Rare Breeds Farm** (A816 Oban–Kilmore) A collection of very visitor-friendly animals. Teas, shop, some disabled access; cl end Oct–end Mar; (01631) 770608; £5.

PORT APPIN NM9045
★ ⌂ An attractive little settlement, very peaceful, where you can pick wild blueberries by the roadside, catch a boat across to Lismore (shoreside walks), or just sit by the water keeping your eyes open for the seals that are so common around here. This is *Kidnapped* country, with the scene of the Appin Murder not far off, and a monument marking where James of the Glens was wrongly hanged at Ballachulish to the N (the Ballachulish Hotel has decent food and wide views).

RIVER LEVEN NN1861
⌂ ☀ The glen gives a fine walk through semi-wooded terrain, from Kinlochleven to the dam of the gigantic Blackwater Reservoir – with a bleak view ahead of empty hills.

SEIL NM7819
☀ ⌂ This little island is linked to the mainland by a short bridge that people call the Bridge over the Atlantic. The Tigh an Truish inn by the bridge is a pleasant stop, and there's an attractive walk over to the anchorage on the far side which looks out to Jura.

TARBERT NR8465
★ Pleasant and quite picturesque small harbourside town; the West Loch Hotel (A83 W) does good local seafood.

TAYNUILT NN0031
↓T **Bonawe Iron Furnace** (off A85) The most complete remaining charcoal-fired ironworks in Britain, worked until 1876. Iron produced here was used for the cannonballs for Nelson's ships. Shop; cl end Nov–Apr with restricted hours in Oct; (01866) 822432; £2.30. The Polfearn Hotel on the lochside does good food.

Inns with decent food, in good places for drivers, walkers or strollers, include the Ardentinny Hotel by Loch Long at Ardentinny NS1887, Galley of Lorne at Ardfern NM8004, Village Inn at Arrochar NN2904, Kilchrenan Inn at Kilchrenan by Loch Awe NN0222, Portsonachan Hotel on the opposite side of that loch NN1227, Whistlefield Hotel by Loch Eck NS1493, Loch Gair Hotel on Loch Gair NR9190 and Oystercatcher at Otter Ferry NR9384.

Where to eat

Many places in the **Where to stay** section, above, also have very good food.

CAIRNDOW NN1710 **Loch Fyne Oyster Bar** *Clachan Farm* (01499) 600264 Relaxed restaurant in converted farm buildings by Loch Fyne, serving good seafood and smoked fish (they have their own smokehouse); reasonably priced wine list and a warm welcome; cl 25–26 Dec, 1 Jan; disabled access. **£22|£6.**

FORT WILLIAM NN1074 **Alexandra** *The Parade* (01397) 702241 Popular hotel in town square with meals and snacks in the Great Food Stop (open all day) and evening restaurant; disabled access. **£17.50 in restaurant|£5.**

KENTALLEN NM9957 **Ardsheal House** (01631) 740227 Particularly good daily-changing evening food in the attractive conservatory dining room of a fine hotel set in 900 acres; very comfortable rooms, antiques, and a relaxed atmosphere; lovely bdrms; cl Christmas. **£30 4-course dinner.**

KENTALLEN NN0057 **Holly Tree** (01631) 740292 Super food in a carefully converted railway station, cosy public rooms, lovely shoreside setting (best to book in winter); bdrms; cl 28 Nov–28 Dec, 9 Jan–4 Feb; disabled access. **£28|£6.50.**

TAYVALLICH NR7487 **Tayvallich Inn** (01546) 870282 Simply refurbished pub overlooking yacht anchorage with super local seafood (other decent dishes too), a dining conservatory (no smoking), and friendly service; cl Mon, Nov–Mar; limited disabled access. £25|£7.

North Scotland

Sensational scenery in the west and on Skye, solitude in the north, empty beaches on the east coast.

The main draw is the scenery, and the feeling of getting away from it all. The west coast has glorious vistas of sea, mountains and islands. Long empty sandy beaches (and good golf courses) make the east coast suit a quiet summer holiday. The north coast is relatively wild and empty: addictive to some people, harsh and inhospitable to others. Skye is idyllic in good weather. There are a few interesting places to visit – but they're not the reason for coming here.

The area is usually at its best between late May and early July, while the days are very long and before the midges have really got into their stride.

Where to stay

ACHILTIBUIE NC0208 **Summer Isles** *Achiltibuie, Ullapool, Ross-shire IV26 2YG (01854) 622282* ***£95;** 13 comfortable rms. Beautifully placed above the sea towards the end of a very long and lonely road, warm, friendly and well furnished hotel with delicious set menus using fresh ingredients (in which it's largely self-sufficient), a choice of superb puddings and excellent array of uncommon cheeses; pretty watercolours and flowers; cl mid-Oct–Easter; children over 6.

APPLECROSS NG7144 **Applecross Inn** *Applecross, Strathcarron, Ross-shire IV54 8LR (01520) 744262* **£45;** 5 rms with breathtaking sea views over the Sound of Raasay, shared bthrms. Gloriously placed informal inn with tables out by the shore, simple, comfortable and friendly bar, log or peat fire in the lounge, a lively landlord, and a small restaurant with excellent fresh fish and seafood.

ARISAIG NM6984 **Arisaig House** *Beasdale, Arisaig, Inverness-shire PH39 4NR (01687) 450622* **£160,** plus special breaks; 12 most attractive, recently refurbished rms with wonderful views. Beautifully furnished extremely comfortable hotel in attractive wooded and terraced grounds nr the shore; elegant drawing room, cosy morning room, lovely flowers, and very good imaginative food using fresh local produce; billiards room, croquet; cl Nov–Easter; children over 10.

AULTIVULLIN NC8168 **Catalina** *Aultivullin, Strathy Point, Thurso, Caithness KW14 7RY (01641) 541279* **£38;** 1 suite. Extended former croft on wild headland just a short walk from the Atlantic ocean; residents have their own wing with private lounge and dining room but owners offer a friendly welcome, good breakfasts, and enjoyable 3-course meals – bring your own wine and they will serve you at whatever time you wish to eat; no children or dogs, and no smoking; disabled access.

CROMARTY NH7867 **Royal** *Marine Terrace, Cromarty, Ross-shire IV11 8YN (01381) 600217* ***£59.80,** plus special breaks; 10 rms. Traditional waterfront hotel with friendly owners and staff, attractive lounges, bars and sun lounge, and Scottish dishes in the dining room; gets very busy in summer.

DRUMNADROCHIT NH5029 **Benleva** *Drumnadrochit, Inverness IV3 6UH (01456) 450288* **£50;** 8 rms. Run by particularly helpful and friendly owners, this small family-run hotel is in a fine spot nr Loch Ness with plenty of outside pursuits (the owners will help organise fishing trips); comfortable residents' lounge with an open fire, well stocked bar, and homely dining room with a good choice of tasty food using local meat and fish; pets welcome.

DRUMNADROCHIT NH5129 **Borlum Farmhouse** *Drumnadrochit, Inverness IV3 6XN (01456) 450358* **£50;** 6 rms, 2 with own bthrm. Traditional stone farmhouse with marvellous views over Loch Ness, a warm, comfortably furnished sitting room with log fire, summer conservatory sitting room, friendly atmosphere, and good Scottish breakfasts; BHS-approved riding centre and you can help with animals on the farm; good provision for families; self-catering and caravan/camping also; cl Oct–Mar.

DRUMNADROCHIT NH4731 **Polmaily House** *Drumnadrochit, Inverness IV3 6XT (01456) 450343* **£100,* plus special breaks; 11 light, pretty rms. Very relaxing and homely hotel in 18 acres, with a comfortable drawing room and library, open fires, and excellent food in the no smoking restaurant (wonderful packed lunches too); a happy place for families with a well equipped indoor play area with lots of supervised activities, baby sitting and listening, hundreds of children's videos, plenty of ponies and pets, swimming pool, tennis, croquet, fishing, and boating; disabled access.

GARVE NH3969 **Inchbae Lodge** *Inchbae, Garve, Ross-shire IV23 2PH (01997) 455269* **£66,* plus special breaks; 15 rms, some in chalet. Former hunting lodge – under new owners – in a lovely Highland setting with comfortable homely lounges, winter log fires, a small bar (liked by locals), and good fixed-price evening meals using fresh local produce; lots of wildlife, marvellous walks; pets by prior arrangement; cl Christmas; disabled access.

GLENELG NG8119 **Glenelg Inn** *Glenelg, Kyle, Ross-shire IV40 8JR (01599) 522273* **£138 inc dinner,** plus special breaks; 6 individually decorated and comfortable rms, all with fine views. Overlooking Skye across its own beach, this carefully refurbished homely hotel has a relaxed bar, comfortable sofas and blazing fires, friendly staff and locals, good food using local venison, local hill-bred lamb and lots of wonderfully fresh fish and seafood, and quite a few whiskies; the drive to the inn involves spectacular views from the steep road; cl end Oct–Easter but open Christmas and New Year; disabled access.

HARLOSH NG2841 **Harlosh House** *Harlosh, Dunvegan, Isle of Skye IV55 8ZG (01470) 521367* **£160 inc dinner;** 6 rms, 5 with own bthrm, and most with lovely views. One of the oldest buildings on NW Skye, this 18th-c house is on a small peninsula jutting into Loch Bracadale; lochside gardens and lots of wildlife, a wonderfully quiet homely lounge, home-made breads, imaginative cooking using fresh local produce in the evening restaurant, and fine breakfasts; cl late Oct–Easter.

ISLE ORNSAY NG7015 **Kinloch Lodge** *Isle Ornsay, Isle of Skye IV43 8QY (01471) 833214* **£130 inc dinner,** plus special breaks; 15 rms. Surrounded by rugged mountain scenery at the head of Loch Na Dal, this charming little white stone hotel has a relaxed atmosphere in its comfortable and attractive drawing rooms, antiques, portraits, flowers, log fires, and good imaginative food; cookery demonstrations; cl 5 days over Christmas.

ISLE ORNSAY NG6912 **Tigh Osda Eilean Iarmain** *Isle Ornsay, Isle of Skye IV43 8QR (01471) 833332* **£110,* plus winter breaks; 16 individual rms (those in the main hotel best), all with fine views. Sparkling white hotel with Gaelic-speaking staff and locals, a big cheerfully busy bar, pretty dining room with lovely sea views, and very good food; disabled access.

LAIDE NG8990 **Old Smiddy** *Laide, Ashnasheen, Ross-shire IV22 2NB (01445) 731425* **£48;** 3 pretty rms with thoughtful extras. Really welcoming, charming, no smoking cottage in a lovely spot by loch and mountains, with a blazing fire in the comfortable, homely lounge, and a dining room with super breakfasts and delicious evening meals (using local and home-grown produce; bring your own wine); lots of outside pursuits, and pets welcome; cl Nov–Mar; children over 12.

LYBSTER ND2436 **Portland Arms** *Lybster, Caithness KW3 6BS (01593) 721721*

£68; 24 comfortable rms. Staunch old granite hotel with really friendly staff, an attractive dining room, generous helpings of good fresh food and fine breakfasts; small cosy panelled lounge bar, and informal locals' bar; shooting/fishing can be arranged; disabled access.

MELVICH NC8864 **Melvich Hotel** *Melvich, Thurso, Caithness KW14 7YJ* (01641) 531206 **£60,** plus special breaks; 14 rms with showers (4 bthrms in addition). Small traditional hotel in a lovely spot with homely furniture and peat fires in the civilised lounge, cosy bar, very relaxing atmosphere, friendly owners and staff, good food (especially local seafood and wild salmon), and fine views over Melvich Bay.

PLOCKTON NG8033 **Plockton Hotel** (not to be confused with Plockton Inn around the corner) *41 Harbour St, Plockton, Ross-shire IV52 8TN* (01599) 544274 *£66, plus special breaks; 9 rms plus 4 in cottage annexe. Small notably friendly hotel in a row of elegant houses by a shore lined with palm trees and flowering shrubs, looking over the sheltered anchorage to rugged mountains, with a comfortably furnished lively lounge bar, separate public bar, enjoyable food in the little no smoking restaurant, good breakfasts, a good choice of whiskies, and attentive owners; good disabled access.

PORTREE NG4843 **Craiglockhart** *Beaumont Crescent, Portree, Isle of Skye IV51 9DF* (01478) 612233 *£46; 9 rms, 3 with own bthrm. Small family-run guesthouse overlooking the harbour with fine views through picture windows in the lounge and dining room and good breakfasts; cl Nov–Mar.

PORTREE NG4843 **Rosedale** *Beaumont Crescent, Portree, Isle of Skye IV51 9DF* (01478) 613131 **£82,** plus special breaks; 23 rms, many with harbour views. Built from 3 fishermen's cottages with lots of passages and stairs, this waterfront hotel has 2 traditional lounges, a small first-floor restaurant with freshly cooked popular food, lots of whiskies in the cocktail bar, helpful staff, a harbourside garden and marvellous views.

RAASAY NG5641 (off Skye) **Isle of Raasay Hotel** *Raasay, Kyle, Ross-shire IV40 8PB* (01478) 660222 *£55, plus special breaks; 12 rms, plus 6 beds in bunk house. Family-run Victorian hotel with marvellous views over the Sound of Raasay to Skye, popular with walkers and birdwatchers; home-made food with an emphasis on fresh fish; no petrol on the island; disabled access.

SCARISTA NG0192 **Scarista House** *Scarista, Harris, Isle of Harris HS3 3HX* (01859) 550238 *£120; 5 rms, some in annexe. Marvellously wild countryside and empty beaches surround this isolated small hotel with its homely rooms, warm friendly atmosphere, plenty of books and records (no radio, TV or newspapers), and good food in the candlelit dining room using organic home-grown veg and herbs, hand-made cheeses, their own eggs, home-made bread, cakes, biscuits, yoghurt and marmalade, and lots of fish and shellfish; excellent for wildlife, walks and fishing; cl Oct–Apr; dogs allowed; children over 8.

SCOURIE NC1641 **Eddrachilles** *Badcall Bay, Scourie, Lairg, Sutherland IV27 4TH* (01971) 502080 *£80, plus special breaks; 11 comfortable rms. Well run hotel in its own 320 acres overlooking Badcall Bay, with wonderful island views; popular with nature-lovers – bird sanctuary nearby, seals, fishing and walking; cl 25 Oct–21 Mar; children over 3.

SCOURIE NC1641 **Scourie Hotel** *Scourie, Lairg, Sutherland IV27 4SX* (01971) 502396 **£55;** 20 rms with views to Scourie Bay. A haven for anglers with 36 exclusive beats on a 25,000-acre estate; snug bar, 2 comfortable lounges and good food using plenty of local game and fish in the smart no smoking dining room; cl end Oct–mid-Mar.

SHIEL BRIDGE NG9319 **Kintail Lodge** *Shiel Bridge, Kyle of Lochalsh, Ross-shire IV40 8HL* (01599) 511275 **£67,** plus special breaks; 17 good-value big rms, most with own bthrm. Pleasantly informal and fairly simple former shooting lodge on Loch Duich, with magnificent views, 4 acres of walled gardens, residents' lounge bar and a comfortable sitting room; good, well prepared food inc wild salmon, and a fine collection of malt whiskies.

SHIELDAIG NG8153 **Tigh an Eilean** *Shieldaig, Strathcarron, Ross-shire IV54 8XN*

(01520) 755251 **£107.40, 11 rms.** Attractive hotel in outstanding position with lovely view of a pine-covered island and the sea (private fishing and sea fishing arranged), within easy reach of NTS Torridon Estate and Beinn Eighe nature reserve; pretty, comfortable residents' lounge with a well stocked honesty bar, modern dining room with delicious food, warmly friendly owner; cl mid-Oct–Easter; no children.

SKEABOST NG4148 **Skeabost House** *Skeabost, Portree, Isle of Skye IV51 9NP (01470) 532202* **£85,** plus special breaks; 26 rms, 5 in annexe in Garden House. Smart, friendly little hotel with a lawn running down to Loch Snizort (good salmon fishing), spacious no smoking lounge (marvellous buffet table), Victorian-style dining conservatory, lovely afternoon tea, log fires, a high-ceilinged bar off the stately hall, and a billiards room; bog-and-water garden, 9-hole golf course; cl Oct–end Mar.

STRONTIAN NM8161 **Kilcamb Lodge Hotel** *Strontian, Acharacle, Argyll PH36 4HY (01967) 402257* **£110,** plus special breaks; 11 rms. Warmly friendly little hotel in 30 acres by Loch Sunart, with log fires in the 2 lounges, carefully cooked food using fresh local ingredients, a fine choice of malt whiskies in the small bar, and a relaxed atmosphere; cl Christmas; children over 8 in the dining room; disabled access in cottage.

TARBERT NB1301 **Leachin House** *Tarbert, Isle of Harris, Western Isles HS3 3AH (01859) 502157* ***£86,** plus special breaks; 2 comfortable rms. Meaning 'house among the rocks', this neat and peaceful Victorian stone house on the loch shores (wonderful sunsets) is a haven for nature lovers and walkers – guided trips to look for seals, otters and eagles, fishing, and fine wild flowers in spring and early summer; friendly helpful owners, interesting nautical memorabilia, open fire in the drawing room, and particularly good food using delicious local seafood and lamb, served around a communal table in a dining room with original 19th-c hand-painted French wallpaper; cl 18 Dec–18 Jan; children over 10.

TORRIDON NG8854 **Loch Torridon** *Torridon, Ashnasheen, Ross-shire IV22 2EY (01445) 791242* **£110,** plus special breaks; 22 comfortable rms. Built in 1887 as a shooting lodge in 58 acres at the foot of Ben Damph by Upper Loch Torridon, this turreted stone house has unusual ornate ceilings and panelling, log fires and innovative cooking; they also run the Ben Damph Lodge just up the road; children over 12 in dining room; disabled access.

ULLAPOOL NH1192 **Altnaharrie** *Ullapool, Ross-shire IV26 2SS (01854) 633230* ***£350,** inc dinner; 8 rms. Across Loch Broom and reached by a 10-minute boat journey, this carefully restored house was originally built for drovers: 2 lounges with lots of books, an open fire, a mix of Scandinavian and English furnishings, marvellously quiet relaxing atmosphere, room service (they think tea-making facilities in rooms are a sign of neglect), perhaps the best food in Scotland – 5 set courses with much of the food home-grown or caught locally – and a very good wine list; no smoking; cl mid-Nov–Easter; children over 8.

ULLAPOOL NH1293 **Ceilidh Place** *W Argyle St, Ullapool, Ross-shire IV26 2TY (01854) 612103* ***£125,** plus special breaks; 13 rms, most with own bthrm, plus 10 in annexe across the road. White-painted hotel in a quiet side street with an attractive conservatory dining room, stylish café-bar with attractive modern prints and plants, good food, decent wines and cognacs, and a relaxed friendly atmosphere.

To see and do

ACHILTIBUIE NC0208
❀ **Hydroponicum** Bizarre indoor garden of the future – without any soil. Fascinating guided tours show how plants such as figs, lemons and bananas grow quite happily using the nutrients from the soil, but not the soil itself.

Good home-made meals and snacks, shop; hourly tours Easter–Sept (cl Oct–Easter); (01854) 622202; £4.

AUCKENGILL ND3664
⚒ **Northlands Viking Centre** (Old School) Interesting displays on how the Norsemen came from Scandinavia to

Shetland, Orkney and Caithness, with a Viking longship and other relics. Shop, disabled access; cl Oct–May; (01955) 607771; £1.45.

BALMACARA NG8028

⌂ ❀ (A67) Huge crofting estate surrounding the Kyle of Lochalsh, with challenging walks through breathtaking scenery; you can still see traditional crofting at Drumbuie and Duirnish. The landscape is interspersed with lochs and impressive landmarks like the Five Sisters of Kintail (a fine target for hardened walkers) and Beinn Fhada.

❀ **Lochalsh House** (A87 3m E of Kyle of Lochalsh) Wonderful woodland gardens, with peaceful walks, collections of rhododendrons, hydrangeas, fuchsias and other plants, and views towards Skye. Open all year; (01599) 566325; *£2; NTS.

BALNAKIEL NC3967

❀ The most north-westerly part of mainland Britain, wild, remote and spectacular, with a little craft village (some bits cl Sun, and limited opening in winter; (01971) 511277; free).

BEINN EIGHE NG9963

⌂ One of the easier mountain ascents, with a well marked Mountain Trail making a circular route above Loch Maree.

BETTYHILL NC7062

♂ ✙ **Strathnaver Museum** Good informative memorial to the notorious Highlands Clearances; limited disabled access; cl 1–2pm and all day Sun, and Nov–Mar; (01641) 521418; £1.50. The churchyard has a finely carved 9th-c Celtic stone. The Bettyhill Hotel does decent food. Just S is a wonderful **nature reserve**, and the beach nearby is attractive.

CROMARTY NH7867

⚓ ♂ **Dolphin Ecosse** (Bank House) Boat trips out to see the local bottlenose dolphins: they can't guarantee sightings, but nine out of ten of their trips do come across dolphins, and they point out various seabirds and local landmarks along the way. Very friendly and informal, and rated very highly by readers. Whale-watching trips too in Aug and Sept – best to book on (01381) 600323; disabled access. £15. Cromarty itself is a delightfully sleepy place with lots of unspoilt buildings in its

well restored core and a surprisingly good little **museum**. The friendly Royal Hotel has good-value food and lovely views.

DORNIE NG8826

🏰 **Eilean Donan Castle** (off A87) Connected to the mainland by a causeway, and unforgettably beautiful. First built in 1220, destroyed in 1719, and then restored at the beginning of the 20th century, it's perfectly positioned at the meeting point of Lochs Long, Duich and Alsh. Visitor centre with teas and shop, disabled access; cl Nov–Mar; (01599) 555202; *£3.75.

DRUMNADROCHIT NH5130

! ❀ **Official Loch Ness Monster Exhibition** (Drumnadrochit Hotel) Walk-through multi-media experience tracing the legend from its beginnings in Highland folklore to the scientific investigations of recent years. There's a kilt-maker on site. Meals, snacks, shop, disabled access; cl 25–26 Dec, 1 Jan; (01456) 450218; £6.50.

🏰 **Urquhart Castle** (just SE) 14th-c remains, once the biggest castle in Scotland. A piper plays here every day Jun–Sept. Snacks, shop; cl 25–26 Dec, 1–2 Jan; (01456) 450551; £3.80.

DUNCANSBY HEAD ND4073

⌂ ❀ A grand spot on a fine day, with an absorbing cliff walk S for a good view of the spectacular Stacks of Duncansby, 60-metre (200ft) offshore rock pinnacles.

DUNNET HEAD ND2074

❀ Mainland Britain's furthest point N, with views to Orkney. A lovely spot on a clear early summer's day, with spring flowers in the close turf, and puffins pottering around – but wild and unforgiving when the weather changes.

DURNESS NC4067

⚓ ❀ Attractively placed nr the beautiful sea loch, Loch Eriboll; you can join atmospheric boat tours of the **Smoo Cave** and its underground waterfall; cl Nov–May; (01971) 511259; £2.50.

⚓ ♟ **Cape Wrath** In summer you can make an adventurous expedition to this stormy tip of coast, guarded by a lonely lighthouse, by boat across the Kyle of Durness and then along a very long rough track (wear sensible shoes) to the lighthouse itself.

ELPHIN NC2110

🐄 **Highland & Rare Breeds Farm**
▣ (A835) Traditional Scottish farm
animals close up, on a family-worked
croft in attractive setting. They sell
fleeces and hand-spun wool. Snacks,
shop, some disabled access; cl 21
Sept–21 May; (01854) 666204; £3.50.

EVANTON NH5864

ᛏ **Clanland & Sealpoint** ▣ Housed
in an attractive restored building on the
shores of Cromarty Firth, this lively new
visitor centre takes a fresh look at the
area's local heritage and maritime
history. Café, shop, disabled access; cl 25
Dec, 1–2 Jan; (01349) 830000; *£3.75.

FALLS OF GLOMACH NH0125

◠ Tremendous waterfall in a
wilderness setting, a fine destination for
walkers on Kintail.

FALLS OF MEASACH NH1978

◠ ✺ With a mighty drop of 60 metres
(200ft), these are the highlight of the
mile-long, sheer-sided Corrieshalloch
Gorge, owned by the National Trust
for Scotland and equipped with a
viewing platform.

FALLS OF SHIN NH5799

🐟 (B864 S) There's a good chance of
seeing salmon leaping here in June or
early July, especially if there's been a dry
spell followed by rain so that the river is
in spate.

GAIRLOCH NG8076

ᛏ **Gairloch Heritage Museum** ▣
Enthusiastically run, perhaps the best of
the several heritage museums in the
Highlands; new hands-on exhibition
opens in Apr. Meals, snacks, shop,
disabled access; cl Sun, Nov–Mar exc by
arrangement; (01445) 712287; £2.50.
The Old Inn here is good, and Gairloch
is a useful base for hikers.

GLEN AFFRIC NH2124

◠ One of the most majestic glens, with
a walking route along its floor.

GLENFINNAN NM9080

🏛👁 **Jacobite Monument** (A830)
Built in 1815 to commemorate the
Highlanders who fought and died for
Bonnie Prince Charlie, in a commanding
position at the head of Loch Shiel. A
visitor centre has exhibitions on the
prince. Good snacks, shop, limited
disabled access; visitor centre cl
Oct–Easter and some lunchtimes;
£1.50; (01397) 722250; NTS.

GOLSPIE NC8500

🏰 ✺ ▣ **Dunrobin Castle** (A9)
Splendid castle – a gleaming turreted
structure with views out to sea and
gardens modelled on those at
Versailles. The family home of the Earls
and Dukes of Sutherland for longer than
anyone can remember, the site was
named after Earl Robin in the 13th c; he
was responsible for the original square
keep. Drastically renovated in the 19th
c, it has fine collections of furnishings
and art, inc several Canalettos, and a
unique collection of Pictish stones.
Snacks, shop; cl am Sun, and mid-
Oct–Mar, gardens open all year;
(01408) 633177; £5.50.

HELMSDALE ND0315

ᛏ ✺ **Timespan Visitor Centre**
(Dunrobin St) Extended centre with
reconstructions of scenes in Highland
history (with sound effects), art
exhibitions and interesting herb garden.
Riverside café, shop, disabled access; cl
am Sun, mid-Oct–Easter; (01431)
821327; £3.50.

HIGHLAND WALKING NC2617

◠ The Highlands offer ultra-tough
mountain walking, but relatively few
easier routes on defined paths; shorter
circular walks are few and far between.
For non-mountaineers the Highlands
can be tantalising but problematic:
compared to the uplands of England and
Wales there are few obvious walking
routes (OS maps show hardly any), and
the scale of the scenery is often so vast
that you need to walk for hours before
the views change. The high peaks are
mostly for the dedicated (and fit)
enthusiast. There is an informal
tradition of allowing general access to
the mountains, but there are few rights
of way, and areas are often closed for at
least part of the grouse-shooting
season (12 Aug–10 Dec), particularly its
first few weeks, and the deer-stalking
season (1 July–20 Oct for stags, 21
Oct–15 Feb for hinds).

JOHN O' GROATS ND3773

✺ Gets its share of visitors under the
mistaken impression that it's the most
northerly point on mainland Britain.
Increasingly developed for tourists, but
still a pleasant spot. The hotel on the
harbour looking across to the Orkneys
has decent food.

KINLOCHBERVIE NC2156

★ ♨ A friendly village with decent beaches, mountains and scenery nearby; it's most lively around 6pm on Mon–Thurs (2pm Fri), when the fishing boats return to the pier and auction their catch. There may be **boat trips** round the harbour.

KIRKHILL NH5543

🏚 🏰 **Moniack Castle** (A862) Former fortress of the Lovat chiefs, now producing traditional country wines – also meat and game preserves, and an interesting apricot, almond and banana jam. There are tastings and tours. Shop; cl Sun, 25 Dec; (01463) 831283; £2.

KNOYDART NG8100

◁ ❀ A real Highland wilderness on the W coast, glorious roadless country that's irresistible to hardened walkers – given good weather, full equipment and strong legs. There is a ferry 3 days a week from Mallaig to nearby Inverie, where the Old Forge is very hospitable (and open all day).

LOCH NESS NH5330

❀ ♨ Drumnadrochit (see *above*) is the best place to begin exploring this striking 24-mile loch with the largest volume of fresh water of any lake in the British Isles; up to 215 metres (700ft) deep in places, so it's not hard to see why stories sprang up of what was hidden in its waters. You can generally take **boat trips** on the lake, some of the boats are equipped with sonar for monster-spotting.

PLOCKTON NG8033

★ Idyllic waterside village, with palm trees along the village street; the TV series *Hamish Macbeth* was filmed here. The Plockton Hotel has good generous food.

POOLEWE NG8681

❀ **Inverewe Gardens** (A832) Unmissable beautiful gardens full of rare and subtropical plants, with a magnificent background of mountain scenery. The Atlantic Drift is responsible for the special microclimate which lets these unusual plants flourish even though this is further N than Moscow. Guided walks wkdys at 1.30pm, Apr–Sept. Meals, snacks, shop, limited disabled access; visitor centre and restaurant cl Nov–mid-Mar; (01445) 781200; £4;

NTS. Choppys has good well priced food.

RUBHA REIDH NG7391

◁ 🏮 **Rubha Reidh Lighthouse** Remote outpost several miles along a track N of Melvaig; they organise enjoyable walking holidays in the splendidly wild countryside around; B & B or hostel-style rooms – don't worry about the colour of the water, it's just peaty; (01445) 771263.

SKYE NG4829

❀ ♨ ◁ After Lewis, the biggest of the islands off the Scottish coast, now linked to the mainland by a bridge: islanders who'd campaigned for the bridge didn't expect the high tolls (which were later reduced), and others were initially unnerved by the prospect of easier access bringing floods of visitors and the end of the island's unique air of romance – so far neither has happened. The closing of the Kyle of Lochalsh ferry is lamented – though you can still emulate Bonnie Prince Charlie and Flora MacDonald on one from Mallaig, or the tiny summer one to Kylerhea from past Glenelg. The coasts have plenty of opportunities for gentle pottering, and for finding quiet coves and bays, especially on the W coast, where for instance Tarskavaig, or Stein in the N, are lovely spots to watch the sun go down. The jagged teeth of the Cuillin mountain range to the SE of the centre are unforgettable. Besides places mentioned in **Where to stay** and **Where to eat**, the Misty Isle at Dunvegan, Sligachan Inn at the junction of the A850 and A863 in the middle of the island, the Struan Grill at Struan and the waterside Old Inn at Carbost (handy for the Talisker distillery, which can be visited) all do decent food.

🏚 ❀ 🏛 **Armadale Castle, Gardens & Museum of the Isles** The castle was built for Lord Macdonald in 1815; it now houses an excellent visitor centre looking at the history of the clan, and the surrounding 40 acres offer beautiful walks among gardens and woodlands. Sleat, this southern peninsula, is known as the Garden of Skye. Very good restaurant, shop, disabled access; cl Oct–Mar (01471) 844305; £3.85.

🏚 ♨ **Dunvegan Castle** Dramatically set on the sea loch of Dunvegan, this

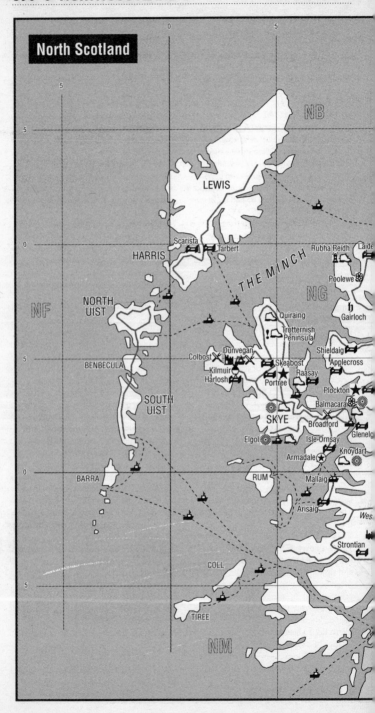

North Scotland

NB

LEWIS

Scarista
Tarbert

Rubha Reidh
Laidé

HARRIS

THE MINCH

Poolewe

NG

NF

NORTH
UIST

Quiraing

Gairloch

Trotternish
Peninsula

BENBECULA

Colbost
Dunvegan

Shieldaig

Applecross

Kilmuir
Harlosh

Skeabost
Portree
Raasay

SOUTH
UIST

SKYE

Plockton
Balmacara

Broadford

Glenelg

Elgol
Isle-Ornsay

Knoydart

Armadale

BARRA

RUM

Mallaig

Arisaig

Wes.

Strontian

COLL

TIREE

NM

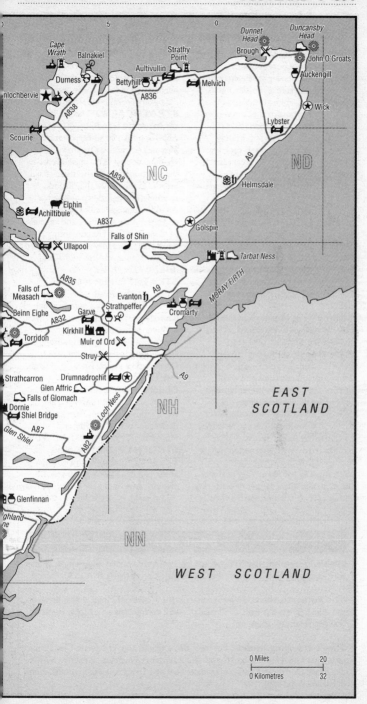

EAST
SCOTLAND

WEST   SCOTLAND

| 0 Miles | 20 |
| 0 Kilometres | 32 |

has been the home of the Chief of Macleod for 800 years; no other Scottish castle has been inhabited by the same family for so long. Among its relics is a lock of Bonnie Prince Charlie's hair. Staying here inspired Walter Scott's *Lord of the Isles*. Meals, snacks, shops, limited disabled access; open daily but best to check in winter; cl 24–25 and 31 Dec, 1 Jan; (01470) 521206; £5,20, £3.70 gardens only. There are several good self-catering cottages in the attractive grounds, and **boat trips** go from the jetty to a nearby colony of brown and great grey Atlantic seals (Easter–Oct; £8).

❀ ♨ ⌂ **Elgol** A peaceful spot for gorgeous sunset views. There may be summer **boat trips** to the lonely and dramatic inlet of Loch Coruisk from Elgol. One of the island's lovely shoreside walks runs from Elgol to Loch na Creitheach at the heart of the formidable Cuillins, a mecca for rock-climbers.

♂ **Kilmuir** The **Museum of Island Life** here is well worth a look; cl Sun, and Oct–Easter; £2.

★ **Portree** Skye's busiest harbour, attractive and quite picturesque, though in summer it tends to swarm with visitors; the harbourside Pier Hotel is right in the thick of the action, the quieter Cuillins View on the outskirts has good-value food in its conservatory.

⌂ **Quiraing** (NE) A fascinating tumbled rock mass, with a surprisingly manageable path through it.

♨ ⌂ **Raasay** (off Skye) Very peaceful island, an ideal place for gentle pottering without lots of competition from other

visitors – and for some quite stiff hill walks if that's what you prefer.

⌂ ! **Trotternish peninsula** (NE) Quite extraordinary rock scenery and formations like the **Old Man of Storr**; the Glenview Hotel at Culnaknock up here has good food, and in season the Flodigarry Hotel serves food all day.

STRATHCARRON NG9338

❀ **Attadale Gardens** 🖼 (on the A890 between Strathcarron and S Strome) Attractive gardens with winding woodland paths, sheltered by the surrounding hills and steep cliffs. Started in the 1830s, they include rhododendrons, azaleas and bamboo. An old sunken garden has been restored along with herb and vegetable gardens, and they are currently developing a nursery garden. Disabled access; cl Sun, and Nov–mid-Apr; (01520) 722217; *£2.

STRATHPEFFER NH4858

Originally a fashionable 19th-c spa resort, this has quite a different feel from the rest of the area, with its rather continental appearance of dignified hotels and villas stepped up among its wooded slopes; some call it the Harrogate of the North.

♂ ✿ **Highland Museum of Childhood** In the restored Victorian railway station, with several craft workshops in summer. Snacks, shop; disabled access; cl am Sun, and Nov–Mar; (01997) 421031; *£1.50.

STRATHY POINT NC8269

♖ ⌂ (W of Thurso) With a lighthouse at the end of a narrow peninsula, a pleasant stroll along the little road from its car park.

Days Out

Highland drama: Beinn Eighe nature reserve/mountain trail; lunch at the Kinlochewe Hotel nr Torridon; the Countryside Centre there; drive to Applecross.

The far north-west: Ullapool; lunch at the Morefield Motel there; drive on the A835 SE to the Falls of Measach; A832 to Inverewe Gardens, Poolewe; Gairloch Heritage Museum.

Skye's changing moods: Portree; drive round the Trotternish peninsula, past the Old Man of Storr and the Quiraing; lunch at Skeabost House, Skeabost; Dunvegan Castle, Armadale; boat trip to spot seals, or the Museum of Island Life (cl Sun).

TARBAT NESS NH9487
△ ⚓ ⛰ Jutting from the S side of
Dornoch Firth, this is rather isolated,
but worth the journey for the walk
around the peninsula, from
Portmahomack, past the lighthouse,
and then along the S coast past a ruined
castle to reach Rockfield.

TORRIDON NG9055
ψ ✳ △ **Torridon Countryside
Centre** (jnctn A896 and Diabaig rd)
Gateway to a huge area of nature
reserve in stunning mountain scenery –
some say the best in Scotland. It has
displays on the scenery and wildlife, as
well as a deer park and deer museum.
Visitor centre cl Sun am, and all
Oct–Apr; £1.50; (01445) 791221; NTS.
Nearby at the Mains there are herds of
red deer. Torridon is wonderful for
challenging walks, and there are a few
outstanding easier ones, based, for
example on Loch Torridon's shores.
The Kinlochewe Hotel (A896 E) has
decent food; to reach anywhere N of
here by car from the S, it's much
quicker to go by Inverness than to make
your way all the way up the W coast.

ULLAPOOL NH1294
⚓ A good centre, with quite a busy
harbour, a lot going on for a small place
– and good eating (besides the places
we've picked out, the fish and chip
restaurant is very good, with
surprisingly presentable white wines,
and the Ferry Boat is useful). You can
get a ferry out to the Summer Isles.

WEST HIGHLAND LINE NM9080
🚂 ✳ A good way of seeing Highlands
scenery between Fort William and
Mallaig: steamtrains in summer, year-
round normal trains. The views are
terrific.

WICK ND3650
★ † This waterside village has
attractive houses and a good church.
🏭 **Caithness Glass Factory** (Wick
Airport Industrial Estate) Glass-making
demonstrations (not wknds), and
factory seconds. Meals, snacks, shop,
disabled access; cl Sun Dec–Mar;
(01955) 602286; free.
⛫ **Castle of Old Wick** (just S) Ruined
four-storey square tower, probably
dating from the 12th c.
🏛 **Wick Heritage Centre** In eight
buildings by the harbour, this very good
centre presents the history of the town;
open Jun–Sept (exc Sun); (01955)
605393; £2.

This is a part of the world where inns
doing a decent bite to eat are very much
at a premium, and a welcome sight
indeed after miles of empty road.
Besides those listed elsewhere, ones we
can recommend for their positions
include the Aultbea Inn at Aultbea
NG8689, Aultguish Hotel NH3570 on
the A835 nr Loch Glascarnoch,
Badachro Inn at Badachro NG7773,
Royal Hotel at Cromarty NH7867,
Northern Sands at Dunnet ND2170,
Lock at Fort Augustus NH3709, Cluanie
by the loch (walks and maybe eagles) in
Glen Shiel NH0711, Garvault Inn
extraordinarily isolated on the B871 N
of Kinbrace NC8732, Kylesku Hotel at
Kylesku NC2234 (the boatman here has
taken readers for fascinating 4-hr boat
tours), Lewiston Arms at Lewiston
NH5029, Loch Carron Hotel on Loch
Carron NG9039, Glenuig Hotel at
Lochailort NM7682, Inver Lodge Hotel
overlooking Lochinver harbour
NC0923, Scrabster Inn at Scrabster
ND0970, Ben View at Strontian
NM8161, Loch Maree Hotel at Talladale
NG8970 and Ben Loyal Hotel at Tongue
NC5957. Almost all these places have
bedrooms.

Where to eat

BROADFORD NG6323 **Fig Tree** *Isle of Skye* (01471) 822616 Enjoyable home-
made food inc fresh fish and vegetarian choices in friendly little place; cl Sun,
Oct–Feb; disabled access. **£20|£5.**
BROUGH ND2273 **Dunnet Head Tearoom/Restaurant** (01847) 851774
Small traditional unpretentious cottage with good reasonably priced food and
snacks served by warmly friendly owners – fair choice of vegetarian dishes, fresh
salmon, local seafood, and local beef; take your own wine; bdrms; open 3–8pm (last
orders then), tearoom cl Oct–Easter; children must be well behaved. **£14|£4.**
COLBOST NG2050 **Three Chimneys** *Isle of Skye* (01470) 511258 No smoking

crofter's cottage nr sea with cosy feel in two stone-walled rooms, open fires, friendly owners, thoughtful wine list, and most enjoyable food with a strong emphasis on fish (though plenty of game and vegetarian choices, too); morning coffee and afternoon teas; bdrm suites; cl am Sun, mid-Jan–mid-Feb; children over 8 in evening restaurant (any age at lunchtime). **£35|£7.50.**

DUNVEGAN NG2449 **Macleod's Table** *Dunvegan Castle, Isle of Skye* (01470) 521310 Decorated with pine throughout, popular family restaurant with very reasonably priced generous morning coffee, snacks and full meals, and afternoon teas; friendly helpful staff; loch cruises, seal colony, castle gardens and craft shops; cl 31 Oct–mid-Mar; disabled access. **£17|£5.**

KINLOCHBERVIE NC2455 **Old School House** *Inshegra* (01971) 521383 Very good food in old school building with school-related items like photographs, maps, notebooks on tables; home-grown veg, local fish and venison, enjoyable puddings, and very good service; bdrms in newish building; disabled access; cl 25 Dec–1 Jan. **£16|£3.75.**

MUIR OF ORD NH5251 **Dower House** (01463) 870090 Very good modern cooking in attractive hotel restaurant, with fine wines, and friendly service; bdrms and lovely gardens; children over 5 in restaurant. **£36.50|£3.50.**

STRUY NH3939 **Struy Inn** (01463) 761219 Clean, pleasant and friendly small inn with very good fairly priced food, and a fine range of malt whiskies; bdrms; cl Mon, and also Tues–Thurs in Jan–Mar; disabled access. **£25|£5.**

ULLAPOOL NH1294 **Morefield Motel** *North Rd* (01854) 612161 Big helpings of exceptionally fresh enterprisingly cooked fish and seafood (owners are former fishermen and divers), Aberdeen Angus steaks and roast beef, and vegetarian dishes in the smart restaurant of basic hotel, also bar food; restaurant cl 25–26 Dec, 1 Jan; disabled access. **£20|£5.**

Special thanks to I and L Cook, Elizabeth Roberts, Lesley Honner, Helen Sandilands, Jean and George Dundas.

Scotland Calendar

Some of these dates were provisional as we went to press. Please check information with the telephone numbers provided.

JANUARY

1 **Edinburgh** Hogmanay Millennium: fireworks, torchlight procession, fire festival, street theatre, Beating the Retreat and lots more – *till 3 January* (09069) 150150

9 **Kilwinning** Millennium Fireworks Display (01294) 311477

12 **Glasgow** Celtic Connections – *till 30 January* (0141) 353 4137

25 **Scotland** Robert Burns Day: commemoration of Scotland's national poet around the country (01387) 260446; **Lerwick** Up-Helly-A': traditional Viking Fire Festival (01595) 693434

FEBRUARY

9 **Inverness** Music Festival – *till 11 March* (01463) 233902

MARCH

2 **Dumfermline** Sound and Light Performance illustrating 2,000 years of Christian history – *till 4 March* (01383) 721271

Scotland Calendar (cont.)

4 Edinburgh Rugby International at Murrayfield: Scotland v France (0131) 346 5000
6 Glenshee Snow Fun Week – *till 11 March* (01575) 582213
25 Blair Atholl World Highland Dancing Competition at Blair Castle (01796) 482376

APRIL

1 Dundee Flower Show at Dick McTaggart Centre – *till 2 April* (01382) 433435; **Edinburgh** Rugby International at Murrayfield: Scotland v England (0131) 346 5000
2 Dundee Easter Fun Day at Camperdown Park (01382) 433435
8 Edinburgh International Science Festival – *till 23 April* (0131) 473 2070
13 Glasgow Art Fair – *till 16 April* (0141) 287 2000
20 Edinburgh Folk Festival – *till 23 April* (0131) 554 3092
27 Isle of Bute Jazz Festival – *till 1 May* (01700) 502151
29 Edinburgh Rugby League Final at Murrayfield (0131) 346 5000; also, Water of Leith Festival – *till 7 May* (0131) 473 3800; **Perth** Central Scotland Horse Trials at Scone Palace – *till 30 April* (01577) 830240

MAY

1 Loch Tay Celtic Fair at the Scottish Crannog Centre – *till 5 May* (0131) 473 3800
5 Perth Play commemorating the assassination of King James I at Perth Theatre and selected outdoor sites – *till 13 May* (01738) 472700
7 Glasgow Highland Games at Gourock Park (01475) 714853; **Stirling** Beltane: May fire festival and fireworks (01786) 443126
17 Perth Festival of the Arts – *till 29 May* (01738) 475295
20 Pathhead Fun Day at Callander Park (01875) 320127
24 Glasgow Big Country: international festival of Americana – *till 3 June* (0141) 445 5079
25 Glasgow BBC Music Live inc concert in George Square – *till 29 May* (0141) 287 4276
27 Blackford Highland Games (01764) 682314; **Blair Atholl** Highlanders Parade at Blair Castle (01796) 481207
28 Blair Atholl Highland Gathering at Blair Castle (01796) 481207

JUNE

2 Glasgow National Gardening Show at Strathclyde Country Park – *till 4 June* (01698) 252565; **Isle of Bute** Regatta – *till 4 June* (01700) 503389
8 Lanark Lanimer Day: street tableaux, beating retreat, checking of old burgh boundaries (01555) 661661
9 Aberfeldy Perthshire and Angus Provincial Mod: festival of Gaelic language and music – *till 10 June* (01567) 820 435
10 Glasgow West End Festival inc Midsummer Carnival Parade – *till 25 June* (0141) 341 0844; **Renfrewshire** Festival – *till 1 July* (0141) 332 6633
12 Tantallon Jousting and Medieval Entertainment at Tantallon Castle – *till 13 June* (0131) 668 8600
13 Linlithgow Marches: traditional boundaries ceremony (01506) 890124
16 Rothesay Regatta (01700) 503734

Scotland Calendar (cont.)

17 **Dundee** Water Festival – *till 25 June* (01382) 227473
22 **Comrie** Festival – *till 5 July* (01764) 670858; **Dunkeld and Birnam** Arts Festival – *till 25 June* (01350) 723205
24 **Edinburgh** Royal Highland Show at Ingliston Showground – *till 25 June* (0131) 333 2444; **Glasgow** Lord Provost's Procession (0141) 287 2000

JULY

1 **Edinburgh** Festival of Scottish Craft at the Royal Museum and Museum of Scotland – *till 31 July* (0131) 332 2433; **Paisley** Sma' Shot Day: celebration of Paisley's weaving heritage (0141) 887 1007; **Perth** Scottish Game Conservancy Fair at Scone Palace – *till 2 July* (01620) 850577
2 **Cupar** The Thrie Estates: large production of Scotland's greatest play on its original outdoor site – *till 9 July* (0141) 339 9210
5 **Glasgow** International Jazz Festival – *till 9 July* (0141) 552 3552
8 **Caerlaverock** Re-creation of the siege of 1300 – *till 9 July* (0131) 668 8685; **Glamis** Scottish Transport Rally at Glamis Castle – *till 9 July* (01307) 462496
13 **Aberdeen** World Corporate Games – *till 16 July* (01733) 380888
15 **Loch Lomond** Highland Games at Balloch Castle Country Park (01387) 752805; **North Uist** Highland Games (01876) 500239; **Stonehaven** Folk Festival – *till 17 July* (01569) 765063
16 **Edinburgh** The Thrie Estates at Carlton Hill: large production of Scotland's greatest play on its original outdoor site – *till 30 July* (0141) 339 9210
20 **St Andrews** Open Golf Championship – *till 23 July* (01334) 472112
22 **Dunoon** Cowal Europe: world's largest Highland games – *till 29 July* (01369) 703206; **Lochearnhead** Highland Gathering (01567) 830229
31 **Turriff** Agricultural Show – *till 1 August* (01224) 288813

AUGUST

1 **Glasgow** AD: theatrical event in three plays retelling the story of Jesus Christ – *till 1 September* (0141) 204 3123
2 **Dundee** Guitar Festival – *till 6 August* (01382) 453353
3 **Speyside** Speyfest: pan-celtic festival of traditional music and song – *till 6 August* (01343) 820951
4 **Edinburgh** Military Tattoo at Edinburgh Castle: massed piped bands, display teams, dancers – *till 26 August* (0131) 225 1188; **Huntly** Gordon Gathering – *till 6 August* (01466) 799178; **Perth** Agricultural Show at Scone Palace – *till 5 August* (01738) 623780; **St Andrews** Lammas Fair – *till 8 August* (01334) 417846
5 **Montrose** Highland Games Festival Weekend (01674) 678802
9 **Glasgow** Strathclyde Police International Tattoo at Scottish Exhibition and Conference Centre – *till 12 August* (0141) 287 7777
12 **Aberfeldy** Atholl and Breadalbane Show and Highland Games (01887) 840224; **Edinburgh** Book Festival – *till 28 August* (0131) 624 5050; **Glasgow** World Pipe Band Championships (0141) 221 5414
13 **Edinburgh** International Film Festival – *till 27 August* (0131) 228 4051; **Edinburgh** International Festival – *till 2 September* (0131) 473 2001; **Perth** Highland Games (01738) 627782
19 **Isle of Bute** Highland Games (0131) 332 2433; **Kinross** Show (01577) 863339; **Kirkmichael** Strathardle Highland Games (01250) 881337

Scotland Calendar (cont.)

20 **Crieff** Highland Games (01738) 627782; **Glenisla** Highland Gathering (01575) 582281

21 **Auchterarder** WPGA Golf Tournament at Gleneagles – *till 28 August* (01764) 694469

23 **Dunoon** Kirn Gala (01369) 706884; **Muir of Ord** Highland Gathering and Games Championships – *till 24 August* (01862) 892600

25 **Blair Atholl** International Horse Trials at Blair Castle – *till 28 August* (01796) 481543; **Dunoon** Cowal Highland Gathering – *till 26 August* (0131) 332 2433

SEPTEMBER

1 **Ayr** Celtic Ceilidh Band Festival – *till 3 September* (01292) 885777; **Dundee** Flower and Food Festival – *till 3 September* (01382) 433435; **Kirriemuir** Festival of Traditional Music and Song – *till 3 September* (01575) 540261

2 **Braemar** Royal Highland Gathering (01339) 755377

3 **Blairgowrie** Highland Games (01828) 627253

9 **Ayr** Festival – *till 24 September* (01292) 885777; **Leuchars** RAF Battle of Britain Airshow: over 100 aircraft (01334) 839000

10 **Perth** Farming Yesteryear and Vintage Rally at Scone Palace (01828) 633214

17 **Perth** Hunter Trial at Scone Palace (01577) 830240

23 **Perth** Scottish Riding Club Championships – *till 24 September* (01334) 840497

OCTOBER

5 **Edinburgh** Flower Festival at St Giles Cathedral – *till 8 October* (01387) 255708

28 **Blair Atholl** Piping Championships at Blair Castle (01698) 843843

NOVEMBER

5 **Dundee** Fireworks (01382) 433435

25 **Dundee** Mountain Film Festival – *till 26 November* (01382) 668193

DECEMBER

29 **Edinburgh** Hogmanay – *till 31 December* (0131) 473 3800

Please let us know what you think of places in the *Guide*. Use the report forms at the back of the book or simply write us a letter.

WALES

North Wales (which gets the lion's share of summer visitors) combines glorious unspoilt mountain and valley scenery with plenty of enjoyable and interesting places to visit. West Wales has a beautiful coastline, with lovely walks along it – even in bad weather when upland areas are more or less a write-off, the coast preserves a gloomy magnificence. Mid Wales has fewer tourist attractions: its strength is the grand scenery, which includes the Brecon Beacons National Park, the empty and lonely Cambrian Mountains (wonderful high-level drives here), and the Elan Valley lakes. South Wales has a very good choice of interesting days out, and some pockets of fine scenery.

Besides the medieval castles and spectacular private railways which are almost a Wales trademark, enjoyable days out run from dramatic show caves to grand houses and gardens, from animal parks to Celtic myth-making, from lively historic re-creations to intriguing alternatives for the future. There are some excellent industrial museums – again, full of life.

We have mentioned a few of the Roman and prehistoric sites in which the area abounds. You can get more information from CADW (Welsh Historic Monuments Commission), (029) 2050 0200, which is also responsible for the care of the great majority of the historic castles and other monuments here: if you plan to visit many of their sites, an Explorer Pass (about £15 for a week, less for three days) from tourist information centres or CADW direct is good value as it admits to all.

You can cut down on transport costs with a seven-day Freedom of Wales Rover train pass (around £60).

North Wales

Plenty of action and outings, dramatic scenery.

The landscape varies richly, from Snowdonia's majestic mountain expanses to the intricate and rather intimate landscapes of Clwyd, the luscious Vale of Conwy and the peace of Anglesey. Snowdonia gives plenty of fine walking, both gentle and taxing – somewhere to justify a walking holiday. The much less visited Berwyn Hills further inland also give memorable scenic drives. There are good long beaches and attractive traditional family resorts, yet it's easy to get away from the crowds even in high summer – particularly on the shores of the very Welsh Lleyn Peninsula.

A wide choice of good family days out includes tremendous castles, lots of picturesque railway lines (our favourite is the one up Snowdon), rewarding great houses such as Erddig, Plas Mawr in Conwy and Bodelwyddan Castle (a family treat). Bodnant Garden at Tal-y-Cafn is glorious, and exciting is not too strong a word for the slate mining museum above Llanberis.

There is a splendid range of places to stay in, many in superb countryside.

Where to stay

ABERSOCH SH3225 **Porth Tocyn** *Bwlch Tocyn, Abersoch, Pwllheli, Gwynedd LL53 7BU* (01758) 713303 **£83,** plus special breaks; 17 attractive rms, some with sea views. On a headland overlooking Cardigan Bay, a lovely place to stay – with a refreshingly sensible and helpful approach to families (though not solely a family hotel); very friendly hard-working owners and staff, several cosy interconnecting sitting rooms with antiques and fresh flowers, most enjoyable traditional cooking in the restaurant (lots of options such as light lunches, high teas for children as they must be over 7 for dinner in the restaurant, and imaginative Sun lunches), and a happy atmosphere; lots of space in the pretty garden, heated swimming pool in summer, hard tennis court; cl mid-Nov–wk before Easter; disabled access.

BEAUMARIS SH6076 **Olde Bulls Head** *Castle St, Beaumaris, Anglesey, Gwynedd LL58 8AP* (01248) 810329 **£81,** plus special breaks; 15 rms with antiques and brass bedsteads. Partly 15th-c pub nr the castle, with snug alcoves, low beams and open fire in the quaint rambling bar, interesting decorations, popular bar food, very good restaurant food (especially fish), fine wines, and cheery service; entrance to pretty courtyard is closed by the biggest single-hinged door in Britain; cl 25–26 Dec, 1 Jan; children over 7 in restaurant in evening.

BEDDGELERT SH5948 **Sygun Fawr Country House** *Beddgelert, Caernarfon, Gwynedd LL55 4NE* (01766) 890258 **£57,** plus special breaks; 9 rms. Marvellous views of Gwynant Valley and the Snowdon range from this secluded 17th-c hotel, and lots of surrounding walks; comfortable sitting room, well-stocked bar, and home cooking in the candlelit, traditionally furnished dining room; sauna.

BETWS-Y-COED SH7955 **Ty Gwyn** *Betws-y-Coed, Gwynedd LL24 0SG* (01690) 710383 ***£56,** plus special breaks; 12 lovely rms, most with own bthrm. Welcoming 17th-c coaching inn with interesting old prints, furniture and bric-à-brac (owners own the antique shop next door), good food and friendly service; pleasant setting overlooking the river and a very good base for the area; children free if sharing parents' rm; cl Mon–Weds in Jan; disabled access.

BLAENAU FFESTINIOG SH7045 **Queens** *1 High St, Blaenau Ffestiniog, Gwynedd LL41 3ES* (01766) 830055 **£50,** plus special breaks; 12 individually decorated rms. By the famous narrow-gauge railway and surrounded by Snowdonia National Park, this most attractively refurbished Victorian hotel has real ales in the convivial lounge bar, good all-day food in the bistro (converts to more formal evening restaurant with imaginative dishes), and swift friendly service; lots to do nearby; cl 25 Dec.

BRYNSIENCYN SH4868 **Plas Trefarthen** *Brynsiencyn, Llanfairpwllgwyngyll, Anglesey, Gwynedd LL61 6SJ* (01248) 430379 **£44;** 7 rms. Happy and comfortable family house with panoramic views of Caernarfon Castle and Snowdonia, full-size snooker table, table tennis, and home-cooked food using produce grown on the farm; Mrs Roberts is a well known soprano soloist for Welsh choirs; self-catering also; cl Christmas.

CAERNARFON SH5163 **Seiont Manor** *Llanrug, Caernarfon, Gwynedd LL55 2AQ* (01286) 673366 **£140,** plus special breaks; 28 luxurious rms. Fine hotel built from the original farmstead of a Georgian manor house, in 150 acres of mature parkland; open fires and comfortable sofas in the lounge, restful atmosphere in the library and drawing room, imaginative food in the restaurant's four interconnecting areas; leisure suite with swimming pool, gym, sauna and solarium.

CAPEL COCH SH4581 **Tre-Ysgawen Hall** *Capel Coch, Llangefni, Anglesey, Gwynedd LL77 7UR* (01248) 750750 **£122,** plus special breaks; 19 lavish rms. Handsome Victorian stone mansion with landscaped gardens, plushly comfortable bar, carefully decorated lounge, friendly staff and fine food in the conservatory-style restaurant; clay-pigeon shooting; cl 24 Dec–2 Jan; disabled access.

CAPEL GARMON SH8156 **Tan-y-Foel Country House** *Capel Garmon, Betws-y-Coed, Gwynedd LL26 0RE (01690) 710507* **£120,** plus special breaks; 7 comfortable rms. Charming, partly 16th-c, no smoking manor house N of village, with mature gardens and marvellous surrounding countryside; two spacious lounges, one with winter log fire, warm, friendly and relaxing atmosphere, very good food using the freshest produce inc local lamb and home-made bread, interesting wine list; cl Christmas, limited opening Dec and Jan; children over 7; no pets.

CAPEL GARMON SH8155 **White Horse** *Capel Garmon, Llanrwst, Gwynedd LL26 0RW (01690) 710271* **£56,** plus special breaks; 6 simple rms (those in newish part are quietest). Comfortable, homely, low-beamed inn with a friendly atmosphere, winter log fires, very good home-made food in both the bar and little no smoking restaurant (some traditional Welsh meals), marvellous breakfasts, magnificent views, delightful surrounding countryside; children over 12

CONWY SH7877 **Castle** *High St, Conwy, Gwynedd LL32 8DB (01492) 592324* **£70,** plus special breaks; 29 rms. In the heart of the historic town, early 16th-c inn with fine original oil paintings in public rooms, good food in the pretty restaurant, a proper pubby bar (popular with locals), friendly helpful staff, decent breakfasts, and car parking.

GELLILYDAN SH6939 **Tyddyn Du Farm** *Gellilydan, Ffestiniog, Gwynedd LL41 4RB (01766) 590281* ***£42;** 5 rms with views of hills and mountains, 2 in private cottage suites. 400-year-old farmhouse on working farm in the heart of Snowdonia; beams and exposed stonework, big inglenook fireplaces in the residents' lounge, and wholesome home-made food using own free-range eggs; you can help with the lambs, goats, ducks, sheep and pony; fine walks, inc short one to their own Roman site; cl 25 Dec; partial disabled access.

LLANABER SH5919 **Llwyndu Farmhouse** *Llanaber, Barmouth, Gwynedd LL42 1RR (01341) 280144* **£60,** plus special breaks; 7 charming rms, some in a nicely converted 18th-c barn. Most attractive 16th-c farmhouse set just above Cardigan Bay, with a warm welcome from the friendly owners, big inglenook fireplaces, oak beams, little mullioned windows, relaxing lounge, enjoyable breakfasts, and good imaginative food in the candlelit dining room; cl 25–26 Dec.

LLANARMON DC SJ1532 **West Arms** *Llanarmon DC, Llangollen, Clwyd LL20 7LD (01691) 600665* **£75,** plus special breaks; 15 rms. Charming and civilised old place with heavy beams and timbers, log fires in inglenook fireplaces, a lounge bar interestingly furnished with antique settles, sofas in the old-fashioned entrance hall, a comfortable locals' bar, good food, and a friendly, quiet atmosphere; the lawn runs down to the River Ceiriog (fishing for residents); disabled access.

LLANDRILLO SJ0337 **Tyddyn Llan** *Llandrillo, Corwen, Clwyd LL21 0ST (01490) 440264* **£100,** plus special breaks; 10 pretty rms. Restful Georgian house with fresh flowers and antiques in the elegantly furnished and comfortable public rooms, charming staff, very good inventive food (using their own herbs) and 3 acres of lovely gardens; fishing on 4 miles of the River Dee (ghillies available) and fine forest walks (guides available) – can arrange riding and shooting too; dogs by prior arrangement; cl 2 wks Jan.

LLANDUDNO SH7979 **Bodysgallen Hall** *Pentywyn Rd, Llandudno, Gwynedd LL30 1RS (01492) 584466* **£175,** plus special breaks; 35 deeply comfortable rms, 19 in hotel, the rest in cottages in grounds. Fine 17th-c house in its own parkland, with mullioned windows, oak panelling, lovely entrance hall and first-floor drawing room, open fires, very good imaginative food in the no smoking dining room, and an 18th-c walled rose garden and knot garden; tennis, croquet, swimming pool, sauna, gym and beauty salon; children over 8; dogs allowed in cottage suites; disabled access.

LLANDUDNO SH7979 **St Tudno** *Promenade, Llandudno, Gwynedd LL30 2LP (01492) 874411* **£150,** plus special breaks; 20 pretty, individually decorated rms, many with sea views. Standing opposite the pier, this well run, smart Victorian seaside hotel has genuinely helpful and friendly staff, Victorian-style décor in the restful, no smoking sitting room, a convivial bar lounge, relaxed coffee lounge for light lunches, and an attractive garden-style restaurant with imaginative modern food; good wine list; small indoor pool.

LLANDYRNOG SJ1264 **Berllan Bach** *Llandyrnog, Denbigh, Clwyd LL16 4LR* (01824) 790732 **£55,** plus special breaks; 3 rms with French windows on to individual patios. Carefully converted cottage and barns at the foot of hills in the Vale of Clwyd, with a woodburner in the comfortable sitting room and good food in the dining conservatory; marvellous walks, well behaved dogs welcome.

LLANERCHYMEDD SH4284 **Llwydiarth Fawr Farm** *Llanerchymedd, Anglesey, Gwynedd LL71 8DF* (01248) 470321 ***£50,** plus special breaks; 3 rms in main house, 2 cottage suites in the grounds. Handsome Georgian farmhouse on 850-acre cattle and sheep farm, with a particularly warm, homely atmosphere and welcome, comfortable lounge with antiques, log fire, books and lovely views, and very good home-made food using farm and other fresh local produce; terrace, lake for private fishing, nature walks, birdwatching; no smoking; cl Christmas–New Year.

LLANFAIR DC SJ1355 **Eyarth Station** *Llanfair DC, Ruthin, Clwyd LL15 2EE* (01824) 703643 ***£44,** plus special breaks; 6 pretty rms. Carefully converted old railway station with quiet gardens and wonderful views, a friendly relaxed atmosphere, log fire in the airy and comfortable beamed lounge, good breakfasts and enjoyable suppers in the dining room (more lovely views); sun terrace and heated swimming pool, and lots of walks; dogs by prior arrangement; disabled access.

LLANFIHANGEL-YNG-NGWYNFA SJ0815 **Cyfie Farm** *Llanfihangel, Llanfyllin, Powys SY22 5JE* (01691) 648451 ***£52,** plus special breaks; 4 rms inc 3 suites with lovely views. Carefully restored 17th-c Welsh stone longhouse on 178 acres of cattle and sheep farm (guests welcome to take an interest in the lambs, shearing and hay-gathering); timbered and beamed rms with fine family furniture, log fire in the residents' lounge, hearty farmhouse cooking in the attractive dining conservatory, and a relaxed, friendly atmosphere; cl Jan/Feb.

LLANGOLLEN SJ2541 **Bryn Howel** *Llangollen, Clwyd LL20 7UW* (01978) 860331 **£90,** plus special breaks; 36 rms. Extended Victorian mansion in the lovely Vale of Llangollen, with comfortable lounges, a panelled bar, small cocktail bar, open fires, and good food using home-grown herbs and fresh local produce in the restaurant; neat grounds, sauna and solarium, and private salmon and trout fishing on the River Dee.

LLANNEFYDD SH9870 **Hawk & Buckle** *Llaneffyd, Denbigh, Clwyd LL16 5ED* (01745) 540249 ***£55;** 10 modern rms, lovely views. Pleasant 17th-c stone inn, 215 metres (700ft) up in the hills with remarkable vistas; decent choice of food using fresh local produce, neatly kept beamed and knocked-through lounge bar; a good base for exploring the area – by horse, car or on foot; cl 25 Dec; children over 8.

LLANSANFFRAID GLAN CONWY SH8075 **Old Rectory** *Llanrwst Rd, Glan Conwy, Colwyn Bay, Clwyd LL28 5LF* (01492) 580611 **£109,** plus special breaks; 6 deeply comfortable rms. Georgian house in pleasant gardens with fine views over the Conwy estuary, Conwy Castle and Snowdonia; delightful public rooms with flowers, antiques and family photos, and after introductions over cocktails you can enjoy the delicious food and marvellous wines; good Welsh breakfasts, and warm, friendly staff; cl 20 Dec–1 Feb; children under 9 months or over 5; small well behaved dogs and smokers are both welcome in the coach house only.

LLANWDDYN SJ0219 **Lake Vyrnwy Hotel** *Llanwddyn, Oswestry, Powys SY10 0LY* (01691) 870692 **£99;** 35 rms, the ones overlooking the lake are the nicest – and quietest. Large, impressive, Tudor-style mansion overlooking the lake from the hillside in 24,000 acres of forestry, with lots of sporting activities (especially fishing); log fires and sporting prints in the comfortable and elegant public rooms, relaxed atmosphere, clubby bar, and good food using home-made preserves, chutneys, mustards and vinegars and home-grown produce from own kitchen garden; nice teas too.

MAENTWROG SH6640 **Grapes** *Maentwrog, Blaenau Ffestiniog, Gwynedd LL41 4HN (01766) 590208* ***£50;** 8 rms. Bustling and cheery, family-run 17th-c pub with interesting lamps, guns and blowlamps, lots of varnished pine and stripped stone walls in the relaxed friendly bars; enjoyable food in both the bar and restaurant, verandah with café bar, big breakfasts, good views from the terrace and garden; can arrange mountain bike wknds.

NANTGWYNANT SH6250 **Pen-y-Gwryd Hotel** *Nantgwynant, Llanberis, Caernarfon, Gwynedd LL55 4NT (01286) 870211* **£54;** 16 rms. Set in 2-acre grounds, this well liked hotel is at the foot of the Llanberis Pass in Snowdonia National Park; warm log fire in the simply furnished panelled residents' lounge, a slate-floored climbers' bar with plenty of memorabilia, friendly, chatty games room (lots of walkers, climbers and fishermen), hearty, enjoyable food, big breakfasts, and packed lunches; cl Nov–Dec and mid-week Jan and Feb; disabled access.

PENMAENPOOL SH6818 **George III** *Penmaenpool, Dolgellau, Gwynedd LL40 1YD (01341) 422525* **£94,** plus special breaks; 11 low-beamed rms, some in an award-winning converted railway station. Cosy 17th-c inn on Mawddach estuary, with good lunchtime food, an imaginative evening restaurant, snug lounge with log fire, a beamed and partly panelled bar (real ales), fine nearby walks, and free salmon and trout fishing permits for residents; disabled access.

PORTMEIRION SH5937 **Portmeirion Hotel** *Penrhyndeudraeth, Porthmadog, Gwynedd LL48 6ET (01766) 770228* **£145** in hotel (14 rms), **£125** in village (26 rms), plus special breaks. On the edge of an estuary and surrounded by beaches and woods (and traffic-free), this is a remarkable place; the hotel down by the water is quite luxurious – elegant rooms with marble, gilt, and rich colourful fabrics – while behind and in the steeply landscaped grounds above it is a well dispersed, very colourful Italianate village, luscious to look at, inc all sorts of characterful cottage bedrooms tucked into the hillside; very romantic when the day visitors have left; lots to do; cl 10–23 Jan; disabled access.

SARON SH4557 **Pengwern** *Saron, Caernarfon, Gwynedd LL54 5UH (01286) 831500* ***£40,** plus special breaks; 3 rms. In 130 acres running down to Foryd Bay, this spacious, no smoking farmhouse has marvellous views of Snowdonia, and delicious food using home-produced beef and lamb, in the attractive dining room; cl Dec–Jan.

TAL-Y-BONT SH7669 **Lodge** *Tal-y-Bont, Conwy, Gwynedd LL32 8YX (01492) 660766* **£70,** plus special breaks; 14 rms – new suites to be opened soon. Friendly little modern hotel in over 3 acres on the edge of Snowdonia, with an open fire, books and magazines in the comfortable lounge, generous helpings of popular food using lots of home-grown produce in the no smoking restaurant, and good service; lots of walks; well behaved pets welcome; good disabled access.

TALSARNAU SH6135 **Maes-y-Neuadd** *Talsarnau, Gwynedd LL47 6YA (01766) 780200* **£173 inc 5-course dinner,** plus special breaks; 16 luxurious rms. Looking out across Snowdonia, this attractive, extended 14th-c mansion is set in 8 acres of landscaped hillside; flowers, plants, antiques and open fires, a peaceful atmosphere, very good food (herbs and vegetables from their own garden), friendly dogs and cats, and charming staff; children over 8 in evening restaurant; disabled access.

TREMEIRCHION SJ0771 **Bach-y-Graig** *Tremeirchion, St Asaph, Clwyd LL17 0UH (01745) 730627* ***£46;** 3 rms, 2 with brass beds. Wales's first brick-built house with a date-stone of 1567, in a 200-acre dairy farm at the foot of the Clwydian Hills; inglenook fireplace in the big lounge, home cooking using home-produced beef and lamb and their own free-range eggs, and a warm welcome; you can join in farm activities or walk their woodland trail; cl Christmas and New Year.

TUDWEILIOG SH2336 **Lion** *Tudweiliog, Pwllheli, Gwynedd LL53 8ND (01758) 770244* **£44;** 4 basic rms. Extended 300-year-old village pub with good-value home-made food in the comfortable bar and dining rooms, a welcome for families, play area, lovely views; 10 minutes' walk to beach.

To see and do

ABERFFRAW SH3270

🏛 **Barclodiad y Gawres** Some 5,000 years old, this 6-metre (20ft) underground passage tomb at the top of the cliff is notable for the patterns carved by the entrance and in the side chambers, shown up by a good torch; it's sealed, but you can ask for a key at the Wayside Café in Llanfaelog, about a mile away. Hard to believe now, but Aberffraw was once the Welsh capital. There are some lovely unspoilt coves and beaches nearby; the beach up the road at Rhosneigr is particularly good (and clean).

BANGOR SH5872

Quiet university town with a pedestrianised High St and a yacht harbour that adds a lively touch in summer; the pier was restored with an EU grant. The Nelson nr the harbour has decent food, as do the Antelope and Union.

† 🏵 ♨ **Bangor Cathedral** Founded 70 years before the one at Canterbury; the present building is restored 13th- to 15th-c, and has an interesting 16th-c carving of Christ bound and seated on a rock, as well as some fine Victorian stained glass. The Bible Garden outside contains only plants mentioned in the Scriptures. Opposite is a little museum of Welsh rural life (cl Mon and Sun; free).

🏛 🖼 🕍 🏵 **Penrhyn Castle** (1m E) Splendid 19th-c neo-Norman fantasy built by a slate magnate: the interior is in suitably grand style, with quite remarkable – and often bizarre – panelling, decoration and furnishings. The cathedral-like great hall is heated by the Roman method of hot air under the floor, and one of the beds weighs over a ton – carved from slate. An unexpectedly rich collection of paintings includes works by Rembrandt and Canaletto. In the stableyard is a museum of unique early locomotives, and

there's a walled garden and adventure playground. Meals, snacks, shop, disabled access; cl am (exc July and Aug), all day Tues, and Nov–Mar; (01248) 353084; £5, garden only £3; NT.

BEAUMARIS SH6076

★ † The most attractive town on Anglesey, with a good deal of character, several old buildings, and a busy waterfront. The 15th-c church of St Mary and St Nicholas – easy to spot by its robust square tower – houses the stone coffin of Joan, daughter of King John and wife of the Welsh leader Llewelyn the Great. The Olde Bull's Head and Sailor's Return are good for lunch.

🏰 **Beaumaris Castle** 🖼 One of the most impressive and complete of those built by Edward I, despite the struggle over it with Owain Glyndwr in the early 1400s, and the plundering of its lead, timber and stone in later ages. Beautifully symmetrical, it took from 1295 to 1312 to build (though the money ran out before it could be finished). Shop, good disabled access; cl 24–26 Dec, 1 Jan; (01248) 810361; £2.20.

🏛 **Beaumaris Courthouse** 🖼 Unique Victorian survival. You can stand in the dock and imagine you're just about to be sentenced. Open Easter–Oct, exc when court in session; (01248) 811691; court £1.50.

🏛 **Beaumaris Gaol** Paints a vivid picture of the harshness of the 19th-c prison system, especially in the dank, poky cells. Shop; open as courthouse, or by appointment, (01248) 810921; £2.75, joint with courthouse £3.50.

🐟 **Marine World** (Seafront) Displays of the sea life of the Menai Strait; Snacks, shop, disabled access; cl 25 Dec; (01248) 810072; £2.25.

BEDDGELERT SH5948

★ ⌂ A quiet village which dreamed up

Please let us know what you think of places in the *Guide*. Use the report forms at the back of the book or simply write us a letter.

the myth that it was the resting place of Llewelyn's faithful mastiff over a hundred years ago and has been living off it ever since. The Prince Llewelyn does good-value food, and there's fine Snowdonia walking around the Aberglaslyn Pass (A498 S).

⛩ ※ **Sygun Copper Mine** 🖼 (A498 NE) Interesting tours through often spectacular underground mine workings, with magnificent stalactites and stalagmites and traces of gold and silver in the copper ore veins. You're greeted by a wonderful view of the mountains when you come up at the end. Snacks, shop, some disabled access; cl wkdys Nov–Feb; (01766) 510101; *£4.75.

BETWS-Y-COED SH7956

🐟 🛏 19th-c inland resort village in a beautiful wooded gorge at the head of the Vale of Conwy, on the road to Bangor (and thence Ireland) as well as to Snowdon. Surrounded by picturesque woodland walks, the village has over a century of catering to visitors behind it. One of the best strolls is along the old riverside railway track by the Afon Llugwy W: the raging Swallow Falls and Fairy Glen just W of the village itself are deservedly regarded as two of the area's finest beauty spots. Several interesting bridges nearby, as well as the bizarre Ugly House, which looks like a series of boulders thrown haphazardly together. The Royal Oak Hotel (open all day – afternoon teas, too), Glan Aber Hotel and Ty Gwyn have good food.

🚂 **Conwy Valley Railway Museum** (Old Goods Yard) Good look at the narrow and standard gauge railways of North Wales, with railway stock and other memorabilia, model railway layouts, a steam-hauled model railway in the 4-acre grounds, and a 15-in-gauge tramway to the woods. Meals, snacks, shop, disabled access; cl wkdys Nov–Feb; (01690) 710568; *£1.

BLAENAU FFESTINIOG SH6946

This straggle of village is dwarfed by the vast spoil slopes from the slate mines all around it – once the slate capital of Wales, now with the passing of the industry like a living museum. The Grapes at Maentwrog is fairly handy for lunch.

⛩ 🛏 🚠 **Llechwedd Slate Caverns** A470) Very busy and popular, with particularly exciting underground train journeys through the caverns; one of the two routes re-creates the world of the Victorian miner, while the other (along Britain's steepest railway) ends with a walk through ten atmospheric chambers, each with its own sound and light show. Plenty on the surface too, inc a railway museum, slate mill and complete Victorian village. Meals, snacks, shop, disabled access with prior warning; cl 25–26 Dec, 1 Jan; (01766) 830306; single tour £6.75; surface attractions free.

🏛 ※ **Pumped Storage Power Station** (Tanygrisiau, off A496 S) Guided tours of the first hydro-electric pumped storage scheme in the country, with dramatic views towards the peaks of Snowdonia. Meals, snacks, shop; cl Sat (exc mid-July–Aug), and all Nov–Easter; (01766) 830310; £2.75. From the information centre there's an attractive (if slightly hairy) drive into the mountains to Stwlan Dam, which also gives super views.

BODELWYDDAN SH9974

🏚 🐝 🖼 **Bodelwyddan Castle** (off A55) The walled gardens surrounding this showy white limestone castle include a glorious mix of woodland walks, flowering plants, aviary and water features. The house (older than its 19th-c exterior suggests) has been very well restored as a Victorian mansion, with furniture from the Victoria & Albert Museum, and photographs and portraits from the National Portrait Gallery. Plenty for children, inc a woodland adventure playground, and entertaining exhibitions of puzzles, games and optical illusions. Snacks, shop, disabled access; cl Fri (exc July and Aug), and Mon too Nov–Mar; (01745) 584060; £4.30, grounds only £1. The Kinmel Arms at St George has good, interesting food.

✝ **Bodelwyddan marble church** 19th-c, built entirely of locally quarried stone: an unusual and quite splendid sight.

BODORGAN SH4272

🐖 🕊 🏚 ! **Henblas Park** (Bodorgan) Good range of family activities, from sheep-shearing, falconry and farm animals, through magic shows and juggling workshops, to tractor rides and a Neolithic burial chamber. Meals, snacks, shop, disabled access (but no facilities); open Easter hols, May bank hol wknd, and Sun–Fri late May–Sept; (01407) 840440; £3.75.

BRYNSIENCYN SH4765

♪ **Anglesey Sea Zoo** 🏷 (A4080 just S) Excellent collection of local marine life, housed in tanks specially designed to provide as unrestricted and natural an environment as possible. Also walk-through shipwreck, touch pools, adventure playground, and home-made fudge and ice-cream. Meals and snacks (their oysters are guaranteed to contain a pearl), shop, disabled access; cl 12–26 Dec, 1 wk in Jan; (01248) 430411; £4.95. The Mermaid at Foel Ferry has decent food.

🐄 **Foel Farm Park** Friendly working farm with daily sheep-milking, tractor rides, and more home-made ice-cream. Snacks, shop, disabled access; cl Nov–Mar; (01248) 430646; £3.95.

🍎 ❀ **Pick-your-own** (Gwydryn Hir farm) Pick fruit and veg while taking in the view of Snowdonia; open Jun–Oct; (01248) 430344.

🏛 **Prehistoric burial chamber** A couple of miles NW by the back road towards Llangaffo is what looks like a Stone Age hut, but is actually a burial chamber from which the covering earth has been eroded over the millennia.

CAERNARFON SH4763

★ ❀ Surviving lengths of its 13th-c town walls still crowd in its quaintly narrow streets (quaint, that is, unless you're trying to drive through them). The town harbour is busy with yachts in summer, and you can explore a restored steam-powered dredger moored here. The Black Boy and Palace Vaults do decent food.

✈ **Air World** (Caernarfon Airport, off A499 nr Llandwrog) They encourage you to climb aboard some of the helicopters and aeroplanes here; also a great many model aeroplanes, and pleasure flights. Meals, snacks, shop, disabled access; cl Nov–Feb (exc by appointment); (01286) 830800; £4.

🏰 **Caernarfon Castle** The largest of Edward I's Welsh castles, built after the defeat of Llewelyn the Last, and still quite spectacular. Finished in 1328, it's unusual both for its octagonal towers and for the bands of colour decorating the walls. Edward's son was born here and presented to the people, setting the precedent for future Princes of Wales. Shop; cl 24–26 Dec, 1 Jan; (01286) 677617; £4.20. In the square outside, around the statue of former PM David Lloyd George, there's a busy Sat market.

🏛🐚 **Segontium Roman Fort & Museum** (A4085) Roman fort dating from AD78; excavations have exposed various rebuildings during its three centuries of importance, and a museum shows some of the finds. There's a tradition that Constantine the Great was born here (and the walls of the nearby castle used to be thought to be modelled partly on the walls of Constantinople). Shop, some disabled access; cl am Sun, 24–26 Dec, 1 Jan; (01286) 675625; £1.25.

CAPEL CURIG SH7258

★ ☁ This attractive village is a useful base for enjoyable Snowdonia rambles around the pleasantly landscaped reservoirs N.

CHIRK SJ2938

The quiet little town, important as a staging post on the former road to Ireland, has something of a bypassed-by-time feel now; the Hand and (on the B5070 S) the Bridge are quite useful for lunch.

🏰 ❀ 🏛 **Chirk Castle** (just W) One of the lucky few of Edward I's castles to survive as an occupied home rather than fall to ruin. The exterior is still much as it was when built 700 years ago, with its high walls and drum towers, though there have been lots of alterations inside: most of the medieval-looking decorations were by Pugin in the 19th c, the elegant stone staircase dates from the 18th c, and the Long Gallery is 17th-c. The wrought-iron entrance gates are particularly fine, and the formal gardens are magnificent. Meals, snacks, shop, some disabled access; cl am, all Mon (exc bank hols) and Tues, and Nov–Mar; (01691) 777701; £4.80; NT. It's right by a well preserved stretch of the earthworks of Offa's Dyke.

COED Y BRENIN SH7226

🏕 ⛺ ◿ **Forest Park & Visitor Centre** (Maesgwn) Excellent introduction to what translates as King's Forest, so called to commemorate the Silver Jubilee of King George V. Some beautifully varied sights and landscapes, as well as wildlife observation hides, and over 50 miles of walks. Bike hire, snacks, shop, disabled access; cl wkdys Nov–Easter, 24–25 Dec; (01341) 440666; free, £1 parking.

COLWYN BAY SH8480

☺ Though this busy summer seaside resort has all that's wanted for a family beach holiday, it's rather eclipsed by Llandudno just along the coast. The quieter end at Rhos-on-Sea has a puppet theatre; mainly open just school hols; (01492) 548166 for programme. The Rhos Fynach opposite the small harbour at this end, once Captain Morgan's home, does decent food.

🐘 ※ ✦ **Welsh Mountain Zoo** (Flagstaff Gardens, Old Highway) Lots of exotic animals in natural-looking habitats, but what really distinguishes this 37-acre zoo from any other is the quite magnificent view over the bay. Also penguin parade and falconry displays. Meals, snacks, shop, mostly disabled access; cl 25 Dec; (01492) 532938; £5.95. In summer a free minibus service usually runs here from the town station. The Mountain View at Mochdre has good-value food.

CONWY SH7877

★ 🏰 ◢ ⚓ Cheerful old town dominated by its castle, the key part of the town's elaborate defensive system – 21 (originally 22) towers linked by walls some 9 metres (30ft) high, still the most complete town wall in Wales, with craggy old town gates. You can walk along some parts, looking down over the narrow little streets that still follow their medieval layout. There's a little **aquarium** by the quay, and you can usually go on summer **boat trips**. The Castle Hotel is a civilised place for lunch.

🏛 **Aberconwy House** 🏠 (Castle St) The only house in the town which survives from the 14th c, once the home of a prosperous merchant. Rooms are furnished in period style and there's an interesting audio-visual show. Shop; cl Tues, and Nov–Mar; (01492) 592246; £2; NT.

🦋 ✦ **Butterfly Jungle** (Bodlondeb Park) By the river, with butterflies and exotic plants and birds in a re-created jungle environment. Shop, snacks, disabled acess; cl Nov–Mar; (01492) 593149; £3.50.

🏰 ※ **Conwy Castle** One of the best-known in Wales, and one of the most important examples of military architecture in the whole of Europe. Built for Edward I in 1283–9, it's very well preserved, still looking exactly as a medieval fortress should – despite the ravages of the Civil War and beyond. There's an exhibition on Edward and the other castles he built, as well as a scale model of the castle and the town in the early 14th c. The top of the turrets offer fine panoramic views; the most dramatic views of the castle itself are from the other side of the estuary. Shop; cl 24–26 Dec, 1 Jan; (01492) 592358; £3.50.

◿ ※ **Conwy Mountain** Just W of the town, pleasant walking; not a real mountain but with views of Anglesey worthy of mountain status.

🏛 **Conwy Suspension Bridge** 🏠 Suspension bridge over the river built by Telford in 1826, and now restored by the National Trust, who have also opened up its toll house, the rooms furnished as they would have been in the last century; cl Tues (exc July and Aug) and all Nov–Mar; (01492) 573282; £1. The other, tubular bridge was built by Stephenson in 1848.

🏛 **Plas Mawr** (High St) Elaborate Tudor mansion, carefully restored, its splendid plasterwork, flagstone floors and huge fireplaces all now looking as good as when they were new. Shop, disabled access; cl Mon (exc bank hols) and all Nov–Apr; (01492) 580167; £4.

🏛 ! **Smallest House** Nicely placed on the quayside is Britain's smallest house, barely 2 metres (6ft) wide and its front wall only 3 metres (10ft) high. Squeezed into the two rooms (one up, one down) are all the comforts of home, or at least most – there's no lavatory. Shop, limited disabled access; cl Nov–Mar, Good Fri; (01492) 593484; 50p.

! **Teapot World** (Castle St) Splendidly silly collection of unusually shaped teapots from the last 300 years – everything from wigwams to cauliflowers. Shop; cl Nov–Mar; (01492) 593429; £1.50.

CORWEN SJ0743

✝ **Derwen church** (off A494, a few miles N) Interesting medieval building with an elaborately carved rood screen and loft, some old wall paintings, and an excellent Celtic cross in the churchyard.

✝ **Llangar church** (B4401 S) Built in the 13th c, with remarkable paintings of the seven deadly sins; it's usually visited only at 2pm, from Rhug chapel (and covered by the same ticket). The Crown in Corwen has good-value food.

✝ **Rhug chapel** (1m N) 17th-c, not inspiring from the outside, but inside is a riot of colour, almost every available piece of woodwork covered with cheery patterns and paintwork. Cl 2–3pm (when the custodian opens nearby Llangar church, see above), all Sun and Mon (exc bank hol wknds), and Oct–Apr; (01490) 412025; £2.

CRICCIETH SH4937

Restrained resort with a good sheltered sandy beach. The Prince of Wales is a reliable food pub.

🏰 ✳ **Criccieth Castle** 13th-c remains on a rocky, mounded peninsula above the little town, giving superb views over Tremadog Bay. Parts of the inner walls are well preserved, and there's an impressive gatehouse. A cartoon video looks at castles of Wales and other Welsh princes. Shop, disabled access; cl Nov–Mar; (01766) 522227; £2.20.

DENBIGH SJ0566

⛉ A museum on the High St has interesting finds from nearby Bronze Age sites, and the riverside Brookhouse Mill is popular for lunch, as is the Lion out at Gwytherin (B5384 W).

🏰 ✝ **Denbigh Castle** Largely ruined, but the 13th-c gatehouse is still impressive, with its trio of towers and a superb archway; the figure on the summit is thought to represent Edward I. Among other remains are what's left of an ambitious church built by the Earl of Leicester, favourite of Elizabeth I. Limited disabled access; cl castle May–Sept, monument 24–26 Dec; £2 (free in winter).

DINAS MAWDDWY SH8513

🚂 **Meirion Mill** Nestling among riverside woods below the mountains on the S fringes of Snowdonia is this charmingly set working woollen mill, in the grounds of the old Mawddwy railway station. Meals, snacks, shop (lots of locally made goods), disabled access; cl Jan–Feb; (01650) 531311; free. Nearby is a picturesque pack-horse bridge, and the waterside Dolbrodmaeth has decent food.

DOLWYDDELAN SH7352

🏰 ✝ **Dolwyddelan Castle** Picturesquely set on a lightly wooded crag, these old ruins were reputedly the birthplace of Llewelyn the Great. You can still see a restored keep from around 1200 and a 13th-c curtain wall. Summer snacks and shop; cl 24–26 Dec, 1 Jan; (01690) 750366; £2. The village church is attractive, and the Gwydr has cheap food.

FLINT SJ2473

🏰 **Flint Castle** Another fine 13th-c castle, the first built by Edward I to subdue the natives. Parts of the walls and corner towers survive, but the most impressive bit is the great tower or donjon, which is separated by the moat. Overlooking the River Dee, it has a role in Shakespeare's *Richard II*. Cl 24–26 Dec, 1 Jan; free. The Britannia in nearby Halkyn is good for lunch, with fine Dee estuary views from its conservatory.

GRESFORD SJ3454

✝ **Gresford church** Has some wonderful medieval stained glass, and its bells are often described as one of the Seven Wonders of Wales. A yew tree outside is reputed to be 1,400 years old. The Pant-yr-Ochain has good food.

HARLECH SH5831

🏰 ✳ **Harlech Castle** Splendid-looking structure built in 1283–90 by Edward I, its rugged glory the massive twin-towered gatehouse. It was starved into capitulation by Owain Glyndwr in 1404, and later dogged defence inspired the song *Men of Harlech*. Before the sea retreated there was a sheer drop into the water on one side, but it now stands above dunes, with wonderful views of Snowdonia from the battlements. Shop; cl 24–26 Dec, 1 Jan; (01766) 780552;

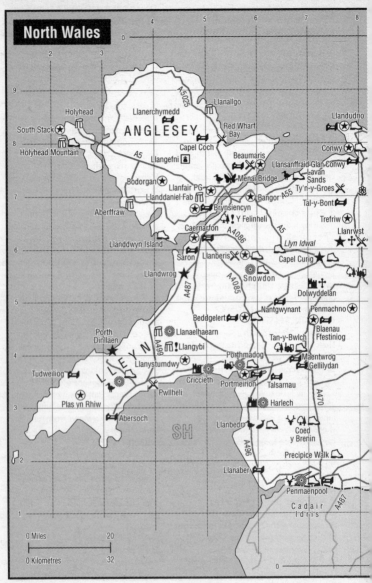

North Wales

£3. The village around it has all that the crowds of summer visitors to the castle and the good beach could want. The riverside Victoria at Llanbedr does decent food.

HOLYHEAD SH2482

Long-established fishing town on little Holy Island, now an unassuming resort with some burial chambers and

ancient sites not far away. The Victorian breakwater protecting the harbour is Britain's longest. Across the old Four Mile Bridge at Valley the Bull has good-value food.

HOLYHEAD MOUNTAIN SH2183

A dramatic hill giving good walks at the W tip of Holy Island, with an Iron Age fort and Roman watchtower site.

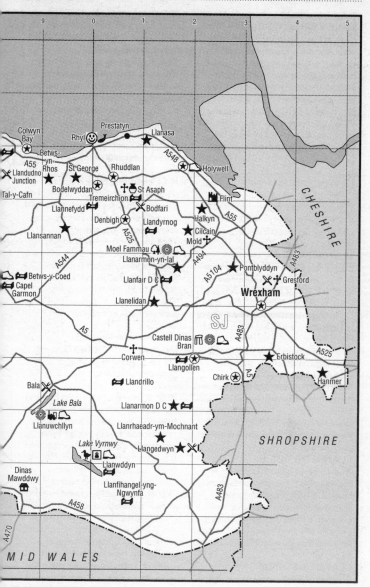

HOLYWELL SJ1977

⚓ ⚓ 🏛 **Greenfield Valley Heritage Centre** 🖼 (A548) Farm museum, and an increasing number of buildings rescued from their original sites and rebuilt here. These include a 17th-c cottage, Victorian farmhouse, and a school, all furnished in period style. Also the remains of a Cistercian abbey and a good few relics of the Industrial Revolution. Snacks, shop, disabled access; cl Nov–Mar; (01352) 714172; £2.

! ⌂ **St Winefride's Well** Source of the holy spring that turned the spot into a centre of pilgrimage – it's supposed to have healing powers. There are pleasant walks from here through the valley to the coast.

LAKE VYRNWY SJ0119

⌂ ❦ 🅴 **Lake Vyrnwy** This massive reservoir, created at the end of the last century, supplies Liverpool with 57 million gallons of water a day. It's an attractive spot to wander, with a visitor centre, waymarked trails, cycle hire, bird hides and a new sculpture trail. When the water is low you can see the remains of the original village of Llanwddyn, drowned long ago; shop (wknds only Jan–Mar), limited disabled access. (01691) 870245; free.

LAVAN SANDS SH6473

⌂ ❦ (nr Aber) Much of the North Wales coast is built on or ribboned by roads, but this is a notable exception: walks by a vast stretch of tidal sands, with flocks of wading birds.

LLANAELHAEARN SH3744

🏛 ✳ **Tre'r Ceiri Hill Fort** Off the B4417, just up the hill, a signed path leads to this evocative place, occupied from the Bronze Age through to the Dark Ages; a massive stone wall, lots of hut foundations, and fine views. At Morfa Nefyn nearby, the Bryncynan and (overlooking a lovely sandy bay) the Cliff Hotel do decent lunches.

LLANALLGO SH4986

🏛 **Din Llugwy ancient village** Remains of a 4th-c village: a pentagonal stone wall surrounds two circular and seven rectangular buildings; free. The Parciau Arms at Marianglas is the best place for a meal.

LLANBEDR SH5526

❦ ♪ ⌂ **Shell Island** (Llanbedr) A causeway leads over the sands to this near-island, appropriately named – after winter storms and high tides it's excellent for beach-combing; there are also wild birds and flowers, and you can fish here. Snacks, shop; (01341) 241453; £4 per car.

LLANBERIS SH5760

⌨ Plenty of B & Bs, small hotels, shops and cafés for the summer visitors here for Snowdon, and there are quite a few craft shops dotted along the High St. Sherpa Buses run a good service up the mountain (you can get it from several of the North Wales resorts). Just N of town is a modern working **pottery**; cl 2 wks at Christmas; (01286) 872529; free.

🏰 **Dolbadarn Castle** (A4086, at the foot of Llanberis Pass) Built in the early 13th c by Llewelyn the Great – it has a fine round keep; free.

🏚 **Electric Mountain** (Llanberis) Various changing exhibitions, then a coach whisks you off for a tour of the spectacular Dinorwic hydro-electric power station (one of Europe's biggest), deep in the mountain. Best to book, (01286) 870636. Snacks, shop, disabled access (with notice); cl Mon–Weds Jan–Easter and 2 wks at Christmas; £5.

🚂 ⌕ **Llanberis Lake Railway** (Padarn Country Park, off A4086) Four-mile trips (they are extending in 2000) along the shore of Llyn Padarn, using steam locomotives dating from 1889 to 1948. Ideal for those who want the steamtrain experience but don't want to spend too long getting it. Snacks, shop, disabled access; cl Nov–Easter; (01286) 870549 for timetable; £4.10. The station is set in a super lakeside park with walks through ancient woodland.

⌂ **Pen-y-Gwryd Hotel** (Nantgwynant, A4086/A498 SE of Llanberis) Another good spot for Snowdon walks; also a good place for lunch.

🚂 ✳ **Snowdon Mountain Railway** (A4086) The best ascent of Snowdon: Britain's only public rack-and-pinion railway, operated by vintage Swiss steam and modern diesel locomotives. It follows the route of an old pony track, and on a good day takes passengers up over 915 metres (3,000ft) right to the summit – where, in clear weather, glorious breathtaking views might include the Isle of Man and the Wicklow Mountains in Ireland. It's without a doubt one of the most spectacular train journeys in the country. Trains leave when there are more than a couple of dozen people on board – so if there aren't many people about you may have to wait for it to start, and if there are you may have to queue (there is a sort of booking service). When trains are running to the summit, you can visit the highest postbox in Britain. The mountain summit is crowned by a café dubbed 'the highest slum in Wales' by one of our most telling architectural critics; certainly one of the less successful works of Portmeirion architect Sir Clough Williams-Ellis, it's likely to be replaced in the next few years. It can be chilly, so wrap up well. Meals, snacks, shop, disabled access (with notice); open mid-Mar–Oct, though always best to ring first – of the 241 operational days in 1996, it was possible to reach the summit on only 138; (01286) 870223; £15 return.

⬇↥ ♓ **Welsh Slate Museum** (Padarn Country Park, off A4086) Lottery-funded improvements have added an extra dimension of fun to this already intriguing place, once one of the biggest quarries in the country, stepped steeply into the mountain. They now have the world's only working incline, carrying wagons up and down a hill, and a row of re-constructed quarrymen's cottages decked out in period furniture from the 1860s, 1900s and 1969. The quarry workshop has been preserved largely in its original state – complete with working craftsmen and machinery. Its water wheel is one of the largest in the world. Snacks, shop, disabled access; cl wknds Oct–Easter; (01286) 870630; £3.50.

LLANDDANIEL FAB SH5069

ⅷ **Bryn Celli Ddu** Restored Neolithic passage burial chamber built over a previous stone circle, at the end of a long tunnel, with a carved stone over a burial pit; locked, but key at the nearby farmhouse; free. Take a torch.

LLANDDWYN ISLAND SH3863

◠ Really a peninsula, making a satisfying walk from Newborough Warren over the lovely beach.

LLANDUDNO SH7882

★ ☺ ♪ ◠ ※ † The main holiday town in the area, and though it does have a long, well sheltered curve of good pebbly beach, a promenade and a range of resort entertainments, it doesn't feel at all brash. There are charming little shops and boutiques, a well restored pier (from where you can fish), and cable-cars as well as the famously steep quaint tramway up the massive Great Orme headland which protects the main beach – there's a quieter but more exposed beach on the far side. You can walk all the way up, too; a café en route

has views to justify stopping. At the top there's a 12th-c church, a visitor centre with local geology, and more good walking. On the way down a dry ski-slope also has a toboggan run. The Queen's Head at Glanwydden, off the Colwyn Bay road, does very good food.

▰※ **Conwy Valley Railway** Railtrack line from Llandudno to Blaenau Ffestiniog, through magnificent scenery, with several useful stops en route.

ⅷ ✆ **Great Orme Mines** 4,000-year-old copper mine nr the summit of Great Orme, the biggest such site so far discovered. It's also the only prehistoric mine open to the public, with displays of finds, and guided underground walks through the cavernous workings themselves. Teas, shop; cl Nov–Jan; (01492) 870447; £4.20.

❗ **Rabbit Hole** (Trinity Sq) Jolly exhibition devoted to Alice in Wonderland, with life-size animated tableaux; the real Alice holidayed in Llandudno as a child. Shop, disabled access; cl winter Suns, Nov–Easter; (01492) 860082; £2.95.

LLANFAIRPWLLGWYNGYLL SH5372

※ The record books and tongue-twisting schoolboys add another 39 letters (gocherychwyrndrobwllllantysili ogogogoch) to this village's name, but locals cut it even shorter, to Llanfair PG, or Llanfairpwll. Excellent views of Snowdonia and the Menai Strait from the top of the Marquess of Anglesey's Column, built in 1816 to commemorate the military achievements of Wellington's second-in-command at the Battle of Waterloo. The nearby village of Penmynydd was the ancient home of the Tudor family. The Liverpool Arms at Menai Bridge is the nearest good place for lunch.

※ ⅷ ▣ ❀ ⛵ **Plas Newydd** (A4080, 2m S) Fine mountain views from the creeper-covered former home of the Marquess of Anglesey, an elegant 18th-c mansion best known for its mural by Rex Whistler. Other works by the painter as well, along with a collection of relics from Waterloo, and a good spring garden with rhododendrons (Apr–Jun only); **boat trips** from the jetty. Meals, snacks, shop, disabled access; cl am, Thurs, Fri, all Nov–Mar; (01248) 714795; £4.20; NT.

LLANGEFNI SH4576

Right in the centre of Anglesey, and its 'capital', with a big open-air market every Thurs.

🖼 **Oriel Ynys Mon** (Rhosmeirch, B5111 N) Excellent gallery with imaginative changing displays on the history of Anglesey, as well as a collection of wildlife paintings by C F Tunnicliffe. You can spend a surprising amount of time here. Meals, snacks, shop, disabled access; cl Mon (exc bank hols), Christmas wk; (01248) 724444; £2.25.

LLANGOLLEN SJ2142

🏰 Not special in itself despite a good few solid and gracious Georgian and Victorian villas; what makes it attractive is its charming valley setting above the River Dee. It has discreet hotels that cater for the generally older people to whom the area most appeals – though it comes vividly alive during the *eisteddfod*. The Abbey Grange, Royal and Wild Pheasant hotels do decent lunches.

🏛 ❋ ⌂ **Castell Dinas Bran** The place for walkers to head for from Llangollen. This hill fort commands views over the vale and is close to the Panorama Walk (actually a surfaced minor road); walks can be linked to the canal towpath below.

⛵ **Horse-drawn boat trips** (Llangollen Wharf) Horse-drawn boat trips along the Vale of Llangollen from here; Apr–Oct; prior notice required for disabled access; (01978) 860702; £3. The Sarah Ponsonby close by has decent food.

🚂 **Llangollen Railway** (Abbey Rd) Now running eight miles, with steam and diesel trains from the pleasantly preserved station to the village of Glyndyfrdwy up the Dee (the Bedwyn Arms, in a lovely setting above the river, does food). Meals, snacks, shop, special coach for the disabled (you have to book); (01978) 860951 for timetable; around £8 full return fare, less for shorter trips.

🎞 **Lower Dee Exhibitions Centre** (Mill St) New centre housing a large display of model railways and a collection of memorabilia from the *Dr Who* series, inc many of the monsters

bent on exterminating him. Meals, snacks, shop; (01978) 860584; £4.50 model railways, £5.50 Dr Who.

🚗 ❋ **Motor Museum & Canal Exhibition** 🏷 Classic cars and motorcycles and an exhibition on the canal network. Snacks, shop, disabled access; cl Mon and all Nov–Feb; (01978) 860324; £2. The Sarah Ponsonby nearby has good-value food.

🏛 ❋ **Plas Newydd** Lady Eleanor Butler and Sarah Ponsonby, the 'Ladies of Llangollen', lived here from 1780 to 1831. The beautiful half-timbered house has stained glass, leather wall coverings and domestic paraphernalia of the period. Pleasant gardens. Shop; cl Nov–Mar; (01978) 861314; £2.50.

❋ **Pontcysyllte Aqueduct** (off A5/A539 E) Very spectacular to cross – by boat or on foot; the Sun Trevor at Trevor Uchaf above here has good food and more views.

🏛 ❋ **Valle Crucis Abbey** (A542 2m N) Substantial remains of the early 13th-c abbey church, and some beautifully carved grave slabs. Shop, limited disabled access; cl Oct–Apr; (01978) 860326; £2. The ruins stand at the bottom of the Horseshoe Pass, a nerve-wrackingly steep but scenic mountain drive; the Britannia Inn just above the abbey has exceptional views.

LLANGYBI SH4241

🏛 ! **St Cybi's Well** Known to the Welsh as Fynnon Gybi, this has been reckoned to have healing properties for over a thousand years. Look out for the corbelled beehive vaulting inside the roofless stone structure, which is ancient Irish in style.

LLANRWST SH7961

★ ✝ Pretty little town with an old stone bridge over the Conwy River, said to be the work of Inigo Jones. **Gwydir Chapel**, added by the influential Wynn family to the parish church in the 17th c, has a stone coffin reputedly that of Llewelyn the Great, as well as a magnificent rood screen from the ruins of Maenan Abbey. The Wynns also constructed the nearby **Gwydir Uchaf Chapel**, with intriguing ceiling paintings.

LLANUWCHLLYN SH8829

🚂 ❋ ⌂ **Bala Lake Railway** 🏷 Some of the carriages on trains using this delightful 4½-mile route are open to the elements, which seems to make the views of the lake and mountains more vivid. The locomotives were once used to haul slate in the local quarries. Snacks, shop, disabled access (but no facilities); cl most Mons and Fris Apr–Jun and Sept, and all Oct–Easter; (01678) 540666 for timetable; £6.50. The Eryrod, with panoramic views, has good-value food; and you can walk along the shores of the lake itself.

LLANYSTUMDWY SH4738

🏠🌊 **Lloyd George Memorial Museum** (A497) Audio-visual displays and memorabilia relating to the life of Lloyd George, whose family moved here from Manchester when he was a boy. They lived in nearby Highgate Cottage, which has been restored to the way it was then, and has a neat Victorian garden. Shop, disabled access; cl wknds (exc in summer), and all Nov–Mar (exc by appointment); (01766) 522071; £3. It's a short stroll from here to the site where he's buried.

🐖 **Rabbit Farm** (just off A497) Children enjoy this: around 700 rabbits, with other animals and pony rides. Cl Oct–Easter; (01766) 523136; £2.75

LLEYN PENINSULA SH3235

△🌊🐦 Very unspoilt, this peninsula has some good coastal walks around its tip, starting W from Aberdaron, with fine windswept views from Mynydd Mawr (bird reserve nearby), and E of here is the spectacular bay of Hell's Mouth; the beaches along here have clean bathing water. For a stiffer walk, try Yr Eifl (the Rivals), a 563-metre (1,849ft) mountain close to the coast.

LLYN IDWAL SH6460

△ This superbly sited Snowdonia lake beneath Glyder Fach gives pleasant walks along a signed nature trail.

MENAI BRIDGE SH5571

The village takes its name from Thomas Telford's magnificent iron suspension bridge linking Anglesey to the mainland, the first such bridge in the world. The waterside Liverpool Arms has good-value fresh food.

🦋🐦 **Butterfly Palace** 🏛 (A5025) Exotic butterflies from all corners of the globe, as well as bird house, insectarium, reptile house, and adventure playground. Meals, snacks,

shop, disabled access; cl Jan and Feb; (01248) 712474; *£4.

MOEL FAMMAU SJ1662

△⚘🌊 The highest point of the Clwydian Range, a bulging massif with clearly marked paths; walk up from the car park on the minor road E of Llanbedr DC through colour-coded forest trails or over open land, for views of much of Snowdonia, the edge of the Peak District and the Wirral.

MOLD SJ2364

✝ A very good theatre, and a richly decorated parish church built to commemorate the victory of Henry Tudor at Bosworth Field in 1485. The Druid Arms, in a lovely setting at Llanferres out on the Ruthin road, has good food.

PENMACHNO SH8052

🍴🐑 **Penmachno Woollen Mill** Timeless watermill powered by the River Machno, with local weavers explaining and demonstrating the history and craft of the cottage weaving industry. The setting is lovely. Snacks, good shop; cl 25 Dec and maybe winter Sun and Mon; (01690) 710545; free.

🏠 **Ty Mawr Wybrnant** (forest road NW) Picturesque, lonely, thick-walled medieval cottage, birthplace of Bishop William Morgan who first translated the Bible into Welsh (see *St Asaph entry*). Shop; open pm Thurs–Sun Apr–Oct (cl Sat in Oct); (01690) 760213; £2; NT.

🏠 **Ty'n-y-Coed Uchaf** Reached by a pleasant walk along the river from the woollen mill's car park, a fully furnished 19th-c farmhouse, good for showing the traditional way of life in this area. Open pm Thurs, Fri and Sun Apr–Oct; (01690) 760229; £2; NT.

PENMAENPOOL SH6717

Ⅴ△🌊 Its small waterside nature reserve has a very useful nature information centre pointing out promising places throughout this whole area, a good region for walks. One is the walk along the old railway track beside the Mawddach estuary to Fairbourne, giving magnificent views. The George III is a pleasant place for lunch.

Abergwynant Farm Trekking Centre (A493, about a mile SW) Will take beginners out on ponies for an hour, over scenic routes; (01341) 422377; from £10. You can stay at the farm too.

PLAS YN RHIW SH2328

🏠 ❀ ♿ Charming if unassuming little manor house, worth a visit for the gardens and woodland, inc a waterfall, spring snowdrop wood and subtropical specimens. Shop, very limited disabled access; cl Tues, all Oct–Mar; (01758) 780219; £3.20; NT. The setting is lovely, overlooking one of the area's wildest coasts. The beautifully placed Sun over at Llanengan does decent food.

PORTHMADOG SH5638

Quite a busy shopping town of low slate-roofed houses, with a spacious harbour and a long causeway road (5p toll) across the estuary. The Ship has decent food, and nearby Black Rock Golden Sands is one of the area's finest beaches.

🚂 △ ❀ **Ffestiniog Railway** (Harbour Station) The famous narrow-gauge railway opened in 1836 to carry slate from Blaenau Ffestiniog to Porthmadog by gravity. Closed in 1946, it reopened in 1955 and has gradually been extended to climb the 13¼ miles to Blaenau Ffestiniog; further extensions are planned. Stop off at stations along the way for good walks and views. The railway links with the main line Cambrian Coast Line, hugging the coast from Pwllheli to Machynlleth, with many stops along the way. Meals, snacks, shop, some disabled access; limited winter service, best to phone; (01766) 512340; full return fare £13.80.

🏺 **Porthmadog Pottery** (Snowdon St) Demonstrations, and the chance to make a pot yourself, as well as try out other crafts, and a mural illustrating the town's history. Snacks, shop, very good disabled access; cl most wknds, best to check winter opening; (01766) 512137; free, though may be charges for some activities.

🚂 **Welsh Highland Railway** 🔄 (opposite the main line station) Overshadowed by its more famous neighbour in size but certainly not in spirit, this enthusiastically restored line runs trains daily in the summer hols and most Suns Apr–Oct; Meals, snacks, shop, disabled access; cl Nov–Easter;

(01766) 513402 for timetable; £2.

PORTMEIRION SH5837

🏠 ❀ ❄ **Plas Brondanw** (Llanfrothen, A4085 N of Penrhyndeudraeth) The ancestral home of Welsh architect Sir Clough Williams-Ellis, and you can visit the architectural garden he designed there – great views; (01766) 771136; £1.50.

★ ❀ ♿ ! **Portmeirion village** On the steep wooded shores of an inlet from Tremadog Bay, this fairy-tale holiday village designed by Williams-Ellis is set in 175 acres of lush coastal cliff and woodland gardens. Quite charming, it's an Italianate folly – pastel-washed cottages interlaced with grottoes and cobbled squares, a bell tower, castle and lighthouse, and long picturesque flights of steps zigzagging down to the water, which at low tide dries to miles of sand. Enveloping the village are the 60 acres of Gwyllt gardens, with fine displays of rhododendrons, azaleas, hydrangeas and subtropical flora; good wild woodlands, too. You have to pay a toll to enter the village, but once in can see the house where Noel Coward wrote *Blithe Spirit* and the locations for the cult TV series *The Prisoner*; children can play in the playground, on a make-believe schooner apparently moored by the hotel, or, tide permitting, on the beach. A lovely relaxing place, quite unlike anywhere else. Meals, snacks, shops (one specialising in Portmeirion pottery), some disabled access; (01766) 770000; £4.50, less Nov–Mar. No dogs – though there's a touching dog cemetery in the woods nearby.

PRECIPICE WALK SH7321

△ Signposted N of Dolgellau, this is an attractive Snowdonia walk.

PRESTATYN SJ0683

Bustling seaside resort standing at one end of the 168-mile route of Offa's Dyke, marked by a stone pillar above the main beach.

RHUDDLAN SJ0478

🏠 ❀ **Bodrhyddan Hall** (A5151 Rhuddlan–Dyserth) Lovely dolls' house front, and some wonderfully elaborate fireplaces in the drawing room. Also a formal French garden and an interesting well-house built by Inigo Jones. Teas, shop, disabled access to ground floor only; open pm Tues and Thurs Jun–Sept; (01745) 590414; *£4.

✝ **Dyserth church** Partly 13th-c, with a Jesse window; not far from a plunging 18-metre (60-ft) waterfall.

🏰 **Rhuddlan Castle** Fine old castle, adapted by Edward I from an earlier Norman structure, to guard what was once a busy port (now a sleepy little town). Overlooking the river, it's a pretty spot. Shop, disabled access; cl 27 Sept– 30 Apr; (01745) 590777; £2.

RHYL SJ0081

☺ Rather brash seaside resort; if you're passing with children, the Knight's Cavern, a lively interpretation of Welsh history, should amuse them.

🐟 **Sea Life Aquarium** (East Parade) One of the very good centres that we've described in several English resorts, with a dramatic Shark Encounter as well as the usual walk-through underwater tunnel. Meals, snacks, shop, disabled access; cl 25 Dec; (01745) 344660; £5.25.

ST ASAPH SJ0374

✝ ☃ **St Asaph Cathedral & Museum** To match its tiny little city, this is the smallest in Britain, founded in 537. A column in the grounds commemorates its most famous cleric Bishop Morgan (see *Penmachno* entry) and his work translating the Bible into Welsh. There's a little museum with finds from the site, open by appointment, Shop, disabled access; (01745) 583429; free. The Farmers Arms (The Waen) does proper food.

SNOWDON SH6455

△ ❀ This whole area has plenty of fine walking, both gentle and taxing, to fill a walking holiday. Snowdonia's main mountain group soars dramatically, many of its peaks having easily identifiable shapes (when you can see them through the mist). Snowdon itself, the highest mountain in England or Wales, has a number of ways up ranging from the easy path alongside the mountain railway to the enthralling Horseshoe Route, which makes its way along knife-edge ridges; the Pyg Track and Watkin Path are among the favourites. For a taste of the mountain without actually going up it, follow the start of the Miners Track (from the Pen-y-pass car park on the A4086), which really is a track as far as Glaslyn, the last of four lakes passed. The National Trust has now bought large areas of the mountain, planning some path improvements alongside careful conservation of the landscape – perhaps with eventual regeneration of some former oak forest.

SOUTH STACK SH2182

🐦 🏚 **Seabird Centre** The spectacular cliffs nr the lighthouse are full of seabird breeding colonies, and this 780-acre RSPB reserve has guillemots, razorbills and puffins (especially around May, Jun and July). Lots of colourful wild flowers too, and maybe the odd seal. The visitor centre has closed-circuit TV pictures of nesting birds; guided walks leave here at 2pm Tues and Sat May–Aug. Visitor centre cl Oct–Easter; (01407) 764973; free. Nearby is a large group of the foundations of **hut circles**, probably around 2,000 years old, still with some visible traces of stone sleeping slabs. The RSPB have now opened a second seabird centre at the South Stack lighthouse; cl Oct–Easter; (01248) 724444; £2.

Days Out

Medieval town and Victorian seaside: Conwy; lunch at the Castle Hotel there, or the Queen's Head, Llandudno Junction; tram up Great Ormes Head from Llandudno, or visit Bodnant Garden.

Snowdon: Caernarfon Castle; lunch at Y Bistro, Llanberis; Snowdon Mountain Railway, Welsh Slate Museum or Electric Mountain there.

Italianate fantasy and slate city: Portmeirion; lunch there, or at the Ship, Porthmadog; Llechwedd Slate Caverns, Blaenau Ffestiniog.

TAL-Y-CAFN SH7972

❀ Bodnant Garden (off A470)
Started in 1875 but improved in 1900
(and indeed ever since, in the hands of
the green-fingered family which has
owned them), these gardens are among
Britain's greatest. Part of the 80-acre
grounds have a beautiful woodland
garden in a sheltered valley, notable for
its rhododendrons and azaleas, while
below the house are five terraces in the
Italian style, with a canal pool,
reconstructed pin mill and an open-air
stage on the lowest. Many fine rare
plants inc unusual trees and shrubs.
Meals, snacks, shop, disabled access
(but it is steep in places); cl Nov–mid-
Mar; (01492) 650460; £4.60; NT. The
Tal-y-Cafn Inn is useful for lunch, and
the Olde Bull, in a delightful setting
perched on the hillside opposite at
Llanbedr-y-Cennin, does good
imaginative food (and is a popular pub
with walkers); the Holland Arms at
Trofarth is also handy for lunch.

TAN-Y-BWLCH SH6945

⚲ ◠ ⛟ Plas Tan-y-Bwlch (off A487)
The grounds of the Snowdonia National
Park's study centre have rewarding
strolls through extensive woodland; in
places the paths cross the Ffestiniog
Railway (and you can buy tickets for it
here). Woods open all year, gardens
summer only; (01766) 590324; £2.50.

TREFRIW SH7863

✝ Used to be a spa, and you can still see
the wells on the northern outskirts of
the village (the water is said to treat
rheumatism, indigestion, and
homesickness). The village also has a
14th-c church; the Princes Arms has
nice food.

☎ ❀ Trefriw Woollen Mill (B5106)
The same family have run this woollen
mill for 135 years; two hydro-electric
turbines are driven by the fast-flowing
Afon Crafnant, and there's a weaver's
garden (best Jun–Sept). Weaving
demonstrations in the turbine house
wkdys all year (even Nov–Easter when
the mill itself is closed), plus wknds in
summer. Maybe spinning
demonstrations too in summer, so
worth checking first to see exactly
what's going on. Snacks, shop (selling
tapestries and tweeds made here),
disabled access; cl 1–2pm, all Sun (exc

bank hols and late May–Sept); (01492)
640462; free.

WREXHAM SJ3350

✝ Mostly an industrial town, but its
15th-c church is worth a look, with its
magnificent steeple.

**ⅰ ⚒ Bersham Industrial Heritage
Centre** (B5099/B5098 W) Well re-
created 18th-c ironworks, with a good
overview of other local industries, and
demonstrations of various traditional
skills. Snacks, shop, limited disabled
access; ironworks cl all Oct–Easter and
wkdys in Apr; (01978) 261529; heritage
centre free, ironworks £1.

⌂ ❀ Erddig (well signed S) Superb
late 17th-c house, especially interesting
for the way you can explore the life of
those 'upstairs' and 'downstairs' equally
as thoroughly; the gallery of servants'
portraits is especially touching.
Enlarged and improved in the early
18th c, the house is filled with splendid
original furnishings, inc a magnificent
state bed in Chinese silk. Restored
outbuildings include a laundry,
bakehouse, estate smithy and sawmill,
and the surrounding parkland is very
pleasant to stroll through. It's one of
the most attractive places to visit in all
of Wales. Meals, snacks, shop, some
disabled access; open pm Sat–Weds
Easter–Nov; (01978) 313333; £6,
garden and below-stairs tour only £4;
NT. The Cross Foxes at Overton
Bridge, a few miles S, has good food.

🐄 Farm World ▣ (adjacent to
Erddig) Well liked by readers, a 300-
acre working dairy farm with all the
necessary ingredients. Cl Nov–Feb;
(01978) 840697; £3.95.

Y FELINHELI SH5367

⚲ ! Greenwood Centre (off B4366
NE of Caernarfon) An unexpected
delight, a lively look at trees and wood
from trunks and rainforests to
Ethiopian wooden pillows. You can
handle most of the exhibits, and there's
17 acres of woodland to explore.
Mostly indoors, so ideal for rainy days,
but worth popping into at any time.
Teas, shop, disabled access; open daily
in summer, best to ring for winter
opening; (01248) 671493; £3.95. The
Vaynol Arms at Pentir has good food.

★ **Other attractive villages**, almost
all with decent pubs and in general

tending to appeal for their surroundings more than for the beauty of their buildings, include Betws-yn-Rhos SH9174, Cilcain SJ1865, Erbistock SJ3542, Halkyn SJ2172, Hanmer SJ4639, Llanarmon DC SJ1633, Llanarmon-yn-Ial SJ1956, Llanasa SJ1082, Llandwrog SH4456, Llanelidan SJ1150, Llangedwyn SJ1924 in the Tanat Valley, Llanrhaeadr-ym-Mochnant SJ1226 (where *An Englishman Who Went Up A Hill* was filmed), Llansannan SH9466, Pontblyddyn SJ2761, Porth Dinllaen SH2741 (an idyllic seaside spot, but you have to walk to it) and St George SH9576.

Other pubs and inns in attractive areas or with notable views include the Porth Tocyn Hotel above the sea at Abersoch SH3226 (excellent clean beach for families here), Castell Cidwm at Betws Garmon SH5458, Sportsman's Arms up on the A543 S of Bylchau SH9863, White Horse and Bryn Tyrch at Capel Garmon SH8255, Grouse at Carrog SJ1144, T'yn y Groes at Ganllwyd SH7224, Eagle & Child in the hilltop village of Gwaenysgor SJ0881, the Druid at Llanferres SJ1961 (doing well under new management), Cross Foxes on the Dee at Overton Bridge SJ3643, the Ship by acres of sand on the shore of Red Wharf Bay SH5281, Cwellyn Arms at Rhyd-ddu SH5753 (big playground), White Eagle on Holy Island at Rhoscolyn SH2676 and Caerffynon Hall at Talsarnau SH6236.

Where to eat

BALA SH9236 **Neuadd-y-Cyfnod** (Old School Restaurant) *High St* (01678) 521269 Relaxed and informal restaurant in the attractive old building (it can trace its history back to 1600) with huge helpings of good-value food (morning coffee, lunch, tea and dinner), pleasant service, and nice furnishings; Welsh lamb a speciality; disabled access; cl beginning Nov–Mar. **£15|£5**.

BEAUMARIS SH6076 **Sailors Return** *Church St* (01248) 811314 Bright and cheerful, more or less open-plan pub, with a collection of car-shaped teapots, naval memorabilia and maps and old prints, comfortable furnishings in rich colours, a good mix of customers, well kept real ales, and enjoyable food inc daily specials. **£18.15|£5.95**.

BODFARI SJ0970 **Dinorben Arms** (01745) 710309 Carefully extended building with warmly welcoming beamed rooms, three open fires, a huge collection of whiskies, well kept real ales and plenty of good wines, popular lunchtime smorgasbord, Fri/Sat carvery, and help-yourself farmhouse buffet Weds/Thurs; disabled access. **£17.50|£4.45**.

GRESFORD SJ3352 **Pant-yr-Ochain** *Chester Rd* (01978) 853525 Attractively and interestingly decorated spacious pub with country furnishings, good open fires, big dining area set out as a library, a no smoking room, consistently interesting food, a decent range of wines, well kept real ales, polite, efficient service, and a civilised atmosphere. **£22|£5.95**.

LLANBERIS SH5760 **Y Bistro** *43–45 High St* (01286) 871278 Friendly, no smoking restaurant with good local produce used in Welsh and English cooking – fine fish and enjoyable puddings; may cl Sun, Mon in winter. **£22**.

LLANDUDNO JUNCTION SH8180 **Queens Head** *Glanwydden* (01492) 546570 Busy but comfortable dining pub with a spacious and comfortable modern lounge bar, carefully prepared, imaginative food using lots of fine seafood, delicious puddings, real ales, and decent wines; cl 25 Dec; children over 7. **£24.50|£5.95**.

LLANGEDWYN SJ1924 **Green** (01691) 828234 Very well run ancient place in a lovely spot in the Tanat Valley, with lots of nooks, alcoves and crannies, blazing log fire, a nice mix of furnishings, and a pleasant upstairs no smoking restaurant; impressive range of tasty bar food, half a dozen real ales, and a good choice of malt whiskies and wines; attractive garden over the road with picnic sets by the river, and fishing permits; disabled access. **£17|£4.90**.

LLANRWST SH7961 **Ty-Hwnt-i'r-Bont** (01492) 640138 Charming little 500-year-old cottage by a bridge, run by the Holt family for 26 years, with nice old country furniture under the beams and joists, interesting knick-knacks, light lunches, home-made cakes, shortbread and scones for enjoyable afternoon teas, and quite a choice of teas, coffees and milk shakes; home-made mustards to take away, and old books and bric-à-brac upstairs; cl Mon (exc bank hols), and Nov–Easter; partial disabled access. £4.50.

PWLLHELI SH3535 **Plas Bodegroes** *off A497 (01758) 612363* Lovely Georgian manor house in tree-filled grounds, with comfortably restful rooms, good food using superb fresh local produce (especially fish) and a very good wine list; bedrooms; cl Mon, Dec–Feb. **£40** for 5 courses.

RED WHARF BAY SH5281 **Ship** *(01248) 852568* Solidly built old pub looking over miles of cockle-sands, with enterprising bar food, big old-fashioned bars, coal fires, friendly and cheerful service, no smoking dining room and cellar room, well kept real ales, quite a few whiskies, and plenty of seats outside. **£21|£5**.

TY'N-Y-GROES SH7772 **Groes** *(01492) 650545* Particularly well run family inn with wonderful views from the airy, no smoking conservatory, rambling low-beamed and thick-walled rooms with welcoming atmosphere and interesting old furnishings, winter log fires, a fine range of good traditional country cooking, well kept real ales, and efficient, friendly service; stylish bdrms; children over 10 in restaurant; disabled access (and one specially equipped bdrm). **£22.50|£6.95**.

West Wales

Unspoilt coastal beauty, great for a quiet holiday.

This quietly appealing area has quite a lot to keep children amused, besides many castles, and a decent spread of other places to visit. Tenby, showing its medieval origins still, is a civilised small resort. St David's is rewarding.

The coast is relatively gentle in the south, with level cliffs, sinuous estuaries and some lovely sandy beaches. In the west and north it's much more rugged, with seals and dolphins. The Pembrokeshire Coast Path snaking around the intricate seaboard makes the most of it.

Where to stay

BROAD HAVEN SM8616 **Druidstone** *Broad Haven, Haverfordwest SA62 3NE (01437) 781221* **£70**, plus special breaks; 9 rms, some with sea view, shared bthrms. Alone on the coast above an effectively private beach with exhilarating cliff walks, this roomy and very informally friendly hotel, with something of a folk-club and Outward Bound feel at times, is extremely winning and relaxing if you take to its unique combination of good wholesome and often memorably inventive food, slightly fend-for-yourself approach amid elderly furniture, and glorious seaside surroundings; self-catering cottages, 2 with wheelchair access. All sorts of unusual sporting activities inc sand-yachting; cl Mon–Weds mid-Nov–mid-Dec (fully open from then on), cl Mon–Thurs end second wknd Nov for one month, and on same days, end first wk Jan–end second wk Feb; disabled access (see above).

CAREW SN0403 **Old Stable Cottage** *Carew, Tenby, Dyfed SA70 8SL (01646) 651889* **£48**; 3 rms. Originally a stable and carthouse for the castle, this attractive place has an inglenook fireplace and original bread oven, games room, conservatory overlooking the garden, and good Aga-cooked food; children over 3.

CRUGYBAR SN6437 **Glanrannell Park** *Crugybar, Llanwrda, Dyfed SA19 8SA (01558) 685230* ***£72**, plus special breaks; 8 rms. Surrounded by lawns and overlooking a small private lake in 23 acres of parkland, this very laid-back, peaceful hotel has two comfortable lounges and a small library, a well stocked bar, especially good, varied food using fresh local produce where possible, and friendly helpful staff; excellent area for walks and birdwatching, also lots of wildlife, pony-trekking, and fishing nearby; cl Nov–Mar.

FISHGUARD SM9736 **Gilfach Goch Farm** *Fishguard, Dyfed SA65 9SR (01348) 873871* ***£52,*** plus special breaks; 6 rms. Traditional, carefully modernised, 18th-c Welsh stone farmhouse on a 10-acre smallholding with sheep, donkeys, Vietnamese pot-bellied pig, dogs, cats, and fowl; lovely views and nr the Pembrokeshire coastal path, log fires, homely lounge, good country cooking using many home-produced ingredients, and a safe garden for children; no smoking; self-catering also; cl Oct–Mar; partial disabled access.

FISHGUARD SM9537 **Manor House** *Fishguard, Dyfed SA65 9HG (01348) 873260* ***£48,*** plus special breaks; 6 comfortable rms, most with sea views. Georgian house with fine views of the harbour from the sheltered garden; well planned basement restaurant with interesting home-made food using fresh local produce; cl Christmas.

GLYNARTHEN SN3049 **Penbontbren Farm** *Glynarthen, Llandysul, Dyfed SA44 6PE (01239) 810248* **£70;** 10 rms in converted stone outbuildings. Run by a friendly Welsh-speaking family, this Victorian farmhouse is in lovely countryside, with nature trails, horse riding, a little farm museum, and nearby beaches; period pine furnishings in the bar, lounge and well liked restaurant, good hearty dinners inc some regional dishes, bar lunches, and decent breakfasts; cl 4 days over Christmas; disabled access.

LLANDELOY SM8527 **Lochmeyler Farm** *Llandeloy, Haverfordwest, Dyfed SA62 6LL (01348) 837724* **£60,** plus special breaks; 16 rms. Attractive 16th-c farmhouse on a 220-acre working dairy farm; two lounges (one no smoking), log fires, traditional farmhouse cooking in the pleasant dining room, mature garden, and Welsh cakes on arrival; you can walk around the farm trails; disabled access.

NEVERN SN0840 **Trewern Arms** *Nevern, Newport, Dyfed SA42 0NB (01239) 820395* **£50;** 10 rms. Creeper-clad old inn in a pleasant riverside hamlet; interestingly decorated slate-floored bar, a comfortable lounge bar, decent food, well kept real ales, quiet garden; disabled access.

PENALLY SS1199 **Penally Abbey** *Penally, Tenby, Dyfed SA70 7PY (01834) 843033* **£100;** 12 pretty rms, many with four-posters, and 4 in coach house. 'Gothick'-style country-house hotel in 5 acres of gardens and woodland, with fine views across the golf course and Carmarthen Bay; open fire in the comfortable lounge, tiny bar, conservatory, very good food in the elegant, candlelit restaurant, delicious breakfasts, small indoor swimming pool, snooker and croquet; children over 7 in restaurant; disabled access.

PONTFAEN SN0533 **Tregynon Country Farmhouse** *Pontfaen, Fishguard, Dyfed SA65 9TU (01239) 820531* **£65,** plus special breaks; 6 rms. Peacefully set 16th-c farmhouse on the edge of the Gwaun Valley, in lovely unspoilt countryside with lots of wildlife and walks; big inglenook fireplace in the beamed lounge, friendly welcome, and very good, imaginative, additive-free food using produce from their own and neighbouring farms; home-smoked meats, and home-made preserves; cl 2 wks winter – best to phone; children over 8.

RHYDLEWIS SN3447 **Broniwan** *Rhydlewis, Llandysul, Dyfed SA44 5PF (01239) 851261* **£43;** 3 pretty rms, 2 with own bthrm. Grey stone house with pine-panelled windows, on a small farm surrounded by beech and pine trees, with fine views of the Prescelly Hills in the distance, lots of wildlife, and you can help with the calves, hens, and cows; stone barn with games, table tennis and books, a woodburner in the comfortable sitting room, a separate dining room, and good, naturally produced food from both the garden and farm; no smoking; children over 10.

ST DAVID'S SM7524 **Warpool Court** *St David's, Haverfordwest, Dyfed SA62 6BN (01437) 720300* ***£138,*** plus special breaks; 25 rms. Originally built as St David's cathedral school in the 1860s and bordering NT land, this popular hotel has lovely views over St Brides Bay; Ada Williams's collection of lovely hand-painted tiles can be seen in the public rooms, food in the spacious, elegant restaurant is imaginative (good for vegetarians too), and staff are helpful and friendly; quiet gardens, heated summer swimming pool, tennis, exercise room, table tennis, pool, croquet, and free golf at St David's golf club; cl Jan.

SPITTAL SM9822 **Lower Haythog** *Spittal, Haverfordwest, Dyfed SA62 5QL (01437) 731279* **£45;** 6 rms. Centuries-old farmhouse on a working dairy farm in 250 acres of unspoilt countryside; with a comfortable lounge, log fire, books and games, traditional breakfasts, good cooking in the dining room, and friendly owners; swing and slide in the garden, trout ponds in the woods.

To see and do

ABERAERON SN4562
★ ⚘ The line of colour-washed houses facing the harbour is very pretty; there's a good craft centre here too, and the Harbourmaster is a useful stop.

AMROTH SN1607
The beach here is lovely, and the New Inn facing it has good home cooking.
🏵 **Colby Woodland Garden** (off A477) Beautiful woodland gardens in a sheltered valley with pretty cascading stream – very pleasant and colourful, especially in autumn. A walled garden has a 'gothick' gazebo and colourful herbaceous plants. Snacks, shop; cl Oct–Apr; (01834) 811885; *£2.80; NT.

BEGELLY SN1109
🐖 ⚘ **Folly Farm** (A478) Busy working dairy farm, with the chance to milk a cow – or watch the more modern methods in the milking parlour. Everyone gets a chance to bottle-feed some of the friendly animals. Also an indoor traditional fairground, good play areas and go-carts. Meals, snacks, shop, disabled access; cl Nov–Feb; (01834) 812731; £3.75. A working pottery is nearby, (01834) 811204.

BURRY PORT SN4100
🏵 ⚘ 🌳 🐾 **Pembrey Country Park** Good for families to unwind, with 100 acres of woodland, summer falconry and orienteering, adventure playground, visitor centre, dry ski slope, toboggan run, a miniature railway and eight miles of clean sandy beach (no dogs in summer). Meals, snacks, shop, disabled access; park open all year, though most attractions cl winter; (01554) 833913; parking £4, considerably less winter, charges for some attractions.

CAREW SN0403
🏰 ✕ 🏚 **Carew Castle & Tidal Mill** 🖼 Magnificent Norman castle (the setting

for the Great Tournament of 1507), with an especially handsome ivy-clad south-east tower. The mill is one of just three restored tidal mills in Britain, with records dating back to 1558. Shop; cl Nov–Easter; (01646) 651782; £2.65 both, £1.70 each. By the good Carew Inn nearby is the Carew Cross, an impressive 4-metre (13-ft) Celtic cross dating from the 11th c.

CARMARTHEN SN4120
🏰 🏚 Busy regional market town, according to legend the birthplace of Merlin, with the remains of a 13th-c castle, and on Priory St an unusual 2nd-c Roman amphitheatre. The Cresselly Arms, along the A40 E in the pretty village of Pont ar Gothi (pleasant riverside walks), is reliable for lunch and has good-value bar food.
♿ 🏵 **Carmarthen Museum** (Abergwili, just E) Good museum in a former palace of the Bishop of St David's, in 7 acres of attractive grounds. Snacks, shop, disabled access to ground floor only; cl Sun, 25–26 Dec, 1 Jan; (01267) 231691; free.
🚂 **Gwili Railway** 🖼 (Bronwydd, A484 N) Short steamtrain trips along a scenic standard-gauge branch line of the old Great Western Railway. Snacks, shop, disabled access; trains daily in Aug, and most Suns and some Weds May–Sept; (01267) 230666 for timetable; £3.50.

CARNINGLI COMMON SN0637
☁ ❋ 🏚 (S of Newport) Pleasant walks with some interesting views, on largely unspoilt moorland capped by ancient cairns and other antiquities.

CASTELL HENLLYS SN1138
🏚 ♃ Signed off the A487 E of Newport, where the Llwyngwair Arms surprises with its authentic Indian food, is this Iron Age hill fort in beautiful

countryside overlooking the River Gwaun, with an interesting reconstruction of three big conical roundhouses. Also a forge, smithy, primitive looms and herb garden. Snacks, shop, some disabled access; cl Oct–Mar; (01239) 891319; £2.60.

CASTLE MORRIS SM9032

🐾 🏠 **Llangloffan Farmhouse Cheese** (Llangloffan Farm, just N) Delicious, traditional farmhouse hard cheeses are hand-made here, and you can watch the whole process (which stage depends on the time of day you visit) and even meet the cows. Before Mr Downey set up the farm (run entirely on organic principles) he was a viola player in the Hallé Orchestra; his award-winning cheeses now go all over the world. Snacks, shop, disabled access; cheese-making am only, phone to check times, farm shop open daily exc Sun; (01348) 891241; *£2. The excellent-value fish restaurant at Letterston is handy.

CEMAES HEAD SN1249

⌂ ☀ Gives walkers good views over the mouth of the Teifi estuary and out over the Irish Sea.

CENARTH SN2641

✾ ☂ **National Coracle Centre** 🔳 Unique collection of small hand-made boats from all over the world; they may have demonstrations of how they're made, and there are also various tools used for poaching. A medieval bridge and a pretty waterfall provide the backdrop. Snacks, shop, disabled access; cl Sat, and all Nov–Mar; (01239) 710980; *£2.50.

★ **Newcastle Emlyn** The attractive main street of this nearby village leads down to an ancient bridge; the Bunch of Grapes and Pelican do decent food.

CILGERRAN SN1943

🏰 ☀ **Cilgerran Castle** (off A484) Picturesquely placed on a crag above the River Teifi, this twin-towered Plantagenet fortress has good views from its towers and high walls, though, as usual, you have to go up a spiral staircase. Shop (not Sat), disabled access; (01239) 615007; £2. The ancient Pendre is good for lunch.

✟ **Welsh Wildlife Centre** (Cilgerran) Covering 350 acres, this is one of the richest areas of wetland in

the district; the reed bed is the second biggest in Wales. You'll probably see more towards dusk, but even then some bashful creatures might not emerge; a video shows the species you may have missed. Meals, snacks, shop, disabled access; open Easter–Oct half-term; (01239) 621600; *£2.50.

DALE SM8104

⌂ ☀ **Dale peninsula** At the entrance to the huge natural harbour of Milford Haven, with gentle, level-topped terrain giving walkers a bird's-eye view of the shipping activities, reducing the giant oil tankers to a pleasantly toy-like scale.

⚓ **Boat trips to Skomer, Skokholm, etc** Dale is the normal base for the National Park boats to the islands of Skomer, Grassholme and Skokholm; sailing times (usually Apr–Oct only) from Dale Sailing Co, (01646) 601636. The Griffin overlooking the anchorage is useful for lunch.

🐦 **Grassholme** The island has 30,000 pairs of gannets: on a clear sunny morning, even from the coast, you can see it's white with them.

🐦 **Skokholm** This island has Britain's first bird observatory, still tracking migrations.

🐦 ✟ 🏚 **Skomer** 720 acres of spectacular wild scenery with countless birds (including breeding pairs of short-eared owls) and flowers, as well as seals playing on the shore – maybe common seals briefly in Jun or July, more likely grey seals and their pups in Sept and Oct; it's also remarkable for the easily traced remains of the Iron Age settlement here – there's a well laid-out trail.

DINAS HEAD SN0039

⌂ The circuit of this nice miniature headland gives about an hour's walk.

DRE-FACH FELINDRE SN3539

🔧 ☂ **Museum of the Welsh Woollen Industry** (off A484) Working museum with textile machinery and tools dating back to the 18th c. Also factory trails, and demonstrations of fabric-making – you may be able to try your hand at spinning. Snacks, shop, disabled access to ground floor; cl Sun, and Sat Nov–Mar; (01559) 370929; £2.60. There are decent places to eat in

Newcastle Emlyn.

FISHGUARD SM9537

★ The old fishing harbour is surrounded by appropriately small streets of terraced cottages (the Ship here has lots of atmosphere); there's an entirely separate big commercial harbour used by the Irish ferries. In between, the upper town has some attractive old buildings and is pleasant to saunter through. In 1997, a 100-ft-long tapestry went on show to commemorate the 200th anniversary of the defeat here of the last army to invade mainland Britain. The Royal Oak (scene of the final surrender) has decent food.

△ ⚔ ✧ **Strumble Head** You can drive or walk up on to the high headland which protects the harbour; its cliffs are quite grand, particularly where the seas boil through the narrow neck cutting off the rock on which Strumble Head lighthouse stands (there's a car park nearby). Down on the rocks there you quite often see seals even in the spring, though they're more common in late summer. The scenery typifies the rocky, big-dipper coastline of North Pembrokeshire.

GWAUN VALLEY SN0034

△ ⚘ Pretty walks along the lushly wooded river either upstream or downstream of Pontfaen.

GWBERT-ON-SEA SN1648

🐑 ❀ △ ✧ **Cardigan Island Coastal Farm Park** Most notable for its fine clifftop setting overlooking Cardigan Island; there are a good few friendly animals for children, as well as plenty of wild flowers, and a coastal walk to caves where seals breed (best Mar–Nov). You may even see dolphins leaping out of the sea. Open all year; (01239) 612196; £1.70.

KIDWELLY SN4007

🏰 **Kidwelly Castle** When this was built, in the 12th c, the sea used to wash against the steep slope below. Four massive towers, the tremendous gatehouse and much of the impressive outer walls still remain, with steps up to the battlements and turrets. From the walls, the narrow medieval street layout of Kidwelly itself is very obvious. Shop, some disabled access; cl 24–26 Dec, 1 Jan; (01554) 890104; *£2.20 (inc audio tour).

⚒ **Kidwelly Industrial Museum** (Mynyddygarreg, NE) Looks at two great Welsh industries, coal- and tin-mining. The original tinplate working buildings are still here, and there's an exhibition of coal-mining with pithead gear and a winding engine. Snacks, shop, disabled access; open Easter, then wkdys and pm wknds May–Aug; (01554) 891078; free. The riverside Gwenllian Court Hotel out this way has decent food.

LAMPHEY SN0101

🏛 **Lamphey Palace** (A4139) Ruined 13th-c palace once belonging to the Bishops of St David's. Shop; cl 25 Dec; (029) 2050 0200; £2.

LAUGHARNE SN3011

△ ❀ The setting on the Taf estuary makes this a rewarding spot for wandering – past Laugharne Castle, Dylan Thomas's Boat House and along the cliff walk (known as Dylan's Walk); in the other direction there's a pleasant walk via Roche Castle. Thomas and his wife are buried in the village churchyard, their grave marked by a simple white cross. Browns Hotel (King St) seems not much changed since Thomas drank there; splendid secondhand bookshop opposite.

🏠 **Dylan Thomas's Boat House** (Dylan's Walk) Wales's best-known recent poet lived here while he was writing *Under Milk Wood*, and there are still some of his family photographs and furniture. The writing shed he used for so many poems is nearby. Snacks, shop; cl 25 Dec; (01994) 427420; *£2.75.

🏰 ⚜ ❀ **Laugharne Castle** The ruin Dylan Thomas described as 'brown as owls' is a massive battlemented compilation of styles from the 12th to the 16th c; it has Victorian and Georgian gardens and good views over the estuary. Cl Oct–Apr; (01994) 427906; £2.

LITTLE HAVEN SM8512

★ △ Attractive village, with boats pulled up on to the sand, and a nice base for seaside walks on the Pembrokeshire Coast Path. There are some attractive sandy-floored rock coves to explore at low tide around here and the Druidstone Hotel to the N, with a good cliff walk northwards from there to the long sweep of sand and surf at Newgale Sands (food all day from the Duke of Edinburgh).

LLANARTHNE SN5320

⚘ National Botanic Garden of Wales This ambitious £43 million horticultural development is the first national botanic garden to be built in Britain for two centuries. The gardens are being landscaped around the 18th-c Middleton Hall, in the heart of the attractive Tywi Valley, and the idea behind them was first conceived at the Earth Summit in Rio de Janeiro, nearly 10 years ago. The impressive Norman Foster-designed Great Glasshouses are already complete, and as we went to press, finishing touches were just being put to fountains, a gatehouse and 220-metre-long herbaceous borders. The gardens will comprise science, leisure and educational facilities, a farm estate committed to commercial organic management, and should be open around spring. When we went to press, they had not yet finalised opening times or admission prices, so best to phone for information on (01558) 668768.

LLANDEILO SN6222

★ An attractive sloping town; the Castle Hotel is home to some splendid beers, and past it, the Plough at Rhosmaen is a favourite local dining pub.

△ ⚘ ⚘ ⛪ ❦ **Dinefwr Park** (20 minutes' walk from riverside lodge on the S edge of Llandeilo; follow Dyfed Wildlife Trust path) Pleasant walks through wooded Capability Brown parkland around an isolated, largely 13th-c castle. Plenty of deer, but no trace of the medieval town which is known to have stood outside the walls. Meals, snacks, shop, disabled access; cl Tues, Weds and Nov–Mar; (01558) 823902; £2.80.

⚘ ⚘ **Gelli Aur Country Park** (3m W, off B4300) Very relaxing: 60 acres of wooded parkland around a splendid mansion, with an arboretum, nature trails, and specimen trees and shrubs. Meals, snacks, shop, disabled access; cl 25–26 Dec; (01558) 668885; £1.20 parking charge.

LLANELLI SN5001

⚘ ⚘ **Parc Howard Art Gallery & Museum** In pleasant parkland, the largest collection of the distinctive local pottery in existence, as well as local history, and pictures by local artist J Dickson Innes. Cl 1–2 pm, and 25–26 Dec; (01554) 772029; free. The Stepney (Park St) is handy for lunch.

❦ **Wildfowl & Wetlands Trust** (3m E) By Wales's main estuary for wildfowl and waders, with plenty of observation hides and special walkways. Many of the birds will feed from your hand, and at their summer duckery you can hear ducklings calling from inside their eggs. Meals, snacks, shop, disabled access; cl 24–25 Dec; (01554) 741087; £4.25.

LLANGRANOG SN3154

★ △ Attractive fishing village with a nice family beach backed by cliffs; there's a pleasant stroll to a headland to the N (otherwise, Cardiganshire lacks a coastal path for much of the way).

LLANSTEPHAN SN3410

⛪ ✳ **Llanstephan Castle** Sprawling 11th/13th-c ruin, majestically overlooking the Tywi estuary and Carmarthen Bay from an isolated ridge high over the water. Impressive gatehouse with fine vaulted ceiling, and you can still see the slots for drenching intruders with boiling fat or lead; free.

LLANYCEFN SN1024

🏠 **Penrhos Cottage** 🖼 (off B4313) There can't have been many housing problems around here if local tradition is to be believed; anyone who built a house overnight on common land was entitled to claim it, and this old cottage was such a one, frantically constructed by friends and family. Small shop, disabled access; open by appointment only, (01437) 731328; donations.

MANORBIER SS0697

⛪ ★ ⚘ **Manorbier Castle** Still in the hands of the family who have owned it for over 300 years, this impressive, partly 12th-c fortress looking down to the beach has massive medieval outer walls and an early round tower, with a 13th-c chapel and other buildings, and more modern constructions within the walls. Snacks, shop; cl Oct–Easter; (01834) 871394; £2. The quiet village is attractive, with a particularly good clean beach, and there's a striking view of the castle from the church. The Castle Inn (open all day in summer) is useful for lunch. Springfields Farm (off A4139) has

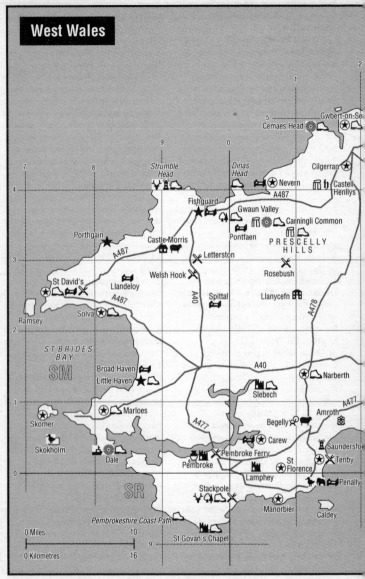

West Wales

pick-your-own strawberries and a decent farm shop; (01834) 871746.
MARLOES SM7508
🏛🐾❋⌂ **Marloes Deer Park** Not actually a deer park, but a wild cliffy headland a couple of miles W of Marloes, joined to the mainland by quite a narrow isthmus showing steep Iron Age defences; a place to watch birds

(choughs breed here) and maybe seals on the offshore rocks. The Lobster Pot in Marloes is a useful informal family pub, and the beaches are safe for bathing as well as gloriously remote.
❋⌂ **Marloes peninsula** Gentle terrain above the cliffs, giving views of Skomer Island, and memorable walkers' routes that need only minimal inland

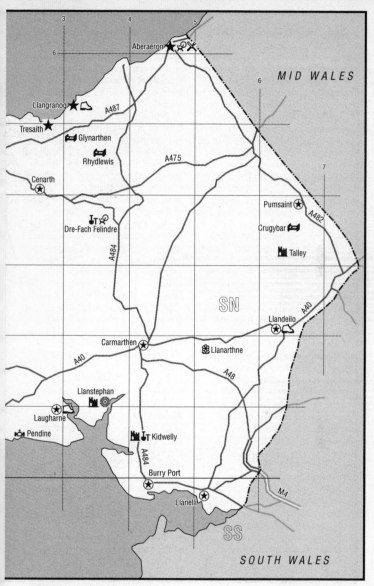

walking to complete the circuit.

NARBERTH SN1014

★ Pleasant little town standing on the imaginary Landsker line separating the 'Little England' of South Pembrokeshire from the more properly Welsh areas to the N. The Angel has good food.

✗ △ **Blackpool Mill** (Canaston Bridge, 3m W) Striking, three-storeyed, former corn mill with working machinery, and pleasant walks along the fish-filled river that powers it; caverns next door. Snacks, shop; cl Nov–Mar; (01437) 541233; £1.

☺ **CC2000** (Canaston Bridge, 3m W) 10-pin bowling, amusements and a reconstruction of TV's *Crystal Maze*; cl 25–26 Dec; (01834) 891622; separate charges for individual attractions.

🐾 **Cwm Deri Vineyard** (Martletwy, off A4075 SW) Self-guided walks, rare breeds, a small collection of teddy bears hidden in a shed, and tastings. Maybe cl winter wkdys, and all Jan and Feb (though worth giving them a ring if you're passing); (01834) 891274; free.

🏰 **Llawhaden Castle** 12th-c ruins, surrounded by a deep moat, with the remains of the 13th/14th-c bishop's hall, kitchen and bakehouse; free. The post office nearby sells guides and postcards.

☺ **Oakwood** (A4075 W) The only real theme park in Wales, and a good one too, especially in the summer holidays when they stay open till 10pm, rounding off every night with a firework display. There's a real mix of things to do, from Europe's biggest wooden rollercoaster to live Wild West saloon shows. Younger children have their own little rollercoaster (there's another medium-sized one aimed at families), as well as a small farm area, and carousels and the like. The real talking point is the sky-coaster, Vertigo, quite the most unpleasant-looking ride we've ever seen: you're strapped in a harness and winched to a height of up to 140ft, then freefall at 60 mph back towards the ground – just before which you'll start swinging like a frantic pendulum. A nightmare cross between bungee-jumping and a parachute drop, this obviously wouldn't suit everyone, so rather than bump up the entry price, there's an extra charge (£30 for up to three people, the maximum number that can go on it at once). This has proved enormously popular, so if you want to try it in peak periods you'll need to get there fairly early to book in. Meals, snacks, shop, disabled access; cl Oct–Easter (exc around Christmas, when special events); (01834) 891373; £10.95.

NEVERN SN0839

★ ✝ Interesting old riverside village with a medieval bridge over the Nyfer. The church has a tall 10th-c carved Celtic cross and other carved stones, some with Viking patterns, in the graveyard, where the massive yew trees are reputed to weep tears of blood if the priest is not Welsh-speaking. The Trewern Arms is handy for lunch.

🏛 ❋ **Pentre Ifan Burial Chamber** (SE towards Brynberian) One of the most impressive ancient monuments in Wales: a striking, former long barrow, with the enormous capstone still held up by three of the four surviving great upright megaliths. Great views over the Nyfer Valley.

PEMBROKE SM9801

🏺 **Museum of the Home** (Westgate Hill) Intriguing private collection of all sorts of everyday objects from the past 300 years, in a pleasant domestic setting. No under-5s; open Mon–Thurs May–Sept; (01646) 681200; *£1.20.

🏰 **Pembroke Castle** The birthplace of Henry VII and thus the Tudor dynasty, this impressive 13th-c castle is largely intact, and its endless passages, tunnels and stairways are great fun to explore. The 23-metre (75-ft) tower is one of the finest in Britain. Summer snacks, shop, disabled access; cl 24–26 Dec, 1 Jan; (01646) 684585; *£3 (guided tours by arrangement, Jun–Aug exc Sat, 50p extra). The Pembroke Ferry pub by the water at the foot of the bridge over the estuary does good fresh fish.

PEMBROKESHIRE COAST PATH SR9294

⌒ Snaking around the intricate Pembrokeshire seaboard, this makes for notable walks.

PENALLY SS1199

🦜 🐾 **Stepaside Bird & Animal Park** (A477) A friendly place with exotic birds, snakes, reptiles and meercats. Lots going on through the day inc crocodile-taming demonstrations and spider and snake handling. Snacks, shop, disabled access; cl Nov–Mar; (01834) 843102; £3.75.

PENDINE SN2307

🏎 **Museum of Speed** The hard flat sand on the beaches here made it a favourite spot for attempting new speed records; in 1926 J G Parry Thomas and his 27-litre car Babs set a short-lived land-speed record of 168 mph, but the careers of both ended the following year in a grisly accident. The car spent the next 40 years buried in the sand but has now been restored, and in July and Aug (maybe longer) forms the centrepiece of this small museum overlooking the beach. Also local and natural history; shop, disabled access; (01994) 453488; free.

PORTHGAIN SM8132

★ Quaint small working harbour in a tiny village carefully preserved by the National Park authorities. Former granite and slate centre – bastions of former stone works still tower over the water. The Sloop is a good pub, and there are fine coastal walks.

PRESCELLY HILLS SN0529

△ 🏛 (Mynydd Preseli) Pleasant walks with interesting views, on largely unspoilt moorland capped by ancient cairns and other antiquities – for example, the intriguing Carn Arthur and a hill fort, both reached from the back road along the E side.

PUMSAINT SN6640

🏴 🏛 ! **Dolaucothi Gold Mines** (off A482) 2,000 years of gold-mining are the focus of this unusual mine, in use since Roman times; tours of both the Roman adits and the deeper 1930s workings, complete with miners' lamps and helmets. Good visitor centre, woodland walks, and the chance to have a go at panning for gold. Stout footwear recommended. Meals, snacks, shop; site open Apr–Sept (cl Thurs and Fri exc July and Aug), underground tours (no under 5s) mid-May–late Sept; (01558) 650359; £2.60, tours £3.60 (£2.60 NT members); NT. Get there early for the underground tours, especially in summer hols. The nearby Brunant Arms, in fine scenery at Caio, has decent food.

ST DAVID'S SM7525

★ ✝ △ 🏛 ♨ ♥ The cathedral here has had a community in residence around it for longer than any other in Britain, but thanks to the relative isolation of the place it's stayed undeveloped, so that St David's today is little more than a village – with lots of colourful flowers in spring. It's a good area for coastal walks, perhaps to ancient sites such as the Neolithic burial chambers up by St David's Head to the S or over towards Solva, to St Non's Chapel, or W to St Justinian (another chapel here, looking over Ramsey Island). The Old Cross Hotel nr the cathedral is a civilised place for lunch, and the Farmers Arms is cheap and cheerful. The beach at Whitesands Bay is good. In summer there are boat trips from the lifeboat station to rocky Ramsey Island, where seabirds nest in great numbers.

! **Adventure Days** Organise well supervised abseiling, canoeing, rock-climbing and other activities – ideal for off-loading active children for the day (over-8s only); (01437) 721611.

🏚 **Bishop's Palace** Impressive ruins, clearly once very grand: plenty of quadrangles, stairways and splendid arcaded walls, with all sorts of intricate and often entertaining details (like the carvings below the arcaded parapets). Atmospheric and tranquil, particularly out of season when you may have it largely to yourself. Shop, limited disabled access; cl am winter Suns, 24–26 Dec, 1 Jan; (01437) 720517; £2.

♩ **Oceanarium** (New St) Excellent insight into sea and shore life; highlights include the shark tank and rock pool. Talks and demonstrations for children during school hols. Snacks, shop, limited disabled access; cl 25–26 Dec; (01437) 720453; £3.

Days Out

Cathedral village: Solva; lunch at the Cambrian Arms there, or the Old Cross Hotel or Farmers Arms, St David's; St David's Cathedral and Bishop's Palace; boat trip to Ramsey Island, or walk from Whitesand Bay to St David's Head.

Lily-ponds behind the beach: Pembroke Castle; lunch at the Armstrong Arms, Stackpole, or the Ferry, Pembroke Ferry; Bosherston lily-ponds, St Govan's Chapel.

Harnessing the tide: Tenby; lunch at the Carew Inn, Carew; Carew Castle and Tidal Mill.

† **St David's Cathedral** The Norman church had largely collapsed by the 15th c and elaborate repairs had to be made; the resulting roof is an impressive lace-like oak affair, and oak features in most of the rest of the church too. There's a fine collection of Celtic sculptured crosses. Shop, disabled access; cl am Sun; donations.

St David's Farm Park (NE edge, off A487) Big collection of rare breeds, as well as rides on either a tractor or one of their shire horses. Highly praised by readers. Meals, snacks, shop (with their own wool, and spinning demonstrations), disabled access; cl Oct–Easter; (01437) 721601; £3.75.

† **St Non's Chapel** (about ½m N) Reputed birthplace of St Non, the mother of St David; there are lovely sea views from the very scant ruins of the simple coastal chapel here, signed down a track from the useful St Non's Hotel, with a holy well nearby. The walk from St David's is pleasant.

ST FLORENCE SN0802

Manor House Wildlife Park (B4318) Around 35 acres of wooded grounds and gardens with exotic birds, reptiles and fish, a pets corner, playground, model railway and falconry displays (2pm); also a new natural history museum. Meals, snacks, shop, disabled access; cl Oct–Easter; (01646) 651201; £4. The Old Parsonage Farm does quick family food.

ST GOVAN'S CHAPEL SR9692

(past Bosherston, towards St Govan's Head) A simple, reroofed, 14th-c ruin, dramatically set halfway down the sea cliffs, and reached via rough rock steps; the former holy well just below has now dried up.

SAUNDERSFOOT SN1304

Quiet, extended, seaside village, with a lighthouse on the spit sheltering the harbour and sandy beach; good fresh fish at the Royal Oak.

SLEBECH SN0215

Slebech church (off A40 5m E of Haverfordwest) Gloriously isolated ruined 12th-c church, formerly a temple of the Knights Hospitaller, by the tidal waters of the East Cleddau. Though there is a track from the main road, it's more enjoyable to turn down the A4075, take the next right turn and

park by the mill, walk over the bridge and down the track through the woods above the river. In Haverfordwest, George's (Market St) does good food.

SOLVA SM8024

★ One of the prettiest villages on the coast, with a great deal of character. From the harbour a good, interesting, shortish path runs E to Dinas Fawr, the opposite headland. This high crag (enclosed by the ramparts of an Iron Age fort) gives pretty views of the attractive little fishing village and the coast. The Cambrian Arms is a reliable dining pub.

STACKPOLE SR9694

Bosherston lily-ponds These ancient elongated lily-ponds are a fine sight when in bloom in summer, and well worth a walk; (there are several car parks).

Stackpole Estate (B4319) This spectacular 2,000-acre estate is a real delight to wander through, with lakes, woodlands, cliffs, dunes and beaches offering a range of landscapes to suit every taste and mood. Barafundle Bay is a lovely relatively undiscovered beach. Footpaths lead past a quarry and assorted wildlife over the lake to Bosherston lily-ponds. Snacks (at Stackpole Quay); (01646) 661359; free, NT. The Armstrong Arms does good food, and the St Govan's pub is useful too.

TALLEY SN6332

Talley Abbey (off B4302) Ruins of a once-magnificent 12th-c abbey, still very fine, especially the two pointed archways; (01558) 685444; free.

TENBY SS1496

★ Pleasantly restrained family seaside resort, with sheltered beaches and rock coves. It's a walled town, the splendidly preserved 13th-c wall still with many of its towers left, as well as a magnificent 14th-c arched barbican gateway; a moat used to run the whole length of what is now a tree-lined street. The medieval Plantagenet House, and Coach & Horses and Lamb are all pleasant lunch places.

† **Caldey Island** Reached by summer boat trips from Tenby harbour (May–Sept wkdys, weather permitting, £6), still a monastic island, where the Cistercian monks have good cream and

honey for sale, as well as more durable crafts and old-fashioned perfume. Besides the modern abbey, there's a 13th-c church with a simple cobbled floor, still in use, on one side of the small cloister of the original priory; these ancient priory buildings (which you can see from outside but not enter) give a better sense of the past than almost anywhere else in West Wales. Sailing times from the tourist information centre, (01834) 842404.

! Dino's Den (Great Wedlock Farm, Gumfreston – B4318 W) Fun for families, and an unusual example of farm diversification. The woods are filled with very well constructed, life-size dinosaurs, some of which roar or spit. A visitor centre is designed to look like fossilised dinosaur ribs. Meals, snacks, shop, disabled access; open daily Easter–Sept, and Oct half-term; (01834) 845272; £3.75.

⊖ 🏛 Hoyle's Mouth Cave (off A4139 just SW, Trefloyne Lane towards St Florence; short path through wood on left after 500 yds) Running more than 30 metres (100ft) back into the hillside, this spooky place has yielded Ice Age mammoth bones, as well as human tools dating back over 10,000 years. Take a torch, but don't go in winter – you'd disturb the hibernating bats.

✝ St Mary's Church (Tenby) Interesting 13th-c building with a huge steeple and a plaque commemorating a local invention that many of us use every day – the equals sign.

🐾 ⊖ 🖼 Tenby Castle Museum There are some remains of the 13th-c castle on the headland above the yachting harbour. Within the castle site is a local history and geology museum, with prehistoric finds and an art gallery with Augustus and Gwen John collections. Shop; cl winter wknds and Christmas wk; (01834) 842809; £1.70.

🏛 Tudor Merchant's House (Quay Hill) Fine example of gabled 15th-c architecture, with a good Flemish chimney and the remains of frescoes on three walls; small herb garden. Shop; cl Weds, and all Nov–Mar; (01834) 842279; *£1.80; NT.

TRESAITH SN2751
★ Attractive coastal village, with a decent pub (and a waterfall to its beach).

Pubs and inns doing food that are noteworthy for their fine positions include the Black Lion at Abergorlech SN5833 (lots of good walks nearby), Forest Arms at Brechfa SN5230, Cresselly Arms by the water at Cresswell Quay SN0406, Stanley Arms on the Cleddau estuary opposite Picton Castle at Landshipping SN0111 and Cennen Arms at Trapp SN6518. The Teifi Netpool at St Dogmaels SN1645 is handy for a walk along to Poppitt Sands.

Where to eat

ABERAERON SN4562 **Hive on the Quay** *Cadwgan Pl* (01545) 570445 Cheerful harbourside place on the wharf, based around a family honey business (their home-made honey ice-cream is delicious), with lunchtime buffet, popular café, and good, unfussy evening meals relying heavily on organic produce – quite an emphasis on fish from their own boat; also a bee exhibition and shop; cl mid-Sept–Spring bank hol. **£18|£6.50.**

LETTERSTON SM9429 **Something Cooking** *A40 5m S of Fishguard* (01348) 840621 Enthusiastically run and very friendly fish restaurant with truly outstanding fresh fish, served by neat uniformed waitresses – very reasonable prices too; cl am Sun, 2 wks Christmas; disabled access. **£13|£4.25.**

PEMBROKE FERRY SM9704 **Ferry** (01646) 682947 Former sailors' haunt by the water below Cleddau Bridge (not by the new ferry), with an extensive range of very fresh fish dishes – non-fishy things too – nautical décor, good views, a relaxed pubby atmosphere, well kept real ales, decent malt whiskies, and efficient service; restaurant cl 25–26 Dec. **£15.45|£4.95.**

ROSEBUSH SN0630 **New Inn** *NW of village* (01437) 532542 Very attractively restored 17th-c drovers' inn with three cosy rooms, simple antique oak country furniture on handsome slate flagstones, a relaxed atmosphere, good, wide-ranging bar food using carefully chosen local ingredients, half a dozen real ales, well chosen wines, and friendly staff; cl second wk Jan. **£22|£6.**

ROSEBUSH SN0729 **Old Post Office** *(01437) 532205* Quaint bistro with lots of local photos, farming tools and teapots on the ceiling, good-value lunches, well prepared traditional cooking in the candlelit dining room, and coffee and afternoon tea; bdrms; some disabled access. **£18|£5.25.**

ST DAVID'S SM7525 **Morgan's Brasserie** *20 Nun St (01437) 720508* Smart little brasserie specialising in good fresh fish, from a shortish menu supplemented by daily specials and using fresh local produce; friendly service; and good-value wines; cl Sun and Mon, Jan–Feb; partial disabled access. **£27.**

STACKPOLE SR9896 **Armstrong Arms** *Jasons Corner (01646) 672324* Charming, rather Swiss-looking dining pub, run by a mother and daughter team, with neat oak furnishings and glossy beams in four rambling areas, particularly good interesting food (inc fresh local fish), well kept real ales, cheerful uniformed waitresses, and seats in the flower-filled garden; must book pm Sat, am Sun; disabled access. **£16|£4.95.**

TENBY SN1300 **Celtic Fare Tearooms** *Vernon House, St Julian St (01834) 845258* Cosy tearoom with jugs and teapots hanging from the beams, an open fire and gas lamps, quite a few teas, and really good home-made cakes, scones, and pastries; may cl winter Mon; disabled access. **£16|£4.25.**

WELSH HOOK SM9327 **Stone Hall** *(01348) 840212* 14th-c house with imaginative French food and fine wines in the beamed restaurant (evenings only), a characterful bar, and lovely grounds; bdrms. **£24.**

Mid Wales

The lonely heart of Wales, great untouched landscapes.

This is one of Britain's best areas for really getting away from it all. The scenery is spectacular. Though it doesn't quite match the very best of Snowdonia or the West Wales coast, you're not sharing it with as many other visitors. It has very good walking, and little-used former drovers' roads give glorious scenic drives, threading through the huge tracts of forest and moorland around the Llyn Briane reservoir, the Cambrian Mountains and the reservoirs above the Elan Valley. Other kinder ranges of hills tempt out more people, most notably the western Black Mountain, the Brecon Beacons and the eastern Black Mountains. The area's river valleys are among the finest in Wales: the friendly Usk, the rather more imposing Upper Wye, and above Aberystwyth, the beautiful Vale of Rheidol.

Sparsely populated, with far more sheep than people, Mid Wales has a few rather pleasantly idiosyncratic places to visit, such as Celtica in Machynlleth and the nearby Centre for Alternative Technology, and King Arthur's Labyrinth at Corris (fun for children). The friendly towns include a string of dignified, slightly old-fashioned, inland spa towns.

There are some very comfortable places to stay in, with glorious countryside more or less on their doorsteps.

Please let us know what you think of places in the *Guide*. Use the report forms at the back of the book or simply write us a letter.

Where to stay

ABERDOVEY SN6195 **Bodfor** *Bodfor Terrace, Aberdovey, Gwynedd LL35 0EA (01654) 767475* **£51.70,** plus special breaks; 15 rms with showers, most with sea views. Small, family-run, seafront hotel with a bar, comfortable lounge, good restaurant food, and helpful service; dogs welcome; cl 20 Dec–1 Jan.

ABERDOVEY SN6195 **Penhelig Arms** *Terrace Rd, Aberdovey, Gwynedd LL35 0LT (01654) 767215* **£69,** plus special breaks; 10 comfortable rms. Carefully refurbished building in a fine spot overlooking the sea; cosy bar, open fires, very good food with emphasis on daily delivered fresh local fish in the no smoking restaurant, extensive wine list with 14 by the glass (champagne, too), splendid breakfasts, and friendly service; lovely views of Dyfy estuary; cl 25–26 Dec.

ABERDOVEY SN6195 **Preswylfa** *Aberdovey, Gwynedd LL35 0LB (01654) 767239* ***£50;** 4 super rms with lovely views. Friendly and relaxed Edwardian house in a pretty, mature garden; courteous, genuinely helpful owners, period drawing room with grand piano (all welcome to play), enjoyable evening meals (by arrangement) using home-grown produce in the dining room with fine views, and a footpath leading to the village and beach (4 minutes); children over 8.

ABERHAFESP SO0595 **Dyffryn** *Aberhafesp, Newtown, Powys SY16 3JD (01686) 688817* ***£50;** 3 rms. Carefully restored half-timbered barn on a 100-acre sheep and beef cattle farm, with a residents' lounge overlooking the stream, traditional cooking in the dining room, and friendly owners; no smoking; children over 10.

CARNO SN9697 **Aleppo Merchant** *Carno, Caersws, Powys SY17 5LL (01686) 420210* ***£45;** 6 rms, most with shower. Warm and friendly 17th-c inn in a rural setting, with a comfortably modernised beamed lounge bar, open fire in the small adjoining lounge, a fair choice of well liked food, helpful service, and well kept real ales; children over 12.

CHURCH STOKE SO2689 **Drewin Farm** *Church Stoke, Montgomery, Powys SY15 6TW (01588) 620325* **£38;** 2 rms. Attractive 17th-c farmhouse with lovely views; a warm welcome, comfortable lounge, traditional cooking in the dining room, and games room with snooker table in the converted granary; Offa's Dyke footpath runs through the mixed farm of sheep, cattle and crops; cl Nov–Feb.

CRICKHOWELL SO2118 **Bear** *Crickhowell, Powys NP8 1BW (01873) 810408* **£61;** 35 rms, the back ones are the best, and some have Jacuzzis. Particularly friendly coaching inn with a calmly civilised atmosphere, excellent food using local produce and home-grown herbs, fine wines and ports, well kept real ales, and prompt, attentive service; lots of antiques, deeply comfortable seats, and a roaring log fire in the heavily beamed lounge, and a partly no smoking family room; children over 5 in restaurant; dogs welcome; disabled access.

CRICKHOWELL SO1719 **Gliffaes Country House** *Crickhowell, Powys NP8 1RH (01874) 730371* **£101.70,** plus special breaks; 22 rms, several refurbished this year. Run by the same family since 1948, this imposing house is set in 33 acres of wonderfully peaceful grounds with fine rare trees; an enjoyably informal and relaxed atmosphere, comfortable big sitting room, elegant drawing room, pleasant conservatory, glorious views from the terrace, good cooking, and cheerful staff; fishing, hard tennis court, golf practice net, and a putting and croquet lawn.

EGLWYSFACH SN6796 **Ynyshir Hall** *Eglwysfach, Machynlleth, Powys SY20 8TA (01654) 781209* ***£150,** plus special breaks; 10 individually decorated, no smoking rms. Carefully run Georgian manor house in 14 acres of landscaped gardens adjoining the Ynyshir coastal bird reserve; particularly good service, antiques, log fires and paintings in the light and airy public rooms, extremely good food using home-grown vegetables, and delicious breakfasts; lots to do nearby; cl 3–23 Jan; children over 9.

GLADESTRY SO2355 **Royal Oak** *Gladestry, Kington, Herefordshire HR5 3NR (01544) 370669* ***£40,** plus special breaks; 5 well equipped rms. Unpretentious and welcoming inn on Offa's Dyke, with beams and flagstones, a quiet relaxing atmosphere, good home-cooked bar food (inc nice breakfasts), comfortable lounge, separate bar, and picnic sets in the lovely secluded garden behind.

GUILSFIELD SJ2110 **Lower Trelydan** *Guilsfield, Welshpool, Powys SY21 9PH (01938) 553105* ***£48; 3** rms. Charming black and white farmhouse on a beef cattle and sheep farm, with lovely heavily beamed ceilings, fine antiques and comfortable seating, a cosy licensed bar, warm and friendly atmosphere, and delicious farmhouse cooking; pretty garden; self-catering also in barn conversion; cl Christmas; disabled access.

HAY-ON-WYE SO2342 **Old Black Lion** *26 Lion St, Hay-on-Wye, Herefordshire HR3 5AD (01497) 820841* ***£57.50,** plus special breaks; 10 rms, some in modern annexe. Smartly civilised old hotel with low beams and black panelling, a convivial bar, wide choice of carefully prepared food in both the bar and candlelit, no smoking, cottagey restaurant, and an extensive wine list; close to fishing (private salmon and trout fishing) and riding; children over 5 and must be over 8 in restaurant.

KNIGHTON SO3172 **Milebrook House** *Stanage, Milebrook, Knighton, Powys LD7 1LT (01547) 528632* ***£73,** plus special breaks; 10 spacious rms, 4 in a newer smart wing. Charming 18th-c house in 3 acres, surrounded by really unspoilt countryside and with River Teme trout fishing; log fires, residents' sitting room, bar (where light lunches are served), and good sound cooking using home-grown vegetables; children over 8; disabled access.

LLANDEFALLE SO1034 **Trehenry Farm** *Llandefalle, Brecon, Powys LD3 0UN (01874) 754312* **£40;** 4 rms. 18th-c farmhouse on a 200-acre farm with lovely views of the Black Mountains and Brecon Beacons; inglenook fireplaces, beams, TV lounge, good food, and large garden; self-catering also; cl Christmas.

LLANDEGLEY SO1263 **Ffaldau Country House** *Llandegley, Llandrindod Wells, Powys LD1 5UD (01597) 851421* ***£48;** 3 rms. Carefully restored, heavily beamed 16th-c country house with flower-filled landscaped gardens; log fire in the comfortable lounge, residents' bar, upstairs sitting room with games and books, enjoyable dinners in the charming dining room, and fine breakfasts; dogs by prior arrangement; children over 12.

LLANEGRYN SH6250 **Cefn Coch** *Llanegryn, Tywyn, Gwynedd LL36 9SD (01654) 712193* ***£46;** 5 rms. Traditional coaching inn set in an acre of gardens with fine views, and on the edge of Snowdonia National Park; beams, slate floors, stripped pine, and fresh flowers, Laura Ashley décor, pictures and a woodburner in the lounge; a homely atmosphere, friendly owners, and enjoyable food – they also have a little tearoom; cl Nov–Jan; no children.

LLANGAMMARCH WELLS SN9447 **Lake** *Llangammarch Wells, Powys LD4 4BS (01591) 620202* **£120;** 19 charming, pretty rms with fruit and a decanter of sherry. Particularly well run, turn-of-the-century half-timbered hotel in 50 acres with plenty of wildlife, well stocked trout lake, clay-pigeon shoots, and tennis; deeply comfortable, tranquil drawing room with antiques, paintings and a log fire, wonderful afternoon teas (in summer under the chestnut tree overlooking the river), courteous discreet service, fine wines and very good modern British cooking in the elegant candlelit dining room, and liberal breakfasts; children over 7 in evening dining room; disabled access.

LLANGORSE SO1327 **Trewalter** *Llangorse, Brecon, Powys LD3 0PS (01874) 658442* **£51;** 4 rms. Only 10 minutes from Hay-on-Wye, this charming and friendly Victorian house has panoramic views across to the Brecon Beacons, an open fire and plenty of games and books in the comfortable sitting room, candlelit dinners taken around one big table, and good breakfasts; watersports on a natural lake by the village; cl Christmas and New Year; children over 4.

LLANWRTYD WELLS SN8746 **Carlton House** *Dolycoed Rd, Llanwrtyd Wells, Powys LD5 4RA (01591) 610248* **£60,** plus special breaks; 7 well equipped rms. Warm, friendly owners run this comfortable, Edwardian restaurant-with-rooms, and there's a relaxing sitting room with original panelling, log fire, plants and antiques, an attractive little dining room serving exceptionally good modern British cooking using top quality local produce (delicious puddings and home-made canapés and petit fours), super breakfasts with home-made bread and marmalade, and a thoughtful wine list; cl 10–27 Dec.

LLYSWEN SO1337 **Griffin** *Llyswen, Brecon, Powys LD3 0UR* (01874) 754241 **£70**, plus special breaks; 7 rms. Old-fashioned and warmly welcoming, family-run sporting inn; imaginative fresh food in the no smoking restaurant (brook trout and salmon caught by the family, local game in season), good breakfasts, an interesting, comfortable bar with a huge inglenook, and helpful service; fishing and shooting courses; cl 25–26 Dec.

LLYSWEN SO1239 **Llangoed Hall** *Llyswen, Brecon, Powys LD3 0YP* (01874) 754525 **£185**, plus special breaks; 23 very pretty rms with luxurious touches. Fine, largely Jacobean mansion beautifully converted into a first-class hotel with a lovely house-party atmosphere, handsome hall, elegant and spacious public rooms with antiques, wonderful pictures, fresh flowers and views over the grounds, imaginative modern cooking in the charming restaurant, and very good Welsh breakfasts; marvellous surrounding countryside; children over 8.

MONTGOMERY SO2296 **Dragon** *Market Sq, Montgomery, Powys SY15 6PA* (01686) 668359 **£74**, plus special breaks; 20 rms. Attractive black and white timbered small hotel with a pleasant grey-stone tiled hall, comfortable residents' lounge, beamed bar, and a restaurant using local produce; indoor swimming pool, live jazz pm Weds.

NEWTOWN SO1292 **Lower Gwestydd** *Aberbechan, Newtown, Powys SY16 3AY* (01686) 626718 *£42; 2 rms. Traditional, 17th-c, black and white half-timbered house on 200 acres of mainly sheep and arable farmland, in lovely countryside; comfortable lounge and dining room, and good food with their own fruit and veg, chicken and lamb; you can wander around the farm; cl Christmas–New Year.

PENNAL SH6799 **Gogarth Hall Farm** *Pennal, Machynlleth, Powys SY20 9LB* (01654) 791235 *£44; 2 rms. 17th-c house on a working farm of suckler cows and sheep, with marvellous views of the Dovey estuary – guests welcome to walk around the farm; dining room and lounge, enjoyable breakfasts and evening meals, and utility room for children to use in wet weather; babysitting available; dogs by arrangement; self-catering also.

PRESTEIGNE SO3164 **Radnorshire Arms** *Presteigne, Powys LD8 2BE* (01544) 267406 **£79**; 16 rms. Rambling, handsomely timbered, 17th-c hotel with old-fashioned charm and an unchanging atmosphere, elegantly moulded beams and fine dark panelling in the lounge bar, latticed windows, enjoyable food (inc morning coffee and afternoon tea), a separate no smoking restaurant, well kept real ales, and politely attentive service.

OLD RADNOR SO2559 **Harp** *Old Radnor, Presteigne, Powys LD8 2RH* (01544) 350655 *£52; 5 pretty rms, most with own bthrm. 15th-c inn in superb, tranquil hilltop position, with lovely views and good walks nearby; attentive and hospitable new licensees, a fine inglenook and elderly seats in the slate-floored lounge, a stripped-stone public bar with a smaller log fire and old-fashioned settles, good-value home cooking, well kept ales, characterful dining room with antique curved settle and other high-backed seats, and enjoyable breakfasts; seats outside with play area; dogs allowed; cl wkdy lunchtimes.

RHANDIRMWYN SN7843 **Royal Oak** *Rhandirmwyn, Llandovery, Dyfed SA20 0NY* (01550) 760201 **£56**; 5 rms, most with own bthrm. Homely, friendly, family-run pub in the foothills of the Cambrian Mountains with fine views, superb walking and RSPB Dinas Bird Reserve nearby; simple furnishings, a log fire, well kept real ale, decent food, and a warm welcome; dogs by prior arrangement.

RHAYADER SN9969 **Beili Neuadd** *Rhayader, Powys LD6 5NS* (01597) 810211 *£40, plus special activity breaks; 3 rms. Charming, partly 16th-c stone-built farmhouse in quiet countryside (they have their own trout pools and woodland), with beams, polished oak floorboards, and log fires in renovated rooms, and evening meals by arrangement; dormitory accommodation for up to 20 in the stone barn with self-catering kitchen; golf, pony-trekking and guided walks nearby; cl Christmas and New Year; children over 8.

To see and do

ABERDOVEY SN6196

★ Attractive, restrained resort with very pleasant sheltered beaches, but none of the crowds or tat they usually bring. Legend has it there's a lost city beneath the sea, inundated by the crashing waves in a great storm 1,500 years ago. Sometimes at night imaginative people can hear the mournful tolling of its bells. Besides the Penhelig Arms Hotel, the Britannia does good food and has great views.

ABERYSTWYTH SN5981

🏨 ☉ 🏛 ⌂ Low-key resort, scarcely changed in 20 years, with long shingle beaches and a sedate cliff railway to the large camera obscura high above. Quite a scholarly university town, too, with a good museum, and one of the very few of Edward I's castles in this part of Wales. The university has a large agricultural college attached and as well as the usual sheep you may see llamas in some of the surrounding fields. There's a pleasant walk along the straight stretch of coast to Borth; you can use the train for the other half of a round trip.

☉ 🏛 National Library of Wales

(Penglais Hill) Imposing neo-classical building looking over the town, with exhibitions of fine early Welsh and Celtic manuscripts and more modern art. Meals, snacks, shop, disabled access; (cl Sun, bank hols and first full wk Oct; free).

🏨 ❀ Vale of Rheidol Railway

(Alexander Rd) The town's main attraction for families, with steamtrains for several miles along the picturesque twists of the Rheidol Valley to the dramatic beauty-spot gorge of Devil's Bridge. You can use the railway for attractive round-trip walks. Snacks, shop; trains run most days Easter–Oct, (01970) 625819 for timetable; £10.50 full return fare.

BLACK MOUNTAIN SN8123

⌂ The westernmost range in the Brecon Beacons National Park – not to be confused with the Black Mountains to the E. Much of the high terrain is a long way from the road, so this part is more the preserve of the committed long-distance walker. The craggy ridge known as Carmarthen Fan protrudes dramatically above the moors and provides the high point of a long but rewarding walk from the N.

BLACK MOUNTAINS SO2632

❀ ⌂ Making up the eastern part of the Brecon Beacons National Park, these finger-shaped ridges have steep-sided valleys between. Most of the best views are from the Offa's Dyke Path along the eastern flanks: the land eastwards slopes abruptly down to low-lying agricultural Herefordshire, and views far into England give you a feeling of true border country. Circular walks here tend to be long and hefty, often with two major ascents to get you up on to the different ridges, but the scenic Gospel Pass road from Hay-on-Wye lets you drive to within reasonable striking distance of Hay Bluff (670 metres, 2,200ft). Twmpa (690 metres, 2,263ft) is better known by its intriguing English name of Lord Hereford's Knob; though it's not itself on the Offa's Dyke Path, it is nearby, and you can combine it with Hay Bluff in a longer walk. Llanthony Abbey, with an atmospheric cellar bar, makes a beautiful objective in the valley below, where diligent map-reading is needed for a cross-fields route from Cwmyoy, with extensions on to the Offa's Dyke Path on the ridge to complete a satisfying circuit.

BRECON SO0428

★ 🏰 ✝ 🏛 ☉ Enjoyable and interesting small town, with some fine old buildings around its main square and narrow streets, and a bustling livestock market on Tues and Fri. The striking Norman priory was grandly restored in the 19th c and became a cathedral in 1923. Also the rather sad remnants of a castle, and a couple of decent little museums. The refurbished Camden Arms (Walton) is a comfortable food stop. Some of the highest peaks in the area are a short drive away.

☉ Brecknock Museum (Captain's

Walk) Has the town's excellently preserved assize court with a new interpretative exhibition, as well as plenty of love spoons and some interesting Celtic crosses. Cl 1–2pm Sat, Sun in winter, Good Fri, 25–26

Dec, 1 Jan; (01874) 624121; £1.

🏠 ☀ 🏠 🐦 **Brecon Beacons Mountain Centre** (Libanus) Useful National Park visitor centre (cl 25 Dec, 1 Jan; free, car parking charge from £1 per hour); they can advise on local walks, inc how to get to the spectacular waterfalls nr Glyn Neath. From the centre there's free access to the surrounding area known as Illtud Common, with fine views of the Beacons and an Iron Age hill fort to make for; this can also be used as a starting-point for walking up to Craig Cerrig-gleisiad, a Fan Frynach National Nature Reserve SN9522, home to arctic/alpine flora and some 80 bird species.

Cantref Trekking & Riding Centre (Upper Cantref, just S) Can organise pony-trekking through this attractive landscape(£8 an hour, £20 a day), and does B & B too; ring Mrs Evans on (01874) 665223.

BRECON BEACONS SO0121
🏠 A pair of graceful pointed summits connected by a short ridge that seems to be visible from most of South Wales, and that gives a magnificent high-level walk along the crest, which has massive drops on the northern side. Pen-y-Fan (886 metres, 2,906ft) is the highest Welsh summit outside Snowdonia, and the main east–west upland spine effectively stretches about 5 miles. The most popular walk up from Pont ar Daf, from the A470 to the W, is straightforward enough although there has been some serious footpath erosion, but the northern approaches are more exciting and surprisingly little walked.

🐦 🏠 **Brecon Beacons National Park** The southern parts of the park, within easy reach of South Wales, have gentle forest walks in large conifer plantations, where waterfalls and a series of attractive reservoirs are the main features. The abrupt transition from the industrial valleys into this empty wildness is startling.

BUILTH WELLS SO0451
★ 🏠 Pleasant small spa town, with good walks in attractive scenery.

CADAIR IDRIS SH7112
🏠 This great peak in the S of the Snowdonia National Park offers

walkers various ways up its friendly slopes. Good spots are the Arthog waterfalls and nearby lakes, on the lower slopes.

CARREG CENNEN SN6619
🏛 ☀ **Carreg Cennen Castle** (nr Trapp, SE of Llandeilo) Few castles can boast as excellent a setting as these old ruins, dramatically dominating their limestone crag high above the river, and overlooking the unspoilt countryside towards the Black Mountains. Rebuilt in the 13th c (and again in the 19th – you can easily distinguish the new stonework), the castle has a mysterious passage in the side of the cliff. Readers enjoy coming here and the staff are very friendly. Meals, snacks, shop; cl 25 Dec; (01558) 822291; £2.50. The Cennen Arms nearby has good, simple food.

CORRIS SH7408
★ Attractive and nicely set beneath the towering crags of Cadair Idris, with lakes and pine forests in the surrounding valley. The whole village seems to be made of slate.

🎨 **Corris Craft Centre** (off A487 towards Corris Uchaf) Craft workshops inc a working potter, toymaker, goldsmith, and candlemaker, with a restaurant, shop, picnic area and play area; best to check winter opening; (01654) 761249; free.

♿ 🌮 ! **King Arthur's Labyrinth** (Upper Corris, off A487 towards Corris Uchaf) Fun for families; a boat trip takes you to the heart of the underground tunnels and caverns, then it's a half-mile walk through passageways punctuated with scenes from the local version of the Arthurian legends. Wrap up well: it can get cold down here. Meals, snacks, shop, disabled access; cl Nov–Mar; (01654) 761584; £4.25.

CRAIG Y NOS SN8316
🦋 🐦 **Craig y Nos Country Park** Ideal for a picnic or a stroll: 40 acres of woodland, lake and meadow, landscaped in the 19th century by the opera singer Adelina Patti. Interactive displays in the visitor centre, and a wild flower maze. Shop, limited disabled access; cl 25 Dec; (01639) 730395; park free, though £1 parking.

🌮 🍴 ! **Dan yr Ogof Showcaves** (A4067 just N) Fascinating series of caves, well lit to emphasise the extraordinary rock formations. The Cathedral Cave is the largest single chamber open to the public in any British showcave, while 3,000 years ago Bone Cave was lived in by humans. There's also a dinosaur park, Iron Age farm, shire horse centre, and artificial ski-slope, so lots to see. Meals, snacks, shops; cl Nov–Apr (though maybe open Christmas and Feb half-term, phone to check); (01639) 730284; £6.95. The Tafarn y Garreg just N does decent food.

CRICKHOWELL SO2118

★ Pleasant village-sized 'town', with an excellent inn in the Bear (can get very busy), and a fine ancient bridge over the Usk (which the good Bridge End Inn overlooks).

DEVIL'S BRIDGE SN7477

✿ Pretty bridges and dramatic waterfall, tucked away in an atmospheric wooded gorge. The oldest bridge gave this beauty spot its name, when it was built by the Devil in order to trap an old woman into giving him her soul; she outwitted him. Wordsworth was inspired to write a sonnet after a visit here. The entertaining Halfway Inn at Pisgah, on the A4120 to Aberystwyth, is good for lunch.

ELAN VALLEY SN9365

❋ ☘ ◠ These four lakes W of Rhayader are the best and most famous of the many man-made reservoirs in Wales. Built at the turn of the last century, they have weathered in well now – even the dams look good, and there are splendid valley and Cambrian Mountain views, especially from high-level trackways. It's a good spot for birdwatching, especially in summer, and among the many species you may see red kites. The Elan Valley Hotel (B4518) has decent food.

◠ **Elan Valley Visitor Centre** (Elan village) Good opening to this attractive area, with an audio-visual show and displays. Meals, snacks, shop, disabled access. Cl Nov–mid-Mar; (01597) 810880; free (voluntary £1 car parking charge). Outside is a statue of Shelley, who lived in a house now lost beneath the water. Low-level walks from here include forest walks and strolls along

the old railway track by the water's edge – very attractive.

FAIRBOURNE SH6112

🚂 **Fairbourne & Barmouth Steam Railway** (Beach Rd) Running the spectacular 2½ miles to the end of the peninsula and the ferry for Barmouth, this started life in 1890 as a horse-drawn railway used to carry building materials for the seaside resort of Fairbourne. Meals, snacks, shop, good disabled access; cl 25 Dec; Nov–Easter, (01341) 250362 for timetable; £4. The Fairbourne Hotel is quite useful for lunch, as is the 15th-c Last Inn on Barmouth Harbour. The attractively set George III along the estuary at Penmaenpool is quite handy too. Fairbourne and Barmouth both have good clean beaches.

HAY-ON-WYE SO2342

★ ◠ This pleasant small town has become a world centre for secondhand and antiquarian books. There is a growing number of print, junk and antique shops too, as well as a rather jolly puzzle and teddy bear shop on Broad St. Hay Bluff nearby has lovely walks, and it's within easy reach of the Black Mountains, the Golden Valley over the English border, and the attractive unspoilt countryside just over the Gwent border that we mention in the South Wales section. Besides the fine Old Black Lion, the Kilvert Court (01497) 821042 can be recommended both for food and as a place to stay. Black Mountain Activities just up the road (technically in Herefordshire) can arrange all sorts of exertions; (01497) 847897.

LLANBISTER SO0974

✝ **Llanbister church** Interesting, with a chimney instead of the usual tower, and presumably a warmer congregation.

✝ **Llananno church** (nearby) Remarkable, with an astonishingly elaborate rood screen that wouldn't be out of place in a cathedral.

LLANDRINDOD WELLS SO0661

★ Civilised inland resort sheltering below the hills, a largely intact gem of the railway age, with imposing buildings on broad avenues and terraces, wrought-iron frills everywhere, elegant flower displays and Victorian parks, antique shop-fronts and little canopies along the shopping streets. It was clearly a resort for temperance – though there are places to drink, they're tucked discreetly away. The former spa pump room has been reopened, and there are sedate walks around a very old-fashioned boating lake. The atmospheric old Llanerch has good home cooking, and the Metropole Hotel generally does some food all day. ⋔ ⌂ **Cefnllys Castle** A good walk from the town to this impressively sited hill fort with a lonely church below, close to Shaky Bridge (no longer shaky); a nature trail here takes you along the banks of the River Ithon.

♨ **National Cycle Exhibition** (Temple St) Over 250 cycles, reconstructions of Victorian and Edwardian cycle shops, and artist exhibitions. Meals, snacks, shop, disabled access; (01597) 825531; £2.50.

♨ **Radnorshire Museum** (Temple St) Charming district museum, well worth a look, with an exhibition centre showing varying exhibits from Welsh blankets to Victorian photography; cl Mon, winter pm Sat and all Sun; (01597) 824513; £1.

LLANFAIR CAEREINION SJ1006

🚂 **Welshpool & Llanfair Railway** (£) (A458) Colonial and Austrian steam locomotives are among the wide variety of engines that run along this pretty eight-mile line, and the Welshpool end has an award-winning station reconstruction. Snacks, shop, disabled access (with prior notice); cl Oct–Mar exc Dec Santa Specials, (01938) 810441 for timetable; £7.50. The Goat is useful for lunch.

LLANIDLOES SN9584

★ ⌂ Attractive small town, with a unique Elizabethan timbered market hall.

LLANWRTYD WELLS SN8746

★ ⌂ Pleasant small spa town, said to be Britain's smallest town, with good walks in attractive scenery, also mountain bike hire. The good Neuadd Arms is the focus for all sorts of activities inc man v horse v mountain bike marathons, and bog-snorkelling championships.

MACHYNLLETH SH7400

★ Wide main street with a handsome 24-metre (78-ft) 19th-c clock tower,

and a very relaxed feel. The White Lion does decent lunches, inc vegetarian.

♨ ⌂ **Celtica** Very enjoyable look at the history and legends of the Celts, in an 18th-c mansion. There's a traditionalish museum upstairs, but more fun is the lively walk-through exhibition on the ground floor, special effects bringing ancient villages and druids' prophecies vividly to life. Also a good themed indoor play area for the under-8s. It's popular with school trips the last couple of weeks of term. Meals, snacks, good shop, disabled access; cl 24–26 Dec, 1 Jan; (01654) 702702; £4.95.

⤒ ! **Centre for Alternative Technology** (A487 3m N) Technologies for the improvement of the environment have been researched and displayed at this enthusiastic place for over 20 years now, with constantly updated demonstrations of wind power, wave power and solar energy – you can even ride a water-powered cliff railway (one of Britain's steepest; Easter–Oct only) There's a fun exhibition on what it's like to be in a mole hole. The site, an old slate quarry, has fine views over neighbouring Snowdonia National Park, and they look after children well. Wholesome vegetarian restaurant, good bookshop, disabled access; cl 24–26 Dec, 1 Jan, and two wks mid-Jan; (01654) 702400; £5.90 inc cliff railway, £4 without. They do good-value family tickets, and you can save 10% off the entry cost if you arrive by bus, or 50% if you come by bike; you can also halve the cost of hiring a bike from Greenstiles in Machynlleth, (01654) 703543.

⋔ ♨ **Parliament House** (Machynlleth) Local history museum in a 16th-c building, with a particular emphasis on the rebellion of Owain Glyndwr (it's on the spot where he held parliament). Brass-rubbing centre, shop, disabled access; cl 12.30–1.30pm, Sun, and all Oct–Easter; (01654) 702827; free.

MONTGOMERY SO2793

★ ⛰ ❀ Tiny town, rewarding for a short exploration on foot, with great views from its castle perched above. Montgomeryshire consists of the quintessential sheep-grazed lands of rural Wales – not prime walking

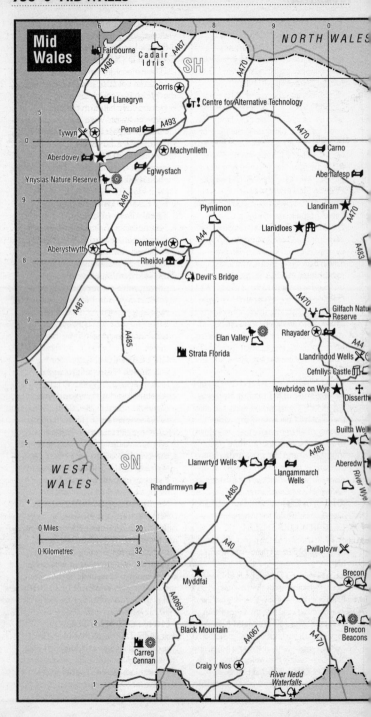

Mid Wales

NORTH WALES

Fairbourne
Cadair Idris
Corris
SH
Centre for Alternative Technology
Llanegryn
Pennal
A493
Carno
Tywyn
Machynlleth
Aberdovey
Aberhafesp
Eglwysfach
Ynyslas Nature Reserve
Plynlimon
Llandinam
Ponterwyd
Llanidloes
Aberystwyth
Rheidol
Devil's Bridge
A44
Gilfach Nature Reserve
Elan Valley
Rhayader
Strata Florida
Llandrindod Wells
Cefnllys Castle
Newbridge on Wye
Disserth
Builth Wells
Llanwrtyd Wells
Aberedw
Llangammarch Wells
Rhandirmwyn
River Wye

WEST WALES
SN

0 Miles   20
0 Kilometres   32

Pwllgloyw
Brecon
Myddfai
Black Mountain
Brecon Beacons
Carreg Cennen
Craig y Nos
River Nedd Waterfalls

country, lacking major objectives for walkers, with few major peaks and fair distances between villages.

OFFA'S DYKE PATH SO2455

⌂ The major walkers' attraction in this part; on its coast-to-coast route over the Welsh Marches it takes in some very attractive hill-farm country between Hay-on-Wye and Knighton, including Hergest Ridge (in Herefordshire, but easily reached from the Welsh side) and some well preserved stretches of Offa's 9th-c boundary marker between Knighton and Kington.

OLD RADNOR SO2559

✝ ※ **Old Radnor church** Handsome screen and roof, Britain's oldest organ-case and font; delightful surroundings, with hilltop views. The Harp up here has good home cooking.

PLYNLIMON SN7687

⌂ These windswept often boggy uplands and the surrounding Cambrian Mountains, though not endowed with the friendliest of climates, can be magnificently exhilarating for hardy walkers.

PONTERWYD SN728I

🍴 ⌂ **Bwlch Nant-yr-Arian Forest Centre** (A44 just W) Good starting point for exploring the forest, with walks and a few activities for children. You may see otters in the adjacent lake and they have a red kite feeding station in winter. Snacks, shop, disabled access to new visitor centre; (01974) 261404; free (parking £1). The Dyffryn Castell in the spectacular valley to the E is nice for lunch.

⚒ **Llywernog Silver Lead Mine** (A434 just W) A busy, lively place, set against a beautiful sweeping mountainside backdrop. Regular displays of silver panning, sound and light tableaux in the caves and tunnels along the expanded underground tour, and working waterwheels; you can try panning for Fool's Gold or dowsing for mineral veins. Wear sensible shoes in wet weather. Snacks, shop, some disabled access; open mid-Mar–Oct (cl Mon exc during July and Aug); (01970) 890620; £4.50.

※ **Mountain drive** There's an eye-opening mountain drive from Ponterwyd N past the partly wooded

Nant-y-moch reservoir below the slopes of Plynlimon, and on to Tal-y-bont.

PRESTEIGNE SO3164

★ † Attractive former county town of Radnorshire, with some fine timbered houses and a handsome church. The Radnorshire Arms is good value.
🏠 **Judge's Lodgings** (Broad St) Good restoration of the judge's living quarters. Unlike in most historic reconstructions, you can sit on the chairs and try out the beds for comfort. There's a lively audio tour which leads you to trial in the Victorian court. Shop, disabled access to ground floor only; cl Nov–Feb; (01544) 260652; *£3.50.

RADNOR FOREST SO2160

🐾 ⌂ Open walking country for the most part, with conifers on the northern slopes. Walks include New Radnor to the modest summit of the quaintly named Whimble, and from the A44 between Llanfihangel-nant-Melan and New Radnor to Water-break-its-neck waterfall (don't miss the path at the top of the fall).

RADNORSHIRE HILLS SO1553

⌂ Away from Offa's Dyke, Radnorshire is less well known than it deserves to be, with old drovers' tracks providing some enjoyable escapist walking, and a reasonable network of field paths. There are few major objectives, but the part between Aberedw, Glascwm and Gladestry (where the Royal Oak is a welcome sight on the Offa's Dyke Path) is all very pleasant walking.

RHAYADER SN9867

★ This is a pleasant little town, and the Bear, Castle and Cornhill are useful food stops.
🍺 ❀ 🐦 **Gigrin Farm** (South Rd, just outside) Farm trail with excellent views; from mid-Oct–mid-Apr also has a red kite centre with hides (the birds are fed daily at 2pm). Also B & B and camping. Snacks, shop, disabled access; cl 25 Dec; (01597) 810243; £2.50.
🐦 ⌂ **Gilfach Nature Reserve** (just N) Includes farmland virtually unchanged in 200 years amid fine craggy mountain backdrops; several paths have been freshly signposted and some new ones opened, inc the Monks' Trod and the nature trail from Gilfach Farm – leading across a defunct railway and close to the otter-populated River Marteg, eventually emerging on the A470 by Pont Marteg, a delightful shady place with a footbridge over the River Wye. Longhouse and visitors' centre, snacks, shop, limited disabled access; £1.50; cl Tues, Oct–Mar; (01597) 870301; £1.50.
🏛 **Welsh Royal Crystal** (Brynberth Industrial Estate) Workshop tours; no glass-making wknds, or some wkdys, best to check first on (01597) 811005, Snacks, shop, disabled access; cl 25–26 Dec, 1 Jan; £1.50 workshop tour, £2 guided tour.

RHEIDOL SN7079

🏛 ♪ **Rheidol Hydro-electric Scheme** (off A44 at Capel Bangor) Guided tours of this power station with an unexpected fish farm. Good nature

---

Days Out

The railway that served the mines: Aberystwyth; snack at the Mill (Mill St) there; Devil's Bridge by the Vale of Rheidol Railway; or by car, then drive via Llywernog silver mine, Ponterwyd, and on past Nant-y-Moch reservoir to Talybont – if time, stroll on the nearby Ynyslas seaside nature reserve.

Ascent from bookshop town: Hay-on-Wye; drive up Gospel Pass; lunch at the Abbey Hotel, Llanthony; walk there (leaflets in car park); Cwmyoy and Partrishow churches.

Brecon Beacons waterfall country: Brecon; A470 past the slopes of Pen-y-fan; walk from Brecon Beacons Mountain Centre on to Mynydd Illtud common, or in the Mellte/Hepste gorges; either picnic en route, or lunch at the Gwyn Arms, Craig y Nos; Dan yr Ogof caves, Craig y Nos.

trails, scenic lakes and reservoirs, trout fishing. Snacks, disabled access; cl Nov–Mar; (01970) 880667; free, fishing permits from £6.

RIVER NEDD WATERFALLS
SN9007

△ ♧ A series of mighty waterfalls with few rivals in Britain grace the deep wooded gorges of the Nedd, Hepste and Mellte, just inside the southern Brecon Beacons park boundary (within easy reach of South Wales, too). An easy path from Pontneddfechan nr Glyn Neath leads along the River Nedd; and the Porth yr Ogof car park nr Ystradfellte is convenient for the Mellte waterfall. Dire warning notices ward you off getting too close to the edge (it is certainly hazardously slippery), but you can accompany the river most of the way to its junction with the Hepste. Here, a path actually crosses the river by going behind the curtain of Sgwd yr Eira waterfall – a rock ledge holds you in safely, but it's an excitingly damp experience. The Angel in nearby Pontneddfechan has good-value food.

RIVER WYE
SO0847

△ Pleasant escapist walks around Aberedw and Boughrood, with a reasonable network of field paths.

STRATA FLORIDA
SN7465

🏚 Strata Florida Abbey Little is left of this once-important centre of learning, except the ruined church and cloister, but the surroundings are lovely. 14th-c poet Dafyd ap Gwilym is thought to be buried here. Teas, shop, disabled access; cl Oct–Easter; (01974) 831261; £2. From Tregaron down the B4343, a steep road climbs through the pine forests into the mountains, eventually reaching the Llyn Brianne reservoir.

TALYBONT-ON-USK
SO1122

★ ⚓ △ Attractive village, with friendly boat hire on the Monmouthshire & Brecon Canal, opposite the Travellers Rest (generous food). It's on the Taff Trail waymarked path.

TRETOWER
SO1821

🏛🏚 Tretower Court & Castle (off A40) The medieval manor house dates from the 14th c, though it has been developed over the centuries; beside it is the substantial ruin of an 11th-c motte and bailey, with massively thick

walls and a three-storey tower. Shop, limited disabled access; cl Nov–Feb; (029) 2050 0200; £2.20. The Nantyffin Cider Mill is handy for lunch.

TYWYN
SH5800

🚂🌼🏚 Tal-y-Llyn Railway This railway journey affords glorious views, climbing from the little seaside resort up the steep sides of the Fathew Valley and stopping for passengers to admire Dolgoch Falls and visit the Nant Gwernol Forest (there's a waterfall two minutes away from the platform at this end). The 27in-gauge railway, the oldest of this gauge in the world, was built in 1865 to serve the slate mine at Abergynolwyn (where the Railway Inn does decent food in a lovely setting). Snacks, shop, disabled access with prior notice; cl Nov–mid-Feb (exc Dec Santa specials); (01654) 710472 for timetable; £8.50 full return. A museum at the Tywyn Station shows locomotives, wagons and signalling equipment whenever the railway is running.

USK VALLEY
SO1519

△ Walkers can enjoy the lusher swathes, along the towpath of the 33-mile Monmouthshire & Brecon canal.

WELSHPOOL
SJ2106

The Raven and Royal Oak both have decent food, and the main railway station is rather unusual.

🏚🏵🏚 Powis Castle (A483, 1m S) Set in magnificent gardens with splendid 18th-c terraces, this dramatic-looking castle was built in the 13th c, but far from falling into decay like so many others, has developed into a grand house over the years. It's been constantly occupied since its construction, once by the son of Clive of India – there are displays about his father's life. Meals, snacks, shop; cl Mon (exc bank hols), Tues (exc July and Aug), and Nov–Mar (castle and museum cl am); (01938) 554336; £7.50, Garden only £5; NT. The King's Head at Guilsfield does good home cooking.

🏚❄ Powysland Museum & Canal Centre (Canal Wharf) Respectable local history museum, with canal material too; disabled access; cl Weds; *£1.

YNYSLAS NATURE RESERVE
SN6094

🌼🦅△ (just N of Borth) A major

scenic highlight of the coast, with watery views across the vast sands of the Dovey estuary, lots of birds, and an important dune system, habitat for orchids. You can walk round the tip of land jutting into the mouth of the Dovey and then along the shore.
★ **Other attractive villages and small towns** in the area, all with decent pubs, include Berriew SJ1801, Llanbedr SO2420, Llandinam SO0388, Llangenny SO2417, Llyswen SO1337, Myddfai SN7730 and Newbridge-on-Wye SO0158.

Other pubs doing food that are particularly worth noting for their positions include the Admiral Rodney at Criggion SJ2915, Farmers Arms at Cwmdu SO1823, Dolfor Inn at Dolfor SO1187, White Swan at Llanfrynach SO0725, Coach & Horses above the canal at Llangynidr SO1519 (lovely walks), Stables Hotel at Neuadd Fawr SO2322 (good hill walking) and the canalside Royal Oak at Pencelli SO0925.
✝ Some unspoilt and humble rustic **churches** in beautiful settings include Aberedw SO0847, Bleddfa SO2168 (the Hundred House is a good base for walkers), Disserth SO0358, Llanbadarn-y-garreg SO1148, Maesyronnen Chapel SO1740 NW of Hay, and Rhulen SO1349.

Where to eat

Many of the places listed in the **Where to stay** section serve very good food, too.

CRICKHOWELL SO1920 **Nantyffin Cider Mill** *(A40 NW)* *(01873) 801775* Handsome pink-washed dining pub with a striking raftered restaurant, smart relaxed atmosphere, fresh and dried flowers, a woodburner, comfortable tables and chairs, beautifully presented, imaginative food (much organic produce), excellent service, well kept real ales, good wines and charming views; cl Mon; disabled access. **£20.65|£5.95.**

HAY-ON-WYE SO2342 **Kilverts** *Bullring (01497) 821042* Friendly town pub with an informal, relaxed atmosphere in the airy high-beamed bar, candles on the good mix of tables, some stripped stone walls and standing timbers, interesting food (especially the daily specials), well kept real ales, local Welsh wines, and efficient, easy-going service; bdrms; cl 25 Dec. **£25|£5.50.**

LLANDRINDOD WELLS SO0561 **Llanerch** *Waterloo Rd (01597) 822086* Welcoming, low-ceilinged 16th-c inn with old-fashioned settles in the cheerful, beamed main bar, communicating lounges (one no smoking), popular bar food, well kept real ales, prompt service, peaceful mountain views from the back terrace, and boules and an orchard in the garden; bdrms; cl Christmas; disabled access. **£20|£3.95.**

LLOWES SO1941 **Radnor Arms** *(01497) 847460* Small, modest and very old place with a log fire in the bar, neat little cottagey dining room, enjoyable food (nice puddings), friendly staff, and tables in the imaginatively planted garden; cl pm Sun, Mon (exc bank hols); partial disabled access. **£20|£6.75.**

PWLLGLOYW SO0333 **Seland Newydd** *Gerhonddu (01874) 690282* Popular with a good mix of people, this former pub has a comfortable lounge, huge fireplace in the bar, and an attractive dining room with most enjoyable, flavoursome food; a thoughtful little wine list; cl am Tues and Weds in winter; disabled access. **£27|£7.50.**

TYWYN SH5800 **Proper Gander** *High St (01654) 711270* Popular little pink tea shop on two floors, with morning coffee, lunches, and good afternoon teas; more elaborate evening restaurant, and good Sun lunch; disabled access. **£24 dinner, £15.50 lunch|£5.60.**

Please let us know what you think of places in the *Guide*. Use the report forms at the back of the book or simply write us a letter.

South Wales

The pick of Wales's places to visit.

Among the abundance of interesting and enjoyable places to visit here, for all age groups and tastes, we'd particularly pick out the highly realistic Rhondda mining re-creation at Porth, the excellent Techniquest in Cardiff, the Welsh Folk Museum just outside, and the entertaining Llancaiach Fawr at Nelson. Cardiff has plenty for visitors, with lots of new development on Cardiff Bay (including its new government building), and its Millennium Stadium, of course. Swansea has several places well worth seeing. Elsewhere are spectacular castles, and small towns of real character such as Monmouth. Children like the friendly animal centres at Penally, Cilfrew and Cwmbran. Even quite close to the built-up and industrialised areas are some unspoilt pockets of attractive scenery.

Where to stay

GILWERN SO2413 **Wenallt Farm** *Twyn-Wenallt, Gilwern, Abergavenny, Gwent NP7 0HP* (01873) 830694 **£48;** 8 rms. Friendly and relaxing 16th-c Welsh longhouse on 50 acres of farmland, with oak beams and an inglenook fireplace in the big drawing room, a TV room, good food, and lots to do nearby; dogs welcome.

GOVILON SO2513 **Llanwenarth House** *Govilon, Abergavenny, Gwent NP7 9SF* (01873) 830289 ***£78,** plus special breaks; 4 spacious, comfortable rms. Fine family-run 16th-c manor house in quiet grounds, with a gracious sitting room, log fires, antiques and fresh flowers, good food using local game and fish and home-produced meat, poultry and garden veg in the elegant candlelit dining room, and friendly, helpful staff; lots to do nearby; croquet; cl part Jan, all Feb except by prior arrangement; children over 10; partial disabled access.

LLANFIHANGEL CRUCORNEY SO3120 **Penyclawdd Court** *Llanfihangel Crucorney, Abergavenny, Gwent NP7 7LB* (01873) 890719 ***£80,** plus special breaks; 3 rms with mountain views. Interesting Tudor manor house below Bryn Arw mountain in the Brecon Beacons, with an Elizabethan knot garden, Norman motte and bailey, and a developing yew hedge maze; careful renovation, underfloor heating and no electricity in the dining room (breakfast and dinner by candlelight), as well as flagstones, beams and sloping floors; decent breakfasts, good evening meals (and Tudor feasts); children over 12.

MONMOUTH SO5012 **Riverside** *Cinderhill St, Monmouth, Gwent NP5 3EY* (01600) 715577 ***£68,** plus special breaks; 16 rms. Comfortably refurbished, welcoming hotel overlooking the River Monnow and 13th-c fortified gatehouse, with good-value bar meals, extensive restaurant menu, and conservatory; disabled access.

MUMBLES SS6087 **Hillcrest House** *Higher Lane, Mumbles, Swansea SA3 4NS* (01792) 363700 **£68,** plus special breaks; 7 individually decorated rms, each themed to represent a different country. Friendly white house with a stone terrace, two minutes from the beach yet handy for Swansea; informal welcoming atmosphere, thoughtful individual service, comfortable lounge, imaginative seasonal dishes, and a new bar-cum-restaurant with African gamehide theme; cl 15 Dec–2 Jan.

OXWICH SS5086 **Oxwich Bay** *Oxwich, Swansea SA3 1LS* (01792) 390329 ***£70,** plus special breaks; 13 rms. Comfortable hotel on the edge of the beach in a lovely area, with dedicated and friendly staff, food served all day, restaurant/lounge bar with panoramic views, summer outdoor dining area with weekend barbecues, and a welcome for families; cl 24–25 Dec.

REYNOLDSTON SS4691 **Fairyhill** *Reynoldston, Swansea, West Glamorgan SA3 1BS (01792) 390139* ***£110,*** plus special breaks; 8 rms. 18th-c hotel in 24 wooded acres with croquet, trout stream and wild duck on the lake; log fire in the comfortable drawing room, cosy bar, lovely food in the attractive dining room, hearty breakfasts, afternoon tea on a leafy terrace, and personal friendly service; cl 24 Dec–6 Jan; children over 9.

ST BRIDES WENTLOOG ST2982 **West Usk Lighthouse** *St Brides Wentloog, Newport, Gwent NP1 9SF (01633) 810126* **£75;** 3 rms. Unusual former lighthouse – squat rather than tall; modern stylish furnishings, lots of framed record sleeves, an informal atmosphere, good big breakfasts, and a small vegan restaurant; flotation tank, aromatherapy and psychotherapy sessions; lots of walks.

TINTERN PARVA SO5301 **Parva Farmhouse** *Tintern Parva, Chepstow, Gwent NP6 6SQ (01291) 689411* **£68,** plus special breaks; 9 comfortable rms. Friendly stone farmhouse rebuilt in the mid-17th c, with leather chesterfields, a woodburner and honesty bar in the large beamed lounge, books (no TV downstairs), and very good food and wine in the cosy restaurant; nr the River Wye and lovely countryside; free accommodation for children in parents' room.

WHITEBROOK SO5306 **Crown at Whitebrook** *Whitebrook, Monmouth, Gwent NP5 4TX (01600) 860254* **£80,** plus special breaks; 10 neat rms. Small modernised hotel with a 17th-c heart in the beautiful Wye Valley; friendly and caring service, a relaxed atmosphere, comfortable lounge and bar; small cosy restaurant with fine wines and excellent food combining Welsh ingredients and French style, very good breakfasts; cl 2 wks Jan and 2 wks Aug; children over 12.

To see and do

WALES Family Attraction of the Year

ⓗ ⓙⓣ ▣ **PORTH** ST0290 **Rhondda Heritage Park** (off A470) The days when coal was king are brought back to life at this well organised centre, based around the last colliery buildings in the area. The highlight of anyone's visit is likely to be the splendidly evocative trip down the mine itself, but you should head first for the Black Gold displays in three restored buildings on the surface. Models and multi-media displays set the scene rather well, tracing the experiences of three generations of a local mining family, taking in pit disasters, riots and the 1920 battle for minimum wages. Displays in the Fan House look at the wider social heritage of the valleys, and particularly their choirs and brass bands; they also cover the role of women in the community. Next stop is the Lamp Room, where it's on with the hard hats and into the cage for a two-minute ride down to Pit Bottom. Former miners lead you through the workings of the Lewis Merthyr Colliery, displayed as they would have been in the 1950s. You can touch the machinery, hear the blasts of explosives, and the noise and heat are uncannily realistic (it may be slightly claustrophobic). The trip back to the surface is fun, on a simulated ride that hurtles you through dark, twisting tunnels. Back above ground there's a gallery with art by locals, a re-created village street, an authentic valley chapel, and from Easter–Oct, an excellent themed adventure play area for children (extra charge). It's a good excursion whatever the weather, and most families spend around three hours here without too much trouble. They do good events around Halloween and Christmas; tickets for their carol concerts usually sell out well in advance. Meals, snacks, shop, good disabled access (even underground); cl Mon from Oct–Easter, and 25–26 Dec; (01443) 682036; £5.50 (£4.25 children). The family ticket, covering two adults and two children, offers a good saving at £16.25.

ABERDULAIS SS7799

Aberdulais Falls (A465) Since the 16th c this splendid waterfall has been used to power a range of industries from copper-smelting to tinplate. A magnificent waterwheel now generates electricity. Wknd snacks, shop, disabled access (right to the top of the falls thanks to a lift powered by the electricity generated on site); open Apr–Oct, and wknds in Mar; (01639) 636674; £2.80; NT.

ABERGAVENNY SO2914

🏛️ ✝ There are some attractive ancient buildings in Nevill St and particularly Market St – where there's a busy Tues and Fri market. The **church** has a remarkable collection of memorials. The Greyhound is a good dining pub, while outside, the Lamb & Flag (B4598 SE) is also popular.

🏰 🍺 **Abergavenny Castle** 12th- and 14th-c remains inc the walls, towers and rebuilt gatehouse; the early 19th-c keep and an adjoining house now contain a local history museum. Shop; cl 1–2pm, all Sun (exc pm in summer); (01873) 854282; *£1.

BARRY ST1166

☺ 🏰 Lively seaside resort which, along with its jutting-out peninsula Barry Island, grew as a centre for the coal industry. Remains of a 13th-c castle, and the usual fairground attractions for children. Nearby, the Star in Dinas Powis is good for lunch.

🦅 **Welsh Hawking Centre** (Weycock Rd) Cheery centre with over 200 birds of prey. Regular flying demonstrations (12 noon, 2.30pm, 4pm), baby birds (May–July), adventure playground; there are also animals for children to pet and fuss over. Snacks, shop, some disabled access; cl 25 Dec; (01446) 734687; £3.

BETTWS NEWYDD SO3605

✝ **Bettws Newydd church** Largely unaltered from the 15th c, with a choir gallery and fine screen. Peaceful village; the Black Bear has enterprising food.

BLAENAVON SO2703

⌂ **Afon Lwyd Valley** Interesting example of post-mining land reclamation between here and Cwmbran New Town, with plantings designed for re-establishment of nature (and for pleasant walking).

🏰 ⬆️ **Big Pit Mining Museum** 📷 (B4248) Sample the life of a miner by donning a safety helmet and descending 90 metres (300ft) in the cage into the Big Pit, which closed as a working coal mine in 1980. Also a reconstructed miner's cottage, and an exhibition in the old pithead baths. Good fun – the guides are former miners so have plenty of anecdotes; you'll need sensible shoes and warm clothing. Children must be over 1 metre tall to go underground. Meals, snacks, shop, disabled access with prior warning; usually cl Dec–Feb – but worth checking; (01495) 790311; £5.75. The Goose & Cuckoo, over the hill at Rhyd-y-Meirch just off the A4042, does good home cooking.

BRIDGEND SS9084

🦋 **Bryngarw Country Park** (just N) Unexpectedly tranquil refuge from the M4, with woodland walks, formal gardens, ornamental lakes and a Japanese garden. Playground, snacks, shop, disabled access; cl 25–26 Dec; (01656) 725155; free (£1.50 parking school hols and wknds).

🏰 **Ewenny Priory** This riverside ruin is one of the finest fortified religious buildings in Britain.

🏰 **Newcastle** Ruined 12th-c castle with surviving rectangular tower, richly carved Norman gateway and massive curtain walls; collect key from the nearby corner shop. The prosperous industrial town below isn't much of a place for visitors, but nearby Merthyr Mawr, with its interesting warren of high sandhills, is attractive, as are Southerndown and Ogmore.

CAERLEON ST3490

🏛️ 🖼️ 🦅 **Roman Fortress Baths, Amphitheatre & Barracks** One of the best examples of an amphitheatre in the country, alongside a similarly well preserved bath-house, now under cover. Also the foundations of barrack lines and parts of the ramparts, and the remains of the cookhouse and latrines. Shop, disabled access; cl 24–26 Dec, 1 Jan; (01554) 890104; £2. Caerleon is reckoned in these parts to have been the site of the court of King Arthur. The tourist information centre on the High St has a little art gallery and various craft workshops; the Hanbury Arms has generous food.

⚬ **Roman Legionary Museum** (High St) Gives some idea of the daily life of the garrison; quite a few hands-on activities at wknds. Shop, disabled access; cl am Sun, 25–26 Dec, 1 Jan; (01633) 423134; *£2.10. You can get a joint ticket for the museum and the baths.

CAERPHILLY ST1587

🏰 **Caerphilly Castle** The largest in Wales, with extensive land and water defences. Rising sheer from its broad outer moat, it's a proper picture-book castle, pleasing for this reason to the most casual visitor. It also enthrals serious students of castle architecture with its remarkably complex design of concentric defences. Look out for the incredible leaning tower, which appears ready to topple any second. Shop, disabled access to ground floor; cl 24–26 Dec, 1 Jan; (029) 2088 3143; £2.50. In the oddly strung-out small town, the ancient Courthouse overlooking the castle has a useful, quick carvery, while the thatched Travellers Rest is good value.

CAERWENT ROMAN WALLS
ST4790

🏛 These massive walls, still some 4½ metres (15ft) high in places, enclosed the large site of Venta Silurum – over 40 acres, enough for a sizeable town, though none of that's left now; free. The Carpenters Arms up in the attractive village of Shirenewton does worthwhile food.

CALDICOT ST4888

🏰⚬🐾 **Caldicot Castle** (off B4245) The well preserved 12th/14th-c castle was restored as a family home in the 1880s, and lived in until 20 years ago – since when it's been a local museum, surrounded by a country park. Snacks, shop, limited disabled access; cl am Sun, lunchtimes Oct and Mar, and all Nov–Feb; (01291) 424447; £1.50.

CARDIFF ST1876

🏨🐾✝ The civic centre has a range of grand 20th-c white stone civic, governmental or museum buildings around formal Cathays Park. The old city centre is closer to Cardiff Castle, which has Capability Brown's 18th-c landscaped park between it and the river. In the centre, parts are pedestrianised (for example around the fine church of St John the Baptist), and there are many covered shopping arcades, Victorian and modern; multi-ride bus tickets are good value for getting around. As we went to press, the magnificent Millennium Stadium was hosting the Rugby World Cup. The Cottage and Philharmonic (both St Mary's St) and Golden Cross (Custom House St) are quite useful for lunch.

🏨 **!** **Cardiff Bay Visitor Centre** (Bute St) This space-age-looking centre explains the ambitious continuing rejuvenation of the Inner Harbour and docklands; cl 24–26 Dec; (029) 2046 3833; free. The area includes Techniquest, a slightly incongruous Norwegian timbered church, and by 2001 it will be home to the Millennium Centre – an arts complex that will house the Welsh National Opera – and the futuristic debating chamber of the newly formed Welsh Assembly. The docklands New Sea Lock (Harrowby St) may be Cardiff's most unspoilt pub, the smarter Wharf (Atlantic Wharf) is right on the water's edge.

🏰🏛⚬ **Cardiff Castle** (Castle St) Despite their fairytale medieval appearance, the main buildings are largely 19th-c, when the Marquess of Bute employed William Burges to rebuild and replace the place, adding richly romantic wall paintings, tapestries and carvings. Some parts are much older, and in the grounds there's even a piece of a 3-metre (10-ft) thick Roman wall. The Norman keep survives, and there's a 13th-c tower – these two look like proper castle architecture, perched on a little mound. Also two military museums. Snacks, shop; cl 25–26 Dec, 1 Jan; (029) 2087 8100; £4.80 for full guided tour, £2.40 grounds only.

🖼 **Centre for the Visual Arts** (Working St, The Hayes) Wales's largest gallery housed in a listed city-centre building; works by Welsh and international artists, plus regularly changing exhibitions of 20th-c art, and a fun interactive art gallery, Fantasmic. Meals, snacks, shop, disabled access; cl Mon (exc bank hols); (029) 2038 8922; £3.50.

🎨 **Craft in the Bay** (Bute St) Demonstrations by potters, jewellers and glass-workers, and a large gallery and shop; cl 25–26 Dec, 1 Jan; free.

✝ **Llandaff Cathedral** (W of centre) Rebuilt several times; it includes some delightful medieval masonry, Pre-Raphaelite works, a marvellous modern timber roof, and a central concrete arch that you may think a mistake. The nearby green has an attractive collection of buildings around it, inc the good Black Lion.

⌖ᴛ **Museum of Welsh Life** (St Fagans, A4232 4m W) Excellent 100-acre open-air museum, with a variety of reconstructed buildings from castles to cottages illustrating styles and living conditions throughout the ages. Buildings have come from all over Wales, and there are some remarkable exhibits, inc a homely gas-lit Edwardian farmhouse and an entire Celtic village. You can buy things from a period grocery store. Also crafts and lots of seasonal events – there's plenty to fascinate here. Meals and snacks (in a 1920s tearoom), shop, disabled access; cl 24–26 Dec; (029) 2057 3500; £5.50. The Plymouth Arms is very handy for good-value food.

⌖▣ **National Museum of Wales** (Cathays Park) Lively these days, with interactive displays and exhibitions on subjects as diverse as ceramics, coins and prehistoric sea monsters. The East Wing has an impressive collection of paintings, with notable French Impressionists, and there's an excellent section on the evolution of the Welsh landscape. Meals, snacks, shop, disabled access; cl Mon exc bank hols, 25 Dec; (029) 2039 7951; *£5.50.

! ☺ **Techniquest** (Stuart St) Fun as well as interest at this hi-tech science centre, with around 160 hands-on exhibits and activities, a planetarium, and even a realistic dragon conjured up by laser. All exceptionally well done, it's an excellent family excursion. Meals, snacks, shop, very good disabled access; cl 23–26 Dec; (029) 2047 5475; £5.

CHEPSTOW ST5294

⌖ ℘ A steep but civilised small town, still with its battlemented 13th-c town gate. Stuart Crystal have a museum and workshop opposite the castle, and there's a working pottery on Lower Church St (cl 1–2 pm). The civilised Bridge and Castle View are useful.

🏰 **Chepstow Castle** The first recorded Norman stone castle, proudly standing on an easily defended spot above the Wye, overlooking the harbour. Splendid gatehouse with portcullis grooves and ancient gates, and exhibitions on siege warfare and the English Civil War. Shop, limited disabled access; cl 24–26 Dec, 1 Jan; *£3.

⌖ **Chepstow Museum** (Bridge St) Good local history exhibits; cl 1–2pm, 25–26 Dec, 1 Jan; £1.

CRYNANT SN7904

⌖ᴛ **Cefn Coed Colliery Museum** (A4109) On the site of former Blaenant Colliery, the story of mining in the Dulais Valley. It still has a steam winding-engine, though the winding gear is now run by electricity. Also a simulated underground mining gallery, boiler house and compressor house. Shop, mostly disabled access; cl Nov–Mar; (01639) 750556; *£3.

CWM DARRAN SO1203

✠ ⌖ ❀ ⌂ (Rhymney Valley, nr Bargoed) Interesting example of post-mining land reclamation, which now provides a wide variety of natural habitats for wildlife and plants, with scenery ranging from the valley floor through forest areas to upland moors giving walkers superb views of the Brecon Beacons.

CWMBRAN ST2795

🐖 ⌖ ℘ **Greenmeadow Community Farm** ▣ (1m W) Founded to protect one of the encroaching new town's last green areas, this friendly farm has a wide range of animals – traditional, rare and cuddly – as well as a deer enclosure, bluebell wood, and craft workshops. Meals, snacks, shop, disabled access; cl 25–26 Dec; (01633) 862202; *£3.25. Up towards Pontypool, the canalside Open Hearth (Griffithstown) has good food.

CYNONVILLE SS8194

⌖ ⌂ **Afan Forest Park** (A4107) 9,000 tranquil acres of forest, with trails for walking or cycling (you can hire mountain bikes in summer), and a visitor centre; free, though £1.15 parking charge.

⌖ᴛ **Welsh Miners' Museum** (Afan Forest Park) Illustrates life as a miner

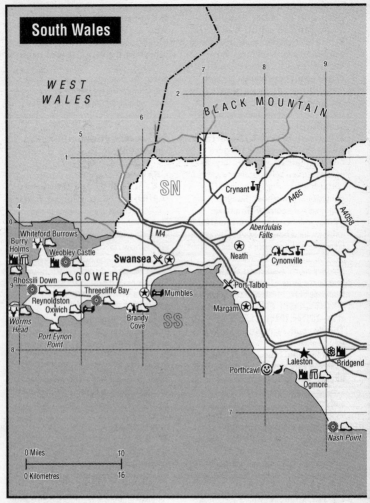

South Wales

WEST WALES

BLACK MOUNTAIN

SN

Crynant

A465

A4058

Aberdulais
Falls

Whiteford Burrows

Burry
Holms

Weobley Castle

M4

Swansea

Neath

Cynonville

Port-Talbot

Rhossili Down

GOWER

Threecliffe Bay

Mumbles

Margam

Reynoldston
Oxwich

Brandy
Cove

SS

Worms
Head

Port Eynon
Point

Porthcawl

Laleston

Bridgend

Ogmore

Nash Point

| 0 Miles | 10 |
| 0 Kilometres | 16 |

with coal faces, pit gear and mining equipment among the displays. Meals, snacks, shop, disabled access and entry free; cl 25–26 Dec; (01639) 850564; *£1.

EBBW VALE SO1508

Victoria Park (Victoria, A4046 2m S) The site of a former Garden Festival, still full of the lakes, gardens, wetlands and woodland from 1992. Much is being developed as an ambitious garden village, and it's interesting watching the project's progress. Pleasant walks and trails, exhibitions, and some quite

extraordinary sculptures, one made from 30,000 individually modelled clay bricks. Also a large factory shopping centre. Snacks, shop, disabled access; centre cl 25 Dec, 1 Jan 2000; (01495) 350010; free (charge for land train).

GOVILON SO2414

△ **Monmouthshire & Brecon Canal** A walk along the canal to Llanfoist SO2813 can tie in with a return along the track of the former Abergavenny–Merthyr Tydfil railway line, making a level 4 miles in all.

GOWER SS4990

△ This peninsula stretching W of

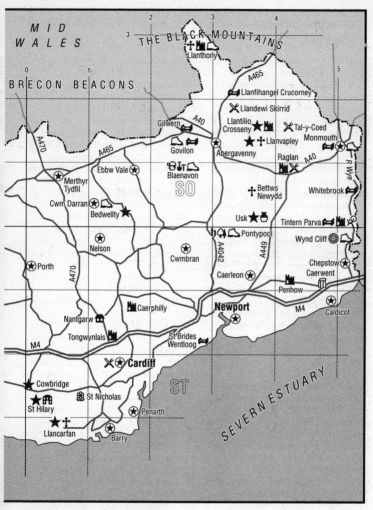

Swansea has quite a bit of off-putting ribbon development along the roads entering it, but it's well worth persevering. Once beyond the creeping urbanisation W of Swansea, it encapsulates on a small scale many different types of Welsh landscape, with lots of walking opportunities, and parts of the coast are lovely (but the N coast is attractive only at its western end). The area tends to be busy in summer (quite a young feel in parts), but even the main places are quiet and virtually empty out of season. The King Arthur at Reynoldston is the best place here for food.

⚓ ⌂ Brandy Cove This tiny cove makes an attractive destination for a walk down the wooded Bishopston Valley.

🏚 🏛 ⌂ Burry Holms Islet with a ruined chapel and an Iron Age fort; you can walk out across the sands at low tide.

★ ♨ Mumbles Pleasantly unspoilt resort with a gallery collection of traditional Welsh love spoons (cl Sun), and a surprisingly active night life; 14 pubs line the stretch of Mumbles Rd nr Mumbles Head, and Swansea students like to 'go mumbling' between them.

The White Rose does good-value food.

🔲 **Oxwich Bay** Dunes and broad sands, presided over by Oxwich Point on its W side; good walking. It's also good for windsurfing – you can hire wet suits from a windsurfing school at Oxwich Bay – though the water will never be more than what might euphemistically be called invigorating.

🏛 **Oystermouth Castle** 🔲 (Mumbles) Very complete ruins of the de Breose family castle, in a small park overlooking the bay. The gatehouse, chapel and great hall date from the 13th–14th c. Cl Oct–Mar; £1.50.

🔲 **Port Eynon Point** Interesting, with a huge medieval rock-dove dovecot in the cliff (birds still use it), and cliff walks on either side; windsurfing below.

❋ 🔲 **Rhossili Down** This rounded, windswept, rough-cropped moorland seems a million miles from Swansea (yet as the crow flies is only about 10 from the outskirts); it offers Gower walkers breathtaking coast views. From Rhossili, walks can also take in the long surfers' sands of the bay. There's an informative NT visitor centre at Rhossili; cl Mon–Tues Nov–Dec, wkdys Feb–Mar, all Jan.

🔲 ❋ **Threecliff Bay** From the NT car park nr Penmaen church, a good walk follows the lane down to this bay, then heads W along the coast as far as Nicholaston Farm to end with the mild ascent of Cefn Bryn, a rounded moorland hill giving breathtaking views of both – or all three – Gower coasts.

🏛 ❋ 🔲 **Weobley Castle** (Llanrhidian) 12th/14th-c fortified manor house with an exhibition on the area's history, and superb views. Cl 24–26 Dec, 1 Jan; (01792) 390012; £2. The Welcome to Town is in a lovely spot above the estuary, and the long, glistening cockle sands are full of interest for walkers.

🌱 🔲 **Whiteford Burrows** An extensive nature reserve, with sand dunes, marshy slacks and pine trees – good walks.

🌱 🔲 **Worms Head** Nature reserve where you may see seals on the tidal rocks in late summer; walks here can also take in Mewslade Bay, where the south-facing sands are enclosed by limestone cliffs.

LLANTHONY SO2923

✝ **Cwmyoy church** (Llanthony Valley road) Repeated landslips have left the medieval church twisted, and its tower leans at an angle that makes the Tower of Pisa look positively sober.

🏛 🔲 **Llanthony Priory** Graceful ruins of a 12th-c priory, the money for its construction put up by Hugh de Lacey when he decided he'd had enough of being a bold bad baron and was thinking of retiring into these lonely hills. It's a very romantic spot, with nothing much but the noise of the sheep to disturb the peace. The remains cover a variety of architectural styles; free. The very ancient crypt bar below the Abbey Hotel, right among the priory buildings, is useful for a snack lunch – a most unusual place. This is a good start or objective for Black Mountains walks.

✝ **Partrishow church** (nr Llanthony) A remarkable building in the Black Mountains, with a musicians' gallery and a mural of a figure of Death wielding a shovel.

LLANTILIO CROSSENY SO3914

★ Attractive village with a lovely view of the 13th-c church from the former moat of Hen Cwrt nearby; the Halfway House and Hostry are good for lunch.

🏛 ★ **White Castle** (NW) The remains of the most substantial of the trio of moated castles Hubert de Burgh built to defend the Welsh Marches; £2. The other ruins stand at Skenfrith (the Bell has good-value food) and Grosmont, an attractive hillside village with another 13th-c church (the Angel here is also good value).

LLANVAPLEY SO3614

★ ✝ Interesting village, with a church dating from 860.

MARGAM SS8086

🔲 🏠 ☺ 🏛 ⭐ 🔲 ⚘ **Margam Park** (A48) Pretty country park based around a splendid 'gothick' mansion, its 850 acres full of natural and historic features and various themed areas, inc a scaled-down nursery-rhyme village for young children. Also a ruined abbey and Iron Age hill fort, marked walks among the parkland and forests, giant maze, deer and cattle, and an adventure playground. Meals, snacks, shop, disabled access; cl winter Mon and Tues; (01639) 871131; £3.75, less in winter, when none of the attractions are open (though they have various special events).

MERTHYR TYDFIL SO0511

🚂 **Brecon Mountain Railway** (off A465) The route of this narrow-gauge railway starts at Pant Station, 3m N of Merthyr Tydfil, where there's a display of various engines inc vintage locomotives and others from around the world. The journey takes you into the beautiful Brecon Beacons as far as the Taf Fechan reservoir. Snacks, shop, disabled access; cl Nov–Easter exc over Christmas; (01685) 722988 for timetable; £6.20. On a disused railway line, the Dowlais Viaduct is a striking sight, well worth a detour.

🏛 🎨 ♨ **Cyfarthfa Castle** (Cyfarthfa Park) Impressive early 19th-c castellated 'gothick' mansion, set in beautiful gardens. Recently restored to their full Regency glory, the state rooms contain a museum with displays on Egyptology and archaeology. Meals, snacks, shop, disabled access; cl am winter wknds, 24 Dec–2 Jan; (01685) 723112; £1.50.

🐾 **Garwnant Forest Centre** (5 m NW, off A470) Looking out over the Llwyn-On reservoir on the southern edge of the Brecon Beacons National Park, carefully restored old farm buildings with displays on forestry, wildlife and conservation, and information on nature trails and cycle routes (you can hire bikes). Also a discovery centre for children. Meals, snacks, shop, disabled access; (01685) 384060; £1 car parking charge.

🏛 **Joseph Parry's Cottage** (Chapel Row, Georgetown) The composer of *Myfanwy* was born here, and the ground floor has been restored and decorated in the style of the 1840s. Shop; open pm Thurs–Sun Easter–Sept; (01685) 723112; 60p. The Butchers Arms up at Pontsticill has good home cooking.

MONMOUTH SO5113

★ 🏛 🏛 Attractive market town of considerable character; below the remains of the 12th-c castle where Henry V was born, and the 17th-c Great Castle House (built with enormous blocks of masonry in its precincts), the main Agincourt Sq is surrounded by handsome buildings, inc the imposing central Shire Hall with its arcaded market floor. The town nestles in the crook formed by the River Wye and the River Monnow, with a splendid 13th-c gatehouse bridge over the Monnow. The Punch House is the most enjoyable place here for lunch, and the Gockett (B4293 towards Trelleck) is also useful (children are welcome and they have bedrooms with bathrooms).

🗻 ❀ **Fairview Rock** This lofty crag nr the Biblins suspension bridge makes a good riverside walk from Monmouth, with a level track giving an easy route along the picturesque Lower Wye gorge.

♨ **Nelson Museum** (Priory St) Tremendous collection relating to Nelson, inc letters, medals and best of all his fighting sword. Nelson has nothing to do with Monmouth, but the collection was originally put together by Lady Llangattock who lived nearby. Shop, some disabled access; cl 1–2pm, am Sun, 24–26 Dec, 1 Jan; (01600) 713519; £1.

Days Out

Lower Wye tour: Chepstow Castle; lunch at the Castle Hotel or Bridge Hotel there; view from Wynd Cliff; Tintern Abbey; Monmouth.

Show and spectacle around Cardiff: Castell Coch, Tongwynlais; Llandaff Cathedral; lunch at the Maltsters Arms there; Museum of Welsh Life, St Fagans (like Llandaff, described under Cardiff).

Industrious past: Stroll along the Monmouthshire & Brecon Canal between Gilwern and Govilon, back along the old railway track; lunch at the Drum & Monkey, Clydach; Big Pit Mining Museum, Blaenavon.

NANTGARW ST1285

🏛 **Nantgarw China Works Museum** (Treforest Industrial Estate, off A470) For a brief period early in the 19th c, Nantgarw porcelain was among the finest in the world. They still make pots and clay pipes, and you can watch the craftsmen at work. Shop; cl Mon, plus winter Tues and Weds, 20 Dec–12 Jan; (01443) 841703; £1.

NASH POINT SS9168

△ ※ The curious striped cliffs of the Glamorgan coast look over the Bristol Channel to Exmoor. It is worth getting down to shore level to see the cliffs in their full glory.

NEATH SS7597

🔾 **Borough Museum** (Gwyn Hall, Orchard St) Includes finds from a nearby Roman fort. Shop, disabled access; cl Sun, Mon (exc bank hols); (01639) 645741; free.

🏵 **Gnoll Estate** (B4434 NE) Landscaped grounds beautifully restored by the local council. The visitor centre will have you believe they're the finest in Europe, and though this is something of an exaggeration, with some of the features it's not too wide of the mark. Snacks, shop, disabled access; cl 24 Dec–2 Jan; (01639) 635808; free.

🏰 **Neath Abbey** Remains of a Cistercian abbey founded in 1130 by Richard de Grainville. Disabled access; cl am Sun, 25–26 Dec; free.

NELSON ST1196

🏠🏚🔾! **Llancaiach Fawr** (B4254) Splendidly entertaining and carefully organised living history museum, the Elizabethan manor's Civil War days brought vividly to life by costumed guides who rarely step out of character – they even speak in 17th-c style. Children don't mind visiting a stately home when it's like this – not only are there no ropes or barriers (it's all firmly hands-on), but they can try on historic clothes, handle armour, or even languish in the stocks for a while. Extra activities summer wknds. Meals, snacks, shop; cl Mon, am Sun in winter, and Christmas wk; (01443) 412248; £4.50.

NEWPORT ST3187

🔾 🖾 **Museum & Art Gallery** (John Frost Sq) Worthwhile collections – inc teapots; cl Sun and bank hols; free.

🏚 🏵 🏴 ⚓ **Tredegar House** (Coedkernew; off A48 SW) Magnificent 17th-c house and gardens set in a 90-acre landscaped park on the edge of this industrial town. The Morgans, later Lords Tredegar, lived here for five centuries, and the household's above and below stairs activities are well illustrated in the 30 or so rooms on show. In the grounds are carriage rides, self-guided trails, craft workshops, an Edwardian sunken garden, as well as boating and an adventure playfarm. Meals, snacks, shop, disabled access; cl Mon and Tues (exc Aug), Oct wkdys, and all Nov–Easter; (01633) 815880; £3.95. Past here on the B4239, the Lighthouse Inn at St Brides Wentlooge has good food upstairs, and great Severn views.

OGMORE SS8876

🏰 △ 🏛 **Ogmore Castle** Three-storeyed 12th-c keep with a preserved hooded fireplace, a dry moat surrounding the inner ward and a surviving 12-metre (40-ft) W wall. The setting of this ruin is attractive: odd to think that what this impressive fortress was built to defend was the row of stepping stones which still cross the river; free. The Pelican is good for lunch, and the cheery Three Golden Cups, along the road at Southerndown, gives sea views to Devon on a clear day. Just past it there's a car park by the interestingly preserved remains of the seaside gardens of entirely demolished Dunraven Castle, with walks by the cliffs over the sands and rock pools, and around to the fragmentary remains of an Iron Age promontory hill fort.

PENARTH ST1971

★ An unspoilt seaside resort of some charm, with the usual attractions.

↓T 🏵 🔾 **Cosmeston Medieval Village** (Lavernock Rd towards Sully) Living museum of medieval life, reconstructed on the site of an actual village which was deserted during the 14th c. Hens and sheep wander between the cottages. Meals, snacks, shop, disabled access; cl 25 Dec; (029) 2070 8686; £3. It's set in the Cosmeston Lakes country park, with lakes, woodland and wildlife.

🔾 🖾 **Turner House** (Plymouth Rd) Changing exhibits from the National

Museum of Wales; disabled access to ground floor; cl am Sun, all day Mon (exc bank hols), and between exhibitions; (029) 2070 8870; £1.25 (free Sun).

PENHOW ST4290

🏰 **Penhow Castle** 🔲 (A48) The oldest lived-in castle in Wales, with tours of the restored rooms taking you from the 12th-c ramparts and Norman bedchamber through the 15th-c Great Hall with its minstrels' gallery to the Victorian housekeeper's room. There's a choice of several good Walkman tours, one specially for children, and others concentrating on a particular topic, such as the musical or domestic history of the building. You can stay here. Snacks, shop; cl Mon (exc bank hols), Tues, and all Oct–Feb exc Weds and pm occasional Suns; (01633) 400800; £3.60. The Rock & Fountain now has good, interesting food.

PONTYPOOL SO2801

🏠 🗘 △ **Valley Inheritance** (Pontypool Park, off A4042) The story of a typical South Wales valley, well shown in the Georgian stable block of Pontypool Park House. Snacks, shop, disabled access; cl am Sun, 25–26 Dec; (01495) 752036; £1.20. The surrounding country park is a microcosm of the Welsh valleys scenery: patches of conifer plantation and rather scrappy moorland rising high above the industrial valleys – not exactly pretty, but its gruff sense of place appeals to some. The Open Hearth, just below the canal at Griffithstown, is a very welcoming place and good for lunch.

PORTH ST0290

🏠 ⬇🚋 🔲 **Rhondda Heritage Park** See *separate family panel on p.944.*

PORTHCAWL SS8176

☺ 🎣 Still developing summer resort, with broad sandy beaches, a well placed golf club, fairground, fishing from the pier, and what's said to be the largest caravan park in Wales (some say Europe); it's quieter on the W side of the harbour.

RAGLAN SO4108

🏰 **Raglan Castle** Quite magnificent ruins of a 15th-c castle, particularly notable for its Yellow Tower of Gwent. Its intricate history is displayed in the

closet tower and two rooms of the gatehouse. Shop, some disabled access; cl 24–26 Dec, 1 Jan; (01291) 690228; £2.40. The Clytha Arms (Abergavenny road) has good food.

ST HILARY ST0171

🏰 ★ **Beaupre Castle** Well preserved ruined Elizabethan courtyard mansion with an extraordinarily elaborate three-storey Italianate porch; free. The genuinely old-fashioned and friendly Bush is good for lunch, and the village with its thatched houses is pretty.

ST NICHOLAS ST0971

🏵 **Dyffryn Gardens** (off A48) Small themed gardens and seasonal bedding displays help break up the 50 acres of rare plants and shrubs which make up these lovely gardens. Also extensive plant houses, inc a large temperate house and a succulent house, and an arboretum. Summer snacks (open-air theatre then too), shop, limited disabled access; open daily in summer, best to check in winter; (029) 2059 3328; £3.

SWANSEA SS6593

🏰 Largely post-industrial and commercial, so there are few buildings of any age or great appeal to visitors, but there's a good fresh-food covered market with cockles and laverbread, and long sandy beaches have made it something of a family summer resort. Among some high spots is the 1934 Guildhall, containing the Brangwyn Hall with its 16 huge British Empire murals painted by Sir Frank Brangwyn for the House of Lords – Wales's gain, as they were judged too controversial. There are some castle ruins (you can't go inside, but can see them from outside), inc a striking 14th-c first-floor arcade. The Dylan Thomas Centre (Somerset Pl, Marina) is devoted to Welsh literature, with exhibitions, restaurant, and a good bookshop café (you can peruse the books over your coffee). The Hanbury in Kingsway is popular for lunch, and the Banker's Draft (Wind St) and Potter's Wheel (Kingsway) have good-value food all day.

👁 **Egypt Centre** (University Campus, off Oystermouth Rd) Recently opened, with an important collection of Egyptian artifacts. Shop, disabled access; cl Sun and Mon; (01792) 295960; free.

⏳🖼 **Glynn Vivian Art Gallery & Museum** (Alexandra Rd) Displays of porcelain from Swansea's all-too-brief but brilliant period of production between 1814 and 1824, and paintings, drawings and sculptures by British, French and, above all, Welsh artists – especially the locally born Ceri Richards. Good changing exhibitions. Shop, some disabled access; cl Mon (exc bank hols), 25–26 Dec, 1 Jan; (01792) 655006; free.

❋ ⬇T **Maritime & Industrial Museum** (Museum Sq, Maritime Quarter) In the heart of the revitalised docks, with its summer collection of historic ships the biggest and most varied assemblage of floating maritime exhibits in Wales. Also a complete working woollen mill. Summer snacks, shop, disabled access; cl Mon (exc bank hols), 25–26 Dec, 1 Jan; (01792) 650351; free.

🦋 ⍦ **Plantasia** (Parc Tawe) Tropical and desert plants in a big, futuristic landscaped glasshouse, also an aviary, reptiles and various creepy-crawlies. Snacks, shop, disabled access; (01792) 474555; cl Mon (exc bank hols and July–Aug), 25–26 Dec; £2.20.

⏳ **Swansea Museum** (Victoria Rd, Maritime Quarter) The oldest in Wales, with local history and replicas of the oldest human bones found in Wales (cl Mon exc bank hols; free).

TINTERN PARVA SO5300
🏰 ⚘ **Tintern Abbey** (off A466) Remarkably well preserved, these 14th-c ruins were considered an essential spot for 18th-c artists and poets to visit, lying as they do in a lovely part of the steeply wooded Wye Valley. Wordsworth was just one of many to find inspiration here. Shop, disabled access; cl 24–26 Dec, 1 Jan; (01291) 689251; £2.40. The **Abbey Mill** nearby has been converted into a little craft centre, with demonstrations and a decent coffee shop; cl 25–26 Dec; free. A visitor centre at Tintern Old Station can help you make the most of the surrounding hills and woodland.

TONGWYNLAIS ST1382
🏰 **Castell Coch** (off A470) This spectacular triangular hillside landmark, designed in 1875 by William Burges for the Marquis of Bute, is actually based on a 13th-c castle in spite of its improbable appearance, something by Disney out of Wagner – red sandstone, conical towers, drawbridge and portcullis. Though never finished, it's a very successful pastiche, and inside is just as impressive: an astonishly elaborate mock medieval idyll of gilt, gorgeous colours, statues, murals and carvings. The bedroom of Lady Bute is decorated on the theme of Sleeping Beauty. Shop, disabled access to ground floor only; cl 24–26 Dec, 1 Jan; (029) 2081 0101; *£2.50.

USK SO3700
⏳ ★ **Gwent Rural Life Museum** (New Market St) Interesting collection, housed in an old barn; cl am wknds and all Nov–Mar; *£2. The little town is attractive, with the Nag's Head currently the best pub.

WYND CLIFF ST5297
❋ ⌂ This viewpoint gives walkers an extensive panorama, a short detour up steps. Elsewhere, the Wye Valley Walk between Chepstow and Tintern gives only occasional views down to the river, which in this picturesque Lower Wye gorge makes the boundary between England and Wales.

★ **Other attractive villages or small towns,** all with decent pubs, include Bedwellty SO1600, Cowbridge SS9974 and Laleston SS8879. The church and churchyard of Llancarfan ST0570 are worth a look.

Pubs or inns elsewhere which are particularly useful for their attractive surroundings or views include the Lamb & Flag out on the Brecon road from Abergavenny SO2515, Bridgend by the canal at Gilwern SO2414, Old Glais at Glais SN7000, Prince of Wales nr the sand dune nature reserve at Kenfig SS8383, Old House at Llangynwyd SS8588, the Greyhound at Llantrisant ST3997, Brynfynnon at Llanwonno ST0295, Plough & Harrow at Monknash SS9270, Rowan Tree at Nelson ST1195, Halfway House at Tal-y-coed SO4115, the Trekkers at The Narth SO5206 and the Fountain at Trelleck Grange SO4902.

Where to eat

CARDIFF ST1876 **Monde** *60 St Mary St (029) 2038 7376* Bustling open-plan restaurant with a big choice of delicious fish and shellfish, decent wines, and friendly, efficient service; cl Sun, 25–26 Dec. **£20**|2-course lunch £5.

LLANDEWI SKIRRID SO3416 **Walnut Tree** *(01873) 852797* Comfortable, stylish dining pub run by the same licensees for over 28 years; marvellously relaxed atmosphere (you can pop in for just a drink or a one-course meal), outstanding, imaginative and carefully prepared food using tip-top quality produce (wonderful puddings and fine cheeses), an attractive choice of wines (particularly strong on Italian ones), and efficient, friendly service; cl Sun, Mon, 1 wk Christmas, 2 wks Feb; disabled access. **£34**|£15.

PORT TALBOT SS7489 **Aberavon Beach Hotel** *(01639) 884949* Popular modern hotel opposite a wide sandy beach, with imaginative modern cooking in the no smoking restaurant, good wine list, helpful staff, and refurbished public rooms; all-weather leisure centre; comfortable bdrms; good disabled access. **£23**|2-course lunch £8.50.

RAGLAN SO3608 **Clytha Arms** *Clytha, (3m W) (01873) 840206* Fine old country inn with a tastefully and solidly comfortable bar, cheerful and helpful staff, good, carefully prepared food inc delicious puddings and good-value Sun lunch in the no smoking restaurant, log fires, well kept real ales, and a neat garden; bdrms; no food pm Sun and Mon. **£24.50**|£5.

SWANSEA SS6592 **Number One Restaurant** *1 Wind St (01792) 456996* Small bistro-style restaurant with a relaxed and friendly atmosphere, helpful staff, and really good food using local produce – lots of fish and game and lovely puddings; cl Sun, Mon, 1 wk Christmas. **£27.50 dinner**, **£17 lunch**|£4.

TAL-Y-COED SO4115 **Halfway House** *(01600) 780269* Pretty, neat and clean 17th-c cottage with a huge wisteria, cosy, little, no smoking dining room, snug main bar, lots of Wills cigarette cards, well kept real ales, carefully presented bar food, welcoming service, and a tidy garden; cl am Mon–Fri; children must be well behaved; disabled access. **£18**|£4.

Special thanks to Mrs J E Ward, Mr and Mrs D Pilgrim, Mr and Mrs Norbury.

Wales Calendar

Some of these dates were provisional as we went to press. Please check information with the telephone numbers provided.

JANUARY

29 **Chirk** Snowdrop Days at Chirk Castle – *till 30 January* (01691) 777701

FEBRUARY

5 **Bangor** Snowdrop Days at Penrhyn Castle – *till 6 February* (01248) 353084; **Chirk** Snowdrop Days at Chirk Castle – *till 6 February* (01691) 777701

12 **Chirk** Snowdrop Days at Chirk Castle – *till 13 February* (01691) 777701

13 **Bangor** Snowdrop Days at Penrhyn Castle – *till 14 February* (01248) 353084

Wales Calendar (cont.)

MARCH

5 Bangor Daffodil Day at Penrhyn Castle (01248) 353084

APRIL

28 St Fagans May Fair Festival at the Museum of Welsh Life – *till 1 May* (029) 2057 3500
29 Llandovery National Town Criers' Championship – *till 30 April* (029) 2057 3500

MAY

12 Llangollen International Jazz Festival – *till 14 May* (0151) 339 3367
16 Welshpool Meet the Gardener Tour at Powis Castle (01938) 554338
24 Welshpool National Gardens Scheme at Powis Castle (01938) 554338
26 Hay-on-Wye Festival of Literature – *till 4 June* (01497) 821217
27 Bangor Victorian Childhood Experience at Penrhyn Castle (01248) 353084; **St David's** St David's Cathedral Music Festival – *till 4 June* (01437) 720271
28 Swansea City and County of Swansea Show – *till 29 May* (01792) 635428
29 Penrhyn Bay National Eisteddfod – *till 3 June* (01248) 670648

JUNE

10 Llanelwedd Smallholder Weekend at the Royal Welsh Showground – *till 11 June* (01454) 299187
11 Amroth Specialist Plant Fair at Colby Woodland Garden (01834) 811885
13 Chirk National Gardens Scheme Open Day at the Castle (01691) 777701
19 Bangor National Gardens Scheme at Penrhyn Castle (01248) 353084; **Welshpool** Meet the Gardener Tour at Powis Castle (01938) 554338
30 Conwy North Wales Bluegrass Music Festival – *till 2 July* (01492) 580454; **St Donats Castle** Welsh International Festival of Storytelling at St Donats Arts Centre – *till 2 July* (01446) 794848

JULY

1 Ely Festival – *till 9 July* (029) 2057 8368
2 St Asaph Fireworks Concert at Bodelwyddan Castle (01625) 575681
4 Llangollen International Musical Eisteddfod: cosmopolitan gathering at the Royal International Pavilion – *till 9 July* (01978) 860236
5 Brecon County Show (01568) 708760
8 Welshpool Mid Wales Festival of Transport at Powis Castle – *till 9 July* (01938) 553680
16 Bangor Vintage and Classic Cars at Penrhyn Castle (01248) 353084; **Welshpool** Country and Western Music Festival at the County Showground (01938) 552563
18 Saundersfoot Flower Festival – *till 22 July* (01834) 812880
20 Cardiff Welsh Proms at St David's Hall – *till 29 July* (029) 2087 8444
21 Welshpool Meet the Gardener Tour at Powis Castle (01938) 554338
22 Aberystwyth International Music Festival – *till 12 August* (01970) 622889

Wales Calendar (cont.)

23 **Fishguard** Music Festival – *till 31 July* (01348) 873612
24 **Llanelwedd** Royal Welsh Show at the Showground – *till 27 July* (01982) 553683
29 **Caernarfon** North Wales Agricultural Show at Wern Ddu Fields (01286) 881632; **Chirk** Elizabethan Open Days at Chirk Castle – *till 30 July* (01691) 777701

AUGUST

5 **Aberystwyth** Celtic Film Festival – *till 15 August* (01970) 622889; **Llanelli** National Eisteddfod of Wales – *till 12 August* (029) 2076 3777; **St Asaph** Gala Day – *till 6 August* (01745) 582746
10 **Carmarthen** United Counties Agricultural Show – *till 11 August* (01267) 232141
11 **Brecon** Jazz Festival: over 80 international performers – *till 13 August* (01874) 625557
12 **Newcastle Emlyn** River Festival – *till 20 August* (01239) 710238
13 **Hay-on-Wye** Vintage Steam Rally at Boatside Farm (01874) 711110
15 **Gwalchmai** Anglesey Show at the Showground – *till 16 August* (01407) 720072; **Haverfordwest** Pembrokeshire County Show at the County Showground – *till 17 August* (01437) 764331
19 **Llandrindod Wells** Victorian Festival – *till 27 August* (01597) 823441; **Llanfairpwllgwyngyll** Open-air Jazz at Plas Newydd (01248) 714795
22 **New Quay** Cardigan Bay Regatta – *till 24 August* (01545) 561019
24 **Chirk** Elizabethan Open Days at Chirk Castle – *till 25 August* (01691) 777701
26 **Croeslan** Orllwyn Teifi Vintage Show – *till 28 August* (01559) 370885
28 **Llanwrtyd Wells** World Bog Snorkel and Mountain Bike Leaping Championships (01591) 610666
31 **Bangor** Medieval Madness Fun Day at Penrhyn Castle (01248) 353084; **Monmouth** Monmouthshire Show at Vauxhall Fields (01291) 691160

SEPTEMBER

1 **Welshpool** Meet the Gardener Tour at Powis Castle (01938) 554338
9 **Gwernesney** Usk Show (01291) 672379
16 **Wales** European Heritage Open Days: free access to up to 90 properties, some rarely open to the public such as Dyffryn Gardens in **Barry**, Cwmgwili House in **Carmarthen**, **Cardiff** Crown Court and Mansion House, **Denby** Town Walls, St David's College in **Lampeter**, Round House Tower in **Nantyglo** and Tredegar House in **Newport** – *till 17 September* (029) 2048 4606
22 **St Fagans** Harvest Festival at the Museum of Welsh Life – *till 23 September* (029) 2057 3500

OCTOBER

1 **Merthyr Tydfil** Tydfil Arts Festival – *till 31 October* (01685) 389995
7 **Swansea** Festival – *till 21 October* (01492) 876886
8 **Bangor** Victorian Childhood Experience at Penrhyn Castle (01248) 353084
13 **Llandudno** October Festival – *till 20 October* (01492) 593922
27 **Swansea** Dylan Thomas Festival at the Dylan Thomas Centre – *till 9 November* (01792) 463980

Wales Calendar (cont.)

NOVEMBER

10 Cardiff Welsh International Film Festival – *till 19 November* (01970) 617995

DECEMBER

6 St Fagans Christmas Tree Festival – *till 9 December* (029) 2057 3500
31 Llanwrtyd Wells New Year Walk-in, *at 11pm* in the square: torchlight walk with a horse's skull (Celtic tradition) (01591) 610236

We welcome reports from readers

This *Guide* depends on readers' reports. Do help us if you can – in return, we offer a discount on the next edition to people who've helped us with reports for it. Tell us what you think about places already in it, and anything extra you think we should say about them. And send us your ideas for inclusion in the next edition: places to visit, eat at or stay in, attractive drives or walks, maybe even unusual interesting shops you know of. Use the card in the middle, the report forms at the end, or just write – no stamp needed: *The Good Britain Guide*, FREEPOST TN1569, Wadhurst, E Sussex TN5 7BR.

INDEX

This index includes the main places in the **To see and Do** sections.
Numbers in *italic* refer to entries included in suggestions for **Days Out**.

REPORT FORMS

Please report to us: you can use the tear-out card in the middle of the book, the forms on the following pages, or just plain paper – whichever's easiest for you. We need to know what you think of the places mentioned in this edition – especially, whether you think we should add to or change our descriptions of them. We need to know about other places worthy of inclusion. We need to know about ones that should not be included. We try to answer all letters, and readers who send us reports will be offered a discount on the price of the next edition that benefits from their help.

If you are recommending a new entry, the more detail you can put into your description, the better. This will help not just us but also your fellow-readers gauge its appeal. A description of its character and even furnishings is a tremendous boon. Imagine you're writing about it for the *Guide* itself, and put in the sorts of things you'd want to know yourself before deciding whether to choose it.

The atmosphere and character of a holiday hotel or simpler place to stay, or of a restaurant, are very important to us – why it would, or would not, appeal to people who don't know it. But, of course, the quality and type of its food matter a lot, too, so please tell us about that as well. A full address and telephone number is an enormous help.

We'd also very much like you to let us know of places you've enjoyed visiting – anything from a little village to a stately home, from a shop selling unusual things to a factory visit, from an outstanding plant nursery to a hot-air balloon festival, from a hidden-away country church to a cathedral, from a peaceful wood or a nature reserve or a stretch of unspoilt coastal cliff to a theme park or a zoo or a pleasure beach. We're also particularly interested in enjoyable walks and drives. Whatever it is, if you've enjoyed it, please tell us about it.

The card in the middle of the book is a general purpose one for any recommendation. There are also different forms on the following pages: one for endorsement of existing entries; and three forms for more detailed descriptions of places to visit, hotels or restaurants.

When you go to a hotel, restaurant, or anywhere else, don't tell them you're a reporter for *The Good Britain Guide*; we do make clear that all inspections are anonymous, and if you declare yourself as a reporter you risk getting special treatment – for better or for worse! When you write to *The Good Britain Guide* , FREEPOST TN1569, WADHURST, E. Sussex TN5 7BR, you don't need a stamp in the UK. We'll gladly send you more forms (free) if you wish. The information you send us will be stored in our computer files.

Though we try to answer letters, we do have other work to do, besides producing this *Guide*. So please understand if there's a delay. And from June well into autumn, when we are fully extended getting the next edition to the printers, we put all letters and reports aside, not answering them until the rush is over (and after our post-press-day autumn holiday). The end of May is pretty much the cut-off date for reasoned consideration of reports for the next edition – and the earlier the better, if they're suggestions of new entries.

We'll assume we can print your name or initials as a recommender unless you tell us otherwise.

The Good Britain Guide: Endorsement Form

I have been to the following hotels/restaurants/attractions/places in *The Good Britain Guide 2000* in the last few months, found them as described, and confirm that they deserve continued inclusion:

Your own name and address (*block capitals please*)

The Good Britain Guide: Report Form

Please use this form to tell us about anything which *you* think should or should not be included in the next edition of *The Good Britain Guide*. Just fill it in and sent it to us – no stamp needed.

ALISDAIR AIRD

☐ *Please tick this box if you would like extra report forms.*

Report on *(its name)*

Its address:

Postcode: Telephone:

What is this? (e.g. *hotel, restaurant, garden, village, drive, walk*)

Description/why it appeals

PLEASE GIVE YOUR NAME AND ADDRESS ON THE BACK OF THIS FORM

Your own name and address (*block capitals please*)

Please return to:
    The Good Britain Guide
    FREEPOST TN1569
    WADHURST
    E. Sussex
    TN5 7BR

The Good Britain Guide: Report Form

Please use this form to tell us about anything which *you* think should or should not be included in the next edition of *The Good Britain Guide*. Just fill it in and sent it to us – no stamp needed.

ALISDAIR AIRD

☐ *Please tick this box if you would like extra report forms.*

Report on *(its name)*

Its address:

Postcode: Telephone:

What is this? (e.g. *hotel, restaurant, garden, village, drive, walk*)

Description/why it appeals

PLEASE GIVE YOUR NAME AND ADDRESS ON THE BACK OF THIS FORM

Your own name and address (*block capitals please*)

Please return to:
The Good Britain Guide
FREEPOST TN1569
WADHURST
E. Sussex
TN5 7BR

The Good Britain Guide: Report Form

Please use this form to tell us about anything which *you* think should or should not be included in the next edition of *The Good Britain Guide*. Just fill it in and sent it to us – no stamp needed.

ALISDAIR AIRD

☐ *Please tick this box if you would like extra report forms.*

Report on *(its name)*

Its address:

Postcode: Telephone:

What is this? (e.g. *hotel, restaurant, garden, village, drive, walk*)

Description/why it appeals

PLEASE GIVE YOUR NAME AND ADDRESS ON THE BACK OF THIS FORM

Your own name and address (*block capitals please*)

Please return to:
   The Good Britain Guide
   FREEPOST TN1569
   WADHURST
   E. Sussex
   TN5 7BR